# BaseBall
# ameríca™

# 1997
# ALMANAC

# A Comprehensive Review
# Of the 1996 Season,
# Featuring Statistics
# And Commentary

Copyright 1996 by Baseball America, Inc.
Distributed by Simon & Schuster

# Baseball america's
# 1997 ALMANAC

**PUBLISHED BY**
Baseball America, Inc.

**EDITOR**
Allan Simpson

**ASSISTANT EDITOR**
John Manuel

**ASSOCIATE EDITORS**
Jim Callis
Will Lingo
John Royster
Alan Schwarz

**CONTRIBUTING WRITERS**
Peter Barrouquere, Wayne Graczyk, Howard Herman, Sean Kernan,
Andrew Linker, Cindy Martinez Rhodes, Javier Morales, Tim Pearrell, John Perrotto,
Curt Rallo, Gene Sapakoff, George Schroeder, Larry Starks, Susan Wade, Chris Wright

**STATISTICAL PRODUCTION CONSULTANT**
Howe Sportsdata International,
Boston, Mass.

## Baseball america

| | | |
|---|---|---|
| **EDITOR** | **PUBLISHER** | **PRODUCTION SUPERVISOR** |
| Allan Simpson | Dave Chase | Jeff Brunk |
| **MANAGING EDITOR** | | **ADVERTISING DIRECTOR** |
| Jim Callis | | Kris Howard |

**EDITOR'S NOTE**
  Major league statistics are based on final, unofficial 1996 averages. Minor league statistics are official.
  The organization statistics, which begin on page 58, include all players who participated in at least one game during the 1996 season. Pitchers' batting statistics are not included, nor are the pitching statistics of field players who pitched on rare occasions. For players who played with more than one team in the same league, the player's cumulative statistics appear on the line immediately after the player's second-team statistics.
  Innings have been rounded off to the nearest full inning.

  *Lefthanded batter, pitcher   #Switch hitter

# CONTENTS

**Cover Photograph:** Yankees by Steve Crandall

# MAJOR
# LEAGUES

# 1996 Year Of The Homer; Labor Strife Lingers

**By ALAN SCHWARZ**

It was the year that saw the Yankees reassert themselves as baseball's elite. It was the year that saw the industry return to normal, with minimal talk of strikes and shortened seasons.

Most of all, though, it was the year of the home run.

There never had been another season like it. Home runs flew out of parks with frightening frequency, at least for opposing pitchers. A record 4,962 home runs were hit, breaking the former mark of 4,458, set in 1987. That increase of 11.3 percent indicated that the game had entered a new era—one in which offense soared, games lasted four hours, and fans simply ate it up.

So many records were set in 1996, statisticians couldn't keep up with it all. But some accomplishments were greeted with appropriate fanfare. A select list:

■ The Orioles set a major league record with 257 team home runs, besting the old mark of 240 set by the legendary 1961 Yankees of Roger Maris and Mickey Mantle. Perhaps most amazing, the Mariners (245) and Athletics (243) also would have broken the Yankees vaunted record had the Orioles not crashed through it first. In all, 10 of the 28 teams set organization marks for home runs.

■ The top gun for the Orioles was Brady Anderson, a player whose previous high in home runs was 21. He hit a phenomenal 50 in 1996, second in the major leagues, and before a midseason bout with appendicitis—surgery for which he put off until the winter—he appeared to have a chance to break Maris' season record of 61.

■ Joining Anderson on the 50-homer level was Oakland's Mark McGwire, who hit 52 despite missing 32 games to injury. Anderson and McGwire became the first players in the same season to hit 50 since 1961 when Maris and Mantle hit 61 and 54, respectively.

■ Perhaps scarier, more players slammed 40 homers and 30 homers than any season in history.

**Pace Setter.** Oakland's Mark McGwire hit 52 homers in 1996, to lead a record onslaught.

The 15 players besides Anderson and McGwire to hit more than 40 were Ken Griffey (49), Albert Belle (48), Juan Gonzalez (47), Andres Galarraga (47), Jay Buhner (44), Mo Vaughn (44), Barry Bonds (42), Gary Sheffield (42), Todd Hundley (41, to set a new major league record for catchers), Greg Vaughn (41), Frank Thomas (40), Vinny Castilla (40), Ken Caminiti (40), Sammy Sosa (40) and Ellis Burks (40).

The 23 players who hit 30-39 were Rafael Palmeiro (39), Cecil Fielder (39), Dean Palmer (38), Jim Thome (38), Ed Sprague (36), Alex Rodriguez (36), Henry Rodriguez (36), Geronimo Berroa (36), John Jaha (34), Eric Karros (34), Ryan Klesko (34), Robin Ventura (34), Barry Larkin (33), Jeff Bagwell (31), Dante Bichette (31), Joe Carter (30), Steve Finley (30), Ron Gant (30), Bernard Gilkey (30), Chipper Jones (30), Jeff King (30), Tim Salmon (30) and Benito Santiago (30).

■ On the pitching side, the results were correspondingly bleak. The Tigers' maligned pitching staff posted a 6.38 ERA. But the effect was felt throughout both leagues. The American League's composite ERA was a neat and not-so-tidy 5.00. The National League, traditionally a pitching sanctuary, still ballooned to 4.22.

Trying to make sense of all the records, experts sought out reasons for the offensive boom. Though no one culprit was apprehended, these were some of the

## PUTTING 1996 IN PERSPECTIVE

### MOST HOME RUNS

| Per Game, All-Time | | Per Club, All-Time | |
|---|---|---|---|
| 1. **1996** 2.20 | | 1. **Baltimore, 1996** | 257 |
| 2. 1987 2.12 | | 2. **Seattle, 1996** | 245 |
| 3. 1994 2.07 | | 3. **Oakland, 1996** | 243 |
| 4. 1995 2.02 | | 4. New York (AL), 1961 | 240 |
| 5. 1993 1.78 | | 5. Minnesota, 1963 | 225 |
| 6. 1970 1.76 | | Detroit, 1987 | 225 |
| 7. 1977 1.73 | | 7. **Colorado, 1996** | 221 |
| 8. 1960 1.72 | | New York (NL), 1947 | 221 |
| 9. 1950 1.67 | | Cincinnati, 1956 | 221 |
| 10. 1991 1.61 | | Minnesota, 1964 | 221 |

THE SPORTS GROUP

suspects:

■ **The Rocketball Theory:** Was the ball juiced in 1996? One National League executive thought so.

"I'll tell you what," he said, "a lot of people think the ball is like a rocket now. And I'm beginning to believe it, too. You see guys who aren't even home run hitters hitting home runs to the opposite field."

Responding to whether his company's baseballs had been changed for the season, Scott Smith, Rawlings Sporting Goods director of marketing services, said, "For Major League Baseball to pull off a conspiracy to change the properties of the ball, that would be pretty outrageous. I mean, they can't even get together to decide whether to have the DH, right?"

■ **The No Pitcher Theory:** With expansion having diluted talent and with cries that children don't throw as much anymore, some theorized that there simply were too few major league-quality pitchers to keep offense on its former levels.

"Did the hitters all of a sudden visit Tony Gwynn's house for the winter? I don't think so," Braves general manager John Schuerholz quipped.

■ **The Jack LaLanne Theory:** There were 10 major leaguers listed at 240 pounds or more, compared with two in 1965. Hitters are bigger and stronger than ever. The result is an ability to hit balls farther more frequently.

"Every team has a weight guy and a strength guy," Pirates coach Rich Donnelly said. "We've got players who lift after the game, before the game, during the game. Pretty soon they'll be taking barbells out there between innings."

■ **The New Stadium Theory:** Several new ballparks, Baltimore's Camden Yards, Colorado's Coors Field and Texas' The Ballpark at Arlington being prime examples, were built as hitters parks. The Oakland Coliseum saw offense soar after being enclosed. These stadiums quickly became home run havens and began to distort offensive performance for their players and those throughout the league as well.

"What they've done, when you think about it, is turn back the clock," ESPN commentator Jon Miller said, "so that the newer parks play the way the old parks played. Most of those old parks were pretty cozy."

■ **The Strize Zone Theory:** Regardless of what the

**Labor Leaders.** Union head Donald Fehr, left, and owners representative Randy Levine worked long and hard to reach accord on a new Basic Agreement.

leagues, the hitters and the umpires say, the strike zone has shrunk throughout the 1990s. That results in more hitters counts and a feeling on the part of pitchers that they have to put a ball right over the plate to get a strike called.

"If the only place a pitcher can throw to get a strike is that area just above the batter's knees," the Elias Sports Bureau's Steve Hirdt said, "it stands to reason that a batter can zone in on that pitch."

None of the above theories could be entirely correct. But all these factors did combine to create one zany 1996 season. And there were no signs that the trend would stop anytime soon.

## Players, Owners Agree

The good news on the labor front in 1996 was that there were no strikes or lockouts. Unlike 1994 and 1995, the full 162-game season and playoffs unfolded as usual. The bad news was that the warring owners and players still went through a season without coming to terms on a labor agreement.

All that ended Nov. 26, however, when club owners met in Rosemont, Ill., and ratified an agreement reached weeks earlier by union head Don Fehr and owners negotiator Randy Levine.

The same deal that was rejected Nov. 6 by an overwhelming 18-12 margin was approved 26-4, with the Chicago White Sox, Cleveland, Kansas City and Oakland dissenting. A three-quarters majority was required for passage.

"A long and winding road has come to an end," acting commissioner Bud Selig said. "Baseball fans can finally look forward to five years of uninterrupted play. We can now work together to bring peace to the game."

Final approval from players was expected a week later.

The owners about-face came exactly a week after White Sox owner Jerry Reinsdorf shattered baseball's salary structure by signing Albert Belle to a record $55 million, five-year deal. That contact provoked criticism from many baseball executives who felt betrayed and those sentiments were largely behind the dramatic swing that saw 14 owners change their vote.

The deal is retroactive to 1996 and runs through 2000. The players have the option of extending it through 2001.

**Bud Selig.** De facto commissioner.

"We wish we would have gotten a better system, but you're not going to conquer the world in one negotiation," Phillies owner Bill Giles said.

The most revolutionary aspect is the start of interleague play in 1997, beginning June 12 when the four National League West teams play the four American League West teams. Teams will play 15 or 16 interleague games, depending on their division.

The core provisions of the agreement (see chart, 'Basic Agreement') are a luxury tax designed to slow the rise in payrolls among large-market teams; and revenue sharing, which will shift at least $70 million a year from the large markets to the small markets.

Fehr and Levine spoke on and off during the year, but just when the two sides appeared to come together in August, owners balked at a key concession Levine had negotiated and blocked the agreement's ratification.

The two leaders again appeared to have an agreement—the same one that was later ratified—when they met during the World Series. The players signed off on the deal, but owners again balked.

The main objection several owners had with Levine's deal was that players would receive service time for the 75 days they were on strike from 1994-95, and one and possibly two years at the end of the agreement that provided for no luxury tax.

Several owners, most notably Reinsdorf, balked at the idea of giving players service time, which players had received in past strikes. Those 75 days would allow 18 players, including key pitchers Alex Fernandez (White Sox) and Mel Rojas (Expos), to become free agents in the offseason.

"(Montreal has) been able to remain competitive by being able to trade those players before they become free agents and get fair value," Reinsdorf said. "If they had known their guys would be free agents this year, they might have traded them. To all of a sudden say to them you no longer have a tradeable commodity is unfair."

While teams did play a full season in 1996, attendance at major league games did not return to pre-strike figures and ratings for postseason play— even for a World Series that featured marquee teams like the New York Yankees and Atlanta Braves—were among the poorest ever.

### ATTENDANCE SLIDE

| Year | Total | Per Game |
|------|-------|----------|
| 1993 | 70,245,237 | 30,972 |
| 1994 | 50,009,023 | 31,611 |
| 1995 | 50,282,795 | 26,202 |
| 1996 | 60,096,451 | 26,889 |

Attendance in 1993 and 1994 (through Aug. 12, the date the players went on strike) averaged more than 31,000 a game. Attendance in 1995 and 1996 averaged less than 27,000 an opening—a drop of about 15 per cent.

## Alomar Sullies Posteason

Alas, baseball wasn't without its share of courtroom fights in 1996. The most publicized came after the ugly Sept. 27 incident in Toronto in which Orioles second baseman Roberto Alomar, incensed over a call by home-plate umpire John Hirschbeck, spat in the umpire's face, and later said that Hirschbeck had become "real bitter" since his 7-year-old son John died in 1993.

American League president Gene Budig immediately suspended Alomar for five games—the last two games of 1996 and the first three of 1997—but after Alomar

# BASIC AGREEMENT

A glance at the terms of the new Basic Agreement that was ratified on Nov. 26, 1996 at a meeting of baseball's club owners in Rosemont, Ill. The owners had originally rejected the same agreement.

### LENGTH

The agreement runs through Oct. 31, 2000. Players have an option to extend to Oct. 31, 2001.

### WHAT THE OWNERS GET

### LUXURY TAX

Teams that have payrolls exceeding set thresholds will be taxed on the portion above the thresholds. Money will be used to fund the owners' 1997 revenue-sharing shortfall.

1997—35 percent tax on amounts above $51 million.
1998—35 percent tax on amounts above $55 million.
1999—34 percent tax on amounts above $58.9 million.
2000—No tax
2001—No tax.

### REVENUE SHARING

The owners' revenue-sharing plan, adopted March 21, 1996. Retroactive to 1996, to be phased in at 60 percent for the first two years of what the maximum pool will be in 1997. The following levels are applicable:

1997—60 percent          2000—100 percent
1998—80 percent          2001—100 percent
1999—85 percent

An estimated 13 teams will give money and 13 teams will receive, with about $70 million to be transferred in 1996. The most a team would give in 1996 is about $6 million, which also is about the most any team would receive.

### PAYROLL TAX

Players pay a tax of 2.5 percent of their salaries in 1996 and 1997, with the money coming from licensing income, special dues or another method determined by the union. The players will pay a minimum of $40 million. Twenty-five man rosters and disabled lists will be used for the calculation.

### POSTSEASON PLAYER POOL

The players' share of the ticketed money from the first three games of each division playoff series will be reduced to 60 percent from 80 percent. Authorization granted to go to a best-of-7 division series, probably implemented in 1998.

### EXPANSION

Owners will have the right to add two expansion franchises, provided that they decide by Dec. 31, 1999, and the teams start play by 2002.

### SALARY ARBITRATION

Three-man panels will be scheduled to hear cases instead of single arbitrators in 50 percent of the cases in 1998, 75 percent in 1999, and 100 percent in 2000 and 2001.

### INTERLEAGUE PLAY

Owners may start interleague play in 1997, with each team playing 15 or 16 interleague games. The designated hitter will be used in American League ballparks. The interleague-play agreement is for 1997 only.

### WHAT THE PLAYERS GET

### MINIMUM SALARY

1997—$150,000
1998—$170,000
1999—$200,000
2000—$200,000 plus cost-of-living adjustment if option isn't exercised.
2001—$200,000 plus cost-of-living adjustment if option isn't exercised.

### SERVICE TIME

All players on major league rosters during the entire 1994-95 strike will receive 75 days service time. Each club that loses a free agent who becomes eligible because of strike service time receives an amateur draft pick between the first and second round.

**Costly Spit.** Baltimore's Roberto Alomar spit in the face of umpire John Hirschbeck, incurring the wrath of the American public.

MORRIS FOSTOFF

active through the playoffs. They threatened to strike during all four Division Series before Major League Baseball received an injunction in Philadelphia federal court Oct. 4 to keep them from doing so.

"With this, you're giving people in the playoffs and World Series almost a free pass if you're not going to enforce suspensions during that period of time," umpires union chief Richie Phillips said. "People see a player commit an outrageous act on one night and then go out and play the next day."

Phillips demanded that Budig hear Alomar's appeal during the playoffs, but when the player dropped his appeal, bylaws allowed baseball no recourse but to have the suspension begin on Opening Day 1997.

Alomar claimed that Hirschbeck had called him an unflattering name after ejecting him for arguing a called third strike. "We didn't understand each other," Alomar said. "What happened was in the heat of the moment."

Alomar, who apologized for the incident, went on to have a standout Division Series. While fans booed loudly and wore spit shields to taunt baseball's newest villain, Alomar hit a home run in the top of the 10th inning in Game Four in Cleveland to beat the Indians 4-3 and send Baltimore to the Championship Series against the Yankees.

"We've had bumpings, we've had fights, we've had sprays when you argue back and forth," umpire Jim McKean said, "but I've never seen a ballplayer try and directly spit in any umpire's face. Only animals spit in people's faces."

Alomar appealed, it was clear that he had deferred the punishment until 1997. Regular-season infractions typically are not punishable by postseason suspensions.

Major league umpires, not to mention most of the public, became enraged at how Alomar would remain

## Cubans Cause Bidding War

After years of concern that expansion has diluted the level of major league talent, there appeared to be some hope for the future when the door to Cuba's closetful

## ATTENDANCE FALLOUT

| | 1994 | | | 1995 | | | 1996 | | |
|---|---|---|---|---|---|---|---|---|---|
| | Dates | Attendance | Average | Dates | Attendance | Average | Dates | Attendance | Average |
| Atlanta | 54 | 2,539,240 | 47,022 | 72 | 2,561,831 | 35,581 | 81 | 2,901,242 | 35,818 |
| Baltimore | 54 | 2,535,359 | 46,951 | 72 | 3,098,475 | 43,034 | 81 | 3,646,950 | 45,024 |
| Boston | 61 | 1,775,826 | 29,111 | 72 | 2,164,378 | 30,061 | 81 | 2,315,233 | 28,583 |
| California | 63 | 1,512,622 | 24,009 | 72 | 1,748,680 | 24,287 | 81 | 1,820,532 | 22,476 |
| Chicago NL | 58 | 1,845,208 | 31,813 | 70 | 1,893,925 | 27,056 | 78 | 2,219,110 | 28,450 |
| Chicago AL | 53 | 1,697,398 | 32,026 | 71 | 1,609,773 | 22,672 | 79 | 1,676,416 | 21,220 |
| Cincinnati | 60 | 1,897,681 | 31,628 | 71 | 1,843,649 | 25,967 | 76 | 1,861,428 | 24,492 |
| Cleveland | 51 | 1,995,174 | 39,121 | 71 | 2,842,725 | 40,038 | 79 | 3,318,174 | 42,002 |
| Colorado | 56 | 3,281,511 | 58,705 | 71 | 3,341,988 | 47,070 | 81 | 3,891,014 | 48,037 |
| Detroit | 57 | 1,184,783 | 20,785 | 71 | 1,180,979 | 16,634 | 81 | 1,168,610 | 14,427 |
| Florida | 59 | 1,937,467 | 32,838 | 69 | 1,670,255 | 24,206 | 80 | 1,746,767 | 21,835 |
| Houston | 59 | 1,561,136 | 26,460 | 71 | 1,363,801 | 19,208 | 81 | 1,975,888 | 24,394 |
| Kansas City | 57 | 1,400,494 | 24,570 | 70 | 1,232,969 | 17,614 | 80 | 1,436,007 | 17,950 |
| Los Angeles | 55 | 2,279,421 | 41,444 | 72 | 2,766,251 | 38,420 | 81 | 3,188,454 | 39,364 |
| Milwaukee | 56 | 1,268,397 | 22,650 | 71 | 1,087,560 | 15,318 | 78 | 1,327,155 | 17,015 |
| Minnesota | 59 | 1,398,565 | 23,705 | 72 | 1,057,667 | 14,690 | 80 | 1,437,352 | 17,967 |
| Montreal | 52 | 1,276,250 | 24,543 | 71 | 1,292,764 | 18,207 | 81 | 1,618,573 | 19,982 |
| New York NL | 52 | 1,151,471 | 22,143 | 70 | 1,254,307 | 17,919 | 78 | 1,588,323 | 20,363 |
| New York AL | 57 | 1,675,557 | 29,396 | 70 | 1,705,257 | 24,361 | 78 | 2,250,839 | 28,857 |
| Oakland | 56 | 1,242,692 | 22,191 | 71 | 1,174,310 | 16,540 | 80 | 1,148,380 | 14,355 |
| Philadelphia | 58 | 2,290,971 | 39,500 | 71 | 2,043,588 | 28,783 | 78 | 1,801,677 | 23,098 |
| Pittsburgh | 60 | 1,222,517 | 20,375 | 70 | 905,517 | 12,936 | 78 | 1,326,640 | 17,008 |
| St. Louis | 54 | 1,866,544 | 34,566 | 71 | 1,727,536 | 24,331 | 81 | 2,659,239 | 32,830 |
| San Diego | 57 | 953,857 | 16,734 | 70 | 1,019,728 | 14,568 | 81 | 2,187,886 | 27,011 |
| San Francisco | 59 | 1,704,614 | 28,892 | 72 | 1,241,497 | 17,243 | 80 | 1,413,687 | 17,671 |
| Seattle | 44 | 1,103,798 | 25,086 | 73 | 1,640,992 | 22,479 | 81 | 2,722,392 | 33,610 |
| Texas | 62 | 2,502,538 | 40,364 | 72 | 1,985,910 | 27,582 | 80 | 2,888,920 | 36,112 |
| Toronto | 59 | 2,907,933 | 49,287 | 72 | 2,826,483 | 39,257 | 81 | 2,559,563 | 31,600 |
| **Total** | **1,582** | **50,009,023** | **31,611** | **1,919** | **50,282,795** | **26,202** | **2,235** | **60,096,451** | **26,889** |

of baseball talent opened a crack with the signing of defectors Livan Hernandez by the Marlins and Osvaldo Fernandez by the Giants.

After weeks of spirited bidding, Hernandez, 20, received the largest contract ever for an amateur player, $4.5 million, on Jan. 13. (That record later was broken with the Diamondbacks' signing of Travis Lee for $10 million.) Hernandez' contract called for a $2.5 million bonus and a guaranteed four-year major league contract. Fernandez signed with the Giants several days later for a $3.2 million three-year deal with a $1.3 million bonus.

The large sums of money afforded these players fueled speculation that several other Cuban players would defect in the future.

Hernandez was considered the better prospect, armed with a

**Record Contract.** Cuban Livan Hernandez signed a $4.5 million free-agent contract with the Marlins.

low-90s fastball and eight years younger than Fernandez. He also was considered a special resource for the Marlins, whose market includes a large Cuban population.

"We hope people understand we're reaching out to the community," Marlins general manager Dave Dombrowski said. "But it's a situation where you don't just sign somebody to try to please people locally if you don't think they have that kind of ability."

Referring to the money his club afforded Fernandez, which many clubs believed was far more than necessary to sign him, Giants GM Bob Quinn said, "Take it to the bank. People in the organization have seen him throw at least five times, and he's a guy who could step into your rotation and help right away."

Fernandez did step into the Giants rotation, but didn't fare as well as he was billed. He went 7-13 with a 4.61 ERA.

Hernandez' season was roughly as disappointing. He was sent to Triple-A Charlotte to start and struggled, allowing 17 runs in 13 innings in his first three starts before a demotion to Double-A Portland. More disturbing to Florida officials, his mid-90s fastball barely was hitting 90, and he was considerably overweight. But he rebounded in Double-A, going 9-2 with a 4.34 ERA and 95 strikeouts in 93 innings.

Fernandez became the first key player ever to defect from the powerful Cuban national team when he left July 29, 1995, before a four-game series against Team USA in Millington, Tenn. Hernandez left the Cuban national team Sept. 27, 1995, in Monterrey, Mexico, while training for the Intercontinental Cup.

Under the guidance of Miami-based agent Joe Cubas, who helped Fernandez and Hernandez defect, the two righthanders sought and were granted residency in the Dominican Republic. Dominicans aren't subject to the draft, so Major League Baseball ruled that Fernandez and Hernandez were free to cut a deal with any team.

Previous Cuban defectors who sought asylum in the

United States were subject either to a special lottery, as were Cardinals righthander Rene Arocha and Mets shortstop Rey Ordonez, or to the June draft, as was Athletics righthander Ariel Prieto.

"The problem we had in Cuba was that there's not access there for all 30 clubs to go in and scout there," said Bill Murray, MLB's executive director of baseball operations. "Some clubs could, some clubs couldn't. Canadian clubs could get a visa, or maybe a team had an employee born in Cuba. It wasn't fair for some clubs to get a leg up."

Speaking of getting a leg up, the Diamondbacks did just that in signing the other two key Cuban talents available in 1996, two years before the expansion team was to begin major league play. Righthanders Vladimir Nunez, 20, and Larry Rodriguez, 21, signed minor league contracts Feb. 1. Nunez received a $1.75 million signing bonus while Rodriguez received $1.25 million.

## McSherry's Death

Roberto Alomar's insolence wasn't anywhere near the worst turn of events regarding umpires in 1996. The most sad and shocking blow came when popular veteran umpire John McSherry collapsed and died during the Expos-Reds game on Opening Day in

**Umpire Dies.** Veteran National League umpire John McSherry, 52, died on the job while umpiring a game in Cincinnati.

# 1996 MAJOR LEAGUE ALL-STAR GAME

## Homeboy Piazza Leads NL To Third Straight Win

Mike Piazza, raised in suburban Norristown, made Philadelphia's Veterans Stadium his own personal showcase in winning MVP honors at the 1996 All-Star Game.

The Dodgers catcher clouted a solo homer and run-scoring double while nine National League hurlers scattered seven hits for a 6-0 victory over the American League.

It was the first shutout in All-Star Game play since the AL's 2-0 win in 1990, and the NL's first whitewash since 1987.

Righthander John Smoltz (Braves) got the win by pitching the first two frames. No other NL pitcher worked more than an inning.

Piazza homered to start the second inning off losing pitcher Charles Nagy (Indians), his second straight All-Star Game homer. He hit one in his last at-bat in the '95 contest.

Neither team walked a batter, while NL pitchers recorded five strikeouts—three at the expense of Indians slugger Albert Belle.

### TOP VOTE GETTERS

#### AMERICAN LEAGUE

**CATCHER:** 1. Ivan Rodriguez, Rangers, 1,441,920; 2. Sandy Alomar, Indians, 1,370,428; 3. Dan Wilson, Mariners, 583,577.

**FIRST BASE:** 1. Frank Thomas, White Sox, 1,215,690; 2. Will Clark, Rangers, 703,775; 3. Eddie Murray, Indians, 531,409.

**SECOND BASE:** 1. Roberto Alomar, Orioles, 2,153,993; 2. Carlos Baerga, Indians, 984,021; 3. Chuck Knoblauch, Twins, 448,601.

**THIRD BASE:** 1. Wade Boggs, Yankees, 1,282,767; 2. Jim Thome, Indians, 954,265; 3. Dean Palmer, Rangers, 559,810.

**SHORTSTOP:** 1. Cal Ripken, Orioles, 2,550,275; 2. Omar Vizquel, Indians, 829,519; 3. Alex Rodriguez, Mariners, 609,679.

**OUTFIELD:** 1. Ken Griffey, Mariners, 3,064,814; 2. Albert Belle, Indians, 1,692,409; 3. Kenny Lofton, Indians, 1,337,262; 4. Brady Anderson, Orioles, 1,153,904; 5. Jay Buhner, Mariners, 768,401; 6. Paul O'Neill, Yankees, 589,754; 7. Kirby Puckett, Twins, 582,859; 8. Bobby Bonilla, Orioles, 570,716; 9. Manny Ramirez, Indians, 504,700.

#### NATIONAL LEAGUE

**CATCHER:** 1. Mike Piazza, Dodgers, 2,272,115; 2. Javier Lopez, Braves, 523,218; 3. Jayhawk Owens, Rockies, 374,184.

**FIRST BASE:** 1. Fred McGriff, Braves, 1,358,094; 2. Jeff Bagwell, Astros, 1,186,569; 3. Andres Galarraga, Rockies, 732,045.

**SECOND BASE:** 1. Craig Biggio, Astros, 1,241,228; 2. Ryne Sandberg, Cubs, 818,035; 3. Eric Young, Rockies, 597,057.

**THIRD BASE:** 1. Matt Williams, Giants, 958,422; 2. Ken Caminiti, Padres, 908,971; 3. Chipper Jones, Braves, 851,000.

**SHORTSTOP:** 1. Barry Larkin, Reds, 1,085,711; 2. Ozzie Smith, Cardinals, 796,316; 3. Walt Weiss, Rockies, 638,504.

**OUTFIELD:** 1. Barry Bonds, Giants, 1,750,498; 2. Tony Gwynn, Padres, 1,485,693; 3. Dante Bichette, Rockies, 980,802; 4. David Justice, Braves, 791,044; 5. Henry Rodriguez, Expos, 755,620; 6. Ryan Klesko, Braves, 693,602; 7. Larry Walker, Rockies, 666,615; 8. Ellis Burks, Rockies, 651,485; 9. Sammy Sosa, Cubs, 636,492.

### ROSTERS

#### AMERICAN LEAGUE

**MANAGER:** Mike Hargrove, Indians.

**PITCHERS:** Chuck Finley, Angels; Roberto Hernandez, White Sox; Jose Mesa, Indians; Jeff Montgomery, Royals; **Charles Nagy, Indians**; Roger Pavlik, Rangers; Troy Percival, Angels; Andy Pettitte, Yankees; John Wetteland, Yankees.

**CATCHERS: Ivan Rodriguez, Rangers**; Sandy Alomar, Indians; Dan Wilson, Mariners.

**INFIELDERS: Roberto Alomar (2b), Orioles**; **Wade Boggs**

**(3b), Yankees**; Travis Fryman, Tigers; Chuck Knoblauch, Twins; Edgar Martinez, Mariners; Mark McGwire, Athletics; **Cal Ripken (ss), Orioles**; Alex Rodriguez, Mariners; x-Frank Thomas (1b), White Sox; y-**Mo Vaughn (1b), Red Sox**.

**OUTFIELDERS:** y-Brady Anderson, Orioles; **Albert Belle (lf), Indians**; Jay Buhner (rf), **Mariners**; Joe Carter, Blue Jays; x-Ken Griffey (cf), Mariners; **Kenny Lofton (cf), Indians**; Greg Vaughn, Brewers.

#### NATIONAL LEAGUE

**MANAGER:** Bobby Cox, Braves.

**PITCHERS:** Ricky Bottalico, Phillies; Kevin Brown, Marlins; Tom Glavine, Braves; Al Leiter, Marlins; Greg Maddux, Braves; Pedro Martinez, Expos; **John Smoltz, Braves**; Steve Trachsel, Cubs; Mark Wohlers, Braves; Todd Worrell, Dodgers.

**CATCHERS:** Todd Hundley, Mets; Jason Kendall, Pirates; **Mike Piazza, Dodgers.**

**INFIELDERS:** Jeff Bagwell, Astros; **Craig Biggio (2b), Astros**; y-Ken Caminiti, Padres; Mark Grudzielanek, Expos; y-**Chipper Jones (3b), Braves**; **Barry Larkin (ss), Reds**; **Fred McGriff (1b), Braves**; Ozzie Smith, Cardinals; x-Matt Williams (3b), Giants; Eric Young, Rockies.

**OUTFIELDERS: Dante Bichette (rf), Rockies; Barry Bonds (lf), Giants**; Ellis Burks, Rockies; x-Tony Gwynn (rf), Padres; **Lance Johnson (cf), Mets**; y-Henry Rodriguez, Expos; Gary Sheffield, Marlins.

Starters in **boldface**.
x-injured, did not play. y-injury replacement.

### July 9 in Philadelphia
### National League 6, American League 0

| American | ab | r | h | bi | bb | so | National | ab | r | h | bi | bb | so |
|---|---|---|---|---|---|---|---|---|---|---|---|---|---|
| Lofton cf | 3 | 0 | 2 | 0 | 0 | 0 | Johnson cf | 4 | 1 | 3 | 0 | 0 | 0 |
| Carter cf | 1 | 0 | 1 | 0 | 0 | 0 | Larkin ss | 3 | 1 | 1 | 0 | 0 | 0 |
| Boggs 3b | 3 | 0 | 0 | 0 | 0 | 0 | Smith ss | 1 | 0 | 0 | 0 | 0 | 0 |
| Fryman ph-3b | 1 | 0 | 0 | 0 | 0 | 1 | Bonds lf | 3 | 0 | 1 | 1 | 0 | 0 |
| R. Alomar 2b | 3 | 0 | 1 | 0 | 0 | 0 | P. Martinez p | 0 | 0 | 0 | 0 | 0 | 0 |
| Knoblauch 2b | 1 | 0 | 1 | 0 | 0 | 0 | Sheffield rf | 1 | 0 | 0 | 0 | 0 | 0 |
| Belle lf | 4 | 0 | 0 | 0 | 0 | 3 | McGriff 1b | 2 | 0 | 0 | 0 | 0 | 2 |
| M. Vaughn 1b | 3 | 0 | 1 | 0 | 0 | 0 | Glavine p | 0 | 0 | 0 | 0 | 0 | 0 |
| McGwire 1b | 1 | 0 | 0 | 0 | 0 | 0 | Caminiti 3b | 2 | 1 | 1 | 1 | 0 | 1 |
| I. Rodriguez c | 2 | 0 | 0 | 0 | 0 | 1 | Worrell p | 0 | 0 | 0 | 0 | 0 | 0 |
| S. Alomar ph-c | 2 | 0 | 0 | 0 | 0 | 0 | Wohlers p | 0 | 0 | 0 | 0 | 0 | 0 |
| Ripken ss | 3 | 0 | 0 | 0 | 0 | 0 | Leiter p | 0 | 0 | 0 | 0 | 0 | 0 |
| Percival p | 0 | 0 | 0 | 0 | 0 | 0 | Piazza c | 3 | 1 | 2 | 2 | 0 | 1 |
| Hernandez p | 0 | 0 | 0 | 0 | 0 | 0 | Hundley c | 1 | 0 | 0 | 0 | 0 | 0 |
| Wilson ph | 1 | 0 | 0 | 0 | 0 | 0 | Kendall c | 0 | 0 | 0 | 0 | 0 | 0 |
| Anderson rf | 2 | 0 | 0 | 0 | 0 | 0 | Bichette rf | 3 | 1 | 1 | 0 | 0 | 1 |
| Pavlik p | 0 | 0 | 0 | 0 | 0 | 0 | Trachsel p | 0 | 0 | 0 | 0 | 0 | 0 |
| A. Rodriguez ss | 1 | 0 | 0 | 0 | 0 | 0 | Grudzielanek 3b | 1 | 0 | 0 | 0 | 0 | 0 |
| Nagy p | 0 | 0 | 0 | 0 | 0 | 0 | Jones 3b | 2 | 1 | 1 | 0 | 0 | 0 |
| E. Martinez ph | 1 | 0 | 0 | 0 | 0 | 0 | Bottalico p | 0 | 0 | 0 | 0 | 0 | 0 |
| Finley p | 0 | 0 | 0 | 0 | 0 | 0 | Burks lf | 2 | 0 | 1 | 0 | 0 | 1 |
| Buhner ph-rf | 2 | 0 | 0 | 0 | 0 | 0 | Biggio 2b | 3 | 0 | 0 | 1 | 0 | 1 |
| | | | | | | | Young pr-2b | 1 | 0 | 0 | 0 | 0 | 0 |
| | | | | | | | Smoltz p | 0 | 0 | 0 | 0 | 0 | 0 |
| | | | | | | | H. Rodriguez ph | 1 | 0 | 1 | 1 | 0 | 0 |
| | | | | | | | Brown p | 0 | 0 | 0 | 0 | 0 | 0 |
| | | | | | | | Bagwell 1b | 2 | 0 | 0 | 0 | 0 | 1 |
| **Totals** | **34** | **0** | **7** | **0** | **0** | **5** | **Totals** | **35** | **6** | **12** | **6** | **0** | **8** |

| | | |
|---|---|---|
| American | 000 000 000 | —0 |
| National | 121 002 00x | —6 |

E—Caminiti. DP—American 1, National 1. LOB—American 7, National 5. 2B—M. Vaughn, Johnson, Piazza, Bichette. 3B—Burks. HR—Piazza, Caminiti. SB—Lofton 2, Johnson. CS—Bonds, Johnson.

| American | ip | h | r | er | bb | so | National | ip | h | r | er | bb | so |
|---|---|---|---|---|---|---|---|---|---|---|---|---|---|
| Nagy L | 2 | 4 | 3 | 3 | 0 | 1 | Smoltz W | 2 | 2 | 0 | 0 | 0 | 1 |
| Finley | 2 | 3 | 1 | 1 | 0 | 4 | Brown | 1 | 0 | 0 | 0 | 0 | 0 |
| Pavlik | 2 | 3 | 2 | 2 | 0 | 2 | Glavine | 1 | 0 | 0 | 0 | 0 | 1 |
| Percival | 1 | 1 | 0 | 0 | 0 | 1 | Bottalico | 1 | 0 | 0 | 0 | 0 | 1 |
| Hernandez | 1 | 1 | 0 | 0 | 0 | 0 | P. Martinez | 1 | 2 | 0 | 0 | 0 | 1 |
| | | | | | | | Trachsel | 1 | 0 | 0 | 0 | 0 | 1 |
| | | | | | | | Worrell | 1 | 2 | 0 | 0 | 0 | 1 |
| | | | | | | | Wohlers | ⅔ | 1 | 0 | 0 | 0 | 0 |
| | | | | | | | Leiter | ⅓ | 0 | 0 | 0 | 0 | 0 |

WP—Pavlik.

Umpires: HP—Randy Marsh; 1B—Larry McCoy; 2B—Charlie Reliford; 3B—Joe Brinkman; LF—Larry Poncino; RF—Chuck Meriwether.

T—2:35. A—62,670.

Cincinnati April 1.

McSherry, 51, spent 25 years as a National League umpire and was one of the game's best-liked arbiters. Calling balls and strikes that day in Cincinnati, he collapsed near home plate and was pronounced dead about an hour later at University Hospital.

"We respected John McSherry," Reds first baseman Hal Morris said. "He never compromised his integrity and he worked hard out there. He was one of the few umpires in the world who will tell you, 'I missed one.'"

McSherry, who appeared healthy before the game, had a series of physical problems. In 1991, he collapsed because of dehydration during a Cardinals-Braves game. In August of 1995, he took a leave of absence after complaining of shortness of breath during a series between the Braves and Cubs.

The sudden death of McSherry, who was listed as weighing 328 pounds, raised concern around baseball that umpires' physical condition needed to be monitored more carefully. McSherry actually weighed closer to 400. Eric Gregg was listed at 325, Ken Kaiser 288 and Joe West 275.

"The outsiders focused entirely on John's weight after his death," veteran umpire Randy Marsh said. "But the people who knew him thought about what a good, hardworking person he was. He probably spent a larger percentage of the day thinking about baseball than any umpire in the league."

## Schott Gets Banned

Reds owner Marge Schott, known for making comments embarrassing to the industry, did just that after McSherry died by complaining that the rescheduling of the game for the next day would hurt her club financially. "I feel cheated," she said. But she saved her most controversial words for later in April during an infamous ESPN interview that prompted her suspension from baseball.

Speaking with the network, Schott discussed Adolf Hitler and said, "Everybody knows he was good at the beginning, but he just went too far." (She had made a virtually identical comment to The New York Times four years before.) The remark touched off a raging controversy over whether she was fit to run a major league team. MLB decided she wasn't June 12, suspending her from day-to-day control of the Reds through the 1998 season.

"Baseball will never condone any type of racism," NL president Len Coleman said.

This was Schott's second such banishment from the game. On Feb. 2, 1993, MLB suspended Schott for one year for bringing "disrepute and embarrassment" to the game with her repeated use of racial and ethnic slurs. She took sensitivity training as part of her suspension.

MLB approved Reds controller John Allen, 47, as Schott's replacement Aug. 9. Among his first moves were instituting special game promotions, flying championship banners at Riverfront Stadium—Schott had packed them away—and reassuring players that money would be spent to upgrade clubhouse facilities. Attendance jumped 10 percent after Allen took control.

"The support for the change has been most rewarding," Allen said. "This shows that if you do what's

**Untimely Remarks.** Cincinnati owner Marge Schott was censured for inappropriate comments about Adolph Hitler.

right from a fan's perspective, things will work out."

## MLB Dips Into Mexico

In a litmus test of how well Major League Baseball might be able to expand internationally, the Mets and Padres participated in the first regular-season series outside the United States and Canada Aug. 16-18 by playing three games in Monterrey, Mexico. From most accounts, the test went rather poorly.

Though fan support at Estadio Monterrey was strong and enthusiastic, players generally disliked the experience.

"You can have this —— place," Mets catcher Todd Hundley said. "It ain't worth coming here."

Hundley, stricken with diarrhea, was one of a handful of players on both clubs who experienced ailments related to the unusual diet and arid summer climate of northern Mexico. Padres third baseman Ken Caminiti suffered from dehydration. New York closer John Franco got a delayed case of diarrhea. Mets infielder Edgardo Alfonzo and outfielder Chris Jones both felt queasy by the final day of the trip.

"Let other teams come here and get sick," Hundley said. "It's like Russian roulette. You might get sick. You might not. You're just taking your chances."

During a weekend billed as La Primera Serie, in which the Padres won two games and the Mets one, stomach ailments were only a secondary issue. The primary complaint for players on both clubs was inadequate lighting and a background that made fly balls almost impossible to see during the first two games, played at night.

"After the first night, I wasn't really looking forward to the second game at all," Mets center fielder Lance Johnson said. "These were probably the hardest conditions I've played in in a long, long time."

San Diego star Tony Gwynn thought expansion to Mexico can occur, but not within the five-year window he had heard some executives discuss. The Padres are planning to play another series in Monterrey in 1997 against the Astros.

"My own opinion is they're quite a bit away," Gwynn said. "Not so much because of the field or the stadium, but in trying to convince people that this is a

## MARCH

**31**—In the first regular-season major league game to be played in March, a crowd of 57,467 watched as the Mariners defeated the White Sox 3-2 in 12 innings at the Kingdome in Seattle.

## APRIL

**1**—The Mets rallied from a 6-0 deficit to post a 7-6 victory over the Cardinals in the biggest opening-day comeback of this century.

**2**—Tigers first baseman Cecil Fielder stole the first base in his 1,097-game career in Detroit's 10-6 victory over the Twins, snapping the longest drought in history.

**21**—Baltimore's Brady Anderson led off his fourth straight game with a home run, a major league record.

**22**—The Mariners set a major league record for homers in the month of April with 39, breaking the White Sox' 1984 mark of 38. Seattle finished the month with 44.

**26**—Florida's Gary Sheffield hit his 11th home run of the month, tying the major league record. Baltimore's Brady Anderson tied the mark on the 28th while San Francisco's Barry Bonds matched the feat on the 30th.

**30**—The Yankees' 13-10 defeat of Baltimore established a major league record for the longest nine-inning game in history: 4 hours, 21 minutes. That broke the mark of 4:18 set by the Dodgers and Giants on Oct. 2, 1962.

## MAY

**4**—Baltimore's Brady Anderson becomes the fastest player ever to reach 15 home runs in a season with a shot off the Brewers' Steve Sparks.

**5**—The Reds' Eric Davis became the 18th player in history to hit a grand slam in consecutive contests.

**11**—Marlins lefthander Al Leiter threw the season's first no-hitter in an 11-0 win against the Colorado Rockies. It was the first no-hitter for Leiter and the Marlins.

**12**—Astros catcher Jerry Goff tied a major league record for passed balls when he committed six in a 7-6 loss to Montreal. He was sent back to the minors a day after the game.

**14**—Righthander Dwight Gooden threw the eighth no-hitter in Yankees history and the first of his career in a 2-0 victory over the Mariners.

**17**—Dave Nilsson of the Brewers hit two homers in the sixth inning, the third time a player hit two homers in an inning. The previous day, Cubs outfielder Sammy Sosa accomplished the feat, making it the first time players had hit two homers in the same frame on consecutive days.

**17**—In the ninth inning of the Orioles' 14-13 win over the Mariners, catcher Chris Hoiles homered to become the 12th player in history to hit a two-out grand slam to decide a contest by one run.

**17**—Braves outfielder Jermaine Dye became the 71st player to homer in his first major league at-bat.

**21**—Ken Griffey became the seventh youngest player to reach 200 career homers in Seattle's 13-7 win against the Red Sox. The other six—Mel Ott, Eddie Mathews, Jimmie Foxx, Mickey Mantle, Frank Robinson and Henry Aaron—are all in the Hall of Fame.

**31**—Expos outfielder Henry Rodriguez hit his 20th homer, setting a NL mark for most home runs by the end of May, in a 7-4 win over the Giants.

## JUNE

**4**—The Pirates made Clemson righthander Kris Benson the top pick in the amateur free-agent draft. The Devil Rays and Diamondbacks made their first ever selections, with Tampa Bay choosing outfielder Paul Wilder and Arizona taking pitcher Nick Bierbrodt.

**6**—In Boston's 7-4 defeat of the White Sox, shortstop John Valentin hit for the cycle to become the first player in history to hit for the cycle and turn an unassisted triple play in a

**Ken Griffey**
Hit 200th career homer May 21

career. He recorded the triple play on July 8, 1994.

**14**—Cal Ripken played in his 2,216 straight game, surpassing the world record formerly owned by Japan's Sachio Kinugasa, who played in 2,215 consecutive games for the Hiroshima Carp from Oct. 19, 1970 to Oct. 22, 1987.

**23**—In a 3-2 loss to Montreal, St. Louis third baseman Gary Gaetti hit his 300th career homer. Two days later, Mark McGwire of Oakland reached the mark with a two-homer game.

**30**—Rockies second baseman Eric Young tied a modern-day major league mark by recording six stolen bases in a 16-15 win over the Dodgers.

## JULY

**6**—New York's John Wetteland set a record by recording his 20th save in 20 consecutive appearances, breaking the mark of 19 set by Lee Smith in 1983.

**9**—In the 67th All-Star Game, played at Veterans Stadium in Philadelphia, the NL defeated the AL 6-0. Dodgers catcher Mike Piazza grabbed the MVP award with a home run, double and two RBIs.

**12**—Twins outfielder Kirby Puckett announced his retirement due to irreversible retina damage in his right eye. The Twins retired his number 34 on Kirby Puckett Night Sept. 7.

**24**—Indians starter Dennis Martinez won the 240th game of his career, 10-0 over Toronto. The victory broke Juan Marichal's mark for most wins by a Latin American pitcher.

**28**—Darryl Strawberry hit a two-run homer to rally the Yankees to a 3-2 victory against Kansas City. It was Strawberry's 300th career homer, making him the fifth player to reach that plateau during the 1996 season.

**29**—One month after suffering a mild heart attack, Tommy Lasorda announced his retirement as manager of the Dodgers after 21 years. Bill Russell assumed managerial duties.

**31**—Rangers outfielder Juan Gonzalez tied a record for homers in July with his 15th in a 9-2 win over the Yankees. The record was shared by Joe DiMaggio (1937), Hank Greenberg (1938) and Joe Adcock (1956).

**31**—The Tigers traded first baseman Cecil Fielder to the Yankees for outfielder Ruben Sierra, marking the first time players with more than 220 home runs had been traded for one another.

## AUGUST

**4**—Former Orioles manager Earl Weaver, pitcher Jim Bunning, Negro League pitcher Bill Foster and early manager Ned Hanlon were inducted into the National Baseball Hall of Fame.

**9**—Padres outfielder Greg Vaughn collected his 100th RBI during a 12-3 win over Pittsburgh, making him the first player in history to register 100 RBIs in a season while playing for teams in both leagues. Vaughn had 95 RBIs with Milwaukee before being traded to San Diego.

**12**—Oakland's Geronimo Berroa became the 10th player in history to record two three-homer games in a season with three blasts in an 11-1 win against the Twins. He also went deep three times against the Yankees May 22.

**16**—The Padres beat the Mets 15-10 in the opening contest of their three-game series played in Monterrey, Mexico. It marked the first major league regular-season game ever played outside the U.S. or Canada.

**16**—Atlanta's John Smoltz became the first 20-game winner of the season, fanning six in seven innings of a 5-4 Atlanta win over Pittsburgh.

**19**—The Rangers established an AL standard by playing their 15th consecutive game without an error in a 10-3 triumph over Cleveland. Texas failed to tie the major league record, held by the 1992 Cardinals, when Kevin Elster committed an error during the team's 10-4 loss to Cleveland the next day.

**21**—Seattle shortstop Alex Rodriguez connected on his 30th homer during the Mariners' 10-5 loss to Baltimore, becoming the fifth shortstop in history to hit 30 in a season. Cal Ripken and Rico Petrocelli did it once each, while Vern Stephens accomplished the feat twice. Ernie Banks had five such seasons.

**25**—Despite an 8-5 loss to the Red Sox, the Mariners set a record by smacking back-to-back homers for the 17th time, snapping a record shared by the 1977 Red Sox and 1982 Brewers. Alex Rodriguez homered off Joe Hudson and Ken Griffey followed with a shot off Eric Gunderson.

**28**—The Rockies tied an NL mark when Vinny Castilla became the fourth Colorado player to reach the 100 RBI plateau for the season. He joined Andres Galarraga, Ellis Burks and Dante Bichette as the Rockies became the first team to achieve the feat since the 1929 Chicago Cubs and Philadelphia Athletics.

**29**—Bobby Bonilla's two-homer performance in a 9-6 loss to Seattle gave the Orioles a major league-record seventh player with 20 or more homers in a season. Bonilla joined teammates Rafael Palmeiro, Brady Anderson, Roberto Alomar, B.J. Surhoff, Cal Ripken and Chris Hoiles in setting the mark. The last team to have six or more players with 20 or more homers was the 1956 Detroit Tigers.

### SEPTEMBER

**2**—Boston's Mike Greenwell set a record by driving in all nine runs in a 9-8, 10-inning win over the Mariners. Greenwell's nine RBIs surpassed George Kelly of the New York Giants (1924) and Bob Johnson of the Philadelphia Athletics (1938) for the most RBIs by a player responsible for all his team's runs.

**2**—The Yankees welcomed righthander David Cone back to their rotation after he missed most of the season because of an aneurysm in his pitching arm. Cone responded with seven no-hit innings, fanning six, to lead New York past Oakland 5-0.

**2**—In an 8-5 loss to the Dodgers, the Mets' Todd Hundley set a single-season home run record for switch-hitters with his 39th round tripper, breaking Howard Johnson's 1991 mark of 38.

**3**—The Cardinals' Todd Stottlemyre earned a 12-3 win against the Astros, giving him and his father Mel the record for most victories by a father-son duo. The Stottlemyres had combined for 259 wins, breaking the old mark of Steve and Dizzy Trout.

**5**—Minnesota's Paul Molitor collected his 200th hit of the year in a 6-2 win over California. Molitor joined Sam Rice of the Washington Senators as the only players in history to have a 200-hit season after their 40th birthday.

**6**—Brett Butler returned to the Dodgers lineup after missing nearly four months because of treatment for tonsil cancer. Butler went 1-for-3 with a walk and scored the winning run in a 2-1 win over the Pirates.

**6**—Baltimore's Eddie Murray became the third player in history to register 3,000 hits and 500 homers when he hit No. 500 off Detroit's Felipe Lira in a 5-4 loss. Murray joined Henry Aaron and Willie Mays as the only players to accomplish the feat.

**8**—Florida's Gary Sheffield hit the majors 4,459th homer of the season, setting a record. The old mark of 4,458 was set in 1987.

**11**—San Diego's Ken Caminiti homered from both sides of the plate for the fourth time, breaking a major league record he set in 1995.

**12**—Colorado's Ellis Burks stole his 30th base of the year, becoming the 15th player in history to hit 30 homers and steal 30 bases in a season.

**12**—Seattle shortstop Alex Rodriguez hit a first-inning double in an 8-5 win against Kansas City, giving him 88 extra-base hits for the season. That broke Robin Yount's record for most extra-base hits in a season by a shortstop.

**13**—The Rockies tied a record when Dante Bichette hit his 30th homer of the season in a 6-3 win over the Astros. The homer gave Colorado four players with 30 or more in a season, the third time a team had accomplished the feat. The others were the 1995 Rockies and the 1977 Dodgers. Bichette's blast also put him in the 30-30 club, making him

and Ellis Burks the first teammates to achieve the feat since Howard Johnson and Darryl Strawberry did it for the 1987 Mets.

**13**—In a 7-4 loss to the Orioles, the Tigers gave up their 227th home run of the season, breaking a record held previously by the 1987 Orioles.

**14**—During a 6-5 victory over Atlanta, the Mets' Todd Hundley hit his 41st home run of the season, breaking Roy Campanella's 43-year-old record for homers by a catcher.

**14**—Oakland's Mark McGwire became the 13th player in history to reach 50 home runs in Oakland's 9-8 win over Cleveland.

**Eddie Murray**
Hit 500th homer Sept. 6

**15**—The Orioles set a record when catcher Mark Parent hit the 241st home run of the season during a 16-6 win over the Tigers. The Orioles eclipsed the 1961 Yankees for most homers by a team in a season.

**16**—Minnesota's Paul Molitor became the 21st player to reach the 3,000-hit mark when he tripled in the fifth inning off the Royals' Jose Rosado in a 6-5 loss.

**16**—Barry Bonds became the third player in history to tally 40 home runs and 30 steals in a season, joining Henry Aaron (1963) and Jose Canseco (1988). Colorado's Ellis Burks joined the club later in the season.

**17**—Righthander Hideo Nomo of the Dodgers threw his first career no-hitter, blanking the Rockies 9-0 at Colorado's Coors Field. It was the 20th no-hitter in Dodgers history.

**17**—The Indians clinched their second consecutive AL Central Division title with a 9-4 win over the White Sox.

**18**—Boston's Roger Clemens equalled his own major league mark with 20 strikeouts in a 4-0 win over Detroit. Clemens, who walked none, also fanned 20 Mariners in 1986.

**21**—During a 13-6 loss to the Brewers, the Tigers fanned eight times to set a record for most strikeouts in a season with 1,208. The previous mark was 1,203 by the 1968 Mets.

**24**—Boston's Mo Vaughn hammered three homers against the Orioles to become the first player since former Red Sox slugger Jim Rice to collect 40 homers and 200 hits in a season.

**24**—The Cardinals clinched the NL Central Division, their first division title since 1987, with a 7-1 win over the Pirates.

**25**—Barry Bonds set an NL mark with his 149th walk of the season, breaking the record shared by Eddie Stanky (1945) and Jim Wynn (1969).

**25**—The Yankees clinched their first AL East title since 1981 with a 19-2 shellacking of the Brewers.

**27**—Barry Bonds joined Jose Canseco as the only players ever to hit 40 homers and steal 40 bases in the same season.

**27**—The Rangers clinched the AL West title, the first playoff berth in team history, when Seattle lost.

**29**—The Rockies became the second team in history to have three 40-homer players when Vinny Castilla hit No. 40, joining Ellis Burks and Andres Galarraga. The 1973 Braves, with Henry Aaron, Darrell Evans and Davey Johnson, first accomplished the feat. The Rockies also tied an NL mark with their 221st homer of the season, equalling the 1947 Giants and the 1956 Reds.

**29**—Baltimore's Brady Anderson set a major league mark with his 12th leadoff home run, breaking Bobby Bonds' 1973 record of 11.

**29**—The Padres clinched the NL West crown by completing a three-game sweep of the Dodgers, their first title since 1984.

**29**—Shortstop Alan Trammel of the Tigers ended his 20-year career with a base hit in his final at-bat.

viable place to live."

At least some players recognized that their temporary discomfort was part of a necessary step toward breaking baseball's stagnation and extending an olive branch to Latin America.

"I was ready to come here," said Mets second baseman Carlos Baerga, a native of Puerto Rico. "Baseball needs to be Spanish. Major League Baseball needs to go international. We're idols in Latin America. A lot of these kids can't come to the States to watch us play.

"Basketball goes everywhere. Football, too. We've got to go other places."

## Cooperstown Welcomes Four

The Veterans Committee made up for whatever work it felt the baseball writers didn't do, choosing four new members for induction to the Hall of Fame.

Jim Bunning, Earl Weaver, Bill Foster and Ned Hanlon were inducted during ceremonies Aug. 4 in Cooperstown. They were the only ones inducted because the Baseball Writers Association of America chose no one in 1996.

Bunning, 64, played 17 seasons with the Tigers and Phillies, compiling a career record of 224-184 and a 3.27 ERA. He also pitched a perfect game for Philadelphia on Father's Day 1964 against the Mets.

Weaver, 65, managed the Baltimore Orioles for 17 seasons, with a career record of 1,480-1,060, six American League East titles, four pennants and the 1970 World Series championship. He managed only one team with a losing record—his last, which went 73-89 in 1986. But he generally is remembered for his irascible attitude and combative behavior toward umpires.

"Those incidents are still kind of embarrassing," he said. "When I see the clips I say, 'How could I do that?' "

The other Baltimore manager inducted was undoubtedly not as well known. Hanlon, who lived from 1857-1937, helped advance the game during his years as a manager, most of them in Baltimore.

Hanlon enjoyed a creditable 13-year career as an outfielder, batting .260 lifetime with 930 runs and 329 stolen bases. He spent 1889-92 as a player-manager with Pittsburgh and Baltimore.

Hanlon managed Baltimore through 1898, moving on to Brooklyn from 1899-1905 and finishing his career with two seasons in Cincinnati. He compiled a career record of 1,313-1,164.

Perhaps more important were his innovations. He traveled around the world after the 1888 season, bringing baseball to several nations, including New Zealand, for the first time. Hanlon also used his home field to get a true home-field advantage. For instance, the foul lines were sloped for bunts and the ground was kept hard for "Baltimore chops."

Foster, who lived from 1904-78, was one of the best lefthanders in the history of the Negro Leagues. The half-brother of Rube Foster, regarded as the father of the Negro Leagues, Foster played from 1923-37 for several teams but he made his name with the Chicago American Giants.

Foster won 137 career games and was occasionally regarded as the best big-game pitcher ever to play in the Negro Leagues. In 1927, he went 32-3 (21-3 in league games) and pitched the American Giants to

**Hall Of Famer.** Former Baltimore skipper Earl Weaver was one of four elected to the Hall of Fame in 1996.

playoff wins over Satchel Paige's Birmingham Black Barons, then to a second consecutive World Series title over the Bacharach Giants.

Foster managed at the end of his career, and after he retired from professional baseball he managed the Harlem Globetrotters for a short time. He was dean of men and baseball coach at Alcorn State University from 1960 until shortly before his death.

## Major League News Roundup

■ Major League Baseball addressed its longstanding marketing void by hiring Gregory Murphy on June 11 as CEO of a new entity, Major League Baseball Enterprises.

"If you don't know where you're going, any road will get you there," Murphy said of MLB's old approach that resulted in the disaster of The Baseball Network. "There's been a lot of that going on. What we need to do is very firmly and very clearly decide what road we're going down—and why."

Murphy, 47, came from outside the sports industry. He was known best for his work with General Foods and Kraft Foods Bakery Companies, where he developed the fat-free Entenmann's line.

Murphy vowed to work with the Players Association to market the game cooperatively.

"The players care passionately about this game," he said. "We need to work with them to focus on the fans. Fans first. Fans first. If we do that, this game will boom."

■ To the surprise of few, the ballyhooed United League went the way of Atlantis, becoming nothing more than a footnote in baseball history.

Founders of the league had presented it in November 1994 as an alternative to the major leagues during the height of hand-wringing over the strike. They said the league would open in 1996 at the latest.

# 1996 MAJOR LEAGUE FREE AGENTS

A total of 147 players were eligible for free agency following the 1996 season. Generally, players become eligible after six full major league seasons.

The number was expected to decrease as players/clubs exercised 1997 options and players elected not to file by the prescribed deadline. In addition, the pending resolution of a new Basic Agreement between the owners and Players Association will affect the status of 18 players whose free agency hinges on players being granted service time for the days lost to the 1994 strike.

Players have been designated as Type A, B and C free agents, as determined by a rating system that examines statistics from the last two years. In order to receive draft-pick compensation for these free agents, teams must have offered them arbitration by Dec. 7, 1996.

Teams signing a Type A free agent (the top 30 percent at each position) must give his former team a first-round pick (or a second-round pick if the signing team owns one of the first 15 selections). The former team also gets a supplemental pick after the first round. Teams signing a Type B free agent (31-50 percent) surrender the same pick as for a Type A, but the former team doesn't receive a bonus pick. Teams losing a Type C free agent (51-60) get a supplemental pick after the second round.

Type A, B and C players who became free agents because of repeater rights don't require compensation in any case.

**Boston's Roger Clemens**

MORRIS FOSTOFF

### ATLANTA (9)
Steve Avery, lhp (B)
Rafael Belliard, ss
Mike Bielecki, rhp (B)
Mark Lemke, 2b (A)
Terry Pendleton, 3b (A)
%#Luis Polonia, of
Dwight Smith, of
John Smoltz, rhp (A)
Jerome Walton, of (B)

### BALTIMORE (11)
%Bobby Bonilla, of (A)
Mike Devereaux, of (B)
Pete Incaviglia, of
Roger McDowell, rhp (B)
%Eddie Murray, 1b (B)
Jimmy Myers, lhp
%Jesse Orosco, lhp (A)
%Mark Parent, c
Bill Ripken, 2b
David Wells, lhp (A)
Todd Zeile, 3b (A)

### BOSTON (5)
Roger Clemens, rhp (A)
Brent Cookson, of
Mike Maddux, rhp (A)
*Tim Naehring, 3b (A)
%Mike Stanley, c (A)

### CALIFORNIA (4)
Shawn Boskie, rhp (B)
David Holdridge, rhp
%Jack Howell, 3b
Rex Hudler, of

### CHICAGO/AL (9)
%#Harold Baines, dh (B)
Pat Borders, c
*Tony Castillo, lhp (A)
*Alex Fernandez, rhp (A)
Marvin Freeman, rhp
Chad Kreuter, c
%Don Slaught, c (B)
Kevin Tapani, rhp (A)
%Danny Tartabull, of (B)

### CHICAGO/NL (5)
*Luis Gonzalez, of (B)
%Dave Magadan, 3b (B)
Jaime Navarro, rhp (A)
%Bob Patterson, lhp (A)
Ryne Sandberg, 2b (B)

### CINCINNATI (8)
Eric Davis, of (B)
Lenny Harris, inf
*Thomas Howard, of (C)
%Kevin Mitchell, of (B)
%Joe Oliver, c (A)
%Chris Sabo, 3b
Lee Smith, rhp (B)

FRANK RAGSDALE

**Cleveland's Albert Belle**

### CLEVELAND (8)
Albert Belle, of (A)
Mark Carreon, of (B)
Scott Leius, 3b
%Dennis Martinez, rhp (A)
Kent Mercker, lhp
%Tony Pena, c
Eric Plunk, rhp (A)
Greg Swindell, lhp

### COLORADO (4)
Eric Anthony, of (C)
Pedro Castellano, 3b
+Jeff Reed, c (B)
Bret Saberhagen, rhp

### DETROIT (0)
No free agents

### FLORIDA (4)
Andre Dawson, of
Craig Grebeck, inf
Alejandro Pena, rhp
Joe Siddall, c

### HOUSTON (8)
%#John Cangelosi, of (C)
Danny Darwin, rhp
%#Doug Drabek, rhp (A)
Xavier Hernandez, rhp (B)
John Johnstone, rhp
Kirt Manwaring, c (B)
Gregg Olson, rhp
Bill Spiers, ss

### KANSAS CITY (0)
No free agents

### LOS ANGELES (6)
Brett Butler, of (B)
Dave Clark, of (B)
Delino DeShields, 2b (C)
Greg Gagne, ss (A)
Mark Guthrie, lhp (A)
Tim Wallach, 3b (B)

### MILWAUKEE (4)
Marshall Boze, rhp
Cris Carpenter, rhp
Doug Jones, rhp (A)
Mark Kiefer, rhp

### MINNESOTA (1)
Tom Quinlan, 3b

### MONTREAL (3)
*Moises Alou, of (A)
Mark Leiter, rhp (B)
*Mel Rojas, rhp (A)

### NEW YORK/AL (7)
Mike Aldrete, of
%#Tony Fernandez, ss
Joe Girardi, c (A)
%Jimmy Key, lhp
Tim McIntosh, c
Melido Perez, rhp
&John Wetteland, rhp (A)

### NEW YORK/NL (3)
Alvaro Espinoza, inf
*Brent Mayne, c (C)
Kevin Roberson, of

### OAKLAND (4)
*Mike Bordick, ss (A)
John Briscoe, rhp
Jim Corsi, rhp (A)
%Terry Steinbach, c (A)

### PHILADELPHIA (6)
%Jim Eisenreich, of (A)
Sid Fernandez, lhp
Jeff Parrett, rhp (B)
J.R. Phillips, 1b
%Benito Santiago, c (A)
David West, lhp

### PITTSBURGH (1)
John Hope, rhp

### ST. LOUIS (8)
Luis Alicea, 2b (B)
+Tony Fossas, lhp (A)
Gary Gaetti, 3b (A)
Mike Gallego, ss
+Rick Honeycutt, lhp (A)
Willie McGee, of
Tom Pagnozzi, c (B)
%#Ozzie Smith, ss

### SAN DIEGO (5)
Chris Gwynn, of
*Craig Shipley, inf (C)
Bob Tewksbury, rhp (B)
Fernando Valenzuela, lhp (B)
Greg Vaughn, of (B)

### SAN FRANCISCO (2)
%Shawon Dunston, ss (A)
%Robby Thompson, 2b

### SEATTLE (8)
%Chris Bosio, rhp
Lee Guetterman, rhp
Greg Hibbard, lhp
Dave Hollins, 3b (B)
Mike Jackson, rhp (A)
Jamie Moyer, lhp (B)
Terry Mulholland, lhp (B)
*Mark Whiten, of (B)

### TEXAS (12)
Dennis Cook, lhp (B)
Kevin Elster, ss (B)
Rene Gonzales, 3b
Kevin Gross, rhp (B)
%Darryl Hamilton, cf (B)
%Mike Henneman, rhp (A)
%Mark McLemore, 2b (A)
%#Jeff Russell, rhp (B)
Mike Stanton, rhp (A)
%#Kurt Stillwell, 2b
Dave Valle, c

### TORONTO (2)
Brian Bohanon, lhp
%Juan Samuel, 1b

*Free agent if granted strike service time in labor agreement.
#Repeater-rights player becomes free agent if club doesn't offer arbitration.
%Repeater-rights free agent doesn't require compensation.
+Team option for 1997. &Player option for 1997.

# MAJOR LEAGUE DEBUTS, 1996

| Player, Pos., Club | Debut |
|---|---|
| Abreu, Bob, of, Astros | Sept. 1 |
| Adamson, Joel, lhp, Marlins | April 10 |
| Adams, Willie, rhp, Athletics | June 11 |
| Allensworth, Jermaine, of, Pirates | July 23 |
| Alston, Garvin, rhp, Rockies | June 6 |
| Arias, George, 3b, Angels | April 2 |
| Aucoin, Derek, rhp, Expos | May 21 |
| Ayrault, Joe, c, Braves | Sept. 1 |
| Banks, Brian, of, Brewers | Sept. 9 |
| Barron, Tony, of, Expos | June 2 |
| Bartee, Kimera, of, Tigers | April 3 |
| Batista, Tony, ss, Athletics | June 3 |
| Beamon, Trey, of, Pirates | Aug. 4 |
| Beckett, Robbie, lhp, Rockies | Sept. 12 |
| Beech, Matt, lhp, Phillies | Aug. 8 |
| Belk, Tim, 1b, Reds | June 25 |
| Bevil, Brian, rhp, Royals | June 17 |
| Blazier, Ron, rhp, Phillies | May 31 |
| Bluma, Jaime, rhp, Royals | Aug. 9 |
| Booty, Josh, 3b, Marlins | Sept. 24 |
| Bourgeois, Steve, rhp, Giants | April 3 |
| Bowers, Brent, of, Orioles | Aug. 16 |
| Boze, Marshall, rhp, Brewers | April 28 |
| Brede, Brent, of, Twins | Sept. 8 |
| Brito, Tilson, ss, Blue Jays | April 1 |
| Brown, Brant, 1b, Cubs | June 15 |
| Brown, Kevin, c, Rangers | Sept. 12 |
| Burke, John, rhp, Rockies | Aug. 13 |
| Busby, Mike, rhp, Cardinals | April 7 |
| Cairo, Miguel, 2b, Blue Jays | April 17 |
| Canizaro, Jay, 2b, Giants | April 28 |
| Carlson, Dan, rhp, Giants | Sept. 15 |
| Casanova, Raul, c, Tigers | May 24 |
| Castillo, Luis, 2b, Marlins | Aug. 8 |
| Chavez, Raul, c, Expos | Aug. 30 |
| Chouinard, Bobby, rhp, Athletics | May 26 |
| Cockrell, Alan, of, Rockies | Sept. 7 |
| Coppinger, Rocky, rhp, Orioles | June 11 |
| Cordova, Francisco, rhp, Pirates | April 2 |
| Crawford, Carlos, rhp, Phillies | June 7 |
| Crespo, Felipe, 2b, Blue Jays | April 28 |
| Cruz, Jacob, of, Giants | July 18 |
| D'Amico, Jeff, rhp, Brewers | June 28 |
| Delgado, Alex, c, Red Sox | April 4 |
| Delgado, Wilson, ss, Giants | Sept. 24 |
| Dessens, Elmer, rhp, Pirates | June 24 |
| Diaz, Einar, c, Indians | Sept. 9 |
| Dickson, Jason, rhp, Angels | Aug. 21 |
| Difelice, Mike, c, Cardinals | Sept. 1 |
| Doster, David, 2b, Phillies | June 15 |
| Dunn, Todd, of, Brewers | Sept. 8 |
| Durant, Mike, c, Twins | April 3 |
| Dye, Jermaine, of, Braves | May 17 |
| Echevarria, Angel, of, Rockies | July 15 |
| Ellis, Robert, rhp, Angels | Sept. 12 |
| Erstad, Darin, of, Angels | June 14 |
| Estalella, Bobby, c, Phillies | Sept. 17 |

**Mets' Rey Ordonez**

| | |
|---|---|
| Farmer, Michael, lhp, Rockies | May 4 |
| Fasano, Sal, c, Royals | April 3 |
| Fernandez, Osvaldo, rhp, Giants | April 5 |
| Fox, Andy, 2b, Yankees | April 7 |
| Fyhrie, Mike, rhp, Mets | Sept. 14 |
| Garciaparra, Nomar, ss, Red Sox | Aug. 31 |
| Garrison, Webster, 2b, Athletics | Aug. 2 |
| Glanville, Doug, of, Cubs | June 9 |
| Graffanino, Tony, 2b, Braves | April 19 |
| Graves, Danny, rhp, Indians | July 13 |
| Greene, Charlie, c, Mets | Sept. 15 |
| Greene, Todd, c, Angels | July 30 |
| Grundt, Ken, lhp, Red Sox | Aug. 8 |
| Guerrero, Vladimir, of, Expos | Sept. 19 |
| Guerrero, Wilton, ss, Dodgers | Sept. 4 |
| Hancock, Ryan, rhp, Angels | June 8 |
| Hardtke, Jason, 2b, Mets | Sept. 8 |
| Harris, Pep, rhp, Angels | Aug. 14 |
| Hawblitzel, Ryan, rhp, Rockies | June 9 |
| Heflin, Bronson, rhp, Phillies | Aug. 1 |
| Heredia, Felix, lhp, Marlins | Aug. 9 |
| Hernandez, Livan, rhp, Marlins | Sept. 24 |
| Holbert, Aaron, 2b, Cardinals | April 14 |
| Holt, Chris, rhp, Astros | Sept. 1 |
| Holtz, Mike, lhp, Angels | July 11 |
| Houston, Tyler, c, Braves | April 3 |
| Howard, Matt, 2b, Yankees | May 17 |
| Hunter, Rich, rhp, Phillies | April 6 |
| Hurst, Bill, rhp, Marlins | Sept. 18 |
| Ibanez, Raul, of, Mariners | Aug. 1 |
| Jackson, Damian, ss, Indians | Sept. 12 |
| Janzen, Marty, rhp, Blue Jays | May 12 |
| Jennings, Robin, of, Cubs | April 18 |
| Jensen, Marcus, c, Giants | April 14 |
| Jones, Andruw, of, Braves | Aug. 15 |
| Jones, Dax, of, Giants | July 11 |
| Jones, Terry, of, Rockies | Sept. 9 |
| Keagle, Greg, rhp, Tigers | April 1 |
| Kendall, Jason, c, Pirates | April 1 |
| Kieschnick, Brooks, of, Cubs | April 3 |
| Lacy, Kerry, rhp, Red Sox | Aug. 16 |
| Larkin, Andy, rhp, Marlins | Sept. 29 |
| Lesher, Brian, of, Athletics | Aug. 25 |
| Levine, Alan, rhp, White Sox | June 22 |
| Loiselle, Rich, rhp, Pirates | Sept. 7 |
| Ludwick, Eric, rhp, Cardinals | Sept. 1 |
| Lukachyk, Rob, of, Expos | July 5 |
| Luke, Matt, of, Yankees | April 3 |
| Lyons, Curt, rhp, Reds | Sept. 19 |
| Machado, Robert, c, White Sox | July 24 |
| Maduro, Calvin, rhp, Phillies | Sept. 2 |
| Magee, Wendell, of, Phillies | Aug. 16 |
| Malave, Jose, of, Red Sox | May 23 |
| Martinez, Manny, of, Mariners | June 15 |
| Martinez, Pablo, ss, Braves | July 20 |
| Mashore, Damon, of, Athletics | June 5 |
| McCarthy, Greg, lhp, Mariners | Aug. 28 |
| McKeel, Walt, c, Red Sox | Sept. 14 |

| | |
|---|---|
| McMillon, Billy, of, Marlins | July 26 |
| Mejia, Miguel, of, Cardinals | April 4 |
| Mendoza, Ramiro, rhp, Yankees | May 25 |
| Milchin, Mike, lhp, Twins | May 14 |
| Miller, Travis, lhp, Twins | Aug. 25 |
| Miller, Trever, lhp, Tigers | Sept. 4 |
| Milliard, Ralph, 2b, Marlins | May 10 |
| Mirabelli, Doug, c, Giants | Aug. 27 |
| Mitchell, Larry, rhp, Phillies | Aug. 11 |
| Moehler, Brian, rhp, Tigers | Sept. 22 |
| Molina, Izzy, c, Athletics | Aug. 15 |
| Montgomery, Ray, of, Astros | July 3 |
| Montgomery, Steve, rhp, Athletics | April 3 |
| Moore, Kerwin, of, Athletics | Aug. 30 |
| Morman, Alvin, lhp, Astros | April 2 |
| Mosquera, Julio, c, Blue Jays | Aug. 17 |
| Mottola, Chad, of, Reds | April 22 |
| Mueller, Bill, 3b, Giants | April 18 |
| Mulligan, Sean, c, Padres | Sept. 1 |
| Munoz, Jose, 2b, White Sox | April 7 |
| Murray, Glenn, of, Phillies | May 10 |
| Myers, Jimmy, rhp, Orioles | April 6 |
| Myers, Rod, rhp, Cubs | April 3 |
| Myers, Roderick, of, Royals | June 21 |
| Naulty, Dan, rhp, Twins | April 2 |
| Nixon, Trot, of, Red Sox | Sept. 21 |
| Norton, Greg, 3b, White Sox | Aug. 18 |
| Ordonez, Rey, ss, Mets | April 1 |
| Osik, Keith, c, Pirates | April 5 |
| Pacheco, Alex, rhp, Expos | April 17 |
| Paniagua, Jose, rhp, Expos | April 4 |
| Patterson, Danny, rhp, Rangers | July 26 |
| Perez, Danny, of, Brewers | June 30 |
| Perez, Neifi, ss, Rockies | Aug. 31 |
| Peters, Chris, lhp, Pirates | July 19 |
| Polley, Dale, lhp, Yankees | June 23 |
| Potts, Mike, lhp, Brewers | April 6 |
| Pritchett, Chris, 1b, Angels | Sept. 6 |
| Quirico, Rafael, lhp, Phillies | June 25 |
| Relaford, Desi, ss, Phillies | Aug. 1 |
| Renteria, Edgar, ss, Marlins | May 10 |
| Robertson, Mike, 1b, White Sox | Sept. 6 |
| Rodriguez, Nerio, rhp, Orioles | Aug. 17 |
| Rodriguez, Tony, 2b, Red Sox | July 12 |
| Rolen, Scott, 3b, Phillies | Aug. 1 |
| Rosado, Jose, lhp, Royals | June 12 |
| Ruebel, Matt, lhp, Pirates | May 21 |
| Sackinsky, Brian, rhp, Orioles | April 20 |
| Schmidt, Jeff, rhp, Angels | May 17 |
| Schutz, Carl, lhp, Braves | Sept. 3 |
| Selby, Bill, 3b, Red Sox | April 19 |
| Serafini, Dan, lhp, Twins | June 25 |
| Sheets, Andy, ss, Mariners | April 22 |
| Silva, Jose, rhp, Blue Jays | Sept. 10 |
| Small, Mark, rhp, Astros | April 5 |
| Soderstrom, Steve, rhp, Giants | Sept. 17 |
| Spiezio, Scott, 3b, Athletics | Sept. 15 |
| Stephenson, Garrett, rhp, Orioles | July 25 |
| Suzuki, Mac, rhp, Mariners | July 7 |
| Telemaco, Amaury, rhp, Cubs | May 16 |
| Thompson, Jason, 1b, Padres | June 9 |
| Thompson, Justin, lhp, Tigers | May 27 |
| Valdes, Pedro, of, Cubs | May 15 |
| VanRyn, Ben, lhp, Angels | May 9 |
| Veras, Dario, rhp, Padres | July 31 |
| Wagner, Matt, rhp, Mariners | June 5 |
| Walker, Todd, 3b, Twins | Aug. 30 |
| Wallace, Derek, rhp, Mets | Aug. 13 |
| Wilkins, Marc, rhp, Pirates | May 13 |
| Williams, Keith, of, Giants | June 7 |
| Williams, Shad, rhp, Angels | May 18 |
| Wilson, Desi, 1b, Giants | Aug. 7 |
| Wilson, Paul, rhp, Mets | April 4 |
| Witasick, Jay, rhp, Athletics | July 7 |
| Wright, Jamey, rhp, Rockies | July 3 |
| Yan, Esteban, rhp, Orioles | May 20 |
| Young, Dmitri, 1b, Cardinals | Aug. 29 |
| Zuber, Jon, 1b, Phillies | April 19 |

**Pittsburgh's Jason Kendall**

# ROOKIE OF THE YEAR
## Yankees' Jeter Earns First-Year Honor

Behind the sweet inside-out swing, the soft hands and the dazzling statistics is an uncommon maturity that allowed Derek Jeter to excel in the toughest sports town in America, in a uniform packed with tradition and expectation. And he did it in the heat of a pennant race, in the spotlight of a World Series, with performances that belied his rookie status.

And for those reasons, among others, Jeter, 22, earned recognition as Baseball America's 1996 Rookie of the Year.

Only someone with Jeter's maturity could have handled the assignment he received back in spring training, when manager Joe Torre stuck the rookie into the Yankee's $50-million lineup.

"Hit .250 and make the routine plays," Torre said. "That's all I was looking for."

Right from Opening Day, when he homered off Cleveland's Dennis Martinez to key a 7-1 Yankees win, Jeter did more than hold his own. Ask any teammate about him, and he'll fill notebooks with praise reserved for perennial all-stars.

"If you ask me, he has been the

### PREVIOUS WINNERS
**1989**—Gregg Olson, rhp, Orioles
**1990**—Sandy Alomar, c, Indians
**1991**—Jeff Bagwell, 1b, Astros
**1992**—Pat Listach, ss, Brewers
**1993**—Mike Piazza, c, Dodgers
**1994**—Raul Mondesi, of, Dodgers
**1995**—Hideo Nomo, rhp, Dodgers

**Derek Jeter**

MVP of this team," second baseman Mariano Duncan said. "I can't tell you how impressed I am with this kid and what he's done for this team."

Jeter was born in Pequannock, N.J., and even after the family moved to Michigan, he stayed loyal to the Yankees, dreaming someday of playing shortstop in the Bronx.

The dream stayed on course when the Yankees selected Jeter with the sixth overall pick in 1992 draft out of Kalamazoo Central High, the first high school player drafted. After spending parts of four seasons in the minors—earning Baseball America's 1994 Minor League Player of

## TOP 20 ROOKIES
### Selected by Baseball America

1. Derek Jeter, ss, Yankees
2. Todd Hollandsworth, of, Dodgers
3. Edgar Renteria, ss, Marlins
4. Jason Kendall, c, Pirates
5. Rey Ordonez, ss, Mets
6. Tony Clark, 1b, Tigers
7. James Baldwin, rhp, White Sox
8. Ugueth Urbina, rhp, Expos
9. Alan Benes, rhp, Cardinals
10. Billy Wagner, lhp, Astros
11. F.P. Santangelo, of-3b, Expos
12. Jose Rosado, lhp, Royals
13. Jermaine Dye, of, Braves
14. Joe Randa, 3b, Royals
15. Donne Wall, rhp, Astros
16. Quinton McCracken, of, Rockies
17. Alex Ochoa, of, Mets
18. Chan Ho Park, rhp, Dodgers
19. Terrell Wade, lhp, Braves
20. Rocky Coppinger, rhp, Orioles

the Year award—Jeter blossomed in New York in 1996. He hit .314 with 10 homers and 78 RBIs, while swiping 14 bases and scoring 104 runs. He was a stabilizing force in the postseason as the Yankees won their first World Series in 18 years.

In a year of the rookie shortstop, Mets phenom Rey Ordonez hogged the preseason ink. Ordonez made more highlight reel plays, but Jeter was more consistent, making 22 errors to Ordonez' 27. Jeter's durability was also remarkable—he missed only five regular-season games, including two after the division title had been clinched.

Jeter was the 22-year-old kid who dreamed of being a great Yankee shortstop—then became one.

**—JIM SALISBURY**

---

Officials said the league was killed by a television deal that fell through and problems getting stadium leases. The league had a deal with Liberty Sports. But Liberty merged with Fox, which already had agreed to a broadcast agreement with Major League Baseball.

The United League planned to field 10 teams. Proposed sites for its franchises included Los Angeles, New Orleans, New York, Puerto Rico, Vancouver and Washington.

■ Baseball lost another icon from its golden age when Mel Allen, the voice of the Yankees and later "This Week In Baseball," died June 16 in Greenwich, Conn. He was 83.

Allen, whose lilting Alabama drawl became one of the great voices of baseball broacasting, was a broadcaster for 58 years.

"How about that?" became Allen's familiar signature phrase for millions. He was the only announcer to call baseball games in seven decades.

"Mel Allen meant as much to Yankee tradition as legends like Ruth, Gehrig, DiMaggio and Mantle," Yankees owner George Steinbrenner said. "He was the voice of the Yankees."

Allen was elected to the broadcasters' wing of the Hall of Fame in 1978.

■ The Phillies had quite a down year, going 67-95 to finish last in the National League East, but they got a smile when owner Bill Giles finished second in a country-wide search for a lookalike for Dave Thomas, the founder and pitchman of Wendy's.

Giles, who was chosen from among 1,678 entrants, received a glass statue of Thomas, a certificate and $100 in Wendy's gift certificates.

"People stare at me or stop me and they say, 'I know you,' " Giles said. "And I tell them I'm the guy on the TV commercial. When the team is doing bad, I tell them I'm Dave Thomas. When the team is winning, I say I'm Bill Giles. These days, I say I'm Dave Thomas."

# 40-MAN ROSTERS

Major league clubs are required to finalize their 40-man winter rosters, effective Nov. 20 each year. Those left unprotected become subject to the Rule 5 draft at the Winter Meetings.

Players requiring protection include those with (a.) four years of professional experience who were 18 or younger on June 5 preceding the signing of their first contract, or (b.) three years of professional experience who were 19 and older.

Forty-man rosters, effective Nov. 20, 1996:

## ATLANTA

**Manager:** Bobby Cox.
**Coaches:** Jim Beauchamp, Pat Corrales, Clarence Jones, Leo Mazzone, Ned Yost.
**Pitchers (17):** Pedro Borbon, Joe Borowski, Scott Brow, Paul Byrd, Brad Clontz, Tom Glavine, Dean Hartgraves, John LeRoy, Greg Maddux, Kevin Millwood, Denny Neagle, Carl Schutz, John Smoltz, Ben VanRyn, Terrell Wade, Mark Wohlers, Brad Woodall.
**Catchers (3):** Joe Ayrault, Javier Lopez, Eduardo Perez.
**Infielders (9):** Jeff Blauser (ss), Ed Giovanola (2b), Tony Graffanino (2b), Chipper Jones (3b), Marty Malloy (2b), Fred McGriff (1b), Mike Mordecai (ss), Randall Simon (1b), Robert Smith (ss).
**Outfielders (9):** Danny Bautista, Jermaine Dye, Marquis Grissom, Damon Hollins, Andruw Jones, Dave Justice, Ryan Klesko, Marc Lewis, Wonderful Monds.

## BALTIMORE

**Manager:** Dave Johnson.
**Coaches:** Rick Down, Andy Etchebarren, Elrod Hendricks, Ray Miller, Sam Perlozzo, John Stearns.
**Pitchers (17):** Armando Benitez, Rocky Coppinger, Archie Corbin, Scott Erickson, Jimmy Haynes, Rick Krivda, Terry Mathews, Alan Mills, Julio Moreno, Mike Mussina, Randy Myers, Jesse Orosco, William Percibal, Arthur Rhodes, Nerio Rodriguez, Francisco Saneaux, Esteban Yan.
**Catchers (3):** Cesar Devarez, Chris Hoiles, B.J. Waszgis.
**Infielders (9):** Manny Alexander (ss), Roberto Alomar (2b), Juan Bautista (ss), Domingo Martinez (1b), Scott McClain (3b), Willis Otanez (3b), Rafael Palmeiro (1b), Cal Ripken (ss), B.J. Surhoff (3b).
**Outfielders (6):** Wady Almonte, Brady Anderson, Danny Clyburn, Jeffrey Hammonds, Eugene Kingsale, Tony Tarasco.

## BOSTON

**Manager:** Jimy Williams.
**Coaches:** Dave Jauss, Joe Kerrigan, Wendell Kim, Grady Little, Jim Rice, Herm Starrette.
**Pitchers (17):** Rick Betti, Mark Brandenburg, Vaughn Eshelman, Rich Garces, Tom Gordon, Greg Hansell, Reggie Harris, Butch Henry, Joe Hudson, Kerry Lacy, Pat Mahomes, Rafael Orellano, Aaron Sele, Heathcliff Slocumb, Jeff Suppan, Ricky Trlicek, Tim Wakefield.
**Catchers (4):** Bill Haselman, Scott Hatteberg, Walt McKeel, Mike Stanley.
**Infielders (11):** Wil Cordero (2b), Bo Dodson (1b), Jeff Frye (2b), Nomar Garciaparra (ss), Reggie Jefferson (1b), Roberto Mejia (2b), Tim Naehring (3b), Arquimedez Pozo (2b), Tony Rodriguez (2b), John Valentin (ss), Mo Vaughn (1b).
**Outfielders (8):** Darren Bragg, Jose Canseco, Adam Hyzdu, Jose Malave, Trot Nixon, Troy O'Leary, Roy Padilla, Rudy Pemberton.

## CALIFORNIA

**Manager:** Terry Collins.
**Coaches:** Marcel Lachemann; Others unavailable.
**Pitchers (22):** Jim Abbott, Jason Dickson, Geoff Edsell, Robert Ellis, Chuck Finley, Mike Freehill, Greg Gohr, Mark Gubicza, Ryan Hancock, Pep Harris, Mike Holtz, Mike James, Pete Janicki, Mark Langston, Darrell May, Chuck McElroy, Troy Percival, Matt Perisho, Jeff Schmidt, Dennis Springer, Todd Van Poppel, Shad Williams.
**Catchers (5):** Jorge Fabregas, Todd Greene, Bret Hemphill, Chris Turner, Scott Vollmer.
**Infielders (7):** George Arias (3b), Gary DiSarcina (ss), Robert Eenhoorn (ss), Dave Hollins (3b), Chris Pritchett (1b), J.T. Snow (1b), Randy Velarde (2b).
**Outfielders (5):** Garret Anderson, Jim Edmonds, Darin Erstad, Orlando Palmeiro, Tim Salmon.

## CHICAGO-AL

**Manager:** Terry Bevington.
**Coaches:** Bill Buckner, Ron Jackson, Art Kusyner, Joe Nossek, Mike Pazik, Doug Rader, Mark Salas.
**Pitchers (21):** Wilson Alvarez, James Baldwin, Jason Bere, Mike Bertotti, Carlos Castillo, Tony Castillo, Chris Clemons, Nelson Cruz, Jeff Darwin, Alex Fernandez, Tom Fordham, Roberto Hernandez, Stacy Jones, Matt Karchner, Brian Keyser, Al Levine, Scott Ruffcorn, Bill Simas, Mike Sirotka, Larry Thomas, Brian Woods.
**Catchers (2):** Ron Karkovice, Robert Machado.
**Infielders (9):** Domingo Cedeno (ss), Ray Durham (2b), Ozzie Guillen (ss), Norberto Martin (2b), Greg Norton (3b), Olmedo Saenz (3b), Chris Snopek (3b), Frank Thomas (1b), Robin Ventura (3b).
**Outfielders (8):** Jeff Abbott, Albert Belle, Mike Cameron, Jimmy Hurst, Darren Lewis, Dave Martinez, Lyle Mouton, Tony Phillips.

## CHICAGO-NL

**Manager:** Jim Riggleman.
**Coaches:** Dave Bialas, Tony Muser, Mako Oliveras, Dan Radison, Phil Regan, Billy Williams.
**Pitchers (16):** Terry Adams, Kent Bottenfield, Jim Bullinger, Larry Casian, Frank Castillo, Kevin Foster, Jeremi Gonzalez, Rodney Myers, Bob Patterson, Marc Pisciotta, Steve Rain, Brian Stephenson, Dave Swartzbaugh, Amaury Telemaco, Steve Trachsel, Turk Wendell.
**Catchers (4):** Pat Cline, Tyler Houston, Mike Hubbard, Scott Servais.
**Infielders (9):** Brant Brown (1b), Miguel Cairo (2b), Leo Gomez (3b), Mark Grace (1b), Jose Hernandez (ss), Jason Maxwell (ss), Bobby Morris (2b), Kevin Orie (3b), Rey Sanchez (ss).
**Outfielders (10):** Scott Bullett, Doug Glanville, Luis Gonzalez, Vee Hightower, Robin Jennings, Brooks Kieschnick, Brian McRae, Sammy Sosa, Ozzie Timmons, Pedro Valdes.

## CINCINNATI

**Manager:** Ray Knight.
**Coaches:** Ken Griffey Sr., Don Gullett, Tom Hume, Denis Menke, Ron Oester, Joel Youngblood.
**Pitchers (17):** Jeff Brantley, Dave Burba, Hector Carrasco, Kevin Jarvis, Curt Lyons, Mike Morgan, Mike Remlinger, Jose Rijo, Johnny Ruffin, Roger Salkeld, Pete Schourek, Scott Service, Tim Scott, Tim Shaw, John Smiley, Scott Sullivan, Gabe White.
**Catchers (4):** Paul Bako, Brook Fordyce, Eddie Taubensee, Justin Towle.
**Infielders (11):** Tim Belk (1b), Aaron Boone (3b), Bret Boone (2b), Jeff Branson (3b), Willie Greene (3b), Lenny Harris (2b), Barry Larkin (ss), Hal Morris (1b), Eric Owens (2b), Eduardo Perez (3b), Pokey Reese (ss).
**Outfielders (8):** Steve Gibralter, Curtis Goodwin, Mike Kelly, Chad Mottola, Glenn Murray, Reggie Sanders, Ruben Sierra, Pat Watkins.

## CLEVELAND

**Manager:** Mike Hargrove.
**Coaches:** John Goryl, Luis Isaac, Charlie Manuel, Dave Nelson, Jeff Newman, Mark Wiley.
**Pitchers (20):** Brian Anderson, Paul Assenmacher, Bartolo Colon, Maximo De la Rosa, Travis Driskill, Alan Embree, Danny Graves, Daron Kirkreit, Steve Kline, Albie Lopez, Mike Matthews, Jack McDowell, Jose Mesa, Charles Nagy, Chad Ogea, Joe Roa, Paul Shuey, Teddy Warrecker, Casey Whitten.
**Catchers (2):** Sandy Alomar, Einar Diaz.
**Infielders (9):** Julio Franco (1b), Damian Jackson (2b), Herbert Perry (1b), Kevin Seitzer (3b), Richie Sexson (1b), Jim Thome (3b), Omar Vizquel (ss), Matt Williams (3b), Enrique Wilson (ss).
**Outfielders (7):** Bruce Aven, Brian Giles, Kenny Lofton, Alex Ramirez, Manny Ramirez, Ryan Thomson, Nigel Wilson.

## COLORADO

**Manager:** Don Baylor.
**Coaches:** P.J. Carey, Frank Funk, Gene Glynn, Clint Hurdle, Jackie Moore.
**Pitchers (20):** Garvin Alston, Roger Bailey, Robbie Beckett, John Burke, Mike DeJean, Luther Hackman, Darren Holmes, Bobby Jones, Curtis Leskanic, Mike Munoz, Lance Painter, Steve Reed, Bryan Rekar, Armando Reynoso, Kevin Ritz, Bruce Ruffin, Bill Swift, Mark Thompson, John Thomson, Jamey Wright.
**Catchers (3):** Steve Decker, Jayhawk Owens, Jeff Reed.
**Infielders (8):** Jason Bates (ss), Vinny Castilla (3b), Craig Counsell (ss), Andres Galarraga (1b), Jeff Huson (2b), Neifi

Perez (ss), Walt Weiss (ss), Eric Young (2b).

**Outfielders (9):** Dante Bichette, Ellis Burks, Angel Echevarria, Derrick Gibson, Terry Jones, Quinton McCracken, John Vander Wal, Edgard Velazquez, Larry Walker.

## DETROIT

**Manager:** Buddy Bell.
**Coaches:** Rick Adair, Larry Herndon, Perry Hill, Fred Kendall, Larry Parrish, Jerry White.
**Pitchers (23):** Bryan Corey, John Cummings, Glenn Dishman, Joey Eischen, Ramon Fermin, Scott Gentile, Rick Greene, Fernando Hernandez, Greg Keagle, Jose Lima, Felipe Lira, Dan Miceli, Trever Miller, Brian Moehler, Mike Myers, C.J. Nitkowski, Omar Olivares, Willis Roberts, John Rosengren, A.J. Sager, Cameron Smith, Justin Thompson, Greg Whiteman.
**Catchers (2):** Brad Ausmus, Raul Casanova.
**Infielders (8):** Richard Almanzar (2b), Tony Clark (1b), Damion Easley (2b), Travis Fryman (3b), Luis Garcia (ss), Dave Hajek (2b), Mark Lewis (2b), Phil Nevin (3b).
**Outfielders (7):** Kimera Bartee, Decomba Conner, Juan Encarnacion, Bobby Higginson, Melvin Nieves, Curtis Pride, Bubba Trammell.

## FLORIDA

**Manager:** Jim Leyland.
**Coaches:** Larry Rothschild, Rich Donnelly, Milt May, Tommy Sandt, Jerry Manuel, Bruce Kimm.
**Pitchers (23):** Antonio Alfonseca, Miguel Batista, Kevin Brown, Vic Darensborg, Rich Heredia, Felix Heredia, Dustin Hermanson, Livan Hernandez, Bill Hurst, Mark Hutton, Andy Larkin, Al Leiter, Matt Mantei, Kurt Miller, Robb Nen, Yorkis Perez, Jay Powell, Pat Rapp, Tony Saunders, Rob Stanifer, Marc Valdes, Bryan Ward, Matt Whisenant.
**Catchers (2):** Charles Johnson, Gregg Zaun.
**Infielders (8):** Kurt Abbott (ss), Alex Arias (ss), Bobby Bonilla (3b), Josh Booty (3b), Luis Castillo (2b), Greg Colbrunn (1b), Ralph Milliard (2b), Edgar Renteria (ss).
**Outfielders (7):** Jeff Conine, Todd Dunwoody, Billy McMillon, Joe Orsulak, Gary Sheffield, Jesus Tavarez, Devon White.

## HOUSTON

**Manager:** Larry Dierker.
**Coaches:** Alan Ashby, Jose Cruz Sr., Tom McCraw, Vern Ruhle, Bill Virdon.
**Pitchers (19):** Manuel Barrios, Doug Brocail, Ryan Creek, Mike Grzanich, Mike Hampton, Oscar Henriquez, Chris Holt, John Hudek, Todd Jones, Darryl Kile, Tom Martin, Doug Mlicki, Alvin Morman, Shane Reynolds, Mark Small, Jeff Tabaka, Billy Wagner, Donne Wall, Mike Walter.
**Catchers (2):** Tony Eusebio, Randy Knorr.
**Infielders (8):** Jeff Bagwell (1b), Sean Berry (3b), Craig Biggio (2b), Andujar Cedeno (ss), Carlos Guillen (ss), Ricky Gutierrez (ss), Orlando Miller (ss), Bill Spiers (ss).
**Outfielders (7):** Bob Abreu, Derek Bell, Richard Hidalgo, Brian Hunter, Derrick May, Ray Montgomery, James Mouton.

## KANSAS CITY

**Manager:** Bob Boone.
**Coaches:** Rich Dauer, Guy Hansen, Bruce Kison, Greg Luzinski, Mitchell Page, Jamie Quirk.
**Pitchers (17):** Kevin Appier, Tim Belcher, Brian Bevil, Jaime Bluma, Melvin Bunch, Jeff Granger, Chris Haney, Rich Huisman, Jason Jacome, Doug Linton, Jeff Montgomery, Hipolito Pichardo, Jim Pittsley, Ken Ray, Jose Rosado, Glendon Rusch, Bob Scanlan.
**Catchers (3):** Sal Fasano, Mike Macfarlane, Mike Sweeney.
**Infielders (14):** Bob Hamelin (1b), Jed Hansen (2b), David Howard (ss), Keith Lockhart (3b), Mendy Lopez (3b), Felix Martinez (ss), Sergio Nunez (2b), Jose Offerman (ss), Craig Paquette (3b), Joe Randa (3b), Bip Roberts (2b), Chris Stynes (2b), Joe Vitiello (1b), Kevin Young (1b).
**Outfielders (6):** Johnny Damon, Chili Davis, Tom Goodwin, Roderick Myers, Jon Nunnally, Michael Tucker.

## LOS ANGELES

**Manager:** Bill Russell.
**Coaches:** Joe Amalfitano, Mark Cresse, Manny Mota, Mike Scioscia, Reggie Smith, Dave Wallace.
**Pitchers (19):** Pedro Astacio, Tom Candiotti, Darren Dreifort, Rick Gorecki, Mark Guthrie, Darren Hall, Matt Herges, Jesus Martinez, Ramon Martinez, Hideo Nomo, Antonio Osuna, Chan Ho Park, Scott Radinsky, Gary Rath, Felix Rodriguez, David Spykstra, Ismael Valdez, Eric Weaver, Todd Worrell.
**Catchers (4):** Henry Blanco, Ken Huckaby, Mike Piazza, Tom Prince.
**Infielders (11):** Mike Busch (3b), Juan Castro (ss), Tripp

Cromer (ss), Chad Fonville (2b), Greg Gagne (ss), Wilton Guerrero (ss), Chip Hale (2b), Garey Ingram (2b), Eric Karros (1b), Nelson Liriano (2b), Adam Riggs (2b), John Wehner (3b).
**Outfielders (6):** Billy Ashley, Roger Cedeno, Karim Garcia, Todd Hollandsworth, Wayne Kirby, Raul Mondesi.

## MILWAUKEE

**Manager:** Phil Garner.
**Coaches:** Chris Bando, Bill Castro, Jim Gantner, Lamar Johnson, Don Rowe.
**Pitchers (17):** Peter Benny, Jeff D'Amico, Valerio De los Santos, Cal Eldred, Mike Fetters, Bryce Florie, Scott Karl, Sean Maloney, Ben McDonald, Jose Mercedes, Angel Miranda, Al Reyes, Henry Santos, Steve Sparks, Tim VanEgmond, Ron Villone, Bob Wickman.
**Catchers (4):** Bobby Hughes, Jesse Levis, Mike Matheny, Kelly Stinnett.
**Infielders (9):** Ron Belliard (2b), Jeff Cirillo (3b), John Jaha (1b), Mark Loretta (ss), Dave Nilsson (1b), Tim Unroe (3b), Jose Valentin (ss), Fernando Vina (2b), Antone Williamson (1b).
**Outfielders (8):** Brian Banks, Jeromy Burnitz, Chuckie Carr, Todd Dunn, Ken Felder, Matt Mieske, Marc Newfield, Gerald Williams.

## MINNESOTA

**Manager:** Tom Kelly.
**Coaches:** Terry Crowley, Ron Gardenhire, Rich Stelmaszek, Dick Such, Scott Ullger.
**Pitchers (16):** Rick Aguilera, Scott Aldred, Eddie Guardado, LaTroy Hawkins, Scott Klingenbeck, Travis Miller, Dan Naulty, Jose Parra, Dan Perkins, Brad Radke, Todd Ritchie, Rich Robertson, Frank Rodriguez, Dan Serafini, Dave Stevens, Mike Trombley.
**Catchers (3):** Greg Myers, Matt Walbeck, Jose Valentin.
**Infielders (11):** David Arias (1b), Ron Coomer (3b), Denny Hocking (ss), Chuck Knoblauch (2b), Corey Koskie (3b), Ryan Lane (ss), Pat Meares (ss), Paul Molitor (1b), Brian Raabe (2b), Scott Stahoviak (1b), Todd Walker (3b).
**Outfielders (10):** Rich Becker, Brent Brede, Marty Cordova, Torii Hunter, J.J. Johnson, Roberto Kelly, Chris Latham, Matt Lawton, Jamie Ogden, Ryan Radmanovich.

## MONTREAL

**Manager:** Felipe Alou.
**Coaches:** Pierre Arsenault, Bobby Cuellar, Tommy Harper, Pete Mackanin, Luis Pujols, Jim Tracy.
**Pitchers (19):** Tavo Alvarez, Derek Aucoin, Jason Baker, Rheal Cormier, Omar Daal, Mike Dyer, Steve Falteisek, Jeff Juden, Barry Manuel, Pedro Martinez, Jose Paniagua, Carlos Perez, Mel Rojas, Everett Stull, Mike Thurman, Ugueth Urbina, Dave Veres, Matt Wagner, Neal Weber.
**Catchers (5):** Raul Chavez, Darrin Fletcher, Bob Henley, Tim Laker, Chris Widger.
**Infielders (7):** Israel Alcantara (3b), Shane Andrews (3b), Orlando Cabrera (ss), Mark Grudzielanek (ss), Mike Lansing (2b), Ryan McGuire (1b), David Segui (1b).
**Outfielders (9):** Moises Alou, Yamil Benitez, Cliff Floyd, Vladimir Guerrero, Sherman Obando, Henry Rodriguez, F.P. Santangelo, DaRond Stovall, Rondell White.

## NEW YORK-AL

**Manager:** Joe Torre.
**Coaches:** Jose Cardenal, Chris Chambliss, Tony Cloninger, Willie Randolph, Mel Stottlemyre, Don Zimmer.
**Pitchers (18):** Brian Boehringer, Billy Brewer, David Cone, Chris Cumberland, Dwight Gooden, Scott Kamienecki, Jimmy Key, Graeme Lloyd, Jim Mecir, Rafael Medina, Ramiro Mendoza, Jeff Nelson, Andy Pettitte, Danny Rios, Mariano Rivera, Kenny Rogers, Tim Rumer, David Weathers.
**Catchers (3):** Mike Figga, Jim Leyritz, Jorge Posada.
**Infielders (12):** Wade Boggs (3b), Mariano Duncan (2b), Cecil Fielder (1b), Andy Fox (3b), Charlie Hayes (3b), Derek Jeter (ss), Pat Kelly (2b), Gabby Martinez (ss), Tino Martinez (1b), Luis Sojo (2b).
**Outfielders (8):** Ricky Ledee, Matt Luke, Paul O'Neill, Tim Raines, Ruben Rivera, Shane Spencer, Darryl Strawberry, Bernie Williams.

## NEW YORK-NL

**Manager:** Bobby Valentine.
**Coaches:** Bob Apodaca; Others unavailable.
**Pitchers (21):** Juan Acevedo, Mark Clark, Joe Crawford, Jerry DiPoto, Octavio Dotel, John Franco, Mark Fyrhie, Pete Harnisch, Doug Henry, Jason Isringhausen, Bobby Jones, Cory Lidle, Greg McMichael, Dave Mlicki, Robert Person, Bill Pulsipher, Hector Ramirez, Jesus Sanchez, Derek Wallace, Mike Welch, Paul Wil-

Welch, Paul Wilson.

**Catchers (4):** Alberto Castillo, Charlie Greene, Todd Hundley, Brent Mayne.

**Infielders (8):** Edgardo Alfonso (2b), Carlos Baerga (2b), Tim Bogar (ss), Rico Brogna (1b), Alvaro Espinoza (3b), Butch Huskey (1b), Rey Ordonez (ss), Roberto Petagine (1b).

**Outfielders (7):** Carl Everett, Bernard Gilkey, Lance Johnson, Carlos Mendoza, Alex Ochoa, Jay Payton, Preston Wilson.

## OAKLAND

**Manager:** Art Howe.

**Coaches:** Bob Alejo, Bob Cluck, Brad Fischer, Denny Walling, Ron Washington.

**Pitchers (20):** Mark Acre, Willie Adams, Bobby Chouinard, Carl Dale, Buddy Groom, Doug Johns, Dane Johnson, Steve Karsay, Mike Mohler, Steve Montgomery, Ariel Prieto, Carlos Reyes, Brad Rigby, Aaron Small, Bill Taylor, Dave Telgheder, Bret Wagner, John Wasdin, Don Wengert, Jay Witasick.

**Catchers (2):** Izzy Molina, George Williams.

**Infielders (10):** Tony Batista (ss), Mike Bordick (ss), Rafael Bournigal (ss), Scott Brosious (3b), Steve Cox (1b), Brent Gates (2b), Jason Giambi (3b), Jason McDonald (2b), Mark McGwire (1b), Scott Spiezio (3b).

**Outfielders (6):** Allen Battle, Geronimo Berroa, Jose Herrera, Brian Lesher, Matt Stairs, Ernie Young.

## PHILADELPHIA

**Manager:** Terry Francona.

**Coaches:** Galen Cisco, Chuck Cottier, Hal McRae, Brad Mills, Joe Rigoli, John Vukovich.

**Pitchers (19):** Matt Beech, Ron Blazier, Toby Borland, Ricky Bottalico, Jason Boyd, Wayne Gomes, Mike Grace, Tyler Green, Rich Hunter, Ricardo Jordan, Calvin Maduro, Michael Mimbs, Larry Mitchell, Bobby Munoz, Ryan Nye, Ken Ryan, Curt Schilling, Russ Springer, Mike Williams.

**Catchers (2):** Bobby Estalella, Mike Lieberthal.

**Infielders (9):** David Doster (2b), Rex Hudler (2b), Kevin Jordan (2b), Mickey Morandini (2b), Desi Relaford (ss), Scott Rolen (3b), Gene Schall (1b), Kevin Sefcik (ss), Kevin Stocker (ss).

**Outfielders (7):** Ruben Amaro, Darren Daulton, Lenny Dykstra, Gregg Jefferies, Tony Longmire, Wendell Magee, Ricky Otero.

## PITTSBURGH

**Manager:** Gene Lamont.

**Coaches:** Joe Jones, Jack Lind, Lloyd McClendon, Rick Renick, Pete Vuckovich, Spin Williams.

**Pitchers (21):** Jason Christiansen, Steve Cooke, Francisco Cordova, Kane Davis, Elmer Dessens, John Dillinger, John Ericks, Jeff Kelly, Jon Lieber, Esteban Loaiza, Rich Loiselle, Ramon Morel, Steve Parris, Chris Peters, Jose Pett, Matt Ruebel, Jason Schmidt, Jose Silva, Clint Sodowsky, Paul Wagner, Marc Wilkins.

**Catchers (3):** Angelo Encarnacion, Jason Kendall, Keith Osik.

**Infielders (7):** Jay Bell (ss), Lou Collier (ss), Brando Cromer (ss), Freddy Garcia (3b), Mark Johnson (1b), Jeff King (2b), Tony Womack (ss).

**Outfielders (9):** Jermaine Allensworth, Trey Beamon, Adrian Brown, Midre Cummings, Jose Guillen, Mike Kingery, Al Martin, Charles Peterson, T.J. Staton.

## ST. LOUIS

**Manager:** Tony La Russa.

**Coaches:** Mark DeJohn, Dave Duncan, George Hendrick, Dave McKay, Tommie Reynolds.

**Pitchers (20):** Manuel Aybar, Cory Bailey, Brian Barber, Rich Batchelor, Alan Benes, Andy Benes, Mike Busby, Dennis Eckersley, Tony Fossas, John Frascatore, Rick Honeycutt, Danny Jackson, Curtis King, Eric Ludwick, T.J. Mathews, Donovan Osborne, Mark Petkovsek, Brady Raggio, Blake Stein, Todd Stottlemyre.

**Catchers (3):** Mike Defelice, Eli Marrero, Danny Sheaffer.

**Infielders (9):** David Bell (2b), Royce Clayton (ss), Delino DeShields (2b), Gary Gaetti (3b), Mike Gulan (3b), Aaron Holbert (3b), John Mabry (1b), Luis Ordaz (ss), Dmitri Young (1b).

**Outfielders (6):** Terry Bradshaw, Ron Gant, Brian Jordan, Ray Lankford, Miguel Mejia, Mark Sweeney.

## SAN DIEGO

**Manager:** Bruce Bochy.

**Coaches:** Tim Flannery, Davey Lopes, Rob Picciolo, Marv Rettenmund, Dan Warthen.

**Pitchers (17):** Andy Ashby, Sean Bergman, Andres Berumen, Willie Blair, Doug Bochtler, Shane Dennis, Todd Erdos, Joey Hamilton, Trevor Hoffman, Brad Kaufman, Marc Kroon, Joey Long, Heath Murray, Scott Sanders, Fernando Valenzuela, Dario Veras, Tim Worrell.

**Catchers (3):** John Flaherty, Brian Johnson, Sean Mulligan.

**Infielders (14):** Homer Bush (2b), Ken Caminiti (3b), Archi Cianfrocco (3b), Chris Gomez (ss), Wally Joyner (1b), Derrek Lee (1b), Scott Livingstone (3b), Luis Lopez (2b), Juan Melo (ss), Jody Reed (2b), Craig Shipley (ss), Jason Thompson (1b), Jorge Velandia (ss), Quilvio Veras (2b).

**Outfielders (5):** Steve Finley, Tony Gwynn, Rickey Henderson, Earl Johnson, Chris Jones.

## SAN FRANCISCO

**Manager:** Dusty Baker.

**Coaches:** Carlos Alfonso, Gene Clines, Sonny Jackson, Ron Perranoski, Dick Pole.

**Pitchers (20):** Rod Beck, Steve Bourgeois, Dan Carlson, Doug Creek, Rich DeLucia, Mark Dewey, Shawn Estes, Osvaldo Fernandez, Keith Foulke, Chad Frontera, Mark Gardner, Fausto Macey, Jim Poole, Kirk Rueter, Steve Soderstrom, Julian Tavarez, Carlos Valdez, William VanLandingham, Mike Villano, Allen Watson.

**Catchers (4):** Marcus Jensen, Tom Lampkin, Doug Mirabelli, Rick Wilkins.

**Infielders (7):** Rich Aurilia (ss), Jay Canizaro (2b), Wilson Delgado (ss), Jeff Kent (3b), Bill Mueller (3b), Jose Vizcaino (2b), Desi Wilson (1b).

**Outfielders (9):** Marvin Benard, Barry Bonds, Jacob Cruz, Glenallen Hill, Trenidad Hubbard, Stan Javier, Dante Powell, Armando Rios, Chris Singleton.

## SEATTLE

**Manager:** Lou Piniella.

**Coaches:** Nardi Contreras, Lee Elia, John McLaren, Sam Mejias, Matt Sinatro, Steve Smith.

**Pitchers (23):** Bobby Ayala, Rafael Carmona, Norm Charlton, Dean Crow, Tim Davis, Scott Davison, Jeff Fassero, Tim Harikkala, Sterling Hitchcock, Edwin Hurtado, Randy Johnson, Derek Lowe, Damaso Marte, Greg McCarthy, Rusty Meacham, Paul Menhart, Ivan Montane, Jamie Moyer, Alex Pacheco, Mac Suzuki, Salomon Torres, Bob Wells, Bob Wolcott.

**Catchers (2):** John Marzano, Dan Wilson.

**Infielders (8):** Joey Cora (2b), Russ Davis (3b), Giomar Guevara (ss), Edgar Martinez (3b), Alex Rodriguez (ss), Andy Sheets (ss), Dave Silvestri (ss), Paul Sorrento (1b).

**Outfielders (6):** Rich Amaral, Jay Buhner, Ken Griffey Jr., Raul Ibanez, Marcus Sturdivant, Mark Whiten.

## TEXAS

**Manager:** Johnny Oates.

**Coaches:** Dick Bosman, Bucky Dent, Larry Hardy, Rudy Jaramillo, Ed Napoleon, Jerry Narron.

**Pitchers (13):** Jose Alberro, John Burkett, Wilson Heredia, Ken Hill, Eric Moody, Darren Oliver, Danny Patterson, Roger Pavlik, Julio Santana, Tanyon Sturtze, Ed Vosberg, Matt Whiteside, Bobby Witt.

**Catchers (4):** Kevin Brown, Henry Mercedes, Ivan Rodriguez, Mickey Tettleton.

**Infielders (9):** Mike Bell (3b), Will Clark (1b), Edwin Diaz (2b), Hanley Frias (ss), Benji Gil (ss), Mark McLemore (2b), Dean Palmer (3b), Lee Stevens (1b), Fernando Tatis (3b).

**Outfielders (9):** Damon Buford, Lou Frazier, Juan Gonzalez, Rusty Greer, Mark Little, Warren Newson, Lonell Roberts, Marc Sagmoen, Andrew Vessel.

## TORONTO

**Manager:** Cito Gaston.

**Coaches:** Alfredo Griffin, Jim Lett, Nick Leyva, Mel Queen, Gene Tenace, Willie Upshaw.

**Pitchers (17):** Luis Andujar, Tim Crabtree, Roberto Duran, Kelvim Escobar, Huck Flener, Juan Guzman, Erik Hanson, Pat Hentgen, Marty Janzen, Dan Plesac, Paul Quantrill, Bill Risley, Mark Sievert, Paul Spoljaric, Mike Timlin, Woody Williams, Joe Young.

**Catchers (3):** Sandy Martinez, Julio Mosquera, Charlie O'Brien.

**Infielders (11):** Tilson Brito (ss), Felipe Crespo (2b), Carlos Delgado (1b), Tom Evans (3b), Carlos Garcia (2b), Alex Gonzalez (ss), Ryan Jones (1b), John Olerud (1b), Jeff Patzke (2b), Tomas Perez (ss), Ed Sprague (3b).

**Outfielders (9):** Jacob Brumfield, Joe Carter, Shawn Green, Orlando Merced, Otis Nixon, Robert Perez, Angel Ramirez, Anthony Sanders, Shannon Stewart.

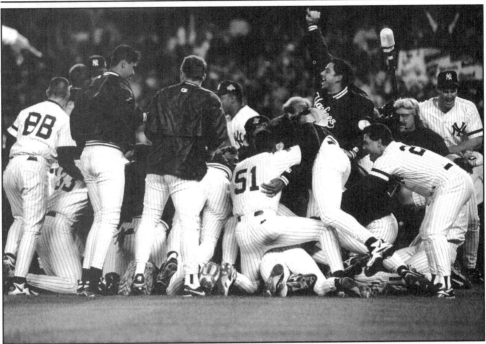

**The Celebration Begins.** Moments after the Yankees beat the Braves 3-2 to win the 1996 World Series, players piled on pitcher John Wetteland, who earned his fourth save of the Series. It was New York's first Series triumph in 18 years.

# Yankees Stage Improbable Comeback

**By JOHN PERROTTO**

The 1996 World Series was a testament to how quickly fortunes change in baseball.

Two games in, the Atlanta Braves were being hailed as one of the greatest teams of all time. The Braves were in the midst of one of the most dominant stretches in post-season history and seemed poised to sweep the New York Yankees.

After rallying from a 3-1 deficit to beat the St. Louis Cardinals in the National League Championship Series, winning the final three games by the ungodly aggregate sum of 32-1, Atlanta seemed well on its way to a second straight World Series title as it dominated the Yankees in the first two games of the Series at New York's Yankee Stadium.

Atlanta won the first two games decisively, 12-1 and 4-0. The "Team of the '90s" inscription on its 1995 World Series rings didn't seem like such a big boast after all.

My, how things changed. Four games later, the Braves were being villified for one of the great collapses of all time.

The Yankees made one of the most incredible comebacks in baseball history, taking three straight games in Atlanta then clinching the Series at home in Game Six

for their record 23rd championship but first since 1978.

While seemingly the entire baseball world had given Atlanta the Series after two games, the Yankees never gave up hope.

"The one thing you have to understand about this club is that it was under pressure all year long," first-year New York manager Joe Torre said. "First of all, when you put on the Yankee pinstripes, you are automatically under a certain amount of pressure in living up to the tradition and expectations that are associated with this franchise.

"We had the pressure of holding off Baltimore in (the American League East) after we built a big lead. Then, we had a lot of pressure in the American League playoffs with two very tough series. Plus, we played in more games decided by two runs or less than any team in the major leagues.

"We were under pressure every day of the season and our guys always responded. That's why I wasn't concerned once we fell behind 2-0 in this series. I knew what these guys had inside and what they were capable of overcoming."

The city of New York embraced the Yankees like no champion before.

# WORLD SERIES
## YEAR-BY-YEAR

| Year | Winner | Manager | Loser | Manager | Result | MVP |
|---|---|---|---|---|---|---|
| 1903 | Boston (AL) | Jimmy Collins | Pittsburgh (NL) | Fred Clarke | 5-3 | None Selected |
| 1904 | NO SERIES | | | | | |
| 1905 | New York (NL) | John McGraw | Philadelphia (AL) | Connie Mack | 4-1 | None Selected |
| 1906 | Chicago (AL) | Fielder Jones | Chicago (NL) | Frank Chance | 4-2 | None Selected |
| 1907 | Chicago (NL) | Frank Chance | Detroit (AL) | Hugh Jennings | 4-0 | None Selected |
| 1908 | Chicago (NL) | Frank Chance | Detroit (AL) | Hugh Jennings | 4-1 | None Selected |
| 1909 | Pittsburgh (NL) | Fred Clarke | Detroit (AL) | Hugh Jennings | 4-3 | None Selected |
| 1910 | Philadelphia (AL) | Connie Mack | Chicago (NL) | Frank Chance | 4-1 | None Selected |
| 1911 | Philadelphia (AL) | Connie Mack | New York (NL) | John McGraw | 4-2 | None Selected |
| 1912 | Boston (AL) | Jake Stahl | New York (NL) | John McGraw | 4-3-1 | None Selected |
| 1913 | Philadelphia (AL) | Connie Mack | New York (NL) | John McGraw | 4-1 | None Selected |
| 1914 | Boston (NL) | George Stallings | Philadelphia (AL) | Connie Mack | 4-0 | None Selected |
| 1915 | Boston (AL) | Bill Carrigan | Philadelphia (NL) | Pat Moran | 4-1 | None Selected |
| 1916 | Boston (AL) | Bill Carrigan | Brooklyn (NL) | Wilbert Robinson | 4-1 | None Selected |
| 1917 | Chicago (AL) | Pants Rowland | New York (NL) | John McGraw | 4-2 | None Selected |
| 1918 | Boston (AL) | Ed Barrow | Chicago (NL) | Fred Mitchell | 4-2 | None Selected |
| 1919 | Cincinnati (NL) | Pat Moran | Chicago (AL) | Kid Gleason | 5-3 | None Selected |
| 1920 | Cleveland (AL) | Tris Speaker | Brooklyn (NL) | Wilbert Robinson | 5-2 | None Selected |
| 1921 | New York (NL) | John McGraw | New York (AL) | Miller Huggins | 5-3 | None Selected |
| 1922 | New York (NL) | John McGraw | New York (AL) | Miller Huggins | 4-0 | None Selected |
| 1923 | New York (AL) | Miller Huggins | New York (NL) | John McGraw | 4-2 | None Selected |
| 1924 | Washington (AL) | Bucky Harris | New York (NL) | John McGraw | 4-3 | None Selected |
| 1925 | Pittsburgh (NL) | Bill McKechnie | Washington (AL) | Bucky Harris | 4-3 | None Selected |
| 1926 | St. Louis (NL) | Rogers Hornsby | New York (AL) | Miller Huggins | 4-3 | None Selected |
| 1927 | New York (AL) | Miller Huggins | Pittsburgh (NL) | Donie Bush | 4-0 | None Selected |
| 1928 | New York (AL) | Miller Huggins | St. Louis (NL) | Bill McKechnie | 4-0 | None Selected |
| 1929 | Philadelphia (AL) | Connie Mack | Chicago (NL) | Joe McCarthy | 4-1 | None Selected |
| 1930 | Philadelphia (AL) | Connie Mack | St. Louis (NL) | Gabby Street | 4-2 | None Selected |
| 1931 | St. Louis (NL) | Gabby Street | Philadelphia (AL) | Connie Mack | 4-3 | None Selected |
| 1932 | New York (AL) | Joe McCarthy | Chicago (NL) | Charlie Grimm | 4-0 | None Selected |
| 1933 | New York (NL) | Bill Terry | Washington (AL) | Joe Cronin | 4-1 | None Selected |
| 1934 | St. Louis (NL) | Frankie Frisch | Detroit (AL) | Mickey Cochrane | 4-3 | None Selected |
| 1935 | Detroit (AL) | Mickey Cochrane | Chicago (NL) | Charlie Grimm | 4-2 | None Selected |
| 1936 | New York (AL) | Joe McCarthy | New York (NL) | Bill Terry | 4-2 | None Selected |
| 1937 | New York (AL) | Joe McCarthy | New York (NL) | Bill Terry | 4-1 | None Selected |
| 1938 | New York (AL) | Joe McCarthy | Chicago (NL) | Gabby Hartnett | 4-0 | None Selected |
| 1939 | New York (AL) | Joe McCarthy | Cincinnati (NL) | Bill McKechnie | 4-0 | None Selected |
| 1940 | Cincinnati (NL) | Bill McKechnie | Detroit (AL) | Del Baker | 4-3 | None Selected |
| 1941 | New York (AL) | Joe McCarthy | Brooklyn (NL) | Leo Durocher | 4-1 | None Selected |
| 1942 | St. Louis (NL) | Billy Southworth | New York (AL) | Joe McCarthy | 4-1 | None Selected |
| 1943 | New York (AL) | Joe McCarthy | St. Louis (NL) | Billy Southworth | 4-1 | None Selected |
| 1944 | St. Louis (NL) | Billy Southworth | St. Louis (AL) | Luke Sewell | 4-2 | None Selected |
| 1945 | Detroit (AL) | Steve O'Neill | Chicago (NL) | Charlie Grimm | 4-3 | None Selected |
| 1946 | St. Louis (NL) | Eddie Dyer | Boston (AL) | Joe Cronin | 4-3 | None Selected |
| 1947 | New York (AL) | Bucky Harris | Brooklyn (NL) | Burt Shotton | 4-3 | None Selected |
| 1948 | Cleveland (AL) | Lou Boudreau | Boston (NL) | Billy Southworth | 4-2 | None Selected |
| 1949 | New York (AL) | Casey Stengel | Brooklyn (NL) | Burt Shotton | 4-1 | None Selected |
| 1950 | New York (AL) | Casey Stengel | Philadelphia (NL) | Eddie Sawyer | 4-0 | None Selected |
| 1951 | New York (AL) | Casey Stengel | New York (NL) | Leo Durocher | 4-2 | None Selected |
| 1952 | New York (AL) | Casey Stengel | Brooklyn (NL) | Chuck Dressen | 4-3 | None Selected |
| 1953 | New York (AL) | Casey Stengel | Brooklyn (NL) | Chuck Dressen | 4-2 | None Selected |
| 1954 | New York (NL) | Leo Durocher | Cleveland (AL) | Al Lopez | 4-0 | None Selected |
| 1955 | Brooklyn (NL) | Walter Alston | New York (AL) | Casey Stengel | 4-3 | Johnny Podres, p, Brooklyn |
| 1956 | New York (AL) | Casey Stengel | Brooklyn (NL) | Walter Alston | 4-3 | Don Larsen, p, New York |
| 1957 | Milwaukee (NL) | Fred Haney | New York (AL) | Casey Stengel | 4-3 | Lew Burdette, p, Milwaukee |
| 1958 | New York (AL) | Casey Stengel | Milwaukee (NL) | Fred Haney | 4-3 | Bob Turley, p, New York |
| 1959 | Los Angeles (NL) | Walter Alston | Chicago (AL) | Al Lopez | 4-2 | Larry Sherry, p, Los Angeles |
| 1960 | Pittsburgh (NL) | Danny Murtaugh | New York (AL) | Casey Stengel | 4-3 | Bobby Richardson, 2b, New York |
| 1961 | New York (AL) | Ralph Houk | Cincinnati (NL) | Fred Hutchinson | 4-1 | Whitey Ford, p, New York |
| 1962 | New York (AL) | Ralph Houk | San Francisco (NL) | Alvin Dark | 4-3 | Ralph Terry, p, New York |
| 1963 | Los Angeles (NL) | Walter Alston | New York (AL) | Ralph Houk | 4-0 | Sandy Koufax, p, Los Angeles |
| 1964 | St. Louis (NL) | Johnny Keene | New York (AL) | Yogi Berra | 4-3 | Bob Gibson, p, St. Louis |
| 1965 | Los Angeles (NL) | Walter Alston | Minnesota (AL) | Sam Mele | 4-3 | Sandy Koufax, p, Los Angeles |
| 1966 | Baltimore (AL) | Hank Bauer | Los Angeles (NL) | Walter Alston | 4-0 | Frank Robinson, of, Baltimore |
| 1967 | St. Louis (NL) | Red Schoendienst | Boston (AL) | Dick Williams | 4-3 | Bob Gibson, p, St. Louis |
| 1968 | Detroit (AL) | Mayo Smith | St. Louis (NL) | Red Schoendienst | 4-3 | Mickey Lolich, p, Detroit |
| 1969 | New York (NL) | Gil Hodges | Baltimore (AL) | Earl Weaver | 4-1 | Donn Clendenon, 1b, New York |
| 1970 | Baltimore (AL) | Earl Weaver | Cincinnati (NL) | Sparky Anderson | 4-1 | Brooks Robinson, 3b, Baltimore |
| 1971 | Pittsburgh (NL) | Danny Murtaugh | Baltimore (AL) | Earl Weaver | 4-3 | Roberto Clemente, of, Pittsburgh |
| 1972 | Oakland (AL) | Dick Williams | Cincinnati (NL) | Sparky Anderson | 4-3 | Gene Tenace, c, Oakland |
| 1973 | Oakland (AL) | Dick Williams | New York (NL) | Yogi Berra | 4-3 | Reggie Jackson, of, Oakland |
| 1974 | Oakland (AL) | Alvin Dark | Los Angeles (NL) | Walter Alston | 4-1 | Rollie Fingers, p, Oakland |
| 1975 | Cincinnati (NL) | Sparky Anderson | Boston (AL) | Darrell Johnson | 4-3 | Pete Rose, 3b, Cincinnati |
| 1976 | Cincinnati (NL) | Sparky Anderson | New York (AL) | Billy Martin | 4-0 | Johnny Bench, c, Cincinnati |
| 1977 | New York (AL) | Billy Martin | Los Angeles (NL) | Tom Lasorda | 4-2 | Reggie Jackson, of, New York |
| 1978 | New York (AL) | Bob Lemon | Los Angeles (NL) | Tom Lasorda | 4-2 | Bucky Dent, ss, New York |
| 1979 | Pittsburgh (NL) | Chuck Tanner | Baltimore (AL) | Earl Weaver | 4-3 | Willie Stargell, 1b, Pittsburgh |
| 1980 | Philadelphia (NL) | Dallas Green | Kansas City (AL) | Jim Frey | 4-2 | Mike Schmidt, 3b, Philadelphia |
| 1981 | Los Angeles (NL) | Tom Lasorda | New York (AL) | Bob Lemon | 4-2 | Cey/Guerrero/Yeager, Los Angeles |
| 1982 | St. Louis (NL) | Whitey Herzog | Milwaukee (AL) | Harvey Kuenn | 4-3 | Darrell Porter, c, St. Louis |
| 1983 | Baltimore (AL) | Joe Altobelli | Philadelphia (NL) | Paul Owens | 4-1 | Rick Dempsey, c, Baltimore |
| 1984 | Detroit (AL) | Sparky Anderson | San Diego (NL) | Dick Williams | 4-1 | Alan Trammell, ss, Detroit |
| 1985 | Kansas City (AL) | Dick Howser | St. Louis (NL) | Whitey Herzog | 4-3 | Bret Saberhagen, p, Kansas City |
| 1986 | New York (NL) | Dave Johnson | Boston (AL) | John McNamara | 4-3 | Ray Knight, 3b, New York |
| 1987 | Minnesota (AL) | Tom Kelly | St. Louis (NL) | Whitey Herzog | 4-3 | Frank Viola, p, Minnesota |
| 1988 | Los Angeles (NL) | Tom Lasorda | Oakland (AL) | Tony La Russa | 4-1 | Orel Hershiser, p, Los Angeles |
| 1989 | Oakland (AL) | Tony La Russa | San Francisco (NL) | Roger Craig | 4-0 | Dave Stewart, p, Oakland |
| 1990 | Cincinnati (NL) | Lou Piniella | Oakland (AL) | Tony La Russa | 4-0 | Jose Rijo, p, Cincinnati |
| 1991 | Minnesota (AL) | Tom Kelly | Atlanta (NL) | Bobby Cox | 4-3 | Jack Morris, p, Minnesota |
| 1992 | Toronto (AL) | Cito Gaston | Atlanta (NL) | Bobby Cox | 4-2 | Pat Borders, c, Toronto |
| 1993 | Toronto (AL) | Cito Gaston | Philadelphia (NL) | Jim Fregosi | 4-2 | Paul Molitor, dh, Toronto |
| 1994 | NO SERIES | | | | | |
| 1995 | Atlanta (NL) | Bobby Cox | Cleveland (AL) | Mike Hargrove | 4-2 | Tom Glavine, p, Atlanta |
| 1996 | New York (AL) | Joe Torre | Atlanta (NL) | Bobby Cox | 4-2 | John Wetteland, p, New York |

Three days after the Yankees humbled the Braves, New Yorkers staged a ticker-tape parade to match the enormity of the team's World Series comeback. A record crowd of 3.5 million fans celebrated the franchise's conquest.

"You could have lit up the whole world with the energy you put out today," Torre told the assembled masses.

## Predicted His Team's Success

The Yankees won the AL East despite seeing a 12-game lead in late July cut to 2½ by mid-September. They went 45-30 in games decided by two runs or less. They fell behind 1-0 to Texas in the AL Division Series then won the next three games, all after trailing at some point, to win the best-of-five series. In the AL Championship Series, they went to Baltimore tied 1-1 then won three in a row at Camden Yards.

That gave Torre so much confidence in his club that he didn't flinch when not-too-happy owner George Steinbrenner dropped by the manager's office after the Game One debacle. In fact, Torre became a clairvoyant.

"I was in one of my goofy moods, probably because I hadn't slept in three weeks," Torre said. "George was kind of embarrassed about what happened in the first game but I just winked at him and told him not to worry. I told him we might lose the second game, too, but I knew we'd be OK once we got to Atlanta because that's my town, I played and managed there. I told George we'd win the three in Atlanta and then come home and wrap it up in Game Six. He looked at me like I had two heads."

But, it's exactly what happened as New York wound up going an unbelievable 8-0 on the road in the postseason.

It was also fitting that the Yankees would become only the third team to win a World Series after losing the first two games at home, joining the 1985 Kansas City Royals and 1986 New York Mets. New York had a roster filled with comeback stories.

First, there was Torre. He was the ultimate story of perserverance, having played and managed in 4,272 games without ever reaching a World Series, more than any person in baseball history.

Torre figured he would never get another chance to manage after St. Louis fired him during the 1995 season. Yet, the Yankees gave the New York native an opportunity.

There was pitcher Dwight Gooden and outfielder Darryl Strawberry. The linchpins of the Mets' championship team in '86, their struggles with drugs had all but destroyed what once seemed to be Hall of Fame careers. Yet, Steinbrenner gave each a last chance and they became key

**Outstanding Player.** Reliever John Wetteland earned Series MVP honors by saving all four Yankee wins.

MORRIS FOSTOFF

players again.

There was pitcher David Cone. He underwent career-threatening surgery in mid-May to remove an aneurysm from his pitching shoulder but was back on a major-league mound by Labor Day. Cone started the Yankees' Series comeback by winning Game Three.

There was pitcher Jimmy Key. He wasn't expected to be ready until the all-star break after undergoing shoulder surgery the previous year. Yet, Key was in the rotation when the season started and was the winning pitcher in the Game Six clincher.

And there was first-year general manager Bob Watson. He was nearly fired by Steinbrenner in August after acquiring two injured players from the Milwaukee Brewers, lefthanded reliever Graeme Lloyd and utilityman Pat Listach, in a trade for pitcher Bob Wickman and outfielder Gerald Williams. Watson was vindicated in the Series as Lloyd retired all seven batters he faced, striking out four.

"New York is a city of battlers," Steinbrenner said. "You battle to get a cab every morning in this town. I don't think anyone exemplifies what New York City is all about more than this Yankee ballclub."

## Teenager Shines

The Yankees, though, embarrassed the city more than anything in the first two games at home.

In the first World Series game in the Bronx since 1981, delayed a day after a torrential rainstorm, Atlanta rolled to a 12-1 victory in the opener behind rookie phenom Andruw Jones,

**Long Wait.** Yankees manager Joe Torre waited 33 years to make an appearance in the World Series.

DAVID SEELIG

**Dejection.** Braves manager Bobby Cox contemplates his team's four-game losing streak after winning the first two games.

LEE R. SCHMID

who homered in his first two at bats and drove in five runs.

At 19, Jones became the youngest player ever to homer in a World Series. It was just another step on his incredible '96 journey that started at Class A Durham and included pit stops at Double-A Greenville and Triple-A Richmond before ending in the World Series. Jones' hitting was more than enough for winning pitcher John Smoltz, who allowed one run on two hits in six innings.

Atlanta quickly went up 2-0 in the series by posting a 4-0 win in Game Two. Greg Maddux allowed six hits in eight shutout innings while Fred McGriff had three RBIs.

The Braves seemed on the verge of a sweep as the Series shifted to Atlanta but that's when the Yankees took over.

Cone and three relievers combined on a six-hitter as the Yankees posted a 5-2 win in Game Three. Outfielder Bernie Williams, who carried New York to playoffs victories over Texas and Baltimore, homered and drove in three runs.

The momentum then turned for good in Game Four as the Yankees rallied for an 8-6 victory in 10 innings after falling behind 6-0 in the fifth. Jim Leyritz' three-run homer off closer Mark Wohlers in the eighth knotted the score at 6-6. The winning run scored in the 10th when pinch hitter Wade Boggs drew a bases-loaded walk from Steve Avery with one out immediately after Atlanta manager Bobby Cox decided to intentionally walk Williams with runners on first and second.

"I get paid an awful lot of money to get big outs late in the games and I didn't do the job," Wohlers said. "I have big shoulders, though. I take the responsibility for

us losing this series. The entire World Series really turned on Leyritz's homer."

The Yankees pulled ahead in the series as Andy Pettitte outdueled Smoltz in a 1-0 classic in Game Five. After being knocked out in the third inning of Game One, Pettitte scattered five hits in 8⅓ innings before John Wetteland got the final two outs.

Though the visiting team won the first five games of the World Series for the first time since the Cubs and White Sox met in the battle of Chicago in 1906, the law of averages finally worked out in Game Six. Back in the Bronx, the Yankees capped their comeback with a 3-2 win.

The Yankees scored three runs off Maddux in the third inning and made it stand up, though the game did have a dramatic conclusion. Marquis Grissom's two-out RBI single off Wetteland in the ninth cut the New York lead to 3-2 and put runners on first and second. However, Wetteland got Mark Lemke to foul out to third baseman Charlie Hayes, setting off a wild celebration at the mound.

"It was absolute elation, mayhem," Wetteland said. "It was a tremendous feeling. All of a sudden that went to tremendous pain in my ankle. I was screaming for someone to get off—actually 10 to get off. I thought my ankle was going to break, I honestly did. It was scary."

Wetteland survived, though, and was on his feet to accept the Series Most Valuable Player award. Wetteland saved all four victories, breaking the Series record of three held by a pair of Pittsburgh relievers, Elroy Face in 1960 and Kent Tekulve in 1979. Wetteland allowed one run in 3⅔ innings.

## Heroes All Around

Everyone in the New York lineup was a hero, though. Lloyd continually got lefthanded hitters out in tough situations while set-up man supreme Mariano Rivera got many big outs along with fellow righties Jeff Nelson, David Weathers and Brian Boehringer. In 15 post-season games, Yankees relievers were 6-1 with seven saves and a 1.79 ERA.

But the spotlight in this World Series was really on Torre. In addition to the long wait for his first World Series, Torre endured a season of tragedy with his two older brothers.

Torre learned between games of a June day-night doubleheader in Cleveland that Rocco had died of a heart attack. Frank Torre, a first baseman with the Milwaukee Braves and Philadelphia Phillies from 1956-63, spent two months awaiting a heart transplant in a New York hospital before having the operation on the eve of Game Six.

Losing to Torre even took some of the sting out of losing for the Braves.

"If you have to lose, I don't mind losing to Joe," Cox said. "He's a class act."

Still, it was a bitter defeat for the Braves. Atlanta has appeared in four of the past five World Series but won only once. Suddenly those ghosts of falls past, which seemed to be exorcised with the Series win over Cleveland in 1995, came back.

"After going two up on the road, you figure you're going to win one or two at home," Cox said. "The Yankees, though, came right back and showed us what they're made of. You have to tip your hat to them."

# WORLD SERIES
## BOX SCORES

### Game One: October 20
### Braves 12, Yankees 1

| ATLANTA | ab | r | h | bi | bb | so | NEW YORK | ab | r | h | bi | bb | so |
|---|---|---|---|---|---|---|---|---|---|---|---|---|---|
| Grissom cf | 5 | 2 | 2 | 1 | 0 | 0 | Jeter ss | 3 | 1 | 0 | 0 | 1 | 1 |
| Lemke 2b | 4 | 0 | 2 | 1 | 0 | 0 | Boggs 3b | 4 | 0 | 2 | 1 | 0 | 0 |
| C. Jones 3b | 4 | 1 | 1 | 3 | 0 | 0 | Williams cf | 3 | 0 | 0 | 0 | 1 | 1 |
| McGriff 1b | 5 | 2 | 2 | 2 | 0 | 2 | Martinez 1b | 3 | 0 | 1 | 0 | 1 | 1 |
| Lopez c | 4 | 2 | 1 | 0 | 1 | 1 | Fielder dh | 4 | 0 | 0 | 0 | 0 | 1 |
| Perez c | 0 | 0 | 0 | 0 | 0 | 0 | Strawberry lf | 3 | 0 | 0 | 0 | 0 | 0 |
| Dye rf | 5 | 0 | 1 | 0 | 0 | 1 | Raines lf | 1 | 0 | 0 | 0 | 0 | 0 |
| A. Jones lf | 4 | 3 | 3 | 5 | 0 | 0 | O'Neill rf | 2 | 0 | 0 | 0 | 1 | 0 |
| Klesko dh | 4 | 1 | 0 | 0 | 0 | 1 | Aldrete rf | 0 | 0 | 0 | 0 | 0 | 0 |
| Blauser ss | 3 | 1 | 1 | 0 | 0 | 0 | Hayes ph | 1 | 0 | 0 | 0 | 0 | 0 |
| Polonia ph | 1 | 0 | 0 | 0 | 0 | 1 | Duncan 2b | 3 | 0 | 0 | 0 | 0 | 0 |
| Belliard ss | 0 | 0 | 0 | 0 | 0 | 0 | Fox 2b | 0 | 0 | 0 | 0 | 0 | 0 |
| | | | | | | | Sojo ph | 1 | 0 | 0 | 0 | 0 | 0 |
| | | | | | | | Leyritz c | 3 | 0 | 1 | 0 | 1 | 1 |
| **Totals** | **39** | **12** | **13** | **12** | **1** | **6** | **Totals** | **31** | **1** | **4** | **1** | **5** | **5** |

| | |
|---|---|
| **Atlanta** | **026 013 000—12** |
| **New York** | **000 010 000— 1** |

**E**—Duncan (1). **LOB**—Atlanta 3, New York 8. **2B**—Boggs (1). **HR**—McGriff (1), A. Jones 2 (2). **SB**—C. Jones (1). **S**—Lemke. **SF**—C. Jones.

| Atlanta | ip | h | r | er | bb | so | New York | ip | h | r | er | bb | so |
|---|---|---|---|---|---|---|---|---|---|---|---|---|---|
| Smoltz W | 6 | 2 | 1 | 1 | 5 | 4 | Pettitte L | 2⅓ | 6 | 7 | 7 | 1 | 1 |
| McMichael | 1 | 2 | 0 | 0 | 0 | 1 | Boehringer | 3 | 5 | 5 | 3 | 0 | 2 |
| Neagle | 1 | 0 | 0 | 0 | 0 | 0 | Weathers | 1⅔ | 1 | 0 | 0 | 0 | 0 |
| Wade | ⅔ | 0 | 0 | 0 | 0 | 0 | Nelson | 1 | 1 | 0 | 0 | 0 | 1 |
| Clontz | ⅓ | 0 | 0 | 0 | 0 | 0 | Wetteland | 1 | 0 | 0 | 0 | 0 | 2 |

**Umpires: HP**—Evans; **1B**—Tata; **2B**—Welke; **3B**—Rippley; **LF**—Young; **RF**—Davis.

**T**—3:02. **A**—56,365.

### Game Two: October 21
### Braves 4, Yankees 0

| ATLANTA | ab | r | h | bi | bb | so | NEW YORK | ab | r | h | bi | bb | so |
|---|---|---|---|---|---|---|---|---|---|---|---|---|---|
| Grissom cf | 5 | 1 | 2 | 1 | 0 | 1 | Raines lf | 4 | 0 | 2 | 0 | 0 | 0 |
| Lemke 2b | 4 | 2 | 2 | 0 | 0 | 0 | Boggs 3b | 4 | 0 | 1 | 0 | 0 | 0 |
| C. Jones 3b | 3 | 0 | 1 | 0 | 1 | 1 | Williams cf | 4 | 0 | 0 | 0 | 0 | 1 |
| McGriff 1b | 3 | 0 | 2 | 3 | 0 | 1 | Martinez 1b | 4 | 0 | 0 | 0 | 0 | 2 |
| Lopez c | 4 | 0 | 1 | 0 | 0 | 0 | Fielder dh | 4 | 0 | 2 | 0 | 0 | 0 |
| Dye rf | 4 | 0 | 1 | 0 | 0 | 0 | Fox pr | 0 | 0 | 0 | 0 | 0 | 0 |
| A. Jones lf | 3 | 0 | 0 | 0 | 0 | 1 | O'Neill rf | 4 | 0 | 1 | 0 | 0 | 1 |
| Pendleton dh | 4 | 1 | 1 | 0 | 0 | 1 | Duncan 2b | 3 | 0 | 0 | 0 | 0 | 1 |
| Blauser ss | 2 | 0 | 0 | 0 | 1 | 0 | Girardi c | 3 | 0 | 0 | 0 | 0 | 0 |
| Polonia ph | 1 | 0 | 0 | 0 | 0 | 0 | Jeter ss | 2 | 0 | 1 | 0 | 0 | 0 |
| Belliard ss | 0 | 0 | 0 | 0 | 0 | 0 | | | | | | | |
| **Totals** | **33** | **4** | **10** | **4** | **2** | **5** | **Totals** | **32** | **0** | **7** | **0** | **0** | **5** |

| | |
|---|---|
| **Atlanta** | **101 011 000—4** |
| **New York** | **000 000 000—0** |

**E**—Raines (1). **DP**—New York 2, Atlanta 1. **LOB**—New York 6, Atlanta 7. **2B**—Lemke (1), Grissom (1), C. Jones (1), Pendleton (1), O'Neill (1). **CS**—Raines. **S**—Lemke. **SF**—McGriff.

| Atlanta | ip | h | r | er | bb | so | New York | ip | h | r | er | bb | so |
|---|---|---|---|---|---|---|---|---|---|---|---|---|---|
| Maddux W | 8 | 6 | 0 | 0 | 0 | 2 | Key L | 6 | 10 | 4 | 4 | 2 | 0 |
| Wohlers | 1 | 1 | 0 | 0 | 0 | 3 | Lloyd | ⅔ | 0 | 0 | 0 | 0 | 2 |
| | | | | | | | Nelson | 1⅓ | 0 | 0 | 0 | 0 | 2 |
| | | | | | | | M. Rivera | 1 | 0 | 0 | 0 | 0 | 1 |

**HBP**—A. Jones (by Key), Jeter (by Maddux).

**Umpires: HP**—Tata; **1B**—Welke; **2B**—Rippley; **3B**—Young; **LF**—Davis; **RF**—Evans.

**T**—2:44. **A**—56,340.

### Game Three: October 22
### Yankees 5, Braves 2

| NEW YORK | ab | r | h | bi | bb | so | ATLANTA | ab | r | h | bi | bb | so |
|---|---|---|---|---|---|---|---|---|---|---|---|---|---|
| Raines lf | 4 | 1 | 1 | 0 | 1 | 0 | Grissom cf | 4 | 1 | 3 | 0 | 0 | 0 |
| Jeter ss | 3 | 1 | 1 | 0 | 1 | 1 | Lemke 2b | 4 | 0 | 1 | 1 | 0 | 0 |
| Williams cf | 5 | 2 | 2 | 3 | 0 | 1 | C. Jones 3b | 3 | 0 | 1 | 0 | 1 | 1 |
| Fielder 1b | 3 | 0 | 1 | 0 | 1 | 0 | McGriff 1b | 3 | 0 | 0 | 0 | 1 | 0 |
| Fox pr | 0 | 1 | 0 | 0 | 0 | 0 | Klesko lf | 3 | 0 | 0 | 1 | 1 | 2 |
| Martinez 1b | 0 | 0 | 0 | 0 | 1 | 0 | Lopez c | 4 | 0 | 1 | 0 | 0 | 0 |
| Hayes 3b | 5 | 0 | 0 | 0 | 0 | 3 | A. Jones rf | 4 | 0 | 0 | 0 | 0 | 2 |
| Strawberry rf | 3 | 0 | 1 | 1 | 1 | 2 | Blauser ss | 4 | 0 | 0 | 0 | 0 | 2 |
| Duncan 2b | 3 | 0 | 1 | 0 | 0 | 1 | Glavine p | 1 | 1 | 0 | 0 | 1 | 0 |
| Sojo 2b | 1 | 0 | 1 | 1 | 0 | 0 | Polonia ph | 0 | 0 | 0 | 0 | 1 | 0 |
| Girardi c | 2 | 0 | 0 | 0 | 1 | 2 | McMichael p | 0 | 0 | 0 | 0 | 0 | 0 |
| Cone p | 2 | 0 | 0 | 0 | 0 | 1 | Clontz p | 0 | 0 | 0 | 0 | 0 | 0 |
| Leyritz ph | 1 | 0 | 0 | 0 | 0 | 0 | Bielecki p | 0 | 0 | 0 | 0 | 0 | 0 |
| M. Rivera p | 1 | 0 | 0 | 0 | 0 | 0 | Pendleton ph | 1 | 0 | 0 | 0 | 0 | 0 |
| Lloyd p | 0 | 0 | 0 | 0 | 0 | 0 | | | | | | | |
| Wetteland p | 0 | 0 | 0 | 0 | 0 | 0 | | | | | | | |
| **Totals** | **33** | **5** | **8** | **5** | **6** | **11** | **Totals** | **31** | **2** | **6** | **2** | **5** | **7** |

| | |
|---|---|
| **New York** | **100 100 030—5** |
| **Atlanta** | **000 001 010—2** |

**E**—Jeter (1), Blauser (1). **DP**—New York 1, Atlanta 1. **LOB**—New York 9, Atlanta 7. **2B**—Fielder (1). **3B**—Grissom (1). **HR**—Williams (1). **CS**—A. Jones, Polonia. **S**—Jeter, Girardi.

| New York | ip | h | r | er | bb | so | Atlanta | ip | h | r | er | bb | so |
|---|---|---|---|---|---|---|---|---|---|---|---|---|---|
| Cone W | 6 | 4 | 1 | 1 | 4 | 3 | Glavine L | 7 | 4 | 2 | 1 | 3 | 8 |
| M. Rivera | 1⅓ | 2 | 1 | 1 | 1 | 1 | McMichael | 0 | 3 | 3 | 3 | 0 | 0 |
| Lloyd | ⅔ | 0 | 0 | 0 | 0 | 1 | Clontz | 1 | 1 | 0 | 0 | 1 | 1 |
| Wetteland S | 1 | 0 | 0 | 0 | 0 | 2 | Bielecki | 1 | 0 | 0 | 0 | 2 | 2 |

McMichael pitched to three batters in 8th.

**Umpires: HP**—Welke; **1B**—Rippley; **2B**—Young; **3B**—Davis; **LF**—Evans; **RF**—Tata.

**T**—3:22. **A**—51,843.

### Game Four: October 23
### Yankees 8, Braves 6

| NEW YORK | ab | r | h | bi | bb | so | ATLANTA | ab | r | h | bi | bb | so |
|---|---|---|---|---|---|---|---|---|---|---|---|---|---|
| Raines lf | 5 | 1 | 0 | 0 | 1 | 1 | Grissom cf | 5 | 0 | 1 | 2 | 0 | 0 |
| Jeter ss | 4 | 2 | 2 | 0 | 2 | 2 | Lemke 2b | 5 | 0 | 1 | 0 | 0 | 1 |
| Williams cf | 4 | 1 | 0 | 0 | 2 | 1 | C. Jones 3b-ss | 3 | 2 | 1 | 0 | 2 | 0 |
| Fielder 1b | 4 | 1 | 2 | 1 | 1 | 0 | McGriff 1b | 3 | 1 | 2 | 1 | 2 | 0 |
| Fox pr-3b | 0 | 0 | 0 | 0 | 0 | 0 | Clontz p | 0 | 0 | 0 | 0 | 0 | 0 |
| Boggs ph-3b | 0 | 0 | 0 | 1 | 1 | 0 | Lopez c | 2 | 1 | 0 | 1 | 1 | 1 |
| Hayes 3b-1b | 5 | 1 | 3 | 1 | 1 | 0 | Wohlers p | 0 | 0 | 0 | 0 | 0 | 0 |
| Strawberry rf | 5 | 0 | 2 | 0 | 1 | 2 | Avery p | 0 | 0 | 0 | 0 | 0 | 0 |
| Duncan 2b | 5 | 1 | 0 | 0 | 0 | 1 | Klesko 1b | 1 | 0 | 0 | 0 | 0 | 1 |
| Girardi c | 2 | 0 | 0 | 0 | 0 | 0 | A. Jones lf | 4 | 1 | 3 | 1 | 1 | 1 |
| O'Neill ph | 1 | 0 | 0 | 0 | 0 | 1 | Dye rf | 4 | 0 | 0 | 0 | 0 | 0 |
| Leyritz c | 2 | 1 | 1 | 3 | 0 | 0 | Blauser ss | 3 | 1 | 1 | 1 | 0 | 2 |
| Rogers p | 1 | 0 | 1 | 0 | 0 | 0 | Belliard ss | 0 | 0 | 0 | 0 | 0 | 0 |
| Boehringer p | 0 | 0 | 0 | 0 | 0 | 0 | Polonia, ph | 1 | 0 | 0 | 0 | 0 | 1 |
| Sojo ph | 1 | 0 | 1 | 0 | 0 | 0 | Pendleton 3b | 1 | 0 | 0 | 0 | 0 | 0 |
| Weathers p | 0 | 0 | 0 | 0 | 0 | 0 | Neagle p | 1 | 0 | 0 | 0 | 0 | 1 |
| Martinez ph | 1 | 0 | 0 | 0 | 0 | 1 | Wade p | 0 | 0 | 0 | 0 | 0 | 0 |
| Nelson p | 0 | 0 | 0 | 0 | 0 | 0 | Bielecki p | 1 | 0 | 0 | 0 | 0 | 1 |
| Aldrete ph | 1 | 0 | 0 | 0 | 0 | 0 | Perez c | 1 | 0 | 0 | 0 | 0 | 0 |
| M. Rivera p | 0 | 0 | 0 | 0 | 0 | 0 | | | | | | | |
| Lloyd p | 1 | 0 | 0 | 0 | 0 | 0 | | | | | | | |
| Wetteland p | 0 | 0 | 0 | 0 | 0 | 0 | | | | | | | |
| **Totals** | **42** | **8** | **12** | **6** | **9** | **9** | **Totals** | **35** | **6** | **9** | **6** | **6** | **9** |

| | |
|---|---|
| **New York** | **000 003 030 2—8** |
| **Atlanta** | **041 010 000 0—6** |

**E**—Dye (1), Klesko (1). **DP**—New York 1, Atlanta 1. **LOB**—New York 13, Atlanta 8. **2B**—Grissom (2), A. Jones (1). **HR**—McGriff (2), Leyritz (1). **S**—Neagle, Dye. **SF**—Lopez.

| New York | ip | h | r | er | bb | so | Atlanta | ip | h | r | er | bb | so |
|---|---|---|---|---|---|---|---|---|---|---|---|---|---|
| Rogers | 2 | 5 | 5 | 5 | 2 | 0 | Neagle | 5 | 5 | 3 | 2 | 4 | 3 |
| Boehringer | 2 | 0 | 0 | 0 | 0 | 3 | Wade | 0 | 0 | 0 | 0 | 1 | 0 |
| Weathers | 1 | 1 | 1 | 1 | 2 | 2 | Bielecki | 2 | 0 | 0 | 0 | 1 | 4 |
| Nelson | 2 | 0 | 0 | 0 | 1 | 2 | Wohlers | 2 | 6 | 3 | 3 | 0 | 1 |
| M. Rivera | 1⅓ | 2 | 0 | 0 | 1 | 1 | Avery L | ⅔ | 1 | 2 | 1 | 3 | 0 |
| Lloyd W | 1 | 0 | 0 | 0 | 0 | 1 | Clontz | ⅓ | 0 | 0 | 0 | 0 | 1 |
| Wetteland S | ⅔ | 1 | 0 | 0 | 0 | 0 | | | | | | | |

Rogers pitched to two batters in 3rd. Neagle pitched to four batters in 6th. Wade pitched to one batter in 6th.

**Balk**—Weathers. **Umpires: HP**—Rippley; **1B**—Young; **2B**—Davis; **3B**—Evans; **LF**—Tata; **RF**—Welke.

**T**—4:19. **A**—51,881.

### Game Five: October 24
### Yankees 1, Braves 0

| NEW YORK | ab | r | h | bi | bb | so | ATLANTA | ab | r | h | bi | bb | so |
|---|---|---|---|---|---|---|---|---|---|---|---|---|---|
| Jeter ss | 4 | 0 | 0 | 0 | 0 | 1 | Grissom cf | 3 | 0 | 2 | 0 | 1 | 1 |
| Hayes 3b | 4 | 1 | 0 | 0 | 0 | 2 | Lemke 2b | 4 | 0 | 0 | 0 | 0 | 2 |
| Williams cf | 4 | 0 | 0 | 0 | 0 | 2 | C. Jones 3b | 4 | 0 | 1 | 0 | 0 | 0 |
| Fielder 1b | 4 | 0 | 3 | 1 | 0 | 1 | McGriff 1b | 3 | 0 | 0 | 0 | 1 | 1 |
| Martinez 1b | 0 | 0 | 0 | 0 | 0 | 0 | Lopez c | 4 | 0 | 0 | 0 | 0 | 0 |
| Strawberry lf | 3 | 0 | 0 | 0 | 1 | 1 | A. Jones lf | 2 | 0 | 1 | 0 | 1 | 0 |
| O'Neill rf | 2 | 0 | 0 | 0 | 2 | 0 | Klesko ph | 0 | 0 | 0 | 0 | 1 | 0 |
| Duncan 2b | 4 | 0 | 0 | 0 | 0 | 1 | Dye rf | 3 | 0 | 0 | 0 | 0 | 0 |
| Sojo 2b | 0 | 0 | 0 | 0 | 0 | 0 | Polonia ph | 1 | 0 | 0 | 0 | 0 | 0 |
| Leyritz c | 2 | 0 | 1 | 0 | 2 | 1 | Blauser ss | 3 | 0 | 0 | 0 | 0 | 0 |
| Pettitte p | 4 | 0 | 0 | 0 | 0 | 1 | Smoltz p | 2 | 0 | 1 | 0 | 0 | 0 |
| Wetteland p | 0 | 0 | 0 | 0 | 0 | 0 | Mordecai ph | 1 | 0 | 0 | 0 | 0 | 0 |
| | | | | | | | Wohlers p | 0 | 0 | 0 | 0 | 0 | 0 |
| **Totals** | **31** | **1** | **4** | **1** | **5** | **10** | **Totals** | **30** | **0** | **5** | **0** | **4** | **4** |

**Top Hitter.** Atlanta outfielder Marquis Grissom led the Series with a .444 average even though his team lost in six games.

MORRIS FOSTOFF

**Umpires:** HP—Davis; **1B**—Evans; **2B**—Tata; **3B**—Welke; **LF**—Rippley; **RF**—Young.

**T**—2:52. **A**—56,375.

## COMPOSITE BOX

### NEW YORK

| Player, Pos. | AVG | G | AB | R | H | 2B | 3B | HR | RBI | BB | SO | SB |
|---|---|---|---|---|---|---|---|---|---|---|---|---|
| Kenny Rogers, p | 1.000 | 1 | 1 | 0 | 1 | 0 | 0 | 0 | 0 | 0 | 0 | 0 |
| Luis Sojo, 2b | .600 | 5 | 5 | 0 | 3 | 1 | 0 | 0 | 1 | 0 | 0 | 0 |
| Cecil Fielder, dh-1b | .391 | 6 | 23 | 1 | 9 | 2 | 0 | 0 | 2 | 2 | 2 | 0 |
| Jim Leyritz, c | .375 | 4 | 8 | 1 | 3 | 0 | 0 | 1 | 3 | 3 | 2 | 1 |
| Wade Boggs, 3b | .273 | 4 | 11 | 0 | 3 | 1 | 0 | 0 | 2 | 1 | 0 | 0 |
| Derek Jeter, ss | .250 | 6 | 20 | 5 | 5 | 0 | 0 | 0 | 1 | 4 | 6 | 1 |
| Tim Raines, lf | .214 | 4 | 14 | 2 | 3 | 0 | 0 | 0 | 0 | 2 | 1 | 0 |
| Joe Girardi, c | .200 | 4 | 10 | 1 | 2 | 0 | 1 | 0 | 1 | 1 | 2 | 0 |
| Charlie Hayes, 3b-1b | .188 | 5 | 16 | 2 | 3 | 0 | 0 | 0 | 1 | 1 | 5 | 0 |
| D. Strawberry, lf-rf | .188 | 5 | 16 | 0 | 3 | 0 | 0 | 0 | 1 | 4 | 6 | 0 |
| Paul O'Neill, rf | .167 | 5 | 12 | 1 | 2 | 2 | 0 | 0 | 0 | 3 | 2 | 0 |
| Bernie Williams, cf | .167 | 6 | 24 | 3 | 4 | 0 | 0 | 1 | 4 | 3 | 6 | 1 |
| Tino Martinez, 1b | .091 | 6 | 11 | 0 | 1 | 0 | 0 | 0 | 2 | 5 | 0 | 0 |
| Mariano Duncan, 2b | .053 | 6 | 19 | 1 | 1 | 0 | 0 | 0 | 0 | 4 | 1 | 0 |
| Mike Aldrete, rf | .000 | 2 | 1 | 0 | 0 | 0 | 0 | 0 | 0 | 0 | 0 | 0 |
| Graeme Lloyd, p | .000 | 3 | 1 | 0 | 0 | 0 | 0 | 0 | 0 | 0 | 0 | 0 |
| Mariano Rivera, p | .000 | 3 | 1 | 0 | 0 | 0 | 0 | 0 | 0 | 0 | 0 | 0 |
| David Cone, p | .000 | 1 | 2 | 0 | 0 | 0 | 0 | 0 | 0 | 0 | 1 | 0 |
| Andy Pettitte, p | .000 | 1 | 4 | 0 | 0 | 0 | 0 | 0 | 0 | 0 | 1 | 0 |
| Andy Fox, 2b-3b | .000 | 4 | 0 | 1 | 0 | 0 | 0 | 0 | 0 | 0 | 0 | 0 |
| Totals | .216 | 6 | 199 | 18 | 43 | 6 | 1 | 2 | 16 | 26 | 43 | 4 |

| Pitcher | W | L | ERA | G | GS | SV | IP | H | R | ER | BB | SO |
|---|---|---|---|---|---|---|---|---|---|---|---|---|
| Jeff Nelson | 0 | 0 | 0.00 | 3 | 0 | 0 | 4 | 1 | 0 | 0 | 1 | 5 |
| Graeme Lloyd | 1 | 0 | 0.00 | 4 | 0 | 0 | 3 | 0 | 0 | 0 | 0 | 4 |
| David Cone | 1 | 0 | 1.50 | 1 | 1 | 0 | 6 | 4 | 1 | 1 | 4 | 3 |
| Mariano Rivera | 0 | 0 | 1.59 | 4 | 0 | 0 | 6 | 4 | 1 | 1 | 3 | 4 |
| John Wetteland | 0 | 0 | 2.08 | 4 | 0 | 4 | 4 | 4 | 1 | 1 | 1 | 6 |
| David Weathers | 0 | 0 | 3.00 | 3 | 0 | 0 | 3 | 2 | 1 | 1 | 3 | 3 |
| Jimmy Key | 1 | 1 | 3.97 | 2 | 2 | 0 | 11 | 15 | 5 | 5 | 5 | 1 |
| Brian Boehringer | 0 | 0 | 5.40 | 2 | 0 | 0 | 5 | 5 | 5 | 3 | 0 | 5 |
| Andy Pettitte | 1 | 1 | 5.91 | 2 | 2 | 0 | 11 | 11 | 7 | 7 | 4 | 5 |
| Kenny Rogers | 0 | 0 | 22.50 | 1 | 1 | 0 | 2 | 5 | 5 | 5 | 2 | 0 |
| Totals | 4 | 2 | 3.93 | 6 | 6 | 4 | 55 | 51 | 26 | 24 | 23 | 36 |

### ATLANTA

| Player, Pos. | AVG | G | AB | R | H | 2B | 3B | HR | RBI | BB | SO | SB |
|---|---|---|---|---|---|---|---|---|---|---|---|---|
| John Smoltz, p | .500 | 1 | 2 | 0 | 1 | 0 | 0 | 0 | 0 | 0 | 0 | 0 |
| Marquis Grissom, cf | .444 | 6 | 27 | 4 | 12 | 2 | 1 | 0 | 5 | 1 | 2 | 1 |
| Andruw Jones, lf-rf | .400 | 6 | 20 | 4 | 8 | 1 | 0 | 2 | 6 | 3 | 6 | 1 |
| Fred McGriff, 1b | .300 | 6 | 20 | 4 | 6 | 0 | 0 | 2 | 6 | 5 | 4 | 0 |
| Chipper Jones, 3b-ss | .286 | 6 | 21 | 3 | 6 | 3 | 0 | 0 | 3 | 4 | 2 | 1 |
| Mark Lemke, 2b | .231 | 6 | 26 | 2 | 6 | 1 | 0 | 0 | 2 | 0 | 3 | 0 |
| T. Pendleton, dh-3b | .222 | 4 | 9 | 1 | 2 | 1 | 0 | 0 | 0 | 1 | 1 | 0 |
| Javier Lopez, c | .190 | 6 | 21 | 3 | 4 | 0 | 0 | 0 | 1 | 3 | 4 | 0 |
| Jeff Blauser, ss | .167 | 6 | 18 | 2 | 3 | 1 | 0 | 0 | 1 | 4 | 4 | 0 |
| Jermaine Dye, rf | .188 | 5 | 17 | 0 | 2 | 0 | 0 | 0 | 1 | 1 | 1 | 0 |
| R. Klesko, ph-1b-dh | .100 | 5 | 10 | 2 | 1 | 0 | 0 | 0 | 1 | 2 | 4 | 0 |
| Mike Bielecki, p | .000 | 2 | 1 | 0 | 0 | 0 | 0 | 0 | 0 | 0 | 1 | 0 |
| Tom Glavine, p | .000 | 1 | 1 | 1 | 0 | 0 | 0 | 0 | 0 | 0 | 1 | 0 |
| Mike Mordecai, ph | .000 | 1 | 1 | 0 | 0 | 0 | 0 | 0 | 0 | 1 | 0 | 0 |
| Denny Neagle, p | .000 | 1 | 1 | 0 | 0 | 0 | 0 | 0 | 0 | 0 | 1 | 0 |
| Eddie Perez, c | .000 | 2 | 1 | 0 | 0 | 0 | 0 | 0 | 0 | 0 | 0 | 0 |
| Luis Polonia, ph | .000 | 5 | 4 | 0 | 0 | 0 | 0 | 0 | 0 | 1 | 2 | 0 |
| Totals | .254 | 6 | 201 | 26 | 51 | 9 | 1 | 4 | 26 | 23 | 36 | 3 |

| Pitcher | W | L | ERA | G | GS | SV | IP | H | R | ER | BB | SO |
|---|---|---|---|---|---|---|---|---|---|---|---|---|
| Mike Bielecki | 0 | 0 | 0.00 | 2 | 0 | 0 | 3 | 0 | 0 | 0 | 3 | 6 |
| Brad Clontz | 0 | 0 | 0.00 | 3 | 0 | 0 | 2 | 1 | 0 | 0 | 1 | 2 |
| Terrell Wade | 0 | 0 | 0.00 | 2 | 0 | 0 | 1 | 0 | 0 | 0 | 1 | 0 |
| John Smoltz | 1 | 1 | 0.64 | 2 | 2 | 0 | 14 | 6 | 2 | 1 | 8 | 14 |
| Tom Glavine | 0 | 1 | 1.29 | 1 | 1 | 0 | 7 | 4 | 2 | 1 | 3 | 8 |
| Greg Maddux | 1 | 1 | 1.72 | 2 | 2 | 0 | 16 | 14 | 3 | 3 | 1 | 5 |
| Denny Neagle | 0 | 0 | 3.00 | 2 | 1 | 0 | 3 | 3 | 2 | 1 | 2 | 4 |
| Mark Wohlers | 0 | 0 | 6.23 | 4 | 0 | 0 | 4 | 7 | 3 | 3 | 2 | 4 |
| Steve Avery | 0 | 0 | 13.50 | 1 | 0 | 0 | 1 | 1 | 2 | 1 | 5 | 0 |
| Greg McMichael | 0 | 0 | 27.00 | 2 | 0 | 0 | 1 | 5 | 3 | 3 | 0 | 1 |
| Totals | 2 | 4 | 2.33 | 6 | 6 | 0 | 54 | 43 | 18 | 14 | 26 | 43 |

| | | | | |
|---|---|---|---|---|
| New York | 103 | 213 | 060 | 2—18 |
| Atlanta | 168 | 135 | 011 | 0—26 |

**DP**—Atlanta 6, New York 7. **LOB**—Atlanta 41, New York 48.

**E**—Duncan 2, Raines, Jeter 2, Blauser, Dye, Klesko, Raines, Grissom, Hayes, A. Jones 2, Polonia, Pendleton. **S**—Lemke 2, Dye, Jeter, Girardi, Neagle. **SF**—C. Jones, McGriff, Lopez.

**HBP**—Jeter (by Maddux), A. Jones (by Key). **Balk**—Weathers.

**Umpires**—Tim Welke, Terry Tata, Steve Rippley, Jim Evans, Larry Young, Gerry Davis.

---

| New York | | | 000 100 000—1 |
|---|---|---|---|
| Atlanta | | | 000 000 000—0 |

**E**—Jeter(2), Grissom (1). **DP**—Atlanta 1, New York 2. **LOB**—Atlanta 7, New York 8. **2B**—Fielder (2), C. Jones (2). **SB**—Leyritz (1), Duncan (1), A. Jones (1), Grissom (1). **CS**—A. Jones.

| New York | ip | h | r | er | bb | so | Atlanta | ip | h | r | er | bb | so |
|---|---|---|---|---|---|---|---|---|---|---|---|---|---|
| Pettitte W | 8⅓ | 5 | 0 | 0 | 3 | 4 | Smoltz L | 8 | 4 | 1 | 0 | 3 | 10 |
| Wetteland S | ⅔ | 0 | 0 | 0 | 1 | 0 | Wohlers | 1 | 0 | 0 | 0 | 2 | 0 |

**WP**—Wohlers.

**Umpires:** HP—Young; **1B**—Davis; **2B**—Evans; **3B**—Tata; **LF**—Welke; **RF**—Rippley.

**T**—2:54. **A**—51,881.

### Game Six: October 26
### Yankees 3, Braves 2

| ATLANTA | ab | r | h | bi | bb | so | NEW YORK | ab | r | h | bi | bb | so |
|---|---|---|---|---|---|---|---|---|---|---|---|---|---|
| Grissom cf | 5 | 0 | 2 | 1 | 0 | 0 | Jeter ss | 4 | 1 | 1 | 1 | 0 | 1 |
| Lemke 2b | 5 | 0 | 0 | 0 | 0 | 0 | Boggs 3b | 3 | 0 | 0 | 0 | 0 | 0 |
| C. Jones 3b | 4 | 0 | 1 | 0 | 0 | 0 | Hayes 3b | 1 | 0 | 0 | 0 | 0 | 0 |
| McGriff 1b | 3 | 1 | 0 | 0 | 1 | 0 | Williams cf | 4 | 0 | 2 | 1 | 0 | 0 |
| Lopez c | 4 | 0 | 1 | 0 | 1 | 2 | Fielder dh | 4 | 0 | 1 | 0 | 0 | 0 |
| A. Jones lf-rf | 3 | 0 | 1 | 0 | 1 | 2 | Martinez 1b | 3 | 0 | 0 | 0 | 0 | 1 |
| Dye rf | 1 | 0 | 0 | 1 | 1 | 0 | Strawberry lf | 2 | 0 | 0 | 0 | 1 | 1 |
| Klesko ph-lf | 2 | 1 | 1 | 0 | 0 | 0 | O'Neill rf | 3 | 1 | 1 | 0 | 0 | 0 |
| Pendleton dh | 3 | 0 | 1 | 0 | 1 | 0 | Duncan 2b | 1 | 0 | 0 | 0 | 0 | 0 |
| Belliard pr | 0 | 0 | 0 | 0 | 0 | 0 | Sojo 2b | 2 | 0 | 1 | 0 | 0 | 0 |
| Blauser ss | 3 | 0 | 1 | 0 | 0 | 0 | Girardi c | 3 | 1 | 2 | 1 | 0 | 0 |
| Polonia ph | 1 | 0 | 0 | 0 | 0 | 1 | | | | | | | |
| Totals | 33 | 2 | 8 | 2 | 5 | 5 | Totals | 30 | 3 | 8 | 3 | 1 | 3 |

| Atlanta | | 000 100 001—2 |
|---|---|---|
| New York | | 003 000 00x—3 |

**E**—Duncan (2). **DP**—Atlanta 2, New York 1. **LOB**—Atlanta 9, New York 4. **2B**—Blauser (1), C. Jones (3), O'Neill (2), Sojo (1). **3B**—Girardi (1). **SB**—Jeter (1), Williams (1). **CS**—Pendleton.

| Atlanta | ip | h | r | er | bb | so | New York | ip | h | r | er | bb | so |
|---|---|---|---|---|---|---|---|---|---|---|---|---|---|
| Maddux L | 7⅔ | 8 | 3 | 3 | 1 | 3 | Key W | 5⅓ | 5 | 1 | 1 | 3 | 1 |
| Wohlers | ⅓ | 0 | 0 | 0 | 0 | 0 | Weathers | ⅓ | 0 | 0 | 0 | 1 | 1 |
| | | | | | | | Lloyd | ⅓ | 0 | 0 | 0 | 0 | 0 |
| | | | | | | | M. Rivera | 2 | 0 | 0 | 0 | 1 | 1 |
| | | | | | | | Wetteland S | 1 | 3 | 1 | 1 | 0 | 2 |

# New-Look Yankees Storm To AL Title

**By JOHN ROYSTER**

It used to be said that rooting for the New York Yankees was like rooting for U.S. Steel.

The Bronx Bombers were the dominant franchise in baseball from the 1920s through 1981, going to the World Series 33 times and winning it 22 times. To be a Yankee fan was to be accused of being a front-runner.

But then the world turned upside down. The Yankees went 15 years between World Series trips, finally returning in 1996. During that time, U.S. Steel even ceased being U.S. Steel. It changed its name to USX.

Then when the Yankees did make it back to the World Series, they were cast in the role of lovable underdog against the mighty Atlanta Braves. A 12-year-old helped them win a playoff game against Baltimore. One of their regular outfielders began the season in the independent Northern League. One of their starting pitchers had career-threatening surgery in the spring, and was back in the rotation by late summer. Their manager was a walking human-interest story.

This bunch hardly resembled the Bronx Bombers. During the regular season, they were ninth in the 14-team American League in slugging percentage, ninth in runs and 12th in home runs.

They did rank high in batting average and on-base percentage, and had a good pitching staff. In the homer-happy AL, they won by playing like a National League team.

"We don't have a great deal of power, so we have to do the small things," manager Joe Torre said. "You take what they give you. You put the ball in play and move runners."

**Series MVP.** Outfielder Bernie Williams hit .474 in the ALCS to lead the Yankees to the 1996 American League pennant.

Little ball, though, took a holiday when the Yankees faced the Orioles in the AL Championship Series. New York hit 10 home runs, one of them assisted by America's newest child star, and won in five games. The Orioles hit nine dingers, but did little else offensively.

New York won Game One 5-4 in 11 innings, but the headlines were about Derek Jeter's game-tying home run in

**Dwight Gooden**

the eighth inning, not Bernie Williams' game-winner in the 11th.

Jeter's drive was about to fall into the glove of right fielder Tony Tarasco, or maybe bounce off the Yankee Stadium wall, when a 12-year-old middle-school student named Jeffrey Maier reached into play with a gloved hand and deflected the ball into the stands.

Umpire Dave Garcia mistakenly ruled it a home run, tying the game and handing Maier his 15 minutes of fame awfully early in life.

Within 48 hours, Maier found himself on both "Good Morning America" and Regis & Kathie Lee. ABC, which wasn't even televising the games, put him up in an expensive hotel suite. One New York tabloid got him tickets behind the Yankees dugout for Game Two. Another sent nine reporters to follow him around. Presidential candidates have had smaller entourages.

If Maier was a hero in New York, he was a villain in Baltimore. When the Orioles won Game Two 5-3, it meant that if not for Maier's interference and Garcia's bad call, the Orioles might well have won the first two games on the road.

Instead, they lost the next three games at home, and the Yankees won the pennant. New York's hero in those games wasn't as surprising as Maier, but was pretty darn surprising. Darryl Strawberry, who hit three home runs in the last two games, began the season playing for the St. Paul Saints. Before that, the Yankees had declined to re-sign him after the 1995 season. Before that, he had been in drug rehab and in trouble with the IRS. Before that, his career had been threatened by injury while with the Dodgers.

"I was pretty sure it was over," Strawberry said of his time in St. Paul. "I was ready to go home and start a life with my church."

But then Yankees owner George Steinbrenner re-signed him over the objections of general manager

# AMERICAN LEAGUE
## CHAMPIONS, 1901-96

| | Pennant | Pct. | GA |
|---|---|---|---|
| 1901 | Chicago | .610 | 4 |
| 1902 | Philadelphia | .610 | 5 |
| 1903 | Boston | .659 | 14½ |
| 1904 | Boston | .617 | 1½ |
| 1905 | Philadelphia | .622 | 2 |
| 1906 | Chicago | .616 | 3 |
| 1907 | Detroit | .613 | 1½ |
| 1908 | Detroit | .588 | ½ |
| 1909 | Detroit | .645 | 3½ |
| 1910 | Philadelphia | .680 | 14½ |
| 1911 | Philadelphia | .669 | 13½ |
| 1912 | Boston | .691 | 14 |
| 1913 | Philadelphia | .627 | 6½ |
| 1914 | Philadelphia | .651 | 8½ |
| 1915 | Boston | .669 | 2½ |
| 1916 | Boston | .591 | 2 |
| 1917 | Chicago | .649 | 9 |
| 1918 | Boston | .595 | 2½ |
| 1919 | Chicago | .629 | 3½ |
| 1920 | Cleveland | .636 | 2 |
| 1921 | New York | .641 | 4½ |
| 1922 | New York | .610 | 1 |
| 1923 | New York | .645 | 16 |
| 1924 | Washington | .597 | 2 |
| 1925 | Washington | .636 | 8½ |
| 1926 | New York | .591 | 3 |
| 1927 | New York | .714 | 19 |
| 1928 | New York | .656 | 2½ |
| 1929 | Philadelphia | .693 | 18 |
| 1930 | Philadelphia | .662 | 8 |

| | Pennant | Pct. | GA | MVP |
|---|---|---|---|---|
| 1931 | Philadelphia | .704 | 13½ | Lefty Grove, lhp, Philadelphia |
| 1932 | New York | .695 | 13 | Jimmie Foxx, 1b, Philadelphia |
| 1933 | Washington | .651 | 7 | Jimmie Foxx, 1b, Philadelphia |
| 1934 | Detroit | .656 | 7 | Mickey Cochrane, c, Detroit |
| 1935 | Detroit | .616 | 3 | Hank Greenberg, 1b, Detroit |
| 1936 | New York | .667 | 19½ | Lou Gehrig, 1b, New York |
| 1937 | New York | .662 | 13 | Charlie Gehringer, 2b, Detroit |
| 1938 | New York | .651 | 9½ | Jimmie Foxx, 1b, Boston |
| 1939 | New York | .702 | 17 | Joe DiMaggio, of, New York |
| 1940 | Detroit | .584 | 1 | Hank Greenberg, 1b, Detroit |
| 1941 | New York | .656 | 17 | Joe DiMaggio, of, New York |
| 1942 | New York | .669 | 9 | Joe Gordon, 2b, New York |
| 1943 | New York | .636 | 13½ | Spud Chandler, rhp, New York |
| 1944 | St. Louis | .578 | 1 | Hal Newhouser, lhp, Detroit |
| 1945 | Detroit | .575 | 1½ | Hal Newhouher, lhp, Detroit |
| 1946 | Boston | .675 | 12 | Ted Williams, of, Boston |
| 1947 | New York | .630 | 12 | Joe DiMaggio, of, New York |
| 1948 | Cleveland | .626 | 1 | Lou Boudreau, ss, Cleveland |
| 1949 | New York | .630 | 1 | Ted Williams, of, Boston |
| 1950 | New York | .636 | 3 | Phil Rizzuto, ss, New York |
| 1951 | New York | .636 | 5 | Yogi Berra, c, New York |
| 1952 | New York | .617 | 2 | Bobby Shantz, lhp, Philadelphia |
| 1953 | New York | .656 | 8½ | Al Rosen, 3b, Cleveland |
| 1954 | Cleveland | .721 | 8 | Yogi Berra, c, New York |
| 1955 | New York | .623 | 3 | Yogi Berra, c, New York |
| 1956 | New York | .630 | 9 | Mickey Mantle, of, New York |
| 1957 | New York | .636 | 8 | Mickey Mantle, of, New York |
| 1958 | New York | .597 | 10 | Jackie Jensen, of, Boston |
| 1959 | Chicago | .610 | 5 | Nellie Fox, 2b, Chicago |
| 1960 | New York | .630 | 8 | Roger Maris, of, New York |
| 1961 | New York | .673 | 8 | Roger Maris, of, New York |
| 1962 | New York | .593 | 5 | Mickey Mantle, of, New York |
| 1963 | New York | .646 | 10½ | Elston Howard, c, New York |
| 1964 | New York | .611 | 1 | Brooks Robinson, 3b, Baltimore |
| 1965 | Minnesota | .630 | 7 | Zoilo Versalles, ss, Minnesota |
| 1966 | Baltimore | .606 | 9 | Frank Robinson, of, Baltimore |
| 1967 | Boston | .568 | 1 | Carl Yastrzemski, of, Boston |
| 1968 | Detroit | .636 | 12 | Denny McLain, rhp, Detroit |

| | East. Div. | PCT | GA | West. Div. | PCT | GA | Pennant | MVP |
|---|---|---|---|---|---|---|---|---|
| 1969 | Baltimore | .673 | 19 | Minnesota | .599 | 9 | Baltimore 3-0 | Harmon Killebrew, 1b-3b, Minnesota |
| 1970 | Baltimore | .667 | 15 | Minnesota | .605 | 9 | Baltimore 3-0 | Boog Powell, 1b, Baltimore |
| 1971 | Baltimore | .639 | 12 | Oakland | .627 | 16 | Baltimore 3-0 | Vida Blue, lhp, Oakland |
| 1972 | Detroit | .551 | ½ | Oakland | .600 | 5½ | Oakland 3-2 | Dick Allen, 1b, Chicago |
| 1973 | Baltimore | .599 | 8 | Oakland | .580 | 6 | Oakland 3-2 | Reggie Jackson, of, Oakland |
| 1974 | Baltimore | .562 | 2 | Oakland | .556 | 5 | Oakland 3-1 | Jeff Burroughs, of, Texas |
| 1975 | Boston | .594 | 4½ | Oakland | .605 | 7 | Boston 3-0 | Fred Lynn, of, Boston |
| 1976 | New York | .610 | 10½ | Kansas City | .556 | 2½ | New York 3-2 | Thurman Munson, c, New York |
| 1977 | New York | .617 | 2½ | Kansas City | .630 | 8 | New York 3-2 | Rod Carew, 1b, Minnesota |
| 1978 | New York | .613 | 1 | Kansas City | .568 | 5 | New York 3-1 | Jim Rice, of, Boston |
| 1979 | Baltimore | .642 | 8 | California | .543 | 3 | Baltimore 3-1 | Don Baylor, dh, California |
| 1980 | New York | .636 | 3 | Kansas City | .599 | 14 | Kansas City 3-0 | George Brett, 3b, Kansas City |
| 1981 | New York* | .607 | 2 | Oakland** | .587 | — | New York 3-0 | Rollie Fingers, rhp, Milwaukee |
| | Milwaukee | .585 | 1½ | Kansas City | .566 | 1 | | |
| 1982 | Milwaukee | .586 | 1 | California | .574 | 3 | Milwaukee 3-2 | Robin Yount, ss, Milwaukee |
| 1983 | Baltimore | .605 | 6 | Chicago | .611 | 20 | Baltimore 3-1 | Cal Ripken Jr., ss, Baltimore |
| 1984 | Detroit | .642 | 15 | Kansas City | .519 | 3 | Detroit 3-0 | Willie Hernandez, lhp, Detroit |
| 1985 | Toronto | .615 | 2 | Kansas City | .562 | 1 | Kansas City 4-3 | Don Mattingly, 1b, New York |
| 1986 | Boston | .590 | 5½ | California | .568 | 5 | Boston 4-3 | Roger Clemens, rhp, Boston |
| 1987 | Detroit | .605 | 2 | Minnesota | .525 | 2 | Minnesota 4-1 | George Bell, of, Toronto |
| 1988 | Boston | .549 | 1 | Oakland | .642 | 13 | Oakland 4-0 | Jose Canseco, of, Oakland |
| 1989 | Toronto | .549 | 2 | Oakland | .611 | 7 | Oakland 4-1 | Robin Yount, of, Milwaukee |
| 1990 | Boston | .543 | 2 | Oakland | .636 | 9 | Oakland 4-0 | Rickey Henderson, of, Oakland |
| 1991 | Toronto | .562 | 7 | Minnesota | .586 | 8 | Minnesota 4-1 | Cal Ripken Jr., ss, Baltimore |
| 1992 | Toronto | .593 | 4 | Oakland | .593 | 6 | Toronto 4-2 | Dennis Eckersley, rhp, Oakland |
| 1993 | Toronto | .586 | 7 | Chicago | .580 | 8 | Toronto 4-2 | Frank Thomas, 1b, Chicago |

| | East Div. | PCT | GA | Central Div. | PCT | GA | West Div. | PCT | GA | MVP |
|---|---|---|---|---|---|---|---|---|---|---|
| 1994 | New York | .619 | 6½ | Chicago | .593 | 1 | Texas | | .456 | | Frank Thomas, 1b, Chicago |
| 1995 | Boston | .597 | 7 | Cleveland# | .694 | 30 | Seattle | | .545 | 1 | Mo Vaughn, 1b, Boston |
| 1996 | New York@ | .568 | 4 | Cleveland | .615 | 14½ | Texas | | .556 | 4 | Juan Gonzalez, of, Texas |

*Won first half; defeated Milwaukee 3-2 in best-of-5 playoff.    **Won first half, defeated Kansas City 3-0 in best-of-5 playoff.
#Won AL pennant, defeating Seattle 4-2.    @ Won AL pennant, defeating Baltimore 4-1.

| Page | EAST | W | L | PCT | GB | Manager | General Manager | Attend./Dates | Last Penn. |
|---|---|---|---|---|---|---|---|---|---|
| 169 | New York Yankees | 92 | 70 | .568 | — | Joe Torre | Bob Watson | 2,250,124 (78) | 1996 |
| 67 | Baltimore Orioles* | 88 | 74 | .543 | 4 | Dave Johnson | Pat Gillick | 3,646,950 (81) | 1983 |
| 74 | Boston Red Sox | 85 | 77 | .525 | 7 | Kevin Kennedy | Dan Duquette | 2,315,233 (81) | 1986 |
| 234 | Toronto Blue Jays | 74 | 88 | .457 | 18 | Cito Gaston | Gord Ash | 2,559,563 (81) | 1993 |
| 120 | Detroit Tigers | 53 | 109 | .327 | 39 | Buddy Bell | Randy Smith | 1,168,610 (81) | 1984 |

| Page | CENTRAL | W | L | PCT | GB | Manager | General Manager | Attend./Dates | Last Penn. |
|---|---|---|---|---|---|---|---|---|---|
| 108 | Cleveland Indians | 99 | 62 | .615 | — | Mike Hargrove | John Hart | 3,318,174 (79) | 1995 |
| 88 | Chicago White Sox | 85 | 77 | .525 | 14½ | Terry Bevington | Ron Schueler | 1,676,416 (79) | 1959 |
| 151 | Milwaukee Brewers | 80 | 82 | .494 | 19½ | Phil Garner | Sal Bando | 1,327,155 (78) | 1982 |
| 157 | Minnesota Twins | 78 | 84 | .481 | 21½ | Tom Kelly | Terry Ryan | 1,437,352 (80) | 1991 |
| 138 | Kansas City Royals | 75 | 86 | .466 | 24 | Bob Boone | Herk Robinson | 1,436,007 (80) | 1985 |

| Page | WEST | W | L | PCT | GB | Manager(s) | General Manager | Attend./Dates | Last Penn. |
|---|---|---|---|---|---|---|---|---|---|
| 228 | Texas Rangers | 90 | 72 | .556 | — | Johnny Oates | Doug Melvin | 2,888,920 (80) | None |
| 220 | Seattle Mariners | 85 | 76 | .528 | 4½ | Lou Piniella | Woody Woodward | 2,722,054 (81) | None |
| 183 | Oakland Athletics | 78 | 84 | .481 | 12 | Art Howe | Sandy Alderson | 1,148,382 (80) | 1990 |
| 81 | California Angels | 70 | 91 | .435 | 19½ | Lachemann/McNamara | Bill Bavasi | 1,820,532 (81) | None |

*Won wild-card playoff berth
**NOTE:** Team's individual batting, pitching and fielding statistics can be found on page indicated in lefthand column.

Bob Watson. Strawberry went just 3-for-16 in the World Series, but the Yankees beat the Braves in six games.

Considering all he'd been through, Strawberry must have walked away with considerable satisfaction.

## Comebacks Galore

Anywhere you looked in the Yankees' clubhouse, there was a story of courage and redemption.

There was Dwight Gooden, the righthander whose career closely parallels Strawberry's. They were teammates during the Mets' glory years in the mid-1980s. Both endured career-threatening injury and drug problems before reuniting with the Yankees.

At first, it didn't appear that Gooden's story would have the requisite happy ending. He went 0-3 with a 11.48 ERA in his first three starts of 1996. But the Yankees had to keep him in the rotation because an aneurysm developed in Cone's right shoulder.

Cone underwent surgery, and it was uncertain whether he ever would pitch again. Gooden proceeded to go 2-0 with a 1.24 ERA in four starts. His crowning moment was a May 14 no-hitter against Seattle, four days after Cone's operation.

"At this time last year, I didn't know if I'd ever have this opportunity again," said Gooden, who was serving a suspension for violating his drug aftercare program. "To hit rock bottom and then to win again in the big leagues, for me personally is a miracle."

Gooden ran out of gas late in the year, and was left off the Yankees postseason roster. But that was about the time Cone was making a miracle comeback of his own.

On Sept. 2 in Oakland, Cone made his first major league start after surgery and pitched seven no-hit innings. He remained in the rotation through the World

**Juan Gonzalez**

**Yankee Clipper.** Lefthander Andy Pettitte led New York to the AL pennant by winning 21 games.

Series.

All of this was presided over by Torre, who reached the World Series for the first time in 33 years as a major league player and manager. As if that wasn't drama enough, Torre's brother Rocco, a New York police officer, died of a heart attack in June. Another brother, Frank, a former major league mainstay with the Braves, spent the postseason in a New York hospital awaiting a heart transplant.

## Schizoid Orioles Win

Of course, the Yankees weren't the 1996 postseason's only underdog. The Orioles, after all, knocked off the mighty Cleveland Indians in the AL Division

# AMERICAN LEAGUE
## YEAR-BY-YEAR LEADERS: BATTING

| Year | Batting Average | Home Runs | RBIs |
|---|---|---|---|
| 1901 | Nap Lajoie, Philadelphia .422 | Nap Lajoie, Philadelphia 14 | Nap Lajoie, Philadelphia 125 |
| 1902 | Ed Delahanty, Wash. .376 | Socks Seybold, Philadelphia 16 | Buck Freeman, Boston 121 |
| 1903 | Nap Lajoie, Cleveland .355 | Buck Freeman, Boston 13 | Buck Freeman, Boston 104 |
| 1904 | Nap Lajoie, Cleveland .381 | Harry Davis, Philadelphia 10 | Nap Lajoie, Cleveland 102 |
| 1905 | Elmer Flick, Cleveland .306 | Harry Davis, Philadelphia 8 | Harry Davis, Philadelphia 83 |
| 1906 | George Stone, St. Louis .358 | Harry Davis, Philadelphia 12 | Harry Davis, Philadelphia 96 |
| 1907 | Ty Cobb, Detroit .350 | Harry Davis, Philadelphia 8 | Ty Cobb, Detroit 116 |
| 1908 | Ty Cobb, Detroit .324 | Sam Crawford, Detroit 7 | Ty Cobb, Detroit 101 |
| 1909 | Ty Cobb, Detroit .377 | Ty Cobb, Detroit 9 | Ty Cobb, Detroit 115 |
| 1910 | Ty Cobb, Detroit .385 | Jake Stahl, Boston 10 | Sam Crawford, Detroit 115 |
| 1911 | Ty Cobb, Detroit .420 | Frank Baker, Philadelphia 11 | Ty Cobb, Detroit 144 |
| 1912 | Ty Cobb, Detroit .410 | 2 tied at 10 | Frank Baker, Philadelphia 133 |
| 1913 | Ty Cobb, Detroit .390 | Frank Baker, Philadelphia 12 | Frank Baker, Philadelphia 126 |
| 1914 | Ty Cobb, Detroit .368 | Frank Baker, Philadelphia 9 | Sam Crawford, Detroit 112 |
| 1915 | Ty Cobb, Detroit .370 | Braggo Roth, Cleveland 7 | Sam Crawford, Detroit 116 |
| 1916 | Tris Speaker, Cleveland .386 | Wally Pipp, New York 12 | Wally Pipp, New York 99 |
| 1917 | Ty Cobb, Detroit .383 | Wally Pipp, New York 9 | Bob Veach, Detroit 115 |
| 1918 | Ty Cobb, Detroit .382 | 2 tied at 11 | 2 tied at 74 |
| 1919 | Ty Cobb, Detroit .384 | Babe Ruth, Boston 29 | Babe Ruth, Boston 112 |
| 1920 | George Sisler, St. Louis .407 | Babe Ruth, New York 54 | Babe Ruth, New York 137 |
| 1921 | Harry Heilmann, Detroit .394 | Babe Ruth, New York 59 | Babe Ruth, New York 171 |
| 1922 | George Sisler, St. Louis .420 | Kenny Williams, St. Louis 39 | Kenny Williams, St. Louis 155 |
| 1923 | Harry Heilmann, Detroit .403 | Babe Ruth, New York 41 | Babe Ruth, New York 131 |
| 1924 | Babe Ruth, New York .378 | Babe Ruth, New York 46 | Goose Goslin, Wash. 129 |
| 1925 | Harry Heilmann, Detroit .393 | Bob Meusel, New York 33 | Bob Meusel, New York 138 |
| 1926 | Heinie Manush, Detroit .377 | Babe Ruth, New York 47 | Babe Ruth, New York 145 |
| 1927 | Harry Heilmann, Detroit .398 | Babe Ruth, New York 60 | Lou Gehrig, New York 175 |
| 1928 | Goose Goslin, Wash. .379 | Babe Ruth, New York 54 | 2 tied at 142 |
| 1929 | Lew Fonseca, Cleveland .369 | Babe Ruth, New York 46 | Al Simmons, Philadelphia 157 |
| 1930 | Al Simmons, Philadelphia .381 | Babe Ruth, New York 49 | Lou Gehrig, New York 174 |
| 1931 | Al Simmons, Philadelphia .390 | Babe Ruth, New York 46 | Lou Gehrig, New York 184 |
| 1932 | Dale Alexander, Det.-Bos. .367 | Jimmie Foxx, Philadelphia 58 | Jimmie Foxx, Philadelphia 169 |
| 1933 | Jimmie Foxx, Philadelphia .356 | Jimmie Foxx, Philadelphia 48 | Jimmie Foxx, Philadelphia 163 |
| 1934 | Lou Gehrig, New York .363 | Lou Gehrig, New York 49 | Lou Gehrig, New York 165 |
| 1935 | Buddy Myer, Washington .349 | 2 tied at 36 | Hank Greenberg, Detroit 170 |
| 1936 | Luke Appling, Chicago .388 | Lou Gehrig, New York 49 | Hal Trosky, Cleveland 162 |
| 1937 | Charlie Gehringer, Detroit .371 | Joe DiMaggio, New York 46 | Hank Greenberg, Detroit 183 |
| 1938 | Jimmie Foxx, Boston .349 | Hank Greenberg, Detroit 58 | Jimmie Foxx, Boston 175 |
| 1939 | Joe DiMaggio, New York .381 | Jimmie Foxx, Boston 35 | Ted Williams, Boston 145 |
| 1940 | Joe DiMaggio, New York .352 | Hank Greenberg, Detroit 41 | Hank Greenberg, Detroit 150 |
| 1941 | Ted Williams, Boston .406 | Ted Williams, Boston 37 | Joe DiMaggio, New York 125 |
| 1942 | Ted Williams, Boston .356 | Ted Williams, Boston 36 | Ted Williams, Boston 137 |
| 1943 | Luke Appling, Chicago .328 | Rudy York, Detroit 34 | Rudy York, Detroit 118 |
| 1944 | Lou Boudreau, Cleve. .327 | Nick Etten, New York 22 | Vern Stephens, St. Louis 109 |
| 1945 | Snuffy Stirnweiss, N.Y. .309 | Vern Stephens, St. Louis 24 | Nick Etten, New York 111 |
| 1946 | Mickey Vernon, Wash. .352 | Hank Greenberg, Detroit 44 | Hank Greenberg, Detroit 127 |
| 1947 | Ted Williams, Boston .343 | Ted Williams, Boston 32 | Ted Williams, Boston 114 |

| Year | Batting Average | Home Runs | RBIs |
|---|---|---|---|
| 1948 | Ted Williams, Boston .369 | Joe DiMaggio, New York 39 | Joe DiMaggio, New York 155 |
| 1949 | George Kell, Detroit .343 | Ted Williams, Boston 43 | 2 tied at 159 |
| 1950 | Billy Goodman, Boston .354 | Al Rosen, Cleveland 37 | 2 tied at 144 |
| 1951 | Ferris Fain, Philadelphia .344 | Gus Zernial, Chi.-Phil. 33 | Gus Zernial, Chi.-Phil. 129 |
| 1952 | Ferris Fain, Philadelphia .327 | Larry Doby, Cleveland 32 | Al Rosen, Cleveland 105 |
| 1953 | Mickey Vernon, Wash. .337 | Al Rosen, Cleveland 43 | Al Rosen, Cleveland 145 |
| 1954 | Bobby Avila, Cleveland .341 | Larry Doby, Cleveland 32 | Larry Doby, Cleveland 126 |
| 1955 | Al Kaline, Detroit .340 | Mickey Mantle, New York 37 | 2 tied at 116 |
| 1956 | Mickey Mantle, New York .353 | Mickey Mantle, New York 52 | Mickey Mantle, New York 130 |
| 1957 | Ted Williams, Boston .388 | Roy Sievers, Washington 42 | Roy Sievers, Washington 114 |
| 1958 | Ted Williams, Boston .328 | Mickey Mantle, New York 42 | Jackie Jensen, Boston 122 |
| 1959 | Harvey Kuenn, Detroit .353 | 2 tied at 42 | Jackie Jensen, Boston 112 |
| 1960 | Pete Runnels, Boston .320 | Mickey Mantle, New York 40 | Roger Maris, New York 112 |
| 1961 | Norm Cash, Detroit .361 | Roger Maris, New York 61 | Roger Maris, New York 142 |
| 1962 | Pete Runnels, Boston .326 | Harmon Killebrew, Minn. 48 | Harmon Killebrew, Minn. 126 |
| 1963 | Carl Yastrzemski, Boston .321 | Harmon Killebrew, Minn. 45 | Dick Stuart, Boston 118 |
| 1964 | Tony Oliva, Minnesota .323 | Harmon Killebrew, Minn. 49 | Brooks Robinson, Baltimore 118 |
| 1965 | Tony Oliva, Minnesota .321 | Tony Conigliaro, Boston 32 | Rocky Colavito, Cleveland 108 |
| 1966 | Frank Robinson, Balt. .316 | Frank Robinson, Baltimore 49 | Frank Robinson, Baltimore 122 |
| 1967 | Carl Yastrzemski, Boston .326 | 2 tied at 44 | Carl Yastrzemski, Boston 121 |
| 1968 | Carl Yastrzemski, Boston .301 | Frank Howard, Washington 44 | Ken Harrelson, Boston 109 |
| 1969 | Rod Carew, Minnesota .332 | Harmon Killebrew, Minn. 49 | Harmon Killebrew, Minn. 140 |
| 1970 | Alex Johnson, California .329 | Frank Howard, Washington 44 | Frank Howard, Washington 126 |
| 1971 | Tony Oliva, Minnesota .337 | Bill Melton, Chicago 33 | Harmon Killebrew, Minn. 119 |
| 1972 | Rod Carew, Minnesota .318 | Dick Allen, Chicago 37 | Dick Allen, Chicago 113 |
| 1973 | Rod Carew, Minnesota .350 | Reggie Jackson, Oakland 32 | Reggie Jackson, Oakland 117 |
| 1974 | Rod Carew, Minnesota .364 | Dick Allen, Chicago 32 | Jeff Burroughs, Texas 118 |
| 1975 | Rod Carew, Minnesota .359 | 2 tied at 36 | George Scott, Milwaukee 109 |
| 1976 | George Brett, Kansas City .333 | Graig Nettles, New York 32 | Lee May, Baltimore 109 |
| 1977 | Rod Carew, Minnesota .388 | Jim Rice, Boston 39 | Larry Hisle, Minnesota 119 |
| 1978 | Rod Carew, Minnesota .333 | Jim Rice, Boston 46 | Jim Rice, Boston 139 |
| 1979 | Fred Lynn, Boston .333 | Gorman Thomas, Mil. 45 | Don Baylor, California 139 |
| 1980 | George Brett, Kansas City .390 | 2 tied at 41 | Cecil Cooper, Milwaukee 122 |
| 1981 | Carney Lansford, Boston .336 | 4 tied at 22 | Eddie Murray, Baltimore 78 |
| 1982 | Willie Wilson, Kansas City .332 | 2 tied at 39 | Hal McRae, Kansas City 133 |
| 1983 | Wade Boggs, Boston .361 | Jim Rice, Boston 39 | 2 tied at 126 |
| 1984 | Don Mattingly, New York .343 | Tony Armas, Boston 43 | Tony Armas, Boston 123 |
| 1985 | Wade Boggs, Boston .368 | Darrell Evans, Detroit 40 | Don Mattingly, New York 145 |
| 1986 | Wade Boggs, Boston .357 | Jesse Barfield, Toronto 40 | Joe Carter, Cleveland 121 |
| 1987 | Wade Boggs, Boston .363 | Mark McGwire, Oakland 49 | George Bell, Toronto 134 |
| 1988 | Wade Boggs, Boston .366 | Jose Canseco, Oakland 42 | Jose Canseco, Oakland 124 |
| 1989 | Kirby Puckett, Minn. .339 | Fred McGriff, Toronto 36 | Ruben Sierra, Texas 119 |
| 1990 | George Brett, Kansas City .329 | Cecil Fielder, Detroit 51 | Cecil Fielder, Detroit 132 |
| 1991 | Julio Franco, Texas .341 | 2 tied at 44 | Cecil Fielder, Detroit 133 |
| 1992 | Edgar Martinez, Seattle .343 | Juan Gonzalez, Texas 43 | Cecil Fielder, Detroit 124 |
| 1993 | John Olerud, Toronto .363 | Juan Gonzalez, Texas 46 | Albert Belle, Cleveland 129 |
| 1994 | Paul O'Neill, New York .359 | Ken Griffey, Seattle 40 | Kirby Puckett, Minnesota 112 |
| 1995 | Edgar Martinez, Seattle .356 | Albert Belle, Cleveland 50 | 2 tied at 126 |
| 1996 | Alex Rodriguez, Seattle .358 | Mark McGwire Oakland 52 | Albert Belle, Cleveland 148 |

# AMERICAN LEAGUE
## YEAR-BY-YEAR LEADERS: PITCHING

| Year | Wins | ERA | Strikeouts |
|---|---|---|---|
| 1901 | Cy Young, Boston 33 | Cy Young, Boston 1.63 | Cy Young, Boston 158 |
| 1902 | Cy Young, Boston 32 | Ed Siever, Detroit 1.91 | Rube Waddell, Philadelphia 210 |
| 1903 | Cy Young, Boston 28 | Earl Moore, Cleveland 1.77 | Rube Waddell, Philadelphia 302 |
| 1904 | Jack Chesbro, New York 41 | Addie Joss, Cleveland 1.59 | Rube Waddell, Philadelphia 349 |
| 1905 | Rube Waddell, Phil. 26 | Rube Waddell, Philadelphia 1.48 | Rue Waddell, Philadelphia 287 |
| 1906 | Al Orth, New York 27 | Doc White, Chicago 1.52 | Rube Waddell, Philadelphia 196 |
| 1907 | 2 tied at 27 | Ed Walsh, Chicago 1.60 | Rube Waddell, Philadelphia 232 |
| 1908 | Ed Walsh, Chicago 40 | Addie Joss, Cleveland 1.16 | Ed Walsh, Chicago 269 |
| 1909 | George Mullin, Detroit 29 | Harry Krause, Philadelphia 1.39 | Frank Smith, Chicago 177 |
| 1910 | Jack Coombs, Phil. 31 | Ed Walsh, Chicago 1.27 | Walter Johnson, Washington 313 |
| 1911 | Jack Coombs, Phil. 28 | Vean Gregg, Cleveland 1.81 | Ed Walsh, Chicago 255 |
| 1912 | Joe Wood, Boston 34 | Walter Johnson, Washington 1.39 | Walter Johnson, Washington 303 |
| 1913 | Walter Johnson, Wash. 36 | Walter Johnson, Wash. 1.14 | Walter Johnson, Washington 243 |
| 1914 | Walter Johnson, Wash. 28 | Dutch Leonard, Bos. 1.00 | Walter Johnson, Washington 225 |
| 1915 | Walter Johnson, Wash. 27 | Joe Wood, Boston 1.49 | Walter Johnson, Washington 203 |
| 1916 | Walter Johnson, Wash. 25 | Babe Ruth, Boston 1.75 | Walter Johnson, Washington 228 |
| 1917 | Ed Cicotte, Chicago 28 | Ed Cicotte, Chicago 1.53 | Walter Johnson, Washington 188 |
| 1918 | Walter Johnson, Wash. 23 | Walter Johnson, Wash. 1.27 | Walter Johnson, Washington 162 |
| 1919 | Ed Cicotte, Chicago 29 | Walter Johnson, Wash. 1.49 | Walter Johnson, Washington 147 |
| 1920 | Jim Bagby, Cleveland 31 | Bob Shawkey, New York 2.45 | Stan Coveleski, Cleveland 133 |
| 1921 | 2 tied at 27 | Red Faber, Chicago 2.48 | Walter Johnson, Washington 143 |
| 1922 | Eddie Rommel, Phil. 27 | Red Faber, Chicago 2.80 | Urban Shocker, St. Louis 149 |
| 1923 | George Uhle, Cleveland 26 | Stan Coveleski, Claveland 2.76 | Walter Johnson, Washington 130 |
| 1924 | Walter Johnson, Wash. 23 | Walter Johnson, Wash. 2.72 | Walter Johnson, Washington 158 |
| 1925 | 2 tied at 21 | Stan Coveleski, Wash. 2.84 | Lefty Grove, Philadelphia 116 |
| 1926 | George Uhle, Claveland 27 | Lefty Grove, Philadelphia 2.51 | Lefty Grove, Philadelphia 194 |
| 1927 | 2 tied at 22 | Wilcy Moore, New York 2.28 | Lefty Grove, Philadelphia 174 |
| 1928 | 2 tied at 24 | Garland Braxton, Wash. 2.52 | Lefty Grove, Philadelphia 183 |
| 1929 | George Earnshaw, Phil. 24 | Lefty Grove, Philadelphia 2.82 | Lefty Grove, Philadelphia 170 |
| 1930 | Lefty Grove, Philadelphia 28 | Lefty Grove, Philadelphia 2.54 | Lefty Grove, Philadelphia 209 |
| 1931 | Lefty Grove, Philadelphia 31 | Lefty Grove, Philadelphia 2.05 | Lefty Grove, Philadelphia 175 |
| 1932 | General Crowder, Wash. 26 | Lefty Grove, Philadelphia 2.84 | Red Ruffing, New York 190 |
| 1933 | 2 tied at 24 | Monte Pearson, Cleveland 2.33 | Lefty Gomez, New York 163 |
| 1934 | Lefty Gomez, New York 26 | Lefty Gomez, New York 2.33 | Lefty Gomez, New York 158 |
| 1935 | Wes Ferrell, Boston 25 | Lefty Grove, Boston 2.70 | Tommy Bridges, Detroit 163 |
| 1936 | Tommy Bridges, Detroit 23 | Lefty Grove, Boston 2.81 | Tommy Bridges, Detroit 175 |
| 1937 | Lefty Gomez, New York 21 | Lefty Gomez, New York 2.33 | Lefty Gomez, New York 194 |
| 1938 | Red Ruffing, New York 21 | Lefty Grove, Philadelphia 3.07 | Bob Feller, Cleveland 240 |
| 1939 | Bob Feller, Cleveland 24 | Lefty Grove, Cleveland 2.54 | Bob Feller, Cleveland 246 |
| 1940 | Bob Feller, Cleveland 27 | Bob Feller, Cleveland 2.62 | Bob Feller, Cleveland 261 |
| 1941 | Bob Feller, Cleveland 25 | Thornton Lee, Chicago 2.37 | Bob Feller, Cleveland 260 |
| 1942 | Tex Hughson, Boston 22 | Ted Lyons, Chicago 2.10 | 2 tied at 113 |
| 1943 | 2 tied at 20 | Spud Chandler, New York 1.64 | Allie Reynolds, Cleveland 151 |
| 1944 | Hal Newhouser, Detroit 29 | Dizzy Trout, Detroit 2.12 | Hal Newhouser, Detroit 187 |
| 1945 | Hal Newhouser, Detroit 25 | Hal Newhouser, Detroit 1.81 | Hal Newhouser, Detroit 212 |
| 1946 | 2 tied at 26 | Hal Newhouser, Detroit 1.94 | Bob Feller, Cleveland 348 |
| 1947 | Bob Feller, Cleveland 20 | Spud Chandler, New York 2.46 | Bob Feller, Cleveland 196 |
| 1948 | Hal Newhouser, Detroit 21 | Gene Bearden, Cleveland 2.43 | Bob Feller, Cleveland 164 |
| 1949 | Mel Parnell, Boston 25 | Mel Parnell, Boston 2.78 | Virgil Trucks, Detroit 153 |
| 1950 | Bob Lemon, Cleveland 23 | Early Wynn, Cleveland 3.20 | Bob Lemon, Cleveland 170 |
| 1951 | Bob Feller, Cleveland 22 | Saul Rogovin, Det.-Chi. 2.78 | Vic Raschi, New York 164 |
| 1952 | Bobby Shantz, Phil. 24 | Allie Reynolds, New York 2.07 | Allie Reynolds, New York 160 |
| 1953 | Bob Porterfield, Wash. 22 | Eddie Lopat, New York 2.43 | Billy Pierce, Chicago 186 |
| 1954 | 2 tied at 23 | Mike Garcia, Cleveland 2.64 | Bob Turley, Baltimore 185 |
| 1955 | 3 tied at 18 | Billy Pierce, Chicago 1.97 | Herb Score, Cleveland 245 |
| 1956 | Frank Lary, Detroit 21 | Whitey Ford, New York 2.47 | Herb Score, Cleveland 263 |
| 1957 | 2 tied at 20 | Bobby Shantz, New York 2.45 | Early Wynn, Cleveland 184 |
| 1958 | Bob Turley, New York 21 | Whitey Ford, New York 2.01 | Early Wynn, Chicago 179 |
| 1959 | Early Wynn, Chicago 22 | Hoyt Wilhelm, Balt. 2.19 | Jim Bunning, Detroit 201 |
| 1960 | 2 tied at 18 | Frank Baumann, Chicago 2.68 | Jim Bunning, Detroit 201 |
| 1961 | Whitey Ford, New York 25 | Dick Donovan, Washington 2.40 | Camilo Pascual, Minnesota 221 |
| 1962 | Ralph Terry, New York 23 | Hank Aguirre, Detroit 2.21 | Camilo Pascual, Minnesota 206 |
| 1963 | Whitey Ford, New York 24 | Gary Peters, Chicago 2.33 | Camilo Pascual, Minnesota 202 |
| 1964 | 2 tied at 20 | Dean Chance, L.A. 1.65 | Al Downing, New York 217 |
| 1965 | Mudcat Grant, Minnesota 21 | Sam McDowell, Cleveland 2.18 | Sam McDowell, Cleveland 325 |
| 1966 | Jim Kaat, Minnesota 25 | Gary Peters, Chicago 1.98 | Sam McDowell, Cleveland 225 |
| 1967 | 2 tied at 22 | Joel Horlen, Chicago 2.06 | Jim Lonborg, Boston 246 |
| 1968 | Denny McLain, Detroit 31 | Luis Tiant, Cleveland 1.60 | Sam McDowell, Cleveland 283 |
| 1969 | Denny McLain, Detroit 24 | Dick Bosman, Washington 2.19 | Sam McDowell, Cleveland 279 |
| 1970 | 3 tied at 24 | Diego Segui, Oakland 2.56 | Sam McDowell, Cleveland 304 |
| 1971 | Mickey Lolich, Detroit 25 | Vida Blue, Oakland 1.82 | Mickey Lolich, Detroit 308 |
| 1972 | 2 tied at 24 | Luis Tiant, Boston 1.91 | Nolan Ryan, California 329 |
| 1973 | Wilbur Wood, Chicago 24 | Jim Palmer, Baltimore 2.40 | Nolan Ryan, California 383 |
| 1974 | 2 tied at 25 | Catfish Hunter, Oakland 2.49 | Nolan Ryan, California 367 |
| 1975 | 2 tied at 23 | Jim Palmer, Baltimore 2.09 | Frank Tanana, California 269 |
| 1976 | Jim Palmer, Baltimore 22 | Mark Fidrych, Detroit 2.34 | Nolan Ryan, California 327 |
| 1977 | 3 tied at 20 | Frank Tanana, California 2.54 | Nolan Ryan, California 341 |
| 1978 | Ron Guidry, New York 25 | Ron Guidry, New York 1.74 | Nolan Ryan, California 260 |
| 1979 | Mike Flanagan, Baltimore 23 | Ron Guidry, New York 2.78 | Nolan Ryan, California 223 |
| 1980 | Steve Stone, Baltimore 25 | Rudy May, New York 2.47 | Len Barker, Cleveland 187 |
| 1981 | Steve McCatty, Oakland 14 | Steve McCatty, Oak. 2.32 | Len Barker, Cleveland 127 |
| 1982 | LaMarr Hoyt, Chicago 19 | Rick Sutcliffe, Cleveland 2.96 | Floyd Bannister, Seattle 209 |
| 1983 | LaMarr Hoyt, Chicago 24 | Rick Honeycutt, Texas 2.42 | Jack Morris, Detroit 232 |
| 1984 | Mike Boddicker, Balt. 20 | Mike Boddicker, Balt. 2.79 | Mark Langston, Seattle 204 |
| 1985 | Ron Guidry, New York 22 | Dave Stieb, Toronto 2.48 | Bert Blyleven, Cleve.-Minn. 206 |
| 1986 | Roger Clemens, Boston 24 | Roger Clemens, Boston 2.48 | Mark Langston, Seattle 245 |
| 1987 | 2 tied at 20 | Jimmy Key, Toronto 2.76 | Mark Langston, Seattle 262 |
| 1988 | Frank Viola, Minnesota 24 | Allan Anderson, Minnesota 2.45 | Roger Clemens, Boston 291 |
| 1989 | Bret Saberhagen, K.C. 23 | Bret Saberhagen, K.C. 2.16 | Nolan Ryan, Texas 301 |
| 1990 | Bob Welch, Oakland 27 | Roger Clemens, Boston 1.93 | Nolan Ryan, Texas 232 |
| 1991 | 2 tied at 20 | Roger Clemens, Boston 2.62 | Roger Clemens, Boston 241 |
| 1992 | 2 tied at 21 | Roger Clemens, Boston 2.41 | Randy Johnson, Seattle 241 |
| 1993 | Jack McDowell, Chicago 22 | Kevin Appier, Kansas City 2.56 | Randy Johnson, Seattle 308 |
| 1994 | Jimmy Key, New York 17 | Steve Ontiveros, Oakland 2.65 | Randy Johnson, Seattle 204 |
| 1995 | Mike Mussina, Baltimore 19 | Randy Johnson, Seattle 2.48 | Randy Johnson, Seattle 294 |
| 1996 | Andy Pettitte, New York 21 | Juan Guzman, Toronto 2.93 | Roger Clemens, Boston 257 |

Series.

Cleveland was the defending league champion, and had the best record in the majors (99-62) during the regular season. But Baltimore grabbed the best-of-five series by the throat when Brady Anderson led off the first game with a home run. It never let go, and won in four games.

Baltimore took a commanding 2-0 lead in games with help from a controversial play. With the score tied 4-4, the Orioles loaded the bases with nobody out in the eighth inning. B.J. Surhoff hit a comebacker that should have been turned into a double play. Paul Assenmacher threw home for the first out, but catcher Sandy Alomar's throw eluded first baseman Jeff Kent. The winning run scored and the Orioles later added two more and won 7-4.

The Indians contended that Surhoff ran inside the baseline and interfered with Alomar's throw, but their appeal fell on deaf ears.

The Orioles were supposed to be as good as the Indians and Yankees when the 1996 season started. Owner Peter Angelos bought everything except Boardwalk and Park Place in an attempt to win the pennant. But the team he assembled often bore a closer resemblance to Melrose Place.

"This team can win, but there are a lot of things going on," outfielder Luis Polonia said after being designated for assignment by the Orioles in midseason. "They can have a hell of a team. But people are always worrying about what other people do, criticizing instead of just going out and playing the game right."

Nothing the Orioles did in 1996 should have come as a surprise. They opened the season 11-2, then were the second-worst team in the American League from mid-April to the end of July.

By that time, they were 12 games behind the Yankees in the AL East. They closed the deficit to 2½ before losing their division-title hopes in a late-September series against New York. But they won the wild-card spot when Roberto Alomar hit a game-winning home run in Toronto, the day after his celebrated spitting incident.

**Sensational Shortstop.** Seattle's 21-year-old Alex Rodriguez had a banner 1996 season, hitting .358 with 36 homers.

MEL BAILEY

Even in the game in which they eliminated Cleveland, the Orioles struck out a postseason-record 23 times. Alomar saved them again, tying the game with a single in the ninth and winning it with a home run in the 12th.

In the other division series, the Yankees lost Game One to the Rangers before winning three straight. They came from behind all three times, and won on their last at-bat in Games Two and Three.

Jeter scored the winning run in the 12th inning of

# AMERICAN LEAGUE ALL-STARS

Selected by Baseball America

| Pos. | Player, Team | B-T | Ht. | Wt. | Age | '96 Salary | AVG | AB | R | H | 2B | 3B | HR | RBI | SB |
|---|---|---|---|---|---|---|---|---|---|---|---|---|---|---|---|
| C | Ivan Rodriguez, Texas | R-R | 5-9 | 205 | 24 | $4,000,000 | .300 | 639 | 116 | 192 | 47 | 3 | 19 | 86 | 5 |
| 1B | Mo Vaughn, Boston | L-R | 6-1 | 245 | 28 | 5,350,000 | .326 | 635 | 118 | 207 | 29 | 1 | 44 | 143 | 2 |
| 2B | Chuck Knoblauch, Minn. | R-R | 5-9 | 181 | 28 | 4,670,000 | .341 | 578 | 140 | 197 | 35 | 14 | 13 | 72 | 45 |
| 3B | Jim Thome, Cleveland | L-R | 6-4 | 220 | 26 | 1,525,000 | .311 | 505 | 122 | 157 | 28 | 5 | 38 | 116 | 2 |
| SS | Alex Rodriguez, Seattle | R-R | 6-2 | 190 | 21 | 442,334 | .358 | 601 | 141 | 215 | 54 | 1 | 36 | 123 | 15 |
| OF | Albert Belle, Cleveland | R-R | 6-2 | 210 | 30 | 5,500,000 | .311 | 602 | 124 | 187 | 38 | 3 | 48 | 148 | 11 |
| | Juan Gonzalez, Texas | R-R | 6-3 | 210 | 27 | 7,100,000 | .314 | 541 | 89 | 170 | 33 | 2 | 47 | 144 | 2 |
| | Ken Griffey, Seattle | L-L | 6-3 | 220 | 26 | 7,500,000 | .303 | 545 | 125 | 165 | 26 | 2 | 49 | 140 | 16 |
| DH | Paul Molitor, Minnesota | R-R | 6-0 | 190 | 40 | 2,000,000 | .341 | 660 | 99 | 225 | 41 | 8 | 9 | 113 | 18 |

| Pos. | Player, Team | B-T | Ht. | Wt. | | '96 Salary | W | L | ERA | G | SV | IP | H | BB | SO |
|---|---|---|---|---|---|---|---|---|---|---|---|---|---|---|---|
| P | Andy Pettitte, New York | L-L | 6-5 | 235 | 24 | 150,000 | 21 | 8 | 3.87 | 35 | 0 | 221 | 229 | 72 | 162 |
| | Pat Hentgen, Toronto | R-R | 6-2 | 200 | 27 | 2,250,000 | 20 | 10 | 3.22 | 35 | 0 | 266 | 238 | 94 | 177 |
| | Charles Nagy, Cleveland | L-R | 6-3 | 200 | 29 | 3,337,500 | 17 | 5 | 3.41 | 32 | 0 | 222 | 217 | 61 | 167 |
| | Mariano Rivera, New York | R-R | 6-2 | 168 | 26 | 131,125 | 8 | 3 | 2.09 | 61 | 5 | 108 | 73 | 34 | 130 |
| RP | John Wetteland, New York | R-R | 6-2 | 215 | 30 | 4,000,000 | 2 | 3 | 2.83 | 62 | 43 | 64 | 54 | 21 | 69 |

**Player of the Year:** Alex Rodriguez, ss, Seattle. **Pitcher of the Year:** Andy Pettitte, lhp, New York. **Rookie of the Year:** Derek Jeter, ss, New York.

**Manager of the Year:** Joe Torre, New York. **Executive of the Year:** Doug Melvin, Texas.

Game Two when Rangers third baseman Dean Palmer fielded a bunt and threw past first base. In Game Three, Williams and Mariano Duncan drove in ninth-inning runs to turn a 2-1 deficit into a 3-2 victory.

Rangers right fielder Juan Gonzalez capped a brilliant season by hitting five home runs in the four games against the Yankees. Gonzalez hit .314 with 47 homers and 144 RBIs during the regular season, leading the Rangers into the postseason for the first time.

"I've never seen anything like it before," Rangers center fielder Darryl Hamilton said. "It seems like every time he comes up he has guys on base and he does the job. I've never seen anybody who can put up as many RBIs as that guy.

"When we're in the dugout trying to get things going, we say, 'Whoever's in front of Juan, get in scoring position.' That means getting on first base."

The Rangers, though, survived a scare similar to the Yankees' before winning the AL West. Their nine-game lead shrank to one game over Seattle, reviving memories of 1995, when the Mariners overtook the Angels with a September charge. But the Rangers won six of their last eight games and the division, and reached the postseason for the first time in their history.

## A-Rod's Coming-Out Party

Some major league stars emerge gradually. For others, the light comes on suddenly. In the case of Seattle Mariners shortstop Alex Rodriguez, it was more like a lighthouse, piercing bright and visible for miles.

Rodriguez, the first player picked in the 1993 draft, batted .204 in 17 major league games in 1994. The

On The Warpath. Cleveland's Albert Belle had another big season in 1996, hitting .311 with 48 homers and 148 RBIs.

next year, he batted .232 in 48 games.

In the spring of 1996, Rodriguez walked into the office of manager Lou Piniella and pronounced himself ready. He was 20 years old.

And he was right. He proceeded to hit a league-leading .358 with 36 homers and 123 RBIs, with 54 doubles. He helped carry Seattle when one of its other marquee players, Ken Griffey, was out with an injury.

"I hate the word 'potential,'" Rodriguez said. "Potential means you haven't gotten it done. Now I've got to produce. I'm not a prospect anymore."

A couple of guys twice Rodriguez' age made headlines in 1996 as well. Orioles DH Eddie Murray hit his 500th home run, and Twins DH Paul Molitor reached 3,000 hits.

Murray, 40, who got his 3,000th hit in 1995, joined Hank Aaron and Willie Mays as the only players with a 500-3,000 double.

Murray, who was traded from Cleveland back to his original major league team, Baltimore, at midseason, hit his 500th homer Sept. 6 off the Tigers' Felipe Lira. It cleared the fence in right-center field at Camden Yards.

Molitor, 40, entered the season needing 211 hits to reach 3,000. He was coming off the worst season of his career, so his target date for 3,000 was sometime in 1997, if at all.

He finished the season with 225 hits, and on Sept. 16 became the first player to reach 3,000 with something other than a single or double. He tripled off Royals rookie lefthander Jose Rosado.

What's an American League season without some kind of controversy involving Indians outfielder Albert Belle?

Belle had another monster season, batting .311 with 48 homers and 148 RBIs, but his biggest headlines came after he delivered a forearm shiver to Brewers second baseman Fernando Vina while trying to break up a double play.

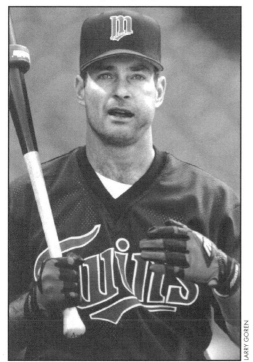

Milestone. Minnesota's Paul Molitor, 40, became the latest member of baseball's 3,000 hit club. He had 225 hits on the year.

# AMERICAN LEAGUE
## DEPARTMENT LEADERS

## BATTING

### GAMES
Cal Ripken, Baltimore...................... 163
Rafael Palmeiro, Baltimore............... 162
Mo Vaughn, Boston........................ 161
Paul Molitor, Minnesota.................... 161
Cecil Fielder, Detroit-New York ........ 160

### AT-BATS
Kenny Lofton, Cleveland .................. 662
Paul Molitor, Minnesota.................... 660
Cal Ripken, Baltimore...................... 640
Ivan Rodriguez, Texas .................... 639
Mo Vaughn, Boston......................... 635

### RUNS
Alex Rodriguez, Seattle.................... 141
Chuck Knoblauch, Minnesota............. 140
Kenny Lofton, Cleveland .................. 132
Roberto Alomar, Baltimore ............... 132
Ken Griffey, Seattle ......................... 125

### HITS
Paul Molitor, Minnesota.................... 225
Alex Rodriguez, Seattle.................... 215
Kenny Lofton, Cleveland .................. 210
Mo Vaughn, Boston......................... 207
Chuck Knoblauch, Minnesota........... 197

### TOTAL BASES
Alex Rodriguez, Seattle.................... 379
Albert Belle, Cleveland .................... 375
Mo Vaughn, Boston......................... 370
Brady Anderson, Baltimore .............. 369
Juan Gonzalez, Texas...................... 348

### EXTRA-BASE HITS
Brady Anderson, Baltimore ................ 92
Alex Rodriguez, Seattle..................... 91
Albert Belle, Cleveland ..................... 89
Juan Gonzalez, Texas....................... 82
Rafael Palmeiro, Baltimore................ 81
Manny Ramirez, Cleveland ................ 81

### DOUBLES
Alex Rodriguez, Seattle..................... 54
Edgar Martinez, Seattle .................... 52
Ivan Rodriguez, Texas ...................... 47
Jeff Cirillo, Milwaukee ...................... 46
Marty Cordova, Minnesota ................ 46

### TRIPLES
Chuck Knoblauch, Minnesota............. 14
Fernando Vina, Milwaukee ................ 10
Jose Offerman, Kansas City................ 8
Dave Martinez, Chicago ...................... 8
Ozzie Guillen, Chicago ........................ 8
Paul Molitor, Minnesota....................... 8

### HOME RUNS
Mark McGwire, Oakland..................... 52
Brady Anderson, Baltimore ............... 50
Ken Griffey, Seattle .......................... 49
Albert Belle, Cleveland ..................... 48

**Chuck Knoblauch**
14 triples

**Cal Ripken**
Played in 163 games

Juan Gonzalez, Texas........................ 47

### HOME RUN RATIO
(At-Bats per Home Runs)
Mark McGwire, Oakland..................... 8.1
Ken Griffey, Seattle ......................... 11.1
Juan Gonzalez, Texas....................... 11.5
Brady Anderson, Baltimore............... 11.6
Albert Belle, Cleveland .................... 12.5

### RUNS BATTED IN
Albert Belle, Cleveland .................... 148
Juan Gonzalez, Texas....................... 144
Mo Vaughn, Boston.......................... 143
Rafael Palmeiro, Baltimore............... 142
Ken Griffey, Seattle ......................... 140

### SACRIFICE BUNTS
Tom Goodwin, Kansas City ................ 21
David Howard, Kansas City................ 17
Gary DiSarcina, California.................. 16
Kevin Elster, Texas........................... 16
Darren Lewis, Chicago ...................... 15

### SACRIFICE FLIES
Bobby Bonilla, Baltimore .................. 17
Roberto Alomar, Baltimore ................ 12
Kevin Elster, Texas........................... 11
Travis Fryman, Detroit ...................... 10
Jay Buhner, Seattle .......................... 10
Rusty Greer, Texas ........................... 10
Eddie Murray, Cleve.-Balt.................. 10

### HIT BY PITCH
Brady Anderson, Baltimore................ 22
Chuck Knoblauch, Minnesota............. 19
Charlie O'Brien, Toronto.................... 17
Mo Vaughn, Boston........................... 14
Dave Hollins, Minn.-Seattle............... 13
Fernando Vina, Milwaukee................. 13

### WALKS
Tony Phillips, Chicago ..................... 125
Jim Thome, Cleveland ..................... 123
Edgar Martinez, Seattle ................... 123
Mark McGwire, Oakland ................... 116
Frank Thomas, Chicago ................... 109

### INTENTIONAL WALKS
Frank Thomas, Chicago ..................... 26
Mo Vaughn, Boston ........................... 19
Mark McGwire, Oakland ..................... 16
Albert Belle, Cleveland ..................... 15
Ken Griffey, Seattle .......................... 13

### STRIKEOUTS
Jay Buhner, Seattle ......................... 159
Melvin Nieves, Detroit....................... 158

Mo Vaughn, Boston.......................... 154
Ed Sprague, Toronto ........................ 146
Jose Valentin, Milwaukee................. 145
Dean Palmer, Texas......................... 145

### TOUGHEST TO STRIKE OUT
(Plate Appearances per SO)
Ozzie Guillen, Chicago .................... 19.6
Joey Cora, Seattle ........................... 18.2
Wade Boggs, New York .................... 17.9
Fernando Vina, Milwaukee ............... 17.6
Gary DiSarcina, California ............... 16.0

### STOLEN BASES
Kenny Lofton, Cleveland .................... 75
Tom Goodwin, Kansas City ................ 66
Otis Nixon, Toronto............................ 54
Chuck Knoblauch, Minnesota............. 45
Omar Vizquel, Cleveland.................... 35

### CAUGHT STEALING
Tom Goodwin, Kansas City ................ 22
Kenny Lofton, Cleveland .................... 17
Chuck Knoblauch, Minnesota............. 14
Otis Nixon, Toronto............................ 13
Kimera Bartee, Detroit ...................... 10
Chad Curtis, Detroit .......................... 10
John Valentin, Milwaukee.................. 10
Jose Offerman, Kansas City.............. 10
Mark McLemore, Texas...................... 10

### GIDP
Cal Ripken, Baltimore........................ 28
Frank Thomas, Chicago ..................... 25
Garret Anderson, California................ 22
Paul O'Neill, New York ...................... 21
Paul Molitor, Minnesota..................... 21

### HITTING STREAKS
Marty Cordova, Minnesota ................ 23
Roberto Alomar, Baltimore ................ 22
Four tied with .................................... 21

### MULTIPLE-HIT GAMES
Paul Molitor, Minnesota..................... 72
Kenny Lofton, Cleveland .................... 67
Alex Rodriguez, Seattle..................... 65
Chuck Knoblauch, Minnesota............. 61
Roberto Alomar, Baltimore ................ 61

### SLUGGING PERCENTAGE
Mark McGwire, Oakland ................. .730
Juan Gonzalez, Texas...................... .643
Brady Anderson, Baltimore.............. .637
Alex Rodriguez, Seattle................... .631
Ken Griffey, Seattle ........................ .628

**Brady Anderson**
92 extra-base hits

**Mark McGwire**
.467 on-base percentage

## ON-BASE PERCENTAGE
Mark McGwire, Oakland .................. .467
Edgar Martinez, Seattle ................. .464
Frank Thomas, Chicago ................. .459
Jim Thome, Cleveland ................... .450
Chuck Knoblauch, Minnesota .......... .448

## PITCHING

### WINS
Andy Pettitte, New York...................... 21
Pat Hentgen, Toronto ......................... 20
Mike Mussina, Baltimore .................... 19
Charles Nagy, Cleveland.................... 17
Alex Fernandez, Chicago ................... 16
Ken Hill, Texas .................................. 16
Bobby Witt, Texas .............................. 16

### LOSSES
Jim Abbott, California ......................... 18
Erik Hanson, Toronto......................... 17
Rich Robertson, Minnesota ................ 17
Chuck Finley, California ..................... 16
Brad Radke, Minnesota ..................... 16

### WINNING PERCENTAGE
Jamie Moyer, Boston-Seattle ........... .813
Charles Nagy, Cleveland.................. .773
Andy Pettitte, New York..................... .724
Darren Oliver, Texas ........................ .700
Pat Hentgen, Toronto ....................... .667

### GAMES
Eddie Guardado, Minnesota............... 83
Mike Myers, Detroit............................ 83
Mike Stanton, Boston-Texas .............. 81
Heathcliff Slocumb, Boston ............... 75
Jeff Nelson, New York ....................... 73
Mike Jackson, Seattle........................ 73

### GAMES STARTED
Mike Mussina, Baltimore .................... 36
Eleven tied with ................................ 35

### COMPLETE GAMES
Pat Hentgen, Toronto ......................... 10
Roger Pavlik, Texas ............................. 7
Ken Hill, Texas .................................... 7
Tim Wakefield, Boston.......................... 6
Alex Fernandez, Chicago ..................... 6
Scott Erickson, Baltimore ..................... 6
Roger Clemens, Boston ........................ 6

### SHUTOUTS
Pat Hentgen, Toronto ........................... 3
Ken Hill, Texas .................................... 3
Rich Robertson, Minnesota ................... 3
Roger Clemens, Boston ........................ 2
Felipe Lira, Detroit ............................... 2

### GAMES FINISHED
Roberto Hernandez, Chicago .............. 61
Heathcliff Slocumb, Boston ................ 60

---

Jose Mesa, Cleveland ........................ 60
John Wetteland, New York................. 58
Mike Timlin, Toronto ......................... 56

### SAVES
John Wetteland, New York................. 43
Jose Mesa, Cleveland ....................... 39
Roberto Hernandez, Chicago............. 38
Troy Percival, California .................... 36
Mike Fetters, Milwaukee ................... 32

### INNINGS PITCHED
Pat Hentgen, Toronto ....................... 266
Alex Fernandez, Chicago ................. 258
Ken Hill, Texas ................................ 251
Mike Mussina, Baltimore ................. 243
Roger Clemens, Boston ................... 243

### HITS ALLOWED
Chris Haney, Kansas City................. 267
Mike Mussina, Baltimore ................. 264
Scott Erickson, Baltimore ................. 262
Tim Belcher, Kansas City ................. 262
Ken Hill, Texas ................................ 250

### RUNS ALLOWED
Tim Wakefield, Boston...................... 151
Tom Gordon, Boston ........................ 143
Erik Hanson, Toronto........................ 143
Mike Mussina, Baltimore ................. 137
Scott Erickson, Baltimore ................. 137

### HOME RUNS ALLOWED
Shawn Boskie, California................... 40
Brad Radke, Minnesota ..................... 40
Tim Wakefield, Boston....................... 38
Alex Fernandez, Chicago .................. 34
Kevin Tapani, Chicago ...................... 34

### WALKS
Rich Robertson, Minnesota .............. 116
Roger Clemens, Boston ................... 106
Tom Gordon, Boston ........................ 105
Erik Hanson, Toronto........................ 102
Wilson Alvarez, Chicago.................... 97

### FEWEST WALKS PER 9 INNINGS
Chris Haney, Kansas City................... 2.0
David Wells, Baltimore ...................... 2.0

**Pat Hentgen**
10 complete games

Brad Radke, Minnesota ..................... 2.2
Charles Nagy, Cleveland.................... 2.5
Alex Fernandez, Chicago .................. 2.5
Orel Hershiser, Cleveland ................. 2.5
Juan Guzman, Toronto ...................... 2.5

### HIT BATSMEN
Shawn Boskie, California................... 13
Jason Grimsley, California.................. 13
Tim Wakefield, Boston....................... 12
Orel Hershiser, Cleveland ................. 12
Scott Karl, Milwaukee ....................... 11
Scott Erickson, Baltimore ................. 11
Chuck Finley, California..................... 11

---

### STRIKEOUTS
Roger Clemens, Boston .................. 257
Chuck Finley, California................... 215
Kevin Appier, Kansas City............... 207
Mike Mussina, Baltimore ................. 204
Alex Fernandez, Chicago ................. 200

### STRIKEOUTS PER 9 INNINGS
Roger Clemens, Boston .................... 9.5
Kevin Appier, Kansas City................. 8.8
Chuck Finley, California...................... 8.1
Juan Guzman, Toronto....................... 7.9
Mike Mussina, Baltimore ................... 7.5

### WILD PITCHES
Chuck Finley, California..................... 17
Richie Lewis, Detroit.......................... 14
Jim Abbott, California ........................ 13
Kevin Tapani, Chicago ...................... 13
Erik Hanson, Toronto......................... 13

### BALKS
Ken Hill, Texas .................................... 4
Eight tied with ..................................... 2

### OPPONENTS BATTING AVERAGE
Juan Guzman, Toronto..................... .238
Roger Clemens, Boston .................. .237
Pat Hentgen, Toronto ...................... .241
Kevin Appier, Kansas City............... .245
Alex Fernandez, Chicago ................ .253

## FIELDING

### PITCHER
| | | |
|---|---|---|
| PCT | Charles Nagy, Cleveland...... | 1.000 |
| PO | Two tied with.............................. | 29 |
| A | Orel Hershiser, Cleveland ........ | 47 |
| E | Ben McDonald, Milwaukee ....... | 6 |
| TC | Scott Erickson, Baltimore ........ | 75 |
| DP | Two tied with.............................. | 7 |

### CATCHER
| | | |
|---|---|---|
| PCT | Jesse Levis, Milwaukee........... | .998 |
| PO | Ivan Rodriguez, Texas............ | 850 |
| A | Ivan Rodriguez, Texas............. | 81 |
| E | Two tied with............................. | 10 |
| TC | Ivan Rodriguez, Texas............. | 941 |
| DP | Ivan Rodriguez, Texas............. | 11 |
| PB | Mike Stanley, Boston............... | 18 |

### FIRST BASE
| | | |
|---|---|---|
| PCT | Tino Martinez, New York ........ | .996 |
| PO | Rafael Palmeiro, Baltimore.... | 1384 |
| A | Rafael Palmeiro, Baltimore...... | 118 |
| E | Mo Vaughn, Boston .................. | 15 |
| TC | Rafael Palmeiro, Baltimore...... | 1510 |
| DP | Rafael Palmeiro, Baltimore...... | 157 |

### SECOND BASE
| | | |
|---|---|---|
| PCT | Chuck Knoblauch, Minn.......... | .988 |
| PO | Fernando Vina, Milwaukee ...... | 333 |
| A | Mark McLemore, Texas........... | 473 |
| E | Fernando Vina, Milwaukee ....... | 16 |
| TC | Mark McLemore, Texas........... | 798 |
| DP | Fernando Vina, Milwaukee ...... | 116 |

### THIRD BASE
| | | |
|---|---|---|
| PCT | Travis Fryman, Detroit............ | .979 |
| PO | Robin Ventura, Chicago ......... | 133 |
| A | Travis Fryman, Detroit............. | 271 |
| E | Jeff Cirillo, Milwaukee.............. | 18 |
| TC | Robin Ventura Chicago .......... | 382 |
| DP | Robin Ventura, Chicago ......... | 34 |

### SHORTSTOP
| | | |
|---|---|---|
| PCT | David Howard, Kansas City.... | .982 |
| PO | Kevin Elster, Texas................ | 285 |
| A | Mike Bordick, Oakland............. | 476 |
| E | Jose Valentin, Milwaukee ........ | 37 |
| TC | Alex Gonzalez, Toronto........... | 766 |
| DP | Alex Gonzalez, Toronto........... | 122 |

### OUTFIELD
| | | |
|---|---|---|
| PCT | Darryl Hamilton, Texas ......... | 1.000 |
| PO | Rich Becker, Minnesota........... | 391 |
| A | Manny Ramirez, Cleveland ...... | 19 |
| E | Melvin Nieves, Detroit.............. | 13 |
| TC | Rich Becker, Minnesota........... | 412 |
| DP | Rich Becker, Minnesota........... | 9 |

Belle initially was suspended for five games, but AL president Gene Budig later reduced it to three, then to two plus a $10,000 contribution to inner-city youth baseball.

## Puckett, Winfield Retire

Baseball lost some considerably more respected players when Kirby Puckett, Alan Trammell and Dave Winfield retired.

Glaucoma appeared in Puckett's right eye in spring training, and he finally announced his retirement from the Twins shortly after the all-star break. Despite laser surgery and medication, the vision in the eye was reduced to 20/400.

It didn't diminish his accomplishments. He made the AL all-star team 10 times in 12 seasons. He won a batting title in 1989 and an RBI title in 1994. He hit better than .300 eight times, won six Gold Gloves and carried the Twins to World Series wins in 1987 and 1991.

"I want to tell the little kids who prayed for me that just because I can't see doesn't mean that God doesn't answer prayers," Puckett said in announcing his retirement. "He does. I can see my beautiful wife and wonderful kids, and I'm still alive."

Puckett won the 1996 Roberto Clemente Award for public service by a major league player.

Trammell was quietly efficient in 20 years as a Tigers infielder, but his retirement was entirely too quiet. There was no big farewell tour, not a lot of media attention and Trammell played his last game before a typically small crowd in Detroit.

**Kirby Puckett**

As the most fundamentally sound shortstop of his era and a six-time all-star, Trammell deserved better. He hit .450 with two home runs as the Tigers won the 1984 World Series.

"Unfortunately, each time one of these guys leaves we're not replacing them with the same kind of class," Brewers manager Phil Garner said. "That's what's missing in our game today."

Winfield, who played his last season with the Indians in 1995, used his retirement announcement in February to deliver a similar critique.

"You can't trash the components of the game and disrespect the people who come to watch us play," he said. "I want people to look at this game like I did, like my brother did, when we were kids. Every chance we got, we had a baseball in our hand. We played

**Alan Trammell**

up against the wall, off the steps, in the schoolyard. That's all we wanted to do. Baseball has fallen behind the other sports."

If so, Winfield didn't contribute to its downfall. He

## AL: BEST TOOLS

A Baseball America survey of American League managers, conducted at midseason 1996, ranked AL players with the best tools:

| BEST HITTER | BEST PICKOFF MOVE |
|---|---|
| 1. Frank Thomas, White Sox | 1. Andy Pettitte, Yankees |
| 2. Roberto Alomar, Orioles | 2. Ed Vosberg, Rangers |
| 3. Edgar Martinez, Mariners | 3. Mark Langston, Angels |
| **BEST POWER HITTER** | **BEST RELIEVER** |
| 1. Albert Belle, Indians | 1. Jose Mesa, Indians |
| 2. Frank Thomas, White Sox | 2. Troy Percival, Angels |
| 3. Mark McGwire, Athletics | 3. R. Hernandez, White Sox |
| **BEST BUNTER** | **BEST DEFENSIVE C** |
| 1. Roberto Alomar, Orioles | 1. Ivan Rodriguez, Rangers |
| 2. Kenny Lofton, Indians | 2. Dan Wilson, Mariners |
| 3. Omar Vizquel, Indians | 3. Ron Karkovice, White Sox |
| **BEST HIT-AND-RUN ARTIST** | **BEST DEFENSIVE 1B** |
| 1. Chuck Knoblauch, Twins | 1. J.T. Snow, Angels |
| 2. Kevin Seitzer, Brewers | 2. Rafael Palmeiro, Orioles |
| 3. Edgar Martinez, Mariners | 2. Will Clark, Rangers |
| **BEST BASERUNNER** | **BEST DEFENSIVE 2B** |
| 1. Roberto Alomar, Blue Jays | 1. Roberto Alomar, Blue Jays |
| 2. Kenny Lofton, Indians | 2. Chuck Knoblauch, Twins |
| 3. Paul Molitor, Twins | 3. Fernando Vina, Brewers |
| **FASTEST BASERUNNER** | **BEST DEFENSIVE 3B** |
| 1. Kenny Lofton, Indians | 1. Wade Boggs, Yankees |
| 2. Tom Goodwin, Royals | 2. Robin Ventura, White Sox |
| 3. Otis Nixon, Blue Jays | 3. Travis Fryman, Tigers |
| **BEST PITCHER** | **BEST DEFENSIVE SS** |
| 1. Mike Mussina, Orioles | 1. Omar Vizquel, Indians |
| 2. Randy Johnson, Mariners | 2. Cal Ripken, Orioles |
| 3. Charles Nagy, Indians | 3. Mike Bordick, Athletics |
| **BEST FASTBALL** | **BEST INFIELD ARM** |
| 1. Randy Johnson, Mariners | 1. Alex Rodriguez, Mariners |
| 2. Troy Percival, Angels | 2. Travis Fryman, Tigers |
| 3. Jose Mesa, Indians | 3. Dean Palmer, Rangers |
| **BEST CURVEBALL** | **BEST DEFENSIVE OF** |
| 1. Tom Gordon, Red Sox | 1. Ken Griffey, Mariners |
| 2. Mike Mussina, Orioles | 2. Kenny Lofton, Indians |
| 3. Mark Langston, Angels | 3. Brady Anderson, Orioles |
| **BEST SLIDER** | **BEST OF ARM** |
| 1. Randy Johnson, Mariners | 1. Jay Buhner, Mariners |
| 2. Kevin Appier, Royals | 2. Ken Griffey, Mariners |
| 3. Juan Guzman, Blue Jays | 3. Tim Salmon, Angels |
| **BEST CHANGEUP** | **MOST EXCITING PLAYER** |
| 1. Mike Mussina, Orioles | 1. Ken Griffey, Mariners |
| 2. Erik Hanson, Blue Jays | 2. Kenny Lofton, Indians |
| 3. Jimmy Key, Yankees | 3. Frank Thomas, White Sox |
| **BEST CONTROL** | **BEST MANAGER** |
| 1. Mike Mussina, Orioles | 1. Lou Piniella, Mariners |
| 2. David Wells, Orioles | 2. Joe Torre, Yankees |
| 3. Charles Nagy, Indians | 3. Johnny Oates, Rangers |

played all 23 of his professional seasons in the big leagues, and made 12 all-star teams. He retired at 44 as the majors' active leader in hits (3,110) and RBIs (1,833).

## Lachemann, Kennedy Leave

Two AL managers left their jobs during or shortly after the season.

Marcel Lachemann left the Angels less than a year after almost leading them to a division title. California lost the AL West to Seattle in a one-game playoff in 1995, but finished last in 1996.

The Angels never contended in '96, and general manager Bill Bavasi talked Lachemann out of quitting in July. Lachemann finally did resign in August, and John McNamara was named interim manager for the balance of the season. The team finished last.

The Red Sox fired Kevin Kennedy shortly after the season. Boston had charged into contention late in the year, but couldn't overcome an awful start.

# AMERICAN LEAGUE
## 1996 BATTING, PITCHING STATISTICS

### CLUB BATTING

| | AVG | G | AB | R | H | 2B | 3B | HR | BB | SO | SB |
|---|---|---|---|---|---|---|---|---|---|---|---|
| Cleveland | .293 | 161 | 5681 | 952 | 1665 | 335 | 23 | 218 | 671 | 844 | 160 |
| New York | .288 | 162 | 5628 | 871 | 1621 | 293 | 28 | 162 | 632 | 909 | 96 |
| Minnesota | .288 | 162 | 5673 | 877 | 1633 | 332 | 47 | 118 | 576 | 958 | 143 |
| Seattle | .287 | 161 | 5668 | 993 | 1625 | 343 | 19 | 245 | 670 | 1052 | 90 |
| Texas | .284 | 163 | 5702 | 928 | 1622 | 323 | 32 | 221 | 660 | 1041 | 83 |
| Boston | .283 | 162 | 5756 | 928 | 1631 | 308 | 31 | 209 | 642 | 1020 | 91 |
| Chicago | .281 | 162 | 5644 | 898 | 1586 | 284 | 33 | 195 | 701 | 927 | 105 |
| Milwaukee | .279 | 162 | 5662 | 894 | 1578 | 304 | 40 | 178 | 624 | 986 | 101 |
| California | .276 | 161 | 5686 | 762 | 1571 | 256 | 24 | 192 | 527 | 974 | 53 |
| Baltimore | .274 | 163 | 5689 | 949 | 1557 | 299 | 29 | 257 | 645 | 915 | 76 |
| Kansas City | .267 | 161 | 5542 | 746 | 1477 | 286 | 38 | 123 | 529 | 943 | 195 |
| Oakland | .265 | 162 | 5630 | 861 | 1492 | 283 | 21 | 243 | 640 | 1114 | 58 |
| Toronto | .259 | 162 | 5599 | 766 | 1451 | 302 | 35 | 177 | 529 | 1105 | 116 |
| Detroit | .256 | 162 | 5530 | 783 | 1413 | 257 | 21 | 204 | 546 | 1268 | 87 |

### CLUB PITCHING

| | ERA | G | CG | SHO | SV | IP | H | R | ER | BB | SO |
|---|---|---|---|---|---|---|---|---|---|---|---|
| Cleveland | 4.34 | 161 | 13 | 9 | 46 | 1452 | 1530 | 769 | 700 | 484 | 1033 |
| Chicago | 4.52 | 162 | 7 | 4 | 43 | 1461 | 1529 | 794 | 734 | 616 | 1039 |
| Kansas City | 4.55 | 161 | 17 | 8 | 35 | 1450 | 1563 | 786 | 733 | 460 | 926 |
| Toronto | 4.57 | 162 | 19 | 7 | 35 | 1446 | 1476 | 809 | 734 | 610 | 1033 |
| New York | 4.65 | 162 | 6 | 9 | 52 | 1440 | 1469 | 787 | 744 | 610 | 1139 |
| Texas | 4.65 | 163 | 19 | 6 | 43 | 1449 | 1569 | 799 | 749 | 582 | 976 |
| Boston | 4.98 | 162 | 17 | 5 | 37 | 1458 | 1606 | 921 | 807 | 722 | 1165 |
| Milwaukee | 5.14 | 162 | 6 | 4 | 42 | 1447 | 1570 | 899 | 826 | 635 | 846 |
| Baltimore | 5.14 | 163 | 13 | 1 | 44 | 1469 | 1604 | 903 | 839 | 597 | 1047 |
| Oakland | 5.20 | 162 | 7 | 5 | 34 | 1456 | 1638 | 900 | 841 | 644 | 884 |
| Seattle | 5.21 | 161 | 4 | 4 | 34 | 1432 | 1562 | 895 | 829 | 605 | 1000 |
| Minnesota | 5.28 | 162 | 13 | 5 | 31 | 1440 | 1561 | 900 | 844 | 581 | 959 |
| California | 5.29 | 161 | 12 | 8 | 38 | 1439 | 1546 | 943 | 847 | 662 | 1052 |
| Detroit | 6.38 | 162 | 10 | 4 | 22 | 1433 | 1699 | 1103 | 1015 | 784 | 957 |

### CLUB FIELDING

| | PCT | PO | A | E | DP | | PCT | PO | A | E | DP |
|---|---|---|---|---|---|---|---|---|---|---|---|
| Texas | .986 | 4348 | 1647 | 87 | 150 | Toronto | .982 | 4337 | 1606 | 110 | 187 |
| New York | .985 | 4320 | 1613 | 91 | 146 | Seattle | .981 | 4295 | 1540 | 110 | 155 |
| Baltimore | .984 | 4406 | 1730 | 97 | 173 | Cleveland | .980 | 4357 | 1765 | 124 | 156 |
| Minnesota | .984 | 4319 | 1519 | 94 | 142 | California | .979 | 4317 | 1702 | 128 | 156 |
| Oakland | .984 | 4369 | 1778 | 103 | 195 | Milwaukee | .978 | 4342 | 1693 | 134 | 180 |
| Chicago | .982 | 4383 | 1574 | 109 | 145 | Boston | .978 | 4374 | 1638 | 135 | 152 |
| Kansas City | .982 | 4350 | 1704 | 111 | 184 | Detroit | .978 | 4298 | 1727 | 137 | 157 |

### INDIVIDUAL BATTING LEADERS
(Minimum 502 Plate Appearances)

| | AVG | G | AB | R | H | 2B | 3B | HR | RBI | BB | SO | SB |
|---|---|---|---|---|---|---|---|---|---|---|---|---|
| Rodriguez, Alex, Seattle | .358 | 146 | 601 | 141 | 215 | 54 | 1 | 36 | 123 | 59 | 104 | 15 |
| Thomas, Frank, Chicago | .349 | 141 | 527 | 110 | 184 | 26 | 0 | 40 | 134 | 109 | 70 | 1 |
| Molitor, Paul, Minnesota | .341 | 161 | 660 | 99 | 225 / 41 | 8 | 9 | 113 | 56 | 72 | 18 |
| Knoblauch, Chuck, Minn. | .341 | 153 | 578 | 140 | 197 | 35 | 14 | 13 | 72 | 98 | 74 | 45 |
| Greer, Rusty, Texas | .332 | 139 | 542 | 96 | 180 | 41 | 6 | 18 | 100 | 62 | 86 | 9 |
| Nilsson, Dave, Milwaukee | .331 | 123 | 453 | 81 | 150 | 33 | 2 | 17 | 84 | 57 | 68 | 2 |
| Alomar, Roberto, Baltimore | .328 | 153 | 588 | 132 | 193 | 43 | 4 | 22 | 94 | 90 | 65 | 17 |
| Martinez, Edgar, Seattle | .327 | 139 | 499 | 121 | 163 | 52 | 2 | 26 | 103 | 123 | 84 | 3 |
| Seitzer, Kevin, Mil.-Cleve. | .326 | 154 | 573 | 85 | 187 | 35 | 3 | 13 | 78 | 87 | 79 | 6 |
| Vaughn, Mo, Boston | .326 | 161 | 635 | 118 | 207 | 29 | 1 | 44 | 143 | 95 | 154 | 2 |

### INDIVIDUAL PITCHING LEADERS
(Minimum 162 Innings)

| | W | L | ERA | G | GS | CG | SV | IP | H | R | ER | BB | SO |
|---|---|---|---|---|---|---|---|---|---|---|---|---|---|
| Guzman, Juan, Toronto | 11 | 8 | 2.93 | 27 | 27 | 4 | 0 | 188 | 158 | 68 | 61 | 53 | 165 |
| Hentgen, Pat, Toronto | 20 | 10 | 3.22 | 35 | 35 | 10 | 0 | 266 | 238 | 105 | 95 | 94 | 177 |
| Nagy, Charles, Cleveland | 17 | 5 | 3.41 | 32 | 32 | 5 | 0 | 222 | 217 | 89 | 84 | 61 | 176 |
| Fernandez, Alex, Chicago | 16 | 10 | 3.45 | 35 | 35 | 6 | 0 | 258 | 248 | 110 | 99 | 72 | 200 |
| Appier, Kevin, Kansas City | 14 | 11 | 3.62 | 32 | 32 | 5 | 0 | 211 | 192 | 87 | 85 | 75 | 207 |
| Hill, Ken, Texas | 16 | 10 | 3.63 | 35 | 35 | 7 | 0 | 251 | 250 | 110 | 101 | 95 | 170 |
| Clemens, Roger, Boston | 10 | 13 | 3.63 | 34 | 34 | 6 | 0 | 243 | 216 | 106 | 98 | 106 | 257 |
| Pettitte, Andy, New York | 21 | 8 | 3.87 | 35 | 34 | 2 | 0 | 221 | 229 | 105 | 95 | 72 | 162 |
| McDonald, Ben, Milwaukee | 12 | 10 | 3.90 | 35 | 35 | 2 | 0 | 221 | 228 | 104 | 96 | 67 | 146 |
| Belcher, Tim, Kansas City | 15 | 11 | 3.92 | 35 | 35 | 4 | 0 | 239 | 262 | 117 | 104 | 68 | 113 |

# AWARD WINNERS

Selected by Baseball Writers Association of America

## MVP

| Player, Team | 1st | 2nd | 3rd | Total |
|---|---|---|---|---|
| Juan Gonzalez, Texas. | 11 | 7 | 5 | 290 |
| Alex Rodriguez, Sea.... | 10 | 10 | 4 | 287 |
| Albert Belle, Cleve. | 2 | 8 | 10 | 228 |
| Ken Griffey, Seattle | 4 | 1 | 2 | 188 |
| Mo Vaughn, Boston | 0 | 1 | 3 | 184 |
| Rafael Palmeiro, Balt... | 0 | 0 | 2 | 104 |
| Mark McGwire, Oak. | 0 | 0 | 2 | 100 |
| Frank Thomas, Chi. | 0 | 0 | 0 | 88 |
| Brady Anderson, Balt.... | 0 | 0 | 0 | 53 |
| Ivan Rodriguez, Texas.. | 1 | 0 | 0 | 52 |
| Kenny Lofton, Cleve. .... | 0 | 0 | 0 | 34 |
| Mariano Rivera, N.Y. .... | 0 | 1 | 0 | 27 |
| Paul Molitor, Minn. ....... | 0 | 0 | 0 | 19 |
| Andy Pettitte, N.Y. ....... | 0 | 0 | 0 | 11 |
| Jim Thome, Cleve. ....... | 0 | 0 | 0 | 9 |
| Chuck Knoblauch, Min... | 0 | 0 | 0 | 8 |
| Jay Buhner, Seattle ...... | 0 | 0 | 0 | 6 |
| Bernie Williams, Sea.... | 0 | 0 | 0 | 6 |
| John Wetteland, N.Y..... | 0 | 0 | 0 | 4 |
| Roberto Alomar, Balt. .... | 0 | 0 | 0 | 3 |
| Terry Steinbach, Oak..... | 0 | 0 | 0 | 1 |

## Cy Young Award

| Player, Team | 1st | 2nd | 3rd | Total |
|---|---|---|---|---|
| Pat Hentgen, Toronto .. | 16 | 9 | 3 | 110 |
| Andy Pettitte, New York. | 11 | 16 | 1 | 104 |
| Mariano Rivera, N.Y. ..... | 1 | 1 | 10 | 18 |
| Charles Nagy, Cleve. ..... | 0 | 1 | 9 | 12 |
| Mike Mussina, Balt. ...... | 0 | 1 | 2 | 5 |
| Alex Fernandez, Chi. ...... | 0 | 0 | 1 | 1 |
| Roberto Hernandez, Chi.. | 0 | 0 | 1 | 1 |
| Ken Hill, Texas ............. | 0 | 0 | 1 | 1 |

## Rookie of the Year

| Player, Team | 1st | 2nd | 3rd | Total |
|---|---|---|---|---|
| Derek Jeter, New York | 28 | 0 | 0 | 140 |
| James Baldwin, Chi..... | 0 | 19 | 7 | 64 |
| Tony Clark, Detroit........ | 0 | 6 | 12 | 30 |
| Rocky Coppinger, Balt... | 0 | 1 | 3 | 6 |
| Jose Rosado, K.C. ....... | 0 | 1 | 3 | 6 |
| Darin Erstad, California.. | 0 | 1 | 0 | 3 |
| Jose Batista, California. | 0 | 0 | 1 | 1 |
| Tim Crabtree, Toronto ... | 0 | 0 | 1 | 1 |
| Jeff D'Amico, Milw. ........ | 0 | 0 | 1 | 1 |

## Manager of the Year

| Manager, Team | 1st | 2nd | 3rd | Total |
|---|---|---|---|---|
| Johnny Oates, Texas... | 12 | 8 | 5 | 89 |
| Joe Torre, New York.... | 10 | 12 | 3 | 89 |
| Lou Piniella, Seattle..... | 3 | 4 | 8 | 35 |
| Mike Hargrove, Cleve. ... | 2 | 3 | 3 | 22 |
| Buddy Bell, Detroit......... | 1 | 0 | 0 | 5 |
| Dave Johnson, Balt. ...... | 0 | 0 | 4 | 4 |
| Tom Kelly, Minnesota .... | 0 | 0 | 4 | 4 |
| Art Howe, Oakland ....... | 0 | 1 | 0 | 3 |
| Kevin Kennedy, Boston . | 0 | 0 | 1 | 1 |

**NOTE:** MVP balloting based on 14 points for first-place vote, nine for second, eight for third, etc.; Cy Young Award, Rookie of the Year and Manager of the Year balloting based on five points for first-place vote, three for second and one for third.

## Gold Glove Awards

Selected by AL managers

C—Ivan Rodriguez, Texas. 1B—J.T. Snow, California. 2B—Roberto Alomar, Baltimore. 3B—Robin Ventura, Chicago. SS—Omar Vizquel, Cleveland. OF—Ken Griffey, Seattle; Kenny Lofton, Cleveland; Jay Buhner, Seattle. P—Mike Mussina, Baltimore.

# AMERICAN LEAGUE
## DIVISION SERIES
### TEXAS vs. NEW YORK

## BOX SCORES

**Game One: October 1**
**Rangers 6, Yankees 2**

| TEXAS | ab | r | h | bi | bb | so | NEW YORK | ab | r | h | bi | bb | so |
|---|---|---|---|---|---|---|---|---|---|---|---|---|---|
| Hamilton cf | 4 | 0 | 0 | 0 | 0 | 0 | Raines lf | 5 | 1 | 1 | 0 | 0 | 1 |
| Rodriguez c | 4 | 1 | 1 | 0 | 0 | 1 | Boggs 3b | 5 | 0 | 1 | 0 | 0 | 1 |
| Greer lf | 3 | 1 | 1 | 0 | 1 | 1 | O'Neill rf | 4 | 0 | 0 | 0 | 0 | 1 |
| Gonzalez rf | 4 | 1 | 1 | 3 | 0 | 1 | Williams cf | 4 | 0 | 1 | 1 | 0 | 0 |
| Clark 1b | 4 | 1 | 1 | 0 | 0 | 0 | Martinez 1b | 4 | 1 | 3 | 0 | 0 | 0 |
| Tettleton dh | 3 | 1 | 0 | 0 | 1 | 3 | Strawberry dh | 4 | 0 | 0 | 0 | 0 | 2 |
| Palmer 3b | 4 | 1 | 2 | 2 | 0 | 1 | Duncan 2b | 4 | 0 | 2 | 1 | 0 | 1 |
| McLemore 2b | 4 | 0 | 1 | 1 | 0 | 1 | Girardi c | 3 | 0 | 1 | 0 | 1 | 0 |
| Elster ss | 4 | 0 | 1 | 0 | 0 | 2 | Jeter ss | 4 | 0 | 1 | 0 | 0 | 1 |
| **Totals** | **34** | **6** | **8** | **6** | **2** | **10** | **Totals** | **37** | **2** | **10** | **2** | **1** | **7** |

| | |
|---|---|
| **Texas** | **000 501 000—6** |
| **New York** | **100 100 000—2** |

**DP**—New York 1. **LOB**—Texas 3, New York 9. **2B**—Elster (1), Boggs (1), Martinez 2 (2). **HR**—Gonzalez (1), Palmer (1). **CS**—McLemore (1).

| Texas | ip | h | r | er | bb | so | New York | ip | h | r | er | bb | so |
|---|---|---|---|---|---|---|---|---|---|---|---|---|---|
| Burkett W | 9 | 10 | 2 | 2 | 1 | 7 | Cone L | 6 | 8 | 6 | 6 | 2 | 8 |
| | | | | | | | Lloyd | 1 | 0 | 0 | 0 | 0 | 0 |
| | | | | | | | Weathers | 2 | 0 | 0 | 0 | 0 | 2 |

**Umpires: HP**—Evans; **1B**—Kaiser; **2B**—Merrill; **3B**—Young; **LF**—Clark; **RF**—Johnson.

**T**—2:50. **A**—57,205.

**Game Two: October 2**
**Yankees 5, Rangers 4**

| TEXAS | ab | r | h | bi | bb | so | NEW YORK | ab | r | h | bi | bb | so |
|---|---|---|---|---|---|---|---|---|---|---|---|---|---|
| Hamilton cf | 6 | 0 | 2 | 0 | 0 | 0 | Raines lf | 4 | 0 | 1 | 0 | 1 | 0 |
| Rodriguez c | 4 | 0 | 0 | 0 | 1 | 2 | Boggs 3b | 3 | 0 | 0 | 0 | 0 | 0 |
| Greer lf | 5 | 1 | 0 | 0 | 1 | 1 | Hayes ph-3b | 1 | 0 | 0 | 1 | 0 | 0 |
| Gonzalez rf | 5 | 2 | 3 | 4 | 1 | 0 | O'Neill rf | 5 | 0 | 1 | 0 | 0 | 0 |
| Clark 1b | 4 | 0 | 1 | 0 | 2 | 0 | Williams cf | 3 | 1 | 1 | 0 | 2 | 0 |
| Palmer 3b | 6 | 0 | 1 | 0 | 0 | 1 | Martinez 1b | 4 | 1 | 0 | 0 | 1 | 1 |
| Tettleton dh | 3 | 0 | 0 | 0 | 2 | 2 | Fielder dh | 3 | 1 | 2 | 2 | 1 | 0 |
| McLemore 2b | 4 | 0 | 0 | 0 | 0 | 2 | Fox pr-dh | 0 | 0 | 0 | 0 | 0 | 0 |
| Elster ss | 4 | 1 | 1 | 0 | 1 | 0 | Strawberry ph-dh | 1 | 0 | 0 | 0 | 0 | 0 |
| | | | | | | | Duncan 2b | 5 | 0 | 0 | 0 | 0 | 1 |
| | | | | | | | Leyritz c | 2 | 0 | 0 | 1 | 0 | 0 |
| | | | | | | | Girardi pr-c | 1 | 1 | 0 | 0 | 1 | 0 |
| | | | | | | | Jeter ss | 5 | 1 | 3 | 0 | 0 | 0 |
| **Totals** | **41** | **4** | **8** | **4** | **8** | **8** | **Totals** | **37** | **5** | **8** | **4** | **6** | **2** |

| | |
|---|---|
| **Texas** | **013 000 000 000—4** |
| **New York** | **010 100 110 001—5** |

None out when winning run scored

**E**—Palmer (1). **DP**—Texas 1, New York 1. **LOB**—Texas 11, New York 9. **2B**—Elster (2), Jeter (1). **HR**—Gonzalez 2 (3), Fielder (1). **S**—Raines, Hayes, Rodriguez, McLemore. **SF**—Hayes.

| Texas | ip | h | r | er | bb | so | New York | ip | h | r | er | bb | so |
|---|---|---|---|---|---|---|---|---|---|---|---|---|---|
| Hill | 6 | 5 | 3 | 3 | 3 | 1 | Pettitte | 6⅓ | 4 | 4 | 4 | 6 | 3 |
| Cook | 1 | 0 | 0 | 0 | 0 | 0 | M. Rivera | 2⅔ | 0 | 0 | 0 | 0 | 1 |
| Russell | 2⅓ | 2 | 1 | 1 | 0 | 0 | Wetteland | 2 | 2 | 0 | 0 | 1 | 2 |
| Stanton L | 1⅔ | 1 | 1 | 0 | 3 | 1 | Lloyd | 0 | 1 | 0 | 0 | 0 | 0 |
| Henneman | 0 | 0 | 0 | 0 | 0 | 0 | Nelson | ⅔ | 1 | 0 | 0 | 0 | 2 |
| | | | | | | | Rogers | 0 | 0 | 0 | 0 | 1 | 0 |
| | | | | | | | Boehringer W | ⅓ | 0 | 0 | 0 | 0 | 0 |

Hill pitched to two batters in 7th; Lloyd pitched to one batter in 12th; Rogers pitched to one batter in 12th; Stanton pitched to two batters in 12th.

**WP**—Pettitte. **HBP**—Leyritz (by Hill).

**Umpires: HP**—Kaiser; **1B**—Merrill; **2B**—Young; **3B**—Clark. **LF**—Johnson. **RF**—Evans.

**T**—4:25. **A**—57,156.

**Game Three: October 4**
**Yankees 3, Rangers 2**

| NEW YORK | ab | r | h | bi | bb | so | TEXAS | ab | r | h | bi | bb | so |
|---|---|---|---|---|---|---|---|---|---|---|---|---|---|
| Jeter ss | 4 | 1 | 2 | 0 | 0 | 1 | Hamilton cf | 5 | 0 | 1 | 0 | 0 | 1 |
| Raines lf | 3 | 1 | 1 | 0 | 1 | 0 | Rodriguez c | 4 | 0 | 2 | 1 | 0 | 0 |
| Williams cf | 3 | 1 | 2 | 2 | 0 | 0 | Greer lf | 4 | 0 | 1 | 0 | 0 | 0 |
| Fielder dh | 4 | 0 | 0 | 0 | 0 | 1 | Gonzalez rf | 4 | 1 | 2 | 1 | 0 | 0 |
| Martinez 1b | 3 | 0 | 0 | 0 | 1 | 0 | Clark 1b | 3 | 0 | 0 | 0 | 1 | 2 |
| Duncan 2b | 3 | 0 | 2 | 1 | 0 | 0 | Palmer 3b | 4 | 0 | 0 | 0 | 0 | 2 |
| Sojo 2b | 0 | 0 | 0 | 0 | 0 | 0 | Tettleton dh | 3 | 0 | 0 | 0 | 1 | 1 |
| O'Neill rf | 3 | 0 | 0 | 0 | 0 | 1 | Buford pr | 0 | 0 | 0 | 0 | 0 | 0 |
| R. Rivera ph-rf | 1 | 0 | 0 | 0 | 0 | 1 | McLemore 2b | 3 | 0 | 0 | 0 | 0 | 1 |
| Hayes 3b | 3 | 0 | 0 | 0 | 0 | 0 | Elster ss | 1 | 1 | 0 | 0 | 2 | 0 |
| Girardi c | 2 | 0 | 0 | 0 | 1 | 0 | Newson ph | 1 | 0 | 0 | 0 | 0 | 0 |
| **Totals** | **29** | **3** | **7** | **3** | **3** | **4** | **Totals** | **32** | **2** | **6** | **2** | **4** | **7** |

| | |
|---|---|
| **New York** | **100 000 002—3** |
| **Texas** | **000 110 000—2** |

**E**—Girardi (1), Elster (1). **DP**—Texas 3. **LOB**—New York 4, Texas 8. **2B**—Rodriguez (1). **HR**—Gonzalez (4), Williams (1). **SB**—Elster (1). **CS**—Williams (1), Hayes (1), Raines (1). **S**—McLemore. **SF**—Williams.

| New York | ip | h | er | r | bb | so | Texas | ip | h | er | r | bb | so |
|---|---|---|---|---|---|---|---|---|---|---|---|---|---|
| Key | 5 | 5 | 2 | 2 | 1 | 3 | Oliver L | 8 | 6 | 3 | 3 | 2 | 3 |
| Nelson W | 3 | 1 | 0 | 0 | 2 | 3 | Henneman | ⅔ | 1 | 0 | 0 | 1 | 0 |
| Wetteland S | 1 | 0 | 0 | 0 | 1 | 1 | Stanton | ⅓ | 0 | 0 | 0 | 0 | 1 |

Oliver pitched to two batters in 9th.

**HBP**—Duncan (by Oliver).

**Umpires: HP**—Tschida; **1B**—Welke; **2B**—Shulock; **3B**—Hendry; **LF**—Coble; **RF**—Kosc.

**T**—3:09. **A**—50,860.

**Game Four: October 5**
**Yankees 6, Rangers 4**

| NEW YORK | ab | r | h | bi | bb | so | TEXAS | ab | r | h | bi | bb | so |
|---|---|---|---|---|---|---|---|---|---|---|---|---|---|
| Raines lf | 4 | 1 | 1 | 0 | 1 | 0 | Hamilton cf | 4 | 0 | 0 | 0 | 0 | 1 |
| Boggs 3b | 4 | 0 | 0 | 0 | 0 | 1 | Rodriguez c | 4 | 0 | 3 | 1 | 1 | 0 |
| Williams cf | 5 | 3 | 3 | 2 | 0 | 1 | Greer lf | 4 | 0 | 0 | 0 | 1 | 1 |
| Martinez 1b | 4 | 1 | 1 | 0 | 1 | 0 | Gonzalez rf | 3 | 1 | 1 | 1 | 2 | 1 |
| Fielder dh | 4 | 1 | 2 | 2 | 0 | 1 | Clark 1b | 5 | 0 | 0 | 0 | 0 | 0 |
| Fox pr-dh | 0 | 0 | 0 | 0 | 0 | 0 | Palmer 3b | 5 | 2 | 1 | 0 | 0 | 1 |
| Leyritz ph-dh | 1 | 0 | 0 | 0 | 0 | 1 | Tettleton dh | 3 | 0 | 1 | 1 | 1 | 1 |
| O'Neill rf | 3 | 0 | 1 | 0 | 0 | 0 | McLemore 2b | 4 | 1 | 1 | 1 | 0 | 0 |
| Hayes ph | 1 | 0 | 1 | 0 | 0 | 0 | Elster ss | 3 | 0 | 2 | 0 | 0 | 0 |
| R. Rivera rf | 0 | 0 | 0 | 0 | 0 | 0 | Newson ph | 0 | 0 | 0 | 0 | 1 | 0 |
| Duncan 2b | 4 | 0 | 1 | 1 | 0 | 2 | Buford pr | 0 | 0 | 0 | 0 | 0 | 0 |
| Sojo 2b | 0 | 0 | 0 | 0 | 0 | 0 | Gonzales ss | 0 | 0 | 0 | 0 | 0 | 0 |
| Girardi c | 3 | 0 | 1 | 0 | 1 | 1 | | | | | | | |
| Jeter ss | 4 | 0 | 1 | 1 | 0 | 0 | | | | | | | |
| **Totals** | **37** | **6** | **12** | **6** | **3** | **7** | **Totals** | **35** | **4** | **9** | **4** | **6** | **5** |

| | |
|---|---|
| **New York** | **000 310 101—6** |
| **Texas** | **022 000 000—4** |

**E**—Jeter (1). **DP**—New York 1, Texas 1. **LOB**—New York 8, Texas 11. **2B**—Palmer (1). **HR**—Gonzalez (5), Williams 2 (3). **SB**—Williams (1). **S**—Boggs, Hamilton.

| New York | ip | h | r | er | bb | so | Texas | ip | h | r | er | bb | so |
|---|---|---|---|---|---|---|---|---|---|---|---|---|---|
| Rogers | 2 | 5 | 2 | 2 | 1 | 1 | Witt | 3⅓ | 4 | 3 | 3 | 2 | 3 |
| Boehringer | 1 | 3 | 2 | 1 | 2 | 0 | Patterson | ⅓ | 1 | 0 | 0 | 0 | 0 |
| Weathers W | 3 | 1 | 0 | 0 | 0 | 3 | Cook | ⅓ | 0 | 0 | 0 | 1 | 0 |
| M. Rivera | 2 | 0 | 0 | 0 | 1 | 0 | Pavlik L | 2⅔ | 4 | 2 | 2 | 0 | 1 |
| Wetteland S | 1 | 0 | 0 | 0 | 2 | 1 | Vosberg | 0 | 1 | 0 | 0 | 0 | 0 |
| | | | | | | | Russell | ⅔ | 1 | 0 | 0 | 0 | 1 |
| | | | | | | | Stanton | 1⅓ | 1 | 1 | 1 | 0 | 1 |
| | | | | | | | Henneman | ⅓ | 0 | 0 | 0 | 0 | 1 |

Boehringer pitched to two batters in 4th; Vosberg pitched to one batter in 7th.

**WP**—Witt.

**Umpires: HP**—Welke; **1B**—Shulock; **2B**—Hendry; **3B**—Coble; **LF**—Kosc; **RF**—Tschida.

**T**—3:57. **A**—50,056.

## COMPOSITE BOX

**TEXAS**

| Player Pos. | AVG | G | AB | R | H | 2B | 3B | HR | RBI | BB | SO | SB |
|---|---|---|---|---|---|---|---|---|---|---|---|---|
| Juan Gonzalez, rf | .438 | 4 | 16 | 5 | 7 | 0 | 0 | 5 | 9 | 3 | 2 | 0 |
| Ivan Rodriguez, c | .375 | 4 | 16 | 1 | 6 | 1 | 0 | 0 | 2 | 2 | 3 | 0 |
| Kevin Elster, ss | .333 | 4 | 12 | 2 | 4 | 2 | 0 | 0 | 0 | 3 | 2 | 1 |
| Dean Palmer, 3b | .211 | 4 | 19 | 3 | 4 | 1 | 0 | 1 | 2 | 0 | 5 | 0 |
| Daryl Hamilton, cf | .158 | 4 | 19 | 0 | 3 | 0 | 0 | 0 | 0 | 0 | 2 | 0 |
| Mark McLemore, 2b | .133 | 4 | 15 | 1 | 2 | 0 | 0 | 0 | 2 | 0 | 4 | 0 |
| Will Clark, 1b | .125 | 4 | 16 | 1 | 2 | 0 | 0 | 0 | 0 | 3 | 2 | 0 |
| Rusty Greer, lf | .125 | 4 | 16 | 2 | 2 | 0 | 0 | 0 | 0 | 3 | 3 | 0 |
| Mickey Tettleton, dh | .083 | 4 | 12 | 1 | 1 | 0 | 0 | 0 | 1 | 5 | 7 | 0 |
| Warren Newson, ph | .000 | 3 | 1 | 0 | 0 | 0 | 0 | 0 | 0 | 1 | 0 | 0 |
| Damon Buford, pr | .000 | 3 | 0 | 0 | 0 | 0 | 0 | 0 | 0 | 0 | 0 | 0 |
| **Totals** | **.218** | **4** | **142** | **16** | **31** | **4** | **0** | **6** | **16** | **20** | **30** | **1** |

| Pitcher | W | L | ERA | G | GS | SV | IP | H | R | ER | BB | SO |
|---|---|---|---|---|---|---|---|---|---|---|---|---|
| Dennis Cook | 0 | 0 | 0.00 | 2 | 0 | 0 | 1 | 0 | 0 | 0 | 1 | 0 |
| Mike Henneman | 0 | 0 | 0.00 | 3 | 0 | 0 | 1 | 1 | 0 | 0 | 1 | 1 |
| Danny Patterson | 0 | 0 | 0.00 | 1 | 0 | 0 | 1 | 1 | 0 | 0 | 0 | 0 |
| John Burkett | 1 | 0 | 2.00 | 1 | 1 | 0 | 9 | 10 | 2 | 2 | 1 | 7 |
| Mike Stanton | 0 | 1 | 2.70 | 3 | 0 | 0 | 3 | 2 | 2 | 1 | 3 | 3 |
| Jeff Russell | 0 | 0 | 3.00 | 2 | 0 | 0 | 3 | 3 | 1 | 1 | 0 | 1 |

| Pitcher | W | L | ERA | G | GS | SV | IP | H | R | ER | BB | SO |
|---|---|---|---|---|---|---|---|---|---|---|---|---|
| Darren Oliver | 0 | 1 | 3.38 | 1 | 1 | 0 | 8 | 6 | 3 | 3 | 2 | 3 |
| Ken Hill | 0 | 0 | 4.50 | 1 | 1 | 0 | 6 | 5 | 3 | 3 | 3 | 1 |
| Roger Pavlik | 0 | 1 | 6.75 | 1 | 0 | 0 | 3 | 4 | 2 | 2 | 0 | 1 |
| Bobby Witt | 0 | 0 | 8.10 | 1 | 1 | 0 | 3 | 4 | 3 | 3 | 2 | 3 |
| Ed Vosberg | 0 | 0 | — | 1 | 0 | 0 | 0 | 1 | 0 | 0 | 0 | 0 |
| **Totals** | 1 | 3 | 3.55 | 4 | 4 | 0 | 38 | 37 | 16 | 15 | 13 | 20 |

## NEW YORK

| Player, Pos. | AVG | G | AB | R | H | 2B | 3B | HR | RBI | BB | SO | SB |
|---|---|---|---|---|---|---|---|---|---|---|---|---|
| Bernie Williams, cf | .467 | 4 | 15 | 5 | 7 | 0 | 0 | 3 | 5 | 2 | 1 | 1 |
| Derek Jeter, ss | .412 | 4 | 17 | 2 | 7 | 1 | 0 | 0 | 1 | 0 | 2 | 0 |
| Cecil Fielder, dh | .364 | 3 | 11 | 2 | 4 | 0 | 0 | 1 | 4 | 1 | 2 | 0 |
| Mariano Duncan, 2b | .313 | 4 | 16 | 0 | 5 | 0 | 0 | 0 | 3 | 0 | 4 | 0 |
| Tino Martinez, 1b | .267 | 4 | 15 | 3 | 4 | 2 | 0 | 0 | 3 | 1 | 0 |  |
| Tim Raines, lf | .250 | 4 | 16 | 3 | 4 | 0 | 0 | 0 | 3 | 1 | 0 |  |
| Joe Girardi, c | .222 | 4 | 9 | 1 | 2 | 0 | 0 | 0 | 1 | 4 | 1 | 0 |
| Charlie Hayes, 3b-ph | .200 | 3 | 5 | 0 | 1 | 0 | 0 | 0 | 1 | 0 | 0 | 0 |
| Paul O'Neill, rf | .133 | 4 | 15 | 0 | 2 | 0 | 0 | 0 | 0 | 2 | 0 |  |
| Wade Boggs, 3b | .083 | 3 | 12 | 0 | 1 | 1 | 0 | 0 | 0 | 2 | 0 |  |
| Darryl Strawberry, dh | .000 | 2 | 5 | 0 | 0 | 0 | 0 | 0 | 0 | 0 | 0 | 0 |
| Jim Leyritz, c-ph | .000 | 2 | 3 | 0 | 0 | 0 | 0 | 0 | 0 | 0 | 1 | 0 |
| Ruben Rivera, rf-ph | .000 | 2 | 1 | 0 | 0 | 0 | 0 | 0 | 0 | 0 | 1 | 0 |
| Andy Fox, dh-pr | .000 | 2 | 0 | 0 | 0 | 0 | 0 | 0 | 0 | 0 | 0 | 0 |
| Luis Sojo, 2b | .000 | 2 | 0 | 0 | 0 | 0 | 0 | 0 | 0 | 0 | 0 | 0 |
| **Totals** | .264 | 4 | 140 | 16 | 37 | 4 | 0 | 4 | 15 | 13 | 20 | 1 |

| Pitcher | W | L | ERA | G | GS | SV | IP | H | R | ER | BB | SO |
|---|---|---|---|---|---|---|---|---|---|---|---|---|
| David Weathers | 1 | 0 | 0.00 | 2 | 0 | 0 | 5 | 1 | 0 | 0 | 0 | 5 |
| Mariano Rivera | 0 | 0 | 0.00 | 2 | 0 | 0 | 5 | 0 | 0 | 0 | 1 | 1 |
| John Wetteland | 0 | 0 | 0.00 | 3 | 0 | 2 | 4 | 2 | 0 | 0 | 4 | 4 |
| Jeff Nelson | 1 | 0 | 0.00 | 2 | 0 | 0 | 4 | 2 | 0 | 0 | 2 | 5 |
| Graeme Lloyd | 0 | 0 | 0.00 | 2 | 0 | 0 | 1 | 1 | 0 | 0 | 0 | 0 |
| Jimmy Key | 0 | 0 | 3.60 | 1 | 1 | 0 | 5 | 5 | 2 | 2 | 1 | 3 |
| Andy Pettitte | 0 | 0 | 5.68 | 1 | 1 | 0 | 6 | 4 | 4 | 4 | 6 | 3 |
| Brian Boehringer | 1 | 0 | 6.75 | 2 | 0 | 0 | 1 | 3 | 2 | 1 | 2 | 0 |
| David Cone | 0 | 1 | 9.00 | 1 | 1 | 0 | 6 | 8 | 6 | 6 | 2 | 8 |
| Kenny Rogers | 0 | 0 | 9.00 | 2 | 1 | 0 | 2 | 5 | 2 | 2 | 2 | 1 |
| **Totals** | 3 | 1 | 3.46 | 4 | 4 | 2 | 39 | 31 | 16 | 15 | 20 | 30 |

| Texas | 035 | 611 | 000 | 000—16 |
|---|---|---|---|---|
| New York | 210 | 510 | 213 | 001—16 |

DP—Texas 4, New York 3. LOB—Texas 5, New York 30.
E—Elster, Girardi, Jeter, Palmer. CS—Williams, Hayes, McLemore. S—McLemore 2, Boggs, Hamilton, Hayes, Raines, Rodriguez. SF—Williams, Hayes.
HBP—Leyritz (by Hill), Duncan (by Oliver). WP—Pettitte, Witt.
Umpires—Al Clark, Drew Coble, Jim Evans, Ted Hendry, Mark Johnson, Ken Kaiser, Greg Kosc, Durwood Merrill, John Shulock, Tim Tschida, Tim Welke, Larry Young,.

## CLEVELAND vs. BALTIMORE

# BOX SCORES

### Game One: October 1
### Orioles 10, Indians 4

| CLEVELAND | ab | r | h | bi | bb | so | BALTIMORE | ab | r | h | bi | bb | so |
|---|---|---|---|---|---|---|---|---|---|---|---|---|---|
| Lofton cf | 5 | 0 | 1 | 1 | 0 | 1 | Anderson cf | 5 | 2 | 2 | 1 | 0 | 0 |
| Seitzer dh | 5 | 0 | 1 | 0 | 0 | 2 | Zeile 3b | 4 | 2 | 2 | 0 | 1 | 1 |
| Thome 3b | 4 | 0 | 1 | 0 | 0 | 2 | R. Alomar 2b | 4 | 0 | 1 | 1 | 0 | 0 |
| Belle lf | 4 | 0 | 0 | 0 | 0 | 0 | Palmeiro 1b | 4 | 2 | 1 | 1 | 0 | 1 |
| Franco 1b | 4 | 0 | 1 | 0 | 0 | 0 | Bonilla rf | 3 | 1 | 1 | 4 | 2 | 1 |
| Ramirez rf | 4 | 2 | 3 | 1 | 0 | 0 | Devereaux pr-rf | 0 | 0 | 0 | 0 | 0 | 0 |
| Kent 2b | 4 | 1 | 1 | 0 | 0 | 0 | C. Ripken ss | 5 | 0 | 3 | 1 | 0 | 0 |
| S. Alomar c | 3 | 0 | 1 | 1 | 0 | 0 | Murray dh | 4 | 0 | 0 | 0 | 0 | 1 |
| Giles ph | 1 | 0 | 0 | 0 | 0 | 1 | Surhoff lf | 4 | 2 | 2 | 2 | 0 | 0 |
| Pena c | 0 | 0 | 0 | 0 | 0 | 0 | Hoiles c | 2 | 1 | 0 | 0 | 1 | 0 |
| Alicea 2b | 5 | 1 | 4 | 1 | 0 | 0 | Parent c | 0 | 0 | 0 | 0 | 0 | 0 |
| Vizquel ss | 2 | 1 | 1 | 1 | 1 | 0 |  |  |  |  |  |  |  |
| **Totals** | 48 | 4 | 11 | 4 | 1 | 6 | **Totals** | 35 | 10 | 12 | 10 | 4 | 4 |

| Cleveland | 010 | 200 | 100— 4 |
|---|---|---|---|
| Baltimore | 112 | 005 | 10x—10 |

E—Zeile (1). LOB—Cleveland 8, Baltimore 8. 2B—Kent (1), Vizquel (1), Palmeiro (1), C. Ripken (1). HR—Anderson (1), Bonilla (1), Surhoff 2 (2), Ramirez (1). SB—Vizquel (1). CS—Vizquel. SF—Vizquel, R. Alomar.

| Cleveland | ip | h | r | er | bb | so | Baltimore | ip | h | r | er | bb | so |
|---|---|---|---|---|---|---|---|---|---|---|---|---|---|
| Nagy L | 5⅓ | 9 | 7 | 7 | 3 | 1 | Wells W | 6⅔ | 8 | 4 | 4 | 1 | 3 |
| Embree | ⅓ | 0 | 1 | 1 | 0 | 0 | Orosco | 0 | 0 | 0 | 0 | 0 | 0 |
| Shuey | 1⅓ | 3 | 2 | 2 | 0 | 2 | Mathews | ⅔ | 2 | 0 | 0 | 0 | 1 |
| Tavarez | 1 | 0 | 0 | 0 | 1 | 1 | Rhodes | ⅔ | 0 | 0 | 0 | 0 | 1 |
|  |  |  |  |  |  |  | Myers | 1 | 0 | 0 | 0 | 0 | 2 |

Orosco pitched to one batter in 7th.
HBP—Palmeiro (by Embree); Hoiles (by Nagy); Thome (by Orosco). WP—Mathews.
Umpires—HP—Coble; 1B—Kosc; 2B—Tschida; 3B—Welke; LF—Hendry; RF—Shulock.
T—3:25. A—47,644.

### Game Two: October 2
### Orioles 7, Indians 4

| CLEVELAND | ab | r | h | bi | bb | so | BALTIMORE | ab | r | h | bi | bb | so |
|---|---|---|---|---|---|---|---|---|---|---|---|---|---|
| Lofton cf | 5 | 1 | 2 | 0 | 0 | 1 | Anderson cf | 4 | 1 | 2 | 2 | 0 | 2 |
| Seitzer 1b | 4 | 0 | 2 | 1 | 0 | 0 | Zeile 3b | 4 | 0 | 0 | 0 | 1 | 0 |
| Kent pr-1b | 0 | 1 | 0 | 0 | 0 | 0 | R. Alomar 2b | 4 | 1 | 1 | 1 | 1 | 0 |
| Thome 3b | 4 | 1 | 2 | 0 | 0 | 2 | Palmeiro 1b | 3 | 1 | 1 | 0 | 0 | 1 |
| Belle lf | 3 | 1 | 1 | 2 | 1 | 0 | Bonilla rf | 2 | 1 | 0 | 0 | 2 | 0 |
| Franco dh | 3 | 0 | 0 | 1 | 0 | 2 | Devereaux pr-rf | 0 | 0 | 0 | 0 | 0 | 0 |
| Ramirez rf | 4 | 0 | 0 | 0 | 0 | 2 | C. Ripken ss | 3 | 1 | 2 | 1 | 0 | 0 |
| S. Alomar c | 4 | 0 | 0 | 0 | 0 | 0 | Murray dh | 3 | 0 | 2 | 1 | 1 | 1 |
| Vizquel ss | 3 | 0 | 0 | 0 | 1 | 0 | Alexander pr | 0 | 1 | 0 | 0 | 0 | 0 |
| Vizcaino 2b | 3 | 0 | 1 | 0 | 1 | 1 | Surhoff lf | 4 | 0 | 0 | 0 | 0 | 0 |
|  |  |  |  |  |  |  | Incaviglia pr-lf | 0 | 1 | 0 | 0 | 0 | 0 |
|  |  |  |  |  |  |  | Parent c | 3 | 0 | 1 | 0 | 0 | 1 |
|  |  |  |  |  |  |  | Hoiles ph-c | 0 | 0 | 0 | 0 | 1 | 0 |
| **Totals** | 33 | 4 | 8 | 4 | 3 | 8 | **Totals** | 30 | 7 | 9 | 5 | 7 | 5 |

| Cleveland | 000 | 003 | 010—4 |
|---|---|---|---|
| Baltimore | 100 | 030 | 03x—7 |

E—Seitzer (1), S. Alomar (1). DP—Cleveland 1, Baltimore 1. LOB—Cleveland 6, Baltimore 8. 2B—Seitzer (1), Murray (1), C. Ripken (2). HR—Anderson 2 (2), Belle (1). SB—Lofton 2 (2), Vizquel (2). SF—Anderson, Franco.

| Cleveland | ip | h | r | er | bb | so | Baltimore | ip | h | r | er | bb | so |
|---|---|---|---|---|---|---|---|---|---|---|---|---|---|
| Hershiser | 5 | 7 | 4 | 3 | 3 | 3 | Erickson | 6⅔ | 6 | 3 | 3 | 2 | 6 |
| Plunk L | 2 | 1 | 3 | 3 | 2 | 2 | Orosco | ⅓ | 2 | 1 | 1 | 0 | 1 |
| Assenmacher | ⅔ | 0 | 0 | 0 | 1 | 0 | Benitez W | 1 | 0 | 0 | 0 | 1 | 1 |
| Tavarez | ⅓ | 1 | 0 | 0 | 1 | 0 | Myers | 1 | 0 | 0 | 0 | 0 | 0 |

Orosco pitched to two batters in 8th. Plunk pitched to three batters in 8th.
HBP—C. Ripken (by Hershiser).
Umpires—HP—Kosc; 1B—Tschida; 2B—Welke; 3B—Shulock; LF—Hendry; RF—Coble.
T—3:27. A—48,970.

### Game Three: October 4
### Indians 9, Orioles 4

| BALTIMORE | ab | r | h | bi | bb | so | CLEVELAND | ab | r | h | bi | bb | so |
|---|---|---|---|---|---|---|---|---|---|---|---|---|---|
| Anderson cf | 3 | 0 | 0 | 1 | 1 | 0 | Lofton cf | 3 | 2 | 0 | 0 | 2 | 0 |
| Zeile 3b | 5 | 0 | 1 | 0 | 0 | 3 | Seitzer 1b | 4 | 1 | 2 | 3 | 1 | 0 |
| R. Alomar 2b | 3 | 0 | 0 | 1 | 2 |  | Thome 3b | 2 | 0 | 0 | 0 | 1 | 1 |
| Palmeiro 1b | 4 | 0 | 0 | 0 | 1 | 0 | Candaele ph | 0 | 1 | 0 | 0 | 1 | 0 |
| Bonilla rf | 4 | 1 | 1 | 0 | 0 | 1 | Kent 3b | 1 | 0 | 0 | 0 | 0 | 0 |
| C. Ripken ss | 4 | 1 | 1 | 0 | 0 | 1 | Belle lf | 4 | 1 | 2 | 4 | 1 | 1 |
| Murray dh | 4 | 1 | 2 | 0 | 0 | 1 | Franco 1b | 4 | 0 | 0 | 0 | 0 | 2 |
| Surhoff lf | 4 | 1 | 2 | 3 | 0 | 1 | Ramirez rf | 4 | 1 | 1 | 1 | 0 | 1 |
| Devereaux pr | 0 | 0 | 0 | 0 | 0 | 0 | S. Alomar c | 4 | 0 | 0 | 0 | 0 | 1 |
| Hoiles c | 2 | 0 | 1 | 0 | 1 | 0 | Vizquel ss | 4 | 3 | 3 | 0 | 0 | 1 |
| Alexander pr | 0 | 0 | 0 | 0 | 0 | 0 | Vizcaino 2b | 4 | 0 | 2 | 1 | 0 | 0 |
| Parent c | 1 | 0 | 0 | 0 | 0 | 0 |  |  |  |  |  |  |  |
| **Totals** | 34 | 4 | 8 | 4 | 3 | 8 | **Totals** | 34 | 9 | 10 | 9 | 6 | 8 |

| Baltimore | 010 | 300 | 000—4 |
|---|---|---|---|
| Cleveland | 120 | 100 | 41x—9 |

E—Zeile (2), Bonilla (1). DP—Baltimore 1, Cleveland 1. LOB—Baltimore 7, Cleveland 7. 2B—Vizcaino 2 (2). HR—Belle (2), Ramirez (2), Surhoff (3). SB—Murray (1), Lofton 3 (5), Belle (1), Vizquel.

| Baltimore | ip | h | r | er | bb | so | Cleveland | ip | h | r | er | bb | so |
|---|---|---|---|---|---|---|---|---|---|---|---|---|---|
| Mussina | 6 | 7 | 4 | 3 | 2 | 6 | McDowell | 5⅔ | 6 | 4 | 4 | 1 | 5 |
| Orosco L | 0 | 0 | 3 | 3 | 3 | 0 | Embree | ⅓ | 0 | 0 | 0 | 0 | 0 |
| Benitez | 1 | 0 | 1 | 1 | 0 | 1 | Shuey | ⅔ | 1 | 0 | 0 | 2 | 0 |
| Rhodes | ⅓ | 1 | 1 | 1 | 1 | 0 | Assenmacher W | ⅓ | 0 | 0 | 0 | 0 | 0 |
| Mathews | ⅔ | 1 | 0 | 0 | 0 | 1 | Plunk | 1 | 0 | 0 | 0 | 0 | 2 |
|  |  |  |  |  |  |  | Mesa | 1 | 1 | 0 | 0 | 0 | 1 |

Orosco pitched to three batters in 7th.
HBP—Anderson (by McDowell).
Umpires—HP—Merrill; 1B—Young; 2B—Clark; 3B—Johnson; LF—Evans; RF—Kaiser.
T—3:44. A—44,250.

### Game Four: October 5
### Orioles 4, Indians 3

| BALTIMORE | ab | r | h | bi | bb | so | CLEVELAND | ab | r | h | bi | bb | so |
|---|---|---|---|---|---|---|---|---|---|---|---|---|---|
| Anderson cf | 5 | 0 | 1 | 0 | 1 | 1 | Lofton cf | 5 | 0 | 0 | 0 | 0 | 1 |
| Zeile 3b | 5 | 0 | 0 | 0 | 1 | 1 | Vizquel ss | 5 | 0 | 2 | 1 | 1 | 3 |
| R. Alomar 2b | 6 | 1 | 3 | 2 | 0 | 1 | Seitzer dh | 4 | 0 | 0 | 0 | 1 | 2 |
| Palmeiro 1b | 6 | 1 | 1 | 1 | 0 | 4 | Candaele pr-dh | 0 | 0 | 0 | 0 | 0 | 0 |
| Bonilla rf | 6 | 1 | 1 | 1 | 0 | 4 | Belle lf | 4 | 0 | 0 | 0 | 1 | 2 |
| C. Ripken ss | 6 | 0 | 2 | 0 | 0 | 2 | Franco 1b | 4 | 1 | 1 | 0 | 1 | 2 |
| Murray dh | 4 | 0 | 2 | 0 | 2 | 2 | Ramirez rf | 4 | 1 | 2 | 0 | 1 | 1 |
| Incaviglia lf | 5 | 0 | 1 | 0 | 0 | 4 | Kent 3b | 3 | 0 | 0 | 0 | 0 | 0 |

| | ab | r | h | bi | bb | so | | ab | r | h | bi | bb | so |
|---|---|---|---|---|---|---|---|---|---|---|---|---|---|
| Devereaux lf | 1 | 0 | 0 | 0 | 0 | 0 | Wilson ph | 1 | 0 | 0 | 0 | 0 | 0 |
| Hoiles c | 3 | 0 | 0 | 0 | 0 | 3 | Thome 3b | 0 | 0 | 0 | 0 | 0 | 0 |
| Surhoff ph | 1 | 0 | 1 | 0 | 0 | 0 | S. Alomar c | 5 | 0 | 1 | 2 | 0 | 0 |
| Alexander pr | 0 | 1 | 0 | 0 | 0 | 0 | Vizcaino 2b | 5 | 1 | 1 | 0 | 0 | 0 |
| Parent c | 1 | 0 | 0 | 0 | 0 | 1 | | | | | | | |
| **Totals** | 50 | 4 | 14 | 4 | 3 | 23 | **Totals** | 40 | 3 | 7 | 3 | 5 | 10 |

| | |
|---|---|
| **Baltimore** | **020 000 001 001—4** |
| **Cleveland** | **000 210 000 000—3** |

**E**—Palmeiro (1), Vizcaino (1). **LOB**—Baltimore 13, Cleveland 8. **2B**—Zeile (1), C. Ripken (3), Ramirez 2 (2). **HR**—R. Alomar (1), Palmeiro (1), Bonilla (2). **SB**—Vizquel (4), Seitzer (1). **CS**—Anderson, Vizquel, S. Alomar. **S**—Lofton, Kent.

| **Baltimore** | ip | h | r | er | bb | so | **Clevaland** | ip | h | r | er | bb | so |
|---|---|---|---|---|---|---|---|---|---|---|---|---|---|
| Wells | 7 | 7 | 3 | 3 | 3 | 3 | Nagy | 6 | 6 | 2 | 2 | 2 | 12 |
| Mathews | 1⅓ | 0 | 0 | 0 | 1 | 1 | Embree | ⅓ | 0 | 0 | 0 | 0 | 1 |
| Orosco | ⅔ | 0 | 0 | 0 | 0 | 1 | Shuey | 0 | 1 | 0 | 0 | 0 | 0 |
| Benitez W | 2 | 0 | 0 | 0 | 1 | 4 | Assenmacher | ⅔ | 0 | 0 | 0 | 0 | 2 |
| Myers S | 1 | 0 | 0 | 0 | 0 | 1 | Plunk | 1 | 0 | 0 | 0 | 0 | 2 |
| | | | | | | | Mesa L | 3⅔ | 7 | 2 | 2 | 0 | 6 |
| | | | | | | | Ogea | ⅓ | 0 | 0 | 0 | 1 | 0 |

**Umpires: HP**—Young; **1B**—Clark; **2B**—Johnson; **3B**—Evans; **LF**—Kaiser; **RF**—Merrill.

**T**—4:41. **A**—44,280.

## COMPOSITE BOX

### BALTIMORE

| Player, Pos. | AVG | G | AB | R | H | 2B | 3B | HR | RBI | BB | SO | SB |
|---|---|---|---|---|---|---|---|---|---|---|---|---|
| Cal Ripken, ss | .444 | 4 | 18 | 2 | 8 | 3 | 0 | 0 | 2 | 0 | 3 | 0 |
| Eddie Murray, dh | .400 | 4 | 15 | 1 | 6 | 1 | 0 | 0 | 1 | 3 | 4 | 1 |
| B.J. Surhoff, lf | .385 | 4 | 13 | 3 | 5 | 0 | 0 | 3 | 5 | 0 | 1 | 0 |
| Roberto Alomar, 2b | .294 | 4 | 17 | 2 | 5 | 0 | 0 | 1 | 4 | 2 | 3 | 0 |
| Brady Anderson, cf | .294 | 4 | 17 | 3 | 5 | 0 | 0 | 2 | 4 | 2 | 3 | 0 |
| Todd Zeile, 3b | .263 | 4 | 19 | 2 | 5 | 1 | 0 | 0 | 0 | 2 | 5 | 0 |
| Bobby Bonilla, rf | .200 | 4 | 15 | 4 | 3 | 0 | 0 | 2 | 5 | 4 | 6 | 0 |
| Pete Incaviglia, lf | .200 | 2 | 5 | 1 | 1 | 0 | 0 | 0 | 0 | 0 | 4 | 0 |
| Mark Parent, c | .200 | 4 | 5 | 0 | 1 | 0 | 0 | 0 | 0 | 0 | 2 | 0 |
| Rafael Palmeiro, 1b | .176 | 4 | 17 | 4 | 3 | 1 | 0 | 1 | 2 | 1 | 6 | 0 |
| Chris Hoiles, c | .143 | 4 | 7 | 1 | 1 | 0 | 0 | 0 | 0 | 3 | 3 | 0 |
| Manny Alexander, pr | .000 | 3 | 0 | 2 | 0 | 0 | 0 | 0 | 0 | 0 | 0 | 0 |
| Mike Devereaux, pr-rf | .000 | 4 | 1 | 0 | 0 | 0 | 0 | 0 | 0 | 0 | 0 | 0 |
| **Totals** | **.289** | **4** | **149** | **25** | **43** | **6** | **0** | **9** | **23** | **17** | **40** | **1** |

| Pitcher | W | L | ERA | G | GS | SV | IP | H | R | ER | BB | SO |
|---|---|---|---|---|---|---|---|---|---|---|---|---|
| Randy Myers | 0 | 0 | 0.00 | 3 | 0 | 2 | 3 | 0 | 0 | 0 | 0 | 3 |
| Terry Mathews | 0 | 0 | 0.00 | 3 | 0 | 0 | 3 | 3 | 0 | 0 | 1 | 2 |
| Armando Benitez | 2 | 0 | 2.25 | 3 | 0 | 0 | 4 | 1 | 1 | 1 | 2 | 6 |
| Scott Erickson | 0 | 0 | 4.05 | 1 | 1 | 0 | 7 | 6 | 3 | 3 | 2 | 6 |
| Mike Mussina | 0 | 0 | 4.50 | 1 | 1 | 0 | 6 | 7 | 4 | 3 | 2 | 6 |
| David Wells | 1 | 0 | 4.61 | 2 | 2 | 0 | 14 | 15 | 7 | 7 | 4 | 6 |
| Arthur Rhodes | 0 | 0 | 9.00 | 2 | 0 | 0 | 1 | 1 | 1 | 1 | 1 | 1 |
| Jesse Orosco | 0 | 1 | 36.00 | 4 | 0 | 0 | 1 | 2 | 4 | 4 | 3 | 2 |
| **Totals** | **3** | **1** | **4.50** | **4** | **4** | **2** | **38** | **35** | **20** | **19** | **15** | **32** |

### CLEVELAND

| Player Pos. | AVG | G | AB | R | H | 2B | 3B | HR | RBI | BB | SO | SB |
|---|---|---|---|---|---|---|---|---|---|---|---|---|
| Omar Vizquel, ss | .429 | 4 | 14 | 4 | 6 | 1 | 0 | 0 | 2 | 3 | 4 | 4 |
| Manny Ramirez, rf | .375 | 4 | 16 | 4 | 6 | 2 | 0 | 2 | 2 | 1 | 4 | 0 |
| Jose Vizcaino, 2b | .333 | 3 | 12 | 1 | 4 | 2 | 0 | 0 | 1 | 1 | 1 | 0 |
| Jim Thome, 3b | .300 | 4 | 10 | 1 | 3 | 0 | 0 | 0 | 0 | 1 | 5 | 0 |
| Kevin Seitzer, 1b-dh | .294 | 4 | 17 | 1 | 5 | 1 | 0 | 0 | 4 | 2 | 4 | 1 |
| Albert Belle, lf | .200 | 4 | 15 | 2 | 3 | 0 | 0 | 2 | 6 | 3 | 2 | 1 |
| Kenny Lofton, cf | .167 | 4 | 18 | 3 | 3 | 0 | 0 | 0 | 1 | 2 | 3 | 5 |
| Julio Franco, 1b-dh | .133 | 4 | 15 | 1 | 2 | 0 | 0 | 0 | 1 | 1 | 6 | 0 |
| Jeff Kent, 2b-1b-3b | .125 | 4 | 8 | 2 | 1 | 1 | 0 | 0 | 0 | 0 | 0 | 0 |
| Sandy Alomar, c | .125 | 4 | 16 | 0 | 2 | 0 | 0 | 0 | 3 | 0 | 2 | 0 |
| Casey Candaele, pr-dh | .000 | 2 | 0 | 1 | 0 | 0 | 0 | 0 | 0 | 1 | 0 | 0 |
| Brian Giles, ph | .000 | 1 | 1 | 0 | 0 | 0 | 0 | 0 | 0 | 0 | 1 | 0 |
| Nigel Wilson, ph | .000 | 1 | 1 | 0 | 0 | 0 | 0 | 0 | 0 | 0 | 0 | 0 |
| Tony Pena, c | .000 | 1 | 0 | 0 | 0 | 0 | 0 | 0 | 0 | 0 | 0 | 0 |
| **Totals** | **.245** | **4** | **143** | **20** | **35** | **7** | **0** | **4** | **20** | **15** | **32** | **11** |

| Pitcher | W | L | ERA | G | GS | SV | IP | H | R | ER | BB | SO |
|---|---|---|---|---|---|---|---|---|---|---|---|---|
| Paul Assenmacher | 1 | 0 | 0.00 | 3 | 0 | 0 | 2 | 0 | 0 | 0 | 1 | 2 |
| Chad Ogea | 0 | 0 | 0.00 | 1 | 0 | 0 | 0 | 0 | 0 | 0 | 1 | 0 |
| Julian Tavarez | 0 | 0 | 0.00 | 2 | 0 | 0 | 1 | 1 | 0 | 0 | 2 | 1 |
| Jose Mesa | 0 | 1 | 3.86 | 2 | 0 | 0 | 5 | 8 | 2 | 2 | 0 | 7 |
| Orel Hershiser | 0 | 0 | 5.40 | 1 | 1 | 0 | 5 | 7 | 4 | 3 | 3 | 3 |
| Jack McDowell | 0 | 0 | 6.35 | 1 | 1 | 0 | 6 | 6 | 4 | 4 | 1 | 5 |
| Eric Plunk | 0 | 1 | 6.75 | 3 | 0 | 0 | 4 | 1 | 3 | 3 | 2 | 6 |
| Charles Nagy | 0 | 1 | 7.15 | 2 | 2 | 0 | 11 | 15 | 9 | 9 | 5 | 13 |
| Paul Shuey | 0 | 0 | 9.00 | 3 | 0 | 0 | 2 | 5 | 2 | 2 | 2 | 2 |
| Alan Embree | 0 | 0 | 9.00 | 3 | 0 | 0 | 1 | 0 | 1 | 1 | 0 | 1 |
| **Totals** | **1** | **3** | **5.84** | **4** | **4** | **0** | **37** | **43** | **25** | **24** | **17** | **40** |

| | |
|---|---|
| **Cleveland** | **130 513 520 000—20** |
| **Baltimore** | **242 335 131 001—25** |

**DP**—Cleveland 2, Baltimore 2. **LOB**—Cleveland 29, Baltimore 36. **E**—Zeile 2, Seitzer, S. Alomar, Bonilla, Palmeiro, Vizcaino. **CS**—Vizquel. **S**—Kent, Lofton. **SF**—Vizquel 2, R. Alomar, S. Alomar, Franco, Anderson.

**HBP**—Palmeiro (by Embree), Hoiles (by Nagy), Thome (by Orosco), Ripken (by Hershiser), Anderson (by McDowell). **WP**—Mathews.

**Umpires**—Al Clark, Drew Coble, Jim Evans, Ted Hendry, Mark Johnson, Ken Kaiser, Greg Kosc, Durwood Merrill, John Shulock, Tim Tschida, Tim Welke, Larry Young,.

# CHAMPIONSHIP SERIES

## BALTIMORE vs. NEW YORK

## BOX SCORES

### Game One: October 9
### Yankees 5, Orioles 4

| **BALTIMORE** | ab | r | h | bi | bb | so | **NEW YORK** | ab | r | h | bi | bb | so |
|---|---|---|---|---|---|---|---|---|---|---|---|---|---|
| Anderson cf | 5 | 1 | 2 | 1 | 1 | 1 | Raines lf | 6 | 1 | 2 | 0 | 0 | 0 |
| Zeile 3b | 6 | 0 | 1 | 0 | 0 | 1 | Boggs 3b | 5 | 1 | 0 | 0 | 1 | 1 |
| Alomar 2b | 6 | 0 | 1 | 0 | 0 | 3 | Williams cf | 4 | 1 | 2 | 2 | 2 | 1 |
| Palmeiro 1b | 3 | 3 | 3 | 1 | 2 | 0 | Martinez 1b | 5 | 0 | 1 | 0 | 0 | 1 |
| Bonilla rf | 4 | 0 | 0 | 0 | 0 | 0 | Fielder dh | 2 | 1 | 0 | 0 | 3 | 0 |
| Tarasco rf | 1 | 0 | 0 | 0 | 0 | 1 | Fox pr | 0 | 0 | 0 | 0 | 0 | 0 |
| C. Ripken ss | 5 | 0 | 2 | 0 | 0 | 1 | O'Neill rf | 3 | 0 | 0 | 0 | 0 | 0 |
| Murray dh | 4 | 0 | 1 | 1 | 1 | 0 | Hayes ph | 0 | 0 | 0 | 0 | 0 | 0 |
| Surhoff lf | 3 | 0 | 0 | 1 | 0 | 1 | Strawberry ph-rf | 1 | 0 | 0 | 1 | 1 | 0 |
| Devereaux lf | 1 | 0 | 0 | 0 | 0 | 0 | Duncan 2b | 4 | 0 | 1 | 0 | 0 | 1 |
| Parent c | 5 | 0 | 1 | 0 | 0 | 2 | Leyritz c | 4 | 0 | 1 | 1 | 0 | 2 |
| | | | | | | | Aldrete ph | 0 | 0 | 0 | 0 | 0 | 0 |
| | | | | | | | Girardi ph-c | 1 | 0 | 0 | 0 | 0 | 0 |
| | | | | | | | Jeter ss | 5 | 1 | 4 | 1 | 0 | 0 |
| **Totals** | 43 | 4 | 11 | 4 | 4 | 10 | **Totals** | 40 | 5 | 11 | 5 | 7 | 6 |

| | |
|---|---|
| **Baltimore** | **011 101 000 00—4** |
| **New York** | **110 000 110 01—5** |

No outs when winning run scored.

**E**—Alomar (1). **DP**—Baltimore 2. **LOB**—Baltimore 11, New York 13. **2B**—C. Ripken (1), Anderson (1), Raines (1), Williams (1). **HR**—Anderson (1), Palmeiro (1), Jeter (1), Williams (1). **SB**—Jeter (1). **SF**—Surhoff.

| **Baltimore** | ip | h | r | er | bb | so | **New York** | ip | h | r | er | bb | so |
|---|---|---|---|---|---|---|---|---|---|---|---|---|---|
| Erickson | 6⅓ | 7 | 3 | 2 | 3 | 3 | Pettitte | 7 | 7 | 4 | 4 | 4 | 4 |
| Orosco | ⅓ | 0 | 0 | 0 | 1 | 1 | Nelson | 1 | 0 | 0 | 0 | 0 | 1 |
| Benitez | 1 | 2 | 1 | 1 | 2 | 2 | Wetteland | 1 | 1 | 0 | 0 | 0 | 2 |
| Rhodes | ⅓ | 0 | 0 | 0 | 0 | 0 | M. Rivera W | 2 | 3 | 0 | 0 | 0 | 3 |
| Mathews | ⅓ | 0 | 0 | 0 | 1 | 0 | | | | | | | |
| Myers L | 1⅔ | 2 | 1 | 1 | 0 | 0 | | | | | | | |

Myers pitched to one batter in 11th.

**Umpires: HP**—Barnett; **1B**—Scott; **2B**—Reilly; **3B**—Morrison; **LF**—Roe; **RF**—Garcia.

**T**—4:23. **A**—56,495.

### Game Two: October 10
### Orioles 5, Yankees 3

| **BALTIMORE** | ab | r | h | bi | bb | so | **NEW YORK** | ab | r | h | bi | bb | so |
|---|---|---|---|---|---|---|---|---|---|---|---|---|---|
| Anderson cf | 4 | 2 | 1 | 0 | 1 | 1 | Jeter ss | 5 | 1 | 2 | 0 | 0 | 2 |
| Zeile 3b | 4 | 1 | 2 | 2 | 1 | 0 | Raines lf | 4 | 1 | 1 | 0 | 1 | 1 |
| Alomar 2b | 4 | 1 | 2 | 1 | 0 | 0 | Williams cf | 3 | 0 | 2 | 1 | 2 | 1 |
| Palmeiro 1b | 4 | 1 | 1 | 2 | 1 | 1 | Fielder dh | 5 | 0 | 1 | 1 | 0 | 0 |
| Bonilla rf | 4 | 0 | 0 | 0 | 1 | 4 | Martinez 1b | 4 | 0 | 0 | 0 | 0 | 0 |
| Tarasco rf | 0 | 0 | 0 | 0 | 0 | 0 | Duncan 2b | 4 | 0 | 1 | 0 | 0 | 1 |
| C. Ripken ss | 5 | 0 | 2 | 0 | 0 | 0 | O'Neill rf | 2 | 0 | 1 | 0 | 1 | 1 |
| Murray dh | 4 | 0 | 1 | 0 | 0 | 1 | Leyritz ph-rf | 1 | 0 | 0 | 0 | 0 | 0 |
| Surhoff lf | 4 | 0 | 1 | 0 | 0 | 0 | Hayes 3b | 4 | 0 | 1 | 0 | 0 | 2 |
| Devereaux lf | 0 | 0 | 0 | 0 | 0 | 0 | Girardi c | 4 | 1 | 2 | 0 | 0 | 0 |
| Hoiles c | 3 | 0 | 0 | 0 | 1 | 0 | | | | | | | |
| **Totals** | 36 | 5 | 10 | 5 | 5 | 7 | **Totals** | 36 | 3 | 11 | 2 | 4 | 8 |

| | |
|---|---|
| **Baltimore** | **002 000 210 —5** |
| **New York** | **200 000 100 —3** |

**E**—Duncan (1). **DP**— Baltimore 2, New York 1. **LOB**—Baltimore 10, New York 11. **2B**—Alomar (1), Duncan (1). **3B**— Girardi (1). **HR**—Zeile (1), Palmeiro (2). **SF**—Alomar.

| **Baltimore** | ip | h | r | er | bb | so | **New York** | ip | h | r | er | bb | so |
|---|---|---|---|---|---|---|---|---|---|---|---|---|---|
| Wells W | 6⅔ | 8 | 3 | 3 | 3 | 6 | Cone | 6 | 5 | 2 | 2 | 5 | 5 |
| Mills | 0 | 1 | 0 | 0 | 0 | 0 | Nelson L | 1⅓ | 5 | 3 | 3 | 0 | 1 |
| Orosco | 1⅓ | 1 | 0 | 0 | 0 | 1 | Lloyd | 1⅓ | 0 | 0 | 0 | 0 | 1 |
| Myers | ⅓ | 1 | 0 | 0 | 1 | 1 | Weathers | ⅓ | 0 | 0 | 0 | 0 | 0 |
| Benitez S | ⅔ | 0 | 0 | 0 | 0 | 0 | | | | | | | |

**HBP**—Martinez (by Wells). **WP**—Cone.

**Umpires: HP**—Scott; **1B**—Reilly; **2B**—Morrison; **3B**—Roe; **LF**—Garcia; **RF**—Barnett.

**T**—4:13. **A**—56,432.

### Game Three: October 11
### Yankees 5, Orioles 2

| NEW YORK | ab | r | h | bi | bb | so | BALTIMORE | ab | r | h | bi | bb | so |
|---|---|---|---|---|---|---|---|---|---|---|---|---|---|
| Raines lf | 5 | 0 | 1 | 0 | 0 | 0 | Anderson cf | 4 | 1 | 1 | 0 | 0 | 2 |
| Jeter ss | 4 | 1 | 1 | 0 | 0 | 1 | Zeile 3b | 4 | 1 | 1 | 2 | 0 | 0 |
| Williams cf | 3 | 2 | 1 | 1 | 1 | 1 | Alomar 2b | 4 | 0 | 0 | 0 | 0 | 0 |
| Martinez 1b | 4 | 1 | 2 | 0 | 0 | 0 | Palmeiro 1b | 3 | 0 | 0 | 0 | 0 | 0 |
| Fielder dh | 4 | 1 | 1 | 3 | 0 | 2 | Bonilla rf | 3 | 0 | 0 | 0 | 0 | 0 |
| Strawberry rf | 4 | 0 | 1 | 0 | 0 | 1 | C. Ripken ss | 3 | 0 | 0 | 0 | 0 | 1 |
| Duncan 2b | 4 | 0 | 0 | 0 | 0 | 1 | Murray dh | 2 | 0 | 0 | 0 | 1 | 1 |
| Sojo 2b | 0 | 0 | 0 | 0 | 0 | 0 | Surhoff lf | 3 | 0 | 1 | 0 | 0 | 1 |
| Hayes 3b | 2 | 0 | 0 | 0 | 2 | 0 | Hoiles c | 3 | 0 | 0 | 0 | 0 | 1 |
| Girardi c | 4 | 0 | 1 | 0 | 0 | 1 | | | | | | | |
| **Totals** | **34** | **5** | **8** | **4** | **3** | **7** | **Totals** | **29** | **2** | **3** | **2** | **1** | **6** |

| | |
|---|---|
| **New York** | **000 100 040—5** |
| **Baltimore** | **200 000 000—2** |

**E**—C. Ripken (1), Zeile (1). **DP**—New York 1, Baltimore 2. **LOB**—New York 5, Baltimore 1. **2B**—Jeter (1), Martinez (1). **HR**—Zeile (2), Fielder (1).

| New York | ip | h | r | er | bb | so | Baltimore | ip | h | r | er | bb | so |
|---|---|---|---|---|---|---|---|---|---|---|---|---|---|
| Key W | 8 | 3 | 2 | 2 | 1 | 5 | Mussina L | 7⅔ | 8 | 5 | 5 | 2 | 6 |
| Wetteland S | 1 | 0 | 0 | 0 | 0 | 1 | Orosco | ⅓ | 0 | 0 | 0 | 0 | 0 |
| | | | | | | | Mathews | 1 | 0 | 0 | 0 | 1 | 1 |

**Umpires: HP**—Reilly; **1B**—Morrison; **2B**—Roe; **3B**—Garcia; **LF**—Barnett; **RF**—Scott.

**T**—2:50. **A**—48,635.

### Game Four: October 12
### Yankees 8, Orioles 4

| NEW YORK | ab | r | h | bi | bb | so | BALTIMORE | ab | r | h | bi | bb | so |
|---|---|---|---|---|---|---|---|---|---|---|---|---|---|
| Jeter ss | 5 | 1 | 1 | 0 | 0 | 2 | Anderson cf | 4 | 1 | 0 | 0 | 1 | 1 |
| Boggs 3b | 5 | 0 | 0 | 0 | 0 | 1 | Zeile 3b | 5 | 0 | 2 | 0 | 0 | 0 |
| Williams cf | 4 | 2 | 2 | 2 | 0 | 0 | Alomar 2b | 5 | 0 | 2 | 0 | 0 | 1 |
| Martinez 1b | 4 | 1 | 1 | 0 | 0 | 0 | Palmeiro 1b | 3 | 0 | 0 | 1 | 1 | 2 |
| Fielder dh | 4 | 0 | 0 | 1 | 0 | 1 | Bonilla rf | 5 | 0 | 0 | 0 | 0 | 0 |
| Strawberry lf | 4 | 3 | 3 | 3 | 0 | 1 | C. Ripken ss | 3 | 1 | 1 | 0 | 1 | 0 |
| Raines lf | 0 | 0 | 0 | 0 | 0 | 0 | Incaviglia dh | 2 | 1 | 1 | 0 | 0 | 0 |
| O'Neill rf | 3 | 1 | 1 | 2 | 1 | 1 | Murray ph-dh | 2 | 0 | 1 | 0 | 0 | 0 |
| Duncan 2b | 3 | 0 | 1 | 0 | 0 | 0 | Devereaux lf | 1 | 0 | 0 | 0 | 0 | 1 |
| Sojo 2b | 1 | 0 | 0 | 0 | 0 | 0 | Surhoff ph-lf | 3 | 0 | 2 | 1 | 0 | 0 |
| Girardi c | 3 | 0 | 0 | 0 | 1 | 2 | Hoiles c | 4 | 1 | 2 | 2 | 0 | 1 |
| **Totals** | **36** | **8** | **9** | **8** | **2** | **8** | **Totals** | **37** | **4** | **11** | **4** | **3** | **6** |

| | |
|---|---|
| **New York** | **210 200 030—8** |
| **Baltimore** | **101 200 00x—4** |

**LOB**—New York 3, Baltimore 10. **2B**—Jeter (2), Duncan (2), Williams (2), Alomar (2). **HR**—Williams (2), Strawberry 2 (2), O'Neill (1), Hoiles (1). **SF**—Palmeiro.

| New York | ip | h | r | er | bb | so | Baltimore | ip | h | r | er | bb | so |
|---|---|---|---|---|---|---|---|---|---|---|---|---|---|
| Rogers | 3 | 5 | 4 | 4 | 2 | 3 | Coppinger L | 5⅓ | 6 | 5 | 5 | 1 | 3 |
| Weathers W | 2⅔ | 3 | 0 | 0 | 0 | 0 | Rhodes | ⅔ | 0 | 0 | 0 | 0 | 1 |
| Lloyd | ⅓ | 0 | 0 | 0 | 0 | 0 | Mills | 1⅓ | 1 | 1 | 1 | 0 | 2 |
| M. Rivera | 2 | 3 | 0 | 0 | 1 | 2 | Orosco | 0 | 1 | 1 | 1 | 0 | 0 |
| Wetteland | 1 | 0 | 0 | 0 | 0 | 1 | Benitez | ⅔ | 1 | 1 | 1 | 1 | 0 |
| | | | | | | | Mathews | 1 | 0 | 0 | 0 | 0 | 2 |

Rogers pitched to two batters in 4th. Orsoco pitched to one batter in 8th.

**WP**—Rogers.

**Umpires: HP**—Morrison; **1B**—Roe; **2B**—Garcia; **3B**—Barnett; **LF**—Scott; **RF**—Reilly.

**T**—3:45. **A**—48,974.

### Game Five: October 13
### Yankees 6, Orioles 4

| NEW YORK | ab | r | h | bi | bb | so | BALTIMORE | ab | r | h | bi | bb | so |
|---|---|---|---|---|---|---|---|---|---|---|---|---|---|
| Jeter ss | 5 | 1 | 2 | 0 | 0 | 0 | Anderson cf | 4 | 0 | 0 | 0 | 0 | 0 |
| Boggs 3b | 5 | 0 | 2 | 0 | 0 | 1 | Zeile 3b | 3 | 1 | 2 | 1 | 1 | 0 |
| Williams cf | 5 | 1 | 2 | 0 | 0 | 1 | Alomar 2b | 4 | 1 | 0 | 0 | 0 | 0 |
| Martinez 1b | 5 | 1 | 0 | 0 | 0 | 1 | Palmeiro 1b | 4 | 0 | 0 | 0 | 0 | 1 |
| Fielder dh | 3 | 1 | 1 | 3 | 1 | 2 | Bonilla rf | 4 | 1 | 1 | 2 | 0 | 0 |
| Fox pr-dh | 0 | 0 | 0 | 0 | 0 | 0 | C. Ripken ss | 4 | 0 | 0 | 0 | 0 | 2 |
| Hayes ph-dh | 1 | 0 | 0 | 0 | 0 | 0 | Murray dh | 3 | 1 | 1 | 1 | 0 | 0 |
| Strawberry lf | 3 | 1 | 1 | 1 | 1 | 0 | Surhoff lf | 2 | 0 | 0 | 0 | 1 | 0 |
| Raines lf | 0 | 0 | 0 | 0 | 0 | 0 | Parent c | 1 | 0 | 0 | 0 | 0 | 0 |
| O'Neill rf | 3 | 0 | 1 | 0 | 1 | 0 | Hoiles ph-c | 2 | 0 | 0 | 0 | 0 | 1 |
| Leyritz c | 3 | 1 | 1 | 1 | 1 | 2 | | | | | | | |
| Sojo 2b | 4 | 0 | 1 | 0 | 0 | 1 | | | | | | | |
| **Totals** | **37** | **6** | **11** | **5** | **4** | **8** | **Totals** | **31** | **4** | **4** | **4** | **2** | **4** |

| | |
|---|---|
| **New York** | **006 000 000—6** |
| **Baltimore** | **000 001 012—4** |

**E**—Alomar (2). **DP**—Baltimore 1. **LOB**—New York 8, Baltimore 2. **2B**—Williams (3). **HR**—Zeile (3), Bonilla (1), Murray (1), Fielder (2), Strawberry (3), Leyritz (1). **SB**—Jeter (2), Williams (1).

| New York | ip | h | r | er | bb | so | Baltimore | ip | h | r | er | bb | so |
|---|---|---|---|---|---|---|---|---|---|---|---|---|---|
| Pettite W | 8 | 3 | 2 | 2 | 1 | 3 | Erickson L | 5 | 7 | 6 | 1 | 1 | 5 |
| Wetteland | 1 | 1 | 2 | 2 | 1 | 1 | Rhodes | 1 | 2 | 0 | 0 | 0 | 1 |
| | | | | | | | Mills | 1 | 1 | 0 | 0 | 1 | 1 |
| | | | | | | | Myers | 2 | 1 | 0 | 0 | 2 | 1 |

Mills pitched to one batter in 8th.

**Umpires: HP**—Roe; **1B**—Garcia; **2B**—Barnett; **3B**—Scott; **LF**—Reilly; **RF**—Morrison.

**T**—2:57. **A**—48,718.

## COMPOSITE BOX

### BALTIMORE

| Player, Pos. | AVG | G | AB | R | H | 2B | 3B | HR | RBI | BB | SO | SB |
|---|---|---|---|---|---|---|---|---|---|---|---|---|
| Pete Incaviglia, dh | .500 | 1 | 2 | 1 | 1 | 0 | 0 | 0 | 0 | 0 | 0 | 0 |
| Todd Zeile, 3b | .364 | 5 | 22 | 3 | 8 | 0 | 0 | 3 | 5 | 2 | 1 | 0 |
| Eddie Murray, dh-ph | .267 | 5 | 15 | 1 | 4 | 0 | 0 | 1 | 2 | 2 | 2 | 0 |
| B.J. Surhoff, lf-ph | .267 | 5 | 15 | 0 | 4 | 0 | 0 | 0 | 2 | 1 | 2 | 0 |
| Cal Ripken Jr., ss | .250 | 5 | 20 | 1 | 5 | 1 | 0 | 0 | 0 | 1 | 4 | 0 |
| Rafael Palmeiro, 1b | .235 | 5 | 17 | 4 | 4 | 0 | 0 | 2 | 4 | 4 | 4 | 0 |
| Roberto Alomar, 2b | .217 | 5 | 23 | 2 | 5 | 2 | 0 | 0 | 1 | 0 | 4 | 0 |
| Brady Anderson, cf | .190 | 5 | 21 | 5 | 4 | 1 | 0 | 1 | 1 | 3 | 5 | 0 |
| Chris Hoiles, c | .167 | 4 | 12 | 1 | 2 | 0 | 0 | 1 | 2 | 1 | 3 | 0 |
| Mark Parent, c | .167 | 2 | 6 | 0 | 1 | 0 | 0 | 0 | 0 | 0 | 2 | 0 |
| Bobby Bonilla, rf | .050 | 5 | 20 | 1 | 1 | 0 | 0 | 1 | 2 | 1 | 4 | 0 |
| Tony Tarasco, rf | .000 | 2 | 1 | 0 | 0 | 0 | 0 | 0 | 0 | 0 | 1 | 0 |
| Mike Devereaux, lf | .000 | 3 | 2 | 0 | 0 | 0 | 0 | 0 | 0 | 0 | 1 | 0 |
| **Totals** | **.222** | **5** | **176** | **19** | **39** | **4** | **0** | **9** | **19** | **15** | **33** | **0** |

| Pitcher | W | L | ERA | G | GS | SV | IP | H | R | ER | BB | SO |
|---|---|---|---|---|---|---|---|---|---|---|---|---|
| Terry Mathews | 0 | 0 | 0.00 | 3 | 0 | 0 | 2 | 0 | 0 | 0 | 2 | 3 |
| Arthur Rhodes | 0 | 0 | 0.00 | 3 | 0 | 0 | 2 | 2 | 0 | 0 | 0 | 2 |
| Randy Myers | 0 | 1 | 2.25 | 3 | 0 | 0 | 4 | 4 | 1 | 1 | 3 | 2 |
| Scott Erickson | 0 | 1 | 2.38 | 2 | 2 | 0 | 11 | 14 | 9 | 3 | 4 | 8 |
| Alan Mills | 0 | 0 | 3.86 | 3 | 0 | 0 | 2 | 3 | 1 | 1 | 1 | 3 |
| David Wells | 1 | 0 | 4.05 | 1 | 1 | 0 | 7 | 8 | 3 | 3 | 3 | 6 |
| Jesse Orosco | 0 | 0 | 4.50 | 4 | 0 | 0 | 2 | 2 | 1 | 1 | 1 | 2 |
| Mike Mussina | 0 | 1 | 5.87 | 1 | 1 | 0 | 8 | 8 | 5 | 5 | 2 | 6 |
| Armando Benitez | 0 | 0 | 7.71 | 3 | 0 | 1 | 2 | 3 | 2 | 2 | 3 | 2 |
| Rocky Coppinger | 0 | 1 | 8.44 | 1 | 1 | 0 | 5 | 6 | 5 | 5 | 1 | 3 |
| **Totals** | **1** | **4** | **4.11** | **5** | **5** | **1** | **46** | **50** | **27** | **21** | **20** | **37** |

### NEW YORK

| Player, Pos. | AVG | G | AB | R | H | 2B | 3B | HR | RBI | BB | SO | SB |
|---|---|---|---|---|---|---|---|---|---|---|---|---|
| Bernie Williams, cf | .474 | 5 | 19 | 6 | 9 | 3 | 0 | 2 | 6 | 5 | 4 | 1 |
| Derek Jeter, ss | .417 | 5 | 24 | 5 | 10 | 2 | 0 | 1 | 1 | 0 | 5 | 2 |
| Darryl Strawberry, rf-lf | .417 | 4 | 12 | 4 | 5 | 0 | 0 | 3 | 5 | 2 | 2 | 0 |
| Paul O'Neill, rf | .273 | 4 | 11 | 1 | 3 | 0 | 0 | 1 | 2 | 3 | 2 | 0 |
| Tim Raines, lf | .267 | 5 | 15 | 2 | 4 | 1 | 0 | 0 | 0 | 1 | 1 | 0 |
| Joe Girardi, c | .250 | 4 | 12 | 1 | 3 | 0 | 1 | 0 | 0 | 1 | 3 | 0 |
| Jim Leyritz, c-ph-rf | .250 | 3 | 8 | 1 | 2 | 0 | 0 | 1 | 2 | 1 | 4 | 0 |
| Mariano Duncan, 2b | .200 | 4 | 15 | 0 | 3 | 2 | 0 | 0 | 0 | 0 | 3 | 0 |
| Luis Sojo, 2b | .200 | 3 | 5 | 0 | 1 | 0 | 0 | 0 | 0 | 0 | 1 | 0 |
| Tino Martinez, 1b | .182 | 5 | 22 | 3 | 4 | 1 | 0 | 0 | 0 | 0 | 2 | 0 |
| Cecil Fielder, dh | .167 | 5 | 18 | 3 | 3 | 0 | 0 | 2 | 8 | 4 | 5 | 0 |
| Charlie Hayes, ph-3b | .143 | 4 | 7 | 0 | 1 | 0 | 0 | 0 | 0 | 2 | 2 | 0 |
| Wade Boggs, 3b | .133 | 3 | 15 | 1 | 2 | 0 | 0 | 0 | 0 | 1 | 1 | 0 |
| Mike Aldrete, ph | .000 | 1 | 0 | 0 | 0 | 0 | 0 | 0 | 0 | 0 | 0 | 0 |
| Andy Fox, pr | .000 | 2 | 0 | 0 | 0 | 0 | 0 | 0 | 0 | 0 | 0 | 0 |
| **Totals** | **.273** | **5** | **183** | **27** | **50** | **9** | **1** | **10** | **24** | **20** | **37** | **3** |

| Pitcher | W | L | ERA | G | GS | SV | IP | H | R | ER | BB | SO |
|---|---|---|---|---|---|---|---|---|---|---|---|---|
| Mariano Rivera | 1 | 0 | 0.00 | 2 | 0 | 0 | 4 | 6 | 0 | 0 | 1 | 5 |
| Graeme Lloyd | 0 | 0 | 0.00 | 2 | 0 | 0 | 2 | 0 | 0 | 0 | 0 | 1 |
| David Weathers | 1 | 0 | 0.00 | 2 | 0 | 0 | 3 | 3 | 0 | 0 | 0 | 0 |
| Jimmy Key | 1 | 0 | 2.25 | 1 | 1 | 0 | 8 | 3 | 2 | 2 | 1 | 5 |
| David Cone | 0 | 0 | 3.00 | 1 | 1 | 0 | 6 | 5 | 2 | 2 | 5 | 5 |
| Andy Pettitte | 1 | 0 | 3.60 | 2 | 2 | 0 | 15 | 10 | 6 | 6 | 5 | 7 |
| John Wetteland | 0 | 0 | 4.50 | 4 | 0 | 1 | 4 | 2 | 2 | 2 | 1 | 5 |
| Jeff Nelson | 0 | 1 | 11.57 | 2 | 0 | 0 | 2 | 5 | 3 | 3 | 0 | 2 |
| Kenny Rogers | 0 | 0 | 12.00 | 1 | 1 | 0 | 3 | 5 | 4 | 4 | 2 | 3 |
| **Totals** | **4** | **1** | **3.64** | **5** | **5** | **1** | **47** | **39** | **19** | **19** | **15** | **33** |

| | |
|---|---|
| **Baltimore** | **314 302 222 00—19** |
| **New York** | **526 300 280 01—27** |

**DP**—Baltimore 7, New York 2. **LOB**—Baltimore 34, New York 40.

**E**—Alomar 2, Duncan, Ripken, Zeile. **SF**—Surhoff, Alomar, Palmeiro.

**HBP**—Martinez (by Wells), Duncan (by Mathews). **BK**—Pettitte.

**Umpires**—Rocky Roe, Rich Garcia, Larry Barnett, Dale Scott, Mike Reilly, Dan Morrison.

# Braves Blitz Cards To Win NLCS Title

**By WILL LINGO**

If there's a World Series in the 1990s, chances are the Atlanta Braves will be there.

And 1996 was no exception, as the Braves spotted the St. Louis Cardinals a 3-1 lead in the National League Championship Series, then blitzed the Cardinals in three straight games to take another pennant.

Since their worst-to-first season in 1991, the Braves have been in the playoffs every year there have been playoffs. And they've gone on to the World Series every year except 1993, when the upstart Philadelphia Phillies beat them in the LCS in six games.

The 1996 NLCS started out looking like another cruise to the World Series for the Braves, but the Cardinals responded with three surprising victories. Unfortunately for them, the Braves had John Smoltz, Greg Maddux and Tom Glavine to bail them out, and their bats came alive.

The series opened true to form, with the Braves winning 4-2 behind eight innings from Smoltz and two RBIs each from second baseman Mark Lemke and catcher Javy Lopez, who went on to become the series MVP.

But the next night in Atlanta, the Cardinals exploded for eight runs (three earned) off Maddux, including a back-breaking grand slam by third baseman Gary Gaetti in the seventh.

That gave the Cardinals the jolt of confidence they needed returning home to St. Louis. With loud, enthusiastic crowds behind them, the Cardinals scratched out 3-2 and 4-3 victories in the next two games.

In Game Three, former Braves outfielder Ron Gant haunted his old team, hitting two home runs and driving in all three St. Louis runs. Starter Donovan Osborne pitched seven solid innings, and the Cardinals bullpen shut down the Braves, as it did in all three of the Cardinals victories.

The Braves appeared to have Game Four in hand, leading 3-0 after six innings and recent Pirates acquisition Denny Neagle doing his job. But Neagle tired in the seventh, giving up two runs on a two-out triple by Cardinals rookie Dmitri Young.

Then Bobby Cox brought in Greg McMichael, who pitched ineffectively. McMichael gave up one run in the seventh, then gave up the game-winner in the eighth, a solo home run by Brian Jordan. Again the Cardinals bullpen combo of Rick Honeycutt and closer Dennis Eckersley handcuffed the Braves, and the Cardinals took a commanding 3-1 lead.

But when Eckersley pumped his fist after that victory,

**Career Year.** Braves righthander John Smoltz won 24 games in 1996 to capture the NL Cy Young Award.

LARRY GOREN

**Dennis Eckersley**

it seemed to ignite the Braves, who accused the Cardinals of beginning their celebration too early. Cardinals manager Tony La Russa said simply that his team was enthusiastic.

Whatever it was that motivated the Braves, they came out on fire in Game Five, hammering the Cardinals 14-0 in a game that was never in doubt. Cardinals starter Todd Stottlemyre, who won Game Two and came back on three days' rest, was tired and ineffective, but the Braves hit whoever was on the mound.

The Braves pounded out 22 hits, including home runs by Lopez and first baseman Fred McGriff, and Lopez and Lemke both were 4-for-5. The game put a jolt into the Braves' bats, which had been quiet throughout the postseason.

Lost in the onslaught was Smoltz' seven innings of shutout pitching, giving him a 1.13 ERA for the NL playoffs.

Rookie Alan Benes stepped up in Game Six as the series shifted back to Atlanta and La Russa abandoned his three-man rotation. The Braves manufactured two runs against Benes, but he pitched well.

| Page | EAST | W | L | PCT | GB | Manager(s) | General Manager | Attend./Dates | Last Pennant |
|---|---|---|---|---|---|---|---|---|---|
| 60 | Atlanta Braves | 96 | 66 | .593 | — | Bobby Cox | John Schuerholz | 2,901,242 (81) | 1996 |
| 163 | Montreal Expos | 88 | 74 | .543 | 8 | Felipe Alou | Jim Beattie | 1,618,573 (81) | None |
| 126 | Florida Marlins | 80 | 82 | .494 | 16 | Lachemann/Boles | Dave Dombrowski | 1,746,757 (80) | None |
| 176 | New York Mets | 71 | 91 | .438 | 25 | Green/Valentine | Joe McIlvaine | 1,588,323 (78) | 1986 |
| 189 | Philadelphia Phillies | 67 | 95 | .414 | 29 | Jim Fregosi | Lee Thomas | 1,801,677 (78) | 1993 |
| **Page** | **CENTRAL** | **W** | **L** | **PCT** | **GB** | **Manager** | **General Manager** | **Attend./Dates** | **Last Pennant** |
| 202 | St. Louis Cardinals | 88 | 74 | .543 | — | Tony La Russa | Walt Jocketty | 2,659,251 (81) | 1987 |
| 132 | Houston Astros | 82 | 80 | .506 | 6 | Terry Collins | Gerry Hunsicker | 1,975,888 (81) | None |
| 102 | Cincinnati Reds | 81 | 81 | .500 | 7 | Ray Knight | Jim Bowden | 1,861,428 (76) | 1990 |
| 95 | Chicago Cubs | 76 | 86 | .469 | 12 | Jim Riggleman | Ed Lynch | 2,219,110 (78) | 1945 |
| 195 | Pittsburgh Pirates | 73 | 89 | .451 | 15 | Jim Leyland | Cam Bonifay | 1,332,150 (78) | 1979 |
| **Page** | **WEST** | **W** | **L** | **PCT** | **GB** | **Manager(s)** | **General Manager** | **Attend./Dates** | **Last Pennant** |
| 208 | San Diego Padres | 91 | 71 | .562 | — | Bruce Bochy | Kevin Towers | 2,187,884 (81) | 1984 |
| 144 | Los Angeles Dodgers* | 90 | 72 | .556 | 1 | Lasorda/Russell | Fred Claire | 3,188,454 (81) | 1988 |
| 114 | Colorado Rockies | 83 | 79 | .512 | 8 | Don Baylor | Bob Gebhard | 3,891,014 (81) | None |
| 214 | San Francisco Giants | 68 | 94 | .420 | 23 | Dusty Baker | Bob Quinn | 1,413,687 (80) | 1989 |

*Won wild-card playoff berth

**NOTE:** Team's individual batting, pitching and fielding statistics can be found on page indicated in lefthand column.

But the Braves again got great pitching, with Maddux and Mark Wohlers combining on a six-hitter in a 3-1 win. That set the stage for Game Seven, Osborne against Glavine.

The Braves bats again came alive, and a six-run first inning paved the way for a 15-0 whitewash. Osborne recorded only two outs, while Glavine pitched seven scoreless innings.

Highlights of the Braves' outburst included home runs from McGriff, who had four RBIs, and Lopez, who had three.

After dropping three straight to the Cardinals, the awakened Braves outscored St. Louis 32-1 in the last three games, giving up 17 hits while pounding out 46.

## Brooms Aplenty

The Braves and Cardinals had proven in the National League Division Series that they were the best teams in the league, with both teams sweeping into the NLCS.

The Cardinals continued their resurgence under La Russa, who along with general manager Walt Jocketty overhauled the team before the season, to good effect.

The Cardinals won the NL Central and faced NL West champion San Diego in the Divison Series. All three games in the series were close, but the Padres always seemed to make the mistake that cost them, and the Cardinals always seemd to make the little plays to pull out the victory.

Stottlemyre gave up one run in 6⅔ innings in Game One, and the bullpen closed the door behind him. Gaetti's three-run homer in the first provided all the runs the Cardinals needed in the 3-1 victory.

Righthander Andy Benes pitched seven gritty innings in Game Two, giving up four runs but keeping the Car-

**Big Fly.** Brian Jordan's ninth-inning homer lifted the Cards over the Padres in decisive Game Three.

dinals in it. He handed a 4-4 tie over to the bullpen, and they again closed out the Padres. The Cardinals scratched out a run in the eighth to win 5-4.

The series moved to San Diego for Game Three, and the Padres jumped out to a 4-1 lead. The Cardinals scored three runs in the sixth, led by a solo home run from Gant, to tie it, and both teams scored single runs to make it 5-5 in the ninth. Then Jordan came through with a two-run homer to win it. Eckersley picked up the save, as he did in all three games. He gave up no runs and only three hits in 3⅔ innings of work in the Division Series.

The other Division Series was a sweep as well, with the Braves stifling the Dodgers and giving up only five runs (three earned) and 14 hits in the three games.

It was a familiar story for the Braves—and the Dodgers, who were swept by Cincinnati in 1995 as well. Their pitching was masterful and their hitting was good enough. Pitching dominated the series, as the Dodgers batted just .147 and the Braves .180. But the Braves had four home runs to make the difference.

Smoltz went nine innings in Game One, but he was matched by the Dodgers pitchers, and the game went to extra innings. Lopez' solo shot off Antonio Osuna gave the Braves a 2-1 win.

It was Maddux' turn in Game Two. He gave up two unearned runs in seven innings, but solo home runs by Ryan Klesko, McGriff and Jermaine Dye gave the Braves a 3-2 win.

The Braves bludgeoned Dodgers starter Hideo Nomo in Game Three, scoring five runs on him in 3⅔ innings. Dodgers relievers stopped the bleeding, but Glavine and the Braves bullpen made those runs stand up in a 5-2

# NATIONAL LEAGUE
## CHAMPIONS, 1901-96

NOTE: Most Valuable Player award formally recognized in 1931
GA—Games ahead of second-place team

| | Pennant | Pct. | GA |
|---|---|---|---|
| 1901 | Pittsburgh | .647 | 1½ |
| 1902 | Pittsburgh | .741 | 27½ |
| 1903 | Pittsburgh | .650 | 6½ |
| 1904 | New York | .693 | 13 |
| 1905 | New York | .686 | 9 |
| 1906 | Chicago | .763 | 20 |
| 1907 | Chicago | .704 | 17 |
| 1908 | Chicago | .643 | 1 |
| 1909 | Pittsburgh | .724 | 6½ |
| 1910 | Chicago | .675 | 13 |
| 1911 | New York | .647 | 7½ |
| 1912 | New York | .682 | 10 |
| 1913 | New York | .664 | 12½ |
| 1914 | Boston | .614 | 10½ |
| 1915 | Philadelphia | .592 | 7 |
| 1916 | Brooklyn | .610 | 2½ |
| 1917 | New York | .636 | 10 |
| 1918 | Chicago | .651 | 10½ |
| 1919 | Cincinnati | .686 | 9 |
| 1920 | Brooklyn | .604 | 7 |
| 1921 | New York | .614 | 4 |
| 1922 | New York | .604 | 7 |
| 1923 | New York | .621 | 4½ |
| 1924 | New York | .608 | 1½ |
| 1925 | Pittsburgh | .621 | 8½ |
| 1926 | St. Louis | .578 | 2 |
| 1927 | Pittsburgh | .610 | 1½ |
| 1928 | St. Louis | .617 | 2 |
| 1929 | Chicago | .645 | 10½ |
| 1930 | St. Louis | .597 | 2 |

| | Pennant | Pct. | GA | MVP |
|---|---|---|---|---|
| 1931 | St. Louis | .656 | 13 | Frankie Frisch, 2b, St.Louis |
| 1932 | Chicago | .584 | 4 | Chuck Klein, of, Philadelphia |
| 1933 | New York | .599 | 5 | Carl Hubbell, lhp, New York |
| 1934 | St. Louis | .621 | 2 | Dizzy Dean, rhp, St.Louis |
| 1935 | Chicago | .649 | 4 | Gabby Hartnett, c, Chicago |
| 1936 | New York | .597 | 5 | Carl Hubbell, lhp, New York |
| 1937 | New York | .625 | 3 | Joe Medwick, of, St. Louis |
| 1938 | Chicago | .586 | 2 | Ernie Lombardi, c, Cincinnati |
| 1939 | Cincinnati | .630 | 4½ | Bucky Walters, rhp, Cincinnati |
| 1940 | Cincinnati | .654 | 12 | Frank McCormick, 1b, Cincinnati |
| 1941 | Brooklyn | .649 | 2½ | Dolf Camilli, 1b, Brooklyn |
| 1942 | St. Louis | .688 | 2 | Mort Cooper, rhp, St. Louis |
| 1943 | St. Louis | .682 | 18 | Stan Musial, of, St. Louis |
| 1944 | St. Louis | .682 | 14½ | Marty Marion, ss, St. Louis |
| 1945 | Chicago | .636 | 3 | Phil Cavarretta, 1b, Chicago |
| 1946 | St. Louis | .628 | 2 | Stan Musial, 1b, St. Louis |
| 1947 | Brooklyn | .610 | 5 | Bob Elliott, 3b, Boston |
| 1948 | Boston | .595 | 6½ | Stan Musial, of, St. Louis |
| 1949 | Brooklyn | .630 | 1 | Jackie Robinson, 2b, Brooklyn |
| 1950 | Philadelphia | .591 | 2 | Jim Konstanty, rhp, Philadelphia |
| 1951 | New York | .624 | 1 | Roy Campanella, c, Brooklyn |
| 1952 | Brooklyn | .627 | 4½ | Hank Sauer, of, Chicago |
| 1953 | Brooklyn | .682 | 13 | Roy Campanella, c, Brooklyn |
| 1954 | New York | .630 | 5 | Willie Mays, of, New York |
| 1955 | Brooklyn | .641 | 13½ | Roy Campanella, c, Brooklyn |
| 1956 | Brooklyn | .604 | 1 | Don Newcombe, rhp, Brooklyn |
| 1957 | Milwaukee | .617 | 8 | Hank Aaron, of, Milwaukee |
| 1958 | Milwaukee | .597 | 8 | Ernie Banks, ss, Chicago |
| 1959 | Los Angeles | .564 | 2 | Ernie Banks, ss, Chicago |
| 1960 | Pittsburgh | .617 | 7 | Dick Groat, ss, Pittsburgh |
| 1961 | Cincinnati | .604 | 4 | Frank Robinson, of, Cincinnati |
| 1962 | San Francisco | .624 | 1 | Maury Wills, ss, Los Angeles |
| 1963 | Los Angeles | .611 | 6 | Sandy Koufax, lhp, Los Angeles |
| 1964 | St. Louis | .574 | 1 | Ken Boyer, 3b, St. Louis |
| 1965 | Los Angeles | .599 | 2 | Willie Mays, of, San Francisco |
| 1966 | Los Angeles | .586 | 1½ | Roberto Clemente, of, Pittsburgh |
| 1967 | St. Louis | .627 | 10½ | Orlando Cepeda, 1b, St. Louis |
| 1968 | St. Louis | .599 | 9 | Bob Gibson, rhp, St. Louis |

| | East. Div. | PCT | GA | West. Div. | PCT | GA | Pennant | | MVP |
|---|---|---|---|---|---|---|---|---|---|
| 1969 | New York | .617 | 8 | Atlanta | .574 | 3 | New York | 3-0 | Willie McCovey, 1b, San Francisco |
| 1970 | Pittsburgh | .549 | 5 | Cincinnati | .630 | 14½ | Cincinnati | 3-0 | Johnny Bench, c, Cincinnati |
| 1971 | Pittsburgh | .599 | 7 | San Francisco | .556 | 1 | Pittsburgh | 3-1 | Joe Torre, 3b, St. Louis |
| 1972 | Pittsburgh | .619 | 11 | Cincinnati | .617 | 10½ | Cincinnati | 3-2 | Johnny Bench, c, Cincinnati |
| 1973 | New York | .509 | 1½ | Cincinnati | .611 | 3½ | New York | 3-2 | Pete Rose, of, Cincinnati |
| 1974 | Pittsburgh | .543 | 1½ | Los Angeles | .630 | 4 | Los Angeles | 3-1 | Steve Garvey, 1b, Los Angeles |
| 1975 | Pittsburgh | .571 | 6½ | Cincinnati | .667 | 20 | Cincinnati | 3-0 | Joe Morgan, 2b, Cincinnati |
| 1976 | Philadelphia | .623 | 9 | Cincinnati | .630 | 10 | Cincinnati | 3-0 | Joe Morgan, 2b, Cincinnati |
| 1977 | Philadelphia | .623 | 5 | Los Angeles | .605 | 10 | Los Angeles | 3-1 | George Foster, of, Cincinnati |
| 1978 | Philadelphia | .556 | 1½ | Los Angeles | .586 | 2½ | Los Angeles | 3-1 | Dave Parker, of, Pittsburgh |
| 1979 | Pittsburgh | .605 | 2 | Cincinnati | .559 | 1½ | Pittsburgh | 3-0 | Hernandez, St. Louis; Stargell, Pittsburgh |
| 1980 | Philadelphia | .562 | 1 | Houston | .571 | 1 | Philadelphia | 3-2 | Mike Schmidt, 3b, Philadelphia |
| 1981 | Montreal* | .566 | ½ | Los Angeles** | .632 | ½ | Los Angeles | 3-2 | Mike Schmidt, 3b, Philadelphia |
| | Philadelphia | .618 | 1½ | Houston | .623 | 1 | | | |
| 1982 | St. Louis | .568 | 3 | Atlanta | .549 | 1 | St. Louis | 3-0 | Dale Murphy, of, Atlanta |
| 1983 | Philadelphia | .556 | 6 | Los Angeles | .562 | 3 | Philadelphia | 3-1 | Dale Murphy, of, Atlanta |
| 1984 | Chicago | .596 | 6½ | San Diego | .568 | 12 | San Diego | 3-2 | Ryne Sandberg, 2b, Chicago |
| 1985 | St. Louis | .623 | 3 | Los Angeles | .586 | 5½ | St. Louis | 4-2 | Willie McGee, of, St. Louis |
| 1986 | New York | .667 | 21½ | Houston | .593 | 10 | New York | 4-2 | Mike Schmidt, 3b, Philadelphia |
| 1987 | St. Louis | .586 | 3 | San Francisco | .556 | 6 | St. Louis | 4-3 | Andre Dawson, of, Chicago |
| 1988 | New York | .625 | 15 | Los Angeles | .584 | 7 | Los Angeles | 4-3 | Kirk Gibson, of, Los Angeles |
| 1989 | Chicago | .571 | 6 | San Francisco | .568 | 3 | San Francisco | 4-1 | Kevin Mitchell, of, San Francisco |
| 1990 | Pittsburgh | .586 | 4 | Cincinnati | .562 | 5 | Cincinnati | 4-2 | Barry Bonds, of, Pittsburgh |
| 1991 | Pittsburgh | .605 | 14 | Atlanta | .580 | 1 | Atlanta | 4-3 | Terry Pendleton, 3b, Atlanta |
| 1992 | Pittsburgh | .593 | 9 | Atlanta | .605 | 8 | Atlanta | 4-3 | Barry Bonds, of, Pittsburgh |
| 1993 | Philadelphia | .599 | 3 | Atlanta | .642 | 1 | Philadelphia | 4-2 | Barry Bonds, of, San Francisco |

| | East Div. | PCT | GA | Central Div. | PCT | GA | West Div. | PCT | GA | MVP |
|---|---|---|---|---|---|---|---|---|---|---|
| 1994 | Montreal | .649 | 6 | Cincinnati | .593 | ½ | Los Angeles | .509 | 3½ | Jeff Bagwell, 1b, Houston |
| 1995 | Atlanta# | .625 | 21 | Cincinnati | .590 | 9 | Los Angeles | .542 | 1 | Barry Larkin, ss, Cincinnati |
| 1996 | Atlanta@ | .593 | 8 | St. Louis | .543 | 6 | San Diego | .562 | 1 | Ken Caminiti, 3b, San Diego |

*Won second half; defeated Philadelphia 3-2 in best-of-5 playoff.   **Won first half; defeated Houston 3-2 in best-of-5 playoff.
#Won NL pennant, defeating Cincinnati 4-2.   @ Won NL pennant, defeating St. Louis 4-3.

win. Wohlers picked up the save, his third of the series.

## Dodger Dilemma

The playoff fold ended a tumultuous season for the Dodgers, who played their way out of a division title and saw longtime manager Tommy Lasorda retire in July.

Lasorda had an angioplasty procedure in June after doctors determined he had a heart attack. Lasorda said he had been cleared medically to return to the dugout, but he thought it better to retire.

"For me to get into a uniform again, as excitable as I am, I could not continue," said Lasorda, 68. "I decided it's best for me and the organization to step down. That's quite a decision."

Former Dodgers shortstop Bill Russell, who moved up from the coaching staff to fill in for Lasorda after the heart attack, stayed on to guide the team through the rest of the season.

Lasorda had been the Dodgers' manager since September 1976 and was in his 47th year in the organiza-

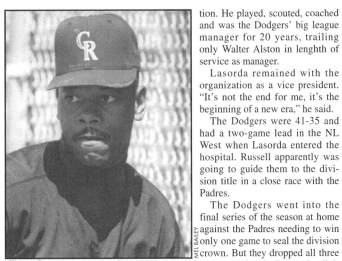

**Ellis Burks.** Monster season: .344-40-128

tion. He played, scouted, coached and was the Dodgers' big league manager for 20 years, trailing only Walter Alston in lenghth of service as manager.

Lasorda remained with the organization as a vice president. "It's not the end for me, it's the beginning of a new era," he said.

The Dodgers were 41-35 and had a two-game lead in the NL West when Lasorda entered the hospital. Russell apparently was going to guide them to the division title in a close race with the Padres.

The Dodgers went into the final series of the season at home against the Padres needing to win only one game to seal the division crown. But they dropped all three games, giving the Padres the divi-

sion title.

"We wanted to win one ballgame, and we did everything we could to win," Russell said. "We tried everything."

The series did lack some drama, because the loser was assured of a wild-card playoff berth. But the failure of the Dodgers' bats foretold their disappointing playoff performance.

## Division Darlings

The Cardinals endured a similarly eventful year, winning the NL Central after an offseason makeover and ushering out one of the team's fixtures, shortstop Ozzie Smith.

La Russa came over to the National League and brought in a crew of veteran players as well as pitching coach Dave Duncan.

The pitching staff was made over with proven veterans including Eckersley, Honeycutt, Stottlemyre and Benes, and a rookie, Andy Benes' younger brother Alan.

Veteran hitters boosted the team as well, including

**Tommy Lasorda.** Parting shot

# NATIONAL LEAGUE ALL-STARS

Selected by Baseball America

| Pos. | Player, Team | B-T | Ht. | Wt. | Age | '96 Salary | AVG | AB | R | H | 2B | 3B | HR | RBI | SB |
|------|--------------|-----|-----|-----|-----|-----------|-----|-----|-----|-----|-----|-----|-----|-----|-----|
| C | Mike Piazza, Los Angeles... | R-R | 6-3 | 220 | 28 | $2,700,000 | .336 | 547 | 87 | 184 | 16 | 0 | 36 | 105 | 3 |
| 1B | Jeff Bagwell, Houston......... | R-R | 6-0 | 195 | 28 | 4,875,000 | .315 | 568 | 111 | 179 | 48 | 2 | 31 | 120 | 21 |
| 2B | Eric Young, Colorado.......... | R-R | 5-9 | 180 | 29 | 1,050,000 | .317 | 568 | 113 | 184 | 23 | 4 | 8 | 74 | 53 |
| 3B | Ken Caminiti, San Diego..... | B-R | 6-0 | 200 | 33 | 3,050,000 | .326 | 546 | 109 | 178 | 37 | 2 | 40 | 130 | 11 |
| SS | Barry Larkin, Cincinnati...... | R-R | 6-0 | 195 | 32 | 5,600,000 | .298 | 517 | 117 | 154 | 32 | 4 | 33 | 89 | 36 |
| OF | Ellis Burks, Colorado.......... | R-R | 6-2 | 205 | 32 | 3,000,000 | .344 | 613 | 142 | 211 | 45 | 8 | 40 | 128 | 32 |
| | Barry Bonds, San Francisco | L-L | 6-1 | 185 | 32 | 8,266,859 | .308 | 517 | 122 | 159 | 27 | 3 | 42 | 129 | 40 |
| | Steve Finley, San Diego...... | L-L | 6-2 | 180 | 31 | 2,800,526 | .298 | 655 | 126 | 195 | 45 | 9 | 30 | 95 | 22 |

| | | | | | | | W | L | ERA | G | SV | IP | H | BB | SO |
|------|--------------|-----|-----|-----|-----|-----------|-----|-----|-----|-----|-----|-----|-----|-----|-----|
| P | John Smoltz, Atlanta.......... | R-R | 6-3 | 185 | 29 | 5,500,000 | 24 | 8 | 2.94 | 35 | 0 | 253 | 199 | 55 | 276 |
| | Kevin Brown, Florida........... | R-R | 6-4 | 215 | 24 | 3,300,000 | 17 | 11 | 1.89 | 32 | 0 | 233 | 187 | 33 | 159 |
| | Andy Benes, St. Louis........ | R-R | 6-6 | 238 | 29 | 4,000,000 | 18 | 10 | 3.83 | 36 | 0 | 230 | 215 | 77 | 160 |
| | Greg Maddux, Atlanta......... | R-R | 6-0 | 175 | 30 | 6,500,000 | 15 | 11 | 2.72 | 35 | 0 | 245 | 225 | 28 | 172 |
| RP | Trevor Hoffman, San Diego. | R-R | 6-0 | 195 | 29 | 955,000 | 9 | 5 | 2.25 | 70 | 42 | 88 | 50 | 31 | 111 |

**Player of the Year:** Ken Caminiti, 3b, San Diego. **Pitcher of the Year:** John Smoltz, rhp, Atlanta. **Rookie of the Year:** Todd Hollandsworth, of, Los Angeles.
**Manager of the Year:** Felipe Alou, Montreal. **Executive of the Year:** Walt Jocketty, St. Louis.

# NATIONAL LEAGUE
## YEAR-BY-YEAR LEADERS: BATTING

| Year | Batting Average | Home Runs | RBIs |
|---|---|---|---|
| 1901 | Jesse Burkett, St. Louis....382 | Sam Crawford, Cincinnati....16 | Honus Wagner, Pittsburgh....126 |
| 1902 | Ginger Beaumont, Pitt....357 | Tom Leach, Pittsburgh....6 | Honus Wagner, Pittsburgh....91 |
| 1903 | Honus Wagner, Pitt....355 | Jim Sheckard, Brooklyn....9 | Sam Mertes, New York....104 |
| 1904 | Honus Wagner, Pitt....349 | Harry Lumley, Brooklyn....9 | Bill Dahlen, New York....80 |
| 1905 | Cy Seymour, Cincinnati....377 | Fred Odwell, Cincinnati....9 | Cy Seymour, Cincinnati....121 |
| 1906 | Honus Wagner, Pitt....339 | Tim Jordan, Brooklyn....12 | 2 tied at....83 |
| 1907 | Honus Wagner, Pitt....350 | Dave Brain, Boston....10 | Sherry Magee, Philadelphia....85 |
| 1908 | Honus Wagner, Pitt....354 | Tim Jordan, Brooklyn....12 | Honus Wagner, Pittsburgh....109 |
| 1909 | Honus Wagner, Pitt....339 | Red Murray, New York....7 | Honus Wagner, Pittsburgh....100 |
| 1910 | Sherry Magee, Phil....331 | 2 tied at....10 | Sherry Magee, Philadelphia....123 |
| 1911 | Honus Wagner, Pitt....334 | Wildfire Schulte, Chicago....21 | Wildfire Schulte, Chicago....121 |
| 1912 | Heinie Zimmerman, Chi....372 | Heinie Zimmerman, Chicago....14 | Heinie Zimmerman, Chi....103 |
| 1913 | Jake Daubert, Brooklyn....350 | Gavvy Cravath, Philadelphia....19 | Gavvy Cravath, Phil....128 |
| 1914 | Jake Daubert, Brooklyn....329 | Gavvy Cravath, Philadelphia....19 | Sherry Magee, Phil....103 |
| 1915 | Larry Doyle, New York....320 | Gavvy Cravath, Philadelphia....24 | Gavvy Cravath, Phil....115 |
| 1916 | Hal Chase, Cincinnati....339 | 2 tied at....12 | Heinie Zimmerman, Chi.-N.Y...83 |
| 1917 | Edd Roush, Cincinnati....341 | Gavvy Cravath, Philadelphia....12 | Heinie Zimmerman, N.Y....102 |
| 1918 | Zack Wheat, Brooklyn....335 | Gavvy Cravath, Philadelphia....8 | Sherry Magee, Cincinnati....76 |
| 1919 | Edd Roush, Cincinnati....321 | Gavvy Cravath, Philadelphia....12 | Hy Myers, Brooklyn....73 |
| 1920 | Rogers Hornsby, St.L....370 | Cy Williams, Philadelphia....15 | 2 tied at....94 |
| 1921 | Rogers Hornsby, St.L....397 | George Kelly, New York....23 | Rogers Hornsby, St. Louis....126 |
| 1922 | Rogers Hornsby, St.L....401 | Rogers Hornsby, St. Louis....42 | Rogers Hornsby, St. Louis....155 |
| 1923 | Rogers Hornsby, St.L....384 | Cy Williams, Philadelphia....41 | Emil Meusel, New York....125 |
| 1924 | Rogers Hornsby, St.L....424 | Jack Fournier, Brooklyn....27 | George Kelly, New York....136 |
| 1925 | Rogers Hornsby, St.L....403 | Rogers Hornsby, St. Louis....39 | Rogers Hornsby, St. Louis....143 |
| 1926 | Bubbles Hargrave, Cinc....353 | Hack Wilson, Chicago....21 | Jim Bottomley, St. Louis....120 |
| 1927 | Paul Waner, Pittsburgh....380 | 2 tied at....30 | Paul Waner, Pittsburgh....131 |
| 1928 | Rogers Hornsby, St.L....387 | Jim Bottomley, St. Louis....31 | Jim Bottomley, St. Louis....136 |
| 1929 | Lefty ODoul, Philadelphia....398 | Chuck Klein, Philadelphia....43 | Hack Wilson, Chicago....159 |
| 1930 | Bill Terry, New York....401 | Hack Wilson, Chicago....56 | Hack Wilson, Chicago....190 |
| 1931 | Chick Hafey, St. Louis....349 | Chuck Klein, Philadelphia....31 | Chuck Klein, Philadelphia....121 |
| 1932 | Lefty ODoul, Brooklyn....368 | 2 tied at....38 | Frank Hurst, Philadelphia....143 |
| 1933 | Chuck Klein, Philadelphia....368 | Chuck Klein, Philadelphia....28 | Chuck Klein, Philadelphia....120 |
| 1934 | Paul Waner, Pittsburgh....362 | Mel Ott, New York....35 | Mel Ott, New York....135 |
| 1935 | Arky Vaughan, Pittsburgh....385 | Wally Berger, Boston....34 | Wally Berger, Boston....130 |
| 1936 | Paul Waner, Pittsburgh....373 | Mel Ott, New York....33 | Joe Medwick, St. Louis....138 |
| 1937 | Joe Medwick, St. Louis....374 | 2 tied at....31 | Joe Medwick, St. Louis....154 |
| 1938 | Ernie Lombardi, Cincinnati....342 | Mel Ott, New York....36 | Joe Medwick, St. Louis....122 |
| 1939 | Johnny Mize, St. Louis....349 | Johnny Mize, St. Louis....28 | Frank McCormick, Cinc....128 |
| 1940 | Debs Garms, Pittsburgh....355 | Johnny Mize, St. Louis....43 | Johnny Mize, St. Louis....137 |
| 1941 | Pete Reiser, Brooklyn....343 | Dolf Camilli, Brooklyn....34 | Dolf Camilli, Brooklyn....120 |
| 1942 | Ernie Lombardi, Boston....330 | Mel Ott, New York....30 | Johnny Mize, New York....110 |
| 1943 | Stan Musial, St. Louis....357 | Bill Nicholson, Chicago....29 | Bill Nicholson, Chicago....128 |
| 1944 | Dixie Walker, Brooklyn....357 | Bill Nicholson, Chicago....33 | Bill Nicholson, Chicago....122 |
| 1945 | Phil Cavarretta, Chicago....355 | Tommy Holmes, Boston....28 | Dixie Walker, Brooklyn....124 |
| 1946 | Stan Musial, St. Louis....365 | Ralph Kiner, Pittsburgh....23 | Enos Slaughter, St. Louis....130 |
| 1947 | Harry Walker, St.L-Phil....363 | 2 tied at....51 | Johnny Mize, New York....138 |
| 1948 | Stan Musial, St. Louis....376 | Ralph Kiner, Pittsburgh....40 | Stan Musial, St. Louis....131 |
| 1949 | Jackie Robinson, Brook....342 | Ralph Kiner, Pittsburgh....54 | Ralph Kiner, Pittsburgh....127 |
| 1950 | Stan Musial, St. Louis....346 | Ralph Kiner, Pittsburgh....47 | Del Ennis, Philadelphia....126 |
| 1951 | Stan Musial, St. Louis....355 | Ralph Kiner, Pittsburgh....42 | Monte Irvin, New York....121 |
| 1952 | Stan Musial, St. Louis....336 | 2 tied at....37 | Hank Sauer, Chicago....121 |
| 1953 | Carl Furillo, Brooklyn....344 | Eddie Mathews, Milwaukee....47 | Roy Campanella, Brooklyn....142 |
| 1954 | Willie Mays, New York....345 | Ted Kluszewski, Cincinnati....49 | Ted Kluszewski, Cincinnati....141 |
| 1955 | Richie Ashburn, Phil....338 | Willie Mays, New York....51 | Duke Snider, Brooklyn....136 |
| 1956 | Hank Aaron, Milwaukee....328 | Duke Snider, Brooklyn....43 | Stan Musial, St. Louis....109 |
| 1957 | Stan Musial, St. Louis....351 | Hank Aaron, Milwaukee....44 | Hank Aaron, Milwaukee....132 |
| 1958 | Richie Ashburn, Phil....350 | Ernie Banks, Chicago....47 | Ernie Banks, Chicago....129 |
| 1959 | Hank Aaron, Milwaukee....355 | Eddie Mathews, Milwaukee....46 | Ernie Banks, Chicago....143 |
| 1960 | Dick Groat, Pittsburgh....325 | Ernie Banks, Chicago....41 | Hank Aaron, Milwaukee....126 |
| 1961 | Roberto Clemente, Pitt....351 | Orlando Cepeda, San Fran....46 | Orlando Cepeda, San Fran....142 |
| 1962 | Tommy Davis, L.A....346 | Willie Mays, San Francisco....49 | Tommy Davis, Los Angeles....153 |
| 1963 | Tommy Davis, L.A....326 | Hank Aaron, Milwaukee....44 | Hank Aaron, Milwaukee....130 |
| 1964 | Roberto Clemente, Pitt....339 | Willie Mays, San Francisco....47 | Ken Boyer, St. Louis....119 |
| 1965 | Roberto Clemente, Pitt....329 | Willie Mays, San Francisco....52 | Deron Johnson, Cincinnati....130 |
| 1966 | Matty Alou, Pittsburgh....342 | Hank Aaron, Atlanta....44 | Hank Aaron, Atlanta....127 |
| 1967 | Roberto Clemente, Pitt....357 | Hank Aaron, Atlanta....39 | Orlando Cepeda, San Fran....111 |
| 1968 | Pete Rose, Cincinnati....335 | Willie McCovey, San Fran....36 | Willie McCovey, San Fran....105 |
| 1969 | Pete Rose, Cincinnati....348 | Willie McCovey, San Fran....45 | Willie McCovey, San Fran....126 |
| 1970 | Rico Carty, Atlanta....366 | Johnny Bench, Cincinnati....45 | Johnny Bench, Cincinnati....148 |
| 1971 | Joe Torre, St. Louis....363 | Willie Stargell, Pittsburgh....48 | Joe Torre, St. Louis....137 |
| 1972 | Billy Williams, Chicago....333 | Johnny Bench, Cincinnati....40 | Johnny Bench, Cincinnati....125 |
| 1973 | Pete Rose, Cincinnati....338 | Willie Stargell, Pittsburgh....44 | Willie Stargell, Pittsburgh....119 |
| 1974 | Ralph Garr, Atlanta....353 | Mike Schmidt, Philadelphia....36 | Johnny Bench, Cincinnati....129 |
| 1975 | Bill Madlock, Chicago....354 | Mike Schmidt, Philadelphia....38 | Greg Luzinski, Phil....120 |
| 1976 | Bill Madlock, Chicago....339 | Mike Schmidt, Philadelphia....38 | George Foster, Cincinnati....121 |
| 1977 | Dave Parker, Pittsburgh....338 | George Foster, Cincinnati....52 | George Foster, Cincinnati....149 |
| 1978 | Dave Parker, Pittsburgh....334 | George Foster, Cincinnati....40 | George Foster, Cincinnati....120 |
| 1979 | Keith Hernandez, St.L....344 | Dave Kingman, Chicago....48 | Dave Winfield, San Diego....118 |
| 1980 | Bill Buckner, Chicago....324 | Mike Schmidt, Philadelphia....48 | Mike Schmidt, Philadelphia....121 |
| 1981 | Bill Madlock, Pittsburgh....341 | Mike Schmidt, Philadelphia....31 | Mike Schmidt, Philadelphia....91 |
| 1982 | Al Oliver, Montreal....331 | Dave Kingman, New York....37 | Dale Murphy, Atlanta....109 |
| 1983 | Bill Madlock, Pittsburgh....323 | Mike Schmidt, Philadelphia....40 | Dale Murphy, Atlanta....121 |
| 1984 | Tony Gwynn, San Diego....351 | Dale Murphy, Atlanta....36 | 2 tied at....106 |
| 1985 | Willie McGee, St. Louis....353 | Dale Murphy, Atlanta....37 | Dave Parker, Cincinnati....125 |
| 1986 | Tim Raines, Montreal....334 | Mike Schmidt, Philadelphia....37 | Mike Schmidt, Philadelphia....119 |
| 1987 | Tony Gwynn, San Diego....370 | Andre Dawson, Chicago....49 | Andre Dawson, Chicago....137 |
| 1988 | Tony Gwynn, San Diego....313 | Darryl Strawberry, New York....39 | Will Clark, San Francisco....109 |
| 1989 | Tony Gwynn, San Diego....336 | Kevin Mitchell, S.F....47 | Kevin Mitchell, S.F....125 |
| 1990 | Willie McGee, Chicago....335 | Ryne Sandberg, Chicago....40 | Matt Williams, S.F....122 |
| 1991 | Terry Pendleton, Atlanta....319 | Howard Johnson, New York....38 | Howard Johnson, N.Y....117 |
| 1992 | Gary Sheffield, S.D....330 | Fred McGriff, San Diego....35 | Darren Daulton, Phil....109 |
| 1993 | Andres Galarraga, Colo....370 | Barry Bonds, San Francisco....46 | Barry Bonds, S.F....123 |
| 1994 | Tony Gwynn, San Diego....394 | Matt Williams, S.F....43 | Jeff Bagwell, Houston....116 |
| 1995 | Tony Gwynn, San Diego....368 | Dante Bichette, Colorado....40 | Dante Bichette, Colorado....128 |
| 1996 | Tony Gwynn, San Diego....353 | Andres Galarraga, Colorado....47 | Andres Galarraga, Colo....150 |

# NATIONAL LEAGUE
## YEAR-BY-YEAR LEADERS: PITCHING

| Year | Wins | ERA | Strikeouts |
|---|---|---|---|
| 1901 | Bill Donovan, Brooklyn 25 | Jesse Tannehill, Pittsburgh 2.18 | Noodles Hahn, Cin. 233 |
| 1902 | Jack Chesbro, Pittsburgh 28 | Jack Taylor, Chicago 1.33 | Vic Willis, Boston 226 |
| 1903 | Joe McGinnity, New York 31 | Sam Leever, Pittsburgh 2.06 | Christy Mathewson, N.Y. 267 |
| 1904 | Joe McGinnity, New York 35 | Joe McGinnity, New York 1.61 | Christy Mathewson, N.Y. 212 |
| 1905 | Christy Mathewson, N.Y. 32 | Christy Mathewson, N.Y. 1.27 | Christy Mathewson, N.Y. 206 |
| 1906 | Joe McGinnity, New York 27 | Mordecai Brown, Chicago 1.04 | Fred Beebe, Chi.-St.L. 171 |
| 1907 | Christy Mathewson, N.Y. 24 | Jack Pfiester, Chicago 1.15 | Christy Mathewson, N.Y. 178 |
| 1908 | Christy Mathewson, N.Y. 37 | Christy Mathewson, N.Y. 1.43 | Christy Mathewson, N.Y. 259 |
| 1909 | Mordecai Brown, Chicago 27 | Christy Mathewson, N.Y. 1.14 | Orval Overall, Chicago 205 |
| 1910 | Christy Mathewson, N.Y. 27 | George McQuillan, Phil. 1.60 | Christy Mathewson, N.Y. 190 |
| 1911 | Grover Alexander, Phil. 28 | Christy Mathewson, N.Y. 1.99 | Rube Marquard, New York 237 |
| 1912 | 2 tied at 26 | Jeff Tesreau, New York 1.96 | Grover Alexander, Phil. 195 |
| 1913 | Tom Seaton, Philadelphia 27 | Christy Mathewson, N.Y. 2.06 | Tom Seaton, Philadelphia 168 |
| 1914 | 2 tied at 27 | Bill Doak, St. Louis 1.72 | Grover Alexander, Phil. 214 |
| 1915 | Grover Alexander, Phil. 31 | Grover Alexander, Phil. 1.22 | Grover Alexander, Phil. 241 |
| 1916 | Grover Alexander, Phil. 33 | Grover Alexander, Phil. 1.55 | Grover Alexander, Phil. 167 |
| 1917 | Grover Alexander, Phil. 30 | Grover Alexander, Phil. 1.85 | Grover Alexander, Phil. 200 |
| 1918 | Hippo Vaughn, Chicago 22 | Hippo Vaughn, Chicago 1.74 | Hippo Vaughn, Chicago 148 |
| 1919 | Jesse Barnes, New York 25 | Grover Alexander, Chicago 1.72 | Hippo Vaughn, Chicago 141 |
| 1920 | Grover Alexander, Chicago 27 | Grover Alexander, Chicago 1.91 | Grover Alexander, Chicago 173 |
| 1921 | 2 tied at 22 | Bill Doak, St. Louis 2.58 | Burleigh Grimes, Brooklyn 136 |
| 1922 | Eppa Rixey, Cincinnati 25 | Rosy Ryan, New York 3.00 | Dazzy Vance, Brooklyn 134 |
| 1923 | Dolf Luque, Cincinnati 27 | Dolf Luque, Cincinnati 1.93 | Dazzy Vance, Brooklyn 197 |
| 1924 | Dazzy Vance, Brooklyn 28 | Dazzy Vance, Brooklyn 2.16 | Dazzy Vance, Brooklyn 262 |
| 1925 | Dazzy Vance, Brooklyn 22 | Dolf Luque, Cincinnati 2.63 | Dazzy Vance, Brooklyn 221 |
| 1926 | 4 tied at 20 | Ray Kremer, Pittsburgh 2.61 | Dazzy Vance, Brooklyn 140 |
| 1927 | Charlie Root, Chicago 26 | Ray Kremer, Pittsburgh 2.47 | Dazzy Vance, Brooklyn 184 |
| 1928 | 2 tied at 25 | Dazzy Vance, Brooklyn 2.09 | Dazzy Vance, Brooklyn 200 |
| 1929 | Pat Malone, Chicago 22 | Bill Walker, New York 3.08 | Pat Malone, Chicago 166 |
| 1930 | 2 tied at 20 | Dazzy Vance, Brooklyn 2.61 | Bill Hallahan, St. Louis 177 |
| 1931 | 3 tied at 19 | Bill Walker, New York 2.26 | Bill Hallahan, St. Louis 159 |
| 1932 | Lon Warneke, Chicago 22 | Lon Warneke, Chicago 2.37 | Dizzy Dean, St. Louis 191 |
| 1933 | Carl Hubbell, New York 23 | Carl Hubbell, New York 1.66 | Dizzy Dean, St. Louis 199 |
| 1934 | Dizzy Dean, St. Louis 30 | Carl Hubbell, New York 2.30 | Dizzy Dean, St. Louis 195 |
| 1935 | Dizzy Dean, St. Louis 28 | Cy Blanton, Pittsburgh 2.59 | Dizzy Dean, St. Louis 182 |
| 1936 | Carl Hubbell, New York 26 | Carl Hubbell, New York 2.31 | Van Lingle Mungo, Bklyn. 238 |
| 1937 | Carl Hubbell, New York 22 | Jim Turner, Boston 2.38 | Carl Hubbell, New York 159 |
| 1938 | Bill Lee, Chicago 22 | Bill Lee, Chicago 2.66 | Clay Bryant, Chicago 135 |
| 1939 | Bucky Walters, Cincinnati 27 | Bucky Walters, Cincinnati 2.29 | Bucky Walters, Cincinnati 137 |
| 1940 | Bucky Walters, Cincinnati 22 | Bucky Walters, Cincinnati 2.48 | Kirby Higbe, Philadelphia 137 |
| 1941 | 2 tied at 22 | Elmer Riddle, Cincinnati 2.24 | Johnny Vander Meer, Cin. 202 |
| 1942 | Mort Cooper, St. Louis 22 | Mort Cooper, St. Louis 1.77 | Johnny Vander Meer, Cin. 186 |
| 1943 | 3 tied at 21 | Howie Pollet, St. Louis 1.75 | Johnny Vander Meer, Cin. 174 |
| 1944 | Bucky Walters, Cincinnati 23 | Ed Heusser, Cincinnati 2.38 | Bill Voiselle, New York 161 |
| 1945 | Red Barrett, Bos.-St.L. 23 | Hank Borowy, Chicago 2.14 | Preacher Roe, Pittsburgh 148 |
| 1946 | Howie Pollet, St. Louis 21 | Howie Pollet, St. Louis 2.10 | John Schmitz, Chicago 135 |
| 1947 | Ewell Blackwell, Cincinnati 22 | Warren Spahn, Boston 2.33 | Ewell Blackwell, Cincinnati 193 |
| 1948 | Johnny Sain, Boston 24 | Harry Brecheen, St. Louis 2.24 | Harry Brecheen, St. Louis 149 |
| 1949 | Warren Spahn, Boston 21 | Dave Koslo, New York 2.50 | Warren Spahn, Boston 151 |
| 1950 | Warren Spahn, Boston 21 | Jim Hearn, St.L.-New York 2.49 | Warren Spahn, Boston 191 |
| 1951 | 2 tied at 23 | Chet Nichols, Boston 2.88 | 2 tied at 164 |
| 1952 | Robin Roberts, Phil. 28 | Hoyt Wilhelm, New York 2.43 | Warren Spahn, Boston 183 |
| 1953 | 2 tied at 23 | Warren Spahn, Milwaukee 2.10 | Robin Roberts, Phil. 198 |
| 1954 | Robin Roberts, Phil. 23 | John Antonelli, New York 2.29 | Robin Roberts, Phil. 185 |
| 1955 | Robin Roberts, Phil. 23 | Bob Friend, Pittsburgh 2.84 | Sam Jones, Chicago 198 |
| 1956 | Don Newcombe, Brooklyn 27 | Lew Burdette, Milwaukee 2.71 | Sam Jones, Chicago 176 |
| 1957 | Warren Spahn, Milwaukee 21 | Johnny Podres, Brooklyn 2.66 | Jack Sanford, Philadelphia 188 |
| 1958 | 2 tied 22 | Stu Miller, San Francisco 2.47 | Sam Jones, St. Louis 225 |
| 1959 | 3 tied at 21 | Sam Jones, San Francisco 2.82 | Don Drysdale, L. A. 242 |
| 1960 | 2 tied at 21 | Mike McCormick, San Fran. 2.70 | Don Drysdale, L. A. 246 |
| 1961 | 2 tied at 21 | Warren Spahn, Milwaukee 3.01 | Sandy Koufax, L. A. 269 |
| 1962 | Don Drysdale, L. A. 25 | Sandy Koufax, L. A. 2.54 | Don Drysdale, L. A. 232 |
| 1963 | Sandy Koufax, L. A. 25 | Sandy Koufax, L. A. 1.88 | Sandy Koufax, L. A. 306 |
| 1964 | Larry Jackson, Chicago 24 | Sandy Koufax, L. A. 1.74 | Bob Veale, Pittsburgh 250 |
| 1965 | Sandy Koufax, L. A. 26 | Sandy Koufax, L. A. 2.04 | Sandy Koufax, L. A. 382 |
| 1966 | Sandy Koufax, L. A. 27 | Sandy Koufax, L. A. 1.73 | Sandy Koufax, L. A. 317 |
| 1967 | Mike McCormick, S. F. 22 | Phil Niekro, Atlanta 1.87 | Jim Bunning, Philadelphia 253 |
| 1968 | Juan Marichal, S. F. 26 | Bob Gibson, St. Louis 1.12 | Bob Gibson, St. Louis 268 |
| 1969 | Tom Seaver, New York 25 | Juan Marichal, San Fran. 2.10 | Ferguson Jenkins, Chicago 273 |
| 1970 | 2 tied at 23 | Tom Seaver, New York 2.81 | Tom Seaver, New York 283 |
| 1971 | Ferguson Jenkins, Chicago 24 | Tom Seaver, New York 1.76 | Tom Seaver, New York 289 |
| 1972 | Steve Carlton, Phil. 27 | Steve Carlton, Philadelphia 1.98 | Steve Carlton, Phil. 310 |
| 1973 | Ron Bryant, S. F. 24 | Tom Seaver, New York 2.08 | Tom Seaver, New York 251 |
| 1974 | 2 tied at 20 | Buzz Capra, Atlanta 2.28 | Steve Carlton, Phil. 240 |
| 1975 | Tom Seaver, New York 22 | Randy Jones, San Diego 2.24 | Tom Seaver, New York 243 |
| 1976 | Randy Jones, San Diego 22 | John Denny, St. Louis 2.52 | Tom Seaver, New York 235 |
| 1977 | Steve Carlton, Phil. 23 | John Candelaria, Pittsburgh 2.34 | Phil Niekro, Atlanta 262 |
| 1978 | Gaylord Perry, San Diego 21 | Craig Swan, New York 2.43 | J.R. Richard, Houston 303 |
| 1979 | 2 tied at 21 | J.R. Richard, Houston 2.71 | J.R. Richard, Houston 313 |
| 1980 | Steve Carlton, Phil. 24 | Don Sutton, Los Angeles 2.21 | Steve Carlton, Phil. 286 |
| 1981 | Tom Seaver, Cincinnati 14 | Nolan Ryan, Houston 1.69 | Fernando Valenzuela, L.A. 180 |
| 1982 | Steve Carlton, Phil. 23 | Steve Rogers, Montreal 2.40 | Steve Carlton, Phil. 286 |
| 1983 | John Denny, Phil. 19 | Atlee Hammaker, S. F. 2.25 | Steve Carlton, Phil. 275 |
| 1984 | Joaquin Andujar, St. Louis 20 | Alejandro Pena, L. A. 2.48 | Dwight Gooden, New York 276 |
| 1985 | Dwight Gooden, New York 24 | Dwight Gooden, New York 1.53 | Dwight Gooden, New York 268 |
| 1986 | Fernando Valenzuela, L.A. 21 | Mike Scott, Houston 2.22 | Mike Scott, Houston 306 |
| 1987 | Rick Sutcliffe, Chicago 18 | Nolan Ryan, Houston 2.76 | Nolan Ryan, Houston 270 |
| 1988 | 2 tied at 23 | Joe Magrane, St. Louis 2.18 | Nolan Ryan, Houston 228 |
| 1989 | Mike Scott, Houston 20 | Scott Garrelts, S. F. 2.28 | Jose DeLeon, St. Louis 201 |
| 1990 | Doug Drabek, Pittsburgh 22 | Danny Darwin, Houston 2.21 | David Cone, New York 233 |
| 1991 | 2 tied at 20 | Dennis Martinez, Mon. 2.39 | David Cone, New York 241 |
| 1992 | 2 tied at 20 | Bill Swift, San Francisco 2.08 | John Smoltz, Atlanta 215 |
| 1993 | 2 tied at 22 | Greg Maddux, Atlanta 2.36 | Jose Rijo, Cincinnati 227 |
| 1994 | Greg Maddux, Atlanta 16 | Greg Maddux, Atlanta 1.56 | Andy Benes, San Diego 189 |
| 1995 | Greg Maddux, Atlanta 19 | Greg Maddux, Atlanta 1.63 | Hideo Nomo, Los Angeles 236 |
| 1996 | John Smoltz, Atlanta 24 | Kevin Brown, Florida 1.89 | John Smoltz, Atlanta 276 |

# NATIONAL LEAGUE
## DEPARTMENT LEADERS

## BATTING

### GAMES
Jeff Bagwell, Houston ...................... 162
Craig Biggio, Houston ...................... 162
Steve Finley, San Diego .................. 161
Gary Sheffield, Florida ..................... 161
Vinny Castilla, Colorado .................. 160
Lance Johnson, New York ............... 160

### AT-BATS
Lance Johnson, New York ............... 682
Marquis Grissom, Atlanta ................ 671
Mark Grudzielanek, Montreal .......... 657
Steve Finley, San Diego .................. 655
Mike Lansing, Montreal ................... 641

### RUNS
Ellis Burks, Colorado ...................... 142
Steve Finley, San Diego .................. 126
Barry Bonds, San Francisco ............ 122
Andres Galarraga, Colorado ........... 119
Gary Sheffield, Florida .................... 118

### HITS
Lance Johnson, New York ............... 227
Ellis Burks, Colorado ...................... 211
Marquis Grissom, Atlanta ................ 207
Mark Grudzielanek, Montreal .......... 201
Dante Bichette, Colorado ............... 198

### TOTAL BASES
Ellis Burks, Colorado ...................... 392
Andres Galarraga, Colorado ........... 376
Steve Finley, San Diego .................. 348
Vinny Castilla, Colorado .................. 345
Ken Caminiti, San Diego ................. 339

### EXTRA-BASE HITS
Ellis Burks, Colorado ........................ 93
Andres Galarraga, Colorado ............. 89
Steve Finley, San Diego .................... 84
Jeff Bagwell, Houston ....................... 81
Henry Rodriguez, Montreal ............... 79
Ken Caminiti, San Diego ................... 79

### DOUBLES
Jeff Bagwell, Houston ....................... 48
Steve Finley, San Diego .................... 45
Ellis Burks, Colorado ........................ 45
Bernard Gilkey, New York ................. 44
Henry Rodriguez, Montreal ............... 42

### TRIPLES
Lance Johnson, New York ................. 21
Marquis Grissom, Atlanta .................. 10

**Lance Johnson**
21 triples

**Barry Bonds**
151 walks

Thomas Howard, Cincinnati ............... 10
Steve Finley, San Diego ...................... 9
Delino DeShields, Los Angeles ............ 8
Ray Lankford, St. Louis ........................ 8
Ellis Burks, Colorado ........................... 8

### HOME RUNS
Andres Galarraga, Colorado .............. 47
Gary Sheffield, Florida ...................... 42
Barry Bonds, San Francisco .............. 42
Todd Hundley, New York .................... 41
Vinny Castilla, Colorado .................... 40
Sammy Sosa, Chicago ...................... 40
Ken Caminiti, San Diego ................... 40
Ellis Burks, Colorado ........................ 40

### HOME RUN RATIO
(At-Bats per Home Runs)
Barry Bonds, San Francisco ............ 12.3
Gary Sheffield, Florida ..................... 12.4
Sammy Sosa, Chicago ..................... 12.5
Todd Hundley, New York ................... 13.2
Andres Galarraga, Colorado ............ 13.3

### RUNS BATTED IN
Andres Galarraga, Colorado ............ 150
Dante Bichette, Colorado ................. 141
Ken Caminiti, San Diego .................. 130
Barry Bonds, San Francisco ............ 129
Ellis Burks, Colorado ...................... 128

### SACRIFICE BUNTS
Pedro Martinez, Montreal ................... 16
Denny Neagle, Pitts.-Atlanta .............. 16
John Smoltz, Atlanta .......................... 15
Tom Glavine, Atlanta .......................... 15
Shane Reynolds, Houston .................. 14
Walt Weiss, Colorado ......................... 14
Jeff Fassero, Montreal ....................... 14

### SACRIFICE FLIES
Rick Wilkins, Houston-S.F. ................. 10
Ken Caminiti, San Diego .................... 10
Dante Bichette, Colorado ................... 10
Bret Boone, Cincinnati ........................ 9
Brian Jordan, St. Louis ........................ 9
Derek Bell, Houston ............................. 9
Devon White, Florida ........................... 9

### HIT BY PITCH
Craig Biggio, Houston ......................... 27
Eric Young, Colorado .......................... 21
Andres Galarraga, Colorado ............... 17
Jason Kendall, Pittsburgh ................... 15
Greg Colbrunn, Florida ....................... 14
Scott Servais, Chicago ....................... 14

### WALKS
Barry Bonds, San Francisco ............. 151
Gary Sheffield, Florida ..................... 142
Jeff Bagwell, Houston ...................... 135
Rickey Henderson, San Diego ......... 125
Barry Larkin, Cincinnati ..................... 96

### INTENTIONAL WALKS
Barry Bonds, San Francisco ............... 30
Mike Piazza, Los Angeles .................. 21
Jeff Bagwell, Houston ........................ 20
Gary Sheffield, Florida ...................... 19
Ken Caminiti, San Diego .................... 16

### STRIKEOUTS
Henry Rodriguez, Montreal ............... 160
Andres Galarraga, Colorado ............ 157
Todd Hundley, New York ................... 146
Sammy Sosa, Chicago ..................... 134
Ray Lankford, St. Louis .................... 133

### TOUGHEST TO STRIKE OUT
(Plate Appearances per SO)
Eric Young, Colorado ...................... 20.7
Lance Johnson, New York ............... 18.1
Mark Grace, Chicago ...................... 15.0
Barry Larkin, Cincinnati ................... 12.1
Mark Lemke, Atlanta ....................... 11.7

### STOLEN BASES
Eric Young, Colorado ......................... 53
Lance Johnson, New York .................. 50
Delino DeShields, Los Angeles .......... 48
Barry Bonds, San Francisco .............. 40
Al Martin, Pittsburgh .......................... 38

### CAUGHT STEALING
Eric Young, Colorado .......................... 19
Royce Clayton, St. Louis .................... 15

**Eric Young**
53 steals

Rickey Henderson, San Diego ........... 15
Al Martin, Pittsburgh .......................... 12
Lance Johnson, New York .................. 12
Dante Bichette, Colorado ................... 12

### GIDP
Eric Karros, Los Angeles .................... 27
Greg Colbrunn, Florida ....................... 22
Mike Piazza, Los Angeles .................. 21
John Mabry, St. Louis ......................... 21
Charles Johnson, Florida .................... 20
Vinny Castilla, Colorado ..................... 20
Steve Finley, San Diego ..................... 20
Barry Larkin, Cincinnati ..................... 20
Fred McGriff, Atlanta .......................... 20

## HITTING STREAKS

| | |
|---|---|
| Hal Morris, Cincinnati | 29 |
| Marquis Grissom, Atlanta | 28 |
| John Flaherty, San Diego | 27 |
| Edgar Renteria, Florida | 22 |
| Two tied with | 21 |

## MULTIPLE-HIT GAMES

| | |
|---|---|
| Lance Johnson, New York | 75 |
| Ellis Burks, Colorado | 65 |
| Mark Grudzielanek, Montreal | 65 |
| Andres Galarraga, Colorado | 64 |
| Marquis Grissom, Atlanta | 58 |
| Dante Bichette, Colorado | 58 |

## SLUGGING PERCENTAGE

| | |
|---|---|
| Ellis Burks, Colorado | .639 |
| Gary Sheffield, Florida | .624 |
| Ken Caminiti, San Diego | .621 |
| Barry Bonds, San Francisco | .615 |
| Andres Galarraga, Colorado | .601 |

## ON-BASE PERCENTAGE

| | |
|---|---|
| Gary Sheffield, Florida | .465 |
| Barry Bonds, San Francisco | .461 |
| Jeff Bagwell, Houston | .451 |
| Mike Piazza, Los Angeles | .422 |
| Rickey Henderson, San Diego | .410 |
| Barry Larkin, Cincinnati | .410 |

# PITCHING

## WINS

| | |
|---|---|
| John Smoltz, Atlanta | 24 |
| Andy Benes, St. Louis | 18 |
| Kevin Ritz, Colorado | 17 |
| Kevin Brown, Florida | 17 |
| Hideo Nomo, Los Angeles | 16 |
| Shane Reynolds, Houston | 16 |
| Denny Neagle, Pitts.-Atlanta | 16 |
| Al Leiter, Florida | 16 |

## LOSSES

| | |
|---|---|
| Patt Rapp, Florida | 16 |
| Frank Castillo, Chicago | 16 |
| Mike Williams, Philadelphia | 14 |
| Jason Isringhausen, New York | 14 |
| John Smiley, Cincinnati | 14 |
| William VanLandingham, San Francisco | 14 |

## WINNING PERCENTAGE

| | |
|---|---|
| John Smoltz, Atlanta | .750 |
| Ramon Martinez, Los Angeles | .714 |
| Ismael Valdes, Los Angeles | .682 |
| Ugueth Urbina, Montreal | .667 |
| Andy Benes, St. Louis | .643 |

## GAMES

| | |
|---|---|
| Brad Clontz, Atlanta | 81 |
| Bob Patterson, Chicago | 79 |
| Mark Dewey, San Francisco | 78 |
| Jeff Shaw, Cincinnati | 78 |
| Mark Wohlers, Atlanta | 77 |

## GAMES STARTED

| | |
|---|---|
| Tom Glavine, Atlanta | 36 |
| Shane Reynolds, Houston | 35 |
| Jaime Navarro, Chicago | 35 |
| Kevin Ritz, Colorado | 35 |
| John Smoltz, Atlanta | 35 |
| Greg Maddux ,Atlanta | 35 |

## COMPLETE GAMES

| | |
|---|---|
| Curt Schilling, Philadelphia | 8 |
| John Smoltz, Atlanta | 6 |
| Todd Stottlemyre, St. Louis | 5 |
| Jeff Fassero, Montreal | 5 |
| Kevin Brown, Florida | 5 |
| Greg Maddux, Atlanta | 5 |

## SHUTOUTS

| | |
|---|---|
| Kevin Brown, Florida | 3 |
| Seven tied with | 2 |

## GAMES FINISHED

| | |
|---|---|
| Todd Worrell, Los Angeles | 67 |
| Robb Nen, Florida | 66 |
| Mark Wohlers, Atlanta | 64 |

| | |
|---|---|
| Mel Rojas, Montreal | 64 |
| Trevor Hoffman, San Diego | 62 |

## SAVES

| | |
|---|---|
| Jeff Brantley, Cincinnati | 44 |
| Todd Worrell, Los Angeles | 44 |
| Trevor Hoffman, San Diego | 42 |
| Mark Wohlers, Atlanta | 39 |
| Mel Rojas, Montreal | 36 |

## INNINGS PITCHED

| | |
|---|---|
| John Smoltz, Atlanta | 254 |
| Greg Maddux, Atlanta | 245 |
| Shane Reynolds, Houston | 239 |
| Jaime Navarro, Chicago | 237 |
| Tom Glavine, Atlanta | 235 |

## HITS ALLOWED

| | |
|---|---|
| Jaime Navarro, Chicago | 244 |
| Kevin Ritz, Colorado | 236 |
| Darryl Kile, Houston | 233 |
| Shane Reynolds, Houston | 227 |
| Denny Neagle, Pitts.-Atlanta | 226 |

## RUNS ALLOWED

| | |
|---|---|
| Kevin Ritz, Colorado | 135 |
| Mark Leiter, Montreal | 128 |
| William VanLandingham, S.F. | 123 |
| Alan Benes, St. Louis | 120 |
| Jaime Navarro, Chicago | 116 |
| Bob Tewksbury, San Diego | 116 |

## HOME RUNS ALLOWED

| | |
|---|---|
| Mark Leiter, S.F.-Montreal | 37 |
| Pete Harnisch, New York | 30 |
| Todd Stottlemyre, St. Louis | 30 |
| Steve Trachsel, Chicago | 30 |
| Andy Benes, St. Louis | 28 |
| Mark Gardner, San Francisco | 28 |
| Allen Watson, San Francisco | 28 |
| Frank Castillo, Chicago | 28 |

## WALKS

| | |
|---|---|
| Al Leiter, Florida | 119 |
| Kevin Ritz, Colorado | 105 |
| Darryl Kile, Houston | 97 |
| Dave Burba,Cincinnati | 97 |
| Todd Stottlemyre, St. Louis | 93 |

## FEWEST WALKS PER 9 INNINGS

| | |
|---|---|
| Greg Maddux, Atlanta | 1.0 |
| Kevin Brown, Florida | 1.3 |
| Danny Darwin, Pitts,-Houston | 1.5 |
| Shane Reynolds, Houston | 1.7 |
| Bob Tewksbury, San Diego | 1.9 |

## HIT BATSMEN

| | |
|---|---|
| Darryl Kile, Houston | 16 |
| Kevin Brown, Florida | 16 |
| Mark Leiter, S.F.-Montreal | 16 |
| Mark Thompson, Colorado | 13 |
| Kevin Ritz, Colorado | 12 |
| Danny Darwin, Pitts.-Houston | 12 |

## STRIKEOUTS

| | |
|---|---|
| John Smoltz, Atlanta | 276 |
| Hideo Nomo, Los Angeles | 234 |
| Pedro Martinez, Montreal | 222 |
| Jeff Fassero, Montreal | 222 |
| Darryl Kile, Houston | 219 |

## STRIKEOUTS PER 9 INNINGS

| | |
|---|---|
| John Smoltz, Atlanta | 9.8 |
| Hideo Nomo, Los Angeles | 9.2 |
| Pedro Martinez, Montreal | 9.2 |
| Darryl Kile, Houston | 9.0 |
| Curt Schilling, Philadelphia | 8.9 |

## WILD PITCHES

| | |
|---|---|
| Mike Williams, Philadelphia | 16 |
| Jason Isringhausen, New York | 14 |
| Joey Hamilton, San Diego | 14 |
| Pat Rapp, Florida | 13 |
| Darryl Kile, Houston | 13 |
| Marvin Freeman, Colorado | 13 |

## BALKS

| | |
|---|---|
| Ismael Valdes, Los Angeles | 5 |
| Mark Leiter, S.F.-Montreal | 4 |
| Eleven tied with | 3 |

**Jeff Brantley**
44 saves

## OPPONENTS BATTING AVERAGE

| | |
|---|---|
| Al Leiter, Florida | .202 |
| John Smoltz, Atlanta | .216 |
| Hideo Nomo, Los Angeles | .218 |
| Kevin Brown, Florida | .220 |
| Curt Schilling, Philadelphia | .223 |

# FIELDING

## CATCHER

| | | |
|---|---|---|
| PCT | Charles Johnson, Florida | .995 |
| PO | Mike Piazza, Los Angeles | 1056 |
| A | Javier Lopez, Atlanta | 80 |
| E | Jason Kendall, Pittsburgh | 18 |
| TC | Mike Piazza, Los Angeles | 1135 |
| DP | Charles Johnson, Florida | 12 |

## FIRST BASE

| | | |
|---|---|---|
| PCT | Wally Joyner, San Diego | .997 |
| PO | Andres Galarraga, Colorado | 1527 |
| A | Jeff Bagwell, Houston | 136 |
| E | Jeff Bagwell, Houston | 16 |
| TC | Andres Galarraga, Colorado | 1657 |
| DP | Andres Galarraga, Colorado | 154 |

## SECOND BASE

| | | |
|---|---|---|
| PCT | Bret Boone, Cincinnati | .991 |
| PO | Craig Biggio, Houston | 361 |
| A | Craig Biggio, Houston | 440 |
| E | Luis Alicea, St. Louis | 24 |
| TC | Craig Biggio, Houston | 811 |
| DP | Mickey Morandini, Phil. | 87 |

## THIRD BASE

| | | |
|---|---|---|
| PCT | Leo Gomez, Chicago | .972 |
| PO | Terry Pendleton, Fla.-Atlanta | 109 |
| A | Vinny Castilla, Colorado | 389 |
| E | Sean Berry, Houston | 22 |
| TC | Vinny Castilla, Colorado | 506 |
| DP | Vinny Castilla, Colorado | 43 |

## SHORTSTOP

| | | |
|---|---|---|
| PCT | Jay Bell, Pittsburgh | .986 |
| PO | Barry Larkin, Cincinnati | 230 |
| A | Jay Bell, Pittsburgh | 478 |
| E | Walt Weiss, Colorado | 30 |
| TC | Rey Ordonez, New York | 705 |
| DP | Rey Ordonez, New York | 102 |

## OUTFIELD

| | | |
|---|---|---|
| PCT | Ray Lankford, St. Louis | .997 |
| PO | Lance Johnson, New York | 391 |
| A | Bernard Gilkey, New York | 18 |
| E | Three tied with | 12 |
| TC | Lance Johnson, New York | 412 |
| DP | Orlando Merced, Pittsburgh | 5 |

Gant and Gaetti, who combined for 162 RBIs.

The team got off to a slow start but played better and better as the season wore on, especially once it put the Smith distraction behind it.

La Russa played newcomer Royce Clayton at shortstop more than Smith, a 14-time all-star and St. Louis favorite who is considered baseball's best-ever defensive shortstop.

Smith was quiet about it for most of the season, but he did speak out at midseason, and his playing time increased in the second half of the season, as National League fans bid farewell to him. In the last game of road series, La Russa would pinch-hit Smith if he wasn't already in the game to get him one more ovation in each city. Smith also started the game in which the Cardinals clinched the division title.

"Tony knew how much I wanted to be out there," Smith said. "I thank Tony for giving me that opportunity."

The Cardinals were in a hot race with the Astros for the division crown, but the Astros faded and the Cardinals went on to win the division by six games.

The Braves' division title was more workmanlike, as they overcame an early, surprising charge by the Expos and cruised to the division title with the National League's best record.

The most notable aspect of the Braves' regular season was their extended road trip when the Olympics came to Atlanta. They went on a 19-day, 17-game trip that covered 5,592 miles.

The Padres' surge to the NL West title represented the completion of a heartening turnaround for the franchise, which hadn't been to the postseason since 1984 and had

**Ozzie Smith**

**Padre Power.** San Diego's Ken Caminiti won MVP honors in the National League by hitting .326 with 40 homers and 130 RBIs.

LARRY GOREN

endured years of fire sales and failed rebuilding efforts.

Only Tony Gwynn remained from the '84 team, and his two-run single in the clinching game against the Dodgers put the Padres ahead for good.

"It's been a long wait," said Gwynn, who also won his seventh NL batting crown.

Gwynn got considerable help from third baseman Ken Caminiti, who broke the club record for home runs with 40 and RBIs with 130. Steve Finley, who came over with Caminiti before the 1995 season in a trade with the Astros, also contributed 30 home runs and a team-record 125 runs.

# NL: BEST TOOLS

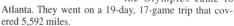

A Baseball America survey of National League managers, conducted at midseason 1996, ranked NL players with the best tools:

**BEST HITTER**
1. Tony, Gwynn, Padres
2. Mike Piazza, Dodgers
3. Jeff Bagwell, Astros

**BEST POWER HITTER**
1. Mike Piazza, Dodgers
2. Jeff Bagwell, Astros
3. Barry Bonds, Giants

**BEST BUNTER**
1. Brett Butler, Dodgers
2. Jay Bell, Pirates
3. Steve Finley, Padres

**BEST HIT-AND-RUN ARTIST**
1. Tony Gwynn, Padres
2. Craig Biggio, Astros
3. Mark Grace, Cubs

**BEST BASERUNNER**
1. Brian McRae, Cubs
2. Barry Larkin, Reds
3. Barry Bonds, Giants

**FASTEST BASERUNNER**
1. Brian Hunter, Astros
2. Lance Johnson, Mets
3. Roger Cedeno, Dodgers

**BEST PITCHER**
1. John Smoltz, Braves
2. Greg Maddux, Braves
3. Kevin Brown, Marlins

**BEST FASTBALL**
1. Mark Wohlers, Braves
2. Robb Nenn, Marlins
3. Antonio Osuna, Dodgers

**BEST CURVEBALL**
1. Darryl Kile, Astros
2. John Smoltz, Braves
3. Jason Isringhausen, Mets

**BEST SLIDER**
1. John Smoltz, Braves
2. Al Leiter, Marlins
3. Todd Worrell, Dodgers

**BEST CHANGEUP**
1. Tom Glavine, Braves
2. Greg Maddux, Braves
3. Denny Neagle, Pirates

**BEST CONTROL**
1. Greg Maddux, Braves
2. Tom Glavine, Braves
3. Bob Tewksbury, Padres

**BEST PICKOFF MOVE**
1. Armando Reynoso, Rockies
2. Terry Mulholland, Phillies
3. Steve Avery, Braves

**BEST RELIEVER**
1. Todd Worrell, Dodgers
2. Mark Wohlers, Braves
3. Rod Beck, Giants

**BEST DEFENSIVE C**
1. Charles Johnson, Marlins
2. Todd Hundley, Mets
3. Kirt Manwaring, Giants

**BEST DEFENSIVE 1B**
1. Mark Grace, Cubs
2. Jeff Bagwell, Astros
3. Andres Galarraga, Rockies

**BEST DEFENSIVE 2B**
1. Craig Biggio, Astros
2. Mark Lemke, Braves
3. Bret Boone, Reds

**BEST DEFENSIVE 3B**
1. Ken Caminiti, Padres
2. Matt Williams, Giants
3. Chipper Jones, Braves

**BEST DEFENSIVE SS**
1. Barry Larkin, Reds
2. Rey Ordonez, Mets
3. Jay Bell, Pirates

**BEST INFIELD ARM**
1. Ken Caminiti, Padres
2. Shawon Dunston, Giants
3. Mike Blowers, Dodgers

**BEST DEFENSIVE OF**
1. Marquis Grissom, Braves
2. Devon White, Marlins
3. Barry Bonds, Giants

**BEST OF ARM**
1. Raul Mondesi, Dodgers
2. Mark Whiten, Braves
3. Sammy Sosa, Cubs

**MOST EXCITING PLAYER**
1. Barry Bonds, Giants
2. Mike Piazza, Dodgers
3. Jeff Bagwell, Astros

**BEST MANAGER**
1. Jim Leyland, Pirates
2. Felipe Alou, Expos
3. Bobby Cox, Braves

# NATIONAL LEAGUE
## 1996 BATTING, PITCHING STATISTICS

### CLUB BATTING

| | AVG | G | AB | R | H | 2B | 3B | HR | BB | SO | SB |
|---|---|---|---|---|---|---|---|---|---|---|---|
| Colorado | .287 | 162 | 5590 | 961 | 1607 | 297 | 37 | 221 | 527 | 1108 | 201 |
| Atlanta | .270 | 162 | 5614 | 773 | 1514 | 264 | 28 | 197 | 530 | 1032 | 83 |
| New York | .270 | 162 | 5618 | 746 | 1515 | 267 | 47 | 147 | 445 | 1069 | 97 |
| St. Louis | .267 | 162 | 5502 | 759 | 1468 | 281 | 31 | 142 | 495 | 1089 | 149 |
| Pittsburgh | .266 | 162 | 5665 | 776 | 1509 | 319 | 33 | 138 | 510 | 989 | 126 |
| San Diego | .265 | 162 | 5655 | 771 | 1499 | 285 | 24 | 147 | 601 | 1015 | 109 |
| Houston | .262 | 162 | 5508 | 753 | 1445 | 297 | 29 | 129 | 554 | 1057 | 180 |
| Montreal | .262 | 162 | 5505 | 741 | 1441 | 297 | 27 | 148 | 492 | 1077 | 108 |
| Florida | .257 | 162 | 5498 | 688 | 1413 | 240 | 30 | 150 | 553 | 1122 | 99 |
| Cincinnati | .256 | 162 | 5455 | 778 | 1398 | 259 | 36 | 191 | 604 | 1134 | 171 |
| Philadelphia | .256 | 162 | 5499 | 650 | 1405 | 249 | 39 | 132 | 536 | 1092 | 117 |
| San Francisco | .253 | 162 | 5533 | 752 | 1400 | 245 | 21 | 153 | 615 | 1189 | 113 |
| Los Angeles | .252 | 162 | 5538 | 703 | 1396 | 215 | 33 | 150 | 516 | 1190 | 124 |
| Chicago | .251 | 162 | 5531 | 772 | 1388 | 267 | 19 | 175 | 523 | 1090 | 108 |

### CLUB PITCHING

| | ERA | G | CG | SHO | SV | IP | H | R | ER | BB | SO |
|---|---|---|---|---|---|---|---|---|---|---|---|
| Los Angeles | 3.46 | 162 | 6 | 9 | 50 | 1466 | 1378 | 652 | 564 | 534 | 1213 |
| Atlanta | 3.52 | 162 | 14 | 9 | 46 | 1469 | 1372 | 648 | 575 | 451 | 1245 |
| San Diego | 3.72 | 162 | 5 | 11 | 47 | 1489 | 1395 | 682 | 616 | 506 | 1194 |
| Montreal | 3.78 | 162 | 11 | 7 | 43 | 1441 | 1353 | 668 | 605 | 482 | 1206 |
| Florida | 3.95 | 162 | 8 | 13 | 41 | 1443 | 1386 | 703 | 634 | 598 | 1050 |
| St. Louis | 3.97 | 162 | 13 | 11 | 43 | 1452 | 1380 | 706 | 641 | 539 | 1050 |
| New York | 4.22 | 162 | 10 | 10 | 41 | 1440 | 1517 | 779 | 675 | 532 | 999 |
| Cincinnati | 4.31 | 162 | 6 | 8 | 52 | 1443 | 1447 | 773 | 692 | 591 | 1089 |
| Chicago | 4.36 | 162 | 10 | 10 | 34 | 1456 | 1447 | 771 | 705 | 546 | 1027 |
| Houston | 4.36 | 162 | 13 | 4 | 35 | 1447 | 1541 | 792 | 702 | 539 | 1163 |
| Philadelphia | 4.48 | 162 | 12 | 6 | 42 | 1423 | 1463 | 790 | 708 | 510 | 1044 |
| Pittsburgh | 4.61 | 162 | 5 | 7 | 37 | 1453 | 1602 | 833 | 744 | 479 | 1044 |
| San Francisco | 4.71 | 162 | 9 | 8 | 35 | 1442 | 1520 | 862 | 755 | 570 | 997 |
| Colorado | 5.59 | 162 | 5 | 4 | 34 | 1423 | 1597 | 964 | 884 | 624 | 932 |

### CLUB FIELDING

| | PCT | PO | A | E | DP | | PCT | PO | A | E | DP |
|---|---|---|---|---|---|---|---|---|---|---|---|
| Chicago | .983 | 4369 | 1768 | 104 | 147 | St. Louis | .980 | 4357 | 1666 | 125 | 139 |
| Florida | .982 | 4329 | 1796 | 111 | 187 | Montreal | .980 | 4324 | 1713 | 126 | 121 |
| San Diego | .981 | 4467 | 1768 | 118 | 136 | Atlanta | .980 | 4407 | 1808 | 130 | 143 |
| Philadelphia | .981 | 4270 | 1582 | 116 | 145 | San Francisco | .978 | 4327 | 1637 | 136 | 165 |
| Cincinnati | .980 | 4329 | 1694 | 121 | 145 | Houston | .978 | 4341 | 1692 | 138 | 130 |
| Pittsburgh | .980 | 4360 | 1868 | 128 | 144 | Colorado | .976 | 4268 | 1901 | 149 | 167 |
| Los Angeles | .980 | 4399 | 1636 | 125 | 143 | New York | .974 | 4320 | 1717 | 159 | 163 |

### INDIVIDUAL BATTING LEADERS
(Minimum 502 Plate Appearances)

| | AVG | G | AB | R | H | 2B | 3B | HR | RBI | BB | SO | SB |
|---|---|---|---|---|---|---|---|---|---|---|---|---|
| Gwynn, Tony, San Diego | .353 | 116 | 451 | 67 | 159 | 27 | 2 | 3 | 50 | 39 | 17 | 11 |
| Burks, Ellis, Colorado | .344 | 156 | 613 | 142 | 211 | 45 | 8 | 40 | 128 | 61 | 114 | 32 |
| Piazza, Mike, Los Angeles | .336 | 148 | 547 | 87 | 184 | 16 | 0 | 36 | 105 | 81 | 93 | 0 |
| Johnson, Lance, N.Y. | .333 | 160 | 682 | 117 | 227 | 31 | 21 | 9 | 69 | 33 | 40 | 50 |
| Grace, Mark, Chicago | .331 | 142 | 547 | 88 | 181 | 39 | 1 | 9 | 75 | 62 | 41 | 2 |
| Caminiti, Ken, San Diego | .326 | 146 | 546 | 109 | 178 | 37 | 2 | 40 | 130 | 78 | 99 | 11 |
| Young, Eric, Colorado | .324 | 141 | 568 | 113 | 184 | 23 | 4 | 8 | 74 | 47 | 31 | 53 |
| Gilkey, Bernard, N.Y. | .317 | 153 | 571 | 108 | 181 | 44 | 3 | 30 | 117 | 73 | 125 | 17 |
| Bagwell, Jeff, Houston | .315 | 162 | 568 | 111 | 179 | 48 | 2 | 31 | 120 | 135 | 114 | 21 |
| Sheffield, Gary, Florida | .314 | 161 | 519 | 118 | 163 | 33 | 1 | 42 | 120 | 142 | 66 | 16 |

### INDIVIDUAL PITCHING LEADERS
(Minimum 162 Innings)

| | W | L | ERA | G | GS | CG | SV | IP | H | R | ER | BB | SO |
|---|---|---|---|---|---|---|---|---|---|---|---|---|---|
| Brown, Kevin, Florida | 17 | 11 | 1.89 | 32 | 32 | 5 | 0 | 233 | 187 | 60 | 49 | 33 | 159 |
| Maddux, Greg, Atlanta | 15 | 11 | 2.72 | 35 | 35 | 5 | 0 | 245 | 225 | 85 | 74 | 28 | 172 |
| Leiter, Al, Florida | 16 | 12 | 2.93 | 33 | 33 | 2 | 0 | 215 | 153 | 74 | 70 | 119 | 200 |
| Smoltz, John, Atlanta | 24 | 8 | 2.94 | 35 | 35 | 6 | 0 | 254 | 199 | 93 | 83 | 55 | 276 |
| Glavine, Tom, Atlanta | 15 | 10 | 2.98 | 36 | 36 | 1 | 0 | 235 | 222 | 91 | 78 | 85 | 181 |
| Trachsel, Steve, Chicago | 13 | 9 | 3.03 | 31 | 31 | 3 | 0 | 205 | 181 | 82 | 69 | 62 | 132 |
| Schilling, Curt, Philadelphia | 9 | 10 | 3.19 | 26 | 26 | 8 | 0 | 183 | 149 | 69 | 65 | 50 | 182 |
| Nomo, Hideo, Los Angeles | 16 | 11 | 3.19 | 33 | 33 | 3 | 0 | 228 | 180 | 93 | 81 | 85 | 234 |
| Fassero, Jeff, Montreal | 15 | 11 | 3.30 | 34 | 34 | 5 | 0 | 232 | 217 | 95 | 85 | 55 | 222 |
| Valdes, Ismael, Los Angeles | 15 | 7 | 3.32 | 33 | 33 | 0 | 0 | 225 | 219 | 94 | 83 | 54 | 173 |

# AWARD WINNERS
Selected by Baseball Writers Association of America

## MVP

| Player, Team | 1st | 2nd | 3rd | Total |
|---|---|---|---|---|
| Ken Caminiti, S.D. | 28 | 0 | 0 | 392 |
| Mike Piazza, L.A. | 0 | 18 | 7 | 237 |
| Ellis Burks, Colorado | 0 | 5 | 4 | 186 |
| Chipper Jones, Atlanta | 0 | 2 | 7 | 158 |
| Barry Bonds, S.F. | 0 | 0 | 4 | 132 |
| Andres Galarraga, Colo. | 0 | 1 | 2 | 112 |
| Gary Sheffield, Florida | 0 | 1 | 2 | 112 |
| Brian Jordan, St. Louis | 0 | 1 | 1 | 69 |
| Jeff Bagwell, Houston | 0 | 0 | 0 | 59 |
| Steve Finley, S.D. | 0 | 0 | 0 | 38 |
| John Smoltz, Atlanta | 0 | 0 | 1 | 33 |
| Barry Larkin, Cinc. | 0 | 0 | 0 | 29 |
| Marquis Grissom, Atl. | 0 | 0 | 0 | 23 |
| Bernard Gilkey, N.Y. | 0 | 0 | 0 | 13 |
| Sammy Sosa, Chicago | 0 | 0 | 0 | 12 |
| Eric Karros, L.A. | 0 | 0 | 0 | 10 |
| Henry Rodriguez, Mon. | 0 | 0 | 0 | 9 |
| Todd Hundley, N.Y. | 0 | 0 | 0 | 7 |
| Lance Johnson, N.Y. | 0 | 0 | 0 | 7 |
| Dante Bichette, Colo. | 0 | 0 | 0 | 6 |
| Todd Worrell, L.A. | 0 | 0 | 0 | 3 |
| Kevin Brown, Florida | 0 | 0 | 0 | 2 |
| Trevor Hoffman, S.D. | 0 | 0 | 0 | 2 |
| Moises Alou, Mon. | 0 | 0 | 0 | 1 |

## Cy Young Award

| Player, Team | 1st | 2nd | 3rd | Total |
|---|---|---|---|---|
| John Smoltz, Atlanta | 26 | 2 | 0 | 136 |
| Kevin Brown, Florida | 2 | 26 | 0 | 88 |
| Andy Benes, St. Louis | 0 | 0 | 9 | 9 |
| Hideo Nomo, L.A. | 0 | 0 | 5 | 5 |
| Trevor Hoffman, S.D. | 0 | 0 | 3 | 3 |
| Todd Worrell, L.A. | 0 | 0 | 3 | 3 |
| Denny Neagle, Pitt.-Atl. | 0 | 0 | 2 | 2 |
| Jeff Fassero, Mon. | 0 | 0 | 1 | 1 |
| Al Leiter, Florida | 0 | 0 | 1 | 1 |
| Shane Reynolds, Hous. | 0 | 0 | 1 | 1 |

## Rookie of the Year

| Player, Team | 1st | 2nd | 3rd | Total |
|---|---|---|---|---|
| Todd Hollandsworth, L.A. | 15 | 9 | 3 | 105 |
| Edgar Renteria, Fla. | 10 | 10 | 4 | 84 |
| Jason Kendall, Pitt. | 1 | 5 | 10 | 30 |
| F.P. Santangelo, Mon. | 1 | 2 | 4 | 15 |
| Rey Ordonez, N.Y. | 1 | 0 | 2 | 7 |
| Jermaine Dye, Atlanta | 0 | 2 | 0 | 6 |
| Alan Benes, St. Louis | 0 | 0 | 5 | 5 |

## Manager of the Year

| Manager, Team | 1st | 2nd | 3rd | Total |
|---|---|---|---|---|
| Bruce Bochy, S.D. | 10 | 7 | 5 | 76 |
| Felipe Alou, Montreal | 8 | 9 | 7 | 74 |
| Tony La Russa, St.L. | 7 | 10 | 10 | 69 |
| Bobby Cox, Atlanta | 3 | 2 | 3 | 24 |
| Bill Russell, L.A. | 0 | 1 | 3 | 6 |
| Terry Collins, Hous. | 0 | 1 | 0 | 3 |

NOTE: MVP balloting based on 14 points for first-place vote, nine for second, eight for third, etc. Cy Young Award, Rookie of the Year and Manager of the Year balloting based on five points for first-place vote, three for second and one for third.

## Gold Glove Awards
Selected by NL managers

**C**—Charles Johnson, Florida. **1B**—Mark Grace, Chicago. **2B**—Craig Biggio, Houston. **3B**—Ken Caminiti, San Diego. **SS**—Barry Larkin, Cincinnati. **OF**—Barry Bonds, San Francisco; Marquis Grissom, Atlanta; Steve Finley, San Diego. **P**—Greg Maddux, Atlanta.

## Notable Numbers

In addition to team achievements, though, lots of individuals put up big numbers, or at least big games.

■ Perhaps none was more surprising than Mets catcher Todd Hundley, who broke Roy Campanella's record for most home runs by a catcher with 41.

Hundley had 50 home runs for his career coming into the season, in 1,468 career at-bats. His 41 for 1996 came in 540 at-bats and marked him as a rising star. That also set a Mets franchise record, passing Darryl Strawberry's 39, and the league record for home runs by a switch-hitter.

Hundley and outfielders Lance Johnson and Bernard Gilkey, acquired in preseason trades with the White Sox and Cardinals, respectively, were the most pleasant surprises for the Mets, who saw their bally-hooed young pitching staff fall on its face, thanks to inexperience and injuries.

■ Barry Bonds continued to excel in the face of a continued decline by the San Francisco Giants. Playing for a team that lost 94 games and offered him little lineup protection, Bonds became the second player in major league history to hit 40 home runs and steal 40 bases.

Jose Canseco did it first with the Athletics in 1988. Bonds hit .308 with 42 homers and 129 RBIs. He stole his 40th base on Sept. 27. Making his feat all the more impressive, Bonds drew a league-record 151 walks on the season.

■ Rockies continued to put up big numbers at Coors Field. Left felder Ellis Burks had a career year, becoming the second player in history to collect 40 homers, 30 steals and 200 hits in a season. Hank Aaron also did it for the 1963 Milwaukee Braves.

Burks hit .344 and drove in 128 runs, and his 32nd stolen base made the Rockies the first team to hit 200 homers and steal 200 bases in a season.

Helping out in that effort was right fielder Dante Bichette, who had a 30-30 season, or to be exact, a 31-31 season. Bichette also drove in 141 runs.

First baseman Andres Galarraga contributed to the Rockies offensive onslaught by leading the league with 47 homers and 150 RBIs.

■ The continued offensive explosion at Coors Field made Hideo Nomo's no-hitter there that much more astounding.

Nomo threw the 20th no-hitter in Dodgers history, but the first at Coors Field, on Sept. 17, in the midst of a pennant race against a fearsome lineup.

"It's one of the most incredible things I've ever seen in baseball," Dodgers reliever Mark Guthrie said. "You'll never see it again. You can sit there and say all the superlatives, but people don't understand what a feat that was."

The air was heavier in Denver that night, but the Dodgers still scored nine runs. And Nomo had an 11.18 ERA in his two previous starts there.

■ The Rockies were on the wrong end of the season's other no-hitter as well, as the Marlins got the first no-hitter in their short history from Al Leiter.

Leiter shut down the Rockies 11-0 on May 11 at Joe Robbie Stadium in front of 31,549 enthusiastic fans. He needed just 103 pitches, retiring five batters on five pitches in a stretch in the eighth and ninth innings.

# NATIONAL LEAGUE
## DIVISION SERIES
### ATLANTA vs. LOS ANGELES
## BOX SCORES

### Game One: October 2
### Braves 2, Dodgers 1

| ATLANTA | ab | r | h | bi | bb | so | L. A. | ab | r | h | bi | bb | so |
|---|---|---|---|---|---|---|---|---|---|---|---|---|---|
| Grissom cf | 4 | 1 | 1 | 0 | 0 | 0 | Kirby cf | 4 | 0 | 1 | 0 | 1 | 0 |
| Lemke 2b | 4 | 0 | 0 | 0 | 0 | 0 | Holl'worth lf | 4 | 0 | 1 | 1 | 0 | 1 |
| C. Jones 3b | 2 | 0 | 0 | 0 | 2 | 2 | Piazza c | 4 | 0 | 1 | 0 | 0 | 2 |
| McGriff 1b | 3 | 0 | 1 | 1 | 0 | 0 | Karros 1b | 3 | 0 | 0 | 0 | 1 | 0 |
| Klesko lf | 1 | 0 | 0 | 0 | 2 | 1 | Mondesi rf | 4 | 0 | 0 | 0 | 0 | 1 |
| Pendleton ph | 1 | 0 | 0 | 0 | 0 | 1 | Wallach 3b | 4 | 0 | 0 | 0 | 0 | 0 |
| A. Jones lf | 0 | 0 | 0 | 0 | 0 | 0 | DeShields 2b | 4 | 0 | 0 | 0 | 0 | 1 |
| Lopez c | 4 | 1 | 1 | 1 | 0 | 0 | Gagne ss | 4 | 1 | 2 | 0 | 0 | 1 |
| Dye rf | 4 | 0 | 0 | 0 | 0 | 3 | Martinez p | 3 | 0 | 0 | 0 | 0 | 2 |
| Blauser ss | 3 | 0 | 1 | 0 | 0 | 1 | Radinsky p | 0 | 0 | 0 | 0 | 0 | 0 |
| Wohlers p | 0 | 0 | 0 | 0 | 0 | 0 | Osuna p | 0 | 0 | 0 | 0 | 0 | 0 |
| Smoltz p | 2 | 0 | 0 | 0 | 0 | 0 | Clark ph | 1 | 0 | 0 | 0 | 0 | 0 |
| Polonia ph | 1 | 0 | 0 | 0 | 0 | 1 | | | | | | | |
| Belliard ss | 0 | 0 | 0 | 0 | 0 | 0 | | | | | | | |
| Totals | 29 | 2 | 4 | 2 | 4 | 9 | Totals | 35 | 1 | 5 | 1 | 2 | 9 |

| | | | | |
|---|---|---|---|---|
| Atlanta | 000 100 000 | 1—2 |
| Los Angeles | 000 010 000 | 0—1 |

**E**—Lopez (1). **DP**—Los Angeles 2. **LOB**—Atlanta 4, Los Angeles 6. **2B**—Hollandsworth (1), Gagne (1). **HR**—Lopez (1). **SB**—Grissom (1), Klesko (1). **CS**—C. Jones (1), McGriff (1), Blauser (1), Kirby (1). **S**—Smoltz. **SF**—McGriff.

| Atlanta | ip | h | r | er | bb | so | Los Angeles | ip | h | r | er | bb | so |
|---|---|---|---|---|---|---|---|---|---|---|---|---|---|
| Smoltz W | 9 | 4 | 1 | 1 | 2 | 7 | Martinez | 8 | 3 | 1 | 1 | 3 | 6 |
| Wohlers S | 1 | 1 | 0 | 0 | 0 | 2 | Radinsky | ⅓ | 0 | 0 | 0 | 1 | 0 |
| | | | | | | | Osuna L | 1⅔ | 1 | 1 | 1 | 0 | 3 |

**HBP**—Blauser (by Osuna).
**Umpires: HP**—Rippley; **1B**—Gregg; **2B**—Hallion; **3B**—Tata; **LF**—Froemming; **RF**—Hohn.
**T**—3:08. **A**—47,428.

**Series MVP.** Braves catcher Jary Lopez hit .542 with a pair of homers to lift Atlanta over St. Louis in the NLCS.

LARRY KINKER

## Game Two: October 3
### Braves 3, Dodgers 2

| ATLANTA | ab | r | h | bi | bb | so | L. A. | ab | r | h | bi | bb | so |
|---|---|---|---|---|---|---|---|---|---|---|---|---|---|
| Grissom cf | 4 | 0 | 0 | 0 | 0 | 1 | Holl'worth lf | 4 | 1 | 1 | 0 | 0 | 2 |
| Lemke 2b | 4 | 0 | 1 | 0 | 0 | 0 | Kirby cf | 4 | 0 | 0 | 0 | 0 | 1 |
| C. Jones 3b | 4 | 0 | 0 | 0 | 0 | 1 | Piazza c | 4 | 1 | 1 | 1 | 0 | 0 |
| McGriff 1b | 4 | 1 | 1 | 1 | 0 | 1 | Karros 1b | 3 | 0 | 0 | 0 | 0 | 2 |
| Klesko lf | 3 | 1 | 1 | 1 | 1 | 1 | Mondesi rf | 3 | 0 | 1 | 1 | 0 | 2 |
| A. Jones pr-lf | 0 | 0 | 0 | 0 | 0 | 0 | Wallach 3b | 3 | 0 | 0 | 0 | 0 | 0 |
| Dye rf | 3 | 1 | 1 | 1 | 0 | 1 | Gagne ss | 3 | 0 | 0 | 0 | 0 | 0 |
| Perez c | 3 | 0 | 1 | 0 | 0 | 0 | Castro 2b | 2 | 0 | 0 | 0 | 0 | 0 |
| Blauser ss | 3 | 0 | 0 | 0 | 0 | 1 | Hansen ph | 1 | 0 | 0 | 0 | 0 | 0 |
| Belliard ss | 0 | 0 | 0 | 0 | 0 | 0 | DeShields 2b | 0 | 0 | 0 | 0 | 0 | 0 |
| Maddux p | 2 | 0 | 0 | 0 | 0 | 1 | Valdes p | 2 | 0 | 0 | 0 | 0 | 0 |
| Polonia ph | 1 | 0 | 0 | 0 | 0 | 0 | Astacio p | 0 | 0 | 0 | 0 | 0 | 0 |
| McMichael p | 0 | 0 | 0 | 0 | 0 | 0 | Ashley ph | 1 | 0 | 0 | 0 | 0 | 1 |
| Wohlers p | 0 | 0 | 0 | 0 | 0 | 0 | Worrell p | 0 | 0 | 0 | 0 | 0 | 0 |
| **Totals** | **31** | **3** | **5** | **3** | **1** | **7** | **Totals** | **30** | **2** | **3** | **2** | **0** | **10** |

| Atlanta | 010 000 200—3 |
|---|---|
| Los Angeles | 100 100 000—2 |

E—Klesko (1). LOB—Atlanta 2, Los Angeles 1. 2B—Mondesi (1). HR—Klesko (1), McGriff (1), Dye (1).

| Atlanta | ip | h | r | er | bb | so | Los Angeles | ip | h | r | er | bb | so |
|---|---|---|---|---|---|---|---|---|---|---|---|---|---|
| Maddux W | 7 | 3 | 2 | 0 | 0 | 7 | Valdes L | 6⅓ | 5 | 3 | 3 | 0 | 5 |
| McMichael | 1 | 0 | 0 | 0 | 0 | 2 | Astacio | 1⅔ | 0 | 0 | 0 | 0 | 1 |
| Wohlers S | 1 | 0 | 0 | 0 | 1 | 1 | Worrell | 1 | 0 | 0 | 0 | 1 | 1 |

Umpires: HP—Gregg; 1B—Hallion; 2B—Tata; 3B—Froemming; LF—Hohn; RF—Rippley.
T—2:08. A—51,916.

## Game Three: October 5
### Braves 5, Dodgers 2

| L. A. | ab | r | h | bi | bb | so | ATLANTA | ab | r | h | bi | bb | so |
|---|---|---|---|---|---|---|---|---|---|---|---|---|---|
| Curtis cf | 2 | 0 | 0 | 0 | 1 | 1 | Grissom cf | 4 | 1 | 0 | 0 | 1 | 1 |
| Kirby cf | 0 | 1 | 0 | 0 | 1 | 0 | Lemke 2b | 4 | 1 | 1 | 2 | 0 | 1 |
| Holl'worth lf | 4 | 0 | 2 | 0 | 0 | 0 | C. Jones 3b | 3 | 2 | 2 | 2 | 1 | 1 |
| Piazza c | 2 | 0 | 1 | 1 | 1 | 0 | McGriff 1b | 2 | 0 | 1 | 1 | 2 | 0 |
| Karros 1b | 3 | 0 | 0 | 1 | 1 | 1 | Klesko lf | 4 | 0 | 0 | 0 | 0 | 2 |
| Mondesi rf | 4 | 0 | 1 | 0 | 0 | 1 | Wohlers p | 0 | 0 | 0 | 0 | 0 | 0 |
| Wallach 3b | 4 | 0 | 0 | 0 | 0 | 0 | Lopez c | 3 | 0 | 1 | 0 | 1 | 0 |
| Osuna p | 0 | 0 | 0 | 0 | 0 | 0 | Dye rf | 4 | 0 | 1 | 0 | 0 | 2 |
| Dreifort p | 0 | 0 | 0 | 0 | 0 | 0 | Blauser ss | 3 | 0 | 0 | 0 | 1 | 1 |
| Gagne ss | 4 | 1 | 1 | 0 | 0 | 2 | Belliard ss | 0 | 0 | 0 | 0 | 0 | 0 |
| Castro 2b | 3 | 0 | 1 | 1 | 1 | 1 | Glavine p | 2 | 1 | 1 | 0 | 0 | 0 |
| Nomo p | 1 | 0 | 0 | 0 | 0 | 1 | McMichael p | 0 | 0 | 0 | 0 | 0 | 0 |
| Guthrie p | 0 | 0 | 0 | 0 | 0 | 0 | Bielecki p | 0 | 0 | 0 | 0 | 0 | 0 |
| Clark ph | 1 | 0 | 0 | 0 | 0 | 1 | A. Jones lf | 0 | 0 | 0 | 0 | 1 | 0 |
| Ashley ph | 1 | 0 | 0 | 0 | 0 | 1 | | | | | | | |
| Candiotti p | 0 | 0 | 0 | 0 | 0 | 0 | | | | | | | |
| Radinsky p | 0 | 0 | 0 | 0 | 0 | 0 | | | | | | | |
| Hansen 3b | 1 | 0 | 0 | 0 | 0 | 0 | | | | | | | |
| **Totals** | **30** | **2** | **6** | **2** | **5** | **10** | **Totals** | **29** | **5** | **7** | **5** | **7** | **8** |

| Los Angeles | 000 000 110—2 |
|---|---|
| Atlanta | 100 400 00x—5 |

E—Wallach (1). DP—Los Angeles 2, Atlanta 1. LOB—Los Angeles 7, Atlanta 8. 2B—Hollandsworth 2 (3), Mondesi (2), Castro (1), Lemke (1), McGriff (1), Glavine (1). HR—C. Jones (1). SB—C. Jones (1), Lopez (1), Dye (1). S—Glavine (1). SF—Piazza.

| Los Angeles | ip | h | r | er | bb | so | Atlanta | ip | h | r | er | bb | so |
|---|---|---|---|---|---|---|---|---|---|---|---|---|---|
| Nomo L | 3⅔ | 5 | 5 | 5 | 3 | 3 | Glavine W | 6⅔ | 5 | 1 | 1 | 3 | 7 |
| Guthrie | ⅓ | 0 | 0 | 0 | 1 | 1 | McMichael | ⅓ | 1 | 1 | 1 | 1 | 1 |
| Candiotti | 2 | 0 | 0 | 0 | 0 | 1 | Bielecki | ⅔ | 0 | 0 | 0 | 1 | 1 |
| Radinsky | 1 | 0 | 0 | 0 | 0 | 2 | Wohlers S | 1⅓ | 0 | 0 | 0 | 0 | 1 |
| Osuna | ⅓ | 2 | 0 | 0 | 1 | 1 | | | | | | | |
| Dreifort | ⅔ | 0 | 0 | 0 | 0 | 0 | | | | | | | |

Umpires: HP—DeMuth; 1B—Pulli; 2B—Wendelstedt; 3B—Bonin; LF—Quick; RF—Davis.
T—3:19. A—52,529.

## COMPOSITE BOX
### ATLANTA

| Player Pos. | AVG | G | AB | R | H | 2B | 3B | HR | RBI | BB | SO | SB |
|---|---|---|---|---|---|---|---|---|---|---|---|---|
| Tom Glavine, p | .500 | 1 | 2 | 1 | 1 | 1 | 0 | 0 | 0 | 0 | 0 | 0 |
| Fred McGriff, 1b | .333 | 3 | 9 | 1 | 3 | 1 | 0 | 1 | 3 | 2 | 1 | 0 |
| Eddie Perez, c | .333 | 1 | 3 | 0 | 1 | 0 | 0 | 0 | 0 | 0 | 0 | 0 |
| Javier Lopez, c | .286 | 2 | 7 | 1 | 2 | 0 | 0 | 1 | 1 | 1 | 0 | 1 |
| Chipper Jones, 3b | .222 | 3 | 9 | 2 | 2 | 0 | 0 | 1 | 2 | 3 | 4 | 1 |
| Jermaine Dye, rf | .182 | 3 | 11 | 2 | 2 | 0 | 0 | 1 | 1 | 0 | 6 | 1 |
| Mark Lemke, 2b | .167 | 3 | 12 | 1 | 2 | 1 | 0 | 0 | 2 | 0 | 1 | 0 |
| Ryan Klesko, lf | .125 | 3 | 8 | 1 | 1 | 0 | 0 | 1 | 1 | 3 | 4 | 1 |
| Jeff Blauser, ss | .111 | 3 | 9 | 1 | 0 | 0 | 0 | 0 | 0 | 1 | 3 | 0 |
| Marquis Grissom, cf | .083 | 3 | 12 | 2 | 1 | 0 | 0 | 0 | 0 | 1 | 2 | 1 |
| Terry Pendleton, 3b | .000 | 1 | 1 | 0 | 0 | 0 | 0 | 0 | 0 | 0 | 1 | 0 |
| Greg Maddux, p | .000 | 1 | 2 | 0 | 0 | 0 | 0 | 0 | 0 | 0 | 1 | 0 |

---

| | AVG | 2 | | | | | | | | 0 | 1 | 0 |
|---|---|---|---|---|---|---|---|---|---|---|---|---|

| Luis Polonia, ph | .000 | 2 | 2 | 0 | 0 | 0 | 0 | 0 | 0 | 0 | 1 | 0 |
| John Smoltz, p | .000 | 1 | 2 | 0 | 0 | 0 | 0 | 0 | 0 | 0 | 0 | 0 |
| Rafael Belliard, ss | .000 | 3 | 0 | 0 | 0 | 0 | 0 | 0 | 0 | 0 | 0 | 0 |
| Andruw Jones, lf-ph | .000 | 3 | 0 | 0 | 0 | 0 | 0 | 0 | 0 | 1 | 0 | 0 |
| **Totals** | **.180** | **3** | **89** | **10** | **16** | **3** | **0** | **4** | **10** | **12** | **24** | **5** |

| Pitcher | W | L | ERA | G | GS | SV | IP | H | R | ER | BB | SO |
|---|---|---|---|---|---|---|---|---|---|---|---|---|
| Greg Maddux | 1 | 0 | 0.00 | 1 | 1 | 0 | 7 | 3 | 2 | 0 | 0 | 7 |
| Mark Wohlers | 0 | 0 | 0.00 | 3 | 0 | 2 | 3 | 1 | 0 | 0 | 0 | 4 |
| Mike Bielecki | 0 | 0 | 0.00 | 1 | 0 | 0 | 1 | 0 | 0 | 0 | 1 | 1 |
| John Smoltz | 1 | 0 | 1.00 | 1 | 1 | 0 | 9 | 4 | 1 | 1 | 2 | 7 |
| Tom Glavine | 1 | 0 | 1.35 | 1 | 1 | 0 | 7 | 5 | 1 | 1 | 3 | 7 |
| Greg McMichael | 0 | 0 | 6.75 | 2 | 0 | 0 | 1 | 1 | 1 | 1 | 1 | 3 |
| **Totals** | **3** | **0** | **0.96** | **3** | **3** | **2** | **28** | **14** | **5** | **3** | **7** | **29** |

### LOS ANGELES

| Player Pos. | AVG | G | AB | R | H | 2B | 3B | HR | RBI | BB | SO | SB |
|---|---|---|---|---|---|---|---|---|---|---|---|---|
| Todd Holl'worth, lf | .333 | 3 | 12 | 1 | 4 | 3 | 0 | 0 | 1 | 0 | 3 | 0 |
| Mike Piazza, c | .300 | 3 | 10 | 1 | 3 | 0 | 0 | 0 | 2 | 1 | 2 | 0 |
| Greg Gagne, ss | .273 | 3 | 11 | 2 | 3 | 1 | 0 | 0 | 0 | 0 | 5 | 0 |
| Juan Castro, 2b | .200 | 2 | 5 | 0 | 1 | 1 | 0 | 0 | 1 | 1 | 1 | 0 |
| Raul Mondesi, rf | .182 | 3 | 11 | 0 | 2 | 2 | 0 | 0 | 1 | 0 | 4 | 0 |
| Wayne Kirby, cf | .125 | 3 | 8 | 1 | 1 | 0 | 0 | 0 | 0 | 2 | 1 | 0 |
| Hideo Nomo, p | .000 | 1 | 1 | 0 | 0 | 0 | 0 | 0 | 0 | 0 | 1 | 0 |
| Billy Ashley, ph | .000 | 2 | 2 | 0 | 0 | 0 | 0 | 0 | 0 | 0 | 2 | 0 |
| Dave Clark, ph | .000 | 2 | 2 | 0 | 0 | 0 | 0 | 0 | 0 | 0 | 1 | 0 |
| Dave Hansen, ph | .000 | 2 | 2 | 0 | 0 | 0 | 0 | 0 | 0 | 0 | 0 | 0 |
| Chad Curtis, cf | .000 | 1 | 2 | 0 | 0 | 0 | 0 | 0 | 0 | 1 | 1 | 0 |
| Ismael Valdes, p | .000 | 1 | 2 | 0 | 0 | 0 | 0 | 0 | 0 | 0 | 0 | 0 |
| Ramon Martinez, p | .000 | 1 | 3 | 0 | 0 | 0 | 0 | 0 | 0 | 0 | 2 | 0 |
| Delino DeShields, 2b | .000 | 2 | 4 | 0 | 0 | 0 | 0 | 0 | 0 | 1 | 0 | 0 |
| Eric Karros, 1b | .000 | 3 | 9 | 0 | 0 | 0 | 0 | 0 | 2 | 2 | 3 | 0 |
| Tim Wallach, 3b | .000 | 3 | 11 | 0 | 0 | 0 | 0 | 0 | 0 | 0 | 0 | 0 |
| **Totals** | **.147** | **3** | **95** | **5** | **14** | **7** | **0** | **0** | **5** | **7** | **29** | **0** |

| Pitcher | W | L | ERA | G | GS | SV | IP | H | R | ER | BB | SO |
|---|---|---|---|---|---|---|---|---|---|---|---|---|
| Tom Candiotti | 0 | 0 | 0.00 | 1 | 0 | 0 | 2 | 0 | 0 | 0 | 0 | 1 |
| Pedro Astacio | 0 | 0 | 0.00 | 1 | 0 | 0 | 2 | 0 | 0 | 0 | 0 | 1 |
| Scott Radinsky | 0 | 0 | 0.00 | 2 | 0 | 0 | 1 | 0 | 0 | 0 | 1 | 2 |
| Todd Worrell | 0 | 0 | 0.00 | 1 | 0 | 0 | 1 | 0 | 0 | 0 | 1 | 1 |
| Darren Dreifort | 0 | 0 | 0.00 | 1 | 0 | 0 | 1 | 0 | 0 | 0 | 0 | 0 |
| Mark Guthrie | 0 | 0 | 0.00 | 1 | 0 | 0 | 1 | 0 | 0 | 0 | 1 | 1 |
| Ramon Martinez | 0 | 0 | 1.12 | 1 | 1 | 0 | 8 | 3 | 1 | 1 | 3 | 6 |
| Ismael Valdes | 0 | 1 | 4.26 | 1 | 1 | 0 | 6 | 5 | 3 | 3 | 0 | 5 |
| Antonio Osuna | 0 | 0 | 4.50 | 2 | 0 | 0 | 2 | 3 | 1 | 1 | 4 | 4 |
| Hideo Nomo | 0 | 1 | 12.27 | 1 | 1 | 0 | 4 | 5 | 5 | 5 | 3 | 3 |
| **Totals** | **0** | **3** | **3.33** | **3** | **3** | **0** | **27** | **16** | **10** | **10** | **12** | **24** |

DP—Atlanta 1, Los Angeles 4. LOB—Atlanta 14, Los Angeles 14. E—Lopez, Grissom, Klesko, Wallach. CS—C. Jones, McGriff, Blauser, Kirby. S—Smoltz, Glavine. SF—McGriff, Piazza.

HBP—Blauser (by Osuna). Umpires—Greg Bonin, Gerry Davis, Dana DeMuth, Bruce Froemming, Eric Gregg, Tom Hallion, Bill Hohn, Frank Pulli, Jim Quick, Steve Rippley, Terry Tata, Harry Wendelstedt.

## ST. LOUIS vs. SAN DIEGO

# BOX SCORES

### Game One: October 1
### Cardinals 3, Padres 1

| SAN DIEGO | ab | r | h | bi | bb | so | ST. LOUIS | ab | r | h | bi | bb | so |
|---|---|---|---|---|---|---|---|---|---|---|---|---|---|
| Henderson lf | 4 | 1 | 2 | 1 | 1 | 0 | Clayton ss | 3 | 0 | 1 | 0 | 1 | 1 |
| T. Gwynn rf | 5 | 0 | 2 | 0 | 0 | 0 | McGee cf | 4 | 0 | 0 | 0 | 0 | 0 |
| Finley cf | 3 | 0 | 1 | 0 | 0 | 1 | Gant lf | 2 | 1 | 1 | 0 | 1 | 0 |
| Caminiti 3b | 3 | 0 | 0 | 1 | 3 | 0 | Jordan rf | 4 | 1 | 1 | 0 | 0 | 1 |
| Joyner 1b | 3 | 0 | 1 | 0 | 0 | 0 | Gaetti 3b | 3 | 1 | 1 | 3 | 0 | 1 |
| Vaughn ph | 1 | 0 | 0 | 0 | 0 | 0 | Mabry 1b | 3 | 0 | 0 | 0 | 0 | 0 |
| Cianfrocco 1b | 0 | 0 | 0 | 0 | 0 | 0 | Pagnozzi c | 3 | 0 | 0 | 0 | 0 | 2 |
| Gomez ss | 4 | 0 | 0 | 0 | 0 | 2 | Alicea 2b | 3 | 0 | 2 | 0 | 0 | 0 |
| Johnson c | 4 | 0 | 0 | 0 | 0 | 1 | Stottlemyre p | 2 | 0 | 0 | 0 | 0 | 2 |
| Reed 2b | 4 | 0 | 1 | 0 | 0 | 0 | Honeycutt p | 1 | 0 | 0 | 0 | 0 | 1 |
| Hamilton p | 2 | 0 | 0 | 0 | 0 | 2 | Eckersley p | 0 | 0 | 0 | 0 | 0 | 0 |
| Livingstone ph | 1 | 0 | 0 | 0 | 0 | 0 | | | | | | | |
| Blair p | 0 | 0 | 0 | 0 | 0 | 0 | | | | | | | |
| C. Gwynn ph | 1 | 0 | 1 | 0 | 0 | 0 | | | | | | | |
| **Totals** | **35** | **1** | **8** | **1** | **2** | **9** | **Totals** | **28** | **3** | **6** | **3** | **2** | **9** |

| St. Louis | 000 001 200—3 |
|---|---|
| San Diego | 300 000 000—3 |

E—Caminiti (1). DP—San Diego 2. LOB—San Diego 10, St. Louis 4. 2B—T.Gwynn (1), Alicea 2 (2). HR—Henderson (1), Gaetti (1). SB—Gwynn (1), Finley (1), Gant 2 (2). CS—Clayton.

| San Diego | ip | h | r | er | bb | so | St. Louis | ip | h | r | er | bb | so |
|---|---|---|---|---|---|---|---|---|---|---|---|---|---|
| Hamilton L | 6 | 5 | 3 | 3 | 0 | 6 | Stottlemyre W | 6⅔ | 5 | 1 | 1 | 2 | 7 |
| Blair | 2 | 1 | 0 | 0 | 2 | 3 | Honeycutt | ⅔ | 1 | 0 | 0 | 0 | 1 |
| | | | | | | | Eckersley S | 1⅔ | 2 | 0 | 0 | 0 | 1 |

HBP—Gant (by Hamilton), Finley (by Stottlmyre).
**Umpires: HP**—Quick; **1B**—Davis; **2B**—DeMuth; **3B**—Pulli; **LF**—Wendelstedt; **RF**—Bonin.
**T**—2:39. **A**—54,193.

### Game Two: October 4
### Cardinals 5, Padres 4

| SAN DIEGO | ab | r | h | bi | bb | so | ST. LOUIS | ab | r | h | bi | bb | so |
|---|---|---|---|---|---|---|---|---|---|---|---|---|---|
| Henderson lf | 3 | 1 | 1 | 0 | 1 | 2 | Smith ss | 2 | 1 | 1 | 0 | 2 | 0 |
| T. Gwynn rf | 3 | 0 | 1 | 1 | 0 | 0 | McGee cf | 3 | 1 | 1 | 1 | 1 | 1 |
| Finley cf | 4 | 0 | 0 | 0 | 0 | 2 | Gant lf | 4 | 0 | 1 | 3 | 0 | 0 |
| Caminiti 3b | 3 | 1 | 1 | 1 | 1 | 1 | Jordan rf | 3 | 1 | 0 | 0 | 1 | 2 |
| Joyner 1b | 4 | 0 | 0 | 0 | 0 | 2 | Gaetti 3b | 4 | 0 | 0 | 0 | 0 | 0 |
| Hoffman p | 0 | 0 | 0 | 0 | 0 | 0 | Mabry 1b | 3 | 0 | 0 | 0 | 1 | 1 |
| Flaherty c | 4 | 0 | 0 | 0 | 0 | 1 | Pagnozzi c | 4 | 0 | 1 | 1 | 0 | 1 |
| Gomez ss | 4 | 0 | 1 | 0 | 0 | 1 | Alicea 2b | 3 | 1 | 0 | 0 | 1 | 1 |
| Reed 2b | 3 | 0 | 0 | 0 | 0 | 1 | Eckersley p | 0 | 0 | 0 | 0 | 0 | 0 |
| Vaughn ph | 1 | 0 | 0 | 0 | 0 | 0 | Andy Benes p | 2 | 1 | 1 | 0 | 0 | 1 |
| Sanders p | 1 | 0 | 0 | 0 | 0 | 0 | Honeycutt p | 0 | 0 | 0 | 0 | 0 | 0 |
| Veras p | 0 | 0 | 0 | 0 | 0 | 0 | Gallego 2b | 0 | 0 | 0 | 0 | 0 | 0 |
| C. Gwynn ph | 1 | 1 | 1 | 0 | 0 | 0 | | | | | | | |
| Worrell p | 0 | 0 | 0 | 0 | 0 | 0 | | | | | | | |
| Livingstone ph | 1 | 1 | 1 | 0 | 0 | 0 | | | | | | | |
| Bochtler p | 0 | 0 | 0 | 0 | 0 | 0 | | | | | | | |
| Cianfrocco 1b | 0 | 0 | 0 | 0 | 0 | 0 | | | | | | | |
| **Totals** | 32 | 4 | 6 | 3 | 2 | 10 | **Totals** | 28 | 5 | 5 | 5 | 6 | 7 |

| | | |
|---|---|---|
| San Diego | | 000 012 010—4 |
| St. Louis | | 001 030 01x—5 |

**E**—McGee (1). **LOB**—San Diego 4, St. Louis 6. **2B**—Gant (1). **HR**—Caminiti (1). **S**—T. Gwynn, Benes.

| San Diego | ip | h | r | er | bb | so | St. Louis | ip | h | r | er | bb | so |
|---|---|---|---|---|---|---|---|---|---|---|---|---|---|
| Sanders | 4⅓ | 3 | 4 | 4 | 4 | 4 | Benes | 7 | 6 | 4 | 4 | 1 | 9 |
| Veras | ⅔ | 1 | 0 | 0 | 1 | 0 | Honeycutt W | 1 | 0 | 0 | 0 | 1 | 0 |
| Worrell | 2 | 1 | 0 | 0 | 0 | 2 | Eckersley S | 1 | 0 | 0 | 0 | 0 | 1 |
| Bochtler L | ⅓ | 0 | 1 | 1 | 2 | 0 | | | | | | | |
| Hoffman | ⅔ | 0 | 0 | 0 | 0 | 0 | | | | | | | |

Benes pitched to two batters in 8th.
**WP**—Bochtler.
**Umpires: HP**—Davis; **1B**—DeMuth; **2B**—Pulli; **3B**—Wendelstedt; **LF**—Bonin; **RF**—Quick.
**T**—2:55. **A**—56,752.

### Game Three: October 5
### Cardinals 7, Padres 5

| ST. LOUIS | ab | r | h | bi | bb | so | SAN DIEGO | ab | r | h | bi | bb | so |
|---|---|---|---|---|---|---|---|---|---|---|---|---|---|
| Clayton ss | 3 | 1 | 1 | 0 | 2 | 0 | Henderson lf | 5 | 0 | 1 | 0 | 0 | 1 |
| McGee cf | 3 | 0 | 0 | 0 | 0 | 1 | T. Gwynn rf | 5 | 0 | 1 | 0 | 0 | 2 |
| Petkovsek p | 0 | 0 | 0 | 0 | 0 | 0 | Finley cf | 5 | 0 | 0 | 0 | 0 | 1 |
| Sweeney ph | 1 | 0 | 1 | 0 | 0 | 0 | Caminiti 3b | 4 | 2 | 2 | 2 | 0 | 1 |
| Honeycutt p | 0 | 0 | 0 | 0 | 0 | 0 | Cianfrocco 1b | 3 | 1 | 1 | 0 | 0 | 1 |
| Mathews p | 0 | 0 | 0 | 0 | 0 | 0 | Worrell p | 0 | 0 | 0 | 0 | 0 | 0 |
| Smith ph | 1 | 0 | 0 | 0 | 0 | 0 | Valenzuela p | 0 | 0 | 0 | 0 | 0 | 0 |
| Eckersley p | 0 | 0 | 0 | 0 | 0 | 0 | Veras p | 0 | 0 | 0 | 0 | 0 | 0 |
| Gant lf | 4 | 2 | 2 | 1 | 1 | 0 | Vaughn ph | 1 | 0 | 0 | 0 | 0 | 1 |
| Jordan rf | 5 | 2 | 3 | 3 | 0 | 0 | Flaherty c | 4 | 0 | 0 | 0 | 0 | 0 |
| Gaetti 3b | 4 | 0 | 0 | 0 | 0 | 2 | Johnson c | 4 | 2 | 3 | 0 | 0 | 0 |
| Mejia pr | 0 | 0 | 0 | 0 | 0 | 0 | Lopez pr | 0 | 0 | 0 | 0 | 0 | 0 |
| Gallego 2b | 1 | 0 | 0 | 0 | 0 | 1 | Hoffman p | 0 | 0 | 0 | 0 | 0 | 0 |
| Mabry 1b | 4 | 1 | 3 | 1 | 0 | 0 | Gomez ss | 4 | 0 | 1 | 1 | 0 | 1 |
| Pagnozzi c | 4 | 0 | 2 | 1 | 1 | 0 | Reed 2b | 4 | 0 | 2 | 2 | 0 | 0 |
| Alicea 2b | 5 | 0 | 0 | 3 | 0 | 3 | Ashby p | 1 | 0 | 0 | 0 | 0 | 1 |
| Osborne p | 1 | 0 | 0 | 0 | 0 | 0 | Joyner 1b | 2 | 0 | 0 | 0 | 0 | 0 |
| Lankford ph-cf | 2 | 1 | 1 | 0 | 1 | 0 | | | | | | | |
| **Totals** | 38 | 7 | 13 | 6 | 5 | 7 | **Totals** | 38 | 5 | 11 | 5 | 0 | 9 |

| | | |
|---|---|---|
| St. Louis | | 100 003 102—7 |
| San Diego | | 021 100 010—5 |

**E**—Alicea (1), Caminiti 2 (3). **DP**—San Diego 2. **LOB**—St. Louis 10, San Diego 7. **2B**—Johnson (1), Reed (1). **3B**—Mabry (1). **HR**—Gant (1), Jordan (1), Caminiti 2 (3). **SB**—Jordan (1). **CS**—Alicea. **S**—Mabry, Ashby.

| St. Louis | ip | h | r | er | bb | so | San Diego | ip | h | r | er | bb | so |
|---|---|---|---|---|---|---|---|---|---|---|---|---|---|
| Osborne | 4 | 7 | 4 | 4 | 0 | 5 | Ashby | 5⅓ | 4 | 1 | 1 | 4 | 5 |
| Petkovsek | 2 | 0 | 0 | 0 | 0 | 1 | Worrell | 1⅓ | 3 | 1 | 1 | 1 | 0 |
| Honeycutt | 1 | 2 | 1 | 1 | 0 | 1 | Valenzuela | ⅔ | 0 | 0 | 0 | 2 | 0 |
| Mathews W | 1 | 1 | 0 | 0 | 0 | 2 | Veras | ⅓ | 0 | 0 | 0 | 0 | 0 |
| Eckersley S | 1 | 1 | 0 | 0 | 0 | 0 | Hoffman L | 1 | 3 | 2 | 2 | 1 | 2 |

Worrell pitched to one batter in 8th. Honeycutt pitched to one batter in 8th.
**WP**—Ashby.
**Umpires: HP**—Hallion; **1B**—Tata; **2B**—Froemming; **3B**—Hohn; **LF**—Rippley; **RF**—Gregg.
**T**—3:32. **A**—53,899.

## COMPOSITE BOX

### SAN DIEGO

| Player Pos. | AVG | G | AB | R | H | 2B | 3B | HR | RBI | BB | SO | SB |
|---|---|---|---|---|---|---|---|---|---|---|---|---|
| Chris Gwynn, ph | 1.000 | 2 | 2 | 1 | 2 | 0 | 0 | 0 | 0 | 0 | 0 | 0 |
| Scott Livingstone, ph | .500 | 2 | 2 | 1 | 1 | 0 | 0 | 0 | 0 | 0 | 0 | 0 |
| Brian Johnson, c | .375 | 2 | 8 | 2 | 3 | 1 | 0 | 0 | 0 | 0 | 1 | 0 |
| Rickey Henderson, lf | .333 | 3 | 12 | 4 | 4 | 0 | 0 | 1 | 2 | 3 | 0 | 0 |
| Archi Cianfrocco, 1b | .333 | 3 | 3 | 1 | 1 | 0 | 0 | 0 | 0 | 0 | 1 | 0 |
| Tony Gwynn, rf | .308 | 3 | 13 | 0 | 4 | 1 | 0 | 0 | 1 | 0 | 2 | 1 |
| Ken Caminiti, 3b | .300 | 3 | 10 | 3 | 3 | 0 | 0 | 3 | 3 | 2 | 5 | 0 |
| Jody Reed, 2b | .273 | 3 | 11 | 0 | 3 | 1 | 0 | 0 | 2 | 0 | 1 | 0 |
| Chris Gomez, ss | .167 | 3 | 12 | 0 | 2 | 0 | 0 | 0 | 1 | 0 | 4 | 0 |
| Wally Joyner, 1b | .111 | 3 | 9 | 0 | 1 | 0 | 0 | 0 | 0 | 0 | 2 | 0 |
| Steve Finley, cf | .083 | 3 | 12 | 0 | 1 | 0 | 0 | 0 | 0 | 0 | 4 | 1 |
| Andy Ashby, p | .000 | 1 | 1 | 0 | 0 | 0 | 0 | 0 | 0 | 0 | 1 | 0 |
| Scott Sanders, p | .000 | 1 | 1 | 0 | 0 | 0 | 0 | 0 | 0 | 0 | 0 | 0 |
| Joey Hamilton, p | .000 | 1 | 2 | 0 | 0 | 0 | 0 | 0 | 0 | 0 | 2 | 0 |
| Greg Vaughn, lf-ph | .000 | 3 | 3 | 0 | 0 | 0 | 0 | 0 | 0 | 0 | 3 | 0 |
| John Flaherty, c | .000 | 2 | 4 | 0 | 0 | 0 | 0 | 0 | 0 | 0 | 1 | 0 |
| Luis Lopez, pr | .000 | 1 | 0 | 0 | 0 | 0 | 0 | 0 | 0 | 0 | 0 | 0 |
| **Totals** | .238 | 3 | 105 | 10 | 25 | 3 | 0 | 3 | 9 | 4 | 28 | 2 |

| Pitcher | W | L | ERA | G | GS | SV | IP | H | R | ER | BB | SO |
|---|---|---|---|---|---|---|---|---|---|---|---|---|
| Willie Blair | 0 | 0 | 0.00 | 1 | 0 | 0 | 2 | 1 | 0 | 0 | 2 | 3 |
| Dario Veras | 0 | 0 | 0.00 | 2 | 0 | 0 | 1 | 1 | 0 | 0 | 1 | 0 |
| Fernando Valenzuela | 0 | 0 | 0.00 | 1 | 0 | 0 | 1 | 0 | 0 | 0 | 2 | 0 |
| Tim Worrell | 0 | 0 | 2.45 | 2 | 0 | 0 | 4 | 4 | 1 | 1 | 1 | 2 |
| Joey Hamilton | 0 | 1 | 4.50 | 1 | 1 | 0 | 6 | 5 | 3 | 3 | 0 | 6 |
| Andy Ashby | 0 | 0 | 6.75 | 1 | 1 | 0 | 5 | 7 | 4 | 4 | 1 | 5 |
| Scott Sanders | 0 | 0 | 8.31 | 1 | 1 | 0 | 4 | 3 | 4 | 4 | 4 | 4 |
| Trevor Hoffman | 0 | 1 | 10.00 | 2 | 0 | 0 | 2 | 3 | 2 | 2 | 1 | 2 |
| Doug Bochtler | 0 | 1 | 27.00 | 1 | 0 | 0 | 0 | 1 | 1 | 2 | 0 | 0 |
| **Totals** | 0 | 3 | 5.40 | 3 | 3 | 0 | 25 | 24 | 15 | 15 | 13 | 23 |

### ST. LOUIS

| Player Pos. | AVG | G | AB | R | H | 2B | 3B | HR | RBI | BB | SO | SB |
|---|---|---|---|---|---|---|---|---|---|---|---|---|
| Mark Sweeney, ph | 1.000 | 1 | 1 | 0 | 1 | 0 | 0 | 0 | 0 | 0 | 0 | 0 |
| Ray Lankford, cf | .500 | 1 | 2 | 1 | 1 | 0 | 0 | 0 | 0 | 1 | 0 | 0 |
| Andy Benes, p | .500 | 1 | 2 | 1 | 1 | 0 | 0 | 0 | 0 | 0 | 1 | 0 |
| Ron Gant, lf | .400 | 3 | 10 | 3 | 4 | 1 | 0 | 1 | 4 | 2 | 0 | 2 |
| Brian Jordan, rf | .333 | 3 | 12 | 4 | 4 | 0 | 0 | 1 | 3 | 1 | 3 | 1 |
| Royce Clayton, ss | .333 | 2 | 6 | 1 | 2 | 0 | 0 | 0 | 0 | 3 | 1 | 0 |
| Ozzie Smith, ss | .333 | 2 | 3 | 1 | 1 | 0 | 0 | 0 | 0 | 2 | 0 | 0 |
| John Mabry, 1b | .300 | 3 | 10 | 1 | 3 | 0 | 1 | 0 | 1 | 1 | 1 | 0 |
| Tom Pagnozzi, c | .273 | 3 | 11 | 0 | 3 | 0 | 0 | 0 | 2 | 1 | 3 | 0 |
| Luis Alicea, 2b | .182 | 3 | 11 | 1 | 2 | 2 | 0 | 0 | 1 | 4 | 0 | 0 |
| Willie McGee, cf | .091 | 3 | 10 | 1 | 1 | 0 | 0 | 0 | 1 | 1 | 3 | 0 |
| Gary Gaetti, 3b | .091 | 3 | 11 | 1 | 1 | 0 | 0 | 0 | 1 | 3 | 0 | 0 |
| Rick Honeycutt, p | .000 | 3 | 1 | 0 | 0 | 0 | 0 | 0 | 0 | 0 | 1 | 0 |
| Mike Gallego, 2b | .000 | 2 | 1 | 0 | 0 | 0 | 0 | 0 | 0 | 0 | 1 | 0 |
| Donovan Osborne, p | .000 | 1 | 0 | 0 | 0 | 0 | 0 | 0 | 0 | 0 | 0 | 0 |
| Todd Stottlmyre, p | .000 | 1 | 2 | 0 | 0 | 0 | 0 | 0 | 0 | 0 | 1 | 0 |
| **Totals** | .255 | 3 | 94 | 15 | 24 | 3 | 1 | 3 | 14 | 13 | 23 | 3 |

| Pitcher | W | L | ERA | G | GS | SV | IP | H | R | ER | BB | SO |
|---|---|---|---|---|---|---|---|---|---|---|---|---|
| Dennis Eckersley | 0 | 0 | 0.00 | 3 | 0 | 3 | 4 | 3 | 0 | 0 | 0 | 2 |
| Mark Petkovsek | 0 | 0 | 0.00 | 1 | 0 | 0 | 2 | 0 | 0 | 0 | 0 | 1 |
| T.J. Mathews | 1 | 0 | 0.00 | 1 | 0 | 0 | 1 | 1 | 0 | 0 | 0 | 2 |
| Todd Stottlmyre | 1 | 0 | 1.35 | 1 | 1 | 0 | 7 | 5 | 1 | 1 | 2 | 7 |
| Rick Honeycutt | 1 | 0 | 3.38 | 3 | 0 | 0 | 3 | 3 | 1 | 1 | 1 | 2 |
| Andy Benes | 0 | 0 | 5.14 | 1 | 1 | 0 | 7 | 6 | 4 | 4 | 1 | 9 |
| Donovan Osborne | 0 | 0 | 9.00 | 1 | 1 | 0 | 4 | 7 | 4 | 4 | 0 | 5 |
| **Totals** | 3 | 0 | 3.33 | 3 | 3 | 3 | 27 | 25 | 10 | 10 | 4 | 28 |

**DP**—San Diego 4. **LOB**—San Diego 21, St. Louis 20.
**E**—Caminiti 3, Alicea, McGee. **CS**—Alicea 2, Clayton. **S**—Andy Benes, T. Gwynn, Mabry, Ashby.
**HBP**—Gant (by Hamilton), Finley (by Stottlmyre). **Umpires**—Greg Bonin, Gerry Davis, Dana DeMuth, Bruce Froemming, Eric Gregg, Tom Hallion, Bill Hohn, Frank Pulli, Jim Quick, Steve Rippley, Terry Tata, Harry Wendelstedt.

## CHAMPIONSHIP SERIES

### ATLANTA vs. ST. LOUIS

## BOX SCORES

### Game One: October 9
### Braves 4, Cardinals 2

| ST. LOUIS | ab | r | h | bi | bb | so | ATLANTA | ab | r | h | bi | bb | so |
|---|---|---|---|---|---|---|---|---|---|---|---|---|---|
| Smith ss | 4 | 0 | 0 | 0 | 0 | 0 | Grissom cf | 4 | 1 | 1 | 0 | 0 | 2 |
| Lankford cf | 4 | 0 | 0 | 0 | 0 | 1 | Lemke 2b | 3 | 0 | 1 | 2 | 1 | 0 |
| Gant lf | 4 | 0 | 0 | 0 | 0 | 1 | A. Jones pr-lf | 0 | 1 | 0 | 0 | 0 | 0 |
| Jordan rf | 4 | 1 | 1 | 0 | 0 | 1 | C. Jones 3b | 4 | 1 | 4 | 0 | 0 | 0 |
| Gaetti 3b | 3 | 0 | 1 | 0 | 0 | 1 | McGriff 1b | 4 | 0 | 0 | 0 | 0 | 1 |
| Mejia pr | 0 | 1 | 0 | 0 | 0 | 0 | Klesko lf | 3 | 0 | 1 | 0 | 0 | 1 |

| St. Louis | ab | r | h | bi | bb | so | Atlanta | ab | r | h | bi | bb | so |
|---|---|---|---|---|---|---|---|---|---|---|---|---|---|
| Gallego 3b | 0 | 0 | 0 | 0 | 0 | 0 | Pendleton ph | 0 | 0 | 0 | 0 | 1 | 0 |
| Sweeney ph | 1 | 0 | 0 | 0 | 0 | 1 | Belliard 2b | 0 | 0 | 0 | 0 | 0 | 0 |
| Mabry 1b | 4 | 0 | 1 | 0 | 0 | 1 | Lopez c | 4 | 0 | 1 | 2 | 0 | 0 |
| Pagnozzi c | 4 | 0 | 1 | 1 | 0 | 1 | Dye rf | 4 | 0 | 0 | 0 | 0 | 0 |
| Alicea 2b | 2 | 0 | 0 | 0 | 1 | 0 | Blauser ss | 4 | 1 | 1 | 0 | 0 | 2 |
| An. Benes p | 1 | 0 | 1 | 0 | 1 | 0 | Smoltz p | 3 | 0 | 0 | 0 | 0 | 3 |
| McGee ph | 1 | 0 | 0 | 0 | 0 | 0 | Wohlers p | 0 | 0 | 0 | 0 | 0 | 0 |
| Petkovsek p | 0 | 0 | 0 | 0 | 0 | 0 | | | | | | | |
| Fossas p | 0 | 0 | 0 | 0 | 0 | 0 | | | | | | | |
| Mathews p | 0 | 0 | 0 | 0 | 0 | 0 | | | | | | | |
| **Totals** | **32** | **2** | **5** | **1** | **2** | **7** | **Totals** | **33** | **4** | **9** | **4** | **2** | **11** |

**St. Louis** 010 000 100—2
**Atlanta** 000 020 02x—4

E—Alicea (1). LOB—St. Louis 5, Atlanta 7. 2B—An. Benes (1), Grissom (1). 3B—Jordan (1). SB—C. Jones (1).

| St. Louis | ip | h | r | er | bb | so | Atlanta | ip | h | r | er | bb | so |
|---|---|---|---|---|---|---|---|---|---|---|---|---|---|
| An. Benes | 6 | 7 | 2 | 2 | 0 | 7 | Smoltz W | 8 | 5 | 2 | 2 | 2 | 6 |
| Petkovsek L | 1 | 1 | 2 | 2 | 1 | 2 | Wohlers S | 1 | 0 | 0 | 0 | 0 | 1 |
| Fossas | ⅓ | 0 | 0 | 0 | 0 | 0 | | | | | | | |
| Mathews | ⅔ | 1 | 0 | 0 | 1 | 2 | | | | | | | |

Petkovsek pitched to two batters in 8th.
WP: Smoltz 2.
Umpires: HP—Runge; 1B—Hirschbeck; 2B—Davidson; 3B—West; LF—Crawford; RF—Montague.
T—2:35. A—48,686.

### Game Two: October 10
### Cardinals 8, Braves 3

| ST. LOUIS | ab | r | h | bi | bb | so | ATLANTA | ab | r | h | bi | bb | so |
|---|---|---|---|---|---|---|---|---|---|---|---|---|---|
| Clayton ss | 4 | 2 | 2 | 0 | 1 | 1 | Grissom cf | 5 | 2 | 2 | 2 | 0 | 0 |
| Lankford cf | 3 | 1 | 0 | 1 | 1 | 1 | Lemke 2b | 3 | 0 | 1 | 0 | 1 | 1 |
| Gant lf | 5 | 1 | 3 | 1 | 0 | 2 | C. Jones 3b | 4 | 0 | 0 | 0 | 0 | 0 |
| Jordan rf | 4 | 1 | 2 | 1 | 0 | 1 | Avery p | 0 | 0 | 0 | 0 | 0 | 0 |
| Gaetti 3b | 5 | 1 | 1 | 4 | 0 | 1 | McGriff 1b | 3 | 0 | 0 | 0 | 1 | 1 |
| Mabry 1b | 4 | 0 | 1 | 0 | 0 | 0 | Klesko lf | 4 | 0 | 1 | 1 | 0 | 1 |
| Pagnozzi c | 4 | 0 | 1 | 0 | 0 | 1 | Dye rf | 4 | 0 | 0 | 0 | 0 | 1 |
| Gallego 2b | 4 | 1 | 1 | 0 | 0 | 1 | Perez c | 1 | 0 | 0 | 0 | 1 | 0 |
| Stottlemyre p | 2 | 0 | 0 | 0 | 0 | 0 | Pendleton ph | 1 | 0 | 0 | 0 | 0 | 0 |
| Sweeney ph | 0 | 1 | 0 | 0 | 0 | 0 | Lopez c | 1 | 0 | 1 | 0 | 0 | 0 |
| Petkovsek p | 0 | 0 | 0 | 0 | 0 | 0 | Blauser ss | 4 | 1 | 0 | 0 | 0 | 0 |
| Young p | 1 | 0 | 0 | 0 | 0 | 0 | Maddux p | 2 | 0 | 0 | 0 | 0 | 2 |
| Honeycutt p | 0 | 0 | 0 | 0 | 0 | 0 | McMichael p | 0 | 0 | 0 | 0 | 0 | 0 |
| Eckersley p | 0 | 0 | 0 | 0 | 0 | 0 | Polonia ph | 1 | 0 | 0 | 0 | 0 | 0 |
| | | | | | | | Neagle p | 0 | 0 | 0 | 0 | 0 | 0 |
| | | | | | | | Mordecai 3b | 1 | 0 | 0 | 0 | 0 | 1 |
| **Totals** | **36** | **8** | **11** | **7** | **3** | **7** | **Totals** | **34** | **3** | **5** | **3** | **3** | **10** |

**St. Louis** 102 000 500—8
**Atlanta** 002 001 000—3

E—Grissom (1), C. Jones (1), Clayton (1), Gallego (1). DP—Atlanta 1. LOB—St. Louis 6, Atlanta 7. 2B—Gant (1), Jordan (1), Pagnozzi (1). HR—Gaetti (1), Grissom (1). SB—Clayton (1), Grissom (1). S—Sweeney. SF—Lankford.

| St. Louis | ip | h | r | er | bb | so | Atlanta | ip | h | r | er | bb | so |
|---|---|---|---|---|---|---|---|---|---|---|---|---|---|
| Stottlemyre W | 6 | 4 | 3 | 3 | 3 | 8 | Maddux L | 6⅔ | 9 | 8 | 3 | 2 | 3 |
| Petkovsek | 1 | 0 | 0 | 0 | 0 | 0 | McMichael | ⅓ | 1 | 0 | 0 | 0 | 1 |
| Honeycutt | ⅔ | 0 | 0 | 0 | 0 | 1 | Neagle | 1 | 0 | 0 | 0 | 0 | 2 |
| Eckersley | 1⅓ | 1 | 0 | 0 | 0 | 1 | Avery | 1 | 1 | 0 | 0 | 1 | 1 |

WP—Maddux.
Umpires: HP—Hirschbeck; 1B—Davidson; 2B—West; 3B—Crawford; LF—Montague; RF—Runge.
T—2:53. A—52,067.

### Game Three: October 12
### Cardinals 3, Braves 2

| ATLANTA | ab | r | h | bi | bb | so | ST. LOUIS | ab | r | h | bi | bb | so |
|---|---|---|---|---|---|---|---|---|---|---|---|---|---|
| Grissom cf | 5 | 1 | 2 | 0 | 0 | 2 | Clayton ss | 4 | 1 | 2 | 0 | 0 | 0 |
| Lemke 2b | 4 | 0 | 1 | 0 | 1 | 0 | Lankford cf | 4 | 0 | 0 | 0 | 0 | 1 |
| C. Jones 3b | 3 | 1 | 1 | 1 | 0 | 0 | Honeycutt p | 0 | 0 | 0 | 0 | 0 | 0 |
| McGriff 1b | 3 | 0 | 1 | 0 | 1 | 1 | Eckersley p | 0 | 0 | 0 | 0 | 0 | 0 |
| Lopez c | 4 | 0 | 3 | 0 | 0 | 0 | Gant lf | 4 | 2 | 2 | 3 | 0 | 1 |
| Dye rf | 3 | 0 | 0 | 1 | 0 | 0 | Jordan rf | 4 | 0 | 0 | 0 | 0 | 1 |
| A. Jones rf | 2 | 0 | 0 | 0 | 1 | 1 | Gaetti 3b | 3 | 0 | 2 | 0 | 0 | 1 |
| Pendleton ph | 1 | 0 | 0 | 0 | 0 | 0 | Mabry 1b | 2 | 0 | 1 | 0 | 0 | 0 |
| McMichael p | 0 | 0 | 0 | 0 | 0 | 0 | Pagnozzi c | 3 | 0 | 0 | 0 | 0 | 0 |
| Blauser ss | 4 | 0 | 0 | 0 | 0 | 2 | Gallego 2b | 3 | 0 | 0 | 0 | 0 | 0 |
| Glavine p | 2 | 0 | 0 | 0 | 0 | 1 | Osborne p | 3 | 0 | 0 | 0 | 0 | 3 |
| Mordecai ph | 1 | 0 | 0 | 0 | 0 | 0 | Petkovsek p | 0 | 0 | 0 | 0 | 0 | 0 |
| Bielecki p | 0 | 0 | 0 | 0 | 0 | 0 | McGee cf | 0 | 0 | 0 | 0 | 0 | 0 |
| Klesko lf | 1 | 0 | 0 | 0 | 0 | 0 | | | | | | | |
| **Totals** | **33** | **2** | **8** | **2** | **3** | **8** | **Totals** | **30** | **3** | **7** | **3** | **0** | **8** |

**Atlanta** 100 000 010—2
**St. Louis** 200 001 00x—3

E—Blauser (1). DP—Atlanta 1. LOB—Atlanta 9, St. Louis 4. 2B—Lopez (1). HR—Gant 2 (2). SF—Dye, C. Jones.

| Atlanta | ip | h | r | er | bb | so | St. Louis | ip | h | r | er | bb | so |
|---|---|---|---|---|---|---|---|---|---|---|---|---|---|
| Glavine L | 6 | 7 | 3 | 3 | 0 | 5 | Osborne W | 7 | 7 | 2 | 2 | 3 | 6 |
| Bielecki | 1 | 0 | 0 | 0 | 0 | 1 | Petkovsek | 1 | 1 | 0 | 0 | 0 | 1 |
| McMichael | 1 | 0 | 0 | 0 | 0 | 2 | Honeycutt | ⅓ | 0 | 0 | 0 | 0 | 0 |
| | | | | | | | Eckersley S | ⅔ | 0 | 0 | 0 | 0 | 1 |

Osborne pitched to two batters in 8th.
HBP—Mabry (by Glavine). WP—Osborne.
Umpires: HP—Davidson; 1B—West; 2B—Crawford; 3B—Montague; LF—Runge; RF—Hirschbeck.
T—2:46. A—56,769.

### Game Four: October 13
### Cardinals 4, Braves 3

| ATLANTA | ab | r | h | bi | bb | so | ST. LOUIS | ab | r | h | bi | bb | so |
|---|---|---|---|---|---|---|---|---|---|---|---|---|---|
| Grissom cf | 5 | 0 | 0 | 0 | 0 | 1 | Clayton ss | 4 | 0 | 1 | 1 | 0 | 2 |
| Lemke 2b | 4 | 1 | 1 | 0 | 0 | 0 | McGee cf | 4 | 0 | 1 | 0 | 0 | 0 |
| C.Jones 3b | 3 | 1 | 2 | 0 | 1 | 0 | Gant lf | 2 | 0 | 0 | 0 | 2 | 0 |
| McGriff 1b | 3 | 0 | 0 | 0 | 1 | 0 | Jordan rf | 4 | 1 | 1 | 1 | 0 | 0 |
| Klesko lf | 3 | 1 | 1 | 1 | 1 | 0 | Gaetti 3b | 4 | 0 | 0 | 0 | 0 | 2 |
| Lopez c | 3 | 0 | 0 | 0 | 1 | 0 | Mabry 1b | 4 | 1 | 1 | 0 | 0 | 1 |
| Wohlers p | 0 | 0 | 0 | 0 | 0 | 0 | Pagnozzi c | 2 | 1 | 0 | 0 | 1 | 1 |
| Dye rf | 4 | 0 | 3 | 1 | 0 | 0 | Gallego 2b | 2 | 0 | 0 | 0 | 0 | 1 |
| Blauser ss | 3 | 0 | 1 | 0 | 0 | 1 | Young ph | 1 | 1 | 1 | 2 | 0 | 0 |
| Polonia ph | 1 | 0 | 0 | 0 | 0 | 0 | Honeycutt p | 0 | 0 | 0 | 0 | 0 | 0 |
| Neagle p | 2 | 0 | 1 | 0 | 0 | 0 | Eckersley p | 0 | 0 | 0 | 0 | 0 | 0 |
| McMichael p | 0 | 0 | 0 | 0 | 0 | 0 | An. Benes p | 2 | 0 | 0 | 0 | 0 | 1 |
| Perez c | 0 | 0 | 0 | 0 | 0 | 0 | Fossas p | 0 | 0 | 0 | 0 | 0 | 0 |
| Pendleton ph | 1 | 0 | 0 | 0 | 0 | 1 | Mathews p | 0 | 0 | 0 | 0 | 0 | 0 |
| | | | | | | | Al. Benes p | 0 | 0 | 0 | 0 | 0 | 0 |
| | | | | | | | Alicea ph-2b | 0 | 0 | 0 | 0 | 1 | 0 |
| **Totals** | **32** | **3** | **9** | **3** | **4** | **3** | **Totals** | **29** | **4** | **5** | **4** | **4** | **8** |

**Atlanta** 010 002 000—3
**St. Louis** 000 000 31x—4

E—McGriff (1). DP—Atlanta 1, St. Louis 2. LOB—Atlanta 7, St. Louis 5. 2B—C. Jones (1), Dye (1). 3B—Young (1). HR—Jordan (1), Lemke (1), Klesko (1). CS—Dye. S—Neagle.

| Atlanta | ip | h | r | er | bb | so | St. Louis | ip | h | r | er | bb | so |
|---|---|---|---|---|---|---|---|---|---|---|---|---|---|
| Neagle | 6⅔ | 2 | 2 | 2 | 3 | 6 | An. Benes | 5 | 7 | 3 | 3 | 1 | 0 |
| McMichael L | ⅔ | 3 | 2 | 2 | 1 | 0 | Fossas | ⅔ | 0 | 0 | 0 | 2 | 0 |
| Wohlers | ⅔ | 0 | 0 | 0 | 0 | 2 | Mathews | | 0 | 1 | 0 | 0 | 0 |
| | | | | | | | Al. Benes | 1⅓ | 0 | 0 | 0 | 0 | 1 |
| | | | | | | | Honeycutt | ⅔ | 0 | 0 | 0 | 1 | 0 |
| | | | | | | | Eckersley W | 1⅓ | 1 | 0 | 0 | 0 | 2 |

An. Benes pitched to two batters in 6th. Mathews pitched to one batter in 6th.
Umpires: HP—West; 1B—Crawford; 2B—Montague; 3B—Runge; LF—Hirschbeck; RF—Davidson.
T—3:17. A—56,764.

### Game Five: October 14
### Braves 14, Cardinals 0

| ATLANTA | ab | r | h | bi | bb | so | ST. LOUIS | ab | r | h | bi | bb | so |
|---|---|---|---|---|---|---|---|---|---|---|---|---|---|
| Grissom cf | 6 | 2 | 3 | 1 | 0 | 0 | Smith ss | 4 | 0 | 0 | 0 | 0 | 1 |
| Lemke 2b | 5 | 2 | 4 | 1 | 0 | 0 | McGee cf | 3 | 0 | 1 | 0 | 0 | 2 |
| Mordecai 2b | 1 | 1 | 1 | 0 | 0 | 0 | Mejia cf | 1 | 0 | 0 | 0 | 0 | 0 |
| C. Jones 3b | 3 | 1 | 2 | 3 | 1 | 0 | Gant lf | 3 | 0 | 1 | 0 | 0 | 0 |
| Pendleton ph-3b | 2 | 0 | 0 | 0 | 0 | 1 | Gallego 3b | 0 | 0 | 0 | 0 | 1 | 0 |
| McGriff 1b | 6 | 1 | 2 | 3 | 0 | 1 | Jordan rf | 2 | 0 | 1 | 0 | 0 | 0 |
| Klesko lf | 4 | 0 | 1 | 1 | 0 | 3 | Fossas p | 0 | 0 | 0 | 0 | 0 | 0 |
| A. Jones ph-lf | 1 | 0 | 0 | 0 | 1 | 0 | Young ph-1b | 2 | 0 | 1 | 0 | 0 | 1 |
| Lopez c | 5 | 4 | 4 | 1 | 0 | 0 | Gaetti 3b | 2 | 0 | 2 | 0 | 1 | 0 |
| Wade p | 0 | 0 | 0 | 0 | 0 | 0 | Petkovsek p | 0 | 0 | 0 | 0 | 0 | 0 |
| Clontz p | 0 | 0 | 0 | 0 | 0 | 0 | Lankford ph | 1 | 0 | 0 | 0 | 0 | 1 |
| Dye rf | 6 | 1 | 1 | 0 | 0 | 2 | Honeycutt p | 0 | 0 | 0 | 0 | 0 | 0 |
| Blauser ss | 2 | 1 | 1 | 2 | 2 | 0 | Mabry 1b-rf | 4 | 0 | 1 | 0 | 0 | 0 |
| Belliard pr-ss | 1 | 0 | 1 | 1 | 0 | 0 | Pagnozzi c | 1 | 0 | 0 | 0 | 0 | 0 |
| Smoltz p | 4 | 1 | 2 | 1 | 0 | 0 | Sheaffer ph-c | 3 | 0 | 0 | 0 | 0 | 1 |
| Polonia ph | 1 | 0 | 0 | 0 | 0 | 0 | Alicea 2b | 4 | 0 | 0 | 0 | 0 | 1 |
| Bielecki p | 0 | 0 | 0 | 0 | 0 | 0 | Stottlemyre p | 0 | 0 | 0 | 0 | 0 | 0 |
| Perez c | 0 | 0 | 0 | 0 | 0 | 0 | Jackson p | 1 | 0 | 0 | 0 | 0 | 1 |
| | | | | | | | Sweeney rf-lf | 2 | 0 | 0 | 0 | 0 | 1 |
| **Totals** | **47** | **14** | **22** | **14** | **5** | **7** | **Totals** | **26** | **0** | **7** | **0** | **2** | **9** |

**Atlanta** 520 310 012—14
**St. Louis** 000 000 000— 0

DP—Atlanta 1, St. Louis 2. LOB—Atlanta 11, St. Louis 8. 2B—C. Jones (2), Lemke (1), Lopez 2 (3). 3B—Blauser (1). HR—McGriff (1), Lopez (1). SB—Grissom (2).

| Atlanta | ip | h | r | er | bb | so | St. Louis | ip | h | r | er | bb | so |
|---|---|---|---|---|---|---|---|---|---|---|---|---|---|
| Smoltz W | 7 | 7 | 0 | 0 | 1 | 6 | Stottlemyre L | 1 | 9 | 7 | 7 | 0 | 1 |
| Bielecki | 1 | 0 | 0 | 0 | 1 | 2 | Jackson | 3 | 7 | 3 | 3 | 3 | 3 |

| | | | | | | | | | | | | |
|---|---|---|---|---|---|---|---|---|---|---|---|---|
| Wade | ⅓ | 0 | 0 | 0 | 0 | 1 | Fossas | 2 | 1 | 1 | 1 | 1 | 1 |
| Clontz | ⅔ | 0 | 0 | 0 | 0 | 0 | Petkovsek | 2 | 2 | 1 | 1 | 0 | 1 |
| | | | | | | | Honeycutt | 1 | 3 | 2 | 2 | 1 | 1 |

Stottlemyre pitched to three batters in 2nd.

**Umpires: HP**—Crawford; **1B**—Montague; **2B**—Runge; **3B**—Hirschbeck; **LF**—Davidson; **RF**—West.

**T**—2:57. **A**—56, 782.

### Game Six: October 16
### Braves 3, Cardinals 1

| ST. LOUIS | ab | r | h | bi | bb | so | ATLANTA | ab | r | h | bi | bb | so |
|---|---|---|---|---|---|---|---|---|---|---|---|---|---|
| Clayton ss | 4 | 1 | 1 | 0 | 0 | 1 | Grissom cf | 4 | 0 | 0 | 0 | 0 | 3 |
| McGee rf | 4 | 0 | 2 | 0 | 0 | 0 | Lemke 2b | 4 | 0 | 2 | 1 | 0 | 0 |
| Gant lf | 4 | 0 | 0 | 0 | 0 | 2 | C. Jones 3b | 4 | 0 | 0 | 0 | 0 | 0 |
| Jordan cf | 4 | 0 | 1 | 0 | 0 | 1 | McGriff 1b | 4 | 1 | 1 | 0 | 0 | 1 |
| Gaetti 3b | 4 | 0 | 1 | 0 | 0 | 0 | Klesko lf | 1 | 0 | 0 | 0 | 1 | 1 |
| Mabry 1b | 4 | 0 | 1 | 0 | 0 | 2 | A. Jones ph-lf | 2 | 0 | 0 | 0 | 0 | 1 |
| Pagnozzi c | 3 | 0 | 0 | 0 | 0 | 0 | Lopez c | 3 | 1 | 2 | 0 | 0 | 1 |
| Gallego 2b | 2 | 0 | 0 | 0 | 0 | 0 | Dye rf | 2 | 0 | 1 | 1 | 1 | 0 |
| Sweeney ph | 1 | 0 | 0 | 0 | 0 | 0 | Blauser ss | 0 | 1 | 0 | 0 | 2 | 0 |
| Stottlemyre p | 0 | 0 | 0 | 0 | 0 | 0 | Belliard ss | 1 | 0 | 1 | 1 | 0 | 0 |
| Al. Benes p | 1 | 0 | 0 | 0 | 0 | 1 | Maddux p | 2 | 0 | 0 | 0 | 0 | 0 |
| Lankford ph | 1 | 0 | 0 | 0 | 0 | 0 | Wohlers p | 1 | 0 | 0 | 0 | 0 | 1 |
| Fossas p | 0 | 0 | 0 | 0 | 0 | 0 | | | | | | | |
| Petkovsek p | 0 | 0 | 0 | 0 | 0 | 0 | | | | | | | |
| Alicea ph-2b | 1 | 0 | 0 | 0 | 0 | 1 | | | | | | | |
| **Totals** | **33** | **1** | **6** | **0** | **0** | **8** | **Totals** | **28** | **3** | **7** | **3** | **4** | **8** |

| | |
|---|---|
| **St. Louis** | **000 000 010—1** |
| **Atlanta** | **010 010 01x—3** |

**E**—Petkovsek (1). **DP**—St. Louis 1. **LOB**—St. Louis 5, Atlanta 9. **2B**—Lopez (4). **SB**—Lopez (1). **S**—Maddux. **SF**—Dye.

| St. Louis | ip | h | r | er | bb | so | Atlanta | ip | h | r | er | bb | so |
|---|---|---|---|---|---|---|---|---|---|---|---|---|---|
| Al. Benes L | 5 | 3 | 2 | 2 | 2 | 4 | Maddux W | 7⅔ | 6 | 1 | 1 | 0 | 7 |
| Fossas | ⅓ | 0 | 0 | 0 | 0 | 0 | Wohlers | 1⅓ | 0 | 0 | 0 | 0 | 1 |
| Petkovsek | 1⅔ | 2 | 0 | 0 | 2 | 2 | | | | | | | |
| Stottlemyre | 1 | 2 | 1 | 1 | 0 | 2 | | | | | | | |

**HBP**—Lopez (by Stottlemyre), Blauser (by Al. Benes). **WP**—Petkovsek, Wohlers.

**Umpires: HP**—Montague; **1B**—Runge; **2B**—M. Hirschbeck; **3B**—Davidson; **LF**—West; **RF**—Crawford.

**T**—2:41. **A**—52,067.

### Game Seven: October 17
### Braves 15, Cardinals 0

| ST. LOUIS | ab | r | h | bi | bb | so | ATLANTA | ab | r | h | bi | bb | so |
|---|---|---|---|---|---|---|---|---|---|---|---|---|---|
| Clayton ss | 4 | 0 | 1 | 0 | 0 | 0 | Grissom cf | 6 | 1 | 2 | 0 | 0 | 0 |
| McGee rf | 3 | 0 | 1 | 0 | 0 | 1 | Lemke 2b | 4 | 1 | 2 | 0 | 1 | 1 |
| Sweeney lf | 0 | 0 | 0 | 0 | 0 | 0 | Mordecai ph-2b | 1 | 0 | 0 | 0 | 0 | 0 |
| Gant lf | 3 | 0 | 0 | 0 | 0 | 0 | C. Jones 3b | 4 | 2 | 2 | 0 | 1 | 0 |
| Sheaffer c | 0 | 0 | 0 | 0 | 0 | 0 | Perez 1b | 0 | 0 | 0 | 0 | 0 | 0 |
| Jordan cf | 3 | 0 | 0 | 0 | 0 | 0 | McGriff 1b | 5 | 4 | 3 | 4 | 0 | 0 |
| Mejia cf | 0 | 0 | 0 | 0 | 0 | 0 | Bielecki p | 0 | 0 | 0 | 0 | 0 | 0 |
| Gaetti 3b | 3 | 0 | 0 | 0 | 0 | 0 | Avery p | 0 | 0 | 0 | 0 | 0 | 0 |
| Young 1b | 3 | 0 | 0 | 0 | 0 | 2 | Lopez c | 4 | 3 | 2 | 3 | 1 | 0 |
| Pagnozzi c | 2 | 0 | 1 | 0 | 0 | 0 | Dye rf | 5 | 1 | 1 | 1 | 0 | 1 |
| Mabry rf | 1 | 0 | 0 | 0 | 0 | 1 | A. Jones lf | 4 | 2 | 2 | 3 | 1 | 0 |
| Gallego 2b | 3 | 0 | 1 | 0 | 0 | 1 | Blauser ss | 0 | 1 | 0 | 0 | 0 | 0 |
| Osborne p | 0 | 0 | 0 | 0 | 0 | 0 | Belliard ss | 4 | 0 | 2 | 0 | 0 | 0 |
| An. Benes p | 1 | 0 | 0 | 0 | 0 | 1 | Glavine p | 4 | 0 | 1 | 3 | 0 | 2 |
| Smith ph | 1 | 0 | 0 | 0 | 0 | 0 | Pendleton 3b | 1 | 0 | 0 | 0 | 0 | 0 |
| Petkovsek p | 0 | 0 | 0 | 0 | 0 | 0 | | | | | | | |
| Honeycutt p | 0 | 0 | 0 | 0 | 0 | 0 | | | | | | | |
| Fossas p | 0 | 0 | 0 | 0 | 0 | 0 | | | | | | | |
| Alicea ph | 1 | 0 | 0 | 0 | 0 | 0 | | | | | | | |
| **Totals** | **28** | **0** | **4** | **0** | **0** | **6** | **Totals** | **28** | **3** | **7** | **3** | **4** | **8** |

| | |
|---|---|
| **St. Louis** | **000 000 000— 0** |
| **Atlanta** | **600 403 20x—15** |

**E**—McGee (1), Clayton (2). **DP**—Atlanta 2. **LOB**—St. Louis 1, Atlanta 8. **2B**—Lopez (5), Lemke (2). **3B**—McGriff (1), Glavine (1). **HR**—McGriff (2), Lopez (2), A. Jones (1). **CS**—Clayton.

| St. Louis | ip | h | r | er | bb | so | Atlanta | ip | h | r | er | bb | so |
|---|---|---|---|---|---|---|---|---|---|---|---|---|---|
| Osborne L | ⅔ | 5 | 6 | 6 | 1 | 0 | Glavine W | 7 | 3 | 0 | 0 | 0 | 4 |
| An. Benes | 4⅓ | 5 | 4 | 4 | 2 | 2 | Bielecki | 1 | 0 | 0 | 0 | 0 | 2 |
| Petkovsek | ⅔ | 5 | 3 | 3 | 0 | 1 | Avery | 1 | 1 | 0 | 0 | 0 | 0 |
| Honeycutt | 1⅓ | 2 | 2 | 2 | 1 | 1 | | | | | | | |
| Fossas | 1 | 0 | 0 | 0 | 0 | 0 | | | | | | | |

**HBP**—Blauser (by Osborne).

**Umpires: HP**—Runge; **1B**—Hirschbeck; **2B**—Davidson; **3B**—West; **LF**—Crawford; **RF**—Montague.

**T**—2:25. **A**—52,067.

## COMPOSITE BOX

### ST. LOUIS

| Player, Pos. | AVG | G | AB | R | H | 2B | 3B | HR | RBI | BB | SO | SB |
|---|---|---|---|---|---|---|---|---|---|---|---|---|
| Royce Clayton, ss | .350 | 5 | 20 | 4 | 7 | 0 | 0 | 0 | 1 | 1 | 4 | 1 |
| Willie McGee, cf | .333 | 6 | 15 | 0 | 5 | 0 | 0 | 0 | 0 | 0 | 3 | 0 |
| Gary Gaetti, 3b | .292 | 7 | 24 | 1 | 7 | 0 | 0 | 1 | 4 | 1 | 5 | 0 |
| Dmitri Young, ph-1b | .286 | 4 | 7 | 1 | 2 | 0 | 1 | 0 | 2 | 0 | 2 | 0 |
| John Mabry, rf-1b | .261 | 7 | 23 | 1 | 6 | 0 | 0 | 0 | 0 | 0 | 6 | 0 |
| Andy Benes, p | .250 | 3 | 4 | 0 | 1 | 1 | 0 | 0 | 0 | 1 | 2 | 0 |
| Ron Gant, lf | .240 | 7 | 25 | 3 | 6 | 1 | 0 | 2 | 4 | 2 | 6 | 0 |
| Brian Jordan, rf-cf | .240 | 7 | 25 | 3 | 6 | 1 | 1 | 1 | 2 | 1 | 3 | 0 |
| Tom Pagnozzi, c | .158 | 7 | 19 | 1 | 3 | 1 | 0 | 0 | 1 | 1 | 4 | 0 |
| Mike Gallego, 2b-3b | .143 | 7 | 14 | 1 | 2 | 0 | 0 | 0 | 0 | 1 | 3 | 0 |
| Miguel Mejia, cf-pr | .000 | 3 | 1 | 1 | 0 | 0 | 0 | 0 | 0 | 0 | 1 | 0 |
| Alan Benes, p | .000 | 2 | 1 | 0 | 0 | 0 | 0 | 0 | 0 | 0 | 1 | 0 |
| Danny Jackson, p | .000 | 1 | 1 | 0 | 0 | 0 | 0 | 0 | 0 | 0 | 1 | 0 |
| Todd Stottlemyre, p | .000 | 2 | 2 | 0 | 0 | 0 | 0 | 0 | 0 | 0 | 0 | 0 |
| Donovan Osborne, p | .000 | 2 | 3 | 0 | 0 | 0 | 0 | 0 | 0 | 0 | 3 | 0 |
| Danny Sheaffer, c | .000 | 2 | 3 | 0 | 0 | 0 | 0 | 0 | 0 | 0 | 1 | 0 |
| Mark Sweeney, ph-rf | .000 | 5 | 4 | 1 | 0 | 0 | 0 | 0 | 0 | 0 | 2 | 0 |
| Luis Alicea, 2b | .000 | 5 | 8 | 0 | 0 | 0 | 0 | 0 | 0 | 2 | 1 | 0 |
| Ozzie Smith, ss | .000 | 3 | 9 | 0 | 0 | 0 | 0 | 0 | 0 | 0 | 1 | 0 |
| Ray Lankford, cf-ph | .000 | 5 | 13 | 1 | 0 | 0 | 0 | 0 | 1 | 1 | 4 | 0 |
| **Totals** | **.204** | **7** | **221** | **18** | **45** | **4** | **2** | **4** | **15** | **11** | **53** | **1** |

| Pitcher | W | L | ERA | G | GS | SV | IP | H | R | ER | BB | SO |
|---|---|---|---|---|---|---|---|---|---|---|---|---|
| Dennis Eckersley | 1 | 0 | 0.00 | 3 | 0 | 1 | 3 | 2 | 0 | 0 | 0 | 4 |
| T.J. Mathews | 0 | 0 | 0.00 | 2 | 0 | 0 | 1 | 2 | 0 | 0 | 1 | 2 |
| Tony Fossas | 0 | 0 | 2.08 | 5 | 0 | 0 | 4 | 1 | 1 | 1 | 3 | 1 |
| Alan Benes | 0 | 1 | 2.84 | 2 | 1 | 0 | 6 | 3 | 2 | 2 | 2 | 5 |
| Andy Benes | 0 | 0 | 5.28 | 3 | 2 | 0 | 15 | 19 | 9 | 9 | 3 | 9 |
| Mark Petkovsek | 0 | 1 | 7.36 | 6 | 0 | 0 | 7 | 11 | 6 | 6 | 3 | 7 |
| Rick Honeycutt | 0 | 0 | 9.00 | 5 | 0 | 0 | 4 | 5 | 4 | 4 | 3 | 3 |
| Danny Jackson | 0 | 0 | 9.00 | 1 | 0 | 0 | 3 | 7 | 3 | 3 | 3 | 3 |
| Donovan Osborne | 1 | 1 | 9.39 | 2 | 2 | 0 | 8 | 12 | 8 | 8 | 4 | 6 |
| Todd Stottlemyre | 1 | 1 | 12.38 | 3 | 2 | 0 | 8 | 15 | 11 | 11 | 3 | 11 |
| **Totals** | **3** | **4** | **6.60** | **7** | **7** | **1** | **60** | **77** | **44** | **44** | **25** | **51** |

### ATLANTA

| Player, Pos. | AVG | G | AB | R | H | 2B | 3B | HR | RBI | BB | SO | SB |
|---|---|---|---|---|---|---|---|---|---|---|---|---|
| Rafael Belliard, ss | .667 | 4 | 6 | 0 | 4 | 0 | 0 | 0 | 2 | 0 | 0 | 0 |
| Javier Lopez, c | .542 | 7 | 24 | 8 | 13 | 5 | 0 | 2 | 6 | 3 | 1 | 1 |
| Denny Neagle, p | .500 | 2 | 2 | 0 | 1 | 0 | 0 | 0 | 0 | 0 | 0 | 0 |
| Mark Lemke, 2b | .444 | 7 | 27 | 4 | 12 | 2 | 0 | 1 | 5 | 3 | 2 | 0 |
| Chipper Jones, 3b | .440 | 7 | 25 | 6 | 11 | 2 | 0 | 0 | 4 | 4 | 1 | 1 |
| Marquis Grissom, cf | .286 | 7 | 35 | 7 | 10 | 1 | 0 | 1 | 3 | 0 | 8 | 2 |
| John Smoltz, p | .286 | 2 | 7 | 1 | 2 | 0 | 0 | 0 | 1 | 0 | 3 | 0 |
| Ryan Klesko, lf | .250 | 6 | 16 | 1 | 4 | 0 | 0 | 1 | 3 | 2 | 6 | 0 |
| Mike Mordecai, ph-3b | .250 | 4 | 4 | 1 | 1 | 0 | 0 | 0 | 0 | 0 | 1 | 0 |
| Fred McGriff, 1b | .250 | 7 | 28 | 6 | 7 | 0 | 1 | 2 | 7 | 3 | 5 | 0 |
| Andruw Jones, lf | .222 | 5 | 9 | 3 | 2 | 0 | 0 | 1 | 3 | 3 | 2 | 0 |
| Jermaine Dye, rf | .214 | 7 | 28 | 2 | 6 | 1 | 0 | 0 | 4 | 1 | 7 | 0 |
| Jeff Blauser, ss | .176 | 7 | 17 | 5 | 3 | 0 | 1 | 0 | 2 | 4 | 6 | 0 |
| Tom Glavine, p | .167 | 2 | 6 | 0 | 1 | 0 | 1 | 0 | 3 | 0 | 3 | 0 |
| Eddie Perez, c-1b | .000 | 4 | 1 | 0 | 0 | 0 | 0 | 0 | 0 | 1 | 0 | 0 |
| Mark Wohlers, p | .000 | 3 | 1 | 0 | 0 | 0 | 0 | 0 | 0 | 0 | 1 | 0 |
| Luis Polonia, ph | .000 | 3 | 3 | 0 | 0 | 0 | 0 | 0 | 0 | 0 | 0 | 0 |
| Greg Maddux, p | .000 | 2 | 4 | 0 | 0 | 0 | 0 | 0 | 0 | 0 | 2 | 0 |
| Terry Pendleton, ph | .000 | 6 | 6 | 0 | 0 | 0 | 0 | 0 | 0 | 1 | 3 | 0 |
| **Totals** | **.309** | **7** | **249** | **44** | **77** | **11** | **3** | **8** | **43** | **25** | **51** | **4** |

| Pitcher | W | L | ERA | G | GS | SV | IP | H | R | ER | BB | SO |
|---|---|---|---|---|---|---|---|---|---|---|---|---|
| Mark Wohlers | 0 | 0 | 0.00 | 3 | 0 | 2 | 3 | 0 | 0 | 0 | 0 | 4 |
| Mike Bielecki | 0 | 0 | 0.00 | 3 | 0 | 0 | 3 | 0 | 0 | 0 | 1 | 5 |
| Steve Avery | 0 | 0 | 0.00 | 2 | 0 | 0 | 2 | 2 | 0 | 0 | 1 | 1 |
| Brad Clontz | 0 | 0 | 0.00 | 1 | 0 | 0 | 1 | 0 | 0 | 0 | 0 | 0 |
| Terrell Wade | 0 | 0 | 0.00 | 1 | 0 | 0 | 0 | 0 | 0 | 0 | 0 | 1 |
| John Smoltz | 2 | 0 | 1.20 | 2 | 2 | 0 | 15 | 12 | 2 | 2 | 3 | 12 |
| Tom Glavine | 1 | 1 | 2.08 | 2 | 2 | 0 | 13 | 10 | 3 | 3 | 0 | 9 |
| Denny Neagle | 0 | 0 | 2.35 | 2 | 1 | 0 | 8 | 2 | 2 | 2 | 3 | 8 |
| Greg Maddux | 1 | 1 | 2.51 | 2 | 2 | 0 | 14 | 15 | 9 | 4 | 2 | 10 |
| Greg McMichael | 0 | 1 | 9.00 | 3 | 0 | 0 | 2 | 4 | 2 | 2 | 1 | 3 |
| **Totals** | **4** | **3** | **1.92** | **7** | **7** | **2** | **61** | **45** | **18** | **13** | **11** | **53** |

| | |
|---|---|
| **St. Louis** | **312 001 920 —18** |
| **Atlanta** | **(12)42 746 252 —44** |

**DP**—St. Louis 5, Atlanta 6. **LOB**—St. Louis 34, Atlanta 58.

**E**—Clayton 2, Gallego, Petkovsek, McGee, Alicea, McGriff, Blauser, Grissom, C. Jones. **CS**—Dye. **S**—Sweeney, Neagle, Maddux. **SF**—Dye 2, C. Jones, Lankford.

**HBP**—Blauser 2 (by Osborne, Alan Benes), Lopez (by Stottlemyre), Mabry (by Glavine). **WP**—Smoltz 2, Maddux, Osborne.

**Umpires**—Gerry Crawford, Joe West, Paul Runge, Mark Hirschbeck, Bob Davidson, Ed Montague.

# ORGANIZATION STATISTICS

# ARIZONA
## DIAMONDBACKS

### FARM SYSTEM

**Director of Field Operations:** Tommy Jones

| Class | Farm Team | League | W | L | Pct. | Finish* | Manager | First Yr |
|---|---|---|---|---|---|---|---|---|
| #A | Visalia (Calif.) Oaks@ | California | 59 | 90 | .357 | 9th (10) | Tim Torricelli | 1996 |
| #R | Lethbridge (Alta.) Black Diamonds | Pioneer | 50 | 22 | .694 | 1st (8) | Chris Speier | 1996 |
| R | Phoenix Diamondbacks | Arizona | 20 | 36 | .357 | 6th (6) | Dwayne Murphy | 1996 |

*Finish in overall standings (No. of teams in league) #Advanced level @Shared club with Detroit Tigers

### BAKERSFIELD
Class A/Co-Op
#### CALIFORNIA LEAGUE

| BATTING | AVG | G | AB | R | H | 2B | 3B | HR | RBI | BB | SO | SB | CS | B | T | HT | WT | DOB | 1st Yr | Resides |
|---|---|---|---|---|---|---|---|---|---|---|---|---|---|---|---|---|---|---|---|---|
| Herider, Jeremy | .196 | 29 | 107 | 18 | 21 | 4 | 0 | 0 | 12 | 26 | 32 | 1 | 1 | S | R | 5-10 | 180 | 4-9-72 | 1995 | Lancaster, Calif. |
| 2-team (49 Visalia) | .218 | 78 | 252 | 40 | 55 | 10 | 0 | 1 | 26 | 59 | 68 | 3 | 7 | | | | | | | |
| Kinard, Kirk | .198 | 37 | 116 | 16 | 23 | 3 | 2 | 0 | 5 | 13 | 44 | 3 | 1 | R | R | 6-0 | 175 | 3-7-74 | 1996 | Pascagoula, Miss. |
| Kliner, Josh | .308 | 43 | 156 | 37 | 48 | 6 | 1 | 5 | 33 | 37 | 25 | 0 | 3 | S | R | 5-11 | 180 | 12-27-72 | 1996 | Placentia, Calif. |
| Stoner, Mike | .293 | 36 | 147 | 25 | 43 | 6 | 1 | 6 | 22 | 8 | 18 | 1 | 1 | R | R | 6-0 | 200 | 5-23-73 | 1996 | Simpsonville, Ky. |

**GAMES BY POSITION: 1B**—Kliner 3, Stoner 36. **2B**— Herider 1, Kinard 20, Kliner 24. **3B**— Herider 1, Kinard 2, Kliner 1. **SS**— Herider 24, Kinard 16. **OF**—Herider 4, Kliner 17, Stoner 1.

### VISALIA
Class A/Co-Op
#### CALIFORNIA LEAGUE

| BATTING | AVG | G | AB | R | H | 2B | 3B | HR | RBI | BB | SO | SB | CS | B | T | HT | WT | DOB | 1st Yr | Resides |
|---|---|---|---|---|---|---|---|---|---|---|---|---|---|---|---|---|---|---|---|---|
| Barajas, Rod | .162 | 27 | 74 | 6 | 12 | 3 | 0 | 0 | 8 | 7 | 21 | 0 | 0 | R | R | 6-2 | 220 | 9-5-75 | 1996 | Norwalk, Calif. |
| Brissey, Jason | .226 | 83 | 234 | 32 | 53 | 15 | 3 | 7 | 34 | 18 | 80 | 2 | 4 | R | R | 5-8 | 165 | 8-7-72 | 1994 | Huntington Beach, Calif. |
| Darnell, Bryce | .077 | 7 | 13 | 1 | 1 | 0 | 0 | 0 | 1 | 0 | 2 | 0 | 0 | L | R | 6-2 | 215 | 9-13-72 | 1996 | Brooklyn Center, Minn. |
| Durkac, Bo | .298 | 126 | 453 | 67 | 135 | 29 | 2 | 4 | 81 | 79 | 84 | 6 | 3 | S | R | 6-1 | 205 | 12-12-72 | 1995 | Kittanning, Pa. |
| Herider, Jeremy | .234 | 49 | 145 | 22 | 34 | 6 | 0 | 1 | 14 | 33 | 36 | 2 | 6 | S | R | 5-10 | 180 | 4-9-72 | 1995 | Lancaster, Calif. |
| Martinez, Tony | .193 | 31 | 83 | 7 | 16 | 6 | 0 | 0 | 11 | 7 | 20 | 0 | 0 | R | R | 6-2 | 185 | 11-27-73 | 1996 | Fullerton, Calif. |

**GAMES BY POSITION: C**—Barajas 17, Darnell 5. **1B**—Durkac 3, Herider 1, Martinez 23. **2B**—Brissey 3, Herider 17. **3B**—Durkac 122, Herider 5, Martinez 4. **SS**—Brissey 64, Herider 24. **OF**—Brissey 3.

| PITCHING | W | L | ERA | G | GS | CG | SV | IP | H | R | ER | BB | SO | B | T | HT | WT | DOB | 1st Yr | Resides |
|---|---|---|---|---|---|---|---|---|---|---|---|---|---|---|---|---|---|---|---|---|
| Duffy, Ryan | 0 | 0 | 1.17 | 15 | 0 | 0 | 0 | 15 | 6 | 3 | 2 | 6 | 9 | R | L | 6-3 | 185 | 6-1-73 | 1994 | Mooretown, Ontario |
| Gomez, Javier | 1 | 3 | 3.68 | 22 | 0 | 0 | 0 | 37 | 32 | 17 | 15 | 18 | 40 | R | R | 6-1 | 195 | 12-10-73 | 1995 | Miami, Fla. |
| Hernandez, Jeremy | 2 | 9 | 5.96 | 24 | 15 | 0 | 0 | 103 | 133 | 89 | 68 | 30 | 88 | R | R | 6-7 | 210 | 7-6-66 | 1987 | Yuma, Ariz. |
| Nunez, Vladimir | 1 | 6 | 5.43 | 12 | 10 | 0 | 0 | 53 | 64 | 45 | 32 | 17 | 37 | R | R | 6-5 | 240 | 3-15-75 | 1996 | Santo Domingo, D.R. |
| Rodriguez, Larry | 2 | 5 | 5.24 | 13 | 10 | 0 | 0 | 57 | 72 | 49 | 33 | 19 | 37 | R | R | 6-2 | 195 | 9-9-74 | 1996 | Santo Domingo, D.R. |
| Southall, Pete | 1 | 1 | 9.17 | 32 | 0 | 0 | 0 | 54 | 83 | 64 | 55 | 27 | 26 | R | R | 6-2 | 210 | 8-23-72 | 1995 | Gainesville, Fla. |

### LETHBRIDGE
Rookie
#### PIONEER LEAGUE

| BATTING | AVG | G | AB | R | H | 2B | 3B | HR | RBI | BB | SO | SB | CS | B | T | HT | WT | DOB | 1st Yr | Resides |
|---|---|---|---|---|---|---|---|---|---|---|---|---|---|---|---|---|---|---|---|---|
| Allison, Brad | .209 | 25 | 43 | 7 | 9 | 0 | 0 | 1 | 6 | 9 | 16 | 0 | 1 | R | R | 5-11 | 220 | 11-24-73 | 1996 | Cynthiana, Ky. |
| Baltzell, Beau | .135 | 19 | 37 | 1 | 5 | 2 | 0 | 0 | 5 | 4 | 9 | 0 | 0 | R | R | 5-11 | 215 | 8-2-73 | 1996 | Omaha, Neb. |
| Barajas, Rod | .337 | 51 | 175 | 47 | 59 | 9 | 3 | 10 | 50 | 12 | 24 | 2 | 1 | R | R | 6-2 | 220 | 9-5-75 | 1996 | Norwalk, Calif. |
| Boughton, Mike | .286 | 62 | 224 | 32 | 64 | 7 | 2 | 1 | 29 | 16 | 50 | 4 | 6 | S | R | 6-3 | 170 | 11-8-74 | 1996 | Lewisville, Texas |
| Conti, Jason | .367 | 63 | 226 | 63 | 83 | 15 | 1 | 4 | 49 | 30 | 29 | 30 | 7 | L | R | 5-11 | 175 | 1-27-75 | 1996 | Cranberry Township, Pa. |
| Davis, Reggie | .315 | 31 | 89 | 18 | 28 | 7 | 1 | 1 | 18 | 13 | 19 | 0 | 2 | R | R | 5-10 | 210 | 11-2-74 | 1996 | Winston, Ga. |
| Gann, Jamie | .287 | 49 | 129 | 19 | 37 | 10 | 1 | 2 | 22 | 10 | 42 | 3 | 3 | R | R | 6-1 | 185 | 5-1-75 | 1996 | Norman, Okla. |
| Glasser, Scott | .296 | 9 | 27 | 7 | 8 | 1 | 1 | 0 | 3 | 5 | 7 | 0 | 0 | R | R | 6-1 | 180 | 12-9-75 | 1996 | Huntington Beach, Calif. |
| Hardy, Brett | .367 | 30 | 90 | 28 | 33 | 3 | 0 | 1 | 15 | 22 | 14 | 2 | 0 | L | L | 6-0 | 180 | 12-22-73 | 1996 | Laguna Beach, Calif. |
| Hartman, Ron | .326 | 66 | 258 | 69 | 84 | 23 | 0 | 16 | 72 | 36 | 42 | 5 | 2 | R | R | 6-1 | 200 | 12-17-74 | 1996 | Baltimore, Md. |
| Hayman, David | .313 | 63 | 233 | 68 | 73 | 8 | 4 | 17 | 59 | 43 | 78 | 4 | 0 | R | R | 5-10 | 197 | 7-9-74 | 1996 | Terry, Miss. |
| Kinard, Kirk | .000 | 5 | 13 | 0 | 0 | 0 | 0 | 0 | 0 | 0 | 7 | 0 | 0 | R | R | 6-0 | 175 | 3-7-74 | 1996 | Pascagoula, Miss. |
| Kliner, Josh | .250 | 12 | 28 | 6 | 7 | 1 | 0 | 0 | 2 | 3 | 3 | 1 | 0 | S | R | 5-11 | 180 | 12-27-72 | 1996 | Placentia, Calif. |
| Moore, Jason | .245 | 47 | 151 | 34 | 37 | 6 | 0 | 8 | 35 | 27 | 61 | 1 | 3 | R | R | 6-3 | 240 | 7-16-75 | 1996 | Hurricane, W.Va. |
| Nunez, Jose | .311 | 40 | 122 | 43 | 38 | 5 | 2 | 3 | 24 | 24 | 25 | 5 | 0 | R | R | 5-9 | 180 | 3-4-76 | 1996 | Brooklyn, N.Y. |
| Rhea, Chip | .252 | 43 | 139 | 25 | 35 | 5 | 2 | 3 | 22 | 15 | 47 | 1 | 2 | S | R | 6-1 | 190 | 7-24-73 | 1996 | Johnson City, Tenn. |
| Ryan, Rob | .303 | 59 | 211 | 55 | 64 | 8 | 1 | 4 | 37 | 43 | 33 | 23 | 6 | L | L | 5-11 | 180 | 6-24-73 | 1996 | Spokane, Wash. |
| Spivey, Ernest | .336 | 31 | 107 | 30 | 36 | 3 | 4 | 2 | 25 | 23 | 24 | 8 | 3 | R | R | 6-0 | 185 | 1-28-75 | 1996 | Oklahoma City, Okla. |
| Stoner, Mike | .321 | 24 | 78 | 13 | 25 | 1 | 2 | 1 | 13 | 12 | 13 | 1 | 0 | R | R | 6-0 | 200 | 5-23-73 | 1996 | Simpsonville, Ky. |
| Sweeney, Kevin | .424 | 63 | 203 | 72 | 86 | 19 | 1 | 14 | 72 | 60 | 36 | 3 | 0 | L | L | 5-11 | 185 | 3-30-74 | 1996 | Cheektowaga, N.Y. |

**GAMES BY POSITION: C**—Allison 24, Baltzell 16, Barajas 42, Davis 21. **1B**—Barajas 3, Hardy 11, Hartman 1, Hayman 12, Kliner 1, Moore 42, Rhea 5, Stoner 11. **2B**—Glasser 1, Kliner 5, Nunez 21, Rhea 27, Spivey 30. **3B**—Conti 1, Glasser 4, Hartman 58, Kinard 1, Kliner 3, Nunez 11, Rhea 6. **SS**—Boughton 62, Glasser 1, Kinard 4, Nunez 7, Spivey 4. **OF**—Conti 56, Gann 45, Hardy 15, Hayman 34, Rhea 3, Ryan 56, Sweeney 51.

| PITCHING | W | L | ERA | G | GS | CG | SV | IP | H | R | ER | BB | SO | B | T | HT | WT | DOB | 1st Yr | Resides |
|---|---|---|---|---|---|---|---|---|---|---|---|---|---|---|---|---|---|---|---|---|
| Anderson, Dallas | 1 | 0 | 4.15 | 16 | 0 | 0 | 0 | 17 | 15 | 10 | 8 | 20 | 15 | R | R | 6-4 | 210 | 2-27-74 | 1996 | Taber, Alberta |
| Bice, Justin | 2 | 3 | 5.15 | 17 | 6 | 0 | 0 | 44 | 54 | 34 | 25 | 18 | 49 | R | R | 6-3 | 210 | 4-17-75 | 1996 | Mesa, Ariz. |
| Bierbrodt, Nick | 2 | 0 | 0.50 | 3 | 3 | 0 | 0 | 18 | 12 | 4 | 1 | 5 | 23 | L | L | 6-5 | 180 | 5-16-78 | 1996 | Long Beach, Calif. |
| Chavez, Mark | 1 | 2 | 3.60 | 24 | 0 | 0 | 4 | 30 | 35 | 20 | 12 | 4 | 26 | R | R | 5-11 | 185 | 5-1-73 | 1996 | Wilmington, Calif. |
| Crews, Jason | 1 | 1 | 2.50 | 25 | 1 | 0 | 5 | 40 | 30 | 12 | 11 | 15 | 37 | R | R | 6-2 | 200 | 8-28-73 | 1996 | Plantation, Fla. |
| Crossan, Clay | 4 | 1 | 4.73 | 19 | 4 | 0 | 0 | 40 | 55 | 29 | 21 | 18 | 27 | R | R | 6-1 | 175 | 8-30-73 | 1996 | Loomis, Calif. |
| Done, Johnny | 2 | 1 | 1.95 | 22 | 0 | 0 | 1 | 37 | 41 | 16 | 8 | 8 | 30 | R | R | 5-11 | 165 | 11-25-75 | 1993 | Santo Domingo, D.R. |
| Duffy, Ryan | 6 | 2 | 2.64 | 25 | 0 | 0 | 1 | 31 | 24 | 11 | 9 | 20 | 30 | R | L | 6-3 | 185 | 6-1-73 | 1994 | Mooretown, Ontario |
| Gomez, Javier | 3 | 2 | 4.50 | 19 | 0 | 0 | 1 | 42 | 41 | 25 | 21 | 17 | 35 | R | R | 6-1 | 195 | 12-10-73 | 1995 | Miami, Fla. |
| Norris, Ben | 0 | 0 | 6.35 | 3 | 3 | 0 | 0 | 11 | 14 | 9 | 8 | 5 | 12 | L | L | 6-3 | 185 | 12-6-77 | 1996 | Austin, Texas |
| Nunez, Vladimir | 10 | 0 | 2.22 | 14 | 13 | 0 | 0 | 85 | 78 | 25 | 21 | 10 | 93 | R | R | 6-5 | 240 | 3-15-75 | 1996 | Santo Domingo, D.R. |
| Oleksik, George | 6 | 1 | 6.58 | 14 | 14 | 0 | 0 | 67 | 82 | 53 | 49 | 36 | 30 | R | R | 6-4 | 205 | 4-19-74 | 1996 | McMinnville, Tenn. |
| Rodriguez, Larry | 7 | 1 | 3.83 | 10 | 10 | 1 | 0 | 54 | 56 | 31 | 23 | 9 | 46 | R | R | 6-2 | 195 | 9-9-74 | 1996 | Santo Domingo, D.R. |
| Sabel, Eric | 1 | 4 | 2.79 | 20 | 3 | 0 | 1 | 42 | 43 | 23 | 13 | 7 | 41 | R | R | 6-3 | 186 | 10-14-74 | 1996 | West Lafayette, Ind. |
| Samboy, Javier | 1 | 1 | 4.33 | 17 | 3 | 0 | 0 | 27 | 26 | 15 | 13 | 17 | 19 | L | L | 6-2 | 160 | 2-13-75 | 1992 | Santo Domingo, D.R. |
| Verplancke, Joe | 3 | 3 | 3.00 | 12 | 12 | 0 | 0 | 48 | 44 | 22 | 16 | 25 | 63 | R | R | 6-2 | 185 | 5-11-75 | 1996 | Ontario, Calif. |

# PHOENIX — Rookie

## ARIZONA LEAGUE

| BATTING | AVG | G | AB | R | H | 2B | 3B | HR | RBI | BB | SO | SB | CS | B | T | HT | WT | DOB | 1st Yr | Resides |
|---|---|---|---|---|---|---|---|---|---|---|---|---|---|---|---|---|---|---|---|---|
| Bautista, Juan | .200 | 49 | 140 | 14 | 28 | 3 | 1 | 0 | 14 | 11 | 51 | 5 | 2 | R | R | 6-1 | 157 | 7-20-78 | 1996 | San Fran. de Macorís, D.R. |
| Chapman, David | .119 | 37 | 118 | 12 | 14 | 2 | 2 | 0 | 12 | 10 | 28 | 0 | 1 | R | R | 6-2 | 185 | 12-15-77 | 1996 | Alta Loma, Calif. |
| Garcia, Juan | .255 | 36 | 110 | 25 | 28 | 3 | 3 | 3 | 14 | 24 | 26 | 16 | 6 | R | R | 5-9 | 160 | 9-25-78 | 1996 | San Fran. de Macorís, D.R. |
| Glasser, Scott | .297 | 41 | 128 | 25 | 38 | 0 | 4 | 0 | 10 | 14 | 16 | 13 | 2 | R | R | 6-1 | 180 | 12-9-75 | 1996 | Huntington Beach, Calif. |
| Hardy, Brett | .000 | 4 | 3 | 0 | 0 | 0 | 0 | 0 | 0 | 2 | 3 | 0 | 0 | L | L | 6-0 | 180 | 12-22-73 | 1996 | Laguna Beach, Calif. |
| Hudson, Bert | .277 | 35 | 112 | 12 | 31 | 5 | 4 | 0 | 20 | 8 | 33 | 2 | 0 | R | R | 5-11 | 185 | 10-6-77 | 1996 | Jay, Fla. |
| Leyba, Jhonathan | .258 | 24 | 31 | 2 | 8 | 1 | 0 | 0 | 0 | 6 | 11 | 0 | 0 | R | R | 5-11 | 180 | 8-6-78 | 1996 | Santo Domingo, D.R. |
| Martinez, Jorge | .161 | 20 | 31 | 6 | 5 | 0 | 0 | 1 | 4 | 6 | 12 | 0 | 0 | S | R | 5-11 | 185 | 3-13-78 | 1996 | New York, N.Y. |
| McAffee, Josh | .147 | 39 | 102 | 13 | 15 | 5 | 0 | 0 | 7 | 18 | 39 | 1 | 1 | R | R | 6-0 | 198 | 11-4-77 | 1996 | Rock Springs, Wyom. |
| Mouton, Aaron | .250 | 1 | 4 | 0 | 1 | 1 | 0 | 0 | 0 | 1 | 0 | 0 | 0 | S | R | 5-11 | 165 | 3-12-77 | 1996 | Richmond, Calif. |
| Nunez, Jose | .176 | 4 | 17 | 1 | 3 | 0 | 0 | 0 | 2 | 1 | 2 | 1 | 0 | R | R | 5-9 | 180 | 3-4-76 | 1996 | Brooklyn, N.Y. |
| Osborne, Mark | .267 | 31 | 105 | 15 | 28 | 6 | 3 | 1 | 16 | 9 | 24 | 0 | 0 | L | R | 6-4 | 204 | 2-1-78 | 1996 | Sanford, N.C. |
| Panaro, Carmen | .242 | 28 | 33 | 6 | 8 | 2 | 0 | 0 | 4 | 7 | 8 | 0 | 1 | L | R | 6-0 | 195 | 9-21-75 | 1996 | Buffalo, N.Y. |
| Proctor, Jerry | .202 | 45 | 163 | 14 | 33 | 5 | 4 | 0 | 9 | 8 | 60 | 2 | 0 | R | R | 6-5 | 200 | 3-5-78 | 1996 | Pasadena, Calif. |
| Rexrode, Jackie | .329 | 48 | 140 | 28 | 46 | 2 | 0 | 1 | 17 | 44 | 27 | 8 | 5 | L | R | 5-10 | 165 | 9-16-78 | 1996 | Laurel, Md. |
| Rodriguez, Diogenes | .217 | 32 | 106 | 8 | 23 | 7 | 1 | 0 | 11 | 7 | 40 | 2 | 0 | R | R | 6-3 | 194 | 12-6-78 | 1996 | Santo Domingo, D.R. |
| Rodriguez, Miguel | .232 | 23 | 56 | 9 | 13 | 2 | 3 | 2 | 7 | 4 | 18 | 1 | 0 | R | R | 5-10 | 170 | 5-27-78 | 1996 | El Sombrero, Venez. |
| Rottman, Paul | .140 | 17 | 43 | 3 | 6 | 2 | 0 | 0 | 2 | 4 | 13 | 1 | 1 | R | R | 6-3 | 185 | 12-11-77 | 1996 | Albuquerque, N.M. |
| Sandoval, Jhensy | .289 | 38 | 149 | 22 | 43 | 11 | 0 | 2 | 26 | 7 | 41 | 1 | 1 | R | R | 6-0 | 160 | 9-11-78 | 1996 | Santo Domingo, D.R. |
| Spivey, Ernest | .333 | 20 | 69 | 13 | 23 | 0 | 0 | 0 | 3 | 12 | 16 | 11 | 2 | R | R | 6-0 | 185 | 1-28-75 | 1996 | Oklahoma City, Okla. |
| Torres, Jose | .315 | 29 | 54 | 13 | 17 | 1 | 3 | 0 | 5 | 4 | 18 | 5 | 3 | R | R | 6-0 | 170 | 11-26-77 | 1996 | Guaynabo, P.R. |
| Vinas, Alex | .218 | 18 | 55 | 5 | 12 | 2 | 0 | 0 | 7 | 4 | 20 | 2 | 0 | S | R | 6-1 | 170 | 4-6-78 | 1996 | Santo Domingo, D.R. |
| Wilson, Keith | .266 | 42 | 143 | 19 | 38 | 5 | 0 | 2 | 20 | 12 | 21 | 1 | 1 | R | R | 5-11 | 175 | 12-31-73 | 1996 | Buckeye, Ariz. |

**GAMES BY POSITION: C**—Hudson 1, Leyba 24, McAffee 36, Osborne 15, Panaro 13. **1B**—D. Rodriguez 31, Wilson 33. **2B**—Glasser 3, Martinez 5, Nunez 1, Rexrode 43, Spivey 10. **3B**—Glasser 34, Hudson 2, Martinez 5, Nunez 3, D. Rodriguez 1, Spivey 3, Vina 18, Wilson 7. **SS**—Bautista 48, Glasser 9, Martinez 1, Mouton 1, Spivey 8. **OF**—Chapman 35, Garcia 23, Hardy 2, Hudson 15, Martinez 3, Proctor 42, M. Rodriguez 16, Rottman 12, Sandoval 33, Torres 22.

| PITCHING | W | L | ERA | G | GS | CG | SV | IP | H | R | ER | BB | SO | B | T | HT | WT | DOB | 1st Yr | Resides |
|---|---|---|---|---|---|---|---|---|---|---|---|---|---|---|---|---|---|---|---|---|
| Bell, Matthew | 1 | 4 | 4.68 | 18 | 0 | 0 | 0 | 33 | 36 | 27 | 17 | 11 | 24 | R | R | 6-5 | 190 | 1-8-78 | 1996 | Joplin, Mo. |
| Bido, Jose | 2 | 3 | 4.83 | 11 | 11 | 0 | 0 | 50 | 51 | 30 | 27 | 22 | 24 | R | R | 6-0 | 170 | 12-20-78 | 1996 | San Fran. de Macorís, D.R. |
| Bierbrodt, Nick | 1 | 1 | 1.66 | 8 | 8 | 0 | 0 | 38 | 25 | 9 | 7 | 13 | 46 | L | L | 6-5 | 180 | 5-16-78 | 1996 | Long Beach, Calif. |
| Escalante, Piter | 0 | 1 | 6.20 | 15 | 0 | 0 | 0 | 25 | 35 | 17 | 17 | 5 | 24 | R | R | 6-0 | 187 | 4-5-78 | 1996 | Santo Domingo, D.R. |
| Fleming, John | 1 | 4 | 4.02 | 10 | 5 | 0 | 0 | 31 | 33 | 17 | 14 | 17 | 29 | R | R | 6-3 | 185 | 1-20-78 | 1996 | Chula Vista, Calif. |
| Frias, Miguel | 1 | 1 | 2.35 | 19 | 0 | 0 | 2 | 31 | 28 | 18 | 8 | 17 | 30 | L | L | 5-11 | 165 | 12-27-77 | 1996 | Santo Domingo, D.R. |
| Kempton, Ryan | 0 | 3 | 3.12 | 14 | 0 | 0 | 1 | 26 | 29 | 14 | 9 | 7 | 14 | R | R | 6-3 | 210 | 8-4-76 | 1996 | Post Falls, Idaho |
| McCall, Travis | 3 | 2 | 4.06 | 16 | 0 | 0 | 0 | 38 | 45 | 21 | 17 | 11 | 38 | L | L | 5-11 | 180 | 12-20-77 | 1996 | Chino Hills, Calif. |
| McCutcheon, Mike | 0 | 1 | 0.49 | 14 | 0 | 0 | 2 | 18 | 9 | 3 | 1 | 7 | 18 | L | L | 6-0 | 170 | 7-5-77 | 1996 | Mauna Loa, Hawaii |
| Norris, Ben | 2 | 2 | 4.60 | 8 | 7 | 0 | 0 | 31 | 33 | 21 | 16 | 4 | 37 | L | L | 6-3 | 185 | 12-6-77 | 1996 | Austin, Texas |
| Ortiz, Edickson | 2 | 2 | 3.60 | 7 | 0 | 0 | 0 | 15 | 13 | 10 | 6 | 7 | 15 | R | R | 6-1 | 170 | 5-15-77 | 1996 | La Romana, D.R. |
| Paredes, Vladimir | 1 | 1 | 3.95 | 17 | 0 | 0 | 0 | 27 | 18 | 15 | 12 | 27 | 20 | L | L | 6-0 | 180 | 5-11-78 | 1996 | Santo Domingo, D.R. |
| Penny, Brad | 2 | 2 | 2.36 | 11 | 8 | 0 | 0 | 50 | 36 | 18 | 13 | 14 | 52 | R | R | 6-4 | 195 | 5-24-78 | 1996 | Broken Arrow, Okla. |
| Putt, Eric | 3 | 3 | 4.60 | 12 | 8 | 0 | 0 | 45 | 45 | 37 | 23 | 22 | 29 | R | R | 6-3 | 175 | 6-29-78 | 1996 | De Bary, Fla. |
| Van Wormer, Marc | 1 | 5 | 7.26 | 10 | 9 | 0 | 0 | 31 | 42 | 33 | 25 | 13 | 25 | R | R | 6-7 | 220 | 8-21-77 | 1996 | Prescott, Ariz. |

# ATLANTA BRAVES

**Manager:** Bobby Cox.  **1996 Record:** 96-66, .593 (1st, NL East).

| BATTING | AVG | G | AB | R | H | 2B | 3B | HR | RBI | BB | SO | SB | CS | B | T | HT | WT | DOB | 1st Yr | Resides |
|---|---|---|---|---|---|---|---|---|---|---|---|---|---|---|---|---|---|---|---|---|
| Ayrault, Joe | .200 | 7 | 5 | 0 | 1 | 0 | 0 | 0 | 0 | 0 | 1 | 0 | 0 | R | R | 6-3 | 190 | 10-8-71 | 1990 | Sarasota, Fla. |
| Bautista, Danny | .150 | 17 | 20 | 1 | 3 | 0 | 0 | 1 | 2 | 5 | 0 | 0 | 0 | R | R | 5-11 | 170 | 5-24-72 | 1989 | Santo Domingo, D.R. |
| Belliard, Rafael | .169 | 87 | 142 | 9 | 24 | 7 | 0 | 0 | 3 | 2 | 22 | 3 | 1 | R | R | 5-6 | 160 | 10-24-61 | 1980 | Boca Raton, Fla. |
| Blauser, Jeff | .245 | 83 | 265 | 48 | 65 | 14 | 1 | 10 | 35 | 40 | 54 | 6 | 0 | R | R | 6-1 | 180 | 11-8-65 | 1984 | Alpharetta, Ga. |
| Dye, Jermaine | .281 | 98 | 292 | 32 | 82 | 16 | 0 | 12 | 37 | 8 | 67 | 1 | 4 | R | R | 6-0 | 195 | 1-28-74 | 1993 | Vacaville, Calif. |
| Giovanola, Ed | .232 | 43 | 82 | 10 | 19 | 2 | 0 | 0 | 7 | 8 | 13 | 1 | 0 | L | R | 5-10 | 170 | 3-4-69 | 1990 | San Jose, Calif. |
| Graffanino, Tony | .174 | 22 | 46 | 7 | 8 | 1 | 1 | 0 | 2 | 4 | 13 | 0 | 0 | R | R | 6-1 | 200 | 6-6-72 | 1990 | Seneca, S.C. |
| Grissom, Marquis | .308 | 158 | 671 | 106 | 207 | 32 | 10 | 23 | 74 | 41 | 73 | 28 | 11 | R | R | 5-11 | 192 | 4-17-67 | 1988 | Red Oak, Ga. |
| Houston, Tyler | .222 | 33 | 27 | 3 | 6 | 2 | 1 | 1 | 8 | 1 | 9 | 0 | 0 | L | R | 6-2 | 210 | 1-17-71 | 1989 | Las Vegas, Nev. |
| Jones, Andruw | .217 | 31 | 106 | 11 | 23 | 7 | 1 | 5 | 13 | 7 | 29 | 3 | 0 | R | R | 6-1 | 170 | 4-23-77 | 1994 | Willemstad, Curacao |
| Jones, Chipper | .309 | 157 | 598 | 114 | 185 | 32 | 5 | 30 | 110 | 87 | 88 | 14 | 1 | S | R | 6-3 | 195 | 4-24-72 | 1990 | New Smyrna Beach, Fla. |
| Justice, Dave | .321 | 40 | 140 | 23 | 45 | 9 | 0 | 6 | 25 | 21 | 22 | 1 | 1 | L | L | 6-3 | 200 | 4-14-66 | 1985 | Atlanta, Ga. |
| Klesko, Ryan | .282 | 153 | 528 | 90 | 149 | 21 | 4 | 34 | 93 | 68 | 129 | 6 | 3 | L | L | 6-3 | 220 | 6-12-71 | 1989 | Boynton Beach, Fla. |
| Lemke, Mark | .255 | 135 | 498 | 64 | 127 | 17 | 0 | 5 | 37 | 53 | 48 | 5 | 2 | S | R | 5-9 | 167 | 8-13-65 | 1983 | Atlanta, Ga. |
| Lopez, Javy | .282 | 138 | 489 | 56 | 138 | 19 | 1 | 23 | 69 | 28 | 84 | 1 | 6 | R | R | 6-3 | 185 | 11-5-70 | 1988 | Ponce, P.R. |
| Martinez, Pablo | .500 | 4 | 2 | 1 | 1 | 0 | 0 | 0 | 0 | 0 | 0 | 0 | 1 | S | R | 5-10 | 155 | 6-29-69 | 1989 | San Juan Baron, D.R. |
| McGriff, Fred | .295 | 159 | 617 | 81 | 182 | 37 | 1 | 28 | 107 | 68 | 116 | 7 | 3 | L | L | 6-3 | 215 | 10-31-63 | 1981 | Tampa, Fla. |
| Mordecai, Mike | .241 | 66 | 108 | 12 | 26 | 5 | 0 | 2 | 8 | 9 | 24 | 1 | 0 | R | R | 5-11 | 175 | 12-13-67 | 1989 | Pinson, Ala. |
| Pendleton, Terry | .204 | 42 | 162 | 21 | 33 | 6 | 0 | 4 | 17 | 15 | 36 | 2 | 1 | S | R | 5-9 | 195 | 7-16-60 | 1982 | Duluth, Ga. |
| 2-team (111 Florida). | .238 | 153 | 568 | 51 | 135 | 26 | 1 | 11 | 75 | 41 | 111 | 2 | 3 | | | | | | | |
| Perez, Eddie | .256 | 68 | 156 | 19 | 40 | 9 | 1 | 4 | 17 | 8 | 19 | 0 | 0 | R | R | 6-1 | 175 | 5-4-68 | 1987 | Maracaibo, Venez. |
| Polonia, Luis | .419 | 22 | 31 | 3 | 13 | 0 | 0 | 0 | 2 | 1 | 3 | 1 | 1 | L | L | 5-8 | 150 | 10-27-64 | 1984 | Santiago, D.R. |
| Smith, Dwight | .203 | 101 | 153 | 16 | 31 | 5 | 0 | 3 | 16 | 17 | 42 | 1 | 3 | L | R | 5-11 | 177 | 11-8-63 | 1984 | Atlanta, Ga. |
| Walton, Jerome | .340 | 37 | 47 | 9 | 16 | 5 | 0 | 1 | 4 | 5 | 10 | 0 | 0 | R | R | 6-1 | 175 | 7-8-65 | 1986 | Fairburn, Ga. |
| Whiten, Mark | .256 | 36 | 90 | 12 | 23 | 5 | 1 | 3 | 17 | 16 | 25 | 2 | 5 | S | R | 6-3 | 215 | 11-25-66 | 1986 | Pensacola, Fla. |
| 2-team (59 Phil.) | .243 | 96 | 272 | 45 | 66 | 13 | 1 | 10 | 38 | 49 | 87 | 15 | 8 | | | | | | | |

| PITCHING | W | L | ERA | G | GS | CG | SV | IP | H | R | ER | BB | SO | B | T | HT | WT | DOB | 1st Yr | Resides |
|---|---|---|---|---|---|---|---|---|---|---|---|---|---|---|---|---|---|---|---|---|
| Avery, Steve | 7 | 10 | 4.47 | 24 | 23 | 1 | 0 | 131 | 146 | 70 | 65 | 40 | 86 | L | L | 6-4 | 205 | 4-14-70 | 1988 | Taylor, Mich. |
| Bielecki, Mike | 4 | 3 | 2.63 | 40 | 5 | 0 | 2 | 75 | 63 | 24 | 22 | 33 | 71 | R | R | 6-3 | 195 | 7-31-59 | 1979 | Crownsville, Md. |
| Borbon, Pedro | 3 | 0 | 2.75 | 43 | 0 | 0 | 1 | 36 | 26 | 12 | 11 | 7 | 31 | L | L | 6-1 | 205 | 11-15-67 | 1988 | Houston, Texas |
| Borowski, Joe | 2 | 4 | 4.85 | 22 | 0 | 0 | 0 | 26 | 33 | 15 | 14 | 13 | 15 | R | R | 6-2 | 225 | 5-4-71 | 1989 | Bayonne, N.J. |
| Clontz, Brad | 6 | 3 | 5.69 | 81 | 0 | 0 | 1 | 81 | 78 | 53 | 51 | 33 | 49 | R | R | 6-1 | 180 | 4-25-71 | 1992 | Patrick Spring, Va. |
| Glavine, Tom | 15 | 10 | 2.98 | 36 | 36 | 1 | 0 | 235 | 222 | 91 | 78 | 85 | 181 | L | L | 6-1 | 185 | 3-25-66 | 1984 | Alpharetta, Ga. |
| Hartgraves, Dean | 1 | 0 | 4.34 | 20 | 0 | 0 | 0 | 19 | 16 | 10 | 9 | 7 | 14 | R | L | 6-0 | 185 | 8-12-66 | 1987 | Central Point, Ore. |
| 2-team (19 Houston) | 1 | 0 | 4.78 | 39 | 0 | 0 | 0 | 38 | 34 | 21 | 20 | 23 | 30 | | | | | | | |
| Lomon, Kevin | 0 | 0 | 4.91 | 6 | 0 | 0 | 0 | 7 | 7 | 4 | 4 | 3 | 1 | R | R | 6-1 | 195 | 11-20-71 | 1991 | Cameron, Okla. |
| Maddux, Greg | 15 | 11 | 2.72 | 35 | 35 | 5 | 0 | 245 | 225 | 85 | 74 | 28 | 172 | R | R | 6-0 | 175 | 4-14-66 | 1984 | Las Vegas, Nev. |
| McMichael, Greg | 5 | 3 | 3.22 | 73 | 0 | 0 | 2 | 87 | 84 | 37 | 31 | 27 | 78 | R | R | 6-3 | 215 | 12-1-66 | 1988 | Alpharetta, Ga. |
| Neagle, Denny | 2 | 3 | 5.59 | 6 | 6 | 1 | 0 | 39 | 40 | 26 | 24 | 14 | 18 | L | L | 6-2 | 215 | 9-13-68 | 1989 | Gambrills, Md. |
| 2-team (27 Pitt.) | 16 | 9 | 3.50 | 33 | 33 | 2 | 0 | 221 | 226 | 93 | 86 | 48 | 149 | | | | | | | |
| Schmidt, Jason | 3 | 4 | 6.75 | 13 | 11 | 0 | 0 | 59 | 69 | 48 | 44 | 32 | 48 | R | R | 6-5 | 185 | 1-29-73 | 1991 | Kelso, Wash. |
| Schutz, Carl | 0 | 0 | 2.70 | 4 | 0 | 0 | 0 | 3 | 3 | 1 | 1 | 2 | 5 | L | L | 5-11 | 200 | 8-22-71 | 1993 | Paulina, La. |
| Smoltz, John | 24 | 8 | 2.94 | 35 | 35 | 6 | 0 | 254 | 199 | 93 | 83 | 55 | 276 | R | R | 6-3 | 185 | 5-15-67 | 1986 | Duluth, Ga. |
| Thobe, Tom | 0 | 1 | 1.50 | 4 | 0 | 0 | 0 | 6 | 5 | 2 | 1 | 0 | 1 | L | L | 6-5 | 195 | 9-3-69 | 1988 | Huntington Beach, Calif. |
| Wade, Terrell | 5 | 0 | 2.97 | 44 | 8 | 0 | 1 | 70 | 57 | 28 | 23 | 47 | 79 | L | L | 6-3 | 204 | 1-25-73 | 1991 | Rembert, S.C. |
| Wohlers, Mark | 2 | 4 | 3.03 | 77 | 0 | 0 | 39 | 77 | 71 | 30 | 26 | 21 | 100 | R | R | 6-4 | 207 | 1-23-70 | 1988 | Atlanta, Ga. |
| Woodall, Brad | 2 | 2 | 7.32 | 8 | 3 | 0 | 0 | 20 | 28 | 19 | 16 | 4 | 20 | S | L | 6-0 | 175 | 6-25-69 | 1991 | Blythewood, S.C. |

## FIELDING

| Catcher | PCT | G | PO | A | E | DP | PB |
|---|---|---|---|---|---|---|---|
| Ayrault | 1.000 | 7 | 14 | 0 | 0 | 0 | 0 |
| Lopez | .994 | 135 | 994 | 80 | 6 | 9 | 11 |
| Perez | .993 | 54 | 250 | 19 | 2 | 4 | 0 |

| First Base | PCT | G | PO | A | E | DP |
|---|---|---|---|---|---|---|
| Houston | 1.000 | 11 | 16 | 1 | 0 | 1 |
| Klesko | 1.000 | 2 | 13 | 2 | 0 | 2 |
| McGriff | .992 | 158 | 1416 | 124 | 12 | 118 |
| Mordecai | 1.000 | 1 | 2 | 1 | 0 | 0 |
| Perez | .971 | 7 | 31 | 3 | 1 | 7 |

| Second Base | PCT | G | PO | A | E | DP |
|---|---|---|---|---|---|---|
| Belliard | .951 | 15 | 14 | 25 | 2 | 7 |
| Giovanola | 1.000 | 5 | 5 | 10 | 0 | 2 |
| Graffanino | .969 | 18 | 24 | 39 | 2 | 9 |
| Lemke | .977 | 133 | 228 | 410 | 15 | 71 |
| Mordecai | .985 | 20 | 26 | 38 | 1 | 8 |

| Third Base | PCT | G | PO | A | E | DP |
|---|---|---|---|---|---|---|
| Giovanola | 1.000 | 6 | 1 | 7 | 0 | 1 |
| C. Jones | .947 | 118 | 48 | 185 | 13 | 9 |
| Mordecai | .944 | 10 | 4 | 13 | 1 | 0 |
| Pendleton | .938 | 41 | 26 | 79 | 7 | 5 |

| Shortstop | PCT | G | PO | A | E | DP |
|---|---|---|---|---|---|---|
| Belliard | .983 | 63 | 51 | 125 | 3 | 25 |
| Blauser | .926 | 79 | 83 | 205 | 23 | 40 |
| Giovanola | .983 | 25 | 18 | 39 | 1 | 9 |
| C. Jones | .975 | 38 | 53 | 104 | 4 | 27 |
| Martinez | 1.000 | 1 | 0 | 2 | 0 | 1 |
| Mordecai | 1.000 | 6 | 1 | 1 | 0 | 0 |

| Outfield | PCT | G | PO | A | E | DP |
|---|---|---|---|---|---|---|
| Bautista | 1.000 | 14 | 10 | 0 | 0 | 0 |
| Dye | .950 | 92 | 150 | 2 | 8 | 1 |
| Grissom | .997 | 158 | 338 | 10 | 1 | 1 |
| A. Jones | .975 | 29 | 73 | 4 | 2 | 0 |
| C. Jones | 1.000 | 1 | 2 | 0 | 0 | 0 |
| Justice | 1.000 | 40 | 88 | 3 | 0 | 1 |
| Klesko | .975 | 144 | 191 | 6 | 5 | 1 |
| Polonia | .800 | 7 | 4 | 0 | 1 | 0 |
| Smith | .962 | 29 | 49 | 1 | 2 | 0 |
| Walton | 1.000 | 28 | 34 | 0 | 0 | 0 |
| Whiten | .933 | 29 | 41 | 1 | 3 | 0 |

**Marquis Grissom**

BRAVES

Third baseman Chipper Jones led the Braves with a .309 average and 110 RBIs

Braves minor league Player of the Year Andruw Jones

LARRY GOREN

MEL BAILEY

## FARM SYSTEM

**Director, Minor League Operations:** Rod Gilbreath

| Class | Farm Team | League | W | L | Pct. | Finish* | Manager | First Yr |
|---|---|---|---|---|---|---|---|---|
| AAA | Richmond (Va.) Braves | International | 62 | 79 | .440 | T-8th (10) | Bill Dancy | 1966 |
| AA | Greenville (S.C.) Braves | Southern | 58 | 82 | .414 | 9th (10) | Jeff Cox | 1984 |
| #A | Durham (N.C.) Bulls | Carolina | 73 | 66 | .525 | 4th (8) | Randy Ingle | 1980 |
| A | Macon (Ga.) Braves | South Atlantic | 61 | 79 | .436 | 11th (14) | Paul Runge | 1991 |
| A | Eugene (Ore.) Emeralds | Northwest | 49 | 27 | .645 | 1st (8) | Jim Saul | 1995 |
| #R | Danville (Va.) Braves | Appalachian | 37 | 29 | .561 | 5th (9) | Brian Snitker | 1993 |
| R | West Palm Beach (Fla.) Braves | Gulf Coast | 14 | 45 | .237 | 16th (16) | Lucas/ Cadahia | 1976 |

*Finish in overall standings (No. of teams in league)   #Advanced level

## ORGANIZATION LEADERS

### MAJOR LEAGUERS

**BATTING**
- *AVG Chipper Jones........ .309
- R Chipper Jones......... 114
- H Marquis Grissom..... 207
- TB Marquis Grissom..... 328
- 2B Fred McGriff.............. 37
- 3B Marquis Grissom....... 10
- HR Ryan Klesko.............. 34
- RBI Chipper Jones........... 110
- BB Chipper Jones........... 87
- SO Ryan Klesko............ 129
- SB Marquis Grissom....... 28

**PITCHING**
- W John Smoltz.............. 24
- L Greg Maddux ........... 11
- #ERA Mike Bielecki.......... 2.63
- G Brad Clontz .............. 81
- CG John Smoltz.............. 6
- SV Mark Wohlers........... 39
- IP John Smoltz ........... 254
- BB Tom Glavine ............ 85
- SO John Smoltz ........... 276

THE SPORTS GROUP

**Mark Wohlers.** 39 saves

### MINOR LEAGUERS

**BATTING**
- *AVG Andruw Jones, Durham/Green./Rich.... .339
- R Andruw Jones, Durham/Green./Rich..... 115
- H Marc Lewis, Macon/Durham................. 154
- TB Andruw Jones, Durham/Green./Rich..... 290
- 2B Rob Sasser, Macon ........................... 35
- 3B Adam Johnson, Eugene ........................... 9
- HR Ron Wright, Durham/Greenville ............. 36
- RBI Ron Wright, Durham/Greenville ............ 114
- BB Ron Wright, Durham/Greenville ............. 77
- SO Ron Wright, Durham/Greenville ............ 151
- SB Marc Lewis, Macon/Durham.................. 50

**PITCHING**
- W Derrin Ebert, Durham ............................ 12
- L Two tied at.................................... 11
- #ERA Kevin McGlinchy, Danville/Eugene ...... 1.49
- G Adam Butler, Macon/Durham/Green. ...... 59
- CG Brad Woodall, Richmond......................... 5
- SV Adam Butler, Macon/Durham/Green. ...... 30
- IP Derrin Ebert, Durham ........................... 166
- BB Billy Blythe, Macon .............................. 107
- SO John Rocker, Macon/Durham............... 150

*Minimum 250 At-Bats   #Minimum 75 Innings

## TOP 10 PROSPECTS

**How the Braves Top 10 prospects, as judged by Baseball America prior to the 1996 season, fared in 1996:**

LARRY GOREN

**Jermaine Dye**

| Player, Pos. | Club (Class—League) | AVG | AB | R | H | 2B | 3B | HR | RBI | SB |
|---|---|---|---|---|---|---|---|---|---|---|
| 1. Andruw Jones, of | Durham (A—Carolina) | .313 | 243 | 65 | 76 | 14 | 3 | 17 | 43 | 16 |
| | Greenville (AA—Southern) | .369 | 157 | 39 | 58 | 10 | 1 | 12 | 37 | 12 |
| | Richmond (AAA—International) | .378 | 45 | 11 | 17 | 3 | 1 | 5 | 12 | 2 |
| | Atlanta | .217 | 106 | 11 | 23 | 7 | 1 | 5 | 13 | 3 |
| 3. Jermaine Dye, of | Richmond (AAA—International) | .232 | 142 | 25 | 33 | 7 | 1 | 6 | 19 | 3 |
| | Atlanta | .281 | 292 | 32 | 82 | 16 | 0 | 12 | 37 | 1 |
| 4. Robert Smith, 3b | Richmond (AAA—International) | .256 | 445 | 49 | 114 | 27 | 0 | 8 | 58 | 15 |
| 6. Damon Hollins, of | Richmond (AAA—International) | .199 | 146 | 16 | 29 | 9 | 0 | 0 | 8 | 2 |
| 7. George Lombard, of | Macon (A—South Atlantic) | .245 | 444 | 76 | 109 | 16 | 8 | 15 | 51 | 24 |
| 8. *Ron Wright, 1b | Durham (A—Carolina) | .275 | 240 | 47 | 66 | 15 | 2 | 20 | 62 | 1 |
| | Greenville (AA—Southern) | .254 | 232 | 39 | 59 | 11 | 1 | 16 | 52 | 1 |
| | Carolina (AA—Southern) | .143 | 14 | 1 | 2 | 0 | 0 | 0 | 0 | 0 |
| 9. Glenn Williams, ss | Macon (A—South Atlantic) | .193 | 181 | 14 | 35 | 7 | 3 | 3 | 18 | 4 |

| | | W | L | ERA | G | SV | IP | H | BB | SO |
|---|---|---|---|---|---|---|---|---|---|---|
| 2. *Jason Schmidt, rhp | Atlanta | 3 | 4 | 6.75 | 13 | 0 | 59 | 69 | 32 | 48 |
| | Richmond (AAA—International) | 3 | 0 | 2.56 | 7 | 0 | 46 | 36 | 19 | 41 |
| | Pittsburgh | 2 | 2 | 4.06 | 6 | 0 | 37 | 38 | 21 | 26 |
| 5. Terrell Wade, lhp | Atlanta | 5 | 0 | 2.97 | 44 | 1 | 70 | 57 | 47 | 79 |
| 10. Damian Moss, lhp | Durham (A—Carolina) | 9 | 1 | 2.25 | 14 | 0 | 84 | 52 | 40 | 89 |
| | Greenville (AA—Southern) | 2 | 5 | 4.97 | 11 | 0 | 58 | 57 | 35 | 48 |

*Traded to Pirates

## INTERNATIONAL LEAGUE

| BATTING | AVG | G | AB | R | H | 2B | 3B | HR | RBI | BB | SO | SB | CS | B | T | HT | WT | DOB | 1st Yr | Resides |
|---|---|---|---|---|---|---|---|---|---|---|---|---|---|---|---|---|---|---|---|---|
| Ayrault, Joe | .229 | 98 | 314 | 23 | 72 | 15 | 0 | 5 | 34 | 26 | 57 | 1 | 1 | R | R | 6-3 | 190 | 10-8-71 | 1990 | Sarasota, Fla. |
| Beltre, Esteban | .250 | 10 | 28 | 3 | 7 | 3 | 0 | 0 | 0 | 1 | 2 | 0 | 0 | R | R | 5-10 | 172 | 12-26-67 | 1984 | San Pedro de Macoris, D.R. |
| 2-team (4 Scranton) | .209 | 14 | 43 | 4 | 9 | 3 | 0 | 0 | 1 | 1 | 3 | 0 | 0 | | | | | | | |
| Benbow, Lou | .232 | 91 | 250 | 21 | 58 | 8 | 0 | 1 | 23 | 16 | 65 | 3 | 4 | R | R | 6-0 | 167 | 1-12-71 | 1991 | Laguna Hills, Calif. |
| Cox, Darron | .238 | 55 | 168 | 19 | 40 | 9 | 0 | 3 | 20 | 5 | 22 | 1 | 0 | R | R | 6-1 | 205 | 11-21-67 | 1989 | Norman, Okla. |
| Dye, Jermaine | .232 | 36 | 142 | 25 | 33 | 7 | 1 | 6 | 19 | 5 | 25 | 3 | 0 | R | R | 6-0 | 195 | 1-28-74 | 1993 | Vacaville, Calif. |
| Garcia, Omar | .264 | 93 | 311 | 36 | 82 | 15 | 1 | 4 | 35 | 9 | 32 | 4 | 4 | R | R | 6-0 | 192 | 11-16-71 | 1989 | Carolina, P.R. |
| Giovanola, Ed | .295 | 62 | 210 | 29 | 62 | 15 | 1 | 3 | 16 | 37 | 34 | 2 | 6 | L | R | 5-10 | 170 | 3-4-69 | 1990 | San Jose, Calif. |
| Graffanino, Tony | .283 | 96 | 353 | 57 | 100 | 29 | 2 | 7 | 33 | 34 | 72 | 11 | 7 | R | R | 6-1 | 200 | 6-6-72 | 1990 | Seneca, S.C. |
| Grijak, Kevin | .367 | 13 | 30 | 3 | 11 | 3 | 0 | 1 | 8 | 5 | 7 | 0 | 1 | L | R | 6-2 | 195 | 8-6-70 | 1991 | Sterling Heights, Mich. |
| Hollins, Damon | .199 | 42 | 146 | 16 | 29 | 9 | 0 | 0 | 8 | 16 | 37 | 2 | 3 | R | L | 5-11 | 180 | 6-12-74 | 1992 | Vallejo, Calif. |
| Jones, Andruw | .378 | 12 | 45 | 11 | 17 | 3 | 1 | 5 | 12 | 1 | 9 | 2 | 2 | R | R | 6-1 | 170 | 4-23-77 | 1994 | Willemstad, Curacao |
| Malloy, Marty | .203 | 18 | 64 | 7 | 13 | 2 | 1 | 0 | 8 | 5 | 7 | 3 | 0 | L | R | 5-10 | 160 | 7-6-72 | 1992 | Trenton, Fla. |
| Martinez, Pablo | .270 | 77 | 263 | 29 | 71 | 12 | 3 | 1 | 18 | 12 | 58 | 14 | 7 | S | R | 5-10 | 155 | 6-29-69 | 1989 | San Juan Baron, D.R. |
| Moore, Bobby | .270 | 67 | 200 | 29 | 54 | 10 | 0 | 3 | 14 | 15 | 11 | 9 | 2 | R | R | 5-11 | 165 | 10-27-65 | 1987 | Cincinnati, Ohio |
| Mordecai, Mike | .182 | 3 | 11 | 2 | 2 | 0 | 0 | 1 | 2 | 3 | 0 | 0 | 0 | R | R | 5-11 | 175 | 12-13-67 | 1989 | Pinson, Ala. |
| Pecorilli, Aldo | .290 | 122 | 403 | 61 | 117 | 27 | 0 | 15 | 62 | 31 | 87 | 5 | 6 | R | R | 5-11 | 185 | 9-12-70 | 1992 | Sterling Heights, Mich. |
| Pegues, Steve | .341 | 52 | 167 | 31 | 57 | 10 | 1 | 7 | 30 | 6 | 43 | 0 | 0 | R | R | 6-2 | 190 | 5-21-68 | 1987 | Pontotoc, Miss. |
| Rodarte, Raul | .338 | 61 | 219 | 30 | 74 | 12 | 2 | 9 | 46 | 19 | 43 | 4 | 2 | R | R | 5-11 | 190 | 4-9-70 | 1991 | Diamond Bar, Calif. |
| Smith, Robert | .256 | 124 | 445 | 49 | 114 | 27 | 0 | 8 | 58 | 32 | 114 | 15 | 9 | R | R | 6-3 | 190 | 4-10-74 | 1992 | Oakland, Calif. |
| Swann, Pedro | .250 | 93 | 296 | 42 | 74 | 11 | 4 | 4 | 35 | 22 | 56 | 7 | 7 | L | R | 6-0 | 195 | 10-27-70 | 1991 | Townsend, Del. |
| Walton, Jerome | .444 | 6 | 18 | 3 | 8 | 2 | 1 | 1 | 5 | 1 | 5 | 0 | 0 | R | R | 6-1 | 175 | 7-8-65 | 1986 | Fairburn, Ga. |
| Warner, Mike | .207 | 7 | 29 | 4 | 6 | 1 | 0 | 0 | 1 | 1 | 8 | 1 | 2 | L | L | 5-10 | 170 | 5-9-71 | 1992 | Palm Beach Gardens, Fla. |
| Williams, Juan | .272 | 119 | 357 | 55 | 97 | 22 | 2 | 15 | 52 | 51 | 127 | 5 | 4 | L | R | 6-0 | 180 | 10-9-72 | 1990 | Riverside, Calif. |

| PITCHING | W | L | ERA | G | GS | CG | SV | IP | H | R | ER | BB | SO | B | T | HT | WT | DOB | 1st Yr | Resides |
|---|---|---|---|---|---|---|---|---|---|---|---|---|---|---|---|---|---|---|---|---|
| Borowski, Joe | 1 | 5 | 3.71 | 34 | 0 | 0 | 7 | 53 | 42 | 25 | 22 | 30 | 40 | R | R | 6-2 | 225 | 5-4-71 | 1989 | Bayonne, N.J. |
| Brock, Chris | 10 | 11 | 4.67 | 26 | 25 | 3 | 0 | 150 | 137 | 95 | 78 | 61 | 112 | R | R | 6-0 | 175 | 2-5-70 | 1992 | Altamonte Springs, Fla. |
| Dettmer, John | 3 | 5 | 3.92 | 19 | 6 | 0 | 0 | 60 | 69 | 27 | 26 | 9 | 26 | R | R | 6-0 | 185 | 3-4-70 | 1992 | Glencoe, Mo. |
| Fox, Chad | 3 | 10 | 4.73 | 18 | 18 | 1 | 0 | 93 | 91 | 57 | 49 | 49 | 87 | R | R | 6-2 | 180 | 9-3-70 | 1992 | Houston, Texas |
| Harrison, Tommy | 0 | 0 | 5.21 | 10 | 0 | 0 | 0 | 19 | 16 | 12 | 11 | 12 | 12 | R | R | 6-2 | 180 | 9-30-71 | 1993 | Miamisburg, Ohio |
| Hartgraves, Dean | 0 | 0 | 2.08 | 4 | 0 | 0 | 0 | 9 | 4 | 2 | 2 | 2 | 8 | R | L | 6-0 | 185 | 8-12-66 | 1987 | Central Point, Ore. |
| Hostetler, Mike | 11 | 9 | 4.38 | 27 | 24 | 2 | 0 | 148 | 168 | 80 | 72 | 41 | 81 | R | R | 6-2 | 195 | 6-5-70 | 1991 | Marietta, Ga. |
| 2-team (33 Norfolk) | 4 | 5 | 2.69 | 53 | 0 | 0 | 1 | 57 | 69 | 23 | 20 | 17 | 71 | | | | | | | |
| Lomon, Kevin | 9 | 8 | 4.33 | 26 | 26 | 2 | 0 | 141 | 151 | 82 | 68 | 44 | 102 | R | R | 6-1 | 195 | 11-20-71 | 1991 | Cameron, Okla. |
| Murray, Matt | 1 | 2 | 6.00 | 5 | 2 | 0 | 0 | 12 | 12 | 8 | 8 | 14 | 9 | L | R | 6-6 | 235 | 9-26-70 | 1988 | Swampscott, Mass. |
| 2-team (13 Scranton) | 2 | 10 | 7.38 | 18 | 15 | 0 | 0 | 68 | 75 | 60 | 56 | 63 | 43 | | | | | | | |
| Nichols, Rod | 3 | 3 | 1.99 | 57 | 0 | 0 | 20 | 72 | 54 | 20 | 16 | 20 | 64 | R | R | 6-2 | 190 | 12-29-64 | 1985 | Columbus, Ga. |
| Schmidt, Jason | 3 | 0 | 2.56 | 7 | 7 | 0 | 0 | 46 | 36 | 17 | 13 | 19 | 41 | R | R | 6-5 | 185 | 1-29-73 | 1991 | Kelso, Wash. |
| Schutz, Carl | 4 | 3 | 5.30 | 41 | 7 | 0 | 3 | 70 | 86 | 46 | 41 | 26 | 52 | L | L | 5-11 | 200 | 8-22-71 | 1993 | Paulina, La. |
| Schwarz, Jeff | 0 | 1 | 27.00 | 2 | 0 | 0 | 0 | 1 | 4 | 4 | 4 | 4 | 1 | R | R | 6-5 | 190 | 5-20-64 | 1982 | Fort Pierce, Fla. |
| Steph, Rod | 2 | 3 | 3.84 | 38 | 0 | 0 | 1 | 80 | 75 | 34 | 34 | 17 | 41 | R | R | 5-11 | 185 | 8-27-69 | 1991 | Plano, Texas |
| Thobe, Tom | 1 | 8 | 6.13 | 31 | 6 | 1 | 3 | 72 | 89 | 60 | 49 | 37 | 40 | L | L | 6-5 | 195 | 9-3-69 | 1988 | Huntington Beach, Calif. |
| Woodall, Brad | 9 | 7 | 3.38 | 21 | 21 | 5 | 0 | 133 | 124 | 59 | 50 | 36 | 74 | S | L | 6-0 | 175 | 6-25-69 | 1991 | Blythewood, S.C. |

### FIELDING

| Catcher | PCT | G | PO | A | E | DP | PB |
|---|---|---|---|---|---|---|---|
| Ayrault | .982 | 97 | 546 | 61 | 11 | 7 | 11 |
| Cox | 1.000 | 49 | 310 | 29 | 0 | 5 | 4 |
| Pecorilli | .714 | 2 | 5 | 0 | 2 | 0 | 0 |

| First Base | PCT | G | PO | A | E | DP |
|---|---|---|---|---|---|---|
| Benbow | 1.000 | 1 | 1 | 0 | 0 | 0 |
| Cox | 1.000 | 3 | 9 | 0 | 0 | 1 |
| Garcia | .997 | 83 | 604 | 35 | 2 | 57 |
| Grijak | 1.000 | 9 | 69 | 7 | 0 | 5 |
| Pecorilli | .984 | 59 | 394 | 32 | 7 | 36 |

| Second Base | PCT | G | PO | A | E | DP |
|---|---|---|---|---|---|---|
| Benbow | .969 | 18 | 27 | 35 | 2 | 13 |
| Giovanola | .959 | 17 | 30 | 41 | 3 | 11 |
| Graffanino | .977 | 93 | 215 | 216 | 10 | 47 |
| Malloy | .973 | 17 | 33 | 39 | 2 | 8 |

| Third Base | PCT | G | PO | A | E | DP |
|---|---|---|---|---|---|---|
| Beltre | .833 | 2 | 2 | 3 | 1 | 0 |
| Benbow | .913 | 44 | 28 | 67 | 9 | 5 |
| Giovanola | 1.000 | 8 | 5 | 24 | 0 | 3 |
| Martinez | 1.000 | 14 | 4 | 22 | 0 | 3 |
| Pecorilli | .875 | 2 | 2 | 5 | 1 | 0 |
| Rodarte | .714 | 9 | 2 | 8 | 4 | 1 |
| Smith | .935 | 77 | 63 | 125 | 13 | 10 |

| Shortstop | PCT | G | PO | A | E | DP |
|---|---|---|---|---|---|---|
| Beltre | .909 | 7 | 7 | 13 | 2 | 4 |
| Benbow | .853 | 12 | 11 | 18 | 5 | 5 |
| Giovanola | .941 | 28 | 37 | 90 | 8 | 17 |
| Malloy | 1.000 | 1 | 1 | 1 | 0 | 1 |
| Martinez | .933 | 62 | 79 | 158 | 17 | 29 |
| Mordecai | 1.000 | 3 | 3 | 13 | 0 | 1 |
| Smith | .934 | 43 | 53 | 103 | 11 | 21 |

| Outfield | PCT | G | PO | A | E | DP |
|---|---|---|---|---|---|---|
| Dye | .955 | 36 | 83 | 2 | 4 | 0 |
| Giovanola | 1.000 | 5 | 5 | 0 | 0 | 0 |
| Grijak | .000 | 1 | 0 | 0 | 0 | 0 |
| Hollins | .976 | 41 | 116 | 6 | 3 | 0 |
| Jones | .972 | 12 | 34 | 1 | 1 | 0 |
| Moore | .983 | 59 | 117 | 2 | 2 | 1 |
| Pecorilli | .960 | 20 | 23 | 1 | 1 | 0 |
| Pegues | .973 | 36 | 68 | 3 | 2 | 0 |
| Rodarte | .944 | 52 | 94 | 7 | 6 | 3 |
| Swann | .983 | 86 | 171 | 5 | 3 | 0 |
| Walton | 1.000 | 5 | 12 | 0 | 0 | 0 |
| Warner | 1.000 | 7 | 14 | 0 | 0 | 0 |
| Williams | .965 | 111 | 239 | 8 | 9 | 0 |

## SOUTHERN LEAGUE

| BATTING | AVG | G | AB | R | H | 2B | 3B | HR | RBI | BB | SO | SB | CS | B | T | HT | WT | DOB | 1st Yr | Resides |
|---|---|---|---|---|---|---|---|---|---|---|---|---|---|---|---|---|---|---|---|---|
| Brito, Luis | .116 | 19 | 43 | 4 | 5 | 0 | 0 | 0 | 4 | 1 | 6 | 1 | 1 | S | R | 6-0 | 155 | 4-12-71 | 1989 | San Pedro de Macoris, D.R. |
| Correa, Miguel | .222 | 64 | 225 | 20 | 50 | 13 | 2 | 5 | 25 | 11 | 65 | 2 | 2 | S | R | 6-2 | 165 | 9-10-71 | 1990 | Arroyo, P.R. |
| Helms, Wes | .255 | 64 | 231 | 24 | 59 | 13 | 2 | 4 | 22 | 13 | 48 | 2 | 1 | R | R | 6-4 | 210 | 5-12-76 | 1994 | Gastonia, N.C. |
| Hicks, Jamie | .167 | 3 | 6 | 0 | 1 | 0 | 0 | 0 | 0 | 0 | 0 | 0 | 0 | R | R | 6-2 | 200 | 11-15-71 | 1994 | Hermitage, Tenn. |
| Jimenez, Manny | .274 | 131 | 474 | 68 | 130 | 21 | 2 | 3 | 57 | 28 | 67 | 12 | 7 | R | R | 5-11 | 160 | 7-4-71 | 1990 | Pueblo Nuevo, D.R. |
| Jones, Andruw | .369 | 38 | 157 | 39 | 58 | 10 | 1 | 12 | 37 | 17 | 34 | 12 | 4 | R | R | 6-1 | 170 | 4-23-77 | 1994 | Willemstad, Curacao |
| Malloy, Marty | .312 | 111 | 429 | 82 | 134 | 27 | 2 | 4 | 36 | 54 | 50 | 11 | 10 | L | R | 5-10 | 160 | 7-6-72 | 1992 | Trenton, Fla. |
| Martinez, Pablo | .324 | 9 | 37 | 7 | 12 | 2 | 2 | 1 | 11 | 2 | 6 | 3 | 0 | S | R | 5-10 | 155 | 6-29-69 | 1989 | San Juan Baron, D.R. |
| McBride, Gator | .268 | 85 | 291 | 38 | 78 | 17 | 5 | 4 | 50 | 27 | 75 | 4 | 3 | R | R | 5-10 | 170 | 8-12-73 | 1993 | Hurricane, W.Va. |
| McFarlin, Jason | .230 | 79 | 244 | 40 | 56 | 14 | 0 | 4 | 21 | 29 | 60 | 6 | 2 | L | L | 6-0 | 175 | 6-28-70 | 1989 | Pensacola, Fla. |
| Monds, Wonderful | .300 | 32 | 110 | 17 | 33 | 9 | 1 | 2 | 14 | 9 | 17 | 7 | 3 | R | R | 6-3 | 190 | 1-11-73 | 1993 | Fort Pierce, Fla. |
| Newell, Brett | .219 | 103 | 297 | 23 | 65 | 5 | 0 | 1 | 21 | 19 | 98 | 0 | 6 | R | R | 6-0 | 180 | 10-25-72 | 1994 | El Segundo, Calif. |
| Nunez, Raymond | .201 | 58 | 169 | 15 | 34 | 6 | 0 | 4 | 26 | 9 | 43 | 1 | 2 | R | R | 6-0 | 150 | 9-22-72 | 1990 | Manzanillo, D.R. |

## BATTING

| BATTING | AVG | G | AB | R | H | 2B | 3B | HR | RBI | BB | SO | SB | CS | B | T | HT | WT | DOB | 1st Yr | Resides |
|---|---|---|---|---|---|---|---|---|---|---|---|---|---|---|---|---|---|---|---|---|
| Rippelmeyer, Brad | .067 | 7 | 15 | 2 | 1 | 0 | 0 | 0 | 1 | 1 | 6 | 0 | 0 | R | R | 6-2 | 190 | 2-6-70 | 1991 | Valmeyer, Ill. |
| Rodarte, Raul | .330 | 48 | 176 | 33 | 58 | 11 | 0 | 6 | 28 | 16 | 23 | 0 | 3 | R | R | 5-11 | 190 | 4-9-70 | 1991 | Diamond Bar, Calif. |
| 2-team (20 Carolina) | .306 | 68 | 219 | 39 | 67 | 12 | 0 | 6 | 34 | 28 | 35 | 2 | 4 | | | | | | | |
| Simon, Randall | .279 | 134 | 498 | 74 | 139 | 26 | 2 | 18 | 77 | 37 | 61 | 4 | 9 | L | L | 6-0 | 180 | 5-26-75 | 1993 | Willemstad, Curacao |
| Stricklin, Scott | .145 | 45 | 131 | 14 | 19 | 4 | 0 | 0 | 11 | 16 | 29 | 1 | 1 | L | R | 5-11 | 180 | 2-17-72 | 1993 | The Plains, Ohio |
| Swann, Pedro | .310 | 35 | 129 | 15 | 40 | 5 | 0 | 3 | 20 | 18 | 23 | 4 | 4 | L | R | 6-0 | 195 | 10-27-70 | 1991 | Townsend, Del. |
| Toth, David | .266 | 120 | 376 | 63 | 100 | 31 | 1 | 10 | 55 | 58 | 61 | 2 | 3 | R | R | 6-1 | 195 | 12-8-69 | 1990 | West Keansburg, N.J. |
| Walton, Jerome | .200 | 3 | 5 | 0 | 1 | 0 | 1 | 0 | 0 | 3 | 1 | 0 | 0 | R | R | 6-1 | 175 | 7-8-65 | 1986 | Fairburn, Ga. |
| Warner, Mike | .259 | 64 | 205 | 39 | 53 | 19 | 2 | 6 | 33 | 47 | 45 | 10 | 7 | L | L | 5-10 | 170 | 5-9-71 | 1992 | Palm Beach Gardens, Fla. |
| Wright, Ron | .254 | 63 | 232 | 39 | 59 | 11 | 1 | 16 | 52 | 38 | 73 | 1 | 0 | R | R | 6-0 | 215 | 1-21-76 | 1994 | Kennewick, Wash. |

## PITCHING

| PITCHING | W | L | ERA | G | GS | CG | SV | IP | H | R | ER | BB | SO | B | T | HT | WT | DOB | 1st Yr | Resides |
|---|---|---|---|---|---|---|---|---|---|---|---|---|---|---|---|---|---|---|---|---|
| Arnold, Jamie | 7 | 7 | 4.92 | 23 | 23 | 2 | 0 | 128 | 149 | 79 | 70 | 44 | 64 | R | R | 6-2 | 188 | 3-24-74 | 1992 | Kissimmee, Fla. |
| Avery, Steve | 0 | 0 | 0.00 | 1 | 1 | 0 | 0 | 1 | 0 | 0 | 0 | 0 | 1 | L | L | 6-4 | 205 | 4-14-70 | 1988 | Taylor, Mich. |
| Bock, Jeff | 6 | 5 | 5.35 | 20 | 19 | 0 | 0 | 106 | 136 | 67 | 63 | 41 | 51 | R | R | 6-5 | 200 | 4-26-71 | 1993 | Cary, N.C. |
| Borbon, Pedro | 0 | 0 | 0.00 | 1 | 0 | 0 | 0 | 1 | 0 | 0 | 0 | 0 | 0 | L | L | 6-1 | 205 | 11-15-67 | 1988 | Houston, Texas |
| Butler, Adam | 1 | 4 | 5.09 | 38 | 0 | 0 | 17 | 35 | 36 | 22 | 20 | 16 | 31 | L | L | 6-2 | 225 | 8-17-73 | 1995 | Burke, Va. |
| Byrd, Matt | 4 | 9 | 6.97 | 51 | 4 | 0 | 2 | 90 | 108 | 77 | 70 | 40 | 66 | S | R | 6-2 | 200 | 5-17-71 | 1993 | Brighton, Mich. |
| Carper, Mark | 0 | 0 | 0.00 | 4 | 0 | 0 | 0 | 6 | 4 | 1 | 0 | 5 | 1 | R | R | 6-2 | 200 | 9-29-68 | 1991 | Highland, Md. |
| Cather, Mike | 3 | 4 | 3.70 | 53 | 0 | 0 | 5 | 88 | 89 | 42 | 36 | 29 | 61 | R | R | 6-2 | 180 | 12-17-70 | 1993 | Folsom, Calif. |
| Daniels, Lee | 0 | 2 | 2.65 | 16 | 0 | 0 | 9 | 17 | 10 | 5 | 5 | 14 | 23 | R | R | 6-4 | 180 | 3-31-71 | 1990 | Rochelle, Ga. |
| Dettmer, John | 3 | 3 | 2.88 | 26 | 0 | 0 | 0 | 41 | 43 | 19 | 13 | 6 | 28 | R | R | 6-0 | 185 | 3-4-70 | 1992 | Glencoe, Mo. |
| Duncan, Chip | 0 | 2 | 11.48 | 8 | 1 | 0 | 0 | 13 | 23 | 17 | 17 | 11 | 10 | R | R | 5-11 | 185 | 6-27-65 | 1987 | Fort Myers, Fla. |
| Etheridge, Roger | 4 | 2 | 6.89 | 49 | 1 | 0 | 2 | 67 | 71 | 55 | 51 | 55 | 43 | L | L | 6-5 | 215 | 5-31-72 | 1992 | Linden, Ala. |
| Gray, Dennis | 1 | 2 | 4.85 | 7 | 0 | 0 | 0 | 13 | 11 | 8 | 7 | 9 | 13 | L | L | 6-6 | 225 | 12-24-69 | 1991 | Banning, Calif. |
| 2-team (21 Port City) | 3 | 2 | 6.99 | 28 | 1 | 0 | 0 | 46 | 45 | 40 | 36 | 51 | 37 | | | | | | | |
| Harrison, Tommy | 8 | 4 | 4.71 | 20 | 16 | 0 | 0 | 99 | 88 | 55 | 52 | 34 | 82 | R | R | 6-2 | 180 | 9-30-71 | 1993 | Miamisburg, Ohio |
| Hollinger, Adrian | 2 | 1 | 5.46 | 20 | 0 | 0 | 0 | 30 | 30 | 19 | 18 | 17 | 24 | L | R | 6-0 | 180 | 9-23-70 | 1991 | Mira Loma, Calif. |
| Jacobs, Ryan | 3 | 9 | 6.68 | 21 | 21 | 0 | 0 | 100 | 127 | 83 | 74 | 57 | 64 | R | L | 6-2 | 175 | 2-3-74 | 1992 | Winston-Salem, N.C. |
| Koller, Jerry | 2 | 10 | 5.50 | 14 | 13 | 0 | 0 | 74 | 83 | 50 | 45 | 27 | 45 | R | R | 6-3 | 190 | 6-30-72 | 1990 | Martinsville, Ind. |
| LeRoy, John | 1 | 1 | 2.98 | 8 | 8 | 0 | 0 | 45 | 43 | 18 | 15 | 18 | 38 | R | R | 6-3 | 175 | 4-19-75 | 1993 | Bellevue, Wash. |
| Moss, Damian | 2 | 5 | 4.97 | 11 | 10 | 0 | 0 | 58 | 57 | 41 | 32 | 35 | 48 | R | L | 6-0 | 187 | 11-24-76 | 1994 | Sadler, Australia |
| Schmidt, Jason | 0 | 0 | 9.00 | 1 | 1 | 0 | 0 | 2 | 4 | 2 | 2 | 0 | 2 | R | R | 6-5 | 185 | 1-29-73 | 1991 | Kelso, Wash. |
| Steed, Rick | 6 | 9 | 3.92 | 33 | 9 | 0 | 0 | 101 | 100 | 51 | 44 | 44 | 70 | R | R | 6-2 | 185 | 9-8-70 | 1989 | West Covina, Calif. |
| Steph, Rod | 0 | 0 | 0.00 | 2 | 0 | 0 | 0 | 3 | 1 | 0 | 0 | 0 | 3 | R | R | 5-11 | 185 | 8-27-69 | 1991 | Plano, Texas |
| Stewart, Rachaad | 3 | 5 | 6.06 | 24 | 13 | 0 | 0 | 71 | 89 | 55 | 48 | 48 | 74 | L | L | 6-4 | 212 | 10-8-74 | 1994 | Elgin, Ill. |
| Thomas, Royal | 0 | 0 | 9.00 | 2 | 0 | 0 | 0 | 2 | 2 | 2 | 2 | 4 | 0 | R | R | 6-2 | 187 | 9-3-69 | 1987 | Beaumont, Texas |

## FIELDING

| Catcher | PCT | G | PO | A | E | DP | PB |
|---|---|---|---|---|---|---|---|
| Hicks | 1.000 | 1 | 1 | 0 | 0 | 0 | 0 |
| Rippelmeyer | 1.000 | 1 | 2 | 0 | 0 | 0 | 0 |
| Stricklin | .996 | 44 | 238 | 30 | 1 | 5 | 4 |
| Toth | .981 | 107 | 600 | 83 | 13 | 5 | 9 |

| First Base | PCT | G | PO | A | E | DP |
|---|---|---|---|---|---|---|
| Jimenez | 1.000 | 1 | 3 | 0 | 0 | 0 |
| Newell | 1.000 | 1 | 8 | 0 | 0 | 0 |
| Nunez | 1.000 | 6 | 60 | 2 | 0 | 8 |
| Simon | .983 | 81 | 664 | 50 | 12 | 61 |
| Wright | .988 | 54 | 434 | 45 | 6 | 34 |

| Second Base | PCT | G | PO | A | E | DP |
|---|---|---|---|---|---|---|
| Brito | 1.000 | 2 | 3 | 3 | 0 | 1 |
| Jimenez | .968 | 35 | 58 | 91 | 5 | 20 |
| Malloy | .972 | 105 | 209 | 278 | 14 | 53 |
| Newell | .000 | 1 | 0 | 0 | 0 | 0 |

| Third Base | PCT | G | PO | A | E | DP |
|---|---|---|---|---|---|---|
| Helms | .924 | 64 | 50 | 96 | 12 | 6 |
| Jimenez | .917 | 44 | 29 | 82 | 10 | 5 |
| Newell | 1.000 | 4 | 3 | 8 | 0 | 0 |
| Nunez | .848 | 23 | 10 | 29 | 7 | 2 |
| Rippelmeyer | .667 | 2 | 0 | 2 | 1 | 0 |
| Rodarte | .902 | 19 | 18 | 28 | 5 | 4 |
| Toth | .000 | 1 | 0 | 0 | 0 | 0 |

| Shortstop | PCT | G | PO | A | E | DP |
|---|---|---|---|---|---|---|
| Brito | .936 | 13 | 13 | 31 | 3 | 6 |
| Jimenez | .939 | 56 | 78 | 139 | 14 | 27 |
| Martinez | .957 | 9 | 9 | 35 | 2 | 7 |
| Newell | .955 | 84 | 116 | 201 | 15 | 44 |

| Outfield | PCT | G | PO | A | E | DP |
|---|---|---|---|---|---|---|
| Correa | .981 | 60 | 150 | 6 | 3 | 1 |
| Jimenez | .000 | 1 | 0 | 0 | 0 | 0 |

| | PCT | G | PO | A | E | DP |
|---|---|---|---|---|---|---|
| Jones | .993 | 38 | 129 | 7 | 1 | 1 |
| McBride | .977 | 80 | 127 | 3 | 3 | 0 |
| McFarlin | .983 | 71 | 111 | 3 | 2 | 1 |
| Monds | .970 | 32 | 62 | 2 | 2 | 1 |
| Nunez | .000 | 1 | 0 | 0 | 0 | 0 |
| Rippelmeyer | 1.000 | 1 | 3 | 0 | 0 | 0 |
| Rodarte | .980 | 26 | 42 | 7 | 1 | 2 |
| Simon | .941 | 36 | 59 | 5 | 4 | 0 |
| Swann | .949 | 34 | 55 | 1 | 3 | 0 |
| Toth | 1.000 | 1 | 1 | 0 | 0 | 0 |
| Walton | 1.000 | 3 | 2 | 0 | 0 | 0 |
| Warner | .994 | 60 | 153 | 6 | 1 | 3 |

# DURHAM — Class A
## CAROLINA LEAGUE

| BATTING | AVG | G | AB | R | H | 2B | 3B | HR | RBI | BB | SO | SB | CS | B | T | HT | WT | DOB | 1st Yr | Resides |
|---|---|---|---|---|---|---|---|---|---|---|---|---|---|---|---|---|---|---|---|---|
| Brito, Luis | .286 | 81 | 315 | 35 | 90 | 16 | 1 | 3 | 34 | 10 | 33 | 6 | 3 | S | R | 6-0 | 155 | 4-12-71 | 1989 | San Pedro de Macoris, D.R. |
| Cordero, Edward | .198 | 68 | 177 | 27 | 35 | 6 | 1 | 0 | 12 | 15 | 59 | 1 | 3 | R | R | 6-0 | 155 | 6-6-75 | 1992 | Santo Domingo, D.R. |
| Correa, Miguel | .258 | 65 | 248 | 39 | 64 | 17 | 2 | 7 | 27 | 14 | 46 | 15 | 6 | S | R | 6-2 | 165 | 9-10-71 | 1990 | Arroyo, P.R. |
| Eaglin, Mike | .253 | 131 | 466 | 84 | 118 | 26 | 2 | 11 | 54 | 50 | 88 | 23 | 12 | S | R | 5-10 | 170 | 4-25-73 | 1992 | San Pablo, Calif. |
| French, Anton | .248 | 52 | 210 | 25 | 52 | 10 | 2 | 5 | 22 | 13 | 42 | 23 | 3 | S | R | 5-10 | 170 | 7-25-75 | 1993 | St. Louis, Mo. |
| Helms, Wes | .322 | 67 | 258 | 40 | 83 | 19 | 2 | 13 | 54 | 12 | 51 | 1 | 1 | R | R | 6-4 | 210 | 5-12-76 | 1994 | Gastonia, N.C. |
| Jones, Andruw | .313 | 66 | 243 | 65 | 76 | 14 | 3 | 17 | 43 | 42 | 54 | 16 | 4 | R | R | 6-1 | 170 | 4-23-77 | 1994 | Willemstad, Curacao |
| Kennedy, Gus | .210 | 116 | 348 | 52 | 73 | 11 | 2 | 19 | 50 | 58 | 124 | 6 | 6 | R | R | 5-10 | 195 | 12-26-73 | 1994 | Seligman, Ariz. |
| Lewis, Marc | .298 | 68 | 262 | 43 | 78 | 12 | 2 | 6 | 26 | 24 | 37 | 25 | 9 | R | R | 6-2 | 175 | 5-20-75 | 1994 | Decatur, Ala. |
| Magee, Danny | .299 | 95 | 344 | 59 | 103 | 19 | 3 | 12 | 40 | 20 | 70 | 17 | 5 | R | R | 6-0 | 175 | 11-25-74 | 1993 | Denham Springs, La. |
| Mahoney, Mike | .259 | 101 | 363 | 52 | 94 | 24 | 2 | 9 | 46 | 23 | 64 | 4 | 3 | R | R | 6-0 | 185 | 12-5-72 | 1995 | Des Moines, Iowa |
| Matos, Julius | .224 | 67 | 219 | 24 | 49 | 9 | 3 | 6 | 28 | 7 | 70 | 6 | 6 | R | R | 6-2 | 160 | 12-23-74 | 1992 | Barahona, D.R. |
| McBride, Gator | .245 | 14 | 49 | 7 | 12 | 4 | 0 | 2 | 6 | 5 | 14 | 1 | 0 | R | R | 5-10 | 170 | 8-12-73 | 1993 | Hurricane, W.Va. |
| Nunez, Raymond | .309 | 65 | 243 | 30 | 75 | 18 | 1 | 10 | 55 | 12 | 45 | 2 | 2 | R | R | 6-0 | 185 | 9-22-72 | 1990 | Manzanillo, D.R. |
| Smith, Sean | .227 | 87 | 278 | 18 | 63 | 9 | 1 | 8 | 34 | 32 | 59 | 3 | 1 | L | R | 5-10 | 185 | 2-15-74 | 1992 | Oconomowoc, Wis. |
| Trippy, Joe | .250 | 5 | 20 | 3 | 5 | 0 | 0 | 1 | 3 | 2 | 3 | 1 | 2 | L | L | 5-10 | 185 | 7-31-73 | 1995 | Seattle, Wash. |
| Warner, Mike | .111 | 3 | 9 | 1 | 1 | 0 | 0 | 0 | 2 | 2 | 2 | 1 | 0 | L | L | 5-10 | 170 | 5-9-71 | 1992 | Palm Beach Gardens, Fla. |
| Whatley, Gabe | .331 | 49 | 160 | 29 | 53 | 11 | 0 | 3 | 26 | 32 | 23 | 7 | 6 | L | R | 6-0 | 180 | 12-29-71 | 1993 | Stone Mountain, Ga. |
| Wood, Tony | .144 | 60 | 118 | 11 | 17 | 1 | 0 | 0 | 5 | 5 | 38 | 5 | 4 | R | R | 5-9 | 170 | 7-6-72 | 1994 | Tacoma, Wash. |
| Wright, Ron | .275 | 66 | 240 | 47 | 66 | 15 | 2 | 20 | 62 | 37 | 71 | 1 | 0 | R | R | 6-0 | 215 | 1-21-76 | 1994 | Kennewick, Wash. |
| Wright, Terry | .191 | 49 | 131 | 11 | 25 | 4 | 1 | 0 | 8 | 9 | 14 | 4 | 4 | L | L | 6-0 | 175 | 11-1-70 | 1994 | Ellenboro, N.C. |
| 2-team (9 W-S) | .200 | 58 | 160 | 15 | 32 | 4 | 1 | 0 | 11 | 12 | 18 | 4 | 5 | | | | | | | |

**GAMES BY POSITION: C**—Mahoney 90, Matos 55, Smith 3. **1B**—Nunez 60, Smith 5, Whatley 7, Wood 14, R. Wright 66, T. Wright 2. **2B**—Brito 2, Cordero 11, Eaglin 128, Nunez 1, Wood 4. **3B**—Brito 1, Cordero 10, Helms 67, Magee 43, Whatley 17, Wood 17. **SS**—Brito

JEFF GOLDEN

DAVID SEELIG

**Home Run Leaders.** First baseman Ron Wright, left, and outfielder Ryan Klesko led Braves minor and major leaguers in home runs in 1996. Klesko hit 34 home runs for Atlanta, Wright 36 for Class A Durham and Class AA Greenville before being traded to Pittsburgh.

67, Cordero 40, French 1, Magee 39, Wood 7. **OF**—Brito 8, Cordero 1, Correa 63, French 45, Jones 66, Kennedy 106, Lewis 67, McBride 13, Trippy 5, Warner 1, Whatley 28, Wood 5, T. Wright 42.

| PITCHING | W | L | ERA | G | GS | CG | SV | IP | H | R | ER | BB | SO | B | T | HT | WT | DOB | 1st Yr | Resides |
|---|---|---|---|---|---|---|---|---|---|---|---|---|---|---|---|---|---|---|---|---|
| Bowie, Micah | 3 | 6 | 3.66 | 13 | 13 | 0 | 0 | 66 | 55 | 29 | 27 | 33 | 65 | L | L | 6-4 | 185 | 11-10-74 | 1993 | Humble, Texas |
| Briggs, Anthony | 9 | 10 | 4.40 | 31 | 18 | 1 | 0 | 125 | 131 | 84 | 61 | 60 | 76 | R | R | 6-1 | 162 | 9-14-73 | 1994 | Manning, S.C. |
| Brooks, Antone | 0 | 0 | 0.00 | 2 | 0 | 0 | 0 | 3 | 1 | 0 | 0 | 0 | 6 | L | L | 6-0 | 176 | 12-20-73 | 1995 | Florence, S.C. |
| Butler, Adam | 0 | 0 | 0.00 | 9 | 0 | 0 | 5 | 11 | 2 | 0 | 0 | 7 | 14 | L | L | 6-2 | 225 | 8-17-73 | 1995 | Burke, Va. |
| Cruz, Charlie | 1 | 1 | 5.79 | 8 | 0 | 0 | 0 | 19 | 15 | 12 | 12 | 7 | 12 | L | L | 5-10 | 175 | 10-22-73 | 1995 | Miami, Fla. |
| Ebert, Derrin | 12 | 9 | 4.00 | 27 | 27 | 2 | 0 | 166 | 189 | 102 | 74 | 37 | 99 | L | L | 6-3 | 175 | 8-21-76 | 1994 | Hesperia, Calif. |
| Giard, Ken | 3 | 5 | 5.16 | 42 | 0 | 0 | 1 | 68 | 69 | 44 | 39 | 43 | 93 | R | R | 6-3 | 210 | 4-2-73 | 1991 | Warwick, R.I. |
| Jones, Mike | 0 | 2 | 4.79 | 7 | 3 | 0 | 0 | 21 | 21 | 14 | 11 | 14 | 16 | S | L | 6-0 | 187 | 8-9-72 | 1996 | San Diego, Calif. |
| King, Raymond | 3 | 6 | 4.46 | 14 | 14 | 2 | 0 | 83 | 104 | 54 | 41 | 15 | 52 | L | L | 6-1 | 221 | 1-15-74 | 1995 | Ripley, Tenn. |
| LeRoy, John | 7 | 4 | 3.50 | 19 | 19 | 0 | 0 | 111 | 91 | 47 | 43 | 52 | 94 | R | R | 6-3 | 175 | 4-19-75 | 1993 | Bellevue, Wash. |
| Ligtenberg, Kerry | 7 | 4 | 2.41 | 49 | 0 | 0 | 20 | 60 | 58 | 20 | 16 | 16 | 76 | R | R | 6-2 | 185 | 5-11-71 | 1994 | St. Paul, Minn. |
| Mathews, Del | 4 | 3 | 4.43 | 42 | 2 | 0 | 5 | 65 | 74 | 39 | 32 | 26 | 46 | L | L | 6-3 | 200 | 10-31-74 | 1993 | Fernandina Beach, Fla. |
| Millwood, Kevin | 6 | 9 | 4.28 | 33 | 20 | 1 | 1 | 149 | 138 | 77 | 71 | 58 | 139 | R | R | 6-4 | 205 | 12-24-74 | 1993 | Bessemer City, N.C. |
| Moss, Damian | 9 | 1 | 2.25 | 14 | 14 | 0 | 0 | 84 | 52 | 25 | 21 | 40 | 89 | R | L | 6-0 | 187 | 11-24-76 | 1994 | Sadler, Australia |
| Olszewski, Eric | 2 | 2 | 1.88 | 32 | 0 | 0 | 4 | 53 | 34 | 12 | 11 | 21 | 69 | L | R | 6-3 | 205 | 11-4-74 | 1993 | Spring, Texas |
| Rocker, John | 4 | 3 | 3.39 | 9 | 9 | 0 | 0 | 58 | 63 | 24 | 22 | 25 | 43 | R | L | 6-4 | 205 | 10-17-74 | 1994 | Macon, Ga. |
| Schmitt, Chris | 3 | 1 | 4.40 | 42 | 0 | 0 | 0 | 74 | 80 | 47 | 36 | 45 | 65 | L | L | 5-11 | 180 | 1-1-71 | 1993 | Sarasota, Fla. |

## MACON — Class A

### SOUTH ATLANTIC LEAGUE

| BATTING | AVG | G | AB | R | H | 2B | 3B | HR | RBI | BB | SO | SB | CS | B | T | HT | WT | DOB | 1st Yr | Resides |
|---|---|---|---|---|---|---|---|---|---|---|---|---|---|---|---|---|---|---|---|---|
| Bass, Jayson | .364 | 5 | 22 | 2 | 8 | 0 | 0 | 1 | 1 | 0 | 5 | 3 | 1 | S | R | 6-0 | 175 | 6-2-76 | 1994 | Fayette, Ala. |
| Brown, Roosevelt | .278 | 113 | 413 | 61 | 115 | 27 | 0 | 19 | 64 | 33 | 60 | 21 | 11 | L | R | 5-10 | 190 | 8-3-75 | 1993 | Vicksburg, Miss. |
| Daugherty, Keith | .232 | 106 | 327 | 38 | 76 | 17 | 2 | 10 | 39 | 26 | 89 | 5 | 3 | R | R | 6-4 | 230 | 7-11-73 | 1995 | Opelika, Ala. |
| Delgado, Jose | .293 | 102 | 345 | 43 | 101 | 16 | 0 | 0 | 50 | 27 | 56 | 23 | 11 | S | R | 5-11 | 155 | 3-20-75 | 1993 | Carolina, P.R. |
| Foote, Derek | .236 | 107 | 330 | 29 | 78 | 10 | 1 | 17 | 45 | 30 | 141 | 3 | 1 | L | R | 6-4 | 235 | 11-18-74 | 1994 | Smithfield, N.C. |
| Hicks, Jamie | .220 | 68 | 186 | 17 | 41 | 7 | 0 | 3 | 17 | 9 | 33 | 3 | 1 | R | R | 6-2 | 200 | 11-15-71 | 1994 | Hermitage, Tenn. |
| Hodges, Randy | .241 | 101 | 278 | 36 | 67 | 12 | 1 | 2 | 28 | 18 | 42 | 10 | 10 | L | R | 6-0 | 185 | 1-20-73 | 1995 | Ocala, Fla. |
| Lewis, Marc | .315 | 66 | 241 | 36 | 76 | 14 | 3 | 5 | 28 | 21 | 31 | 25 | 8 | R | R | 6-2 | 175 | 5-20-75 | 1994 | Decatur, Ala. |
| Lombard, George | .245 | 116 | 444 | 76 | 109 | 16 | 8 | 15 | 51 | 36 | 122 | 24 | 17 | L | R | 6-0 | 208 | 9-14-75 | 1994 | Atlanta, Ga. |
| Lunar, Fernando | .184 | 104 | 343 | 33 | 63 | 9 | 0 | 7 | 33 | 20 | 65 | 3 | 2 | R | R | 6-2 | 205 | 5-25-77 | 1994 | Anaco, Venez. |
| Pendergrass, Tyrone | .267 | 12 | 45 | 8 | 12 | 1 | 1 | 1 | 3 | 4 | 12 | 5 | 3 | S | R | 6-1 | 174 | 7-31-76 | 1995 | Hartsville, S.C. |
| Person, Wilt | .156 | 40 | 122 | 9 | 19 | 0 | 0 | 0 | 7 | 4 | 23 | 2 | 3 | R | R | 6-3 | 175 | 8-16-73 | 1994 | Starkville, Miss. |
| Pointer, Corey | .240 | 8 | 25 | 4 | 6 | 1 | 0 | 1 | 2 | 0 | 9 | 2 | 1 | R | R | 6-2 | 205 | 9-2-75 | 1994 | Waxahachie, Texas |
| Ross, Jason | .158 | 5 | 19 | 2 | 3 | 0 | 0 | 1 | 3 | 2 | 7 | 1 | 0 | R | R | 6-4 | 215 | 6-10-74 | 1996 | Augusta, Ga. |
| Rust, Brian | .111 | 7 | 9 | 2 | 1 | 0 | 0 | 0 | 2 | 2 | 2 | 0 | 0 | R | R | 6-3 | 205 | 8-1-74 | 1995 | Portland, Ore. |
| Sasser, Rob | .262 | 135 | 465 | 64 | 122 | 35 | 3 | 8 | 64 | 65 | 108 | 38 | 8 | R | R | 6-4 | 190 | 3-6-75 | 1993 | Oakland, Calif. |
| Trippy, Joe | .271 | 128 | 439 | 78 | 119 | 22 | 8 | 4 | 42 | 55 | 48 | 47 | 20 | L | L | 5-10 | 185 | 7-31-73 | 1995 | Seattle, Wash. |
| Utting, Ben | .227 | 119 | 330 | 36 | 75 | 12 | 2 | 0 | 19 | 22 | 68 | 16 | 5 | L | R | 6-1 | 160 | 12-25-75 | 1993 | Melbourne, Australia |
| Williams, Glenn | .193 | 51 | 181 | 14 | 35 | 7 | 3 | 3 | 18 | 18 | 47 | 4 | 2 | S | R | 6-1 | 185 | 7-18-77 | 1994 | Ingleburn, Australia |

**GAMES BY POSITION: C**—Foote 47, Hicks 11, Hodges 1, Lunar 90, Pointer 7. **1B**—Daugherty 82, Foote 33, Hicks 24, Person 4, Rust 1, Sasser 28. **2B**—Delgado 84, Hodges 58, Sasser 1, Utting 9. **3B**—Daugherty 2, Hicks 2, Hodges 21, Sasser 110, Utting 20. **SS**—Delgado

2, Sasser 11, Utting 88, Williams 51. **OF**—Bass 5, Brown 83, Daugherty 2, Hicks 8, Hodges 9, Lewis 64, Lombard 108, Pendergrass 12, Person 20, Ross 5, Sasser 1, Trippy 121.

| PITCHING | W | L | ERA | G | GS | CG | SV | IP | H | R | ER | BB | SO | B | T | HT | WT | DOB | 1st Yr | Resides |
|---|---|---|---|---|---|---|---|---|---|---|---|---|---|---|---|---|---|---|---|---|
| Abreu, Winston | 4 | 3 | 3.00 | 12 | 12 | 0 | 0 | 60 | 51 | 29 | 20 | 25 | 60 | R | R | 6-2 | 155 | 4-5-77 | 1994 | Cotui, D.R. |
| Blythe, Billy | 4 | 12 | 5.36 | 26 | 26 | 0 | 0 | 123 | 128 | 98 | 73 | 107 | 85 | R | R | 6-2 | 190 | 1-25-76 | 1994 | Lexington, Ky. |
| Brooks, Antone | 9 | 4 | 2.24 | 43 | 0 | 0 | 10 | 80 | 57 | 24 | 20 | 36 | 101 | L | L | 6-0 | 176 | 12-20-73 | 1995 | Florence, S.C. |
| Butler, Adam | 0 | 1 | 1.23 | 12 | 0 | 0 | 8 | 15 | 5 | 3 | 2 | 3 | 23 | L | L | 6-2 | 225 | 8-17-73 | 1995 | Burke, Va. |
| Case, Chris | 2 | 4 | 4.08 | 23 | 4 | 0 | 0 | 53 | 52 | 35 | 24 | 25 | 36 | L | L | 6-5 | 170 | 12-23-74 | 1996 | Hendersonville, N.C. |
| Christmas, Maurice | 5 | 4 | 4.10 | 39 | 1 | 0 | 1 | 83 | 89 | 45 | 38 | 21 | 62 | R | R | 6-4 | 190 | 2-26-74 | 1992 | Winchester, Mass. |
| Cochran, Andrew | 0 | 3 | 4.94 | 13 | 0 | 0 | 0 | 24 | 19 | 16 | 13 | 14 | 17 | L | L | 6-2 | 205 | 10-8-74 | 1995 | Richmond, B.C. |
| Corba, Lisandro | 0 | 0 | 1.80 | 2 | 0 | 0 | 0 | 5 | 3 | 1 | 1 | 5 | 1 | R | R | 6-3 | 200 | 9-2-75 | 1995 | Santa Fe, Argentina |
| Cruz, Charlie | 5 | 4 | 3.72 | 35 | 0 | 0 | 4 | 77 | 70 | 40 | 32 | 34 | 89 | L | L | 5-10 | 175 | 10-22-73 | 1995 | Miami, Fla. |
| Daugherty, Keith | 0 | 0 | 0.00 | 4 | 0 | 0 | 0 | 5 | 0 | 0 | 0 | 0 | 2 | R | R | 6-4 | 230 | 7-11-73 | 1995 | Opelika, Ala. |
| Garcia, Jose | 8 | 4 | 4.19 | 32 | 19 | 0 | 0 | 122 | 108 | 64 | 57 | 58 | 109 | R | R | 6-1 | 165 | 2-26-75 | 1994 | Santo Domingo, D.R. |
| Giard, Ken | 1 | 0 | 1.59 | 5 | 0 | 0 | 1 | 6 | 3 | 1 | 1 | 1 | 9 | R | R | 6-3 | 210 | 4-2-73 | 1991 | Warwick, R.I. |
| Howard, Jamie | 0 | 4 | 7.86 | 8 | 6 | 0 | 0 | 26 | 37 | 26 | 23 | 16 | 11 | R | R | 6-5 | 200 | 12-7-73 | 1992 | Lafayette, La. |
| Jacobs, Dwayne | 2 | 7 | 6.80 | 26 | 15 | 0 | 0 | 82 | 85 | 82 | 62 | 76 | 76 | R | R | 6-8 | 195 | 7-17-76 | 1994 | Jacksonville, Fla. |
| Jacobs, Mike | 0 | 4 | 5.26 | 11 | 2 | 0 | 0 | 26 | 31 | 26 | 15 | 19 | 21 | R | R | 6-6 | 235 | 5-3-73 | 1994 | Stockbridge, Ga. |
| Kahlon, Bobby | 2 | 1 | 3.52 | 14 | 0 | 0 | 4 | 23 | 21 | 10 | 9 | 10 | 25 | R | R | 6-0 | 175 | 9-15-72 | 1995 | El Sobrante, Calif. |
| King, Raymond | 3 | 5 | 2.80 | 18 | 10 | 1 | 0 | 71 | 63 | 34 | 22 | 30 | 63 | L | L | 6-1 | 221 | 1-15-74 | 1995 | Ripley, Tenn. |
| Pinales, Aquiles | 3 | 1 | 5.72 | 18 | 0 | 0 | 0 | 28 | 26 | 23 | 18 | 21 | 22 | R | R | 5-11 | 190 | 9-26-74 | 1996 | La Romana, D.R. |
| Rocker, John | 5 | 3 | 3.89 | 20 | 19 | 2 | 0 | 106 | 85 | 60 | 46 | 63 | 107 | R | L | 6-4 | 205 | 10-17-74 | 1994 | Macon, Ga. |
| Sanchez, Martin | 5 | 5 | 3.97 | 31 | 13 | 0 | 1 | 107 | 109 | 60 | 47 | 53 | 92 | R | R | 6-2 | 175 | 1-19-77 | 1994 | Santo Domingo, D.R. |
| Shumate, Jacob | 0 | 0 | 12.00 | 1 | 1 | 0 | 0 | 3 | 5 | 5 | 4 | 2 | 2 | R | R | 6-2 | 180 | 1-22-76 | 1994 | Hartsville, S.C. |
| Snead, George | 0 | 1 | 11.05 | 3 | 0 | 0 | 0 | 7 | 13 | 10 | 9 | 0 | 3 | R | R | 6-3 | 210 | 1-30-74 | 1996 | Soperton, Ga. |
| Villegas, Ismael | 3 | 7 | 5.00 | 12 | 12 | 2 | 0 | 72 | 80 | 46 | 40 | 19 | 60 | R | R | 6-0 | 177 | 8-12-76 | 1995 | Caguas, P.R. |

## EUGENE — Class A
### NORTHWEST LEAGUE

| BATTING | AVG | G | AB | R | H | 2B | 3B | HR | RBI | BB | SO | SB | CS | B | T | HT | WT | DOB | 1st Yr | Resides |
|---|---|---|---|---|---|---|---|---|---|---|---|---|---|---|---|---|---|---|---|---|
| Arnold, John | .256 | 31 | 78 | 16 | 20 | 5 | 0 | 5 | 19 | 14 | 25 | 1 | 0 | R | R | 6-0 | 185 | 2-12-75 | 1996 | Albuquerque, N.M. |
| Brown, Gavin | .262 | 58 | 206 | 31 | 54 | 6 | 1 | 6 | 34 | 22 | 33 | 0 | 2 | R | R | 6-4 | 211 | 5-12-75 | 1996 | Newport Beach, Calif. |
| Cross, Adam | .255 | 55 | 196 | 34 | 50 | 12 | 0 | 3 | 24 | 27 | 41 | 9 | 5 | R | R | 6-1 | 180 | 8-22-73 | 1995 | Bluff City, Tenn. |
| DeRosa, Mark | .259 | 70 | 255 | 43 | 66 | 13 | 1 | 2 | 28 | 38 | 48 | 3 | 4 | R | R | 6-1 | 185 | 2-26-75 | 1996 | Carlstadt, N.J. |
| Ellison, Skeeter | .350 | 7 | 20 | 4 | 7 | 3 | 1 | 1 | 6 | 3 | 6 | 0 | 1 | S | R | 5-10 | 177 | 9-15-75 | 1995 | Provo, Utah |
| Espada, Angel | .245 | 24 | 98 | 15 | 24 | 4 | 0 | 0 | 5 | 3 | 11 | 13 | 5 | R | R | 5-9 | 150 | 8-15-75 | 1994 | Salinas, P.R. |
| Hacker, Steve | .250 | 75 | 292 | 45 | 73 | 15 | 1 | 21 | 61 | 26 | 64 | 0 | 0 | R | R | 6-5 | 240 | 9-6-74 | 1995 | St. Louis, Mo. |
| Hines, Pooh | .352 | 21 | 88 | 20 | 31 | 5 | 5 | 2 | 8 | 7 | 18 | 3 | 4 | R | R | 5-11 | 185 | 9-13-74 | 1995 | Atlanta, Ga. |
| Johnson, Adam | .314 | 76 | 318 | 58 | 100 | 22 | 9 | 7 | 56 | 19 | 32 | 4 | 1 | L | L | 6-0 | 185 | 7-18-75 | 1996 | Naples, Fla. |
| Katz, Jason | .179 | 7 | 28 | 3 | 5 | 1 | 0 | 0 | 2 | 4 | 11 | 0 | 0 | S | R | 5-10 | 180 | 10-7-73 | 1996 | Bayside, N.Y. |
| Norris, Dax | .289 | 60 | 232 | 31 | 67 | 17 | 0 | 7 | 37 | 18 | 32 | 2 | 0 | R | R | 5-10 | 190 | 11-14-73 | 1996 | LaGrange, Ga. |
| Pickett, Eric | .224 | 61 | 214 | 32 | 48 | 7 | 4 | 6 | 25 | 25 | 77 | 1 | 4 | L | R | 6-2 | 190 | 10-16-75 | 1994 | San Jose, Calif. |
| Pointer, Corey | .245 | 65 | 233 | 46 | 57 | 12 | 3 | 14 | 39 | 35 | 88 | 10 | 2 | R | R | 6-2 | 205 | 9-2-75 | 1994 | Waxahachie, Texas |
| Rust, Brian | .287 | 71 | 275 | 52 | 79 | 24 | 3 | 10 | 43 | 20 | 74 | 4 | 2 | R | R | 6-3 | 205 | 8-1-74 | 1995 | Portland, Ore. |
| Vecchioni, Jerry | .137 | 26 | 51 | 7 | 7 | 2 | 0 | 1 | 4 | 8 | 21 | 0 | 0 | R | R | 6-0 | 180 | 3-18-77 | 1995 | Baltimore, Md. |
| Wong, Jerrod | .262 | 28 | 84 | 10 | 22 | 2 | 0 | 1 | 6 | 3 | 20 | 0 | 0 | R | R | 6-0 | 185 | 5-29-74 | 1996 | Boise, Idaho |

**GAMES BY POSITION: C**—Arnold 17, Brown 12, Norris 56, Pointer 1. **1B**—Hacker 64, Pointer 1, Rust 6, Wong 14. **2B**—Cross 39, Ellison 3, Espada 23, Hines 14, Katz 2, Vecchioni 3. **3B**—Cross 7, Hines 6, Katz 2, Rust 65, Vecchioni 3. **SS**—Cross 1, DeRosa 70, Katz 1, Vecchioni 9. **OF**—Brown 34, Cross 1, Ellison 1, Johnson 76, Pickett 52, Pointer 64, Rust 1, Vecchioni 1, Wong 3.

| PITCHING | W | L | ERA | G | GS | CG | SV | IP | H | R | ER | BB | SO | B | T | HT | WT | DOB | 1st Yr | Resides |
|---|---|---|---|---|---|---|---|---|---|---|---|---|---|---|---|---|---|---|---|---|
| Allen, Rodney | 2 | 1 | 3.50 | 22 | 1 | 0 | 6 | 44 | 47 | 21 | 17 | 13 | 39 | R | R | 6-2 | 210 | 6-29-74 | 1996 | Lindside, W.Va. |
| Bauldree, Joe | 0 | 0 | 9.00 | 3 | 1 | 0 | 0 | 7 | 10 | 8 | 7 | 4 | 5 | R | R | 6-6 | 185 | 3-23-77 | 1995 | Wake Forest, N.C. |
| Beasley, Earl | 0 | 0 | 0.00 | 3 | 0 | 0 | 0 | 4 | 4 | 2 | 0 | 2 | 7 | R | L | 5-11 | 168 | 1-10-76 | 1996 | Lake City, Fla. |
| Bell, Rob | 5 | 6 | 5.11 | 16 | 16 | 0 | 0 | 81 | 89 | 49 | 46 | 29 | 74 | R | R | 6-5 | 225 | 1-17-77 | 1995 | Marlboro, N.Y. |
| Blanco, Roger | 2 | 1 | 6.46 | 5 | 3 | 0 | 0 | 15 | 17 | 13 | 11 | 12 | 12 | R | R | 6-6 | 220 | 8-29-76 | 1993 | La Sabana, Venez. |
| 2-team (11 Everett) ... | 3 | 8 | 6.23 | 16 | 14 | 0 | 0 | 65 | 79 | 59 | 45 | 40 | 47 | | | | | | | |
| Chen, Bruce | 4 | 1 | 2.27 | 11 | 8 | 0 | 0 | 36 | 23 | 13 | 9 | 14 | 55 | L | L | 6-2 | 180 | 6-19-77 | 1994 | Panama City, Panama |
| Cochran, Andrew | 6 | 0 | 3.55 | 15 | 7 | 0 | 0 | 58 | 54 | 33 | 23 | 26 | 51 | L | L | 6-2 | 205 | 10-8-74 | 1995 | Richmond, B.C. |
| Cortes, David | 2 | 1 | 0.73 | 15 | 0 | 0 | 4 | 25 | 13 | 2 | 2 | 6 | 33 | R | R | 5-11 | 195 | 10-15-73 | 1996 | El Centro, Calif. |
| Flach, Jason | 4 | 1 | 2.26 | 27 | 0 | 0 | 11 | 60 | 45 | 18 | 15 | 17 | 68 | R | R | 6-0 | 165 | 11-25-73 | 1996 | Davenport, Iowa |
| Giuliano, Joe | 4 | 5 | 3.55 | 26 | 1 | 0 | 3 | 66 | 61 | 39 | 26 | 26 | 58 | R | R | 6-2 | 180 | 1-1-76 | 1994 | Hamilton, Ohio |
| Jones, Michael | 5 | 4 | 3.98 | 13 | 2 | 0 | 0 | 41 | 40 | 24 | 18 | 17 | 41 | S | L | 6-0 | 187 | 8-9-72 | 1996 | San Diego, Calif. |
| Koehler, P.K. | 4 | 2 | 3.63 | 17 | 11 | 0 | 0 | 74 | 74 | 38 | 30 | 23 | 54 | L | L | 6-8 | 215 | 8-10-73 | 1994 | Medford, Ore. |
| McGlinchy, Kevin | 0 | 0 | 5.40 | 2 | 2 | 0 | 0 | 7 | 7 | 5 | 4 | 1 | 5 | R | R | 6-5 | 220 | 6-28-77 | 1996 | Ocala, Fla. |
| Milburn, Adam | 3 | 1 | 2.98 | 24 | 0 | 0 | 7 | 42 | 28 | 17 | 14 | 21 | 33 | R | L | 6-1 | 195 | 4-17-74 | 1996 | Springfield, Ky. |
| Nelson, Joe | 5 | 3 | 4.37 | 14 | 13 | 0 | 0 | 70 | 69 | 43 | 34 | 29 | 67 | R | R | 6-2 | 180 | 10-25-74 | 1996 | Alameda, Calif. |
| Osting, Jimmy | 2 | 1 | 2.59 | 5 | 5 | 0 | 0 | 24 | 14 | 11 | 7 | 13 | 35 | R | L | 6-5 | 200 | 4-7-77 | 1995 | Louisville, Ky. |
| Perez, Odalis | 2 | 1 | 3.80 | 10 | 6 | 0 | 0 | 24 | 26 | 16 | 10 | 11 | 38 | L | L | 6-1 | 175 | 6-7-78 | 1994 | Las Matas de Farfan, D.R. |
| Pinales, Aquiles | 0 | 0 | 3.38 | 3 | 0 | 0 | 1 | 5 | 4 | 3 | 2 | 2 | 4 | R | R | 5-11 | 190 | 9-26-74 | 1996 | La Romana, D.R. |

## DANVILLE — Rookie
### APPALACHIAN LEAGUE

| BATTING | AVG | G | AB | R | H | 2B | 3B | HR | RBI | BB | SO | SB | CS | B | T | HT | WT | DOB | 1st Yr | Resides |
|---|---|---|---|---|---|---|---|---|---|---|---|---|---|---|---|---|---|---|---|---|
| Arnold, John | .231 | 7 | 26 | 3 | 6 | 1 | 0 | 0 | 1 | 1 | 8 | 0 | 0 | R | R | 6-0 | 185 | 2-12-75 | 1996 | Albuquerque, N.M. |
| Bass, Jayson | .242 | 57 | 207 | 41 | 50 | 11 | 6 | 2 | 23 | 34 | 32 | 22 | 5 | S | R | 6-0 | 175 | 6-2-76 | 1994 | Fayette, Ala. |
| Borges, Alex | .154 | 5 | 13 | 1 | 2 | 0 | 0 | 0 | 2 | 2 | 4 | 1 | 0 | R | R | 6-1 | 185 | 7-2-74 | 1996 | Miramar, Fla. |
| Brooks, Anthony | .250 | 2 | 8 | 0 | 2 | 1 | 0 | 0 | 1 | 0 | 3 | 0 | 0 | R | R | 6-0 | 190 | 1-25-77 | 1996 | Pensacola, Fla. |
| Castaldo, Eric | .229 | 26 | 83 | 11 | 19 | 3 | 0 | 1 | 12 | 13 | 27 | 2 | 3 | R | R | 6-1 | 180 | 8-16-74 | 1996 | Apopka, Fla. |
| Champion, Jeff | .273 | 4 | 11 | 2 | 3 | 0 | 0 | 0 | 1 | 0 | 3 | 0 | 0 | R | R | 6-3 | 215 | 4-16-76 | 1996 | Chicago, Ill. |
| Ellison, Skeeter | .263 | 58 | 190 | 29 | 50 | 7 | 5 | 8 | 34 | 40 | 71 | 8 | 6 | S | R | 5-10 | 177 | 9-15-75 | 1995 | Provo, Utah |
| Katz, Jason | .237 | 45 | 139 | 20 | 33 | 8 | 1 | 1 | 17 | 22 | 38 | 7 | 5 | S | R | 5-10 | 180 | 10-7-73 | 1996 | Bayside, N.Y. |
| Pendergrass, Tyrone | .309 | 54 | 220 | 50 | 68 | 8 | 7 | 3 | 23 | 24 | 39 | 40 | 6 | S | R | 6-1 | 174 | 7-31-76 | 1995 | Hartsville, S.C. |

| Name | AVG | G | AB | R | H | 2B | 3B | HR | RBI | BB | SO | SB | CS | B | T | HT | WT | DOB | 1st Yr | Resides |
|---|---|---|---|---|---|---|---|---|---|---|---|---|---|---|---|---|---|---|---|---|
| Pugh, Josh | .143 | 6 | 21 | 0 | 3 | 0 | 0 | 0 | 1 | 0 | 3 | 0 | 0 | R | R | 6-0 | 200 | 9-10-77 | 1996 | Lexington, Ky. |
| Ross, Jason | .268 | 43 | 149 | 26 | 40 | 8 | 1 | 3 | 20 | 11 | 42 | 6 | 3 | R | R | 6-4 | 215 | 6-10-74 | 1996 | Augusta, Ga. |
| Scharrer, Jim | .227 | 62 | 242 | 31 | 55 | 17 | 2 | 3 | 32 | 22 | 74 | 3 | 4 | R | R | 6-4 | 220 | 11-5-76 | 1995 | Erie, Pa. |
| Shy, Jason | .243 | 11 | 37 | 5 | 9 | 1 | 0 | 1 | 3 | 1 | 8 | 1 | 1 | R | R | 5-11 | 200 | 11-17-73 | 1995 | Chico, Calif. |
| Spencer, Jeff | .237 | 64 | 241 | 40 | 57 | 21 | 3 | 9 | 41 | 31 | 61 | 6 | 3 | R | R | 6-2 | 170 | 6-25-77 | 1995 | Melbourne, Australia |
| Strangfeld, Aaron | .236 | 31 | 106 | 15 | 25 | 5 | 0 | 2 | 15 | 17 | 19 | 1 | 0 | S | R | 6-1 | 215 | 10-27-77 | 1996 | Lemon Grove, Calif. |
| Terhune, Mike | .280 | 56 | 214 | 32 | 60 | 9 | 5 | 2 | 27 | 23 | 26 | 6 | 3 | S | R | 6-1 | 185 | 10-14-75 | 1996 | Pocono Manor, Pa. |
| Thorpe, A.D. | .230 | 43 | 148 | 23 | 34 | 1 | 2 | 0 | 11 | 33 | 25 | 18 | 6 | S | R | 5-11 | 160 | 6-19-77 | 1996 | Rougemont, N.C. |
| Torrealba, Steve | .200 | 2 | 5 | 1 | 1 | 0 | 0 | 0 | 0 | 0 | 2 | 0 | 1 | R | R | 6-0 | 175 | 2-24-78 | 1995 | Barquisimeto, Venez. |
| Vecchioni, Jerry | .105 | 12 | 38 | 3 | 4 | 0 | 1 | 0 | 2 | 6 | 11 | 0 | 0 | R | R | 6-0 | 180 | 3-18-77 | 1995 | Baltimore, Md. |
| Walker, Corey | .198 | 30 | 91 | 15 | 18 | 3 | 1 | 2 | 19 | 12 | 30 | 2 | 2 | R | L | 6-2 | 195 | 6-1-74 | 1996 | St. Louis, Mo. |

**GAMES BY POSITION: C**—Arnold 7, Borges 5, Castaldo 22, Ellison 2, Pugh 6, Strangfeld 26, Torrealba 2. **1B**—Scharrer 62, Strangfeld 3, Terhune 1. **2B**—Brooks 1, Katz 14, Terhune 52. **3B**—Katz 7, Spencer 60. **SS**—Katz 18, Thorpe 43, Vecchioni 11. **OF**—Bass 54, Champion 2, Ellison 45, Pendergrass 53, Ross 34, Shy 4, Walker 14.

| PITCHING | W | L | ERA | G | GS | CG | SV | IP | H | R | ER | BB | SO | B | T | HT | WT | DOB | 1st Yr | Resides |
|---|---|---|---|---|---|---|---|---|---|---|---|---|---|---|---|---|---|---|---|---|
| Bauldree, Joe | 3 | 2 | 1.41 | 23 | 0 | 0 | 5 | 45 | 32 | 14 | 7 | 18 | 52 | R | R | 6-6 | 185 | 3-23-77 | 1995 | Wake Forest, N.C. |
| Beasley, Earl | 1 | 2 | 1.72 | 27 | 0 | 0 | 12 | 37 | 28 | 8 | 7 | 10 | 47 | R | L | 5-11 | 168 | 1-12-76 | 1996 | Lake City, Fla. |
| Birrell, Simon | 0 | 2 | 7.20 | 5 | 0 | 0 | 0 | 5 | 5 | 6 | 4 | 8 | 2 | R | R | 6-6 | 185 | 10-7-77 | 1995 | Ephrata, Wash. |
| Fowler, Ben | 0 | 0 | 14.29 | 4 | 0 | 0 | 0 | 6 | 8 | 13 | 9 | 5 | 2 | S | R | 6-4 | 185 | 1-21-77 | 1995 | Alpharetta, Ga. |
| LaGrandeur, Yan | 3 | 1 | 4.10 | 19 | 2 | 0 | 0 | 37 | 39 | 19 | 17 | 19 | 34 | R | R | 6-2 | 197 | 9-21-76 | 1996 | Grandy, Quebec |
| Marquis, Jason | 1 | 1 | 4.63 | 7 | 4 | 0 | 0 | 23 | 30 | 18 | 12 | 7 | 24 | L | R | 6-1 | 185 | 8-21-78 | 1996 | Coral Springs, Fla. |
| McGlinchy, Kevin | 3 | 2 | 1.13 | 13 | 13 | 0 | 0 | 72 | 52 | 21 | 9 | 11 | 77 | R | R | 6-5 | 220 | 6-28-77 | 1996 | Ocala, Fla. |
| Onley, Shawn | 3 | 2 | 3.80 | 13 | 12 | 0 | 0 | 64 | 53 | 31 | 27 | 23 | 59 | R | R | 6-5 | 190 | 9-10-74 | 1996 | Mt. Pleasant, Texas |
| Pacheco, Delvis | 8 | 1 | 2.64 | 13 | 12 | 0 | 0 | 65 | 56 | 28 | 19 | 21 | 60 | R | R | 6-2 | 180 | 6-25-78 | 1995 | Maracay, Venez. |
| Schurman, Ryan | 2 | 4 | 4.96 | 21 | 1 | 0 | 1 | 45 | 45 | 30 | 25 | 18 | 49 | R | R | 6-4 | 180 | 8-28-76 | 1995 | Tualatin, Ore. |
| Shiell, Jason | 1 | 1 | 1.97 | 12 | 12 | 0 | 0 | 59 | 44 | 14 | 13 | 19 | 57 | R | R | 6-0 | 180 | 10-19-76 | 1995 | Savannah, Ga. |
| Snead, George | 2 | 1 | 7.50 | 10 | 0 | 0 | 0 | 18 | 26 | 17 | 15 | 8 | 4 | R | R | 6-3 | 210 | 1-30-74 | 1996 | Soperton, Ga. |
| Villegas, Ismael | 0 | 0 | 3.00 | 1 | 0 | 0 | 0 | 3 | 2 | 1 | 1 | 1 | 4 | R | R | 6-0 | 177 | 8-12-76 | 1995 | Caguas, P.R. |
| Winkelsas, Joe | 1 | 1 | 7.15 | 8 | 0 | 0 | 2 | 11 | 11 | 10 | 9 | 4 | 9 | R | R | 6-3 | 188 | 9-14-73 | 1996 | Buffalo, N.Y. |
| Wise, William | 2 | 6 | 6.95 | 21 | 0 | 1 | 0 | 34 | 40 | 39 | 26 | 26 | 25 | R | R | 6-4 | 203 | 9-10-75 | 1994 | Plains, Ga. |
| Wyatt, Ben | 5 | 3 | 4.42 | 10 | 10 | 0 | 0 | 53 | 50 | 27 | 26 | 19 | 31 | L | L | 6-4 | 170 | 11-14-76 | 1995 | Little Rock, Ark. |

# WEST PALM BEACH                                                Rookie
## GULF COAST LEAGUE

| BATTING | AVG | G | AB | R | H | 2B | 3B | HR | RBI | BB | SO | SB | CS | B | T | HT | WT | DOB | 1st Yr | Resides |
|---|---|---|---|---|---|---|---|---|---|---|---|---|---|---|---|---|---|---|---|---|
| Borges, Alex | .385 | 5 | 13 | 1 | 5 | 0 | 0 | 0 | 1 | 4 | 1 | 1 | 0 | R | R | 6-1 | 185 | 7-2-74 | 1996 | Miramar, Fla. |
| Brignac, Junior | .194 | 53 | 191 | 15 | 37 | 7 | 0 | 0 | 8 | 9 | 60 | 3 | 7 | R | R | 6-3 | 175 | 2-15-78 | 1996 | Sun Valley, Calif. |
| Brooks, Anthony | .220 | 43 | 164 | 15 | 36 | 8 | 1 | 0 | 10 | 11 | 33 | 2 | 9 | R | R | 6-0 | 190 | 1-25-77 | 1996 | Pensacola, Fla. |
| Champion, Jeff | .170 | 29 | 88 | 6 | 15 | 1 | 2 | 0 | 2 | 8 | 23 | 2 | 2 | R | R | 6-3 | 215 | 4-16-76 | 1996 | Chicago, Ill. |
| Colson, Julian | .268 | 15 | 41 | 5 | 11 | 4 | 0 | 1 | 2 | 2 | 13 | 0 | 0 | R | R | 5-11 | 190 | 3-24-77 | 1996 | Lutz, Fla. |
| Crespo, Jesse | .217 | 44 | 129 | 11 | 28 | 4 | 0 | 0 | 9 | 8 | 28 | 4 | 0 | R | R | 6-3 | 200 | 9-18-77 | 1996 | Camuy, P.R. |
| Hessman, Michael | .216 | 53 | 190 | 13 | 41 | 10 | 1 | 1 | 15 | 12 | 41 | 1 | 1 | R | R | 6-5 | 220 | 3-5-78 | 1996 | Westminster, Calif. |
| Monds, Wonderful | .400 | 3 | 5 | 3 | 2 | 0 | 0 | 2 | 3 | 2 | 1 | 0 | 0 | R | R | 6-3 | 190 | 1-11-73 | 1993 | Fort Pierce, Fla. |
| Otero, Oscar | .246 | 54 | 191 | 15 | 47 | 9 | 2 | 1 | 24 | 8 | 18 | 4 | 5 | R | R | 6-1 | 165 | 5-28-77 | 1995 | Cayey, P.R. |
| Pugh, Josh | .258 | 30 | 89 | 8 | 23 | 4 | 0 | 1 | 12 | 7 | 23 | 1 | 0 | R | R | 6-0 | 200 | 9-10-77 | 1996 | Lexington, Ky. |
| Ramos, Isandel | .221 | 49 | 149 | 9 | 33 | 4 | 0 | 0 | 12 | 21 | 31 | 0 | 1 | L | R | 6-0 | 200 | 10-28-76 | 1996 | Carolina, P.R. |
| Thorpe, A.D. | .268 | 12 | 41 | 9 | 11 | 1 | 0 | 0 | 1 | 4 | 7 | 5 | 2 | S | R | 5-11 | 160 | 6-19-77 | 1996 | Rougemont, N.C. |
| Torrealba, Steve | .171 | 52 | 146 | 9 | 25 | 2 | 0 | 0 | 7 | 16 | 19 | 1 | 2 | R | R | 6-0 | 175 | 2-24-78 | 1995 | Barquisimeto, Venez. |
| Walker, Corey | .375 | 3 | 8 | 2 | 3 | 2 | 0 | 0 | 0 | 1 | 0 | 0 | 0 | R | L | 6-2 | 195 | 6-1-74 | 1996 | St. Louis, Mo. |
| Ward, Greg | .000 | 3 | 5 | 0 | 0 | 0 | 0 | 0 | 1 | 3 | 0 | 0 | 0 | R | R | 6-5 | 215 | 4-8-78 | 1996 | Avon, Conn. |
| Wilson, Heath | .167 | 3 | 6 | 1 | 1 | 0 | 0 | 0 | 0 | 0 | 2 | 0 | 0 | R | R | 6-2 | 190 | 8-9-78 | 1996 | Torquay, Australia |
| Wong, Jerrod | .289 | 13 | 45 | 7 | 13 | 6 | 0 | 0 | 4 | 1 | 7 | 0 | 1 | L | L | 6-3 | 200 | 5-29-74 | 1996 | Boise, Idaho |
| Zapp, A.J. | .149 | 47 | 161 | 9 | 24 | 9 | 0 | 0 | 5 | 15 | 58 | 0 | 0 | L | R | 6-2 | 190 | 4-24-78 | 1996 | Greenwood, Ind. |
| Zydowsky, John | .190 | 52 | 174 | 15 | 33 | 3 | 0 | 1 | 12 | 10 | 38 | 3 | 3 | R | R | 5-11 | 175 | 4-18-78 | 1996 | Pardeeville, Wis. |

**GAMES BY POSITION: C**—Borges 3, Crespo 8, Pugh 17, Torrealba 41, Wilson 2. **1B**—Crespo 6, Hessman 16, Torrealba 1, Zapp 29. **2B**—Brignac 1, Otero 8, Zydowsky 51. **3B**—Champion 2, Hessman 23, Otero 5, Ramos 36. **SS**—Brignac 49, Otero 3, Thorpe 9. **OF**—Brooks 43, Champion 25, Colson 15, Crespo 29, Bowler 8, Hessman 10, Monds 3, Otero 39, Ramos 1, Torrealba 1, Walker 3, Ward 3, Wilson 1, Wong 4, Zydowsky 1.

| PITCHING | W | L | ERA | G | GS | CG | SV | IP | H | R | ER | BB | SO | B | T | HT | WT | DOB | 1st Yr | Resides |
|---|---|---|---|---|---|---|---|---|---|---|---|---|---|---|---|---|---|---|---|---|
| Armenta, Alfredo | 2 | 4 | 4.22 | 14 | 2 | 0 | 1 | 43 | 38 | 23 | 20 | 20 | 39 | L | L | 6-1 | 185 | 8-23-78 | 1996 | Juarez, Mexico |
| Birrell, Simon | 0 | 4 | 2.40 | 10 | 10 | 0 | 0 | 56 | 50 | 18 | 15 | 22 | 32 | R | R | 6-6 | 185 | 10-7-77 | 1995 | Ephrata, Wash. |
| Canciobello, Anthony | 1 | 1 | 2.29 | 15 | 0 | 0 | 3 | 35 | 30 | 10 | 9 | 15 | 16 | R | R | 6-1 | 185 | 8-21-76 | 1996 | Carol City, Fla. |
| Ceasar, Donald | 1 | 1 | 4.44 | 10 | 3 | 0 | 0 | 24 | 25 | 12 | 12 | 15 | 17 | R | R | 6-6 | 197 | 10-25-78 | 1996 | Lake Charles, La. |
| Fowler, Ben | 1 | 4 | 3.34 | 8 | 6 | 0 | 0 | 30 | 27 | 21 | 11 | 11 | 22 | S | R | 6-4 | 185 | 1-21-77 | 1995 | Alpharetta, Ga. |
| Galban, Julian | 0 | 2 | 13.50 | 5 | 1 | 0 | 0 | 6 | 14 | 14 | 9 | 9 | 3 | R | L | 6-2 | 205 | 1-8-74 | 1996 | Miami, Fla. |
| Harden, Nathan | 2 | 2 | 4.62 | 14 | 2 | 0 | 0 | 39 | 32 | 29 | 20 | 15 | 30 | R | R | 6-2 | 185 | 1-13-78 | 1996 | Dripping Springs, Texas |
| Lee, Winston | 1 | 2 | 2.77 | 13 | 3 | 0 | 1 | 39 | 32 | 12 | 12 | 3 | 36 | R | R | 6-5 | 210 | 8-17-76 | 1996 | Montrose, Calif. |
| Lindemann, Jeff | 2 | 1 | 1.13 | 4 | 2 | 0 | 0 | 16 | 12 | 4 | 2 | 3 | 12 | R | R | 6-4 | 185 | 4-13-78 | 1996 | Tinley Park, Ill. |
| Quevedo, Ruben | 2 | 6 | 2.29 | 10 | 10 | 0 | 0 | 55 | 50 | 19 | 14 | 9 | 49 | R | R | 6-1 | 180 | 1-5-79 | 1996 | Valencia, Venez. |
| Reeder, Galen | 1 | 2 | 4.50 | 16 | 0 | 0 | 1 | 32 | 38 | 20 | 16 | 11 | 26 | L | L | 6-2 | 194 | 2-14-76 | 1996 | Loganville, Ga. |
| Rivera, Luis | 1 | 2 | 2.59 | 8 | 6 | 0 | 0 | 24 | 18 | 9 | 7 | 6 | 16 | R | R | 6-2 | 145 | 6-21-78 | 1995 | Chihuahua, Mexico |
| Serrano, Liosvany | 1 | 2 | 7.33 | 12 | 2 | 0 | 0 | 27 | 29 | 27 | 22 | 22 | 7 | R | R | 6-0 | 190 | 12-16-75 | 1996 | Miami, Fla. |
| Snead, George | 0 | 1 | 3.86 | 3 | 0 | 0 | 0 | 7 | 7 | 6 | 3 | 4 | 5 | R | R | 6-3 | 210 | 1-30-74 | 1996 | Soperton, Ga. |
| Taylor, Aaron | 0 | 9 | 7.74 | 13 | 9 | 0 | 0 | 52 | 68 | 54 | 45 | 28 | 33 | R | R | 6-7 | 205 | 8-20-77 | 1996 | Hahira, Ga. |
| Vergara, Luis | 0 | 2 | 6.19 | 4 | 3 | 0 | 0 | 16 | 21 | 14 | 11 | 4 | 10 | R | R | 6-0 | 180 | 3-31-78 | 1996 | Panama City, Panama |

# BALTIMORE ORIOLES

**Manager:** Dave Johnson.  **1996 Record:** 88-74, .543 (2nd, AL East).

| BATTING | AVG | G | AB | R | H | 2B | 3B | HR | RBI | BB | SO | SB | CS | B | T | HT | WT | DOB | 1st Yr | Resides |
|---|---|---|---|---|---|---|---|---|---|---|---|---|---|---|---|---|---|---|---|---|
| Alexander, Manny | .103 | 54 | 68 | 6 | 7 | 0 | 0 | 0 | 4 | 3 | 27 | 3 | 3 | R | R | 5-10 | 165 | 3-20-71 | 1988 | San Pedro de Macoris, D.R. |
| Alomar, Roberto | .328 | 153 | 588 | 132 | 193 | 43 | 4 | 22 | 94 | 90 | 65 | 17 | 6 | S | R | 6-0 | 175 | 2-5-68 | 1985 | Salinas, P.R. |
| Anderson, Brady | .297 | 149 | 579 | 117 | 172 | 37 | 5 | 50 | 110 | 76 | 106 | 21 | 8 | L | L | 6-1 | 195 | 1-18-64 | 1985 | Newport Beach, Calif. |
| Bonilla, Bobby | .287 | 159 | 595 | 107 | 171 | 27 | 5 | 28 | 116 | 75 | 85 | 1 | 3 | S | R | 6-3 | 240 | 2-23-63 | 1981 | Bradenton, Fla. |
| Bowers, Brent | .308 | 21 | 39 | 6 | 12 | 2 | 0 | 0 | 3 | 0 | 7 | 0 | 0 | L | R | 6-3 | 200 | 5-2-71 | 1989 | Bridgeview, Ill. |
| Devarez, Cesar | .111 | 10 | 18 | 3 | 2 | 0 | 1 | 0 | 0 | 1 | 3 | 0 | 0 | R | R | 5-10 | 175 | 9-22-69 | 1988 | San Pedro de Macoris, D.R. |
| Devereaux, Mike | .229 | 127 | 323 | 49 | 74 | 11 | 2 | 8 | 34 | 34 | 53 | 8 | 2 | R | R | 6-0 | 195 | 4-10-63 | 1985 | Tampa, Fla. |
| Hammonds, Jeffrey | .226 | 71 | 248 | 38 | 56 | 10 | 1 | 9 | 27 | 23 | 53 | 3 | 3 | R | R | 6-0 | 180 | 3-5-71 | 1992 | Scotch Plains, N.J. |
| Hoiles, Chris | .258 | 127 | 407 | 64 | 105 | 13 | 0 | 25 | 73 | 57 | 97 | 0 | 1 | R | R | 6-0 | 213 | 3-20-65 | 1986 | Cockeysville, Md. |
| Huson, Jeff | .321 | 17 | 28 | 5 | 9 | 1 | 0 | 0 | 2 | 1 | 3 | 0 | 0 | L | R | 6-3 | 180 | 8-15-64 | 1986 | Bedford, Texas |
| Incaviglia, Pete | .303 | 12 | 33 | 4 | 10 | 2 | 0 | 2 | 8 | 0 | 7 | 0 | 0 | R | R | 6-1 | 225 | 4-2-64 | 1986 | Collegeville, Texas |
| Murray, Eddie | .257 | 64 | 230 | 36 | 59 | 12 | 0 | 10 | 34 | 27 | 42 | 1 | 0 | S | R | 6-2 | 220 | 2-24-56 | 1973 | Canyon Country, Calif. |
| 2-team (88 Cleve.) | .260 | 152 | 566 | 69 | 147 | 21 | 1 | 22 | 79 | 61 | 87 | 4 | 0 | | | | | | | |
| Palmeiro, Rafael | .289 | 162 | 626 | 110 | 181 | 40 | 2 | 39 | 142 | 95 | 96 | 8 | 0 | L | L | 6-0 | 188 | 9-24-64 | 1985 | Arlington, Texas |
| Parent, Mark | .182 | 18 | 33 | 4 | 6 | 1 | 0 | 2 | 6 | 2 | 10 | 0 | 0 | R | R | 6-5 | 225 | 9-16-61 | 1979 | San Diego, Calif. |
| 2-team (38 Detroit) | .226 | 56 | 137 | 17 | 31 | 7 | 0 | 9 | 23 | 5 | 37 | 0 | 0 | | | | | | | |
| Polonia, Luis | .240 | 58 | 175 | 25 | 42 | 4 | 1 | 2 | 14 | 10 | 20 | 8 | 6 | L | L | 5-8 | 150 | 10-27-64 | 1984 | Santiago, D.R. |
| Ripken, Billy | .230 | 57 | 135 | 19 | 31 | 8 | 0 | 2 | 12 | 9 | 18 | 0 | 0 | R | R | 6-1 | 188 | 12-16-64 | 1982 | Cockeysville, Md. |
| Ripken, Cal | .278 | 163 | 640 | 94 | 178 | 40 | 1 | 26 | 102 | 59 | 78 | 1 | 2 | R | R | 6-4 | 220 | 8-24-60 | 1978 | Reisterstown, Md. |
| Smith, Mark | .244 | 27 | 78 | 9 | 19 | 2 | 0 | 4 | 10 | 3 | 20 | 0 | 2 | R | R | 6-3 | 205 | 5-7-70 | 1991 | Arcadia, Calif. |
| Surhoff, B.J. | .292 | 143 | 537 | 74 | 157 | 27 | 6 | 21 | 82 | 47 | 79 | 0 | 1 | L | R | 6-1 | 200 | 8-4-64 | 1985 | Franklin, Wis. |
| Tarasco, Tony | .238 | 31 | 84 | 14 | 20 | 3 | 0 | 1 | 9 | 7 | 15 | 5 | 3 | L | R | 6-1 | 205 | 12-9-70 | 1988 | Santa Monica, Calif. |
| Zaun, Greg | .231 | 50 | 108 | 16 | 25 | 8 | 1 | 1 | 13 | 11 | 15 | 0 | 0 | S | R | 5-10 | 170 | 4-14-71 | 1989 | Glendale, Calif. |
| Zeile, Todd | .239 | 29 | 117 | 17 | 28 | 8 | 0 | 5 | 19 | 15 | 16 | 0 | 0 | R | R | 6-1 | 185 | 9-9-65 | 1986 | Valencia, Calif. |

| PITCHING | W | L | ERA | G | GS | CG | SV | IP | H | R | ER | BB | SO | B | T | HT | WT | DOB | 1st Yr | Resides |
|---|---|---|---|---|---|---|---|---|---|---|---|---|---|---|---|---|---|---|---|---|
| Benitez, Armando | 1 | 0 | 3.77 | 18 | 0 | 0 | 4 | 14 | 7 | 6 | 6 | 6 | 20 | R | R | 6-4 | 220 | 11-3-72 | 1990 | San Pedro de Macoris, D.R. |
| Coppinger, Rocky | 10 | 6 | 5.18 | 23 | 22 | 0 | 0 | 125 | 126 | 76 | 72 | 60 | 104 | R | R | 6-5 | 245 | 3-19-74 | 1994 | El Paso, Texas |
| Corbin, Archie | 2 | 0 | 2.30 | 18 | 0 | 0 | 0 | 27 | 22 | 7 | 7 | 22 | 20 | R | R | 6-4 | 187 | 12-30-67 | 1986 | Beaumont, Texas |
| Erickson, Scott | 13 | 12 | 5.02 | 34 | 34 | 6 | 0 | 222 | 262 | 137 | 124 | 66 | 100 | R | R | 6-4 | 225 | 2-2-68 | 1989 | Sunnyvale, Calif. |
| Haynes, Jimmy | 3 | 6 | 8.29 | 26 | 11 | 0 | 1 | 89 | 122 | 84 | 82 | 58 | 65 | R | R | 6-4 | 185 | 9-5-72 | 1991 | LaGrange, Ga. |
| Krivda, Rick | 3 | 5 | 4.96 | 22 | 11 | 0 | 0 | 82 | 89 | 48 | 45 | 39 | 54 | R | L | 6-1 | 180 | 1-19-70 | 1991 | McKeesport, Pa. |
| Mathews, Terry | 2 | 2 | 3.38 | 14 | 0 | 0 | 0 | 19 | 20 | 7 | 7 | 7 | 13 | L | R | 6-2 | 225 | 10-5-64 | 1987 | Boyce, La. |
| McDowell, Roger | 1 | 1 | 4.25 | 41 | 0 | 0 | 4 | 59 | 69 | 32 | 28 | 23 | 20 | R | R | 6-1 | 195 | 12-21-60 | 1982 | Stuart, Fla. |
| Mercker, Kent | 3 | 6 | 7.76 | 14 | 12 | 0 | 0 | 58 | 73 | 56 | 50 | 35 | 22 | L | L | 6-2 | 195 | 2-1-68 | 1986 | Dublin, Ohio |
| Milchin, Mike | 1 | 0 | 5.73 | 13 | 0 | 0 | 0 | 11 | 13 | 7 | 7 | 5 | 10 | L | L | 6-3 | 190 | 2-28-68 | 1989 | Richmond, Va. |
| 2-team (26 Minnesota) | 3 | 1 | 7.44 | 39 | 0 | 0 | 0 | 33 | 44 | 28 | 27 | 17 | 29 | | | | | | | |
| Mills, Alan | 3 | 2 | 4.28 | 49 | 0 | 0 | 3 | 55 | 40 | 26 | 26 | 35 | 50 | S | R | 6-1 | 192 | 10-18-66 | 1986 | Lakeland, Fla. |
| Mussina, Mike | 19 | 11 | 4.81 | 36 | 36 | 4 | 0 | 243 | 264 | 137 | 130 | 69 | 204 | R | R | 6-2 | 185 | 12-8-68 | 1990 | Montoursville, Pa. |
| Myers, Jimmy | 0 | 0 | 7.07 | 11 | 0 | 0 | 0 | 14 | 18 | 13 | 11 | 3 | 6 | R | R | 6-1 | 195 | 4-28-69 | 1987 | Crowder, Okla. |
| Myers, Randy | 4 | 4 | 3.53 | 62 | 0 | 0 | 31 | 59 | 60 | 24 | 23 | 29 | 74 | L | L | 6-1 | 210 | 9-19-62 | 1982 | Vancouver, Wash. |
| Orosco, Jesse | 3 | 1 | 3.40 | 66 | 0 | 0 | 0 | 56 | 42 | 22 | 21 | 28 | 52 | R | L | 6-2 | 205 | 4-21-57 | 1978 | Poway, Calif. |
| Rhodes, Arthur | 9 | 1 | 4.08 | 28 | 2 | 0 | 1 | 53 | 48 | 28 | 24 | 23 | 62 | L | L | 6-2 | 204 | 10-24-69 | 1988 | Sarasota, Fla. |
| Rodriguez, Nerio | 0 | 1 | 4.32 | 8 | 1 | 0 | 0 | 17 | 18 | 11 | 8 | 7 | 12 | R | R | 6-1 | 195 | 3-22-73 | 1991 | San Pedro de Macoris, D.R. |
| Sackinsky, Brian | 0 | 0 | 3.86 | 3 | 0 | 0 | 0 | 5 | 6 | 2 | 2 | 3 | 2 | R | R | 6-4 | 220 | 6-22-71 | 1992 | Library, Pa. |
| Shepherd, Keith | 0 | 0 | 8.71 | 13 | 0 | 0 | 0 | 21 | 31 | 27 | 20 | 18 | 17 | R | R | 6-2 | 197 | 1-21-68 | 1986 | Wabash, Ind. |
| Stephenson, Garrett | 0 | 1 | 12.79 | 3 | 0 | 0 | 0 | 6 | 13 | 9 | 9 | 3 | 3 | R | R | 6-4 | 185 | 1-2-72 | 1992 | Kimberly, Md. |
| Wells, David | 11 | 14 | 5.14 | 34 | 34 | 3 | 0 | 224 | 247 | 132 | 128 | 51 | 130 | L | L | 6-4 | 225 | 5-20-63 | 1982 | Palm Harbor, Fla. |
| Yan, Esteban | 0 | 0 | 5.79 | 4 | 0 | 0 | 0 | 9 | 13 | 7 | 6 | 3 | 7 | R | R | 6-4 | 180 | 6-22-74 | 1991 | La Higuera, D.R. |

## FIELDING

| Catcher | PCT | G | PO | A | E | DP | PB |
|---|---|---|---|---|---|---|---|
| Devarez | 1.000 | 10 | 38 | 1 | 0 | 0 | 1 |
| Hoiles | .992 | 126 | 777 | 42 | 7 | 3 | 7 |
| Parent | .987 | 18 | 73 | 3 | 1 | 1 | 2 |
| Zaun | .987 | 49 | 215 | 10 | 3 | 3 | 4 |

| First Base | PCT | G | PO | A | E | DP |
|---|---|---|---|---|---|---|
| Bonilla | .966 | 9 | 27 | 1 | 1 | 4 |
| Hoiles | .000 | 1 | 0 | 0 | 0 | 0 |
| Murray | 1.000 | 1 | 10 | 1 | 0 | 0 |
| Palmeiro | .995 | 159 | 1384 | 118 | 8 | 157 |
| Parent | 1.000 | 1 | 1 | 0 | 0 | 0 |
| B. Ripken | 1.000 | 1 | 3 | 0 | 0 | 1 |
| Surhoff | 1.000 | 2 | 11 | 2 | 0 | 0 |

| Second Base | PCT | G | PO | A | E | DP |
|---|---|---|---|---|---|---|
| Alexander | 1.000 | 7 | 6 | 4 | 0 | 1 |
| Alomar | .985 | 141 | 278 | 445 | 11 | 107 |
| Huson | .973 | 12 | 20 | 16 | 1 | 6 |
| B. Ripken | .968 | 30 | 34 | 57 | 3 | 15 |

| Third Base | PCT | G | PO | A | E | DP |
|---|---|---|---|---|---|---|
| Alexander | .923 | 7 | 3 | 9 | 1 | 1 |
| Bonilla | 1.000 | 4 | 1 | 3 | 0 | 0 |

| | PCT | G | PO | A | E | DP |
|---|---|---|---|---|---|---|
| Huson | 1.000 | 3 | 0 | 1 | 0 | 0 |
| B. Ripken | 1.000 | 25 | 3 | 38 | 0 | 1 |
| C. Ripken | 1.000 | 6 | 5 | 16 | 0 | 1 |
| Surhoff | .948 | 106 | 79 | 175 | 14 | 22 |
| Zeile | .963 | 29 | 24 | 55 | 3 | 9 |

| Shortstop | PCT | G | PO | A | E | DP |
|---|---|---|---|---|---|---|
| Alexander | .940 | 21 | 14 | 33 | 3 | 6 |
| C. Ripken | .980 | 158 | 231 | 468 | 14 | 109 |

| Outfield | PCT | G | PO | A | E | DP |
|---|---|---|---|---|---|---|
| Alexander | .750 | 3 | 2 | 1 | 1 | 0 |
| Anderson | .992 | 143 | 341 | 10 | 3 | 1 |
| Bonilla | .975 | 108 | 187 | 8 | 5 | 1 |
| Bowers | 1.000 | 21 | 22 | 2 | 0 | 0 |
| Devereaux | .983 | 112 | 170 | 7 | 3 | 3 |
| Hammonds | .980 | 70 | 145 | 3 | 3 | 0 |
| Incaviglia | 1.000 | 7 | 9 | 1 | 0 | 0 |
| Polonia | .983 | 34 | 56 | 1 | 1 | 0 |
| Smith | .980 | 20 | 50 | 0 | 1 | 0 |
| Surhoff | .979 | 27 | 45 | 1 | 1 | 0 |
| Tarasco | 1.000 | 23 | 50 | 1 | 0 | 0 |

**Mike Mussina**

MORRIS FOSTOFF

Outfielder Brady Anderson led the Orioles with 50 homers

Orioles minor league Player of the Year Chris Kirgan

LARRY GOREN

# ORIOLES

## FARM SYSTEM

**Director of Player Development:** Syd Thrift

| Class | Farm Team | League | W | L | Pct. | Finish* | Manager(s) | First Yr |
|---|---|---|---|---|---|---|---|---|
| AAA | Rochester (N.Y.) Red Wings | International | 72 | 69 | .511 | 4th (10) | Marv Foley | 1961 |
| AA | Bowie (Md.) Baysox | Eastern | 54 | 88 | .380 | 10th (10) | Miscik/Blackwell | 1993 |
| #A | Frederick (Md.) Keys | Carolina | 67 | 72 | .482 | 5th (8) | Blackwell/Garcia | 1989 |
| #A | High Desert (Calif.) Mevericks | California | 76 | 64 | .543 | 4th (10) | Joe Ferguson | 1995 |
| #R | Bluefield (W.Va.) Orioles | Appalachian | 42 | 26 | .618 | +2nd (9) | Bobby Dickerson | 1958 |
| R | Sarasota (Fla.) Orioles | Gulf Coast | 36 | 24 | .600 | 4th (16) | Tommy Shields | 1991 |

*Finish in overall standings (No. of teams in league)   #Advanced level   +Won league championship

## ORGANIZATION LEADERS

### MAJOR LEAGUERS

**BATTING**
*AVG Roberto Alomar...... .328
R Roberto Alomar........ 132
H Roberto Alomar........ 193
TB Brady Anderson...... 369
2B Roberto Alomar........ 43
3B B.J. Surhoff................ 6
HR Brady Anderson...... 50
RBI Rafael Palmeiro ...... 142
BB Rafael Palmeiro ...... 95
SO Brady Anderson...... 106
SB Brady Anderson........ 21

**PITCHING**
W Mike Mussina.............19
L David Wells............... 14
#ERA Mike Mussina....... 4.81
G Jesse Orosco............ 66
CG Scott Erickson........... 6
SV Randy Myers............ 31
IP Mike Mussina.......... 243
BB Mike Mussina........... 69
SO Mike Mussina.......... 204

LARRY GOREN

**Rafael Palmeiro.** 142 RBIs

### MINOR LEAGUERS

**BATTING**
*AVG Mike Berry, High Desert/Bowie ............ .354
R Mike Berry, High Desert/Bowie ............112
H Rolando Avila, High Desert/Bowie ........ 174
TB Chris Kirgan, High Desert..................... 287
2B Mike Berry, High Desert/Bowie ............ 44
3B Two tied at................................................ 10
HR Chris Kirgan, High Desert...................... 35
RBI Chris Kirgan, High Desert.................... 131
BB Mike Berry, High Desert/Bowie ............ 103
SO Chris Kirgan, High Desert.................... 162
SB Curtis Charles, Bluefield......................... 31

**PITCHING**
W Calvin Maduro, Bowie/Rochester........... 12
L Shane Hale, Bowie................................... 13
#ERA Nerio Rodriguez, Frederick/Roch. ....... 2.21
G Matt Snyder, High Desert ....................... 58
CG Calvin Maduro, Bowie/Rochester ........... 4
SV Matt Snyder, High Desert ...................... 20
IP Matt Marenghi, High Desert ................. 171
BB Francisco Saneaux, Fred./H.D. .............. 97
SO Julio Moreno, Frederick........................ 147

*Minimum 250 At-Bats   #Minimum 75 Innings

## TOP 10 PROSPECTS

How the Orioles Top 10 prospects, as judged by Baseball America prior to the 1996 season, fared in 1996:

**Rocky Coppinger**

| Player, Pos. | Club (Class—League) | AVG | AB | R | H | 2B | 3B | HR | RBI | SB |
|---|---|---|---|---|---|---|---|---|---|---|
| 5. Eddy Martinez, ss | Bluefield (R—Appalachian) | .221 | 122 | 18 | 27 | 3 | 0 | 1 | 15 | 15 |
| | Frederick (A—Carolina) | .221 | 244 | 21 | 54 | 4 | 0 | 2 | 25 | 13 |
| 6. Eugene Kingsale, of | Frederick (A—Carolina) | .271 | 166 | 26 | 45 | 6 | 4 | 0 | 9 | 23 |
| 7. Tommy Davis, 1b | Bowie (AA—Eastern) | .261 | 524 | 75 | 137 | 32 | 2 | 14 | 54 | 5 |
| 8. *Kimera Bartee, of | Detroit | .253 | 217 | 32 | 55 | 6 | 1 | 1 | 14 | 20 |
| 10. Scott McClain, 3b | Rochester (AAA—International) | .281 | 463 | 76 | 130 | 23 | 4 | 17 | 69 | 8 |

| Player, Pos. | Club (Class—League) | W | L | ERA | G | SV | IP | H | BB | SO |
|---|---|---|---|---|---|---|---|---|---|---|
| 1. Rocky Coppinger, rhp | Rochester (AAA—International) | 6 | 4 | 4.19 | 12 | 0 | 73 | 65 | 39 | 81 |
| | Baltimore | 10 | 6 | 5.18 | 23 | 0 | 125 | 126 | 60 | 104 |
| 2. Jimmy Haynes, rhp | Rochester (AAA—International) | 1 | 1 | 5.65 | 5 | 0 | 29 | 31 | 18 | 24 |
| | Baltimore | 3 | 6 | 8.29 | 26 | 1 | 89 | 122 | 58 | 65 |
| 3. Billy Percibal, rhp | Did not play — Injured | | | | | | | | | |
| 4. Chris Fussell, rhp | Frederick (A—Carolina) | 5 | 2 | 2.81 | 15 | 0 | 86 | 71 | 44 | 94 |
| 9. Alvie Shepherd, rhp | Frederick (A—Carolina) | 6 | 5 | 5.59 | 41 | 10 | 97 | 112 | 47 | 104 |

*Claimed on waivers by Tigers

## INTERNATIONAL LEAGUE

| BATTING | AVG | G | AB | R | H | 2B | 3B | HR | RBI | BB | SO | SB | CS | B | T | HT | WT | DOB | 1st Yr | Resides |
|---|---|---|---|---|---|---|---|---|---|---|---|---|---|---|---|---|---|---|---|---|
| Avila, Rolando | .298 | 12 | 47 | 7 | 14 | 2 | 1 | 0 | 6 | 3 | 4 | 2 | 0 | R | R | 5-8 | 170 | 8-10-73 | 1994 | Paramount, Calif. |
| Bellinger, Clay | .301 | 125 | 459 | 68 | 138 | 34 | 4 | 15 | 78 | 33 | 90 | 8 | 4 | R | R | 6-3 | 195 | 11-18-68 | 1989 | Oneonta, N.Y. |
| Blosser, Greg | .235 | 38 | 115 | 11 | 27 | 6 | 1 | 2 | 12 | 12 | 29 | 2 | 1 | L | L | 6-3 | 205 | 6-26-71 | 1989 | Sarasota, Fla. |
| Bowers, Brent | .325 | 49 | 206 | 40 | 67 | 8 | 4 | 4 | 19 | 14 | 41 | 9 | 3 | L | R | 6-3 | 200 | 5-2-71 | 1989 | Bridgeview, Ill. |
| Brown, Jarvis | .211 | 57 | 204 | 28 | 43 | 6 | 6 | 4 | 19 | 19 | 36 | 9 | 1 | R | R | 5-7 | 170 | 3-26-67 | 1986 | Mt. Zion, Ill. |
| Cookson, Brent | .265 | 30 | 113 | 22 | 30 | 7 | 0 | 6 | 21 | 9 | 20 | 2 | 1 | R | R | 5-11 | 200 | 9-7-69 | 1991 | Santa Paula, Calif. |
| 2-team (73 Pawtucket) | .269 | 103 | 368 | 73 | 99 | 20 | 1 | 25 | 71 | 33 | 92 | 4 | 5 | | | | | | | |
| Denson, Drew | .350 | 16 | 60 | 14 | 21 | 7 | 1 | 2 | 10 | 7 | 12 | 0 | 0 | R | R | 6-5 | 220 | 11-16-65 | 1984 | Cincinnati, Ohio |
| Devarez, Cesar | .287 | 67 | 223 | 24 | 64 | 9 | 1 | 4 | 27 | 9 | 26 | 5 | 1 | R | R | 5-10 | 175 | 9-22-69 | 1988 | San Pedro de Macoris, D.R. |
| Figueroa, Bien | .312 | 50 | 154 | 25 | 48 | 7 | 0 | 1 | 16 | 14 | 11 | 3 | 1 | R | R | 5-10 | 167 | 2-7-64 | 1986 | Tallahassee, Fla. |
| Gordon, Keith | .250 | 33 | 104 | 15 | 26 | 4 | 1 | 5 | 19 | 9 | 27 | 0 | 3 | R | R | 6-1 | 205 | 1-22-69 | 1990 | Olney, Md. |
| Hall, Joe | .288 | 131 | 479 | 96 | 138 | 26 | 10 | 19 | 95 | 67 | 69 | 15 | 9 | R | R | 6-0 | 180 | 3-6-66 | 1988 | Paducah, Ky. |
| Hammonds, Jeffrey | .272 | 34 | 125 | 24 | 34 | 4 | 2 | 3 | 19 | 19 | 19 | 3 | 1 | R | R | 6-0 | 180 | 3-5-71 | 1992 | Scotch Plains, N.J. |
| Huson, Jeff | .250 | 2 | 8 | 0 | 2 | 0 | 0 | 0 | 1 | 0 | 2 | 0 | 0 | L | R | 6-3 | 180 | 8-15-64 | 1986 | Bedford, Texas |
| Martinez, Domingo | .362 | 29 | 116 | 18 | 42 | 7 | 0 | 7 | 38 | 10 | 17 | 0 | 1 | R | R | 6-2 | 185 | 8-4-67 | 1985 | Santo Domingo, D.R. |
| McClain, Scott | .281 | 131 | 463 | 76 | 130 | 23 | 4 | 17 | 69 | 61 | 109 | 8 | 6 | R | R | 6-3 | 209 | 5-19-72 | 1990 | Glendale, Ariz. |
| Owens, Billy | .254 | 61 | 201 | 19 | 51 | 14 | 0 | 5 | 30 | 10 | 35 | 2 | 2 | S | R | 6-1 | 210 | 4-12-71 | 1992 | Fresno, Calif. |
| Polonia, Luis | .240 | 13 | 50 | 9 | 12 | 2 | 0 | 0 | 3 | 7 | 8 | 5 | 0 | L | L | 5-8 | 150 | 10-27-64 | 1984 | Santiago, D.R. |
| Rosario, Mel | .000 | 3 | 2 | 0 | 0 | 0 | 0 | 0 | 0 | 0 | 1 | 0 | 0 | R | R | 6-0 | 191 | 5-25-73 | 1992 | Miami, Fla. |
| Smith, Mark | .348 | 39 | 132 | 24 | 46 | 14 | 1 | 8 | 32 | 14 | 22 | 10 | 1 | R | R | 6-3 | 205 | 5-7-70 | 1991 | Arcadia, Calif. |
| Tarasco, Tony | .262 | 29 | 103 | 18 | 27 | 6 | 0 | 2 | 9 | 17 | 20 | 4 | 4 | L | R | 6-1 | 205 | 12-9-70 | 1988 | Santa Monica, Calif. |
| Tyler, Brad | .270 | 118 | 382 | 68 | 103 | 18 | 10 | 13 | 52 | 67 | 95 | 19 | 7 | L | R | 6-2 | 175 | 3-3-69 | 1990 | Aurora, Ind. |
| Waszgis, B.J. | .266 | 96 | 304 | 37 | 81 | 16 | 0 | 11 | 48 | 41 | 87 | 2 | 3 | R | R | 6-2 | 210 | 8-24-70 | 1991 | Omaha, Neb. |
| Wawruck, Jim | .284 | 59 | 204 | 31 | 58 | 14 | 6 | 0 | 15 | 14 | 29 | 4 | 2 | L | L | 5-11 | 185 | 4-23-70 | 1991 | Glastonbury, Conn. |
| Zaun, Greg | .319 | 14 | 47 | 11 | 15 | 2 | 0 | 0 | 4 | 11 | 6 | 2 | 0 | S | R | 5-10 | 170 | 4-14-71 | 1989 | Glendale, Calif. |
| Zosky, Eddie | .256 | 95 | 340 | 42 | 87 | 22 | 4 | 3 | 34 | 21 | 40 | 5 | 2 | R | R | 6-0 | 175 | 2-10-68 | 1989 | Whittier, Calif. |

| PITCHING | W | L | ERA | G | GS | CG | SV | IP | H | R | ER | BB | SO | B | T | HT | WT | DOB | 1st Yr | Resides |
|---|---|---|---|---|---|---|---|---|---|---|---|---|---|---|---|---|---|---|---|---|
| Benitez, Armando | 0 | 0 | 2.25 | 2 | 0 | 0 | 0 | 4 | 3 | 1 | 1 | 1 | 5 | R | R | 6-4 | 220 | 11-3-72 | 1990 | San Pedro de Macoris, D.R. |
| Coppinger, Rocky | 6 | 4 | 4.19 | 12 | 12 | 0 | 0 | 73 | 65 | 36 | 34 | 39 | 81 | R | R | 6-5 | 245 | 3-19-74 | 1994 | El Paso, Texas |
| Corbin, Archie | 0 | 2 | 4.74 | 20 | 5 | 0 | 1 | 44 | 44 | 25 | 23 | 25 | 47 | R | R | 6-4 | 187 | 12-30-67 | 1986 | Beaumont, Texas |
| Dedrick, Jim | 6 | 3 | 6.51 | 39 | 3 | 0 | 4 | 66 | 88 | 59 | 48 | 41 | 37 | S | R | 6-0 | 185 | 4-4-68 | 1990 | Everett, Wash. |
| Dixon, Steve | 0 | 2 | 3.41 | 32 | 0 | 0 | 2 | 34 | 27 | 15 | 13 | 23 | 32 | L | L | 6-0 | 195 | 8-3-69 | 1989 | Louisville, Ky. |
| Edens, Tom | 4 | 6 | 5.19 | 20 | 10 | 0 | 0 | 68 | 73 | 43 | 39 | 23 | 36 | L | R | 6-2 | 185 | 6-9-61 | 1983 | Clarkston, Wash. |
| Florence, Don | 4 | 4 | 6.14 | 36 | 8 | 0 | 0 | 85 | 111 | 62 | 58 | 30 | 53 | R | L | 6-0 | 195 | 3-16-67 | 1988 | New Boston, N.H. |
| Flynt, Will | 1 | 1 | 8.27 | 4 | 4 | 0 | 0 | 16 | 26 | 15 | 15 | 13 | 9 | L | L | 6-5 | 215 | 11-23-67 | 1991 | San Diego, Calif. |
| Frohwirth, Todd | 0 | 2 | 4.50 | 9 | 0 | 0 | 0 | 16 | 11 | 8 | 8 | 5 | 16 | R | R | 6-4 | 204 | 9-28-62 | 1984 | Milwaukee, Wis. |
| Grott, Matt | 0 | 0 | 3.86 | 5 | 1 | 0 | 0 | 9 | 13 | 10 | 4 | 7 | 5 | L | L | 6-1 | 205 | 12-5-67 | 1989 | Glendale, Ariz. |
| 2-team (27 Scranton) | 1 | 3 | 4.78 | 32 | 13 | 0 | 0 | 96 | 105 | 58 | 51 | 29 | 68 | | | | | | | |
| Harris, Doug | 2 | 3 | 4.08 | 7 | 3 | 0 | 0 | 18 | 22 | 19 | 8 | 6 | 4 | R | R | 6-4 | 205 | 9-27-69 | 1990 | Carlisle, Pa. |
| Haynes, Jimmy | 1 | 1 | 5.65 | 5 | 5 | 0 | 0 | 29 | 31 | 19 | 18 | 18 | 24 | R | R | 6-4 | 185 | 9-5-72 | 1991 | LaGrange, Ga. |
| Krivda, Rick | 3 | 1 | 4.30 | 8 | 8 | 0 | 0 | 44 | 51 | 24 | 21 | 15 | 34 | R | L | 6-1 | 180 | 1-19-70 | 1991 | McKeesport, Pa. |
| Lane, Ryan | 1 | 0 | 5.64 | 9 | 0 | 0 | 1 | 22 | 31 | 16 | 14 | 8 | 13 | L | L | 6-1 | 180 | 6-2-71 | 1992 | Taylorville, Ill. |
| Maduro, Calvin | 3 | 5 | 4.74 | 8 | 8 | 0 | 0 | 44 | 49 | 25 | 23 | 18 | 40 | R | R | 6-0 | 175 | 9-5-74 | 1992 | Santa Cruz, Aruba |
| Munoz, Oscar | 6 | 7 | 4.23 | 21 | 17 | 1 | 0 | 113 | 100 | 60 | 53 | 37 | 85 | R | R | 6-2 | 205 | 9-25-69 | 1990 | Hialeah, Fla. |
| Myers, Jimmy | 7 | 5 | 2.89 | 39 | 0 | 0 | 12 | 53 | 53 | 19 | 17 | 12 | 21 | R | R | 6-1 | 185 | 4-28-69 | 1987 | Crowder, Okla. |
| Powell, Dennis | 0 | 1 | 1.35 | 5 | 0 | 0 | 1 | 7 | 4 | 1 | 1 | 1 | 4 | R | L | 6-3 | 200 | 8-13-63 | 1983 | Norman Park, Ga. |
| Revenig, Todd | 2 | 0 | 7.50 | 3 | 0 | 0 | 0 | 6 | 8 | 5 | 5 | 0 | 4 | R | R | 6-1 | 185 | 6-28-69 | 1990 | Baxter, Minn. |
| Rodriguez, Nerio | 1 | 0 | 1.80 | 2 | 2 | 0 | 0 | 15 | 10 | 3 | 3 | 2 | 6 | R | R | 6-1 | 195 | 3-22-73 | 1991 | San Pedro de Macoris, D.R. |
| Sackinsky, Brian | 7 | 3 | 3.46 | 14 | 13 | 1 | 0 | 68 | 75 | 28 | 26 | 15 | 38 | R | R | 6-4 | 220 | 6-22-71 | 1992 | Library, Pa. |
| Shepherd, Keith | 4 | 7 | 4.01 | 27 | 11 | 2 | 9 | 94 | 91 | 54 | 42 | 37 | 98 | R | R | 6-2 | 197 | 1-21-68 | 1986 | Wabash, Ind. |
| Shouse, Brian | 1 | 2 | 4.50 | 30 | 0 | 0 | 2 | 50 | 53 | 27 | 25 | 16 | 45 | L | L | 5-11 | 180 | 9-26-68 | 1990 | Effingham, Ill. |
| Stephenson, Garrett | 7 | 6 | 4.81 | 23 | 21 | 3 | 0 | 122 | 123 | 66 | 65 | 44 | 86 | R | R | 6-4 | 185 | 1-2-72 | 1992 | Kimberly, Md. |
| Williams, Jeff | 1 | 1 | 1.13 | 8 | 0 | 0 | 0 | 8 | 11 | 7 | 1 | 4 | 4 | R | R | 6-4 | 230 | 4-16-69 | 1990 | Arlington, Texas |
| Yan, Esteban | 5 | 4 | 4.27 | 22 | 10 | 0 | 1 | 72 | 75 | 37 | 34 | 18 | 61 | R | R | 6-4 | 180 | 6-22-74 | 1991 | La Higuera, D.R. |

### FIELDING

| Catcher | PCT | G | PO | A | E | DP | PB |
|---|---|---|---|---|---|---|---|
| Devarez | .991 | 61 | 421 | 44 | 4 | 3 | 3 |
| Rosario | .875 | 3 | 7 | 0 | 1 | 0 | 0 |
| Waszgis | .988 | 75 | 443 | 46 | 6 | 2 | 6 |
| Zaun | .965 | 8 | 52 | 3 | 2 | 0 | 0 |

| First Base | PCT | G | PO | A | E | DP |
|---|---|---|---|---|---|---|
| Bellinger | .992 | 42 | 338 | 13 | 3 | 27 |
| Figueroa | .971 | 5 | 30 | 4 | 1 | 0 |
| Martinez | .992 | 29 | 233 | 13 | 2 | 24 |
| Owens | .998 | 53 | 416 | 26 | 1 | 35 |
| Tyler | 1.000 | 8 | 49 | 3 | 0 | 8 |
| Waszgis | 1.000 | 10 | 68 | 7 | 0 | 5 |

| Second Base | PCT | G | PO | A | E | DP |
|---|---|---|---|---|---|---|
| Bellinger | .916 | 25 | 40 | 58 | 9 | 9 |

| | PCT | G | PO | A | E | DP |
|---|---|---|---|---|---|---|
| Figueroa | .975 | 32 | 49 | 67 | 3 | 11 |
| Tyler | .954 | 92 | 161 | 229 | 19 | 59 |
| Zosky | .944 | 5 | 8 | 9 | 1 | 3 |

| Third Base | PCT | G | PO | A | E | DP |
|---|---|---|---|---|---|---|
| Figueroa | .909 | 11 | 6 | 14 | 2 | 2 |
| McClain | .954 | 131 | 96 | 255 | 17 | 30 |
| Tyler | .667 | 2 | 0 | 2 | 1 | 1 |
| Zosky | 1.000 | 1 | 0 | 3 | 0 | 1 |

| Shortstop | PCT | G | PO | A | E | DP |
|---|---|---|---|---|---|---|
| Bellinger | .959 | 55 | 77 | 157 | 10 | 37 |
| Figueroa | 1.000 | 1 | 2 | 5 | 0 | 0 |
| Zosky | .952 | 89 | 151 | 245 | 20 | 36 |

| Outfield | PCT | G | PO | A | E | DP |
|---|---|---|---|---|---|---|
| Avila | 1.000 | 12 | 29 | 3 | 0 | 0 |
| Blosser | .895 | 19 | 15 | 2 | 2 | 0 |
| Bowers | .979 | 43 | 89 | 3 | 2 | 0 |
| Brown | .992 | 57 | 124 | 5 | 1 | 2 |
| Cookson | 1.000 | 28 | 44 | 0 | 0 | 0 |
| Gordon | .970 | 26 | 64 | 1 | 2 | 0 |
| Hall | .978 | 119 | 203 | 15 | 5 | 0 |
| Hammonds | .987 | 28 | 75 | 1 | 1 | 0 |
| Huson | 1.000 | 2 | 4 | 0 | 0 | 0 |
| Polonia | 1.000 | 8 | 18 | 0 | 0 | 0 |
| Smith | .966 | 32 | 55 | 1 | 2 | 0 |
| Tarasco | 1.000 | 3 | 4 | 0 | 0 | 0 |
| Tyler | 1.000 | 9 | 20 | 1 | 0 | 0 |
| Wawruck | 1.000 | 47 | 85 | 1 | 0 | 0 |

## EASTERN LEAGUE

| BATTING | AVG | G | AB | R | H | 2B | 3B | HR | RBI | BB | SO | SB | CS | B | T | HT | WT | DOB | 1st Yr | Resides |
|---|---|---|---|---|---|---|---|---|---|---|---|---|---|---|---|---|---|---|---|---|
| Avila, Rolando | .266 | 60 | 233 | 31 | 62 | 12 | 1 | 2 | 17 | 19 | 34 | 8 | 5 | R | R | 5-8 | 170 | 8-10-73 | 1994 | Paramount, Calif. |
| Bautista, Juan | .234 | 129 | 441 | 35 | 103 | 18 | 3 | 3 | 33 | 21 | 102 | 15 | 12 | R | R | 6-1 | 185 | 6-24-75 | 1992 | San Pedro de Macoris, D.R. |
| Berrios, Harry | .187 | 37 | 123 | 19 | 23 | 4 | 0 | 6 | 17 | 16 | 24 | 7 | 2 | R | R | 5-11 | 205 | 12-2-71 | 1993 | Grand Rapids, Mich. |
| Berry, Mike | .143 | 2 | 7 | 1 | 1 | 0 | 0 | 0 | 2 | 0 | 4 | 0 | 0 | R | R | 5-10 | 185 | 8-12-70 | 1993 | Rolling Hills, Calif. |
| Bowers, Brent | .311 | 58 | 228 | 37 | 71 | 11 | 1 | 9 | 25 | 17 | 40 | 10 | 4 | L | R | 6-3 | 200 | 5-2-71 | 1989 | Bridgeview, Ill. |

## BATTING

| BATTING | AVG | G | AB | R | H | 2B | 3B | HR | RBI | BB | SO | SB | CS | B | T | HT | WT | DOB | 1st Yr | Resides |
|---|---|---|---|---|---|---|---|---|---|---|---|---|---|---|---|---|---|---|---|---|
| Castaneda, Hector | .216 | 14 | 51 | 6 | 11 | 1 | 0 | 1 | 5 | 3 | 12 | 2 | 0 | L | R | 6-2 | 190 | 11-1-71 | 1990 | Mexico City, Mexico |
| Clark, Howie | .272 | 127 | 449 | 55 | 122 | 29 | 3 | 4 | 52 | 59 | 54 | 2 | 8 | L | R | 5-10 | 171 | 2-13-74 | 1992 | Huntington Beach, Calif. |
| Clyburn, Danny | .252 | 95 | 365 | 51 | 92 | 14 | 5 | 18 | 55 | 17 | 88 | 4 | 3 | R | R | 6-3 | 217 | 4-6-74 | 1992 | Lancaster, S.C. |
| Curtis, Kevin | .246 | 129 | 460 | 69 | 113 | 21 | 2 | 18 | 58 | 54 | 95 | 2 | 1 | R | R | 6-2 | 210 | 8-19-72 | 1993 | Upland, Calif. |
| Davis, Tommy | .261 | 137 | 524 | 75 | 137 | 32 | 2 | 14 | 54 | 41 | 113 | 5 | 8 | R | R | 6-1 | 195 | 5-21-73 | 1994 | Semmes, Ala. |
| Dellucci, David | .291 | 66 | 251 | 27 | 73 | 14 | 1 | 2 | 33 | 28 | 56 | 2 | 7 | L | L | 5-10 | 180 | 10-31-73 | 1995 | Baton Rouge, La. |
| Foster, Jim | .303 | 9 | 33 | 7 | 10 | 1 | 2 | 2 | 9 | 7 | 6 | 0 | 0 | R | R | 6-4 | 220 | 8-18-71 | 1993 | Warwick, R.I. |
| Gordon, Keith | .261 | 82 | 306 | 38 | 80 | 13 | 2 | 5 | 28 | 22 | 80 | 13 | 11 | R | R | 6-1 | 205 | 1-22-69 | 1990 | Olney, Md. |
| Gresham, Kris | .202 | 42 | 129 | 12 | 26 | 7 | 0 | 0 | 6 | 10 | 28 | 1 | 2 | R | R | 6-2 | 206 | 8-30-70 | 1991 | Mt. Pleasant, N.C. |
| Huson, Jeff | .385 | 3 | 13 | 3 | 5 | 2 | 0 | 0 | 1 | 0 | 0 | 0 | 1 | L | R | 6-3 | 180 | 8-15-64 | 1986 | Bedford, Texas |
| Millares, Jose | .186 | 25 | 70 | 3 | 13 | 3 | 0 | 0 | 1 | 4 | 6 | 1 | 1 | R | R | 5-11 | 190 | 3-24-68 | 1990 | Palmdale, Calif. |
| O'Toole, Bobby | .000 | 6 | 10 | 0 | 0 | 0 | 0 | 0 | 0 | 0 | 5 | 0 | 0 | R | R | 6-0 | 195 | 5-19-74 | 1995 | Newton, Mass. |
| Otanez, Willis | .265 | 138 | 506 | 60 | 134 | 27 | 2 | 24 | 75 | 45 | 97 | 3 | 7 | R | R | 5-11 | 150 | 4-19-73 | 1990 | Las Matas de Cotui, D.R. |
| Raleigh, Matt | .250 | 4 | 8 | 0 | 2 | 1 | 0 | 0 | 2 | 1 | 3 | 0 | 0 | R | R | 5-11 | 205 | 7-18-70 | 1992 | Swanton, Ver. |
| Rice, Lance | .213 | 55 | 164 | 8 | 35 | 4 | 0 | 2 | 17 | 13 | 19 | 0 | 0 | S | R | 6-1 | 195 | 10-19-66 | 1988 | Salem, Ore. |
| Rosario, Melvin | .210 | 47 | 162 | 14 | 34 | 10 | 0 | 2 | 17 | 6 | 43 | 3 | 2 | S | R | 6-0 | 191 | 5-25-73 | 1992 | Miami, Fla. |
| Smith, Mark | .091 | 6 | 22 | 1 | 2 | 0 | 0 | 1 | 2 | 1 | 6 | 0 | 0 | R | R | 6-3 | 205 | 5-7-70 | 1991 | Arcadia, Calif. |
| Thompson, Fletcher | .256 | 59 | 172 | 30 | 44 | 4 | 1 | 1 | 19 | 32 | 52 | 8 | 4 | L | R | 5-11 | 180 | 9-14-68 | 1990 | Jackson, Miss. |

## PITCHING

| PITCHING | W | L | ERA | G | GS | CG | SV | IP | H | R | ER | BB | SO | B | T | HT | WT | DOB | 1st Yr | Resides |
|---|---|---|---|---|---|---|---|---|---|---|---|---|---|---|---|---|---|---|---|---|
| Benitez, Armando | 0 | 0 | 4.50 | 4 | 4 | 0 | 0 | 6 | 7 | 3 | 3 | 0 | 8 | R | R | 6-4 | 220 | 11-3-72 | 1990 | San Pedro de Macoris, D.R. |
| Bennett, Joel | 2 | 3 | 3.29 | 10 | 8 | 0 | 0 | 55 | 36 | 21 | 20 | 17 | 48 | R | R | 6-1 | 161 | 1-31-70 | 1991 | Kirkwood, N.Y. |
| 2-team (3 Trenton) | 3 | 3 | 3.66 | 13 | 8 | 0 | 0 | 59 | 39 | 25 | 24 | 19 | 56 | | | | | | | |
| Brewer, Brian | 2 | 4 | 4.89 | 11 | 11 | 0 | 0 | 57 | 61 | 40 | 31 | 27 | 35 | L | L | 5-11 | 210 | 12-10-71 | 1993 | Fairfield, Calif. |
| Cafaro, Rocco | 4 | 8 | 4.96 | 27 | 15 | 1 | 0 | 103 | 130 | 67 | 57 | 36 | 55 | R | R | 6-0 | 175 | 12-2-72 | 1993 | Brandon, Fla. |
| Chavez, Carlos | 4 | 6 | 4.34 | 56 | 1 | 0 | 7 | 83 | 69 | 44 | 40 | 52 | 80 | R | R | 6-1 | 200 | 8-25-72 | 1992 | El Paso, Texas |
| Clayton, Royal | 0 | 1 | 10.80 | 3 | 2 | 0 | 0 | 8 | 12 | 10 | 10 | 4 | 5 | R | R | 6-2 | 210 | 11-25-65 | 1987 | Inglewood, Calif. |
| Conner, Scott | 1 | 5 | 5.05 | 21 | 11 | 0 | 0 | 82 | 86 | 54 | 46 | 36 | 59 | R | R | 6-2 | 192 | 3-22-72 | 1991 | Irvine, Calif. |
| Courtright, John | 0 | 0 | 6.46 | 9 | 0 | 0 | 0 | 15 | 19 | 15 | 11 | 8 | 10 | L | L | 6-2 | 185 | 5-30-70 | 1991 | Columbus, Ohio |
| 2-team (3 Hard. City) | 1 | 1 | 6.56 | 23 | 3 | 0 | 0 | 48 | 61 | 40 | 35 | 24 | 22 | | | | | | | |
| Dean, Greg | 0 | 3 | 8.53 | 3 | 3 | 0 | 0 | 13 | 21 | 15 | 12 | 13 | 4 | R | R | 6-2 | 220 | 4-16-74 | 1995 | Ada, Okla. |
| Dedrick, Jim | 1 | 1 | 3.38 | 13 | 0 | 0 | 0 | 27 | 28 | 10 | 10 | 14 | 21 | S | R | 6-0 | 185 | 4-4-68 | 1990 | Everett, Wash. |
| Grott, Matt | 2 | 1 | 4.98 | 9 | 0 | 0 | 0 | 22 | 26 | 15 | 12 | 5 | 15 | L | L | 6-1 | 205 | 12-5-67 | 1989 | Glendale, Ariz. |
| Hale, Shane | 5 | 13 | 5.00 | 24 | 24 | 0 | 0 | 135 | 146 | 81 | 75 | 51 | 86 | R | L | 6-1 | 180 | 12-30-68 | 1990 | Mobile, Ala. |
| Harris, Doug | 0 | 2 | 11.08 | 3 | 3 | 0 | 0 | 13 | 17 | 16 | 16 | 7 | 5 | R | R | 6-4 | 205 | 9-27-69 | 1990 | Carlisle, Pa. |
| Hill, Milt | 5 | 7 | 6.67 | 25 | 16 | 2 | 1 | 88 | 126 | 73 | 65 | 18 | 66 | R | R | 6-0 | 180 | 8-22-65 | 1987 | Cumming, Ga. |
| Hostetler, Marcus | 3 | 0 | 3.32 | 32 | 0 | 0 | 1 | 57 | 51 | 29 | 21 | 22 | 44 | R | R | 6-3 | 210 | 7-4-69 | 1993 | Kalona, Iowa |
| Jarvis, Matt | 1 | 3 | 7.45 | 6 | 4 | 0 | 0 | 19 | 31 | 17 | 16 | 7 | 13 | R | L | 6-4 | 185 | 2-22-72 | 1991 | Albuquerque, N.M. |
| Lane, Aaron | 3 | 5 | 4.59 | 13 | 8 | 1 | 2 | 51 | 44 | 37 | 26 | 24 | 35 | L | L | 6-1 | 190 | 6-2-71 | 1992 | Taylorville, Ill. |
| Lemp, Chris | 1 | 3 | 4.72 | 27 | 1 | 0 | 1 | 48 | 53 | 27 | 25 | 24 | 35 | R | R | 6-0 | 175 | 7-23-71 | 1991 | Sacramento, Calif. |
| Maduro, Calvin | 9 | 7 | 3.26 | 19 | 19 | 4 | 0 | 124 | 116 | 50 | 45 | 36 | 87 | R | R | 6-0 | 175 | 9-5-74 | 1992 | Santa Cruz, Aruba |
| Maine, Dalton | 1 | 5 | 5.06 | 11 | 0 | 0 | 0 | 21 | 24 | 14 | 12 | 11 | 18 | R | R | 6-3 | 185 | 3-22-72 | 1995 | Framingham, Mass. |
| O'Donoghue, John | 1 | 3 | 4.38 | 7 | 7 | 0 | 0 | 37 | 42 | 21 | 18 | 16 | 26 | L | L | 6-6 | 210 | 5-26-69 | 1990 | Elkton, Md. |
| Plaster, Allen | 0 | 0 | 13.50 | 1 | 0 | 0 | 0 | 2 | 5 | 3 | 3 | 1 | 3 | R | R | 6-3 | 210 | 8-13-70 | 1991 | Kernersville, N.C. |
| Revenig, Todd | 3 | 4 | 2.63 | 38 | 0 | 0 | 7 | 62 | 42 | 18 | 18 | 18 | 39 | R | R | 6-1 | 185 | 6-28-69 | 1990 | Baxter, Minn. |
| Rhodes, Joey | 2 | 1 | 1.50 | 4 | 1 | 0 | 0 | 12 | 6 | 2 | 2 | 5 | 9 | R | R | 6-3 | 205 | 1-8-75 | 1994 | Hendersonville, N.C. |
| Ryan, Kevin | 1 | 9 | 9.00 | 2 | 1 | 0 | 0 | 3 | 7 | 4 | 3 | 1 | 2 | R | R | 6-1 | 187 | 9-23-70 | 1991 | Oklahoma City, Okla. |
| Schuermann, Lance | 0 | 0 | 3.18 | 6 | 0 | 0 | 0 | 6 | 7 | 5 | 2 | 2 | 6 | L | L | 6-2 | 200 | 2-7-70 | 1991 | St. Louis, Mo. |
| Strange, Don | 2 | 1 | 2.45 | 12 | 0 | 0 | 3 | 15 | 11 | 4 | 4 | 5 | 10 | R | R | 6-0 | 195 | 5-26-67 | 1989 | Springfield, Mass. |
| Tranbarger, Mark | 3 | 3 | 5.40 | 40 | 2 | 0 | 3 | 55 | 67 | 37 | 33 | 35 | 45 | L | L | 6-2 | 205 | 9-17-69 | 1991 | Cincinnati, Ohio |
| Yan, Esteban | 0 | 2 | 5.63 | 9 | 1 | 0 | 0 | 16 | 18 | 12 | 10 | 6 | 10 | R | R | 6-4 | 180 | 6-22-74 | 1991 | La Higuera, D.R. |

## FIELDING

### Catcher

| Catcher | PCT | G | PO | A | E | DP | PB |
|---|---|---|---|---|---|---|---|
| Castaneda | 1.000 | 8 | 59 | 3 | 0 | 0 | 0 |
| Clark | 1.000 | 1 | 1 | 0 | 0 | 0 | 0 |
| Foster | .988 | 8 | 77 | 5 | 1 | 1 | 2 |
| Gresham | .993 | 41 | 239 | 38 | 2 | 7 | 5 |
| O'Toole | 1.000 | 6 | 19 | 0 | 0 | 0 | 0 |
| Rice | .994 | 52 | 302 | 45 | 2 | 2 | 3 |
| Rosario | .973 | 38 | 219 | 38 | 7 | 3 | 6 |

### First Base

| First Base | PCT | G | PO | A | E | DP |
|---|---|---|---|---|---|---|
| Clark | 1.000 | 1 | 1 | 0 | 0 | 0 |
| Curtis | 1.000 | 8 | 78 | 1 | 0 | 5 |
| Davis | .995 | 134 | 1158 | 95 | 6 | 79 |
| Millares | 1.000 | 1 | 1 | 0 | 0 | 0 |
| Raleigh | 1.000 | 1 | 1 | 0 | 0 | 0 |

### Second Base

| Second Base | PCT | G | PO | A | E | DP |
|---|---|---|---|---|---|---|
| Bautista | .000 | 1 | 0 | 0 | 1 | 0 |

| | PCT | G | PO | A | E | DP |
|---|---|---|---|---|---|---|
| Clark | .974 | 123 | 249 | 286 | 14 | 52 |
| Millares | .975 | 17 | 44 | 33 | 2 | 10 |
| Thompson | 1.000 | 6 | 6 | 4 | 0 | 0 |

### Third Base

| Third Base | PCT | G | PO | A | E | D |
|---|---|---|---|---|---|---|
| Castaneda | 1.000 | 1 | 0 | 0 | 0 | 0 |
| Clark | 1.000 | 1 | 0 | 1 | 0 | 0 |
| Huson | 1.000 | 1 | 1 | 4 | 0 | 1 |
| Millares | .000 | 1 | 0 | 0 | 0 | 0 |
| Otanez | .941 | 133 | 106 | 278 | 24 | 18 |
| Thompson | .920 | 12 | 6 | 17 | 2 | 2 |

### Shortstop

| Shortstop | PCT | G | PO | A | E | DP |
|---|---|---|---|---|---|---|
| Bautista | .951 | 127 | 203 | 354 | 29 | 55 |
| Clark | .000 | 1 | 0 | 0 | 0 | 0 |
| Millares | .800 | 2 | 1 | 3 | 1 | 0 |
| Otanez | 1.000 | 1 | 0 | 1 | 0 | 0 |

| | PCT | G | PO | A | E | DP |
|---|---|---|---|---|---|---|
| Thompson | .933 | 20 | 26 | 57 | 6 | 8 |

### Outfield

| Outfield | PCT | G | PO | A | E | DP |
|---|---|---|---|---|---|---|
| Avila | .977 | 58 | 127 | 3 | 3 | 0 |
| Berrios | .946 | 34 | 52 | 1 | 3 | 0 |
| Bowers | .992 | 55 | 116 | 4 | 1 | 0 |
| Clark | .000 | 2 | 0 | 0 | 0 | 0 |
| Clyburn | .899 | 59 | 103 | 4 | 12 | 0 |
| Curtis | .984 | 90 | 179 | 11 | 3 | 1 |
| Davis | .000 | 1 | 0 | 0 | 0 | 0 |
| Dellucci | .979 | 60 | 134 | 5 | 3 | 0 |
| Foster | .000 | 1 | 0 | 0 | 0 | 0 |
| Gordon | .938 | 73 | 117 | 5 | 8 | 1 |
| Huson | 1.000 | 2 | 3 | 0 | 0 | 0 |
| Millares | 1.000 | 1 | 0 | 0 | 0 | 0 |
| Raleigh | 1.000 | 1 | 1 | 0 | 0 | 0 |
| Thompson | .750 | 4 | 3 | 0 | 1 | 0 |

## BAKERSFIELD

Class A/Co-Op

## CALIFORNIA LEAGUE

### BATTING

| BATTING | AVG | G | AB | R | H | 2B | 3B | HR | RBI | BB | SO | SB | CS | B | T | HT | WT | DOB | 1st Yr | Resides |
|---|---|---|---|---|---|---|---|---|---|---|---|---|---|---|---|---|---|---|---|---|
| Daedelow, Craig | .235 | 86 | 298 | 37 | 70 | 17 | 1 | 1 | 28 | 31 | 60 | 10 | 4 | R | R | 5-11 | 175 | 4-3-76 | 1994 | Huntington Beach, Calif. |
| Harmer, Frank | .179 | 28 | 67 | 6 | 12 | 2 | 0 | 0 | 4 | 8 | 16 | 0 | 1 | S | R | 6-3 | 210 | 5-21-75 | 1994 | Altamonte Springs, Fla. |
| Hendricks, Ryan | .160 | 30 | 94 | 13 | 15 | 1 | 0 | 3 | 8 | 12 | 31 | 1 | 0 | L | R | 6-3 | 205 | 8-3-72 | 1994 | Randallstown, Md. |
| 2-team (14 H. D.) | .179 | 44 | 123 | 16 | 22 | 3 | 0 | 3 | 12 | 17 | 42 | 2 | 0 | | | | | | | |
| Paxton, Chris | .249 | 85 | 269 | 30 | 67 | 14 | 0 | 11 | 39 | 35 | 89 | 0 | 0 | L | R | 6-2 | 195 | 12-11-76 | 1995 | Palmdale, Calif. |

**GAMES BY POSITION: C**—Harmer 25, Paxton 39. **1B**—Hendricks 26, Paxton 20. **2B**—Daedelow 1. **SS**—Daedelow 84.

### PITCHING

| PITCHING | W | L | ERA | G | GS | CG | SV | IP | H | R | ER | BB | SO | B | T | HT | WT | DOB | 1st Yr | Resides |
|---|---|---|---|---|---|---|---|---|---|---|---|---|---|---|---|---|---|---|---|---|
| Bates, Shawn | 1 | 1 | 12.60 | 4 | 0 | 0 | 0 | 5 | 13 | 8 | 7 | 4 | 1 | L | L | 6-3 | 202 | 2-27-75 | 1994 | Wichita Falls, Texas |
| Bray, Chris | 0 | 2 | 12.68 | 17 | 0 | 0 | 1 | 22 | 28 | 34 | 31 | 38 | 15 | R | R | 6-4 | 200 | 10-28-74 | 1995 | Currituck, N.C. |
| Maine, Dalton | 2 | 3 | 3.23 | 23 | 2 | 0 | 6 | 47 | 42 | 25 | 17 | 14 | 58 | R | R | 6-3 | 185 | 3-22-72 | 1995 | Framingham, Mass. |

| PITCHING | W | L | ERA | G | GS | CG | SV | IP | H | R | ER | BB | SO | B | T | HT | WT | DOB | 1st Yr | Resides |
|---|---|---|---|---|---|---|---|---|---|---|---|---|---|---|---|---|---|---|---|---|
| Reed, Dan | 2 | 4 | 5.00 | 20 | 7 | 0 | 0 | 68 | 83 | 52 | 38 | 36 | 48 | R | L | 6-4 | 210 | 10-20-74 | 1995 | McLean, Va. |
| Sellner, Aaron | 0 | 2 | 7.71 | 16 | 0 | 0 | 0 | 26 | 33 | 32 | 22 | 20 | 26 | L | R | 6-1 | 193 | 9-6-73 | 1994 | West Haven, Conn. |

# HIGH DESERT — Class A

## CALIFORNIA LEAGUE

| BATTING | AVG | G | AB | R | H | 2B | 3B | HR | RBI | BB | SO | SB | CS | B | T | HT | WT | DOB | 1st Yr | Resides |
|---|---|---|---|---|---|---|---|---|---|---|---|---|---|---|---|---|---|---|---|---|
| Akins, Carlos | .208 | 11 | 24 | 4 | 5 | 1 | 0 | 0 | 2 | 6 | 8 | 1 | 0 | R | R | 6-0 | 180 | 7-12-74 | 1995 | Oklahoma City, Okla. |
| Avila, Rolando | .331 | 68 | 296 | 54 | 98 | 17 | 2 | 4 | 33 | 22 | 32 | 15 | 7 | R | R | 5-8 | 170 | 8-10-73 | 1994 | Paramount, Calif. |
| Berry, Mike | .361 | 121 | 463 | 109 | 167 | 44 | 5 | 13 | 113 | 99 | 67 | 7 | 4 | R | R | 5-10 | 185 | 8-12-70 | 1993 | Rolling Hills, Calif. |
| Bogle, Bryan | .317 | 126 | 495 | 86 | 157 | 32 | 6 | 22 | 92 | 35 | 142 | 14 | 9 | R | R | 6-1 | 205 | 5-18-73 | 1994 | Merritt Island, Fla. |
| Bryant, Chris | .299 | 68 | 234 | 53 | 70 | 10 | 2 | 5 | 41 | 32 | 55 | 3 | 2 | R | R | 6-2 | 195 | 12-15-72 | 1995 | Middlesex, N.C. |
| Carney, Bartt | .250 | 47 | 116 | 31 | 29 | 3 | 3 | 1 | 11 | 15 | 26 | 6 | 4 | S | R | 5-11 | 170 | 12-16-73 | 1994 | Parnell, Iowa |
| D'Aquila, Tom | .063 | 6 | 16 | 2 | 1 | 0 | 1 | 0 | 1 | 1 | 7 | 0 | 0 | R | R | 6-1 | 190 | 4-15-73 | 1994 | Middletown, Conn. |
| Eaddy, Keith | .080 | 12 | 25 | 1 | 2 | 0 | 0 | 0 | 0 | 0 | 7 | 2 | 1 | R | R | 5-9 | 180 | 11-23-70 | 1992 | Newark, N.J. |
| Garcia, Jesse | .266 | 137 | 459 | 94 | 122 | 21 | 5 | 10 | 66 | 57 | 81 | 25 | 7 | R | R | 5-9 | 165 | 9-24-73 | 1993 | Robstown, Texas |
| Gresham, Kris | .375 | 2 | 8 | 2 | 3 | 0 | 0 | 2 | 4 | 0 | 1 | 0 | 0 | R | R | 6-2 | 206 | 8-30-70 | 1991 | Mt. Pleasant, N.C. |
| Harmer, Frank | .242 | 36 | 95 | 20 | 23 | 5 | 0 | 3 | 16 | 22 | 25 | 1 | 0 | S | R | 6-3 | 210 | 5-21-75 | 1994 | Altamonte Springs, Fla. |
| 2-team (28 Bakers.) | .216 | 64 | 162 | 26 | 35 | 7 | 0 | 3 | 20 | 30 | 41 | 1 | 1 | | | | | | | |
| Hendricks, Ryan | .241 | 14 | 29 | 3 | 7 | 2 | 0 | 0 | 4 | 5 | 11 | 1 | 0 | L | R | 6-3 | 205 | 8-3-72 | 1994 | Randallstown, Md. |
| Hodge, Roy | .280 | 112 | 393 | 71 | 110 | 21 | 2 | 8 | 54 | 47 | 58 | 9 | 7 | R | R | 6-2 | 191 | 6-22-71 | 1990 | St. Thomas, V.I. |
| Hugo, Sean | .154 | 18 | 39 | 3 | 6 | 1 | 0 | 2 | 5 | 4 | 11 | 0 | 2 | L | L | 6-1 | 195 | 9-7-72 | 1994 | Oklahoma City, Okla. |
| Kirgan, Chris | .297 | 136 | 529 | 96 | 157 | 23 | 1 | 35 | 131 | 54 | 162 | 2 | 3 | L | L | 6-4 | 235 | 6-29-73 | 1994 | Littleton, Colo. |
| Lamb, David | .257 | 116 | 460 | 63 | 118 | 24 | 3 | 3 | 55 | 50 | 68 | 5 | 6 | S | R | 6-3 | 175 | 6-6-75 | 1993 | Newbury Park, Calif. |
| LeCronier, Jason | .237 | 52 | 135 | 20 | 32 | 3 | 1 | 4 | 25 | 6 | 37 | 1 | 0 | L | R | 5-11 | 200 | 3-30-73 | 1995 | Bay City, Mich. |
| Michael, Jeff | .286 | 3 | 7 | 2 | 2 | 0 | 0 | 0 | 0 | 2 | 1 | 0 | 1 | R | R | 6-1 | 185 | 8-8-71 | 1993 | Hamilton, Ohio |
| Newstrom, Doug | .313 | 122 | 403 | 84 | 126 | 30 | 3 | 11 | 75 | 73 | 62 | 15 | 8 | L | R | 6-1 | 195 | 9-18-71 | 1993 | Goodyear, Ariz. |
| O'Toole, Bobby | .171 | 16 | 35 | 8 | 6 | 1 | 0 | 0 | 3 | 8 | 10 | 0 | 0 | R | R | 6-0 | 195 | 5-19-74 | 1995 | Newton, Mass. |
| Paz, Richard | .176 | 7 | 17 | 2 | 3 | 1 | 0 | 0 | 0 | 1 | 4 | 0 | 0 | R | R | 5-8 | 130 | 7-30-77 | 1994 | Los Teques, Venez. |
| Raleigh, Matt | .286 | 27 | 84 | 17 | 24 | 6 | 0 | 7 | 13 | 14 | 33 | 2 | 0 | R | R | 5-11 | 205 | 7-18-70 | 1992 | Swanton, Ver. |
| Rosario, Melvin | .319 | 42 | 163 | 35 | 52 | 9 | 1 | 10 | 34 | 21 | 45 | 4 | 0 | S | R | 6-0 | 191 | 5-25-73 | 1992 | Miami, Fla. |
| 2-team (10 R.C.) | .311 | 52 | 196 | 42 | 61 | 12 | 1 | 13 | 44 | 24 | 53 | 5 | 0 | | | | | | | |
| Russin, Tom | .000 | 6 | 6 | 0 | 0 | 0 | 0 | 0 | 0 | 0 | 2 | 0 | 0 | R | R | 6-2 | 200 | 9-9-73 | 1995 | Sarasota, Fla. |
| Suplee, Ray | .298 | 112 | 352 | 54 | 105 | 16 | 2 | 6 | 56 | 32 | 72 | 3 | 3 | R | R | 6-3 | 200 | 12-15-70 | 1992 | Sarasota, Fla. |
| Thompson, Fletcher | .292 | 25 | 72 | 10 | 21 | 4 | 1 | 0 | 8 | 10 | 6 | 3 | 2 | L | R | 5-11 | 180 | 9-14-68 | 1990 | Jackson, Miss. |

**GAMES BY POSITION: C**—Carney 1, Gresham 2, Harmer 33, Newstrom 79, O'Toole 14, Russin 32. **1B**—Bryant 1, Hendricks 6, Kirgan 135, Michael 1, Newstrom 2, Raleigh 5, Russin 4. **2B**—Berry 8, Bryant 1, Garcia 137, LeCronier 1, Suplee 1, Thompson 4. **3B**—Berry 98, Bogle 8, Bryant 31, Michael 2, Raleigh 2, Thompson 17. **SS**—Bryant 22, Garcia 1, Lamb 116, Paz 7, Thompson 4. **OF**—Akins 10, Avila 68, Bogle 111, Carney 46, D'Aquila 5, Eaddy 9, Hodge 106, Hugo 2, Kirgan 1, LeCronier 39, Newstrom 1, Suplee 82.

| PITCHING | W | L | ERA | G | GS | CG | SV | IP | H | R | ER | BB | SO | B | T | HT | WT | DOB | 1st Yr | Resides |
|---|---|---|---|---|---|---|---|---|---|---|---|---|---|---|---|---|---|---|---|---|
| Brewer, Brian | 5 | 4 | 5.16 | 18 | 13 | 0 | 0 | 75 | 77 | 53 | 43 | 48 | 57 | L | L | 5-11 | 210 | 12-10-71 | 1993 | Fairfield, Calif. |
| Crills, Brad | 2 | 4 | 4.68 | 14 | 14 | 1 | 0 | 77 | 79 | 45 | 40 | 26 | 45 | R | R | 6-0 | 195 | 10-16-71 | 1994 | East Stroudsburg, Pa. |
| Daigle, Tim | 1 | 0 | 9.82 | 4 | 0 | 0 | 0 | 4 | 7 | 4 | 4 | 1 | 2 | L | L | 5-11 | 170 | 2-4-72 | 1994 | Thibodaux, La. |
| Darley, Ned | 2 | 1 | 6.38 | 30 | 1 | 0 | 1 | 42 | 44 | 34 | 30 | 29 | 34 | L | R | 6-4 | 225 | 2-27-71 | 1990 | Alcolu, S.C. |
| Dean, Greg | 10 | 7 | 4.36 | 37 | 12 | 0 | 3 | 105 | 110 | 68 | 51 | 71 | 76 | R | R | 6-2 | 220 | 4-16-74 | 1995 | Ada, Okla. |
| Eibey, Scott | 1 | 0 | 8.49 | 11 | 0 | 0 | 0 | 12 | 17 | 16 | 11 | 10 | 7 | L | L | 6-4 | 210 | 1-19-74 | 1995 | Waterloo, Iowa |
| Falkenborg, Brian | 0 | 0 | 0.00 | 1 | 0 | 0 | 0 | 1 | 1 | 0 | 0 | 0 | 1 | R | R | 6-6 | 187 | 1-18-78 | 1996 | Redmond, Wash. |
| Hacen, Abraham | 0 | 0 | 32.40 | 3 | 0 | 0 | 0 | 3 | 12 | 13 | 12 | 7 | 2 | R | R | 6-2 | 175 | 1-22-76 | 1993 | La Romana, D.R. |
| Hackett, Jason | 0 | 0 | 4.70 | 5 | 0 | 0 | 0 | 8 | 9 | 4 | 4 | 15 | 4 | L | L | 6-1 | 176 | 3-10-75 | 1994 | Worton, Md. |
| Huntsman, Brandon | 1 | 1 | 9.55 | 13 | 2 | 0 | 0 | 27 | 36 | 29 | 29 | 27 | 25 | R | R | 6-4 | 205 | 11-19-75 | 1994 | Pleasant Grove, Utah |
| Lehman, Toby | 1 | 2 | 6.46 | 6 | 5 | 0 | 0 | 24 | 24 | 19 | 17 | 22 | 18 | R | R | 6-0 | 200 | 8-12-71 | 1992 | Vista, Calif. |
| Maine, Dalton | 1 | 0 | 1.50 | 10 | 0 | 0 | 2 | 12 | 8 | 2 | 2 | 2 | 9 | R | R | 6-3 | 185 | 3-22-72 | 1995 | Framingham, Mass. |
| 2-team (23 Bakers.) | 3 | 2 | 3.88 | 33 | 2 | 0 | 8 | 59 | 50 | 27 | 19 | 16 | 67 | | | | | | | |
| Marenghi, Matt | 9 | 7 | 5.85 | 33 | 23 | 1 | 1 | 171 | 205 | 119 | 111 | 54 | 114 | R | R | 6-2 | 185 | 1-22-73 | 1994 | Las Vegas, Nev. |
| Montgomery, Steve | 5 | 6 | 5.27 | 44 | 3 | 0 | 2 | 72 | 85 | 54 | 42 | 34 | 79 | R | R | 6-7 | 230 | 2-21-74 | 1994 | Warren, Ohio |
| Olszewski, Tim | 5 | 6 | 6.61 | 49 | 0 | 0 | 0 | 64 | 78 | 53 | 47 | 41 | 38 | R | R | 6-2 | 200 | 2-24-74 | 1995 | Germantown, Wis. |
| Reed, Dan | 4 | 0 | 4.76 | 17 | 6 | 0 | 0 | 51 | 53 | 28 | 27 | 22 | 43 | R | L | 6-4 | 210 | 10-20-74 | 1995 | McLean, Va. |
| 2-team (20 Bakers.) | 6 | 4 | 4.90 | 37 | 13 | 0 | 0 | 119 | 136 | 80 | 65 | 58 | 91 | | | | | | | |
| Reich, Steve | 0 | 2 | 10.80 | 2 | 2 | 0 | 0 | 7 | 14 | 11 | 8 | 3 | 0 | L | L | 5-11 | 185 | 5-22-71 | 1996 | Washington, Conn. |
| Rhodes, Joe | 5 | 9 | 5.11 | 25 | 21 | 0 | 0 | 123 | 133 | 85 | 70 | 66 | 81 | R | R | 6-3 | 205 | 1-8-75 | 1994 | Hendersonville, N.C. |
| Saneaux, Francisco | 4 | 5 | 5.56 | 20 | 19 | 0 | 0 | 102 | 98 | 71 | 63 | 91 | 101 | R | R | 6-4 | 180 | 3-3-74 | 1991 | Santo Domingo, D.R. |
| Sauritch, Chris | 4 | 1 | 5.68 | 35 | 0 | 0 | 0 | 52 | 52 | 33 | 33 | 33 | 41 | S | R | 5-10 | 175 | 3-24-72 | 1994 | Lake Forest, Calif. |
| Seaver, Mark | 2 | 1 | 3.42 | 4 | 4 | 0 | 0 | 24 | 19 | 12 | 9 | 10 | 16 | R | R | 6-8 | 240 | 4-6-75 | 1996 | Hickory, Pa. |
| Sellner, Aaron | 1 | 1 | 7.56 | 4 | 0 | 0 | 0 | 8 | 11 | 9 | 7 | 5 | 5 | L | R | 6-1 | 193 | 9-6-73 | 1994 | West Haven, Conn. |
| 2-team (16 Bakers.) | 0 | 3 | 7.68 | 20 | 0 | 0 | 0 | 34 | 44 | 41 | 29 | 25 | 31 | | | | | | | |
| Smith, Hut | 3 | 4 | 5.36 | 10 | 7 | 1 | 0 | 50 | 59 | 34 | 30 | 16 | 34 | S | R | 6-3 | 195 | 6-8-73 | 1992 | Kannapolis, N.C. |
| Snyder, Matt | 6 | 2 | 3.75 | 58 | 0 | 0 | 20 | 72 | 60 | 34 | 30 | 38 | 93 | R | R | 5-11 | 190 | 7-7-74 | 1995 | Newtown, Pa. |
| White, Gary | 4 | 2 | 5.82 | 16 | 8 | 0 | 0 | 51 | 62 | 36 | 33 | 26 | 34 | L | L | 6-2 | 215 | 8-14-72 | 1995 | Fort Myers, Fla. |

## VISALIA — Class A/Co-Op

## CALIFORNIA LEAGUE

| PITCHING | W | L | ERA | G | GS | CG | SV | IP | H | R | ER | BB | SO | B | T | HT | WT | DOB | 1st Yr | Resides |
|---|---|---|---|---|---|---|---|---|---|---|---|---|---|---|---|---|---|---|---|---|
| Pena, Alex | 1 | 3 | 5.73 | 44 | 2 | 0 | 0 | 71 | 94 | 53 | 45 | 31 | 30 | R | R | 6-0 | 175 | 9-9-72 | 1993 | El Paso, Texas |

# FREDERICK — Class A

## CAROLINA LEAGUE

| BATTING | AVG | G | AB | R | H | 2B | 3B | HR | RBI | BB | SO | SB | CS | B | T | HT | WT | DOB | 1st Yr | Resides |
|---|---|---|---|---|---|---|---|---|---|---|---|---|---|---|---|---|---|---|---|---|
| Akins, Carlos | .290 | 42 | 145 | 36 | 42 | 7 | 1 | 5 | 14 | 34 | 31 | 9 | 5 | R | R | 6-0 | 180 | 7-12-74 | 1995 | Oklahoma City, Okla. |
| Almonte, Wady | .286 | 85 | 287 | 45 | 82 | 12 | 2 | 12 | 44 | 21 | 59 | 1 | 5 | R | R | 6-0 | 180 | 4-20-75 | 1993 | Higuey, D.R. |
| Berrios, Harry | .230 | 43 | 161 | 25 | 37 | 9 | 1 | 4 | 20 | 12 | 21 | 8 | 3 | R | R | 5-11 | 205 | 12-2-71 | 1993 | Grand Rapids, Mich. |
| Berry, Mike | .125 | 3 | 8 | 2 | 1 | 0 | 0 | 1 | 1 | 4 | 2 | 0 | 0 | R | R | 5-10 | 185 | 8-12-70 | 1993 | Rolling Hills, Calif. |

## BATTING

| | AVG | G | AB | R | H | 2B | 3B | HR | RBI | BB | SO | SB | CS | B | T | HT | WT | DOB | 1st Yr | Resides |
|---|---|---|---|---|---|---|---|---|---|---|---|---|---|---|---|---|---|---|---|---|
| Bryant, Chris | .000 | 3 | 8 | 0 | 0 | 0 | 0 | 0 | 0 | 0 | 4 | 0 | 0 | R | R | 6-2 | 195 | 12-15-72 | 1995 | Middlesex, N.C. |
| Chavez, Eric | .279 | 122 | 416 | 60 | 116 | 29 | 1 | 18 | 64 | 72 | 101 | 5 | 3 | R | R | 5-11 | 212 | 9-7-70 | 1992 | Carlsbad, N.M. |
| D'Aquila, Tom | .146 | 45 | 130 | 21 | 19 | 3 | 0 | 1 | 11 | 25 | 55 | 9 | 4 | R | R | 6-1 | 190 | 4-15-72 | 1994 | Middletown, Conn. |
| Daedelow, Craig | .208 | 26 | 72 | 13 | 15 | 4 | 0 | 0 | 6 | 8 | 9 | 2 | 0 | R | R | 5-11 | 175 | 4-3-76 | 1994 | Huntington Beach, Calif. |
| Dellucci, David | .324 | 59 | 185 | 33 | 60 | 11 | 1 | 4 | 28 | 38 | 34 | 5 | 6 | L | L | 5-10 | 180 | 10-31-73 | 1995 | Baton Rouge, La. |
| Foster, Jim | .252 | 82 | 278 | 35 | 70 | 20 | 2 | 7 | 42 | 39 | 32 | 6 | 3 | R | R | 6-4 | 220 | 8-18-71 | 1993 | Warwick, R.I. |
| Fowler, Maleke | .182 | 5 | 11 | 3 | 2 | 0 | 0 | 0 | 1 | 3 | 2 | 1 | 1 | R | R | 5-11 | 180 | 8-11-75 | 1996 | Baton Rouge, La. |
| Gabriel, Denio | .180 | 40 | 133 | 12 | 24 | 1 | 1 | 0 | 5 | 11 | 29 | 6 | 9 | S | R | 6-0 | 150 | 10-25-75 | 1993 | La Romana, D.R. |
| Gargiulo, Mike | .199 | 51 | 161 | 14 | 32 | 9 | 0 | 2 | 16 | 15 | 35 | 2 | 1 | L | R | 6-1 | 175 | 1-22-75 | 1993 | Harrisburg, Pa. |
| Hodge, Roy | .000 | 4 | 12 | 2 | 0 | 0 | 0 | 0 | 0 | 3 | 5 | 1 | 0 | R | R | 6-2 | 191 | 6-22-71 | 1990 | St. Thomas, V.I. |
| Huson, Jeff | .438 | 4 | 16 | 4 | 7 | 2 | 0 | 1 | 1 | 2 | 0 | 0 | 1 | L | R | 6-3 | 180 | 8-15-64 | 1986 | Bedford, Texas |
| Isom, Johnny | .290 | 124 | 486 | 69 | 141 | 27 | 3 | 18 | 104 | 40 | 87 | 8 | 6 | R | R | 5-11 | 210 | 8-9-73 | 1995 | Fort Worth, Texas |
| Kingsale, Eugene | .271 | 49 | 166 | 26 | 45 | 6 | 4 | 0 | 9 | 19 | 32 | 23 | 4 | S | R | 6-3 | 170 | 8-20-76 | 1994 | Aruba, Aruba |
| Lawrence, Chip | .235 | 43 | 132 | 9 | 31 | 1 | 1 | 0 | 14 | 8 | 13 | 6 | 3 | R | R | 6-2 | 182 | 11-14-74 | 1996 | St. Petersburg, Fla. |
| LeCronier, Jason | .228 | 29 | 92 | 13 | 21 | 3 | 0 | 1 | 12 | 10 | 29 | 0 | 0 | L | R | 5-11 | 200 | 3-30-73 | 1995 | Bay City, Mich. |
| Martin, Lincoln | .266 | 114 | 421 | 77 | 112 | 17 | 7 | 2 | 31 | 50 | 66 | 22 | 7 | S | R | 5-10 | 170 | 10-20-71 | 1993 | Douglasville, Ga. |
| Martinez, Eddy | .221 | 74 | 244 | 21 | 54 | 4 | 0 | 2 | 25 | 21 | 48 | 13 | 8 | R | R | 6-2 | 150 | 10-23-77 | 1995 | San Pedro de Macoris, D.R. |
| McCollough, Adam | .000 | 4 | 10 | 0 | 0 | 0 | 0 | 0 | 0 | 0 | 4 | 0 | 0 | R | R | 6-1 | 190 | 8-26-73 | 1996 | Lawton, Okla. |
| O'Toole, Bobby | .143 | 3 | 7 | 0 | 1 | 0 | 0 | 0 | 0 | 0 | 2 | 0 | 0 | R | R | 6-0 | 195 | 5-19-74 | 1995 | Newton, Mass. |
| Raleigh, Matt | .228 | 21 | 57 | 8 | 13 | 0 | 1 | 1 | 8 | 12 | 22 | 3 | 0 | R | R | 5-11 | 205 | 7-18-70 | 1992 | Swanton, Ver. |
| Russin, Tom | .200 | 19 | 65 | 2 | 13 | 4 | 0 | 0 | 6 | 1 | 16 | 2 | 2 | R | R | 6-2 | 200 | 9-9-73 | 1995 | Sarasota, Fla. |
| Short, Rick | .312 | 126 | 474 | 68 | 148 | 33 | 0 | 3 | 54 | 29 | 44 | 12 | 7 | R | R | 6-0 | 190 | 12-6-72 | 1994 | South Elgin, Ill. |
| Smith, Mark | .000 | 1 | 1 | 0 | 0 | 0 | 0 | 0 | 0 | 0 | 0 | 0 | 0 | R | R | 6-3 | 205 | 5-7-70 | 1991 | Arcadia, Calif. |
| Tarasco, Tony | .229 | 9 | 35 | 6 | 8 | 3 | 0 | 1 | 5 | 4 | 4 | 0 | 1 | L | R | 6-1 | 205 | 12-9-70 | 1988 | Santa Monica, Calif. |
| Utting, Andrew | .333 | 1 | 3 | 0 | 1 | 0 | 0 | 0 | 1 | 0 | 1 | 0 | 0 | S | R | 6-1 | 175 | 9-9-77 | 1995 | Melbourne, Australia |
| Wolff, Mike | .253 | 105 | 352 | 44 | 89 | 21 | 0 | 7 | 50 | 16 | 32 | 6 | 3 | L | L | 6-3 | 205 | 2-17-73 | 1994 | Granger, Ind. |

**GAMES BY POSITION: C**—Chavez 13, Foster 78, Gargiulo 9, McCollough 3, O'Toole 3. **1B**—Chavez 35, Raleigh 14, Russin 18, Short 1, Wolff 88. **2B**—Akins 1, Daedelow 14, Fowler 2, Gabriel 24, Martin 85, Short 20. **3B**—Berry 2, Bryant 2, Chavez 41, Daedelow 1, Gabriel 3, Raleigh 2, Short 99. **SS**—Daedelow 11, Fowler 1, Gabriel 13, Lawrence 42, Martinez 74, Short 7. **OF**—Akins 42, Almonte 84, Berrios 43, Chavez 3, D'Aquila 42, Dellucci 55, Fowler 2, Hodge 3, Huson 4, Isom 85, Kingsale 50, LeCronier 20.

## PITCHING

| | W | L | ERA | G | GS | CG | SV | IP | H | R | ER | BB | SO | B | T | HT | WT | DOB | 1st Yr | Resides |
|---|---|---|---|---|---|---|---|---|---|---|---|---|---|---|---|---|---|---|---|---|
| Bigham, Dave | 4 | 6 | 5.64 | 29 | 9 | 0 | 2 | 69 | 82 | 52 | 43 | 14 | 56 | L | L | 5-11 | 190 | 9-20-70 | 1989 | Mankato, Minn. |
| Brown, Derek | 0 | 1 | 9.00 | 1 | 1 | 0 | 0 | 4 | 6 | 4 | 4 | 3 | 0 | R | R | 6-0 | 170 | 7-23-76 | 1994 | Hagerstown, Md. |
| Cafaro, Rocco | 1 | 3 | 4.50 | 8 | 0 | 0 | 2 | 20 | 19 | 10 | 10 | 6 | 16 | R | R | 6-0 | 175 | 12-2-72 | 1993 | Brandon, Fla. |
| Conner, Scott | 1 | 2 | 3.65 | 12 | 10 | 0 | 0 | 62 | 52 | 29 | 25 | 27 | 47 | R | R | 6-2 | 192 | 3-22-72 | 1991 | Irvine, Calif. |
| Dyess, Todd | 4 | 7 | 5.25 | 20 | 17 | 0 | 0 | 96 | 99 | 63 | 56 | 39 | 90 | R | R | 6-3 | 192 | 3-20-73 | 1994 | Florence, Miss. |
| Dykhoff, Radhames | 2 | 6 | 5.66 | 33 | 0 | 0 | 3 | 62 | 77 | 45 | 39 | 22 | 75 | L | L | 6-0 | 205 | 9-27-74 | 1993 | Oranjestad, Aruba |
| Fussell, Chris | 5 | 2 | 2.81 | 15 | 14 | 1 | 0 | 86 | 71 | 36 | 27 | 44 | 94 | R | R | 6-3 | 185 | 5-19-76 | 1994 | Oregon, Ohio |
| Hernandez, Francisco | 4 | 3 | 4.57 | 37 | 0 | 0 | 12 | 45 | 44 | 26 | 23 | 21 | 39 | R | R | 6-0 | 160 | 12-17-76 | 1994 | San Pedro de Macoris, D.R. |
| Moreno, Julio | 9 | 10 | 3.50 | 28 | 26 | 0 | 0 | 162 | 167 | 89 | 63 | 38 | 147 | R | R | 6-1 | 145 | 10-23-75 | 1994 | Los Llanos, D.R. |
| Morseman, Robert | 0 | 6 | 6.10 | 29 | 0 | 0 | 3 | 49 | 56 | 36 | 33 | 31 | 50 | L | L | 6-4 | 190 | 6-10-74 | 1995 | Westfield, Pa. |
| Paronto, Chad | 0 | 1 | 4.80 | 8 | 1 | 0 | 0 | 15 | 11 | 9 | 8 | 8 | 6 | R | R | 6-5 | 255 | 7-28-75 | 1996 | North Haverhill, N.H. |
| Pena, Alex | 0 | 1 | 13.50 | 2 | 0 | 0 | 0 | 2 | 3 | 3 | 3 | 1 | 1 | R | R | 6-0 | 175 | 9-9-72 | 1993 | El Paso, Texas |
| Ponson, Sidney | 7 | 6 | 3.45 | 18 | 16 | 3 | 0 | 107 | 98 | 56 | 41 | 28 | 110 | R | R | 6-1 | 200 | 11-2-76 | 1994 | Aruba, Aruba |
| Rodriguez, Nerio | 8 | 7 | 2.26 | 24 | 17 | 1 | 2 | 111 | 83 | 42 | 28 | 40 | 114 | R | R | 6-1 | 195 | 3-22-73 | 1991 | San Pedro de Macoris, D.R. |
| Rogers, Jason | 0 | 8 | 5.48 | 31 | 18 | 1 | 0 | 115 | 136 | 87 | 70 | 62 | 87 | L | L | 6-6 | 215 | 4-5-73 | 1994 | Reno, Nev. |
| Saneaux, Francisco | 0 | 0 | 37.13 | 2 | 1 | 0 | 0 | 3 | 9 | 11 | 11 | 6 | 3 | R | R | 6-4 | 180 | 3-3-74 | 1991 | Santo Domingo, D.R. |
| Shepherd, Alvie | 6 | 5 | 5.59 | 41 | 6 | 0 | 10 | 97 | 112 | 67 | 60 | 47 | 104 | R | R | 6-7 | 245 | 5-12-74 | 1996 | Bellwood, Ill. |
| Trimarco, Mike | 5 | 3 | 4.94 | 43 | 0 | 0 | 3 | 78 | 96 | 52 | 43 | 23 | 47 | R | R | 6-0 | 170 | 12-22-71 | 1993 | Aurora, Ill. |
| Weglarz, John | 0 | 0 | 7.71 | 2 | 0 | 0 | 0 | 2 | 3 | 2 | 2 | 1 | 2 | R | R | 6-1 | 180 | 11-12-70 | 1992 | Franklin Square, N.Y. |
| Wegmann, Tom | 1 | 1 | 1.80 | 3 | 3 | 0 | 0 | 15 | 13 | 9 | 3 | 5 | 16 | R | R | 6-0 | 190 | 8-29-68 | 1990 | Dyersville, Iowa |

# BLUEFIELD    Rookie

## APPALACHIAN LEAGUE

### BATTING

| | AVG | G | AB | R | H | 2B | 3B | HR | RBI | BB | SO | SB | CS | B | T | HT | WT | DOB | 1st Yr | Resides |
|---|---|---|---|---|---|---|---|---|---|---|---|---|---|---|---|---|---|---|---|---|
| Ahrendt, Jay | .500 | 3 | 4 | 1 | 2 | 0 | 0 | 0 | 2 | 1 | 1 | 0 | 0 | L | R | 6-2 | 210 | 1-23-74 | 1996 | Homewood, Ill. |
| Akins, Carlos | .298 | 18 | 57 | 19 | 17 | 4 | 0 | 0 | 14 | 15 | 11 | 15 | 0 | R | R | 6-0 | 180 | 7-12-74 | 1995 | Oklahoma City, Okla. |
| Alley, Chip | .194 | 24 | 67 | 7 | 13 | 4 | 0 | 0 | 4 | 15 | 16 | 0 | 2 | S | R | 6-3 | 190 | 12-20-76 | 1995 | West Palm Beach, Fla. |
| Casimiro, Carlos | .276 | 62 | 239 | 51 | 66 | 16 | 0 | 10 | 33 | 20 | 52 | 22 | 9 | R | R | 6-0 | 155 | 11-8-76 | 1994 | San Pedro de Macoris, D.R. |
| Charles, Curtis | .203 | 60 | 182 | 36 | 37 | 7 | 1 | 6 | 17 | 32 | 76 | 31 | 6 | R | R | 6-1 | 179 | 3-15-95 | 1995 | Caracas, Venez. |
| Dent, Darrell | .223 | 59 | 193 | 40 | 43 | 6 | 2 | 0 | 14 | 28 | 49 | 30 | 9 | L | L | 6-2 | 172 | 5-26-77 | 1995 | Van Nuys, Calif. |
| DeCinces, Tim | .297 | 39 | 128 | 24 | 38 | 8 | 0 | 7 | 32 | 24 | 28 | 3 | 1 | L | R | 6-2 | 195 | 4-26-74 | 1996 | Newport Beach, Calif. |
| Fowler, Maleke | .372 | 26 | 86 | 23 | 32 | 5 | 0 | 0 | 8 | 14 | 16 | 17 | 3 | R | R | 5-11 | 180 | 8-11-75 | 1996 | Baton Rouge, La. |
| Lawrence, Chip | .206 | 15 | 34 | 6 | 7 | 0 | 0 | 1 | 4 | 4 | 4 | 0 | 0 | R | R | 6-2 | 182 | 11-14-74 | 1996 | St. Petersburg, Fla. |
| Martinez, Eddy | .221 | 37 | 122 | 18 | 27 | 3 | 0 | 1 | 15 | 13 | 29 | 15 | 5 | R | R | 6-2 | 150 | 10-23-77 | 1995 | San Pedro de Macoris, D.R. |
| McCollough, Adam | .301 | 31 | 93 | 16 | 28 | 7 | 1 | 4 | 23 | 5 | 20 | 2 | 0 | R | R | 6-1 | 190 | 8-26-73 | 1996 | Lawton, Okla. |
| Minor, Ryan | .253 | 25 | 87 | 14 | 22 | 6 | 0 | 4 | 9 | 7 | 32 | 1 | 0 | R | R | 6-7 | 225 | 1-5-74 | 1996 | Edmond, Okla. |
| O'Toole, Bobby | .263 | 8 | 19 | 2 | 5 | 1 | 0 | 1 | 4 | 4 | 7 | 2 | 0 | R | R | 6-0 | 195 | 5-19-74 | 1995 | Newton, Mass. |
| Paz, Richard | .294 | 50 | 170 | 42 | 50 | 7 | 0 | 1 | 21 | 42 | 24 | 9 | 4 | R | R | 5-8 | 152 | 7-30-77 | 1994 | Los Teques, Venez. |
| Pedrosa, Alex | .247 | 34 | 77 | 12 | 19 | 9 | 0 | 0 | 15 | 13 | 22 | 0 | 1 | L | L | 5-10 | 198 | 5-15-75 | 1996 | Miami, Fla. |
| Pickering, Calvin | .325 | 60 | 200 | 45 | 65 | 14 | 1 | 18 | 66 | 28 | 64 | 8 | 2 | L | L | 6-3 | 283 | 9-29-76 | 1995 | Temple Terrace, Fla. |
| Ribaudo, Mike | .091 | 7 | 22 | 1 | 2 | 0 | 0 | 0 | 1 | 2 | 7 | 0 | 0 | R | R | 6-2 | 175 | 6-21-75 | 1995 | Sarasota, Fla. |
| Rivera, Roberto | .215 | 46 | 158 | 20 | 34 | 8 | 0 | 5 | 26 | 10 | 54 | 14 | 4 | R | R | 6-2 | 160 | 11-25-76 | 1994 | La Romana, D.R. |
| Russin, Tom | .258 | 57 | 190 | 32 | 49 | 15 | 1 | 8 | 40 | 17 | 38 | 1 | 2 | R | R | 6-2 | 200 | 9-9-73 | 1995 | Sarasota, Fla. |
| Stephens, Joel | .248 | 41 | 101 | 14 | 25 | 5 | 0 | 0 | 9 | 15 | 17 | 8 | 3 | R | R | 6-2 | 175 | 3-15-76 | 1995 | Tioga, Pa. |

**GAMES BY POSITION: C**—Ahrendt 3, Alley 24, DeCinces 17, McCollough 27, O'Toole 7, Rivera 1. **1B**—DeCinces 1, Pickering 53, Russin 24. **2B**—Casimiro 60, Fowler 4, Paz 8. **3B**—Casimiro 1, DeCinces 10, Fowler 1, Lawrence 9, Minor 22, Paz 17, Ribaudo 3, Russin 18. **SS**—Lawrence 6, Martinez 37, Minor 3, Paz 27, Pickering 1. **OF**—Akins 13, Casimiro 1, Charles 58, Dent 56, Fowler 16, Pedrosa 16, Rivera 37, Stephens 30.

### PITCHING

| | W | L | ERA | G | GS | CG | SV | IP | H | R | ER | BB | SO | B | T | HT | WT | DOB | 1st Yr | Resides |
|---|---|---|---|---|---|---|---|---|---|---|---|---|---|---|---|---|---|---|---|---|
| Achilles, Matt | 3 | 2 | 3.80 | 13 | 0 | 0 | 0 | 24 | 20 | 16 | 10 | 19 | 22 | R | R | 6-3 | 175 | 8-18-76 | 1996 | Moline, Ill. |
| Bray, Chris | 0 | 0 | 9.90 | 7 | 0 | 0 | 1 | 10 | 9 | 13 | 11 | 12 | 9 | R | R | 6-4 | 200 | 10-28-74 | 1995 | Currituck, N.C. |

| PITCHING | W | L | ERA | G | GS | CG | SV | IP | H | R | ER | BB | SO | B | T | HT | WT | DOB | 1st Yr | Resides |
|---|---|---|---|---|---|---|---|---|---|---|---|---|---|---|---|---|---|---|---|---|
| Brown, Derek | 0 | 1 | 16.88 | 2 | 2 | 0 | 0 | 5 | 12 | 10 | 10 | 2 | 3 | R | R | 6-0 | 170 | 7-23-76 | 1994 | Hagerstown, Md. |
| Eibey, Scott | 5 | 1 | 2.80 | 24 | 0 | 0 | 2 | 45 | 30 | 19 | 14 | 17 | 59 | L | L | 6-4 | 210 | 1-19-74 | 1995 | Waterloo, Iowa |
| Fisher, Louis | 3 | 4 | 4.40 | 14 | 13 | 1 | 0 | 72 | 58 | 43 | 35 | 48 | 52 | R | R | 6-1 | 189 | 10-14-76 | 1995 | Oakland, Calif. |
| Hacen, Abraham | 8 | 3 | 3.41 | 15 | 12 | 2 | 0 | 63 | 54 | 29 | 24 | 36 | 69 | R | R | 6-2 | 175 | 1-22-76 | 1993 | La Romana, D.R. |
| Hackett, Jason | 1 | 1 | 5.48 | 19 | 5 | 0 | 1 | 46 | 47 | 33 | 28 | 28 | 56 | L | L | 6-1 | 176 | 3-10-75 | 1994 | Worton, Md. |
| Huntsman, Brandon | 4 | 5 | 4.08 | 14 | 13 | 0 | 0 | 68 | 54 | 37 | 31 | 38 | 79 | R | R | 6-4 | 205 | 11-19-75 | 1994 | Pleasant Grove, Utah |
| McNatt, Josh | 0 | 1 | 8.53 | 2 | 1 | 0 | 0 | 6 | 10 | 6 | 6 | 6 | 7 | L | L | 6-4 | 200 | 7-23-77 | 1996 | Jackson, Tenn. |
| Mercedes, Carlos | 1 | 2 | 5.18 | 14 | 0 | 0 | 1 | 24 | 24 | 24 | 14 | 9 | 18 | R | R | 6-0 | 175 | 3-29-76 | 1994 | El Seibo, D.R. |
| Molina, Gabe | 4 | 0 | 3.60 | 23 | 0 | 0 | 7 | 30 | 29 | 12 | 12 | 13 | 33 | R | R | 5-11 | 190 | 5-3-75 | 1996 | Denver, Colo. |
| Paronto, Chad | 1 | 1 | 1.69 | 9 | 2 | 0 | 1 | 21 | 16 | 4 | 4 | 5 | 24 | R | R | 6-5 | 255 | 7-28-75 | 1996 | North Haverhill, N.H. |
| Parrish, John | 2 | 1 | 2.70 | 8 | 0 | 0 | 1 | 13 | 11 | 6 | 4 | 9 | 18 | L | L | 5-11 | 165 | 11-26-77 | 1996 | Lancaster, Pa. |
| Peguero, Americo | 4 | 2 | 2.82 | 9 | 9 | 0 | 0 | 51 | 38 | 24 | 16 | 22 | 54 | R | R | 6-0 | 140 | 5-20-77 | 1995 | La Romana, D.R. |
| Santos, Juan Carlos | 0 | 1 | 6.20 | 16 | 0 | 0 | 0 | 25 | 32 | 19 | 17 | 11 | 20 | R | R | 6-2 | 160 | 2-23-76 | 1993 | Ramon Santana, D.R. |
| Seaver, Mark | 1 | 0 | 1.20 | 3 | 2 | 0 | 0 | 15 | 4 | 2 | 2 | 5 | 18 | R | R | 6-8 | 240 | 4-6-75 | 1996 | Hickory, Pa. |
| Towers, Josh | 4 | 1 | 5.24 | 14 | 9 | 0 | 0 | 55 | 63 | 35 | 32 | 5 | 61 | R | R | 6-1 | 150 | 2-26-77 | 1996 | Port Hueneme, Calif. |

## SARASOTA — Rookie

### GULF COAST LEAGUE

| BATTING | AVG | G | AB | R | H | 2B | 3B | HR | RBI | BB | SO | SB | CS | B | T | HT | WT | DOB | 1st Yr | Resides |
|---|---|---|---|---|---|---|---|---|---|---|---|---|---|---|---|---|---|---|---|---|
| Ahrendt, Jay | .318 | 25 | 66 | 9 | 21 | 4 | 0 | 1 | 11 | 14 | 15 | 0 | 2 | L | R | 6-2 | 210 | 1-23-74 | 1996 | Homewood, Ill. |
| Almonte, Wady | .333 | 1 | 3 | 2 | 1 | 0 | 0 | 0 | 1 | 1 | 0 | 1 | 0 | R | R | 6-0 | 180 | 4-20-75 | 1993 | Higuey, D.R. |
| Bello, Jilberto | .157 | 40 | 134 | 10 | 21 | 5 | 1 | 0 | 9 | 11 | 48 | 8 | 4 | R | R | 6-3 | 150 | 2-26-77 | 1994 | San Pedro de Macoris, D.R. |
| Butkus, Ben | .146 | 20 | 41 | 1 | 6 | 0 | 1 | 0 | 3 | 1 | 13 | 0 | 1 | R | R | 6-2 | 170 | 2-24-76 | 1996 | Windermere, Fla. |
| Carney, Bartt | .250 | 6 | 12 | 4 | 3 | 0 | 0 | 0 | 1 | 5 | 1 | 1 | 0 | S | R | 5-11 | 170 | 12-16-73 | 1994 | Parnell, Iowa |
| Coffie, Evanon | .218 | 56 | 193 | 29 | 42 | 8 | 4 | 0 | 20 | 23 | 26 | 6 | 2 | L | R | 6-1 | 170 | 5-16-77 | 1995 | Curacao, Neth. Antilles |
| Davison, Ashanti | .263 | 31 | 76 | 13 | 20 | 2 | 0 | 0 | 4 | 11 | 14 | 9 | 2 | R | R | 5-10 | 170 | 10-31-78 | 1996 | Stockton, Calif. |
| Figueroa, Francisco | .340 | 43 | 150 | 22 | 51 | 8 | 1 | 0 | 23 | 8 | 25 | 3 | 0 | R | R | 6-6 | 225 | 2-9-77 | 1996 | Hialeah, Fla. |
| Hooper, Daren | .250 | 33 | 104 | 22 | 26 | 4 | 0 | 3 | 12 | 16 | 30 | 1 | 0 | R | R | 6-1 | 215 | 5-15-77 | 1996 | Woodside, Calif. |
| King, Brion | .115 | 9 | 26 | 5 | 3 | 1 | 0 | 0 | 1 | 2 | 5 | 2 | 0 | R | R | 6-0 | 200 | 9-1-76 | 1995 | Oviedo, Fla. |
| Kirkpatrick, Michael | .226 | 17 | 31 | 3 | 7 | 0 | 0 | 0 | 2 | 0 | 5 | 2 | 3 | L | L | 6-0 | 180 | 11-12-77 | 1996 | New Castle, Del. |
| Matos, Luis | .292 | 43 | 130 | 21 | 38 | 2 | 0 | 0 | 13 | 15 | 18 | 12 | 7 | R | R | 6-1 | 155 | 10-30-78 | 1996 | Bayamon, P.R. |
| Morales, Domingo | .386 | 19 | 70 | 9 | 27 | 5 | 3 | 0 | 15 | 2 | 4 | 6 | 2 | R | R | 6-0 | 160 | 8-15-76 | 1994 | Hato Mayor, D.R. |
| Morgan, Todd | .172 | 18 | 29 | 2 | 5 | 0 | 0 | 0 | 0 | 4 | 7 | 1 | 1 | R | R | 6-1 | 185 | 10-8-77 | 1996 | Pompano Beach, Fla. |
| Ortiz, Pedro | .246 | 43 | 126 | 16 | 31 | 8 | 0 | 3 | 6 | 4 | 33 | 5 | 0 | R | R | 6-0 | 175 | 10-29-76 | 1994 | Levittown, P.R. |
| Owens, Billy | .167 | 6 | 18 | 0 | 3 | 0 | 0 | 0 | 3 | 0 | 4 | 0 | 0 | S | R | 6-1 | 210 | 4-12-71 | 1992 | Fresno, Calif. |
| Pedrosa, Alex | .308 | 3 | 13 | 0 | 4 | 1 | 0 | 0 | 0 | 0 | 1 | 1 | 0 | L | L | 5-10 | 198 | 5-15-75 | 1996 | Miami, Fla. |
| Perez, Jesse | .173 | 36 | 104 | 9 | 18 | 3 | 0 | 0 | 10 | 7 | 33 | 2 | 3 | S | R | 6-4 | 175 | 7-19-78 | 1996 | Mayaguez, P.R. |
| Perez, Richard | .254 | 41 | 138 | 25 | 35 | 5 | 2 | 3 | 18 | 12 | 34 | 10 | 5 | R | R | 6-0 | 155 | 2-18-78 | 1995 | San Pedro de Macoris, D.R. |
| Ramirez, Luis | .160 | 41 | 131 | 13 | 21 | 4 | 3 | 0 | 12 | 7 | 47 | 1 | 2 | R | R | 6-3 | 180 | 9-26-78 | 1996 | Arroyo, P.R. |
| Ramos, Noel | .217 | 18 | 46 | 4 | 10 | 3 | 0 | 2 | 6 | 4 | 17 | 0 | 0 | R | R | 6-1 | 230 | 10-25-76 | 1994 | Isabella, P.R. |
| Rivera, Roberto | .625 | 4 | 8 | 7 | 5 | 1 | 1 | 0 | 2 | 3 | 1 | 3 | 0 | R | R | 6-2 | 160 | 11-25-76 | 1994 | La Romana, D.R. |
| Robertson, Dean | .302 | 53 | 179 | 32 | 54 | 11 | 2 | 2 | 25 | 28 | 17 | 16 | 7 | R | R | 6-1 | 166 | 2-19-76 | 1994 | Geelong, Australia |
| Tarasco, Tony | .375 | 3 | 8 | 2 | 3 | 1 | 0 | 0 | 3 | 2 | 1 | 0 | 0 | L | R | 6-1 | 205 | 12-9-70 | 1988 | Santa Monica, Calif. |
| Taylor, Avery | .160 | 9 | 25 | 0 | 4 | 0 | 0 | 0 | 2 | 0 | 8 | 2 | 1 | R | R | 6-0 | 202 | 11-30-75 | 1995 | Long Beach, Miss. |
| Utting, Andrew | .263 | 36 | 114 | 10 | 30 | 7 | 2 | 1 | 19 | 17 | 16 | 4 | 0 | S | R | 6-1 | 175 | 9-9-77 | 1995 | Melbourne, Australia |
| Zosky, Eddie | .333 | 1 | 3 | 1 | 1 | 1 | 0 | 0 | 0 | 1 | 0 | 0 | 0 | R | R | 6-0 | 185 | 2-10-68 | 1989 | Whittier, Calif. |

**GAMES BY POSITION: C**—Ahrendt 8, Bello 35, Utting 21. **1B**—Ahrendt 2, Figueroa 38, Owens 5, Ramos 17, Robertson 2, Utting 11. **2B**—Butkus 6, J. Perez 2, Robertson 47, Taylor 9. **3B**—Butkus 3, Coffie 1, King 8, Ortiz 26, J. Perez 31. **SS**—Butkus 12, Coffie 56, J. Perez 3, Robertson 2, Zosky 1. **OF**—Ahrendt 1, Almonte 1, Carney 6, Davison 28, Hooper 10, Kirkpatrick 13, Matos 41, Morales 16, Morgan 13, Ortiz 9, J. Perez 5, R. Perez 35, Ramirez 36, Rivera 3.

| PITCHING | W | L | ERA | G | GS | CG | SV | IP | H | R | ER | BB | SO | B | T | HT | WT | DOB | 1st Yr | Resides |
|---|---|---|---|---|---|---|---|---|---|---|---|---|---|---|---|---|---|---|---|---|
| Achilles, Matt | 0 | 1 | 2.25 | 5 | 5 | 0 | 0 | 20 | 16 | 6 | 5 | 10 | 12 | R | R | 6-3 | 175 | 8-18-76 | 1996 | Moline, Ill. |
| Andrade, Jancy | 3 | 2 | 2.68 | 18 | 3 | 0 | 5 | 37 | 30 | 13 | 11 | 13 | 30 | R | R | 6-2 | 165 | 6-29-78 | 1995 | Cumana, Venez. |
| Benitez, Armando | 0 | 0 | 0.00 | 1 | 0 | 0 | 0 | 2 | 1 | 0 | 0 | 0 | 5 | R | R | 6-4 | 220 | 11-3-72 | 1990 | San Pedro de Macoris, D.R. |
| Brown, Derek | 6 | 1 | 3.11 | 9 | 8 | 1 | 1 | 55 | 50 | 19 | 19 | 11 | 37 | R | R | 6-0 | 170 | 7-23-76 | 1994 | Hagerstown, Md. |
| Cruz, Charlie | 1 | 0 | 4.50 | 9 | 0 | 0 | 0 | 14 | 19 | 10 | 7 | 6 | 7 | R | R | 6-4 | 225 | 2-12-77 | 1995 | Santiago, D.R. |
| Falkenborg, Brian | 3 | 2 | 3.57 | 8 | 6 | 0 | 0 | 28 | 21 | 13 | 8 | 8 | 36 | R | R | 6-6 | 187 | 1-18-78 | 1996 | Redmond, Wash. |
| Forbes, Cameron | 4 | 5 | 4.34 | 13 | 13 | 0 | 0 | 77 | 73 | 48 | 37 | 22 | 71 | R | R | 6-0 | 175 | 2-28-77 | 1996 | Lara, Australia |
| Heredia, Maximo | 3 | 1 | 2.88 | 17 | 0 | 0 | 4 | 34 | 22 | 15 | 11 | 12 | 25 | R | R | 6-1 | 145 | 9-27-76 | 1994 | San Pedro de Macoris, D.R. |
| Jimenez, Ricardo | 5 | 3 | 2.01 | 12 | 12 | 0 | 0 | 63 | 46 | 22 | 14 | 34 | 44 | R | R | 6-0 | 160 | 5-23-78 | 1995 | La Higuera, D.R. |
| Johnson, Jeremiah | 0 | 0 | 0.00 | 4 | 0 | 0 | 0 | 6 | 4 | 0 | 0 | 1 | 10 | R | R | 6-6 | 210 | 7-19-77 | 1996 | Litchfield, Mich. |
| LaRocca, Todd | 1 | 0 | 12.71 | 4 | 0 | 0 | 0 | 6 | 8 | 8 | 8 | 2 | 9 | R | R | 6-1 | 185 | 9-21-72 | 1994 | Atlanta, Ga. |
| McNatt, Josh | 2 | 2 | 2.18 | 12 | 8 | 0 | 0 | 54 | 36 | 15 | 13 | 12 | 42 | L | L | 6-4 | 200 | 7-23-77 | 1996 | Jackson, Tenn. |
| Mercedes, Carlos | 1 | 2 | 5.40 | 5 | 1 | 0 | 1 | 8 | 15 | 7 | 5 | 2 | 6 | R | R | 6-0 | 175 | 3-29-76 | 1994 | El Seibo, D.R. |
| Munoz, Oscar | 0 | 0 | 0.00 | 2 | 0 | 0 | 1 | 3 | 0 | 0 | 0 | 0 | 1 | R | R | 6-2 | 205 | 9-25-69 | 1990 | Hialeah, Fla. |
| Parrish, John | 0 | 0 | 1.86 | 11 | 0 | 0 | 2 | 19 | 13 | 5 | 4 | 11 | 33 | L | L | 5-11 | 165 | 11-26-77 | 1996 | Lancaster, Pa. |
| Phipps, Jeff | 3 | 1 | 5.93 | 17 | 0 | 0 | 2 | 27 | 30 | 20 | 18 | 12 | 23 | R | R | 6-8 | 225 | 2-5-75 | 1996 | Blythe, Calif. |
| Ryan, Kevin | 1 | 0 | 0.00 | 2 | 0 | 0 | 0 | 3 | 2 | 1 | 0 | 0 | 2 | R | R | 6-1 | 187 | 9-23-70 | 1991 | Oklahoma City, Okla. |
| Sackinsky, Brian | 0 | 0 | 5.19 | 3 | 1 | 0 | 0 | 9 | 11 | 6 | 5 | 1 | 3 | R | R | 6-4 | 220 | 6-22-71 | 1992 | Library, Pa. |
| Santana, Orlando | 1 | 1 | 3.16 | 16 | 0 | 0 | 2 | 26 | 24 | 12 | 9 | 6 | 19 | R | R | 6-3 | 160 | 12-12-78 | 1995 | Los Llanos, D.R. |
| Santos, Juan | 0 | 0 | 3.86 | 6 | 0 | 0 | 2 | 9 | 9 | 4 | 4 | 2 | 4 | R | R | 6-2 | 160 | 2-23-76 | 1993 | Ramon Santana, D.R. |
| Sims, Ken | 0 | 2 | 4.96 | 11 | 2 | 0 | 2 | 16 | 22 | 12 | 9 | 8 | 20 | R | R | 6-4 | 187 | 7-24-75 | 1996 | Union, S.C. |
| Wegmann, Tom | 0 | 0 | 0.00 | 4 | 1 | 0 | 0 | 9 | 4 | 2 | 0 | 2 | 12 | R | R | 6-0 | 190 | 8-29-68 | 1990 | Dyersville, Iowa |

# BOSTON RED SOX

**Manager:** Kevin Kennedy.    **1996 Record:** 85-77, .525 (3rd, AL East).

| BATTING | AVG | G | AB | R | H | 2B | 3B | HR | RBI | BB | SO | SB | CS | B | T | HT | WT | DOB | 1st Yr | Resides |
|---|---|---|---|---|---|---|---|---|---|---|---|---|---|---|---|---|---|---|---|---|
| Beltre, Esteban | .258 | 27 | 62 | 6 | 16 | 2 | 0 | 0 | 6 | 4 | 14 | 1 | 0 | R | R | 5-10 | 172 | 12-26-67 | 1984 | San Pedro de Macoris, D.R. |
| Bragg, Darren | .252 | 58 | 222 | 38 | 56 | 14 | 1 | 3 | 22 | 36 | 39 | 6 | 4 | L | R | 5-9 | 180 | 9-7-69 | 1991 | Wolcott, Conn. |
| 2-team (69 Seattle) | .261 | 127 | 417 | 74 | 109 | 26 | 2 | 10 | 47 | 69 | 74 | 14 | 9 | | | | | | | |
| Canseco, Jose | .289 | 96 | 360 | 68 | 104 | 22 | 1 | 28 | 82 | 63 | 82 | 3 | 1 | R | R | 6-3 | 185 | 7-2-64 | 1982 | Miami, Fla. |
| Clark, Phil | .000 | 3 | 3 | 0 | 0 | 0 | 0 | 0 | 0 | 0 | 1 | 0 | 0 | R | R | 6-0 | 180 | 5-6-68 | 1986 | Toledo, Ohio |
| Cole, Alex | .222 | 24 | 72 | 13 | 16 | 5 | 1 | 0 | 7 | 8 | 11 | 5 | 3 | L | L | 6-2 | 183 | 8-17-65 | 1985 | St. Petersburg, Fla. |
| Cordero, Wil | .288 | 59 | 198 | 29 | 57 | 14 | 0 | 3 | 37 | 11 | 31 | 2 | 1 | R | R | 6-2 | 185 | 10-3-71 | 1988 | Mayaguez, P.R. |
| Cuyler, Milt | .200 | 50 | 110 | 19 | 22 | 1 | 2 | 2 | 12 | 13 | 19 | 7 | 3 | S | R | 5-10 | 185 | 10-7-68 | 1986 | Lakeland, Fla. |
| Delgado, Alex | .250 | 26 | 20 | 5 | 5 | 0 | 0 | 0 | 1 | 3 | 3 | 0 | 0 | R | R | 6-0 | 160 | 1-11-71 | 1988 | Palmerejo, Venez. |
| Frye, Jeff | .286 | 105 | 419 | 74 | 120 | 27 | 2 | 4 | 41 | 54 | 57 | 18 | 4 | R | R | 5-9 | 180 | 8-31-66 | 1988 | Las Vegas, Nev. |
| Garciaparra, Nomar | .241 | 24 | 87 | 11 | 21 | 2 | 3 | 4 | 16 | 4 | 14 | 5 | 0 | R | R | 6-0 | 165 | 7-23-73 | 1994 | Whittier, Calif. |
| Greenwell, Mike | .295 | 77 | 295 | 35 | 87 | 20 | 1 | 7 | 44 | 18 | 27 | 4 | 0 | L | R | 6-0 | 205 | 7-18-63 | 1982 | Cape Coral, Fla. |
| Haselman, Bill | .274 | 77 | 237 | 33 | 65 | 13 | 1 | 8 | 34 | 19 | 52 | 4 | 2 | R | R | 6-3 | 215 | 5-25-66 | 1987 | Saratoga, Calif. |
| Hatteberg, Scott | .182 | 10 | 11 | 3 | 2 | 1 | 0 | 0 | 0 | 3 | 2 | 0 | 0 | L | R | 6-1 | 185 | 12-14-69 | 1991 | Yakima, Wash. |
| Hosey, Dwayne | .218 | 28 | 78 | 13 | 17 | 2 | 2 | 1 | 3 | 7 | 17 | 6 | 3 | S | R | 5-10 | 170 | 3-11-67 | 1987 | Altadena, Calif. |
| Jefferson, Reggie | .347 | 122 | 386 | 67 | 134 | 30 | 4 | 19 | 74 | 25 | 89 | 0 | 0 | L | L | 6-4 | 215 | 9-25-68 | 1986 | Tallahassee, Fla. |
| Malave, Jose | .235 | 41 | 102 | 12 | 24 | 3 | 0 | 4 | 17 | 2 | 25 | 0 | 0 | R | R | 6-2 | 195 | 5-31-71 | 1990 | Cumana, Venez. |
| Manto, Jeff | .208 | 22 | 48 | 8 | 10 | 3 | 1 | 2 | 6 | 8 | 12 | 0 | 0 | R | R | 6-3 | 210 | 8-23-64 | 1985 | Bristol, Pa. |
| 2-team (21 Seattle) | .197 | 43 | 102 | 15 | 20 | 6 | 1 | 3 | 10 | 17 | 24 | 0 | 1 | | | | | | | |
| Mitchell, Kevin | .304 | 27 | 92 | 9 | 28 | 4 | 0 | 2 | 13 | 11 | 14 | 0 | 0 | R | R | 5-11 | 210 | 1-13-62 | 1981 | Chula Vista, Calif. |
| Naehring, Tim | .288 | 116 | 430 | 77 | 124 | 16 | 0 | 17 | 65 | 49 | 63 | 2 | 1 | R | R | 6-2 | 200 | 2-1-67 | 1988 | Cincinnati, Ohio |
| Nixon, Trot | .500 | 2 | 4 | 2 | 2 | 1 | 0 | 0 | 0 | 0 | 1 | 1 | 0 | L | L | 6-1 | 195 | 4-11-74 | 1993 | Wilmington, N.C. |
| O'Leary, Troy | .260 | 149 | 497 | 68 | 129 | 28 | 5 | 15 | 81 | 47 | 80 | 3 | 2 | L | L | 6-0 | 190 | 8-4-69 | 1987 | Rialto, Calif. |
| Pemberton, Rudy | .512 | 13 | 41 | 11 | 21 | 8 | 0 | 1 | 10 | 2 | 4 | 3 | 1 | R | R | 6-1 | 185 | 12-17-69 | 1987 | San Pedro de Macoris, D.R. |
| Pirkl, Greg | .000 | 2 | 2 | 0 | 0 | 0 | 0 | 0 | 0 | 0 | 1 | 0 | 0 | R | R | 6-5 | 225 | 8-7-70 | 1988 | Phoenix, Ariz. |
| 2-team (7 Seattle) | .174 | 9 | 23 | 2 | 4 | 1 | 0 | 1 | 1 | 0 | 4 | 0 | 0 | | | | | | | |
| Pozo, Arquimedez | .172 | 21 | 58 | 4 | 10 | 3 | 1 | 1 | 11 | 2 | 10 | 1 | 0 | R | R | 5-10 | 160 | 8-24-73 | 1991 | Santo Domingo, D.R. |
| Rodriguez, Tony | .239 | 27 | 67 | 7 | 16 | 1 | 0 | 1 | 9 | 4 | 8 | 0 | 0 | R | R | 5-11 | 165 | 8-15-70 | 1991 | Cidra, P.R. |
| Selby, Bill | .274 | 40 | 95 | 12 | 26 | 4 | 0 | 3 | 6 | 9 | 11 | 1 | 1 | L | R | 5-9 | 190 | 6-11-70 | 1992 | Walls, Miss. |
| Stanley, Mike | .270 | 121 | 397 | 73 | 107 | 20 | 1 | 24 | 69 | 69 | 62 | 2 | 0 | R | R | 6-0 | 190 | 6-25-63 | 1985 | Oviedo, Fla. |
| Tatum, Jimmy | .125 | 2 | 8 | 1 | 1 | 0 | 0 | 0 | 0 | 0 | 2 | 0 | 0 | R | R | 6-2 | 200 | 10-9-67 | 1985 | Lakeside, Calif. |
| Tinsley, Lee | .245 | 92 | 192 | 28 | 47 | 6 | 1 | 3 | 14 | 13 | 56 | 6 | 8 | S | R | 5-10 | 180 | 3-4-69 | 1987 | Shelbyville, Ky. |
| Valentin, John | .296 | 131 | 527 | 84 | 156 | 29 | 3 | 13 | 59 | 63 | 59 | 9 | 10 | R | R | 6-0 | 185 | 2-18-67 | 1988 | Braintree, Mass. |
| Vaughn, Mo | .326 | 161 | 635 | 118 | 207 | 29 | 1 | 44 | 143 | 95 | 154 | 2 | 0 | L | R | 6-1 | 230 | 12-15-67 | 1989 | Braintree, Mass. |

| PITCHING | W | L | ERA | G | GS | CG | SV | IP | H | R | ER | BB | SO | B | T | HT | WT | DOB | 1st Yr | Resides |
|---|---|---|---|---|---|---|---|---|---|---|---|---|---|---|---|---|---|---|---|---|
| Belinda, Stan | 2 | 1 | 6.59 | 31 | 0 | 0 | 2 | 29 | 31 | 22 | 21 | 20 | 18 | R | R | 6-3 | 215 | 8-6-66 | 1985 | Alexandria, Pa. |
| Brandenburg, Mark | 4 | 2 | 3.81 | 29 | 0 | 0 | 0 | 28 | 28 | 13 | 12 | 8 | 29 | R | R | 6-0 | 170 | 7-14-70 | 1992 | Humble, Texas |
| 2-team (26 Texas) | 5 | 5 | 3.43 | 55 | 0 | 0 | 0 | 76 | 76 | 35 | 29 | 33 | 66 | | | | | | | |
| Clemens, Roger | 10 | 13 | 3.63 | 34 | 34 | 6 | 0 | 243 | 216 | 106 | 98 | 106 | 257 | R | R | 6-4 | 220 | 8-4-62 | 1983 | Houston, Texas |
| Doherty, John | 0 | 0 | 5.68 | 3 | 0 | 0 | 0 | 6 | 8 | 10 | 4 | 4 | 3 | R | R | 6-4 | 210 | 6-11-67 | 1989 | Tuckahoe, N.Y. |
| Eshelman, Vaughn | 6 | 3 | 7.08 | 39 | 10 | 0 | 0 | 88 | 112 | 79 | 69 | 58 | 59 | L | L | 6-3 | 205 | 5-22-69 | 1991 | Houston, Texas |
| Garces, Rich | 3 | 2 | 4.91 | 37 | 0 | 0 | 0 | 44 | 42 | 26 | 24 | 33 | 55 | R | R | 6-0 | 230 | 5-18-71 | 1988 | Maracay, Venez. |
| Gordon, Tom | 12 | 9 | 5.59 | 34 | 34 | 4 | 0 | 216 | 249 | 143 | 134 | 105 | 171 | R | R | 5-9 | 180 | 11-18-67 | 1986 | Avon Park, Fla. |
| Grundt, Ken | 0 | 0 | 27.00 | 1 | 0 | 0 | 0 | 1 | 1 | 1 | 1 | 0 | 0 | L | L | 6-4 | 195 | 8-26-69 | 1991 | Chicago, Ill. |
| Gunderson, Eric | 0 | 1 | 8.31 | 28 | 0 | 0 | 0 | 17 | 21 | 17 | 16 | 8 | 7 | R | L | 6-0 | 195 | 3-29-66 | 1987 | Portland, Ore. |
| Harris, Reggie | 0 | 0 | 12.46 | 4 | 0 | 0 | 0 | 4 | 7 | 6 | 6 | 5 | 4 | R | R | 6-1 | 190 | 8-12-68 | 1987 | Waynesboro, Va. |
| Hudson, Joe | 3 | 5 | 5.40 | 36 | 0 | 0 | 1 | 45 | 57 | 35 | 27 | 32 | 19 | R | R | 6-1 | 180 | 9-29-70 | 1992 | Medford, N.J. |
| Knackert, Brent | 0 | 1 | 9.00 | 8 | 0 | 0 | 0 | 10 | 16 | 12 | 10 | 7 | 5 | R | R | 6-3 | 195 | 8-1-69 | 1987 | Huntington Beach, Calif. |
| Lacy, Kerry | 2 | 0 | 3.38 | 11 | 0 | 0 | 1 | 15 | 15 | 5 | 4 | 8 | 9 | R | R | 6-2 | 195 | 8-7-72 | 1991 | Higdon, Ala. |
| Maddux, Mike | 3 | 2 | 4.48 | 23 | 7 | 0 | 0 | 64 | 76 | 37 | 32 | 27 | 32 | L | R | 6-2 | 188 | 8-27-61 | 1982 | Las Vegas, Nev. |
| Mahomes, Pat | 2 | 0 | 5.84 | 11 | 0 | 0 | 2 | 12 | 9 | 8 | 8 | 6 | 6 | R | R | 6-4 | 210 | 8-9-70 | 1988 | Lindale, Texas |
| 2-team (20 Minn.) | 3 | 4 | 6.91 | 31 | 5 | 0 | 2 | 57 | 72 | 46 | 44 | 33 | 36 | | | | | | | |
| Minchey, Nate | 0 | 2 | 15.00 | 2 | 2 | 0 | 0 | 6 | 16 | 11 | 10 | 5 | 4 | R | R | 6-7 | 225 | 8-31-69 | 1987 | San Antonio, Texas |
| Moyer, Jamie | 7 | 1 | 4.50 | 23 | 10 | 0 | 0 | 90 | 111 | 50 | 45 | 27 | 50 | L | L | 6-0 | 170 | 11-18-62 | 1984 | Granger, Ill. |
| Pennington, Brad | 0 | 2 | 2.77 | 14 | 0 | 0 | 0 | 13 | 6 | 5 | 4 | 15 | 13 | L | L | 6-6 | 215 | 4-14-69 | 1989 | Salem, Ind. |
| Sele, Aaron | 7 | 11 | 5.32 | 29 | 29 | 1 | 0 | 157 | 192 | 110 | 93 | 67 | 137 | R | R | 6-5 | 218 | 6-25-70 | 1991 | Poulsbo, Wash. |
| Slocumb, Heathcliff | 5 | 5 | 3.02 | 75 | 0 | 0 | 31 | 83 | 68 | 31 | 28 | 55 | 88 | R | R | 6-3 | 180 | 6-7-66 | 1984 | Jamaica, N.Y. |
| Stanton, Mike | 4 | 3 | 3.83 | 59 | 0 | 0 | 1 | 56 | 58 | 24 | 24 | 23 | 46 | L | L | 6-1 | 190 | 6-2-67 | 1987 | Houston, Texas |
| Suppan, Jeff | 1 | 1 | 7.54 | 8 | 4 | 0 | 0 | 23 | 29 | 19 | 19 | 13 | 13 | R | R | 6-2 | 210 | 1-2-75 | 1993 | West Hills, Calif. |
| Wakefield, Tim | 14 | 13 | 5.14 | 32 | 32 | 6 | 0 | 212 | 238 | 151 | 121 | 90 | 140 | R | R | 6-2 | 204 | 8-2-66 | 1988 | Melbourne, Fla. |

First baseman Mo Vaughn led Boston with 44 homers and 143 RBIs

Red Sox minor league Player of the Year Carl Pavano

MORRIS FOSTOFF

MEL BAILEY

## FARM SYSTEM

**Director of Player Development and Administration:** Ed Kenney

| Class | Farm Team | League | W | L | Pct. | Finish* | Manager | First Yr |
|---|---|---|---|---|---|---|---|---|
| AAA | Pawtucket (R.I.) Red Sox | International | 78 | 64 | .549 | 3rd (10) | Buddy Bailey | 1973 |
| AA | Trenton (N.J.) Thunder | Eastern | 86 | 56 | .606 | 1st (10) | Ken Macha | 1995 |
| #A | Sarasota (Fla.) Red Sox | Florida State | 67 | 69 | .493 | 9th (14) | DeMarlo Hale | 1994 |
| A | Michigan Battle Cats | Midwest | 60 | 78 | .435 | 13th (14) | Tommy Barrett | 1995 |
| A | Lowell (Mass.) Spinners | New York-Penn | 33 | 41 | .446 | 9th (14) | Billy Gardner Jr. | 1996 |
| R | Fort Myers (Fla.) Red Sox | Gulf Coast | 24 | 36 | .400 | 14th (16) | Bob Geren | 1993 |

*Finish in overall standings (No. of teams in league)   #Advanced level

## ORGANIZATION LEADERS

### MAJOR LEAGUERS

**BATTING**
| | | |
|---|---|---|
| *AVG | Reggie Jefferson | .347 |
| R | Mo Vaughn | 118 |
| H | Mo Vaughn | 207 |
| TB | Mo Vaughn | 370 |
| 2B | Reggie Jefferson | 30 |
| 3B | Troy O'Leary | 5 |
| HR | Mo Vaughn | 44 |
| RBI | Mo Vaughn | 143 |
| BB | Mo Vaughn | 95 |
| SO | Mo Vaughn | 154 |
| SB | Jeff Frye | 18 |

**PITCHING**
| | | |
|---|---|---|
| W | Tim Wakefield | 14 |
| L | Two tied at | 13 |
| #ERA | Heathcliff Slocumb | 3.02 |
| G | Heathcliff Slocumb | 75 |
| CG | Two tied at | 6 |
| SV | Heathcliff Slocumb | 31 |
| IP | Roger Clemens | 243 |
| BB | Roger Clemens | 106 |
| SO | Roger Clemens | 257 |

**Roger Clemens.** 257 strikeouts

LARRY GOREN

### MINOR LEAGUERS

**BATTING**
| | | |
|---|---|---|
| *AVG | Bo Dodson, Pawtucket | .344 |
| R | Walt McKeel, Trenton | 86 |
| H | Walt McKeel, Trenton | 140 |
| TB | Rudy Pemberton, Pawtucket | 244 |
| 2B | Andy Abad, Sarasota/Trenton | 37 |
| 3B | Three tied at | 8 |
| HR | Rudy Pemberton, Pawtucket | 27 |
| RBI | Rudy Pemberton, Pawtucket | 92 |
| BB | Andy Abad, Sarasota/Trenton | 70 |
| SO | Two tied at | 123 |
| SB | Rick Holifield, Trenton/Pawtucket | 36 |

**PITCHING**
| | | |
|---|---|---|
| W | Carl Pavano, Trenton | 16 |
| L | Two tied at | 12 |
| #ERA | Bobby Rodgers, Lowell | 1.90 |
| G | Chuck Ricci, Pawtucket | 60 |
| CG | Jeff Suppan, Pawtucket | 7 |
| SV | Scott Jones, Michigan | 18 |
| IP | Juan Pena, Michigan | 188 |
| BB | Jared Fernandez, Trenton | 83 |
| SO | Juan Pena, Michigan | 156 |

*Minimum 250 At-Bats   #Minimum 75 Innings

## TOP 10 PROSPECTS

How the Red Sox Top 10 prospects, as judged by Baseball America prior to the 1996 season, fared in 1996:

**Donnie Sadler**

STEWART SMITH

| Player, Pos. | Club (Class—League) | AVG | AB | R | H | 2B | 3B | HR | RBI | SB |
|---|---|---|---|---|---|---|---|---|---|---|
| 1. Donnie Sadler, ss | Trenton (AA—Eastern) | .267 | 454 | 68 | 121 | 20 | 8 | 6 | 46 | 34 |
| 3. Trot Nixon, of | Trenton (AA—Eastern) | .251 | 438 | 55 | 110 | 11 | 4 | 11 | 63 | 7 |
| | Boston | .500 | 4 | 2 | 2 | 1 | 0 | 0 | 0 | 1 |
| 4. Nomar Garciaparra,ss | Pawtucket (AAA—International) | .343 | 172 | 40 | 59 | 15 | 2 | 16 | 46 | 3 |
| | Boston | .241 | 87 | 11 | 21 | 2 | 3 | 4 | 16 | 5 |
| 7. Michael Coleman, of | Sarasota (A—Florida State) | .246 | 407 | 54 | 100 | 20 | 5 | 1 | 36 | 24 |

| Player, Pos. | Club (Class—League) | W | L | ERA | G | SV | IP | H | BB | SO |
|---|---|---|---|---|---|---|---|---|---|---|
| 2. Jeff Suppan, rhp | Pawtucket (AAA—International) | 10 | 6 | 3.22 | 22 | 0 | 145 | 130 | 25 | 142 |
| | Boston | 1 | 1 | 7.54 | 8 | 0 | 23 | 29 | 13 | 13 |
| 5. Andy Yount, rhp | Lowell (A—New York-Penn) | 1 | 2 | 6.29 | 8 | 0 | 34 | 38 | 38 | 30 |
| 6. Brian Rose, rhp | Trenton (AA—Eastern) | 12 | 7 | 4.01 | 27 | 0 | 164 | 157 | 45 | 115 |
| 8. Carl Pavano, rhp | Trenton (AA—Eastern) | 16 | 5 | 2.63 | 27 | 0 | 185 | 154 | 47 | 146 |
| 9. Rafael Orellano, lhp | Pawtucket (AAA—International) | 4 | 11 | 7.88 | 22 | 0 | 99 | 124 | 62 | 66 |
| 10. Peter Munro, rhp | Sarasota (A—Florida State) | 11 | 6 | 3.60 | 27 | 1 | 155 | 153 | 62 | 115 |

## FIELDING

| Catcher | PCT | G | PO | A | E | DP | PB |
|---|---|---|---|---|---|---|---|
| Delgado | .889 | 14 | 16 | 0 | 2 | 1 | 0 |
| Haselman | .994 | 69 | 494 | 33 | 3 | 6 | 5 |
| Hatteberg | 1.000 | 10 | 32 | 2 | 0 | 0 | 0 |
| Stanley | .985 | 105 | 654 | 19 | 10 | 3 | 18 |

| First Base | PCT | G | PO | A | E | DP |
|---|---|---|---|---|---|---|
| Clark | 1.000 | 1 | 2 | 0 | 0 | 0 |
| Cordero | 1.000 | 1 | 7 | 0 | 0 | 2 |
| Delgado | 1.000 | 1 | 1 | 1 | 0 | 0 |
| Haselman | 1.000 | 2 | 13 | 0 | 0 | 2 |
| Jefferson | .993 | 16 | 117 | 16 | 1 | 8 |
| Manto | 1.000 | 1 | 1 | 0 | 0 | 0 |
| Pirkl | 1.000 | 2 | 14 | 2 | 0 | 2 |
| Vaughn | .988 | 146 | 1208 | 73 | 15 | 123 |

| Second Base | PCT | G | PO | A | E | DP |
|---|---|---|---|---|---|---|
| Beltre | .963 | 8 | 16 | 10 | 1 | 4 |
| Cordero | .949 | 37 | 75 | 110 | 10 | 19 |
| Delgado | 1.000 | 1 | 0 | 1 | 0 | 0 |
| Frye | .983 | 100 | 200 | 317 | 9 | 70 |
| Garciaparra | 1.000 | 1 | 2 | 1 | 0 | 0 |
| Manto | .963 | 4 | 10 | 16 | 1 | 3 |

| | PCT | G | PO | A | E | DP |
|---|---|---|---|---|---|---|
| Naehring | .000 | 1 | 0 | 0 | 0 | 0 |
| Pozo | .930 | 10 | 18 | 22 | 3 | 3 |
| Selby | .980 | 14 | 22 | 28 | 1 | 5 |

| Third Base | PCT | G | PO | A | E | DP |
|---|---|---|---|---|---|---|
| Beltre | 1.000 | 13 | 11 | 13 | 0 | 1 |
| Clark | 1.000 | 1 | 0 | 1 | 0 | 0 |
| Delgado | .000 | 4 | 0 | 0 | 0 | 0 |
| Manto | .960 | 10 | 7 | 17 | 1 | 1 |
| Naehring | .963 | 116 | 82 | 206 | 11 | 17 |
| Pozo | .957 | 10 | 5 | 17 | 1 | 1 |
| Rodriguez | .800 | 5 | 2 | 2 | 1 | 0 |
| Selby | .875 | 14 | 6 | 15 | 3 | 0 |
| Tatum | 1.000 | 2 | 3 | 2 | 0 | 0 |
| Valentin | .947 | 118 | 194 | 347 | 16 | 87 |

| Shortstop | PCT | G | PO | A | E | DP |
|---|---|---|---|---|---|---|
| Beltre | 1.000 | 6 | 4 | 3 | 0 | 0 |
| Frye | 1.000 | 3 | 1 | 0 | 0 | 0 |
| Garciaparra | .988 | 22 | 35 | 50 | 1 | 11 |
| Manto | .913 | 4 | 7 | 14 | 2 | 3 |
| Rodriguez | .979 | 21 | 30 | 62 | 2 | 11 |

| | PCT | G | PO | A | E | DP |
|---|---|---|---|---|---|---|
| Valentin | .971 | 118 | 194 | 347 | 16 | 87 |

| Outfield | PCT | G | PO | A | E | DP |
|---|---|---|---|---|---|---|
| Bragg | .986 | 58 | 136 | 5 | 2 | 2 |
| Canseco | 1.000 | 11 | 17 | 1 | 0 | 0 |
| Cole | .974 | 24 | 37 | 1 | 1 | 1 |
| Cuyler | .972 | 45 | 104 | 0 | 3 | 0 |
| Delgado | 1.000 | 6 | 5 | 1 | 0 | 0 |
| Frye | 1.000 | 5 | 10 | 0 | 0 | 0 |
| Greenwell | .973 | 76 | 137 | 9 | 4 | 2 |
| Hosey | .984 | 26 | 60 | 2 | 1 | 1 |
| Jefferson | .969 | 45 | 61 | 1 | 2 | 0 |
| Malave | .978 | 38 | 43 | 1 | 1 | 0 |
| Manto | .000 | 1 | 0 | 0 | 0 | 0 |
| Mitchell | .935 | 21 | 29 | 0 | 2 | 0 |
| Nixon | 1.000 | 2 | 3 | 0 | 0 | 0 |
| O'Leary | .971 | 146 | 227 | 8 | 7 | 0 |
| Pemberton | 1.000 | 13 | 9 | 0 | 0 | 0 |
| Selby | 1.000 | 6 | 2 | 0 | 0 | 0 |
| Tinsley | .993 | 83 | 132 | 8 | 1 | 1 |

# PAWTUCKET                                    Class AAA
## INTERNATIONAL LEAGUE

### BATTING

| | AVG | G | AB | R | H | 2B | 3B | HR | RBI | BB | SO | SB | CS | B | T | HT | WT | DOB | 1st Yr | Resides |
|---|---|---|---|---|---|---|---|---|---|---|---|---|---|---|---|---|---|---|---|---|
| Bell, Juan | .248 | 68 | 210 | 28 | 52 | 13 | 2 | 5 | 23 | 22 | 43 | 2 | 2 | S | R | 5-11 | 175 | 3-29-68 | 1985 | San Pedro de Macoris, D.R. |
| Brown, Randy | .167 | 3 | 6 | 0 | 1 | 0 | 0 | 0 | 1 | 1 | 1 | 0 | 0 | R | R | 5-11 | 160 | 5-1-70 | 1989 | Houston, Texas |
| Canseco, Jose | .200 | 2 | 5 | 0 | 1 | 0 | 0 | 0 | 3 | 0 | 0 | 0 | 0 | R | R | 6-3 | 185 | 7-2-64 | 1982 | Miami, Fla. |
| Clark, Phil | .325 | 97 | 369 | 57 | 120 | 36 | 2 | 12 | 69 | 17 | 32 | 3 | 6 | R | R | 6-0 | 180 | 5-6-68 | 1986 | Toledo, Ohio |
| Cole, Alex | .296 | 82 | 304 | 57 | 90 | 14 | 8 | 4 | 39 | 50 | 47 | 11 | 7 | L | L | 6-2 | 183 | 8-17-65 | 1985 | St. Petersburg, Fla. |
| Cookson, Brent | .271 | 73 | 255 | 51 | 69 | 13 | 1 | 19 | 50 | 24 | 72 | 2 | 4 | R | R | 5-11 | 200 | 9-7-69 | 1991 | Santa Paula, Calif. |
| Cordero, Wil | .300 | 10 | 2 | 3 | 1 | 0 | 1 | 2 | 2 | 3 | 0 | 0 | 0 | R | R | 6-2 | 185 | 10-3-71 | 1988 | Mayaguez, P.R. |
| Delgado, Alex | .216 | 27 | 88 | 15 | 19 | 3 | 0 | 1 | 6 | 7 | 11 | 0 | 0 | R | R | 6-0 | 160 | 1-11-71 | 1988 | Palmerejo, Venez. |
| Dodson, Bo | .344 | 82 | 276 | 37 | 95 | 20 | 0 | 11 | 43 | 32 | 50 | 4 | 0 | L | L | 6-2 | 195 | 12-7-70 | 1989 | West Sacramento, Calif. |
| Fuller, Aaron | .500 | 1 | 2 | 0 | 1 | 0 | 0 | 0 | 0 | 0 | 0 | 0 | 0 | S | R | 5-10 | 170 | 9-7-71 | 1993 | Sacramento, Calif. |
| Garciaparra, Nomar | .343 | 43 | 172 | 40 | 59 | 15 | 2 | 16 | 46 | 14 | 21 | 3 | 1 | R | R | 6-0 | 165 | 7-23-73 | 1994 | Whittier, Calif. |
| Greenwell, Mike | .273 | 3 | 11 | 3 | 3 | 0 | 0 | 2 | 2 | 1 | 0 | 0 | 0 | L | R | 6-0 | 205 | 7-18-63 | 1982 | Cape Coral, Fla. |
| Hatteberg, Scott | .268 | 90 | 287 | 52 | 77 | 16 | 0 | 12 | 49 | 58 | 66 | 1 | 1 | L | R | 6-1 | 185 | 12-14-69 | 1991 | Yakima, Wash. |
| Holifield, Rick | .069 | 9 | 29 | 1 | 2 | 1 | 0 | 0 | 1 | 1 | 12 | 1 | 1 | L | L | 6-2 | 165 | 3-25-70 | 1988 | Montclair, Calif. |
| Hosey, Dwayne | .297 | 93 | 367 | 77 | 109 | 25 | 4 | 14 | 53 | 40 | 67 | 20 | 7 | S | R | 5-10 | 170 | 3-11-67 | 1987 | Altadena, Calif. |
| Jackson, Gavin | .250 | 15 | 44 | 5 | 11 | 2 | 0 | 1 | 3 | 8 | 0 | 1 | 5 | R | R | 6-1 | 170 | 7-19-73 | 1993 | Sylvester, Ga. |
| Jose, Felix | .219 | 11 | 32 | 3 | 7 | 3 | 0 | 2 | 5 | 3 | 10 | 0 | 0 | S | R | 6-1 | 220 | 5-8-65 | 1984 | Boca Raton, Fla. |
| LeVangie, Dana | .250 | 2 | 4 | 1 | 1 | 0 | 0 | 0 | 0 | 0 | 1 | 0 | 0 | R | R | 5-10 | 185 | 8-11-69 | 1991 | Whitman, Mass. |
| Lewis, T.R. | .314 | 79 | 274 | 55 | 86 | 23 | 1 | 14 | 52 | 34 | 50 | 2 | 2 | R | R | 6-0 | 180 | 4-17-71 | 1989 | Jacksonville, Fla. |
| Malave, Jose | .271 | 41 | 155 | 30 | 42 | 6 | 0 | 8 | 29 | 12 | 37 | 2 | 1 | R | R | 6-2 | 195 | 5-31-71 | 1990 | Cumana, Venez. |
| Manto, Jeff | .244 | 12 | 45 | 6 | 11 | 5 | 0 | 2 | 6 | 5 | 8 | 1 | 0 | R | R | 6-3 | 210 | 8-23-64 | 1985 | Bristol, Pa. |
| Mejia, Roberto | .257 | 21 | 74 | 9 | 19 | 4 | 0 | 0 | 4 | 5 | 18 | 4 | 1 | R | R | 5-11 | 180 | 4-14-72 | 1989 | Hato Mayor, D.R. |
| Merloni, Lou | .252 | 38 | 115 | 19 | 29 | 6 | 0 | 1 | 12 | 10 | 20 | 0 | 1 | R | R | 5-11 | 188 | 4-6-71 | 1993 | Framingham, Mass. |
| Mitchell, Kevin | .125 | 5 | 16 | 1 | 2 | 0 | 0 | 0 | 0 | 5 | 3 | 0 | 0 | R | R | 5-11 | 210 | 1-13-62 | 1981 | Chula Vista, Calif. |
| Pemberton, Rudy | .326 | 102 | 396 | 77 | 129 | 28 | 3 | 27 | 92 | 18 | 63 | 16 | 7 | R | R | 6-1 | 185 | 12-17-69 | 1987 | San Pedro de Macoris, D.R. |
| Pough, Pork Chop | .236 | 74 | 242 | 43 | 57 | 17 | 2 | 12 | 40 | 32 | 68 | 2 | 2 | R | R | 6-0 | 173 | 12-25-69 | 1988 | Avon Park, Fla. |
| Pozo, Arquimedez | .243 | 11 | 37 | 6 | 9 | 1 | 0 | 1 | 3 | 3 | 6 | 0 | 0 | R | R | 5-10 | 160 | 8-24-73 | 1991 | Santo Domingo, D.R. |
| Rodriguez, Tony | .245 | 72 | 265 | 37 | 65 | 14 | 1 | 3 | 28 | 15 | 32 | 3 | 1 | R | R | 5-11 | 185 | 8-15-70 | 1991 | Cidra, P.R. |
| Selby, Bill | .254 | 71 | 260 | 39 | 66 | 14 | 5 | 11 | 47 | 22 | 39 | 0 | 3 | L | R | 5-9 | 190 | 6-11-70 | 1992 | Walls, Miss. |
| Tatum, Jim | .273 | 19 | 66 | 11 | 18 | 2 | 0 | 5 | 16 | 7 | 12 | 2 | 0 | R | R | 6-2 | 200 | 10-9-67 | 1985 | Lakeside, Calif. |
| Zambrano, Eddie | .111 | 3 | 9 | 0 | 1 | 0 | 0 | 0 | 1 | 0 | 4 | 0 | 0 | R | R | 6-2 | 175 | 2-1-66 | 1985 | Maracaibo, Venez. |
| Zinter, Alan | .269 | 108 | 357 | 78 | 96 | 19 | 5 | 26 | 69 | 58 | 123 | 5 | 1 | S | R | 6-2 | 190 | 5-19-68 | 1989 | El Paso, Texas |

### PITCHING

| | W | L | ERA | G | GS | CG | SV | IP | H | R | ER | BB | SO | B | T | HT | WT | DOB | 1st Yr | Resides |
|---|---|---|---|---|---|---|---|---|---|---|---|---|---|---|---|---|---|---|---|---|
| Austin, Jim | 0 | 1 | 9.00 | 10 | 0 | 0 | 0 | 14 | 15 | 14 | 14 | 9 | 7 | R | R | 6-2 | 200 | 12-7-63 | 1986 | Richmond, Va. |
| Bakkum, Scott | 4 | 2 | 6.09 | 14 | 2 | 0 | 0 | 44 | 51 | 33 | 30 | 8 | 25 | R | R | 6-4 | 205 | 11-20-69 | 1992 | LaCrosse, Wis. |
| Belinda, Stan | 1 | 0 | 0.00 | 6 | 0 | 0 | 0 | 8 | 2 | 2 | 0 | 2 | 7 | R | R | 6-3 | 215 | 8-6-66 | 1985 | Alexandria, Pa. |
| Cain, Tim | 1 | 0 | 1.86 | 11 | 0 | 0 | 0 | 19 | 15 | 4 | 4 | 6 | 10 | S | R | 6-1 | 180 | 10-9-69 | 1990 | Piscataway, N.J. |
| Cederblad, Brett | 0 | 0 | 3.60 | 10 | 0 | 0 | 0 | 20 | 26 | 10 | 8 | 4 | 19 | R | R | 6-5 | 195 | 3-6-73 | 1995 | Parkwood, Australia |
| DeSilva, John | 4 | 3 | 5.21 | 16 | 16 | 0 | 0 | 85 | 99 | 55 | 49 | 27 | 68 | R | R | 6-0 | 193 | 9-30-67 | 1989 | Fort Bragg, Calif. |
| Doherty, John | 1 | 4 | 6.62 | 19 | 7 | 0 | 1 | 50 | 79 | 39 | 37 | 8 | 13 | R | R | 6-4 | 210 | 6-11-67 | 1989 | Tuckahoe, N.Y. |
| Eshelman, Vaughn | 1 | 2 | 4.33 | 7 | 1 | 0 | 0 | 44 | 40 | 21 | 21 | 19 | 28 | L | L | 6-3 | 195 | 5-22-69 | 1991 | Houston, Texas |
| Finnvold, Gar | 3 | 2 | 6.62 | 8 | 8 | 0 | 0 | 35 | 50 | 29 | 26 | 11 | 35 | R | R | 6-5 | 195 | 3-11-68 | 1990 | Boca Raton, Fla. |
| Garces, Rich | 4 | 0 | 2.30 | 10 | 0 | 0 | 0 | 16 | 10 | 4 | 4 | 5 | 13 | R | R | 6-0 | 230 | 5-18-71 | 1988 | Maracay, Venez. |
| Grundt, Ken | 9 | 4 | 4.20 | 44 | 0 | 0 | 2 | 64 | 72 | 32 | 30 | 16 | 46 | L | L | 6-4 | 195 | 8-26-69 | 1991 | Chicago, Ill. |
| Gunderson, Eric | 2 | 1 | 3.48 | 26 | 1 | 0 | 2 | 34 | 38 | 15 | 13 | 9 | 34 | R | L | 6-0 | 195 | 3-29-66 | 1987 | Portland, Ore. |
| Hansen, Brent | 1 | 0 | 6.23 | 2 | 2 | 0 | 0 | 9 | 8 | 6 | 6 | 3 | 3 | R | R | 6-2 | 195 | 8-4-70 | 1992 | Carlsbad, Calif. |
| Hudson, Joe | 1 | 1 | 3.51 | 25 | 0 | 0 | 5 | 33 | 29 | 19 | 13 | 21 | 18 | R | R | 6-1 | 180 | 9-29-70 | 1992 | Medford, N.J. |
| Knackert, Brent | 2 | 3 | 5.17 | 19 | 5 | 0 | 2 | 47 | 48 | 32 | 27 | 26 | 34 | R | R | 6-3 | 195 | 8-1-69 | 1987 | Huntington Beach, Calif. |
| Lacy, Kerry | 0 | 0 | 0.00 | 1 | 0 | 0 | 0 | 1 | 1 | 0 | 0 | 2 | 8 | R | R | 6-2 | 195 | 8-7-72 | 1991 | Higdon, Ala. |
| Looney, Brian | 5 | 6 | 4.81 | 27 | 9 | 1 | 1 | 82 | 78 | 55 | 44 | 27 | 78 | L | L | 5-10 | 180 | 9-26-69 | 1991 | Cheshire, Conn. |
| Maddux, Mike | 2 | 0 | 3.21 | 3 | 3 | 0 | 0 | 14 | 13 | 5 | 5 | 2 | 9 | L | R | 6-2 | 188 | 8-27-61 | 1982 | Las Vegas, Nev. |
| Minchey, Nate | 7 | 4 | 2.96 | 14 | 13 | 6 | 0 | 97 | 89 | 32 | 32 | 21 | 61 | R | R | 6-7 | 215 | 8-31-69 | 1987 | San Antonio, Texas |
| Orellano, Rafael | 4 | 11 | 7.88 | 22 | 20 | 0 | 0 | 99 | 124 | 94 | 87 | 62 | 66 | L | L | 6-2 | 160 | 4-28-73 | 1993 | Humacao, P.R. |
| Pierce, Jeff | 2 | 1 | 4.94 | 12 | 3 | 0 | 0 | 31 | 37 | 18 | 17 | 8 | 22 | R | R | 6-1 | 200 | 6-7-69 | 1991 | Staatsburg, N.Y. |
| Ricci, Chuck | 8 | 4 | 3.01 | 60 | 0 | 0 | 13 | 81 | 56 | 30 | 27 | 32 | 79 | R | R | 6-2 | 180 | 11-20-68 | 1987 | Laurel, Md. |
| Schullstrom, Erik | 1 | 4 | 5.01 | 15 | 10 | 0 | 0 | 56 | 57 | 37 | 31 | 28 | 62 | R | R | 6-5 | 220 | 3-25-69 | 1990 | San Leandro, Calif. |

| PITCHING | W | L | ERA | G | GS | CG | SV | IP | H | R | ER | BB | SO | B | T | HT | WT | DOB | 1st Yr | Resides |
|---|---|---|---|---|---|---|---|---|---|---|---|---|---|---|---|---|---|---|---|---|
| Sele, Aaron | 0 | 0 | 6.00 | 1 | 1 | 0 | 0 | 3 | 3 | 2 | 2 | 1 | 4 | R | R | 6-5 | 218 | 6-25-70 | 1991 | Poulsbo, Wash. |
| Suppan, Jeff | 10 | 6 | 3.22 | 22 | 22 | 7 | 0 | 145 | 130 | 66 | 52 | 25 | 142 | R | R | 6-2 | 210 | 1-2-75 | 1993 | West Hills, Calif. |
| Tomlin, Randy | 0 | 2 | 8.31 | 5 | 2 | 0 | 1 | 13 | 17 | 12 | 12 | 5 | 5 | L | L | 5-10 | 182 | 6-14-66 | 1988 | Mars, Pa. |
| VanEgmond, Tim | 5 | 3 | 4.38 | 11 | 11 | 1 | 0 | 62 | 66 | 37 | 30 | 24 | 46 | R | R | 6-2 | 185 | 5-31-69 | 1991 | Senoia, Ga. |

### FIELDING

| Catcher | PCT | G | PO | A | E | DP | PB |
|---|---|---|---|---|---|---|---|
| Clark | .965 | 15 | 72 | 10 | 3 | 0 | 2 |
| Delgado | .990 | 10 | 7 | 2 | 1 | 1 | 2 |
| Hatteberg | .990 | 86 | 566 | 42 | 6 | 0 | 10 |
| LeVangie | .923 | 2 | 11 | 1 | 1 | 0 | 1 |
| Zinter | .993 | 25 | 140 | 9 | 1 | 1 | 2 |

| First Base | PCT | G | PO | A | E | DP |
|---|---|---|---|---|---|---|
| Clark | .974 | 4 | 37 | 0 | 1 | 4 |
| Delgado | 1.000 | 1 | 4 | 1 | 0 | 0 |
| Dodson | .995 | 73 | 562 | 48 | 3 | 51 |
| Lewis | 1.000 | 2 | 7 | 1 | 0 | 0 |
| Pough | 1.000 | 26 | 206 | 10 | 0 | 19 |
| Tatum | 1.000 | 1 | 7 | 0 | 0 | 1 |
| Zinter | .989 | 49 | 407 | 24 | 5 | 37 |

| Second Base | PCT | G | PO | A | E | DP |
|---|---|---|---|---|---|---|
| Bell | .981 | 57 | 108 | 146 | 5 | 31 |
| Clark | .000 | 2 | 0 | 0 | 0 | 0 |
| Cordero | 1.000 | 3 | 2 | 6 | 0 | 1 |
| Manto | 1.000 | 2 | 4 | 8 | 0 | 1 |
| Mejia | .963 | 20 | 25 | 52 | 3 | 9 |
| Merloni | .962 | 11 | 21 | 30 | 2 | 3 |

| | PCT | G | PO | A | E | DP |
|---|---|---|---|---|---|---|
| Rodriguez | 1.000 | 5 | 13 | 13 | 0 | 2 |
| Selby | .942 | 50 | 82 | 113 | 12 | 31 |
| Tatum | 1.000 | 6 | 8 | 18 | 0 | 2 |

| Third Base | PCT | G | PO | A | E | DP |
|---|---|---|---|---|---|---|
| Bell | .000 | 1 | 0 | 0 | 0 | 0 |
| Clark | .872 | 38 | 23 | 52 | 11 | 5 |
| Delgado | 1.000 | 1 | 1 | 1 | 0 | 0 |
| Manto | .938 | 10 | 9 | 21 | 2 | 2 |
| Merloni | .917 | 17 | 6 | 38 | 4 | 1 |
| Pough | .909 | 46 | 27 | 83 | 11 | 7 |
| Pozo | .886 | 11 | 11 | 20 | 4 | 1 |
| Rodriguez | 1.000 | 1 | 1 | 0 | 0 | 0 |
| Selby | .902 | 10 | 14 | 27 | 4 | 3 |
| Tatum | .875 | 12 | 5 | 16 | 3 | 1 |
| Zinter | .000 | 1 | 0 | 0 | 0 | 0 |

| Shortstop | PCT | G | PO | A | E | DP |
|---|---|---|---|---|---|---|
| Bell | .964 | 13 | 15 | 39 | 2 | 9 |
| Brown | .833 | 2 | 2 | 3 | 1 | 1 |
| Garciaparra | .973 | 43 | 63 | 120 | 5 | 24 |
| Jackson | .947 | 15 | 21 | 50 | 4 | 8 |

| | PCT | G | PO | A | E | DP |
|---|---|---|---|---|---|---|
| Merloni | .915 | 11 | 12 | 31 | 4 | 7 |
| Rodriguez | .976 | 69 | 83 | 198 | 7 | 39 |

| Outfield | PCT | G | PO | A | E | DP |
|---|---|---|---|---|---|---|
| Brown | 1.000 | 1 | 0 | 1 | 0 | 0 |
| Clark | 1.000 | 2 | 2 | 0 | 0 | 0 |
| Cole | .964 | 79 | 153 | 6 | 6 | 1 |
| Cookson | 1.000 | 47 | 73 | 4 | 0 | 0 |
| Fuller | 1.000 | 1 | 1 | 0 | 0 | 0 |
| Greenwell | 1.000 | 2 | 3 | 0 | 0 | 0 |
| Holifield | .929 | 9 | 13 | 0 | 1 | 0 |
| Hosey | .985 | 91 | 197 | 4 | 3 | 0 |
| Jose | .889 | 3 | 8 | 0 | 1 | 0 |
| Lewis | .991 | 67 | 111 | 3 | 1 | 0 |
| Malave | .986 | 34 | 68 | 0 | 1 | 0 |
| Mejia | 1.000 | 1 | 2 | 0 | 0 | 0 |
| Mitchell | .667 | 2 | 2 | 0 | 1 | 0 |
| Pemberton | .973 | 95 | 180 | 1 | 5 | 0 |
| Selby | 1.000 | 2 | 3 | 0 | 0 | 0 |
| Tatum | .857 | 2 | 6 | 0 | 1 | 0 |
| Zambrano | .909 | 3 | 9 | 1 | 1 | 0 |

# TRENTON
## Class AA
## EASTERN LEAGUE

| BATTING | AVG | G | AB | R | H | 2B | 3B | HR | RBI | BB | SO | SB | CS | B | T | HT | WT | DOB | 1st Yr | Resides |
|---|---|---|---|---|---|---|---|---|---|---|---|---|---|---|---|---|---|---|---|---|
| Abad, Andy | .277 | 65 | 213 | 33 | 59 | 22 | 1 | 4 | 39 | 33 | 41 | 5 | 3 | L | L | 6-1 | 185 | 8-25-72 | 1993 | Jupiter, Fla. |
| Allison, Chris | .230 | 109 | 357 | 49 | 82 | 7 | 1 | 0 | 22 | 28 | 61 | 14 | 11 | R | R | 5-10 | 165 | 10-22-71 | 1994 | Rock Island, Ill. |
| Borrero, Richie | .310 | 26 | 71 | 12 | 22 | 5 | 2 | 3 | 26 | 8 | 16 | 2 | 1 | R | R | 6-1 | 195 | 1-5-73 | 1990 | Hormigueros, P.R. |
| Brown, Randy | .298 | 72 | 245 | 46 | 73 | 15 | 2 | 11 | 38 | 27 | 56 | 9 | 4 | R | R | 5-11 | 160 | 5-1-70 | 1989 | Houston, Texas |
| Carey, Todd | .250 | 125 | 440 | 78 | 110 | 34 | 3 | 20 | 78 | 48 | 123 | 4 | 4 | L | R | 6-1 | 180 | 8-14-71 | 1992 | Cumberland, R.I. |
| Collier, Dan | .213 | 28 | 94 | 12 | 20 | 3 | 0 | 4 | 9 | 9 | 36 | 2 | 1 | R | R | 6-3 | 200 | 8-13-70 | 1991 | Ozark, Ala. |
| Coughlin, Kevin | .271 | 52 | 170 | 24 | 46 | 2 | 1 | 0 | 18 | 22 | 24 | 5 | 4 | L | L | 6-0 | 175 | 9-7-70 | 1989 | Clarksburg, Md. |
| Delgado, Alex | .222 | 21 | 81 | 7 | 18 | 4 | 0 | 3 | 14 | 9 | 8 | 1 | 0 | R | R | 6-0 | 160 | 1-11-71 | 1988 | Palmerejo, Venez. |
| Holifield, Rick | .267 | 109 | 375 | 73 | 100 | 20 | 4 | 10 | 38 | 52 | 98 | 35 | 18 | L | L | 6-2 | 165 | 3-25-70 | 1988 | Montclair, Calif. |
| Hyzdu, Adam | .337 | 109 | 374 | 71 | 126 | 24 | 3 | 25 | 80 | 56 | 75 | 1 | 8 | R | R | 6-2 | 210 | 12-6-71 | 1990 | Mesa, Ariz. |
| Jackson, Gavin | .250 | 6 | 20 | 2 | 5 | 2 | 0 | 0 | 3 | 2 | 3 | 0 | 1 | R | R | 5-10 | 170 | 7-19-73 | 1993 | Sylvester, Ga. |
| LeVangie, Dana | .218 | 23 | 55 | 5 | 12 | 3 | 0 | 2 | 7 | 12 | 11 | 2 | 2 | R | R | 5-10 | 185 | 8-11-69 | 1991 | Whitman, Mass. |
| Manto, Jeff | .286 | 6 | 21 | 3 | 6 | 0 | 0 | 0 | 5 | 1 | 5 | 0 | 0 | R | R | 6-3 | 210 | 8-23-64 | 1985 | Bristol, Pa. |
| McKeel, Walt | .302 | 128 | 464 | 86 | 140 | 19 | 1 | 16 | 78 | 60 | 52 | 2 | 4 | R | R | 6-2 | 200 | 1-17-72 | 1990 | Stantonsburg, N.C. |
| Merloni, Lou | .232 | 28 | 95 | 11 | 22 | 6 | 1 | 3 | 16 | 9 | 18 | 0 | 2 | R | R | 5-10 | 180 | 4-6-71 | 1993 | Framingham, Mass. |
| Naehring, Tim | .222 | 3 | 9 | 2 | 2 | 1 | 0 | 1 | 2 | 1 | 3 | 0 | 0 | R | R | 6-2 | 200 | 2-1-67 | 1988 | Cincinnati, Ohio |
| Nixon, Trot | .251 | 123 | 438 | 55 | 110 | 11 | 4 | 11 | 63 | 50 | 65 | 7 | 9 | L | L | 6-1 | 195 | 4-11-74 | 1993 | Wilmington, N.C. |
| Ortiz, Nick | .223 | 38 | 130 | 20 | 29 | 4 | 0 | 3 | 13 | 13 | 28 | 2 | 2 | R | R | 6-0 | 165 | 7-9-73 | 1991 | Cidra, P.R. |
| Patton, Greg | .188 | 6 | 16 | 3 | 3 | 1 | 0 | 0 | 1 | 4 | 4 | 0 | 1 | R | R | 6-4 | 190 | 3-8-72 | 1993 | Springfield, Va. |
| Rappoli, Paul | .212 | 69 | 193 | 16 | 41 | 8 | 0 | 3 | 22 | 27 | 54 | 4 | 5 | L | R | 6-1 | 195 | 10-4-71 | 1990 | Stoughton, Mass. |
| Romano, Scott | .167 | 1 | 6 | 0 | 1 | 0 | 0 | 0 | 1 | 2 | 0 | 0 | 0 | R | R | 6-1 | 185 | 8-3-71 | 1989 | Tampa, Fla. |
| Sadler, Donnie | .267 | 115 | 454 | 68 | 121 | 20 | 8 | 6 | 46 | 38 | 75 | 34 | 8 | R | R | 5-6 | 165 | 6-17-75 | 1994 | Valley Mills, Texas |
| Woods, Tyrone | .312 | 99 | 356 | 75 | 111 | 16 | 2 | 25 | 71 | 56 | 66 | 5 | 4 | R | R | 6-1 | 190 | 8-19-69 | 1988 | Brooksville, Fla. |

| PITCHING | W | L | ERA | G | GS | CG | SV | IP | H | R | ER | BB | SO | B | T | HT | WT | DOB | 1st Yr | Resides |
|---|---|---|---|---|---|---|---|---|---|---|---|---|---|---|---|---|---|---|---|---|
| Barkley, Brian | 8 | 8 | 5.72 | 22 | 21 | 0 | 0 | 120 | 126 | 79 | 76 | 56 | 89 | L | L | 6-2 | 170 | 12-8-75 | 1994 | Waco, Texas |
| Bennett, Joel | 1 | 0 | 8.31 | 3 | 0 | 0 | 0 | 4 | 3 | 4 | 4 | 2 | 8 | R | R | 6-1 | 161 | 1-31-70 | 1991 | Kirkwood, N.Y. |
| Betti, Rick | 9 | 1 | 3.67 | 31 | 8 | 0 | 1 | 81 | 70 | 39 | 33 | 44 | 65 | R | L | 5-11 | 170 | 9-16-73 | 1993 | Milford, Mass. |
| Blais, Mike | 10 | 3 | 3.94 | 53 | 0 | 0 | 5 | 78 | 74 | 37 | 34 | 23 | 52 | R | R | 6-5 | 226 | 10-2-71 | 1993 | East Lyme, Conn. |
| Cederblad, Brett | 1 | 3 | 3.72 | 27 | 3 | 0 | 2 | 58 | 59 | 27 | 24 | 16 | 49 | S | R | 6-5 | 195 | 3-6-73 | 1995 | Parkwood, Australia |
| Doherty, John | 1 | 1 | 1.85 | 4 | 4 | 0 | 0 | 24 | 20 | 8 | 5 | 2 | 14 | R | R | 6-4 | 210 | 6-11-67 | 1989 | Tuckahoe, N.Y. |
| Emerson, Scott | 1 | 0 | 5.85 | 19 | 0 | 0 | 0 | 32 | 34 | 24 | 21 | 26 | 23 | S | L | 6-5 | 175 | 12-22-71 | 1992 | Phoenix, Ariz. |
| Eversgerd, Bryan | 1 | 0 | 2.57 | 4 | 0 | 0 | 0 | 7 | 6 | 2 | 2 | 4 | 2 | R | L | 6-1 | 185 | 2-11-69 | 1989 | Centralia, Ill. |
| Fernandez, Jared | 9 | 9 | 5.08 | 30 | 29 | 3 | 0 | 179 | 185 | 115 | 101 | 83 | 94 | R | R | 6-2 | 225 | 2-2-72 | 1994 | West Valley, Utah |
| Grundt, Ken | 1 | 0 | 0.00 | 12 | 0 | 0 | 0 | 13 | 6 | 0 | 0 | 6 | 13 | L | L | 6-4 | 195 | 8-26-69 | 1991 | Chicago, Ill. |
| Harris, Reggie | 2 | 1 | 1.46 | 33 | 0 | 0 | 17 | 37 | 17 | 6 | 6 | 19 | 43 | R | R | 6-1 | 190 | 8-12-68 | 1987 | Waynesboro, Va. |
| Hecker, Doug | 0 | 1 | 2.25 | 13 | 0 | 0 | 2 | 20 | 18 | 5 | 5 | 5 | 12 | R | R | 6-4 | 210 | 1-21-71 | 1992 | Wantagh, N.Y. |
| Knackert, Brent | 0 | 0 | 1.38 | 11 | 0 | 0 | 10 | 13 | 6 | 2 | 2 | 6 | 21 | R | R | 6-3 | 195 | 8-1-69 | 1988 | Huntington Beach, Calif. |
| Mahay, Ron | 0 | 1 | 29.45 | 1 | 1 | 0 | 0 | 4 | 12 | 13 | 12 | 6 | 0 | L | L | 6-2 | 185 | 6-28-71 | 1991 | Crestwood, Ill. |
| McGraw, Tom | 3 | 4 | 3.18 | 30 | 0 | 0 | 1 | 34 | 34 | 15 | 12 | 19 | 32 | L | L | 6-2 | 195 | 12-8-67 | 1990 | Yacolt, Wash. |
| Merrill, Ethan | 3 | 6 | 7.05 | 13 | 10 | 1 | 0 | 60 | 71 | 55 | 47 | 26 | 42 | L | L | 6-3 | 200 | 4-21-72 | 1994 | South Burlington, Ver. |
| Pavano, Carl | 16 | 5 | 2.63 | 27 | 26 | 6 | 0 | 185 | 154 | 66 | 54 | 47 | 146 | R | R | 6-5 | 230 | 1-8-76 | 1994 | Southington, Conn. |
| Pierce, Jeff | 0 | 0 | 1.00 | 4 | 0 | 0 | 0 | 9 | 6 | 1 | 1 | 4 | 5 | R | R | 6-1 | 200 | 6-7-69 | 1991 | Staatsburg, N.Y. |
| Rose, Brian | 12 | 7 | 4.01 | 27 | 27 | 4 | 0 | 164 | 157 | 82 | 73 | 45 | 115 | R | R | 6-3 | 205 | 2-13-76 | 1995 | Dartmouth, Mass. |
| Schullstrom, Erik | 3 | 0 | 2.54 | 19 | 0 | 0 | 1 | 28 | 23 | 11 | 8 | 13 | 22 | R | R | 6-5 | 220 | 3-25-69 | 1990 | San Leandro, Calif. |
| Senior, Shawn | 5 | 6 | 4.72 | 16 | 13 | 1 | 0 | 82 | 89 | 53 | 43 | 42 | 49 | L | L | 6-1 | 195 | 3-17-72 | 1993 | Cherry Hill, N.J. |

## FIELDING

| Catcher | PCT | G | PO | A | E | DP | PB |
|---|---|---|---|---|---|---|---|
| Borrero | .982 | 25 | 157 | 9 | 3 | 1 | 7 |
| Delgado | 1.000 | 13 | 94 | 11 | 0 | 1 | 2 |
| Hyzdu | 1.000 | 1 | 3 | 0 | 0 | 0 | |
| LeVangie | .993 | 23 | 129 | 14 | 1 | 2 | 0 |
| McKeel | .992 | 93 | 552 | 76 | 5 | 11 | 17 |

| First Base | PCT | G | PO | A | E | DP |
|---|---|---|---|---|---|---|
| Abad | .997 | 41 | 326 | 18 | 1 | 33 |
| Carey | .976 | 16 | 121 | 2 | 3 | 9 |
| Coughlin | .995 | 25 | 196 | 14 | 1 | 17 |
| Delgado | 1.000 | 6 | 67 | 2 | 0 | 7 |
| McKeel | .984 | 38 | 283 | 23 | 5 | 26 |
| Merloni | 1.000 | 1 | 7 | 1 | 0 | 0 |
| Patton | 1.000 | 1 | 1 | 1 | 0 | 0 |
| Rappoli | 1.000 | 2 | 3 | 2 | 0 | 1 |
| Romano | 1.000 | 1 | 15 | 0 | 0 | 0 |
| Woods | 1.000 | 27 | 220 | 14 | 0 | 23 |

| Second Base | PCT | G | PO | A | E | DP |
|---|---|---|---|---|---|---|
| Allison | .959 | 106 | 237 | 253 | 21 | 62 |
| Brown | .910 | 19 | 29 | 32 | 6 | 7 |
| Carey | .895 | 4 | 8 | 9 | 2 | 2 |
| Manto | .000 | 1 | 0 | 0 | 2 | 0 |
| Merloni | .947 | 7 | 10 | 8 | 1 | 1 |
| Ortiz | .971 | 20 | 35 | 31 | 2 | 9 |
| Patton | .833 | 1 | 1 | 4 | 1 | 1 |

| Third Base | PCT | G | PO | A | E | DP |
|---|---|---|---|---|---|---|
| Brown | .895 | 8 | 6 | 11 | 2 | 1 |
| Carey | .941 | 103 | 67 | 238 | 19 | 21 |
| Delgado | 1.000 | 2 | 0 | 4 | 0 | 0 |
| Manto | 1.000 | 3 | 3 | 2 | 0 | 1 |
| McKeel | 1.000 | 2 | 0 | 1 | 0 | 0 |
| Merloni | .923 | 20 | 22 | 50 | 6 | 5 |
| Naehring | .750 | 2 | 1 | 2 | 1 | 0 |
| Ortiz | .947 | 10 | 9 | 9 | 1 | 0 |
| Patton | 1.000 | 3 | 2 | 6 | 0 | 1 |

| Shortstop | PCT | G | PO | A | E | DP |
|---|---|---|---|---|---|---|
| Brown | .941 | 46 | 61 | 115 | 11 | 27 |
| Carey | 1.000 | 4 | 7 | 16 | 0 | 7 |
| Jackson | .957 | 6 | 8 | 14 | 1 | 3 |
| Manto | .833 | 1 | 2 | 3 | 1 | 0 |
| Merloni | .889 | 2 | 0 | 8 | 1 | 1 |
| Ortiz | .981 | 11 | 10 | 41 | 1 | 3 |
| Sadler | .930 | 79 | 117 | 231 | 26 | 42 |

| Outfield | PCT | G | PO | A | E | DP |
|---|---|---|---|---|---|---|
| Abad | 1.000 | 28 | 42 | 2 | 0 | 1 |
| Brown | .000 | 2 | 0 | 0 | 0 | 0 |
| Collier | 1.000 | 9 | 14 | 1 | 0 | 0 |
| Coughlin | 1.000 | 20 | 29 | 2 | 0 | 1 |
| Holifield | .984 | 104 | 240 | 8 | 4 | 1 |
| Hyzdu | .979 | 79 | 132 | 9 | 3 | 1 |
| Nixon | .979 | 120 | 224 | 14 | 5 | 4 |
| Rappoli | 1.000 | 60 | 75 | 3 | 0 | 1 |
| Sadler | .987 | 30 | 68 | 6 | 1 | 2 |

## BAKERSFIELD

Class A/Co-Op

## CALIFORNIA LEAGUE

### BATTING

| | AVG | G | AB | R | H | 2B | 3B | HR | RBI | BB | SO | SB | CS | B | T | HT | WT | DOB | 1st Yr | Resides |
|---|---|---|---|---|---|---|---|---|---|---|---|---|---|---|---|---|---|---|---|---|
| Bazzani, Matt | .203 | 20 | 69 | 5 | 14 | 3 | 0 | 2 | 8 | 7 | 21 | 0 | 0 | R | R | 6-1 | 205 | 9-17-73 | 1994 | Foster City, Calif. |
| Collier, Dan | .274 | 56 | 212 | 22 | 58 | 15 | 1 | 5 | 40 | 6 | 63 | 9 | 3 | R | R | 6-3 | 200 | 8-13-70 | 1991 | Ozark, Ala. |
| Martin, Jeff | .182 | 5 | 22 | 2 | 4 | 0 | 0 | 0 | 1 | 0 | 10 | 0 | 0 | R | R | 6-3 | 230 | 7-14-70 | 1992 | Nashville, Tenn. |
| Sheffield, Tony | .233 | 49 | 172 | 14 | 40 | 8 | 1 | 3 | 13 | 13 | 73 | 8 | 5 | L | L | 6-1 | 195 | 2-17-74 | 1992 | Tullahoma, Tenn. |
| Smith, Dave | .239 | 35 | 117 | 25 | 28 | 9 | 1 | 3 | 18 | 20 | 36 | 1 | 0 | R | R | 5-10 | 180 | 2-18-72 | 1993 | Cheektowaga, N.Y. |

**GAMES BY POSITION: C**—Bazzani 10, Martin 5. **1B**—Smith 18. **2B**—Smith 9. **SS**—Smith 6. **OF**—Bazzani 6, Collier 46, Sheffield 39, Smith 2.

### PITCHING

| | W | L | ERA | G | GS | CG | SV | IP | H | R | ER | BB | SO | B | T | HT | WT | DOB | 1st Yr | Resides |
|---|---|---|---|---|---|---|---|---|---|---|---|---|---|---|---|---|---|---|---|---|
| Bush, Craig | 4 | 6 | 4.98 | 41 | 0 | 0 | 8 | 72 | 84 | 44 | 40 | 36 | 80 | R | R | 6-3 | 235 | 8-13-73 | 1991 | Lancaster, Ohio |
| Symmonds, Maika | 0 | 2 | 8.88 | 7 | 2 | 1 | 0 | 24 | 34 | 32 | 24 | 21 | 3 | L | L | 5-9 | 180 | 3-13-75 | 1995 | Bellefonte, Pa. |

## SARASOTA

Class A

## FLORIDA STATE LEAGUE

### BATTING

| | AVG | G | AB | R | H | 2B | 3B | HR | RBI | BB | SO | SB | CS | B | T | HT | WT | DOB | 1st Yr | Resides |
|---|---|---|---|---|---|---|---|---|---|---|---|---|---|---|---|---|---|---|---|---|
| Abad, Andy | .287 | 58 | 202 | 28 | 58 | 15 | 1 | 2 | 41 | 37 | 28 | 10 | 3 | L | L | 6-1 | 185 | 8-25-72 | 1993 | Jupiter, Fla. |
| Bazzani, Matt | .270 | 12 | 37 | 5 | 10 | 1 | 1 | 1 | 4 | 2 | 6 | 0 | 0 | R | R | 6-1 | 205 | 9-17-73 | 1994 | Foster City, Calif. |
| Borrero, Richie | .250 | 27 | 92 | 15 | 23 | 5 | 0 | 3 | 13 | 6 | 17 | 1 | 1 | R | R | 6-1 | 195 | 1-5-73 | 1990 | Hormigueros, P.R. |
| Bowles, John | .183 | 33 | 93 | 17 | 17 | 3 | 0 | 1 | 8 | 13 | 18 | 2 | 2 | L | R | 5-11 | 188 | 9-6-74 | 1992 | Rockville, Md. |
| Braddy, Junior | .241 | 98 | 345 | 37 | 83 | 20 | 5 | 7 | 36 | 26 | 97 | 7 | 2 | R | R | 6-3 | 205 | 10-4-71 | 1994 | Lexington, Ky. |
| Coleman, Michael | .246 | 110 | 407 | 54 | 100 | 20 | 5 | 1 | 36 | 38 | 86 | 24 | 5 | R | R | 5-11 | 180 | 8-16-75 | 1994 | Nashville, Tenn. |
| DePastino, Joe | .262 | 97 | 344 | 35 | 90 | 16 | 2 | 6 | 44 | 29 | 71 | 2 | 3 | R | R | 6-2 | 210 | 9-4-73 | 1992 | Sarasota, Fla. |
| DeRosso, Tony | .257 | 116 | 416 | 64 | 107 | 19 | 5 | 14 | 60 | 31 | 84 | 15 | 2 | R | R | 6-3 | 215 | 11-7-75 | 1994 | Moultrie, Ga. |
| Faggett, Ethan | .275 | 110 | 408 | 48 | 112 | 12 | 8 | 4 | 35 | 35 | 118 | 24 | 10 | L | L | 6-0 | 190 | 8-21-74 | 1992 | Burleson, Texas |
| Fuller, Aaron | .300 | 115 | 434 | 74 | 130 | 20 | 5 | 5 | 49 | 63 | 60 | 33 | 12 | S | R | 5-10 | 170 | 9-7-71 | 1993 | Sacramento, Calif. |
| Gibralter, David | .285 | 120 | 452 | 47 | 129 | 34 | 3 | 12 | 70 | 30 | 101 | 8 | 7 | R | R | 6-3 | 215 | 6-19-75 | 1993 | Duncanville, Texas |
| Goligoski, Jason | .385 | 4 | 13 | 1 | 5 | 0 | 0 | 0 | 3 | 2 | 2 | 0 | 1 | L | R | 6-1 | 180 | 10-2-71 | 1993 | Hamilton, Mon. |
| Jackson, Gavin | .239 | 87 | 276 | 26 | 66 | 13 | 2 | 0 | 24 | 33 | 47 | 4 | 6 | R | R | 5-10 | 170 | 7-19-73 | 1993 | Sylvester, Ga. |
| Metzger, Erik | .333 | 1 | 3 | 0 | 1 | 0 | 0 | 0 | 0 | 0 | 2 | 0 | 0 | R | R | 6-0 | 205 | 7-27-74 | 1996 | Brentwood, Tenn. |
| Padilla, Roy | .296 | 8 | 27 | 2 | 8 | 2 | 0 | 0 | 2 | 2 | 3 | 4 | 0 | L | L | 6-7 | 230 | 8-4-75 | 1993 | Panama City, Panama |
| Patton, Greg | .244 | 80 | 275 | 31 | 67 | 16 | 2 | 3 | 24 | 35 | 64 | 2 | 3 | R | R | 6-4 | 190 | 3-8-72 | 1993 | Springfield, Va. |
| Rodriguez, Tony | .286 | 8 | 21 | 0 | 6 | 0 | 0 | 0 | 1 | 2 | 0 | 0 | 0 | R | R | 5-11 | 165 | 8-15-70 | 1991 | Cidra, P.R. |
| Rojas, Mo | .000 | 2 | 5 | 0 | 0 | 0 | 0 | 0 | 0 | 0 | 2 | 0 | 0 | R | R | 5-11 | 180 | 11-25-76 | 1995 | Hialeah, Fla. |
| Sanchez, Orlando | .333 | 5 | 15 | 2 | 5 | 2 | 0 | 0 | 4 | 1 | 3 | 0 | 0 | R | R | 6-0 | 160 | 7-19-78 | 1996 | Sinaloa, Mexico |
| Smith, David | .250 | 45 | 124 | 24 | 31 | 3 | 1 | 3 | 12 | 23 | 27 | 6 | 3 | R | R | 5-10 | 180 | 2-18-72 | 1993 | Cheektowaga, N.Y. |
| Tebbs, Nathan | .250 | 116 | 420 | 44 | 105 | 11 | 2 | 1 | 34 | 24 | 68 | 17 | 4 | S | S | 5-11 | 175 | 9-19-74 | 1993 | Riverton, Utah |
| Underwood, Devin | .269 | 27 | 67 | 12 | 18 | 3 | 0 | 1 | 13 | 8 | 9 | 0 | 0 | S | R | 6-1 | 180 | 4-22-74 | 1994 | Anaheim, Calif. |

**GAMES BY POSITION: C**—Bazzani 10, Borrero 24, Bowles 8, DePastino 82, Underwood 20. **1B**—Abad 29, Braddy 1, DePastino 1, DeRosso 18, Gibralter 93, Patton 2. **2B**—Bowles 11, Jackson 10, Rodriguez 3, Sanchez 5, Smith 24, Tebbs 88. **3B**—DeRosso 83, Fuller 1, Gibralter 17, Patton 42, Rodriguez 2, Smith 2. **SS**—Bowles 1, Goligoski 4, Jackson 78, Patton 30, Rodriguez 1, Tebbs 25. **OF**—Abad 26, Braddy 73, Coleman 108, DeRosso 3, Faggett 92, Fuller 107, Padilla 8, Patton 1, Rodriguez 1, Rojas 1, Tebbs 4.

### PITCHING

| | W | L | ERA | G | GS | CG | SV | IP | H | R | ER | BB | SO | B | T | HT | WT | DOB | 1st Yr | Resides |
|---|---|---|---|---|---|---|---|---|---|---|---|---|---|---|---|---|---|---|---|---|
| Barksdale, Joe | 2 | 7 | 7.79 | 19 | 11 | 0 | 0 | 65 | 88 | 62 | 56 | 41 | 37 | R | R | 6-3 | 200 | 9-6-73 | 1993 | Augusta, Ga. |
| Belinda, Stan | 0 | 1 | 45.00 | 1 | 1 | 0 | 0 | 1 | 6 | 5 | 5 | 1 | 1 | R | R | 6-3 | 215 | 8-6-66 | 1985 | Alexandria, Pa. |
| Betti, Rick | 0 | 2 | 2.87 | 13 | 0 | 0 | 7 | 16 | 13 | 6 | 5 | 7 | 21 | R | L | 5-11 | 170 | 9-16-73 | 1993 | Milford, Mass. |
| Cannon, Kevan | 0 | 0 | 0.00 | 2 | 0 | 0 | 0 | 1 | 1 | 0 | 0 | 0 | 3 | L | L | 6-3 | 215 | 8-24-74 | 1995 | Columbus, Ohio |
| Cook, Jake | 2 | 9 | 5.38 | 20 | 13 | 1 | 1 | 85 | 100 | 67 | 51 | 44 | 49 | R | R | 6-6 | 220 | 8-31-74 | 1993 | Greenville, Ohio |
| Emerson, Scott | 0 | 0 | 5.40 | 4 | 0 | 0 | 0 | 7 | 11 | 4 | 4 | 7 | 7 | S | L | 6-5 | 175 | 12-22-71 | 1992 | Phoenix, Ariz. |
| Farrell, Jim | 9 | 8 | 3.51 | 21 | 21 | 3 | 0 | 133 | 116 | 58 | 52 | 34 | 92 | R | R | 6-1 | 180 | 11-1-73 | 1995 | Hartville, Ohio |
| Festa, Chris | 0 | 2 | 8.55 | 6 | 2 | 0 | 0 | 20 | 37 | 24 | 19 | 11 | 12 | R | R | 6-2 | 190 | 9-7-72 | 1995 | Holliston, Mass. |
| Graham, Rich | 0 | 2 | 3.57 | 11 | 0 | 0 | 0 | 23 | 23 | 13 | 9 | 7 | 21 | R | R | 6-1 | 175 | 2-26-70 | 1994 | Northboro, Mass. |
| Hale, Chad | 3 | 0 | 3.12 | 42 | 0 | 0 | 7 | 61 | 56 | 33 | 21 | 17 | 37 | R | L | 6-2 | 245 | 8-3-71 | 1994 | Thornville, Ohio |
| Hansen, Brent | 2 | 4 | 5.51 | 8 | 8 | 1 | 0 | 47 | 54 | 36 | 29 | 21 | 25 | R | R | 6-2 | 195 | 8-4-70 | 1992 | Carlsbad, Calif. |
| Hartgrove, Lyle | 2 | 0 | 4.66 | 15 | 0 | 0 | 0 | 19 | 30 | 12 | 10 | 3 | 7 | R | R | 6-1 | 160 | 2-2-74 | 1994 | Asheboro, N.C. |
| Hecker, Doug | 2 | 2 | 4.97 | 26 | 3 | 0 | 6 | 42 | 46 | 25 | 23 | 12 | 39 | R | R | 6-4 | 210 | 1-21-71 | 1992 | Wantagh, N.Y. |
| Mahay, Ron | 2 | 2 | 3.82 | 31 | 4 | 0 | 2 | 71 | 61 | 33 | 30 | 35 | 66 | L | L | 6-2 | 185 | 6-28-71 | 1991 | Crestwood, Ill. |
| Martinez, Cesar | 3 | 4 | 4.72 | 35 | 0 | 0 | 1 | 69 | 82 | 40 | 36 | 40 | 50 | L | L | 6-2 | 200 | 4-29-73 | 1993 | San Diego, Calif. |
| Merrill, Ethan | 5 | 6 | 4.31 | 14 | 14 | 0 | 0 | 88 | 96 | 50 | 42 | 26 | 54 | L | L | 6-3 | 200 | 4-21-72 | 1994 | South Burlington, Ver. |
| Munro, Peter | 11 | 6 | 3.60 | 27 | 25 | 2 | 1 | 155 | 153 | 76 | 62 | 62 | 115 | R | R | 6-2 | 185 | 6-14-75 | 1994 | Little Neck, N.Y. |
| Peterson, Dean | 2 | 7 | 3.05 | 26 | 3 | 0 | 3 | 62 | 45 | 30 | 21 | 21 | 58 | R | R | 6-3 | 200 | 8-3-72 | 1993 | Cortland, Ohio |

| PITCHING | W | L | ERA | G | GS | CG | SV | IP | H | R | ER | BB | SO | B | T | HT | WT | DOB | 1st Yr | Resides |
|---|---|---|---|---|---|---|---|---|---|---|---|---|---|---|---|---|---|---|---|---|
| Ramirez, Felix | 1 | 0 | 3.27 | 5 | 0 | 0 | 0 | 11 | 10 | 8 | 4 | 8 | 7 | L | L | 5-11 | 170 | 1-7-75 | 1996 | Beverly Hills, Calif. |
| Ramsay, Rob | 2 | 2 | 6.09 | 12 | 7 | 0 | 0 | 34 | 42 | 23 | 23 | 27 | 32 | L | L | 6-4 | 220 | 12-3-73 | 1996 | Washougal, Wash. |
| Tillmon, Darrell | 7 | 6 | 3.20 | 18 | 18 | 1 | 0 | 112 | 104 | 41 | 40 | 28 | 59 | L | L | 6-2 | 170 | 3-30-73 | 1995 | Wadesboro, N.C. |
| Tweedlie, Brad | 2 | 0 | 0.79 | 11 | 0 | 0 | 7 | 11 | 6 | 1 | 1 | 3 | 9 | R | R | 6-2 | 215 | 12-9-71 | 1993 | Enfield, Conn. |
| Tyrell, Jim | 1 | 2 | 5.27 | 8 | 0 | 0 | 0 | 14 | 11 | 9 | 8 | 8 | 14 | R | L | 5-11 | 170 | 10-14-72 | 1992 | Poughkeepsie, N.Y. |
| Wimberly, Larry | 2 | 4 | 6.90 | 6 | 6 | 0 | 0 | 30 | 38 | 26 | 23 | 16 | 16 | L | L | 6-2 | 185 | 8-22-75 | 1994 | Winter Garden, Fla. |

# MICHIGAN — Class A
## MIDWEST LEAGUE

| BATTING | AVG | G | AB | R | H | 2B | 3B | HR | RBI | BB | SO | SB | CS | B | T | HT | WT | DOB | 1st Yr | Resides |
|---|---|---|---|---|---|---|---|---|---|---|---|---|---|---|---|---|---|---|---|---|
| Betancourt, Rafael | .167 | 62 | 168 | 14 | 28 | 1 | 2 | 3 | 14 | 12 | 39 | 5 | 2 | R | R | 6-1 | 187 | 4-29-75 | 1994 | Cumana, Venez. |
| Borrero, Richie | .167 | 11 | 30 | 3 | 5 | 1 | 0 | 0 | 1 | 2 | 5 | 0 | 1 | R | R | 6-1 | 195 | 1-5-73 | 1990 | Hormigueros, P.R. |
| Chamblee, James | .218 | 100 | 303 | 31 | 66 | 15 | 2 | 1 | 39 | 16 | 75 | 2 | 2 | R | R | 6-4 | 175 | 5-6-75 | 1995 | Denton, Texas |
| Chevalier, Virgil | .248 | 126 | 483 | 61 | 120 | 31 | 3 | 8 | 62 | 33 | 69 | 11 | 4 | R | R | 6-2 | 230 | 10-31-73 | 1995 | Burnt Hills, N.Y. |
| Clark, Kevin | .276 | 126 | 474 | 53 | 131 | 32 | 3 | 10 | 56 | 30 | 94 | 4 | 5 | R | R | 6-1 | 200 | 4-30-73 | 1993 | Henderson, Nev. |
| Ferguson, Dwight | .111 | 10 | 36 | 2 | 4 | 0 | 0 | 0 | 4 | 14 | 0 | 1 | 1 | L | L | 6-1 | 170 | 12-9-76 | 1995 | Carol City, Fla. |
| Goodwin, Keith | .273 | 66 | 238 | 40 | 65 | 18 | 0 | 1 | 28 | 25 | 52 | 11 | 6 | R | R | 6-2 | 188 | 2-5-75 | 1994 | Sulphur, La. |
| Hamilton, Joe | .262 | 108 | 389 | 54 | 102 | 20 | 2 | 13 | 58 | 45 | 117 | 3 | 5 | L | R | 6-0 | 185 | 7-12-74 | 1992 | Rehoboth, Mass. |
| Lebron, Ruben | .178 | 38 | 107 | 17 | 19 | 5 | 0 | 0 | 6 | 7 | 18 | 3 | 0 | S | R | 5-10 | 140 | 8-10-75 | 1992 | San Pedro de Macoris, D.R. |
| Liniak, Cole | .263 | 121 | 437 | 65 | 115 | 26 | 2 | 3 | 46 | 59 | 59 | 7 | 6 | R | R | 6-1 | 181 | 8-23-76 | 1995 | Encinitas, Calif. |
| Morgan, Scooby | .143 | 7 | 7 | 1 | 1 | 0 | 0 | 0 | 0 | 0 | 2 | 0 | 0 | L | L | 5-10 | 190 | 11-23-74 | 1996 | Lake Placid, Fla. |
| Ortiz, Nick | .302 | 73 | 242 | 37 | 73 | 14 | 4 | 2 | 25 | 20 | 44 | 1 | 1 | R | R | 6-0 | 165 | 7-9-73 | 1991 | Cidra, P.R. |
| Padilla, Roy | .280 | 103 | 386 | 58 | 108 | 20 | 6 | 2 | 40 | 34 | 56 | 21 | 8 | L | L | 6-7 | 230 | 8-4-75 | 1993 | Panama City, Panama |
| Prodanov, Peter | .231 | 44 | 147 | 21 | 34 | 7 | 1 | 3 | 14 | 18 | 23 | 2 | 1 | R | R | 6-1 | 200 | 9-4-73 | 1995 | Princeton Junction, N.J. |
| Raifstanger, John | .290 | 111 | 345 | 55 | 100 | 17 | 1 | 5 | 41 | 62 | 48 | 5 | 4 | R | R | 6-0 | 190 | 6-2-73 | 1994 | Great Barrington, Mass. |
| Rathmell, Lance | .130 | 20 | 54 | 5 | 7 | 1 | 1 | | 5 | 3 | 9 | 0 | 0 | R | R | 6-1 | 185 | 8-1-73 | 1995 | Williamsport, Pa. |
| Rivera, Wilfredo | .248 | 65 | 149 | 17 | 37 | 9 | 2 | 2 | 18 | 7 | 32 | 1 | 0 | R | R | 6-2 | 200 | 5-12-74 | 1993 | Vega Alta, P.R. |
| Sapp, Damian | .322 | 90 | 335 | 55 | 108 | 21 | 4 | 18 | 52 | 38 | 88 | 3 | 2 | R | R | 6-3 | 225 | 5-20-76 | 1994 | Pleasant Grove, Utah |
| Sheffield, Tony | .233 | 48 | 133 | 20 | 31 | 10 | 1 | 5 | 31 | 12 | 38 | 3 | 2 | L | L | 6-1 | 190 | 2-17-74 | 1992 | Tullahoma, Tenn. |
| Tippin, Greg | .271 | 93 | 229 | 29 | 62 | 12 | 1 | 7 | 31 | 16 | 62 | 1 | 0 | L | L | 6-0 | 190 | 3-4-73 | 1995 | Anaheim, Calif. |

GAMES BY POSITION: C—Borrero 11, Chevalier 76, Clark 8, Prodanov 3, Sapp 55. 1B—Chevalier 23, Clark 72, Prodanov 2, Raifstanger 8, Rathmell 7, Sapp 9, Tippin 39. 2B—Betancourt 14, Lebron 33, Liniak 1, Ortiz 43, Prodanov 5, Raifstanger 54, Rathmell 4, Tippin 1. 3B—Betancourt 6, Chamblee 1, Clark 7, Liniak 116, Ortiz 5, Prodanov 13, Raifstanger 5, Rathmell 5. SS—Betancourt 46, Chamblee 92, Liniak 1, Ortiz 21, Prodanov 1, Sheffield 1. OF—Chamblee 7, Chevalier 8, Ferguson 10, Goodwin 62, Hamilton 102, Padilla 98, Prodanov 24, Raifstanger 38, Rivera 41, Sheffield 48, Tippin 20.

| PITCHING | W | L | ERA | G | GS | CG | SV | IP | H | R | ER | BB | SO | B | T | HT | WT | DOB | 1st Yr | Resides |
|---|---|---|---|---|---|---|---|---|---|---|---|---|---|---|---|---|---|---|---|---|
| Barksdale, Joe | 2 | 5 | 5.32 | 8 | 8 | 0 | 0 | 44 | 42 | 30 | 26 | 33 | 16 | R | R | 6-3 | 200 | 9-6-73 | 1993 | Augusta, Ga. |
| Bush, Craig | 1 | 1 | 3.38 | 4 | 0 | 0 | 0 | 8 | 11 | 3 | 3 | 2 | 7 | R | R | 6-3 | 235 | 8-13-73 | 1991 | Lancaster, Ohio |
| Cannon, Kevan | 2 | 6 | 2.59 | 37 | 0 | 0 | 5 | 73 | 70 | 24 | 21 | 21 | 72 | L | L | 6-3 | 215 | 8-24-74 | 1995 | Columbus, Ohio |
| Crawford, Paxton | 6 | 11 | 3.58 | 22 | 22 | 1 | 0 | 128 | 120 | 62 | 51 | 42 | 105 | R | R | 6-3 | 190 | 8-4-77 | 1995 | Carlsbad, N.M. |
| Farrell, Jim | 6 | 1 | 2.45 | 7 | 7 | 2 | 0 | 44 | 39 | 15 | 12 | 17 | 32 | R | R | 6-1 | 180 | 11-1-73 | 1995 | Hartville, Ohio |
| Jones, Scott | 0 | 3 | 5.44 | 48 | 0 | 0 | 18 | 45 | 32 | 33 | 27 | 45 | 41 | R | R | 6-0 | 200 | 3-1-73 | 1995 | Union, Ohio |
| McLaughlin, Denis | 2 | 4 | 6.25 | 39 | 0 | 0 | 0 | 59 | 59 | 47 | 41 | 43 | 45 | R | R | 6-5 | 215 | 11-19-72 | 1994 | Warwick, N.Y. |
| Morgan, Scooby | 0 | 1 | 5.87 | 5 | 1 | 0 | 0 | 15 | 16 | 13 | 10 | 12 | 3 | L | L | 5-10 | 190 | 11-23-74 | 1996 | Lake Placid, Fla. |
| Noffke, Andrew | 5 | 3 | 4.86 | 28 | 7 | 0 | 3 | 74 | 74 | 51 | 40 | 57 | 34 | R | R | 6-6 | 220 | 6-19-73 | 1995 | Springfield, Ohio |
| Pena, Juan | 12 | 10 | 2.97 | 26 | 26 | 4 | 0 | 188 | 149 | 70 | 62 | 34 | 156 | R | R | 6-2 | 210 | 6-27-77 | 1995 | Hialeah, Fla. |
| Rivera, Wilfredo | 1 | 4 | 4.86 | 16 | 5 | 0 | 0 | 46 | 42 | 27 | 25 | 36 | 28 | R | R | 6-2 | 200 | 5-12-74 | 1993 | Vega Alta, P.R. |
| Romboli, Curtis | 3 | 5 | 4.22 | 41 | 2 | 0 | 0 | 79 | 78 | 43 | 37 | 45 | 75 | L | L | 6-0 | 190 | 2-7-73 | 1995 | Randolph, Mass. |
| Sauve, Jeff | 0 | 3 | 4.09 | 36 | 0 | 0 | 0 | 62 | 51 | 34 | 28 | 26 | 55 | R | R | 6-1 | 200 | 6-27-75 | 1995 | Camp Hill, Pa. |
| Spinelli, Mike | 3 | 4 | 5.25 | 11 | 11 | 0 | 0 | 60 | 58 | 43 | 35 | 39 | 41 | L | L | 6-2 | 220 | 10-5-76 | 1996 | Revere, Mass. |
| Symmonds, Maika | 0 | 0 | 11.88 | 5 | 0 | 0 | 0 | 8 | 12 | 11 | 11 | 10 | 4 | L | S | 5-9 | 180 | 3-13-73 | 1995 | Bellefonte, Pa. |
| Tillmon, Darrell | 4 | 3 | 5.21 | 7 | 7 | 0 | 0 | 38 | 28 | 25 | 22 | 17 | 27 | L | L | 6-2 | 170 | 3-30-73 | 1995 | Wadesboro, N.C. |
| Wimberly, Larry | 3 | 4 | 2.85 | 14 | 14 | 2 | 0 | 66 | 58 | 27 | 21 | 24 | 41 | L | L | 6-2 | 185 | 8-22-75 | 1994 | Winter Garden, Fla. |
| Yennaco, Joe | 10 | 10 | 4.61 | 28 | 28 | 4 | 0 | 170 | 195 | 112 | 87 | 68 | 117 | S | R | 6-2 | 220 | 11-17-75 | 1995 | Windham, N.H. |

# LOWELL — Class A
## NEW YORK-PENN LEAGUE

| BATTING | AVG | G | AB | R | H | 2B | 3B | HR | RBI | BB | SO | SB | CS | B | T | HT | WT | DOB | 1st Yr | Resides |
|---|---|---|---|---|---|---|---|---|---|---|---|---|---|---|---|---|---|---|---|---|
| Alayon, Elvis | .277 | 63 | 213 | 28 | 59 | 3 | 1 | 4 | 20 | 11 | 37 | 10 | 3 | L | R | 5-11 | 170 | 12-14-74 | 1995 | New York, N.Y. |
| Fuentes, Javier | .287 | 46 | 157 | 21 | 45 | 6 | 1 | 2 | 21 | 21 | 23 | 2 | 1 | R | R | 6-1 | 180 | 9-27-74 | 1996 | Austin, Texas |
| Hillenbrand, Shea | .315 | 72 | 279 | 33 | 88 | 18 | 2 | 2 | 38 | 18 | 32 | 4 | 3 | R | R | 6-1 | 185 | 7-27-75 | 1996 | Mesa, Ariz. |
| Hine, Steve | .274 | 27 | 73 | 5 | 20 | 2 | 0 | 3 | 10 | 6 | | 0 | 0 | L | R | 5-10 | 175 | 2-6-74 | 1996 | Milford, Conn. |
| Jenkins, Corey | .224 | 65 | 228 | 37 | 51 | 7 | 2 | 8 | 29 | 28 | 81 | 5 | 0 | R | R | 6-2 | 195 | 8-25-76 | 1995 | Columbia, S.C. |
| Johnson, Rontrez | .222 | 35 | 135 | 27 | 30 | 4 | | 4 | 12 | 21 | 30 | 7 | 3 | R | R | 5-10 | 160 | 12-12-76 | 1995 | Marshall, Texas |
| Keaveney, Jeff | .249 | 49 | 169 | 15 | 42 | 13 | 1 | 4 | 20 | 10 | 65 | 1 | 1 | R | R | 6-5 | 240 | 10-7-75 | 1996 | Framingham, Mass. |
| Kingsbury, Willy | .159 | 19 | 63 | 3 | 10 | 1 | 0 | 1 | 5 | 2 | 28 | 0 | 1 | L | R | 6-2 | 218 | 1-5-74 | 1996 | East Corinth, Ver. |
| Kratochvil, Tim | .304 | 44 | 158 | 20 | 48 | 11 | 0 | 3 | 19 | 8 | 31 | 1 | 1 | R | R | 6-2 | 220 | 4-2-74 | 1996 | Mt. Olive, Ill. |
| Lebron, Ruben | .220 | 46 | 159 | 24 | 35 | 5 | 1 | 0 | 7 | 7 | 31 | 11 | 3 | S | R | 5-10 | 140 | 8-10-75 | 1992 | San Pedro de Macoris, D.R. |
| Lomasney, Steve | .139 | 59 | 173 | 26 | 24 | 10 | 0 | 4 | 21 | 42 | 63 | 2 | 0 | R | R | 6-0 | 185 | 8-9-77 | 1995 | Peabody, Mass. |
| McKinley, Michael | .188 | 30 | 64 | 10 | 12 | 4 | 0 | 0 | 6 | 9 | 22 | 1 | 4 | R | R | 6-0 | 180 | 11-30-74 | 1996 | Mesa, Ariz. |
| Metzger, Erik | .115 | 9 | 26 | 2 | 3 | 1 | 0 | 2 | 3 | 4 | 6 | 0 | 1 | R | R | 6-0 | 205 | 7-27-74 | 1996 | Brentwood, Tenn. |
| Olmeda, Jose | .225 | 27 | 89 | 6 | 20 | | 0 | 2 | 10 | 12 | 27 | 1 | 2 | S | R | 6-1 | 165 | 7-7-77 | 1996 | Fajardo, P.R. |
| Sanchez, Orlando | .183 | 33 | 115 | 15 | 21 | 2 | 0 | | 5 | 10 | 29 | 3 | 0 | R | R | 6-0 | 160 | 7-19-78 | 1996 | Sinaloa, Mex |
| Thompson, Andre | .168 | 35 | 107 | 12 | 18 | 4 | 1 | 2 | 8 | 7 | 35 | 1 | 0 | R | R | 6-0 | 185 | 12-23-74 | 1996 | Jackson, Miss. |
| Veras, Wilton | .240 | 67 | 250 | 22 | 60 | 15 | 0 | 0 | 19 | 13 | 29 | 2 | 1 | R | R | 6-1 | 180 | 1-19-78 | 1995 | Santo Domingo, D.R. |

GAMES BY POSITION: C—Kingsbury 10, Kratochvil 9, Lomasney 54, Metzger 7. 1B—Fuentes 3, Hillenbrand 52, Kratochvil 18. 2B—Hine 22, Lebron 38, Sanchez 23. 3B—Fuentes 6, Hillenbrand 4, Veras 65. SS—Fuentes 27, Hillenbrand 11, Lebron 3, Olmeda 26, Sanchez 10. OF—Alayon 61, Jenkins 65, Johnson 35, Keaveney 17, Kratochvil 1, McKinley 28, Thompson 34.

| PITCHING | W | L | ERA | G | GS | CG | SV | IP | H | R | ER | BB | SO | B | T | HT | WT | DOB | 1st Yr | Resides |
|---|---|---|---|---|---|---|---|---|---|---|---|---|---|---|---|---|---|---|---|---|
| Austin, Kevie | 2 | 0 | 5.87 | 8 | 0 | 0 | 0 | 15 | 14 | 11 | 10 | 10 | 15 | R | R | 6-0 | 185 | 7-12-73 | 1995 | Marietta, Ga. |
| Beale, Chuck | 0 | 0 | 1.24 | 28 | 0 | 0 | 16 | 29 | 16 | 7 | 4 | 7 | 33 | R | R | 6-0 | 180 | 3-19-74 | 1996 | Dublin, Ga. |

| PITCHING | W | L | ERA | G | GS | CG | SV | IP | H | R | ER | BB | SO | B | T | HT | WT | DOB | 1st Yr | Resides |
|---|---|---|---|---|---|---|---|---|---|---|---|---|---|---|---|---|---|---|---|---|
| Cressend, Jack | 3 | 2 | 2.36 | 9 | 8 | 0 | 0 | 46 | 37 | 15 | 12 | 17 | 57 | R | R | 6-1 | 185 | 5-13-75 | 1996 | Covington, La. |
| Duffy, John | 3 | 4 | 5.66 | 29 | 0 | 0 | 0 | 41 | 56 | 32 | 26 | 27 | 32 | L | L | 6-2 | 185 | 12-4-73 | 1996 | Audubon, Pa. |
| Festa, Chris | 2 | 5 | 5.10 | 20 | 9 | 1 | 0 | 72 | 94 | 53 | 41 | 20 | 43 | R | R | 6-2 | 190 | 9-7-72 | 1995 | Holliston, Mass. |
| Kinney, Matt | 3 | 9 | 2.68 | 15 | 15 | 0 | 0 | 87 | 68 | 51 | 26 | 44 | 72 | R | R | 6-4 | 190 | 12-16-76 | 1995 | Bangor, Maine |
| Montemayor, Humberto | 1 | 2 | 6.20 | 5 | 5 | 0 | 0 | 25 | 30 | 20 | 17 | 6 | 19 | R | R | 6-0 | 174 | 10-12-77 | 1996 | Nuevo Leon, Mexico |
| Morgan, Scooby | 1 | 1 | 4.76 | 13 | 1 | 0 | 0 | 23 | 25 | 18 | 12 | 20 | 19 | L | L | 5-10 | 190 | 11-23-74 | 1996 | Lake Placid, Fla. |
| Musgrave, Brian | 0 | 0 | 0.00 | 1 | 0 | 0 | 0 | 5 | 4 | 1 | 0 | 2 | 7 | L | L | 6-2 | 200 | 4-24-74 | 1996 | Princeton, N.C. |
| Rodgers, Bobby | 7 | 4 | 1.90 | 14 | 14 | 2 | 0 | 90 | 60 | 33 | 19 | 31 | 108 | R | R | 6-3 | 225 | 7-22-74 | 1996 | St. Charles, Mo. |
| Smetana, Steve | 5 | 0 | 1.45 | 19 | 0 | 0 | 2 | 31 | 22 | 5 | 5 | 3 | 33 | L | L | 6-0 | 205 | 4-14-73 | 1996 | Chardon, Ohio |
| Symmonds, Maika | 1 | 0 | 10.45 | 5 | 0 | 0 | 0 | 10 | 11 | 12 | 12 | 15 | 10 | L | L | 5-9 | 180 | 3-13-73 | 1995 | Bellefonte, Pa. |
| Thompson, Chris | 2 | 5 | 4.40 | 25 | 0 | 0 | 0 | 47 | 43 | 34 | 23 | 20 | 51 | R | R | 6-2 | 195 | 9-29-72 | 1996 | Elyria, Ohio |
| Welch, Robb | 2 | 7 | 5.09 | 14 | 14 | 1 | 0 | 81 | 85 | 50 | 46 | 37 | 63 | R | R | 6-4 | 190 | 12-30-75 | 1994 | Twin Falls, Idaho |
| Yount, Andy | 1 | 2 | 6.29 | 8 | 8 | 0 | 0 | 34 | 38 | 30 | 24 | 38 | 30 | R | R | 6-2 | 185 | 2-14-77 | 1995 | Kingwood, Texas |

# FORT MYERS                                               Rookie

## GULF COAST LEAGUE

| BATTING | AVG | G | AB | R | H | 2B | 3B | HR | RBI | BB | SO | SB | CS | B | T | HT | WT | DOB | 1st Yr | Resides |
|---|---|---|---|---|---|---|---|---|---|---|---|---|---|---|---|---|---|---|---|---|
| Ahumada, Alejandro | .279 | 37 | 122 | 14 | 34 | 6 | 0 | 0 | 15 | 3 | 32 | 1 | 5 | R | R | 6-1 | 155 | 1-20-79 | 1996 | Sinaloa, Mexico |
| Barnes, John | .277 | 30 | 101 | 9 | 28 | 4 | 0 | 1 | 17 | 5 | 17 | 4 | 0 | R | R | 6-2 | 205 | 4-24-76 | 1996 | El Cajon, Calif. |
| Barrientos, Edgar | .122 | 23 | 41 | 6 | 5 | 0 | 0 | 0 | 1 | 6 | 14 | 0 | 0 | S | R | 6-1 | 160 | 12-3-78 | 1996 | Barquisimeto, Venez. |
| Bazzani, Matt | .400 | 11 | 25 | 7 | 10 | 5 | 0 | 1 | 3 | 3 | 4 | 0 | 0 | R | R | 6-1 | 205 | 9-17-73 | 1994 | Foster City, Calif. |
| Brito, Bobby | .252 | 33 | 115 | 10 | 29 | 10 | 0 | 0 | 14 | 5 | 21 | 5 | 0 | R | R | 5-9 | 180 | 12-23-77 | 1996 | Cypress, Calif. |
| Cardona, Luis | .133 | 29 | 75 | 5 | 10 | 2 | 0 | 1 | 5 | 0 | 18 | 1 | 1 | R | R | 6-1 | 198 | 9-14-77 | 1995 | San Sebastian, P.R. |
| Chaidez, Juan | .128 | 22 | 47 | 1 | 6 | 0 | 1 | 0 | 0 | 2 | 16 | 0 | 1 | S | R | 6-2 | 205 | 3-29-77 | 1996 | Hialeah, Fla. |
| Cordero, Wil | .300 | 3 | 10 | 1 | 3 | 0 | 0 | 1 | 3 | 0 | 2 | 0 | 0 | R | R | 6-2 | 185 | 10-3-71 | 1988 | Mayaguez, P.R. |
| Ferguson, Dwight | .324 | 36 | 68 | 23 | 22 | 2 | 1 | 2 | 11 | 15 | 22 | 10 | 5 | L | L | 6-1 | 170 | 12-9-76 | 1995 | Carol City, Fla. |
| Flores, Oswaldo | .300 | 37 | 120 | 22 | 36 | 7 | 2 | 0 | 9 | 8 | 28 | 14 | 2 | S | R | 6-3 | 180 | 4-24-78 | 1995 | Caracas, Venez. |
| Garciaparra, Nomar | .286 | 5 | 14 | 4 | 4 | 2 | 1 | 0 | 5 | 1 | 0 | 0 | 0 | R | R | 6-0 | 165 | 7-23-73 | 1994 | Whittier, Calif. |
| Goligoski, Jason | .000 | 3 | 8 | 0 | 0 | 0 | 0 | 0 | 1 | 1 | 2 | 0 | 0 | L | R | 6-1 | 180 | 10-2-71 | 1993 | Hamilton, Mon. |
| Gruber, Nick | .167 | 5 | 6 | 0 | 1 | 0 | 0 | 0 | 1 | 1 | 1 | 0 | 0 | R | R | 6-0 | 185 | 10-14-76 | 1995 | Westmont, N.J. |
| Hamilton, Joe | .250 | 1 | 4 | 1 | 1 | 0 | 0 | 0 | 0 | 0 | 1 | 0 | 0 | R | R | 6-0 | 185 | 7-12-74 | 1992 | Rehoboth, Mass. |
| Johnson, Rontrez | .294 | 28 | 85 | 20 | 25 | 6 | 0 | 0 | 9 | 17 | 11 | 6 | 2 | R | R | 5-10 | 160 | 12-12-76 | 1995 | Marshall, Texas |
| Kingsbury, Willy | .333 | 28 | 93 | 7 | 31 | 9 | 0 | 2 | 22 | 10 | 18 | 3 | 0 | L | R | 6-2 | 218 | 1-5-74 | 1996 | East Corinth, Ver. |
| LoCurto, Gary | .314 | 36 | 137 | 35 | 43 | 8 | 0 | 4 | 22 | 18 | 44 | 5 | 4 | S | R | 6-2 | 200 | 5-25-78 | 1996 | Safety Harbor, Fla. |
| Mendoza, Angel | .269 | 49 | 160 | 17 | 43 | 13 | 2 | 2 | 13 | 9 | 42 | 3 | 4 | R | R | 6-2 | 165 | 11-30-78 | 1996 | San Pedro de Macoris, D.R. |
| Merloni, Lou | .250 | 1 | 4 | 1 | 1 | 0 | 0 | 0 | 1 | 0 | 0 | 0 | 0 | R | R | 5-10 | 188 | 4-6-71 | 1993 | Framingham, Mass. |
| Metzger, Erik | .232 | 19 | 56 | 4 | 13 | 3 | 0 | 0 | 5 | 4 | 14 | 0 | 0 | R | R | 6-0 | 205 | 7-27-74 | 1996 | Brentwood, Tenn. |
| Nova, Geraldo | .190 | 33 | 84 | 15 | 16 | 3 | 2 | 0 | 10 | 17 | 32 | 3 | 2 | S | R | 6-1 | 168 | 3-1-78 | 1995 | Santo Domingo, D.R. |
| Olmeda, Jose | .291 | 15 | 55 | 8 | 16 | 4 | 0 | 2 | 5 | 3 | 13 | 1 | 1 | S | R | 6-1 | 165 | 7-7-77 | 1995 | Fajardo, P.R. |
| Perez, Alejandro | .233 | 15 | 43 | 6 | 10 | 3 | 1 | 0 | 3 | 1 | 10 | 1 | 0 | R | R | 6-2 | 175 | 3-18-79 | 1996 | Santiago D.R. |
| Perini, Mike | .170 | 34 | 94 | 8 | 16 | 1 | 1 | 0 | 7 | 13 | 27 | 3 | 2 | L | R | 6-2 | 200 | 4-27-78 | 1996 | Carlsbad, N.M. |
| Prodanov, Peter | .120 | 9 | 25 | 5 | 3 | 1 | 0 | 0 | 1 | 2 | 3 | 0 | 0 | R | R | 5-11 | 180 | 9-4-73 | 1995 | Princeton Junction, N.J. |
| Rojas, Moises | .228 | 39 | 114 | 21 | 26 | 4 | 1 | 3 | 9 | 9 | 17 | 3 | 1 | R | R | 6-3 | 199 | 12-17-76 | 1995 | Hialeah, Fla. |
| Roman, Felipe | .272 | 47 | 162 | 15 | 44 | 7 | 1 | 1 | 17 | 7 | 35 | 2 | 5 | R | R | 6-3 | 199 | 12-17-76 | 1995 | Rio Piedras, P.R. |
| Sanchez, Orlando | .268 | 16 | 56 | 8 | 15 | 1 | 1 | 0 | 3 | 6 | 9 | 2 | 0 | R | R | 6-0 | 160 | 7-19-78 | 1996 | Sinaloa, Mexico |
| Smith, Dave | .333 | 3 | 9 | 0 | 3 | 1 | 0 | 0 | 0 | 1 | 1 | 0 | 0 | L | L | 5-10 | 180 | 2-18-72 | 1993 | Cheektowaga, N.Y. |
| Stenson, Dernell | .216 | 32 | 97 | 16 | 21 | 3 | 1 | 2 | 15 | 16 | 26 | 4 | 3 | L | L | 6-1 | 215 | 6-17-78 | 1996 | La Grange, Ga. |
| Tardiff, Jeremy | .200 | 4 | 5 | 0 | 1 | 0 | 0 | 0 | 0 | 1 | 1 | 0 | 0 | R | R | 6-1 | 195 | 11-27-76 | 1995 | Mechanic Falls, Maine |

**GAMES BY POSITION: C**—Bazzani 5, Brito 11, Cardona 16, Chaidez 21, Gruber 4, Kingsbury 17, Metzger 16. **1B**—Bazzani 2, Cardona 12, Chaidez 2, Ferguson 1, Kingsbury 7, LoCurto 19, Metzger 1, Prodanov 4, Rojas 1, Roman 33. **2B**—Ahumada 14, Barrientos 20, Cordero 1, Merloni 1, Nova 25, Sanchez 13, Smith 3. **3B**—Ahumada 7, Cardona 1, LoCurto 13, Mendoza 22, Nova 5, Prodanov 3, Roman 16, Sanchez 4. **SS**—Ahumada 19, Garciaparra 5, Goligoski 3, Mendoza 31, Olmeda 4, Sanchez 1. **OF**—Barnes 26, Ferguson 21, Flores 33, Hamilton 1, Johnson 25, Perez 15, Perini 29, Prodanov 3, Rojas 34, Roman 1, Stenson 25, Tardiff 4.

| PITCHING | W | L | ERA | G | GS | CG | SV | IP | H | R | ER | BB | SO | B | T | HT | WT | DOB | 1st Yr | Resides |
|---|---|---|---|---|---|---|---|---|---|---|---|---|---|---|---|---|---|---|---|---|
| Arias, Rafael | 1 | 6 | 4.93 | 13 | 5 | 0 | 0 | 49 | 68 | 39 | 27 | 8 | 20 | R | R | 6-5 | 168 | 2-4-77 | 1994 | San Pedro de Macoris, D.R. |
| Austin, Kevie | 3 | 4 | 3.18 | 16 | 0 | 0 | 1 | 23 | 24 | 17 | 8 | 13 | 26 | R | R | 6-0 | 185 | 7-12-73 | 1995 | Marietta, Ga. |
| Benzing, Skipp | 2 | 2 | 4.33 | 12 | 9 | 0 | 0 | 52 | 55 | 31 | 25 | 16 | 51 | L | R | 6-2 | 180 | 11-29-76 | 1996 | Gays Mills, Wis. |
| Berroa, Oliver | 1 | 2 | 5.12 | 17 | 0 | 0 | 1 | 32 | 21 | 28 | 18 | 23 | 28 | R | R | 6-1 | 180 | 3-24-78 | 1996 | San Pedro de Macoris, D.R. |
| Calvert, Neal | 1 | 4 | 5.30 | 20 | 3 | 0 | 0 | 36 | 41 | 29 | 21 | 17 | 34 | R | R | 6-5 | 180 | 11-30-76 | 1996 | Beaudesert, Australia |
| Duchscherer, Justin | 0 | 2 | 3.13 | 13 | 8 | 0 | 1 | 55 | 52 | 26 | 19 | 14 | 45 | R | R | 6-3 | 165 | 11-19-77 | 1996 | Lubbock, Texas |
| Garrett, Josh | 1 | 1 | 1.67 | 7 | 5 | 0 | 0 | 27 | 22 | 8 | 5 | 5 | 17 | R | R | 6-4 | 190 | 1-12-78 | 1996 | Richland, Ind. |
| Montanez, Jorge | 0 | 0 | 2.03 | 10 | 0 | 0 | 0 | 13 | 15 | 12 | 3 | 5 | 7 | R | R | 6-2 | 184 | 6-8-77 | 1996 | Lara, Venez. |
| Montemayor, Humberto | 4 | 3 | 2.78 | 10 | 2 | 0 | 0 | 32 | 30 | 14 | 10 | 11 | 19 | R | R | 6-0 | 174 | 10-12-77 | 1996 | Nuevo Leon, Mexico |
| Peterson, Dean | 0 | 0 | 0.00 | 2 | 2 | 0 | 0 | 6 | 4 | 0 | 0 | 0 | 7 | R | R | 6-3 | 200 | 8-3-72 | 1993 | Cortland, Ohio |
| Pierce, Jeff | 0 | 0 | 0.79 | 5 | 4 | 0 | 1 | 11 | 12 | 1 | 1 | 1 | 10 | R | R | 6-1 | 200 | 6-7-69 | 1991 | Staatsburg, N.Y. |
| Ramirez, Felix | 0 | 0 | 9.00 | 1 | 0 | 0 | 0 | 1 | 1 | 2 | 1 | 2 | 1 | L | L | 5-11 | 170 | 1-7-75 | 1996 | Beverly Hills, Calif. |
| Ramsay, Rob | 0 | 1 | 4.91 | 2 | 0 | 0 | 0 | 4 | 5 | 2 | 2 | 3 | 5 | L | L | 6-4 | 220 | 12-3-73 | 1996 | Washougal, Wash. |
| Reitsma, Chris | 1 | 1 | 1.35 | 7 | 6 | 0 | 0 | 27 | 24 | 7 | 4 | 1 | 32 | R | R | 6-5 | 200 | 12-31-77 | 1996 | Calgary, Alberta |
| Santana, Pedro | 5 | 3 | 1.89 | 13 | 8 | 0 | 0 | 71 | 59 | 24 | 15 | 12 | 33 | R | R | 6-3 | 186 | 11-22-77 | 1995 | San Pedro de Macoris, D.R. |
| Sekany, Jason | 0 | 0 | 2.31 | 5 | 2 | 0 | 1 | 12 | 14 | 3 | 3 | 3 | 16 | R | R | 6-4 | 175 | 7-20-75 | 1996 | Pleasanton, Calif. |
| Silva, Juan | 0 | 3 | 5.26 | 14 | 0 | 0 | 2 | 26 | 34 | 16 | 15 | 12 | 31 | L | L | 6-5 | 190 | 11-30-77 | 1996 | Bolivar, Venez. |
| Spinelli, Mike | 1 | 0 | 2.25 | 1 | 0 | 0 | 0 | 4 | 4 | 1 | 1 | 0 | 2 | L | L | 6-2 | 220 | 10-5-76 | 1996 | Revere, Mass. |
| Stallings, Ben | 1 | 4 | 4.89 | 11 | 6 | 0 | 0 | 42 | 45 | 33 | 23 | 22 | 36 | R | R | 6-1 | 200 | 9-30-76 | 1995 | Owensboro, Ky. |
| Tyrell, Jim | 0 | 0 | 81.00 | 1 | 0 | 0 | 0 | 1 | 5 | 6 | 6 | 2 | 1 | R | L | 5-11 | 170 | 10-14-72 | 1992 | Poughkeepsie, N.Y. |

# CALIFORNIA ANGELS

**Managers:** Marcel Lachemann, Joe Maddon, John McNamara.
**1996 Record:** 70-91, .435 (4th, AL West).

| BATTING | AVG | G | AB | R | H | 2B | 3B | HR | RBI | BB | SO | SB | CS | B | T | HT | WT | DOB | 1st Yr | Resides |
|---|---|---|---|---|---|---|---|---|---|---|---|---|---|---|---|---|---|---|---|---|
| Aldrete, Mike | .150 | 31 | 40 | 5 | 6 | 1 | 0 | 3 | 8 | 5 | 4 | 0 | 0 | L | L | 5-11 | 180 | 1-29-61 | 1983 | Monterey, Calif. |
| Anderson, Garret | .285 | 150 | 607 | 79 | 173 | 33 | 2 | 12 | 72 | 27 | 84 | 7 | 9 | L | L | 6-3 | 190 | 6-30-72 | 1990 | Granada Hills, Calif. |
| Arias, George | .238 | 84 | 252 | 19 | 60 | 8 | 1 | 6 | 28 | 16 | 50 | 2 | 0 | R | R | 5-11 | 190 | 3-12-72 | 1993 | Tucson, Ariz. |
| Borders, Pat | .228 | 19 | 57 | 6 | 13 | 3 | 0 | 2 | 8 | 3 | 11 | 0 | 1 | R | R | 6-2 | 195 | 5-14-63 | 1982 | Lake Wales, Fla. |
| Davis, Chili | .292 | 145 | 530 | 73 | 155 | 24 | 0 | 28 | 95 | 86 | 99 | 5 | 2 | S | R | 6-3 | 217 | 1-17-60 | 1978 | Scottsdale, Ariz. |
| DiSarcina, Gary | .256 | 150 | 536 | 62 | 137 | 26 | 4 | 5 | 48 | 21 | 36 | 2 | 1 | R | R | 6-1 | 178 | 11-19-67 | 1988 | East Sandwich, Mass. |
| Easley, Damion | .156 | 28 | 45 | 4 | 7 | 1 | 0 | 2 | 7 | 6 | 12 | 0 | 0 | R | R | 5-11 | 155 | 11-11-69 | 1989 | Glendale, Ariz. |
| Edmonds, Jim | .304 | 114 | 431 | 73 | 131 | 28 | 3 | 27 | 66 | 46 | 101 | 4 | 0 | L | L | 6-1 | 190 | 6-27-70 | 1988 | Diamond Bar, Calif. |
| Eenhoorn, Robert | .267 | 6 | 15 | 1 | 4 | 0 | 0 | 0 | 0 | 0 | 2 | 0 | 0 | R | R | 6-3 | 175 | 2-9-68 | 1990 | Rotterdam, Holland |
|   2-team (12 N.Y.) | .172 | 18 | 29 | 3 | 5 | 0 | 0 | 0 | 2 | 2 | 5 | 0 | 0 | | | | | | | |
| Erstad, Darin | .284 | 57 | 208 | 34 | 59 | 5 | 1 | 4 | 20 | 17 | 29 | 3 | 3 | L | L | 6-2 | 195 | 6-4-74 | 1995 | Jamestown, N.D. |
| Fabregas, Jorge | .287 | 90 | 254 | 18 | 73 | 6 | 0 | 2 | 26 | 17 | 27 | 0 | 1 | L | R | 6-3 | 205 | 3-13-70 | 1991 | Miami, Fla. |
| Greene, Todd | .190 | 29 | 79 | 9 | 15 | 1 | 0 | 2 | 9 | 4 | 11 | 2 | 0 | R | R | 5-10 | 195 | 5-8-71 | 1993 | Martinez, Ga. |
| Howell, Jack | .270 | 66 | 126 | 20 | 34 | 4 | 1 | 8 | 21 | 10 | 30 | 0 | 1 | L | R | 6-0 | 201 | 8-18-61 | 1983 | Tucson, Ariz. |
| Hudler, Rex | .311 | 92 | 302 | 60 | 94 | 20 | 3 | 16 | 40 | 9 | 54 | 14 | 5 | R | R | 6-2 | 180 | 9-2-60 | 1978 | Fresno, Calif. |
| Palmeiro, Orlando | .287 | 50 | 87 | 6 | 25 | 6 | 1 | 0 | 6 | 8 | 13 | 0 | 1 | L | R | 5-11 | 155 | 1-19-69 | 1991 | Miami, Fla. |
| Pritchett, Chris | .154 | 5 | 13 | 1 | 2 | 0 | 0 | 0 | 1 | 0 | 3 | 0 | 0 | L | R | 6-4 | 185 | 1-31-70 | 1991 | Modesto, Calif. |
| Salmon, Tim | .286 | 156 | 581 | 90 | 166 | 27 | 4 | 30 | 98 | 93 | 125 | 4 | 2 | R | R | 6-3 | 220 | 8-24-68 | 1989 | Phoenix, Ariz. |
| Schofield, Dick | .250 | 13 | 16 | 3 | 4 | 0 | 0 | 0 | 0 | 1 | 1 | 1 | 0 | R | R | 5-10 | 178 | 11-21-62 | 1981 | Laguna Hills, Calif. |
| Slaught, Don | .324 | 62 | 207 | 23 | 67 | 9 | 0 | 6 | 32 | 13 | 20 | 0 | 0 | R | R | 6-1 | 190 | 9-11-58 | 1980 | Arlington, Texas |
| Snow, J.T. | .257 | 155 | 575 | 69 | 148 | 20 | 1 | 17 | 67 | 56 | 96 | 1 | 6 | S | L | 6-2 | 202 | 2-26-68 | 1989 | Corona del Mar, Calif. |
| Turner, Chris | .333 | 4 | 3 | 1 | 1 | 0 | 0 | 0 | 1 | 1 | 0 | 0 | 0 | R | R | 6-1 | 190 | 3-23-69 | 1991 | Bowling Green, Ky. |
| Velarde, Randy | .285 | 136 | 530 | 82 | 151 | 27 | 3 | 14 | 54 | 70 | 118 | 7 | 7 | R | R | 6-0 | 185 | 11-24-62 | 1985 | Midland, Texas |
| Wallach, Tim | .237 | 57 | 190 | 23 | 45 | 7 | 0 | 8 | 20 | 18 | 47 | 1 | 0 | R | R | 6-3 | 200 | 9-14-57 | 1979 | Tustin, Calif. |

| PITCHING | W | L | ERA | G | GS | CG | SV | IP | H | R | ER | BB | SO | B | T | HT | WT | DOB | 1st Yr | Resides |
|---|---|---|---|---|---|---|---|---|---|---|---|---|---|---|---|---|---|---|---|---|
| Abbott, Jim | 2 | 18 | 7.48 | 27 | 23 | 1 | 0 | 142 | 171 | 128 | 118 | 78 | 58 | L | L | 6-3 | 210 | 9-19-67 | 1989 | Newport Beach, Calif. |
| Abbott, Kyle | 0 | 1 | 20.25 | 3 | 0 | 0 | 0 | 4 | 10 | 9 | 9 | 5 | 3 | L | L | 6-4 | 195 | 2-18-68 | 1989 | Cherry Hill, N.J. |
| Boskie, Shawn | 12 | 11 | 5.32 | 37 | 28 | 1 | 0 | 189 | 226 | 126 | 112 | 67 | 133 | R | R | 6-3 | 205 | 3-28-67 | 1986 | Reno, Nev. |
| Dickson, Jason | 1 | 4 | 4.57 | 7 | 7 | 0 | 0 | 43 | 52 | 22 | 22 | 18 | 20 | L | R | 6-0 | 190 | 3-30-73 | 1994 | Chatham, N.B. |
| Edenfield, Ken | 0 | 0 | 10.38 | 2 | 0 | 0 | 0 | 4 | 10 | 5 | 5 | 2 | 4 | R | R | 6-1 | 165 | 3-18-67 | 1990 | Knoxville, Tenn. |
| Eichhorn, Mark | 1 | 2 | 5.04 | 24 | 0 | 0 | 0 | 30 | 36 | 17 | 17 | 11 | 24 | R | R | 6-3 | 210 | 11-21-60 | 1979 | Aptos, Calif. |
| Ellis, Robert | 0 | 0 | 0.00 | 3 | 0 | 0 | 0 | 5 | 0 | 0 | 0 | 4 | 5 | R | R | 6-5 | 220 | 12-15-70 | 1990 | Baton Rouge, La. |
| Finley, Chuck | 15 | 16 | 4.16 | 35 | 35 | 4 | 0 | 238 | 241 | 124 | 110 | 94 | 215 | L | L | 6-6 | 214 | 11-26-62 | 1985 | Newport Beach, Calif. |
| Frohwirth, Todd | 0 | 0 | 11.12 | 4 | 0 | 0 | 0 | 6 | 10 | 11 | 7 | 4 | 1 | R | R | 6-4 | 204 | 9-28-62 | 1984 | Milwaukee, Wis. |
| Gohr, Greg | 1 | 1 | 7.50 | 15 | 0 | 0 | 1 | 24 | 34 | 20 | 20 | 10 | 15 | R | R | 6-3 | 205 | 10-29-67 | 1989 | Campbell, Calif. |
|   2-year (17 Detroit) | 5 | 9 | 7.24 | 32 | 16 | 0 | 1 | 116 | 163 | 96 | 93 | 44 | 75 | | | | | | | |
| Grimsley, Jason | 5 | 7 | 6.84 | 35 | 20 | 2 | 0 | 130 | 150 | 110 | 99 | 74 | 82 | R | R | 6-3 | 180 | 8-7-67 | 1985 | Cleveland, Texas |
| Hancock, Ryan | 4 | 1 | 7.48 | 11 | 4 | 0 | 0 | 28 | 34 | 23 | 23 | 17 | 19 | R | R | 6-2 | 220 | 11-11-71 | 1993 | Cupertino, Calif. |
| Harris, Pep | 2 | 0 | 3.90 | 11 | 3 | 0 | 0 | 32 | 31 | 16 | 14 | 17 | 20 | R | R | 6-2 | 185 | 9-23-72 | 1991 | Lancaster, S.C. |
| Holtz, Mike | 3 | 3 | 2.45 | 30 | 0 | 0 | 0 | 29 | 21 | 11 | 8 | 19 | 31 | L | L | 5-9 | 172 | 10-10-72 | 1994 | Ebensburg, Pa. |
| Holzemer, Mark | 1 | 0 | 8.76 | 25 | 0 | 0 | 0 | 25 | 35 | 28 | 24 | 8 | 20 | L | L | 6-0 | 165 | 8-20-69 | 1988 | Littleton, Colo. |
| James, Mike | 5 | 5 | 2.67 | 69 | 0 | 0 | 1 | 81 | 62 | 27 | 24 | 42 | 65 | R | R | 6-3 | 180 | 8-15-67 | 1988 | Mary Esther, Fla. |
| Langston, Mark | 6 | 5 | 4.82 | 18 | 18 | 2 | 0 | 123 | 116 | 68 | 66 | 45 | 83 | R | L | 6-2 | 184 | 8-20-60 | 1981 | Anaheim Hills, Calif. |
| Leftwich, Phil | 0 | 1 | 7.36 | 2 | 2 | 0 | 0 | 7 | 12 | 9 | 6 | 3 | 4 | R | R | 6-5 | 205 | 5-19-69 | 1990 | Mesa, Ariz. |
| May, Darrell | 0 | 0 | 10.13 | 5 | 0 | 0 | 0 | 3 | 3 | 3 | 3 | 2 | 1 | L | L | 6-2 | 170 | 6-13-72 | 1992 | Rogue River, Ore. |
| McElroy, Chuck | 5 | 1 | 2.95 | 40 | 0 | 0 | 0 | 37 | 32 | 12 | 12 | 13 | 32 | L | L | 6-0 | 195 | 10-1-67 | 1986 | Friendswood, Texas |
| Monteleone, Rich | 0 | 3 | 5.87 | 12 | 0 | 0 | 0 | 15 | 23 | 11 | 10 | 2 | 5 | R | R | 6-2 | 217 | 3-22-63 | 1982 | Tampa, Fla. |
| Pennington, Brad | 0 | 0 | 12.27 | 8 | 0 | 0 | 0 | 7 | 5 | 10 | 10 | 16 | 7 | L | L | 6-6 | 215 | 4-14-69 | 1989 | Salem, Ind. |
|   2-team (14 Boston) | 0 | 2 | 6.20 | 22 | 0 | 0 | 0 | 20 | 11 | 15 | 14 | 31 | 20 | | | | | | | |
| Percival, Troy | 0 | 2 | 2.31 | 62 | 0 | 0 | 36 | 74 | 38 | 20 | 19 | 31 | 100 | R | R | 6-3 | 200 | 8-9-69 | 1990 | Moreno Valley, Calif. |
| Sanderson, Scott | 0 | 2 | 7.50 | 5 | 4 | 0 | 0 | 18 | 39 | 21 | 15 | 4 | 7 | R | R | 6-5 | 192 | 7-22-56 | 1977 | Northbrook, Ill. |
| Schmidt, Jeff | 2 | 0 | 7.88 | 9 | 0 | 0 | 0 | 8 | 13 | 9 | 7 | 8 | 2 | R | R | 6-5 | 210 | 2-21-71 | 1992 | La Crosse, Wis. |
| Smith, Lee | 0 | 0 | 2.45 | 11 | 0 | 0 | 0 | 11 | 8 | 4 | 3 | 3 | 6 | R | R | 6-6 | 269 | 12-4-57 | 1975 | Castor, La. |
| Springer, Dennis | 5 | 6 | 5.51 | 20 | 15 | 2 | 0 | 95 | 91 | 65 | 58 | 43 | 64 | R | R | 5-10 | 185 | 2-12-65 | 1987 | Fresno, Calif. |
| VanRyn, Ben | 0 | 0 | 0.00 | 1 | 0 | 0 | 1 | 1 | 1 | 0 | 0 | 1 | 0 | L | L | 6-5 | 195 | 8-9-71 | 1990 | Kendallville, Ind. |
| Williams, Shad | 0 | 2 | 8.89 | 13 | 2 | 0 | 0 | 28 | 42 | 34 | 28 | 21 | 26 | R | R | 6-0 | 185 | 3-10-71 | 1991 | Fresno, Calif. |

Reliever Troy Percival led the Angels with 36 saves

MEL BAILEY

Angels minor league
Player of the Year
Larry Barnes

# ANGELS

## FARM SYSTEM

**Director of Player Development:** Ken Forsch

| Class | Farm Team | League | W | L | Pct. | Finish* | Manager | First Yr |
|---|---|---|---|---|---|---|---|---|
| AAA | Vancouver (B.C.) Canadians | Pacific Coast | 68 | 70 | .493 | 5th (10) | Don Long | 1993 |
| AA | Midland (Texas) Angels | Texas | 58 | 82 | .414 | 8th (8) | Mario Mendoza | 1985 |
| #A | Lake Elsinore (Calif.) Storm | California | 75 | 65 | .536 | +5th (10) | Mitch Seoane | 1994 |
| A | Cedar Rapids (Iowa) Kernels | Midwest | 63 | 72 | .467 | 12th (14) | Tom Lawless | 1993 |
| A | Boise (Idaho) Hawks | Northwest | 43 | 33 | .566 | 2nd (8) | Tom Kotchman | 1990 |
| R | Mesa (Ariz.) Angels | Arizona | 24 | 32 | .429 | 5th (6) | Bruce Hines | 1989 |

*Finish in overall standings (No. of teams in league)   #Advanced level   +Won league championship

## ORGANIZATION LEADERS

### MAJOR LEAGUERS

**BATTING**
| | | |
|---|---|---|
| *AVG | Rex Hudler | .311 |
| R | Tim Salmon | 90 |
| H | Garret Anderson | 173 |
| TB | Tim Salmon | 291 |
| 2B | Garret Anderson | 33 |
| 3B | Two tied at | 4 |
| HR | Tim Salmon | 30 |
| RBI | Tim Salmon | 98 |
| BB | Tim Salmon | 93 |
| SO | Tim Salmon | 125 |
| SB | Rex Hudler | 14 |

**PITCHING**
| | | |
|---|---|---|
| W | Chuck Finley | 15 |
| L | Jim Abbott | 18 |
| #ERA | Mike James | 2.67 |
| G | Mike James | 69 |
| CG | Chuck Finley | 4 |
| SV | Troy Percival | 36 |
| IP | Chuck Finley | 238 |
| BB | Chuck Finley | 94 |
| SO | Chuck Finley | 215 |

THE SPORTS GROUP

**Chuck Finley.** 15 wins

### MINOR LEAGUERS

**BATTING**
| | | |
|---|---|---|
| *AVG | Greg Shockey, Midland | .317 |
| R | Joe Urso, Lake Elsinore | 106 |
| H | Larry Barnes, Cedar Rapids | 155 |
| TB | Larry Barnes, Cedar Rapids | 282 |
| 2B | Joe Urso, Lake Elsinore | 47 |
| 3B | Norm Hutchins, Cedar Rapids | 16 |
| HR | Larry Barnes, Cedar Rapids | 27 |
| RBI | Larry Barnes, Cedar Rapids | 112 |
| BB | Joe Urso, Lake Elsinore | 75 |
| SO | Jon Vander Griend, Cedar Rapids | 142 |
| SB | Justin Baughman, Cedar Rapids | 50 |

**PITCHING**
| | | |
|---|---|---|
| W | Jason Dickson, Midland/Vancouver | 12 |
| L | Matt Beaumont, Midland | 16 |
| #ERA | Ramon Ortiz, AZL Angels/Boise | 2.46 |
| G | Grant Vermillion, C.R./Lake Elsinore | 56 |
| CG | Jason Dickson, Midland/Vancouver | 10 |
| SV | Jeff Schmidt, Vancouver | 19 |
| IP | Geoff Edsell, Midland/Vancouver | 193 |
| BB | Geoff Edsell, Midland/Vancouver | 92 |
| SO | Jarrod Washburn, L.E./Midland | 156 |

*Minimum 250 At-Bats   #Minimum 75 Innings

## TOP 10 PROSPECTS

**How the Angels Top 10 prospects, as judged by Baseball America prior to the 1996 season, fared in 1996:**

MEL BAILEY

**Todd Greene**

| Player, Pos. | Club (Class—League) | AVG | AB | R | H | 2B | 3B | HR | RBI | SB |
|---|---|---|---|---|---|---|---|---|---|---|
| 1. Darin Erstad, of | Vancouver (AAA—Pacific Coast) | .305 | 351 | 63 | 107 | 22 | 5 | 6 | 41 | 11 |
| | California | .284 | 208 | 34 | 59 | 5 | 1 | 4 | 20 | 3 |
| 2. Todd Greene, c | Vancouver (AAA—Pacific Coast) | .305 | 223 | 27 | 68 | 18 | 0 | 5 | 33 | 0 |
| | California | .190 | 79 | 9 | 15 | 1 | 0 | 2 | 9 | 2 |
| 4. Norm Hutchins, of | Cedar Rapids (A—Midwest) | .225 | 466 | 59 | 105 | 13 | 16 | 2 | 52 | 22 |
| 5. George Arias, 3b | Vancouver (AAA—Pacific Coast) | .337 | 243 | 49 | 82 | 24 | 0 | 9 | 55 | 2 |
| | California | .238 | 252 | 19 | 60 | 8 | 1 | 6 | 28 | 2 |
| 8. *Marquis Riley, of | Vancouver (AAA—Pacific Coast) | .234 | 47 | 8 | 11 | 2 | 0 | 0 | 0 | 3 |
| | Charlotte (AAA—International) | .227 | 300 | 43 | 68 | 10 | 0 | 0 | 13 | 16 |
| 10. Danny Buxbaum, 1b | Lake Elsinore (A—California) | .292 | 298 | 53 | 87 | 17 | 2 | 14 | 60 | 1 |

| Player, Pos. | Club (Class—League) | W | L | ERA | G | SV | IP | H | BB | SO |
|---|---|---|---|---|---|---|---|---|---|---|
| 3. Jarrod Washburn, lhp | Lake Elsinore (A—California) | 6 | 3 | 3.30 | 14 | 0 | 93 | 79 | 33 | 93 |
| | Midland (AA—Texas) | 5 | 6 | 4.40 | 13 | 0 | 88 | 77 | 25 | 68 |
| | Vancouver (AAA—Pacific Coast) | 0 | 2 | 10.80 | 2 | 0 | 8 | 12 | 12 | 5 |
| 6. Jason Dickson, rhp | Midland (AA—Texas) | 5 | 2 | 3.58 | 8 | 0 | 55 | 55 | 10 | 40 |
| | Vancouver (AAA—Pacific Coast) | 7 | 11 | 3.80 | 18 | 0 | 130 | 134 | 40 | 70 |
| | California | 1 | 4 | 4.57 | 7 | 0 | 43 | 52 | 18 | 20 |
| 7. Pete Janicki, rhp | Vancouver (AAA—Pacific Coast) | 2 | 9 | 6.75 | 31 | 1 | 104 | 135 | 37 | 86 |
| | Midland (AA—Texas) | 1 | 3 | 6.39 | 5 | 0 | 31 | 37 | 10 | 17 |
| 9. Jeremy Blevins, rhp | Boise (A—Northwest) | 2 | 3 | 6.60 | 14 | 0 | 59 | 54 | 58 | 39 |

*Claimed on waivers by Marlins

| Catcher | PCT | G | PO | A | E | DP | PB |
|---|---|---|---|---|---|---|---|
| Borders | .984 | 19 | 111 | 14 | 2 | 1 | 1 |
| Fabregas | .989 | 89 | 502 | 46 | 6 | 3 | 5 |
| Greene | 1.000 | 26 | 119 | 19 | 0 | 1 | 1 |
| Slaught | .992 | 59 | 338 | 27 | 3 | 2 | 5 |
| Turner | 1.000 | 3 | 2 | 2 | 0 | 0 | 0 |

| First Base | PCT | G | PO | A | E | DP |
|---|---|---|---|---|---|---|
| Aldrete | .000 | 1 | 0 | 0 | 0 | 0 |
| Howell | .917 | 2 | 11 | 0 | 1 | 1 |
| Hudler | .978 | 7 | 44 | 0 | 1 | 3 |
| Pritchett | 1.000 | 5 | 29 | 1 | 0 | 3 |
| Snow | .993 | 154 | 1274 | 103 | 10 | 134 |
| Wallach | .958 | 3 | 20 | 3 | 1 | 2 |

| Second Base | PCT | G | PO | A | E | DP |
|---|---|---|---|---|---|---|
| Easley | .960 | 9 | 13 | 11 | 1 | 2 |
| Eenhoorn | .889 | 2 | 4 | 4 | 1 | 1 |

| | PCT | G | PO | A | E | DP |
|---|---|---|---|---|---|---|
| Howell | .000 | 1 | 0 | 0 | 0 | 0 |
| Hudler | .982 | 53 | 97 | 116 | 4 | 35 |
| Schofield | 1.000 | 2 | 4 | 6 | 0 | 1 |
| Velarde | .982 | 114 | 236 | 251 | 9 | 80 |

| Third Base | PCT | G | PO | A | E | DP |
|---|---|---|---|---|---|---|
| Arias | .960 | 83 | 50 | 190 | 10 | 19 |
| Easley | 1.000 | 3 | 0 | 4 | 0 | 0 |
| Eenhoorn | 1.000 | 2 | 2 | 1 | 0 | 0 |
| Howell | .884 | 43 | 17 | 44 | 8 | 5 |
| Schofield | 1.000 | 1 | 0 | 1 | 0 | 0 |
| Velarde | .908 | 28 | 13 | 46 | 6 | 4 |
| Wallach | .941 | 46 | 27 | 85 | 7 | 4 |

| Shortstop | PCT | G | PO | A | E | DP |
|---|---|---|---|---|---|---|
| DiSarcina | .971 | 150 | 212 | 460 | 20 | 93 |
| Easley | .943 | 13 | 9 | 24 | 2 | 10 |

| | PCT | G | PO | A | E | DP |
|---|---|---|---|---|---|---|
| Eenhoorn | .875 | 4 | 1 | 6 | 1 | 1 |
| Schofield | .889 | 7 | 5 | 3 | 1 | 1 |
| Velarde | .938 | 7 | 6 | 9 | 1 | 2 |

| Outfield | PCT | G | PO | A | E | DP |
|---|---|---|---|---|---|---|
| Aldrete | .750 | 6 | 3 | 0 | 1 | 0 |
| Anderson | .979 | 146 | 316 | 5 | 7 | 1 |
| Edmonds | .997 | 111 | 280 | 6 | 1 | 2 |
| Erstad | .976 | 48 | 121 | 2 | 3 | 0 |
| Hudler | .971 | 21 | 32 | 1 | 1 | 0 |
| Palmeiro | 1.000 | 31 | 33 | 0 | 0 | 0 |
| Salmon | .975 | 153 | 299 | 13 | 8 | 0 |
| Turner | 1.000 | 1 | 1 | 0 | 0 | 0 |

MEL BAILEY

DAVID SEELIG

**Two Bright Lights.** The Angels finished last in the American League West, despite the efforts of former No. 1 draft pick Darin Erstad (.284-4-20), left, and outfielder Tim Salmon (.286-30-98)

# VANCOUVER

Class AAA

## PACIFIC COAST LEAGUE

| BATTING | AVG | G | AB | R | H | 2B | 3B | HR | RBI | BB | SO | SB | CS | B | T | HT | WT | DOB | 1st Yr | Resides |
|---|---|---|---|---|---|---|---|---|---|---|---|---|---|---|---|---|---|---|---|---|
| Arias, George | .337 | 59 | 243 | 49 | 82 | 24 | 0 | 9 | 55 | 20 | 38 | 2 | 1 | R | R | 5-11 | 190 | 3-12-72 | 1993 | Tucson, Ariz. |
| Burke, Jamie | .250 | 41 | 156 | 12 | 39 | 5 | 0 | 1 | 14 | 7 | 18 | 2 | 1 | R | R | 6-0 | 195 | 9-24-71 | 1993 | Roseburg, Ore. |
| Carvajal, Jovino | .239 | 77 | 272 | 29 | 65 | 6 | 2 | 4 | 31 | 14 | 38 | 17 | 7 | S | R | 6-1 | 160 | 9-2-68 | 1987 | La Romana, D.R. |
| Coleman, Vince | .207 | 21 | 87 | 9 | 18 | 2 | 1 | 0 | 5 | 9 | 15 | 4 | 1 | S | R | 6-1 | 185 | 9-22-61 | 1982 | St. Louis, Mo. |
| Diaz, Freddy | .260 | 34 | 123 | 19 | 32 | 9 | 2 | 3 | 23 | 14 | 25 | 0 | 0 | S | R | 5-11 | 175 | 9-10-72 | 1992 | El Monte, Calif. |
| Easley, Damion | .313 | 12 | 48 | 13 | 15 | 2 | 1 | 2 | 8 | 9 | 6 | 4 | 1 | R | R | 5-11 | 155 | 11-11-69 | 1989 | Glendale, Ariz. |
| Erstad, Darin | .305 | 85 | 351 | 63 | 107 | 22 | 5 | 6 | 41 | 44 | 53 | 11 | 6 | L | L | 6-2 | 195 | 6-4-74 | 1995 | Jamestown, N.D. |
| Fabregas, Jorge | .297 | 10 | 37 | 4 | 11 | 3 | 0 | 0 | 5 | 4 | 4 | 0 | 0 | L | R | 6-3 | 205 | 3-13-70 | 1991 | Miami, Fla. |
| Forbes, P.J. | .274 | 117 | 409 | 58 | 112 | 24 | 2 | 0 | 46 | 42 | 44 | 4 | 3 | R | R | 5-10 | 160 | 9-22-67 | 1990 | Pittsburg, Kan. |
| Grebeck, Brian | .232 | 78 | 237 | 25 | 55 | 10 | 3 | 1 | 27 | 34 | 27 | 1 | 1 | R | R | 5-7 | 160 | 8-31-67 | 1990 | Cerritos, Calif. |
| Greene, Todd | .305 | 60 | 223 | 27 | 68 | 18 | 0 | 5 | 33 | 16 | 36 | 0 | 2 | R | R | 5-10 | 195 | 5-8-71 | 1993 | Martinez, Ga. |
| Ledesma, Aaron | .305 | 109 | 440 | 60 | 134 | 27 | 4 | 1 | 51 | 32 | 59 | 2 | 3 | R | R | 6-2 | 200 | 6-3-71 | 1990 | Union City, Calif. |
| Martinez, Ray | .253 | 24 | 87 | 8 | 22 | 5 | 2 | 0 | 10 | 1 | 13 | 1 | 0 | R | R | 6-0 | 165 | 10-1-68 | 1987 | Highland Park, Calif. |
| Orton, John | .056 | 6 | 18 | 0 | 1 | 0 | 0 | 0 | 0 | 2 | 5 | 0 | 0 | R | R | 6-1 | 192 | 12-8-65 | 1987 | Atascadero, Calif. |
| Palmeiro, Orlando | .306 | 62 | 245 | 40 | 75 | 13 | 4 | 0 | 33 | 30 | 19 | 7 | 3 | L | R | 5-11 | 155 | 1-19-69 | 1991 | Miami, Fla. |
| Pennyfeather, William | .283 | 108 | 413 | 56 | 117 | 36 | 3 | 5 | 63 | 19 | 71 | 19 | 11 | R | R | 6-2 | 215 | 5-25-68 | 1988 | Perth Amboy, N.J. |
| Pritchett, Chris | .295 | 130 | 485 | 78 | 143 | 39 | 1 | 16 | 73 | 71 | 96 | 5 | 4 | L | R | 6-4 | 185 | 1-31-70 | 1991 | Modesto, Calif. |
| Riley, Marquis | .234 | 12 | 47 | 8 | 11 | 2 | 0 | 0 | 0 | 3 | 12 | 3 | 0 | R | R | 5-10 | 170 | 12-27-70 | 1992 | Ashdown, Ark. |
| Takayoshi, Todd | .286 | 3 | 7 | 1 | 2 | 0 | 0 | 0 | 2 | 0 | 0 | 0 | 0 | L | R | 6-1 | 190 | 10-4-70 | 1993 | Honolulu, Hawaii |
| Tejero, Fausto | .200 | 54 | 155 | 21 | 31 | 4 | 1 | 1 | 12 | 22 | 41 | 0 | 1 | R | R | 6-2 | 205 | 10-26-68 | 1990 | Hialeah, Fla. |
| Turner, Chris | .256 | 113 | 390 | 51 | 100 | 19 | 1 | 2 | 47 | 61 | 85 | 1 | 3 | R | R | 6-1 | 190 | 3-23-69 | 1991 | Bowling Green, Ky. |
| Wolff, Mike | .250 | 71 | 256 | 46 | 64 | 15 | 3 | 10 | 38 | 34 | 69 | 6 | 4 | R | R | 6-1 | 195 | 12-19-70 | 1992 | Wilmington, N.C. |

| PITCHING | W | L | ERA | G | GS | CG | SV | IP | H | R | ER | BB | SO | B | T | HT | WT | DOB | 1st Yr | Resides |
|---|---|---|---|---|---|---|---|---|---|---|---|---|---|---|---|---|---|---|---|---|
| Abbott, Jim | 0 | 2 | 3.41 | 4 | 4 | 1 | 0 | 29 | 16 | 12 | 11 | 20 | 20 | L | L | 6-3 | 210 | 9-19-67 | 1989 | Newport Beach, Calif. |
| Dickson, Jason | 7 | 11 | 3.80 | 18 | 18 | 7 | 0 | 130 | 134 | 73 | 55 | 40 | 70 | L | R | 6-0 | 190 | 3-30-73 | 1994 | Chatham, N.B. |
| Edenfield, Ken | 2 | 4 | 2.81 | 19 | 0 | 0 | 0 | 32 | 26 | 13 | 10 | 20 | 18 | R | R | 6-1 | 165 | 3-18-67 | 1990 | Knoxville, Tenn. |
| Edsell, Geoff | 4 | 6 | 3.43 | 15 | 15 | 3 | 0 | 105 | 93 | 45 | 40 | 45 | 48 | R | R | 6-2 | 195 | 12-10-71 | 1993 | Muncy, Pa. |
| Ellis, Robert | 2 | 3 | 3.25 | 7 | 7 | 1 | 0 | 44 | 30 | 19 | 16 | 28 | 29 | R | R | 6-5 | 220 | 12-15-70 | 1990 | Baton Rouge, La. |
| Freehill, Mike | 1 | 1 | 9.90 | 7 | 0 | 0 | 0 | 10 | 16 | 11 | 11 | 8 | 5 | R | R | 6-3 | 177 | 6-2-71 | 1994 | Phoenix, Ariz. |
| Frohwirth, Todd | 0 | 1 | 3.21 | 9 | 0 | 0 | 2 | 14 | 11 | 5 | 5 | 3 | 13 | R | R | 6-4 | 204 | 9-28-62 | 1984 | Milwaukee, Wis. |
| Grimsley, Jason | 2 | 0 | 1.20 | 2 | 2 | 1 | 0 | 15 | 8 | 2 | 2 | 3 | 13 | R | R | 6-3 | 180 | 8-7-67 | 1985 | Cleveland, Texas |
| Hancock, Ryan | 4 | 6 | 3.70 | 19 | 11 | 1 | 0 | 80 | 69 | 38 | 33 | 38 | 65 | R | R | 6-2 | 220 | 11-11-71 | 1993 | Cupertino, Calif. |
| Harris, Pep | 9 | 3 | 4.56 | 18 | 18 | 1 | 0 | 118 | 135 | 67 | 60 | 46 | 61 | R | R | 6-2 | 185 | 9-23-72 | 1991 | Lancaster, S.C. |
| Holdridge, David | 2 | 1 | 4.63 | 29 | 0 | 0 | 1 | 35 | 39 | 19 | 18 | 23 | 26 | R | R | 6-3 | 195 | 2-5-69 | 1988 | Huntington Beach, Calif. |
| Janicki, Pete | 2 | 9 | 6.75 | 31 | 14 | 0 | 1 | 104 | 135 | 82 | 78 | 37 | 86 | R | R | 6-4 | 190 | 1-26-71 | 1992 | Mesa, Ariz. |
| Leftwich, Phil | 6 | 6 | 5.15 | 19 | 19 | 3 | 0 | 110 | 113 | 75 | 63 | 41 | 87 | R | R | 6-5 | 205 | 5-19-69 | 1990 | Mesa, Ariz. |
| Novoa, Rafael | 1 | 1 | 7.11 | 13 | 0 | 0 | 1 | 13 | 19 | 10 | 10 | 5 | 10 | L | L | 6-1 | 180 | 10-26-67 | 1989 | Phoenix, Ariz. |
| Pennington, Brad | 3 | 0 | 4.23 | 11 | 2 | 0 | 1 | 28 | 20 | 20 | 13 | 22 | 43 | L | L | 6-6 | 215 | 4-14-69 | 1989 | Salem, Ind. |
| Rosselli, Joe | 2 | 3 | 2.91 | 47 | 0 | 0 | 3 | 59 | 53 | 22 | 19 | 26 | 37 | R | L | 6-1 | 170 | 5-28-72 | 1990 | Woodland Hills, Calif. |
| Schmidt, Jeff | 0 | 1 | 2.87 | 35 | 0 | 0 | 19 | 38 | 29 | 12 | 12 | 25 | 19 | R | R | 6-5 | 210 | 2-21-71 | 1992 | La Crosse, Wis. |
| Springer, Dennis | 10 | 3 | 2.72 | 16 | 12 | 6 | 0 | 109 | 89 | 35 | 33 | 36 | 78 | R | R | 5-10 | 185 | 2-12-65 | 1987 | Fresno, Calif. |
| Swingle, Paul | 2 | 2 | 3.00 | 15 | 0 | 0 | 1 | 24 | 20 | 10 | 8 | 11 | 24 | R | R | 6-0 | 185 | 12-21-66 | 1989 | Mesa, Ariz. |
| VanRyn, Ben | 3 | 3 | 3.89 | 18 | 1 | 0 | 0 | 35 | 35 | 17 | 15 | 13 | 28 | L | L | 6-5 | 195 | 8-9-71 | 1990 | Kendallville, Ind. |
| Washburn, Jarrod | 0 | 2 | 10.80 | 2 | 2 | 0 | 0 | 8 | 12 | 16 | 10 | 12 | 5 | L | L | 6-1 | 185 | 8-13-74 | 1995 | Webster, Wis. |
| Williams, Shad | 6 | 2 | 3.96 | 15 | 13 | 1 | 0 | 75 | 73 | 36 | 33 | 28 | 57 | R | R | 6-0 | 185 | 3-10-71 | 1991 | Fresno, Calif. |

## FIELDING

| Catcher | PCT | G | PO | A | E | DP | PB |
|---|---|---|---|---|---|---|---|
| Burke | .969 | 5 | 28 | 3 | 1 | 2 | 0 |
| Fabregas | 1.000 | 3 | 13 | 1 | 0 | 0 | 0 |
| Greene | .988 | 42 | 219 | 37 | 3 | 6 | 8 |
| Orton | 1.000 | 3 | 21 | 2 | 0 | 2 | 0 |
| Takayoshi | 1.000 | 3 | 15 | 0 | 0 | 0 | 0 |
| Tejero | .988 | 49 | 287 | 49 | 4 | 7 | 2 |
| Turner | .987 | 42 | 267 | 27 | 4 | 3 | 3 |

| First Base | PCT | G | PO | A | E | DP |
|---|---|---|---|---|---|---|
| Erstad | 1.000 | 3 | 25 | 6 | 0 | 5 |
| Fabregas | 1.000 | 1 | 14 | 1 | 0 | 0 |
| Pritchett | .995 | 125 | 1107 | 98 | 6 | 107 |
| Tejero | 1.000 | 1 | 10 | 0 | 0 | 0 |
| Turner | 1.000 | 9 | 85 | 6 | 0 | 9 |

| Second Base | PCT | G | PO | A | E | DP |
|---|---|---|---|---|---|---|
| Diaz | .981 | 9 | 24 | 29 | 1 | 8 |
| Easley | 1.000 | 2 | 6 | 4 | 0 | 0 |

| | PCT | G | PO | A | E | DP |
|---|---|---|---|---|---|---|
| Forbes | .986 | 107 | 221 | 281 | 7 | 67 |
| Grebeck | 1.000 | 15 | 30 | 44 | 0 | 10 |
| Martinez | .981 | 10 | 26 | 26 | 1 | 12 |

| Third Base | PCT | G | PO | A | E | DP |
|---|---|---|---|---|---|---|
| Arias | .969 | 59 | 50 | 135 | 6 | 14 |
| Burke | .938 | 21 | 9 | 52 | 4 | 4 |
| Diaz | .960 | 10 | 5 | 19 | 1 | 3 |
| Easley | .000 | 1 | 0 | 0 | 0 | 0 |
| Forbes | .938 | 8 | 10 | 20 | 2 | 3 |
| Grebeck | .978 | 27 | 19 | 69 | 2 | 2 |
| Ledesma | .917 | 3 | 3 | 8 | 1 | 2 |
| Turner | .875 | 12 | 6 | 22 | 4 | 4 |

| Shortstop | PCT | G | PO | A | E | DP |
|---|---|---|---|---|---|---|
| Diaz | .900 | 8 | 12 | 24 | 4 | 8 |
| Easley | .947 | 10 | 14 | 22 | 2 | 4 |
| Forbes | 1.000 | 1 | 4 | 7 | 0 | 1 |

| | PCT | G | PO | A | E | DP |
|---|---|---|---|---|---|---|
| Grebeck | .951 | 22 | 33 | 64 | 5 | 20 |
| Ledesma | .955 | 93 | 147 | 253 | 19 | 55 |
| Martinez | .857 | 12 | 17 | 25 | 7 | 6 |

| Outfield | PCT | G | PO | A | E | DP |
|---|---|---|---|---|---|---|
| Burke | 1.000 | 7 | 8 | 0 | 0 | 0 |
| Carvajal | .955 | 61 | 102 | 4 | 5 | 2 |
| Coleman | .960 | 12 | 24 | 0 | 1 | 0 |
| Diaz | 1.000 | 1 | 6 | 0 | 0 | 0 |
| Erstad | .994 | 81 | 159 | 4 | 1 | 1 |
| Forbes | .000 | 1 | 0 | 0 | 0 | 0 |
| Grebeck | 1.000 | 4 | 11 | 1 | 0 | 0 |
| Palmeiro | .959 | 62 | 113 | 4 | 5 | 0 |
| Pennyfeather | .972 | 90 | 198 | 13 | 6 | 6 |
| Pritchett | 1.000 | 3 | 9 | 0 | 0 | 0 |
| Riley | 1.000 | 12 | 18 | 1 | 0 | 0 |
| Turner | 1.000 | 22 | 38 | 2 | 0 | 0 |
| Wolff | .985 | 67 | 130 | 5 | 2 | 1 |

# MIDLAND — Class AA
## TEXAS LEAGUE

| BATTING | AVG | G | AB | R | H | 2B | 3B | HR | RBI | BB | SO | SB | CS | B | T | HT | WT | DOB | 1st Yr | Resides |
|---|---|---|---|---|---|---|---|---|---|---|---|---|---|---|---|---|---|---|---|---|
| Alfonzo, Edgar | .274 | 83 | 310 | 37 | 85 | 22 | 1 | 4 | 40 | 24 | 45 | 1 | 2 | R | R | 6-0 | 167 | 6-10-67 | 1985 | Santa Teresa, Venez. |
| Betten, Randy | .171 | 28 | 82 | 5 | 14 | 2 | 0 | 0 | 5 | 5 | 19 | 3 | 1 | R | R | 5-11 | 170 | 7-28-71 | 1995 | Highland, Calif. |
| Boykin, Tyrone | .252 | 49 | 127 | 27 | 32 | 10 | 1 | 6 | 30 | 36 | 28 | 0 | 2 | R | R | 6-0 | 195 | 4-25-68 | 1991 | Columbia, S.C. |
| Bryant, Ralph | .208 | 60 | 216 | 33 | 45 | 16 | 0 | 9 | 26 | 19 | 75 | 1 | 1 | L | R | 6-2 | 225 | 5-20-61 | 1993 | Leesburg, Ga. |
| Burke, Jamie | .319 | 45 | 144 | 24 | 46 | 8 | 2 | 2 | 16 | 20 | 22 | 1 | 1 | R | R | 6-0 | 195 | 9-24-71 | 1993 | Roseburg, Ore. |
| Carvajal, Jovino | .269 | 41 | 160 | 20 | 43 | 5 | 2 | 2 | 22 | 10 | 24 | 7 | 7 | S | R | 6-1 | 160 | 9-2-68 | 1987 | La Romana, D.R. |
| Christian, Eddie | .305 | 107 | 426 | 59 | 130 | 30 | 5 | 5 | 46 | 36 | 72 | 7 | 9 | S | L | 5-11 | 180 | 8-26-71 | 1992 | Richmond, Calif. |
| Davalillo, David | .171 | 25 | 82 | 6 | 14 | 1 | 0 | 0 | 5 | 4 | 16 | 2 | 0 | R | R | 5-8 | 170 | 8-17-74 | 1993 | Santa Teresa, Venez. |
| Diaz, Freddy | .199 | 54 | 156 | 23 | 31 | 7 | 2 | 3 | 18 | 13 | 43 | 1 | 1 | S | R | 5-11 | 175 | 9-10-72 | 1992 | El Monte, Calif. |
| Doty, Derrin | .272 | 50 | 158 | 32 | 43 | 10 | 3 | 5 | 25 | 25 | 29 | 3 | 5 | R | R | 6-2 | 220 | 6-3-70 | 1993 | Oak Harbor, Wash. |
| Easley, Damion | .429 | 4 | 14 | 1 | 6 | 2 | 0 | 0 | 2 | 0 | 1 | 0 | 0 | R | R | 5-11 | 155 | 11-11-69 | 1989 | Glendale, Calif. |
| Glenn, Leon | .213 | 94 | 319 | 30 | 68 | 14 | 2 | 10 | 53 | 23 | 86 | 8 | 9 | R | R | 6-2 | 200 | 9-16-69 | 1988 | Louisville, Miss. |
| Guiel, Aaron | .269 | 129 | 439 | 72 | 118 | 29 | 7 | 10 | 48 | 56 | 71 | 11 | 7 | L | R | 5-10 | 190 | 10-5-72 | 1993 | Langley, B.C. |
| Luuloa, Keith | .260 | 134 | 531 | 80 | 138 | 24 | 2 | 7 | 44 | 47 | 54 | 4 | 6 | R | R | 6-1 | 175 | 12-24-74 | 1994 | Kaunakakai, Hawaii |
| McNeely, Jeff | .240 | 36 | 125 | 11 | 30 | 8 | 1 | 0 | 18 | 19 | 27 | 2 | 1 | R | R | 6-2 | 200 | 10-18-69 | 1989 | Monroe, N.C. |
| Moeder, Tony | .224 | 23 | 85 | 19 | 19 | 3 | 1 | 5 | 7 | 12 | 30 | 0 | 0 | R | R | 6-2 | 205 | 7-14-71 | 1994 | San Diego, Calif. |
| Molina, Ben | .274 | 108 | 365 | 45 | 100 | 21 | 2 | 8 | 54 | 25 | 25 | 0 | 1 | R | R | 5-11 | 190 | 7-20-74 | 1993 | Vega Alta, P.R. |
| Monzon, Jose | .279 | 43 | 140 | 15 | 39 | 4 | 0 | 3 | 22 | 9 | 22 | 1 | 0 | R | R | 5-11 | 178 | 11-8-68 | 1987 | Municipio Vargas, Venez. |
| Ortiz, Bo | .296 | 127 | 507 | 73 | 150 | 32 | 5 | 11 | 64 | 32 | 80 | 12 | 7 | R | R | 5-11 | 170 | 4-4-70 | 1991 | Hartford, Conn. |
| Shockey, Greg | .317 | 98 | 325 | 58 | 103 | 26 | 6 | 7 | 58 | 40 | 63 | 2 | 2 | L | L | 6-1 | 190 | 4-11-70 | 1992 | Huntington Beach, Calif. |

| PITCHING | W | L | ERA | G | GS | CG | SV | IP | H | R | ER | BB | SO | B | T | HT | WT | DOB | 1st Yr | Resides |
|---|---|---|---|---|---|---|---|---|---|---|---|---|---|---|---|---|---|---|---|---|
| Abbott, Kyle | 3 | 5 | 4.50 | 15 | 15 | 0 | 0 | 88 | 93 | 52 | 44 | 34 | 48 | L | L | 6-4 | 195 | 2-18-68 | 1989 | Cherry Hill, N.J. |
| Beaumont, Matt | 7 | 16 | 5.85 | 28 | 28 | 2 | 0 | 162 | 198 | 124 | 105 | 71 | 132 | L | L | 6-3 | 210 | 4-22-73 | 1994 | Rittman, Ohio |
| Bonanno, Pete | 1 | 2 | 5.32 | 23 | 6 | 1 | 2 | 64 | 79 | 44 | 38 | 23 | 52 | R | R | 6-0 | 195 | 1-5-71 | 1994 | Tampa, Fla. |
| Brown, Willard | 0 | 6 | 11.61 | 9 | 8 | 0 | 0 | 33 | 58 | 45 | 43 | 9 | 16 | R | R | 6-4 | 215 | 4-14-72 | 1993 | Marblehead, Mass. |
| Castillo, Carlos | 2 | 3 | 4.26 | 25 | 0 | 0 | 1 | 38 | 37 | 19 | 18 | 21 | 15 | R | R | 6-2 | 225 | 5-9-71 | 1991 | Anaheim, Calif. |
| Chavez, Tony | 2 | 4 | 4.21 | 31 | 0 | 0 | 1 | 73 | 81 | 40 | 34 | 25 | 52 | R | R | 5-11 | 180 | 10-22-70 | 1992 | Merced, Calif. |
| DeClue, Jon | 6 | 9 | 5.32 | 32 | 15 | 2 | 0 | 112 | 137 | 83 | 66 | 51 | 76 | R | R | 6-2 | 198 | 9-17-70 | 1994 | Apopka, Fla. |
| Dickson, Jason | 5 | 2 | 3.58 | 8 | 8 | 3 | 0 | 55 | 55 | 27 | 22 | 10 | 40 | L | R | 6-0 | 190 | 3-30-73 | 1994 | Chatham, N.B. |
| Doorneweerd, Dave | 1 | 2 | 5.79 | 9 | 1 | 0 | 0 | 19 | 25 | 15 | 12 | 12 | 20 | R | R | 6-2 | 195 | 9-29-72 | 1991 | New Port Richey, Fla. |
| Edsell, Geoff | 5 | 5 | 4.70 | 14 | 14 | 0 | 0 | 88 | 84 | 53 | 46 | 47 | 60 | R | R | 6-2 | 195 | 12-10-71 | 1993 | Muncy, Pa. |
| Freehill, Mike | 7 | 6 | 3.42 | 47 | 0 | 0 | 17 | 50 | 49 | 25 | 19 | 21 | 48 | R | R | 6-3 | 177 | 6-2-71 | 1994 | Phoenix, Ariz. |
| Goedhart, Darrell | 0 | 1 | 3.86 | 3 | 2 | 0 | 0 | 14 | 15 | 9 | 6 | 4 | 5 | R | R | 6-3 | 210 | 7-18-70 | 1989 | San Jacinto, Calif. |
| Harris, Pep | 2 | 2 | 5.31 | 6 | 6 | 1 | 0 | 39 | 47 | 27 | 23 | 9 | 28 | R | R | 6-2 | 185 | 9-23-72 | 1991 | Lancaster, S.C. |
| Hollinger, Adrian | 1 | 1 | 4.32 | 13 | 0 | 0 | 2 | 17 | 18 | 11 | 8 | 11 | 8 | L | R | 6-0 | 180 | 9-23-70 | 1991 | Mira Loma, Calif. |
| Holtz, Mike | 2 | 4 | 4.17 | 33 | 0 | 0 | 2 | 41 | 52 | 34 | 19 | 9 | 41 | L | L | 5-9 | 172 | 10-10-72 | 1994 | Ebensburg, Pa. |
| Ingram, Todd | 0 | 1 | 7.94 | 15 | 0 | 0 | 0 | 23 | 25 | 22 | 20 | 11 | 11 | R | R | 6-4 | 200 | 4-1-68 | 1991 | Bellevue, Wash. |

| PITCHING | W | L | ERA | G | GS | CG | SV | IP | H | R | ER | BB | SO | B | T | HT | WT | DOB | 1st Yr | Resides |
|---|---|---|---|---|---|---|---|---|---|---|---|---|---|---|---|---|---|---|---|---|
| Janicki, Pete | 1 | 3 | 6.39 | 5 | 5 | 0 | 0 | 31 | 37 | 28 | 22 | 10 | 17 | R | R | 6-4 | 190 | 1-26-71 | 1992 | Mesa, Ariz. |
| Keling, Korey | 0 | 1 | 6.90 | 17 | 1 | 0 | 1 | 30 | 42 | 29 | 23 | 14 | 13 | R | R | 6-5 | 210 | 11-24-68 | 1991 | Shawnee, Kan. |
| Leftwich, Phil | 4 | 2 | 2.90 | 6 | 6 | 1 | 0 | 40 | 33 | 14 | 13 | 4 | 33 | R | R | 6-5 | 205 | 5-19-69 | 1990 | Mesa, Ariz. |
| Novoa, Rafael | 1 | 0 | 6.66 | 19 | 0 | 0 | 2 | 24 | 28 | 20 | 18 | 12 | 16 | L | L | 6-1 | 180 | 10-26-67 | 1989 | Phoenix, Ariz. |
| Perisho, Matt | 3 | 2 | 3.21 | 8 | 8 | 0 | 0 | 53 | 48 | 22 | 19 | 20 | 50 | L | L | 6-0 | 190 | 6-8-75 | 1993 | Chandler, Ariz. |
| Sebach, Kyle | 2 | 0 | 7.59 | 4 | 4 | 0 | 0 | 21 | 31 | 20 | 18 | 15 | 11 | R | R | 6-4 | 195 | 9-6-71 | 1991 | Santee, Calif. |
| Washburn, Jarrod | 5 | 6 | 4.40 | 13 | 13 | 1 | 0 | 88 | 77 | 44 | 43 | 25 | 58 | L | L | 6-1 | 185 | 8-13-74 | 1995 | Webster, Wis. |

### FIELDING

| Catcher | PCT | G | PO | A | E | DP | PB |
|---|---|---|---|---|---|---|---|
| Burke | 1.000 | 8 | 42 | 6 | 0 | 0 | 0 |
| Glenn | 1.000 | 1 | 8 | 0 | 0 | 0 | 0 |
| Molina | .990 | 97 | 615 | 81 | 7 | 9 | 10 |
| Monzon | .967 | 40 | 214 | 48 | 9 | 4 | 11 |

| First Base | PCT | G | PO | A | E | DP |
|---|---|---|---|---|---|---|
| Betten | 1.000 | 8 | 30 | 1 | 0 | 2 |
| Boykin | .981 | 33 | 246 | 18 | 5 | 22 |
| Burke | .969 | 5 | 31 | 0 | 1 | 2 |
| Glenn | .991 | 90 | 716 | 45 | 7 | 82 |
| Moeder | .966 | 23 | 217 | 11 | 8 | 20 |

| Second Base | PCT | G | PO | A | E | DP |
|---|---|---|---|---|---|---|
| Alfonzo | 1.000 | 2 | 3 | 4 | 0 | 2 |
| Davalillo | 1.000 | 4 | 8 | 5 | 0 | 3 |
| Diaz | .000 | 1 | 0 | 0 | 0 | 0 |
| Guiel | .957 | 38 | 72 | 85 | 7 | 24 |

| | PCT | G | PO | A | E | DP |
|---|---|---|---|---|---|---|
| Luuloa | .968 | 100 | 267 | 278 | 18 | 83 |
| Ortiz | 1.000 | 3 | 5 | 6 | 0 | 3 |

| Third Base | PCT | G | PO | A | E | DP |
|---|---|---|---|---|---|---|
| Alfonzo | .929 | 39 | 21 | 84 | 8 | 3 |
| Betten | .935 | 14 | 9 | 34 | 3 | 5 |
| Burke | .929 | 16 | 14 | 25 | 3 | 1 |
| Diaz | .000 | 2 | 0 | 0 | 1 | 0 |
| Easley | .833 | 2 | 2 | 3 | 1 | 0 |
| Glenn | .800 | 4 | 1 | 3 | 1 | 0 |
| Guiel | .914 | 81 | 55 | 169 | 21 | 24 |

| Shortstop | PCT | G | PO | A | E | DP |
|---|---|---|---|---|---|---|
| Alfonzo | .945 | 36 | 45 | 110 | 9 | 14 |
| Betten | .944 | 9 | 8 | 26 | 2 | 4 |
| Davalillo | .947 | 21 | 33 | 57 | 5 | 20 |
| Diaz | .943 | 42 | 63 | 118 | 11 | 25 |

| | PCT | G | PO | A | E | DP |
|---|---|---|---|---|---|---|
| Easley | 1.000 | 2 | 3 | 9 | 0 | 2 |
| Luuloa | .903 | 39 | 40 | 119 | 17 | 27 |

| Outfield | PCT | G | PO | A | E | DP |
|---|---|---|---|---|---|---|
| Boykin | 1.000 | 3 | 2 | 0 | 0 | 0 |
| Bryant | .897 | 18 | 26 | 0 | 3 | 0 |
| Burke | .970 | 16 | 30 | 2 | 1 | 1 |
| Carvajal | 1.000 | 38 | 66 | 2 | 0 | 0 |
| Christian | .968 | 97 | 172 | 8 | 6 | 0 |
| Diaz | .000 | 1 | 0 | 0 | 0 | 0 |
| Doty | .947 | 39 | 51 | 3 | 3 | 0 |
| Glenn | .000 | 2 | 0 | 0 | 0 | 0 |
| Guiel | 1.000 | 6 | 11 | 0 | 0 | 0 |
| McNeely | .986 | 31 | 67 | 2 | 1 | 1 |
| Ortiz | .985 | 122 | 252 | 6 | 4 | 1 |
| Shockey | .992 | 61 | 118 | 8 | 1 | 4 |

# LAKE ELSINORE

**Class A**

## CALIFORNIA LEAGUE

| BATTING | AVG | G | AB | R | H | 2B | 3B | HR | RBI | BB | SO | SB | CS | B | T | HT | WT | DOB | 1st Yr | Resides |
|---|---|---|---|---|---|---|---|---|---|---|---|---|---|---|---|---|---|---|---|---|
| Betten, Randy | .259 | 74 | 274 | 32 | 71 | 15 | 3 | 3 | 34 | 22 | 49 | 11 | 3 | R | R | 5-11 | 170 | 7-28-71 | 1995 | Highland, Calif. |
| Bilderback, Ty | .267 | 42 | 150 | 21 | 40 | 10 | 0 | 3 | 22 | 17 | 38 | 4 | 2 | L | L | 6-2 | 180 | 10-29-73 | 1995 | El Centro, Calif. |
| Buxbaum, Danny | .292 | 74 | 298 | 53 | 87 | 17 | 2 | 14 | 60 | 31 | 41 | 1 | 0 | R | R | 6-4 | 217 | 1-17-73 | 1995 | Alachua, Fla. |
| Carter, Cale | .292 | 38 | 113 | 12 | 33 | 9 | 0 | 1 | 15 | 14 | 21 | 4 | 4 | L | R | 5-10 | 185 | 9-18-73 | 1996 | Tustin, Calif. |
| Christian, Eddie | .397 | 16 | 58 | 10 | 23 | 5 | 0 | 2 | 9 | 12 | 10 | 1 | 2 | S | L | 5-11 | 180 | 8-26-71 | 1992 | Richmond, Calif. |
| Dalton, Jed | .256 | 38 | 121 | 19 | 31 | 4 | 2 | 1 | 15 | 11 | 19 | 6 | 3 | R | R | 6-1 | 190 | 4-3-73 | 1995 | Omaha, Neb. |
| Dauphin, Phil | .229 | 67 | 245 | 43 | 56 | 13 | 1 | 8 | 38 | 36 | 52 | 8 | 3 | L | L | 6-1 | 180 | 5-11-69 | 1990 | Worthington, Ohio |
| Edmonds, Jim | .400 | 5 | 15 | 4 | 6 | 2 | 0 | 1 | 4 | 1 | 1 | 0 | 0 | L | L | 6-1 | 190 | 6-27-70 | 1988 | Diamond Bar, Calif. |
| Failla, Paul | .207 | 91 | 285 | 39 | 59 | 11 | 4 | 1 | 32 | 50 | 66 | 13 | 8 | S | R | 6-2 | 195 | 12-8-72 | 1994 | Sewickley, Pa. |
| Hemphill, Bret | .263 | 108 | 399 | 64 | 105 | 21 | 3 | 17 | 64 | 52 | 93 | 4 | 3 | S | R | 6-3 | 210 | 12-17-71 | 1994 | Santa Clara, Calif. |
| Henderson, Juan | .197 | 50 | 142 | 24 | 29 | 7 | 2 | 0 | 17 | 31 | 47 | 13 | 8 | R | R | 5-10 | 175 | 4-17-74 | 1993 | Santo Domingo, D.R. |
| Herrick, Jason | .319 | 58 | 210 | 35 | 67 | 13 | 2 | 6 | 30 | 25 | 52 | 5 | 4 | L | L | 6-0 | 175 | 7-29-73 | 1991 | Franklin, Wis. |
| Howell, Jack | .167 | 4 | 12 | 2 | 2 | 1 | 0 | 1 | 3 | 3 | 4 | 0 | 0 | L | R | 6-0 | 201 | 8-18-61 | 1983 | Tucson, Ariz. |
| Merullo, Matt | .222 | 9 | 36 | 8 | 8 | 2 | 0 | 1 | 6 | 5 | 7 | 0 | 0 | L | R | 6-2 | 200 | 8-4-65 | 1986 | Ridgefield, Conn. |
| Moeder, Tony | .307 | 94 | 339 | 57 | 104 | 21 | 2 | 14 | 66 | 38 | 92 | 3 | 3 | R | R | 6-2 | 205 | 7-14-71 | 1994 | San Diego, Calif. |
| Morris, Greg | .252 | 62 | 234 | 26 | 59 | 20 | 1 | 2 | 31 | 23 | 50 | 1 | 3 | R | R | 6-4 | 210 | 1-29-72 | 1994 | Carmichael, Calif. |
| Parker, Allan | .194 | 51 | 134 | 13 | 26 | 3 | 0 | 1 | 10 | 10 | 29 | 1 | 2 | R | R | 5-11 | 165 | 5-27-72 | 1994 | Hernando, Calif. |
| Reese, Mat | .500 | 2 | 2 | 1 | 1 | 0 | 0 | 0 | 2 | 0 | 0 | 0 | 0 | L | L | 6-3 | 205 | 5-3-71 | 1993 | Maricopa, Ariz. |
| Schofield, Dick | .250 | 2 | 4 | 1 | 1 | 0 | 0 | 0 | 1 | 1 | 0 | 1 | 0 | R | R | 5-10 | 178 | 11-21-62 | 1981 | Laguna Hills, Calif. |
| Smith, Chris | .266 | 63 | 241 | 38 | 64 | 12 | 2 | 10 | 45 | 24 | 35 | 1 | 1 | R | R | 5-11 | 180 | 1-14-74 | 1992 | Vallejo, Calif. |
| Takayoshi, Todd | .310 | 99 | 310 | 58 | 96 | 18 | 0 | 11 | 61 | 74 | 50 | 0 | 1 | L | R | 6-1 | 190 | 10-4-70 | 1993 | Honolulu, Hawaii |
| Tingley, Ron | .308 | 13 | 39 | 6 | 12 | 1 | 1 | 1 | 10 | 9 | 6 | 0 | 0 | R | R | 6-2 | 194 | 5-27-59 | 1977 | Riverside, Calif. |
| Urso, Joe | .291 | 125 | 474 | 106 | 138 | 47 | 2 | 9 | 66 | 75 | 57 | 6 | 2 | R | R | 5-7 | 160 | 7-28-70 | 1992 | Tampa, Fla. |
| Van Burkleo, Ty | .312 | 61 | 202 | 44 | 63 | 14 | 3 | 14 | 50 | 58 | 42 | 4 | 1 | L | L | 6-5 | 210 | 10-7-63 | 1982 | Mesa, Ariz. |
| Wolff, Mike | .286 | 12 | 42 | 12 | 12 | 3 | 0 | 2 | 7 | 9 | 10 | 3 | 0 | R | R | 6-1 | 195 | 12-19-70 | 1992 | Wilmington, N.C. |
| Young, Kevin | .290 | 114 | 462 | 78 | 134 | 17 | 3 | 2 | 39 | 50 | 58 | 24 | 14 | R | R | 6-0 | 195 | 1-22-72 | 1994 | Northville, Mich. |

**GAMES BY POSITION: C**—Hemphill 108, Merullo 8, Takayoshi 15, Tingley 10. **1B**—Betten 2, Buxbaum 73, Moeder 22, Morris 24, Takayoshi 12, Tingley 1, Van Burkleo 7, Wolff 5. **2B**—Failla 66, Henderson 20, Parker 2, Smith 27, Urso 37. **3B**—Betten 36, Howell 3, Morris 38, Parker 2, Smith 25, Urso 47. **SS**—Betten 22, Failla 20, Henderson 27, Parker 45, Schofield 2, Smith 5, Urso 42. **OF**—Betten 11, Bilderback 38, Carter 34, Christian 16, Dalton 34, Dauphin 67, Edmonds 3, Herrick 57, Moeder 68, Reese 1, Wolff 7, Young 113.

| PITCHING | W | L | ERA | G | GS | CG | SV | IP | H | R | ER | BB | SO | B | T | HT | WT | DOB | 1st Yr | Resides |
|---|---|---|---|---|---|---|---|---|---|---|---|---|---|---|---|---|---|---|---|---|
| Bonanno, Rob | 3 | 2 | 2.20 | 13 | 2 | 0 | 1 | 33 | 34 | 11 | 8 | 10 | 34 | R | R | 6-0 | 195 | 1-5-71 | 1994 | Tampa, Fla. |
| Castillo, Carlos | 2 | 3 | 3.68 | 27 | 0 | 0 | 13 | 29 | 26 | 16 | 12 | 8 | 27 | R | R | 6-2 | 225 | 5-9-71 | 1991 | Anaheim, Calif. |
| Chavez, Tony | 3 | 0 | 1.98 | 10 | 0 | 0 | 4 | 14 | 8 | 4 | 3 | 3 | 16 | R | R | 5-11 | 180 | 10-22-70 | 1992 | Merced, Calif. |
| Cooper, Brian | 7 | 9 | 4.21 | 26 | 23 | 1 | 0 | 162 | 177 | 100 | 76 | 39 | 155 | R | R | 6-1 | 175 | 8-19-74 | 1995 | Glendora, Calif. |
| Deakman, Josh | 8 | 10 | 5.02 | 27 | 25 | 2 | 0 | 163 | 188 | 109 | 91 | 56 | 115 | R | R | 6-5 | 185 | 2-25-74 | 1995 | Beaverton, Ore. |
| De la Cruz, Fernando | 0 | 0 | 8.59 | 5 | 0 | 0 | 0 | 7 | 8 | 12 | 7 | 10 | 3 | R | R | 6-0 | 175 | 1-25-71 | 1993 | La Romana, D.R. |
| Doorneweerd, Dave | 1 | 1 | 6.00 | 11 | 2 | 0 | 0 | 21 | 23 | 17 | 14 | 18 | 24 | R | R | 6-2 | 195 | 9-29-72 | 1991 | New Port Richey, Fla. |
| Eichhorn, Mark | 1 | 0 | 4.70 | 12 | 4 | 0 | 0 | 15 | 15 | 9 | 8 | 2 | 21 | R | R | 6-3 | 210 | 11-21-60 | 1979 | Aptos, Calif. |
| Goedhart, Darrell | 2 | 1 | 1.35 | 4 | 2 | 0 | 0 | 13 | 17 | 6 | 2 | 4 | 12 | R | R | 6-3 | 210 | 7-18-70 | 1989 | San Jacinto, Calif. |
| Harris, Bryan | 0 | 7 | 4.38 | 20 | 2 | 0 | 0 | 37 | 29 | 20 | 18 | 26 | 31 | L | L | 6-2 | 205 | 9-11-73 | 1993 | Peachtree City, Ga. |
| Haynes, Heath | 5 | 1 | 1.64 | 31 | 0 | 0 | 2 | 38 | 29 | 9 | 7 | 2 | 44 | R | R | 6-0 | 175 | 11-30-68 | 1991 | Wheeling, W.Va. |
| Hermanson, Mike | 0 | 3 | 4.11 | 29 | 0 | 0 | 0 | 35 | 40 | 25 | 16 | 22 | 30 | R | R | 6-3 | 195 | 11-26-71 | 1992 | Chicago, Ill. |
| Hill, Jason | 4 | 3 | 2.50 | 32 | 0 | 0 | 0 | 40 | 39 | 16 | 11 | 14 | 28 | R | L | 5-11 | 175 | 4-14-72 | 1994 | Redding, Calif. |
| Holdridge, David | 0 | 2 | 2.08 | 12 | 0 | 0 | 6 | 13 | 11 | 3 | 3 | 2 | 21 | R | R | 6-3 | 195 | 2-5-69 | 1988 | Huntington Beach, Calif. |
| Hollinger, Adrian | 1 | 0 | 1.56 | 12 | 0 | 0 | 0 | 17 | 15 | 6 | 3 | 11 | 15 | L | R | 6-0 | 180 | 9-23-70 | 1991 | Mira Loma, Calif. |
| Holzemer, Mark | 0 | 1 | 2.38 | 9 | 3 | 0 | 0 | 11 | 10 | 3 | 3 | 4 | 12 | L | L | 6-0 | 165 | 8-20-69 | 1988 | Littleton, Colo. |
| Keling, Korey | 0 | 0 | 6.60 | 12 | 0 | 0 | 0 | 15 | 21 | 15 | 11 | 14 | 10 | R | R | 6-5 | 210 | 11-24-68 | 1991 | Shawnee, Kan. |
| Langston, Mark | 0 | 0 | 0.00 | 1 | 1 | 0 | 0 | 4 | 3 | 0 | 0 | 0 | 5 | R | L | 6-2 | 184 | 8-20-60 | 1981 | Anaheim Hills, Calif. |
| Novoa, Rafael | 2 | 2 | 4.39 | 16 | 0 | 0 | 1 | 27 | 29 | 14 | 13 | 12 | 31 | L | L | 6-1 | 180 | 10-26-67 | 1989 | Phoenix, Ariz. |
| Ontiveros, Steve | 1 | 1 | 2.25 | 2 | 2 | 0 | 0 | 8 | 12 | 3 | 2 | 0 | 8 | R | R | 6-0 | 180 | 3-5-61 | 1982 | Stafford, Texas |
| Pennington, Brad | 0 | 0 | 0.00 | 2 | 0 | 0 | 0 | 3 | 0 | 0 | 0 | 2 | 5 | L | L | 6-6 | 215 | 4-14-69 | 1989 | Salem, Ind. |
| Perisho, Matt | 7 | 5 | 4.20 | 21 | 18 | 1 | 0 | 129 | 131 | 72 | 60 | 58 | 97 | L | L | 6-0 | 190 | 6-8-75 | 1993 | Chandler, Ariz. |

| PITCHING | W | L | ERA | G | GS | CG | SV | IP | H | R | ER | BB | SO | B | T | HT | WT | DOB | 1st Yr | Resides |
|---|---|---|---|---|---|---|---|---|---|---|---|---|---|---|---|---|---|---|---|---|
| Sanderson, Scott | 1 | 0 | 3.00 | 1 | 1 | 0 | 0 | 6 | 8 | 3 | 2 | 0 | 4 | R | R | 6-5 | 192 | 7-22-56 | 1977 | Northbrook, Ill. |
| Schoeneweis, Scott | 8 | 3 | 3.94 | 14 | 12 | 0 | 0 | 94 | 86 | 47 | 41 | 27 | 83 | L | L | 6-0 | 180 | 10-2-73 | 1996 | Mt. Laurel, N.J. |
| Sebach, Kyle | 8 | 4 | 5.58 | 26 | 13 | 0 | 0 | 110 | 124 | 73 | 68 | 31 | 105 | R | R | 6-4 | 195 | 9-6-71 | 1991 | Santee, Calif. |
| Sick, David | 1 | 0 | 7.15 | 16 | 0 | 0 | 1 | 23 | 25 | 19 | 18 | 14 | 17 | R | R | 6-2 | 195 | 10-31-71 | 1994 | Wilmington, N.C. |
| Skuse, Nick | 0 | 3 | 6.47 | 6 | 6 | 0 | 0 | 32 | 36 | 27 | 23 | 22 | 18 | R | R | 6-7 | 240 | 1-9-72 | 1994 | Los Gatos, Calif. |
| Smith, Lee | 0 | 0 | 9.00 | 1 | 1 | 0 | 0 | 1 | 1 | 2 | 1 | 1 | 1 | R | R | 6-6 | 269 | 12-4-57 | 1975 | Castor, La. |
| Thurmond, Travis | 2 | 2 | 3.93 | 6 | 5 | 0 | 0 | 37 | 36 | 18 | 16 | 17 | 39 | R | R | 6-3 | 200 | 12-8-73 | 1992 | Hillsboro, Ore. |
| Vermillion, Grant | 2 | 1 | 7.78 | 18 | 0 | 0 | 0 | 20 | 29 | 18 | 17 | 7 | 9 | R | R | 6-0 | 195 | 10-7-71 | 1995 | Sun City, Calif. |
| Washburn, Jarrod | 6 | 3 | 3.30 | 14 | 14 | 3 | 0 | 93 | 79 | 38 | 34 | 33 | 93 | L | L | 6-1 | 185 | 8-13-74 | 1995 | Webster, Wis. |

## CEDAR RAPIDS — Class A
### MIDWEST LEAGUE

| BATTING | AVG | G | AB | R | H | 2B | 3B | HR | RBI | BB | SO | SB | CS | B | T | HT | WT | DOB | 1st Yr | Resides |
|---|---|---|---|---|---|---|---|---|---|---|---|---|---|---|---|---|---|---|---|---|
| Barnes, Larry | .317 | 131 | 489 | 84 | 155 | 36 | 5 | 27 | 112 | 58 | 101 | 9 | 6 | L | L | 6-1 | 195 | 7-23-74 | 1995 | Bakersfield, Calif. |
| Baughman, Justin | .248 | 127 | 464 | 78 | 115 | 17 | 8 | 5 | 48 | 45 | 78 | 50 | 17 | R | R | 5-11 | 175 | 8-1-74 | 1995 | Reno, Nev. |
| Dalton, Jed | .280 | 79 | 304 | 52 | 85 | 16 | 1 | 12 | 47 | 23 | 38 | 20 | 8 | R | R | 6-1 | 190 | 4-3-73 | 1995 | Omaha, Neb. |
| Davalillo, David | .275 | 98 | 378 | 63 | 104 | 22 | 0 | 3 | 34 | 28 | 51 | 4 | 6 | R | R | 5-8 | 170 | 8-17-74 | 1993 | Santa Teresa, Venez. |
| Durrington, Trent | .250 | 25 | 76 | 12 | 19 | 1 | 0 | 0 | 4 | 33 | 20 | 15 | 2 | R | R | 5-10 | 185 | 8-27-75 | 1994 | Broadbeach, Australia |
| Graves, Bryan | .224 | 83 | 228 | 27 | 51 | 5 | 2 | 4 | 27 | 46 | 59 | 4 | 2 | R | R | 6-0 | 200 | 10-8-74 | 1995 | Bogalusa, La. |
| Ham, Kevin | .215 | 100 | 326 | 38 | 70 | 14 | 0 | 10 | 35 | 29 | 102 | 4 | 4 | R | R | 6-1 | 195 | 9-14-74 | 1993 | El Paso, Texas |
| Hutchins, Norm | .225 | 126 | 466 | 59 | 105 | 13 | 16 | 2 | 52 | 28 | 110 | 22 | 8 | S | L | 6-2 | 185 | 11-20-75 | 1994 | Greenburgh, N.Y. |
| Kane, Ryan | .258 | 125 | 485 | 56 | 125 | 29 | 2 | 14 | 75 | 40 | 120 | 5 | 5 | R | R | 6-4 | 210 | 1-25-74 | 1995 | Acton, Mass. |
| McAninch, John | .248 | 86 | 298 | 43 | 74 | 16 | 1 | 10 | 42 | 21 | 81 | 0 | 2 | R | R | 6-0 | 205 | 8-1-73 | 1995 | Oak Harbor, Wash. |
| Mota, Alfonso | .222 | 35 | 63 | 7 | 14 | 3 | 0 | 2 | 4 | 12 | 15 | 1 | 2 | L | R | 5-7 | 165 | 2-25-74 | 1992 | San Pedro de Macoris, D.R. |
| Reese, Mat | .071 | 9 | 14 | 0 | 1 | 0 | 0 | 0 | 0 | 0 | 5 | 0 | 0 | L | L | 6-3 | 205 | 5-3-71 | 1993 | Maricopa, Ariz. |
| Rodriguez, Juan | .240 | 8 | 25 | 3 | 6 | 0 | 1 | 0 | 3 | 1 | 6 | 2 | 1 | S | R | 5-10 | 185 | 12-16-74 | 1994 | Arecibo, P.R. |
| Ryder, Derek | .235 | 62 | 153 | 11 | 36 | 5 | 2 | 0 | 11 | 21 | 31 | 0 | 2 | R | R | 6-1 | 190 | 3-30-73 | 1995 | Wallingford, Pa. |
| Saucedo, Robert | .000 | 3 | 3 | 0 | 0 | 0 | 0 | 0 | 0 | 1 | 0 | 0 | 0 | R | R | 6-0 | 205 | 9-26-75 | 1994 | Guadalupe, Mexico |
| Stuart, Rich | .286 | 39 | 133 | 19 | 38 | 5 | 1 | 2 | 15 | 11 | 33 | 5 | 1 | R | R | 5-10 | 175 | 7-31-76 | 1994 | Arecibo, P.R. |
| Vallone, Gar | .225 | 66 | 151 | 21 | 34 | 4 | 0 | 1 | 14 | 30 | 55 | 2 | 5 | S | R | 6-00 | 175 | 5-9-73 | 1995 | Placentia, Calif. |
| Vander Griend, Jon | .263 | 122 | 434 | 72 | 114 | 32 | 2 | 9 | 64 | 51 | 142 | 9 | 5 | R | R | 6-4 | 225 | 4-25-72 | 1995 | Lynden, Wash. |

**GAMES BY POSITION: C**—Barnes 1, Davalillo 1, Graves 81, McAninch 13, Ryder 62. **1B**—Barnes 122, McAninch 9, Vallone 1, Vander Griend 8. **2B**—Davalillo 87, Durrington 24, Graves 1, Mota 15, Vallone 21. **3B**—Davalillo 4, Kane 120, Vallone 17. **SS**—Baughman 126, Davalillo 8, Vallone 2. **OF**—Barnes 1, Dalton 76, Ham 83, Hutchins 104, Mota 3, Reese 2, Rodriguez 8, Stuart 27, Vander Griend 91.

| PITCHING | W | L | ERA | G | GS | CG | SV | IP | H | R | ER | BB | SO | B | T | HT | WT | DOB | 1st Yr | Resides |
|---|---|---|---|---|---|---|---|---|---|---|---|---|---|---|---|---|---|---|---|---|
| Agosto, Stevenson | 8 | 10 | 4.42 | 28 | 28 | 1 | 0 | 157 | 143 | 91 | 77 | 86 | 121 | L | L | 5-10 | 175 | 9-2-75 | 1994 | Rio Grande, P.R. |
| Alvarez, Juan | 1 | 2 | 3.40 | 40 | 0 | 0 | 3 | 53 | 50 | 25 | 20 | 30 | 53 | L | L | 6-1 | 180 | 8-9-73 | 1995 | Miami, Fla. |
| Cintron, Jose | 10 | 8 | 3.88 | 28 | 28 | 1 | 0 | 179 | 192 | 88 | 77 | 41 | 127 | R | R | 6-2 | 185 | 9-12-75 | 1993 | Yabucoa, P.R. |
| Coe, Keith | 0 | 1 | 10.80 | 6 | 0 | 0 | 0 | 7 | 9 | 10 | 8 | 9 | 5 | R | R | 6-4 | 195 | 8-28-73 | 1994 | Jamesburg, N.J. |
| De la Cruz, Fernando | 0 | 5 | 8.00 | 6 | 6 | 0 | 0 | 27 | 35 | 25 | 24 | 21 | 18 | R | R | 6-0 | 175 | 1-25-71 | 1993 | La Romana, D.R. |
| Farfan, David | 0 | 1 | 2.35 | 5 | 0 | 0 | 1 | 8 | 8 | 9 | 2 | 6 | 4 | R | R | 5-7 | 185 | 5-30-74 | 1995 | Livermore, Calif. |
| Grenert, Geoff | 3 | 7 | 5.88 | 14 | 12 | 1 | 0 | 67 | 73 | 52 | 44 | 30 | 57 | R | R | 6-3 | 181 | 2-18-71 | 1993 | Scottsdale, Ariz. |
| Henderson, Juan | 3 | 0 | 3.15 | 19 | 0 | 0 | 2 | 34 | 25 | 14 | 12 | 19 | 22 | R | R | 5-10 | 175 | 4-17-74 | 1993 | Santo Domingo, D.R. |
| Hermanson, Mike | 0 | 0 | 5.74 | 4 | 3 | 0 | 0 | 16 | 15 | 11 | 10 | 9 | 12 | R | R | 6-3 | 195 | 11-26-71 | 1992 | Chicago, Ill. |
| Hill, Jason | 2 | 2 | 3.09 | 18 | 6 | 0 | 1 | 44 | 38 | 19 | 15 | 31 | 26 | R | L | 5-11 | 175 | 4-14-72 | 1994 | Redding, Calif. |
| Lloyd, John | 8 | 7 | 3.97 | 27 | 17 | 1 | 1 | 100 | 98 | 62 | 44 | 58 | 63 | R | R | 6-2 | 190 | 11-30-73 | 1992 | Jacksonville, Fla. |
| Mayer, Aaron | 1 | 4 | 4.13 | 18 | 5 | 0 | 4 | 48 | 53 | 28 | 22 | 20 | 31 | R | R | 6-6 | 230 | 8-13-74 | 1993 | San Ramon, Calif. |
| O'Quinn, James | 2 | 4 | 5.66 | 41 | 0 | 0 | 6 | 56 | 52 | 40 | 35 | 41 | 58 | L | L | 6-0 | 190 | 8-27-75 | 1995 | Jacksonville, Fla. |
| Petroff, Dan | 2 | 3 | 3.81 | 9 | 9 | 2 | 0 | 50 | 44 | 34 | 21 | 34 | 29 | R | R | 6-4 | 220 | 4-5-74 | 1994 | Punxsutawney, Pa. |
| Scutero, Brian | 10 | 5 | 3.27 | 53 | 0 | 0 | 3 | 88 | 74 | 38 | 32 | 43 | 52 | R | R | 6-1 | 190 | 8-15-73 | 1995 | Winter Park, Fla. |
| Sick, Dave | 1 | 2 | 2.00 | 26 | 0 | 0 | 16 | 27 | 27 | 10 | 6 | 13 | 19 | R | R | 6-2 | 195 | 10-31-71 | 1994 | Wilmington, N.C. |
| Skuse, Nick | 5 | 6 | 4.09 | 18 | 16 | 0 | 0 | 95 | 77 | 47 | 43 | 58 | 50 | R | R | 6-7 | 240 | 1-9-72 | 1994 | Los Gatos, Calif. |
| Stephens, Jason | 2 | 3 | 3.46 | 21 | 0 | 0 | 6 | 26 | 27 | 12 | 10 | 14 | 19 | R | R | 6-0 | 180 | 9-10-75 | 1996 | Springhill, La. |
| Sumter, Kevin | 0 | 0 | 6.75 | 3 | 0 | 0 | 0 | 3 | 4 | 2 | 2 | 1 | 4 | R | R | 6-0 | 185 | 9-4-72 | 1995 | Oakdale, Calif. |
| Thurmond, Travis | 2 | 0 | 1.55 | 4 | 4 | 1 | 0 | 29 | 20 | 6 | 5 | 14 | 29 | R | R | 6-3 | 200 | 12-8-73 | 1992 | Hillsboro, Ore. |
| Vermillion, Grant | 3 | 2 | 4.72 | 38 | 1 | 0 | 2 | 61 | 59 | 34 | 32 | 32 | 54 | R | R | 6-0 | 195 | 10-7-71 | 1995 | Sun City, Calif. |

## BOISE — Class A
### NORTHWEST LEAGUE

| BATTING | AVG | G | AB | R | H | 2B | 3B | HR | RBI | BB | SO | SB | CS | B | T | HT | WT | DOB | 1st Yr | Resides |
|---|---|---|---|---|---|---|---|---|---|---|---|---|---|---|---|---|---|---|---|---|
| Abbott, Chuck | .198 | 70 | 268 | 41 | 53 | 9 | 2 | 0 | 20 | 24 | 59 | 11 | 5 | R | R | 6-1 | 180 | 1-26-75 | 1996 | Schaumburg, Ill. |
| Byers, Scott | .280 | 66 | 257 | 31 | 72 | 19 | 1 | 6 | 39 | 27 | 21 | 0 | 0 | L | L | 6-1 | 210 | 9-9-73 | 1996 | Smyrna, Ga. |
| Castro, Nelson | .000 | 1 | 1 | 0 | 0 | 0 | 0 | 0 | 0 | 0 | 0 | 0 | 0 | S | R | 5-11 | 182 | 6-4-76 | 1994 | Villa Vasquez, D.R. |
| Curtis, Matt | .305 | 75 | 305 | 57 | 93 | 29 | 3 | 12 | 62 | 37 | 47 | 2 | 1 | S | R | 6-0 | 195 | 8-14-74 | 1996 | Visalia, Calif. |
| Durrington, Trent | .279 | 40 | 154 | 38 | 43 | 7 | 2 | 0 | 14 | 31 | 32 | 24 | 5 | R | R | 5-10 | 185 | 8-27-75 | 1994 | Broadbeach, Australia |
| Fefee, Theo | .301 | 41 | 156 | 23 | 47 | 3 | 3 | 3 | 25 | 7 | 44 | 1 | 2 | L | L | 6-3 | 190 | 4-26-74 | 1996 | Chicago, Ill. |
| Ferrer, Eduardo | .262 | 54 | 183 | 31 | 48 | 8 | 2 | 1 | 19 | 32 | 21 | 4 | 4 | R | R | 5-10 | 170 | 11-28-73 | 1996 | Rio Piedras, P.R. |
| Gillespie, Eric | .276 | 61 | 192 | 28 | 53 | 11 | 5 | 3 | 38 | 25 | 50 | 0 | 1 | L | R | 5-10 | 200 | 6-6-75 | 1996 | Long Beach, Calif. |
| Hobbie, Matt | .252 | 51 | 127 | 26 | 32 | 6 | 1 | 2 | 22 | 20 | 24 | 5 | 1 | L | L | 6-0 | 190 | 12-12-74 | 1993 | Bradenton, Fla. |
| Jackson, Wade | .282 | 43 | 117 | 11 | 33 | 5 | 2 | 2 | 25 | 17 | 25 | 5 | 1 | R | R | 5-11 | 190 | 1-25-74 | 1996 | Lake Forest, Calif. |
| Johnson, Patrick | .200 | 27 | 75 | 2 | 15 | 0 | 0 | 0 | 4 | 8 | 12 | 0 | 0 | R | R | 6-3 | 200 | 4-18-75 | 1996 | Taylorsville, Utah |
| Murphy, Nate | .286 | 67 | 266 | 58 | 76 | 18 | 1 | 7 | 41 | 41 | 63 | 12 | 4 | L | L | 6-1 | 190 | 4-15-75 | 1996 | Montague, Mass. |
| Neal, Rob | .289 | 47 | 173 | 36 | 50 | 13 | 1 | 5 | 35 | 20 | 40 | 3 | 1 | R | R | 6-0 | 195 | 1-28-73 | 1996 | Thousand Oaks, Calif. |
| Quesada, Travis | .100 | 10 | 20 | 3 | 2 | 0 | 1 | 0 | 0 | 7 | 7 | 0 | 1 | R | R | 6-4 | 200 | 4-18-75 | 1994 | Guatire, Venez. |
| Rodriguez, Juan | .297 | 52 | 192 | 24 | 57 | 9 | 0 | 2 | 28 | 12 | 52 | 3 | 3 | S | R | 5-10 | 185 | 12-16-74 | 1994 | Arecibo, P.R. |
| Saucedo, Robert | .500 | 1 | 2 | 2 | 1 | 0 | 0 | 0 | 1 | 3 | 0 | 0 | 0 | R | R | 6-0 | 205 | 9-26-75 | 1994 | Guadalupe, Mexico |
| Serrano, Danny | .143 | 8 | 7 | 3 | 1 | 0 | 0 | 0 | 1 | 2 | 0 | 0 | 0 | S | R | 5-10 | 190 | 2-16-75 | 1996 | Arecibo, P.R. |
| Soriano, Jacobo | .000 | 1 | 1 | 0 | 0 | 0 | 0 | 0 | 0 | 0 | 1 | 0 | 0 | R | R | 5-11 | 175 | 11-28-74 | 1992 | San Pedro de Macoris, D.R. |
| Stuart, Rich | .312 | 22 | 93 | 36 | 29 | 6 | 1 | 8 | 24 | 12 | 15 | 8 | 2 | R | R | 5-10 | 175 | 7-31-76 | 1994 | Arecibo, P.R. |
| t'Hoen, E.J. | .200 | 18 | 60 | 6 | 12 | 1 | 0 | 2 | 4 | 4 | 17 | 0 | 0 | R | R | 6-2 | 184 | 11-8-75 | 1996 | Alphen, Holland |
| Ussery, Brian | .261 | 39 | 115 | 15 | 30 | 5 | 0 | 0 | 18 | 31 | 1 | 0 | 0 | S | R | 6-0 | 180 | 2-25-74 | 1996 | Brandon, Fla. |

GAMES BY POSITION: C—Curtis 25, Johnson 26, Saucedo 1, Serrano 5, Ussery 38. 1B—Byers 64, Curtis 12, Rodriguez 12. 2B—Abbott 13, Durrington 35, Ferrer 32, Jackson 1, Quesada 8, Serrano 1, t'Hoen 3. 3B—Curtis 14, Durrington 4, Gillespie 52, Jackson 25. SS—Abbott 59, Castro 1, Durrington 8, t'Hoen 15. OF—Fefee 40, Ferrer 1, Hobbie 43, Jackson 6, Murphy 66, Neal 38, Rodriguez 42, Stuart 20.

| PITCHING | W | L | ERA | G | GS | CG | SV | IP | H | R | ER | BB | SO | B | T | HT | WT | DOB | 1st Yr | Resides |
|---|---|---|---|---|---|---|---|---|---|---|---|---|---|---|---|---|---|---|---|---|
| Blevins, Jeremy | 2 | 3 | 6.60 | 14 | 13 | 0 | 0 | 59 | 54 | 49 | 43 | 58 | 39 | R | R | 6-3 | 195 | 10-5-77 | 1995 | Bristol, Tenn. |
| Cowsill, Brendon | 1 | 0 | 1.57 | 16 | 0 | 0 | 6 | 23 | 19 | 5 | 4 | 9 | 26 | R | R | 6-3 | 190 | 1-7-75 | 1994 | Chula Vista, Calif. |
| Darrell, Tommy | 8 | 1 | 3.48 | 15 | 15 | 1 | 0 | 101 | 114 | 56 | 39 | 13 | 76 | R | R | 6-6 | 210 | 7-21-76 | 1995 | Dunbar, Pa. |
| De la Cruz, Fernando | 6 | 3 | 4.94 | 15 | 15 | 0 | 0 | 86 | 85 | 55 | 47 | 51 | 61 | R | R | 6-0 | 175 | 1-25-71 | 1993 | La Romana, D.R. |
| Greene, Danny | 0 | 3 | 3.86 | 9 | 0 | 0 | 1 | 12 | 12 | 6 | 5 | 8 | 12 | R | R | 6-3 | 220 | 2-24-73 | 1996 | Nashua, N.H. |
| Harriger, Mark | 0 | 0 | 8.31 | 7 | 0 | 0 | 0 | 4 | 9 | 5 | 4 | 3 | 3 | R | R | 6-2 | 196 | 4-29-75 | 1996 | Lakewood, Calif. |
| Hughes, Mike | 0 | 0 | 4.86 | 13 | 0 | 0 | 1 | 17 | 16 | 12 | 9 | 13 | 20 | R | R | 6-3 | 190 | 9-25-76 | 1996 | Fresno, Calif. |
| Humphreys, Kevin | 3 | 2 | 1.99 | 19 | 0 | 0 | 10 | 45 | 32 | 17 | 10 | 15 | 34 | R | R | 6-0 | 180 | 8-21-73 | 1996 | Panama City, Fla. |
| Johnson, Greg | 0 | 0 | 10.24 | 8 | 0 | 0 | 10 | 17 | 11 | 11 | 2 | 6 | L | L | 6-0 | 185 | 4-28-74 | 1995 | Frostburg, Md. |
| Mayer, Aaron | 1 | 0 | 1.00 | 5 | 0 | 0 | 0 | 9 | 6 | 2 | 1 | 3 | 11 | R | R | 6-6 | 230 | 8-13-74 | 1993 | San Ramon, Calif. |
| Ortiz, Ramon | 1 | 1 | 3.66 | 3 | 3 | 0 | 0 | 20 | 21 | 10 | 8 | 6 | 18 | R | R | 6-0 | 150 | 5-23-76 | 1995 | Cotui, D.R. |
| Patino, Leonardo | 6 | 5 | 1.61 | 30 | 0 | 0 | 6 | 56 | 37 | 15 | 10 | 21 | 71 | L | L | 6-2 | 190 | 11-24-73 | 1994 | Cali, Colombia |
| Plooy, Eric | 1 | 1 | 4.63 | 20 | 0 | 0 | 0 | 35 | 39 | 23 | 18 | 15 | 31 | R | R | 6-0 | 215 | 4-6-75 | 1996 | Hanford, Calif. |
| Puffer, Brandon | 2 | 0 | 4.45 | 16 | 0 | 0 | 1 | 30 | 27 | 19 | 15 | 11 | 22 | R | R | 6-3 | 172 | 10-5-75 | 1994 | Mission Viejo, Calif. |
| Riggan, Jerrod | 3 | 5 | 4.63 | 15 | 15 | 1 | 0 | 89 | 90 | 62 | 46 | 38 | 80 | R | R | 6-4 | 185 | 5-16-74 | 1996 | Brewster, Wash. |
| Rodriguez, Hector | 1 | 1 | 3.70 | 20 | 0 | 0 | 0 | 24 | 27 | 13 | 10 | 11 | 25 | R | R | 6-2 | 205 | 3-21-75 | 1996 | Caguas, P.R. |
| Stephens, Jason | 2 | 0 | 8.10 | 3 | 0 | 0 | 1 | 3 | 4 | 3 | 3 | 1 | 5 | R | R | 6-0 | 180 | 9-10-75 | 1996 | Springhill, La. |
| Stockstill, Jason | 0 | 0 | 12.38 | 2 | 2 | 0 | 0 | 8 | 12 | 11 | 11 | 10 | 7 | L | L | 6-5 | 200 | 11-13-76 | 1995 | Anaheim, Calif. |
| Volkman, Keith | 5 | 8 | 6.59 | 16 | 13 | 0 | 0 | 68 | 74 | 66 | 50 | 46 | 38 | L | L | 6-2 | 215 | 1-13-76 | 1994 | Pasadena, Md. |

## MESA — Rookie

### ARIZONA LEAGUE

| BATTING | AVG | G | AB | R | H | 2B | 3B | HR | RBI | BB | SO | SB | CS | B | T | HT | WT | DOB | 1st Yr | Resides |
|---|---|---|---|---|---|---|---|---|---|---|---|---|---|---|---|---|---|---|---|---|
| Antunez, Francisco | .214 | 5 | 14 | 2 | 3 | 0 | 0 | 1 | 1 | 1 | 6 | 0 | 0 | R | R | 5-10 | 180 | 2-11-73 | 1996 | Daytona Beach, Fla. |
| Castro, Nelson | .204 | 53 | 186 | 31 | 38 | 4 | 3 | 3 | 14 | 32 | 42 | 25 | 8 | S | R | 5-11 | 182 | 6-4-76 | 1994 | Villa Vasquez, D.R. |
| Charvel, Ali | .390 | 11 | 41 | 7 | 16 | 4 | 1 | 0 | 2 | 0 | 9 | 1 | 0 | L | L | 6-1 | 195 | 8-11-76 | 1994 | Mexicali, Mexico |
| Collier, Marc | .207 | 30 | 87 | 9 | 18 | 6 | 0 | 0 | 7 | 7 | 22 | 4 | 2 | R | R | 5-11 | 170 | 3-25-78 | 1996 | Hummelstown, Calif. |
| Delgado, Ariel | .229 | 47 | 166 | 21 | 38 | 6 | 1 | 1 | 11 | 20 | 38 | 15 | 2 | L | L | 6-2 | 193 | 9-11-76 | 1994 | Carolina, P.R. |
| DeJesus, Eddie | .264 | 48 | 178 | 27 | 47 | 11 | 3 | 1 | 25 | 7 | 35 | 12 | 3 | R | R | 6-4 | 230 | 4-29-75 | 1996 | Boca Chica, D.R. |
| Fefee, Theo | .286 | 13 | 49 | 14 | 14 | 2 | 3 | 1 | 8 | 6 | 9 | 4 | 0 | L | L | 6-3 | 190 | 4-26-74 | 1996 | Chicago, Ill. |
| Geronimo, Cesar | .281 | 33 | 121 | 9 | 34 | 9 | 1 | 0 | 16 | 8 | 11 | 3 | 1 | R | R | 6-0 | 180 | 12-19-75 | 1995 | Santo Domingo, D.R. |
| Knight, Marcus | .291 | 54 | 203 | 36 | 59 | 16 | 5 | 3 | 30 | 28 | 50 | 10 | 7 | S | R | 5-11 | 185 | 9-10-78 | 1996 | Pembroke Pines, Fla. |
| Lawrence, Mike | .179 | 38 | 117 | 9 | 21 | 2 | 0 | 0 | 12 | 11 | 28 | 1 | 3 | R | R | 6-5 | 200 | 2-18-76 | 1995 | Chico, Calif. |
| Llanos, Alex | .281 | 51 | 203 | 31 | 57 | 9 | 3 | 1 | 26 | 14 | 48 | 10 | 5 | S | R | 6-1 | 170 | 9-20-76 | 1995 | Carolina, P.R. |
| Russoniello, Mike | .080 | 13 | 25 | 1 | 2 | 0 | 0 | 0 | 1 | 1 | 10 | 0 | 1 | R | R | 6-0 | 195 | 5-29-77 | 1996 | Scottsdale, Ariz. |
| Saucedo, Robert | .281 | 18 | 64 | 5 | 18 | 5 | 0 | 1 | 13 | 8 | 11 | 1 | 1 | R | R | 6-0 | 205 | 9-26-75 | 1994 | Guadalupe, Mexico |
| Sears, Jayson | .214 | 4 | 14 | 4 | 3 | 0 | 1 | 0 | 2 | 3 | 4 | 1 | 0 | R | R | 6-0 | 200 | 2-17-76 | 1994 | Henderson, Texas |
| Serrano, Danny | .258 | 19 | 62 | 11 | 16 | 6 | 0 | 0 | 5 | 7 | 11 | 2 | 3 | S | R | 5-10 | 190 | 2-16-75 | 1996 | Arecibo, P.R. |
| Starkey, Nate | .246 | 42 | 138 | 15 | 34 | 9 | 1 | 1 | 22 | 14 | 39 | 3 | 2 | R | R | 6-0 | 205 | 10-8-76 | 1996 | Kaunakakai, Hawaii |
| Tolentino, Juan | .282 | 49 | 170 | 30 | 48 | 9 | 6 | 2 | 14 | 11 | 33 | 21 | 2 | R | R | 5-11 | 175 | 3-12-76 | 1995 | Bronx, N.Y. |
| Ventura, Jose | .169 | 32 | 59 | 13 | 10 | 2 | 1 | 0 | 5 | 13 | 26 | 11 | 1 | L | R | 5-11 | 180 | 11-29-77 | 1995 | San Fran. de Macoris, D.R. |

GAMES BY POSITION: C—Antunez 5, Russoniello 13, Saucedo 15, Sears 4, Serrano 18, Starkey 10. 1B—Delgado 26, DeJesus 11, Lawrence 23. 2B—Collier 23, Llanos 39. 3B—Collier 2, Lawrence 16, Llanos 14, Starkey 33. SS—Castro 53, Collier 5, Llanos 3. OF—Charvel 3, Delgado 24, DeJesus 32, Fefee 10, Geronimo 3, Knight 54, Serrano 1, Tolentino 40, Ventura 19.

| PITCHING | W | L | ERA | G | GS | CG | SV | IP | H | R | ER | BB | SO | B | T | HT | WT | DOB | 1st Yr | Resides |
|---|---|---|---|---|---|---|---|---|---|---|---|---|---|---|---|---|---|---|---|---|
| Ashley, Antonio | 3 | 0 | 5.26 | 17 | 0 | 0 | 1 | 26 | 32 | 17 | 15 | 7 | 21 | R | R | 6-4 | 242 | 11-15-76 | 1995 | Vallejo, Calif. |
| Leach, Jim | 0 | 0 | 9.82 | 5 | 0 | 0 | 0 | 4 | 3 | 5 | 4 | 5 | 3 | R | L | 6-3 | 165 | 1-25-78 | 1996 | Pinellas Park, Fla. |
| Leyva, Edgar | 4 | 7 | 3.94 | 14 | 13 | 1 | 0 | 82 | 79 | 53 | 36 | 27 | 74 | R | R | 6-1 | 195 | 7-27-77 | 1996 | Guasave, Mexico |
| Lopez, Jose | 1 | 2 | 6.75 | 6 | 4 | 0 | 0 | 31 | 30 | 24 | 23 | 18 | 27 | R | R | 6-1 | 170 | 9-30-76 | 1994 | Navojoa, Mexico |
| Margaritis, John | 0 | 1 | 6.57 | 7 | 0 | 0 | 0 | 12 | 19 | 10 | 9 | 3 | 11 | R | R | 6-1 | 195 | 8-12-76 | 1996 | Victoria, B.C. |
| McGuire, Brandon | 0 | 0 | 31.15 | 4 | 0 | 0 | 0 | 4 | 8 | 16 | 15 | 6 | 3 | S | R | 6-4 | 230 | 8-10-77 | 1995 | Big Spring, Texas |
| Ortiz, Jose | 2 | 1 | 6.20 | 14 | 0 | 0 | 2 | 25 | 23 | 17 | 17 | 21 | 32 | R | R | 6-1 | 185 | 1-10-78 | 1996 | Hayward, Calif. |
| Ortiz, Ramon | 5 | 4 | 2.12 | 16 | 8 | 2 | 1 | 68 | 55 | 28 | 16 | 27 | 78 | R | R | 6-0 | 150 | 5-23-76 | 1995 | Cotui, D.R. |
| Padilla, Charly | 1 | 0 | 9.00 | 9 | 0 | 0 | 0 | 10 | 12 | 10 | 10 | 4 | 7 | R | R | 6-4 | 165 | 9-11-78 | 1996 | San Felipe, Venez. |
| Puffer, Brandon | 0 | 1 | 3.60 | 1 | 1 | 0 | 0 | 5 | 7 | 2 | 2 | 1 | 3 | R | R | 6-3 | 172 | 10-5-75 | 1994 | Mission Viejo, Calif. |
| Rojas, Renney | 2 | 0 | 3.58 | 10 | 1 | 1 | 1 | 28 | 23 | 14 | 11 | 8 | 28 | R | R | 6-0 | 170 | 11-7-78 | 1996 | Maracaibo, Venez. |
| Romero, John | 2 | 3 | 4.03 | 14 | 11 | 0 | 1 | 67 | 63 | 43 | 30 | 27 | 53 | R | R | 6-2 | 175 | 9-5-78 | 1996 | Sylmar, Calif. |
| Soriano, Jacobo | 1 | 3 | 5.03 | 15 | 0 | 0 | 5 | 20 | 17 | 13 | 11 | 12 | 22 | R | R | 5-11 | 175 | 11-28-74 | 1992 | San Pedro de Macoris, D.R. |
| Steele, Brandon | 1 | 3 | 4.39 | 7 | 4 | 0 | 1 | 27 | 31 | 18 | 13 | 13 | 19 | R | R | 6-3 | 178 | 8-21-78 | 1996 | Huntington Beach, Calif. |
| Stockstill, Jason | 2 | 6 | 4.17 | 13 | 13 | 0 | 0 | 73 | 74 | 45 | 34 | 34 | 61 | L | L | 6-5 | 200 | 11-13-76 | 1995 | Anaheim, Calif. |
| Swingle, Paul | 0 | 1 | 0.00 | 1 | 1 | 0 | 0 | 1 | 6 | 9 | 0 | 1 | 1 | R | R | 6-0 | 185 | 12-21-66 | 1989 | Mesa, Ariz. |
| Torrealba, Aquiles | 0 | 0 | 8.44 | 5 | 0 | 0 | 0 | 5 | 9 | 5 | 5 | 1 | 0 | R | R | 6-5 | 180 | 9-29-78 | 1996 | San Mateo, Venez. |

# CHICAGO WHITE SOX

**Manager:** Terry Bevington.  **1996 Record:** 85-77, .525 (2nd, AL Central)

| BATTING | AVG | G | AB | R | H | 2B | 3B | HR | RBI | BB | SO | SB | CS | B | T | HT | WT | DOB | 1st Yr | Resides |
|---|---|---|---|---|---|---|---|---|---|---|---|---|---|---|---|---|---|---|---|---|
| Baines, Harold | .311 | 143 | 495 | 80 | 154 | 29 | 0 | 22 | 95 | 73 | 62 | 3 | 1 | L | L | 6-2 | 195 | 3-15-59 | 1977 | St. Michaels, Md. |
| Borders, Pat | .277 | 31 | 94 | 6 | 26 | 1 | 0 | 3 | 6 | 5 | 18 | 0 | 0 | R | R | 6-2 | 195 | 5-14-63 | 1982 | Lake Wales, Fla. |
| 2-team (19 Calif.) | .258 | 50 | 151 | 12 | 39 | 4 | 0 | 5 | 14 | 8 | 29 | 0 | 1 | | | | | | | |
| Cameron, Mike | .091 | 11 | 11 | 1 | 1 | 0 | 0 | 0 | 0 | 1 | 3 | 0 | 1 | R | R | 6-1 | 170 | 1-8-73 | 1991 | LaGrange, Ga. |
| Cedeno, Domingo | .158 | 12 | 19 | 2 | 3 | 2 | 0 | 0 | 3 | 0 | 4 | 1 | 0 | S | R | 6-1 | 170 | 11-4-68 | 1988 | La Romana, D.R. |
| 2-team (77 Toronto) | .272 | 89 | 301 | 46 | 82 | 12 | 2 | 2 | 20 | 15 | 64 | 6 | 3 | | | | | | | |
| Durham, Ray | .275 | 156 | 557 | 79 | 153 | 33 | 5 | 10 | 65 | 58 | 95 | 30 | 4 | S | R | 5-8 | 170 | 11-30-71 | 1990 | Charlotte, N.C. |
| Guillen, Ozzie | .263 | 150 | 499 | 62 | 131 | 24 | 8 | 4 | 45 | 10 | 27 | 6 | 5 | L | R | 5-11 | 164 | 1-20-64 | 1981 | Guarenas, Venez. |
| Karkovice, Ron | .220 | 111 | 355 | 44 | 78 | 22 | 0 | 10 | 38 | 24 | 93 | 0 | 0 | R | R | 6-1 | 215 | 8-8-63 | 1982 | Orlando, Fla. |
| Kreuter, Chad | .219 | 46 | 114 | 14 | 25 | 8 | 0 | 3 | 18 | 13 | 29 | 0 | 0 | S | R | 6-2 | 190 | 8-26-64 | 1985 | Arlington, Texas |
| Lewis, Darren | .228 | 141 | 337 | 55 | 77 | 12 | 2 | 4 | 53 | 45 | 40 | 21 | 5 | R | R | 6-0 | 180 | 8-28-67 | 1988 | San Mateo, Calif. |
| Machado, Robert | .667 | 4 | 6 | 1 | 4 | 1 | 0 | 0 | 2 | 0 | 0 | 0 | 0 | R | R | 6-1 | 150 | 6-3-73 | 1991 | Carabobo, Venez. |
| Martin, Norberto | .350 | 70 | 140 | 30 | 49 | 7 | 0 | 1 | 14 | 6 | 17 | 10 | 2 | S | R | 5-10 | 164 | 12-10-66 | 1984 | Hato Rey, P.R. |
| Martinez, Dave | .318 | 146 | 440 | 85 | 140 | 20 | 8 | 10 | 53 | 52 | 52 | 15 | 7 | L | L | 5-10 | 175 | 9-26-64 | 1983 | Safety Harbor, Fla. |
| Mouton, Lyle | .294 | 87 | 214 | 25 | 63 | 8 | 1 | 7 | 39 | 22 | 50 | 3 | 0 | R | R | 6-4 | 240 | 5-13-69 | 1991 | Lafayette, La. |
| Munoz, Jose | .259 | 17 | 27 | 7 | 7 | 0 | 0 | 0 | 1 | 4 | 1 | 0 | 0 | S | R | 5-11 | 165 | 11-11-67 | 1987 | Yabucoa, P.R. |
| Norton, Greg | .217 | 11 | 23 | 4 | 5 | 0 | 0 | 2 | 3 | 4 | 6 | 0 | 1 | S | R | 6-1 | 182 | 7-6-72 | 1993 | Walnut Creek, Calif. |
| Phillips, Tony | .277 | 153 | 581 | 119 | 161 | 29 | 3 | 12 | 63 | 125 | 132 | 13 | 8 | S | R | 5-10 | 175 | 4-25-59 | 1978 | Scottsdale, Ariz. |
| Robertson, Mike | .143 | 6 | 7 | 0 | 1 | 0 | 0 | 0 | 0 | 0 | 1 | 0 | 0 | L | L | 6-0 | 180 | 10-9-70 | 1991 | Placentia, Calif. |
| Slaught, Don | .250 | 14 | 36 | 2 | 9 | 1 | 0 | 0 | 4 | 2 | 2 | 0 | 0 | R | R | 6-1 | 190 | 9-11-58 | 1980 | Arlington, Texas |
| 2-team (62 Calif.) | .313 | 76 | 243 | 25 | 76 | 10 | 0 | 6 | 36 | 15 | 22 | 0 | 0 | | | | | | | |
| Snopek, Chris | .260 | 46 | 104 | 18 | 27 | 6 | 1 | 6 | 18 | 6 | 16 | 0 | 1 | R | R | 6-1 | 185 | 9-20-70 | 1992 | Cynthiana, Ky. |
| Tartabull, Danny | .254 | 132 | 472 | 58 | 120 | 23 | 3 | 27 | 101 | 64 | 128 | 1 | 2 | R | R | 6-1 | 210 | 10-30-62 | 1980 | Malibu, Calif. |
| Thomas, Frank | .349 | 141 | 527 | 110 | 184 | 26 | 0 | 40 | 134 | 109 | 70 | 1 | 1 | R | R | 6-5 | 257 | 5-27-68 | 1989 | Burr Ridge, Ill. |
| Ventura, Robin | .287 | 158 | 586 | 96 | 168 | 31 | 2 | 34 | 105 | 78 | 81 | 1 | 3 | L | R | 6-1 | 185 | 7-14-67 | 1989 | Santa Maria, Calif. |

| PITCHING | W | L | ERA | G | GS | CG | SV | IP | H | R | ER | BB | SO | B | T | HT | WT | DOB | 1st Yr | Resides |
|---|---|---|---|---|---|---|---|---|---|---|---|---|---|---|---|---|---|---|---|---|
| Alvarez, Wilson | 15 | 10 | 4.22 | 35 | 35 | 0 | 0 | 217 | 216 | 106 | 102 | 97 | 181 | L | L | 6-1 | 235 | 3-24-70 | 1987 | Maracaibo, Venez. |
| Andujar, Luis | 0 | 2 | 8.22 | 5 | 4 | 0 | 0 | 23 | 32 | 22 | 21 | 15 | 6 | R | R | 6-2 | 175 | 11-22-72 | 1991 | Bani, D.R. |
| Baldwin, James | 11 | 6 | 4.42 | 28 | 28 | 0 | 0 | 169 | 168 | 88 | 83 | 57 | 127 | R | R | 6-4 | 210 | 7-15-71 | 1990 | Southern Pines, N.C. |
| Bere, Jason | 0 | 1 | 10.26 | 5 | 5 | 0 | 0 | 17 | 26 | 19 | 19 | 18 | 19 | R | R | 6-3 | 185 | 5-26-71 | 1990 | Wilmington, Mass. |
| Bertotti, Mike | 2 | 0 | 5.14 | 15 | 2 | 0 | 0 | 28 | 28 | 18 | 16 | 20 | 19 | L | L | 6-1 | 185 | 1-18-70 | 1991 | Highland Mills, N.Y. |
| Castillo, Tony | 3 | 1 | 1.59 | 15 | 0 | 0 | 1 | 23 | 23 | 7 | 4 | 9 | 15 | L | L | 5-10 | 190 | 3-1-63 | 1983 | Lara, Venez. |
| 2-team (40 Toronto) | 5 | 4 | 3.60 | 55 | 0 | 0 | 2 | 95 | 95 | 45 | 38 | 24 | 57 | | | | | | | |
| Darwin, Jeff | 0 | 1 | 2.93 | 22 | 0 | 0 | 0 | 31 | 26 | 10 | 10 | 9 | 15 | R | R | 6-3 | 180 | 7-6-69 | 1989 | Gainesville, Texas |
| Fernandez, Alex | 16 | 10 | 3.45 | 35 | 35 | 6 | 0 | 258 | 248 | 110 | 99 | 72 | 200 | R | R | 6-0 | 195 | 8-13-69 | 1990 | Hialeah, Fla. |
| Freeman, Marvin | 0 | 0 | 13.50 | 1 | 1 | 0 | 0 | 2 | 4 | 3 | 3 | 1 | 1 | R | R | 6-7 | 222 | 4-10-63 | 1984 | Country Club Hills, Ill. |
| Hernandez, Roberto | 6 | 5 | 1.91 | 72 | 0 | 0 | 38 | 85 | 65 | 21 | 18 | 38 | 85 | R | R | 6-4 | 235 | 11-11-64 | 1986 | Cobo Rojo, P.R. |
| Jones, Stacy | 0 | 0 | 0.00 | 2 | 0 | 0 | 0 | 2 | 0 | 0 | 0 | 1 | 1 | R | R | 6-6 | 225 | 5-26-67 | 1988 | Attalla, Ala. |
| Karchner, Matt | 7 | 4 | 5.76 | 50 | 0 | 0 | 1 | 59 | 61 | 42 | 38 | 41 | 46 | R | R | 6-4 | 245 | 6-28-67 | 1989 | Berwick, Pa. |
| Keyser, Brian | 1 | 2 | 4.98 | 28 | 0 | 0 | 1 | 60 | 78 | 35 | 33 | 28 | 19 | R | R | 6-1 | 180 | 10-31-66 | 1989 | Walnut Creek, Calif. |
| Levine, Alan | 0 | 1 | 5.40 | 16 | 0 | 0 | 0 | 18 | 22 | 14 | 11 | 7 | 12 | L | R | 6-3 | 180 | 5-22-68 | 1991 | Hanover Park, Ill. |
| Magrane, Joe | 1 | 5 | 6.88 | 19 | 8 | 0 | 0 | 54 | 70 | 45 | 41 | 25 | 21 | R | L | 6-6 | 230 | 7-2-64 | 1985 | Chesterfield, Mo. |
| McCaskill, Kirk | 5 | 5 | 6.97 | 29 | 4 | 0 | 0 | 52 | 72 | 41 | 40 | 31 | 28 | R | R | 6-1 | 205 | 4-9-61 | 1982 | Corona del Mar, Calif. |
| Ruffcorn, Scott | 0 | 1 | 11.37 | 3 | 1 | 0 | 0 | 6 | 10 | 8 | 8 | 6 | 3 | R | R | 6-4 | 215 | 12-29-69 | 1991 | Austin, Texas |
| Sauveur, Rich | 0 | 0 | 15.00 | 3 | 0 | 0 | 0 | 3 | 3 | 5 | 5 | 5 | 1 | L | L | 6-4 | 170 | 11-23-63 | 1983 | Falls Church, Va. |
| Simas, Bill | 2 | 8 | 4.58 | 64 | 0 | 0 | 2 | 73 | 75 | 39 | 37 | 39 | 65 | L | R | 6-3 | 220 | 11-28-71 | 1992 | Fresno, Calif. |
| Sirotka, Mike | 1 | 2 | 7.18 | 15 | 4 | 0 | 0 | 26 | 34 | 27 | 21 | 12 | 11 | L | L | 6-1 | 190 | 5-13-71 | 1993 | Houston, Texas |
| Tapani, Kevin | 13 | 10 | 4.59 | 34 | 34 | 1 | 0 | 225 | 236 | 123 | 115 | 76 | 150 | R | R | 6-0 | 175 | 2-18-64 | 1986 | Eden Prairie, Minn. |
| Thomas, Larry | 2 | 3 | 3.23 | 57 | 0 | 0 | 0 | 31 | 32 | 11 | 11 | 14 | 20 | R | L | 6-1 | 190 | 10-25-69 | 1991 | Mobile, Ala. |

## FIELDING

| Catcher | PCT | G | PO | A | E | DP | PB |
|---|---|---|---|---|---|---|---|
| Borders | .982 | 30 | 144 | 16 | 3 | 1 | 2 |
| Karkovice | .993 | 111 | 680 | 45 | 5 | 5 | 4 |
| Kreuter | .990 | 38 | 181 | 12 | 2 | 4 | 1 |
| Machado | 1.000 | 4 | 6 | 0 | 0 | 0 | 1 |
| Slaught | .986 | 12 | 70 | 0 | 1 | 0 | 0 |

| First Base | PCT | G | PO | A | E | DP |
|---|---|---|---|---|---|---|
| Kreuter | 1.000 | 2 | 1 | 0 | 0 | 0 |
| Martinez | .980 | 23 | 132 | 12 | 3 | 8 |
| Phillips | 1.000 | 1 | 2 | 0 | 0 | 0 |
| Robertson | 1.000 | 2 | 11 | 1 | 0 | 2 |
| Thomas | .992 | 139 | 1098 | 85 | 9 | 111 |
| Ventura | .985 | 14 | 56 | 8 | 1 | 7 |

| Second Base | PCT | G | PO | A | E | DP |
|---|---|---|---|---|---|---|
| Cedeno | .000 | 2 | 0 | 0 | 0 | 0 |

| | PCT | G | PO | A | E | DP |
|---|---|---|---|---|---|---|
| Durham | .984 | 150 | 236 | 423 | 11 | 87 |
| Martin | .982 | 10 | 22 | 34 | 1 | 7 |
| Munoz | .923 | 7 | 12 | 12 | 2 | 2 |
| Phillips | 1.000 | 2 | 4 | 5 | 0 | 2 |

| Third Base | PCT | G | PO | A | E | DP |
|---|---|---|---|---|---|---|
| Cedeno | 1.000 | 6 | 5 | 13 | 0 | 2 |
| Martin | 1.000 | 3 | 0 | 1 | 0 | 0 |
| Munoz | .000 | 1 | 0 | 0 | 0 | 0 |
| Norton | 1.000 | 2 | 4 | 2 | 0 | 1 |
| Snopek | .939 | 27 | 12 | 34 | 3 | 5 |
| Ventura | .974 | 150 | 133 | 239 | 10 | 34 |

| Shortstop | PCT | G | PO | A | E | DP |
|---|---|---|---|---|---|---|
| Cedeno | .909 | 2 | 6 | 4 | 1 | 2 |
| Guillen | .981 | 146 | 220 | 348 | 11 | 69 |

| | PCT | G | PO | A | E | DP |
|---|---|---|---|---|---|---|
| Martin | .943 | 24 | 39 | 44 | 5 | 17 |
| Munoz | 1.000 | 2 | 0 | 1 | 0 | 0 |
| Norton | .778 | 6 | 4 | 3 | 2 | 0 |
| Snopek | .957 | 12 | 13 | 31 | 2 | 5 |

| Outfield | PCT | G | PO | A | E | DP |
|---|---|---|---|---|---|---|
| Cameron | 1.000 | 8 | 7 | 0 | 0 | 0 |
| Guillen | 1.000 | 2 | 2 | 0 | 0 | 0 |
| Lewis | .990 | 138 | 287 | 0 | 3 | 0 |
| Martinez | .988 | 121 | 236 | 4 | 3 | 1 |
| Mouton | .970 | 47 | 64 | 1 | 2 | 0 |
| Munoz | .000 | 1 | 0 | 0 | 0 | 0 |
| Phillips | .981 | 150 | 345 | 13 | 7 | 2 |
| Tartabull | .973 | 122 | 253 | 4 | 7 | 1 |

Alex Fernandez led the
White Sox with 16 wins

Minor league Player of the
Year Mike Cameron

## FARM SYSTEM

Director of Player Development: Steve Noworyta

| Class | Farm Team | League | W | L | Pct. | Finish* | Manager | First Yr |
|---|---|---|---|---|---|---|---|---|
| AAA | Nashville (Tenn.) Sounds | American Assoc. | 77 | 67 | .535 | 4th (8) | Rick Renick | 1993 |
| AA | Birmingham (Ala.) Barons | Southern | 74 | 65 | .532 | 5th (10) | Mike Heath | 1986 |
| #A | Prince William (Va.) Cannons | Carolina | 58 | 80 | .420 | 8th (8) | Dave Huppert | 1994 |
| A | South Bend (Ill.) Silver Hawks | Midwest | 54 | 82 | .397 | 14th (14) | Dave Keller | 1988 |
| A | Hickory (N.C.) Crawdads | South Atlantic | 55 | 85 | .393 | 14th (14) | Chris Cron | 1993 |
| #R | Bristol (Va.) White Sox | Appalachian | 17 | 51 | .250 | 9th (9) | Nick Capra | 1995 |
| R | Sarasota (Fla.) White Sox | Gulf Coast | 20 | 40 | .333 | 15th (16) | Hector Rincones | 1964 |

*Finish in overall standings (No. of teams in league)   #Advanced level

## ORGANIZATION LEADERS

### MAJOR LEAGUERS

**BATTING**

| | | |
|---|---|---|
| *AVG | Frank Thomas | .349 |
| R | Tony Phillips | 119 |
| H | Frank Thomas | 184 |
| TB | Frank Thomas | 330 |
| 2B | Ray Durham | 33 |
| 3B | Two tied at | 8 |
| HR | Frank Thomas | 40 |
| RBI | Frank Thomas | 134 |
| BB | Tony Phillips | 125 |
| SO | Tony Phillips | 132 |
| SB | Ray Durham | 30 |

**PITCHING**

| | | |
|---|---|---|
| W | Alex Fernandez | 16 |
| L | Three tied at | 10 |
| #ERA | Roberto Hernandez | 1.91 |
| G | Roberto Hernandez | 72 |
| CG | Alex Fernandez | 6 |
| SV | Roberto Hernandez | 38 |
| IP | Alex Fernandez | 258 |
| BB | Wilson Alvarez | 97 |
| SO | Alex Fernandez | 200 |

Tony Phillips. 119 runs

### MINOR LEAGUERS

**BATTING**

| | | |
|---|---|---|
| *AVG | Mario Valdez, South Bend/Birm. | .330 |
| R | Mike Cameron, Birmingham | 120 |
| H | Carlos Lee, Hickory | 150 |
| TB | Mike Cameron, Birmingham | 284 |
| 2B | Magglio Ordonez, Birmingham | 41 |
| 3B | Mike Cameron, Birmingham | 12 |
| HR | Mike Cameron, Birmingham | 28 |
| RBI | Jimmy Hurst, Birm./Nashville | 90 |
| BB | Brandon Moore, Prince William | 82 |
| SO | Josh Fauske, Hickory | 132 |
| SB | Ramon Gomez, Hickory | 57 |

**PITCHING**

| | | |
|---|---|---|
| W | Two tied at | 13 |
| L | Maximo Nunez, Hickory | 16 |
| #ERA | Barry Johnson, Birm./Nashville | 2.53 |
| G | Rich Sauveur, Nashville | 61 |
| CG | Carlos Castillo, South Bend/P.W. | 6 |
| SV | Stacy Jones, Birm./Nashville | 26 |
| IP | Carlos Chantres, Hickory/South Bend | 185 |
| BB | Tom Fordham, Birm./Nashville | 83 |
| SO | Carlos Castillo, South Bend/P.W. | 158 |

*Minimum 250 At-Bats   #Minimum 75 Innings

## TOP 10 PROSPECTS

How the White Sox Top 10 prospects, as judged by Baseball America prior to the 1996 season, fared in 1996:

Chris Snopek

| Player, Pos. | Club (Class—League) | AVG | AB | R | H | 2B | 3B | HR | RBI | SB |
|---|---|---|---|---|---|---|---|---|---|---|
| 1. Chris Snopek, 3b-ss | Chicago | .260 | 104 | 18 | 27 | 6 | 1 | 6 | 18 | 0 |
| | Nashville (AAA—Amer. Assoc.) | .248 | 153 | 18 | 38 | 8 | 0 | 2 | 12 | 2 |
| 2. Jeff Abbott, of | Nashville (AAA—Amer. Assoc.) | ..325 | 440 | 64 | 143 | 27 | 1 | 14 | 60 | 12 |
| 5. Jeff Liefer, 3b-dh | South Bend (A—Midwest) | .325 | 277 | 60 | 90 | 14 | 0 | 15 | 58 | 6 |
| | Prince William (A—Carolina) | .224 | 147 | 17 | 33 | 6 | 0 | 1 | 13 | 0 |
| 6. Mike Cameron, of | Birmingham (AA—Southern) | .300 | 473 | 120 | 142 | 34 | 12 | 28 | 77 | 39 |
| | Chicago | .091 | 11 | 1 | 1 | 0 | 0 | 0 | 0 | 0 |
| 7. Jimmy Hurst, of | Birmingham (AA—Southern) | .265 | 472 | 62 | 125 | 23 | 1 | 18 | 88 | 19 |
| | Nashville (AAA—Amer. Assoc.) | .333 | 6 | 2 | 2 | 1 | 0 | 1 | 2 | 0 |
| 9. McKay Christensen, of | Sarasota (R—Gulf Coast) | .263 | 133 | 17 | 35 | 7 | 5 | 1 | 16 | 10 |
| | Hickory (A—South Atlantic) | .000 | 11 | 0 | 0 | 0 | 0 | 0 | 0 | 0 |
| 10. Greg Norton, 3b-ss | Birmingham (AA—Southern) | .282 | 287 | 40 | 81 | 14 | 3 | 8 | 44 | 5 |
| | Nashville (AAA—Amer. Assoc.) | .287 | 164 | 28 | 47 | 14 | 2 | 7 | 26 | 2 |
| | Chicago | .217 | 23 | 4 | 5 | 0 | 0 | 2 | 3 | 0 |

| | | W | L | ERA | G | SV | IP | H | BB | SO |
|---|---|---|---|---|---|---|---|---|---|---|
| 3. Scott Ruffcorn, rhp | Nashville (AAA—Amer. Assoc.) | 13 | 4 | 3.87 | 24 | 0 | 149 | 142 | 61 | 129 |
| | Chicago | 0 | 1 | 11.37 | 3 | 0 | 6 | 10 | 6 | 3 |
| 4. James Baldwin, rhp | Nashville (AAA—Amer. Assoc.) | 1 | 1 | 0.64 | 2 | 0 | 14 | 5 | 4 | 15 |
| | Chicago | 11 | 6 | 4.42 | 28 | 0 | 169 | 168 | 57 | 127 |
| 8. *Luis Andujar, rhp | Nashville (AAA—Amer. Assoc.) | 1 | 4 | 5.92 | 8 | 0 | 38 | 50 | 8 | 24 |
| | Syracuse (AAA—International) | 0 | 0 | 2.25 | 2 | 0 | 12 | 17 | 2 | 10 |
| | Toronto | 1 | 3 | 6.99 | 8 | 0 | 37 | 46 | 16 | 11 |

*Traded to Blue Jays

## AMERICAN ASSOCIATION

| BATTING | AVG | G | AB | R | H | 2B | 3B | HR | RBI | BB | SO | SB | CS | B | T | HT | WT | DOB | 1st Yr | Resides |
|---|---|---|---|---|---|---|---|---|---|---|---|---|---|---|---|---|---|---|---|---|
| Abbott, Jeff | .325 | 113 | 440 | 64 | 143 | 27 | 1 | 14 | 60 | 32 | 50 | 12 | 4 | R | L | 6-2 | 190 | 8-17-72 | 1994 | Atlanta, Ga. |
| Brady, Doug | .241 | 115 | 427 | 59 | 103 | 18 | 7 | 6 | 42 | 31 | 61 | 20 | 6 | S | R | 5-11 | 165 | 11-23-69 | 1991 | Las Vegas, Nev. |
| Cappuccio, Carmine | .273 | 120 | 407 | 55 | 111 | 22 | 3 | 10 | 61 | 25 | 48 | 1 | 3 | L | R | 6-3 | 185 | 2-1-70 | 1992 | Malden, Mass. |
| DiSarcina, Glenn | .237 | 38 | 97 | 8 | 23 | 9 | 0 | 0 | 11 | 5 | 20 | 1 | 1 | L | R | 6-1 | 180 | 4-29-70 | 1991 | Billerica, Mass. |
| Hall, Mel | .267 | 4 | 15 | 1 | 4 | 0 | 0 | 1 | 1 | 1 | 1 | 0 | 0 | L | L | 6-1 | 215 | 9-18-60 | 1978 | Parkland, Fla. |
| Hurst, Jimmy | .333 | 3 | 6 | 2 | 2 | 1 | 0 | 1 | 2 | 1 | 3 | 0 | 0 | R | R | 6-6 | 225 | 3-1-72 | 1991 | Tuscaloosa, Ala. |
| Martin, Norberto | .206 | 17 | 68 | 9 | 14 | 3 | 0 | 2 | 8 | 4 | 10 | 1 | 0 | S | R | 5-10 | 164 | 12-10-66 | 1984 | Hato Rey, P.R. |
| Merchant, Mark | .214 | 42 | 131 | 21 | 28 | 6 | 0 | 4 | 15 | 17 | 29 | 1 | 1 | S | R | 6-2 | 185 | 1-23-69 | 1987 | Chuluota, Fla. |
| Munoz, Jose | .234 | 78 | 295 | 30 | 69 | 17 | 1 | 6 | 34 | 20 | 37 | 8 | 1 | S | R | 5-11 | 165 | 11-11-67 | 1987 | Yabucoa, P.R. |
| Norton, Greg | .287 | 43 | 164 | 28 | 47 | 14 | 2 | 7 | 26 | 17 | 42 | 2 | 3 | S | R | 6-1 | 182 | 7-6-72 | 1993 | Walnut Creek, Calif. |
| Ramsey, Fernando | .218 | 110 | 395 | 42 | 86 | 3 | 0 | 7 | 24 | 10 | 57 | 12 | 10 | R | R | 6-2 | 175 | 12-20-65 | 1987 | Ciudad Arcoiris, Panama |
| Robertson, Mike | .258 | 138 | 450 | 64 | 116 | 16 | 4 | 21 | 74 | 38 | 83 | 1 | 2 | L | L | 6-0 | 180 | 10-9-70 | 1991 | Placentia, Calif. |
| Robledo, Nilson | .100 | 9 | 10 | 0 | 1 | 0 | 0 | 0 | 0 | 1 | 7 | 0 | 0 | R | R | 6-1 | 165 | 11-3-68 | 1989 | Entrega, Panama |
| Saenz, Olmedo | .261 | 134 | 476 | 86 | 124 | 29 | 1 | 18 | 63 | 53 | 80 | 4 | 2 | R | R | 6-2 | 185 | 10-8-70 | 1990 | Chitre Herrera, Panama |
| Snopek, Chris | .248 | 40 | 153 | 18 | 38 | 8 | 0 | 2 | 12 | 21 | 24 | 2 | 2 | R | R | 6-1 | 185 | 9-20-70 | 1992 | Cynthiana, Ky. |
| Tremie, Chris | .219 | 70 | 215 | 17 | 47 | 10 | 1 | 0 | 26 | 18 | 48 | 2 | 0 | R | R | 6-0 | 200 | 10-17-69 | 1992 | Houston, Texas |
| Valrie, Kerry | .273 | 138 | 498 | 59 | 136 | 32 | 5 | 13 | 66 | 28 | 94 | 10 | 9 | R | R | 5-10 | 195 | 10-31-68 | 1990 | Loxley, Ala. |
| Vinas, Julio | .237 | 104 | 338 | 48 | 80 | 18 | 2 | 11 | 52 | 36 | 63 | 1 | 4 | R | R | 6-0 | 200 | 2-14-73 | 1991 | Hialeah, Fla. |
| Wilson, Craig | .179 | 44 | 123 | 13 | 22 | 4 | 1 | 1 | 6 | 10 | 15 | 0 | 0 | R | R | 6-1 | 190 | 9-3-70 | 1992 | Phoenix, Ariz. |

| PITCHING | W | L | ERA | G | GS | CG | SV | IP | H | R | ER | BB | SO | B | T | HT | WT | DOB | 1st Yr | Resides |
|---|---|---|---|---|---|---|---|---|---|---|---|---|---|---|---|---|---|---|---|---|
| Andujar, Luis | 1 | 4 | 5.92 | 8 | 7 | 1 | 0 | 38 | 50 | 26 | 25 | 8 | 24 | R | R | 6-2 | 175 | 11-22-72 | 1991 | Bani, D.R. |
| Baldwin, James | 1 | 1 | 0.64 | 2 | 2 | 1 | 0 | 14 | 5 | 1 | 1 | 4 | 15 | R | R | 6-4 | 210 | 7-15-71 | 1990 | Southern Pines, N.C. |
| Bere, Jason | 0 | 0 | 1.42 | 3 | 3 | 0 | 0 | 13 | 9 | 2 | 2 | 4 | 15 | R | R | 6-3 | 185 | 5-26-71 | 1990 | Wilmington, Mass. |
| Bertotti, Mike | 5 | 3 | 4.37 | 28 | 9 | 1 | 1 | 82 | 80 | 43 | 40 | 42 | 73 | L | L | 6-1 | 185 | 1-18-70 | 1991 | Highland Mills, N.Y. |
| Darwin, Jeff | 5 | 2 | 3.55 | 25 | 6 | 0 | 3 | 63 | 52 | 31 | 25 | 17 | 33 | R | R | 6-3 | 180 | 7-6-69 | 1989 | Gainesville, Texas |
| Ellis, Robert | 3 | 8 | 6.01 | 19 | 13 | 1 | 0 | 70 | 78 | 49 | 47 | 45 | 35 | R | R | 6-5 | 220 | 12-15-70 | 1990 | Baton Rouge, La. |
| Fordham, Tom | 10 | 8 | 3.45 | 22 | 22 | 3 | 0 | 141 | 117 | 60 | 54 | 69 | 118 | L | L | 6-2 | 210 | 2-20-74 | 1993 | El Cajon, Calif. |
| Gajkowski, Steve | 5 | 6 | 3.94 | 49 | 8 | 0 | 2 | 107 | 113 | 61 | 47 | 41 | 47 | R | R | 6-2 | 200 | 12-30-69 | 1990 | Bellevue, Wash. |
| Johnson, Barry | 7 | 2 | 2.80 | 38 | 8 | 0 | 0 | 103 | 93 | 38 | 32 | 39 | 68 | R | R | 6-4 | 200 | 8-21-69 | 1991 | Joliet, Ill. |
| Jones, Stacy | 3 | 0 | 0.83 | 19 | 0 | 0 | 12 | 22 | 17 | 3 | 2 | 6 | 18 | R | R | 6-6 | 225 | 5-26-67 | 1988 | Attalla, Ala. |
| 2-team (9 New Orleans) | 3 | 1 | 3.15 | 28 | 0 | 0 | 12 | 34 | 35 | 13 | 12 | 13 | 28 | | | | | | | |
| Karchner, Matt | 0 | 0 | 0.00 | 1 | 0 | 0 | 0 | 1 | 0 | 0 | 0 | 0 | 0 | R | R | 6-4 | 245 | 6-28-67 | 1989 | Berwick, Pa. |
| Keyser, Brian | 3 | 3 | 2.01 | 6 | 6 | 2 | 0 | 45 | 38 | 11 | 10 | 13 | 22 | R | R | 6-1 | 180 | 10-31-66 | 1989 | Walnut Creek, Calif. |
| Levine, Alan | 4 | 5 | 3.65 | 43 | 0 | 0 | 12 | 62 | 58 | 27 | 25 | 24 | 45 | L | R | 6-3 | 180 | 5-22-68 | 1991 | Hanover Park, Ill. |
| Magrane, Joe | 1 | 1 | 5.47 | 21 | 1 | 0 | 1 | 26 | 29 | 17 | 16 | 8 | 16 | R | L | 6-6 | 230 | 7-2-64 | 1985 | Chesterfield, Mo. |
| Ruffcorn, Scott | 13 | 4 | 3.87 | 24 | 24 | 2 | 0 | 149 | 142 | 71 | 64 | 61 | 129 | R | R | 6-4 | 215 | 12-29-69 | 1991 | Austin, Texas |
| Sauveur, Rich | 4 | 3 | 3.70 | 61 | 3 | 0 | 8 | 73 | 63 | 34 | 30 | 28 | 69 | L | L | 6-4 | 170 | 11-23-63 | 1983 | Falls Church, Va. |
| Schrenk, Steve | 4 | 10 | 4.42 | 16 | 15 | 1 | 0 | 96 | 93 | 54 | 47 | 29 | 58 | R | R | 6-3 | 185 | 11-20-68 | 1987 | Aurora, Ore. |
| Sirotka, Mike | 7 | 5 | 3.60 | 15 | 15 | 1 | 0 | 90 | 90 | 44 | 36 | 24 | 58 | L | L | 6-1 | 180 | 5-13-71 | 1993 | Houston, Texas |
| Smith, Chuck | 0 | 0 | 27.00 | 1 | 0 | 0 | 0 | 1 | 2 | 2 | 2 | 1 | 1 | R | R | 6-1 | 175 | 10-21-69 | 1991 | Cleveland, Ohio |
| Thigpen, Bobby | 0 | 1 | 7.11 | 4 | 0 | 0 | 0 | 6 | 8 | 5 | 5 | 2 | 6 | R | R | 6-3 | 195 | 7-17-63 | 1985 | St. Petersburg, Fla. |
| Worrell, Steve | 1 | 1 | 3.15 | 11 | 2 | 0 | 0 | 20 | 19 | 8 | 7 | 5 | 11 | L | L | 6-2 | 180 | 11-25-69 | 1992 | Cape May, N.J. |
| Zappelli, Mark | 0 | 0 | 0.68 | 9 | 0 | 0 | 1 | 13 | 11 | 3 | 1 | 2 | 9 | R | R | 6-0 | 185 | 7-21-66 | 1989 | Santa Rosa, Calif. |

### FIELDING

| Catcher | PCT | G | PO | A | E | DP | PB |
|---|---|---|---|---|---|---|---|
| Robledo | 1.000 | 1 | 1 | 0 | 0 | 0 | 0 |
| Tremie | .996 | 70 | 433 | 52 | 2 | 6 | 5 |
| Vinas | .992 | 82 | 461 | 46 | 4 | 1 | 5 |

| First Base | PCT | G | PO | A | E | DP |
|---|---|---|---|---|---|---|
| Robertson | .996 | 137 | 1074 | 54 | 4 | 89 |
| Robledo | 1.000 | 5 | 9 | 0 | 0 | 0 |
| Vinas | .992 | 16 | 120 | 8 | 1 | 17 |

| Second Base | PCT | G | PO | A | E | DP |
|---|---|---|---|---|---|---|
| Brady | .971 | 109 | 227 | 273 | 15 | 65 |
| Martin | .957 | 9 | 19 | 26 | 2 | 7 |
| Munoz | .974 | 25 | 49 | 63 | 3 | 12 |
| Wilson | 1.000 | 5 | 9 | 6 | 0 | 4 |

| Third Base | PCT | G | PO | A | E | DP |
|---|---|---|---|---|---|---|
| DiSarcina | .938 | 5 | 2 | 13 | 1 | 1 |
| Martin | 1.000 | 2 | 3 | 1 | 0 | 0 |
| Munoz | .931 | 8 | 7 | 20 | 2 | 3 |
| Norton | .889 | 3 | 1 | 7 | 1 | 1 |
| Saenz | .939 | 120 | 97 | 244 | 22 | 24 |
| Snopek | 1.000 | 5 | 5 | 15 | 0 | 1 |
| Vinas | .909 | 5 | 3 | 7 | 1 | 1 |

| Shortstop | PCT | G | PO | A | E | DP |
|---|---|---|---|---|---|---|
| DiSarcina | .952 | 27 | 40 | 78 | 6 | 16 |
| Martin | 1.000 | 6 | 5 | 16 | 0 | 0 |
| Munoz | .930 | 10 | 14 | 26 | 3 | 5 |
| Norton | .915 | 37 | 42 | 88 | 12 | 10 |

| | PCT | G | PO | A | E | DP |
|---|---|---|---|---|---|---|
| Snopek | .954 | 34 | 33 | 92 | 6 | 16 |
| Wilson | .933 | 40 | 43 | 97 | 10 | 19 |

| Outfield | PCT | G | PO | A | E | DP |
|---|---|---|---|---|---|---|
| Abbott | .990 | 104 | 186 | 5 | 2 | 1 |
| Cappuccio | .991 | 104 | 215 | 11 | 2 | 2 |
| Hurst | 1.000 | 3 | 2 | 0 | 0 | 0 |
| Merchant | 1.000 | 2 | 1 | 0 | 0 | 0 |
| Munoz | 1.000 | 1 | 1 | 0 | 0 | 0 |
| Ramsey | .980 | 107 | 232 | 7 | 5 | 4 |
| Valrie | .981 | 123 | 309 | 7 | 6 | 2 |

## SOUTHERN LEAGUE

| BATTING | AVG | G | AB | R | H | 2B | 3B | HR | RBI | BB | SO | SB | CS | B | T | HT | WT | DOB | 1st Yr | Resides |
|---|---|---|---|---|---|---|---|---|---|---|---|---|---|---|---|---|---|---|---|---|
| Cameron, Mike | .300 | 123 | 473 | 120 | 142 | 34 | 12 | 28 | 77 | 71 | 117 | 39 | 15 | R | R | 6-1 | 170 | 1-8-73 | 1991 | LaGrange, Ga. |
| DiSarcina, Glenn | .366 | 43 | 175 | 25 | 64 | 10 | 3 | 7 | 36 | 7 | 45 | 4 | 0 | L | R | 6-1 | 180 | 4-29-70 | 1991 | Billerica, Mass. |
| Duross, Gabe | .221 | 37 | 140 | 14 | 31 | 3 | 0 | 0 | 15 | 7 | 17 | 1 | 1 | L | L | 6-1 | 195 | 4-6-72 | 1992 | Kingston, N.Y. |
| 2-team (17 Orlando) | .202 | 54 | 198 | 16 | 40 | 3 | 1 | 0 | 21 | 9 | 20 | 1 | 1 | | | | | | | |
| Fryman, Troy | .204 | 14 | 49 | 8 | 10 | 2 | 0 | 1 | 3 | 5 | 11 | 0 | 0 | L | R | 6-4 | 195 | 10-2-71 | 1991 | Pensacola, Fla. |
| Hurst, Jimmy | .265 | 126 | 472 | 62 | 125 | 23 | 1 | 18 | 88 | 53 | 128 | 19 | 11 | R | R | 6-6 | 225 | 3-1-72 | 1991 | Tuscaloosa, Ala. |
| Larregui, Ed | .239 | 65 | 213 | 26 | 51 | 9 | 1 | 0 | 14 | 16 | 31 | 1 | 1 | R | R | 6-0 | 185 | 12-1-72 | 1990 | Carolina, P.R. |
| 2-team (17 Orlando) | .245 | 82 | 282 | 38 | 69 | 14 | 1 | 1 | 19 | 22 | 40 | 1 | 3 | | | | | | | |
| Machado, Robert | .239 | 87 | 309 | 35 | 74 | 10 | 6 | 28 | 20 | 56 | 1 | 4 | | R | R | 6-1 | 185 | 6-3-73 | 1991 | Caracas, Venez. |
| Menechino, Frank | .292 | 125 | 415 | 77 | 121 | 25 | 3 | 12 | 62 | 64 | 84 | 7 | 9 | R | R | 5-9 | 175 | 1-7-71 | 1993 | Staten Island, N.Y. |
| Norton, Greg | .282 | 76 | 287 | 40 | 81 | 14 | 3 | 8 | 44 | 33 | 55 | 5 | 5 | S | R | 6-1 | 182 | 7-6-72 | 1993 | Walnut Creek, Calif. |
| Ordonez, Magglio | .263 | 130 | 499 | 66 | 126 | 41 | 0 | 18 | 67 | 39 | 74 | 9 | 10 | R | R | 5-11 | 155 | 1-28-74 | 1991 | Caracas, Venez. |
| Pearson, Eddie | .223 | 85 | 323 | 38 | 72 | 20 | 0 | 8 | 40 | 31 | 57 | 2 | 2 | L | R | 6-3 | 225 | 1-31-74 | 1992 | Mobile, Ala. |
| Polidor, Wil | .235 | 25 | 81 | 7 | 19 | 3 | 0 | 0 | 6 | 2 | 13 | 0 | 0 | S | R | 5-11 | 158 | 9-23-73 | 1991 | Caracas, Venez. |
| Robledo, Nilson | .231 | 7 | 26 | 3 | 6 | 1 | 0 | 0 | 6 | 2 | 6 | 1 | 0 | R | R | 6-1 | 165 | 11-3-68 | 1989 | Entrega, Panama |
| Rose, Pete | .243 | 108 | 399 | 40 | 97 | 13 | 1 | 3 | 44 | 32 | 54 | 1 | 3 | L | R | 6-1 | 180 | 11-16-69 | 1989 | Cincinnati, Ohio |
| Sawkiw, Warren | .232 | 20 | 56 | 7 | 13 | 2 | 0 | 0 | 5 | 11 | 17 | 2 | 3 | S | R | 5-11 | 180 | 1-19-68 | 1990 | Lakeland, Fla. |

MICHAEL YELMAN

LEE R. SCHMID

**Key Contributors.** The White Sox finished second in the AL Central, thanks largely to the efforts of first baseman Frank Thomas, left, who hit .349 with 134 RBIs, and reliever Roberto Hernandez, who had 38 saves.

| BATTING | AVG | G | AB | R | H | 2B | 3B | HR | RBI | BB | SO | SB | CS | B | T | HT | WT | DOB | 1st Yr | Resides |
|---|---|---|---|---|---|---|---|---|---|---|---|---|---|---|---|---|---|---|---|---|
| Valdez, Mario | .274 | 50 | 168 | 22 | 46 | 10 | 2 | 3 | 28 | 32 | 34 | 0 | 0 | L | R | 6-2 | 190 | 11-19-74 | 1994 | Hialeah, Fla. |
| Vollmer, Scott | .260 | 98 | 361 | 41 | 94 | 21 | 0 | 4 | 31 | 32 | 60 | 0 | 0 | R | R | 6-1 | 175 | 2-9-71 | 1993 | Thousand Oaks, Calif. |
| Williams, Harold | .283 | 14 | 46 | 3 | 13 | 4 | 0 | 0 | 4 | 4 | 12 | 1 | 1 | L | L | 6-4 | 200 | 2-14-71 | 1993 | Garyville, La. |
| Wilson, Craig | .282 | 58 | 202 | 36 | 57 | 9 | 0 | 3 | 26 | 40 | 28 | 1 | 1 | R | R | 6-1 | 190 | 9-3-70 | 1992 | Phoenix, Ariz. |

| PITCHING | W | L | ERA | G | GS | CG | SV | IP | H | R | ER | BB | SO | B | T | HT | WT | DOB | 1st Yr | Resides |
|---|---|---|---|---|---|---|---|---|---|---|---|---|---|---|---|---|---|---|---|---|
| Bere, Jason | 0 | 0 | 4.15 | 1 | 1 | 0 | 0 | 4 | 4 | 2 | 2 | 4 | 5 | R | R | 6-3 | 185 | 5-26-71 | 1990 | Wilmington, Mass. |
| Clemons, Chris | 5 | 2 | 3.15 | 19 | 16 | 1 | 0 | 94 | 91 | 39 | 33 | 40 | 69 | R | R | 6-4 | 220 | 10-31-72 | 1994 | McGregor, Texas |
| Cruz, Nelson | 6 | 6 | 3.20 | 37 | 18 | 2 | 1 | 149 | 150 | 65 | 53 | 41 | 142 | R | R | 6-1 | 160 | 9-13-72 | 1990 | Puerto Plata, D.R. |
| Ellis, Robert | 0 | 1 | 11.05 | 2 | 2 | 0 | 0 | 7 | 6 | 9 | 9 | 8 | 8 | R | R | 6-5 | 220 | 12-15-70 | 1990 | Baton Rouge, La. |
| Eyre, Scott | 12 | 7 | 4.38 | 27 | 27 | 0 | 0 | 158 | 170 | 90 | 77 | 79 | 137 | L | L | 6-1 | 160 | 5-30-72 | 1991 | Magna, Utah |
| Fordham, Tom | 2 | 1 | 2.65 | 6 | 6 | 0 | 0 | 37 | 26 | 13 | 11 | 14 | 37 | L | L | 6-2 | 210 | 2-20-74 | 1993 | El Cajon, Calif. |
| Heathcott, Mike | 11 | 8 | 4.02 | 23 | 23 | 1 | 0 | 148 | 138 | 72 | 66 | 55 | 108 | R | R | 6-3 | 180 | 5-16-69 | 1991 | Chicago, Ill. |
| Johnson, Barry | 0 | 0 | 0.00 | 9 | 0 | 0 | 4 | 11 | 2 | 0 | 0 | 1 | 15 | R | R | 6-4 | 200 | 8-21-69 | 1991 | Joliet, Ill. |
| Jones, Stacy | 1 | 1 | 2.57 | 27 | 0 | 0 | 14 | 28 | 25 | 11 | 8 | 6 | 31 | R | R | 6-6 | 225 | 5-26-67 | 1988 | Attalla, Ala. |
| Moore, Tim | 1 | 4 | 8.54 | 9 | 6 | 0 | 0 | 26 | 43 | 31 | 25 | 6 | 23 | R | R | 6-4 | 190 | 9-4-70 | 1992 | Irving, Texas |
| Perschke, Greg | 2 | 1 | 2.25 | 9 | 0 | 0 | 0 | 12 | 12 | 6 | 3 | 3 | 12 | R | R | 6-3 | 180 | 8-3-67 | 1989 | Laporte, Ind. |
| Place, Mike | 2 | 3 | 7.09 | 22 | 0 | 0 | 1 | 33 | 43 | 26 | 26 | 18 | 20 | R | R | 6-4 | 190 | 8-13-70 | 1990 | Seminole, Fla. |
| Pratt, Rich | 13 | 9 | 3.86 | 27 | 27 | 5 | 0 | 177 | 180 | 87 | 76 | 40 | 122 | L | L | 6-3 | 201 | 5-7-71 | 1993 | East Hartford, Conn. |
| Rizzo, Todd | 4 | 4 | 2.75 | 46 | 0 | 0 | 10 | 69 | 61 | 28 | 21 | 40 | 48 | R | L | 6-3 | 220 | 5-24-71 | 1992 | Aston, Pa. |
| Smith, Chuck | 2 | 1 | 2.64 | 7 | 3 | 0 | 1 | 31 | 25 | 11 | 9 | 15 | 30 | R | R | 6-1 | 175 | 10-21-69 | 1991 | Cleveland, Ohio |
| Snyder, John | 3 | 5 | 4.83 | 9 | 9 | 0 | 0 | 54 | 59 | 35 | 29 | 16 | 58 | R | R | 6-3 | 185 | 8-16-74 | 1992 | Thousand Oaks, Calif. |
| Vazquez, Archie | 0 | 6 | 6.61 | 31 | 1 | 0 | 1 | 65 | 68 | 53 | 48 | 48 | 51 | R | R | 6-4 | 233 | 4-11-72 | 1991 | Hialeah, Fla. |
| Woods, Brian | 5 | 5 | 3.76 | 53 | 0 | 0 | 5 | 67 | 59 | 32 | 28 | 38 | 46 | L | R | 6-6 | 212 | 6-7-71 | 1993 | West Caldwell, N.J. |
| Worrell, Steve | 5 | 1 | 2.12 | 35 | 0 | 0 | 3 | 51 | 28 | 14 | 12 | 21 | 55 | L | L | 6-2 | 190 | 11-25-69 | 1992 | Cape May, N.J. |

### FIELDING

| Catcher | PCT | G | PO | A | E | DP | PB |
|---|---|---|---|---|---|---|---|
| Machado | .991 | 70 | 502 | 67 | 5 | 10 | 11 |
| Robledo | 1.000 | 2 | 8 | 3 | 0 | 0 | 0 |
| Vollmer | .975 | 71 | 543 | 46 | 15 | 2 | 10 |

| First Base | PCT | G | PO | A | E | DP |
|---|---|---|---|---|---|---|
| DiSarcina | 1.000 | 3 | 19 | 3 | 0 | 2 |
| Duross | .989 | 28 | 242 | 22 | 3 | 17 |
| Pearson | .984 | 68 | 529 | 42 | 9 | 32 |
| Robledo | .941 | 3 | 27 | 5 | 2 | 1 |
| Rose | .967 | 8 | 58 | 1 | 2 | 7 |
| Valdez | .993 | 33 | 273 | 25 | 2 | 31 |
| Vollmer | .000 | 1 | 0 | 0 | 0 | 0 |

| Second Base | PCT | G | PO | A | E | DP |
|---|---|---|---|---|---|---|
| DiSarcina | 1.000 | 5 | 12 | 10 | 0 | 4 |
| Menechino | .978 | 123 | 273 | 308 | 13 | 74 |

| | PCT | G | PO | A | E | DP |
|---|---|---|---|---|---|---|
| Polidor | 1.000 | 5 | 8 | 11 | 0 | 1 |
| Rose | 1.000 | 2 | 1 | 4 | 0 | 0 |
| Sawkiw | .947 | 5 | 6 | 12 | 1 | 0 |
| Vollmer | 1.000 | 1 | 1 | 0 | 0 | 0 |
| Wilson | .909 | 2 | 4 | 6 | 1 | 3 |

| Third Base | PCT | G | PO | A | E | DP |
|---|---|---|---|---|---|---|
| DiSarcina | .941 | 25 | 16 | 48 | 4 | 3 |
| Polidor | .941 | 6 | 4 | 12 | 1 | 2 |
| Rose | .942 | 97 | 73 | 201 | 17 | 12 |
| Sawkiw | .000 | 1 | 0 | 0 | 0 | 0 |
| Vollmer | 1.000 | 7 | 2 | 14 | 0 | 1 |
| Wilson | .939 | 11 | 6 | 25 | 2 | 3 |

| Shortstop | PCT | G | PO | A | E | DP |
|---|---|---|---|---|---|---|
| DiSarcina | .941 | 4 | 7 | 9 | 1 | 1 |

| | PCT | G | PO | A | E | DP |
|---|---|---|---|---|---|---|
| Norton | .949 | 76 | 104 | 214 | 17 | 34 |
| Polidor | .975 | 12 | 9 | 30 | 1 | 5 |
| Rose | .750 | 1 | 1 | 2 | 1 | 0 |
| Sawkiw | .929 | 12 | 16 | 23 | 3 | 5 |
| Wilson | .930 | 40 | 57 | 117 | 13 | 28 |

| Outfield | PCT | G | PO | A | E | DP |
|---|---|---|---|---|---|---|
| Cameron | .973 | 120 | 249 | 8 | 7 | 1 |
| Fryman | 1.000 | 8 | 14 | 0 | 0 | 0 |
| Hurst | .972 | 119 | 234 | 11 | 7 | 2 |
| Larregui | .983 | 45 | 56 | 1 | 1 | 0 |
| Ordonez | .976 | 129 | 231 | 12 | 6 | 3 |
| Sawkiw | 1.000 | 2 | 2 | 0 | 0 | 0 |
| Valdez | 1.000 | 7 | 11 | 1 | 0 | 0 |

## CAROLINA LEAGUE

| BATTING | AVG | G | AB | R | H | 2B | 3B | HR | RBI | BB | SO | SB | CS | B | T | HT | WT | DOB | 1st Yr | Resides |
|---|---|---|---|---|---|---|---|---|---|---|---|---|---|---|---|---|---|---|---|---|
| Antczak, Chuck | .091 | 5 | 11 | 2 | 1 | 0 | 0 | 0 | 0 | 1 | 2 | 0 | 0 | R | R | 6-0 | 185 | 10-8-73 | 1995 | Sarasota, Fla. |
| Avery, Mark | .237 | 75 | 270 | 33 | 64 | 16 | 2 | 9 | 31 | 32 | 66 | 0 | 0 | R | R | 6-2 | 215 | 7-26-70 | 1993 | Sterling Heights, Mich. |
| Boulware, Ben | .253 | 117 | 443 | 41 | 112 | 18 | 1 | 5 | 52 | 28 | 51 | 16 | 6 | R | R | 5-11 | 185 | 2-25-72 | 1993 | Los Gatos, Calif. |
| Carone, Rick | .111 | 7 | 27 | 1 | 3 | 1 | 0 | 1 | 3 | 3 | 7 | 0 | 1 | R | R | 6-0 | 195 | 1-17-71 | 1993 | Cary, Ill. |
| Evans, Jason | .264 | 95 | 329 | 41 | 87 | 24 | 2 | 4 | 41 | 58 | 80 | 4 | 3 | S | R | 5-11 | 187 | 2-11-71 | 1992 | Chatsworth, Calif. |
| Fraraccio, Dan | .275 | 44 | 149 | 16 | 41 | 9 | 0 | 0 | 20 | 12 | 20 | 1 | 0 | R | R | 5-11 | 175 | 9-18-70 | 1992 | Bradenton, Fla. |
| Hayes, Darren | .212 | 66 | 189 | 28 | 40 | 8 | 2 | 1 | 19 | 29 | 64 | 5 | 2 | R | R | 6-1 | 195 | 11-12-72 | 1995 | Lenoir, N.C. |
| Johnson, Mark | .241 | 18 | 58 | 9 | 14 | 3 | 0 | 0 | 3 | 13 | 6 | 0 | 0 | L | R | 6-0 | 185 | 9-12-75 | 1994 | Warner Robins, Ga. |
| Kopriva, Dan | .252 | 91 | 337 | 53 | 85 | 21 | 1 | 8 | 39 | 59 | 44 | 0 | 0 | R | R | 5-11 | 190 | 11-6-69 | 1992 | Traer, Iowa |
| Levias, Andres | .100 | 15 | 40 | 3 | 4 | 1 | 0 | 0 | 1 | 4 | 15 | 0 | 1 | S | R | 6-1 | 175 | 10-1-73 | 1992 | Lakewood, Calif. |
| Liefer, Jeff | .224 | 37 | 147 | 17 | 33 | 6 | 0 | 1 | 13 | 11 | 27 | 0 | 0 | L | R | 6-3 | 195 | 8-17-74 | 1996 | Upland, Calif. |
| McKinnon, Sandy | .263 | 113 | 410 | 56 | 108 | 28 | 5 | 8 | 60 | 23 | 68 | 20 | 10 | R | R | 5-8 | 175 | 9-20-73 | 1993 | Nicholls, Ga. |
| Moore, Brandon | .241 | 125 | 439 | 56 | 106 | 13 | 2 | 1 | 42 | 82 | 70 | 9 | 11 | R | R | 5-11 | 175 | 8-23-72 | 1994 | Springville, Ala. |
| Polidor, Wil | .232 | 72 | 276 | 26 | 64 | 7 | 3 | 2 | 26 | 15 | 34 | 2 | 4 | S | R | 6-1 | 158 | 9-23-73 | 1991 | Caracas, Venez. |
| Robledo, Nilson | .259 | 80 | 313 | 37 | 81 | 16 | 0 | 8 | 46 | 21 | 55 | 0 | 0 | R | R | 6-1 | 165 | 11-3-68 | 1989 | Entrega, Panama |
| Simmons, Brian | .198 | 33 | 131 | 17 | 26 | 4 | 3 | 4 | 14 | 9 | 39 | 2 | 0 | S | R | 6-2 | 191 | 9-4-73 | 1995 | McMurray, Pa. |
| Strasser, John | .200 | 18 | 55 | 7 | 11 | 0 | 0 | 1 | 2 | 8 | 18 | 0 | 0 | R | R | 5-10 | 165 | 11-28-74 | 1995 | Glendale, Ariz. |
| Thomas, Juan | .299 | 134 | 495 | 88 | 148 | 28 | 6 | 20 | 71 | 54 | 129 | 9 | 3 | R | R | 6-5 | 240 | 4-17-72 | 1991 | Ashland, Ky. |
| Walker, Joe | .199 | 54 | 161 | 22 | 32 | 9 | 0 | 5 | 14 | 18 | 65 | 0 | 0 | S | R | 6-3 | 210 | 11-15-71 | 1995 | Saginaw, Mich. |
| Whittaker, Jerry | .257 | 83 | 303 | 50 | 78 | 12 | 3 | 10 | 42 | 24 | 70 | 13 | 4 | R | R | 6-2 | 190 | 11-17-94 | 1994 | Long Beach, Calif. |

**GAMES BY POSITION: C**—Antczak 3, Avery 37, Carone 7, Johnson 16, Robledo 40, Walker 40. **1B**—Kopriva 2, Robledo 18, Thomas 118. **2B**—Boulware 87, Moore 7, Polidor 39, Strasser 13. **3B**—Fraraccio 21, Kopriva 89, Polidor 30. **SS**—Fraraccio 16, Moore 117, Polidor 8, Strasser 2. **OF**—Boulware 33, Evans 94, Fraraccio 4, Hayes 65, Levias 14, McKinnon 107, Simmons 4, Whittaker 82.

| PITCHING | W | L | ERA | G | GS | CG | SV | IP | H | R | ER | BB | SO | B | T | HT | WT | DOB | 1st Yr | Resides |
|---|---|---|---|---|---|---|---|---|---|---|---|---|---|---|---|---|---|---|---|---|
| Broome, Curtis | 3 | 3 | 5.46 | 27 | 2 | 0 | 0 | 56 | 68 | 41 | 34 | 38 | 33 | R | R | 6-2 | 195 | 4-30-72 | 1993 | Gary, Ind. |
| Buteaux, Shane | 2 | 3 | 3.35 | 23 | 0 | 0 | 2 | 40 | 34 | 18 | 15 | 22 | 29 | R | R | 6-3 | 202 | 12-28-71 | 1994 | New Iberia, La. |
| Castillo, Carlos | 2 | 4 | 3.95 | 6 | 6 | 4 | 0 | 43 | 45 | 22 | 19 | 4 | 30 | R | R | 6-2 | 230 | 4-21-75 | 1994 | Miami, Fla. |
| Christman, Scott | 1 | 0 | 0.00 | 1 | 1 | 0 | 0 | 5 | 4 | 0 | 0 | 3 | 4 | L | L | 6-3 | 190 | 12-3-71 | 1993 | Vancouver, Wash. |
| Clemons, Chris | 1 | 4 | 2.25 | 6 | 6 | 0 | 0 | 36 | 36 | 16 | 9 | 8 | 26 | R | R | 6-4 | 220 | 10-31-72 | 1994 | McGregor, Texas |
| Desrosiers, Erik | 1 | 1 | 5.63 | 7 | 7 | 1 | 0 | 40 | 47 | 29 | 25 | 9 | 25 | R | R | 6-4 | 210 | 9-21-74 | 1995 | Fountain Hills, Ariz. |
| Dixon, Jim | 5 | 7 | 4.79 | 38 | 2 | 0 | 4 | 73 | 71 | 46 | 39 | 31 | 56 | R | R | 6-3 | 195 | 10-7-72 | 1993 | Raton, N.M. |
| Duncan, Sean | 0 | 0 | 5.74 | 6 | 0 | 0 | 1 | 16 | 17 | 11 | 10 | 9 | 13 | L | L | 6-2 | 195 | 4-9-74 | 1994 | Arlington, Texas |
| Ford, Jack | 3 | 4 | 4.18 | 36 | 0 | 0 | 1 | 75 | 78 | 40 | 35 | 29 | 59 | L | L | 6-0 | 170 | 11-30-71 | 1992 | Paris, Texas |
| Halley, Allen | 7 | 12 | 3.54 | 24 | 24 | 4 | 0 | 137 | 123 | 69 | 54 | 49 | 131 | S | R | 6-1 | 195 | 9-7-71 | 1995 | St. Maarten, Neth. Antilles |
| Hasselhoff, Derek | 1 | 1 | 5.23 | 5 | 0 | 0 | 1 | 10 | 14 | 7 | 6 | 6 | 9 | R | R | 6-2 | 185 | 10-10-73 | 1995 | Pasadena, Md. |
| Herbert, Russ | 6 | 10 | 3.38 | 25 | 25 | 1 | 0 | 144 | 129 | 73 | 54 | 62 | 148 | R | R | 6-4 | 200 | 4-21-72 | 1994 | Mentor, Ohio |
| Lundquist, David | 0 | 2 | 5.67 | 5 | 5 | 0 | 0 | 27 | 31 | 17 | 17 | 14 | 23 | R | R | 6-2 | 200 | 6-4-73 | 1993 | Carson City, Nev. |
| Olsen, Jim | 6 | 4 | 3.87 | 12 | 12 | 0 | 0 | 79 | 74 | 39 | 34 | 31 | 55 | R | R | 6-4 | 210 | 3-16-75 | 1995 | Fairfield, Calif. |
| Place, Mike | 6 | 2 | 2.31 | 23 | 0 | 0 | 7 | 39 | 30 | 17 | 10 | 7 | 31 | R | R | 6-4 | 190 | 8-13-70 | 1990 | Seminole, Fla. |
| Portillo, Alex | 1 | 1 | 5.29 | 25 | 0 | 0 | 2 | 49 | 55 | 35 | 29 | 16 | 30 | L | L | 6-1 | 175 | 12-27-74 | 1992 | El Hatillo, Venez. |
| Quirk, John | 1 | 2 | 6.21 | 18 | 3 | 0 | 0 | 42 | 52 | 34 | 29 | 28 | 22 | L | L | 6-4 | 210 | 11-20-70 | 1993 | Bronx, N.Y. |
| Smith, Chuck | 6 | 6 | 4.01 | 20 | 20 | 2 | 0 | 123 | 125 | 65 | 55 | 49 | 99 | R | R | 6-1 | 175 | 10-21-69 | 1991 | Cleveland, Ohio |
| Theodile, Robert | 7 | 9 | 4.30 | 25 | 22 | 1 | 1 | 132 | 133 | 73 | 63 | 56 | 91 | R | R | 6-3 | 190 | 9-16-72 | 1992 | Jeanerette, La. |
| Zappelli, Mark | 0 | 2 | 5.84 | 4 | 3 | 1 | 0 | 25 | 28 | 16 | 16 | 8 | 9 | R | R | 6-0 | 185 | 7-21-66 | 1989 | Santa Rosa, Calif. |

## MIDWEST LEAGUE

| BATTING | AVG | G | AB | R | H | 2B | 3B | HR | RBI | BB | SO | SB | CS | B | T | HT | WT | DOB | 1st Yr | Resides |
|---|---|---|---|---|---|---|---|---|---|---|---|---|---|---|---|---|---|---|---|---|
| Anderson, Frank | .155 | 68 | 213 | 8 | 33 | 5 | 3 | 4 | 19 | 10 | 89 | 1 | 2 | R | R | 6-1 | 200 | 9-1-75 | 1995 | Stockbridge, Ga. |
| Antczak, Chuck | .097 | 16 | 31 | 3 | 3 | 2 | 0 | 0 | 1 | 1 | 9 | 0 | 0 | R | R | 6-0 | 185 | 10-8-73 | 1995 | Sarasota, Fla. |
| Bowness, Brian | .202 | 65 | 203 | 19 | 41 | 4 | 1 | 0 | 18 | 18 | 36 | 1 | 2 | R | R | 6-3 | 205 | 5-23-74 | 1995 | East Hanover, N.J. |
| Cancel, David | .251 | 96 | 315 | 30 | 79 | 7 | 2 | 2 | 29 | 13 | 37 | 12 | 8 | S | R | 5-11 | 168 | 3-3-74 | 1994 | San Sebastian, P.R. |
| Drent, Brian | .189 | 93 | 291 | 37 | 55 | 17 | 1 | 2 | 23 | 44 | 107 | 12 | 6 | R | R | 6-3 | 205 | 7-27-73 | 1994 | Worthington, Minn. |
| Friedrich, Steve | .264 | 133 | 545 | 51 | 144 | 25 | 6 | 3 | 46 | 20 | 114 | 18 | 11 | R | R | 6-0 | 175 | 5-29-73 | 1993 | Yorba Linda, Calif. |
| Garcia, Luis | .217 | 58 | 221 | 23 | 48 | 9 | 1 | 1 | 16 | 9 | 29 | 3 | 4 | R | R | 6-3 | 200 | 9-22-75 | 1995 | Hermosillo, Mexico |
| Hayes, Darren | .071 | 9 | 28 | 5 | 2 | 0 | 0 | 1 | 5 | 4 | 14 | 1 | 1 | R | R | 6-1 | 195 | 11-12-72 | 1995 | Lenoir, N.C. |
| Heintz, Chris | .265 | 64 | 230 | 25 | 61 | 12 | 1 | 1 | 22 | 23 | 46 | 1 | 1 | R | R | 6-1 | 200 | 8-6-74 | 1996 | Clearwater, Fla. |
| Izquierdo, Sergio | .000 | 2 | 2 | 0 | 0 | 0 | 0 | 0 | 0 | 1 | 0 | 0 | 0 | R | R | 5-9 | 182 | 8-11-72 | 1994 | Hialeah, Fla. |
| Johnson, Jeff | .180 | 102 | 345 | 27 | 62 | 13 | 0 | 2 | 39 | 22 | 49 | 10 | 7 | R | R | 5-10 | 175 | 6-8-73 | 1995 | Clinton, Miss. |
| Johnson, Mark | .257 | 67 | 214 | 29 | 55 | 14 | 3 | 2 | 27 | 39 | 25 | 3 | 3 | L | R | 6-0 | 185 | 9-12-75 | 1994 | Warner Robins, Ga. |
| Klee, Chuck | .236 | 18 | 55 | 8 | 13 | 0 | 0 | 2 | 4 | 7 | 13 | 2 | 2 | R | R | 6-3 | 175 | 5-15-77 | 1995 | Lighthouse Point, Fla. |
| Liefer, Jeff | .325 | 74 | 277 | 60 | 90 | 14 | 0 | 15 | 58 | 30 | 62 | 6 | 5 | L | R | 6-3 | 195 | 8-17-74 | 1996 | Upland, Calif. |
| Sheppard, Greg | .268 | 54 | 142 | 17 | 38 | 5 | 1 | 0 | 9 | 11 | 40 | 5 | 2 | R | R | 6-0 | 190 | 3-1-75 | 1996 | Lancaster, Calif. |
| Simmons, Brian | .298 | 92 | 356 | 72 | 106 | 29 | 6 | 17 | 58 | 48 | 69 | 14 | 9 | S | R | 6-2 | 191 | 9-4-73 | 1995 | McMurray, Pa. |
| Strasser, John | .125 | 2 | 8 | 0 | 1 | 0 | 0 | 0 | 0 | 0 | 4 | 0 | 0 | R | R | 5-10 | 165 | 11-28-74 | 1995 | Glendale, Ariz. |
| Topham, Ryan | .232 | 114 | 392 | 50 | 91 | 17 | 7 | 5 | 39 | 53 | 106 | 18 | 9 | L | L | 6-3 | 200 | 12-17-73 | 1995 | Portage, Mich. |
| Valdez, Mario | .376 | 61 | 202 | 44 | 76 | 19 | 0 | 10 | 43 | 36 | 42 | 2 | 4 | L | R | 6-2 | 190 | 11-19-74 | 1994 | Hialeah, Fla. |
| Wilhelm, Brent | .242 | 107 | 380 | 55 | 92 | 21 | 4 | 4 | 38 | 57 | 55 | 8 | 8 | R | R | 6-0 | 185 | 1-22-73 | 1995 | Independence, Mo. |

**GAMES BY POSITION: C**—Anderson 68, Antczak 11, Izquierdo 1, M. Johnson 65, Sheppard 4. **1B**—Bowness 51, Heintz 11, Sheppard 26, Valdez 52, Wilhelm 6. **2B**—Friedrich 109, Heintz 1, J. Johnson 28, Sheppard 1, Wilhelm 5. **3B**—Antczak 2, Friedrich 5, Heintz 49, Klee 2, Liefer 36, Sheppard 2, Wilhelm 43. **SS**—Friedrich 19, J. Johnson 74, Klee 16, Strasser 2, Wilhelm 33. **OF**—Cancel 79, Drent 78, Friedrich 1, Garcia 45, Hayes 9, Sheppard 10, Simmons 91, Topham 102.

| PITCHING | W | L | ERA | G | GS | CG | SV | IP | H | R | ER | BB | SO | B | T | HT | WT | DOB | 1st Yr | Resides |
|---|---|---|---|---|---|---|---|---|---|---|---|---|---|---|---|---|---|---|---|---|
| Beirne, Kevin | 11 | 4 | 4.15 | 26 | 25 | 1 | 0 | 145 | 153 | 85 | 67 | 60 | 110 | L | R | 6-4 | 210 | 1-7-74 | 1995 | The Woodlands, Texas |
| Buteaux, Shane | 3 | 4 | 3.23 | 25 | 0 | 0 | 2 | 39 | 37 | 21 | 14 | 15 | 33 | R | R | 6-3 | 202 | 12-28-71 | 1994 | New Iberia, La. |
| Castillo, Carlos | 9 | 9 | 4.05 | 20 | 19 | 5 | 0 | 133 | 131 | 74 | 60 | 29 | 128 | R | R | 6-2 | 230 | 4-21-75 | 1994 | Miami, Fla. |
| Chantres, Carlos | 3 | 5 | 3.60 | 10 | 10 | 1 | 0 | 65 | 61 | 31 | 26 | 19 | 41 | R | R | 6-3 | 175 | 4-1-76 | 1994 | Miami, Fla. |
| Desrosiers, Erik | 3 | 5 | 4.72 | 14 | 12 | 0 | 1 | 69 | 68 | 41 | 36 | 19 | 39 | R | R | 6-4 | 210 | 9-21-74 | 1995 | Fountain Hills, Ariz. |
| Duncan, Sean | 2 | 5 | 3.38 | 43 | 0 | 0 | 3 | 56 | 43 | 29 | 21 | 23 | 54 | L | L | 6-2 | 195 | 6-9-73 | 1994 | Arlington, Texas |

| PITCHING | W | L | ERA | G | GS | CG | SV | IP | H | R | ER | BB | SO | B | T | HT | WT | DOB | 1st Yr | Resides |
|---|---|---|---|---|---|---|---|---|---|---|---|---|---|---|---|---|---|---|---|---|
| Filbeck, Ryan | 1 | 4 | 3.63 | 19 | 2 | 0 | 3 | 35 | 27 | 16 | 14 | 11 | 20 | R | R | 6-2 | 200 | 12-23-72 | 1993 | El Toro, Calif. |
| Garber, Joel | 0 | 5 | 5.10 | 14 | 7 | 0 | 0 | 48 | 60 | 40 | 27 | 15 | 27 | L | L | 6-4 | 200 | 10-14-73 | 1995 | Manhattan Beach, Calif. |
| Garcia, Ariel | 6 | 10 | 4.58 | 26 | 26 | 0 | 0 | 151 | 159 | 96 | 77 | 48 | 76 | R | R | 6-0 | 158 | 10-3-75 | 1993 | Panama City, Panama |
| Hasselhoff, Derek | 6 | 3 | 3.02 | 35 | 0 | 0 | 10 | 48 | 46 | 18 | 16 | 17 | 39 | R | R | 6-2 | 185 | 10-10-73 | 1995 | Pasadena, Md. |
| Kraus, Tim | 3 | 4 | 2.67 | 35 | 5 | 0 | 0 | 81 | 82 | 42 | 24 | 31 | 48 | L | R | 6-1 | 190 | 12-26-72 | 1995 | Cincinnati, Ohio |
| Kruse, Kelly | 1 | 2 | 4.89 | 26 | 0 | 0 | 2 | 35 | 36 | 21 | 19 | 20 | 16 | R | R | 6-3 | 210 | 5-1-72 | 1995 | Russellville, Mo. |
| Olsen, Jason | 4 | 1 | 1.75 | 9 | 9 | 0 | 0 | 57 | 39 | 16 | 11 | 13 | 55 | R | R | 6-4 | 210 | 3-16-75 | 1995 | Fairfield, Calif. |
| Portillo, Alex | 0 | 0 | 2.89 | 7 | 0 | 0 | 0 | 9 | 9 | 4 | 3 | 1 | 9 | L | L | 6-1 | 175 | 12-27-74 | 1992 | El Hatillo, Venez. |
| Quirk, John | 0 | 0 | 4.26 | 5 | 0 | 0 | 0 | 6 | 8 | 3 | 3 | 7 | 1 | L | L | 6-4 | 210 | 11-20-70 | 1993 | Bronx, N.Y. |
| Secoda, Jason | 6 | 12 | 3.97 | 31 | 21 | 0 | 1 | 134 | 132 | 84 | 59 | 75 | 94 | R | R | 6-4 | 195 | 9-2-74 | 1995 | Fullerton, Calif. |
| Vota, Michael | 2 | 2 | 4.57 | 34 | 0 | 0 | 0 | 65 | 79 | 41 | 33 | 23 | 35 | R | R | 6-4 | 175 | 12-29-72 | 1995 | Dubois, Pa. |

# HICKORY | Class A

## SOUTH ATLANTIC LEAGUE

| BATTING | AVG | G | AB | R | H | 2B | 3B | HR | RBI | BB | SO | SB | CS | B | T | HT | WT | DOB | 1st Yr | Resides |
|---|---|---|---|---|---|---|---|---|---|---|---|---|---|---|---|---|---|---|---|---|
| Albert, Rashad | .235 | 49 | 179 | 31 | 42 | 7 | 3 | 2 | 10 | 14 | 51 | 18 | 6 | R | R | 6-1 | 165 | 9-18-75 | 1994 | Fernandina Beach, Fla. |
| Antczak, Chuck | .154 | 9 | 13 | 0 | 2 | 0 | 0 | 0 | 1 | 3 | 2 | 0 | 0 | R | R | 6-0 | 185 | 10-8-73 | 1995 | Sarasota, Fla. |
| Baugh, Darren | .285 | 68 | 267 | 46 | 76 | 5 | 2 | 2 | 24 | 27 | 48 | 17 | 5 | R | R | 6-3 | 175 | 9-3-75 | 1996 | San Mateo, Calif. |
| Bearden, Doug | .219 | 49 | 169 | 12 | 37 | 7 | 0 | 1 | 11 | 3 | 35 | 0 | 3 | R | R | 6-2 | 170 | 9-11-75 | 1994 | Lexington, S.C. |
| Christensen, McKay | .000 | 6 | 11 | 0 | 0 | 0 | 0 | 0 | 0 | 1 | 4 | 0 | 0 | L | L | 5-11 | 178 | 8-14-75 | 1995 | Clovis, Calif. |
| Downs, Brian | .208 | 84 | 279 | 23 | 58 | 10 | 0 | 3 | 28 | 15 | 78 | 0 | 1 | R | R | 6-2 | 210 | 4-10-75 | 1995 | Chino, Calif. |
| Fauske, Josh | .243 | 115 | 412 | 43 | 100 | 20 | 0 | 9 | 62 | 51 | 132 | 1 | 1 | R | R | 6-4 | 230 | 3-16-74 | 1995 | Mercer Island, Wash. |
| Garcia, Luis | .273 | 76 | 289 | 31 | 79 | 18 | 3 | 3 | 38 | 14 | 41 | 9 | 6 | R | R | 6-3 | 200 | 9-22-75 | 1995 | Hermosillo, Mexico |
| Gomez, Ramon | .249 | 116 | 418 | 73 | 104 | 8 | 3 | 1 | 30 | 44 | 99 | 57 | 19 | R | R | 6-2 | 175 | 10-6-75 | 1994 | San Pedro de Macoris, D.R. |
| Hollins, Darontaye | .167 | 37 | 132 | 10 | 22 | 2 | 0 | 0 | 6 | 10 | 41 | 3 | 3 | R | R | 6-0 | 200 | 9-6-74 | 1995 | Roseville, Calif. |
| Inglin, Jeff | .361 | 22 | 83 | 12 | 30 | 6 | 2 | 2 | 15 | 4 | 11 | 2 | 1 | R | R | 5-11 | 185 | 10-8-75 | 1996 | Petaluma, Calif. |
| Klee, Chuck | .202 | 38 | 109 | 7 | 22 | 2 | 1 | 0 | 7 | 5 | 31 | 2 | 2 | R | R | 6-3 | 175 | 5-15-77 | 1995 | Lighthouse Point, Fla. |
| Lee, Carlos | .313 | 119 | 480 | 65 | 150 | 23 | 6 | 8 | 70 | 23 | 50 | 18 | 13 | R | R | 6-2 | 202 | 6-20-76 | 1994 | Aguadulce, Panama |
| Lutz, Manuel | .238 | 44 | 143 | 10 | 34 | 2 | 0 | 1 | 12 | 9 | 46 | 0 | 1 | L | R | 6-2 | 230 | 6-14-76 | 1995 | Spring Valley, Calif. |
| McClure, Craig | .203 | 59 | 212 | 21 | 43 | 8 | 3 | 2 | 19 | 20 | 62 | 6 | 2 | R | R | 6-1 | 175 | 8-4-75 | 1993 | Littleton, Colo. |
| Olson, Dan | .249 | 57 | 193 | 25 | 48 | 8 | 2 | 2 | 19 | 31 | 65 | 2 | 3 | L | L | 6-2 | 215 | 4-14-75 | 1996 | Cape May, N.J. |
| Paul, Josh | .327 | 59 | 226 | 41 | 74 | 16 | 0 | 8 | 37 | 21 | 53 | 13 | 4 | R | R | 6-1 | 185 | 5-19-75 | 1996 | Buffalo Grove, Ill. |
| Pryor, Pete | .307 | 59 | 205 | 37 | 63 | 18 | 1 | 6 | 37 | 36 | 43 | 3 | 2 | L | L | 6-4 | 265 | 9-3-75 | 1996 | Sacramento, Calif. |
| Rodriguez, Liu | .249 | 122 | 430 | 57 | 107 | 18 | 0 | 0 | 30 | 60 | 77 | 15 | 14 | S | R | 5-9 | 170 | 11-5-76 | 1995 | Caracas, Venez |
| Romero, Marty | .111 | 5 | 18 | 2 | 2 | 0 | 0 | 0 | 1 | 1 | 4 | 0 | 0 | L | R | 6-1 | 180 | 9-13-76 | 1994 | Cape Coral, Fla. |
| Shelton, Barry | .211 | 47 | 161 | 15 | 34 | 9 | 0 | 3 | 13 | 12 | 52 | 1 | 2 | R | R | 5-11 | 210 | 8-4-73 | 1995 | Roanoke, Va. |
| Stevens, Clayton | .212 | 35 | 113 | 6 | 24 | 4 | 1 | 2 | 14 | 7 | 47 | 0 | 1 | R | R | 6-3 | 210 | 7-28-75 | 1995 | Bay Minette, Ala. |
| Strasser, John | .149 | 41 | 101 | 10 | 15 | 3 | 0 | 1 | 8 | 11 | 24 | 2 | 5 | R | R | 5-10 | 165 | 11-28-74 | 1995 | Glendale, Ariz. |
| Thomas, Allen | .250 | 36 | 100 | 19 | 25 | 6 | 0 | 1 | 20 | 11 | 31 | 3 | 0 | L | L | 6-0 | 190 | 2-4-74 | 1996 | Morganton, N.C. |

**GAMES BY POSITION: C**—Antczak 8, Downs 84, Fauske 32, Lutz 1, Paul 27, Romero 5. **1B**—Fauske 43, Lee 9, Inglin 19, Pryor 55, Shelton 26. **2B**—Bearden 29, Rodriguez 91, Strasser 31. **3B**—Bearden 6, Lee 113, Lutz 17, Shelton 5, Strasser 9. **SS**—Baugh 68, Bearden 16, Klee 37, Rodriguez 33. **OF**—Albert 46, Christensen 5, Garcia 57, Gomez 111, Hollins 34, Inglin 16, McClure 43, Olson 49, Olson 21, Stevens 32, Thomas 26.

| PITCHING | W | L | ERA | G | GS | CG | SV | IP | H | R | ER | BB | SO | B | T | HT | WT | DOB | 1st Yr | Resides |
|---|---|---|---|---|---|---|---|---|---|---|---|---|---|---|---|---|---|---|---|---|
| Bales, Joe | 1 | 1 | 8.35 | 15 | 2 | 0 | 0 | 32 | 45 | 35 | 30 | 29 | 24 | R | R | 6-5 | 175 | 9-13-74 | 1993 | Reno, Nev. |
| Bere, Jason | 1 | 0 | 0.00 | 1 | 1 | 0 | 0 | 7 | 0 | 0 | 0 | 0 | 5 | R | R | 6-3 | 185 | 5-26-71 | 1990 | Wilmington, Mass. |
| Bradford, Chad | 0 | 2 | 0.90 | 28 | 0 | 0 | 18 | 30 | 21 | 7 | 3 | 7 | 27 | R | R | 6-5 | 205 | 9-14-74 | 1996 | Jackson, Miss. |
| Buckman, Tom | 0 | 3 | 2.57 | 16 | 0 | 0 | 1 | 28 | 36 | 16 | 8 | 7 | 15 | R | R | 6-6 | 200 | 6-28-74 | 1995 | Pembroke Pines, Fla. |
| Chantres, Carlos | 6 | 7 | 3.76 | 18 | 18 | 0 | 0 | 120 | 108 | 63 | 50 | 38 | 93 | R | R | 6-3 | 175 | 4-1-76 | 1994 | Miami, Fla. |
| Demorejon, Pete | 1 | 2 | 4.43 | 17 | 1 | 0 | 0 | 43 | 45 | 26 | 21 | 22 | 34 | R | R | 6-1 | 180 | 10-16-74 | 1995 | Miami, Fla. |
| Farley, Joe | 3 | 0 | 2.10 | 4 | 4 | 0 | 0 | 26 | 21 | 6 | 6 | 5 | 15 | L | L | 6-3 | 185 | 9-12-74 | 1996 | Montoursville, Pa. |
| Garber, Joel | 1 | 1 | 4.03 | 17 | 1 | 0 | 2 | 51 | 60 | 26 | 23 | 16 | 46 | L | L | 6-4 | 200 | 10-14-73 | 1995 | Manhattan Beach, Calif. |
| Gray, Jason | 3 | 8 | 4.59 | 13 | 13 | 1 | 0 | 69 | 67 | 45 | 35 | 28 | 61 | R | R | 6-2 | 185 | 4-28-77 | 1995 | North Lauderdale, Fla. |
| Hunt, Jon | 7 | 10 | 3.78 | 25 | 25 | 3 | 0 | 143 | 136 | 85 | 60 | 70 | 80 | L | L | 6-1 | 190 | 5-17-74 | 1995 | Ironton, Ohio |
| Iglesias, Mario | 3 | 4 | 4.93 | 10 | 5 | 0 | 1 | 35 | 45 | 19 | 19 | 6 | 31 | R | R | 6-3 | 195 | 6-2-74 | 1996 | Castro Valley, Calif. |
| Lakman, Jason | 0 | 6 | 6.79 | 13 | 13 | 0 | 0 | 64 | 66 | 55 | 48 | 43 | 43 | R | R | 6-4 | 220 | 10-17-76 | 1995 | Woodinville, Wash. |
| Nichols, James | 0 | 4 | 2.70 | 20 | 1 | 0 | 1 | 50 | 52 | 30 | 15 | 18 | 45 | R | R | 6-4 | 215 | 1-22-76 | 1995 | Bear, Del. |
| Nunez, Maximo | 5 | 16 | 4.67 | 31 | 24 | 3 | 0 | 152 | 173 | 93 | 79 | 45 | 105 | R | R | 6-5 | 165 | 1-15-73 | 1991 | Villa Mella, D.R. |
| Olsen, Jason | 2 | 1 | 1.37 | 4 | 4 | 1 | 0 | 26 | 19 | 5 | 4 | 6 | 32 | R | R | 6-4 | 210 | 3-16-75 | 1995 | Fairfield, Calif. |
| Reimers, Tom | 2 | 2 | 6.43 | 14 | 12 | 0 | 0 | 56 | 66 | 43 | 40 | 25 | 53 | R | R | 6-2 | 185 | 5-27-75 | 1996 | Santa Ana, Calif. |
| Roberts, Mark | 4 | 6 | 4.88 | 13 | 13 | 0 | 0 | 72 | 70 | 42 | 39 | 19 | 62 | R | R | 6-2 | 190 | 9-29-75 | 1996 | Zephyrhills, Fla. |
| Ruiz, Rafael | 1 | 2 | 3.35 | 34 | 0 | 0 | 0 | 51 | 58 | 32 | 19 | 13 | 52 | L | L | 6-0 | 170 | 2-17-75 | 1992 | Caracas, Venez. |
| Sauget, Rich | 2 | 1 | 3.99 | 25 | 0 | 0 | 1 | 47 | 48 | 24 | 21 | 9 | 39 | R | R | 6-4 | 220 | 1-28-73 | 1996 | Sauget, Ill. |
| Schmack, Brian | 4 | 2 | 2.31 | 43 | 0 | 0 | 5 | 62 | 61 | 24 | 16 | 16 | 56 | R | R | 6-2 | 195 | 12-7-73 | 1995 | Barrington, Ill. |
| Virchis, Adam | 8 | 6 | 3.27 | 26 | 3 | 0 | 0 | 83 | 82 | 38 | 30 | 25 | 42 | R | R | 6-3 | 180 | 10-15-73 | 1995 | Chula Vista, Calif. |

# BRISTOL | Rookie

## APPALACHIAN LEAGUE

| BATTING | AVG | G | AB | R | H | 2B | 3B | HR | RBI | BB | SO | SB | CS | B | T | HT | WT | DOB | 1st Yr | Resides |
|---|---|---|---|---|---|---|---|---|---|---|---|---|---|---|---|---|---|---|---|---|
| Albert, Rashad | .230 | 55 | 204 | 23 | 47 | 4 | 2 | 5 | 22 | 9 | 51 | 16 | 8 | R | R | 6-1 | 165 | 9-18-75 | 1994 | Fernandina Beach, Fla. |
| Antczak, Chuck | .304 | 7 | 23 | 2 | 7 | 0 | 0 | 0 | 2 | 5 | 0 | 0 | 0 | R | R | 6-0 | 185 | 10-8-73 | 1995 | Sarasota, Fla. |
| Bearden, Doug | .157 | 40 | 127 | 6 | 20 | 1 | 0 | 1 | 6 | 7 | 29 | 2 | 1 | R | R | 6-2 | 170 | 9-11-75 | 1994 | Lexington, S.C. |
| Connolly, Sean | .155 | 39 | 116 | 10 | 18 | 4 | 0 | 1 | 13 | 10 | 44 | 2 | 2 | R | R | 6-2 | 195 | 1-4-74 | 1996 | East Sandwich, Mass. |
| Heintz, Chris | .345 | 8 | 29 | 7 | 10 | 7 | 0 | 2 | 8 | 4 | 2 | 1 | 1 | R | R | 6-1 | 200 | 8-6-74 | 1996 | Clearwater, Fla. |
| Hollins, Darontaye | .172 | 16 | 58 | 8 | 10 | 2 | 0 | 0 | 6 | 6 | 20 | 5 | 2 | R | R | 6-0 | 200 | 9-6-74 | 1995 | Roseville, Calif. |
| Horn, Marv | .091 | 20 | 55 | 6 | 5 | 1 | 0 | 3 | 9 | 9 | 28 | 0 | 0 | L | L | 6-4 | 195 | 8-2-74 | 1995 | Hawthorne, Calif. |
| Inglin, Jeff | .290 | 50 | 193 | 27 | 56 | 10 | 0 | 8 | 24 | 11 | 25 | 9 | 6 | R | R | 5-11 | 185 | 10-8-75 | 1996 | Petaluma, Calif. |
| Klee, Chuck | .207 | 48 | 184 | 22 | 38 | 6 | 0 | 4 | 17 | 7 | 38 | 2 | 2 | R | R | 6-3 | 175 | 5-15-77 | 1995 | Lighthouse Point, Fla. |
| Lopes, Omar | .216 | 55 | 171 | 19 | 37 | 8 | 1 | 1 | 14 | 27 | 30 | 6 | 4 | R | R | 6-0 | 180 | 1-3-77 | 1996 | Valencia, Venez. |
| Lutz, Manuel | .252 | 55 | 202 | 26 | 51 | 12 | 1 | 6 | 23 | 17 | 53 | 1 | 2 | L | R | 6-2 | 230 | 6-14-76 | 1995 | Spring Valley, Calif. |
| McClure, Craig | .257 | 66 | 253 | 30 | 65 | 13 | 1 | 2 | 23 | 20 | 48 | 7 | 3 | R | R | 6-1 | 175 | 8-4-75 | 1993 | Littleton, Colo. |
| Romero, Marty | .225 | 36 | 111 | 10 | 25 | 8 | 0 | 1 | 10 | 11 | 34 | 2 | 1 | L | R | 6-1 | 180 | 9-13-76 | 1994 | Cape Coral, Fla. |
| Shelton, Barry | .247 | 45 | 154 | 19 | 38 | 8 | 0 | 2 | 13 | 8 | 50 | 2 | 2 | R | R | 5-11 | 210 | 8-4-73 | 1995 | Roanoke, Va. |

| BATTING | AVG | G | AB | R | H | 2B | 3B | HR | RBI | BB | SO | SB | CS | B | T | HT | WT | DOB | 1st Yr | Resides |
|---|---|---|---|---|---|---|---|---|---|---|---|---|---|---|---|---|---|---|---|---|
| Solano, Angel | .216 | 37 | 134 | 10 | 29 | 2 | 0 | 0 | 5 | 6 | 11 | 6 | 4 | R | R | 5-11 | 160 | 5-9-76 | 1995 | Villa Magdella, D.R. |
| Stevens, Clay | .215 | 48 | 149 | 19 | 32 | 3 | 2 | 5 | 23 | 24 | 69 | 5 | 4 | R | R | 6-3 | 210 | 7-28-75 | 1995 | Bay Minette, Ala. |

**GAMES BY POSITION: C**—Antczak 6, Connolly 38, Romero 30. **1B**—Heintz 8, Horn 5, Lutz 41, Romero 2, Shelton 16. **2B**—Bearden 38, Inglin 8, Solano 23. **3B**—Bearden 2, Inglin 11, Klee 17, Lopes 26, Lutz 2, Shelton 10, Solano 4. **SS**—Klee 32, Lopes 29, Solano 8. **OF**—Albert 54, Hollins 16, Inglin 18, Lutz 1, McClure 60, Shelton 17, Stevens 17.

| PITCHING | W | L | ERA | G | GS | CG | SV | IP | H | R | ER | BB | SO | B | T | HT | WT | DOB | 1st Yr | Resides |
|---|---|---|---|---|---|---|---|---|---|---|---|---|---|---|---|---|---|---|---|---|
| Bales, Joe | 1 | 10 | 5.15 | 13 | 12 | 1 | 0 | 72 | 74 | 49 | 41 | 39 | 55 | R | R | 6-5 | 175 | 9-13-74 | 1993 | Reno, Nev. |
| Buckman, Tom | 1 | 6 | 4.88 | 17 | 7 | 1 | 0 | 52 | 62 | 39 | 28 | 21 | 51 | R | R | 6-6 | 200 | 6-28-74 | 1995 | Pembroke Pines, Fla. |
| Cardona, Steve | 0 | 1 | 5.40 | 6 | 0 | 0 | 0 | 5 | 7 | 3 | 3 | 4 | 7 | R | R | 6-2 | 190 | 2-18-74 | 1996 | Stockton, Calif. |
| Carlson, Garret | 0 | 0 | 12.21 | 16 | 0 | 0 | 0 | 24 | 43 | 48 | 33 | 29 | 20 | R | R | 6-3 | 195 | 10-15-73 | 1995 | Spokane, Wash. |
| Demorejon, Pete | 1 | 2 | 6.99 | 18 | 1 | 0 | 1 | 37 | 49 | 33 | 29 | 22 | 39 | R | R | 6-1 | 180 | 10-16-74 | 1995 | Miami, Fla. |
| Farley, Joe | 3 | 6 | 3.48 | 10 | 10 | 3 | 0 | 65 | 73 | 34 | 25 | 11 | 54 | L | L | 6-3 | 185 | 9-12-74 | 1996 | Montoursville, Pa. |
| Heineman, Rick | 2 | 1 | 4.50 | 23 | 0 | 0 | 4 | 36 | 37 | 25 | 18 | 22 | 34 | R | R | 6-4 | 210 | 7-15-73 | 1996 | Culver City, Calif. |
| Hodges, Reid | 0 | 2 | 11.22 | 16 | 3 | 0 | 0 | 30 | 38 | 41 | 37 | 25 | 24 | R | R | 6-3 | 215 | 12-25-74 | 1996 | Stone Mountain, Ga. |
| Iglesias, Mario | 0 | 0 | 2.16 | 3 | 0 | 0 | 1 | 8 | 6 | 2 | 2 | 1 | 2 | R | R | 6-3 | 195 | 6-2-74 | 1996 | Castro Valley, Calif. |
| Irvine, Kirk | 0 | 0 | 4.87 | 11 | 5 | 1 | 0 | 41 | 49 | 30 | 22 | 10 | 39 | R | R | 6-0 | 185 | 1-27-75 | 1996 | Chino Hills, Calif. |
| Lakman, Jason | 4 | 4 | 5.67 | 13 | 13 | 1 | 0 | 67 | 70 | 48 | 42 | 38 | 64 | R | R | 6-4 | 220 | 10-17-76 | 1995 | Woodinville, Wash. |
| Nichols, James | 4 | 3 | 4.10 | 12 | 4 | 0 | 1 | 42 | 31 | 21 | 19 | 17 | 36 | R | R | 6-4 | 215 | 1-22-76 | 1995 | Bear, Del. |
| Schorzman, Steve | 0 | 9 | 4.57 | 14 | 13 | 1 | 0 | 69 | 73 | 43 | 35 | 31 | 50 | R | R | 6-3 | 190 | 7-6-74 | 1996 | Cambridge, Idaho |
| Stanley, Todd | 1 | 3 | 5.31 | 17 | 0 | 0 | 1 | 20 | 23 | 21 | 12 | 19 | 13 | R | R | 6-2 | 195 | 1-23-74 | 1996 | San Antonio, Texas |

## SARASOTA — GULF COAST LEAGUE — Rookie

| BATTING | AVG | G | AB | R | H | 2B | 3B | HR | RBI | BB | SO | SB | CS | B | T | HT | WT | DOB | 1st Yr | Resides |
|---|---|---|---|---|---|---|---|---|---|---|---|---|---|---|---|---|---|---|---|---|
| Bulheller, Greg | .100 | 9 | 20 | 0 | 2 | 1 | 0 | 0 | 1 | 0 | 4 | 0 | 0 | R | R | 6-2 | 210 | 4-14-74 | 1996 | Highland Springs, Va. |
| Carmona, Antonio | .234 | 47 | 154 | 15 | 36 | 5 | 1 | 0 | 15 | 7 | 26 | 4 | 2 | R | R | 5-11 | 175 | 12-8-76 | 1994 | San Pedro de Macoris, D.R. |
| Christensen, McKay | .263 | 35 | 133 | 17 | 35 | 7 | 5 | 1 | 16 | 10 | 23 | 10 | 3 | L | L | 5-11 | 178 | 8-14-75 | 1995 | Clovis, Calif. |
| Cochran, Ed | .174 | 53 | 144 | 20 | 25 | 5 | 1 | 0 | 12 | 11 | 45 | 6 | 1 | R | R | 6-2 | 185 | 1-3-78 | 1996 | Arroyo, P.R. |
| Crede, Joe | .299 | 56 | 221 | 30 | 66 | 17 | 1 | 4 | 32 | 9 | 41 | 1 | 1 | R | R | 6-3 | 185 | 4-26-78 | 1996 | Westphalia, Mo. |
| Fennell, Jason | .239 | 56 | 197 | 24 | 47 | 8 | 0 | 2 | 19 | 27 | 39 | 4 | 0 | S | R | 6-3 | 205 | 11-15-77 | 1996 | Butler, Pa. |
| Gonzalez, Jose | .277 | 51 | 166 | 22 | 46 | 6 | 3 | 0 | 14 | 12 | 31 | 4 | 6 | R | R | 5-10 | 170 | 9-24-77 | 1996 | Barcelona, Venez. |
| Horn, Marv | .250 | 9 | 28 | 4 | 7 | 0 | 0 | 0 | 2 | 6 | 3 | 1 | 0 | L | L | 6-4 | 195 | 8-2-74 | 1995 | Hawthorne, Calif. |
| McDermott, Mike | .250 | 44 | 144 | 17 | 36 | 11 | 0 | 2 | 18 | 11 | 38 | 1 | 3 | R | R | 6-3 | 195 | 11-7-76 | 1996 | Moraga, Calif. |
| Nova, Fernando | .300 | 58 | 203 | 24 | 61 | 12 | 1 | 1 | 22 | 18 | 48 | 9 | 6 | R | R | 6-0 | 168 | 2-9-76 | 1995 | San Pedro de Macoris, D.R. |
| Olson, Dan | .364 | 3 | 11 | 4 | 4 | 3 | 0 | 0 | 5 | 4 | 4 | 0 | 0 | L | L | 6-2 | 215 | 4-14-75 | 1996 | Cape May, N.J. |
| Parra, Alejandro | .116 | 39 | 86 | 12 | 10 | 0 | 0 | 0 | 3 | 21 | 28 | 2 | 2 | R | R | 5-10 | 165 | 11-19-77 | 1996 | Cumana, Venez. |
| Paul, Josh | .000 | 1 | 0 | 0 | 0 | 0 | 0 | 0 | 0 | 1 | 0 | 0 | 0 | R | R | 6-1 | 185 | 5-19-75 | 1996 | Buffalo Grove, Ill. |
| Pryor, Pete | .111 | 3 | 9 | 0 | 1 | 0 | 0 | 0 | 0 | 0 | 2 | 0 | 0 | L | L | 6-4 | 265 | 9-3-73 | 1996 | Sacramento, Calif. |
| Solano, Angel | .294 | 9 | 34 | 6 | 10 | 0 | 0 | 0 | 3 | 3 | 4 | 1 | 2 | R | R | 5-11 | 160 | 5-9-76 | 1996 | Villa Magdella, D.R. |
| Sutton, Joe | .221 | 40 | 113 | 10 | 25 | 7 | 1 | 1 | 11 | 15 | 33 | 1 | 0 | R | R | 6-3 | 225 | 10-17-74 | 1996 | West Union, W.Va. |
| Terrell, Jimmy | .223 | 56 | 220 | 21 | 49 | 7 | 0 | 2 | 9 | 13 | 45 | 3 | 4 | L | R | 6-2 | 175 | 9-8-77 | 1996 | Blue Springs, Mo. |
| Thomas, Allen | .208 | 7 | 24 | 4 | 5 | 1 | 2 | 0 | 2 | 1 | 8 | 0 | 0 | L | L | 6-0 | 190 | 2-4-74 | 1996 | Morganton, N.C. |
| Valenzuela, Mario | .260 | 21 | 73 | 6 | 19 | 3 | 2 | 1 | 8 | 4 | 20 | 0 | 0 | R | R | 6-2 | 190 | 3-10-77 | 1996 | San Marcos, Mexico |

**GAMES BY POSITION: C**—Bulheller 5, Carmona 31, Sutton 31. **1B**—Bulheller 3, Carmona 11, Cochran 4, Horn 9, McDermott 33, Pryor 2. **2B**—Cochran 1, Gonzalez 39, Parra 24, Solano 8, Sutton 1. **3B**—Crede 53, Gonzalez 4, McDermott 5. **SS**—Cochran 1, McDermott 2, Parra 12, Solano 2, Terrell 49. **OF**—Carmona 4, Christensen 26, Cochran 40, Fennell 46, Gonzalez 2, Nova 58, Olson 3, Thomas 5, Valenzuela 6.

| PITCHING | W | L | ERA | G | GS | CG | SV | IP | H | R | ER | BB | SO | B | T | HT | WT | DOB | 1st Yr | Resides |
|---|---|---|---|---|---|---|---|---|---|---|---|---|---|---|---|---|---|---|---|---|
| Andujar, Luis | 1 | 0 | 0.00 | 1 | 1 | 0 | 0 | 6 | 3 | 0 | 0 | 0 | 3 | R | R | 6-2 | 175 | 11-22-72 | 1991 | Bani, D.R. |
| Barry, Chad | 0 | 1 | 10.22 | 10 | 0 | 0 | 0 | 12 | 17 | 15 | 14 | 9 | 15 | R | R | 6-2 | 190 | 9-24-73 | 1996 | Santee, Calif. |
| Bere, Jason | 0 | 1 | 6.00 | 1 | 1 | 0 | 0 | 3 | 3 | 2 | 2 | 1 | 3 | R | R | 6-3 | 185 | 5-26-71 | 1990 | Wilmington, Mass. |
| Bullock, Brian | 0 | 0 | 0.00 | 1 | 0 | 0 | 0 | 1 | 0 | 0 | 0 | 2 | 1 | R | R | 6-1 | 205 | 7-4-76 | 1996 | Smyrna, Tenn. |
| Cardona, Steve | 1 | 1 | 2.63 | 15 | 0 | 0 | 0 | 24 | 28 | 10 | 7 | 9 | 31 | R | R | 6-2 | 190 | 2-18-74 | 1996 | Stockton, Calif. |
| Christman, Scott | 1 | 1 | 3.75 | 4 | 4 | 0 | 0 | 12 | 13 | 8 | 5 | 4 | 13 | L | L | 6-3 | 190 | 12-3-71 | 1993 | Vancouver, Wash. |
| De la Rosa, Raul | 0 | 2 | 6.92 | 18 | 1 | 0 | 1 | 26 | 43 | 31 | 20 | 9 | 16 | R | R | 6-2 | 168 | 6-3-76 | 1993 | San Pedro de Macoris, D.R. |
| Felix, Miguel | 3 | 6 | 3.31 | 12 | 12 | 1 | 0 | 73 | 73 | 39 | 27 | 19 | 64 | R | R | 6-1 | 155 | 12-30-76 | 1995 | San Pedro de Macoris, D.R. |
| Forti, Gene | 4 | 2 | 3.65 | 12 | 8 | 0 | 1 | 57 | 50 | 28 | 23 | 20 | 44 | L | L | 6-2 | 210 | 9-2-77 | 1996 | El Paso, Texas |
| Lopez, Jose | 0 | 3 | 4.18 | 16 | 1 | 0 | 0 | 24 | 21 | 12 | 11 | 6 | 13 | S | R | 6-2 | 185 | 4-16-76 | 1996 | Ridgewood, N.Y. |
| Lundquist, Dave | 1 | 1 | 2.63 | 3 | 3 | 0 | 0 | 14 | 8 | 4 | 4 | 2 | 16 | R | R | 6-2 | 200 | 6-4-73 | 1993 | Carson City, Nev. |
| Mendoza, Geronimo | 1 | 8 | 9.78 | 12 | 7 | 0 | 0 | 39 | 55 | 49 | 42 | 26 | 29 | R | R | 6-4 | 160 | 1-23-78 | 1995 | Santo Domingo, D.R. |
| Perez, Elvis | 0 | 0 | 11.66 | 14 | 0 | 0 | 0 | 15 | 27 | 26 | 19 | 12 | 9 | L | L | 6-2 | 185 | 2-9-78 | 1996 | Hialeah, Fla. |
| Reimers, Tom | 0 | 0 | 0.00 | 1 | 0 | 0 | 1 | 3 | 3 | 0 | 0 | 1 | 1 | R | R | 6-2 | 185 | 5-27-75 | 1996 | Santa Ana, Calif. |
| Rodgers, Marcus | 1 | 3 | 3.35 | 10 | 6 | 1 | 0 | 38 | 44 | 17 | 14 | 16 | 29 | R | R | 6-3 | 225 | 11-7-76 | 1996 | Saraland, Ala. |
| Simmons, Mike | 2 | 2 | 3.51 | 17 | 1 | 0 | 1 | 41 | 46 | 22 | 16 | 12 | 32 | R | R | 6-5 | 215 | 3-12-74 | 1996 | Hastings, Neb. |
| Snyder, John | 1 | 0 | 1.65 | 4 | 4 | 0 | 0 | 16 | 5 | 3 | 3 | 4 | 23 | R | R | 6-3 | 185 | 8-16-74 | 1992 | Thousand Oaks, Calif. |
| Stanley, Todd | 0 | 0 | 0.00 | 1 | 0 | 0 | 0 | 2 | 0 | 0 | 0 | 0 | 3 | R | R | 6-2 | 195 | 1-23-74 | 1996 | San Antonio, Texas |
| Stinson, Kevin | 1 | 5 | 2.29 | 24 | 0 | 0 | 6 | 35 | 39 | 16 | 9 | 11 | 34 | R | R | 6-2 | 190 | 1-31-76 | 1996 | Kirkland, Wash. |
| Tellez, Eloy | 3 | 4 | 2.94 | 11 | 11 | 2 | 0 | 70 | 57 | 30 | 23 | 27 | 34 | L | R | 6-3 | 215 | 1-29-76 | 1996 | El Paso, Texas |

# CHICAGO CUBS

**Manager:** Jim Riggleman.  **1996** Record: 76-86, .469 (4th, NL Central)

| BATTING | AVG | G | AB | R | H | 2B | 3B | HR | RBI | BB | SO | SB | CS | B | T | HT | WT | DOB | 1st Yr | Resides |
|---|---|---|---|---|---|---|---|---|---|---|---|---|---|---|---|---|---|---|---|---|
| Barberie, Bret | .034 | 15 | 29 | 4 | 1 | 0 | 0 | 1 | 2 | 5 | 11 | 0 | 1 | S | R | 5-11 | 180 | 8-16-67 | 1989 | Cerritos, Calif. |
| Brown, Brant | .304 | 29 | 69 | 11 | 21 | 1 | 0 | 5 | 9 | 2 | 17 | 3 | 3 | L | L | 6-3 | 220 | 6-22-71 | 1992 | Porterville, Calif. |
| Bullett, Scott | .212 | 109 | 165 | 26 | 35 | 5 | 0 | 3 | 16 | 10 | 54 | 7 | 3 | L | L | 6-2 | 190 | 12-25-68 | 1988 | Martinsburg, W.Va. |
| Dorsett, Brian | .122 | 17 | 41 | 3 | 5 | 0 | 0 | 1 | 3 | 4 | 8 | 0 | 0 | R | R | 6-4 | 222 | 4-9-61 | 1983 | Terre Haute, Ind. |
| Fermin, Felix | .125 | 11 | 16 | 4 | 2 | 1 | 0 | 0 | 1 | 2 | 0 | 0 | 0 | R | R | 5-11 | 170 | 10-9-63 | 1983 | Santiago, D.R. |
| Glanville, Doug | .241 | 49 | 83 | 10 | 20 | 5 | 1 | 1 | 10 | 3 | 11 | 2 | 0 | R | R | 6-2 | 170 | 8-25-70 | 1991 | Teaneck, N.J. |
| Gomez, Leo | .238 | 136 | 362 | 44 | 86 | 19 | 0 | 17 | 56 | 53 | 94 | 1 | 4 | R | R | 6-0 | 208 | 3-2-67 | 1986 | Canovanas, P.R. |
| Gonzalez, Luis | .271 | 146 | 483 | 70 | 131 | 30 | 4 | 15 | 79 | 61 | 49 | 9 | 6 | L | R | 6-2 | 180 | 9-3-67 | 1988 | Houston, Texas |
| Grace, Mark | .331 | 142 | 547 | 88 | 181 | 39 | 1 | 9 | 75 | 62 | 41 | 2 | 3 | L | L | 6-2 | 190 | 6-28-64 | 1986 | Pacific Palisades, Calif. |
| Haney, Todd | .134 | 49 | 82 | 11 | 11 | 1 | 0 | 0 | 3 | 7 | 15 | 1 | 0 | R | R | 5-9 | 165 | 7-30-65 | 1987 | Waco, Texas |
| Hernandez, Jose | .242 | 131 | 331 | 52 | 80 | 14 | 1 | 10 | 41 | 24 | 97 | 4 | 0 | R | R | 6-0 | 180 | 7-14-69 | 1987 | Vega Alta, P.R. |
| Houston, Tyler | .339 | 46 | 115 | 18 | 39 | 7 | 0 | 2 | 19 | 8 | 18 | 3 | 2 | L | R | 6-2 | 210 | 1-17-71 | 1989 | Las Vegas, Nev. |
| 2-team (33 Atlanta) | .317 | 79 | 142 | 21 | 45 | 9 | 1 | 3 | 27 | 9 | 27 | 3 | 2 | | | | | | | |
| Hubbard, Mike | .105 | 21 | 38 | 1 | 4 | 0 | 0 | 1 | 4 | 0 | 15 | 0 | 0 | R | R | 6-1 | 180 | 2-16-71 | 1992 | Madison Heights, Va. |
| Jennings, Robin | .224 | 31 | 58 | 7 | 13 | 5 | 0 | 4 | 4 | 3 | 9 | 1 | 0 | L | L | 6-2 | 200 | 4-11-72 | 1992 | Miami, Fla. |
| Kieschnick, Brooks | .345 | 25 | 29 | 6 | 10 | 2 | 0 | 1 | 6 | 3 | 8 | 0 | 0 | L | R | 6-4 | 228 | 6-6-72 | 1993 | Caldwell, Texas |
| Magadan, Dave | .254 | 78 | 169 | 23 | 43 | 10 | 0 | 3 | 17 | 29 | 23 | 0 | 2 | L | R | 6-3 | 200 | 9-30-62 | 1983 | Tampa, Fla. |
| McRae, Brian | .276 | 157 | 624 | 111 | 172 | 32 | 5 | 17 | 66 | 73 | 84 | 37 | 9 | S | R | 6-0 | 185 | 8-27-67 | 1985 | Leawood, Kan. |
| Sanchez, Rey | .211 | 95 | 289 | 28 | 61 | 9 | 0 | 1 | 12 | 22 | 42 | 7 | 1 | R | R | 5-10 | 180 | 10-5-67 | 1986 | Rio Piedras, P.R. |
| Sandberg, Ryne | .244 | 150 | 554 | 85 | 135 | 28 | 4 | 25 | 92 | 54 | 116 | 12 | 8 | R | R | 6-1 | 175 | 9-18-59 | 1978 | Phoenix, Ariz. |
| Servais, Scott | .265 | 129 | 445 | 42 | 118 | 20 | 0 | 11 | 63 | 30 | 75 | 0 | 2 | R | R | 6-2 | 195 | 6-4-67 | 1989 | Coon Valley, Wis. |
| Shumpert, Terry | .226 | 27 | 31 | 5 | 7 | 1 | 0 | 2 | 6 | 2 | 11 | 0 | 1 | R | R | 5-11 | 185 | 8-16-66 | 1987 | Paducah, Ky. |
| Sosa, Sammy | .273 | 124 | 498 | 84 | 136 | 21 | 2 | 40 | 100 | 34 | 134 | 18 | 5 | R | R | 6-0 | 165 | 11-12-68 | 1986 | San Pedro de Macoris, D.R. |
| Timmons, Ozzie | .200 | 65 | 140 | 18 | 28 | 4 | 0 | 7 | 16 | 15 | 30 | 1 | 0 | R | R | 6-2 | 205 | 9-18-70 | 1991 | Tampa, Fla. |
| Valdes, Pedro | .125 | 9 | 8 | 2 | 1 | 1 | 0 | 0 | 1 | 1 | 5 | 0 | 0 | L | L | 6-1 | 160 | 6-29-73 | 1991 | Loiza, P.R. |

| PITCHING | W | L | ERA | G | GS | CG | SV | IP | H | R | ER | BB | SO | B | T | HT | WT | DOB | 1st Yr | Resides |
|---|---|---|---|---|---|---|---|---|---|---|---|---|---|---|---|---|---|---|---|---|
| Adams, Terry | 3 | 6 | 2.94 | 69 | 0 | 0 | 4 | 101 | 84 | 36 | 33 | 49 | 78 | R | R | 6-3 | 180 | 3-6-73 | 1991 | Semmes, Ala. |
| Bottenfield, Kent | 3 | 5 | 2.63 | 48 | 0 | 0 | 1 | 62 | 59 | 25 | 18 | 19 | 33 | R | R | 6-2 | 225 | 11-14-68 | 1986 | Royal Palm Beach, Fla. |
| Bullinger, Jim | 6 | 10 | 6.54 | 37 | 20 | 1 | 1 | 129 | 144 | 101 | 94 | 68 | 90 | R | R | 6-2 | 180 | 8-21-65 | 1986 | Sarasota, Fla. |
| Campbell, Mike | 3 | 1 | 4.46 | 13 | 5 | 0 | 0 | 36 | 29 | 19 | 18 | 10 | 19 | R | R | 6-3 | 210 | 2-17-64 | 1985 | Kirkland, Wash. |
| Casian, Larry | 1 | 1 | 1.88 | 35 | 0 | 0 | 0 | 24 | 14 | 5 | 5 | 11 | 15 | R | L | 6-0 | 173 | 10-28-65 | 1987 | Salem, Ore. |
| Castillo, Frank | 7 | 16 | 5.28 | 33 | 33 | 1 | 0 | 182 | 209 | 112 | 107 | 46 | 139 | R | R | 6-1 | 185 | 4-1-69 | 1987 | El Paso, Texas |
| Foster, Kevin | 7 | 6 | 6.21 | 17 | 16 | 1 | 0 | 87 | 98 | 63 | 60 | 35 | 53 | R | R | 6-1 | 160 | 1-13-69 | 1988 | Evanston, Ill. |
| Jones, Doug | 2 | 2 | 5.01 | 28 | 0 | 0 | 2 | 32 | 41 | 20 | 18 | 7 | 26 | R | R | 6-2 | 195 | 6-24-57 | 1978 | Tucson, Ariz. |
| Myers, Rodney | 2 | 1 | 4.68 | 45 | 0 | 0 | 0 | 67 | 61 | 38 | 35 | 38 | 50 | R | R | 6-1 | 190 | 6-26-69 | 1990 | Rockford, Ill. |
| Navarro, Jaime | 15 | 12 | 3.92 | 35 | 35 | 4 | 0 | 237 | 244 | 116 | 103 | 72 | 158 | R | R | 6-4 | 225 | 3-27-67 | 1987 | Orlando, Fla. |
| Patterson, Bob | 3 | 3 | 3.13 | 79 | 0 | 0 | 8 | 55 | 46 | 19 | 19 | 22 | 53 | R | L | 6-2 | 185 | 5-16-59 | 1982 | Hickory, N.C. |
| Perez, Mike | 0 | 1 | 4.67 | 24 | 0 | 0 | 0 | 27 | 29 | 14 | 14 | 13 | 22 | R | R | 6-0 | 187 | 10-19-64 | 1986 | Yauco, P.R. |
| Sturtze, Tanyon | 1 | 0 | 9.00 | 6 | 0 | 0 | 0 | 11 | 16 | 11 | 11 | 5 | 7 | R | R | 6-5 | 190 | 10-12-70 | 1990 | Worcester, Mass. |
| Swartzbaugh, Dave | 0 | 2 | 6.38 | 6 | 5 | 0 | 0 | 24 | 26 | 17 | 17 | 14 | 13 | R | R | 6-2 | 195 | 2-11-68 | 1989 | Middletown, Ohio |
| Telemaco, Amaury | 5 | 7 | 5.46 | 25 | 17 | 0 | 0 | 97 | 108 | 67 | 59 | 31 | 64 | R | R | 6-3 | 180 | 1-19-74 | 1991 | La Romana, D.R. |
| Trachsel, Steve | 13 | 9 | 3.03 | 31 | 31 | 3 | 0 | 205 | 181 | 82 | 69 | 62 | 132 | R | R | 6-4 | 185 | 10-31-70 | 1991 | Yorba Linda, Calif. |
| Wendell, Turk | 4 | 5 | 2.84 | 70 | 0 | 0 | 18 | 79 | 58 | 26 | 25 | 44 | 75 | S | R | 6-2 | 175 | 5-19-67 | 1988 | Dalton, Mass. |

## FIELDING

| Catcher | PCT | G | PO | A | E | DP | PB |
|---|---|---|---|---|---|---|---|
| Dorsett | 1.000 | 15 | 79 | 5 | 0 | 1 | 1 |
| Houston | .986 | 27 | 130 | 9 | 2 | 0 | 2 |
| Hubbard | 1.000 | 14 | 53 | 3 | 0 | 1 | 1 |
| Servais | .988 | 128 | 797 | 72 | 11 | 11 | 9 |

| First Base | PCT | G | PO | A | E | DP |
|---|---|---|---|---|---|---|
| Brown | 1.000 | 18 | 126 | 17 | 0 | 4 |
| Gomez | 1.000 | 8 | 41 | 5 | 0 | 1 |
| Gonzalez | 1.000 | 2 | 13 | 1 | 0 | 0 |
| Grace | .997 | 141 | 1260 | 107 | 4 | 120 |
| Houston | 1.000 | 1 | 1 | 1 | 0 | 0 |
| Magadan | 1.000 | 10 | 59 | 4 | 0 | 4 |
| Servais | 1.000 | 1 | 1 | 1 | 0 | 0 |

| Second Base | PCT | G | PO | A | E | DP |
|---|---|---|---|---|---|---|
| Barberie | 1.000 | 6 | 5 | 17 | 0 | 1 |
| Fermin | .875 | 6 | 2 | 5 | 1 | 1 |
| Haney | .978 | 23 | 29 | 60 | 2 | 12 |
| Hernandez | 1.000 | 1 | 0 | 1 | 0 | 0 |
| Houston | 1.000 | 2 | 2 | 6 | 0 | 2 |
| Sandberg | .991 | 146 | 227 | 422 | 6 | 82 |
| Shumpert | 1.000 | 4 | 2 | 2 | 0 | 0 |

| Third Base | PCT | G | PO | A | E | DP |
|---|---|---|---|---|---|---|
| Barberie | 1.000 | 2 | 1 | 2 | 0 | 0 |
| Gomez | .972 | 124 | 69 | 176 | 7 | 17 |
| Haney | .889 | 4 | 3 | 5 | 1 | 0 |

| | PCT | G | PO | A | E | DP |
|---|---|---|---|---|---|---|
| Hernandez | .978 | 43 | 13 | 32 | 1 | 2 |
| Houston | .938 | 9 | 6 | 9 | 1 | 0 |
| Magadan | .963 | 51 | 16 | 63 | 3 | 4 |
| Shumpert | .923 | 10 | 8 | 4 | 1 | 0 |

| Shortstop | PCT | G | PO | A | E | DP |
|---|---|---|---|---|---|---|
| Barberie | .000 | 1 | 0 | 0 | 0 | 0 |
| Fermin | 1.000 | 2 | 3 | 2 | 0 | 0 |
| Gomez | 1.000 | 1 | 0 | 1 | 0 | 1 |
| Haney | .000 | 3 | 0 | 0 | 0 | 0 |
| Hernandez | .948 | 87 | 134 | 215 | 19 | 51 |
| Sanchez | .977 | 92 | 151 | 307 | 11 | 55 |
| Shumpert | 1.000 | 1 | 1 | 3 | 0 | 2 |

| Outfield | PCT | G | PO | A | E | DP |
|---|---|---|---|---|---|---|
| Bullett | .986 | 58 | 70 | 2 | 1 | 1 |
| Glanville | .973 | 35 | 35 | 1 | 1 | 0 |
| Gonzalez | .988 | 139 | 231 | 6 | 3 | 2 |
| Hernandez | 1.000 | 1 | 1 | 0 | 0 | 0 |
| Houston | .000 | 1 | 0 | 0 | 0 | 0 |
| Jennings | 1.000 | 11 | 19 | 2 | 0 | 0 |
| Kieschnick | .833 | 8 | 5 | 0 | 1 | 0 |
| McRae | .986 | 155 | 345 | 2 | 5 | 1 |
| Sosa | .964 | 124 | 253 | 15 | 10 | 1 |
| Timmons | 1.000 | 47 | 65 | 1 | 0 | 1 |
| Valdes | 1.000 | 2 | 1 | 0 | 0 | 0 |

**Ryne Sandberg**

Outfielder Sammy Sosa topped the Cubs with 40 homers

Cubs minor league Player of the Year Kerry Wood

# CUBS

## FARM SYSTEM

**Director, Minor Leagues:** David Wilder

| Class | Farm Team | League | W | L | Pct. | Finish* | Manager | First Yr |
|---|---|---|---|---|---|---|---|---|
| AAA | Iowa Cubs | American Assoc. | 64 | 78 | .451 | 6th (8) | Ron Clark | 1981 |
| AA | Orlando (Fla.) Cubs | Southern | 60 | 78 | .439 | 8th (10) | Bruce Kimm | 1993 |
| #A | Daytona (Fla.) Cubs | Florida State | 71 | 66 | .518 | 6th (14) | Dave Trembley | 1993 |
| A | Rockford (Ill.) Cubbies | Midwest | 70 | 65 | .519 | 5th (14) | Steve Roadcap | 1995 |
| A | Williamsport (Pa.) Cubs | New York-Penn | 43 | 32 | .573 | 5th (14) | Ruben Amaro Sr. | 1994 |
| R | Fort Myers (Fla.) Cubs | Gulf Coast | 34 | 26 | .567 | 6th (16) | Sandy Alomar Sr. | 1993 |

*Finish in overall standings (No. of teams in league)    #Advanced level

## ORGANIZATION LEADERS

### MAJOR LEAGUERS

**BATTING**

| | | |
|---|---|---|
| *AVG | Mark Grace | .331 |
| R | Brian McRae | 111 |
| H | Mark Grace | 181 |
| TB | Sammy Sosa | 281 |
| 2B | Mark Grace | 39 |
| 3B | Brian McRae | 5 |
| HR | Sammy Sosa | 40 |
| RBI | Sammy Sosa | 100 |
| BB | Brian McRae | 73 |
| SO | Sammy Sosa | 134 |
| SB | Brian McRae | 37 |

**PITCHING**

| | | |
|---|---|---|
| W | Jaime Navarro | 15 |
| L | Frank Castillo | 16 |
| #ERA | Turk Wendell | 2.84 |
| G | Bob Patterson | 79 |
| CG | Jaime Navarro | 4 |
| SV | Turk Wendell | 18 |
| IP | Jaime Navarro | 237 |
| BB | Jaime Navarro | 72 |
| SO | Jaime Navarro | 158 |

GEROGE GOJKOVICH

**Jaime Navarro.** 15 wins

### MINOR LEAGUERS

**BATTING**

| | | |
|---|---|---|
| *AVG | Scott Vieira, Rockford | .324 |
| R | Terry Joseph, Rockford | 98 |
| H | Ricky Freeman, Daytona | 145 |
| TB | Ricky Freeman, Daytona | 232 |
| 2B | Ricky Freeman, Daytona | 36 |
| 3B | Kelvin Barnes, Rockford | 8 |
| HR | Three tied at | 18 |
| RBI | Terry Joseph, Rockford | 94 |
| BB | Scott Vieira, Rockford | 84 |
| SO | Bo Porter, Rockford/Daytona | 131 |
| SB | Elinton Jasco, Rockford | 48 |

**PITCHING**

| | | |
|---|---|---|
| W | Jeff Yoder, Rockford | 12 |
| L | Wade Walker, Orlando | 14 |
| #ERA | Courtney Duncan, Williamsport | 2.19 |
| G | Steve Rain, Orlando/Iowa | 61 |
| CG | Two tied at | 3 |
| SV | Brandon Hammack, Rockford/Daytona | 29 |
| IP | Wade Walker, Orlando | 188 |
| BB | Wade Walker, Orlando | 76 |
| SO | Kerry Wood, Daytona | 136 |

*Minimum 250 At-Bats    #Minimum 75 Innings

## TOP 10 PROSPECTS

**How the Cubs Top 10 prospects, as judged by Baseball America prior to the 1996 season, fared in 1996:**

**Brooks Kieschnick**

| Player, Pos. | Club (Class—League) | AVG | AB | R | H | 2B | 3B | HR | RBI | SB |
|---|---|---|---|---|---|---|---|---|---|---|
| 1. Brooks Kieschnick, of | Iowa (AAA—American Assoc.) | .259 | 441 | 47 | 114 | 20 | 1 | 18 | 64 | 0 |
| | Chicago | .345 | 29 | 6 | 10 | 2 | 0 | 1 | 6 | 0 |
| 5. Pat Cline, c | Daytona (A—Florida State) | .279 | 434 | 75 | 121 | 30 | 2 | 17 | 76 | 10 |
| 9. Kevin Orie, 3b | Orlando (AA—Southern) | .314 | 296 | 42 | 93 | 25 | 0 | 8 | 58 | 2 |
| | Iowa (AAA—American Assoc.) | .208 | 48 | 5 | 10 | 1 | 0 | 2 | 6 | 0 |
| 10. Robin Jennings, of | Iowa (AAA—American Assoc.) | .284 | 331 | 53 | 94 | 15 | 6 | 18 | 56 | 2 |
| | Chicago | .224 | 58 | 7 | 13 | 5 | 0 | 0 | 4 | 1 |

| | | W | L | ERA | G | SV | IP | H | BB | SO |
|---|---|---|---|---|---|---|---|---|---|---|
| 2. Kerry Wood, rhp | Daytona (A—Florida State) | 10 | 2 | 2.91 | 22 | 0 | 114 | 72 | 70 | 136 |
| 3. Terry Adams, rhp | Chicago | 3 | 6 | 2.94 | 69 | 4 | 101 | 84 | 49 | 78 |
| 4. Amaury Telemaco, rhp | Iowa (AAA—American Assoc.) | 3 | 1 | 3.06 | 8 | 0 | 50 | 38 | 18 | 42 |
| | Chicago | 5 | 7 | 5.46 | 25 | 0 | 97 | 108 | 31 | 64 |
| 6. Jason Ryan rhp | Daytona (A—Florida State) | 1 | 8 | 5.24 | 17 | 1 | 67 | 72 | 33 | 49 |
| | Orlando (AA—Southern) | 2 | 5 | 5.71 | 7 | 0 | 35 | 39 | 24 | 25 |
| 7. Brian Stephenson, rhp | Orlando (AA—Southern) | 5 | 13 | 4.69 | 32 | 1 | 129 | 130 | 61 | 106 |
| 8. Wade Walker, rhp | Orlando (AA—Southern) | 8 | 14 | 4.41 | 29 | 0 | 188 | 205 | 76 | 117 |

## AMERICAN ASSOCIATION

| BATTING | AVG | G | AB | R | H | 2B | 3B | HR | RBI | BB | SO | SB | CS | B | T | HT | WT | DOB | 1st Yr | Resides |
|---|---|---|---|---|---|---|---|---|---|---|---|---|---|---|---|---|---|---|---|---|
| Barberie, Bret | .233 | 68 | 210 | 26 | 49 | 8 | 0 | 5 | 24 | 31 | 23 | 3 | 2 | S | R | 5-11 | 180 | 8-16-67 | 1989 | Cerritos, Calif. |
| Brown, Brant | .304 | 94 | 342 | 48 | 104 | 25 | 3 | 10 | 43 | 19 | 65 | 6 | 6 | L | L | 6-3 | 220 | 6-22-71 | 1992 | Porterville, Calif. |
| Campos, Miguel | .250 | 2 | 4 | 0 | 1 | 0 | 0 | 0 | 0 | 0 | 2 | 0 | 0 | R | R | 6-1 | 185 | 3-28-76 | 1994 | Carabobo, Venez. |
| Carter, Michael | .266 | 113 | 384 | 41 | 102 | 13 | 1 | 2 | 18 | 10 | 42 | 4 | 6 | R | R | 5-9 | 170 | 5-5-69 | 1990 | Vicksburg, Miss. |
| Cholowsky, Dan | .173 | 26 | 52 | 10 | 9 | 5 | 0 | 2 | 5 | 11 | 18 | 0 | 0 | R | R | 6-0 | 195 | 10-30-70 | 1991 | San Jose, Calif. |
| 2-team (17 Louis.) | .176 | 43 | 108 | 13 | 19 | 7 | 0 | 3 | 11 | 15 | 34 | 1 | 2 | | | | | | | |
| Dorsett, Brian | .207 | 9 | 29 | 2 | 6 | 2 | 0 | 1 | 2 | 0 | 4 | 0 | 0 | R | R | 6-4 | 222 | 4-9-61 | 1983 | Terre Haute, Ind. |
| Erdman, Brad | .175 | 57 | 171 | 18 | 30 | 6 | 0 | 2 | 16 | 16 | 38 | 1 | 0 | R | R | 6-3 | 190 | 2-23-70 | 1989 | Casper, Wyom. |
| Faries, Paul | .261 | 37 | 115 | 14 | 30 | 4 | 2 | 0 | 8 | 14 | 12 | 6 | 1 | R | R | 5-10 | 170 | 2-20-65 | 1987 | San Diego, Calif. |
| Fermin, Felix | .286 | 39 | 119 | 8 | 34 | 4 | 1 | 0 | 8 | 3 | 7 | 1 | 0 | R | R | 5-11 | 170 | 10-9-63 | 1983 | Santiago, D.R. |
| Finn, John | .273 | 17 | 55 | 10 | 15 | 1 | 0 | 1 | 5 | 4 | 7 | 1 | 1 | R | R | 5-8 | 168 | 10-18-67 | 1989 | Oakland, Calif. |
| Glanville, Doug | .308 | 90 | 373 | 53 | 115 | 23 | 3 | 3 | 34 | 12 | 35 | 15 | 10 | R | R | 6-2 | 170 | 8-25-70 | 1991 | Teaneck, N.J. |
| Haney, Todd | .246 | 66 | 240 | 20 | 59 | 13 | 0 | 2 | 19 | 19 | 24 | 3 | 1 | R | R | 5-9 | 165 | 7-30-65 | 1987 | Waco, Texas |
| Hubbard, Mike | .293 | 67 | 232 | 38 | 68 | 12 | 0 | 7 | 33 | 10 | 56 | 2 | 0 | R | R | 6-1 | 180 | 2-16-71 | 1992 | Madison Heights, Va. |
| Jennings, Robin | .284 | 86 | 331 | 53 | 94 | 15 | 6 | 18 | 56 | 32 | 53 | 2 | 0 | L | L | 6-2 | 200 | 4-11-72 | 1992 | Miami, Fla. |
| Kessinger, Keith | .239 | 55 | 184 | 19 | 44 | 8 | 0 | 4 | 26 | 22 | 30 | 0 | 1 | S | R | 6-2 | 185 | 2-19-67 | 1989 | Oxford, Miss. |
| Kieschnick, Brooks | .259 | 117 | 441 | 47 | 114 | 20 | 1 | 18 | 64 | 37 | 108 | 0 | 1 | L | R | 6-4 | 228 | 6-6-72 | 1993 | Caldwell, Texas |
| Kosco, Bryn | .253 | 29 | 79 | 8 | 20 | 2 | 0 | 2 | 7 | 5 | 22 | 0 | 0 | L | R | 6-1 | 185 | 3-9-67 | 1988 | Poland, Ohio |
| Magadan, Dave | .222 | 3 | 9 | 0 | 2 | 1 | 0 | 0 | 1 | 1 | 2 | 0 | 0 | L | R | 6-3 | 200 | 9-30-62 | 1983 | Tampa, Fla. |
| Merullo, Matt | .236 | 30 | 89 | 8 | 21 | 8 | 0 | 1 | 10 | 8 | 15 | 1 | 0 | L | R | 6-2 | 200 | 8-4-65 | 1986 | Ridgefield, Conn. |
| Orie, Kevin | .208 | 14 | 48 | 5 | 10 | 1 | 0 | 2 | 6 | 6 | 10 | 0 | 0 | R | R | 6-4 | 215 | 9-1-72 | 1993 | Pittsburgh, Pa. |
| Ortiz, Hector | .241 | 27 | 79 | 6 | 19 | 2 | 0 | 0 | 3 | 3 | 16 | 0 | 0 | R | R | 6-0 | 178 | 10-14-69 | 1988 | Canovanas, P.R. |
| Petersen, Chris | .247 | 63 | 194 | 12 | 48 | 6 | 3 | 2 | 23 | 12 | 46 | 1 | 2 | R | R | 5-10 | 160 | 11-6-70 | 1992 | Southington, Conn. |
| Sanchez, Rey | .167 | 3 | 12 | 2 | 2 | 0 | 0 | 0 | 1 | 1 | 2 | 2 | 0 | R | R | 5-10 | 180 | 10-5-67 | 1986 | Rio Piedras, P.R. |
| Shumpert, Terry | .276 | 72 | 246 | 45 | 68 | 13 | 4 | 5 | 32 | 24 | 44 | 13 | 3 | R | R | 5-11 | 185 | 8-16-66 | 1987 | Paducah, Ky. |
| Timmons, Ozzie | .249 | 59 | 213 | 32 | 53 | 7 | 0 | 17 | 40 | 28 | 42 | 1 | 1 | R | R | 6-2 | 205 | 9-18-70 | 1991 | Tampa, Fla. |
| Valdes, Pedro | .295 | 103 | 397 | 61 | 117 | 23 | 0 | 15 | 60 | 31 | 57 | 2 | 0 | L | L | 6-1 | 160 | 6-29-73 | 1991 | Loiza, P.R. |
| Woodson, Tracy | .184 | 10 | 38 | 2 | 7 | 3 | 0 | 2 | 8 | 2 | 8 | 0 | 0 | R | R | 6-3 | 215 | 10-5-62 | 1984 | Raleigh, N.C. |

| PITCHING | W | L | ERA | G | GS | CG | SV | IP | H | R | ER | BB | SO | B | T | HT | WT | DOB | 1st Yr | Resides |
|---|---|---|---|---|---|---|---|---|---|---|---|---|---|---|---|---|---|---|---|---|
| Bottenfield, Kent | 1 | 2 | 2.19 | 28 | 0 | 0 | 18 | 25 | 19 | 9 | 6 | 8 | 14 | R | R | 6-2 | 225 | 11-14-68 | 1986 | Royal Palm Beach, Fla. |
| Burlingame, Ben | 5 | 6 | 4.30 | 27 | 11 | 0 | 0 | 98 | 104 | 49 | 47 | 20 | 66 | R | R | 6-5 | 210 | 1-31-70 | 1991 | Newton, Mass. |
| Campbell, Mike | 8 | 2 | 2.73 | 16 | 16 | 1 | 0 | 96 | 75 | 31 | 29 | 23 | 87 | R | R | 6-3 | 210 | 2-17-64 | 1985 | Kirkland, Wash. |
| Casian, Larry | 3 | 2 | 1.71 | 24 | 4 | 0 | 1 | 47 | 37 | 13 | 9 | 11 | 32 | R | L | 6-0 | 173 | 10-28-65 | 1987 | Salem, Ore. |
| Dabney, Fred | 2 | 3 | 4.34 | 33 | 3 | 1 | 0 | 64 | 76 | 38 | 31 | 24 | 33 | R | L | 6-3 | 190 | 11-20-67 | 1988 | Sarasota, Fla. |
| Foster, Kevin | 7 | 6 | 4.30 | 18 | 18 | 3 | 0 | 115 | 106 | 56 | 55 | 46 | 87 | R | R | 6-1 | 160 | 1-13-69 | 1988 | Evanston, Ill. |
| Guzman, Jose | 1 | 6 | 8.45 | 8 | 8 | 0 | 0 | 38 | 51 | 39 | 36 | 19 | 24 | R | R | 6-3 | 195 | 4-9-63 | 1981 | Arlington, Texas |
| Moten, Scott | 1 | 2 | 9.21 | 21 | 1 | 0 | 0 | 42 | 55 | 47 | 43 | 18 | 18 | R | R | 6-1 | 198 | 4-12-72 | 1992 | Bellflower, Calif. |
| Perez, Mike | 0 | 4 | 6.53 | 23 | 0 | 0 | 0 | 30 | 42 | 24 | 22 | 15 | 19 | R | R | 6-0 | 187 | 10-19-64 | 1986 | Yauco, P.R. |
| Pulido, Carlos | 2 | 8 | 5.31 | 28 | 17 | 0 | 0 | 102 | 133 | 64 | 60 | 36 | 48 | L | L | 6-0 | 182 | 8-5-71 | 1989 | Caracas, Venez. |
| Rain, Steve | 2 | 1 | 3.12 | 26 | 0 | 0 | 10 | 26 | 17 | 9 | 9 | 8 | 23 | R | R | 6-6 | 225 | 6-2-75 | 1993 | Walnut, Calif. |
| Ratliff, Jon | 4 | 8 | 5.28 | 32 | 13 | 0 | 1 | 94 | 107 | 63 | 55 | 31 | 59 | R | R | 6-5 | 200 | 12-22-71 | 1993 | Clay, N.Y. |
| Renko, Steve | 2 | 0 | 2.57 | 3 | 3 | 1 | 0 | 21 | 16 | 6 | 6 | 5 | 11 | R | R | 6-3 | 205 | 8-1-67 | 1990 | Overland Park, Kan. |
| Rivera, Roberto | 1 | 0 | 2.70 | 35 | 0 | 0 | 2 | 33 | 26 | 10 | 10 | 8 | 18 | L | L | 6-0 | 175 | 1-1-69 | 1988 | Bayamon, P.R. |
| Steenstra, Kennie | 8 | 12 | 5.01 | 26 | 26 | 1 | 0 | 158 | 170 | 96 | 88 | 47 | 101 | R | R | 6-5 | 220 | 10-13-70 | 1992 | Lynchburg, Mo. |
| Sturtze, Tanyon | 6 | 4 | 4.85 | 51 | 1 | 0 | 4 | 72 | 80 | 42 | 39 | 33 | 51 | R | R | 6-5 | 190 | 10-12-70 | 1990 | Worcester, Mass. |
| Swartzbaugh, Dave | 8 | 11 | 3.88 | 44 | 13 | 0 | 0 | 118 | 106 | 61 | 51 | 33 | 103 | R | R | 6-2 | 195 | 2-11-68 | 1989 | Middletown, Ohio |
| Telemaco, Amaury | 3 | 1 | 3.06 | 8 | 8 | 1 | 0 | 50 | 37 | 16 | 17 | 11 | 47 | R | R | 6-3 | 180 | 1-19-74 | 1991 | La Romana, D.R. |

### FIELDING

| Catcher | PCT | G | PO | A | E | DP | PB |
|---|---|---|---|---|---|---|---|
| Campos | 1.000 | 2 | 10 | 2 | 0 | 0 | 0 |
| Cholowsky | 1.000 | 3 | 1 | 0 | 0 | 0 | 0 |
| Dorsett | 1.000 | 7 | 46 | 2 | 0 | 1 | 0 |
| Erdman | .991 | 52 | 310 | 20 | 3 | 2 | 3 |
| Hubbard | .988 | 62 | 370 | 25 | 5 | 5 | 5 |
| Merullo | 1.000 | 1 | 3 | 0 | 0 | 0 | 0 |
| Ortiz | .987 | 25 | 139 | 9 | 2 | 0 | 1 |

| First Base | PCT | G | PO | A | E | DP |
|---|---|---|---|---|---|---|
| Brown | .990 | 92 | 762 | 66 | 8 | 74 |
| Erdman | 1.000 | 1 | 11 | 0 | 0 | 2 |
| Kieschnick | .984 | 52 | 417 | 23 | 7 | 34 |
| Kosco | 1.000 | 3 | 23 | 0 | 0 | 1 |
| Shumpert | 1.000 | 1 | 4 | 0 | 0 | 0 |

| Second Base | PCT | G | PO | A | E | DP |
|---|---|---|---|---|---|---|
| Barberie | .990 | 20 | 35 | 61 | 1 | 14 |
| Carter | .667 | 1 | 1 | 1 | 1 | 0 |
| Cholowsky | 1.000 | 5 | 8 | 13 | 0 | 4 |
| Faries | .935 | 14 | 33 | 39 | 5 | 8 |
| Fermin | .750 | 1 | 1 | 2 | 1 | 0 |

| | PCT | G | PO | A | E | DP |
|---|---|---|---|---|---|---|
| Finn | .900 | 2 | 4 | 5 | 1 | 0 |
| Haney | .963 | 53 | 95 | 138 | 9 | 28 |
| Kessinger | .857 | 2 | 3 | 3 | 1 | 0 |
| Petersen | 1.000 | 7 | 15 | 22 | 0 | 4 |
| Shumpert | .982 | 46 | 97 | 127 | 4 | 31 |

| Third Base | PCT | G | PO | A | E | DP |
|---|---|---|---|---|---|---|
| Barberie | .951 | 38 | 25 | 72 | 5 | 7 |
| Cholowsky | .818 | 11 | 7 | 20 | 6 | 1 |
| Erdman | .000 | 1 | 0 | 0 | 0 | 0 |
| Faries | 1.000 | 2 | 2 | 4 | 0 | 0 |
| Fermin | .944 | 11 | 3 | 14 | 1 | 0 |
| Finn | .943 | 14 | 8 | 25 | 2 | 2 |
| Haney | .857 | 8 | 4 | 8 | 2 | 1 |
| Hubbard | 1.000 | 3 | 2 | 2 | 0 | 0 |
| Kessinger | 1.000 | 5 | 2 | 4 | 0 | 1 |
| Kosco | .920 | 17 | 5 | 18 | 2 | 1 |
| Magadan | 1.000 | 3 | 3 | 3 | 0 | 2 |
| Orie | .974 | 14 | 11 | 26 | 1 | 0 |
| Petersen | 1.000 | 3 | 2 | 1 | 0 | 0 |

| | PCT | G | PO | A | E | DP |
|---|---|---|---|---|---|---|
| Shumpert | .945 | 24 | 14 | 38 | 3 | 2 |
| Woodson | .963 | 10 | 6 | 20 | 1 | 1 |

| Shortstop | PCT | G | PO | A | E | DP |
|---|---|---|---|---|---|---|
| Faries | .988 | 20 | 32 | 47 | 1 | 12 |
| Fermin | .989 | 22 | 31 | 63 | 1 | 16 |
| Haney | 1.000 | 6 | 9 | 12 | 0 | 3 |
| Kessinger | .979 | 45 | 61 | 123 | 4 | 27 |
| Petersen | .979 | 53 | 91 | 140 | 5 | 30 |
| Sanchez | .933 | 3 | 4 | 10 | 1 | 2 |
| Shumpert | 1.000 | 1 | 4 | 0 | 0 | 0 |

| Outfield | PCT | G | PO | A | E | DP |
|---|---|---|---|---|---|---|
| Carter | .977 | 82 | 169 | 3 | 4 | 1 |
| Glanville | .987 | 86 | 217 | 6 | 3 | 3 |
| Haney | .000 | 1 | 0 | 0 | 0 | 0 |
| Hubbard | .000 | 1 | 0 | 0 | 0 | 0 |
| Jennings | .982 | 77 | 156 | 5 | 3 | 1 |
| Kieschnick | .989 | 52 | 81 | 5 | 1 | 0 |
| Timmons | .971 | 50 | 98 | 1 | 3 | 0 |
| Valdes | .974 | 88 | 183 | 7 | 5 | 1 |

## SOUTHERN LEAGUE

| BATTING | AVG | G | AB | R | H | 2B | 3B | HR | RBI | BB | SO | SB | CS | B | T | HT | WT | DOB | 1st Yr | Resides |
|---|---|---|---|---|---|---|---|---|---|---|---|---|---|---|---|---|---|---|---|---|
| Bullett, Scott | .182 | 3 | 11 | 2 | 2 | 0 | 0 | 0 | 0 | 1 | 2 | 2 | 0 | L | L | 6-2 | 190 | 12-25-68 | 1988 | Martinsburg, W.Va. |
| Cholowsky, Dan | .238 | 45 | 143 | 21 | 34 | 4 | 0 | 4 | 14 | 23 | 38 | 2 | 4 | R | R | 6-0 | 195 | 10-30-70 | 1991 | San Jose, Calif. |
| Dowler, Dee | .278 | 113 | 352 | 59 | 98 | 15 | 6 | 6 | 47 | 47 | 42 | 25 | 5 | R | R | 5-9 | 175 | 7-23-71 | 1993 | Indianapolis, Ind. |
| Duross, Gabe | .155 | 17 | 58 | 2 | 9 | 0 | 1 | 0 | 6 | 2 | 3 | 0 | 0 | L | L | 6-1 | 195 | 4-6-72 | 1992 | Kingston, N.Y. |
| Forkerway, Trey | .242 | 59 | 161 | 22 | 39 | 9 | 1 | 3 | 20 | 11 | 24 | 0 | 2 | R | R | 5-11 | 175 | 5-17-71 | 1993 | Abilene, Texas |

GEORGE GOJKOVICH

MORRIS FOSTOFF

**Stalwarts.** Outfielder Brian McRae, left, and first baseman Mark Grace enjoyed solid 1996 seasons for the Cubs. McRae led the team with 111 runs and 37 stolen bases; Grace hit a team-best .331.

| BATTING | AVG | G | AB | R | H | 2B | 3B | HR | RBI | BB | SO | SB | CS | B | T | HT | WT | DOB | 1st Yr | Resides |
|---|---|---|---|---|---|---|---|---|---|---|---|---|---|---|---|---|---|---|---|---|
| Fryman, Troy ............. | .230 | 54 | 200 | 27 | 46 | 16 | 1 | 1 | 25 | 20 | 50 | 2 | 2 | L | R | 6-4 | 195 | 10-2-71 | 1991 | Pensacola, Fla. |
| 2-team (14 Birm.)..... | .225 | 68 | 249 | 35 | 56 | 18 | 1 | 2 | 28 | 25 | 61 | 2 | 2 | | | | | | | |
| Hightower, Vee .......... | .067 | 19 | 75 | 2 | 5 | 0 | 0 | 0 | 4 | 4 | 24 | 3 | 0 | S | R | 6-5 | 205 | 4-26-72 | 1993 | Mt. Lebanon, Pa. |
| Hughes, Troy ............. | .273 | 123 | 450 | 75 | 123 | 26 | 3 | 18 | 93 | 50 | 86 | 3 | 4 | R | R | 6-4 | 212 | 1-3-71 | 1989 | Mt. Vernon, Ill. |
| Kingston, Mark ........... | .205 | 60 | 122 | 21 | 25 | 9 | 0 | 3 | 17 | 22 | 39 | 1 | 1 | S | R | 6-4 | 210 | 5-16-70 | 1992 | Midland, Ga. |
| Larregui, Ed .............. | .261 | 17 | 69 | 12 | 18 | 5 | 0 | 1 | 5 | 6 | 9 | 0 | 2 | R | R | 6-0 | 185 | 12-1-72 | 1990 | Carolina, P.R. |
| Livsey, Shawn ............ | .257 | 75 | 257 | 36 | 66 | 15 | 2 | 2 | 33 | 27 | 39 | 13 | 8 | S | R | 5-11 | 180 | 7-21-73 | 1991 | Chicago, Ill. |
| Maxwell, Jason .......... | .266 | 126 | 433 | 64 | 115 | 20 | 1 | 9 | 45 | 56 | 77 | 19 | 4 | R | R | 6-0 | 175 | 3-21-72 | 1993 | Lewisburg, Tenn. |
| Morris, Bobby .......... | .262 | 131 | 465 | 72 | 122 | 29 | 3 | 8 | 62 | 65 | 73 | 12 | 14 | L | R | 6-0 | 180 | 11-22-72 | 1993 | Munster, Ind. |
| Orie, Kevin ................ | .314 | 82 | 296 | 42 | 93 | 25 | 0 | 8 | 58 | 48 | 52 | 2 | 0 | R | R | 6-4 | 215 | 9-1-72 | 1993 | Pittsburgh, Pa. |
| Ortiz, Hector ............. | .218 | 78 | 216 | 16 | 47 | 8 | 0 | 0 | 15 | 26 | 23 | 1 | 2 | R | R | 6-0 | 178 | 10-14-69 | 1988 | Canovanas, P.R. |
| Perez, Richard ........... | .167 | 10 | 18 | 0 | 3 | 0 | 0 | 0 | 1 | 1 | 3 | 0 | 0 | R | R | 6-2 | 175 | 1-30-73 | 1991 | Lara, Venez. |
| Petersen, Chris .......... | .296 | 47 | 152 | 21 | 45 | 3 | 4 | 2 | 12 | 18 | 31 | 3 | 5 | R | R | 5-10 | 160 | 11-6-70 | 1992 | Southington, Conn. |
| Samuels, Scott ........... | .260 | 106 | 342 | 62 | 89 | 19 | 5 | 2 | 33 | 62 | 81 | 21 | 10 | L | R | 5-11 | 190 | 5-19-70 | 1992 | San Jose, Calif. |
| Thurston, Jerrey ......... | .209 | 67 | 177 | 16 | 37 | 6 | 1 | 3 | 23 | 14 | 57 | 0 | 0 | R | R | 6-4 | 200 | 4-17-72 | 1990 | Longwood, Fla. |
| Walker, Steve ............ | .254 | 54 | 224 | 31 | 57 | 7 | 4 | 4 | 21 | 18 | 65 | 6 | 9 | S | R | 6-1 | 180 | 2-11-72 | 1991 | Leesburg, Ga. |
| Williams, Harold ........ | .263 | 80 | 255 | 33 | 67 | 6 | 0 | 10 | 36 | 27 | 55 | 1 | 2 | L | L | 6-4 | 200 | 2-14-71 | 1993 | Garyville, La. |
| 2-team (14 Birm.)..... | .266 | 94 | 301 | 36 | 80 | 10 | 0 | 10 | 40 | 31 | 67 | 2 | 3 | | | | | | | |

| PITCHING | W | L | ERA | G | GS | CG | SV | IP | H | R | ER | BB | SO | B | T | HT | WT | DOB | 1st Yr | Resides |
|---|---|---|---|---|---|---|---|---|---|---|---|---|---|---|---|---|---|---|---|---|
| Bogle, Sean ................ | 0 | 0 | 0.00 | 4 | 0 | 0 | 0 | 6 | 2 | 0 | 0 | 6 | 6 | R | R | 6-2 | 195 | 10-3-73 | 1994 | Indianapolis, Ind. |
| Burlingame, Ben .......... | 1 | 1 | 3.71 | 11 | 0 | 0 | 0 | 17 | 21 | 7 | 7 | 10 | 16 | R | R | 6-5 | 210 | 1-31-70 | 1991 | Newton, Mass. |
| Byrne, Earl ............... | 1 | 2 | 5.59 | 11 | 6 | 1 | 0 | 37 | 36 | 28 | 23 | 26 | 30 | L | L | 6-1 | 165 | 7-2-72 | 1994 | Melbourne, Australia |
| Ciccarella, Joe ........... | 0 | 0 | 0.00 | 1 | 0 | 0 | 0 | 1 | 1 | 0 | 0 | 2 | 0 | L | L | 6-3 | 190 | 12-29-69 | 1991 | Huntington Beach, Calif. |
| Connolly, Matt ........... | 7 | 3 | 3.31 | 31 | 10 | 1 | 2 | 87 | 79 | 45 | 32 | 35 | 80 | R | R | 6-8 | 230 | 10-1-68 | 1991 | Richmond Hill, N.Y. |
| Dabney, Fred ............. | 0 | 0 | 2.57 | 12 | 0 | 0 | 0 | 14 | 15 | 5 | 4 | 5 | 16 | R | L | 6-3 | 190 | 11-20-67 | 1988 | Sarasota, Fla. |
| Gambs, Chris .............. | 0 | 0 | 5.40 | 2 | 0 | 0 | 0 | 5 | 3 | 3 | 3 | 5 | 3 | R | R | 6-2 | 210 | 10-26-73 | 1991 | Richmond, Calif. |
| Garcia, Al ............... | 6 | 7 | 4.85 | 23 | 16 | 1 | 0 | 119 | 149 | 71 | 64 | 32 | 66 | R | R | 6-0 | 175 | 6-11-74 | 1993 | Buena Park, Calif. |
| Gonzalez, Jeremi ......... | 6 | 3 | 3.34 | 17 | 14 | 0 | 0 | 97 | 95 | 39 | 36 | 28 | 85 | R | R | 6-1 | 180 | 1-8-75 | 1992 | Maracaibo, Venez. |
| Graves, Ryan ............ | 0 | 2 | 12.00 | 4 | 1 | 0 | 1 | 9 | 16 | 15 | 12 | 9 | 3 | L | L | 6-2 | 185 | 2-15-74 | 1996 | Riverside, Calif. |
| Hart, Jason ............... | 3 | 5 | 3.21 | 51 | 0 | 0 | 4 | 73 | 59 | 29 | 26 | 28 | 78 | R | R | 6-0 | 195 | 11-14-71 | 1994 | Round Rock, Texas |
| Hutcheson, David ........ | 4 | 3 | 3.51 | 19 | 13 | 0 | 0 | 85 | 82 | 43 | 33 | 28 | 60 | R | R | 6-2 | 185 | 8-29-71 | 1993 | Tampa, Fla. |
| Moten, Scott ............. | 2 | 6 | 5.63 | 18 | 7 | 1 | 1 | 54 | 59 | 40 | 34 | 31 | 35 | R | R | 6-1 | 198 | 4-12-72 | 1992 | Bellflower, Calif. |
| Pulido, Carlos ........... | 2 | 2 | 7.45 | 6 | 0 | 0 | 0 | 10 | 17 | 9 | 8 | 3 | 12 | L | L | 6-0 | 182 | 8-5-71 | 1989 | Caracas, Venez |
| Rain, Steve .............. | 1 | 0 | 2.56 | 35 | 0 | 0 | 10 | 39 | 32 | 15 | 11 | 12 | 48 | R | R | 6-6 | 225 | 6-2-75 | 1993 | Walnut, Calif. |
| Rivera, Roberto .......... | 1 | 2 | 6.35 | 9 | 0 | 0 | 1 | 17 | 20 | 13 | 12 | 8 | 14 | L | L | 6-0 | 175 | 1-1-69 | 1988 | Bayamon, P.R. |
| Ryan, Jason ................ | 2 | 5 | 5.71 | 7 | 7 | 0 | 0 | 35 | 39 | 30 | 22 | 24 | 25 | S | R | 6-2 | 180 | 1-23-76 | 1994 | Bound Brook, N.J. |
| Speier, Justin ............ | 4 | 1 | 2.05 | 24 | 0 | 0 | 6 | 26 | 23 | 7 | 6 | 5 | 14 | R | R | 6-4 | 195 | 11-6-73 | 1995 | Scottsdale, Ariz. |
| Stephenson, Brian ........ | 5 | 13 | 4.69 | 32 | 20 | 0 | 1 | 129 | 130 | 82 | 67 | 61 | 106 | R | R | 6-3 | 205 | 7-17-73 | 1994 | Fullerton, Calif. |
| Thomas, Royal ........... | 3 | 2 | 6.23 | 8 | 8 | 0 | 0 | 43 | 55 | 37 | 30 | 14 | 20 | R | R | 6-2 | 187 | 9-3-69 | 1987 | Beaumont, Texas |
| 2-team (2 Greenville)... | 3 | 2 | 6.35 | 10 | 8 | 0 | 0 | 45 | 57 | 39 | 32 | 18 | 20 | | | | | | | |
| Trachsel, Steve ........... | 0 | 1 | 2.77 | 2 | 2 | 0 | 0 | 13 | 11 | 6 | 4 | 0 | 12 | R | R | 6-3 | 185 | 10-31-70 | 1991 | Yorba Linda, Calif. |
| Twiggs, Greg ............. | 4 | 2 | 3.95 | 44 | 0 | 0 | 1 | 55 | 53 | 27 | 24 | 33 | 40 | R | L | 5-10 | 155 | 10-15-71 | 1993 | Winter Springs, Fla. |
| Walker, Wade ............ | 8 | 14 | 4.41 | 29 | 29 | 2 | 0 | 188 | 205 | 112 | 92 | 76 | 117 | R | R | 6-1 | 190 | 9-18-71 | 1993 | Gonzales, La. |
| Ward, Duane ............ | 0 | 1 | 27.00 | 2 | 0 | 0 | 0 | 1 | 4 | 4 | 4 | 2 | 0 | R | R | 6-4 | 210 | 5-28-64 | 1982 | Las Vegas, Nev. |
| Williams, Greg ............ | 0 | 0 | 4.26 | 12 | 2 | 0 | 0 | 19 | 21 | 12 | 9 | 13 | 11 | L | L | 6-1 | 195 | 4-30-72 | 1993 | Portland, Ore. |
| Winslett, Dax ............. | 1 | 3 | 7.84 | 4 | 4 | 0 | 0 | 21 | 31 | 19 | 18 | 7 | 13 | R | R | 6-1 | 200 | 1-1-72 | 1993 | Houston, Texas |

## FIELDING

**Catcher**

| | PCT | G | PO | A | E | DP | PB |
|---|---|---|---|---|---|---|---|
| Cholowsky | .940 | 16 | 61 | 2 | 4 | 0 | 4 |
| Kingston | .971 | 13 | 60 | 7 | 2 | 1 | 1 |
| Ortiz | .988 | 76 | 475 | 32 | 6 | 2 | 5 |
| Thurston | .987 | 63 | 354 | 21 | 5 | 5 | 8 |

**First Base**

| | PCT | G | PO | A | E | DP |
|---|---|---|---|---|---|---|
| Cholowsky | .992 | 15 | 114 | 12 | 1 | 11 |
| Duross | .993 | 17 | 130 | 12 | 1 | 12 |
| Fryman | 1.000 | 10 | 58 | 5 | 0 | 4 |
| Kingston | 1.000 | 4 | 23 | 1 | 0 | 3 |
| Morris | .982 | 73 | 564 | 38 | 11 | 49 |
| Perez | .973 | 5 | 31 | 5 | 1 | 3 |
| Williams | .980 | 34 | 232 | 19 | 5 | 21 |

**Second Base**

| | PCT | G | PO | A | E | DP |
|---|---|---|---|---|---|---|
| Forkerway | 1.000 | 11 | 13 | 34 | 0 | 7 |
| Livsey | .963 | 63 | 118 | 167 | 11 | 27 |
| Maxwell | .947 | 26 | 39 | 68 | 6 | 17 |
| Morris | .915 | 36 | 41 | 66 | 10 | 14 |
| Perez | .833 | 2 | 2 | 3 | 1 | 0 |
| Petersen | .982 | 24 | 48 | 60 | 2 | 15 |

**Third Base**

| | PCT | G | PO | A | E | DP |
|---|---|---|---|---|---|---|
| Cholowsky | .884 | 21 | 13 | 25 | 5 | 3 |
| Forkerway | .913 | 14 | 3 | 18 | 2 | 2 |
| Kingston | .912 | 32 | 20 | 32 | 5 | 2 |
| Maxwell | 1.000 | 5 | 3 | 10 | 0 | 2 |
| Morris | .909 | 4 | 2 | 8 | 1 | 1 |
| Orie | .936 | 79 | 60 | 144 | 14 | 14 |
| Perez | .000 | 1 | 0 | 0 | 0 | 0 |

**Shortstop**

| | PCT | G | PO | A | E | DP |
|---|---|---|---|---|---|---|
| Forkerway | .966 | 28 | 35 | 79 | 4 | 15 |
| Livsey | .000 | 1 | 0 | 0 | 0 | 0 |
| Maxwell | .946 | 97 | 146 | 258 | 23 | 40 |
| Petersen | .904 | 24 | 43 | 61 | 11 | 15 |

**Outfield**

| | PCT | G | PO | A | E | DP |
|---|---|---|---|---|---|---|
| Bullett | 1.000 | 2 | 1 | 0 | 0 | 0 |
| Dowler | .991 | 101 | 209 | 5 | 2 | 0 |
| Forkerway | 1.000 | 4 | 1 | 0 | 0 | 0 |
| Fryman | .959 | 46 | 67 | 4 | 3 | 0 |
| Hightower | .978 | 18 | 44 | 0 | 1 | 0 |
| Hughes | .961 | 113 | 211 | 11 | 9 | 3 |
| Larregui | 1.000 | 13 | 24 | 1 | 0 | 0 |
| Samuels | .981 | 96 | 149 | 7 | 3 | 1 |
| Walker | .975 | 54 | 114 | 5 | 3 | 0 |

## BAKERSFIELD — Class A/Co-Op

### CALIFORNIA LEAGUE

| BATTING | AVG | G | AB | R | H | 2B | 3B | HR | RBI | BB | SO | SB | CS | B | T | HT | WT | DOB | 1st Yr | Resides |
|---|---|---|---|---|---|---|---|---|---|---|---|---|---|---|---|---|---|---|---|---|
| Bentley, Kevin | .274 | 22 | 84 | 19 | 23 | 3 | 1 | 5 | 21 | 9 | 30 | 7 | 1 | R | R | 6-2 | 210 | 9-21-72 | 1995 | Bedford, Texas |
| Cabrera, Alex | .281 | 89 | 345 | 45 | 97 | 18 | 1 | 15 | 53 | 14 | 80 | 0 | 1 | R | R | 6-2 | 217 | 12-24-71 | 1991 | El Tigre, Venez. |

**GAMES BY POSITION: 1B**—Cabrera 37. **OF**—Bentley 19, Cabrera 46.

## DAYTONA — Class A

### FLORIDA STATE LEAGUE

| BATTING | AVG | G | AB | R | H | 2B | 3B | HR | RBI | BB | SO | SB | CS | B | T | HT | WT | DOB | 1st Yr | Resides |
|---|---|---|---|---|---|---|---|---|---|---|---|---|---|---|---|---|---|---|---|---|
| Avalos, Gilbert | .253 | 90 | 285 | 38 | 72 | 12 | 0 | 0 | 25 | 20 | 49 | 23 | 8 | R | R | 5-11 | 175 | 3-26-73 | 1993 | Houston, Texas |
| Bentley, Kevin | .272 | 78 | 254 | 32 | 69 | 9 | 2 | 5 | 30 | 19 | 79 | 9 | 3 | R | R | 6-2 | 210 | 9-21-72 | 1995 | Bedford, Texas |
| Bustos, Saul | .188 | 100 | 298 | 35 | 56 | 7 | 2 | 5 | 29 | 22 | 76 | 5 | 4 | R | R | 5-11 | 170 | 9-30-72 | 1994 | Odessa, Texas |
| Campos, Miguel | .417 | 8 | 12 | 1 | 5 | 0 | 0 | 0 | 1 | 1 | 1 | 0 | 0 | R | R | 6-1 | 185 | 3-28-76 | 1994 | Carabobo, Venez. |
| Carter, Quincy | .000 | 1 | 0 | 1 | 0 | 0 | 0 | 0 | 0 | 0 | 0 | 0 | 0 | R | R | 6-3 | 200 | 10-13-77 | 1996 | Elkwood, Ga. |
| Cline, Pat | .279 | 124 | 434 | 75 | 121 | 30 | 2 | 17 | 76 | 54 | 79 | 10 | 2 | R | R | 6-3 | 220 | 10-9-74 | 1993 | Bradenton, Fla. |
| Dowler, Dee | .404 | 12 | 47 | 5 | 19 | 3 | 0 | 0 | 8 | 5 | 5 | 4 | 1 | R | R | 5-9 | 175 | 7-23-71 | 1993 | Indianapolis, Ind. |
| Ellis, Kevin | .272 | 128 | 481 | 69 | 131 | 23 | 2 | 16 | 89 | 25 | 64 | 5 | 4 | R | R | 6-0 | 210 | 11-21-71 | 1993 | Waco, Texas |
| Forkerway, Trey | .280 | 49 | 143 | 27 | 40 | 6 | 1 | 0 | 13 | 17 | 17 | 7 | 6 | R | R | 5-11 | 175 | 5-17-71 | 1993 | Abilene, Texas |
| Freeman, Ricky | .304 | 127 | 477 | 70 | 145 | 36 | 6 | 13 | 64 | 36 | 72 | 10 | 8 | R | R | 6-4 | 205 | 2-3-72 | 1994 | Houston, Texas |
| Gazarek, Marty | .278 | 129 | 472 | 68 | 131 | 31 | 4 | 11 | 77 | 28 | 52 | 15 | 13 | R | R | 6-2 | 190 | 6-1-73 | 1994 | North Baltimore, Ohio |
| Hightower, Vee | .324 | 87 | 293 | 59 | 95 | 13 | 5 | 6 | 27 | 52 | 44 | 25 | 7 | S | R | 6-5 | 205 | 4-26-72 | 1993 | Mt. Lebanon, Pa. |
| Jackson, Jeff | .245 | 16 | 53 | 5 | 13 | 2 | 1 | 0 | 4 | 8 | 18 | 7 | 1 | R | R | 6-2 | 180 | 1-2-72 | 1989 | Chicago, Ill. |
| Lantigua, Eddie | .196 | 43 | 143 | 10 | 28 | 1 | 0 | 5 | 14 | 3 | 31 | 3 | 1 | R | R | 6-0 | 198 | 1-9-73 | 1991 | Moca, D.R. |
| Livsey, Shawn | .325 | 50 | 194 | 39 | 63 | 14 | 3 | 2 | 28 | 24 | 32 | 17 | 6 | S | R | 5-11 | 180 | 7-21-73 | 1991 | Chicago, Ill. |
| Magadan, Dave | .300 | 7 | 20 | 5 | 6 | 1 | 0 | 0 | 3 | 7 | 2 | 0 | 0 | L | R | 6-3 | 200 | 9-30-62 | 1983 | Tampa, Fla. |
| Micucci, Mike | .183 | 39 | 82 | 6 | 15 | 0 | 0 | 0 | 3 | 5 | 16 | 0 | 3 | L | R | 5-11 | 185 | 12-15-72 | 1994 | Emerson, N.J. |
| Perez, Richard | .228 | 52 | 184 | 20 | 42 | 7 | 1 | 0 | 8 | 12 | 24 | 4 | 3 | R | R | 6-2 | 175 | 1-30-73 | 1991 | Lara, Venez. |
| Pico, Brandon | .194 | 19 | 67 | 10 | 13 | 0 | 1 | 1 | 8 | 5 | 9 | 1 | 0 | L | L | 6-1 | 185 | 1-2-74 | 1992 | Newport, R.I. |
| Porter, Bo | .175 | 20 | 63 | 9 | 11 | 4 | 1 | 0 | 6 | 6 | 24 | 5 | 1 | R | R | 6-1 | 188 | 7-5-72 | 1994 | Newark, N.J. |
| Rivera, Santiago | .150 | 10 | 20 | 3 | 3 | 1 | 1 | 0 | 1 | 4 | 5 | 0 | 0 | S | R | 5-11 | 180 | 12-15-72 | 1993 | Rio Piedras, P.R. |
| Seidel, Ryan | .118 | 9 | 17 | 0 | 2 | 1 | 0 | 0 | 1 | 3 | 5 | 0 | 0 | R | R | 6-0 | 180 | 5-21-73 | 1995 | Westlake Village, Calif. |
| Snyder, Jared | .207 | 12 | 29 | 5 | 6 | 0 | 0 | 0 | 4 | 2 | 6 | 0 | 0 | R | R | 6-2 | 215 | 3-8-70 | 1993 | Saugus, Calif. |
| Valette, Ramon | .194 | 14 | 31 | 5 | 6 | 2 | 1 | 0 | 2 | 3 | 5 | 1 | 0 | R | R | 6-1 | 160 | 1-20-72 | 1990 | Sabana Grande, D.R. |
| Walker, Steve | .316 | 58 | 225 | 39 | 71 | 17 | 2 | 9 | 39 | 17 | 53 | 21 | 4 | S | R | 6-1 | 180 | 2-11-72 | 1991 | Leesburg, Ga. |
| Whatley, Gabe | .226 | 56 | 146 | 24 | 42 | 14 | 1 | 2 | 25 | 26 | 27 | 9 | 1 | L | R | 6-0 | 180 | 12-29-71 | 1993 | Stone Mountain, Ga. |

**GAMES BY POSITION: C**—Campos 7, Cline 104, Micucci 37, Snyder 10. **1B**—Ellis 46, Freeman 95. **2B**—Avalos 73, Forkerway 6, Livsey 46, Perez 20, Rivera 2. **3B**—Avalos 15, Forkerway 16, Freeman 35, Lantigua 37, Magadan 4, Perez 29, Whatley 16. **SS**—Bustos 100, Forkerway 30, Jackson 1, Perez 2, Rivera 8, Valette 13. **OF**—Bentley 64, Carter 1, Dowler 12, Ellis 8, Gazarek 126, Hightower 81, Jackson 16, Lantigua 2, Pico 18, Porter 19, Seidel 9, Walker 55, Whatley 24.

| PITCHING | W | L | ERA | G | GS | CG | SV | IP | H | R | ER | BB | SO | B | T | HT | WT | DOB | 1st Yr | Resides |
|---|---|---|---|---|---|---|---|---|---|---|---|---|---|---|---|---|---|---|---|---|
| Bair, Dennis | 9 | 8 | 3.67 | 29 | 28 | 2 | 0 | 174 | 167 | 82 | 71 | 42 | 127 | L | R | 6-5 | 215 | 11-17-74 | 1995 | Monhall, Pa. |
| Barker, Richie | 4 | 0 | 5.67 | 17 | 0 | 0 | 0 | 27 | 34 | 23 | 17 | 18 | 14 | R | R | 6-2 | 195 | 10-29-72 | 1994 | Malden, Mass. |
| Bogle, Sean | 3 | 1 | 7.13 | 13 | 0 | 0 | 0 | 18 | 28 | 17 | 14 | 13 | 18 | R | R | 6-2 | 195 | 10-3-73 | 1994 | Indianapolis, Ind. |
| Booker, Chris | 0 | 0 | 0.00 | 1 | 1 | 0 | 0 | 2 | 1 | 0 | 0 | 3 | 2 | R | R | 6-3 | 205 | 12-9-76 | 1995 | Monroeville, Ala. |
| Box, Shawn | 6 | 2 | 4.27 | 14 | 9 | 0 | 0 | 53 | 38 | 28 | 25 | 12 | 32 | R | R | 5-11 | 180 | 3-13-73 | 1994 | Mereta, Texas |
| Brown, Darold | 4 | 4 | 2.73 | 35 | 0 | 0 | 4 | 53 | 42 | 20 | 16 | 20 | 43 | L | L | 6-0 | 175 | 8-16-73 | 1993 | Atlanta, Ga. |
| Byrne, Earl | 1 | 4 | 3.38 | 18 | 3 | 1 | 1 | 45 | 44 | 22 | 17 | 21 | 47 | L | L | 6-1 | 165 | 7-2-72 | 1994 | Melbourne, Australia |
| Carl, Todd | 1 | 1 | 7.27 | 5 | 0 | 0 | 0 | 9 | 19 | 11 | 7 | 6 | 2 | R | R | 6-5 | 220 | 1-3-73 | 1993 | Stitzer, Wis. |
| Diaz, Jairo | 1 | 1 | 3.08 | 8 | 3 | 0 | 0 | 26 | 31 | 14 | 9 | 14 | 18 | R | R | 6-2 | 198 | 8-21-75 | 1994 | Maracay, Venez. |
| Faulkner, Neal | 1 | 1 | 7.82 | 11 | 0 | 0 | 2 | 13 | 17 | 11 | 11 | 5 | 10 | R | R | 6-9 | 230 | 4-16-75 | 1994 | Montgomery, Ala. |
| Gambs, Chris | 0 | 2 | 6.26 | 13 | 0 | 0 | 0 | 23 | 28 | 22 | 16 | 21 | 17 | R | R | 6-2 | 210 | 10-26-73 | 1991 | Richmond, Calif. |
| Garcia, Al | 4 | 1 | 2.87 | 7 | 7 | 0 | 0 | 47 | 48 | 20 | 15 | 5 | 28 | S | R | 6-2 | 175 | 6-11-74 | 1993 | Buena Park, Calif. |
| Graves, Ryan | 0 | 0 | 5.25 | 6 | 0 | 0 | 0 | 12 | 16 | 8 | 7 | 5 | 9 | L | L | 6-2 | 185 | 2-15-74 | 1996 | Riverside, Calif. |
| Green, Jason | 0 | 3 | 10.93 | 5 | 4 | 0 | 0 | 14 | 13 | 17 | 17 | 29 | 13 | R | R | 6-2 | 195 | 11-15-73 | 1993 | Hercules, Calif. |
| Greene, Brian | 5 | 2 | 3.07 | 26 | 1 | 0 | 1 | 56 | 51 | 26 | 19 | 18 | 37 | R | R | 6-2 | 200 | 11-30-73 | 1995 | Ft. Thomas, Ky. |
| Guzman, Jose | 1 | 0 | 2.45 | 2 | 2 | 0 | 0 | 11 | 8 | 3 | 3 | 7 | 14 | R | R | 6-3 | 195 | 4-9-63 | 1981 | Arlington, Texas |
| Hammack, Brandon | 2 | 1 | 2.30 | 27 | 0 | 0 | 16 | 31 | 27 | 10 | 8 | 10 | 36 | R | R | 6-5 | 240 | 3-5-73 | 1995 | San Antonio, Texas |
| Licciardi, Ron | 1 | 0 | 1.13 | 2 | 1 | 0 | 0 | 8 | 3 | 2 | 1 | 2 | 3 | L | L | 6-2 | 190 | 3-26-76 | 1995 | Oakdale, Conn. |
| McNeese, John | 1 | 1 | 5.14 | 9 | 0 | 0 | 0 | 14 | 18 | 8 | 8 | 7 | 10 | R | L | 6-0 | 180 | 11-25-71 | 1995 | Columbia, Miss. |
| McNichol, Brian | 1 | 1 | 4.67 | 8 | 7 | 0 | 0 | 35 | 39 | 24 | 18 | 14 | 22 | L | L | 6-6 | 210 | 5-20-74 | 1993 | Woodbridge, Va. |
| Montelongo, Joe | 6 | 6 | 3.10 | 19 | 14 | 1 | 0 | 102 | 84 | 53 | 35 | 36 | 77 | R | R | 6-0 | 190 | 9-12-73 | 1994 | Cleveland, Ga. |
| Mosley, Tim | 0 | 3 | 11.42 | 6 | 0 | 0 | 0 | 9 | 16 | 15 | 11 | 6 | 7 | R | R | 6-0 | 180 | 10-16-74 | 1995 | New Castle, Pa. |
| Peterson, Jayson | 0 | 2 | 6.51 | 8 | 7 | 0 | 0 | 28 | 35 | 29 | 20 | 21 | 15 | S | R | 6-4 | 185 | 11-2-75 | 1994 | Commerce City, Colo. |

| PITCHING | W | L | ERA | G | GS | CG | SV | IP | H | R | ER | BB | SO | B | T | HT | WT | DOB | 1st Yr | Resides |
|---|---|---|---|---|---|---|---|---|---|---|---|---|---|---|---|---|---|---|---|---|
| Ryan, Jason ................ | 1 | 8 | 5.24 | 17 | 10 | 0 | 1 | 67 | 72 | 42 | 39 | 33 | 49 | S | R | 6-2 | 180 | 1-23-76 | 1994 | Bound Brook, N.J. |
| Speier, Justin ............... | 2 | 4 | 3.76 | 33 | 0 | 0 | 13 | 38 | 32 | 19 | 16 | 19 | 34 | R | R | 6-4 | 195 | 11-6-73 | 1995 | Scottsdale, Ariz. |
| Stevenson, Jason ......... | 8 | 5 | 3.54 | 27 | 17 | 2 | 0 | 122 | 136 | 56 | 48 | 22 | 86 | R | R | 6-3 | 180 | 8-11-74 | 1994 | Phenix City, Ala. |
| Ward, Duane ............... | 0 | 1 | 6.35 | 6 | 0 | 0 | 0 | 6 | 5 | 4 | 4 | 4 | 3 | R | R | 6-4 | 210 | 5-28-64 | 1982 | Las Vegas, Nev. |
| Winslett, Dax ............... | 0 | 1 | 13.50 | 2 | 1 | 0 | 0 | 6 | 10 | 10 | 9 | 5 | 3 | R | R | 6-1 | 200 | 1-1-72 | 1993 | Houston, Texas |
| Wood, Kerry ............... | 10 | 2 | 2.91 | 22 | 22 | 0 | 0 | 114 | 72 | 51 | 37 | 70 | 136 | R | R | 6-5 | 190 | 6-16-77 | 1995 | Grand Prairie, Texas |

## ROCKFORD — Class A
### MIDWEST LEAGUE

| BATTING | AVG | G | AB | R | H | 2B | 3B | HR | RBI | BB | SO | SB | CS | B | T | HT | WT | DOB | 1st Yr | Resides |
|---|---|---|---|---|---|---|---|---|---|---|---|---|---|---|---|---|---|---|---|---|
| Barnes, Kelvin ............. | .235 | 125 | 429 | 59 | 101 | 19 | 8 | 11 | 63 | 42 | 100 | 23 | 3 | R | R | 6-2 | 183 | 9-4-74 | 1994 | Battleboro, N.C. |
| Bly, Derrick ................. | .286 | 4 | 7 | 1 | 2 | 0 | 0 | 1 | 4 | 2 | 5 | 0 | 0 | R | R | 6-0 | 205 | 9-19-74 | 1996 | Tucson, Ariz. |
| Catlett, David ............. | .232 | 78 | 224 | 31 | 52 | 18 | 1 | 1 | 30 | 23 | 73 | 5 | 3 | R | R | 6-0 | 195 | 4-6-74 | 1993 | Berkeley, Calif. |
| Colon, Jose ................. | .250 | 8 | 12 | 1 | 3 | 0 | 0 | 0 | 1 | 3 | 5 | 0 | 2 | R | R | 6-2 | 190 | 1-25-76 | 1995 | Melbourne, Fla. |
| Ellison, Tony ............... | .170 | 31 | 94 | 7 | 16 | 3 | 0 | 2 | 7 | 3 | 30 | 0 | 2 | R | R | 6-0 | 195 | 7-12-74 | 1995 | Grifton, N.C. |
| Jasco, Elinton ............. | .293 | 120 | 464 | 95 | 136 | 11 | 7 | 1 | 43 | 62 | 97 | 48 | 14 | R | R | 5-10 | 150 | 5-11-75 | 1993 | San Pedro de Macoris, D.R. |
| Jefferson, David .......... | .233 | 93 | 301 | 35 | 70 | 8 | 2 | 1 | 40 | 37 | 53 | 15 | 6 | R | R | 6-2 | 190 | 6-18-75 | 1993 | Palo Alto, Calif. |
| Joseph, Terry .............. | .305 | 128 | 449 | 98 | 137 | 23 | 6 | 9 | 94 | 69 | 88 | 28 | 15 | R | R | 5-9 | 185 | 11-20-73 | 1995 | Harvey, La. |
| Kinnie, Donald ............ | .231 | 31 | 65 | 12 | 15 | 4 | 0 | 0 | 3 | 3 | 20 | 7 | 0 | R | R | 6-2 | 185 | 10-4-73 | 1995 | Tuscaloosa, Ala. |
| Lewis, Jeremy ............. | .247 | 105 | 365 | 50 | 90 | 23 | 4 | 5 | 61 | 46 | 85 | 13 | 3 | R | R | 6-1 | 186 | 9-7-72 | 1995 | Cedar Rapids, Iowa |
| Maleski, Tom .............. | .125 | 6 | 8 | 1 | 1 | 0 | 0 | 0 | 1 | 2 | 3 | 0 | 0 | R | R | 6-0 | 200 | 12-23-77 | 1995 | Richardson, Texas |
| McDonald, Ashanti ...... | .233 | 76 | 202 | 19 | 47 | 6 | 2 | 0 | 17 | 21 | 40 | 6 | 2 | L | R | 6-0 | 185 | 4-25-73 | 1995 | Chicago, Ill. |
| Molina, Jose ............... | .226 | 96 | 305 | 35 | 69 | 10 | 1 | 2 | 27 | 36 | 71 | 2 | 4 | R | R | 6-1 | 180 | 6-3-75 | 1993 | Vega Alta, P.R. |
| Nieves, Jose ............... | .242 | 113 | 396 | 55 | 96 | 20 | 4 | 5 | 57 | 33 | 59 | 17 | 9 | R | R | 6-0 | 153 | 6-16-75 | 1992 | Guacara, Venez. |
| Perez, Richard ........... | .253 | 33 | 83 | 12 | 21 | 6 | 0 | 3 | 13 | 10 | 17 | 2 | 0 | R | R | 6-2 | 175 | 1-30-73 | 1991 | Lara, Venez. |
| Pico, Brandon ............. | .314 | 12 | 35 | 3 | 11 | 0 | 1 | 0 | 7 | 3 | 3 | 0 | 0 | L | L | 6-1 | 185 | 1-2-74 | 1992 | Newport, R.I. |
| Porter, Bo ................... | .241 | 105 | 378 | 83 | 91 | 22 | 3 | 7 | 44 | 72 | 107 | 30 | 14 | R | R | 6-1 | 188 | 7-5-72 | 1994 | Newark, N.J. |
| Seidel, Ryan ............... | .190 | 47 | 105 | 14 | 20 | 3 | 0 | 0 | 10 | 6 | 25 | 6 | 3 | R | R | 6-0 | 180 | 5-21-73 | 1995 | Westlake Village, Calif. |
| Turlais, John ............... | .154 | 11 | 26 | 2 | 4 | 1 | 0 | 0 | 2 | 4 | 9 | 0 | 0 | L | R | 6-3 | 200 | 12-30-73 | 1992 | Flora, Ill. |
| Vieira, Scott ............... | .324 | 134 | 442 | 81 | 143 | 30 | 4 | 8 | 81 | 84 | 89 | 9 | 8 | R | R | 5-11 | 185 | 8-17-73 | 1995 | San Ramon, Calif. |

GAMES BY POSITION: C—Lewis 37, Maleski 3, Molina 96, Turlais 8. 1B—Catlett 24, Lewis 1, McDonald 1, Perez 4, Vieira 121. 2B—Jasco 120, Lewis 2, McDonald 7, Nieves 12, Perez 3. 3B—Barnes 117, Bly 1, Lewis 2, McDonald 3, Nieves 11, Perez 28. SS—McDonald 51, Nieves 97, Perez 4, Vieira 1. OF—Colon 7, Ellison 27, Jefferson 93, Joseph 126, Kinnie 20, Lewis 9, Pico 3, Porter 105, Seidel 43, Vieira 8.

| PITCHING | W | L | ERA | G | GS | CG | SV | IP | H | R | ER | BB | SO | B | T | HT | WT | DOB | 1st Yr | Resides |
|---|---|---|---|---|---|---|---|---|---|---|---|---|---|---|---|---|---|---|---|---|
| Ames, Skip ................. | 3 | 3 | 5.95 | 22 | 0 | 0 | 9 | 20 | 25 | 16 | 13 | 17 | 18 | R | R | 6-2 | 175 | 11-9-74 | 1996 | Bellaire, Texas |
| Barker, Richie .............. | 1 | 1 | 5.18 | 19 | 0 | 0 | 1 | 33 | 42 | 24 | 19 | 15 | 23 | R | R | 6-2 | 195 | 10-29-72 | 1994 | Malden, Mass. |
| Birsner, Roark ............ | 0 | 0 | 12.46 | 5 | 0 | 0 | 0 | 4 | 6 | 6 | 6 | 5 | 4 | R | R | 6-4 | 180 | 12-2-75 | 1994 | Berlin, N.J. |
| Bogle, Sean ................ | 0 | 0 | 4.24 | 16 | 0 | 0 | 0 | 23 | 26 | 23 | 11 | 24 | 15 | R | R | 6-2 | 195 | 10-3-73 | 1994 | Indianapolis, Ind. |
| Bryant, Chris ............... | 4 | 7 | 5.65 | 43 | 4 | 0 | 1 | 72 | 87 | 54 | 45 | 37 | 51 | L | L | 6-1 | 180 | 8-13-75 | 1993 | Tampa, Fla. |
| DeWitt, Chris .............. | 6 | 4 | 4.00 | 15 | 13 | 0 | 0 | 81 | 88 | 48 | 36 | 21 | 45 | R | R | 6-5 | 215 | 3-24-74 | 1995 | Ozark, Mo. |
| Diaz, Jairo ................. | 6 | 3 | 3.16 | 25 | 11 | 0 | 0 | 88 | 80 | 33 | 31 | 26 | 84 | R | R | 6-2 | 198 | 8-21-75 | 1994 | Maracay, Venez. |
| Farnsworth, Kyle ......... | 9 | 6 | 3.70 | 20 | 20 | 1 | 0 | 112 | 122 | 62 | 46 | 35 | 82 | R | R | 6-4 | 190 | 4-14-76 | 1995 | Roswell, Ga. |
| Hammack, Brandon ... | 2 | 3 | 2.27 | 30 | 0 | 0 | 13 | 32 | 22 | 13 | 8 | 19 | 45 | R | R | 6-5 | 240 | 3-5-73 | 1995 | San Antonio, Texas |
| Hammons, Matt ........... | 1 | 3 | 6.12 | 5 | 5 | 0 | 0 | 25 | 24 | 19 | 17 | 8 | 22 | R | R | 6-3 | 195 | 4-9-77 | 1995 | San Diego, Calif. |
| Lopez, Orlando ............ | 0 | 0 | 10.80 | 1 | 0 | 0 | 0 | 2 | 6 | 5 | 2 | 0 | 1 | L | L | 6-0 | 185 | 3-28-73 | 1992 | Isabella, P.R. |
| Markey, Barry ............. | 6 | 2 | 3.15 | 15 | 13 | 2 | 0 | 97 | 97 | 43 | 34 | 16 | 39 | R | R | 6-5 | 195 | 7-20-76 | 1995 | St. Petersburg, Fla. |
| Marshall, Gary ............ | 4 | 1 | 3.33 | 50 | 0 | 0 | 2 | 46 | 39 | 20 | 17 | 19 | 35 | R | L | 6-5 | 215 | 9-22-73 | 1996 | La Mesa, Calif. |
| Martinez, Javier .......... | 4 | 3 | 3.36 | 10 | 10 | 3 | 0 | 59 | 49 | 26 | 22 | 30 | 53 | R | R | 6-2 | 195 | 2-5-77 | 1994 | Bayamon, P.R. |
| Mosley, Tim ................ | 3 | 4 | 5.02 | 37 | 0 | 0 | 1 | 57 | 74 | 47 | 32 | 32 | 36 | R | R | 6-0 | 180 | 10-16-74 | 1995 | New Castle, Pa. |
| Peterson, Jayson ........ | 4 | 7 | 3.45 | 15 | 15 | 0 | 0 | 94 | 82 | 50 | 36 | 39 | 87 | S | R | 6-4 | 185 | 11-2-75 | 1994 | Commerce City, Colo. |
| Ricketts, Chad ............ | 3 | 8 | 5.03 | 37 | 9 | 0 | 4 | 88 | 89 | 60 | 49 | 29 | 70 | R | R | 6-5 | 195 | 2-12-75 | 1995 | St. Petersburg, Fla. |
| Tribe, Byron ............... | 0 | 0 | 2.45 | 9 | 1 | 0 | 0 | 15 | 10 | 4 | 4 | 12 | 22 | R | R | 6-3 | 195 | 3-21-75 | 1996 | Katy, Texas |
| Villegas, Ismael ........... | 2 | 5 | 5.13 | 10 | 10 | 1 | 0 | 47 | 63 | 40 | 27 | 25 | 30 | R | R | 6-0 | 177 | 8-12-76 | 1995 | Caguas, P.R. |
| Yoder, Jeff ................. | 12 | 5 | 3.44 | 25 | 24 | 2 | 0 | 154 | 139 | 70 | 59 | 48 | 124 | L | R | 6-2 | 210 | 2-16-76 | 1996 | Pottsville, Pa. |

## WILLIAMSPORT — Class A
### NEW YORK-PENN LEAGUE

| BATTING | AVG | G | AB | R | H | 2B | 3B | HR | RBI | BB | SO | SB | CS | B | T | HT | WT | DOB | 1st Yr | Resides |
|---|---|---|---|---|---|---|---|---|---|---|---|---|---|---|---|---|---|---|---|---|
| Andersen, Ryan .......... | .267 | 25 | 75 | 6 | 20 | 2 | 0 | 0 | 8 | 5 | 11 | 2 | 2 | R | R | 6-1 | 175 | 7-18-73 | 1996 | Huntington Beach, Calif. |
| Blessing, Chad ............ | .238 | 38 | 105 | 15 | 25 | 3 | 0 | 1 | 12 | 14 | 25 | 5 | 2 | R | R | 6-1 | 185 | 10-17-75 | 1996 | Lake Jackson, Texas |
| Campos, Miguel .......... | .150 | 6 | 20 | 1 | 3 | 1 | 0 | 0 | 1 | 0 | 11 | 0 | 0 | R | R | 6-1 | 185 | 3-28-76 | 1994 | Carabobo, Venez. |
| Colon, Jose ................ | .216 | 36 | 125 | 13 | 27 | 5 | 1 | 0 | 15 | 11 | 31 | 3 | 3 | R | R | 6-2 | 190 | 1-25-76 | 1995 | Melbourne, Fla. |
| Connell, Jerry ............. | .000 | 2 | 6 | 0 | 0 | 0 | 0 | 0 | 0 | 0 | 0 | 0 | 0 | R | R | 6-2 | 197 | 7-17-77 | 1995 | Avenel, N.J. |
| Ellison, Tony ............... | .284 | 63 | 229 | 33 | 65 | 10 | 1 | 7 | 35 | 20 | 51 | 4 | 0 | R | R | 6-0 | 195 | 7-12-74 | 1995 | Grifton, N.C. |
| Gordon, Buck .............. | .223 | 32 | 94 | 13 | 21 | 6 | 0 | 0 | 7 | 6 | 35 | 1 | 3 | R | R | 6-1 | 220 | 9-29-74 | 1995 | Shenandoah, Va. |
| Hall, Doug ................. | .264 | 67 | 227 | 35 | 60 | 5 | 3 | 2 | 19 | 20 | 58 | 12 | 11 | L | L | 6-0 | 175 | 12-12-74 | 1996 | Gallatin, Tenn. |
| Jefferies, Daryl ........... | .257 | 34 | 101 | 12 | 26 | 2 | 1 | 0 | 11 | 10 | 18 | 12 | 2 | R | R | 5-10 | 172 | 2-16-74 | 1996 | St. Peters, Mo. |
| Kiefer, Dax ................. | .227 | 64 | 229 | 36 | 52 | 7 | 3 | 3 | 20 | 27 | 50 | 12 | 2 | R | R | 5-11 | 185 | 12-4-73 | 1996 | Deer Park, Texas |
| King, Brad ................. | .171 | 23 | 70 | 7 | 12 | 2 | 1 | 0 | 8 | 4 | 20 | 0 | 1 | R | R | 6-2 | 190 | 12-3-74 | 1996 | Austin, Texas |
| Lewis, Keith ............... | .191 | 60 | 188 | 25 | 36 | 4 | 2 | 0 | 13 | 17 | 46 | 10 | 3 | S | R | 5-10 | 175 | 7-30-74 | 1996 | Alpharetta, Ga. |
| Lisanti, Bob ............... | .193 | 43 | 119 | 10 | 23 | 7 | 0 | 0 | 15 | 13 | 27 | 0 | 3 | R | R | 5-10 | 180 | 1-3-74 | 1996 | Chicago, Ill. |
| Manning, Nate ............ | .317 | 62 | 240 | 28 | 76 | 14 | 1 | 4 | 32 | 14 | 62 | 4 | 0 | R | R | 6-2 | 180 | 12-20-73 | 1996 | Keosauqua, Iowa |
| Meyers, Chad ............. | .243 | 67 | 230 | 46 | 56 | 9 | 2 | 2 | 26 | 33 | 39 | 27 | 6 | R | R | 6-0 | 180 | 8-8-75 | 1996 | Papillon, Neb. |
| Nova, Jose ................. | .232 | 60 | 203 | 27 | 47 | 7 | 3 | 4 | 38 | 25 | 62 | 5 | 2 | R | R | 6-2 | 190 | 5-23-75 | 1995 | Tempe, Ariz. |
| Zuleta, Julio ............... | .258 | 62 | 221 | 35 | 57 | 12 | 2 | 1 | 29 | 19 | 36 | 7 | 4 | R | R | 6-6 | 230 | 3-28-75 | 1993 | Juan Diaz, Panama |

GAMES BY POSITION: C—Campos 6, Gordon 18, King 22, Lisanti 43. 1B—Blessing 31, Gordon 4, King 1, Manning 7, Zuleta 43. 2B—Jefferies 2, Lewis 19, Meyers 57, Nova 2. 3B—Anderson 1, Blessing 3, Jefferies 2, Manning 37, Nova 42. SS—Anderson 20, Jefferies 24, Lewis 41, Nova 2. OF—Colon 36, Connell 2, Ellison 57, Gordon 2, Hall 67, Kiefer 64, Meyers 11, Nova 2.

| PITCHING | W | L | ERA | G | GS | CG | SV | IP | H | R | ER | BB | SO | B | T | HT | WT | DOB | 1st Yr | Resides |
|---|---|---|---|---|---|---|---|---|---|---|---|---|---|---|---|---|---|---|---|---|
| Birsner, Roark ............ | 2 | 4 | 5.47 | 31 | 0 | 0 | 1 | 51 | 53 | 33 | 31 | 27 | 58 | R | R | 6-4 | 180 | 12-2-75 | 1994 | Berlin, N.J. |
| Booker, Chris .............. | 4 | 6 | 5.31 | 14 | 14 | 0 | 0 | 61 | 57 | 51 | 36 | 51 | 52 | R | R | 6-3 | 205 | 12-9-76 | 1995 | Monroeville, Ala. |

| PITCHING | W | L | ERA | G | GS | CG | SV | IP | H | R | ER | BB | SO | B | T | HT | WT | DOB | 1st Yr | Resides |
|---|---|---|---|---|---|---|---|---|---|---|---|---|---|---|---|---|---|---|---|---|
| Brookens, Casey | 3 | 1 | 3.33 | 25 | 1 | 0 | 2 | 51 | 50 | 20 | 19 | 20 | 42 | R | R | 6-0 | 185 | 11-24-73 | 1996 | Fayetteville, Pa. |
| Cannon, Jon | 6 | 4 | 3.02 | 14 | 13 | 0 | 0 | 83 | 61 | 31 | 28 | 26 | 66 | R | L | 6-3 | 185 | 1-1-75 | 1996 | Los Altos, Calif. |
| Crawford, Jim | 0 | 3 | 9.67 | 21 | 0 | 0 | 1 | 27 | 40 | 35 | 29 | 20 | 31 | R | R | 6-0 | 190 | 12-31-74 | 1996 | De Mansion, Calif. |
| Duncan, Courtney | 11 | 1 | 2.19 | 15 | 15 | 1 | 0 | 90 | 58 | 28 | 22 | 34 | 91 | L | R | 5-11 | 175 | 10-9-74 | 1996 | Daphne, Ala. |
| Graves, Ryan | 0 | 0 | 0.00 | 4 | 0 | 0 | 0 | 5 | 4 | 0 | 0 | 2 | 3 | L | L | 6-2 | 185 | 2-15-74 | 1996 | Riverside, Calif. |
| Hart, Lendon | 2 | 3 | 1.44 | 28 | 0 | 0 | 2 | 31 | 15 | 6 | 5 | 24 | 26 | L | L | 5-11 | 185 | 10-8-73 | 1996 | Oak Ridge, Tenn. |
| Holobinko, Mike | 1 | 0 | 1.56 | 4 | 2 | 0 | 0 | 17 | 11 | 4 | 3 | 7 | 9 | L | L | 6-2 | 210 | 12-4-76 | 1995 | Rahway, N.J. |
| Licciardi, Ron | 3 | 5 | 4.50 | 15 | 15 | 0 | 0 | 76 | 78 | 51 | 38 | 38 | 53 | L | L | 6-2 | 190 | 3-26-76 | 1995 | Oakdale, Conn. |
| Nall, John | 0 | 0 | 6.08 | 9 | 0 | 0 | 0 | 13 | 13 | 11 | 9 | 3 | 9 | L | L | 6-5 | 205 | 3-16-74 | 1996 | Arcadia, Calif. |
| Norton, Phillip | 7 | 4 | 2.54 | 15 | 13 | 2 | 0 | 85 | 68 | 33 | 24 | 33 | 77 | R | L | 6-1 | 180 | 2-1-76 | 1996 | Texarkana, Texas |
| Shaffer, Trevor | 2 | 0 | 1.69 | 25 | 0 | 0 | 8 | 32 | 25 | 6 | 6 | 16 | 29 | R | R | 6-3 | 210 | 1-13-74 | 1996 | Menlo Park, Calif. |
| Tribe, Byron | 2 | 1 | 2.49 | 15 | 0 | 0 | 4 | 22 | 16 | 10 | 6 | 13 | 33 | R | R | 6-3 | 195 | 3-21-75 | 1996 | Katy, Texas |
| Velez, Jeff | 0 | 0 | 13.50 | 1 | 1 | 0 | 0 | 2 | 4 | 4 | 3 | 4 | 1 | R | R | 5-11 | 175 | 10-19-74 | 1996 | Greenwich, Conn. |
| Villegas, Ismael | 0 | 0 | 2.57 | 2 | 2 | 0 | 0 | 7 | 7 | 3 | 2 | 4 | 5 | R | R | 6-0 | 177 | 8-12-76 | 1995 | Caguas, P.R. |

## FORT MYERS — Rookie

### GULF COAST LEAGUE

| BATTING | AVG | G | AB | R | H | 2B | 3B | HR | RBI | BB | SO | SB | CS | B | T | HT | WT | DOB | 1st Yr | Resides |
|---|---|---|---|---|---|---|---|---|---|---|---|---|---|---|---|---|---|---|---|---|
| Abreu, Dennis | .313 | 56 | 192 | 32 | 60 | 5 | 0 | 0 | 15 | 21 | 20 | 35 | 9 | R | R | 6-0 | 165 | 4-22-78 | 1995 | Aragua, Venez. |
| Abreu, Nelson | .221 | 44 | 136 | 15 | 30 | 2 | 3 | 1 | 11 | 19 | 31 | 15 | 4 | R | R | 6-0 | 170 | 8-16-76 | 1994 | Maracay, Venez. |
| Bly, Derrick | .282 | 53 | 195 | 37 | 55 | 11 | 2 | 13 | 32 | 21 | 54 | 8 | 3 | R | R | 6-0 | 205 | 9-19-74 | 1996 | Tucson, Ariz. |
| Carter, Quincy | .215 | 55 | 181 | 31 | 39 | 6 | 1 | 3 | 37 | 35 | 36 | 18 | 6 | R | R | 6-3 | 200 | 10-13-77 | 1996 | Elkwood, Ga. |
| Connell, Jerry | .333 | 21 | 72 | 7 | 24 | 3 | 0 | 2 | 12 | 7 | 14 | 5 | 1 | R | R | 6-2 | 197 | 7-17-77 | 1995 | Avenel, N.J. |
| Font, Franklin | .301 | 59 | 239 | 43 | 72 | 5 | 4 | 0 | 18 | 17 | 36 | 31 | 9 | R | R | 5-10 | 175 | 11-4-77 | 1995 | Maracaibo, Venez. |
| Grubbs, Chris | .150 | 30 | 80 | 11 | 12 | 2 | 1 | 0 | 3 | 8 | 27 | 5 | 4 | R | R | 6-3 | 195 | 12-27-75 | 1996 | Ocoee, Fla. |
| Hammons, Matt | .000 | 1 | 0 | 0 | 0 | 0 | 0 | 0 | 0 | 0 | 0 | 1 | 0 | R | R | 6-3 | 195 | 4-9-77 | 1995 | San Diego, Calif. |
| Heredia, Rafael | .224 | 23 | 76 | 12 | 17 | 4 | 1 | 1 | 8 | 9 | 21 | 11 | 1 | R | R | 6-0 | 172 | 12-3-75 | 1994 | Santo Domingo, D.R. |
| Jimenez, Felipe | .246 | 49 | 171 | 18 | 42 | 4 | 0 | 0 | 10 | 5 | 44 | 20 | 9 | R | R | 6-3 | 185 | 12-22-76 | 1994 | Camatagua, Venez. |
| Kinnie, Donald | .308 | 19 | 39 | 6 | 12 | 3 | 1 | 1 | 7 | 2 | 6 | 3 | 1 | R | R | 6-2 | 185 | 10-4-73 | 1995 | Tuscaloosa, Ala. |
| Longmire, Marcel | .191 | 34 | 115 | 11 | 22 | 2 | 1 | 2 | 7 | 8 | 35 | 6 | 4 | R | R | 6-2 | 205 | 4-18-78 | 1996 | Vallejo, Calif. |
| Payano, Alexi | .253 | 28 | 83 | 15 | 21 | 5 | 1 | 0 | 10 | 4 | 12 | 3 | 1 | R | R | 6-2 | 185 | 4-8-77 | 1994 | Bani, D.R. |
| Pressley, Kasey | .137 | 35 | 124 | 9 | 17 | 1 | 0 | 1 | 13 | 13 | 49 | 1 | 1 | L | R | 6-4 | 220 | 9-5-76 | 1995 | Orlando, Fla. |
| Salazar, Juan | .296 | 52 | 186 | 32 | 55 | 16 | 1 | 6 | 31 | 22 | 40 | 12 | 2 | S | R | 6-4 | 200 | 10-31-77 | 1994 | Valencia, Venez. |
| Stewart, Courteney | .256 | 21 | 78 | 6 | 20 | 3 | 0 | 0 | 5 | 2 | 28 | 4 | 1 | R | R | 6-2 | 195 | 4-10-76 | 1996 | Atlanta, Ga. |

**GAMES BY POSITION: C**—Grubbs 29, Longmire 3, Payano 21, Salazar 15. **1B**—Bly 11, Longmire 2, Pressley 26, Salazar 26. **2B**—D. Abreu 56, N. Abreu 6, Font 4. **3B**—N. Abreu 25, Bly 38, Salazar 1. **SS**—N. Abreu 5, Font 57. **OF**—N. Abreu 10, Carter 50, Connell 16, Grubbs 1, Heredia 16, Jimenez 46, Kinnie 11, Longmire 27, Pressley 1, Stewart 13.

| PITCHING | W | L | ERA | G | GS | CG | SV | IP | H | R | ER | BB | SO | B | T | HT | WT | DOB | 1st Yr | Resides |
|---|---|---|---|---|---|---|---|---|---|---|---|---|---|---|---|---|---|---|---|---|
| Alvino, Royel | 2 | 2 | 4.42 | 13 | 1 | 0 | 3 | 18 | 10 | 10 | 9 | 17 | 23 | R | R | 6-4 | 175 | 9-23-75 | 1993 | Bani, D.R. |
| Connell, Brian | 2 | 1 | 10.54 | 7 | 5 | 0 | 0 | 14 | 12 | 18 | 16 | 15 | 11 | L | L | 6-2 | 185 | 8-4-77 | 1996 | Clearwater, Fla. |
| Crane, Randy | 0 | 3 | 1.86 | 15 | 0 | 0 | 1 | 29 | 17 | 11 | 6 | 16 | 35 | R | R | 6-2 | 180 | 7-4-75 | 1996 | McMinnville, Ore. |
| Feliz, Jose | 4 | 1 | 2.21 | 11 | 7 | 0 | 0 | 61 | 46 | 20 | 15 | 18 | 57 | R | R | 6-1 | 175 | 8-31-76 | 1994 | Santo Domingo, D.R. |
| Fennell, Barry | 0 | 4 | 2.95 | 10 | 7 | 0 | 1 | 43 | 37 | 19 | 14 | 12 | 42 | R | L | 6-4 | 200 | 9-30-76 | 1994 | Pennsauken, N.J. |
| Gissell, Chris | 4 | 2 | 2.35 | 11 | 10 | 0 | 0 | 61 | 54 | 23 | 16 | 8 | 64 | R | R | 6-4 | 180 | 1-4-78 | 1996 | Vancouver, Wash. |
| Holobinko, Mike | 0 | 0 | 0.52 | 11 | 0 | 0 | 3 | 17 | 10 | 1 | 1 | 7 | 22 | L | L | 6-2 | 210 | 12-4-76 | 1995 | Rahway, N.J. |
| Kelley, Jason | 2 | 3 | 5.96 | 8 | 7 | 0 | 0 | 26 | 18 | 22 | 17 | 16 | 29 | R | R | 6-1 | 225 | 11-14-75 | 1994 | Live Oak, Fla. |
| Mallory, Andrew | 0 | 3 | 3.86 | 12 | 7 | 0 | 0 | 54 | 49 | 31 | 23 | 22 | 33 | R | R | 6-2 | 165 | 9-25-76 | 1996 | St. Petersburg, Fla. |
| Martinez, Javier | 2 | 1 | 0.60 | 3 | 3 | 0 | 0 | 15 | 11 | 4 | 1 | 6 | 15 | R | R | 6-2 | 195 | 2-5-77 | 1994 | Bayamon, P.R. |
| McNichol, Brian | 0 | 0 | 0.00 | 1 | 1 | 0 | 0 | 3 | 4 | 2 | 0 | 0 | 2 | L | L | 6-6 | 210 | 5-20-74 | 1995 | Woodbridge, Va. |
| Nall, John | 2 | 0 | 2.59 | 10 | 1 | 0 | 1 | 24 | 25 | 12 | 7 | 4 | 11 | L | L | 6-5 | 205 | 3-16-74 | 1996 | Arcadia, Calif. |
| Noel, Todd | 0 | 0 | 6.75 | 3 | 0 | 0 | 0 | 4 | 4 | 4 | 3 | 2 | 4 | R | R | 6-4 | 185 | 9-28-78 | 1996 | Maurice, La. |
| Norton, Phillip | 0 | 0 | 0.00 | 1 | 0 | 0 | 0 | 3 | 1 | 0 | 0 | 0 | 6 | R | L | 6-1 | 180 | 2-1-76 | 1996 | Texarkana, Texas |
| Pitt, Jye | 1 | 2 | 1.84 | 12 | 0 | 0 | 0 | 29 | 21 | 8 | 6 | 9 | 38 | L | R | 6-2 | 190 | 2-21-78 | 1996 | Dapto, Australia |
| Polanco, Elvis | 6 | 3 | 2.59 | 14 | 7 | 1 | 2 | 56 | 55 | 28 | 16 | 18 | 37 | R | R | 6-2 | 164 | 3-10-78 | 1994 | Puerto Cabello, Venez. |
| Vizcaino, Edward | 5 | 0 | 1.62 | 14 | 4 | 0 | 2 | 44 | 34 | 8 | 8 | 8 | 24 | R | R | 6-0 | 160 | 4-17-77 | 1994 | Bani, D.R. |
| Ward, Brandon | 2 | 1 | 2.81 | 16 | 0 | 0 | 2 | 26 | 16 | 9 | 8 | 10 | 32 | R | R | 6-5 | 170 | 1-21-76 | 1996 | Fontana, Calif. |

# CINCINNATI REDS

**Manager:** Ray Knight.    **1996 Record:** 81-81, .500 (3rd, NL Central)

| BATTING | AVG | G | AB | R | H | 2B | 3B | HR | RBI | BB | SO | SB | CS | B | T | HT | WT | DOB | 1st Yr | Resides |
|---|---|---|---|---|---|---|---|---|---|---|---|---|---|---|---|---|---|---|---|---|
| Anthony, Eric | .244 | 47 | 123 | 22 | 30 | 6 | 0 | 8 | 13 | 22 | 36 | 0 | 1 | L | L | 6-2 | 195 | 11-8-67 | 1986 | Houston, Texas |
| Belk, Tim | .200 | 7 | 15 | 2 | 3 | 0 | 0 | 0 | 0 | 1 | 2 | 0 | 0 | R | R | 6-3 | 200 | 4-6-70 | 1992 | Houston, Texas |
| Boone, Bret | .233 | 142 | 520 | 56 | 121 | 21 | 3 | 12 | 69 | 31 | 100 | 3 | 2 | R | R | 5-10 | 180 | 4-6-69 | 1990 | Villa Park, Calif. |
| Branson, Jeff | .244 | 129 | 311 | 34 | 76 | 16 | 4 | 9 | 37 | 31 | 67 | 2 | 0 | L | R | 6-0 | 180 | 1-26-67 | 1989 | Silas, Ala. |
| Coleman, Vince | .155 | 33 | 84 | 10 | 13 | 1 | 1 | 1 | 4 | 9 | 31 | 12 | 2 | S | R | 6-1 | 185 | 9-22-61 | 1982 | St. Louis, Mo. |
| Davis, Eric | .287 | 129 | 415 | 81 | 119 | 20 | 0 | 26 | 83 | 70 | 121 | 23 | 9 | R | R | 6-3 | 185 | 5-29-62 | 1980 | Woodland Hills, Calif. |
| Fordyce, Brook | .286 | 4 | 7 | 0 | 2 | 1 | 0 | 0 | 1 | 3 | 1 | 0 | 0 | R | R | 6-1 | 185 | 5-7-70 | 1989 | Old Lyme, Conn. |
| Gibralter, Steve | .000 | 2 | 2 | 0 | 0 | 0 | 0 | 0 | 0 | 0 | 2 | 0 | 0 | R | R | 6-0 | 170 | 10-9-72 | 1990 | Duncanville, Texas |
| Goodwin, Curtis | .228 | 49 | 136 | 20 | 31 | 3 | 0 | 0 | 5 | 19 | 34 | 15 | 6 | L | L | 5-11 | 180 | 9-30-72 | 1991 | San Leandro, Calif. |
| Greene, Willie | .244 | 115 | 287 | 48 | 70 | 5 | 5 | 19 | 63 | 36 | 88 | 0 | 1 | L | R | 5-11 | 184 | 9-23-71 | 1989 | Haddock, Ga. |
| Harris, Lenny | .285 | 125 | 302 | 33 | 86 | 17 | 2 | 5 | 32 | 21 | 31 | 14 | 6 | L | R | 5-10 | 205 | 10-28-64 | 1983 | Miami, Fla. |
| Howard, Thomas | .272 | 121 | 360 | 50 | 98 | 19 | 10 | 6 | 42 | 17 | 51 | 6 | 5 | S | R | 6-2 | 205 | 12-11-64 | 1986 | Elk Grove, Calif. |
| Kelly, Mike | .184 | 19 | 49 | 5 | 9 | 4 | 0 | 1 | 7 | 9 | 11 | 4 | 0 | R | R | 6-4 | 195 | 6-2-70 | 1991 | Los Alamitos, Calif. |
| Larkin, Barry | .298 | 152 | 517 | 117 | 154 | 32 | 4 | 33 | 89 | 96 | 52 | 36 | 10 | R | R | 6-0 | 190 | 4-28-64 | 1985 | Cincinnati, Ohio |
| Mitchell, Kevin | .267 | 11 | 15 | 2 | 4 | 1 | 0 | 1 | 3 | 1 | 3 | 0 | 0 | R | R | 5-11 | 210 | 1-13-62 | 1981 | Chula Vista, Calif. |
| Morris, Hal | .313 | 142 | 528 | 82 | 165 | 32 | 4 | 16 | 80 | 50 | 76 | 7 | 5 | L | L | 6-4 | 215 | 4-9-65 | 1986 | Union, Ky. |
| Mottola, Chad | .215 | 35 | 79 | 10 | 17 | 3 | 0 | 3 | 6 | 6 | 16 | 2 | 2 | R | R | 6-3 | 215 | 10-15-71 | 1992 | Pembroke Pines, Fla. |
| Oliver, Joe | .242 | 106 | 289 | 31 | 70 | 12 | 1 | 11 | 46 | 28 | 54 | 2 | 0 | R | R | 6-3 | 220 | 7-24-65 | 1983 | Orlando, Fla. |
| Owens, Eric | .200 | 88 | 205 | 26 | 41 | 6 | 0 | 0 | 9 | 23 | 38 | 16 | 2 | R | R | 6-1 | 184 | 2-3-71 | 1992 | Danville, Va. |
| Perez, Eduardo | .222 | 18 | 36 | 8 | 8 | 0 | 0 | 3 | 5 | 5 | 9 | 0 | 0 | R | R | 6-4 | 215 | 9-11-69 | 1991 | Santurce, P.R. |
| Sabo, Chris | .256 | 54 | 125 | 15 | 32 | 7 | 1 | 3 | 16 | 18 | 27 | 2 | 0 | R | R | 6-0 | 185 | 1-19-62 | 1983 | Sarasota, Fla. |
| Sanders, Reggie | .251 | 81 | 287 | 49 | 72 | 17 | 1 | 14 | 33 | 44 | 86 | 24 | 8 | R | R | 6-1 | 180 | 12-1-67 | 1988 | Cincinnati, Ohio |
| Taubensee, Eddie | .291 | 108 | 327 | 46 | 95 | 20 | 0 | 12 | 48 | 26 | 64 | 3 | 4 | L | R | 6-4 | 205 | 10-31-68 | 1986 | Houston, Texas |

| PITCHING | W | L | ERA | G | GS | CG | SV | IP | H | R | ER | BB | SO | B | T | HT | WT | DOB | 1st Yr | Resides |
|---|---|---|---|---|---|---|---|---|---|---|---|---|---|---|---|---|---|---|---|---|
| Brantley, Jeff | 1 | 2 | 2.41 | 66 | 0 | 0 | 44 | 71 | 54 | 21 | 19 | 28 | 76 | R | R | 5-10 | 189 | 9-5-63 | 1985 | Clinton, Miss. |
| Burba, Dave | 11 | 13 | 3.83 | 34 | 33 | 0 | 0 | 195 | 179 | 96 | 83 | 97 | 148 | R | R | 6-4 | 240 | 7-7-66 | 1987 | Springfield, Ohio |
| Carrara, Giovanni | 1 | 0 | 5.87 | 8 | 5 | 0 | 0 | 23 | 31 | 17 | 15 | 13 | 13 | R | R | 6-2 | 210 | 3-4-68 | 1990 | Anzoategui, Venez. |
| Carrasco, Hector | 4 | 3 | 3.75 | 56 | 0 | 0 | 0 | 74 | 58 | 37 | 31 | 45 | 59 | R | R | 6-2 | 175 | 10-22-69 | 1988 | San Pedro de Macoris, D.R. |
| Hernandez, Xavier | 0 | 0 | 13.50 | 3 | 0 | 0 | 0 | 3 | 8 | 6 | 5 | 2 | 3 | L | R | 6-2 | 185 | 8-16-65 | 1986 | Missouri City, Texas |
| Jarvis, Kevin | 8 | 9 | 5.98 | 24 | 20 | 2 | 0 | 120 | 152 | 93 | 80 | 43 | 63 | L | R | 6-2 | 200 | 8-1-69 | 1991 | Lexington, Ky. |
| Lilliquist, Derek | 0 | 0 | 7.36 | 5 | 0 | 0 | 0 | 4 | 5 | 3 | 3 | 0 | 1 | L | L | 5-10 | 195 | 2-20-66 | 1987 | Vero Beach, Fla. |
| Lyons, Curt | 2 | 0 | 4.50 | 3 | 3 | 0 | 0 | 16 | 17 | 8 | 8 | 7 | 14 | R | R | 6-5 | 228 | 10-17-74 | 1992 | Richmond, Ky. |
| Martinez, Pedro A. | 0 | 0 | 6.00 | 4 | 0 | 0 | 0 | 3 | 5 | 2 | 2 | 1 | 3 | L | L | 6-2 | 155 | 11-29-68 | 1987 | Villa Mella, D.R. |
| 2-team (5 New York) | 0 | 0 | 6.30 | 9 | 0 | 0 | 0 | 10 | 13 | 9 | 7 | 8 | 9 | | | | | | | |
| McElroy, Chuck | 2 | 0 | 6.57 | 12 | 0 | 0 | 0 | 12 | 13 | 10 | 9 | 10 | 13 | L | L | 6-0 | 195 | 10-1-67 | 1986 | Friendswood, Texas |
| Moore, Marcus | 3 | 3 | 5.81 | 23 | 0 | 0 | 2 | 26 | 26 | 21 | 17 | 22 | 27 | S | R | 6-5 | 204 | 11-2-70 | 1989 | Oakland, Calif. |
| Morgan, Mike | 2 | 3 | 2.30 | 5 | 5 | 0 | 0 | 27 | 28 | 9 | 7 | 7 | 19 | R | R | 6-2 | 222 | 10-8-59 | 1978 | Ogden, Utah |
| 2-team (18 St. Louis) | 6 | 11 | 4.63 | 23 | 23 | 0 | 0 | 130 | 146 | 72 | 67 | 47 | 74 | | | | | | | |
| Portugal, Mark | 8 | 9 | 3.98 | 27 | 26 | 1 | 0 | 156 | 146 | 77 | 69 | 42 | 93 | R | R | 6-0 | 190 | 10-30-62 | 1981 | Missouri City, Texas |
| Pugh, Tim | 1 | 1 | 11.49 | 10 | 0 | 0 | 0 | 16 | 24 | 20 | 20 | 11 | 9 | R | R | 6-6 | 225 | 1-26-67 | 1989 | Florence, Ky. |
| Remlinger, Mike | 0 | 1 | 5.60 | 19 | 4 | 0 | 0 | 27 | 24 | 17 | 17 | 19 | 19 | L | L | 6-0 | 195 | 3-23-66 | 1987 | Plymouth, Mass. |
| Ruffin, Johnny | 1 | 3 | 5.49 | 49 | 0 | 0 | 0 | 62 | 71 | 42 | 38 | 37 | 69 | R | R | 6-3 | 170 | 7-29-71 | 1988 | Butler, Ala. |
| Salkeld, Roger | 8 | 5 | 5.20 | 29 | 19 | 1 | 0 | 116 | 114 | 69 | 67 | 54 | 82 | R | R | 6-5 | 215 | 3-6-71 | 1989 | Saugus, Calif. |
| Schourek, Pete | 4 | 5 | 6.01 | 12 | 12 | 0 | 0 | 67 | 79 | 48 | 45 | 24 | 54 | L | L | 6-5 | 195 | 5-10-69 | 1987 | Falls Church, Va. |
| Service, Scott | 1 | 0 | 3.94 | 34 | 1 | 0 | 0 | 48 | 51 | 21 | 21 | 18 | 46 | R | R | 6-6 | 226 | 2-26-67 | 1986 | Cincinnati, Ohio |
| Shaw, Jeff | 8 | 6 | 2.49 | 78 | 0 | 0 | 4 | 105 | 99 | 34 | 29 | 29 | 69 | R | R | 6-2 | 185 | 7-7-66 | 1986 | Washington Courthouse, Ohio |
| Smiley, John | 13 | 14 | 3.64 | 35 | 34 | 2 | 0 | 217 | 207 | 100 | 88 | 54 | 171 | L | L | 6-4 | 215 | 3-17-65 | 1983 | Warrendale, Pa. |
| Smith, Lee | 3 | 4 | 4.06 | 43 | 0 | 0 | 2 | 44 | 49 | 20 | 20 | 23 | 35 | R | R | 6-6 | 269 | 12-4-57 | 1975 | Castor, La. |
| Spradlin, Jerry | 0 | 0 | 0.00 | 1 | 0 | 0 | 0 | 0 | 0 | 0 | 0 | 0 | 0 | S | R | 6-7 | 240 | 6-14-67 | 1988 | Anaheim, Calif. |
| Sullivan, Scott | 0 | 0 | 2.25 | 7 | 0 | 0 | 0 | 8 | 7 | 2 | 2 | 5 | 3 | R | R | 6-3 | 210 | 3-13-71 | 1993 | Carrollton, Ala. |

## FIELDING

| Catcher | PCT | G | PO | A | E | DP | PB |
|---|---|---|---|---|---|---|---|
| Fordyce | 1.000 | 4 | 18 | 0 | 0 | 0 | 0 |
| Oliver | .992 | 97 | 572 | 44 | 5 | 7 | 4 |
| Taubensee | .981 | 94 | 538 | 42 | 11 | 7 | 3 |

| First Base | PCT | G | PO | A | E | DP |
|---|---|---|---|---|---|---|
| Belk | 1.000 | 6 | 28 | 0 | 0 | 2 |
| Davis | 1.000 | 1 | 7 | 0 | 0 | 0 |
| Greene | 1.000 | 2 | 1 | 0 | 0 | 0 |
| Harris | .993 | 16 | 123 | 12 | 1 | 10 |
| Mitchell | .968 | 3 | 28 | 2 | 1 | 4 |
| Morris | .993 | 140 | 1129 | 91 | 8 | 103 |
| Oliver | 1.000 | 3 | 9 | 1 | 0 | 0 |
| Perez | 1.000 | 8 | 56 | 7 | 0 | 6 |

| Second Base | PCT | G | PO | A | E | DP |
|---|---|---|---|---|---|---|
| Boone | .991 | 141 | 315 | 381 | 6 | 84 |
| Branson | .976 | 31 | 36 | 45 | 2 | 11 |

| | PCT | G | PO | A | E | DP |
|---|---|---|---|---|---|---|
| Greene | 1.000 | 1 | 1 | 1 | 0 | 1 |
| Harris | .960 | 7 | 10 | 14 | 1 | 3 |
| Owens | .944 | 6 | 10 | 7 | 1 | 0 |

| Third Base | PCT | G | PO | A | E | DP |
|---|---|---|---|---|---|---|
| Branson | .932 | 64 | 31 | 93 | 9 | 12 |
| Greene | .927 | 73 | 45 | 146 | 15 | 13 |
| Harris | .935 | 24 | 21 | 37 | 4 | 2 |
| Owens | 1.000 | 5 | 1 | 4 | 0 | 0 |
| Perez | 1.000 | 3 | 3 | 4 | 0 | 0 |
| Sabo | .961 | 43 | 27 | 72 | 4 | 6 |

| Shortstop | PCT | G | PO | A | E | DP |
|---|---|---|---|---|---|---|
| Branson | .969 | 38 | 30 | 63 | 3 | 17 |
| Greene | 1.000 | 1 | 0 | 2 | 0 | 0 |
| Larkin | .975 | 151 | 230 | 426 | 17 | 80 |

| Outfield | PCT | G | PO | A | E | DP |
|---|---|---|---|---|---|---|
| Anthony | .949 | 37 | 35 | 2 | 2 | 0 |
| Coleman | .968 | 20 | 28 | 2 | 1 | 0 |
| Davis | .989 | 126 | 272 | 3 | 3 | 0 |
| Gibralter | .000 | 2 | 0 | 0 | 1 | 0 |
| Goodwin | .970 | 42 | 64 | 0 | 2 | 0 |
| Greene | .909 | 10 | 10 | 0 | 1 | 0 |
| Harris | 1.000 | 37 | 44 | 2 | 0 | 0 |
| Howard | .982 | 103 | 160 | 7 | 3 | 1 |
| Kelly | .972 | 17 | 34 | 1 | 1 | 1 |
| Mitchell | .978 | 31 | 45 | 0 | 1 | 0 |
| Mottola | 1.000 | 31 | 42 | 2 | 0 | 0 |
| Oliver | 1.000 | 3 | 2 | 0 | 0 | 0 |
| Owens | .986 | 52 | 65 | 3 | 1 | 1 |
| Sanders | .988 | 80 | 160 | 7 | 2 | 2 |

**Shortstop Barry Larkin led the Reds with 33 homers and 36 stolen bases**

LARRY GOREN

**Reds minor league Player of the Year Aaron Boone**

ROBERT GURGANUS

REDS

## FARM SYSTEM

**Director of Player Development:** Chief Bender

| Class | Farm Team | League | W | L | Pct. | Finish* | Manager | First Yr |
|-------|-----------|--------|---|---|------|---------|---------|----------|
| AAA | Indianapolis (Ind.) Indians | American Assoc. | 78 | 66 | .542 | 3rd (8) | Dave Miley | 1993 |
| AA | Chattanooga (Tenn.) Lookouts | Southern | 81 | 59 | .579 | 2nd (10) | Mark Berry | 1988 |
| #A | Winston-Salem (N.C.) Warthogs | Carolina | 74 | 65 | .532 | 3rd (8) | Phillip Wellman | 1993 |
| A | Charleston (W.Va.) Alley Cats | South Atlantic | 58 | 84 | .408 | 12th (14) | Thompson/Scott | 1990 |
| #R | Billings (Mont.) Mustangs | Pioneer | 23 | 49 | .319 | 7th (8) | Matt Martin | 1974 |
| #R | Princeton (W.Va.) Reds | Appalachian | 28 | 40 | .412 | 7th (9) | Mark Wagner | 1991 |

*Finish in overall standings (No. of teams in league)   #Advanced level

## ORGANIZATION LEADERS

### MAJOR LEAGUERS

**BATTING**
| | | |
|---|---|---|
| *AVG | Hal Morris | .313 |
| R | Barry Larkin | 117 |
| H | Hal Morris | 165 |
| TB | Barry Larkin | 293 |
| 2B | Two tied at | 32 |
| 3B | Thomas Howard | 10 |
| HR | Barry Larkin | 33 |
| RBI | Barry Larkin | 89 |
| BB | Barry Larkin | 96 |
| SO | Eric Davis | 121 |
| SB | Barry Larkin | 36 |

**PITCHING**
| | | |
|---|---|---|
| W | John Smiley | 13 |
| L | John Smiley | 14 |
| #ERA | Jeff Shaw | 2.49 |
| G | Jeff Shaw | 78 |
| CG | Two tied at | 2 |
| SV | Jeff Brantley | 44 |
| IP | John Smiley | 217 |
| BB | Dave Burba | 97 |
| SO | John Smiley | 171 |

MORRIS FOSTOFF

**Hal Morris.** .313 average

### MINOR LEAGUERS

**BATTING**
| | | |
|---|---|---|
| *AVG | Wylie Campbell, Billings | .371 |
| R | Aaron Boone, Chattanooga | 86 |
| H | Aaron Boone, Chattanooga | 158 |
| TB | Aaron Boone, Chattanooga | 267 |
| 2B | Aaron Boone, Chattanooga | 44 |
| 3B | Roberto Mejia, Indianapolis | 9 |
| HR | Eduardo Perez, Indianapolis | 21 |
| RBI | Aaron Boone, Chattanooga | 95 |
| BB | Steve Goodhart, Charleston | 94 |
| SO | Thomas Scott, Charleston | 156 |
| SB | Curtis Goodwin, Indianapolis | 40 |

**PITCHING**
| | | |
|---|---|---|
| W | Travis Buckley, Chattanooga/Indy | 14 |
| L | Three tied at | 11 |
| #ERA | Curt Lyons, Chattanooga | 2.41 |
| G | James Nix, Chattanooga | 62 |
| CG | Clint Koppe, Winston-Salem/Chatt. | 4 |
| SV | Domingo Jean, Chatt./Indy | 31 |
| IP | Chris Reed, Chattanooga | 176 |
| BB | Chris Reed, Chattanooga | 91 |
| SO | Curt Lyons, Chattanooga | 176 |

*Minimum 250 At-Bats   #Minimum 75 Innings

## TOP 10 PROSPECTS

**How the Reds Top 10 prospects, as judged by Baseball America prior to the 1996 season, fared in 1996:**

STAN DENNY

**Pokey Reese**

| Player, Pos. | Club (Class—League) | AVG | AB | R | H | 2B | 3B | HR | RBI | SB |
|--------------|---------------------|-----|-----|-----|-----|-----|-----|-----|-----|-----|
| 1. Pokey Reese, ss | Indianapolis (AAA—Amer. Assoc.) | .232 | 280 | 26 | 65 | 16 | 0 | 1 | 23 | 5 |
| 2. Steve Gibralter, of | Indianapolis (AAA—Amer. Assoc.) | .255 | 447 | 58 | 114 | 29 | 2 | 11 | 54 | 2 |
| | Cincinnati | .000 | 2 | 0 | 0 | 0 | 0 | 0 | 0 | 0 |
| 3. Eric Owens, 2b-3b | Indianapolis (AAA—Amer. Assoc.) | .320 | 128 | 24 | 41 | 8 | 2 | 4 | 14 | 6 |
| | Cincinnati | .200 | 206 | 26 | 41 | 6 | 0 | 0 | 9 | 16 |
| 4. Pat Watkins, of | Chattanooga (AA—Southern) | .276 | 492 | 63 | 136 | 31 | 2 | 8 | 59 | 15 |
| 6. Aaron Boone, 3b | Chattanooga (AA—Southern) | .288 | 548 | 86 | 158 | 44 | 7 | 17 | 95 | 21 |
| 7. Chad Mottola, of | Indianapolis (AAA—Amer. Assoc.) | .262 | 362 | 45 | 95 | 24 | 3 | 9 | 47 | 9 |
| | Cincinnati | .215 | 79 | 10 | 17 | 3 | 0 | 3 | 6 | 2 |
| 8. Decomba Conner, of | Winston-Salem (A—Carolina) | .281 | 512 | 77 | 144 | 18 | 5 | 20 | 64 | 33 |
| 9. Tim Belk, 1b | Indianapolis (AAA—Amer. Assoc.) | .287 | 436 | 63 | 125 | 27 | 3 | 15 | 63 | 5 |
| | Cincinnati | .200 | 15 | 2 | 3 | 0 | 0 | 0 | 0 | 0 |

| | | W | L | ERA | G | SV | IP | H | BB | SO |
|--------------|---------------------|-----|-----|-----|-----|-----|-----|-----|-----|-----|
| 5. Brett Tomko, rhp | Chattanooga (AA—Southern) | 11 | 7 | 3.88 | 27 | 0 | 158 | 131 | 54 | 164 |
| 10. *Chad Fox, rhp | Richmond (AAA—International) | 3 | 10 | 4.73 | 18 | 0 | 93 | 91 | 49 | 87 |

*Traded to Braves

## AMERICAN ASSOCIATION

| BATTING | AVG | G | AB | R | H | 2B | 3B | HR | RBI | BB | SO | SB | CS | B | T | HT | WT | DOB | 1st Yr | Resides |
|---|---|---|---|---|---|---|---|---|---|---|---|---|---|---|---|---|---|---|---|---|
| Anthony, Eric | .238 | 7 | 21 | 4 | 5 | 1 | 0 | 2 | 7 | 7 | 8 | 0 | 1 | L | L | 6-2 | 195 | 11-8-67 | 1986 | Houston, Texas |
| Arias, Amador | .000 | 1 | 3 | 0 | 0 | 0 | 0 | 0 | 0 | 0 | 1 | 0 | 0 | S | R | 5-10 | 160 | 5-28-72 | 1990 | Maracay, Venez. |
| Belk, Tim | .287 | 120 | 436 | 63 | 125 | 27 | 3 | 15 | 63 | 27 | 72 | 5 | 2 | R | R | 6-3 | 200 | 4-6-70 | 1992 | Houston, Texas |
| Coleman, Vince | .077 | 7 | 26 | 2 | 2 | 0 | 0 | 0 | 1 | 1 | 5 | 0 | 0 | S | R | 6-1 | 185 | 9-22-61 | 1982 | St. Louis, Mo. |
| Fordyce, Brook | .275 | 107 | 374 | 48 | 103 | 20 | 3 | 16 | 64 | 25 | 56 | 2 | 1 | R | R | 6-1 | 185 | 5-7-70 | 1989 | Old Lyme, Conn. |
| Garcia, Guillermo | .255 | 16 | 47 | 4 | 12 | 2 | 0 | 0 | 0 | 2 | 6 | 0 | 0 | R | R | 6-3 | 190 | 4-4-72 | 1990 | Santo Domingo, D.R. |
| Gibralter, Steve | .255 | 126 | 447 | 58 | 114 | 29 | 2 | 11 | 54 | 26 | 114 | 2 | 3 | R | R | 6-0 | 170 | 10-9-72 | 1990 | Duncanville, Texas |
| Goodwin, Curtis | .261 | 91 | 337 | 57 | 88 | 19 | 4 | 2 | 30 | 54 | 67 | 40 | 12 | L | L | 5-11 | 180 | 9-30-72 | 1991 | San Leandro, Calif. |
| Howard, Tom | .400 | 1 | 5 | 2 | 2 | 0 | 0 | 1 | 2 | 0 | 0 | 0 | 0 | S | R | 6-2 | 205 | 12-11-64 | 1986 | Elk Grove, Calif. |
| Howitt, Dann | .276 | 50 | 156 | 19 | 43 | 6 | 1 | 4 | 22 | 14 | 35 | 0 | 3 | L | R | 6-5 | 205 | 2-13-64 | 1986 | Medford, Ore. |
| 2-team (46 Louisville) | .266 | 96 | 297 | 38 | 79 | 12 | 2 | 8 | 40 | 30 | 66 | 4 | 4 | | | | | | | |
| Kelly, Mike | .209 | 88 | 292 | 43 | 61 | 10 | 1 | 8 | 30 | 30 | 80 | 13 | 2 | R | R | 6-4 | 195 | 6-2-70 | 1991 | Los Alamitos, Calif. |
| Kmak, Joe | .280 | 48 | 143 | 20 | 40 | 3 | 0 | 2 | 19 | 26 | 35 | 3 | 0 | R | R | 6-0 | 185 | 5-3-63 | 1985 | Foster City, Calif. |
| Kremblas, Frank | .198 | 23 | 91 | 14 | 18 | 5 | 0 | 0 | 8 | 7 | 30 | 3 | 1 | R | R | 5-11 | 180 | 10-25-66 | 1989 | Carroll, Ohio |
| Ladell, Cleveland | .000 | 8 | 7 | 0 | 0 | 0 | 0 | 0 | 0 | 1 | 1 | 0 | 0 | R | R | 5-11 | 170 | 9-19-70 | 1992 | Dallas, Texas |
| Mejia, Roberto | .291 | 101 | 374 | 55 | 109 | 24 | 9 | 13 | 58 | 29 | 79 | 13 | 5 | R | R | 5-11 | 160 | 4-14-72 | 1989 | Hato Mayor, D.R. |
| Mitchell, Keith | .300 | 112 | 357 | 60 | 107 | 21 | 3 | 16 | 66 | 64 | 68 | 9 | 1 | R | R | 5-10 | 180 | 8-6-69 | 1987 | San Diego, Calif. |
| Morris, Hal | .500 | 1 | 4 | 1 | 2 | 1 | 0 | 1 | 0 | 1 | 0 | 0 | 0 | L | L | 6-4 | 215 | 4-9-65 | 1986 | Union, Ky. |
| Mottola, Chad | .262 | 103 | 362 | 45 | 95 | 24 | 3 | 9 | 47 | 21 | 93 | 9 | 6 | R | R | 6-3 | 215 | 10-15-71 | 1992 | Pembroke Pines, Fla. |
| Owens, Eric | .320 | 33 | 128 | 24 | 41 | 8 | 2 | 4 | 14 | 11 | 16 | 6 | 3 | R | R | 5-11 | 184 | 2-3-71 | 1992 | Danville, Va. |
| Perez, Eduardo | .293 | 122 | 451 | 84 | 132 | 29 | 5 | 21 | 84 | 51 | 69 | 11 | 0 | R | R | 6-4 | 215 | 9-11-69 | 1991 | Santurce, P.R. |
| Reese, Pokey | .232 | 79 | 280 | 26 | 65 | 16 | 0 | 1 | 23 | 21 | 46 | 5 | 2 | R | R | 6-0 | 160 | 6-10-73 | 1991 | Columbia, S.C. |
| Sabo, Chris | .290 | 8 | 31 | 0 | 9 | 1 | 0 | 0 | 1 | 0 | 6 | 0 | 0 | R | R | 6-0 | 185 | 1-19-62 | 1983 | Sarasota, Fla. |
| Sanchez, Yuri | .000 | 1 | 4 | 0 | 0 | 0 | 0 | 0 | 0 | 0 | 2 | 0 | 0 | L | R | 6-1 | 165 | 11-11-73 | 1992 | Lynn, Mass. |
| Sanders, Reggie | .417 | 4 | 12 | 3 | 5 | 2 | 0 | 0 | 1 | 1 | 4 | 0 | 1 | R | R | 6-1 | 180 | 12-1-67 | 1988 | Cincinnati, Ohio |
| Santana, Ruben | .118 | 6 | 17 | 4 | 2 | 1 | 0 | 0 | 2 | 3 | 3 | 0 | 0 | R | R | 6-2 | 175 | 3-7-70 | 1990 | Santo Domingo, D.R. |
| Valdez, Trovin | .000 | 1 | 1 | 0 | 0 | 0 | 0 | 0 | 0 | 0 | 1 | 0 | 0 | S | R | 5-10 | 163 | 11-18-73 | 1993 | New York, N.Y. |
| Wilson, Brandon | .233 | 95 | 305 | 48 | 71 | 7 | 3 | 4 | 31 | 39 | 53 | 10 | 6 | R | R | 6-1 | 180 | 2-26-69 | 1990 | Owensboro, Ky. |

| PITCHING | W | L | ERA | G | GS | CG | SV | IP | H | R | ER | BB | SO | B | T | HT | WT | DOB | 1st Yr | Resides |
|---|---|---|---|---|---|---|---|---|---|---|---|---|---|---|---|---|---|---|---|---|
| Buckley, Travis | 11 | 7 | 4.50 | 22 | 20 | 1 | 0 | 122 | 126 | 68 | 61 | 32 | 58 | R | R | 6-4 | 208 | 6-15-70 | 1989 | Overland Park, Kan. |
| Carrara, Giovanni | 4 | 0 | 0.76 | 9 | 6 | 1 | 1 | 48 | 25 | 6 | 4 | 9 | 45 | R | R | 6-2 | 210 | 3-4-68 | 1990 | Anzoategui, Venez. |
| Carrasco, Hector | 0 | 1 | 2.14 | 13 | 2 | 0 | 0 | 21 | 18 | 7 | 5 | 13 | 17 | R | R | 6-2 | 175 | 10-22-69 | 1988 | San Pedro de Macoris, D.R. |
| Doyle, Tom | 0 | 1 | 3.86 | 1 | 0 | 0 | 0 | 2 | 2 | 1 | 1 | 1 | 1 | L | L | 6-3 | 205 | 1-20-70 | 1988 | Redondo Beach, Calif. |
| Drahman, Brian | 0 | 0 | 7.20 | 3 | 0 | 0 | 0 | 5 | 7 | 6 | 4 | 4 | 1 | R | R | 6-3 | 231 | 11-7-66 | 1986 | Fort Lauderdale, Fla. |
| Fortugno, Tim | 5 | 5 | 3.41 | 41 | 5 | 0 | 2 | 58 | 55 | 27 | 22 | 25 | 46 | L | L | 6-0 | 185 | 4-11-62 | 1986 | Huntington Beach, Calif. |
| Frazier, Ron | 0 | 1 | 11.05 | 2 | 2 | 0 | 0 | 7 | 8 | 11 | 9 | 3 | 4 | R | R | 6-2 | 185 | 6-13-69 | 1990 | Otis, Mass. |
| Jarvis, Kevin | 4 | 3 | 5.06 | 8 | 8 | 0 | 0 | 43 | 45 | 27 | 24 | 12 | 32 | L | R | 6-2 | 200 | 8-1-69 | 1991 | Lexington, Ky. |
| Jean, Domingo | 1 | 1 | 8.68 | 7 | 0 | 0 | 0 | 9 | 13 | 11 | 9 | 8 | 5 | R | R | 6-2 | 175 | 1-9-69 | 1990 | San Pedro de Macoris, D.R. |
| Lilliquist, Derek | 4 | 1 | 2.60 | 47 | 0 | 0 | 1 | 52 | 47 | 17 | 15 | 7 | 51 | L | L | 5-10 | 195 | 2-20-66 | 1987 | Vero Beach, Fla. |
| Luebbers, Larry | 5 | 4 | 3.91 | 14 | 11 | 0 | 0 | 71 | 76 | 44 | 31 | 23 | 35 | R | R | 6-6 | 190 | 10-11-69 | 1990 | Florence, Ky. |
| McElroy, Chuck | 1 | 1 | 2.70 | 5 | 3 | 0 | 0 | 13 | 11 | 4 | 4 | 4 | 10 | L | L | 6-0 | 195 | 10-1-67 | 1986 | Friendswood, Texas |
| Moore, Marcus | 4 | 7 | 3.45 | 15 | 15 | 0 | 0 | 89 | 72 | 41 | 34 | 38 | 70 | S | R | 6-5 | 204 | 11-2-70 | 1989 | Oakland, Calif. |
| Ojala, Kirt | 7 | 7 | 3.77 | 22 | 21 | 3 | 0 | 134 | 143 | 67 | 56 | 31 | 92 | L | L | 6-2 | 200 | 12-24-68 | 1990 | Portage, Mich. |
| Olson, Gregg | 0 | 0 | 4.26 | 7 | 0 | 0 | 4 | 6 | 6 | 4 | 3 | 6 | 4 | R | R | 6-4 | 212 | 10-11-66 | 1988 | Reisterstown, Md. |
| Powell, Ross | 6 | 3 | 6.03 | 12 | 11 | 0 | 0 | 60 | 74 | 41 | 40 | 26 | 51 | L | L | 6-0 | 180 | 1-24-68 | 1989 | Antioch, Tenn. |
| 2-team (5 Louisville) | 6 | 3 | 5.56 | 17 | 11 | 0 | 0 | 68 | 82 | 43 | 42 | 28 | 61 | | | | | | | |
| Pugh, Tim | 2 | 1 | 2.45 | 4 | 4 | 1 | 0 | 26 | 19 | 7 | 7 | 4 | 18 | R | R | 6-6 | 225 | 1-26-67 | 1989 | Florence, Ky. |
| Remlinger, Mike | 4 | 3 | 2.52 | 28 | 13 | 0 | 0 | 89 | 64 | 29 | 25 | 44 | 97 | L | L | 6-0 | 195 | 3-23-66 | 1987 | Plymouth, Mass. |
| Service, Scott | 1 | 4 | 3.00 | 35 | 1 | 0 | 15 | 48 | 34 | 18 | 16 | 10 | 58 | R | R | 6-6 | 226 | 2-26-67 | 1986 | Cincinnati, Ohio |
| Spradlin, Jerry | 6 | 8 | 3.33 | 49 | 8 | 0 | 15 | 100 | 94 | 49 | 37 | 23 | 79 | S | R | 6-7 | 240 | 6-14-67 | 1988 | Anaheim, Calif. |
| Sullivan, Scott | 5 | 2 | 2.73 | 53 | 3 | 0 | 1 | 109 | 95 | 38 | 33 | 37 | 77 | R | R | 6-3 | 210 | 3-13-71 | 1993 | Carrollton, Ala. |
| Warren, Brian | 2 | 3 | 3.90 | 50 | 0 | 0 | 0 | 65 | 68 | 30 | 28 | 25 | 40 | R | R | 6-1 | 165 | 4-26-67 | 1990 | Bridgewater, Mass. |
| White, Gabe | 6 | 3 | 2.77 | 11 | 11 | 0 | 0 | 68 | 69 | 25 | 21 | 9 | 51 | L | L | 6-2 | 200 | 11-20-71 | 1990 | Sebring, Fla. |

### FIELDING

| Catcher | PCT | G | PO | A | E | DP | PB |
|---|---|---|---|---|---|---|---|
| Fordyce | .994 | 96 | 610 | 49 | 4 | 9 | 4 |
| Garcia | 1.000 | 8 | 48 | 2 | 0 | 0 | 2 |
| Kmak | .988 | 46 | 313 | 30 | 4 | 3 | 7 |
| Kremblas | 1.000 | 1 | 5 | 3 | 0 | 0 | 0 |

| First Base | PCT | G | PO | A | E | DP |
|---|---|---|---|---|---|---|
| Belk | .986 | 113 | 930 | 44 | 14 | 75 |
| Fordyce | 1.000 | 2 | 10 | 0 | 0 | 1 |
| Garcia | .824 | 2 | 11 | 3 | 3 | 3 |
| Howitt | .979 | 6 | 44 | 3 | 1 | 6 |
| Kmak | .000 | 1 | 0 | 0 | 0 | 0 |
| Mitchell | .989 | 27 | 172 | 13 | 2 | 21 |
| Morris | 1.000 | 1 | 2 | 0 | 0 | 0 |
| Perez | 1.000 | 6 | 35 | 4 | 0 | 2 |

| Second Base | PCT | G | PO | A | E | DP |
|---|---|---|---|---|---|---|
| Garcia | .913 | 5 | 7 | 14 | 2 | 4 |
| Kremblas | .990 | 22 | 52 | 50 | 1 | 8 |
| Mejia | .975 | 98 | 208 | 261 | 12 | 52 |

| | PCT | G | PO | A | E | DP |
|---|---|---|---|---|---|---|
| Owens | 1.000 | 8 | 17 | 20 | 0 | 7 |
| Wilson | .944 | 17 | 37 | 48 | 5 | 10 |

| Third Base | PCT | G | PO | A | E | DP |
|---|---|---|---|---|---|---|
| Belk | .000 | 2 | 0 | 0 | 3 | 0 |
| Howitt | 1.000 | 1 | 2 | 3 | 0 | 0 |
| Mejia | .000 | 1 | 0 | 0 | 0 | 0 |
| Owens | .778 | 9 | 5 | 9 | 4 | 1 |
| Perez | .932 | 114 | 75 | 211 | 21 | 19 |
| Reese | .880 | 7 | 9 | 13 | 3 | 1 |
| Sabo | 1.000 | 8 | 6 | 16 | 0 | 1 |
| Santana | .909 | 5 | 4 | 6 | 1 | 0 |
| Wilson | .889 | 7 | 2 | 6 | 1 | 2 |

| Shortstop | PCT | G | PO | A | E | DP |
|---|---|---|---|---|---|---|
| Arias | 1.000 | 1 | 0 | 3 | 0 | 0 |
| Owens | .980 | 14 | 15 | 34 | 1 | 5 |
| Reese | .948 | 73 | 122 | 226 | 19 | 48 |
| Sanchez | 1.000 | 1 | 2 | 2 | 0 | 0 |

| | PCT | G | PO | A | E | DP |
|---|---|---|---|---|---|---|
| Wilson | .935 | 63 | 74 | 141 | 15 | 27 |

| Outfield | PCT | G | PO | A | E | DP |
|---|---|---|---|---|---|---|
| Anthony | .750 | 3 | 3 | 0 | 1 | 0 |
| Belk | 1.000 | 6 | 2 | 0 | 0 | 0 |
| Coleman | 1.000 | 6 | 6 | 0 | 0 | 0 |
| Gibralter | .975 | 113 | 262 | 10 | 7 | 2 |
| Goodwin | .978 | 82 | 172 | 4 | 4 | 1 |
| Howard | 1.000 | 1 | 3 | 0 | 0 | 0 |
| Howitt | 1.000 | 16 | 20 | 1 | 0 | 1 |
| Kelly | .971 | 72 | 132 | 2 | 4 | 1 |
| Ladell | 1.000 | 2 | 1 | 0 | 0 | 0 |
| Mitchell | .963 | 46 | 75 | 4 | 3 | 0 |
| Mottola | .968 | 95 | 176 | 8 | 6 | 1 |
| Owens | .889 | 3 | 7 | 1 | 1 | 0 |
| Sanders | 1.000 | 3 | 4 | 1 | 0 | 0 |
| Wilson | .833 | 5 | 5 | 0 | 1 | 0 |

## SOUTHERN LEAGUE

| BATTING | AVG | G | AB | R | H | 2B | 3B | HR | RBI | BB | SO | SB | CS | B | T | HT | WT | DOB | 1st Yr | Resides |
|---|---|---|---|---|---|---|---|---|---|---|---|---|---|---|---|---|---|---|---|---|
| Arias, Amador | .000 | 1 | 1 | 0 | 0 | 0 | 0 | 0 | 0 | 0 | 0 | 0 | 0 | S | R | 5-10 | 160 | 5-28-72 | 1990 | Maracay, Venez. |
| Bako, Paul | .294 | 110 | 360 | 53 | 106 | 27 | 0 | 8 | 48 | 48 | 93 | 1 | 0 | L | R | 6-2 | 205 | 6-20-72 | 1993 | Lafayette, La. |
| Boone, Aaron | .288 | 136 | 548 | 86 | 158 | 44 | 7 | 17 | 95 | 38 | 77 | 21 | 10 | R | R | 6-2 | 190 | 3-9-73 | 1994 | Villa Park, Calif. |
| Broach, Donald | .261 | 110 | 349 | 58 | 91 | 10 | 2 | 6 | 37 | 39 | 51 | 20 | 9 | R | R | 6-0 | 185 | 7-18-71 | 1993 | Cincinnati, Ohio |
| Brown, Ray | .327 | 115 | 364 | 68 | 119 | 26 | 5 | 13 | 52 | 52 | 62 | 2 | 1 | L | R | 6-2 | 205 | 7-30-72 | 1994 | Redding, Calif. |
| Garcia, Guillermo | .315 | 60 | 203 | 25 | 64 | 12 | 0 | 6 | 36 | 12 | 32 | 3 | 3 | R | R | 6-3 | 190 | 4-4-72 | 1990 | Santo Domingo, D.R. |
| Hall, Billy | .295 | 117 | 461 | 80 | 136 | 24 | 3 | 2 | 43 | 57 | 72 | 34 | 11 | S | R | 5-9 | 180 | 6-17-69 | 1991 | Wichita, Kan. |
| Howard, Tom | .333 | 8 | 30 | 4 | 10 | 1 | 0 | 1 | 2 | 2 | 7 | 1 | 1 | S | R | 6-2 | 205 | 12-11-64 | 1986 | Elk Grove, Calif. |
| King, Andre | .070 | 13 | 43 | 1 | 3 | 0 | 1 | 0 | 3 | 1 | 21 | 0 | 1 | R | R | 6-1 | 190 | 11-26-73 | 1993 | Fort Lauderdale, Fla. |
| Ladell, Cleveland | .252 | 121 | 405 | 59 | 102 | 15 | 7 | 4 | 41 | 31 | 88 | 31 | 14 | R | R | 5-11 | 170 | 9-19-70 | 1992 | Dallas, Texas |
| Magdaleno, Ricky | .222 | 132 | 424 | 60 | 94 | 21 | 1 | 17 | 63 | 64 | 135 | 2 | 7 | R | R | 6-1 | 170 | 7-6-74 | 1993 | Baldwin Park, Calif. |
| Meggers, Mike | .198 | 38 | 111 | 13 | 22 | 6 | 0 | 5 | 18 | 16 | 33 | 1 | 2 | R | R | 6-2 | 200 | 7-6-70 | 1992 | Sacramento, Calif. |
| Morrow, Nick | 1.000 | 1 | 1 | 1 | 1 | 0 | 0 | 0 | 0 | 0 | 0 | 0 | 0 | R | R | 5-11 | 180 | 4-17-72 | 1994 | Lexington, Ky. |
| Rumfield, Toby | .280 | 113 | 364 | 49 | 102 | 25 | 1 | 9 | 53 | 37 | 51 | 2 | 1 | R | R | 6-3 | 190 | 9-4-72 | 1991 | Belton, Texas |
| Santana, Ruben | .309 | 98 | 343 | 47 | 106 | 21 | 2 | 8 | 56 | 26 | 39 | 5 | 3 | R | R | 6-2 | 175 | 3-7-70 | 1990 | Santo Domingo, D.R. |
| Thomas, Keith | .095 | 9 | 21 | 3 | 2 | 1 | 0 | 0 | 3 | 0 | 8 | 0 | 0 | S | R | 6-1 | 180 | 9-12-68 | 1986 | Chicago, Ill. |
| Watkins, Pat | .276 | 127 | 492 | 63 | 136 | 31 | 2 | 8 | 59 | 30 | 64 | 15 | 11 | R | R | 6-2 | 185 | 9-2-72 | 1993 | Garner, N.C. |
| White, Jimmy | .132 | 15 | 38 | 5 | 5 | 1 | 1 | 0 | 2 | 4 | 12 | 0 | 0 | L | R | 6-1 | 170 | 12-1-72 | 1990 | Tampa, Fla. |

| PITCHING | W | L | ERA | G | GS | CG | SV | IP | H | R | ER | BB | SO | B | T | HT | WT | DOB | 1st Yr | Resides |
|---|---|---|---|---|---|---|---|---|---|---|---|---|---|---|---|---|---|---|---|---|
| Allen, Cedric | 1 | 2 | 6.51 | 12 | 3 | 1 | 0 | 28 | 31 | 23 | 20 | 11 | 12 | L | L | 5-10 | 183 | 1-13-72 | 1994 | Belton, Texas |
| Beltran, Alonso | 0 | 1 | 8.10 | 3 | 3 | 0 | 0 | 13 | 18 | 13 | 12 | 6 | 10 | R | R | 6-3 | 180 | 3-4-72 | 1991 | El Paso, Texas |
| Bryant, Adam | 0 | 0 | 0.00 | 1 | 0 | 0 | 0 | 1 | 0 | 0 | 0 | 1 | 0 | R | R | 6-6 | 225 | 12-27-71 | 1994 | Levittown, Pa. |
| Buckley, Travis | 3 | 4 | 4.86 | 8 | 2 | 0 | 0 | 54 | 57 | 40 | 29 | 13 | 41 | R | R | 6-4 | 208 | 6-15-70 | 1989 | Overland Park, Kan. |
| Courtright, John | 1 | 2 | 2.39 | 9 | 9 | 0 | 0 | 60 | 52 | 18 | 16 | 11 | 36 | L | L | 6-2 | 185 | 5-30-70 | 1991 | Columbus, Ohio |
| Donnelly, Brendan | 1 | 2 | 5.52 | 22 | 0 | 0 | 0 | 29 | 27 | 21 | 18 | 17 | 22 | R | R | 6-3 | 200 | 7-4-71 | 1992 | Albuquerque, N.M. |
| Doyle, Tom | 4 | 2 | 4.80 | 53 | 0 | 0 | 0 | 54 | 54 | 34 | 29 | 39 | 32 | L | L | 6-3 | 205 | 1-20-70 | 1988 | Redondo Beach, Calif. |
| Fortugno, Tim | 2 | 0 | 0.00 | 11 | 0 | 0 | 6 | 11 | 4 | 0 | 0 | 4 | 10 | L | L | 6-0 | 185 | 4-11-62 | 1986 | Huntington Beach, Calif. |
| Frazier, Ron | 2 | 5 | 5.83 | 31 | 4 | 0 | 0 | 71 | 91 | 51 | 46 | 25 | 54 | R | R | 6-2 | 185 | 6-13-69 | 1990 | Otis, Mass. |
| Giron, Emiliano | 0 | 0 | 2.25 | 4 | 0 | 0 | 0 | 8 | 5 | 3 | 2 | 5 | 8 | R | R | 6-2 | 165 | 1-5-72 | 1990 | Santo Domingo, D.R. |
| Jean, Domingo | 2 | 3 | 4.08 | 39 | 0 | 0 | 31 | 40 | 34 | 19 | 18 | 17 | 33 | R | R | 6-2 | 175 | 1-9-69 | 1990 | San Pedro de Macoris, D.R. |
| Koppe, Clint | 4 | 2 | 3.49 | 10 | 9 | 1 | 1 | 57 | 54 | 27 | 22 | 18 | 30 | R | R | 6-2 | 190 | 8-14-73 | 1994 | Lake Jackson, Texas |
| Lister, Marty | 0 | 1 | 5.31 | 19 | 0 | 0 | 0 | 20 | 25 | 13 | 12 | 11 | 10 | L | L | 6-2 | 210 | 6-12-72 | 1992 | Pensacola, Fla. |
| Luebbers, Larry | 3 | 5 | 3.63 | 11 | 11 | 0 | 0 | 69 | 64 | 32 | 28 | 26 | 38 | R | R | 6-6 | 190 | 10-11-69 | 1990 | Florence, Ky. |
| Lyons, Curt | 13 | 4 | 2.41 | 24 | 24 | 1 | 0 | 142 | 113 | 48 | 38 | 52 | 176 | R | R | 6-5 | 228 | 10-17-74 | 1992 | Richmond, Ky. |
| McKenzie, Scott | 2 | 4 | 3.40 | 27 | 0 | 0 | 0 | 48 | 51 | 25 | 18 | 23 | 28 | R | R | 6-0 | 185 | 9-30-70 | 1993 | Arlington, Texas |
| Nix, James | 7 | 2 | 3.34 | 62 | 0 | 0 | 11 | 89 | 80 | 43 | 33 | 46 | 93 | R | R | 5-11 | 175 | 9-6-70 | 1992 | Burton, Texas |
| Reed, Chris | 13 | 10 | 4.09 | 28 | 27 | 2 | 1 | 176 | 157 | 89 | 80 | 91 | 135 | R | R | 6-3 | 206 | 8-25-73 | 1991 | Anaheim, Calif. |
| Robbins, Jason | 5 | 3 | 4.72 | 25 | 12 | 0 | 1 | 76 | 81 | 46 | 40 | 43 | 72 | R | R | 6-3 | 195 | 12-20-72 | 1993 | South Bend, Ind. |
| Roper, John | 0 | 2 | 9.75 | 3 | 3 | 0 | 0 | 12 | 19 | 18 | 13 | 7 | 6 | R | R | 6-0 | 175 | 11-21-71 | 1990 | Raeford, N.C. |
| Sparks, Jeff | 0 | 0 | 4.50 | 3 | 0 | 0 | 0 | 2 | 5 | 1 | 1 | 2 | 2 | R | R | 6-3 | 210 | 4-4-72 | 1995 | Houston, Texas |
| Tomko, Brett | 11 | 7 | 3.88 | 27 | 27 | 0 | 0 | 158 | 131 | 73 | 68 | 54 | 164 | R | R | 6-4 | 205 | 4-7-73 | 1995 | Tampa, Fla. |

### FIELDING

| Catcher | PCT | G | PO | A | E | DP | PB |
|---|---|---|---|---|---|---|---|
| Bako | .984 | 102 | 694 | 84 | 13 | 8 | 7 |
| Garcia | .993 | 32 | 248 | 22 | 2 | 3 | 4 |
| Rumfield | 1.000 | 15 | 80 | 7 | 0 | 0 | 2 |

| First Base | PCT | G | PO | A | E | DP |
|---|---|---|---|---|---|---|
| Brown | .981 | 72 | 584 | 50 | 12 | 47 |
| Garcia | 1.000 | 2 | 4 | 0 | 0 | 0 |
| Rumfield | .992 | 73 | 554 | 56 | 5 | 71 |

| Second Base | PCT | G | PO | A | E | DP |
|---|---|---|---|---|---|---|
| Arias | 1.000 | 1 | 2 | 1 | 0 | 0 |
| Garcia | .933 | 14 | 24 | 32 | 4 | 5 |

| | PCT | G | PO | A | E | DP |
|---|---|---|---|---|---|---|
| Hall | .971 | 117 | 223 | 314 | 16 | 71 |
| Santana | 1.000 | 16 | 27 | 44 | 0 | 14 |

| Third Base | PCT | G | PO | A | E | DP |
|---|---|---|---|---|---|---|
| Boone | .939 | 126 | 101 | 225 | 21 | 28 |
| Garcia | 1.000 | 7 | 4 | 11 | 0 | 3 |
| Santana | .893 | 14 | 9 | 16 | 3 | 2 |

| Shortstop | PCT | G | PO | A | E | DP |
|---|---|---|---|---|---|---|
| Boone | .982 | 14 | 22 | 32 | 1 | 9 |
| Magdaleno | .937 | 131 | 187 | 337 | 35 | 74 |

| Outfield | PCT | G | PO | A | E | DP |
|---|---|---|---|---|---|---|
| Broach | .983 | 104 | 165 | 12 | 3 | 0 |
| Howard | 1.000 | 5 | 8 | 0 | 0 | 0 |
| King | 1.000 | 13 | 28 | 0 | 0 | 0 |
| Ladell | .977 | 117 | 246 | 7 | 6 | 3 |
| Meggers | .981 | 27 | 50 | 1 | 1 | 0 |
| Morrow | 1.000 | 1 | 1 | 0 | 0 | 0 |
| Rumfield | 1.000 | 4 | 4 | 1 | 0 | 0 |
| Santana | 1.000 | 40 | 60 | 0 | 0 | 0 |
| Thomas | 1.000 | 5 | 10 | 0 | 0 | 0 |
| Watkins | .984 | 126 | 220 | 21 | 4 | 2 |
| White | .833 | 6 | 4 | 1 | 1 | 1 |

## CAROLINA LEAGUE

| BATTING | AVG | G | AB | R | H | 2B | 3B | HR | RBI | BB | SO | SB | CS | B | T | HT | WT | DOB | 1st Yr | Resides |
|---|---|---|---|---|---|---|---|---|---|---|---|---|---|---|---|---|---|---|---|---|
| Allen, Marlon | .237 | 121 | 426 | 57 | 101 | 19 | 1 | 17 | 82 | 32 | 133 | 8 | 2 | R | R | 6-6 | 228 | 3-28-73 | 1994 | Columbus, Ga. |
| Arias, Amador | .288 | 116 | 378 | 53 | 109 | 17 | 1 | 10 | 57 | 40 | 72 | 30 | 10 | S | R | 5-10 | 160 | 5-28-72 | 1990 | Maracay, Venez. |
| Conner, Decomba | .281 | 129 | 512 | 77 | 144 | 18 | 5 | 20 | 63 | 43 | 117 | 33 | 11 | R | R | 5-10 | 184 | 7-17-73 | 1994 | Mooresville, N.C. |
| Eddie, Steve | .272 | 137 | 497 | 56 | 135 | 23 | 2 | 9 | 64 | 45 | 78 | 14 | 5 | R | R | 6-1 | 185 | 1-6-71 | 1993 | Storm Lake, Iowa |
| Jenkins, Dee | .268 | 108 | 380 | 52 | 102 | 20 | 2 | 9 | 59 | 54 | 96 | 15 | 7 | L | R | 5-9 | 175 | 6-28-73 | 1991 | Columbia, S.C. |
| King, Andre | .192 | 82 | 261 | 43 | 50 | 9 | 3 | 8 | 29 | 34 | 88 | 16 | 7 | R | R | 6-1 | 190 | 11-26-73 | 1993 | Fort Lauderdale, Fla. |
| Larkin, Stephen | .179 | 39 | 117 | 13 | 21 | 2 | 0 | 3 | 6 | 14 | 25 | 6 | 1 | L | L | 6-0 | 190 | 7-24-73 | 1994 | Cincinnati, Ohio |
| Lofton, James | .224 | 82 | 277 | 27 | 62 | 9 | 0 | 3 | 33 | 27 | 55 | 14 | 8 | S | R | 5-9 | 170 | 3-6-74 | 1993 | Los Angeles, Calif. |
| Morrow, Nick | .258 | 123 | 422 | 78 | 109 | 19 | 3 | 18 | 54 | 59 | 93 | 28 | 6 | R | R | 5-11 | 180 | 4-17-72 | 1994 | Lexington, Ky. |
| Parsons, Jason | .348 | 14 | 46 | 4 | 16 | 3 | 0 | 0 | 7 | 2 | 5 | 0 | 2 | S | R | 6-3 | 220 | 9-2-72 | 1995 | Newport Beach, Calif. |
| Sanchez, Yuri | .215 | 100 | 353 | 48 | 76 | 15 | 3 | 5 | 39 | 43 | 103 | 9 | 6 | L | R | 6-1 | 165 | 11-11-73 | 1992 | Lynn, Mass. |
| Sharp, Scott | .232 | 34 | 95 | 14 | 22 | 8 | 0 | 0 | 8 | 13 | 39 | 3 | 1 | R | R | 6-2 | 200 | 10-16-72 | 1994 | Sykesville, Md. |
| Thomas, Rod | .000 | 3 | 7 | 0 | 0 | 0 | 0 | 0 | 0 | 4 | 4 | 0 | 0 | R | R | 6-1 | 195 | 8-22-73 | 1991 | Reddick, Fla. |
| Towle, Justin | .256 | 116 | 351 | 60 | 90 | 19 | 1 | 16 | 47 | 93 | 96 | 17 | 3 | R | R | 6-3 | 210 | 2-21-74 | 1992 | Seattle, Wash. |
| Valdez, Trovin | .254 | 90 | 342 | 49 | 87 | 11 | 3 | 3 | 30 | 22 | 62 | 26 | 14 | S | R | 5-10 | 163 | 11-18-73 | 1993 | New York, N.Y. |
| Wright, Terry | .241 | 9 | 29 | 4 | 7 | 0 | 0 | 3 | 3 | 4 | 0 | 1 | 1 | L | L | 5-11 | 170 | 1-9-74 | 1994 | Ellenboro, N.C. |

**GAMES BY POSITION: C**—Sharp 34, Towle 112. **1B**—Allen 117, Eddie 1, Larkin 19, Parsons 9, Towle 1. **2B**—Arias 66, Jenkins 22, Lofton 58. **3B**—Arias 4, Eddie 134, Jenkins 1, Lofton 1. **SS**—Arias 40, Eddie 2, Sanchez 100. **OF**—Conner 124, King 75, Larkin 15, Lofton 1, Morrow 114, Parsons 1, Thomas 1, Valdez 89, Wright 7.

| PITCHING | W | L | ERA | G | GS | CG | SV | IP | H | R | ER | BB | SO | B | T | HT | WT | DOB | 1st Yr | Resides |
|---|---|---|---|---|---|---|---|---|---|---|---|---|---|---|---|---|---|---|---|---|
| Allen, Cedric | 7 | 3 | 3.82 | 12 | 12 | 1 | 0 | 68 | 73 | 33 | 29 | 28 | 40 | L | L | 5-10 | 183 | 1-13-72 | 1994 | Belton, Texas |
| Atchley, Justin | 3 | 3 | 5.09 | 12 | 12 | 0 | 0 | 69 | 74 | 48 | 39 | 16 | 50 | L | L | 6-2 | 205 | 9-5-73 | 1995 | Sedro Woolley, Wash. |
| Bailey, Ben | 7 | 4 | 2.85 | 16 | 15 | 2 | 0 | 101 | 91 | 34 | 32 | 32 | 78 | R | R | 6-2 | 220 | 8-31-74 | 1995 | Howe, Ind. |
| Beltran, Alonso | 2 | 1 | 1.88 | 14 | 1 | 0 | 0 | 38 | 26 | 9 | 8 | 10 | 26 | R | R | 6-3 | 180 | 3-4-72 | 1991 | El Paso, Texas |
| Bryant, Adam | 4 | 3 | 2.38 | 28 | 0 | 0 | 8 | 34 | 39 | 13 | 9 | 10 | 16 | R | R | 6-6 | 225 | 12-27-71 | 1994 | Levittown, Pa. |
| Caruthers, Clay | 10 | 10 | 4.37 | 28 | 28 | 2 | 0 | 169 | 179 | 93 | 82 | 60 | 105 | S | R | 6-2 | 200 | 11-20-72 | 1994 | North Richland Hills, Texas |
| Etler, Todd | 4 | 5 | 3.49 | 33 | 1 | 0 | 2 | 77 | 72 | 30 | 30 | 17 | 59 | R | R | 6-0 | 205 | 4-18-74 | 1992 | Villa Hills, Ky. |
| Giron, Emiliano | 0 | 0 | 7.41 | 12 | 0 | 0 | 0 | 17 | 21 | 14 | 14 | 11 | 17 | R | R | 6-2 | 165 | 1-5-72 | 1990 | Santo Domingo, D.R. |
| Koppe, Clint | 8 | 2 | 3.30 | 16 | 15 | 3 | 0 | 95 | 87 | 41 | 35 | 25 | 46 | R | R | 6-4 | 220 | 8-14-73 | 1994 | Lake Jackson, Texas |
| Lister, Marty | 0 | 0 | 5.40 | 7 | 0 | 0 | 0 | 10 | 9 | 7 | 6 | 9 | 9 | L | L | 6-2 | 210 | 6-12-72 | 1992 | Pensacola, Fla. |
| Lott, Brian | 8 | 11 | 4.34 | 26 | 26 | 2 | 0 | 147 | 169 | 99 | 71 | 49 | 85 | R | R | 6-0 | 200 | 5-15-72 | 1994 | Cleveland, Texas |
| Magre, Pete | 2 | 2 | 2.58 | 37 | 0 | 0 | 1 | 59 | 44 | 22 | 17 | 32 | 33 | R | R | 6-1 | 180 | 10-31-70 | 1993 | Cameron, Texas |
| Murphy, Chris | 8 | 11 | 5.09 | 29 | 19 | 1 | 1 | 124 | 164 | 87 | 70 | 36 | 80 | L | L | 6-8 | 235 | 2-16-72 | 1995 | Cincinnati, Ohio |
| Nieto, Tony | 3 | 2 | 5.14 | 37 | 0 | 0 | 4 | 56 | 66 | 37 | 32 | 22 | 30 | S | R | 6-1 | 170 | 4-19-73 | 1994 | Monterey Park, Calif. |
| Priest, Eddie | 1 | 0 | 0.73 | 4 | 4 | 0 | 0 | 12 | 5 | 2 | 1 | 6 | 9 | R | L | 6-1 | 200 | 4-8-74 | 1994 | Horton, Ala. |
| Runyan, Paul | 3 | 1 | 2.41 | 6 | 5 | 0 | 0 | 37 | 38 | 11 | 10 | 8 | 11 | R | R | 6-2 | 200 | 8-5-71 | 1994 | San Antonio, Texas |
| Solomon, David | 3 | 2 | 4.56 | 38 | 0 | 0 | 0 | 53 | 56 | 32 | 27 | 27 | 28 | R | L | 5-10 | 185 | 9-30-71 | 1994 | Saginaw, Mich. |
| Tweedlie, Brad | 1 | 5 | 6.67 | 33 | 0 | 0 | 11 | 30 | 35 | 23 | 22 | 22 | 22 | R | R | 6-2 | 215 | 12-9-71 | 1993 | Enfield, Conn. |
| Wright, Scott | 0 | 0 | 7.71 | 1 | 1 | 0 | 0 | 5 | 7 | 4 | 4 | 3 | 2 | R | R | 6-2 | 205 | 10-15-72 | 1995 | Medford, Wis. |

## CHARLESTON — Class A

### SOUTH ATLANTIC LEAGUE

| BATTING | AVG | G | AB | R | H | 2B | 3B | HR | RBI | BB | SO | SB | CS | B | T | HT | WT | DOB | 1st Yr | Resides |
|---|---|---|---|---|---|---|---|---|---|---|---|---|---|---|---|---|---|---|---|---|
| Claybrook, Steve | .262 | 123 | 439 | 62 | 115 | 18 | 3 | 4 | 40 | 69 | 144 | 37 | 11 | L | R | 6-0 | 170 | 12-30-72 | 1995 | Robstown, Texas |
| Concepcion, David | .198 | 40 | 116 | 9 | 23 | 3 | 1 | 0 | 11 | 10 | 31 | 3 | 1 | S | R | 5-10 | 175 | 4-28-75 | 1995 | Miami, Fla. |
| Davis, James | .288 | 84 | 313 | 42 | 90 | 14 | 1 | 3 | 38 | 32 | 57 | 8 | 3 | R | R | 6-4 | 205 | 4-14-73 | 1995 | Franklin, Ky. |
| Goodhart, Steve | .216 | 115 | 380 | 61 | 82 | 16 | 3 | 0 | 26 | 94 | 95 | 16 | 12 | R | R | 6-0 | 170 | 2-14-73 | 1995 | Heath, Ohio |
| Hampton, Mike | .217 | 134 | 475 | 69 | 103 | 22 | 4 | 13 | 68 | 61 | 120 | 22 | 6 | R | R | 6-7 | 195 | 1-17-72 | 1994 | Colorado Springs, Colo. |
| Ingram, Darron | .188 | 15 | 48 | 5 | 9 | 3 | 0 | 1 | 6 | 8 | 19 | 0 | 0 | R | R | 6-3 | 225 | 6-7-76 | 1994 | Lexington, Ky. |
| Johnson, Anthony | .231 | 9 | 26 | 3 | 6 | 1 | 0 | 1 | 5 | 6 | 9 | 1 | 2 | R | R | 6-3 | 210 | 2-17-73 | 1995 | Neptune, N.J. |
| Larkin, Stephen | .271 | 58 | 203 | 30 | 55 | 7 | 2 | 5 | 33 | 35 | 40 | 5 | 4 | L | L | 6-0 | 175 | 7-24-73 | 1994 | Cincinnati, Ohio |
| LaRue, Jason | .211 | 37 | 123 | 17 | 26 | 8 | 0 | 2 | 14 | 11 | 28 | 3 | 0 | R | R | 5-11 | 195 | 3-19-74 | 1995 | Spring Branch, Texas |
| Lewis, Dwayne | .180 | 22 | 61 | 12 | 11 | 0 | 2 | 0 | 7 | 4 | 13 | 5 | 2 | L | R | 5-9 | 160 | 5-18-73 | 1995 | Brooklyn, N.Y. |
| Mason, Lamont | .216 | 68 | 190 | 24 | 41 | 2 | 1 | 1 | 16 | 28 | 48 | 11 | 6 | R | R | 5-9 | 169 | 7-10-72 | 1995 | Lexington, Ky. |
| Parsons, Jason | .284 | 48 | 162 | 18 | 46 | 11 | 0 | 3 | 24 | 15 | 25 | 3 | 1 | S | R | 6-3 | 220 | 9-2-72 | 1995 | Newport Beach, Calif. |
| Patellis, Anthony | .181 | 61 | 227 | 23 | 41 | 9 | 1 | 2 | 13 | 13 | 72 | 4 | 3 | R | R | 5-10 | 190 | 3-1-74 | 1995 | Campbell, Ohio |
| Rojas, Christian | .218 | 129 | 468 | 71 | 102 | 27 | 3 | 12 | 70 | 46 | 147 | 6 | 9 | R | R | 6-1 | 170 | 6-3-75 | 1994 | Santo Domingo, D.R. |
| Scott, Thomas | .221 | 123 | 429 | 54 | 95 | 27 | 6 | 11 | 52 | 66 | 156 | 19 | 7 | R | R | 6-0 | 185 | 3-29-73 | 1995 | Canby, Ore. |
| Sorg, Jay | .247 | 72 | 275 | 30 | 68 | 7 | 0 | 1 | 27 | 27 | 70 | 3 | 6 | L | R | 6-3 | 195 | 5-10-73 | 1994 | Louisville, Ky. |
| Thomas, Rod | .206 | 81 | 257 | 34 | 53 | 9 | 1 | 4 | 24 | 41 | 92 | 6 | 5 | R | R | 6-1 | 195 | 8-22-73 | 1991 | Reddick, Fla. |
| Ward, Chris | .138 | 34 | 109 | 5 | 15 | 5 | 0 | 0 | 7 | 4 | 44 | 0 | 0 | R | R | 6-4 | 225 | 10-17-74 | 1996 | Richardson, Texas |
| Wilson, Brian | .205 | 101 | 303 | 31 | 62 | 11 | 0 | 1 | 26 | 34 | 89 | 10 | 8 | R | R | 6-1 | 185 | 7-14-72 | 1994 | Albany, Texas |

GAMES BY POSITION: C—Davis 80, J. LaRue 34, Ward 33. 1B—Davis 3, Hampton 5, Johnson 3, Larkin 44, J. LaRue 2, Parsons 17, Sorg 71. 2B—Concepcion 10, Goodhart 114, Lewis 15, Mason 8, Patellis 2, Sorg 1, Wilson 4. 3B—Concepcion 8, Hampton 81, Patellis 52, Wilson 12. SS—Hampton 1, Lewis 8, Mason 57, Thomas 1, Wilson 85. OF—Claybrook 117, Hampton 30, Ingram 3, Larkin 2, Patellis 1, Rojas 123, Scott 115, Thomas 51.

| PITCHING | W | L | ERA | G | GS | CG | SV | IP | H | R | ER | BB | SO | B | T | HT | WT | DOB | 1st Yr | Resides |
|---|---|---|---|---|---|---|---|---|---|---|---|---|---|---|---|---|---|---|---|---|
| Atchley, Justin | 3 | 3 | 3.46 | 17 | 16 | 0 | 1 | 91 | 98 | 42 | 35 | 23 | 78 | L | L | 6-2 | 205 | 9-5-73 | 1995 | Sedro Woolley, Wash. |
| Bailey, Ben | 3 | 7 | 3.88 | 11 | 11 | 0 | 0 | 63 | 58 | 33 | 27 | 25 | 66 | R | R | 6-2 | 220 | 8-31-74 | 1995 | Howe, Ind. |
| Bryant, Adam | 1 | 1 | 2.12 | 22 | 0 | 0 | 7 | 30 | 22 | 7 | 7 | 2 | 25 | R | R | 6-6 | 225 | 12-27-71 | 1994 | Levittown, Pa. |
| Callahan, Damon | 5 | 8 | 5.26 | 27 | 19 | 0 | 1 | 103 | 112 | 66 | 60 | 39 | 85 | R | R | 6-4 | 190 | 12-10-75 | 1994 | Cleveland, Tenn. |
| Cushman, Dwayne | 5 | 3 | 2.10 | 55 | 0 | 0 | 15 | 73 | 70 | 29 | 17 | 13 | 57 | R | R | 6-0 | 175 | 11-27-71 | 1995 | Port Salerno, Fla. |
| Davis, Lance | 1 | 0 | 2.45 | 4 | 0 | 0 | 0 | 4 | 4 | 1 | 1 | 2 | 5 | R | L | 6-0 | 165 | 9-1-76 | 1995 | Polk City, Fla. |
| Garcia, Eddy | 7 | 6 | 3.03 | 30 | 11 | 1 | 1 | 107 | 91 | 48 | 36 | 58 | 74 | R | R | 6-2 | 205 | 5-31-76 | 1994 | San Cristobal, D.R. |
| Giron, Emiliano | 1 | 2 | 2.76 | 32 | 1 | 0 | 5 | 46 | 33 | 17 | 14 | 23 | 63 | R | R | 6-2 | 165 | 1-5-72 | 1990 | Santo Domingo, D.R. |
| Horne, Jeff | 0 | 2 | 9.00 | 3 | 3 | 0 | 0 | 12 | 18 | 16 | 12 | 8 | 8 | R | R | 6-4 | 205 | 11-13-74 | 1996 | Gastonia, N.C. |
| Lapka, Rick | 4 | 10 | 4.78 | 29 | 18 | 0 | 0 | 98 | 101 | 67 | 52 | 55 | 63 | R | R | 6-4 | 195 | 11-18-71 | 1994 | Cicero, Ill. |
| LaRue, Shaun | 0 | 0 | 7.94 | 4 | 0 | 0 | 0 | 6 | 7 | 5 | 5 | 2 | 4 | L | R | 6-2 | 225 | 10-30-71 | 1995 | Spring Branch, Texas |
| LeBlanc, Eric | 1 | 2 | 4.97 | 6 | 5 | 0 | 0 | 29 | 33 | 18 | 16 | 13 | 28 | L | R | 6-1 | 195 | 7-6-73 | 1996 | North Troy, Ver. |
| MacRae, Scott | 8 | 7 | 3.35 | 29 | 20 | 1 | 0 | 124 | 118 | 61 | 46 | 53 | 82 | R | R | 6-3 | 205 | 8-13-74 | 1995 | Marietta, Ga. |
| Mattox, Gene | 1 | 2 | 6.59 | 22 | 0 | 0 | 1 | 27 | 35 | 22 | 20 | 18 | 15 | R | R | 6-2 | 205 | 3-24-75 | 1995 | Jacksonville, Fla. |
| Montgomery, Joe | 0 | 1 | 4.50 | 14 | 0 | 0 | 0 | 24 | 23 | 17 | 12 | 19 | 16 | R | R | 6-0 | 155 | 10-15-72 | 1995 | Richmond, Ky. |
| Riedling, John | 6 | 10 | 3.99 | 26 | 26 | 0 | 0 | 140 | 135 | 85 | 62 | 66 | 90 | R | R | 5-11 | 190 | 8-29-75 | 1994 | Pompano Beach, Fla. |
| Roberts, Randy | 0 | 2 | 9.00 | 5 | 1 | 0 | 0 | 10 | 20 | 18 | 10 | 14 | 7 | R | R | 6-3 | 180 | 1-19-74 | 1992 | San Cristobal, D.R. |
| Runyan, Paul | 7 | 5 | 3.83 | 29 | 7 | 0 | 2 | 80 | 81 | 47 | 34 | 19 | 41 | R | R | 6-2 | 200 | 8-5-71 | 1994 | San Antonio, Texas |
| Sparks, Jeff | 2 | 7 | 4.74 | 46 | 3 | 0 | 0 | 89 | 79 | 51 | 47 | 46 | 94 | R | R | 6-3 | 210 | 4-4-72 | 1995 | Houston, Texas |
| Wright, Scott | 5 | 4 | 2.70 | 28 | 1 | 1 | 1 | 67 | 54 | 24 | 20 | 20 | 53 | R | R | 6-2 | 205 | 10-15-72 | 1995 | Medford, Wis. |

## PRINCETON — Rookie

### APPALACHIAN LEAGUE

| BATTING | AVG | G | AB | R | H | 2B | 3B | HR | RBI | BB | SO | SB | CS | B | T | HT | WT | DOB | 1st Yr | Resides |
|---|---|---|---|---|---|---|---|---|---|---|---|---|---|---|---|---|---|---|---|---|
| Boyette, Tony | .267 | 5 | 15 | 0 | 4 | 0 | 0 | 0 | 2 | 2 | 3 | 0 | 0 | R | R | 6-0 | 200 | 12-7-75 | 1994 | Alachua, Fla. |
| Bracho, Darwin | .245 | 14 | 53 | 5 | 13 | 1 | 0 | 0 | 5 | 2 | 13 | 0 | 0 | S | R | 5-10 | 175 | 4-10-75 | 1995 | Maracaibo, Venez. |
| Clark, John | .250 | 58 | 196 | 30 | 49 | 5 | 2 | 0 | 17 | 38 | 41 | 7 | 2 | L | R | 6-0 | 175 | 6-23-74 | 1996 | Prestonsburg, Ky. |
| Concepcion, David | .250 | 4 | 16 | 2 | 4 | 1 | 0 | 0 | 2 | 3 | 2 | 0 | 0 | S | R | 5-10 | 175 | 4-28-75 | 1995 | Miami, Fla. |
| Denman, Demond | .222 | 55 | 203 | 21 | 45 | 12 | 1 | 3 | 27 | 11 | 70 | 0 | 2 | R | R | 6-3 | 210 | 4-22-75 | 1996 | Crockett, Texas |
| Fehrenbach, Todd | .153 | 19 | 59 | 8 | 9 | 3 | 0 | 1 | 5 | 2 | 34 | 0 | 0 | L | R | 6-0 | 203 | 5-5-76 | 1995 | Inverness, Fla. |
| Goodman, Herbert | .223 | 39 | 121 | 15 | 27 | 4 | 0 | 1 | 12 | 11 | 39 | 5 | 8 | R | R | 6-0 | 190 | 3-25-75 | 1995 | Florence, S.C. |
| Herrera, Jesus | .221 | 25 | 68 | 8 | 15 | 6 | 0 | 0 | 7 | 2 | 17 | 0 | 0 | S | R | 6-2 | 160 | 8-25-76 | 1995 | Maracaibo, Venez. |
| Hucks, Brian | .295 | 34 | 122 | 25 | 36 | 4 | 1 | 6 | 25 | 23 | 21 | 2 | 1 | R | R | 5-10 | 190 | 3-7-73 | 1996 | Lexington, S.C. |
| Martinez, Alejandro | .213 | 38 | 108 | 17 | 23 | 3 | 0 | 0 | 13 | 14 | 33 | 2 | 1 | R | R | 5-11 | 175 | 10-30-78 | 1996 | Santo Domingo, D.R. |

| BATTING | AVG | G | AB | R | H | 2B | 3B | HR | RBI | BB | SO | SB | CS | B | T | HT | WT | DOB | 1st Yr | Resides |
|---|---|---|---|---|---|---|---|---|---|---|---|---|---|---|---|---|---|---|---|---|
| Montgomery, Andre | .286 | 41 | 133 | 24 | 38 | 6 | 3 | 4 | 18 | 20 | 29 | 5 | 2 | R | R | 5-10 | 160 | 6-27-77 | 1995 | Louisville, Ky. |
| O'Hearn, Brandon | .277 | 65 | 235 | 33 | 65 | 17 | 2 | 13 | 52 | 29 | 88 | 2 | 0 | R | R | 6-3 | 200 | 6-24-75 | 1996 | Butler, Ga. |
| Oliver, John | .203 | 41 | 143 | 20 | 29 | 5 | 0 | 2 | 13 | 11 | 31 | 3 | 1 | R | R | 6-3 | 190 | 5-14-78 | 1996 | Dallas, Pa. |
| Parsons, Jason | .407 | 23 | 91 | 22 | 37 | 9 | 0 | 5 | 17 | 5 | 9 | 0 | 2 | S | R | 6-3 | 220 | 9-2-72 | 1995 | Newport Beach, Calif. |
| Presto, Nick | .262 | 12 | 42 | 12 | 11 | 2 | 1 | 0 | 1 | 6 | 4 | 1 | 2 | R | R | 5-10 | 175 | 7-8-74 | 1996 | Jupiter, Fla. |
| Skeens, Jeremy | .271 | 54 | 188 | 34 | 51 | 3 | 7 | 1 | 12 | 25 | 49 | 19 | 2 | R | R | 6-2 | 175 | 11-13-77 | 1996 | Middletown, Ohio |
| Solano, Manuel | .215 | 57 | 209 | 41 | 45 | 11 | 3 | 5 | 23 | 18 | 40 | 7 | 2 | R | R | 5-11 | 172 | 5-17-78 | 1995 | Villa Mella, D.R. |
| Terry, Tony | .213 | 55 | 174 | 14 | 37 | 5 | 0 | 3 | 21 | 13 | 59 | 5 | 4 | S | R | 6-1 | 185 | 8-2-75 | 1994 | Abbeville, S.C. |
| Ward, Chris | .167 | 8 | 24 | 3 | 4 | 1 | 0 | 1 | 6 | 2 | 8 | 0 | 0 | R | R | 6-4 | 225 | 10-17-74 | 1996 | Richardson, Texas |

**GAMES BY POSITION: C**—Bracho 13, Fehrenbach 19, Hucks 32, Ward 7. **1B**—Denman 43, O'Hearn 10, Parsons 16. **2B**—Clark 29, Montgomery 40, Solano 1. **3B**—Clark 30, Concepcion 4, Martinez 38, Montgomery 1, Solano 1. **SS**—Martinez 1, Presto 12, Solano 56. **OF**—Goodman 4, Herrera 21, O'Hearn 54, Oliver 33, Skeens 55, Terry 53.

| PITCHING | W | L | ERA | G | GS | CG | SV | IP | H | R | ER | BB | SO | B | T | HT | WT | DOB | 1st Yr | Resides |
|---|---|---|---|---|---|---|---|---|---|---|---|---|---|---|---|---|---|---|---|---|
| Altman, Gene | 2 | 0 | 4.10 | 18 | 1 | 0 | 3 | 42 | 34 | 24 | 19 | 15 | 36 | R | R | 6-7 | 209 | 9-1-78 | 1996 | Lynchburg, S.C. |
| Caddell, Carl | 2 | 5 | 6.68 | 9 | 9 | 0 | 0 | 31 | 33 | 31 | 23 | 32 | 33 | R | R | 6-3 | 185 | 10-13-75 | 1996 | Fort Worth, Texas |
| Carlyle, Buddy | 2 | 4 | 4.66 | 10 | 9 | 1 | 0 | 46 | 47 | 33 | 24 | 16 | 42 | S | R | 6-2 | 175 | 12-21-77 | 1996 | Bellevue, Neb. |
| Davis, Lance | 2 | 0 | 1.20 | 2 | 2 | 1 | 0 | 15 | 6 | 4 | 2 | 3 | 19 | R | L | 6-0 | 165 | 9-1-76 | 1995 | Polk City, Fla. |
| Giron, Roberto | 1 | 3 | 3.10 | 22 | 1 | 0 | 7 | 41 | 34 | 18 | 14 | 11 | 44 | R | R | 6-2 | 175 | 3-24-76 | 1994 | Villa Mella, D.R. |
| Horne, Jeff | 3 | 3 | 3.47 | 10 | 8 | 3 | 0 | 47 | 42 | 30 | 18 | 21 | 45 | R | R | 6-4 | 205 | 11-13-74 | 1996 | Gastonia, N.C. |
| Hurtado, Omar | 1 | 2 | 6.15 | 15 | 0 | 0 | 0 | 26 | 24 | 22 | 18 | 17 | 19 | R | R | 6-0 | 187 | 10-24-78 | 1996 | Aragua, Venez. |
| Lawrence, Rich | 0 | 0 | 0.00 | 1 | 0 | 0 | 0 | 1 | 3 | 1 | 0 | 2 | 6 | R | R | 6-0 | 185 | 9-22-74 | 1995 | Naples, Fla. |
| LeBlanc, Eric | 4 | 1 | 4.53 | 9 | 6 | 0 | 1 | 46 | 39 | 29 | 23 | 16 | 51 | L | R | 6-1 | 195 | 7-6-73 | 1996 | North Troy, Ver. |
| Mallard, Randi | 2 | 7 | 3.68 | 13 | 11 | 1 | 0 | 66 | 66 | 42 | 27 | 38 | 72 | R | R | 6-1 | 185 | 8-11-75 | 1996 | Tampa, Fla. |
| Mattox, Gene | 0 | 0 | 0.00 | 3 | 0 | 0 | 0 | 4 | 1 | 1 | 0 | 4 | 3 | R | R | 6-2 | 205 | 3-24-75 | 1995 | Jacksonville, Fla. |
| Phillips, Jon | 3 | 4 | 4.29 | 23 | 0 | 0 | 2 | 42 | 40 | 25 | 20 | 28 | 53 | R | R | 6-5 | 205 | 1-23-75 | 1996 | Hiram, Ga. |
| Roberts, Randy | 3 | 2 | 2.66 | 12 | 4 | 1 | 0 | 51 | 33 | 20 | 15 | 29 | 49 | R | R | 6-3 | 180 | 1-19-74 | 1992 | San Cristobal, D.R. |
| Rose, Ted | 3 | 5 | 6.22 | 11 | 11 | 1 | 0 | 59 | 70 | 44 | 41 | 21 | 53 | L | R | 6-1 | 180 | 8-23-73 | 1996 | St. Clairsville, Ohio |
| Vicentino, Andy | 0 | 4 | 6.50 | 11 | 6 | 0 | 0 | 46 | 52 | 38 | 33 | 25 | 41 | L | L | 6-1 | 184 | 1-10-76 | 1992 | Maracaibo, Venez. |

## BILLINGS — Rookie

### PIONEER LEAGUE

| BATTING | AVG | G | AB | R | H | 2B | 3B | HR | RBI | BB | SO | SB | CS | B | T | HT | WT | DOB | 1st Yr | Resides |
|---|---|---|---|---|---|---|---|---|---|---|---|---|---|---|---|---|---|---|---|---|
| Burress, Andy | .318 | 27 | 107 | 23 | 34 | 5 | 2 | 5 | 25 | 7 | 16 | 4 | 1 | R | R | 6-0 | 190 | 7-18-77 | 1995 | McRae, Ga. |
| Campbell, Wylie | .371 | 70 | 259 | 69 | 96 | 15 | 7 | 0 | 30 | 45 | 29 | 24 | 6 | S | R | 5-11 | 170 | 3-27-75 | 1996 | Fort Worth, Texas |
| Dresch, Michael | .243 | 34 | 115 | 15 | 28 | 6 | 1 | 2 | 17 | 13 | 26 | 3 | 3 | L | R | 6-1 | 180 | 11-30-73 | 1996 | San Antonio, Texas |
| Garrett, Scott | .184 | 41 | 136 | 14 | 25 | 6 | 0 | 2 | 17 | 9 | 41 | 0 | 1 | R | R | 6-5 | 225 | 3-8-74 | 1996 | Denver, N.C. |
| Griggs, Rod | .272 | 49 | 151 | 24 | 41 | 3 | 0 | 0 | 20 | 19 | 29 | 6 | 1 | R | R | 5-10 | 185 | 3-18-74 | 1996 | Bolivar, Tenn. |
| Guthrie, David | .227 | 48 | 181 | 45 | 41 | 6 | 3 | 4 | 28 | 26 | 48 | 10 | 1 | S | R | 6-2 | 185 | 5-21-74 | 1995 | Raleigh, N.C. |
| Hucks, Brian | .322 | 20 | 59 | 10 | 19 | 6 | 0 | 2 | 12 | 12 | 14 | 0 | 0 | R | R | 5-10 | 190 | 3-7-73 | 1996 | Lexington, S.C. |
| Ingram, Darron | .295 | 65 | 251 | 49 | 74 | 13 | 0 | 17 | 56 | 34 | 88 | 7 | 3 | R | R | 6-3 | 225 | 6-7-76 | 1994 | Lexington, Ky. |
| Jenkins, Daniel | .222 | 55 | 126 | 21 | 28 | 7 | 2 | 0 | 14 | 16 | 39 | 0 | 3 | R | R | 6-2 | 175 | 10-28-74 | 1996 | Beaumont, Texas |
| Keller, Jeremy | .241 | 59 | 237 | 39 | 57 | 12 | 0 | 7 | 39 | 24 | 52 | 0 | 2 | L | R | 6-0 | 190 | 1-24-74 | 1996 | Mobile, Ala. |
| Kirby, Doug | .236 | 57 | 182 | 29 | 43 | 10 | 1 | 3 | 20 | 39 | 48 | 4 | 1 | R | R | 6-0 | 195 | 6-27-75 | 1996 | Hesperia, Calif. |
| Mapp, Eric | .263 | 55 | 175 | 21 | 46 | 10 | 6 | 3 | 34 | 13 | 41 | 1 | 3 | S | R | 6-2 | 205 | 11-10-72 | 1995 | Douglas, Ariz. |
| Marn, Kevin | .277 | 66 | 271 | 48 | 75 | 11 | 1 | 1 | 38 | 24 | 49 | 19 | 3 | R | R | 6-4 | 205 | 3-23-74 | 1996 | Broadview Heights, Ohio |
| Patellis, Anthony | .285 | 44 | 172 | 35 | 49 | 9 | 5 | 8 | 32 | 22 | 45 | 3 | 2 | R | R | 5-10 | 190 | 3-1-74 | 1995 | Campbell, Ohio |
| Presto, Nick | .125 | 4 | 16 | 2 | 2 | 0 | 0 | 0 | 1 | 2 | 6 | 0 | 1 | R | R | 5-10 | 175 | 7-8-74 | 1996 | Jupiter, Fla. |
| Price, Corey | .191 | 49 | 131 | 18 | 25 | 3 | 0 | 0 | 16 | 24 | 32 | 2 | 2 | S | R | 6-0 | 170 | 9-18-76 | 1996 | Mt. Pleasant, Texas |

**GAMES BY POSITION: C**—Burress 24, Garrett 36, Hucks 18. **1B**—Burress 1, Dresch 26, Garrett 5, Keller 43, Mapp 6. **2B**—Campbell 68, Mapp 2, Patellis 1, Price 9. **3B**—Dresch 3, Griggs 1, Guthrie 10, Keller 19, Patellis 42, Price 5. **SS**—Campbell 1, Griggs 1, Guthrie 39, Kirby 1, Presto 4, Price 33. **OF**—Burress 2, Dresch 2, Griggs 45, Ingram 52, Jenkins 52, Kirby 49, Mapp 28, Marn 66.

| PITCHING | W | L | ERA | G | GS | CG | SV | IP | H | R | ER | BB | SO | B | T | HT | WT | DOB | 1st Yr | Resides |
|---|---|---|---|---|---|---|---|---|---|---|---|---|---|---|---|---|---|---|---|---|
| Angerhofer, Chad | 1 | 7 | 8.09 | 13 | 13 | 0 | 0 | 62 | 93 | 71 | 56 | 33 | 48 | L | L | 6-1 | 190 | 10-5-75 | 1995 | Gainesville, Fla. |
| Buckley, Matt | 1 | 2 | 5.00 | 24 | 0 | 0 | 0 | 45 | 55 | 36 | 25 | 22 | 37 | R | R | 6-6 | 185 | 11-17-73 | 1996 | Charlotte, N.C. |
| Cloud, Tony | 0 | 5 | 6.37 | 12 | 11 | 0 | 0 | 54 | 69 | 53 | 38 | 34 | 44 | R | R | 5-11 | 185 | 8-12-75 | 1995 | Lancaster, Calif. |
| Davis, Lance | 2 | 3 | 6.70 | 16 | 5 | 0 | 0 | 46 | 59 | 41 | 34 | 33 | 43 | R | L | 6-0 | 165 | 9-1-76 | 1995 | Polk City, Fla. |
| Fonceca, Chad | 1 | 4 | 10.22 | 22 | 0 | 0 | 1 | 37 | 58 | 50 | 42 | 18 | 36 | L | R | 6-0 | 185 | 1-2-76 | 1995 | Victorville, Calif. |
| Harris, Josh | 1 | | 6.31 | 20 | 2 | 0 | 0 | 41 | 58 | 33 | 29 | 21 | 30 | R | R | 6-3 | 230 | 10-23-77 | 1996 | Canyon Lake, Texas |
| Herrera, Desmond | 2 | 2 | 8.83 | 30 | 0 | 0 | 2 | 35 | 61 | 38 | 34 | 11 | 32 | R | R | 6-2 | 210 | 5-12-74 | 1996 | Ontario, Calif. |
| Marine, Justin | 0 | 1 | 7.36 | 21 | 0 | 0 | 0 | 33 | 46 | 32 | 27 | 20 | 22 | R | R | 6-4 | 230 | 11-14-74 | 1995 | Canoga Park, Calif. |
| Merrell, Phil | 4 | 7 | 7.04 | 14 | 13 | 1 | 1 | 69 | 83 | 63 | 54 | 48 | 54 | R | R | 6-1 | 190 | 3-11-78 | 1996 | Nampa, Idaho |
| Needham, Kevin | 1 | 2 | 5.75 | 26 | 0 | 0 | 2 | 36 | 44 | 23 | 23 | 18 | 37 | L | L | 6-0 | 190 | 1-30-75 | 1996 | Burlington, Ontario |
| Shepard, David | 6 | 7 | 5.91 | 15 | 14 | 1 | 0 | 81 | 109 | 69 | 53 | 21 | 80 | R | R | 6-1 | 190 | 2-6-74 | 1996 | Hornell, N.Y. |
| Smith, Stephen | 2 | 2 | 4.26 | 24 | 0 | 0 | 3 | 32 | 39 | 20 | 15 | 16 | 23 | R | R | 6-2 | 190 | 6-23-73 | 1996 | Burkburnett, Texas |
| Zwemke, Bryan | 2 | 6 | 7.49 | 14 | 14 | 0 | 0 | 64 | 101 | 74 | 53 | 28 | 35 | R | R | 6-3 | 185 | 3-21-74 | 1996 | Aurora, Colo. |

# CLEVELAND INDIANS

**Manager:** Mike Hargrove  **1996 Record:** 99-62, .615 (1st, AL Central)

| BATTING WT | AVG | G | AB | R | H | 2B | 3B | HR | RBI | BB | SO | SB | CS | B | T | HT | DOB | 1st Yr | Resides |
|---|---|---|---|---|---|---|---|---|---|---|---|---|---|---|---|---|---|---|---|
| Alomar, Sandy | .263 | 127 | 418 | 53 | 110 | 23 | 0 | 11 | 50 | 19 | 42 | 1 | 0 | R | R | 6-5 | 215 | 6-18-66 | 1984 | Westlake, Ohio |
| Baerga, Carlos | .267 | 100 | 424 | 54 | 113 | 25 | 0 | 10 | 55 | 16 | 25 | 1 | 1 | S | R | 5-11 | 200 | 11-4-68 | 1986 | Westlake, Ohio |
| Belle, Albert | .311 | 158 | 602 | 124 | 187 | 38 | 3 | 48 | 148 | 99 | 87 | 11 | 0 | R | R | 6-2 | 210 | 8-25-66 | 1987 | Euclid, Ohio |
| Burnitz, Jeromy | .281 | 71 | 128 | 30 | 36 | 10 | 0 | 7 | 26 | 25 | 31 | 2 | 1 | L | R | 6-0 | 190 | 4-14-69 | 1990 | Key Largo, Fla. |
| Candaele, Casey | .250 | 24 | 44 | 8 | 11 | 2 | 0 | 1 | 4 | 1 | 9 | 0 | 0 | S | R | 5-9 | 165 | 1-12-61 | 1983 | San Luis Obispo, Calif. |
| Carreon, Mark | .324 | 38 | 142 | 16 | 46 | 12 | 0 | 2 | 14 | 11 | 9 | 1 | 1 | R | L | 6-0 | 195 | 7-9-63 | 1981 | Tucson, Ariz. |
| Diaz, Einar | .000 | 4 | 1 | 0 | 0 | 0 | 0 | 0 | 0 | 0 | 0 | 0 | 0 | R | R | 5-10 | 165 | 12-28-72 | 1991 | Chiriqui, Panama |
| Espinoza, Alvaro | .223 | 59 | 112 | 12 | 25 | 4 | 2 | 4 | 11 | 6 | 18 | 1 | 1 | R | R | 6-0 | 190 | 2-19-62 | 1979 | Bergenfield, N.J. |
| Franco, Julio | .322 | 112 | 432 | 72 | 139 | 20 | 1 | 14 | 76 | 61 | 82 | 8 | 8 | R | R | 6-1 | 188 | 8-23-61 | 1978 | Arlington, Texas |
| Giles, Brian | .355 | 51 | 121 | 26 | 43 | 14 | 1 | 5 | 27 | 19 | 13 | 3 | 0 | L | L | 5-11 | 195 | 1-20-71 | 1989 | El Cajon, Calif. |
| Jackson, Damian | .300 | 5 | 10 | 2 | 3 | 2 | 0 | 0 | 1 | 1 | 4 | 0 | 0 | R | R | 5-10 | 160 | 8-16-73 | 1992 | Concord, Calif. |
| Kent, Jeff | .265 | 39 | 102 | 16 | 27 | 7 | 0 | 3 | 16 | 10 | 22 | 2 | 1 | R | R | 6-1 | 185 | 3-7-68 | 1989 | Huntington Beach, Calif. |
| Kirby, Wayne | .250 | 27 | 16 | 3 | 4 | 1 | 0 | 0 | 1 | 2 | 2 | 0 | 1 | L | R | 5-10 | 185 | 1-22-64 | 1983 | Yorktown, Va. |
| Leius, Scott | .140 | 27 | 43 | 3 | 6 | 4 | 0 | 1 | 3 | 2 | 8 | 0 | 0 | R | R | 6-3 | 208 | 9-24-65 | 1986 | Minnetonka, Minn. |
| Lofton, Kenny | .317 | 154 | 662 | 132 | 210 | 35 | 4 | 14 | 67 | 61 | 82 | 75 | 17 | L | L | 6-0 | 180 | 5-31-67 | 1988 | Tucson, Ariz. |
| Murray, Eddie | .262 | 88 | 336 | 33 | 88 | 9 | 1 | 12 | 45 | 34 | 45 | 3 | 0 | S | R | 6-2 | 220 | 2-24-56 | 1973 | Canyon Country, Calif. |
| Pena, Geronimo | .111 | 5 | 9 | 1 | 1 | 0 | 0 | 1 | 2 | 1 | 4 | 0 | 0 | S | R | 6-1 | 170 | 3-29-67 | 1985 | Los Alcarrizos, D.R. |
| Pena, Tony | .195 | 67 | 174 | 14 | 34 | 4 | 0 | 1 | 27 | 15 | 25 | 0 | 1 | R | R | 6-0 | 184 | 6-4-57 | 1976 | Santiago, D.R. |
| Perry, Herbert | .083 | 7 | 12 | 1 | 1 | 1 | 0 | 0 | 0 | 1 | 2 | 1 | 0 | R | R | 6-2 | 210 | 9-15-69 | 1991 | Mayo, Fla. |
| Ramirez, Manny | .309 | 152 | 550 | 94 | 170 | 45 | 3 | 33 | 112 | 85 | 104 | 8 | 5 | R | R | 6-0 | 190 | 5-30-72 | 1991 | Brooklyn, N.Y. |
| Seitzer, Kevin | .386 | 22 | 83 | 11 | 32 | 10 | 0 | 1 | 16 | 14 | 11 | 0 | 0 | R | R | 5-11 | 190 | 3-26-62 | 1983 | Overland Park, Kan. |
| 2-team (132 Mil.) | .326 | 154 | 573 | 85 | 187 | 35 | 3 | 13 | 78 | 87 | 79 | 6 | 1 | | | | | | |
| Thome, Jim | .311 | 151 | 505 | 122 | 157 | 28 | 5 | 38 | 116 | 123 | 141 | 2 | 2 | L | R | 6-4 | 220 | 8-27-70 | 1989 | Peoria, Ill. |
| Thompson, Ryan | .318 | 8 | 22 | 2 | 7 | 0 | 0 | 1 | 5 | 1 | 6 | 0 | 0 | R | R | 6-3 | 200 | 11-4-67 | 1987 | Edesville, Md. |
| Vizcaino, Jose | .285 | 48 | 179 | 23 | 51 | 5 | 2 | 0 | 13 | 7 | 24 | 6 | 2 | S | R | 6-1 | 180 | 3-26-68 | 1987 | El Cajon, Calif. |
| Vizquel, Omar | .297 | 151 | 542 | 98 | 161 | 36 | 1 | 9 | 64 | 56 | 42 | 35 | 9 | S | R | 5-9 | 165 | 4-24-67 | 1984 | Caracas, Venez. |
| Wilson, Nigel | .250 | 10 | 12 | 2 | 3 | 0 | 0 | 2 | 5 | 1 | 6 | 0 | 0 | L | L | 6-1 | 170 | 1-12-70 | 1988 | Ajax, Ontario |

| PITCHING | W | L | ERA | G | GS | CG | SV | IP | H | R | ER | BB | SO | B | T | HT | WT | DOB | 1st Yr | Resides |
|---|---|---|---|---|---|---|---|---|---|---|---|---|---|---|---|---|---|---|---|---|
| Anderson, Brian | 3 | 1 | 4.91 | 10 | 9 | 0 | 0 | 51 | 58 | 29 | 28 | 14 | 21 | S | L | 6-1 | 180 | 4-26-72 | 1993 | Geneva, Ohio |
| Assenmacher, Paul | 4 | 2 | 3.09 | 63 | 0 | 0 | 1 | 47 | 46 | 18 | 16 | 14 | 44 | L | L | 6-3 | 195 | 12-10-60 | 1983 | Stone Mountain, Ga. |
| Embree, Alan | 1 | 1 | 6.39 | 24 | 0 | 0 | 0 | 31 | 30 | 26 | 22 | 21 | 33 | L | L | 6-2 | 190 | 1-23-70 | 1990 | Brush Prairie, Wash. |
| Graves, Danny | 2 | 0 | 4.55 | 15 | 0 | 0 | 0 | 30 | 29 | 18 | 15 | 10 | 22 | R | R | 5-11 | 200 | 8-7-73 | 1995 | Valrico, Fla. |
| Hershiser, Orel | 15 | 9 | 4.24 | 33 | 33 | 1 | 0 | 206 | 238 | 115 | 97 | 58 | 125 | R | R | 6-3 | 193 | 9-16-58 | 1979 | Pasadena, Calif. |
| Lopez, Albie | 5 | 4 | 6.39 | 13 | 10 | 0 | 0 | 62 | 80 | 47 | 44 | 22 | 45 | R | R | 6-2 | 205 | 8-18-71 | 1991 | Mesa, Ariz. |
| Martinez, Dennis | 9 | 6 | 4.50 | 20 | 20 | 1 | 0 | 112 | 122 | 63 | 56 | 37 | 48 | R | R | 6-1 | 183 | 5-14-55 | 1974 | Miami, Fla. |
| McDowell, Jack | 13 | 9 | 5.11 | 30 | 30 | 5 | 0 | 192 | 214 | 119 | 109 | 67 | 141 | R | R | 6-5 | 185 | 1-16-66 | 1987 | Chicago, Ill. |
| Mercker, Kent | 1 | 0 | 3.09 | 10 | 0 | 0 | 0 | 12 | 10 | 4 | 4 | 3 | 7 | L | L | 6-2 | 195 | 2-1-68 | 1986 | Dublin, Ohio |
| 2-team (14 Baltimore) | 4 | 6 | 6.98 | 24 | 12 | 0 | 0 | 70 | 83 | 60 | 54 | 38 | 29 | | | | | | | |
| Mesa, Jose | 2 | 7 | 3.73 | 69 | 0 | 0 | 39 | 72 | 69 | 32 | 30 | 28 | 64 | R | R | 6-3 | 225 | 5-22-66 | 1982 | Westlake, Ohio |
| Nagy, Charles | 17 | 5 | 3.41 | 32 | 32 | 5 | 0 | 222 | 217 | 89 | 84 | 61 | 167 | L | R | 6-3 | 200 | 5-5-67 | 1989 | Westlake, Ohio |
| Ogea, Chad | 10 | 6 | 4.79 | 29 | 21 | 1 | 0 | 147 | 151 | 82 | 78 | 42 | 101 | R | R | 6-2 | 200 | 11-9-70 | 1991 | Lake Charles, La. |
| Plunk, Eric | 3 | 2 | 2.43 | 56 | 0 | 0 | 2 | 78 | 56 | 21 | 21 | 34 | 85 | R | R | 6-6 | 220 | 9-3-63 | 1981 | Riverside, Calif. |
| Poole, Jim | 4 | 0 | 3.04 | 32 | 0 | 0 | 0 | 27 | 29 | 15 | 9 | 14 | 19 | L | L | 6-2 | 203 | 4-28-66 | 1988 | Ellicott City, Md. |
| Roa, Joe | 0 | 0 | 10.80 | 1 | 0 | 0 | 0 | 2 | 4 | 2 | 2 | 3 | 0 | R | R | 6-1 | 194 | 10-11-71 | 1989 | Hazel Park, Mich. |
| Shuey, Paul | 5 | 2 | 2.85 | 42 | 0 | 0 | 4 | 54 | 45 | 19 | 17 | 26 | 44 | R | R | 6-3 | 215 | 9-16-70 | 1992 | Raleigh, N.C. |
| Swindell, Greg | 1 | 1 | 6.59 | 13 | 2 | 0 | 0 | 29 | 31 | 21 | 21 | 8 | 21 | R | L | 6-3 | 225 | 1-2-65 | 1986 | Houston, Texas |
| Tavarez, Julian | 4 | 7 | 5.36 | 51 | 4 | 0 | 0 | 81 | 101 | 49 | 48 | 22 | 46 | R | R | 6-2 | 165 | 5-22-73 | 1990 | Santiago, D.R. |

## FIELDING

| Catcher | PCT | G | PO | A | E | DP | PB |
|---|---|---|---|---|---|---|---|
| Alomar | .988 | 124 | 724 | 48 | 9 | 5 | 7 |
| Diaz | 1.000 | 4 | 4 | 0 | 0 | 0 | |
| T. Pena | .992 | 67 | 336 | 27 | 3 | 6 | 4 |

| First Base | PCT | G | PO | A | E | DP |
|---|---|---|---|---|---|---|
| Alomar | .000 | 1 | 0 | 0 | 0 | 0 |
| Carreon | .994 | 34 | 305 | 19 | 2 | 23 |
| Espinoza | 1.000 | 18 | 97 | 8 | 0 | 10 |
| Franco | .990 | 97 | 852 | 77 | 9 | 89 |
| Kent | .992 | 20 | 112 | 9 | 1 | 13 |
| Leius | .976 | 7 | 39 | 2 | 1 | 1 |
| Perry | 1.000 | 5 | 29 | 2 | 0 | 3 |
| Seitzer | 1.000 | 5 | 31 | 9 | 0 | 1 |

| Second Base | PCT | G | PO | A | E | DP |
|---|---|---|---|---|---|---|
| Baerga | .971 | 100 | 191 | 308 | 15 | 63 |
| Candaele | 1.000 | 11 | 20 | 30 | 0 | 11 |

| | PCT | G | PO | A | E | DP |
|---|---|---|---|---|---|---|
| Espinoza | .941 | 5 | 5 | 11 | 1 | 5 |
| Kent | 1.000 | 9 | 11 | 30 | 0 | 2 |
| Leius | 1.000 | 6 | 3 | 8 | 0 | 1 |
| G. Pena | 1.000 | 1 | 2 | 3 | 0 | 1 |
| Vizcaino | .981 | 45 | 79 | 125 | 4 | 27 |

| Third Base | PCT | G | PO | A | E | DP |
|---|---|---|---|---|---|---|
| Candaele | 1.000 | 3 | 1 | 3 | 0 | 1 |
| Espinoza | .947 | 20 | 7 | 11 | 1 | 1 |
| Kent | 1.000 | 6 | 2 | 7 | 0 | 1 |
| Leius | 1.000 | 8 | 3 | 6 | 0 | 0 |
| G. Pena | .000 | 3 | 0 | 0 | 0 | 0 |
| Perry | .000 | 1 | 0 | 0 | 0 | 0 |
| Seitzer | .903 | 12 | 9 | 19 | 3 | 2 |
| Thome | .953 | 150 | 86 | 262 | 17 | 24 |

| Shortstop | PCT | G | PO | A | E | DP |
|---|---|---|---|---|---|---|
| Candaele | 1.000 | 1 | 1 | 0 | 0 | 0 |
| Espinoza | .978 | 16 | 16 | 29 | 1 | 12 |
| Jackson | 1.000 | 5 | 3 | 13 | 0 | 4 |
| Vizcaino | 1.000 | 4 | 3 | 10 | 0 | 4 |
| Vizquel | .971 | 150 | 226 | 447 | 20 | 91 |

| Outfield | PCT | G | PO | A | E | DP |
|---|---|---|---|---|---|---|
| Belle | .970 | 152 | 309 | 11 | 10 | 0 |
| Burnitz | 1.000 | 30 | 44 | 0 | 0 | 0 |
| Carreon | 1.000 | 5 | 6 | 0 | 0 | 0 |
| Giles | 1.000 | 16 | 26 | 0 | 0 | 0 |
| Kirby | 1.000 | 18 | 8 | 0 | 0 | 0 |
| Lofton | .975 | 152 | 376 | 13 | 10 | 3 |
| Ramirez | .970 | 149 | 272 | 19 | 9 | 4 |
| Thompson | 1.000 | 8 | 5 | 0 | 0 | 0 |
| Wilson | .000 | 1 | 0 | 0 | 0 | 0 |

Jim Thome hit .311 with 38 homers for the Indians

Indians minor league Player of the Year Russ Branyan

DAVID SEELIG

BILL SETLIFF

# INDIANS

## FARM SYSTEM

**Director of Minor League Operations:** Mark Shapiro

| Class | Farm Team | League | W | L | Pct. | Finish* | Manager | First Yr |
|---|---|---|---|---|---|---|---|---|
| AAA | Buffalo (N.Y.) Bisons | American Assoc. | 84 | 60 | .583 | 1st (8) | Brian Graham | 1995 |
| AA | Canton-Akron (Ohio) Indians | Eastern | 71 | 71 | .500 | 6th (10) | Jeff Datz | 1989 |
| #A | Kinston (N.C.) Indians | Carolina | 76 | 62 | .551 | 2nd (8) | Jack Mull | 1987 |
| A | Columbus (Ga.) RedStixx | South Atlantic | 79 | 63 | .556 | 4th (14) | Joel Skinner | 1991 |
| A | Watertown (N.Y.) Indians | New York-Penn | 45 | 30 | .600 | 3rd (14) | Ted Kubiak | 1989 |
| #R | Burlington (N.C.) Indians | Appalachian | 29 | 38 | .433 | 6th (10) | Harry Spilman | 1986 |

*Finish in overall standings (No. of teams in league)    #Advanced level

## ORGANIZATION LEADERS

### MAJOR LEAGUERS

**BATTING**
*AVG Julio Franco ........... .322
R Kenny Lofton........... 132
H Kenny Lofton........... 210
TB Albert Belle ............. 375
2B Manny Ramirez........ 45
3B Jim Thome ................. 5
HR Albert Belle .............. 48
RBI Albert Belle ............ 148
BB Jim Thome .............. 123
SO Jim Thome .............. 141
SB Kenny Lofton............. 75

**PITCHING**
W Charles Nagy ........... 17
L Two tied at ................. 9
#ERA Eric Plunk ........... 2.43
G Jose Mesa ................ 69
CG Two tied at ................ 5
SV Jose Mesa ............... 39
IP Charles Nagy ......... 222
BB Jack McDowell ..........67
SO Charles Nagy ......... 167

**Kenny Lofton.** 75 *stolen bases*

LARRY GOREN

### MINOR LEAGUERS

**BATTING**
*AVG Sean Casey, Kinston ........................... .331
R Russ Branyan, Columbus..................... 102
H Alex Ramirez, Canton-Akron ............... 169
TB Russ Branyan, Columbus..................... 277
2B Richie Sexson, Canton-Akron ............... 33
3B Alex Ramirez, Canton-Akron ................. 12
HR Russ Branyan, Columbus..................... 40
RBI Russ Branyan, Columbus..................... 106
BB Russ Branyan, Columbus..................... 62
SO Russ Branyan, Columbus..................... 166
SB Patricio Claudio, Kinston ........................ 36

**PITCHING**
W Three tied at ........................................... 13
L Igor Oropeza, Bakersfield/Kinston........... 16
#ERA Danny Graves, Buffalo ........................ 1.48
G Wilmer Montoya, Kinston/Canton ........... 54
CG Joe Roa, Buffalo ...................................... 5
SV Scott Winchester, Columbus .................. 26
IP Travis Driskill, Canton-Akron ............... 172
BB Igor Oropeza, Bakersfield/Kinston ....... 110
SO Travis Driskill, Canton-Akron ............... 148

*Minimum 250 At-Bats    #Minimum 75 Innings

## TOP 10 PROSPECTS

**How the Indians Top 10 prospects, as judged by Baseball America prior to the 1996 season, fared in 1996:**

RODGER WOOD

**Bartolo Colon**

| Player, Pos. | Club (Class—League) | AVG | AB | R | H | 2B | 3B | HR | RBI | SB |
|---|---|---|---|---|---|---|---|---|---|---|
| 4. Richie Sexson, 1b | Canton-Akron (AA—Eastern) | .276 | 518 | 85 | 143 | 33 | 3 | 16 | 76 | 2 |
| 6. Enrique Wilson, ss | Canton-Akron (AA—Eastern) | .304 | 484 | 70 | 147 | 17 | 5 | 5 | 50 | 23 |
| | Buffalo (AAA—American Assoc.) | .500 | 8 | 1 | 4 | 1 | 0 | 0 | 0 | 0 |
| 8. Russ Branyan, 3b | Columbus (A—South Atlantic) | .268 | 482 | 102 | 129 | 20 | 4 | 40 | 106 | 7 |
| 9. David Miller, of-1b | Kinston (A—Carolina) | .254 | 488 | 71 | 124 | 23 | 1 | 7 | 54 | 14 |
| 10. Damian Jackson, ss | Buffalo (AAA—American Assoc.) | .257 | 452 | 77 | 116 | 15 | 1 | 12 | 49 | 24 |
| | Cleveland | .300 | 10 | 2 | 3 | 2 | 0 | 0 | 1 | 0 |

| | | W | L | ERA | G | SV | IP | H | BB | SO |
|---|---|---|---|---|---|---|---|---|---|---|
| 1. Bartolo Colon, rhp | Canton-Akron (AA—Eastern) | 2 | 2 | 1.74 | 13 | 0 | 62 | 44 | 25 | 56 |
| | Buffalo (AAA—American Assoc.) | 0 | 0 | 6.00 | 8 | 0 | 15 | 16 | 8 | 19 |
| 2. Jaret Wright, rhp | Kinston (A—Carolina) | 7 | 4 | 2.50 | 19 | 0 | 101 | 65 | 55 | 109 |
| 3. Alan Embree, lhp | Buffalo (AAA—American Assoc.) | 4 | 1 | 3.93 | 20 | 5 | 34 | 26 | 14 | 46 |
| | Cleveland | 1 | 1 | 6.39 | 24 | 0 | 31 | 30 | 21 | 33 |
| 5. Danny Graves, rhp | Buffalo (AAA—American Assoc.) | 4 | 3 | 1.48 | 43 | 19 | 79 | 57 | 24 | 46 |
| | Cleveland | 2 | 0 | 4.58 | 15 | 0 | 30 | 29 | 10 | 22 |
| 7. Paul Shuey, rhp | Buffalo (AAA—American Assoc.) | 3 | 2 | 0.81 | 19 | 4 | 33 | 14 | 9 | 57 |
| | Cleveland | 5 | 2 | 2.85 | 42 | 4 | 54 | 45 | 26 | 44 |

## AMERICAN ASSOCIATION

| BATTING | AVG | G | AB | R | H | 2B | 3B | HR | RBI | BB | SO | SB | CS | B | T | HT | WT | DOB | 1st Yr | Resides |
|---|---|---|---|---|---|---|---|---|---|---|---|---|---|---|---|---|---|---|---|---|
| Aven, Bruce | .667 | 3 | 9 | 5 | 6 | 0 | 0 | 1 | 2 | 1 | 1 | 0 | 1 | R | R | 5-9 | 180 | 3-4-72 | 1994 | Orange, Texas |
| Bryant, Pat | .172 | 27 | 64 | 6 | 11 | 1 | 0 | 0 | 0 | 5 | 20 | 0 | 2 | R | R | 5-11 | 182 | 10-27-72 | 1990 | Sherman Oaks, Calif. |
| Candaele, Casey | .311 | 94 | 392 | 66 | 122 | 22 | 2 | 6 | 37 | 27 | 35 | 3 | 5 | S | R | 5-9 | 165 | 1-12-61 | 1983 | San Luis Obispo, Calif. |
| Costo, Tim | .214 | 83 | 252 | 25 | 54 | 12 | 0 | 8 | 28 | 19 | 59 | 1 | 2 | R | R | 6-5 | 230 | 2-16-69 | 1990 | Glen Ellyn, Ill. |
| Dunn, Steve | .290 | 92 | 300 | 35 | 87 | 20 | 1 | 12 | 48 | 30 | 74 | 2 | 1 | L | L | 6-4 | 220 | 4-18-70 | 1988 | Fairfax, Va. |
| Faries, Paul | .250 | 49 | 172 | 24 | 43 | 9 | 1 | 2 | 15 | 12 | 24 | 3 | 1 | R | R | 5-10 | 170 | 2-20-65 | 1987 | San Diego, Calif. |
| 3-team (37 la./35 N.O.) | .247 | 121 | 397 | 45 | 98 | 14 | 4 | 3 | 31 | 37 | 49 | 10 | 3 | | | | | | | |
| Giles, Brian | .314 | 83 | 318 | 65 | 100 | 17 | 6 | 20 | 64 | 42 | 29 | 1 | 0 | L | L | 5-11 | 195 | 1-20-71 | 1989 | El Cajon, Calif. |
| Helfand, Eric | .209 | 90 | 258 | 31 | 54 | 10 | 0 | 5 | 22 | 46 | 51 | 0 | 3 | L | R | 6-0 | 210 | 3-25-69 | 1990 | San Diego, Calif. |
| Jackson, Damian | .257 | 133 | 452 | 77 | 116 | 15 | 1 | 12 | 49 | 48 | 78 | 24 | 7 | R | R | 5-10 | 160 | 8-16-73 | 1992 | Concord, Calif. |
| Leius, Scott | .268 | 35 | 123 | 22 | 33 | 3 | 1 | 4 | 17 | 12 | 16 | 0 | 0 | R | R | 6-3 | 208 | 9-24-65 | 1986 | Minnetonka, Minn. |
| Lis, Joe | .233 | 51 | 146 | 21 | 34 | 8 | 0 | 6 | 22 | 18 | 19 | 0 | 0 | R | R | 5-10 | 170 | 11-3-68 | 1991 | Newburgh, Ind. |
| Marsh, Tom | .235 | 112 | 395 | 45 | 93 | 16 | 1 | 10 | 49 | 16 | 58 | 9 | 5 | R | R | 6-2 | 180 | 12-27-65 | 1988 | Toledo, Ohio |
| Pena, Geronimo | .348 | 24 | 89 | 15 | 31 | 9 | 1 | 4 | 17 | 12 | 27 | 0 | 0 | S | R | 6-1 | 170 | 3-29-67 | 1985 | Los Alcarrizos, D.R. |
| 2-team (19 Louisville) | .313 | 51 | 195 | 32 | 61 | 15 | 3 | 10 | 35 | 24 | 52 | 0 | 0 | | | | | | | |
| Perry, Herbert | .338 | 40 | 151 | 21 | 51 | 7 | 1 | 5 | 30 | 7 | 19 | 4 | 0 | R | R | 6-2 | 210 | 9-15-69 | 1991 | Mayo, Fla. |
| Sparks, Don | .295 | 137 | 511 | 69 | 151 | 32 | 5 | 8 | 68 | 54 | 72 | 2 | 2 | R | R | 6-2 | 185 | 6-19-66 | 1988 | Long Beach, Calif. |
| Thompson, Ryan | .259 | 138 | 540 | 79 | 140 | 26 | 4 | 21 | 83 | 21 | 119 | 12 | 5 | R | R | 6-3 | 200 | 11-4-67 | 1987 | Edesville, Md. |
| Wilson, Enrique | .500 | 3 | 8 | 1 | 4 | 1 | 0 | 0 | 0 | 1 | 1 | 0 | 2 | S | R | 5-11 | 160 | 7-27-75 | 1992 | Santo Domingo, D.R. |
| Wilson, Nigel | .299 | 128 | 482 | 88 | 144 | 23 | 6 | 30 | 95 | 50 | 117 | 4 | 4 | L | L | 6-1 | 170 | 1-12-70 | 1988 | Ajax, Ontario |
| Wilson, Tom | .269 | 72 | 208 | 28 | 56 | 14 | 2 | 9 | 30 | 35 | 66 | 0 | 1 | R | R | 6-3 | 185 | 12-19-70 | 1991 | Yorba Linda, Calif. |

| PITCHING | W | L | ERA | G | GS | CG | SV | IP | H | R | ER | BB | SO | B | T | HT | WT | DOB | 1st Yr | Resides |
|---|---|---|---|---|---|---|---|---|---|---|---|---|---|---|---|---|---|---|---|---|
| Anderson, Brian | 11 | 5 | 3.59 | 19 | 19 | 2 | 0 | 128 | 125 | 57 | 51 | 28 | 85 | S | L | 6-1 | 180 | 4-26-72 | 1993 | Geneva, Ohio |
| Butcher, Mike | 1 | 2 | 8.18 | 12 | 2 | 0 | 0 | 22 | 31 | 24 | 20 | 13 | 21 | R | R | 6-1 | 200 | 5-10-65 | 1986 | Phoenix, Ariz. |
| Cadaret, Greg | 1 | 5 | 3.66 | 32 | 3 | 0 | 2 | 64 | 59 | 28 | 26 | 29 | 44 | L | L | 6-3 | 215 | 2-27-62 | 1983 | Mesa, Ariz. |
| Colon, Bartolo | 0 | 0 | 6.00 | 8 | 0 | 0 | 0 | 15 | 16 | 10 | 10 | 8 | 19 | R | R | 6-0 | 185 | 5-24-75 | 1994 | Puerto Plata, D.R. |
| Cornelius, Reid | 5 | 7 | 5.60 | 20 | 18 | 0 | 0 | 90 | 101 | 64 | 56 | 49 | 62 | R | R | 6-0 | 190 | 6-2-70 | 1989 | Thomasville, Ala. |
| Embree, Alan | 4 | 1 | 3.93 | 20 | 0 | 0 | 5 | 34 | 26 | 16 | 15 | 14 | 46 | L | L | 6-2 | 190 | 1-23-70 | 1990 | Brush Prairie, Wash. |
| Farrell, John | 3 | 0 | 3.67 | 4 | 4 | 0 | 0 | 27 | 20 | 11 | 11 | 7 | 14 | R | R | 6-4 | 210 | 8-4-62 | 1984 | Westlake, Ohio |
| Graves, Danny | 4 | 3 | 1.48 | 43 | 0 | 0 | 19 | 79 | 57 | 14 | 13 | 24 | 46 | R | R | 5-11 | 200 | 8-7-73 | 1995 | Valrico, Fla. |
| Grigsby, Benji | 0 | 0 | 5.40 | 8 | 0 | 0 | 0 | 13 | 18 | 13 | 8 | 4 | 3 | R | R | 6-1 | 200 | 12-2-70 | 1992 | Lafayette, La. |
| Lewis, James | 9 | 6 | 5.01 | 21 | 21 | 2 | 0 | 120 | 134 | 79 | 67 | 49 | 71 | R | R | 6-4 | 190 | 1-31-70 | 1991 | Jacksonville, Fla. |
| Lopez, Albie | 10 | 2 | 3.87 | 17 | 17 | 2 | 0 | 105 | 90 | 54 | 45 | 40 | 89 | R | R | 6-2 | 205 | 8-18-71 | 1991 | Mesa, Ariz. |
| Mercker, Kent | 0 | 2 | 3.94 | 3 | 3 | 0 | 0 | 16 | 11 | 7 | 7 | 9 | 11 | L | L | 6-2 | 195 | 2-1-68 | 1986 | Dublin, Ohio |
| Ogea, Chad | 0 | 1 | 5.26 | 5 | 5 | 0 | 0 | 26 | 27 | 15 | 15 | 6 | 20 | R | R | 6-2 | 200 | 11-9-70 | 1991 | Lake Charles, La. |
| Plantenberg, Erik | 2 | 2 | 3.74 | 17 | 1 | 0 | 1 | 34 | 35 | 16 | 14 | 14 | 29 | S | L | 6-1 | 180 | 10-30-68 | 1990 | Bellevue, Wash. |
| Roa, Joe | 11 | 8 | 3.27 | 26 | 24 | 5 | 0 | 165 | 161 | 66 | 60 | 36 | 82 | R | R | 6-1 | 194 | 10-11-71 | 1989 | Hazel Park, Mich. |
| Scott, Darryl | 3 | 5 | 2.89 | 50 | 1 | 0 | 9 | 81 | 61 | 29 | 26 | 24 | 73 | R | R | 6-1 | 185 | 8-6-68 | 1990 | Prior Lake, Minn. |
| Shuey, Paul | 3 | 2 | 0.81 | 19 | 0 | 0 | 4 | 33 | 14 | 4 | 3 | 9 | 57 | R | R | 6-3 | 215 | 9-16-70 | 1992 | Raleigh, N.C. |
| Tavarez, Julian | 1 | 0 | 1.29 | 2 | 2 | 0 | 0 | 14 | 10 | 2 | 2 | 3 | 10 | R | R | 6-2 | 165 | 5-22-73 | 1990 | Santiago, D.R. |
| Wertz, Bill | 1 | 2 | 4.71 | 17 | 1 | 0 | 0 | 29 | 32 | 16 | 15 | 19 | 22 | R | R | 6-6 | 220 | 1-15-67 | 1989 | Cleveland, Ohio |
| Whitten, Casey | 3 | 4 | 8.04 | 12 | 10 | 0 | 0 | 44 | 54 | 47 | 39 | 24 | 35 | L | L | 6-0 | 175 | 5-23-72 | 1993 | Terre Haute, Ind. |
| Williams, Jimmy | 12 | 3 | 4.04 | 35 | 13 | 0 | 0 | 114 | 116 | 60 | 51 | 45 | 96 | L | L | 6-7 | 232 | 5-18-65 | 1984 | Butler, Ala. |

### Catcher

| Catcher | PCT | G | PO | A | E | DP | PB |
|---|---|---|---|---|---|---|---|
| Helfand | .992 | 87 | 573 | 34 | 5 | 3 | 16 |
| T. Wilson | .988 | 66 | 386 | 26 | 5 | 3 | 8 |

### First Base

| First Base | PCT | G | PO | A | E | DP |
|---|---|---|---|---|---|---|
| Costo | .998 | 54 | 417 | 35 | 1 | 39 |
| Dunn | .995 | 52 | 385 | 27 | 2 | 37 |
| Helfand | 1.000 | 1 | 4 | 0 | 0 | 1 |
| Leius | .979 | 14 | 92 | 3 | 2 | 8 |
| Pena | 1.000 | 5 | 41 | 1 | 0 | 5 |
| Perry | .987 | 29 | 209 | 19 | 3 | 20 |
| Sparks | 1.000 | 10 | 81 | 7 | 0 | 8 |

### Second Base

| Second Base | PCT | G | PO | A | E | DP |
|---|---|---|---|---|---|---|
| Candaele | .979 | 56 | 98 | 131 | 5 | 37 |
| Costo | .833 | 1 | 1 | 4 | 1 | 0 |
| Faries | .984 | 44 | 79 | 107 | 3 | 28 |
| Leius | .957 | 10 | 16 | 28 | 2 | 9 |
| Lis | .985 | 36 | 68 | 63 | 2 | 24 |

### FIELDING

| | PCT | G | PO | A | E | DP |
|---|---|---|---|---|---|---|
| Pena | .917 | 11 | 13 | 20 | 3 | 0 |
| Sparks | .900 | 3 | 7 | 2 | 1 | 1 |
| T. Wilson | 1.000 | 1 | 1 | 0 | 0 | 0 |

### Third Base

| Third Base | PCT | G | PO | A | E | DP |
|---|---|---|---|---|---|---|
| Bryant | .000 | 1 | 0 | 0 | 0 | 0 |
| Costo | .778 | 4 | 2 | 5 | 2 | 1 |
| Faries | 1.000 | 3 | 2 | 5 | 0 | 1 |
| Leius | .750 | 3 | 1 | 5 | 2 | 0 |
| Lis | .909 | 4 | 0 | 10 | 1 | 0 |
| Pena | .950 | 5 | 5 | 14 | 1 | 1 |
| Perry | .889 | 7 | 3 | 5 | 1 | 0 |
| Sparks | .952 | 129 | 66 | 250 | 16 | 21 |
| E. Wilson | .667 | 2 | 0 | 2 | 1 | 0 |
| T. Wilson | .500 | 1 | 1 | 1 | 2 | 0 |

### Shortstop

| Shortstop | PCT | G | PO | A | E | DP |
|---|---|---|---|---|---|---|
| Candaele | .949 | 13 | 15 | 41 | 3 | 8 |

| | PCT | G | PO | A | E | DP |
|---|---|---|---|---|---|---|
| Faries | 1.000 | 2 | 5 | 5 | 0 | 1 |
| Jackson | .954 | 131 | 203 | 403 | 29 | 84 |
| Pena | 1.000 | 1 | 2 | 2 | 0 | 0 |
| E. Wilson | 1.000 | 1 | 1 | 2 | 0 | 0 |
| T. Wilson | .000 | 1 | 0 | 0 | 0 | 0 |

### Outfield

| Outfield | PCT | G | PO | A | E | DP |
|---|---|---|---|---|---|---|
| Aven | 1.000 | 3 | 7 | 0 | 0 | 0 |
| Bryant | .979 | 22 | 45 | 2 | 1 | 0 |
| Candaele | 1.000 | 35 | 75 | 3 | 0 | 0 |
| Costo | .667 | 3 | 2 | 0 | 1 | 0 |
| Dunn | 1.000 | 1 | 3 | 0 | 0 | 0 |
| Giles | .986 | 83 | 132 | 5 | 2 | 0 |
| Leius | .500 | 1 | 1 | 0 | 1 | 0 |
| Marsh | .986 | 107 | 203 | 11 | 3 | 0 |
| Perry | 1.000 | 4 | 5 | 0 | 0 | 0 |
| Thompson | .973 | 136 | 317 | 8 | 9 | 3 |
| N. Wilson | .982 | 65 | 104 | 4 | 2 | 1 |

## EASTERN LEAGUE

| BATTING | AVG | G | AB | R | H | 2B | 3B | HR | RBI | BB | SO | SB | CS | B | T | HT | WT | DOB | 1st Yr | Resides |
|---|---|---|---|---|---|---|---|---|---|---|---|---|---|---|---|---|---|---|---|---|
| Aven, Bruce | .297 | 131 | 481 | 91 | 143 | 31 | 4 | 23 | 79 | 43 | 101 | 22 | 6 | R | R | 5-9 | 180 | 3-4-72 | 1994 | Orange, Texas |
| Betts, Todd | .252 | 77 | 238 | 35 | 60 | 13 | 0 | 1 | 26 | 38 | 51 | 0 | 1 | L | R | 6-0 | 190 | 6-24-73 | 1993 | Scarborough, Ontario |
| Betzsold, Jim | .239 | 84 | 268 | 35 | 64 | 11 | 5 | 3 | 35 | 30 | 74 | 4 | 1 | R | R | 6-3 | 210 | 8-7-72 | 1994 | Orange, Calif. |
| Bryant, Pat | .193 | 34 | 109 | 13 | 21 | 2 | 1 | 3 | 17 | 17 | 24 | 8 | 2 | R | R | 5-11 | 182 | 10-27-72 | 1990 | Sherman Oaks, Calif. |
| Diaz, Einar | .281 | 104 | 395 | 47 | 111 | 26 | 2 | 3 | 35 | 12 | 32 | 3 | 2 | R | R | 5-10 | 165 | 12-28-72 | 1991 | Chiriqui, Panama |
| Gutierrez, Ricky | .252 | 119 | 484 | 69 | 122 | 11 | 3 | 7 | 55 | 37 | 56 | 18 | 9 | R | R | 6-0 | 170 | 3-23-70 | 1994 | Long Beach, Calif. |
| Harvey, Ray | .353 | 5 | 17 | 3 | 6 | 3 | 0 | 0 | 0 | 2 | 2 | 0 | 0 | L | L | 6-1 | 185 | 1-1-69 | 1991 | Brentwood, Tenn. |
| McCall, Rod | .300 | 120 | 440 | 80 | 132 | 29 | 2 | 27 | 85 | 52 | 118 | 2 | 0 | L | R | 6-7 | 235 | 11-4-71 | 1990 | Stanton, Calif. |
| Neal, Mike | .224 | 94 | 254 | 42 | 57 | 9 | 3 | 4 | 32 | 39 | 53 | 2 | 3 | R | R | 6-1 | 180 | 11-5-71 | 1993 | Hammond, La. |
| Ramirez, Alex | .329 | 131 | 513 | 79 | 169 | 28 | 12 | 14 | 85 | 16 | 74 | 18 | 10 | R | R | 5-11 | 176 | 10-3-74 | 1991 | Miranda, Venez. |
| Raven, Luis | .302 | 74 | 268 | 57 | 81 | 17 | 0 | 21 | 64 | 38 | 73 | 0 | 0 | R | R | 6-4 | 230 | 11-19-68 | 1989 | La Guaira, Venez. |
| Sexson, Richie | .276 | 133 | 518 | 85 | 143 | 33 | 3 | 16 | 76 | 39 | 118 | 2 | 1 | R | R | 6-6 | 206 | 12-29-74 | 1993 | Brush Prairie, Wash. |

| BATTING | AVG | G | AB | R | H | 2B | 3B | HR | RBI | BB | SO | SB | CS | B | T | HT | WT | DOB | 1st Yr | Resides |
|---|---|---|---|---|---|---|---|---|---|---|---|---|---|---|---|---|---|---|---|---|
| Soliz, Steve ............... | .259 | 46 | 143 | 18 | 37 | 4 | 2 | 15 | 11 | 28 | 1 | 2 | R | R | 5-10 | 180 | 1-27-71 | 1993 | Oxnard, Calif. |
| Thomas, Greg ........... | .279 | 97 | 301 | 44 | 84 | 14 | 4 | 13 | 55 | 26 | 56 | 2 | 1 | L | L | 6-3 | 200 | 7-19-72 | 1993 | Orlando, Fla. |
| Wilson, Enrique .......... | .304 | 117 | 484 | 70 | 147 | 17 | 5 | 5 | 50 | 31 | 46 | 23 | 16 | S | R | 5-11 | 160 | 7-27-75 | 1992 | Santo Domingo, D.R. |

| PITCHING | W | L | ERA | G | GS | CG | SV | IP | H | R | ER | BB | SO | B | T | HT | WT | DOB | 1st Yr | Resides |
|---|---|---|---|---|---|---|---|---|---|---|---|---|---|---|---|---|---|---|---|---|
| Brown, Dickie .............. | 0 | 2 | 8.03 | 6 | 0 | 0 | 0 | 12 | 13 | 12 | 11 | 9 | 11 | R | R | 5-9 | 170 | 8-13-70 | 1990 | North Little Rock, Ark. |
| Bullard, Jason ............. | 1 | 1 | 2.45 | 9 | 0 | 0 | 0 | 11 | 7 | 3 | 3 | 6 | 12 | R | R | 6-2 | 185 | 10-23-68 | 1991 | Sweeny, Texas |
| 2-team (8 Binghamton) . | 1 | 1 | 2.57 | 17 | 0 | 0 | 0 | 21 | 18 | 7 | 6 | 11 | 22 | | | | | | | |
| Cabrera, Jose ............. | 4 | 3 | 5.63 | 15 | 9 | 1 | 0 | 62 | 78 | 45 | 39 | 17 | 40 | R | R | 6-0 | 197 | 3-24-72 | 1991 | Santiago, D.R. |
| Colon, Bartolo ............. | 2 | 2 | 1.74 | 13 | 12 | 0 | 0 | 62 | 44 | 17 | 12 | 25 | 56 | R | R | 6-0 | 185 | 5-24-75 | 1994 | Puerto Plata, D.R. |
| Delamaza, Roland ........ | 9 | 7 | 4.38 | 40 | 14 | 0 | 1 | 140 | 122 | 75 | 68 | 49 | 132 | R | R | 6-2 | 195 | 11-11-71 | 1993 | Arleta, Calif. |
| De la Rosa, Maximo ... | 11 | 5 | 3.91 | 40 | 15 | 0 | 3 | 120 | 104 | 60 | 52 | 81 | 109 | R | R | 5-11 | 170 | 7-12-71 | 1990 | Villa Mella, D.R. |
| Dougherty, Tony .......... | 0 | 0 | 9.00 | 3 | 0 | 0 | 0 | 5 | 3 | 5 | 5 | 8 | 6 | R | R | 6-2 | 205 | 4-12-73 | 1994 | Slippery Rock, Pa. |
| Driskill, Travis ............. | 13 | 7 | 3.61 | 29 | 24 | 4 | 0 | 172 | 169 | 89 | 69 | 63 | 148 | R | R | 6-0 | 185 | 8-1-71 | 1993 | Austin, Texas |
| Grigsby, Benji ............. | 1 | 2 | 1.26 | 16 | 0 | 0 | 2 | 29 | 22 | 11 | 4 | 11 | 21 | R | R | 6-2 | 200 | 12-2-70 | 1992 | Lafayette, La. |
| Kline, Steve ................ | 8 | 12 | 5.46 | 25 | 24 | 0 | 0 | 147 | 168 | 98 | 89 | 55 | 107 | S | L | 6-2 | 200 | 8-22-72 | 1993 | Winfield, Pa. |
| Martinez, Johnny ......... | 0 | 1 | 5.40 | 5 | 0 | 0 | 0 | 8 | 9 | 6 | 5 | 4 | 3 | R | R | 6-3 | 168 | 11-25-72 | 1991 | Guayabin, D.R. |
| Matthews, Mike ........... | 9 | 11 | 4.66 | 27 | 27 | 3 | 0 | 162 | 178 | 96 | 84 | 74 | 112 | L | L | 6-2 | 175 | 10-24-73 | 1992 | Woodbridge, Va. |
| McCormack, Andy ........ | 0 | 1 | 27.00 | 1 | 0 | 0 | 0 | 1 | 3 | 3 | 3 | 2 | 0 | R | L | 6-1 | 205 | 2-4-74 | 1993 | Raynham, Mass. |
| Montoya, Wilmer ......... | 2 | 5 | 3.38 | 43 | 0 | 0 | 23 | 51 | 41 | 24 | 19 | 28 | 42 | R | R | 5-10 | 165 | 3-15-74 | 1993 | Carabobo, Venez. |
| Plantenberg, Erik ........ | 0 | 0 | 3.00 | 19 | 0 | 0 | 0 | 21 | 21 | 7 | 7 | 2 | 26 | S | L | 6-1 | 180 | 10-30-68 | 1990 | Bellevue, Wash. |
| Sexton, Jeff ................. | 2 | 4 | 5.11 | 9 | 9 | 0 | 0 | 49 | 45 | 29 | 28 | 23 | 34 | R | R | 6-2 | 190 | 10-4-71 | 1993 | Indianola, Okla. |
| Tolar, Kevin ................ | 1 | 3 | 2.62 | 50 | 0 | 0 | 1 | 45 | 42 | 19 | 13 | 26 | 39 | R | L | 6-3 | 225 | 1-28-71 | 1989 | Panama City, Fla. |
| Vaught, Jay ................. | 5 | 4 | 4.77 | 51 | 0 | 0 | 3 | 94 | 101 | 58 | 50 | 35 | 78 | L | R | 6-1 | 185 | 12-21-71 | 1994 | Deer Park, Texas |
| Whitten, Casey ............ | 3 | 1 | 1.67 | 8 | 8 | 0 | 0 | 38 | 23 | 8 | 7 | 13 | 44 | L | L | 6-0 | 175 | 5-23-72 | 1993 | Terre Haute, Ind. |

### FIELDING

| Catcher | PCT | G | PO | A | E | DP | PB |
|---|---|---|---|---|---|---|---|
| Diaz ................ | .983 | 103 | 762 | 87 | 15 | 4 | 10 |
| Soliz .............. | .987 | 45 | 276 | 31 | 4 | 6 | 2 |

| First Base | PCT | G | PO | A | E | DP |
|---|---|---|---|---|---|---|
| Betts ............. | 1.000 | 1 | 3 | 0 | 0 | 0 |
| McCall ............ | .993 | 34 | 250 | 19 | 2 | 25 |
| Raven ............. | .929 | 3 | 13 | 0 | 1 | 1 |
| Sexson ............ | .989 | 104 | 892 | 76 | 11 | 91 |
| Thomas .......... | .953 | 8 | 36 | 5 | 2 | 3 |

| Second Base | PCT | G | PO | A | E | DP |
|---|---|---|---|---|---|---|
| Betts .............. | .000 | 1 | 0 | 0 | 0 | 0 |

| | PCT | G | PO | A | E | DP |
|---|---|---|---|---|---|---|
| Gutierrez ........ | .975 | 99 | 197 | 263 | 12 | 63 |
| Neal ............... | .973 | 43 | 76 | 101 | 5 | 24 |
| Wilson ........... | 1.000 | 1 | 0 | 2 | 0 | 1 |

| Third Base | PCT | G | PO | A | E | DP |
|---|---|---|---|---|---|---|
| Betts ............. | .899 | 72 | 34 | 117 | 17 | 12 |
| Diaz .............. | 1.000 | 3 | 3 | 1 | 0 | 0 |
| Neal .............. | .898 | 24 | 12 | 41 | 6 | 5 |
| Raven ........... | .885 | 64 | 32 | 114 | 19 | 9 |

| Shortstop | PCT | G | PO | A | E | DP |
|---|---|---|---|---|---|---|
| Betts ............. | 1.000 | 2 | 2 | 3 | 0 | 1 |

| | PCT | G | PO | A | E | DP |
|---|---|---|---|---|---|---|
| Gutierrez ........ | .969 | 20 | 26 | 68 | 3 | 10 |
| Neal ............... | .860 | 12 | 19 | 30 | 8 | 7 |
| Wilson ........... | .949 | 113 | 179 | 342 | 28 | 74 |

| Outfield | PCT | G | PO | A | E | DP |
|---|---|---|---|---|---|---|
| Aven ............. | .979 | 130 | 280 | 3 | 6 | 0 |
| Betzsold ......... | .966 | 84 | 140 | 4 | 5 | 0 |
| Bryant ........... | .980 | 33 | 47 | 1 | 1 | 0 |
| Harvey .......... | 1.000 | 4 | 6 | 0 | 0 | 0 |
| Neal .............. | 1.000 | 7 | 11 | 0 | 0 | 0 |
| Ramirez .......... | .977 | 131 | 209 | 4 | 5 | 0 |
| Thomas .......... | .989 | 67 | 83 | 7 | 1 | 1 |

## BAKERSFIELD
**Class A/Co-Op**

## CALIFORNIA LEAGUE

| BATTING | AVG | G | AB | R | H | 2B | 3B | HR | RBI | BB | SO | SB | CS | B | T | HT | WT | DOB | 1st Yr | Resides |
|---|---|---|---|---|---|---|---|---|---|---|---|---|---|---|---|---|---|---|---|---|
| Johnson, Todd ........... | .238 | 110 | 369 | 45 | 88 | 23 | 0 | 2 | 31 | 32 | 90 | 1 | 1 | R | R | 5-11 | 205 | 12-18-70 | 1993 | Fresno, Calif. |
| Lewis, Andreaus ......... | .244 | 62 | 205 | 40 | 50 | 13 | 0 | 3 | 16 | 22 | 78 | 9 | 2 | S | R | 6-2 | 215 | 1-22-74 | 1993 | Decatur, Ga. |

**GAMES BY POSITION: C**—Johnson 73. **OF**—Johnson 38.

| PITCHING | W | L | ERA | G | GS | CG | SV | IP | H | R | ER | BB | SO | B | T | HT | WT | DOB | 1st Yr | Resides |
|---|---|---|---|---|---|---|---|---|---|---|---|---|---|---|---|---|---|---|---|---|
| Cabrera, Jose .............. | 2 | 2 | 3.92 | 7 | 7 | 0 | 0 | 41 | 40 | 25 | 18 | 21 | 52 | R | R | 6-0 | 197 | 3-24-72 | 1991 | Santiago, D.R. |
| Hritz, Derrick .............. | 4 | 6 | 5.86 | 31 | 7 | 0 | 2 | 81 | 100 | 68 | 53 | 50 | 60 | L | L | 6-1 | 188 | 9-21-72 | 1993 | Gahanna, Ohio |
| Oldham, Bob .............. | 2 | 10 | 9.69 | 41 | 17 | 0 | 0 | 143 | 224 | 187 | 154 | 105 | 107 | R | R | 6-5 | 220 | 4-4-74 | 1994 | Connellsville, Pa. |
| Oropeza, Igor ............. | 1 | 14 | 6.80 | 23 | 21 | 4 | 0 | 138 | 160 | 113 | 104 | 92 | 94 | R | R | 6-4 | 183 | 7-11-72 | 1992 | La Guaira, Venez. |
| Palmer, Brett .............. | 2 | 6 | 7.42 | 12 | 11 | 2 | 0 | 61 | 91 | 63 | 50 | 45 | 37 | L | L | 6-3 | 180 | 3-8-75 | 1993 | Idaho Falls, Idaho |
| Runion, Tony .............. | 0 | 6 | 11.36 | 7 | 6 | 1 | 0 | 36 | 61 | 56 | 45 | 27 | 20 | R | R | 6-3 | 220 | 12-6-71 | 1993 | Florence, Ky. |

## KINSTON
**Class A**

## CAROLINA LEAGUE

| BATTING | AVG | G | AB | R | H | 2B | 3B | HR | RBI | BB | SO | SB | CS | B | T | HT | WT | DOB | 1st Yr | Resides |
|---|---|---|---|---|---|---|---|---|---|---|---|---|---|---|---|---|---|---|---|---|
| Berrios, Harry .............. | .192 | 24 | 73 | 7 | 14 | 5 | 0 | 2 | 11 | 9 | 16 | 2 | 0 | R | R | 5-11 | 205 | 12-2-71 | 1993 | Grand Rapids, Mich. |
| 2-team (43 Frederick) | .218 | 67 | 234 | 32 | 51 | 14 | 1 | 6 | 31 | 21 | 37 | 10 | 3 | | | | | | | |
| Casey, Sean ............... | .331 | 92 | 344 | 62 | 114 | 31 | 3 | 12 | 57 | 36 | 47 | 1 | 1 | L | R | 6-4 | 215 | 7-2-74 | 1995 | Pittsburgh, Pa. |
| Cawhorn, Gerad .......... | .236 | 53 | 174 | 29 | 41 | 14 | 1 | 2 | 23 | 22 | 35 | 2 | 1 | R | R | 6-1 | 185 | 8-27-71 | 1993 | Brea, Calif. |
| Claudio, Patricio ......... | .291 | 100 | 361 | 67 | 105 | 15 | 2 | 1 | 38 | 47 | 74 | 36 | 14 | R | R | 6-0 | 173 | 4-12-72 | 1991 | Santiago, D.R. |
| Evans, Pat ................... | .259 | 21 | 27 | 5 | 7 | 3 | 1 | 0 | 6 | 4 | 12 | 0 | 1 | S | R | 5-10 | 175 | 12-5-72 | 1994 | San Ramon, Calif. |
| Glass, Chip ................. | .267 | 134 | 479 | 64 | 128 | 18 | 9 | 5 | 52 | 40 | 67 | 11 | 6 | L | L | 5-11 | 180 | 6-24-71 | 1994 | Ukiah, Calif. |
| Hagy, Gary ................. | .218 | 74 | 174 | 30 | 38 | 10 | 1 | 5 | 22 | 40 | 50 | 4 | 3 | R | R | 6-3 | 195 | 4-7-69 | 1991 | Ephrata, Wash. |
| Harriss, Robin ............. | .218 | 89 | 262 | 25 | 57 | 7 | 1 | 5 | 32 | 16 | 57 | 1 | 2 | R | R | 6-1 | 205 | 8-7-71 | 1994 | San Angelo, Texas |
| Harvey, Ray ............... | .281 | 32 | 114 | 14 | 32 | 7 | 0 | 2 | 16 | 12 | 26 | 0 | 0 | L | L | 6-1 | 185 | 1-1-69 | 1991 | Brentwood, Tenn. |
| Jorgensen, Tim ........... | .216 | 119 | 412 | 56 | 89 | 24 | 0 | 17 | 64 | 41 | 103 | 1 | 2 | L | R | 6-3 | 200 | 11-30-72 | 1995 | Luxemburg, Wis. |
| Mercedes, Guillermo ... | .246 | 117 | 382 | 45 | 94 | 12 | 1 | 0 | 27 | 30 | 41 | 3 | 3 | S | R | 5-11 | 155 | 1-17-74 | 1993 | La Romana, D.R. |
| Miller, David .............. | .254 | 129 | 488 | 71 | 124 | 23 | 1 | 7 | 54 | 38 | 94 | 14 | 7 | L | L | 6-4 | 200 | 12-9-73 | 1996 | Philadelphia, Pa. |
| Moyle, Mike ............... | .269 | 61 | 197 | 37 | 53 | 12 | 1 | 7 | 34 | 30 | 32 | 3 | 2 | R | R | 6-2 | 200 | 9-8-71 | 1992 | Perth, Australia |
| Perry, Chan ................ | .291 | 96 | 358 | 44 | 104 | 27 | 1 | 10 | 62 | 36 | 33 | 2 | 3 | R | R | 6-2 | 200 | 9-13-72 | 1994 | Mayo, Fla. |
| Ramirez, Omar ............ | .400 | 2 | 5 | 1 | 2 | 0 | 0 | 1 | 3 | 1 | 0 | 0 | 0 | R | R | 5-9 | 170 | 11-2-70 | 1990 | Santiago, D.R. |
| Taylor, Jerry ............... | .260 | 64 | 146 | 19 | 38 | 9 | 1 | 1 | 19 | 48 | 37 | 1 | 1 | R | R | 5-10 | 210 | 12-19-72 | 1995 | Goliad, Texas |
| Warner, Bryan ............. | .225 | 43 | 111 | 9 | 25 | 2 | 0 | 1 | 12 | 8 | 23 | 2 | 1 | L | L | 5-9 | 185 | 8-7-74 | 1994 | Monrovia, Calif. |
| White, Eric ................. | .239 | 114 | 422 | 50 | 101 | 26 | 1 | 4 | 52 | 32 | 65 | 3 | 4 | R | R | 6-1 | 180 | 10-13-72 | 1992 | Diamond Bar, Calif. |

**GAMES BY POSITION: C**—Evans 20, Harriss 87, Moyle 54. **1B**—Casey 70, Hagy 5, Harvey 6, Miller 35, Perry 27. **2B**—Cawhorn 43, Hagy 28, White 81. **3B**—Cawhorn 11, Hagy 3, Jorgensen 118, Perry 1, White 12. **SS**—Hagy 37, Mercedes 117. **OF**—Berrios 22, Claudio 79, Glass 131, Harvey 2, Miller 88, Perry 19, Taylor 53, Warner 39, White 19.

| PITCHING | W | L | ERA | G | GS | CG | SV | IP | H | R | ER | BB | SO | B | T | HT | WT | DOB | 1st Yr | Resides |
|---|---|---|---|---|---|---|---|---|---|---|---|---|---|---|---|---|---|---|---|---|
| Brabant, Daniel ............. | 1 | 1 | 4.35 | 26 | 1 | 0 | 2 | 60 | 52 | 34 | 29 | 29 | 50 | R | R | 6-1 | 211 | 4-16-73 | 1993 | Longueuil, Quebec |

| PITCHING | W | L | ERA | G | GS | CG | SV | IP | H | R | ER | BB | SO | B | T | HT | WT | DOB | 1st Yr | Resides |
|---|---|---|---|---|---|---|---|---|---|---|---|---|---|---|---|---|---|---|---|---|
| Cabrera, Jose | 1 | 1 | 1.02 | 4 | 3 | 0 | 0 | 18 | 7 | 2 | 2 | 8 | 19 | R | R | 6-0 | 197 | 3-24-72 | 1991 | Santiago, D.R. |
| Caldwell, David | 13 | 9 | 3.30 | 23 | 23 | 0 | 0 | 139 | 142 | 66 | 51 | 37 | 80 | L | L | 6-3 | 190 | 11-14-74 | 1994 | Brooklyn, N.Y. |
| Donovan, Scot | 2 | 2 | 5.26 | 28 | 0 | 0 | 0 | 53 | 60 | 39 | 31 | 25 | 36 | L | R | 6-3 | 195 | 7-3-72 | 1994 | Dunwoody, Ga. |
| Dougherty, Tony | 3 | 1 | 1.62 | 18 | 0 | 0 | 8 | 33 | 29 | 6 | 6 | 11 | 32 | R | R | 6-2 | 205 | 4-12-73 | 1994 | Slippery Rock, Pa. |
| Granata, Chris | 7 | 6 | 4.34 | 35 | 6 | 1 | 0 | 95 | 105 | 51 | 46 | 43 | 57 | R | R | 6-0 | 205 | 2-26-72 | 1994 | Columbus, Ohio |
| Hanson, Kris | 2 | 5 | 5.36 | 9 | 8 | 0 | 0 | 47 | 46 | 31 | 28 | 16 | 26 | R | R | 6-5 | 240 | 1-5-71 | 1993 | Stevens Point, Wis. |
| Harvey, Terry | 2 | 4 | 4.00 | 12 | 12 | 0 | 0 | 70 | 80 | 38 | 31 | 16 | 34 | R | R | 6-1 | 180 | 1-29-73 | 1995 | Dacula, Ga. |
| Kirkreit, Daron | 2 | 0 | 1.93 | 6 | 6 | 0 | 0 | 33 | 23 | 7 | 7 | 10 | 19 | R | R | 6-6 | 225 | 8-7-72 | 1993 | Norco, Calif. |
| McCormack, Andy | 0 | 0 | 0.00 | 5 | 0 | 0 | 1 | 10 | 4 | 0 | 0 | 2 | 8 | R | L | 6-1 | 205 | 2-4-74 | 1993 | Raynham, Mass. |
| Mesa, Rafael | 8 | 3 | 2.32 | 45 | 1 | 0 | 15 | 81 | 58 | 26 | 21 | 28 | 56 | R | R | 6-4 | 175 | 10-9-73 | 1991 | Azua, D.R. |
| Montoya, Wilmer | 1 | 2 | 1.20 | 11 | 0 | 0 | 2 | 15 | 10 | 5 | 2 | 6 | 12 | R | R | 5-10 | 165 | 3-15-74 | 1993 | Carabobo, Venez. |
| Najera, Noe | 12 | 2 | 2.70 | 24 | 24 | 1 | 0 | 140 | 124 | 52 | 42 | 62 | 131 | L | L | 6-2 | 190 | 12-9-70 | 1992 | Norwalk, Calif. |
| Negrette, Richard | 0 | 1 | 23.14 | 1 | 1 | 0 | 0 | 2 | 9 | 7 | 6 | 4 | 0 | S | R | 6-2 | 175 | 3-6-76 | 1994 | Maracaibo, Venez. |
| Oropeza, Igor | 1 | 2 | 3.81 | 8 | 4 | 0 | 0 | 26 | 23 | 13 | 11 | 18 | 20 | R | R | 6-4 | 183 | 7-11-72 | 1992 | LaGuaira, Venez. |
| Perez, Julio | 1 | 2 | 3.09 | 24 | 0 | 0 | 3 | 44 | 44 | 22 | 15 | 17 | 21 | R | R | 6-1 | 163 | 5-18-74 | 1993 | San Cristobal, D.R. |
| Runion, Tony | 1 | 1 | 5.79 | 6 | 1 | 0 | 0 | 14 | 16 | 10 | 9 | 11 | 11 | R | R | 6-3 | 220 | 12-6-71 | 1993 | Florence, Ky. |
| Warrecker, Teddy | 9 | 11 | 6.03 | 27 | 26 | 1 | 0 | 131 | 137 | 105 | 88 | 88 | 88 | L | R | 6-5 | 215 | 10-1-72 | 1994 | Santa Barbara, Calif. |
| Weber, Lenny | 2 | 4 | 1.83 | 36 | 0 | 0 | 6 | 59 | 44 | 12 | 12 | 36 | 49 | R | R | 6-1 | 180 | 8-6-72 | 1994 | Jeanerette, La. |
| Wright, Jaret | 7 | 4 | 2.50 | 19 | 19 | 0 | 0 | 101 | 65 | 32 | 28 | 55 | 109 | R | R | 6-2 | 220 | 12-29-75 | 1994 | Anaheim, Calif. |
| Zubiri, John | 1 | 1 | 3.21 | 3 | 3 | 0 | 0 | 14 | 14 | 8 | 5 | 9 | 11 | R | R | 6-2 | 170 | 11-15-74 | 1992 | Hanford, Calif. |

# COLUMBUS — Class A

## SOUTH ATLANTIC LEAGUE

| BATTING | AVG | G | AB | R | H | 2B | 3B | HR | RBI | BB | SO | SB | CS | B | T | HT | WT | DOB | 1st Yr | Resides |
|---|---|---|---|---|---|---|---|---|---|---|---|---|---|---|---|---|---|---|---|---|
| Anderson, Milt | .231 | 81 | 251 | 46 | 58 | 12 | 2 | 5 | 27 | 42 | 53 | 29 | 10 | S | R | 5-10 | 175 | 9-7-72 | 1995 | Fitzgerald, Ga. |
| Branyan, Russ | .268 | 130 | 482 | 102 | 129 | 20 | 4 | 40 | 106 | 62 | 166 | 7 | 4 | L | R | 6-3 | 195 | 12-19-75 | 1994 | Warner Robins, Ga. |
| Budzinski, Mark | .262 | 74 | 260 | 42 | 68 | 12 | 4 | 3 | 38 | 59 | 68 | 12 | 3 | L | L | 6-2 | 175 | 3-26-73 | 1995 | Severna Park, Md. |
| Donati, John | .283 | 40 | 145 | 23 | 41 | 6 | 1 | 6 | 28 | 10 | 27 | 1 | 0 | R | R | 6-1 | 200 | 5-4-73 | 1991 | Concord, Calif. |
| Evans, Pat | .125 | 6 | 16 | 0 | 2 | 0 | 0 | 0 | 2 | 5 | 0 | 0 | 0 | S | R | 5-10 | 175 | 12-5-72 | 1994 | San Ramon, Calif. |
| Glavine, Mike | .277 | 38 | 119 | 17 | 33 | 5 | 0 | 6 | 16 | 28 | 33 | 0 | 0 | L | L | 6-3 | 210 | 1-24-73 | 1995 | Billerica, Mass. |
| Gonzalez, Mauricio | .242 | 25 | 95 | 13 | 23 | 4 | 0 | 1 | 7 | 1 | 18 | 0 | 1 | S | R | 5-11 | 170 | 2-13-72 | 1990 | Santo Domingo, D.R. |
| Gonzalez, Ricky | .235 | 75 | 247 | 19 | 58 | 11 | 0 | 1 | 12 | 17 | 42 | 0 | 0 | R | R | 6-0 | 185 | 11-13-74 | 1995 | Miami, Fla. |
| Hayes, Heath | .233 | 104 | 348 | 51 | 81 | 14 | 0 | 22 | 57 | 36 | 106 | 2 | 1 | R | R | 6-3 | 195 | 2-29-72 | 1994 | Citrus Heights, Calif. |
| Lewis, Andreaus | .078 | 23 | 64 | 6 | 5 | 2 | 0 | 1 | 7 | 31 | 2 | 0 | 0 | S | R | 6-2 | 215 | 1-22-74 | 1993 | Decatur, Ga. |
| Minici, Jason | .213 | 98 | 334 | 37 | 71 | 18 | 2 | 4 | 23 | 31 | 84 | 9 | 4 | R | R | 6-0 | 190 | 10-29-73 | 1995 | Irvine, Calif. |
| Morgan, Scott | .311 | 87 | 305 | 62 | 95 | 25 | 1 | 22 | 80 | 46 | 70 | 9 | 5 | R | R | 6-7 | 230 | 7-19-73 | 1995 | Spokane, Wash. |
| Mota, Cristian | .213 | 32 | 122 | 17 | 26 | 4 | 0 | 3 | 10 | 10 | 31 | 1 | 2 | S | R | 5-11 | 165 | 3-31-76 | 1994 | San Pedro de Macoris, D.R. |
| Scutaro, Marcos | .251 | 85 | 315 | 66 | 79 | 12 | 3 | 10 | 45 | 38 | 86 | 6 | 3 | R | R | 5-10 | 170 | 10-30-75 | 1995 | San Felipe, Venez. |
| Stumberger, Darren | .310 | 129 | 471 | 77 | 146 | 30 | 3 | 22 | 89 | 53 | 72 | 0 | 1 | R | R | 6-3 | 205 | 4-11-73 | 1994 | Boca Raton, Fla. |
| Thornhill, Chad | .181 | 52 | 160 | 34 | 29 | 1 | 2 | 2 | 18 | 30 | 32 | 1 | 2 | S | R | 6-3 | 180 | 8-22-72 | 1995 | Fresno, Calif. |
| Valera, Willy | .214 | 116 | 393 | 47 | 84 | 16 | 2 | 4 | 34 | 19 | 88 | 11 | 7 | R | R | 6-0 | 155 | 7-23-75 | 1993 | San Cristobal, D.R. |
| Warner, Bryan | .265 | 81 | 328 | 38 | 87 | 14 | 0 | 4 | 34 | 19 | 44 | 7 | 4 | L | L | 5-9 | 185 | 8-7-74 | 1994 | Monrovia, Calif. |
| Whitaker, Chad | .235 | 66 | 234 | 32 | 55 | 10 | 1 | 12 | 29 | 25 | 80 | 2 | 2 | R | R | 6-2 | 190 | 9-16-76 | 1995 | Fort Lauderdale, Fla. |

**GAMES BY POSITION: C**—Evans 6, R. Gonzalez 75, Hayes 68. **1B**—Glavine 3, M. Gonzalez 1, Hayes 16, Stumberger 128, Thornhill 3. **2B**—M. Gonzalez 11, Mota 31, Scutaro 78, Thornhill 25. **3B**—Branyan 118, Hayes 17, Scutaro 3, Thornhill 7. **SS**—M. Gonzalez 13, Scutero 5, Thornhill 17, Valera 114. **OF**—Anderson 74, Budzinski 65, Hayes 3, Lewis 7, Minici 81, Morgan 73, Warner 80, Whitaker 63.

| PITCHING | W | L | ERA | G | GS | CG | SV | IP | H | R | ER | BB | SO | B | T | HT | WT | DOB | 1st Yr | Resides |
|---|---|---|---|---|---|---|---|---|---|---|---|---|---|---|---|---|---|---|---|---|---|
| Adge, Jason | 0 | 4 | 6.85 | 16 | 0 | 0 | 0 | 24 | 37 | 23 | 18 | 11 | 21 | L | R | 6-0 | 195 | 10-18-71 | 1995 | Sacramento, Calif. |
| Atkins, Dannon | 11 | 10 | 3.93 | 28 | 28 | 2 | 0 | 170 | 156 | 85 | 74 | 64 | 129 | R | R | 6-3 | 195 | 8-7-73 | 1995 | Miami, Fla. |
| Bennett, Jason | 3 | 4 | 3.49 | 40 | 0 | 0 | 1 | 70 | 51 | 31 | 27 | 25 | 51 | R | R | 6-0 | 200 | 7-15-74 | 1995 | Montoursville, Pa. |
| Crowell, Jim | 7 | 10 | 4.14 | 28 | 28 | 3 | 0 | 165 | 163 | 89 | 76 | 69 | 104 | L | L | 6-4 | 220 | 5-14-74 | 1995 | Indianapolis, Ind. |
| Deschenes, Marc | 5 | 2 | 3.40 | 16 | 16 | 0 | 0 | 77 | 70 | 38 | 29 | 41 | 67 | R | R | 6-0 | 175 | 1-6-73 | 1994 | Dracut, Mass. |
| Dougherty, Tony | 3 | 1 | 2.94 | 19 | 1 | 0 | 2 | 49 | 30 | 16 | 16 | 22 | 44 | R | R | 6-2 | 205 | 4-12-73 | 1994 | Slippery Rock, Pa. |
| Granger, Greg | 8 | 4 | 3.31 | 20 | 12 | 0 | 2 | 84 | 90 | 42 | 31 | 28 | 67 | R | R | 6-5 | 200 | 3-7-73 | 1993 | Ellettsville, Ind. |
| Grife, Rich | 2 | 4 | 3.88 | 36 | 0 | 0 | 3 | 58 | 56 | 29 | 25 | 20 | 42 | R | R | 6-6 | 235 | 2-3-72 | 1995 | Des Moines, Iowa |
| Horn, Keith | 5 | 5 | 3.91 | 25 | 12 | 0 | 0 | 90 | 80 | 48 | 39 | 24 | 78 | R | R | 5-11 | 185 | 5-17-74 | 1995 | Jonesboro, Ark. |
| Hritz, Derrick | 0 | 0 | 11.57 | 5 | 0 | 0 | 0 | 7 | 17 | 9 | 9 | 0 | 2 | L | L | 6-1 | 188 | 9-21-72 | 1993 | Gahanna, Ohio |
| Loudermilk, Darren | 0 | 0 | 3.00 | 3 | 0 | 0 | 0 | 6 | 5 | 2 | 2 | 4 | 8 | R | R | 6-3 | 220 | 10-11-74 | 1995 | Oklahoma City, Okla. |
| Mathis, Sammie | 8 | 3 | 4.01 | 31 | 4 | 1 | 2 | 85 | 84 | 43 | 38 | 31 | 67 | R | R | 5-11 | 195 | 12-16-72 | 1995 | El Dorado, Ark. |
| Merrick, Brett | 6 | 2 | 2.82 | 44 | 0 | 0 | 1 | 54 | 36 | 21 | 17 | 24 | 51 | L | L | 6-0 | 180 | 5-30-74 | 1995 | Lynwood, Wash. |
| Palmer, Brett | 0 | 2 | 6.23 | 5 | 3 | 0 | 0 | 13 | 19 | 12 | 9 | 10 | 14 | L | L | 6-3 | 180 | 3-8-75 | 1993 | Idaho Falls, Idaho |
| Rakers, Jason | 5 | 4 | 3.61 | 14 | 14 | 1 | 0 | 77 | 84 | 37 | 31 | 17 | 68 | R | R | 6-2 | 197 | 6-29-73 | 1995 | Pittsburgh, Pa. |
| Sanders, Frankie | 9 | 3 | 2.52 | 22 | 22 | 0 | 0 | 121 | 103 | 52 | 34 | 37 | 109 | R | R | 5-11 | 165 | 8-27-75 | 1995 | Sarasota, Fla. |
| Thobe, J.J. | 0 | 2 | 7.71 | 2 | 2 | 0 | 0 | 7 | 11 | 6 | 6 | 6 | 4 | R | R | 6-6 | 200 | 11-19-70 | 1992 | Huntington Beach, Calif. |
| Winchester, Scott | 7 | 3 | 3.23 | 52 | 0 | 0 | 26 | 61 | 50 | 27 | 22 | 16 | 60 | R | R | 6-2 | 210 | 4-20-73 | 1995 | Midland, Mich. |

# WATERTOWN — Class A

## NEW YORK-PENN LEAGUE

| BATTING | AVG | G | AB | R | H | 2B | 3B | HR | RBI | BB | SO | SB | CS | B | T | HT | WT | DOB | 1st Yr | Resides |
|---|---|---|---|---|---|---|---|---|---|---|---|---|---|---|---|---|---|---|---|---|
| Afenir, Tom | .222 | 3 | 9 | 0 | 2 | 0 | 0 | 0 | 1 | 0 | 3 | 0 | 0 | R | R | 6-0 | 180 | 8-9-71 | 1995 | San Diego, Calif. |
| Coats, Nathan | .265 | 31 | 102 | 13 | 27 | 5 | 1 | 0 | 7 | 8 | 20 | 1 | 1 | R | R | 5-11 | 185 | 5-1-74 | 1995 | Sparks, Nev. |
| Huelsmann, Mike | .262 | 41 | 130 | 21 | 34 | 5 | 1 | 0 | 21 | 17 | 14 | 14 | 4 | S | R | 5-11 | 165 | 11-21-74 | 1996 | St. Louis, Mo. |
| Kent, Troy | .251 | 72 | 263 | 34 | 66 | 20 | 2 | 3 | 32 | 33 | 54 | 1 | 5 | R | R | 6-0 | 200 | 9-11-73 | 1996 | Oldsmar, Fla. |
| Konrady, Dennis | .251 | 60 | 183 | 23 | 46 | 10 | 1 | 0 | 30 | 42 | 32 | 2 | 5 | L | R | 5-11 | 185 | 9-21-74 | 1996 | Eugene, Ore. |
| Landstad, Rob | .300 | 6 | 20 | 3 | 6 | 2 | 1 | 0 | 3 | 2 | 6 | 0 | 0 | L | R | 6-0 | 230 | 4-17-73 | 1996 | Canora, Sask. |
| McDonald, John | .270 | 75 | 278 | 48 | 75 | 11 | 0 | 2 | 26 | 32 | 49 | 11 | 1 | R | R | 5-11 | 170 | 9-24-74 | 1996 | East Lyme, Conn. |
| Motley, Mel | .246 | 61 | 199 | 24 | 49 | 8 | 2 | 1 | 27 | 24 | 55 | 5 | 5 | R | R | 6-4 | 195 | 2-5-74 | 1996 | Riverside, Calif. |
| Peoples, Danny | .239 | 35 | 117 | 20 | 28 | 7 | 0 | 3 | 26 | 28 | 36 | 3 | 1 | R | R | 6-1 | 207 | 1-20-75 | 1996 | Round Rock, Texas |
| Petke, Jon | .246 | 63 | 224 | 35 | 55 | 10 | 0 | 1 | 26 | 44 | 36 | 8 | 4 | R | R | 6-1 | 195 | 1-14-73 | 1996 | Mission Viejo, Calif. |
| Rodriguez, Chris | .000 | 2 | 5 | 0 | 0 | 0 | 0 | 0 | 0 | 0 | 1 | 0 | 0 | S | R | 5-11 | 175 | 11-4-73 | 1996 | Davidsonville, Md. |
| Rodriguez, Gary | .235 | 67 | 247 | 45 | 58 | 7 | 0 | 0 | 17 | 44 | 70 | 20 | 7 | L | R | 5-11 | 165 | 7-17-76 | 1996 | Keller, Texas |

| BATTING | AVG | G | AB | R | H | 2B | 3B | HR | RBI | BB | SO | SB | CS | B | T | HT | WT | DOB | 1st Yr | Resides |
|---|---|---|---|---|---|---|---|---|---|---|---|---|---|---|---|---|---|---|---|---|
| Stanton, Rob .............. | .185 | 44 | 146 | 19 | 27 | 5 | 0 | 3 | 20 | 15 | 49 | 0 | 0 | R | R | 6-5 | 225 | 4-18-75 | 1996 | Winter Park, Fla. |
| Taylor, Adam .............. | .184 | 49 | 147 | 25 | 27 | 5 | 0 | 7 | 27 | 36 | 57 | 1 | 0 | R | R | 5-11 | 195 | 3-14-74 | 1996 | Grass Lake, Mich. |
| Tiller, Brad .................. | .233 | 55 | 202 | 26 | 47 | 5 | 3 | 3 | 24 | 10 | 50 | 7 | 5 | R | R | 5-10 | 165 | 11-21-75 | 1994 | Inez, Ky. |
| Whitlock, Brian ........... | .217 | 47 | 152 | 23 | 33 | 5 | 2 | 3 | 14 | 23 | 49 | 2 | 0 | R | R | 6-1 | 180 | 9-16-74 | 1996 | Sarasota, Fla. |

**GAMES BY POSITION: C**—Stanton 33, Coats 29, Taylor 45. **1B**—Kent 71, Konrady 6, Petke 3. **2B**—Konrady 11, Tiller 55, Whitlock 14. **3B**—Kent 2, Konrady 42, C. Rodriguez 1, Whitlock 37. **SS**—McDonald 75. **OF**—Huelsmann 26, Landstad, Motley 52, Petke 59, , C. Rodriguez 1, G. Rodriguez 66, Stanton 33.

| PITCHING | W | L | ERA | G | GS | CG | SV | IP | H | R | ER | BB | SO | B | T | HT | WT | DOB | 1st Yr | Resides |
|---|---|---|---|---|---|---|---|---|---|---|---|---|---|---|---|---|---|---|---|---|
| Brammer, J.D. .............. | 5 | 0 | 3.55 | 17 | 0 | 0 | 1 | 38 | 27 | 22 | 15 | 28 | 49 | R | R | 6-4 | 235 | 1-30-75 | 1996 | Logan, W.Va. |
| Calmus, Lance ............ | 1 | 3 | 6.41 | 11 | 11 | 0 | 0 | 46 | 53 | 40 | 33 | 18 | 51 | R | R | 6-5 | 225 | 1-19-73 | 1996 | Jenks, Okla. |
| Camp, Jared ............... | 10 | 2 | 1.69 | 15 | 15 | 1 | 0 | 96 | 68 | 29 | 18 | 30 | 99 | R | R | 6-1 | 195 | 5-4-75 | 1995 | Huntington, W.Va. |
| DePaula, Sean ............. | 0 | 0 | 0.00 | 1 | 0 | 0 | 0 | 2 | 0 | 0 | 0 | 0 | 5 | R | R | 6-4 | 215 | 11-7-73 | 1996 | Derry, N.H. |
| Edwards, Jon ............... | 1 | 3 | 3.15 | 23 | 0 | 0 | 4 | 34 | 26 | 12 | 12 | 14 | 37 | R | R | 6-0 | 175 | 6-15-73 | 1995 | Walla Walla, Wash. |
| Feliz, Bienvenido ......... | 5 | 6 | 3.89 | 13 | 11 | 2 | 0 | 72 | 59 | 37 | 31 | 26 | 56 | R | R | 6-0 | 175 | 6-4-77 | 1994 | Santo Domingo, D.R. |
| Fleetwood, Tony .......... | 0 | 0 | 5.00 | 12 | 0 | 0 | 1 | 18 | 22 | 13 | 10 | 6 | 19 | L | L | 6-3 | 200 | 12-31-71 | 1995 | Marlow, Okla. |
| Martinez, Dennis ......... | 4 | 2 | 2.44 | 12 | 6 | 0 | 0 | 44 | 30 | 14 | 12 | 20 | 37 | S | R | 6-3 | 170 | 11-16-73 | 1995 | Miami, Fla. |
| Martinez, Willie ........... | 6 | 5 | 2.40 | 14 | 14 | 1 | 0 | 90 | 79 | 25 | 24 | 21 | 92 | R | R | 6-2 | 165 | 1-4-78 | 1995 | Barquisimeto, Venez. |
| Mays, Jarrod ............... | 5 | 2 | 3.34 | 12 | 12 | 0 | 0 | 59 | 62 | 29 | 22 | 18 | 56 | R | R | 6-4 | 190 | 10-8-74 | 1996 | El Dorado Springs, Mo. |
| Minter, Matt ................. | 2 | 1 | 2.50 | 21 | 3 | 0 | 3 | 36 | 29 | 14 | 10 | 13 | 38 | L | L | 6-0 | 185 | 2-22-73 | 1996 | Bellaire, Texas |
| Palmer, Brett .............. | 1 | 1 | 2.53 | 2 | 2 | 0 | 0 | 11 | 6 | 3 | 3 | 6 | 12 | L | L | 6-3 | 180 | 3-8-75 | 1993 | Idaho Falls, Idaho |
| Rigdon, Paul ............... | 2 | 2 | 4.08 | 22 | 0 | 0 | 6 | 40 | 41 | 24 | 18 | 10 | 46 | R | R | 6-3 | 200 | 12-31-75 | 1995 | Jacksonville, Fla. |
| Taylor, Mark ............... | 1 | 0 | 3.54 | 12 | 0 | 0 | 0 | 20 | 18 | 9 | 8 | 16 | 17 | L | L | 6-3 | 185 | 10-30-74 | 1996 | St. Petersburg, Fla. |
| Wagner, Ken ............... | 2 | 3 | 2.20 | 21 | 1 | 0 | 5 | 45 | 32 | 12 | 11 | 20 | 47 | R | R | 6-4 | 218 | 8-3-74 | 1995 | West Palm Beach, Fla. |

# BURLINGTON
**Rookie**

## APPALACHIAN LEAGUE

| BATTING | AVG | G | AB | R | H | 2B | 3B | HR | RBI | BB | SO | SB | CS | B | T | HT | WT | DOB | 1st Yr | Resides |
|---|---|---|---|---|---|---|---|---|---|---|---|---|---|---|---|---|---|---|---|---|
| Afenir, Tom ................. | .240 | 26 | 96 | 4 | 23 | 5 | 0 | 1 | 7 | 0 | 22 | 1 | 1 | R | R | 6-0 | 180 | 8-9-71 | 1995 | San Diego, Calif. |
| Allison, Cody .............. | .260 | 27 | 96 | 10 | 25 | 2 | 0 | 1 | 14 | 12 | 17 | 1 | 0 | L | R | 6-1 | 200 | 8-8-74 | 1995 | Odessa, Texas |
| Edwards, Mike ............ | .282 | 58 | 206 | 31 | 58 | 13 | 1 | 1 | 17 | 37 | 26 | 5 | 4 | R | R | 6-1 | 185 | 11-24-76 | 1995 | Mechanicsburg, Pa. |
| Hardy, Bryan .............. | .156 | 52 | 186 | 16 | 29 | 10 | 0 | 6 | 25 | 9 | 84 | 0 | 0 | L | R | 6-4 | 240 | 3-26-77 | 1995 | Arlington, Texas |
| Hernandez, Jesus ......... | .227 | 19 | 66 | 15 | 15 | 2 | 0 | 2 | 6 | 13 | 8 | 5 | 0 | L | L | 6-2 | 170 | 6-6-77 | 1994 | Laguna Salada, D.R. |
| Jackson, William ......... | .126 | 35 | 103 | 15 | 13 | 1 | 0 | 1 | 3 | 9 | 38 | 6 | 2 | S | R | 6-2 | 190 | 10-5-73 | 1996 | Waco, Texas |
| Landstad, Rob ............ | .293 | 53 | 167 | 31 | 49 | 10 | 3 | 7 | 27 | 40 | 34 | 9 | 3 | L | R | 6-0 | 230 | 4-17-73 | 1996 | Canora, Sask. |
| Messner, Jake ............ | .250 | 47 | 164 | 20 | 41 | 7 | 1 | 3 | 20 | 11 | 41 | 6 | 3 | L | L | 6-0 | 192 | 5-18-77 | 1995 | Sacramento, Calif. |
| Mota, Cristian ............ | .267 | 63 | 251 | 36 | 67 | 14 | 1 | 3 | 34 | 19 | 56 | 13 | 6 | S | R | 5-11 | 165 | 3-31-76 | 1994 | San Pedro de Macoris, D.R. |
| Murphy, Quinn ............ | .153 | 18 | 59 | 7 | 9 | 1 | 0 | 0 | 3 | 6 | 30 | 2 | 1 | L | R | 6-1 | 195 | 9-28-75 | 1994 | Moline, Ill. |
| Perez, Edwin .............. | .233 | 51 | 176 | 22 | 41 | 4 | 0 | 9 | 31 | 15 | 48 | 5 | 4 | R | R | 5-10 | 165 | 5-10-75 | 1993 | Navarrete, D.R. |
| Rodriguez, Aurelio ........ | .132 | 18 | 76 | 12 | 10 | 3 | 1 | 0 | 3 | 4 | 10 | 2 | 3 | R | R | 5-10 | 165 | 12-10-73 | 1996 | Los Mochis, Mexico |
| Rodriguez, Chris ......... | .061 | 19 | 49 | 5 | 3 | 0 | 0 | 0 | 1 | 8 | 20 | 0 | 0 | S | R | 5-11 | 175 | 11-4-73 | 1996 | Davidsonville, Md. |
| Sharpe, Grant ............ | .244 | 26 | 82 | 14 | 20 | 6 | 1 | 4 | 17 | 18 | 26 | 1 | 1 | R | R | 6-4 | 215 | 12-4-77 | 1996 | Laurel, Miss. |
| Siponmaa, Ryan ........... | .154 | 6 | 13 | 3 | 2 | 0 | 0 | 0 | 0 | 5 | 7 | 1 | 0 | R | R | 6-2 | 230 | 1-12-75 | 1996 | Lunenberg, Mass. |
| Taveras, Frank ........... | .236 | 46 | 161 | 18 | 38 | 4 | 0 | 3 | 15 | 6 | 50 | 6 | 3 | L | R | 6-1 | 158 | 9-6-75 | 1993 | Santiago, D.R. |
| Williams, Jewell ........... | .237 | 64 | 236 | 44 | 56 | 10 | 1 | 7 | 35 | 25 | 83 | 16 | 4 | R | R | 6-2 | 185 | 6-25-77 | 1995 | Las Vegas, Nev. |

**GAMES BY POSITION: C**—Afenir 26, Allison 27, Landstad 12, Siponmaa 4. **1B**—Hardy 39, Sharpe 10, Taveras 19. **2B**—Mota 37, Murphy 13, Perez 2, A. Rodriguez 1, C. Rodriguez 15. **3B**—Edwards 40, Mota 27, Murphy 1, Perez 3. **SS**—Edwards 3, Landstad 1, Perez 42, A. Rodriguez 18. **OF**—Hernandez 19, Jackson 30, Landstad 28, Messner 46, Mota 2, Siponmaa 2, Taveras 19, Williams 60.

| PITCHING | W | L | ERA | G | GS | CG | SV | IP | H | R | ER | BB | SO | B | T | HT | WT | DOB | 1st Yr | Resides |
|---|---|---|---|---|---|---|---|---|---|---|---|---|---|---|---|---|---|---|---|---|
| Aracena, Juan ............ | 3 | 4 | 5.48 | 13 | 5 | 0 | 0 | 43 | 61 | 38 | 26 | 7 | 28 | R | R | 6-0 | 150 | 12-17-76 | 1994 | La Vega, D.R. |
| Bacsik, Mike ............... | 4 | 2 | 2.20 | 13 | 13 | 1 | 0 | 70 | 49 | 23 | 17 | 14 | 61 | L | L | 6-3 | 190 | 11-11-77 | 1996 | Duncanville, Texas |
| DePaula, Sean ............ | 4 | 2 | 3.82 | 23 | 0 | 0 | 1 | 35 | 31 | 16 | 15 | 13 | 42 | R | R | 6-4 | 215 | 11-7-73 | 1996 | Derry, N.H. |
| Garza, Alberto ............ | 2 | 4 | 5.45 | 9 | 9 | 0 | 0 | 40 | 34 | 24 | 24 | 15 | 34 | R | R | 6-3 | 195 | 5-25-77 | 1996 | Wapato, Wash. |
| Hamilton, Jim .............. | 1 | 3 | 4.00 | 10 | 10 | 0 | 0 | 45 | 45 | 22 | 20 | 16 | 50 | R | L | 6-3 | 185 | 8-1-75 | 1996 | Weyers Cave, W. Va. |
| Horgan, Joe ............... | 1 | 2 | 4.19 | 23 | 0 | 0 | 7 | 34 | 37 | 25 | 16 | 9 | 48 | L | L | 6-1 | 200 | 6-7-77 | 1996 | Rancho Cordova, Calif. |
| Koeman, Matt ............. | 5 | 2 | 3.72 | 13 | 3 | 0 | 1 | 39 | 33 | 18 | 16 | 10 | 49 | R | R | 6-3 | 200 | 10-13-73 | 1996 | Grand Junction, Colo. |
| Loudermilk, Darren ....... | 1 | 0 | 4.68 | 16 | 0 | 0 | 0 | 33 | 35 | 23 | 17 | 8 | 29 | R | R | 6-3 | 220 | 10-11-74 | 1995 | Oklahoma City, Okla. |
| McDermott, Ryan ......... | 2 | 8 | 4.61 | 13 | 13 | 0 | 0 | 55 | 55 | 38 | 28 | 40 | 38 | R | R | 6-9 | 225 | 6-28-78 | 1996 | Alamogordo, N.M. |
| Mojica, Gonzalo .......... | 1 | 0 | 8.54 | 14 | 1 | 0 | 0 | 26 | 28 | 25 | 25 | 28 | 35 | R | R | 6-1 | 170 | 8-4-76 | 1994 | Yabucoa, P.R. |
| Negrette, Richard ........ | 2 | 6 | 5.16 | 14 | 13 | 0 | 0 | 59 | 57 | 50 | 34 | 36 | 52 | S | R | 6-2 | 175 | 3-6-76 | 1994 | Maracaibo, Venez. |
| Pelton, Brad ............... | 0 | 3 | 2.81 | 15 | 0 | 0 | 3 | 26 | 19 | 11 | 8 | 9 | 21 | R | R | 6-3 | 202 | 8-4-74 | 1995 | Pensacola, Fla. |
| Reichow, Robert ......... | 2 | 2 | 4.53 | 21 | 0 | 0 | 1 | 44 | 51 | 23 | 22 | 10 | 41 | R | R | 6-5 | 220 | 10-10-73 | 1996 | Temperance, Mich. |
| Spiegel, Mike .............. | 1 | 0 | 3.74 | 14 | 0 | 0 | 0 | 22 | 19 | 12 | 9 | 12 | 14 | L | L | 6-5 | 200 | 11-24-75 | 1996 | Carmichael, Calif. |

# COLORADO ROCKIES

**Manager:** Don Baylor   **1996 Record:** 83-79, .512 (3rd, NL West).

| BATTING | AVG | G | AB | R | H | 2B | 3B | HR | RBI | BB | SO | SB | CS | B | T | HT | WT | DOB | 1st Yr | Resides |
|---|---|---|---|---|---|---|---|---|---|---|---|---|---|---|---|---|---|---|---|---|
| Anthony, Eric | .242 | 32 | 62 | 10 | 15 | 2 | 0 | 4 | 9 | 10 | 20 | 0 | 1 | L | L | 6-2 | 195 | 11-8-67 | 1986 | Houston, Texas |
| 2-team (47 Cincinnati) | .243 | 79 | 185 | 32 | 45 | 8 | 0 | 12 | 22 | 32 | 56 | 0 | 2 | | | | | | | |
| Bates, Jason | .206 | 88 | 160 | 19 | 33 | 8 | 1 | 1 | 9 | 23 | 34 | 2 | 1 | S | R | 5-11 | 170 | 1-5-71 | 1992 | Norwalk, Calif. |
| Bichette, Dante | .313 | 159 | 633 | 114 | 198 | 39 | 3 | 31 | 141 | 45 | 105 | 31 | 12 | R | R | 6-3 | 235 | 11-18-63 | 1984 | Palm Beach Gardens, Fla. |
| Brito, Jorge | .071 | 8 | 14 | 1 | 1 | 0 | 0 | 0 | 0 | 1 | 8 | 0 | 0 | R | R | 6-1 | 188 | 6-22-66 | 1986 | Athens, Ala. |
| Burks, Ellis | .344 | 156 | 613 | 142 | 211 | 45 | 8 | 40 | 128 | 61 | 114 | 32 | 6 | R | R | 6-2 | 205 | 9-11-64 | 1983 | Denver, Colo. |
| Castellano, Pedro | .118 | 13 | 17 | 1 | 2 | 0 | 0 | 0 | 2 | 3 | 6 | 0 | 0 | R | R | 6-1 | 195 | 3-11-70 | 1988 | Lara, Venez. |
| Castilla, Vinny | .304 | 160 | 629 | 97 | 191 | 34 | 0 | 40 | 113 | 35 | 88 | 7 | 2 | R | R | 6-1 | 185 | 7-4-67 | 1990 | Oaxaca, Mexico |
| Cockrell, Alan | .250 | 9 | 8 | 0 | 2 | 1 | 0 | 0 | 2 | 0 | 4 | 0 | 0 | R | R | 6-2 | 210 | 12-5-62 | 1984 | Galena, Kan. |
| Decker, Steve | .320 | 10 | 25 | 8 | 8 | 2 | 0 | 1 | 8 | 3 | 3 | 1 | 0 | R | R | 6-3 | 205 | 10-25-65 | 1988 | Keizer, Ore. |
| 2-team (57 S.F.) | .245 | 67 | 147 | 24 | 36 | 3 | 0 | 2 | 20 | 18 | 29 | 1 | 0 | | | | | | | |
| Echevarria, Angel | .286 | 26 | 21 | 2 | 6 | 0 | 0 | 0 | 6 | 2 | 5 | 0 | 0 | R | R | 6-4 | 215 | 5-25-71 | 1992 | Bridgeport, Conn. |
| Galarraga, Andres | .304 | 159 | 626 | 119 | 190 | 39 | 3 | 47 | 150 | 40 | 157 | 18 | 8 | R | R | 6-3 | 245 | 6-18-61 | 1979 | Caracas, Venez. |
| Hubbard, Trenidad | .217 | 45 | 60 | 12 | 13 | 5 | 1 | 1 | 12 | 9 | 22 | 2 | 0 | R | R | 5-8 | 180 | 5-11-66 | 1986 | Houston, Texas |
| Jones, Terry | .300 | 12 | 10 | 6 | 3 | 0 | 0 | 0 | 0 | 3 | 6 | 0 | 0 | S | R | 5-10 | 160 | 2-15-71 | 1993 | Pinson, Ala. |
| McCracken, Quinton | .290 | 124 | 283 | 50 | 82 | 13 | 6 | 3 | 40 | 32 | 62 | 17 | 6 | S | R | 5-8 | 170 | 3-16-70 | 1992 | Southport, N.C. |
| Owens, Jayhawk | .239 | 73 | 180 | 31 | 43 | 9 | 1 | 4 | 17 | 27 | 56 | 4 | 1 | R | R | 6-0 | 200 | 2-10-69 | 1990 | Sardinia, Ohio |
| Perez, Neifi | .156 | 17 | 45 | 4 | 7 | 2 | 0 | 0 | 3 | 0 | 8 | 2 | 2 | S | R | 6-0 | 175 | 6-2-75 | 1993 | Villa Mella, D.R. |
| Pulliam, Harvey | .133 | 10 | 15 | 2 | 2 | 0 | 0 | 0 | 0 | 2 | 6 | 0 | 0 | R | R | 6-0 | 205 | 10-20-67 | 1986 | San Francisco, Calif. |
| Reed, Jeff | .284 | 116 | 341 | 34 | 97 | 20 | 1 | 8 | 37 | 43 | 65 | 2 | 2 | L | R | 6-2 | 190 | 11-12-62 | 1980 | Elizabethton, Tenn. |
| Vander Wal, John | .252 | 104 | 151 | 20 | 38 | 6 | 2 | 5 | 31 | 19 | 38 | 2 | 2 | L | L | 6-1 | 180 | 4-29-66 | 1987 | Hudsonville, Mich. |
| Walker, Larry | .276 | 83 | 272 | 58 | 75 | 18 | 4 | 18 | 58 | 20 | 58 | 18 | 2 | L | R | 6-2 | 185 | 12-1-66 | 1985 | Maple Ridge, B.C. |
| Weiss, Walt | .282 | 155 | 517 | 89 | 146 | 20 | 2 | 8 | 48 | 80 | 78 | 10 | 2 | S | R | 6-0 | 178 | 11-28-63 | 1985 | Danville, Calif. |
| Young, Eric | .324 | 141 | 568 | 113 | 184 | 23 | 4 | 8 | 74 | 47 | 31 | 53 | 19 | R | R | 5-9 | 017 | 5-18-67 | 1989 | New Brunswick, N.J. |

| PITCHING | W | L | ERA | G | GS | CG | SV | IP | H | R | ER | BB | SO | B | T | HT | WT | DOB | 1st Yr | Resides |
|---|---|---|---|---|---|---|---|---|---|---|---|---|---|---|---|---|---|---|---|---|
| Alston, Garvin | 1 | 0 | 9.00 | 6 | 0 | 0 | 0 | 6 | 9 | 6 | 6 | 3 | 5 | R | R | 6-2 | 188 | 12-8-71 | 1992 | Mt. Vernon, N.Y. |
| Bailey, Roger | 2 | 3 | 6.24 | 24 | 11 | 0 | 1 | 84 | 94 | 64 | 58 | 52 | 45 | R | R | 6-1 | 180 | 10-3-70 | 1992 | Tallahassee, Fla. |
| Beckett, Robbie | 0 | 0 | 13.50 | 5 | 0 | 0 | 0 | 5 | 6 | 8 | 8 | 9 | 6 | R | L | 6-5 | 235 | 7-16-72 | 1990 | Austin, Texas |
| Burke, John | 2 | 1 | 7.47 | 11 | 0 | 0 | 0 | 16 | 21 | 13 | 13 | 7 | 19 | S | R | 6-4 | 220 | 2-9-70 | 1992 | Highlands Ranch, Colo. |
| Farmer, Mike | 0 | 1 | 7.71 | 7 | 4 | 0 | 0 | 28 | 32 | 25 | 24 | 13 | 16 | S | L | 6-1 | 200 | 7-3-68 | 1990 | Gary, Ind. |
| Freeman, Marvin | 7 | 9 | 6.04 | 26 | 23 | 0 | 0 | 130 | 151 | 100 | 87 | 57 | 71 | R | R | 6-7 | 222 | 4-10-63 | 1984 | Country Club Hills, Ill. |
| Habyan, John | 1 | 1 | 7.13 | 19 | 0 | 0 | 0 | 24 | 34 | 19 | 19 | 14 | 25 | R | R | 6-2 | 195 | 1-29-64 | 1982 | Bel Air, Md. |
| Hawblitzel, Ryan | 0 | 1 | 6.00 | 8 | 0 | 0 | 0 | 15 | 18 | 12 | 10 | 6 | 7 | R | R | 6-2 | 170 | 4-30-71 | 1990 | Lake Worth, Fla. |
| Holmes, Darren | 5 | 4 | 3.97 | 62 | 0 | 0 | 1 | 77 | 78 | 41 | 34 | 28 | 73 | R | R | 6-0 | 190 | 4-25-66 | 1984 | Fletcher, N.C. |
| Leskanic, Curtis | 7 | 5 | 6.23 | 70 | 0 | 0 | 6 | 74 | 82 | 51 | 51 | 38 | 76 | R | R | 6-0 | 180 | 4-2-68 | 1990 | Pineville, La. |
| Munoz, Mike | 2 | 2 | 6.65 | 54 | 0 | 0 | 0 | 45 | 55 | 33 | 33 | 16 | 45 | L | L | 6-2 | 190 | 7-12-65 | 1986 | West Covina, Calif. |
| Nied, David | 0 | 2 | 13.50 | 6 | 1 | 0 | 0 | 5 | 5 | 8 | 8 | 4 | 4 | R | R | 6-2 | 185 | 12-22-68 | 1988 | Denver, Colo. |
| Painter, Lance | 4 | 2 | 5.86 | 34 | 1 | 0 | 0 | 51 | 56 | 37 | 33 | 25 | 48 | L | L | 6-1 | 195 | 7-21-67 | 1990 | Milwaukee, Wis. |
| Reed, Steve | 4 | 3 | 3.96 | 70 | 0 | 0 | 0 | 75 | 66 | 38 | 33 | 19 | 51 | R | R | 6-2 | 195 | 3-11-66 | 1988 | Lewiston, Idaho |
| Rekar, Bryan | 2 | 4 | 8.95 | 14 | 11 | 0 | 0 | 58 | 87 | 61 | 58 | 26 | 25 | R | R | 6-3 | 205 | 6-3-72 | 1993 | Orland Park, Ill. |
| Reynoso, Armando | 8 | 9 | 4.96 | 30 | 30 | 0 | 0 | 169 | 195 | 97 | 93 | 49 | 88 | R | R | 6-0 | 196 | 5-1-66 | 1989 | Lagos de Moreno, Mexico |
| Ritz, Kevin | 17 | 11 | 5.28 | 35 | 35 | 2 | 0 | 213 | 236 | 135 | 125 | 105 | 105 | R | R | 6-4 | 220 | 6-8-65 | 1986 | Cambridge, Ohio |
| Ruffin, Bruce | 7 | 5 | 4.00 | 71 | 0 | 0 | 24 | 70 | 55 | 35 | 31 | 29 | 74 | S | L | 6-2 | 213 | 10-4-63 | 1985 | Austin, Texas |
| Swift, Billy | 1 | 1 | 5.40 | 7 | 3 | 0 | 2 | 18 | 23 | 12 | 11 | 5 | 5 | R | R | 6-0 | 191 | 10-27-61 | 1985 | South Portland, Maine |
| Thompson, Mark | 9 | 11 | 5.30 | 34 | 28 | 3 | 0 | 170 | 189 | 109 | 100 | 74 | 99 | R | R | 6-2 | 205 | 4-7-71 | 1992 | Russellville, Ky. |
| Wright, Jamey | 4 | 4 | 4.93 | 16 | 15 | 0 | 0 | 91 | 105 | 60 | 50 | 41 | 45 | R | R | 6-6 | 205 | 12-24-74 | 1993 | Moore, Okla. |

## FIELDING

| Catcher | PCT | G | PO | A | E | DP | PB |
|---|---|---|---|---|---|---|---|
| Brito | 1.000 | 8 | 36 | 7 | 0 | 1 | 1 |
| Decker | 1.000 | 10 | 51 | 6 | 0 | 0 | 0 |
| Owens | .974 | 68 | 312 | 27 | 9 | 3 | 7 |
| Reed | .982 | 111 | 546 | 51 | 11 | 4 | 11 |

| First Base | PCT | G | PO | A | E | DP |
|---|---|---|---|---|---|---|
| Decker | 1.000 | 3 | 18 | 3 | 0 | 1 |
| Galarraga | .992 | 159 | 1527 | 116 | 14 | 154 |
| Vanderwal | .976 | 10 | 38 | 2 | 1 | 2 |

| Second Base | PCT | G | PO | A | E | DP |
|---|---|---|---|---|---|---|
| Bates | .978 | 37 | 58 | 78 | 3 | 16 |
| Castellano | 1.000 | 3 | 3 | 10 | 0 | 2 |
| Perez | .933 | 4 | 6 | 8 | 1 | 3 |
| Young | .985 | 139 | 340 | 431 | 12 | 109 |

| Third Base | PCT | G | PO | A | E | DP |
|---|---|---|---|---|---|---|
| Bates | .818 | 12 | 0 | 9 | 2 | 1 |
| Castellano | 1.000 | 1 | 0 | 1 | 0 | 0 |
| Castilla | .960 | 160 | 97 | 389 | 20 | 43 |
| Decker | 1.000 | 2 | 2 | 2 | 0 | 0 |
| Galarraga | .000 | 1 | 0 | 0 | 0 | 0 |

| Shortstop | PCT | G | PO | A | E | DP |
|---|---|---|---|---|---|---|
| Bates | .938 | 18 | 8 | 22 | 2 | 1 |
| Perez | .972 | 14 | 15 | 20 | 1 | 8 |
| Weiss | .957 | 155 | 220 | 450 | 30 | 90 |

| Outfield | PCT | G | PO | A | E | DP |
|---|---|---|---|---|---|---|
| Anthony | 1.000 | 19 | 20 | 2 | 0 | 0 |
| Bichette | .967 | 156 | 255 | 5 | 9 | 1 |
| Burks | .983 | 152 | 279 | 6 | 5 | 2 |
| Castellano | .000 | 1 | 0 | 0 | 0 | 0 |
| Cockrell | .000 | 1 | 0 | 0 | 0 | 0 |
| Echevarria | 1.000 | 11 | 1 | 0 | 0 | 0 |
| Hubbard | 1.000 | 19 | 32 | 0 | 0 | 0 |
| Jones | 1.000 | 4 | 5 | 0 | 0 | 0 |
| McCracken | .957 | 93 | 131 | 3 | 6 | 0 |
| Pulliam | 1.000 | 3 | 4 | 0 | 0 | 0 |
| Thompson | 1.000 | 1 | 2 | 0 | 0 | 0 |
| Vanderwal | 1.000 | 26 | 34 | 0 | 0 | 0 |
| Walker | .994 | 83 | 153 | 4 | 1 | 0 |

**Ellis Burks**

MORRIS FOSTOFF

Outfielder Dante Bichette had another solid season for the Rockies, hitting .313

Rockies minor league Player of the Year Neifi Perez

MORRIS FOSTOFF

THE SPORTS GROUP

## FARM SYSTEM

**Vice President, Player Personnel:** Dick Balderson

| Class | Farm Team | League | W | L | Pct. | Finish* | Manager | First Yr |
|---|---|---|---|---|---|---|---|---|
| AAA | Colo. Springs (Colo.) Sky Sox | Pacific Coast | 58 | 83 | .411 | 10th (10) | Brad Mills | 1993 |
| AA | New Haven (Conn.) Ravens | Eastern | 66 | 75 | .468 | T-7th (10) | Bill Hayes | 1994 |
| #A | Salem (Va.) Avalanche | Carolina | 62 | 76 | .449 | 7th (8) | Bill McGuire | 1995 |
| A | Asheville (N.C.) Tourists | South Atlantic | 84 | 52 | .618 | 1st (14) | P.J. Carey | 1994 |
| A | Portland (Ore.) Rockies | Northwest | 33 | 43 | .434 | 7th (8) | Ron Gideon | 1995 |
| R | Chandler (Ariz.) Rockies | Arizona | 26 | 30 | .464 | 4th (6) | Jim Eppard | 1992 |

*Finish in overall standings (No. of teams in league)   #Advanced level

## ORGANIZATION LEADERS

### MAJOR LEAGUERS

**BATTING**

| | | |
|---|---|---|
| *AVG | Ellis Burks | .344 |
| R | Ellis Burks | 142 |
| H | Ellis Burks | 211 |
| TB | Ellis Burks | 392 |
| 2B | Ellis Burks | 45 |
| 3B | Ellis Burks | 8 |
| HR | Andres Galarraga | 47 |
| RBI | Andres Galarraga | 150 |
| BB | Walt Weiss | 80 |
| SO | Andres Galarraga | 157 |
| SB | Eric Young | 53 |

**PITCHING**

| | | |
|---|---|---|
| W | Kevin Ritz | 17 |
| L | Two tied at | 11 |
| #ERA | Steve Reed | 3.96 |
| G | Bruce Ruffin | 71 |
| CG | Mark Thompson | 3 |
| SV | Bruce Ruffin | 24 |
| IP | Kevin Ritz | 213 |
| BB | Kevin Ritz | 105 |
| SO | Kevin Ritz | 105 |

**Andres Galarraga.** 47 homers

THE SPORTS GROUP

### MINOR LEAGUERS

**BATTING**

| | | |
|---|---|---|
| *AVG | Two tied at | .337 |
| R | Neifi Perez, Colorado Springs | 77 |
| H | Neifi Perez, Colorado Springs | 180 |
| TB | Neifi Perez, Colorado Springs | 253 |
| 2B | John Giudice, Salem/New Haven | 34 |
| 3B | Neifi Perez, Colorado Springs | 12 |
| HR | Tal Light, Asheville/Salem | 25 |
| RBI | Tal Light, Asheville/Salem | 87 |
| BB | Ben Petrick, Asheville | 75 |
| SO | Justin Drizos, Asheville | 126 |
| SB | Garrett Neubart, Asheville/Salem | 42 |

**PITCHING**

| | | |
|---|---|---|
| W | Scott Randall, Asheville | 14 |
| L | Two tied at | 13 |
| #ERA | Heath Bost, Asheville/New Haven | 1.32 |
| G | Bobby Jones, Colorado Springs | 57 |
| CG | Rodney Pedraza, NH/Colo. Spr. | 3 |
| SV | Chris Macca, Asheville/New Haven | 30 |
| IP | John Thomson, New Haven/Colo. Spr. | 167 |
| BB | Doug Million, Salem/New Haven | 100 |
| SO | Mark Brownson, New Haven | 155 |

*Minimum 250 At-Bats   #Minimum 75 Innings

## TOP 10 PROSPECTS

**How the Rockies Top 10 prospects, as judged by Baseball America prior to the 1996 season, fared in 1996:**

**Derrick Gibson**

THE SPORTS GROUP

| Player, Pos. | Club (Class—League) | AVG | AB | R | H | 2B | 3B | HR | RBI | SB |
|---|---|---|---|---|---|---|---|---|---|---|
| 1. Derrick Gibson, of | New Haven (AA—Eastern) | .256 | 449 | 58 | 115 | 21 | 4 | 15 | 62 | 3 |
| 3. Todd Helton, 1b | New Haven (AA—Eastern) | .332 | 319 | 46 | 106 | 24 | 2 | 7 | 51 | 2 |
| | Colo. Spr. (AAA—Pacific Coast) | .352 | 71 | 13 | 25 | 4 | 1 | 2 | 13 | 0 |
| 4. Neifi Perez, ss | Colo. Spr. (AAA—Pacific Coast) | .316 | 570 | 77 | 180 | 28 | 12 | 7 | 72 | 16 |
| | Colorado | .156 | 45 | 4 | 7 | 2 | 0 | 0 | 3 | 2 |
| 6. Ben Petrick, c | Asheville (A—South Atlantic) | .235 | 446 | 74 | 105 | 24 | 2 | 14 | 52 | 19 |
| 7. Edgard Velazquez, of | New Haven (AA—Eastern) | .290 | 486 | 72 | 141 | 29 | 4 | 19 | 62 | 6 |
| 10. Quinton McCracken, of | Colorado | .290 | 283 | 50 | 82 | 13 | 6 | 3 | 40 | 17 |

| Player, Pos. | Club (Class—League) | W | L | ERA | G | SV | IP | H | BB | SO |
|---|---|---|---|---|---|---|---|---|---|---|
| 2. Jamey Wright, rhp | New Haven (AA—Eastern) | 5 | 1 | 0.81 | 7 | 0 | 45 | 27 | 12 | 54 |
| | Colo. Springs (AAA—Pacific Coast) | 4 | 2 | 2.72 | 9 | 0 | 60 | 53 | 22 | 40 |
| | Colorado | 4 | 4 | 4.93 | 16 | 0 | 91 | 105 | 41 | 45 |
| 5. Doug Million, lhp | Salem (A—Carolina) | 7 | 5 | 2.53 | 17 | 0 | 107 | 84 | 60 | 99 |
| | New Haven (AA—Eastern) | 3 | 3 | 3.15 | 10 | 0 | 54 | 54 | 40 | 40 |
| 8. John Burke, rhp | Colo. Springs (AAA—Pacific Coast) | 2 | 4 | 5.94 | 24 | 1 | 64 | 75 | 28 | 54 |
| | Salem (A—Carolina) | 0 | 1 | 6.00 | 3 | 0 | 12 | 10 | 9 | 12 |
| | Colorado | 2 | 1 | 7.47 | 11 | 0 | 16 | 21 | 7 | 19 |
| 9. Mike Kusiewicz, lhp | Salem (A—Carolina) | 0 | 1 | 5.09 | 5 | 1 | 23 | 19 | 12 | 18 |
| | New Haven (AA—Eastern) | 2 | 4 | 3.30 | 14 | 0 | 76 | 83 | 27 | 64 |

## PACIFIC COAST LEAGUE

| BATTING | AVG | G | AB | R | H | 2B | 3B | HR | RBI | BB | SO | SB | CS | B | T | HT | WT | DOB | 1st Yr | Resides |
|---|---|---|---|---|---|---|---|---|---|---|---|---|---|---|---|---|---|---|---|---|
| Brito, Jorge | .340 | 53 | 159 | 32 | 54 | 17 | 0 | 7 | 31 | 24 | 37 | 0 | 1 | R | R | 6-1 | 188 | 6-22-66 | 1986 | Athens, Ala. |
| Carter, Jeff | .255 | 50 | 161 | 19 | 41 | 9 | 0 | 1 | 12 | 23 | 33 | 3 | 6 | S | R | 5-10 | 160 | 10-20-63 | 1985 | Evanston, Ill. |
| Castellano, Pete | .337 | 94 | 362 | 56 | 122 | 30 | 3 | 13 | 59 | 40 | 46 | 0 | 2 | R | R | 6-1 | 195 | 3-11-70 | 1988 | Lara, Venez. |
| Cockrell, Alan | .300 | 109 | 357 | 55 | 107 | 25 | 3 | 14 | 60 | 52 | 88 | 1 | 2 | R | R | 6-2 | 210 | 12-5-62 | 1984 | Galena, Kan. |
| Counsell, Craig | .240 | 25 | 75 | 17 | 18 | 3 | 0 | 2 | 10 | 24 | 7 | 4 | 3 | L | R | 6-0 | 177 | 8-21-70 | 1992 | Whitefish Bay, Wis. |
| Decker, Steve | .400 | 7 | 25 | 4 | 10 | 1 | 0 | 0 | 3 | 4 | 3 | 0 | 0 | R | R | 6-3 | 205 | 10-25-65 | 1988 | Keizer, Ore. |
| Echevarria, Angel | .337 | 110 | 415 | 67 | 140 | 19 | 2 | 16 | 74 | 38 | 81 | 4 | 3 | R | R | 6-4 | 215 | 5-25-71 | 1992 | Bridgeport, Conn. |
| Figueroa, Bien | .207 | 10 | 29 | 2 | 6 | 2 | 0 | 0 | 6 | 1 | 3 | 0 | 0 | R | R | 5-10 | 167 | 2-7-64 | 1986 | Tallahassee, Fla. |
| Gainer, Jay | .234 | 109 | 333 | 51 | 78 | 16 | 0 | 14 | 49 | 36 | 71 | 6 | 2 | L | L | 6-0 | 188 | 10-8-66 | 1990 | Ellsburg, Va. |
| Giannelli, Ray | .222 | 44 | 117 | 14 | 26 | 8 | 0 | 2 | 13 | 23 | 19 | 1 | 2 | L | R | 6-0 | 195 | 2-5-66 | 1988 | Lindenhurst, N.Y. |
|   2-team (10 Salt Lake) | .230 | 54 | 148 | 16 | 34 | 9 | 0 | 2 | 17 | 25 | 27 | 1 | 2 | | | | | | | |
| Gonzalez, Pete | .174 | 36 | 86 | 10 | 15 | 7 | 0 | 2 | 13 | 17 | 20 | 1 | 1 | R | R | 6-0 | 190 | 11-24-69 | 1989 | Hialeah, Fla. |
| Helton, Todd | .352 | 21 | 71 | 13 | 25 | 4 | 1 | 2 | 13 | 11 | 12 | 0 | 0 | L | L | 6-2 | 195 | 8-20-73 | 1995 | Powell, Tenn. |
| Hubbard, Trenidad | .314 | 50 | 188 | 41 | 59 | 15 | 5 | 6 | 16 | 28 | 14 | 6 | 8 | R | R | 5-8 | 180 | 5-11-66 | 1986 | Houston, Texas |
| Huson, Jeff | .295 | 14 | 61 | 10 | 18 | 4 | 0 | 0 | 8 | 3 | 1 | 6 | 0 | L | R | 6-3 | 180 | 8-15-64 | 1986 | Bedford, Texas |
| Jones, Terry | .288 | 128 | 497 | 75 | 143 | 7 | 4 | 0 | 33 | 37 | 80 | 26 | 14 | S | R | 5-10 | 160 | 2-15-71 | 1993 | Pinson, Ala. |
| Kennedy, David | .255 | 117 | 333 | 46 | 85 | 27 | 0 | 11 | 50 | 36 | 82 | 1 | 2 | R | R | 6-4 | 215 | 9-3-70 | 1992 | Glen Ridge, N.J. |
| List, Lou | .083 | 7 | 12 | 1 | 1 | 0 | 0 | 1 | 0 | 6 | 0 | 0 | 0 | R | R | 6-3 | 200 | 11-17-65 | 1987 | North Hollywood, Calif. |
| Miller, Roger | .000 | 1 | 2 | 0 | 0 | 0 | 0 | 0 | 0 | 0 | 0 | 0 | 0 | R | R | 6-0 | 190 | 4-4-67 | 1989 | Sarasota, Fla. |
| Owens, Jayhawk | .227 | 6 | 22 | 6 | 5 | 3 | 0 | 0 | 6 | 3 | 6 | 0 | 0 | R | R | 6-0 | 200 | 2-10-69 | 1990 | Sardinia, Ohio |
| Perez, Neifi | .316 | 133 | 570 | 77 | 180 | 28 | 12 | 7 | 72 | 21 | 48 | 16 | 13 | S | R | 6-0 | 175 | 6-2-75 | 1993 | Villa Mella, D.R. |
| Pozo, Yohel | .277 | 20 | 47 | 8 | 13 | 2 | 0 | 1 | 5 | 2 | 8 | 0 | 0 | R | R | 6-2 | 188 | 10-17-73 | 1992 | Maracaibo, Venez. |
| Pulliam, Harvey | .276 | 79 | 283 | 46 | 78 | 13 | 1 | 10 | 58 | 32 | 49 | 2 | 3 | R | R | 6-0 | 205 | 10-20-67 | 1986 | San Francisco, Calif. |
| Strittmatter, Mark | .233 | 58 | 159 | 21 | 37 | 8 | 1 | 2 | 18 | 17 | 30 | 2 | 1 | R | R | 6-1 | 200 | 4-4-69 | 1992 | Ridgewood, N.J. |
| Walker, Larry | .364 | 3 | 11 | 2 | 4 | 0 | 0 | 2 | 8 | 1 | 4 | 0 | 0 | L | R | 6-2 | 185 | 12-1-66 | 1985 | Maple Ridge, B.C. |
| White, Billy | .243 | 103 | 284 | 24 | 69 | 11 | 2 | 3 | 26 | 32 | 80 | 2 | 2 | R | R | 6-0 | 185 | 7-3-68 | 1989 | Louisville, Ky. |
| Young, Eric | .261 | 7 | 23 | 4 | 6 | 1 | 1 | 0 | 3 | 5 | 1 | 0 | 0 | R | R | 5-9 | 017 | 5-18-67 | 1989 | New Brunswick, N.J. |

| PITCHING | W | L | ERA | G | GS | CG | SV | IP | H | R | ER | BB | SO | B | T | HT | WT | DOB | 1st Yr | Resides |
|---|---|---|---|---|---|---|---|---|---|---|---|---|---|---|---|---|---|---|---|---|
| Alston, Garvin | 1 | 4 | 5.77 | 35 | 0 | 0 | 14 | 34 | 47 | 23 | 22 | 27 | 36 | R | R | 6-2 | 188 | 12-8-71 | 1992 | Mt. Vernon, N.Y. |
| Ausanio, Joe | 1 | 1 | 4.34 | 13 | 1 | 0 | 0 | 19 | 18 | 10 | 9 | 10 | 18 | R | R | 6-1 | 205 | 12-9-65 | 1988 | Kingston, N.Y. |
| Bailey, Roger | 4 | 4 | 6.29 | 9 | 9 | 0 | 0 | 49 | 60 | 34 | 34 | 20 | 27 | R | R | 6-0 | 180 | 10-3-70 | 1992 | Tallahassee, Fla. |
| Beckett, Robbie | 0 | 2 | 2.19 | 12 | 0 | 0 | 1 | 12 | 6 | 6 | 3 | 11 | 15 | R | L | 6-5 | 235 | 7-16-72 | 1990 | Austin, Texas |
| Burke, John | 2 | 4 | 5.94 | 24 | 9 | 0 | 1 | 64 | 75 | 46 | 42 | 28 | 54 | S | R | 6-4 | 220 | 2-9-70 | 1992 | Highlands Ranch, Colo. |
| Bustillos, Albert | 6 | 10 | 5.23 | 33 | 22 | 1 | 1 | 145 | 167 | 91 | 84 | 44 | 95 | R | R | 6-1 | 230 | 4-8-68 | 1988 | San Jose, Calif. |
| DeJean, Mike | 0 | 2 | 5.13 | 30 | 0 | 0 | 1 | 40 | 52 | 24 | 23 | 21 | 31 | R | R | 6-2 | 205 | 9-28-70 | 1992 | Denham Springs, La. |
| Farmer, Mike | 3 | 3 | 3.30 | 9 | 9 | 2 | 0 | 57 | 51 | 27 | 21 | 25 | 28 | S | L | 6-1 | 200 | 7-3-68 | 1990 | Gary, Ind. |
| Fredrickson, Scott | 2 | 2 | 6.64 | 55 | 0 | 0 | 2 | 64 | 71 | 56 | 47 | 40 | 66 | R | R | 6-3 | 215 | 8-19-67 | 1990 | San Antonio, Texas |
| Habyan, John | 0 | 0 | 4.50 | 1 | 1 | 0 | 0 | 4 | 2 | 2 | 2 | 1 | 4 | R | R | 6-2 | 195 | 1-29-64 | 1982 | Bel Air, Md. |
| Hawblitzel, Ryan | 7 | 6 | 5.00 | 26 | 18 | 0 | 1 | 117 | 131 | 76 | 65 | 27 | 75 | R | R | 6-2 | 170 | 4-30-71 | 1990 | Lake Worth, Fla. |
| Henry, Dwayne | 1 | 4 | 7.71 | 28 | 0 | 0 | 0 | 40 | 43 | 38 | 34 | 33 | 38 | R | R | 6-3 | 205 | 2-16-62 | 1980 | Middleton, Del. |
| Jones, Bobby | 2 | 8 | 4.97 | 57 | 0 | 0 | 3 | 89 | 88 | 54 | 49 | 63 | 78 | R | L | 6-0 | 175 | 4-11-72 | 1992 | Rutherford, N.J. |
| Kramer, Tom | 8 | 4 | 5.37 | 41 | 10 | 0 | 4 | 112 | 129 | 74 | 67 | 47 | 79 | 1 | R | 6-0 | 205 | 1-9-68 | 1987 | St. Bernard, Ohio |
| Leskanic, Curtis | 0 | 0 | 3.00 | 3 | 0 | 0 | 0 | 3 | 5 | 1 | 1 | 1 | 2 | R | R | 6-0 | 180 | 4-2-68 | 1990 | Pineville, La. |
| Munoz, Mike | 1 | 1 | 2.03 | 10 | 0 | 0 | 3 | 13 | 8 | 3 | 3 | 6 | 13 | L | L | 6-2 | 190 | 7-12-65 | 1986 | West Covina, Calif. |
| Nied, David | 3 | 8 | 12.27 | 16 | 16 | 0 | 0 | 62 | 116 | 92 | 85 | 32 | 53 | R | R | 6-2 | 185 | 12-22-68 | 1988 | Denver, Colo. |
| Pedraza, Rod | 1 | 1 | 8.36 | 6 | 5 | 0 | 0 | 28 | 39 | 26 | 26 | 4 | 13 | R | R | 6-2 | 210 | 12-28-69 | 1991 | Cuero, Texas |
| Rekar, Bryan | 8 | 8 | 4.46 | 19 | 19 | 0 | 0 | 123 | 138 | 68 | 61 | 36 | 75 | R | R | 6-3 | 205 | 6-3-72 | 1993 | Orland Park, Ill. |
| Thomson, John | 4 | 7 | 5.04 | 11 | 11 | 0 | 0 | 70 | 76 | 45 | 39 | 26 | 62 | R | R | 6-3 | 175 | 10-1-73 | 1993 | Sulphur, La. |
| Viano, Jacob | 0 | 2 | 10.89 | 7 | 3 | 0 | 0 | 21 | 33 | 25 | 25 | 13 | 12 | R | R | 5-11 | 180 | 9-4-73 | 1993 | Long Beach, Calif. |
| Wright, Jamey | 4 | 2 | 2.72 | 9 | 9 | 0 | 0 | 60 | 53 | 20 | 18 | 22 | 40 | R | R | 6-2 | 205 | 12-24-74 | 1993 | Moore, Okla. |

### FIELDING

| Catcher | PCT | G | PO | A | E | DP | PB |
|---|---|---|---|---|---|---|---|
| Brito | .977 | 50 | 313 | 25 | 8 | 1 | 3 |
| Decker | .984 | 7 | 56 | 4 | 1 | 0 | 2 |
| Gonzalez | .985 | 34 | 179 | 16 | 3 | 2 | 4 |
| Hubbard | 1.000 | 1 | 1 | 0 | 0 | 0 | 0 |
| Miller | 1.000 | 1 | 7 | 0 | 0 | 0 | 0 |
| Owens | 1.000 | 5 | 35 | 3 | 0 | 0 | 1 |
| Pozo | .971 | 13 | 62 | 4 | 2 | 1 | 0 |
| Strittmatter | .982 | 56 | 302 | 34 | 6 | 4 | 1 |

| First Base | PCT | G | PO | A | E | DP |
|---|---|---|---|---|---|---|
| Gainer | .984 | 59 | 467 | 29 | 8 | 41 |
| Giannelli | 1.000 | 2 | 13 | 2 | 0 | 2 |
| Helton | .988 | 20 | 143 | 16 | 2 | 16 |
| Kennedy | .987 | 78 | 582 | 42 | 8 | 64 |

| Second Base | PCT | G | PO | A | E | DP |
|---|---|---|---|---|---|---|
| Carter | .967 | 41 | 76 | 99 | 6 | 25 |
| Counsell | .962 | 16 | 27 | 48 | 3 | 9 |

| | PCT | G | PO | A | E | DP |
|---|---|---|---|---|---|---|
| Giannelli | 1.000 | 1 | 0 | 1 | 0 | 0 |
| Hubbard | .963 | 17 | 29 | 48 | 3 | 13 |
| Huson | 1.000 | 9 | 24 | 27 | 0 | 4 |
| White | .954 | 63 | 89 | 160 | 12 | 21 |
| Young | .917 | 7 | 15 | 18 | 3 | 8 |

| Third Base | PCT | G | PO | A | E | DP |
|---|---|---|---|---|---|---|
| Castellano | .963 | 93 | 49 | 185 | 9 | 17 |
| Counsell | 1.000 | 6 | 2 | 9 | 0 | 1 |
| Figueroa | .929 | 9 | 2 | 11 | 1 | 1 |
| Giannelli | .824 | 14 | 10 | 18 | 6 | 1 |
| Gonzalez | .000 | 1 | 0 | 0 | 0 | 0 |
| Hubbard | .750 | 1 | 0 | 3 | 1 | 0 |
| White | .953 | 25 | 8 | 33 | 2 | 3 |

| Shortstop | PCT | G | PO | A | E | DP |
|---|---|---|---|---|---|---|
| Counsell | .929 | 5 | 6 | 7 | 1 | 0 |
| Huson | .964 | 5 | 12 | 15 | 1 | 3 |

| | PCT | G | PO | A | E | DP |
|---|---|---|---|---|---|---|
| Perez | .963 | 132 | 244 | 409 | 25 | 91 |
| White | .923 | 4 | 5 | 7 | 1 | 2 |

| Outfield | PCT | G | PO | A | E | DP |
|---|---|---|---|---|---|---|
| Carter | 1.000 | 4 | 6 | 1 | 0 | 1 |
| Cockrell | .973 | 95 | 173 | 7 | 5 | 2 |
| Echevarria | .978 | 105 | 168 | 8 | 4 | 0 |
| Gainer | .857 | 8 | 6 | 0 | 1 | 0 |
| Giannelli | 1.000 | 9 | 15 | 0 | 0 | 0 |
| Helton | 1.000 | 2 | 1 | 1 | 0 | 0 |
| Hubbard | 1.000 | 27 | 59 | 3 | 0 | 1 |
| Jones | .949 | 124 | 281 | 14 | 16 | 2 |
| List | 1.000 | 2 | 1 | 0 | 0 | 0 |
| Pulliam | .935 | 74 | 124 | 6 | 9 | 0 |
| Walker | 1.000 | 3 | 6 | 2 | 0 | 0 |

## EASTERN LEAGUE

| BATTING | AVG | G | AB | R | H | 2B | 3B | HR | RBI | BB | SO | SB | CS | B | T | HT | WT | DOB | 1st Yr | Resides |
|---|---|---|---|---|---|---|---|---|---|---|---|---|---|---|---|---|---|---|---|---|
| Bernhardt, Steve | .286 | 32 | 84 | 5 | 24 | 3 | 0 | 0 | 10 | 4 | 14 | 0 | 2 | R | R | 6-0 | 180 | 10-9-70 | 1993 | Timonium, Md. |
| Garcia, Vicente | .214 | 87 | 295 | 32 | 63 | 10 | 1 | 3 | 18 | 28 | 43 | 1 | 2 | R | R | 6-0 | 170 | 2-14-75 | 1993 | Maracaibo, Venez. |
| Gibson, Derrick | .256 | 122 | 449 | 58 | 115 | 21 | 4 | 15 | 62 | 31 | 125 | 3 | 12 | R | R | 6-2 | 238 | 2-5-75 | 1993 | Winter Haven, Fla. |
| Giudice, John | .254 | 32 | 118 | 13 | 30 | 4 | 1 | 4 | 13 | 10 | 25 | 2 | 4 | R | R | 6-1 | 205 | 6-19-71 | 1993 | New Britain, Conn. |
| Goligoski, Jason | .172 | 30 | 64 | 6 | 11 | 0 | 1 | 0 | 3 | 8 | 12 | 0 | 2 | L | R | 6-1 | 180 | 10-2-71 | 1993 | Hamilton, Mon. |
| Gonzalez, Pete | .185 | 42 | 119 | 9 | 22 | 1 | 0 | 2 | 8 | 14 | 19 | 1 | 2 | R | R | 6-0 | 190 | 11-24-69 | 1989 | Hialeah, Fla. |

## BATTING

| BATTING | AVG | G | AB | R | H | 2B | 3B | HR | RBI | BB | SO | SB | CS | B | T | HT | WT | DOB | 1st Yr | Resides |
|---|---|---|---|---|---|---|---|---|---|---|---|---|---|---|---|---|---|---|---|---|
| Grunewald, Keith | .227 | 111 | 352 | 27 | 80 | 13 | 2 | 3 | 28 | 25 | 98 | 2 | 1 | S | R | 6-1 | 185 | 10-15-71 | 1993 | Marietta, Ga. |
| Helton, Todd | .332 | 93 | 319 | 46 | 106 | 24 | 2 | 7 | 51 | 51 | 37 | 2 | 5 | L | L | 6-2 | 195 | 8-20-73 | 1995 | Powell, Tenn. |
| Higgins, Mike | .181 | 22 | 72 | 6 | 13 | 2 | 1 | 0 | 5 | 2 | 14 | 1 | 1 | R | R | 6-0 | 205 | 6-3-71 | 1993 | Nutley, N.J. |
| Holdren, Nate | .167 | 10 | 36 | 3 | 6 | 1 | 0 | 1 | 6 | 2 | 11 | 1 | 1 | R | R | 6-4 | 240 | 12-8-71 | 1993 | Richland, Wash. |
| Jarrett, Link | .195 | 56 | 164 | 18 | 32 | 6 | 0 | 1 | 9 | 14 | 23 | 1 | 1 | S | R | 5-10 | 165 | 1-26-72 | 1994 | Tallahassee, Fla. |
| Miller, Roger | .242 | 85 | 256 | 23 | 62 | 8 | 1 | 3 | 29 | 26 | 32 | 0 | 1 | R | R | 6-0 | 190 | 4-4-67 | 1989 | Sarasota, Fla. |
| Myrow, John | .251 | 122 | 406 | 46 | 102 | 11 | 3 | 4 | 36 | 30 | 61 | 11 | 3 | R | R | 6-0 | 177 | 2-11-72 | 1993 | Pacific Palisades, Calif. |
| Scalzitti, Will | .231 | 7 | 26 | 1 | 6 | 2 | 0 | 0 | 1 | 0 | 3 | 0 | 0 | R | R | 6-0 | 190 | 8-29-72 | 1992 | Hollywood, Fla. |
| Sexton, Chris | .216 | 127 | 444 | 50 | 96 | 12 | 2 | 0 | 28 | 71 | 68 | 8 | 5 | R | R | 5-11 | 180 | 8-3-71 | 1993 | Cincinnati, Ohio |
| Taylor, Jamie | .243 | 124 | 362 | 46 | 88 | 20 | 1 | 8 | 37 | 45 | 74 | 1 | 2 | L | R | 6-2 | 220 | 10-10-70 | 1992 | Bloomingdale, Ohio |
| Velazquez, Edgard | .290 | 132 | 486 | 72 | 141 | 29 | 4 | 19 | 62 | 53 | 114 | 6 | 2 | R | R | 6-0 | 170 | 12-15-75 | 1993 | Guaynabo, P.R. |
| Wells, Forry | .230 | 108 | 304 | 44 | 70 | 19 | 1 | 7 | 43 | 46 | 73 | 1 | 2 | L | R | 6-4 | 205 | 3-21-71 | 1994 | Belleville, Ill. |
| Young, Eric | .067 | 3 | 15 | 0 | 1 | 0 | 0 | 0 | 0 | 0 | 3 | 0 | 0 | R | R | 5-9 | 017 | 5-18-67 | 1989 | New Brunswick, N.J. |

| PITCHING | W | L | ERA | G | GS | CG | SV | IP | H | R | ER | BB | SO | B | T | HT | WT | DOB | 1st Yr | Resides |
|---|---|---|---|---|---|---|---|---|---|---|---|---|---|---|---|---|---|---|---|---|
| Beckett, Robbie | 6 | 3 | 4.81 | 30 | 4 | 0 | 0 | 49 | 38 | 30 | 26 | 46 | 55 | R | L | 6-5 | 235 | 7-16-72 | 1990 | Austin, Texas |
| 2-team (3 Portland) | 7 | 3 | 5.11 | 33 | 7 | 0 | 0 | 62 | 55 | 39 | 35 | 59 | 62 | | | | | | | |
| Bost, Heath | 1 | 0 | 1.50 | 4 | 0 | 0 | 0 | 6 | 5 | 1 | 1 | 2 | 7 | R | R | 6-4 | 200 | 10-13-74 | 1995 | Taylorsville, N.C. |
| Brownson, Mark | 8 | 13 | 3.50 | 37 | 19 | 1 | 3 | 144 | 141 | 73 | 56 | 43 | 155 | R | R | 6-0 | 175 | 6-17-75 | 1994 | Wellington, Fla. |
| Cimorelli, Frank | 0 | 1 | 5.00 | 5 | 0 | 0 | 0 | 9 | 10 | 6 | 5 | 4 | 9 | R | R | 6-0 | 175 | 8-2-68 | 1989 | Hyde Park, N.Y. |
| Crowther, Brent | 3 | 7 | 6.20 | 25 | 12 | 0 | 1 | 86 | 109 | 64 | 59 | 30 | 54 | R | R | 6-4 | 220 | 5-15-72 | 1994 | North Vancouver, B.C. |
| DeJean, Mike | 0 | 0 | 3.22 | 16 | 0 | 0 | 11 | 22 | 20 | 9 | 8 | 8 | 12 | R | R | 6-2 | 205 | 9-28-70 | 1992 | Denham Springs, La. |
| Eden, Bill | 1 | 1 | 5.23 | 29 | 0 | 0 | 0 | 41 | 48 | 26 | 24 | 24 | 41 | L | L | 6-2 | 205 | 4-4-73 | 1994 | Franklin, Tenn. |
| Kusiewicz, Mike | 2 | 4 | 3.30 | 14 | 14 | 0 | 0 | 76 | 83 | 38 | 28 | 27 | 64 | R | L | 6-2 | 185 | 11-1-76 | 1995 | Nepean, Ontario |
| Macca, Chris | 3 | 1 | 1.30 | 28 | 0 | 0 | 15 | 35 | 18 | 6 | 5 | 18 | 34 | R | R | 6-4 | 185 | 11-14-74 | 1995 | Plant City, Fla. |
| Martin, Chandler | 1 | 0 | 7.20 | 1 | 1 | 0 | 0 | 5 | 6 | 4 | 4 | 3 | 4 | R | R | 6-1 | 180 | 10-23-73 | 1995 | Salem, Ore. |
| Million, Doug | 3 | 3 | 3.15 | 10 | 10 | 0 | 0 | 54 | 54 | 23 | 19 | 40 | 40 | L | L | 6-4 | 175 | 10-13-75 | 1994 | Sarasota, Fla. |
| Moore, Joel | 0 | 5 | 4.60 | 6 | 6 | 0 | 0 | 31 | 35 | 18 | 16 | 5 | 15 | L | R | 6-2 | 200 | 8-13-72 | 1993 | Elgin, Ill. |
| Neier, Chris | 1 | 7 | 4.98 | 55 | 0 | 0 | 2 | 81 | 99 | 63 | 45 | 44 | 54 | R | R | 6-4 | 205 | 11-19-71 | 1992 | Palo Alto, Calif. |
| Pedraza, Rodney | 7 | 3 | 2.95 | 19 | 18 | 3 | 0 | 122 | 115 | 49 | 40 | 21 | 74 | R | R | 6-2 | 210 | 12-28-69 | 1991 | Cuero, Texas |
| Pool, Matt | 0 | 1 | 2.70 | 4 | 0 | 0 | 0 | 7 | 9 | 2 | 2 | 1 | 7 | S | R | 6-6 | 190 | 7-8-73 | 1994 | Fresno, Calif. |
| Saipe, Mike | 10 | 7 | 3.07 | 32 | 19 | 1 | 3 | 138 | 114 | 53 | 47 | 42 | 126 | R | R | 6-1 | 190 | 9-10-73 | 1994 | San Diego, Calif. |
| Sobkoviak, Jeff | 0 | 1 | 5.40 | 4 | 0 | 0 | 0 | 7 | 5 | 4 | 4 | 5 | 4 | R | R | 6-7 | 225 | 8-22-71 | 1992 | Iroquois, Ill. |
| Thomson, John | 9 | 4 | 2.86 | 16 | 16 | 1 | 0 | 98 | 82 | 35 | 31 | 27 | 86 | R | R | 6-3 | 175 | 10-1-73 | 1993 | Sulphur, La. |
| Viano, Jacob | 4 | 3 | 4.84 | 23 | 5 | 0 | 0 | 45 | 39 | 28 | 24 | 24 | 32 | R | R | 5-11 | 180 | 9-4-73 | 1993 | Long Beach, Calif. |
| Voisard, Mark | 0 | 2 | 9.35 | 8 | 0 | 0 | 0 | 9 | 10 | 9 | 9 | 5 | 7 | R | R | 6-5 | 210 | 11-4-69 | 1992 | Sidney, Ohio |
| Wright, Jamey | 5 | 1 | 0.81 | 7 | 7 | 1 | 0 | 45 | 27 | 7 | 4 | 12 | 54 | R | R | 6-6 | 205 | 12-24-74 | 1993 | Moore, Okla. |
| Zolecki, Mike | 2 | 8 | 5.46 | 47 | 10 | 0 | 2 | 91 | 82 | 60 | 55 | 68 | 83 | R | R | 6-2 | 195 | 12-6-71 | 1993 | South Milwaukee, Wis. |

### FIELDING

| Catcher | PCT | G | PO | A | E | DP | PB |
|---|---|---|---|---|---|---|---|
| Gonzalez | .966 | 37 | 231 | 24 | 9 | 0 | 1 |
| Higgins | .987 | 21 | 140 | 13 | 2 | 0 | 2 |
| Miller | .991 | 82 | 611 | 69 | 6 | 8 | 6 |
| Scalzitti | .984 | 6 | 58 | 3 | 1 | 0 | 1 |

| First Base | PCT | G | PO | A | E | DP |
|---|---|---|---|---|---|---|
| Bernhardt | 1.000 | 2 | 14 | 1 | 0 | 1 |
| Grunewald | 1.000 | 13 | 102 | 7 | 0 | 9 |
| Helton | .994 | 92 | 788 | 61 | 5 | 58 |
| Holdren | .987 | 9 | 68 | 6 | 1 | 9 |
| Taylor | 1.000 | 1 | 2 | 0 | 0 | 0 |
| Wells | .980 | 27 | 218 | 22 | 5 | 28 |

| Second Base | PCT | G | PO | A | E | DP |
|---|---|---|---|---|---|---|
| Bernhardt | 1.000 | 5 | 4 | 8 | 0 | 2 |

| | PCT | G | PO | A | E | DP |
|---|---|---|---|---|---|---|
| Garcia | .985 | 72 | 148 | 182 | 5 | 42 |
| Goligoski | 1.000 | 10 | 10 | 21 | 0 | 8 |
| Grunewald | .966 | 20 | 37 | 49 | 3 | 10 |
| Jarrett | .966 | 47 | 77 | 96 | 6 | 17 |
| Young | 1.000 | 3 | 9 | 5 | 0 | 0 |

| Third Base | PCT | G | PO | A | E | DP |
|---|---|---|---|---|---|---|
| Bernhardt | .881 | 21 | 12 | 40 | 7 | 3 |
| Grunewald | .898 | 27 | 13 | 40 | 6 | 1 |
| Taylor | .934 | 110 | 79 | 258 | 24 | 30 |

| Shortstop | PCT | G | PO | A | E | DP |
|---|---|---|---|---|---|---|
| Goligoski | 1.000 | 10 | 10 | 23 | 0 | 1 |
| Grunewald | .935 | 19 | 20 | 38 | 4 | 6 |
| Jarrett | 1.000 | 7 | 6 | 16 | 0 | 4 |

| | PCT | G | PO | A | E | DP |
|---|---|---|---|---|---|---|
| Sexton | .954 | 116 | 178 | 294 | 23 | 58 |

| Outfield | PCT | G | PO | A | E | DP |
|---|---|---|---|---|---|---|
| Gibson | .932 | 117 | 168 | 10 | 13 | 0 |
| Giudice | .944 | 30 | 46 | 5 | 3 | 0 |
| Goligoski | 1.000 | 2 | 2 | 0 | 0 | 0 |
| Grunewald | 1.000 | 1 | 2 | 0 | 0 | 0 |
| Myrow | .939 | 107 | 159 | 10 | 11 | 2 |
| Sexton | 1.000 | 10 | 12 | 0 | 0 | 0 |
| Velazquez | .978 | 123 | 215 | 9 | 5 | 1 |
| Wells | .962 | 47 | 75 | 1 | 3 | 1 |

# SALEM

Class A

## CAROLINA LEAGUE

| BATTING | AVG | G | AB | R | H | 2B | 3B | HR | RBI | BB | SO | SB | CS | B | T | HT | WT | DOB | 1st Yr | Resides |
|---|---|---|---|---|---|---|---|---|---|---|---|---|---|---|---|---|---|---|---|---|
| Barthol, Blake | .285 | 109 | 375 | 58 | 107 | 17 | 2 | 13 | 67 | 36 | 48 | 12 | 5 | R | R | 6-0 | 200 | 4-7-73 | 1995 | Emmaus, Pa. |
| Bernhardt, Steve | .300 | 63 | 203 | 17 | 61 | 12 | 2 | 1 | 19 | 12 | 23 | 4 | 4 | R | R | 6-0 | 180 | 10-9-70 | 1995 | Timonium, Md. |
| Culp, Brian | .198 | 36 | 121 | 8 | 24 | 4 | 0 | 1 | 15 | 16 | 14 | 3 | 1 | R | R | 6-0 | 195 | 7-5-70 | 1993 | Overland Park, Kan. |
| Cunningham, Earl | .172 | 29 | 87 | 9 | 15 | 1 | 0 | 1 | 6 | 9 | 24 | 3 | 0 | R | R | 6-2 | 250 | 6-3-70 | 1989 | Lancaster, S.C. |
| Fantauzzi, John | .284 | 62 | 95 | 10 | 27 | 10 | 0 | 0 | 11 | 17 | 25 | 2 | 0 | L | L | 6-6 | 220 | 11-26-71 | 1992 | Lakeland, Fla. |
| Gambill, Chad | .296 | 115 | 406 | 61 | 120 | 22 | 2 | 7 | 41 | 33 | 83 | 6 | 6 | R | R | 6-2 | 190 | 11-27-74 | 1993 | Clearwater, Fla. |
| Giudice, John | .292 | 101 | 373 | 58 | 109 | 30 | 1 | 16 | 67 | 45 | 66 | 10 | 8 | R | R | 6-1 | 205 | 6-19-71 | 1993 | New Britain, Conn. |
| Gordon, Gary | .371 | 10 | 35 | 5 | 13 | 3 | 0 | 0 | 1 | 3 | 6 | 2 | 1 | R | R | 5-10 | 190 | 12-13-76 | 1995 | Willingboro, N.J. |
| Grunewald, Keith | .243 | 10 | 37 | 1 | 9 | 1 | 0 | 0 | 4 | 2 | 12 | 0 | 3 | S | R | 6-1 | 185 | 10-15-71 | 1993 | Marietta, Ga. |
| Hall, Ronnie | .151 | 14 | 53 | 7 | 8 | 2 | 0 | 0 | 2 | 4 | 8 | 1 | 1 | R | R | 6-4 | 195 | 10-14-75 | 1993 | Tustin, Calif. |
| Hamlin, Mark | .143 | 9 | 28 | 1 | 4 | 0 | 0 | 1 | 2 | 4 | 3 | 0 | 0 | R | R | 6-3 | 220 | 2-9-74 | 1996 | Augusta, Ga. |
| Higgins, Mike | .237 | 66 | 219 | 24 | 52 | 11 | 0 | 5 | 18 | 24 | 50 | 1 | 4 | R | R | 6-0 | 205 | 6-3-71 | 1993 | Nutley, N.J. |
| Holdren, Nate | .277 | 114 | 426 | 53 | 118 | 24 | 1 | 16 | 64 | 29 | 109 | 15 | 5 | R | R | 6-4 | 240 | 12-8-71 | 1993 | Richland, Wash. |
| Houser, Kyle | .239 | 117 | 436 | 59 | 104 | 12 | 3 | 1 | 48 | 68 | 47 | 13 | 9 | R | R | 6-0 | 150 | 1-21-75 | 1993 | Dallas, Texas |
| Jarrett, Link | .224 | 38 | 98 | 9 | 22 | 3 | 1 | 0 | 8 | 8 | 14 | 1 | 2 | S | R | 5-10 | 165 | 1-26-72 | 1994 | Tallahassee, Fla. |
| Jones, Pookie | .281 | 102 | 335 | 45 | 94 | 18 | 1 | 6 | 40 | 29 | 76 | 16 | 6 | R | R | 6-1 | 190 | 7-13-71 | 1994 | Killen, Ala. |
| Light, Tal | .235 | 64 | 234 | 29 | 55 | 10 | 0 | 13 | 36 | 19 | 59 | 3 | 1 | R | R | 6-3 | 205 | 11-28-73 | 1995 | Lumberton, Texas |
| Mayber, Chan | .208 | 97 | 264 | 35 | 55 | 5 | 0 | 1 | 20 | 27 | 50 | 22 | 9 | R | R | 5-11 | 160 | 10-7-72 | 1994 | Pueblo, Colo. |
| Neubart, Garrett | .365 | 24 | 85 | 16 | 31 | 2 | 2 | 0 | 6 | 12 | 13 | 8 | 6 | R | R | 5-10 | 160 | 11-7-73 | 1995 | Livingston, N.J. |
| Pena, Elvis | .223 | 102 | 341 | 48 | 76 | 9 | 4 | 0 | 28 | 61 | 70 | 30 | 16 | S | R | 5-11 | 155 | 9-15-76 | 1994 | Santo Domingo, D.R. |
| Scalzitti, Will | .196 | 81 | 270 | 24 | 53 | 14 | 0 | 6 | 23 | 16 | 33 | 0 | 2 | R | R | 6-0 | 190 | 8-29-72 | 1992 | Hollywood, Fla. |
| Walker, Larry | .500 | 2 | 8 | 3 | 4 | 3 | 0 | 1 | 1 | 0 | 1 | 0 | 0 | L | R | 6-2 | 185 | 12-1-66 | 1985 | Maple Ridge, B.C. |
| Young, Eric | .300 | 3 | 10 | 2 | 3 | 3 | 0 | 0 | 3 | 1 | 2 | 0 | 0 | R | R | 5-9 | 017 | 5-18-67 | 1989 | New Brunswick, N.J. |

**GAMES BY POSITION: C**—Barthol 92, Higgins 47, Scalzitti 5. **1B**—Bernhardt 1, Fantauzzi 59, Holdren 94, Light 4, Scalzitti 23. **2B**—Grunewald 10, Jarrett 19, Mayber 15, Pena 97, Young 3. **3B**—Barthol 1, Bernhardt 61, Jarrett 7, Light 58, Mayber 28, Neubart 1, Pena 1, Scalzitti 1. **SS**—Houser 117, Jarrett 10, Mayber 18. **OF**—Culp 13, Cunningham 22, Gambill 114, Giudice 100, Gordon 10, Hall 5, Hamlin 5, Higgins 1, Jarrett 1, Jones 8, Mayber 38, Neubart 23, Pena 1, Scalzitti 20.

## PITCHING

| PITCHING | W | L | ERA | G | GS | CG | SV | IP | H | R | ER | BB | SO | B | T | HT | WT | DOB | 1st Yr | Resides |
|---|---|---|---|---|---|---|---|---|---|---|---|---|---|---|---|---|---|---|---|---|
| Barnes, Keith | 1 | 0 | 3.38 | 4 | 0 | 0 | 0 | 8 | 10 | 3 | 3 | 2 | 9 | L | L | 6-3 | 189 | 8-9-74 | 1992 | Hixson, Tenn. |
| Burke, John | 0 | 1 | 6.00 | 3 | 3 | 0 | 0 | 12 | 10 | 12 | 8 | 9 | 12 | S | R | 6-4 | 220 | 2-9-70 | 1992 | Highlands Ranch, Colo. |
| Colmenares, Luis | 4 | 5 | 5.23 | 32 | 0 | 0 | 12 | 33 | 28 | 21 | 19 | 22 | 45 | R | R | 5-11 | 189 | 11-25-76 | 1994 | Valencia, Venez. |
| Crowther, Brent | 3 | 3 | 4.03 | 8 | 8 | 1 | 0 | 51 | 52 | 23 | 23 | 14 | 28 | R | R | 6-4 | 220 | 5-15-72 | 1994 | North Vancouver, B.C. |
| Eden, Bill | 0 | 1 | 2.70 | 11 | 0 | 0 | 1 | 13 | 8 | 4 | 4 | 7 | 15 | L | L | 6-2 | 205 | 4-4-73 | 1994 | Franklin, Tenn. |
| Garrett, Neil | 0 | 1 | 5.14 | 1 | 1 | 0 | 0 | 7 | 8 | 4 | 4 | 2 | 8 | R | R | 6-1 | 170 | 7-4-74 | 1992 | Joliet, Ill. |
| Genke, Todd | 8 | 7 | 3.53 | 41 | 1 | 0 | 3 | 87 | 88 | 41 | 34 | 28 | 55 | R | R | 6-1 | 190 | 4-8-71 | 1993 | Greenfield, Wis. |
| Hackman, Luther | 5 | 7 | 4.24 | 21 | 21 | 1 | 0 | 110 | 93 | 60 | 52 | 69 | 83 | R | R | 6-4 | 195 | 10-10-74 | 1994 | Columbus, Miss. |
| Kusiewicz, Mike | 0 | 1 | 5.09 | 5 | 3 | 0 | 1 | 23 | 19 | 15 | 13 | 12 | 18 | R | L | 6-2 | 185 | 11-1-76 | 1995 | Nepean, Ontario |
| LaRock, Scott | 3 | 2 | 3.65 | 39 | 1 | 0 | 1 | 81 | 72 | 38 | 33 | 31 | 57 | R | R | 6-1 | 195 | 9-17-72 | 1994 | Cheshire, Conn. |
| Lee, David | 0 | 2 | 2.25 | 8 | 0 | 0 | 1 | 12 | 14 | 6 | 3 | 6 | 10 | R | R | 6-2 | 200 | 3-12-73 | 1995 | Pittsburgh, Pa. |
| Martin, Chandler | 2 | 8 | 5.87 | 13 | 13 | 1 | 0 | 69 | 80 | 56 | 45 | 53 | 59 | R | R | 6-1 | 180 | 10-23-73 | 1995 | Salem, Ore. |
| McClinton, Patrick | 3 | 1 | 2.09 | 39 | 0 | 0 | 1 | 65 | 58 | 28 | 15 | 21 | 47 | L | L | 6-5 | 210 | 8-9-71 | 1993 | Louisville, Ky. |
| Million, Doug | 7 | 5 | 2.53 | 17 | 16 | 1 | 0 | 107 | 84 | 37 | 30 | 60 | 99 | L | L | 6-4 | 175 | 10-13-75 | 1994 | Sarasota, Fla. |
| Murphy, Sean | 0 | 1 | 5.68 | 3 | 0 | 0 | 1 | 6 | 9 | 5 | 4 | 1 | 4 | R | R | 6-1 | 180 | 12-7-72 | 1995 | Hays, Kan. |
| Nied, David | 3 | 3 | 2.95 | 7 | 6 | 1 | 0 | 43 | 37 | 25 | 14 | 18 | 42 | R | R | 6-2 | 185 | 12-22-68 | 1988 | Denver, Colo. |
| Pool, Matt | 5 | 6 | 4.64 | 27 | 21 | 0 | 0 | 136 | 158 | 80 | 70 | 41 | 93 | S | R | 6-6 | 190 | 7-8-73 | 1994 | Fresno, Calif. |
| Rose, Brian | 0 | 0 | 6.14 | 5 | 0 | 0 | 0 | 7 | 10 | 7 | 5 | 2 | 2 | R | R | 6-1 | 195 | 10-7-72 | 1994 | Potsdam, N.Y. |
| Sawyer, Zack | 0 | 1 | 13.50 | 4 | 0 | 0 | 1 | 2 | 6 | 3 | 3 | 1 | 2 | R | R | 6-4 | 215 | 3-19-73 | 1991 | Clinton, Mass. |
| Shoemaker, Steve | 2 | 7 | 4.69 | 25 | 13 | 0 | 1 | 86 | 63 | 49 | 45 | 63 | 105 | L | R | 6-1 | 195 | 2-3-73 | 1994 | Phoenixville, Pa. |
| Sobkoviak, Jeff | 6 | 6 | 3.14 | 46 | 1 | 0 | 9 | 77 | 67 | 31 | 27 | 26 | 52 | R | R | 6-7 | 225 | 8-22-71 | 1992 | Iroquois, Ill. |
| Swift, Bill | 0 | 0 | 4.50 | 2 | 2 | 0 | 0 | 6 | 9 | 4 | 3 | 1 | 4 | R | R | 6-0 | 191 | 10-27-61 | 1985 | South Portland, Maine |
| Vavrek, Mike | 10 | 8 | 4.87 | 26 | 25 | 2 | 0 | 150 | 167 | 92 | 81 | 59 | 103 | L | L | 6-2 | 185 | 4-23-74 | 1995 | Glendale Heights, Ill. |
| Walls, Doug | 0 | 0 | 7.07 | 5 | 3 | 0 | 1 | 14 | 17 | 12 | 11 | 10 | 17 | L | R | 6-3 | 200 | 3-21-74 | 1993 | Union, Ohio |

# ASHEVILLE                                    Class A
## SOUTH ATLANTIC LEAGUE

| BATTING | AVG | G | AB | R | H | 2B | 3B | HR | RBI | BB | SO | SB | CS | B | T | HT | WT | DOB | 1st Yr | Resides |
|---|---|---|---|---|---|---|---|---|---|---|---|---|---|---|---|---|---|---|---|---|
| Alamo, Efrain | .220 | 67 | 250 | 34 | 55 | 13 | 0 | 6 | 18 | 23 | 68 | 8 | 10 | R | R | 6-2 | 190 | 10-5-76 | 1994 | Canovanas, P.R. |
| Arias, Rogelio | .167 | 27 | 84 | 7 | 14 | 0 | 0 | 0 | 5 | 3 | 12 | 1 | 3 | S | R | 6-0 | 165 | 6-9-76 | 1993 | Santo Domingo, D.R. |
| Bryant, Clint | .246 | 68 | 228 | 33 | 56 | 9 | 2 | 5 | 30 | 36 | 45 | 10 | 10 | R | R | 6-0 | 180 | 8-29-73 | 1996 | Lubbock, Texas |
| Clifford, John | .215 | 94 | 317 | 29 | 68 | 14 | 1 | 1 | 27 | 25 | 69 | 19 | 8 | R | R | 6-1 | 185 | 8-18-73 | 1995 | Shrewsbury, Mass. |
| Cunningham, Earl | .256 | 35 | 133 | 19 | 34 | 11 | 0 | 9 | 30 | 7 | 42 | 5 | 1 | R | R | 6-2 | 250 | 6-3-70 | 1989 | Lancaster, S.C. |
| Drizos, Justin | .265 | 127 | 438 | 64 | 116 | 29 | 2 | 18 | 76 | 70 | 126 | 7 | 3 | L | L | 6-2 | 200 | 12-8-73 | 1995 | Irvine, Calif. |
| Duverge, Salvador | .198 | 103 | 349 | 38 | 69 | 12 | 1 | 3 | 31 | 32 | 84 | 8 | 12 | R | R | 6-0 | 165 | 5-14-76 | 1994 | San Cristobal, D.R. |
| Elam, Brett | .243 | 122 | 412 | 49 | 100 | 12 | 2 | 5 | 37 | 49 | 100 | 5 | 5 | R | R | 6-0 | 170 | 8-1-72 | 1995 | Council Bluffs, Iowa |
| Feuerstein, David | .286 | 130 | 514 | 84 | 147 | 27 | 7 | 1 | 69 | 42 | 68 | 21 | 10 | R | R | 6-2 | 200 | 7-19-73 | 1995 | Scarsdale, N.Y. |
| Groseclose, David | .244 | 84 | 250 | 40 | 61 | 9 | 0 | 0 | 31 | 43 | 55 | 13 | 12 | R | R | 5-11 | 165 | 10-4-72 | 1995 | Covington, Va. |
| Hallead, John | .162 | 38 | 136 | 17 | 22 | 4 | 1 | 0 | 9 | 17 | 39 | 5 | 4 | L | L | 5-10 | 180 | 2-4-76 | 1994 | Ellensburg, Wash. |
| Light, Tal | .327 | 52 | 205 | 34 | 67 | 15 | 0 | 12 | 51 | 21 | 58 | 8 | 4 | R | R | 6-3 | 205 | 11-28-73 | 1995 | Lumberton, Texas |
| Neubart, Garrett | .280 | 71 | 282 | 60 | 79 | 11 | 3 | 0 | 22 | 31 | 45 | 34 | 5 | R | R | 5-10 | 160 | 11-7-73 | 1995 | Livingston, N.J. |
| Petrick, Ben | .235 | 122 | 446 | 74 | 105 | 24 | 2 | 14 | 52 | 75 | 98 | 19 | 9 | R | R | 6-0 | 195 | 4-7-77 | 1996 | Hillsboro, Ore. |
| Pozo, Yohel | .141 | 27 | 85 | 5 | 12 | 1 | 0 | 0 | 4 | 5 | 20 | 0 | 1 | R | R | 6-2 | 188 | 10-17-73 | 1992 | Maracaibo, Venez. |
| Whitley, Matt | .255 | 104 | 368 | 40 | 94 | 12 | 1 | 0 | 33 | 44 | 38 | 10 | 14 | R | R | 6-0 | 170 | 3-29-72 | 1995 | Dunwoody, Ga. |

**GAMES BY POSITION: C**—Arias 25, Clifford 10, Petrick 94, Pozo 14. **1B**—Clifford 19, Drizos 125. **2B**—Groseclose 71, Whitley 69. **3B**—Arias 1, Bryant 67, Clifford 2, Elam 23, Light 50. **SS**—Bryant 1, Elam 103, Whitley 37. **OF**—Alamo 62, Clifford 31, Cunningham 3, Duverge 96, Feuerstein 128, Hallead 34, Neubart 66.

| PITCHING | W | L | ERA | G | GS | CG | SV | IP | H | R | ER | BB | SO | B | T | HT | WT | DOB | 1st Yr | Resides |
|---|---|---|---|---|---|---|---|---|---|---|---|---|---|---|---|---|---|---|---|---|
| Barnes, Keith | 4 | 5 | 2.96 | 17 | 16 | 1 | 0 | 97 | 83 | 43 | 32 | 31 | 76 | L | L | 6-3 | 189 | 8-9-74 | 1992 | Hixson, Tenn. |
| Bevel, Bobby | 4 | 2 | 3.18 | 41 | 0 | 0 | 0 | 68 | 61 | 25 | 24 | 30 | 60 | L | L | 5-10 | 180 | 10-10-73 | 1995 | West Plains, Md. |
| Bost, Heath | 5 | 2 | 1.30 | 41 | 0 | 0 | 15 | 76 | 45 | 13 | 11 | 19 | 102 | R | R | 6-4 | 200 | 10-13-74 | 1995 | Taylorsville, N.C. |
| Colmenares, Luis | 2 | 6 | 4.43 | 12 | 12 | 1 | 0 | 65 | 58 | 36 | 32 | 25 | 56 | R | R | 5-11 | 189 | 11-25-76 | 1994 | Valencia, Venez. |
| D'Alessandro, Marc | 7 | 13 | 3.52 | 28 | 28 | 1 | 0 | 158 | 182 | 92 | 62 | 56 | 118 | L | L | 6-2 | 195 | 7-23-75 | 1994 | Ocean, N.J. |
| Dietrich, Jason | 1 | 0 | 1.46 | 7 | 0 | 0 | 1 | 12 | 7 | 2 | 2 | 6 | 21 | R | R | 5-11 | 190 | 11-15-72 | 1994 | Garden Grove, Calif. |
| Emiliano, Jamie | 1 | 1 | 9.53 | 6 | 0 | 0 | 1 | 6 | 7 | 6 | 6 | 2 | 7 | R | R | 5-10 | 210 | 8-2-74 | 1995 | Andrews, Texas |
| Garrett, Neil | 12 | 4 | 3.59 | 22 | 22 | 1 | 0 | 135 | 131 | 61 | 54 | 37 | 120 | R | R | 6-1 | 170 | 7-4-74 | 1992 | Joliet, Ill. |
| Gonzalez, Laril | 1 | 1 | 3.60 | 35 | 0 | 0 | 4 | 45 | 37 | 21 | 18 | 37 | 53 | R | R | 6-4 | 180 | 5-25-76 | 1994 | San Cristobal, D.R. |
| Kammerer, James | 4 | 2 | 3.14 | 9 | 8 | 0 | 0 | 43 | 36 | 18 | 15 | 18 | 44 | L | L | 6-3 | 205 | 7-21-73 | 1995 | Winona, Minn. |
| Keehn, Drew | 3 | 2 | 6.05 | 26 | 1 | 0 | 0 | 55 | 61 | 51 | 37 | 42 | 35 | R | R | 6-4 | 185 | 9-19-74 | 1994 | Chandler, Ariz. |
| Macca, Chris | 1 | 1 | 1.07 | 26 | 0 | 0 | 15 | 34 | 18 | 5 | 4 | 11 | 46 | R | R | 6-2 | 185 | 11-14-74 | 1995 | Plant City, Fla. |
| Martin, Chandler | 9 | 0 | 2.20 | 14 | 14 | 0 | 0 | 86 | 65 | 26 | 21 | 31 | 73 | R | R | 6-1 | 180 | 10-23-73 | 1995 | Salem, Ore. |
| Murphy, Sean | 9 | 4 | 2.71 | 35 | 6 | 0 | 2 | 83 | 58 | 35 | 25 | 43 | 80 | R | R | 6-1 | 180 | 12-7-72 | 1995 | Hays, Kan. |
| Randall, Scott | 14 | 4 | 2.74 | 24 | 24 | 1 | 0 | 154 | 121 | 53 | 47 | 50 | 136 | R | R | 6-3 | 178 | 10-29-75 | 1995 | Goleta, Calif. |
| Rose, Brian | 4 | 5 | 3.56 | 38 | 1 | 0 | 3 | 68 | 53 | 30 | 27 | 16 | 73 | R | R | 6-1 | 195 | 10-7-72 | 1994 | Potsdam, N.Y. |
| Schroeffel, Scott | 1 | 0 | 3.86 | 2 | 2 | 0 | 0 | 12 | 10 | 7 | 5 | 6 | 15 | S | R | 6-0 | 190 | 12-30-73 | 1996 | Wexford, Pa. |
| Stepka, Tom | 2 | 0 | 0.56 | 2 | 2 | 1 | 0 | 16 | 6 | 2 | 1 | 1 | 16 | R | R | 6-2 | 185 | 11-29-75 | 1996 | Williamsville, N.Y. |

# PORTLAND                                    Class A
## NORTHWEST LEAGUE

| BATTING | AVG | G | AB | R | H | 2B | 3B | HR | RBI | BB | SO | SB | CS | B | T | HT | WT | DOB | 1st Yr | Resides |
|---|---|---|---|---|---|---|---|---|---|---|---|---|---|---|---|---|---|---|---|---|
| Anderson, Blake | .231 | 39 | 134 | 24 | 31 | 5 | 2 | 3 | 16 | 26 | 27 | 1 | 1 | S | R | 6-0 | 195 | 9-22-73 | 1996 | Dallas, Texas |
| Anthony, Brian | .140 | 30 | 107 | 6 | 15 | 5 | 0 | 1 | 5 | 10 | 30 | 1 | 0 | L | R | 6-2 | 218 | 10-22-73 | 1996 | Walnut Creek, Calif. |
| Arias, Rogelio | .238 | 44 | 168 | 15 | 40 | 3 | 1 | 1 | 15 | 5 | 24 | 1 | 1 | S | R | 6-0 | 165 | 6-9-76 | 1993 | Santo Domingo, D.R. |
| Bair, Rod | .217 | 56 | 221 | 34 | 48 | 11 | 2 | 4 | 33 | 17 | 29 | 9 | 4 | R | R | 5-11 | 190 | 10-29-74 | 1996 | Tempe, Ariz. |
| Cespedes, Angel | .188 | 27 | 80 | 8 | 15 | 1 | 1 | 1 | 3 | 10 | 28 | 1 | 1 | S | R | 5-11 | 168 | 10-25-77 | 1995 | Azua, D.R. |
| Clark, John | .204 | 58 | 211 | 17 | 43 | 8 | 3 | 2 | 19 | 12 | 62 | 0 | 2 | R | R | 6-4 | 195 | 10-17-76 | 1995 | Cibolo, Texas |
| Hallead, John | .243 | 52 | 181 | 22 | 44 | 9 | 0 | 1 | 21 | 15 | 42 | 6 | 1 | L | L | 5-10 | 180 | 2-4-76 | 1994 | Ellensburg, Wash. |
| Hamlin, Mark | .272 | 54 | 202 | 22 | 55 | 8 | 2 | 4 | 26 | 16 | 53 | 5 | 3 | R | R | 6-3 | 220 | 2-9-74 | 1996 | Augusta, Ga. |
| Hutchison, Bernard | .260 | 51 | 192 | 29 | 50 | 6 | 0 | 0 | 13 | 16 | 34 | 20 | 3 | R | R | 5-10 | 160 | 5-2-74 | 1996 | Tallassee, Ala. |
| Keck, Brian | .263 | 43 | 156 | 29 | 41 | 1 | 2 | 0 | 20 | 22 | 23 | 7 | 2 | R | R | 6-3 | 185 | 1-15-74 | 1996 | Dodge City, Kan. |
| Lindsey, John | .255 | 57 | 208 | 32 | 53 | 11 | 1 | 2 | 22 | 26 | 63 | 1 | 1 | R | R | 6-3 | 215 | 1-30-77 | 1995 | Hattiesburg, Miss. |

| BATTING | AVG | G | AB | R | H | 2B | 3B | HR | RBI | BB | SO | SB | CS | B | T | HT | WT | DOB | 1st Yr | Resides |
|---|---|---|---|---|---|---|---|---|---|---|---|---|---|---|---|---|---|---|---|---|
| Livingston, Doug | .299 | 57 | 224 | 36 | 67 | 18 | 4 | 5 | 34 | 23 | 45 | 6 | 0 | R | R | 5-8 | 160 | 4-9-74 | 1996 | Thonotosassa, Fla. |
| Marnell, Dean | .298 | 38 | 131 | 20 | 39 | 7 | 0 | 0 | 23 | 9 | 12 | 0 | 1 | R | R | 5-11 | 185 | 1-9-76 | 1996 | West Footscray, Australia |
| Myers, Aaron | .276 | 72 | 290 | 52 | 80 | 24 | 3 | 5 | 46 | 25 | 48 | 1 | 2 | R | R | 6-1 | 200 | 5-14-76 | 1994 | Santa Maria, Calif. |
| Vidal, Carlos | .226 | 32 | 106 | 16 | 24 | 8 | 1 | 1 | 11 | 18 | 20 | 0 | 1 | R | R | 5-10 | 188 | 4-21-75 | 1995 | Hialeah, Fla. |
| Zweifel, Kent | .471 | 4 | 17 | 5 | 8 | 3 | 1 | 0 | 4 | 0 | 4 | 0 | 0 | R | R | 6-3 | 210 | 3-21-77 | 1996 | Klamath Falls, Ore. |

**GAMES BY POSITION: C**—Anderson 24, Arias 38, Vidal 16. **1B**—Anderson 3, Anthony 23, Lindsey 50, Myers 1, Vidal 3. **2B**—Cespedes 23, Keck 9, Livingston 48. **3B**—Keck 6, Myers 70. **SS**—Clark 53, Keck 24. **OF**—Anthony 1, Bair 54, Hallead 49, Hamlin 50, Hutchison 44, Livingston 2, Marnell 34, Vidal 1, Zweifel 4.

| PITCHING | W | L | ERA | G | GS | CG | SV | IP | H | R | ER | BB | SO | B | T | HT | WT | DOB | 1st Yr | Resides |
|---|---|---|---|---|---|---|---|---|---|---|---|---|---|---|---|---|---|---|---|---|
| Brueggemann, Dean | 1 | 1 | 4.37 | 8 | 2 | 0 | 0 | 23 | 21 | 15 | 11 | 8 | 12 | L | L | 6-4 | 195 | 3-11-76 | 1996 | Smithton, Ill. |
| Brzozoski, Marc | 1 | 3 | 4.56 | 18 | 0 | 0 | 4 | 26 | 27 | 15 | 13 | 10 | 22 | R | R | 6-1 | 195 | 7-27-73 | 1995 | Calhoun, Ga. |
| Chacon, Shawn | 0 | 2 | 6.86 | 4 | 4 | 0 | 0 | 20 | 24 | 18 | 15 | 9 | 17 | R | R | 6-3 | 195 | 12-23-77 | 1996 | Greeley, Colo. |
| Christman, Tim | 1 | 2 | 4.28 | 21 | 0 | 0 | 2 | 40 | 30 | 23 | 19 | 23 | 56 | L | L | 6-2 | 180 | 3-31-75 | 1996 | Oneonta, N.Y. |
| Druckrey, Chris | 0 | 1 | 7.94 | 6 | 0 | 0 | 0 | 17 | 29 | 20 | 15 | 12 | 19 | R | R | 6-5 | 220 | 8-18-74 | 1995 | St. Anne, Ill. |
| Ford, Jason | 0 | 2 | 10.13 | 13 | 0 | 0 | 1 | 19 | 22 | 21 | 21 | 14 | 29 | L | L | 6-0 | 175 | 3-9-74 | 1996 | Richland, Wash. |
| Hinchy, Brian | 0 | 3 | 7.36 | 9 | 0 | 0 | 0 | 11 | 13 | 16 | 9 | 9 | 5 | R | R | 6-3 | 250 | 7-8-75 | 1996 | Federal Way, Wash. |
| Lee, David | 5 | 1 | 0.78 | 17 | 0 | 0 | 7 | 23 | 13 | 3 | 2 | 16 | 24 | R | R | 6-2 | 200 | 3-12-73 | 1995 | Pittsburgh, Pa. |
| Mahlberg, John | 2 | 7 | 5.43 | 17 | 10 | 0 | 1 | 56 | 67 | 43 | 34 | 15 | 47 | R | R | 6-2 | 197 | 10-21-76 | 1995 | Coquille, Ore. |
| Matcuk, Steven | 5 | 3 | 4.29 | 10 | 10 | 0 | 0 | 57 | 52 | 31 | 27 | 15 | 49 | R | R | 6-2 | 185 | 4-8-76 | 1996 | Pasadena, Md. |
| Nicholson, John | 0 | 1 | 4.20 | 3 | 3 | 0 | 0 | 15 | 12 | 8 | 7 | 10 | 11 | S | R | 6-4 | 205 | 12-6-77 | 1996 | Houston, Texas |
| Romine, Jason | 4 | 1 | 2.73 | 16 | 5 | 0 | 2 | 59 | 48 | 18 | 18 | 20 | 53 | R | R | 6-5 | 215 | 4-11-75 | 1995 | Omak, Wash. |
| Rosa, Cristy | 0 | 1 | 6.75 | 3 | 3 | 0 | 0 | 9 | 14 | 10 | 7 | 3 | 5 | R | R | 6-1 | 165 | 10-5-77 | 1995 | Guanica, P.R. |
| Schmidt, Donnie | 2 | 2 | 3.36 | 19 | 5 | 0 | 0 | 59 | 53 | 31 | 22 | 20 | 51 | R | R | 6-1 | 175 | 2-18-75 | 1996 | Sherwood, Ore. |
| Schroeffel, Scott | 1 | 1 | 1.66 | 16 | 6 | 0 | 1 | 60 | 36 | 15 | 11 | 17 | 61 | S | R | 6-0 | 190 | 12-30-73 | 1996 | Wexford, Pa. |
| Sebring, Jeff | 5 | 5 | 3.79 | 16 | 12 | 0 | 0 | 76 | 78 | 38 | 32 | 28 | 49 | L | L | 6-2 | 185 | 11-6-74 | 1996 | Boone, Iowa |
| Stepka, Tom | 5 | 4 | 3.71 | 12 | 12 | 0 | 0 | 68 | 74 | 42 | 28 | 10 | 48 | R | R | 6-2 | 185 | 11-29-75 | 1996 | Williamsville, N.Y. |
| Thompson, Travis | 0 | 2 | 5.94 | 9 | 0 | 0 | 0 | 17 | 21 | 11 | 11 | 6 | 8 | R | R | 6-4 | 190 | 1-10-75 | 1996 | Milwaukee, Wis. |
| Westbrook, Jake | 1 | 1 | 2.55 | 4 | 4 | 0 | 0 | 25 | 22 | 8 | 7 | 5 | 19 | R | R | 6-3 | 180 | 9-29-77 | 1996 | Danielsville, Ga. |

## CHANDLER     Rookie
## ARIZONA LEAGUE

| BATTING | AVG | G | AB | R | H | 2B | 3B | HR | RBI | BB | SO | SB | CS | B | T | HT | WT | DOB | 1st Yr | Resides |
|---|---|---|---|---|---|---|---|---|---|---|---|---|---|---|---|---|---|---|---|---|
| Castro, Juan | .247 | 22 | 77 | 10 | 19 | 3 | 2 | 0 | 6 | 2 | 10 | 3 | 1 | R | R | 6-1 | 205 | 4-21-75 | 1996 | Turmero, Venez. |
| Gordon, Gary | .291 | 47 | 179 | 35 | 52 | 5 | 0 | 0 | 10 | 33 | 54 | 23 | 6 | R | R | 5-10 | 190 | 12-13-76 | 1995 | Willingboro, N.J. |
| Hudde, Alejandro | .215 | 26 | 93 | 9 | 20 | 3 | 2 | 0 | 8 | 2 | 25 | 4 | 0 | R | R | 6-0 | 195 | 6-20-75 | 1994 | Caracas, Venez. |
| Kirkpatrick, Brian | .156 | 11 | 32 | 2 | 5 | 1 | 0 | 0 | 2 | 1 | 7 | 0 | 1 | R | R | 6-3 | 185 | 9-7-76 | 1995 | King City, Calif. |
| Landaeta, Luis | .278 | 44 | 176 | 27 | 49 | 9 | 1 | 0 | 20 | 5 | 22 | 7 | 2 | L | L | 5-9 | 180 | 3-4-77 | 1996 | Valencia, Venez. |
| Mahoney, Ricardo | .256 | 23 | 82 | 12 | 21 | 5 | 0 | 0 | 12 | 8 | 20 | 1 | 1 | R | R | 6-1 | 180 | 10-13-78 | 1996 | Panama City, Panama |
| Mitchell, Andres | .177 | 51 | 175 | 23 | 31 | 1 | 1 | 0 | 13 | 23 | 54 | 17 | 7 | R | R | 6-1 | 185 | 5-26-76 | 1996 | Brentwood, Tenn. |
| Petersen, Mike | .322 | 52 | 205 | 26 | 66 | 12 | 2 | 1 | 25 | 11 | 25 | 3 | 2 | R | R | 6-4 | 190 | 10-15-76 | 1996 | Missouri City, Texas |
| Rodriguez, Chris | .173 | 31 | 98 | 13 | 17 | 4 | 0 | 0 | 6 | 11 | 16 | 1 | 1 | R | R | 6-2 | 190 | 5-10-76 | 1996 | Modesto, Calif. |
| Rosario, Carlos | .286 | 50 | 199 | 27 | 57 | 7 | 5 | 2 | 34 | 12 | 42 | 9 | 7 | S | R | 6-0 | 180 | 5-10-77 | 1996 | Santo Domingo, D.R. |
| Schwartzbauer, Brad | .344 | 43 | 154 | 20 | 53 | 9 | 2 | 1 | 18 | 19 | 30 | 4 | 3 | L | R | 6-1 | 195 | 5-4-77 | 1996 | White Bear Lake, Minn. |
| Selga, Andres | .170 | 30 | 100 | 13 | 17 | 5 | 0 | 0 | 5 | 2 | 32 | 0 | 1 | R | R | 6-2 | 173 | 7-29-75 | 1995 | Valencia, Venez. |
| Torres, Wolf | .230 | 49 | 187 | 29 | 43 | 5 | 1 | 0 | 22 | 22 | 46 | 4 | 2 | S | R | 5-9 | 190 | 5-28-77 | 1996 | Turmero, Venez. |
| Zweifel, Kent | .230 | 40 | 148 | 13 | 34 | 5 | 4 | 2 | 19 | 13 | 54 | 1 | 1 | R | R | 6-3 | 210 | 3-21-77 | 1996 | Klamath Falls, Ore. |

**GAMES BY POSITION: C**—Castro 21, Mahoney 8, Rodriguez 31. **1B**—Petersen 46, Schwartzbauer 3, Zewifel 12. **2B**—Hudde 13, Torres 44. **3B**—Hudde 13, Kirkpatrick 8, Petersen 2, Schwartzbauer 34. **SS**—Mitchell 51, Petersen 1, Torres 4. **OF**—Gordon 46, Landaeta 40, Rosario 47, Selga 28, Zweifel 10.

| PITCHING | W | L | ERA | G | GS | CG | SV | IP | H | R | ER | BB | SO | B | T | HT | WT | DOB | 1st Yr | Resides |
|---|---|---|---|---|---|---|---|---|---|---|---|---|---|---|---|---|---|---|---|---|
| Barboza, Carlos | 1 | 2 | 3.00 | 18 | 0 | 0 | 1 | 30 | 34 | 18 | 10 | 12 | 18 | R | R | 6-1 | 170 | 2-21-78 | 1996 | Maracaibo, Venez. |
| Bruegge mann, Dean | 1 | 2 | 3.63 | 3 | 3 | 0 | 0 | 22 | 22 | 10 | 9 | 3 | 11 | L | L | 6-4 | 195 | 3-11-76 | 1996 | Smithton, Ill. |
| Chacon, Shawn | 1 | 2 | 1.60 | 11 | 11 | 1 | 0 | 56 | 46 | 17 | 10 | 15 | 64 | R | R | 6-3 | 195 | 12-23-77 | 1996 | Greeley, Colo. |
| Contreras, Orlando | 3 | 4 | 4.55 | 16 | 0 | 0 | 1 | 30 | 28 | 21 | 15 | 15 | 26 | R | R | 6-1 | 162 | 9-17-76 | 1995 | Maracaibo, Venez. |
| Douglas, Reggie | 0 | 0 | 12.86 | 12 | 0 | 0 | 0 | 14 | 23 | 20 | 20 | 16 | 13 | R | R | 6-5 | 220 | 2-2-77 | 1995 | Los Angeles, Calif. |
| Hinchy, Brian | | 1 | 3.00 | 14 | 0 | 0 | 4 | 15 | 15 | 8 | 5 | 5 | 7 | R | R | 6-3 | 250 | 7-8-75 | 1996 | Federal Way, Wash. |
| Kennedy, Ryan | 0 | 4 | 5.57 | 18 | 3 | 0 | 3 | 32 | 40 | 27 | 20 | 18 | 41 | R | R | 6-4 | 215 | 10-29-75 | 1996 | Shubuta, Miss. |
| Martino, Wil | 1 | 3 | 4.38 | 17 | 0 | 0 | 4 | 25 | 26 | 21 | 12 | 8 | 29 | L | L | 6-4 | 188 | 12-6-77 | 1995 | Santo Domingo, D.R. |
| Moore, Joel | 1 | 0 | 1.00 | 4 | 4 | 0 | 0 | 18 | 13 | 2 | 2 | 0 | 19 | L | R | 6-2 | 200 | 8-13-72 | 1993 | Elgin, Ill. |
| Nicholson, John | 3 | 5 | 1.64 | 11 | 11 | 1 | 0 | 66 | 42 | 16 | 12 | 14 | 65 | S | R | 6-4 | 205 | 12-6-77 | 1996 | Houston, Texas |
| Rivera, Alvin | 4 | 2 | 3.28 | 11 | 7 | 0 | 1 | 49 | 48 | 22 | 18 | 12 | 44 | R | R | 6-2 | 195 | 8-30-78 | 1996 | Yabucoa, P.R. |
| Rodriguez, Humberto | 1 | 2 | 6.75 | 17 | 0 | 0 | 0 | 21 | 30 | 23 | 16 | 12 | 18 | R | R | 6-2 | 250 | 3-13-78 | 1996 | Municipio Vargas, Venez. |
| Rosa, Cristy | 1 | 0 | 5.82 | 6 | 3 | 0 | 0 | 17 | 22 | 11 | 11 | 4 | 12 | R | R | 6-1 | 165 | 10-5-77 | 1995 | Guanica, P.R. |
| Slamka, John | 0 | 0 | 0.00 | 1 | 0 | 0 | 0 | 1 | 0 | 0 | 0 | 2 | 3 | R | L | 6-3 | 190 | 4-2-74 | 1994 | Phoenix, Ariz. |
| Thompson, Travis | 4 | 1 | 3.30 | 9 | 3 | 0 | 0 | 30 | 34 | 12 | 11 | 5 | 25 | R | R | 6-4 | 190 | 1-10-75 | 1996 | Milwaukee, Wis. |
| Westbrook, Jake | 4 | 2 | 2.87 | 11 | 11 | 0 | 0 | 63 | 66 | 33 | 20 | 14 | 57 | R | R | 6-3 | 180 | 9-29-77 | 1996 | Danielsville, Ga. |

# DETROIT TIGERS

**Manager:** Buddy Bell.  **1996 Record:** 53-109, .327 (5th, AL East)

| BATTING | AVG | G | AB | R | H | 2B | 3B | HR | RBI | BB | SO | SB | CS | B | T | HT | WT | DOB | 1st Yr | Resides |
|---|---|---|---|---|---|---|---|---|---|---|---|---|---|---|---|---|---|---|---|---|
| Ausmus, Brad | .248 | 75 | 226 | 30 | 56 | 12 | 0 | 4 | 22 | 26 | 45 | 3 | 4 | R | R | 5-11 | 185 | 4-14-69 | 1988 | Cheshire, Conn. |
| Bartee, Kimera | .253 | 110 | 217 | 32 | 55 | 6 | 1 | 1 | 14 | 17 | 77 | 20 | 10 | S | R | 6-0 | 180 | 7-21-72 | 1993 | Omaha, Neb. |
| Bautista, Danny | .250 | 25 | 64 | 12 | 16 | 2 | 0 | 2 | 8 | 9 | 15 | 1 | 2 | R | R | 5-11 | 170 | 5-24-72 | 1989 | Santo Domingo, D.R. |
| Casanova, Raul | .188 | 25 | 85 | 6 | 16 | 1 | 0 | 4 | 9 | 6 | 18 | 0 | 0 | R | R | 6-0 | 192 | 8-24-72 | 1990 | Ponce, P.R. |
| Cedeno, Andujar | .196 | 52 | 179 | 19 | 35 | 4 | 2 | 7 | 20 | 4 | 37 | 2 | 1 | R | R | 6-1 | 168 | 8-21-69 | 1987 | La Romana, D.R. |
| Clark, Tony | .250 | 100 | 376 | 56 | 94 | 14 | 0 | 27 | 72 | 29 | 127 | 0 | 1 | S | R | 6-8 | 240 | 6-15-72 | 1990 | El Cajon, Calif. |
| Cruz, Fausto | .237 | 14 | 38 | 5 | 9 | 2 | 0 | 0 | 1 | 1 | 11 | 0 | 0 | R | R | 5-11 | 165 | 1-5-72 | 1990 | Villa Vasquez, D.R. |
| Curtis, Chad | .263 | 104 | 400 | 65 | 105 | 20 | 1 | 10 | 37 | 53 | 73 | 16 | 10 | R | R | 5-10 | 175 | 11-6-68 | 1989 | Middleville, Mich. |
| Easley, Damion | .343 | 21 | 67 | 10 | 23 | 1 | 0 | 2 | 10 | 4 | 13 | 3 | 1 | R | R | 5-11 | 155 | 11-11-69 | 1989 | Glendale, Ariz. |
|   2-team (28 Calif.) | .268 | 49 | 112 | 14 | 30 | 2 | 0 | 4 | 17 | 10 | 25 | 3 | 1 |  |  |  |  |  |  |  |
| Fielder, Cecil | .248 | 107 | 391 | 55 | 97 | 12 | 0 | 26 | 80 | 63 | 91 | 2 | 0 | R | R | 6-3 | 250 | 9-21-63 | 1982 | Grosse Point Farms, Mich. |
| Flaherty, John | .250 | 47 | 152 | 18 | 38 | 12 | 0 | 4 | 23 | 8 | 25 | 1 | 0 | R | R | 6-1 | 202 | 10-21-67 | 1988 | West Nyack, N.Y. |
| Fryman, Travis | .268 | 157 | 616 | 90 | 165 | 32 | 3 | 22 | 100 | 57 | 118 | 4 | 3 | R | R | 6-1 | 194 | 3-25-69 | 1987 | Cantonment, Fla. |
| Gomez, Chris | .242 | 48 | 128 | 21 | 31 | 5 | 0 | 1 | 16 | 18 | 20 | 1 | 1 | R | R | 6-1 | 183 | 6-16-71 | 1992 | Lakewood, Calif. |
| Hiatt, Phil | .190 | 7 | 21 | 3 | 4 | 0 | 1 | 0 | 1 | 2 | 11 | 0 | 0 | R | R | 6-3 | 200 | 5-1-69 | 1990 | Pensacola, Fla. |
| Higginson, Bob | .320 | 130 | 440 | 75 | 141 | 35 | 0 | 26 | 81 | 65 | 66 | 6 | 3 | L | R | 5-11 | 180 | 8-18-70 | 1992 | Philadelphia, Pa. |
| Hyers, Tim | .077 | 17 | 26 | 1 | 2 | 1 | 0 | 0 | 0 | 4 | 5 | 0 | 0 | L | L | 6-1 | 180 | 10-3-71 | 1990 | Covington, Ga. |
| Lewis, Mark | .270 | 145 | 545 | 69 | 147 | 30 | 3 | 11 | 55 | 42 | 109 | 6 | 1 | R | R | 6-1 | 190 | 11-30-69 | 1988 | Hamilton, Ohio |
| Nevin, Phil | .292 | 38 | 120 | 15 | 35 | 5 | 0 | 8 | 19 | 8 | 39 | 1 | 0 | R | R | 6-2 | 185 | 1-19-71 | 1992 | Placentia, Calif. |
| Nieves, Melvin | .246 | 120 | 431 | 71 | 106 | 23 | 4 | 24 | 60 | 44 | 158 | 1 | 2 | S | R | 6-2 | 186 | 12-28-71 | 1988 | Bayamon, P.R. |
| Parent, Mark | .240 | 38 | 104 | 13 | 25 | 6 | 0 | 7 | 17 | 3 | 27 | 0 | 0 | R | R | 6-5 | 225 | 9-16-61 | 1979 | San Diego, Calif. |
| Penn, Shannon | .071 | 6 | 14 | 0 | 1 | 0 | 0 | 0 | 1 | 0 | 3 | 0 | 0 | S | R | 5-10 | 163 | 9-11-69 | 1989 | Cincinnati, Ohio |
| Pride, Curtis | .300 | 95 | 267 | 52 | 80 | 17 | 5 | 10 | 31 | 31 | 63 | 11 | 6 | L | R | 5-11 | 195 | 12-17-68 | 1986 | Silver Spring, Md. |
| Sierra, Ruben | .222 | 46 | 158 | 22 | 35 | 9 | 1 | 1 | 20 | 20 | 25 | 3 | 1 | S | R | 6-1 | 200 | 10-6-65 | 1983 | Carolina, P.R. |
|   2-team (96 N.Y.) | .247 | 142 | 518 | 61 | 128 | 26 | 2 | 12 | 72 | 60 | 83 | 4 | 4 |  |  |  |  |  |  |  |
| Singleton, Duane | .161 | 18 | 56 | 5 | 9 | 1 | 0 | 0 | 3 | 4 | 15 | 0 | 2 | L | R | 6-1 | 170 | 8-6-72 | 1990 | Staten Island, N.Y. |
| Trammell, Alan | .233 | 66 | 193 | 16 | 45 | 2 | 0 | 1 | 16 | 10 | 27 | 6 | 0 | R | R | 6-0 | 185 | 2-21-58 | 1976 | Bloomfield Hills, Mich. |
| Williams, Eddie | .200 | 77 | 215 | 22 | 43 | 5 | 0 | 6 | 26 | 18 | 50 | 0 | 2 | R | R | 6-0 | 175 | 11-1-64 | 1983 | La Mesa, Calif. |

| PITCHING | W | L | ERA | G | GS | CG | SV | IP | H | R | ER | BB | SO | B | T | HT | WT | DOB | 1st Yr | Resides |
|---|---|---|---|---|---|---|---|---|---|---|---|---|---|---|---|---|---|---|---|---|
| Aldred, Scott | 0 | 4 | 9.35 | 11 | 8 | 0 | 0 | 43 | 60 | 52 | 45 | 26 | 36 | L | L | 6-4 | 195 | 6-12-68 | 1987 | Lakeland, Fla. |
| Christopher, Mike | 1 | 1 | 9.30 | 13 | 0 | 0 | 0 | 30 | 47 | 36 | 31 | 11 | 19 | R | R | 6-5 | 205 | 11-3-63 | 1985 | Petersburg, Va. |
| Cummings, John | 3 | 3 | 5.12 | 21 | 0 | 0 | 0 | 32 | 36 | 20 | 18 | 20 | 24 | L | L | 6-3 | 200 | 5-10-69 | 1990 | Laguna Niguel, Calif. |
| Eischen, Joey | 1 | 1 | 3.24 | 24 | 0 | 0 | 0 | 25 | 27 | 11 | 9 | 14 | 15 | L | L | 6-1 | 190 | 5-25-70 | 1989 | West Covina, Calif. |
| Farrell, John | 0 | 2 | 14.21 | 2 | 2 | 0 | 0 | 6 | 11 | 10 | 10 | 5 | 0 | R | R | 6-4 | 210 | 8-4-62 | 1984 | Westlake, Ohio |
| Gohr, Greg | 4 | 8 | 7.17 | 17 | 16 | 0 | 0 | 92 | 129 | 76 | 73 | 34 | 60 | R | R | 6-3 | 205 | 10-29-67 | 1989 | Campbell, Calif. |
| Keagle, Greg | 3 | 6 | 7.39 | 26 | 6 | 0 | 0 | 88 | 104 | 76 | 72 | 68 | 70 | R | R | 6-2 | 185 | 6-28-71 | 1993 | Horseheads, N.Y. |
| Lewis, Richie | 4 | 6 | 4.18 | 72 | 0 | 0 | 2 | 90 | 78 | 45 | 42 | 65 | 78 | R | R | 5-10 | 175 | 1-25-66 | 1987 | Losantville, Ind. |
| Lima, Jose | 5 | 6 | 5.70 | 39 | 4 | 0 | 3 | 73 | 87 | 48 | 46 | 22 | 59 | R | R | 6-2 | 170 | 9-30-72 | 1989 | Santiago, D.R. |
| Lira, Felipe | 6 | 14 | 5.22 | 32 | 32 | 3 | 0 | 195 | 204 | 123 | 113 | 66 | 113 | R | R | 6-0 | 170 | 4-26-72 | 1990 | Miranda, Venez. |
| Maxcy, Brian | 0 | 0 | 13.50 | 2 | 0 | 0 | 0 | 3 | 8 | 5 | 5 | 2 | 1 | R | R | 6-1 | 170 | 5-4-71 | 1992 | Amory, Miss. |
| McCurry, Jeff | 0 | 0 | 24.30 | 2 | 0 | 0 | 0 | 3 | 9 | 9 | 9 | 2 | 0 | R | R | 6-7 | 210 | 1-21-70 | 1991 | Houston, Texas |
| Miller, Trever | 0 | 4 | 9.18 | 5 | 4 | 0 | 0 | 17 | 28 | 17 | 17 | 9 | 8 | R | L | 6-3 | 175 | 5-29-73 | 1991 | Louisville, Ky. |
| Moehler, Brian | 0 | 1 | 4.35 | 2 | 2 | 0 | 0 | 10 | 11 | 10 | 5 | 8 | 2 | R | R | 6-3 | 195 | 12-31-71 | 1993 | Rockingham, N.C. |
| Myers, Mike | 1 | 5 | 5.01 | 83 | 0 | 0 | 6 | 65 | 70 | 41 | 36 | 34 | 69 | L | L | 6-3 | 197 | 6-26-69 | 1990 | Wheeling, Ill. |
| Nitkowski, C.J. | 2 | 3 | 8.08 | 11 | 8 | 0 | 0 | 46 | 62 | 44 | 41 | 38 | 36 | L | L | 6-2 | 185 | 3-9-73 | 1994 | Milford, Pa. |
| Olivares, Omar | 7 | 11 | 4.89 | 25 | 25 | 4 | 0 | 160 | 169 | 90 | 87 | 75 | 81 | R | R | 6-1 | 183 | 7-6-67 | 1987 | San German, P.R. |
| Olson, Gregg | 3 | 0 | 5.02 | 43 | 0 | 0 | 8 | 43 | 43 | 25 | 24 | 28 | 29 | R | R | 6-4 | 212 | 10-11-66 | 1988 | Reisterstown, Md. |
| Sager, A.J. | 4 | 5 | 5.01 | 22 | 9 | 0 | 0 | 79 | 91 | 46 | 44 | 29 | 52 | R | R | 6-4 | 220 | 3-3-65 | 1988 | Kirkersville, Ohio |
| Scanlan, Bob | 0 | 0 | 10.64 | 8 | 0 | 0 | 0 | 11 | 16 | 15 | 13 | 9 | 3 | R | R | 6-8 | 215 | 8-9-66 | 1984 | Beverly Hills, Calif. |
| Sodowsky, Clint | 1 | 3 | 11.84 | 7 | 7 | 0 | 0 | 24 | 40 | 34 | 32 | 20 | 9 | L | R | 6-3 | 180 | 7-13-72 | 1991 | Ponca City, Okla. |
| Thompson, Justin | 1 | 6 | 4.58 | 11 | 11 | 0 | 0 | 59 | 62 | 35 | 30 | 31 | 44 | L | L | 6-3 | 175 | 3-8-73 | 1991 | Spring, Texas |
| Urbani, Tom | 2 | 2 | 8.37 | 16 | 2 | 0 | 0 | 24 | 31 | 22 | 22 | 14 | 20 | L | L | 6-1 | 190 | 1-21-68 | 1990 | Santa Cruz, Calif. |
| Van Poppel, Todd | 2 | 4 | 11.39 | 9 | 9 | 1 | 0 | 36 | 53 | 51 | 46 | 29 | 16 | R | R | 6-5 | 210 | 12-9-71 | 1990 | Arlington, Texas |
|   2-team (28 Oakland) | 3 | 9 | 9.06 | 37 | 15 | 1 | 1 | 99 | 139 | 107 | 100 | 62 | 53 |  |  |  |  |  |  |  |
| Veres, Randy | 0 | 4 | 8.31 | 25 | 0 | 0 | 0 | 30 | 38 | 29 | 28 | 14 | 14 | R | R | 6-3 | 187 | 11-25-65 | 1985 | Rancho Cordova, Calif. |
| Walker, Mike | 0 | 0 | 8.46 | 20 | 0 | 0 | 1 | 28 | 40 | 26 | 26 | 17 | 13 | R | R | 6-1 | 195 | 10-4-66 | 1986 | Brooksville, Fla. |
| Williams, Brian | 3 | 10 | 6.77 | 40 | 17 | 2 | 2 | 121 | 145 | 107 | 91 | 85 | 72 | R | R | 6-2 | 195 | 2-15-69 | 1990 | Cayce, S.C. |

## FIELDING

| Catcher | PCT | G | PO | A | E | DP | PB |
|---|---|---|---|---|---|---|---|
| Ausmus | .992 | 73 | 452 | 35 | 4 | 4 | 2 |
| Casanova | .978 | 22 | 123 | 12 | 3 | 0 | 3 |
| Flaherty | .981 | 46 | 243 | 13 | 5 | 1 | 1 |
| Nevin | 1.000 | 4 | 12 | 1 | 0 | 0 | 1 |
| Parent | .994 | 33 | 158 | 14 | 1 | 4 | 2 |

| First Base | PCT | G | PO | A | E | DP |
|---|---|---|---|---|---|---|
| Clark | .993 | 86 | 766 | 54 | 6 | 82 |
| Fielder | .989 | 71 | 589 | 59 | 7 | 51 |
| Hyers | 1.000 | 9 | 30 | 1 | 0 | 6 |
| Williams | 1.000 | 7 | 22 | 1 | 0 | 7 |

| Second Base | PCT | G | PO | A | E | DP |
|---|---|---|---|---|---|---|
| Cruz | .906 | 8 | 9 | 20 | 3 | 3 |
| Easley | .974 | 8 | 14 | 24 | 1 | 4 |
| Lewis | .987 | 144 | 264 | 414 | 9 | 94 |
| Trammell | .950 | 11 | 15 | 23 | 2 | 6 |

| Third Base | PCT | G | PO | A | E | DP |
|---|---|---|---|---|---|---|
| Cedeno | 1.000 | 1 | 0 | 2 | 0 | 0 |
| Easley | .857 | 2 | 2 | 4 | 1 | 2 |
| Fryman | .979 | 128 | 96 | 271 | 8 | 25 |
| Hiatt | 1.000 | 3 | 2 | 7 | 0 | 1 |
| Nevin | .943 | 24 | 17 | 49 | 4 | 6 |
| Trammell | 1.000 | 8 | 7 | 13 | 0 | 1 |
| Williams | 1.000 | 3 | 0 | 1 | 0 | 0 |

| Shortstop | PCT | G | PO | A | E | DP |
|---|---|---|---|---|---|---|
| Cedeno | .948 | 51 | 68 | 149 | 12 | 27 |
| Cruz | .824 | 4 | 4 | 10 | 3 | 2 |
| Easley | .962 | 8 | 6 | 19 | 1 | 6 |
| Fryman | .985 | 29 | 53 | 82 | 2 | 18 |
| Gomez | .970 | 47 | 77 | 114 | 6 | 34 |
| Trammell | .976 | 43 | 52 | 108 | 4 | 15 |

| Outfield | PCT | G | PO | A | E | DP |
|---|---|---|---|---|---|---|
| Bartee | .991 | 99 | 217 | 1 | 2 | 0 |
| Bautista | .974 | 22 | 38 | 0 | 1 | 0 |
| Curtis | .965 | 104 | 243 | 6 | 9 | 1 |
| Easley | 1.000 | 2 | 1 | 0 | 0 | 0 |
| Hiatt | 1.000 | 2 | 1 | 1 | 0 | 0 |
| Higginson | .963 | 123 | 227 | 9 | 9 | 1 |
| Hyers | 1.000 | 1 | 3 | 0 | 0 | 0 |
| Nevin | .944 | 9 | 16 | 1 | 1 | 0 |
| Nieves | .943 | 105 | 207 | 9 | 13 | 2 |
| Penn | .000 | 1 | 0 | 0 | 0 | 0 |
| Pride | .967 | 48 | 89 | 0 | 3 | 0 |
| Sierra | .914 | 23 | 52 | 1 | 5 | 1 |
| Singleton | 1.000 | 15 | 29 | 3 | 0 | 2 |
| Trammell | 1.000 | 1 | 1 | 0 | 0 | 0 |
| Williams | 1.000 | 2 | 3 | 0 | 0 | 0 |

**Third baseman Travis Fryman drove in 100 runs for the last-place Tigers**

RON VESELY

Tigers minor league Player of the Year Bubba Trammell

MEL BAILEY

# TIGERS

**Assistant General Manager:** Steve Lubratich

| Class | Farm Team | League | W | L | Pct. | Finish* | Manager(s) | First Yr |
|-------|-----------|--------|---|---|------|---------|-----------|----------|
| AAA | Toledo (Ohio) Mud Hens | International | 70 | 72 | .493 | T-5th (10) | Tom Runnells | 1987 |
| AA | Jacksonville (Fla.) Suns | Southern | 75 | 63 | .543 | +3rd (10) | Plummer/Parrish | 1995 |
| #A | Visalia (Calif.) Oaks@ | California | 50 | 90 | .357 | 9th (10) | Tim Torricelli | 1996 |
| #A | Lakeland (Fla.) Tigers | Florida State | 61 | 77 | .442 | 13th (14) | Dave Anderson | 1960 |
| A | Fayetteville (N.C.) Generals | South Atlantic | 76 | 63 | .547 | 5th (14) | Dwight Lowry | 1987 |
| A | Jamestown (N.Y.) Jammers | New York-Penn | 39 | 36 | .520 | 7th (14) | Bruce Fields | 1994 |
| R | Lakeland (Fla.) Tigers | Gulf Coast | 26 | 34 | .433 | 12th (16) | Kevin Bradshaw | 1995 |

*Finish in overall standings (No. of teams)  #Advanced level  +Won championship  @Shared club with Diamondbacks

### MAJOR LEAGUERS

**BATTING**
*AVG Bob Higginson ....... .320
R Travis Fryman........... 90
H Travis Fryman......... 165
TB Travis Fryman......... 269
2B Bob Higginson ........ 35
3B Curtis Pride ................ 5
HR Tony Clark .............. 27
RBI Travis Fryman .......... 100
BB Bob Higginson .......... 65
SO Melvin Nieves ........ 158
SB Kimera Bartee.......... 20

**PITCHING**
W Omar Olivares............ 7
L Felipe Lira ............... 14
#ERA Richie Lewis.......... 4.18
G Mike Myers ............. 83
CG Omar Olivares........... 4
SV Gregg Olson ............. 8
IP Felipe Lira.............. 195
BB Brian Williams........... 85
SO Felipe Lira.............. 113

**Bob Higginson.** .320 average

MORRIS FOSTOFF

### MINOR LEAGUERS

**BATTING**
*AVG Bubba Trammell, Jacksonville/Toledo.. .316
R Dave Roberts, Visalia/Jacksonville ....... 112
H Gabe Kapler, Fayetteville ...................... 157
TB Phil Hiatt, Toledo .................................. 304
2B Gabe Kapler, Fayetteville ...................... 45
3B Lonny Landry, Lakeland/Visalia ............... 9
HR Phil Hiatt, Toledo .................................. 42
RBI Phil Hiatt, Toledo .................................. 119
BB Dave Roberts, Visalia/Jacksonville ......... 99
SO Keith Kimsey, Visalia/Jacksonville ........ 190
SB Dave Roberts, Visalia/Jacksonville ......... 65

**PITCHING**
W Brian Moehler, Jacksonville..................... 15
L Brian Powell, Lakeland ........................... 13
#ERA Bryan Corey, Fayetteville ....................1.21
G Two tied at.............................................. 60
CG Two tied at.............................................. 5
SV Bryan Corey, Fayetteville ........................ 34
IP Dave Borkowski, Fayetteville ............... 178
BB John Kelly, Visalia/Jacksonville.............. 98
SO Clay Bruner, Fayetteville ...................... 152

*Minimum 250 At-Bats  #Minimum 75 Innings

How the Tigers Top 10 prospects, as judged by Baseball America prior to the 1996 season, fared in 1996:

**Mike Drumright**

| Player, Pos. | Club (Class—League) | AVG | AB | R | H | 2B | 3B | HR | RBI | SB |
|--------------|---------------------|-----|----|---|---|----|----|----|----|----|
| 3. Tony Clark, 1b | Toledo (AAA—International) | .299 | 194 | 42 | 58 | 7 | 1 | 14 | 36 | 1 |
| | Detroit | .250 | 376 | 56 | 94 | 14 | 0 | 27 | 72 | 0 |
| 5. Juan Encarnacion, of | Lakeland (A—Florida State) | .240 | 499 | 54 | 120 | 31 | 2 | 15 | 58 | 11 |
| 7. Mike Darr, of | Lakeland (A—Florida State) | .248 | 311 | 26 | 77 | 14 | 7 | 0 | 38 | 7 |
| 8. Luis Garcia, ss-2b | Jacksonville (AA—Southern) | .245 | 522 | 68 | 128 | 22 | 4 | 9 | 46 | 15 |

| Player, Pos. | Club (Class—League) | W | L | ERA | G | SV | IP | H | BB | SO |
|--------------|---------------------|---|---|-----|---|----|----|---|----|----|
| 1. Mike Drumright, rhp | Jacksonville (AA—Southern) | 6 | 4 | 3.97 | 18 | 0 | 100 | 80 | 48 | 109 |
| 2. Justin Thompson, lhp | Toledo (AAA—International) | 6 | 3 | 3.42 | 13 | 0 | 84 | 74 | 26 | 69 |
| | Detroit | 1 | 6 | 4.58 | 11 | 0 | 59 | 62 | 31 | 44 |
| | Fayetteville (A—South Atlantic) | 0 | 0 | 3.00 | 1 | 0 | 3 | 1 | 0 | 5 |
| 4. Cam Smith, rhp | Lakeland (A—Florida State) | 5 | 8 | 4.59 | 22 | 0 | 114 | 93 | 71 | 114 |
| 6. *Cade Gaspar, rhp | Rancho Cucamonga (A—California) | 7 | 4 | 5.05 | 24 | 0 | 112 | 121 | 50 | 106 |
| 9. Greg Whiteman, lhp | Lakeland (A—Florida State) | 11 | 10 | 3.71 | 27 | 0 | 150 | 134 | 89 | 122 |
| 10. Trever Miller, lhp | Toledo (AAA—International) | 13 | 6 | 4.90 | 27 | 0 | 165 | 167 | 65 | 115 |
| | Detroit | 0 | 4 | 9.18 | 5 | 0 | 17 | 28 | 9 | 8 |

*Traded to Padres

## INTERNATIONAL LEAGUE

| BATTING | AVG | G | AB | R | H | 2B | 3B | HR | RBI | BB | SO | SB | CS | B | T | HT | WT | DOB | 1st Yr | Resides |
|---|---|---|---|---|---|---|---|---|---|---|---|---|---|---|---|---|---|---|---|---|
| Baez, Kevin | .245 | 98 | 302 | 34 | 74 | 12 | 3 | 11 | 44 | 24 | 53 | 3 | 0 | R | R | 6-0 | 170 | 1-10-67 | 1988 | Brooklyn, N.Y. |
| Barker, Glen | .250 | 24 | 80 | 13 | 20 | 2 | 1 | 0 | 2 | 9 | 25 | 6 | 6 | R | R | 5-10 | 180 | 5-10-71 | 1993 | Albany, N.Y. |
| Casanova, Raul | .273 | 49 | 161 | 23 | 44 | 11 | 0 | 8 | 28 | 20 | 24 | 0 | 1 | R | R | 6-0 | 192 | 8-24-72 | 1990 | Ponce, P.R. |
| Clark, Tony | .299 | 55 | 194 | 42 | 58 | 7 | 1 | 14 | 36 | 31 | 58 | 1 | 1 | S | R | 6-8 | 240 | 6-15-72 | 1990 | El Cajon, Calif. |
| Cotton, John | .187 | 50 | 171 | 14 | 32 | 7 | 1 | 4 | 19 | 7 | 64 | 4 | 4 | L | R | 6-0 | 170 | 10-30-70 | 1989 | Huntsville, Texas |
| Cruz, Fausto | .250 | 107 | 384 | 49 | 96 | 18 | 2 | 12 | 59 | 33 | 81 | 11 | 10 | R | R | 5-11 | 165 | 1-5-72 | 1990 | Villa Vasquez, D.R. |
| Franklin, Micah | .246 | 53 | 179 | 32 | 44 | 10 | 1 | 7 | 21 | 27 | 60 | 3 | 2 | S | R | 6-0 | 195 | 4-25-72 | 1990 | San Francisco, Calif. |
| Hansen, Terrel | .125 | 5 | 16 | 2 | 2 | 0 | 0 | 1 | 1 | 1 | 8 | 1 | 0 | R | R | 6-3 | 210 | 9-25-66 | 1987 | Bremerton, Wash. |
| Hiatt, Phil | .261 | 142 | 555 | 99 | 145 | 27 | 3 | 42 | 119 | 50 | 180 | 17 | 6 | R | R | 6-3 | 200 | 5-1-69 | 1990 | Pensacola, Fla. |
| Higginson, Bob | .308 | 3 | 13 | 4 | 4 | 0 | 1 | 0 | 1 | 3 | 0 | 0 | 0 | L | R | 5-11 | 180 | 8-18-70 | 1992 | Philadelphia, Pa. |
| Hyers, Tim | .259 | 117 | 437 | 55 | 113 | 17 | 6 | 7 | 59 | 40 | 57 | 7 | 1 | L | L | 6-1 | 180 | 10-3-71 | 1990 | Covington, Ga. |
| Kowitz, Brian | .191 | 24 | 68 | 9 | 13 | 5 | 0 | 0 | 3 | 9 | 12 | 2 | 2 | L | L | 5-10 | 175 | 8-7-69 | 1990 | Owings Mills, Md. |
| Mitchell, Tony | .278 | 82 | 288 | 45 | 80 | 10 | 4 | 12 | 43 | 41 | 89 | 3 | 2 | S | R | 6-4 | 225 | 10-14-70 | 1989 | Detroit, Mich. |
| Penn, Shannon | .287 | 97 | 356 | 65 | 102 | 12 | 4 | 6 | 42 | 26 | 59 | 22 | 11 | S | R | 5-10 | 163 | 9-11-69 | 1989 | Cincinnati, Ohio |
| Pride, Curtis | .231 | 9 | 26 | 4 | 6 | 1 | 0 | 1 | 2 | 9 | 7 | 4 | 1 | L | R | 5-11 | 195 | 12-17-68 | 1986 | Silver Spring, Md. |
| Rodriguez, Steve | .285 | 96 | 333 | 49 | 95 | 18 | 2 | 4 | 30 | 23 | 43 | 18 | 3 | R | R | 5-9 | 170 | 11-29-70 | 1992 | Las Vegas, Nev. |
| Singleton, Duane | .221 | 88 | 294 | 42 | 65 | 15 | 6 | 8 | 30 | 36 | 84 | 17 | 7 | L | R | 6-1 | 170 | 8-6-72 | 1990 | Staten Island, N.Y. |
| Tackett, Jeff | .237 | 89 | 283 | 41 | 67 | 10 | 3 | 7 | 49 | 36 | 54 | 4 | 2 | R | R | 6-2 | 206 | 12-1-65 | 1984 | Cockeysville, Md. |
| Trammell, Bubba | .294 | 51 | 180 | 32 | 53 | 14 | 1 | 6 | 24 | 22 | 44 | 5 | 1 | R | R | 6-2 | 205 | 11-6-71 | 1994 | Knoxville, Tenn. |
| Ward, Daryle | .174 | 6 | 23 | 1 | 4 | 0 | 0 | 0 | 1 | 0 | 3 | 0 | 0 | L | L | 6-2 | 230 | 6-27-75 | 1994 | Riverside, Calif. |
| Wedge, Eric | .235 | 96 | 332 | 61 | 78 | 25 | 0 | 15 | 57 | 43 | 81 | 2 | 2 | R | R | 6-3 | 215 | 1-27-68 | 1989 | Fort Wayne, Ind. |

| PITCHING | W | L | ERA | G | GS | CG | SV | IP | H | R | ER | BB | SO | B | T | HT | WT | DOB | 1st Yr | Resides |
|---|---|---|---|---|---|---|---|---|---|---|---|---|---|---|---|---|---|---|---|---|
| Barnes, Brian | 6 | 6 | 3.99 | 14 | 13 | 2 | 0 | 88 | 85 | 49 | 39 | 29 | 70 | L | L | 5-9 | 170 | 3-25-67 | 1989 | Smyrna, Ga. |
| Blomdahl, Ben | 2 | 6 | 6.22 | 53 | 0 | 0 | 2 | 59 | 77 | 42 | 41 | 18 | 34 | R | R | 6-2 | 185 | 12-30-70 | 1991 | Riverside, Calif. |
| Christopher, Mike | 4 | 1 | 3.92 | 39 | 0 | 0 | 22 | 39 | 50 | 21 | 17 | 5 | 40 | R | R | 6-5 | 205 | 11-3-63 | 1985 | Petersburg, Va. |
| Farrell, John | 2 | 4 | 8.10 | 6 | 6 | 1 | 0 | 30 | 38 | 29 | 27 | 9 | 21 | R | R | 6-4 | 210 | 8-4-62 | 1984 | Westlake, Ohio |
| Gallaher, Kevin | 0 | 0 | 21.00 | 2 | 0 | 0 | 0 | 3 | 9 | 7 | 7 | 4 | 4 | R | R | 6-3 | 190 | 8-1-68 | 1991 | Vienna, Va. |
| Gohr, Greg | 0 | 0 | 7.50 | 2 | 2 | 0 | 0 | 12 | 17 | 10 | 10 | 5 | 15 | R | R | 6-3 | 205 | 10-29-67 | 1989 | Campbell, Calif. |
| Guilfoyle, Mike | 5 | 5 | 5.14 | 54 | 0 | 0 | 1 | 49 | 59 | 35 | 28 | 31 | 42 | L | L | 5-11 | 187 | 4-29-68 | 1990 | Bayonne, N.J. |
| Henry, Dwayne | 1 | 0 | 7.23 | 18 | 0 | 0 | 1 | 19 | 21 | 19 | 15 | 12 | 23 | R | R | 6-3 | 205 | 2-16-62 | 1980 | Middleton, Del. |
| Keagle, Greg | 2 | 3 | 10.00 | 6 | 6 | 0 | 0 | 27 | 42 | 32 | 30 | 11 | 24 | R | R | 6-2 | 185 | 6-28-71 | 1993 | Horseheads, N.Y. |
| Lewis, Richie | 0 | 0 | 2.25 | 2 | 0 | 0 | 0 | 4 | 1 | 1 | 1 | 1 | 4 | R | R | 5-10 | 175 | 1-25-66 | 1987 | Losantville, Ind. |
| Lima, Jose | 5 | 4 | 6.78 | 12 | 12 | 0 | 0 | 69 | 93 | 53 | 52 | 12 | 57 | R | R | 6-2 | 170 | 9-30-72 | 1989 | Santiago, D.R. |
| Marshall, Randy | 3 | 5 | 4.15 | 29 | 11 | 0 | 0 | 95 | 97 | 49 | 44 | 25 | 60 | L | L | 6-3 | 170 | 10-12-66 | 1989 | Ypsilanti, Mich. |
| Maxcy, Brian | 3 | 1 | 3.97 | 15 | 0 | 0 | 0 | 23 | 24 | 11 | 10 | 9 | 8 | R | R | 6-1 | 170 | 5-4-71 | 1992 | Amory, Miss. |
| McCurry, Jeff | 1 | 4 | 4.76 | 39 | 0 | 0 | 2 | 59 | 66 | 37 | 31 | 26 | 56 | R | R | 6-7 | 210 | 1-21-70 | 1991 | Houston, Texas |
| Miller, Trever | 13 | 6 | 4.90 | 27 | 27 | 0 | 0 | 165 | 167 | 98 | 90 | 65 | 115 | R | L | 6-3 | 175 | 5-29-73 | 1991 | Louisville, Ky. |
| Nitkowski, C.J. | 4 | 6 | 4.46 | 19 | 19 | 1 | 0 | 111 | 104 | 60 | 55 | 53 | 103 | L | L | 6-2 | 185 | 3-9-73 | 1994 | Milford, Pa. |
| Olivares, Omar | 1 | 0 | 8.44 | 1 | 1 | 0 | 0 | 5 | 4 | 5 | 5 | 3 | 5 | R | R | 6-1 | 183 | 7-6-67 | 1987 | San German, P.R. |
| Sager, A.J. | 1 | 0 | 2.63 | 18 | 2 | 0 | 0 | 38 | 38 | 14 | 11 | 3 | 24 | R | R | 6-4 | 220 | 3-3-65 | 1988 | Kirkersville, Ohio |
| Scanlan, Bob | 1 | 3 | 7.50 | 14 | 5 | 0 | 0 | 36 | 46 | 35 | 30 | 15 | 18 | R | R | 6-8 | 215 | 8-9-66 | 1984 | Beverly Hills, Calif. |
| Sodowsky, Clint | 6 | 8 | 3.94 | 19 | 19 | 1 | 0 | 119 | 128 | 67 | 52 | 51 | 59 | L | R | 6-3 | 180 | 7-13-72 | 1991 | Ponca City, Okla. |
| Thompson, Justin | 6 | 3 | 3.42 | 13 | 13 | 3 | 0 | 84 | 74 | 36 | 32 | 26 | 69 | L | L | 6-3 | 175 | 3-8-73 | 1991 | Spring, Texas |
| Urbani, Tom | 0 | 3 | 6.43 | 4 | 0 | 0 | 0 | 14 | 18 | 15 | 10 | 7 | 10 | L | L | 6-1 | 190 | 1-21-68 | 1990 | Santa Cruz, Calif. |
| Walker, Mike | 3 | 2 | 3.83 | 28 | 0 | 0 | 6 | 45 | 37 | 23 | 19 | 27 | 37 | R | R | 6-1 | 195 | 10-4-66 | 1986 | Brooksville, Fla. |
| Williams, Brian | 1 | 2 | 5.49 | 3 | 3 | 1 | 0 | 20 | 22 | 13 | 12 | 9 | 21 | R | R | 6-2 | 195 | 2-15-69 | 1990 | Cayce, S.C. |

### FIELDING

| Catcher | PCT | G | PO | A | E | DP | PB |
|---|---|---|---|---|---|---|---|
| Casanova | .992 | 36 | 234 | 15 | 2 | 2 | 5 |
| Tackett | .993 | 86 | 561 | 35 | 4 | 7 | 7 |
| Wedge | 1.000 | 27 | 147 | 13 | 0 | 0 | 3 |

| First Base | PCT | G | PO | A | E | DP |
|---|---|---|---|---|---|---|
| Clark | .993 | 44 | 400 | 28 | 3 | 36 |
| Hyers | .996 | 88 | 786 | 68 | 3 | 85 |
| Tackett | .909 | 2 | 9 | 1 | 1 | 0 |
| Ward | .979 | 6 | 42 | 5 | 1 | 5 |
| Wedge | .970 | 5 | 62 | 2 | 2 | 5 |

| Second Base | PCT | G | PO | A | E | DP |
|---|---|---|---|---|---|---|
| Baez | .981 | 42 | 74 | 135 | 4 | 28 |
| Cotton | .917 | 8 | 9 | 13 | 2 | 3 |

| | PCT | G | PO | A | E | DP |
|---|---|---|---|---|---|---|
| Cruz | .974 | 7 | 17 | 21 | 1 | 7 |
| Penn | .931 | 5 | 14 | 13 | 2 | 2 |
| Rodriguez | .984 | 90 | 176 | 252 | 7 | 63 |

| Third Base | PCT | G | PO | A | E | DP |
|---|---|---|---|---|---|---|
| Baez | 1.000 | 2 | 1 | 3 | 0 | 0 |
| Cotton | .000 | 1 | 0 | 0 | 0 | 0 |
| Hiatt | .943 | 141 | 85 | 345 | 26 | 39 |

| Shortstop | PCT | G | PO | A | E | DP |
|---|---|---|---|---|---|---|
| Baez | .934 | 51 | 69 | 157 | 16 | 33 |
| Cotton | 1.000 | 1 | 1 | 0 | 0 | 0 |
| Cruz | .954 | 93 | 161 | 296 | 22 | 61 |

| Outfield | PCT | G | PO | A | E | DP |
|---|---|---|---|---|---|---|
| Barker | .982 | 22 | 51 | 3 | 1 | 0 |
| Cotton | .975 | 36 | 75 | 4 | 2 | 1 |
| Franklin | 1.000 | 52 | 93 | 2 | 0 | 1 |
| Hansen | 1.000 | 4 | 2 | 1 | 0 | 0 |
| Higginson | 1.000 | 3 | 3 | 0 | 0 | 0 |
| Hyers | .947 | 28 | 35 | 1 | 2 | 0 |
| Kowitz | .913 | 22 | 20 | 1 | 2 | 1 |
| Mitchell | .983 | 59 | 108 | 5 | 2 | 2 |
| Penn | .969 | 84 | 117 | 6 | 4 | 0 |
| Pride | 1.000 | 3 | 3 | 0 | 0 | 0 |
| Rodriguez | 1.000 | 1 | 2 | 0 | 0 | 0 |
| Singleton | .973 | 83 | 134 | 8 | 4 | 0 |
| Trammell | .987 | 47 | 72 | 5 | 1 | 1 |

## SOUTHERN LEAGUE

| BATTING | AVG | G | AB | R | H | 2B | 3B | HR | RBI | BB | SO | SB | CS | B | T | HT | WT | DOB | 1st Yr | Resides |
|---|---|---|---|---|---|---|---|---|---|---|---|---|---|---|---|---|---|---|---|---|
| Barker, Glen | .158 | 43 | 120 | 9 | 19 | 2 | 1 | 0 | 8 | 8 | 36 | 6 | 4 | R | R | 5-10 | 180 | 5-10-71 | 1993 | Albany, N.Y. |
| Bream, Scott | .241 | 36 | 108 | 18 | 26 | 3 | 1 | 3 | 12 | 10 | 31 | 2 | 1 | R | R | 6-0 | 185 | 11-4-70 | 1989 | Omaha, Neb. |
| Brock, Tarrik | .127 | 37 | 102 | 14 | 13 | 2 | 0 | 0 | 6 | 10 | 36 | 3 | 3 | L | L | 6-3 | 170 | 12-25-73 | 1991 | Hawthorne, Calif. |
| Casanova, Raul | .333 | 8 | 30 | 5 | 10 | 2 | 0 | 4 | 9 | 2 | 7 | 0 | 0 | R | R | 6-0 | 192 | 8-24-72 | 1990 | Ponce, P.R. |
| Catalanotto, Frank | .298 | 132 | 497 | 105 | 148 | 34 | 6 | 17 | 67 | 74 | 69 | 15 | 14 | L | R | 6-0 | 170 | 4-27-74 | 1992 | Smithtown, N.Y. |
| Cotton, John | .240 | 63 | 217 | 34 | 52 | 7 | 4 | 13 | 39 | 19 | 66 | 15 | 3 | L | R | 6-0 | 170 | 10-30-70 | 1989 | Huntsville, Texas |
| Dismuke, Jamie | .266 | 29 | 79 | 7 | 21 | 4 | 1 | 4 | 12 | 14 | 14 | 0 | 0 | L | R | 6-1 | 210 | 10-17-69 | 1989 | Syracuse, N.Y. |
| Freeman, Sean | .267 | 124 | 412 | 72 | 110 | 18 | 1 | 25 | 74 | 66 | 117 | 3 | 4 | L | L | 6-3 | 205 | 9-10-71 | 1994 | Andover, Ohio |
| Garcia, Luis | .245 | 131 | 522 | 68 | 128 | 22 | 4 | 9 | 46 | 12 | 90 | 15 | 12 | R | R | 6-0 | 174 | 5-20-75 | 1993 | San Fran. de Macoris, D.R. |
| Hansen, Terrel | .264 | 104 | 367 | 49 | 97 | 18 | 2 | 25 | 66 | 19 | 107 | 5 | 2 | R | R | 6-3 | 210 | 9-25-66 | 1987 | Bremerton, Wash. |
| Kimsey, Keith | .179 | 31 | 106 | 8 | 19 | 0 | 1 | 2 | 6 | 13 | 50 | 2 | 4 | R | R | 6-7 | 200 | 8-15-72 | 1991 | Lakeland, Fla. |
| Lidle, Kevin | .250 | 4 | 8 | 2 | 2 | 0 | 0 | 1 | 2 | 1 | 2 | 1 | 0 | R | R | 5-11 | 170 | 3-22-72 | 1992 | West Covina, Calif. |
| Makarewicz, Scott | .314 | 83 | 258 | 42 | 81 | 16 | 1 | 14 | 49 | 18 | 46 | 4 | 3 | R | R | 6-0 | 200 | 3-1-67 | 1989 | Grand Rapids, Mich. |
| Mashore, Justin | .285 | 120 | 453 | 67 | 129 | 27 | 8 | 7 | 50 | 33 | 97 | 17 | 13 | R | R | 5-9 | 190 | 2-14-72 | 1991 | Concord, Calif. |

| BATTING | AVG | G | AB | R | H | 2B | 3B | HR | RBI | BB | SO | SB | CS | B | T | HT | WT | DOB | 1st Yr | Resides |
|---|---|---|---|---|---|---|---|---|---|---|---|---|---|---|---|---|---|---|---|---|
| Mitchell, Tony | .312 | 51 | 173 | 30 | 54 | 13 | 0 | 11 | 41 | 21 | 45 | 1 | 0 | S | R | 6-4 | 225 | 10-14-70 | 1989 | Detroit, Mich. |
| Nevin, Phil | .294 | 98 | 344 | 77 | 101 | 18 | 1 | 24 | 69 | 60 | 83 | 6 | 2 | R | R | 6-2 | 185 | 1-19-71 | 1992 | Placentia, Calif. |
| Pough, Pork Chop | .500 | 2 | 4 | 1 | 2 | 0 | 0 | 0 | 0 | 0 | 2 | 0 | 0 | R | R | 6-0 | 173 | 12-25-69 | 1988 | Avon Park, Fla. |
| Roberts, Dave | .222 | 3 | 9 | 0 | 2 | 0 | 0 | 0 | 0 | 1 | 0 | 0 | 1 | L | L | 5-10 | 172 | 5-31-72 | 1994 | Oceanside, Calif. |
| Schmidt, Tom | .221 | 115 | 385 | 45 | 85 | 24 | 2 | 11 | 45 | 31 | 91 | 4 | 1 | R | R | 6-3 | 200 | 2-12-73 | 1992 | Perry Hall, Md. |
| Thompson, Billy | .232 | 41 | 112 | 9 | 26 | 5 | 0 | 3 | 10 | 7 | 31 | 1 | 2 | R | R | 5-11 | 185 | 11-5-70 | 1993 | Wayne, W.Va. |
| Trammell, Bubba | .328 | 83 | 311 | 63 | 102 | 23 | 2 | 27 | 75 | 32 | 61 | 3 | 2 | R | R | 6-2 | 205 | 11-6-71 | 1994 | Knoxville, Tenn. |

| PITCHING | W | L | ERA | G | GS | CG | SV | IP | H | R | ER | BB | SO | B | T | HT | WT | DOB | 1st Yr | Resides |
|---|---|---|---|---|---|---|---|---|---|---|---|---|---|---|---|---|---|---|---|---|
| Barnes, Brian | 4 | 6 | 3.74 | 13 | 12 | 1 | 0 | 75 | 74 | 37 | 31 | 25 | 74 | L | L | 5-9 | 170 | 3-25-67 | 1989 | Smyrna, Ga. |
| Carlyle, Buddy | 8 | 5 | 4.05 | 27 | 26 | 1 | 0 | 156 | 167 | 92 | 70 | 51 | 89 | R | R | 6-1 | 185 | 9-16-69 | 1992 | Cordova, Tenn. |
| Cedeno, Blas | 0 | 0 | 5.40 | 26 | 2 | 0 | 0 | 47 | 63 | 34 | 28 | 26 | 30 | R | R | 6-0 | 165 | 11-15-72 | 1991 | Carabobo, Venez. |
| Drews, Matt | 0 | 4 | 4.35 | 6 | 6 | 1 | 0 | 31 | 26 | 18 | 15 | 19 | 40 | R | R | 6-8 | 205 | 8-29-74 | 1994 | Sarasota, Fla. |
| Drumright, Mike | 6 | 4 | 3.97 | 18 | 18 | 1 | 0 | 100 | 80 | 51 | 44 | 48 | 109 | L | R | 6-4 | 210 | 4-19-74 | 1995 | Valley Center, Kan. |
| Fermin, Ramon | 6 | 6 | 4.50 | 46 | 6 | 0 | 3 | 84 | 82 | 56 | 42 | 46 | 48 | R | R | 6-3 | 180 | 11-25-72 | 1990 | San Fran. de Macoris, D.R. |
| Gaillard, Eddie | 9 | 6 | 3.38 | 56 | 0 | 0 | 1 | 88 | 82 | 40 | 33 | 50 | 76 | R | R | 6-1 | 180 | 8-13-70 | 1993 | West Palm Beach, Fla. |
| Greene, Rick | 2 | 7 | 4.98 | 57 | 0 | 0 | 30 | 56 | 67 | 44 | 31 | 39 | 42 | R | R | 6-5 | 200 | 1-2-71 | 1992 | Miami, Fla. |
| Gutierrez, Jim | 8 | 6 | 3.76 | 51 | 10 | 0 | 1 | 105 | 98 | 55 | 44 | 54 | 71 | R | R | 6-2 | 190 | 11-28-70 | 1989 | Burlington, Wash. |
| Kelly, John | 2 | 2 | 4.58 | 9 | 9 | 1 | 0 | 55 | 54 | 38 | 28 | 35 | 29 | R | R | 6-4 | 210 | 7-3-67 | 1990 | Buford, Ga. |
| Moehler, Brian | 15 | 6 | 3.48 | 28 | 28 | 1 | 0 | 173 | 186 | 80 | 67 | 50 | 120 | R | R | 6-3 | 195 | 12-31-71 | 1993 | Rockingham, N.C. |
| Norman, Scott | 6 | 5 | 4.82 | 27 | 14 | 0 | 0 | 97 | 122 | 58 | 52 | 37 | 30 | R | R | 6-0 | 195 | 9-1-72 | 1993 | Sarasota, Fla. |
| Reed, Brandon | 1 | 0 | 2.08 | 7 | 3 | 0 | 1 | 26 | 18 | 6 | 6 | 3 | 18 | R | R | 6-4 | 185 | 12-18-74 | 1994 | Lapeer, Mich. |
| Rosengren, John | 5 | 1 | 4.55 | 60 | 0 | 0 | 1 | 55 | 48 | 36 | 28 | 37 | 47 | L | L | 6-4 | 190 | 8-10-72 | 1992 | Rye, N.Y. |
| Salazar, Mike | 2 | 5 | 4.30 | 16 | 4 | 0 | 0 | 29 | 34 | 25 | 14 | 14 | 19 | L | L | 6-4 | 200 | 4-16-71 | 1993 | Clovis, Calif. |
| Skrmetta, Matt | 0 | 0 | 4.50 | 4 | 0 | 0 | 0 | 6 | 4 | 3 | 3 | 5 | 7 | S | R | 6-3 | 220 | 11-6-72 | 1993 | Satellite Beach, Fla. |
| Whiteside, Sean | 1 | 0 | 5.84 | 8 | 0 | 0 | 0 | 12 | 11 | 9 | 8 | 9 | 9 | L | L | 6-4 | 190 | 4-19-71 | 1992 | Cordele, Ga. |

### FIELDING

| Catcher | PCT | G | PO | A | E | DP | PB |
|---|---|---|---|---|---|---|---|
| Casanova | 1.000 | 4 | 21 | 1 | 0 | 0 | 1 |
| Lidle | 1.000 | 1 | 5 | 0 | 0 | 0 | 1 |
| Makarewicz | .987 | 66 | 392 | 51 | 6 | 4 | 12 |
| Nevin | .978 | 62 | 354 | 50 | 9 | 6 | 17 |
| Thompson | .977 | 23 | 118 | 11 | 3 | 1 | 5 |

| First Base | PCT | G | PO | A | E | DP |
|---|---|---|---|---|---|---|
| Cotton | 1.000 | 1 | 7 | 0 | 0 | 1 |
| Dismuke | 1.000 | 3 | 26 | 1 | 0 | 2 |
| Freeman | .994 | 116 | 1064 | 81 | 7 | 106 |
| Hansen | .996 | 24 | 200 | 27 | 1 | 22 |
| Nevin | 1.000 | 1 | 7 | 0 | 0 | 1 |
| Schmidt | 1.000 | 1 | 2 | 1 | 0 | 0 |
| Thompson | 1.000 | 1 | 2 | 0 | 0 | 0 |

| Second Base | PCT | G | PO | A | E | DP |
|---|---|---|---|---|---|---|
| Bream | .950 | 5 | 8 | 11 | 1 | 2 |

| Third Base | PCT | G | PO | A | E | DP |
|---|---|---|---|---|---|---|
| Bream | .750 | 5 | 4 | 8 | 4 | 0 |
| Cotton | .838 | 23 | 7 | 24 | 6 | 2 |
| Lidle | 1.000 | 2 | 0 | 1 | 0 | 0 |
| Nevin | .943 | 12 | 7 | 26 | 2 | 3 |
| Pough | 1.000 | 2 | 0 | 2 | 0 | 0 |
| Schmidt | .904 | 109 | 80 | 230 | 33 | 21 |

| Shortstop | PCT | G | PO | A | E | DP |
|---|---|---|---|---|---|---|
| Bream | .955 | 4 | 9 | 12 | 1 | 0 |
| Cotton | 1.000 | 9 | 6 | 15 | 0 | 5 |
| Garcia | .947 | 131 | 205 | 435 | 36 | 93 |
| Schmidt | .923 | 3 | 9 | 3 | 1 | 1 |

| Catalanotto | PCT | G | PO | A | E | DP |
|---|---|---|---|---|---|---|
| Catalanotto | .968 | 132 | 246 | 421 | 22 | 99 |
| Cotton | .926 | 6 | 7 | 18 | 2 | 4 |

| Outfield | PCT | G | PO | A | E | DP |
|---|---|---|---|---|---|---|
| Barker | .979 | 41 | 91 | 2 | 2 | 0 |
| Bream | 1.000 | 18 | 20 | 2 | 0 | 0 |
| Brock | .930 | 34 | 48 | 5 | 4 | 0 |
| Cotton | 1.000 | 35 | 42 | 5 | 0 | 0 |
| Dismuke | 1.000 | 7 | 6 | 0 | 0 | 0 |
| Hansen | 1.000 | 46 | 50 | 1 | 0 | 0 |
| Kimsey | .966 | 31 | 50 | 6 | 2 | 4 |
| Makarewicz | .000 | 1 | 0 | 0 | 0 | 0 |
| Mashore | .984 | 113 | 228 | 19 | 4 | 3 |
| Mitchell | .949 | 27 | 35 | 2 | 2 | 0 |
| Nevin | 1.000 | 11 | 16 | 0 | 0 | 0 |
| Roberts | 1.000 | 3 | 5 | 0 | 0 | 0 |
| Thompson | .947 | 15 | 16 | 2 | 1 | 0 |
| Trammell | .955 | 70 | 100 | 6 | 5 | 1 |

**VISALIA**     Class A/Co-Op

## CALIFORNIA LEAGUE

| BATTING | AVG | G | AB | R | H | 2B | 3B | HR | RBI | BB | SO | SB | CS | B | T | HT | WT | DOB | 1st Yr | Resides |
|---|---|---|---|---|---|---|---|---|---|---|---|---|---|---|---|---|---|---|---|---|
| Arano, Eloy | .229 | 43 | 140 | 19 | 32 | 6 | 0 | 0 | 16 | 17 | 30 | 4 | 2 | S | R | 5-11 | 170 | 3-5-74 | 1993 | Veracruz, Mexico |
| Danapilis, Eric | .257 | 105 | 377 | 58 | 97 | 29 | 1 | 10 | 64 | 66 | 122 | 2 | 1 | R | R | 6-2 | 220 | 6-11-71 | 1993 | St. Joseph, Mich. |
| De la Rosa, Elvis | .221 | 69 | 204 | 33 | 45 | 10 | 1 | 6 | 27 | 24 | 76 | 2 | 2 | R | R | 5-11 | 210 | 5-5-75 | 1993 | Elias Pina, D.R. |
| DeJesus, Malvin | .241 | 124 | 485 | 66 | 117 | 24 | 4 | 6 | 51 | 63 | 107 | 34 | 13 | R | R | 5-9 | 160 | 9-16-71 | 1992 | Carolina, P.R. |
| Facione, Chris | .258 | 78 | 310 | 50 | 80 | 16 | 6 | 7 | 38 | 22 | 60 | 9 | 11 | R | R | 6-3 | 190 | 9-21-70 | 1993 | Millbrae, Calif. |
| Kimsey, Keith | .274 | 99 | 394 | 64 | 108 | 17 | 3 | 21 | 72 | 43 | 140 | 13 | 4 | R | R | 6-7 | 200 | 8-15-72 | 1991 | Lakeland, Fla. |
| Lackey, Steve | .266 | 46 | 184 | 27 | 49 | 11 | 1 | 4 | 29 | 16 | 44 | 7 | 1 | R | R | 5-11 | 165 | 9-25-74 | 1992 | Riverside, Calif. |
| Landry, Lonny | .215 | 51 | 191 | 23 | 41 | 7 | 2 | 2 | 10 | 9 | 54 | 10 | 2 | R | R | 5-10 | 185 | 11-2-72 | 1993 | Broussard, La. |
| Lemonis, Chris | .278 | 126 | 482 | 69 | 134 | 27 | 3 | 14 | 82 | 35 | 99 | 12 | 5 | L | R | 5-11 | 185 | 8-21-73 | 1995 | New York, N.Y. |
| Marine, Del | .257 | 105 | 378 | 58 | 97 | 20 | 1 | 16 | 69 | 47 | 121 | 8 | 2 | R | R | 6-0 | 205 | 10-18-71 | 1992 | Woodland Hills, Calif. |
| Neikirk, Derick | .148 | 9 | 27 | 3 | 4 | 0 | 0 | 0 | 2 | 2 | 9 | 0 | 0 | R | R | 6-3 | 214 | 9-5-74 | 1996 | Glendale, Ariz. |
| Roberts, Dave | .272 | 126 | 482 | 112 | 131 | 24 | 7 | 5 | 37 | 98 | 105 | 65 | 21 | L | L | 5-10 | 172 | 5-31-72 | 1994 | Oceanside, Calif. |
| Sanchez, Yuri | .237 | 18 | 59 | 9 | 14 | 1 | 0 | 3 | 6 | 7 | 19 | 1 | 1 | L | R | 6-1 | 165 | 11-11-73 | 1992 | Lynn, Mass. |

**GAMES BY POSITION: C**—De la Rosa 66, Marine 67, Neikirk 6.**1B**—Danapilis 96, Marine 28. **2B**—Arano 9, Lackey 28, Lemonis 77. **3B**—Arano 6, Lackey 4, Lemonis 3, Marine 2. **SS**—Arano 20, Lackey 14, Sanchez 17. **OF**—Arano 8, Danapilis 3, DeJesus 85, Facione 78, Kimsey 99, Landry 51, Roberts 99.

| PITCHING | W | L | ERA | G | GS | CG | SV | IP | H | R | ER | BB | SO | B | T | HT | WT | DOB | 1st Yr | Resides |
|---|---|---|---|---|---|---|---|---|---|---|---|---|---|---|---|---|---|---|---|---|
| Dalton, Brian | 1 | 1 | 5.40 | 13 | 0 | 0 | 0 | 27 | 26 | 16 | 16 | 19 | 19 | R | R | 6-1 | 190 | 6-24-72 | 1994 | Brooksville, Fla. |
| 2-team (6 Stockton) | .1 | 2 | 5.84 | 19 | 0 | 0 | 0 | 37 | 38 | 25 | 24 | 29 | 28 | | | | | | | |
| Goldsmith, Gary | 10 | 11 | 4.98 | 28 | 27 | 0 | 0 | 170 | 188 | 108 | 94 | 76 | 120 | R | R | 6-2 | 205 | 7-4-71 | 1993 | Alamogordo, N.M. |
| Granger, Greg | 2 | 0 | 4.87 | 4 | 4 | 0 | 0 | 20 | 24 | 12 | 11 | 10 | 13 | R | R | 6-5 | 200 | 3-7-73 | 1993 | Ellettsville, Ind. |
| Harper, David | 0 | 0 | 19.73 | 12 | 0 | 0 | 0 | 9 | 15 | 19 | 19 | 10 | 5 | R | R | 6-3 | 185 | 9-14-74 | 1996 | Mansfield, Texas |
| Johnson, Carl | 3 | 5 | 15.55 | 15 | 5 | 0 | 0 | 22 | 35 | 44 | 38 | 35 | 16 | R | R | 6-4 | 195 | 9-8-70 | 1990 | Lacey, Wash. |
| Jordan, Jason | 6 | 10 | 4.85 | 30 | 20 | 1 | 0 | 145 | 175 | 89 | 78 | 54 | 110 | R | R | 6-3 | 220 | 10-2-72 | 1994 | Wichita, Kan. |
| Kelly, John | 2 | 10 | 7.13 | 19 | 18 | 1 | 1 | 96 | 115 | 100 | 76 | 63 | 89 | R | R | 6-4 | 210 | 7-3-67 | 1990 | Buford, Ga. |
| Salazar, Mike | 0 | 2 | 5.40 | 4 | 0 | 0 | 0 | 25 | 31 | 19 | 15 | 11 | 14 | L | L | 6-4 | 200 | 4-16-71 | 1993 | Clovis, Calif. |
| Thompson, Justin | 0 | 0 | 0.00 | 1 | 1 | 0 | 0 | 3 | 2 | 0 | 0 | 2 | 7 | L | L | 6-3 | 175 | 3-8-73 | 1991 | Spring, Texas |
| Tuttle, Dave | 7 | 9 | 3.71 | 55 | 0 | 0 | 21 | 70 | 71 | 39 | 29 | 33 | 56 | R | R | 6-3 | 190 | 9-29-69 | 1992 | Los Gatos, Calif. |

**LAKELAND**     Class A

## FLORIDA STATE LEAGUE

| BATTING | AVG | G | AB | R | H | 2B | 3B | HR | RBI | BB | SO | SB | CS | B | T | HT | WT | DOB | 1st Yr | Resides |
|---|---|---|---|---|---|---|---|---|---|---|---|---|---|---|---|---|---|---|---|---|
| Almanzar, Richard | .306 | 124 | 471 | 81 | 144 | 22 | 2 | 1 | 36 | 49 | 49 | 53 | 19 | R | R | 5-10 | 155 | 4-3-76 | 1993 | San Fran. de Macoris, D.R. |
| Arano, Eloy | .232 | 46 | 155 | 15 | 36 | 3 | 1 | 0 | 7 | 8 | 23 | 0 | 1 | S | R | 5-11 | 170 | 3-5-74 | 1993 | Veracruz, Mexico |
| Balfe, Ryan | .277 | 92 | 347 | 48 | 96 | 21 | 1 | 11 | 65 | 24 | 66 | 3 | 0 | S | R | 6-1 | 180 | 11-14-75 | 1994 | Cornwall, N.Y. |

| BATTING | AVG | G | AB | R | H | 2B | 3B | HR | RBI | BB | SO | SB | CS | B | T | HT | WT | DOB | 1st Yr | Resides |
|---|---|---|---|---|---|---|---|---|---|---|---|---|---|---|---|---|---|---|---|---|
| Borel, Jamie | .227 | 31 | 44 | 10 | 10 | 1 | 0 | 0 | 1 | 7 | 8 | 1 | 2 | R | R | 5-11 | 170 | 9-20-71 | 1994 | Raleigh, N.C. |
| Boryczewski, Marty | .188 | 13 | 16 | 1 | 3 | 1 | 0 | 0 | 2 | 4 | 7 | 0 | 0 | R | R | 6-2 | 195 | 8-17-73 | 1994 | Parsippany, N.J. |
| Brock, Tarrik | .278 | 53 | 212 | 42 | 59 | 11 | 4 | 5 | 27 | 17 | 61 | 9 | 2 | L | L | 6-3 | 170 | 12-25-73 | 1991 | Hawthorne, Calif. |
| Darr, Mike | .248 | 85 | 311 | 26 | 77 | 14 | 7 | 0 | 38 | 28 | 64 | 7 | 3 | L | R | 6-3 | 205 | 3-21-76 | 1994 | Corona, Calif. |
| Encarnacion, Juan | .240 | 131 | 499 | 54 | 120 | 31 | 2 | 15 | 58 | 24 | 104 | 11 | 5 | R | R | 6-2 | 160 | 3-8-76 | 1993 | Las Matas de Farfan, D.R. |
| French, Anton | .277 | 61 | 253 | 36 | 70 | 10 | 6 | 0 | 14 | 12 | 37 | 24 | 10 | S | R | 5-10 | 175 | 7-25-75 | 1993 | St. Louis, Mo. |
| Landry, Jacques | .086 | 11 | 35 | 2 | 3 | 1 | 0 | 0 | 2 | 3 | 15 | 0 | 0 | R | R | 6-3 | 205 | 8-15-73 | 1996 | LaMarque, Texas |
| Landry, Lonny | .236 | 75 | 292 | 35 | 69 | 9 | 7 | 3 | 21 | 24 | 72 | 19 | 3 | R | R | 5-10 | 185 | 11-2-72 | 1993 | Broussard, La. |
| Lidle, Kevin | .216 | 97 | 320 | 37 | 69 | 18 | 1 | 8 | 41 | 30 | 90 | 1 | 1 | R | R | 5-11 | 170 | 3-22-72 | 1992 | West Covina, Calif. |
| Moore, Tris | .152 | 11 | 33 | 6 | 5 | 2 | 0 | 0 | 4 | 7 | 11 | 2 | 0 | R | R | 6-0 | 185 | 1-15-74 | 1996 | Miami, Fla. |
| Perez, Santiago | .251 | 122 | 418 | 33 | 105 | 18 | 2 | 1 | 27 | 16 | 88 | 6 | 5 | S | R | 6-2 | 150 | 12-30-75 | 1993 | Santo Domingo, D.R. |
| Rodriguez, Adam | .238 | 57 | 160 | 18 | 38 | 7 | 1 | 3 | 25 | 20 | 37 | 0 | 0 | R | R | 5-10 | 195 | 3-16-71 | 1993 | Tucson, Ariz. |
| Salzano, Jerry | .263 | 123 | 426 | 52 | 112 | 28 | 4 | 6 | 60 | 38 | 66 | 6 | 7 | R | R | 6-0 | 175 | 10-27-74 | 1992 | Trenton, N.J. |
| Waggoner, Jay | .237 | 64 | 194 | 17 | 46 | 7 | 0 | 0 | 21 | 11 | 44 | 1 | 2 | L | R | 5-11 | 195 | 10-2-71 | 1995 | Birmingham, Ala. |
| Ward, Daryle | .291 | 128 | 464 | 65 | 135 | 29 | 4 | 10 | 68 | 57 | 77 | 1 | 1 | L | L | 6-2 | 230 | 6-27-75 | 1994 | Riverside, Calif. |

**GAMES BY POSITION: C**—Boryczewski 13, Lidle 96, Rodriguez 43. **1B**—Rodriguez 8, Salzano 1, Waggoner 23, Ward 123. **2B**—Almanzar 124, Arano 19, Salzano 3. **3B**—Arano 7, Balfe 81, Landry 11, Salzano 42. **SS**—Arano 16, Perez 122, Salzano 2. **OF**—Arano 2, Borel 17, Brock 51, Darr 82, French 59, Landry 65, Moore 10, Salzano 14.

| PITCHING | W | L | ERA | G | GS | CG | SV | IP | H | R | ER | BB | SO | B | T | HT | WT | DOB | 1st Yr | Resides |
|---|---|---|---|---|---|---|---|---|---|---|---|---|---|---|---|---|---|---|---|---|
| Cedeno, Blas | 1 | 1 | 5.51 | 10 | 0 | 0 | 0 | 16 | 17 | 10 | 10 | 7 | 11 | R | R | 6-0 | 165 | 11-15-72 | 1991 | Carabobo, Venez. |
| Dinyar, Eric | 3 | 3 | 1.92 | 58 | 0 | 0 | 27 | 66 | 45 | 20 | 14 | 35 | 55 | R | R | 6-6 | 210 | 8-13-73 | 1994 | Johnstown, Pa. |
| Eby, Mike | 0 | 0 | 4.50 | 17 | 0 | 0 | 0 | 28 | 28 | 16 | 14 | 24 | 27 | L | L | 6-1 | 190 | 2-25-72 | 1995 | Westlake, Calif. |
| Gonzalez, Gener | 0 | 0 | 4.50 | 1 | 0 | 0 | 0 | 2 | 3 | 5 | 1 | 2 | 1 | R | R | 6-4 | 170 | 2-19-76 | 1993 | Santo Domingo, D.R. |
| Granger, Greg | 1 | 0 | 1.42 | 5 | 0 | 0 | 0 | 6 | 7 | 1 | 1 | 3 | 4 | R | R | 6-5 | 200 | 3-7-73 | 1993 | Ellettsville, Ind. |
| Jacobson, K.J. | 0 | 4 | 3.67 | 26 | 3 | 0 | 1 | 56 | 53 | 30 | 23 | 36 | 44 | R | R | 6-3 | 205 | 2-17-71 | 1994 | Seattle, Wash. |
| Marrero, Kenny | 2 | 3 | 2.30 | 34 | 0 | 0 | 0 | 67 | 60 | 26 | 17 | 25 | 82 | R | R | 6-3 | 208 | 5-13-70 | 1991 | Dorado, P.R. |
| Powell, Brian | 8 | 13 | 4.90 | 29 | 27 | 5 | 0 | 174 | 195 | 106 | 95 | 47 | 84 | R | R | 6-2 | 205 | 10-10-73 | 1995 | Bainbridge, Ga. |
| Roberts, Willis | 9 | 7 | 2.89 | 23 | 22 | 2 | 0 | 149 | 133 | 60 | 48 | 69 | 105 | R | R | 6-3 | 175 | 6-19-75 | 1992 | San Cristobal, D.R. |
| Salazar, Mike | 1 | 1 | 2.50 | 19 | 1 | 0 | 0 | 36 | 31 | 16 | 10 | 6 | 24 | L | L | 6-4 | 200 | 4-16-71 | 1993 | Clovis, Calif. |
| Santos, Victor | 2 | 2 | 2.22 | 5 | 4 | 0 | 0 | 28 | 19 | 11 | 7 | 9 | 25 | R | R | 6-3 | 175 | 10-2-76 | 1995 | Garfield, N.J. |
| Scanlan, Bob | 0 | 1 | 5.00 | 2 | 2 | 0 | 0 | 9 | 9 | 6 | 5 | 3 | 4 | R | R | 6-8 | 215 | 8-9-66 | 1984 | Beverly Hills, Calif. |
| Siler, Jeff | 6 | 3 | 2.64 | 37 | 0 | 0 | 1 | 58 | 52 | 20 | 17 | 18 | 45 | L | L | 6-0 | 180 | 10-1-70 | 1994 | Merrill, Mich. |
| Skrmetta, Matt | 5 | 5 | 3.59 | 40 | 0 | 0 | 5 | 53 | 44 | 23 | 21 | 19 | 52 | S | R | 6-3 | 220 | 11-6-72 | 1993 | Satellite Beach, Fla. |
| Smith, Cam | 5 | 8 | 4.59 | 22 | 21 | 0 | 0 | 114 | 93 | 64 | 58 | 71 | 114 | R | R | 6-3 | 190 | 9-20-73 | 1993 | Selkirk, N.Y. |
| Sobik, Trad | 4 | 6 | 4.43 | 13 | 13 | 2 | 0 | 81 | 79 | 51 | 40 | 48 | 49 | R | R | 6-2 | 175 | 1-29-76 | 1994 | Palm Harbor, Fla. |
| Whiteman, Greg | 11 | 10 | 3.71 | 27 | 27 | 1 | 0 | 150 | 134 | 66 | 62 | 89 | 122 | L | L | 6-2 | 185 | 6-12-73 | 1994 | Wileyford, W.Va. |
| Whiteside, Sean | 4 | 10 | 3.86 | 19 | 18 | 0 | 0 | 103 | 104 | 51 | 44 | 32 | 63 | L | L | 6-4 | 190 | 4-19-71 | 1992 | Cordele, Ga. |

# FAYETTEVILLE — Class A
## SOUTH ATLANTIC LEAGUE

| BATTING | AVG | G | AB | R | H | 2B | 3B | HR | RBI | BB | SO | SB | CS | B | T | HT | WT | DOB | 1st Yr | Resides |
|---|---|---|---|---|---|---|---|---|---|---|---|---|---|---|---|---|---|---|---|---|
| Barker, Glen | .288 | 37 | 132 | 23 | 38 | 1 | 0 | 1 | 9 | 16 | 34 | 20 | 6 | R | R | 5-10 | 180 | 5-10-71 | 1993 | Albany, N.Y. |
| Bass, Jason | .231 | 104 | 295 | 44 | 68 | 12 | 3 | 11 | 43 | 54 | 118 | 19 | 10 | L | L | 6-3 | 212 | 6-22-74 | 1993 | Seattle, Wash. |
| Brock, Tarrik | .294 | 32 | 119 | 21 | 35 | 5 | 2 | 1 | 11 | 14 | 31 | 4 | 5 | L | L | 6-3 | 170 | 12-25-73 | 1991 | Hawthorne, Calif. |
| Capellan, Rene | .260 | 72 | 250 | 26 | 65 | 10 | 0 | 1 | 31 | 12 | 47 | 1 | 1 | R | R | 5-11 | 160 | 4-24-78 | 1995 | Santo Domingo, D.R. |
| Cardona, Javier | .282 | 97 | 348 | 42 | 98 | 21 | 0 | 4 | 28 | 28 | 53 | 1 | 5 | R | R | 6-0 | 185 | 9-15-75 | 1994 | Dorado, P.R. |
| De la Cruz, Carlos | .226 | 98 | 318 | 34 | 72 | 21 | 4 | 5 | 39 | 21 | 100 | 18 | 8 | R | R | 6-2 | 175 | 7-24-75 | 1994 | Santo Domingo, D.R. |
| Engleka, Matt | .229 | 93 | 262 | 28 | 60 | 18 | 0 | 1 | 25 | 48 | 36 | 6 | 6 | R | R | 5-10 | 170 | 10-6-72 | 1995 | Dayton, Ohio |
| Fuller, Brian | .251 | 76 | 239 | 48 | 60 | 12 | 3 | 10 | 30 | 32 | 50 | 2 | 2 | R | R | 6-2 | 205 | 11-5-72 | 1995 | Plover, Wis. |
| Garcia, Apostol | .194 | 74 | 242 | 33 | 47 | 7 | 1 | 2 | 17 | 21 | 77 | 12 | 3 | S | R | 6-0 | 155 | 8-3-76 | 1994 | Las Matas de Farfan, D.R. |
| Inzunza, Miguel | .250 | 68 | 232 | 24 | 58 | 12 | 0 | 0 | 31 | 27 | 19 | 2 | 3 | R | R | 5-10 | 175 | 7-16-72 | 1995 | Ontario, Calif. |
| Kapler, Gabe | .300 | 138 | 524 | 81 | 157 | 45 | 0 | 26 | 99 | 62 | 73 | 14 | 4 | R | R | 6-1 | 190 | 7-31-75 | 1996 | Reseda, Calif. |
| Koonce, Graham | .238 | 133 | 487 | 61 | 116 | 22 | 3 | 8 | 59 | 58 | 97 | 7 | 7 | L | L | 6-3 | 195 | 5-15-74 | 1994 | Julian, Calif. |
| Kopacz, Derek | .231 | 49 | 186 | 25 | 43 | 11 | 3 | 3 | 14 | 14 | 49 | 2 | 2 | R | R | 5-10 | 185 | 4-2-75 | 1995 | Orland Park, Ill. |
| Lackey, Steve | .216 | 82 | 310 | 38 | 67 | 13 | 0 | 4 | 43 | 28 | 58 | 24 | 6 | R | R | 5-11 | 165 | 9-25-74 | 1992 | Riverside, Calif. |
| Landry, Jacques | .188 | 31 | 101 | 10 | 19 | 4 | 0 | 1 | 3 | 5 | 36 | 1 | 0 | R | R | 6-3 | 205 | 8-15-73 | 1996 | LaMarque, Texas |
| Ruiz, Cesar | .097 | 10 | 31 | 0 | 3 | 1 | 0 | 0 | 1 | 2 | 9 | 1 | 0 | S | R | 6-1 | 150 | 9-14-74 | 1992 | Haina, D.R. |
| Sosa, Franklin | .178 | 34 | 90 | 6 | 16 | 3 | 0 | 0 | 4 | 8 | 17 | 1 | 3 | R | R | 5-11 | 170 | 2-27-76 | 1994 | Los Llanos, D.R. |
| Weaver, Scott | .235 | 115 | 430 | 68 | 101 | 20 | 0 | 2 | 43 | 60 | 59 | 28 | 20 | L | L | 5-11 | 190 | 9-21-73 | 1995 | Sault Ste. Marie, Mich. |

**GAMES BY POSITION: C**—Cardona 85, Engleka 1, Fuller 38, Sosa 29. **1B**—Engleka 13, Koonce 132, Ruiz 3, Sosa 3. **2B**—Capellan 5, Engleka 38, Garcia 1, Inzunza 68, Lackey 36, Landry 1, Ruiz 3. **3B**—Capellan 55, Engleka 15, Kapler 1, Kopacz 45, Lackey 1, Landry 32. **SS**—Engleka 31, Garcia 73, Inzunza 1, Lackey 44. **OF**—Barker 36, Bass 84, Brock 32, Capellan 1, De la Cruz 77, Engleka 5, Kapler 129, Koonce 1, Weaver 70.

| PITCHING | W | L | ERA | G | GS | CG | SV | IP | H | R | ER | BB | SO | B | T | HT | WT | DOB | 1st Yr | Resides |
|---|---|---|---|---|---|---|---|---|---|---|---|---|---|---|---|---|---|---|---|---|
| Bettencourt, Justin | 7 | 11 | 3.24 | 26 | 26 | 2 | 0 | 153 | 127 | 78 | 55 | 58 | 148 | L | L | 6-2 | 198 | 12-19-73 | 1994 | Capitola, Calif. |
| Borkowski, Dave | 10 | 10 | 3.33 | 27 | 27 | 5 | 0 | 178 | 158 | 85 | 66 | 54 | 117 | R | R | 6-1 | 200 | 2-7-77 | 1995 | Sterling Heights, Mich. |
| Bruner, Clay | 14 | 5 | 2.59 | 27 | 26 | 0 | 0 | 157 | 124 | 64 | 45 | 77 | 152 | R | R | 6-3 | 190 | 10-16-76 | 1995 | Weatherford, Okla. |
| Cordero, Francisco | 0 | 0 | 2.57 | 2 | 1 | 0 | 0 | 7 | 2 | 2 | 2 | 6 | 7 | R | R | 6-1 | 170 | 8-11-77 | 1994 | Santo Domingo, D.R. |
| Corey, Bryan | 6 | 4 | 1.21 | 60 | 0 | 0 | 34 | 82 | 50 | 19 | 11 | 17 | 101 | R | R | 6-1 | 170 | 10-21-73 | 1993 | Newbury Park, Calif. |
| Dalton, Brian | 0 | 0 | 1.00 | 7 | 0 | 0 | 0 | 9 | 5 | 2 | 1 | 5 | 7 | R | R | 6-1 | 190 | 6-24-72 | 1994 | Brooksville, Fla. |
| Darwin, David | 5 | 2 | 3.20 | 17 | 9 | 0 | 0 | 59 | 54 | 22 | 21 | 12 | 49 | L | L | 6-0 | 185 | 12-19-73 | 1996 | Cornelius, N.C. |
| Durkovic, Peter | 3 | 3 | 4.61 | 53 | 0 | 0 | 3 | 53 | 54 | 35 | 27 | 16 | 67 | L | L | 6-4 | 215 | 7-9-73 | 1995 | Flushing, N.Y. |
| Eby, Mike | 3 | 1 | 1.07 | 27 | 0 | 0 | 4 | 51 | 27 | 11 | 6 | 30 | 58 | L | L | 6-1 | 190 | 2-25-72 | 1995 | Westlake, Calif. |
| Foran, John | 4 | 7 | 4.14 | 35 | 17 | 0 | 0 | 111 | 107 | 57 | 51 | 53 | 82 | R | R | 6-1 | 185 | 10-22-73 | 1995 | Alford, Fla. |
| Gonzalez, Gener | 5 | 3 | 3.06 | 17 | 0 | 0 | 0 | 32 | 27 | 17 | 11 | 23 | 32 | R | R | 6-4 | 170 | 2-19-76 | 1993 | Santo Domingo, D.R. |
| Jacobson, Kelton | 0 | 1 | 3.12 | 6 | 0 | 0 | 0 | 9 | 7 | 3 | 3 | 3 | 8 | R | R | 6-3 | 205 | 2-17-71 | 1994 | Seattle, Wash. |
| Malenfant, Dave | 5 | 5 | 5.34 | 23 | 1 | 0 | 2 | 30 | 29 | 26 | 18 | 25 | 34 | R | R | 6-3 | 205 | 4-30-75 | 1996 | Flint, Mich. |
| Melendez, David | 11 | 4 | 2.62 | 27 | 21 | 1 | 0 | 131 | 114 | 56 | 38 | 40 | 121 | S | R | 6-0 | 168 | 6-25-76 | 1996 | Caguas, P.R. |
| Perusek, William | 0 | 0 | 6.55 | 39 | 1 | 0 | 1 | 45 | 51 | 38 | 33 | 51 | 50 | R | R | 6-2 | 210 | 10-6-73 | 1996 | Cleveland, Ohio |
| Ramirez, Jose | 1 | 1 | 4.15 | 15 | 1 | 0 | 0 | 26 | 35 | 15 | 12 | 14 | 30 | L | L | 6-1 | 170 | 9-1-75 | 1994 | Santo Domingo, D.R. |
| Stentz, Brent | 7 | 8 | 3.49 | 45 | 8 | 0 | 2 | 98 | 91 | 51 | 38 | 27 | 92 | R | R | 6-5 | 225 | 7-24-75 | 1995 | Brooksville, Fla. |
| Thompson, Justin | 0 | 0 | 3.00 | 1 | 1 | 0 | 0 | 3 | 1 | 1 | 1 | 0 | 5 | L | L | 6-3 | 175 | 3-8-71 | 1991 | Spring, Texas |

## NEW YORK-PENN LEAGUE

| BATTING | AVG | G | AB | R | H | 2B | 3B | HR | RBI | BB | SO | SB | CS | B | T | HT | WT | DOB | 1st Yr | Resides |
|---|---|---|---|---|---|---|---|---|---|---|---|---|---|---|---|---|---|---|---|---|
| Airoso, Kurt | .282 | 27 | 78 | 12 | 22 | 5 | 2 | 2 | 12 | 10 | 31 | 3 | 1 | R | R | 6-2 | 190 | 2-12-75 | 1996 | Tulare, Calif. |
| Cedeno, Jesus | .280 | 74 | 236 | 43 | 66 | 16 | 2 | 9 | 39 | 31 | 57 | 7 | 6 | R | R | 5-11 | 160 | 6-24-76 | 1994 | Santo Domingo, D.R. |
| Ciminiello, Mike | .111 | 10 | 18 | 1 | 2 | 0 | 0 | 0 | 1 | 0 | 2 | 0 | 0 | R | R | 6-2 | 205 | 5-15-74 | 1996 | St. James, N.Y. |
| DeDonatis, Don | .298 | 42 | 141 | 21 | 42 | 4 | 0 | 0 | 17 | 17 | 15 | 9 | 4 | L | R | 5-11 | 190 | 6-23-75 | 1996 | Sterling Heights, Mich. |
| Fick, Robert | .248 | 43 | 133 | 18 | 33 | 6 | 0 | 1 | 14 | 12 | 25 | 3 | 1 | L | R | 6-1 | 195 | 3-15-74 | 1996 | Thousand Oaks, Calif. |
| Kopacz, Derek | .236 | 68 | 242 | 34 | 57 | 17 | 4 | 7 | 40 | 21 | 74 | 2 | 5 | R | R | 5-10 | 185 | 4-2-75 | 1995 | Orland Park, Ill. |
| Lindstrom, David | .248 | 52 | 165 | 19 | 41 | 10 | 0 | 5 | 13 | 10 | 29 | 1 | 0 | R | R | 6-3 | 185 | 8-6-74 | 1996 | Brooklyn Park, Minn. |
| Mitchell, Derek | .245 | 56 | 184 | 25 | 45 | 10 | 2 | 2 | 25 | 18 | 38 | 7 | 4 | R | R | 6-1 | 180 | 3-9-75 | 1996 | Gurnee, Ill. |
| Moore, Tris | .271 | 13 | 48 | 9 | 13 | 2 | 0 | 1 | 13 | 5 | 10 | 2 | 3 | R | R | 6-0 | 185 | 1-15-74 | 1996 | Miami, Fla. |
| Ramirez, Frank | .054 | 19 | 37 | 5 | 2 | 1 | 0 | 0 | 3 | 2 | 17 | 1 | 0 | R | R | 6-2 | 195 | 1-21-76 | 1994 | Santo Domingo, D.R. |
| Restovich, George | .179 | 48 | 151 | 25 | 27 | 5 | 0 | 6 | 22 | 30 | 55 | 1 | 1 | L | R | 6-1 | 205 | 9-12-73 | 1996 | Rochester, Minn. |
| Rios, Brian | .304 | 36 | 102 | 19 | 31 | 6 | 2 | 1 | 17 | 19 | 15 | 4 | 1 | R | R | 6-3 | 190 | 7-15-74 | 1996 | Corona, Calif. |
| Sollmann, Scott | .281 | 67 | 253 | 49 | 71 | 5 | 5 | 0 | 19 | 34 | 47 | 35 | 14 | L | L | 5-9 | 167 | 5-2-75 | 1996 | Cincinnati, Ohio |
| Tagliaferri, Jeff | .246 | 72 | 252 | 42 | 62 | 12 | 3 | 9 | 36 | 42 | 61 | 2 | 2 | L | R | 6-1 | 200 | 8-3-75 | 1996 | Granada Hills, Calif. |
| Wakeland, Chris | .309 | 70 | 220 | 38 | 68 | 14 | 5 | 10 | 49 | 43 | 83 | 8 | 3 | L | L | 6-0 | 190 | 6-15-74 | 1996 | St. Helens, Ore. |
| Zapata, Alexis | .283 | 15 | 8 | 15 | 1 | 2 | 2 | 7 | 3 | 19 | 0 | 0 | | R | R | 6-3 | 190 | 5-20-77 | 1996 | Santo Domingo, D.R. |
| Zepeda, Jesse | .208 | 54 | 178 | 23 | 37 | 3 | 2 | 0 | 17 | 21 | 31 | 6 | 3 | S | R | 5-10 | 165 | 5-4-74 | 1996 | Santa Maria, Calif. |

**GAMES BY POSITION: C**—Ciminiello 3, Fick 23, Lindstrom 42, Restovich 15, **1B**—Ciminiello 6, Lindstrom 4, Tagliaferri 72. **2B**—DeDonatis 39, Zepeda 45. **3B**—Kopacz 61, Lindstrom 1, Mitchell 11, Zepeda 5. **SS**—Mitchell 45, Rios 32, Zepeda 3. **OF**—Airoso 17, Cedeno 71, Lindstrom 1, Moore 9, Ramirez 6, Sollmann 65, Wakefield 59, Zapata 14.

| PITCHING | W | L | ERA | G | GS | CG | SV | IP | H | R | ER | BB | SO | B | T | HT | WT | DOB | 1st Yr | Resides |
|---|---|---|---|---|---|---|---|---|---|---|---|---|---|---|---|---|---|---|---|---|
| Bauer, Chris | 3 | 4 | 4.08 | 11 | 11 | 0 | 0 | 57 | 65 | 31 | 26 | 15 | 35 | R | R | 6-4 | 185 | 12-28-73 | 1996 | Tulsa, Okla. |
| Browning, Tom | 0 | 1 | 8.10 | 5 | 1 | 0 | 0 | 7 | 13 | 7 | 6 | 6 | 5 | L | L | 6-2 | 200 | 1-16-73 | 1996 | Noblesville, Ind. |
| Cordero, Francisco | 0 | 0 | 0.82 | 2 | 2 | 0 | 0 | 11 | 5 | 1 | 1 | 2 | 10 | R | R | 6-2 | 170 | 8-11-77 | 1994 | Santo Domingo, D.R. |
| Gonzalez, Gener | 0 | 0 | 5.40 | 6 | 0 | 0 | 0 | 10 | 16 | 8 | 6 | 4 | 10 | R | R | 6-4 | 170 | 2-19-76 | 1993 | Santo Domingo, D.R. |
| Kauflin, David | 6 | 2 | 3.09 | 22 | 7 | 0 | 0 | 64 | 55 | 25 | 22 | 26 | 56 | R | R | 6-4 | 230 | 5-20-76 | 1994 | Clinton Township, Mich. |
| Malenfant, Dave | 0 | 0 | 0.00 | 2 | 0 | 0 | 0 | 3 | 1 | 1 | 0 | 2 | 0 | R | R | 6-3 | 205 | 4-30-75 | 1996 | Flint, Mich. |
| Miller, Matt | 1 | 3 | 4.62 | 6 | 6 | 0 | 0 | 25 | 33 | 16 | 13 | 13 | 20 | L | L | 6-3 | 175 | 8-2-74 | 1996 | Lubbock, Texas |
| Mitchell, Chris | 1 | 5 | 3.97 | 25 | 7 | 0 | 1 | 57 | 54 | 33 | 25 | 30 | 43 | R | R | 6-3 | 215 | 12-18-74 | 1996 | Phoenixville, Pa. |
| Oakley, Matt | 4 | 2 | 2.22 | 24 | 1 | 0 | 1 | 49 | 30 | 18 | 12 | 34 | 54 | R | R | 6-3 | 225 | 7-12-73 | 1995 | Raleigh, N.C. |
| Ortiz, Rosario | 2 | 0 | 0.00 | 6 | 0 | 0 | 0 | 8 | 3 | 0 | 0 | 6 | 6 | R | R | 6-4 | 215 | 3-1-75 | 1996 | Globe, Ariz. |
| Persails, Mark | 1 | 4 | 4.24 | 13 | 13 | 0 | 0 | 64 | 53 | 35 | 30 | 29 | 37 | R | R | 6-3 | 185 | 10-25-75 | 1995 | Vassar, Mich. |
| Quintal, Craig | 4 | 8 | 3.44 | 15 | 15 | 0 | 0 | 86 | 93 | 51 | 33 | 23 | 49 | R | R | 6-0 | 200 | 1-21-75 | 1996 | New Orleans, La. |
| Reinfelder, Dave | 2 | 2 | 2.83 | 28 | 0 | 0 | 2 | 57 | 46 | 24 | 18 | 14 | 52 | R | L | 6-1 | 180 | 4-24-74 | 1995 | Vassar, Mich. |
| Romo, Greg | 4 | 2 | 2.35 | 6 | 6 | 1 | 0 | 38 | 35 | 17 | 10 | 6 | 39 | L | R | 6-3 | 175 | 5-14-75 | 1995 | Wasco, Calif. |
| Schroeder, Chad | 5 | 0 | 1.40 | 31 | 0 | 0 | 6 | 39 | 29 | 15 | 6 | 6 | 41 | R | R | 6-3 | 200 | 9-21-73 | 1996 | Elgin, Ill. |
| Spear, Russ | 2 | 1 | 5.19 | 8 | 7 | 0 | 0 | 35 | 39 | 24 | 20 | 15 | 28 | R | R | 6-3 | 190 | 8-30-77 | 1995 | Albanvale, Australia |
| Zamarripa, Mark | 4 | 2 | 2.03 | 29 | 0 | 0 | 4 | 49 | 25 | 13 | 11 | 14 | 61 | R | R | 6-0 | 180 | 7-28-74 | 1996 | Los Angeles, Calif. |

## GULF COAST LEAGUE

| BATTING | AVG | G | AB | R | H | 2B | 3B | HR | RBI | BB | SO | SB | CS | B | T | HT | WT | DOB | 1st Yr | Resides |
|---|---|---|---|---|---|---|---|---|---|---|---|---|---|---|---|---|---|---|---|---|
| Alvarez, Julio | .261 | 28 | 92 | 13 | 24 | 2 | 0 | 0 | 10 | 11 | 22 | 5 | 1 | S | R | 6-0 | 160 | 3-2-79 | 1996 | Santiago, D.R. |
| Aybar, Ramon | .286 | 43 | 154 | 30 | 44 | 7 | 1 | 0 | 16 | 19 | 38 | 32 | 3 | L | R | 5-9 | 150 | 5-10-76 | 1994 | Bani, D.R. |
| Hazelton, Justin | .128 | 47 | 141 | 15 | 18 | 3 | 0 | 1 | 12 | 21 | 45 | 1 | 2 | R | R | 6-2 | 180 | 7-9-78 | 1996 | Philipsburg, Pa. |
| Jamison, Nick | .105 | 31 | 95 | 11 | 10 | 1 | 1 | 0 | 9 | 12 | 18 | 1 | 2 | L | L | 6-1 | 175 | 7-11-78 | 1996 | Greenwood, Ind. |
| Lignitz, Jeremiah | .176 | 46 | 153 | 9 | 27 | 2 | 2 | 1 | 13 | 18 | 53 | 2 | 1 | L | R | 6-2 | 210 | 5-18-77 | 1995 | Davidson, Mich. |
| McKinney, Antonio | .211 | 44 | 147 | 27 | 31 | 4 | 2 | 1 | 13 | 15 | 44 | 8 | 0 | R | R | 5-10 | 175 | 1-2-78 | 1996 | Portland, Ore. |
| Meran, Jorge | .315 | 54 | 168 | 25 | 53 | 13 | 3 | 2 | 32 | 13 | 42 | 7 | 2 | R | R | 6-0 | 175 | 2-14-75 | 1991 | Santo Domingo, D.R. |
| Mercedes, Matia | .200 | 16 | 50 | 9 | 10 | 6 | 0 | 0 | 6 | 7 | 10 | 2 | 1 | R | R | 5-11 | 135 | 3-24-76 | 1994 | San Pedro de Macoris, D.R. |
| Moore, Tris | .259 | 16 | 54 | 9 | 14 | 1 | 0 | 2 | 12 | 8 | 12 | 2 | 0 | R | R | 6-0 | 185 | 1-15-74 | 1996 | Miami, Fla. |
| Neikirk, Derick | .211 | 18 | 38 | 4 | 8 | 0 | 0 | 0 | 1 | 5 | 7 | 0 | 0 | R | R | 6-3 | 214 | 9-5-74 | 1996 | Glendale, Ariz. |
| Peniche, Fray | .193 | 40 | 119 | 17 | 23 | 6 | 2 | 0 | 5 | 12 | 39 | 2 | 3 | R | R | 6-2 | 185 | 11-2-76 | 1995 | Santiago, D.R. |
| Reyes, Deurys | .143 | 5 | 7 | 3 | 1 | 0 | 1 | 0 | 0 | 2 | 3 | 0 | 0 | L | L | 5-11 | 155 | 8-8-79 | 1996 | Santo Domingo, D.R. |
| Shipman, Nate | .204 | 35 | 113 | 16 | 23 | 6 | 1 | 1 | 12 | 7 | 37 | 7 | 2 | S | R | 6-0 | 190 | 2-22-77 | 1995 | New Port Richey, Fla. |
| Stevenson, Chad | .291 | 46 | 158 | 13 | 46 | 18 | 0 | 0 | 16 | 9 | 47 | 1 | 0 | R | R | 6-4 | 215 | 2-3-76 | 1994 | Henderson, Nev. |
| Tanaka, Shuta | .164 | 44 | 116 | 16 | 19 | 7 | 1 | 0 | 11 | 18 | 21 | 5 | 1 | L | R | 5-10 | 160 | 2-23-77 | 1996 | Nishinomiya, Japan |
| Whitner, Keith | .202 | 43 | 124 | 13 | 25 | 2 | 0 | 1 | 8 | 15 | 40 | 8 | 2 | R | R | 6-3 | 195 | 9-26-75 | 1996 | Los Angeles, Calif. |
| Zapata, Alexis | .333 | 51 | 189 | 34 | 63 | 13 | 5 | 6 | 41 | 12 | 35 | 8 | 4 | R | R | 6-3 | 190 | 5-20-77 | 1996 | Santo Domingo, D.R. |

| PITCHING | W | L | ERA | G | GS | CG | SV | IP | H | R | ER | BB | SO | B | T | HT | WT | DOB | 1st Yr | Resides |
|---|---|---|---|---|---|---|---|---|---|---|---|---|---|---|---|---|---|---|---|---|
| Adachi, Tomo | 0 | 1 | 8.38 | 5 | 0 | 0 | 0 | 10 | 15 | 15 | 9 | 7 | 7 | R | L | 6-1 | 170 | 8-21-74 | 1996 | Nishinomiya, Japan |
| Alvord, Aaron | 4 | 3 | 4.85 | 16 | 0 | 0 | 2 | 43 | 60 | 28 | 23 | 6 | 21 | R | R | 6-1 | 180 | 6-21-77 | 1996 | Canton, Kan. |
| Donastorg, Raul | 1 | 2 | 3.96 | 20 | 0 | 0 | 4 | 25 | 24 | 13 | 11 | 9 | 17 | R | R | 6-4 | 230 | 10-22-77 | 1996 | San Pedro de Macoris, D.R. |
| Gonzalez, Gener | 2 | 1 | 3.32 | 4 | 4 | 0 | 0 | 19 | 17 | 9 | 7 | 9 | 19 | R | R | 6-4 | 170 | 2-19-76 | 1993 | Santo Domingo, D.R. |
| Keller, Kris | 1 | 2 | 2.38 | 8 | 6 | 0 | 0 | 34 | 23 | 12 | 9 | 21 | 23 | R | R | 6-2 | 220 | 3-1-78 | 1996 | Atlantic Beach, Fla. |
| Martinez, Romulo | 1 | 6 | 2.73 | 12 | 12 | 0 | 0 | 63 | 67 | 28 | 19 | 9 | 51 | R | R | 6-1 | 170 | 12-5-76 | 1994 | Santiago, D.R. |
| McFarlane, Joseph | 2 | 0 | 3.93 | 15 | 2 | 0 | 2 | 37 | 32 | 21 | 16 | 14 | 34 | R | R | 6-3 | 185 | 2-20-77 | 1995 | Anacortes, Wash. |
| Ramirez, Jose | 2 | 7 | 3.92 | 13 | 11 | 0 | 0 | 60 | 69 | 49 | 26 | 23 | 47 | L | L | 6-1 | 170 | 9-1-75 | 1994 | Santo Domingo, D.R. |
| Reed, Aaron | 0 | 1 | 6.00 | 18 | 0 | 0 | 0 | 27 | 34 | 25 | 18 | 17 | 26 | R | R | 6-3 | 180 | 12-4-77 | 1996 | Brisbane, Australia |
| Reed, Brandon | 0 | 0 | 0.00 | 1 | 1 | 0 | 0 | 2 | 0 | 0 | 0 | 2 | 7 | R | R | 6-4 | 185 | 12-18-74 | 1994 | Lapeer, Mich. |
| Romo, Greg | 1 | 0 | 1.57 | 8 | 1 | 0 | 1 | 23 | 19 | 7 | 4 | 4 | 29 | L | R | 6-3 | 175 | 5-14-75 | 1995 | Wasco, Calif. |
| Santamaria, Juan | 2 | 7 | 5.34 | 12 | 12 | 0 | 0 | 56 | 52 | 47 | 33 | 25 | 43 | R | R | 6-1 | 165 | 5-6-77 | 1995 | Santo Domingo, D.R. |
| Santos, Victor | 3 | 2 | 1.98 | 9 | 9 | 0 | 0 | 50 | 44 | 12 | 11 | 13 | 39 | R | R | 6-3 | 175 | 10-2-76 | 1995 | Garfield, N.J. |
| Seebode, Michael | 4 | 2 | 3.75 | 12 | 2 | 0 | 0 | 36 | 34 | 22 | 15 | 11 | 25 | L | L | 6-1 | 200 | 11-6-77 | 1996 | Valatie, N.Y. |
| Van Winkle, Judd | 3 | 1 | 6.95 | 8 | 0 | 0 | 1 | 22 | 37 | 17 | 17 | 4 | 22 | L | L | 6-2 | 190 | 12-17-75 | 1996 | Spartanburg, S.C. |

# FLORIDA MARLINS

**Managers:** Rene Lachemann, John Boles.  **1996 Record:** 80-82, .494 (3rd, NL East).

| BATTING | AVG | G | AB | R | H | 2B | 3B | HR | RBI | BB | SO | SB | CS | B | T | HT | WT | DOB | 1st Yr | Resides |
|---|---|---|---|---|---|---|---|---|---|---|---|---|---|---|---|---|---|---|---|---|
| Abbott, Kurt | .253 | 109 | 320 | 37 | 81 | 18 | 7 | 8 | 33 | 22 | 99 | 3 | 3 | R | R | 6-0 | 170 | 6-2-69 | 1989 | St. Petersburg, Fla. |
| Arias, Alex | .277 | 100 | 224 | 27 | 62 | 11 | 2 | 3 | 26 | 17 | 28 | 2 | 0 | R | R | 6-3 | 185 | 11-20-67 | 1987 | New York, N.Y. |
| Booty, Josh | .500 | 2 | 2 | 1 | 1 | 0 | 0 | 0 | 0 | 0 | 0 | 0 | 0 | R | R | 6-3 | 210 | 4-29-75 | 1994 | Shreveport, La. |
| Brooks, Jerry | .400 | 8 | 5 | 2 | 2 | 0 | 1 | 0 | 3 | 1 | 1 | 0 | 0 | R | R | 6-0 | 195 | 3-23-67 | 1988 | Syracuse, N.Y. |
| Castillo, Luis | .262 | 41 | 164 | 26 | 43 | 2 | 1 | 1 | 8 | 14 | 46 | 17 | 4 | S | R | 5-11 | 146 | 9-12-75 | 1993 | San Pedro de Macoris, D.R. |
| Colbrunn, Greg | .286 | 141 | 511 | 60 | 146 | 26 | 2 | 16 | 69 | 25 | 76 | 4 | 5 | R | R | 6-0 | 200 | 7-26-69 | 1988 | Fontana, Calif. |
| Conine, Jeff | .293 | 157 | 597 | 84 | 175 | 32 | 2 | 26 | 95 | 62 | 121 | 1 | 4 | R | R | 6-1 | 220 | 6-27-66 | 1988 | Rialto, Calif. |
| Dawson, Andre | .276 | 42 | 58 | 6 | 16 | 2 | 0 | 2 | 14 | 2 | 13 | 0 | 0 | R | R | 6-3 | 195 | 7-10-54 | 1975 | Miami, Fla. |
| Grebeck, Craig | .211 | 50 | 95 | 8 | 20 | 1 | 0 | 1 | 9 | 4 | 14 | 0 | 0 | R | R | 5-7 | 148 | 12-29-64 | 1987 | Cerritos, Calif. |
| Johnson, Charles | .218 | 120 | 386 | 34 | 84 | 13 | 1 | 13 | 37 | 40 | 91 | 1 | 0 | R | R | 6-2 | 215 | 7-20-71 | 1992 | Fort Pierce, Fla. |
| McMillon, Billy | .216 | 28 | 51 | 4 | 11 | 0 | 0 | 4 | 5 | 14 | 0 | 0 | 0 | L | L | 5-11 | 172 | 11-17-71 | 1993 | Sumter, S.C. |
| Milliard, Ralph | .161 | 24 | 62 | 7 | 10 | 2 | 0 | 1 | 14 | 16 | 2 | 0 | 0 | R | R | 5-10 | 160 | 12-30-73 | 1993 | Soest, Neth. Antilles |
| Morman, Russ | .167 | 6 | 6 | 0 | 1 | 1 | 0 | 0 | 1 | 2 | 0 | 0 | 0 | R | R | 6-4 | 215 | 4-28-62 | 1983 | Blue Springs, Mo. |
| Natal, Rob | .133 | 44 | 90 | 4 | 12 | 1 | 1 | 0 | 2 | 15 | 31 | 0 | 1 | R | R | 6-0 | 195 | 11-13-65 | 1987 | Chula Vista, Calif. |
| Orsulak, Joe | .221 | 120 | 217 | 23 | 48 | 6 | 1 | 2 | 19 | 16 | 38 | 1 | 1 | L | L | 6-1 | 203 | 5-31-62 | 1981 | Cockeysville, Md. |
| Pendleton, Terry | .251 | 111 | 406 | 30 | 102 | 20 | 1 | 7 | 58 | 26 | 75 | 0 | 2 | S | R | 5-9 | 195 | 7-16-60 | 1982 | Duluth, Ga. |
| Renteria, Edgar | .309 | 106 | 431 | 68 | 133 | 18 | 3 | 5 | 31 | 33 | 68 | 16 | 2 | R | R | 6-1 | 172 | 8-7-75 | 1992 | Barranquilla, Colombia |
| Sheffield, Gary | .314 | 161 | 519 | 118 | 163 | 33 | 1 | 42 | 120 | 142 | 66 | 16 | 9 | R | R | 5-11 | 190 | 11-18-68 | 1986 | St. Petersburg, Fla. |
| Siddall, Joe | .149 | 18 | 47 | 0 | 7 | 1 | 0 | 0 | 3 | 2 | 8 | 0 | 0 | L | R | 6-1 | 197 | 10-25-67 | 1988 | Windsor, Ontario |
| Tavarez, Jesus | .219 | 98 | 114 | 14 | 25 | 3 | 0 | 0 | 6 | 7 | 18 | 5 | 1 | S | R | 6-0 | 170 | 3-26-71 | 1993 | Santo Domingo, D.R. |
| Veras, Quilvio | .253 | 73 | 253 | 40 | 64 | 8 | 1 | 4 | 14 | 51 | 42 | 8 | 8 | S | R | 5-8 | 168 | 4-3-71 | 1990 | Santo Domingo, D.R. |
| Weathers, David | .158 | 32 | 19 | 1 | 3 | 0 | 0 | 1 | 2 | 0 | 13 | 0 | 0 | R | R | 6-3 | 205 | 9-25-69 | 1988 | Leoma, Tenn. |
| White, Devon | .274 | 146 | 552 | 77 | 151 | 37 | 6 | 17 | 84 | 38 | 99 | 22 | 6 | S | R | 6-2 | 178 | 12-29-62 | 1981 | Mesa, Ariz. |
| Zaun, Greg | .290 | 10 | 31 | 4 | 9 | 1 | 0 | 1 | 2 | 3 | 5 | 1 | 0 | S | R | 5-10 | 170 | 4-14-71 | 1989 | Glendale, Calif. |

| PITCHING | W | L | ERA | G | GS | CG | SV | IP | H | R | ER | BB | SO | B | T | HT | WT | DOB | 1st Yr | Resides |
|---|---|---|---|---|---|---|---|---|---|---|---|---|---|---|---|---|---|---|---|---|
| Adamson, Joel | 0 | 0 | 7.36 | 9 | 0 | 0 | 0 | 11 | 18 | 9 | 9 | 7 | 7 | L | L | 6-4 | 180 | 7-2-71 | 1990 | Lakewood, Calif. |
| Batista, Miguel | 0 | 0 | 5.56 | 9 | 0 | 0 | 0 | 11 | 9 | 8 | 7 | 7 | 6 | R | R | 6-0 | 160 | 2-19-71 | 1988 | San Pedro de Macoris, D.R. |
| Brown, Kevin | 17 | 11 | 1.89 | 32 | 32 | 5 | 0 | 233 | 187 | 60 | 49 | 33 | 159 | R | R | 6-4 | 195 | 3-14-65 | 1986 | Macon, Ga. |
| Burkett, John | 6 | 10 | 4.32 | 24 | 24 | 1 | 0 | 154 | 154 | 84 | 74 | 42 | 108 | R | R | 6-3 | 205 | 11-28-64 | 1983 | Scottsdale, Ariz. |
| Hammond, Chris | 5 | 8 | 6.56 | 38 | 9 | 0 | 0 | 81 | 104 | 65 | 59 | 27 | 50 | L | L | 6-1 | 195 | 1-21-66 | 1986 | Birmingham, Ala. |
| Helling, Rick | 2 | 1 | 1.95 | 5 | 4 | 0 | 0 | 28 | 14 | 6 | 6 | 7 | 26 | R | R | 6-3 | 215 | 12-15-70 | 1992 | West Fargo, N.D. |
| Heredia, Felix | 1 | 1 | 4.32 | 21 | 0 | 0 | 0 | 17 | 21 | 8 | 8 | 10 | 10 | L | L | 6-0 | 160 | 6-18-76 | 1993 | Barahona, D.R. |
| Hernandez, Livan | 0 | 0 | 0.00 | 1 | 0 | 0 | 0 | 3 | 3 | 0 | 0 | 2 | 2 | R | R | 6-2 | 220 | 2-20-75 | 1996 | Miami, Fla. |
| Hurst, Bill | 0 | 0 | 0.00 | 2 | 0 | 0 | 0 | 2 | 3 | 0 | 0 | 1 | 1 | R | R | 6-7 | 220 | 4-28-70 | 1990 | Miami, Fla. |
| Hutton, Mark | 5 | 1 | 3.67 | 13 | 9 | 0 | 0 | 56 | 47 | 23 | 23 | 18 | 31 | R | R | 6-6 | 225 | 2-6-70 | 1989 | West Lakes, Australia |
| Larkin, Andy | 0 | 0 | 1.80 | 1 | 1 | 0 | 0 | 5 | 3 | 1 | 1 | 4 | 4 | R | R | 6-4 | 181 | 6-27-74 | 1992 | Medford, Ore. |
| Leiter, Al | 16 | 12 | 2.93 | 33 | 33 | 2 | 0 | 215 | 153 | 74 | 70 | 119 | 200 | L | L | 6-1 | 190 | 10-23-65 | 1984 | Plantation, Fla. |
| Mantei, Matt | 1 | 0 | 6.38 | 14 | 0 | 0 | 0 | 18 | 13 | 13 | 13 | 21 | 25 | R | R | 6-1 | 181 | 7-7-73 | 1991 | Sawyer, Mich. |
| Mathews, Terry | 2 | 4 | 4.91 | 57 | 0 | 0 | 4 | 55 | 59 | 33 | 30 | 27 | 49 | L | R | 6-2 | 225 | 10-5-64 | 1987 | Boyce, La. |
| Miller, Kurt | 1 | 3 | 6.80 | 26 | 5 | 0 | 0 | 46 | 57 | 41 | 35 | 33 | 30 | R | R | 6-5 | 200 | 8-24-72 | 1990 | Bakersfield, Calif. |
| Nen, Robb | 5 | 1 | 1.95 | 75 | 0 | 0 | 35 | 83 | 67 | 21 | 18 | 21 | 92 | R | R | 6-4 | 190 | 11-28-69 | 1987 | Seal Beach, Calif. |
| Pall, Donn | 1 | 1 | 5.79 | 12 | 0 | 0 | 0 | 19 | 16 | 15 | 12 | 9 | 9 | R | R | 6-1 | 180 | 1-11-62 | 1985 | Bloomingdale, Ill. |
| Pena, Alejandro | 0 | 1 | 4.50 | 4 | 0 | 0 | 0 | 4 | 4 | 5 | 2 | 1 | 5 | R | R | 6-1 | 200 | 6-25-59 | 1979 | Roswell, Ga. |
| Perez, Yorkis | 3 | 4 | 5.29 | 64 | 0 | 0 | 0 | 48 | 51 | 28 | 28 | 31 | 47 | L | L | 6-0 | 160 | 9-30-67 | 1983 | Haina, D.R. |
| Powell, Jay | 4 | 3 | 4.54 | 67 | 0 | 0 | 2 | 71 | 71 | 41 | 36 | 36 | 52 | R | R | 6-4 | 220 | 1-9-72 | 1993 | Collinsville, Tenn. |
| Rapp, Pat | 8 | 16 | 5.10 | 30 | 29 | 0 | 0 | 162 | 184 | 95 | 92 | 91 | 86 | R | R | 6-3 | 210 | 7-13-67 | 1989 | Sulphur, La. |
| Valdes, Marc | 1 | 3 | 4.81 | 11 | 8 | 0 | 0 | 49 | 63 | 32 | 26 | 23 | 13 | R | R | 6-0 | 170 | 12-20-71 | 1993 | Tampa, Fla. |

## FIELDING

| Catcher | PCT | G | PO | A | E | DP | PB |
|---|---|---|---|---|---|---|---|
| Johnson | .995 | 120 | 751 | 70 | 4 | 12 | 5 |
| Natal | .976 | 43 | 187 | 14 | 5 | 2 | 6 |
| Siddall | .977 | 18 | 78 | 8 | 2 | 1 | 1 |
| Zaun | 1.000 | 10 | 60 | 6 | 0 | 0 | 0 |

| First Base | PCT | G | PO | A | E | DP |
|---|---|---|---|---|---|---|
| Arias | 1.000 | 1 | 1 | 0 | 0 | 0 |
| Brooks | .000 | 1 | 0 | 0 | 1 | 0 |
| Colbrunn | .995 | 134 | 1169 | 101 | 6 | 130 |
| Conine | .991 | 48 | 292 | 40 | 3 | 33 |
| Morman | 1.000 | 2 | 2 | 0 | 0 | 1 |
| Orsulak | 1.000 | 2 | 4 | 1 | 0 | 1 |

| Second Base | PCT | G | PO | A | E | DP |
|---|---|---|---|---|---|---|
| Abbott | 1.000 | 20 | 35 | 39 | 0 | 6 |
| Arias | 1.000 | 1 | 0 | 2 | 0 | 0 |
| Castillo | .986 | 41 | 99 | 118 | 3 | 37 |
| Grebeck | .985 | 29 | 67 | 65 | 2 | 24 |
| Milliard | .955 | 24 | 42 | 65 | 5 | 14 |
| Veras | .986 | 67 | 174 | 191 | 5 | 54 |

| Third Base | PCT | G | PO | A | E | DP |
|---|---|---|---|---|---|---|
| Abbott | .914 | 33 | 22 | 42 | 6 | 3 |
| Arias | .956 | 59 | 21 | 66 | 4 | 8 |
| Booty | .000 | 1 | 0 | 0 | 0 | 0 |
| Grebeck | .000 | 1 | 0 | 0 | 0 | 0 |
| Pendleton | .961 | 108 | 83 | 216 | 12 | 22 |

| Shortstop | PCT | G | PO | A | E | DP |
|---|---|---|---|---|---|---|
| Abbott | .969 | 44 | 66 | 123 | 6 | 34 |
| Arias | .966 | 20 | 26 | 59 | 3 | 15 |
| Grebeck | 1.000 | 2 | 0 | 1 | 0 | 0 |
| Renteria | .979 | 106 | 163 | 345 | 11 | 77 |

| Outfield | PCT | G | PO | A | E | DP |
|---|---|---|---|---|---|---|
| Brooks | 1.000 | 2 | 2 | 0 | 0 | 0 |
| Conine | .975 | 128 | 186 | 8 | 5 | 2 |
| Dawson | .833 | 6 | 5 | 0 | 1 | 0 |
| McMillon | 1.000 | 15 | 17 | 0 | 0 | 0 |
| Orsulak | .956 | 59 | 80 | 6 | 4 | 0 |
| Sheffield | .976 | 161 | 238 | 8 | 6 | 0 |
| Tavarez | 1.000 | 65 | 58 | 0 | 0 | 0 |
| White | .987 | 139 | 296 | 5 | 4 | 1 |

**Gary Sheffield**

LARRY GOREN

Closer Robb Nen led the Marlins with 35 saves in 1996

Marlins minor league Player of the Year Billy McMillon

DAVID SEELIG

MORRIS FOSTOFF

## FARM SYSTEM

**Director of Player Development:** John Boles

| Class | Farm Team | League | W | L | Pct. | Finish* | Manager | First Yr |
|---|---|---|---|---|---|---|---|---|
| AAA | Charlotte (N.C.) Knights | International | 62 | 79 | .440 | T-8th (10) | Sal Rende | 1995 |
| AA | Portland (Maine) Sea Dogs | Eastern | 83 | 58 | .589 | 2nd (10) | Carlos Tosca | 1994 |
| #A | Brevard County (Fla.) Manatees | Florida State | 47 | 92 | .338 | 14th (14) | Fredi Gonzalez | 1994 |
| A | Kane County (Ill.) Cougars | Midwest | 65 | 68 | .489 | 9th (14) | Lynn Jones | 1993 |
| A | Utica (N.Y.) Blue Marlins | New York-Penn | 29 | 47 | .382 | 13th (14) | Steve McFarland | 1996 |
| R | Melbourne (Fla.) Marlins | Gulf Coast | 34 | 25 | .576 | 5th (16) | Juan Bustabad | 1992 |

*Finish in overall standings (No. of teams in league)   #Advanced level

## ORGANIZATION LEADERS

### MAJOR LEAGUERS

**BATTING**

| | | |
|---|---|---|
| *AVG | Gary Sheffield | .314 |
| R | Gary Sheffield | 118 |
| H | Jeff Conine | 175 |
| TB | Gary Sheffield | 324 |
| 2B | Devon White | 37 |
| 3B | Kurt Abbott | 7 |
| HR | Gary Sheffield | 42 |
| RBI | Gary Sheffield | 120 |
| BB | Gary Sheffield | 142 |
| SO | Jeff Conine | 121 |
| SB | Devon White | 22 |

**PITCHING**

| | | |
|---|---|---|
| W | Kevin Brown | 17 |
| L | Pat Rapp | 16 |
| #ERA | Kevin Brown | 1.89 |
| G | Robb Nen | 75 |
| CG | Kevin Brown | 5 |
| SV | Robb Nen | 35 |
| IP | Kevin Brown | 233 |
| BB | Al Leiter | 119 |
| SO | Al Leiter | 200 |

MORRIS FOSTOFF

**Kevin Brown.** 17 wins, 1.89 ERA

### MINOR LEAGUERS

**BATTING**

| | | |
|---|---|---|
| *AVG | Billy McMillon, Charlotte | .352 |
| R | Randy Winn, Kane County | 90 |
| H | Todd Dunwoody, Portland | 153 |
| TB | Jerry Brooks, Charlotte | 269 |
| 2B | Two tied at | 32 |
| 3B | Hayward Cook, Brevard/Portland | 9 |
| HR | Jerry Brooks, Charlotte | 34 |
| RBI | Jerry Brooks, Charlotte | 107 |
| BB | John Roskos, Portland | 67 |
| SO | Josh Booty, Kane County | 195 |
| SB | Luis Castillo, Portland | 51 |

**PITCHING**

| | | |
|---|---|---|
| W | Victor Hurtado, Kane County | 15 |
| L | Dan Ehler, Brevard County | 16 |
| #ERA | Gabe Gonzalez, Char./Brevard Co. | 1.82 |
| G | Dan Chergey, Charlotte/Portland | 58 |
| CG | Victor Hurtado, Kane County | 5 |
| SV | Bill Hurst, Portland | 30 |
| IP | Victor Hurtado, Kane County | 176 |
| BB | Matt Whisenant, Charlotte | 101 |
| SO | Tony Saunders, Portland | 156 |

*Minimum 250 At-Bats   #Minimum 75 Innings

## TOP 10 PROSPECTS

**How the Marlins Top 10 prospects, as judged by Baseball America prior to the 1996 season, fared in 1996:**

STEVE MOORE

**Edgar Renteria**

| Player, Pos. | Club (Class—League) | AVG | AB | R | H | 2B | 3B | HR | RBI | SB |
|---|---|---|---|---|---|---|---|---|---|---|
| 1. Edgar Renteria, ss | Charlotte (AAA—International) | .280 | 132 | 17 | 37 | 8 | 0 | 2 | 16 | 10 |
| | Florida | .309 | 431 | 68 | 133 | 18 | 3 | 5 | 31 | 16 |
| 2. Luis Castillo, 2b | Portland (AA—Eastern) | .317 | 420 | 83 | 133 | 15 | 7 | 1 | 35 | 51 |
| | Florida | .262 | 164 | 26 | 43 | 2 | 1 | 1 | 8 | 17 |
| 4. Jaime Jones, of | Kane County (A—Midwest) | .249 | 237 | 29 | 59 | 17 | 1 | 8 | 45 | 7 |
| 5. Josh Booty, 3b | Kane County (A—Midwest) | .206 | 475 | 62 | 98 | 25 | 1 | 21 | 87 | 2 |
| | Florida | .500 | 2 | 1 | 1 | 0 | 0 | 0 | 0 | 0 |
| 7. Billy McMillon, of | Charlotte (AAA—International) | .352 | 347 | 72 | 122 | 32 | 2 | 17 | 70 | 5 |
| | Florida | .216 | 51 | 4 | 11 | 0 | 0 | 0 | 4 | 0 |
| 8. Randy Winn, of | Kane County (A—Midwest) | .270 | 514 | 90 | 139 | 16 | 3 | 0 | 35 | 30 |
| 9. Ralph Milliard, 2b | Portland (AA—Eastern) | .200 | 20 | 2 | 4 | 0 | 1 | 0 | 2 | 1 |
| | Charlotte (AAA—International) | .276 | 250 | 47 | 69 | 15 | 2 | 6 | 26 | 8 |
| | Florida | .161 | 62 | 7 | 10 | 2 | 0 | 0 | 1 | 2 |
| 10. Alex Gonzalez, ss | Kane County (A—Midwest) | .200 | 10 | 2 | 2 | 0 | 0 | 0 | 0 | 0 |
| | Portland (AA—Eastern) | .235 | 34 | 4 | 8 | 0 | 1 | 0 | 1 | 0 |

| | | | W | L | ERA | G | SV | IP | H | BB | SO |
|---|---|---|---|---|---|---|---|---|---|---|---|
| 3. Jay Powell, rhp | Brevard County (A—Florida State) | | 0 | 0 | 0.00 | 1 | 0 | 2 | 0 | 0 | 4 |
| | Florida | | 4 | 3 | 4.54 | 67 | 2 | 71 | 71 | 36 | 52 |
| 6. Will Cunnane, rhp | Portland (AA—Eastern) | | 10 | 12 | 3.74 | 25 | 0 | 152 | 156 | 30 | 101 |

## INTERNATIONAL LEAGUE

| BATTING | AVG | G | AB | R | H | 2B | 3B | HR | RBI | BB | SO | SB | CS | B | T | HT | WT | DOB | 1st Yr | Resides |
|---|---|---|---|---|---|---|---|---|---|---|---|---|---|---|---|---|---|---|---|---|
| Abbott, Kurt | .377 | 18 | 69 | 20 | 26 | 10 | 1 | 5 | 11 | 7 | 18 | 2 | 0 | R | R | 6-0 | 170 | 6-2-69 | 1989 | St. Petersburg, Fla. |
| Brooks, Jerry | .288 | 136 | 466 | 72 | 134 | 29 | 2 | 34 | 107 | 32 | 78 | 5 | 5 | R | R | 6-0 | 195 | 3-23-67 | 1988 | Syracuse, N.Y. |
| Clapinski, Chris | .285 | 105 | 362 | 74 | 103 | 20 | 1 | 10 | 39 | 47 | 54 | 13 | 6 | S | R | 6-0 | 165 | 8-20-71 | 1992 | Rancho Mirage, Calif. |
| Fagley, Dan | .000 | 2 | 1 | 1 | 0 | 0 | 0 | 0 | 0 | 0 | 0 | 0 | 0 | R | R | 5-10 | 185 | 12-18-74 | 1994 | Riverton, N.J. |
| Gregg, Tommy | .286 | 119 | 405 | 69 | 116 | 24 | 0 | 22 | 80 | 49 | 62 | 10 | 1 | L | L | 6-1 | 190 | 7-29-63 | 1985 | Smyrna, N.C. |
| Halter, Shane | .293 | 16 | 41 | 3 | 12 | 1 | 0 | 0 | 4 | 2 | 8 | 0 | 0 | R | R | 5-10 | 160 | 11-8-69 | 1991 | Papillion, Neb. |
| Johnson, Erik | .178 | 67 | 185 | 19 | 33 | 6 | 0 | 0 | 10 | 8 | 35 | 0 | 2 | R | R | 5-11 | 175 | 10-11-65 | 1987 | San Ramon, Calif. |
| Lucca, Lou | .260 | 87 | 273 | 26 | 71 | 14 | 1 | 7 | 35 | 11 | 62 | 0 | 3 | R | R | 5-11 | 210 | 10-13-70 | 1992 | San Francisco, Calif. |
| McMillon, Billy | .352 | 97 | 347 | 72 | 122 | 32 | 2 | 17 | 70 | 36 | 76 | 5 | 3 | L | L | 5-11 | 172 | 11-17-71 | 1993 | Sumter, S.C. |
| Milliard, Ralph | .276 | 69 | 250 | 47 | 69 | 15 | 2 | 6 | 26 | 38 | 43 | 8 | 4 | R | R | 5-10 | 160 | 12-30-73 | 1993 | Soest, Neth. Antilles |
| Morman, Russ | .332 | 80 | 289 | 59 | 96 | 18 | 1 | 18 | 77 | 29 | 51 | 2 | 4 | R | R | 6-4 | 215 | 4-28-62 | 1983 | Blue Springs, Mo. |
| Olmeda, Jose | .320 | 115 | 375 | 52 | 120 | 26 | 1 | 9 | 49 | 21 | 58 | 7 | 6 | S | R | 5-9 | 155 | 6-20-68 | 1989 | Gurabo, P.R. |
| Renteria, Edgar | .280 | 35 | 132 | 17 | 37 | 8 | 0 | 2 | 16 | 9 | 17 | 10 | 4 | R | R | 6-1 | 172 | 8-7-75 | 1992 | Barranquilla, Colombia |
| Riley, Marquis | .227 | 92 | 300 | 43 | 68 | 10 | 0 | 0 | 13 | 26 | 31 | 16 | 5 | R | R | 5-10 | 170 | 12-27-70 | 1992 | Ashdown, Ark. |
| Robertson, Jason | .040 | 11 | 25 | 2 | 1 | 0 | 0 | 1 | 2 | 2 | 12 | 0 | 1 | L | L | 6-2 | 200 | 3-24-71 | 1989 | Country Club Hills, Ill. |
| Ronan, Marc | .305 | 79 | 220 | 23 | 67 | 10 | 0 | 4 | 20 | 16 | 37 | 3 | 4 | L | R | 6-2 | 190 | 9-19-69 | 1990 | Tallahassee, Fla. |
| Sheff, Chris | .264 | 92 | 284 | 41 | 75 | 15 | 1 | 12 | 49 | 21 | 55 | 7 | 1 | R | R | 6-3 | 210 | 2-4-71 | 1992 | Laguna Hills, Calif. |
| Siddall, Joe | .280 | 65 | 189 | 22 | 53 | 13 | 1 | 3 | 20 | 11 | 36 | 1 | 2 | L | R | 6-1 | 197 | 10-25-67 | 1988 | Windsor, Ontario |
| Torres, Tomas | .250 | 5 | 4 | 0 | 1 | 0 | 0 | 0 | 1 | 0 | 0 | 0 | 0 | R | R | 5-11 | 165 | 9-29-74 | 1992 | Azua, D.R. |
| Veras, Quilvio | .327 | 28 | 104 | 22 | 34 | 5 | 2 | 2 | 8 | 13 | 14 | 8 | 3 | S | R | 5-8 | 168 | 4-3-71 | 1990 | Santo Domingo, D.R. |
| Whitmore, Darrell | .304 | 55 | 204 | 27 | 62 | 13 | 0 | 11 | 36 | 7 | 43 | 2 | 5 | L | R | 6-1 | 210 | 11-18-68 | 1990 | Front Royal, Va. |

| PITCHING | W | L | ERA | G | GS | CG | SV | IP | H | R | ER | BB | SO | B | T | HT | WT | DOB | 1st Yr | Resides |
|---|---|---|---|---|---|---|---|---|---|---|---|---|---|---|---|---|---|---|---|---|
| Adamson, Joel | 6 | 6 | 3.78 | 44 | 8 | 0 | 3 | 98 | 108 | 48 | 41 | 28 | 84 | L | L | 6-4 | 180 | 7-2-71 | 1990 | Lakewood, Calif. |
| Alfonseca, Antonio | 4 | 4 | 5.53 | 14 | 13 | 0 | 1 | 72 | 86 | 47 | 44 | 22 | 51 | R | R | 6-5 | 160 | 4-16-72 | 1990 | La Romana, D.R. |
| Batista, Miguel | 4 | 3 | 5.38 | 47 | 2 | 0 | 4 | 77 | 93 | 57 | 46 | 39 | 56 | R | R | 6-0 | 160 | 2-19-71 | 1988 | San Pedro de Macoris, D.R. |
| Brito, Mario | 1 | 0 | 1.80 | 6 | 0 | 0 | 4 | 5 | 3 | 1 | 1 | 2 | 10 | R | R | 6-3 | 179 | 4-9-66 | 1985 | Bonao, D.R. |
| Chergey, Dan | 0 | 1 | 6.21 | 45 | 1 | 0 | 1 | 75 | 86 | 55 | 52 | 28 | 43 | R | R | 6-2 | 195 | 1-29-71 | 1993 | Thousand Oaks, Calif. |
| Darensbourg, Vic | 1 | 5 | 3.69 | 47 | 0 | 0 | 7 | 63 | 61 | 30 | 26 | 32 | 66 | L | L | 5-10 | 165 | 11-13-70 | 1992 | Los Angeles, Calif. |
| Gonzalez, Gabe | 0 | 0 | 3.00 | 2 | 0 | 0 | 0 | 3 | 4 | 1 | 1 | 2 | 3 | S | L | 6-1 | 160 | 5-24-72 | 1995 | Long Beach, Calif. |
| Hammond, Chris | 1 | 0 | 7.20 | 1 | 1 | 0 | 0 | 5 | 5 | 4 | 4 | 0 | 3 | L | L | 6-1 | 195 | 1-21-66 | 1986 | Birmingham, Ala. |
| Harris, Doug | 0 | 0 | 3.00 | 3 | 0 | 0 | 0 | 3 | 3 | 1 | 1 | 0 | 1 | R | R | 6-4 | 205 | 9-27-69 | 1990 | Carlisle, Pa. |
|   2-team (7 Rochester) | 2 | 3 | 3.92 | 10 | 3 | 0 | 0 | 21 | 25 | 20 | 9 | 6 | 5 | | | | | | | |
| Hernandez, Livan | 2 | 4 | 5.14 | 10 | 10 | 0 | 0 | 49 | 61 | 32 | 28 | 34 | 45 | R | R | 6-2 | 220 | 2-20-75 | 1996 | Miami, Fla. |
| Juelsgaard, Jarod | 4 | 2 | 3.48 | 26 | 5 | 0 | 1 | 44 | 43 | 23 | 17 | 21 | 29 | R | R | 6-3 | 190 | 6-27-68 | 1991 | Elk Horn, Iowa |
| Mantei, Matt | 0 | 2 | 4.70 | 7 | 0 | 0 | 2 | 8 | 6 | 4 | 4 | 7 | 8 | R | R | 6-1 | 181 | 7-7-73 | 1991 | Sawyer, Mich. |
| Mendoza, Reynol | 7 | 4 | 5.64 | 15 | 14 | 2 | 0 | 91 | 112 | 67 | 57 | 33 | 41 | R | R | 6-0 | 215 | 10-27-70 | 1992 | San Antonio, Texas |
| Miller, Kurt | 3 | 5 | 4.66 | 12 | 12 | 2 | 0 | 66 | 77 | 39 | 34 | 26 | 38 | R | R | 6-5 | 200 | 8-24-72 | 1990 | Bakersfield, Calif. |
| Mix, Greg | 1 | 3 | 6.87 | 4 | 4 | 0 | 0 | 18 | 27 | 15 | 14 | 7 | 9 | R | R | 6-4 | 230 | 8-21-71 | 1993 | Albuquerque, N.M. |
| Pall, Donn | 3 | 3 | 2.96 | 38 | 0 | 0 | 17 | 52 | 42 | 21 | 17 | 12 | 53 | R | R | 6-1 | 180 | 1-11-62 | 1985 | Bloomingdale, Ill. |
| Perez, Yorkis | 3 | 0 | 4.22 | 9 | 0 | 0 | 0 | 11 | 6 | 5 | 5 | 3 | 13 | L | L | 6-0 | 160 | 9-30-67 | 1983 | Haina, D.R. |
| Rapp, Pat | 1 | 1 | 8.18 | 2 | 2 | 0 | 0 | 11 | 18 | 12 | 10 | 4 | 9 | R | R | 6-3 | 210 | 7-13-67 | 1989 | Sulphur, La. |
| Rojas, Euclides | 0 | 0 | 6.00 | 6 | 0 | 0 | 0 | 9 | 12 | 6 | 6 | 3 | 8 | R | R | 6-0 | 190 | 8-25-67 | 1995 | Miami, Fla. |
| Seelbach, Chris | 6 | 13 | 7.35 | 25 | 25 | 1 | 0 | 138 | 167 | 123 | 113 | 76 | 98 | R | R | 6-4 | 180 | 12-18-72 | 1991 | Lufkin, Texas |
| Valdes, Marc | 4 | 4 | 5.12 | 8 | 8 | 1 | 0 | 51 | 66 | 32 | 29 | 15 | 24 | R | R | 6-0 | 170 | 12-20-71 | 1993 | Tampa, Fla. |
| Weathers, David | 0 | 0 | 7.71 | 1 | 1 | 0 | 0 | 2 | 5 | 2 | 2 | 3 | 0 | R | R | 6-3 | 205 | 9-25-69 | 1988 | Leoma, Tenn. |
| Weston, Mickey | 5 | 9 | 5.78 | 31 | 14 | 0 | 1 | 104 | 131 | 73 | 67 | 39 | 47 | R | R | 6-1 | 180 | 3-26-61 | 1982 | Fenton, Mich. |
| Whisenant, Matt | 8 | 10 | 6.92 | 28 | 22 | 1 | 0 | 121 | 149 | 107 | 93 | 101 | 97 | S | L | 6-3 | 215 | 6-8-71 | 1990 | La Canada, Calif. |

### FIELDING

| Catcher | PCT | G | PO | A | E | DP | PB |
|---|---|---|---|---|---|---|---|
| Brooks | .982 | 31 | 155 | 11 | 3 | 0 | 4 |
| Fagley | 1.000 | 1 | 1 | 0 | 0 | 0 | 0 |
| Ronan | .991 | 74 | 389 | 49 | 4 | 4 | 10 |
| Siddall | .984 | 62 | 316 | 43 | 6 | 4 | 6 |

| First Base | PCT | G | PO | A | E | DP |
|---|---|---|---|---|---|---|
| Brooks | .974 | 20 | 168 | 16 | 5 | 13 |
| Gregg | .996 | 65 | 522 | 45 | 2 | 46 |
| Halter | 1.000 | 1 | 4 | 0 | 0 | 0 |
| Johnson | 1.000 | 1 | 7 | 2 | 0 | 0 |
| Morman | .993 | 61 | 533 | 25 | 4 | 40 |
| Olmeda | 1.000 | 1 | 6 | 2 | 0 | 1 |

| Second Base | PCT | G | PO | A | E | DP |
|---|---|---|---|---|---|---|
| Abbott | .929 | 5 | 10 | 16 | 2 | 6 |
| Clapinski | 1.000 | 4 | 8 | 11 | 0 | 1 |
| Halter | 1.000 | 3 | 1 | 6 | 0 | 0 |
| Johnson | .991 | 24 | 49 | 64 | 1 | 15 |

| Third Base | PCT | G | PO | A | E | DP |
|---|---|---|---|---|---|---|
| Abbott | 1.000 | 2 | 0 | 1 | 0 | 0 |
| Brooks | .000 | 1 | 0 | 0 | 0 | 0 |
| Clapinski | .917 | 12 | 6 | 16 | 2 | 1 |
| Halter | 1.000 | 2 | 0 | 2 | 0 | 0 |
| Johnson | .974 | 16 | 6 | 31 | 1 | 2 |
| Lucca | .913 | 85 | 38 | 151 | 18 | 10 |
| Olmeda | .929 | 46 | 33 | 84 | 9 | 6 |
| Siddall | .667 | 1 | 0 | 2 | 1 | 0 |
| Torres | .000 | 1 | 0 | 0 | 0 | 0 |

| Shortstop | PCT | G | PO | A | E | DP |
|---|---|---|---|---|---|---|
| Abbott | 1.000 | 11 | 21 | 43 | 0 | 10 |
| Clapinski | .963 | 85 | 122 | 238 | 14 | 41 |

| | PCT | G | PO | A | E | DP |
|---|---|---|---|---|---|---|
| Johnson | .939 | 12 | 14 | 17 | 2 | 8 |
| Olmeda | .917 | 4 | 4 | 7 | 1 | 0 |
| Renteria | .959 | 35 | 48 | 114 | 7 | 15 |
| Torres | .000 | 1 | 0 | 0 | 0 | 0 |

| Outfield | PCT | G | PO | A | E | DP |
|---|---|---|---|---|---|---|
| Brooks | .989 | 52 | 82 | 9 | 1 | 1 |
| Clapinski | 1.000 | 3 | 7 | 0 | 0 | 0 |
| Gregg | .980 | 32 | 47 | 1 | 1 | 0 |
| Halter | .923 | 7 | 10 | 2 | 1 | 0 |
| McMillon | .973 | 94 | 135 | 10 | 4 | 0 |
| Olmeda | 1.000 | 37 | 55 | 1 | 0 | 0 |
| Riley | .990 | 86 | 184 | 5 | 2 | 0 |
| Robertson | .933 | 10 | 14 | 0 | 1 | 0 |
| Sheff | .986 | 83 | 133 | 8 | 2 | 0 |
| Whitmore | .943 | 54 | 114 | 2 | 7 | 0 |

## EASTERN LEAGUE

| BATTING | AVG | G | AB | R | H | 2B | 3B | HR | RBI | BB | SO | SB | CS | B | T | HT | WT | DOB | 1st Yr | Resides |
|---|---|---|---|---|---|---|---|---|---|---|---|---|---|---|---|---|---|---|---|---|
| Aversa, Joe | .244 | 54 | 135 | 22 | 33 | 8 | 0 | 0 | 21 | 23 | 22 | 2 | 3 | S | R | 5-10 | 155 | 5-20-68 | 1990 | Huntington Beach, Calif. |
|   2-team (13 Bing.) | .234 | 67 | 167 | 25 | 39 | 8 | 0 | 0 | 22 | 30 | 30 | 2 | 3 | | | | | | | |
| Berg, David | .302 | 109 | 414 | 64 | 125 | 28 | 5 | 9 | 73 | 42 | 60 | 17 | 7 | R | R | 5-11 | 185 | 9-3-70 | 1993 | Roseville, Calif. |
| Brown, Ron | .100 | 4 | 10 | 1 | 1 | 0 | 0 | 0 | 1 | 3 | 2 | 1 | 0 | R | R | 6-3 | 185 | 1-17-70 | 1993 | Tampa, Fla. |
| Castillo, Luis | .317 | 109 | 420 | 83 | 133 | 15 | 7 | 1 | 35 | 66 | 68 | 51 | 28 | S | R | 5-11 | 146 | 9-12-75 | 1993 | San Pedro de Macoris, D.R. |
| Clapinski, Chris | .260 | 23 | 73 | 15 | 19 | 7 | 0 | 3 | 11 | 13 | 13 | 3 | 1 | S | R | 6-0 | 165 | 8-20-71 | 1992 | Rancho Mirage, Calif. |
| Cook, Hayward | .304 | 14 | 46 | 7 | 14 | 3 | 0 | 0 | 3 | 6 | 13 | 2 | 1 | R | R | 5-11 | 195 | 6-24-72 | 1994 | San Jose, Calif. |
| Dunwoody, Todd | .277 | 138 | 552 | 88 | 153 | 30 | 6 | 24 | 93 | 45 | 149 | 24 | 19 | L | L | 6-2 | 185 | 4-11-75 | 1993 | West Lafayette, Ind. |
| Gonzalez, Alex | .235 | 11 | 34 | 4 | 8 | 0 | 1 | 0 | 1 | 2 | 10 | 0 | 0 | R | R | 6-0 | 150 | 2-15-77 | 1994 | Turmero, Venez. |

## BATTING

| BATTING | AVG | G | AB | R | H | 2B | 3B | HR | RBI | BB | SO | SB | CS | B | T | HT | WT | DOB | 1st Yr | Resides |
|---|---|---|---|---|---|---|---|---|---|---|---|---|---|---|---|---|---|---|---|---|
| Hastings, Lionel | .232 | 97 | 293 | 30 | 68 | 12 | 1 | 6 | 44 | 15 | 50 | 5 | 2 | R | R | 5-9 | 175 | 1-26-73 | 1994 | Orange, Calif. |
| Mack, Quinn | .216 | 36 | 111 | 12 | 24 | 5 | 0 | 3 | 19 | 7 | 20 | 3 | 3 | L | L | 5-10 | 180 | 9-11-65 | 1987 | Cerritos, Calif. |
| Millar, Kevin | .318 | 130 | 472 | 69 | 150 | 32 | 0 | 18 | 86 | 37 | 53 | 6 | 5 | R | R | 6-1 | 195 | 9-24-71 | 1993 | Encino, Calif. |
| Milliard, Ralph | .200 | 6 | 20 | 2 | 4 | 0 | 1 | 0 | 2 | 1 | 5 | 1 | 0 | R | R | 5-10 | 160 | 12-30-73 | 1993 | Soest, Neth. Antilles |
| O'Neill, Doug | .257 | 72 | 241 | 39 | 62 | 10 | 2 | 7 | 26 | 26 | 64 | 8 | 4 | R | R | 5-10 | 200 | 6-29-70 | 1991 | Campbell, Calif. |
| Redmond, Mike | .287 | 120 | 394 | 43 | 113 | 22 | 0 | 4 | 44 | 26 | 45 | 3 | 4 | R | R | 6-0 | 190 | 5-5-71 | 1993 | Spokane, Wash. |
| Robertson, Jason | .272 | 99 | 338 | 65 | 92 | 17 | 3 | 12 | 48 | 31 | 91 | 12 | 6 | L | L | 6-2 | 200 | 3-24-71 | 1989 | Country Club Hills, Ill. |
| Rodriguez, Maximo | .176 | 6 | 17 | 1 | 3 | 0 | 0 | 0 | 1 | 1 | 6 | 0 | 1 | R | R | 6-0 | 170 | 11-18-73 | 1993 | La Romana, D.R. |
| Roskos, John | .275 | 121 | 396 | 53 | 109 | 26 | 3 | 9 | 58 | 67 | 102 | 3 | 4 | R | R | 5-11 | 198 | 11-19-74 | 1993 | Rio Rancho, N.M. |
| Sheff, Chris | .295 | 27 | 105 | 16 | 31 | 12 | 2 | 2 | 17 | 13 | 23 | 3 | 2 | R | R | 6-3 | 210 | 2-4-71 | 1992 | Laguna Hills, Calif. |
| Torres, Tony | .270 | 47 | 126 | 21 | 34 | 11 | 0 | 1 | 13 | 14 | 24 | 3 | 1 | R | R | 5-9 | 165 | 6-1-70 | 1992 | San Pablo, Calif. |
| Wilson, Pookie | .256 | 113 | 375 | 46 | 96 | 16 | 5 | 6 | 35 | 33 | 49 | 7 | 10 | L | L | 5-10 | 180 | 10-24-70 | 1992 | Sylacauga, Ala. |

## PITCHING

| PITCHING | W | L | ERA | G | GS | CG | SV | IP | H | R | ER | BB | SO | B | T | HT | WT | DOB | 1st Yr | Resides |
|---|---|---|---|---|---|---|---|---|---|---|---|---|---|---|---|---|---|---|---|---|
| Alkire, Jeff | 0 | 2 | 6.41 | 11 | 0 | 0 | 0 | 20 | 26 | 15 | 14 | 7 | 24 | R | L | 6-1 | 200 | 11-15-69 | 1992 | San Jose, Calif. |
| Beckett, Robbie | 1 | 0 | 6.23 | 3 | 3 | 0 | 0 | 13 | 17 | 9 | 9 | 13 | 7 | R | L | 6-5 | 235 | 7-16-72 | 1990 | Austin, Texas |
| Chergey, Dan | 0 | 2 | 4.00 | 13 | 0 | 0 | 2 | 18 | 18 | 9 | 8 | 6 | 16 | R | R | 6-2 | 195 | 1-29-71 | 1993 | Thousand Oaks, Calif. |
| Cunnane, Will | 10 | 12 | 3.74 | 25 | 25 | 4 | 0 | 152 | 156 | 73 | 63 | 30 | 101 | R | R | 6-2 | 165 | 4-24-74 | 1993 | Congers, N.Y. |
| Harris, Doug | 6 | 3 | 3.57 | 20 | 0 | 0 | 1 | 35 | 33 | 15 | 14 | 14 | 26 | R | R | 6-4 | 205 | 9-27-69 | 1990 | Carlisle, Pa. |
|   2-team (3 Bowie) | 6 | 5 | 5.59 | 23 | 3 | 0 | 1 | 48 | 50 | 31 | 30 | 21 | 31 | | | | | | | |
| Heredia, Felix | 8 | 1 | 1.50 | 55 | 0 | 0 | 5 | 60 | 48 | 11 | 10 | 15 | 42 | L | L | 6-0 | 160 | 6-18-76 | 1993 | Barahona, D.R. |
| Hernandez, Livan | 9 | 2 | 4.34 | 15 | 15 | 0 | 0 | 93 | 81 | 48 | 45 | 34 | 95 | R | R | 6-2 | 220 | 2-20-75 | 1996 | Miami, Fla. |
| Hurst, Bill | 2 | 3 | 2.20 | 45 | 0 | 0 | 30 | 49 | 45 | 22 | 12 | 31 | 46 | R | R | 6-7 | 220 | 4-28-70 | 1990 | Miami, Fla. |
| Larkin, Andy | 4 | 1 | 3.10 | 8 | 8 | 0 | 0 | 49 | 45 | 18 | 17 | 10 | 40 | R | R | 6-4 | 181 | 6-27-74 | 1992 | Medford, Ore. |
| Meadows, Brian | 0 | 1 | 4.33 | 4 | 4 | 1 | 0 | 27 | 26 | 15 | 13 | 4 | 13 | R | R | 6-4 | 210 | 11-21-75 | 1994 | Troy, Ala. |
| Mendoza, Reynol | 4 | 2 | 3.43 | 10 | 0 | 2 | 0 | 63 | 60 | 27 | 24 | 14 | 41 | R | R | 6-0 | 215 | 10-27-70 | 1992 | San Antonio, Texas |
| Mix, Greg | 3 | 0 | 4.52 | 25 | 5 | 0 | 1 | 66 | 80 | 40 | 33 | 19 | 57 | R | R | 6-4 | 210 | 8-21-71 | 1993 | Albuquerque, N.M. |
| Nunez, Clemente | 2 | 7 | 5.47 | 32 | 10 | 0 | 0 | 97 | 119 | 74 | 59 | 31 | 52 | R | R | 5-11 | 181 | 2-10-75 | 1992 | Bonao, D.R. |
| Saunders, Tony | 13 | 4 | 2.63 | 26 | 26 | 2 | 0 | 168 | 121 | 51 | 49 | 62 | 156 | L | L | 6-1 | 189 | 4-29-74 | 1992 | Ellicott City, Md. |
| Stanifer, Robby | 3 | 1 | 1.57 | 18 | 0 | 0 | 2 | 34 | 27 | 11 | 6 | 9 | 33 | R | R | 6-2 | 195 | 3-10-72 | 1994 | Easley, S.C. |
| Thornton, Paul | 3 | 6 | 4.17 | 52 | 0 | 0 | 4 | 78 | 74 | 45 | 36 | 44 | 64 | R | R | 6-2 | 210 | 6-21-70 | 1993 | Callahan, Fla. |
| Valdes, Marc | 6 | 2 | 2.66 | 10 | 10 | 1 | 0 | 64 | 60 | 25 | 19 | 12 | 49 | R | R | 6-0 | 170 | 12-20-71 | 1993 | Tampa, Fla. |
| Ward, Bryan | 9 | 9 | 4.91 | 28 | 25 | 2 | 0 | 147 | 170 | 97 | 80 | 32 | 124 | L | L | 6-2 | 210 | 1-28-72 | 1993 | Mt. Holly, N.J. |

### FIELDING

| Catcher | PCT | G | PO | A | E | DP | PB |
|---|---|---|---|---|---|---|---|
| Redmond | .996 | 119 | 814 | 88 | 4 | 10 | 8 |
| Rodriguez | 1.000 | 6 | 44 | 5 | 0 | 0 | |
| Roskos | .988 | 29 | 147 | 11 | 2 | 0 | 7 |

| First Base | PCT | G | PO | A | E | DP |
|---|---|---|---|---|---|---|
| Berg | 1.000 | 1 | 1 | 0 | 0 | 0 |
| Millar | .987 | 87 | 739 | 48 | 10 | 79 |
| Roskos | .987 | 67 | 572 | 39 | 8 | 61 |
| Wilson | 1.000 | 1 | 9 | 2 | 0 | 2 |

| Second Base | PCT | G | PO | A | E | DP |
|---|---|---|---|---|---|---|
| Aversa | 1.000 | 2 | 2 | 5 | 0 | 0 |
| Castillo | .975 | 108 | 217 | 326 | 14 | 87 |
| Hastings | .981 | 19 | 49 | 52 | 2 | 18 |
| Milliard | 1.000 | 5 | 12 | 18 | 0 | 6 |

| | PCT | G | PO | A | E | DP |
|---|---|---|---|---|---|---|
| Torres | .924 | 13 | 29 | 32 | 5 | 7 |
| **Third Base** | **PCT** | **G** | **PO** | **A** | **E** | **DP** |
| Aversa | .911 | 34 | 15 | 57 | 7 | 8 |
| Berg | .903 | 19 | 20 | 45 | 7 | 4 |
| Hastings | .902 | 68 | 33 | 152 | 20 | 16 |
| Millar | .952 | 34 | 14 | 86 | 5 | 9 |
| Torres | .881 | 13 | 7 | 30 | 5 | 1 |
| **Shortstop** | **PCT** | **G** | **PO** | **A** | **E** | **DP** |
| Aversa | .915 | 12 | 19 | 35 | 5 | 8 |
| Berg | .958 | 90 | 123 | 313 | 19 | 65 |
| Clapinski | .980 | 23 | 29 | 68 | 2 | 13 |
| Gonzalez | .887 | 11 | 17 | 38 | 7 | 12 |
| Hastings | .750 | 1 | 1 | 2 | 1 | 0 |

| | PCT | G | PO | A | E | DP |
|---|---|---|---|---|---|---|
| Torres | .811 | 9 | 7 | 23 | 7 | 3 |
| **Outfield** | **PCT** | **G** | **PO** | **A** | **E** | **DP** |
| Aversa | 1.000 | 7 | 12 | 2 | 0 | 0 |
| Brown | 1.000 | 2 | 2 | 0 | 0 | 0 |
| Cook | 1.000 | 13 | 18 | 1 | 0 | 0 |
| Dunwoody | .996 | 138 | 254 | 2 | 1 | 2 |
| Hastings | 1.000 | 6 | 2 | 0 | 0 | 0 |
| Mack | .929 | 28 | 39 | 0 | 3 | 0 |
| O'Neill | .960 | 68 | 96 | 1 | 4 | 1 |
| Robertson | .949 | 54 | 74 | 0 | 4 | 0 |
| Sheff | 1.000 | 27 | 37 | 0 | 0 | 0 |
| Wilson | .982 | 104 | 153 | 8 | 3 | 0 |

# BREVARD COUNTY — Class A
## FLORIDA STATE LEAGUE

| BATTING | AVG | G | AB | R | H | 2B | 3B | HR | RBI | BB | SO | SB | CS | B | T | HT | WT | DOB | 1st Yr | Resides |
|---|---|---|---|---|---|---|---|---|---|---|---|---|---|---|---|---|---|---|---|---|
| Alaimo, Jason | .238 | 6 | 21 | 1 | 5 | 0 | 0 | 0 | 0 | 1 | 4 | 0 | 0 | R | R | 5-8 | 200 | 7-31-75 | 1996 | Holbrook, N.Y. |
| Babin, Brady | .200 | 2 | 5 | 0 | 1 | 0 | 0 | 0 | 0 | 0 | 2 | 0 | 0 | R | R | 6-0 | 170 | 9-17-75 | 1993 | Gonzales, La. |
| Baugh, Gavin | .121 | 19 | 33 | 5 | 4 | 1 | 0 | 0 | 1 | 2 | 17 | 1 | 2 | R | R | 6-3 | 205 | 7-26-73 | 1992 | San Mateo, Calif. |
| Brunson, Matt | .205 | 127 | 396 | 51 | 81 | 13 | 1 | 0 | 29 | 66 | 89 | 28 | 11 | S | R | 5-11 | 165 | 9-2-74 | 1993 | Englewood, Colo. |
| Cady, Todd | .215 | 101 | 340 | 34 | 73 | 10 | 1 | 7 | 34 | 38 | 83 | 3 | 6 | S | R | 6-4 | 222 | 11-25-72 | 1994 | La Mesa, Calif. |
| Camilo, Jose | .182 | 12 | 44 | 6 | 8 | 0 | 1 | 2 | 4 | 3 | 11 | 2 | 0 | L | L | 5-11 | 175 | 9-28-76 | 1994 | Trujillo Alto, P.R. |
| Castro, Dennis | .258 | 67 | 225 | 15 | 58 | 11 | 2 | 3 | 27 | 16 | 56 | 0 | 4 | L | R | 6-2 | 195 | 11-25-72 | 1994 | Gilroy, Calif. |
| Cook, Hayward | .292 | 80 | 284 | 45 | 83 | 11 | 9 | 7 | 47 | 29 | 87 | 14 | 7 | R | R | 5-10 | 195 | 6-24-72 | 1994 | San Jose, Calif. |
| Darden, Tony | .241 | 108 | 390 | 37 | 94 | 21 | 4 | 1 | 43 | 28 | 55 | 6 | 11 | R | R | 6-0 | 170 | 5-29-74 | 1994 | Gilmer, Texas |
| Erwin, Mat | .278 | 60 | 212 | 24 | 59 | 13 | 1 | 1 | 31 | 22 | 30 | 0 | 2 | R | R | 6-0 | 195 | 2-28-73 | 1995 | Fair Oaks, Calif. |
| Fagley, Dan | .094 | 20 | 53 | 1 | 5 | 2 | 0 | 0 | 2 | 5 | 19 | 0 | 0 | R | R | 5-10 | 185 | 12-18-74 | 1994 | Riverton, N.J. |
| Glozier, Larry | .154 | 5 | 13 | 0 | 2 | 0 | 0 | 0 | 0 | 1 | 3 | 1 | 0 | R | R | 5-10 | 180 | 9-2-73 | 1996 | Chicago, Ill. |
| Goodell, Steve | .250 | 1 | 4 | 0 | 1 | 0 | 0 | 0 | 0 | 0 | 0 | 0 | 0 | R | R | 6-3 | 196 | 4-23-75 | 1995 | Danville, Calif. |
| Harvey, Aaron | .261 | 99 | 360 | 37 | 94 | 18 | 3 | 5 | 40 | 21 | 55 | 13 | 8 | L | R | 5-10 | 180 | 6-11-73 | 1994 | Donvale, Australia |
| Jackson, Ryan | .308 | 6 | 26 | 4 | 8 | 2 | 0 | 1 | 4 | 1 | 7 | 1 | 0 | L | L | 6-2 | 195 | 11-15-71 | 1994 | Sarasota, Fla. |
| Owen, Tom | .210 | 49 | 124 | 14 | 26 | 2 | 1 | 1 | 9 | 27 | 22 | 2 | 2 | R | R | 6-0 | 180 | 2-13-73 | 1995 | Elkhart, Iowa |
| Podsednik, Scott | .261 | 108 | 383 | 39 | 100 | 9 | 2 | 0 | 30 | 45 | 65 | 20 | 10 | L | L | 6-0 | 170 | 3-18-76 | 1994 | West, Texas |
| Ramirez, Julio | .246 | 17 | 61 | 11 | 15 | 0 | 1 | 0 | 2 | 4 | 18 | 2 | 3 | R | R | 5-11 | 160 | 8-10-77 | 1994 | Santo Domingo, D.R. |
| Rascon, Rene | .258 | 10 | 31 | 3 | 8 | 1 | 0 | 1 | 6 | 6 | 10 | 0 | 2 | L | L | 6-3 | 210 | 9-27-73 | 1995 | Watsonville, Calif. |
| Reeves, Glenn | .299 | 123 | 478 | 72 | 143 | 29 | 4 | 6 | 41 | 63 | 82 | 8 | 5 | R | R | 6-0 | 175 | 1-19-74 | 1993 | Victoria, Australia |
| Reynoso, Ismael | .114 | 11 | 35 | 5 | 4 | 0 | 0 | 0 | 1 | 1 | 11 | 2 | 1 | R | R | 5-10 | 165 | 6-17-78 | 1995 | La Romana, D.R. |
| Rodriguez, Maximo | .227 | 84 | 273 | 19 | 62 | 16 | 0 | 3 | 39 | 18 | 62 | 3 | 3 | R | R | 6-0 | 170 | 11-18-73 | 1993 | La Romana, D.R. |
| Rodriguez, Victor | .274 | 114 | 438 | 54 | 120 | 14 | 4 | 0 | 26 | 32 | 42 | 20 | 7 | R | R | 6-2 | 175 | 10-25-76 | 1994 | Guayama, P.R. |
| Shanahan, Jason | .205 | 102 | 371 | 39 | 76 | 19 | 2 | 2 | 32 | 36 | 63 | 2 | 1 | S | R | 6-2 | 210 | 8-27-73 | 1993 | Missoula, Mon. |
| Wilkes, Brian | .364 | 4 | 11 | 4 | 4 | 0 | 0 | 0 | 2 | 2 | 3 | 0 | 1 | R | R | 6-1 | 195 | 4-12-75 | 1996 | Jacksonville, Fla. |

**GAMES BY POSITION: C**—Alaimo 6, Cady 2, Erwin 45, Fagley 20, M. Rodriguez 77, Wilkes 4. **1B**—Cady 56, Castro 1, Jackson 3, Owen 1, Shanahan 83. **2B**—Brunson 117, Darden 20, Glozier 3, Owen 7, Reynoso 2. **3B**—Baugh 2, Cady 1, Castro 50, Darden 65, Owen 36, Shanahan 1. **SS**—Babin 2, Baugh 10, Brunson 13, Glozier 1, Goodell 1, V. Rodriguez 114. **OF**—Camilo 10, Cook 77, Darden 23, Harvey 75, Podsednik 105, Ramirez 17, Rascon 9, Reeves 114, M. Rodriguez 1, Shanahan 1.

| PITCHING | W | L | ERA | G | GS | CG | SV | IP | H | R | ER | BB | SO | B | T | HT | WT | DOB | 1st Yr | Resides |
|---|---|---|---|---|---|---|---|---|---|---|---|---|---|---|---|---|---|---|---|---|
| Alejo, Nigel | 1 | 6 | 4.58 | 37 | 0 | 0 | 11 | 39 | 47 | 23 | 20 | 13 | 35 | R | R | 6-0 | 171 | 1-12-75 | 1993 | Palo Negro, Venez. |
| Altman, Heath | 0 | 1 | 11.96 | 16 | 0 | 0 | 0 | 23 | 31 | 38 | 31 | 27 | 7 | S | R | 6-5 | 200 | 6-2-71 | 1993 | Hamlet, N.C. |
| Bowen, Mitchel | 0 | 2 | 4.67 | 29 | 0 | 0 | 2 | 54 | 66 | 33 | 28 | 14 | 29 | R | R | 6-5 | 225 | 10-24-72 | 1993 | La Crescenta, Calif. |
| Caravelli, Mike | 4 | 3 | 2.27 | 47 | 0 | 0 | 1 | 71 | 69 | 20 | 18 | 16 | 46 | R | L | 6-2 | 200 | 7-27-72 | 1995 | Santa Monica, Calif. |
| Darensbourg, Vic | 0 | 0 | 0.00 | 2 | 0 | 0 | 0 | 3 | 1 | 0 | 0 | 1 | 5 | L | L | 5-10 | 165 | 11-13-70 | 1992 | Los Angeles, Calif. |
| Ehler, Dan | 5 | 16 | 4.74 | 28 | 23 | 1 | 0 | 150 | 176 | 88 | 79 | 41 | 88 | R | R | 6-3 | 180 | 2-17-75 | 1993 | Covina, Calif. |
| Enard, Tony | 0 | 1 | 5.79 | 2 | 0 | 0 | 0 | 5 | 2 | 3 | 3 | 4 | 6 | R | R | 6-4 | 220 | 8-16-74 | 1995 | Sparks, Nev. |
| Filbeck, Ryan | 1 | 1 | 8.44 | 9 | 0 | 0 | 0 | 11 | 16 | 13 | 10 | 5 | 9 | R | R | 6-2 | 200 | 12-23-72 | 1993 | El Toro, Calif. |
| Garagozzo, Keith | 0 | 1 | 10.80 | 2 | 2 | 0 | 0 | 5 | 9 | 6 | 6 | 4 | 1 | L | L | 6-0 | 170 | 10-25-69 | 1991 | Maple Shade, N.J. |
| Gonzalez, Gabe | 2 | 7 | 1.77 | 47 | 0 | 0 | 9 | 76 | 56 | 20 | 15 | 23 | 62 | S | L | 6-1 | 160 | 5-24-72 | 1995 | Long Beach, Calif. |
| Gonzalez, Juan | 1 | 9 | 5.32 | 23 | 17 | 0 | 0 | 86 | 102 | 57 | 51 | 27 | 48 | R | R | 6-1 | 188 | 1-28-75 | 1992 | Bani, D.R. |
| Hammond, Chris | 0 | 0 | 0.00 | 1 | 1 | 0 | 0 | 4 | 3 | 0 | 0 | 0 | 8 | L | L | 6-1 | 195 | 1-21-66 | 1986 | Birmingham, Ala. |
| Larkin, Andy | 0 | 4 | 4.23 | 6 | 6 | 0 | 0 | 28 | 34 | 20 | 13 | 7 | 18 | R | R | 6-4 | 181 | 6-27-74 | 1992 | Medford, Ore. |
| Meadows, Brian | 8 | 7 | 3.58 | 24 | 23 | 3 | 0 | 146 | 129 | 73 | 58 | 25 | 69 | R | R | 6-4 | 210 | 11-21-75 | 1994 | Troy, Ala. |
| Miles, David | 1 | 5 | 5.48 | 27 | 7 | 0 | 0 | 71 | 90 | 57 | 43 | 31 | 37 | L | L | 6-3 | 195 | 2-26-73 | 1994 | Renton, Wash. |
| Miller, David | 4 | 5 | 4.76 | 26 | 11 | 0 | 0 | 85 | 94 | 51 | 45 | 26 | 40 | R | R | 6-7 | 220 | 8-31-73 | 1995 | Sanford, N.C. |
| Miranda, Walter | 0 | 1 | 9.95 | 2 | 2 | 0 | 0 | 6 | 8 | 7 | 7 | 6 | 1 | R | R | 6-4 | 190 | 1-6-75 | 1992 | Cartagena, Colombia |
| Parisi, Mike | 6 | 8 | 4.15 | 21 | 19 | 1 | 0 | 119 | 117 | 59 | 55 | 39 | 65 | R | R | 6-3 | 195 | 6-18-73 | 1994 | Arcadia, Calif. |
| Powell, Jay | 0 | 0 | 0.00 | 1 | 1 | 0 | 0 | 2 | 0 | 0 | 0 | 0 | 0 | R | R | 6-4 | 220 | 1-9-72 | 1993 | Collinsville, Tenn. |
| Press, Gregg | 9 | 9 | 2.75 | 28 | 23 | 0 | 0 | 150 | 134 | 62 | 46 | 37 | 90 | R | R | 6-3 | 200 | 9-21-71 | 1994 | Santa Cruz, Calif. |
| Stanifer, Rob | 4 | 2 | 2.39 | 22 | 0 | 0 | 0 | 49 | 54 | 17 | 13 | 9 | 32 | R | R | 6-2 | 195 | 3-10-72 | 1994 | Easley, S.C. |
| Stephens, Shannon | 0 | 6 | 6.29 | 4 | 4 | 0 | 0 | 24 | 33 | 22 | 17 | 9 | 12 | R | R | 6-2 | 205 | 8-28-73 | 1995 | Grover Beach, Calif. |
| Thornton, Paul | 0 | 0 | 0.00 | 1 | 0 | 0 | 0 | 3 | 4 | 0 | 0 | 0 | 2 | R | R | 6-2 | 210 | 6-21-70 | 1993 | Callahan, Fla. |
| Treend, Pat | 1 | 0 | 0.00 | 1 | 0 | 0 | 0 | 1 | 0 | 0 | 0 | 0 | 1 | R | R | 6-4 | 220 | 11-1-71 | 1995 | West Hills, Calif. |

# KANE COUNTY — Class A
## MIDWEST LEAGUE

| BATTING | AVG | G | AB | R | H | 2B | 3B | HR | RBI | BB | SO | SB | CS | B | T | HT | WT | DOB | 1st Yr | Resides |
|---|---|---|---|---|---|---|---|---|---|---|---|---|---|---|---|---|---|---|---|---|
| Agnoly, Earl | .246 | 63 | 203 | 19 | 50 | 8 | 2 | 1 | 20 | 14 | 40 | 2 | 4 | R | R | 6-0 | 170 | 11-18-75 | 1993 | Cativa, Panama |
| Booty, Josh | .206 | 128 | 475 | 62 | 98 | 25 | 1 | 21 | 87 | 46 | 195 | 2 | 3 | R | R | 6-3 | 210 | 4-29-75 | 1994 | Shreveport, La. |
| Brown, Roosevelt | .150 | 11 | 40 | 1 | 6 | 2 | 0 | 0 | 3 | 1 | 10 | 0 | 1 | L | R | 5-10 | 190 | 8-3-75 | 1993 | Vicksburg, Miss. |
| Camilo, Jose | .177 | 30 | 96 | 10 | 17 | 0 | 2 | 5 | 14 | 10 | 26 | 7 | 0 | L | L | 5-11 | 175 | 9-28-76 | 1994 | Trujillo Alto, P.R. |
| Funaro, Joe | .309 | 89 | 291 | 57 | 90 | 20 | 2 | 7 | 43 | 40 | 42 | 5 | 3 | R | R | 5-9 | 170 | 3-20-73 | 1995 | Hamden, Conn. |
| Garcia, Amaury | .263 | 106 | 395 | 65 | 104 | 19 | 7 | 6 | 36 | 62 | 84 | 37 | 19 | R | R | 5-10 | 160 | 5-20-75 | 1993 | Santo Domingo, D.R. |
| Glozier, Larry | .215 | 26 | 79 | 13 | 17 | 3 | 1 | 0 | 4 | 18 | 17 | 1 | 3 | R | R | 5-10 | 180 | 9-2-73 | 1996 | Chicago, Ill. |
| Gonzalez, Alex | .200 | 4 | 10 | 2 | 2 | 0 | 0 | 0 | 2 | 4 | 0 | 0 | 0 | R | R | 6-0 | 150 | 2-15-77 | 1994 | Turmero, Venez. |
| Goodell, Steve | .280 | 86 | 282 | 34 | 79 | 17 | 2 | 9 | 39 | 30 | 68 | 1 | 1 | R | R | 6-3 | 196 | 4-23-75 | 1995 | Danville, Calif. |
| Jones, Jaime | .249 | 62 | 237 | 29 | 59 | 17 | 1 | 8 | 45 | 19 | 74 | 7 | 2 | L | L | 6-3 | 190 | 8-2-76 | 1995 | Poway, Calif. |
| Kotsay, Mark | .283 | 17 | 60 | 16 | 17 | 5 | 0 | 2 | 8 | 16 | 8 | 3 | 0 | L | L | 6-0 | 180 | 12-2-75 | 1996 | Santa Fe Springs, Calif. |
| Kuilan, Hector | .201 | 94 | 308 | 28 | 62 | 12 | 1 | 6 | 30 | 22 | 52 | 1 | 3 | R | R | 5-11 | 190 | 4-3-76 | 1994 | Vega Alta, P.R. |
| McCartney, Sommer | .300 | 51 | 160 | 21 | 48 | 14 | 0 | 5 | 19 | 14 | 50 | 1 | 1 | R | R | 6-0 | 200 | 8-2-74 | 1994 | San Jose, Calif. |
| Rascon, Rene | .170 | 56 | 188 | 23 | 32 | 6 | 0 | 4 | 20 | 17 | 61 | 0 | 1 | L | L | 6-3 | 210 | 9-27-73 | 1995 | Watsonville, Calif. |
| Robertson, Ryan | .231 | 55 | 160 | 21 | 37 | 8 | 0 | 3 | 16 | 37 | 31 | 0 | 1 | L | R | 6-4 | 210 | 9-30-72 | 1995 | Port Neches, Texas |
| Rolison, Nate | .243 | 131 | 474 | 63 | 115 | 28 | 1 | 14 | 75 | 66 | 170 | 3 | 3 | L | R | 6-5 | 225 | 3-27-77 | 1995 | Petal, Miss. |
| White, Walter | .175 | 95 | 308 | 26 | 54 | 15 | 3 | 1 | 24 | 35 | 90 | 1 | 4 | R | R | 6-0 | 180 | 12-12-71 | 1994 | Rohnert Park, Calif. |
| Winn, Randy | .270 | 130 | 514 | 90 | 139 | 16 | 3 | 0 | 35 | 47 | 115 | 30 | 18 | S | R | 6-2 | 175 | 6-9-74 | 1995 | Danville, Calif. |

**GAMES BY POSITION: C**—Kuilan 94, McCartney 7, Robertson 40. **1B**—Agnoly 4, Robertson 1, Rolison 131. **2B**—Funaro 4, Garcia 105, Glozier 24, White 1. **3B**—Booty 121, Glozier 1, Goodell 7, White 5. **SS**—Funaro 1, Glozier 1, Gonzalez 4, Goodell 41, White 90. **OF**—Agnoly 23, Brown 11, Camilo 2, Funaro 80, Goodell 22, Jones 59, Kotsay 17, Rascon 49, Winn 128.

| PITCHING | W | L | ERA | G | GS | CG | SV | IP | H | R | ER | BB | SO | B | T | HT | WT | DOB | 1st Yr | Resides |
|---|---|---|---|---|---|---|---|---|---|---|---|---|---|---|---|---|---|---|---|---|
| Burgus, Travis | 5 | 4 | 1.78 | 30 | 7 | 1 | 4 | 96 | 80 | 29 | 19 | 39 | 111 | L | L | 6-2 | 185 | 11-6-72 | 1995 | Mission Viejo, Calif. |
| Castro, Antonio | 6 | 7 | 3.53 | 39 | 0 | 0 | 7 | 66 | 55 | 38 | 26 | 31 | 63 | R | R | 6-2 | 175 | 7-9-71 | 1993 | Phoenix, Ariz. |
| Dempster, Ryan | 2 | 1 | 2.73 | 4 | 4 | 1 | 0 | 26 | 18 | 10 | 8 | 18 | 16 | R | R | 6-2 | 195 | 5-3-77 | 1995 | Gibsons, B.C. |
| DeWitt, Scott | 10 | 11 | 4.72 | 27 | 27 | 1 | 0 | 149 | 151 | 96 | 78 | 59 | 119 | R | L | 6-0 | 200 | 10-6-74 | 1995 | Springfield, Ore. |
| Duvall, Michael | 4 | 1 | 2.06 | 41 | 0 | 0 | 8 | 48 | 43 | 20 | 11 | 21 | 46 | R | L | 6-0 | 185 | 10-11-74 | 1995 | Centerville, Calif. |
| Enard, Tony | 0 | 0 | 6.75 | 3 | 0 | 0 | 0 | 3 | 1 | 2 | 2 | 4 | 1 | R | R | 6-4 | 220 | 8-16-74 | 1995 | Sparks, Nev. |
| Evans, Mike | 0 | 0 | 10.80 | 2 | 0 | 0 | 0 | 2 | 3 | 2 | 2 | 4 | 1 | R | R | 6-4 | 210 | 7-24-68 | 1991 | New Port Richey, Fla. |
| Garcia, Rick | 0 | 4 | 6.28 | 32 | 2 | 0 | 0 | 57 | 63 | 48 | 40 | 41 | 47 | R | R | 6-4 | 210 | 8-25-73 | 1995 | El Paso, Texas |
| Getz, Rod | 3 | 14 | 5.01 | 25 | 25 | 1 | 0 | 120 | 146 | 79 | 67 | 41 | 85 | R | R | 6-5 | 180 | 2-17-76 | 1995 | Lawrenceberg, Ind. |
| Hurtado, Victor | 15 | 7 | 3.27 | 27 | 27 | 5 | 0 | 176 | 167 | 79 | 64 | 56 | 126 | R | R | 6-1 | 155 | 6-14-77 | 1994 | Santo Domingo, D.R. |
| Pailthorpe, Bob | 4 | 5 | 3.48 | 43 | 0 | 0 | 2 | 72 | 76 | 36 | 28 | 30 | 74 | R | R | 6-1 | 210 | 12-6-72 | 1995 | Fremont, Calif. |
| Santoro, Gary | 1 | 2 | 2.76 | 31 | 0 | 0 | 9 | 33 | 30 | 13 | 10 | 12 | 35 | R | R | 6-3 | 205 | 12-15-72 | 1995 | Watertown, Conn. |
| Stephens, Shannon | 8 | 3 | 2.88 | 17 | 17 | 1 | 0 | 106 | 92 | 41 | 34 | 25 | 85 | R | R | 6-2 | 205 | 8-28-73 | 1995 | Grover Beach, Calif. |
| Treend, Pat | 0 | 2 | 4.44 | 27 | 0 | 0 | 0 | 49 | 46 | 32 | 24 | 23 | 40 | R | R | 6-4 | 220 | 11-1-71 | 1995 | West Hills, Calif. |
| Vardijan, Dan | 7 | 7 | 3.35 | 24 | 24 | 2 | 0 | 145 | 128 | 71 | 54 | 55 | 92 | R | R | 6-5 | 193 | 12-1-76 | 1995 | Glenview, Ill. |

# UTICA — Class A
## NEW YORK-PENN LEAGUE

| BATTING | AVG | G | AB | R | H | 2B | 3B | HR | RBI | BB | SO | SB | CS | B | T | HT | WT | DOB | 1st Yr | Resides |
|---|---|---|---|---|---|---|---|---|---|---|---|---|---|---|---|---|---|---|---|---|
| Ammirato, Zak | .221 | 74 | 262 | 26 | 58 | 13 | 2 | 6 | 36 | 39 | 80 | 3 | 2 | S | R | 6-1 | 190 | 4-17-74 | 1996 | Spokane, Wash. |
| Arenas, Pete | .192 | 66 | 182 | 25 | 35 | 5 | 0 | 0 | 12 | 31 | 61 | 1 | 3 | L | R | 5-11 | 180 | 12-7-73 | 1996 | Waukegen, Ill. |
| Braughler, Matt | .216 | 42 | 125 | 15 | 27 | 4 | 0 | 1 | 5 | 11 | 33 | 0 | 0 | L | R | 6-2 | 200 | 5-12-73 | 1996 | Morehead, Ky. |
| Cole, Abdul | .213 | 67 | 202 | 21 | 43 | 15 | 1 | 2 | 27 | 24 | 78 | 7 | 2 | R | R | 6-1 | 185 | 8-4-75 | 1994 | San Francisco, Calif. |
| Diaz, Alain | .213 | 46 | 141 | 14 | 30 | 6 | 1 | 1 | 11 | 16 | 25 | 1 | 1 | R | R | 6-0 | 185 | 12-3-74 | 1996 | Hialeah, Fla. |
| Fagley, Dan | .000 | 1 | 3 | 0 | 0 | 0 | 0 | 0 | 0 | 1 | 2 | 0 | 0 | R | R | 5-10 | 185 | 12-18-74 | 1996 | Riverton, N.J. |
| Forchic, Derek | .287 | 27 | 87 | 12 | 25 | 5 | 1 | 2 | 10 | 5 | 20 | 0 | 0 | L | R | 6-2 | 210 | 11-22-73 | 1996 | Almonesson, N.J. |
| Foster, Quincy | .221 | 73 | 240 | 34 | 53 | 7 | 1 | 1 | 22 | 30 | 71 | 24 | 6 | L | R | 6-2 | 175 | 10-30-74 | 1996 | Hendersonville, N.C. |
| Garrett, Jason | .276 | 68 | 243 | 34 | 67 | 8 | 4 | 4 | 35 | 25 | 53 | 1 | 2 | R | R | 6-2 | 180 | 6-10-73 | 1995 | Manchaca, Texas |
| Glozier, Larry | .000 | 2 | 3 | 0 | 0 | 0 | 0 | 0 | 0 | 1 | 2 | 0 | 0 | R | R | 5-10 | 180 | 9-2-73 | 1996 | Chicago, Ill. |
| Harris, Mike | .283 | 38 | 92 | 9 | 26 | 8 | 0 | 1 | 8 | 11 | 25 | 0 | 0 | R | R | 6-1 | 190 | 5-25-74 | 1996 | Mt. Ephraim, N.J. |
| Jones, Jay | .284 | 37 | 116 | 9 | 33 | 6 | 0 | 0 | 9 | 6 | 17 | 0 | 1 | L | R | 6-0 | 195 | 10-24-74 | 1996 | Trussville, Ala. |

| BATTING | AVG | G | AB | R | H | 2B | 3B | HR | RBI | BB | SO | SB | CS | B | T | HT | WT | DOB | 1st Yr | Resides |
|---|---|---|---|---|---|---|---|---|---|---|---|---|---|---|---|---|---|---|---|---|
| Kleinz, Larry | .242 | 73 | 256 | 21 | 62 | 14 | 1 | 0 | 34 | 20 | 44 | 1 | 0 | R | R | 6-1 | 195 | 3-3-74 | 1996 | Hamilton Square, N.J. |
| Sime, Rafael | .241 | 67 | 216 | 26 | 52 | 9 | 5 | 3 | 31 | 28 | 62 | 10 | 4 | L | L | 6-1 | 155 | 9-30-76 | 1994 | Valverde Mao, D.R. |
| Venghaus, Jeff | .229 | 75 | 258 | 53 | 59 | 12 | 2 | 1 | 24 | 60 | 70 | 16 | 12 | S | R | 6-0 | 185 | 9-17-74 | 1996 | Spring, Texas |

**GAMES BY POSITION: C**—Braughler 30, Fagley 1, Forchic 18, Jones 32. **1B**—Ammirato 11, Garrett 66, Jones 3. **2B**—Ammirato 1, Arenas 2, Glozier 2, Venghaus 74. **3B**—Ammirato 6, Harris 1, Kleinz 72. **SS**—Arenas 64, Harris 26, Kleinz 2. **OF**—Ammirato 27, Arenas 1, Cole 62, Diaz 23, Foster 72, Sime 63, Venghaus 1.

| PITCHING | W | L | ERA | G | GS | CG | SV | IP | H | R | ER | BB | SO | B | T | HT | WT | DOB | 1st Yr | Resides |
|---|---|---|---|---|---|---|---|---|---|---|---|---|---|---|---|---|---|---|---|---|
| Albrecht, Dan | 0 | 0 | 7.59 | 13 | 0 | 0 | 0 | 21 | 25 | 19 | 18 | 25 | 19 | R | L | 6-0 | 190 | 12-22-73 | 1996 | Liberal, Kan. |
| Beagle, Chad | 0 | 1 | 81.00 | 1 | 0 | 0 | 0 | 0 | 3 | 3 | 3 | 2 | 0 | L | L | 6-5 | 195 | 3-31-71 | 1996 | Roanoke, Va. |
| Billingsley, Brent | 4 | 5 | 4.01 | 15 | 15 | 0 | 0 | 90 | 83 | 46 | 40 | 28 | 82 | L | L | 6-2 | 200 | 4-19-75 | 1996 | Chino Hills, Calif. |
| Cames, Aaron | 6 | 2 | 2.81 | 18 | 9 | 1 | 0 | 74 | 60 | 28 | 23 | 18 | 77 | R | R | 6-1 | 192 | 11-21-75 | 1996 | Woodland, Calif. |
| Duncan, Geoff | 2 | 5 | 3.79 | 24 | 1 | 0 | 2 | 40 | 46 | 23 | 17 | 19 | 52 | R | R | 6-2 | 175 | 4-1-75 | 1996 | Roswell, Ga. |
| Eason, Michael | 0 | 1 | 6.75 | 9 | 0 | 0 | 1 | 15 | 21 | 12 | 11 | 7 | 9 | R | R | 6-2 | 185 | 4-3-74 | 1996 | Riverside, Calif. |
| Ferrell, Dan | 2 | 5 | 4.71 | 14 | 13 | 1 | 1 | 71 | 74 | 40 | 37 | 17 | 61 | L | L | 6-1 | 190 | 8-24-74 | 1996 | Portland, Ind. |
| Johannsen, Jeff | 4 | 5 | 4.33 | 14 | 14 | 0 | 0 | 79 | 68 | 40 | 38 | 22 | 73 | L | L | 6-3 | 200 | 6-10-73 | 1996 | Eldridge, Iowa |
| Lewis, Ron | 2 | 2 | 3.96 | 20 | 0 | 0 | 2 | 36 | 36 | 17 | 16 | 15 | 42 | R | R | 6-3 | 205 | 7-14-73 | 1996 | Stockton, Calif. |
| Moore, Joe | 0 | 5 | 3.78 | 11 | 0 | 0 | 1 | 17 | 22 | 15 | 7 | 10 | 14 | R | R | 6-2 | 190 | 11-21-73 | 1996 | Corpus Christi, Texas |
| Santiago, Derek | 2 | 2 | 4.45 | 12 | 10 | 0 | 0 | 55 | 57 | 30 | 27 | 28 | 41 | R | R | 6-1 | 155 | 10-10-75 | 1996 | Aurora, Ill. |
| Stadelhofer, Mike | 0 | 0 | 9.31 | 4 | 0 | 0 | 0 | 10 | 15 | 12 | 10 | 5 | 9 | R | R | 6-3 | 225 | 6-4-74 | 1993 | Calistoga, Calif. |
| Townsend, Dave | 3 | 6 | 3.59 | 14 | 14 | 2 | 0 | 78 | 69 | 38 | 31 | 18 | 51 | R | R | 6-3 | 230 | 8-2-74 | 1996 | Canton, Miss. |
| Wyckoff, Travis | 2 | 5 | 2.95 | 24 | 0 | 0 | 1 | 37 | 39 | 21 | 12 | 14 | 16 | S | L | 6-0 | 180 | 9-30-73 | 1996 | Wichita, Kan. |
| Zaleski, Kevin | 2 | 3 | 3.91 | 26 | 0 | 0 | 7 | 25 | 30 | 16 | 11 | 8 | 21 | R | R | 6-2 | 215 | 8-18-73 | 1996 | Glendale Heights, Ill. |

# MELBOURNE — Rookie

## GULF COAST LEAGUE

| BATTING | AVG | G | AB | R | H | 2B | 3B | HR | RBI | BB | SO | SB | CS | B | T | HT | WT | DOB | 1st Yr | Resides |
|---|---|---|---|---|---|---|---|---|---|---|---|---|---|---|---|---|---|---|---|---|
| Abreu, Miguel | .210 | 23 | 62 | 4 | 13 | 1 | 0 | 0 | 1 | 4 | 14 | 3 | 0 | R | R | 6-1 | 160 | 8-15-78 | 1994 | San Pedro de Macoris, D.R. |
| Alaimo, Jason | .272 | 47 | 173 | 20 | 47 | 11 | 0 | 0 | 24 | 15 | 43 | 2 | 1 | R | R | 5-8 | 200 | 7-31-75 | 1996 | Holbrooke, N.Y. |
| Bautista, Jorge | .265 | 47 | 151 | 23 | 40 | 4 | 1 | 7 | 24 | 26 | 28 | 4 | 2 | R | R | 5-9 | 165 | 7-12-76 | 1995 | San Cristobal, D.R. |
| Conway, Scott | .238 | 30 | 101 | 7 | 24 | 6 | 0 | 2 | 15 | 7 | 23 | 3 | 1 | L | L | 6-4 | 200 | 10-18-78 | 1996 | Mt. Laurel, N.J. |
| Franco, Raul | .278 | 60 | 241 | 40 | 67 | 14 | 2 | 0 | 15 | 13 | 30 | 16 | 7 | R | R | 5-11 | 150 | 1-14-76 | 1994 | San Pedro de Macoris, D.R. |
| Gonzalez, Alex | .390 | 10 | 41 | 6 | 16 | 3 | 0 | 0 | 6 | 2 | 4 | 1 | 0 | R | R | 6-0 | 150 | 2-15-77 | 1997 | Turmero, Venez. |
| Jackson, Quantaa | .138 | 27 | 80 | 5 | 11 | 3 | 0 | 0 | 6 | 8 | 31 | 2 | 0 | R | R | 6-2 | 215 | 10-19-77 | 1996 | Wharton, Texas |
| Jackson, Ramona | .346 | 8 | 26 | 5 | 9 | 0 | 0 | 0 | 7 | 1 | 3 | 2 | 0 | L | L | 6-2 | 195 | 11-15-71 | 1994 | Sarasota, Fla. |
| Maduro, Remy | .226 | 24 | 84 | 8 | 19 | 2 | 0 | 0 | 14 | 15 | 9 | 2 | 0 | L | R | 6-1 | 176 | 9-18-76 | 1996 | Hooffdorp, Neth. Antilles |
| Morales, Steve | .167 | 29 | 84 | 8 | 14 | 2 | 0 | 1 | 7 | 5 | 13 | 0 | 0 | S | R | 6-3 | 210 | 10-24-70 | 1994 | Downey, Calif. |
| Pass, Patrick | .244 | 29 | 90 | 14 | 22 | 4 | 0 | 0 | 8 | 15 | 27 | 5 | 2 | R | R | 6-1 | 202 | 12-31-77 | 1996 | Tucker, Ga. |
| Pimentel, Marino | .125 | 15 | 40 | 4 | 5 | 1 | 0 | 0 | 1 | 1 | 17 | 0 | 3 | S | R | 6-3 | 155 | 12-25-77 | 1996 | San Francisco de Macoris, D.R. |
| Polonia, Isreal | .310 | 50 | 171 | 22 | 53 | 6 | 2 | 4 | 31 | 10 | 50 | 6 | 7 | R | R | 6-0 | 160 | 10-10-77 | 1995 | San Pedro de Macoris, D.R. |
| Ramirez, Julio | .287 | 43 | 174 | 35 | 50 | 5 | 4 | 0 | 16 | 15 | 34 | 26 | 7 | R | R | 5-11 | 160 | 8-10-77 | 1994 | Santo Domingo, D.R. |
| Reynoso, Ismael | .155 | 30 | 97 | 8 | 15 | 4 | 0 | 0 | 9 | 3 | 22 | 3 | 2 | R | R | 5-10 | 165 | 6-17-78 | 1995 | La Romana, D.R. |
| Roneberg, Brett | .213 | 50 | 174 | 23 | 37 | 8 | 0 | 1 | 15 | 11 | 39 | 0 | 0 | L | L | 6-1 | 183 | 2-5-79 | 1996 | Cairns, Australia |
| Washington, Cory | .239 | 41 | 134 | 26 | 32 | 2 | 0 | 1 | 11 | 17 | 25 | 10 | 2 | R | R | 5-11 | 175 | 12-23-77 | 1996 | Fayetteville, N.C. |
| Wilkes, Brian | .162 | 17 | 37 | 4 | 6 | 0 | 0 | 0 | 1 | 9 | 9 | 1 | 0 | R | R | 6-1 | 195 | 4-12-75 | 1996 | Jacksonville, Fla. |

**GAMES BY POSITION: C**—Alaimo 28, Q. Jackson 1, Morales 28, Wilkes 7. **1B**—Conway 30, R. Jackson 4, Pimentel 1, Roneberg 30. **2B**—Franco 59. **3B**—Bautista 45, Reynoso 15, Wilkes 4. **SS**—Abreu 1, Gonzalez 7, Polonia 43, Reynoso 16. **OF**—Abreu 18, Q. Jackson 9, R. Jackson 2, Maduro 23, Pass 29, Pimentel 11, Ramirez 42, Roneberg 17, Washington 36.

| PITCHING | W | L | ERA | G | GS | CG | SV | IP | H | R | ER | BB | SO | B | T | HT | WT | DOB | 1st Yr | Resides |
|---|---|---|---|---|---|---|---|---|---|---|---|---|---|---|---|---|---|---|---|---|
| Blanco, Pablo | 3 | 5 | 4.57 | 12 | 11 | 2 | 0 | 65 | 58 | 43 | 33 | 36 | 42 | R | R | 6-2 | 170 | 1-15-78 | 1995 | Santo Domingo, D.R. |
| Casey, Shaw | 2 | 3 | 3.49 | 15 | 0 | 0 | 2 | 28 | 22 | 12 | 11 | 18 | 25 | R | R | 6-2 | 190 | 3-27-75 | 1996 | Las Vegas, Nev. |
| Enard, Tony | 0 | 0 | 0.00 | 2 | 0 | 0 | 0 | 7 | 3 | 0 | 0 | 3 | 5 | R | R | 6-4 | 220 | 8-16-74 | 1995 | Sparks, Nev. |
| Evans, Mike | 0 | 1 | 1.27 | 19 | 0 | 0 | 3 | 35 | 24 | 8 | 5 | 13 | 40 | L | L | 5-11 | 185 | 4-1-76 | 1996 | West Palm Beach, Fla. |
| Izquierdo, Hansel | 3 | 2 | 2.70 | 12 | 0 | 0 | 3 | 13 | 7 | 4 | 4 | 5 | 17 | R | R | 6-2 | 200 | 1-2-77 | 1995 | Miami, Fla. |
| Knotts, Gary | 4 | 2 | 2.04 | 12 | 9 | 1 | 0 | 57 | 35 | 16 | 13 | 17 | 46 | R | R | 6-4 | 200 | 2-12-77 | 1996 | Decatur, Ala. |
| Lara, Nelson | 1 | 2 | 5.59 | 7 | 0 | 0 | 0 | 10 | 6 | 11 | 6 | 12 | 3 | R | R | 6-4 | 165 | 7-15-78 | 1995 | Santo Domingo, D.R. |
| Levan, Matthew | 1 | 3 | 3.42 | 9 | 6 | 0 | 0 | 26 | 24 | 14 | 10 | 11 | 26 | L | L | 6-3 | 180 | 6-24-95 | 1996 | Coatesville, Pa. |
| Lugo, Marcelino | 5 | 0 | 1.85 | 8 | 0 | 0 | 0 | 24 | 9 | 5 | 5 | 7 | 13 | R | R | 6-0 | 180 | 4-24-76 | 1996 | Miami, Fla. |
| McClaskey, Tim | 4 | 3 | 2.59 | 12 | 12 | 2 | 0 | 73 | 58 | 28 | 21 | 13 | 63 | R | R | 6-1 | 170 | 1-11-76 | 1996 | Wilton, Iowa |
| Medina, Carlos | 0 | 1 | 3.72 | 4 | 1 | 0 | 0 | 10 | 16 | 7 | 4 | 1 | 9 | L | L | 6-2 | 160 | 5-16-77 | 1994 | La Vega, D.R. |
| Morris, Alex | 2 | 0 | 1.21 | 14 | 2 | 0 | 2 | 37 | 20 | 11 | 5 | 8 | 36 | L | R | 6-4 | 220 | 12-31-76 | 1996 | Austin, Texas |
| Neal, Blaine | 1 | 1 | 4.60 | 7 | 5 | 0 | 1 | 29 | 32 | 18 | 15 | 6 | 15 | L | R | 6-5 | 205 | 4-6-78 | 1996 | Port Richey, Fla. |
| Parks, Wes | 2 | 1 | 0.00 | 6 | 2 | 0 | 0 | 25 | 10 | 1 | 0 | 8 | 19 | R | R | 6-0 | 215 | 10-18-77 | 1996 | Duluth, Ga. |
| Tejera, Michael | 1 | 0 | 3.60 | 2 | 0 | 0 | 0 | 5 | 6 | 2 | 2 | 0 | 2 | L | L | 5-9 | 175 | 10-18-76 | 1995 | Miami, Fla. |
| Wesolowski, David | 0 | 0 | 6.00 | 2 | 2 | 0 | 0 | 9 | 11 | 8 | 6 | 2 | 4 | R | R | 6-3 | 180 | 1-15-78 | 1996 | Williamsville, N.Y. |
| Widerski, Jonathan | 8 | 2 | 2.55 | 12 | 10 | 0 | 0 | 67 | 59 | 26 | 19 | 22 | 55 | R | R | 6-4 | 190 | 5-17-77 | 1995 | Minneapolis, Minn. |

# HOUSTON ASTROS

**Manager:** Terry Collins.    **1996 Record:** 82-80, .506 (2nd, NL Central)

| BATTING | AVG | G | AB | R | H | 2B | 3B | HR | RBI | BB | SO | SB | CS | B | T | HT | WT | DOB | 1st Yr | Resides |
|---|---|---|---|---|---|---|---|---|---|---|---|---|---|---|---|---|---|---|---|---|
| Abreu, Bob | .227 | 15 | 22 | 1 | 5 | 1 | 0 | 0 | 1 | 2 | 3 | 0 | 0 | L | R | 6-0 | 160 | 3-11-74 | 1991 | Turmero, Venez. |
| Bagwell, Jeff | .315 | 162 | 568 | 111 | 179 | 48 | 2 | 31 | 120 | 135 | 114 | 21 | 7 | R | R | 6-0 | 195 | 5-27-68 | 1989 | Houston, Texas |
| Bell, Derek | .263 | 158 | 627 | 84 | 165 | 40 | 3 | 17 | 113 | 40 | 123 | 29 | 3 | R | R | 6-2 | 200 | 12-11-68 | 1987 | Tampa, Fla. |
| Berry, Sean | .281 | 132 | 431 | 55 | 121 | 38 | 1 | 17 | 95 | 23 | 58 | 12 | 6 | R | R | 5-11 | 210 | 3-22-66 | 1986 | Rolling Hills Estates, Calif. |
| Biggio, Craig | .288 | 162 | 605 | 113 | 174 | 24 | 4 | 15 | 75 | 75 | 72 | 25 | 7 | R | R | 5-11 | 180 | 12-14-65 | 1987 | Houston, Texas |
| Cangelosi, John | .263 | 108 | 262 | 49 | 69 | 11 | 4 | 1 | 16 | 44 | 41 | 17 | 9 | S | L | 5-8 | 160 | 3-10-63 | 1982 | Chicago, Ill. |
| Cedeno, Andujar | .000 | 3 | 2 | 1 | 0 | 0 | 0 | 0 | 0 | 2 | 1 | 0 | 0 | R | R | 6-1 | 168 | 8-21-69 | 1987 | La Romana, D.R. |
| 2-team (49 S.D.) | .231 | 52 | 156 | 11 | 36 | 2 | 1 | 3 | 18 | 11 | 33 | 3 | 2 | | | | | | | |
| Eusebio, Tony | .270 | 58 | 152 | 15 | 41 | 7 | 2 | 1 | 19 | 18 | 20 | 0 | 1 | R | R | 6-2 | 180 | 4-27-67 | 1985 | Kissimmee, Fla. |
| Goff, Jerry | .500 | 1 | 4 | 1 | 2 | 0 | 0 | 1 | 2 | 0 | 1 | 0 | 0 | L | R | 6-3 | 207 | 4-12-64 | 1986 | San Rafael, Calif. |
| Gutierrez, Ricky | .284 | 89 | 218 | 28 | 62 | 8 | 1 | 1 | 15 | 23 | 42 | 6 | 1 | R | R | 6-1 | 175 | 5-23-70 | 1988 | Miami, Fla. |
| Hajek, Dave | .300 | 8 | 10 | 3 | 3 | 1 | 0 | 0 | 2 | 0 | 0 | 0 | 0 | R | R | 5-10 | 165 | 10-14-67 | 1990 | Colorado Springs, Colo. |
| Hunter, Brian | .276 | 132 | 526 | 74 | 145 | 27 | 2 | 5 | 35 | 17 | 92 | 35 | 9 | R | R | 6-4 | 180 | 3-5-71 | 1989 | Vancouver, Wash. |
| Knorr, Randy | .195 | 37 | 87 | 7 | 17 | 5 | 0 | 1 | 7 | 5 | 18 | 0 | 1 | R | R | 6-2 | 212 | 11-12-68 | 1986 | Covina, Calif. |
| Manwaring, Kirt | .220 | 37 | 82 | 5 | 18 | 3 | 0 | 0 | 4 | 3 | 16 | 0 | 0 | R | R | 5-11 | 203 | 7-15-65 | 1986 | Scottsdale, Ariz. |
| 2-team (49 S.F.) | .229 | 86 | 227 | 14 | 52 | 9 | 0 | 1 | 18 | 19 | 40 | 0 | 1 | | | | | | | |
| May, Derrick | .251 | 109 | 259 | 24 | 65 | 12 | 3 | 5 | 33 | 30 | 33 | 2 | 2 | L | R | 6-4 | 200 | 7-14-68 | 1986 | Newark, Del. |
| Miller, Orlando | .256 | 139 | 468 | 43 | 120 | 26 | 2 | 15 | 58 | 14 | 116 | 3 | 7 | R | R | 6-1 | 180 | 1-13-69 | 1988 | El Dorado, Panama |
| Montgomery, Ray | .214 | 12 | 14 | 4 | 3 | 1 | 0 | 1 | 4 | 1 | 5 | 0 | 0 | R | R | 6-3 | 195 | 8-8-69 | 1990 | Bronxville, N.Y. |
| Mouton, James | .263 | 122 | 300 | 40 | 79 | 15 | 1 | 3 | 34 | 38 | 55 | 21 | 9 | R | R | 5-9 | 175 | 12-29-68 | 1991 | Sacramento, Calif. |
| Simms, Mike | .176 | 49 | 68 | 6 | 12 | 2 | 1 | 1 | 8 | 4 | 16 | 1 | 0 | R | R | 6-4 | 185 | 1-12-67 | 1985 | Houston, Texas |
| Spiers, Bill | .252 | 122 | 218 | 27 | 55 | 10 | 1 | 6 | 26 | 20 | 34 | 7 | 0 | L | R | 6-2 | 190 | 6-5-66 | 1987 | Ellorbee, S.C. |
| Wilkins, Rick | .213 | 84 | 254 | 34 | 54 | 8 | 2 | 6 | 23 | 46 | 81 | 0 | 1 | L | R | 6-2 | 210 | 6-4-67 | 1987 | Jacksonville, Fla. |

| PITCHING | W | L | ERA | G | GS | CG | SV | IP | H | R | ER | BB | SO | B | T | HT | WT | DOB | 1st Yr | Resides |
|---|---|---|---|---|---|---|---|---|---|---|---|---|---|---|---|---|---|---|---|---|
| Brocail, Doug | 1 | 5 | 4.58 | 23 | 4 | 0 | 0 | 53 | 58 | 31 | 27 | 23 | 34 | L | R | 6-5 | 190 | 5-16-67 | 1986 | Lamar, Colo. |
| Clark, Terry | 0 | 2 | 11.37 | 5 | 0 | 0 | 0 | 6 | 16 | 10 | 8 | 2 | 5 | R | R | 6-2 | 196 | 10-10-60 | 1979 | La Puente, Ca. |
| Darwin, Danny | 3 | 2 | 5.95 | 15 | 6 | 0 | 0 | 42 | 43 | 31 | 28 | 11 | 27 | R | R | 6-3 | 202 | 10-25-55 | 1976 | Valley View, Texas |
| 2-team (19 Pitt.) | 10 | 11 | 3.77 | 34 | 25 | 0 | 0 | 165 | 160 | 79 | 69 | 27 | 96 | | | | | | | |
| Dougherty, Jim | 0 | 2 | 9.00 | 12 | 0 | 0 | 0 | 13 | 14 | 14 | 13 | 11 | 6 | R | R | 6-0 | 210 | 3-8-68 | 1991 | Kitty Hawk, N.C. |
| Drabek, Doug | 7 | 9 | 4.57 | 30 | 30 | 1 | 0 | 175 | 208 | 102 | 89 | 60 | 137 | R | R | 6-1 | 185 | 7-25-62 | 1983 | The Woodlands, Texas |
| Hampton, Mike | 10 | 10 | 3.59 | 27 | 27 | 2 | 0 | 160 | 175 | 79 | 64 | 49 | 101 | R | L | 5-10 | 180 | 9-9-72 | 1990 | Homosassa, Fla. |
| Hartgraves, Dean | 0 | 0 | 5.21 | 19 | 0 | 0 | 0 | 19 | 18 | 11 | 11 | 16 | 16 | R | L | 6-0 | 185 | 8-12-66 | 1987 | Central Point, Ore. |
| Hernandez, Xavier | 5 | 5 | 4.22 | 58 | 0 | 0 | 6 | 75 | 69 | 39 | 35 | 26 | 78 | L | R | 6-2 | 185 | 8-16-65 | 1986 | Missouri City, Texas |
| 2-team (3 Cincinnati) | 5 | 5 | 4.62 | 61 | 0 | 0 | 6 | 78 | 77 | 45 | 40 | 28 | 81 | | | | | | | |
| Holt, Chris | 0 | 1 | 5.79 | 4 | 0 | 0 | 0 | 5 | 5 | 3 | 3 | 3 | 0 | R | R | 6-4 | 205 | 9-18-71 | 1992 | Dallas, Texas |
| Hudek, John | 2 | 0 | 2.81 | 15 | 0 | 0 | 2 | 16 | 12 | 5 | 5 | 5 | 14 | S | R | 6-1 | 200 | 8-8-66 | 1988 | Tampa, Fla. |
| Johnstone, John | 1 | 0 | 5.54 | 9 | 0 | 0 | 0 | 13 | 17 | 8 | 8 | 5 | 6 | R | R | 6-3 | 195 | 11-25-68 | 1987 | Liverpool, N.Y. |
| Jones, Todd | 6 | 3 | 4.40 | 51 | 0 | 0 | 17 | 57 | 61 | 30 | 28 | 32 | 44 | L | R | 6-3 | 200 | 4-24-68 | 1989 | Pell City, Ala. |
| Kile, Darryl | 12 | 11 | 4.19 | 35 | 33 | 4 | 0 | 219 | 233 | 113 | 102 | 97 | 219 | R | R | 6-5 | 185 | 12-2-68 | 1988 | Corona, Ca. |
| Morman, Alvin | 4 | 1 | 4.93 | 53 | 0 | 0 | 0 | 42 | 43 | 24 | 23 | 24 | 31 | L | L | 6-3 | 210 | 1-6-69 | 1991 | Rockingham, N.C. |
| Olson, Gregg | 1 | 0 | 4.82 | 9 | 0 | 0 | 0 | 9 | 12 | 5 | 5 | 7 | 8 | R | R | 6-4 | 212 | 10-11-66 | 1988 | Reisterstown, Md. |
| Reynolds, Shane | 16 | 10 | 3.65 | 35 | 35 | 4 | 0 | 239 | 227 | 103 | 97 | 44 | 204 | R | R | 6-3 | 210 | 3-26-68 | 1989 | Houston, Texas |
| Small, Mark | 0 | 1 | 5.92 | 16 | 0 | 0 | 0 | 24 | 33 | 23 | 16 | 13 | 16 | R | R | 6-3 | 205 | 11-12-67 | 1989 | Seattle, Wash. |
| Swindell, Greg | 0 | 3 | 7.83 | 8 | 4 | 0 | 0 | 23 | 35 | 25 | 20 | 11 | 15 | R | L | 6-3 | 225 | 1-2-65 | 1986 | Houston, Texas |
| Tabaka, Jeff | 0 | 2 | 6.64 | 18 | 0 | 0 | 1 | 20 | 28 | 18 | 15 | 14 | 18 | R | L | 6-2 | 195 | 1-17-64 | 1986 | Clinton, Ohio |
| Wagner, Billy | 2 | 2 | 2.44 | 37 | 0 | 0 | 9 | 52 | 28 | 16 | 14 | 30 | 67 | L | L | 5-10 | 180 | 7-25-71 | 1993 | Tannersville, Va. |
| Wall, Donne | 9 | 8 | 4.56 | 26 | 23 | 2 | 0 | 150 | 170 | 84 | 76 | 34 | 99 | R | R | 6-1 | 180 | 7-11-67 | 1989 | Festus, Mo. |
| Young, Anthony | 3 | 3 | 4.59 | 28 | 0 | 0 | 0 | 33 | 36 | 18 | 17 | 22 | 19 | R | R | 6-2 | 200 | 1-19-66 | 1987 | Houston, Texas |

## FIELDING

| Catcher | PCT | G | PO | A | E | DP | PB |
|---|---|---|---|---|---|---|---|
| Eusebio | .996 | 47 | 255 | 24 | 1 | 1 | 1 |
| Goff | 1.000 | 1 | 11 | 0 | 0 | 1 | 6 |
| Knorr | 1.000 | 33 | 204 | 14 | 0 | 1 | 0 |
| Manwaring | .995 | 37 | 171 | 21 | 1 | 3 | 0 |
| Wilkins | .990 | 82 | 550 | 39 | 6 | 3 | 7 |

| First Base | PCT | G | PO | A | E | DP |
|---|---|---|---|---|---|---|
| Bagwell | .989 | 162 | 1336 | 136 | 16 | 117 |
| Simms | 1.000 | 5 | 7 | 1 | 0 | 0 |
| Spiers | 1.000 | 4 | 9 | 1 | 0 | 2 |

| Second Base | PCT | G | PO | A | E | DP |
|---|---|---|---|---|---|---|
| Biggio | .988 | 162 | 361 | 440 | 10 | 76 |
| Gutierrez | .857 | 5 | 3 | 3 | 1 | 1 |
| Hajek | 1.000 | 2 | 2 | 1 | 0 | 0 |
| Spiers | 1.000 | 7 | 7 | 4 | 0 | 2 |

| Third Base | PCT | G | PO | A | E | DP |
|---|---|---|---|---|---|---|
| Berry | .922 | 110 | 67 | 194 | 22 | 13 |
| Cedeno | 1.000 | 1 | 0 | 1 | 0 | 0 |
| Gutierrez | 1.000 | 6 | 1 | 5 | 0 | 0 |
| Hajek | 1.000 | 3 | 1 | 6 | 0 | 0 |

| | PCT | G | PO | A | E | DP |
|---|---|---|---|---|---|---|
| Miller | .949 | 29 | 14 | 23 | 2 | 1 |
| Spiers | .959 | 77 | 22 | 94 | 5 | 9 |

| Shortstop | PCT | G | PO | A | E | DP |
|---|---|---|---|---|---|---|
| Cedeno | 1.000 | 2 | 3 | 6 | 0 | 3 |
| Gutierrez | .953 | 74 | 82 | 141 | 11 | 33 |
| Miller | .958 | 117 | 133 | 297 | 19 | 59 |
| Spiers | 1.000 | 4 | 3 | 9 | 0 | 1 |

| Outfield | PCT | G | PO | A | E | DP |
|---|---|---|---|---|---|---|
| Abreu | 1.000 | 7 | 6 | 0 | 0 | 0 |
| Bell | .977 | 157 | 283 | 16 | 7 | 4 |
| Cangelosi | .975 | 78 | 113 | 5 | 3 | 0 |
| Hunter | .960 | 127 | 279 | 11 | 12 | 1 |
| May | .970 | 71 | 126 | 5 | 4 | 0 |
| Montgomery | 1.000 | 6 | 6 | 0 | 0 | 0 |
| Mouton | .971 | 108 | 158 | 7 | 5 | 1 |
| Simms | 1.000 | 12 | 17 | 0 | 0 | 0 |
| Spiers | 1.000 | 2 | 3 | 0 | 0 | 0 |

**Shane Reynolds**

Jeff Bagwell led the Astros with 31 homers and 120 RBIs

LARRY GOREN

Astros minor league Player of the Year Bob Abreu

STEVE MOORE

## FARM SYSTEM

**Director, Player Development and Scouting:** Dan O'Brien Jr.

| Class | Farm Team | League | W | L | Pct. | Finish* | Manager | First Yr |
|---|---|---|---|---|---|---|---|---|
| AAA | Tucson (Ariz.) Toros | Pacific Coast | 70 | 74 | .486 | 6th (10) | Tim Tolman | 1980 |
| AA | Jackson (Miss.) Generals | Texas | 70 | 70 | .500 | +T-4th (8) | Dave Engle | 1991 |
| #A | Kissimmee (Fla.) Cobras | Florida State | 60 | 75 | .444 | 12th (14) | Alan Ashby | 1985 |
| A | Quad City (Iowa) River Bandits | Midwest | 70 | 61 | .534 | 4th (14) | Jim Pankovits | 1993 |
| A | Auburn (N.Y.) Doubledays | New York-Penn | 37 | 39 | .487 | 8th (14) | Manny Acta | 1982 |
| R | Kissimmee (Fla.) Astros | Gulf Coast | 31 | 28 | .525 | 7th (16) | Bobby Ramos | 1977 |

*Finish in overall standings (No. of teams in league)   #Advanced level   +Won league championship

## ORGANIZATION LEADERS

### MAJOR LEAGUERS

**BATTING**
| | | |
|---|---|---|
| *AVG | Jeff Bagwell | .315 |
| R | Craig Biggio | 113 |
| H | Jeff Bagwell | 179 |
| TB | Jeff Bagwell | 324 |
| 2B | Jeff Bagwell | 48 |
| 3B | Two tied at | 4 |
| HR | Jeff Bagwell | 31 |
| RBI | Jeff Bagwell | 120 |
| BB | Jeff Bagwell | 135 |
| SO | Derek Bell | 123 |
| SB | Brian Hunter | 35 |

**PITCHING**
| | | |
|---|---|---|
| W | Shane Reynolds | 16 |
| L | Two tied at | 11 |
| #ERA | Mike Hampton | 3.59 |
| G | Xavier Hernandez | 61 |
| CG | Two tied at | 4 |
| SV | Todd Jones | 17 |
| IP | Shane Reynolds | 239 |
| BB | Darryl Kile | 97 |
| SO | Darryl Kile | 219 |

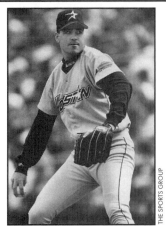

THE SPORTS GROUP

**Darryl Kile.** 219 strikeouts

### MINOR LEAGUERS

**BATTING**
| | | |
|---|---|---|
| *AVG | Mitch Meluskey, Kiss./Jackson | .326 |
| R | Bob Abreu, Tucson | 86 |
| H | Dave Hajek, Tucson | 161 |
| TB | Chris Hatcher, Jackson/Tucson | 286 |
| 2B | Richard Hidalgo, Jackson | 34 |
| 3B | Bob Abreu, Tucson | 16 |
| HR | Chris Hatcher, Jackson/Tucson | 31 |
| RBI | Chris Hatcher, Jackson/Tucson | 97 |
| BB | Bob Abreu, Tucson | 83 |
| SO | Chris Hatcher, Jackson/Tucson | 126 |
| SB | Carlos Hernandez, Quad City | 41 |

**PITCHING**
| | | |
|---|---|---|
| W | Edgar Ramos, Kissimmee/Jackson | 13 |
| L | Dan Lock, Kissimmee | 18 |
| #ERA | Jeriome Robertson, GCL Astros/Kiss. | 1.79 |
| G | Tom Martin, Jackson/Tucson | 62 |
| CG | Two tied at | 4 |
| SV | Manuel Barrios, Jackson | 23 |
| IP | Chris Holt, Tucson | 186 |
| BB | Ryan Creek, Jackson | 121 |
| SO | Brian Sikorski, Quad City | 150 |

*Minimum 250 At-Bats   #Minimum 75 Innings

## TOP 10 PROSPECTS

**How the Astros Top 10 prospects, as judged by Baseball America prior to the 1996 season, fared in 1996:**

STEVE MOORE

**Billy Wagner**

| Player, Pos. | Club (Class—League) | AVG | AB | R | H | 2B | 3B | HR | RBI | SB |
|---|---|---|---|---|---|---|---|---|---|---|
| 2. Richard Hidalgo, of | Jackson (AA—Texas) | .294 | 513 | 66 | 151 | 34 | 2 | 14 | 78 | 11 |
| 3. Bob Abreu, of | Tucson (AAA—Pacific Coast) | .285 | 484 | 86 | 138 | 14 | 16 | 13 | 68 | 24 |
| | Houston | .227 | 22 | 1 | 5 | 1 | 0 | 0 | 1 | 0 |
| 4. Carlos Guillen, ss | Quad City (A—Midwest) | .330 | 112 | 23 | 37 | 7 | 1 | 3 | 17 | 13 |
| 6. Ramon Castro, c | Quad City (A—Midwest) | .248 | 314 | 38 | 78 | 15 | 0 | 7 | 43 | 2 |
| 8. Bryant Nelson, 3b | Kissimmee (A—Florida State) | .252 | 345 | 38 | 87 | 21 | 6 | 3 | 52 | 8 |
| 9. Russ Johnson, ss | Jackson (AA—Texas) | .310 | 496 | 86 | 154 | 24 | 5 | 15 | 74 | 9 |

| | | W | L | ERA | G | SV | IP | H | BB | SO |
|---|---|---|---|---|---|---|---|---|---|---|
| 1. Billy Wagner, lhp | Tucson (AAA—Pacific Coast) | 6 | 2 | 3.28 | 12 | 0 | 74 | 62 | 33 | 86 |
| | Houston | 2 | 2 | 2.44 | 37 | 9 | 52 | 28 | 30 | 67 |
| 5. Scott Elarton, rhp | Kissimmee (A—Florida State) | 12 | 7 | 2.92 | 27 | 0 | 172 | 154 | 54 | 130 |
| 7. Chris Holt, rhp | Tucson (AAA—Pacific Coast) | 9 | 6 | 3.62 | 28 | 0 | 186 | 208 | 38 | 137 |
| | Houston | 0 | 1 | 5.79 | 4 | 0 | 5 | 5 | 3 | 0 |
| 10. Oscar Henriquez, rhp | Kissimmee (A—Florida State) | 0 | 4 | 3.97 | 37 | 15 | 34 | 28 | 29 | 40 |

LARRY GOREN

STAN DENNY

**Killer B's.** Along with first baseman Jeff Bagwell (.315-31-120), outfielder Derek Bell (.263-17-113), left, and second baseman Craig Biggio (.288-15-75, 113 runs scored) contributed to the Astros' second-place finish.

## TUCSON Class AAA

### PACIFIC COAST LEAGUE

| BATTING | AVG | G | AB | R | H | 2B | 3B | HR | RBI | BB | SO | SB | CS | B | T | HT | WT | DOB | 1st Yr | Resides |
|---|---|---|---|---|---|---|---|---|---|---|---|---|---|---|---|---|---|---|---|---|
| Abreu, Bob | .283 | 132 | 484 | 86 | 137 | 14 | 16 | 13 | 68 | 83 | 111 | 24 | 18 | L | R | 6-0 | 160 | 3-11-74 | 1991 | Turmero, Venez. |
| Ball, Jeff | .324 | 116 | 429 | 64 | 139 | 31 | 2 | 19 | 73 | 34 | 83 | 10 | 8 | R | R | 5-10 | 185 | 4-17-69 | 1990 | Merced, Calif. |
| Bridges, Kary | .314 | 42 | 140 | 24 | 44 | 9 | 1 | 1 | 21 | 9 | 8 | 1 | 3 | L | R | 5-10 | 165 | 10-27-71 | 1993 | Hattiesburg, Miss. |
| Brumley, Mike | .234 | 88 | 278 | 40 | 65 | 11 | 7 | 4 | 28 | 40 | 79 | 9 | 3 | S | R | 5-10 | 175 | 4-9-63 | 1983 | Tulsa, Okla. |
| Christopherson, Eric | .287 | 67 | 223 | 31 | 64 | 15 | 3 | 6 | 36 | 21 | 47 | 2 | 0 | R | R | 6-1 | 190 | 4-25-69 | 1990 | Westminster, Calif. |
| Davis, Jay | .337 | 33 | 101 | 18 | 34 | 7 | 1 | 1 | 17 | 5 | 16 | 4 | 1 | L | L | 5-11 | 172 | 10-3-70 | 1989 | Chicago, Ill. |
| Eusebio, Tony | .415 | 15 | 53 | 8 | 22 | 4 | 0 | 0 | 14 | 2 | 7 | 0 | 0 | R | R | 6-2 | 180 | 4-27-67 | 1985 | Kissimmee, Fla. |
| Goff, Jerry | .236 | 96 | 275 | 39 | 65 | 14 | 2 | 9 | 52 | 55 | 97 | 1 | 0 | L | R | 6-3 | 207 | 4-12-64 | 1986 | San Rafael, Calif. |
| Groppuso, Mike | .255 | 50 | 145 | 15 | 37 | 3 | 1 | 5 | 18 | 8 | 45 | 2 | 0 | R | R | 6-3 | 195 | 3-9-70 | 1991 | Lake Katrine, N.Y. |
| Hajek, Dave | .317 | 121 | 508 | 81 | 161 | 31 | 5 | 4 | 64 | 25 | 36 | 9 | 6 | R | R | 5-10 | 165 | 10-14-67 | 1990 | Colorado Springs, Colo. |
| Hatcher, Chris | .302 | 95 | 348 | 53 | 105 | 21 | 4 | 18 | 61 | 14 | 87 | 10 | 8 | R | R | 6-3 | 220 | 1-7-69 | 1990 | Carter Lake, Iowa |
| Holbert, Ray | .247 | 28 | 97 | 13 | 24 | 3 | 2 | 0 | 10 | 7 | 19 | 4 | 1 | R | R | 6-0 | 165 | 9-25-70 | 1988 | Moreno Valley, Calif. |
| Hunter, Brian | .357 | 3 | 14 | 3 | 5 | 0 | 1 | 0 | 1 | 0 | 2 | 3 | 0 | R | R | 6-4 | 180 | 3-5-71 | 1989 | Vancouver, Wash. |
| Kellner, Frank | .272 | 96 | 254 | 37 | 69 | 12 | 5 | 1 | 31 | 22 | 43 | 3 | 6 | S | R | 5-11 | 175 | 1-5-67 | 1990 | Tucson, Ariz. |
| Luce, Roger | .300 | 20 | 50 | 8 | 15 | 2 | 1 | 2 | 8 | 2 | 17 | 0 | 0 | R | R | 6-4 | 215 | 5-7-69 | 1991 | Houston, Texas |
| Montgomery, Ray | .306 | 100 | 359 | 70 | 110 | 20 | 0 | 22 | 75 | 59 | 54 | 7 | 1 | R | R | 6-3 | 195 | 8-8-69 | 1990 | Bronxville, N.Y. |
| Mora, Melvin | .281 | 62 | 228 | 35 | 64 | 11 | 2 | 3 | 26 | 17 | 27 | 3 | 5 | R | R | 5-10 | 160 | 2-2-72 | 1991 | Naquanqua, Venez. |
| Mouton, James | .250 | 1 | 4 | 1 | 1 | 0 | 0 | 0 | 0 | 1 | 0 | 0 | 0 | R | R | 5-9 | 175 | 12-29-68 | 1991 | Sacramento, Calif. |
| Probst, Alan | .286 | 2 | 7 | 0 | 2 | 1 | 0 | 0 | 1 | 1 | 3 | 0 | 0 | R | R | 6-4 | 205 | 10-24-70 | 1992 | Avis, Pa. |
| Pye, Eddie | .258 | 92 | 275 | 39 | 71 | 15 | 6 | 2 | 25 | 29 | 41 | 5 | 3 | R | R | 5-10 | 170 | 2-13-67 | 1988 | Columbia, Tenn. |
| Ramos, Ken | .270 | 104 | 385 | 54 | 104 | 22 | 3 | 4 | 34 | 41 | 41 | 6 | 9 | L | L | 6-1 | 185 | 6-8-67 | 1989 | Pueblo, Colo. |
| Simms, Mike | .297 | 17 | 64 | 11 | 19 | 3 | 0 | 7 | 19 | 9 | 17 | 0 | 3 | R | R | 6-4 | 185 | 1-12-67 | 1985 | Houston, Texas |
| Trammell, Gary | .400 | 3 | 10 | 3 | 4 | 0 | 0 | 1 | 2 | 2 | 2 | 0 | 0 | L | R | 6-0 | 180 | 10-16-72 | 1993 | Garland, Texas |

| PITCHING | W | L | ERA | G | GS | CG | SV | IP | H | R | ER | BB | SO | B | T | HT | WT | DOB | 1st Yr | Resides |
|---|---|---|---|---|---|---|---|---|---|---|---|---|---|---|---|---|---|---|---|---|
| Bell, Eric | 4 | 14 | 5.65 | 30 | 21 | 1 | 0 | 127 | 177 | 114 | 80 | 48 | 58 | L | L | 6-0 | 165 | 10-27-63 | 1982 | Modesto, Calif. |
| Brocail, Doug | 0 | 1 | 7.36 | 5 | 1 | 0 | 0 | 7 | 12 | 6 | 6 | 1 | 4 | L | R | 6-5 | 190 | 5-16-67 | 1986 | Lamar, Colo. |
| Dault, Donnie | 0 | 0 | 9.00 | 1 | 0 | 0 | 0 | 2 | 4 | 2 | 2 | 0 | 2 | R | R | 6-6 | 185 | 4-15-72 | 1991 | Austin, Texas |
| Dougherty, Jim | 4 | 3 | 3.50 | 46 | 0 | 0 | 1 | 62 | 65 | 35 | 24 | 27 | 53 | R | R | 6-0 | 210 | 3-8-68 | 1991 | Kitty Hawk, N.C. |
| Evans, David | 6 | 12 | 5.24 | 43 | 15 | 0 | 1 | 112 | 120 | 77 | 65 | 47 | 80 | R | R | 6-3 | 185 | 1-1-68 | 1990 | Houston, Texas |
| Gallaher, Kevin | 4 | 2 | 4.66 | 35 | 3 | 0 | 1 | 87 | 88 | 50 | 45 | 45 | 81 | R | R | 6-3 | 190 | 8-1-68 | 1991 | Vienna, Va. |
| Hartgraves, Dean | 2 | 1 | 1.89 | 18 | 0 | 0 | 4 | 19 | 17 | 6 | 4 | 8 | 13 | R | L | 6-0 | 185 | 8-12-66 | 1987 | Central Point, Ore. |
| Holt, Chris | 9 | 6 | 3.72 | 28 | 27 | 4 | 0 | 186 | 209 | 87 | 77 | 38 | 137 | R | R | 6-4 | 205 | 9-18-71 | 1992 | Dallas, Texas |
| Hudek, John | 1 | 0 | 3.10 | 17 | 2 | 0 | 4 | 20 | 17 | 8 | 7 | 8 | 26 | S | R | 6-1 | 200 | 8-8-66 | 1988 | Tampa, Fla. |
| Humphrey, Rich | 1 | 1 | 10.80 | 10 | 0 | 0 | 0 | 13 | 23 | 20 | 16 | 7 | 8 | R | R | 6-1 | 185 | 6-24-71 | 1993 | Lakeland, Fla. |
| Johnstone, John | 3 | 3 | 3.42 | 45 | 1 | 0 | 5 | 55 | 59 | 27 | 21 | 22 | 70 | R | R | 6-3 | 195 | 11-25-68 | 1987 | Liverpool, N.Y. |
| Jones, Todd | 0 | 0 | 0.00 | 1 | 0 | 0 | 0 | 2 | 1 | 1 | 0 | 2 | 0 | R | R | 6-3 | 200 | 4-24-68 | 1989 | Pell City, Ala. |
| Kester, Tim | 0 | 1 | 43.20 | 1 | 1 | 0 | 0 | 2 | 8 | 8 | 8 | 1 | 1 | R | R | 6-4 | 185 | 12-1-71 | 1993 | Coral Springs, Fla. |
| Loiselle, Rich | 2 | 2 | 2.43 | 5 | 5 | 1 | 0 | 33 | 28 | 20 | 9 | 11 | 31 | R | R | 6-5 | 225 | 1-12-72 | 1991 | Oshkosh, Wis. |
| Martin, Tom | 0 | 0 | 0.00 | 5 | 0 | 0 | 0 | 6 | 6 | 0 | 0 | 2 | 1 | L | L | 6-1 | 185 | 5-21-70 | 1989 | Panama City, Fla. |

## PITCHING

| | W | L | ERA | G | GS | CG | SV | IP | H | R | ER | BB | SO | B | T | HT | WT | DOB | 1st Yr | Resides |
|---|---|---|---|---|---|---|---|---|---|---|---|---|---|---|---|---|---|---|---|---|
| Mlicki, Doug | 5 | 11 | 4.72 | 26 | 26 | 0 | 0 | 137 | 171 | 89 | 72 | 41 | 98 | R | R | 6-3 | 175 | 4-23-71 | 1992 | Dublin, Ohio |
| Patrick, Bronswell | 7 | 3 | 3.51 | 33 | 15 | 0 | 1 | 118 | 137 | 59 | 46 | 33 | 82 | R | R | 6-1 | 205 | 9-16-70 | 1988 | Greenville, N.C. |
| Simons, Doug | 3 | 4 | 5.40 | 8 | 6 | 0 | 0 | 42 | 53 | 25 | 25 | 15 | 27 | L | L | 6-0 | 160 | 9-15-66 | 1988 | Orlando, Fla. |
| Small, Mark | 3 | 3 | 2.08 | 32 | 0 | 0 | 7 | 39 | 32 | 17 | 9 | 18 | 36 | R | R | 6-3 | 205 | 11-12-67 | 1989 | Seattle, Wash. |
| Tabaka, Jeff | 6 | 2 | 2.93 | 41 | 0 | 0 | 4 | 43 | 40 | 16 | 14 | 21 | 51 | R | L | 6-2 | 195 | 1-17-64 | 1986 | Clinton, Ohio |
| Wagner, Billy | 6 | 2 | 3.28 | 12 | 12 | 1 | 0 | 74 | 62 | 32 | 27 | 33 | 86 | L | L | 5-10 | 180 | 7-25-71 | 1993 | Tannersville, Va. |
| Wall, Donne | 3 | 3 | 4.13 | 8 | 8 | 0 | 0 | 52 | 67 | 30 | 24 | 6 | 36 | R | R | 6-1 | 180 | 7-11-67 | 1989 | Festus, Mo. |
| Young, Anthony | 1 | 0 | 3.86 | 4 | 1 | 0 | 0 | 5 | 3 | 3 | 2 | 5 | 3 | R | R | 6-2 | 200 | 1-19-66 | 1987 | Houston, Texas |

## FIELDING

| Catcher | PCT | G | PO | A | E | DP | PB |
|---|---|---|---|---|---|---|---|
| Christopherson | .990 | 61 | 450 | 34 | 5 | 3 | 6 |
| Eusebio | 1.000 | 10 | 45 | 1 | 0 | 0 | 3 |
| Goff | .978 | 74 | 440 | 49 | 11 | 4 | 12 |
| Luce | 1.000 | 16 | 75 | 7 | 0 | 1 | 2 |
| Probst | 1.000 | 1 | 10 | 2 | 0 | 0 | 0 |

| First Base | PCT | G | PO | A | E | DP |
|---|---|---|---|---|---|---|
| Ball | .986 | 94 | 773 | 64 | 12 | 72 |
| Brumley | .970 | 12 | 88 | 10 | 3 | 5 |
| Goff | .994 | 19 | 142 | 11 | 1 | 14 |
| Groppuso | 1.000 | 4 | 31 | 1 | 0 | 2 |
| Kellner | 1.000 | 11 | 53 | 4 | 0 | 8 |
| Montgomery | 1.000 | 2 | 10 | 1 | 0 | 1 |
| Simms | .967 | 17 | 138 | 9 | 5 | 12 |

| Second Base | PCT | G | PO | A | E | DP |
|---|---|---|---|---|---|---|
| Bridges | .957 | 34 | 54 | 81 | 6 | 21 |

| | PCT | G | PO | A | E | DP |
|---|---|---|---|---|---|---|
| Brumley | 1.000 | 1 | 3 | 1 | 0 | 1 |
| Hajek | .959 | 73 | 146 | 225 | 16 | 52 |
| Kellner | .957 | 7 | 11 | 11 | 1 | 1 |
| Mora | 1.000 | 2 | 3 | 3 | 0 | 2 |
| Pye | .969 | 46 | 74 | 113 | 6 | 23 |

| Third Base | PCT | G | PO | A | E | DP |
|---|---|---|---|---|---|---|
| Ball | .878 | 21 | 9 | 34 | 6 | 3 |
| Brumley | .917 | 15 | 3 | 19 | 2 | 1 |
| Groppuso | .880 | 39 | 27 | 68 | 13 | 8 |
| Hajek | .903 | 26 | 19 | 46 | 7 | 6 |
| Kellner | .929 | 10 | 2 | 11 | 1 | 0 |
| Mora | .889 | 33 | 16 | 64 | 10 | 2 |
| Pye | .952 | 31 | 13 | 46 | 3 | 3 |

| Shortstop | PCT | G | PO | A | E | DP |
|---|---|---|---|---|---|---|
| Brumley | .916 | 49 | 57 | 129 | 17 | 23 |

| | PCT | G | PO | A | E | DP |
|---|---|---|---|---|---|---|
| Hajek | .901 | 27 | 39 | 61 | 11 | 15 |
| Holbert | .919 | 27 | 37 | 65 | 9 | 10 |
| Kellner | .944 | 64 | 79 | 173 | 15 | 36 |
| Pye | .750 | 2 | 2 | 4 | 2 | 2 |

| Outfield | PCT | G | PO | A | E | DP |
|---|---|---|---|---|---|---|
| Abreu | .969 | 128 | 202 | 15 | 7 | 2 |
| Brumley | .933 | 6 | 14 | 0 | 1 | 0 |
| Davis | .958 | 26 | 45 | 1 | 2 | 0 |
| Hatcher | .984 | 75 | 122 | 4 | 2 | 0 |
| Hunter | 1.000 | 3 | 8 | 0 | 0 | 0 |
| Montgomery | .978 | 93 | 172 | 7 | 4 | 1 |
| Mora | .941 | 29 | 61 | 3 | 4 | 0 |
| Mouton | 1.000 | 1 | 2 | 0 | 0 | 0 |
| Ramos | .956 | 92 | 165 | 10 | 8 | 0 |
| Trammell | 1.000 | 4 | 4 | 0 | 0 | 0 |

# JACKSON — Class AA

## TEXAS LEAGUE

### BATTING

| | AVG | G | AB | R | H | 2B | 3B | HR | RBI | BB | SO | SB | CS | B | T | HT | WT | DOB | 1st Yr | Resides |
|---|---|---|---|---|---|---|---|---|---|---|---|---|---|---|---|---|---|---|---|---|
| Bridges, Kary | .325 | 87 | 338 | 51 | 110 | 12 | 2 | 4 | 33 | 32 | 14 | 4 | 5 | L | R | 5-10 | 165 | 10-27-71 | 1993 | Hattiesburg, Miss. |
| Colon, Dennis | .280 | 127 | 432 | 49 | 121 | 23 | 1 | 12 | 58 | 21 | 49 | 0 | 3 | L | R | 5-10 | 165 | 8-4-73 | 1991 | Manati, P.R. |
| Forkner, Tim | .293 | 114 | 379 | 55 | 111 | 20 | 3 | 7 | 46 | 55 | 47 | 0 | 4 | L | R | 5-11 | 180 | 3-28-73 | 1993 | Greeley, Colo. |
| Gonzalez, Jimmy | .200 | 2 | 5 | 1 | 1 | 0 | 0 | 0 | 0 | 1 | 1 | 0 | 0 | R | R | 6-3 | 210 | 3-8-73 | 1991 | Hartford, Conn. |
| Groppuso, Mike | .252 | 33 | 111 | 17 | 28 | 0 | 2 | 3 | 12 | 11 | 35 | 1 | 1 | R | R | 6-3 | 195 | 3-9-70 | 1991 | Lake Katrine, N.Y. |
| Hatcher, Chris | .308 | 41 | 156 | 29 | 48 | 9 | 1 | 13 | 36 | 9 | 32 | 2 | 1 | R | R | 6-3 | 220 | 1-7-69 | 1990 | Carter Lake, Iowa |
| Hidalgo, Richard | .294 | 130 | 513 | 66 | 151 | 34 | 2 | 14 | 78 | 29 | 55 | 11 | 7 | R | R | 6-2 | 175 | 7-2-75 | 1993 | Guarenas, Venez. |
| Johnson, Russ | .310 | 132 | 496 | 86 | 154 | 24 | 5 | 15 | 74 | 56 | 50 | 9 | 4 | R | R | 5-10 | 185 | 2-22-73 | 1994 | Baton Rouge, La. |
| Luce, Roger | .255 | 69 | 243 | 29 | 62 | 11 | 4 | 8 | 36 | 10 | 52 | 0 | 0 | R | R | 6-4 | 215 | 5-7-69 | 1991 | Houston, Texas |
| Magallanes, Bobby | .268 | 12 | 41 | 7 | 11 | 2 | 0 | 2 | 4 | 2 | 8 | 0 | 0 | R | R | 5-8 | 170 | 8-18-69 | 1990 | Downey, Calif. |
| McNabb, Buck | .301 | 88 | 279 | 38 | 84 | 15 | 5 | 0 | 26 | 41 | 37 | 10 | 6 | L | R | 6-0 | 180 | 1-17-73 | 1991 | Fort Walton Beach, Fla. |
| Meluskey, Mitch | .313 | 38 | 134 | 18 | 42 | 11 | 0 | 0 | 21 | 18 | 24 | 0 | 0 | S | R | 6-0 | 185 | 9-18-73 | 1992 | Yakima, Wash. |
| Mitchell, Donovan | .252 | 120 | 408 | 57 | 103 | 22 | 2 | 3 | 32 | 33 | 51 | 11 | 4 | L | R | 5-9 | 175 | 11-27-69 | 1992 | White Plains, N.Y. |
| Mora, Melvin | .286 | 70 | 255 | 36 | 73 | 6 | 1 | 5 | 23 | 14 | 23 | 4 | 7 | R | R | 5-10 | 160 | 2-2-72 | 1991 | Naquanqua, Venez. |
| Mota, Gary | .240 | 12 | 25 | 3 | 6 | 0 | 0 | 0 | 4 | 2 | 2 | 0 | 0 | R | R | 6-0 | 195 | 10-6-70 | 1990 | La Crescenta, Calif. |
| Peterson, Nate | .278 | 114 | 324 | 36 | 90 | 19 | 0 | 2 | 34 | 27 | 49 | 1 | 1 | L | R | 6-2 | 185 | 7-12-71 | 1993 | Melbourne, Australia |
| Probst, Alan | .244 | 63 | 180 | 20 | 44 | 9 | 1 | 7 | 33 | 16 | 43 | 1 | 0 | R | R | 6-4 | 205 | 10-24-70 | 1992 | Avis, Pa. |
| Ross, Tony | .175 | 34 | 80 | 13 | 14 | 0 | 1 | 0 | 3 | 7 | 11 | 2 | 1 | R | R | 5-11 | 175 | 5-11-75 | 1992 | Kansas City, Mo. |
| Sanchez, Victor | .219 | 86 | 210 | 30 | 46 | 9 | 0 | 13 | 34 | 15 | 58 | 4 | 1 | R | R | 5-11 | 175 | 12-20-71 | 1994 | Stockton, Calif. |

### PITCHING

| | W | L | ERA | G | GS | CG | SV | IP | H | R | ER | BB | SO | B | T | HT | WT | DOB | 1st Yr | Resides |
|---|---|---|---|---|---|---|---|---|---|---|---|---|---|---|---|---|---|---|---|---|
| Barrios, Manuel | 6 | 4 | 2.37 | 60 | 0 | 0 | 23 | 68 | 60 | 29 | 18 | 29 | 69 | R | R | 6-0 | 145 | 9-21-74 | 1993 | Cabecera, Panama |
| Brocail, Doug | 0 | 0 | 0.00 | 2 | 2 | 0 | 0 | 4 | 1 | 0 | 0 | 1 | 5 | R | R | 6-5 | 190 | 5-16-67 | 1986 | Lamar, Colo. |
| Creek, Ryan | 7 | 15 | 5.26 | 27 | 26 | 1 | 0 | 142 | 139 | 95 | 83 | 121 | 119 | R | R | 6-1 | 180 | 9-24-72 | 1993 | Martinsburg, W.Va. |
| Dace, Derek | 0 | 0 | 2.25 | 1 | 1 | 0 | 0 | 4 | 5 | 1 | 1 | 5 | 0 | L | L | 6-7 | 200 | 4-9-75 | 1994 | Sullivan, Mo. |
| Dault, Donnie | 0 | 0 | 0.00 | 1 | 0 | 0 | 0 | 2 | 2 | 0 | 0 | 2 | 1 | R | R | 6-6 | 185 | 4-15-72 | 1991 | Austin, Texas |
| Grzanich, Mike | 5 | 4 | 3.98 | 57 | 0 | 0 | 6 | 72 | 60 | 47 | 32 | 43 | 80 | R | R | 6-1 | 180 | 8-24-72 | 1992 | Champaign, Ill. |
| Halama, John | 9 | 10 | 3.21 | 27 | 27 | 0 | 0 | 163 | 151 | 77 | 58 | 59 | 110 | L | L | 6-5 | 195 | 2-22-72 | 1994 | Brooklyn, N.Y. |
| Humphrey, Rich | 4 | 2 | 2.51 | 43 | 0 | 0 | 1 | 65 | 53 | 21 | 18 | 15 | 37 | R | R | 6-1 | 185 | 6-24-71 | 1993 | Lakeland, Fla. |
| Kester, Tim | 2 | 4 | 3.73 | 48 | 4 | 0 | 1 | 104 | 105 | 52 | 43 | 16 | 55 | R | R | 6-5 | 225 | 12-1-71 | 1993 | Coral Springs, Fla. |
| Loiselle, Rich | 7 | 4 | 3.47 | 16 | 16 | 2 | 0 | 99 | 107 | 46 | 38 | 27 | 65 | R | R | 6-5 | 225 | 1-12-72 | 1991 | Oshkosh, Wis. |
| Martin, Tom | 6 | 2 | 3.24 | 57 | 0 | 0 | 3 | 75 | 71 | 35 | 27 | 42 | 58 | L | L | 6-1 | 185 | 5-21-70 | 1989 | Panama City, Fla. |
| Narcisse, Tyrone | 7 | 12 | 5.54 | 27 | 26 | 0 | 0 | 127 | 151 | 92 | 78 | 55 | 88 | R | R | 6-5 | 205 | 2-4-72 | 1990 | Port Arthur, Texas |
| Ramos, Edgar | 4 | 5 | 4.88 | 12 | 12 | 1 | 0 | 66 | 63 | 41 | 36 | 29 | 52 | R | R | 6-4 | 170 | 3-6-75 | 1992 | Cumana, Venez. |
| Simons, Doug | 8 | 7 | 3.48 | 20 | 19 | 1 | 0 | 127 | 132 | 53 | 49 | 30 | 75 | L | L | 6-0 | 160 | 9-15-66 | 1988 | Orlando, Fla. |
| Walker, Jamie | 5 | 1 | 2.50 | 45 | 7 | 0 | 2 | 101 | 94 | 34 | 28 | 35 | 79 | L | L | 6-2 | 190 | 7-1-71 | 1992 | Clarksville, Tenn. |

### FIELDING

| Catcher | PCT | G | PO | A | E | DP | PB |
|---|---|---|---|---|---|---|---|
| Gonzalez | 1.000 | 2 | 19 | 2 | 0 | 0 | 1 |
| Luce | .990 | 66 | 366 | 37 | 4 | 7 | 7 |
| Meluskey | .978 | 30 | 207 | 18 | 5 | 1 | 4 |
| Probst | .983 | 51 | 323 | 32 | 6 | 7 | 3 |

| First Base | PCT | G | PO | A | E | DP |
|---|---|---|---|---|---|---|
| Bridges | 1.000 | 1 | 2 | 0 | 0 | 0 |
| Colon | .982 | 120 | 966 | 97 | 19 | 92 |
| Forkner | .974 | 4 | 32 | 6 | 1 | 1 |
| Groppuso | .833 | 2 | 14 | 1 | 3 | 0 |
| Peterson | 1.000 | 1 | 3 | 0 | 0 | 1 |
| Probst | .000 | 1 | 0 | 0 | 0 | 0 |
| Sanchez | .979 | 34 | 263 | 22 | 6 | 26 |

| Second Base | PCT | G | PO | A | E | DP |
|---|---|---|---|---|---|---|
| Bridges | .953 | 82 | 130 | 196 | 16 | 52 |
| Colon | 1.000 | 2 | 2 | 4 | 0 | 1 |
| Magallanes | 1.000 | 10 | 15 | 23 | 0 | 5 |
| Mitchell | .962 | 47 | 76 | 101 | 7 | 25 |
| Mora | .946 | 10 | 12 | 23 | 2 | 4 |

| Third Base | PCT | G | PO | A | E | DP |
|---|---|---|---|---|---|---|
| Forkner | .924 | 100 | 60 | 256 | 26 | 19 |
| Groppuso | .879 | 20 | 13 | 38 | 7 | 6 |
| Mitchell | .944 | 22 | 18 | 50 | 4 | 3 |
| Mora | .900 | 5 | 3 | 15 | 2 | 0 |

| Shortstop | PCT | G | PO | A | E | DP |
|---|---|---|---|---|---|---|
| Groppuso | 1.000 | 3 | 1 | 5 | 0 | 1 |
| Johnson | .949 | 132 | 219 | 411 | 34 | 87 |

| | PCT | G | PO | A | E | DP |
|---|---|---|---|---|---|---|
| Magallanes | 1.000 | 1 | 2 | 3 | 0 | 0 |
| Mitchell | 1.000 | 2 | 2 | 2 | 0 | 0 |
| Mora | .955 | 6 | 4 | 17 | 1 | 0 |

| Outfield | PCT | G | PO | A | E | DP |
|---|---|---|---|---|---|---|
| Hatcher | .947 | 33 | 53 | 1 | 3 | 0 |
| Hidalgo | .981 | 127 | 302 | 14 | 6 | 6 |
| McNabb | 1.000 | 77 | 111 | 4 | 0 | 0 |
| Mitchell | .946 | 44 | 66 | 4 | 4 | 0 |
| Mora | .978 | 46 | 89 | 1 | 2 | 0 |
| Mota | 1.000 | 8 | 7 | 0 | 0 | 0 |
| Peterson | .923 | 94 | 137 | 7 | 12 | 1 |
| Ross | .956 | 32 | 39 | 4 | 2 | 1 |
| Sanchez | .000 | 1 | 0 | 0 | 0 | 0 |

## FLORIDA STATE LEAGUE

| BATTING | AVG | G | AB | R | H | 2B | 3B | HR | RBI | BB | SO | SB | CS | B | T | HT | WT | DOB | 1st Yr | Resides |
|---|---|---|---|---|---|---|---|---|---|---|---|---|---|---|---|---|---|---|---|---|
| Amezcua, Adan | .284 | 88 | 264 | 24 | 75 | 16 | 1 | 0 | 29 | 25 | 42 | 0 | 1 | R | R | 6-1 | 180 | 3-9-74 | 1993 | Mazatlan, Mexico |
| Barksdale, Shane | .133 | 9 | 15 | 1 | 2 | 0 | 0 | 1 | 0 | 0 | 7 | 0 | 0 | L | R | 6-4 | 195 | 9-6-76 | 1994 | Gallant, Ala. |
| Bowers, R.J. | .246 | 40 | 122 | 19 | 30 | 2 | 1 | 5 | 14 | 16 | 32 | 5 | 2 | R | R | 6-1 | 210 | 2-10-74 | 1992 | West Middlesex, Pa. |
| Freire, Alejandro | .255 | 115 | 384 | 40 | 98 | 24 | 1 | 12 | 42 | 24 | 66 | 11 | 7 | R | R | 6-1 | 170 | 8-23-74 | 1992 | Caracas, Venez. |
| Gonzalez, Jimmy | .168 | 73 | 208 | 19 | 35 | 4 | 1 | 6 | 17 | 25 | 59 | 1 | 0 | R | R | 6-3 | 210 | 3-8-73 | 1991 | Hartford, Conn. |
| Landaker, Dave | .194 | 41 | 108 | 10 | 21 | 2 | 0 | 0 | 7 | 15 | 23 | 1 | 3 | R | R | 6-0 | 185 | 2-20-74 | 1992 | Simi Valley, Calif. |
| Linares, Sendry | .250 | 2 | 4 | 0 | 1 | 0 | 0 | 0 | 0 | 0 | 0 | 0 | 0 | R | R | 5-11 | 180 | 7-7-75 | 1994 | Caracas, Venez |
| Manwarren, Mark | .190 | 74 | 158 | 16 | 30 | 7 | 0 | 1 | 10 | 15 | 58 | 17 | 2 | R | R | 6-1 | 175 | 12-12-72 | 1996 | Dodge City, Kan. |
| McNabb, Buck | .346 | 7 | 26 | 4 | 9 | 1 | 0 | 0 | 3 | 3 | 5 | 3 | 0 | L | R | 6-0 | 180 | 1-17-73 | 1991 | Fort Walton Beach, Fla. |
| Meluskey, Mitch | .333 | 74 | 231 | 29 | 77 | 19 | 0 | 1 | 31 | 29 | 26 | 1 | 1 | S | R | 6-0 | 185 | 9-18-73 | 1992 | Yakima, Wash. |
| Mota, Gary | .329 | 45 | 152 | 17 | 50 | 8 | 3 | 2 | 20 | 5 | 31 | 0 | 3 | R | R | 6-0 | 195 | 10-6-70 | 1990 | La Crescenta, Calif. |
| Nelson, Bryant | .252 | 89 | 345 | 38 | 87 | 21 | 6 | 3 | 52 | 19 | 27 | 8 | 2 | S | R | 5-10 | 170 | 1-27-74 | 1994 | Crossett, Ark. |
| Perez, Jhonny | .270 | 90 | 322 | 54 | 87 | 20 | 2 | 12 | 49 | 26 | 70 | 16 | 16 | R | R | 5-10 | 150 | 10-23-76 | 1994 | Santo Domingo, D.R. |
| Pratt, Wes | .176 | 48 | 142 | 18 | 25 | 6 | 0 | 2 | 15 | 9 | 33 | 2 | 1 | R | R | 6-3 | 180 | 3-5-73 | 1994 | North East, Md. |
| Robles, Oscar | .269 | 125 | 427 | 57 | 115 | 13 | 2 | 0 | 29 | 74 | 37 | 10 | 8 | L | R | 5-11 | 155 | 4-9-76 | 1994 | San Diego, Calif. |
| Rodriguez, Noel | .251 | 82 | 291 | 24 | 73 | 16 | 1 | 5 | 38 | 26 | 31 | 0 | 1 | R | R | 6-3 | 180 | 12-5-73 | 1991 | Yabucoa, P.R. |
| Rose, Mike | .000 | 2 | 1 | 0 | 0 | 0 | 0 | 0 | 0 | 0 | 1 | 0 | 0 | R | R | 6-1 | 190 | 8-25-76 | 1993 | Elk Grove, Calif. |
| Ross, Tony | .223 | 57 | 193 | 22 | 43 | 8 | 2 | 1 | 17 | 15 | 42 | 10 | 2 | R | R | 5-11 | 175 | 5-11-75 | 1992 | Kansas City, Mo. |
| Samboy, Nelson | .253 | 105 | 372 | 43 | 94 | 20 | 2 | 0 | 21 | 20 | 61 | 17 | 7 | R | R | 5-10 | 155 | 9-4-76 | 1994 | Pedernales, D.R. |
| Saylor, Jamie | .204 | 59 | 181 | 17 | 37 | 3 | 3 | 1 | 6 | 10 | 43 | 8 | 6 | L | R | 5-11 | 165 | 9-11-74 | 1993 | Garland, Texas |
| Trammell, Gary | .289 | 118 | 402 | 48 | 116 | 16 | 8 | 0 | 39 | 20 | 52 | 11 | 3 | L | R | 6-0 | 180 | 10-16-72 | 1993 | Texarkana, Texas |

**GAMES BY POSITION: C**—Amezcua 35, Gonzalez 63, Meluskey 52, Rose 1. **1B**—Freire 46, Gonzalez 3, Landaker 2, Rodriguez 77, Trammell 15. **2B**—Robles 29, Samboy 96, Saylor 3, Trammell 16. **3B**—Landaker 1, Nelson 86, Robles 7, Saylor 39, Trammell 7. **SS**—Nelson 1, Perez 44, Robles 90, Saylor 3. **OF**—Barksdale 8, Bowers 37, Freire 70, Landaker 37, Linares 1, Manwarran 63, McNabb 7, Mota 30, Pratt 47, Rodriguez 3, Ross 53, Samboy 1, Saylor 13, Trammell 83.

| PITCHING | W | L | ERA | G | GS | CG | SV | IP | H | R | ER | BB | SO | B | T | HT | WT | DOB | 1st Yr | Resides |
|---|---|---|---|---|---|---|---|---|---|---|---|---|---|---|---|---|---|---|---|---|
| Dace, Derek | 0 | 0 | 2.95 | 12 | 0 | 0 | 1 | 18 | 19 | 6 | 6 | 7 | 11 | L | L | 6-7 | 200 | 4-9-75 | 1994 | Sullivan, Mo. |
| Dault, Donnie | 2 | 2 | 5.08 | 29 | 0 | 0 | 3 | 39 | 33 | 24 | 22 | 20 | 42 | R | R | 6-6 | 185 | 4-15-72 | 1991 | Austin, Texas |
| Elarton, Scott | 12 | 7 | 2.92 | 27 | 27 | 3 | 0 | 172 | 154 | 67 | 56 | 54 | 130 | R | R | 6-8 | 225 | 2-23-76 | 1994 | Lamar, Colo. |
| Garcia, Gabe | 0 | 1 | 0.00 | 3 | 0 | 0 | 0 | 9 | 6 | 2 | 0 | 3 | 4 | R | R | 6-2 | 200 | 3-15-77 | 1996 | Union City, Calif. |
| Hall, Billy | 0 | 0 | 0.00 | 2 | 0 | 0 | 0 | 3 | 2 | 0 | 0 | 0 | 1 | R | R | 6-0 | 200 | 9-4-73 | 1994 | Mannford, Okla. |
| Henriquez, Oscar | 0 | 4 | 3.97 | 31 | 0 | 0 | 15 | 34 | 28 | 18 | 15 | 29 | 40 | R | R | 6-4 | 175 | 1-28-74 | 1991 | LaGuaira, Venez |
| Hudek, John | 0 | 0 | 0.00 | 2 | 1 | 0 | 0 | 3 | 2 | 0 | 0 | 0 | 2 | S | R | 6-1 | 200 | 8-8-66 | 1988 | Tampa, Fla. |
| Humphrey, Rich | 0 | 1 | 2.08 | 5 | 0 | 0 | 2 | 9 | 6 | 3 | 2 | 1 | 5 | R | R | 6-1 | 185 | 6-24-71 | 1993 | Lakeland, Fla. |
| Lock, Dan | 4 | 4 | 4.75 | 27 | 2 | 1 | 0 | 148 | 166 | 109 | 78 | 62 | 72 | R | L | 6-5 | 210 | 3-27-73 | 1994 | Brighton, Mich. |
| Lopez, Johann | 3 | 10 | 3.75 | 19 | 19 | 2 | 0 | 98 | 114 | 50 | 41 | 35 | 70 | R | R | 6-2 | 170 | 4-4-75 | 1992 | Agua Negra, Venez. |
| McFerrin, Chris | 0 | 0 | 10.13 | 4 | 0 | 0 | 0 | 3 | 7 | 7 | 3 | 3 | 2 | L | R | 6-5 | 175 | 6-30-76 | 1995 | Fresno, Calif. |
| Medina, Tomas | 1 | 0 | 7.50 | 9 | 0 | 0 | 0 | 12 | 16 | 11 | 10 | 9 | 7 | R | R | 6-2 | 165 | 4-12-75 | 1994 | Barquisimeto, Venez. |
| Mercado, Hector | 3 | 5 | 4.16 | 56 | 0 | 0 | 3 | 80 | 78 | 43 | 37 | 48 | 68 | L | L | 6-3 | 205 | 4-29-74 | 1992 | Dorado, P.R. |
| Mounce, Tony | 9 | 9 | 2.25 | 25 | 25 | 4 | 0 | 156 | 139 | 65 | 39 | 68 | 102 | L | L | 6-2 | 185 | 2-8-75 | 1994 | Kennewick, Wash. |
| Ramos, Edgar | 9 | 0 | 1.51 | 11 | 11 | 1 | 0 | 78 | 51 | 17 | 13 | 15 | 81 | R | R | 6-4 | 170 | 3-6-75 | 1992 | Cumana, Venez. |
| Robertson, Jeriome | 0 | 0 | 2.57 | 1 | 1 | 0 | 0 | 7 | 4 | 4 | 2 | 1 | 2 | L | L | 6-1 | 178 | 3-30-77 | 1996 | Exeter, Calif. |
| Shaver, Tony | 4 | 4 | 2.39 | 42 | 0 | 0 | 4 | 64 | 57 | 24 | 17 | 23 | 35 | R | R | 5-11 | 185 | 2-15-72 | 1994 | Orlando, Fla. |
| Stachler, Eric | 4 | 3 | 3.83 | 30 | 0 | 0 | 0 | 56 | 50 | 35 | 24 | 39 | 41 | R | R | 6-3 | 215 | 4-18-73 | 1995 | Coldwater, Ohio |
| Steinke, Brock | 4 | 3 | 6.41 | 16 | 8 | 0 | 1 | 46 | 62 | 39 | 33 | 31 | 22 | R | R | 6-2 | 180 | 6-27-75 | 1993 | Cedar Rapids, Iowa |
| Tucker, Julien | 4 | 8 | 4.27 | 32 | 16 | 0 | 1 | 116 | 131 | 79 | 55 | 41 | 55 | L | R | 6-7 | 200 | 4-19-73 | 1993 | Chataeuguay, Quebec |

## MIDWEST LEAGUE

| BATTING | AVG | G | AB | R | H | 2B | 3B | HR | RBI | BB | SO | SB | CS | B | T | HT | WT | DOB | 1st Yr | Resides |
|---|---|---|---|---|---|---|---|---|---|---|---|---|---|---|---|---|---|---|---|---|
| Adams, Jason | .265 | 74 | 226 | 35 | 60 | 14 | 0 | 2 | 27 | 29 | 36 | 6 | 6 | L | L | 6-1 | 180 | 6-22-73 | 1995 | Rose Hill, Kan. |
| Alexander, Chad | .264 | 118 | 435 | 68 | 115 | 25 | 4 | 13 | 69 | 57 | 108 | 16 | 11 | R | R | 6-0 | 190 | 5-24-74 | 1995 | Lufkin, Texas |
| Bovender, Andy | .260 | 76 | 269 | 41 | 70 | 18 | 2 | 8 | 36 | 31 | 61 | 4 | 7 | R | R | 6-3 | 190 | 4-10-73 | 1995 | Charlotte, N.C. |
| Bowers, R.J. | .257 | 64 | 226 | 35 | 58 | 23 | 0 | 4 | 20 | 33 | 59 | 6 | 10 | R | R | 6-1 | 210 | 2-10-74 | 1992 | West Middlesex, Pa. |
| Castro, Ramon | .248 | 96 | 314 | 38 | 78 | 15 | 0 | 7 | 43 | 31 | 61 | 2 | 0 | R | R | 6-3 | 195 | 3-1-76 | 1994 | Vega Baja, P.R. |
| Chavera, Arnie | .245 | 77 | 184 | 22 | 45 | 16 | 1 | 3 | 34 | 19 | 46 | 0 | 1 | L | R | 5-10 | 195 | 9-24-73 | 1994 | Arlington, Texas |
| Coe, Ryan | .293 | 77 | 246 | 38 | 72 | 10 | 1 | 14 | 47 | 18 | 56 | 0 | 0 | R | R | 5-10 | 200 | 1-16-73 | 1995 | East Ridge, Tenn. |
| Guillen, Carlos | .330 | 29 | 112 | 23 | 37 | 7 | 1 | 3 | 17 | 16 | 25 | 13 | 6 | R | R | 6-0 | 150 | 9-30-75 | 1993 | Aragua, Venez. |
| Hernandez, Carlos | .270 | 112 | 456 | 67 | 123 | 15 | 7 | 5 | 49 | 27 | 71 | 41 | 14 | R | R | 5-9 | 160 | 12-12-75 | 1993 | Caracas, Venez. |
| Johnson, Ric | .236 | 95 | 318 | 36 | 75 | 9 | 3 | 3 | 39 | 16 | 47 | 10 | 4 | R | R | 6-2 | 185 | 3-18-74 | 1995 | Chicago, Ill. |
| Lugo, Julio | .295 | 101 | 393 | 66 | 116 | 18 | 2 | 10 | 50 | 32 | 75 | 24 | 11 | R | R | 5-11 | 155 | 11-16-75 | 1995 | Brooklyn, N.Y. |
| Robinson, Hassan | .271 | 106 | 373 | 53 | 101 | 11 | 2 | 1 | 34 | 35 | | 15 | 6 | R | R | 6-3 | 180 | 9-22-72 | 1994 | Queens Village, N.Y. |
| Roche, Marlon | .273 | 85 | 275 | 34 | 75 | 5 | 4 | 4 | 25 | 26 | 60 | 5 | 12 | R | R | 6-1 | 172 | 4-11-75 | 1992 | Caracas, Venez. |
| Rodriguez, Noel | .271 | 39 | 144 | 26 | 39 | 10 | 0 | 4 | 19 | 14 | 18 | 1 | 0 | R | R | 6-3 | 180 | 12-5-73 | 1991 | Yabucoa, P.R. |
| Saylor, Jamie | .121 | 23 | 58 | 8 | 7 | 1 | 0 | 0 | 5 | 3 | 13 | 4 | 2 | L | R | 5-11 | 165 | 9-11-74 | 1993 | Garland, Texas |
| Truby, Chris | .251 | 109 | 362 | 45 | 91 | 15 | 3 | 8 | 37 | 28 | 74 | 6 | 10 | R | R | 6-2 | 185 | 12-9-73 | 1993 | Mukilteo, Wash. |

**GAMES BY POSITION: C**—Castro 96, Chavera 10, Coe 45. **1B**—Bovender 27, Chavera 18, Rodriguez 36, Truby 61. **2B**—Adams 20, Hernandez 106, Lugo 8. **3B**—Bovender 44, Bowers 45, Lugo 1, Truby 45. **SS**—Guillen 29, Hernandez 5, Lugo 82, Saylor 18. **OF**—Alexander 96, Bowers 52, Johnson 88, Robinson 96, Roche 68, Saylor 2.

| PITCHING | W | L | ERA | G | GS | CG | SV | IP | H | R | ER | BB | SO | B | T | HT | WT | DOB | 1st Yr | Resides |
|---|---|---|---|---|---|---|---|---|---|---|---|---|---|---|---|---|---|---|---|---|
| Blanco, Alberto | 2 | 2 | 3.47 | 11 | 11 | 0 | 0 | 47 | 42 | 25 | 18 | 15 | 58 | L | L | 6-1 | 170 | 3-3-73 | 1993 | Miranda, Venez. |
| Garcia, Freddy | 5 | 4 | 3.12 | 13 | 13 | 0 | 0 | 61 | 57 | 27 | 21 | 27 | 50 | R | R | 6-3 | 180 | 10-6-76 | 1994 | Miranda, Venez. |
| Gunderson, Mike | 4 | 4 | 5.15 | 34 | 7 | 0 | 3 | 80 | 80 | 60 | 46 | 64 | 59 | R | R | 6-4 | 235 | 3-24-73 | 1994 | Detroit Lakes, Minn. |
| Hill, Chris | 6 | 5 | 6.24 | 18 | 5 | 0 | 0 | 49 | 48 | 39 | 34 | 15 | 39 | R | R | 6-0 | 165 | 10-25-74 | 1996 | Huntington Beach , Calif. |
| Loiz, Niuman | 8 | 6 | 4.93 | 28 | 14 | 1 | 1 | 115 | 121 | 75 | 63 | 53 | 75 | R | R | 6-2 | 180 | 12-12-73 | 1991 | Caracas, Venez. |
| Lynch, Jim | 1 | 1 | 4.01 | 31 | 1 | 0 | 1 | 61 | 51 | 28 | 27 | 50 | 51 | R | R | 6-4 | 195 | 12-12-75 | 1994 | Evansville, Ind. |
| O'Malley, Paul | 11 | 9 | 3.34 | 26 | 26 | 1 | 0 | 178 | 173 | 80 | 66 | 51 | 111 | R | R | 6-3 | 180 | 12-20-72 | 1994 | Skokie, Ill. |
| Root, Derek | 5 | 3 | 3.00 | 40 | 2 | 0 | 7 | 63 | 55 | 25 | 21 | 26 | 47 | L | L | 6-5 | 190 | 5-26-75 | 1993 | Lakewood, Ohio |
| Runyan, Sean | 9 | 4 | 3.88 | 29 | 17 | 0 | 0 | 132 | 128 | 61 | 57 | 30 | 104 | L | L | 6-3 | 200 | 6-21-74 | 1992 | Urbandale, Iowa |

| PITCHING | W | L | ERA | G | GS | CG | SV | IP | H | R | ER | BB | SO | B | T | HT | WT | DOB | 1st Yr | Resides |
|---|---|---|---|---|---|---|---|---|---|---|---|---|---|---|---|---|---|---|---|---|
| Sikorski, Brian ...........11 | 11 | 8 | 3.13 | 26 | 25 | 1 | 0 | 167 | 140 | 79 | 58 | 70 | 150 | R | R | 6-1 | 190 | 7-27-74 | 1995 | Roseville, Mich. |
| Smith, Eric ................. | 6 | 3 | 3.11 | 26 | 7 | 0 | 1 | 75 | 66 | 32 | 26 | 26 | 59 | R | R | 6-0 | 185 | 5-17-74 | 1995 | Garden City, Kan. |
| Steinke, Brock ............. | 2 | 4 | 6.10 | 24 | 3 | 0 | 2 | 49 | 53 | 38 | 33 | 36 | 55 | R | R | 6-2 | 180 | 6-27-75 | 1993 | Cedar Rapids, Iowa |
| Tickell, Brian ............... | 0 | 2 | 9.72 | 7 | 0 | 0 | 0 | 8 | 17 | 10 | 9 | 5 | 4 | R | R | 6-2 | 185 | 11-9-74 | 1995 | Grand Prairie, Texas |
| Walter, Michael ........... | 3 | 6 | 2.04 | 52 | 0 | 0 | 21 | 62 | 37 | 20 | 14 | 34 | 85 | R | R | 6-1 | 190 | 10-23-74 | 1993 | San Diego, Calif. |

## AUBURN  —  Class A
### NEW YORK-PENN LEAGUE

| BATTING | AVG | G | AB | R | H | 2B | 3B | HR | RBI | BB | SO | SB | CS | B | T | HT | WT | DOB | 1st Yr | Resides |
|---|---|---|---|---|---|---|---|---|---|---|---|---|---|---|---|---|---|---|---|---|
| Barr, Tucker ............... | .218 | 44 | 165 | 16 | 36 | 12 | 0 | 4 | 22 | 5 | 39 | 1 | 1 | R | R | 6-1 | 205 | 5-26-75 | 1996 | Atlanta, Ga. |
| Burns, Kevin ................ | .264 | 71 | 269 | 27 | 71 | 19 | 3 | 11 | 55 | 15 | 77 | 2 | 1 | L | L | 6-5 | 210 | 9-9-75 | 1995 | El Dorado, Ark. |
| Cole, Eric ................... | .172 | 46 | 151 | 9 | 26 | 4 | 0 | 1 | 10 | 6 | 46 | 3 | 1 | R | R | 6-1 | 180 | 11-15-75 | 1995 | Lancaster, Calif. |
| Cook, John ................. | .086 | 10 | 35 | 0 | 3 | 0 | 0 | 0 | 1 | 0 | 7 | 1 | 0 | R | R | 6-0 | 210 | 1-2-73 | 1995 | Elmira, N.Y. |
| Dallimore, Brian .......... | .266 | 74 | 290 | 50 | 77 | 17 | 3 | 5 | 30 | 18 | 38 | 7 | 5 | R | R | 6-1 | 185 | 11-15-73 | 1996 | Las Vegas, Nev. |
| Farraez, Jesus ............ | .225 | 42 | 129 | 13 | 29 | 4 | 4 | 2 | 11 | 10 | 34 | 2 | 2 | R | R | 6-1 | 180 | 10-18-72 | 1994 | La Virginia, Venez. |
| Hyers, Matt ................ | .255 | 63 | 231 | 50 | 59 | 13 | 1 | 1 | 20 | 36 | 50 | 14 | 4 | L | R | 5-11 | 170 | 8-8-75 | 1996 | Covington, Ga. |
| Mansavage, Jay .......... | .169 | 49 | 148 | 17 | 25 | 7 | 2 | 1 | 17 | 18 | 33 | 5 | 2 | S | R | 6-1 | 185 | 7-11-75 | 1996 | Riverwoods, Ill. |
| Mejia, Marlon .............. | .206 | 34 | 107 | 11 | 22 | 3 | 2 | 1 | 8 | 0 | 20 | 1 | 0 | R | R | 6-1 | 175 | 11-17-74 | 1995 | Jersey City, N.J. |
| Pratt, Wes ................. | .313 | 70 | 246 | 43 | 77 | 22 | 1 | 5 | 35 | 39 | 37 | 11 | 3 | R | R | 6-3 | 180 | 3-5-73 | 1994 | North East, Md. |
| Reeder, Jim ................ | .282 | 69 | 241 | 24 | 68 | 8 | 4 | 0 | 25 | 23 | 32 | 6 | 1 | L | R | 6-1 | 200 | 3-18-75 | 1996 | Evanston, Ill. |
| Rose, Mike ................. | .250 | 61 | 180 | 20 | 45 | 5 | 1 | 2 | 11 | 30 | 41 | 9 | 3 | R | R | 6-1 | 190 | 8-25-76 | 1995 | Elk Grove, Calif. |
| Wesson, Barry ............ | .159 | 55 | 176 | 11 | 28 | 7 | 0 | 0 | 12 | 12 | 46 | 5 | 3 | R | R | 6-2 | 180 | 11-24-77 | 1995 | Glen Allan, Miss. |
| Young, Randy .............. | .229 | 40 | 131 | 17 | 30 | 2 | 0 | 0 | 4 | 9 | 22 | 13 | 6 | R | R | 5-11 | 165 | 12-13-72 | 1996 | Belle Plaine, Kan. |

**GAMES BY POSITION : C**—Barr 22, Cook 4, Rose 56. **1B**—Burns 67, Cole 11, Mejia 1. **2B**—Dallimore 19, Hyers 16, Mansavage 41. **3B**—Cole 25, Dallimore 52, Mejia 1. **SS**—Dallimore 1, Hyers 46, Mansavage 1, Mejia 32. **OF**—Farraez 41, Pratt 61, Reeder 49, Wesson 51, Young 36.

| PITCHING | W | L | ERA | G | GS | CG | SV | IP | H | R | ER | BB | SO | B | T | HT | WT | DOB | 1st Yr | Resides |
|---|---|---|---|---|---|---|---|---|---|---|---|---|---|---|---|---|---|---|---|---|
| Bernhard, David ........... | 3 | 2 | 4.78 | 24 | 2 | 0 | 1 | 49 | 56 | 31 | 26 | 23 | 27 | R | R | 6-7 | 220 | 8-19-74 | 1996 | Carmel Valley, Calif. |
| Braswell, Bryan .......... | 4 | 8 | 4.32 | 15 | 14 | 0 | 0 | 73 | 70 | 40 | 35 | 29 | 77 | L | L | 6-1 | 195 | 6-30-75 | 1996 | Springboro, Ohio |
| Crawford, Chris ........... | 2 | 4 | 4.12 | 12 | 9 | 0 | 0 | 59 | 51 | 28 | 27 | 29 | 36 | R | R | 6-8 | 225 | 5-13-75 | 1994 | Kalamazoo, Mich. |
| Dace, Derek ................ | 3 | 4 | 3.25 | 15 | 15 | 0 | 0 | 97 | 89 | 41 | 35 | 35 | 87 | L | L | 6-7 | 200 | 4-9-75 | 1996 | Sullivan, Mo. |
| Fuller, Duane .............. | 1 | 0 | 8.66 | 11 | 2 | 0 | 0 | 18 | 17 | 18 | 17 | 21 | 16 | R | R | 6-1 | 180 | 12-9-74 | 1996 | St. Petersburg, Fla. |
| Fuller, Stephen ............ | 2 | 6 | 5.66 | 18 | 9 | 0 | 0 | 70 | 80 | 52 | 44 | 38 | 45 | R | R | 6-5 | 195 | 7-8-74 | 1994 | St. Charles, Ill. |
| Green, Jason ............... | 0 | 0 | 0.00 | 2 | 2 | 0 | 0 | 6 | 4 | 1 | 0 | 1 | 2 | R | R | 6-2 | 195 | 11-15-73 | 1993 | Hercules, Calif. |
| Maldonado, Esteban .... | 0 | 1 | 5.17 | 6 | 6 | 0 | 0 | 16 | 20 | 14 | 9 | 9 | 9 | R | R | 6-4 | 210 | 8-3-75 | 1996 | Villa Carolina, P.R. |
| McFerrin, Chris ........... | 4 | 2 | 1.71 | 33 | 0 | 0 | 20 | 42 | 23 | 16 | 8 | 24 | 45 | L | R | 6-5 | 175 | 6-30-76 | 1995 | Fresno, Calif. |
| Miller, Wade ............... | 1 | 1 | 5.00 | 2 | 2 | 0 | 0 | 9 | 8 | 9 | 5 | 4 | 11 | R | R | 6-2 | 185 | 9-13-76 | 1996 | Topton, Pa. |
| Rijo, Jose ................... | 1 | 3 | 3.54 | 33 | 0 | 0 | 3 | 53 | 65 | 29 | 21 | 16 | 39 | R | R | 6-1 | 150 | 5-4-76 | 1993 | La Romana, D.R. |
| Turley, Jason .............. | 3 | 0 | 5.56 | 19 | 0 | 0 | 0 | 44 | 39 | 35 | 27 | 36 | 31 | R | R | 6-2 | 190 | 2-13-75 | 1994 | Evanston, Wyom. |
| Wilmot, Toby ............... | 3 | 2 | 3.57 | 13 | 0 | 0 | 0 | 23 | 23 | 11 | 9 | 17 | 19 | L | L | 6-0 | 180 | 4-16-74 | 1996 | Pauls Valley, Okla. |
| Yanez, Luis ................ | 5 | 5 | 2.45 | 15 | 15 | 2 | 0 | 99 | 85 | 38 | 27 | 31 | 73 | R | R | 6-2 | 187 | 12-1-77 | 1995 | Anzoategui, Venez. |

## KISSIMMEE  —  Rookie
### GULF COAST LEAGUE

| BATTING | AVG | G | AB | R | H | 2B | 3B | HR | RBI | BB | SO | SB | CS | B | T | HT | WT | DOB | 1st Yr | Resides |
|---|---|---|---|---|---|---|---|---|---|---|---|---|---|---|---|---|---|---|---|---|
| Alleyne, Roberto .......... | .331 | 48 | 151 | 32 | 50 | 9 | 0 | 7 | 27 | 20 | 32 | 4 | 4 | R | R | 6-4 | 195 | 5-15-77 | 1994 | Panama City, Panama |
| Byrd, Brandon ............. | .194 | 37 | 124 | 7 | 24 | 11 | 1 | 1 | 20 | 12 | 41 | 0 | 2 | R | R | 6-5 | 225 | 5-22-78 | 1996 | Montgomery, Ala. |
| Chapman, Scott ........... | .261 | 45 | 142 | 17 | 37 | 8 | 1 | 2 | 19 | 18 | 25 | 3 | 1 | R | R | 6-3 | 205 | 1-30-78 | 1995 | Albany, Ohio |
| Deshazer, Jeremy ....... | .235 | 52 | 170 | 20 | 40 | 5 | 4 | 0 | 12 | 9 | 49 | 5 | 5 | S | R | 5-10 | 175 | 8-18-76 | 1995 | Kirkland, Wash. |
| De la Espada, Miguel .. | .211 | 42 | 123 | 14 | 26 | 8 | 0 | 2 | 9 | 7 | 40 | 1 | 2 | R | R | 6-4 | 204 | 7-8-76 | 1994 | Colon, Panama |
| Escalona, Felix ........... | .147 | 28 | 75 | 8 | 11 | 2 | 0 | 1 | 9 | 8 | 31 | 1 | 2 | R | R | 6-0 | 170 | 3-12-79 | 1996 | Carbello, Venez. |
| Hill, Jason ................. | .286 | 42 | 140 | 22 | 40 | 13 | 2 | 4 | 31 | 13 | 21 | 7 | 5 | R | R | 5-11 | 205 | 2-25-75 | 1996 | Crestline, Calif. |
| Linares, Sendry ........... | .207 | 23 | 58 | 5 | 12 | 6 | 0 | 0 | 6 | 3 | 10 | 1 | 0 | R | R | 5-11 | 180 | 7-7-75 | 1994 | Caracas, Venez. |
| McNeal, Aaron ............. | .250 | 55 | 200 | 22 | 50 | 10 | 2 | 2 | 31 | 13 | 52 | 0 | 2 | R | R | 6-3 | 220 | 4-28-78 | 1996 | Castro Valley, Calif. |
| Miles, Aaron ............... | .294 | 55 | 214 | 48 | 63 | 3 | 2 | 0 | 15 | 20 | 18 | 14 | 7 | L | R | 5-9 | 160 | 12-15-76 | 1995 | Antioch, Calif. |
| Nicely, Dru ................. | .106 | 25 | 66 | 4 | 7 | 0 | 0 | 0 | 3 | 7 | 20 | 2 | 0 | R | R | 6-3 | 195 | 6-29-78 | 1996 | Burley, Idaho |
| Robertson, Geoff ......... | .136 | 38 | 81 | 8 | 11 | 1 | 0 | 0 | 2 | 15 | 38 | 7 | 4 | L | L | 6-1 | 180 | 3-3-77 | 1996 | Landrum, S.C. |
| Santana, Pedro ........... | .271 | 56 | 207 | 40 | 56 | 6 | 5 | 1 | 20 | 21 | 44 | 33 | 4 | R | R | 5-11 | 160 | 9-21-76 | 1995 | San Pedro de Macoris, D.R. |
| Ubaldo, Nelson ........... | .059 | 5 | 17 | 0 | 1 | 1 | 0 | 0 | 2 | 1 | 7 | 0 | 0 | R | R | 6-2 | 200 | 6-27-74 | 1995 | Cambridge, Mass. |
| Wheeler, Michael ......... | .264 | 39 | 129 | 16 | 34 | 9 | 1 | 0 | 18 | 4 | 40 | 7 | 1 | R | R | 6-1 | 180 | 10-25-77 | 1996 | Cincinnati, Ohio |

**GAMES BY POSITION: C**—Chapman 31, Hill 18, Linares 21, McNeal 1. **1B**—Alleyne 15, Byrd 2, Hill 1, McNeal 46. **2B**—Escalona 6, Miles 47, Santana 7. **3B**—Escalona 20, Nicely 22, Santa 5, Wheeler 16. **SS**—Escalona 1, Nicely 1, Santana 38, Wheeler 16. **OF**—Alleyne 24, Byrd 28, Deshazer 48, De la Espada 40, Hill 18, Robertson 30, Santana 1, Ubaldo 5.

| PITCHING | W | L | ERA | G | GS | CG | SV | IP | H | R | ER | BB | SO | B | T | HT | WT | DOB | 1st Yr | Resides |
|---|---|---|---|---|---|---|---|---|---|---|---|---|---|---|---|---|---|---|---|---|
| Barksdale, Shane ........ | 0 | 2 | 3.00 | 12 | 0 | 0 | 1 | 18 | 14 | 6 | 6 | 8 | 16 | L | R | 6-4 | 195 | 9-6-76 | 1994 | Gallant, Ala. |
| Blackmore, John .......... | 1 | 0 | 3.46 | 16 | 1 | 0 | 0 | 26 | 22 | 15 | 10 | 17 | 17 | R | R | 6-3 | 190 | 11-5-77 | 1996 | Plainville, Conn. |
| Celta, Nicolas ............. | 2 | 2 | 3.38 | 17 | 0 | 0 | 0 | 27 | 30 | 19 | 10 | 8 | 30 | L | L | 6-0 | 160 | 8-15-77 | 1994 | Maracay, Venez. |
| Crawford, Chris ........... | 0 | 0 | 9.00 | 1 | 0 | 0 | 0 | 2 | 3 | 2 | 2 | 1 | 3 | R | R | 6-8 | 225 | 5-13-75 | 1994 | Kalamazoo, Mich. |
| Garcia, Gabe ............... | 3 | 4 | 2.48 | 13 | 5 | 0 | 1 | 36 | 30 | 12 | 10 | 10 | 50 | R | R | 6-2 | 200 | 3-15-77 | 1996 | Union City, Calif. |
| Hamulack, Tim ............ | 1 | 4 | 2.33 | 22 | 0 | 0 | 2 | 27 | 23 | 9 | 7 | 13 | 24 | R | L | 6-4 | 225 | 11-14-76 | 1996 | Edgewood, Md. |
| Huber, John ............... | 1 | 2 | 4.04 | 10 | 6 | 0 | 0 | 36 | 33 | 20 | 16 | 23 | 37 | R | R | 6-3 | 200 | 4-18-78 | 1996 | West Chester, Ohio |
| Ireland, Eric ............... | 3 | 4 | 4.70 | 12 | 11 | 0 | 0 | 54 | 54 | 33 | 28 | 23 | 43 | R | R | 6-1 | 165 | 3-11-77 | 1996 | Long Beach, Calif. |
| McCarter, Jason .......... | 0 | 1 | 1.21 | 21 | 0 | 0 | 8 | 22 | 13 | 6 | 3 | 14 | 26 | R | R | 6-3 | 196 | 9-26-76 | 1995 | Watsonville, Calif. |
| McKnight, Tony ........... | 2 | 2 | 6.66 | 9 | 6 | 0 | 0 | 24 | 34 | 26 | 18 | 7 | 17 | L | R | 6-5 | 205 | 6-27-77 | 1995 | Texarkana, Ark. |
| Medina, Tom ............... | 1 | 1 | 4.15 | 8 | 0 | 0 | 2 | 13 | 13 | 7 | 6 | 6 | 10 | R | R | 6-2 | 165 | 4-12-75 | 1994 | Barquisimeto, Venez. |
| Miller, Wade ............... | 3 | 4 | 3.79 | 11 | 10 | 0 | 0 | 57 | 49 | 26 | 24 | 12 | 53 | R | R | 6-2 | 185 | 9-13-76 | 1996 | Topton, Pa. |
| Pascarella, Josh .......... | 1 | 0 | 4.78 | 15 | 4 | 0 | 0 | 38 | 35 | 29 | 20 | 24 | 43 | R | R | 6-0 | 175 | 11-7-76 | 1996 | San Diego, Calif. |
| Prestash, J.D. ............. | 0 | 0 | 1.59 | 4 | 0 | 0 | 0 | 6 | 9 | 4 | 1 | 0 | 5 | L | L | 6-4 | 195 | 8-14-75 | 1995 | Phillipsburg, Pa. |
| Robertson, Jeriome ....... | 5 | 3 | 1.72 | 13 | 13 | 1 | 0 | 78 | 51 | 20 | 15 | 15 | 98 | L | L | 6-1 | 178 | 3-30-77 | 1996 | Exeter, Calif. |
| Shearn, Thomas .......... | 5 | 2 | 1.73 | 17 | 3 | 0 | 0 | 42 | 34 | 13 | 8 | 10 | 43 | R | R | 6-5 | 200 | 8-28-77 | 1996 | Columbus, Ohio |

# KANSAS CITY ROYALS

**Manager:** Bob Boone.  **1996 Record:** 75-86, .466 (5th, AL Central).

| BATTING | AVG | G | AB | R | H | 2B | 3B | HR | RBI | BB | SO | SB | CS | B | T | HT | WT | DOB | 1st Yr | Resides |
|---|---|---|---|---|---|---|---|---|---|---|---|---|---|---|---|---|---|---|---|---|
| Damon, Johnny | .271 | 145 | 517 | 61 | 140 | 22 | 5 | 6 | 50 | 31 | 64 | 25 | 5 | L | L | 6-0 | 175 | 11-5-73 | 1992 | Orlando, Fla. |
| Fasano, Sal | .203 | 51 | 143 | 20 | 29 | 2 | 0 | 6 | 19 | 14 | 25 | 1 | 1 | R | R | 6-2 | 220 | 8-10-71 | 1993 | Hanover Park, Ill. |
| Goodwin, Tom | .282 | 143 | 524 | 80 | 148 | 14 | 4 | 1 | 35 | 39 | 79 | 66 | 22 | L | R | 6-1 | 165 | 7-27-68 | 1989 | Fresno, Calif. |
| Hamelin, Bob | .255 | 89 | 239 | 31 | 61 | 14 | 1 | 9 | 40 | 54 | 58 | 5 | 2 | L | L | 6-0 | 235 | 11-29-67 | 1988 | Charlotte, N.C. |
| Howard, Dave | .219 | 143 | 420 | 51 | 92 | 14 | 5 | 4 | 48 | 40 | 74 | 5 | 6 | S | R | 6-0 | 175 | 2-26-67 | 1987 | Sarasota, Fla. |
| Lennon, Patrick | .233 | 14 | 30 | 5 | 7 | 3 | 0 | 0 | 1 | 7 | 10 | 0 | 0 | R | R | 6-2 | 200 | 4-27-68 | 1986 | Whiteville, N.C. |
| Lockhart, Keith | .273 | 138 | 433 | 49 | 118 | 33 | 3 | 7 | 55 | 30 | 40 | 11 | 6 | L | R | 5-10 | 170 | 11-10-64 | 1986 | Largo, Fla. |
| Macfarlane, Mike | .274 | 112 | 379 | 58 | 104 | 24 | 2 | 19 | 54 | 31 | 57 | 3 | 3 | R | R | 6-1 | 205 | 4-12-64 | 1985 | Overland Park, Kan. |
| Mercedes, Henry | .250 | 4 | 4 | 1 | 1 | 0 | 0 | 0 | 0 | 0 | 1 | 0 | 0 | R | R | 5-11 | 185 | 7-23-69 | 1988 | Santo Domingo, D.R. |
| Myers, Rod | .286 | 22 | 63 | 9 | 18 | 7 | 0 | 1 | 11 | 7 | 16 | 3 | 2 | L | L | 6-0 | 190 | 1-14-73 | 1991 | Conroe, Texas |
| Norman, Les | .122 | 54 | 49 | 9 | 6 | 0 | 0 | 0 | 6 | 14 | 1 | 1 | R | R | 6-1 | 185 | 2-25-69 | 1991 | Greenfield, Ill. |
| Nunnally, Jon | .211 | 35 | 90 | 16 | 19 | 5 | 1 | 5 | 17 | 13 | 25 | 0 | 0 | L | R | 5-10 | 188 | 11-9-71 | 1992 | Pelham, N.C. |
| Offerman, Jose | .303 | 151 | 561 | 85 | 170 | 33 | 8 | 5 | 47 | 74 | 98 | 24 | 10 | S | R | 6-0 | 160 | 11-8-68 | 1988 | San Pedro de Macoris, D.R. |
| Paquette, Craig | .259 | 118 | 429 | 61 | 111 | 15 | 1 | 22 | 67 | 23 | 101 | 5 | 3 | R | R | 6-0 | 190 | 3-28-69 | 1989 | Garden Grove, Calif. |
| Randa, Joe | .303 | 110 | 337 | 36 | 102 | 24 | 1 | 6 | 47 | 26 | 47 | 13 | 4 | R | R | 5-11 | 190 | 12-18-69 | 1991 | Delafield, Wis. |
| Roberts, Bip | .283 | 90 | 339 | 39 | 96 | 21 | 2 | 0 | 52 | 25 | 38 | 12 | 9 | S | R | 5-7 | 160 | 10-27-63 | 1982 | San Diego, Calif. |
| Stynes, Chris | .293 | 36 | 92 | 8 | 27 | 6 | 0 | 0 | 6 | 2 | 5 | 5 | 2 | R | R | 5-9 | 170 | 1-19-73 | 1991 | Boca Raton, Fla. |
| Sweeney, Mike | .279 | 50 | 165 | 23 | 46 | 10 | 0 | 4 | 24 | 18 | 21 | 1 | 2 | R | R | 6-1 | 195 | 7-22-73 | 1991 | Ontario, Calif. |
| Tucker, Michael | .260 | 108 | 339 | 55 | 88 | 18 | 4 | 12 | 53 | 40 | 69 | 10 | 4 | L | R | 6-2 | 185 | 6-25-71 | 1992 | Chase City, Va. |
| Vitiello, Joe | .241 | 85 | 257 | 29 | 62 | 15 | 1 | 8 | 40 | 38 | 69 | 2 | 0 | R | R | 6-2 | 215 | 4-11-70 | 1991 | Stoneham, Mass. |
| Young, Kevin | .242 | 55 | 132 | 20 | 32 | 6 | 0 | 8 | 23 | 11 | 32 | 3 | 3 | R | R | 6-2 | 219 | 6-16-69 | 1990 | Kansas City, Kan. |

| PITCHING | W | L | ERA | G | GS | CG | SV | IP | H | R | ER | BB | SO | B | T | HT | WT | DOB | 1st Yr | Resides |
|---|---|---|---|---|---|---|---|---|---|---|---|---|---|---|---|---|---|---|---|---|
| Appier, Kevin | 14 | 11 | 3.62 | 32 | 32 | 5 | 0 | 211 | 192 | 87 | 85 | 75 | 207 | R | R | 6-2 | 195 | 12-6-67 | 1987 | Overland Park, Kan. |
| Belcher, Tim | 15 | 11 | 3.92 | 35 | 35 | 4 | 0 | 239 | 262 | 117 | 104 | 68 | 113 | R | R | 6-3 | 220 | 10-19-61 | 1984 | Mt. Gilead, Ohio |
| Bevil, Brian | 1 | 0 | 5.73 | 3 | 1 | 0 | 0 | 11 | 9 | 7 | 7 | 5 | 7 | R | R | 6-3 | 190 | 9-5-71 | 1991 | Houston, Texas |
| Bluma, Jaime | 0 | 0 | 3.60 | 17 | 0 | 0 | 5 | 20 | 18 | 9 | 8 | 4 | 14 | R | R | 5-11 | 195 | 5-18-72 | 1994 | Owasso, Okla. |
| Clark, Terry | 1 | 1 | 7.79 | 12 | 0 | 0 | 0 | 17 | 28 | 15 | 15 | 7 | 12 | R | R | 6-2 | 196 | 10-10-60 | 1979 | La Puente, Calif. |
| Granger, Jeff | 0 | 0 | 6.61 | 15 | 0 | 0 | 0 | 16 | 21 | 13 | 12 | 10 | 11 | R | L | 6-4 | 200 | 12-16-71 | 1993 | Orange, Texas |
| Gubicza, Mark | 4 | 12 | 5.13 | 19 | 19 | 2 | 0 | 119 | 132 | 70 | 68 | 34 | 55 | R | R | 6-5 | 230 | 8-14-62 | 1981 | Northridge, Calif. |
| Haney, Chris | 10 | 14 | 4.70 | 35 | 35 | 4 | 0 | 228 | 267 | 136 | 119 | 51 | 115 | L | L | 6-3 | 195 | 11-16-68 | 1990 | Barboursville, Va. |
| Huisman, Rick | 2 | 1 | 4.60 | 22 | 0 | 0 | 1 | 29 | 25 | 15 | 15 | 18 | 23 | R | R | 6-3 | 200 | 5-17-69 | 1990 | Bensenville, Ill. |
| Jacome, Jason | 0 | 4 | 4.72 | 49 | 2 | 0 | 1 | 48 | 67 | 27 | 25 | 22 | 32 | L | L | 6-0 | 180 | 11-24-70 | 1991 | Tucson, Ariz. |
| Linton, Doug | 7 | 9 | 5.02 | 21 | 18 | 0 | 0 | 104 | 111 | 65 | 58 | 26 | 87 | R | R | 6-1 | 190 | 9-22-67 | 1987 | Kingsport, Tenn. |
| Magnante, Mike | 2 | 2 | 5.67 | 38 | 0 | 0 | 0 | 54 | 58 | 38 | 34 | 24 | 32 | L | L | 6-1 | 190 | 6-17-65 | 1988 | Burbank, Calif. |
| Montgomery, Jeff | 4 | 6 | 4.26 | 48 | 0 | 0 | 24 | 63 | 19 | 9 | 8 | 19 | 45 | R | R | 5-11 | 180 | 1-7-62 | 1983 | Leawood, Kan. |
| Pichardo, Hipolito | 3 | 5 | 5.43 | 57 | 0 | 0 | 3 | 68 | 74 | 41 | 41 | 26 | 43 | R | R | 6-1 | 185 | 8-22-69 | 1988 | Esperanza, D.R. |
| Pugh, Tim | 0 | 1 | 5.45 | 19 | 1 | 0 | 0 | 36 | 42 | 24 | 22 | 12 | 27 | R | R | 6-6 | 225 | 1-26-67 | 1989 | Florence, Ky. |
| Robinson, Ken | 1 | 0 | 6.00 | 5 | 0 | 0 | 0 | 6 | 9 | 4 | 4 | 3 | 5 | R | R | 5-9 | 175 | 11-3-69 | 1991 | Akron, Ohio |
| Rosado, Jose | 8 | 6 | 3.21 | 16 | 16 | 2 | 0 | 107 | 101 | 39 | 38 | 26 | 64 | L | L | 6-0 | 175 | 11-9-74 | 1994 | Dorado, P.R. |
| Scanlan, Bob | 0 | 1 | 3.18 | 9 | 0 | 0 | 0 | 11 | 13 | 4 | 4 | 3 | 3 | R | R | 6-8 | 215 | 8-9-66 | 1984 | Beverly Hills, Calif. |
| 2-team (8 Detroit) | 0 | 1 | 6.85 | 17 | 0 | 0 | 0 | 22 | 29 | 19 | 17 | 12 | 6 | | | | | | | |
| Valera, Julio | 3 | 2 | 6.46 | 31 | 2 | 0 | 1 | 61 | 75 | 44 | 44 | 27 | 31 | R | R | 6-2 | 215 | 10-13-68 | 1986 | San Sebastian, P.R. |

## FIELDING

| Catcher | PCT | G | PO | A | E | DP | PB |
|---|---|---|---|---|---|---|---|
| Fasano | .984 | 51 | 291 | 14 | 5 | 2 | 2 |
| Macfarlane | .993 | 99 | 511 | 35 | 4 | 2 | 5 |
| Mercedes | 1.000 | 4 | 2 | 0 | 0 | 0 | 0 |
| Sweeney | .994 | 26 | 158 | 7 | 1 | 3 | 4 |

| First Base | PCT | G | PO | A | E | DP |
|---|---|---|---|---|---|---|
| Hamelin | .984 | 33 | 232 | 20 | 4 | 25 |
| Howard | 1.000 | 2 | 4 | 0 | 0 | 0 |
| Offerman | 1.000 | 96 | 796 | 68 | 5 | 82 |
| Paquette | 1.000 | 19 | 149 | 12 | 0 | 24 |
| Randa | 1.000 | 7 | 21 | 3 | 0 | 2 |
| Tucker | 1.000 | 9 | 52 | 3 | 0 | 6 |
| Vitiello | 1.000 | 9 | 40 | 5 | 0 | 4 |
| Young | 1.000 | 27 | 182 | 16 | 0 | 25 |

| Second Base | PCT | G | PO | A | E | DP |
|---|---|---|---|---|---|---|
| Howard | 1.000 | 3 | 9 | 10 | 0 | 3 |
| Lockhart | .975 | 84 | 110 | 206 | 8 | 54 |
| Offerman | .993 | 38 | 64 | 81 | 1 | 29 |
| Randa | .976 | 15 | 15 | 26 | 1 | 5 |
| Roberts | .986 | 63 | 101 | 189 | 4 | 42 |
| Stynes | 1.000 | 5 | 8 | 5 | 0 | 2 |

| Third Base | PCT | G | PO | A | E | DP |
|---|---|---|---|---|---|---|
| Lockhart | .953 | 55 | 27 | 75 | 5 | 5 |
| Paquette | .891 | 51 | 20 | 70 | 11 | 4 |

| | PCT | G | PO | A | E | DP |
|---|---|---|---|---|---|---|
| Randa | .951 | 92 | 44 | 131 | 9 | 11 |
| Stynes | .667 | 2 | 0 | 2 | 1 | 0 |
| Young | 1.000 | 7 | 3 | 2 | 0 | 0 |

| Shortstop | PCT | G | PO | A | E | DP |
|---|---|---|---|---|---|---|
| Howard | .982 | 135 | 197 | 401 | 11 | 109 |
| Offerman | .933 | 36 | 54 | 85 | 10 | 30 |
| Paquette | .968 | 11 | 14 | 16 | 1 | 5 |

| Outfield | PCT | G | PO | A | E | DP |
|---|---|---|---|---|---|---|
| Damon | .983 | 144 | 350 | 5 | 6 | 4 |
| Goodwin | .984 | 136 | 303 | 7 | 5 | 1 |
| Howard | .000 | 1 | 0 | 0 | 0 | 0 |
| Lennon | .947 | 11 | 18 | 0 | 1 | 0 |
| Myers | 1.000 | 19 | 33 | 0 | 0 | 0 |
| Norman | 1.000 | 38 | 44 | 1 | 0 | 0 |
| Nunnally | .968 | 29 | 61 | 0 | 2 | 0 |
| Offerman | 1.000 | 1 | 6 | 0 | 0 | 0 |
| Paquette | .976 | 47 | 79 | 3 | 2 | 1 |
| Roberts | 1.000 | 11 | 14 | 1 | 0 | 1 |
| Stynes | .939 | 19 | 30 | 1 | 2 | 0 |
| Tucker | .989 | 98 | 183 | 5 | 2 | 1 |
| Vitiello | .000 | 1 | 0 | 0 | 0 | 0 |
| Young | .938 | 17 | 14 | 1 | 1 | 0 |

**Tim Belcher**

MEL BAILEY

Shortstop Jose Offerman led the Royals in batting, runs and hits

Royals minor league Player of the Year Mike Sweeney

LARRY GOREN

# ROYALS

## FARM SYSTEM

**Director of Minor League Operations:** Bob Hegman

| Class | Farm Team | League | W | L | Pct. | Finish* | Manager | First Yr |
|-------|-----------|--------|---|---|------|---------|---------|----------|
| AAA | Omaha (Neb.) Royals | American Assoc. | 79 | 65 | .549 | 2nd (8) | Mike Jirschele | 1969 |
| AA | Wichita (Kan.) Wranglers | Texas | 70 | 70 | .500 | T-4th (8) | Ron Johnson | 1995 |
| #A | Wilmington (Del.) Blue Rocks | Carolina | 80 | 60 | .571 | +1st (8) | John Mizerock | 1993 |
| A | Lansing (Mich.) Lugnuts | Midwest | 68 | 71 | .489 | 8th (14) | Brian Poldberg | 1996 |
| A | Spokane (Wash.) Indians | Northwest | 37 | 39 | .487 | 5th (8) | Bob Herold | 1995 |
| R | Fort Myers (Fla.) Royals | Gulf Coast | 30 | 29 | .508 | 8th (16) | Al Pedrique | 1993 |

*Finish in overall standings (No. of teams in league)   #Advanced level   +Won league championship

## ORGANIZATION LEADERS

### MAJOR LEAGUERS

**BATTING**

| | | |
|---|---|---|
| *AVG | Two tied at | .303 |
| R | Jose Offerman | 85 |
| H | Jose Offerman | 170 |
| TB | Jose Offerman | 234 |
| 2B | Two tied at | 33 |
| 3B | Jose Offerman | 8 |
| HR | Craig Paquette | 22 |
| RBI | Craig Paquette | 67 |
| BB | Jose Offerman | 74 |
| SO | Craig Paquette | 101 |
| SB | Tom Goodwin | 66 |

**PITCHING**

| | | |
|---|---|---|
| W | Tim Belcher | 15 |
| L | Chris Haney | 14 |
| #ERA | Jose Rosado | 3.21 |
| G | Hipolito Pichardo | 57 |
| CG | Kevin Appier | 5 |
| SV | Jeff Montgomery | 24 |
| IP | Tim Belcher | 239 |
| BB | Kevin Appier | 75 |
| SO | Kevin Appier | 207 |

**Kevin Appier.** 207 strikeouts

THE SPORTS GROUP

### MINOR LEAGUERS

**BATTING**

| | | |
|---|---|---|
| *AVG | Chris Stynes, Omaha | .356 |
| R | Jose Cepeda, Lansing | 87 |
| H | Jose Cepeda, Lansing | 161 |
| TB | Larry Sutton, Wichita | 229 |
| 2B | Three tied at | 31 |
| 3B | Juan Rocha, Lansing | 8 |
| HR | Jon Nunnally, Omaha | 25 |
| RBI | Larry Sutton, Wichita | 84 |
| BB | Larry Sutton, Wichita | 77 |
| SO | Al Shirley, Wilmington | 149 |
| SB | Sergio Nunez, Wilmington | 44 |

**PITCHING**

| | | |
|---|---|---|
| W | Brian Bevil, Wichita/Omaha | 16 |
| L | Ken Ray, Wichita | 12 |
| #ERA | Steve Prihoda, Wilmington | 1.47 |
| G | Allen McDill, Wichita/Omaha | 56 |
| CG | Two tied at | 3 |
| SV | Two tied at | 25 |
| IP | Mike Bovee, Wichita | 177 |
| BB | Carlos Paredes, Lansing | 69 |
| SO | Brian Bevil, Wichita/Omaha | 147 |

*Minimum 250 At-Bats   #Minimum 75 Innings

## TOP 10 PROSPECTS

How the Royals Top 10 prospects, as judged by Baseball America prior to the 1996 season, fared in 1996:

**Jim Pittsley**

| Player, Pos. | Club (Class—League) | AVG | AB | R | H | 2B | 3B | HR | RBI | SB |
|--------------|---------------------|-----|----|---|---|----|----|----|----|----|
| 2. Joe Vitiello, 1b | Omaha (AAA—American Assoc.) | .280 | 132 | 26 | 37 | 7 | 0 | 9 | 31 | 1 |
| | Kansas City | .241 | 257 | 29 | 62 | 15 | 1 | 8 | 40 | 2 |
| 4. Carlos Beltran, of | Lansing (A—Midwest) | .143 | 42 | 3 | 6 | 2 | 0 | 0 | 0 | 1 |
| | Spokane (A—Northwest) | .270 | 215 | 29 | 58 | 8 | 3 | 7 | 29 | 10 |
| 5. Felix Martinez, ss | Omaha (AAA—American Assoc.) | .235 | 395 | 54 | 93 | 13 | 3 | 5 | 35 | 18 |
| 6. Mike Sweeney, c | Wichita (AA—Texas) | .319 | 235 | 45 | 75 | 18 | 1 | 14 | 51 | 3 |
| | Omaha (AAA—American Assoc.) | .257 | 101 | 14 | 26 | 9 | 0 | 3 | 16 | 0 |
| | Kansas City | .279 | 165 | 23 | 46 | 10 | 0 | 4 | 24 | 1 |
| 7. Sal Fasano, c | Omaha (AAA—American Assoc.) | .231 | 104 | 12 | 24 | 4 | 0 | 4 | 15 | 0 |
| | Kansas City | .203 | 143 | 20 | 29 | 2 | 0 | 6 | 19 | 1 |
| 8. Gary Coffee, 1b | Lansing (A—Midwest) | .232 | 393 | 52 | 91 | 17 | 2 | 11 | 59 | 6 |

| | | W | L | ERA | G | SV | IP | H | BB | SO |
|--------------|---------------------|---|---|-----|---|----|----|---|----|----|
| 1. Jim Pittsley, rhp | Wilmington (A—Carolina) | 0 | 1 | 11.00 | 2 | 0 | 9 | 13 | 5 | 10 |
| | Wichita (AA—Texas) | 3 | 0 | 0.41 | 3 | 0 | 22 | 9 | 5 | 7 |
| | Omaha (AAA—American Assoc.) | 7 | 1 | 3.97 | 13 | 0 | 70 | 74 | 39 | 53 |
| 3. Glendon Rusch, lhp | Omaha (AAA—American Assoc.) | 11 | 9 | 3.98 | 28 | 0 | 170 | 177 | 40 | 117 |
| 9. Jaime Bluma, rhp | Omaha (AAA—American Assoc.) | 1 | 2 | 3.12 | 52 | 25 | 58 | 57 | 20 | 40 |
| | Kansas City | 0 | 0 | 3.60 | 17 | 5 | 20 | 18 | 4 | 14 |
| 10. Jeff Martin, rhp | Wilmington (A—Carolina) | 0 | 1 | 4.87 | 5 | 0 | 20 | 24 | 5 | 12 |

— **Class AAA**

## AMERICAN ASSOCIATION

| BATTING | AVG | G | AB | R | H | 2B | 3B | HR | RBI | BB | SO | SB | CS | B | T | HT | WT | DOB | 1st Yr | Resides |
|---|---|---|---|---|---|---|---|---|---|---|---|---|---|---|---|---|---|---|---|---|
| Burton, Darren | .270 | 129 | 463 | 75 | 125 | 28 | 5 | 15 | 67 | 59 | 82 | 7 | 7 | S | R | 6-1 | 185 | 9-16-72 | 1990 | Somerset, Ky. |
| Diaz, Lino | .271 | 75 | 266 | 32 | 72 | 13 | 2 | 3 | 28 | 17 | 29 | 0 | 3 | R | R | 5-11 | 182 | 7-22-70 | 1993 | Altoona, Pa. |
| Fasano, Sal | .231 | 29 | 104 | 12 | 24 | 4 | 0 | 4 | 15 | 6 | 21 | 0 | 1 | R | R | 6-2 | 220 | 8-10-71 | 1993 | Hanover Park, Ill. |
| Grotewold, Jeff | .278 | 98 | 338 | 63 | 94 | 20 | 0 | 10 | 51 | 58 | 84 | 1 | 3 | L | R | 6-0 | 215 | 12-8-65 | 1987 | Lake Arrowhead, Calif. |
| Halter, Shane | .258 | 93 | 299 | 43 | 77 | 24 | 0 | 3 | 33 | 31 | 49 | 7 | 2 | R | R | 5-10 | 160 | 11-8-69 | 1991 | Papillion, Neb. |
| Hamelin, Bob | .313 | 4 | 16 | 4 | 5 | 1 | 1 | 0 | 0 | 1 | 4 | 1 | 0 | L | L | 6-0 | 235 | 11-29-67 | 1988 | Charlotte, N.C. |
| Hansen, Jed | .232 | 29 | 99 | 14 | 23 | 4 | 0 | 3 | 9 | 12 | 22 | 2 | 0 | R | R | 6-1 | 195 | 8-19-72 | 1994 | Olympia, Wash. |
| Martinez, Felix | .235 | 118 | 395 | 54 | 93 | 13 | 3 | 5 | 35 | 44 | 79 | 18 | 10 | S | R | 6-0 | 168 | 5-18-74 | 1993 | Nagua, D.R. |
| Martinez, Ramon | .253 | 85 | 320 | 35 | 81 | 12 | 3 | 6 | 41 | 21 | 34 | 3 | 2 | R | R | 6-1 | 170 | 10-10-72 | 1993 | Toa Alta, P.R. |
| Mercedes, Henry | .215 | 72 | 223 | 28 | 48 | 9 | 1 | 8 | 35 | 28 | 60 | 0 | 0 | R | R | 5-11 | 185 | 7-23-69 | 1988 | Santo Domingo, D.R. |
| Merchant, Mark | .280 | 38 | 118 | 18 | 33 | 7 | 0 | 4 | 21 | 22 | 26 | 1 | 0 | S | R | 6-2 | 185 | 1-23-69 | 1987 | Chuluota, Fla. |
| 2-team (42 Nash.) | .245 | 80 | 249 | 39 | 61 | 13 | 0 | 8 | 36 | 39 | 55 | 2 | 1 | | | | | | | |
| Mota, Jose | .245 | 72 | 229 | 24 | 56 | 5 | 2 | 3 | 20 | 17 | 28 | 7 | 6 | S | R | 5-9 | 155 | 3-16-65 | 1985 | Glendale, Calif. |
| Myers, Rod | .292 | 112 | 411 | 68 | 120 | 27 | 1 | 16 | 54 | 49 | 106 | 37 | 8 | L | L | 6-0 | 190 | 1-14-73 | 1991 | Conroe, Texas |
| Norman, Les | .260 | 24 | 77 | 8 | 20 | 6 | 0 | 1 | 13 | 6 | 8 | 0 | 1 | R | R | 6-1 | 185 | 2-25-69 | 1991 | Greenfield, Ill. |
| Nunnally, Jon | .281 | 103 | 345 | 76 | 97 | 21 | 4 | 25 | 77 | 47 | 100 | 10 | 9 | L | R | 5-10 | 188 | 11-9-71 | 1992 | Pelham, N.C. |
| Paquette, Craig | .333 | 18 | 63 | 9 | 21 | 3 | 0 | 4 | 13 | 8 | 14 | 1 | 0 | R | R | 6-0 | 190 | 3-28-69 | 1989 | Garden Grove, Calif. |
| Randa, Joe | .111 | 3 | 9 | 1 | 1 | 0 | 1 | 0 | 0 | 1 | 1 | 0 | 0 | R | R | 5-11 | 190 | 12-18-69 | 1991 | Delafield, Wis. |
| Stewart, Andy | .215 | 50 | 181 | 23 | 39 | 10 | 2 | 2 | 13 | 15 | 25 | 0 | 2 | R | R | 6-1 | 205 | 12-5-70 | 1990 | Oshawa, Ontario |
| Stynes, Chris | .356 | 72 | 284 | 50 | 101 | 22 | 6 | 10 | 40 | 18 | 17 | 7 | 3 | R | R | 5-9 | 170 | 1-19-73 | 1991 | Boca Raton, Fla. |
| Sweeney, Mike | .257 | 25 | 101 | 14 | 26 | 9 | 0 | 3 | 16 | 6 | 13 | 0 | 0 | R | R | 6-1 | 195 | 7-22-73 | 1991 | Ontario, Calif. |
| Tucker, Scooter | .162 | 24 | 74 | 5 | 12 | 2 | 0 | 1 | 4 | 2 | 12 | 0 | 0 | R | R | 6-2 | 215 | 11-18-66 | 1988 | Cantonment, Fla. |
| Vitiello, Joe | .280 | 36 | 132 | 26 | 37 | 7 | 0 | 9 | 31 | 16 | 32 | 1 | 0 | R | R | 6-2 | 215 | 4-11-70 | 1991 | Stoneham, Mass. |
| Young, Kevin | .306 | 50 | 186 | 29 | 57 | 11 | 1 | 13 | 46 | 12 | 41 | 3 | 0 | R | R | 6-2 | 219 | 6-16-69 | 1990 | Kansas City, Kan. |
| Zupcic, Bob | .143 | 4 | 7 | 1 | 1 | 0 | 0 | 0 | 1 | 0 | 5 | 0 | 0 | R | R | 6-4 | 220 | 8-18-66 | 1987 | Charlotte, N.C. |

| PITCHING | W | L | ERA | G | GS | CG | SV | IP | H | R | ER | BB | SO | B | T | HT | WT | DOB | 1st Yr | Resides |
|---|---|---|---|---|---|---|---|---|---|---|---|---|---|---|---|---|---|---|---|---|
| Bevil, Brian | 7 | 5 | 4.12 | 12 | 12 | 0 | 0 | 68 | 62 | 36 | 31 | 19 | 73 | R | R | 6-3 | 190 | 9-5-71 | 1991 | Houston, Texas |
| Bluma, Jaime | 1 | 2 | 3.12 | 52 | 0 | 0 | 25 | 58 | 57 | 22 | 20 | 20 | 40 | R | R | 5-11 | 195 | 5-18-72 | 1994 | Owasso, Okla. |
| Bunch, Melvin | 8 | 9 | 6.08 | 33 | 27 | 0 | 0 | 147 | 181 | 106 | 99 | 59 | 94 | R | R | 6-1 | 165 | 11-4-71 | 1992 | Texarkana, Texas |
| Clark, Terry | 3 | 1 | 2.56 | 16 | 2 | 0 | 2 | 46 | 42 | 15 | 13 | 13 | 36 | R | R | 6-2 | 196 | 10-10-60 | 1979 | La Puente, Calif. |
| Granger, Jeff | 5 | 3 | 2.34 | 45 | 0 | 0 | 4 | 77 | 65 | 24 | 20 | 29 | 68 | R | L | 6-4 | 200 | 12-16-71 | 1993 | Orange, Texas |
| Huisman, Rich | 2 | 4 | 4.87 | 27 | 4 | 0 | 0 | 57 | 54 | 32 | 31 | 24 | 50 | R | R | 6-3 | 200 | 5-17-69 | 1990 | Bensenville, Ill. |
| Kiefer, Mark | 3 | 2 | 4.93 | 8 | 7 | 0 | 0 | 46 | 49 | 31 | 25 | 9 | 33 | R | R | 6-4 | 184 | 11-13-68 | 1988 | Kingsland, Texas |
| 2-team (22 N.O.) | 6 | 8 | 4.56 | 30 | 17 | 1 | 0 | 118 | 109 | 71 | 60 | 42 | 99 | | | | | | | |
| Linton, Doug | 1 | 1 | 4.76 | 4 | 4 | 0 | 0 | 23 | 26 | 13 | 12 | 7 | 14 | R | R | 6-1 | 190 | 9-22-67 | 1987 | Kingsport, Tenn. |
| Magnante, Mike | 1 | 0 | 0.00 | 1 | 0 | 0 | 0 | 3 | 3 | 1 | 0 | 0 | 6 | L | L | 6-1 | 190 | 6-17-65 | 1988 | Burbank, Calif. |
| McDill, Allen | 0 | 1 | 54.00 | 2 | 0 | 0 | 0 | 0 | 3 | 2 | 2 | 1 | 1 | L | L | 6-1 | 160 | 8-23-71 | 1992 | Hot Springs, Ark. |
| Meacham, Rusty | 3 | 3 | 4.82 | 23 | 4 | 0 | 2 | 52 | 56 | 30 | 28 | 18 | 39 | R | R | 6-2 | 175 | 1-27-68 | 1988 | Palm City, Fla. |
| Olsen, Steve | 7 | 4 | 5.07 | 24 | 4 | 1 | 0 | 66 | 70 | 39 | 37 | 23 | 41 | R | R | 6-4 | 225 | 11-2-69 | 1991 | La Grange, Ky. |
| Patterson, Ken | 0 | 1 | 1.80 | 16 | 0 | 0 | 1 | 20 | 16 | 5 | 4 | 4 | 13 | L | L | 6-4 | 222 | 7-8-64 | 1985 | McGregor, Texas |
| Pittsley, Jim | 7 | 1 | 3.97 | 13 | 13 | 0 | 0 | 70 | 74 | 34 | 31 | 39 | 53 | R | R | 6-7 | 215 | 4-3-74 | 1992 | Dubois, Pa. |
| Ralston, Kris | 0 | 0 | 3.00 | 1 | 0 | 0 | 0 | 3 | 3 | 1 | 1 | 0 | 1 | R | R | 6-2 | 205 | 8-8-71 | 1993 | Carthage, Mo. |
| Robinson, Ken | 2 | 0 | 0.79 | 6 | 0 | 0 | 0 | 11 | 7 | 1 | 1 | 4 | 9 | R | R | 5-9 | 175 | 11-3-69 | 1991 | Akron, Ohio |
| Rodriguez, Rich | 2 | 3 | 3.99 | 47 | 0 | 0 | 3 | 70 | 75 | 40 | 31 | 18 | 39 | L | L | 5-11 | 200 | 3-1-63 | 1984 | Knoxville, Tenn. |
| Rosado, Jose | 8 | 3 | 3.17 | 15 | 15 | 1 | 0 | 97 | 80 | 38 | 34 | 38 | 82 | L | L | 6-0 | 175 | 11-9-74 | 1994 | Dorado, P.R. |
| Rusch, Glendon | 11 | 9 | 3.98 | 28 | 28 | 1 | 0 | 170 | 177 | 88 | 75 | 40 | 117 | L | L | 6-2 | 170 | 11-7-74 | 1993 | Seattle, Wash. |
| Scanlan, Bob | 0 | 0 | 0.73 | 12 | 0 | 0 | 5 | 12 | 10 | 2 | 1 | 3 | 9 | R | R | 6-8 | 215 | 8-9-66 | 1984 | Beverly Hills, Calif. |
| Torres, Dilson | 4 | 7 | 4.60 | 16 | 14 | 2 | 0 | 86 | 102 | 54 | 44 | 19 | 36 | R | R | 6-2 | 215 | 5-31-70 | 1991 | Suredo, Venez. |
| Toth, Robert | 3 | 3 | 7.04 | 11 | 8 | 0 | 0 | 46 | 63 | 40 | 36 | 17 | 20 | R | R | 6-2 | 180 | 7-30-72 | 1990 | Cypress, Calif. |
| Valera, Julio | 1 | 3 | 5.17 | 6 | 2 | 0 | 0 | 16 | 22 | 13 | 9 | 5 | 9 | R | R | 6-2 | 215 | 10-13-68 | 1986 | San Sebastian, P.R. |

### FIELDING

| Catcher | PCT | G | PO | A | E | DP | PB |
|---|---|---|---|---|---|---|---|
| Fasano | .980 | 25 | 179 | 18 | 4 | 4 | 1 |
| Mercedes | .993 | 66 | 400 | 49 | 3 | 6 | 6 |
| Stewart | 1.000 | 14 | 83 | 6 | 0 | 1 | 0 |
| Sweeney | 1.000 | 23 | 167 | 8 | 0 | 2 | 3 |
| Tucker | .992 | 23 | 122 | 10 | 1 | 1 | 3 |

| First Base | PCT | G | PO | A | E | DP |
|---|---|---|---|---|---|---|
| Fasano | 1.000 | 2 | 18 | 1 | 0 | 5 |
| Grotewold | .993 | 32 | 259 | 14 | 2 | 25 |
| Hamelin | 1.000 | 4 | 37 | 1 | 0 | 6 |
| Merchant | 1.000 | 8 | 40 | 3 | 0 | 6 |
| Norman | .923 | 3 | 23 | 1 | 2 | 1 |
| Paquette | 1.000 | 2 | 13 | 2 | 0 | 2 |
| Stewart | .996 | 28 | 240 | 20 | 1 | 30 |
| Tucker | 1.000 | 1 | 6 | 0 | 0 | 1 |
| Vitiello | .990 | 36 | 281 | 20 | 3 | 27 |
| Young | .990 | 31 | 269 | 21 | 3 | 23 |

| Second Base | PCT | G | PO | A | E | DP |
|---|---|---|---|---|---|---|
| Halter | 1.000 | 7 | 15 | 13 | 0 | 4 |
| Hansen | .953 | 29 | 66 | 75 | 7 | 21 |
| R. Martinez | .969 | 85 | 163 | 207 | 12 | 53 |
| Mota | .952 | 22 | 37 | 43 | 4 | 13 |
| Stynes | .971 | 7 | 18 | 15 | 1 | 6 |

| Third Base | PCT | G | PO | A | E | DP |
|---|---|---|---|---|---|---|
| Diaz | .959 | 65 | 42 | 120 | 7 | 6 |
| Fasano | 1.000 | 1 | 1 | 2 | 0 | 0 |
| Halter | .846 | 20 | 9 | 24 | 6 | 3 |
| Mota | .962 | 26 | 12 | 39 | 2 | 6 |
| Paquette | .857 | 4 | 5 | 7 | 2 | 1 |
| Randa | 1.000 | 3 | 1 | 10 | 0 | 1 |
| Stynes | .934 | 28 | 13 | 58 | 5 | 2 |
| Young | .946 | 11 | 11 | 24 | 2 | 3 |

| Shortstop | PCT | G | PO | A | E | DP |
|---|---|---|---|---|---|---|
| Halter | .921 | 18 | 25 | 33 | 5 | 5 |
| F. Martinez | .929 | 117 | 177 | 374 | 42 | 79 |
| Mota | .949 | 12 | 18 | 38 | 3 | 14 |

| Outfield | PCT | G | PO | A | E | DP |
|---|---|---|---|---|---|---|
| Burton | .986 | 121 | 262 | 11 | 4 | 3 |
| Halter | .977 | 51 | 81 | 5 | 2 | 0 |
| Merchant | .500 | 3 | 1 | 0 | 1 | 0 |
| Mota | 1.000 | 5 | 9 | 0 | 0 | 0 |
| Myers | .993 | 112 | 263 | 5 | 2 | 2 |
| Norman | .943 | 16 | 33 | 0 | 2 | 0 |
| Nunnally | .980 | 99 | 182 | 12 | 4 | 5 |
| Paquette | .857 | 2 | 6 | 0 | 1 | 0 |
| Stynes | .959 | 35 | 67 | 4 | 3 | 0 |
| Zupcic | 1.000 | 3 | 6 | 1 | 0 | 0 |

## WICHITA — **Class AA**

### TEXAS LEAGUE

| BATTING | AVG | G | AB | R | H | 2B | 3B | HR | RBI | BB | SO | SB | CS | B | T | HT | WT | DOB | 1st Yr | Resides |
|---|---|---|---|---|---|---|---|---|---|---|---|---|---|---|---|---|---|---|---|---|
| Cameron, Stanton | .143 | 2 | 7 | 0 | 1 | 0 | 0 | 0 | 2 | 0 | 4 | 0 | 0 | R | R | 6-5 | 195 | 7-5-69 | 1987 | Powell, Tenn. |
| Carr, Jeremy | .260 | 129 | 453 | 68 | 118 | 23 | 2 | 6 | 40 | 47 | 64 | 41 | 9 | R | R | 5-10 | 170 | 3-30-71 | 1993 | Boise, Idaho |
| Delaney, Sean | .208 | 23 | 48 | 5 | 10 | 3 | 0 | 2 | 5 | 5 | 15 | 2 | 0 | R | R | 5-11 | 190 | 5-22-70 | 1992 | Berwyn, Ill. |
| Diaz, Lino | .252 | 44 | 159 | 18 | 40 | 8 | 1 | 3 | 19 | 9 | 11 | 2 | 1 | R | R | 5-11 | 182 | 7-22-70 | 1993 | Altoona, Pa. |
| Gonzalez, Raul | .286 | 23 | 84 | 17 | 24 | 5 | 1 | 1 | 9 | 5 | 12 | 1 | 2 | R | R | 5-8 | 175 | 12-27-73 | 1991 | Carolina, P.R. |
| Hansen, Jed | .286 | 99 | 405 | 60 | 116 | 27 | 4 | 12 | 50 | 29 | 72 | 14 | 8 | R | R | 6-1 | 195 | 8-19-72 | 1994 | Olympia, Wash. |
| Long, Kevin | .273 | 128 | 436 | 62 | 119 | 31 | 3 | 3 | 48 | 56 | 36 | 9 | 14 | L | L | 5-9 | 165 | 12-30-66 | 1989 | Phoenix, Ariz. |

| BATTING | AVG | G | AB | R | H | 2B | 3B | HR | RBI | BB | SO | SB | CS | B | T | HT | WT | DOB | 1st Yr | Resides |
|---|---|---|---|---|---|---|---|---|---|---|---|---|---|---|---|---|---|---|---|---|
| Long, Ryan | .283 | 122 | 442 | 64 | 125 | 29 | 1 | 20 | 78 | 17 | 71 | 6 | 5 | R | R | 6-2 | 185 | 2-3-73 | 1991 | Houston, Texas |
| Lopez, Mendy | .281 | 93 | 327 | 47 | 92 | 20 | 5 | 6 | 32 | 26 | 67 | 14 | 4 | R | R | 6-2 | 165 | 10-15-74 | 1992 | Santo Domingo, D.R. |
| Martinez, Ramon | .344 | 26 | 93 | 16 | 32 | 4 | 1 | 1 | 8 | 7 | 8 | 4 | 1 | R | R | 6-1 | 170 | 10-10-72 | 1993 | Toa Alta, P.R. |
| Medrano, Anthony | .274 | 125 | 474 | 59 | 130 | 26 | 1 | 8 | 55 | 18 | 36 | 10 | 8 | R | R | 5-11 | 155 | 12-8-74 | 1993 | Long Beach, Calif. |
| Morillo, Cesar | .235 | 45 | 119 | 8 | 28 | 3 | 1 | 2 | 7 | 7 | 18 | 3 | 0 | S | R | 5-11 | 180 | 7-21-73 | 1990 | Eugene, Ore. |
| Rodriguez, Boi | .063 | 16 | 32 | 0 | 2 | 1 | 0 | 0 | 1 | 4 | 15 | 0 | 0 | L | R | 6-0 | 180 | 4-14-66 | 1987 | Dorado Beach, P.R. |
| Sheppard, Don | .216 | 45 | 97 | 12 | 21 | 2 | 0 | 3 | 12 | 9 | 24 | 3 | 4 | R | R | 6-2 | 180 | 5-2-71 | 1989 | Pittsburg, Calif. |
| Sisco, Steve | .297 | 122 | 462 | 80 | 137 | 24 | 1 | 13 | 74 | 40 | 69 | 4 | 2 | R | R | 5-9 | 180 | 12-2-69 | 1992 | Thousand Oaks, Calif. |
| Stewart, Andy | .302 | 58 | 202 | 29 | 61 | 17 | 3 | 3 | 32 | 14 | 25 | 3 | 2 | R | R | 5-11 | 205 | 12-5-70 | 1990 | Oshawa, Ontario |
| Strickland, Chad | .226 | 77 | 239 | 35 | 54 | 15 | 2 | 5 | 34 | 16 | 23 | 1 | 1 | R | R | 6-1 | 185 | 3-16-72 | 1990 | Midwest City, Okla. |
| Sutton, Larry | .296 | 125 | 463 | 84 | 137 | 22 | 2 | 22 | 84 | 77 | 66 | 4 | 1 | L | L | 5-11 | 175 | 5-14-70 | 1992 | Temecula, Calif. |
| Sweeney, Mike | .319 | 66 | 235 | 45 | 75 | 18 | 1 | 14 | 51 | 32 | 29 | 3 | 2 | R | R | 6-1 | 195 | 7-22-73 | 1991 | Ontario, Calif. |
| Tucker, Michael | .450 | 6 | 20 | 4 | 9 | 1 | 0 | 0 | 7 | 5 | 4 | 0 | 2 | L | R | 6-2 | 185 | 6-25-71 | 1992 | Chase City, Va. |

| PITCHING | W | L | ERA | G | GS | CG | SV | IP | H | R | ER | BB | SO | B | T | HT | WT | DOB | 1st Yr | Resides |
|---|---|---|---|---|---|---|---|---|---|---|---|---|---|---|---|---|---|---|---|---|
| Bevil, Brian | 9 | 2 | 2.02 | 13 | 13 | 2 | 0 | 76 | 56 | 22 | 17 | 26 | 74 | R | R | 6-3 | 190 | 9-5-71 | 1991 | Houston, Texas |
| Bovee, Mike | 10 | 11 | 4.84 | 27 | 27 | 3 | 0 | 177 | 223 | 113 | 95 | 40 | 102 | R | R | 5-10 | 200 | 8-21-73 | 1991 | Mira Mesa, Calif. |
| Byrdak, Tim | 5 | 7 | 6.91 | 15 | 15 | 0 | 0 | 85 | 112 | 73 | 65 | 44 | 47 | L | L | 5-11 | 170 | 10-31-73 | 1994 | Oak Forest, Ill. |
| Eddy, Chris | 0 | 0 | 2.97 | 30 | 0 | 0 | 0 | 30 | 33 | 16 | 10 | 18 | 22 | L | L | 6-3 | 200 | 11-27-69 | 1992 | Duncanville, Texas |
| Evans, Bart | 1 | 2 | 11.84 | 9 | 7 | 0 | 0 | 24 | 31 | 38 | 32 | 36 | 16 | R | R | 6-1 | 190 | 12-30-70 | 1992 | Ozark, Mo. |
| Gamboa, Javier | 5 | 5 | 5.93 | 15 | 15 | 0 | 0 | 91 | 118 | 68 | 60 | 33 | 39 | R | R | 6-1 | 185 | 3-17-74 | 1994 | Paso Robles, Calif. |
| Grundy, Phil | 1 | 0 | 1.29 | 1 | 1 | 0 | 0 | 7 | 4 | 1 | 1 | 2 | 0 | R | R | 6-2 | 195 | 9-8-72 | 1993 | Somerset, Ky. |
| Harrison, Brian | 9 | 2 | 3.66 | 49 | 7 | 0 | 6 | 118 | 118 | 54 | 48 | 14 | 80 | R | R | 6-1 | 175 | 12-18-68 | 1992 | Bryan, Texas |
| McDill, Allen | 1 | 5 | 5.54 | 54 | 0 | 0 | 11 | 65 | 79 | 43 | 40 | 21 | 62 | L | L | 6-1 | 160 | 8-23-71 | 1992 | Hot Springs, Ark. |
| Morones, Geno | 1 | 5 | 6.93 | 13 | 4 | 1 | 0 | 38 | 50 | 32 | 29 | 19 | 24 | R | R | 5-11 | 197 | 3-26-71 | 1991 | San Leandro, Calif. |
| Olsen, Steve | 6 | 0 | 2.77 | 15 | 3 | 0 | 1 | 55 | 40 | 18 | 17 | 14 | 39 | R | R | 6-4 | 225 | 11-2-69 | 1991 | La Grange, Ky. |
| Pittsley, Jim | 3 | 0 | 0.41 | 3 | 3 | 0 | 0 | 22 | 9 | 1 | 1 | 5 | 7 | R | R | 6-7 | 215 | 4-3-74 | 1992 | Dubois, Pa. |
| Rawitzer, Kevin | 0 | 6 | 4.74 | 42 | 0 | 0 | 3 | 68 | 77 | 52 | 36 | 39 | 48 | L | L | 5-10 | 185 | 2-28-71 | 1993 | Danville, Calif. |
| Ray, Ken | 4 | 12 | 6.12 | 22 | 22 | 1 | 0 | 121 | 151 | 94 | 82 | 57 | 79 | R | R | 6-2 | 160 | 11-27-74 | 1993 | Roswell, Ga. |
| Rosado, Jose | 2 | 0 | 0.00 | 2 | 2 | 0 | 0 | 13 | 10 | 0 | 0 | 1 | 12 | L | L | 6-0 | 175 | 11-9-74 | 1994 | Dorado, P.R. |
| Smith, Toby | 4 | 2 | 4.13 | 42 | 0 | 0 | 8 | 52 | 46 | 25 | 24 | 19 | 44 | R | R | 6-6 | 225 | 11-16-71 | 1993 | Guthrie, Okla. |
| Telgheder, Jim | 0 | 2 | 3.43 | 13 | 0 | 0 | 0 | 21 | 23 | 9 | 8 | 6 | 11 | R | R | 6-3 | 210 | 3-22-71 | 1993 | Slate Hill, N.Y. |
| Torres, Dilson | 5 | 3 | 3.88 | 9 | 8 | 0 | 1 | 56 | 62 | 27 | 24 | 13 | 27 | R | R | 6-1 | 215 | 5-31-70 | 1991 | Suredo, Venez. |
| Toth, Robert | 4 | 6 | 3.78 | 19 | 13 | 2 | 4 | 105 | 100 | 48 | 44 | 24 | 51 | R | R | 6-2 | 180 | 7-30-72 | 1990 | Cypress, Calif. |

**FIELDING**

| Catcher | PCT | G | PO | A | E | DP | PB |
|---|---|---|---|---|---|---|---|
| Delaney | .976 | 23 | 75 | 7 | 2 | 1 | 2 |
| Stewart | .977 | 43 | 216 | 35 | 6 | 3 | 4 |
| Strickland | .986 | 64 | 317 | 48 | 5 | 6 | 3 |
| Sweeney | .995 | 30 | 201 | 13 | 1 | 0 | 2 |

| First Base | PCT | G | PO | A | E | DP |
|---|---|---|---|---|---|---|
| Sisco | .988 | 17 | 157 | 3 | 2 | 18 |
| Stewart | .000 | 1 | 0 | 0 | 0 | 0 |
| Sutton | .989 | 124 | 1105 | 76 | 13 | 118 |
| Tucker | 1.000 | 2 | 6 | 1 | 0 | 1 |

| Second Base | PCT | G | PO | A | E | DP |
|---|---|---|---|---|---|---|
| Hansen | .979 | 96 | 196 | 276 | 10 | 72 |
| Martinez | .956 | 26 | 47 | 84 | 6 | 20 |
| Morillo | 1.000 | 8 | 9 | 21 | 0 | 3 |

| | PCT | G | PO | A | E | DP |
|---|---|---|---|---|---|---|
| Sisco | 1.000 | 16 | 34 | 37 | 0 | 13 |

| Third Base | PCT | G | PO | A | E | DP |
|---|---|---|---|---|---|---|
| Diaz | .922 | 44 | 36 | 82 | 10 | 12 |
| Lopez | .933 | 91 | 75 | 261 | 24 | 28 |
| Morillo | .909 | 6 | 1 | 9 | 1 | 0 |
| Sisco | .929 | 10 | 10 | 16 | 2 | 2 |

| Shortstop | PCT | G | PO | A | E | DP |
|---|---|---|---|---|---|---|
| Lopez | 1.000 | 2 | 5 | 4 | 0 | 1 |
| Medrano | .934 | 121 | 188 | 324 | 36 | 79 |
| Morillo | .943 | 26 | 23 | 59 | 5 | 11 |
| Sisco | 1.000 | 1 | 1 | 1 | 0 | 1 |

| Outfield | PCT | G | PO | A | E | DP |
|---|---|---|---|---|---|---|
| Cameron | .000 | 2 | 0 | 0 | 0 | 0 |
| Carr | .982 | 127 | 262 | 12 | 5 | 5 |
| Gonzalez | .969 | 23 | 30 | 1 | 1 | 0 |
| Hansen | .000 | 1 | 0 | 0 | 0 | 0 |
| K. Long | .980 | 121 | 238 | 11 | 5 | 1 |
| R. Long | .969 | 74 | 150 | 6 | 5 | 1 |
| Morillo | 1.000 | 1 | 1 | 0 | 0 | 0 |
| Rodriguez | 1.000 | 5 | 9 | 0 | 0 | 0 |
| Sheppard | .972 | 38 | 65 | 5 | 2 | 1 |
| Sisco | .967 | 61 | 115 | 4 | 4 | 1 |
| Stewart | 1.000 | 1 | 1 | 0 | 0 | 0 |
| Strickland | 1.000 | 5 | 8 | 1 | 0 | 0 |
| Sutton | .000 | 2 | 0 | 0 | 0 | 0 |
| Tucker | 1.000 | 6 | 11 | 0 | 0 | 0 |

# WILMINGTON                    Class A
## CAROLINA LEAGUE

| BATTING | AVG | G | AB | R | H | 2B | 3B | HR | RBI | BB | SO | SB | CS | B | T | HT | WT | DOB | 1st Yr | Resides |
|---|---|---|---|---|---|---|---|---|---|---|---|---|---|---|---|---|---|---|---|---|
| Brooks, Ramy | .251 | 111 | 363 | 54 | 91 | 24 | 2 | 15 | 66 | 45 | 80 | 4 | 3 | R | R | 6-2 | 180 | 4-12-70 | 1990 | Blanchard, Okla. |
| Byington, Jimmie | .296 | 105 | 297 | 46 | 88 | 20 | 2 | 1 | 32 | 19 | 44 | 12 | 8 | R | R | 6-0 | 170 | 8-22-73 | 1993 | Tulsa, Okla. |
| Cedeno, Eduardo | .209 | 78 | 163 | 28 | 34 | 7 | 0 | 1 | 18 | 14 | 65 | 11 | 5 | R | R | 6-0 | 150 | 8-2-72 | 1990 | La Romana, D.R. |
| Delaney, Donovan | .272 | 124 | 386 | 45 | 105 | 17 | 4 | 4 | 38 | 21 | 63 | 18 | 7 | R | R | 5-11 | 200 | 3-24-74 | 1994 | Haughton, La. |
| Evans, Michael | .191 | 98 | 278 | 36 | 53 | 9 | 1 | 10 | 40 | 56 | 78 | 1 | 2 | L | R | 6-0 | 190 | 8-7-72 | 1993 | Houston, Texas |
| McNally, Sean | .276 | 126 | 428 | 49 | 118 | 27 | 1 | 8 | 63 | 57 | 83 | 3 | 1 | R | R | 6-4 | 205 | 12-14-72 | 1994 | Rye, N.Y. |
| Mendez, Carlos | .293 | 109 | 406 | 40 | 119 | 25 | 3 | 4 | 59 | 22 | 39 | 3 | 1 | R | R | 6-1 | 195 | 6-18-74 | 1991 | Caracas, Venez. |
| Montilla, Julio | .260 | 49 | 150 | 22 | 39 | 10 | 0 | 0 | 12 | 9 | 18 | 3 | 1 | S | R | 5-10 | 170 | 6-9-73 | 1992 | Caracas, Venez. |
| Nunez, Sergio | .271 | 105 | 402 | 60 | 109 | 23 | 6 | 3 | 40 | 38 | 52 | 44 | 11 | R | R | 5-11 | 155 | 1-3-75 | 1992 | Santo Domingo, D.R. |
| Prieto, Alejandro | .284 | 119 | 447 | 65 | 127 | 19 | 6 | 1 | 40 | 31 | 66 | 26 | 15 | S | R | 5-11 | 150 | 6-19-76 | 1993 | Caracas, Venez. |
| Rackley, Keifer | .279 | 95 | 290 | 47 | 81 | 13 | 2 | 10 | 47 | 46 | 55 | 4 | 2 | L | R | 6-1 | 200 | 2-27-71 | 1993 | Birmingham, Ala. |
| Shirley, Al | .229 | 116 | 340 | 54 | 78 | 13 | 2 | 17 | 47 | 57 | 149 | 8 | 7 | R | R | 6-1 | 209 | 10-18-73 | 1991 | Danville, Va. |
| Smith, Matt | .248 | 125 | 451 | 48 | 112 | 17 | 2 | 5 | 59 | 42 | 110 | 3 | 4 | L | L | 6-4 | 215 | 6-2-76 | 1994 | Grants Pass, Ore. |
| Strickland, Chad | .061 | 11 | 33 | 2 | 2 | 1 | 0 | 0 | 3 | 3 | 5 | 1 | 0 | R | R | 6-1 | 185 | 3-16-72 | 1990 | Midwest City, Okla. |
| Teeters, Brian | .215 | 61 | 172 | 41 | 37 | 9 | 3 | 2 | 17 | 33 | 50 | 19 | 3 | L | L | 5-10 | 175 | 11-12-72 | 1992 | Bakersfield, Calif. |

**GAMES BY POSITION: C**—Brooks 105, Byington 1, Cedeno 1, Evans 8, Mendez 34, Smith 1, Strickland 10. **1B**— Byington 2, Evans 1, Mendez 28, Nunez 1, Smith 120. **2B**—Byington 4, Cedeno 36, Montilla 8, Nunez 103. **3B**—Byington 10, Cedeno 20, McNally 124, Montilla 5. **SS**—Byington 2, Cedeno 5, Montilla 31, Nunez 119. **OF**—Byington 90, Cedeno 4, Delaney 121, Evans 37, Rackley 96, Shirley 111, Teeters 49.

| PITCHING | W | L | ERA | G | GS | CG | SV | IP | H | R | ER | BB | SO | B | T | HT | WT | DOB | 1st Yr | Resides |
|---|---|---|---|---|---|---|---|---|---|---|---|---|---|---|---|---|---|---|---|---|
| Anderson, Eric | 12 | 5 | 3.69 | 27 | 26 | 1 | 0 | 158 | 161 | 81 | 65 | 44 | 69 | R | R | 6-1 | 190 | 10-20-74 | 1993 | Blue Springs, Mo. |
| Brixey, Dustin | 10 | 5 | 3.44 | 34 | 12 | 1 | 1 | 115 | 109 | 58 | 44 | 50 | 95 | R | R | 6-4 | 190 | 10-16-73 | 1993 | Jay, Okla. |
| Carter, Lance | 3 | 6 | 6.34 | 16 | 12 | 0 | 0 | 65 | 81 | 50 | 46 | 17 | 49 | R | R | 6-1 | 170 | 12-18-74 | 1994 | Bradenton, Fla. |
| Flury, Pat | 7 | 2 | 1.92 | 45 | 0 | 0 | 5 | 84 | 66 | 22 | 18 | 29 | 67 | R | R | 6-2 | 205 | 3-14-73 | 1993 | Sparks, Nev. |
| Gamboa, Javier | 3 | 1 | 3.15 | 6 | 6 | 0 | 0 | 34 | 36 | 12 | 12 | 2 | 24 | R | R | 6-1 | 185 | 3-17-74 | 1994 | Paso Robles, Calif. |
| Grieve, Tim | 4 | 1 | 1.31 | 22 | 0 | 0 | 4 | 34 | 28 | 9 | 5 | 13 | 30 | R | R | 6-0 | 180 | 8-17-71 | 1994 | Arlington, Texas |
| Grundy, Phil | 7 | 11 | 3.55 | 27 | 26 | 3 | 0 | 165 | 155 | 87 | 65 | 49 | 117 | R | R | 6-2 | 195 | 9-8-72 | 1993 | Somerset, Ky. |
| Hodges, Kevin | 2 | 4 | 5.35 | 8 | 8 | 0 | 0 | 39 | 45 | 30 | 23 | 18 | 15 | R | R | 6-4 | 200 | 6-24-73 | 1991 | Spring, Texas |
| Martin, Jeff | 0 | 1 | 4.87 | 5 | 0 | 0 | 0 | 20 | 24 | 11 | 11 | 5 | 12 | R | R | 6-1 | 199 | 1-25-74 | 1995 | Las Vegas, Nev. |
| Morones, Geno | 6 | 3 | 3.09 | 19 | 14 | 0 | 0 | 96 | 86 | 40 | 33 | 27 | 60 | R | R | 5-11 | 197 | 3-26-71 | 1991 | San Leandro, Calif. |

| PITCHING | W | L | ERA | G | GS | CG | SV | IP | H | R | ER | BB | SO | B | T | HT | WT | DOB | 1st Yr | Resides |
|---|---|---|---|---|---|---|---|---|---|---|---|---|---|---|---|---|---|---|---|---|
| Phillips, Marc | 2 | 0 | 5.26 | 31 | 0 | 0 | 0 | 50 | 59 | 33 | 29 | 19 | 19 | L | L | 6-2 | 195 | 5-30-72 | 1994 | Waynesboro, Va. |
| Pittsley, Jim | 0 | 1 | 11.00 | 2 | 2 | 0 | 0 | 9 | 13 | 12 | 11 | 5 | 10 | R | R | 6-7 | 215 | 4-3-74 | 1992 | Dubois, Pa. |
| Prihoda, Steve | 6 | 6 | 1.47 | 47 | 0 | 0 | 25 | 79 | 50 | 17 | 13 | 22 | 89 | R | L | 6-6 | 220 | 12-7-72 | 1995 | Weimer, Texas |
| Saier, Matt | 9 | 9 | 4.03 | 26 | 26 | 0 | 0 | 134 | 136 | 74 | 60 | 52 | 129 | R | R | 6-2 | 192 | 1-29-73 | 1995 | Gulf Breeze, Fla. |
| Telgheder, Jim | 8 | 3 | 2.42 | 31 | 2 | 0 | 2 | 74 | 60 | 24 | 20 | 14 | 50 | R | R | 6-3 | 210 | 3-22-71 | 1993 | Slate Hill, N.Y. |
| Wolff, Bryan | 1 | 2 | 3.61 | 42 | 0 | 0 | 4 | 62 | 49 | 35 | 25 | 38 | 56 | R | R | 6-1 | 195 | 3-16-72 | 1993 | St. Louis, Mo. |

# LANSING — Class A
## MIDWEST LEAGUE

| BATTING | AVG | G | AB | R | H | 2B | 3B | HR | RBI | BB | SO | SB | CS | B | T | HT | WT | DOB | 1st Yr | Resides |
|---|---|---|---|---|---|---|---|---|---|---|---|---|---|---|---|---|---|---|---|---|
| Amado, Jose | .349 | 57 | 212 | 39 | 74 | 18 | 1 | 5 | 47 | 17 | 17 | 8 | 4 | R | R | 6-1 | 194 | 1-1-75 | 1994 | San Cristobal, Venez. |
| 2-team (61 Wisconsin) | .318 | 118 | 444 | 82 | 141 | 31 | 1 | 10 | 83 | 37 | 37 | 14 | 9 | | | | | | | |
| Arrollado, Courtney | .256 | 17 | 39 | 5 | 10 | 1 | 0 | 0 | 6 | 7 | 13 | 2 | 1 | R | R | 6-1 | 190 | 9-5-74 | 1993 | San Diego, Calif. |
| Beltran, Carlos | .143 | 11 | 42 | 3 | 6 | 2 | 0 | 0 | 0 | 1 | 11 | 1 | 0 | S | R | 6-1 | 175 | 4-24-77 | 1995 | Manati, P.R. |
| Blosser, Doug | .205 | 36 | 117 | 14 | 24 | 5 | 0 | 5 | 18 | 15 | 38 | 2 | 0 | L | R | 6-3 | 215 | 10-1-76 | 1995 | Sarasota, Fla. |
| Cepeda, Jose | .289 | 135 | 558 | 87 | 161 | 29 | 3 | 3 | 81 | 38 | 44 | 10 | 3 | R | R | 6-0 | 185 | 8-1-74 | 1995 | Fajardo, P.R. |
| Coffee, Gary | .232 | 105 | 393 | 52 | 91 | 17 | 2 | 11 | 59 | 53 | 141 | 6 | 1 | R | R | 6-3 | 235 | 3-13-75 | 1994 | Atlanta, Ga. |
| Escandon, Emiliano | .272 | 107 | 372 | 51 | 101 | 18 | 5 | 4 | 52 | 46 | 47 | 8 | 3 | S | R | 5-10 | 170 | 11-6-74 | 1995 | Ontario, Calif. |
| Febles, Carlos | .295 | 102 | 363 | 84 | 107 | 23 | 5 | 5 | 43 | 66 | 64 | 30 | 14 | R | R | 5-11 | 165 | 5-24-76 | 1994 | La Romana, D.R. |
| Finnieston, Adam | .181 | 60 | 193 | 19 | 35 | 3 | 3 | 2 | 13 | 13 | 61 | 4 | 1 | R | R | 6-0 | 190 | 10-11-72 | 1995 | Miami, Fla. |
| Hallmark, Patrick | .280 | 118 | 453 | 68 | 127 | 23 | 5 | 1 | 53 | 34 | 80 | 33 | 9 | R | R | 6-0 | 170 | 12-31-73 | 1995 | Houston, Texas |
| Layne, Jason | .253 | 25 | 91 | 11 | 23 | 4 | 0 | 1 | 16 | 13 | 23 | 1 | 0 | L | R | 6-2 | 215 | 5-17-73 | 1996 | Tyler, Texas |
| Longueira, Tony | .190 | 45 | 153 | 14 | 29 | 2 | 1 | 1 | 15 | 14 | 23 | 4 | 3 | R | R | 6-0 | 170 | 9-24-74 | 1995 | Pembroke Pines, Fla. |
| Melito, Mark | .254 | 59 | 201 | 39 | 51 | 12 | 1 | 1 | 18 | 27 | 28 | 8 | 3 | R | R | 6-1 | 175 | 2-4-72 | 1995 | Glen Ridge, N.J. |
| Miranda, Tony | .287 | 39 | 136 | 28 | 39 | 6 | 1 | 2 | 23 | 17 | 24 | 3 | 0 | R | R | 5-10 | 175 | 5-23-73 | 1995 | Lynwood, Calif. |
| Montas, Ricardo | .292 | 8 | 24 | 1 | 7 | 0 | 0 | 0 | 2 | 4 | 0 | 0 | 0 | R | R | 6-1 | 160 | 3-9-77 | 1994 | Santo Domingo, D.R. |
| Murray, Doug | .143 | 18 | 35 | 2 | 5 | 0 | 0 | 0 | 4 | 1 | 11 | 0 | 0 | L | R | 6-3 | 215 | 10-9-74 | 1996 | Orland Park, Ill. |
| Pitts, Rick | .208 | 13 | 48 | 7 | 10 | 1 | 0 | 0 | 2 | 5 | 14 | 2 | 1 | R | R | 6-1 | 180 | 3-13-76 | 1994 | Seattle, Wash. |
| Quinn, Mark | .302 | 113 | 437 | 63 | 132 | 23 | 3 | 9 | 71 | 43 | 54 | 14 | 8 | R | R | 6-1 | 185 | 5-21-74 | 1995 | San Dimas, Calif. |
| Robles, Juan | .269 | 27 | 67 | 11 | 18 | 4 | 0 | 1 | 5 | 6 | 10 | 2 | 0 | R | R | 5-10 | 190 | 3-17-72 | 1994 | Hermosillo, Mexico |
| Rocha, Juan | .268 | 131 | 459 | 79 | 123 | 22 | 8 | 14 | 83 | 68 | 116 | 15 | 9 | R | R | 5-11 | 175 | 9-8-73 | 1995 | Santa Fe, Calif. |
| Schafer, Brett | .255 | 15 | 47 | 5 | 12 | 2 | 1 | 0 | 3 | 7 | 7 | 3 | 2 | R | R | 5-11 | 175 | 7-3-73 | 1995 | Malibu, Calif. |
| Treanor, Matt | .260 | 119 | 384 | 56 | 100 | 18 | 2 | 6 | 33 | 35 | 63 | 5 | 3 | R | R | 6-1 | 188 | 3-3-76 | 1994 | Anaheim, Calif. |

**GAMES BY POSITION: C**—Hallmark 13, Murray 15, Robles 24, Treanor 111. **1B**—Amado 3, Arrollado 2, Blosser 7, Cepeda 7, Coffee 100, Layne 25. **2B**—Arrollado 5, Escandon 43, Febles 96, Hallmark 1, Longueira 6, Melito 2, Montas 2. **3B**—Amado 39, Arrollado 3, Cepeda 88, Escandon 7, Hallmark 4, Longueira 4, Melito 1, Schafer 2. **SS**—Arrollado 4, Cepeda 30, Escandon 18, Febles 1, Longueira 34, Melito 55, Montas 6. **OF**—Amado 2, Arrollado 2, Beltran 11, Escandon 6, Finnieston 39, Hallmark 101, Longueira 3, Miranda 18, Pitts 12, Quinn 111, Rocha 127, Schafer 14, Treanor 2.

| PITCHING | W | L | ERA | G | GS | CG | SV | IP | H | R | ER | BB | SO | B | T | HT | WT | DOB | 1st Yr | Resides |
|---|---|---|---|---|---|---|---|---|---|---|---|---|---|---|---|---|---|---|---|---|---|
| Adam, Justin | 3 | 7 | 5.18 | 46 | 0 | 0 | 1 | 80 | 84 | 59 | 46 | 58 | 61 | R | R | 6-4 | 218 | 8-22-74 | 1992 | Windsor, Ontario |
| Bernal, Manuel | 2 | 4 | 4.55 | 34 | 6 | 0 | 2 | 95 | 123 | 55 | 48 | 16 | 41 | R | R | 6-2 | 163 | 4-29-74 | 1994 | Los Mochis, Mexico |
| Boring, Richard | 0 | 0 | 3.00 | 3 | 0 | 0 | 0 | 3 | 4 | 1 | 1 | 2 | 2 | R | R | 6-5 | 210 | 7-23-75 | 1996 | Nacogdoches, Texas |
| Grieve, Tim | 0 | 1 | 3.00 | 3 | 0 | 0 | 0 | 3 | 0 | 1 | 1 | 6 | 5 | R | R | 6-0 | 180 | 8-17-71 | 1994 | Arlington, Texas |
| Hodges, Kevin | 1 | 2 | 4.66 | 9 | 9 | 0 | 0 | 48 | 47 | 32 | 25 | 19 | 23 | R | R | 6-4 | 200 | 6-24-73 | 1991 | Spring, Texas |
| Kaysner, Brent | 2 | 3 | 5.08 | 38 | 0 | 0 | 0 | 44 | 38 | 34 | 25 | 57 | 39 | R | R | 6-6 | 235 | 4-23-74 | 1994 | Bothell, Wash. |
| Key, Scott | 1 | 5 | 5.40 | 42 | 0 | 0 | 5 | 62 | 51 | 45 | 37 | 46 | 60 | R | R | 5-10 | 162 | 10-4-76 | 1995 | Cantonment, Fla. |
| Matos, Luis | 1 | 1 | 6.35 | 8 | 0 | 0 | 0 | 17 | 23 | 13 | 12 | 9 | 10 | R | R | 6-2 | 185 | 9-18-74 | 1992 | Cabo Rojo, P.R. |
| Mull, Blaine | 15 | 8 | 3.25 | 28 | 28 | 1 | 0 | 175 | 186 | 91 | 63 | 40 | 114 | R | R | 6-4 | 186 | 8-14-76 | 1994 | Morganton, N.C. |
| Paredes, Carlos | 7 | 8 | 4.85 | 23 | 23 | 0 | 0 | 119 | 138 | 75 | 64 | 69 | 72 | R | R | 6-0 | 170 | 5-10-76 | 1995 | Sabana de la Mar, D.R. |
| Ritter, Jason | 0 | 0 | 9.53 | 13 | 0 | 0 | 0 | 17 | 35 | 24 | 18 | 10 | 8 | R | R | 6-2 | 185 | 7-16-74 | 1994 | Tulsa, Okla. |
| Robbins, Michael | 9 | 6 | 3.40 | 25 | 15 | 0 | 0 | 116 | 122 | 56 | 44 | 37 | 76 | L | L | 6-1 | 190 | 2-7-74 | 1995 | Oakland, Calif. |
| Sanders, Allen | 3 | 0 | 4.31 | 5 | 5 | 0 | 0 | 31 | 38 | 18 | 15 | 2 | 5 | R | R | 6-3 | 195 | 4-15-75 | 1995 | Deer Park, Texas |
| Sanders, Craig | 2 | 1 | 4.80 | 8 | 0 | 0 | 0 | 15 | 10 | 13 | 8 | 17 | 15 | S | R | 6-3 | 185 | 7-31-72 | 1995 | Lincoln, Neb. |
| Santiago, Jose | 7 | 6 | 2.57 | 54 | 0 | 0 | 19 | 70 | 78 | 34 | 22 | 21 | 55 | R | R | 6-3 | 200 | 11-5-74 | 1994 | Loiza, P.R. |
| Thorn, Todd | 11 | 5 | 3.11 | 27 | 27 | 2 | 0 | 171 | 161 | 70 | 59 | 34 | 107 | L | L | 6-1 | 175 | 11-4-76 | 1995 | Stratford, Ontario |
| Villarreal, Modesto | 0 | 5 | 6.21 | 15 | 5 | 0 | 0 | 42 | 54 | 37 | 29 | 12 | 29 | R | R | 6-3 | 195 | 10-29-75 | 1993 | Panama City, Panama |
| Wallace, Jeff | 4 | 9 | 5.30 | 30 | 21 | 0 | 0 | 122 | 140 | 79 | 72 | 66 | 84 | L | L | 6-2 | 237 | 4-12-76 | 1995 | Paris, Ohio |

# SPOKANE — Class A
## NORTHWEST LEAGUE

| BATTING | AVG | G | AB | R | H | 2B | 3B | HR | RBI | BB | SO | SB | CS | B | T | HT | WT | DOB | 1st Yr | Resides |
|---|---|---|---|---|---|---|---|---|---|---|---|---|---|---|---|---|---|---|---|---|
| Arrollado, Courtney | .213 | 22 | 47 | 2 | 10 | 1 | 0 | 0 | 2 | 1 | 13 | 2 | 0 | R | R | 6-1 | 190 | 9-5-74 | 1993 | San Diego, Calif. |
| Beltran, Carlos | .270 | 59 | 215 | 29 | 58 | 8 | 3 | 7 | 29 | 31 | 65 | 10 | 2 | S | R | 6-1 | 175 | 4-24-77 | 1995 | Manati, P.R. |
| Berger, Brandon | .307 | 71 | 283 | 46 | 87 | 12 | 1 | 13 | 58 | 31 | 64 | 17 | 5 | R | R | 6-0 | 205 | 2-21-75 | 1996 | Fort Mitchell, Ky. |
| Blosser, Doug | .255 | 16 | 47 | 10 | 12 | 4 | 1 | 3 | 8 | 6 | 14 | 0 | 0 | L | R | 6-3 | 215 | 10-1-76 | 1995 | Sarasota, Fla. |
| Didion, Kris | .219 | 61 | 201 | 30 | 44 | 7 | 4 | 6 | 32 | 26 | 60 | 7 | 2 | R | R | 5-11 | 198 | 12-23-75 | 1996 | Santa Ana, Calif. |
| Escamilla, Roman | .217 | 46 | 152 | 11 | 33 | 7 | 0 | 2 | 21 | 12 | 22 | 1 | 0 | R | R | 6-0 | 193 | 1-21-74 | 1996 | Corpus Christi, Texas |
| Giambi, Jeremy | .273 | 67 | 231 | 58 | 63 | 17 | 0 | 6 | 39 | 61 | 32 | 22 | 5 | L | L | 6-0 | 185 | 9-30-74 | 1996 | Covina, Calif. |
| Harp, Scott | .275 | 55 | 178 | 31 | 49 | 10 | 1 | 2 | 16 | 21 | 28 | 6 | 1 | R | R | 5-10 | 165 | 12-11-73 | 1996 | Dallas, Texas |
| Layne, Jason | .286 | 41 | 126 | 24 | 36 | 9 | 3 | 5 | 27 | 17 | 34 | 0 | 0 | L | R | 6-2 | 215 | 5-17-73 | 1996 | Tyler, Texas |
| Miranda, Tony | .170 | 21 | 53 | 11 | 9 | 3 | 0 | 2 | 8 | 9 | 13 | 2 | 1 | R | R | 5-10 | 175 | 5-23-73 | 1995 | Lynwood, Calif. |
| Moore, Kenderick | .260 | 52 | 204 | 37 | 53 | 6 | 1 | 2 | 25 | 23 | 29 | 19 | 3 | R | R | 5-10 | 175 | 5-17-73 | 1996 | Ardmore, Okla. |
| Pellow, Kit | .287 | 71 | 279 | 48 | 80 | 18 | 2 | 18 | 66 | 20 | 52 | 8 | 3 | R | R | 6-1 | 200 | 8-28-73 | 1996 | Olathe, Kan. |
| Pitts, Rick | .193 | 55 | 135 | 23 | 26 | 2 | 0 | 2 | 11 | 18 | 37 | 14 | 5 | R | R | 6-1 | 180 | 3-13-76 | 1994 | Seattle, Wash. |
| Robles, Juan | .275 | 53 | 178 | 27 | 49 | 6 | 1 | 2 | 20 | 17 | 37 | 4 | 1 | R | R | 5-10 | 190 | 3-17-72 | 1994 | Hermosillo, Mexico |
| Sees, Eric | .202 | 59 | 168 | 25 | 34 | 7 | 1 | 0 | 8 | 21 | 36 | 8 | 5 | R | R | 6-2 | 185 | 11-9-74 | 1996 | Bothell, Wash. |
| Taft, Brent | .190 | 42 | 126 | 21 | 24 | 6 | 1 | 1 | 8 | 14 | 27 | 3 | 0 | R | R | 5-7 | 170 | 11-9-73 | 1996 | Hueytown, Ala. |

**GAMES BY POSITION: C**—Didion 1, Escamilla 36, Pellow 4, Robles 48. **1B**—Arrollado 4, Berger 1, Blosser 8, Didion 1, Layne 26, Pellow 44. **2B**—Arrollado 5, Didion 3, Harp 21, Moore 51, Taft 6. **3B**—Arrollado 11, Didion 54, Escamilla 3, Harp 1, Moore 1, Pellow 10, Sees 8, Taft 2. **SS**—Pitts 1, Sees 52, Taft 37. **OF**—Beltran 52, Berger 68, Giambi 58, Harp 18, Miranda 1, Pellow 12, Pitts 43, Robles 1.

| PITCHING | W | L | ERA | G | GS | CG | SV | IP | H | R | ER | BB | SO | B | T | HT | WT | DOB | 1st Yr | Resides |
|---|---|---|---|---|---|---|---|---|---|---|---|---|---|---|---|---|---|---|---|---|
| Aguilar, Alonzo | 2 | 2 | 4.05 | 15 | 0 | 0 | 1 | 20 | 20 | 14 | 9 | 11 | 22 | R | R | 6-0 | 185 | 12-15-74 | 1995 | Los Angeles, Calif. |
| Baird, Brandon | 1 | 1 | 4.76 | 5 | 1 | 0 | 0 | 11 | 10 | 8 | 6 | 8 | 13 | L | L | 5-11 | 175 | 9-18-73 | 1996 | Enid, Okla. |
| Brewer, Ryan | 3 | 2 | 3.35 | 17 | 2 | 0 | 5 | 43 | 41 | 20 | 16 | 16 | 39 | L | R | 6-2 | 180 | 10-31-73 | 1996 | Denton, Texas |
| Burton, Jamie | 0 | 1 | 5.40 | 11 | 0 | 0 | 0 | 13 | 11 | 11 | 8 | 13 | 12 | R | L | 6-5 | 198 | 5-28-75 | 1995 | Central Point, Ore. |
| Calero, Enrique | 4 | 2 | 2.52 | 17 | 11 | 0 | 1 | 75 | 77 | 34 | 21 | 18 | 61 | R | R | 6-2 | 175 | 1-9-75 | 1996 | Rio Piedras, P.R. |
| Carcamo, Kevin | 0 | 0 | 6.33 | 10 | 0 | 0 | 0 | 21 | 31 | 19 | 15 | 7 | 13 | R | R | 5-11 | 185 | 10-27-75 | 1993 | Panama City, Panama |
| Chapman, Jake | 7 | 1 | 2.37 | 19 | 7 | 0 | 1 | 68 | 44 | 19 | 18 | 20 | 71 | R | L | 6-1 | 180 | 1-11-74 | 1996 | Rensselaer, Ind. |
| Hueston, Steve | 3 | 2 | 3.08 | 13 | 13 | 0 | 0 | 64 | 54 | 27 | 22 | 31 | 60 | R | R | 6-0 | 195 | 9-25-73 | 1996 | Pacifica, Calif. |
| Lineweaver, Aaron | 3 | 4 | 7.53 | 21 | 5 | 0 | 1 | 49 | 62 | 43 | 41 | 23 | 34 | R | R | 6-1 | 200 | 7-26-73 | 1996 | Denton, Texas |
| Mullen, Scott | 5 | 6 | 3.92 | 15 | 15 | 0 | 0 | 80 | 78 | 45 | 35 | 29 | 78 | R | L | 6-2 | 185 | 1-17-75 | 1996 | Beuafort, S.C. |
| Quigley, Don | 0 | 1 | 6.26 | 19 | 0 | 0 | 1 | 27 | 41 | 24 | 19 | 18 | 18 | R | R | 6-0 | 185 | 11-17-74 | 1996 | Fremont, Calif. |
| Rodriguez, Chad | 0 | 2 | 5.23 | 15 | 0 | 0 | 3 | 21 | 22 | 16 | 12 | 8 | 24 | R | R | 6-2 | 210 | 10-16-73 | 1996 | Topeka, Kan. |
| Sanders, Allen | 5 | 2 | 4.53 | 13 | 5 | 0 | 0 | 44 | 49 | 25 | 22 | 9 | 19 | R | R | 6-3 | 195 | 4-15-75 | 1996 | Deer Park, Texas |
| Sanders, Craig | 0 | 1 | 10.32 | 6 | 0 | 0 | 1 | 11 | 14 | 16 | 13 | 15 | 5 | S | R | 6-4 | 225 | 7-31-72 | 1995 | Lincoln, Neb. |
| Simontacchi, Jason | 2 | 5 | 5.17 | 14 | 6 | 0 | 2 | 47 | 59 | 37 | 27 | 15 | 43 | R | R | 6-2 | 185 | 11-13-73 | 1996 | Sunnyvale, Calif. |
| Stein, Ethan | 0 | 3 | 6.34 | 9 | 8 | 0 | 0 | 38 | 48 | 27 | 27 | 12 | 20 | R | R | 6-6 | 210 | 11-11-74 | 1996 | Cary, N.C. |
| Villarreal, Modesto | 2 | 4 | 5.74 | 19 | 3 | 0 | 3 | 47 | 57 | 33 | 30 | 11 | 35 | R | R | 6-3 | 195 | 10-29-75 | 1993 | Panama City, Panama |

## FORT MYERS — Rookie

### GULF COAST LEAGUE

| BATTING | AVG | G | AB | R | H | 2B | 3B | HR | RBI | BB | SO | SB | CS | B | T | HT | WT | DOB | 1st Yr | Resides |
|---|---|---|---|---|---|---|---|---|---|---|---|---|---|---|---|---|---|---|---|---|
| Bautista, Francisco | .292 | 29 | 89 | 11 | 26 | 3 | 0 | 0 | 8 | 8 | 24 | 3 | 3 | R | R | 6-1 | 175 | 4-22-76 | 1994 | El Seybo, D.R. |
| Benes, Richard | .147 | 29 | 68 | 6 | 10 | 2 | 0 | 0 | 2 | 3 | 16 | 1 | 2 | S | R | 5-8 | 155 | 2-20-78 | 1996 | Bronx, N.Y. |
| Blosser, Doug | .216 | 12 | 37 | 4 | 8 | 0 | 0 | 0 | 4 | 4 | 10 | 0 | 0 | L | R | 6-3 | 215 | 10-1-76 | 1995 | Sarasota, Fla. |
| Brambilla, Mike | .271 | 49 | 166 | 21 | 45 | 13 | 1 | 5 | 25 | 9 | 32 | 0 | 0 | R | R | 6-3 | 210 | 5-7-76 | 1996 | Brea, Calif. |
| Bronson, Ben | .309 | 27 | 94 | 19 | 29 | 8 | 1 | 0 | 8 | 16 | 16 | 9 | 3 | L | R | 5-10 | 175 | 9-9-72 | 1996 | Jasper, Texas |
| Brown, Dermal | .050 | 7 | 20 | 1 | 1 | 1 | 0 | 0 | 1 | 0 | 6 | 0 | 2 | L | R | 6-1 | 210 | 3-27-78 | 1996 | Newburgh, N.Y. |
| Dasher, Melvin | .269 | 17 | 52 | 10 | 14 | 3 | 1 | 1 | 6 | 5 | 14 | 1 | 0 | R | R | 6-2 | 195 | 9-9-76 | 1995 | Palatka, Fla. |
| Filardi, Wladimir | .179 | 21 | 39 | 3 | 7 | 2 | 0 | 1 | 5 | 2 | 15 | 0 | 1 | R | R | 6-1 | 170 | 6-27-78 | 1996 | Caracas, Venez. |
| Herrera, Pedro | .253 | 31 | 99 | 8 | 25 | 4 | 0 | 0 | 10 | 3 | 21 | 1 | 2 | R | R | 6-1 | 169 | 5-24-79 | 1996 | Santo Domingo, D.R. |
| Hill, Jeremy | .178 | 31 | 90 | 4 | 16 | 6 | 0 | 0 | 4 | 12 | 17 | 0 | 0 | R | R | 6-0 | 190 | 8-8-77 | 1996 | Dallas, Texas |
| Lebron, Juan | .288 | 58 | 215 | 19 | 62 | 9 | 2 | 3 | 30 | 6 | 34 | 1 | 2 | R | R | 6-4 | 195 | 6-7-77 | 1995 | Arroyo, P.R. |
| Ligons, Merrell | .185 | 48 | 130 | 18 | 24 | 4 | 1 | 0 | 5 | 15 | 24 | 2 | 1 | S | R | 5-10 | 165 | 6-22-77 | 1996 | Culver City, Calif. |
| Medrano, Steve | .273 | 46 | 154 | 24 | 42 | 10 | 0 | 1 | 11 | 19 | 21 | 3 | 1 | S | R | 6-0 | 160 | 10-8-77 | 1996 | La Puente, Calif. |
| Montas, Richard | .264 | 50 | 182 | 25 | 48 | 6 | 1 | 2 | 22 | 20 | 31 | 5 | 1 | R | R | 6-1 | 160 | 3-9-77 | 1994 | Santo Domingo, D.R. |
| Radcliff, Vic | .309 | 48 | 165 | 24 | 51 | 11 | 2 | 3 | 20 | 15 | 34 | 1 | 1 | R | R | 5-10 | 180 | 9-23-76 | 1995 | Beech Island, S.C. |
| Ramirez, Juan | .231 | 34 | 91 | 10 | 21 | 4 | 0 | 1 | 8 | 4 | 22 | 0 | 0 | R | R | 6-3 | 190 | 7-14-77 | 1995 | La Vega, D.R. |
| Stafford, Kimani | .051 | 21 | 39 | 5 | 2 | 0 | 0 | 0 | 3 | 8 | 16 | 1 | 1 | R | R | 5-11 | 170 | 6-17-76 | 1995 | Richmond, Calif. |
| Taveras, Jose | .191 | 13 | 47 | 3 | 9 | 2 | 0 | 0 | 4 | 1 | 7 | 0 | 2 | R | R | 6-0 | 160 | 12-17-76 | 1994 | Nagua, D.R. |
| Tillero, Jackson | .228 | 40 | 127 | 12 | 29 | 4 | 0 | 1 | 12 | 10 | 18 | 1 | 0 | R | R | 6-0 | 165 | 4-26-78 | 1995 | Petare, Venez. |

**GAMES BY POSITION: C**—Brambilla 5, Herrera 30, Hill 30. **1B**—Blosser 4, Brambilla 28, Montas 3, Ramirez 33. **2B**—Benes 25, Ligons 29, Montas 11, Stafford 3. **3B**—Montas 37, Radcliff 27, Ramirez 1. **SS**—Benes 1, Ligons 16, Medrano 46, Montas 2. **OF**—Bautista 23, Bronson 25, Brown 1, Dasher 14, Filardi 18, Lebron 47, Ligons 1, Radcliff 16, Stafford 14, Taveras 11, Tillero 34.

| PITCHING | W | L | ERA | G | GS | CG | SV | IP | H | R | ER | BB | SO | B | T | HT | WT | DOB | 1st Yr | Resides |
|---|---|---|---|---|---|---|---|---|---|---|---|---|---|---|---|---|---|---|---|---|
| Boring, Richard | 1 | 1 | 1.95 | 15 | 0 | 0 | 4 | 28 | 21 | 10 | 6 | 5 | 10 | R | R | 6-5 | 210 | 7-23-75 | 1996 | Nacogdoches, Texas |
| Cantu, Alvin | 4 | 2 | 3.70 | 9 | 9 | 0 | 0 | 49 | 54 | 24 | 20 | 12 | 42 | L | L | 6-1 | 190 | 9-23-76 | 1996 | Lamesa, Texas |
| Carcamo, Kevin | 2 | 0 | 2.55 | 9 | 0 | 0 | 2 | 25 | 15 | 9 | 7 | 5 | 22 | R | R | 5-11 | 185 | 10-27-75 | 1993 | Panama City, Panama |
| Durbin, Chad | 3 | 2 | 4.26 | 11 | 8 | 1 | 0 | 44 | 34 | 22 | 21 | 25 | 43 | R | R | 6-2 | 177 | 12-3-77 | 1996 | Baton Rouge, La. |
| Gonzalez, Edwin | 5 | 3 | 3.75 | 12 | 8 | 1 | 1 | 58 | 60 | 32 | 24 | 14 | 39 | R | R | 5-11 | 184 | 8-13-77 | 1995 | Santo Domingo, D.R. |
| Grieve, Tim | 1 | 0 | 0.00 | 2 | 0 | 0 | 0 | 3 | 1 | 1 | 0 | 1 | 2 | R | R | 6-0 | 180 | 8-17-71 | 1994 | Arlington, Texas |
| Kauffman, George | 0 | 0 | 0.00 | 1 | 0 | 0 | 0 | 1 | 1 | 0 | 0 | 0 | 1 | R | R | 6-4 | 215 | 2-25-75 | 1996 | Kansas City, Mo. |
| Kyzar, Cory | 0 | 2 | 8.27 | 8 | 0 | 2 | 0 | 16 | 21 | 16 | 15 | 10 | 19 | R | R | 6-1 | 190 | 9-4-77 | 1996 | Ellisville, Miss. |
| McDaniel, Denton | 1 | 1 | 3.72 | 7 | 5 | 0 | 0 | 19 | 15 | 11 | 8 | 10 | 25 | L | L | 6-3 | 200 | 8-12-76 | 1996 | Austin, Texas |
| Meady, Todd | 2 | 5 | 3.39 | 11 | 10 | 1 | 0 | 58 | 58 | 31 | 22 | 16 | 47 | R | R | 6-4 | 216 | 9-13-76 | 1995 | Middlebury, Conn. |
| Moreno, Orber | 5 | 1 | 1.36 | 12 | 7 | 0 | 1 | 46 | 37 | 15 | 7 | 10 | 50 | R | R | 6-1 | 140 | 4-27-77 | 1996 | Los Autos, Venez. |
| Naranjo, Ivan | 1 | 0 | 4.40 | 15 | 0 | 0 | 1 | 29 | 33 | 16 | 14 | 9 | 18 | S | L | 6-1 | 170 | 11-20-77 | 1996 | Caracas, Venez. |
| Penny, Tony | 3 | 1 | 2.59 | 14 | 0 | 0 | 2 | 24 | 22 | 8 | 7 | 4 | 20 | R | R | 6-4 | 168 | 3-23-76 | 1995 | Newberry, S.C. |
| Roeder, Jason | 0 | 1 | 9.00 | 3 | 0 | 0 | 0 | 4 | 6 | 4 | 4 | 3 | 3 | R | R | 6-2 | 210 | 2-26-74 | 1996 | Seymour, Ind. |
| Roup, Randall | 0 | 0 | 12.46 | 8 | 0 | 0 | 0 | 9 | 15 | 13 | 12 | 7 | 8 | S | R | 6-3 | 190 | 12-29-76 | 1996 | Houston, Texas |
| Shannon, Bobby | 0 | 0 | 0.00 | 2 | 0 | 0 | 0 | 2 | 2 | 0 | 0 | 0 | 0 | R | L | 5-11 | 185 | 9-21-77 | 1995 | Shippensburg, Pa. |
| Thurman, Corey | 1 | 6 | 6.08 | 11 | 11 | 0 | 0 | 47 | 53 | 32 | 32 | 28 | 52 | R | R | 6-2 | 215 | 11-5-78 | 1996 | Wake Village, Texas |
| Torres, Michael | 2 | 3 | 6.48 | 18 | 0 | 0 | 2 | 33 | 47 | 35 | 24 | 6 | 26 | R | R | 5-11 | 180 | 1-11-78 | 1996 | Fontana, Calif. |

# LOS ANGELES DODGERS

**Managers:** Tom Lasorda, Bill Russell.  **1996 Record:** 90-72, .556 (2nd, NL West).

| BATTING | AVG | G | AB | R | H | 2B | 3B | HR | RBI | BB | SO | SB | CS | B | T | HT | WT | DOB | 1st Yr | Resides |
|---|---|---|---|---|---|---|---|---|---|---|---|---|---|---|---|---|---|---|---|---|
| Ashley, Billy | .200 | 71 | 110 | 18 | 22 | 2 | 1 | 9 | 25 | 21 | 44 | 0 | 0 | R | R | 6-7 | 230 | 7-11-70 | 1988 | Belleville, Mich. |
| Blowers, Mike | .265 | 92 | 317 | 31 | 84 | 19 | 2 | 6 | 38 | 37 | 77 | 0 | 0 | R | R | 6-2 | 210 | 4-24-65 | 1986 | Tacoma, Wash. |
| Busch, Mike | .217 | 38 | 83 | 8 | 18 | 4 | 0 | 4 | 17 | 5 | 33 | 0 | 0 | R | R | 6-5 | 241 | 7-7-68 | 1990 | Donahue, Iowa |
| Butler, Brett | .267 | 34 | 131 | 22 | 35 | 1 | 1 | 0 | 8 | 9 | 22 | 8 | 3 | L | L | 5-10 | 160 | 6-15-57 | 1979 | Atlanta, Ga. |
| Castro, Juan | .197 | 70 | 132 | 16 | 26 | 5 | 3 | 0 | 5 | 10 | 27 | 1 | 0 | R | R | 5-10 | 163 | 6-20-72 | 1991 | Los Mochis, Mexico |
| Cedeno, Roger | .246 | 86 | 211 | 26 | 52 | 11 | 1 | 2 | 18 | 24 | 47 | 5 | 1 | S | R | 6-1 | 165 | 8-16-74 | 1992 | Carabobo, Venez. |
| Clark, Dave | .200 | 15 | 15 | 0 | 3 | 0 | 0 | 1 | 3 | 2 | 0 | 0 | | L | R | 6-2 | 210 | 9-3-62 | 1983 | Tupelo, Miss. |
| 2-team (92 Pittsburgh) | .270 | 107 | 226 | 28 | 61 | 12 | 2 | 8 | 36 | 34 | 53 | 2 | 1 | | | | | | | |
| Curtis, Chad | .212 | 43 | 104 | 20 | 22 | 5 | 0 | 2 | 9 | 17 | 15 | 2 | 1 | R | R | 5-10 | 175 | 11-6-68 | 1989 | Middleville, Mich. |
| DeShields, Delino | .224 | 154 | 581 | 75 | 130 | 12 | 8 | 5 | 41 | 53 | 124 | 48 | 11 | L | R | 6-1 | 175 | 1-15-69 | 1987 | West Palm Beach, Fla. |
| Fonville, Chad | .204 | 103 | 201 | 34 | 41 | 4 | 1 | 0 | 13 | 17 | 31 | 7 | 2 | S | R | 5-7 | 155 | 3-5-71 | 1992 | Midway Park, N.C. |
| Gagne, Greg | .255 | 128 | 428 | 48 | 109 | 13 | 2 | 10 | 55 | 50 | 93 | 4 | 2 | R | R | 5-11 | 180 | 11-12-61 | 1979 | Rehoboth, Mass. |
| Garcia, Karim | .000 | 1 | 1 | 0 | 0 | 0 | 0 | 0 | 0 | 0 | 1 | 0 | 0 | L | L | 6-0 | 172 | 10-29-75 | 1993 | Obregon, Mexico |
| Guerrero, Wilton | .000 | 5 | 2 | 1 | 0 | 0 | 0 | 0 | 0 | 0 | 2 | 0 | 0 | R | R | 5-11 | 145 | 10-24-74 | 1992 | Nizao, D.R. |
| Hansen, Dave | .221 | 80 | 104 | 7 | 23 | 1 | 0 | 0 | 6 | 11 | 22 | 0 | 0 | L | R | 6-0 | 195 | 11-24-68 | 1986 | Laguna Hills, Calif. |
| Hernandez, Carlos | .286 | 13 | 14 | 1 | 4 | 0 | 0 | 0 | 2 | 2 | 0 | 0 | 0 | R | R | 5-11 | 185 | 5-24-67 | 1985 | Caracas,Venez. |
| Hollandsworth, Todd | .291 | 149 | 478 | 64 | 139 | 26 | 4 | 12 | 59 | 41 | 93 | 21 | 6 | L | L | 6-2 | 193 | 4-20-73 | 1991 | San Ramon, Calif. |
| Karros, Eric | .260 | 154 | 608 | 84 | 158 | 29 | 1 | 34 | 111 | 53 | 121 | 8 | 0 | R | R | 6-4 | 222 | 11-4-67 | 1988 | Manhattan Beach, Calif. |
| Kirby, Wayne | .271 | 65 | 188 | 23 | 51 | 10 | 1 | 1 | 11 | 17 | 17 | 4 | 2 | L | R | 5-10 | 185 | 1-22-64 | 1983 | Yorktown, Va. |
| Marrero, Oreste | .375 | 10 | 8 | 2 | 3 | 1 | 0 | 0 | 1 | 1 | 3 | 0 | 0 | L | L | 6-0 | 205 | 10-31-69 | 1987 | Bayamon, P.R. |
| Mondesi, Raul | .297 | 157 | 634 | 98 | 188 | 40 | 7 | 24 | 88 | 32 | 122 | 14 | 7 | R | R | 5-11 | 210 | 3-12-71 | 1988 | New York, N.Y. |
| Parker, Rick | .286 | 16 | 14 | 2 | 4 | 1 | 0 | 0 | 1 | 0 | 2 | 1 | 0 | R | R | 6-0 | 185 | 3-20-63 | 1985 | Independence, Mo. |
| Piazza, Mike | .336 | 148 | 547 | 87 | 184 | 16 | 0 | 36 | 105 | 81 | 93 | 0 | 3 | R | R | 6-3 | 200 | 9-4-68 | 1989 | Manhattan Beach, Calif. |
| Prince, Tom | .297 | 40 | 64 | 6 | 19 | 6 | 0 | 1 | 11 | 6 | 15 | 0 | 0 | R | R | 5-11 | 185 | 8-13-64 | 1984 | Bradenton, Fla. |
| Thompson, Milt | .118 | 48 | 51 | 2 | 6 | 1 | 0 | 0 | 1 | 6 | 10 | 1 | 1 | L | R | 5-11 | 170 | 1-5-59 | 1979 | Ballwin, Mo. |
| Wallach, Tim | .228 | 45 | 162 | 14 | 37 | 3 | 1 | 4 | 22 | 12 | 32 | 0 | 1 | R | R | 6-3 | 200 | 9-14-57 | 1979 | Tustin, Calif. |

| PITCHING | W | L | ERA | G | GS | CG | SV | IP | H | R | ER | BB | SO | B | T | HT | WT | DOB | 1st Yr | Resides |
|---|---|---|---|---|---|---|---|---|---|---|---|---|---|---|---|---|---|---|---|---|
| Astacio, Pedro | 9 | 8 | 3.44 | 35 | 32 | 0 | 0 | 212 | 207 | 86 | 81 | 67 | 130 | R | R | 6-2 | 195 | 11-28-69 | 1988 | Miami, Fla. |
| Bruske, Jim | 0 | 0 | 5.68 | 11 | 0 | 0 | 0 | 13 | 17 | 8 | 8 | 3 | 12 | R | R | 6-1 | 185 | 10-7-64 | 1986 | Palmdale, Calif. |
| Candiotti, Tom | 9 | 11 | 4.49 | 28 | 27 | 1 | 0 | 152 | 172 | 91 | 76 | 43 | 79 | R | R | 6-2 | 220 | 8-31-57 | 1979 | Concord, Calif. |
| Cummings, John | 0 | 1 | 6.75 | 4 | 0 | 0 | 0 | 5 | 12 | 7 | 4 | 2 | 5 | L | L | 6-3 | 200 | 5-10-69 | 1990 | Laguna Niguel, Calif. |
| Dreifort, Darren | 1 | 4 | 4.94 | 19 | 0 | 0 | 0 | 24 | 23 | 13 | 13 | 12 | 24 | R | R | 6-2 | 205 | 5-18-72 | 1994 | Wichita, Kan. |
| Eischen, Joey | 0 | 1 | 4.78 | 28 | 0 | 0 | 0 | 43 | 48 | 25 | 23 | 20 | 36 | L | L | 6-1 | 190 | 5-25-70 | 1989 | West Covina, Calif. |
| Guthrie, Mark | 2 | 3 | 3.22 | 66 | 0 | 0 | 1 | 73 | 65 | 21 | 18 | 22 | 56 | L | L | 6-4 | 205 | 9-22-65 | 1987 | Bradenton, Fla. |
| Hall, Darren | 0 | 2 | 6.00 | 9 | 0 | 0 | 0 | 12 | 13 | 9 | 8 | 5 | 12 | R | R | 6-3 | 205 | 7-14-64 | 1986 | Irving, Texas |
| Martinez, Ramon | 15 | 6 | 3.42 | 28 | 27 | 2 | 0 | 169 | 153 | 76 | 64 | 86 | 134 | S | R | 6-4 | 173 | 3-22-68 | 1985 | Santo Domingo, D.R. |
| Nomo, Hideo | 16 | 11 | 3.19 | 33 | 33 | 3 | 0 | 228 | 180 | 93 | 81 | 85 | 234 | R | R | 6-2 | 210 | 8-31-68 | 1995 | Kobe, Japan |
| Osuna, Antonio | 9 | 6 | 3.00 | 73 | 0 | 0 | 4 | 84 | 65 | 33 | 28 | 32 | 85 | R | R | 5-11 | 160 | 4-12-73 | 1991 | Sinaloa, Mexico |
| Park, Chan Ho | 5 | 5 | 3.64 | 48 | 10 | 0 | 0 | 109 | 82 | 48 | 44 | 71 | 119 | R | R | 6-2 | 185 | 6-30-73 | 1994 | Glendale, Calif. |
| Radinsky, Scott | 5 | 1 | 2.41 | 58 | 0 | 0 | 1 | 52 | 52 | 19 | 14 | 17 | 48 | L | L | 6-3 | 204 | 3-3-68 | 1986 | Simi Valley, Calif. |
| Valdes, Ismael | 15 | 7 | 3.32 | 33 | 33 | 0 | 0 | 225 | 219 | 94 | 83 | 54 | 173 | R | R | 6-3 | 207 | 8-21-73 | 1991 | Victoria, Mexico |
| Worrell, Todd | 4 | 6 | 3.03 | 72 | 0 | 0 | 44 | 65 | 70 | 29 | 22 | 15 | 66 | R | R | 6-5 | 200 | 9-28-59 | 1982 | St. Louis, Mo. |

## FIELDING

| Catcher | PCT | G | PO | A | E | DP | PB |
|---|---|---|---|---|---|---|---|
| Hernandez | 1.000 | 9 | 31 | 1 | 0 | 0 | 0 |
| Piazza | .992 | 146 | 1056 | 70 | 9 | 6 | 12 |
| Prince | .994 | 35 | 161 | 11 | 1 | 1 | 3 |

| First Base | PCT | G | PO | A | E | DP |
|---|---|---|---|---|---|---|
| Blowers | 1.000 | 6 | 20 | 2 | 0 | 0 |
| Busch | 1.000 | 1 | 2 | 0 | 0 | 0 |
| Hansen | 1.000 | 8 | 54 | 4 | 0 | 3 |
| Karros | .990 | 154 | 1314 | 121 | 15 | 133 |
| Marrero | 1.000 | 1 | 1 | 0 | 0 | 0 |

| Second Base | PCT | G | PO | A | E | DP |
|---|---|---|---|---|---|---|
| Castro | 1.000 | 9 | 7 | 12 | 0 | 1 |
| DeShields | .975 | 154 | 274 | 400 | 17 | 79 |
| Fonville | .982 | 23 | 20 | 34 | 1 | 8 |

| Third Base | PCT | G | PO | A | E | DP |
|---|---|---|---|---|---|---|
| Blowers | .951 | 90 | 56 | 120 | 9 | 9 |
| Busch | .932 | 23 | 16 | 25 | 3 | 1 |
| Castro | .889 | 23 | 5 | 3 | 1 | 0 |
| Fonville | 1.000 | 2 | 2 | 2 | 0 | 0 |

| | PCT | G | PO | A | E | DP |
|---|---|---|---|---|---|---|
| Hansen | .962 | 19 | 6 | 19 | 1 | 1 |
| Wallach | .971 | 45 | 38 | 62 | 3 | 3 |
| **Shortstop** | **PCT** | **G** | **PO** | **A** | **E** | **DP** |
| Blowers | .000 | 1 | 0 | 0 | 0 | 0 |
| Castro | .982 | 30 | 40 | 69 | 2 | 21 |
| Fonville | .936 | 20 | 11 | 33 | 3 | 5 |
| Gagne | .965 | 127 | 183 | 404 | 21 | 87 |
| **Outfield** | **PCT** | **G** | **PO** | **A** | **E** | **DP** |
| Ashley | .952 | 38 | 38 | 2 | 2 | 1 |
| Butler | .987 | 34 | 74 | 1 | 1 | 0 |
| Castro | 1.000 | 1 | 2 | 0 | 0 | 0 |
| Cedeno | .983 | 71 | 117 | 2 | 2 | 0 |
| Clark | .000 | 1 | 0 | 0 | 0 | 0 |
| Curtis | .985 | 40 | 62 | 2 | 1 | 1 |
| Fonville | .964 | 35 | 51 | 2 | 2 | 1 |
| Hollandsworth | .978 | 142 | 217 | 7 | 5 | 1 |
| Kirby | .969 | 53 | 93 | 2 | 3 | 0 |
| Mondesi | .967 | 157 | 337 | 11 | 12 | 4 |
| Parker | 1.000 | 4 | 1 | 0 | 0 | 0 |
| Thompson | 1.000 | 17 | 13 | 0 | 0 | 0 |

Ramon Martinez

Dodgers outfielder Raul Mondesi hit .297 with 24 homers

Dodgers minor league Player of the Year Paul Konerko

GEORGE GOJKOVICH

LEE SCHMID

## FARM SYSTEM

**Director of Minor League Operations:** Charlie Blaney

| Class | Farm Team | League | W | L | Pct. | Finish* | Manager | First Yr |
|---|---|---|---|---|---|---|---|---|
| AAA | Albuquerque (N.M.) Dukes | Pacific Coast | 67 | 76 | .469 | 9th (10) | Phil Regan | 1963 |
| AA | San Antonio (Texas) Missions | Texas | 69 | 70 | .496 | 6th (8) | John Shelby | 1977 |
| #A | San Bernardino (Calif.) Spirit | California | 70 | 70 | .500 | 7th (10) | Del Crandall | 1995 |
| #A | Vero Beach (Fla.) Dodgers | Florida State | 65 | 66 | .496 | 8th (14) | Jon Debus | 1980 |
| A | Savannah (Ga.) Sand Gnats | South Atlantic | 72 | 69 | .511 | +7th (14) | John Shoemaker | 1996 |
| A | Yakima (Wash.) Bears | Northwest | 40 | 36 | .526 | +3rd (8) | Joe Vavra | 1988 |
| #R | Great Falls (Mont.) Dodgers | Pioneer | 33 | 39 | .458 | 6th (8) | John Shoemaker | 1984 |

*Finish in overall standings (No. of teams in league)  #Advanced level  +Won league championship

## ORGANIZATION LEADERS

### MAJOR LEAGUERS

**BATTING**
| | | |
|---|---|---|
| *AVG | Mike Piazza | .336 |
| R | Raul Mondesi | 98 |
| H | Raul Mondesi | 188 |
| TB | Raul Mondesi | 314 |
| 2B | Raul Mondesi | 40 |
| 3B | Delino DeShields | 8 |
| HR | Mike Piazza | 36 |
| RBI | Eric Karros | 111 |
| BB | Mike Piazza | 81 |
| SO | Delino DeShields | 124 |
| SB | Delino DeShields | 48 |

**PITCHING**
| | | |
|---|---|---|
| W | Hideo Nomo | 16 |
| L | Two tied at | 11 |
| #ERA | Antonio Osuna | 3.00 |
| G | Antonio Osuna | 73 |
| CG | Hideo Nomo | 3 |
| SV | Todd Worrell | 44 |
| IP | Hideo Nomo | 228 |
| BB | Ramon Martinez | 86 |
| SO | Hideo Nomo | 234 |

**Hideo Nomo.** 16 wins

LARRY GOREN

### MINOR LEAGUERS

**BATTING**
| | | |
|---|---|---|
| *AVG | Wilton Guerrero, Albuquerque | .344 |
| R | Eric Stuckenschneider, Savannah | 111 |
| H | Two tied at | 147 |
| TB | Eddie Davis, San Bernardino | 265 |
| 2B | Willie Romero, S.A./Albuquerque | 36 |
| 3B | Two tied at | 12 |
| HR | Paul Konerko, S.A./Albuquerque | 30 |
| RBI | Adrian Beltre, Savannah/San Bern. | 99 |
| BB | Eric Stuckenschneider, Savannah | 111 |
| SO | Eddie Davis, San Bernardino | 150 |
| SB | Kevin Gibbs, Vero Beach | 60 |

**PITCHING**
| | | |
|---|---|---|
| W | Billy Neal, Vero Beach | 16 |
| L | Mike Iglesias, Sav./V.B./San Bern. | 15 |
| #ERA | Dan Ricabal, Savannah/Vero Beach | 1.90 |
| G | Rich Linares, San Bernardino | 60 |
| CG | Four tied at | 2 |
| SV | Rich Linares, San Bernardino | 33 |
| IP | Gary Rath, Albuquerque | 180 |
| BB | Dan Camacho, V.B./San Bern./S.A. | 98 |
| SO | Dennis Reyes, San Bernardino | 176 |

*Minimum 250 At-Bats  #Minimum 75 Innings

## TOP 10 PROSPECTS

How the Dodgers Top 10 prospects, as judged by Baseball America prior to the 1996 season, fared in 1996:

**Karim Garcia**

LARRY GOREN

| Player, Pos. | Club (Class—League) | AVG | AB | R | H | 2B | 3B | HR | RBI | SB |
|---|---|---|---|---|---|---|---|---|---|---|
| 1. Karim Garcia, of | San Antonio (AA—Texas) | .248 | 129 | 21 | 32 | 6 | 1 | 5 | 22 | 1 |
| | Albuquerque (AAA—Pacific Coast) | .297 | 327 | 54 | 97 | 17 | 10 | 13 | 58 | 6 |
| | Los Angeles | .000 | 1 | 0 | 0 | 0 | 0 | 0 | 0 | 0 |
| 3. Todd Hollandsworth, of | Los Angeles | .291 | 478 | 64 | 139 | 26 | 4 | 12 | 59 | 21 |
| 4. Paul Konerko, 1b | San Antonio (AA—Texas) | .300 | 470 | 78 | 141 | 23 | 2 | 29 | 86 | 1 |
| | Albuquerque (AAA—Pacific Coast) | .429 | 14 | 2 | 6 | 0 | 0 | 1 | 2 | 0 |
| 5. Wilton Guerrero, 2b-ss | Albuquerque (AAA—Pacific Coast) | .344 | 425 | 79 | 146 | 17 | 12 | 2 | 38 | 26 |
| | Los Angeles | .000 | 2 | 1 | 0 | 0 | 0 | 0 | 0 | 0 |
| 6. Roger Cedeno, of | Albuquerque (AAA—Pacific Coast) | .224 | 125 | 16 | 28 | 2 | 3 | 1 | 10 | 6 |
| | Los Angeles | .246 | 211 | 26 | 52 | 11 | 1 | 2 | 18 | 5 |
| 10. Adam Riggs, 2b | San Antonio (AA—Texas) | .283 | 506 | 68 | 143 | 31 | 6 | 14 | 66 | 16 |

| | | W | L | ERA | G | SV | IP | H | BB | SO |
|---|---|---|---|---|---|---|---|---|---|---|
| 2. Chan Ho Park, rhp | Los Angeles | 5 | 5 | 3.64 | 48 | 0 | 109 | 82 | 71 | 119 |
| 7. David Yocum, lhp | Vero Beach (A—Florida State) | 0 | 2 | 6.14 | 7 | 0 | 15 | 22 | 7 | 6 |
| 8. Onan Masaoka, lhp | Savannah (A—South Atlantic) | 2 | 5 | 4.29 | 13 | 0 | 65 | 55 | 35 | 80 |
| 9. Felix Rodriguez, rhp | Albuquerque (AAA—Pacific Coast) | 3 | 9 | 5.53 | 27 | 0 | 107 | 111 | 60 | 65 |

## PACIFIC COAST LEAGUE

| BATTING | AVG | G | AB | R | H | 2B | 3B | HR | RBI | BB | SO | SB | CS | B | T | HT | WT | DOB | 1st Yr | Resides |
|---|---|---|---|---|---|---|---|---|---|---|---|---|---|---|---|---|---|---|---|---|
| Anderson, Cliff | .269 | 64 | 186 | 19 | 50 | 9 | 2 | 4 | 17 | 21 | 53 | 3 | 3 | L | R | 5-8 | 165 | 7-4-70 | 1992 | Kodiak, Alaska |
| Ashley, Billy | .348 | 7 | 23 | 6 | 8 | 1 | 0 | 1 | 9 | 7 | 9 | 2 | 0 | R | R | 6-7 | 230 | 7-11-70 | 1988 | Belleville, Mich. |
| Blanco, Henry | .167 | 2 | 6 | 1 | 1 | 0 | 0 | 0 | 0 | 3 | 0 | 0 | 0 | R | R | 5-11 | 168 | 8-29-71 | 1990 | Guarenas, Venez. |
| Busch, Mike | .303 | 38 | 142 | 30 | 43 | 6 | 1 | 12 | 36 | 22 | 45 | 0 | 1 | R | R | 6-5 | 241 | 7-7-68 | 1990 | Donahue, Iowa |
| Castro, Juan | .375 | 17 | 56 | 12 | 21 | 4 | 2 | 1 | 8 | 6 | 7 | 1 | 1 | R | R | 5-10 | 163 | 6-20-72 | 1991 | Los Mochis, Mexico |
| Cedeno, Roger | .224 | 33 | 125 | 16 | 28 | 2 | 3 | 1 | 10 | 15 | 22 | 6 | 5 | S | R | 6-1 | 165 | 8-16-74 | 1992 | Carabobo, Venez. |
| Dandridge, Brad | .263 | 30 | 80 | 14 | 21 | 4 | 0 | 2 | 7 | 3 | 7 | 0 | 0 | R | R | 6-0 | 190 | 11-29-71 | 1993 | Santa Maria, Calif. |
| Demetral, Chris | .263 | 99 | 209 | 30 | 55 | 8 | 0 | 4 | 26 | 40 | 35 | 4 | 3 | L | R | 5-11 | 175 | 12-8-69 | 1991 | Sterling Heights, Mich. |
| Fonville, Chad | .240 | 25 | 96 | 17 | 23 | 1 | 0 | 0 | 5 | 8 | 13 | 7 | 0 | S | R | 5-7 | 155 | 3-5-71 | 1992 | Midway Park, N.C. |
| Fox, Eric | .330 | 30 | 91 | 8 | 30 | 6 | 1 | 0 | 2 | 4 | 20 | 1 | 2 | S | L | 5-10 | 180 | 8-15-63 | 1986 | Paso Robles, Calif. |
| Gagne, Greg | .273 | 4 | 11 | 1 | 3 | 1 | 0 | 0 | 1 | 1 | 1 | 0 | 0 | R | R | 5-11 | 180 | 11-12-61 | 1979 | Rehoboth, Mass. |
| Garcia, Karim | .297 | 84 | 327 | 54 | 97 | 17 | 10 | 13 | 58 | 29 | 67 | 6 | 4 | L | L | 6-0 | 172 | 10-29-75 | 1993 | Ciudad Obregon, Mexico |
| Guerrero, Wilton | .344 | 98 | 425 | 79 | 146 | 17 | 12 | 2 | 38 | 26 | 48 | 26 | 15 | R | R | 5-11 | 145 | 10-24-74 | 1992 | Nizao, D.R. |
| Hernandez, Carlos | .240 | 66 | 233 | 19 | 56 | 11 | 0 | 5 | 30 | 11 | 49 | 5 | 4 | R | R | 5-11 | 185 | 5-24-67 | 1985 | Caracas, Venez. |
| Huckaby, Ken | .276 | 103 | 286 | 37 | 79 | 16 | 2 | 3 | 41 | 17 | 35 | 0 | 0 | R | R | 6-1 | 205 | 1-27-71 | 1991 | Philadelphia, Pa. |
| Ingram, Garey | .100 | 6 | 10 | 1 | 1 | 0 | 0 | 0 | 0 | 1 | 2 | 0 | 0 | R | R | 5-11 | 185 | 7-25-70 | 1990 | Columbus, Ga. |
| Johnson, Keith | .250 | 4 | 16 | 2 | 4 | 1 | 0 | 0 | 2 | 1 | 1 | 0 | 0 | R | R | 5-11 | 190 | 4-17-71 | 1992 | Stockton, Calif. |
| Kirkpatrick, Jay | .243 | 51 | 107 | 12 | 26 | 5 | 0 | 0 | 9 | 10 | 35 | 0 | 0 | L | R | 6-4 | 220 | 7-10-69 | 1991 | Tallahassee, Fla. |
| Konerko, Paul | .429 | 4 | 14 | 2 | 6 | 0 | 0 | 1 | 2 | 1 | 2 | 0 | 1 | R | R | 6-3 | 210 | 3-5-76 | 1994 | Paradise Valley, Ariz. |
| Lott, Billy | .266 | 114 | 418 | 67 | 111 | 20 | 1 | 19 | 66 | 46 | 124 | 6 | 7 | R | R | 6-4 | 210 | 8-16-70 | 1989 | Petal, Miss. |
| Luzinski, Ryan | .143 | 9 | 14 | 0 | 2 | 0 | 0 | 0 | 1 | 0 | 6 | 0 | 0 | R | R | 6-1 | 215 | 8-22-73 | 1992 | Medford, N.J. |
| Marrero, Oreste | .283 | 121 | 441 | 50 | 125 | 29 | 1 | 13 | 76 | 36 | 119 | 2 | 6 | L | L | 6-0 | 205 | 10-31-69 | 1987 | Bayamon, P.R. |
| Maurer, Ron | .275 | 80 | 222 | 32 | 61 | 14 | 1 | 5 | 30 | 30 | 50 | 2 | 4 | R | R | 5-11 | 185 | 6-10-68 | 1990 | Beachwood, N.J. |
| Melendez, Dan | .152 | 31 | 46 | 5 | 7 | 2 | 0 | 0 | 2 | 8 | 14 | 0 | 0 | L | L | 6-4 | 195 | 1-4-71 | 1992 | Los Angeles, Calif. |
| Parker, Rick | .303 | 50 | 175 | 26 | 53 | 7 | 3 | 0 | 23 | 23 | 27 | 7 | 6 | R | R | 6-0 | 185 | 3-20-63 | 1985 | Independence, Mo. |
| Prince, Tom | .411 | 32 | 95 | 24 | 39 | 5 | 1 | 7 | 22 | 15 | 14 | 0 | 2 | R | R | 5-11 | 185 | 8-13-64 | 1984 | Bradenton, Fla. |
| Richardson, Brian | .245 | 105 | 355 | 52 | 87 | 17 | 2 | 9 | 43 | 32 | 89 | 4 | 1 | R | R | 6-2 | 190 | 8-31-75 | 1992 | Diamond Bar, Calif. |
| Rios, Eduardo | .069 | 15 | 29 | 3 | 2 | 0 | 0 | 0 | 1 | 3 | 6 | 1 | 0 | R | R | 5-10 | 160 | 10-13-72 | 1991 | Charallave, Venez. |
| Roberge, J.P. | .321 | 53 | 156 | 17 | 50 | 6 | 1 | 4 | 17 | 14 | 28 | 3 | 0 | R | R | 6-0 | 190 | 9-12-72 | 1994 | Arcadia, Calif. |
| Romero, Willie | .385 | 4 | 13 | 1 | 5 | 0 | 0 | 1 | 3 | 1 | 1 | 1 | 0 | R | R | 5-11 | 158 | 8-5-74 | 1991 | Candelaria, Venez. |
| Williams, Reggie | .287 | 92 | 352 | 60 | 101 | 25 | 2 | 6 | 42 | 37 | 72 | 17 | 7 | S | R | 6-1 | 180 | 5-5-66 | 1988 | Laurens, S.C. |

| PITCHING | W | L | ERA | G | GS | CG | SV | IP | H | R | ER | BB | SO | B | T | HT | WT | DOB | 1st Yr | Resides |
|---|---|---|---|---|---|---|---|---|---|---|---|---|---|---|---|---|---|---|---|---|
| Brewer, Billy | 2 | 2 | 3.13 | 31 | 0 | 0 | 2 | 32 | 28 | 13 | 11 | 22 | 33 | L | L | 6-1 | 175 | 4-15-68 | 1990 | Waco, Texas |
| Brunson, Will | 3 | 4 | 4.47 | 9 | 9 | 1 | 0 | 54 | 53 | 29 | 27 | 23 | 47 | L | L | 6-4 | 185 | 3-20-70 | 1992 | DeSoto, Texas |
| Bruske, Jim | 5 | 2 | 4.06 | 36 | 0 | 0 | 4 | 62 | 63 | 34 | 28 | 21 | 51 | R | R | 6-1 | 185 | 10-7-64 | 1986 | Palmdale, Calif. |
| Correa, Ramser | 0 | 3 | 5.75 | 23 | 0 | 0 | 1 | 36 | 44 | 29 | 23 | 22 | 30 | R | R | 6-5 | 225 | 11-13-70 | 1987 | Carolina, P.R. |
| Cummings, John | 2 | 6 | 4.14 | 27 | 9 | 0 | 2 | 78 | 91 | 47 | 36 | 28 | 49 | L | L | 6-3 | 200 | 5-10-69 | 1990 | Laguna Niguel, Calif. |
| Dreifort, Darren | 5 | 6 | 4.17 | 18 | 18 | 0 | 0 | 86 | 88 | 49 | 40 | 52 | 75 | R | R | 6-2 | 205 | 5-18-72 | 1994 | Wichita, Kan. |
| Elvira, Narciso | 1 | 1 | 4.76 | 3 | 3 | 0 | 0 | 17 | 19 | 12 | 9 | 9 | 14 | L | L | 5-10 | 160 | 10-29-67 | 1986 | Veracruz, Mexico |
| Garcia, Jose | 6 | 1 | 4.71 | 44 | 0 | 0 | 0 | 78 | 97 | 49 | 41 | 40 | 34 | R | R | 6-3 | 146 | 6-12-72 | 1991 | Monte Cristi, D.R. |
| Harkey, Mike | 7 | 11 | 5.38 | 49 | 13 | 0 | 13 | 119 | 146 | 79 | 71 | 39 | 90 | R | R | 6-5 | 235 | 10-25-66 | 1987 | Chino Hills, Calif. |
| Henderson, Ryan | 0 | 0 | 7.94 | 3 | 0 | 0 | 0 | 6 | 5 | 9 | 5 | 8 | 4 | R | R | 6-1 | 190 | 9-30-69 | 1992 | Dana Point, Calif. |
| Herges, Matt | 4 | 1 | 2.60 | 10 | 4 | 2 | 0 | 35 | 33 | 11 | 10 | 14 | 15 | R | R | 6-0 | 200 | 4-1-70 | 1992 | Champaign, Ill. |
| Hubbs, Jim | 7 | 1 | 4.76 | 49 | 0 | 0 | 2 | 76 | 89 | 51 | 40 | 47 | 82 | R | R | 6-2 | 200 | 1-23-71 | 1993 | Renton, Wash. |
| Jones, Calvin | 0 | 0 | 4.50 | 10 | 0 | 0 | 0 | 12 | 11 | 6 | 6 | 12 | 15 | R | R | 6-3 | 185 | 9-26-63 | 1984 | Perris, Calif. |
| Lagarde, Joe | 0 | 0 | 5.25 | 10 | 0 | 0 | 0 | 12 | 14 | 7 | 7 | 9 | 11 | R | R | 5-9 | 180 | 1-17-75 | 1993 | Washington, D.C. |
| Mimbs, Mark | 8 | 8 | 4.59 | 34 | 23 | 1 | 0 | 151 | 165 | 93 | 77 | 43 | 136 | L | L | 6-2 | 180 | 2-13-69 | 1990 | Macon, Ga. |
| Osuna, Antonio | 0 | 0 | 0.00 | 1 | 0 | 0 | 0 | 1 | 2 | 0 | 0 | 0 | 1 | R | R | 5-11 | 160 | 4-12-73 | 1991 | Sinaloa, Mexico |
| Pyc, Dave | 2 | 3 | 9.17 | 13 | 4 | 0 | 0 | 35 | 53 | 39 | 36 | 19 | 27 | L | L | 6-3 | 235 | 2-11-71 | 1992 | Depew, N.Y. |
| Rath, Gary | 10 | 11 | 4.19 | 30 | 30 | 1 | 0 | 180 | 177 | 97 | 84 | 89 | 125 | L | L | 6-2 | 185 | 1-10-73 | 1994 | Long Beach, Miss. |
| Rodriguez, Felix | 3 | 9 | 5.53 | 27 | 19 | 0 | 0 | 107 | 111 | 70 | 66 | 60 | 65 | R | R | 6-1 | 190 | 12-5-72 | 1990 | Monte Cristi, D.R. |
| Seanez, Rudy | 0 | 2 | 6.52 | 20 | 0 | 0 | 6 | 19 | 27 | 18 | 14 | 11 | 20 | R | R | 5-10 | 185 | 10-20-68 | 1986 | El Centro, Calif. |
| Treadwell, Jody | 1 | 1 | 7.85 | 5 | 3 | 0 | 0 | 18 | 30 | 18 | 16 | 10 | 16 | R | R | 6-0 | 190 | 12-14-68 | 1990 | Jacksonville, Fla. |
| Weaver, Eric | 1 | 4 | 5.40 | 13 | 8 | 0 | 0 | 47 | 63 | 39 | 28 | 22 | 38 | R | R | 6-5 | 230 | 8-4-73 | 1991 | Illiopolis, Ill. |

### FIELDING

| Catcher | PCT | G | PO | A | E | DP | PB |
|---|---|---|---|---|---|---|---|
| Blanco | 1.000 | 2 | 11 | 0 | 0 | 0 | 0 |
| Dandridge | .967 | 8 | 28 | 1 | 1 | 0 | 0 |
| Hernandez | .978 | 50 | 320 | 35 | 8 | 5 | 3 |
| Huckaby | .990 | 94 | 557 | 63 | 6 | 11 | 10 |
| Kirkpatrick | .000 | 1 | 0 | 0 | 0 | 0 | 0 |
| Luzinski | 1.000 | 2 | 5 | 0 | 0 | 0 | 0 |
| Prince | .990 | 19 | 86 | 18 | 1 | 2 | 2 |

| First Base | PCT | G | PO | A | E | DP |
|---|---|---|---|---|---|---|
| Busch | .987 | 25 | 216 | 15 | 3 | 22 |
| Hernandez | .933 | 2 | 11 | 3 | 1 | 3 |
| Kirkpatrick | .987 | 27 | 145 | 12 | 2 | 18 |
| Konerko | 1.000 | 4 | 30 | 0 | 0 | 2 |
| Marrero | .991 | 89 | 689 | 63 | 7 | 71 |
| Maurer | 1.000 | 7 | 42 | 4 | 0 | 2 |
| Melendez | .985 | 27 | 119 | 9 | 2 | 13 |
| Parker | .875 | 2 | 13 | 1 | 2 | 4 |
| Roberge | 1.000 | 2 | 5 | 3 | 0 | 2 |

| Second Base | PCT | G | PO | A | E | DP |
|---|---|---|---|---|---|---|
| Castro | 1.000 | 1 | 5 | 1 | 0 | 1 |
| Demetral | .971 | 56 | 75 | 123 | 6 | 23 |
| Fonville | .958 | 6 | 9 | 14 | 1 | 2 |
| Guerrero | .973 | 66 | 137 | 188 | 9 | 49 |

| | PCT | G | PO | A | E | DP |
|---|---|---|---|---|---|---|
| Ingram | .800 | 2 | 3 | 1 | 1 | 1 |
| Maurer | 1.000 | 6 | 15 | 14 | 0 | 4 |
| Parker | .959 | 20 | 34 | 60 | 4 | 20 |
| Richardson | 1.000 | 3 | 1 | 1 | 0 | 0 |
| Rios | .955 | 12 | 15 | 27 | 2 | 9 |

| Third Base | PCT | G | PO | A | E | DP |
|---|---|---|---|---|---|---|
| Busch | 1.000 | 9 | 3 | 19 | 0 | 0 |
| Castro | .931 | 12 | 6 | 21 | 2 | 4 |
| Dandridge | .000 | 1 | 0 | 0 | 1 | 0 |
| Demetral | .000 | 2 | 0 | 0 | 0 | 0 |
| Hernandez | .000 | 1 | 0 | 0 | 0 | 0 |
| Lott | 1.000 | 1 | 0 | 1 | 0 | 0 |
| Maurer | .951 | 32 | 10 | 48 | 3 | 6 |
| Parker | .833 | 7 | 3 | 7 | 2 | 1 |
| Prince | 1.000 | 3 | 2 | 2 | 0 | 0 |
| Richardson | .908 | 95 | 63 | 183 | 25 | 14 |
| Rios | 1.000 | 1 | 1 | 3 | 0 | 1 |
| Roberge | .900 | 4 | 1 | 8 | 1 | 1 |

| Shortstop | PCT | G | PO | A | E | DP |
|---|---|---|---|---|---|---|
| Anderson | .951 | 60 | 74 | 180 | 13 | 36 |
| Castro | 1.000 | 4 | 6 | 11 | 0 | 2 |
| Fonville | .944 | 18 | 30 | 55 | 5 | 7 |

| | PCT | G | PO | A | E | DP |
|---|---|---|---|---|---|---|
| Gagne | 1.000 | 4 | 7 | 9 | 0 | 5 |
| Guerrero | .943 | 34 | 46 | 118 | 10 | 24 |
| Johnson | 1.000 | 4 | 8 | 11 | 0 | 1 |
| Maurer | .932 | 35 | 50 | 115 | 12 | 28 |
| Parker | .000 | 1 | 0 | 0 | 0 | 0 |
| Richardson | 1.000 | 1 | 2 | 2 | 0 | 1 |
| Rios | .875 | 1 | 3 | 4 | 1 | 1 |

| Outfield | PCT | G | PO | A | E | DP |
|---|---|---|---|---|---|---|
| Ashley | .917 | 7 | 11 | 0 | 1 | 0 |
| Cedeno | 1.000 | 32 | 71 | 2 | 0 | 1 |
| Dandridge | 1.000 | 11 | 12 | 0 | 0 | 0 |
| Fonville | 1.000 | 2 | 3 | 1 | 0 | 0 |
| Fox | .980 | 28 | 46 | 2 | 1 | 0 |
| Garcia | .921 | 80 | 148 | 4 | 13 | 0 |
| Lott | .940 | 112 | 196 | 6 | 13 | 1 |
| Marrero | .970 | 28 | 31 | 1 | 1 | 0 |
| Maurer | 1.000 | 3 | 3 | 0 | 0 | 0 |
| Parker | .972 | 24 | 32 | 3 | 1 | 0 |
| Prince | .000 | 1 | 0 | 0 | 0 | 0 |
| Roberge | .970 | 45 | 60 | 4 | 2 | 1 |
| Romero | 1.000 | 4 | 10 | 0 | 0 | 0 |
| Williams | .981 | 89 | 197 | 10 | 4 | 5 |

### TEXAS LEAGUE

| BATTING | AVG | G | AB | R | H | 2B | 3B | HR | RBI | BB | SO | SB | CS | B | T | HT | WT | DOB | 1st Yr | Resides |
|---|---|---|---|---|---|---|---|---|---|---|---|---|---|---|---|---|---|---|---|---|
| Anderson, Cliff | .231 | 7 | 26 | 2 | 6 | 0 | 1 | 0 | 2 | 1 | 7 | 0 | 1 | L | R | 5-8 | 165 | 7-4-70 | 1992 | Kodiak, Alaska |
| Blanco, Henry | .267 | 92 | 307 | 39 | 82 | 14 | 1 | 5 | 40 | 28 | 38 | 2 | 3 | R | R | 5-11 | 168 | 8-29-71 | 1990 | Guarenas, Venez. |
| Dandridge, Brad | .282 | 47 | 177 | 22 | 50 | 7 | 0 | 3 | 25 | 12 | 19 | 4 | 3 | R | R | 6-0 | 190 | 11-29-71 | 1993 | Santa Maria, Calif. |
| Durkin, Chris | .300 | 8 | 30 | 6 | 9 | 2 | 0 | 1 | 3 | 4 | 9 | 0 | 0 | L | L | 6-6 | 247 | 8-12-70 | 1991 | Youngstown, Ohio |
| Garcia, Karim | .248 | 35 | 129 | 21 | 32 | 6 | 1 | 5 | 22 | 9 | 38 | 1 | 1 | L | L | 6-0 | 172 | 10-29-75 | 1993 | Ciudad Obregon, Mexico |
| Johnson, Keith | .274 | 127 | 521 | 74 | 143 | 28 | 6 | 10 | 57 | 17 | 82 | 15 | 8 | R | R | 5-11 | 190 | 4-17-71 | 1992 | Stockton, Calif. |
| Kirkpatrick, Jay | .242 | 30 | 91 | 6 | 22 | 4 | 0 | 3 | 10 | 11 | 26 | 1 | 0 | L | R | 6-4 | 220 | 7-10-69 | 1991 | Tallahassee, Fla. |
| Konerko, Paul | .300 | 133 | 470 | 78 | 141 | 23 | 2 | 29 | 86 | 72 | 85 | 1 | 3 | R | R | 6-3 | 210 | 3-5-76 | 1994 | Paradise Valley, Ariz. |
| Luzinski, Ryan | .291 | 32 | 103 | 12 | 30 | 6 | 0 | 0 | 10 | 11 | 19 | 2 | 0 | R | R | 6-1 | 215 | 8-22-73 | 1992 | Medford, N.J. |
| Martin, James | .211 | 38 | 114 | 9 | 24 | 6 | 1 | 1 | 8 | 9 | 42 | 2 | 2 | L | R | 6-1 | 210 | 12-10-70 | 1991 | Eufaula, Okla. |
| Maurer, Ron | .263 | 6 | 19 | 3 | 5 | 0 | 0 | 0 | 3 | 7 | 0 | 0 | 0 | R | R | 6-1 | 185 | 6-10-68 | 1990 | Beachwood, N.J. |
| Melendez, Dan | .238 | 67 | 189 | 19 | 45 | 10 | 0 | 1 | 29 | 20 | 31 | 0 | 0 | L | L | 6-4 | 195 | 1-4-71 | 1992 | Los Angeles, Calif. |
| Moore, Michael | .240 | 64 | 200 | 21 | 48 | 10 | 4 | 2 | 21 | 17 | 64 | 8 | 4 | R | R | 6-4 | 200 | 3-7-71 | 1992 | Beverly Hills, Calif. |
| Richardson, Brian | .323 | 19 | 62 | 10 | 20 | 1 | 1 | 0 | 7 | 2 | 10 | 0 | 2 | R | R | 6-2 | 190 | 8-31-75 | 1992 | Diamond Bar, Calif. |
| Riggs, Adam | .283 | 134 | 506 | 68 | 143 | 31 | 6 | 14 | 66 | 37 | 82 | 16 | 6 | R | R | 6-0 | 190 | 10-4-72 | 1994 | Andover, N.J. |
| Rios, Eddie | .277 | 75 | 242 | 29 | 67 | 11 | 2 | 5 | 37 | 20 | 32 | 2 | 2 | R | R | 5-10 | 160 | 10-13-72 | 1991 | Charallave, Venez. |
| Roberge, J.P. | .293 | 62 | 232 | 28 | 68 | 14 | 2 | 6 | 27 | 14 | 39 | 9 | 3 | R | R | 6-0 | 180 | 9-12-72 | 1994 | Arcadia, Calif. |
| Romero, Willie | .295 | 122 | 444 | 66 | 131 | 36 | 6 | 6 | 48 | 34 | 52 | 21 | 15 | R | R | 5-11 | 158 | 8-5-74 | 1991 | Candelaria, Venez. |
| Spearman, Vernon | .257 | 123 | 471 | 66 | 121 | 15 | 9 | 1 | 30 | 35 | 38 | 26 | 17 | L | L | 5-10 | 160 | 12-17-69 | 1991 | Union City, Calif. |
| Stare, Lonny | .224 | 32 | 67 | 7 | 15 | 2 | 0 | 0 | 4 | 11 | 11 | 2 | 2 | R | R | 5-11 | 185 | 5-20-71 | 1994 | San Diego, Calif. |
| Steed, Dave | .118 | 7 | 17 | 0 | 2 | 1 | 0 | 0 | 2 | 1 | 6 | 0 | 0 | R | R | 6-1 | 205 | 2-25-73 | 1993 | Starkville, Miss. |
| Yard, Bruce | .314 | 48 | 153 | 25 | 48 | 15 | 1 | 1 | 13 | 7 | 11 | 0 | 0 | L | R | 6-0 | 175 | 10-17-71 | 1993 | McIntyre, Pa. |

| PITCHING | W | L | ERA | G | GS | CG | SV | IP | H | R | ER | BB | SO | B | T | HT | WT | DOB | 1st Yr | Resides |
|---|---|---|---|---|---|---|---|---|---|---|---|---|---|---|---|---|---|---|---|---|
| Ahearne, Pat | 2 | 4 | 5.76 | 8 | 8 | 0 | 0 | 45 | 59 | 34 | 29 | 18 | 21 | R | R | 6-3 | 195 | 12-10-69 | 1992 | Atascadero, Calif. |
| Brunson, Will | 3 | 1 | 2.14 | 11 | 8 | 0 | 0 | 42 | 32 | 13 | 10 | 15 | 38 | L | L | 6-4 | 185 | 3-20-70 | 1992 | DeSoto, Texas |
| Camacho, Dan | 1 | 1 | 2.70 | 4 | 2 | 0 | 0 | 17 | 11 | 5 | 5 | 17 | 11 | R | R | 5-11 | 200 | 11-11-73 | 1992 | San Diego, Calif. |
| Colon, Julio | 2 | 3 | 4.46 | 6 | 6 | 0 | 0 | 36 | 35 | 20 | 18 | 17 | 14 | R | R | 6-2 | 202 | 10-30-72 | 1993 | Los Angeles, Calif. |
| Correa, Ramser | 4 | 1 | 2.88 | 31 | 0 | 0 | 9 | 34 | 26 | 12 | 11 | 16 | 29 | R | R | 6-5 | 225 | 11-13-70 | 1987 | Carolina, P.R. |
| Garcia, Jose | 2 | 0 | 0.00 | 8 | 0 | 0 | 2 | 11 | 4 | 0 | 0 | 0 | 8 | R | R | 6-3 | 146 | 6-12-72 | 1991 | Monte Cristi, D.R. |
| Henderson, Ryan | 3 | 3 | 3.82 | 39 | 0 | 0 | 6 | 64 | 59 | 29 | 27 | 29 | 46 | R | R | 6-1 | 190 | 9-30-69 | 1992 | Dana Point, Calif. |
| Herges, Matt | 3 | 2 | 2.71 | 30 | 6 | 0 | 3 | 83 | 83 | 38 | 25 | 28 | 45 | R | R | 6-0 | 200 | 4-1-70 | 1992 | Champaign, Ill. |
| Hollis, Ron | 0 | 3 | 3.43 | 25 | 0 | 0 | 1 | 39 | 38 | 21 | 15 | 19 | 36 | L | R | 6-3 | 205 | 8-13-73 | 1994 | Brighton, Mich. |
| Jacobsen, Joe | 1 | 4 | 4.19 | 38 | 0 | 0 | 5 | 58 | 62 | 33 | 27 | 24 | 36 | R | R | 6-3 | 225 | 12-26-71 | 1992 | Clovis, Calif. |
| Lagarde, Joe | 3 | 1 | 1.74 | 24 | 0 | 0 | 9 | 31 | 28 | 7 | 6 | 10 | 22 | R | R | 5-9 | 180 | 1-17-75 | 1993 | Washington, D.C. |
| Martinez, Jesus | 10 | 13 | 4.40 | 27 | 27 | 0 | 0 | 162 | 157 | 90 | 79 | 92 | 124 | L | L | 6-2 | 145 | 3-13-74 | 1991 | Santo Domingo, D.R. |
| Martinez, Ramon | 0 | 0 | 0.00 | 1 | 1 | 0 | 0 | 3 | 0 | 0 | 0 | 3 | 1 | S | R | 6-4 | 173 | 3-22-68 | 1985 | Santo Domingo, D.R. |
| Pincavitch, Kevin | 0 | 0 | 5.63 | 11 | 0 | 0 | 0 | 16 | 26 | 14 | 10 | 10 | 11 | R | R | 5-11 | 180 | 7-5-70 | 1992 | Greensboro, Pa. |
| Prado, Jose | 2 | 1 | 5.01 | 18 | 1 | 0 | 1 | 32 | 32 | 21 | 18 | 24 | 20 | R | R | 6-2 | 195 | 5-9-72 | 1993 | Miami, Fla. |
| Price, Tom | 0 | 4 | 9.36 | 7 | 5 | 0 | 0 | 25 | 50 | 30 | 26 | 13 | 11 | L | L | 6-0 | 190 | 3-19-72 | 1994 | Edwardsville, Ill. |
| Pyc, Dave | 7 | 5 | 2.98 | 14 | 14 | 1 | 0 | 97 | 106 | 45 | 32 | 24 | 62 | L | L | 6-3 | 235 | 2-11-71 | 1992 | Depew, N.Y. |
| Roach, Petie | 6 | 3 | 3.82 | 13 | 13 | 1 | 0 | 75 | 81 | 41 | 32 | 34 | 40 | L | L | 6-2 | 180 | 9-19-70 | 1991 | Redding, Calif. |
| Watts, Brandon | 6 | 10 | 4.50 | 22 | 22 | 2 | 0 | 126 | 136 | 69 | 63 | 70 | 75 | R | R | 6-3 | 173 | 3-24-72 | 1991 | Ruston, La. |
| Weaver, Eric | 10 | 5 | 3.30 | 18 | 18 | 1 | 0 | 123 | 106 | 51 | 45 | 44 | 69 | R | R | 6-5 | 230 | 8-4-73 | 1991 | Illiopolis, Ill. |
| Zerbe, Chad | 4 | 6 | 4.50 | 17 | 11 | 1 | 1 | 86 | 98 | 52 | 43 | 37 | 38 | L | L | 6-0 | 190 | 4-27-72 | 1991 | Tampa, Fla. |

| FIELDING | | | | | | | | | |
|---|---|---|---|---|---|---|---|---|---|

**Catcher**

| | PCT | G | PO | A | E | DP | PB |
|---|---|---|---|---|---|---|---|
| Blanco | .979 | 91 | 532 | 65 | 13 | 8 | 17 |
| Dandridge | 1.000 | 10 | 46 | 5 | 0 | 0 | 3 |
| Luzinski | .995 | 31 | 173 | 22 | 1 | 3 | 2 |
| Maurer | 1.000 | 6 | 23 | 2 | 0 | 0 | 0 |
| Steed | .960 | 6 | 23 | 1 | 1 | 0 | 0 |
| Yard | .000 | 1 | 0 | 0 | 0 | 0 | 0 |

**First Base**

| | PCT | G | PO | A | E | DP |
|---|---|---|---|---|---|---|
| Kirkpatrick | 1.000 | 6 | 47 | 4 | 0 | 2 |
| Konerko | .989 | 120 | 1114 | 92 | 14 | 107 |
| Melendez | .994 | 19 | 162 | 9 | 1 | 21 |
| Roberge | 1.000 | 1 | 1 | 0 | 0 | 0 |

**Second Base**

| | PCT | G | PO | A | E | DP |
|---|---|---|---|---|---|---|
| Riggs | .962 | 125 | 295 | 395 | 27 | 91 |

| | PCT | G | PO | A | E | DP |
|---|---|---|---|---|---|---|
| Rios | .970 | 13 | 25 | 39 | 2 | 11 |
| Roberge | .933 | 3 | 5 | 9 | 1 | 1 |

**Third Base**

| | PCT | G | PO | A | E | DP |
|---|---|---|---|---|---|---|
| Blanco | .000 | 2 | 0 | 0 | 0 | 0 |
| Johnson | .964 | 43 | 34 | 101 | 5 | 13 |
| Richardson | .925 | 19 | 11 | 38 | 4 | 3 |
| Rios | .886 | 41 | 18 | 83 | 13 | 8 |
| Roberge | .948 | 41 | 17 | 93 | 6 | 10 |
| Yard | 1.000 | 2 | 1 | 4 | 0 | 0 |

**Shortstop**

| | PCT | G | PO | A | E | DP |
|---|---|---|---|---|---|---|
| Anderson | .956 | 7 | 10 | 33 | 2 | 3 |
| Johnson | .964 | 86 | 128 | 301 | 16 | 54 |
| Rios | .955 | 4 | 5 | 16 | 1 | 1 |

| | PCT | G | PO | A | E | DP |
|---|---|---|---|---|---|---|
| Yard | .934 | 45 | 67 | 146 | 15 | 32 |

**Outfield**

| | PCT | G | PO | A | E | DP |
|---|---|---|---|---|---|---|
| Dandridge | .982 | 38 | 52 | 3 | 1 | 0 |
| Durkin | 1.000 | 5 | 10 | 1 | 0 | 1 |
| Garcia | .971 | 33 | 60 | 6 | 2 | 1 |
| Martin | .974 | 34 | 35 | 2 | 1 | 0 |
| Melendez | 1.000 | 1 | 2 | 0 | 0 | 0 |
| Moore | .960 | 47 | 111 | 8 | 5 | 2 |
| Roberge | .960 | 20 | 22 | 2 | 1 | 0 |
| Romero | .970 | 120 | 246 | 14 | 8 | 3 |
| Spearman | .963 | 118 | 250 | 7 | 10 | 2 |
| Stare | 1.000 | 24 | 29 | 1 | 0 | 0 |

### CALIFORNIA LEAGUE

| BATTING | AVG | G | AB | R | H | 2B | 3B | HR | RBI | BB | SO | SB | CS | B | T | HT | WT | DOB | 1st Yr | Resides |
|---|---|---|---|---|---|---|---|---|---|---|---|---|---|---|---|---|---|---|---|---|
| Anderson, Cliff | .296 | 55 | 230 | 43 | 68 | 16 | 2 | 11 | 44 | 15 | 50 | 7 | 5 | L | R | 5-8 | 165 | 7-4-70 | 1992 | Kodiak, Alaska |
| Baker, Jason | .103 | 19 | 29 | 2 | 3 | 0 | 0 | 1 | 0 | 10 | 0 | 0 | 0 | R | L | 6-0 | 185 | 12-31-73 | 1995 | Rome, N.Y. |
| Beltre, Adrian | .261 | 63 | 238 | 40 | 62 | 13 | 1 | 10 | 40 | 19 | 44 | 3 | 4 | R | R | 5-11 | 200 | 4-7-78 | 1994 | Santo Domingo, D.R. |
| Carpentier, Mike | .214 | 15 | 42 | 5 | 9 | 1 | 0 | 0 | 7 | 4 | 4 | 2 | 3 | R | R | 5-11 | 180 | 8-1-74 | 1995 | Redlands, Calif. |
| Cooney, Kyle | .273 | 107 | 406 | 57 | 111 | 20 | 0 | 14 | 67 | 28 | 78 | 9 | 8 | R | R | 6-2 | 200 | 3-31-73 | 1994 | Meriden, Conn. |
| Davis, Eddie | .256 | 136 | 546 | 107 | 140 | 34 | 2 | 29 | 89 | 62 | 150 | 31 | 23 | R | R | 6-0 | 202 | 12-22-72 | 1993 | New Orleans, La. |
| Demetral, Chris | .281 | 11 | 32 | 5 | 9 | 3 | 0 | 1 | 4 | 6 | 5 | 0 | 3 | L | R | 5-11 | 175 | 12-8-69 | 1993 | Sterling Heights, Mich. |
| Faircloth, Kevin | .298 | 56 | 171 | 30 | 51 | 6 | 3 | 4 | 23 | 20 | 30 | 9 | 8 | R | R | 6-2 | 170 | 6-6-73 | 1994 | Winston-Salem, N.C. |
| Gonzalez, Manuel | .304 | 43 | 168 | 29 | 51 | 7 | 3 | 0 | 21 | 12 | 32 | 10 | 8 | S | R | 6-2 | 192 | 5-30-76 | 1994 | Santo Domingo, D.R. |
| Gross, Rafael | .235 | 112 | 362 | 58 | 85 | 18 | 2 | 6 | 43 | 18 | 68 | 31 | 14 | R | R | 5-11 | 185 | 8-15-74 | 1993 | Santo Domingo, D.R. |
| Jones, Jack | .241 | 10 | 29 | 5 | 7 | 3 | 0 | 1 | 6 | 6 | 8 | 1 | 1 | R | R | 5-11 | 165 | 11-7-74 | 1996 | Modesto, Calif. |
| Landrum, Tito | .268 | 51 | 157 | 29 | 42 | 7 | 0 | 3 | 20 | 21 | 38 | 8 | 4 | R | R | 6-4 | 210 | 8-26-70 | 1991 | Sweetwater, Ala. |
| Lewis, Tyrone | .263 | 67 | 217 | 30 | 57 | 14 | 2 | 5 | 30 | 14 | 51 | 6 | 2 | R | R | 5-10 | 185 | 1-22-74 | 1992 | Waco, Texas |
| Luzinski, Ryan | .347 | 30 | 118 | 24 | 41 | 10 | 0 | 5 | 21 | 11 | 33 | 6 | 1 | R | R | 6-1 | 215 | 8-22-73 | 1992 | Medford, N.J. |
| Martin, James | .243 | 50 | 152 | 26 | 37 | 1 | 1 | 6 | 23 | 16 | 53 | 9 | 4 | L | R | 6-1 | 210 | 12-10-70 | 1992 | Eufaula, Okla. |

| BATTING | AVG | G | AB | R | H | 2B | 3B | HR | RBI | BB | SO | SB | CS | B | T | HT | WT | DOB | 1st Yr | Resides |
|---|---|---|---|---|---|---|---|---|---|---|---|---|---|---|---|---|---|---|---|---|
| McCarty, Matt | .236 | 38 | 110 | 30 | 26 | 2 | 2 | 6 | 19 | 14 | 35 | 5 | 2 | R | R | 6-0 | 172 | 2-2-76 | 1995 | Crawfordsville, Ind. |
| Mikesell, Steve | .067 | 6 | 15 | 2 | 1 | 0 | 1 | 0 | 1 | 2 | 6 | 0 | 0 | R | R | 6-1 | 220 | 8-13-73 | 1996 | Covina, Calif. |
| Morimoto, Ken | .250 | 24 | 92 | 13 | 23 | 3 | 0 | 0 | 8 | 12 | 28 | 14 | 3 | R | R | 6-1 | 163 | 9-22-74 | 1995 | Eleele, Hawaii |
| Richardson, Scott | .306 | 128 | 458 | 80 | 140 | 30 | 0 | 13 | 69 | 46 | 71 | 31 | 14 | R | R | 6-1 | 175 | 2-19-71 | 1992 | Rialto, Calif. |
| Roberge, J.P. | .364 | 12 | 44 | 8 | 16 | 3 | 1 | 1 | 6 | 3 | 9 | 1 | 2 | R | R | 6-0 | 180 | 9-12-72 | 1994 | Arcadia, Calif. |
| Sell, Chip | .280 | 95 | 321 | 47 | 90 | 12 | 0 | 1 | 23 | 27 | 68 | 13 | 5 | L | R | 6-2 | 195 | 6-19-71 | 1994 | Woodburn, Ore. |
| Sowards, Ryan | .000 | 5 | 2 | 0 | 0 | 0 | 0 | 0 | 0 | 2 | 1 | 0 | 0 | L | R | 6-0 | 180 | 8-11-73 | 1994 | Bothell, Wash. |
| Steed, David | .299 | 28 | 87 | 11 | 26 | 6 | 0 | 1 | 13 | 14 | 19 | 2 | 3 | R | R | 6-1 | 205 | 2-25-73 | 1993 | Starkville, Miss. |
| Townsend, Chad | .295 | 116 | 421 | 63 | 124 | 18 | 1 | 22 | 72 | 50 | 100 | 3 | 2 | L | L | 6-5 | 235 | 7-4-71 | 1992 | Palm Desert, Calif. |
| Wallach, Tim | .300 | 5 | 20 | 3 | 6 | 0 | 1 | 6 | 2 | 7 | 0 | 0 | 0 | R | R | 6-3 | 200 | 9-14-57 | 1979 | Tustin, Calif. |
| Wingate, Ervan | .324 | 115 | 383 | 60 | 124 | 16 | 0 | 12 | 55 | 32 | 75 | 7 | 9 | R | R | 6-0 | 185 | 2-4-74 | 1992 | Redlands, Calif. |

**GAMES BY POSITION: C**—Cooney 92, Luzinski 20, Mikesell 5, Steed 27. **1B**—Cooney 1, Richardson 1, Roberge 9, Sell 22, Sowards 1, Townsend 36. **2B**—Anderson 5, Carpentier 10, Demetral 2, Faircloth 4, Gross 85, Richardson 4, Wingate 23. **3B**—Beltre 58, Carpentier 1, Demetral 2, Gross 22, McCarty 35, Sell 1, Sowards 1, Wingate 23. **SS**—Anderson 52, Carpentier 3, Cooney 1, Faircloth 52, Gross 5, Jones 10, Morimoto 24, Wingate 4. **OF**—Baker 16, Cooney 1, Davis 135, Gonzalez 43, Landrum 38, Martin 22, Richardson 114, Roberge 4, Sell 57, Wingate 22.

| PITCHING | W | L | ERA | G | GS | CG | SV | IP | H | R | ER | BB | SO | B | T | HT | WT | DOB | 1st Yr | Resides |
|---|---|---|---|---|---|---|---|---|---|---|---|---|---|---|---|---|---|---|---|---|
| Babineaux, Darrin | 1 | 3 | 14.29 | 5 | 5 | 0 | 0 | 17 | 34 | 27 | 27 | 14 | 16 | R | R | 6-4 | 210 | 7-10-74 | 1995 | Rayne, La. |
| Backowski, Lance | 0 | 0 | 18.00 | 1 | 0 | 0 | 0 | 1 | 2 | 2 | 2 | 2 | 0 | R | R | 6-0 | 180 | 6-8-75 | 1995 | Fresno, Calif. |
| Brown, Alvin | 2 | 4 | 3.80 | 42 | 2 | 0 | 2 | 69 | 43 | 40 | 29 | 62 | 84 | R | R | 6-1 | 200 | 9-2-70 | 1989 | Los Angeles, Calif. |
| Camacho, Dan | 4 | 5 | 6.69 | 14 | 13 | 0 | 1 | 74 | 81 | 56 | 55 | 52 | 72 | R | R | 5-11 | 200 | 11-11-73 | 1992 | San Diego, Calif. |
| Candiotti, Tom | 0 | 1 | 5.00 | 2 | 2 | 0 | 0 | 9 | 11 | 6 | 5 | 4 | 10 | R | R | 6-2 | 220 | 8-31-57 | 1979 | Concord, Calif. |
| Castro, Nelson | 2 | 4 | 6.30 | 12 | 0 | 0 | 1 | 20 | 25 | 14 | 14 | 9 | 22 | R | R | 6-1 | 185 | 12-10-71 | 1990 | Los Angeles, Calif. |
| Deskins, Casey | 3 | 3 | 6.07 | 12 | 7 | 0 | 0 | 43 | 61 | 38 | 29 | 12 | 26 | R | L | 6-3 | 220 | 4-5-72 | 1993 | Yakima, Wash. |
| Foster, Kris | 3 | 5 | 3.86 | 30 | 8 | 0 | 2 | 82 | 66 | 46 | 35 | 54 | 78 | R | R | 6-1 | 200 | 8-30-74 | 1993 | Lehigh Acres, Fla. |
| Kenady, Jake | 2 | 3 | 6.40 | 45 | 0 | 0 | 0 | 70 | 83 | 65 | 50 | 68 | 81 | L | L | 6-4 | 205 | 9-21-73 | 1991 | Scottsdale, Ariz. |
| Keppen, Jeff | 3 | 1 | 5.82 | 24 | 1 | 0 | 0 | 56 | 56 | 44 | 36 | 46 | 45 | R | R | 6-2 | 190 | 1-31-74 | 1995 | Lawrenceville, Ga. |
| Linares, Rich | 4 | 3 | 3.36 | 60 | 0 | 0 | 33 | 62 | 59 | 30 | 23 | 19 | 59 | R | R | 5-11 | 200 | 8-31-72 | 1992 | Long Beach, Calif. |
| McDonald, Matt | 0 | 0 | 12.00 | 4 | 0 | 0 | 0 | 9 | 14 | 14 | 12 | 11 | 11 | L | L | 6-4 | 200 | 6-10-74 | 1994 | Princeton, Ill. |
| Moreno, Claudio | 1 | 2 | 7.82 | 6 | 6 | 0 | 0 | 25 | 41 | 28 | 22 | 9 | 27 | R | R | 6-2 | 188 | 9-16-73 | 1996 | San Diego, Calif. |
| Oropesa, Eddie | 11 | 6 | 3.34 | 33 | 19 | 0 | 1 | 156 | 133 | 74 | 58 | 77 | 133 | L | L | 6-2 | 200 | 11-23-71 | 1993 | Miami, Fla. |
| Paluk, Jeff | 4 | 3 | 5.06 | 50 | 0 | 0 | 5 | 69 | 79 | 47 | 39 | 31 | 70 | R | R | 6-4 | 215 | 9-28-72 | 1994 | Plymouth, Mich. |
| Pincavitch, Kevin | 8 | 8 | 4.88 | 20 | 17 | 0 | 0 | 101 | 95 | 66 | 55 | 75 | 79 | R | R | 5-11 | 180 | 7-5-70 | 1992 | Greensboro, Pa. |
| Price, Tom | 5 | 3 | 3.84 | 15 | 11 | 1 | 0 | 82 | 94 | 42 | 35 | 5 | 60 | L | L | 6-0 | 190 | 3-19-72 | 1994 | Edwardsville, Ill. |
| Radinsky, Scott | 0 | 0 | 2.08 | 3 | 0 | 0 | 0 | 4 | 2 | 1 | 1 | 2 | 4 | L | L | 6-3 | 204 | 3-3-68 | 1986 | Simi Valley, Calif. |
| Reyes, Dennis | 11 | 12 | 4.17 | 29 | 28 | 0 | 0 | 166 | 166 | 106 | 77 | 77 | 176 | L | L | 6-3 | 220 | 4-19-77 | 1994 | Zaragoza, Mexico |
| Sanchez, Mike | 0 | 0 | 8.22 | 11 | 0 | 0 | 0 | 23 | 23 | 30 | 21 | 28 | 29 | R | R | 6-3 | 175 | 11-23-75 | 1995 | Riverside, Calif. |
| Sikes, Ken | 6 | 3 | 4.81 | 17 | 17 | 0 | 0 | 92 | 89 | 58 | 49 | 56 | 65 | R | R | 6-5 | 240 | 1-25-73 | 1993 | Perry, Ga. |
| Urbina, Dan | 0 | 0 | 5.91 | 3 | 3 | 0 | 0 | 11 | 11 | 8 | 7 | 9 | 13 | R | R | 6-0 | 195 | 11-13-74 | 1992 | Miranda, Venez. |

# VERO BEACH                                                                 Class A

## FLORIDA STATE LEAGUE

| BATTING | AVG | G | AB | R | H | 2B | 3B | HR | RBI | BB | SO | SB | CS | B | T | HT | WT | DOB | 1st Yr | Resides |
|---|---|---|---|---|---|---|---|---|---|---|---|---|---|---|---|---|---|---|---|---|
| Asencio, Alex | .266 | 115 | 402 | 56 | 107 | 12 | 6 | 2 | 49 | 29 | 68 | 15 | 6 | L | L | 6-0 | 155 | 5-30-74 | 1991 | San Cristobal, D.R. |
| Barlok, Todd | .258 | 116 | 384 | 63 | 99 | 19 | 4 | 4 | 47 | 55 | 94 | 7 | 6 | R | R | 6-4 | 220 | 8-8-71 | 1995 | Bristol, Conn. |
| Carpentier, Mike | .226 | 64 | 208 | 28 | 47 | 9 | 0 | 4 | 23 | 19 | 34 | 3 | 4 | R | R | 5-11 | 180 | 8-1-74 | 1995 | Redlands, Calif. |
| Cora, Alex | .257 | 61 | 214 | 26 | 55 | 5 | 4 | 0 | 26 | 12 | 36 | 5 | 5 | L | R | 6-0 | 180 | 10-18-75 | 1996 | Caguas, P.R. |
| Coston, Sean | .227 | 10 | 22 | 4 | 5 | 1 | 0 | 0 | 0 | 1 | 9 | 0 | 0 | S | R | 6-2 | 205 | 3-9-72 | 1996 | Altadena, Calif. |
| Durkin, Chris | .267 | 56 | 202 | 49 | 54 | 11 | 0 | 16 | 34 | 28 | 54 | 4 | 0 | L | L | 6-6 | 247 | 8-12-70 | 1991 | Youngstown, Ohio |
| Faircloth, Kevin | .333 | 4 | 9 | 4 | 3 | 0 | 0 | 1 | 3 | 2 | 1 | 0 | 0 | R | R | 6-2 | 170 | 6-6-73 | 1994 | Winston-Salem, N.C. |
| Gibbs, Kevin | .270 | 118 | 423 | 69 | 114 | 9 | 11 | 0 | 33 | 65 | 80 | 60 | 19 | S | R | 6-2 | 182 | 4-3-74 | 1995 | Davidsonville, Md. |
| Landrum, Tito | .238 | 44 | 122 | 12 | 29 | 5 | 0 | 2 | 14 | 10 | 33 | 2 | 0 | R | R | 6-4 | 210 | 8-26-70 | 1991 | Sweetwater, Ala. |
| LoDuca, Paul | .305 | 124 | 439 | 54 | 134 | 22 | 0 | 3 | 66 | 70 | 38 | 8 | 2 | R | R | 5-10 | 193 | 4-12-72 | 1993 | Phoenix, Ariz. |
| Majeski, Brian | .249 | 69 | 205 | 30 | 51 | 9 | 1 | 0 | 14 | 29 | 56 | 16 | 7 | R | R | 6-0 | 180 | 1-10-72 | 1994 | Plantsville, Conn. |
| Martinez, Rafael | .198 | 116 | 354 | 38 | 70 | 8 | 3 | 5 | 45 | 40 | 105 | 1 | 5 | L | L | 6-3 | 185 | 8-24-75 | 1992 | Santo Domingo, D.R. |
| Metcalfe, Mike | .000 | 2 | 5 | 0 | 0 | 0 | 0 | 0 | 0 | 0 | 0 | 0 | 0 | S | R | 5-10 | 175 | 1-2-73 | 1996 | Orlando, Fla. |
| Meyer, Travis | .242 | 12 | 33 | 6 | 8 | 1 | 0 | 3 | 8 | 3 | 6 | 0 | 0 | R | R | 6-0 | 205 | 9-18-73 | 1995 | Westerville, Ohio |
| Morimoto, Ken | .000 | 6 | 11 | 1 | 0 | 0 | 0 | 0 | 1 | 4 | 0 | 0 | 0 | R | R | 6-1 | 163 | 9-22-74 | 1995 | Eleele, Hawaii |
| Owen, Andy | .272 | 101 | 342 | 35 | 93 | 21 | 2 | 3 | 54 | 34 | 63 | 5 | 5 | L | L | 5-10 | 180 | 7-12-73 | 1995 | Escondido, Calif. |
| Ozuna, Rafael | .221 | 33 | 113 | 16 | 25 | 1 | 1 | 0 | 9 | 14 | 21 | 3 | 2 | S | R | 5-11 | 176 | 7-11-74 | 1993 | San Cristobal, D.R. |
| Schaaf, Ben | .220 | 61 | 186 | 23 | 41 | 8 | 1 | 0 | 11 | 12 | 47 | 4 | 2 | R | R | 5-10 | 170 | 10-15-72 | 1994 | Frankfort, Ill. |
| Sotelo, Danilo | .238 | 72 | 239 | 39 | 57 | 14 | 4 | 4 | 32 | 28 | 56 | 3 | 2 | R | R | 5-8 | 160 | 3-25-75 | 1996 | Managua, Nicaragua |
| Sowards, Ryan | .200 | 7 | 15 | 0 | 3 | 1 | 0 | 0 | 2 | 3 | 5 | 0 | 0 | L | R | 6-0 | 180 | 8-11-73 | 1994 | Bothell, Wash. |
| Steed, David | .288 | 22 | 73 | 6 | 21 | 3 | 0 | 1 | 10 | 6 | 15 | 1 | 0 | R | R | 6-1 | 205 | 2-25-73 | 1993 | Starkville, Miss. |
| Walkanoff, A.J. | .282 | 29 | 85 | 15 | 24 | 5 | 2 | 3 | 19 | 11 | 15 | 0 | 0 | R | R | 6-4 | 220 | 3-4-74 | 1995 | Zion, Ill. |
| Yard, Bruce | .266 | 59 | 192 | 24 | 51 | 7 | 2 | 1 | 15 | 18 | 19 | 2 | 2 | L | R | 6-0 | 175 | 10-17-71 | 1993 | McIntyre, Pa. |

**GAMES BY POSITION: C**—LoDuca 98, Meyer 11, Steed 20, Walkanoff 15. **1B**—LoDuca 12, Martinez 111, Schaaf 23. **2B**—Carpentier 32, Gibbs 1, Ozuna 33, Schaaf 3, Sotelo 67, Yard 1. **3B**—Barlock 110, Carpentier 11, LoDuca 12, Schaaf 12, Yard 4. **SS**—Carpentier 20, Cora 58, Faircloth 3, Ozuna 1, Yard 55. **OF**—Asencio 108, Cora 1, Coston 3, Durkin 20, Gibbs 115, Landrum 23, Majeski 55, Morimoto 4, Owen 83, Schaaf 13.

| PITCHING | W | L | ERA | G | GS | CG | SV | IP | H | R | ER | BB | SO | B | T | HT | WT | DOB | 1st Yr | Resides |
|---|---|---|---|---|---|---|---|---|---|---|---|---|---|---|---|---|---|---|---|---|
| Ahearne, Pat | 3 | 2 | 2.11 | 6 | 6 | 1 | 0 | 47 | 38 | 16 | 11 | 5 | 26 | R | R | 6-3 | 195 | 12-10-69 | 1992 | Atascadero, Calif. |
| Babineaux, Darrin | 1 | 7 | 3.29 | 10 | 10 | 1 | 0 | 63 | 56 | 30 | 23 | 23 | 41 | R | R | 6-4 | 210 | 7-10-74 | 1995 | Rayne, La. |
| Bland, Nate | 10 | 4 | 3.09 | 17 | 17 | 0 | 0 | 96 | 99 | 42 | 33 | 35 | 91 | L | L | 6-5 | 195 | 12-27-74 | 1993 | Birmingham, Ala. |
| Camacho, Dan | 5 | 1 | 2.48 | 10 | 10 | 0 | 0 | 54 | 38 | 16 | 15 | 29 | 50 | R | R | 5-11 | 200 | 11-11-73 | 1992 | San Diego, Calif. |
| Chambers, Scott | 0 | 0 | 2.25 | 10 | 0 | 0 | 0 | 12 | 7 | 6 | 3 | 5 | 20 | L | L | 5-10 | 175 | 7-10-75 | 1995 | Benton, Ky. |
| Colon, Julio | 3 | 2 | 2.61 | 8 | 8 | 0 | 0 | 41 | 44 | 21 | 12 | 19 | 49 | R | R | 6-2 | 202 | 10-30-72 | 1993 | Los Angeles, Calif. |
| Eaddy, Brad | 0 | 1 | 5.91 | 12 | 0 | 0 | 0 | 11 | 9 | 8 | 7 | 4 | 8 | L | L | 6-5 | 200 | 6-6-70 | 1994 | Florence, S.C. |
| Hollis, Ron | 0 | 1 | 2.95 | 19 | 0 | 0 | 11 | 21 | 20 | 10 | 7 | 7 | 27 | L | R | 6-3 | 205 | 8-13-73 | 1994 | Brighton, Mich. |
| Iglesias, Mike | 5 | 8 | 5.11 | 31 | 16 | 0 | 7 | 104 | 112 | 68 | 59 | 37 | 101 | R | R | 6-5 | 215 | 11-9-72 | 1991 | Castro Valley, Calif. |
| Lagarde, Joe | 4 | 3 | 2.44 | 14 | 4 | 0 | 1 | 44 | 41 | 17 | 12 | 22 | 46 | R | R | 5-9 | 180 | 1-17-75 | 1993 | Washington, D.C. |
| Martinez, Ramon | 1 | 0 | 0.00 | 1 | 1 | 0 | 0 | 7 | 5 | 1 | 0 | 0 | 10 | S | R | 6-4 | 173 | 3-22-68 | 1985 | Santo Domingo, D.R. |

| PITCHING | W | L | ERA | G | GS | CG | SV | IP | H | R | ER | BB | SO | B | T | HT | WT | DOB | 1st Yr | Resides |
|---|---|---|---|---|---|---|---|---|---|---|---|---|---|---|---|---|---|---|---|---|
| McNeely, Mitch | 1 | 1 | 2.08 | 23 | 1 | 1 | 2 | 48 | 32 | 13 | 11 | 12 | 34 | L | L | 6-6 | 190 | 2-14-74 | 1995 | New Albany, Miss. |
| Mitchell, Kendrick | 3 | 8 | 5.47 | 39 | 6 | 0 | 1 | 81 | 75 | 61 | 49 | 51 | 58 | R | R | 6-4 | 210 | 12-6-73 | 1992 | Portland, Ore. |
| Nakashima, Tony | 0 | 0 | 0.00 | 2 | 0 | 0 | 1 | 3 | 4 | 1 | 0 | 0 | 2 | L | L | 5-9 | 160 | 3-17-78 | 1995 | Sao Paulo, Brazil |
| Neal, Billy | 16 | 6 | 2.28 | 51 | 0 | 0 | 1 | 111 | 94 | 37 | 28 | 39 | 75 | R | R | 6-0 | 201 | 9-20-71 | 1995 | Scottsdale, Ariz. |
| Parra, Julio | 0 | 0 | 1.27 | 12 | 0 | 0 | 1 | 21 | 12 | 3 | 3 | 5 | 17 | R | R | 6-1 | 245 | 9-2-74 | 1995 | Los Mochis, Mexico |
| Pivaral, Hugo | 1 | 1 | 4.44 | 7 | 6 | 0 | 0 | 26 | 34 | 15 | 13 | 8 | 16 | R | R | 6-5 | 220 | 1-2-77 | 1994 | Guatemala City, Guatemala |
| Ricabal, Dan | 0 | 2 | 1.20 | 13 | 1 | 0 | 1 | 30 | 14 | 7 | 4 | 17 | 36 | R | R | 6-1 | 185 | 7-8-72 | 1994 | Rosemead, Calif. |
| Roach, Petie | 3 | 4 | 3.65 | 17 | 10 | 0 | 0 | 69 | 56 | 30 | 28 | 17 | 52 | L | L | 6-2 | 180 | 9-19-70 | 1992 | Redding, Calif. |
| Rolocut, Brian | 1 | 7 | 5.51 | 33 | 6 | 0 | 0 | 65 | 69 | 50 | 40 | 53 | 52 | R | R | 6-1 | 195 | 4-8-74 | 1993 | Gambrills, Md. |
| Scheffler, Craig | 0 | 0 | 6.53 | 31 | 1 | 0 | 1 | 41 | 50 | 33 | 30 | 27 | 23 | S | L | 6-2 | 195 | 9-13-71 | 1993 | Wausau, Wis. |
| Stone, Ricky | 8 | 6 | 3.83 | 21 | 21 | 1 | 0 | 113 | 115 | 58 | 48 | 46 | 74 | R | R | 6-2 | 173 | 2-28-75 | 1994 | Hamilton, Ohio |
| Yocum, David | 0 | 2 | 6.14 | 7 | 7 | 0 | 0 | 15 | 22 | 11 | 10 | 7 | 8 | L | L | 6-0 | 175 | 6-10-74 | 1995 | Miami, Fla. |

# SAVANNAH     Class A
## SOUTH ATLANTIC LEAGUE

| BATTING | AVG | G | AB | R | H | 2B | 3B | HR | RBI | BB | SO | SB | CS | B | T | HT | WT | DOB | 1st Yr | Resides |
|---|---|---|---|---|---|---|---|---|---|---|---|---|---|---|---|---|---|---|---|---|
| Backowski, Lance | .122 | 30 | 49 | 7 | 6 | 0 | 0 | 0 | 0 | 7 | 19 | 0 | 2 | R | R | 6-0 | 180 | 6-8-75 | 1995 | Fresno, Calif. |
| Beltre, Adrian | .307 | 68 | 244 | 48 | 75 | 14 | 3 | 16 | 59 | 35 | 46 | 4 | 3 | R | R | 5-11 | 200 | 4-7-78 | 1994 | Santo Domingo, D.R. |
| Cuevas, Trent | .152 | 15 | 46 | 2 | 7 | 1 | 0 | 0 | 6 | 0 | 14 | 0 | 0 | R | R | 5-11 | 175 | 12-25-76 | 1995 | Placentia, Calif. |
| Garcia, Miguel | .152 | 17 | 66 | 8 | 10 | 3 | 0 | 0 | 5 | 8 | 15 | 4 | 3 | R | R | 6-2 | 205 | 2-15-75 | 1992 | Santiago, D.R. |
| Gil, Geronimo | .243 | 79 | 276 | 29 | 67 | 13 | 1 | 7 | 38 | 8 | 69 | 0 | 2 | R | R | 6-2 | 195 | 8-7-75 | 1993 | Oaxaca, Mexico |
| Gonzalez, Manuel | .229 | 65 | 231 | 30 | 53 | 10 | 2 | 1 | 19 | 20 | 52 | 15 | 8 | S | R | 6-2 | 192 | 5-30-76 | 1994 | Santo Domingo, D.R. |
| Harmon, Brian | .217 | 85 | 230 | 36 | 50 | 11 | 0 | 10 | 37 | 50 | 56 | 0 | 3 | R | R | 6-2 | 215 | 3-21-76 | 1994 | Palos Heights, Ill. |
| Hernaiz, Juan | .278 | 132 | 492 | 68 | 137 | 19 | 8 | 14 | 73 | 21 | 96 | 42 | 15 | R | R | 5-11 | 185 | 2-15-75 | 1992 | Carolina, P.R. |
| Malave, Joshua | .250 | 6 | 16 | 2 | 4 | 0 | 0 | 0 | 5 | 3 | 0 | 0 | 0 | R | R | 6-0 | 196 | 3-22-75 | 1995 | Fort Lauderdale, Fla. |
| Mateo, Jose | .162 | 111 | 308 | 33 | 50 | 3 | 1 | 2 | 16 | 34 | 89 | 15 | 5 | S | R | 6-0 | 160 | 12-23-76 | 1994 | Santo Domingo, D.R. |
| Meyer, Travis | .292 | 68 | 185 | 23 | 54 | 8 | 2 | 3 | 20 | 22 | 42 | 0 | 0 | R | R | 6-2 | 205 | 9-18-73 | 1995 | Westerville, Ohio |
| Morrison, Greg | .254 | 94 | 299 | 32 | 76 | 11 | 4 | 4 | 39 | 19 | 65 | 4 | 7 | L | L | 6-1 | 185 | 2-23-76 | 1995 | Medicine Hat, Alberta |
| Ozuna, Rafael | .244 | 87 | 307 | 41 | 75 | 12 | 5 | 5 | 27 | 28 | 69 | 9 | 3 | S | R | 5-11 | 176 | 7-11-74 | 1993 | San Cristobal, D.R. |
| Pena, Angel | .205 | 36 | 127 | 13 | 26 | 4 | 0 | 6 | 16 | 7 | 37 | 1 | 1 | R | R | 6-0 | 220 | 2-16-75 | 1993 | San Pedro de Macoris, D.R. |
| Pimentel, Jose | .278 | 123 | 461 | 66 | 128 | 21 | 4 | 7 | 54 | 28 | 100 | 50 | 19 | R | R | 6-0 | 160 | 12-3-74 | 1993 | San Cristobal, D.R. |
| Prokopec, Luke | .216 | 82 | 245 | 34 | 53 | 12 | 1 | 4 | 29 | 27 | 78 | 0 | 5 | L | R | 6-0 | 180 | 2-23-78 | 1995 | Renmark, South Australia |
| Roney, Chad | .341 | 24 | 41 | 3 | 14 | 2 | 0 | 0 | 4 | 5 | 6 | 0 | 0 | R | R | 6-0 | 180 | 9-3-74 | 1996 | Fort Myers, Fla. |
| Sosa, Juan | .254 | 112 | 370 | 58 | 94 | 21 | 2 | 7 | 38 | 30 | 64 | 14 | 12 | R | R | 6-1 | 175 | 8-19-75 | 1993 | San Fran. de Macoris, D.R. |
| Sotelo, Danilo | .211 | 10 | 38 | 5 | 8 | 2 | 2 | 0 | 3 | 5 | 6 | 2 | 0 | R | R | 5-8 | 160 | 3-25-75 | 1996 | Managua, Nicaragua |
| Stuckenschneider, Eric | .277 | 140 | 470 | 111 | 130 | 28 | 6 | 16 | 63 | 111 | 96 | 50 | 18 | R | R | 6-0 | 190 | 8-24-71 | 1994 | Freeburg, Mo. |
| Tucker, Jon | .319 | 14 | 47 | 8 | 15 | 2 | 1 | 1 | 12 | 6 | 7 | 1 | 0 | L | L | 6-4 | 200 | 12-17-76 | 1995 | Northridge, Calif. |
| Weekley, Jason | .000 | 1 | 4 | 0 | 0 | 0 | 0 | 0 | 0 | 1 | 0 | 0 | 0 | R | R | 6-3 | 190 | 8-20-73 | 1996 | Hercules, Calif. |
| Zaun, Brian | .204 | 52 | 147 | 14 | 30 | 5 | 0 | 0 | 11 | 7 | 41 | 1 | 0 | R | R | 6-2 | 195 | 5-14-74 | 1996 | Maple Grove, Minn. |

**GAMES BY POSITION: C**—Gil 63, Malave 3, Meyer 51, Pena 30, Roney 17. **1B**—Harmon 72, Hernaiz 1, Meyer 1, Morrison 71, Tucker 14. **2B**—Backowski 18, Beltre 1, Cuevas 1, Morrison 1, Ozuna 80, Sosa 45, Sotello 10. **3B**—Backowski 4, Beltre 67, Cuevas 3, Malave 1, Roney 1, Sosa 31, Zaun 52. **SS**—Backowski 2, Cuevas 9, Mateo 109, Ozuna 3, Prokopec 1, Sosa 41, Stuckenschneider 1, Zaun 1. **OF**—Garcia 11, Gonzalez 39, Hernaiz 123, Morrison 3, Pimentel 116, Prokopec 54, Sosa 4, Stuckenschneider 105, Weekley 1.

| PITCHING | W | L | ERA | G | GS | CG | SV | IP | H | R | ER | BB | SO | B | T | HT | WT | DOB | 1st Yr | Resides |
|---|---|---|---|---|---|---|---|---|---|---|---|---|---|---|---|---|---|---|---|---|---|
| Allen, Craig | 0 | 0 | 2.45 | 1 | 1 | 0 | 0 | 4 | 4 | 4 | 1 | 3 | 2 | R | R | 6-3 | 200 | 12-22-72 | 1996 | Franklin, Ky. |
| Babineaux, Darrin | 5 | 5 | 4.82 | 13 | 12 | 1 | 0 | 71 | 70 | 45 | 38 | 30 | 48 | R | R | 6-4 | 210 | 7-10-74 | 1995 | Rayne, La. |
| Bland, Mike | 1 | 0 | 1.63 | 5 | 5 | 0 | 0 | 28 | 24 | 8 | 5 | 10 | 24 | L | L | 6-5 | 195 | 12-27-74 | 1993 | Birmingham, Ala. |
| Charbonneau, Marc | 4 | 6 | 4.71 | 25 | 9 | 0 | 0 | 80 | 84 | 52 | 42 | 31 | 82 | R | L | 6-3 | 185 | 9-29-75 | 1995 | Ottawa, Ontario |
| Davis, John | 9 | 5 | 2.74 | 38 | 10 | 2 | 1 | 112 | 72 | 39 | 34 | 58 | 123 | R | R | 6-4 | 218 | 8-31-73 | 1995 | Swainsboro, Ga. |
| Gagne, Eric | 7 | 6 | 3.28 | 23 | 21 | 1 | 0 | 115 | 94 | 48 | 42 | 43 | 131 | R | R06-2 | 6-2 | 190 | 1-7-76 | 1996 | Mascouche, Quebec |
| Judd, Mike | 4 | 2 | 2.44 | 15 | 8 | 1 | 3 | 55 | 40 | 21 | 15 | 15 | 62 | R | R | 6-2 | 200 | 6-30-75 | 1995 | La Mesa, Calif. |
|    2-team (29 G'boro.) | .. 6 | 4 | 2.90 | 44 | 8 | 1 | 13 | 84 | 62 | 35 | 27 | 23 | 98 | | | | | | | |
| Keppen, Jeff | 0 | 1 | 2.25 | 12 | 0 | 0 | 0 | 20 | 13 | 10 | 5 | 20 | 26 | R | R | 6-2 | 190 | 1-31-74 | 1995 | Lawrenceville, Ga. |
| Masaoka, Onan | 2 | 5 | 4.29 | 13 | 13 | 0 | 0 | 65 | 55 | 35 | 31 | 35 | 80 | R | L | 6-0 | 188 | 10-27-77 | 1995 | Hilo, Hawaii |
| McDonald, Matt | 5 | 6 | 4.73 | 28 | 13 | 0 | 3 | 84 | 66 | 56 | 44 | 50 | 85 | L | L | 6-4 | 200 | 6-10-74 | 1994 | Princeton, Ill. |
| Nakashima, Tony | 3 | 2 | 2.45 | 27 | 0 | 0 | 2 | 37 | 20 | 11 | 10 | 19 | 39 | L | L | 5-9 | 160 | 3-17-78 | 1995 | Sao Paulo, Brazil |
| Ochsenfeld, Chris | 6 | 7 | 4.19 | 26 | 18 | 0 | 1 | 110 | 118 | 66 | 51 | 52 | 79 | L | L | 6-2 | 210 | 8-21-76 | 1994 | Hampton, Va. |
| Parra, Julio | 1 | 1 | 2.30 | 12 | 0 | 0 | 2 | 16 | 8 | 4 | 4 | 6 | 19 | R | R | 6-1 | 245 | 9-2-74 | 1994 | Los Mochis, Mexico |
| Pearsall, J.J. | 6 | 5 | 3.29 | 45 | 2 | 0 | 3 | 88 | 76 | 48 | 32 | 46 | 88 | L | L | 6-2 | 202 | 9-9-73 | 1995 | Burnt Hills, N.Y. |
| Reed, Jason | 0 | 0 | 7.15 | 5 | 0 | 0 | 0 | 11 | 14 | 10 | 9 | 7 | 8 | L | L | 6-3 | 215 | 6-8-73 | 1994 | Lakeside, Calif. |
| Ricabal, Dan | 2 | 4 | 2.08 | 40 | 0 | 0 | 24 | 55 | 32 | 19 | 14 | 17 | 78 | R | R | 6-1 | 185 | 7-8-72 | 1994 | Rosemead, Calif. |
| South, Carl | 6 | 5 | 4.13 | 33 | 10 | 0 | 0 | 96 | 85 | 58 | 44 | 42 | 84 | R | R | 6-5 | 210 | 4-14-75 | 1994 | Roswell, Ga. |
| Spykstra, Dave | 6 | 4 | 3.31 | 28 | 14 | 2 | 0 | 101 | 83 | 47 | 37 | 44 | 104 | R | R | 6-2 | 200 | 8-26-73 | 1992 | Denver, Colo. |
| Stone, Ricky | 2 | 1 | 3.98 | 5 | 5 | 0 | 0 | 32 | 34 | 15 | 14 | 9 | 31 | R | R | 6-2 | 173 | 2-28-75 | 1994 | Hamilton, Ohio |
| Torres, Jackson | 3 | 4 | 4.28 | 42 | 0 | 0 | 3 | 61 | 52 | 39 | 29 | 29 | 32 | R | R | 6-2 | 198 | 8-19-74 | 1992 | Azua, D.R. |

# YAKIMA     Class A
## NORTHWEST LEAGUE

| BATTING | AVG | G | AB | R | H | 2B | 3B | HR | RBI | BB | SO | SB | CS | B | T | HT | WT | DOB | 1st Yr | Resides |
|---|---|---|---|---|---|---|---|---|---|---|---|---|---|---|---|---|---|---|---|---|
| Bergeron, Peter | .254 | 61 | 232 | 36 | 59 | 5 | 3 | 5 | 21 | 28 | 59 | 13 | 9 | L | R | 6-1 | 185 | 11-9-77 | 1996 | Greenfield, Mass. |
| Brown, Eric | .234 | 53 | 171 | 19 | 40 | 9 | 0 | 7 | 21 | 16 | 68 | 5 | 2 | R | R | 6-1 | 205 | 2-28-77 | 1995 | La Place, La. |
| Flores, Eric | .190 | 38 | 100 | 7 | 19 | 4 | 0 | 0 | 8 | 12 | 42 | 0 | 0 | R | R | 6-3 | 190 | 7-7-76 | 1995 | Oxnard, Calif. |
| Glassey, Josh | .219 | 50 | 137 | 11 | 30 | 5 | 0 | 0 | 20 | 26 | 44 | 0 | 0 | L | R | 6-1 | 190 | 5-6-77 | 1996 | Del Mar, Calif. |
| King, William | .154 | 24 | 39 | 4 | 6 | 0 | 0 | 1 | 7 | 16 | 0 | 0 | 1 | L | R | 6-1 | 195 | 5-31-78 | 1996 | Brooklyn, N.Y. |
| Malave, Jaime | .204 | 40 | 108 | 14 | 22 | 6 | 0 | 5 | 16 | 6 | 33 | 0 | 0 | R | R | 6-0 | 196 | 3-22-75 | 1995 | Fort Lauderdale, Fla. |
| Marshall, Monte | .191 | 17 | 68 | 9 | 13 | 1 | 1 | 0 | 7 | 7 | 14 | 0 | 1 | S | R | 5-7 | 155 | 12-6-73 | 1996 | Meridian, Miss. |
| Meyer, Bobby | .213 | 33 | 80 | 12 | 17 | 5 | 0 | 1 | 7 | 12 | 25 | 2 | 0 | R | R | 6-0 | 170 | 9-17-74 | 1995 | Dubuque, Iowa |
| Meyer, Matt | .302 | 66 | 235 | 40 | 71 | 14 | 6 | 4 | 28 | 27 | 73 | 6 | 0 | L | R | 6-2 | 205 | 3-28-74 | 1996 | Yakima, Wash. |
| Morrison, Scott | .207 | 60 | 184 | 22 | 38 | 11 | 1 | 1 | 26 | 32 | 42 | 2 | 1 | R | R | 6-0 | 180 | 9-24-72 | 1996 | Galveston, Texas |
| Mota, Tony | .276 | 60 | 225 | 29 | 62 | 11 | 3 | 3 | 29 | 13 | 37 | 13 | 7 | S | R | 6-1 | 200 | 10-31-77 | 1996 | Miami, Fla. |
| Newton, Kimani | .156 | 33 | 45 | 8 | 7 | 1 | 0 | 0 | 3 | 6 | 13 | 1 | 2 | R | R | 6-0 | 185 | 6-16-79 | 1996 | Christiansted, V.I. |

| BATTING | AVG | G | AB | R | H | 2B | 3B | HR | RBI | BB | SO | SB | CS | B | T | HT | WT | DOB | 1st Yr | Resides |
|---|---|---|---|---|---|---|---|---|---|---|---|---|---|---|---|---|---|---|---|---|
| Rolls, Damian | .265 | 66 | 257 | 31 | 68 | 11 | 1 | 4 | 27 | 7 | 46 | 8 | 3 | R | R | 6-2 | 205 | 9-15-77 | 1996 | Kansas City, Kan. |
| Saitta, Rich | .248 | 44 | 165 | 17 | 41 | 5 | 0 | 1 | 17 | 11 | 34 | 7 | 5 | R | R | 5-10 | 170 | 7-28-75 | 1996 | Marlboro, N.J. |
| Sankey, Brian | .294 | 72 | 255 | 40 | 75 | 19 | 2 | 11 | 52 | 34 | 53 | 2 | 0 | L | L | 6-1 | 195 | 6-12-74 | 1996 | North Attleboro, Mass. |
| Stearns, Randy | .257 | 57 | 183 | 29 | 47 | 8 | 3 | 0 | 10 | 17 | 60 | 17 | 6 | L | R | 6-0 | 190 | 10-22-74 | 1996 | Bloomer, Wis. |
| Wilson, Steve | .177 | 42 | 113 | 9 | 20 | 5 | 0 | 1 | 8 | 5 | 44 | 3 | 0 | R | R | 5-11 | 200 | 6-12-74 | 1996 | Marietta, Ga. |

**GAMES BY POSITION: C**—Glassey 37, Malave 22, M. Meyer 1, Newton 1, Stearns 1, Wilson 41. **1B**—King 11, Malave 6, M. Meyer 1, Sankey 71. **2B**—Marshall 17, B. Meyer 20, Morrison 1, Saitta 42. **3B**—Flores 9, Malave 5, B. Meyer 6, Morrison 1, Rolls 65. **SS**—Flores 27, Morrison 57. **OF**—Bergeron 54, Brown 42, B. Meyer 1, M. Meyer 56, Mota 40, Newton 18, Stearsn 39.

| PITCHING | W | L | ERA | G | GS | CG | SV | IP | H | R | ER | BB | SO | B | T | HT | WT | DOB | 1st Yr | Resides |
|---|---|---|---|---|---|---|---|---|---|---|---|---|---|---|---|---|---|---|---|---|
| Culmo, Kevin | 4 | 2 | 2.27 | 17 | 5 | 0 | 2 | 63 | 47 | 18 | 16 | 22 | 60 | R | R | 6-2 | 190 | 11-13-74 | 1996 | Sacramento, Calif. |
| Deskins, Casey | 4 | 5 | 4.76 | 15 | 9 | 0 | 0 | 62 | 69 | 40 | 33 | 20 | 43 | R | L | 6-3 | 220 | 4-5-72 | 1993 | Yakima, Wash. |
| Franklin, Wayne | 1 | 0 | 2.52 | 20 | 0 | 0 | 1 | 25 | 32 | 10 | 7 | 12 | 22 | L | L | 6-2 | 195 | 3-9-74 | 1996 | North East, Md. |
| Hall, Darren | 0 | 1 | 3.00 | 2 | 2 | 0 | 0 | 3 | 5 | 2 | 1 | 0 | 4 | R | R | 6-3 | 205 | 7-14-64 | 1986 | Irving, Texas |
| Hannah, Michael | 1 | 1 | 5.70 | 18 | 0 | 0 | 1 | 24 | 25 | 26 | 15 | 22 | 13 | R | R | 6-2 | 190 | 4-1-75 | 1996 | Bremen, Ga. |
| Kramer, Matt | 2 | 0 | 2.61 | 12 | 5 | 0 | 0 | 38 | 36 | 13 | 11 | 21 | 31 | R | R | 6-2 | 210 | 4-4-76 | 1996 | Simi Valley, Calif. |
| Kubenka, Jeff | 5 | 1 | 2.51 | 28 | 0 | 0 | 14 | 32 | 20 | 11 | 9 | 10 | 61 | R | L | 6-0 | 195 | 8-24-74 | 1996 | Schulenburg, Texas |
| Lilly, Ted | 4 | 0 | 0.84 | 13 | 8 | 0 | 0 | 54 | 25 | 9 | 5 | 14 | 75 | L | L | 6-1 | 180 | 1-4-76 | 1996 | Fresno, Calif. |
| Lovinger, Eric | 0 | 1 | 1.80 | 4 | 0 | 0 | 0 | 5 | 4 | 3 | 1 | 2 | 3 | R | R | 6-3 | 205 | 1-2-73 | 1996 | Portland, Ore. |
| Maestas, Mickey | 0 | 6 | 9.20 | 14 | 6 | 0 | 0 | 30 | 44 | 34 | 31 | 17 | 25 | R | R | 6-3 | 195 | 8-24-75 | 1996 | Key Largo, Fla. |
| Mayo, Blake | 5 | 2 | 1.20 | 20 | 6 | 0 | 1 | 67 | 44 | 15 | 9 | 12 | 68 | R | R | 6-2 | 210 | 12-18-72 | 1996 | Gadsden, Ala. |
| Mitchell, Dean | 2 | 2 | 3.44 | 15 | 5 | 0 | 2 | 52 | 53 | 25 | 20 | 25 | 61 | R | R | 5-11 | 175 | 3-19-74 | 1996 | Waco, Texas |
| O'Shaughnessy, Jay | 4 | 3 | 3.23 | 13 | 11 | 0 | 1 | 56 | 26 | 24 | 20 | 36 | 85 | R | R | 6-3 | 220 | 8-14-74 | 1995 | Belmont, Mass. |
| Paluk, Brian | 4 | 1 | 3.40 | 20 | 5 | 0 | 0 | 45 | 36 | 24 | 17 | 17 | 37 | R | R | 6-6 | 225 | 10-5-75 | 1996 | Plymouth, Mich. |
| Simon, Ben | 2 | 6 | 3.66 | 15 | 10 | 0 | 1 | 66 | 59 | 34 | 27 | 21 | 62 | R | R | 6-1 | 198 | 11-12-74 | 1996 | Berlin Heights, Ohio |
| Stover, C.D. | 1 | 4 | 5.57 | 15 | 4 | 0 | 1 | 32 | 36 | 23 | 20 | 16 | 25 | R | R | 6-5 | 225 | 12-8-75 | 1996 | Citrus Heights, Calif. |
| Taczy, Craig | 1 | 1 | 7.48 | 16 | 0 | 0 | 1 | 22 | 27 | 22 | 18 | 16 | 14 | L | L | 6-6 | 225 | 4-15-77 | 1995 | Crestwood, Ill. |

## GREAT FALLS — Rookie
### PIONEER LEAGUE

| BATTING | AVG | G | AB | R | H | 2B | 3B | HR | RBI | BB | SO | SB | CS | B | T | HT | WT | DOB | 1st Yr | Resides |
|---|---|---|---|---|---|---|---|---|---|---|---|---|---|---|---|---|---|---|---|---|
| Auterson, Jeff | .206 | 51 | 165 | 22 | 34 | 4 | 1 | 4 | 12 | 20 | 72 | 6 | 8 | R | R | 6-1 | 190 | 2-22-78 | 1996 | Riverside, Calif. |
| Bramlett, Jeff | .261 | 56 | 222 | 42 | 58 | 14 | 6 | 7 | 41 | 17 | 62 | 12 | 3 | R | R | 6-0 | 200 | 4-27-76 | 1995 | Cleveland, Tenn. |
| Cripps, Bobby | .309 | 49 | 139 | 23 | 43 | 4 | 3 | 2 | 28 | 9 | 19 | 6 | 5 | L | R | 6-2 | 200 | 5-9-77 | 1996 | Powell River, B.C. |
| Cuevas, Trent | .258 | 51 | 155 | 24 | 40 | 12 | 1 | 3 | 20 | 11 | 30 | 2 | 5 | R | R | 5-11 | 175 | 12-25-76 | 1995 | Placentia, Calif. |
| Falcon, David | .321 | 20 | 53 | 6 | 17 | 3 | 0 | 1 | 8 | 12 | 8 | 2 | 0 | R | R | 6-1 | 200 | 8-28-78 | 1996 | Bayamon, P.R. |
| Foulks, Brian | .314 | 35 | 121 | 14 | 38 | 7 | 1 | 1 | 9 | 1 | 24 | 4 | 2 | R | R | 6-3 | 205 | 12-26-73 | 1996 | Lexington, S.C. |
| Illig, Brett | .227 | 44 | 119 | 15 | 27 | 3 | 0 | 1 | 11 | 6 | 36 | 4 | 2 | R | R | 6-3 | 185 | 9-4-77 | 1995 | Phoenixville, Pa. |
| Leach, Nick | .251 | 58 | 199 | 42 | 50 | 8 | 1 | 9 | 25 | 36 | 33 | 2 | 4 | L | R | 6-1 | 190 | 12-7-77 | 1996 | Madera, Calif. |
| Marshall, Monte | .265 | 52 | 181 | 36 | 48 | 7 | 1 | 0 | 22 | 19 | 34 | 10 | 7 | S | R | 5-7 | 155 | 12-6-73 | 1996 | Meridian, Miss. |
| McCarty, Matt | .284 | 58 | 208 | 40 | 59 | 7 | 10 | 3 | 32 | 24 | 56 | 16 | 2 | R | R | 6-0 | 172 | 2-2-76 | 1995 | Crawfordsville, Ind. |
| Meyer, Bobby | .377 | 14 | 53 | 12 | 20 | 2 | 3 | 0 | 4 | 10 | 16 | 7 | 4 | R | R | 6-0 | 170 | 9-17-74 | 1995 | Dubuque, Iowa |
| Morimoto, Ken | .285 | 32 | 123 | 40 | 35 | 3 | 1 | 1 | 12 | 19 | 26 | 27 | 4 | R | R | 6-1 | 163 | 9-22-74 | 1995 | Eleele, Hawaii |
| Richey, Mikal | .108 | 34 | 65 | 8 | 7 | 1 | 0 | 0 | 0 | 8 | 25 | 4 | 1 | R | R | 5-10 | 185 | 8-3-78 | 1996 | Decatur, Ga. |
| Riley, Cash | .303 | 44 | 145 | 23 | 44 | 8 | 1 | 3 | 26 | 14 | 30 | 6 | 6 | R | R | 6-2 | 190 | 6-4-77 | 1996 | Irving, Texas |
| Snow, Casey | .269 | 43 | 130 | 19 | 35 | 6 | 0 | 2 | 23 | 13 | 33 | 1 | 4 | S | R | 5-10 | 185 | 12-8-74 | 1996 | Canoga Park, Calif. |
| Tucker, Jon | .345 | 48 | 174 | 39 | 60 | 12 | 1 | 12 | 54 | 15 | 30 | 13 | 5 | L | L | 6-4 | 200 | 12-17-76 | 1995 | Northridge, Calif. |
| Weekley, Jason | .366 | 64 | 238 | 35 | 87 | 12 | 5 | 7 | 43 | 18 | 63 | 8 | 12 | R | R | 6-3 | 190 | 8-20-73 | 1996 | Hercules, Calif. |

**GAMES BY POSITION: C**—Cripps 43, Falcon 8, Snow 30. **1B**—Bramlett 37, Tucker 35. **2B**—Cuevas 19, Marshall 48, Meyer 14. **3B**—Cuevas 14, Illig 21, Leach 52, McCarty 5. **SS**—Cuevas 24, Illig 24, McCarty 4, Morimoto 29, Snow 1. **OF**—Auterson 50, Bramlett 8, Foulks 24, McCarty 48, Richey 23, Riley 38, Weekley 54.

| PITCHING | W | L | ERA | G | GS | CG | SV | IP | H | R | ER | BB | SO | B | T | HT | WT | DOB | 1st Yr | Resides |
|---|---|---|---|---|---|---|---|---|---|---|---|---|---|---|---|---|---|---|---|---|
| Allen, Craig | 4 | 2 | 3.84 | 13 | 12 | 0 | 0 | 61 | 52 | 38 | 26 | 31 | 46 | R | R | 6-3 | 200 | 12-22-72 | 1996 | Franklin, Ky. |
| Bohman, John | 1 | 0 | 12.27 | 12 | 0 | 0 | 0 | 18 | 24 | 28 | 25 | 15 | 5 | R | R | 6-2 | 210 | 8-6-75 | 1996 | San Fernando, Calif. |
| Bourbakis, Michael | 4 | 2 | 8.93 | 17 | 5 | 0 | 0 | 41 | 47 | 45 | 41 | 39 | 36 | R | R | 6-3 | 195 | 11-19-76 | 1995 | Brooklyn, N.Y. |
| Burnside, Adrian | 1 | 3 | 6.80 | 14 | 5 | 0 | 0 | 41 | 44 | 35 | 31 | 38 | 33 | R | L | 6-4 | 168 | 3-15-77 | 1996 | Alice Springs, Australia |
| Cervantes, Peter | 3 | 4 | 2.98 | 9 | 8 | 1 | 0 | 51 | 52 | 29 | 17 | 11 | 40 | L | R | 6-3 | 195 | 10-13-74 | 1995 | Los Angeles, Calif. |
| Correa, Elvis | 1 | 0 | 10.00 | 16 | 1 | 0 | 1 | 27 | 41 | 32 | 30 | 11 | 25 | R | R | 6-3 | 185 | 11-10-78 | 1996 | Milwaukee, Wis. |
| Dollar, Toby | 1 | 6 | 8.39 | 14 | 7 | 0 | 0 | 49 | 72 | 54 | 46 | 24 | 42 | R | R | 6-3 | 215 | 12-27-74 | 1996 | Graham, Texas |
| Feliciano, Pedro | 2 | 3 | 5.71 | 22 | 1 | 0 | 3 | 41 | 50 | 36 | 26 | 26 | 39 | L | L | 5-11 | 165 | 8-25-76 | 1995 | Dorado, P.R. |
| Flores, Pedro | 4 | 2 | 5.79 | 18 | 3 | 0 | 0 | 47 | 44 | 37 | 30 | 28 | 24 | L | L | 6-0 | 205 | 3-30-77 | 1996 | Baldwin Park, Calif. |
| Garcia, Miguel | 3 | 5 | 5.18 | 22 | 5 | 0 | 3 | 40 | 53 | 27 | 23 | 17 | 29 | R | R | 6-2 | 205 | 2-15-75 | 1992 | Santiago, D.R. |
| Ishimaru, Taisuke | 0 | 1 | 5.14 | 9 | 2 | 0 | 2 | 21 | 22 | 13 | 12 | 14 | 11 | R | R | 6-1 | 155 | 9-18-77 | 1996 | Tokyo, Japan |
| Jacobson, Brian | 4 | 2 | 5.45 | 29 | 0 | 0 | 7 | 38 | 56 | 37 | 23 | 13 | 31 | S | L | 6-0 | 190 | 10-12-74 | 1996 | Perris, Calif. |
| Sanchez, Mike | 0 | 0 | 9.64 | 9 | 0 | 0 | 1 | 9 | 8 | 11 | 10 | 10 | 7 | R | R | 6-3 | 175 | 11-23-75 | 1995 | Riverside, Calif. |
| Soto, Seferino | 2 | 4 | 6.14 | 15 | 11 | 0 | 1 | 56 | 56 | 45 | 38 | 35 | 51 | R | R | 6-1 | 175 | 8-26-75 | 1995 | Escondido, Calif. |
| Thomas, Brad | 3 | 2 | 6.31 | 11 | 5 | 0 | 0 | 36 | 48 | 27 | 25 | 11 | 28 | L | L | 6-3 | 192 | 10-27-77 | 1996 | Sydney, Australia |
| Thompson, Frank | 0 | 3 | 8.62 | 14 | 7 | 0 | 0 | 47 | 60 | 50 | 45 | 25 | 39 | R | R | 6-1 | 190 | 4-10-73 | 1996 | Daytona Beach, Fla. |

# MILWAUKEE BREWERS

**Manager:** Phil Garner.  **1996 Record:** 80-82, .481 (3rd, AL Central).

| BATTING | AVG | G | AB | R | H | 2B | 3B | HR | RBI | BB | SO | SB | CS | B | T | HT | WT | DOB | 1st Yr | Resides |
|---|---|---|---|---|---|---|---|---|---|---|---|---|---|---|---|---|---|---|---|---|
| Banks, Brian | .571 | 4 | 7 | 2 | 4 | 2 | 0 | 1 | 2 | 1 | 2 | 0 | 0 | S | R | 6-3 | 200 | 9-28-70 | 1993 | Mesa, Ariz. |
| Burnitz, Jeromy | .236 | 23 | 72 | 8 | 17 | 4 | 0 | 2 | 14 | 8 | 16 | 2 | 0 | L | R | 6-0 | 190 | 4-14-69 | 1990 | Key Largo, Fla. |
| 2-team (71 Cleve.) | .265 | 94 | 200 | 38 | 53 | 14 | 0 | 9 | 40 | 33 | 47 | 4 | 1 | | | | | | | |
| Carr, Chuck | .274 | 27 | 106 | 18 | 29 | 6 | 1 | 1 | 11 | 6 | 21 | 5 | 4 | S | R | 5-10 | 165 | 8-10-68 | 1986 | Tucson, Ariz. |
| Cirillo, Jeff | .325 | 158 | 566 | 101 | 184 | 46 | 5 | 15 | 83 | 58 | 69 | 4 | 9 | R | R | 6-2 | 180 | 9-23-69 | 1991 | Van Nuys, Calif. |
| Dunn, Todd | .300 | 6 | 10 | 2 | 3 | 1 | 0 | 0 | 1 | 0 | 3 | 0 | 0 | R | R | 6-5 | 220 | 7-29-70 | 1993 | Jacksonville, Fla. |
| Hulse, David | .222 | 81 | 117 | 18 | 26 | 3 | 0 | 0 | 6 | 8 | 16 | 4 | 1 | L | L | 5-11 | 170 | 2-25-68 | 1990 | San Angelo, Texas |
| Jaha, John | .300 | 148 | 543 | 108 | 163 | 28 | 1 | 34 | 118 | 85 | 118 | 3 | 1 | R | R | 6-1 | 205 | 5-27-66 | 1985 | Portland, Ore. |
| Koslofski, Kevin | .214 | 25 | 42 | 5 | 9 | 3 | 2 | 0 | 6 | 4 | 12 | 0 | 0 | L | R | 5-8 | 175 | 9-24-66 | 1984 | Maroa, Ill. |
| Levis, Jesse | .236 | 104 | 233 | 27 | 55 | 6 | 1 | 1 | 21 | 38 | 15 | 0 | 0 | L | R | 5-9 | 180 | 4-14-68 | 1989 | Philadelphia, Pa. |
| Listach, Pat | .240 | 87 | 317 | 51 | 76 | 16 | 2 | 1 | 33 | 36 | 51 | 25 | 5 | S | R | 5-9 | 170 | 9-12-67 | 1988 | Woodway, Texas |
| Loretta, Mark | .279 | 73 | 154 | 20 | 43 | 3 | 0 | 1 | 13 | 14 | 15 | 2 | 1 | R | R | 6-0 | 175 | 8-14-71 | 1993 | Laguna Niguel, Calif. |
| Matheny, Mike | .204 | 106 | 313 | 31 | 64 | 15 | 2 | 8 | 46 | 14 | 80 | 3 | 2 | R | R | 6-3 | 205 | 9-22-70 | 1991 | Reynoldsburg, Ohio |
| Mieske, Matt | .278 | 127 | 374 | 46 | 104 | 24 | 3 | 14 | 64 | 26 | 76 | 1 | 5 | R | R | 6-0 | 185 | 2-13-68 | 1990 | Livonia, Mich. |
| Newfield, Marc | .307 | 49 | 179 | 21 | 55 | 15 | 0 | 7 | 31 | 11 | 26 | 0 | 1 | R | R | 6-4 | 205 | 10-19-72 | 1990 | Huntington Beach, Calif. |
| Nilsson, Dave | .331 | 123 | 453 | 81 | 150 | 33 | 2 | 17 | 84 | 57 | 68 | 2 | 3 | L | R | 6-3 | 215 | 12-14-69 | 1987 | Everton Hills, Australia |
| Perez, Danny | .000 | 4 | 4 | 0 | 0 | 0 | 0 | 0 | 0 | 0 | 0 | 0 | 0 | R | R | 5-10 | 188 | 2-26-71 | 1992 | El Paso, Texas |
| Seitzer, Kevin | .316 | 132 | 490 | 74 | 155 | 25 | 3 | 12 | 62 | 73 | 68 | 6 | 1 | R | R | 5-11 | 190 | 3-26-62 | 1983 | Overland Park, Kan. |
| Stinnett, Kelly | .077 | 14 | 26 | 1 | 2 | 0 | 0 | 0 | 0 | 2 | 11 | 0 | 0 | R | R | 5-11 | 195 | 2-14-70 | 1990 | Lawton, Okla. |
| Unroe, Tim | .188 | 14 | 16 | 5 | 3 | 0 | 0 | 0 | 0 | 4 | 5 | 0 | 1 | R | R | 6-3 | 200 | 10-7-70 | 1992 | Round Lake Beach, Ill. |
| Valentin, Jose | .259 | 154 | 552 | 90 | 143 | 33 | 7 | 24 | 95 | 66 | 145 | 17 | 4 | S | R | 5-10 | 175 | 10-12-69 | 1987 | Manati, P.R. |
| Vaughn, Greg | .280 | 12 | 375 | 78 | 105 | 16 | 0 | 31 | 95 | 58 | 99 | 5 | 3 | R | R | 6-0 | 205 | 7-3-65 | 1986 | Elk Grove, Calif. |
| Vina, Fernando | .283 | 140 | 554 | 94 | 157 | 19 | 10 | 7 | 46 | 38 | 35 | 16 | 7 | L | R | 5-9 | 170 | 4-16-69 | 1990 | Sacramento, Calif. |
| Ward, Turner | .179 | 43 | 67 | 7 | 12 | 2 | 1 | 2 | 10 | 13 | 17 | 3 | 0 | S | R | 6-2 | 182 | 4-11-65 | 1986 | Saraland, Ala. |
| Williams, Gerald | .207 | 26 | 92 | 6 | 19 | 4 | 0 | 0 | 4 | 4 | 18 | 1 | 1 | R | R | 6-2 | 185 | 8-10-66 | 1987 | La Place, La. |
| 2-team (99 N.Y.) | .252 | 125 | 325 | 43 | 82 | 19 | 4 | 5 | 34 | 19 | 57 | 10 | 9 | | | | | | | |

| PITCHING | W | L | ERA | G | GS | CG | SV | IP | H | R | ER | BB | SO | B | T | HT | WT | DOB | 1st Yr | Resides |
|---|---|---|---|---|---|---|---|---|---|---|---|---|---|---|---|---|---|---|---|---|
| Bones, Ricky | 7 | 14 | 5.83 | 32 | 23 | 0 | 0 | 145 | 170 | 104 | 94 | 62 | 59 | R | R | 6-0 | 190 | 4-7-69 | 1986 | Guayama, P.R. |
| Boze, Marshall | 0 | 2 | 7.79 | 25 | 0 | 0 | 1 | 32 | 47 | 29 | 28 | 25 | 19 | R | R | 6-1 | 212 | 5-23-71 | 1990 | Springfield, Ill. |
| Burrows, Terry | 2 | 0 | 2.84 | 8 | 0 | 0 | 0 | 13 | 12 | 4 | 4 | 10 | 5 | L | L | 6-1 | 185 | 11-28-68 | 1990 | Lake Charles, La. |
| Carpenter, Cris | 0 | 0 | 7.56 | 8 | 0 | 0 | 0 | 8 | 12 | 8 | 7 | 2 | 2 | R | R | 6-1 | 185 | 4-5-65 | 1988 | Gainesville, Ga. |
| D'Amico, Jeff | 6 | 6 | 5.44 | 17 | 17 | 0 | 0 | 86 | 88 | 53 | 52 | 31 | 53 | R | R | 6-7 | 250 | 12-27-75 | 1993 | Pinellas Park, Fla. |
| Eldred, Cal | 4 | 4 | 4.46 | 15 | 15 | 0 | 0 | 85 | 82 | 43 | 42 | 38 | 50 | R | R | 6-4 | 235 | 11-24-67 | 1989 | Center Point, Iowa |
| Fetters, Mike | 3 | 3 | 3.38 | 61 | 0 | 0 | 32 | 61 | 65 | 28 | 23 | 26 | 53 | R | R | 6-4 | 215 | 12-19-64 | 1986 | Gilbert, Ariz. |
| Florie, Bryce | 0 | 1 | 6.63 | 15 | 0 | 0 | 0 | 19 | 20 | 16 | 14 | 13 | 12 | R | R | 6-0 | 170 | 5-21-70 | 1988 | Hanahan, S.C. |
| Garcia, Ramon | 4 | 4 | 6.66 | 37 | 2 | 0 | 4 | 76 | 84 | 58 | 56 | 21 | 40 | R | R | 6-2 | 200 | 12-9-69 | 1987 | Guanare, Venez. |
| Givens, Brian | 1 | 3 | 12.86 | 4 | 4 | 0 | 0 | 14 | 32 | 22 | 20 | 7 | 10 | R | L | 6-6 | 220 | 11-6-65 | 1984 | Aurora, Colo. |
| Jones, Doug | 5 | 0 | 3.41 | 24 | 0 | 0 | 1 | 32 | 31 | 13 | 12 | 13 | 34 | R | R | 6-2 | 195 | 6-24-57 | 1978 | Tucson, Ariz. |
| Karl, Scott | 13 | 9 | 4.86 | 32 | 32 | 3 | 0 | 207 | 220 | 124 | 112 | 72 | 121 | L | L | 6-2 | 195 | 8-9-71 | 1992 | Carlsbad, Calif. |
| Kiefer, Mark | 0 | 0 | 8.10 | 7 | 0 | 0 | 0 | 10 | 15 | 9 | 9 | 5 | 5 | R | R | 6-4 | 184 | 11-13-68 | 1988 | Kingsland, Texas |
| Lloyd, Graeme | 2 | 4 | 2.82 | 52 | 0 | 0 | 0 | 51 | 49 | 19 | 16 | 17 | 24 | L | L | 6-7 | 230 | 4-9-67 | 1988 | Gnarwarre, Australia |
| McDonald, Ben | 12 | 10 | 3.90 | 35 | 35 | 2 | 0 | 221 | 228 | 104 | 96 | 67 | 146 | R | R | 6-7 | 210 | 11-24-67 | 1989 | Denham Springs, La. |
| Mercedes, Jose | 0 | 2 | 9.18 | 11 | 0 | 0 | 0 | 17 | 20 | 18 | 17 | 5 | 6 | R | R | 6-1 | 180 | 3-5-71 | 1990 | Las Palmillas, D.R. |
| Miranda, Angel | 7 | 6 | 4.94 | 46 | 12 | 0 | 1 | 109 | 116 | 68 | 60 | 69 | 78 | L | L | 6-1 | 195 | 11-9-69 | 1987 | Arecibo, P.R. |
| Potts, Mike | 1 | 2 | 7.15 | 24 | 0 | 0 | 1 | 45 | 58 | 39 | 36 | 30 | 21 | L | L | 5-9 | 170 | 9-5-70 | 1990 | Lithonia, Ga. |
| Reyes, Alberto | 1 | 0 | 7.94 | 5 | 0 | 0 | 0 | 6 | 8 | 5 | 5 | 2 | 2 | R | R | 6-0 | 165 | 4-10-71 | 1988 | Santo Domingo, D.R. |
| Sparks, Steve | 4 | 7 | 6.60 | 20 | 13 | 1 | 0 | 89 | 103 | 66 | 65 | 52 | 21 | R | R | 6-0 | 180 | 7-2-65 | 1987 | Tulsa, Okla. |
| VanEgmond, Tim | 3 | 5 | 5.27 | 12 | 9 | 0 | 0 | 55 | 58 | 35 | 32 | 23 | 33 | R | R | 6-2 | 185 | 5-31-69 | 1991 | Senoia, Ga. |
| Villone, Ron | 0 | 0 | 3.28 | 23 | 0 | 0 | 2 | 25 | 14 | 9 | 9 | 18 | 19 | L | L | 6-3 | 235 | 1-16-70 | 1992 | Bergenfield, N.J. |
| Wickander, Kevin | 2 | 0 | 4.97 | 21 | 0 | 0 | 0 | 25 | 26 | 16 | 14 | 17 | 19 | L | L | 6-3 | 200 | 1-4-65 | 1986 | Glendale, Ariz. |
| Wickman, Bob | 3 | 0 | 3.24 | 12 | 0 | 0 | 0 | 17 | 12 | 9 | 6 | 10 | 14 | R | R | 6-1 | 220 | 2-6-69 | 1990 | Abrams, Wis. |
| 2-team (58 N.Y.) | 7 | 1 | 4.42 | 70 | 0 | 0 | 0 | 96 | 106 | 50 | 47 | 44 | 75 | | | | | | | |

## FIELDING

| Catcher | PCT | G | PO | A | E | DP | PB |
|---|---|---|---|---|---|---|---|
| Levis | .998 | 90 | 373 | 26 | 1 | 5 | 5 |
| Matheny | .985 | 104 | 475 | 40 | 8 | 5 | 3 |
| Nilsson | 1.000 | 2 | 2 | 1 | 0 | 0 | 0 |
| Stinnett | .960 | 14 | 46 | 2 | 2 | 1 | 1 |

| First Base | PCT | G | PO | A | E | DP |
|---|---|---|---|---|---|---|
| Banks | 1.000 | 1 | 14 | 1 | 0 | 0 |
| Cirillo | 1.000 | 2 | 5 | 0 | 0 | 0 |
| Jaha | .992 | 85 | 676 | 58 | 6 | 84 |
| Nilsson | .981 | 24 | 145 | 13 | 3 | 16 |
| Seitzer | .996 | 65 | 489 | 47 | 2 | 52 |
| Unroe | .976 | 11 | 41 | 0 | 1 | 4 |

| Second Base | PCT | G | PO | A | E | DP |
|---|---|---|---|---|---|---|
| Cirillo | 1.000 | 1 | 2 | 4 | 0 | 1 |

| | PCT | G | PO | A | E | DP |
|---|---|---|---|---|---|---|
| Loretta | .989 | 28 | 32 | 61 | 1 | 13 |
| Vina | .979 | 137 | 333 | 412 | 16 | 116 |

| Third Base | PCT | G | PO | A | E | DP |
|---|---|---|---|---|---|---|
| Cirillo | .950 | 154 | 105 | 238 | 18 | 18 |
| Loretta | 1.000 | 23 | 9 | 23 | 0 | 4 |
| Unroe | 1.000 | 3 | 0 | 10 | 0 | 0 |

| Shortstop | PCT | G | PO | A | E | DP |
|---|---|---|---|---|---|---|
| Loretta | .982 | 21 | 22 | 32 | 1 | 12 |
| Valentin | .950 | 151 | 243 | 460 | 37 | 113 |

| Outfield | PCT | G | PO | A | E | DP |
|---|---|---|---|---|---|---|
| Banks | 1.000 | 3 | 1 | 0 | 0 | 0 |
| Burnitz | .976 | 22 | 39 | 1 | 1 | 0 |
| Carr | 1.000 | 27 | 76 | 4 | 0 | 1 |

| | PCT | G | PO | A | E | DP |
|---|---|---|---|---|---|---|
| Dunn | 1.000 | 6 | 6 | 0 | 0 | 0 |
| Hulse | .990 | 68 | 94 | 1 | 1 | 1 |
| Koslofski | .972 | 22 | 35 | 0 | 1 | 0 |
| Mieske | .996 | 122 | 250 | 7 | 1 | 1 |
| Newfield | .990 | 49 | 96 | 3 | 1 | 1 |
| Nilsson | .965 | 61 | 105 | 5 | 4 | 1 |
| Perez | 1.000 | 3 | 5 | 0 | 0 | 0 |
| Unroe | .000 | 1 | 0 | 0 | 0 | 0 |
| Vaughn | .980 | 100 | 192 | 5 | 4 | 1 |
| Ward | 1.000 | 32 | 54 | 1 | 0 | 0 |
| Williams | .987 | 26 | 74 | 3 | 1 | 1 |

Jeff Cirillo led the Brewers with 184 hits and 46 doubles

Brewers minor league Player of the Year Todd Dunn

MIKE PONZINI

THE SPORTS GROUP

## FARM SYSTEM

**Director of Player Development:** Fred Stanley

| Class | Farm Team | League | W | L | Pct. | Finish* | Manager | First Yr |
|---|---|---|---|---|---|---|---|---|
| AAA | New Orleans (La.) Zephyrs | American Assoc. | 58 | 84 | .408 | 8th (8) | Tim Ireland | 1993 |
| AA | El Paso (Texas) Diablos | Texas | 76 | 63 | .547 | 1st (8) | Dave Machemer | 1981 |
| #A | Stockton (Calif.) Ports | California | 79 | 61 | .564 | 3rd (10) | Greg Mahlberg | 1979 |
| A | Beloit (Wis.) Brewers | Midwest | 69 | 67 | .507 | T-6th (14) | Luis Salazar | 1982 |
| #R | Helena (Mont.) Brewers | Pioneer | 43 | 29 | .597 | +2nd (8) | Alex Morales | 1985 |
| #R | Ogden (Utah) Raptors | Pioneer | 42 | 30 | .583 | 3rd (8) | Bernie Moncallo | 1996 |

*Finish in overall standings (No. of teams in league)   #Advanced level   +Won league championship

## ORGANIZATION LEADERS

### MAJOR LEAGUERS

**BATTING**
| | | |
|---|---|---|
| *AVG | Dave Nilsson | .331 |
| R | John Jaha | 108 |
| H | Jeff Cirillo | 184 |
| TB | John Jaha | 295 |
| 2B | Jeff Cirillo | 46 |
| 3B | Fernando Vina | 10 |
| HR | John Jaha | 34 |
| RBI | John Jaha | 118 |
| BB | John Jaha | 85 |
| SO | Jose Valentin | 145 |
| SB | Pat Listach | 25 |

**PITCHING**
| | | |
|---|---|---|
| W | Scott Karl | 13 |
| L | Ricky Bones | 14 |
| #ERA | Ben McDonald | 3.90 |
| G | Bob Wickman | 70 |
| CG | Scott Karl | 3 |
| SV | Mike Fetters | 32 |
| IP | Ben McDonald | 221 |
| BB | Scott Karl | 72 |
| SO | Ben McDonald | 146 |

**John Jaha.** 118 RBIs

MIKE PONZINI

### MINOR LEAGUERS

**BATTING**
| | | |
|---|---|---|
| *AVG | Todd Dunn, El Paso | .340 |
| R | Mike Kinkade, Beloit | 104 |
| H | Scott Krause, Stockton/El Paso | 155 |
| TB | Two tied at | 260 |
| 2B | Jonas Hamlin, El Paso | 35 |
| 3B | Three tied at | 8 |
| HR | Kelly Stinnett, New Orleans | 27 |
| RBI | Mike Rennhack, Stockton | 103 |
| BB | Lauro Felix, El Paso/New Orleans | 92 |
| SO | Kenny Felder, New Orleans | 129 |
| SB | Greg Martinez, Stockton/El Paso | 44 |

**PITCHING**
| | | |
|---|---|---|
| W | Travis Smith, Stockton/El Paso | 13 |
| L | Two tied at | 11 |
| #ERA | Jason Dawsey, Beloit | 1.51 |
| G | Sean Maloney, El Paso | 51 |
| CG | Valerio de los Santos, Beloit | 5 |
| SV | Sean Maloney, El Paso | 38 |
| IP | Steve Woodard, Stockton | 181 |
| BB | Two tied at | 87 |
| SO | Peter Benny, Beloit | 150 |

*Minimum 250 At-Bats   #Minimum 75 Innings

## TOP 10 PROSPECTS

**How the Brewers Top 10 prospects, as judged by Baseball America prior to the 1996 season, fared in 1996:**

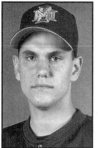

**Jeff D'Amico**

| Player, Pos. | Club (Class—League) | AVG | AB | R | H | 2B | 3B | HR | RBI | SB |
|---|---|---|---|---|---|---|---|---|---|---|
| 2. Geoff Jenkins, of-dh | Stockton (A—California) | .348 | 138 | 27 | 48 | 8 | 4 | 3 | 25 | 3 |
| | El Paso (AA—Texas) | .286 | 77 | 17 | 22 | 5 | 4 | 1 | 11 | 1 |
| 3. Antone Williamson, 3b | New Orleans (AAA—Amer. Assoc.) | .261 | 199 | 23 | 52 | 10 | 1 | 5 | 23 | 1 |
| 4. Mark Loretta, ss | New Orleans (AAA—Amer. Assoc.) | .254 | 71 | 10 | 18 | 5 | 1 | 0 | 11 | 1 |
| | Milwaukee | .279 | 154 | 20 | 43 | 3 | 0 | 1 | 13 | 2 |
| 6. Danny Klassen, ss | Stockton (A—California) | .269 | 432 | 58 | 116 | 22 | 4 | 2 | 46 | 14 |
| 7. Todd Dunn, of | El Paso (AA—Texas) | .340 | 359 | 72 | 122 | 24 | 5 | 19 | 78 | 13 |
| | Milwaukee | .300 | 10 | 2 | 3 | 1 | 0 | 0 | 1 | 0 |
| 8. Ron Belliard, 2b | El Paso (AA—Texas) | .279 | 416 | 73 | 116 | 20 | 8 | 3 | 57 | 26 |
| 10. Brian Banks, of | New Orleans (AAA—Amer. Assoc.) | .271 | 487 | 71 | 132 | 29 | 7 | 16 | 64 | 17 |
| | Milwaukee | .571 | 7 | 2 | 4 | 2 | 0 | 1 | 2 | 0 |

| Player, Pos. | Club (Class—League) | W | L | ERA | G | SV | IP | H | BB | SO |
|---|---|---|---|---|---|---|---|---|---|---|
| 1. Jeff D'Amico, rhp | El Paso (AA—Texas) | 5 | 4 | 3.19 | 13 | 0 | 96 | 89 | 13 | 76 |
| | Milwaukee | 6 | 6 | 5.44 | 17 | 0 | 86 | 88 | 31 | 53 |
| 5. Byron Browne, rhp | New Orleans (AAA—Amer. Assoc.) | 3 | 9 | 6.20 | 23 | 0 | 107 | 104 | 73 | 80 |
| 9. Doug Webb, rhp | El Paso (AA—Texas) | 1 | 0 | 6.75 | 10 | 0 | 8 | 4 | 10 | 3 |

## AMERICAN ASSOCIATION

| BATTING | AVG | G | AB | R | H | 2B | 3B | HR | RBI | BB | SO | SB | CS | B | T | HT | WT | DOB | 1st Yr | Resides |
|---|---|---|---|---|---|---|---|---|---|---|---|---|---|---|---|---|---|---|---|---|
| Banks, Brian | .271 | 137 | 487 | 71 | 132 | 29 | 7 | 16 | 64 | 66 | 105 | 17 | 8 | S | R | 6-3 | 200 | 9-28-70 | 1993 | Mesa, Ariz. |
| Caceres, Edgar | .270 | 115 | 397 | 40 | 107 | 10 | 2 | 4 | 29 | 23 | 32 | 8 | 5 | S | R | 6-1 | 170 | 6-6-64 | 1984 | Barquisimeto, Venez. |
| Carr, Chuck | .385 | 4 | 13 | 2 | 5 | 1 | 0 | 0 | 1 | 2 | 1 | 2 | 0 | S | R | 5-10 | 165 | 8-10-68 | 1986 | Tucson, Ariz. |
| Faries, Paul | .227 | 35 | 110 | 7 | 25 | 1 | 1 | 1 | 8 | 11 | 13 | 1 | 1 | R | R | 5-10 | 170 | 2-20-65 | 1987 | San Diego, Calif. |
| Felder, Ken | .216 | 122 | 430 | 55 | 93 | 20 | 1 | 17 | 45 | 28 | 129 | 2 | 4 | R | R | 6-3 | 235 | 2-9-71 | 1992 | Niceville, Fla. |
| Felix, Lauro | .000 | 2 | 4 | 0 | 0 | 0 | 0 | 0 | 0 | 0 | 2 | 0 | 0 | R | R | 5-9 | 160 | 6-24-70 | 1992 | El Paso, Texas |
| Harris, Mike | .193 | 40 | 150 | 17 | 29 | 2 | 1 | 2 | 11 | 6 | 30 | 1 | 2 | L | L | 5-11 | 195 | 4-30-70 | 1991 | Lexington, Ky. |
| Hughes, Bobby | .200 | 37 | 125 | 11 | 25 | 5 | 0 | 4 | 15 | 4 | 31 | 1 | 1 | R | R | 6-4 | 220 | 3-10-71 | 1992 | North Hollywood, Calif. |
| Hulse, David | .276 | 8 | 29 | 2 | 8 | 2 | 0 | 0 | 1 | 1 | 6 | 0 | 0 | L | L | 5-11 | 170 | 2-25-68 | 1990 | San Angelo, Texas |
| James, Dion | .290 | 11 | 31 | 0 | 9 | 0 | 0 | 0 | 3 | 3 | 5 | 0 | 1 | L | L | 6-1 | 175 | 11-9-62 | 1980 | Sacramento, Calif. |
| Jenkins, Brett | .225 | 26 | 71 | 9 | 16 | 3 | 0 | 6 | 11 | 3 | 17 | 0 | 1 | R | R | 6-1 | 195 | 4-5-70 | 1991 | Rancho Cordova, Calif. |
| Koslofski, Kevin | .231 | 75 | 238 | 39 | 55 | 8 | 3 | 4 | 25 | 31 | 64 | 5 | 2 | L | R | 5-8 | 175 | 9-24-66 | 1984 | Maroa, Ill. |
| Landry, Todd | .240 | 113 | 391 | 41 | 94 | 19 | 2 | 5 | 44 | 32 | 61 | 14 | 4 | R | L | 6-4 | 215 | 8-21-72 | 1993 | Donaldsonville, La. |
| Lopez, Pedro | .218 | 34 | 87 | 7 | 19 | 4 | 0 | 0 | 3 | 13 | 22 | 0 | 0 | R | R | 6-0 | 160 | 3-29-69 | 1988 | Vega Baja, P.R. |
| Lopez, Roberto | .233 | 129 | 438 | 50 | 102 | 20 | 3 | 7 | 39 | 62 | 67 | 8 | 6 | S | R | 5-9 | 150 | 11-15-71 | 1994 | Bayamon, P.R. |
| Loretta, Mark | .254 | 19 | 71 | 10 | 18 | 5 | 1 | 0 | 11 | 9 | 8 | 1 | 1 | R | R | 6-0 | 175 | 8-14-71 | 1993 | Laguna Niguel, Calif. |
| Maas, Kevin | .256 | 36 | 117 | 18 | 30 | 8 | 0 | 8 | 22 | 14 | 18 | 0 | 0 | L | L | 6-3 | 205 | 1-20-65 | 1986 | Berkeley, Calif. |
| Matheny, Mike | .227 | 20 | 66 | 3 | 15 | 4 | 0 | 1 | 6 | 2 | 17 | 1 | 0 | R | R | 6-3 | 205 | 9-22-70 | 1991 | Reynoldsburg, Ohio |
| Nilsson, Dave | .269 | 7 | 26 | 3 | 7 | 1 | 0 | 1 | 2 | 4 | 3 | 0 | 0 | L | R | 6-3 | 215 | 12-14-69 | 1987 | Everton Hills, Australia |
| Ortega, Hector | .556 | 5 | 18 | 2 | 10 | 0 | 1 | 0 | 2 | 0 | 2 | 0 | 0 | R | R | 6-3 | 183 | 8-31-72 | 1989 | Puerto Cabello, Venez. |
| Perez, Danny | .187 | 65 | 198 | 25 | 37 | 5 | 0 | 2 | 15 | 32 | 57 | 4 | 2 | R | R | 5-10 | 188 | 2-26-71 | 1992 | El Paso, Texas |
| Stinnett, Kelly | .287 | 95 | 334 | 63 | 96 | 21 | 1 | 27 | 70 | 31 | 83 | 3 | 3 | R | R | 5-11 | 195 | 2-14-70 | 1990 | Lawton, Okla. |
| Talanoa, Scott | .188 | 32 | 80 | 9 | 15 | 1 | 0 | 2 | 11 | 8 | 26 | 2 | 0 | R | R | 6-5 | 240 | 11-12-69 | 1991 | Lawndale, Calif. |
| Unroe, Tim | .270 | 109 | 404 | 72 | 109 | 26 | 4 | 25 | 67 | 36 | 121 | 8 | 3 | R | R | 6-3 | 200 | 10-7-70 | 1992 | Round Lake Beach, Ill. |
| Wakamatsu, Don | .000 | 1 | 0 | 0 | 0 | 0 | 0 | 0 | 0 | 0 | 0 | 0 | 0 | R | R | 6-2 | 200 | 2-22-63 | 1985 | Hayward, Calif. |
| Ward, Turner | .348 | 9 | 23 | 4 | 8 | 1 | 0 | 1 | 1 | 7 | 4 | 0 | 0 | S | R | 6-2 | 182 | 4-11-65 | 1986 | Saraland, Ala. |
| Weger, Wes | .210 | 64 | 210 | 23 | 44 | 11 | 0 | 4 | 23 | 18 | 33 | 0 | 0 | R | R | 6-0 | 170 | 10-3-70 | 1992 | Longwood, Fla. |
| Williamson, Antone | .261 | 55 | 199 | 23 | 52 | 10 | 1 | 5 | 23 | 19 | 40 | 1 | 0 | L | R | 6-1 | 195 | 7-18-73 | 1994 | Torrance, Calif. |

| PITCHING | W | L | ERA | G | GS | CG | SV | IP | H | R | ER | BB | SO | B | T | HT | WT | DOB | 1st Yr | Resides |
|---|---|---|---|---|---|---|---|---|---|---|---|---|---|---|---|---|---|---|---|---|
| Archer, Kurt | 1 | 3 | 5.46 | 4 | 0 | 0 | 0 | 31 | 39 | 20 | 19 | 9 | 15 | R | R | 6-4 | 230 | 4-27-69 | 1990 | Burlington, Wash. |
| Bowen, Ryan | 2 | 2 | 4.94 | 6 | 6 | 0 | 0 | 27 | 27 | 18 | 15 | 19 | 23 | R | R | 6-0 | 185 | 2-10-68 | 1987 | Houston, Texas |
| Boze, Marshall | 4 | 3 | 4.89 | 25 | 2 | 0 | 3 | 39 | 35 | 22 | 21 | 29 | 32 | R | R | 6-1 | 212 | 5-23-71 | 1990 | Springfield, Ill. |
| Browne, Byron | 3 | 9 | 6.20 | 23 | 21 | 1 | 0 | 107 | 104 | 79 | 74 | 73 | 80 | R | R | 6-7 | 200 | 8-8-70 | 1991 | Phoenix, Ariz. |
| Burrows, Terry | 3 | 0 | 2.51 | 18 | 0 | 0 | 6 | 29 | 19 | 9 | 8 | 8 | 17 | L | L | 6-1 | 185 | 11-28-68 | 1990 | Lake Charles, La. |
| Carpenter, Cris | 1 | 0 | 2.52 | 40 | 0 | 0 | 8 | 50 | 46 | 16 | 14 | 7 | 41 | R | R | 6-1 | 185 | 4-5-65 | 1988 | Gainesville, Ga. |
| Eddy, Chris | 0 | 0 | 9.72 | 12 | 0 | 0 | 0 | 8 | 13 | 9 | 9 | 11 | 11 | L | L | 6-3 | 200 | 11-27-69 | 1992 | Duncanville, Texas |
| Eldred, Cal | 2 | 2 | 3.34 | 6 | 6 | 0 | 0 | 32 | 24 | 12 | 12 | 17 | 30 | R | R | 6-4 | 235 | 11-24-67 | 1989 | Center Point, Iowa |
| Farrell, Mike | 5 | 3 | 4.20 | 29 | 4 | 0 | 2 | 64 | 72 | 31 | 30 | 13 | 39 | L | L | 6-2 | 184 | 1-28-69 | 1991 | Logansport, Ind. |
| Ganote, Joe | 6 | 11 | 5.19 | 41 | 12 | 0 | 0 | 109 | 121 | 77 | 63 | 44 | 65 | R | R | 6-1 | 185 | 1-22-68 | 1990 | Lake Wylie, S.C. |
| Garcia, Ramon | 2 | 1 | 1.88 | 11 | 5 | 0 | 0 | 38 | 31 | 10 | 8 | 12 | 32 | R | R | 6-2 | 200 | 12-9-69 | 1987 | Guanare, Venez. |
| Givens, Brian | 10 | 9 | 3.02 | 29 | 22 | 3 | 1 | 137 | 124 | 60 | 46 | 57 | 117 | R | L | 6-6 | 220 | 11-6-65 | 1984 | Aurora, Colo. |
| Jones, Doug | 0 | 3 | 3.75 | 13 | 0 | 0 | 6 | 24 | 28 | 10 | 10 | 6 | 17 | R | R | 6-2 | 195 | 6-24-57 | 1978 | Tucson, Ariz. |
| Jones, Stacy | 0 | 1 | 7.11 | 9 | 0 | 0 | 0 | 13 | 18 | 10 | 10 | 7 | 10 | R | R | 6-6 | 225 | 5-26-67 | 1988 | Attalla, Ala. |
| Kiefer, Mark | 3 | 6 | 4.33 | 22 | 10 | 1 | 0 | 73 | 60 | 40 | 35 | 33 | 66 | R | R | 6-4 | 184 | 11-13-68 | 1988 | Kingsland, Texas |
| Kloek, Kevin | 0 | 0 | 9.00 | 1 | 0 | 0 | 0 | 1 | 3 | 1 | 1 | 1 | 0 | R | R | 6-3 | 175 | 8-15-70 | 1992 | Santa Barbara, Calif. |
| Mercedes, Jose | 3 | 7 | 3.56 | 25 | 15 | 0 | 1 | 101 | 109 | 58 | 40 | 28 | 47 | R | R | 6-1 | 180 | 3-5-71 | 1990 | Las Palmillas, D.R. |
| Misuraca, Mike | 2 | 7 | 4.13 | 23 | 12 | 0 | 2 | 81 | 93 | 42 | 37 | 31 | 57 | R | R | 6-0 | 188 | 8-21-68 | 1989 | Covina, Calif. |
| Montoya, Norm | 2 | 1 | 8.53 | 11 | 0 | 0 | 2 | 13 | 23 | 16 | 12 | 5 | 8 | L | L | 6-1 | 190 | 9-24-70 | 1990 | Newark, Calif. |
| Phillips, Tony | 2 | 1 | 2.92 | 20 | 6 | 0 | 0 | 52 | 51 | 25 | 17 | 7 | 32 | R | R | 6-4 | 195 | 6-9-69 | 1991 | Hattiesburg, Miss. |
| Potts, Mike | 0 | 1 | 6.75 | 11 | 1 | 0 | 0 | 16 | 23 | 15 | 12 | 11 | 8 | L | L | 5-9 | 170 | 9-5-70 | 1990 | Lithonia, Ga. |
| Roberson, Sid | 0 | 1 | 4.91 | 2 | 2 | 0 | 0 | 11 | 10 | 6 | 6 | 9 | 3 | L | L | 5-9 | 170 | 9-7-71 | 1992 | Orange Park, Fla. |
| Rodriguez, Frankie | 0 | 2 | 6.75 | 13 | 1 | 0 | 0 | 19 | 24 | 15 | 14 | 11 | 16 | R | R | 5-9 | 170 | 1-6-73 | 1992 | Brea, Calif. |
| Slusarski, Joe | 2 | 4 | 4.95 | 40 | 0 | 0 | 1 | 60 | 70 | 38 | 33 | 24 | 36 | R | R | 6-4 | 195 | 12-19-66 | 1989 | Springfield, Ill. |
| Sparks, Steve | 2 | 6 | 4.99 | 11 | 10 | 3 | 0 | 58 | 64 | 43 | 32 | 35 | 27 | R | R | 6-0 | 180 | 7-2-65 | 1987 | Tulsa, Okla. |
| VanEgmond, Tim | 5 | 1 | 1.50 | 7 | 7 | 0 | 0 | 48 | 28 | 8 | 8 | 11 | 32 | R | R | 6-2 | 185 | 5-31-69 | 1991 | Senoia, Ga. |
| Wickander, Kevin | 0 | 1 | 12.79 | 8 | 0 | 0 | 0 | 6 | 9 | 12 | 9 | 5 | 9 | L | L | 6-3 | 200 | 1-4-65 | 1986 | Glendale, Ariz. |

### FIELDING

| Catcher | PCT | G | PO | A | E | DP | PB |
|---|---|---|---|---|---|---|---|
| Banks | 1.000 | 3 | 7 | 0 | 0 | 1 | |
| Hughes | .980 | 32 | 175 | 24 | 4 | 3 | 4 |
| P. Lopez | .988 | 27 | 151 | 14 | 2 | 3 | 6 |
| Matheny | 1.000 | 18 | 87 | 6 | 0 | 0 | 5 |
| Stinnett | .982 | 81 | 485 | 48 | 10 | 9 | 6 |
| Wakamatsu | .000 | 1 | 0 | 0 | 0 | 0 | |

| First Base | PCT | G | PO | A | E | DP |
|---|---|---|---|---|---|---|
| Caceres | 1.000 | 2 | 12 | 0 | 0 | 1 |
| Harris | 1.000 | 4 | 20 | 1 | 0 | 1 |
| Hughes | .000 | 1 | 0 | 0 | 0 | 0 |
| Landry | .992 | 91 | 756 | 86 | 7 | 79 |
| Maas | .989 | 12 | 85 | 7 | 1 | 8 |
| Nilsson | 1.000 | 3 | 25 | 3 | 0 | 4 |
| Talanoa | 1.000 | 1 | 2 | 0 | 0 | 0 |
| Unroe | .966 | 22 | 104 | 11 | 4 | 15 |
| Williamson | .979 | 29 | 268 | 16 | 6 | 26 |

| Second Base | PCT | G | PO | A | E | DP |
|---|---|---|---|---|---|---|
| Caceres | 1.000 | 5 | 8 | 9 | 0 | 2 |

| | PCT | G | PO | A | E | DP |
|---|---|---|---|---|---|---|
| Faries | 1.000 | 3 | 8 | 7 | 0 | 3 |
| Jenkins | .875 | 3 | 2 | 5 | 1 | 1 |
| R. Lopez | .976 | 121 | 252 | 307 | 14 | 88 |
| Weger | .979 | 26 | 35 | 60 | 2 | 11 |

| Third Base | PCT | G | PO | A | E | DP |
|---|---|---|---|---|---|---|
| Banks | .778 | 6 | 1 | 6 | 2 | 1 |
| Caceres | 1.000 | 4 | 1 | 2 | 0 | 1 |
| Faries | .945 | 19 | 17 | 52 | 4 | 4 |
| Hughes | .800 | 1 | 1 | 3 | 1 | 0 |
| Jenkins | .833 | 8 | 1 | 9 | 2 | 1 |
| Ortega | 1.000 | 5 | 3 | 6 | 0 | 1 |
| Stinnett | .800 | 4 | 0 | 4 | 1 | 0 |
| Unroe | .932 | 94 | 68 | 218 | 21 | 22 |
| Weger | .904 | 25 | 15 | 32 | 5 | 2 |
| Williamson | .778 | 5 | 3 | 4 | 2 | 1 |

| Shortstop | PCT | G | PO | A | E | DP |
|---|---|---|---|---|---|---|
| Caceres | .964 | 105 | 147 | 308 | 17 | 65 |
| Faries | .967 | 14 | 19 | 39 | 2 | 10 |

| | PCT | G | PO | A | E | DP |
|---|---|---|---|---|---|---|
| Felix | 1.000 | 2 | 4 | 5 | 0 | 1 |
| R. Lopez | .882 | 2 | 10 | 5 | 2 | 2 |
| Loretta | .948 | 19 | 31 | 60 | 5 | 15 |
| Unroe | 1.000 | 3 | 1 | 1 | 0 | 0 |
| Weger | .884 | 13 | 11 | 27 | 5 | 3 |

| Outfield | PCT | G | PO | A | E | DP |
|---|---|---|---|---|---|---|
| Banks | .977 | 130 | 248 | 12 | 6 | 3 |
| Carr | 1.000 | 4 | 6 | 2 | 0 | 1 |
| Felder | .962 | 114 | 163 | 14 | 7 | 5 |
| Harris | .973 | 38 | 72 | 0 | 2 | 0 |
| Hulse | 1.000 | 5 | 11 | 0 | 0 | 0 |
| James | .958 | 10 | 23 | 0 | 1 | 0 |
| Jenkins | 1.000 | 1 | 1 | 0 | 0 | 0 |
| Koslofski | .988 | 71 | 154 | 4 | 2 | 2 |
| Landry | .935 | 27 | 27 | 2 | 2 | 0 |
| Perez | .976 | 63 | 120 | 1 | 3 | 0 |
| Unroe | 1.000 | 2 | 2 | 1 | 0 | 0 |

## TEXAS LEAGUE

### BATTING

| | AVG | G | AB | R | H | 2B | 3B | HR | RBI | BB | SO | SB | CS | B | T | HT | WT | DOB | 1st Yr | Resides |
|---|---|---|---|---|---|---|---|---|---|---|---|---|---|---|---|---|---|---|---|---|
| Belliard, Ronnie | .279 | 109 | 416 | 73 | 116 | 20 | 8 | 3 | 57 | 60 | 51 | 26 | 10 | R | R | 5-9 | 176 | 4-7-75 | 1994 | Miami, Fla. |
| Dobrolsky, Bill | .282 | 68 | 202 | 26 | 57 | 11 | 1 | 2 | 21 | 17 | 37 | 1 | 4 | R | R | 6-2 | 205 | 3-16-70 | 1991 | Orwigsburg, Pa. |
| Dunn, Todd | .340 | 98 | 359 | 72 | 122 | 24 | 5 | 19 | 78 | 45 | 84 | 13 | 4 | R | R | 6-5 | 220 | 7-29-70 | 1993 | Jacksonville, Fla. |
| Felix, Lauro | .269 | 101 | 301 | 71 | 81 | 15 | 2 | 10 | 59 | 74 | 69 | 11 | 5 | R | R | 5-9 | 160 | 6-24-70 | 1992 | El Paso, Texas |
| Hamlin, Jonas | .283 | 131 | 515 | 81 | 146 | 35 | 8 | 21 | 94 | 37 | 101 | 9 | 7 | R | R | 6-4 | 210 | 4-18-70 | 1990 | West Valley City, Utah |
| Harris, Mike | .308 | 76 | 260 | 47 | 80 | 15 | 5 | 7 | 35 | 29 | 29 | 5 | 2 | L | L | 5-11 | 195 | 4-30-70 | 1991 | Lexington, Ky. |
| Hughes, Bobby | .304 | 67 | 237 | 43 | 72 | 18 | 1 | 15 | 39 | 30 | 40 | 3 | 3 | R | R | 6-4 | 220 | 3-10-71 | 1992 | North Hollywood, Calif. |
| Jenkins, Geoff | .286 | 22 | 77 | 17 | 22 | 5 | 4 | 1 | 11 | 12 | 21 | 1 | 2 | L | L | 6-1 | 205 | 7-21-74 | 1995 | Stateline, Nev. |
| Krause, Scott | .318 | 24 | 85 | 16 | 27 | 5 | 2 | 3 | 11 | 2 | 19 | 2 | 0 | R | R | 6-1 | 195 | 8-16-73 | 1994 | Willowick, Ohio |
| Lopez, Pedro | .306 | 46 | 144 | 22 | 44 | 10 | 1 | 2 | 20 | 17 | 24 | 2 | 2 | R | R | 6-0 | 160 | 3-29-69 | 1988 | Vega Baja, P.R. |
| Martinez, Gabby | .251 | 91 | 338 | 44 | 85 | 11 | 8 | 0 | 37 | 18 | 57 | 8 | 9 | S | R | 6-2 | 170 | 1-7-74 | 1992 | Santurce, P.R. |
| Martinez, Greg | .313 | 41 | 166 | 27 | 52 | 2 | 2 | 1 | 21 | 13 | 19 | 14 | 4 | S | R | 5-10 | 168 | 1-27-72 | 1993 | Las Vegas, Nev. |
| McKamie, Sean | .000 | 1 | 0 | 0 | 0 | 0 | 0 | 0 | 0 | 0 | 0 | 0 | 0 | R | R | 6-2 | 160 | 9-27-69 | 1989 | St. Paul, Minn. |
| Nicholas, Darrell | .274 | 70 | 237 | 46 | 65 | 12 | 4 | 2 | 24 | 27 | 57 | 7 | 9 | R | R | 6-0 | 180 | 5-26-72 | 1994 | Garyville, La. |
| Ortega, Hector | .242 | 99 | 351 | 52 | 85 | 12 | 4 | 7 | 53 | 27 | 74 | 11 | 6 | R | R | 6-3 | 183 | 8-31-72 | 1989 | Puerto Cabello, Venez. |
| Perez, Danny | .351 | 38 | 154 | 31 | 54 | 16 | 6 | 2 | 19 | 13 | 30 | 5 | 1 | R | R | 5-10 | 188 | 2-26-71 | 1992 | El Paso, Texas |
| Rodriques, Cecil | .283 | 119 | 389 | 63 | 110 | 23 | 6 | 5 | 50 | 32 | 92 | 5 | 8 | R | R | 6-0 | 175 | 9-3-71 | 1991 | Fort Pierce, Fla. |
| Seitzer, Brad | .319 | 115 | 433 | 78 | 138 | 31 | 1 | 17 | 87 | 51 | 67 | 6 | 4 | R | R | 6-2 | 195 | 2-2-70 | 1991 | Lincoln, Ill. |

### PITCHING

| | W | L | ERA | G | GS | CG | SV | IP | H | R | ER | BB | SO | B | T | HT | WT | DOB | 1st Yr | Resides |
|---|---|---|---|---|---|---|---|---|---|---|---|---|---|---|---|---|---|---|---|---|
| D'Amico, Jeff | 5 | 4 | 3.19 | 13 | 13 | 3 | 0 | 96 | 89 | 42 | 34 | 13 | 76 | R | R | 6-7 | 250 | 12-27-75 | 1993 | Pinellas Park, Fla. |
| Farrell, Mike | 1 | 0 | 0.66 | 11 | 0 | 0 | 1 | 14 | 6 | 3 | 1 | 2 | 13 | L | L | 6-2 | 184 | 1-28-69 | 1991 | Logansport, Ind. |
| Ganote, Joe | 0 | 0 | 5.79 | 1 | 1 | 0 | 0 | 5 | 9 | 3 | 3 | 1 | 5 | R | R | 6-1 | 185 | 1-22-68 | 1990 | Lake Wylie, S.C. |
| Gavaghan, Sean | 4 | 1 | 5.11 | 24 | 0 | 0 | 0 | 37 | 48 | 27 | 21 | 15 | 24 | R | R | 6-1 | 194 | 12-19-69 | 1992 | Fort Washington, Pa. |
| Kloek, Kevin | 3 | 1 | 4.02 | 9 | 9 | 0 | 0 | 54 | 58 | 29 | 24 | 18 | 46 | R | R | 6-3 | 175 | 8-15-70 | 1992 | Santa Barbara, Calif. |
| Kramer, Jeff | 3 | 4 | 6.34 | 21 | 5 | 0 | 1 | 60 | 76 | 57 | 42 | 29 | 36 | R | R | 5-11 | 180 | 10-6-73 | 1994 | Rincon, Ga. |
| Maloney, Sean | 3 | 2 | 1.43 | 51 | 0 | 0 | 38 | 57 | 49 | 11 | 9 | 12 | 57 | R | R | 6-7 | 210 | 5-25-71 | 1993 | North Kingstown, R.I. |
| Montoya, Norm | 9 | 8 | 4.67 | 24 | 17 | 1 | 1 | 125 | 153 | 74 | 65 | 28 | 73 | L | L | 6-1 | 190 | 9-24-70 | 1990 | Newark, Calif. |
| Mullins, Greg | 1 | 5 | 7.07 | 23 | 1 | 0 | 2 | 28 | 30 | 25 | 22 | 17 | 28 | L | L | 6-0 | 160 | 12-13-71 | 1995 | Palatka, Fla. |
| Paul, Andy | 5 | 6 | 4.72 | 38 | 7 | 0 | 3 | 95 | 105 | 60 | 50 | 43 | 72 | R | R | 6-4 | 205 | 9-4-71 | 1992 | Whitehouse Station, N.J. |
| Rodriguez, Frank | 3 | 4 | 6.82 | 16 | 7 | 0 | 0 | 34 | 45 | 32 | 26 | 24 | 39 | R | R | 5-9 | 170 | 1-6-73 | 1992 | Brea, Calif. |
| Sadler, Aldren | 3 | 3 | 4.71 | 26 | 0 | 0 | 1 | 42 | 39 | 28 | 22 | 40 | 31 | R | R | 6-6 | 192 | 2-10-72 | 1992 | Conyers, Ga. |
| Salazar, Luis | 1 | 0 | 11.81 | 3 | 0 | 0 | 0 | 5 | 14 | 8 | 7 | 1 | 2 | R | R | 6-0 | 185 | 9-16-74 | 1995 | Barcelona, Venez. |
| Santos, Henry | 7 | 7 | 6.10 | 35 | 12 | 0 | 0 | 100 | 126 | 76 | 68 | 50 | 74 | L | L | 6-1 | 175 | 1-17-73 | 1990 | Santiago, D.R. |
| Smith, Travis | 7 | 4 | 4.18 | 17 | 17 | 3 | 0 | 108 | 119 | 56 | 50 | 39 | 68 | R | R | 5-10 | 170 | 11-7-72 | 1995 | Bend, Ore. |
| Taylor, Tommy | 2 | 1 | 4.67 | 14 | 0 | 0 | 0 | 17 | 24 | 9 | 9 | 6 | 20 | R | R | 6-1 | 180 | 7-16-70 | 1989 | Louisa, Va. |
| Tollberg, Brian | 7 | 5 | 4.90 | 26 | 26 | 0 | 0 | 154 | 183 | 90 | 84 | 23 | 109 | R | R | 6-3 | 195 | 9-16-72 | 1994 | Bradenton, Fla. |
| Webb, Doug | 1 | 0 | 6.75 | 10 | 0 | 0 | 0 | 8 | 4 | 6 | 6 | 1 | 0 | R | R | 6-3 | 205 | 8-25-73 | 1994 | Draper, Utah |
| Whitaker, Steve | 11 | 7 | 4.58 | 25 | 24 | 2 | 0 | 145 | 157 | 92 | 74 | 87 | 85 | L | L | 6-6 | 225 | 4-15-70 | 1991 | Atwater, Calif. |
| Wilstead, Judd | 0 | 1 | 8.47 | 7 | 0 | 0 | 0 | 17 | 19 | 18 | 16 | 7 | 11 | L | R | 6-4 | 205 | 3-14-73 | 1991 | Washington, Utah |

### FIELDING

| Catcher | PCT | G | PO | A | E | DP | PB |
|---|---|---|---|---|---|---|---|
| Dobrolsky | .983 | 59 | 369 | 37 | 7 | 0 | 5 |
| Hughes | .979 | 44 | 250 | 32 | 6 | 4 | 9 |
| Lopez | .969 | 45 | 248 | 32 | 9 | 5 | 5 |

| First Base | PCT | G | PO | A | E | DP |
|---|---|---|---|---|---|---|
| Hamlin | .988 | 127 | 1189 | 71 | 15 | 122 |
| Harris | 1.000 | 1 | 11 | 1 | 0 | 1 |
| Ortega | .957 | 5 | 44 | 0 | 2 | 4 |
| Seitzer | .957 | 7 | 61 | 6 | 3 | 6 |

| Second Base | PCT | G | PO | A | E | DP |
|---|---|---|---|---|---|---|
| Belliard | .972 | 107 | 246 | 314 | 16 | 89 |
| Felix | .943 | 26 | 50 | 66 | 7 | 21 |

| | PCT | G | PO | A | E | DP |
|---|---|---|---|---|---|---|
| Seitzer | 1.000 | 17 | 28 | 41 | 0 | 9 |

| Third Base | PCT | G | PO | A | E | DP |
|---|---|---|---|---|---|---|
| Dobrolsky | .857 | 5 | 1 | 5 | 1 | 0 |
| Felix | 1.000 | 3 | 3 | 4 | 0 | 0 |
| Hamlin | .333 | 1 | 0 | 1 | 2 | 0 |
| Ortega | .913 | 61 | 37 | 131 | 16 | 14 |
| Seitzer | .928 | 79 | 52 | 205 | 20 | 24 |

| Shortstop | PCT | G | PO | A | E | DP |
|---|---|---|---|---|---|---|
| Felix | .923 | 59 | 82 | 159 | 20 | 43 |
| Ga. Martinez | .914 | 85 | 102 | 239 | 32 | 48 |
| Ortega | 1.000 | 1 | 0 | 2 | 0 | 0 |

| | PCT | G | PO | A | E | DP |
|---|---|---|---|---|---|---|
| Seitzer | .917 | 3 | 5 | 6 | 1 | 1 |

| Outfield | PCT | G | PO | A | E | DP |
|---|---|---|---|---|---|---|
| Dunn | .940 | 72 | 108 | 2 | 7 | 0 |
| Felix | 1.000 | 17 | 37 | 2 | 0 | 0 |
| Harris | .971 | 54 | 96 | 4 | 3 | 1 |
| Krause | 1.000 | 24 | 36 | 4 | 0 | 2 |
| Gr. Martinez | .980 | 41 | 99 | 0 | 2 | 0 |
| Nicholas | .962 | 67 | 144 | 6 | 6 | 0 |
| Ortega | .857 | 14 | 12 | 0 | 2 | 0 |
| Perez | .947 | 38 | 67 | 5 | 4 | 1 |
| Rodriques | .947 | 113 | 170 | 8 | 10 | 3 |

## CALIFORNIA LEAGUE

### BATTING

| | AVG | G | AB | R | H | 2B | 3B | HR | RBI | BB | SO | SB | CS | B | T | HT | WT | DOB | 1st Yr | Resides |
|---|---|---|---|---|---|---|---|---|---|---|---|---|---|---|---|---|---|---|---|---|
| Andreopoulos, Alex | .302 | 87 | 291 | 52 | 88 | 17 | 2 | 5 | 41 | 40 | 33 | 10 | 3 | L | R | 5-10 | 190 | 8-19-72 | 1995 | Toronto, Ontario |
| Betances, Junior | .253 | 125 | 458 | 69 | 116 | 9 | 7 | 1 | 41 | 51 | 61 | 14 | 11 | R | R | 5-10 | 170 | 5-26-73 | 1991 | La Vega, D.R. |
| Campillo, Rob | .241 | 46 | 145 | 11 | 35 | 4 | 1 | 0 | 18 | 15 | 27 | 2 | 3 | R | R | 6-0 | 195 | 11-2-71 | 1992 | Tucson, Ariz. |
| DeBerry, Joe | .268 | 54 | 190 | 33 | 51 | 7 | 2 | 7 | 25 | 23 | 55 | 3 | 0 | L | L | 6-2 | 195 | 6-30-70 | 1991 | Colorado Springs, Colo. |
| Felix, Lauro | .182 | 12 | 33 | 5 | 6 | 0 | 0 | 2 | 5 | 18 | 9 | 1 | 2 | R | R | 5-9 | 160 | 6-24-70 | 1992 | El Paso, Texas |
| James, Dion | .188 | 4 | 16 | 5 | 3 | 0 | 0 | 0 | 0 | 5 | 3 | 3 | 0 | L | L | 6-1 | 175 | 11-9-62 | 1980 | Sacramento, Calif. |
| Jenkins, Geoff | .348 | 37 | 138 | 27 | 48 | 8 | 4 | 3 | 25 | 20 | 32 | 3 | 3 | L | L | 6-1 | 205 | 7-21-74 | 1995 | Stateline, Nev. |
| Klassen, Danny | .269 | 118 | 432 | 58 | 116 | 22 | 4 | 2 | 46 | 34 | 77 | 14 | 8 | R | R | 6-0 | 175 | 9-22-75 | 1993 | Port St Lucie, Fla. |
| Kominek, Toby | .296 | 100 | 358 | 76 | 106 | 17 | 7 | 7 | 47 | 49 | 97 | 10 | 7 | R | R | 6-2 | 205 | 6-13-73 | 1995 | Erie, Mich. |
| Krause, Scott | .300 | 108 | 427 | 82 | 128 | 22 | 4 | 19 | 83 | 32 | 101 | 25 | 6 | R | R | 6-1 | 195 | 8-16-73 | 1994 | Willowick, Ohio |
| Lopez, Mickey | .281 | 64 | 217 | 30 | 61 | 10 | 1 | 0 | 25 | 23 | 36 | 6 | 4 | S | R | 5-9 | 165 | 11-17-73 | 1995 | Miami, Fla. |
| Martinez, Greg | .287 | 73 | 286 | 51 | 82 | 5 | 1 | 0 | 26 | 29 | 34 | 30 | 9 | S | R | 5-10 | 168 | 1-27-72 | 1993 | Las Vegas, Nev. |
| McGonigle, Bill | .269 | 74 | 227 | 29 | 61 | 12 | 0 | 1 | 25 | 18 | 27 | 2 | 4 | R | R | 6-1 | 175 | 11-13-71 | 1994 | Glendale, Ariz. |
| Morreale, John | .236 | 50 | 148 | 19 | 35 | 7 | 0 | 2 | 19 | 16 | 33 | 3 | 3 | R | R | 6-1 | 195 | 8-29-71 | 1994 | New Orleans, La. |
| Rennhack, Mike | .320 | 121 | 456 | 67 | 146 | 32 | 4 | 17 | 103 | 53 | 66 | 8 | 10 | S | R | 6-3 | 190 | 8-25-74 | 1992 | Orlando, Fla. |
| Reynolds, Chance | .164 | 20 | 67 | 3 | 11 | 2 | 0 | 0 | 7 | 8 | 10 | 1 | 2 | S | R | 5-10 | 185 | 7-14-73 | 1993 | Byromville, Ga. |
| Swinton, Jermaine | .280 | 40 | 164 | 30 | 46 | 9 | 0 | 10 | 35 | 13 | 72 | 0 | 0 | R | R | 6-4 | 250 | 10-9-72 | 1990 | Brooklyn, N.Y. |
| Tyler, Josh | .322 | 75 | 273 | 42 | 88 | 14 | 2 | 2 | 33 | 25 | 35 | 4 | 8 | R | R | 6-1 | 185 | 9-6-73 | 1994 | Green Lane, Pa. |
| Williams, Drew | .305 | 112 | 433 | 78 | 132 | 28 | 3 | 24 | 85 | 64 | 86 | 8 | 1 | L | R | 5-11 | 200 | 2-3-72 | 1994 | Jacksonville, Fla. |

**GAMES BY POSITION: C**—Andreopoulos 86, Campillo 46, Reynolds 17, Tyler 1. **1B**—DeBerry 32, Krause 7, Tyler 1, Williams 102. **2B**—Betances 2, Felix 4, Lopez 60, Morreale 49, Tyler 37. **3B**—Betances 113, Reynolds 3, Tyler 30, Williams 2. **SS**—Betances 13, Felix 8, Klassen 118, Lopez 4, Morreale 1. **OF**—James 4, Jenkins 3, Kominek 94, Krause 99, Martinez 69, McGonigle 64, Rennhack 95, Reynolds 1, Swinton 7, Tyler 1.

| PITCHING | W | L | ERA | G | GS | CG | SV | IP | H | R | ER | BB | SO | B | T | HT | WT | DOB | 1st Yr | Resides |
|---|---|---|---|---|---|---|---|---|---|---|---|---|---|---|---|---|---|---|---|---|
| Beck, Greg | 9 | 11 | 6.14 | 28 | 28 | 0 | 0 | 152 | 197 | 119 | 104 | 53 | 96 | R | R | 6-4 | 215 | 10-21-72 | 1994 | Fort Myers, Fla. |
| Brown, Dickie | 0 | 0 | 5.68 | 5 | 0 | 0 | 0 | 6 | 9 | 5 | 4 | 4 | 7 | R | R | 5-9 | 170 | 8-13-70 | 1990 | North Little Rock, Ark. |
| Burt, Chris | 0 | 0 | 54.00 | 1 | 0 | 0 | 0 | 3 | 2 | 2 | 1 | 0 | 1 | R | R | 6-3 | 200 | 1-11-73 | 1994 | Beloit, Wis. |
| Cana, Nelson | 4 | 4 | 4.44 | 29 | 0 | 0 | 2 | 53 | 47 | 30 | 26 | 36 | 36 | L | L | 6-2 | 190 | 7-17-75 | 1993 | Cumana, Venez. |
| Caridad, Ron | 1 | 0 | 1.50 | 18 | 0 | 0 | 1 | 30 | 29 | 9 | 5 | 13 | 19 | R | R | 5-10 | 180 | 3-22-72 | 1990 | Miami, Fla. |
| Dalton, Brian | 0 | 1 | 6.97 | 6 | 0 | 0 | 0 | 10 | 12 | 9 | 8 | 10 | 9 | R | R | 6-1 | 190 | 6-24-72 | 1994 | Brooksville, Fla. |
| Drysdale, Brooks | 6 | 1 | 5.13 | 35 | 0 | 0 | 0 | 60 | 61 | 35 | 34 | 28 | 61 | R | R | 5-10 | 175 | 6-15-71 | 1993 | Petaluma, Calif. |
| Estrada, Horacio | 1 | 3 | 4.59 | 29 | 0 | 0 | 3 | 51 | 43 | 29 | 26 | 21 | 62 | L | L | 6-1 | 185 | 10-19-75 | 1992 | Valencia, Venez. |
| Gardner, Scott | 10 | 8 | 4.13 | 27 | 21 | 3 | 0 | 144 | 127 | 77 | 66 | 52 | 148 | S | R | 6-5 | 225 | 9-30-71 | 1990 | Fenton, Mich. |
| Hill, Tyrone | 0 | 2 | 5.03 | 5 | 5 | 0 | 0 | 20 | 18 | 14 | 11 | 9 | 11 | L | L | 6-6 | 220 | 3-7-72 | 1991 | Yucaipa, Calif. |
| Hommel, Brian | 0 | 0 | 0.00 | 4 | 0 | 0 | 0 | 5 | 2 | 1 | 0 | 4 | 4 | L | L | 5-10 | 170 | 10-26-72 | 1995 | Indianapolis, Ind. |
| Huber, Jeff | 1 | 1 | 1.83 | 18 | 0 | 0 | 6 | 20 | 24 | 9 | 4 | 3 | 12 | R | L | 6-4 | 220 | 12-17-70 | 1990 | Scottsdale, Ariz. |
| Huntsman, Scott | 4 | 3 | 2.79 | 43 | 0 | 0 | 12 | 48 | 37 | 21 | 15 | 27 | 56 | R | R | 6-2 | 230 | 10-28-72 | 1994 | Zanesville, Ohio |
| Kramer, Jeff | 6 | 4 | 4.42 | 15 | 7 | 0 | 0 | 59 | 62 | 43 | 29 | 31 | 46 | R | R | 5-11 | 180 | 10-6-73 | 1994 | Rincon, Ga. |
| Mullins, Greg | 0 | 0 | 3.97 | 10 | 0 | 0 | 1 | 11 | 13 | 5 | 5 | 4 | 12 | L | L | 6-0 | 160 | 12-13-71 | 1995 | Palatka, Fla. |
| Pasqualicchio, Mike | 3 | 3 | 3.53 | 18 | 17 | 0 | 0 | 71 | 67 | 35 | 28 | 36 | 69 | R | L | 6-1 | 205 | 8-17-74 | 1995 | Astoria, N.Y. |
| Sadler, Al | 1 | 2 | 2.70 | 18 | 0 | 0 | 7 | 20 | 12 | 7 | 6 | 7 | 19 | R | R | 6-6 | 192 | 2-10-72 | 1992 | Conyers, Ga. |
| Salazar, Luis | 3 | 2 | 3.49 | 44 | 0 | 0 | 6 | 57 | 46 | 23 | 22 | 16 | 34 | R | R | 6-0 | 185 | 9-16-74 | 1995 | Barcelona, Venez. |
| Smith, Travis | 6 | 1 | 1.84 | 14 | 6 | 0 | 1 | 59 | 56 | 17 | 12 | 21 | 48 | R | R | 5-10 | 170 | 11-7-72 | 1995 | Bend, Ore. |
| Wagner, Joe | 12 | 6 | 4.79 | 28 | 28 | 0 | 0 | 167 | 171 | 102 | 89 | 86 | 103 | R | R | 6-1 | 195 | 12-8-71 | 1993 | Janesville, Wis. |
| Woodard, Steve | 12 | 9 | 4.02 | 28 | 28 | 3 | 0 | 181 | 201 | 89 | 81 | 33 | 142 | L | R | 6-4 | 225 | 5-15-75 | 1994 | Hartselle, Ala. |

## BELOIT — Class A

### MIDWEST LEAGUE

| BATTING | AVG | G | AB | R | H | 2B | 3B | HR | RBI | BB | SO | SB | CS | B | T | HT | WT | DOB | 1st Yr | Resides |
|---|---|---|---|---|---|---|---|---|---|---|---|---|---|---|---|---|---|---|---|---|
| Campusano, Carlos | .246 | 108 | 337 | 33 | 83 | 17 | 4 | 1 | 20 | 10 | 63 | 4 | 3 | R | R | 5-11 | 155 | 9-2-75 | 1994 | Palave, D.R. |
| Cancel, Robinson | .220 | 72 | 218 | 26 | 48 | 3 | 1 | 1 | 29 | 14 | 31 | 13 | 5 | R | R | 5-11 | 195 | 5-4-76 | 1994 | Lajas, P.R. |
| Carrasquel, Domingo | .168 | 73 | 190 | 16 | 32 | 6 | 0 | 0 | 10 | 21 | 14 | 1 | 1 | R | R | 5-11 | 168 | 8-18-71 | 1991 | Barquisimeto, Venez. |
| Elliott, David | .268 | 112 | 365 | 65 | 98 | 12 | 3 | 12 | 58 | 62 | 80 | 17 | 10 | R | R | 6-2 | 192 | 8-10-73 | 1995 | Gladstone, Mich. |
| Iapoce, Anthony | .290 | 78 | 269 | 63 | 78 | 6 | 3 | 1 | 11 | 44 | 54 | 23 | 13 | S | L | 5-10 | 178 | 8-23-73 | 1994 | Ridgewood, N.Y. |
| Kinkade, Mike | .304 | 135 | 496 | 104 | 151 | 33 | 4 | 15 | 100 | 46 | 68 | 23 | 12 | R | R | 6-1 | 210 | 5-6-73 | 1995 | Tigard, Ore. |
| Listach, Pat | .400 | 1 | 5 | 2 | 2 | 0 | 0 | 0 | 0 | 0 | 1 | 0 | 0 | S | R | 5-9 | 170 | 9-12-67 | 1988 | Woodway, Texas |
| Lopez, Mickey | .271 | 61 | 236 | 35 | 64 | 10 | 2 | 0 | 14 | 28 | 36 | 12 | 8 | S | R | 5-9 | 165 | 11-17-73 | 1995 | Miami, Fla. |
| Lopiccolo, Jamie | .263 | 96 | 304 | 44 | 80 | 19 | 2 | 4 | 57 | 39 | 48 | 4 | 6 | R | R | 6-3 | 200 | 5-18-73 | 1995 | Sterling Heights, Mich. |
| Mealing, Al | .259 | 88 | 274 | 41 | 71 | 15 | 4 | 6 | 24 | 20 | 66 | 13 | 12 | L | R | 6-2 | 195 | 12-30-73 | 1993 | Edgefield, S.C. |
| Noriega, Kevin | .268 | 115 | 414 | 55 | 111 | 22 | 2 | 4 | 59 | 39 | 69 | 5 | 5 | S | R | 6-1 | 175 | 1-28-74 | 1992 | Caracas, Venez |
| O'Neal, Troy | .243 | 74 | 206 | 18 | 50 | 4 | 0 | 0 | 20 | 16 | 28 | 1 | 2 | R | R | 5-11 | 190 | 4-24-72 | 1995 | Greenville, Del. |
| Parent, Gerald | .211 | 40 | 95 | 12 | 20 | 6 | 1 | 0 | 12 | 18 | 19 | 2 | 3 | L | R | 6-2 | 210 | 12-7-73 | 1995 | Assonet, Mass. |
| Peters, Tony | .257 | 71 | 179 | 20 | 46 | 13 | 3 | 2 | 23 | 18 | 47 | 5 | 1 | R | R | 6-2 | 210 | 10-28-74 | 1995 | Parkman, Ohio |
| Phair, Kelly | .212 | 30 | 99 | 16 | 21 | 5 | 0 | 0 | 12 | 13 | 18 | 3 | 1 | R | R | 6-2 | 185 | 6-2-73 | 1995 | Cincinnati, Ohio |
| Ritter, Ryan | .239 | 99 | 347 | 43 | 83 | 12 | 6 | 7 | 42 | 24 | 103 | 20 | 6 | R | R | 6-0 | 190 | 11-26-73 | 1995 | Marietta, Ga. |
| Smith, Rick | .245 | 114 | 372 | 41 | 91 | 27 | 1 | 7 | 57 | 39 | 81 | 4 | 5 | L | R | 6-2 | 205 | 1-5-72 | 1995 | Big Rapids, Mich. |
| Zwisler, Josh | .074 | 8 | 27 | 3 | 2 | 0 | 0 | 0 | 1 | 5 | 9 | 0 | 0 | R | R | 5-11 | 185 | 9-30-74 | 1993 | Cuyahoga Falls, Ohio |

**GAMES BY POSITION: C**—Cancel 72, Kinkade 7, O'Neal 74, Peters 3. **1B**—Kinkade 1, Noriega 56, Peters 5, Smith 83, Zwisler 2. **2B**—Campusano 24, Carrasquel 36, Lopez 58, Ritter 35. **3B**—Campusano 4, Carrasquel 4, Kinkade 129, Ritter 7. **SS**—Campusano 79, Carrasquel 34, Listach 1, Lopez 7, Phair 30. **OF**—Elliott 110, Iapoce 76, Kinkade 1, Lopiccolo 56, Mealing 69, Noriega 43, Parent 35, Peters 61. Ritter 9, Zwisler 6.

| PITCHING | W | L | ERA | G | GS | CG | SV | IP | H | R | ER | BB | SO | B | T | HT | WT | DOB | 1st Yr | Resides |
|---|---|---|---|---|---|---|---|---|---|---|---|---|---|---|---|---|---|---|---|---|
| Arias, Wagner | 3 | 4 | 2.74 | 21 | 5 | 0 | 2 | 69 | 52 | 26 | 21 | 24 | 58 | R | R | 6-1 | 180 | 11-24-74 | 1992 | Bani, D.R. |
| Barnes, Larry | 0 | 5 | 7.02 | 9 | 9 | 0 | 0 | 33 | 30 | 30 | 26 | 34 | 34 | S | R | 6-5 | 230 | 8-11-76 | 1994 | Jacksonville, Fla. |
| Benny, Peter | 7 | 10 | 3.79 | 26 | 26 | 2 | 0 | 157 | 136 | 80 | 66 | 87 | 150 | R | R | 6-3 | 196 | 11-9-75 | 1993 | Tempe, Ariz. |
| Berninger, Darren | 2 | 3 | 5.40 | 41 | 0 | 0 | 5 | 62 | 69 | 48 | 37 | 28 | 39 | R | R | 6-3 | 225 | 1-4-73 | 1995 | Baton Rouge, La. |
| Bishop, Joshua | 12 | 9 | 3.86 | 29 | 29 | 4 | 0 | 170 | 177 | 84 | 73 | 62 | 111 | R | R | 6-4 | 180 | 7-16-74 | 1995 | Sedalia, Mo. |
| Camp, Jared | 3 | 5 | 5.43 | 11 | 11 | 0 | 0 | 53 | 56 | 42 | 32 | 39 | 47 | R | R | 6-1 | 195 | 5-4-75 | 1995 | Huntington, W.Va. |
| Cana, Nelson | 3 | 0 | 2.83 | 21 | 0 | 0 | 4 | 35 | 34 | 15 | 11 | 21 | 38 | L | L | 6-2 | 190 | 7-17-75 | 1993 | Cumana, Venez. |
| Collins, Edward | 6 | 5 | 4.70 | 38 | 3 | 0 | 3 | 67 | 79 | 44 | 35 | 37 | 50 | R | R | 6-3 | 225 | 8-26-76 | 1994 | Union, N.J. |
| Dawsey, Jason | 4 | 4 | 1.51 | 31 | 14 | 1 | 2 | 101 | 71 | 21 | 17 | 42 | 119 | L | L | 5-8 | 165 | 5-27-74 | 1995 | Lexington, S.C. |
| De los Santos, Valerio | 10 | 8 | 3.55 | 33 | 23 | 5 | 4 | 165 | 164 | 83 | 65 | 59 | 137 | L | L | 6-1 | 185 | 10-19-75 | 1992 | Valencia, Venez. |
| Estrada, Horacio | 2 | 1 | 1.23 | 17 | 0 | 0 | 1 | 29 | 21 | 8 | 4 | 11 | 34 | L | L | 6-1 | 185 | 10-19-75 | 1992 | Valencia, Venez. |
| Fieldbinder, Mick | 1 | 0 | 3.39 | 12 | 12 | 1 | 0 | 77 | 74 | 33 | 29 | 18 | 66 | R | R | 6-4 | 200 | 10-2-73 | 1996 | Rochester, Ill. |
| Gooda, David | 1 | 3 | 10.43 | 4 | 4 | 0 | 0 | 15 | 24 | 21 | 17 | 11 | 6 | L | L | 6-3 | 196 | 8-17-76 | 1995 | Brisbane, Australia |
| Housley, Adam | 2 | 4 | 2.99 | 34 | 0 | 0 | 4 | 69 | 74 | 33 | 23 | 28 | 49 | S | R | 6-3 | 198 | 8-13-71 | 1994 | Napa, Calif. |
| Pavlovich, Tony | 2 | 3 | 3.21 | 28 | 0 | 0 | 4 | 34 | 26 | 12 | 12 | 15 | 31 | R | R | 5-11 | 185 | 8-23-74 | 1994 | Pavo, Ga. |
| Reyes, Alberto | 1 | 0 | 1.83 | 13 | 0 | 0 | 0 | 20 | 17 | 7 | 4 | 6 | 22 | R | R | 6-0 | 165 | 4-10-71 | 1988 | Santo Domingo, D.R. |
| Steinert, Rob | 0 | 0 | 4.50 | 3 | 0 | 0 | 0 | 2 | 2 | 1 | 1 | 4 | 1 | R | R | 6-2 | 195 | 9-29-71 | 1993 | Greenlawn, N.Y. |
| Tijerina, Tano | 0 | 1 | 11.37 | 5 | 0 | 0 | 0 | 13 | 31 | 17 | 16 | 8 | 4 | R | R | 6-4 | 225 | 6-23-74 | 1993 | Waco, Texas |

## HELENA — Rookie

### PIONEER LEAGUE

| BATTING | AVG | G | AB | R | H | 2B | 3B | HR | RBI | BB | SO | SB | CS | B | T | HT | WT | DOB | 1st Yr | Resides |
|---|---|---|---|---|---|---|---|---|---|---|---|---|---|---|---|---|---|---|---|---|
| Cafaro, Nick | .350 | 49 | 157 | 34 | 55 | 7 | 2 | 0 | 22 | 20 | 36 | 15 | 8 | R | R | 6-0 | 170 | 3-29-74 | 1996 | Brandon, Fla. |
| Fernandez, Ramon | .000 | 3 | 6 | 0 | 0 | 0 | 0 | 0 | 0 | 0 | 3 | 0 | 0 | R | R | 6-0 | 185 | 9-21-77 | 1996 | Cayey, P.R. |
| Fink, Marc | .355 | 37 | 107 | 18 | 38 | 8 | 0 | 9 | 28 | 26 | 27 | 0 | 0 | L | L | 6-3 | 230 | 7-27-76 | 1994 | Jackson, N.J. |
| Guerrero, Sergio | .318 | 57 | 217 | 48 | 69 | 13 | 0 | 2 | 40 | 25 | 14 | 6 | 3 | R | R | 5-9 | 180 | 12-22-74 | 1995 | McAllen, Texas |
| Hemphill, James | .313 | 51 | 128 | 26 | 40 | 8 | 1 | 2 | 18 | 21 | 31 | 4 | 2 | R | R | 6-3 | 210 | 4-6-74 | 1996 | Hammond, La. |
| Jenkins, Pete | .143 | 7 | 21 | 3 | 3 | 2 | 0 | 0 | 2 | 5 | 5 | 0 | 0 | R | R | 6-1 | 220 | 4-25-76 | 1996 | Redlands, Calif. |
| 2-team (14 Ogden) | .174 | 21 | 46 | 7 | 8 | 2 | 0 | 1 | 5 | 11 | 13 | 0 | 0 | | | | | | | |
| Johnson, Ledowick | .341 | 59 | 208 | 70 | 71 | 8 | 3 | 7 | 33 | 58 | 43 | 19 | 6 | L | R | 5-11 | 170 | 10-21-72 | 1995 | Greenville, N.C. |
| Kirby, Scott | .200 | 47 | 145 | 26 | 29 | 4 | 0 | 4 | 21 | 19 | 42 | 0 | 3 | R | R | 6-2 | 190 | 7-18-77 | 1996 | Lakeland, Fla. |
| Klimek, Josh | .296 | 67 | 253 | 56 | 75 | 17 | 0 | 6 | 51 | 42 | 39 | 5 | 1 | L | R | 6-1 | 175 | 2-2-74 | 1996 | St. Louis, Mo. |
| Osilka, Garret | .212 | 53 | 165 | 34 | 35 | 2 | 1 | 2 | 19 | 25 | 33 | 6 | 6 | R | R | 6-1 | 180 | 9-14-77 | 1996 | Jacksonville, Fla. |

| BATTING | AVG | G | AB | R | H | 2B | 3B | HR | RBI | BB | SO | SB | CS | B | T | HT | WT | DOB | 1st Yr | Resides |
|---|---|---|---|---|---|---|---|---|---|---|---|---|---|---|---|---|---|---|---|---|
| Rogue, Francisco ........ | .229 | 30 | 109 | 14 | 25 | 3 | 0 | 0 | 8 | 8 | 19 | 1 | 0 | R | R | 6-2 | 170 | 11-22-75 | 1993 | Santo Domingo, D.R. |
| Schaub, Greg .............. | .265 | 63 | 245 | 39 | 65 | 13 | 6 | 9 | 50 | 19 | 38 | 4 | 3 | R | R | 6-1 | 185 | 3-30-77 | 1995 | Oxford, Pa. |
| Suero, Ignacio ............. | .338 | 55 | 210 | 46 | 71 | 11 | 1 | 12 | 63 | 23 | 29 | 3 | 4 | R | R | 5-11 | 190 | 7-19-73 | 1994 | Villa Blanca, D.R. |
| Thompson, Dan ........... | .338 | 50 | 145 | 29 | 49 | 6 | 1 | 6 | 30 | 9 | 28 | 3 | 2 | L | R | 6-3 | 205 | 9-3-73 | 1996 | Lexington, Ky. |
| Washam, Jason ............ | .327 | 60 | 226 | 56 | 74 | 10 | 1 | 8 | 51 | 38 | 39 | 3 | 4 | R | R | 6-1 | 190 | 8-18-74 | 1996 | Lincoln, Ill. |
| Wetmore, Mike ............ | .277 | 50 | 202 | 44 | 56 | 10 | 3 | 1 | 23 | 24 | 38 | 11 | 6 | S | R | 5-9 | 170 | 6-16-75 | 1996 | Coupeville, Wash. |

**GAMES BY POSITION: C**—Jenkins 7, Roque 23, Suero 41, Washam 8. **1B**—Fink 11, Kirby 16, Roque 7, Washam 45. **2B**—Guerrero 52, Osilka 6, Wetmore 17. **3B**—Kirby 26, Klimek 51. **SS**—Osilka 43, Wetmore 33. **OF**—Cafaro 47, Fernandez 3, Hemphill 39, Johnson 55, Schaub 62, Thompson 39.

| PITCHING | W | L | ERA | G | GS | CG | SV | IP | H | R | ER | BB | SO | B | T | HT | WT | DOB | 1st Yr | Resides |
|---|---|---|---|---|---|---|---|---|---|---|---|---|---|---|---|---|---|---|---|---|
| Arnold, Jay ................... | 0 | 1 | 54.00 | 1 | 1 | 0 | 0 | 1 | 3 | 4 | 4 | 3 | 1 | R | R | 6-5 | 210 | 8-2-76 | 1996 | Cave Creek, Ariz. |
| 2-team (6 Ogden) ..... | 1 | 1 | 5.60 | 7 | 4 | 0 | 0 | 18 | 15 | 16 | 11 | 15 | 8 | | | | | | | |
| Fieldbinder, Michael ..... | 2 | 0 | 3.60 | 2 | 2 | 0 | 0 | 10 | 8 | 4 | 4 | 1 | 12 | R | R | 6-4 | 200 | 10-2-73 | 1996 | Rochester, Ill. |
| Garcia, Jose ................ | 0 | 0 | 16.20 | 2 | 0 | 0 | 0 | 2 | 1 | 3 | 3 | 3 | 2 | R | R | 6-4 | 215 | 4-29-78 | 1996 | Las Vegas, Nev. |
| Gnirk, Mark ................. | 1 | 0 | 3.42 | 10 | 2 | 0 | 1 | 24 | 26 | 12 | 9 | 4 | 26 | R | R | 6-3 | 195 | 8-21-74 | 1996 | Phoenix, Ariz. |
| Guzman, Jonathan ........ | 3 | 7 | 7.43 | 20 | 5 | 0 | 0 | 50 | 64 | 48 | 41 | 32 | 40 | L | L | 6-2 | 216 | 8-26-77 | 1995 | Levittown, P.R. |
| Hardwick, Bubba ........... | 0 | 1 | 9.00 | 3 | 3 | 0 | 0 | 5 | 8 | 5 | 5 | 6 | 4 | L | L | 5-10 | 170 | 1-18-72 | 1992 | Lakeland, Fla. |
| Hedley, Brian ............... | 1 | 2 | 10.36 | 14 | 0 | 0 | 1 | 24 | 38 | 29 | 28 | 15 | 19 | R | R | 5-11 | 195 | 10-11-74 | 1996 | San Bruno, Calif. |
| Kendall, Phil ................. | 0 | 0 | 20.25 | 2 | 0 | 0 | 0 | 1 | 3 | 4 | 3 | 5 | 3 | R | R | 6-4 | 190 | 8-22-77 | 1996 | Jasper, Ind. |
| Leshay, Maney ............. | 2 | 0 | 3.50 | 4 | 4 | 0 | 0 | 18 | 17 | 14 | 7 | 12 | 11 | R | R | 6-1 | 190 | 3-15-73 | 1996 | Tequesta, Fla. |
| Levrault, Allen ............. | 4 | 3 | 5.32 | 18 | 11 | 0 | 1 | 71 | 70 | 43 | 42 | 22 | 68 | R | R | 6-3 | 238 | 8-15-77 | 1996 | Westport, Mass. |
| Lorenzo, Martin ............ | 0 | 1 | 5.58 | 23 | 1 | 0 | 1 | 40 | 45 | 29 | 25 | 22 | 31 | R | R | 6-2 | 210 | 12-4-76 | 1995 | Bani, D.R. |
| Norris, McKenzie .......... | 3 | 2 | 5.26 | 18 | 6 | 0 | 4 | 39 | 43 | 31 | 23 | 33 | 36 | R | R | 6-7 | 218 | 3-19-76 | 1995 | Mesa, Ariz. |
| Paredes, Roberto .......... | 3 | 1 | 2.67 | 25 | 0 | 0 | 6 | 30 | 23 | 13 | 9 | 16 | 41 | R | R | 6-3 | 170 | 10-16-73 | 1993 | Santo Domingo, D.R. |
| Passini, Brian ............... | 7 | 2 | 3.48 | 15 | 14 | 1 | 0 | 78 | 91 | 37 | 30 | 27 | 71 | L | L | 6-3 | 195 | 1-24-75 | 1996 | Hennepin, Ill. |
| Podjan, Jimmy ............. | 1 | 1 | 5.40 | 4 | 0 | 0 | 0 | 7 | 11 | 5 | 4 | 3 | 5 | R | R | 6-2 | 180 | 3-4-75 | 1995 | St. Joseph, Mich. |
| 2-team (16 Ogden) ... | 1 | 2 | 4.85 | 20 | 0 | 0 | 3 | 30 | 30 | 20 | 16 | 19 | 21 | | | | | | | |
| Prempas, Lyle ............. | 2 | 1 | 9.07 | 21 | 2 | 0 | 2 | 43 | 51 | 47 | 43 | 46 | 52 | L | L | 6-7 | 205 | 12-3-74 | 1993 | Westchester, Ill. |
| Tank, Travis ................. | 7 | 3 | 3.22 | 29 | 0 | 0 | 3 | 64 | 65 | 38 | 23 | 30 | 74 | R | R | 6-2 | 220 | 3-27-75 | 1996 | Sheboygan Falls, Wis. |
| Thompson, Dan ............ | 0 | 0 | 8.44 | 4 | 0 | 0 | 0 | 5 | 7 | 5 | 5 | 1 | 4 | L | R | 6-3 | 205 | 9-3-73 | 1996 | Lexington, Ky. |
| Tijerina, Tano .............. | 3 | 6 | 8.74 | 19 | 8 | 0 | 1 | 58 | 93 | 65 | 56 | 27 | 33 | R | R | 6-4 | 225 | 6-23-74 | 1993 | Waco, Texas |
| Watson, Mark .............. | 5 | 4 | 4.77 | 13 | 13 | 0 | 0 | 60 | 59 | 43 | 32 | 28 | 68 | R | L | 6-4 | 215 | 1-23-74 | 1996 | Atlanta, Ga. |

# OGDEN — Rookie

## PIONEER LEAGUE

| BATTING | AVG | G | AB | R | H | 2B | 3B | HR | RBI | BB | SO | SB | CS | B | T | HT | WT | DOB | 1st Yr | Resides |
|---|---|---|---|---|---|---|---|---|---|---|---|---|---|---|---|---|---|---|---|---|
| Alfano, Jeff ................. | .283 | 45 | 159 | 29 | 45 | 9 | 0 | 4 | 29 | 12 | 30 | 2 | 2 | R | R | 6-3 | 190 | 8-16-76 | 1996 | Visalia, Calif. |
| Barker, Kevin .............. | .317 | 71 | 281 | 61 | 89 | 19 | 4 | 9 | 56 | 46 | 54 | 0 | 2 | L | L | 6-3 | 205 | 7-26-75 | 1996 | Mendota, Va. |
| Darula, Bobby ............. | .274 | 45 | 106 | 19 | 29 | 4 | 0 | 4 | 23 | 17 | 22 | 2 | 2 | L | R | 5-10 | 175 | 10-29-74 | 1996 | Greenwich, Conn. |
| Faurot, Adam ............. | .235 | 67 | 238 | 41 | 56 | 9 | 0 | 2 | 18 | 26 | 35 | 18 | 10 | R | R | 5-11 | 170 | 8-7-74 | 1996 | Blountstown, Fla. |
| Fernandez, Ramon ..... | .078 | 38 | 64 | 7 | 5 | 2 | 0 | 0 | 3 | 7 | 28 | 0 | 2 | R | R | 6-0 | 185 | 9-21-77 | 1996 | Cayey, P.R. |
| 2-team (3 Helena) ... | .071 | 41 | 70 | 7 | 5 | 2 | 0 | 0 | 3 | 7 | 31 | 0 | 2 | | | | | | | |
| Glover, Jason .............. | .289 | 58 | 194 | 42 | 56 | 10 | 4 | 8 | 35 | 32 | 52 | 8 | 4 | R | R | 6-0 | 195 | 5-21-74 | 1996 | Stone Mountain, Ga. |
| Green, Chad ............... | .358 | 21 | 81 | 22 | 29 | 4 | 1 | 3 | 8 | 15 | 23 | 12 | 3 | S | R | 5-10 | 185 | 6-28-75 | 1996 | Cincinnati, Ohio |
| Jenkins, Pete .............. | .200 | 14 | 25 | 4 | 5 | 0 | 0 | 1 | 3 | 6 | 8 | 0 | 0 | R | R | 6-1 | 220 | 4-25-75 | 1996 | Redlands, Calif. |
| Macalutas, Jon ........... | .343 | 54 | 178 | 41 | 61 | 10 | 0 | 3 | 24 | 18 | 21 | 8 | 2 | R | R | 6-0 | 190 | 8-21-74 | 1996 | Stockton, Calif. |
| Martinez, David .......... | .330 | 35 | 103 | 25 | 34 | 6 | 1 | 0 | 13 | 26 | 30 | 0 | 3 | R | R | 6-0 | 165 | 5-28-76 | 1993 | Santo Domingo, D.R. |
| Moore, Donald ............ | .271 | 50 | 85 | 16 | 23 | 0 | 3 | 1 | 13 | 7 | 30 | 5 | 1 | R | R | 6-2 | 184 | 6-12-76 | 1995 | York, Pa. |
| Parent, Gerald ............ | .385 | 62 | 218 | 42 | 84 | 18 | 0 | 6 | 42 | 37 | 34 | 5 | 1 | L | R | 6-2 | 210 | 12-7-73 | 1995 | Assonet, Mass. |
| Parmenter, Ross ......... | .305 | 45 | 141 | 21 | 43 | 9 | 0 | 2 | 18 | 21 | 31 | 0 | 3 | R | R | 6-1 | 185 | 11-23-74 | 1996 | Ben Lomond, Calif. |
| Phair, Kelly ................. | .294 | 41 | 163 | 41 | 48 | 12 | 1 | 2 | 24 | 27 | 36 | 17 | 4 | R | R | 6-2 | 185 | 6-2-73 | 1995 | Cincinnati, Ohio |
| Rodriguez, Miguel ........ | .285 | 69 | 274 | 66 | 78 | 18 | 2 | 17 | 65 | 21 | 44 | 22 | 5 | R | R | 6-1 | 205 | 5-14-75 | 1993 | El Seybo, D.R. |
| Walther, Chris ............ | .351 | 63 | 239 | 47 | 84 | 16 | 4 | 6 | 54 | 14 | 21 | 3 | 2 | R | R | 6-2 | 200 | 8-28-76 | 1995 | Odessa, Fla. |

**GAMES BY POSITION: C**—Alfano 33, Darula 12, Jenkins 10, Rodriguez 28, Walther 1. **1B**—Barker 69, Darula 7, Rodrigueua 4, Walther 2. **2B**—Darula 1, Faurot 23, Glover 1, Macalutas 13, Parmenter 2, Phair 39. **3B**—Alfano 1, Darula 1, Faurot 35, Fernandez 1, Glover 8, Martinez 6, Parmenter 2, Phair 1, Walther 31. **SS**—Faurot 11, Martinez 29, Parmenter 40, Phair 4. **OF**—Darula 3, Fernandez 37, Glover 31, Green 21, Macalutas 33, Moore 44, Parent 62, Walther 36.

| PITCHING | W | L | ERA | G | GS | CG | SV | IP | H | R | ER | BB | SO | B | T | HT | WT | DOB | 1st Yr | Resides |
|---|---|---|---|---|---|---|---|---|---|---|---|---|---|---|---|---|---|---|---|---|
| Arnold, Jay ................... | 1 | 0 | 3.71 | 6 | 3 | 0 | 0 | 17 | 12 | 12 | 7 | 12 | 7 | R | R | 6-5 | 210 | 8-2-76 | 1996 | Cave Creek, Ariz. |
| Barnes, Larry .............. | 4 | 4 | 5.19 | 11 | 10 | 0 | 0 | 50 | 45 | 45 | 29 | 31 | 54 | S | R | 6-5 | 230 | 8-11-76 | 1994 | Jacksonville, Fla. |
| Boker, John ................ | 5 | 1 | 4.35 | 15 | 6 | 0 | 0 | 50 | 53 | 29 | 24 | 41 | 70 | R | R | 6-3 | 195 | 1-1-75 | 1996 | Huber Heights, Ohio |
| Fulcher, John .............. | 2 | 3 | 5.43 | 13 | 10 | 0 | 0 | 58 | 67 | 45 | 35 | 15 | 65 | L | L | 6-3 | 190 | 9-18-74 | 1996 | Manassas, Va. |
| Glick, Dave ................. | 3 | 1 | 3.41 | 24 | 0 | 0 | 0 | 34 | 31 | 15 | 13 | 21 | 41 | L | L | 6-1 | 190 | 4-2-76 | 1995 | Palmdale, Calif. |
| Gutierrez, Alfredo ........ | 0 | 3 | 4.22 | 19 | 0 | 0 | 9 | 21 | 18 | 12 | 10 | 11 | 18 | R | R | 6-1 | 190 | 3-22-76 | 1994 | Riverside, Calif. |
| Hawkins, Al ................. | 3 | 3 | 3.21 | 9 | 5 | 0 | 0 | 34 | 31 | 16 | 12 | 13 | 23 | R | R | 6-2 | 210 | 1-1-78 | 1996 | Elizabeth, N.J. |
| Hook, Jeff .................... | 0 | 0 | 8.44 | 3 | 0 | 0 | 0 | 5 | 7 | 5 | 5 | 8 | 3 | L | R | 6-4 | 195 | 8-26-74 | 1994 | Newbury Park, Calif. |
| Ishee, Gabe ................ | 6 | 4 | 4.73 | 15 | 14 | 1 | 0 | 86 | 94 | 55 | 45 | 42 | 83 | S | R | 6-2 | 195 | 8-14-74 | 1995 | Biloxi, Miss. |
| Ledeit, Richard ............ | 0 | 1 | 3.92 | 11 | 1 | 0 | 0 | 21 | 24 | 12 | 9 | 9 | 16 | R | R | 6-2 | 215 | 3-12-73 | 1996 | San Jose, Calif. |
| Miller, Shawn .............. | 3 | 1 | 2.41 | 17 | 0 | 0 | 3 | 41 | 41 | 14 | 11 | 15 | 43 | R | R | 6-4 | 221 | 5-7-74 | 1995 | Bensenville, Ill. |
| O'Leary, Kevin ............. | 1 | 0 | 5.63 | 2 | 2 | 0 | 0 | 8 | 7 | 5 | 5 | 2 | 8 | R | R | 6-3 | 195 | 1-24-74 | 1996 | West Roxbury, Mass. |
| O'Reilly, John .............. | 7 | 1 | 3.96 | 13 | 12 | 0 | 0 | 64 | 66 | 34 | 28 | 27 | 82 | R | R | 6-3 | 200 | 8-11-74 | 1996 | Oakland, N.J. |
| Perez, Jesse ................ | 2 | 1 | 2.57 | 19 | 0 | 0 | 3 | 21 | 19 | 12 | 6 | 11 | 16 | S | R | 5-11 | 185 | 8-15-75 | 1995 | Cantil, Calif. |
| Podjan, Jimmy ............. | 1 | 1 | 4.70 | 16 | 0 | 0 | 3 | 23 | 19 | 15 | 12 | 16 | 16 | R | R | 6-2 | 180 | 3-4-75 | 1995 | St. Joseph, Mich. |
| Richardson, Brad ......... | 1 | 1 | 10.72 | 19 | 0 | 0 | 1 | 23 | 28 | 37 | 27 | 28 | 25 | R | L | 6-0 | 195 | 2-11-76 | 1996 | Saginaw, Texas |
| Stewart, Paul .............. | 1 | 4 | 7.83 | 12 | 9 | 0 | 0 | 44 | 47 | 49 | 38 | 26 | 39 | R | R | 6-6 | 205 | 10-21-78 | 1996 | Raleigh, N.C. |
| Warren, DeShawn ........ | 1 | 0 | 6.75 | 3 | 0 | 0 | 0 | 3 | 2 | 3 | 2 | 3 | 7 | L | L | 6-0 | 172 | 5-5-74 | 1992 | Butler, Ala. |
| Zapata, Juan .............. | 2 | 1 | 6.06 | 20 | 0 | 0 | 0 | 36 | 43 | 26 | 24 | 11 | 32 | R | R | 6-2 | 205 | 9-3-73 | 1993 | Rio Arriba, D.R. |

# MINNESOTA TWINS

**Manager:** Tom Kelly.     **1996 Record:** 78-84, .481 (4th, AL Central).

| BATTING | AVG | G | AB | R | H | 2B | 3B | HR | RBI | BB | SO | SB | CS | B | T | HT | WT | DOB | 1st Yr | Resides |
|---|---|---|---|---|---|---|---|---|---|---|---|---|---|---|---|---|---|---|---|---|
| Becker, Rich | .291 | 148 | 525 | 92 | 153 | 31 | 4 | 12 | 71 | 68 | 118 | 19 | 5 | L | L | 5-10 | 180 | 2-1-72 | 1990 | Cape Coral, Fla. |
| Brede, Brent | .300 | 10 | 20 | 2 | 6 | 0 | 1 | 0 | 2 | 1 | 5 | 0 | 0 | L | L | 6-4 | 190 | 9-13-71 | 1990 | Trenton, Ill. |
| Coomer, Ron | .296 | 95 | 233 | 34 | 69 | 12 | 1 | 12 | 41 | 17 | 24 | 3 | 0 | R | R | 5-11 | 195 | 11-18-66 | 1987 | Crest Hill, Ill. |
| Cordova, Marty | .309 | 145 | 569 | 97 | 176 | 46 | 1 | 16 | 111 | 53 | 96 | 11 | 5 | R | R | 6-0 | 190 | 7-10-69 | 1989 | Henderson, Nev. |
| Durant, Mike | .210 | 40 | 81 | 15 | 17 | 3 | 0 | 0 | 5 | 10 | 15 | 3 | 0 | R | R | 6-2 | 198 | 9-14-69 | 1991 | Columbus, Ohio |
| Hale, Chip | .276 | 85 | 87 | 8 | 24 | 5 | 0 | 1 | 16 | 10 | 6 | 0 | 0 | L | R | 5-10 | 175 | 12-2-64 | 1987 | Tucson, Ariz. |
| Hocking, Denny | .197 | 49 | 127 | 16 | 25 | 6 | 0 | 1 | 10 | 8 | 24 | 3 | 3 | S | R | 5-10 | 174 | 4-2-70 | 1990 | Torrance, Calif. |
| Hollins, Dave | .242 | 121 | 422 | 71 | 102 | 26 | 0 | 13 | 53 | 71 | 102 | 6 | 4 | S | R | 6-1 | 207 | 5-25-66 | 1987 | Orchard Park, N.Y. |
| Kelly, Roberto | .323 | 98 | 322 | 41 | 104 | 17 | 4 | 6 | 47 | 23 | 53 | 10 | 2 | R | R | 6-2 | 202 | 10-1-64 | 1982 | Panama City, Panama |
| Knoblauch, Chuck | .341 | 153 | 578 | 140 | 197 | 35 | 14 | 13 | 72 | 98 | 74 | 45 | 14 | R | R | 5-9 | 181 | 7-7-68 | 1989 | Houston, Texas |
| Lawton, Matt | .258 | 79 | 252 | 34 | 65 | 7 | 1 | 6 | 42 | 28 | 28 | 4 | 4 | L | R | 5-9 | 180 | 11-3-71 | 1991 | Lyman, Miss. |
| Meares, Pat | .267 | 152 | 517 | 66 | 138 | 26 | 7 | 8 | 67 | 17 | 90 | 9 | 4 | R | R | 6-0 | 180 | 9-6-68 | 1990 | Wichita, Kan. |
| Molitor, Paul | .341 | 161 | 660 | 99 | 225 | 41 | 8 | 9 | 113 | 56 | 72 | 18 | 6 | R | R | 6-0 | 185 | 8-22-56 | 1977 | Edina, Wis. |
| Myers, Greg | .286 | 97 | 329 | 37 | 94 | 22 | 3 | 6 | 47 | 19 | 52 | 0 | 0 | L | R | 6-2 | 215 | 4-14-66 | 1984 | Riverside, Calif. |
| Quinlan, Tom | .000 | 4 | 6 | 0 | 0 | 0 | 0 | 0 | 0 | 0 | 3 | 0 | 0 | R | R | 6-3 | 210 | 3-27-68 | 1987 | Maplewood, Minn. |
| Raabe, Brian | .222 | 7 | 9 | 0 | 2 | 0 | 0 | 0 | 1 | 0 | 1 | 0 | 0 | R | R | 5-9 | 170 | 11-5-67 | 1990 | Blaine, Minn. |
| Reboulet, Jeff | .222 | 107 | 234 | 20 | 52 | 9 | 0 | 0 | 23 | 25 | 34 | 4 | 2 | R | R | 6-0 | 168 | 4-30-64 | 1986 | Kettering, Ohio |
| Stahoviak, Scott | .284 | 130 | 405 | 72 | 115 | 30 | 3 | 13 | 61 | 59 | 114 | 3 | 3 | L | R | 6-5 | 222 | 3-6-70 | 1991 | Grayslake, Ill. |
| Walbeck, Matt | .223 | 63 | 215 | 25 | 48 | 10 | 0 | 2 | 24 | 9 | 34 | 3 | 1 | S | R | 5-11 | 188 | 10-2-69 | 1987 | Sacramento, Calif. |
| Walker, Todd | .256 | 25 | 82 | 8 | 21 | 6 | 0 | 0 | 6 | 4 | 13 | 2 | 0 | L | R | 6-0 | 180 | 5-25-73 | 1994 | Bossier City, La. |

| PITCHING | W | L | ERA | G | GS | CG | SV | IP | H | R | ER | BB | SO | B | T | HT | WT | DOB | 1st Yr | Resides |
|---|---|---|---|---|---|---|---|---|---|---|---|---|---|---|---|---|---|---|---|---|
| Aguilera, Rick | 8 | 6 | 5.42 | 19 | 19 | 2 | 0 | 111 | 124 | 69 | 67 | 27 | 83 | R | R | 6-5 | 203 | 12-31-61 | 1983 | Chanhassen, Minn. |
| Aldred, Scott | 6 | 5 | 5.09 | 25 | 17 | 0 | 0 | 122 | 134 | 73 | 69 | 42 | 75 | L | L | 6-4 | 195 | 6-12-68 | 1987 | Lakeland, Fla. |
| 2-team (11 Detroit) | 6 | 9 | 6.21 | 36 | 25 | 0 | 0 | 165 | 194 | 125 | 114 | 68 | 111 | | | | | | | |
| Bennett, Erik | 2 | 0 | 7.90 | 24 | 0 | 0 | 1 | 27 | 33 | 24 | 24 | 16 | 13 | R | R | 6-2 | 205 | 9-13-68 | 1989 | Yreka, Calif. |
| Guardado, Eddie | 6 | 5 | 5.25 | 83 | 0 | 0 | 4 | 74 | 61 | 45 | 43 | 33 | 74 | R | L | 6-0 | 187 | 10-2-70 | 1991 | Stockton, Calif. |
| Hansell, Greg | 3 | 0 | 5.69 | 50 | 0 | 0 | 3 | 74 | 83 | 48 | 47 | 31 | 46 | R | R | 6-5 | 215 | 3-12-71 | 1989 | Gig Harbor, Wash. |
| Hawkins, LaTroy | 1 | 1 | 8.20 | 7 | 6 | 0 | 0 | 26 | 42 | 24 | 24 | 9 | 24 | R | R | 6-5 | 195 | 12-21-72 | 1991 | Gary, Ind. |
| Klingenbeck, Scott | 1 | 1 | 7.85 | 10 | 3 | 0 | 0 | 29 | 42 | 28 | 25 | 10 | 15 | R | R | 6-2 | 205 | 2-3-71 | 1992 | Cincinnati, Ohio |
| Mahomes, Pat | 1 | 4 | 7.20 | 20 | 5 | 0 | 0 | 45 | 63 | 38 | 36 | 27 | 30 | R | R | 6-4 | 210 | 8-9-70 | 1988 | Lindale, Texas |
| Milchin, Mike | 2 | 1 | 8.31 | 26 | 0 | 0 | 0 | 22 | 31 | 21 | 20 | 12 | 19 | L | L | 6-3 | 190 | 2-28-68 | 1989 | Richmond, Va. |
| Miller, Travis | 1 | 2 | 9.23 | 7 | 7 | 0 | 0 | 26 | 45 | 29 | 27 | 9 | 15 | R | L | 6-3 | 205 | 11-2-72 | 1994 | West Manchester, Ohio |
| Naulty, Dan | 3 | 2 | 3.79 | 49 | 0 | 0 | 4 | 57 | 43 | 26 | 24 | 35 | 56 | R | R | 6-6 | 211 | 1-6-70 | 1992 | Huntington Beach, Calif. |
| Parra, Jose | 5 | 5 | 6.04 | 27 | 5 | 0 | 0 | 70 | 88 | 48 | 47 | 27 | 50 | R | R | 5-11 | 160 | 11-28-72 | 1990 | Santiago, D.R. |
| Radke, Brad | 11 | 16 | 4.46 | 35 | 35 | 3 | 0 | 232 | 231 | 125 | 115 | 57 | 148 | R | R | 6-2 | 180 | 10-27-72 | 1991 | Tampa, Fla. |
| Robertson, Rich | 7 | 17 | 5.12 | 36 | 31 | 5 | 0 | 186 | 197 | 113 | 106 | 116 | 114 | L | L | 6-4 | 175 | 9-15-68 | 1990 | Waller, Texas |
| Rodriguez, Frank | 13 | 14 | 5.05 | 38 | 33 | 3 | 2 | 207 | 218 | 129 | 116 | 78 | 110 | R | R | 6-0 | 175 | 12-11-72 | 1991 | Brooklyn, N.Y. |
| Serafini, Dan | 0 | 1 | 10.38 | 1 | 1 | 0 | 0 | 4 | 7 | 5 | 5 | 2 | 1 | S | L | 6-1 | 185 | 1-25-74 | 1992 | San Bruno, Calif. |
| Stevens, Dave | 3 | 3 | 4.66 | 49 | 0 | 0 | 11 | 58 | 58 | 31 | 30 | 25 | 29 | R | R | 6-3 | 210 | 3-4-70 | 1990 | La Habra, Calif. |
| Trombley, Mike | 5 | 1 | 3.01 | 43 | 0 | 0 | 6 | 69 | 61 | 24 | 23 | 25 | 57 | R | R | 6-2 | 200 | 4-14-67 | 1989 | Fort Myers, Fla. |

## FIELDING

| Catcher | PCT | G | PO | A | E | DP | PB |
|---|---|---|---|---|---|---|---|
| Durant | .975 | 37 | 183 | 13 | 5 | 1 | 0 |
| Myers | .985 | 90 | 488 | 27 | 8 | 5 | 6 |
| Walbeck | .994 | 61 | 326 | 18 | 2 | 2 | 5 |

| First Base | PCT | G | PO | A | E | DP |
|---|---|---|---|---|---|---|
| Coomer | .993 | 57 | 244 | 39 | 2 | 26 |
| Hale | 1.000 | 6 | 7 | 1 | 0 | 1 |
| Hocking | 1.000 | 1 | 1 | 0 | 0 | 0 |
| Molitor | .993 | 17 | 138 | 13 | 1 | 13 |
| Reboulet | 1.000 | 13 | 57 | 8 | 0 | 7 |
| Stahoviak | .994 | 114 | 801 | 92 | 5 | 79 |

| Second Base | PCT | G | PO | A | E | DP |
|---|---|---|---|---|---|---|
| Hale | 1.000 | 14 | 8 | 13 | 0 | 2 |
| Hocking | 1.000 | 2 | 1 | 2 | 0 | 1 |
| Knoblauch | .988 | 151 | 271 | 390 | 8 | 93 |
| Raabe | .000 | 1 | 0 | 0 | 0 | 0 |
| Reboulet | 1.000 | 22 | 24 | 22 | 0 | 4 |
| Walker | 1.000 | 4 | 5 | 7 | 0 | 1 |

| Third Base | PCT | G | PO | A | E | DP |
|---|---|---|---|---|---|---|
| Coomer | 1.000 | 9 | 2 | 3 | 0 | 0 |
| Hale | 1.000 | 3 | 2 | 0 | 0 | 1 |

| | PCT | G | PO | A | E | DP |
|---|---|---|---|---|---|---|
| Hollins | .953 | 116 | 81 | 206 | 14 | 16 |
| Quinlan | .667 | 4 | 0 | 2 | 1 | 0 |
| Raabe | .857 | 6 | 2 | 4 | 1 | 1 |
| Reboulet | .984 | 36 | 19 | 41 | 1 | 5 |
| Walker | .956 | 20 | 11 | 32 | 2 | 3 |

| Shortstop | PCT | G | PO | A | E | DP |
|---|---|---|---|---|---|---|
| Hocking | 1.000 | 6 | 3 | 3 | 0 | 0 |
| Meares | .965 | 150 | 257 | 344 | 22 | 85 |
| Reboulet | .987 | 37 | 34 | 41 | 1 | 13 |

| Outfield | PCT | G | PO | A | E | DP |
|---|---|---|---|---|---|---|
| Becker | .993 | 146 | 391 | 18 | 3 | 9 |
| Brede | 1.000 | 7 | 12 | 1 | 0 | 0 |
| Coomer | .935 | 23 | 29 | 0 | 2 | 0 |
| Cordova | .991 | 145 | 328 | 9 | 3 | 1 |
| Hale | .000 | 3 | 0 | 0 | 0 | 0 |
| Hocking | .985 | 33 | 62 | 4 | 1 | 0 |
| Kelly | .990 | 93 | 203 | 4 | 2 | 0 |
| Lawton | .985 | 75 | 196 | 4 | 3 | 1 |
| Meares | .000 | 1 | 0 | 0 | 0 | 0 |
| Reboulet | 1.000 | 7 | 4 | 2 | 0 | 0 |

**Paul Molitor**

**Chuck Knoblauch hit .341 for the Twins with 140 runs scored**

STAN DENNY

Twins minor league
Player of the Year
Todd Walker

LARRY GOREN

## FARM SYSTEM

**Director of Minor Leagues:** Jim Rantz

| Class | Farm Team | League | W | L | Pct. | Finish* | Manager | First Yr |
|---|---|---|---|---|---|---|---|---|
| AAA | Salt Lake (Utah) Buzz | Pacific Coast | 78 | 66 | .542 | 2nd (10) | Phil Roof | 1994 |
| AA | Hardware City (Conn.) Rock Cats | Eastern | 61 | 81 | .430 | 9th (10) | Al Newman | 1995 |
| #A | Fort Myers (Fla.) Miracle | Florida State | 79 | 58 | .577 | 2nd (14) | John Russell | 1993 |
| A | Fort Wayne (Ind.) Wizards | Midwest | 69 | 67 | .536 | 6th (14) | Dan Rohn | 1993 |
| #R | Elizabethton (Tenn.) Twins | Appalachian | 40 | 27 | .597 | 4th (9) | Jose Marzan | 1974 |
| R | Fort Myers (Fla.) Twins | Gulf Coast | 30 | 30 | .500 | 9th (16) | Mike Boulanger | 1989 |

*Finish in overall standings (No. of teams in league)   #Advanced level

## ORGANIZATION LEADERS

### MAJOR LEAGUERS

**BATTING**
| | | |
|---|---|---|
| *AVG | Two tied at | .341 |
| R | Chuck Knoblauch | 140 |
| H | Paul Molitor | 225 |
| TB | Paul Molitor | 309 |
| 2B | Marty Cordova | 46 |
| 3B | Chuck Knoblauch | 14 |
| HR | Marty Cordova | 16 |
| RBI | Paul Molitor | 113 |
| BB | Chuck Knoblauch | 98 |
| SO | Rich Becker | 118 |
| SB | Chuck Knoblauch | 45 |

**PITCHING**
| | | |
|---|---|---|
| W | Frank Rodriguez | 13 |
| L | Rich Robertson | 17 |
| #ERA | Brad Radke | 4.46 |
| G | Eddie Guardado | 83 |
| CG | Rich Robertson | 5 |
| SV | Dave Stevens | 11 |
| IP | Brad Radke | 232 |
| BB | Rich Robertson | 116 |
| SO | Brad Radke | 148 |

KEVIN REECE

**Marty Cordova.** 46 doubles

### MINOR LEAGUERS

**BATTING**
| | | |
|---|---|---|
| *AVG | Brian Raabe, Salt Lake | .351 |
| R | Brian Raabe, Salt Lake | 103 |
| H | Todd Walker, Salt Lake | 187 |
| TB | Todd Walker, Salt Lake | 330 |
| 2B | Todd Walker, Salt Lake | 41 |
| 3B | Two tied at | 9 |
| HR | Todd Walker, Salt Lake | 28 |
| RBI | Todd Walker, Salt Lake | 111 |
| BB | Brent Brede, Salt Lake | 87 |
| SO | Ryan Lane, Fort Myers/Hard. City | 125 |
| SB | Armann Brown, Fort Myers | 36 |

**PITCHING**
| | | |
|---|---|---|
| W | Two tied at | 13 |
| L | Robert Boggs, Fort Wayne | 12 |
| #ERA | Trevor Cobb, Fort Myers | 2.64 |
| G | Fred Rath, Ft. Wayne/Ft. Myers | 54 |
| CG | Scott Klingenbeck, Salt Lake | 5 |
| SV | Fred Rath, Ft. Wayne/Ft. Myers | 18 |
| IP | Mark Redman, Hard. City/Salt Lake | 193 |
| BB | Mark Redman, Hard. City/Salt Lake | 86 |
| SO | Jason Bell, Ft. Myers/Hard. City | 177 |

*Minimum 250 At-Bats   #Minimum 75 Innings

## TOP 10 PROSPECTS

**How the Twins Top 10 prospects, as judged by Baseball America prior to the 1996 season, fared in 1996:**

STEVE MOORE

**Jose Valentin**

| Player, Pos. | Club (Class—League) | AVG | AB | R | H | 2B | 3B | HR | RBI | SB |
|---|---|---|---|---|---|---|---|---|---|---|
| 1. Todd Walker, 3b | Salt Lake (AAA—Pacific Coast) | .339 | 551 | 94 | 187 | 41 | 9 | 28 | 111 | 13 |
| | Minnesota | .256 | 82 | 8 | 21 | 6 | 0 | 0 | 6 | 2 |
| 2. Jose Valentin, c | Fort Myers (A—Florida State) | .263 | 338 | 34 | 89 | 26 | 1 | 7 | 54 | 1 |
| | Hardware City (AA—Eastern) | .236 | 165 | 22 | 39 | 8 | 0 | 3 | 14 | 0 |
| 6. Torii Hunter, of | Hardware City (AA—Eastern) | .263 | 342 | 49 | 90 | 20 | 3 | 7 | 33 | 7 |
| | Fort Myers (A—Florida State) | .188 | 16 | 1 | 3 | 0 | 0 | 0 | 1 | 1 |
| 8. Matt Lawton, of | Salt Lake (AAA—Pacific Coast) | .297 | 212 | 40 | 63 | 16 | 1 | 7 | 33 | 2 |
| | Minnesota | .258 | 252 | 34 | 65 | 7 | 1 | 6 | 42 | 4 |

| | | W | L | ERA | G | SV | IP | H | BB | SO |
|---|---|---|---|---|---|---|---|---|---|---|
| 3. LaTroy Hawkins, rhp | Salt Lake (AAA—Pacific Coast) | 9 | 8 | 3.92 | 20 | 0 | 138 | 138 | 31 | 99 |
| | Minnesota | 1 | 1 | 8.20 | 7 | 0 | 26 | 42 | 9 | 24 |
| 4. Dan Serafini, lhp | Salt Lake (AAA—Pacific Coast) | 7 | 7 | 5.58 | 25 | 0 | 131 | 164 | 58 | 109 |
| | Minnesota | 0 | 1 | 10.38 | 1 | 0 | 4 | 7 | 2 | 1 |
| 5. Travis Miller, lhp | Salt Lake (AAA—Pacific Coast) | 8 | 10 | 4.83 | 27 | 0 | 160 | 187 | 57 | 143 |
| 7. Jason Bell, rhp | Hardware City (AA—Eastern) | 2 | 6 | 4.40 | 16 | 0 | 94 | 93 | 38 | 94 |
| | Fort Myers (A—Florida State) | 6 | 3 | 1.69 | 13 | 0 | 90 | 61 | 22 | 83 |
| 9. Mark Redman, lhp | Salt Lake (AAA—Pacific Coast) | 0 | 0 | 9.00 | 1 | 0 | 4 | 7 | 2 | 4 |
| | Hardware City (AA—Eastern) | 7 | 7 | 3.81 | 16 | 0 | 106 | 101 | 50 | 96 |
| | Fort Myers (A—Florida State) | 3 | 4 | 1.85 | 13 | 0 | 83 | 63 | 34 | 75 |
| 10. Marc Barcelo, rhp | Salt Lake (AAA—Pacific Coast) | 2 | 2 | 6.52 | 12 | 0 | 59 | 82 | 17 | 34 |
| | Hardware City (AA—Eastern) | 3 | 8 | 5.06 | 14 | 0 | 80 | 98 | 38 | 59 |

## PACIFIC COAST LEAGUE

| BATTING | AVG | G | AB | R | H | 2B | 3B | HR | RBI | BB | SO | SB | CS | B | T | HT | WT | DOB | 1st Yr | Resides |
|---|---|---|---|---|---|---|---|---|---|---|---|---|---|---|---|---|---|---|---|---|
| Brede, Brent | .348 | 132 | 483 | 102 | 168 | 38 | 8 | 11 | 86 | 87 | 87 | 14 | 6 | L | L | 6-4 | 190 | 9-13-71 | 1990 | Trenton, Ill. |
| Durant, Mike | .287 | 31 | 101 | 21 | 29 | 7 | 0 | 1 | 12 | 11 | 21 | 7 | 2 | R | R | 6-2 | 198 | 9-14-69 | 1991 | Columbus, Ohio |
| Giannelli, Ray | .258 | 10 | 31 | 2 | 8 | 1 | 0 | 0 | 4 | 2 | 8 | 0 | 0 | L | R | 6-0 | 195 | 2-5-66 | 1988 | Lindenhurst, N.Y. |
| Hazlett, Steve | .203 | 101 | 44 | 61 | 14 | 4 | 10 | 41 | 33 | 85 | 7 | 2 | | R | R | 5-11 | 190 | 3-30-70 | 1991 | Longmont, Colo. |
| Hocking, Denny | .277 | 37 | 130 | 18 | 36 | 6 | 2 | 3 | 22 | 10 | 17 | 2 | 2 | S | R | 5-10 | 174 | 4-2-70 | 1990 | Torrance, Calif. |
| Horn, Jeff | .337 | 25 | 83 | 14 | 28 | 5 | 0 | 3 | 13 | 12 | 5 | 0 | 1 | R | R | 6-1 | 197 | 8-23-70 | 1992 | Las Vegas, Nev. |
| Johnson, J.J. | .339 | 13 | 56 | 8 | 19 | 3 | 1 | 1 | 13 | 1 | 11 | 0 | 1 | R | R | 6-0 | 195 | 8-31-73 | 1991 | Pine Plains, N.Y. |
| Latham, Chris | .274 | 115 | 376 | 59 | 103 | 16 | 6 | 9 | 50 | 36 | 91 | 26 | 9 | S | R | 6-0 | 188 | 5-26-73 | 1991 | Las Vegas, Nev. |
| Lawton, Matt | .297 | 53 | 212 | 40 | 63 | 16 | 1 | 7 | 33 | 26 | 34 | 2 | 4 | L | R | 5-9 | 180 | 11-3-71 | 1991 | Lyman, Miss. |
| Leonard, Mark | .250 | 59 | 192 | 25 | 48 | 6 | 2 | 5 | 27 | 41 | 39 | 0 | 2 | L | R | 6-0 | 212 | 8-14-64 | 1986 | San Jose, Calif. |
| Lopez, Rene | .241 | 22 | 58 | 5 | 14 | 4 | 0 | 0 | 14 | 5 | 10 | 1 | 0 | R | R | 5-11 | 195 | 12-10-71 | 1992 | Downey, Calif. |
| Miller, Damian | .286 | 104 | 385 | 54 | 110 | 27 | 1 | 7 | 55 | 25 | 58 | 1 | 4 | R | R | 6-2 | 190 | 10-13-69 | 1990 | West Salem, Wis. |
| Ogden, Jamie | .263 | 123 | 448 | 80 | 118 | 22 | 2 | 18 | 74 | 45 | 105 | 17 | 2 | L | L | 6-5 | 233 | 1-19-72 | 1990 | White Bear Lake, Minn. |
| Quinlan, Tom | .283 | 121 | 491 | 81 | 139 | 38 | 1 | 15 | 81 | 38 | 121 | 4 | 8 | R | R | 6-3 | 210 | 3-27-68 | 1987 | Maplewood, Minn. |
| Raabe, Brian | .351 | 116 | 482 | 103 | 169 | 39 | 4 | 18 | 69 | 47 | 19 | 8 | 8 | R | R | 5-9 | 170 | 11-5-67 | 1990 | Blaine, Minn. |
| Reimer, Kevin | .285 | 54 | 193 | 29 | 55 | 9 | 0 | 10 | 33 | 11 | 31 | 4 | 1 | L | R | 6-2 | 230 | 6-28-64 | 1985 | Enderby, B.C. |
| Simons, Mitch | .264 | 129 | 512 | 76 | 135 | 27 | 8 | 5 | 59 | 43 | 59 | 35 | 11 | R | R | 5-9 | 170 | 12-13-68 | 1991 | Midwest City, Okla. |
| Walker, Todd | .339 | 135 | 551 | 94 | 187 | 41 | 9 | 28 | 111 | 57 | 91 | 13 | 8 | L | R | 6-0 | 180 | 5-25-73 | 1994 | Bossier City, La. |

| PITCHING | W | L | ERA | G | GS | CG | SV | IP | H | R | ER | BB | SO | B | T | HT | WT | DOB | 1st Yr | Resides |
|---|---|---|---|---|---|---|---|---|---|---|---|---|---|---|---|---|---|---|---|---|
| Barcelo, Marc | 2 | 2 | 6.52 | 12 | 9 | 0 | 0 | 59 | 82 | 45 | 43 | 17 | 34 | R | R | 6-3 | 210 | 1-10-72 | 1993 | Tucson, Ariz. |
| Bennett, Erik | 3 | 1 | 6.38 | 17 | 0 | 0 | 0 | 24 | 27 | 17 | 17 | 14 | 10 | R | R | 6-2 | 205 | 9-13-68 | 1989 | Yreka, Calif. |
| Hawkins, LaTroy | 9 | 8 | 3.92 | 20 | 20 | 4 | 0 | 138 | 138 | 66 | 60 | 31 | 99 | R | R | 6-5 | 195 | 12-21-72 | 1991 | Gary, Ind. |
| Klingenbeck, Scott | 9 | 3 | 3.11 | 22 | 22 | 5 | 0 | 151 | 159 | 64 | 52 | 41 | 100 | R | R | 6-2 | 205 | 2-3-71 | 1992 | Cincinnati, Ohio |
| Konieczki, Dom | 0 | 0 | 18.00 | 4 | 0 | 0 | 0 | 3 | 8 | 7 | 6 | 5 | 2 | R | L | 6-1 | 170 | 6-16-69 | 1991 | Lehigh Acres, Fla. |
| Legault, Kevin | 5 | 4 | 5.36 | 50 | 0 | 0 | 0 | 81 | 100 | 51 | 48 | 24 | 57 | R | R | 6-1 | 185 | 3-5-71 | 1992 | Watervliet, N.Y. |
| Mahomes, Pat | 1 | 3 | 3.74 | 22 | 2 | 0 | 7 | 34 | 32 | 14 | 14 | 12 | 41 | R | R | 6-4 | 210 | 8-9-70 | 1988 | Lindale, Texas |
| Milchin, Mike | 0 | 0 | 3.68 | 19 | 0 | 0 | 2 | 22 | 21 | 9 | 9 | 11 | 18 | L | L | 6-3 | 190 | 2-28-68 | 1989 | Richmond, Va. |
| Miller, Travis | 8 | 10 | 4.83 | 27 | 27 | 1 | 0 | 160 | 187 | 97 | 86 | 57 | 143 | R | L | 6-3 | 205 | 11-2-72 | 1994 | West Manchester, Ohio |
| Misuraca, Mike | 1 | 2 | 6.27 | 18 | 2 | 0 | 1 | 37 | 50 | 33 | 26 | 16 | 25 | R | R | 6-0 | 188 | 8-21-68 | 1989 | Covina, Calif. |
| Norris, Joe | 1 | 1 | 5.79 | 21 | 0 | 0 | 2 | 37 | 48 | 27 | 24 | 17 | 38 | R | R | 6-4 | 215 | 11-29-70 | 1989 | Oswego, S.C. |
| Parra, Jose | 5 | 3 | 5.11 | 23 | 1 | 0 | 8 | 44 | 51 | 25 | 25 | 13 | 26 | R | R | 5-11 | 160 | 11-28-72 | 1990 | Santiago, D.R. |
| Redman, Mark | 0 | 0 | 9.00 | 1 | 1 | 0 | 0 | 4 | 7 | 4 | 4 | 2 | 4 | L | L | 6-5 | 220 | 1-5-74 | 1995 | Del Mar, Calif. |
| Ritchie, Todd | 0 | 4 | 5.47 | 16 | 0 | 0 | 0 | 25 | 27 | 15 | 15 | 11 | 19 | R | R | 6-3 | 205 | 11-7-71 | 1990 | Duncanville, Texas |
| Roberts, Brett | 9 | 7 | 5.40 | 31 | 30 | 2 | 0 | 168 | 211 | 115 | 101 | 71 | 86 | R | R | 6-7 | 225 | 3-24-70 | 1991 | South Webster, Ohio |
| Serafini, Dan | 7 | 7 | 5.58 | 25 | 23 | 1 | 0 | 131 | 164 | 84 | 81 | 58 | 109 | S | L | 6-1 | 185 | 1-25-74 | 1992 | San Bruno, Calif. |
| Stidham, Phil | 10 | 5 | 6.78 | 33 | 7 | 0 | 0 | 78 | 100 | 63 | 59 | 40 | 54 | R | R | 6-0 | 180 | 11-18-68 | 1991 | Tulsa, Okla. |
| Trombley, Mike | 2 | 2 | 2.45 | 24 | 0 | 0 | 10 | 37 | 24 | 12 | 10 | 10 | 38 | R | R | 6-2 | 200 | 4-14-67 | 1989 | Fort Myers, Fla. |
| Watkins, Scott | 4 | 6 | 7.69 | 47 | 0 | 0 | 1 | 50 | 60 | 46 | 43 | 34 | 43 | L | L | 6-3 | 180 | 5-15-70 | 1992 | Sand Springs, Okla. |

### FIELDING

| Catcher | PCT | G | PO | A | E | DP | PB |
|---|---|---|---|---|---|---|---|
| Durant | .982 | 17 | 100 | 12 | 2 | 1 | 0 |
| Horn | .994 | 24 | 155 | 13 | 1 | 1 | 2 |
| Lopez | .989 | 16 | 88 | 6 | 1 | 2 | 1 |
| Miller | .991 | 95 | 619 | 70 | 6 | 9 | 7 |

| First Base | PCT | G | PO | A | E | DP |
|---|---|---|---|---|---|---|
| Brede | .996 | 28 | 249 | 20 | 1 | 28 |
| Durant | 1.000 | 1 | 1 | 0 | 0 | 0 |
| Giannelli | 1.000 | 1 | 8 | 1 | 0 | 2 |
| Hocking | 1.000 | 1 | 10 | 0 | 0 | 0 |
| Miller | 1.000 | 2 | 11 | 1 | 0 | 1 |
| Ogden | .990 | 83 | 759 | 44 | 8 | 58 |
| Quinlan | .997 | 38 | 333 | 22 | 1 | 28 |

| Second Base | PCT | G | PO | A | E | DP |
|---|---|---|---|---|---|---|
| Hocking | 1.000 | 1 | 0 | 1 | 0 | 0 |

| | PCT | G | PO | A | E | DP |
|---|---|---|---|---|---|---|
| Quinlan | .965 | 12 | 22 | 33 | 2 | 10 |
| Raabe | .995 | 83 | 163 | 252 | 2 | 56 |
| Simons | .978 | 19 | 41 | 49 | 2 | 12 |
| Walker | .977 | 36 | 72 | 99 | 4 | 20 |

| Third Base | PCT | G | PO | A | E | DP |
|---|---|---|---|---|---|---|
| Giannelli | 1.000 | 5 | 1 | 7 | 0 | 1 |
| Hocking | .667 | 1 | 0 | 2 | 1 | 0 |
| Quinlan | .949 | 52 | 43 | 126 | 9 | 7 |
| Raabe | 1.000 | 5 | 5 | 6 | 0 | 1 |
| Walker | .940 | 87 | 57 | 177 | 15 | 12 |

| Shortstop | PCT | G | PO | A | E | DP |
|---|---|---|---|---|---|---|
| Hocking | .978 | 22 | 26 | 65 | 2 | 12 |
| Quinlan | .921 | 17 | 31 | 51 | 7 | 13 |
| Raabe | .961 | 11 | 12 | 37 | 2 | 7 |

| | PCT | G | PO | A | E | DP |
|---|---|---|---|---|---|---|
| Simons | .970 | 101 | 153 | 329 | 15 | 66 |

| Outfield | PCT | G | PO | A | E | DP |
|---|---|---|---|---|---|---|
| Brede | .964 | 97 | 155 | 4 | 6 | 1 |
| Giannelli | 1.000 | 1 | 2 | 0 | 0 | 0 |
| Hazlett | .975 | 99 | 137 | 17 | 4 | 2 |
| Hocking | 1.000 | 13 | 15 | 1 | 0 | 0 |
| Johnson | .952 | 12 | 20 | 0 | 1 | 0 |
| Latham | .964 | 110 | 235 | 9 | 9 | 2 |
| Lawton | .936 | 41 | 88 | 0 | 6 | 0 |
| Leonard | .971 | 23 | 32 | 2 | 1 | 1 |
| Ogden | .977 | 44 | 81 | 3 | 2 | 0 |
| Reimer | .953 | 27 | 40 | 1 | 2 | 0 |
| Simons | 1.000 | 8 | 13 | 0 | 0 | 0 |

## EASTERN LEAGUE

| BATTING | AVG | G | AB | R | H | 2B | 3B | HR | RBI | BB | SO | SB | CS | B | T | HT | WT | DOB | 1st Yr | Resides |
|---|---|---|---|---|---|---|---|---|---|---|---|---|---|---|---|---|---|---|---|---|
| Byrd, Anthony | .247 | 59 | 194 | 23 | 48 | 8 | 1 | 1 | 10 | 18 | 35 | 11 | 9 | S | R | 5-11 | 190 | 11-13-70 | 1993 | Atlanta, Ga. |
| Caraballo, Gary | .240 | 85 | 292 | 32 | 70 | 16 | 0 | 7 | 32 | 27 | 62 | 1 | 3 | R | R | 5-11 | 205 | 7-11-71 | 1989 | Yauco, P.R. |
| Ferguson, Jeff | .285 | 89 | 284 | 46 | 81 | 16 | 2 | 5 | 20 | 37 | 67 | 5 | 4 | R | R | 5-10 | 175 | 6-18-73 | 1994 | Placentia, Calif. |
| Hilt, Scott | .194 | 70 | 180 | 19 | 35 | 5 | 1 | 2 | 19 | 34 | 53 | 3 | 2 | L | R | 6-2 | 215 | 12-9-72 | 1994 | Westfield, Mass. |
| Horn, Jeff | .267 | 12 | 45 | 4 | 12 | 2 | 0 | 0 | 3 | 6 | 7 | 0 | 1 | R | R | 6-1 | 197 | 8-23-70 | 1992 | Las Vegas, Nev. |
| Hunter, Torii | .263 | 99 | 342 | 49 | 90 | 20 | 3 | 7 | 33 | 28 | 60 | 7 | 7 | R | R | 6-2 | 205 | 7-18-75 | 1993 | Pine Bluff, Ark. |
| Johnson, J.J. | .273 | 119 | 440 | 62 | 120 | 23 | 3 | 16 | 59 | 40 | 90 | 10 | 11 | R | R | 6-0 | 195 | 8-31-73 | 1991 | Pine Plains, N.Y. |
| Lane, Ryan | .222 | 33 | 117 | 13 | 26 | 5 | 1 | 2 | 12 | 8 | 29 | 3 | 4 | R | R | 6-1 | 185 | 7-6-74 | 1993 | Bellefontaine, Ohio |
| Lewis, Anthony | .253 | 134 | 458 | 58 | 116 | 15 | 2 | 24 | 95 | 47 | 99 | 6 | 9 | L | L | 5-11 | 185 | 2-2-71 | 1989 | North Las Vegas, Nev. |
| Lopez, Rene | .233 | 61 | 180 | 23 | 42 | 9 | 0 | 3 | 16 | 21 | 28 | 0 | 3 | R | R | 5-11 | 195 | 12-10-71 | 1992 | Downey, Calif. |
| Nevers, Tom | .264 | 127 | 459 | 65 | 121 | 27 | 7 | 7 | 44 | 46 | 87 | 3 | 10 | R | R | 6-1 | 175 | 9-13-71 | 1990 | Edina, Minn. |
| Radmanovich, Ryan | .280 | 125 | 453 | 77 | 127 | 31 | 2 | 25 | 86 | 49 | 122 | 4 | 11 | L | R | 6-2 | 185 | 8-9-71 | 1993 | Calgary, Alberta |
| Roper, Chad | .251 | 128 | 466 | 59 | 117 | 18 | 2 | 10 | 48 | 42 | 73 | 4 | 7 | R | R | 6-1 | 212 | 3-29-74 | 1992 | Belton, S.C. |
| Rupp, Chad | .252 | 77 | 278 | 38 | 70 | 14 | 0 | 18 | 48 | 13 | 56 | 3 | 2 | R | R | 6-2 | 215 | 9-30-71 | 1993 | Charlotte, N.C. |
| Turner, Brian | .242 | 48 | 157 | 19 | 38 | 8 | 0 | 6 | 18 | 13 | 35 | 5 | 2 | L | L | 6-2 | 210 | 6-9-71 | 1989 | Orwell, Ohio |
| 2-team (32 Bing.) | .223 | 80 | 241 | 27 | 55 | 13 | 2 | 8 | 30 | 22 | 53 | 6 | 3 | | | | | | | |
| Valentin, Jose | .236 | 48 | 165 | 22 | 39 | 8 | 0 | 3 | 14 | 16 | 35 | 0 | 3 | S | R | 5-10 | 191 | 9-19-75 | 1993 | Manati, P.R. |
| Valette, Ramon | .239 | 23 | 71 | 7 | 17 | 2 | 2 | 1 | 6 | 0 | 11 | 6 | 0 | R | R | 6-1 | 160 | 1-20-72 | 1990 | Sabana, D.R. |
| Walbeck, Matt | .208 | 7 | 24 | 1 | 5 | 0 | 0 | 0 | 0 | 1 | 1 | 0 | 0 | S | R | 5-11 | 188 | 10-2-69 | 1987 | Sacramento, Calif. |

| PITCHING | W | L | ERA | G | GS | CG | SV | IP | H | R | ER | BB | SO | B | T | HT | WT | DOB | 1st Yr | Resides |
|---|---|---|---|---|---|---|---|---|---|---|---|---|---|---|---|---|---|---|---|---|
| Barcelo, Marc | 3 | 8 | 5.06 | 14 | 13 | 3 | 0 | 80 | 98 | 53 | 45 | 38 | 59 | R | R | 6-3 | 210 | 1-10-72 | 1993 | Tucson, Ariz. |
| Bell, Jason | 2 | 6 | 4.40 | 16 | 16 | 2 | 0 | 94 | 93 | 54 | 46 | 38 | 94 | R | R | 6-3 | 208 | 9-30-74 | 1995 | Orlando, Fla. |
| Bowers, Shane | 6 | 8 | 4.19 | 27 | 22 | 1 | 0 | 131 | 134 | 71 | 61 | 42 | 96 | R | R | 6-6 | 215 | 7-27-71 | 1993 | Covina, Calif. |
| Caridad, Ron | 0 | 2 | 5.01 | 20 | 0 | 0 | 0 | 32 | 29 | 21 | 18 | 24 | 21 | R | R | 5-10 | 180 | 3-22-72 | 1990 | Miami, Fla. |
| Carrasco, Troy | 6 | 9 | 5.07 | 34 | 17 | 1 | 0 | 110 | 113 | 74 | 62 | 66 | 69 | S | L | 5-11 | 172 | 1-27-75 | 1993 | Tampa, Fla. |
| Courtright, John | 1 | 1 | 6.61 | 14 | 3 | 0 | 0 | 33 | 42 | 25 | 24 | 16 | 12 | L | L | 6-2 | 185 | 5-30-70 | 1991 | Columbus, Ohio |
| Gavaghan, Sean | 2 | 2 | 6.46 | 28 | 0 | 0 | 6 | 39 | 42 | 28 | 28 | 29 | 44 | R | R | 6-1 | 194 | 12-19-69 | 1992 | Fort Washington, Pa. |
| Konieczki, Dom | 1 | 3 | 4.98 | 28 | 0 | 0 | 2 | 34 | 32 | 19 | 19 | 23 | 23 | R | L | 6-1 | 170 | 6-16-69 | 1991 | Lehigh Acres, Fla. |
| Linebarger, Keith | 7 | 5 | 3.27 | 42 | 4 | 1 | 4 | 99 | 98 | 53 | 36 | 32 | 69 | R | R | 6-6 | 220 | 5-11-71 | 1992 | Ringgold, Ga. |
| Morse, Paul | 6 | 4 | 5.34 | 35 | 1 | 0 | 4 | 56 | 55 | 36 | 33 | 26 | 48 | R | R | 6-2 | 185 | 2-27-73 | 1995 | Danville, Ky. |
| Ohme, Kevin | 5 | 6 | 4.33 | 51 | 0 | 0 | 3 | 81 | 83 | 49 | 39 | 33 | 42 | L | L | 6-1 | 175 | 4-13-71 | 1993 | Brandon, Fla. |
| Redman, Mark | 7 | 7 | 3.81 | 16 | 16 | 3 | 0 | 106 | 101 | 51 | 45 | 50 | 96 | L | L | 6-5 | 220 | 1-5-74 | 1995 | Del Mar, Calif. |
| Ritchie, Todd | 3 | 7 | 5.44 | 29 | 10 | 0 | 4 | 83 | 101 | 55 | 50 | 30 | 53 | R | R | 6-3 | 205 | 11-7-71 | 1990 | Duncanville, Texas |
| Sampson, Benj | 5 | 7 | 5.73 | 16 | 16 | 1 | 0 | 75 | 108 | 54 | 48 | 25 | 51 | L | L | 6-0 | 197 | 4-27-75 | 1993 | Bondurant, Iowa |
| Stidham, Phil | 1 | 0 | 2.63 | 12 | 0 | 0 | 1 | 14 | 11 | 5 | 4 | 8 | 16 | R | R | 6-0 | 180 | 11-18-68 | 1991 | Tulsa, Okla. |
| Trinidad, Hector | 6 | 6 | 3.84 | 25 | 24 | 1 | 0 | 138 | 137 | 75 | 59 | 31 | 93 | R | R | 6-2 | 190 | 9-8-73 | 1991 | Whittier, Calif. |

## FIELDING

| Catcher | PCT | G | PO | A | E | DP | PB |
|---|---|---|---|---|---|---|---|
| Hilt | .985 | 54 | 307 | 29 | 5 | 4 | 7 |
| Horn | 1.000 | 12 | 75 | 9 | 0 | 0 | 2 |
| Lopez | .987 | 59 | 330 | 43 | 5 | 8 | 6 |
| Valentin | .980 | 31 | 177 | 15 | 4 | 0 | 2 |
| Walbeck | 1.000 | 3 | 11 | 2 | 0 | 0 | 1 |

| First Base | PCT | G | PO | A | E | DP |
|---|---|---|---|---|---|---|
| Caraballo | .981 | 18 | 140 | 13 | 3 | 10 |
| Lewis | .991 | 16 | 104 | 3 | 1 | 10 |
| Roper | .979 | 6 | 45 | 2 | 1 | 4 |
| Rupp | .985 | 68 | 573 | 35 | 9 | 47 |
| Turner | .991 | 41 | 310 | 34 | 3 | 24 |

| Second Base | PCT | G | PO | A | E | DP |
|---|---|---|---|---|---|---|
| Caraballo | .951 | 24 | 48 | 49 | 5 | 6 |

| | PCT | G | PO | A | E | DP |
|---|---|---|---|---|---|---|
| Ferguson | .966 | 88 | 170 | 229 | 14 | 43 |
| Lane | .966 | 12 | 25 | 31 | 2 | 7 |
| Nevers | 1.000 | 20 | 43 | 39 | 0 | 7 |
| Valette | 1.000 | 7 | 16 | 12 | 0 | 1 |

| Third Base | PCT | G | PO | A | E | DP |
|---|---|---|---|---|---|---|
| Caraballo | .945 | 25 | 19 | 67 | 5 | 7 |
| Nevers | .667 | 3 | 2 | 6 | 4 | 0 |
| Roper | .918 | 108 | 64 | 205 | 24 | 16 |
| Valentin | .970 | 15 | 11 | 21 | 1 | 5 |

| Shortstop | PCT | G | PO | A | E | DP |
|---|---|---|---|---|---|---|
| Caraballo | .842 | 5 | 4 | 12 | 3 | 1 |
| Lane | .894 | 22 | 30 | 46 | 9 | 7 |
| Nevers | .951 | 106 | 153 | 310 | 24 | 54 |

| | PCT | G | PO | A | E | DP |
|---|---|---|---|---|---|---|
| Roper | .933 | 5 | 4 | 10 | 1 | 2 |
| Valette | .947 | 15 | 21 | 33 | 3 | 3 |

| Outfield | PCT | G | PO | A | E | DP |
|---|---|---|---|---|---|---|
| Byrd | .952 | 49 | 98 | 2 | 5 | 1 |
| Caraballo | .900 | 8 | 26 | 1 | 3 | 0 |
| Hunter | .982 | 96 | 207 | 11 | 4 | 0 |
| Johnson | .959 | 115 | 201 | 9 | 9 | 1 |
| Lewis | .947 | 41 | 71 | 1 | 4 | 0 |
| Radmanovich | .984 | 118 | 246 | 3 | 4 | 0 |
| Turner | 1.000 | 8 | 12 | 0 | 0 | 0 |

## CALIFORNIA LEAGUE

| PITCHING | W | L | ERA | G | GS | CG | SV | IP | H | R | ER | BB | SO | B | T | HT | WT | DOB | 1st Yr | Resides |
|---|---|---|---|---|---|---|---|---|---|---|---|---|---|---|---|---|---|---|---|---|
| Nartker, Mike | 1 | 1 | 6.75 | 3 | 3 | 0 | 0 | 12 | 22 | 10 | 9 | 7 | 11 | R | R | 6-2 | 205 | 11-26-71 | 1995 | Hillsboro, Ohio |
| Ruch, Rob | 2 | 7 | 4.13 | 37 | 5 | 0 | 3 | 96 | 94 | 57 | 44 | 47 | 75 | R | R | 6-3 | 205 | 7-5-72 | 1994 | Westville, Ill. |

# FORT MYERS     Class A

## FLORIDA STATE LEAGUE

| BATTING | AVG | G | AB | R | H | 2B | 3B | HR | RBI | BB | SO | SB | CS | B | T | HT | WT | DOB | 1st Yr | Resides |
|---|---|---|---|---|---|---|---|---|---|---|---|---|---|---|---|---|---|---|---|---|
| Alvarez, Rafael | .136 | 6 | 22 | 1 | 3 | 0 | 0 | 0 | 1 | 1 | 7 | 0 | 1 | L | L | 5-11 | 165 | 1-22-77 | 1994 | Valencia, Venez. |
| Borrego, Ramon | .196 | 16 | 56 | 10 | 11 | 2 | 1 | 0 | 5 | 4 | 13 | 1 | 4 | S | R | 5-7 | 150 | 6-7-78 | 1996 | Mariara, Venez. |
| Brown, Armann | .248 | 112 | 403 | 75 | 100 | 14 | 8 | 3 | 27 | 65 | 75 | 36 | 15 | R | R | 6-1 | 163 | 9-10-72 | 1992 | Houston, Texas |
| Cranford, Joe | .219 | 30 | 105 | 9 | 23 | 3 | 1 | 0 | 17 | 7 | 21 | 3 | 1 | R | R | 6-1 | 180 | 2-10-75 | 1996 | Macon, Ga. |
| Fortin, Troy | .249 | 104 | 358 | 40 | 89 | 11 | 2 | 7 | 52 | 29 | 29 | 1 | 1 | R | R | 5-11 | 200 | 2-24-75 | 1993 | Lundar, Manitoba |
| Garcia, Carlos | .144 | 26 | 90 | 10 | 13 | 2 | 0 | 1 | 8 | 6 | 26 | 9 | 2 | R | R | 5-11 | 165 | 5-21-76 | 1993 | Coraballeda, Venez. |
| Gunderson, Shane | .251 | 117 | 410 | 61 | 103 | 20 | 5 | 5 | 50 | 63 | 85 | 12 | 8 | R | R | 6-0 | 205 | 10-16-73 | 1995 | Faribault, Minn. |
| Hunter, Torii | .188 | 4 | 16 | 1 | 3 | 0 | 0 | 0 | 1 | 2 | 5 | 1 | 1 | R | R | 6-2 | 205 | 7-18-75 | 1993 | Pine Bluff, Ark. |
| Jones, Ben | .210 | 56 | 162 | 22 | 34 | 1 | 0 | 0 | 8 | 17 | 26 | 17 | 3 | R | R | 5-10 | 175 | 9-15-73 | 1992 | Alexandria, La. |
| Jones, Ivory | .236 | 48 | 144 | 20 | 34 | 7 | 1 | 0 | 10 | 21 | 32 | 9 | 7 | L | L | 5-10 | 160 | 2-28-73 | 1995 | Vallejo, Calif. |
| Jones, Jacque | .667 | 1 | 3 | 0 | 2 | 1 | 0 | 0 | 1 | 0 | 0 | 0 | 1 | L | L | 5-10 | 175 | 4-25-75 | 1996 | San Diego, Calif. |
| Knauss, Tom | .188 | 36 | 117 | 11 | 22 | 1 | 0 | 5 | 12 | 12 | 28 | 2 | 1 | R | R | 6-2 | 218 | 6-16-74 | 1992 | Arlington Heights, Ill. |
| Koskie, Corey | .260 | 95 | 338 | 43 | 88 | 19 | 4 | 9 | 55 | 40 | 76 | 1 | 1 | L | R | 6-3 | 215 | 6-28-73 | 1994 | Dugold, Manitoba |
| Lane, Ryan | .272 | 106 | 404 | 74 | 110 | 20 | 7 | 9 | 62 | 60 | 96 | 21 | 9 | R | R | 6-1 | 185 | 7-6-74 | 1993 | Bellefontaine, Ohio |
| Legree, Keith | .273 | 58 | 198 | 39 | 54 | 8 | 2 | 5 | 37 | 42 | 52 | 2 | 2 | L | R | 6-2 | 195 | 12-26-71 | 1991 | Statesboro, Ga. |
| McCalmont, Jim | .202 | 30 | 89 | 8 | 18 | 3 | 0 | 0 | 6 | 4 | 15 | 1 | 0 | R | R | 6-0 | 185 | 10-6-71 | 1994 | Scottsdale, Ariz. |
| Mientkiewicz, Doug | .291 | 133 | 492 | 69 | 143 | 36 | 4 | 5 | 79 | 66 | 47 | 12 | 2 | L | R | 6-2 | 190 | 6-19-74 | 1995 | Miami, Fla. |
| Moriarty, Mike | .250 | 133 | 428 | 76 | 107 | 18 | 2 | 3 | 39 | 59 | 67 | 14 | 15 | R | R | 6-0 | 169 | 3-8-74 | 1995 | Clayton, N.J. |
| Mucker, Kelcey | .239 | 100 | 331 | 34 | 79 | 9 | 3 | 2 | 32 | 36 | 66 | 5 | 2 | L | R | 6-4 | 235 | 2-17-75 | 1993 | Lawrenceburg, Ind. |
| Valentin, Jose | .263 | 87 | 338 | 34 | 89 | 26 | 1 | 7 | 54 | 32 | 65 | 1 | 0 | S | R | 5-10 | 191 | 9-19-75 | 1993 | Manati, P.R. |
| Walbeck, Matt | .273 | 9 | 33 | 4 | 9 | 1 | 1 | 0 | 9 | 4 | 2 | 0 | 1 | S | R | 5-11 | 188 | 10-2-69 | 1987 | Sacramento, Calif. |

**GAMES BY POSITION: C**—Fortin 76, Mientkiewicz 8, Valentin 53, Walbeck 3. **1B**—Fortin 13, Gunderson 2, Mientkiewica 126. **2B**—Borrego 7, Cranford 25, Garcia 1, Lane 105, McCalmont 4. **3B**—Borrego 8, Cranford 6, Garcia 19, Koskie 87, McCalmont 18, Valentin 5. **SS**—Garcia 4, Lane 2, Moiarty 133. **OF**—Alvarez 5, Brown 95, Fortin 1, Gunderson 112, Hunter 4, B. Jones 41, I. Jones 37, J. Jones 1, Knauss 13, Legree 49, Mucker 84.

| PITCHING | W | L | ERA | G | GS | CG | SV | IP | H | R | ER | BB | SO | B | T | HT | WT | DOB | 1st Yr | Resides |
|---|---|---|---|---|---|---|---|---|---|---|---|---|---|---|---|---|---|---|---|---|
| Aguilera, Rick | 2 | 0 | 3.75 | 2 | 2 | 0 | 0 | 12 | 13 | 5 | 5 | 1 | 12 | R | R | 6-5 | 203 | 12-31-61 | 1983 | Chanhassen, Minn. |
| Bell, Jason | 6 | 3 | 1.69 | 13 | 13 | 0 | 0 | 90 | 61 | 20 | 17 | 22 | 83 | R | R | 6-3 | 208 | 9-30-74 | 1995 | Orlando, Fla. |
| Cobb, Trevor | 4 | 5 | 2.64 | 31 | 14 | 1 | 0 | 126 | 101 | 44 | 37 | 43 | 98 | L | L | 6-2 | 185 | 7-13-73 | 1992 | Marysville, Wash. |
| Dowhower, Deron | 2 | 4 | 3.70 | 39 | 2 | 0 | 1 | 75 | 63 | 37 | 31 | 45 | 83 | R | R | 6-2 | 206 | 2-14-72 | 1993 | Nashville, Tenn. |
| Gandarillas, Gus | 0 | 0 | 9.00 | 4 | 0 | 0 | 1 | 6 | 9 | 7 | 6 | 8 | 3 | R | R | 6-0 | 180 | 7-19-71 | 1992 | Hialeah, Fla. |
| Gourdin, Tom | 4 | 6 | 4.26 | 52 | 1 | 0 | 16 | 63 | 63 | 37 | 30 | 29 | 44 | R | R | 6-3 | 205 | 5-24-72 | 1993 | Murray, Utah |
| Konieczki, Dom | 0 | 0 | 0.64 | 14 | 0 | 0 | 1 | 14 | 7 | 1 | 1 | 6 | 22 | R | L | 6-1 | 170 | 6-16-69 | 1991 | Lehigh Acres, Fla. |
| Lincoln, Mike | 5 | 2 | 4.07 | 12 | 11 | 0 | 0 | 60 | 64 | 31 | 27 | 25 | 24 | R | R | 6-2 | 200 | 4-10-75 | 1996 | Citrus Heights, Calif. |
| Morse, Paul | 0 | 0 | 2.57 | 13 | 0 | 0 | 9 | 14 | 8 | 4 | 4 | 5 | 10 | R | R | 6-2 | 185 | 2-27-73 | 1995 | Danville, Ky. |
| Mott, Tom | 7 | 5 | 4.82 | 14 | 14 | 0 | 0 | 75 | 80 | 43 | 40 | 37 | 48 | R | R | 6-3 | 222 | 10-9-73 | 1993 | San Luis Obispo, Calif. |
| Pavicich, Paul | 2 | 3 | 5.06 | 29 | 0 | 0 | 0 | 43 | 49 | 30 | 24 | 13 | 29 | L | L | 6-2 | 196 | 1-10-73 | 1994 | Los Gatos, Calif. |
| Perkins, Dan | 13 | 7 | 2.96 | 39 | 13 | 3 | 2 | 137 | 125 | 52 | 45 | 37 | 111 | R | R | 6-2 | 184 | 3-15-75 | 1993 | Miami, Fla. |

| PITCHING | W | L | ERA | G | GS | CG | SV | IP | H | R | ER | BB | SO | B | T | HT | WT | DOB | 1st Yr | Resides |
|---|---|---|---|---|---|---|---|---|---|---|---|---|---|---|---|---|---|---|---|---|
| Peters, Tim | 0 | 3 | 3.54 | 28 | 0 | 0 | 1 | 28 | 31 | 11 | 11 | 5 | 23 | L | L | 6-0 | 190 | 12-1-72 | 1995 | Houston, Texas |
| Radlosky, Rob | 4 | 6 | 5.45 | 28 | 16 | 1 | 1 | 104 | 116 | 70 | 63 | 46 | 80 | R | R | 6-2 | 200 | 1-7-74 | 1994 | Lantana, Fla. |
| Rath, Fred | 2 | 5 | 2.79 | 22 | 0 | 0 | 4 | 29 | 25 | 10 | 9 | 10 | 29 | R | R | 6-3 | 205 | 1-5-73 | 1995 | Tampa, Fla. |
| Redman, Mark | 3 | 4 | 1.85 | 13 | 13 | 1 | 0 | 83 | 63 | 24 | 17 | 34 | 75 | L | L | 6-5 | 220 | 1-5-74 | 1995 | Del Mar, Calif. |
| Richardson, Kasey | 1 | 0 | 6.32 | 3 | 3 | 0 | 0 | 16 | 18 | 11 | 11 | 8 | 12 | L | L | 6-4 | 180 | 8-27-76 | 1994 | Huntingtown, Md. |
| Rushing, Will | 13 | 6 | 3.49 | 28 | 25 | 2 | 1 | 165 | 157 | 72 | 64 | 74 | 111 | L | L | 6-3 | 193 | 11-8-72 | 1995 | Statesboro, Ga. |
| Sampson, Benj | 7 | 1 | 3.47 | 11 | 11 | 2 | 0 | 70 | 55 | 28 | 27 | 26 | 65 | L | L | 6-0 | 197 | 4-27-75 | 1993 | Bondurant, Iowa |
| Tatar, Jason | 0 | 0 | 9.82 | 4 | 0 | 0 | 0 | 4 | 6 | 4 | 4 | 4 | 4 | R | R | 6-0 | 194 | 8-15-74 | 1992 | Rantoul, Ill. |

# FORT WAYNE — Class A
## MIDWEST LEAGUE

| BATTING | AVG | G | AB | R | H | 2B | 3B | HR | RBI | BB | SO | SB | CS | B | T | HT | WT | DOB | 1st Yr | Resides |
|---|---|---|---|---|---|---|---|---|---|---|---|---|---|---|---|---|---|---|---|---|
| Allen, Chad | .429 | 7 | 21 | 2 | 9 | 0 | 0 | 0 | 2 | 3 | 2 | 1 | 1 | R | R | 6-1 | 190 | 2-6-75 | 1996 | DeSoto, Texas |
| Alvarez, Rafael | .302 | 119 | 473 | 61 | 143 | 30 | 7 | 4 | 58 | 43 | 55 | 11 | 9 | L | L | 5-11 | 165 | 1-22-77 | 1994 | Valencia, Venez. |
| Bunkley, Antuan | .233 | 58 | 172 | 19 | 40 | 11 | 1 | 1 | 12 | 16 | 39 | 1 | 0 | R | R | 6-1 | 205 | 9-20-75 | 1994 | West Palm Beach, Fla. |
| Cey, Dan | .259 | 27 | 85 | 8 | 22 | 4 | 0 | 0 | 6 | 8 | 11 | 2 | 1 | R | R | 6-1 | 175 | 11-8-75 | 1996 | Woodland Hills, Calif. |
| Davidson, Cleatus | .177 | 59 | 203 | 20 | 36 | 8 | 3 | 0 | 30 | 23 | 45 | 2 | 3 | S | R | 5-10 | 160 | 11-1-76 | 1994 | Lake Wales, Fla. |
| Felston, Anthony | .313 | 62 | 201 | 53 | 63 | 4 | 1 | 0 | 18 | 43 | 36 | 22 | 4 | L | L | 5-9 | 170 | 11-26-74 | 1996 | Leland, Miss. |
| Fraser, Joe | .224 | 101 | 331 | 42 | 74 | 17 | 1 | 6 | 43 | 26 | 60 | 7 | 2 | R | R | 6-1 | 200 | 8-23-74 | 1995 | Westminster, Calif. |
| Garcia, Carlos | .211 | 40 | 128 | 18 | 27 | 2 | 0 | 1 | 9 | 20 | 24 | 14 | 5 | R | R | 5-11 | 165 | 5-21-76 | 1993 | Coraballeda, Venez. |
| Gordon, Adrian | .297 | 110 | 343 | 58 | 102 | 15 | 7 | 1 | 47 | 47 | 90 | 9 | 9 | R | R | 6-3 | 217 | 3-8-74 | 1992 | Alexandria, La. |
| Herdman, Eli | .190 | 7 | 21 | 2 | 4 | 0 | 0 | 1 | 8 | 7 | 7 | 0 | 1 | L | R | 6-0 | 196 | 3-24-76 | 1994 | Bremerton, Wash. |
| Huls, Steve | .214 | 60 | 201 | 21 | 43 | 3 | 1 | 1 | 11 | 12 | 53 | 2 | 2 | S | R | 6-1 | 170 | 10-11-74 | 1996 | Cold Spring, Minn. |
| Johnson, Heath | .160 | 8 | 25 | 4 | 4 | 1 | 0 | 0 | 1 | 6 | 9 | 0 | 0 | L | R | 6-3 | 210 | 8-25-76 | 1994 | Lakefield, Minn. |
| Johnson, Travis | .328 | 57 | 183 | 32 | 60 | 18 | 2 | 3 | 18 | 32 | 49 | 5 | 5 | L | R | 6-0 | 210 | 11-23-73 | 1995 | Grand Rapids, N.D. |
| Juarez, Raul | .224 | 54 | 170 | 24 | 38 | 6 | 0 | 2 | 21 | 20 | 51 | 1 | 2 | R | R | 6-3 | 185 | 10-28-75 | 1994 | Caraboba, Venez. |
| Knauss, Tom | .300 | 56 | 207 | 30 | 62 | 18 | 2 | 7 | 39 | 25 | 46 | 1 | 0 | R | R | 6-2 | 218 | 6-16-74 | 1992 | Arlington Heights, Ill. |
| Lakovic, Greg | .255 | 36 | 94 | 12 | 24 | 3 | 0 | 0 | 11 | 16 | 22 | 2 | 2 | L | R | 6-2 | 178 | 1-31-75 | 1994 | Coquitlam, B.C. |
| Paez, Israel | .266 | 128 | 451 | 86 | 120 | 22 | 5 | 5 | 50 | 51 | 76 | 11 | 8 | S | R | 5-10 | 182 | 12-23-76 | 1994 | Caraboba, Venez. |
| Peterman, Tommy | .251 | 58 | 175 | 17 | 44 | 11 | 0 | 3 | 28 | 10 | 30 | 0 | 1 | L | L | 6-0 | 215 | 5-21-75 | 1996 | Marietta, Ga. |
| Pierzynski, A.J. | .274 | 114 | 431 | 48 | 118 | 30 | 3 | 7 | 70 | 22 | 53 | 0 | 4 | L | R | 6-3 | 202 | 12-30-76 | 1994 | Orlando, Fla. |
| Schroeder, John | .264 | 111 | 425 | 54 | 112 | 20 | 2 | 14 | 58 | 18 | 119 | 3 | 5 | L | R | 6-4 | 224 | 10-9-75 | 1994 | Coeur D'Alene, Idaho |
| Smith, Jeff | .236 | 63 | 208 | 20 | 49 | 6 | 0 | 2 | 26 | 22 | 32 | 2 | 1 | L | R | 6-3 | 211 | 6-17-74 | 1996 | Naples, Fla. |

**GAMES BY POSITION: C**—Lakovic 3, Pierzynski 95, Smith 50. **1B**—Bunkley 6, Garcia 1, Lakovic 1, Peterman 31, Schroeder 106. **2B**—Fraser 97, Garcia 1, Huls 14, Paez 35. **3B**—Bunkley 20, Fraser 1, Garcia 26, Herdman 7, Huls 1, Lakovic 7, Paez 89, Schroeder 1. **SS**—Cey 27, Davidson 59, Garcia 4, Huls 47, Paez 9, Peterman 1. **OF**—Allen 4, Alvarez 115, Felston 59, Fraser 1, Garcia 7, Gordon 80, H. Johnson 6, T. Johnson 51, Juarez 50, Knauss 56, Paez 3, Pierzynski 3.

| PITCHING | W | L | ERA | G | GS | CG | SV | IP | H | R | ER | BB | SO | B | T | HT | WT | DOB | 1st Yr | Resides |
|---|---|---|---|---|---|---|---|---|---|---|---|---|---|---|---|---|---|---|---|---|---|
| Bartels, Todd | 2 | 3 | 4.10 | 11 | 10 | 0 | 0 | 53 | 51 | 29 | 24 | 11 | 34 | R | R | 6-4 | 215 | 11-16-73 | 1995 | Omaha, Neb. |
| Boggs, Robert | 9 | 12 | 4.02 | 28 | 27 | 1 | 0 | 150 | 153 | 81 | 67 | 64 | 134 | R | R | 6-3 | 185 | 8-30-74 | 1995 | Lizemore, W.Va. |
| Chapman, Walker | 6 | 8 | 4.73 | 19 | 18 | 1 | 0 | 97 | 107 | 61 | 51 | 41 | 61 | R | R | 6-3 | 219 | 2-25-76 | 1994 | Frostburg, Md. |
| Gillian, Charlie | 0 | 0 | 3.18 | 20 | 0 | 0 | 5 | 23 | 24 | 9 | 8 | 5 | 14 | R | R | 6-2 | 196 | 5-29-74 | 1996 | Beckley, W.Va. |
| Haigler, Phil | 4 | 5 | 5.27 | 15 | 13 | 0 | 0 | 68 | 80 | 42 | 40 | 25 | 35 | R | R | 6-3 | 220 | 6-13-74 | 1996 | Pascagoula, Miss. |
| Harris, Jeff | 8 | 3 | 3.11 | 42 | 0 | 0 | 3 | 90 | 90 | 35 | 31 | 33 | 85 | R | R | 6-1 | 190 | 7-4-74 | 1995 | San Pablo, Calif. |
| Hooten, David | 4 | 1 | 2.41 | 21 | 0 | 0 | 2 | 37 | 30 | 11 | 10 | 13 | 39 | R | R | 6-0 | 175 | 5-8-75 | 1996 | Atlanta, Ga. |
| LaRosa, Tom | 7 | 3 | 3.53 | 15 | 13 | 2 | 0 | 89 | 77 | 46 | 35 | 33 | 90 | R | L | 5-10 | 180 | 6-28-75 | 1994 | Henderson, Nev. |
| Mahaffey, Alan | 7 | 10 | 4.84 | 30 | 19 | 2 | 0 | 126 | 139 | 84 | 68 | 35 | 75 | L | L | 6-3 | 200 | 2-2-74 | 1995 | Springfield, Mo. |
| McBride, Rodney | 0 | 5 | 8.08 | 16 | 10 | 0 | 0 | 46 | 69 | 47 | 41 | 24 | 44 | R | R | 6-1 | 205 | 11-15-74 | 1994 | Memphis, Tenn. |
| McKenzie, Jason | 1 | 1 | 5.17 | 17 | 0 | 0 | 0 | 38 | 38 | 24 | 22 | 14 | 29 | R | R | 6-0 | 190 | 6-21-74 | 1996 | Hernando, Miss. |
| Niedermaier, Brad | 6 | 4 | 3.25 | 32 | 3 | 0 | 2 | 69 | 64 | 39 | 25 | 29 | 72 | R | R | 6-3 | 205 | 2-9-73 | 1995 | Niles, Ill. |
| Peters, Tim | 2 | 0 | 1.31 | 13 | 0 | 0 | 0 | 21 | 15 | 5 | 3 | 4 | 10 | L | L | 6-0 | 190 | 12-1-72 | 1995 | Houston, Texas |
| Rath, Fred | 1 | 2 | 1.51 | 32 | 0 | 0 | 14 | 42 | 26 | 12 | 7 | 10 | 63 | R | R | 6-3 | 205 | 1-5-73 | 1995 | Tampa, Fla. |
| Richardson, Kasey | 6 | 8 | 3.47 | 30 | 13 | 1 | 1 | 112 | 113 | 56 | 43 | 39 | 81 | L | L | 6-4 | 180 | 8-27-76 | 1994 | Huntingtown, Md. |
| Spiers, Corey | 0 | 1 | 6.75 | 2 | 1 | 0 | 0 | 4 | 6 | 3 | 3 | 5 | 2 | L | L | 6-1 | 195 | 6-19-75 | 1996 | Houston, Texas |
| Splittorff, Jamie | 2 | 1 | 4.23 | 8 | 6 | 0 | 0 | 28 | 28 | 14 | 13 | 12 | 21 | L | R | 6-3 | 185 | 10-12-73 | 1995 | Blue Springs, Mo. |
| Tanksley, Scott | 2 | 1 | 3.14 | 16 | 0 | 0 | 0 | 29 | 24 | 16 | 10 | 8 | 25 | S | R | 5-11 | 185 | 11-1-73 | 1995 | Kemp, Texas |
| Vanderbush, Matt | 2 | 1 | 5.32 | 35 | 3 | 0 | 1 | 66 | 92 | 47 | 39 | 35 | 55 | L | L | 6-5 | 230 | 6-3-74 | 1995 | Glenwood, N.J. |

# ELIZABETHTON — Rookie
## APPALACHIAN LEAGUE

| BATTING | AVG | G | AB | R | H | 2B | 3B | HR | RBI | BB | SO | SB | CS | B | T | HT | WT | DOB | 1st Yr | Resides |
|---|---|---|---|---|---|---|---|---|---|---|---|---|---|---|---|---|---|---|---|---|
| Brown, Jerome | .267 | 50 | 165 | 32 | 44 | 10 | 2 | 4 | 25 | 21 | 58 | 4 | 1 | S | R | 5-10 | 168 | 1-19-76 | 1994 | Smithville, Okla. |
| Buchman, Tom | .353 | 6 | 17 | 3 | 6 | 3 | 0 | 1 | 3 | 4 | 4 | 0 | 0 | R | R | 5-11 | 205 | 12-4-74 | 1996 | Lenexa, Kan. |
| Cranford, Joe | .281 | 32 | 121 | 20 | 34 | 6 | 3 | 4 | 18 | 13 | 28 | 2 | 1 | R | R | 6-1 | 180 | 2-10-75 | 1996 | Macon, Ga. |
| Davidson, Cleatus | .286 | 65 | 248 | 53 | 71 | 10 | 6 | 6 | 31 | 39 | 45 | 17 | 6 | S | R | 5-10 | 160 | 11-1-76 | 1994 | Lake Wales, Fla. |
| Herdman, Eli | .242 | 62 | 198 | 31 | 48 | 12 | 1 | 8 | 37 | 48 | 70 | 1 | 2 | L | R | 6-0 | 196 | 3-24-76 | 1994 | Bremerton, Wash. |
| Irvis, Damon | .169 | 56 | 172 | 30 | 29 | 5 | 1 | 0 | 15 | 26 | 62 | 8 | 3 | R | R | 5-9 | 156 | 1-18-76 | 1994 | Lake Wales, Fla. |
| Johnson, Heath | .242 | 48 | 149 | 24 | 36 | 9 | 0 | 7 | 32 | 30 | 60 | 2 | 0 | L | R | 6-3 | 210 | 8-25-76 | 1994 | Lakefield, Minn. |
| McHenry, Joe | .164 | 51 | 159 | 24 | 26 | 5 | 2 | 0 | 9 | 29 | 58 | 6 | 1 | L | R | 6-1 | 175 | 5-24-76 | 1995 | Murfreesboro, Tenn. |
| Moeller, Chad | .356 | 17 | 59 | 17 | 21 | 4 | 0 | 4 | 13 | 18 | 9 | 1 | 2 | R | R | 6-3 | 210 | 2-18-75 | 1996 | Upland, Calif. |
| Moss, Rick | .353 | 32 | 116 | 21 | 41 | 10 | 0 | 5 | 18 | 14 | 17 | 3 | 1 | R | R | 6-0 | 185 | 9-18-75 | 1996 | Lockport, Ill. |
| Orndorff, Dave | .319 | 13 | 47 | 8 | 15 | 2 | 1 | 2 | 6 | 1 | 10 | 4 | 1 | R | R | 5-10 | 175 | 8-10-77 | 1995 | Shippensburg, Pa. |
| Pena, Francisco | .167 | 35 | 84 | 12 | 14 | 1 | 0 | 0 | 9 | 18 | 29 | 0 | 0 | R | R | 6-1 | 194 | 8-22-76 | 1994 | Santo Domingo, D.R. |
| Peterman, Tommy | .300 | 3 | 10 | 5 | 3 | 0 | 0 | 1 | 4 | 5 | 1 | 0 | 0 | L | L | 6-0 | 215 | 5-21-75 | 1996 | Marietta, Ga. |
| Reyes, Freddy | .321 | 65 | 252 | 46 | 81 | 20 | 1 | 8 | 55 | 19 | 49 | 0 | 1 | R | R | 6-1 | 214 | 4-9-75 | 1995 | Lafayette, Ind. |
| Shotwell, Robert | .237 | 25 | 76 | 8 | 18 | 1 | 0 | 0 | 3 | 5 | 13 | 0 | 1 | R | R | 6-5 | 190 | 8-15-74 | 1994 | Antioch, Tenn. |
| Thieleke, C.J. | .295 | 43 | 146 | 18 | 43 | 4 | 1 | 0 | 16 | 27 | 26 | 4 | 3 | L | R | 5-11 | 175 | 3-22-75 | 1996 | Iowa City, Iowa |
| Vilchez, Jose | .295 | 126 | 45 | 134 | 20 | 9 | 1 | 16 | 15 | 27 | 8 | 2 | S | R | 5-11 | 180 | 4-20-76 | 1994 | Maracaibo, Venez. |

**GAMES BY POSITION: C**—Buchman 6, Moeller 12, Orndorff 5, Pena 34, Shotwell 22. **1B**—Cranford 1, Herdman 3, Peterman 1, Reyes 62. **2B**—Craford 24, Moss 12, Orndorff 2, Thieleke 32. **3B**—Herdman 54, Moss 12, Thieleke 2. **SS**—Cranford 5, Davidson 65. **OF**—Brown 41, Irvis 53, Johnson 37, McHenry 41, Moss 2, Vilchez 42.

| PITCHING | W | L | ERA | G | GS | CG | SV | IP | H | R | ER | BB | SO | B | T | HT | WT | DOB | 1st Yr | Resides |
|---|---|---|---|---|---|---|---|---|---|---|---|---|---|---|---|---|---|---|---|---|
| Bauder, Mike | 1 | 1 | 4.50 | 18 | 2 | 0 | 2 | 36 | 31 | 22 | 18 | 13 | 41 | L | L | 5-10 | 160 | 5-13-75 | 1996 | Las Vegas, Nev. |
| Blank, Dave | 1 | 1 | 8.18 | 16 | 0 | 0 | 0 | 22 | 31 | 22 | 20 | 9 | 36 | L | L | 6-4 | 205 | 10-22-73 | 1995 | Jennings, La. |
| Dose, Gary | 1 | 0 | 4.15 | 17 | 0 | 0 | 0 | 22 | 22 | 13 | 10 | 19 | 24 | R | R | 6-0 | 184 | 8-22-73 | 1996 | Elgin, Minn. |
| Forster, Pete | 2 | 2 | 7.04 | 4 | 4 | 0 | 0 | 23 | 23 | 19 | 18 | 12 | 20 | L | L | 6-4 | 185 | 6-4-75 | 1994 | Gladstone, Mo. |
| Garff, Jeff | 6 | 5 | 4.58 | 12 | 12 | 2 | 0 | 73 | 71 | 44 | 37 | 13 | 38 | R | R | 6-4 | 195 | 12-3-75 | 1995 | Bountiful, Utah |
| Garza, Chris | 4 | 0 | 1.98 | 22 | 0 | 0 | 5 | 36 | 26 | 8 | 8 | 12 | 44 | L | L | 5-11 | 185 | 7-23-75 | 1996 | Los Angeles, Calif. |
| Hooten, David | 1 | 0 | 4.32 | 6 | 0 | 0 | 1 | 8 | 6 | 4 | 4 | 5 | 15 | R | R | 6-0 | 175 | 5-8-75 | 1996 | Atlanta, Ga. |
| Lynch, Ryan | 3 | 2 | 3.40 | 11 | 9 | 0 | 0 | 45 | 43 | 19 | 17 | 22 | 35 | L | L | 6-4 | 225 | 8-10-74 | 1996 | Solano Beach, Calif. |
| Malko, Bryan | 5 | 3 | 4.59 | 12 | 12 | 1 | 0 | 67 | 73 | 36 | 34 | 27 | 54 | R | R | 6-3 | 185 | 1-23-77 | 1995 | Piscataway, N.J. |
| McBride, Rodney | 3 | 2 | 2.43 | 12 | 12 | 1 | 0 | 74 | 60 | 29 | 20 | 28 | 83 | R | R | 6-1 | 205 | 11-15-74 | 1994 | Memphis, Tenn. |
| Nye, Richie | 1 | 2 | 7.30 | 15 | 1 | 0 | 0 | 25 | 34 | 25 | 20 | 6 | 24 | R | R | 6-3 | 185 | 2-19-75 | 1996 | Pocolan, Okla. |
| Opipari, Mario | 3 | 1 | 1.95 | 19 | 1 | 0 | 6 | 32 | 15 | 7 | 7 | 9 | 36 | S | R | 6-0 | 185 | 1-24-75 | 1996 | Henderson, Nev. |
| Spiers, Corey | 6 | 5 | 3.34 | 17 | 8 | 0 | 0 | 59 | 69 | 45 | 22 | 26 | 67 | L | L | 6-1 | 195 | 6-19-75 | 1996 | Houston, Texas |
| Yeskie, Nate | 3 | 3 | 5.23 | 7 | 6 | 0 | 0 | 33 | 38 | 27 | 19 | 8 | 28 | R | R | 6-2 | 195 | 8-13-74 | 1996 | Carson City, Nev. |

## TWINS     Rookie

### GULF COAST LEAGUE

| BATTING | AVG | G | AB | R | H | 2B | 3B | HR | RBI | BB | SO | SB | CS | B | T | HT | WT | DOB | 1st Yr | Resides |
|---|---|---|---|---|---|---|---|---|---|---|---|---|---|---|---|---|---|---|---|---|
| Ayuso, Julio | .214 | 33 | 98 | 15 | 21 | 3 | 0 | 3 | 11 | 15 | 29 | 1 | 2 | R | R | 6-3 | 180 | 6-23-77 | 1995 | Carolina, P.R. |
| Bolivar, Ceasar | .342 | 41 | 155 | 30 | 53 | 7 | 1 | 1 | 18 | 8 | 32 | 26 | 6 | R | R | 5-10 | 168 | 10-18-78 | 1996 | Catia la Mar, Venez. |
| Borrego, Ramon | .357 | 19 | 70 | 16 | 25 | 5 | 1 | 0 | 4 | 9 | 4 | 7 | 3 | S | R | 5-7 | 150 | 6-7-78 | 1996 | Mariara, Venez. |
| Brosam, Eric | .182 | 21 | 55 | 6 | 10 | 2 | 1 | 0 | 8 | 7 | 11 | 1 | 0 | L | R | 6-1 | 200 | 12-4-77 | 1996 | Redwood Falls, Minn. |
| Cruz, Andres | .218 | 28 | 78 | 14 | 17 | 4 | 1 | 1 | 9 | 16 | 13 | 1 | 0 | R | R | 5-11 | 175 | 6-11-77 | 1995 | Salinas, P.R. |
| Daniels, Deion | .111 | 4 | 9 | 0 | 1 | 0 | 0 | 0 | 0 | 0 | 4 | 0 | 0 | R | R | 6-5 | 210 | 9-22-75 | 1996 | Sanford, Fla. |
| Felston, Anthony | .500 | 2 | 4 | 2 | 2 | 0 | 0 | 0 | 0 | 2 | 0 | 0 | 0 | L | L | 5-9 | 170 | 11-26-74 | 1996 | Leland, Miss. |
| Johnson, Carlisle | .158 | 26 | 76 | 8 | 12 | 1 | 0 | 0 | 6 | 12 | 29 | 0 | 0 | R | R | 6-3 | 220 | 9-14-76 | 1995 | Pierson, Fla. |
| Kennedy, Brian | .218 | 37 | 110 | 8 | 24 | 2 | 1 | 0 | 16 | 13 | 30 | 3 | 4 | L | R | 6-1 | 190 | 8-9-77 | 1996 | Lafayette, Ind. |
| Lopez, Henry | .254 | 34 | 122 | 24 | 31 | 5 | 6 | 5 | 26 | 15 | 25 | 9 | 2 | R | R | 5-11 | 185 | 3-20-78 | 1996 | El Portal, D.R. |
| Lorenzo, Juan | .254 | 37 | 134 | 23 | 34 | 5 | 0 | 3 | 15 | 2 | 20 | 4 | 1 | S | R | 6-0 | 155 | 6-10-78 | 1995 | Cambito Garabitos, D.R. |
| Moss, Rick | .346 | 28 | 107 | 18 | 37 | 8 | 2 | 0 | 23 | 7 | 7 | 2 | 2 | L | R | 6-0 | 185 | 9-18-75 | 1996 | Lockport, Ill. |
| Nelson, Kevin | .238 | 34 | 122 | 8 | 29 | 4 | 0 | 1 | 11 | 7 | 27 | 0 | 0 | R | R | 6-3 | 200 | 2-9-77 | 1995 | Alexander, Ark. |
| Orndorff, Dave | .091 | 8 | 22 | 4 | 2 | 1 | 0 | 0 | 1 | 6 | 10 | 0 | 0 | R | R | 5-10 | 175 | 8-10-77 | 1995 | Shippensburg, Pa. |
| Prada, Nelson | .243 | 41 | 144 | 16 | 35 | 11 | 1 | 2 | 16 | 6 | 30 | 1 | 0 | R | R | 6-0 | 185 | 2-22-76 | 1995 | Barquisimeto, Venez. |
| Rivas, Luis | .259 | 53 | 201 | 29 | 52 | 12 | 1 | 1 | 13 | 18 | 37 | 35 | 10 | R | R | 5-10 | 155 | 8-30-79 | 1996 | La Guira, Vz |
| Ryan, Mike | .197 | 43 | 157 | 13 | 31 | 8 | 2 | 0 | 13 | 13 | 20 | 3 | 0 | L | R | 6-0 | 175 | 7-6-77 | 1996 | Indiana, Pa. |
| Silva, Carlos | .189 | 24 | 53 | 4 | 10 | 2 | 0 | 0 | 6 | 8 | 16 | 2 | 3 | R | R | 5-10 | 160 | 3-14-79 | 1996 | Aragua, Venez. |
| Smith, Marcus | .186 | 33 | 102 | 11 | 19 | 2 | 3 | 0 | 12 | 9 | 29 | 7 | 2 | L | R | 6-0 | 180 | 6-7-76 | 1996 | Hammond, Ind. |
| Torres, Gabriel | .348 | 22 | 66 | 9 | 23 | 4 | 1 | 1 | 5 | 7 | 10 | 1 | 2 | R | R | 6-1 | 185 | 3-20-78 | 1996 | Acarigua Portuges, Venez. |
| Vilorio, Leonel | .156 | 10 | 32 | 5 | 5 | 0 | 1 | 0 | 1 | 3 | 6 | 0 | 1 | R | R | 6-1 | 180 | 3-10-78 | 1996 | Santo Domingo, D.R. |

**GAMES BY POSITION: C**—Cruz 1, Orndorff 4, Prada 41, Torres 19. **1B**—Brosam 20, Cruz 18, Nelson 25. **2B**—Borrego 19, Lorenzo 27, Orndorff 2, Silva 20. **3B**—Moss 12, Nelson 5, Ryan 35, Silva 1, Vilorio 10. **SS**—Lorenzo 11, Rivas 51, Silva 1. **OF**—Ayuso 29, Bolivar 25, Daniels 2, Felston 2, Kennedy 32, Lopez 34, Moss 14, Smith 30.

| PITCHING | W | L | ERA | G | GS | CG | SV | IP | H | R | ER | BB | SO | B | T | HT | WT | DOB | 1st Yr | Resides |
|---|---|---|---|---|---|---|---|---|---|---|---|---|---|---|---|---|---|---|---|---|
| Blanco, Edgar | 1 | 1 | 4.35 | 12 | 0 | 0 | 0 | 21 | 16 | 10 | 10 | 13 | 19 | R | R | 6-2 | 182 | 3-4-78 | 1996 | Palo Negro, Venez. |
| Clark, Greg | 6 | 4 | 3.39 | 13 | 12 | 0 | 0 | 66 | 84 | 42 | 25 | 19 | 37 | R | R | 6-4 | 194 | 8-19-77 | 1995 | Sydney, Australia |
| Espina, Rendy | 0 | 2 | 9.26 | 7 | 1 | 0 | 0 | 12 | 18 | 12 | 12 | 8 | 10 | L | L | 6-0 | 180 | 5-11-78 | 1996 | Cabimas, Venez. |
| Gandarillas, Gus | 0 | 0 | 1.00 | 3 | 1 | 0 | 2 | 9 | 10 | 3 | 1 | 3 | 14 | R | R | 6-0 | 180 | 7-19-71 | 1992 | Hialeah, Fla. |
| Gholar, Antonio | 1 | 2 | 1.72 | 15 | 7 | 0 | 2 | 52 | 30 | 18 | 10 | 30 | 50 | R | R | 6-2 | 195 | 3-13-74 | 1996 | Bassfield, Miss. |
| Jacobs, Jake | 1 | 2 | 5.74 | 6 | 6 | 0 | 0 | 27 | 31 | 22 | 17 | 7 | 29 | R | R | 6-6 | 230 | 3-28-78 | 1996 | Pensacola, Fla. |
| Juarez, Raul | 3 | 2 | 6.94 | 11 | 0 | 0 | 0 | 12 | 12 | 11 | 9 | 7 | 9 | R | R | 6-3 | 185 | 10-28-75 | 1994 | Carabobo, Venez. |
| Loonam, Rick | 5 | 3 | 1.76 | 22 | 1 | 0 | 4 | 46 | 46 | 16 | 9 | 8 | 35 | R | R | 6-4 | 215 | 11-7-75 | 1996 | Lakewood, Colo. |
| Marshall, Lee | 4 | 4 | 2.31 | 12 | 12 | 3 | 0 | 70 | 59 | 31 | 18 | 18 | 39 | R | R | 6-5 | 205 | 9-25-76 | 1996 | Ariton, Ala. |
| Moylan, Peter | 1 | 1 | 4.08 | 13 | 0 | 0 | 1 | 29 | 34 | 16 | 13 | 9 | 16 | R | R | 6-2 | 200 | 12-2-78 | 1996 | Lesmerdle, Australia |
| Mundine, John | 2 | 1 | 5.20 | 14 | 0 | 0 | 1 | 28 | 31 | 19 | 16 | 13 | 21 | S | R | 5-11 | 185 | 9-6-77 | 1996 | Luling, Texas |
| Nye, Richie | 0 | 0 | 1.80 | 1 | 1 | 0 | 0 | 5 | 4 | 1 | 1 | 1 | 4 | R | R | 6-3 | 185 | 2-19-75 | 1996 | Pocolan, Okla. |
| Opipari, Mario | 0 | 0 | 0.00 | 4 | 0 | 0 | 1 | 6 | 2 | 0 | 0 | 3 | 6 | S | R | 6-0 | 185 | 1-24-75 | 1996 | Henderson, Nev. |
| Perez, Pablo | 5 | 4 | 3.02 | 12 | 10 | 2 | 0 | 60 | 54 | 23 | 20 | 17 | 43 | R | R | 6-0 | 170 | 8-27-73 | 1991 | Santo Domingo, D.R. |
| Reilly, Sean | 1 | 2 | 5.48 | 12 | 1 | 0 | 1 | 21 | 23 | 15 | 13 | 11 | 25 | R | L | 6-3 | 180 | 6-10-77 | 1995 | Burlington, Ontario |
| Tatar, Jason | 0 | 0 | 1.80 | 2 | 0 | 0 | 0 | 5 | 2 | 1 | 1 | 1 | 7 | R | R | 6-0 | 194 | 8-15-74 | 1992 | Rantoul, Ill. |
| Vallis, Jamie | 1 | 3 | 3.52 | 12 | 8 | 0 | 0 | 38 | 37 | 18 | 15 | 15 | 25 | R | L | 6-6 | 180 | 5-22-77 | 1996 | Bedford, N.S. |

# MONTREAL EXPOS

**Manager:** Felipe Alou.  **1996 Record:** 88-74, .543 (2nd, NL East).

| BATTING | AVG | G | AB | R | H | 2B | 3B | HR | RBI | BB | SO | SB | CS | B | T | HT | WT | DOB | 1st Yr | Resides |
|---|---|---|---|---|---|---|---|---|---|---|---|---|---|---|---|---|---|---|---|---|
| Alou, Moises | .281 | 143 | 540 | 87 | 152 | 28 | 2 | 21 | 96 | 49 | 83 | 9 | 4 | R | R | 6-3 | 195 | 7-3-66 | 1986 | Redwood City, Calif. |
| Andrews, Shane | .227 | 127 | 375 | 43 | 85 | 15 | 2 | 19 | 64 | 35 | 119 | 3 | 1 | R | R | 6-1 | 205 | 8-28-71 | 1990 | Carlsbad, N.M. |
| Barron, Tony | .000 | 1 | 1 | 0 | 0 | 0 | 0 | 0 | 0 | 0 | 1 | 0 | 0 | R | R | 6-0 | 185 | 8-17-66 | 1987 | Tacoma, Wash. |
| Benitez, Yamil | .167 | 11 | 12 | 0 | 2 | 0 | 0 | 0 | 2 | 0 | 4 | 0 | 0 | R | R | 6-2 | 180 | 10-5-72 | 1990 | San Juan, P.R. |
| Chavez, Raul | .200 | 4 | 5 | 1 | 1 | 0 | 0 | 0 | 0 | 1 | 1 | 0 | 0 | R | R | 5-11 | 175 | 3-18-73 | 1990 | Valencia, Venez. |
| Fletcher, Darrin | .266 | 127 | 394 | 41 | 105 | 22 | 0 | 12 | 57 | 27 | 42 | 0 | 0 | L | R | 6-2 | 195 | 10-3-66 | 1987 | Oakwood, Ill. |
| Floyd, Cliff | .242 | 117 | 227 | 29 | 55 | 15 | 4 | 6 | 26 | 30 | 52 | 7 | 1 | L | R | 6-4 | 220 | 12-5-72 | 1991 | Markham, Ill. |
| Grudzielanek, Mark | .306 | 153 | 657 | 99 | 201 | 34 | 4 | 6 | 49 | 26 | 83 | 33 | 7 | R | R | 6-1 | 170 | 6-30-70 | 1991 | El Paso, Texas |
| Guerrero, Vladimir | .185 | 9 | 27 | 2 | 5 | 0 | 0 | 1 | 1 | 0 | 3 | 0 | 0 | R | R | 6-2 | 158 | 2-9-76 | 1993 | Nizao Bani, D.R. |
| Lansing, Mike | .285 | 159 | 641 | 99 | 183 | 40 | 2 | 11 | 53 | 44 | 85 | 23 | 8 | R | R | 6-0 | 175 | 4-3-68 | 1990 | Casper, Wyom. |
| Lukachyk, Rob | .000 | 2 | 2 | 0 | 0 | 0 | 0 | 0 | 0 | 0 | 1 | 0 | 0 | L | R | 6-0 | 185 | 7-24-68 | 1987 | Sarasota, Fla. |
| Obando, Sherman | .247 | 89 | 178 | 30 | 44 | 9 | 0 | 8 | 22 | 22 | 48 | 2 | 0 | R | R | 6-4 | 215 | 1-23-70 | 1988 | Changuinola, Panama |
| Rodriguez, Henry | .276 | 145 | 532 | 81 | 147 | 42 | 1 | 36 | 103 | 37 | 160 | 2 | 0 | L | L | 6-1 | 210 | 11-8-67 | 1986 | New York, N.Y. |
| Santangelo, F.P. | .277 | 152 | 393 | 54 | 109 | 20 | 5 | 7 | 56 | 49 | 61 | 5 | 2 | S | R | 5-10 | 165 | 10-24-67 | 1989 | El Dorado Hills, Calif. |
| Schu, Rick | .000 | 1 | 4 | 0 | 0 | 0 | 0 | 0 | 0 | 0 | 0 | 0 | 0 | R | R | 6-0 | 185 | 1-26-62 | 1981 | Carmichael, Calif. |
| Segui, David | .286 | 115 | 416 | 69 | 119 | 30 | 1 | 11 | 58 | 60 | 54 | 4 | 4 | S | L | 6-1 | 202 | 7-19-66 | 1988 | Kansas City, Kan. |
| Silvestri, Dave | .204 | 86 | 162 | 16 | 33 | 4 | 0 | 1 | 17 | 34 | 41 | 2 | 1 | R | R | 6-0 | 180 | 9-29-67 | 1989 | St. Louis, Mo. |
| Spehr, Tim | .091 | 63 | 44 | 4 | 4 | 1 | 0 | 1 | 3 | 3 | 15 | 1 | 0 | R | R | 6-2 | 205 | 7-2-66 | 1988 | Waco, Texas |
| Stankiewicz, Andy | .286 | 64 | 77 | 12 | 22 | 5 | 1 | 0 | 9 | 6 | 12 | 1 | 0 | R | R | 5-9 | 165 | 8-10-64 | 1986 | La Habra, Calif. |
| Webster, Lenny | .230 | 78 | 174 | 18 | 40 | 10 | 0 | 2 | 17 | 25 | 21 | 0 | 0 | R | R | 5-9 | 195 | 2-10-65 | 1986 | Charlotte, N.C. |
| White, Rondell | .293 | 88 | 334 | 35 | 98 | 19 | 4 | 6 | 41 | 22 | 53 | 14 | 6 | R | R | 6-1 | 193 | 2-23-72 | 1990 | Gray, Ga. |

| PITCHING | W | L | ERA | G | GS | CG | SV | IP | H | R | ER | BB | SO | B | T | HT | WT | DOB | 1st Yr | Resides |
|---|---|---|---|---|---|---|---|---|---|---|---|---|---|---|---|---|---|---|---|---|
| Alvarez, Tavo | 2 | 1 | 3.00 | 11 | 5 | 0 | 0 | 21 | 19 | 10 | 7 | 12 | 9 | R | R | 6-3 | 183 | 11-25-71 | 1990 | Tucson, Ariz. |
| Aucoin, Derek | 0 | 1 | 3.38 | 2 | 0 | 0 | 0 | 3 | 3 | 1 | 1 | 1 | 1 | R | R | 6-7 | 226 | 3-27-70 | 1989 | Montreal, Quebec |
| Cormier, Rheal | 7 | 10 | 4.17 | 33 | 27 | 1 | 0 | 160 | 165 | 80 | 74 | 41 | 100 | L | L | 5-10 | 185 | 4-23-67 | 1989 | Saint John, N.B. |
| Daal, Omar | 4 | 5 | 4.02 | 64 | 6 | 0 | 0 | 87 | 74 | 40 | 39 | 37 | 82 | L | L | 6-3 | 185 | 3-1-72 | 1990 | Valencia, Venez. |
| Dyer, Mike | 5 | 5 | 4.40 | 70 | 1 | 0 | 2 | 76 | 79 | 40 | 37 | 34 | 51 | R | R | 6-3 | 200 | 9-8-66 | 1986 | Fullerton, Calif. |
| Fassero, Jeff | 15 | 11 | 3.30 | 34 | 34 | 5 | 0 | 232 | 217 | 95 | 85 | 55 | 222 | L | L | 6-1 | 180 | 1-5-63 | 1984 | Springfield, Ill. |
| Juden, Jeff | 1 | 0 | 2.20 | 22 | 0 | 0 | 0 | 33 | 22 | 12 | 8 | 14 | 26 | R | R | 6-7 | 245 | 1-19-71 | 1989 | Salem, Mass. |
| 2-team (36 S.F.) | 5 | 0 | 3.27 | 58 | 0 | 0 | 0 | 74 | 61 | 35 | 27 | 34 | 61 | | | | | | | |
| Leiper, Dave | 0 | 1 | 11.25 | 7 | 0 | 0 | 0 | 4 | 9 | 5 | 5 | 2 | 3 | L | L | 6-1 | 160 | 6-18-62 | 1982 | Plano, Texas |
| 2-team (26 Phil.) | 2 | 1 | 7.20 | 33 | 0 | 0 | 0 | 25 | 40 | 21 | 20 | 9 | 13 | | | | | | | |
| Leiter, Mark | 4 | 2 | 4.39 | 12 | 12 | 1 | 0 | 70 | 68 | 35 | 34 | 19 | 46 | R | R | 6-3 | 210 | 4-13-63 | 1983 | West Caldwell, N.J. |
| 2-team (23 S.F.) | 8 | 12 | 4.92 | 35 | 34 | 2 | 0 | 205 | 219 | 128 | 112 | 69 | 164 | | | | | | | |
| Manuel, Barry | 4 | 1 | 3.24 | 53 | 0 | 0 | 0 | 86 | 70 | 34 | 31 | 26 | 62 | R | R | 5-11 | 185 | 8-12-65 | 1987 | Mamou, La. |
| Martinez, Pedro | 13 | 10 | 3.70 | 33 | 33 | 4 | 0 | 217 | 189 | 100 | 89 | 70 | 222 | R | R | 5-11 | 150 | 7-25-71 | 1988 | Santo Domingo, D.R. |
| Pacheco, Alex | 0 | 0 | 11.12 | 5 | 0 | 0 | 0 | 6 | 8 | 7 | 7 | 1 | 7 | R | R | 6-3 | 170 | 7-19-73 | 1990 | Caracas, Venez. |
| Paniagua, Jose | 2 | 4 | 3.53 | 13 | 11 | 0 | 0 | 51 | 55 | 24 | 20 | 23 | 27 | R | R | 6-1 | 160 | 8-20-73 | 1991 | Santo Domingo, D.R. |
| Rojas, Mel | 7 | 4 | 3.22 | 74 | 0 | 0 | 36 | 81 | 56 | 30 | 29 | 28 | 92 | R | R | 5-11 | 165 | 12-10-66 | 1986 | Santo Domingo, D.R. |
| Rueter, Kirk | 5 | 6 | 4.58 | 16 | 16 | 0 | 0 | 79 | 91 | 44 | 40 | 22 | 30 | L | L | 6-3 | 190 | 12-1-70 | 1991 | Hoyleton, Ill. |
| Scott, Tim | 3 | 5 | 3.11 | 45 | 0 | 0 | 1 | 46 | 41 | 18 | 16 | 21 | 37 | R | R | 6-2 | 205 | 11-16-66 | 1984 | Hanford, Calif. |
| Urbina, Ugueth | 10 | 5 | 3.71 | 33 | 17 | 0 | 0 | 114 | 102 | 54 | 47 | 44 | 108 | R | R | 6-2 | 170 | 2-15-74 | 1991 | Caracas, Venez. |
| Veres, Dave | 6 | 3 | 4.17 | 68 | 0 | 0 | 4 | 78 | 85 | 39 | 36 | 32 | 81 | R | R | 6-2 | 195 | 10-19-66 | 1986 | Gresham, Ore. |

## FIELDING

| Catcher | PCT | G | PO | A | E | DP | PB |
|---|---|---|---|---|---|---|---|
| Chavez | 1.000 | 3 | 14 | 0 | 0 | 0 | 0 |
| Fletcher | .992 | 112 | 721 | 30 | 6 | 5 | 6 |
| Spehr | .985 | 58 | 121 | 7 | 2 | 0 | 1 |
| Webster | .998 | 63 | 390 | 25 | 1 | 3 | 3 |

| First Base | PCT | G | PO | A | E | DP |
|---|---|---|---|---|---|---|
| Floyd | .941 | 2 | 16 | 0 | 1 | 1 |
| Rodriguez | .989 | 51 | 426 | 28 | 5 | 28 |
| Segui | .993 | 113 | 945 | 90 | 7 | 79 |
| Silvestri | 1.000 | 1 | 3 | 0 | 0 | 0 |

| Second Base | PCT | G | PO | A | E | DP |
|---|---|---|---|---|---|---|
| Lansing | .985 | 159 | 347 | 393 | 11 | 85 |
| Santangelo | 1.000 | 5 | 5 | 7 | 0 | 2 |
| Silvestri | .000 | 1 | 0 | 0 | 0 | 0 |
| Stankiewicz | .969 | 19 | 12 | 19 | 1 | 2 |

| Third Base | PCT | G | PO | A | E | DP |
|---|---|---|---|---|---|---|
| Andrews | .955 | 123 | 64 | 256 | 15 | 13 |
| Santangelo | .960 | 23 | 14 | 34 | 2 | 2 |
| Schu | .667 | 1 | 0 | 2 | 1 | 0 |
| Silvestri | .913 | 47 | 20 | 85 | 10 | 5 |

| | PCT | G | PO | A | E | DP |
|---|---|---|---|---|---|---|
| Stankiewicz | .500 | 1 | 0 | 1 | 1 | 0 |

| Shortstop | PCT | G | PO | A | E | DP |
|---|---|---|---|---|---|---|
| Grudzielanek | .959 | 153 | 180 | 453 | 27 | 78 |
| Lansing | 1.000 | 2 | 2 | 2 | 0 | 1 |
| Santangelo | .000 | 1 | 0 | 0 | 0 | 0 |
| Silvestri | 1.000 | 10 | 0 | 7 | 0 | 0 |
| Stankiewicz | .964 | 13 | 4 | 23 | 1 | 4 |

| Outfield | PCT | G | PO | A | E | DP |
|---|---|---|---|---|---|---|
| Alou | .989 | 142 | 258 | 8 | 3 | 2 |
| Benitez | .500 | 4 | 1 | 0 | 1 | 0 |
| Floyd | .960 | 85 | 93 | 2 | 4 | 0 |
| Guerrero | 1.000 | 8 | 11 | 0 | 0 | 0 |
| Obando | .962 | 47 | 74 | 2 | 3 | 0 |
| Rodriguez | .947 | 89 | 102 | 5 | 6 | 0 |
| Santangelo | .983 | 124 | 232 | 4 | 4 | 1 |
| Silvestri | .000 | 2 | 0 | 0 | 0 | 0 |
| Spehr | .000 | 1 | 0 | 0 | 0 | 0 |
| White | .990 | 86 | 186 | 5 | 2 | 1 |

MORRIS FOSTOFF

**Jeff Fassero**

**EXPOS**

Henry Rodriguez topped the Expos with 35 homers and 103 RBIs

GEORGE GOJKOVICH

MORRIS FOSTOFF

Expos minor league
Player of the Year
Vladimir Guerrero

## FARM SYSTEM

**Director of Player Development:** Bill Geivett

| Class | Farm Team | League | W | L | Pct. | Finish* | Manager | First Yr |
|---|---|---|---|---|---|---|---|---|
| AAA | Ottawa (Ontario) Lynx | International | 60 | 82 | .423 | 10th (10) | Pete Mackanin | 1993 |
| AA | Harrisburg (Pa.) Senators | Eastern | 74 | 68 | .521 | +4th (10) | Pat Kelly | 1991 |
| #A | West Palm Beach (Fla.) Expos | Florida State | 68 | 67 | .504 | 7th (14) | Rick Sofield | 1969 |
| A | Delmarva (Md.) Shorebirds | South Atlantic | 83 | 59 | .585 | 3rd (14) | Doug Sisson | 1996 |
| A | Vermont Expos | New York-Penn | 48 | 26 | .649 | 1st (14) | Kevin Higgins | 1994 |
| R | West Palm Beach (Fla.) Expos | Gulf Coast | 41 | 18 | .695 | 1st (16) | Jim Gabella | 1986 |

*Finish in overall standings (No. of teams in league)   #Advanced level   +Won league championship

## ORGANIZATION LEADERS

### MAJOR LEAGUERS

**BATTING**
*AVG Mark Grudzielanek. .306
R Two tied at ................ 99
H Mark Grudzielanek.. 201
TB Henry Rodriguez......299
2B Henry Rodriguez...... 42
3B F.P. Santangelo .......... 5
HR Henry Rodriguez....... 36
RBI Henry Rodriguez... 103
BB David Segui ............. 60
SO Henry Rodriguez..... 160
SB Mark Grudzielanek.... 33

**PITCHING**
W Jeff Fassero ............. 15
L Jeff Fassero ............. 12
#ERA Mel Rojas ............. 3.22
G Mel Rojas................. 74
CG Jeff Fassero ............... 5
SV Mel Rojas ................ 36
IP Jeff Fassero ........... 232
BB Pedro Martinez ......... 70
SO Two tied at ............. 222

GEORGE GOJKOVICH

**Mark Grudzielanek.** .306 average

### MINOR LEAGUERS

**BATTING**
*AVG Vladimir Guerrero, W.P.B./Harris. ........ .360
R Vladimir Guerrero, W.P.B./Harris. ......... 100
H Vladimir Guerrero, W.P.B./Harris. ......... 179
TB Vladimir Guerrero, W.P.B./Harris. ......... 307
2B Vladimir Guerrero, W.P.B./Harris. ......... 40
3B Chris Stowers, Vermont .......................... 9
HR Vladimir Guerrero, W.P.B./Harris. .......... 24
RBI Vladimir Guerrero, W.P.B./Harris. .......... 96
BB Jon Saffer, Harrisburg ............................ 78
SO Chris Schwab, Delmarva...................... 135
SB Orlando Cabrera, Delmarva .................. 51

**PITCHING**
W Javier Vazquez, Delmarva ..................... 14
L Two tied at....................................... 11
#ERA Peter Fortune, GCL Expos/Vermont .... 2.02
G Kirk Bullinger, Ottawa/Harrisburg ........... 57
CG Troy Mattes, Delmarva ........................... 5
SV Ben Fleetham, Delmarva/WPB/Harr. ...... 31
IP Scott Forster, Harrisburg ...................... 176
BB Everett Stull, Ottawa/Harrisburg............. 91
SO Javier Vazquez, Delmarva ................... 173

*Minimum 250 At-Bats   #Minimum 75 Innings

## TOP 10 PROSPECTS

**How the Expos Top 10 prospects, as judged by Baseball America prior to the 1996 season, fared in 1996:**

**Ugueth Urbina**

| Player, Pos. | Club (Class—League) | AVG | AB | R | H | 2B | 3B | HR | RBI | SB |
|---|---|---|---|---|---|---|---|---|---|---|
| 1. Vladimir Guerrero, of | West Palm Beach (A—Florida State) | .363 | 80 | 16 | 29 | 8 | 0 | 5 | 18 | 2 |
| | Harrisburg (AA—Eastern) | .360 | 417 | 84 | 150 | 32 | 8 | 19 | 78 | 17 |
| | Montreal | .185 | 27 | 2 | 5 | 0 | 0 | 1 | 1 | 0 |
| 3. Hiram Bocachica, ss | West Palm Beach (A—Florida State) | .337 | 267 | 50 | 90 | 17 | 5 | 2 | 26 | 21 |
| | West Palm Beach (R—Gulf Coast) | .250 | 32 | 11 | 8 | 3 | 0 | 0 | 2 | 2 |
| 4. Brad Fullmer, of | Harrisburg (AA—Eastern) | .276 | 98 | 11 | 27 | 4 | 1 | 4 | 14 | 0 |
| | West Palm Beach (A—Florida State) | .303 | 380 | 52 | 115 | 29 | 1 | 5 | 63 | 4 |
| 6. Yamil Benitez, of | Ottawa (AAA—International) | .278 | 439 | 56 | 122 | 20 | 2 | 23 | 81 | 11 |
| | Montreal | .167 | 12 | 0 | 2 | 0 | 0 | 0 | 2 | 0 |
| 9. Michael Barrett, c | Delmarva (A—South Atlantic) | .238 | 474 | 57 | 113 | 29 | 4 | 4 | 62 | 5 |

| | | W | L | ERA | G | SV | IP | H | BB | SO |
|---|---|---|---|---|---|---|---|---|---|---|
| 2. Ugueth Urbina, rhp | Ottawa (AAA—International) | 2 | 0 | 2.66 | 5 | 0 | 24 | 17 | 6 | 28 |
| | Montreal | 10 | 5 | 3.71 | 33 | 0 | 114 | 102 | 44 | 108 |
| 5. Everett Stull, rhp | Ottawa (AAA—International) | 2 | 6 | 6.33 | 13 | 0 | 70 | 87 | 39 | 69 |
| | Harrisburg (AA—Eastern) | 6 | 3 | 3.15 | 14 | 0 | 80 | 64 | 52 | 81 |
| 7. Jose Paniagua, rhp | Harrisburg (AA—Eastern) | 3 | 0 | 0.00 | 3 | 0 | 18 | 12 | 2 | 16 |
| | Ottawa (AAA—International) | 9 | 5 | 3.18 | 15 | 0 | 85 | 72 | 23 | 61 |
| | Montreal | 2 | 4 | 3.53 | 11 | 0 | 51 | 55 | 23 | 27 |
| 8. Neil Weber, lhp | Harrisburg (AA—Eastern) | 7 | 4 | 3.03 | 18 | 0 | 107 | 90 | 44 | 74 |
| 10. Jason Baker, rhp | Delmarva (A—South Atlantic) | 9 | 7 | 2.81 | 27 | 0 | 160 | 127 | 77 | 147 |

## INTERNATIONAL LEAGUE

| BATTING | AVG | G | AB | R | H | 2B | 3B | HR | RBI | BB | SO | SB | CS | B | T | HT | WT | DOB | 1st Yr | Resides |
|---|---|---|---|---|---|---|---|---|---|---|---|---|---|---|---|---|---|---|---|---|
| Barron, Tony | .320 | 105 | 394 | 58 | 126 | 29 | 2 | 14 | 59 | 20 | 74 | 9 | 4 | R | R | 6-0 | 185 | 8-17-66 | 1987 | Tacoma, Wash. |
| Benitez, Yamil | .278 | 114 | 439 | 56 | 122 | 20 | 2 | 23 | 81 | 28 | 120 | 11 | 4 | R | R | 6-2 | 180 | 10-5-72 | 1990 | San Juan, P.R. |
| Bieser, Steve | .322 | 123 | 382 | 63 | 123 | 24 | 4 | 1 | 32 | 35 | 55 | 27 | 7 | S | R | 5-10 | 170 | 8-4-67 | 1989 | St. Genevieve, Mo. |
| Buccheri, Jim | .257 | 65 | 206 | 40 | 53 | 3 | 4 | 1 | 12 | 33 | 28 | 33 | 6 | R | R | 5-11 | 165 | 11-12-68 | 1988 | Fountain Valley, Calif. |
| Castleberry, Kevin | .280 | 66 | 193 | 27 | 54 | 8 | 3 | 3 | 22 | 21 | 27 | 9 | 5 | L | R | 5-10 | 170 | 4-22-68 | 1989 | Midwest City, Okla. |
| Chavez, Raul | .247 | 60 | 198 | 15 | 49 | 10 | 0 | 2 | 24 | 11 | 31 | 0 | 2 | R | R | 5-11 | 175 | 3-18-73 | 1990 | Valencia, Venez. |
| Coolbaugh, Scott | .208 | 58 | 173 | 20 | 36 | 12 | 1 | 3 | 22 | 23 | 37 | 2 | 2 | R | R | 5-11 | 195 | 6-13-66 | 1987 | Seguin, Texas |
| Floyd, Cliff | .303 | 20 | 76 | 7 | 23 | 3 | 1 | 1 | 8 | 7 | 20 | 2 | 2 | L | R | 6-4 | 220 | 12-5-72 | 1991 | Markham, Ill. |
| Heffernan, Bert | .303 | 64 | 198 | 20 | 60 | 8 | 1 | 1 | 27 | 14 | 15 | 1 | 4 | L | R | 5-10 | 185 | 3-3-65 | 1988 | Stony Brook, N.Y. |
| Leach, Jalal | .317 | 37 | 101 | 12 | 32 | 4 | 0 | 3 | 9 | 8 | 17 | 0 | 0 | L | L | 6-2 | 200 | 3-14-69 | 1990 | Novato, Calif. |
| Lukachyk, Rob | .264 | 70 | 246 | 38 | 65 | 15 | 4 | 9 | 39 | 13 | 54 | 10 | 2 | L | R | 6-0 | 185 | 7-24-68 | 1987 | Sarasota, Fla. |
| Martin, Chris | .264 | 122 | 451 | 68 | 119 | 30 | 1 | 8 | 54 | 33 | 54 | 25 | 12 | R | R | 6-1 | 170 | 1-25-68 | 1990 | Los Angeles, Calif. |
| Matos, Francisco | .238 | 100 | 307 | 30 | 73 | 15 | 3 | 2 | 23 | 16 | 35 | 4 | 5 | R | R | 6-1 | 160 | 4-8-70 | 1988 | Azua, D.R. |
| McDavid, Ray | .155 | 18 | 58 | 7 | 9 | 1 | 0 | 0 | 2 | 9 | 11 | 6 | 2 | L | R | 6-3 | 195 | 7-20-71 | 1989 | San Diego, Calif. |
| McGuire, Ryan | .257 | 134 | 451 | 62 | 116 | 21 | 2 | 12 | 60 | 59 | 80 | 11 | 4 | L | L | 6-1 | 195 | 11-23-71 | 1993 | Woodland Hills, Calif. |
| Montoyo, Charlie | .351 | 22 | 57 | 10 | 20 | 5 | 1 | 0 | 5 | 7 | 6 | 0 | 0 | R | R | 5-10 | 170 | 10-17-65 | 1987 | Florida, P.R. |
| Reyes, Gilberto | .182 | 17 | 44 | 5 | 8 | 3 | 0 | 3 | 5 | 8 | 12 | 0 | 0 | R | R | 6-2 | 200 | 12-10-63 | 1980 | Santo Domingo, D.R. |
| Schu, Rick | .271 | 116 | 395 | 48 | 107 | 24 | 3 | 12 | 54 | 41 | 51 | 9 | 3 | R | R | 6-0 | 185 | 1-26-62 | 1981 | Carmichael, Calif. |
| Yan, Julian | .184 | 48 | 136 | 17 | 25 | 3 | 1 | 4 | 21 | 10 | 40 | 0 | 0 | R | R | 6-4 | 190 | 7-24-65 | 1985 | El Seibo, D.R. |

| PITCHING | W | L | ERA | G | GS | CG | SV | IP | H | R | ER | BB | SO | B | T | HT | WT | DOB | 1st Yr | Resides |
|---|---|---|---|---|---|---|---|---|---|---|---|---|---|---|---|---|---|---|---|---|
| Alvarez, Tavo | 4 | 9 | 4.70 | 20 | 20 | 2 | 0 | 113 | 128 | 66 | 59 | 25 | 86 | R | R | 6-3 | 183 | 11-25-71 | 1990 | Tucson, Ariz. |
| Aucoin, Derek | 3 | 5 | 3.96 | 52 | 0 | 0 | 3 | 75 | 74 | 37 | 33 | 53 | 69 | R | R | 6-7 | 226 | 3-27-70 | 1989 | Montreal, Quebec |
| Baxter, Bob | 3 | 3 | 5.51 | 54 | 2 | 0 | 3 | 82 | 104 | 55 | 50 | 23 | 60 | L | L | 6-1 | 180 | 2-17-69 | 1990 | Norwood, Mass. |
| Boucher, Denis | 3 | 7 | 9.30 | 17 | 11 | 0 | 0 | 61 | 90 | 63 | 63 | 40 | 24 | R | L | 6-1 | 195 | 3-7-68 | 1988 | Lachine, Quebec |
| Bullinger, Kirk | 2 | 1 | 3.52 | 10 | 0 | 0 | 0 | 15 | 10 | 6 | 6 | 9 | 9 | R | R | 6-2 | 170 | 10-28-69 | 1992 | Hammond, La. |
| Dorlarque, Aaron | 1 | 1 | 13.27 | 14 | 0 | 0 | 0 | 20 | 39 | 30 | 29 | 11 | 13 | R | R | 6-3 | 180 | 2-16-70 | 1992 | Vancouver, Wash. |
| Falteisek, Steve | 2 | 5 | 6.36 | 12 | 12 | 0 | 0 | 58 | 75 | 45 | 41 | 25 | 26 | R | R | 6-2 | 200 | 1-28-72 | 1992 | Floral Park, N.Y. |
| Gray, Dennis | 0 | 0 | 6.75 | 3 | 0 | 0 | 0 | 5 | 9 | 4 | 4 | 5 | 3 | L | L | 6-6 | 225 | 12-24-69 | 1991 | Banning, Calif. |
| Habyan, John | 0 | 1 | 2.45 | 7 | 0 | 0 | 1 | 7 | 7 | 2 | 2 | 2 | 8 | R | R | 6-2 | 195 | 1-29-64 | 1982 | Bel Air, Md. |
| Henderson, Rod | 4 | 11 | 5.19 | 25 | 23 | 3 | 0 | 121 | 117 | 75 | 70 | 52 | 83 | R | R | 6-4 | 195 | 3-11-71 | 1992 | Glasgow, Ky. |
| Ilsley, Blaise | 5 | 2 | 5.16 | 20 | 4 | 0 | 0 | 45 | 49 | 27 | 26 | 15 | 22 | L | L | 6-1 | 185 | 4-9-64 | 1985 | Alpena, Mich. |
| Leiper, Dave | 3 | 1 | 1.93 | 25 | 0 | 0 | 6 | 33 | 29 | 7 | 7 | 6 | 26 | L | L | 6-1 | 160 | 6-18-62 | 1982 | Plano, Texas |
| Pacheco, Alex | 2 | 2 | 6.48 | 33 | 0 | 0 | 6 | 42 | 47 | 32 | 30 | 18 | 34 | R | R | 6-3 | 170 | 7-19-73 | 1990 | Caracas, Venez. |
| Paniagua, Jose | 9 | 5 | 3.18 | 15 | 14 | 2 | 0 | 85 | 72 | 39 | 30 | 23 | 61 | R | R | 6-1 | 160 | 8-20-73 | 1991 | Santo Domingo, D.R. |
| Rivera, Ben | 4 | 9 | 6.46 | 31 | 15 | 0 | 1 | 100 | 112 | 74 | 72 | 47 | 87 | R | R | 6-6 | 230 | 1-11-69 | 1986 | San Pedro de Macoris, D.R. |
| Rueter, Kirk | 1 | 2 | 4.20 | 3 | 3 | 1 | 0 | 15 | 21 | 7 | 7 | 3 | 3 | L | L | 6-3 | 190 | 12-1-70 | 1991 | Hoyleton, Ill. |
| Schmidt, Curt | 1 | 5 | 2.43 | 54 | 0 | 0 | 13 | 70 | 60 | 27 | 19 | 22 | 45 | R | R | 6-3 | 223 | 3-16-70 | 1992 | Miles City, Mon. |
| Stull, Everett | 2 | 6 | 6.33 | 13 | 13 | 1 | 0 | 70 | 87 | 57 | 49 | 39 | 69 | R | R | 6-3 | 195 | 8-24-71 | 1992 | Stone Mountain, Ga. |
| Telford, Anthony | 7 | 2 | 4.11 | 30 | 15 | 1 | 0 | 118 | 128 | 62 | 54 | 34 | 69 | R | R | 6-0 | 175 | 3-6-66 | 1987 | Pinellas Park, Fla. |
| Urbina, Ugueth | 2 | 0 | 2.66 | 5 | 0 | 0 | 0 | 24 | 17 | 9 | 7 | 6 | 28 | R | R | 6-2 | 170 | 2-15-74 | 1991 | Caracas, Venez. |
| Whitehurst, Wally | 2 | 4 | 4.37 | 15 | 5 | 0 | 3 | 35 | 41 | 17 | 17 | 13 | 35 | R | R | 6-3 | 185 | 4-11-64 | 1985 | Madisonville, La. |

### FIELDING

| Catcher | PCT | G | PO | A | E | DP | PB |
|---|---|---|---|---|---|---|---|
| Bieser | .983 | 33 | 159 | 17 | 3 | 1 | 2 |
| Chavez | .990 | 60 | 363 | 50 | 4 | 3 | 4 |
| Heffernan | .993 | 48 | 277 | 19 | 2 | 1 | 2 |
| Reyes | 1.000 | 15 | 85 | 15 | 0 | 1 | 3 |

| First Base | PCT | G | PO | A | E | DP |
|---|---|---|---|---|---|---|
| Coolbaugh | 1.000 | 3 | 11 | 2 | 0 | 1 |
| Lukachyk | 1.000 | 6 | 31 | 4 | 0 | 4 |
| Martin | .000 | 1 | 0 | 0 | 0 | 0 |
| McGuire | .993 | 120 | 984 | 73 | 7 | 86 |
| Schu | 1.000 | 6 | 23 | 1 | 0 | 4 |
| Yan | .969 | 23 | 144 | 13 | 5 | 10 |

| Second Base | PCT | G | PO | A | E | DP |
|---|---|---|---|---|---|---|
| Bieser | 1.000 | 1 | 0 | 1 | 0 | 0 |
| Buccheri | 1.000 | 8 | 9 | 6 | 0 | 1 |
| Castleberry | .974 | 60 | 94 | 166 | 7 | 27 |
| Heffernan | 1.000 | 2 | 0 | 2 | 0 | 1 |

| Third Base | PCT | G | PO | A | E | DP |
|---|---|---|---|---|---|---|
| Martin | 1.000 | 1 | 2 | 6 | 0 | 1 |
| Matos | .977 | 72 | 108 | 150 | 6 | 37 |
| Montoyo | .000 | 4 | 0 | 0 | 0 | 0 |
| Schu | .978 | 26 | 42 | 46 | 2 | 13 |

| Third Base | PCT | G | PO | A | E | DP |
|---|---|---|---|---|---|---|
| Castleberry | 1.000 | 4 | 0 | 2 | 0 | 0 |
| Coolbaugh | .971 | 51 | 37 | 95 | 4 | 6 |
| Floyd | .000 | 1 | 0 | 0 | 0 | 0 |
| Heffernan | .857 | 4 | 2 | 4 | 1 | 1 |
| Martin | .917 | 11 | 7 | 15 | 2 | 2 |
| Matos | 1.000 | 1 | 2 | 4 | 0 | 0 |
| Montoyo | .917 | 5 | 6 | 5 | 1 | 2 |
| Schu | .928 | 79 | 52 | 140 | 15 | 11 |

| Shortstop | PCT | G | PO | A | E | DP |
|---|---|---|---|---|---|---|
| Coolbaugh | .000 | 1 | 0 | 0 | 0 | 0 |
| Martin | .965 | 110 | 178 | 341 | 19 | 62 |

| | PCT | G | PO | A | E | DP |
|---|---|---|---|---|---|---|
| Matos | .977 | 24 | 27 | 57 | 2 | 12 |
| Montoyo | .939 | 13 | 26 | 36 | 4 | 8 |
| Schu | .933 | 4 | 3 | 11 | 1 | 1 |

| Outfield | PCT | G | PO | A | E | DP |
|---|---|---|---|---|---|---|
| Barron | 1.000 | 92 | 154 | 7 | 0 | 0 |
| Benitez | .968 | 111 | 197 | 14 | 7 | 2 |
| Bieser | .973 | 81 | 178 | 5 | 5 | 1 |
| Buccheri | 1.000 | 55 | 121 | 2 | 0 | 0 |
| Floyd | .951 | 19 | 38 | 1 | 2 | 0 |
| Heffernan | .000 | 1 | 0 | 0 | 0 | 0 |
| Leach | 1.000 | 21 | 27 | 1 | 0 | 0 |
| Lukachyk | .971 | 57 | 99 | 3 | 3 | 0 |
| McDavid | 1.000 | 17 | 29 | 0 | 0 | 0 |
| McGuire | .750 | 3 | 3 | 0 | 1 | 0 |
| Schu | 1.000 | 1 | 2 | 0 | 0 | 0 |

## EASTERN LEAGUE

| BATTING | AVG | G | AB | R | H | 2B | 3B | HR | RBI | BB | SO | SB | CS | B | T | HT | WT | DOB | 1st Yr | Resides |
|---|---|---|---|---|---|---|---|---|---|---|---|---|---|---|---|---|---|---|---|---|
| Alcantara, Israel | .211 | 62 | 218 | 26 | 46 | 5 | 0 | 8 | 19 | 14 | 62 | 1 | 1 | R | R | 6-2 | 165 | 5-6-73 | 1991 | Santo Domingo, D.R. |
| Barron, Tony | .284 | 18 | 67 | 12 | 19 | 3 | 1 | 5 | 12 | 6 | 19 | 1 | 0 | R | R | 6-0 | 185 | 8-17-66 | 1987 | Tacoma, Wash. |
| Blum, Geoff | .240 | 120 | 396 | 47 | 95 | 22 | 2 | 1 | 41 | 59 | 51 | 6 | 7 | S | R | 6-3 | 193 | 4-26-73 | 1994 | Chino, Calif. |
| Cabrera, Jolbert | .240 | 107 | 354 | 40 | 85 | 18 | 2 | 3 | 29 | 23 | 63 | 10 | 5 | R | R | 6-0 | 177 | 12-8-72 | 1991 | Cartagena, Colombia |
| Campos, Jesus | .260 | 73 | 208 | 15 | 54 | 4 | 0 | 0 | 17 | 9 | 17 | 5 | 9 | R | R | 5-9 | 145 | 10-12-73 | 1991 | San Pedro de Macoris, D.R. |
| Carvajal, Jhonny | .300 | 16 | 60 | 7 | 18 | 3 | 2 | 0 | 4 | 5 | 10 | 1 | 1 | R | R | 5-10 | 165 | 7-24-74 | 1993 | Barcelona, Venez. |
| Crosby, Mike | .202 | 31 | 99 | 3 | 20 | 4 | 0 | 1 | 6 | 3 | 25 | 0 | 0 | L | R | 6-1 | 200 | 2-24-69 | 1992 | Warwick, R.I. |
| Fullmer, Brad | .276 | 24 | 98 | 11 | 27 | 4 | 1 | 4 | 14 | 3 | 8 | 0 | 0 | L | R | 6-1 | 185 | 1-17-75 | 1994 | Chatsworth, Calif. |
| Guerrero, Vladimir | .360 | 118 | 417 | 84 | 150 | 32 | 8 | 19 | 78 | 51 | 42 | 17 | 10 | R | R | 6-2 | 158 | 2-6-76 | 1993 | Nizao Bani, D.R. |
| Henley, Bob | .228 | 103 | 289 | 33 | 66 | 12 | 1 | 3 | 27 | 70 | 78 | 1 | 2 | R | R | 6-2 | 190 | 1-30-73 | 1993 | Grand Bay, Ala. |
| Koeyers, Ramsey | .208 | 25 | 77 | 6 | 16 | 3 | 0 | 1 | 9 | 2 | 27 | 0 | 1 | R | R | 6-1 | 187 | 8-7-74 | 1991 | Brievengst, Curacao |
| Leach, Jalal | .328 | 83 | 268 | 38 | 88 | 22 | 3 | 6 | 48 | 21 | 55 | 3 | 7 | L | L | 6-2 | 200 | 3-14-69 | 1990 | Novato, Calif. |
| Lukachyk, Rob | .326 | 27 | 92 | 22 | 30 | 6 | 0 | 5 | 24 | 12 | 18 | 4 | 1 | L | R | 6-0 | 185 | 7-24-68 | 1987 | Sarasota, Fla. |
| Masteller, Dan | .328 | 44 | 128 | 21 | 42 | 11 | 0 | 2 | 21 | 18 | 11 | 0 | 0 | L | L | 6-0 | 185 | 3-17-68 | 1989 | Lyndhurst, Ohio |

| BATTING | AVG | G | AB | R | H | 2B | 3B | HR | RBI | BB | SO | SB | CS | B | T | HT | WT | DOB | 1st Yr | Resides |
|---|---|---|---|---|---|---|---|---|---|---|---|---|---|---|---|---|---|---|---|---|
| Montoyo, Charlie | .224 | 74 | 183 | 21 | 41 | 3 | 1 | 0 | 18 | 32 | 23 | 1 | 0 | R | R | 5-10 | 170 | 10-17-65 | 1987 | Florida, P.R. |
| Rendina, Mike | .143 | 16 | 42 | 4 | 6 | 2 | 0 | 0 | 3 | 11 | 0 | 0 | 0 | L | L | 6-4 | 215 | 9-28-70 | 1988 | El Cajon, Calif. |
| Renteria, Dave | .236 | 24 | 72 | 7 | 17 | 6 | 0 | 0 | 4 | 5 | 13 | 0 | 0 | R | R | 6-0 | 175 | 12-1-72 | 1992 | Belen, N.M. |
| Saffer, Jon | .300 | 134 | 487 | 96 | 146 | 26 | 4 | 10 | 52 | 78 | 77 | 8 | 16 | L | R | 6-2 | 200 | 7-6-73 | 1992 | Tucson, Ariz. |
| Stovall, DaRond | .221 | 74 | 272 | 38 | 60 | 7 | 1 | 10 | 36 | 32 | 86 | 10 | 5 | S | L | 6-1 | 185 | 1-3-73 | 1991 | East St. Louis, Ill. |
| Talanoa, Scott | .210 | 50 | 138 | 20 | 29 | 5 | 0 | 11 | 23 | 31 | 50 | 0 | 0 | R | R | 6-5 | 240 | 11-12-69 | 1991 | Lawndale, Calif. |
| Thoutsis, Paul | .200 | 5 | 20 | 1 | 4 | 3 | 0 | 0 | 3 | 2 | 6 | 0 | 0 | L | R | 6-1 | 185 | 10-23-65 | 1983 | Worcester, Mass. |
| Vidro, Jose | .259 | 126 | 452 | 57 | 117 | 25 | 3 | 18 | 82 | 29 | 71 | 3 | 1 | S | R | 5-11 | 175 | 8-27-74 | 1992 | Sabana Grande, P.R. |
| White, Rondell | .350 | 5 | 20 | 5 | 7 | 1 | 0 | 3 | 6 | 1 | 1 | 1 | 1 | R | R | 6-1 | 193 | 2-23-72 | 1990 | Gray, Ga. |

| PITCHING | W | L | ERA | G | GS | CG | SV | IP | H | R | ER | BB | SO | B | T | HT | WT | DOB | 1st Yr | Resides |
|---|---|---|---|---|---|---|---|---|---|---|---|---|---|---|---|---|---|---|---|---|
| Bennett, Shayne | 8 | 8 | 2.53 | 53 | 0 | 0 | 12 | 93 | 83 | 32 | 26 | 35 | 89 | R | R | 6-5 | 200 | 4-10-72 | 1993 | Modbury, Australia |
| Benz, Jake | 1 | 4 | 5.97 | 34 | 0 | 0 | 4 | 38 | 42 | 30 | 25 | 27 | 25 | L | L | 5-9 | 162 | 2-27-71 | 1994 | Pleasant Hill, Calif. |
| Boucher, Denis | 1 | 0 | 1.50 | 1 | 1 | 0 | 0 | 6 | 2 | 1 | 1 | 2 | 6 | R | L | 6-1 | 195 | 3-7-68 | 1988 | Lachine, Quebec |
| Bullinger, Kirk | 3 | 4 | 1.97 | 47 | 0 | 0 | 22 | 46 | 46 | 16 | 10 | 18 | 29 | R | R | 6-2 | 170 | 10-28-69 | 1992 | Hammond, La. |
| DeHart, Rick | 1 | 2 | 2.68 | 30 | 2 | 0 | 1 | 44 | 46 | 19 | 13 | 19 | 30 | L | L | 6-1 | 180 | 3-21-70 | 1992 | Topeka, Kan. |
| Dorlarque, Aaron | 1 | 0 | 6.00 | 13 | 0 | 0 | 0 | 24 | 32 | 17 | 16 | 7 | 14 | R | R | 6-3 | 180 | 2-16-70 | 1992 | Vancouver, Wash. |
| Falteisek, Steve | 6 | 5 | 3.81 | 17 | 17 | 1 | 0 | 116 | 111 | 60 | 49 | 48 | 62 | R | R | 6-2 | 200 | 1-28-72 | 1992 | Floral Park, N.Y. |
| Fleetham, Ben | 0 | 0 | 0.00 | 4 | 0 | 0 | 1 | 6 | 2 | 0 | 0 | 5 | 6 | R | R | 6-1 | 205 | 8-3-72 | 1994 | Minneapolis, Minn. |
| Forster, Scott | 10 | 7 | 3.78 | 28 | 28 | 0 | 0 | 176 | 164 | 92 | 74 | 67 | 97 | R | L | 6-1 | 194 | 10-27-71 | 1994 | Flourtown, Pa. |
| Gentile, Scott | 2 | 2 | 2.63 | 15 | 0 | 0 | 1 | 24 | 14 | 8 | 7 | 14 | 23 | R | R | 5-11 | 210 | 12-21-70 | 1992 | Berlin, Conn. |
| Gray, Dennis | 0 | 0 | 7.59 | 9 | 0 | 0 | 0 | 11 | 12 | 9 | 9 | 14 | 10 | L | L | 6-6 | 225 | 12-24-69 | 1991 | Banning, Calif. |
| Hmielewski, Chris | 1 | 2 | 12.00 | 3 | 0 | 0 | 0 | 3 | 4 | 4 | 4 | 3 | 2 | L | L | 6-4 | 210 | 7-18-70 | 1991 | Franklin Park, Ill. |
| Kendrena, Ken | 0 | 4 | 4.63 | 7 | 0 | 0 | 0 | 12 | 10 | 6 | 6 | 2 | 4 | R | R | 5-11 | 170 | 10-29-70 | 1992 | Rancho Cucamonga, Calif. |
| Martinez, Ramiro | 0 | 4 | 4.50 | 8 | 5 | 0 | 0 | 24 | 23 | 13 | 12 | 15 | 10 | L | L | 6-2 | 185 | 1-28-72 | 1992 | Los Angeles, Calif. |
| McCommon, Jason | 10 | 10 | 3.94 | 30 | 24 | 1 | 0 | 153 | 169 | 88 | 67 | 44 | 92 | R | R | 6-0 | 190 | 8-9-71 | 1994 | Memphis, Tenn. |
| Pacheco, Alex | 5 | 2 | 2.73 | 18 | 0 | 0 | 0 | 26 | 26 | 10 | 8 | 12 | 27 | R | R | 6-3 | 170 | 7-19-73 | 1990 | Caracas, Venez |
| Paniagua, Jose | 3 | 0 | 0.00 | 3 | 3 | 0 | 0 | 18 | 12 | 1 | 0 | 2 | 16 | R | R | 6-1 | 160 | 8-20-73 | 1991 | Santo Domingo, D.R. |
| Phelps, Tom | 2 | 2 | 2.47 | 8 | 8 | 2 | 0 | 47 | 43 | 16 | 13 | 19 | 23 | L | L | 6-3 | 192 | 3-4-74 | 1993 | Tampa, Fla. |
| Pisciotta, Scott | 2 | 1 | 5.50 | 27 | 0 | 0 | 1 | 36 | 35 | 22 | 22 | 27 | 18 | R | R | 6-7 | 225 | 6-8-73 | 1991 | Marietta, Ga. |
| Pote, Lou | 1 | 7 | 5.07 | 25 | 18 | 0 | 1 | 105 | 114 | 66 | 59 | 48 | 61 | R | R | 6-3 | 190 | 8-27-71 | 1991 | Chicago, Ill. |
| Stull, Everett | 6 | 3 | 3.15 | 14 | 14 | 0 | 0 | 80 | 64 | 31 | 28 | 52 | 81 | R | R | 6-3 | 195 | 8-24-71 | 1992 | Stone Mountain, Ga. |
| Thurman, Mike | 3 | 1 | 5.11 | 4 | 4 | 0 | 0 | 25 | 25 | 14 | 14 | 5 | 14 | R | R | 6-5 | 190 | 7-22-73 | 1994 | Philomath, Ore. |
| Weber, Neil | 7 | 4 | 3.03 | 18 | 18 | 1 | 0 | 107 | 90 | 37 | 36 | 44 | 74 | L | L | 6-5 | 205 | 12-6-72 | 1993 | Irvine, Calif. |

### FIELDING

| Catcher | PCT | G | PO | A | E | DP | PB |
|---|---|---|---|---|---|---|---|
| Crosby | .988 | 27 | 142 | 17 | 2 | 1 | 4 |
| Henley | .986 | 99 | 565 | 92 | 9 | 11 | 7 |
| Koeyers | .965 | 24 | 131 | 8 | 5 | 0 | 6 |

| First Base | PCT | G | PO | A | E | DP |
|---|---|---|---|---|---|---|
| Barron | .964 | 3 | 26 | 1 | 1 | 3 |
| Blum | 1.000 | 1 | 2 | 0 | 0 | 0 |
| Fullmer | .923 | 1 | 11 | 1 | 1 | 1 |
| Leach | 1.000 | 1 | 2 | 1 | 0 | 0 |
| Lukachyk | .978 | 24 | 206 | 21 | 5 | 19 |
| Masteller | .993 | 39 | 286 | 13 | 2 | 28 |
| Montoyo | .991 | 32 | 224 | 9 | 2 | 21 |
| Rendina | 1.000 | 14 | 99 | 5 | 0 | 14 |
| Talanoa | .983 | 42 | 308 | 31 | 6 | 34 |
| Thoutsis | 1.000 | 5 | 44 | 2 | 0 | 2 |
| Vidro | 1.000 | 1 | 8 | 1 | 0 | 2 |

| Second Base | PCT | G | PO | A | E | DP |
|---|---|---|---|---|---|---|
| Blum | .984 | 85 | 223 | 207 | 7 | 55 |
| Carvajal | .980 | 16 | 42 | 57 | 2 | 14 |
| Montoyo | .959 | 10 | 27 | 20 | 2 | 11 |
| Renteria | .962 | 6 | 13 | 12 | 1 | 1 |
| Vidro | .987 | 34 | 78 | 74 | 2 | 21 |

| Third Base | PCT | G | PO | A | E | DP |
|---|---|---|---|---|---|---|
| Alcantara | .912 | 57 | 33 | 133 | 16 | 12 |
| Cabrera | 1.000 | 1 | 0 | 1 | 0 | 0 |
| Montoyo | .970 | 16 | 8 | 24 | 1 | 1 |
| Renteria | .500 | 1 | 0 | 1 | 1 | 0 |
| Vidro | .952 | 77 | 46 | 193 | 12 | 17 |

| Shortstop | PCT | G | PO | A | E | DP |
|---|---|---|---|---|---|---|
| Blum | .982 | 30 | 34 | 74 | 2 | 19 |
| Cabrera | .950 | 102 | 173 | 305 | 25 | 59 |
| Renteria | .895 | 15 | 23 | 28 | 6 | 4 |

| | PCT | G | PO | A | E | DP |
|---|---|---|---|---|---|---|
| Vidro | .857 | 2 | 3 | 3 | 1 | 1 |

| Outfield | PCT | G | PO | A | E | DP |
|---|---|---|---|---|---|---|
| Barron | 1.000 | 11 | 18 | 4 | 0 | 0 |
| Blum | .000 | 1 | 0 | 0 | 0 | 0 |
| Cabrera | 1.000 | 3 | 6 | 0 | 0 | 0 |
| Campos | .961 | 58 | 117 | 6 | 5 | 2 |
| Fullmer | .970 | 19 | 32 | 0 | 1 | 0 |
| Guerrero | .961 | 106 | 184 | 13 | 8 | 3 |
| Leach | .976 | 61 | 121 | 2 | 3 | 0 |
| Lukachyk | 1.000 | 2 | 6 | 1 | 0 | 0 |
| Saffer | .940 | 106 | 154 | 3 | 10 | 0 |
| Stovall | .983 | 72 | 171 | 4 | 3 | 1 |
| White | 1.000 | 5 | 12 | 0 | 0 | 0 |

# WEST PALM BEACH                                                          Class A
## FLORIDA STATE LEAGUE

| BATTING | AVG | G | AB | R | H | 2B | 3B | HR | RBI | BB | SO | SB | CS | B | T | HT | WT | DOB | 1st Yr | Resides |
|---|---|---|---|---|---|---|---|---|---|---|---|---|---|---|---|---|---|---|---|---|
| Alcantara, Israel | .311 | 15 | 61 | 11 | 19 | 2 | 0 | 4 | 14 | 3 | 13 | 0 | 0 | R | R | 6-2 | 165 | 5-6-73 | 1991 | Santo Domingo, D.R. |
| Bady, Edward | .281 | 128 | 484 | 62 | 136 | 9 | 3 | 1 | 34 | 42 | 93 | 42 | 17 | S | R | 5-11 | 170 | 2-5-73 | 1994 | Queens, N.Y. |
| Blakeney, Mo | .176 | 7 | 17 | 1 | 3 | 0 | 1 | 0 | 2 | 0 | 0 | 0 | 0 | R | R | 5-10 | 185 | 1-17-73 | 1995 | Kannapolis, N.C. |
| Bocachica, Hiram | .337 | 71 | 267 | 50 | 90 | 17 | 5 | 2 | 26 | 34 | 47 | 21 | 3 | R | R | 5-11 | 165 | 3-4-76 | 1994 | Bayamon, P.R. |
| Bravo, Danny | .197 | 48 | 137 | 15 | 27 | 2 | 2 | 0 | 12 | 14 | 30 | 3 | 4 | S | R | 5-11 | 175 | 5-27-76 | 1996 | Maracaibo, Venez. |
| Brinkley, Josh | .261 | 87 | 268 | 34 | 70 | 11 | 2 | 5 | 27 | 26 | 44 | 1 | 2 | R | R | 5-11 | 175 | 8-5-73 | 1993 | Raleigh, N.C. |
| Brown, Nate | .214 | 95 | 285 | 39 | 61 | 12 | 1 | 3 | 25 | 30 | 68 | 12 | 4 | L | L | 6-5 | 225 | 2-3-71 | 1993 | Berkeley, Calif. |
| Campos, Jesus | .250 | 44 | 148 | 24 | 37 | 6 | 1 | 0 | 20 | 12 | 24 | 8 | 3 | R | R | 5-9 | 145 | 10-12-73 | 1991 | San Pedro de Macoris, D.R. |
| Carvajal, Jhonny | .237 | 114 | 426 | 50 | 101 | 18 | 0 | 2 | 38 | 44 | 73 | 14 | 16 | R | R | 5-10 | 165 | 7-24-74 | 1993 | Barcelona, Venez. |
| Coquillette, Trace | .252 | 72 | 266 | 39 | 67 | 17 | 4 | 1 | 27 | 27 | 72 | 9 | 7 | R | R | 5-11 | 185 | 6-4-74 | 1993 | Orangevale, Calif. |
| Foster, Jeff | .154 | 3 | 13 | 0 | 2 | 0 | 0 | 0 | 1 | 0 | 6 | 1 | 0 | L | R | 6-2 | 175 | 2-25-72 | 1993 | Knoxville, Tenn. |
| Fullmer, Brad | .303 | 102 | 380 | 52 | 115 | 29 | 1 | 5 | 63 | 32 | 43 | 4 | 6 | L | R | 6-1 | 195 | 1-17-75 | 1994 | Chatsworth, Calif. |
| Giardi, Mike | .253 | 48 | 150 | 19 | 38 | 6 | 1 | 5 | 19 | 27 | 33 | 2 | 1 | R | R | 6-2 | 205 | 7-14-72 | 1994 | Salem, Mass. |
|   2-team (5 Tampa) | .245 | 53 | 163 | 22 | 40 | 6 | 1 | 5 | 20 | 31 | 36 | 2 | 1 | | | | | | | |
| Guerrero, Vladimir | .363 | 20 | 80 | 16 | 29 | 8 | 0 | 5 | 18 | 3 | 10 | 2 | 2 | R | R | 6-2 | 158 | 2-9-76 | 1993 | Nizao Bani, D.R. |
| Haas, Matt | .266 | 77 | 207 | 22 | 55 | 7 | 1 | 1 | 26 | 22 | 27 | 4 | 2 | L | R | 6-1 | 175 | 2-1-72 | 1994 | Paducah, Ky. |
| Hacopian, Derek | .268 | 43 | 157 | 23 | 42 | 12 | 0 | 2 | 22 | 13 | 11 | 0 | 3 | R | R | 6-0 | 200 | 1-1-70 | 1992 | Potomac, Md. |
| Koeyers, Ramsey | .121 | 10 | 33 | 2 | 4 | 2 | 0 | 0 | 2 | 0 | 8 | 0 | 0 | R | R | 5-11 | 175 | 8-7-74 | 1991 | Brievengst, Curacao |
| Mathews, Byron | .263 | 10 | 19 | 4 | 5 | 0 | 0 | 0 | 4 | 5 | 0 | 0 | 0 | S | R | 6-2 | 175 | 11-30-70 | 1992 | Ballwin, Mo. |
| McDavid, Ray | .375 | 4 | 16 | 2 | 6 | 2 | 0 | 1 | 3 | 3 | 1 | 1 | 0 | L | R | 6-3 | 195 | 7-20-71 | 1989 | San Diego, Calif. |
| Morales, Francisco | .274 | 75 | 259 | 32 | 71 | 20 | 2 | 3 | 42 | 19 | 79 | 3 | 1 | R | R | 6-3 | 180 | 1-31-73 | 1991 | San Pedro de Macoris, D.R. |
|   2-team (21 St. Pete.) | .261 | 96 | 326 | 38 | 85 | 25 | 3 | 4 | 48 | 24 | 104 | 3 | 1 | | | | | | | |
| Ottavinia, Paul | .213 | 45 | 141 | 15 | 30 | 2 | 1 | 1 | 10 | 12 | 20 | 2 | 1 | L | L | 6-1 | 190 | 4-22-73 | 1994 | Flanders, N.J. |
| Pachot, John | .190 | 44 | 163 | 8 | 31 | 9 | 0 | 0 | 19 | 2 | 19 | 0 | 1 | R | R | 6-2 | 168 | 11-11-74 | 1993 | Ponce, P.R. |
| Post, Dave | .279 | 59 | 258 | 42 | 72 | 15 | 6 | 5 | 35 | 37 | 32 | 8 | 4 | R | R | 5-11 | 170 | 9-3-73 | 1992 | Kingston, N.Y. |
| Renteria, David | .187 | 31 | 107 | 10 | 20 | 2 | 1 | 0 | 9 | 3 | 26 | 1 | 0 | R | R | 6-0 | 175 | 12-1-72 | 1992 | Belen, N.M. |
| Roberts, John | .134 | 28 | 67 | 7 | 9 | 1 | 2 | 2 | 8 | 7 | 26 | 1 | 0 | R | R | 5-9 | 185 | 9-30-73 | 1991 | Pine Bluff, Ark. |

| BATTING | AVG | G | AB | R | H | 2B | 3B | HR | RBI | BB | SO | SB | CS | B | T | HT | WT | DOB | 1st Yr | Resides |
|---|---|---|---|---|---|---|---|---|---|---|---|---|---|---|---|---|---|---|---|---|
| Stovall, Darond | .452 | 8 | 31 | 8 | 14 | 4 | 0 | 1 | 8 | 6 | 7 | 2 | 2 | S | L | 6-1 | 185 | 1-3-73 | 1991 | East St. Louis, Ill. |
| White, Rondell | .200 | 3 | 10 | 0 | 2 | 1 | 0 | 0 | 2 | 0 | 4 | 0 | 1 | R | R | 6-1 | 193 | 2-23-92 | 1990 | Gray, Ga. |

**GAMES BY POSITION: C**—Brinkley 23, Brown 1, Haas 27, Koeyers 9, Morales 55, Pachot 40. **1B**—Brown 63, Campos 1, Fullmer 9, Giardi 7, Haas 18, Hacopian 29, Morales 1, Post 20. **2B**—Bravo 44, Carvajal 33, Coquillette 36, Giardi 2, Post 30. **3B**—Alcantara 14, Brinkley 30, Carvajal 22, Coquillette 33, Foster 2, Giardi 30, Post 14, Renteria 1. **SS**—Bocachica 27, Bravo 4, Carvajal 64, Post 15, Renteria 30. **OF**—Bady 127, Blakeney 6, Brinkley 10, Brown 33, Campos 43, Fullmer 81, Giardi 9, Guerrero 20, Haas 18, Mathews 8, McDavid 4, Ottavinia 45, Post 5, Roberts 24, Stovall 8, White 1.

| PITCHING | W | L | ERA | G | GS | CG | SV | IP | H | R | ER | BB | SO | B | T | HT | WT | DOB | 1st Yr | Resides |
|---|---|---|---|---|---|---|---|---|---|---|---|---|---|---|---|---|---|---|---|---|
| Bell, Mike | 0 | 1 | 8.80 | 13 | 0 | 0 | 0 | 15 | 27 | 19 | 15 | 11 | 11 | L | L | 6-2 | 195 | 10-14-72 | 1995 | Sarasota, Fla. |
| Benz, Jake | 2 | 4 | 2.21 | 16 | 0 | 0 | 2 | 20 | 19 | 10 | 5 | 11 | 14 | L | L | 5-9 | 162 | 2-27-72 | 1994 | Pleasant Hill, Calif. |
| Boucher, Denis | 1 | 0 | 2.84 | 2 | 2 | 0 | 0 | 13 | 12 | 4 | 4 | 2 | 5 | R | L | 6-1 | 195 | 3-7-68 | 1988 | Lachine, Quebec |
| Centeno, Jose | 4 | 4 | 3.90 | 37 | 0 | 0 | 4 | 60 | 64 | 30 | 26 | 19 | 47 | L | L | 6-1 | 168 | 11-9-72 | 1993 | Anzoategui, Venez. |
| Cole, Jason | 6 | 1 | 2.31 | 39 | 0 | 0 | 3 | 62 | 57 | 25 | 16 | 20 | 40 | R | R | 6-3 | 198 | 9-8-72 | 1994 | Coventry, R.I. |
| DaSilva, Fernando | 4 | 2 | 2.57 | 40 | 0 | 0 | 0 | 67 | 58 | 23 | 19 | 20 | 45 | R | R | 6-2 | 194 | 9-6-71 | 1991 | Brossard, Quebec |
| Dixon, Tim | 5 | 11 | 2.90 | 37 | 16 | 0 | 2 | 124 | 126 | 55 | 40 | 35 | 87 | L | L | 6-2 | 215 | 2-26-72 | 1995 | San Jose, Calif. |
| Durocher, Jayson | 7 | 6 | 3.34 | 23 | 23 | 1 | 0 | 129 | 118 | 65 | 48 | 44 | 101 | R | R | 6-3 | 195 | 8-18-74 | 1993 | Scottsdale, Ariz. |
| Fleetham, Ben | 1 | 2 | 2.05 | 31 | 0 | 0 | 17 | 31 | 15 | 8 | 7 | 15 | 48 | R | R | 6-1 | 205 | 8-3-72 | 1994 | Minneapolis, Minn. |
| Franko, Kris | 2 | 1 | 3.75 | 9 | 0 | 0 | 0 | 12 | 10 | 6 | 5 | 4 | 3 | L | L | 6-0 | 185 | 9-26-70 | 1993 | Cumberland, Ohio |
| Gentile, Scott | 0 | 0 | .00 | 7 | 0 | 0 | 1 | 10 | 8 | 0 | 0 | 2 | 5 | R | R | 5-11 | 210 | 12-21-70 | 1992 | Berlin, Conn. |
| Handy, Russell | 2 | 4 | 9.09 | 14 | 5 | 0 | 0 | 32 | 43 | 40 | 32 | 28 | 12 | R | R | 6-4 | 200 | 8-4-74 | 1993 | Bakersfield, Calif. |
| Marquez, Robert | 1 | 1 | 7.36 | 11 | 0 | 0 | 6 | 11 | 14 | 10 | 9 | 5 | 8 | R | R | 6-0 | 180 | 4-21-73 | 1995 | Houston, Texas |
| Martinez, Ramiro | 1 | 0 | 3.40 | 9 | 7 | 0 | 0 | 42 | 47 | 20 | 16 | 14 | 44 | L | L | 6-2 | 185 | 1-28-72 | 1992 | Los Angeles, Calif. |
| Moraga, David | 7 | 10 | 4.58 | 29 | 20 | 1 | 0 | 126 | 138 | 74 | 64 | 50 | 96 | L | L | 6-0 | 184 | 7-8-75 | 1994 | Suisun City, Calif. |
| Phelps, Tommy | 10 | 2 | 2.89 | 18 | 18 | 1 | 0 | 112 | 105 | 42 | 36 | 35 | 71 | L | L | 6-3 | 192 | 3-4-74 | 1993 | Tampa, Fla. |
| Rhodriguez, Rory | 5 | 2 | 4.10 | 35 | 2 | 0 | 0 | 68 | 57 | 33 | 31 | 37 | 48 | R | R | 5-10 | 175 | 2-26-71 | 1991 | Carol City, Fla. |
| Stubbs, Jerry | 0 | 0 | 6.00 | 7 | 0 | 0 | 0 | 9 | 11 | 7 | 6 | 5 | 3 | R | R | 6-2 | 180 | 3-4-72 | 1994 | Hutchinson, Kan. |
| Thurman, Mike | 6 | 8 | 3.40 | 19 | 19 | 1 | 0 | 114 | 122 | 53 | 43 | 23 | 68 | R | R | 6-5 | 190 | 7-22-73 | 1994 | Philomath, Ore. |
| Urbina, Ugueth | 1 | 1 | 1.29 | 3 | 3 | 0 | 0 | 14 | 13 | 3 | 2 | 3 | 21 | R | R | 6-2 | 170 | 2-15-74 | 1991 | Caracas, Venez. |
| Weidert, Chris | 3 | 8 | 3.40 | 20 | 20 | 1 | 0 | 106 | 106 | 54 | 40 | 37 | 64 | R | R | 6-3 | 210 | 4-3-74 | 1994 | Emporia, Kan. |

# DELMARVA    Class A
## SOUTH ATLANTIC LEAGUE

| BATTING | AVG | G | AB | R | H | 2B | 3B | HR | RBI | BB | SO | SB | CS | B | T | HT | WT | DOB | 1st Yr | Resides |
|---|---|---|---|---|---|---|---|---|---|---|---|---|---|---|---|---|---|---|---|---|
| Acosta, Ed | .191 | 32 | 68 | 11 | 13 | 0 | 1 | 0 | 5 | 3 | 20 | 0 | 0 | R | R | 6-1 | 160 | 12-5-71 | 1993 | Rock Falls, Ill. |
| Adolfo, Carlos | .272 | 132 | 492 | 82 | 134 | 20 | 8 | 10 | 71 | 47 | 106 | 18 | 6 | R | R | 5-11 | 160 | 4-20-76 | 1994 | Santo Domingo, D.R. |
| Alvarado, Basilio | .308 | 6 | 13 | 1 | 4 | 0 | 0 | 0 | 1 | 0 | 2 | 0 | 0 | R | R | 5-11 | 199 | 7-20-74 | 1992 | Santo Domingo, D.R. |
| Barrett, Michael | .238 | 129 | 474 | 57 | 113 | 29 | 4 | 4 | 62 | 18 | 42 | 5 | 11 | R | R | 6-3 | 185 | 10-22-76 | 1995 | Alpharetta, Ga. |
| Blakeney, Mo | .255 | 41 | 110 | 13 | 28 | 7 | 0 | 1 | 11 | 7 | 20 | 3 | 5 | R | R | 5-10 | 165 | 1-17-73 | 1995 | Kannapolis, N.C. |
| Bravo, Danny | .230 | 18 | 61 | 10 | 14 | 6 | 1 | 0 | 7 | 2 | 14 | 1 | 0 | S | R | 5-11 | 175 | 5-27-77 | 1996 | Maracaibo, Venez. |
| Cabrera, Orlando | .252 | 134 | 512 | 86 | 129 | 28 | 4 | 14 | 65 | 54 | 63 | 51 | 18 | R | R | 5-11 | 165 | 3-2-74 | 1994 | Cartagena, Colombia |
| Camilli, Jason | .223 | 119 | 426 | 53 | 95 | 13 | 2 | 3 | 36 | 63 | 89 | 26 | 17 | R | R | 6-0 | 178 | 10-18-75 | 1994 | Phoenix, Ariz. |
| Denning, Wes | .221 | 115 | 349 | 60 | 77 | 17 | 8 | 4 | 37 | 43 | 63 | 31 | 10 | L | R | 5-11 | 180 | 12-30-72 | 1995 | St. Paul, Minn. |
| Fernandez, Jose | .273 | 126 | 421 | 72 | 115 | 23 | 6 | 12 | 70 | 50 | 76 | 23 | 10 | R | R | 6-2 | 210 | 11-2-74 | 1993 | Santiago, D.R. |
| Garcia, Jaime | .236 | 62 | 182 | 27 | 43 | 14 | 1 | 5 | 19 | 22 | 51 | 1 | 4 | R | R | 5-8 | 180 | 5-8-72 | 1995 | Tolleson, Ariz. |
| Macias, Jose | .247 | 116 | 369 | 64 | 91 | 13 | 4 | 1 | 33 | 56 | 48 | 38 | 15 | S | R | 5-10 | 173 | 1-25-74 | 1992 | Panama, Panama |
| Oliveras, Ricardo | .250 | 4 | 4 | 0 | 1 | 1 | 0 | 0 | 0 | 0 | 2 | 0 | 0 | R | R | 6-0 | 175 | 1-11-75 | 1993 | Caracas, Venez |
| Olsen, D.C. | .213 | 91 | 291 | 26 | 62 | 13 | 1 | 5 | 42 | 24 | 60 | 3 | 2 | R | R | 6-0 | 220 | 5-3-72 | 1995 | Oakhurst, Calif. |
| Schneider, Brian | .333 | 5 | 9 | 0 | 3 | 0 | 0 | 0 | 1 | 1 | 1 | 0 | 0 | L | R | 6-1 | 180 | 11-26-76 | 1995 | Cherryville, Pa. |
| Schwab, Chris | .224 | 119 | 428 | 52 | 96 | 30 | 3 | 9 | 64 | 45 | 135 | 3 | 4 | R | L | 6-3 | 215 | 7-25-74 | 1993 | Eagan, Minn. |
| Seguignol, Fernando | .239 | 118 | 410 | 59 | 98 | 14 | 5 | 8 | 55 | 48 | 126 | 12 | 13 | S | R | 6-5 | 179 | 1-19-75 | 1993 | Panama City, Panama |

**GAMES BY POSITION: C**—Barrett 83, Garcia 56, Oliveras 3, Schneider 5. **1B**—Olsen 76, Schwab 72. **2B**—Acosta 13, Bravo 1, Cabrera 64, Camilli 49, Macias 29. **3B**—Acosta 13, Barrett 1, Bravo 7, Fernandez 124, Macias 10. **SS**—Acosta 2, Bravo 8, Cabrera 67, Camilli 69. **OF**—Acosta 3, Adolfo 126, Blakeney 35, Denning 112, Fernandez 1, Macias 70, Schwab 5, Seguignol 106.

| PITCHING | W | L | ERA | G | GS | CG | SV | IP | H | R | ER | BB | SO | B | T | HT | WT | DOB | 1st Yr | Resides |
|---|---|---|---|---|---|---|---|---|---|---|---|---|---|---|---|---|---|---|---|---|
| Baker, Jason | 9 | 7 | 2.81 | 27 | 27 | 2 | 0 | 160 | 127 | 70 | 50 | 77 | 147 | R | R | 6-4 | 195 | 11-21-74 | 1993 | Midland, Texas |
| Bell, Mike | 6 | 1 | 1.36 | 40 | 0 | 0 | 5 | 60 | 39 | 13 | 9 | 18 | 59 | L | L | 6-2 | 195 | 10-14-72 | 1995 | Sarasota, Fla. |
| Centeno, Jose | 1 | 0 | 2.28 | 11 | 0 | 0 | 0 | 24 | 20 | 7 | 6 | 4 | 22 | L | L | 6-1 | 168 | 11-9-72 | 1993 | Anzoategui, Venez. |
| Civit, Xavier | 3 | 4 | 3.68 | 34 | 0 | 0 | 0 | 51 | 42 | 31 | 21 | 20 | 57 | R | R | 6-2 | 175 | 5-17-73 | 1993 | Barcelona, Spain |
| Cole, Jason | 1 | 2 | 1.02 | 10 | 0 | 0 | 1 | 18 | 11 | 4 | 2 | 1 | 20 | R | R | 6-3 | 198 | 9-8-72 | 1994 | Coventry, R.I. |
| Fleetham, Ben | 1 | 1 | 1.37 | 16 | 0 | 0 | 13 | 20 | 9 | 4 | 3 | 7 | 34 | R | R | 6-1 | 205 | 8-3-72 | 1994 | Minneapolis, Minn. |
| Handy, Russell | 2 | 3 | 5.45 | 24 | 0 | 0 | 4 | 38 | 40 | 38 | 23 | 36 | 28 | R | R | 6-4 | 200 | 8-4-74 | 1993 | Bakersfield, Calif. |
| Leslie, Sean | 1 | 2 | 2.63 | 18 | 4 | 1 | 0 | 38 | 25 | 13 | 11 | 9 | 23 | R | L | 6-2 | 212 | 12-15-73 | 1996 | Willits, Calif. |
| Marquez, Robert | 1 | 2 | 3.66 | 29 | 0 | 0 | 1 | 47 | 44 | 23 | 19 | 22 | 49 | R | R | 6-0 | 180 | 4-21-73 | 1995 | Houston, Texas |
| Mattes, Troy | 10 | 9 | 2.86 | 27 | 27 | 5 | 0 | 173 | 142 | 77 | 55 | 50 | 151 | R | R | 6-7 | 185 | 8-26-75 | 1994 | Sarasota, Fla. |
| Mitchell, Scott | 5 | 6 | 2.35 | 33 | 5 | 1 | 1 | 77 | 69 | 29 | 20 | 24 | 76 | R | R | 5-11 | 170 | 3-19-73 | 1995 | Citrus Heights, Calif. |
| Powell, Jeremy | 12 | 9 | 3.03 | 27 | 27 | 1 | 0 | 158 | 127 | 68 | 53 | 66 | 109 | R | R | 6-5 | 230 | 6-18-76 | 1994 | Sacramento, Calif. |
| Smart, J.D. | 9 | 8 | 3.39 | 25 | 25 | 3 | 0 | 157 | 155 | 75 | 59 | 31 | 109 | L | R | 6-2 | 185 | 11-12-73 | 1995 | Austin, Texas |
| Vazquez, Javier | 14 | 3 | 2.68 | 27 | 27 | 1 | 0 | 164 | 138 | 64 | 49 | 57 | 173 | R | R | 6-2 | 175 | 6-25-76 | 1994 | Ponce, P.R. |
| Woodring, Jason | 8 | 3 | 1.84 | 46 | 0 | 0 | 12 | 59 | 42 | 17 | 12 | 17 | 43 | R | R | 6-3 | 190 | 4-2-74 | 1993 | Trinidad, Colo. |

# VERMONT    Class A
## NEW YORK-PENN LEAGUE

| BATTING | AVG | G | AB | R | H | 2B | 3B | HR | RBI | BB | SO | SB | CS | B | T | HT | WT | DOB | 1st Yr | Resides |
|---|---|---|---|---|---|---|---|---|---|---|---|---|---|---|---|---|---|---|---|---|
| Alvarado, Basilio | .234 | 49 | 171 | 16 | 40 | 8 | 1 | 1 | 22 | 3 | 37 | 0 | 3 | R | R | 5-11 | 199 | 7-20-74 | 1992 | Santo Domingo, D.R. |
| Barlow, Ethan | .250 | 42 | 116 | 18 | 29 | 1 | 0 | 0 | 8 | 14 | 20 | 8 | 5 | L | L | 5-7 | 170 | 4-24-74 | 1996 | Cambridge, Mass. |
| Blandford, Paul | .247 | 64 | 231 | 39 | 57 | 11 | 7 | 1 | 39 | 34 | 37 | 11 | 9 | R | R | 5-10 | 175 | 3-29-74 | 1996 | Elk Grove, Calif. |
| Buirley, Matt | .174 | 35 | 115 | 10 | 20 | 4 | 0 | 1 | 8 | 9 | 46 | 1 | 2 | R | R | 6-3 | 210 | 7-21-75 | 1996 | Gambier, Ohio |
| Carroll, Jamey | .276 | 54 | 203 | 40 | 56 | 6 | 1 | 0 | 17 | 29 | 25 | 16 | 11 | R | R | 5-11 | 165 | 2-18-75 | 1996 | Newburgh, N.Y. |
| Chatman, Karl | .265 | 72 | 260 | 47 | 69 | 11 | 3 | 1 | 38 | 27 | 52 | 16 | 6 | R | R | 6-1 | 190 | 1-17-75 | 1996 | Nacogdoches, Texas |
| De la Rosa, Tomas | .250 | 3 | 8 | 1 | 2 | 0 | 0 | 0 | 1 | 0 | 3 | 0 | 0 | R | R | 5-10 | 155 | 1-28-78 | 1996 | La Victoria, D.R. |
| Gonzalez, Freddy | .209 | 14 | 43 | 7 | 9 | 2 | 1 | 0 | 6 | 7 | 12 | 2 | 0 | S | R | 5-11 | 175 | 12-2-73 | 1993 | Barcelona, Venez. |

| BATTING | AVG | G | AB | R | H | 2B | 3B | HR | RBI | BB | SO | SB | CS | B | T | HT | WT | DOB | 1st Yr | Resides |
|---|---|---|---|---|---|---|---|---|---|---|---|---|---|---|---|---|---|---|---|---|
| MacKay, Tripp | .244 | 46 | 172 | 29 | 42 | 4 | 0 | 1 | 12 | 25 | 29 | 9 | 7 | S | R | 5-10 | 170 | 8-15-73 | 1996 | Mt. Pleasant, Texas |
| Oropeza, William | .297 | 37 | 128 | 13 | 38 | 9 | 1 | 1 | 26 | 3 | 20 | 1 | 1 | R | R | 6-1 | 175 | 10-16-75 | 1994 | LaGuaira, Venez. |
| Pond, Simon | .300 | 69 | 253 | 37 | 76 | 16 | 1 | 3 | 40 | 26 | 26 | 9 | 3 | L | R | 6-1 | 175 | 10-27-76 | 1994 | North Vancouver, B.C. |
| Stowers, Chris | .319 | 72 | 282 | 58 | 90 | 21 | 9 | 7 | 44 | 21 | 37 | 16 | 5 | L | L | 6-3 | 195 | 8-18-74 | 1996 | Marietta, Ga. |
| Swaino, Shannon | .284 | 50 | 155 | 20 | 44 | 10 | 1 | 0 | 21 | 23 | 31 | 0 | 2 | L | R | 6-0 | 205 | 9-26-74 | 1996 | Akron, Ohio |
| Tracy, Andrew | .269 | 57 | 175 | 26 | 47 | 11 | 1 | 4 | 24 | 32 | 37 | 1 | 1 | L | R | 6-3 | 220 | 12-11-73 | 1996 | Bowling Green, Ohio |
| Ware, Jeremy | .191 | 32 | 94 | 12 | 18 | 2 | 0 | 0 | 6 | 15 | 25 | 5 | 3 | R | R | 6-1 | 190 | 10-23-75 | 1995 | Guelph, Ontario |

**GAMES BY POSITION: C**—Alvarado 48, Buirley 14, Swaino 17. **1B**—Oropeza 22, Swaino 6, Tracy 52. **2B**—Blandford 56, Carroll 2, MacKay 18. **3B**—Carroll 2, Oropeza 7, Pond 67, Tracy 1. **SS**—Carroll 49, De la Rosa 3, Mackay 26. **OF**—Barlow 39, Buirley 5, Chatman 72, Gonzales 13, Stowers 70, Ware 31.

| PITCHING | W | L | ERA | G | GS | CG | SV | IP | H | R | ER | BB | SO | B | T | HT | WT | DOB | 1st Yr | Resides |
|---|---|---|---|---|---|---|---|---|---|---|---|---|---|---|---|---|---|---|---|---|
| Figueroa, Julio | 5 | 3 | 3.30 | 14 | 14 | 1 | 0 | 79 | 78 | 37 | 29 | 32 | 59 | R | R | 6-1 | 179 | 6-29-74 | 1992 | La Romana, D.R. |
| Fortune, Peter | 0 | 1 | 3.86 | 2 | 0 | 0 | 0 | 2 | 3 | 2 | 1 | 2 | 2 | L | L | 6-2 | 190 | 3-4-75 | 1995 | Valley Cottage, N.Y. |
| Garsky, Brian | 5 | 1 | 3.18 | 25 | 0 | 0 | 1 | 28 | 25 | 13 | 10 | 15 | 34 | R | R | 6-1 | 172 | 10-14-75 | 1995 | Clinton Township, Mich. |
| Lara, Giovanni | 6 | 3 | 4.68 | 15 | 15 | 2 | 0 | 92 | 95 | 54 | 48 | 27 | 63 | R | R | 6-2 | 163 | 9-20-75 | 1993 | San Cristobal, D.R. |
| Leslie, Sean | 2 | 4 | 4.12 | 17 | 7 | 0 | 0 | 55 | 52 | 28 | 25 | 14 | 46 | R | L | 6-2 | 212 | 12-15-73 | 1996 | Willits, Calif. |
| Matz, Brian | 5 | 3 | 2.60 | 14 | 9 | 0 | 0 | 55 | 41 | 20 | 16 | 18 | 53 | L | L | 6-1 | 195 | 9-23-74 | 1996 | Towson, Md. |
| Morris, Chad | 2 | 1 | 3.69 | 20 | 0 | 0 | 0 | 32 | 20 | 13 | 13 | 10 | 44 | R | R | 6-3 | 193 | 7-6-72 | 1995 | Florence, S.C. |
| Parker, Christian | 7 | 1 | 2.48 | 14 | 14 | 2 | 0 | 80 | 63 | 26 | 22 | 22 | 61 | R | R | 6-1 | 200 | 7-3-75 | 1996 | Albuquereque, N.M. |
| Quezada, Edward | 6 | 5 | 2.33 | 14 | 14 | 2 | 0 | 93 | 82 | 32 | 24 | 20 | 79 | R | R | 6-2 | 150 | 1-15-75 | 1993 | Santana Nizao, D.R. |
| Rosado, Juan | 1 | 0 | 3.32 | 12 | 0 | 0 | 0 | 19 | 20 | 9 | 7 | 9 | 19 | L | L | 5-11 | 180 | 8-6-74 | 1994 | Camuy, P.R. |
| Stevenson, Rodney | 5 | 2 | 2.84 | 22 | 0 | 0 | 1 | 32 | 24 | 11 | 10 | 13 | 46 | R | R | 6-2 | 210 | 3-21-74 | 1996 | Columbus, Ga. |
| Westover, Richard | 3 | 2 | 2.41 | 18 | 1 | 0 | 0 | 34 | 24 | 10 | 9 | 8 | 23 | R | R | 6-3 | 210 | 6-11-96 | 1996 | Brooklyn, N.Y. |
| Young, Tim | 1 | 0 | 0.31 | 27 | 0 | 0 | 18 | 29 | 14 | 1 | 1 | 4 | 46 | L | L | 5-9 | 170 | 10-15-73 | 1996 | Bristol, Fla. |

# WEST PALM BEACH · Rookie

## GULF COAST LEAGUE

| BATTING | AVG | G | AB | R | H | 2B | 3B | HR | RBI | BB | SO | SB | CS | B | T | HT | WT | DOB | 1st Yr | Resides |
|---|---|---|---|---|---|---|---|---|---|---|---|---|---|---|---|---|---|---|---|---|
| Alcantara, Israel | .300 | 7 | 30 | 4 | 9 | 2 | 0 | 2 | 10 | 3 | 6 | 0 | 1 | R | R | 6-2 | 165 | 5-6-73 | 1991 | Santo Domingo, D.R. |
| Bagley, Sean | .246 | 42 | 118 | 27 | 29 | 7 | 0 | 0 | 12 | 11 | 29 | 9 | 2 | R | R | 6-3 | 195 | 6-20-76 | 1994 | Gig Harbor, Wash. |
| Besford, Tim | .083 | 10 | 12 | 1 | 1 | 0 | 0 | 0 | 0 | 1 | 5 | 0 | 0 | S | R | 6-2 | 170 | 7-1-77 | 1996 | Melbourne,Australia |
| Bocachica, Hiram | .250 | 9 | 32 | 11 | 8 | 3 | 0 | 0 | 2 | 5 | 3 | 2 | 1 | R | R | 5-11 | 165 | 3-4-76 | 1994 | Bayamon, P.R. |
| Bradley, Milton | .241 | 32 | 112 | 18 | 27 | 7 | 1 | 1 | 12 | 13 | 15 | 7 | 4 | S | R | 6-0 | 170 | 4-15-78 | 1996 | Long Beach, Calif. |
| Coquillette, Trace | .160 | 7 | 25 | 4 | 4 | 1 | 0 | 0 | 0 | 4 | 6 | 1 | 0 | R | R | 5-11 | 165 | 6-4-74 | 1993 | Orangevale, Calif. |
| Daniels, Ronny | .208 | 46 | 159 | 29 | 33 | 6 | 4 | 3 | 28 | 18 | 44 | 9 | 2 | R | L | 6-3 | 210 | 9-17-76 | 1995 | Lake Wales, Fla. |
| Davis, Torrance | .255 | 27 | 55 | 13 | 14 | 1 | 0 | 0 | 7 | 4 | 7 | 1 | 4 | R | R | 6-1 | 180 | 12-25-75 | 1995 | Texarkana, Texas |
| De la Rosa, Tomas | .251 | 54 | 187 | 35 | 47 | 7 | 1 | 0 | 21 | 22 | 25 | 8 | 5 | R | R | 5-10 | 155 | 1-28-78 | 1996 | La Victoria, D.R. |
| Hall, Noah | .248 | 42 | 137 | 25 | 34 | 5 | 3 | 1 | 18 | 19 | 22 | 6 | 2 | R | R | 5-11 | 200 | 6-9-77 | 1996 | Aptos, Calif. |
| Hernandez, Rafael | .210 | 37 | 100 | 13 | 21 | 2 | 1 | 0 | 12 | 10 | 30 | 6 | 4 | R | R | 5-10 | 155 | 9-23-75 | 1995 | San Pedro de Macoris, D.R. |
| James, Kenny | .208 | 45 | 168 | 24 | 35 | 5 | 2 | 0 | 12 | 15 | 34 | 4 | 3 | S | R | 6-0 | 198 | 10-9-76 | 1995 | Sebring, Fla. |
| Koeyers, Ramsey | .158 | 7 | 19 | 2 | 3 | 1 | 0 | 0 | 0 | 3 | 6 | 0 | 0 | R | R | 5-11 | 187 | 8-7-74 | 1991 | Brievengst, Curacao |
| Leidens, Enrique | .221 | 27 | 77 | 8 | 17 | 1 | 0 | 1 | 6 | 8 | 14 | 6 | 2 | R | R | 5-11 | 165 | 2-6-78 | 1995 | Aragua, Venez. |
| Llanos, Francisco | .176 | 27 | 74 | 5 | 13 | 5 | 0 | 0 | 10 | 7 | 23 | 0 | 1 | R | R | 6-2 | 218 | 10-20-76 | 1995 | Carolina, P.R. |
| Mateo, Henry | .250 | 14 | 44 | 8 | 11 | 3 | 0 | 0 | 3 | 5 | 11 | 5 | 1 | S | R | 5-11 | 170 | 10-14-76 | 1995 | Santurce, P.R. |
| McDavid, Ray | .273 | 4 | 11 | 2 | 3 | 0 | 1 | 0 | 0 | 3 | 3 | 1 | 0 | L | R | 6-3 | 195 | 7-20-71 | 1989 | San Diego, Calif. |
| Oliveros, Ricardo | .000 | 1 | 0 | 0 | 0 | 0 | 0 | 0 | 0 | 0 | 0 | 0 | 0 | R | R | 6-0 | 175 | 1-11-75 | 1993 | Caracas, Venez. |
| Oropeza, William | .167 | 5 | 18 | 2 | 3 | 0 | 0 | 0 | 1 | 5 | 0 | 0 | 0 | R | R | 6-1 | 175 | 10-16-75 | 1994 | LaGuaira, Venez. |
| Ottavinia, Paul | .400 | 3 | 10 | 1 | 4 | 0 | 0 | 0 | 1 | 2 | 1 | 0 | 0 | L | L | 6-1 | 190 | 4-22-73 | 1994 | Flanders, N.J. |
| Ovalles, Homy | .255 | 48 | 161 | 19 | 41 | 7 | 4 | 0 | 30 | 7 | 24 | 4 | 6 | R | R | 5-10 | 160 | 7-6-76 | 1994 | Miranda, Venez. |
| Pachot, John | .300 | 8 | 30 | 3 | 9 | 1 | 1 | 0 | 3 | 1 | 0 | 0 | 0 | R | R | 6-2 | 168 | 11-11-74 | 1993 | Ponce, P.R. |
| Post, Dave | .080 | 8 | 25 | 3 | 2 | 0 | 0 | 1 | 1 | 4 | 6 | 1 | 0 | R | R | 5-11 | 170 | 9-3-73 | 1992 | Kingston, N.Y. |
| Rivera, Luis | .059 | 22 | 51 | 2 | 3 | 0 | 0 | 0 | 2 | 5 | 13 | 0 | 1 | R | R | 6-3 | 185 | 12-21-77 | 1996 | Bayamon, P.R. |
| Schneider, Brian | .268 | 52 | 164 | 26 | 44 | 5 | 2 | 0 | 23 | 24 | 15 | 2 | 3 | L | R | 6-1 | 180 | 11-26-76 | 1995 | Cherryville, Pa. |
| Stovall, DaRond | .441 | 9 | 34 | 5 | 15 | 3 | 2 | 0 | 7 | 3 | 6 | 3 | 0 | S | L | 6-1 | 185 | 1-3-73 | 1991 | East St. Louis, Ill. |
| Ware, Jeremy | .364 | 15 | 44 | 10 | 16 | 3 | 3 | 0 | 17 | 9 | 4 | 6 | 1 | R | R | 6-1 | 190 | 10-23-75 | 1995 | Guelph, Ontario |
| White, Rondell | .250 | 3 | 12 | 3 | 3 | 0 | 0 | 2 | 4 | 0 | 1 | 1 | 0 | R | R | 6-1 | 193 | 2-23-72 | 1990 | Gray, Ga. |

**GAMES BY POSITION: C**—Besford 5, Koeyers 7, Pachot 4, Rivera 20, Schneider 41. **1B**—Bagley 42, Llanos 26, Oropeza 1. **2B**—Coquillette 4, Hernandez 1, Leidens 17, Mateo 14, Ovalles 21, Post 8. **3B**—Alcantara 5, Bagley 1, Coquillette 3, Hernandez 33, Ovalles 25. **SS**—De la Rosa 53, Leidens 10. **OF**—Bradley 30, Daniels 42, Davis 25, Hall 26, James 44, McDavid 1, Ottavinia 3, Ovalles 1, Stovall 7, Ware 14, White 3.

| PITCHING | W | L | ERA | G | GS | CG | SV | IP | H | R | ER | BB | SO | B | T | HT | WT | DOB | 1st Yr | Resides |
|---|---|---|---|---|---|---|---|---|---|---|---|---|---|---|---|---|---|---|---|---|
| Fortune, Peter | 6 | 0 | 1.96 | 13 | 13 | 0 | 0 | 73 | 52 | 23 | 16 | 21 | 66 | L | L | 6-2 | 190 | 3-4-75 | 1995 | Valley Cottage, N.Y. |
| Fraser, Joe | 4 | 0 | 1.81 | 11 | 10 | 0 | 0 | 50 | 35 | 14 | 10 | 18 | 45 | R | R | 6-1 | 195 | 10-23-77 | 1996 | Anaheim, Calif. |
| Gentile, Scott | 1 | 1 | 4.91 | 5 | 1 | 0 | 1 | 7 | 5 | 4 | 4 | 4 | 5 | R | R | 5-11 | 210 | 12-21-70 | 1992 | Berlin, Conn. |
| Martin, Curtis | 2 | 0 | 2.40 | 8 | 1 | 0 | 0 | 15 | 13 | 4 | 4 | 2 | 6 | L | L | 6-2 | 190 | 11-22-77 | 1996 | Merritt Island, Fla. |
| Martin, Trey | 6 | 0 | 5.44 | 13 | 8 | 1 | 2 | 51 | 50 | 36 | 31 | 14 | 35 | R | R | 6-2 | 175 | 10-2-76 | 1995 | Phoenix, Ariz. |
| Orta, Juan | 3 | 0 | 2.53 | 20 | 0 | 0 | 1 | 32 | 21 | 10 | 9 | 11 | 15 | R | R | 6-2 | 175 | 4-13-78 | 1995 | Maracay, Venez. |
| Powley, Greg | 1 | 3 | 3.65 | 13 | 6 | 0 | 0 | 44 | 37 | 19 | 18 | 11 | 34 | R | R | 6-2 | 170 | 4-12-76 | 1996 | Carmel Mountain, Calif. |
| Rivera, Marcos | 4 | 2 | 2.12 | 18 | 1 | 0 | 3 | 34 | 33 | 9 | 8 | 7 | 16 | L | L | 5-11 | 160 | 2-28-77 | 1996 | Arecibo, P.R. |
| Sadler, William | 2 | 2 | 3.89 | 17 | 3 | 0 | 1 | 37 | 41 | 24 | 16 | 12 | 24 | L | L | 6-2 | 180 | 10-11-76 | 1996 | Perry, Fla. |
| Salyers, Jeremy | 1 | 4 | 4.26 | 11 | 9 | 2 | 1 | 57 | 47 | 36 | 27 | 26 | 30 | R | R | 6-3 | 205 | 1-31-76 | 1996 | Pound, Va. |
| Sanchez, Bienvenido | 1 | 2 | 6.10 | 6 | 0 | 0 | 0 | 10 | 20 | 12 | 7 | 2 | 5 | R | R | 6-1 | 185 | 10-14-75 | 1995 | Arecibo, P.R. |
| Sorzano, Ronnie | 3 | 2 | 2.60 | 15 | 5 | 0 | 3 | 45 | 39 | 16 | 13 | 8 | 27 | R | R | 6-3 | 180 | 3-7-76 | 1994 | Caracas, Venez. |
| Sparks, Eric | 4 | 0 | 2.76 | 14 | 1 | 0 | 3 | 29 | 25 | 10 | 9 | 5 | 10 | S | L | 6-1 | 210 | 6-2-74 | 1996 | Hoosick Falls, N.Y. |
| Stading, Kris | 2 | 1 | 1.80 | 12 | 1 | 0 | 0 | 20 | 11 | 4 | 4 | 9 | 20 | L | L | 6-7 | 235 | 12-24-76 | 1995 | Phoenix, Ariz. |
| Weidert, Chris | 0 | 0 | 1.80 | 2 | 1 | 0 | 0 | 5 | 2 | 1 | 1 | 0 | 2 | R | R | 6-3 | 210 | 4-3-74 | 1994 | Emporia, Kan. |
| Westover, Richard | 0 | 0 | 0.00 | 1 | 0 | 0 | 0 | 1 | 0 | 0 | 0 | 0 | 1 | R | R | 6-3 | 210 | 6-11-96 | 1996 | Brooklyn, N.Y. |

# NEW YORK YANKEES

**Manager:** Joe Torre.  **1996 Record:** 92-70, .568 (1st, AL East).

| BATTING | AVG | G | AB | R | H | 2B | 3B | HR | RBI | BB | SO | SB | CS | B | T | HT | WT | DOB | 1st Yr | Resides |
|---|---|---|---|---|---|---|---|---|---|---|---|---|---|---|---|---|---|---|---|---|
| Aldrete, Mike | .250 | 32 | 68 | 11 | 17 | 5 | 0 | 3 | 12 | 9 | 15 | 0 | 1 | L | L | 5-11 | 180 | 1-29-61 | 1983 | Monterey, Calif. |
| 2-team (31 Calif.) | .213 | 63 | 108 | 16 | 23 | 6 | 0 | 6 | 20 | 14 | 19 | 0 | 1 | | | | | | | |
| Boggs, Wade | .311 | 132 | 501 | 80 | 156 | 29 | 2 | 2 | 41 | 67 | 32 | 1 | 2 | L | R | 6-2 | 197 | 6-15-58 | 1976 | Tampa, Fla. |
| Duncan, Mariano | .340 | 109 | 400 | 62 | 136 | 34 | 3 | 8 | 56 | 9 | 77 | 4 | 3 | R | R | 6-0 | 185 | 3-13-63 | 1982 | Cherry Hill, N.J. |
| Eenhoorn, Robert | .071 | 12 | 14 | 2 | 1 | 0 | 0 | 0 | 2 | 2 | 3 | 0 | 0 | R | R | 6-3 | 175 | 2-9-68 | 1990 | Rotterdam, Holland |
| Fielder, Cecil | .260 | 53 | 200 | 30 | 52 | 8 | 0 | 13 | 37 | 24 | 48 | 0 | 0 | R | R | 6-3 | 250 | 9-21-63 | 1982 | Grosse Pte. Farms, Mich. |
| 2-team (107 Detroit) | .252 | 160 | 591 | 85 | 149 | 20 | 0 | 39 | 117 | 87 | 139 | 2 | 0 | | | | | | | |
| Fox, Andy | .196 | 113 | 189 | 26 | 37 | 4 | 0 | 3 | 13 | 20 | 28 | 11 | 3 | L | R | 6-4 | 185 | 1-12-71 | 1989 | Sacramento, Calif. |
| Girardi, Joe | .294 | 124 | 422 | 55 | 124 | 22 | 3 | 2 | 45 | 30 | 55 | 13 | 4 | R | R | 5-11 | 195 | 10-14-64 | 1986 | Lake Forest, Ill. |
| Hayes, Charlie | .284 | 20 | 67 | 7 | 19 | 3 | 0 | 2 | 13 | 1 | 12 | 0 | 0 | R | R | 6-0 | 224 | 5-29-65 | 1983 | Hattiesburg, Miss. |
| Howard, Matt | .204 | 35 | 54 | 9 | 11 | 1 | 0 | 1 | 9 | 2 | 8 | 1 | 0 | R | R | 5-10 | 170 | 9-22-67 | 1989 | San Diego, Calif. |
| James, Dion | .167 | 6 | 12 | 1 | 2 | 0 | 0 | 0 | 1 | 2 | 1 | 0 | 0 | L | L | 6-1 | 175 | 11-9-62 | 1980 | Sacramento, Calif. |
| Jeter, Derek | .314 | 157 | 582 | 104 | 183 | 25 | 6 | 10 | 78 | 48 | 102 | 14 | 7 | R | R | 6-3 | 175 | 6-26-74 | 1992 | Kalamazoo, Mich. |
| Kelly, Pat | .143 | 13 | 21 | 4 | 3 | 0 | 0 | 0 | 2 | 2 | 9 | 0 | 1 | R | R | 6-0 | 180 | 10-14-67 | 1988 | Bangor, Pa. |
| Leyritz, Jim | .264 | 88 | 265 | 23 | 70 | 10 | 0 | 7 | 40 | 30 | 68 | 2 | 0 | R | R | 6-0 | 190 | 12-27-63 | 1986 | Plantation, Fla. |
| Listach, Pat | .240 | 87 | 317 | 51 | 76 | 16 | 2 | 1 | 33 | 36 | 51 | 25 | 5 | S | R | 5-9 | 170 | 9-12-67 | 1988 | Woodway, Texas |
| Luke, Matt | .000 | 1 | 0 | 1 | 0 | 0 | 0 | 0 | 0 | 0 | 0 | 0 | 0 | L | L | 6-5 | 225 | 2-26-71 | 1992 | Brea, Calif. |
| Martinez, Tino | .292 | 155 | 595 | 82 | 174 | 28 | 0 | 25 | 117 | 68 | 85 | 2 | 1 | L | R | 6-2 | 210 | 12-7-67 | 1989 | Tampa, Fla. |
| McIntosh, Tim | .000 | 3 | 3 | 0 | 0 | 0 | 0 | 0 | 0 | 0 | 0 | 0 | 0 | R | R | 5-11 | 195 | 3-21-65 | 1986 | Herald, Calif. |
| O'Neill, Paul | .302 | 150 | 546 | 89 | 165 | 35 | 1 | 19 | 91 | 102 | 76 | 0 | 1 | L | L | 6-4 | 215 | 2-25-63 | 1981 | Cincinnati, Ohio |
| Posada, Jorge | .071 | 8 | 14 | 1 | 1 | 0 | 0 | 0 | 0 | 1 | 6 | 0 | 0 | S | R | 6-0 | 167 | 8-17-71 | 1991 | Rio Piedras, P.R. |
| Raines, Tim | .284 | 59 | 201 | 45 | 57 | 10 | 0 | 9 | 33 | 34 | 29 | 10 | 1 | S | R | 5-8 | 185 | 9-16-59 | 1977 | Heathrow, Fla. |
| Rivera, Ruben | .284 | 46 | 88 | 17 | 25 | 6 | 1 | 2 | 16 | 13 | 26 | 6 | 2 | R | R | 6-3 | 190 | 11-14-73 | 1992 | Chorrera, Panama |
| Sierra, Ruben | .258 | 96 | 360 | 39 | 93 | 17 | 1 | 11 | 52 | 40 | 58 | 1 | 3 | S | R | 6-1 | 200 | 10-6-65 | 1983 | Carolina, P.R. |
| Sojo, Luis | .275 | 18 | 40 | 3 | 11 | 2 | 0 | 0 | 5 | 1 | 4 | 0 | 0 | R | R | 5-11 | 174 | 1-3-66 | 1987 | Barquisimeto, Venez. |
| 2-team (77 Seattle) | .220 | 95 | 287 | 23 | 63 | 10 | 1 | 1 | 21 | 11 | 17 | 2 | 2 | | | | | | | |
| Strawberry, Darryl | .262 | 63 | 202 | 35 | 53 | 13 | 0 | 11 | 36 | 31 | 55 | 6 | 5 | L | L | 6-6 | 215 | 3-12-62 | 1980 | Glendale, Calif. |
| Williams, Bernie | .305 | 143 | 551 | 108 | 168 | 26 | 7 | 29 | 102 | 82 | 72 | 17 | 4 | S | R | 6-2 | 196 | 9-13-68 | 1986 | Vega Alta, P.R. |
| Williams, Gerald | .270 | 99 | 233 | 37 | 63 | 15 | 4 | 5 | 30 | 15 | 39 | 7 | 8 | R | R | 6-2 | 185 | 8-10-66 | 1987 | La Place, La. |

| PITCHING | W | L | ERA | G | GS | CG | SV | IP | H | R | ER | BB | SO | B | T | HT | WT | DOB | 1st Yr | Resides |
|---|---|---|---|---|---|---|---|---|---|---|---|---|---|---|---|---|---|---|---|---|
| Boehringer, Brian | 2 | 4 | 5.44 | 15 | 3 | 0 | 0 | 46 | 46 | 28 | 28 | 21 | 37 | S | R | 6-2 | 180 | 1-8-69 | 1991 | Fenton, Mo. |
| Bones, Ricky | 0 | 0 | 14.14 | 4 | 1 | 0 | 0 | 7 | 14 | 11 | 11 | 6 | 4 | R | R | 6-0 | 190 | 4-7-69 | 1986 | Guayama, P.R. |
| 2-team (32 Milw.) | 7 | 14 | 6.22 | 36 | 24 | 0 | 0 | 152 | 184 | 115 | 105 | 68 | 63 | | | | | | | |
| Brewer, Billy | 1 | 0 | 9.53 | 4 | 0 | 0 | 0 | 6 | 7 | 6 | 6 | 8 | 8 | L | L | 6-1 | 175 | 4-15-68 | 1990 | Waco, Texas |
| Cone, David | 7 | 2 | 2.88 | 11 | 11 | 1 | 0 | 72 | 50 | 25 | 23 | 34 | 71 | L | R | 6-1 | 190 | 1-2-63 | 1981 | Leawood, Kan. |
| Gibson, Paul | 0 | 0 | 6.23 | 4 | 0 | 0 | 0 | 4 | 6 | 3 | 3 | 3 | 0 | L | L | 6-0 | 185 | 1-4-60 | 1978 | Center Moriches, N.Y. |
| Gooden, Dwight | 11 | 7 | 5.01 | 29 | 29 | 1 | 0 | 171 | 169 | 101 | 95 | 88 | 126 | R | R | 6-2 | 210 | 11-16-64 | 1982 | St. Petersburg, Fla. |
| Howe, Steve | 0 | 1 | 6.35 | 25 | 0 | 0 | 1 | 17 | 19 | 12 | 12 | 6 | 5 | L | L | 5-11 | 195 | 3-10-58 | 1979 | Whitefish, Mon. |
| Hutton, Mark | 0 | 2 | 5.04 | 12 | 2 | 0 | 0 | 30 | 32 | 19 | 17 | 18 | 25 | R | R | 6-6 | 225 | 2-6-70 | 1989 | West Lakes, Australia |
| Kamieniecki, Scott | 1 | 2 | 11.12 | 7 | 5 | 0 | 0 | 23 | 36 | 30 | 28 | 19 | 15 | R | R | 6-0 | 190 | 4-19-64 | 1987 | Flint, Mich. |
| Key, Jimmy | 12 | 11 | 4.68 | 30 | 30 | 0 | 0 | 169 | 171 | 93 | 88 | 58 | 116 | R | L | 6-1 | 185 | 4-22-61 | 1982 | Tarpon Springs, Fla. |
| Lloyd, Graeme | 0 | 2 | 17.47 | 13 | 0 | 0 | 0 | 6 | 12 | 11 | 11 | 5 | 6 | L | L | 6-7 | 230 | 4-9-67 | 1988 | Gnarwarre, Australia |
| 2-team (52 Milw.) | 2 | 6 | 4.29 | 65 | 0 | 0 | 0 | 57 | 61 | 30 | 27 | 22 | 30 | | | | | | | |
| Mecir, Jim | 1 | 1 | 5.13 | 26 | 0 | 0 | 0 | 40 | 42 | 24 | 23 | 23 | 38 | S | R | 6-1 | 195 | 5-16-70 | 1991 | St. James, N.Y. |
| Mendoza, Ramiro | 4 | 5 | 6.79 | 12 | 11 | 0 | 0 | 53 | 80 | 43 | 40 | 10 | 34 | R | R | 6-2 | 154 | 6-15-72 | 1992 | Los Santos, Panama |
| Nelson, Jeff | 4 | 4 | 4.36 | 73 | 0 | 0 | 2 | 74 | 75 | 38 | 36 | 36 | 91 | R | R | 6-8 | 225 | 11-17-66 | 1984 | Baltimore, Md. |
| Pavlas, Dave | 0 | 0 | 2.35 | 16 | 0 | 0 | 1 | 23 | 23 | 7 | 6 | 7 | 18 | R | R | 6-7 | 195 | 8-12-62 | 1985 | Phoenix, Ariz. |
| Pettitte, Andy | 21 | 8 | 3.87 | 35 | 34 | 2 | 0 | 221 | 229 | 105 | 95 | 72 | 162 | L | L | 6-5 | 220 | 6-15-72 | 1991 | Deer Park, Texas |
| Polley, Dale | 1 | 3 | 7.89 | 32 | 0 | 0 | 0 | 22 | 23 | 20 | 19 | 11 | 14 | R | L | 6-0 | 165 | 8-9-65 | 1987 | Frankfort, Ky. |
| Rivera, Mariano | 8 | 3 | 2.09 | 61 | 0 | 0 | 5 | 108 | 73 | 25 | 25 | 34 | 130 | R | R | 6-4 | 168 | 11-29-69 | 1990 | Puerto Caimito, Panama |
| Rogers, Kenny | 12 | 8 | 4.68 | 30 | 30 | 2 | 0 | 179 | 179 | 97 | 93 | 83 | 92 | L | L | 6-1 | 205 | 11-10-64 | 1982 | Arlington, Texas |
| Weathers, David | 0 | 2 | 9.35 | 11 | 4 | 0 | 0 | 17 | 23 | 19 | 18 | 14 | 13 | R | R | 6-3 | 205 | 9-25-69 | 1988 | Leoma, Tenn. |
| Wetteland, John | 2 | 3 | 2.83 | 62 | 0 | 0 | 43 | 64 | 54 | 23 | 20 | 21 | 69 | R | R | 6-2 | 195 | 8-21-66 | 1985 | Cedar, N.M. |
| Whitehurst, Wally | 1 | 1 | 6.75 | 2 | 2 | 0 | 0 | 8 | 11 | 6 | 6 | 2 | 1 | R | R | 6-3 | 185 | 4-11-64 | 1985 | Madisonville, La. |
| Wickman, Bob | 4 | 1 | 4.67 | 58 | 0 | 0 | 0 | 79 | 94 | 41 | 41 | 34 | 61 | R | R | 6-1 | 220 | 2-6-69 | 1990 | Abrams, Wis. |

## FIELDING

| Catcher | PCT | G | PO | A | E | DP | PB |
|---|---|---|---|---|---|---|---|
| Girardi | .996 | 120 | 803 | 45 | 3 | 8 | 10 |
| Leyritz | .995 | 55 | 363 | 19 | 2 | 2 | 7 |
| McIntosh | .000 | 1 | 0 | 0 | 0 | 0 | 0 |
| Posada | 1.000 | 4 | 17 | 2 | 0 | 0 | 0 |

| First Base | PCT | G | PO | A | E | DP |
|---|---|---|---|---|---|---|
| Aldrete | 1.000 | 8 | 38 | 0 | 0 | 4 |
| Fielder | 1.000 | 9 | 74 | 4 | 0 | 8 |
| Leyritz | 1.000 | 5 | 16 | 0 | 0 | 2 |
| Martinez | .996 | 151 | 1238 | 83 | 5 | 118 |
| McIntosh | 1.000 | 1 | 6 | 1 | 0 | 1 |
| O'Neill | .000 | 1 | 0 | 0 | 0 | 0 |

| Second Base | PCT | G | PO | A | E | DP |
|---|---|---|---|---|---|---|
| Duncan | .975 | 104 | 183 | 238 | 11 | 57 |
| Eenhoorn | 1.000 | 10 | 15 | 11 | 0 | 5 |
| Fox | .958 | 72 | 78 | 104 | 8 | 21 |
| Howard | .976 | 30 | 14 | 27 | 1 | 5 |
| Kelly | .970 | 10 | 8 | 24 | 1 | 3 |
| Leyritz | 1.000 | 2 | 2 | 1 | 0 | 0 |
| Listach | .982 | 12 | 29 | 26 | 1 | 8 |
| Sojo | 1.000 | 14 | 14 | 28 | 0 | 8 |

| Third Base | PCT | G | PO | A | E | DP |
|---|---|---|---|---|---|---|
| Boggs | .974 | 123 | 62 | 201 | 7 | 24 |
| Duncan | .667 | 3 | 1 | 1 | 1 | 1 |
| Fox | .980 | 31 | 10 | 38 | 1 | 3 |
| Hayes | 1.000 | 19 | 14 | 30 | 0 | 4 |
| Howard | 1.000 | 6 | 3 | 4 | 0 | 0 |
| Leyritz | .778 | 13 | 3 | 11 | 4 | 0 |
| McIntosh | .000 | 1 | 0 | 0 | 0 | 0 |
| Sojo | 1.000 | 1 | 0 | 1 | 0 | 0 |

| Shortstop | PCT | G | PO | A | E | DP |
|---|---|---|---|---|---|---|
| Fox | .889 | 9 | 8 | 16 | 3 | 3 |
| Jeter | .969 | 157 | 244 | 444 | 22 | 83 |
| Listach | .938 | 7 | 5 | 10 | 1 | 1 |
| Sojo | 1.000 | 4 | 2 | 8 | 0 | 2 |

| Outfield | PCT | G | PO | A | E | DP |
|---|---|---|---|---|---|---|
| Aldrete | 1.000 | 9 | 8 | 0 | 0 | 0 |
| Duncan | 1.000 | 3 | 3 | 0 | 0 | 0 |
| Fox | .000 | 1 | 0 | 0 | 0 | 0 |
| James | 1.000 | 4 | 3 | 0 | 0 | 0 |
| Leyritz | 1.000 | 3 | 3 | 0 | 0 | 0 |
| Listach | .982 | 68 | 158 | 6 | 3 | 1 |
| O'Neill | 1.000 | 146 | 293 | 7 | 0 | 3 |
| Raines | .988 | 50 | 79 | 3 | 1 | 0 |
| Sierra | .984 | 33 | 56 | 5 | 1 | 1 |
| Strawberry | 1.000 | 34 | 45 | 1 | 0 | 0 |
| B. Williams | .986 | 140 | 334 | 10 | 5 | 3 |
| G. Williams | .978 | 92 | 132 | 1 | 3 | 1 |

**YANKEES**

**Outfielder Bernie Williams led the Yankees with 29 homers and 17 stolen bases**

FPO

DAVID SEELIG

**Yankees minor league Player of the Year Ricky Ledee**

RICH ABEL

## FARM SYSTEM

**Director of Player Development:** Mark Newman

| Class | Farm Team | League | W | L | Pct. | Finish* | Manager(s) | First Yr |
|---|---|---|---|---|---|---|---|---|
| AAA | Columbus (Ohio) Clippers | International | 85 | 57 | .599 | +1st (10) | Stump Merrill | 1979 |
| AA | Norwich (Conn.) Navigators | Eastern | 71 | 70 | .504 | 5th (10) | Jim Essian | 1995 |
| #A | Tampa (Fla.) Yankees | Florida State | 84 | 50 | .627 | 1st (14) | Trey Hillman | 1994 |
| A | Greensboro (N.C.) Bats | South Atlantic | 56 | 86 | .394 | 13th (14) | Patterson/Johnson | 1990 |
| A | Oneonta (N.Y.) Yankees | New York-Penn | 31 | 45 | .408 | 13th (14) | Gary Tuck | 1967 |
| R | Tampa (Fla.) Yankees | Gulf Coast | 37 | 21 | .638 | +2nd (16) | Ken Dominguez | 1980 |

*Finish in overall standings (No. of teams in league)   #Advanced level   +Won league championship

## ORGANIZATION LEADERS

### MAJOR LEAGUERS

**BATTING**
| | | |
|---|---|---|
| *AVG | Mariano Duncan | .340 |
| R | Bernie Williams | 108 |
| H | Derek Jeter | 183 |
| TB | Bernie Williams | 295 |
| 2B | Paul O'Neill | 35 |
| 3B | Bernie Williams | 7 |
| HR | Bernie Williams | 29 |
| RBI | Tino Martinez | 117 |
| BB | Paul O'Neill | 102 |
| SO | Derek Jeter | 139 |
| SB | Bernie Williams | 17 |

**PITCHING**
| | | |
|---|---|---|
| W | Andy Pettitte | 21 |
| L | Jimmy Key | 11 |
| #ERA | Mariano Rivera | 2.09 |
| G | Jeff Nelson | 73 |
| CG | Two tied at | 2 |
| SV | John Wetteland | 43 |
| IP | Andy Pettitte | 221 |
| BB | Dwight Gooden | 88 |
| SO | Andy Pettitte | 162 |

STAN DENNY

**Tino Martinez.** 117 RBIs

### MINOR LEAGUERS

**BATTING**
| | | |
|---|---|---|
| *AVG | Ricky Ledee, Norwich/Columbus | .305 |
| R | Ricky Ledee, Norwich/Columbus | 106 |
| H | Ricky Ledee, Norwich/Columbus | 151 |
| TB | Ricky Ledee, Norwich/Columbus | 285 |
| 2B | Mike Lowell, Greensboro/Tampa | 38 |
| 3B | Two tied at | 10 |
| HR | Shane Spencer, Norwich/Columbus | 32 |
| RBI | Ricky Ledee, Norwich/Columbus | 101 |
| BB | Kevin Riggs, Norwich | 81 |
| SO | Cody Samuel, Greensboro | 165 |
| SB | Rod Smith, Greensboro | 57 |

**PITCHING**
| | | |
|---|---|---|
| W | Three tied at | 12 |
| L | Three tied at | 14 |
| #ERA | Jay Tessmer, Tampa | 1.48 |
| G | Jay Tessmer, Tampa | 68 |
| CG | Mike Buddie, Norwich | 4 |
| SV | Jay Tessmer, Tampa | 35 |
| IP | Chris Corn, Tampa | 170 |
| BB | Stephen Randolph, Greensboro | 96 |
| SO | Brian Boehringer, Columbus | 132 |

*Minimum 250 At-Bats   #Minimum 75 Innings

## TOP 10 PROSPECTS

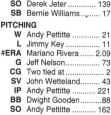

MLE BAILEY

**Ruben Rivera**

**How the Yankees Top 10 prospects, as judged by Baseball America prior to the 1996 season, fared in 1996:**

| Player, Pos. | Club (Class—League) | AVG | AB | R | H | 2B | 3B | HR | RBI | SB |
|---|---|---|---|---|---|---|---|---|---|---|
| 1. Ruben Rivera, of | Columbus (AAA—International) | .235 | 362 | 59 | 85 | 20 | 4 | 10 | 46 | 15 |
| | New York | .284 | 88 | 17 | 25 | 6 | 1 | 2 | 16 | 6 |
| 2. Derek Jeter, ss | New York | .314 | 582 | 104 | 183 | 25 | 6 | 10 | 78 | 14 |
| 4. Andy Fox, 3b | New York | .196 | 189 | 26 | 37 | 4 | 0 | 3 | 13 | 11 |
| 5. D'Angelo Jimenez, ss | Greensboro (A—South Atlantic) | .244 | 537 | 68 | 131 | 25 | 5 | 6 | 48 | 15 |
| 7. Shea Morenz, of | Greensboro (A—South Atlantic) | .249 | 338 | 40 | 84 | 14 | 4 | 2 | 48 | 13 |
| 9. Mike Figga, c | Columbus (AAA—International) | .273 | 11 | 3 | 3 | 1 | 0 | 0 | 0 | 0 |
| 10. Tate Seefried, 1b | Norwich (AA—Eastern) | .208 | 361 | 52 | 75 | 17 | 0 | 14 | 47 | 2 |

| | | W | L | ERA | G | SV | IP | H | BB | SO |
|---|---|---|---|---|---|---|---|---|---|---|
| 3. *Matt Drews, rhp | Columbus (AAA—International) | 0 | 4 | 8.41 | 7 | 0 | 20 | 18 | 27 | 7 |
| | Norwich (AA—Eastern) | 1 | 3 | 4.50 | 9 | 0 | 46 | 40 | 33 | 37 |
| | Tampa (A—Florida State) | 0 | 3 | 7.13 | 4 | 0 | 18 | 26 | 12 | 12 |
| | Jacksonville (AA—Southern) | 0 | 4 | 4.35 | 6 | 0 | 31 | 26 | 19 | 40 |
| 6. Ray Ricken, rhp | Columbus (AAA—International) | 4 | 5 | 4.76 | 20 | 1 | 68 | 62 | 37 | 58 |
| | Norwich (AA—Eastern) | 5 | 2 | 4.47 | 8 | 0 | 46 | 42 | 20 | 42 |
| 8. Chris Cumberland, lhp | Columbus (AAA—International) | 2 | 7 | 6.52 | 12 | 0 | 58 | 86 | 23 | 35 |
| | Norwich (AA—Eastern) | 5 | 7 | 5.27 | 16 | 0 | 96 | 112 | 37 | 44 |

*Traded to Tigers

## INTERNATIONAL LEAGUE

| BATTING | AVG | G | AB | R | H | 2B | 3B | HR | RBI | BB | SO | SB | CS | B | T | HT | WT | DOB | 1st Yr | Resides |
|---|---|---|---|---|---|---|---|---|---|---|---|---|---|---|---|---|---|---|---|---|
| Barker, Tim | .266 | 116 | 402 | 71 | 107 | 27 | 8 | 2 | 45 | 56 | 57 | 24 | 8 | R | R | 6-0 | 175 | 6-30-68 | 1989 | Salisbury, Md. |
| Benavides, Freddie | .000 | 1 | 4 | 0 | 0 | 0 | 0 | 0 | 1 | 0 | 0 | 0 | 0 | R | R | 6-2 | 180 | 4-7-66 | 1987 | Laredo, Texas |
| Carpenter, Bubba | .245 | 132 | 466 | 55 | 114 | 23 | 3 | 7 | 48 | 48 | 80 | 10 | 7 | L | L | 6-1 | 185 | 7-23-68 | 1991 | Winslow, Ark. |
| Cruz, Ivan | .258 | 130 | 446 | 84 | 115 | 26 | 0 | 28 | 96 | 48 | 99 | 2 | 4 | L | L | 6-3 | 210 | 5-3-68 | 1989 | Fajardo, P.R. |
| Dalesandro, Mark | .282 | 78 | 255 | 34 | 72 | 29 | 4 | 2 | 38 | 17 | 31 | 2 | 0 | R | R | 6-0 | 185 | 5-14-68 | 1990 | Chicago, Ill. |
| Delvecchio, Nick | 1.000 | 2 | 1 | 0 | 1 | 0 | 0 | 0 | 0 | 3 | 0 | 0 | 0 | L | R | 6-5 | 203 | 1-23-70 | 1992 | Natick, Mass. |
| Diaz, Mario | .262 | 16 | 61 | 9 | 16 | 3 | 0 | 2 | 11 | 1 | 6 | 0 | 2 | R | R | 5-10 | 160 | 1-10-62 | 1979 | Yabucoa, P.R. |
| Duncan, Mariano | .200 | 2 | 5 | 0 | 1 | 0 | 0 | 0 | 2 | 0 | 2 | 0 | 0 | R | R | 6-0 | 185 | 3-13-63 | 1982 | Cherry Hill, N.J. |
| Eenhoorn, Robert | .337 | 55 | 172 | 28 | 58 | 14 | 1 | 1 | 16 | 21 | 18 | 7 | 2 | R | R | 6-3 | 175 | 2-9-68 | 1990 | Rotterdam, Holland |
| Fermin, Felix | .211 | 7 | 19 | 3 | 4 | 0 | 0 | 0 | 3 | 3 | 1 | 0 | 0 | R | R | 5-11 | 170 | 10-9-63 | 1983 | Santiago, D.R. |
| Figga, Mike | .273 | 4 | 11 | 3 | 3 | 1 | 0 | 0 | 0 | 1 | 3 | 0 | 0 | R | R | 6-0 | 200 | 7-31-70 | 1990 | Tampa, Fla. |
| Hinds, Robert | .087 | 11 | 23 | 4 | 2 | 0 | 0 | 0 | 1 | 4 | 3 | 1 | 0 | R | R | 6-1 | 180 | 4-26-71 | 1992 | Cerritos, Calif. |
| Howard, Matt | .347 | 51 | 202 | 36 | 70 | 12 | 2 | 2 | 16 | 18 | 9 | 9 | 3 | R | R | 5-10 | 170 | 9-22-67 | 1989 | San Diego, Calif. |
| Katzaroff, Robbie | .444 | 2 | 9 | 0 | 4 | 0 | 0 | 0 | 0 | 0 | 0 | 0 | 1 | R | R | 5-8 | 170 | 7-29-68 | 1990 | Phoenix, Ariz. |
| Kelly, Pat | .378 | 8 | 37 | 6 | 14 | 1 | 1 | 2 | 7 | 2 | 11 | 3 | 0 | R | R | 6-0 | 180 | 10-14-67 | 1988 | Bangor, Pa. |
| Ledee, Ricky | .282 | 96 | 358 | 79 | 101 | 22 | 6 | 21 | 64 | 44 | 95 | 6 | 3 | L | L | 6-2 | 160 | 11-22-73 | 1990 | Salinas, P.R. |
| Long, R.D. | .226 | 61 | 124 | 18 | 28 | 3 | 2 | 0 | 9 | 15 | 36 | 5 | 2 | S | R | 6-1 | 183 | 4-2-71 | 1992 | Penfield, N.Y. |
| Luke, Matt | .280 | 74 | 264 | 46 | 74 | 14 | 2 | 19 | 70 | 17 | 52 | 1 | 1 | L | L | 6-5 | 225 | 2-26-71 | 1992 | Brea, Calif. |
| Marini, Marc | .267 | 46 | 135 | 23 | 36 | 11 | 0 | 2 | 23 | 10 | 23 | 1 | 0 | L | L | 6-1 | 185 | 3-17-70 | 1991 | Tunkhannock, Pa. |
| Martindale, Ryan | .263 | 7 | 19 | 3 | 5 | 2 | 1 | 0 | 3 | 3 | 5 | 0 | 0 | R | R | 6-3 | 215 | 12-2-68 | 1991 | Omaha, Neb. |
| McIntosh, Tim | .277 | 67 | 206 | 30 | 57 | 11 | 1 | 10 | 28 | 11 | 40 | 0 | 0 | R | R | 5-11 | 195 | 3-21-65 | 1986 | Herald, Calif. |
| Motuzas, Jeff | .250 | 5 | 12 | 1 | 3 | 0 | 1 | 0 | 1 | 0 | 7 | 0 | 0 | R | R | 6-2 | 205 | 10-1-71 | 1990 | Nashua, N.H. |
| Northrup, Kevin | .286 | 56 | 168 | 22 | 48 | 13 | 1 | 4 | 20 | 12 | 25 | 4 | 2 | R | R | 6-1 | 190 | 1-27-70 | 1992 | Sanford, N.C. |
| Posada, Jorge | .271 | 106 | 354 | 76 | 96 | 22 | 6 | 11 | 62 | 79 | 86 | 3 | 3 | S | R | 6-0 | 167 | 8-17-71 | 1991 | Rio Piedras, P.R. |
| Raines, Tim | .250 | 4 | 12 | 3 | 3 | 1 | 0 | 0 | 0 | 1 | 3 | 1 | 0 | S | R | 5-8 | 185 | 9-16-59 | 1977 | Heathrow, Fla. |
| Rivera, Ruben | .235 | 101 | 362 | 59 | 85 | 20 | 4 | 10 | 46 | 40 | 96 | 15 | 10 | R | R | 6-3 | 190 | 11-14-73 | 1992 | Chorrera, Panama |
| Romano, Scott | .150 | 18 | 40 | 5 | 6 | 2 | 0 | 0 | 4 | 5 | 6 | 1 | 0 | R | R | 6-1 | 185 | 8-3-71 | 1989 | Tampa, Fla. |
| Spencer, Shane | .355 | 9 | 31 | 7 | 11 | 4 | 0 | 3 | 6 | 5 | 5 | 0 | 1 | R | R | 5-11 | 182 | 2-20-72 | 1990 | El Cajon, Calif. |
| Strawberry, Darryl | .375 | 2 | 8 | 3 | 3 | 0 | 0 | 3 | 5 | 0 | 3 | 0 | 0 | L | L | 6-6 | 215 | 3-12-62 | 1980 | Glendale, Calif. |
| Torres, Jaime | .270 | 12 | 37 | 5 | 10 | 3 | 0 | 1 | 7 | 2 | 4 | 1 | 0 | R | R | 6-0 | 176 | 3-12-73 | 1992 | Aragua, Venez. |
| Wilson, Tom | .000 | 1 | 1 | 0 | 0 | 0 | 0 | 0 | 0 | 1 | 0 | 0 | 0 | R | R | 6-3 | 185 | 12-19-70 | 1991 | Yorba Linda, Calif. |
| Woodson, Tracy | .288 | 114 | 420 | 53 | 121 | 34 | 3 | 21 | 81 | 16 | 52 | 4 | 0 | R | R | 6-3 | 215 | 10-5-62 | 1984 | Raleigh, N.C. |

| PITCHING | W | L | ERA | G | GS | CG | SV | IP | H | R | ER | BB | SO | B | T | HT | WT | DOB | 1st Yr | Resides |
|---|---|---|---|---|---|---|---|---|---|---|---|---|---|---|---|---|---|---|---|---|
| Boehringer, Brian | 11 | 7 | 4.00 | 25 | 25 | 3 | 0 | 153 | 155 | 79 | 68 | 56 | 132 | S | R | 6-2 | 180 | 1-8-69 | 1991 | Fenton, Mo. |
| Brewer, Billy | 0 | 2 | 7.20 | 13 | 4 | 0 | 0 | 25 | 27 | 21 | 20 | 19 | 27 | L | L | 6-1 | 175 | 4-15-68 | 1990 | Waco, Texas |
| Brock, Russ | 0 | 0 | 9.00 | 1 | 0 | 0 | 0 | 1 | 2 | 1 | 1 | 0 | 2 | R | R | 6-5 | 210 | 10-13-69 | 1991 | Lockland, Ohio |
| Burrows, Terry | 1 | 0 | 5.96 | 23 | 0 | 0 | 0 | 23 | 24 | 16 | 15 | 11 | 20 | L | L | 6-1 | 185 | 11-28-68 | 1990 | Lake Charles, La. |
| Carper, Mark | 1 | 2 | 6.62 | 15 | 4 | 0 | 0 | 35 | 43 | 30 | 26 | 16 | 16 | R | R | 6-2 | 200 | 9-29-68 | 1991 | Highland, Md. |
| Croghan, Andy | 2 | 0 | 8.46 | 14 | 0 | 0 | 0 | 22 | 27 | 24 | 21 | 13 | 21 | R | R | 6-5 | 205 | 10-26-69 | 1991 | Yorba Linda, Calif. |
| Cumberland, Chris | 2 | 7 | 6.52 | 12 | 12 | 1 | 0 | 58 | 86 | 45 | 42 | 23 | 35 | R | L | 6-1 | 185 | 1-15-73 | 1993 | Safety Harbor, Fla. |
| DeJesus, Jose | 0 | 0 | 14.40 | 3 | 0 | 0 | 0 | 5 | 9 | 8 | 8 | 1 | 6 | R | R | 6-5 | 225 | 1-6-65 | 1983 | Cidra, P.R. |
| Drews, Matt | 0 | 4 | 8.41 | 7 | 7 | 0 | 0 | 20 | 18 | 27 | 19 | 27 | 7 | R | R | 6-8 | 205 | 8-29-74 | 1994 | Sarasota, Fla. |
| Dunbar, Matt | 2 | 0 | 1.74 | 14 | 0 | 0 | 0 | 21 | 12 | 6 | 4 | 13 | 16 | L | L | 6-0 | 160 | 10-15-68 | 1990 | Tallahassee, Fla. |
| Edenfield, Ken | 4 | 1 | 2.34 | 33 | 0 | 0 | 3 | 42 | 32 | 12 | 11 | 15 | 28 | R | R | 6-1 | 165 | 3-18-67 | 1990 | Knoxville, Tenn. |
| Eiland, Dave | 8 | 4 | 2.92 | 15 | 15 | 3 | 0 | 92 | 77 | 37 | 30 | 13 | 76 | R | R | 6-3 | 205 | 7-5-66 | 1987 | Dade City, Fla. |
| Gibson, Paul | 1 | 0 | 7.04 | 9 | 0 | 0 | 0 | 8 | 8 | 6 | 6 | 9 | 4 | R | L | 6-0 | 185 | 1-4-60 | 1978 | Center Moriches, N.Y. |
| Hines, Rich | 6 | 3 | 5.16 | 32 | 5 | 0 | 0 | 66 | 70 | 42 | 38 | 37 | 48 | L | L | 6-1 | 185 | 5-20-69 | 1990 | Milton, Fla. |
| Hutton, Mark | 0 | 0 | 0.00 | 2 | 0 | 0 | 0 | 2 | 0 | 0 | 0 | 2 | 3 | R | R | 6-6 | 225 | 2-6-70 | 1989 | West Lakes, Australia |
| Jerzembeck, Mike | 0 | 0 | 5.40 | 1 | 0 | 0 | 0 | 2 | 1 | 1 | 1 | 1 | 0 | R | R | 6-1 | 185 | 5-18-72 | 1993 | Queens Village, N.Y. |
| Kamienicki, Scott | 2 | 1 | 5.64 | 5 | 5 | 2 | 0 | 30 | 33 | 21 | 19 | 8 | 27 | R | R | 6-0 | 190 | 4-19-64 | 1987 | Flint, Mich. |
| Kotarski, Mike | 0 | 0 | 6.75 | 1 | 1 | 0 | 0 | 4 | 3 | 4 | 3 | 2 | 5 | L | L | 6-1 | 195 | 9-18-70 | 1992 | Peabody, Mass. |
| Mecir, Jim | 3 | 3 | 2.27 | 33 | 0 | 0 | 7 | 48 | 37 | 14 | 12 | 15 | 52 | S | R | 6-1 | 195 | 5-16-70 | 1991 | St. James, N.Y. |
| Melendez, Jose | 1 | 0 | 6.52 | 8 | 1 | 0 | 0 | 10 | 9 | 10 | 7 | 2 | 7 | R | R | 6-2 | 190 | 9-2-65 | 1984 | Naguabo, P.R. |
| Mendoza, Ramiro | 6 | 2 | 2.51 | 15 | 15 | 0 | 0 | 97 | 96 | 30 | 27 | 19 | 61 | R | R | 6-2 | 154 | 6-15-72 | 1992 | Los Santos, Panama |
| Monteleone, Rich | 4 | 3 | 3.60 | 21 | 1 | 0 | 0 | 35 | 42 | 17 | 14 | 7 | 21 | R | R | 6-2 | 217 | 3-22-63 | 1982 | Tampa, Fla. |
| Pavlas, Dave | 8 | 2 | 1.99 | 57 | 0 | 0 | 26 | 77 | 64 | 20 | 17 | 13 | 65 | R | R | 6-7 | 195 | 8-12-62 | 1985 | Phoenix, Ariz. |
| Polley, Dale | 2 | 2 | 3.13 | 31 | 0 | 0 | 1 | 32 | 29 | 11 | 11 | 9 | 29 | R | L | 6-0 | 165 | 8-9-65 | 1987 | Frankfort, Ky. |
| Ricken, Ray | 4 | 5 | 4.76 | 20 | 11 | 1 | 1 | 68 | 62 | 44 | 36 | 37 | 58 | R | R | 6-5 | 225 | 8-11-73 | 1994 | Warren, Mich. |
| Rios, Dan | 4 | 1 | 1.95 | 24 | 0 | 0 | 0 | 28 | 22 | 7 | 6 | 6 | 22 | R | R | 6-2 | 208 | 11-11-72 | 1993 | Hialeah, Fla. |
| Rumer, Tim | 3 | 1 | 2.72 | 12 | 8 | 0 | 0 | 50 | 39 | 20 | 15 | 14 | 35 | L | L | 6-3 | 205 | 8-8-69 | 1990 | Princeton, N.J. |
| Wallace, Kent | 4 | 2 | 4.68 | 13 | 12 | 2 | 0 | 67 | 69 | 37 | 35 | 15 | 34 | L | R | 6-3 | 192 | 8-22-70 | 1992 | Paducah, Ky. |
| Weathers, David | 0 | 2 | 5.40 | 3 | 3 | 0 | 0 | 17 | 20 | 13 | 10 | 5 | 7 | R | R | 6-3 | 205 | 9-25-69 | 1988 | Leoma, Tenn. |
| 2-team (1 Charlotte) | 0 | 2 | 5.68 | 4 | 4 | 0 | 0 | 19 | 25 | 15 | 12 | 8 | 7 | | | | | | | |
| Whitehurst, Wally | 6 | 3 | 2.47 | 13 | 13 | 2 | 0 | 73 | 60 | 25 | 20 | 12 | 48 | R | R | 6-3 | 185 | 4-11-64 | 1985 | Madisonville, La. |
| 2-team (15 Ottawa) | 8 | 7 | 3.08 | 28 | 18 | 2 | 3 | 108 | 101 | 42 | 37 | 25 | 83 | | | | | | | |

## FIELDING

### Catcher

| Catcher | PCT | G | PO | A | E | DP | PB |
|---|---|---|---|---|---|---|---|
| Dalesandro | .979 | 15 | 86 | 6 | 2 | 0 | 1 |
| Figga | 1.000 | 3 | 17 | 2 | 0 | 1 | 0 |
| Martindale | .973 | 7 | 35 | 1 | 1 | 0 | 1 |
| McIntosh | .993 | 24 | 139 | 11 | 1 | 1 | 2 |
| Motuzas | .955 | 5 | 19 | 2 | 1 | 0 | 0 |
| Posada | .985 | 94 | 598 | 51 | 10 | 3 | 10 |
| Torres | 1.000 | 7 | 30 | 3 | 0 | 1 | 0 |

### First Base

| First Base | PCT | G | PO | A | E | DP |
|---|---|---|---|---|---|---|
| Cruz | .996 | 125 | 1028 | 94 | 5 | 88 |
| Luke | .989 | 10 | 87 | 6 | 1 | 3 |
| McIntosh | 1.000 | 11 | 73 | 3 | 0 | 5 |
| Torres | 1.000 | 1 | 2 | 0 | 0 | 0 |
| Woodson | 1.000 | 10 | 58 | 4 | 0 | 5 |

### Second Base

| Second Base | PCT | G | PO | A | E | DP |
|---|---|---|---|---|---|---|
| Barker | .976 | 67 | 133 | 193 | 8 | 43 |
| Dalesandro | .980 | 11 | 19 | 30 | 1 | 5 |
| Diaz | 1.000 | 1 | 0 | 2 | 0 | 1 |
| Duncan | 1.000 | 2 | 1 | 5 | 0 | 1 |

| | PCT | G | PO | A | E | DP |
|---|---|---|---|---|---|---|
| Eenhoorn | 1.000 | 1 | 3 | 2 | 0 | 0 |
| Fermin | 1.000 | 5 | 9 | 21 | 0 | 5 |
| Hinds | .957 | 11 | 27 | 18 | 2 | 3 |
| Howard | 1.000 | 7 | 15 | 17 | 0 | 3 |
| Kelly | 1.000 | 8 | 19 | 19 | 0 | 2 |
| Long | .952 | 40 | 63 | 96 | 8 | 21 |
| Romano | 1.000 | 6 | 7 | 17 | 0 | 1 |

### Third Base

| Third Base | PCT | G | PO | A | E | DP |
|---|---|---|---|---|---|---|
| Barker | 1.000 | 4 | 1 | 2 | 0 | 0 |
| Dalesandro | .887 | 20 | 10 | 37 | 6 | 0 |
| Diaz | 1.000 | 8 | 5 | 19 | 0 | 0 |
| Long | .714 | 5 | 0 | 5 | 2 | 0 |
| McIntosh | .778 | 10 | 7 | 14 | 6 | 1 |
| Northrup | 1.000 | 1 | 0 | 3 | 0 | 0 |
| Romano | 1.000 | 4 | 0 | 6 | 0 | 0 |
| Woodson | .956 | 108 | 73 | 188 | 12 | 19 |

### Shortstop

| Shortstop | PCT | G | PO | A | E | DP |
|---|---|---|---|---|---|---|
| Barker | .947 | 43 | 64 | 133 | 11 | 24 |

| | PCT | G | PO | A | E | DP |
|---|---|---|---|---|---|---|
| Benavides | .667 | 1 | 0 | 2 | 1 | 0 |
| Eenhoorn | .947 | 53 | 73 | 158 | 13 | 23 |
| Fermin | 1.000 | 2 | 4 | 5 | 0 | 1 |
| Howard | .962 | 46 | 53 | 147 | 8 | 30 |
| Long | .875 | 2 | 3 | 4 | 1 | 1 |

### Outfield

| Outfield | PCT | G | PO | A | E | DP |
|---|---|---|---|---|---|---|
| Carpenter | .987 | 123 | 225 | 8 | 3 | 1 |
| Dalesandro | .938 | 13 | 13 | 2 | 1 | 0 |
| Katzaroff | 1.000 | 2 | 2 | 0 | 0 | 0 |
| Ledee | .952 | 68 | 97 | 3 | 5 | 0 |
| Luke | .987 | 50 | 72 | 2 | 1 | 1 |
| Marini | .975 | 24 | 38 | 1 | 1 | 0 |
| McIntosh | 1.000 | 4 | 4 | 0 | 0 | 0 |
| Northrup | .973 | 50 | 67 | 6 | 2 | 1 |
| Posada | .000 | 1 | 0 | 0 | 0 | 0 |
| Raines | 1.000 | 2 | 2 | 0 | 0 | 0 |
| Rivera | .972 | 101 | 239 | 6 | 7 | 1 |
| Romano | 1.000 | 5 | 2 | 0 | 0 | 0 |
| Spencer | .963 | 9 | 25 | 1 | 1 | 1 |

# NORWICH — Class AA
## EASTERN LEAGUE

### BATTING

| BATTING | AVG | G | AB | R | H | 2B | 3B | HR | RBI | BB | SO | SB | CS | B | T | HT | WT | DOB | 1st Yr | Resides |
|---|---|---|---|---|---|---|---|---|---|---|---|---|---|---|---|---|---|---|---|---|
| Delafield, Wil | .196 | 22 | 46 | 3 | 9 | 1 | 0 | 0 | 3 | 2 | 15 | 1 | 1 | R | R | 6-2 | 185 | 2-15-72 | 1992 | Baton Rouge, La. |
| Delvecchio, Nick | .278 | 12 | 36 | 7 | 10 | 3 | 0 | 2 | 7 | 6 | 9 | 1 | 0 | L | R | 6-3 | 203 | 1-23-70 | 1992 | Natick, Mass. |
| DeBerry, Joe | .154 | 9 | 26 | 1 | 4 | 0 | 0 | 0 | 6 | 0 | 7 | 0 | 0 | L | L | 6-2 | 195 | 6-30-70 | 1991 | Colorado Springs, Colo. |
| Donato, Dan | .285 | 134 | 459 | 47 | 131 | 27 | 1 | 2 | 48 | 34 | 51 | 5 | 6 | L | R | 6-1 | 205 | 11-15-72 | 1995 | Dedham, Mass. |
| Fithian, Grant | .197 | 63 | 178 | 19 | 35 | 7 | 1 | 5 | 26 | 11 | 46 | 1 | 0 | R | R | 6-0 | 192 | 11-20-71 | 1994 | Rockwall, Texas |
| Fleming, Carlton | .321 | 15 | 28 | 4 | 9 | 0 | 0 | 0 | 1 | 5 | 1 | 0 | 1 | S | R | 5-11 | 175 | 8-25-71 | 1992 | Freeport, N.Y. |
| Hinds, Robert | .228 | 85 | 180 | 25 | 41 | 3 | 1 | 2 | 15 | 20 | 48 | 9 | 5 | R | R | 6-1 | 180 | 4-26-71 | 1992 | Cerritos, Calif. |
| Imrisek, Jason | .333 | 2 | 6 | 2 | 2 | 1 | 0 | 0 | 2 | 0 | 1 | 0 | 0 | R | R | 5-11 | 185 | 6-10-74 | 1995 | Orland Park, Ill. |
| Katzaroff, Robbie | .274 | 23 | 84 | 11 | 23 | 4 | 0 | 0 | 5 | 7 | 9 | 0 | 2 | R | R | 5-8 | 170 | 7-29-68 | 1990 | Phoenix, Ariz. |
| Kelly, Pat | .294 | 4 | 17 | 3 | 5 | 2 | 1 | 0 | 0 | 0 | 2 | 1 | 0 | R | R | 6-0 | 180 | 10-14-67 | 1988 | Bangor, Pa. |
| Knowles, Eric | .245 | 126 | 396 | 56 | 97 | 23 | 1 | 7 | 42 | 32 | 92 | 9 | 6 | R | R | 6-0 | 190 | 10-21-73 | 1991 | Miami, Fla. |
| Ledee, Ricky | .365 | 39 | 137 | 27 | 50 | 11 | 1 | 8 | 37 | 16 | 25 | 2 | 2 | L | L | 6-2 | 160 | 11-22-73 | 1990 | Salinas, P.R. |
| Long, R.D. | .300 | 6 | 10 | 4 | 3 | 0 | 0 | 0 | 3 | 4 | 2 | 0 | 0 | S | R | 6-1 | 183 | 4-2-71 | 1992 | Penfield, N.Y. |
| McNair, Fred | .276 | 69 | 246 | 31 | 68 | 10 | 1 | 5 | 43 | 11 | 53 | 2 | 0 | R | R | 6-4 | 215 | 1-31-70 | 1989 | Mesa, Ariz. |
| Motuzas, Jeff | .333 | 5 | 9 | 1 | 3 | 0 | 0 | 0 | 2 | 0 | 4 | 0 | 0 | R | R | 6-2 | 205 | 11-1-71 | 1990 | Nashua, N.H. |
| Northrup, Kevin | .243 | 63 | 235 | 36 | 57 | 10 | 2 | 7 | 37 | 26 | 36 | 3 | 1 | R | R | 6-1 | 190 | 1-27-70 | 1992 | Sanford, N.C. |
| Norton, Chris | .279 | 47 | 172 | 24 | 48 | 12 | 1 | 7 | 28 | 15 | 43 | 3 | 2 | R | R | 6-2 | 215 | 9-21-70 | 1992 | Maitland, Fla. |
| Pichardo, Sandy | .353 | 6 | 17 | 3 | 6 | 1 | 0 | 1 | 3 | 1 | 5 | 1 | 0 | S | R | 5-11 | 173 | 11-26-74 | 1991 | Santiago, D.R. |
| Pledger, Kinnis | .265 | 131 | 445 | 80 | 118 | 27 | 6 | 19 | 67 | 65 | 123 | 20 | 5 | L | R | 6-4 | 215 | 7-17-68 | 1987 | Benton, Ark. |
| Raines, Tim | .185 | 8 | 27 | 8 | 5 | 1 | 0 | 1 | 1 | 9 | 2 | 2 | 0 | S | R | 5-8 | 185 | 9-16-59 | 1977 | Heathrow, Fla. |
| Riggs, Kevin | .290 | 118 | 403 | 75 | 117 | 24 | 1 | 2 | 37 | 81 | 66 | 9 | 9 | L | R | 5-11 | 190 | 2-3-69 | 1990 | East Hartford, Conn. |
| Romano, Scott | .290 | 30 | 107 | 14 | 31 | 3 | 0 | 3 | 8 | 10 | 24 | 2 | 0 | R | R | 6-1 | 185 | 8-3-71 | 1989 | Tampa, Fla. |
| 2-team (1 Trenton) | .283 | 31 | 113 | 14 | 32 | 4 | 0 | 3 | 8 | 11 | 26 | 2 | 0 | | | | | | | |
| Seefried, Tate | .208 | 115 | 361 | 52 | 75 | 17 | 0 | 14 | 47 | 47 | 128 | 2 | 3 | L | R | 6-4 | 180 | 4-22-72 | 1990 | El Segundo, Calif. |
| Smith, Sloan | .218 | 60 | 202 | 27 | 44 | 10 | 2 | 2 | 20 | 30 | 96 | 4 | 1 | S | R | 6-4 | 215 | 11-29-72 | 1993 | Evanston, Ill. |
| Spencer, Shane | .253 | 126 | 450 | 70 | 114 | 19 | 0 | 29 | 89 | 68 | 99 | 4 | 2 | R | R | 5-11 | 182 | 2-20-72 | 1990 | El Cajon, Calif. |
| Torres, Jaime | .251 | 100 | 334 | 42 | 84 | 19 | 2 | 6 | 40 | 21 | 28 | 1 | 3 | R | R | 6-0 | 176 | 3-12-73 | 1992 | Aragua, Venez. |
| Troilo, Jason | .500 | 3 | 8 | 3 | 4 | 0 | 2 | 0 | 2 | 0 | 1 | 0 | 0 | R | R | 6-1 | 195 | 9-7-72 | 1994 | Avondale, Pa. |

### PITCHING

| PITCHING | W | L | ERA | G | GS | CG | SV | IP | H | R | ER | BB | SO | B | T | HT | WT | DOB | 1st Yr | Resides |
|---|---|---|---|---|---|---|---|---|---|---|---|---|---|---|---|---|---|---|---|---|
| Beverlin, Jason | 0 | 3 | 8.44 | 8 | 4 | 0 | 0 | 16 | 25 | 21 | 15 | 6 | 17 | L | R | 6-5 | 230 | 11-27-73 | 1994 | Royal Oak, Calif. |
| Brock, Russ | 0 | 1 | 8.18 | 4 | 0 | 0 | 0 | 11 | 14 | 10 | 10 | 5 | 14 | R | R | 6-5 | 210 | 10-13-69 | 1991 | Lockland, Ohio |
| Brown, Charlie | 0 | 0 | 0.00 | 1 | 0 | 0 | 0 | 2 | 1 | 0 | 0 | 0 | 1 | R | R | 6-3 | 178 | 9-13-73 | 1992 | Fort Pierce, Fla. |
| Buddie, Mike | 7 | 12 | 4.45 | 29 | 26 | 4 | 0 | 160 | 176 | 101 | 79 | 71 | 103 | R | R | 6-3 | 210 | 12-12-70 | 1992 | Berea, Ohio |
| Cone, David | 0 | 0 | 0.90 | 2 | 2 | 0 | 0 | 10 | 9 | 3 | 1 | 1 | 13 | L | R | 6-1 | 190 | 1-2-63 | 1981 | Leawood, Kan. |
| Croghan, Andy | 9 | 5 | 3.07 | 35 | 0 | 0 | 4 | 41 | 41 | 23 | 14 | 16 | 49 | R | R | 6-5 | 205 | 10-26-69 | 1991 | Yorba Linda, Calif. |
| Cumberland, Chris | 5 | 7 | 5.27 | 16 | 16 | 2 | 0 | 96 | 112 | 73 | 56 | 37 | 44 | R | L | 6-1 | 185 | 1-15-73 | 1993 | Safety Harbor, Fla. |
| Drews, Matt | 1 | 3 | 4.50 | 9 | 9 | 0 | 0 | 46 | 40 | 26 | 23 | 33 | 37 | R | R | 6-8 | 205 | 8-29-74 | 1994 | Sarasota, Fla. |
| Dunbar, Matt | 4 | 2 | 1.78 | 33 | 6 | 0 | 1 | 71 | 59 | 33 | 14 | 28 | 59 | L | L | 6-0 | 160 | 10-15-68 | 1990 | Tallahassee, Fla. |
| Henthorne, Kevin | 5 | 3 | 3.26 | 12 | 8 | 0 | 0 | 60 | 50 | 25 | 15 | 22 | 47 | S | R | 6-2 | 182 | 12-9-69 | 1994 | San Antonio, Texas |
| Hubbard, Mark | 2 | 0 | 5.49 | 4 | 4 | 0 | 0 | 20 | 19 | 13 | 12 | 10 | 14 | L | L | 6-2 | 190 | 2-2-70 | 1991 | Dover, Fla. |
| Jerzembeck, Mike | 3 | 6 | 4.52 | 14 | 13 | 1 | 0 | 70 | 74 | 38 | 35 | 26 | 65 | R | R | 6-1 | 185 | 5-18-72 | 1993 | Queens Village, N.Y. |
| Kotarski, Mike | 1 | 2 | 4.35 | 42 | 1 | 0 | 3 | 72 | 73 | 40 | 35 | 29 | 66 | L | L | 6-1 | 195 | 9-18-70 | 1992 | Peabody, Mass. |
| Lankford, Frank | 7 | 8 | 2.66 | 61 | 0 | 0 | 4 | 88 | 82 | 42 | 26 | 40 | 61 | R | R | 6-2 | 190 | 3-26-71 | 1993 | Atlanta, Ga. |
| Maeda, Katsuhiro | 3 | 2 | 4.05 | 9 | 9 | 1 | 0 | 53 | 49 | 25 | 24 | 21 | 30 | R | R | 6-2 | 190 | 6-23-71 | 1996 | Kobe, Japan |
| Medina, Rafael | 5 | 8 | 3.06 | 19 | 19 | 1 | 0 | 103 | 78 | 48 | 35 | 55 | 112 | R | R | 6-3 | 194 | 2-15-75 | 1993 | Panama City, Panama |
| Meyer, David | 0 | 0 | 4.71 | 19 | 0 | 0 | 1 | 21 | 20 | 12 | 11 | 11 | 13 | L | L | 6-5 | 215 | 12-15-71 | 1994 | Grapevine, Texas |
| Musselman, Jim | 2 | 1 | 2.25 | 5 | 5 | 1 | 0 | 36 | 28 | 9 | 9 | 10 | 25 | R | R | 6-1 | 190 | 10-25-71 | 1993 | Apopka, Fla. |
| Perez, Melido | 1 | 0 | 0.00 | 1 | 1 | 0 | 0 | 8 | 4 | 0 | 0 | 1 | 7 | R | R | 6-4 | 180 | 2-15-66 | 1984 | San Cristobal, D.R. |
| Quirico, Rafael | 1 | 0 | 4.05 | 4 | 0 | 0 | 0 | 7 | 5 | 3 | 3 | 3 | 9 | L | L | 6-3 | 170 | 9-7-69 | 1987 | Santo Domingo, D.R. |
| 2-team (5 Reading) | 2 | 0 | 2.21 | 9 | 5 | 0 | 0 | 37 | 27 | 9 | 9 | 14 | 32 | | | | | | | |
| Resz, Greg | 1 | 1 | 2.54 | 19 | 2 | 0 | 2 | 39 | 38 | 17 | 11 | 18 | 37 | L | R | 6-5 | 215 | 12-25-71 | 1993 | Springfield, Mo. |
| Ricken, Ray | 5 | 2 | 4.47 | 8 | 8 | 1 | 0 | 46 | 42 | 26 | 23 | 20 | 42 | R | R | 6-5 | 225 | 8-11-73 | 1994 | Warren, Mich. |
| Rios, Dan | 3 | 1 | 2.09 | 38 | 0 | 0 | 17 | 43 | 34 | 14 | 10 | 21 | 38 | R | R | 6-2 | 208 | 11-11-72 | 1993 | Hialeah, Fla. |
| Rumer, Tim | 3 | 1 | 2.25 | 8 | 7 | 0 | 0 | 40 | 32 | 12 | 10 | 18 | 44 | L | L | 6-3 | 205 | 8-8-69 | 1990 | Princeton, N.J. |
| Sutherland, John | 3 | 2 | 2.74 | 26 | 0 | 0 | 1 | 43 | 37 | 15 | 13 | 19 | 31 | R | R | 6-2 | 185 | 10-11-68 | 1991 | Walnut Creek, Calif. |
| Wallace, Kent | 0 | 0 | 6.00 | 1 | 1 | 0 | 0 | 6 | 10 | 4 | 4 | 0 | 1 | L | R | 6-3 | 192 | 8-22-70 | 1992 | Paducah, Ky. |

| Catcher | PCT | G | PO | A | E | DP | PB |
|---|---|---|---|---|---|---|---|
| Fithian | .986 | 42 | 259 | 30 | 4 | 4 | 5 |
| Imrisek | .923 | 2 | 11 | 1 | 1 | 0 | 1 |
| Motuzas | .941 | 4 | 12 | 4 | 1 | 1 | 1 |
| Norton | .981 | 20 | 92 | 9 | 2 | 0 | 7 |
| Torres | .983 | 90 | 624 | 75 | 12 | 6 | 11 |
| Troilo | 1.000 | 3 | 13 | 2 | 0 | 0 | 0 |

| First Base | PCT | G | PO | A | E | DP |
|---|---|---|---|---|---|---|
| Delvecchio | 1.000 | 1 | 2 | 0 | 0 | 0 |
| DeBerry | .968 | 3 | 25 | 5 | 1 | 2 |
| Donato | 1.000 | 1 | 2 | 0 | 0 | 1 |
| McNair | .982 | 38 | 285 | 38 | 6 | 24 |
| Norton | .962 | 15 | 89 | 11 | 4 | 15 |
| Riggs | 1.000 | 1 | 6 | 0 | 0 | 0 |
| Seefried | .985 | 88 | 659 | 58 | 11 | 48 |
| Spencer | 1.000 | 12 | 86 | 5 | 0 | 5 |
| Torres | .964 | 9 | 51 | 2 | 2 | 4 |

| Second Base | PCT | G | PO | A | E | DP |
|---|---|---|---|---|---|---|
| Donato | 1.000 | 1 | 1 | 4 | 0 | 1 |
| Fleming | 1.000 | 7 | 5 | 6 | 0 | 1 |
| Hinds | .932 | 60 | 112 | 108 | 16 | 32 |
| Kelly | .952 | 4 | 7 | 13 | 1 | 3 |
| Knowles | 1.000 | 13 | 14 | 30 | 0 | 3 |
| Long | .750 | 2 | 2 | 1 | 1 | 0 |
| Riggs | .958 | 79 | 125 | 174 | 13 | 36 |
| Romano | 1.000 | 1 | 9 | 6 | 0 | 1 |

| Third Base | PCT | G | PO | A | E | DP |
|---|---|---|---|---|---|---|
| Donato | .911 | 107 | 54 | 201 | 25 | 10 |
| Fithian | 1.000 | 1 | 1 | 2 | 0 | 0 |
| Fleming | .500 | 3 | 0 | 1 | 1 | 0 |
| Hinds | .583 | 6 | 2 | 5 | 5 | 0 |
| Knowles | .816 | 13 | 5 | 26 | 7 | 2 |
| Long | 1.000 | 3 | 2 | 6 | 0 | 1 |
| McNair | .867 | 7 | 3 | 10 | 2 | 0 |
| Norton | .750 | 3 | 1 | 2 | 1 | 1 |
| Romano | .866 | 21 | 19 | 39 | 9 | 3 |
| Spencer | 1.000 | 4 | 2 | 9 | 0 | 0 |
| Torres | 1.000 | 1 | 0 | 1 | 0 | 0 |

| Shortstop | PCT | G | PO | A | E | DP |
|---|---|---|---|---|---|---|
| Donato | .935 | 39 | 55 | 88 | 10 | 16 |
| Fleming | 1.000 | 3 | 5 | 4 | 0 | 0 |
| Hinds | .947 | 7 | 7 | 11 | 1 | 1 |
| Knowles | .940 | 103 | 131 | 262 | 25 | 53 |
| Long | .875 | 1 | 3 | 4 | 1 | 1 |
| Pichardo | .853 | 6 | 14 | 15 | 5 | 6 |
| Romano | 1.000 | 2 | 1 | 6 | 0 | 0 |

| Outfield | PCT | G | PO | A | E | DP |
|---|---|---|---|---|---|---|
| Delafield | 1.000 | 19 | 15 | 2 | 0 | 0 |
| DeBerry | .500 | 3 | 1 | 0 | 1 | 0 |
| Fithian | .000 | 1 | 0 | 0 | 0 | 0 |
| Hinds | 1.000 | 4 | 2 | 0 | 0 | 0 |
| Katzaroff | .967 | 21 | 27 | 2 | 1 | 1 |
| Ledee | .980 | 35 | 48 | 2 | 1 | 0 |
| McNair | .846 | 10 | 10 | 1 | 2 | 0 |
| Northrup | 1.000 | 63 | 109 | 4 | 0 | 2 |
| Norton | .923 | 10 | 11 | 1 | 1 | 0 |
| Pledger | .969 | 122 | 244 | 3 | 8 | 0 |
| Raines | 1.000 | 7 | 4 | 0 | 0 | 0 |
| Riggs | 1.000 | 3 | 2 | 0 | 0 | 0 |
| Romano | 1.000 | 4 | 4 | 0 | 0 | 0 |
| Seefried | .938 | 8 | 15 | 0 | 1 | 0 |
| Smith | .975 | 58 | 116 | 3 | 3 | 0 |
| Spencer | .979 | 95 | 130 | 10 | 3 | 1 |

# TAMPA — Class A

## FLORIDA STATE LEAGUE

### BATTING

| | AVG | G | AB | R | H | 2B | 3B | HR | RBI | BB | SO | SB | CS | B | T | HT | WT | DOB | 1st Yr | Resides |
|---|---|---|---|---|---|---|---|---|---|---|---|---|---|---|---|---|---|---|---|---|
| Ashby, Chris | .246 | 100 | 325 | 55 | 80 | 28 | 0 | 6 | 46 | 71 | 78 | 16 | 4 | R | R | 6-3 | 185 | 12-15-74 | 1993 | Boca Raton, Fla. |
| Beeney, Ryan | .205 | 13 | 39 | 7 | 8 | 1 | 0 | 0 | 4 | 7 | 12 | 0 | 0 | R | R | 6-3 | 200 | 8-22-72 | 1994 | Newark, Ohio |
| Bierek, Kurt | .303 | 88 | 320 | 48 | 97 | 14 | 2 | 11 | 55 | 41 | 40 | 6 | 3 | L | R | 6-4 | 200 | 9-13-72 | 1993 | Hillsboro, Ore. |
| Brown, Vick | .202 | 35 | 89 | 17 | 18 | 3 | 0 | 0 | 7 | 14 | 22 | 2 | 0 | R | R | 6-2 | 165 | 11-14-72 | 1993 | Cypress, Fla. |
| Buchanan, Brian | .260 | 131 | 526 | 65 | 137 | 22 | 4 | 10 | 58 | 37 | 108 | 23 | 8 | R | R | 6-4 | 220 | 7-21-73 | 1994 | Clifton, Va. |
| Camfield, Eric | .220 | 13 | 41 | 4 | 9 | 1 | 0 | 0 | 0 | 2 | 7 | 0 | 1 | L | L | 6-2 | 185 | 1-7-73 | 1995 | Fairborn, Ohio |
| Delvecchio, Nick | .269 | 17 | 52 | 9 | 14 | 2 | 0 | 2 | 4 | 17 | 15 | 2 | 1 | L | R | 6-3 | 203 | 1-23-70 | 1992 | Natick, Mass. |
| Dukart, Derek | .314 | 59 | 194 | 19 | 61 | 17 | 0 | 2 | 27 | 8 | 28 | 1 | 2 | L | R | 6-4 | 205 | 8-17-71 | 1994 | Lincoln, Neb. |
| Emmons, Scott | .204 | 36 | 98 | 6 | 20 | 2 | 1 | 1 | 10 | 10 | 26 | 0 | 1 | R | R | 6-2 | 205 | 7-14-72 | 1995 | Norco, Calif. |
| Giardi, Mike | .154 | 5 | 13 | 3 | 2 | 0 | 0 | 0 | 1 | 4 | 3 | 0 | 0 | R | R | 6-2 | 205 | 7-14-72 | 1994 | Salem, Mass. |
| Gomez, Rudy | .292 | 40 | 130 | 15 | 38 | 9 | 1 | 1 | 24 | 26 | 12 | 4 | 1 | R | R | 5-11 | 180 | 4-19-74 | 1996 | Miami, Fla. |
| Hawkins, Kraig | .299 | 75 | 268 | 41 | 80 | 2 | 5 | 1 | 21 | 35 | 41 | 13 | 6 | S | R | 6-2 | 170 | 12-4-71 | 1992 | Lake Charles, La. |
| Imrisek, Jason | .000 | 4 | 3 | 0 | 0 | 0 | 0 | 0 | 0 | 1 | 0 | 0 | 0 | R | R | 5-11 | 185 | 6-10-74 | 1995 | Orland Park, Ill. |
| Kelly, Pat | .273 | 6 | 22 | 6 | 6 | 0 | 0 | 1 | 2 | 1 | 7 | 0 | 0 | R | R | 6-0 | 180 | 10-14-67 | 1988 | Bangor, Pa. |
| Lobaton, Jose | .232 | 113 | 375 | 39 | 87 | 16 | 5 | 5 | 37 | 34 | 74 | 11 | 7 | R | R | 5-11 | 154 | 3-29-74 | 1992 | Acarigua, Venez. |
| Lowell, Mike | .282 | 24 | 78 | 8 | 22 | 5 | 0 | 0 | 11 | 3 | 13 | 1 | 1 | R | R | 6-4 | 195 | 2-24-74 | 1995 | Coral Gables, Fla. |
| Luke, Matt | .286 | 2 | 7 | 1 | 2 | 0 | 0 | 0 | 1 | 1 | 1 | 0 | 0 | L | L | 6-5 | 225 | 2-26-71 | 1992 | Brea, Calif. |
| McLamb, Brian | .211 | 85 | 266 | 31 | 56 | 13 | 0 | 2 | 25 | 23 | 62 | 7 | 5 | S | R | 6-3 | 185 | 12-13-72 | 1993 | Jacksonville, Fla. |
| Motuzas, Jeff | .000 | 2 | 3 | 0 | 0 | 0 | 0 | 0 | 0 | 0 | 3 | 0 | 0 | R | R | 6-2 | 205 | 10-1-71 | 1990 | Nashua, N.H. |
| Pichardo, Sandy | .252 | 84 | 294 | 40 | 74 | 7 | 7 | 2 | 33 | 21 | 49 | 4 | 6 | S | R | 5-11 | 173 | 11-26-74 | 1991 | Santiago, D.R. |
| Raines, Tim | .361 | 9 | 36 | 9 | 13 | 2 | 0 | 2 | 11 | 8 | 3 | 0 | 0 | S | R | 5-8 | 185 | 9-16-59 | 1977 | Heathrow, Fla. |
| Smith, Sloan | .222 | 61 | 194 | 25 | 43 | 10 | 1 | 4 | 21 | 46 | 60 | 5 | 6 | S | R | 6-4 | 215 | 11-29-72 | 1993 | Evanston, Ill. |
| Troilo, Jason | .200 | 11 | 25 | 2 | 5 | 1 | 0 | 1 | 5 | 1 | 7 | 0 | 0 | R | R | 6-1 | 195 | 9-7-72 | 1994 | Avondale, Pa. |
| Twombley, Dennis | .276 | 28 | 76 | 7 | 21 | 4 | 0 | 1 | 8 | 12 | 18 | 0 | 0 | R | R | 6-2 | 218 | 6-8-75 | 1996 | San Diego, Calif. |
| Wilcox, Luke | .283 | 119 | 470 | 72 | 133 | 32 | 5 | 11 | 76 | 40 | 71 | 14 | 10 | L | R | 6-4 | 190 | 11-15-73 | 1995 | St Johns, Mich. |
| Yedo, Carlos | .227 | 131 | 463 | 58 | 105 | 21 | 1 | 11 | 55 | 64 | 131 | 1 | 0 | L | L | 6-4 | 210 | 2-24-74 | 1994 | Miami, Fla. |

GAMES BY POSITION: C—Ashby 85, Emmons 30, Imrisek 4, Motuzas 1, Troilo 6, Twombley 28. 1B—Delvecchio 1, Emmons 3, Giardi 1, McLamb 4, Yedo 130. 2B—Beeney 2, Brown 24, Gomez 40, Kelly 6, McLamb 1, Pichardo 71. 3B—Beeney 3, Brown 5, Dukart 53, Giardi 3, Lowell 24, McLamb 57, Troilo 1. SS—Beeney 8, Brown 2, Dukart 1, Lobaton 113, McLamb 14. OF—Bierek 58, Buchanan 96, Camfield 3, Hawkins 72, Luke 2, McLamb 4, Pichardo 5, Raines 7, Smith 59, Wilcox 106.

### PITCHING

| | W | L | ERA | G | GS | CG | SV | IP | H | R | ER | BB | SO | B | T | HT | WT | DOB | 1st Yr | Resides |
|---|---|---|---|---|---|---|---|---|---|---|---|---|---|---|---|---|---|---|---|---|
| Beverlin, Jason | 2 | 0 | 3.50 | 25 | 1 | 0 | 1 | 46 | 43 | 22 | 18 | 17 | 38 | L | R | 6-5 | 230 | 11-27-73 | 1994 | Royal Oak, Calif. |
| Bracho, Alejandro | 0 | 0 | 5.40 | 2 | 0 | 0 | 0 | 2 | 2 | 1 | 1 | 2 | 0 | L | L | 6-2 | 185 | 3-10-76 | 1994 | Cabudare, Venez. |
| Brown, Charlie | 0 | 0 | 3.45 | 12 | 0 | 0 | 0 | 16 | 16 | 9 | 6 | 5 | 16 | R | R | 6-3 | 178 | 9-13-73 | 1992 | Fort Pierce, Fla. |
| Corn, Chris | 12 | 4 | 2.91 | 26 | 25 | 2 | 0 | 170 | 145 | 67 | 55 | 38 | 109 | R | R | 6-2 | 170 | 10-4-71 | 1994 | Louisville, Ky. |
| Drews, Matt | 0 | 3 | 7.13 | 4 | 4 | 0 | 0 | 18 | 26 | 20 | 14 | 12 | 12 | R | R | 6-8 | 205 | 8-29-74 | 1994 | Sarasota, Fla. |
| Drumheller, Al | 9 | 3 | 2.28 | 36 | 0 | 0 | 1 | 51 | 34 | 15 | 13 | 33 | 57 | R | L | 6-0 | 185 | 7-31-71 | 1993 | Shenandoah, Pa. |
| Henthorne, Kevin | 7 | 4 | 2.60 | 19 | 13 | 0 | 0 | 93 | 88 | 31 | 27 | 12 | 82 | S | R | 6-2 | 182 | 12-9-69 | 1994 | San Antonio, Texas |
| Hubbard, Mark | 1 | 2 | 5.73 | 4 | 4 | 0 | 0 | 22 | 27 | 17 | 14 | 6 | 12 | L | L | 6-2 | 190 | 2-2-70 | 1991 | Dover, Fla. |
| Hutton, Mark | 0 | 0 | 1.80 | 3 | 2 | 0 | 0 | 5 | 2 | 1 | 1 | 1 | 6 | R | R | 6-5 | 225 | 2-6-70 | 1989 | West Lakes, Australia |
| Jerzembeck, Mike | 4 | 2 | 2.95 | 12 | 12 | 0 | 0 | 73 | 67 | 26 | 24 | 13 | 60 | R | R | 6-1 | 185 | 5-18-72 | 1993 | Queens Village, N.Y. |
| Kamieniecki, Scott | 2 | 1 | 1.17 | 3 | 3 | 1 | 0 | 23 | 20 | 6 | 3 | 4 | 17 | R | R | 6-0 | 190 | 4-19-64 | 1987 | Flint, Mich. |
| Key, Jimmy | 0 | 0 | 2.77 | 2 | 2 | 0 | 0 | 13 | 10 | 4 | 4 | 1 | 11 | R | L | 6-1 | 185 | 4-22-61 | 1982 | Tarpon Springs, Fla. |
| Lail, Denny | 4 | 0 | 2.55 | 31 | 0 | 0 | 1 | 35 | 37 | 11 | 10 | 14 | 21 | R | R | 6-0 | 185 | 9-10-74 | 1995 | Taylorsville, N.C. |
| Maeda, Katsuhiro | 0 | 0 | 4.22 | 2 | 2 | 0 | 0 | 11 | 11 | 5 | 5 | 6 | 8 | R | R | 6-2 | 215 | 6-23-71 | 1996 | Kobe, Japan |
| Meyer, David | 2 | 3 | 2.11 | 11 | 6 | 0 | 0 | 38 | 46 | 16 | 9 | 17 | 18 | L | L | 6-5 | 215 | 12-15-71 | 1994 | Grapevine, Texas |
| Mittauer, Casey | 1 | 1 | 2.01 | 21 | 0 | 0 | 4 | 31 | 28 | 10 | 7 | 5 | 23 | R | R | 6-5 | 225 | 9-1-72 | 1993 | Cooper City, Fla. |
| Musselwhite, Jim | 0 | 2 | 7.80 | 3 | 3 | 0 | 0 | 15 | 24 | 16 | 13 | 5 | 5 | R | R | 6-1 | 190 | 10-25-71 | 1993 | Apopka, Fla. |
| Resz, Greg | 0 | 0 | 2.52 | 20 | 0 | 0 | 4 | 25 | 20 | 11 | 7 | 12 | 31 | L | R | 6-5 | 215 | 12-25-71 | 1993 | Springfield, Mo. |
| Santiago, Sandi | 0 | 1 | 5.11 | 9 | 1 | 0 | 1 | 12 | 18 | 9 | 7 | 4 | 11 | R | R | 6-1 | 175 | 3-16-70 | 1989 | Bani, D.R. |
| Schlomann, Brett | 11 | 8 | 4.26 | 26 | 26 | 1 | 0 | 146 | 152 | 81 | 69 | 49 | 103 | R | R | 6-1 | 185 | 7-31-74 | 1994 | Collinsville, Okla. |
| Shelby, Anthony | 2 | 2 | 1.80 | 24 | 0 | 0 | 1 | 30 | 24 | 9 | 6 | 7 | 18 | L | L | 6-3 | 200 | 12-11-73 | 1993 | Sarasota, Fla. |
| Spence, Cam | 2 | 4 | 5.80 | 8 | 8 | 0 | 0 | 40 | 51 | 31 | 26 | 12 | 20 | R | R | 6-2 | 195 | 10-11-74 | 1996 | Lithonia, Ga. |
| St. Pierre, Bob | 12 | 6 | 3.21 | 29 | 22 | 0 | 1 | 140 | 133 | 69 | 50 | 38 | 107 | R | R | 6-1 | 190 | 4-11-74 | 1995 | Huntington, Md. |
| Stewart, Stan | 0 | 0 | 2.70 | 14 | 0 | 0 | 0 | 27 | 29 | 14 | 8 | 5 | 23 | R | R | 6-5 | 191 | 12-9-72 | 1995 | Gainesville, Fla. |
| Tessmer, Jay | 12 | 4 | 1.48 | 68 | 0 | 0 | 35 | 97 | 68 | 18 | 16 | 19 | 104 | R | R | 6-3 | 190 | 12-26-72 | 1995 | Cochranton, Pa. |

## SOUTH ATLANTIC LEAGUE

| BATTING | AVG | G | AB | R | H | 2B | 3B | HR | RBI | BB | SO | SB | CS | B | T | HT | WT | DOB | 1st Yr | Resides |
|---|---|---|---|---|---|---|---|---|---|---|---|---|---|---|---|---|---|---|---|---|
| Antrim, Pat | .083 | 15 | 12 | 2 | 1 | 0 | 0 | 0 | 0 | 1 | 7 | 1 | 1 | S | R | 6-2 | 170 | 8-18-73 | 1995 | Mission Viejo, Calif. |
| Brown, Vick | .319 | 25 | 91 | 8 | 29 | 6 | 0 | 1 | 9 | 11 | 23 | 9 | 2 | R | R | 6-1 | 165 | 11-14-72 | 1993 | Cypress, Fla. |
| Camfield, Eric | .176 | 76 | 238 | 19 | 42 | 2 | 2 | 0 | 24 | 18 | 63 | 13 | 5 | L | L | 6-2 | 185 | 1-7-73 | 1995 | Fairborn, Ohio |
| Delafield, Wil | .255 | 30 | 98 | 16 | 25 | 4 | 1 | 2 | 11 | 6 | 30 | 1 | 0 | R | R | 6-2 | 185 | 2-15-72 | 1992 | Baton Rouge, La. |
| Dennis, Les | .253 | 33 | 75 | 15 | 19 | 3 | 0 | 1 | 9 | 11 | 27 | 1 | 2 | R | R | 6-0 | 175 | 6-3-73 | 1995 | West Linn, Ore. |
| Emmons, Scott | .239 | 15 | 46 | 7 | 11 | 1 | 0 | 1 | 9 | 2 | 6 | 0 | 1 | R | R | 6-4 | 205 | 12-25-73 | 1995 | Norco, Calif. |
| Giardi, Mike | .222 | 20 | 63 | 11 | 14 | 5 | 0 | 3 | 5 | 10 | 13 | 0 | 1 | R | R | 6-2 | 205 | 7-14-72 | 1994 | Salem, Mass. |
| Hairston, John | .216 | 59 | 194 | 19 | 42 | 5 | 1 | 5 | 19 | 19 | 81 | 4 | 2 | S | R | 6-1 | 185 | 11-15-67 | 1989 | Portland, Ore. |
| Jimenez, D'Angelo | .244 | 138 | 537 | 68 | 131 | 25 | 5 | 6 | 48 | 56 | 113 | 15 | 17 | S | R | 6-0 | 160 | 12-21-77 | 1995 | Santo Domingo, D.R. |
| Keech, Erik | .229 | 16 | 35 | 4 | 8 | 2 | 0 | 0 | 2 | 3 | 4 | 0 | 0 | L | R | 6-2 | 195 | 9-7-74 | 1995 | Sarasota, Fla. |
| Lowell, Mike | .282 | 113 | 433 | 58 | 122 | 33 | 0 | 8 | 64 | 46 | 43 | 10 | 3 | R | R | 6-4 | 195 | 2-24-74 | 1995 | Coral Gables, Fla. |
| McCormick, Cody | .197 | 65 | 173 | 16 | 34 | 9 | 0 | 6 | 20 | 12 | 46 | 0 | 1 | R | R | 6-3 | 200 | 7-30-74 | 1995 | Berkeley, Calif. |
| Morenz, Shea | .249 | 91 | 338 | 40 | 84 | 14 | 4 | 2 | 48 | 38 | 92 | 13 | 3 | L | R | 6-2 | 205 | 1-22-74 | 1995 | San Angelo, Texas |
| Pinto, Rene | .206 | 52 | 165 | 13 | 34 | 9 | 1 | 1 | 14 | 5 | 41 | 2 | 1 | R | R | 6-0 | 195 | 7-17-77 | 1994 | Palo Negra, Venez |
| Rosado, Luis | .250 | 7 | 12 | 2 | 3 | 0 | 0 | 0 | 1 | 6 | 0 | 0 | 0 | R | R | 6-2 | 183 | 10-4-75 | 1994 | San Pedro de Macoris, D.R. |
| Saffer, Jeff | .273 | 45 | 154 | 17 | 42 | 10 | 3 | 3 | 16 | 7 | 60 | 0 | 0 | R | R | 6-4 | 220 | 6-30-75 | 1995 | Tucson, Ariz. |
| Samuel, Cody | .254 | 126 | 477 | 50 | 121 | 19 | 0 | 19 | 86 | 37 | 165 | 0 | 2 | R | R | 6-1 | 210 | 4-10-74 | 1992 | Redondo Beach, Calif. |
| Shumpert, Derek | .253 | 141 | 522 | 76 | 132 | 20 | 10 | 3 | 45 | 57 | 144 | 28 | 18 | S | R | 6-2 | 185 | 9-30-75 | 1993 | St. Louis, Mo. |
| Smith, Rod | .212 | 132 | 481 | 71 | 102 | 15 | 8 | 4 | 32 | 64 | 128 | 57 | 13 | S | R | 6-0 | 185 | 9-2-75 | 1994 | Lexington, Ky. |
| Troilo, Jason | .191 | 67 | 199 | 19 | 38 | 10 | 0 | 3 | 17 | 9 | 62 | 2 | 1 | R | R | 6-1 | 195 | 9-7-72 | 1994 | Avondale, Pa. |
| Velazquez, Jose | .246 | 116 | 415 | 55 | 102 | 17 | 2 | 6 | 43 | 36 | 75 | 4 | 3 | R | R | 6-3 | 205 | 8-24-75 | 1994 | Guayama, P.R. |

**GAMES BY POSITION: C**—Emmons 14, Keech 11, McCormick 25, Pinto 50, Troilo 66. **1B**—Camfield 1, Giardi 5, McCormick 1, Saffer 1, Samuel 98, Velazquez 42. **2B**—Antrim 2, Camfield 1, Dennis 16, Smith 131. **3B**—Antrim 1, Brown 25, Dennis 2, Giardi 3, Lowell 112, Rosado 2. **SS**—Antrim 3, Dennis 4, Jimenez 136, Lowell 1. **OF**—Camfield 67, Delafield 29, Dennis 4, Giardi 13, Hairston 56, Morenz 91, Saffer 36, Shumpert 141, Velazquez 2.

| PITCHING | W | L | ERA | G | GS | CG | SV | IP | H | R | ER | BB | SO | B | T | HT | WT | DOB | 1st Yr | Resides |
|---|---|---|---|---|---|---|---|---|---|---|---|---|---|---|---|---|---|---|---|---|
| Becker, Tom | 6 | 9 | 3.69 | 40 | 14 | 1 | 0 | 127 | 116 | 69 | 52 | 75 | 97 | R | R | 6-3 | 205 | 1-13-75 | 1994 | Adelaide, Australia |
| Bracho, Alejandro | 4 | 4 | 3.80 | 34 | 5 | 0 | 1 | 92 | 96 | 47 | 39 | 34 | 70 | L | L | 6-2 | 185 | 3-10-76 | 1994 | Cabudare, Venez. |
| Brown, Charlie | 2 | 2 | 1.59 | 23 | 0 | 0 | 8 | 28 | 13 | 6 | 5 | 13 | 33 | R | R | 6-3 | 178 | 9-13-73 | 1992 | Fort Pierce, Fla. |
| Coleman, Billy | 0 | 0 | 4.91 | 4 | 0 | 0 | 0 | 7 | 5 | 4 | 4 | 3 | 9 | R | R | 6-1 | 185 | 1-18-69 | 1991 | Roanoke, Texas |
| De los Santos, Luis | 4 | 1 | 4.83 | 7 | 6 | 0 | 0 | 32 | 39 | 17 | 17 | 11 | 21 | R | R | 6-2 | 187 | 11-1-77 | 1995 | San Pedro de Macoris, D.R. |
| Dunbar, Matt | 1 | 1 | 1.93 | 2 | 2 | 0 | 0 | 14 | 6 | 3 | 3 | 4 | 19 | L | L | 6-0 | 160 | 10-15-68 | 1990 | Tallahassee, Fla. |
| Einerston, Darrell | 3 | 9 | 2.70 | 48 | 0 | 0 | 8 | 70 | 69 | 29 | 21 | 19 | 48 | R | R | 6-2 | 190 | 9-4-72 | 1995 | Urbandale, Iowa |
| Ford, Ben | 2 | 6 | 4.26 | 43 | 0 | 0 | 2 | 82 | 75 | 48 | 39 | 33 | 84 | R | R | 6-7 | 200 | 8-15-75 | 1994 | Cedar Rapids, Iowa |
| Frazier, Harold | 0 | 0 | 27.00 | 2 | 0 | 0 | 0 | 1 | 3 | 3 | 2 | 1 | 0 | L | L | 6-1 | 190 | 8-26-73 | 1996 | Morris, Okla. |
| Judd, Mike | 2 | 2 | 3.81 | 29 | 0 | 0 | 10 | 28 | 22 | 14 | 12 | 8 | 36 | R | R | 6-2 | 200 | 6-30-75 | 1995 | La Mesa, Calif. |
| Lail, Denny | 1 | 0 | 4.70 | 11 | 0 | 0 | 0 | 23 | 19 | 16 | 12 | 11 | 24 | R | R | 6-0 | 185 | 9-10-74 | 1995 | Taylorsville, N.C. |
| Meyer, David | 1 | 0 | 0.00 | 6 | 0 | 0 | 0 | 19 | 9 | 0 | 0 | 1 | 24 | L | L | 6-5 | 215 | 12-15-71 | 1994 | Grapevine, Texas |
| Militello, Sam | 0 | 2 | 8.53 | 3 | 3 | 0 | 0 | 6 | 1 | 7 | 6 | 15 | 5 | R | R | 6-3 | 200 | 11-26-69 | 1990 | Tampa, Fla. |
| Musslewhite, Jim | 2 | 1 | 3.15 | 4 | 4 | 0 | 0 | 20 | 26 | 9 | 7 | 3 | 15 | R | R | 6-1 | 190 | 10-25-71 | 1993 | Apopka, Fla. |
| Olivier, Rich | 3 | 2 | 4.24 | 9 | 9 | 0 | 0 | 47 | 51 | 28 | 22 | 23 | 44 | R | R | 6-0 | 155 | 11-22-74 | 1992 | Santo Domingo, D.R. |
| Parotte, Frisco | 0 | 0 | 2.55 | 24 | 0 | 0 | 0 | 53 | 35 | 24 | 15 | 35 | 41 | R | R | 6-3 | 180 | 9-10-75 | 1994 | Levittown, P.R. |
| Randolph, Stephen | 4 | 7 | 3.77 | 32 | 17 | 0 | 0 | 100 | 64 | 46 | 42 | 96 | 111 | L | L | 6-3 | 185 | 5-1-74 | 1995 | Austin, Texas |
| Robbins, Jake | 1 | 8 | 6.45 | 18 | 12 | 0 | 0 | 74 | 80 | 59 | 53 | 49 | 50 | R | R | 6-5 | 195 | 5-23-76 | 1994 | Charlotte, N.C. |
| Robinson, Martin | 1 | 8 | 5.73 | 10 | 10 | 1 | 0 | 49 | 60 | 43 | 31 | 30 | 38 | L | L | 6-1 | 180 | 9-13-76 | 1994 | Cape Coral, Fla. |
| Schaffner, Eric | 3 | 7 | 5.03 | 27 | 12 | 0 | 0 | 91 | 97 | 65 | 51 | 62 | 62 | R | R | 6-4 | 190 | 10-19-74 | 1994 | Keizer, Ore. |
| Shelby, Anthony | 2 | 1 | 1.38 | 16 | 0 | 0 | 1 | 26 | 16 | 5 | 4 | 10 | 25 | L | L | 6-3 | 200 | 12-11-73 | 1993 | Sarasota, Fla. |
| Spence, Cam | 6 | 6 | 3.85 | 19 | 19 | 0 | 0 | 115 | 108 | 66 | 49 | 38 | 89 | R | R | 6-2 | 195 | 10-11-74 | 1996 | Lithonia, Ga. |
| Stewart, Stan | 3 | 3 | 6.16 | 10 | 10 | 1 | 0 | 57 | 64 | 43 | 39 | 26 | 51 | R | R | 6-5 | 191 | 12-9-72 | 1995 | Gainesville, Fla. |
| Taylor, Brien | 0 | 5 | 18.73 | 9 | 9 | 0 | 0 | 16 | 21 | 40 | 34 | 43 | 11 | L | L | 6-4 | 215 | 12-26-71 | 1991 | Beaufort, N.C. |
| Verdin, Cesar | 5 | 2 | 2.42 | 14 | 10 | 1 | 0 | 67 | 56 | 34 | 18 | 24 | 71 | L | L | 6-3 | 210 | 11-11-76 | 1995 | San Diego, Calif. |

## NEW YORK-PENN LEAGUE

| BATTING | AVG | G | AB | R | H | 2B | 3B | HR | RBI | BB | SO | SB | CS | B | T | HT | WT | DOB | 1st Yr | Resides |
|---|---|---|---|---|---|---|---|---|---|---|---|---|---|---|---|---|---|---|---|---|
| Antrim, Pat | .224 | 14 | 49 | 4 | 11 | 0 | 0 | 0 | 2 | 5 | 14 | 3 | 3 | S | R | 6-2 | 170 | 8-18-73 | 1995 | Mission Viejo, Calif. |
| Aylor, Brian | .440 | 8 | 25 | 9 | 11 | 3 | 3 | 0 | 5 | 2 | 5 | 3 | 1 | L | L | 6-2 | 200 | 4-6-74 | 1996 | Midwest City, Okla. |
| Ayotte, Scott | .202 | 27 | 89 | 9 | 18 | 5 | 1 | 0 | 8 | 8 | 32 | 2 | 1 | L | L | 6-1 | 195 | 9-30-73 | 1996 | Lake Port, Mich. |
| Beaumont, Hamil | .000 | 1 | 3 | 0 | 0 | 0 | 0 | 0 | 0 | 0 | 0 | 0 | 0 | R | R | 6-3 | 200 | 1-3-75 | 1993 | Panama City, Panama |
| Beeney, Ryan | .500 | 2 | 4 | 1 | 2 | 0 | 0 | 0 | 0 | 0 | 0 | 0 | 0 | R | R | 6-3 | 200 | 8-22-72 | 1994 | Newark, Ohio |
| Butler, Allen | .217 | 72 | 249 | 32 | 54 | 7 | 2 | 1 | 24 | 32 | 66 | 0 | 1 | L | R | 6-3 | 190 | 1-22-75 | 1996 | Clinchport, Va. |
| Butler, Garrett | .280 | 69 | 207 | 36 | 58 | 3 | 1 | 0 | 16 | 30 | 46 | 29 | 7 | S | R | 6-2 | 165 | 5-20-76 | 1994 | Miami, Fla. |
| Dennis, Les | .243 | 72 | 276 | 36 | 67 | 3 | 2 | 0 | 43 | 33 | 76 | 20 | 9 | R | R | 6-0 | 175 | 6-3-73 | 1995 | West Linn, Ore. |
| De la Cruz, Wilfredo | .400 | 4 | 15 | 3 | 6 | 1 | 0 | 0 | 0 | 1 | 2 | 0 | 0 | R | R | 6-0 | 160 | 2-2-76 | 1994 | Santo Domingo, D.R. |
| Huffman, Ryan | .197 | 23 | 61 | 8 | 12 | 4 | 1 | 0 | 6 | 6 | 24 | 0 | 0 | R | R | 6-2 | 215 | 8-7-73 | 1996 | Cleburne, Texas |
| Kane, Kevin | .250 | 4 | 4 | 1 | 1 | 0 | 0 | 0 | 0 | 0 | 1 | 0 | 0 | R | R | 5-10 | 160 | 11-27-73 | 1996 | Tampa, Fla. |
| Kofler, Eric | .227 | 46 | 176 | 18 | 40 | 8 | 0 | 3 | 22 | 10 | 33 | 3 | 1 | L | L | 6-1 | 170 | 2-11-76 | 1994 | Palm Harbor, Fla. |
| McDonald, Donzell | .277 | 74 | 282 | 57 | 78 | 8 | 10 | 2 | 30 | 43 | 62 | 54 | 4 | S | R | 6-0 | 165 | 2-20-75 | 1995 | Glendale, Colo. |
| Phillips, Blaine | .209 | 47 | 148 | 12 | 31 | 2 | 0 | 0 | 12 | 11 | 51 | 0 | 2 | R | R | 6-1 | 200 | 6-28-73 | 1996 | Sheridan, Wyom. |
| Pinto, Rene | .206 | 53 | 199 | 15 | 41 | 1 | 2 | 2 | 20 | 5 | 54 | 1 | 1 | R | R | 6-0 | 195 | 7-17-77 | 1994 | Palo Negra, Venez |
| Saffer, Jeff | .249 | 53 | 197 | 18 | 49 | 4 | 1 | 4 | 27 | 22 | 62 | 2 | 1 | R | R | 6-4 | 220 | 6-30-75 | 1995 | Tucson, Ariz. |
| Seabol, Scott | .211 | 43 | 142 | 16 | 30 | 9 | 1 | 3 | 10 | 15 | 30 | 2 | 3 | R | R | 6-4 | 200 | 5-17-75 | 1996 | McKeesport, Pa. |
| Twombley, Dennis | .211 | 6 | 19 | 2 | 4 | 1 | 0 | 1 | 3 | 4 | 5 | 0 | 0 | R | R | 6-2 | 185 | 6-8-75 | 1996 | San Diego, Calif. |
| Valencia, Victor | .195 | 72 | 261 | 30 | 51 | 8 | 0 | 3 | 25 | 21 | 86 | 3 | 0 | R | R | 6-2 | 185 | 5-30-77 | 1994 | Maracay, Venez. |
| Wheeler, Ryan | .308 | 24 | 65 | 12 | 20 | 3 | 1 | 0 | 5 | 1 | 11 | 4 | 0 | R | R | 5-10 | 175 | 1-27-74 | 1996 | Elizabethtown, Ky. |

**GAMES BY POSITION: C**—Phillips 3, Pinto 26, Twombley 2, Valencia 47. **1B**—Huffman 6, Saffer 53, Seabol 22. **2B**—Antrim 13, Beeney 2, Kane 1, Phillips 39, Seabol 15, Wheeler 13. **3B**—Butler 71, Phillips 2, Seabol 3. **SS**—Antrim 2, Dennis 72, Seabol 3. **OF**—Aylor 8, Ayotte 25, Butler 69, Dennis 1, De la Cruz 2, Huffman 15, Kofler 37, McDonald 74, Phillips 2, Wheeler 6.

| PITCHING | W | L | ERA | G | GS | CG | SV | IP | H | R | ER | BB | SO | B | T | HT | WT | DOB | 1st Yr | Resides |
|---|---|---|---|---|---|---|---|---|---|---|---|---|---|---|---|---|---|---|---|---|
| Aguilar, Carlos | 0 | 4 | 3.62 | 23 | 0 | 0 | 0 | 50 | 44 | 29 | 20 | 27 | 43 | R | R | 6-1 | 165 | 11-7-75 | 1993 | Carabobo, Venez. |
| Armas, Antonio | 1 | 1 | 5.74 | 3 | 3 | 0 | 0 | 16 | 14 | 12 | 10 | 11 | 14 | R | R | 6-4 | 175 | 4-29-78 | 1994 | Puerto Piritu, Venez. |
| Biehle, Mike | 2 | 3 | 3.96 | 20 | 0 | 0 | 0 | 36 | 37 | 22 | 16 | 18 | 42 | L | L | 6-1 | 215 | 1-17-74 | 1996 | South Lebanon, Ohio |
| Bracho, Alejandro | 0 | 2 | 7.20 | 4 | 1 | 0 | 1 | 10 | 8 | 8 | 8 | 13 | 11 | L | L | 6-2 | 185 | 3-10-76 | 1994 | Cabudare, Venez. |
| Brand, Scott | 1 | 2 | 3.70 | 9 | 1 | 0 | 0 | 24 | 20 | 17 | 10 | 19 | 22 | R | R | 6-3 | 200 | 1-1-76 | 1995 | Lubbock, Texas |
| Coleman, Billy | 1 | 0 | 14.73 | 3 | 0 | 0 | 0 | 4 | 4 | 6 | 6 | 6 | 4 | R | R | 6-1 | 185 | 1-18-69 | 1991 | Roanoke, Texas |
| De los Santos, Luis | 4 | 4 | 3.72 | 10 | 10 | 3 | 0 | 58 | 44 | 28 | 24 | 21 | 62 | R | R | 6-2 | 187 | 11-1-77 | 1995 | San Pedro de Macoris, D.R. |
| Dingman, Craig | 0 | 2 | 2.04 | 20 | 0 | 0 | 9 | 35 | 17 | 11 | 8 | 9 | 52 | R | R | 6-4 | 190 | 3-12-74 | 1994 | Wichita, Kan. |
| Ellison, Jason | 0 | 0 | 9.00 | 1 | 0 | 0 | 0 | 1 | 2 | 1 | 1 | 0 | 2 | R | R | 6-4 | 180 | 7-24-75 | 1996 | Buffalo, Texas |
| Frazier, Harold | 2 | 1 | 2.70 | 5 | 0 | 0 | 0 | 7 | 2 | 2 | 2 | 2 | 7 | L | L | 6-1 | 190 | 8-26-73 | 1996 | Morris, Okla. |
| Hendrikx, Brandon | 3 | 2 | 1.33 | 17 | 0 | 0 | 1 | 27 | 17 | 6 | 4 | 15 | 23 | R | R | 6-1 | 210 | 12-5-75 | 1996 | Lake Forest, Calif. |
| Ingerick, Rhett | 1 | 1 | 5.85 | 11 | 0 | 0 | 0 | 20 | 26 | 16 | 13 | 11 | 21 | R | R | 6-6 | 195 | 10-16-74 | 1996 | Hendersonville, N.C. |
| Krall, Eric | 0 | 5 | 2.42 | 15 | 6 | 0 | 0 | 45 | 43 | 27 | 12 | 25 | 29 | L | L | 6-4 | 215 | 2-27-74 | 1996 | Apopka, Fla. |
| Mota, Daniel | 4 | 4 | 4.50 | 10 | 0 | 0 | 7 | 10 | 10 | 5 | 5 | 2 | 11 | R | R | 6-0 | 170 | 10-9-75 | 1994 | Santo Domingo, D.R. |
| Phillips, Ben | 3 | 4 | 2.97 | 14 | 14 | 0 | 0 | 79 | 58 | 40 | 26 | 41 | 56 | R | R | 6-3 | 195 | 7-28-75 | 1996 | Sheridan, Wyom. |
| Rangel, Julio | 7 | 2 | 2.96 | 15 | 14 | 0 | 0 | 85 | 64 | 35 | 28 | 36 | 79 | R | R | 6-3 | 190 | 9-28-75 | 1994 | Panama City, Panama |
| Rayment, Justin | 0 | 1 | 18.00 | 1 | 1 | 0 | 0 | 2 | 3 | 4 | 4 | 3 | 0 | L | L | 6-8 | 230 | 5-28-74 | 1996 | Sedro Woolley, Wash. |
| Robbins, Jake | 3 | 4 | 4.50 | 11 | 11 | 0 | 0 | 66 | 64 | 42 | 33 | 35 | 47 | R | R | 6-5 | 195 | 5-23-76 | 1994 | Charlotte, N.C. |
| Robinson, Martin | 3 | 6 | 3.90 | 15 | 15 | 1 | 0 | 81 | 83 | 49 | 35 | 43 | 50 | L | L | 6-1 | 180 | 9-13-76 | 1994 | Cape Coral, Fla. |
| Trunk, Todd | 0 | 0 | 36.00 | 1 | 0 | 0 | 0 | 1 | 5 | 4 | 4 | 1 | 1 | R | R | 6-4 | 190 | 7-13-73 | 1996 | Oak Forest, Ill. |

# TAMPA — Rookie

## GULF COAST LEAGUE

| BATTING | AVG | G | AB | R | H | 2B | 3B | HR | RBI | BB | SO | SB | CS | B | T | HT | WT | DOB | 1st Yr | Resides |
|---|---|---|---|---|---|---|---|---|---|---|---|---|---|---|---|---|---|---|---|---|
| Brown, Richard | .287 | 47 | 164 | 33 | 47 | 8 | 3 | 0 | 23 | 23 | 32 | 2 | 1 | L | L | 6-1 | 190 | 4-28-77 | 1996 | Plantation, Fla. |
| Candelaria, Vidal | .279 | 25 | 68 | 8 | 19 | 3 | 0 | 0 | 11 | 6 | 11 | 0 | 0 | L | R | 6-0 | 170 | 5-9-78 | 1996 | Manati, P.R. |
| Carey, Orlando | .249 | 57 | 213 | 32 | 53 | 4 | 3 | 0 | 20 | 14 | 47 | 5 | 3 | R | R | 6-1 | 185 | 2-25-76 | 1996 | Gallatin, Tenn. |
| Cruz, Alain | .255 | 45 | 165 | 33 | 42 | 13 | 2 | 3 | 26 | 16 | 46 | 3 | 0 | R | R | 5-11 | 185 | 7-3-75 | 1996 | Hialeah, Fla. |
| De la Cruz, Wilfredo | .163 | 16 | 43 | 3 | 7 | 0 | 0 | 0 | 6 | 4 | 9 | 1 | 0 | R | R | 6-0 | 160 | 2-2-76 | 1994 | Santo Domingo, D.R. |
| Delvecchio, Nick | .611 | 5 | 18 | 4 | 11 | 4 | 0 | 2 | 8 | 6 | 1 | 1 | 0 | L | R | 6-5 | 203 | 1-23-70 | 1992 | Natick, Mass. |
| Gomez, Rudy | .276 | 16 | 58 | 12 | 16 | 6 | 0 | 0 | 10 | 9 | 7 | 0 | 1 | R | R | 5-11 | 180 | 9-14-74 | 1996 | Miami, Fla. |
| Guzman, Christian | .294 | 42 | 170 | 37 | 50 | 8 | 2 | 1 | 21 | 10 | 31 | 7 | 6 | S | R | 6-0 | 150 | 3-21-78 | 1995 | Santo Domingo, D.R. |
| Johnson, Nick | .287 | 47 | 157 | 31 | 45 | 11 | 1 | 2 | 33 | 30 | 35 | 0 | 0 | L | L | 6-3 | 195 | 6-14-96 | 1996 | Sacramento, Calif. |
| Katzaroff, Robbie | .407 | 7 | 27 | 9 | 11 | 2 | 0 | 0 | 3 | 6 | 0 | 3 | 1 | R | R | 5-8 | 170 | 7-29-68 | 1990 | Phoenix, Ariz. |
| Kelly, Pat | .353 | 5 | 17 | 7 | 6 | 2 | 0 | 1 | 1 | 3 | 2 | 3 | 0 | R | R | 6-0 | 180 | 10-14-67 | 1988 | Bangor, Pa. |
| Leon, Donny | .361 | 53 | 191 | 30 | 69 | 14 | 4 | 6 | 46 | 9 | 30 | 1 | 2 | S | R | 6-2 | 180 | 5-7-76 | 1995 | Ponce, P.R. |
| Mateo, Victor | .315 | 32 | 127 | 25 | 40 | 1 | 3 | 0 | 15 | 9 | 29 | 0 | 2 | S | R | 6-0 | 170 | 11-23-76 | 1995 | Santo Domingo, D.R. |
| Matos, Wellington | .247 | 35 | 97 | 13 | 24 | 5 | 0 | 0 | 14 | 11 | 29 | 0 | 0 | L | L | 6-4 | 205 | 8-11-76 | 1995 | Santo Domingo, D.R. |
| Meier, Bob | .333 | 3 | 3 | 0 | 1 | 1 | 0 | 0 | 0 | 0 | 1 | 0 | 0 | R | R | 6-0 | 170 | 9-5-78 | 1996 | Cinnaminson, N.J. |
| Munson, Nestor | .300 | 19 | 40 | 6 | 12 | 2 | 0 | 1 | 4 | 2 | 9 | 0 | 0 | R | R | 5-9 | 200 | 7-29-75 | 1995 | Canton, Ohio |
| Olivares, Teuris | .300 | 9 | 20 | 3 | 6 | 1 | 0 | 0 | 4 | 1 | 2 | 0 | 0 | R | R | 6-0 | 164 | 12-15-78 | 1996 | San Fran. de Macoris, D.R. |
| Ozuna, Pedro | .306 | 34 | 108 | 24 | 33 | 3 | 1 | 0 | 20 | 11 | 17 | 3 | 1 | R | R | 6-1 | 170 | 5-3-76 | 1994 | Santo Domingo, D.R. |
| Preciado, Victor | .250 | 45 | 164 | 15 | 41 | 7 | 2 | 0 | 22 | 11 | 27 | 1 | 2 | S | R | 6-4 | 205 | 9-3-76 | 1995 | David Chirriqui, Panama |
| Quintero, Christian | .265 | 21 | 68 | 13 | 18 | 4 | 0 | 1 | 8 | 4 | 13 | 1 | 0 | R | R | 6-1 | 154 | 3-2-76 | 1996 | Sinaloa, Mexico |
| Raines, Tim | .600 | 1 | 5 | 2 | 3 | 0 | 0 | 0 | 3 | 1 | 0 | 0 | 0 | S | R | 5-8 | 185 | 9-16-59 | 1977 | Heathrow, Fla. |
| Smith, Nestor | .240 | 14 | 25 | 5 | 6 | 0 | 0 | 0 | 4 | 9 | 1 | 1 | 0 | S | R | 6-1 | 175 | 1-21-78 | 1995 | Maturin, Venez. |

**GAMES BY POSITION: C**—Candelaria 25, Leon 31, Munson 18. **1B**—De la Cruz 1, Delvecchio 3, Johnson 36, Leon 4, Matos 21. **2B**—Cruz 1, Gomez 13, Kelly 3, Mateo 12, Olivares 3, Ozuna 33. **3B**—Cruz 44, De la Cruz 1, Leon 13, Mateo 2, Ozuna 1. **SS**—Guzman 41, Mateo 15, Olivares 6. **OF**—Brown 47, Carey 57, De la Cruz 12, Katzaroff 7, Preciado 40, Quintero 13.

| PITCHING | W | L | ERA | G | GS | CG | SV | IP | H | R | ER | BB | SO | B | T | HT | WT | DOB | 1st Yr | Resides |
|---|---|---|---|---|---|---|---|---|---|---|---|---|---|---|---|---|---|---|---|---|
| Armas, Antonio | 4 | 1 | 3.15 | 8 | 7 | 0 | 1 | 46 | 41 | 18 | 16 | 13 | 45 | R | R | 6-4 | 175 | 4-29-78 | 1994 | Puerto Piritu, Venez. |
| Buchanan, Brian | 4 | 1 | 3.02 | 12 | 11 | 1 | 0 | 60 | 47 | 26 | 20 | 29 | 45 | L | L | 6-2 | 190 | 4-23-77 | 1995 | Oviedo, Fla. |
| Coble, Jason | 1 | 1 | 2.48 | 9 | 9 | 0 | 0 | 33 | 23 | 11 | 9 | 20 | 40 | R | L | 6-3 | 185 | 2-28-76 | 1996 | Fayetteville, Tenn. |
| Coriolan, Roberto | 2 | 1 | 4.30 | 12 | 0 | 0 | 1 | 29 | 27 | 18 | 14 | 16 | 26 | R | R | 6-0 | 190 | 3-27-77 | 1994 | Santo Domingo, D.R. |
| Cremer, Rick | 0 | 1 | 11.57 | 2 | 1 | 0 | 0 | 5 | 3 | 7 | 6 | 4 | 4 | L | L | 6-4 | 180 | 4-19-77 | 1996 | West Frankfort, Ill. |
| Day, Zach | 5 | 2 | 5.61 | 7 | 5 | 0 | 0 | 34 | 41 | 26 | 21 | 3 | 23 | R | R | 6-4 | 185 | 6-15-78 | 1996 | West Harrison, Ind. |
| Ellison, Jason | 3 | 0 | 1.25 | 21 | 3 | 0 | 7 | 36 | 24 | 8 | 5 | 15 | 42 | R | R | 6-4 | 180 | 7-24-75 | 1996 | Buffalo, Texas |
| Fajardo, Alexis | 0 | 0 | 0.00 | 2 | 0 | 0 | 0 | 4 | 2 | 0 | 0 | 4 | 8 | L | L | 6-3 | 215 | 11-4-76 | 1995 | Miami, Fla. |
| Hendrikx, Brandon | 0 | 0 | 3.86 | 7 | 0 | 0 | 1 | 9 | 9 | 10 | 4 | 3 | 10 | R | R | 6-1 | 210 | 12-5-75 | 1996 | Lake Forest, Calif. |
| Key, Jimmy | 1 | 0 | 0.00 | 1 | 1 | 0 | 0 | 5 | 3 | 2 | 0 | 0 | 10 | R | L | 6-1 | 185 | 4-22-61 | 1982 | Tarpon Springs, Fla. |
| Maeda, Katsuhiro | 1 | 1 | 3.00 | 2 | 2 | 1 | 0 | 9 | 4 | 3 | 3 | 2 | 7 | R | R | 6-2 | 215 | 6-23-71 | 1996 | Kobe, Japan |
| Martinez, Oscar | 0 | 0 | 14.90 | 7 | 0 | 0 | 0 | 10 | 22 | 19 | 16 | 4 | 3 | R | R | 6-2 | 185 | 10-7-78 | 1996 | Araure, Venez. |
| McBride, Jason | 3 | 4 | 4.06 | 23 | 0 | 0 | 2 | 31 | 35 | 15 | 14 | 8 | 27 | R | R | 6-1 | 175 | 2-10-76 | 1996 | Pace, Fla. |
| Moreno, Willy | 0 | 1 | 9.56 | 11 | 0 | 0 | 0 | 16 | 27 | 24 | 17 | 8 | 8 | R | R | 6-4 | 185 | 3-31-77 | 1994 | Santo Domingo, D.R. |
| Olivier, Rich | 0 | 0 | 0.00 | 4 | 0 | 0 | 1 | 9 | 4 | 0 | 0 | 1 | 7 | R | R | 6-0 | 155 | 11-22-74 | 1992 | Santo Domingo, D.R. |
| Paraqueima, Jesus | 3 | 2 | 2.01 | 11 | 9 | 0 | 0 | 49 | 43 | 24 | 11 | 15 | 49 | R | R | 6-4 | 185 | 2-24-78 | 1996 | El Tigere, Venez. |
| Perez, Melido | 1 | 0 | 1.64 | 2 | 2 | 0 | 0 | 11 | 9 | 4 | 2 | 3 | 7 | R | R | 6-4 | 180 | 2-15-66 | 1984 | San Cristobal, D.R. |
| Reith, Brian | 2 | 3 | 4.13 | 10 | 4 | 0 | 0 | 33 | 31 | 16 | 15 | 16 | 21 | R | R | 6-5 | 190 | 2-28-78 | 1996 | Fort Wayne, Ind. |
| Rodriguez, Jorge | 0 | 0 | 13.50 | 1 | 0 | 0 | 0 | 1 | 3 | 1 | 1 | 0 | 0 | R | R | 6-2 | 170 | 10-11-76 | 1996 | Penuelas, P.R. |
| Rumer, Tim | 0 | 0 | 0.00 | 2 | 1 | 0 | 0 | 8 | 1 | 0 | 0 | 2 | 15 | L | L | 6-4 | 190 | 8-8-69 | 1990 | Princeton, N.J. |
| Schnautz, Brad | 2 | 0 | 5.16 | 10 | 0 | 0 | 0 | 23 | 28 | 13 | 13 | 5 | 31 | L | L | 6-4 | 190 | 4-6-76 | 1996 | Bryan, Texas |
| Stewart, Don | 0 | 3 | 3.86 | 1 | 0 | 0 | 0 | 2 | 1 | 1 | 1 | 4 | R | R | 6-5 | 191 | 12-9-72 | 1995 | Gainesville, Fla. |
| Trunk, Todd | 0 | 0 | 0.00 | 1 | 0 | 0 | 0 | 1 | 0 | 0 | 0 | 1 | 1 | R | R | 6-4 | 190 | 7-13-73 | 1996 | Oak Forest, Ill. |
| Valle, Yoiset | 3 | 0 | 2.55 | 7 | 1 | 0 | 0 | 18 | 20 | 9 | 5 | 1 | 15 | L | L | 6-3 | 190 | 6-9-78 | 1996 | Miami Lakes, Fla. |
| Wallace, Kent | 1 | 0 | 1.80 | 1 | 1 | 0 | 0 | 5 | 3 | 1 | 1 | 0 | 5 | L | R | 6-3 | 192 | 8-22-70 | 1992 | Paducah, Ky. |

# NEW YORK METS

**Managers:** Dallas Green, Bobby Valentine.  **1996 Record:** 71-91, .438 (4th, NL East).

| BATTING | AVG | G | AB | R | H | 2B | 3B | HR | RBI | BB | SO | SB | CS | B | T | HT | WT | DOB | 1st Yr | Resides |
|---|---|---|---|---|---|---|---|---|---|---|---|---|---|---|---|---|---|---|---|---|
| Alfonzo, Edgardo | .261 | 123 | 368 | 36 | 96 | 15 | 2 | 4 | 40 | 25 | 56 | 2 | 0 | R | R | 5-11 | 185 | 8-11-73 | 1991 | Caracas, Venez. |
| Baerga, Carlos | .193 | 26 | 83 | 5 | 16 | 3 | 0 | 2 | 11 | 5 | 2 | 0 | 0 | S | R | 5-11 | 200 | 11-4-68 | 1986 | Westlake, Ohio |
| Bogar, Tim | .213 | 91 | 89 | 17 | 19 | 4 | 0 | 0 | 6 | 8 | 20 | 1 | 3 | R | R | 6-2 | 198 | 10-28-66 | 1987 | Kankakee, Ill. |
| Brogna, Rico | .255 | 55 | 188 | 18 | 48 | 10 | 1 | 7 | 30 | 19 | 50 | 0 | 0 | L | L | 6-2 | 200 | 4-18-70 | 1988 | Watertown, Conn. |
| Castillo, Alberto | .364 | 6 | 11 | 1 | 4 | 0 | 0 | 0 | 0 | 0 | 4 | 0 | 0 | R | R | 6-0 | 184 | 2-10-70 | 1987 | Las Matas de Far Fan, D.R. |
| Espinoza, Alvaro | .306 | 48 | 134 | 19 | 41 | 7 | 2 | 4 | 16 | 4 | 19 | 0 | 2 | R | R | 6-0 | 190 | 2-19-62 | 1979 | Bergenfield, N.J. |
| Everett, Carl | .240 | 101 | 192 | 29 | 46 | 8 | 1 | 1 | 16 | 21 | 53 | 6 | 0 | S | R | 6-0 | 190 | 6-3-71 | 1990 | Tampa, Fla. |
| Franco, Matt | .194 | 14 | 31 | 3 | 6 | 1 | 0 | 1 | 2 | 1 | 5 | 0 | 0 | L | R | 6-3 | 195 | 8-19-69 | 1987 | Thousand Oaks, Calif. |
| Gilkey, Bernard | .317 | 153 | 571 | 108 | 181 | 44 | 3 | 30 | 117 | 73 | 125 | 17 | 9 | R | R | 6-0 | 170 | 9-24-66 | 1985 | St. Louis, Mo. |
| Greene, Charlie | .000 | 2 | 1 | 0 | 0 | 0 | 0 | 0 | 0 | 0 | 0 | 0 | 0 | R | R | 6-1 | 177 | 1-23-71 | 1991 | Miami, Fla. |
| Hardtke, Jason | .193 | 19 | 57 | 3 | 11 | 5 | 0 | 0 | 6 | 2 | 12 | 0 | 0 | S | R | 5-10 | 175 | 9-15-71 | 1990 | San Jose, Calif. |
| Hundley, Todd | .259 | 153 | 540 | 85 | 140 | 32 | 1 | 41 | 112 | 79 | 146 | 1 | 3 | S | R | 5-11 | 185 | 5-27-69 | 1987 | Port St. Lucie, Fla. |
| Huskey, Butch | .278 | 118 | 414 | 43 | 115 | 16 | 2 | 15 | 60 | 27 | 77 | 1 | 2 | R | R | 6-3 | 240 | 11-10-71 | 1989 | Lawton, Okla. |
| Johnson, Lance | .333 | 160 | 682 | 117 | 227 | 31 | 21 | 9 | 69 | 33 | 40 | 50 | 12 | L | L | 5-11 | 160 | 7-6-63 | 1984 | Mobile, Ala. |
| Jones, Chris | .242 | 89 | 149 | 22 | 36 | 7 | 0 | 4 | 18 | 12 | 42 | 1 | 0 | R | R | 6-2 | 205 | 11-16-65 | 1984 | Cedar Rapids, Iowa |
| Kent, Jeff | .290 | 89 | 335 | 45 | 97 | 20 | 1 | 9 | 39 | 21 | 56 | 4 | 3 | R | R | 6-1 | 185 | 3-7-68 | 1989 | Huntington Beach, Calif. |
| Mayne, Brent | .263 | 70 | 99 | 9 | 26 | 6 | 0 | 1 | 6 | 12 | 22 | 0 | 1 | L | R | 6-1 | 190 | 4-19-68 | 1989 | Costa Mesa, Calif. |
| Ochoa, Alex | .294 | 82 | 282 | 37 | 83 | 19 | 3 | 4 | 33 | 17 | 30 | 4 | 3 | R | R | 6-0 | 185 | 3-29-72 | 1991 | Miami Lakes, Fla. |
| Ordonez, Rey | .257 | 151 | 502 | 51 | 129 | 12 | 4 | 1 | 30 | 22 | 53 | 1 | 3 | R | R | 5-9 | 159 | 1-11-72 | 1993 | Miami, Fla. |
| Petagine, Roberto | .232 | 50 | 99 | 10 | 23 | 3 | 0 | 4 | 17 | 9 | 27 | 0 | 2 | L | L | 6-1 | 172 | 6-7-71 | 1990 | Nueva Esparta, Venez. |
| Roberson, Kevin | .222 | 27 | 36 | 8 | 8 | 1 | 0 | 3 | 9 | 7 | 17 | 0 | 0 | S | R | 6-4 | 210 | 1-29-68 | 1988 | Decatur, Ill. |
| Tomberlin, Andy | .258 | 63 | 66 | 12 | 17 | 4 | 0 | 3 | 10 | 9 | 27 | 0 | 0 | L | L | 5-11 | 160 | 11-7-66 | 1986 | Monroe, N.C. |
| Vizcaino, Jose | .303 | 96 | 363 | 47 | 110 | 12 | 6 | 1 | 32 | 28 | 58 | 9 | 5 | S | R | 6-1 | 180 | 3-26-68 | 1987 | El Cajon, Calif. |

| PITCHING | W | L | ERA | G | GS | CG | SV | IP | H | R | ER | BB | SO | B | T | HT | WT | DOB | 1st Yr | Resides |
|---|---|---|---|---|---|---|---|---|---|---|---|---|---|---|---|---|---|---|---|---|
| Byrd, Paul | 1 | 2 | 4.24 | 38 | 0 | 0 | 0 | 47 | 48 | 22 | 22 | 21 | 31 | R | R | 6-1 | 185 | 12-3-70 | 1991 | Louisville, Ky. |
| Clark, Mark | 14 | 11 | 3.43 | 32 | 32 | 2 | 0 | 212 | 217 | 98 | 81 | 48 | 142 | R | R | 6-5 | 225 | 5-12-68 | 1988 | Bath, Ill. |
| DiPoto, Jerry | 7 | 2 | 4.19 | 57 | 0 | 0 | 0 | 77 | 91 | 44 | 36 | 45 | 52 | R | R | 6-2 | 200 | 5-24-68 | 1989 | North Olmstead, Ohio |
| Franco, John | 4 | 3 | 1.83 | 51 | 0 | 0 | 28 | 54 | 54 | 15 | 11 | 21 | 48 | L | L | 5-10 | 185 | 9-17-60 | 1981 | Brooklyn, N.Y. |
| Fyhrie, Mike | 0 | 1 | 15.43 | 2 | 0 | 0 | 0 | 2 | 4 | 4 | 4 | 3 | 0 | R | R | 6-2 | 190 | 12-9-69 | 1991 | Westminster, Calif. |
| Harnisch, Pete | 8 | 12 | 4.21 | 31 | 31 | 2 | 0 | 195 | 195 | 103 | 91 | 61 | 114 | R | R | 6-0 | 207 | 9-23-66 | 1987 | Freehold, N.J. |
| Henry, Doug | 2 | 8 | 4.68 | 58 | 0 | 0 | 9 | 75 | 82 | 48 | 39 | 36 | 58 | R | R | 6-4 | 205 | 12-10-63 | 1986 | Hartland, Wis. |
| Isringhausen, Jason | 6 | 14 | 4.77 | 27 | 27 | 2 | 0 | 172 | 190 | 103 | 91 | 73 | 114 | R | R | 6-3 | 196 | 9-7-72 | 1992 | Brighton, Ill. |
| Jones, Bobby | 12 | 8 | 4.42 | 31 | 31 | 3 | 0 | 196 | 219 | 102 | 96 | 46 | 116 | R | R | 6-4 | 205 | 2-10-70 | 1991 | Kerman, Calif. |
| MacDonald, Bob | 0 | 2 | 4.26 | 20 | 0 | 0 | 0 | 19 | 16 | 10 | 9 | 9 | 12 | L | L | 6-2 | 208 | 4-27-65 | 1987 | Toms River, N.J. |
| Martinez, Pedro A. | 0 | 0 | 6.43 | 5 | 0 | 0 | 0 | 7 | 8 | 7 | 5 | 7 | 6 | L | L | 6-2 | 155 | 11-29-68 | 1987 | Villa Mella, D.R. |
| Minor, Blas | 0 | 0 | 3.51 | 17 | 0 | 0 | 0 | 26 | 23 | 11 | 10 | 6 | 20 | R | R | 6-3 | 200 | 3-20-66 | 1988 | Gilbert, Ariz. |
| Mlicki, Dave | 6 | 7 | 3.30 | 51 | 2 | 0 | 1 | 90 | 95 | 46 | 33 | 33 | 83 | R | R | 6-4 | 190 | 6-8-68 | 1990 | Galloway, Ohio |
| Person, Robert | 4 | 5 | 4.52 | 27 | 13 | 0 | 0 | 90 | 86 | 50 | 45 | 35 | 76 | R | R | 5-11 | 180 | 1-8-69 | 1989 | St. Louis, Mo. |
| Trlicek, Rick | 0 | 1 | 3.38 | 5 | 0 | 0 | 0 | 5 | 3 | 2 | 2 | 3 | 3 | R | R | 6-3 | 200 | 4-26-69 | 1987 | Houston, Texas |
| Wallace, Derek | 2 | 3 | 4.01 | 19 | 0 | 0 | 3 | 25 | 29 | 12 | 11 | 14 | 15 | R | R | 6-3 | 200 | 9-1-71 | 1992 | Oxnard, Calif. |
| Wilson, Paul | 5 | 12 | 5.38 | 26 | 26 | 1 | 0 | 149 | 157 | 102 | 89 | 71 | 109 | R | R | 6-5 | 235 | 3-28-73 | 1994 | Orlando, Fla. |

## FIELDING

| Catcher | PCT | G | PO | A | E | DP | PB |
|---|---|---|---|---|---|---|---|
| Castillo | 1.000 | 6 | 23 | 0 | 0 | 0 | 0 |
| Greene | 1.000 | 1 | 1 | 0 | 0 | 0 | 0 |
| Hundley | .992 | 150 | 911 | 72 | 8 | 7 | 10 |
| Mayne | 1.000 | 21 | 85 | 3 | 0 | 2 | 0 |

| First Base | PCT | G | PO | A | E | DP |
|---|---|---|---|---|---|---|
| Baerga | .990 | 16 | 98 | 5 | 1 | 8 |
| Bogar | 1.000 | 32 | 77 | 4 | 0 | 7 |
| Brogna | .996 | 52 | 440 | 31 | 2 | 46 |
| Espinoza | .000 | 1 | 0 | 0 | 0 | 0 |
| Franco | 1.000 | 2 | 12 | 1 | 0 | 1 |
| Huskey | .984 | 75 | 569 | 43 | 10 | 57 |
| Jones | 1.000 | 5 | 16 | 1 | 0 | 1 |
| Petagine | .996 | 40 | 209 | 23 | 1 | 20 |
| Tomberlin | .000 | 1 | 0 | 0 | 0 | 0 |

| Second Base | PCT | G | PO | A | E | DP |
|---|---|---|---|---|---|---|
| Alfonzo | .974 | 66 | 122 | 174 | 8 | 42 |
| Baerga | 1.000 | 1 | 3 | 3 | 0 | 1 |
| Bogar | 1.000 | 8 | 4 | 11 | 0 | 4 |
| Espinoza | 1.000 | 2 | 0 | 1 | 0 | 0 |
| Hardtke | 1.000 | 18 | 26 | 34 | 0 | 9 |
| Vizcaino | .986 | 93 | 179 | 259 | 6 | 70 |

| Third Base | PCT | G | PO | A | E | DP |
|---|---|---|---|---|---|---|
| Alfonzo | .957 | 36 | 17 | 50 | 3 | 5 |
| Baerga | .667 | 6 | 2 | 4 | 3 | 0 |
| Bogar | .972 | 25 | 13 | 22 | 1 | 0 |
| Espinoza | .900 | 38 | 20 | 52 | 8 | 2 |
| Franco | .824 | 8 | 3 | 11 | 3 | 0 |
| Huskey | .933 | 6 | 5 | 9 | 1 | 1 |
| Kent | .925 | 89 | 75 | 184 | 21 | 19 |

| Shortstop | PCT | G | PO | A | E | DP |
|---|---|---|---|---|---|---|
| Alfonzo | 1.000 | 15 | 7 | 22 | 0 | 5 |
| Bogar | 1.000 | 19 | 10 | 24 | 0 | 6 |
| Espinoza | 1.000 | 7 | 4 | 13 | 0 | 3 |
| Ordonez | .962 | 150 | 228 | 450 | 27 | 102 |

| Outfield | PCT | G | PO | A | E | DP |
|---|---|---|---|---|---|---|
| Everett | .935 | 55 | 97 | 4 | 7 | 1 |
| Gilkey | .982 | 151 | 309 | 18 | 6 | 4 |
| Huskey | .943 | 40 | 64 | 2 | 4 | 2 |
| Johnson | .971 | 157 | 391 | 9 | 12 | 3 |
| Jones | .957 | 66 | 67 | 0 | 3 | 0 |
| Ochoa | .966 | 76 | 134 | 8 | 5 | 3 |
| Roberson | 1.000 | 10 | 12 | 0 | 0 | 0 |
| Tomberlin | 1.000 | 17 | 8 | 1 | 0 | 0 |

**John Franco**

Lance Johnson led the
Mets in average, runs
and hits

Mets minor league
Player of the Year
Terrence Long

LARRY GOREN

AL SOLOMON

## METS

## FARM SYSTEM

**Director of Minor League Operations:** Jack Zduriencik

| Class | Farm Team | League | W | L | Pct. | Finish* | Manager(s) | First Yr |
|-------|-----------|--------|---|---|------|---------|-----------|----------|
| AAA | Norfolk (Va.) Tides | International | 82 | 59 | .582 | 2nd (10) | Valentine/Benedict | 1969 |
| AA | Binghamton (N.Y.) Mets | Eastern | 76 | 66 | .535 | 3rd (10) | John Tamargo | 1992 |
| #A | St. Lucie (Fla.) Mets | Florida State | 71 | 62 | +5th (14) | John Gibbons | 1988 |
| A | Capital City (S.C.) Bombers | South Atlantic | 82 | 57 | .590 | 2nd (14) | Howie Freiling | 1983 |
| A | Pittsfield (Mass.) Mets | New York-Penn | 46 | 29 | .613 | 2nd (14) | Doug Davis | 1989 |
| #R | Kingsport (Tenn.) Mets | Appalachian | 48 | 19 | .716 | 1st (10) | John Stephenson | 1980 |
| R | St. Lucie (Fla.) Mets | Gulf Coast | 29 | 30 | .492 | 10th (16) | Mickey Brantley | 1988 |

*Finish in overall standings (No. of teams in league)   #Advanced level   +Won league championship

## ORGANIZATION LEADERS

**Todd Hundley.** 41 homers

MORRIS FOSTOFF

### MAJOR LEAGUERS

**BATTING**
| | | |
|---|---|---|
| *AVG | Lance Johnson | .333 |
| R | Lance Johnson | 117 |
| H | Lance Johnson | 227 |
| TB | Lance Johnson | 321 |
| 2B | Bernard Gilkey | 44 |
| 3B | Lance Johnson | 21 |
| HR | Todd Hundley | 41 |
| RBI | Bernard Gilkey | 117 |
| BB | Todd Hundley | 79 |
| SO | Todd Hundley | 146 |
| SB | Lance Johnson | 50 |

**PITCHING**
| | | |
|---|---|---|
| W | Mark Clark | 14 |
| L | Jason Isringhausen | 14 |
| #ERA | Dave Mlicki | 3.30 |
| G | Doug Henry | 58 |
| CG | Bobby Jones | 3 |
| SV | John Franco | 28 |
| IP | Mark Clark | 212 |
| BB | Jason Isringhausen | 73 |
| SO | Mark Clark | 142 |

### MINOR LEAGUERS

**BATTING**
| | | |
|---|---|---|
| *AVG | Carlos Mendoza, Capital City | .337 |
| R | Brian Daubach, Binghamton/Norfolk | 87 |
| H | Matt Franco, Norfolk | 164 |
| TB | Chris Saunders, Binghamton | 236 |
| 2B | Matt Franco, Norfolk | 40 |
| 3B | Fletcher Bates, Capital City | 13 |
| HR | Brian Daubach, Binghamton/Norfolk | 22 |
| RBI | Chris Saunders, Binghamton | 105 |
| BB | Brian Daubach, Binghamton/Norfolk | 80 |
| SO | Bryon Gainey, Capital City | 169 |
| SB | Scott Hunter, St. Lucie | 49 |

**PITCHING**
| | | |
|---|---|---|
| W | Mike Fyrhie, Norfolk | 15 |
| L | Arnold Gooch, St. Lucie | 12 |
| #ERA | Brett Herbison, Pittsfield/Kingsport | 1.83 |
| G | Ricky Trlicek, Norfolk | 62 |
| CG | Nelson Figueroa, Capital City | 8 |
| SV | Mike Welch, Binghamton/Norfolk | 29 |
| IP | Cory Lidle, Binghamton | 190 |
| BB | Rafael Roque, St. Lucie/Binghamton | 78 |
| SO | Nelson Figueroa, Capital City | 200 |

*Minimum 250 At-Bats    #Minimum 75 Innings

## TOP 10 PROSPECTS

**How the Mets Top 10 prospects, as judged by Baseball America prior to the 1996 season, fared in 1996:**

TOM DiPACE

**Paul Wilson**

| Player, Pos. | Club (Class—League) | AVG | AB | R | H | 2B | 3B | HR | RBI | SB |
|--------------|---------------------|-----|----|---|---|----|----|----|-----|-----|
| 2. Jay Payton, of | GCL Mets (R—Gulf Coast) | .385 | 13 | 3 | 5 | 1 | 0 | 1 | 2 | 1 |
| | St. Lucie (A—Florida State) | 308 | 26 | 4 | 8 | 2 | 0 | 0 | 1 | 2 |
| | Binghamton (AA—Eastern) | .200 | 10 | 0 | 2 | 0 | 0 | 0 | 2 | 0 |
| | Norfolk (AAA—International) | .307 | 153 | 30 | 47 | 6 | 3 | 6 | 26 | 10 |
| 3. Rey Ordonez, ss | New York | .257 | 502 | 51 | 129 | 12 | 4 | 1 | 30 | 1 |
| 5. Alex Ochoa, of | Norfolk (AAA—International) | .339 | 233 | 45 | 79 | 12 | 4 | 8 | 39 | 5 |
| | New York | .294 | 282 | 37 | 83 | 19 | 3 | 4 | 33 | 4 |
| 6. Preston Wilson, of | St. Lucie (A—Florida State) | .176 | 85 | 6 | 15 | 3 | 0 | 1 | 7 | 1 |
| 7. Terrence Long, of | Capital City (A—South Atlantic) | .288 | 473 | 66 | 136 | 26 | 9 | 12 | 78 | 32 |
| 10. Bryon Gainey, 1b | Capital City (A—South Atlantic) | .217 | 446 | 53 | 97 | 23 | 0 | 14 | 62 | 5 |

| | | W | L | ERA | G | SV | IP | H | BB | SO |
|---|---|---|---|-----|---|----|----|---|----|----|
| 1. Paul Wilson, rhp | St. Lucie (A—Florida State) | 0 | 1 | 3.38 | 2 | 0 | 8 | 6 | 4 | 5 |
| | Binghamton (AA—Eastern) | 0 | 1 | 7.20 | 1 | 0 | 5 | 6 | 5 | 5 |
| | New York | 5 | 12 | 5.38 | 26 | 0 | 149 | 157 | 71 | 109 |
| 4. Juan Acevedo, rhp | Norfolk (AAA—International) | 4 | 8 | 5.96 | 19 | 0 | 103 | 116 | 53 | 83 |
| 8. Sean Johnston, lhp | | | | Did not play—Injured | | | | | | |
| 9. *Eric Ludwick, rhp | Louisville (AAA—Amer. Assoc.) | 3 | 4 | 2.83 | 11 | 0 | 60 | 55 | 24 | 73 |
| | St. Louis | 0 | 1 | 9.00 | 6 | 0 | 10 | 11 | 3 | 12 |

*Traded to Cardinals

## INTERNATIONAL LEAGUE

| BATTING | AVG | G | AB | R | H | 2B | 3B | HR | RBI | BB | SO | SB | CS | B | T | HT | WT | DOB | 1st Yr | Resides |
|---|---|---|---|---|---|---|---|---|---|---|---|---|---|---|---|---|---|---|---|---|
| Agbayani, Benny | .278 | 99 | 331 | 43 | 92 | 13 | 9 | 7 | 56 | 30 | 57 | 14 | 5 | R | R | 5-11 | 175 | 12-28-71 | 1993 | Aiea, Hawaii |
| Castillo, Alberto | .208 | 113 | 341 | 34 | 71 | 12 | 1 | 11 | 39 | 39 | 67 | 2 | 2 | R | R | 6-0 | 184 | 2-10-70 | 1987 | Los Matas de Farfan, D.R. |
| Chimelis, Joel | .382 | 25 | 76 | 9 | 29 | 6 | 0 | 0 | 4 | 5 | 12 | 1 | 0 | R | R | 6-0 | 165 | 7-27-67 | 1988 | Brooklyn, N.Y. |
| Daubach, Brian | .204 | 17 | 54 | 7 | 11 | 2 | 0 | 0 | 6 | 6 | 14 | 1 | 1 | L | R | 6-1 | 201 | 2-11-72 | 1990 | Belleville, Ill. |
| Flora, Kevin | .222 | 46 | 135 | 20 | 30 | 8 | 1 | 3 | 15 | 11 | 40 | 9 | 2 | R | R | 6-0 | 185 | 6-10-69 | 1987 | Chandler, Ariz. |
| Franco, Matt | .323 | 133 | 508 | 74 | 164 | 40 | 2 | 7 | 81 | 36 | 55 | 5 | 2 | L | R | 6-3 | 195 | 8-19-69 | 1987 | Thousand Oaks, Calif. |
| Gilbert, Shawn | .256 | 131 | 493 | 76 | 126 | 28 | 1 | 9 | 50 | 46 | 97 | 17 | 9 | R | R | 5-9 | 170 | 3-12-65 | 1987 | Glendale, Ariz. |
| Hardtke, Jason | .300 | 71 | 257 | 49 | 77 | 17 | 2 | 9 | 35 | 29 | 29 | 4 | 6 | S | R | 5-10 | 175 | 9-15-71 | 1990 | San Jose, Calif. |
| Howard, Chris | .160 | 56 | 119 | 8 | 19 | 6 | 0 | 2 | 15 | 5 | 30 | 0 | 0 | R | R | 6-2 | 200 | 2-27-66 | 1988 | Houston, Texas |
| Lowery, Terrell | .233 | 62 | 193 | 25 | 45 | 7 | 2 | 4 | 21 | 22 | 44 | 6 | 3 | R | R | 6-3 | 175 | 10-25-70 | 1991 | Oakland, Calif. |
| Mahalik, John | .235 | 8 | 17 | 1 | 4 | 0 | 0 | 0 | 0 | 0 | 1 | 0 | 0 | R | R | 6-2 | 190 | 7-28-71 | 1993 | Irving, Texas |
| McCoy, Trey | .191 | 25 | 47 | 2 | 9 | 1 | 0 | 1 | 7 | 8 | 5 | 0 | 0 | R | R | 6-3 | 215 | 10-12-66 | 1988 | Virginia Beach, Va. |
| Morgan, Kevin | .134 | 29 | 82 | 7 | 11 | 3 | 0 | 0 | 3 | 9 | 14 | 3 | 1 | R | R | 6-1 | 170 | 3-3-70 | 1991 | Duson, La. |
| Ochoa, Alex | .339 | 67 | 233 | 45 | 79 | 12 | 4 | 8 | 39 | 32 | 22 | 5 | 11 | R | R | 6-0 | 185 | 3-29-72 | 1991 | Miami Lakes, Fla. |
| Payton, Jay | .307 | 55 | 153 | 30 | 47 | 6 | 3 | 6 | 26 | 11 | 25 | 10 | 1 | R | R | 5-10 | 190 | 11-22-72 | 1994 | Zanesville, Ohio |
| Petagine, Roberto | .318 | 95 | 314 | 49 | 100 | 24 | 3 | 12 | 65 | 51 | 75 | 4 | 1 | L | L | 6-1 | 172 | 6-7-71 | 1990 | Nueva Esparta, Venez. |
| Rivera, Luis | .225 | 114 | 356 | 34 | 80 | 23 | 3 | 6 | 39 | 31 | 58 | 1 | 3 | R | R | 5-10 | 172 | 1-3-64 | 1982 | Cidra, P.R. |
| Roberson, Kevin | .265 | 70 | 215 | 26 | 57 | 13 | 3 | 7 | 33 | 14 | 65 | 0 | 1 | S | R | 6-4 | 210 | 1-29-68 | 1988 | Decatur, Ill. |
| Thurman, Gary | .267 | 127 | 449 | 81 | 120 | 24 | 6 | 9 | 39 | 40 | 108 | 25 | 12 | R | R | 5-10 | 180 | 11-12-64 | 1983 | Indianapolis, Ind. |
| Tomberlin, Andy | .326 | 38 | 129 | 17 | 42 | 6 | 1 | 8 | 18 | 8 | 29 | 1 | 3 | L | L | 5-11 | 160 | 11-7-66 | 1986 | Monroe, N.C. |

| PITCHING | W | L | ERA | G | GS | CG | SV | IP | H | R | ER | BB | SO | B | T | HT | WT | DOB | 1st Yr | Resides |
|---|---|---|---|---|---|---|---|---|---|---|---|---|---|---|---|---|---|---|---|---|
| Acevedo, Juan | 4 | 8 | 5.96 | 19 | 19 | 2 | 0 | 103 | 116 | 70 | 68 | 53 | 83 | R | R | 6-2 | 195 | 5-5-70 | 1992 | Carpentersville, Ill. |
| Ahearne, Pat | 1 | 2 | 4.62 | 5 | 4 | 0 | 0 | 25 | 26 | 14 | 13 | 9 | 14 | R | R | 6-3 | 195 | 12-10-69 | 1992 | Atascadero, Calif. |
| Ausanio, Joe | 3 | 3 | 5.86 | 35 | 0 | 0 | 4 | 43 | 38 | 31 | 28 | 29 | 40 | R | R | 6-1 | 205 | 12-9-65 | 1988 | Kingston, N.Y. |
| Bark, Brian | 1 | 0 | 4.63 | 12 | 0 | 0 | 0 | 12 | 9 | 6 | 6 | 6 | 13 | L | L | 5-9 | 170 | 8-26-68 | 1990 | Baltimore, Md. |
| Bullard, Jason | 0 | 3 | 4.89 | 24 | 0 | 0 | 0 | 39 | 45 | 23 | 21 | 16 | 24 | R | R | 6-2 | 185 | 10-23-68 | 1991 | Sweeny, Texas |
| Byrd, Paul | 2 | 0 | 3.52 | 5 | 0 | 0 | 1 | 8 | 4 | 3 | 3 | 4 | 8 | R | R | 6-1 | 185 | 12-3-70 | 1991 | Louisville, Ky. |
| Crawford, Joe | 6 | 5 | 3.44 | 20 | 16 | 2 | 0 | 97 | 98 | 45 | 37 | 20 | 68 | L | L | 6-3 | 225 | 5-2-70 | 1991 | Hillsboro, Ohio |
| Fyhrie, Mike | 15 | 6 | 3.04 | 27 | 27 | 2 | 0 | 169 | 150 | 61 | 57 | 33 | 103 | R | R | 6-2 | 190 | 12-9-69 | 1991 | Westminster, Calif. |
| Gardiner, Mike | 13 | 3 | 3.21 | 24 | 24 | 2 | 0 | 146 | 125 | 58 | 52 | 38 | 125 | S | R | 6-0 | 200 | 10-19-65 | 1987 | Canton, Mass. |
| Larson, Toby | 1 | 0 | 4.76 | 1 | 1 | 0 | 0 | 6 | 6 | 3 | 3 | 1 | 1 | R | R | 6-3 | 210 | 2-22-73 | 1994 | Olympia, Wash. |
| Lee, Mark | 2 | 1 | 2.53 | 33 | 0 | 0 | 1 | 32 | 39 | 11 | 9 | 6 | 35 | L | L | 6-3 | 195 | 7-20-64 | 1985 | Colorado Springs, Colo. |
| MacDonald, Bob | 4 | 1 | 3.13 | 27 | 0 | 0 | 0 | 32 | 27 | 14 | 11 | 12 | 36 | L | L | 6-2 | 208 | 4-27-65 | 1987 | Toms River, N.J. |
| Martinez, Pedro A. | 4 | 4 | 3.02 | 34 | 5 | 0 | 2 | 57 | 45 | 29 | 19 | 20 | 37 | L | L | 6-2 | 155 | 11-29-68 | 1987 | Villa Mella, D.R. |
| McCready, Jim | 0 | 0 | 4.15 | 6 | 0 | 0 | 0 | 9 | 11 | 4 | 4 | 0 | 1 | R | R | 6-1 | 187 | 11-25-69 | 1991 | Norwood, Mass. |
| Person, Robert | 5 | 0 | 3.35 | 8 | 8 | 0 | 0 | 43 | 33 | 16 | 16 | 21 | 32 | R | R | 5-11 | 180 | 1-8-69 | 1989 | St. Louis, Mo. |
| Ramirez, Hector | 1 | 0 | 3.38 | 3 | 1 | 0 | 0 | 11 | 13 | 7 | 4 | 3 | 8 | R | R | 6-3 | 218 | 12-15-71 | 1988 | El Seybo, D.R. |
| Reed, Rick | 8 | 10 | 3.16 | 28 | 28 | 1 | 0 | 182 | 164 | 72 | 64 | 33 | 128 | R | R | 6-0 | 200 | 8-16-64 | 1986 | Huntington, W.Va. |
| Rogers, Bryan | 0 | 2 | 3.38 | 20 | 0 | 0 | 0 | 24 | 20 | 11 | 9 | 11 | 23 | R | R | 5-11 | 210 | 10-30-67 | 1988 | Hollister, Calif. |
| Trlicek, Rick | 4 | 5 | 1.87 | 62 | 0 | 0 | 10 | 77 | 52 | 18 | 16 | 16 | 54 | R | R | 6-3 | 200 | 4-26-69 | 1987 | Houston, Texas |
| Wallace, Derek | 5 | 2 | 1.72 | 49 | 0 | 0 | 26 | 58 | 37 | 20 | 11 | 17 | 52 | R | R | 6-3 | 200 | 9-1-71 | 1992 | Oxnard, Calif. |
| Welch, Mike | 0 | 1 | 4.15 | 10 | 0 | 0 | 2 | 9 | 8 | 4 | 4 | 2 | 6 | L | R | 6-2 | 207 | 8-25-72 | 1993 | Nashua, N.H. |
| Withem, Shannon | 3 | 3 | 4.64 | 8 | 8 | 0 | 0 | 43 | 56 | 25 | 22 | 6 | 30 | R | R | 6-3 | 185 | 9-21-72 | 1990 | Ypsilanti, Mich. |

### FIELDING

| Catcher | PCT | G | PO | A | E | DP | PB |
|---|---|---|---|---|---|---|---|
| Castillo | .990 | 111 | 747 | 72 | 8 | 9 | 7 |
| Howard | .992 | 51 | 213 | 22 | 2 | 2 | 4 |

| First Base | PCT | G | PO | A | E | DP |
|---|---|---|---|---|---|---|
| Agbayani | 1.000 | 3 | 27 | 1 | 0 | 3 |
| Chimelis | 1.000 | 2 | 6 | 1 | 0 | 1 |
| Daubach | 1.000 | 9 | 72 | 3 | 0 | 7 |
| Franco | .994 | 42 | 330 | 29 | 2 | 25 |
| Howard | .000 | 1 | 0 | 0 | 0 | 0 |
| McCoy | 1.000 | 3 | 18 | 3 | 0 | 0 |
| Petagine | .982 | 94 | 743 | 67 | 15 | 60 |

| Second Base | PCT | G | PO | A | E | DP |
|---|---|---|---|---|---|---|
| Chimelis | .958 | 6 | 9 | 14 | 1 | 4 |

| | PCT | G | PO | A | E | DP |
|---|---|---|---|---|---|---|
| Gilbert | .976 | 48 | 90 | 113 | 5 | 22 |
| Hardtke | .985 | 70 | 149 | 175 | 5 | 39 |
| Mahalik | 1.000 | 2 | 2 | 2 | 0 | 1 |
| Morgan | .976 | 26 | 49 | 73 | 3 | 15 |

| Third Base | PCT | G | PO | A | E | DP |
|---|---|---|---|---|---|---|
| Chimelis | 1.000 | 3 | 3 | 0 | 0 | 0 |
| Franco | .905 | 91 | 53 | 138 | 20 | 9 |
| Gilbert | .930 | 61 | 33 | 127 | 12 | 6 |
| Rivera | .833 | 2 | 1 | 4 | 1 | 0 |

| Shortstop | PCT | G | PO | A | E | DP |
|---|---|---|---|---|---|---|
| Chimelis | .943 | 13 | 15 | 35 | 3 | 4 |
| Gilbert | .942 | 29 | 41 | 72 | 7 | 15 |

| | PCT | G | PO | A | E | DP |
|---|---|---|---|---|---|---|
| Mahalik | .750 | 3 | 3 | 6 | 3 | 0 |
| Rivera | .958 | 110 | 125 | 326 | 20 | 56 |

| Outfield | PCT | G | PO | A | E | DP |
|---|---|---|---|---|---|---|
| Agbayani | .987 | 81 | 145 | 7 | 2 | 2 |
| Flora | .978 | 34 | 43 | 2 | 1 | 0 |
| Gilbert | .909 | 6 | 10 | 0 | 1 | 0 |
| Lowery | .991 | 57 | 106 | 4 | 1 | 1 |
| Ochoa | .960 | 62 | 110 | 9 | 5 | 3 |
| Payton | 1.000 | 6 | 7 | 1 | 0 | 0 |
| Roberson | .981 | 55 | 99 | 3 | 2 | 2 |
| Thurman | .982 | 122 | 262 | 7 | 5 | 2 |
| Tomberlin | .985 | 32 | 66 | 1 | 1 | 0 |

## EASTERN LEAGUE

| BATTING | AVG | G | AB | R | H | 2B | 3B | HR | RBI | BB | SO | SB | CS | B | T | HT | WT | DOB | 1st Yr | Resides |
|---|---|---|---|---|---|---|---|---|---|---|---|---|---|---|---|---|---|---|---|---|
| Agbayani, Benny | .170 | 21 | 53 | 7 | 9 | 1 | 0 | 2 | 8 | 11 | 13 | 1 | 0 | R | R | 5-11 | 175 | 12-28-71 | 1993 | Aiea, Hawaii |
| Aversa, Joe | .188 | 13 | 32 | 3 | 6 | 0 | 0 | 0 | 1 | 7 | 8 | 0 | 0 | S | R | 5-10 | 155 | 5-20-68 | 1990 | Huntington Beach, Calif. |
| Azuaje, Jesus | .237 | 86 | 249 | 36 | 59 | 16 | 0 | 2 | 26 | 45 | 33 | 5 | 6 | R | R | 5-10 | 170 | 1-16-73 | 1992 | Bolivar, Venez. |
| Daubach, Brian | .296 | 122 | 436 | 80 | 129 | 24 | 1 | 22 | 76 | 74 | 103 | 7 | 9 | L | R | 6-1 | 201 | 2-11-72 | 1990 | Belleville, Ill. |
| Geisler, Phil | .251 | 107 | 355 | 47 | 89 | 17 | 2 | 11 | 59 | 33 | 96 | 5 | 4 | L | L | 6-3 | 200 | 10-23-69 | 1991 | Springfield, Ore. |
| Greene, Charlie | .244 | 100 | 336 | 35 | 82 | 17 | 0 | 2 | 27 | 17 | 52 | 2 | 0 | R | R | 6-1 | 177 | 1-23-71 | 1991 | Miami, Fla. |
| Grifol, Pedro | .238 | 64 | 202 | 22 | 48 | 3 | 0 | 7 | 28 | 13 | 29 | 0 | 0 | R | R | 6-1 | 205 | 11-28-69 | 1991 | Miami, Fla. |
| Hardtke, Jason | .263 | 35 | 137 | 23 | 36 | 11 | 0 | 3 | 16 | 16 | 16 | 0 | 1 | S | R | 5-10 | 175 | 9-15-71 | 1990 | San Jose, Calif. |
| Horne, Tyrone | .272 | 43 | 125 | 17 | 34 | 10 | 0 | 3 | 19 | 15 | 39 | 3 | 0 | L | L | 5-10 | 185 | 11-2-70 | 1989 | Troy, N.C. |
| Leiper, Tim | .167 | 6 | 6 | 0 | 1 | 0 | 0 | 0 | 0 | 1 | 0 | 0 | 0 | L | R | 5-11 | 175 | 7-19-66 | 1985 | Cary, N.C. |
| Lowery, Terrell | .275 | 62 | 211 | 34 | 58 | 13 | 4 | 7 | 32 | 44 | 44 | 5 | 6 | R | R | 6-3 | 175 | 10-25-70 | 1991 | Oakland, Calif. |
| Mahalik, John | .241 | 78 | 216 | 37 | 52 | 11 | 2 | 3 | 22 | 27 | 35 | 6 | 2 | R | R | 6-2 | 190 | 7-28-71 | 1993 | Irving, Texas |
| Maness, Dwight | .243 | 130 | 399 | 65 | 97 | 14 | 7 | 6 | 47 | 52 | 80 | 25 | 8 | R | R | 6-3 | 180 | 4-3-74 | 1992 | New Castle, Del. |
| Morgan, Kevin | .252 | 107 | 409 | 61 | 103 | 11 | 2 | 6 | 35 | 53 | 59 | 13 | 4 | R | R | 6-1 | 170 | 3-3-70 | 1991 | Duson, La. |
| Pagano, Scott | .259 | 126 | 464 | 63 | 120 | 15 | 3 | 1 | 46 | 43 | 55 | 26 | 16 | S | R | 5-11 | 175 | 4-26-71 | 1993 | Dania, Fla. |
| Payton, Jay | .200 | 4 | 10 | 0 | 2 | 0 | 0 | 0 | 2 | 2 | 2 | 0 | 1 | R | R | 5-10 | 190 | 11-22-72 | 1994 | Zanesville, Ohio |

STAN DENNY

THE SPORTS GROUP

**Key Acquisitions.** The Mets traded with St. Louis for outfielder Bernard Gilkey, left, and with Cleveland for righthander Mark Clark prior to the 1996 season. Gilkey led the Mets with 117 RBIs; Clark led with 14 wins.

| BATTING | AVG | G | AB | R | H | 2B | 3B | HR | RBI | BB | SO | SB | CS | B | T | HT | WT | DOB | 1st Yr | Resides |
|---|---|---|---|---|---|---|---|---|---|---|---|---|---|---|---|---|---|---|---|---|
| Saunders, Chris | .298 | 141 | 510 | 82 | 152 | 27 | 3 | 17 | 105 | 73 | 88 | 5 | 4 | R | R | 6-1 | 203 | 7-19-70 | 1992 | Clovis, Calif. |
| Turner, Brian | .202 | 32 | 84 | 8 | 17 | 5 | 2 | 2 | 12 | 9 | 18 | 1 | 1 | L | L | 6-2 | 210 | 6-9-71 | 1989 | Orwell, Ohio |
| White, Don | .192 | 82 | 219 | 29 | 42 | 6 | 1 | 6 | 22 | 26 | 61 | 5 | 4 | R | R | 5-10 | 180 | 3-13-72 | 1991 | Rock Island, Ill. |

| PITCHING | W | L | ERA | G | GS | CG | SV | IP | H | R | ER | BB | SO | B | T | HT | WT | DOB | 1st Yr | Resides |
|---|---|---|---|---|---|---|---|---|---|---|---|---|---|---|---|---|---|---|---|---|
| Bullard, Jason | 0 | 0 | 2.70 | 8 | 0 | 0 | 0 | 10 | 11 | 4 | 3 | 5 | 10 | R | R | 6-2 | 185 | 10-23-68 | 1991 | Sweeny, Texas |
| Carter, John | 9 | 3 | 4.23 | 19 | 19 | 3 | 0 | 111 | 120 | 60 | 52 | 54 | 48 | R | R | 6-1 | 195 | 2-16-72 | 1991 | Chicago, Ill. |
| Crawford, Joe | 5 | 1 | 1.45 | 7 | 7 | 1 | 0 | 50 | 34 | 10 | 8 | 9 | 34 | L | L | 6-3 | 225 | 5-2-70 | 1991 | Hillsboro, Ohio |
| Dixon, Steve | 0 | 1 | 5.40 | 5 | 0 | 0 | 0 | 8 | 10 | 5 | 5 | 8 | 11 | L | L | 6-0 | 195 | 8-3-69 | 1989 | Louisville, Ky. |
| Edmondson, Brian | 6 | 6 | 4.25 | 39 | 13 | 1 | 0 | 114 | 130 | 69 | 54 | 38 | 83 | R | R | 6-2 | 165 | 1-29-73 | 1991 | Riverside, Calif. |
| Fuller, Mark | 5 | 4 | 4.18 | 51 | 0 | 0 | 1 | 75 | 86 | 41 | 35 | 22 | 43 | L | R | 6-6 | 216 | 8-5-70 | 1992 | Melbourne, Fla. |
| Guerra, Mark | 7 | 6 | 3.53 | 27 | 20 | 1 | 0 | 140 | 143 | 60 | 55 | 34 | 84 | R | R | 6-2 | 185 | 11-4-71 | 1994 | Grand Ridge, Fla. |
| Larson, Toby | 2 | 4 | 6.00 | 11 | 8 | 1 | 0 | 48 | 57 | 36 | 32 | 14 | 25 | R | R | 6-3 | 210 | 2-22-73 | 1994 | Olympia, Wash. |
| Lidle, Cory | 14 | 10 | 3.31 | 27 | 27 | 6 | 0 | 190 | 186 | 78 | 70 | 49 | 141 | R | R | 6-0 | 175 | 3-22-72 | 1991 | West Covina, Calif. |
| McCready, Jim | 0 | 0 | 0.00 | 1 | 0 | 0 | 0 | 1 | 0 | 0 | 0 | 0 | 0 | R | R | 6-1 | 187 | 11-25-69 | 1991 | Norwood, Mass. |
| Pierson, Jason | 5 | 3 | 3.38 | 34 | 5 | 0 | 1 | 53 | 56 | 21 | 20 | 15 | 42 | R | L | 6-0 | 190 | 1-6-71 | 1992 | Berwyn, Pa. |
| Ramirez, Hector | 1 | 5 | 5.14 | 38 | 0 | 0 | 6 | 56 | 51 | 34 | 32 | 23 | 49 | R | R | 6-3 | 218 | 12-15-71 | 1988 | El Seybo, D.R. |
| Roberts, Chris | 2 | 7 | 7.24 | 9 | 9 | 1 | 0 | 46 | 55 | 40 | 37 | 37 | 30 | R | L | 5-10 | 185 | 6-25-71 | 1992 | Middleburg, Fla. |
| Roque, Rafael | 0 | 4 | 7.27 | 13 | 13 | 0 | 0 | 61 | 71 | 57 | 49 | 39 | 46 | L | L | 6-4 | 186 | 1-1-72 | 1991 | Santo Domingo, D.R. |
| Sauerbeck, Scott | 3 | 3 | 3.47 | 8 | 8 | 2 | 0 | 47 | 48 | 24 | 18 | 12 | 30 | R | L | 6-3 | 190 | 11-9-71 | 1994 | Cincinnati, Ohio |
| Tam, Jeff | 6 | 2 | 2.44 | 49 | 0 | 0 | 2 | 63 | 51 | 19 | 17 | 16 | 48 | R | R | 6-1 | 185 | 8-19-70 | 1993 | Tallahassee, Fla. |
| Turrentine, Rich | 1 | 1 | 2.89 | 8 | 0 | 0 | 3 | 9 | 12 | 3 | 3 | 5 | 10 | R | R | 6-0 | 175 | 5-21-71 | 1989 | Texarkana, Ark. |
| Welch, Mike | 4 | 2 | 4.59 | 46 | 0 | 0 | 27 | 51 | 55 | 29 | 26 | 10 | 53 | L | R | 6-2 | 207 | 8-25-72 | 1993 | Nashua, N.H. |
| Wilson, Paul | 0 | 1 | 7.20 | 1 | 1 | 0 | 0 | 5 | 6 | 4 | 4 | 5 | 5 | R | R | 6-5 | 235 | 3-28-73 | 1994 | Orlando, Fla. |
| Withem, Shannon | 6 | 3 | 3.24 | 12 | 12 | 1 | 0 | 86 | 86 | 32 | 31 | 17 | 59 | R | R | 6-3 | 185 | 9-21-72 | 1990 | Ypsilanti, Mich. |

## FIELDING

| Catcher | PCT | G | PO | A | E | DP | PB |
|---|---|---|---|---|---|---|---|
| Greene | .995 | 98 | 550 | 75 | 3 | 8 | 3 |
| Grifol | .987 | 53 | 336 | 32 | 5 | 2 | 5 |

| First Base | PCT | G | PO | A | E | DP |
|---|---|---|---|---|---|---|
| Daubach | .991 | 121 | 1108 | 115 | 11 | 109 |
| Geisler | .984 | 9 | 55 | 7 | 1 | 6 |
| Saunders | 1.000 | 2 | 8 | 1 | 0 | 1 |
| Turner | 1.000 | 18 | 163 | 16 | 0 | 10 |

| Second Base | PCT | G | PO | A | E | DP |
|---|---|---|---|---|---|---|
| Aversa | 1.000 | 1 | 1 | 4 | 0 | 0 |
| Azuaje | .978 | 79 | 154 | 249 | 9 | 56 |
| Hardtke | .964 | 34 | 61 | 100 | 6 | 25 |

| | PCT | G | PO | A | E | DP |
|---|---|---|---|---|---|---|
| Leiper | 1.000 | 1 | 1 | 3 | 0 | 1 |
| Mahalik | .987 | 33 | 69 | 85 | 2 | 18 |

| Third Base | PCT | G | PO | A | E | DP |
|---|---|---|---|---|---|---|
| Daubach | .000 | 1 | 0 | 0 | 0 | 0 |
| Leiper | .000 | 1 | 0 | 0 | 0 | 0 |
| Mahalik | .933 | 9 | 1 | 13 | 1 | 3 |
| Saunders | .941 | 137 | 74 | 327 | 25 | 25 |

| Shortstop | PCT | G | PO | A | E | DP |
|---|---|---|---|---|---|---|
| Aversa | .940 | 12 | 16 | 31 | 3 | 5 |
| Azuaje | 1.000 | 1 | 1 | 3 | 0 | 0 |
| Mahalik | .933 | 24 | 28 | 69 | 7 | 15 |

| | PCT | G | PO | A | E | DP |
|---|---|---|---|---|---|---|
| Morgan | .956 | 107 | 170 | 330 | 23 | 65 |

| Outfield | PCT | G | PO | A | E | DP |
|---|---|---|---|---|---|---|
| Agbayani | .952 | 11 | 19 | 1 | 1 | 0 |
| Geisler | .990 | 70 | 93 | 5 | 1 | 1 |
| Horne | 1.000 | 22 | 23 | 2 | 0 | 0 |
| Lowery | .971 | 53 | 97 | 3 | 3 | 0 |
| Maness | .981 | 122 | 244 | 9 | 5 | 0 |
| Pagano | .976 | 116 | 194 | 10 | 5 | 0 |
| Turner | .000 | 2 | 0 | 0 | 0 | 0 |
| White | .941 | 62 | 91 | 4 | 6 | 0 |

---

## BAKERSFIELD
Class A/Co-Op

## CALIFORNIA LEAGUE

| PITCHING | W | L | ERA | G | GS | CG | SV | IP | H | R | ER | BB | SO | B | T | HT | WT | DOB | 1st Yr | Resides |
|---|---|---|---|---|---|---|---|---|---|---|---|---|---|---|---|---|---|---|---|---|
| Arffa, Steve | 5 | 6 | 6.81 | 15 | 11 | 1 | 0 | 73 | 98 | 61 | 55 | 22 | 71 | R | L | 6-2 | 195 | 1-26-73 | 1994 | Glendora, Calif. |

### FLORIDA STATE LEAGUE

| BATTING | AVG | G | AB | R | H | 2B | 3B | HR | RBI | BB | SO | SB | CS | B | T | HT | WT | DOB | 1st Yr | Resides |
|---|---|---|---|---|---|---|---|---|---|---|---|---|---|---|---|---|---|---|---|---|
| Daly, Bob | .273 | 53 | 183 | 18 | 50 | 8 | 0 | 2 | 24 | 12 | 22 | 1 | 3 | R | R | 6-1 | 205 | 10-8-72 | 1992 | Downers Grove, Ill. |
| Diaz, Cesar | .239 | 74 | 247 | 29 | 59 | 15 | 1 | 7 | 34 | 18 | 72 | 9 | 2 | R | R | 6-3 | 185 | 7-12-74 | 1990 | Maracay, Venez. |
| Farrell, Jon | .000 | 1 | 1 | 0 | 0 | 0 | 0 | 0 | 0 | 0 | 1 | 0 | 0 | R | R | 6-0 | 185 | 7-30-71 | 1991 | Jacksonville, Fla. |
| Flora, Kevin | .154 | 11 | 39 | 8 | 6 | 0 | 2 | 0 | 3 | 9 | 14 | 2 | 0 | R | R | 6-0 | 185 | 6-10-69 | 1987 | Chandler, Ariz. |
| Gomez, Paul | .375 | 7 | 24 | 3 | 9 | 2 | 0 | 2 | 7 | 2 | 5 | 0 | 0 | R | R | 5-11 | 190 | 3-8-73 | 1992 | Miami, Fla. |
| Guerrero, Rafael | .246 | 83 | 260 | 32 | 64 | 12 | 0 | 2 | 26 | 20 | 37 | 4 | 0 | R | R | 6-2 | 191 | 12-3-74 | 1991 | Santo Domingo, D.R. |
| Hunter, Scott | .257 | 127 | 475 | 71 | 122 | 19 | 1 | 2 | 38 | 38 | 68 | 49 | 12 | R | R | 6-1 | 195 | 12-17-75 | 1994 | Philadelphia, Pa. |
| Jaime, Angel | .257 | 98 | 288 | 38 | 74 | 10 | 1 | 3 | 21 | 34 | 47 | 12 | 6 | R | R | 6-0 | 160 | 3-6-73 | 1992 | Santo Domingo, D.R. |
| Lopez, Jose | .291 | 121 | 419 | 63 | 122 | 17 | 5 | 11 | 60 | 39 | 103 | 18 | 10 | R | R | 6-1 | 175 | 8-4-75 | 1994 | Santiago, D.R. |
| Miller, Ryan | .255 | 86 | 310 | 32 | 79 | 8 | 3 | 2 | 23 | 22 | 51 | 8 | 5 | R | R | 6-0 | 175 | 10-22-72 | 1994 | Tulare, Calif. |
| Mota, Guillermo | .234 | 102 | 304 | 34 | 71 | 10 | 3 | 1 | 21 | 34 | 90 | 8 | 8 | R | R | 6-5 | 185 | 7-25-73 | 1991 | San Pedro de Macoris, D.R. |
| Naples, Brandon | .000 | 3 | 8 | 0 | 0 | 0 | 0 | 0 | 0 | 0 | 0 | 0 | 0 | R | L | 6-0 | 190 | 11-5-72 | 1995 | Reading, Pa. |
| Patterson, Jarrod | .180 | 17 | 61 | 6 | 11 | 2 | 0 | 1 | 6 | 3 | 19 | 1 | 0 | L | R | 6-0 | 190 | 9-7-73 | 1993 | Clanton, Ala. |
| Payton, Jay | .308 | 9 | 26 | 4 | 8 | 2 | 0 | 0 | 1 | 4 | 5 | 2 | 1 | R | R | 5-10 | 190 | 11-22-72 | 1994 | Zanesville, Ohio |
| Sanderson, David | .239 | 50 | 163 | 17 | 39 | 2 | 3 | 1 | 13 | 22 | 42 | 8 | 3 | L | L | 6-3 | 185 | 10-2-72 | 1994 | Fulton, Mo. |
| Simpson, Jeramie | .216 | 59 | 222 | 25 | 48 | 7 | 5 | 0 | 19 | 17 | 55 | 21 | 11 | L | R | 5-10 | 160 | 11-28-74 | 1994 | Edmond, Okla. |
| Tijerina, Tony | .071 | 19 | 42 | 1 | 3 | 0 | 1 | 0 | 3 | 5 | 7 | 1 | 0 | S | R | 5-11 | 190 | 12-19-69 | 1991 | Georgetown, Texas |
| Turner, Brian | .202 | 33 | 99 | 15 | 20 | 3 | 0 | 2 | 15 | 11 | 27 | 1 | 0 | L | L | 6-2 | 210 | 6-9-71 | 1989 | Orwell, Ohio |
| Warner, Randy | .277 | 109 | 386 | 43 | 107 | 20 | 3 | 8 | 69 | 23 | 65 | 5 | 1 | R | R | 6-2 | 200 | 8-5-73 | 1991 | Seattle, Wash. |
| Wilson, Preston | .176 | 23 | 85 | 6 | 15 | 3 | 0 | 1 | 7 | 8 | 21 | 1 | 1 | R | R | 6-2 | 193 | 7-19-74 | 1992 | Eastover, S.C. |
| Wilson, Vance | .244 | 93 | 311 | 29 | 76 | 14 | 2 | 6 | 44 | 31 | 41 | 2 | 4 | R | R | 5-11 | 190 | 3-17-73 | 1994 | Mesa, Ariz. |
| Zorrilla, Julio | .248 | 110 | 403 | 43 | 100 | 7 | 1 | 0 | 27 | 25 | 72 | 24 | 17 | S | R | 5-11 | 156 | 2-20-75 | 1993 | San Pedro de Macoris, D.R. |

GAMES BY POSITION: C—Diaz 44, Tijerina 16, V. Wilson 81. 1B—Daly 50, Guerrero 3, Maples 3, Patterson 14, Turner 20, Warner 55. 2B—Miller 32, Zorrilla 108. 3B—Gomez 1, Lopez 118, Mota 22. SS—Jaime 6, Miller 58, Zorrilla 1. OF—Daly 1, Farrell 1, Flora 11, Guerrero 74, Hunter 121, Jaime 86, Sanderson 47, Simpson 56, Turner 4, Warner 1, P. Wilson 20.

| PITCHING | W | L | ERA | G | GS | CG | SV | IP | H | R | ER | BB | SO | B | T | HT | WT | DOB | 1st Yr | Resides |
|---|---|---|---|---|---|---|---|---|---|---|---|---|---|---|---|---|---|---|---|---|
| Arffa, Steve | 1 | 2 | 3.31 | 11 | 4 | 0 | 1 | 33 | 29 | 14 | 12 | 8 | 18 | R | L | 6-2 | 195 | 1-26-73 | 1994 | Glendora, Calif. |
| Arroyo, Luis | 1 | 0 | 3.00 | 22 | 0 | 0 | 2 | 42 | 36 | 17 | 14 | 15 | 28 | L | L | 6-0 | 175 | 9-29-73 | 1992 | Arecibo, P.R. |
| Atwater, Joe | 2 | 6 | 4.38 | 19 | 16 | 1 | 0 | 86 | 79 | 47 | 42 | 39 | 66 | L | L | 6-3 | 160 | 2-12-75 | 1993 | Graham, N.C. |
| Bullock, Craig | 0 | 2 | 7.94 | 7 | 0 | 0 | 0 | 6 | 8 | 6 | 5 | 5 | 4 | R | R | 6-3 | 222 | 2-11-72 | 1990 | Houston, Texas |
| Carter, John | 1 | 2 | 7.20 | 4 | 4 | 0 | 0 | 20 | 26 | 18 | 16 | 11 | 6 | R | R | 6-1 | 195 | 2-16-72 | 1991 | Chicago, Ill. |
| Cosman, Jeff | 0 | 1 | 8.59 | 3 | 2 | 0 | 0 | 7 | 11 | 7 | 7 | 2 | 5 | R | R | 6-4 | 193 | 2-8-71 | 1993 | Memphis, Tenn. |
| Cox, Robert | 1 | 0 | 6.75 | 4 | 0 | 0 | 0 | 5 | 4 | 4 | 3 | 6 | 6 | R | R | 6-1 | 176 | 11-11-75 | 1994 | Culver City, Calif. |
| Gooch, Arnold | 12 | 12 | 2.58 | 26 | 26 | 2 | 0 | 168 | 131 | 74 | 48 | 51 | 141 | R | R | 6-2 | 195 | 11-12-76 | 1994 | Levittown, Pa. |
| Harnisch, Pete | 1 | 0 | 2.77 | 2 | 2 | 0 | 0 | 13 | 11 | 4 | 4 | 0 | 12 | R | R | 6-0 | 207 | 9-23-66 | 1987 | Freehold, N.J. |
| Kelly, John | 0 | 0 | 3.00 | 1 | 0 | 0 | 0 | 3 | 3 | 1 | 1 | 0 | 6 | R | R | 6-0 | 180 | 12-13-72 | 1994 | Leominster, Mass. |
| Larson, Toby | 4 | 3 | 4.69 | 9 | 9 | 1 | 0 | 48 | 60 | 28 | 25 | 10 | 36 | R | R | 6-3 | 210 | 2-22-73 | 1994 | Olympia, Wash. |
| Marquardt, Scott | 0 | 0 | 0.00 | 1 | 0 | 0 | 0 | 1 | 1 | 0 | 0 | 1 | 1 | R | R | 6-2 | 195 | 8-25-72 | 1993 | Baytown, Texas |
| McCready, Jim | 1 | 2 | 3.86 | 10 | 0 | 0 | 0 | 16 | 18 | 8 | 7 | 2 | 12 | R | R | 6-1 | 185 | 11-25-69 | 1991 | Norwood, Mass. |
| Murray, Dan | 7 | 5 | 4.25 | 33 | 13 | 0 | 0 | 102 | 114 | 60 | 48 | 53 | 56 | R | R | 6-1 | 185 | 11-21-73 | 1995 | Garden Grove, Calif. |
| Olson, Phil | 1 | 5 | 4.32 | 15 | 7 | 0 | 1 | 50 | 63 | 26 | 24 | 18 | 27 | R | R | 6-3 | 225 | 10-24-73 | 1995 | Sarasota, Fla. |
| Pack, Steve | 0 | 0 | 3.63 | 23 | 0 | 0 | 0 | 35 | 41 | 20 | 14 | 10 | 16 | R | R | 6-5 | 185 | 8-6-73 | 1993 | Fallbrook, Calif. |
| Roberts, Chris | 1 | 0 | 0.00 | 1 | 1 | 0 | 0 | 6 | 1 | 0 | 0 | 3 | 2 | R | L | 5-10 | 185 | 6-25-71 | 1992 | Middleburg, Fla. |
| Rogers, Bryan | 2 | 0 | 1.54 | 9 | 0 | 0 | 0 | 12 | 12 | 2 | 2 | 4 | 11 | R | R | 5-11 | 170 | 10-30-67 | 1988 | Hollister, Calif. |
| Roque, Rafael | 6 | 4 | 2.12 | 14 | 12 | 1 | 0 | 76 | 57 | 22 | 18 | 39 | 59 | L | L | 6-4 | 186 | 1-1-72 | 1991 | Santo Domingo, D.R. |
| Sanchez, Jesus | 9 | 3 | 1.96 | 16 | 16 | 2 | 0 | 92 | 53 | 22 | 20 | 24 | 81 | L | L | 5-10 | 153 | 10-11-74 | 1992 | Nizao Bani, D.R. |
| Sauerbeck, Scott | 6 | 6 | 2.27 | 17 | 16 | 2 | 0 | 99 | 101 | 37 | 25 | 27 | 62 | R | L | 6-3 | 190 | 11-9-71 | 1994 | Cincinnati, Ohio |
| Short, Barry | 6 | 2 | 2.34 | 58 | 0 | 0 | 10 | 88 | 70 | 28 | 23 | 18 | 70 | R | R | 6-3 | 182 | 12-15-73 | 1994 | Mansfield, Mo. |
| Tatis, Ramon | 4 | 2 | 3.39 | 46 | 1 | 0 | 6 | 74 | 71 | 35 | 28 | 38 | 46 | L | L | 6-2 | 180 | 1-5-73 | 1991 | Guayubin, D.R. |
| Turrentine, Rich | 4 | 4 | 2.28 | 45 | 0 | 0 | 21 | 51 | 31 | 18 | 13 | 45 | 63 | R | R | 6-0 | 175 | 5-21-71 | 1989 | Texarkana, Ark. |
| Wilson, Paul | 0 | 1 | 3.38 | 2 | 2 | 0 | 0 | 8 | 6 | 5 | 3 | 4 | 5 | R | R | 6-5 | 235 | 3-28-73 | 1994 | Orlando, Fla. |
| Withem, Shannon | 1 | 0 | 1.29 | 2 | 2 | 0 | 0 | 14 | 8 | 2 | 2 | 1 | 13 | R | R | 6-3 | 185 | 9-21-72 | 1990 | Ypsilanti, Mich. |

## CAPITAL CITY      Class A

### SOUTH ATLANTIC LEAGUE

| BATTING | AVG | G | AB | R | H | 2B | 3B | HR | RBI | BB | SO | SB | CS | B | T | HT | WT | DOB | 1st Yr | Resides |
|---|---|---|---|---|---|---|---|---|---|---|---|---|---|---|---|---|---|---|---|---|
| Arvelo, Tom | .202 | 72 | 218 | 35 | 44 | 3 | 0 | 0 | 14 | 17 | 42 | 8 | 8 | R | R | 6-1 | 170 | 12-11-73 | 1991 | Santo Domingo, D.R. |
| Azuaje, Jesus | .667 | 1 | 3 | 1 | 2 | 1 | 0 | 0 | 1 | 0 | 0 | 0 | 0 | R | R | 5-10 | 170 | 1-16-73 | 1992 | Bolivar, Venez. |
| Bates, Fletcher | .259 | 132 | 491 | 84 | 127 | 21 | 13 | 15 | 72 | 64 | 162 | 16 | 6 | S | R | 6-1 | 193 | 3-24-74 | 1994 | Wilmington, N.C. |
| Black, Brandon | .190 | 25 | 63 | 3 | 12 | 6 | 1 | 0 | 12 | 8 | 16 | 0 | 3 | L | R | 6-0 | 185 | 12-16-74 | 1995 | Florence, Ky. |
| Boyd, Quincy | .000 | 2 | 6 | 0 | 0 | 0 | 0 | 0 | 0 | 1 | 3 | 0 | 0 | R | R | 6-0 | 180 | 2-24-71 | 1994 | Prosperity, S.C. |
| Daly, Bob | .300 | 44 | 140 | 20 | 42 | 7 | 1 | 2 | 17 | 18 | 19 | 1 | 2 | R | R | 6-1 | 205 | 10-8-72 | 1992 | Downers Grove, Ill. |
| Edmondson, Tracy | .190 | 93 | 273 | 43 | 52 | 12 | 0 | 2 | 21 | 55 | 64 | 5 | 5 | R | R | 6-0 | 165 | 6-10-75 | 1995 | Riverside, Calif. |
| Engle, Beau | .000 | 3 | 2 | 0 | 0 | 0 | 0 | 0 | 0 | 0 | 0 | 0 | 0 | R | R | 6-1 | 180 | 11-9-74 | 1994 | Altus, Okla. |
| Erickson, Corey | .220 | 58 | 209 | 16 | 46 | 14 | 0 | 1 | 17 | 19 | 57 | 5 | 3 | R | R | 5-11 | 185 | 1-10-77 | 1995 | Springfield, Ill. |
| Gainey, Bryon | .217 | 122 | 446 | 53 | 97 | 23 | 0 | 14 | 62 | 41 | 169 | 5 | 2 | L | R | 6-5 | 209 | 1-23-76 | 1994 | Mobile, Ala. |
| Gomez, Paul | .150 | 11 | 20 | 2 | 3 | 0 | 0 | 0 | 2 | 4 | 6 | 0 | 0 | R | R | 5-11 | 190 | 3-8-73 | 1992 | Miami, Fla. |
| Long, Terrence | .288 | 123 | 473 | 66 | 136 | 26 | 9 | 12 | 78 | 36 | 120 | 32 | 7 | L | L | 6-1 | 179 | 2-29-76 | 1994 | Millbrook, Ala. |
| Mendoza, Carlos | .337 | 85 | 300 | 61 | 101 | 10 | 2 | 0 | 37 | 57 | 46 | 31 | 13 | L | L | 5-11 | 160 | 11-4-74 | 1994 | Bolivar, Venez. |
| Morales, Eric | .231 | 45 | 121 | 10 | 28 | 3 | 0 | 0 | 14 | 7 | 22 | 0 | 3 | S | R | 5-11 | 171 | 9-26-73 | 1992 | Moca, P.R. |
| Nolte, Bruce | .059 | 16 | 17 | 0 | 1 | 0 | 0 | 0 | 1 | 0 | 2 | 0 | 0 | R | R | 6-0 | 160 | 4-4-74 | 1993 | Pennsauken, N.J. |
| Parsons, Jeff | .184 | 51 | 147 | 13 | 27 | 3 | 2 | 0 | 9 | 22 | 43 | 7 | 4 | R | R | 5-10 | 160 | 11-16-75 | 1995 | Dale, Okla. |
| Patterson, Jarrod | .230 | 70 | 213 | 26 | 49 | 9 | 1 | 3 | 37 | 33 | 65 | 1 | 1 | L | R | 6-0 | 190 | 9-7-73 | 1993 | Clanton, Ala. |
| Polanco, Enohel | .217 | 92 | 299 | 34 | 65 | 12 | 1 | 1 | 24 | 18 | 78 | 6 | 3 | R | R | 5-11 | 140 | 8-11-75 | 1992 | Puerto Plata, D.R. |
| Ramirez, Daniel | .231 | 47 | 143 | 20 | 33 | 5 | 0 | 1 | 13 | 11 | 30 | 6 | 4 | R | R | 5-11 | 175 | 2-22-74 | 1992 | San Pedro de Macoris, D.R. |
| Sanderson, David | .213 | 33 | 61 | 13 | 13 | 3 | 2 | 0 | 3 | 12 | 12 | 1 | 2 | L | L | 6-3 | 185 | 10-2-72 | 1994 | Fulton, Mo. |
| Simpson, Jeramie | .260 | 58 | 204 | 31 | 53 | 2 | 5 | 1 | 25 | 21 | 45 | 11 | 9 | L | R | 5-10 | 160 | 11-28-74 | 1994 | Edmond, Okla. |
| Soriano, Carlos | .237 | 52 | 177 | 22 | 42 | 4 | 0 | 1 | 17 | 17 | 34 | 5 | 2 | R | R | 6-0 | 165 | 10-24-74 | 1992 | San Pedro de Macoris, D.R. |
| Stanton, Thomas | .667 | 1 | 3 | 1 | 2 | 0 | 0 | 0 | 0 | 1 | 1 | 0 | 0 | S | R | 6-1 | 200 | 2-3-76 | 1996 | Middleburg, Fla. |

| BATTING | AVG | G | AB | R | H | 2B | 3B | HR | RBI | BB | SO | SB | CS | B | T | HT | WT | DOB | 1st Yr | Resides |
|---|---|---|---|---|---|---|---|---|---|---|---|---|---|---|---|---|---|---|---|---|
| Valera, Yohanny | .212 | 108 | 372 | 38 | 79 | 18 | 0 | 6 | 38 | 17 | 78 | 2 | 4 | R | R | 6-1 | 170 | 8-17-76 | 1993 | San Cristobal, D.R. |
| Vickers, Randy | .188 | 4 | 16 | 1 | 3 | 0 | 0 | 0 | 0 | 0 | 5 | 0 | 0 | R | R | 6-3 | 200 | 7-21-75 | 1994 | West Covina, Calif. |
| Zamora, Junior | .000 | 1 | 4 | 0 | 0 | 0 | 0 | 0 | 0 | 0 | 3 | 0 | 0 | R | R | 6-2 | 168 | 5-3-76 | 1994 | San Pedro de Macoris, D.R. |

GAMES BY POSITION: C—Engle 3, Gomez 3, Mendoza 1, Morales 1, Morales 42, Valera 108. 1B—Daly 9, Edmondson 1, Gainey 108, Patterson 26. 2B—Arvelo 69, Edmondson 56, Erickson 4, Nolte 1, Parsons 16. 3B—Boyd 1, Daly 1, Edmondson 25, Erickson 58, Gomez 4, Soriano 52, Vickers 3, Zamora 1. SS—Azuaje 1, Edmondson 12, Nolte 5, Parsons 34, Polanco 93. OF—Bates 133, Black 13, Long 119, Mendoza 47, Ramirez 47, Sanderson 22, Simpson 49.

| PITCHING | W | L | ERA | G | GS | CG | SV | IP | H | R | ER | BB | SO | B | T | HT | WT | DOB | 1st Yr | Resides |
|---|---|---|---|---|---|---|---|---|---|---|---|---|---|---|---|---|---|---|---|---|
| Coronado, Osvaldo | 8 | 10 | 4.53 | 32 | 16 | 0 | 1 | 111 | 120 | 68 | 56 | 28 | 96 | R | R | 6-2 | 185 | 12-30-73 | 1992 | Puerto Plata, D.R. |
| DeWitt, Chris | 3 | 0 | 2.35 | 13 | 0 | 0 | 1 | 31 | 22 | 9 | 8 | 11 | 31 | R | R | 6-5 | 215 | 3-24-74 | 1995 | Ozark, Mo. |
| Dotel, Octavio | 11 | 3 | 3.59 | 22 | 19 | 0 | 0 | 115 | 89 | 49 | 46 | 49 | 142 | R | R | 6-5 | 160 | 11-25-73 | 1993 | Santo Domingo, D.R. |
| Figueroa, Nelson | 14 | 7 | 2.04 | 26 | 25 | 8 | 0 | 185 | 119 | 55 | 42 | 58 | 200 | S | R | 6-1 | 165 | 5-18-74 | 1995 | Brooklyn, N.Y. |
| Gulin, Lindsay | 7 | 7 | 2.64 | 19 | 19 | 1 | 0 | 112 | 88 | 40 | 33 | 57 | 134 | L | L | 6-3 | 160 | 11-22-76 | 1995 | Issaquah, Wash. |
| Howatt, Jeff | 4 | 4 | 2.61 | 37 | 0 | 0 | 7 | 69 | 49 | 23 | 20 | 19 | 61 | R | R | 6-6 | 225 | 1-30-74 | 1995 | Fillmore, Calif. |
| Larson, Toby | 1 | 0 | 1.29 | 1 | 1 | 1 | 0 | 7 | 6 | 1 | 1 | 4 | 4 | R | R | 6-3 | 210 | 2-22-73 | 1994 | Olympia, Wash. |
| Lisio, Joseph | 2 | 5 | 2.03 | 40 | 0 | 0 | 18 | 44 | 40 | 16 | 10 | 15 | 42 | R | R | 6-2 | 205 | 8-5-73 | 1994 | West Hempstead, N.Y. |
| McEntire, Ethan | 9 | 6 | 2.22 | 27 | 27 | 1 | 0 | 174 | 123 | 51 | 43 | 61 | 190 | L | L | 5-11 | 195 | 7-19-75 | 1993 | Clarkesville, Ga. |
| Ojeda, Erick | 3 | 5 | 3.99 | 35 | 0 | 0 | 4 | 59 | 55 | 31 | 26 | 14 | 51 | L | L | 5-10 | 177 | 10-15-75 | 1993 | Valencia, Venez. |
| Olson, Phil | 7 | 6 | 2.54 | 16 | 13 | 1 | 0 | 92 | 55 | 34 | 26 | 32 | 63 | R | R | 6-3 | 225 | 10-24-73 | 1995 | Sarasota, Fla. |
| Pack, Steve | 0 | 0 | 2.45 | 6 | 0 | 0 | 0 | 7 | 8 | 2 | 2 | 2 | 8 | R | R | 6-3 | 185 | 8-6-73 | 1993 | Fallbrook, Calif. |
| Poupart, Melvin | 1 | 0 | 2.79 | 5 | 1 | 0 | 0 | 10 | 8 | 3 | 3 | 3 | 13 | R | R | 6-0 | 193 | 7-1-75 | 1994 | Humacao, P.R. |
| Santamaria, Bill | 2 | 0 | 3.58 | 31 | 0 | 0 | 1 | 50 | 43 | 22 | 20 | 26 | 28 | R | R | 6-2 | 223 | 1-6-76 | 1994 | Lakewood, N.J. |
| Trumpour, Andy | 10 | 4 | 2.29 | 26 | 18 | 4 | 1 | 134 | 91 | 47 | 34 | 37 | 105 | R | R | 6-4 | 185 | 10-22-73 | 1992 | Anaheim, Calif. |

## PITTSFIELD — Class A
### NEW YORK-PENN LEAGUE

| BATTING | AVG | G | AB | R | H | 2B | 3B | HR | RBI | BB | SO | SB | CS | B | T | HT | WT | DOB | 1st Yr | Resides |
|---|---|---|---|---|---|---|---|---|---|---|---|---|---|---|---|---|---|---|---|---|
| Bennett, Ryan | .241 | 27 | 79 | 11 | 19 | 2 | 1 | 0 | 14 | 13 | 21 | 0 | 0 | R | R | 6-0 | 195 | 7-26-74 | 1996 | Waukegan, Ill. |
| Bishop, Tim | .000 | 3 | 6 | 1 | 0 | 0 | 0 | 0 | 1 | 0 | 1 | 0 | 0 | R | R | 6-0 | 168 | 5-25-74 | 1994 | Valparaiso, Ind. |
| Cox, Robert | .000 | 4 | 8 | 0 | 0 | 0 | 0 | 0 | 3 | 5 | 0 | 0 | 0 | R | R | 6-1 | 176 | 11-11-75 | 1994 | Culver City, Calif. |
| Erickson, Corey | .264 | 73 | 258 | 49 | 68 | 19 | 1 | 11 | 49 | 43 | 71 | 6 | 3 | R | R | 5-11 | 185 | 1-10-77 | 1995 | Springfield, Ill. |
| Haltiwanger, Garrick | .256 | 60 | 203 | 36 | 52 | 9 | 2 | 9 | 37 | 24 | 55 | 9 | 4 | R | L | 6-2 | 190 | 3-3-75 | 1996 | Irmo, S.C. |
| Huff, B.J. | .196 | 42 | 138 | 19 | 27 | 4 | 2 | 2 | 14 | 7 | 36 | 3 | 1 | R | R | 6-1 | 185 | 8-1-75 | 1996 | Chandler, Ind. |
| Lopez, Pee Wee | .429 | 5 | 14 | 2 | 6 | 0 | 1 | 0 | 3 | 1 | 1 | 0 | 0 | R | R | 6-0 | 195 | 10-22-76 | 1996 | Miami, Fla. |
| Martinez, Roger | .246 | 41 | 126 | 14 | 31 | 4 | 1 | 2 | 14 | 22 | 40 | 1 | 5 | R | R | 5-10 | 175 | 12-6-72 | 1995 | Corpus Christi, Texas |
| Morrison, Ryan | .151 | 39 | 86 | 11 | 13 | 3 | 0 | 0 | 6 | 11 | 26 | 4 | 2 | L | R | 6-2 | 188 | 3-29-75 | 1995 | Liverpool, N.Y. |
| Naples, Brandon | .304 | 71 | 263 | 44 | 80 | 7 | 4 | 0 | 29 | 28 | 45 | 13 | 5 | R | L | 6-0 | 190 | 11-5-72 | 1995 | Reading, Pa. |
| Nolte, Bruce | .319 | 31 | 91 | 16 | 29 | 2 | 1 | 0 | 10 | 6 | 23 | 1 | 0 | R | R | 6-0 | 160 | 4-4-74 | 1993 | Pennsauken, N.J. |
| Parsons, Jeff | .241 | 72 | 274 | 46 | 66 | 5 | 1 | 1 | 14 | 39 | 60 | 20 | 7 | R | R | 5-10 | 160 | 11-16-73 | 1995 | Dale, Okla. |
| Perez, Jersen | .333 | 1 | 3 | 1 | 1 | 0 | 0 | 0 | 0 | 1 | 1 | 0 | 0 | R | R | 5-8 | 175 | 1-20-76 | 1996 | Lynn, Mass. |
| Ramirez, Danny | .281 | 70 | 260 | 28 | 73 | 5 | 5 | 1 | 22 | 14 | 45 | 24 | 9 | R | R | 6-0 | 175 | 2-22-74 | 1992 | San Pedro de Macoris, D.R. |
| Rodriguez, Sammy | .194 | 32 | 93 | 8 | 18 | 3 | 0 | 1 | 10 | 11 | 25 | 1 | 0 | R | R | 5-10 | 180 | 8-20-75 | 1995 | New York, N.Y. |
| Tamargo, John | .223 | 55 | 184 | 26 | 41 | 5 | 3 | 0 | 19 | 35 | 34 | 5 | 3 | R | R | 5-9 | 165 | 5-3-75 | 1996 | Tampa, Fla. |
| Vickers, Randy | .241 | 35 | 133 | 22 | 32 | 5 | 1 | 11 | 30 | 4 | 52 | 1 | 1 | R | R | 6-3 | 200 | 7-21-75 | 1994 | West Covina, Calif. |
| Yoder, P.J. | .242 | 63 | 182 | 26 | 44 | 9 | 3 | 2 | 27 | 39 | 52 | 5 | 6 | L | R | 6-0 | 190 | 8-25-74 | 1995 | Bethlehem, Pa. |

GAMES BY POSITION: C—Bennett 25, Lopez 1, Martinez 38, Morrison 1, Rodriguez 16. 1B—Cox 1, Lopez 1, Naples 55, Vickers 20, Yoder 1. 2B—Erickson 2, Nolte 23, Parsons 4, Tamargo 49. 3B—Cox 1, Erickson 70, Nolte 6, Vickers 3. SS—Nolte 2, Parsons 68, Perez 1, Tamargo 5. OF—Bishop 3, Haltiwanger 55, Huff 36, Morrison 27, Naples 2, Ramirez 70, Yoder 44.

| PITCHING | W | L | ERA | G | GS | CG | SV | IP | H | R | ER | BB | SO | B | T | HT | WT | DOB | 1st Yr | Resides |
|---|---|---|---|---|---|---|---|---|---|---|---|---|---|---|---|---|---|---|---|---|
| Beebe, Hans | 6 | 5 | 3.09 | 14 | 14 | 2 | 0 | 99 | 94 | 39 | 34 | 17 | 74 | L | L | 6-4 | 175 | 4-30-75 | 1994 | Berlin, N.J. |
| Brittan, Corey | 8 | 3 | 2.30 | 14 | 14 | 2 | 0 | 98 | 74 | 30 | 25 | 20 | 84 | R | R | 6-6 | 197 | 2-23-75 | 1996 | Scott City, Kan. |
| Cutchins, Todd | 2 | 1 | 4.62 | 6 | 3 | 0 | 0 | 25 | 24 | 15 | 13 | 10 | 29 | R | L | 6-0 | 190 | 7-14-75 | 1996 | Westlake, La. |
| Ferullo, Matt | 4 | 1 | 4.68 | 11 | 4 | 0 | 2 | 33 | 38 | 20 | 17 | 9 | 22 | L | L | 6-5 | 225 | 5-16-73 | 1995 | Revere, Mass. |
| Herbison, Brett | 0 | 1 | 22.50 | 1 | 1 | 0 | 0 | 2 | 4 | 6 | 5 | 4 | 1 | R | R | 6-5 | 175 | 6-13-77 | 1995 | Elgin, Ill. |
| Kessel, Kyle | 2 | 6 | 4.74 | 13 | 13 | 0 | 0 | 80 | 80 | 44 | 42 | 19 | 67 | L | L | 6-0 | 160 | 6-2-76 | 1994 | Mundelein, Ill. |
| Patterson, Casey | 1 | 3 | 5.32 | 17 | 0 | 0 | 0 | 24 | 30 | 14 | 14 | 10 | 20 | R | R | 6-2 | 165 | 6-18-73 | 1995 | Clovis, Calif. |
| Poupart, Melvin | 2 | 2 | 3.14 | 23 | 0 | 0 | 7 | 29 | 25 | 12 | 10 | 14 | 30 | R | R | 6-0 | 193 | 7-1-75 | 1994 | Humacao, P.R. |
| Presley, Kirk | 1 | 0 | 3.00 | 5 | 5 | 0 | 0 | 18 | 19 | 9 | 6 | 10 | 14 | R | R | 6-3 | 195 | 4-17-75 | 1994 | Tupelo, Miss. |
| Pumphrey, Kenny | 7 | 2 | 3.21 | 14 | 14 | 1 | 0 | 87 | 68 | 41 | 31 | 41 | 61 | R | R | 6-6 | 195 | 9-10-76 | 1994 | Glen Burnie, Md. |
| Pyrtle, Joe | 0 | 1 | 3.45 | 8 | 0 | 0 | 0 | 16 | 18 | 8 | 6 | 4 | 17 | R | R | 6-1 | 200 | 11-21-73 | 1995 | Wilmington, N.C. |
| Rosenbohm, Jim | 1 | 1 | 3.38 | 20 | 0 | 0 | 1 | 27 | 22 | 10 | 10 | 26 | 37 | R | R | 6-1 | 170 | 9-19-73 | 1992 | Omaha, Neb. |
| Splawn, Matt | 4 | 1 | 0.99 | 22 | 0 | 0 | 8 | 36 | 26 | 5 | 4 | 10 | 44 | L | R | 6-1 | 190 | 1-2-73 | 1996 | Waxahachie, Texas |
| Villafuerte, Brandon | 8 | 3 | 3.02 | 18 | 7 | 1 | 1 | 63 | 53 | 21 | 21 | 27 | 59 | R | R | 5-11 | 165 | 12-17-75 | 1995 | Morgan Hill, Calif. |

## KINGSPORT — Rookie
### APPALACHIAN LEAGUE

| BATTING | AVG | G | AB | R | H | 2B | 3B | HR | RBI | BB | SO | SB | CS | B | T | HT | WT | DOB | 1st Yr | Resides |
|---|---|---|---|---|---|---|---|---|---|---|---|---|---|---|---|---|---|---|---|---|
| Bishop, Tim | .325 | 61 | 237 | 47 | 77 | 6 | 4 | 4 | 29 | 20 | 42 | 23 | 10 | R | R | 6-0 | 168 | 5-25-74 | 1994 | Valparaiso, Ind. |
| Black, Brandon | .256 | 62 | 219 | 39 | 56 | 4 | 1 | 3 | 31 | 32 | 38 | 1 | 1 | L | R | 6-0 | 185 | 12-16-74 | 1995 | Florence, Ky. |
| Bruce, Maurice | .184 | 11 | 38 | 5 | 7 | 0 | 1 | 0 | 4 | 0 | 7 | 2 | 1 | R | R | 5-10 | 180 | 5-1-75 | 1996 | Kansas City, Mo. |
| Chancey, Bailey | .269 | 59 | 197 | 44 | 53 | 6 | 3 | 0 | 25 | 42 | 35 | 30 | 5 | S | R | 5-8 | 160 | 8-25-74 | 1996 | Millbrook, Ala. |
| Chancey, Robert | .263 | 6 | 19 | 4 | 5 | 0 | 0 | 1 | 3 | 2 | 5 | 1 | 0 | R | R | 5-11 | 243 | 9-7-72 | 1992 | Millbrook, Ala. |
| Davila, Angel | .000 | 2 | 0 | 1 | 0 | 0 | 0 | 0 | 0 | 2 | 0 | 0 | 0 | R | R | 5-9 | 155 | 5-1-75 | 1996 | East Hartford, Conn. |
| Frost, Robert | .278 | 6 | 18 | 1 | 5 | 2 | 0 | 0 | 3 | 0 | 3 | 0 | 0 | R | R | 6-0 | 215 | 1-14-73 | 1995 | Florissant, Mo. |
| Guerrero, Hamlet | .250 | 6 | 16 | 0 | 4 | 0 | 1 | 0 | 2 | 3 | 3 | 0 | 0 | R | R | 6-0 | 180 | 1-7-75 | 1993 | Peravia, D.R. |
| Jaroncyk, Ryan | .235 | 57 | 221 | 35 | 52 | 5 | 5 | 1 | 21 | 27 | 59 | 4 | 2 | R | R | 6-0 | 160 | 3-26-77 | 1995 | Escondido, Calif. |
| Kushma, John | .287 | 45 | 129 | 20 | 37 | 7 | 1 | 2 | 20 | 16 | 27 | 2 | 1 | R | R | 6-0 | 175 | 9-17-73 | 1996 | Wescosville, Pa. |
| Lopez, Pee Wee | .316 | 65 | 250 | 53 | 79 | 22 | 4 | 7 | 58 | 31 | 25 | 0 | 1 | R | R | 6-0 | 195 | 10-22-76 | 1996 | Miami, Fla. |
| McCarthy, Kevin | .289 | 64 | 235 | 46 | 68 | 14 | 1 | 6 | 43 | 28 | 41 | 10 | 1 | L | L | 6-4 | 198 | 7-5-76 | 1994 | Pittsburgh, Pa. |
| Patton, Cory | .129 | 24 | 31 | 13 | 4 | 0 | 0 | 0 | 1 | 12 | 10 | 4 | 0 | R | R | 6-2 | 185 | 10-18-75 | 1996 | Harrisburg, Ill. |
| Penalver, Juan | .299 | 36 | 107 | 24 | 32 | 5 | 1 | 2 | 17 | 21 | 20 | 0 | 2 | R | R | 6-1 | 175 | 7-15-75 | 1994 | Maturin, Venez. |

| BATTING | AVG | G | AB | R | H | 2B | 3B | HR | RBI | BB | SO | SB | CS | B | T | HT | WT | DOB | 1st Yr | Resides |
|---|---|---|---|---|---|---|---|---|---|---|---|---|---|---|---|---|---|---|---|---|
| Perez, Jersen | .176 | 6 | 17 | 4 | 3 | 0 | 0 | 0 | 3 | 5 | 6 | 0 | 0 | R | R | 5-8 | 175 | 1-20-76 | 1996 | Lynn, Mass. |
| Rodriguez, Mark | .250 | 8 | 24 | 3 | 6 | 0 | 0 | 0 | 3 | 0 | 5 | 0 | 0 | R | R | 5-11 | 215 | 2-4-74 | 1996 | Miami, Fla. |
| Tessmar, Tim | .283 | 65 | 247 | 36 | 70 | 10 | 1 | 5 | 46 | 26 | 32 | 3 | 2 | L | L | 6-3 | 185 | 1-22-74 | 1995 | Rochester Hills, Mich. |
| Zamora, Junior | .242 | 97 | 247 | 37 | 55 | 13 | 0 | 7 | 41 | 11 | 59 | 2 | 1 | R | R | | 168 | 5-3-76 | 1994 | San Pedro de Macoris, D.R. |

**GAMES BY POSITION: C**—Black 12, Frost 5, Lopez 51, Rodriguez 4. **1B**—McCarthy 5, Patton 1, Tessmar 65. **2B**—Bruce 10, Kushma 29, Penalver 36. **3B**—Kushma 6, Lopez 1, Penalver 1, Zamora 60. **SS**—Davila 2, Jaroncyk 57, Kushma 7, Perez 6. **OF**—Bishop 61, Black 10, B. Chancey 55, R. Chancey 7, Guerrero 6, Kushma 1, McCarthy 60, Patton 20.

| PITCHING | W | L | ERA | G | GS | CG | SV | IP | H | R | ER | BB | SO | B | T | HT | WT | DOB | 1st Yr | Resides |
|---|---|---|---|---|---|---|---|---|---|---|---|---|---|---|---|---|---|---|---|---|
| Ballew, Preston | 2 | 1 | 3.10 | 5 | 5 | 0 | 0 | 20 | 22 | 9 | 7 | 2 | 15 | L | L | 5-10 | 175 | 5-13-77 | 1995 | Carlsbad, N.M. |
| Bohannon, Jason | 2 | 1 | 6.92 | 19 | 1 | 0 | 0 | 26 | 34 | 23 | 20 | 16 | 26 | L | L | 6-0 | 175 | 12-12-73 | 1996 | Bella Vista, Ark. |
| Burke, Ethan | 0 | 3 | 17.10 | 9 | 0 | 0 | 0 | 10 | 25 | 20 | 19 | 6 | 5 | R | R | 6-4 | 205 | 9-6-75 | 1994 | Baker, Ore. |
| Burnett, A.J. | 4 | 0 | 3.88 | 12 | 12 | 0 | 0 | 58 | 31 | 26 | 25 | 54 | 68 | R | R | 6-5 | 204 | 1-3-77 | 1995 | North Little Rock, Ark. |
| Cooper, Chadwick | 1 | 1 | 12.79 | 5 | 2 | 0 | 0 | 13 | 21 | 20 | 18 | 8 | 9 | R | R | 6-2 | 205 | 5-15-75 | 1995 | Petersburg, W.Va. |
| Davis, Mike | 1 | 0 | 4.08 | 11 | 0 | 0 | 1 | 18 | 15 | 13 | 8 | 7 | 15 | R | R | 5-11 | 180 | 8-30-75 | 1996 | Rocky Face, Ga. |
| Estrella, Leoncio | 6 | 3 | 3.88 | 15 | 7 | 1 | 0 | 58 | 54 | 32 | 25 | 24 | 52 | R | R | 6-1 | 165 | 2-20-75 | 1994 | Puerto Plata, D.R. |
| Ferullo, Matt | 0 | 0 | 7.11 | 1 | 1 | 0 | 0 | 6 | 9 | 5 | 5 | 1 | 7 | L | R | 6-5 | 225 | 5-16-73 | 1995 | Revere, Mass. |
| Gonzalez, Dicky | 1 | 0 | 1.80 | 1 | 1 | 0 | 0 | 5 | 4 | 2 | 1 | 0 | 7 | R | R | 5-11 | 155 | 10-21-78 | 1996 | Bayamon, P.R. |
| Hafer, Jeff | 0 | 2 | 2.14 | 24 | 0 | 0 | 6 | 34 | 29 | 9 | 8 | 8 | 43 | R | R | 6-1 | 175 | 10-27-74 | 1996 | Springfield, Va. |
| Herbison, Brett | 6 | 2 | 1.29 | 13 | 12 | 0 | 0 | 77 | 43 | 18 | 11 | 31 | 86 | R | R | 6-5 | 175 | 6-13-77 | 1995 | Elgin, Ill. |
| Jelsovsky, Craig | 4 | 1 | 2.59 | 13 | 1 | 0 | 2 | 24 | 18 | 9 | 7 | 10 | 20 | R | R | 6-1 | 165 | 6-2-76 | 1994 | El Cajon, Calif. |
| Lovingood, Jeromie | 0 | 1 | 6.75 | 1 | 1 | 0 | 0 | 4 | 3 | 3 | 3 | 1 | 2 | L | L | 6-6 | 190 | 4-8-78 | 1996 | Riceville, Tenn. |
| Lyons, Mike | 3 | 2 | 1.89 | 25 | 0 | 0 | 5 | 38 | 27 | 14 | 8 | 14 | 52 | R | R | 6-3 | 205 | 5-20-75 | 1996 | Altamonte Springs, Fla. |
| Pyrtle, Joe | 0 | 0 | 0.00 | 3 | 0 | 0 | 0 | 6 | 4 | 0 | 0 | 1 | 4 | R | R | 6-1 | 200 | 11-21-73 | 1996 | Wilmington, N.C. |
| Roberts, Grant | 9 | 1 | 2.10 | 13 | 13 | 2 | 0 | 69 | 43 | 18 | 16 | 37 | 92 | R | R | 6-3 | 187 | 9-13-77 | 1995 | El Cajon, Calif. |
| Tull, Bill | 1 | 0 | 0.83 | 20 | 0 | 0 | 6 | 33 | 18 | 3 | 3 | 8 | 40 | R | R | 6-0 | 170 | 12-4-75 | 1996 | Westville, N.J. |
| Zwirchitz, Andy | 8 | 1 | 1.55 | 12 | 11 | 1 | 0 | 75 | 51 | 22 | 13 | 19 | 76 | R | R | 6-1 | 180 | 5-3-76 | 1996 | Appleton, Wis. |

# PORT ST. LUCIE — Rookie
## GULF COAST LEAGUE

| BATTING | AVG | G | AB | R | H | 2B | 3B | HR | RBI | BB | SO | SB | CS | B | T | HT | WT | DOB | 1st Yr | Resides |
|---|---|---|---|---|---|---|---|---|---|---|---|---|---|---|---|---|---|---|---|---|
| Bruce, Maurice | .285 | 31 | 123 | 16 | 35 | 6 | 3 | 0 | 9 | 4 | 15 | 6 | 1 | R | R | 5-10 | 180 | 5-1-75 | 1996 | Kansas City, Mo. |
| Burns, Patrick | .222 | 43 | 144 | 17 | 32 | 8 | 0 | 0 | 13 | 18 | 32 | 1 | 3 | S | L | 6-1 | 190 | 9-16-77 | 1996 | Denton, Texas |
| Colon, Ariel | .108 | 23 | 65 | 8 | 7 | 1 | 0 | 0 | 5 | 7 | 23 | 1 | 1 | R | R | 6-1 | 185 | 9-17-77 | 1995 | Carolina, P.R. |
| Copeland, Brandon | .237 | 46 | 135 | 31 | 32 | 9 | 2 | 3 | 17 | 36 | 32 | 3 | 0 | R | R | 6-0 | 205 | 3-31-77 | 1996 | Topeka, Kan. |
| Davila, Angel | .179 | 9 | 28 | 3 | 5 | 0 | 0 | 0 | 2 | 1 | 8 | 0 | 1 | R | R | 5-9 | 155 | 5-1-75 | 1996 | East Hartford, Conn. |
| Durick, Chad | .218 | 43 | 133 | 14 | 29 | 6 | 0 | 0 | 12 | 8 | 27 | 6 | 2 | R | R | 6-0 | 175 | 12-28-76 | 1996 | Port St. Lucie, Fla. |
| Engle, Beau | .000 | 2 | 2 | 1 | 0 | 0 | 0 | 0 | 0 | 1 | 2 | 0 | 0 | R | R | 6-1 | 180 | 11-9-74 | 1994 | Altus, Okla. |
| Escobar, Alex | .360 | 24 | 75 | 15 | 27 | 4 | 0 | 0 | 10 | 4 | 9 | 7 | 1 | R | R | 6-1 | 170 | 9-6-78 | 1996 | Valencia, Venez. |
| Guerrero, Hamlet | .260 | 34 | 127 | 16 | 33 | 8 | 2 | 2 | 14 | 9 | 12 | 0 | 2 | R | R | 6-0 | 180 | 1-7-75 | 1993 | Peravia, D.R. |
| Johnson, Tom | .261 | 32 | 115 | 19 | 30 | 5 | 1 | 1 | 9 | 6 | 26 | 6 | 2 | R | R | 6-5 | 210 | 1-25-76 | 1996 | Elizabeth, N.J. |
| Johnson, Tony | .244 | 48 | 164 | 18 | 40 | 6 | 2 | 7 | 27 | 24 | 42 | 5 | 3 | S | R | 5-11 | 180 | 10-17-77 | 1996 | Oakland, Calif. |
| Meadows, Mike | .200 | 8 | 30 | 1 | 6 | 0 | 0 | 0 | 3 | 1 | 9 | 0 | 0 | R | R | 6-1 | 175 | 10-19-78 | 1996 | Sanford, Fla. |
| Moreno, Juan | .264 | 16 | 53 | 7 | 14 | 4 | 1 | 0 | 7 | 4 | 11 | 2 | 0 | R | R | 6-2 | 165 | 3-19-76 | 1996 | Monte Plata, D.R. |
| Mulvehill, Brandon | .169 | 22 | 65 | 9 | 11 | 1 | 3 | 0 | 3 | 3 | 11 | 1 | 1 | R | R | 6-2 | 180 | 2-24-78 | 1996 | Pell City, Ala. |
| Nunez, Jose | .233 | 41 | 120 | 11 | 28 | 3 | 1 | 0 | 15 | 16 | 28 | 4 | 9 | R | R | 5-10 | 155 | 10-3-76 | 1996 | Miami, Fla. |
| Payton, Jay | .385 | 3 | 13 | 3 | 5 | 1 | 0 | 1 | 2 | 0 | 1 | 1 | 0 | R | R | 5-10 | 190 | 11-22-72 | 1994 | Zanesville, Ohio |
| Penalver, Juan | .346 | 15 | 52 | 9 | 18 | 3 | 0 | 0 | 7 | 11 | 10 | 2 | 0 | R | R | 6-1 | 175 | 7-15-75 | 1994 | Maturin, Venez. |
| Perez, Jersen | .278 | 40 | 151 | 24 | 42 | 5 | 3 | 0 | 12 | 17 | 18 | 7 | 2 | R | R | 5-8 | 175 | 1-20-76 | 1996 | Lynn, Mass. |
| Ramos, Kelly | .186 | 20 | 59 | 3 | 11 | 0 | 1 | 0 | 7 | 3 | 10 | 2 | 2 | S | R | 6-0 | 168 | 10-15-76 | 1996 | San Pedro de Macoris, D.R. |
| Stanton, Thomas | .217 | 43 | 152 | 19 | 33 | 6 | 1 | 4 | 19 | 14 | 36 | 0 | 3 | S | R | 6-1 | 200 | 2-3-76 | 1996 | Middleburg, Fla. |
| Stratton, Robert | .254 | 17 | 59 | 5 | 15 | 2 | 0 | 2 | 9 | 2 | 22 | 3 | 2 | R | R | 6-2 | 220 | 10-7-77 | 1996 | Santa Barbara, Calif. |

**GAMES BY POSITION: C**—Engle 2, Guerrero 1, Ramos 19, Stanton 42. **1B**—Burns 40, Colon 18, Copeland 2, Mulvehill 1, Ramos 1. **2B**—Bruce 11, Davila 5, Nunez 36, Penalver 12. **3B**—Bruce 11, Burns 1, Colon 1, Davila 1, Durick 41, Meadows 5, Mulvehill 1, Penalver 3. **SS**—Bruce 11, Davila 3, Durick 3, Escobar 1, Meadows 3, Nunez 5, Penalver 1, Perez 39. **OF**—Burns 1, Copeland 40, Escobar 21, Guerrero 33, Tom Johnson 25, Tony Johnson 36, Moreno 13, Mulvehill 1, Ramos 1.

| PITCHING | W | L | ERA | G | GS | CG | SV | IP | H | R | ER | BB | SO | B | T | HT | WT | DOB | 1st Yr | Resides |
|---|---|---|---|---|---|---|---|---|---|---|---|---|---|---|---|---|---|---|---|---|
| Borkowski, Bob | 3 | 3 | 4.60 | 12 | 7 | 1 | 0 | 43 | 44 | 24 | 22 | 17 | 33 | R | R | 6-2 | 190 | 11-10-76 | 1994 | Wilmington, Del. |
| Carr, Tim | 0 | 3 | 3.86 | 16 | 2 | 0 | 6 | 40 | 34 | 20 | 17 | 13 | 34 | R | R | 6-2 | 180 | 12-20-77 | 1996 | Westlake Village, Calif. |
| Comer, Scott | 2 | 2 | 2.16 | 13 | 8 | 0 | 0 | 50 | 40 | 16 | 12 | 3 | 40 | L | L | 6-5 | 195 | 6-23-77 | 1996 | Klamath Falls, Ore. |
| Cope, Craig | 0 | 0 | 0.00 | 1 | 0 | 0 | 0 | 2 | 0 | 0 | 0 | 2 | 3 | L | L | 6-1 | 174 | 3-21-76 | 1994 | Windsor, Ontario |
| Cosman, Jeff | 0 | 0 | 0.00 | 2 | 1 | 0 | 1 | 6 | 4 | 0 | 0 | 3 | 10 | R | R | 6-4 | 193 | 2-8-71 | 1993 | Memphis, Tenn. |
| Cox, Robert | 0 | 0 | 2.00 | 5 | 0 | 0 | 1 | 9 | 11 | 4 | 2 | 4 | 8 | R | R | 6-1 | 185 | 11-11-75 | 1994 | Culver City, Calif. |
| Ferullo, Matt | 1 | 0 | 4.91 | 2 | 2 | 0 | 0 | 11 | 11 | 6 | 6 | 2 | 13 | L | R | 6-5 | 225 | 5-16-73 | 1995 | Revere, Mass. |
| Garmon, Adam | 2 | 1 | 2.49 | 12 | 2 | 0 | 1 | 25 | 18 | 7 | 7 | 19 | 31 | R | R | 6-4 | 200 | 8-5-77 | 1996 | St. Augustine, Fla. |
| Gonzalez, Dicky | 4 | 2 | 2.66 | 11 | 8 | 2 | 0 | 47 | 50 | 19 | 14 | 3 | 51 | R | R | 5-11 | 155 | 10-21-78 | 1996 | Bayamon, P.R. |
| Lovingood, Jeromie | 4 | 3 | 0.98 | 10 | 8 | 1 | 0 | 46 | 28 | 11 | 5 | 18 | 32 | L | L | 6-6 | 190 | 4-8-78 | 1996 | Riceville, Tenn. |
| Manley, Kevin | 0 | 1 | 17.36 | 10 | 1 | 0 | 1 | 14 | 23 | 32 | 27 | 30 | 13 | R | R | 6-4 | 195 | 10-29-75 | 1994 | Frostproof, Fla. |
| Marquardt, Scott | 0 | 0 | 2.70 | 4 | 1 | 0 | 0 | 10 | 5 | 3 | 3 | 4 | 8 | R | R | 6-2 | 195 | 8-25-72 | 1993 | Baytown, Texas |
| McCready, Jim | 1 | 1 | 1.13 | 5 | 1 | 0 | 0 | 8 | 4 | 3 | 1 | 2 | 8 | R | R | 6-1 | 187 | 11-25-69 | 1991 | Norwood, Mass. |
| Payne, William | 1 | 2 | 5.00 | 11 | 0 | 0 | 2 | 18 | 17 | 14 | 10 | 8 | 17 | R | L | 6-1 | 180 | 10-11-77 | 1996 | Panama City, Fla. |
| Pyrtle, Joe | 0 | 0 | 1.29 | 4 | 0 | 0 | 0 | 7 | 3 | 1 | 1 | 3 | 9 | R | R | 6-1 | 200 | 11-21-73 | 1996 | Wilmington, N.C. |
| Queen, Mike | 3 | 3 | 3.48 | 11 | 3 | 0 | 0 | 34 | 33 | 15 | 13 | 15 | 28 | L | L | 6-4 | 205 | 12-5-77 | 1996 | Gravette, Ark. |
| Roberts, Chris | 0 | 0 | 1.38 | 3 | 3 | 0 | 0 | 13 | 15 | 2 | 2 | 0 | 12 | R | L | 5-10 | 185 | 6-25-71 | 1992 | Middleburg, Fla. |
| Santana, Humberto | 3 | 2 | 3.22 | 10 | 9 | 0 | 0 | 53 | 45 | 16 | 13 | 7 | 40 | L | L | 5-11 | 175 | 3-10-77 | 1995 | Espailla, D.R. |
| Suggs, Willie | 3 | 2 | 4.30 | 10 | 3 | 0 | 0 | 29 | 28 | 15 | 14 | 17 | 22 | R | R | 6-3 | 180 | 8-25-78 | 1996 | Mt. Vernon, Ill. |
| Torres, Eric | 0 | 4 | 7.40 | 20 | 0 | 0 | 5 | 24 | 34 | 24 | 20 | 9 | 20 | R | R | 6-2 | 198 | 6-11-77 | 1995 | Mayaguez, P.R. |
| Tull, Bill | 0 | 0 | 0.00 | 1 | 0 | 0 | 0 | 2 | 3 | 0 | 0 | 1 | 2 | R | R | 6-0 | 170 | 12-4-75 | 1996 | Westville, N.J. |

# OAKLAND ATHLETICS

**Manager:** Art Howe.          **1996 Record:** 78-84, .481 (3rd, AL West).

| BATTING | AVG | G | AB | R | H | 2B | 3B | HR | RBI | BB | SO | SB | CS | B | T | HT | WT | DOB | 1st Yr | Resides |
|---|---|---|---|---|---|---|---|---|---|---|---|---|---|---|---|---|---|---|---|---|
| Batista, Tony | .298 | 74 | 238 | 38 | 71 | 10 | 2 | 6 | 25 | 19 | 49 | 7 | 3 | R | R | 6-0 | 180 | 12-9-73 | 1992 | Mao Valverde, D.R. |
| Battle, Allen | .192 | 47 | 130 | 20 | 25 | 3 | 0 | 1 | 5 | 17 | 26 | 10 | 2 | R | R | 6-0 | 170 | 11-29-68 | 1991 | Mt. Olive, N.C. |
| Berroa, Geronimo | .290 | 153 | 586 | 101 | 170 | 32 | 1 | 36 | 106 | 47 | 122 | 0 | 3 | R | R | 6-0 | 165 | 3-18-65 | 1984 | Santo Domingo, D.R. |
| Bordick, Mike | .240 | 155 | 525 | 46 | 126 | 18 | 4 | 5 | 54 | 52 | 59 | 5 | 6 | R | R | 5-11 | 170 | 7-21-65 | 1986 | Winterport, Maine |
| Bournigal, Rafael | .242 | 88 | 252 | 33 | 61 | 14 | 2 | 0 | 18 | 16 | 19 | 4 | 3 | R | R | 5-11 | 165 | 5-12-66 | 1987 | Santo Domingo, D.R. |
| Brosius, Scott | .304 | 114 | 428 | 73 | 130 | 25 | 0 | 22 | 71 | 59 | 85 | 7 | 2 | R | R | 6-1 | 190 | 8-15-66 | 1987 | McMinnville, Ore. |
| Garrison, Webster | .000 | 5 | 9 | 0 | 0 | 0 | 0 | 0 | 0 | 1 | 0 | 0 | 0 | R | R | 5-11 | 170 | 8-24-65 | 1984 | Marrero, La. |
| Gates, Brent | .263 | 64 | 247 | 26 | 65 | 19 | 2 | 2 | 30 | 18 | 35 | 1 | 1 | S | R | 6-1 | 180 | 3-14-70 | 1991 | Grandville, Mich. |
| Giambi, Jason | .291 | 140 | 536 | 84 | 156 | 40 | 1 | 20 | 79 | 51 | 95 | 0 | 1 | L | R | 6-2 | 200 | 1-8-71 | 1992 | Covina, Calif. |
| Herrera, Jose | .269 | 108 | 320 | 44 | 86 | 15 | 1 | 6 | 30 | 20 | 59 | 8 | 2 | L | L | 6-0 | 164 | 8-30-72 | 1991 | Santo Domingo, D.R. |
| Lesher, Brian | .232 | 26 | 82 | 11 | 19 | 3 | 0 | 5 | 16 | 5 | 17 | 0 | 0 | R | L | 6-5 | 205 | 3-5-71 | 1992 | Newark, Del. |
| Lovullo, Torey | .220 | 65 | 82 | 15 | 18 | 4 | 0 | 3 | 9 | 11 | 17 | 1 | 2 | S | R | 6-0 | 185 | 7-25-65 | 1987 | Northridge, Calif. |
| Mashore, Damon | .267 | 50 | 105 | 20 | 28 | 7 | 1 | 3 | 12 | 16 | 31 | 4 | 0 | R | R | 5-11 | 195 | 10-31-69 | 1991 | Concord, Calif. |
| McGwire, Mark | .312 | 130 | 423 | 104 | 132 | 21 | 0 | 52 | 113 | 116 | 112 | 0 | 0 | R | R | 6-5 | 225 | 10-1-63 | 1984 | Claremont, Calif. |
| Molina, Izzy | .200 | 14 | 25 | 0 | 5 | 2 | 0 | 0 | 1 | 1 | 3 | 0 | 0 | R | R | 6-0 | 200 | 6-3-71 | 1990 | Miami, Fla. |
| Moore, Kerwin | .063 | 22 | 16 | 4 | 1 | 1 | 0 | 0 | 0 | 2 | 6 | 1 | 0 | S | R | 6-1 | 190 | 10-29-70 | 1988 | Detroit, Mich. |
| Munoz, Pedro | .256 | 34 | 121 | 17 | 31 | 5 | 0 | 6 | 18 | 9 | 31 | 0 | 0 | R | R | 5-11 | 203 | 9-19-68 | 1985 | Ponce, P.R. |
| Plantier, Phil | .212 | 73 | 231 | 29 | 49 | 8 | 1 | 7 | 31 | 28 | 56 | 2 | 2 | L | R | 5-11 | 195 | 1-27-69 | 1987 | San Diego, Calif. |
| Spiezio, Scott | .310 | 9 | 29 | 6 | 9 | 2 | 0 | 2 | 8 | 4 | 4 | 0 | 1 | S | R | 6-2 | 205 | 9-21-72 | 1993 | Morris, Ill. |
| Stairs, Matt | .277 | 61 | 137 | 21 | 38 | 5 | 1 | 10 | 23 | 19 | 23 | 1 | 1 | L | R | 5-9 | 175 | 2-27-69 | 1989 | Stanley, N.B. |
| Steinbach, Terry | .272 | 145 | 514 | 79 | 140 | 25 | 1 | 35 | 100 | 49 | 115 | 0 | 1 | R | R | 6-1 | 175 | 3-2-62 | 1983 | Plymouth, Minn. |
| Williams, George | .152 | 56 | 132 | 17 | 20 | 5 | 0 | 3 | 10 | 28 | 32 | 0 | 0 | S | R | 5-10 | 190 | 4-22-69 | 1991 | LaCrosse, Wis. |
| Young, Ernie | .242 | 141 | 462 | 72 | 112 | 19 | 4 | 19 | 64 | 52 | 118 | 7 | 5 | R | R | 6-1 | 190 | 7-8-69 | 1990 | Chicago, Ill. |

| PITCHING | W | L | ERA | G | GS | CG | SV | IP | H | R | ER | BB | SO | B | T | HT | WT | DOB | 1st Yr | Resides |
|---|---|---|---|---|---|---|---|---|---|---|---|---|---|---|---|---|---|---|---|---|
| Acre, Mark | 1 | 3 | 6.12 | 22 | 0 | 0 | 2 | 25 | 38 | 17 | 17 | 9 | 18 | R | R | 6-8 | 235 | 9-16-68 | 1991 | Corning, Calif. |
| Adams, Willie | 3 | 4 | 4.01 | 12 | 12 | 1 | 0 | 76 | 76 | 39 | 34 | 23 | 68 | R | R | 6-7 | 215 | 10-8-72 | 1993 | La Mirada, Calif. |
| Briscoe, John | 0 | 1 | 3.76 | 17 | 0 | 0 | 1 | 26 | 18 | 11 | 11 | 24 | 14 | R | R | 6-3 | 195 | 9-22-67 | 1988 | Richardson, Texas |
| Chouinard, Bobby | 4 | 2 | 6.10 | 13 | 11 | 0 | 0 | 59 | 75 | 41 | 40 | 32 | 32 | R | R | 6-1 | 188 | 5-1-72 | 1990 | Forest Grove, Ore. |
| Corsi, Jim | 6 | 0 | 4.03 | 56 | 0 | 0 | 3 | 74 | 71 | 33 | 33 | 34 | 43 | R | R | 6-1 | 220 | 9-9-61 | 1982 | Natick, Mass. |
| Fletcher, Paul | 0 | 0 | 20.25 | 1 | 0 | 0 | 0 | 1 | 6 | 3 | 3 | 1 | 0 | R | R | 6-1 | 185 | 1-14-67 | 1988 | Ravenswood, W.Va. |
| Groom, Buddy | 5 | 0 | 3.84 | 72 | 1 | 0 | 2 | 77 | 85 | 37 | 33 | 34 | 57 | L | L | 6-2 | 200 | 7-10-65 | 1987 | Red Oak, Texas |
| Johns, Doug | 6 | 12 | 5.98 | 40 | 23 | 1 | 1 | 158 | 187 | 112 | 105 | 69 | 71 | L | R | 6-2 | 185 | 12-19-67 | 1990 | Plantation, Fla. |
| Mohler, Mike | 6 | 3 | 3.67 | 72 | 0 | 0 | 7 | 81 | 79 | 36 | 33 | 41 | 64 | L | R | 6-2 | 195 | 7-26-68 | 1990 | Gonzales, La. |
| Montgomery, Steve | 1 | 0 | 9.22 | 8 | 0 | 0 | 0 | 14 | 18 | 14 | 14 | 13 | 8 | R | R | 6-4 | 200 | 12-25-70 | 1992 | Corona del Mar, Calif. |
| Prieto, Ariel | 6 | 7 | 4.15 | 21 | 21 | 2 | 0 | 126 | 130 | 66 | 58 | 54 | 75 | R | R | 6-3 | 220 | 10-22-66 | 1995 | Naples, Fla. |
| Reyes, Carlos | 7 | 10 | 4.78 | 46 | 10 | 0 | 0 | 122 | 134 | 71 | 65 | 61 | 78 | S | R | 6-1 | 190 | 4-19-69 | 1991 | Macon, Ga. |
| Small, Aaron | 1 | 3 | 8.16 | 12 | 3 | 0 | 0 | 29 | 37 | 28 | 26 | 22 | 17 | R | R | 6-5 | 200 | 11-23-71 | 1989 | Victorville, Calif. |
| Taylor, Billy | 3 | 4 | 4.33 | 55 | 0 | 0 | 17 | 60 | 52 | 30 | 29 | 25 | 67 | R | R | 6-8 | 200 | 10-16-61 | 1980 | Thomasville, Ga. |
| Telgheder, Dave | 4 | 7 | 4.65 | 16 | 14 | 1 | 0 | 79 | 92 | 42 | 41 | 26 | 43 | R | R | 6-3 | 212 | 11-11-66 | 1989 | Slate Hill, N.Y. |
| Van Poppel, Todd | 1 | 5 | 7.71 | 28 | 6 | 0 | 1 | 63 | 86 | 56 | 54 | 33 | 37 | R | R | 6-5 | 210 | 12-9-71 | 1990 | Arlington, Texas |
| Wasdin, John | 8 | 7 | 5.96 | 25 | 21 | 1 | 0 | 131 | 145 | 96 | 87 | 50 | 75 | R | R | 6-2 | 195 | 8-5-72 | 1993 | Tallahassee, Fla. |
| Wengert, Don | 7 | 11 | 5.58 | 36 | 25 | 1 | 0 | 161 | 200 | 102 | 100 | 60 | 75 | R | R | 6-3 | 205 | 11-6-69 | 1992 | Sioux City, Iowa |
| Witasick, Jay | 1 | 1 | 6.23 | 12 | 0 | 0 | 0 | 13 | 12 | 9 | 9 | 5 | 12 | R | R | 6-4 | 205 | 8-28-72 | 1993 | Bel Air, Md. |
| Wojciechowski, Steve | 5 | 5 | 5.65 | 16 | 15 | 0 | 0 | 80 | 97 | 57 | 50 | 28 | 30 | L | L | 6-2 | 185 | 7-29-70 | 1991 | Calumet City, Ill. |

## FIELDING

| Catcher | PCT | G | PO | A | E | DP | PB |
|---|---|---|---|---|---|---|---|
| Molina | 1.000 | 12 | 31 | 1 | 0 | 1 | 0 |
| Steinbach | .991 | 137 | 731 | 46 | 7 | 7 | 6 |
| Williams | .982 | 43 | 154 | 12 | 3 | 1 | 5 |

| First Base | PCT | G | PO | A | E | DP |
|---|---|---|---|---|---|---|
| Brosius | 1.000 | 10 | 37 | 2 | 0 | 1 |
| Garrison | 1.000 | 1 | 1 | 1 | 0 | 0 |
| Giambi | .993 | 45 | 379 | 32 | 3 | 38 |
| Lesher | 1.000 | 1 | 7 | 0 | 0 | 0 |
| Lovullo | 1.000 | 42 | 120 | 9 | 0 | 21 |
| McGwire | .990 | 109 | 913 | 60 | 10 | 118 |
| Stairs | 1.000 | 1 | 6 | 3 | 0 | 1 |
| Steinbach | 1.000 | 1 | 1 | 0 | 0 | 0 |

| Second Base | PCT | G | PO | A | E | DP |
|---|---|---|---|---|---|---|
| Batista | .988 | 52 | 83 | 162 | 3 | 36 |
| Bournigal | .993 | 64 | 115 | 175 | 2 | 40 |
| Garrison | .875 | 3 | 3 | 4 | 1 | 1 |
| Gates | .973 | 63 | 140 | 183 | 9 | 48 |
| Lovullo | 1.000 | 2 | 4 | 1 | 0 | 1 |

| Third Base | PCT | G | PO | A | E | DP |
|---|---|---|---|---|---|---|
| Batista | .931 | 18 | 9 | 18 | 2 | 3 |
| Brosius | .969 | 109 | 83 | 232 | 10 | 25 |
| Giambi | .932 | 39 | 31 | 79 | 8 | 10 |
| Lovullo | .952 | 11 | 9 | 11 | 1 | 3 |
| Spiezio | .833 | 5 | 5 | 5 | 2 | 0 |

| Shortstop | PCT | G | PO | A | E | DP |
|---|---|---|---|---|---|---|
| Batista | 1.000 | 4 | 4 | 11 | 0 | 1 |
| Bordick | .979 | 155 | 266 | 476 | 16 | 121 |
| Bournigal | 1.000 | 23 | 13 | 33 | 0 | 6 |
| Lovullo | .000 | 1 | 0 | 0 | 0 | 0 |

| Outfield | PCT | G | PO | A | E | DP |
|---|---|---|---|---|---|---|
| Battle | .988 | 47 | 82 | 2 | 1 | 0 |
| Berroa | .980 | 61 | 91 | 6 | 2 | 1 |
| Brosius | 1.000 | 4 | 8 | 0 | 0 | 0 |
| Giambi | 1.000 | 45 | 68 | 6 | 0 | 1 |
| Herrera | .970 | 100 | 190 | 2 | 6 | 0 |
| Lesher | .976 | 25 | 39 | 2 | 1 | 0 |
| Lovullo | 1.000 | 1 | 1 | 0 | 0 | 0 |
| Mashore | .985 | 48 | 65 | 1 | 1 | 0 |
| Moore | 1.000 | 18 | 20 | 0 | 0 | 0 |
| Munoz | 1.000 | 14 | 15 | 0 | 0 | 0 |
| Plantier | .973 | 68 | 138 | 8 | 4 | 2 |
| Stairs | .985 | 44 | 58 | 8 | 1 | 3 |
| Young | .997 | 140 | 353 | 8 | 1 | 5 |

**Mark McGwire**

LARRY GOREN

Scott Brosius had his best season in 1996, hitting .304 with 22 homers

A's minor league Player of the Year Miguel Tejada

THE SPORTS GROUP

LARRY GOREN

## FARM SYSTEM

**Director of Player Development:** Keith Lieppman

| Class | Farm Team | League | W | L | Pct. | Finish* | Manager | First Yr |
|---|---|---|---|---|---|---|---|---|
| AAA | Edmonton (Alta.) Trappers | Pacific Coast | 84 | 58 | .592 | +1st (10) | Gary Jones | 1995 |
| AA | Huntsville (Ala.) Stars | Southern | 66 | 74 | .471 | 7th (10) | Dick Scott | 1985 |
| #A | Modesto (Calif.) A's | California | 82 | 58 | .586 | 2nd (10) | Jim Colborn | 1975 |
| A | West Michigan Whitecaps | Midwest | 77 | 61 | .558 | +3rd (14) | Mike Quade | 1994 |
| A | Southern Oregon A's | Northwest | 29 | 47 | .382 | 8th (8) | Tony DeFrancesco | 1979 |
| R | Phoenix (Ariz.) Athletics | Arizona | 33 | 23 | .589 | 2nd (6) | Juan Navarrete | 1988 |

*Finish in overall standings (No. of teams in league)   #Advanced level   +Won league championship

## ORGANIZATION LEADERS

### MAJOR LEAGUERS

**BATTING**
- *AVG  Mark McGwire........ .312
- R  Mark McGwire........ 104
- H  Geronimo Berroa .... 170
- TB  Geronimo Berroa .... 312
- 2B  Jason Giambi ....... 40
- 3B  Two tied at ................ 4
- HR  Mark McGwire......... 52
- RBI  Mark McGwire......... 113
- BB  Mark McGwire......... 116
- SO  Geronimo Berroa .... 122
- SB  Allen Battle .............. 10

**PITCHING**
- W  John Wasdin .............. 8
- L  Doug Johns.............. 12
- #ERA  Mike Mohler ......... 3.67
- G  Two tied at ............... 72
- CG  Ariel Prieto ................ 2
- SV  Billy Taylor ............. 17
- IP  Don Wengert.......... 161
- BB  Doug Johns ............. 69
- SO  Carlos Reyes ........... 78

Geronimo Berroa. 170 hits

THE SPORTS GROUP

### MINOR LEAGUERS

**BATTING**
- *AVG  Mike Neill, Modesto/Edmonton..............331
- R  Mike Neill, Modesto/Edmonton............ 105
- H  D.T. Cromer, Modesto........................ 166
- TB  D.T. Cromer, Modesto ........................ 316
- 2B  D.T. Cromer, Modesto......................... 40
- 3B  Demond Smith, Huntsville/Edmonton...... 14
- HR  D.T. Cromer, Modesto ......................... 30
- RBI  D.T. Cromer, Modesto ....................... 130
- BB  Dane Walker, West Michigan .............. 112
- SO  Juan Dilone, Modesto........................... 138
- SB  Kerwin Moore, Edmonton...................... 38

**PITCHING**
- W  Bill King, Modesto................................. 16
- L  Brad Rigby, Huntsville ......................... 12
- #ERA  Tim Kubinski, Huntsville/Edmonton....... 2.36
- G  Two tied at........................................... 52
- CG  Three tied at .........................................3
- SV  Robert Kazmirski, West Michigan .......... 28
- IP  Bill King, Modesto............................... 163
- BB  Bret Wagner, Huntsville......................... 77
- SO  Scott Rivette, West Michigan ............... 142

*Minimum 250 At-Bats   #Minimum 75 Innings

## TOP 10 PROSPECTS

How the Athletics Top 10 prospects, as judged by Baseball America prior to the 1996 season, fared in 1996:

Ben Grieve

LARRY GOREN

| Player, Pos. | Club (Class—League) | AVG | AB | R | H | 2B | 3B | HR | RBI | SB |
|---|---|---|---|---|---|---|---|---|---|---|
| 1. Ben Grieve, of | Modesto (A—California) | .356 | 281 | 61 | 100 | 20 | 1 | 11 | 51 | 8 |
| | Huntsville (AA—Southern) | .237 | 232 | 34 | 55 | 8 | 1 | 8 | 32 | 0 |
| 4. Steve Cox, 1b | Huntsville (AA—Southern) | .281 | 351 | 59 | 107 | 21 | 1 | 12 | 61 | 2 |
| 5. Ramon Hernandez, c | West Michigan (A—Midwest) | .255 | 447 | 62 | 114 | 26 | 2 | 12 | 68 | 2 |
| 6. Miguel Tejada, ss | Modesto (A—California) | .279 | 458 | 97 | 128 | 12 | 5 | 20 | 72 | 27 |
| 7. Mario Encarnacion, of | West Michigan (A—Midwest) | .229 | 401 | 55 | 92 | 14 | 3 | 7 | 43 | 23 |

| Player, Pos. | Club (Class—League) | W | L | ERA | G | SV | IP | H | BB | SO |
|---|---|---|---|---|---|---|---|---|---|---|
| 2. John Wasdin, rhp | Edmonton (AAA—Pacific Coast) | 2 | 1 | 4.14 | 9 | 0 | 50 | 52 | 17 | 30 |
| | Oakland | 8 | 7 | 5.96 | 25 | 0 | 131 | 145 | 50 | 75 |
| 3. Brad Rigby, rhp | Huntsville (AA—Southern) | 9 | 12 | 3.95 | 26 | 0 | 159 | 161 | 59 | 127 |
| 8. Bret Wagner, lhp | Huntsville (AA—Southern) | 8 | 8 | 4.23 | 27 | 0 | 134 | 125 | 77 | 98 |
| 9. Willie Adams, rhp | Edmonton (AAA—Pacific Coast) | 10 | 4 | 3.78 | 19 | 0 | 112 | 95 | 39 | 80 |
| | Oakland | 3 | 4 | 4.01 | 12 | 0 | 76 | 76 | 23 | 68 |
| 10. Tom Bennett, rhp | Phoenix (R—Arizona) | 0 | 0 | 1.38 | 4 | 0 | 13 | 2 | 11 | 12 |
| | West Michigan (A—Midwest) | 0 | 1 | 3.92 | 6 | 0 | 21 | 17 | 18 | 17 |

## PACIFIC COAST LEAGUE

| BATTING | AVG | G | AB | R | H | 2B | 3B | HR | RBI | BB | SO | SB | CS | B | T | HT | WT | DOB | 1st Yr | Resides |
|---|---|---|---|---|---|---|---|---|---|---|---|---|---|---|---|---|---|---|---|---|
| Batista, Tony | .322 | 57 | 205 | 33 | 66 | 17 | 4 | 8 | 40 | 15 | 30 | 2 | 1 | R | R | 6-0 | 180 | 12-9-73 | 1992 | Mao Valverde, D.R. |
| Battle, Allen | .304 | 62 | 224 | 53 | 68 | 12 | 4 | 3 | 33 | 37 | 37 | 9 | 3 | R | R | 6-0 | 170 | 11-29-68 | 1991 | Mt. Olive, N.C. |
| Brosius, Scott | .625 | 3 | 8 | 5 | 5 | 1 | 0 | 0 | 0 | 3 | 1 | 0 | 0 | R | R | 6-1 | 190 | 8-15-66 | 1987 | McMinnville, Ore. |
| Correia, Rod | .087 | 8 | 23 | 1 | 2 | 0 | 0 | 0 | 0 | 0 | 2 | 1 | 0 | R | R | 5-11 | 185 | 9-13-67 | 1988 | Rehoboth, Mass. |
| Garrison, Webster | .303 | 80 | 294 | 56 | 89 | 18 | 0 | 10 | 49 | 41 | 47 | 2 | 1 | R | R | 5-11 | 170 | 8-24-65 | 1984 | Marrero, La. |
| Gubanich, Creighton | .248 | 34 | 117 | 14 | 29 | 7 | 1 | 4 | 19 | 6 | 33 | 3 | 0 | R | R | 6-4 | 220 | 3-27-72 | 1991 | Phoenixville, Pa. |
| Horne, Tyrone | .230 | 67 | 204 | 28 | 47 | 7 | 2 | 4 | 16 | 32 | 53 | 5 | 3 | L | R | 5-10 | 185 | 11-2-70 | 1989 | Troy, N.C. |
| Lee, Derek | .200 | 9 | 25 | 3 | 5 | 1 | 0 | 0 | 1 | 6 | 2 | 0 | 1 | L | R | 6-1 | 200 | 7-28-66 | 1988 | Reston, Va. |
| Lennon, Patrick | .327 | 68 | 251 | 37 | 82 | 16 | 2 | 12 | 42 | 28 | 82 | 3 | 3 | R | R | 6-2 | 200 | 4-27-68 | 1986 | Whiteville, N.C. |
| Lesher, Brian | .287 | 109 | 414 | 57 | 119 | 29 | 2 | 18 | 75 | 36 | 108 | 6 | 5 | R | L | 6-5 | 205 | 3-5-71 | 1992 | Newark, Del. |
| Lovullo, Torey | .280 | 26 | 93 | 18 | 26 | 4 | 0 | 4 | 19 | 18 | 12 | 0 | 0 | S | R | 6-0 | 185 | 7-25-65 | 1987 | Northridge, Calif. |
| Mashore, Damon | .268 | 50 | 183 | 32 | 49 | 9 | 1 | 8 | 29 | 19 | 48 | 6 | 2 | R | R | 5-11 | 195 | 10-31-69 | 1991 | Concord, Calif. |
| McDonald, Jason | .238 | 137 | 479 | 71 | 114 | 7 | 5 | 8 | 46 | 63 | 82 | 33 | 13 | S | R | 5-8 | 175 | 3-20-72 | 1993 | Elk Grove, Calif. |
| Molina, Izzy | .263 | 98 | 342 | 45 | 90 | 12 | 3 | 12 | 56 | 25 | 55 | 2 | 5 | R | R | 6-0 | 200 | 6-3-71 | 1990 | Miami, Fla. |
| Moore, Kerwin | .230 | 119 | 452 | 90 | 104 | 12 | 11 | 2 | 32 | 95 | 115 | 38 | 12 | S | R | 6-1 | 190 | 10-29-70 | 1988 | Detroit, Mich. |
| Neill, Mike | .150 | 6 | 20 | 4 | 3 | 1 | 0 | 1 | 4 | 2 | 3 | 0 | 0 | L | L | 6-2 | 200 | 4-27-70 | 1991 | Langhorne, Pa. |
| Plantier, Phil | .352 | 34 | 122 | 25 | 43 | 7 | 1 | 9 | 45 | 12 | 25 | 1 | 0 | L | R | 5-11 | 195 | 1-27-69 | 1987 | San Diego, Calif. |
| Poe, Charles | .200 | 3 | 15 | 2 | 3 | 0 | 0 | 0 | 0 | 1 | 5 | 0 | 0 | R | R | 6-0 | 185 | 11-9-71 | 1990 | West Covina, Calif. |
| Sheldon, Scott | .300 | 98 | 350 | 61 | 105 | 27 | 3 | 10 | 60 | 43 | 83 | 5 | 3 | R | R | 6-3 | 185 | 11-28-68 | 1991 | Houston, Texas |
| Smith, Demond | .333 | 2 | 3 | 0 | 1 | 0 | 0 | 0 | 0 | 0 | 2 | 0 | 0 | S | R | 5-11 | 170 | 11-6-72 | 1990 | Rialto, Calif. |
| Spiezio, Scott | .262 | 140 | 523 | 87 | 137 | 30 | 4 | 20 | 91 | 56 | 66 | 6 | 5 | S | R | 6-2 | 205 | 9-21-72 | 1993 | Morris, Ill. |
| Stairs, Matt | .344 | 51 | 180 | 35 | 62 | 16 | 1 | 8 | 41 | 21 | 34 | 0 | 0 | L | R | 5-9 | 175 | 2-27-69 | 1989 | Stanley, N.B. |
| Tomberlin, Andy | .283 | 17 | 60 | 12 | 17 | 2 | 1 | 0 | 5 | 8 | 15 | 1 | 0 | L | L | 5-11 | 160 | 11-7-66 | 1986 | Monroe, N.C. |
| Ventura, Wilfredo | .250 | 2 | 4 | 1 | 1 | 0 | 0 | 0 | 0 | 0 | 1 | 0 | 0 | R | R | 5-11 | 210 | 10-11-76 | 1993 | Santo Domingo, D.R. |
| Walters, Dan | .250 | 25 | 64 | 5 | 16 | 5 | 0 | 1 | 8 | 4 | 7 | 0 | 0 | R | R | 6-2 | 190 | 8-15-66 | 1985 | Santee, Calif. |
| Williams, George | .404 | 14 | 57 | 10 | 23 | 5 | 0 | 5 | 18 | 6 | 11 | 0 | 1 | S | R | 5-10 | 190 | 4-22-69 | 1991 | LaCrosse, Wis. |
| Wood, Jason | .000 | 3 | 12 | 0 | 0 | 0 | 0 | 0 | 0 | 5 | 6 | 0 | 1 | R | R | 6-1 | 170 | 12-16-69 | 1991 | Fresno, Calif. |

| PITCHING | W | L | ERA | G | GS | CG | SV | IP | H | R | ER | BB | SO | B | T | HT | WT | DOB | 1st Yr | Resides |
|---|---|---|---|---|---|---|---|---|---|---|---|---|---|---|---|---|---|---|---|---|
| Acre, Mark | 6 | 2 | 2.09 | 39 | 0 | 0 | 8 | 43 | 33 | 11 | 10 | 16 | 50 | R | R | 6-8 | 235 | 9-16-68 | 1991 | Corning, Calif. |
| Adams, Willie | 10 | 4 | 3.78 | 19 | 19 | 3 | 0 | 112 | 95 | 49 | 47 | 39 | 80 | R | R | 6-7 | 215 | 10-8-72 | 1993 | La Mirada, Calif. |
| Briscoe, John | 5 | 2 | 4.77 | 30 | 1 | 0 | 1 | 55 | 69 | 33 | 29 | 23 | 62 | R | R | 6-3 | 195 | 9-22-67 | 1988 | Richardson, Texas |
| Chouinard, Bobby | 10 | 2 | 2.77 | 15 | 15 | 0 | 0 | 84 | 70 | 32 | 26 | 24 | 45 | R | R | 6-1 | 188 | 5-1-72 | 1990 | Forest Grove, Ore. |
| Daspit, Jamie | 4 | 5 | 4.12 | 33 | 9 | 0 | 0 | 90 | 96 | 50 | 41 | 29 | 76 | R | R | 6-7 | 210 | 8-10-69 | 1990 | Sacramento, Calif. |
| Dressendorfer, Kirk | 0 | 1 | 5.54 | 10 | 0 | 0 | 0 | 13 | 23 | 11 | 8 | 3 | 10 | R | R | 5-11 | 180 | 4-8-69 | 1990 | Pearland, Texas |
| Fletcher, Paul | 4 | 6 | 2.70 | 38 | 0 | 0 | 1 | 83 | 66 | 28 | 25 | 41 | 76 | R | R | 6-1 | 185 | 1-14-67 | 1988 | Ravenswood, W.Va. |
| Grigsby, Benji | 0 | 0 | 7.25 | 11 | 3 | 0 | 0 | 22 | 29 | 20 | 18 | 7 | 15 | R | R | 6-2 | 200 | 12-2-70 | 1992 | Lafayette, La. |
| Kubinski, Tim | 0 | 0 | 0.00 | 1 | 0 | 0 | 0 | 1 | 1 | 0 | 0 | 1 | 0 | L | L | 6-4 | 205 | 1-20-72 | 1993 | San Luis Obispo, Calif. |
| Lorraine, Andrew | 8 | 10 | 5.68 | 30 | 25 | 0 | 0 | 141 | 181 | 95 | 89 | 46 | 73 | L | L | 6-3 | 195 | 8-11-72 | 1993 | Valencia, Calif. |
| Montgomery, Steve | 2 | 0 | 2.89 | 36 | 0 | 0 | 1 | 56 | 51 | 19 | 18 | 12 | 40 | R | R | 6-4 | 200 | 12-25-70 | 1992 | Corona del Mar, Calif. |
| Prieto, Ariel | 3 | 0 | 0.57 | 3 | 3 | 0 | 0 | 16 | 11 | 1 | 1 | 6 | 18 | R | R | 6-3 | 220 | 10-22-66 | 1995 | Naples, Fla. |
| Rose, Scott | 4 | 4 | 2.91 | 50 | 0 | 0 | 10 | 56 | 57 | 21 | 18 | 16 | 20 | R | R | 6-3 | 200 | 5-20-70 | 1990 | Tampa, Fla. |
| Shaw, Curtis | 0 | 0 | 18.00 | 1 | 1 | 0 | 0 | 3 | 6 | 6 | 6 | 2 | 1 | L | L | 6-2 | 205 | 8-16-69 | 1990 | Lawrence, Kan. |
| Small, Aaron | 8 | 6 | 4.29 | 25 | 19 | 1 | 1 | 120 | 111 | 65 | 57 | 28 | 83 | R | R | 6-5 | 200 | 11-23-71 | 1989 | Victorville, Calif. |
| Taylor, Billy | 0 | 0 | 0.79 | 7 | 0 | 0 | 4 | 11 | 10 | 1 | 1 | 3 | 13 | R | R | 6-8 | 200 | 10-16-61 | 1980 | Thomasville, Ga. |
| Telgheder, Dave | 8 | 6 | 4.17 | 17 | 17 | 1 | 0 | 101 | 102 | 53 | 47 | 23 | 59 | R | R | 6-3 | 212 | 11-11-66 | 1989 | Slate Hill, N.Y. |
| Wasdin, John | 2 | 1 | 4.14 | 9 | 9 | 0 | 0 | 50 | 52 | 23 | 23 | 17 | 30 | R | R | 6-2 | 195 | 8-5-72 | 1993 | Tallahassee, Fla. |
| Williams, Todd | 5 | 3 | 5.50 | 35 | 10 | 0 | 0 | 92 | 125 | 71 | 56 | 37 | 33 | R | R | 6-3 | 185 | 2-13-71 | 1991 | East Syracuse, N.Y. |
| Witasick, Jay | 0 | 0 | 4.15 | 6 | 0 | 0 | 2 | 9 | 9 | 4 | 4 | 6 | 9 | R | R | 6-4 | 205 | 8-28-72 | 1993 | Belair, Md. |
| Wojciechowski, Steve | 4 | 3 | 3.73 | 11 | 11 | 1 | 0 | 60 | 56 | 32 | 25 | 21 | 46 | L | L | 6-2 | 185 | 7-29-70 | 1991 | Calumet City, Ill. |

### FIELDING

| Catcher | PCT | G | PO | A | E | DP | PB |
|---|---|---|---|---|---|---|---|
| Gubanich | .992 | 18 | 113 | 13 | 1 | 1 | 1 |
| Molina | .991 | 95 | 562 | 64 | 6 | 7 | 11 |
| Ventura | 1.000 | 4 | 2 | 0 | 0 | 0 | |
| Walters | 1.000 | 21 | 96 | 6 | 0 | 1 | 1 |
| Williams | 1.000 | 12 | 76 | 0 | 0 | 0 | 1 |

| First Base | PCT | G | PO | A | E | DP |
|---|---|---|---|---|---|---|
| Garrison | .983 | 24 | 211 | 15 | 4 | 16 |
| Gubanich | .983 | 9 | 52 | 5 | 1 | 4 |
| Lesher | .990 | 71 | 634 | 41 | 7 | 52 |
| Lovullo | .991 | 13 | 96 | 11 | 1 | 8 |
| Molina | .955 | 4 | 20 | 1 | 1 | 2 |
| Sheldon | .977 | 19 | 163 | 10 | 4 | 19 |
| Spiezio | .966 | 11 | 83 | 2 | 3 | 5 |
| Stairs | .947 | 4 | 17 | 1 | 1 | 2 |
| Wood | .976 | 3 | 39 | 1 | 1 | 3 |

| Second Base | PCT | G | PO | A | E | DP |
|---|---|---|---|---|---|---|
| Garrison | 1.000 | 17 | 33 | 41 | 0 | 7 |
| Lovullo | .970 | 8 | 10 | 22 | 1 | 6 |

| | PCT | G | PO | A | E | DP |
|---|---|---|---|---|---|---|
| McDonald | .962 | 122 | 254 | 352 | 24 | 75 |
| Sheldon | 1.000 | 3 | 6 | 10 | 0 | 1 |

| Third Base | PCT | G | PO | A | E | DP |
|---|---|---|---|---|---|---|
| Brosius | .667 | 3 | 0 | 4 | 2 | 0 |
| Garrison | .947 | 9 | 4 | 14 | 1 | 1 |
| Lovullo | 1.000 | 3 | 4 | 6 | 0 | 0 |
| Sheldon | 1.000 | 3 | 2 | 7 | 0 | 1 |
| Spiezio | .970 | 129 | 91 | 302 | 12 | 18 |

| Shortstop | PCT | G | PO | A | E | DP |
|---|---|---|---|---|---|---|
| Batista | .973 | 57 | 75 | 213 | 8 | 41 |
| Correia | .963 | 6 | 16 | 10 | 1 | 2 |
| Garrison | .938 | 15 | 15 | 46 | 4 | 8 |
| Lovullo | .000 | 1 | 0 | 0 | 0 | 0 |
| Sheldon | .954 | 65 | 86 | 203 | 14 | 39 |

| Outfield | PCT | G | PO | A | E | DP |
|---|---|---|---|---|---|---|
| Battle | .952 | 62 | 116 | 3 | 6 | 0 |
| Fletcher | .000 | 1 | 0 | 0 | 0 | 0 |

| | PCT | G | PO | A | E | DP |
|---|---|---|---|---|---|---|
| Garrison | 1.000 | 3 | 2 | 0 | 0 | 0 |
| Horne | .978 | 45 | 86 | 1 | 2 | 1 |
| Lee | .846 | 9 | 11 | 0 | 2 | 0 |
| Lennon | .939 | 37 | 57 | 5 | 4 | 0 |
| Lesher | .971 | 44 | 65 | 3 | 2 | 2 |
| Lovullo | .667 | 2 | 2 | 0 | 1 | 0 |
| Mashore | .988 | 48 | 74 | 7 | 1 | 1 |
| McDonald | .980 | 18 | 48 | 0 | 1 | 0 |
| Moore | .977 | 118 | 284 | 8 | 7 | 1 |
| Neill | 1.000 | 4 | 10 | 0 | 0 | 0 |
| Plantier | .864 | 20 | 18 | 1 | 3 | 0 |
| Poe | 1.000 | 3 | 5 | 1 | 0 | 0 |
| Sheldon | 1.000 | 1 | 2 | 0 | 0 | 0 |
| Smith | 1.000 | 2 | 3 | 0 | 0 | 0 |
| Stairs | .943 | 18 | 32 | 1 | 2 | 0 |
| Tomberlin | .963 | 17 | 25 | 1 | 1 | 1 |
| Williams | .000 | 1 | 0 | 0 | 0 | 0 |

## SOUTHERN LEAGUE

| BATTING | AVG | G | AB | R | H | 2B | 3B | HR | RBI | BB | SO | SB | CS | B | T | HT | WT | DOB | 1st Yr | Resides |
|---|---|---|---|---|---|---|---|---|---|---|---|---|---|---|---|---|---|---|---|---|
| Bellhorn, Mark | .250 | 131 | 468 | 84 | 117 | 24 | 5 | 10 | 71 | 73 | 124 | 19 | 2 | S | R | 6-1 | 195 | 8-23-74 | 1995 | Oviedo, Fla. |
| Bowles, Justin | .333 | 1 | 3 | 12 | 1 | 4 | 0 | 0 | 2 | 0 | 5 | 0 | 0 | L | L | 6-0 | 195 | 8-20-73 | 1996 | Lake Jackson, Texas |
| Correia, Rod | .253 | 66 | 241 | 38 | 61 | 9 | 1 | 2 | 30 | 28 | 24 | 11 | 1 | R | R | 5-11 | 185 | 9-13-67 | 1988 | Rehoboth, Mass. |
| Cox, Steve | .281 | 104 | 381 | 59 | 107 | 21 | 1 | 12 | 61 | 51 | 65 | 2 | 2 | L | L | 6-4 | 225 | 10-31-74 | 1992 | Strathmore, Calif. |

| BATTING | AVG | G | AB | R | H | 2B | 3B | HR | RBI | BB | SO | SB | CS | B | T | HT | WT | DOB | 1st Yr | Resides |
|---|---|---|---|---|---|---|---|---|---|---|---|---|---|---|---|---|---|---|---|---|
| DeBoer, Rob | .279 | 44 | 122 | 24 | 34 | 6 | 0 | 5 | 21 | 25 | 45 | 1 | 3 | R | R | 5-10 | 205 | 2-4-71 | 1994 | Omaha, Neb. |
| Francisco, David | .259 | 114 | 386 | 59 | 100 | 12 | 1 | 3 | 28 | 28 | 72 | 13 | 4 | R | R | 6-0 | 165 | 2-27-72 | 1991 | Santiago, D.R. |
| Garrison, Webster | .281 | 47 | 178 | 28 | 50 | 12 | 2 | 7 | 31 | 22 | 33 | 1 | 1 | R | R | 5-11 | 170 | 8-24-65 | 1984 | Marrero, La. |
| Grieve, Ben | .237 | 63 | 232 | 34 | 55 | 8 | 1 | 8 | 32 | 35 | 53 | 0 | 3 | L | R | 6-4 | 220 | 5-4-76 | 1994 | Arlington, Texas |
| Gubanich, Creighton | .276 | 62 | 217 | 40 | 60 | 19 | 0 | 9 | 43 | 31 | 71 | 1 | 0 | R | R | 6-4 | 205 | 3-27-72 | 1991 | Phoenixville, Pa. |
| Herrera, Jose | .286 | 23 | 84 | 18 | 24 | 4 | 0 | 1 | 7 | 14 | 15 | 3 | 2 | L | L | 6-0 | 164 | 8-30-72 | 1991 | Santo Domingo, D.R. |
| Hust, Gary | .223 | 60 | 197 | 22 | 44 | 11 | 0 | 3 | 26 | 18 | 64 | 3 | 0 | R | R | 6-4 | 215 | 3-15-72 | 1990 | Petal, Miss. |
| Martins, Eric | .255 | 111 | 388 | 61 | 99 | 23 | 2 | 1 | 34 | 47 | 77 | 7 | 7 | R | R | 5-10 | 175 | 11-19-72 | 1994 | Rowland Heights, Calif. |
| Morales, Willie | .292 | 108 | 377 | 54 | 110 | 24 | 0 | 18 | 73 | 38 | 67 | 0 | 2 | R | R | 5-10 | 182 | 9-7-72 | 1993 | Tucson, Ariz. |
| Poe, Charles | .264 | 122 | 416 | 74 | 110 | 18 | 3 | 12 | 68 | 46 | 99 | 5 | 4 | R | R | 6-0 | 185 | 11-9-71 | 1990 | West Covina, Calif. |
| Smith, Demond | .260 | 123 | 447 | 75 | 116 | 17 | 14 | 9 | 62 | 55 | 89 | 30 | 15 | S | R | 5-11 | 170 | 11-6-72 | 1990 | Rialto, Calif. |
| Wood, Jason | .261 | 133 | 491 | 77 | 128 | 21 | 1 | 20 | 84 | 72 | 87 | 2 | 5 | R | R | 6-1 | 170 | 12-16-69 | 1991 | Fresno, Calif. |

| PITCHING | W | L | ERA | G | GS | CG | SV | IP | H | R | ER | BB | SO | B | T | HT | WT | DOB | 1st Yr | Resides |
|---|---|---|---|---|---|---|---|---|---|---|---|---|---|---|---|---|---|---|---|---|
| Bennett, Bob | 5 | 3 | 5.27 | 38 | 2 | 0 | 0 | 84 | 92 | 55 | 49 | 36 | 83 | R | R | 6-4 | 205 | 12-30-70 | 1992 | Rapid City, S.D. |
| Dressendorfer, Kirk | 4 | 4 | 4.99 | 30 | 1 | 0 | 2 | 52 | 54 | 38 | 29 | 21 | 43 | R | R | 5-11 | 180 | 4-8-69 | 1990 | Pearland, Texas |
| Gogolin, Al | 0 | 0 | 0.00 | 5 | 0 | 0 | 0 | 6 | 3 | 0 | 0 | 2 | 4 | R | R | 6-5 | 215 | 1-14-72 | 1994 | Marietta, Ga. |
| Haught, Gary | 3 | 2 | 3.90 | 45 | 0 | 0 | 4 | 67 | 67 | 33 | 29 | 24 | 52 | S | R | 6-2 | 190 | 9-29-70 | 1992 | Choctaw, Okla. |
| Hollins, Stacy | 9 | 9 | 5.11 | 28 | 26 | 3 | 0 | 141 | 149 | 100 | 80 | 56 | 102 | R | R | 6-3 | 195 | 7-31-72 | 1992 | Willis, Texas |
| Jimenez, Miguel | 0 | 0 | 8.84 | 19 | 2 | 0 | 0 | 38 | 43 | 37 | 37 | 27 | 28 | R | R | 6-2 | 205 | 8-19-69 | 1991 | New York, N.Y. |
| Kubinski, Tim | 8 | 7 | 2.38 | 43 | 3 | 0 | 3 | 102 | 84 | 41 | 27 | 36 | 78 | L | L | 6-4 | 220 | 1-20-72 | 1993 | San Luis Obispo, Calif. |
| Manning, Derek | 0 | 4 | 6.75 | 18 | 12 | 0 | 1 | 72 | 96 | 59 | 54 | 22 | 51 | L | L | 6-4 | 220 | 7-21-70 | 1993 | Wilmington, N.C. |
| Martins, Eric | 1 | 0 | 3.86 | 2 | 0 | 0 | 0 | 2 | 4 | 1 | 1 | 3 | 2 | R | R | 5-10 | 175 | 11-19-72 | 1994 | Rowland Heights, Calif. |
| Maurer, Mike | 4 | 6 | 3.76 | 52 | 0 | 0 | 8 | 65 | 67 | 31 | 27 | 35 | 46 | R | R | 6-2 | 195 | 7-4-72 | 1994 | Burnsville, Minn. |
| Michalak, Chris | 4 | 0 | 7.71 | 21 | 0 | 0 | 0 | 23 | 32 | 29 | 20 | 26 | 15 | L | L | 6-2 | 195 | 1-4-71 | 1993 | Lemont, Ill. |
| Rigby, Brad | 9 | 12 | 3.95 | 26 | 26 | 3 | 0 | 159 | 161 | 89 | 70 | 59 | 127 | R | R | 6-6 | 203 | 5-14-73 | 1993 | Longwood, Fla. |
| Rossiter, Mike | 8 | 9 | 4.84 | 27 | 25 | 2 | 0 | 145 | 167 | 92 | 78 | 44 | 116 | R | R | 6-6 | 230 | 6-20-73 | 1991 | Burbank, Calif. |
| Silva, Luis | 0 | 0 | 13.50 | 1 | 0 | 0 | 0 | 3 | 5 | 4 | 4 | 2 | 2 | R | R | 6-4 | 200 | 4-18-75 | 1994 | Guatire, Venez. |
| Wagner, Bret | 8 | 8 | 4.23 | 27 | 27 | 0 | 0 | 134 | 125 | 77 | 63 | 77 | 98 | L | L | 6-0 | 190 | 4-17-73 | 1994 | New Cumberland, Pa. |
| Witasick, Jay | 0 | 3 | 2.30 | 25 | 6 | 0 | 4 | 67 | 47 | 21 | 17 | 26 | 63 | R | R | 6-4 | 205 | 8-28-72 | 1993 | Bel Air, Md. |
| Zancanaro, Dave | 3 | 3 | 5.61 | 10 | 10 | 0 | 0 | 43 | 54 | 32 | 27 | 26 | 36 | S | L | 6-1 | 180 | 1-8-69 | 1990 | Carmichael, Calif. |

### FIELDING

| Catcher | PCT | G | PO | A | E | DP | PB |
|---|---|---|---|---|---|---|---|
| DeBoer | .980 | 32 | 172 | 26 | 4 | 4 | 6 |
| Gubanich | .982 | 29 | 198 | 16 | 4 | 1 | 11 |
| Morales | .982 | 86 | 577 | 77 | 12 | 4 | 17 |

| First Base | PCT | G | PO | A | E | DP |
|---|---|---|---|---|---|---|
| Correia | 1.000 | 2 | 18 | 4 | 0 | 0 |
| Cox | .985 | 101 | 909 | 72 | 15 | 79 |
| Gubanich | 1.000 | 4 | 41 | 9 | 0 | 5 |
| Morales | .976 | 11 | 74 | 6 | 2 | 7 |
| Wood | 1.000 | 27 | 225 | 18 | 0 | 25 |

| Second Base | PCT | G | PO | A | E | DP |
|---|---|---|---|---|---|---|
| Bellhorn | .961 | 57 | 114 | 158 | 11 | 40 |

| | PCT | G | PO | A | E | DP |
|---|---|---|---|---|---|---|
| Garrison | .968 | 37 | 51 | 99 | 5 | 25 |
| Martins | .967 | 48 | 89 | 116 | 7 | 26 |

| Third Base | PCT | G | PO | A | E | DP |
|---|---|---|---|---|---|---|
| Bellhorn | .848 | 12 | 6 | 22 | 5 | 1 |
| Gubanich | .875 | 5 | 5 | 9 | 2 | 2 |
| Martins | .884 | 50 | 31 | 106 | 18 | 9 |
| Wood | .943 | 82 | 62 | 187 | 15 | 22 |

| Shortstop | PCT | G | PO | A | E | DP |
|---|---|---|---|---|---|---|
| Bellhorn | .940 | 55 | 88 | 164 | 16 | 27 |
| Correia | .925 | 62 | 104 | 180 | 23 | 40 |
| Wood | .965 | 26 | 50 | 87 | 5 | 14 |

| Outfield | PCT | G | PO | A | E | DP |
|---|---|---|---|---|---|---|
| Bowles | 1.000 | 3 | 2 | 0 | 0 | 0 |
| Francisco | .978 | 108 | 217 | 7 | 5 | 1 |
| Garrison | 1.000 | 4 | 2 | 0 | 0 | 0 |
| Grieve | .953 | 59 | 79 | 2 | 4 | 0 |
| Herrera | .972 | 20 | 34 | 1 | 1 | 1 |
| Hust | .973 | 44 | 67 | 6 | 2 | 0 |
| Poe | .957 | 84 | 127 | 5 | 6 | 0 |
| Smith | .955 | 111 | 187 | 4 | 9 | 1 |
| Wood | .000 | 1 | 0 | 0 | 0 | 0 |

## MODESTO  — Class A
### CALIFORNIA LEAGUE

| BATTING | AVG | G | AB | R | H | 2B | 3B | HR | RBI | BB | SO | SB | CS | B | T | HT | WT | DOB | 1st Yr | Resides |
|---|---|---|---|---|---|---|---|---|---|---|---|---|---|---|---|---|---|---|---|---|
| Ardoin, Danny | .262 | 91 | 317 | 55 | 83 | 13 | 3 | 6 | 34 | 47 | 81 | 5 | 7 | R | R | 6-0 | 195 | 7-8-74 | 1995 | Ville Platte, La. |
| Brown, Emil | .303 | 57 | 211 | 50 | 64 | 10 | 1 | 10 | 47 | 32 | 51 | 13 | 5 | R | R | 6-2 | 200 | 12-29-74 | 1994 | Chicago, Ill. |
| Castro, Jose | .226 | 95 | 363 | 58 | 82 | 16 | 1 | 8 | 48 | 42 | 124 | 25 | 12 | S | R | 5-10 | 165 | 10-15-74 | 1994 | Villa Vasquez, D.R. |
| Cesar, Dionys | .200 | 22 | 60 | 5 | 12 | 2 | 0 | 0 | 4 | 7 | 19 | 1 | 3 | S | R | 5-10 | 167 | 9-27-76 | 1994 | Santo Domingo, D.R. |
| Cromer, D.T. | .329 | 124 | 505 | 100 | 166 | 40 | 10 | 30 | 130 | 32 | 67 | 20 | 7 | L | L | 6-2 | 205 | 3-19-71 | 1992 | Murrells Inlet, S.C. |
| D'Amico, Jeff | .267 | 47 | 172 | 28 | 46 | 7 | 1 | 4 | 21 | 19 | 31 | 3 | 1 | R | R | 6-3 | 200 | 11-9-74 | 1993 | Redmond, Wash. |
| DeBoer, Rob | .285 | 73 | 249 | 68 | 71 | 8 | 6 | 12 | 52 | 74 | 75 | 12 | 5 | R | R | 5-10 | 205 | 2-4-71 | 1994 | Omaha, Neb. |
| Dilone, Juan | .265 | 111 | 404 | 78 | 107 | 17 | 1 | 14 | 66 | 45 | 138 | 31 | 10 | S | R | 6-1 | 188 | 5-10-73 | 1990 | Higuey, D.R. |
| Grieve, Ben | .356 | 72 | 281 | 61 | 100 | 20 | 1 | 11 | 51 | 38 | 52 | 8 | 7 | L | R | 6-4 | 220 | 5-4-76 | 1994 | Arlington, Texas |
| Hust, Gary | .238 | 12 | 42 | 6 | 10 | 2 | 0 | 2 | 10 | 10 | 14 | 0 | 2 | R | R | 6-4 | 215 | 3-15-72 | 1990 | Petal, Miss. |
| Madsen, Dave | .241 | 52 | 174 | 25 | 42 | 7 | 0 | 4 | 19 | 31 | 31 | 2 | 0 | R | R | 6-2 | 195 | 6-14-72 | 1993 | St. George, Utah |
| Maxwell, Pat | .455 | 4 | 11 | 1 | 5 | 1 | 0 | 0 | 1 | 1 | 0 | 0 | 0 | L | R | 6-0 | 190 | 3-28-70 | 1991 | Wichita Falls, Texas |
| Moore, Mark | .179 | 31 | 95 | 13 | 17 | 6 | 0 | 4 | 24 | 17 | 37 | 0 | 0 | R | R | 6-2 | 215 | 7-22-70 | 1992 | Prairie Village, Kan. |
| Neill, Mike | .339 | 114 | 442 | 101 | 150 | 20 | 6 | 19 | 78 | 68 | 123 | 28 | 7 | L | L | 6-2 | 200 | 4-27-70 | 1991 | Langhorne, Pa. |
| Newhan, David | .301 | 117 | 455 | 96 | 137 | 27 | 3 | 25 | 75 | 62 | 106 | 17 | 8 | L | R | 5-11 | 180 | 9-7-73 | 1995 | Yorba Linda, Calif. |
| Ortega, Randy | .246 | 23 | 65 | 8 | 16 | 2 | 1 | 1 | 5 | 9 | 11 | 1 | 2 | R | R | 6-1 | 205 | 7-5-72 | 1993 | Stockton, Calif. |
| Ortiz, Jose | .250 | 1 | 4 | 0 | 1 | 0 | 0 | 0 | 0 | 0 | 1 | 0 | 0 | R | R | 5-11 | 160 | 6-13-77 | 1995 | Capotillo, D.R. |
| Polanco, Juan | .214 | 8 | 28 | 4 | 6 | 2 | 0 | 1 | 2 | 3 | 7 | 1 | 2 | R | R | 6-0 | 190 | 1-6-75 | 1993 | Bani, D.R. |
| Slemmer, Dave | .294 | 26 | 85 | 17 | 25 | 9 | 0 | 3 | 13 | 11 | 15 | 2 | 2 | R | R | 6-0 | 187 | 3-29-73 | 1995 | Edwardsville, Ill. |
| Soriano, Fred | .262 | 33 | 126 | 24 | 33 | 3 | 0 | 2 | 19 | 14 | 33 | 14 | 3 | S | R | 5-9 | 160 | 8-5-74 | 1992 | Bani, D.R. |
| Tejada, Miguel | .279 | 114 | 458 | 97 | 128 | 12 | 5 | 20 | 72 | 51 | 93 | 27 | 16 | R | R | 5-11 | 180 | 5-25-76 | 1994 | Bani, D.R. |
| Ventura, Wilfredo | .260 | 32 | 100 | 15 | 26 | 3 | 1 | 4 | 23 | 8 | 37 | 1 | 0 | R | R | 5-11 | 210 | 10-11-76 | 1993 | Santo Domingo, D.R. |
| White, Derrick | .294 | 54 | 197 | 45 | 58 | 15 | 1 | 7 | 39 | 29 | 41 | 8 | 3 | R | R | 6-1 | 215 | 10-12-69 | 1991 | San Rafael, Calif. |

**GAMES BY POSITION: C**—Ardoin 76, DeBoer 43, Moore 6, Ortega 13, Ventura 16. **1B**—Ardoin 4, Cromer 59, Dilone 14, Madsen 30, Moore 10, Ortega 3, Ventura 2, White 30. **2B**—Castro 22, Cesar 21, D'Amico 5, Dilone 30, Madsen 1, Maxwell 3, Moore 1, Newhan 27, Ortiz 1, Slemmer 12, Soriano 31. **3B**—Ardoin 8, Castro 48, Cesar 1, D'Amico 39, Dilone 12, Madsen 15, Ortega 3, Polanco 2, Slemmer 13, Tejada 1, White 17. **SS**—Castro 31, D'Amico 3, Maxwell 1, Soriano 1, Tejada 110. **OF**—Brown 56, Castro 1, Cromer 46, DeBoer 1, Dilone 50, Grieve 69, Hust 12, Neill 98, Newhan 93, Polanco 6, White 6.

| PITCHING | W | L | ERA | G | GS | CG | SV | IP | H | R | ER | BB | SO | B | T | HT | WT | DOB | 1st Yr | Resides |
|---|---|---|---|---|---|---|---|---|---|---|---|---|---|---|---|---|---|---|---|---|
| Cochrane, Chris | 5 | 4 | 4.00 | 21 | 10 | 0 | 0 | 74 | 74 | 38 | 33 | 21 | 68 | R | R | 6-3 | 215 | 12-21-72 | 1994 | South Plainfield, N.J. |
| Connelly, Steven | 4 | 3 | 3.76 | 52 | 0 | 0 | 14 | 65 | 58 | 33 | 27 | 32 | 65 | R | R | 6-3 | 210 | 4-27-74 | 1995 | Long Beach, Calif. |
| Corsi, Jim | 0 | 0 | 0.00 | 1 | 1 | 0 | 0 | 1 | 0 | 0 | 0 | 0 | 2 | R | R | 6-1 | 220 | 9-9-61 | 1982 | Natick, Mass. |
| Dale, Carl | 8 | 2 | 4.28 | 26 | 24 | 0 | 0 | 128 | 124 | 79 | 61 | 72 | 102 | R | R | 6-2 | 215 | 12-7-72 | 1994 | Algood, Tenn. |

| | W | L | ERA | G | GS | CG | SV | IP | H | R | ER | BB | SO | B | T | HT | WT | DOB | 1st Yr | Resides |
|---|---|---|---|---|---|---|---|---|---|---|---|---|---|---|---|---|---|---|---|---|
| Hause, Brendan .......... | 0 | 0 | 13.50 | 1 | 0 | 0 | 0 | 2 | 4 | 3 | 3 | 1 | 2 | L | L | 6-1 | 185 | 10-21-74 | 1992 | San Diego, Calif. |
| Holden, Jason .......... | 0 | 0 | 13.50 | 1 | 0 | 0 | 0 | 2 | 5 | 3 | 3 | 0 | 1 | R | R | 6-2 | 190 | 8-5-73 | 1994 | Southaven, Miss. |
| Jimenez, Miguel .......... | 7 | 1 | 4.58 | 13 | 12 | 0 | 0 | 71 | 87 | 40 | 36 | 28 | 75 | R | R | 6-2 | 205 | 8-19-69 | 1991 | New York, N.Y. |
| Karsay, Steve .......... | 0 | 1 | 2.65 | 14 | 14 | 0 | 0 | 34 | 35 | 16 | 10 | 1 | 31 | R | R | 6-3 | 210 | 3-24-72 | 1990 | Tempe, Ariz. |
| King, Bill ...................... | 16 | 4 | 4.75 | 29 | 27 | 0 | 1 | 163 | 193 | 102 | 86 | 40 | 100 | R | R | 6-5 | 225 | 2-18-73 | 1994 | Chipley, Fla. |
| Lemke, Steve .......... | 4 | 5 | 5.68 | 12 | 6 | 0 | 0 | 44 | 65 | 34 | 28 | 17 | 29 | R | R | 6-1 | 185 | 1-4-70 | 1992 | Lincolnshire, Ill. |
| Michalak, Chris .......... | 2 | 2 | 3.03 | 21 | 0 | 0 | 4 | 39 | 37 | 21 | 13 | 17 | 39 | L | L | 6-2 | 195 | 1-4-71 | 1993 | Lemont, Ill. |
| Nelson, Chris .......... | 3 | 5 | 5.40 | 14 | 13 | 0 | 0 | 63 | 86 | 50 | 38 | 17 | 62 | R | R | 6-3 | 180 | 1-26-73 | 1995 | San Diego, Calif. |
| O'Dell, Jake .......... | 1 | 0 | 5.40 | 1 | 1 | 0 | 0 | 5 | 6 | 4 | 3 | 0 | 4 | R | R | 6-1 | 205 | 9-22-73 | 1996 | Round Rock, Texas |
| Perez, Juan .......... | 2 | 4 | 5.02 | 38 | 8 | 0 | 4 | 99 | 120 | 68 | 55 | 34 | 89 | L | L | 6-0 | 178 | 3-28-73 | 1992 | La Romana, D.R. |
| Prieto, Ariel .......... | 0 | 0 | 3.00 | 2 | 1 | 0 | 1 | 9 | 9 | 4 | 3 | 2 | 8 | R | R | 6-3 | 220 | 10-22-66 | 1995 | Naples, Fla. |
| Rajotte, Jason .......... | 3 | 6 | 2.52 | 47 | 0 | 0 | 7 | 75 | 50 | 24 | 21 | 28 | 57 | L | L | 6-0 | 185 | 12-15-72 | 1993 | West Warwick, R.I. |
| Shaw, Curtis .......... | 10 | 5 | 3.77 | 39 | 10 | 0 | 1 | 107 | 101 | 63 | 45 | 63 | 89 | L | L | 6-2 | 205 | 8-16-69 | 1990 | Lawrence, Kan. |
| Silva, Luis .......... | 0 | 0 | 0.00 | 1 | 0 | 0 | 0 | 1 | 0 | 0 | 0 | 1 | 1 | R | R | 6-4 | 200 | 4-18-75 | 1994 | Guatire, Venez. |
| Telgheder, Dave .......... | 1 | 0 | 1.50 | 1 | 1 | 0 | 0 | 6 | 4 | 3 | 1 | 1 | 3 | R | R | 6-3 | 212 | 11-11-66 | 1989 | Slate Hill, N.Y. |
| Walsh, Matt .......... | 3 | 1 | 3.49 | 38 | 0 | 0 | 4 | 70 | 54 | 38 | 27 | 31 | 68 | S | R | 6-2 | 190 | 12-11-72 | 1993 | Melrose, Mass. |
| Whitaker, Ryan .......... | 6 | 8 | 4.99 | 37 | 9 | 0 | 0 | 114 | 142 | 83 | 63 | 39 | 87 | R | R | 6-0 | 175 | 2-3-72 | 1993 | Broken Arrow, Okla. |
| Zancanaro, Dave .......... | 7 | 3 | 3.38 | 20 | 3 | 0 | 3 | 77 | 61 | 38 | 29 | 37 | 66 | S | L | 6-1 | 180 | 1-8-69 | 1990 | Carmichael, Calif. |

## WEST MICHIGAN — Class A
### MIDWEST LEAGUE

| BATTING | AVG | G | AB | R | H | 2B | 3B | HR | RBI | BB | SO | SB | CS | B | T | HT | WT | DOB | 1st Yr | Resides |
|---|---|---|---|---|---|---|---|---|---|---|---|---|---|---|---|---|---|---|---|---|
| Christenson, Ryan ...... | .311 | 33 | 122 | 21 | 38 | 2 | 2 | 2 | 18 | 13 | 22 | 2 | 4 | R | R | 5-11 | 175 | 3-28-74 | 1995 | Apple Valley, Calif. |
| DaVanon, Jeff .......... | .242 | 89 | 289 | 43 | 70 | 13 | 4 | 2 | 33 | 49 | 66 | 5 | 7 | S | R | 6-0 | 185 | 12-8-73 | 1995 | Del Mar, Calif. |
| Encarnacion, Mario ...... | .229 | 118 | 401 | 55 | 92 | 14 | 3 | 7 | 43 | 49 | 131 | 23 | 8 | R | R | 6-2 | 187 | 9-24-77 | 1994 | Bani, D.R. |
| Espada, Josue .......... | .270 | 23 | 74 | 9 | 20 | 2 | 0 | 0 | 13 | 11 | 3 | 1 | R | R | 5-10 | 175 | 8-30-75 | 1996 | Carolina, P.R. |
| Filchner, Duane .......... | .264 | 133 | 477 | 66 | 126 | 24 | 3 | 7 | 82 | 73 | 82 | 2 | 0 | L | L | 6-1 | 185 | 2-28-73 | 1995 | Northampton, Pa. |
| Hernandez, Ramon ...... | .255 | 123 | 447 | 62 | 114 | 26 | 2 | 12 | 68 | 69 | 62 | 2 | 3 | R | R | 6-0 | 170 | 5-20-76 | 1994 | Caracas, Venez. |
| Lara, Edward .......... | .216 | 87 | 259 | 29 | 56 | 7 | 1 | 0 | 16 | 25 | 39 | 16 | 6 | R | R | 5-9 | 145 | 10-30-75 | 1993 | Bani, D.R. |
| Miranda, Alex .......... | .222 | 123 | 414 | 57 | 92 | 18 | 2 | 5 | 48 | 86 | 84 | 3 | 0 | L | L | 6-2 | 205 | 5-14-72 | 1994 | Miami, Fla. |
| Ortega, Randy .......... | .252 | 49 | 139 | 15 | 35 | 4 | 0 | 2 | 21 | 25 | 34 | 0 | 1 | R | R | 6-1 | 205 | 7-5-72 | 1993 | Stockton, Calif. |
| Paulino, Arturo .......... | .221 | 87 | 231 | 27 | 51 | 7 | 1 | 2 | 19 | 24 | 46 | 9 | 10 | R | R | 5-11 | 170 | 7-18-74 | 1993 | San Cristobal, D.R. |
| Rauer, Troy .......... | .045 | 13 | 22 | 3 | 1 | 0 | 0 | 0 | 1 | 3 | 13 | 0 | 0 | R | R | 6-4 | 225 | 11-18-72 | 1995 | Scottsdale, Ariz. |
| Rondon, Alex .......... | .213 | 19 | 47 | 3 | 10 | 1 | 1 | 0 | 7 | 4 | 15 | 1 | 0 | R | R | 6-0 | 175 | 7-4-74 | 1994 | Guatire, Venez. |
| Soriano, Jose .......... | .247 | 126 | 434 | 57 | 107 | 20 | 3 | 4 | 44 | 31 | 86 | 20 | 11 | R | R | 6-0 | 165 | 4-4-74 | 1992 | Bani, D.R. |
| Valenti, Jon .......... | .260 | 125 | 462 | 46 | 120 | 19 | 4 | 11 | 57 | 33 | 91 | 5 | 3 | R | R | 6-1 | 195 | 11-26-73 | 1994 | Bakersfield, Calif. |
| Walker, Dane .......... | .277 | 127 | 477 | 97 | 132 | 25 | 3 | 7 | 47 | 112 | 75 | 14 | 10 | L | R | 5-10 | 180 | 11-16-69 | 1991 | Lake Oswego, Ore. |
| White, Derrick .......... | .262 | 73 | 263 | 49 | 69 | 17 | 0 | 10 | 43 | 44 | 63 | 12 | 3 | R | R | 6-1 | 215 | 10-12-69 | 1991 | San Rafael, Calif. |

**GAMES BY POSITION: C**—Hernandez 109, Ortega 24, Rondon 13. **1B**—DaVanon 4, Filchner 1, Hernandez 5, Miranda 118, Ortega 11, Rauer 1, Valenti 3, White 13. **2B**—DaVanon 1, Lara 17, Paulino 11, Walker 120. **3B**—Christenson 1, Ortega 1, Paulino 23, Valenti 113, White 12. **SS**—Espada 23, Lara 70, Paulino 48, Valenti 9. **OF**—Christenson 32, DaVanon 51, Encarnacion 112, Filchner 82, Ortega 4, Paulino 3, Rauer 6, Soriano 118, Walker 2, White 23.

| PITCHING | W | L | ERA | G | GS | CG | SV | IP | H | R | ER | BB | SO | B | T | HT | WT | DOB | 1st Yr | Resides |
|---|---|---|---|---|---|---|---|---|---|---|---|---|---|---|---|---|---|---|---|---|
| Abbott, Todd .......... | 11 | 7 | 3.98 | 32 | 13 | 0 | 1 | 131 | 135 | 66 | 58 | 41 | 104 | R | R | 6-4 | 200 | 9-13-73 | 1995 | North Little Rock, Ark. |
| Baez, Benito .......... | 8 | 4 | 3.47 | 32 | 20 | 0 | 4 | 130 | 123 | 60 | 50 | 52 | 92 | L | L | 6-0 | 180 | 5-6-77 | 1994 | Bonao, D.R. |
| Bennett, Tom .......... | 0 | 1 | 3.92 | 6 | 5 | 0 | 0 | 21 | 17 | 11 | 9 | 18 | 17 | R | R | 6-4 | 180 | 5-13-76 | 1995 | Alameda, Calif. |
| Gunther, Kevin .......... | 5 | 5 | 2.92 | 43 | 0 | 0 | 6 | 96 | 83 | 37 | 31 | 25 | 90 | R | R | 6-0 | 200 | 2-6-73 | 1995 | Olympia, Wash. |
| Kazmirski, Robert ...... | 3 | 5 | 2.68 | 51 | 0 | 0 | 28 | 54 | 45 | 19 | 16 | 28 | 37 | R | R | 6-3 | 200 | 6-24-72 | 1995 | Agoura Hills, Calif. |
| Mlodik, Kevin .......... | 8 | 6 | 2.77 | 31 | 22 | 0 | 1 | 136 | 118 | 53 | 42 | 53 | 135 | R | R | 6-1 | 205 | 8-21-74 | 1995 | Rosholt, Wis. |
| Moreno, Juan .......... | 4 | 6 | 4.37 | 38 | 11 | 0 | 0 | 107 | 98 | 60 | 52 | 69 | 97 | L | L | 6-1 | 190 | 2-28-75 | 1994 | Cagua, Venez. |
| Morrison, Chris .......... | 5 | 5 | 4.32 | 40 | 0 | 0 | 1 | 58 | 64 | 38 | 28 | 20 | 51 | R | R | 6-0 | 195 | 4-3-72 | 1995 | Lithonia, Ga. |
| Nelson, Chris .......... | 3 | 1 | 2.42 | 16 | 9 | 0 | 1 | 71 | 53 | 19 | 19 | 20 | 79 | R | R | 6-3 | 180 | 1-26-73 | 1995 | San Diego, Calif. |
| Price, Jamey .......... | 4 | 1 | 1.71 | 20 | 16 | 0 | 0 | 89 | 80 | 22 | 17 | 19 | 88 | R | R | 6-7 | 205 | 2-11-72 | 1996 | Pine Bluff, Ark. |
| Rivette, Scott .......... | 8 | 9 | 3.52 | 32 | 29 | 0 | 1 | 153 | 145 | 80 | 60 | 51 | 142 | S | R | 6-2 | 200 | 2-8-74 | 1995 | Upland, Calif. |
| Smith, Andy .......... | 10 | 7 | 4.58 | 37 | 13 | 0 | 1 | 116 | 112 | 71 | 59 | 68 | 94 | R | R | 6-5 | 220 | 1-29-75 | 1993 | Kannapolis, N.C. |
| Weinberg, Todd .......... | 6 | 4 | 3.45 | 43 | 0 | 0 | 1 | 57 | 48 | 25 | 22 | 31 | 64 | L | R | 6-3 | 225 | 6-13-72 | 1993 | Somerset, Mass. |

## SOUTHERN OREGON — Class A
### NORTHWEST LEAGUE

| BATTING | AVG | G | AB | R | H | 2B | 3B | HR | RBI | BB | SO | SB | CS | B | T | HT | WT | DOB | 1st Yr | Resides |
|---|---|---|---|---|---|---|---|---|---|---|---|---|---|---|---|---|---|---|---|---|
| Bowles, Justin .......... | .285 | 56 | 214 | 41 | 61 | 20 | 1 | 11 | 45 | 31 | 53 | 8 | 3 | L | L | 6-0 | 195 | 8-20-73 | 1996 | Lake Jackson, Texas |
| Byers, MacGregor ........ | .302 | 34 | 126 | 28 | 38 | 9 | 1 | 1 | 20 | 23 | 32 | 5 | 2 | R | R | 6-0 | 185 | 7-22-74 | 1996 | Houston, Texas |
| Cesar, Dionys .......... | .271 | 52 | 203 | 37 | 55 | 7 | 4 | 1 | 12 | 19 | 46 | 18 | 6 | S | R | 5-10 | 167 | 9-27-76 | 1994 | Santo Domingo, D.R. |
| Christenson, Ryan ...... | .287 | 36 | 136 | 31 | 39 | 11 | 0 | 5 | 21 | 19 | 21 | 8 | 6 | R | R | 5-11 | 175 | 3-28-74 | 1995 | Apple Valley, Calif. |
| Espada, Josue .......... | .222 | 15 | 54 | 7 | 12 | 1 | 0 | 1 | 5 | 5 | 10 | 0 | 0 | R | R | 5-10 | 175 | 8-30-75 | 1996 | Carolina, P.R. |
| Freeman, Terrance ..... | .234 | 56 | 167 | 26 | 39 | 5 | 1 | 0 | 18 | 23 | 29 | 21 | 7 | S | R | 5-10 | 170 | 1-24-75 | 1995 | Brandon, Fla. |
| Johnson, Jace .......... | .228 | 36 | 114 | 13 | 26 | 9 | 0 | 1 | 8 | 14 | 29 | 3 | 1 | R | R | 6-0 | 175 | 7-24-74 | 1995 | Phoenix, Ariz. |
| Jones, Tim .......... | .202 | 62 | 173 | 25 | 35 | 8 | 0 | 6 | 18 | 27 | 69 | 7 | 5 | L | R | 6-0 | 208 | 9-13-77 | 1995 | Buena Park, Calif. |
| Kieffer, Brian .......... | .000 | 2 | 2 | 0 | 0 | 0 | 0 | 0 | 0 | 3 | 2 | 0 | 0 | L | R | 6-1 | 190 | 7-23-73 | 1996 | Chicago Ridge, Ill. |
| Marcinczyk, T.R. .......... | .222 | 63 | 216 | 29 | 48 | 13 | 2 | 7 | 38 | 22 | 57 | 3 | 3 | R | R | 6-2 | 195 | 10-11-73 | 1996 | Plainville, Conn. |
| McKay, Cody .......... | .268 | 69 | 254 | 33 | 68 | 13 | 0 | 3 | 30 | 25 | 42 | 0 | 5 | L | R | 6-0 | 190 | 1-11-74 | 1996 | Scottsdale, Ariz. |
| Mensik, Todd .......... | .240 | 59 | 192 | 21 | 46 | 8 | 0 | 0 | 14 | 19 | 39 | 2 | 0 | L | L | 6-2 | 195 | 2-27-75 | 1996 | Orland Park, Ill. |
| Polanco, Juan .......... | .216 | 56 | 208 | 22 | 45 | 7 | 2 | 4 | 24 | 15 | 57 | 13 | 3 | R | R | 6-0 | 190 | 1-6-75 | 1993 | Bani, D.R. |
| Rauer, Troy .......... | .205 | 62 | 215 | 29 | 44 | 10 | 0 | 8 | 24 | 21 | 85 | 7 | 1 | R | R | 6-4 | 225 | 11-18-72 | 1995 | Scottsdale, Ariz. |
| Rondon, Alex .......... | .213 | 49 | 174 | 15 | 37 | 10 | 0 | 5 | 20 | 14 | 43 | 0 | 1 | R | R | 6-0 | 175 | 7-4-74 | 1994 | Guatire, Venez. |
| Slemmer, Dave .......... | .273 | 35 | 139 | 17 | 38 | 6 | 3 | 1 | 12 | 10 | 25 | 11 | 0 | R | R | 6-1 | 187 | 3-29-73 | 1995 | Edwardsville, Ill. |

**GAMES BY POSITION: C**—McKay 48, Rondon 35. **1B**—Marcinczyk 46, Mensik 38, Polanco 3. **2B**—Cesar 13, Freeman 42, Polanco 9, Slemmer 17. **3B**—Byers 30, Cesar 2, McKay 18, Polanco 24, Slemmer 9. **SS**—Cesar 38, Espada 15, Freeman 11, Jones 1, Kieffer 2, Polanco 4, Slemmer 12. **OF**—Bowles 54, Byers 4, Christenson 36, Freeman 1, Johnson 30, Jones 53, Marcinczyk 9, Polanco 20, Rauer 42.

| PITCHING | W | L | ERA | G | GS | CG | SV | IP | H | R | ER | BB | SO | B | T | HT | WT | DOB | 1st Yr | Resides |
|---|---|---|---|---|---|---|---|---|---|---|---|---|---|---|---|---|---|---|---|---|
| Batchelder, Bill | 0 | 0 | 8.71 | 6 | 0 | 0 | 0 | 10 | 19 | 17 | 10 | 12 | 10 | R | R | 6-3 | 190 | 10-19-72 | 1995 | North Andover, Mass. |
| Blumenstock, Brad | 3 | 1 | 9.87 | 23 | 1 | 0 | 0 | 35 | 48 | 49 | 38 | 34 | 20 | R | R | 6-6 | 225 | 2-19-75 | 1996 | Marion, Ill. |
| Costello, T.J. | 0 | 0 | 6.00 | 9 | 0 | 0 | 0 | 12 | 15 | 8 | 8 | 11 | 9 | L | L | 6-2 | 195 | 12-29-73 | 1995 | North Long Branch, N.J. |
| DellaRatta, Pete | 0 | 5 | 7.19 | 22 | 0 | 0 | 2 | 41 | 45 | 34 | 33 | 24 | 41 | R | R | 6-4 | 220 | 2-14-74 | 1996 | Gulf Breeze, Fla. |
| Glaze, Randy | 1 | 2 | 6.35 | 19 | 1 | 0 | 3 | 28 | 23 | 22 | 20 | 23 | 26 | R | R | 6-3 | 185 | 2-11-74 | 1996 | Carthage, Texas |
| Gogolin, Al | 1 | 1 | 8.68 | 6 | 0 | 0 | 0 | 9 | 10 | 9 | 9 | 14 | 3 | R | R | 6-5 | 215 | 1-14-72 | 1994 | Marietta, Ga. |
| Hilton, Willy | 2 | 1 | 5.84 | 26 | 2 | 0 | 2 | 62 | 71 | 44 | 40 | 27 | 38 | R | R | 6-2 | 190 | 12-26-72 | 1995 | Forrest City, Ark. |
| Holden, Jason | 3 | 5 | 5.79 | 9 | 8 | 0 | 0 | 33 | 39 | 27 | 21 | 14 | 21 | R | R | 6-2 | 190 | 8-5-73 | 1994 | Southaven, Miss. |
| Kjos, Ryan | 0 | 3 | 3.72 | 24 | 1 | 0 | 0 | 48 | 41 | 33 | 20 | 26 | 64 | R | R | 6-5 | 230 | 3-4-73 | 1995 | Hopkins, Minn. |
| Knickerbocker, Tom | 1 | 1 | 4.71 | 13 | 1 | 0 | 1 | 21 | 22 | 11 | 11 | 17 | 11 | L | L | 6-4 | 215 | 7-15-75 | 1995 | Prairie Du Chien, Wis. |
| Lagattuta, Rico | 3 | 3 | 2.82 | 28 | 0 | 0 | 3 | 54 | 49 | 23 | 17 | 23 | 31 | L | L | 6-2 | 205 | 1-14-74 | 1996 | Thousand Oaks, Calif. |
| Laxton, Brett | 0 | 5 | 7.71 | 13 | 8 | 0 | 0 | 33 | 39 | 34 | 28 | 26 | 38 | L | R | 6-2 | 205 | 10-5-73 | 1996 | Audubon, N.J. |
| Noriega, Ray | 4 | 4 | 3.54 | 17 | 14 | 0 | 0 | 61 | 61 | 28 | 24 | 22 | 50 | R | L | 5-10 | 175 | 3-28-74 | 1996 | Tucson, Ariz. |
| O'Dell, Jake | 2 | 3 | 3.33 | 13 | 10 | 0 | 0 | 49 | 41 | 25 | 18 | 16 | 46 | R | R | 6-1 | 205 | 9-22-73 | 1996 | Round Rock, Texas |
| Paulino, Jose | 4 | 1 | 3.10 | 10 | 8 | 0 | 0 | 41 | 43 | 20 | 14 | 9 | 21 | R | R | 6-4 | 180 | 1-2-77 | 1994 | San Cristobal, D.R. |
| Robertson, Doug | 3 | 2 | 6.02 | 23 | 4 | 0 | 0 | 52 | 69 | 44 | 35 | 17 | 48 | R | R | 6-0 | 205 | 10-17-74 | 1994 | Bath, Ill. |
| Silva, Luis | 1 | 3 | 9.50 | 5 | 4 | 0 | 0 | 18 | 25 | 22 | 19 | 10 | 18 | R | R | 6-4 | 200 | 4-18-75 | 1994 | Guatire, Venez. |
| Wallace, Flint | 2 | 6 | 4.22 | 17 | 14 | 0 | 0 | 70 | 86 | 34 | 33 | 15 | 45 | R | R | 6-1 | 185 | 7-21-74 | 1996 | Clyde, Texas |

# PHOENIX — Rookie

## ARIZONA LEAGUE

| BATTING | AVG | G | AB | R | H | 2B | 3B | HR | RBI | BB | SO | SB | CS | B | T | HT | WT | DOB | 1st Yr | Resides |
|---|---|---|---|---|---|---|---|---|---|---|---|---|---|---|---|---|---|---|---|---|
| Brown, Emil | .267 | 4 | 15 | 5 | 4 | 3 | 0 | 0 | 2 | 3 | 2 | 1 | 1 | R | R | 6-2 | 200 | 12-29-74 | 1994 | Chicago, Ill. |
| Byers, MacGregor | .325 | 21 | 77 | 15 | 25 | 9 | 1 | 1 | 13 | 18 | 20 | 2 | 0 | R | R | 6-0 | 185 | 7-22-74 | 1996 | Houston, Texas |
| Clifton, Rodney | .207 | 42 | 164 | 27 | 34 | 4 | 1 | 2 | 11 | 13 | 34 | 10 | 2 | R | R | 6-2 | 175 | 11-7-76 | 1996 | Elgin, Ill. |
| Davis, Monte | .286 | 52 | 206 | 40 | 59 | 9 | 4 | 1 | 20 | 21 | 27 | 7 | 8 | R | R | 6-1 | 180 | 12-25-77 | 1996 | Vernon, B.C. |
| Figueroa, Jose | .153 | 49 | 157 | 18 | 24 | 8 | 0 | 1 | 17 | 23 | 38 | 8 | 1 | R | R | 6-4 | 200 | 12-24-75 | 1995 | Santo Domingo, D.R. |
| Goris, Braulio | .244 | 49 | 172 | 24 | 42 | 10 | 3 | 2 | 34 | 31 | 52 | 5 | 2 | L | L | 6-3 | 207 | 10-5-76 | 1995 | New York, N.Y. |
| Hernandez, Victor | .236 | 46 | 144 | 27 | 34 | 5 | 1 | 5 | 22 | 20 | 29 | 11 | 2 | R | R | 6-0 | 167 | 2-28-77 | 1995 | Ciales, P.R. |
| Luderer, Jason | .308 | 6 | 13 | 1 | 4 | 0 | 0 | 0 | 2 | 0 | 1 | 0 | 0 | R | R | 5-11 | 160 | 8-19-78 | 1996 | Tarzana, Calif. |
| Martinez, Hipolito | .265 | 48 | 185 | 29 | 49 | 8 | 3 | 5 | 34 | 19 | 39 | 9 | 0 | R | R | 6-1 | 200 | 1-30-77 | 1994 | Bani, D.R. |
| Nova, Kelvin | .268 | 47 | 164 | 37 | 44 | 12 | 3 | 0 | 18 | 21 | 43 | 14 | 3 | S | R | 5-11 | 175 | 6-15-77 | 1994 | Bani, D.R. |
| Ortiz, Jose | .330 | 52 | 200 | 43 | 66 | 12 | 8 | 4 | 25 | 20 | 34 | 16 | 5 | R | R | 5-11 | 160 | 6-13-77 | 1995 | Capotillo, D.R. |
| Sosa, Nick | .206 | 46 | 165 | 22 | 34 | 8 | 1 | 1 | 26 | 20 | 52 | 2 | 1 | R | R | 6-3 | 205 | 7-18-77 | 1996 | Longwood, Fla. |
| Tegland, Ron | .282 | 27 | 85 | 10 | 24 | 6 | 0 | 3 | 18 | 4 | 25 | 6 | 0 | R | R | 6-2 | 212 | 10-18-73 | 1996 | Oxnard, Calif. |
| Vasquez, Jose | .221 | 46 | 145 | 19 | 32 | 6 | 2 | 1 | 20 | 17 | 42 | 7 | 4 | S | R | 6-2 | 185 | 10-26-77 | 1994 | Bani, D.R. |
| Ventura, Wilfredo | .160 | 8 | 25 | 5 | 4 | 1 | 0 | 0 | 2 | 6 | 8 | 1 | 0 | R | R | 5-11 | 210 | 10-11-76 | 1993 | Santo Domingo, D.R. |

**GAMES BY POSITION: C**—Figueroa 49, Luderer 6, Tegland 1, Ventura 6. **1B**—Byers 1, Goris 21, Sosa 36, Tegland 2. **2B**—Davis 4, Hernandez 16, Nova 42. **3B**—Byers 14, Davis 28, Nova 1, Sosa 1, Tegland 16. **SS**—Davis 9, Ortiz 48. **OF**—Brown 3, Byers 2, Clifton 41, Goris 22, Hernandez 29, Martinez 43, Sosa 1, Tegland 1, Vasquez 43.

| PITCHING | W | L | ERA | G | GS | CG | SV | IP | H | R | ER | BB | SO | B | T | HT | WT | DOB | 1st Yr | Resides |
|---|---|---|---|---|---|---|---|---|---|---|---|---|---|---|---|---|---|---|---|---|
| Abreu, Oscar | 5 | 3 | 6.48 | 17 | 6 | 0 | 1 | 50 | 47 | 43 | 36 | 37 | 62 | R | R | 6-1 | 208 | 2-21-76 | 1994 | Santo Domingo, D.R. |
| Bennett, Tom | 0 | 0 | 1.38 | 4 | 4 | 0 | 0 | 13 | 2 | 2 | 2 | 11 | 12 | R | R | 6-4 | 180 | 5-13-76 | 1995 | Alameda, Calif. |
| D'Amico, Jeff | 3 | 0 | 1.42 | 8 | 0 | 0 | 0 | 19 | 14 | 3 | 3 | 2 | 15 | R | R | 6-3 | 200 | 11-9-74 | 1993 | Redmond, Wash. |
| Faulk, Eric | 0 | 1 | 3.50 | 6 | 4 | 0 | 0 | 18 | 18 | 8 | 7 | 6 | 19 | R | R | 6-0 | 180 | 2-8-77 | 1996 | Wilmington, N.C. |
| Gallagher, Bryan | 2 | 1 | 3.26 | 16 | 1 | 0 | 0 | 30 | 37 | 14 | 11 | 10 | 27 | L | L | 6-2 | 195 | 10-7-76 | 1996 | Klamath Falls, Ore. |
| Garcia, Bryan | 4 | 2 | 5.47 | 18 | 3 | 0 | 1 | 51 | 58 | 36 | 31 | 11 | 39 | R | R | 6-3 | 165 | 6-21-78 | 1996 | Quartz Hill, Calif. |
| Gogolin, Al | 0 | 2 | 7.80 | 6 | 2 | 0 | 0 | 15 | 24 | 14 | 13 | 10 | 20 | R | R | 6-5 | 215 | 1-14-72 | 1994 | Marietta, Ga. |
| Gorrell, Chris | 1 | 2 | 3.93 | 12 | 2 | 0 | 1 | 37 | 36 | 18 | 16 | 8 | 32 | R | R | 6-2 | 188 | 1-27-76 | 1996 | Las Vegas, Nev. |
| Gregg, Kevin | 3 | 3 | 3.10 | 11 | 9 | 0 | 0 | 41 | 30 | 14 | 14 | 21 | 48 | R | R | 6-6 | 205 | 6-20-78 | 1996 | Corvallis, Ore. |
| Kern, Brian | 0 | 0 | 2.05 | 10 | 4 | 0 | 3 | 26 | 23 | 11 | 6 | 5 | 27 | R | R | 6-0 | 185 | 5-11-74 | 1996 | Ewing, Ill. |
| Knickerbocker, Tom | 0 | 2 | 7.08 | 8 | 0 | 0 | 0 | 20 | 21 | 21 | 16 | 16 | 19 | L | L | 6-4 | 215 | 7-15-75 | 1995 | Prairie du Chien, Wis. |
| Leyva, Julian | 0 | 0 | 0.00 | 1 | 0 | 0 | 0 | 4 | 4 | 0 | 0 | 1 | 2 | L | R | 6-0 | 218 | 2-11-78 | 1996 | Riverside, Calif. |
| Mercedes, Jose | 2 | 2 | 6.97 | 10 | 5 | 0 | 1 | 31 | 42 | 28 | 24 | 14 | 19 | R | R | 6-4 | 200 | 4-12-77 | 1994 | San Pedro de Macoris, D.R. |
| Nova, Kelvin | 0 | 1 | 9.82 | 3 | 0 | 0 | 1 | 4 | 8 | 4 | 4 | 2 | 2 | S | R | 5-11 | 175 | 6-15-77 | 1994 | Bani, D.R. |
| Paulino, Jose | 4 | 0 | 3.68 | 6 | 6 | 0 | 0 | 29 | 32 | 13 | 12 | 0 | 31 | R | R | 6-4 | 180 | 1-2-77 | 1994 | San Cristobal, D.R. |
| Silva, Luis | 1 | 0 | 5.00 | 5 | 0 | 0 | 0 | 9 | 9 | 5 | 5 | 0 | 10 | R | R | 6-4 | 200 | 4-18-75 | 1994 | Guatire, Venez. |
| Vizcaino, Luis | 6 | 3 | 4.07 | 15 | 10 | 0 | 1 | 60 | 58 | 36 | 27 | 24 | 52 | R | R | 6-1 | 180 | 6-1-77 | 1995 | Bani, D.R. |
| Winkleman, Greg | 1 | 1 | 1.72 | 25 | 0 | 0 | 6 | 37 | 31 | 11 | 7 | 15 | 32 | L | L | 5-10 | 170 | 9-7-73 | 1996 | Santa Rosa, Calif. |

# PHILADELPHIA
## PHILLIES

**Manager:** Jim Fregosi.  **1996 Record:** 67-95, .414 (5th, NL East).

| BATTING | AVG | G | AB | R | H | 2B | 3B | HR | RBI | BB | SO | SB | CS | B | T | HT | WT | DOB | 1st Yr | Resides |
|---|---|---|---|---|---|---|---|---|---|---|---|---|---|---|---|---|---|---|---|---|
| Amaro, Ruben | .316 | 61 | 117 | 14 | 37 | 10 | 0 | 2 | 15 | 9 | 18 | 0 | 0 | S | R | 5-10 | 175 | 2-12-65 | 1987 | Philadelphia, Pa. |
| Battle, Howard | .000 | 5 | 5 | 0 | 0 | 0 | 0 | 0 | 0 | 0 | 2 | 0 | 0 | R | R | 6-0 | 197 | 3-25-72 | 1990 | Ocean Springs, Miss. |
| Benjamin, Mike | .223 | 35 | 103 | 13 | 23 | 5 | 1 | 4 | 13 | 12 | 21 | 3 | 1 | R | R | 6-0 | 169 | 11-22-65 | 1987 | Chandler, Ariz. |
| Bennett, Gary | .250 | 6 | 16 | 0 | 4 | 0 | 0 | 0 | 1 | 2 | 6 | 0 | 0 | R | R | 6-0 | 190 | 4-17-72 | 1990 | Waukegan, Ill. |
| Daulton, Darren | .167 | 5 | 12 | 3 | 2 | 0 | 0 | 0 | 0 | 7 | 5 | 0 | 0 | L | R | 6-2 | 201 | 1-3-62 | 1980 | Safety Harbor, Fla. |
| Doster, David | .267 | 39 | 105 | 14 | 28 | 8 | 0 | 1 | 8 | 7 | 21 | 0 | 0 | R | R | 5-10 | 185 | 10-8-70 | 1993 | New Haven, Ind. |
| Dykstra, Lenny | .261 | 40 | 134 | 21 | 35 | 6 | 3 | 3 | 13 | 26 | 25 | 3 | 1 | L | L | 5-10 | 160 | 2-10-63 | 1981 | Philadelphia, Pa. |
| Eisenreich, Jim | .361 | 113 | 338 | 45 | 122 | 24 | 3 | 3 | 41 | 31 | 32 | 11 | 1 | L | L | 5-11 | 200 | 4-18-59 | 1980 | Blue Springs, Mo. |
| Estalella, Bobby | .353 | 7 | 17 | 5 | 6 | 0 | 0 | 2 | 4 | 1 | 6 | 1 | 0 | R | R | 6-1 | 200 | 8-23-74 | 1993 | Pembroke Pines, Fla. |
| Incaviglia, Pete | .234 | 99 | 269 | 33 | 63 | 7 | 2 | 16 | 42 | 30 | 82 | 2 | 0 | R | R | 6-1 | 225 | 4-2-64 | 1986 | Collegeville, Texas |
| Jefferies, Gregg | .292 | 104 | 404 | 59 | 118 | 17 | 3 | 7 | 51 | 36 | 21 | 20 | 6 | S | R | 5-10 | 185 | 8-1-67 | 1985 | Millbrae, Calif. |
| Jordan, Kevin | .282 | 43 | 131 | 15 | 37 | 10 | 0 | 3 | 12 | 5 | 20 | 2 | 1 | R | R | 6-1 | 185 | 10-9-69 | 1990 | San Francisco, Calif. |
| Lieberthal, Mike | .253 | 50 | 166 | 21 | 42 | 8 | 0 | 7 | 23 | 10 | 30 | 0 | 0 | R | R | 6-0 | 170 | 1-18-72 | 1990 | Westlake Village, Calif. |
| Magee, Wendell | .204 | 38 | 142 | 9 | 29 | 7 | 0 | 2 | 14 | 9 | 33 | 0 | 0 | R | R | 6-0 | 225 | 8-3-72 | 1994 | Hattiesburg, Miss. |
| Martinez, Manny | .222 | 13 | 36 | 2 | 8 | 0 | 2 | 0 | 0 | 1 | 11 | 2 | 1 | R | R | 6-2 | 169 | 10-3-70 | 1988 | San Pedro de Macoris, D.R. |
| Morandini, Mickey | .250 | 140 | 539 | 64 | 135 | 24 | 6 | 3 | 32 | 49 | 87 | 26 | 5 | L | R | 5-11 | 171 | 4-22-66 | 1989 | Valparaiso, Ind. |
| Murray, Glenn | .196 | 38 | 97 | 8 | 19 | 3 | 0 | 2 | 6 | 7 | 36 | 1 | 1 | R | R | 6-2 | 200 | 11-23-70 | 1989 | Manning, S.C. |
| Otero, Ricky | .273 | 104 | 411 | 54 | 112 | 11 | 7 | 2 | 32 | 34 | 30 | 16 | 10 | S | R | 5-7 | 150 | 4-15-72 | 1991 | Vega Baja, P.R. |
| Phillips, J.R. | .152 | 35 | 79 | 9 | 12 | 5 | 0 | 5 | 10 | 10 | 38 | 0 | 0 | L | L | 6-1 | 185 | 4-29-70 | 1988 | Moreno Valley, Calif. |
|   2-team (15 S.F.) | .163 | 50 | 104 | 12 | 17 | 5 | 0 | 7 | 15 | 11 | 21 | 0 | 0 | | | | | | | |
| Relaford, Desi | .175 | 15 | 40 | 2 | 7 | 2 | 0 | 0 | 1 | 3 | 9 | 1 | 0 | S | R | 5-8 | 155 | 9-16-73 | 1991 | Jacksonville, Fla. |
| Rolen, Scott | .254 | 37 | 130 | 10 | 33 | 7 | 0 | 4 | 18 | 13 | 27 | 0 | 2 | R | R | 6-4 | 210 | 4-4-75 | 1993 | Jasper, Ind. |
| Santiago, Benito | .264 | 136 | 481 | 71 | 127 | 21 | 2 | 30 | 85 | 49 | 104 | 2 | 0 | R | R | 6-1 | 182 | 3-9-65 | 1983 | La Jolla, Calif. |
| Schall, Gene | .273 | 28 | 66 | 7 | 18 | 5 | 1 | 2 | 10 | 12 | 15 | 0 | 0 | R | R | 6-3 | 190 | 6-5-70 | 1991 | Willow Grove, Pa. |
| Sefcik, Kevin | .284 | 44 | 116 | 10 | 33 | 5 | 3 | 0 | 9 | 9 | 16 | 3 | 0 | R | R | 5-1 | 175 | 2-10-71 | 1993 | Tinley Park, Ill. |
| Stocker, Kevin | .254 | 119 | 394 | 46 | 100 | 22 | 6 | 5 | 41 | 43 | 89 | 6 | 4 | S | R | 6-1 | 175 | 2-13-70 | 1991 | Spokane, Wash. |
| Tinsley, Lee | .135 | 31 | 52 | 1 | 7 | 0 | 0 | 0 | 2 | 4 | 22 | 2 | 4 | S | R | 5-10 | 180 | 3-4-69 | 1987 | Shelbyville, Ky. |
| Whiten, Mark | .236 | 60 | 182 | 33 | 43 | 8 | 0 | 7 | 21 | 33 | 62 | 13 | 3 | S | R | 6-3 | 215 | 11-25-66 | 1986 | Pensacola, Fla. |
| Zeile, Todd | .268 | 134 | 500 | 61 | 134 | 24 | 0 | 20 | 80 | 67 | 88 | 1 | 1 | R | R | 6-1 | 185 | 9-9-65 | 1986 | Valencia, Calif. |
| Zuber, Jon | .253 | 30 | 91 | 7 | 23 | 4 | 0 | 1 | 10 | 6 | 11 | 1 | 0 | L | L | 6-1 | 175 | 12-10-69 | 1992 | Moraga, Calif. |

| PITCHING | W | L | ERA | G | GS | CG | SV | IP | H | R | ER | BB | SO | B | T | HT | WT | DOB | 1st Yr | Resides |
|---|---|---|---|---|---|---|---|---|---|---|---|---|---|---|---|---|---|---|---|---|
| Beech, Matt | 1 | 4 | 6.97 | 8 | 8 | 0 | 0 | 41 | 49 | 32 | 32 | 11 | 33 | L | L | 6-2 | 190 | 1-20-72 | 1994 | San Antonio, Texas |
| Blazier, Ron | 3 | 1 | 5.87 | 27 | 0 | 0 | 0 | 38 | 49 | 30 | 25 | 10 | 25 | R | R | 6-6 | 215 | 7-30-71 | 1990 | Bellwood, Pa. |
| Borland, Toby | 7 | 3 | 4.07 | 69 | 0 | 0 | 0 | 91 | 83 | 51 | 41 | 43 | 76 | R | R | 6-7 | 175 | 5-29-69 | 1989 | Quitman, La. |
| Bottalico, Ricky | 4 | 5 | 3.19 | 61 | 0 | 0 | 34 | 68 | 47 | 24 | 24 | 23 | 74 | L | R | 6-1 | 190 | 8-26-69 | 1991 | Newington, Conn. |
| Crawford, Carlos | 0 | 1 | 4.91 | 1 | 1 | 0 | 0 | 4 | 7 | 10 | 2 | 2 | 4 | R | R | 6-1 | 185 | 10-4-71 | 1990 | Charlotte, N.C. |
| Dishman, Glenn | 0 | 0 | 7.71 | 4 | 1 | 0 | 0 | 7 | 9 | 6 | 6 | 2 | 3 | R | L | 6-1 | 195 | 11-5-70 | 1993 | Fremont, Ca. |
|   2-team (3 San Diego) | 0 | 0 | 7.71 | 7 | 1 | 0 | 0 | 9 | 12 | 8 | 8 | 3 | 3 | | | | | | | |
| Fernandez, Sid | 3 | 6 | 3.43 | 11 | 11 | 0 | 0 | 63 | 50 | 25 | 24 | 26 | 77 | L | L | 6-1 | 220 | 10-12-62 | 1981 | Hawaii Kai, Hawaii |
| Frey, Steve | 0 | 1 | 4.72 | 31 | 0 | 0 | 0 | 34 | 38 | 19 | 18 | 18 | 12 | R | L | 5-9 | 170 | 7-29-63 | 1983 | Newtown, Pa. |
| Grace, Mike | 7 | 2 | 3.49 | 12 | 12 | 1 | 0 | 80 | 72 | 33 | 31 | 16 | 49 | R | R | 6-4 | 210 | 6-20-70 | 1991 | Joliet, Ill. |
| Heflin, Bronson | 0 | 0 | 6.75 | 3 | 0 | 0 | 0 | 7 | 11 | 7 | 5 | 3 | 4 | R | R | 6-3 | 195 | 8-29-71 | 1994 | Clarksville, Tenn. |
| Hunter, Rich | 3 | 7 | 6.49 | 14 | 14 | 0 | 0 | 69 | 84 | 54 | 50 | 33 | 32 | R | R | 6-1 | 180 | 9-25-74 | 1993 | Temecula, Ca. |
| Jordan, Ricardo | 2 | 2 | 1.80 | 26 | 0 | 0 | 0 | 25 | 18 | 6 | 5 | 12 | 17 | L | L | 5-11 | 165 | 6-27-70 | 1990 | Delray Beach, Fla. |
| Leiper, Dave | 2 | 0 | 6.43 | 26 | 0 | 0 | 0 | 21 | 31 | 16 | 15 | 7 | 10 | L | L | 6-1 | 160 | 6-18-62 | 1982 | Plano, Texas |
| Maduro, Calvin | 0 | 0 | 3.52 | 4 | 2 | 0 | 0 | 15 | 13 | 6 | 6 | 3 | 11 | R | R | 6-0 | 175 | 9-5-74 | 1992 | Santa Cruz, Aruba |
| Mimbs, Mike | 3 | 9 | 5.53 | 21 | 17 | 0 | 0 | 99 | 116 | 66 | 61 | 41 | 56 | L | L | 6-2 | 182 | 2-13-69 | 1990 | Macon, Ga. |
| Mitchell, Larry | 0 | 0 | 4.50 | 7 | 0 | 0 | 0 | 12 | 14 | 6 | 6 | 5 | 7 | R | R | 6-1 | 200 | 10-16-71 | 1992 | Charlottesville, Va. |
| Mulholland, Terry | 8 | 7 | 4.66 | 21 | 21 | 3 | 0 | 133 | 157 | 74 | 69 | 21 | 52 | L | L | 6-3 | 200 | 3-9-63 | 1984 | Scottsdale, Ariz. |
| Munoz, Bobby | 0 | 3 | 7.82 | 6 | 6 | 0 | 0 | 25 | 42 | 28 | 22 | 7 | 8 | R | R | 6-7 | 237 | 3-3-68 | 1989 | Hialeah, Fla. |
| Parrett, Jeff | 1 | 1 | 1.88 | 18 | 0 | 0 | 0 | 24 | 24 | 5 | 5 | 11 | 22 | R | R | 6-3 | 185 | 8-26-61 | 1983 | Lexington, Ky. |
|   2-team (33 St. Louis) | 3 | 3 | 3.39 | 51 | 0 | 0 | 0 | 66 | 64 | 25 | 25 | 31 | 64 | | | | | | | |
| Quirico, Rafael | 0 | 1 | 37.80 | 1 | 1 | 0 | 0 | 2 | 4 | 7 | 7 | 5 | 1 | L | L | 6-3 | 170 | 9-7-69 | 1987 | Santo Domingo, D.R. |
| Ryan, Ken | 3 | 5 | 2.43 | 62 | 0 | 0 | 8 | 89 | 71 | 32 | 24 | 45 | 70 | R | R | 6-3 | 215 | 10-24-68 | 1986 | Attleboro, Mass. |
| Schilling, Curt | 9 | 10 | 3.19 | 26 | 26 | 8 | 0 | 183 | 149 | 69 | 65 | 50 | 182 | R | R | 6-4 | 215 | 11-14-66 | 1986 | Marlton, N.J. |
| Springer, Russ | 3 | 10 | 4.66 | 51 | 7 | 0 | 0 | 97 | 106 | 60 | 50 | 38 | 94 | R | R | 6-4 | 195 | 11-7-68 | 1989 | Pollack, La. |
| West, David | 2 | 2 | 4.76 | 7 | 4 | 0 | 0 | 28 | 31 | 17 | 15 | 11 | 22 | L | L | 6-6 | 225 | 9-1-64 | 1983 | Stuart, Fla. |
| Williams, Mike | 6 | 14 | 5.44 | 32 | 29 | 0 | 0 | 167 | 188 | 107 | 101 | 67 | 103 | R | R | 6-2 | 190 | 7-29-69 | 1990 | Newport, Va. |

## FIELDING

| Catcher | PCT | G | PO | A | E | DP | PB |
|---|---|---|---|---|---|---|---|
| Bennett | 1.000 | 5 | 35 | 5 | 0 | 0 | 2 |
| Estalella | 1.000 | 6 | 40 | 4 | 0 | 0 | 0 |
| Lieberthal | .990 | 43 | 284 | 20 | 3 | 4 | 0 |
| Santiago | .987 | 114 | 723 | 61 | 10 | 5 | 8 |

| First Base | PCT | G | PO | A | E | DP |
|---|---|---|---|---|---|---|
| Amaro | .000 | 1 | 0 | 0 | 0 | 0 |
| Jefferies | .998 | 53 | 412 | 38 | 1 | 38 |
| Jordan | 1.000 | 30 | 227 | 12 | 0 | 19 |
| Phillips | 1.000 | 11 | 70 | 3 | 0 | 7 |
| Santiago | .992 | 14 | 111 | 6 | 1 | 9 |
| Schall | .986 | 19 | 135 | 8 | 2 | 16 |
| Zeile | .984 | 28 | 223 | 16 | 4 | 30 |
| Zuber | .987 | 22 | 145 | 11 | 2 | 10 |

| Second Base | PCT | G | PO | A | E | DP |
|---|---|---|---|---|---|---|
| Benjamin | 1.000 | 1 | 1 | 0 | 0 | 0 |

| | PCT | G | PO | A | E | DP |
|---|---|---|---|---|---|---|
| Doster | .973 | 24 | 52 | 56 | 3 | 12 |
| Jordan | 1.000 | 7 | 16 | 14 | 0 | 3 |
| Morandini | .982 | 137 | 286 | 353 | 12 | 87 |
| Relaford | 1.000 | 4 | 8 | 11 | 0 | 4 |
| Sefcik | 1.000 | 1 | 1 | 1 | 0 | 0 |

| Third Base | PCT | G | PO | A | E | DP |
|---|---|---|---|---|---|---|
| Battle | .000 | 1 | 0 | 0 | 0 | 0 |
| Doster | 1.000 | 1 | 0 | 1 | 0 | 0 |
| Jordan | 1.000 | 1 | 0 | 1 | 0 | 1 |
| Rolen | .954 | 37 | 29 | 54 | 4 | 4 |
| Sefcik | .872 | 20 | 7 | 34 | 6 | 3 |
| Zeile | .962 | 106 | 72 | 179 | 10 | 13 |

| Shortstop | PCT | G | PO | A | E | DP |
|---|---|---|---|---|---|---|
| Benjamin | .954 | 31 | 37 | 87 | 6 | 14 |
| Relaford | .933 | 9 | 13 | 15 | 2 | 2 |

| | PCT | G | PO | A | E | DP |
|---|---|---|---|---|---|---|
| Sefcik | .986 | 21 | 22 | 48 | 1 | 9 |
| Stocker | .975 | 119 | 165 | 351 | 13 | 79 |

| Outfield | PCT | G | PO | A | E | DP |
|---|---|---|---|---|---|---|
| Amaro | 1.000 | 35 | 50 | 0 | 0 | 0 |
| Daulton | 1.000 | 5 | 6 | 0 | 0 | 0 |
| Dykstra | 1.000 | 39 | 103 | 3 | 0 | 1 |
| Eisenreich | .977 | 91 | 167 | 3 | 4 | 1 |
| Incaviglia | .969 | 71 | 91 | 4 | 3 | 0 |
| Jefferies | 1.000 | 51 | 110 | 1 | 0 | 0 |
| Magee | .978 | 37 | 88 | 2 | 2 | 1 |
| Martinez | .955 | 11 | 20 | 1 | 1 | 0 |
| Murray | 1.000 | 27 | 52 | 1 | 0 | 0 |
| Otero | .985 | 100 | 247 | 8 | 4 | 2 |
| Phillips | .957 | 15 | 43 | 1 | 2 | 1 |
| Tinsley | .960 | 22 | 24 | 0 | 1 | 0 |
| Whiten | .945 | 51 | 97 | 6 | 6 | 1 |

Benito Santiago
hit a career high
30 homers to lead
the Phillies

Phillies minor league
Player of the Year
Scott Rolen

MEL BAILEY

STAN DENNY

## FARM SYSTEM

**Director of Player Development:** Del Unser

| Class | Farm Team | League | W | L | Pct. | Finish* | Manager | First Yr |
|---|---|---|---|---|---|---|---|---|
| AAA | Scranton/W-B (Pa.) Red Barons | International | 70 | 72 | .493 | T-5th (10) | Hobson/Aviles | 1989 |
| AA | Reading (Pa.) Phillies | Eastern | 66 | 75 | .468 | T-7th (10) | Bill Robinson | 1967 |
| #A | Clearwater (Fla.) Phillies | Florida State | 75 | 62 | .547 | 3rd (14) | Al LeBoeuf | 1985 |
| A | Piedmont (N.C.) Boll Weevils | South Atlantic | 72 | 66 | .522 | 6th (14) | Roy Majtyka | 1995 |
| A | Batavia (N.Y.) Clippers | New York-Penn | 42 | 33 | .560 | 6th (14) | Floyd Rayford | 1988 |
| #R | Martinsville (Va.) Phillies | Appalachian | 20 | 47 | .299 | 8th (9) | Ramon Henderson | 1988 |

*Finish in overall standings (No. of teams in league)   #Advanced level

## ORGANIZATION LEADERS

### MAJOR LEAGUERS

**BATTING**
| | | |
|---|---|---|
| *AVG | Jim Eisenreich | .361 |
| R | Benito Santiago | 71 |
| H | Mickey Morandini | 135 |
| TB | Benito Santiago | 242 |
| 2B | Three tied at | 24 |
| 3B | Ricky Otero | 7 |
| HR | Benito Santiago | 30 |
| RBI | Benito Santiago | 85 |
| BB | Todd Zeile | 67 |
| SO | Benito Santiago | 104 |
| SB | Mickey Morandini | 26 |

**PITCHING**
| | | |
|---|---|---|
| W | Curt Schilling | 9 |
| L | Mike Williams | 14 |
| #ERA | Ken Ryan | 2.43 |
| G | Toby Borland | 69 |
| CG | Curt Schilling | 8 |
| SV | Ricky Bottalico | 34 |
| IP | Curt Schilling | 183 |
| BB | Mike Williams | 67 |
| SO | Curt Schilling | 182 |

**Curt Schilling.** .182 strikeouts

MIKE PONZINI

### MINOR LEAGUERS

**BATTING**
| | | |
|---|---|---|
| *AVG | Scott Rolen, Reading/Scranton | .324 |
| R | Mark Raynor, Piedmont/Clearwater | 81 |
| H | Marlon Anderson, Clear./Reading | 156 |
| TB | Dan Held, Reading/Scranton | 226 |
| 2B | Scott Rolen, Reading/Scranton | 39 |
| 3B | Three tied at | 8 |
| HR | Dan Held, Reading/Scranton | 26 |
| RBI | Dan Held, Reading/Scranton | 92 |
| BB | Bobby Estalella, Reading/Scranton | 72 |
| SO | Dan Held, Reading/Scranton | 147 |
| SB | Essex Burton, Reading/Scranton | 45 |

**PITCHING**
| | | |
|---|---|---|
| W | Two tied at | 13 |
| L | Tony Costa, Reading | 13 |
| #ERA | Brian Miller, Batavia | 2.07 |
| G | Wayne Gomes, Reading | 67 |
| CG | Five tied at | 3 |
| SV | Brian Stumpf, Clearwater | 26 |
| IP | Randy Knoll, Piedmont/Clearwater | 172 |
| BB | Tony Costa, Reading | 92 |
| SO | Rob Burger, Piedmont | 171 |

*Minimum 250 At-Bats   #Minimum 75 Innings

## TOP 10 PROSPECTS

How the Phillies Top 10 prospects, as judged by Baseball America prior to the 1996 season, fared in 1996:

RODGER WOOD

**Dave Coggin**

| Player, Pos. | Club (Class—League) | AVG | AB | R | H | 2B | 3B | HR | RBI | SB |
|---|---|---|---|---|---|---|---|---|---|---|
| 1. Scott Rolen, 3b | Reading (AA—Eastern) | .361 | 230 | 44 | 83 | 22 | 2 | 9 | 42 | 8 |
| | Scranton (AAA—International) | .274 | 168 | 23 | 46 | 17 | 0 | 2 | 19 | 4 |
| | Philadelphia | .254 | 130 | 10 | 33 | 7 | 0 | 4 | 18 | 0 |
| 3. Marlon Anderson, 2b | Reading (AA—Eastern) | .274 | 314 | 38 | 86 | 14 | 3 | 3 | 28 | 17 |
| | Clearwater (A—Florida State) | .272 | 257 | 37 | 70 | 10 | 3 | 2 | 22 | 26 |
| 4. Reggie Taylor, of | Piedmont (A—South Atlantic) | .263 | 499 | 68 | 131 | 20 | 6 | 0 | 31 | 36 |
| 6. Bobby Estalella, c | Reading (AA—Eastern) | .244 | 365 | 48 | 89 | 14 | 2 | 23 | 72 | 2 |
| | Scranton (AAA—International) | .250 | 36 | 7 | 9 | 3 | 0 | 3 | 8 | 0 |
| | Philadelphia | .353 | 17 | 5 | 6 | 0 | 0 | 2 | 4 | 1 |
| 10. Wendell Magee, of | Reading (AA—Eastern) | .293 | 270 | 38 | 79 | 15 | 5 | 6 | 30 | 10 |
| | Scranton (AAA—International) | .284 | 155 | 31 | 44 | 9 | 2 | 10 | 32 | 3 |
| | Philadelphia | .204 | 142 | 9 | 29 | 7 | 0 | 2 | 14 | 0 |

| | | W | L | ERA | G | SV | IP | H | BB | SO |
|---|---|---|---|---|---|---|---|---|---|---|
| 2. Dave Coggin, rhp | Piedmont (A—South Atlantic) | 9 | 12 | 4.31 | 28 | 0 | 169 | 156 | 46 | 129 |
| 5. Mike Grace, rhp | Philadelphia | 7 | 2 | 3.49 | 12 | 0 | 80 | 72 | 16 | 49 |
| 7. Carlton Loewer, rhp | Reading (AA—Eastern) | 7 | 10 | 5.26 | 27 | 0 | 171 | 191 | 57 | 119 |
| 8. Wayne Gomes, rhp | Reading (AA—Eastern) | 0 | 4 | 4.48 | 67 | 24 | 64 | 53 | 48 | 79 |
| 9. *Larry Wimberly, lhp | Sarasota (A—Florida State) | 2 | 4 | 6.90 | 6 | 0 | 30 | 38 | 16 | 16 |
| | Michigan (A—Midwest) | 3 | 4 | 2.85 | 14 | 0 | 66 | 58 | 24 | 41 |

*Traded to Red Sox

| BATTING | AVG | G | AB | R | H | 2B | 3B | HR | RBI | BB | SO | SB | CS | B | T | HT | WT | DOB | 1st Yr | Resides |
|---|---|---|---|---|---|---|---|---|---|---|---|---|---|---|---|---|---|---|---|---|
| Amaro, Ruben | .278 | 52 | 180 | 28 | 50 | 10 | 3 | 2 | 22 | 14 | 29 | 7 | 1 | S | R | 5-10 | 175 | 2-12-65 | 1987 | Philadelphia, Pa. |
| 2-team (16 Syracuse) | .270 | 68 | 230 | 36 | 62 | 11 | 3 | 2 | 24 | 24 | 40 | 13 | 3 | | | | | | | |
| Battle, Howard | .228 | 115 | 391 | 37 | 89 | 24 | 1 | 8 | 44 | 21 | 53 | 3 | 8 | R | R | 6-0 | 197 | 3-25-72 | 1990 | Ocean Springs, Miss. |
| Beltre, Esteban | .133 | 4 | 15 | 1 | 2 | 0 | 0 | 0 | 1 | 0 | 1 | 0 | 0 | R | R | 5-10 | 172 | 12-26-67 | 1984 | San Pedro de Macoris, D.R. |
| Benjamin, Mike | .385 | 4 | 13 | 2 | 5 | 2 | 0 | 0 | 4 | 3 | 0 | 0 | 0 | R | R | 6-0 | 169 | 11-22-65 | 1987 | Chandler, Ariz. |
| Bennett, Gary | .248 | 91 | 286 | 37 | 71 | 15 | 1 | 8 | 37 | 24 | 43 | 1 | 0 | R | R | 6-0 | 190 | 4-17-72 | 1990 | Waukegan, Ill. |
| Burton, Essex | .172 | 16 | 58 | 4 | 10 | 3 | 0 | 0 | 1 | 7 | 16 | 5 | 3 | R | R | 5-9 | 155 | 5-16-69 | 1991 | San Diego, Calif. |
| Butler, Rob | .255 | 91 | 298 | 39 | 76 | 15 | 8 | 4 | 34 | 20 | 45 | 3 | 5 | L | L | 5-11 | 185 | 4-10-70 | 1991 | Toronto, Ontario |
| Diaz, Mario | .278 | 46 | 180 | 20 | 50 | 6 | 0 | 3 | 22 | 11 | 9 | 0 | 0 | R | R | 5-10 | 160 | 1-10-62 | 1979 | Yabucoa, P.R. |
| 2-team (16 Col.) | .274 | 62 | 241 | 29 | 66 | 9 | 0 | 5 | 33 | 12 | 15 | 0 | 2 | | | | | | | |
| Doster, David | .258 | 88 | 322 | 37 | 83 | 20 | 0 | 7 | 48 | 26 | 54 | 7 | 3 | R | R | 5-10 | 185 | 10-8-70 | 1993 | New Haven, Ind. |
| Estalella, Bobby | .250 | 11 | 36 | 7 | 9 | 3 | 0 | 3 | 8 | 5 | 10 | 0 | 0 | R | R | 6-1 | 200 | 8-23-74 | 1993 | Pembroke Pines, Fla. |
| Fisher, David | .156 | 26 | 64 | 6 | 10 | 1 | 0 | 1 | 3 | 7 | 15 | 1 | 1 | R | R | 6-0 | 160 | 2-26-70 | 1992 | Joplin, Mo. |
| Flores, Jose | .257 | 26 | 70 | 10 | 18 | 1 | 0 | 0 | 3 | 12 | 10 | 0 | 1 | R | R | 5-11 | 160 | 6-26-73 | 1994 | New York, N.Y. |
| Held, Dan | .000 | 4 | 14 | 1 | 0 | 0 | 0 | 0 | 0 | 1 | 6 | 0 | 0 | R | R | 6-0 | 200 | 10-7-70 | 1993 | Neosho, Wis. |
| Jefferies, Gregg | .118 | 4 | 17 | 1 | 2 | 0 | 1 | 0 | 1 | 3 | 0 | 0 | 0 | S | R | 5-10 | 185 | 8-1-67 | 1985 | Millbrae, Calif. |
| Magee, Wendell | .284 | 44 | 155 | 31 | 44 | 9 | 2 | 10 | 32 | 21 | 31 | 3 | 1 | R | R | 6-0 | 225 | 8-3-72 | 1994 | Hattiesburg, Miss. |
| Manahan, Anthony | .105 | 17 | 38 | 3 | 4 | 2 | 0 | 0 | 2 | 9 | 0 | 0 | 0 | R | R | 6-0 | 190 | 12-15-68 | 1990 | Scottsdale, Ariz. |
| Martinez, Manny | .209 | 17 | 67 | 8 | 14 | 1 | 1 | 0 | 5 | 4 | 17 | 3 | 0 | R | R | 6-2 | 169 | 10-3-70 | 1988 | San Pedro de Macoris, D.R. |
| McNair, Fred | .160 | 14 | 25 | 3 | 4 | 0 | 0 | 0 | 3 | 8 | 12 | 0 | 0 | R | R | 6-4 | 215 | 1-31-70 | 1989 | Mesa, Ariz. |
| Murray, Glenn | .366 | 41 | 142 | 31 | 52 | 10 | 2 | 7 | 22 | 22 | 29 | 7 | 0 | R | R | 6-2 | 200 | 11-23-70 | 1989 | Manning, S.C. |
| Otero, Ricky | .299 | 46 | 177 | 38 | 53 | 9 | 8 | 1 | 9 | 28 | 13 | 15 | 6 | S | R | 5-7 | 150 | 4-15-72 | 1991 | Vega Baja, P.R. |
| Phillips, J.R. | .285 | 53 | 200 | 33 | 57 | 14 | 2 | 13 | 42 | 19 | 53 | 2 | 2 | L | L | 6-1 | 185 | 4-29-70 | 1988 | Moreno Valley, Calif. |
| Relaford, Desi | .235 | 21 | 85 | 12 | 20 | 4 | 1 | 1 | 11 | 8 | 19 | 7 | 1 | S | R | 5-8 | 155 | 9-16-73 | 1991 | Jacksonville, Fla. |
| Rolen, Scott | .274 | 45 | 168 | 23 | 46 | 17 | 0 | 2 | 19 | 28 | 28 | 4 | 5 | R | R | 6-4 | 210 | 4-4-75 | 1993 | Jasper, Ind. |
| Schall, Gene | .288 | 104 | 371 | 66 | 107 | 16 | 5 | 17 | 67 | 48 | 92 | 1 | 0 | R | R | 6-3 | 190 | 6-5-70 | 1991 | Willow Grove, Pa. |
| Sefcik, Kevin | .333 | 45 | 180 | 34 | 60 | 7 | 5 | 0 | 19 | 15 | 20 | 11 | 3 | R | R | 5-1 | 175 | 2-10-71 | 1993 | Tinley Park, Ill. |
| Stocker, Kevin | .227 | 12 | 44 | 5 | 10 | 3 | 0 | 2 | 6 | 0 | 4 | 1 | 0 | S | R | 6-1 | 175 | 2-13-70 | 1991 | Spokane, Wash. |
| Tokheim, David | .212 | 92 | 255 | 35 | 54 | 10 | 4 | 1 | 21 | 11 | 37 | 5 | 5 | L | L | 6-1 | 185 | 5-25-69 | 1991 | Menlo Park, Calif. |
| Wrona, Rick | .229 | 61 | 175 | 10 | 40 | 8 | 0 | 5 | 20 | 7 | 41 | 1 | 1 | R | R | 6-0 | 180 | 12-10-63 | 1985 | Tulsa, Okla. |
| Zuber, Jon | .311 | 118 | 412 | 62 | 128 | 22 | 5 | 4 | 59 | 58 | 50 | 4 | 2 | L | L | 6-1 | 175 | 12-10-69 | 1992 | Moraga, Calif. |
| Zupcic, Bob | .235 | 44 | 119 | 12 | 28 | 5 | 0 | 2 | 16 | 13 | 20 | 1 | 0 | R | R | 6-4 | 220 | 8-18-66 | 1987 | Charlotte, N.C. |

| PITCHING | W | L | ERA | G | GS | CG | SV | IP | H | R | ER | BB | SO | B | T | HT | WT | DOB | 1st Yr | Resides |
|---|---|---|---|---|---|---|---|---|---|---|---|---|---|---|---|---|---|---|---|---|
| Bakkum, Scott | 1 | 5 | 6.06 | 30 | 2 | 0 | 6 | 49 | 68 | 44 | 33 | 20 | 25 | R | R | 6-4 | 205 | 11-20-69 | 1992 | LaCrosse, Wis. |
| 2-team (14 Pawtucket) | 5 | 7 | 6.08 | 44 | 4 | 0 | 6 | 93 | 119 | 77 | 63 | 28 | 50 | | | | | | | |
| Beech, Matt | 2 | 0 | 2.40 | 2 | 2 | 0 | 0 | 15 | 9 | 4 | 4 | 1 | 14 | L | L | 6-1 | 190 | 1-20-72 | 1994 | San Antonio, Texas |
| Blazier, Ron | 4 | 0 | 2.57 | 33 | 0 | 0 | 12 | 42 | 33 | 15 | 12 | 9 | 38 | R | R | 6-6 | 215 | 7-30-71 | 1990 | Bellwood, Pa. |
| Brumley, Duff | 2 | 1 | 5.85 | 20 | 0 | 0 | 0 | 20 | 19 | 18 | 13 | 22 | 15 | R | R | 6-4 | 195 | 8-25-70 | 1990 | Cleveland, Tenn. |
| Crawford, Carlos | 9 | 10 | 4.54 | 28 | 25 | 3 | 1 | 159 | 169 | 87 | 80 | 63 | 89 | R | R | 6-1 | 185 | 10-4-71 | 1990 | Charlotte, N.C. |
| Dodd, Robert | 0 | 0 | 8.10 | 8 | 2 | 0 | 0 | 20 | 32 | 21 | 18 | 9 | 12 | L | L | 6-3 | 195 | 3-14-73 | 1994 | Plano, Texas |
| Doolan, Blake | 1 | 1 | 6.50 | 18 | 0 | 0 | 1 | 18 | 26 | 15 | 13 | 7 | 8 | R | R | 6-0 | 178 | 2-11-69 | 1992 | Pasadena, Texas |
| Elliott, Donnie | 5 | 11 | 4.79 | 21 | 19 | 1 | 0 | 103 | 105 | 62 | 55 | 59 | 93 | R | R | 6-4 | 190 | 9-20-68 | 1988 | Deer Park, Texas |
| Frey, Steve | 2 | 2 | 5.40 | 10 | 0 | 0 | 0 | 13 | 11 | 8 | 8 | 8 | 9 | R | L | 5-9 | 170 | 7-29-63 | 1983 | Newtown, Pa. |
| Greene, Tommy | 2 | 0 | 3.77 | 5 | 5 | 0 | 0 | 31 | 31 | 13 | 13 | 7 | 26 | R | R | 6-5 | 225 | 4-6-67 | 1985 | Richmond, Va. |
| Grott, Matt | 1 | 3 | 4.88 | 27 | 12 | 0 | 0 | 87 | 92 | 48 | 47 | 22 | 63 | L | L | 6-1 | 205 | 12-5-67 | 1989 | Glendale, Ariz. |
| Heflin, Bronson | 4 | 0 | 2.61 | 30 | 0 | 0 | 12 | 38 | 25 | 11 | 11 | 3 | 23 | R | R | 6-3 | 195 | 8-29-71 | 1994 | Clarksville, Tenn. |
| Holman, Craig | 3 | 2 | 5.89 | 36 | 3 | 0 | 0 | 63 | 77 | 44 | 41 | 34 | 36 | S | R | 6-2 | 200 | 3-13-69 | 1991 | Attalla, Ala. |
| Hunter, Rich | 2 | 4 | 6.69 | 8 | 7 | 1 | 0 | 40 | 39 | 31 | 30 | 22 | 22 | R | R | 6-1 | 180 | 9-25-74 | 1993 | Temecula, Calif. |
| Ilsley, Blaise | 1 | 2 | 6.19 | 5 | 3 | 0 | 0 | 16 | 24 | 12 | 11 | 4 | 9 | L | L | 6-1 | 185 | 4-9-64 | 1985 | Alpena, Mich. |
| 2-team (20 Ottawa) | 4 | 6 | 5.43 | 25 | 7 | 0 | 0 | 61 | 73 | 39 | 37 | 19 | 31 | | | | | | | |
| Jordan, Ricardo | 3 | 3 | 5.26 | 32 | 0 | 0 | 1 | 39 | 40 | 30 | 23 | 22 | 40 | L | L | 5-11 | 165 | 6-27-70 | 1990 | Delray Beach, Fla. |
| Karp, Ryan | 1 | 1 | 3.07 | 7 | 7 | 0 | 0 | 41 | 35 | 14 | 14 | 14 | 30 | L | L | 6-4 | 205 | 4-5-70 | 1992 | Coral Gables, Fla. |
| Mimbs, Mike | 2 | 1 | 2.48 | 7 | 3 | 0 | 0 | 29 | 27 | 8 | 8 | 5 | 20 | L | L | 6-2 | 182 | 2-13-69 | 1990 | Macon, Ga. |
| Mitchell, Larry | 1 | 1 | 2.55 | 11 | 0 | 0 | 1 | 25 | 19 | 8 | 7 | 10 | 24 | R | R | 6-1 | 200 | 10-16-71 | 1992 | Charlottesville, Va. |
| Munoz, Bobby | 4 | 2 | 3.91 | 8 | 8 | 0 | 0 | 51 | 50 | 24 | 22 | 7 | 34 | R | R | 6-7 | 237 | 3-3-68 | 1989 | Hialeah, Fla. |
| Murray, Matt | 1 | 8 | 7.67 | 13 | 13 | 0 | 0 | 56 | 63 | 52 | 48 | 49 | 34 | L | R | 6-6 | 235 | 9-26-70 | 1988 | Swampscott, Mass. |
| Nye, Ryan | 5 | 2 | 5.02 | 14 | 14 | 0 | 0 | 81 | 97 | 52 | 45 | 30 | 51 | R | R | 6-2 | 195 | 6-24-73 | 1994 | Cameron, Okla. |
| Quirico, Rafael | 4 | 4 | 3.32 | 13 | 13 | 1 | 0 | 65 | 48 | 29 | 24 | 26 | 51 | L | L | 6-3 | 170 | 9-7-69 | 1987 | Santo Domingo, D.R. |
| Schilling, Curt | 1 | 0 | 1.38 | 2 | 2 | 0 | 0 | 13 | 9 | 2 | 2 | 5 | 10 | R | R | 6-4 | 215 | 11-14-66 | 1986 | Marlton, N.J. |
| Troutman, Keith | 1 | 1 | 5.14 | 8 | 0 | 0 | 0 | 14 | 19 | 9 | 8 | 5 | 9 | R | R | 6-1 | 200 | 5-29-73 | 1992 | Candler, N.C. |
| West, Dave | 1 | 0 | 5.25 | 2 | 2 | 0 | 0 | 12 | 14 | 8 | 7 | 2 | 12 | L | L | 6-6 | 225 | 9-1-64 | 1983 | Stuart, Fla. |
| Wiegandt, Scott | 5 | 6 | 2.71 | 46 | 0 | 0 | 2 | 63 | 63 | 21 | 19 | 33 | 46 | L | L | 5-11 | 180 | 12-9-67 | 1989 | Louisville, Ky. |
| Williams, Mitch | 2 | 2 | 10.20 | 9 | 0 | 0 | 0 | 15 | 25 | 20 | 17 | 11 | 15 | L | L | 6-4 | 200 | 11-17-64 | 1982 | Hico, Texas |

## FIELDING

| Catcher | PCT | G | PO | A | E | DP | PB |
|---|---|---|---|---|---|---|---|
| Bennett | .988 | 85 | 517 | 61 | 7 | 5 | 8 |
| Estalella | .968 | 10 | 55 | 6 | 2 | 0 | 0 |
| Wrona | .980 | 56 | 311 | 27 | 7 | 1 | 5 |

| First Base | PCT | G | PO | A | E | DP |
|---|---|---|---|---|---|---|
| Battle | 1.000 | 2 | 8 | 0 | 0 | 0 |
| Held | .968 | 4 | 28 | 2 | 1 | 2 |
| Jefferies | .962 | 3 | 22 | 3 | 1 | 0 |
| McNair | 1.000 | 3 | 19 | 2 | 0 | 5 |
| Phillips | .889 | 2 | 6 | 2 | 1 | 1 |
| Schall | .996 | 80 | 626 | 67 | 3 | 42 |
| Zuber | .990 | 60 | 457 | 46 | 5 | 44 |

| Second Base | PCT | G | PO | A | E | DP |
|---|---|---|---|---|---|---|
| Amaro | 1.000 | 3 | 3 | 8 | 0 | 1 |
| Burton | .957 | 16 | 32 | 35 | 3 | 12 |
| Diaz | 1.000 | 28 | 56 | 67 | 0 | 11 |
| Doster | .985 | 87 | 197 | 203 | 6 | 40 |
| Fisher | 1.000 | 1 | 0 | 3 | 0 | 0 |
| Flores | .978 | 13 | 17 | 28 | 1 | 5 |

| | PCT | G | PO | A | E | DP |
|---|---|---|---|---|---|---|
| Manahan | 1.000 | 1 | 1 | 0 | 0 | 0 |
| Sefcik | 1.000 | 1 | 4 | 6 | 0 | 2 |

| Third Base | PCT | G | PO | A | E | DP |
|---|---|---|---|---|---|---|
| Amaro | .000 | 1 | 0 | 0 | 0 | 0 |
| Battle | .919 | 88 | 58 | 146 | 18 | 9 |
| Diaz | .949 | 12 | 15 | 22 | 2 | 2 |
| Fisher | 1.000 | 2 | 1 | 2 | 0 | 0 |
| Manahan | 1.000 | 2 | 1 | 2 | 0 | 0 |
| Rolen | .952 | 45 | 32 | 88 | 6 | 8 |
| Sefcik | 1.000 | 1 | 3 | 3 | 0 | 1 |

| Shortstop | PCT | G | PO | A | E | DP |
|---|---|---|---|---|---|---|
| Battle | .963 | 27 | 35 | 70 | 4 | 11 |
| Beltre | .905 | 4 | 7 | 12 | 2 | 3 |
| Benjamin | 1.000 | 4 | 3 | 12 | 0 | 0 |
| Burton | 1.000 | 1 | 1 | 4 | 0 | 0 |
| Diaz | .000 | 1 | 0 | 0 | 1 | 0 |
| Fisher | .883 | 20 | 22 | 46 | 9 | 10 |

| | PCT | G | PO | A | E | DP |
|---|---|---|---|---|---|---|
| Flores | .929 | 12 | 13 | 26 | 3 | 5 |
| Manahan | 1.000 | 9 | 13 | 24 | 0 | 4 |
| Relaford | .938 | 21 | 25 | 65 | 6 | 7 |
| Sefcik | .950 | 43 | 56 | 134 | 10 | 18 |
| Stocker | .982 | 12 | 17 | 39 | 1 | 7 |

| Outfield | PCT | G | PO | A | E | DP |
|---|---|---|---|---|---|---|
| Amaro | .991 | 48 | 107 | 1 | 1 | 0 |
| Butler | 1.000 | 71 | 130 | 4 | 0 | 1 |
| Magee | .959 | 44 | 92 | 2 | 4 | 0 |
| Martinez | .976 | 17 | 40 | 0 | 1 | 0 |
| Murray | .973 | 37 | 72 | 1 | 2 | 0 |
| Otero | .977 | 46 | 121 | 4 | 3 | 1 |
| Phillips | .965 | 52 | 106 | 4 | 4 | 0 |
| Schall | 1.000 | 1 | 1 | 0 | 0 | 0 |
| Tokheim | 1.000 | 75 | 118 | 2 | 0 | 0 |
| Zuber | .985 | 42 | 65 | 0 | 1 | 0 |
| Zupcic | 1.000 | 38 | 50 | 1 | 0 | 1 |

## EASTERN LEAGUE

| BATTING | AVG | G | AB | R | H | 2B | 3B | HR | RBI | BB | SO | SB | CS | B | T | HT | WT | DOB | 1st Yr | Resides |
|---|---|---|---|---|---|---|---|---|---|---|---|---|---|---|---|---|---|---|---|---|
| Amador, Manuel | .278 | 10 | 18 | 5 | 5 | 2 | 0 | 1 | 3 | 5 | 4 | 0 | 0 | S | R | 6-0 | 165 | 11-21-75 | 1993 | Santo Domingo, D.R. |
| Anderson, Marlon | .274 | 75 | 314 | 38 | 86 | 14 | 3 | 3 | 28 | 26 | 44 | 17 | 9 | L | R | 5-10 | 190 | 1-3-74 | 1995 | Prattville, Ala. |
| Angeli, Doug | .235 | 56 | 187 | 24 | 44 | 9 | 0 | 8 | 29 | 20 | 43 | 3 | 2 | R | R | 5-11 | 183 | 1-7-71 | 1993 | Springfield, Ill. |
| Burton, Essex | .304 | 102 | 381 | 66 | 116 | 19 | 5 | 1 | 30 | 37 | 56 | 40 | 12 | R | R | 5-9 | 155 | 5-16-69 | 1991 | San Diego, Calif. |
| Dawkins, Walter | .268 | 77 | 254 | 40 | 68 | 16 | 3 | 4 | 28 | 37 | 48 | 4 | 4 | R | R | 5-10 | 190 | 8-6-72 | 1995 | Garden Grove, Calif. |
| Estalella, Bobby | .244 | 111 | 365 | 48 | 89 | 14 | 2 | 23 | 72 | 67 | 104 | 2 | 4 | R | R | 6-1 | 200 | 8-23-74 | 1993 | Pembroke Pines, Fla. |
| Fisher, David | .269 | 57 | 171 | 21 | 46 | 9 | 0 | 4 | 24 | 12 | 18 | 5 | 3 | R | R | 6-0 | 160 | 2-26-70 | 1992 | Joplin, Mo. |
| Guiliano, Matt | .200 | 74 | 220 | 19 | 44 | 9 | 3 | 0 | 19 | 25 | 59 | 0 | 0 | R | R | 5-7 | 175 | 6-7-72 | 1994 | Ronkonkoma, N.Y. |
| Gyselman, Jeff | .172 | 49 | 128 | 9 | 22 | 2 | 0 | 0 | 12 | 14 | 36 | 0 | 2 | R | R | 6-3 | 193 | 7-10-70 | 1993 | Bothell, Wash. |
| Haws, Scott | 1.000 | 1 | 1 | 0 | 1 | 0 | 0 | 0 | 0 | 2 | 0 | 0 | 0 | L | R | 6-0 | 190 | 1-11-72 | 1992 | Fairless Hills, Pa. |
| Held, Dan | .243 | 136 | 497 | 77 | 121 | 17 | 5 | 26 | 92 | 60 | 141 | 3 | 8 | R | R | 6-0 | 200 | 10-7-70 | 1993 | Neosho, Wis. |
| Kendall, Jeremey | .168 | 35 | 131 | 23 | 22 | 5 | 1 | 1 | 10 | 12 | 35 | 5 | 5 | R | R | 5-9 | 170 | 9-3-71 | 1992 | East Troy, Wis. |
| Magee, Wendell | .293 | 71 | 270 | 38 | 79 | 15 | 5 | 6 | 30 | 24 | 40 | 10 | 6 | R | R | 6-0 | 225 | 8-3-72 | 1994 | Hattiesburg, Miss. |
| McConnell, Chad | .247 | 116 | 385 | 70 | 95 | 18 | 1 | 12 | 50 | 40 | 119 | 6 | 5 | R | R | 6-1 | 180 | 10-13-70 | 1992 | Sioux Falls, S.D. |
| Moler, Jason | .246 | 109 | 374 | 59 | 92 | 22 | 0 | 18 | 59 | 54 | 50 | 4 | 5 | R | R | 6-1 | 195 | 10-29-69 | 1992 | Yorba Linda, Calif. |
| Rolen, Scott | .361 | 61 | 230 | 44 | 83 | 22 | 2 | 9 | 42 | 34 | 32 | 8 | 3 | R | R | 6-4 | 210 | 4-4-75 | 1993 | Jasper, Ind. |
| Royster, Aaron | .257 | 65 | 230 | 42 | 59 | 11 | 0 | 4 | 20 | 30 | 56 | 4 | 5 | R | R | 6-1 | 220 | 11-30-72 | 1994 | Chicago, Ill. |
| Shores, Scott | .229 | 120 | 398 | 52 | 91 | 19 | 8 | 11 | 51 | 46 | 133 | 19 | 10 | R | R | 6-1 | 190 | 2-4-72 | 1994 | Phoenix, Ariz. |

| PITCHING | W | L | ERA | G | GS | CG | SV | IP | H | R | ER | BB | SO | B | T | HT | WT | DOB | 1st Yr | Resides |
|---|---|---|---|---|---|---|---|---|---|---|---|---|---|---|---|---|---|---|---|---|
| Beech, Matt | 11 | 6 | 3.17 | 21 | 21 | 0 | 0 | 133 | 108 | 57 | 47 | 32 | 132 | L | L | 6-2 | 190 | 1-20-72 | 1994 | San Antonio, Texas |
| Costa, Tony | 5 | 13 | 4.81 | 27 | 26 | 1 | 0 | 153 | 150 | 107 | 82 | 92 | 112 | R | R | 6-4 | 210 | 12-19-70 | 1992 | Lemoore, Calif. |
| Dodd, Robert | 2 | 3 | 3.56 | 18 | 5 | 0 | 0 | 43 | 41 | 21 | 17 | 24 | 35 | L | L | 6-3 | 195 | 3-14-73 | 1994 | Plano, Texas |
| Estavil, Mauricio | 0 | 3 | 11.57 | 20 | 0 | 0 | 0 | 19 | 30 | 28 | 24 | 22 | 19 | L | L | 6-0 | 185 | 6-27-72 | 1994 | Calabasas, Calif. |
| Fiore, Tony | 1 | 2 | 4.35 | 5 | 5 | 0 | 0 | 31 | 32 | 21 | 15 | 18 | 19 | R | R | 6-4 | 200 | 10-12-71 | 1992 | Chicago, Ill. |
| Foster, Mark | 4 | 5 | 5.80 | 50 | 8 | 0 | 0 | 76 | 84 | 54 | 49 | 45 | 56 | L | L | 6-1 | 200 | 12-24-71 | 1993 | Severn, Md. |
| Gomes, Wayne | 0 | 4 | 4.48 | 67 | 0 | 0 | 24 | 64 | 53 | 35 | 32 | 48 | 79 | R | R | 6-0 | 215 | 1-15-73 | 1993 | Hampton, Va. |
| Heflin, Bronson | 2 | 2 | 5.22 | 25 | 0 | 0 | 1 | 29 | 37 | 20 | 17 | 15 | 27 | R | R | 6-3 | 195 | 8-29-71 | 1994 | Clarksville, Tenn. |
| Herrmann, Gary | 1 | 5 | 4.99 | 23 | 5 | 0 | 0 | 40 | 43 | 25 | 22 | 27 | 31 | R | L | 6-4 | 205 | 10-15-69 | 1992 | Houston, Texas |
| Holman, Craig | 6 | 1 | 3.50 | 8 | 8 | 0 | 0 | 46 | 42 | 21 | 18 | 13 | 34 | S | R | 6-2 | 200 | 3-13-69 | 1991 | Attalla, Ala. |
| Hunter, Rich | 4 | 3 | 3.17 | 10 | 10 | 2 | 0 | 71 | 69 | 26 | 25 | 12 | 40 | R | R | 6-1 | 180 | 9-25-74 | 1993 | Temecula, Calif. |
| Juhl, Mike | 1 | 1 | 2.79 | 9 | 0 | 0 | 0 | 10 | 8 | 3 | 3 | 5 | 4 | L | L | 5-9 | 180 | 8-10-69 | 1991 | Lake Katrine, N.Y. |
| Loewer, Carlton | 7 | 10 | 5.26 | 27 | 27 | 3 | 0 | 171 | 191 | 115 | 100 | 57 | 119 | S | R | 6-6 | 220 | 9-24-73 | 1995 | Eunice, La. |
| Metheny, Nelson | 0 | 2 | 5.59 | 26 | 0 | 0 | 0 | 39 | 50 | 30 | 24 | 19 | 17 | R | R | 6-3 | 205 | 6-14-71 | 1993 | Salem, Va. |
| Mitchell, Larry | 3 | 6 | 5.21 | 34 | 2 | 0 | 0 | 57 | 55 | 39 | 33 | 44 | 71 | R | R | 6-1 | 200 | 10-16-71 | 1992 | Charlottesville, Va. |
| Munoz, Bobby | 0 | 1 | 2.93 | 4 | 4 | 0 | 0 | 28 | 24 | 13 | 9 | 8 | 29 | R | R | 6-7 | 237 | 3-3-68 | 1989 | Hialeah, Fla. |
| Nye, Ryan | 8 | 2 | 3.84 | 14 | 14 | 0 | 0 | 87 | 76 | 41 | 37 | 30 | 90 | R | R | 6-2 | 195 | 6-24-73 | 1994 | Cameron, Okla. |
| Quirico, Rafael | 1 | 0 | 1.80 | 5 | 5 | 0 | 0 | 30 | 22 | 6 | 6 | 11 | 23 | L | L | 6-3 | 170 | 9-7-69 | 1987 | Santo Domingo, D.R. |
| Troutman, Keith | 6 | 3 | 3.31 | 52 | 1 | 0 | 1 | 73 | 62 | 36 | 27 | 40 | 73 | R | R | 6-1 | 200 | 5-29-73 | 1992 | Candler, N.C. |
| Westbrook, Destry | 4 | 3 | 3.97 | 25 | 0 | 0 | 0 | 34 | 40 | 15 | 15 | 14 | 15 | R | R | 6-1 | 195 | 12-13-70 | 1992 | Montrose, Colo. |

### FIELDING

| Catcher | PCT | G | PO | A | E | DP | PB |
|---|---|---|---|---|---|---|---|
| Estalella | .984 | 106 | 775 | 84 | 14 | 5 | 16 |
| Gyselman | .987 | 47 | 268 | 29 | 4 | 3 | 11 |

| First Base | PCT | G | PO | A | E | DP |
|---|---|---|---|---|---|---|
| Fisher | .983 | 7 | 53 | 4 | 1 | 2 |
| Held | .990 | 134 | 1115 | 81 | 12 | 111 |
| McConnell | .667 | 2 | 2 | 0 | 1 | 1 |
| Moler | 1.000 | 11 | 36 | 3 | 0 | 5 |

| Second Base | PCT | G | PO | A | E | DP |
|---|---|---|---|---|---|---|
| Amador | 1.000 | 1 | 0 | 2 | 0 | 0 |
| Anderson | .957 | 75 | 166 | 239 | 18 | 61 |
| Burton | .950 | 64 | 124 | 162 | 15 | 27 |

| Fisher | .900 | 4 | 5 | 4 | 1 | 2 |
|---|---|---|---|---|---|---|

| Third Base | PCT | G | PO | A | E | DP |
|---|---|---|---|---|---|---|
| Amador | 1.000 | 1 | 1 | 2 | 0 | 0 |
| Fisher | .944 | 27 | 19 | 48 | 4 | 4 |
| Moler | .898 | 57 | 37 | 112 | 17 | 12 |
| Rolen | .949 | 61 | 41 | 125 | 9 | 10 |

| Shortstop | PCT | G | PO | A | E | DP |
|---|---|---|---|---|---|---|
| Amador | .857 | 3 | 3 | 3 | 1 | 1 |
| Angeli | .929 | 56 | 79 | 156 | 18 | 38 |
| Burton | .750 | 2 | 3 | 6 | 3 | 1 |
| Fisher | .957 | 9 | 10 | 12 | 1 | 7 |

| Guiliano | .969 | 73 | 77 | 177 | 8 | 29 |
|---|---|---|---|---|---|---|
| Moler | .944 | 10 | 14 | 20 | 2 | 6 |

| Outfield | PCT | G | PO | A | E | DP |
|---|---|---|---|---|---|---|
| Dawkins | .962 | 70 | 147 | 4 | 6 | 2 |
| Fisher | 1.000 | 5 | 2 | 1 | 0 | 0 |
| Kendall | .984 | 35 | 62 | 1 | 1 | 0 |
| Magee | .973 | 71 | 101 | 8 | 3 | 0 |
| McConnell | .967 | 104 | 199 | 8 | 7 | 2 |
| Moler | .846 | 9 | 11 | 0 | 2 | 0 |
| Royster | .992 | 65 | 114 | 5 | 1 | 1 |
| Shores | .989 | 88 | 170 | 13 | 2 | 4 |

## FLORIDA STATE LEAGUE

| BATTING | AVG | G | AB | R | H | 2B | 3B | HR | RBI | BB | SO | SB | CS | B | T | HT | WT | DOB | 1st Yr | Resides |
|---|---|---|---|---|---|---|---|---|---|---|---|---|---|---|---|---|---|---|---|---|
| Amador, Manuel | .273 | 52 | 172 | 24 | 47 | 10 | 0 | 5 | 21 | 19 | 46 | 1 | 1 | S | R | 6-0 | 165 | 11-21-75 | 1993 | Santo Domingo, D.R. |
| Anderson, Marlon | .272 | 60 | 257 | 37 | 70 | 10 | 3 | 2 | 21 | 14 | 18 | 26 | 1 | L | R | 5-10 | 190 | 1-3-74 | 1995 | Prattville, Ala. |
| Benjamin, Mike | .174 | 8 | 23 | 3 | 4 | 1 | 0 | 0 | 0 | 3 | 4 | 1 | 0 | R | R | 6-0 | 169 | 11-22-65 | 1987 | Chandler, Ariz. |
| Carver, Steve | .278 | 117 | 436 | 59 | 121 | 32 | 0 | 17 | 79 | 52 | 89 | 1 | 1 | L | R | 6-3 | 215 | 9-27-72 | 1995 | Jacksonville, Fla. |
| Costello, Brian | .206 | 81 | 282 | 28 | 58 | 13 | 2 | 2 | 31 | 17 | 84 | 6 | 4 | R | R | 6-2 | 195 | 10-4-74 | 1993 | Orlando, Fla. |
| Cox, Chuck | .100 | 4 | 10 | 0 | 1 | 1 | 0 | 0 | 2 | 1 | 4 | 0 | 0 | R | R | 6-2 | 190 | 1-28-73 | 1995 | Pasadena, Texas |
| Daulton, Darren | .000 | 1 | 1 | 0 | 0 | 0 | 0 | 0 | 0 | 0 | 0 | 0 | 0 | L | R | 6-2 | 201 | 1-3-62 | 1980 | Safety Harbor, Fla. |
| Dawkins, Walter | .293 | 47 | 174 | 22 | 51 | 13 | 2 | 2 | 23 | 20 | 38 | 4 | 5 | R | R | 5-10 | 190 | 8-6-72 | 1995 | Garden Grove, Calif. |
| Evans, Stan | .241 | 80 | 241 | 42 | 58 | 5 | 2 | 2 | 23 | 33 | 36 | 12 | 5 | L | R | 5-11 | 175 | 12-17-70 | 1992 | Oak Hill, Fla. |
| Flores, Jose | .228 | 84 | 281 | 39 | 64 | 6 | 5 | 1 | 39 | 34 | 42 | 15 | 2 | R | R | 5-11 | 160 | 6-26-73 | 1994 | New York, N.Y. |
| Guiliano, Matt | .229 | 55 | 166 | 13 | 38 | 9 | 2 | 1 | 14 | 6 | 46 | 2 | 3 | R | R | 5-7 | 175 | 6-7-72 | 1994 | Ronkonkoma, N.Y. |
| Haws, Scott | .184 | 37 | 114 | 15 | 21 | 1 | 0 | 1 | 11 | 22 | 21 | 0 | 0 | L | R | 6-0 | 190 | 1-11-72 | 1992 | Fairless Hills, Pa. |
| Huff, Larry | .275 | 128 | 133 | 17 | 5 | 4 | 0 | 0 | 60 | 65 | 37 | 11 | 5 | R | R | 6-0 | 175 | 1-24-72 | 1994 | Las Vegas, Nev. |
| Kendall, Jeremey | .244 | 81 | 291 | 42 | 71 | 15 | 4 | 6 | 40 | 34 | 86 | 22 | 5 | R | R | 5-9 | 170 | 9-3-71 | 1992 | East Troy, Wis. |
| Key, Jeff | .244 | 101 | 348 | 53 | 85 | 15 | 4 | 3 | 34 | 16 | 82 | 15 | 3 | L | R | 6-1 | 200 | 11-22-74 | 1993 | Covington, Ga. |
| McMullen, Jon | .185 | 31 | 119 | 10 | 22 | 4 | 0 | 2 | 9 | 12 | 26 | 0 | 0 | L | R | 6-0 | 240 | 11-30-73 | 1992 | Ventura, Calif. |
| Millan, Adam | .270 | 101 | 348 | 55 | 94 | 21 | 1 | 11 | 55 | 52 | 52 | 1 | 2 | R | R | 6-0 | 195 | 3-26-72 | 1994 | Montebello, Calif. |
| Northeimer, Jamie | .254 | 101 | 327 | 52 | 83 | 21 | 0 | 10 | 42 | 60 | 69 | 0 | 2 | R | R | 5-10 | 174 | 7-5-72 | 1994 | Sacramento, Calif. |
| O'Connor, Rick | .240 | 12 | 25 | 3 | 6 | 1 | 0 | 0 | 2 | 3 | 5 | 0 | 0 | R | R | 6-1 | 185 | 9-23-73 | 1995 | Walkerton, Ind. |
| Pullen, Shane | .267 | 23 | 75 | 11 | 20 | 2 | 0 | 0 | 8 | 8 | 20 | 1 | 0 | L | R | 5-11 | 160 | 6-16-73 | 1994 | Kosciusko, Miss. |
| Raynor, Mark | .200 | 18 | 55 | 8 | 11 | 1 | 1 | 0 | 4 | 17 | 9 | 2 | 1 | R | R | 6-0 | 180 | 4-1-73 | 1995 | Williamston, N.C. |
| Royster, Aaron | .280 | 72 | 289 | 35 | 81 | 10 | 2 | 11 | 60 | 23 | 56 | 4 | 3 | R | R | 6-1 | 220 | 11-30-72 | 1994 | Chicago, Ill. |
| Tinsley, Lee | .294 | 4 | 17 | 4 | 5 | 0 | 1 | 0 | 3 | 2 | 4 | 2 | 0 | S | R | 5-10 | 180 | 3-4-69 | 1987 | Shelbyville, Ky. |

**GAMES BY POSITION: C**—Cox 4, Haws 33, Millan 17, Northeimer 89. **1B**—Carver 67, Daulton 1, Millan 74, Pullen 2. **2B**—Amador 12,

Anderson 60, Flores 26, Huff 41, O'Connor 6. **3B**—Amador 26, Carver 31, Evans 1, Flores 2, Huff 88, O'Connor 1. **SS**—Amador 5, Benjamin 8, Flores 56, Guiliano 55, O'Connor 5, Raynor 18. **OF**—Carver 5, Costello 79, Dawkins 47, Evans 77, Kendall 81, Key 39, Pullen 20, Royster 72, Tinsley 4.

| PITCHING | W | L | ERA | G | GS | CG | SV | IP | H | R | ER | BB | SO | B | T | HT | WT | DOB | 1st Yr | Resides |
|---|---|---|---|---|---|---|---|---|---|---|---|---|---|---|---|---|---|---|---|---|
| Barbao, Joe | 4 | 2 | 3.35 | 28 | 0 | 0 | 1 | 40 | 49 | 19 | 15 | 5 | 14 | R | R | 6-1 | 190 | 4-18-72 | 1994 | Crown Point, Ind. |
| Boyd, Jason | 11 | 8 | 3.90 | 26 | 26 | 2 | 0 | 162 | 160 | 75 | 70 | 49 | 120 | R | R | 6-2 | 165 | 2-23-73 | 1994 | Edwardsville, Ill. |
| Censale, Silvio | 8 | 9 | 3.92 | 24 | 22 | 1 | 0 | 126 | 118 | 65 | 55 | 54 | 100 | L | L | 6-2 | 195 | 11-21-71 | 1993 | Lodi, N.J. |
| Estavil, Mauricio | 5 | 3 | 3.44 | 29 | 0 | 0 | 2 | 34 | 20 | 15 | 13 | 20 | 25 | L | L | 6-0 | 185 | 6-27-72 | 1994 | Calabasas, Calif. |
| Fernandez, Sid | 0 | 0 | 0.00 | 1 | 1 | 0 | 0 | 3 | 0 | 0 | 0 | 0 | 5 | L | L | 6-1 | 220 | 10-12-62 | 1981 | Hawaii Kai, Hawaii |
| Fiore, Tony | 8 | 4 | 3.16 | 22 | 22 | 3 | 0 | 128 | 102 | 61 | 45 | 56 | 80 | R | R | 6-4 | 200 | 10-12-71 | 1992 | Chicago, Ill. |
| Greene, Tommy | 1 | 1 | 2.00 | 7 | 4 | 0 | 0 | 27 | 25 | 8 | 6 | 4 | 23 | R | R | 6-5 | 225 | 4-6-67 | 1985 | Richmond, Va. |
| Humphry, Trevor | 2 | 0 | 1.87 | 16 | 0 | 0 | 0 | 34 | 21 | 8 | 7 | 17 | 12 | R | R | 6-2 | 210 | 10-31-71 | 1992 | Delight, Ark. |
| Knoll, Randy | 1 | 0 | 3.05 | 4 | 4 | 0 | 0 | 21 | 17 | 8 | 7 | 2 | 19 | R | R | 6-4 | 190 | 3-21-77 | 1995 | Corona, Calif. |
| Kosek, Kory | 3 | 4 | 3.77 | 42 | 4 | 0 | 1 | 74 | 84 | 43 | 31 | 32 | 50 | R | R | 6-1 | 185 | 4-8-73 | 1995 | Glencoe, Minn. |
| Leaman, Jeff | 1 | 0 | 3.60 | 3 | 0 | 0 | 0 | 5 | 8 | 4 | 2 | 2 | 3 | R | R | 6-0 | 190 | 12-30-72 | 1995 | Litchfield, Calif. |
| Manning, Len | 3 | 7 | 3.69 | 20 | 18 | 1 | 0 | 102 | 94 | 51 | 42 | 63 | 77 | R | L | 6-2 | 195 | 12-30-71 | 1994 | New Brighton, Minn. |
| Metheney, Nelson | 1 | 0 | 0.79 | 21 | 0 | 0 | 1 | 34 | 29 | 4 | 3 | 6 | 19 | R | R | 6-3 | 205 | 6-14-71 | 1993 | Salem, Va. |
| Munoz, Bobby | 1 | 1 | 1.93 | 2 | 2 | 0 | 0 | 14 | 15 | 4 | 3 | -2 | 7 | R | R | 6-7 | 237 | 3-3-68 | 1989 | Hialeah, Fla. |
| Quirico, Rafael | 1 | 0 | 7.84 | 2 | 2 | 0 | 0 | 10 | 13 | 9 | 9 | 1 | 12 | L | L | 6-3 | 170 | 9-7-69 | 1987 | Santo Domingo, D.R. |
| Rama, Shelby | 7 | 3 | 2.92 | 34 | 7 | 0 | 0 | 83 | 88 | 41 | 27 | 25 | 38 | S | R | 6-6 | 210 | 1-22-72 | 1993 | Phoenix, Ariz. |
| Schilling, Curt | 2 | 0 | 1.29 | 2 | 2 | 0 | 0 | 14 | 9 | 2 | 2 | 1 | 17 | R | R | 6-4 | 215 | 11-14-66 | 1986 | Marlton, N.J. |
| Shumaker, Anthony | 5 | 3 | 5.10 | 31 | 0 | 0 | 3 | 30 | 39 | 17 | 17 | 12 | 24 | L | L | 6-5 | 223 | 5-14-73 | 1995 | Kokomo, Ind. |
| Stumpf, Brian | 1 | 6 | 3.36 | 56 | 0 | 0 | 26 | 59 | 54 | 25 | 22 | 32 | 48 | L | R | 6-3 | 200 | 5-22-72 | 1994 | Springfield, Pa. |
| Swan, Tyrone | 3 | 2 | 3.54 | 10 | 6 | 0 | 0 | 41 | 38 | 21 | 16 | 12 | 22 | R | R | 6-7 | 195 | 5-7-69 | 1993 | Sparks, Nev. |
| Vandemark, John | 0 | 2 | 2.39 | 27 | 0 | 0 | 3 | 26 | 21 | 10 | 7 | 14 | 27 | L | L | 6-1 | 205 | 9-28-71 | 1990 | Lockport, N.Y. |
| Wallace, B.J. | 3 | 4 | 5.83 | 15 | 12 | 0 | 0 | 63 | 71 | 47 | 41 | 41 | 37 | R | L | 6-4 | 195 | 5-18-71 | 1992 | Monroeville, Ala. |
| West, David | 1 | 0 | 3.13 | 5 | 5 | 0 | 0 | 23 | 21 | 8 | 8 | 11 | 17 | L | L | 6-6 | 225 | 9-1-64 | 1983 | Stuart, Fla. |
| Westbrook, Destry | 3 | 3 | 2.08 | 34 | 0 | 0 | 0 | 43 | 35 | 12 | 10 | 11 | 35 | R | R | 6-1 | 195 | 12-13-70 | 1992 | Montrose, Colo. |
| Williams, Mitch | 0 | 0 | 2.25 | 6 | 0 | 0 | 0 | 8 | 10 | 3 | 2 | 1 | 6 | L | L | 6-4 | 200 | 11-17-64 | 1982 | Hico, Texas |

# PIEDMONT     Class A

## SOUTH ATLANTIC LEAGUE

| BATTING | AVG | G | AB | R | H | 2B | 3B | HR | RBI | BB | SO | SB | CS | B | T | HT | WT | DOB | 1st Yr | Resides |
|---|---|---|---|---|---|---|---|---|---|---|---|---|---|---|---|---|---|---|---|---|
| Brito, Domingo | .118 | 43 | 102 | 5 | 12 | 3 | 0 | 0 | 9 | 14 | 36 | 1 | 0 | R | R | 6-0 | 160 | 7-6-75 | 1994 | Santo Domingo, D.R. |
| Buczkowski, Matt | .217 | 5 | 23 | 2 | 5 | 1 | 0 | 0 | 1 | 0 | 8 | 0 | 0 | R | R | 6-2 | 185 | 9-14-73 | 1996 | Granger, Ind. |
| Coburn, Todd | .194 | 46 | 155 | 15 | 30 | 9 | 0 | 1 | 16 | 15 | 34 | 2 | 1 | R | R | 6-2 | 205 | 2-26-72 | 1994 | Carson City, Nev. |
| Cornelius, Jonathon | .233 | 123 | 454 | 41 | 106 | 16 | 2 | 12 | 51 | 33 | 132 | 6 | 5 | R | R | 6-1 | 195 | 11-30-73 | 1995 | Covina, Calif. |
| Cox, Chuck | .202 | 27 | 89 | 8 | 18 | 5 | 0 | 1 | 5 | 6 | 26 | 1 | 1 | R | R | 6-2 | 190 | 1-28-73 | 1995 | Pasadena, Texas |
| Crane, Todd | .217 | 9 | 23 | 4 | 5 | 0 | 0 | 0 | 1 | 6 | 6 | 0 | 1 | R | R | 6-1 | 185 | 7-2-73 | 1995 | Roswell, Ga. |
| Elliott, Zach | .228 | 135 | 470 | 57 | 107 | 23 | 0 | 4 | 41 | 67 | 90 | 20 | 11 | R | R | 6-0 | 180 | 9-1-73 | 1995 | Tustin, Calif. |
| Janke, Jared | .219 | 104 | 388 | 36 | 85 | 21 | 0 | 6 | 46 | 24 | 70 | 2 | 2 | R | R | 6-5 | 225 | 5-17-74 | 1995 | Coeur D'Alene, Idaho |
| Kennedy, Justin | .215 | 27 | 107 | 12 | 23 | 5 | 1 | 0 | 14 | 3 | 24 | 1 | 2 | L | L | 6-1 | 188 | 8-16-77 | 1995 | Bastrop, La. |
| Kimm, Tyson | .198 | 35 | 106 | 11 | 21 | 4 | 0 | 0 | 6 | 9 | 23 | 1 | 0 | S | R | 6-1 | 175 | 11-30-72 | 1995 | Amana, Iowa |
| Nichols, Kevin | .222 | 22 | 72 | 5 | 16 | 6 | 0 | 0 | 5 | 3 | 18 | 1 | 0 | R | R | 6-0 | 195 | 4-16-73 | 1996 | Southport, Fla. |
| O'Connor, Rich | .200 | 23 | 55 | 11 | 11 | 1 | 0 | 0 | 0 | 11 | 13 | 1 | 0 | R | R | 6-1 | 185 | 9-23-73 | 1995 | Walkerton, Ind. |
| Pettiford, Torrey | .208 | 74 | 259 | 26 | 54 | 6 | 2 | 0 | 19 | 18 | 49 | 13 | 3 | R | R | 5-9 | 163 | 5-30-73 | 1994 | Cedar Grove, N.C. |
| Pierce, Kirk | .253 | 67 | 198 | 22 | 50 | 12 | 0 | 2 | 28 | 22 | 43 | 0 | 1 | R | R | 6-3 | 200 | 5-26-73 | 1995 | Murrieta, Calif. |
| Pullen, Shane | .269 | 46 | 171 | 15 | 46 | 9 | 1 | 2 | 28 | 16 | 30 | 1 | 2 | L | R | 5-11 | 160 | 6-16-73 | 1994 | Kosciusko, Miss. |
| Raynor, Mark | .304 | 111 | 428 | 73 | 130 | 21 | 2 | 4 | 62 | 50 | 67 | 16 | 10 | R | R | 6-0 | 180 | 4-1-73 | 1995 | Williamston, N.C. |
| Rivero, Eddie | .270 | 52 | 196 | 27 | 53 | 10 | 4 | 4 | 34 | 19 | 37 | 5 | 3 | L | L | 6-0 | 190 | 7-14-73 | 1996 | Miami, Fla. |
| Robinson, David | .248 | 50 | 149 | 22 | 37 | 8 | 2 | 3 | 13 | 12 | 34 | 5 | 3 | L | L | 5-11 | 195 | 11-29-72 | 1995 | Dayton, Ohio |
| Schreimann, Eric | .252 | 91 | 298 | 44 | 75 | 13 | 1 | 7 | 33 | 29 | 66 | 3 | 1 | R | R | 6-1 | 205 | 4-22-75 | 1994 | Jefferson City, Mo. |
| Snusz, Chris | .091 | 4 | 11 | 2 | 1 | 0 | 0 | 0 | 0 | 2 | 1 | 0 | 1 | R | R | 6-0 | 195 | 11-8-72 | 1995 | Buffalo, N.Y. |
| Taylor, Reggie | .263 | 128 | 499 | 68 | 131 | 20 | 6 | 0 | 31 | 29 | 136 | 36 | 17 | L | R | 6-1 | 180 | 1-12-77 | 1995 | Newberry, S.C. |
| Williams, Ricky | .188 | 84 | 266 | 30 | 50 | 4 | 3 | 3 | 20 | 18 | 87 | 17 | 8 | R | R | 6-1 | 190 | 11-6-73 | 1995 | San Diego, Calif. |

**GAMES BY POSITION: C**—Coburn 15, Cox 25, Pierce 67, Schreimann 36, Snusz 4. **1B**—Coburn 21, Elliott 5, Janke 91, Pullen 21. **2B**—Brito 13, Elliott 26, Kimm 27, O'Connor 9, Pettiford 72. **3B**—Brito 7, Buczkowski 5, Coburn 5, Elliott 96, Kimm 7, Nichols 22, O'Connor 8. **SS**—Brito 23, Elliott 9, O'Connor 5, Raynor 110. **OF**—Cornelius 97, Crane 2, Elliott 1, Kennedy 15, Pullen 11, Rivero 51, Robinson 38, Schreimann 1, Taylor 128, Williams 84.

| PITCHING | W | L | ERA | G | GS | CG | SV | IP | H | R | ER | BB | SO | B | T | HT | WT | DOB | 1st Yr | Resides |
|---|---|---|---|---|---|---|---|---|---|---|---|---|---|---|---|---|---|---|---|---|
| Antonini, Adrian | 0 | 1 | 6.75 | 2 | 2 | 0 | 0 | 8 | 12 | 6 | 6 | 4 | 10 | R | R | 6-3 | 225 | 7-27-72 | 1994 | Miami, Fla. |
| Barbao, Joe | 2 | 0 | 1.06 | 17 | 0 | 0 | 0 | 34 | 30 | 7 | 4 | 8 | 32 | R | R | 6-1 | 190 | 4-18-72 | 1994 | Crown Point, Ind. |
| Burger, Rob | 10 | 12 | 3.38 | 27 | 26 | 2 | 0 | 160 | 129 | 74 | 60 | 61 | 171 | R | R | 6-1 | 190 | 3-25-76 | 1994 | Willow Street, Pa. |
| Coggin, Dave | 9 | 12 | 4.31 | 28 | 28 | 3 | 0 | 169 | 156 | 87 | 81 | 46 | 129 | R | R | 6-4 | 195 | 10-30-76 | 1995 | Upland, Calif. |
| Davis, Jason | 6 | 1 | 1.82 | 19 | 0 | 0 | 2 | 25 | 16 | 6 | 5 | 5 | 22 | L | L | 6-3 | 185 | 8-15-74 | 1996 | Winters, Calif. |
| Ford, Brian | 1 | 4 | 4.66 | 37 | 0 | 0 | 1 | 56 | 73 | 33 | 29 | 18 | 40 | R | L | 6-3 | 210 | 1-7-73 | 1995 | Hope Mills, N.C. |
| Hamilton, Paul | 2 | 2 | 9.45 | 4 | 2 | 0 | 0 | 13 | 16 | 15 | 14 | 9 | 12 | R | R | 6-4 | 185 | 10-31-71 | 1993 | Cleveland, Texas |
| Kershner, Jason | 11 | 9 | 3.75 | 28 | 28 | 2 | 0 | 168 | 154 | 81 | 70 | 59 | 156 | L | L | 6-2 | 160 | 12-19-76 | 1995 | Scottsdale, Ariz. |
| Knoll, Randy | 10 | 7 | 2.09 | 22 | 22 | 3 | 0 | 151 | 111 | 48 | 35 | 31 | 144 | R | R | 6-4 | 190 | 3-21-77 | 1995 | Corona, Calif. |
| Leaman, Jeff | 0 | 2 | 5.26 | 19 | 1 | 0 | 0 | 38 | 46 | 23 | 22 | 10 | 21 | R | R | 6-0 | 190 | 12-30-72 | 1995 | Litchfield, Calif. |
| Mejia, Javier | 0 | 0 | 6.00 | 2 | 0 | 0 | 0 | 3 | 3 | 2 | 2 | 3 | 8 | R | R | 6-0 | 190 | 7-28-74 | 1996 | Los Angeles, Calif. |
| Mendes, Jaime | 3 | 2 | 3.21 | 37 | 0 | 0 | 3 | 70 | 78 | 28 | 25 | 13 | 64 | R | R | 5-10 | 185 | 4-6-73 | 1995 | Las Cruces, N.M. |
| Mensink, Brian | 1 | 3 | 3.35 | 6 | 6 | 0 | 0 | 38 | 33 | 15 | 14 | 13 | 27 | R | R | 6-3 | 200 | 11-1-73 | 1995 | Rochester, Minn. |
| Nyari, Pete | 2 | 3 | 3.61 | 45 | 0 | 0 | 18 | 52 | 40 | 27 | 21 | 21 | 67 | R | R | 5-11 | 200 | 9-4-71 | 1994 | Erie, Pa. |
| Shumaker, Anthony | 3 | 0 | 1.38 | 20 | 0 | 0 | 4 | 33 | 16 | 7 | 5 | 10 | 51 | L | L | 6-5 | 223 | 5-14-73 | 1995 | Kokomo, Ind. |
| Sikes, Jason | 4 | 6 | 5.10 | 17 | 17 | 0 | 0 | 78 | 87 | 60 | 44 | 41 | 47 | R | R | 6-5 | 225 | 6-17-76 | 1994 | Perry, Ga. |
| Tebbetts, Scott | 0 | 2 | 13.50 | 5 | 0 | 0 | 0 | 5 | 8 | 9 | 8 | 2 | 2 | R | R | 6-0 | 200 | 10-8-72 | 1995 | San Diego, Calif. |
| Walton, Tim | 2 | 1 | 1.19 | 8 | 5 | 0 | 0 | 38 | 28 | 7 | 5 | 14 | 19 | R | R | 6-0 | 197 | 8-6-72 | 1996 | Cerritos, Calif. |
| Yeager, Gary | 5 | 2 | 2.68 | 40 | 1 | 0 | 6 | 81 | 73 | 26 | 24 | 19 | 66 | R | R | 6-1 | 190 | 11-6-73 | 1995 | Elizabethtown, Pa. |

# BATAVIA     Class A

## NEW YORK-PENN LEAGUE

| BATTING | AVG | G | AB | R | H | 2B | 3B | HR | RBI | BB | SO | SB | CS | B | T | HT | WT | DOB | 1st Yr | Resides |
|---|---|---|---|---|---|---|---|---|---|---|---|---|---|---|---|---|---|---|---|---|
| Batts, Rodney | .144 | 41 | 153 | 20 | 22 | 5 | 1 | 0 | 15 | 12 | 36 | 7 | 2 | R | R | 5-10 | 170 | 10-13-73 | 1996 | Columbus, Miss. |

| BATTING | AVG | G | AB | R | H | 2B | 3B | HR | RBI | BB | SO | SB | CS | B | T | HT | WT | DOB | 1st Yr | Resides |
|---|---|---|---|---|---|---|---|---|---|---|---|---|---|---|---|---|---|---|---|---|
| Clark, Kirby | .262 | 51 | 183 | 25 | 48 | 11 | 1 | 3 | 24 | 16 | 39 | 1 | 1 | L | R | 6-0 | 200 | 10-6-73 | 1996 | Toomsuba, Miss. |
| Cooley, Shannon | .275 | 62 | 229 | 30 | 63 | 9 | 3 | 2 | 23 | 17 | 40 | 6 | 6 | L | R | 6-1 | 170 | 6-24-74 | 1996 | Hickory, Miss. |
| Crane, Todd | .239 | 36 | 138 | 21 | 33 | 10 | 2 | 3 | 18 | 11 | 31 | 3 | 4 | R | R | 6-1 | 185 | 7-2-73 | 1995 | Roswell, Ga. |
| Crawford, Marty | .269 | 63 | 219 | 26 | 59 | 8 | 1 | 2 | 30 | 18 | 22 | 5 | 2 | L | R | 5-7 | 175 | 2-19-74 | 1996 | Grand Prairie, Texas |
| Crede, Brad | .275 | 75 | 280 | 44 | 77 | 15 | 1 | 8 | 51 | 30 | 85 | 0 | 5 | R | R | 6-5 | 200 | 8-15-74 | 1996 | Westphalia, Mo. |
| Francia, David | .289 | 69 | 280 | 45 | 81 | 14 | 5 | 4 | 29 | 8 | 25 | 16 | 6 | L | L | 5-11 | 175 | 4-16-75 | 1996 | Mobile, Ala. |
| Knupfer, Jason | .280 | 66 | 218 | 32 | 61 | 5 | 1 | 1 | 24 | 25 | 43 | 5 | 5 | R | R | 6-0 | 180 | 9-21-74 | 1996 | Redwood City, Calif. |
| Marsters, Brandon | .232 | 42 | 151 | 15 | 35 | 8 | 2 | 1 | 13 | 8 | 46 | 1 | 0 | R | R | 5-10 | 195 | 3-14-75 | 1996 | Sarasota, Fla. |
| Oliveros, Leonardo | .248 | 42 | 121 | 12 | 30 | 7 | 0 | 0 | 18 | 11 | 22 | 1 | 1 | R | R | 5-10 | 185 | 12-1-75 | 1994 | Maturin, Venez. |
| Rivero, Eddie | .255 | 13 | 55 | 7 | 14 | 1 | 2 | 1 | 6 | 2 | 14 | 1 | 2 | L | L | 6-0 | 190 | 7-14-73 | 1996 | Miami, Fla. |
| Snusz, Chris | .161 | 13 | 31 | 6 | 5 | 0 | 0 | 0 | 6 | 4 | 0 | 0 | 0 | R | R | 6-0 | 195 | 11-8-72 | 1995 | Buffalo, N.Y. |
| Taylor, Greg | .245 | 19 | 53 | 5 | 13 | 0 | 3 | 0 | 5 | 3 | 9 | 1 | 0 | R | R | 6-0 | 170 | 10-30-73 | 1996 | Fort Wayne, Ind. |
| Torti, Mike | .250 | 59 | 216 | 35 | 54 | 14 | 4 | 5 | 44 | 27 | 55 | 7 | 0 | R | R | 5-11 | 190 | 8-29-74 | 1996 | Carrollton, Texas |
| Wesemann, Jason | .218 | 49 | 156 | 21 | 34 | 9 | 0 | 1 | 11 | 8 | 30 | 3 | 1 | R | R | 6-0 | 180 | 3-29-74 | 1996 | Watertown, Wis. |

GAMES BY POSITION: C—Clark 10, Marsters 39, Oliveros 26, Snusz 9. 1B—Crede 74. 2B—Batts 40, Crawford 11, Snusz 9, Wesemann 18. 3B—Torti 54, Wesemann 23. SS—Knupfer 65, Taylor 8, Wesemann 4. OF—Clark 10, Cooley 60, Crane 34, Crawford 43, Francia 67, Rivero 13.

| PITCHING | W | L | ERA | G | GS | CG | SV | IP | H | R | ER | BB | SO | B | T | HT | WT | DOB | 1st Yr | Resides |
|---|---|---|---|---|---|---|---|---|---|---|---|---|---|---|---|---|---|---|---|---|
| Allen, Brandon | 2 | 6 | 3.52 | 13 | 11 | 0 | 0 | 64 | 69 | 36 | 25 | 10 | 39 | L | L | 5-10 | 180 | 9-1-74 | 1996 | Littleton, Colo. |
| Cafferty, Jason | 3 | 4 | 6.42 | 14 | 6 | 0 | 0 | 41 | 44 | 30 | 29 | 14 | 35 | R | R | 6-3 | 200 | 3-11-76 | 1996 | Hastings, Neb. |
| Cotton, Joseph | 2 | 4 | 4.27 | 9 | 9 | 0 | 0 | 46 | 43 | 23 | 22 | 19 | 37 | R | R | 6-2 | 190 | 3-25-75 | 1996 | Uniontown, Ohio |
| Crane, John | 1 | 0 | 3.86 | 21 | 0 | 0 | 0 | 35 | 38 | 20 | 15 | 17 | 31 | L | L | 6-1 | 190 | 7-25-74 | 1995 | Swedesboro, N.J. |
| Frace, Ryan | 4 | 1 | 2.68 | 25 | 1 | 0 | 0 | 54 | 49 | 19 | 16 | 14 | 53 | R | R | 6-2 | 205 | 2-23-72 | 1995 | Fullerton, Calif. |
| Kawabata, Kyle | 1 | 2 | 1.93 | 25 | 0 | 0 | 20 | 28 | 21 | 7 | 6 | 7 | 24 | R | R | 6-0 | 195 | 1-2-74 | 1995 | Kailua, Hawaii |
| Mensink, Brian | 3 | 1 | 3.75 | 8 | 8 | 1 | 0 | 50 | 48 | 22 | 21 | 16 | 35 | R | R | 6-4 | 215 | 11-1-73 | 1995 | Rochester, Minn. |
| Miller, Brian | 8 | 3 | 2.07 | 17 | 10 | 1 | 0 | 83 | 70 | 22 | 19 | 25 | 43 | R | R | 6-0 | 200 | 1-26-73 | 1995 | Two Rivers, Wis. |
| Mitchell, Courtney | 0 | 1 | 1.88 | 24 | 0 | 0 | 0 | 43 | 38 | 14 | 9 | 17 | 49 | S | L | 5-9 | 178 | 11-20-72 | 1994 | Garyville, La. |
| Shadburne, Adam | 2 | 0 | 3.18 | 20 | 0 | 0 | 0 | 34 | 34 | 16 | 12 | 8 | 37 | L | R | 6-3 | 210 | 1-18-74 | 1996 | Louisville, Ky. |
| Stevens, Kris | 1 | 1 | 8.10 | 3 | 3 | 0 | 0 | 13 | 16 | 12 | 12 | 6 | 11 | R | L | 6-2 | 188 | 9-19-77 | 1996 | Fontana, Calif. |
| Thomas, Evan | 10 | 2 | 2.78 | 13 | 13 | 0 | 0 | 81 | 60 | 29 | 25 | 23 | 75 | R | R | 5-10 | 175 | 6-14-74 | 1996 | Pembroke Pines, Fla. |
| Tilton, Ira | 5 | 6 | 5.48 | 14 | 14 | 0 | 0 | 69 | 66 | 47 | 42 | 26 | 40 | R | R | 6-4 | 185 | 10-27-74 | 1996 | Indianapolis, Ind. |
| Tober, Dave | 0 | 2 | 6.00 | 4 | 0 | 0 | 0 | 6 | 8 | 6 | 4 | 5 | 8 | R | R | 5-9 | 175 | 5-11-74 | 1996 | Warwick, R.I. |

# MARTINSVILLE     Rookie
## APPALACHIAN LEAGUE

| BATTING | AVG | G | AB | R | H | 2B | 3B | HR | RBI | BB | SO | SB | CS | B | T | HT | WT | DOB | 1st Yr | Resides |
|---|---|---|---|---|---|---|---|---|---|---|---|---|---|---|---|---|---|---|---|---|
| Buckles, Matt | .257 | 34 | 109 | 13 | 28 | 5 | 2 | 3 | 21 | 7 | 24 | 4 | 0 | L | R | 5-11 | 160 | 12-29-76 | 1996 | East Palatka, Fla. |
| Buczkowski, Matt | .304 | 50 | 158 | 25 | 48 | 12 | 1 | 3 | 23 | 27 | 52 | 2 | 3 | R | R | 6-2 | 185 | 9-14-73 | 1996 | Granger, Ind. |
| Edwards, Lamont | .263 | 54 | 198 | 30 | 52 | 10 | 5 | 1 | 26 | 21 | 35 | 7 | 3 | R | R | 6-2 | 200 | 8-6-73 | 1996 | Clinton, N.C. |
| Ferguson, Ryan | .240 | 44 | 154 | 19 | 37 | 9 | 1 | 6 | 20 | 11 | 52 | 3 | 1 | L | L | 6-2 | 180 | 4-6-75 | 1996 | Hermiston, Ore. |
| Ferrand, Thomas | .171 | 48 | 158 | 20 | 27 | 6 | 3 | 0 | 14 | 18 | 74 | 6 | 4 | L | R | 6-2 | 180 | 6-23-74 | 1996 | Jefferson, La. |
| Jenkins, Ben | .207 | 41 | 140 | 10 | 29 | 6 | 0 | 1 | 14 | 12 | 35 | 4 | 3 | R | R | 6-6 | 225 | 8-28-73 | 1996 | Dallas, Texas |
| Johnson, Jason | .272 | 55 | 213 | 29 | 58 | 5 | 2 | 0 | 13 | 14 | 27 | 20 | 7 | R | R | 6-6 | 225 | 1-7-71 | 1993 | Williamsport, Pa. |
| Livingston, Clyde | .125 | 5 | 16 | 1 | 2 | 0 | 0 | 0 | 2 | 1 | 5 | 0 | 0 | L | R | 5-10 | 190 | 2-28-73 | 1995 | Prosperity, S.C. |
| Mata, Manuel | .122 | 16 | 41 | 3 | 5 | 0 | 0 | 0 | 1 | 3 | 17 | 0 | 0 | L | L | 6-1 | 186 | 7-15-76 | 1995 | Caracas, Venez. |
| Mejia, Juan | .181 | 25 | 72 | 9 | 13 | 4 | 0 | 0 | 5 | 6 | 19 | 4 | 0 | R | R | 6-0 | 150 | 11-22-75 | 1994 | San Pedro de Macoris, D.R. |
| Nichols, Kevin | .253 | 42 | 158 | 21 | 40 | 8 | 0 | 4 | 26 | 6 | 23 | 1 | 1 | R | R | 6-0 | 195 | 4-16-73 | 1996 | Southport, Fla. |
| Rollins, Jimmy | .238 | 49 | 172 | 22 | 41 | 3 | 1 | 1 | 16 | 28 | 20 | 11 | 5 | S | R | 5-9 | 165 | 11-27-78 | 1996 | Alameda, Calif. |
| Schlicher, B.J. | .225 | 54 | 187 | 23 | 42 | 7 | 0 | 4 | 16 | 23 | 63 | 1 | 1 | R | R | 6-4 | 210 | 11-7-77 | 1996 | Crawfordsville, Ind. |
| Serafin, Ricardo | .184 | 34 | 98 | 11 | 18 | 2 | 1 | 0 | 6 | 10 | 28 | 11 | 4 | R | R | 6-0 | 160 | 2-20-77 | 1994 | San Pedro de Macoris, D.R. |
| Thompson, Nick | .234 | 39 | 124 | 15 | 29 | 3 | 0 | 1 | 8 | 12 | 18 | 5 | 1 | R | R | 6-0 | 170 | 8-23-74 | 1996 | Dunwoody, Ga. |
| Van Iten, Bob | .239 | 33 | 113 | 9 | 27 | 4 | 0 | 1 | 9 | 4 | 21 | 0 | 1 | L | R | 6-2 | 170 | 7-1-77 | 1996 | Independence, Mo. |
| Worthy, Thomas | .303 | 31 | 76 | 9 | 23 | 3 | 0 | 0 | 7 | 6 | 13 | 4 | 2 | R | R | 5-11 | 165 | 1-21-77 | 1996 | Attalla, Ala. |

GAMES BY POSITION: C—Buczkowski 1, Livingston 4, Thompson 39, Van Iten 30. 1B—Mata 10, Nichols 20, Schlicher 41. 2B—Edwards 47, Jenkins 17, Mejia 5. 3B—Buczkowski 29, Edwards 6, Jenkins 10, Mejia 3, Nichols 19. SS—Jenkins 7, Mejia 13, Rollins 49. OF—Buckles 20, Ferguson 33, Ferrand 48, Jenkins 6, Johnson 53, Serafin 33, Worthy 23.

| PITCHING | W | L | ERA | G | GS | CG | SV | IP | H | R | ER | BB | SO | B | T | HT | WT | DOB | 1st Yr | Resides |
|---|---|---|---|---|---|---|---|---|---|---|---|---|---|---|---|---|---|---|---|---|
| Aguiar, Doug | 1 | 2 | 6.56 | 15 | 2 | 0 | 1 | 36 | 40 | 32 | 26 | 20 | 42 | R | R | 6-0 | 160 | 2-20-77 | 1995 | Zulia, Venez |
| Arias, Jose | 0 | 0 | 10.97 | 5 | 0 | 0 | 0 | 11 | 21 | 21 | 13 | 10 | 6 | R | R | 6-1 | 180 | 2-11-74 | 1994 | Santo Domingo, D.R. |
| Bishop, Terry | 1 | 8 | 8.59 | 13 | 11 | 0 | 0 | 51 | 82 | 55 | 49 | 33 | 48 | L | L | 6-4 | 210 | 11-15-74 | 1996 | Pittsfield, Mass. |
| Fenus, Justin | 2 | 7 | 6.04 | 14 | 8 | 0 | 0 | 45 | 46 | 33 | 30 | 24 | 26 | R | R | 6-3 | 195 | 5-19-75 | 1996 | Mountain View, Wyom. |
| Mejia, Javier | 2 | 2 | 2.80 | 29 | 0 | 0 | 12 | 35 | 29 | 15 | 11 | 15 | 50 | R | R | 5-11 | 180 | 11-26-78 | 1996 | Azua, D.R. |
| Molta, Salvatore | 1 | 9 | 8.31 | 12 | 12 | 0 | 0 | 43 | 45 | 46 | 40 | 39 | 37 | R | R | 6-2 | 195 | 10-28-77 | 1996 | Wallington, N.J. |
| Montero, Francisco | 0 | 2 | 6.46 | 21 | 0 | 0 | 0 | 39 | 58 | 38 | 28 | 18 | 28 | R | R | 6-2 | 170 | 1-6-76 | 1996 | Barahona, D.R. |
| Mosquea, Alberto | 2 | 1 | 5.53 | 14 | 0 | 0 | 0 | 28 | 25 | 28 | 17 | 22 | 18 | R | R | 6-1 | 151 | 9-4-75 | 1994 | Santo Domingo, D.R. |
| Portillo, Ramon | 4 | 2 | 6.00 | 21 | 0 | 0 | 1 | 45 | 52 | 34 | 30 | 29 | 34 | L | L | 5-11 | 165 | 5-10-78 | 1996 | Carabobo, Venez. |
| Quintana, Urbano | 3 | 5 | 4.09 | 15 | 12 | 0 | 0 | 77 | 71 | 44 | 35 | 27 | 38 | R | R | 6-0 | 160 | 2-9-75 | 1993 | Esperanza Mao, D.R. |
| Shockley, Keith | 2 | 2 | 8.00 | 14 | 6 | 1 | 0 | 45 | 62 | 44 | 40 | 10 | 29 | R | L | 6-4 | 190 | 10-25-76 | 1996 | Wichita, Kan. |
| Silva, Carlos | 0 | 4 | 4.00 | 7 | 1 | 0 | 0 | 18 | 20 | 11 | 8 | 5 | 16 | R | R | 6-4 | 198 | 4-23-79 | 1996 | Guayana, Venez. |
| Stevens, Kris | 1 | 4 | 3.64 | 10 | 10 | 0 | 0 | 47 | 54 | 23 | 19 | 10 | 41 | R | L | 6-2 | 188 | 9-19-77 | 1996 | Fontana, Calif. |
| Tober, Dave | 1 | 0 | 2.30 | 9 | 1 | 0 | 0 | 16 | 12 | 6 | 4 | 6 | 15 | R | R | 5-9 | 175 | 5-11-74 | 1996 | Warwick, R.I. |
| Walton, Tim | 0 | 3 | 5.23 | 4 | 4 | 1 | 0 | 21 | 27 | 19 | 12 | 8 | 20 | R | R | 6-0 | 197 | 8-6-72 | 1996 | Cerritos, Calif. |

# PITTSBURGH
## PIRATES

**Manager:** Jim Leyland.  **1996 Record:** 73-89, .451 (5th, NL Central).

| BATTING | AVG | G | AB | R | H | 2B | 3B | HR | RBI | BB | SO | SB | CS | B | T | HT | WT | DOB | 1st Yr | Resides |
|---|---|---|---|---|---|---|---|---|---|---|---|---|---|---|---|---|---|---|---|---|
| Allensworth, Jermaine . . | .262 | 61 | 229 | 32 | 60 | 9 | 3 | 4 | 31 | 23 | 50 | 11 | 6 | R | R | 5-11 | 180 | 1-11-72 | 1993 | Anderson, Ind. |
| Aude, Rich | .250 | 7 | 16 | 0 | 4 | 0 | 0 | 0 | 1 | 0 | 8 | 0 | 0 | R | R | 6-5 | 220 | 7-13-71 | 1989 | Chatsworth, Calif. |
| Beamon, Trey | .216 | 24 | 51 | 7 | 11 | 2 | 0 | 0 | 6 | 4 | 6 | 1 | 1 | L | R | 6-3 | 195 | 2-11-74 | 1992 | Dallas, Texas |
| Bell, Jay | .250 | 151 | 527 | 65 | 132 | 29 | 3 | 13 | 71 | 54 | 108 | 6 | 4 | R | R | 6-1 | 175 | 12-11-65 | 1984 | Valrico, Fla. |
| Brumfield, Jacob | .250 | 29 | 80 | 11 | 20 | 9 | 0 | 2 | 8 | 5 | 17 | 3 | 1 | R | R | 6-0 | 180 | 5-27-65 | 1983 | Atlanta, Ga. |
| Clark, Dave | .275 | 92 | 211 | 28 | 58 | 12 | 2 | 8 | 35 | 31 | 51 | 2 | 1 | L | R | 6-2 | 210 | 9-3-62 | 1983 | Tupelo, Miss. |
| Cummings, Midre | .224 | 24 | 85 | 11 | 19 | 3 | 1 | 3 | 7 | 0 | 16 | 0 | 0 | L | R | 6-0 | 196 | 10-14-71 | 1990 | St. Croix, V.I. |
| Encarnacion, Angelo | .318 | 7 | 22 | 3 | 7 | 2 | 0 | 0 | 1 | 0 | 5 | 0 | 0 | R | R | 5-8 | 180 | 4-18-73 | 1990 | Santo Domingo, D.R. |
| Garcia, Carlos | .285 | 101 | 390 | 66 | 111 | 18 | 4 | 6 | 44 | 23 | 58 | 16 | 6 | R | R | 6-1 | 193 | 10-15-67 | 1987 | Lancaster, N.Y. |
| Hayes, Charlie | .248 | 128 | 459 | 51 | 114 | 21 | 2 | 10 | 62 | 36 | 78 | 6 | 0 | R | R | 6-0 | 224 | 5-29-65 | 1983 | Hattiesburg, Miss. |
| Johnson, Mark | .274 | 127 | 343 | 55 | 94 | 24 | 0 | 13 | 47 | 44 | 64 | 6 | 4 | L | L | 6-4 | 220 | 10-17-67 | 1990 | Worcester, Mass. |
| Kendall, Jason | .300 | 130 | 414 | 54 | 124 | 23 | 5 | 3 | 42 | 35 | 30 | 5 | 2 | R | R | 6-0 | 170 | 6-26-74 | 1992 | Torrance, Calif. |
| King, Jeff | .271 | 155 | 591 | 91 | 160 | 36 | 4 | 30 | 111 | 70 | 95 | 15 | 1 | R | R | 6-1 | 180 | 12-26-64 | 1986 | Wexford, Pa. |
| Kingery, Mike | .246 | 117 | 276 | 32 | 68 | 12 | 2 | 3 | 27 | 23 | 29 | 2 | 1 | L | L | 6-0 | 185 | 3-29-61 | 1980 | Atwater, Minn. |
| Liriano, Nelson | .267 | 112 | 217 | 23 | 58 | 14 | 2 | 3 | 30 | 14 | 22 | 2 | 0 | S | R | 5-10 | 178 | 6-3-64 | 1983 | Puerta Plata, D.R. |
| Martin, Al | .300 | 155 | 630 | 101 | 189 | 40 | 1 | 18 | 72 | 54 | 116 | 38 | 12 | L | L | 6-2 | 210 | 11-24-67 | 1985 | Scottsdale, Ariz. |
| Merced, Orlando | .287 | 120 | 453 | 69 | 130 | 24 | 1 | 17 | 80 | 51 | 74 | 8 | 4 | L | R | 5-11 | 170 | 11-2-66 | 1985 | Ocala, Fla. |
| Osik, Keith | .293 | 48 | 140 | 18 | 41 | 14 | 1 | 1 | 14 | 14 | 22 | 1 | 0 | R | R | 6-0 | 195 | 10-22-68 | 1990 | Rocky Point, N.Y. |
| Sveum, Dale | .353 | 12 | 34 | 9 | 12 | 5 | 0 | 1 | 5 | 6 | 6 | 0 | 0 | S | R | 6-3 | 185 | 11-23-63 | 1982 | Glendale, Ariz. |
| Wehner, John | .259 | 86 | 139 | 19 | 36 | 9 | 1 | 2 | 13 | 8 | 22 | 1 | 5 | R | R | 6-3 | 205 | 6-29-67 | 1988 | Pittsburgh, Pa. |
| Womack, Tony | .333 | 17 | 30 | 11 | 10 | 3 | 1 | 0 | 7 | 6 | 1 | 2 | 0 | L | R | 5-9 | 153 | 9-25-69 | 1991 | Chatham, Va. |

| PITCHING | W | L | ERA | G | GS | CG | SV | IP | H | R | ER | BB | SO | B | T | HT | WT | DOB | 1st Yr | Resides |
|---|---|---|---|---|---|---|---|---|---|---|---|---|---|---|---|---|---|---|---|---|
| Boever, Joe | 0 | 2 | 5.40 | 13 | 0 | 0 | 2 | 15 | 17 | 11 | 9 | 6 | 6 | R | R | 6-1 | 200 | 10-4-60 | 1982 | Palm Harbor, Fla. |
| Christiansen, Jason | 3 | 3 | 6.70 | 33 | 0 | 0 | 0 | 44 | 56 | 34 | 33 | 19 | 38 | R | L | 6-5 | 235 | 9-21-69 | 1991 | Elkhorn, Neb. |
| Cooke, Steve | 0 | 0 | 7.56 | 3 | 0 | 0 | 0 | 8 | 11 | 7 | 7 | 5 | 7 | R | L | 6-6 | 220 | 1-14-70 | 1990 | Tigard, Ore. |
| Cordova, Francisco | 4 | 7 | 4.09 | 59 | 6 | 0 | 12 | 99 | 103 | 49 | 45 | 20 | 95 | R | R | 5-11 | 163 | 4-26-72 | 1992 | Veracruz, Mexico |
| Darwin, Danny | 7 | 9 | 3.02 | 19 | 19 | 0 | 0 | 122 | 117 | 48 | 41 | 16 | 69 | R | R | 6-3 | 202 | 10-25-55 | 1976 | Valley View, Texas |
| Dessens, Elmer | 0 | 2 | 8.28 | 15 | 3 | 0 | 0 | 25 | 40 | 23 | 23 | 4 | 13 | R | R | 6-0 | 190 | 1-13-72 | 1993 | Hermosillo, Mexico |
| Ericks, John | 4 | 5 | 5.79 | 28 | 4 | 0 | 8 | 47 | 56 | 35 | 30 | 19 | 46 | R | R | 6-7 | 220 | 9-16-67 | 1988 | Tinley Park, Ill. |
| Hancock, Lee | 0 | 0 | 6.38 | 13 | 0 | 0 | 0 | 18 | 21 | 18 | 13 | 10 | 13 | L | L | 6-4 | 215 | 6-27-67 | 1988 | Saratoga, Calif. |
| Hope, John | 1 | 3 | 6.98 | 5 | 4 | 0 | 0 | 19 | 17 | 18 | 15 | 11 | 13 | R | R | 6-3 | 206 | 12-21-70 | 1989 | Fort Lauderdale, Fla. |
| Lieber, Jon | 9 | 5 | 3.99 | 51 | 15 | 0 | 1 | 142 | 156 | 70 | 63 | 28 | 94 | L | R | 6-3 | 205 | 4-2-70 | 1992 | Council Bluffs, Iowa |
| Loaiza, Esteban | 2 | 3 | 4.96 | 10 | 10 | 1 | 0 | 53 | 65 | 32 | 29 | 19 | 32 | R | R | 6-2 | 172 | 12-31-71 | 1991 | Imperial Beach, Calif. |
| Loiselle, Rich | 1 | 0 | 3.05 | 5 | 3 | 0 | 0 | 21 | 22 | 8 | 7 | 8 | 9 | R | R | 6-5 | 225 | 1-12-72 | 1991 | Oshkosh, Wis. |
| May, Darrell | 0 | 1 | 9.35 | 5 | 2 | 0 | 0 | 9 | 15 | 10 | 9 | 4 | 5 | L | L | 6-2 | 170 | 6-13-72 | 1992 | Rogue River, Ore. |
| Miceli, Danny | 2 | 10 | 5.78 | 44 | 9 | 0 | 1 | 86 | 99 | 65 | 55 | 45 | 66 | R | R | 5-11 | 205 | 9-9-70 | 1990 | Orlando, Fla. |
| Morel, Ramon | 2 | 1 | 5.36 | 29 | 0 | 0 | 0 | 42 | 57 | 27 | 25 | 19 | 22 | R | R | 6-2 | 170 | 8-15-74 | 1991 | Villa Gonzalez, D.R. |
| Neagle, Denny | 14 | 6 | 3.05 | 27 | 27 | 1 | 0 | 183 | 186 | 67 | 62 | 34 | 131 | L | L | 6-2 | 215 | 9-13-68 | 1989 | Gambrills, Md. |
| Parris, Steve | 0 | 3 | 7.18 | 8 | 4 | 0 | 0 | 26 | 35 | 22 | 21 | 11 | 27 | R | R | 6-0 | 190 | 12-17-67 | 1988 | Joliet, Ill. |
| Peters, Chris | 2 | 4 | 5.63 | 16 | 10 | 0 | 0 | 64 | 72 | 43 | 40 | 25 | 28 | L | L | 6-1 | 170 | 1-28-72 | 1993 | McMurray, Pa. |
| Plesac, Dan | 6 | 5 | 4.09 | 73 | 0 | 0 | 11 | 70 | 67 | 35 | 32 | 24 | 76 | L | L | 6-5 | 215 | 2-4-62 | 1983 | Hales Corners, Wis. |
| Ruebel, Matt | 1 | 1 | 4.60 | 26 | 7 | 0 | 1 | 59 | 64 | 38 | 30 | 25 | 22 | L | L | 6-2 | 180 | 10-16-69 | 1991 | Ames, Iowa |
| Schmidt, Jason | 2 | 2 | 4.06 | 6 | 6 | 1 | 0 | 38 | 39 | 19 | 17 | 21 | 26 | R | R | 6-5 | 185 | 1-29-73 | 1991 | Kelso, Wash. |
| 2-team (13 Atlanta) | 5 | 5 | 5.70 | 19 | 17 | 1 | 0 | 96 | 108 | 67 | 61 | 53 | 74 | | | | | | | |
| Smith, Zane | 4 | 6 | 5.08 | 16 | 16 | 1 | 0 | 83 | 104 | 53 | 47 | 21 | 47 | L | L | 6-1 | 207 | 12-28-60 | 1982 | Stone Mountain, Ga. |
| Wagner, Paul | 4 | 8 | 5.40 | 16 | 15 | 1 | 0 | 82 | 86 | 49 | 49 | 39 | 81 | R | R | 6-1 | 202 | 11-14-67 | 1989 | Germantown, Wis. |
| Wainhouse, Dave | 1 | 0 | 5.70 | 17 | 0 | 0 | 0 | 24 | 22 | 16 | 15 | 10 | 16 | L | R | 6-2 | 185 | 11-7-67 | 1989 | Mercer Island, Wash. |
| Wilkins, Marc | 4 | 3 | 3.84 | 47 | 2 | 0 | 1 | 75 | 75 | 36 | 32 | 36 | 62 | R | R | 5-11 | 215 | 10-21-70 | 1992 | Mansfield, Ohio |

## FIELDING

| Catcher | PCT | G | PO | A | E | DP | PB |
|---|---|---|---|---|---|---|---|
| Encarnacion | .951 | 7 | 35 | 4 | 2 | 0 | 1 |
| Kendall | .980 | 129 | 797 | 71 | 18 | 10 | 8 |
| Osik | .977 | 41 | 235 | 23 | 6 | 2 | 1 |
| Wehner | 1.000 | 1 | 1 | 0 | 0 | 0 | 0 |

| First Base | PCT | G | PO | A | E | DP |
|---|---|---|---|---|---|---|
| Aude | .969 | 4 | 28 | 3 | 1 | 3 |
| Johnson | .994 | 100 | 777 | 72 | 5 | 64 |
| King | .997 | 92 | 745 | 47 | 2 | 60 |
| Merced | 1.000 | 1 | 1 | 0 | 1 | 1 |

| Second Base | PCT | G | PO | A | E | DP |
|---|---|---|---|---|---|---|
| Garcia | .985 | 77 | 131 | 199 | 5 | 35 |
| King | .979 | 71 | 145 | 181 | 7 | 40 |
| Liriano | .984 | 36 | 50 | 73 | 2 | 13 |

| | PCT | G | PO | A | E | DP |
|---|---|---|---|---|---|---|
| Wehner | .974 | 12 | 19 | 18 | 1 | 3 |
| Womack | .875 | 4 | 6 | 8 | 2 | 0 |
| **Third Base** | **PCT** | **G** | **PO** | **A** | **E** | **DP** |
| Garcia | .930 | 14 | 4 | 36 | 3 | 4 |
| Hayes | .950 | 124 | 66 | 275 | 18 | 24 |
| King | .938 | 17 | 6 | 24 | 2 | 1 |
| Liriano | 1.000 | 9 | 4 | 17 | 0 | 0 |
| Osik | 1.000 | 2 | 1 | 2 | 0 | 1 |
| Sveum | .913 | 10 | 4 | 17 | 2 | 1 |
| Wehner | 1.000 | 24 | 8 | 24 | 0 | 3 |

| Shortstop | PCT | G | PO | A | E | DP |
|---|---|---|---|---|---|---|
| Bell | .986 | 151 | 215 | 478 | 10 | 78 |
| Garcia | .961 | 19 | 25 | 49 | 3 | 13 |

| | PCT | G | PO | A | E | DP |
|---|---|---|---|---|---|---|
| Liriano | .923 | 5 | 4 | 8 | 1 | 2 |
| **Outfield** | **PCT** | **G** | **PO** | **A** | **E** | **DP** |
| Allensworth | .979 | 61 | 139 | 4 | 3 | 1 |
| Beamon | .960 | 14 | 24 | 0 | 1 | 0 |
| Brumfield | .946 | 22 | 34 | 1 | 2 | 1 |
| Clark | .988 | 61 | 80 | 3 | 1 | 1 |
| Cummings | .980 | 21 | 49 | 0 | 1 | 0 |
| Johnson | .667 | 1 | 1 | 1 | 1 | 0 |
| Kingery | .985 | 83 | 133 | 2 | 2 | 0 |
| Martin | .965 | 152 | 217 | 5 | 8 | 0 |
| Merced | .988 | 115 | 241 | 14 | 3 | 5 |
| Osik | 1.000 | 2 | 1 | 0 | 0 | 0 |
| Wehner | .971 | 29 | 32 | 1 | 1 | 0 |
| Womack | 1.000 | 6 | 5 | 0 | 0 | 0 |

MORRIS FOSTOFF

**Al Martin led the Pirates with a .300 average and 101 runs scored**

Pirates minor league Player of the Year Jose Guillen

JEFF GOLDEN

## FARM SYSTEM

**Director of Player Personnel:** Pete Vuckovich

| Class | Farm Team | League | W | L | Pct. | Finish* | Manager | First Yr |
|-------|-----------|--------|---|---|------|---------|---------|----------|
| AAA | Calgary (Alberta) Cannons | Pacific Coast | 74 | 68 | .521 | 4th (10) | Trent Jewett | 1995 |
| AA | Carolina (N.C.) Mudcats | Southern | 70 | 69 | .504 | 6th (10) | Marc Hill | 1991 |
| #A | Lynchburg (Va.) Hillcats | Carolina | 65 | 74 | .468 | 6th (8) | Jeff Banister | 1995 |
| A | Augusta (Ga.) GreenJackets | South Atlantic | 71 | 70 | .504 | 8th (14) | Jay Loviglio | 1988 |
| A | Erie (Pa.) Seawolves | New York-Penn | 30 | 46 | .395 | 14th (14) | Jeff Richardson | 1995 |
| R | Bradenton (Fla.) Pirates | Gulf Coast | 28 | 31 | .475 | 11th (16) | Woody Huyke | 1967 |

*Finish in overall standings (No. of teams in league)   #Advanced level

## ORGANIZATION LEADERS

### MAJOR LEAGUERS

**BATTING**

| | | |
|---|---|---|
| *AVG | Al Martin | .300 |
| R | Al Martin | 101 |
| H | Al Martin | 189 |
| TB | Jeff King | 294 |
| 2B | Al Martin | 40 |
| 3B | Jason Kendall | 5 |
| HR | Jeff King | 30 |
| RBI | Jeff King | 111 |
| BB | Jeff King | 70 |
| SO | Al Martin | 116 |
| SB | Al Martin | 38 |

**PITCHING**

| | | |
|---|---|---|
| W | Denny Neagle | 14 |
| L | Dan Miceli | 10 |
| #ERA | Denny Neagle | 3.05 |
| G | Dan Plesac | 73 |
| CG | Five tied at | 1 |
| SV | Francisco Cordova | 12 |
| IP | Denny Neagle | 183 |
| BB | Danny Miceli | 45 |
| SO | Denny Neagle | 131 |

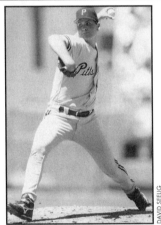

DAVID SEELIG

**Denny Neagle.** 14 wins

### MINOR LEAGUERS

**BATTING**

| | | |
|---|---|---|
| *AVG | Jermaine Allensworth, Calgary | .330 |
| R | Adrian Brown, Lynchburg/Carolina | 87 |
| H | Jose Guillen, Lynchburg | 170 |
| TB | Jose Guillen, Lynchburg | 263 |
| 2B | Freddy Garcia, Lynchburg | 39 |
| 3B | Chance Sanford, Carolina | 13 |
| HR | Chad Hermansen, Augusta/Lynch. | 24 |
| RBI | Jose Guillen, Lynchburg | 94 |
| BB | Three tied at | 72 |
| SO | Chad Hermansen, Augusta/Lynch. | 121 |
| SB | Adrian Brown, Lynchburg/Carolina | 45 |

**PITCHING**

| | | |
|---|---|---|
| W | Elvin Hernandez, Augusta | 17 |
| L | Ryan Young, Augusta | 12 |
| #ERA | Joe Boever, Calgary/Carolina | 2.13 |
| G | Joe Maskivish, Augusta/Lynchburg | 62 |
| CG | Kevin Pickford, Lynchburg | 4 |
| SV | David Wainhouse, Calgary | 25 |
| IP | Kevin Pickford, Carolina | 172 |
| BB | Jimmy Anderson, Lynch./Carolina | 65 |
| SO | Elvin Hernandez, Augusta | 171 |

*Minimum 250 At-Bats   #Minimum 75 Innings

## TOP 10 PROSPECTS

**How the Pirates Top 10 prospects, as judged by Baseball America prior to the 1996 season, fared in 1996:**

GEORGE GOJKOVICH

**Jason Kendall**

| Player, Pos. | Club (Class—League) | AVG | AB | R | H | 2B | 3B | HR | RBI | SB |
|--------------|---------------------|-----|----|---|---|----|----|----|-----|----|
| 1. Jason Kendall, c | Pittsburgh | .300 | 414 | 54 | 124 | 23 | 5 | 3 | 42 | 5 |
| 2. Trey Beamon, of | Calgary (AAA—Pacific Coast) | .288 | 378 | 62 | 109 | 15 | 3 | 5 | 52 | 16 |
| | Pittsburgh | .216 | 51 | 7 | 11 | 2 | 0 | 0 | 6 | 1 |
| 3. Chad Hermansen, ss | Lynchburg (A—Carolina) | .275 | 251 | 40 | 69 | 11 | 3 | 10 | 46 | 5 |
| | Augusta (A—South Atlantic) | .252 | 226 | 41 | 57 | 11 | 3 | 14 | 41 | 11 |
| 4. Freddy Garcia, 3b | Lynchburg (A—Carolina) | .306 | 474 | 79 | 145 | 39 | 3 | 21 | 86 | 4 |
| 5. Charles Peterson, of | Carolina (AA—Southern) | .275 | 462 | 71 | 127 | 24 | 2 | 7 | 63 | 33 |
| 7. Jose Guillen, of | Lynchburg (A—Carolina) | .322 | 528 | 78 | 170 | 30 | 0 | 21 | 94 | 24 |
| 8. Lou Collier, ss | Carolina (AA—Southern) | .280 | 443 | 76 | 124 | 20 | 3 | 3 | 49 | 29 |

| | | W | L | ERA | G | SV | IP | H | BB | SO |
|---|---|---|---|-----|---|----|----|---|----|----|
| 6. Ramon Morel, rhp | Carolina (AA—Southern) | 2 | 5 | 5.09 | 11 | 0 | 64 | 75 | 16 | 44 |
| | Pittsburgh | 2 | 1 | 5.36 | 29 | 0 | 42 | 57 | 19 | 22 |
| 9. Kane Davis, rhp | Lynchburg (A—Carolina) | 11 | 9 | 4.29 | 26 | 0 | 157 | 160 | 56 | 116 |
| 10. Jimmy Anderson, lhp | Lynchburg (A—Carolina) | 5 | 3 | 1.93 | 11 | 0 | 65 | 51 | 21 | 56 |
| | Carolina (AA—Southern) | 8 | 3 | 3.34 | 17 | 0 | 97 | 92 | 44 | 79 |

**Home Run Kings.** Infielders Jeff King (30), left, and Chad Hermansen (24), led Pirates major leaguers and minor leaguers, respectively, in home runs. Hermansen, the Pirates' first-round draft pick in 1995, hit 24 at Class A Augusta and Lynchburg.

JIM McLEAN

## CALGARY — Class AAA

### PACIFIC COAST LEAGUE

| BATTING | AVG | G | AB | R | H | 2B | 3B | HR | RBI | BB | SO | SB | CS | B | T | HT | WT | DOB | 1st Yr | Resides |
|---|---|---|---|---|---|---|---|---|---|---|---|---|---|---|---|---|---|---|---|---|
| Allensworth, Jermaine | .330 | 95 | 352 | 77 | 116 | 23 | 6 | 8 | 43 | 39 | 61 | 25 | 5 | R | R | 5-11 | 180 | 1-11-72 | 1993 | Anderson, Ind. |
| Aude, Rich | .292 | 103 | 394 | 69 | 115 | 29 | 0 | 17 | 81 | 26 | 69 | 4 | 4 | R | R | 6-5 | 220 | 7-13-71 | 1989 | Chatsworth, Calif. |
| Beamon, Trey | .288 | 111 | 378 | 62 | 109 | 15 | 3 | 5 | 52 | 55 | 63 | 16 | 3 | L | R | 6-3 | 195 | 2-11-74 | 1992 | Dallas, Texas |
| Clark, Jerald | .266 | 75 | 248 | 33 | 66 | 20 | 1 | 8 | 45 | 12 | 43 | 0 | 1 | R | R | 6-4 | 202 | 8-10-63 | 1985 | Crockett, Texas |
| Cummings, Midre | .304 | 97 | 368 | 60 | 112 | 24 | 3 | 8 | 55 | 21 | 60 | 6 | 4 | L | R | 6-0 | 196 | 10-14-71 | 1990 | St. Croix, V.I. |
| Edge, Tim | .333 | 12 | 36 | 6 | 12 | 3 | 0 | 2 | 11 | 2 | 9 | 0 | 0 | R | R | 6-0 | 210 | 10-26-68 | 1990 | Snellville, Ga. |
| Encarnacion, Angelo | .319 | 75 | 263 | 38 | 84 | 18 | 0 | 4 | 31 | 10 | 19 | 6 | 2 | R | R | 5-8 | 180 | 4-18-73 | 1990 | Santo Domingo, D.R. |
| Espinosa, Ramon | .282 | 78 | 245 | 37 | 69 | 8 | 8 | 0 | 25 | 6 | 28 | 2 | 3 | R | R | 6-0 | 175 | 2-7-72 | 1990 | San Pedro de Macoris, D.R. |
| Felder, Mike | .284 | 21 | 81 | 14 | 23 | 3 | 0 | 1 | 5 | 3 | 8 | 0 | 0 | S | R | 5-9 | 175 | 11-18-62 | 1981 | Richmond, Calif. |
| Finn, John | .255 | 69 | 192 | 24 | 49 | 13 | 1 | 0 | 32 | 25 | 28 | 2 | 5 | R | R | 5-8 | 168 | 10-18-67 | 1989 | Oakland, Calif. |
| Garcia, Carlos | .333 | 2 | 6 | 0 | 2 | 0 | 1 | 0 | 0 | 0 | 0 | 0 | 0 | R | R | 6-1 | 193 | 10-15-67 | 1987 | Lancaster, N.Y. |
| Marx, Tim | .324 | 95 | 296 | 50 | 96 | 20 | 1 | 1 | 37 | 29 | 50 | 6 | 2 | R | R | 6-2 | 190 | 11-27-68 | 1991 | Evansville, Ind. |
| Millette, Joe | .213 | 53 | 108 | 7 | 23 | 8 | 0 | 0 | 7 | 9 | 19 | 0 | 2 | R | R | 6-1 | 175 | 8-12-66 | 1989 | Lafayette, Calif. |
| Polcovich, Kevin | .274 | 104 | 336 | 53 | 92 | 21 | 3 | 1 | 46 | 18 | 49 | 7 | 6 | R | R | 5-9 | 165 | 6-28-70 | 1992 | Auburn, N.Y. |
| Ratliff, Darryl | .336 | 38 | 131 | 19 | 44 | 3 | 0 | 0 | 12 | 11 | 19 | 4 | 1 | R | R | 6-1 | 180 | 10-15-69 | 1989 | Santa Cruz, Calif. |
| Secrist, Reed | .307 | 128 | 420 | 68 | 129 | 30 | 0 | 17 | 66 | 52 | 105 | 2 | 4 | L | R | 6-1 | 205 | 5-7-70 | 1992 | Farmington, Utah |
| Sveum, Dale | .300 | 101 | 343 | 62 | 103 | 28 | 2 | 23 | 84 | 33 | 71 | 2 | 1 | S | R | 6-3 | 185 | 11-23-63 | 1982 | Glendale, Ariz. |
| Womack, Tony | .300 | 131 | 506 | 75 | 152 | 19 | 11 | 1 | 47 | 31 | 79 | 37 | 12 | L | R | 5-9 | 153 | 9-25-69 | 1991 | Chatham, Va. |

| PITCHING | W | L | ERA | G | GS | CG | SV | IP | H | R | ER | BB | SO | B | T | HT | WT | DOB | 1st Yr | Resides |
|---|---|---|---|---|---|---|---|---|---|---|---|---|---|---|---|---|---|---|---|---|
| Agosto, Juan | 2 | 3 | 3.67 | 24 | 0 | 0 | 0 | 27 | 28 | 16 | 11 | 12 | 10 | L | L | 6-2 | 190 | 2-23-58 | 1975 | Sarasota, Fla. |
| Backlund, Brett | 3 | 2 | 6.00 | 7 | 7 | 0 | 0 | 39 | 47 | 26 | 26 | 16 | 16 | R | R | 6-0 | 195 | 12-16-69 | 1992 | Salem, Ore. |
| Boever, Joe | 12 | 1 | 2.15 | 44 | 0 | 0 | 4 | 84 | 78 | 24 | 20 | 19 | 66 | R | R | 6-1 | 200 | 10-4-60 | 1982 | Palm Harbor, Fla. |
| Bolton, Tom | 12 | 5 | 4.02 | 40 | 14 | 0 | 2 | 116 | 121 | 64 | 52 | 47 | 92 | L | L | 6-3 | 185 | 5-6-62 | 1980 | Smyrna, Tenn. |
| Cadaret, Greg | 0 | 3 | 6.57 | 9 | 0 | 0 | 0 | 12 | 19 | 18 | 9 | 12 | 10 | L | L | 6-3 | 215 | 2-27-62 | 1983 | Mesa, Ariz. |
| Christiansen, Jason | 1 | 0 | 3.27 | 2 | 2 | 0 | 0 | 11 | 9 | 4 | 4 | 1 | 10 | R | L | 6-5 | 235 | 9-21-69 | 1991 | Elkhorn, Neb. |
| Dessens, Elmer | 2 | 2 | 3.15 | 6 | 6 | 0 | 0 | 34 | 40 | 14 | 12 | 15 | 15 | R | R | 6-0 | 180 | 1-13-72 | 1993 | Hermosillo, Mexico |
| Ericks, John | 1 | 2 | 4.20 | 14 | 4 | 0 | 1 | 30 | 31 | 15 | 14 | 15 | 40 | R | R | 6-7 | 220 | 9-16-67 | 1988 | Tinley Park, Ill. |
| Greer, Ken | 5 | 4 | 3.97 | 46 | 1 | 0 | 3 | 68 | 74 | 34 | 30 | 17 | 36 | R | R | 6-2 | 215 | 5-12-67 | 1988 | Hull, Mass. |
| Hancock, Lee | 0 | 0 | 1.80 | 9 | 1 | 0 | 0 | 15 | 9 | 3 | 3 | 5 | 9 | L | L | 6-4 | 215 | 6-27-67 | 1988 | Saratoga, Calif. |
| Hope, John | 4 | 7 | 4.82 | 23 | 21 | 0 | 0 | 125 | 147 | 74 | 67 | 49 | 71 | R | R | 6-3 | 206 | 12-21-70 | 1989 | Fort Lauderdale, Fla. |
| Konuszewski, Dennis | 0 | 0 | 24.30 | 1 | 0 | 0 | 0 | 3 | 13 | 11 | 9 | 5 | 0 | R | R | 6-3 | 210 | 2-4-71 | 1992 | Bridgeport, Mich. |
| Loaiza, Esteban | 3 | 4 | 4.02 | 12 | 11 | 1 | 0 | 69 | 61 | 34 | 31 | 25 | 38 | R | R | 6-2 | 172 | 12-31-71 | 1991 | Imperial Beach, Calif. |
| Loiselle, Rich | 2 | 2 | 4.09 | 8 | 8 | 0 | 0 | 51 | 64 | 28 | 23 | 16 | 41 | R | R | 6-5 | 225 | 1-12-72 | 1991 | Oshkosh, Wis. |
| 2-team (5 Tucson) | 4 | 4 | 3.43 | 13 | 13 | 1 | 0 | 84 | 92 | 48 | 32 | 27 | 72 | | | | | | | |
| May, Darrell | 7 | 6 | 4.10 | 23 | 22 | 1 | 0 | 132 | 146 | 64 | 60 | 36 | 75 | L | L | 6-2 | 170 | 6-13-72 | 1992 | Rogue River, Ore. |
| Peters, Chris | 1 | 1 | 0.98 | 4 | 4 | 0 | 0 | 28 | 18 | 3 | 3 | 8 | 16 | L | L | 6-1 | 170 | 1-28-72 | 1993 | McMurray, Pa. |
| Phoenix, Steve | 1 | 1 | 1.69 | 10 | 1 | 0 | 0 | 16 | 16 | 8 | 3 | 5 | 9 | R | R | 6-3 | 183 | 1-31-68 | 1990 | El Cajon, Calif. |
| Pisciotta, Marc | 2 | 7 | 4.11 | 57 | 0 | 0 | 1 | 66 | 71 | 38 | 30 | 46 | 46 | R | R | 6-5 | 240 | 8-7-70 | 1991 | Charlotte, N.C. |
| Ruebel, Matt | 5 | 3 | 4.60 | 13 | 13 | 1 | 0 | 76 | 89 | 43 | 39 | 28 | 48 | L | L | 6-2 | 180 | 10-16-69 | 1991 | Ames, Iowa |
| Ryan, Matt | 2 | 6 | 5.30 | 51 | 0 | 0 | 20 | 53 | 70 | 39 | 31 | 28 | 35 | R | R | 6-5 | 190 | 3-20-72 | 1993 | Memphis, Tenn. |
| Rychel, Kevin | 2 | 0 | 8.18 | 11 | 0 | 0 | 0 | 11 | 15 | 11 | 10 | 8 | 5 | R | R | 5-9 | 176 | 9-24-71 | 1989 | Midland, Texas |
| Shouse, Brian | 1 | 0 | 10.66 | 12 | 1 | 0 | 0 | 13 | 22 | 15 | 15 | 4 | 12 | L | L | 5-11 | 180 | 9-26-68 | 1990 | Effingham, Ill. |
| Wilson, Gary | 6 | 9 | 5.08 | 27 | 27 | 1 | 0 | 161 | 209 | 105 | 91 | 44 | 88 | R | R | 6-3 | 180 | 1-1-70 | 1992 | Arcata, Calif. |

## FIELDING (top)

| Catcher | PCT | G | PO | A | E | DP | PB |
|---|---|---|---|---|---|---|---|
| Edge ............. | .981 | 11 | 46 | 7 | 1 | 0 | 1 |
| Encarnacion ... | .990 | 63 | 314 | 63 | 4 | 7 | 3 |
| Marx .............. | .994 | 76 | 464 | 51 | 3 | 10 | 6 |
| Secrist ........... | .000 | 1 | 0 | 0 | 0 | 0 | 0 |

| First Base | PCT | G | PO | A | E | DP |
|---|---|---|---|---|---|---|
| Aude .............. | .991 | 97 | 872 | 52 | 8 | 75 |
| Marx .............. | 1.000 | 7 | 20 | 1 | 0 | 2 |
| Secrist ........... | .993 | 30 | 271 | 16 | 2 | 26 |
| Sveum ........... | .994 | 28 | 150 | 10 | 1 | 6 |

| Second Base | PCT | G | PO | A | E | DP |
|---|---|---|---|---|---|---|
| Finn ............... | .987 | 50 | 85 | 139 | 3 | 27 |
| Garcia ........... | 1.000 | 1 | 2 | 2 | 0 | 1 |
| Millette .......... | .920 | 15 | 22 | 24 | 4 | 4 |

| | PCT | G | PO | A | E | DP |
|---|---|---|---|---|---|---|
| Polcovich ........ | .993 | 37 | 56 | 88 | 1 | 16 |
| Sveum ........... | .976 | 28 | 49 | 75 | 3 | 14 |
| Womack .......... | .968 | 40 | 88 | 93 | 6 | 23 |

| Third Base | PCT | G | PO | A | E | DP |
|---|---|---|---|---|---|---|
| Finn ............... | .935 | 16 | 9 | 20 | 2 | 2 |
| Millette .......... | .907 | 19 | 10 | 29 | 4 | 0 |
| Secrist ........... | .910 | 89 | 43 | 169 | 21 | 16 |
| Sveum ........... | .963 | 41 | 27 | 76 | 4 | 9 |

| Shortstop | PCT | G | PO | A | E | DP |
|---|---|---|---|---|---|---|
| Finn ............... | .938 | 2 | 4 | 11 | 1 | 4 |
| Garcia ........... | 1.000 | 1 | 1 | 3 | 0 | 0 |
| Millette .......... | 1.000 | 2 | 0 | 1 | 0 | 0 |
| Polcovich ........ | .948 | 70 | 109 | 204 | 17 | 28 |

| | PCT | G | PO | A | E | DP |
|---|---|---|---|---|---|---|
| Womack .......... | .952 | 79 | 138 | 241 | 19 | 50 |

| Outfield | PCT | G | PO | A | E | DP |
|---|---|---|---|---|---|---|
| Allensworth .... | .971 | 88 | 196 | 4 | 6 | 0 |
| Beamon ......... | .928 | 99 | 161 | 7 | 13 | 0 |
| Clark ............. | .937 | 56 | 99 | 5 | 7 | 1 |
| Cummings ...... | .974 | 80 | 176 | 9 | 5 | 1 |
| Espinosa ........ | .969 | 67 | 114 | 9 | 4 | 1 |
| Felder ............ | .970 | 20 | 30 | 2 | 1 | 0 |
| Millette .......... | .000 | 1 | 0 | 0 | 0 | 0 |
| Ratliff ............ | .955 | 33 | 61 | 3 | 3 | 2 |
| Secrist ........... | 1.000 | 1 | 4 | 0 | 0 | 0 |
| Womack .......... | 1.000 | 16 | 32 | 1 | 0 | 1 |

# CAROLINA                                    Class AA
## SOUTHERN LEAGUE

### BATTING

| BATTING | AVG | G | AB | R | H | 2B | 3B | HR | RBI | BB | SO | SB | CS | B | T | HT | WT | DOB | 1st Yr | Resides |
|---|---|---|---|---|---|---|---|---|---|---|---|---|---|---|---|---|---|---|---|---|
| Beasley, Tony ............. | .312 | 96 | 269 | 40 | 84 | 17 | 5 | 4 | 30 | 30 | 33 | 10 | 9 | R | R | 5-8 | 165 | 12-5-66 | 1989 | Bowling Green, Va. |
| Bonifay, Ken ................ | .243 | 95 | 272 | 33 | 66 | 18 | 2 | 6 | 42 | 41 | 68 | 4 | 3 | L | R | 6-1 | 185 | 9-1-70 | 1991 | Kingsport, Tenn. |
| Boston, D.J. ................ | .280 | 93 | 321 | 47 | 90 | 16 | 4 | 8 | 48 | 49 | 61 | 5 | 3 | L | L | 6-7 | 230 | 9-6-71 | 1991 | Cincinnati, Ohio |
| Brown, Adrian .............. | .296 | 84 | 341 | 48 | 101 | 11 | 3 | 3 | 25 | 25 | 40 | 27 | 11 | S | R | 6-0 | 185 | 2-7-74 | 1992 | Summit, Miss. |
| Collier, Lou ................. | .280 | 119 | 443 | 76 | 124 | 20 | 3 | 3 | 49 | 48 | 73 | 29 | 9 | R | R | 5-10 | 170 | 8-21-73 | 1993 | Chicago, Ill. |
| Conger, Jeff ................. | .230 | 66 | 178 | 19 | 41 | 7 | 1 | 3 | 17 | 17 | 52 | 12 | 4 | L | L | 6-0 | 185 | 8-6-71 | 1990 | Charlotte, N.C. |
| Cranford, Jay .............. | .269 | 90 | 268 | 34 | 72 | 15 | 2 | 2 | 37 | 47 | 68 | 6 | 4 | R | R | 6-3 | 175 | 4-7-71 | 1992 | Macon, Ga. |
| Edge, Tim ................... | .242 | 53 | 153 | 18 | 37 | 10 | 0 | 4 | 21 | 16 | 44 | 1 | 0 | R | R | 6-0 | 210 | 10-26-68 | 1990 | Snellville, Ga. |
| Farrell, Jon ................. | .216 | 22 | 51 | 6 | 11 | 3 | 0 | 0 | 3 | 6 | 22 | 0 | 0 | R | R | 6-2 | 185 | 7-30-71 | 1991 | Jacksonville, Fla. |
| Hanel, Marcus .............. | .178 | 101 | 332 | 22 | 59 | 19 | 1 | 5 | 36 | 16 | 57 | 2 | 2 | R | R | 6-4 | 205 | 10-19-71 | 1989 | Racine, Wis. |
| Leary, Rob .................. | .183 | 32 | 109 | 13 | 20 | 4 | 1 | 4 | 12 | 22 | 31 | 2 | 2 | L | L | 6-3 | 195 | 7-9-71 | 1991 | Bayside, N.Y. |
| Munoz, Omer ............. | 1.000 | 1 | 1 | 0 | 1 | 0 | 0 | 0 | 0 | 0 | 0 | 0 | 0 | R | R | 5-9 | 156 | 3-3-66 | 1985 | Oshkosh, Wis. |
| Peterson, Charles ....... | .275 | 125 | 462 | 71 | 127 | 24 | 2 | 7 | 63 | 50 | 104 | 33 | 10 | R | R | 6-3 | 200 | 5-8-74 | 1993 | Laurens, S.C. |
| Ratliff, Darryl ............. | .274 | 82 | 270 | 39 | 74 | 11 | 0 | 0 | 36 | 25 | 50 | 13 | 8 | R | R | 6-1 | 180 | 10-15-69 | 1989 | Santa Cruz, Calif. |
| Reynolds, Chance ....... | .167 | 4 | 6 | 0 | 1 | 0 | 0 | 0 | 1 | 0 | 2 | 0 | 0 | S | R | 5-10 | 185 | 9-16-71 | 1993 | Byromville, Ga. |
| Rodarte, Raul .............. | .209 | 20 | 43 | 6 | 9 | 1 | 0 | 0 | 6 | 12 | 12 | 2 | 1 | R | R | 5-11 | 190 | 4-9-70 | 1991 | Diamond Bar, Calif. |
| Sanford, Chance ......... | .245 | 131 | 470 | 62 | 115 | 16 | 13 | 4 | 56 | 72 | 108 | 11 | 11 | L | R | 5-10 | 165 | 6-2-72 | 1992 | Houston, Texas |
| Staton, T.J. ................ | .308 | 112 | 386 | 72 | 119 | 24 | 3 | 15 | 57 | 58 | 99 | 17 | 7 | L | L | 6-3 | 200 | 2-17-75 | 1993 | Elyria, Ohio |
| Sweet, Jon ................. | .100 | 20 | 40 | 2 | 4 | 2 | 0 | 0 | 1 | 0 | 3 | 0 | 0 | L | L | 6-0 | 183 | 11-10-71 | 1994 | Columbus, Ohio |
| Wright, Ron ................. | .143 | 4 | 14 | 1 | 2 | 0 | 0 | 0 | 2 | 7 | 0 | 1 | 1 | R | R | 6-0 | 215 | 1-21-76 | 1994 | Kennewick, Wash. |
| 2-team (63 Greenville) . | .248 | 67 | 246 | 40 | 61 | 11 | 1 | 16 | 52 | 40 | 80 | 1 | 1 | | | | | | | |

### PITCHING

| PITCHING | W | L | ERA | G | GS | CG | SV | IP | H | R | ER | BB | SO | B | T | HT | WT | DOB | 1st Yr | Resides |
|---|---|---|---|---|---|---|---|---|---|---|---|---|---|---|---|---|---|---|---|---|
| Anderson, Jimmy ........ | 8 | 3 | 3.34 | 17 | 16 | 0 | 0 | 97 | 92 | 40 | 36 | 44 | 79 | L | L | 6-1 | 180 | 1-22-76 | 1994 | Chesapeake, Va. |
| Backlund, Brett ........... | 4 | 6 | 5.13 | 26 | 9 | 0 | 0 | 81 | 77 | 47 | 46 | 28 | 84 | R | R | 6-0 | 195 | 12-16-69 | 1992 | Salem, Ore. |
| Beatty, Blaine ............. | 11 | 5 | 3.29 | 23 | 22 | 1 | 0 | 145 | 135 | 58 | 53 | 34 | 117 | L | L | 6-2 | 190 | 4-25-64 | 1986 | Victoria, Texas |
| Boever, Joe ................. | 0 | 0 | 0.00 | 1 | 0 | 0 | 0 | 1 | 0 | 0 | 0 | 0 | 1 | R | R | 6-1 | 200 | 10-4-60 | 1982 | Palm Harbor, Fla. |
| Chaves, Rafael ............ | 1 | 2 | 1.37 | 19 | 0 | 0 | 0 | 26 | 21 | 5 | 4 | 8 | 15 | R | R | 6-0 | 195 | 11-1-68 | 1986 | Isabella, P.R. |
| Cooke, Steve ............... | 1 | 5 | 4.53 | 12 | 12 | 0 | 0 | 54 | 56 | 34 | 27 | 26 | 43 | R | L | 6-6 | 220 | 1-14-70 | 1990 | Tigard, Ore. |
| De los Santos, Mariano | 3 | 5 | 3.53 | 52 | 0 | 0 | 1 | 66 | 67 | 28 | 26 | 23 | 79 | R | R | 5-10 | 200 | 7-13-70 | 1989 | Santo Domingo, D.R. |
| Dessens, Elmer ........... | 0 | 1 | 5.40 | 5 | 1 | 0 | 0 | 12 | 15 | 8 | 7 | 4 | 7 | R | R | 6-0 | 190 | 1-13-72 | 1993 | Hermosillo, Mexico |
| Farson, Bryan .............. | 0 | 0 | 16.20 | 4 | 0 | 0 | 0 | 5 | 9 | 10 | 9 | 4 | 3 | L | L | 6-2 | 198 | 7-22-72 | 1994 | Massillon, Ohio |
| Harris, Gene ............... | 0 | 2 | 16.20 | 4 | 0 | 0 | 0 | 3 | 6 | 6 | 6 | 3 | 7 | R | R | 5-11 | 190 | 12-5-64 | 1986 | Okeechobee, Fla. |
| Holman, Shawn ........... | 1 | 0 | 3.12 | 5 | 1 | 0 | 0 | 9 | 11 | 4 | 3 | 6 | 6 | R | R | 6-1 | 200 | 11-10-64 | 1982 | Sewickley, Pa. |
| Konuszewski, Dennis ... | 2 | 8 | 6.30 | 32 | 10 | 0 | 0 | 80 | 103 | 61 | 56 | 36 | 59 | R | R | 6-3 | 210 | 2-4-71 | 1992 | Bridgeport, Mich. |
| Lawrence, Sean .......... | 3 | 5 | 3.95 | 37 | 9 | 0 | 2 | 82 | 80 | 40 | 36 | 36 | 81 | L | L | 6-4 | 215 | 9-2-70 | 1992 | Oak Park, Ill. |
| Miceli, Danny .............. | 1 | 0 | 1.00 | 3 | 0 | 0 | 1 | 9 | 4 | 1 | 1 | 1 | 17 | R | R | 5-11 | 205 | 9-9-70 | 1990 | Orlando, Fla. |
| Morel, Ramon .............. | 2 | 5 | 5.09 | 11 | 11 | 0 | 0 | 64 | 75 | 42 | 36 | 16 | 44 | R | R | 6-2 | 170 | 8-15-74 | 1991 | Villa Gonzalez, D.R. |
| Parris, Steve ............... | 2 | 0 | 3.04 | 5 | 5 | 0 | 0 | 27 | 24 | 11 | 9 | 6 | 22 | R | R | 6-0 | 190 | 12-17-67 | 1989 | Joliet, Ill. |
| Peters, Chris ............... | 7 | 3 | 2.64 | 14 | 14 | 0 | 0 | 92 | 73 | 37 | 27 | 34 | 69 | L | L | 6-1 | 170 | 1-28-72 | 1993 | McMurray, Pa. |
| Phoenix, Steve ............ | 2 | 2 | 4.98 | 20 | 0 | 0 | 5 | 22 | 31 | 12 | 12 | 6 | 16 | R | R | 6-3 | 183 | 1-31-68 | 1990 | El Cajon, Calif. |
| Pontbriant, Matt .......... | 2 | 2 | 5.95 | 45 | 0 | 0 | 0 | 56 | 73 | 40 | 37 | 25 | 36 | L | L | 6-4 | 200 | 5-20-72 | 1991 | Norwich, Conn. |
| Rychel, Kevin .............. | 1 | 1 | 4.46 | 26 | 0 | 0 | 1 | 36 | 32 | 21 | 18 | 11 | 21 | R | R | 5-9 | 176 | 9-24-71 | 1988 | Midland, Texas |
| Taylor, Scott ............... | 11 | 7 | 4.61 | 29 | 25 | 0 | 0 | 158 | 170 | 94 | 81 | 62 | 100 | R | R | 6-3 | 200 | 10-3-66 | 1989 | Wichita, Kan. |
| Wainhouse, Dave ......... | 5 | 3 | 3.16 | 45 | 0 | 0 | 25 | 51 | 43 | 22 | 18 | 31 | 34 | L | R | 6-2 | 185 | 11-7-67 | 1989 | Mercer Island, Wash. |
| White, Rick .................. | 0 | 1 | 11.37 | 2 | 1 | 0 | 0 | 6 | 9 | 8 | 8 | 1 | 7 | R | R | 6-4 | 215 | 12-23-68 | 1990 | Springfield, Ohio |
| Wilkins, Marc ............... | 2 | 3 | 4.01 | 11 | 3 | 0 | 0 | 25 | 19 | 12 | 11 | 11 | 19 | R | R | 5-11 | 210 | 21-10-71 | 1992 | Mansfield, Ohio |

### FIELDING (bottom)

| Catcher | PCT | G | PO | A | E | DP | PB |
|---|---|---|---|---|---|---|---|
| Edge ............. | .994 | 44 | 278 | 39 | 2 | 9 | 4 |
| Hanel ............. | .989 | 91 | 621 | 80 | 8 | 10 | 12 |
| Reynolds ...... | 1.000 | 4 | 10 | 0 | 0 | 0 | 0 |
| Sweet ........... | 1.000 | 16 | 78 | 11 | 0 | 2 | 1 |

| First Base | PCT | G | PO | A | E | DP |
|---|---|---|---|---|---|---|
| Bonifay .......... | .990 | 11 | 98 | 3 | 1 | 9 |
| Boston ........... | .994 | 87 | 743 | 53 | 5 | 57 |
| Edge ............. | 1.000 | 1 | 9 | 3 | 0 | 0 |
| Farrell ........... | 1.000 | 1 | 8 | 0 | 0 | 0 |
| Hanel ............. | 1.000 | 7 | 42 | 6 | 0 | 5 |
| Leary ............. | .982 | 32 | 306 | 16 | 6 | 28 |
| Wright ............ | .941 | 4 | 32 | 0 | 2 | 1 |

| Second Base | PCT | G | PO | A | E | DP |
|---|---|---|---|---|---|---|
| Beasley .......... | .953 | 16 | 26 | 35 | 3 | 11 |
| Sanford .......... | .961 | 127 | 213 | 336 | 22 | 69 |

| Third Base | PCT | G | PO | A | E | DP |
|---|---|---|---|---|---|---|
| Beasley .......... | .833 | 5 | 2 | 3 | 1 | 1 |
| Bonifay .......... | .945 | 59 | 30 | 125 | 9 | 8 |
| Cranford ........ | .928 | 73 | 46 | 159 | 16 | 9 |
| Hanel ............. | .500 | 2 | 0 | 1 | 1 | 0 |
| Rodarte ......... | .913 | 16 | 10 | 32 | 4 | 3 |

| Shortstop | PCT | G | PO | A | E | DP |
|---|---|---|---|---|---|---|
| Beasley .......... | .923 | 15 | 24 | 36 | 5 | 7 |
| Collier ........... | .943 | 117 | 189 | 310 | 30 | 71 |
| Cranford ........ | .955 | 17 | 23 | 41 | 3 | 12 |

| Shortstop | PCT | G | PO | A | E | DP |
|---|---|---|---|---|---|---|
| Munoz ............. | .000 | 1 | 0 | 0 | 0 | 0 |

| Outfield | PCT | G | PO | A | E | DP |
|---|---|---|---|---|---|---|
| Beasley .......... | .885 | 26 | 23 | 0 | 3 | 0 |
| Bonifay .......... | 1.000 | 9 | 10 | 1 | 0 | 1 |
| Brown ............ | .990 | 81 | 185 | 5 | 2 | 2 |
| Conger ........... | .981 | 27 | 49 | 2 | 1 | 0 |
| Farrell ........... | .955 | 13 | 21 | 0 | 1 | 0 |
| Hanel ............. | 1.000 | 3 | 2 | 0 | 0 | 0 |
| Peterson ........ | .948 | 120 | 186 | 16 | 11 | 5 |
| Ratliff ............ | .992 | 57 | 108 | 9 | 1 | 1 |
| Staton ........... | .979 | 106 | 178 | 7 | 4 | 1 |

## CAROLINA LEAGUE

### BATTING

| BATTING | AVG | G | AB | R | H | 2B | 3B | HR | RBI | BB | SO | SB | CS | B | T | HT | WT | DOB | 1st Yr | Resides |
|---|---|---|---|---|---|---|---|---|---|---|---|---|---|---|---|---|---|---|---|---|
| Asche, Mike | .295 | 129 | 498 | 79 | 147 | 25 | 6 | 7 | 54 | 38 | 92 | 26 | 5 | R | R | 6-2 | 190 | 2-13-72 | 1994 | Kearney, Neb. |
| Brooks, Eddie | .267 | 85 | 270 | 41 | 72 | 23 | 1 | 4 | 28 | 15 | 73 | 4 | 2 | R | R | 6-1 | 175 | 11-23-72 | 1994 | Lexington, Ky. |
| Brown, Adrian | .321 | 52 | 215 | 39 | 69 | 9 | 3 | 4 | 25 | 14 | 24 | 18 | 9 | S | R | 6-0 | 185 | 2-7-74 | 1992 | Summit, Miss. |
| Burke, Stoney | .207 | 37 | 92 | 10 | 19 | 4 | 0 | 0 | 9 | 7 | 24 | 0 | 0 | R | R | 6-1 | 200 | 3-27-71 | 1994 | Danville, Ind. |
| Farrell, Jon | .359 | 24 | 78 | 8 | 28 | 3 | 0 | 1 | 11 | 19 | 16 | 0 | 0 | R | R | 6-2 | 185 | 7-30-71 | 1991 | Jacksonville, Fla. |
| Garcia, Freddy | .306 | 129 | 474 | 79 | 145 | 39 | 3 | 21 | 86 | 44 | 86 | 4 | 2 | R | R | 6-2 | 186 | 8-1-72 | 1991 | La Romana, D.R. |
| Guillen, Jose | .322 | 136 | 528 | 78 | 170 | 30 | 0 | 21 | 94 | 20 | 73 | 24 | 13 | R | R | 5-11 | 165 | 5-17-76 | 1993 | San Cristobal, D.R. |
| Harrison, Kenny | .120 | 18 | 50 | 2 | 6 | 3 | 0 | 0 | 3 | 4 | 8 | 0 | 1 | L | R | 6-0 | 195 | 11-8-71 | 1996 | Honolulu, Hawaii |
| Hermansen, Chad | .275 | 66 | 251 | 40 | 69 | 11 | 3 | 10 | 46 | 29 | 56 | 5 | 1 | R | R | 6-2 | 185 | 9-10-77 | 1995 | Henderson, Nev. |
| Kelley, Erskine | .282 | 111 | 344 | 61 | 97 | 22 | 5 | 5 | 43 | 25 | 93 | 13 | 8 | R | R | 6-5 | 210 | 2-27-71 | 1992 | Freeport, N.Y. |
| Martinez, Ramon | .307 | 91 | 306 | 58 | 94 | 10 | 5 | 1 | 30 | 24 | 53 | 12 | 5 | S | R | 6-0 | 170 | 9-8-69 | 1990 | Villa Gonzalez, D.R. |
| Mendez, Sergio | .277 | 39 | 137 | 19 | 38 | 9 | 1 | 4 | 17 | 6 | 24 | 0 | 1 | R | R | 6-0 | 180 | 10-12-73 | 1992 | Santo Domingo, D.R. |
| Munoz, Omer | .300 | 3 | 10 | 0 | 3 | 0 | 0 | 0 | 1 | 0 | 1 | 0 | 0 | R | R | 5-9 | 156 | 3-3-66 | 1985 | Oshkosh, Wis. |
| Robinson, Tony | .172 | 31 | 93 | 13 | 16 | 3 | 0 | 0 | 7 | 17 | 17 | 5 | 3 | R | R | 6-0 | 185 | 6-11-76 | 1994 | Diamond Bar, Calif. |
| Swafford, Derek | .259 | 116 | 433 | 77 | 112 | 18 | 4 | 2 | 48 | 48 | 107 | 35 | 18 | L | R | 5-10 | 175 | 1-21-75 | 1993 | Ventura, Calif. |
| Sweet, Jon | .274 | 72 | 212 | 16 | 58 | 10 | 0 | 0 | 35 | 17 | 26 | 2 | 4 | L | R | 6-0 | 183 | 11-10-71 | 1994 | Columbus, Ohio |
| Thobe, Steve | .228 | 109 | 359 | 49 | 82 | 15 | 0 | 11 | 42 | 29 | 93 | 4 | 4 | R | R | 6-7 | 230 | 5-26-72 | 1994 | Huntington Beach, Calif. |
| Walker, Shon | .303 | 97 | 323 | 61 | 98 | 19 | 3 | 14 | 70 | 49 | 99 | 3 | 4 | L | L | 6-1 | 182 | 6-9-74 | 1992 | Cynthiana, Ky. |

**GAMES BY POSITION: C**—Burke 34, Mendez 36, Sweet 65, Thobe 27. **1B**—Asche 2, Brooks 1, Farrell 4, Harrison 12, Martinez 1, Thobe 91, Walker 50. **2B**—Asche 1, Brooks 29, Martinez 1, Munoz 3, Swafford 112. **3B**—Asche 25, Brooks 10, Garcia 109. **SS**—Brooks 32, Hermansen 64, Martinez 18, Robinson 30. **OF**—Asche 82, Brown 50, Farrell 8, Guillen 125, Kelley 101, Martinez 69, Walker 4.

### PITCHING

| PITCHING | W | L | ERA | G | GS | CG | SV | IP | H | R | ER | BB | SO | B | T | HT | WT | DOB | 1st Yr | Resides |
|---|---|---|---|---|---|---|---|---|---|---|---|---|---|---|---|---|---|---|---|---|
| Anderson, Jimmy | 5 | 3 | 1.93 | 11 | 11 | 1 | 0 | 65 | 51 | 25 | 14 | 21 | 56 | L | L | 6-1 | 180 | 1-22-76 | 1994 | Chesapeake, Va. |
| Blyleven, Todd | 2 | 1 | 2.09 | 23 | 3 | 0 | 1 | 56 | 49 | 18 | 13 | 14 | 33 | R | R | 6-5 | 230 | 9-27-72 | 1993 | Villa Park, Calif. |
| Brown, Michael | 1 | 5 | 7.14 | 34 | 11 | 0 | 0 | 69 | 91 | 66 | 55 | 52 | 62 | L | L | 6-7 | 245 | 11-4-71 | 1989 | Vacaville, Calif. |
| Chaves, Rafael | 1 | 3 | 2.53 | 30 | 0 | 0 | 5 | 32 | 35 | 18 | 9 | 8 | 20 | R | R | 6-0 | 195 | 11-1-68 | 1986 | Isabella, P.R. |
| Collie, Tim | 4 | 1 | 3.60 | 24 | 0 | 0 | 1 | 25 | 26 | 10 | 10 | 10 | 14 | R | R | 5-11 | 185 | 7-5-73 | 1995 | Charlotte, N.C. |
| Davis, Kane | 11 | 9 | 4.29 | 26 | 26 | 3 | 0 | 157 | 160 | 84 | 75 | 56 | 116 | R | R | 6-3 | 180 | 6-25-75 | 1993 | Reedy, W.Va. |
| Dillinger, John | 10 | 5 | 3.74 | 33 | 15 | 2 | 0 | 132 | 101 | 65 | 55 | 58 | 113 | R | R | 6-6 | 230 | 8-28-73 | 1992 | Connellsville, Pa. |
| France, Aaron | 0 | 8 | 6.41 | 13 | 13 | 0 | 0 | 60 | 79 | 53 | 43 | 32 | 40 | L | R | 6-3 | 175 | 4-17-74 | 1994 | Anaheim, Calif. |
| Johnson, Jason | 1 | 4 | 6.50 | 15 | 5 | 0 | 0 | 44 | 56 | 37 | 32 | 12 | 27 | R | R | 6-6 | 220 | 10-27-73 | 1992 | Burlington, Ky. |
| Kelly, Jeff | 3 | 4 | 3.60 | 13 | 13 | 0 | 0 | 75 | 77 | 45 | 30 | 24 | 57 | L | L | 6-5 | 215 | 1-11-75 | 1994 | Staten Island, N.Y. |
| Kelly, John | 0 | 0 | 3.68 | 7 | 0 | 0 | 0 | 7 | 11 | 4 | 3 | 5 | 3 | R | R | 6-0 | 180 | 12-13-72 | 1994 | Leominster, Mass. |
| Maskivish, Joe | 1 | 2 | 6.75 | 12 | 0 | 0 | 4 | 11 | 17 | 9 | 8 | 5 | 10 | R | R | 6-4 | 180 | 8-14-71 | 1994 | Shadyside, Ohio |
| Mattson, Craig | 0 | 0 | 7.71 | 6 | 0 | 0 | 0 | 7 | 10 | 6 | 6 | 5 | 4 | R | R | 6-4 | 205 | 11-25-73 | 1993 | Belvidere, Ill. |
| McDade, Neal | 0 | 1 | 9.00 | 1 | 1 | 0 | 0 | 5 | 6 | 6 | 5 | 1 | 2 | R | R | 6-3 | 165 | 6-16-76 | 1996 | Orange Park, Fla. |
| Paugh, Rick | 1 | 4 | 3.81 | 45 | 0 | 0 | 4 | 52 | 48 | 33 | 22 | 20 | 41 | L | L | 6-1 | 190 | 2-6-72 | 1994 | Bridgeport, W.Va. |
| Phillips, Jason | 5 | 6 | 4.52 | 13 | 13 | 1 | 0 | 74 | 82 | 47 | 37 | 35 | 63 | R | R | 6-6 | 215 | 3-22-74 | 1992 | Muncy, Pa. |
| Pickford, Kevin | 11 | 11 | 4.07 | 28 | 28 | 4 | 0 | 172 | 195 | 99 | 78 | 25 | 100 | L | L | 6-3 | 200 | 3-12-75 | 1993 | Fresno, Calif. |
| Spade, Matt | 6 | 4 | 3.02 | 53 | 0 | 0 | 2 | 80 | 88 | 38 | 27 | 27 | 71 | R | R | 6-0 | 180 | 12-4-72 | 1994 | Boyertown, Pa. |
| Temple, Jason | 2 | 2 | 4.76 | 21 | 0 | 0 | 3 | 23 | 24 | 14 | 12 | 19 | 18 | R | R | 6-1 | 185 | 11-8-74 | 1993 | Woodhaven, Mich. |
| Williams, Matt | 0 | 0 | 5.23 | 23 | 0 | 0 | 0 | 41 | 40 | 27 | 24 | 28 | 45 | S | L | 6-0 | 185 | 4-12-71 | 1992 | Virginia Beach, Va. |

## SOUTH ATLANTIC LEAGUE

### BATTING

| BATTING | AVG | G | AB | R | H | 2B | 3B | HR | RBI | BB | SO | SB | CS | B | T | HT | WT | DOB | 1st Yr | Resides |
|---|---|---|---|---|---|---|---|---|---|---|---|---|---|---|---|---|---|---|---|---|
| Bellenger, Butch | .192 | 8 | 26 | 5 | 5 | 2 | 0 | 0 | 1 | 2 | 6 | 1 | 0 | R | R | 6-0 | 200 | 11-4-73 | 1996 | Lyndhurst, N.J. |
| Bigler, Jeff | .264 | 40 | 121 | 16 | 32 | 10 | 0 | 0 | 14 | 29 | 24 | 0 | 2 | L | L | 6-0 | 190 | 9-13-69 | 1991 | Mequon, Wis. |
| Canetto, John | .357 | 8 | 14 | 1 | 5 | 1 | 0 | 0 | 3 | 1 | 4 | 1 | 0 | S | R | 5-11 | 185 | 9-19-72 | 1995 | Hillsdale, N.Y. |
| Edwards, Aaron | .238 | 40 | 126 | 22 | 30 | 4 | 2 | 1 | 11 | 11 | 28 | 7 | 5 | R | R | 6-2 | 180 | 8-5-73 | 1994 | Ontario, Calif. |
| Farris, Mark | .217 | 78 | 299 | 31 | 65 | 10 | 0 | 2 | 30 | 31 | 66 | 6 | 5 | L | R | 6-3 | 190 | 2-9-75 | 1994 | Angleton, Texas |
| Flanigan, Steve | .208 | 49 | 144 | 14 | 30 | 6 | 0 | 0 | 17 | 5 | 29 | 2 | 1 | R | R | 6-1 | 210 | 10-23-71 | 1995 | Kittanning, Pa. |
| Frias, Ovidio | .266 | 54 | 177 | 18 | 47 | 8 | 0 | 0 | 22 | 25 | 17 | 6 | 8 | R | R | 5-11 | 165 | 3-19-77 | 1995 | Santo Domingo, D.R. |
| Gonzalez, Wikleman | .253 | 118 | 419 | 52 | 106 | 21 | 3 | 4 | 62 | 58 | 41 | 4 | 6 | R | R | 5-11 | 175 | 5-17-74 | 1992 | Palo Negro, Venez. |
| Hermansen, Chad | .252 | 62 | 226 | 41 | 57 | 11 | 3 | 14 | 41 | 38 | 65 | 11 | 3 | R | R | 6-2 | 185 | 9-10-77 | 1995 | Henderson, Nev. |
| May, Freddy | .203 | 123 | 390 | 58 | 79 | 8 | 6 | 5 | 43 | 72 | 119 | 22 | 18 | L | L | 6-2 | 190 | 1-24-76 | 1995 | Seattle, Wash. |
| McSparin, Paul | .071 | 6 | 14 | 1 | 1 | 1 | 0 | 0 | 1 | 0 | 6 | 0 | 0 | R | R | 6-2 | 210 | 4-16-74 | 1994 | Harrisburg, Ill. |
| Mendez, Sergio | .233 | 46 | 172 | 23 | 40 | 9 | 0 | 7 | 26 | 9 | 31 | 3 | 3 | R | R | 6-2 | 180 | 10-12-73 | 1992 | Santo Domingo, D.R. |
| Miyake, Chris | .240 | 101 | 367 | 46 | 88 | 12 | 0 | 2 | 33 | 22 | 55 | 10 | 10 | R | R | 6-2 | 185 | 5-18-74 | 1995 | San Gabriel, Calif. |
| Pena, Alex | .162 | 52 | 167 | 9 | 27 | 4 | 2 | 0 | 12 | 7 | 51 | 2 | 1 | R | R | 6-2 | 175 | 9-9-77 | 1995 | Ensanche Luperon, D.R. |
| Pollock, Elton | .235 | 132 | 452 | 65 | 106 | 13 | 5 | 5 | 47 | 68 | 100 | 29 | 11 | R | R | 5-11 | 185 | 4-17-73 | 1995 | Clinton, S.C. |
| Ramirez, Aramis | .200 | 6 | 20 | 3 | 4 | 1 | 0 | 1 | 2 | 1 | 7 | 0 | 2 | R | R | 6-1 | 176 | 6-25-78 | 1995 | Santo Domingo, D.R. |
| Rice, Andy | .178 | 56 | 185 | 22 | 33 | 5 | 1 | 3 | 13 | 18 | 57 | 4 | 2 | S | R | 6-2 | 220 | 8-31-75 | 1993 | Birmingham, Ala. |
| Schreiber, Stan | .226 | 112 | 367 | 59 | 83 | 10 | 5 | 1 | 31 | 52 | 96 | 20 | 9 | R | R | 5-10 | 175 | 9-8-75 | 1994 | Appleton, Wis. |
| Springfield, Bo | .261 | 59 | 180 | 29 | 47 | 2 | 1 | 0 | 17 | 29 | 47 | 6 | 4 | L | R | 5-10 | 173 | 1-25-76 | 1994 | Denison, Texas |
| Walker, Morgan | .300 | 68 | 253 | 28 | 76 | 15 | 1 | 8 | 50 | 18 | 57 | 5 | 1 | R | L | 6-3 | 215 | 8-7-74 | 1996 | Missouri City, Texas |
| Whipple, Boomer | .236 | 128 | 444 | 75 | 105 | 23 | 0 | 2 | 45 | 72 | 58 | 8 | 7 | R | R | 6-0 | 185 | 2-9-73 | 1995 | Lincolnshire, Ill. |

**GAMES BY POSITION: C**—Canetto 4, Flanigan 35, Gonzalez 98, McSparin 2, Mendez 13. **1B**—Bigler 39, Mendez 11, Walker 47, Whipple 52. **2B**—Bellinger 7, Frias 14, Miyake 85, Schreiber 18, Whipple 26. **3B**—Bellinger 1, Farris 70, Frias 29, Pena 1, Ramirez 6, Schreiber 3, Whipple 36. **SS**—Frias 11, Hermansen 59, Miyake 11, Schreiber 68. **OF**—Edwards 35, May 122, Pena 50, Pollock 121, Rice 36, Schreiber 21, Springfield 56.

### PITCHING

| PITCHING | W | L | ERA | G | GS | CG | SV | IP | H | R | ER | BB | SO | B | T | HT | WT | DOB | 1st Yr | Resides |
|---|---|---|---|---|---|---|---|---|---|---|---|---|---|---|---|---|---|---|---|---|
| Arroyo, Bronson | 8 | 6 | 3.52 | 26 | 26 | 0 | 0 | 136 | 123 | 64 | 53 | 36 | 107 | R | R | 6-5 | 165 | 2-24-77 | 1995 | Brooksville, Fla. |
| Ayers, Mike | 3 | 0 | 4.15 | 27 | 0 | 0 | 0 | 30 | 33 | 21 | 14 | 8 | 31 | L | L | 5-10 | 190 | 12-23-73 | 1996 | Cincinnati, Ohio |
| Blyleven, Todd | 1 | 2 | 3.72 | 12 | 0 | 0 | 2 | 29 | 32 | 15 | 12 | 10 | 27 | R | R | 6-5 | 230 | 9-27-72 | 1993 | Villa Park, Calif. |
| Bullock, Derek | 2 | 4 | 2.08 | 14 | 8 | 2 | 0 | 61 | 55 | 18 | 14 | 16 | 52 | R | R | 6-2 | 186 | 2-24-73 | 1995 | Sioux City, Iowa |
| Collie, Tim | 4 | 2 | 2.12 | 24 | 0 | 0 | 12 | 30 | 28 | 11 | 7 | 4 | 20 | R | R | 5-11 | 185 | 7-5-73 | 1995 | Charlotte, N.C. |
| Daniels, David | 0 | 1 | 5.11 | 11 | 0 | 0 | 3 | 12 | 21 | 8 | 7 | 3 | 14 | R | R | 6-2 | 185 | 7-25-75 | 1995 | Nashville, Tenn. |

| PITCHING | W | L | ERA | G | GS | CG | SV | IP | H | R | ER | BB | SO | B | T | HT | WT | DOB | 1st Yr | Resides |
|---|---|---|---|---|---|---|---|---|---|---|---|---|---|---|---|---|---|---|---|---|
| Dunn, Cordell | 0 | 3 | 12.66 | 3 | 3 | 0 | 0 | 11 | 14 | 15 | 15 | 9 | 7 | R | R | 6-2 | 185 | 11-3-75 | 1994 | Tunica, Miss. |
| Farrow, Jason | 5 | 3 | 2.09 | 46 | 0 | 0 | 3 | 77 | 61 | 26 | 18 | 34 | 81 | R | R | 6-2 | 195 | 7-30-73 | 1995 | Palestine, Texas |
| Fisher, Ryan | 3 | 1 | 3.05 | 14 | 0 | 0 | 0 | 21 | 23 | 14 | 7 | 9 | 16 | L | L | 6-2 | 190 | 4-26-74 | 1995 | Milltown, Wis. |
| France, Aaron | 2 | 1 | 2.52 | 5 | 5 | 0 | 0 | 25 | 23 | 9 | 7 | 7 | 24 | L | R | 6-3 | 175 | 4-17-74 | 1994 | Anaheim, Calif. |
| Havens, Jeff | 1 | 3 | 3.65 | 34 | 1 | 0 | 2 | 44 | 51 | 22 | 18 | 12 | 43 | R | R | 6-1 | 185 | 3-5-73 | 1994 | Beaumont, Texas |
| Hernandez, Elvin | 17 | 5 | 3.14 | 27 | 27 | 2 | 0 | 158 | 140 | 60 | 55 | 16 | 171 | R | R | 6-1 | 165 | 8-20-77 | 1994 | Laguna Salada Monte, D.R. |
| Johnson, Jason | 4 | 4 | 3.11 | 14 | 14 | 1 | 0 | 84 | 82 | 40 | 29 | 25 | 83 | R | R | 6-6 | 220 | 10-27-73 | 1992 | Burlington, Ky. |
| Kelly, Jeff | 6 | 3 | 3.32 | 14 | 14 | 0 | 0 | 84 | 76 | 39 | 31 | 27 | 68 | L | L | 6-6 | 215 | 1-11-75 | 1994 | Staten Island, N.Y. |
| Maskivish, Joe | 1 | 4 | 2.16 | 50 | 0 | 0 | 18 | 50 | 46 | 18 | 12 | 14 | 58 | R | R | 6-4 | 180 | 8-14-71 | 1994 | Shadyside, Ohio |
| Mattson, Craig | 1 | 2 | 1.78 | 18 | 0 | 0 | 0 | 25 | 19 | 6 | 5 | 7 | 18 | R | R | 6-4 | 205 | 11-25-73 | 1993 | Belvidere, Ill. |
| O'Connor, Brian | 0 | 1 | 3.06 | 19 | 0 | 0 | 1 | 35 | 33 | 13 | 12 | 8 | 37 | L | L | 6-2 | 175 | 1-4-77 | 1995 | Cincinnati, Ohio |
| Parris, Steve | 0 | 0 | 0.00 | 1 | 1 | 0 | 0 | 5 | 1 | 0 | 0 | 1 | 6 | R | R | 6-0 | 190 | 12-17-67 | 1989 | Joliet, Ill. |
| Phillips, Jason | 5 | 4 | 2.41 | 14 | 14 | 1 | 0 | 90 | 79 | 35 | 24 | 29 | 75 | R | R | 6-6 | 215 | 3-22-74 | 1992 | Muncy, Pa. |
| Reid, Rayon | 0 | 0 | 2.45 | 3 | 0 | 0 | 0 | 4 | 4 | 5 | 1 | 4 | 3 | R | R | 6-0 | 185 | 7-25-73 | 1993 | North Miami Beach, Fla. |
| Reyes, Jose | 5 | 4 | 6.18 | 23 | 8 | 0 | 0 | 67 | 79 | 51 | 46 | 30 | 57 | R | R | 6-1 | 188 | 5-1-73 | 1993 | Villa Vazquez, D.R. |
| South, Carl | 1 | 0 | 3.00 | 1 | 1 | 0 | 0 | 6 | 5 | 2 | 2 | 2 | 9 | R | R | 6-5 | 210 | 4-14-75 | 1994 | Roswell, Ga. |
| Viegas, Randy | 0 | 0 | 6.27 | 13 | 0 | 0 | 0 | 19 | 16 | 14 | 13 | 14 | 15 | L | L | 6-2 | 175 | 8-22-75 | 1994 | Roseville, Calif. |
| Young, Danny | 0 | 4 | 5.88 | 22 | 1 | 0 | 2 | 34 | 36 | 33 | 22 | 29 | 36 | L | L | 6-5 | 180 | 11-3-71 | 1991 | Woodbury, Tenn. |
| Young, Ryan | 3 | 12 | 5.72 | 21 | 18 | 1 | 0 | 96 | 117 | 66 | 61 | 32 | 48 | R | R | 6-0 | 175 | 6-16-73 | 1995 | Charlotte, N.C. |

## NEW YORK-PENN LEAGUE

| BATTING | AVG | G | AB | R | H | 2B | 3B | HR | RBI | BB | SO | SB | CS | B | T | HT | WT | DOB | 1st Yr | Resides |
|---|---|---|---|---|---|---|---|---|---|---|---|---|---|---|---|---|---|---|---|---|
| Antigua, Nilson | .273 | 57 | 187 | 24 | 51 | 9 | 0 | 4 | 26 | 9 | 26 | 5 | 3 | R | R | 6-2 | 175 | 12-14-75 | 1993 | Monte Plata, D.R. |
| Bellenger, Butch | .238 | 52 | 193 | 21 | 46 | 8 | 0 | 3 | 15 | 9 | 33 | 9 | 4 | R | R | 6-0 | 200 | 11-4-73 | 1996 | Lyndhurst, N.J. |
| Burns, Xavier | .158 | 14 | 38 | 6 | 6 | 1 | 0 | 0 | 2 | 3 | 12 | 2 | 1 | R | R | 5-11 | 185 | 5-8-75 | 1996 | Chicago, Ill. |
| Edwards, Aaron | .170 | 12 | 47 | 4 | 8 | 0 | 0 | 0 | 3 | 2 | 6 | 2 | 0 | R | R | 6-2 | 180 | 8-5-73 | 1994 | Ontario, Calif. |
| Elliott, Dawan | .148 | 39 | 115 | 17 | 17 | 5 | 0 | 2 | 6 | 16 | 42 | 3 | 3 | L | L | 6-3 | 200 | 7-30-76 | 1995 | Long Branch, N.J. |
| Frias, Ovidio | .283 | 12 | 46 | 5 | 13 | 1 | 0 | 0 | 3 | 1 | 7 | 0 | 0 | R | R | 5-11 | 165 | 3-19-77 | 1995 | Santo Domingo, D.R. |
| Hernandez, Alex | .289 | 61 | 225 | 38 | 65 | 13 | 4 | 4 | 30 | 20 | 47 | 7 | 8 | L | L | 6-4 | 190 | 5-28-77 | 1995 | Levittown, P.R. |
| Hundt, Bo | .164 | 20 | 55 | 8 | 9 | 0 | 1 | 1 | 4 | 4 | 11 | 1 | 0 | S | R | 6-2 | 200 | 4-21-75 | 1996 | Bremen, Ind. |
| Larkin, Garrett | .208 | 19 | 53 | 6 | 11 | 2 | 0 | 0 | 4 | 7 | 8 | 0 | 1 | L | R | 6-2 | 185 | 6-20-75 | 1996 | Medfield, Mass. |
| Long, Garrett | .286 | 20 | 70 | 5 | 20 | 2 | 1 | 0 | 7 | 9 | 17 | 1 | 2 | R | R | 6-3 | 195 | 10-5-76 | 1995 | Houston, Texas |
| Lorenzana, Luis | .195 | 44 | 128 | 19 | 25 | 8 | 1 | 0 | 12 | 16 | 26 | 1 | 4 | R | R | 6-0 | 170 | 11-9-78 | 1996 | San Diego, Calif. |
| May, Scott | .250 | 25 | 40 | 5 | 10 | 2 | 0 | 0 | 0 | 7 | 11 | 0 | 0 | L | R | 5-11 | 185 | 6-1-73 | 1996 | Bradenton, Fla. |
| Osik, Keith | .300 | 3 | 10 | 1 | 3 | 1 | 0 | 0 | 2 | 1 | 2 | 0 | 0 | R | R | 6-0 | 195 | 10-22-68 | 1990 | Rocky Point, N.Y. |
| Pena, Adelis | .282 | 66 | 252 | 31 | 71 | 11 | 1 | 1 | 26 | 15 | 41 | 7 | 4 | R | R | 6-1 | 175 | 4-19-77 | 1994 | Cumana, Venez. |
| Pena, Alex | .267 | 74 | 281 | 31 | 75 | 10 | 3 | 4 | 33 | 14 | 52 | 10 | 4 | R | R | 6-2 | 175 | 9-9-77 | 1995 | Ensanche Luperon, D.R. |
| Pointer, Corey | .190 | 5 | 21 | 1 | 4 | 1 | 0 | 0 | 2 | 0 | 9 | 0 | 0 | R | R | 6-2 | 205 | 9-2-75 | 1994 | Waxahachie, Texas |
| Ramirez, Aramis | .305 | 61 | 223 | 37 | 68 | 14 | 4 | 9 | 42 | 31 | 41 | 0 | 0 | R | R | 6-1 | 176 | 6-25-78 | 1995 | Santo Domingo, D.R. |
| Redman, Julian | .294 | 43 | 170 | 31 | 50 | 4 | 6 | 2 | 21 | 17 | 30 | 7 | 3 | L | L | 5-11 | 160 | 3-10-77 | 1996 | Duncanville, Ala. |
| Rice, Andy | .251 | 56 | 187 | 24 | 47 | 12 | 1 | 4 | 19 | 23 | 39 | 6 | 4 | S | R | 6-2 | 220 | 8-31-75 | 1993 | Birmingham, Ala. |
| Shipp, Skip | .254 | 55 | 189 | 19 | 48 | 7 | 0 | 3 | 26 | 16 | 50 | 3 | 2 | R | R | 6-2 | 205 | 1-12-76 | 1995 | Kennesaw, Ga. |

**GAMES BY POSITON: C**—Antigua 47, May 15, Osik 3, Shipp 26. **1B**—Antigua 5, Bellenger 3, Hernandez 29, Hundt 1, Long 20, Shipp 24. **2B**—Bellenger 31, Frias 7, Larkin 4, Ad. Pena 39. **3B**—Bellenger 17, Hundt 1, Larkin 1, May 2, Ad. Pena 2, Ramirez 61. **SS**—Bellenger 1, Larkin 9, Lorenzana 43, Ad. Pena 26. **OF**—Burns 4, Edwards 12, Elliott 37, Frias 2, Hernandez 31, Hundt 7, Al. Pena 73, Pointer 5, Redman 43, Rice 19.

| PITCHING | W | L | ERA | G | GS | CG | SV | IP | H | R | ER | BB | SO | B | T | HT | WT | DOB | 1st Yr | Resides |
|---|---|---|---|---|---|---|---|---|---|---|---|---|---|---|---|---|---|---|---|---|
| Ah Yat, Paul | 1 | 1 | 3.25 | 26 | 0 | 0 | 1 | 28 | 24 | 15 | 10 | 6 | 34 | R | L | 6-1 | 196 | 10-13-73 | 1994 | Honolulu, Hawaii |
| Avila, Jose | 4 | 3 | 4.04 | 14 | 14 | 0 | 0 | 78 | 75 | 37 | 35 | 33 | 74 | R | R | 6-2 | 195 | 3-4-75 | 1994 | Cumana, Venez. |
| Beach, Scott | 0 | 1 | 1.64 | 17 | 0 | 0 | 0 | 22 | 16 | 7 | 4 | 14 | 25 | R | R | 6-4 | 175 | 10-18-73 | 1995 | Prairie Village, Kan. |
| Brooks, Wyatt | 0 | 1 | 1.54 | 15 | 0 | 0 | 1 | 23 | 20 | 5 | 4 | 7 | 24 | R | L | 6-5 | 165 | 12-13-73 | 1996 | Tallahassee, Fla. |
| Campbell, Tedde | 3 | 4 | 3.34 | 27 | 0 | 0 | 4 | 32 | 24 | 17 | 12 | 16 | 30 | R | R | 6-0 | 190 | 7-27-72 | 1995 | Blairsville, Pa. |
| Chaney, Michael | 1 | 1 | 5.28 | 10 | 5 | 0 | 0 | 29 | 27 | 20 | 17 | 14 | 21 | L | L | 6-3 | 200 | 10-3-74 | 1996 | West Chester, Ohio |
| Daniels, David | 1 | 3 | 2.72 | 31 | 0 | 0 | 7 | 36 | 33 | 12 | 11 | 5 | 45 | R | R | 6-2 | 185 | 7-25-73 | 1995 | Nashville, Tenn. |
| Elmore, George | 1 | 0 | 4.78 | 19 | 0 | 0 | 0 | 32 | 38 | 22 | 17 | 21 | 17 | R | R | 6-5 | 245 | 5-31-74 | 1996 | Lucama, N.C. |
| Gonzalez, Luis | 1 | 4 | 5.68 | 21 | 1 | 0 | 0 | 25 | 32 | 19 | 16 | 6 | 19 | R | R | 6-2 | 190 | 5-3-74 | 1996 | El Paso, Texas |
| Haynie, Jason | 3 | 4 | 3.25 | 16 | 12 | 1 | 0 | 80 | 86 | 36 | 29 | 22 | 74 | L | L | 6-0 | 190 | 3-29-74 | 1996 | St. Petersburg Beach, Fla. |
| McDade, Neal | 7 | 3 | 3.40 | 13 | 13 | 3 | 0 | 77 | 76 | 33 | 29 | 21 | 67 | R | R | 6-3 | 165 | 6-16-76 | 1996 | Orange Park, Fla. |
| O'Connor, Brian | 4 | 10 | 5.85 | 15 | 15 | 0 | 0 | 68 | 75 | 60 | 44 | 47 | 60 | L | L | 6-2 | 175 | 1-4-77 | 1995 | Cincinnati, Ohio |
| Pena, Jesus | 2 | 5 | 4.79 | 21 | 3 | 0 | 0 | 36 | 32 | 24 | 19 | 24 | 34 | L | L | 6-0 | 170 | 3-8-75 | 1993 | Santo Domingo, D.R. |
| Santos, Rafael | 1 | 2 | 3.79 | 18 | 4 | 0 | 0 | 55 | 55 | 31 | 23 | 19 | 32 | R | R | 6-2 | 185 | 10-24-75 | 1994 | Haina, D.R. |
| Siciliano, Jess | 0 | 0 | 6.75 | 4 | 0 | 0 | 0 | 5 | 7 | 5 | 4 | 4 | 4 | R | R | 6-2 | 190 | 8-31-76 | 1996 | East White Plains, N.Y. |
| Viegas, Randy | 0 | 0 | 7.36 | 2 | 0 | 0 | 0 | 4 | 4 | 3 | 3 | 4 | 3 | L | L | 6-2 | 175 | 8-22-75 | 1994 | Roseville, Calif. |
| Villar, Maximo | 0 | 5 | 7.22 | 9 | 9 | 0 | 0 | 29 | 46 | 27 | 23 | 9 | 10 | R | R | 6-3 | 175 | 10-11-76 | 1994 | Bani, D.R. |

## GULF COAST LEAGUE

| BATTING | AVG | G | AB | R | H | 2B | 3B | HR | RBI | BB | SO | SB | CS | B | T | HT | WT | DOB | 1st Yr | Resides |
|---|---|---|---|---|---|---|---|---|---|---|---|---|---|---|---|---|---|---|---|---|
| Benjamin, Aljereau | .227 | 45 | 172 | 23 | 39 | 5 | 4 | 3 | 25 | 12 | 35 | 1 | 2 | R | R | 6-1 | 190 | 9-9-77 | 1996 | Houston, Texas |
| Brooks, Ali | .186 | 31 | 97 | 8 | 18 | 0 | 1 | 0 | 9 | 5 | 10 | 8 | 5 | R | R | 5-8 | 160 | 5-14-76 | 1996 | Oakland, Calif. |
| Burns, Xavier | .164 | 22 | 73 | 17 | 12 | 1 | 1 | 0 | 3 | 11 | 24 | 6 | 0 | R | R | 5-11 | 185 | 5-8-75 | 1996 | Chicago, Ill. |
| Delgado, Daniel | .292 | 37 | 96 | 16 | 28 | 2 | 1 | 0 | 11 | 8 | 14 | 3 | 3 | R | R | 5-9 | 165 | 12-29-76 | 1995 | Miami, Fla. |
| Diaz, Diogenes | .233 | 26 | 90 | 7 | 21 | 7 | 2 | 2 | 9 | 5 | 22 | 0 | 0 | R | R | 6-0 | 190 | 10-10-78 | 1996 | Villa Mella, D.R. |
| Elliott, Dawan | .300 | 24 | 90 | 9 | 27 | 7 | 1 | 0 | 18 | 8 | 12 | 5 | 2 | L | L | 6-3 | 200 | 7-30-76 | 1995 | Long Branch, N.J. |
| Evans, Lee | .279 | 32 | 111 | 27 | 31 | 5 | 2 | 3 | 20 | 18 | 26 | 3 | 0 | S | R | 6-1 | 175 | 7-20-77 | 1996 | Northport, Ala. |
| Feliz, Edgar | .000 | 1 | 1 | 0 | 0 | 0 | 0 | 0 | 0 | 0 | 0 | 0 | 0 | S | R | 6-2 | 143 | 12-14-77 | 1994 | Jimani, D.R. |
| Germosen, Julio | .244 | 35 | 123 | 20 | 30 | 4 | 2 | 1 | 11 | 8 | 24 | 2 | 1 | R | R | 6-0 | 150 | 9-28-76 | 1994 | Santo Domingo, D.R. |
| Hundt, Bo | .246 | 20 | 69 | 12 | 17 | 2 | 0 | 1 | 9 | 5 | 9 | 0 | 0 | S | R | 6-2 | 200 | 4-21-75 | 1996 | Bremen, Ind. |
| Jensen, Jacob | .188 | 31 | 96 | 14 | 18 | 4 | 2 | 1 | 13 | 10 | 22 | 2 | 3 | R | R | 6-2 | 185 | 10-31-76 | 1996 | Fresno, Calif. |
| Jordan, Yustin | .247 | 27 | 85 | 10 | 21 | 1 | 0 | 1 | 5 | 10 | 23 | 1 | 0 | R | R | 6-3 | 200 | 8-15-78 | 1996 | Monticello, Ark. |

| | | | | | | | | | | | | | | | | | | | | |
|---|---|---|---|---|---|---|---|---|---|---|---|---|---|---|---|---|---|---|---|---|
| Larkin, Garrett | .377 | 17 | 69 | 7 | 26 | 4 | 2 | 0 | 6 | 2 | 5 | 1 | 1 | L | R | 6-2 | 185 | 6-20-75 | 1996 | Medfield, Mass. |
| Lorenzana, Luis | .151 | 18 | 53 | 4 | 8 | 1 | 0 | 0 | 5 | 12 | 8 | 0 | 1 | R | R | 6-0 | 170 | 11-9-78 | 1996 | San Diego, Calif. |
| Mackowiak, Robert | .267 | 27 | 86 | 8 | 23 | 6 | 1 | 0 | 14 | 13 | 11 | 3 | 1 | L | R | 5-10 | 165 | 6-20-76 | 1996 | Schererville, Ind. |
| McKenzie, Carlton | .307 | 36 | 114 | 14 | 35 | 2 | 2 | 0 | 12 | 8 | 13 | 5 | 5 | L | R | 6-0 | 200 | 5-5-76 | 1996 | Patterson, N.J. |
| Pascual, Edison | .275 | 43 | 149 | 28 | 41 | 15 | 1 | 3 | 20 | 13 | 35 | 7 | 2 | L | L | 6-3 | 170 | 9-10-76 | 1994 | Santo Domingo, D.R. |
| Redman, Julian | .298 | 26 | 104 | 20 | 31 | 4 | 1 | 1 | 16 | 12 | 12 | 15 | 2 | L | L | 5-11 | 160 | 3-10-77 | 1996 | Duncanville, Ala. |
| Rivera, Carlos | .284 | 48 | 183 | 24 | 52 | 8 | 3 | 3 | 26 | 15 | 22 | 1 | 1 | L | L | 6-1 | 200 | 6-10-78 | 1996 | Rio Grande, P.R. |
| Rockow, Jeremy | .222 | 33 | 108 | 13 | 24 | 4 | 1 | 1 | 8 | 9 | 37 | 0 | 3 | L | L | 6-3 | 180 | 10-25-77 | 1996 | North Ft. Myers, Fla. |
| Viera, Rob | .308 | 10 | 26 | 3 | 8 | 0 | 0 | 0 | 1 | 2 | 3 | 0 | 0 | R | R | 6-2 | 215 | 4-19-73 | 1996 | Bradenton, Fla. |

**GAMES BY POSITION: C**—Diaz 26, Evans 29, Hundt 5, Viera 10. **1B**—Hundt 3, Pascual 24, Rivera 35. **2B**—Brooks 28, Delgado 30, Feliz 1, Germosen 6. **3B**—Burns 2, Delgado 1, Germosen 3, Jensen 31, Jordan 27. **SS**— Germosen 27, Larkin 14, Lorenzana 18, Mackowiak 4. **OF**—Benjamin 39, Burns 12, Delgado 1, Elliott 21, Hundt 12, Mackowiak 17, McKenzie 31, Pascual 9, Redman 23, Rockow 29.

| PITCHING | W | L | ERA | G | GS | CG | SV | IP | H | R | ER | BB | SO | B | T | HT | WT | DOB | 1st Yr | Resides |
|---|---|---|---|---|---|---|---|---|---|---|---|---|---|---|---|---|---|---|---|---|
| Alvarado, Carlos | 1 | 1 | 4.94 | 11 | 1 | 0 | 0 | 27 | 32 | 20 | 15 | 10 | 31 | R | R | 6-4 | 195 | 1-24-78 | 1995 | Arecibo, P.R. |
| Alvarado, David | 0 | 0 | 0.00 | 1 | 0 | 0 | 0 | 4 | 0 | 1 | 0 | 1 | 8 | R | R | 6-3 | 170 | 4-29-78 | 1995 | Falcon, Venez. |
| Beach, Scott | 2 | 1 | 10.57 | 7 | 0 | 0 | 0 | 8 | 16 | 9 | 9 | 3 | 4 | R | R | 6-4 | 175 | 10-18-73 | 1995 | Prairie Village, Kan. |
| Bonilla, Miguel | 0 | 0 | 9.00 | 3 | 0 | 0 | 0 | 3 | 6 | 3 | 3 | 1 | 2 | R | R | 6-2 | 195 | 8-23-73 | 1990 | Santo Domingo, D.R. |
| Bravo, Franklin | 5 | 3 | 2.32 | 11 | 11 | 2 | 0 | 62 | 62 | 23 | 16 | 10 | 36 | R | R | 6-2 | 170 | 12-24-78 | 1996 | Santo Domingo, D.R. |
| Classen, Ender | 1 | 1 | 4.70 | 7 | 0 | 0 | 1 | 8 | 12 | 5 | 4 | 3 | 6 | R | R | 6-3 | 185 | 4-1-78 | 1996 | Arecibo, P.R. |
| Cook, O.J. | 5 | 2 | 3.55 | 11 | 6 | 0 | 0 | 51 | 43 | 23 | 20 | 19 | 36 | R | R | 6-3 | 195 | 12-13-76 | 1995 | Bethlehem, Pa. |
| Delgado, Daniel | 1 | 0 | 2.84 | 2 | 0 | 0 | 0 | 6 | 4 | 2 | 2 | 2 | 1 | R | R | 5-9 | 165 | 12-29-76 | 1995 | Miami, Fla. |
| Dunn, Cordell | 0 | 5 | 5.46 | 7 | 6 | 0 | 0 | 28 | 32 | 24 | 17 | 14 | 24 | R | R | 6-2 | 185 | 11-3-75 | 1994 | Tunica, Miss. |
| Finol, Ricardo | 1 | 0 | 9.00 | 6 | 0 | 0 | 0 | 10 | 19 | 10 | 10 | 5 | 9 | S | R | 6-0 | 170 | 5-10-74 | 1996 | San Francisco, Venez. |
| Gaerte, Travis | 1 | 0 | 2.40 | 14 | 0 | 0 | 5 | 30 | 17 | 9 | 8 | 18 | 24 | R | R | 6-3 | 180 | 10-21-76 | 1995 | Fremont, Ind. |
| Gillespie, Ryan | 0 | 0 | 0.00 | 1 | 0 | 0 | 0 | 3 | 4 | 1 | 0 | 0 | 5 | R | R | 6-6 | 200 | 3-29-77 | 1995 | San Diego, Calif. |
| Goedde, Roger | 0 | 2 | 9.10 | 12 | 3 | 0 | 0 | 29 | 45 | 41 | 29 | 11 | 23 | R | R | 6-4 | 180 | 5-19-76 | 1994 | Evansville, Ind. |
| Gresko, Michael | 0 | 1 | 3.00 | 5 | 0 | 0 | 0 | 6 | 3 | 8 | 2 | 5 | 7 | L | L | 6-8 | 200 | 10-27-76 | 1996 | Trenton, N.J. |
| Harris, Gene | 0 | 2 | 3.21 | 9 | 1 | 0 | 1 | 14 | 16 | 7 | 5 | 4 | 14 | R | R | 5-11 | 190 | 12-5-64 | 1986 | Okeechobee, Fla. |
| Heberling, Keith | 0 | 0 | 0.00 | 1 | 0 | 0 | 0 | 1 | 0 | 0 | 0 | 0 | 1 | L | L | 6-3 | 200 | 9-21-72 | 1993 | Vero Beach, Fla. |
| Hlodan, George | 3 | 2 | 2.67 | 7 | 6 | 0 | 0 | 27 | 29 | 12 | 8 | 7 | 15 | R | R | 6-0 | 170 | 6-25-76 | 1996 | Elizabeth, Pa. |
| Hohenstein, Andrew | 2 | 0 | 3.08 | 7 | 5 | 0 | 0 | 26 | 36 | 20 | 9 | 12 | 18 | R | R | 6-4 | 210 | 9-27-77 | 1996 | Riverside, Calif. |
| Mattson, Craig | 0 | 0 | 0.00 | 1 | 0 | 0 | 0 | 1 | 0 | 0 | 0 | 0 | 0 | R | R | 6-4 | 205 | 11-25-73 | 1993 | Belvidere, Ill. |
| Prater, Andrew | 4 | 5 | 3.18 | 12 | 12 | 1 | 0 | 68 | 63 | 24 | 24 | 11 | 53 | R | R | 6-3 | 175 | 9-27-77 | 1996 | Florissant, Mo. |
| Settle, Brian | 1 | 7 | 7.94 | 7 | 0 | 0 | 0 | 11 | 5 | 10 | 10 | 14 | 13 | R | R | 6-5 | 190 | 7-17-77 | 1995 | Portsmouth, Va. |
| Siciliano, Jess | 0 | 0 | 3.60 | 3 | 0 | 0 | 0 | 5 | 4 | 3 | 2 | 2 | 1 | R | R | 6-2 | 190 | 8-31-76 | 1996 | East White Plains, N.Y. |
| Tobias, Daniel | 0 | 1 | 1.59 | 5 | 0 | 0 | 0 | 6 | 4 | 6 | 1 | 4 | 4 | R | R | 6-5 | 200 | 8-20-75 | 1996 | Oregon, Ohio |
| Vogt, Robert | 2 | 3 | 2.95 | 13 | 5 | 0 | 0 | 43 | 36 | 23 | 14 | 19 | 46 | L | L | 6-6 | 200 | 10-19-78 | 1996 | Brandon, Fla. |
| Wagner, Paul | 0 | 0 | 0.00 | 1 | 1 | 0 | 0 | 3 | 2 | 0 | 0 | 0 | 4 | R | R | 6-1 | 202 | 11-14-67 | 1989 | Germantown, Wis. |
| White, Rick | 0 | 0 | 2.25 | 3 | 3 | 0 | 0 | 12 | 8 | 4 | 3 | 3 | 8 | R | R | 6-4 | 215 | 12-23-68 | 1990 | Springfield, Ohio |
| Wright, Jason | 0 | 1 | 1.33 | 13 | 0 | 0 | 7 | 20 | 13 | 3 | 3 | 6 | 25 | R | R | 6-4 | 230 | 8-28-75 | 1996 | Los Alamitos, Calif. |

# ST. LOUIS CARDINALS

**Manager:** Tony La Russa.    **1996 Record:** 88-74, .543 (1st, NL Central).

## BATTING

| | AVG | G | AB | R | H | 2B | 3B | HR | RBI | BB | SO | SB | CS | B | T | HT | WT | DOB | 1st Yr | Resides |
|---|---|---|---|---|---|---|---|---|---|---|---|---|---|---|---|---|---|---|---|---|
| Alicea, Luis | .258 | 129 | 380 | 54 | 98 | 26 | 3 | 5 | 42 | 52 | 78 | 11 | 3 | S | R | 5-9 | 177 | 7-29-65 | 1986 | Loxahatchee, Fla. |
| Bell, David | .214 | 62 | 145 | 12 | 31 | 6 | 0 | 1 | 9 | 10 | 22 | 1 | 1 | R | R | 5-10 | 170 | 9-14-72 | 1990 | Cincinnati, Ohio |
| Borders, Pat | .319 | 26 | 69 | 3 | 22 | 3 | 0 | 0 | 4 | 1 | 14 | 0 | 1 | R | R | 6-2 | 195 | 5-14-63 | 1982 | Lake Wales, Fla. |
| Bradshaw, Terry | .333 | 15 | 21 | 4 | 7 | 1 | 0 | 0 | 3 | 3 | 2 | 0 | 1 | L | R | 6-0 | 180 | 2-3-69 | 1990 | Zuni, Va. |
| Clayton, Royce | .277 | 129 | 491 | 64 | 136 | 20 | 4 | 6 | 35 | 33 | 89 | 33 | 15 | R | R | 6-0 | 183 | 1-2-70 | 1988 | Inglewood, Calif. |
| Difelice, Mike | .286 | 4 | 7 | 0 | 2 | 1 | 0 | 0 | 2 | 0 | 1 | 0 | 0 | R | R | 6-2 | 205 | 5-28-69 | 1991 | Knoxville, Tenn. |
| Gaetti, Gary | .274 | 141 | 522 | 71 | 143 | 27 | 4 | 23 | 80 | 35 | 97 | 2 | 2 | R | R | 6-0 | 200 | 8-19-58 | 1979 | Raleigh, N.C. |
| Gallego, Mike | .210 | 51 | 143 | 12 | 30 | 2 | 0 | 0 | 4 | 12 | 31 | 0 | 0 | R | R | 5-8 | 160 | 10-31-60 | 1981 | Yorba Linda, Calif. |
| Gant, Ron | .246 | 122 | 419 | 74 | 103 | 14 | 2 | 30 | 82 | 73 | 98 | 13 | 4 | R | R | 6-0 | 200 | 3-2-65 | 1983 | Smyrna, Ga. |
| Holbert, Aaron | .000 | 1 | 3 | 0 | 0 | 0 | 0 | 0 | 0 | 0 | 0 | 0 | 0 | R | R | 6-0 | 160 | 1-9-73 | 1990 | Long Beach, Calif. |
| Jordan, Brian | .310 | 140 | 513 | 82 | 159 | 36 | 1 | 17 | 104 | 29 | 84 | 22 | 5 | R | R | 6-1 | 205 | 3-29-67 | 1988 | Baltimore, Md. |
| Lankford, Ray | .275 | 149 | 545 | 100 | 150 | 36 | 8 | 21 | 86 | 79 | 133 | 35 | 7 | L | L | 5-11 | 180 | 6-5-67 | 1987 | Modesto, Calif. |
| Mabry, John | .297 | 151 | 543 | 63 | 161 | 30 | 2 | 13 | 74 | 37 | 84 | 3 | 2 | L | R | 6-4 | 195 | 10-17-70 | 1991 | Warwick, Md. |
| McGee, Willie | .307 | 123 | 309 | 52 | 95 | 15 | 2 | 5 | 41 | 18 | 60 | 5 | 2 | S | R | 6-1 | 185 | 11-2-58 | 1977 | Hercules, Calif. |
| Mejia, Miguel | .087 | 45 | 23 | 10 | 2 | 0 | 0 | 0 | 0 | 0 | 10 | 6 | 3 | R | R | 6-1 | 155 | 3-25-75 | 1992 | San Pedro de Macoris, D.R. |
| Pagnozzi, Tom | .270 | 119 | 407 | 48 | 110 | 23 | 0 | 13 | 55 | 24 | 78 | 4 | 1 | R | R | 6-1 | 190 | 7-30-62 | 1983 | Tucson, Ariz. |
| Sheaffer, Danny | .227 | 79 | 198 | 10 | 45 | 9 | 3 | 2 | 20 | 9 | 25 | 3 | 3 | R | R | 6-0 | 190 | 8-21-61 | 1981 | Winston-Salem, N.C. |
| Smith, Ozzie | .282 | 82 | 227 | 36 | 64 | 10 | 2 | 2 | 18 | 25 | 9 | 7 | 5 | S | R | 5-10 | 150 | 12-26-54 | 1977 | Ladue, Mo. |
| Sweeney, Mark | .265 | 98 | 170 | 32 | 45 | 9 | 0 | 3 | 22 | 33 | 29 | 3 | 0 | L | L | 6-1 | 195 | 10-26-69 | 1991 | Holliston, Mass. |
| Young, Dmitri | .241 | 16 | 29 | 3 | 7 | 0 | 0 | 0 | 2 | 4 | 5 | 0 | 1 | S | R | 6-2 | 215 | 10-11-73 | 1991 | Camarillo, Calif. |

## PITCHING

| | W | L | ERA | G | GS | CG | SV | IP | H | R | ER | BB | SO | B | T | HT | WT | DOB | 1st Yr | Resides |
|---|---|---|---|---|---|---|---|---|---|---|---|---|---|---|---|---|---|---|---|---|
| Bailey, Cory | 5 | 2 | 3.00 | 51 | 0 | 0 | 0 | 57 | 57 | 21 | 19 | 30 | 38 | R | R | 6-1 | 210 | 1-24-71 | 1991 | Marion, Ill. |
| Barber, Brian | 0 | 0 | 15.00 | 1 | 0 | 0 | 3 | 4 | 5 | 5 | 6 | 1 | R | R | 6-1 | 172 | 3-4-73 | 1991 | Orlando, Fla. |
| Batchelor, Richard | 2 | 0 | 1.20 | 11 | 0 | 0 | 0 | 15 | 9 | 2 | 2 | 1 | 11 | R | R | 6-1 | 195 | 4-8-67 | 1990 | Hartsville, S.C. |
| Benes, Alan | 13 | 10 | 4.90 | 34 | 32 | 3 | 0 | 191 | 192 | 120 | 104 | 87 | 131 | R | R | 6-5 | 215 | 1-21-72 | 1993 | Lake Forest, Ill. |
| Benes, Andy | 18 | 10 | 3.83 | 36 | 34 | 3 | 1 | 230 | 215 | 107 | 98 | 77 | 160 | R | R | 6-6 | 238 | 8-20-67 | 1989 | Poway, Calif. |
| Busby, Mike | 0 | 1 | 18.00 | 1 | 1 | 0 | 0 | 4 | 9 | 13 | 8 | 4 | 4 | R | R | 6-4 | 215 | 12-27-72 | 1991 | Wilmington, Calif. |
| Eckersley, Dennis | 0 | 6 | 3.30 | 63 | 0 | 0 | 30 | 60 | 65 | 26 | 22 | 6 | 49 | R | R | 6-2 | 195 | 10-3-54 | 1972 | Sudbury, Mass. |
| Fossas, Tony | 0 | 4 | 2.68 | 65 | 0 | 0 | 2 | 47 | 43 | 19 | 14 | 21 | 36 | L | L | 6-0 | 187 | 9-23-57 | 1979 | Fort Lauderdale, Fla. |
| Honeycutt, Rick | 2 | 1 | 2.85 | 61 | 0 | 0 | 4 | 47 | 42 | 15 | 15 | 7 | 30 | L | L | 6-1 | 192 | 6-29-54 | 1976 | La Habra Heights, Calif. |
| Jackson, Danny | 1 | 1 | 4.46 | 13 | 4 | 0 | 0 | 36 | 33 | 18 | 18 | 16 | 27 | R | L | 6-0 | 205 | 1-5-62 | 1982 | Overland Park, Kan. |
| Ludwick, Eric | 0 | 1 | 9.00 | 6 | 1 | 0 | 0 | 10 | 11 | 11 | 10 | 3 | 12 | R | R | 6-5 | 210 | 12-14-71 | 1993 | Las Vegas, Nev. |
| Mathews, T.J. | 2 | 6 | 3.01 | 67 | 0 | 0 | 6 | 84 | 62 | 32 | 28 | 32 | 80 | R | R | 6-2 | 200 | 1-19-70 | 1992 | Columbia, Ill. |
| Morgan, Mike | 4 | 8 | 5.24 | 18 | 18 | 0 | 0 | 103 | 118 | 63 | 60 | 40 | 55 | R | R | 6-2 | 222 | 10-8-59 | 1978 | Ogden, Utah |
| Osborne, Donovan | 13 | 9 | 3.53 | 30 | 30 | 2 | 0 | 199 | 192 | 87 | 78 | 57 | 134 | L | L | 6-2 | 195 | 6-21-69 | 1990 | Carson City, Nev. |
| Parrett, Jeff | 2 | 2 | 4.25 | 33 | 0 | 0 | 0 | 42 | 40 | 20 | 20 | 20 | 42 | R | R | 6-3 | 185 | 8-26-61 | 1983 | Lexington, Ky. |
| Petkovsek, Mark | 11 | 2 | 3.55 | 48 | 6 | 0 | 0 | 89 | 83 | 37 | 35 | 35 | 45 | R | R | 6-0 | 185 | 11-18-65 | 1987 | Beaumont, Texas |
| Stottlemyre, Todd | 14 | 11 | 3.87 | 34 | 33 | 5 | 0 | 223 | 191 | 100 | 96 | 93 | 194 | L | R | 6-3 | 195 | 5-20-65 | 1986 | Yakima, Wash. |
| Urbani, Tom | 1 | 0 | 7.71 | 3 | 2 | 0 | 0 | 12 | 15 | 10 | 10 | 4 | 1 | L | L | 6-1 | 190 | 1-21-68 | 1990 | Santa Cruz, Calif. |

## FIELDING

| Catcher | PCT | G | PO | A | E | DP | PB |
|---|---|---|---|---|---|---|---|
| Borders | .984 | 17 | 116 | 9 | 2 | 1 | 0 |
| Difelice | 1.000 | 4 | 15 | 1 | 0 | 0 | 0 |
| Pagnozzi | .990 | 116 | 716 | 48 | 8 | 6 | 6 |
| Sheaffer | .983 | 47 | 257 | 27 | 5 | 3 | 1 |

| First Base | PCT | G | PO | A | E | DP |
|---|---|---|---|---|---|---|
| Borders | .500 | 1 | 1 | 0 | 1 | 0 |
| Gaetti | .989 | 14 | 85 | 7 | 1 | 6 |
| Jordan | 1.000 | 1 | 1 | 0 | 0 | 0 |
| Mabry | .994 | 146 | 1170 | 76 | 8 | 107 |
| McGee | 1.000 | 6 | 23 | 4 | 0 | 0 |
| Pagnozzi | 1.000 | 1 | 1 | 0 | 0 | 0 |
| Sheaffer | 1.000 | 6 | 11 | 0 | 0 | 1 |
| Sweeney | .972 | 15 | 67 | 2 | 2 | 7 |
| Young | .976 | 10 | 39 | 1 | 1 | 5 |

| Second Base | PCT | G | PO | A | E | DP |
|---|---|---|---|---|---|---|
| Alicea | .957 | 125 | 241 | 288 | 24 | 70 |
| Bell | .987 | 20 | 23 | 54 | 1 | 9 |
| Gallego | .985 | 43 | 84 | 118 | 3 | 31 |
| Holbert | 1.000 | 1 | 0 | 1 | 0 | 0 |

| Third Base | PCT | G | PO | A | E | DP |
|---|---|---|---|---|---|---|
| Bell | .953 | 45 | 22 | 59 | 4 | 1 |
| Gaetti | .970 | 133 | 63 | 224 | 9 | 16 |
| Gallego | 1.000 | 7 | 3 | 4 | 0 | 0 |
| Sheaffer | .958 | 17 | 6 | 17 | 1 | 0 |

| Shortstop | PCT | G | PO | A | E | DP |
|---|---|---|---|---|---|---|
| Bell | .000 | 1 | 0 | 0 | 0 | 0 |
| Clayton | .972 | 113 | 171 | 347 | 15 | 68 |
| Gallego | 1.000 | 3 | 4 | 0 | 0 | 1 |
| Smith | .969 | 52 | 90 | 162 | 8 | 36 |

| Outfield | PCT | G | PO | A | E | DP |
|---|---|---|---|---|---|---|
| Bradshaw | 1.000 | 7 | 4 | 0 | 0 | 0 |
| Gant | .978 | 116 | 216 | 4 | 5 | 2 |
| Jordan | .994 | 136 | 309 | 9 | 2 | 0 |
| Lankford | .997 | 144 | 356 | 9 | 1 | 0 |
| Mabry | 1.000 | 14 | 12 | 0 | 0 | 0 |
| McGee | .962 | 83 | 119 | 6 | 5 | 3 |
| Mejia | .933 | 21 | 14 | 0 | 1 | 0 |
| Sheaffer | 1.000 | 3 | 3 | 0 | 0 | 0 |
| Sweeney | .984 | 43 | 59 | 1 | 1 | 0 |

**Ron Gant**

DAVID SEELIG

LARRY GOREN

Brian Jordan topped the Cardinals with a .310 average and 104 RBIs

Cardinals minor league Player of the Year Dmitri Young

MEL BAILEY

**CARDINALS**

## FARM SYSTEM

Director of Player Development: Mike Jorgensen

| Class | Farm Team | League | W | L | Pct. | Finish* | Manager | First Yr |
|-------|-----------|--------|---|---|------|---------|---------|----------|
| AAA | Louisville (Ky.) Redbirds | American Assoc. | 60 | 84 | .417 | 7th (8) | Joe Pettini | 1982 |
| AA | Arkansas Travelers | Texas | 67 | 73 | .519 | 7th (8) | Rick Mahler | 1966 |
| #A | St. Petersburg (Fla.) Cardinals | Florida State | 75 | 63 | .543 | 4th (14) | Chris Maloney | 1966 |
| A | Peoria (Ill.) Chiefs | Midwest | 79 | 57 | .581 | 1st (14) | Roy Silver | 1995 |
| A | New Jersey Cardinals | New York-Penn | 28 | 47 | .373 | 14th (14) | Scott Melvin | 1994 |
| #R | Johnson City (Tenn.) Cardinals | Appalachian | 42 | 26 | .618 | T-2nd (9) | Steve Turco | 1975 |

*Finish in overall standings (No. of teams in league)   #Advanced level

## ORGANIZATION LEADERS

### MAJOR LEAGUERS

**BATTING**

| | | |
|---|---|---|
| *AVG | Brian Jordan | .310 |
| R | Ray Lankford | 100 |
| H | John Mabry | 161 |
| TB | Ray Lankford | 265 |
| 2B | Two tied at | 36 |
| 3B | Ray Lankford | 8 |
| HR | Ron Gant | 30 |
| RBI | Brian Jordan | 104 |
| BB | Ray Lankford | 79 |
| SO | Ray Lankford | 133 |
| SB | Ray Lankford | 35 |

**PITCHING**

| | | |
|---|---|---|
| W | Andy Benes | 18 |
| L | Todd Stottlemyre | 11 |
| #ERA | T.J. Mathews | 3.01 |
| G | T.J. Mathews | 67 |
| CG | Todd Stottlemyre | 5 |
| SV | Dennis Eckersley | 30 |
| IP | Andy Benes | 230 |
| BB | Todd Stottlemyre | 93 |
| SO | Todd Stottlemyre | 194 |

MEL BAILEY

**Andy Benes.** 18 wins

### MINOR LEAGUERS

**BATTING**

| | | |
|---|---|---|
| *AVG | Kerry Robinson, Peoria | .359 |
| R | Kerry Robinson, Peoria | 98 |
| H | Kerry Robinson, Peoria | 158 |
| TB | Dmitri Young, Louisville | 245 |
| 2B | Jeff Berblinger, Arkansas | 32 |
| 3B | Kerry Robinson, Peoria | 14 |
| HR | Jose Oliva, Louisville | 31 |
| RBI | Jose Oliva, Louisville | 86 |
| BB | Andy Hall, Peoria | 75 |
| SO | Chris Haas, Peoria | 169 |
| SB | Kerry Robinson, Peoria | 50 |

**PITCHING**

| | | |
|---|---|---|
| W | Blake Stein, St. Petersburg | 16 |
| L | Two tied at | 13 |
| #ERA | Britt Reames, Peoria | 1.90 |
| G | Matt Arrandale, Louisville | 63 |
| CG | Two tied at | 4 |
| SV | Curtis King, St. Pete./Arkansas | 31 |
| IP | Matt Morris, Arkansas/Louisville | 175 |
| BB | Kris Detmers, Arkansas | 70 |
| SO | Britt Reames, Peoria | 167 |

*Minimum 250 At-Bats   #Minimum 75 Innings

## TOP 10 PROSPECTS

How the Cardinals Top 10 prospects, as judged by Baseball America prior to the 1996 season, fared in 1996:

| Player, Pos. | Club (Class—League) | AVG | AB | R | H | 2B | 3B | HR | RBI | SB |
|--------------|---------------------|-----|-----|----|-----|----|----|----|-----|-----|
| 7. Mike Gulan, 3b | Louisville (AAA—Amer. Assoc.) | .255 | 419 | 47 | 107 | 27 | 4 | 17 | 55 | 7 |
| 8. Eli Marrero, c | Arkansas (AA—Texas) | .270 | 374 | 65 | 101 | 17 | 3 | 19 | 65 | 9 |

| Player, Pos. | Club (Class—League) | W | L | ERA | G | SV | IP | H | BB | SO |
|--------------|---------------------|---|---|-----|---|----|-----|-----|-----|-----|
| 1. Alan Benes, rhp | St. Louis | 13 | 10 | 4.90 | 34 | 0 | 191 | 192 | 87 | 131 |
| 2. Matt Morris, rhp | Louisville (AAA—Amer. Assoc.) | 0 | 1 | 3.38 | 1 | 0 | 8 | 8 | 1 | 9 |
| | Arkansas (AA—Texas) | 12 | 12 | 3.88 | 27 | 0 | 167 | 178 | 48 | 120 |
| 3. John Frascatore, rhp | Louisville (AAA—Amer. Assoc.) | 6 | 13 | 5.18 | 36 | 0 | 156 | 180 | 42 | 95 |
| 4. T.J. Mathews, rhp | St. Louis | 2 | 6 | 3.01 | 67 | 6 | 84 | 62 | 32 | 80 |
| 5. *Bret Wagner, lhp | Huntsville (AA—Southern) | 8 | 8 | 4.25 | 27 | 0 | 134 | 125 | 77 | 90 |
| 6. Mike Busby, rhp | Louisville (AAA—Amer. Assoc.) | 2 | 5 | 6.38 | 14 | 0 | 72 | 89 | 44 | 53 |
| | St. Louis | 0 | 1 | 18.00 | 1 | 0 | 4 | 9 | 4 | 4 |
| 9. Kris Detmers, lhp | Arkansas (AA—Texas) | 12 | 8 | 3.35 | 27 | 0 | 164 | 154 | 70 | 97 |
| 10. Brian Barber, rhp | Louisville (AAA—Amer. Assoc.) | 0 | 6 | 5.62 | 11 | 0 | 50 | 49 | 26 | 33 |
| | St. Louis | 0 | 0 | 15.00 | 1 | 0 | 3 | 4 | 6 | 1 |

STEVE MOORE

**Alan Benes**        *Traded to Athletics

## AMERICAN ASSOCIATION

| BATTING | AVG | G | AB | R | H | 2B | 3B | HR | RBI | BB | SO | SB | CS | B | T | HT | WT | DOB | 1st Yr | Resides |
|---|---|---|---|---|---|---|---|---|---|---|---|---|---|---|---|---|---|---|---|---|
| Bell, David | .176 | 42 | 136 | 9 | 24 | 5 | 1 | 0 | 7 | 7 | 15 | 1 | 2 | R | R | 5-10 | 170 | 9-14-72 | 1990 | Cincinnati, Ohio |
| Bradshaw, Terry | .303 | 102 | 389 | 56 | 118 | 23 | 1 | 12 | 44 | 42 | 64 | 21 | 9 | L | R | 6-0 | 180 | 2-3-69 | 1990 | Zuni, Va. |
| Cholowsky, Dan | .179 | 17 | 56 | 3 | 10 | 2 | 0 | 1 | 6 | 4 | 16 | 1 | 2 | R | R | 6-0 | 195 | 10-30-70 | 1991 | San Jose, Calif. |
| Correia, Rod | .159 | 35 | 113 | 7 | 18 | 3 | 0 | 2 | 8 | 3 | 22 | 1 | 2 | R | R | 5-11 | 185 | 9-13-67 | 1988 | Rehoboth, Mass. |
| Cromer, Tripp | .225 | 80 | 244 | 28 | 55 | 4 | 4 | 4 | 25 | 22 | 47 | 3 | 1 | R | R | 6-2 | 160 | 11-21-67 | 1989 | Lexington, S.C. |
| Deak, Darrel | .232 | 70 | 164 | 19 | 38 | 4 | 0 | 8 | 18 | 24 | 47 | 2 | 1 | S | R | 6-0 | 180 | 7-5-69 | 1991 | Scottsdale, Ariz. |
| Difelice, Mike | .285 | 79 | 246 | 25 | 70 | 13 | 0 | 9 | 33 | 20 | 43 | 0 | 3 | R | R | 6-2 | 205 | 5-28-69 | 1991 | Knoxville, Tenn. |
| Diggs, Tony | .205 | 92 | 308 | 35 | 63 | 14 | 2 | 7 | 23 | 33 | 49 | 5 | 5 | S | R | 6-0 | 175 | 4-20-67 | 1989 | Starke, Fla. |
| Franklin, Micah | .232 | 86 | 289 | 43 | 67 | 18 | 3 | 15 | 53 | 40 | 71 | 2 | 3 | S | R | 6-0 | 195 | 4-25-72 | 1990 | San Francisco, Calif. |
| Gulan, Mike | .255 | 123 | 419 | 47 | 107 | 27 | 4 | 17 | 55 | 26 | 119 | 7 | 2 | R | R | 6-1 | 190 | 12-18-70 | 1992 | Steubenville, Ohio |
| Hare, Shawn | .163 | 15 | 49 | 3 | 8 | 1 | 0 | 1 | 3 | 11 | 1 | 0 | L | L | 6-1 | 200 | 3-26-67 | 1989 | Lakeland, Fla. |
| Hemond, Scott | .260 | 50 | 150 | 15 | 39 | 10 | 1 | 3 | 15 | 13 | 35 | 1 | 2 | R | R | 6-0 | 215 | 11-18-65 | 1986 | Dunedin, Fla. |
| Holbert, Aaron | .264 | 112 | 436 | 54 | 115 | 16 | 6 | 4 | 32 | 21 | 61 | 20 | 14 | R | R | 6-0 | 160 | 1-9-73 | 1990 | Long Beach, Calif. |
| Howitt, Dann | .255 | 46 | 141 | 19 | 36 | 6 | 1 | 4 | 18 | 16 | 31 | 4 | 1 | L | R | 6-5 | 205 | 2-13-64 | 1986 | Medford, Ore. |
| McNeely, Jeff | .125 | 3 | 8 | 0 | 1 | 0 | 0 | 0 | 1 | 0 | 2 | 0 | 0 | R | R | 6-2 | 200 | 10-18-69 | 1989 | Monroe, N.C. |
| Oliva, Jose | .242 | 118 | 413 | 52 | 100 | 13 | 0 | 31 | 86 | 34 | 101 | 3 | 3 | R | R | 6-1 | 215 | 3-3-71 | 1988 | San Pedro de Macoris, D.R. |
| Pagnozzi, Tom | .154 | 8 | 26 | 5 | 4 | 0 | 0 | 2 | 3 | 3 | 2 | 0 | 0 | R | R | 6-1 | 190 | 7-30-62 | 1983 | Tucson, Ariz. |
| Pena, Geronimo | .283 | 27 | 106 | 17 | 30 | 6 | 2 | 6 | 18 | 12 | 25 | 0 | 0 | S | R | 6-1 | 170 | 3-29-67 | 1985 | Los Alcarrizos, D.R. |
| Stefanski, Mike | .206 | 53 | 126 | 11 | 26 | 7 | 1 | 2 | 9 | 11 | 11 | 1 | 2 | R | R | 6-2 | 190 | 9-12-69 | 1991 | Redford, Mich. |
| Torres, Paul | .500 | 1 | 2 | 0 | 1 | 0 | 0 | 0 | 0 | 0 | 1 | 0 | 0 | R | R | 6-3 | 210 | 10-19-70 | 1989 | San Lorenzo, Calif. |
| Wimmer, Chris | .249 | 112 | 345 | 40 | 86 | 11 | 2 | 2 | 23 | 16 | 41 | 11 | 3 | R | R | 5-11 | 170 | 9-25-70 | 1992 | Wichita, Kan. |
| Young, Dmitri | .333 | 122 | 459 | 90 | 153 | 31 | 8 | 15 | 64 | 34 | 67 | 16 | 5 | S | R | 6-2 | 215 | 10-11-73 | 1991 | Camarillo, Calif. |

| PITCHING | W | L | ERA | G | GS | CG | SV | IP | H | R | ER | BB | SO | B | T | HT | WT | DOB | 1st Yr | Resides |
|---|---|---|---|---|---|---|---|---|---|---|---|---|---|---|---|---|---|---|---|---|
| Arrandale, Matt | 5 | 4 | 4.78 | 63 | 0 | 0 | 3 | 79 | 83 | 51 | 42 | 33 | 38 | R | R | 6-0 | 165 | 12-14-70 | 1993 | St. Louis, Mo. |
| Aybar, Manuel | 2 | 2 | 3.23 | 5 | 5 | 0 | 0 | 31 | 26 | 12 | 11 | 7 | 25 | R | R | 6-1 | 165 | 10-5-74 | 1991 | Bani, D.R. |
| Badorek, Mike | 0 | 4 | 5.29 | 20 | 6 | 0 | 0 | 49 | 52 | 34 | 29 | 18 | 22 | R | R | 6-5 | 230 | 5-15-69 | 1991 | Mt. Zion, Ill. |
| Bailey, Cory | 2 | 4 | 5.82 | 22 | 0 | 0 | 1 | 34 | 29 | 22 | 22 | 20 | 27 | R | R | 6-1 | 210 | 1-24-71 | 1991 | Marion, Ill. |
| Barber, Brian | 0 | 6 | 5.62 | 11 | 11 | 1 | 0 | 50 | 49 | 37 | 31 | 26 | 33 | R | R | 6-1 | 172 | 3-4-73 | 1991 | Orlando, Fla. |
| Batchelor, Rich | 5 | 2 | 4.12 | 51 | 0 | 0 | 28 | 55 | 59 | 29 | 25 | 19 | 57 | R | R | 6-1 | 195 | 4-8-67 | 1990 | Hartsville, S.C. |
| Beltran, Rigo | 8 | 6 | 4.35 | 38 | 16 | 3 | 0 | 130 | 132 | 67 | 63 | 24 | 132 | L | L | 5-11 | 185 | 11-13-69 | 1991 | San Diego, Calif. |
| Busby, Mike | 2 | 5 | 6.38 | 14 | 14 | 0 | 0 | 72 | 89 | 57 | 51 | 44 | 53 | R | R | 6-4 | 215 | 12-27-72 | 1991 | Wilmington, Calif. |
| Dixon, Steve | 0 | 0 | 10.38 | 8 | 0 | 0 | 0 | 4 | 4 | 5 | 5 | 3 | 2 | L | L | 6-0 | 195 | 8-3-69 | 1989 | Louisville, Ky. |
| Eiland, Dave | 0 | 1 | 5.55 | 8 | 6 | 0 | 0 | 24 | 27 | 17 | 15 | 8 | 17 | R | R | 6-3 | 205 | 7-5-66 | 1987 | Dade City, Fla. |
| Frascatore, John | 6 | 13 | 5.18 | 36 | 21 | 3 | 0 | 156 | 180 | 106 | 90 | 42 | 95 | R | R | 6-1 | 200 | 2-4-70 | 1991 | Oceanside, N.Y. |
| Jackson, Danny | 0 | 0 | 3.46 | 8 | 1 | 0 | 0 | 13 | 14 | 6 | 5 | 6 | 5 | R | L | 6-0 | 205 | 1-5-62 | 1982 | Overland Park, Kan. |
| Lowe, Sean | 8 | 9 | 4.70 | 25 | 18 | 0 | 0 | 115 | 127 | 72 | 60 | 51 | 76 | R | R | 6-2 | 205 | 3-29-71 | 1992 | Mesquite, Texas |
| Ludwick, Eric | 3 | 4 | 2.83 | 11 | 11 | 0 | 0 | 60 | 55 | 24 | 19 | 24 | 73 | R | R | 6-5 | 210 | 12-14-71 | 1993 | Las Vegas, Nev. |
| Maxcy, Brian | 4 | 2 | 4.79 | 36 | 3 | 0 | 1 | 62 | 63 | 34 | 33 | 32 | 52 | R | R | 6-1 | 170 | 5-4-71 | 1992 | Amory, Miss. |
| Morgan, Mike | 1 | 3 | 7.04 | 4 | 4 | 1 | 0 | 23 | 29 | 18 | 18 | 11 | 10 | R | R | 6-2 | 222 | 10-8-59 | 1978 | Ogden, Utah |
| Morris, Matt | 0 | 1 | 3.38 | 1 | 1 | 0 | 0 | 8 | 8 | 3 | 3 | 1 | 9 | R | R | 6-5 | 210 | 8-9-74 | 1995 | Montgomery, N.Y. |
| Mutis, Jeff | 2 | 3 | 5.87 | 32 | 0 | 0 | 1 | 38 | 44 | 26 | 25 | 19 | 21 | L | L | 6-2 | 185 | 12-20-66 | 1988 | Allentown, Pa. |
| Osborne, Donovan | 1 | 0 | 2.57 | 1 | 1 | 0 | 0 | 7 | 6 | 2 | 2 | 2 | 3 | L | L | 6-2 | 195 | 6-21-69 | 1990 | Carson City, Nev. |
| Petkovsek, Mark | 0 | 1 | 9.00 | 2 | 1 | 0 | 0 | 3 | 5 | 4 | 3 | 1 | 4 | R | R | 6-0 | 185 | 11-18-65 | 1987 | Beaumont, Texas |
| Powell, Ross | 0 | 0 | 2.16 | 5 | 0 | 0 | 0 | 8 | 8 | 2 | 2 | 2 | 10 | L | L | 6-0 | 180 | 1-24-68 | 1989 | Antioch, Tenn. |
| Simmons, Scott | 5 | 6 | 4.15 | 30 | 8 | 0 | 1 | 100 | 98 | 51 | 46 | 35 | 58 | R | L | 6-2 | 200 | 8-15-69 | 1991 | St. Charles, Mo. |
| Urbani, Tom | 2 | 2 | 3.27 | 7 | 7 | 0 | 0 | 44 | 40 | 19 | 16 | 12 | 26 | L | L | 6-1 | 190 | 1-21-68 | 1990 | Santa Cruz, Calif. |
| VanRyn, Ben | 4 | 6 | 4.88 | 19 | 10 | 0 | 1 | 66 | 69 | 43 | 36 | 27 | 42 | L | L | 6-5 | 195 | 8-9-71 | 1990 | Kendallville, Ind. |

### FIELDING

| Catcher | PCT | G | PO | A | E | DP | PB |
|---|---|---|---|---|---|---|---|
| Difelice | .984 | 77 | 455 | 48 | 8 | 2 | 7 |
| Hemond | .982 | 37 | 196 | 18 | 4 | 3 | 4 |
| Pagnozzi | 1.000 | 8 | 36 | 5 | 0 | 1 | 1 |
| Stefanski | .981 | 45 | 233 | 20 | 5 | 6 | 3 |

| First Base | PCT | G | PO | A | E | DP |
|---|---|---|---|---|---|---|
| Cholowsky | 1.000 | 1 | 2 | 0 | 0 | 0 |
| Deak | 1.000 | 8 | 43 | 1 | 0 | 0 |
| Gulan | 1.000 | 2 | 3 | 1 | 0 | 0 |
| Oliva | .989 | 21 | 163 | 17 | 2 | 11 |
| Stefanski | 1.000 | 1 | 7 | 0 | 0 | 1 |
| Torres | 1.000 | 1 | 2 | 0 | 0 | 0 |
| Young | .993 | 122 | 1091 | 83 | 8 | 102 |

| Second Base | PCT | G | PO | A | E | DP |
|---|---|---|---|---|---|---|
| Bell | .970 | 34 | 64 | 95 | 5 | 19 |
| Cromer | 1.000 | 2 | 12 | 5 | 0 | 4 |

| | PCT | G | PO | A | E | DP |
|---|---|---|---|---|---|---|
| Deak | 1.000 | 5 | 10 | 13 | 0 | 4 |
| Hemond | 1.000 | 2 | 2 | 7 | 0 | 1 |
| Holbert | .948 | 65 | 119 | 211 | 18 | 31 |
| Pena | .945 | 20 | 51 | 52 | 6 | 14 |
| Wimmer | .982 | 29 | 47 | 62 | 2 | 14 |

| Third Base | PCT | G | PO | A | E | DP |
|---|---|---|---|---|---|---|
| Bell | 1.000 | 8 | 1 | 19 | 0 | 0 |
| Deak | .000 | 1 | 0 | 0 | 0 | 0 |
| Gulan | .927 | 111 | 64 | 239 | 24 | 15 |
| Oliva | .951 | 29 | 21 | 57 | 4 | 5 |
| Wimmer | .833 | 2 | 1 | 4 | 1 | 0 |

| Shortstop | PCT | G | PO | A | E | DP |
|---|---|---|---|---|---|---|
| Bell | 1.000 | 1 | 1 | 0 | 0 | 0 |
| Correia | .953 | 12 | 16 | 25 | 2 | 8 |
| Cromer | .986 | 76 | 112 | 233 | 5 | 45 |

| | PCT | G | PO | A | E | DP |
|---|---|---|---|---|---|---|
| Holbert | .942 | 49 | 66 | 129 | 12 | 28 |
| Wimmer | .986 | 20 | 21 | 47 | 1 | 10 |

| Outfield | PCT | G | PO | A | E | DP |
|---|---|---|---|---|---|---|
| Bradshaw | .967 | 101 | 203 | 5 | 7 | 1 |
| Cholowsky | .952 | 14 | 19 | 1 | 1 | 0 |
| Correia | 1.000 | 24 | 46 | 2 | 0 | 0 |
| Deak | 1.000 | 12 | 14 | 0 | 0 | 0 |
| Diggs | .994 | 89 | 153 | 4 | 1 | 1 |
| Franklin | .977 | 85 | 159 | 11 | 4 | 2 |
| Hare | 1.000 | 14 | 24 | 0 | 0 | 0 |
| Hemond | 1.000 | 1 | 2 | 0 | 0 | 0 |
| Howitt | .975 | 45 | 73 | 6 | 2 | 3 |
| McNeely | 1.000 | 3 | 4 | 0 | 0 | 0 |
| Oliva | 1.000 | 10 | 8 | 0 | 0 | 0 |
| Stefanski | .750 | 3 | 3 | 0 | 1 | 0 |
| Wimmer | .987 | 58 | 74 | 4 | 1 | 0 |

## TEXAS LEAGUE

| BATTING | AVG | G | AB | R | H | 2B | 3B | HR | RBI | BB | SO | SB | CS | B | T | HT | WT | DOB | 1st Yr | Resides |
|---|---|---|---|---|---|---|---|---|---|---|---|---|---|---|---|---|---|---|---|---|
| Anderson, Charlie | .000 | 2 | 1 | 0 | 0 | 0 | 0 | 0 | 0 | 1 | 0 | 0 | 0 | R | R | 6-1 | 190 | 3-18-70 | 1992 | Jacksonville, Fla. |
| Berblinger, Jeff | .288 | 134 | 500 | 78 | 144 | 32 | 7 | 11 | 53 | 52 | 66 | 23 | 10 | R | R | 6-0 | 190 | 11-19-70 | 1993 | Goddard, Kan. |
| Dalton, Dee | .238 | 113 | 345 | 38 | 82 | 17 | 2 | 6 | 42 | 38 | 61 | 4 | 4 | R | R | 5-11 | 170 | 6-17-72 | 1993 | Roanoke, Va. |
| Diggs, Tony | .304 | 35 | 138 | 23 | 42 | 7 | 3 | 3 | 22 | 12 | 16 | 7 | 4 | S | R | 6-0 | 175 | 4-20-67 | 1989 | Starke, Fla. |
| Ellis, Paul | .255 | 65 | 157 | 16 | 40 | 5 | 0 | 3 | 26 | 22 | 20 | 0 | 0 | L | R | 6-1 | 205 | 11-28-68 | 1990 | San Ramon, Calif. |
| Fick, Chris | .257 | 134 | 448 | 64 | 115 | 25 | 2 | 19 | 74 | 67 | 93 | 2 | 5 | L | R | 6-2 | 190 | 10-4-69 | 1994 | Thousand Oaks, Calif. |
| Green, Bert | .200 | 92 | 300 | 45 | 60 | 6 | 3 | 3 | 24 | 38 | 58 | 21 | 8 | R | R | 5-10 | 170 | 6-9-74 | 1993 | Ballwin, Mo. |
| Johns, Keith | .246 | 127 | 447 | 52 | 110 | 17 | 1 | 1 | 40 | 47 | 61 | 8 | 9 | R | R | 6-1 | 175 | 7-19-71 | 1992 | Jacksonville, Fla. |
| Marrero, Eli | .270 | 116 | 374 | 65 | 101 | 17 | 3 | 19 | 65 | 32 | 55 | 9 | 6 | R | R | 6-1 | 180 | 11-17-73 | 1993 | Miami, Fla. |

| BATTING | AVG | G | AB | R | H | 2B | 3B | HR | RBI | BB | SO | SB | CS | B | T | HT | WT | DOB | 1st Yr | Resides |
|---|---|---|---|---|---|---|---|---|---|---|---|---|---|---|---|---|---|---|---|---|
| McEwing, Joe | .208 | 106 | 216 | 27 | 45 | 7 | 3 | 2 | 14 | 13 | 32 | 2 | 4 | R | R | 5-10 | 170 | 10-19-72 | 1992 | Bristol, Pa. |
| Murphy, Jeff | .571 | 2 | 7 | 3 | 4 | 1 | 0 | 0 | 1 | 0 | 2 | 0 | 0 | S | R | 6-2 | 210 | 12-27-70 | 1988 | Las Vegas, Nev. |
| Pages, Javier | .261 | 26 | 46 | 3 | 12 | 2 | 0 | 1 | 7 | 3 | 11 | 0 | 0 | R | R | 6-0 | 190 | 7-27-71 | 1990 | Fort Lauderdale, Fla. |
| Rupp, Brian | .303 | 114 | 353 | 46 | 107 | 17 | 2 | 4 | 41 | 33 | 44 | 5 | 6 | R | R | 6-5 | 185 | 9-20-71 | 1992 | Florissant, Mo. |
| Santucci, Steve | .150 | 11 | 20 | 2 | 3 | 0 | 0 | 0 | 0 | 0 | 5 | 0 | 1 | R | R | 6-1 | 190 | 12-16-71 | 1993 | Leominster, Mass. |
| Torres, Paul | .262 | 102 | 309 | 38 | 81 | 16 | 0 | 11 | 44 | 44 | 62 | 1 | 1 | R | R | 6-3 | 210 | 10-19-70 | 1989 | San Lorenzo, Calif. |
| Velez, Jose | .273 | 86 | 264 | 36 | 72 | 11 | 2 | 2 | 32 | 14 | 29 | 8 | 4 | S | L | 6-1 | 160 | 3-6-73 | 1990 | Mayaguez, P.R. |
| Warner, Ron | .300 | 84 | 233 | 36 | 70 | 22 | 4 | 6 | 39 | 38 | 25 | 5 | 1 | R | R | 6-3 | 185 | 12-2-68 | 1991 | Redlands, Calif. |
| Wolfe, Joel | .215 | 72 | 200 | 29 | 43 | 11 | 2 | 4 | 26 | 28 | 36 | 11 | 7 | R | R | 6-3 | 205 | 6-18-70 | 1991 | Northridge, Calif. |

| PITCHING | W | L | ERA | G | GS | CG | SV | IP | H | R | ER | BB | SO | B | T | HT | WT | DOB | 1st Yr | Resides |
|---|---|---|---|---|---|---|---|---|---|---|---|---|---|---|---|---|---|---|---|---|
| Aybar, Manuel | 8 | 6 | 3.05 | 20 | 20 | 0 | 0 | 121 | 120 | 53 | 41 | 34 | 83 | R | R | 6-1 | 165 | 10-5-74 | 1991 | Bani, D.R. |
| Carpenter, Brian | 1 | 2 | 3.16 | 37 | 6 | 0 | 0 | 74 | 63 | 26 | 26 | 26 | 53 | R | R | 6-0 | 225 | 3-3-71 | 1992 | Marble Falls, Texas |
| Croushore, Rick | 5 | 10 | 4.92 | 34 | 17 | 2 | 3 | 108 | 113 | 75 | 59 | 51 | 85 | R | R | 6-4 | 210 | 8-7-70 | 1993 | Houston, Texas |
| Davis, Ray | 0 | 1 | 5.16 | 12 | 3 | 0 | 0 | 23 | 25 | 15 | 13 | 10 | 15 | R | R | 6-1 | 205 | 2-6-73 | 1991 | East Palatka, Fla. |
| Detmers, Kris | 12 | 8 | 3.35 | 27 | 27 | 0 | 0 | 164 | 154 | 72 | 61 | 70 | 97 | L | L | 6-5 | 215 | 6-22-74 | 1994 | Nokomis, Ill. |
| Garcia, Frank | 0 | 0 | 3.72 | 11 | 0 | 0 | 0 | 19 | 20 | 11 | 8 | 7 | 12 | R | R | 5-11 | 170 | 3-5-74 | 1994 | Azua, D.R. |
| Golden, Matt | 3 | 4 | 4.14 | 52 | 0 | 0 | 18 | 63 | 74 | 40 | 29 | 26 | 43 | R | R | 6-3 | 190 | 1-23-72 | 1994 | Woodbridge, N.J. |
| Hiljus, Erik | 3 | 5 | 6.11 | 10 | 10 | 0 | 0 | 46 | 62 | 37 | 31 | 30 | 21 | R | R | 6-5 | 230 | 12-25-72 | 1991 | Santa Clarita, Calif. |
| King, Curtis | 0 | 1 | 19.80 | 5 | 0 | 0 | 1 | 5 | 15 | 12 | 11 | 6 | 5 | R | R | 6-5 | 205 | 10-25-70 | 1994 | Conshohocken, Pa. |
| Lovingier, Kevin | 2 | 3 | 4.10 | 60 | 0 | 0 | 1 | 64 | 60 | 30 | 29 | 48 | 73 | L | L | 6-1 | 190 | 8-29-71 | 1994 | Mission Viejo, Calif. |
| Lowe, Sean | 2 | 3 | 6.00 | 6 | 6 | 0 | 0 | 33 | 32 | 24 | 22 | 15 | 25 | R | R | 6-2 | 205 | 3-29-71 | 1992 | Mesquite, Texas |
| Matranga, Jeff | 6 | 5 | 2.15 | 62 | 0 | 0 | 4 | 80 | 56 | 22 | 19 | 30 | 82 | R | R | 6-2 | 170 | 12-14-70 | 1992 | Lakeside, Calif. |
| Matulevich, Jeff | 4 | 3 | 3.64 | 41 | 0 | 0 | 1 | 59 | 48 | 33 | 24 | 29 | 51 | R | R | 6-3 | 200 | 4-15-70 | 1992 | Haddam, Conn. |
| Morris, Matt | 12 | 12 | 3.88 | 27 | 27 | 4 | 0 | 167 | 178 | 79 | 72 | 48 | 120 | R | R | 6-5 | 220 | 8-9-74 | 1995 | Montgomery, N.Y. |
| Raggio, Brady | 9 | 10 | 3.22 | 26 | 24 | 4 | 0 | 162 | 160 | 58 | 58 | 40 | 123 | R | R | 6-4 | 210 | 9-17-72 | 1992 | Danville, Calif. |

### FIELDING

| Catcher | PCT | G | PO | A | E | DP | PB |
|---|---|---|---|---|---|---|---|
| Ellis | .991 | 40 | 197 | 18 | 2 | 1 | 5 |
| Marrero | .996 | 107 | 676 | 67 | 3 | 4 | 4 |
| Murphy | 1.000 | 1 | 8 | 0 | 0 | 0 | 1 |
| Pages | 1.000 | 5 | 23 | 0 | 0 | 1 | |

| | PCT | G | PO | A | E | DP |
|---|---|---|---|---|---|---|
| McEwing | .889 | 2 | 4 | 4 | 1 | 1 |
| Warner | 1.000 | 10 | 15 | 27 | 0 | 7 |

| Third Base | PCT | G | PO | A | E | DP |
|---|---|---|---|---|---|---|
| Dalton | .936 | 93 | 58 | 162 | 15 | 11 |
| Rupp | .900 | 5 | 3 | 6 | 1 | 0 |
| Warner | .948 | 52 | 39 | 125 | 9 | 13 |

| Shortstop | PCT | G | PO | A | E | DP |
|---|---|---|---|---|---|---|
| Dalton | 1.000 | 9 | 13 | 34 | 0 | 5 |
| Johns | .951 | 127 | 199 | 348 | 28 | 72 |
| Warner | .821 | 10 | 9 | 14 | 5 | 3 |

| First Base | PCT | G | PO | A | E | DP |
|---|---|---|---|---|---|---|
| Rupp | .996 | 90 | 711 | 56 | 3 | 65 |
| Torres | .973 | 20 | 137 | 6 | 4 | 18 |
| Wolfe | .985 | 44 | 359 | 23 | 6 | 27 |

| Second Base | PCT | G | PO | A | E | DP |
|---|---|---|---|---|---|---|
| Berblinger | .952 | 127 | 241 | 310 | 28 | 73 |
| Dalton | .973 | 7 | 14 | 22 | 1 | 9 |

| Outfield | PCT | G | PO | A | E | DP |
|---|---|---|---|---|---|---|
| Diggs | .988 | 34 | 81 | 1 | 1 | 0 |
| Fick | .965 | 119 | 183 | 8 | 7 | 1 |
| Green | .990 | 89 | 194 | 7 | 2 | 3 |
| McEwing | .993 | 98 | 130 | 11 | 1 | 2 |
| Pages | .000 | 1 | 0 | 0 | 0 | 0 |
| Rupp | 1.000 | 10 | 9 | 0 | 0 | 0 |
| Santucci | 1.000 | 9 | 9 | 0 | 0 | 0 |
| Torres | .971 | 53 | 62 | 4 | 2 | 0 |
| Velez | .978 | 76 | 127 | 7 | 3 | 0 |
| Wolfe | .000 | 1 | 0 | 0 | 0 | 0 |

# ST. PETERSBURG — Class A

## FLORIDA STATE LEAGUE

| BATTING | AVG | G | AB | R | H | 2B | 3B | HR | RBI | BB | SO | SB | CS | B | T | HT | WT | DOB | 1st Yr | Resides |
|---|---|---|---|---|---|---|---|---|---|---|---|---|---|---|---|---|---|---|---|---|
| Biermann, Steve | .123 | 52 | 81 | 13 | 10 | 3 | 0 | 0 | 4 | 8 | 23 | 0 | 0 | S | R | 6-0 | 175 | 9-30-71 | 1993 | St. Louis, Mo. |
| Contreras, Efrain | .152 | 31 | 79 | 6 | 12 | 4 | 1 | 1 | 12 | 10 | 20 | 0 | 0 | L | R | 5-11 | 190 | 12-22-72 | 1994 | Rio Piedras, P.R. |
| Falciglia, Tony | .233 | 16 | 43 | 5 | 10 | 3 | 0 | 0 | 4 | 1 | 16 | 0 | 2 | R | R | 6-0 | 185 | 3-29-72 | 1995 | Bronx, N.Y. |
| Farley, Cordell | .000 | 5 | 4 | 1 | 0 | 0 | 0 | 0 | 0 | 1 | 1 | 0 | 0 | R | R | 5-8 | 160 | 10-31-60 | 1981 | Blackstone, Va. |
| Gallego, Mike | .294 | 14 | 51 | 7 | 15 | 0 | 0 | 0 | 5 | 7 | 4 | 0 | 0 | R | R | 5-8 | 185 | 3-28-73 | 1994 | Yorba Linda, Calif. |
| Green, Bert | .293 | 36 | 140 | 26 | 41 | 4 | 1 | 1 | 11 | 21 | 22 | 13 | 9 | R | R | 5-10 | 170 | 6-9-74 | 1993 | Ballwin, Mo. |
| Hall, Ryan | .213 | 66 | 174 | 7 | 37 | 10 | 0 | 0 | 11 | 19 | 37 | 0 | 0 | L | R | 6-0 | 205 | 2-25-72 | 1994 | Springville, Utah |
| Hogan, Todd | .333 | 2 | 6 | 1 | 2 | 0 | 0 | 0 | 0 | 0 | 3 | 0 | 0 | R | R | 6-2 | 180 | 9-18-75 | 1996 | Dublin, Ga. |
| Jumonville, Joe | .158 | 41 | 101 | 10 | 16 | 3 | 1 | 0 | 7 | 8 | 22 | 0 | 0 | R | R | 6-1 | 205 | 8-18-70 | 1993 | New Iberia, La. |
| LaRiviere, Jason | .300 | 41 | 140 | 27 | 42 | 6 | 0 | 3 | 18 | 18 | 19 | 1 | 1 | R | R | 5-10 | 180 | 9-30-73 | 1995 | Biddeford, Maine |
| Lugo, Jesus | .203 | 19 | 64 | 5 | 13 | 2 | 0 | 0 | 3 | 1 | 7 | 1 | 2 | R | R | 6-3 | 180 | 5-8-75 | 1993 | Puerto la Cruz, Venez. |
| Matvey, Mike | .256 | 127 | 407 | 51 | 104 | 10 | 3 | 1 | 40 | 47 | 90 | 3 | 6 | R | R | 6-0 | 180 | 10-10-71 | 1993 | Charlotte, N.C. |
| McDonald, Keith | .271 | 114 | 410 | 30 | 111 | 25 | 0 | 2 | 52 | 34 | 65 | 1 | 3 | R | R | 6-2 | 215 | 2-8-73 | 1994 | Yorba Linda, Calif. |
| Mejia, Miguel | .115 | 8 | 26 | 2 | 3 | 0 | 0 | 0 | 0 | 1 | 12 | 2 | 0 | R | R | 6-1 | 155 | 3-25-75 | 1992 | San Pedro de Macoris, D.R. |
| Morales, Francisco | .209 | 21 | 67 | 6 | 14 | 5 | 1 | 1 | 6 | 5 | 25 | 0 | 0 | R | R | 6-3 | 180 | 1-31-73 | 1991 | San Pedro de Macoris, D.R. |
| Munoz, Juan | .242 | 90 | 330 | 41 | 80 | 12 | 3 | 1 | 46 | 38 | 35 | 6 | 5 | L | L | 5-9 | 170 | 3-27-74 | 1995 | Maracaibo, Venez |
| Ordaz, Luis | .272 | 126 | 423 | 46 | 115 | 13 | 3 | 3 | 49 | 30 | 53 | 1 | 5 | R | R | 5-11 | 155 | 1-1-75 | 1991 | La Romana, D.R. |
| Ozorio, Yudith | .242 | 136 | 505 | 67 | 122 | 11 | 10 | 1 | 42 | 57 | 110 | 30 | 8 | R | R | 6-0 | 180 | 7-27-71 | 1990 | Miami, Fla. |
| Pages, Javier | .226 | 39 | 106 | 14 | 24 | 7 | 1 | 3 | 8 | 22 | 29 | 1 | 1 | R | R | 6-0 | 190 | 7-27-71 | 1990 | Fort Lauderdale, Fla. |
| Polanco, Placido | .291 | 137 | 540 | 65 | 157 | 29 | 5 | 0 | 51 | 24 | 34 | 4 | 4 | R | R | 5-10 | 168 | 10-10-75 | 1994 | Miami, Fla. |
| Richard, Chris | .283 | 129 | 460 | 65 | 130 | 28 | 6 | 14 | 82 | 57 | 50 | 7 | 3 | L | L | 6-2 | 185 | 6-7-74 | 1995 | San Diego, Calif. |
| Santucci, Steve | .229 | 111 | 349 | 38 | 80 | 10 | 2 | 6 | 29 | 27 | 66 | 3 | 5 | R | R | 6-0 | 175 | 12-16-71 | 1993 | Leominster, Mass. |
| Tanner, Paul | .000 | 1 | 2 | 0 | 0 | 0 | 0 | 0 | 0 | 0 | 0 | 0 | 0 | R | R | 6-0 | 175 | 9-11-74 | 1996 | Albuquerque, N.M. |

**GAMES BY POSITION: C**—Falciglia 10, Hall 2, McDonald 99, Morales 15, Pages 22. **1B**—Hall 19, Jumonville 5, LaRiviere 1, Richard 120. **2B**—Biermann 5, Gallego 12, Matvey 1, Polanco 126. **3B**—Biermann 8, Gallego 1, Jumonville 16, Matvey 122, Tanner 1. **SS**—Biermann 23, Gallego 1, Matvey 4, Ordaz 123. **OF**—Contreras 16, Farley 1, Green 36, LaRiviere 24, Lugo 12, Mejia 6, Munoz 89, Ozorio 135, Richard 9, Santucci 106.

| PITCHING | W | L | ERA | G | GS | CG | SV | IP | H | R | ER | BB | SO | B | T | HT | WT | DOB | 1st Yr | Resides |
|---|---|---|---|---|---|---|---|---|---|---|---|---|---|---|---|---|---|---|---|---|
| Conway, Keith | 7 | 3 | 2.08 | 59 | 0 | 0 | 2 | 69 | 63 | 18 | 16 | 25 | 69 | R | L | 6-2 | 200 | 5-8-73 | 1993 | Philadelphia, Pa. |
| Garcia, Frank | 2 | 0 | 2.53 | 28 | 0 | 0 | 0 | 32 | 35 | 11 | 9 | 18 | 24 | R | R | 5-11 | 170 | 3-5-74 | 1994 | Azua, D.R. |
| Golden, Matt | 0 | 0 | 0.90 | 8 | 0 | 0 | 7 | 10 | 5 | 1 | 1 | 1 | 7 | R | R | 6-3 | 190 | 1-23-72 | 1994 | Woodbridge, N.J. |
| Hall, Yates | 1 | 10 | 5.44 | 26 | 17 | 0 | 1 | 89 | 93 | 62 | 54 | 58 | 58 | R | R | 6-2 | 190 | 3-29-73 | 1994 | Front Royal, Va. |
| Heiserman, Rick | 10 | 8 | 3.24 | 26 | 26 | 1 | 0 | 155 | 168 | 68 | 56 | 41 | 104 | R | R | 6-7 | 220 | 2-22-73 | 1994 | Omaha, Neb. |
| Jackson, Danny | 0 | 0 | 0.00 | 1 | 1 | 0 | 0 | 4 | 2 | 0 | 0 | 0 | 3 | R | L | 6-0 | 205 | 1-5-62 | 1982 | Overland Park, Kan. |
| King, Curtis | 3 | 3 | 2.75 | 48 | 0 | 0 | 30 | 56 | 41 | 20 | 17 | 24 | 27 | R | R | 6-5 | 205 | 10-25-70 | 1994 | Conshohocken, Pa. |
| Logan, Marcus | 7 | 7 | 2.91 | 30 | 19 | 0 | 0 | 133 | 125 | 49 | 43 | 49 | 99 | R | R | 6-0 | 170 | 5-8-72 | 1994 | Evanston, Ill. |
| McNeill, Kevin | 4 | 2 | 2.95 | 45 | 0 | 0 | 0 | 61 | 56 | 28 | 20 | 18 | 44 | R | L | 6-4 | 210 | 12-22-70 | 1994 | Waller, Texas |
| Mendez, Manuel | 4 | 3 | 2.87 | 59 | 0 | 0 | 0 | 69 | 61 | 25 | 22 | 36 | 53 | L | L | 6-0 | 190 | 5-27-74 | 1994 | Fresno, Calif. |
| Morgan, Mike | 1 | 0 | 0.00 | 1 | 1 | 0 | 0 | 6 | 4 | 0 | 0 | 5 | 4 | R | R | 6-2 | 222 | 10-8-59 | 1978 | Ogden, Utah |

| PITCHING | W | L | ERA | G | GS | CG | SV | IP | H | R | ER | BB | SO | B | T | HT | WT | DOB | 1st Yr | Resides |
|---|---|---|---|---|---|---|---|---|---|---|---|---|---|---|---|---|---|---|---|---|
| Osborne, Donovan | 1 | 0 | 0.00 | 1 | 1 | 0 | 0 | 6 | 2 | 0 | 0 | 0 | 2 | L | L | 6-2 | 195 | 6-21-69 | 1990 | Carson City, Nev. |
| Petkovsek, Mark | 0 | 0 | 4.50 | 3 | 0 | 0 | 0 | 6 | 6 | 3 | 3 | 0 | 5 | R | R | 6-0 | 185 | 11-18-65 | 1987 | Beaumont, Texas |
| Pontes, Dan | 7 | 8 | 3.81 | 27 | 22 | 1 | 0 | 120 | 120 | 56 | 51 | 34 | 73 | R | R | 6-3 | 200 | 4-27-71 | 1993 | Geneva, N.Y. |
| Reed, Brian | 5 | 4 | 3.04 | 58 | 0 | 0 | 3 | 68 | 55 | 26 | 23 | 35 | 76 | R | R | 6-2 | 185 | 9-1-71 | 1994 | Lexington, Ky. |
| Stein, Blake | 16 | 5 | 2.15 | 28 | 27 | 2 | 1 | 172 | 122 | 48 | 41 | 54 | 159 | R | R | 6-7 | 210 | 8-3-73 | 1994 | Folsom, La. |
| Windham, Mike | 7 | 10 | 3.13 | 25 | 25 | 1 | 0 | 144 | 153 | 59 | 50 | 57 | 87 | R | R | 6-1 | 185 | 3-8-72 | 1993 | West Palm Beach, Fla. |

## PEORIA — Class A
### MIDWEST LEAGUE

| BATTING | AVG | G | AB | R | H | 2B | 3B | HR | RBI | BB | SO | SB | CS | B | T | HT | WT | DOB | 1st Yr | Resides |
|---|---|---|---|---|---|---|---|---|---|---|---|---|---|---|---|---|---|---|---|---|
| Almond, Greg | .231 | 90 | 273 | 28 | 63 | 14 | 0 | 2 | 41 | 26 | 75 | 2 | 0 | R | R | 6-0 | 195 | 4-14-71 | 1993 | Panama City, Fla. |
| Dishington, Nate | .226 | 75 | 208 | 22 | 47 | 12 | 3 | 3 | 30 | 25 | 73 | 1 | 1 | L | R | 6-3 | 210 | 1-8-75 | 1993 | Glendale, Calif. |
| Farley, Cordell | .232 | 29 | 82 | 10 | 19 | 1 | 1 | 0 | 7 | 4 | 23 | 1 | 4 | R | R | 6-0 | 185 | 3-29-73 | 1996 | Blackstone, Va. |
| Garcia, Ossie | .237 | 120 | 359 | 70 | 85 | 14 | 1 | 0 | 38 | 46 | 68 | 20 | 13 | R | R | 6-1 | 180 | 10-14-73 | 1993 | Hialeah, Fla. |
| Haas, Chris | .240 | 124 | 421 | 56 | 101 | 19 | 1 | 11 | 65 | 64 | 169 | 3 | 2 | L | R | 6-2 | 210 | 10-15-76 | 1995 | Paducah, Ky. |
| Hall, Andy | .300 | 128 | 446 | 80 | 134 | 29 | 5 | 4 | 68 | 75 | 90 | 21 | 7 | S | R | 6-0 | 175 | 4-29-74 | 1995 | Camarillo, Calif. |
| Inzunza, Miguel | .197 | 26 | 61 | 10 | 12 | 1 | 0 | 0 | 8 | 11 | 8 | 0 | 0 | R | R | 5-10 | 170 | 7-16-72 | 1995 | Ontario, Calif. |
| Lariviere, Jason | .249 | 64 | 225 | 33 | 56 | 13 | 1 | 1 | 36 | 25 | 31 | 6 | 5 | R | R | 5-10 | 180 | 9-30-73 | 1995 | Biddeford, Maine |
| McClendon, Travis | .194 | 60 | 155 | 23 | 30 | 8 | 0 | 0 | 23 | 17 | 27 | 1 | 4 | R | R | 5-11 | 185 | 10-22-72 | 1995 | Cottonwood, Ariz. |
| McHugh, Ryan | .253 | 76 | 237 | 46 | 60 | 17 | 4 | 6 | 40 | 33 | 46 | 7 | 4 | R | R | 6-6 | 215 | 7-29-73 | 1995 | Stamford, Conn. |
| McNally, Shawn | .278 | 123 | 431 | 59 | 120 | 19 | 5 | 7 | 75 | 57 | 60 | 9 | 8 | R | R | 6-2 | 215 | 1-29-73 | 1995 | Winder, Ga. |
| Mueller, Brett | .212 | 12 | 33 | 5 | 7 | 3 | 0 | 0 | 3 | 3 | 9 | 1 | 1 | R | R | 6-1 | 195 | 3-26-73 | 1995 | Oakhurst, Calif. |
| Munoz, Juan | .355 | 30 | 107 | 19 | 38 | 9 | 0 | 0 | 18 | 14 | 13 | 4 | 1 | L | L | 5-9 | 170 | 3-27-74 | 1995 | Miami, Fla. |
| Nunez, Isaias | .221 | 108 | 271 | 33 | 60 | 12 | 1 | 1 | 27 | 26 | 53 | 2 | 3 | L | L | 6-2 | 150 | 4-10-74 | 1992 | Bajos de Haina, D.R. |
| Rivera, Miguel | .224 | 72 | 210 | 26 | 47 | 10 | 1 | 1 | 22 | 14 | 33 | 2 | 3 | R | R | 5-10 | 175 | 4-14-74 | 1994 | Racine, Wis. |
| Roberts, Ryan | .200 | 9 | 20 | 0 | 4 | 0 | 0 | 0 | 0 | 1 | 4 | 1 | 0 | R | R | 6-3 | 185 | 3-28-74 | 1996 | Orem, Utah |
| Robinson, Kerry | .359 | 123 | 440 | 98 | 158 | 17 | 14 | 2 | 47 | 51 | 51 | 50 | 27 | L | L | 6-0 | 175 | 10-3-73 | 1994 | Spanish Lake, Mo. |
| Wilders, Paul | .230 | 25 | 61 | 10 | 14 | 4 | 0 | 1 | 9 | 6 | 12 | 0 | 0 | R | R | 6-0 | 200 | 12-29-73 | 1996 | Clifton Park, N.Y. |
| Woolf, Jason | .257 | 108 | 362 | 68 | 93 | 12 | 8 | 1 | 27 | 57 | 87 | 28 | 12 | S | R | 6-1 | 170 | 6-6-77 | 1995 | Miami, Fla. |

**GAMES BY POSITION: C**—Almond 89, Dishington 1, McClendon 55, McNally 13. **1B**—Dishington 24, McNally 40, Munoz 1, Nunez 101, Roberts 1, Wilders 8. **2B**—Hall 108, Inzunza 17, Rivera 20, Roberts 1, Wilders 1. **3B**—Haas 114, Inzunza 1, Rivera 6, Roberts 6, Wilders 14. **SS**—Inzunza 4, Rivera 32, Woolf 106. **OF**—Dishington 2, Farley 24, Garcia 118, Hall 1, LaRiviere 45, McHugh 34, McNally 88, Mueller 2, Munoz 30, Nunez 1, Robinson 115.

| PITCHING | W | L | ERA | G | GS | CG | SV | IP | H | R | ER | BB | SO | B | T | HT | WT | DOB | 1st Yr | Resides |
|---|---|---|---|---|---|---|---|---|---|---|---|---|---|---|---|---|---|---|---|---|
| Almanza, Armando | 8 | 6 | 2.76 | 52 | 1 | 0 | 0 | 62 | 50 | 27 | 19 | 32 | 67 | L | L | 6-3 | 205 | 10-26-72 | 1993 | El Paso, Texas |
| Avrard, Corey | 5 | 9 | 4.24 | 21 | 21 | 2 | 0 | 110 | 105 | 73 | 52 | 58 | 103 | R | R | 6-2 | 195 | 12-6-76 | 1994 | Metairie, La. |
| Benes, Adam | 2 | 2 | 3.74 | 43 | 0 | 0 | 0 | 65 | 58 | 31 | 27 | 28 | 64 | L | R | 6-2 | 195 | 3-12-73 | 1995 | Lake Forest, Ill. |
| Donnelly, Rob | 2 | 2 | 3.43 | 46 | 0 | 0 | 0 | 60 | 45 | 27 | 23 | 24 | 76 | R | R | 6-0 | 180 | 9-27-73 | 1995 | Fresno, Calif. |
| Foderaro, Kevin | 1 | 0 | 3.97 | 32 | 3 | 0 | 0 | 57 | 54 | 25 | 25 | 26 | 41 | R | R | 6-3 | 215 | 10-3-72 | 1994 | Valencia, Calif. |
| Glauber, Keith | 3 | 3 | 3.09 | 54 | 0 | 0 | 14 | 64 | 54 | 31 | 22 | 26 | 80 | R | R | 6-2 | 190 | 1-18-72 | 1994 | Morganville, N.J. |
| Jimenez, Jose | 12 | 9 | 2.92 | 28 | 27 | 3 | 0 | 172 | 158 | 75 | 56 | 53 | 129 | R | R | 6-3 | 170 | 7-7-73 | 1992 | San Pedro de Macoris, D.R. |
| Kast, Nick | 0 | 1 | 17.36 | 5 | 0 | 0 | 0 | 5 | 6 | 11 | 9 | 8 | 8 | R | L | 5-11 | 165 | 8-17-72 | 1995 | Wichita Falls, Texas |
| Kown, John | 9 | 4 | 3.09 | 26 | 11 | 0 | 0 | 79 | 80 | 32 | 27 | 19 | 46 | L | R | 6-5 | 215 | 12-15-72 | 1995 | Marietta, Ga. |
| Montgomery, Greg | 0 | 0 | 2.75 | 14 | 0 | 0 | 0 | 20 | 11 | 6 | 6 | 9 | 22 | R | R | 6-2 | 200 | 5-19-75 | 1996 | Greenbrier, Ark. |
| Politte, Cliff | 14 | 6 | 2.59 | 25 | 25 | 0 | 0 | 150 | 108 | 50 | 43 | 47 | 151 | R | R | 5-11 | 185 | 2-27-74 | 1995 | St. Louis, Mo. |
| Reames, Britt | 15 | 7 | 1.90 | 25 | 25 | 4 | 0 | 161 | 97 | 43 | 34 | 41 | 167 | R | R | 5-11 | 170 | 8-19-73 | 1995 | Seneca, S.C. |
| Roettgen, Mark | 2 | 1 | 5.13 | 6 | 6 | 0 | 0 | 26 | 27 | 22 | 15 | 13 | 24 | R | R | 6-3 | 185 | 8-15-76 | 1994 | Jefferson City, Mo. |
| Wagner, Matt | 4 | 2 | 5.88 | 16 | 12 | 0 | 0 | 64 | 80 | 47 | 42 | 26 | 38 | R | R | 6-5 | 210 | 8-4-74 | 1996 | Brea, Calif. |
| Weibl, Clint | 1 | 2 | 4.85 | 5 | 5 | 0 | 0 | 30 | 27 | 16 | 16 | 7 | 21 | R | R | 6-3 | 180 | 3-17-75 | 1996 | Dawson, Pa. |
| Welch, Travis | 1 | 3 | 3.12 | 34 | 0 | 0 | 17 | 40 | 31 | 17 | 14 | 17 | 34 | R | R | 6-0 | 202 | 1-30-74 | 1993 | Loomis, Calif. |

## NEW JERSEY — Class A
### NEW YORK-PENN LEAGUE

| BATTING | AVG | G | AB | R | H | 2B | 3B | HR | RBI | BB | SO | SB | CS | B | T | HT | WT | DOB | 1st Yr | Resides |
|---|---|---|---|---|---|---|---|---|---|---|---|---|---|---|---|---|---|---|---|---|
| Abell, Antonio | .120 | 7 | 25 | 4 | 3 | 0 | 0 | 0 | 1 | 4 | 11 | 1 | 0 | R | R | 5-10 | 175 | 1-13-75 | 1994 | Ekron, Ky. |
| Betts, Darrell | .102 | 21 | 59 | 6 | 6 | 1 | 0 | 0 | 3 | 8 | 18 | 1 | 0 | S | R | 5-10 | 160 | 2-3-73 | 1995 | Cincinnati, Ohio |
| Britt, Bryan | .239 | 69 | 268 | 28 | 64 | 12 | 1 | 7 | 42 | 19 | 86 | 3 | 5 | R | R | 6-2 | 220 | 4-16-75 | 1996 | Wilmington, N.C. |
| Cameron, Ken | .289 | 53 | 190 | 43 | 55 | 10 | 6 | 0 | 20 | 34 | 37 | 8 | 4 | L | L | 6-0 | 185 | 3-1-73 | 1995 | Pullman, Wash. |
| Deman, Lou | .143 | 8 | 21 | 2 | 3 | 2 | 0 | 0 | 3 | 2 | 6 | 0 | 0 | R | R | 6-2 | 225 | 7-1-73 | 1995 | Egg Harbor, N.J. |
| Falciglia, Tony | .171 | 15 | 41 | 3 | 7 | 2 | 0 | 1 | 6 | 2 | 13 | 0 | 0 | R | R | 5-11 | 185 | 9-29-72 | 1995 | Bronx, N.Y. |
| Finnerty, Keith | .209 | 55 | 172 | 21 | 36 | 7 | 1 | 2 | 16 | 17 | 31 | 7 | 0 | L | R | 5-10 | 170 | 4-10-74 | 1996 | Garnerville, N.Y. |
| Freitas, Joe | .344 | 45 | 163 | 29 | 56 | 10 | 3 | 4 | 37 | 25 | 35 | 0 | 1 | R | R | 6-3 | 195 | 8-2-73 | 1995 | Hanford, Calif. |
| Jimenez, Ruben | .229 | 64 | 236 | 53 | 54 | 5 | 4 | 0 | 12 | 41 | 51 | 20 | 3 | S | R | 5-11 | 155 | 8-18-75 | 1993 | San Pedro de Macoris, D.R. |
| Kennedy, Brad | .211 | 64 | 199 | 24 | 42 | 10 | 4 | 4 | 24 | 30 | 48 | 8 | 0 | L | R | 5-10 | 195 | 11-27-73 | 1996 | Stillwell, Kan. |
| Kleiner, Stacy | .294 | 56 | 177 | 24 | 52 | 10 | 2 | 2 | 23 | 9 | 32 | 2 | 1 | R | R | 6-0 | 185 | 1-12-75 | 1996 | Las Vegas,, Nev. |
| Leon, Jose | .286 | 7 | 28 | 4 | 8 | 3 | 1 | 1 | 3 | 0 | 7 | 0 | 0 | R | R | 6-0 | 160 | 12-8-76 | 1994 | Cayey, P.R. |
| Mazurek, Brian | .310 | 69 | 274 | 31 | 85 | 18 | 1 | 2 | 48 | 16 | 39 | 0 | 2 | L | L | 6-1 | 195 | 4-17-74 | 1996 | Matteson, Ill. |
| McDougal, Mike | .161 | 27 | 31 | 2 | 5 | 0 | 0 | 1 | 5 | 5 | 10 | 0 | 0 | R | R | 6-4 | 210 | 3-22-75 | 1994 | Las Vegas, Nev. |
| McNeal, Pepe | .278 | 19 | 54 | 4 | 15 | 2 | 1 | 1 | 4 | 3 | 14 | 0 | 0 | R | R | 6-3 | 205 | 8-11-75 | 1994 | Thonotosassa, Fla. |
| Roberts, Ryan | .226 | 50 | 190 | 38 | 43 | 8 | 3 | 0 | 18 | 18 | 49 | 1 | 2 | R | R | 6-3 | 185 | 3-28-74 | 1996 | Orem, Utah |
| Schmidt, David | .254 | 57 | 189 | 17 | 48 | 9 | 2 | 1 | 23 | 16 | 55 | 1 | 1 | L | R | 6-1 | 195 | 10-11-73 | 1996 | Kennewick, Wash. |
| Schofield, Andy | .185 | 11 | 27 | 1 | 5 | 0 | 1 | 0 | 1 | 4 | 8 | 0 | 1 | R | R | 5-11 | 185 | 11-11-73 | 1995 | Danville, Ill. |
| Ugueto, Hector | .247 | 52 | 170 | 22 | 42 | 4 | 0 | 0 | 11 | 9 | 40 | 4 | 2 | R | R | 6-0 | 147 | 12-16-73 | 1991 | Catia la Mar, Venez |
| Wilders, Paul | .185 | 10 | 27 | 1 | 5 | 1 | 0 | 0 | 0 | 7 | 9 | 0 | 1 | R | R | 6-0 | 200 | 12-29-73 | 1996 | Clifton Park, N.Y. |

**GAMES BY POSITION: C**—Deman 2, Falciglia 11, McNeal 15, Schmidt 56. **1B**—Kennedy 2, Mazurek 65, McNeal 2. **2B**—Betts 2, Finnerty 43, Roberts 4, Ugueto 3. **3B**—Kennedy 29, Kleiner 1, Leon 6, Roberts 37, Ugueto 4, Wilders 7. **SS**—Betts 13, Jimenez 61, Kleiner 3. **OF**—Abell 7, Betts 3, Britt 53, Cameron 53, Finnerty 7, Freitas 40, Kennedy 19, Schofield 6, Ugueto 47.

| PITCHING | W | L | ERA | G | GS | CG | SV | IP | H | R | ER | BB | SO | B | T | HT | WT | DOB | 1st Yr | Resides |
|---|---|---|---|---|---|---|---|---|---|---|---|---|---|---|---|---|---|---|---|---|
| Clark, Brian | 3 | 5 | 2.86 | 32 | 0 | 0 | 1 | 44 | 42 | 21 | 14 | 15 | 29 | L | L | 6-0 | 190 | 2-20-73 | 1996 | Petal, Miss. |
| Crafton, Kevin | 2 | 3 | 2.18 | 23 | 0 | 0 | 2 | 33 | 28 | 8 | 8 | 6 | 43 | R | R | 6-1 | 185 | 5-10-74 | 1996 | Russellville, Ark. |
| Gallagher, Keith | 1 | 7 | 7.22 | 12 | 12 | 0 | 0 | 52 | 64 | 51 | 42 | 28 | 28 | R | R | 6-2 | 200 | 11-17-73 | 1996 | Orlando, Fla. |

| PITCHING | W | L | ERA | G | GS | CG | SV | IP | H | R | ER | BB | SO | B | T | HT | WT | DOB | 1st Yr | Resides |
|---|---|---|---|---|---|---|---|---|---|---|---|---|---|---|---|---|---|---|---|---|
| Gordon, Andrew | 0 | 0 | 4.22 | 25 | 5 | 0 | 0 | 49 | 67 | 33 | 23 | 9 | 46 | R | R | 6-5 | 205 | 5-4-74 | 1996 | Holbrook, N.Y. |
| Heffernan, Greg | 0 | 1 | 3.42 | 18 | 0 | 0 | 0 | 24 | 24 | 16 | 9 | 13 | 22 | R | R | 6-2 | 180 | 9-18-74 | 1996 | Guelph, Ontario |
| Love, Jeff | 0 | 2 | 6.46 | 17 | 5 | 0 | 0 | 39 | 47 | 35 | 28 | 19 | 29 | R | R | 6-1 | 190 | 11-25-73 | 1996 | Seymour, Conn. |
| McDougal, Mike | 1 | 1 | 7.08 | 14 | 0 | 0 | 0 | 20 | 20 | 17 | 16 | 4 | 25 | R | R | 6-4 | 210 | 3-22-75 | 1994 | Las Vegas, Nev. |
| Montgomery, Greg | 0 | 1 | 1.23 | 11 | 0 | 0 | 1 | 15 | 9 | 5 | 2 | 4 | 22 | R | R | 6-5 | 205 | 5-19-75 | 1996 | Greenbrier, Ark. |
| Nussbeck, Mark | 6 | 3 | 2.94 | 16 | 14 | 0 | 0 | 80 | 72 | 31 | 26 | 16 | 74 | L | R | 6-4 | 180 | 5-25-74 | 1996 | Kansas City, Mo. |
| Pollock, Jason | 3 | 7 | 4.89 | 18 | 10 | 0 | 0 | 57 | 59 | 37 | 31 | 36 | 61 | R | R | 6-3 | 230 | 10-24-74 | 1996 | Martins Ferry, Ohio |
| Reames, Jay | 2 | 2 | 3.32 | 31 | 0 | 0 | 10 | 43 | 42 | 20 | 16 | 18 | 48 | R | R | 6-1 | 205 | 10-31-74 | 1996 | Seneca, S.C. |
| Roque, Jorge | 1 | 2 | 7.02 | 13 | 0 | 0 | 2 | 17 | 15 | 15 | 13 | 23 | 18 | R | R | 6-0 | 195 | 10-15-74 | 1995 | Santurce, P.R. |
| Sheredy, Kevin | 0 | 1 | 4.30 | 8 | 5 | 0 | 0 | 23 | 21 | 15 | 11 | 13 | 13 | R | R | 6-4 | 210 | 1-3-75 | 1996 | Antioch, Calif. |
| Stechschulte, Gene | 1 | 2 | 3.27 | 20 | 1 | 0 | 0 | 33 | 41 | 17 | 12 | 16 | 27 | R | R | 6-6 | 220 | 11-13-74 | 1995 | Kalida, Ohio |
| Ward, Jon | 1 | 6 | 5.80 | 9 | 9 | 0 | 0 | 36 | 56 | 35 | 23 | 21 | 29 | R | R | 6-5 | 210 | 8-12-76 | 1995 | Huntington Beach, Calif. |
| West, Adam | 5 | 4 | 3.70 | 15 | 14 | 0 | 0 | 88 | 82 | 41 | 36 | 29 | 94 | L | L | 6-1 | 185 | 10-10-73 | 1994 | Thousand Oaks, Calif. |

## JOHNSON CITY — Rookie

### APPALACHIAN LEAGUE

| BATTING | AVG | G | AB | R | H | 2B | 3B | HR | RBI | BB | SO | SB | CS | B | T | HT | WT | DOB | 1st Yr | Resides |
|---|---|---|---|---|---|---|---|---|---|---|---|---|---|---|---|---|---|---|---|---|
| Abell, Antonio | .267 | 45 | 131 | 38 | 35 | 6 | 1 | 1 | 9 | 22 | 43 | 10 | 6 | R | R | 5-10 | 175 | 1-13-75 | 1994 | Ekron, Ky. |
| Butler, Brent | .343 | 62 | 248 | 45 | 85 | 21 | 1 | 8 | 50 | 25 | 29 | 8 | 1 | R | R | 6-0 | 180 | 2-11-78 | 1996 | Laurinburg, N.C. |
| Byrd, Issac | .277 | 24 | 94 | 16 | 26 | 6 | 1 | 2 | 15 | 8 | 19 | 5 | 2 | R | R | 6-2 | 185 | 11-16-74 | 1996 | St. Louis, Mo. |
| Clapp, Stubby | .223 | 29 | 94 | 25 | 21 | 3 | 2 | 1 | 15 | 26 | 15 | 9 | 2 | S | R | 5-8 | 175 | 2-24-73 | 1996 | Windsor, Ontario |
| Deck, Billy | .286 | 52 | 182 | 40 | 52 | 14 | 0 | 5 | 33 | 38 | 59 | 5 | 2 | L | L | 6-0 | 180 | 9-16-76 | 1995 | South Venice, Fla. |
| Evans, Brad | .250 | 13 | 32 | 6 | 8 | 0 | 0 | 0 | 4 | 2 | 8 | 0 | 1 | R | R | 6-1 | 190 | 12-18-76 | 1996 | Glenpool, Okla. |
| Farley, Cordell | .286 | 15 | 63 | 17 | 18 | 4 | 3 | 0 | 9 | 4 | 20 | 2 | 2 | R | R | 6-0 | 185 | 3-29-73 | 1996 | Blackstone, Va. |
| Gargiulo, Jimmy | .257 | 46 | 175 | 24 | 45 | 11 | 0 | 3 | 21 | 9 | 28 | 1 | 0 | R | R | 6-1 | 190 | 12-20-75 | 1996 | North Lauderdale, Fla. |
| Harris, Rodger | .369 | 44 | 168 | 38 | 62 | 12 | 2 | 5 | 30 | 10 | 28 | 16 | 6 | S | R | 5-9 | 165 | 8-30-75 | 1995 | Hanford, Calif. |
| Hogan, Todd | .344 | 47 | 183 | 38 | 63 | 7 | 3 | 0 | 32 | 20 | 41 | 18 | 6 | R | R | 6-2 | 180 | 9-18-75 | 1996 | Dublin, Ga. |
| Kritscher, Ryan | .310 | 46 | 168 | 34 | 52 | 19 | 0 | 5 | 33 | 16 | 18 | 3 | 4 | R | R | 5-10 | 180 | 9-29-73 | 1996 | Thousand Oaks, Calif. |
| Lee, Jason | .307 | 36 | 114 | 21 | 35 | 10 | 3 | 2 | 21 | 20 | 25 | 1 | 2 | L | R | 6-1 | 185 | 4-22-77 | 1995 | Burlington, Iowa |
| Leon, Jose | .248 | 59 | 222 | 29 | 55 | 9 | 3 | 10 | 36 | 17 | 92 | 5 | 3 | R | R | 6-0 | 160 | 12-8-76 | 1994 | Cayey, P.R. |
| McNeal, Pepe | .300 | 24 | 90 | 22 | 27 | 6 | 1 | 1 | 11 | 11 | 23 | 0 | 0 | R | R | 6-3 | 205 | 8-11-75 | 1994 | Thonotosassa, Fla. |
| Saturria, Luis | .256 | 57 | 227 | 43 | 58 | 7 | 1 | 5 | 40 | 24 | 61 | 12 | 1 | R | R | 6-2 | 165 | 7-21-76 | 1994 | Boca Chica, D.R. |
| Tanner, Paul | .266 | 41 | 139 | 29 | 37 | 4 | 2 | 1 | 12 | 14 | 37 | 1 | 1 | R | R | 6-0 | 175 | 9-11-74 | 1996 | Albuquerque, N.M. |

GAMES BY POSITION: C—Evans 10, Gargiulo 46, McNeal 17. 1B—Deck 53, Leon 18. 2B—Clapp 20, Harris 27, Hogan 1, Kritscher 24. 3B—Clapp 9, Kritscher 1, Leon 44, Tanner 21. SS—Butler 56, Kritscher 1, Tanner 13. OF—Abell 42, Byrd 23, Farley 15, Harris 2, Hogan 47, Lee 36, Saturria 47.

| PITCHING | W | L | ERA | G | GS | CG | SV | IP | H | R | ER | BB | SO | B | T | HT | WT | DOB | 1st Yr | Resides |
|---|---|---|---|---|---|---|---|---|---|---|---|---|---|---|---|---|---|---|---|---|
| Barfield, Brian | 2 | 2 | 7.36 | 10 | 10 | 0 | 0 | 40 | 53 | 36 | 33 | 29 | 27 | R | R | 6-1 | 190 | 8-26-74 | 1995 | Albany, Ga. |
| DeWitt, Matt | 5 | 5 | 5.42 | 14 | 14 | 0 | 0 | 80 | 96 | 53 | 48 | 26 | 58 | R | R | 6-4 | 220 | 9-4-77 | 1995 | Las Vegas, Nev. |
| DeLeon, Jose | 3 | 1 | 2.12 | 27 | 0 | 0 | 15 | 34 | 28 | 8 | 8 | 10 | 32 | R | R | 6-3 | 152 | 10-2-76 | 1994 | Azua, D.R. |
| Dooley, Chris | 1 | 1 | 4.21 | 13 | 0 | 0 | 1 | 26 | 26 | 14 | 12 | 14 | 28 | L | L | 6-2 | 191 | 12-21-73 | 1996 | Central Square, N.Y. |
| Geis, John | 1 | 0 | 4.50 | 5 | 1 | 0 | 0 | 10 | 8 | 5 | 5 | 4 | 12 | L | L | 6-2 | 180 | 1-31-73 | 1996 | Broken Arrow, Okla. |
| Guzman, Toribio | 2 | 2 | 3.77 | 23 | 0 | 0 | 0 | 31 | 39 | 19 | 13 | 18 | 24 | R | R | 6-3 | 165 | 7-6-76 | 1994 | Bani, D.R. |
| Hogge, Shawn | 0 | 1 | 11.17 | 12 | 0 | 0 | 0 | 10 | 14 | 17 | 12 | 21 | 6 | R | R | 6-3 | 180 | 11-29-77 | 1996 | Puerto La Cruz, Venez. |
| Lugo, Jesus | 0 | 0 | .00 | 3 | 0 | 0 | 0 | 3 | 1 | 0 | 0 | 0 | 2 | R | R | 6-3 | 180 | 5-8-75 | 1993 | Puerto La Cruz, Venez. |
| Mear, Rich | 2 | 2 | 8.31 | 10 | 6 | 0 | 0 | 30 | 35 | 31 | 28 | 37 | 26 | L | L | 6-3 | 218 | 6-30-76 | 1994 | Rowland Heights, Calif. |
| Norris, Steve | 4 | 3 | 6.93 | 16 | 10 | 0 | 0 | 51 | 68 | 49 | 39 | 36 | 36 | L | L | 6-1 | 185 | 2-1-76 | 1996 | Fort Worth, Texas |
| Onofrei, Tim | 1 | 2 | 4.68 | 12 | 7 | 0 | 0 | 42 | 45 | 24 | 22 | 22 | 28 | L | R | 6-2 | 195 | 11-1-74 | 1996 | Vancouver, Wash. |
| Reed, Steve | 5 | 1 | 4.05 | 31 | 0 | 0 | 4 | 40 | 39 | 21 | 18 | 12 | 38 | R | R | 6-2 | 205 | 9-24-75 | 1994 | Juno Beach, Fla. |
| Riegert, Tim | 3 | 0 | 4.19 | 26 | 0 | 0 | 0 | 39 | 41 | 19 | 18 | 16 | 40 | L | L | 6-0 | 180 | 6-29-74 | 1996 | Orlando, Fla. |
| Rosario, Ruben | 7 | 3 | 3.28 | 13 | 13 | 1 | 0 | 71 | 53 | 30 | 26 | 37 | 72 | R | R | 6-3 | 150 | 1-26-75 | 1993 | Boca Chica, D.R. |
| Tuttle, John | 2 | 2 | 4.24 | 21 | 0 | 0 | 0 | 34 | 33 | 22 | 16 | 13 | 25 | L | R | 6-3 | 185 | 11-9-77 | 1996 | San Marino, Calif. |
| Weibl, Clint | 4 | 1 | 2.05 | 7 | 7 | 0 | 0 | 44 | 27 | 12 | 10 | 12 | 51 | R | R | 6-3 | 180 | 3-17-75 | 1996 | Dawson, Pa. |

# SAN DIEGO PADRES

**Manager:** Bruce Bochy.    **1996 Record:** 91-71, .562 (1st, NL West).

| BATTING | AVG | G | AB | R | H | 2B | 3B | HR | RBI | BB | SO | SB | CS | B | T | HT | WT | DOB | 1st Yr | Resides |
|---|---|---|---|---|---|---|---|---|---|---|---|---|---|---|---|---|---|---|---|---|
| Ausmus, Brad | .181 | 50 | 149 | 16 | 27 | 4 | 0 | 1 | 13 | 13 | 27 | 1 | 4 | R | R | 5-11 | 185 | 4-14-69 | 1988 | Cheshire, Conn. |
| Caminiti, Ken | .326 | 146 | 546 | 109 | 178 | 37 | 2 | 40 | 130 | 78 | 99 | 11 | 5 | S | R | 6-0 | 200 | 4-21-63 | 1985 | Richmond, Texas |
| Cedeno, Andujar | .234 | 49 | 154 | 10 | 36 | 2 | 1 | 3 | 18 | 9 | 32 | 3 | 2 | R | R | 6-1 | 168 | 8-21-69 | 1987 | La Romana, D.R. |
| Cianfrocco, Archi | .281 | 79 | 192 | 21 | 54 | 13 | 3 | 2 | 32 | 8 | 56 | 1 | 0 | R | R | 6-5 | 200 | 10-6-66 | 1987 | Rome, N.Y. |
| Dascenzo, Doug | .111 | 21 | 9 | 3 | 1 | 0 | 0 | 0 | 0 | 1 | 2 | 0 | 1 | S | L | 5-8 | 160 | 6-30-64 | 1985 | Labelle, Pa. |
| Deer, Rob | .180 | 25 | 50 | 9 | 9 | 3 | 0 | 4 | 9 | 14 | 30 | 0 | 0 | R | R | 6-3 | 225 | 9-29-60 | 1978 | Scottsdale, Ariz. |
| Finley, Steve | .298 | 161 | 655 | 126 | 195 | 45 | 9 | 30 | 95 | 56 | 88 | 22 | 8 | L | L | 6-2 | 180 | 3-12-65 | 1987 | Houston, Texas |
| Flaherty, John | .303 | 72 | 264 | 22 | 80 | 12 | 0 | 9 | 41 | 9 | 36 | 2 | 3 | R | R | 6-1 | 202 | 10-21-67 | 1988 | West Nyack, N.Y. |
| Gomez, Chris | .262 | 89 | 328 | 32 | 86 | 16 | 1 | 3 | 29 | 39 | 64 | 2 | 2 | R | R | 6-1 | 183 | 6-16-71 | 1992 | Lakewood, Calif. |
| Gwynn, Chris | .178 | 81 | 90 | 8 | 16 | 4 | 0 | 1 | 10 | 10 | 28 | 0 | 0 | L | L | 6-0 | 220 | 10-13-64 | 1985 | Alta Loma, Calif. |
| Gwynn, Tony | .353 | 116 | 451 | 67 | 159 | 27 | 2 | 3 | 50 | 39 | 17 | 11 | 4 | L | L | 5-11 | 210 | 5-9-60 | 1981 | Poway, Calif. |
| Henderson, Rickey | .241 | 148 | 465 | 110 | 112 | 17 | 2 | 9 | 29 | 125 | 90 | 37 | 15 | R | L | 5-10 | 195 | 12-25-58 | 1976 | Oakland, Calif. |
| Johnson, Brian | .272 | 82 | 243 | 18 | 66 | 13 | 1 | 8 | 35 | 4 | 36 | 0 | 0 | R | R | 6-2 | 210 | 1-8-68 | 1989 | Chicago, Ill. |
| Joyner, Wally | .277 | 121 | 433 | 59 | 120 | 29 | 1 | 8 | 65 | 69 | 71 | 5 | 3 | L | L | 6-2 | 200 | 6-16-62 | 1983 | Lee's Summit, Mo. |
| Livingstone, Scott | .297 | 102 | 172 | 20 | 51 | 4 | 1 | 2 | 20 | 9 | 22 | 0 | 1 | L | R | 6-0 | 198 | 7-15-65 | 1988 | Southlake, Texas |
| Lopez, Luis | .180 | 63 | 139 | 10 | 25 | 3 | 0 | 2 | 11 | 9 | 35 | 0 | 0 | S | R | 5-11 | 175 | 9-4-70 | 1988 | Cidra, P.R. |
| Mulligan, Sean | .000 | 2 | 1 | 0 | 0 | 0 | 0 | 0 | 0 | 0 | 0 | 0 | 0 | R | R | 6-2 | 205 | 4-25-70 | 1991 | Diamond Bar, Calif. |
| Newfield, Marc | .251 | 84 | 191 | 27 | 48 | 11 | 0 | 5 | 26 | 16 | 44 | 1 | 1 | R | R | 6-4 | 205 | 10-19-72 | 1990 | Huntington Beach, Calif. |
| Reed, Jody | .244 | 146 | 495 | 45 | 121 | 20 | 0 | 2 | 49 | 59 | 53 | 2 | 5 | R | R | 5-9 | 165 | 7-26-62 | 1984 | Tampa, Fla. |
| Shipley, Craig | .315 | 33 | 92 | 13 | 29 | 5 | 0 | 1 | 7 | 2 | 15 | 7 | 0 | R | R | 6-0 | 168 | 1-7-63 | 1984 | Jupiter, Fla. |
| Steverson, Todd | .000 | 1 | 1 | 0 | 0 | 0 | 0 | 0 | 0 | 0 | 1 | 0 | 0 | R | R | 6-2 | 185 | 11-15-71 | 1992 | Inglewood, Calif. |
| Tatum, Jim | .000 | 5 | 3 | 0 | 0 | 0 | 0 | 0 | 0 | 0 | 1 | 0 | 0 | R | R | 6-2 | 200 | 10-9-67 | 1985 | Lakeside, Calif. |
| Thompson, Jason | .224 | 13 | 49 | 4 | 11 | 4 | 0 | 2 | 6 | 1 | 14 | 0 | 0 | L | L | 6-4 | 200 | 6-13-71 | 1993 | Laguna Hills, Calif. |
| Vaughn, Greg | .206 | 43 | 141 | 20 | 29 | 3 | 1 | 10 | 22 | 24 | 31 | 4 | 1 | R | R | 6-0 | 205 | 7-3-65 | 1986 | Elk Grove, Calif. |

| PITCHING | W | L | ERA | G | GS | CG | SV | IP | H | R | ER | BB | SO | B | T | HT | WT | DOB | 1st Yr | Resides |
|---|---|---|---|---|---|---|---|---|---|---|---|---|---|---|---|---|---|---|---|---|
| Ashby, Andy | 9 | 5 | 3.23 | 24 | 24 | 1 | 0 | 151 | 147 | 60 | 54 | 34 | 85 | R | R | 6-5 | 180 | 7-11-67 | 1986 | Kansas City, Mo. |
| Bergman, Sean | 6 | 8 | 4.37 | 41 | 14 | 0 | 0 | 113 | 119 | 63 | 55 | 33 | 85 | R | R | 6-4 | 205 | 4-11-70 | 1991 | Joliet, Ill. |
| Berumen, Andres | 0 | 0 | 5.40 | 3 | 0 | 0 | 0 | 3 | 3 | 2 | 2 | 2 | 4 | R | R | 6-1 | 205 | 4-5-71 | 1989 | Banning, Calif. |
| Blair, Willie | 2 | 6 | 4.60 | 60 | 0 | 0 | 1 | 88 | 80 | 52 | 45 | 29 | 67 | R | R | 6-1 | 185 | 12-18-65 | 1986 | Lexington, Ky. |
| Bochtler, Doug | 2 | 4 | 3.02 | 63 | 0 | 0 | 3 | 66 | 45 | 25 | 22 | 39 | 68 | R | R | 6-3 | 200 | 7-5-70 | 1989 | West Palm Beach, Fla. |
| Dishman, Glenn | 0 | 0 | 7.71 | 3 | 0 | 0 | 0 | 2 | 3 | 2 | 2 | 1 | 0 | R | L | 6-1 | 195 | 11-5-70 | 1993 | Fremont, Calif. |
| Florie, Bryce | 2 | 2 | 4.01 | 39 | 0 | 0 | 0 | 49 | 45 | 24 | 22 | 27 | 51 | R | R | 6-0 | 170 | 5-21-70 | 1988 | Hanahan, S.C. |
| Hamilton, Joey | 15 | 9 | 4.17 | 34 | 33 | 3 | 0 | 212 | 206 | 100 | 98 | 83 | 184 | R | R | 6-4 | 220 | 9-9-70 | 1991 | Statesboro, Ga. |
| Hermanson, Dustin | 1 | 1 | 8.56 | 8 | 0 | 0 | 0 | 14 | 18 | 15 | 13 | 4 | 11 | R | R | 6-3 | 195 | 12-21-72 | 1994 | Springfield, Ohio |
| Hoffman, Trevor | 9 | 5 | 2.25 | 70 | 0 | 0 | 42 | 88 | 50 | 23 | 22 | 31 | 111 | R | R | 6-0 | 195 | 10-13-67 | 1989 | Williamsville, N.Y. |
| Oquist, Mike | 0 | 0 | 2.35 | 8 | 0 | 0 | 0 | 8 | 6 | 2 | 2 | 4 | 4 | R | R | 6-2 | 170 | 5-30-68 | 1989 | La Junta, Colo. |
| Osuna, Al | 0 | 0 | 2.25 | 10 | 0 | 0 | 0 | 4 | 5 | 1 | 1 | 2 | 4 | R | L | 6-3 | 200 | 8-10-65 | 1987 | Houston, Texas |
| Sanders, Scott | 9 | 5 | 3.38 | 46 | 16 | 0 | 0 | 144 | 117 | 58 | 54 | 48 | 157 | R | R | 6-4 | 220 | 3-25-69 | 1990 | Thibodaux, La. |
| Tewksbury, Bob | 10 | 10 | 4.31 | 36 | 33 | 1 | 0 | 207 | 224 | 116 | 99 | 43 | 126 | R | R | 6-4 | 200 | 11-30-60 | 1981 | Penacook, N.H. |
| Valenzuela, Fernando | 13 | 8 | 3.62 | 33 | 31 | 0 | 0 | 172 | 177 | 78 | 69 | 67 | 95 | L | L | 5-11 | 202 | 11-1-60 | 1978 | Los Angeles, Calif. |
| Veras, Dario | 3 | 1 | 2.79 | 23 | 0 | 0 | 0 | 29 | 24 | 10 | 9 | 10 | 23 | R | R | 6-2 | 165 | 3-13-73 | 1991 | Villa Vasquez, D.R. |
| Villone, Ron | 1 | 1 | 2.95 | 21 | 0 | 0 | 0 | 18 | 17 | 6 | 6 | 7 | 19 | L | L | 6-3 | 235 | 1-16-70 | 1992 | Bergenfield, N.J. |
| Walker, Pete | 0 | 0 | 0.00 | 1 | 0 | 0 | 0 | 1 | 0 | 0 | 0 | 3 | 1 | R | R | 6-2 | 184 | 4-8-69 | 1990 | East Lyme, Conn. |
| Worrell, Tim | 9 | 7 | 3.05 | 50 | 11 | 0 | 1 | 121 | 109 | 45 | 41 | 39 | 99 | R | R | 6-4 | 215 | 7-5-67 | 1990 | Arcadia, Calif. |

## FIELDING

| Catcher | PCT | G | PO | A | E | DP | PB |
|---|---|---|---|---|---|---|---|
| Ausmus | .982 | 46 | 300 | 22 | 6 | 0 | 5 |
| Cianfrocco | .000 | 1 | 0 | 0 | 0 | 0 | 0 |
| Flaherty | .990 | 72 | 471 | 29 | 5 | 3 | 4 |
| Johnson | .989 | 66 | 450 | 21 | 5 | 3 | 5 |

| First Base | PCT | G | PO | A | E | DP |
|---|---|---|---|---|---|---|
| Cianfrocco | 1.000 | 33 | 168 | 15 | 0 | 13 |
| C. Gwynn | 1.000 | 1 | 0 | 1 | 0 | 0 |
| Johnson | 1.000 | 1 | 6 | 0 | 0 | 1 |
| Joyner | .997 | 119 | 1059 | 89 | 3 | 85 |
| Newfield | .909 | 2 | 9 | 1 | 1 | 0 |
| Thompson | .964 | 13 | 94 | 13 | 4 | 6 |

| Second Base | PCT | G | PO | A | E | DP |
|---|---|---|---|---|---|---|
| Cianfrocco | .917 | 6 | 5 | 6 | 1 | 1 |
| Lopez | .962 | 22 | 19 | 32 | 2 | 7 |
| Reed | .987 | 145 | 275 | 411 | 9 | 86 |
| Shipley | .985 | 17 | 26 | 39 | 1 | 6 |

| Third Base | PCT | G | PO | A | E | DP |
|---|---|---|---|---|---|---|
| Caminiti | .954 | 145 | 103 | 310 | 20 | 28 |
| Cedeno | 1.000 | 2 | 1 | 2 | 0 | 0 |
| Cianfrocco | .889 | 11 | 2 | 14 | 2 | 2 |
| Johnson | .000 | 1 | 0 | 0 | 0 | 0 |

| | PCT | G | PO | A | E | DP |
|---|---|---|---|---|---|---|
| Lopez | 1.000 | 2 | 1 | 0 | 0 | 0 |
| Shipley | 1.000 | 4 | 1 | 5 | 0 | 0 |
| Tatum | .000 | 1 | 0 | 0 | 0 | 0 |

| Shortstop | PCT | G | PO | A | E | DP |
|---|---|---|---|---|---|---|
| Cedeno | .946 | 47 | 43 | 131 | 10 | 28 |
| Cianfrocco | 1.000 | 10 | 13 | 16 | 0 | 2 |
| Gomez | .967 | 89 | 124 | 261 | 13 | 54 |
| Lopez | .981 | 35 | 37 | 68 | 2 | 11 |
| Shipley | 1.000 | 7 | 4 | 19 | 0 | 1 |

| Outfield | PCT | G | PO | A | E | DP |
|---|---|---|---|---|---|---|
| Cianfrocco | 1.000 | 8 | 7 | 0 | 0 | 0 |
| Dascenzo | 1.000 | 10 | 3 | 0 | 0 | 0 |
| Deer | 1.000 | 18 | 26 | 0 | 0 | 0 |
| Finley | .982 | 160 | 385 | 7 | 7 | 2 |
| C. Gwynn | 1.000 | 29 | 20 | 0 | 0 | 0 |
| T. Gwynn | .989 | 111 | 182 | 2 | 2 | 0 |
| Henderson | .975 | 134 | 228 | 3 | 6 | 0 |
| Newfield | .970 | 51 | 64 | 0 | 2 | 0 |
| Shipley | 1.000 | 3 | 4 | 1 | 0 | 0 |
| Vaughn | .974 | 39 | 74 | 2 | 2 | 0 |

**Tony Gwynn**

MORRIS FOSTOFF

Outfielder Steve Finley
led San Diego with
126 runs and 195 hits

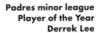

Padres minor league
Player of the Year
Derrek Lee

LARRY GOREN

BILL SETLIFF

# PADRES

## FARM SYSTEM

**Director, Player Development:** Russ Nixon

| Class | Farm Team | League | W | L | Pct. | Finish* | Manager | First Yr |
|---|---|---|---|---|---|---|---|---|
| AAA | Las Vegas (Nev.) Stars | Pacific Coast | 73 | 67 | .521 | 3rd (10) | Jerry Royster | 1983 |
| AA | Memphis (Tenn.) Chicks | Southern | 81 | 58 | .583 | 1st (10) | Ed Romero | 1995 |
| #A | Rancho Cuca. (Calif.) Quakes | California | 69 | 71 | .493 | 8th (10) | Mike Basso | 1993 |
| A | Clinton (Iowa) Lumber Kings | Midwest | 64 | 70 | .478 | 10th (14) | Mike Ramsey | 1995 |
| #R | Idaho Falls (Idaho) Braves | Pioneer | 38 | 34 | .528 | 4th (8) | Don Werner | 1995 |
| R | Peoria (Ariz.) Padres | Arizona | 36 | 20 | .643 | +1st (6) | Larry See | 1988 |

*Finish in overall standings (No. of teams in league)   #Advanced level   +Won league championship

## ORGANIZATION LEADERS

### MAJOR LEAGUERS

**BATTING**

| | | |
|---|---|---|
| *AVG | Tony Gwynn | .353 |
| R | Steve Finley | 126 |
| H | Steve Finley | 195 |
| TB | Steve Finley | 348 |
| 2B | Steve Finley | 45 |
| 3B | Steve Finley | 9 |
| HR | Ken Caminiti | 40 |
| RBI | Ken Caminiti | 130 |
| BB | Rickey Henderson | 125 |
| SO | Ken Caminiti | 99 |
| SB | Rickey Henderson | 37 |

**PITCHING**

| | | |
|---|---|---|
| W | Joey Hamilton | 15 |
| L | Bob Tewksbury | 10 |
| #ERA | Trevor Hoffman | 2.25 |
| G | Trevor Hoffman | 70 |
| CG | Joey Hamilton | 3 |
| SV | Trevor Hoffman | 42 |
| IP | Joey Hamilton | 212 |
| BB | Joey Hamilton | 83 |
| SO | Joey Hamilton | 184 |

**Joey Hamilton.** 15 wins

LARRY GOREN

### MINOR LEAGUERS

**BATTING**

| | | |
|---|---|---|
| *AVG | Ben Reynoso, Idaho Falls | .345 |
| R | Derrek Lee, Memphis | 98 |
| H | Dan Rohrmeier, Memphis | 162 |
| TB | Derrek Lee, Memphis | 285 |
| 2B | Derrek Lee, Memphis | 39 |
| 3B | Gary Matthews, Rancho Cucamonga | 11 |
| HR | Derrek Lee, Memphis | 34 |
| RBI | Derrek Lee, Memphis | 104 |
| BB | Dusty Allen, Clinton/Rancho Cuca. | 105 |
| SO | Derrek Lee, Memphis | 170 |
| SB | James Johnson, Clinton | 44 |

**PITCHING**

| | | |
|---|---|---|
| W | Brandon Kolb, Clinton | 16 |
| L | Keith Davis, Rancho Cucamonga | 15 |
| #ERA | Shane Dennis, R.C./Memphis | 1.85 |
| G | Todd Erdos, Rancho Cucamonga | 55 |
| CG | Three tied at | 4 |
| SV | Marc Kroon, Memphis | 22 |
| IP | Brandon Kolb, Clinton | 181 |
| BB | Fernando Hernandez, Memphis | 85 |
| SO | Shane Dennis, R.C./Memphis | 185 |

*Minimum 250 At-Bats   #Minimum 75 Innings

## TOP 10 PROSPECTS

**How the Padres Top 10 prospects, as judged by Baseball America prior to the 1996 season, fared in 1996:**

| Player, Pos. | Club (Class—League) | AVG | AB | R | H | 2B | 3B | HR | RBI | SB |
|---|---|---|---|---|---|---|---|---|---|---|
| 1. Ben Davis, c | Rancho Cucamonga (A—California) | .201 | 353 | 35 | 71 | 10 | 1 | 6 | 41 | 1 |
| 2. Derrek Lee, 1b | Memphis (AA—Southern) | .280 | 500 | 98 | 140 | 39 | 2 | 34 | 104 | 13 |
| 5. Gabe Alvarez, 3b | Memphis (AA—Southern) | .247 | 368 | 58 | 91 | 23 | 1 | 8 | 40 | 2 |
| 6. *Raul Casanova, c | Jacksonville (AA—Southern) | .333 | 30 | 5 | 10 | 2 | 0 | 4 | 9 | 0 |
| | Toledo (AAA—International) | .273 | 161 | 23 | 44 | 11 | 0 | 8 | 28 | 0 |
| | Detroit | .188 | 85 | 6 | 16 | 1 | 0 | 4 | 9 | 0 |
| 9. Earl Johnson, of | Memphis (AA—Southern) | .252 | 337 | 50 | 85 | 10 | 6 | 2 | 33 | 15 |
| 10. Juan Melo, ss | Rancho Cucamonga (A—California) | .304 | 503 | 75 | 153 | 27 | 6 | 8 | 75 | 6 |

| | | W | L | ERA | G | SV | IP | H | BB | SO |
|---|---|---|---|---|---|---|---|---|---|---|
| 3. Dustin Hermanson, rhp | Las Vegas (AAA—Pacific Coast) | 1 | 4 | 3.13 | 42 | 21 | 46 | 41 | 27 | 54 |
| | San Diego | 1 | 0 | 8.56 | 8 | 0 | 14 | 18 | 4 | 11 |
| 4. #Ron Villone, lhp | Las Vegas (AAA—Pacific Coast) | 2 | 1 | 1.64 | 23 | 3 | 22 | 13 | 9 | 29 |
| | San Diego | 1 | 1 | 2.95 | 21 | 0 | 18 | 17 | 7 | 19 |
| | Milwaukee | 0 | 0 | 3.28 | 23 | 2 | 25 | 14 | 18 | 19 |
| 7. Heath Murray, lhp | Memphis (AA—Southern) | 13 | 9 | 3.21 | 27 | 0 | 174 | 154 | 60 | 156 |
| 8. Marc Kroon, rhp | Memphis (AA—Southern) | 2 | 4 | 2.89 | 44 | 22 | 47 | 33 | 28 | 56 |

**Ben Davis**

LARRY GOREN

*Traded to Tigers;   #Traded to Brewers

## PACIFIC COAST LEAGUE

| BATTING | AVG | G | AB | R | H | 2B | 3B | HR | RBI | BB | SO | SB | CS | B | T | HT | WT | DOB | 1st Yr | Resides |
|---|---|---|---|---|---|---|---|---|---|---|---|---|---|---|---|---|---|---|---|---|
| Barry, Jeff | .083 | 4 | 12 | 1 | 1 | 0 | 0 | 0 | 0 | 3 | 0 | 0 | 0 | S | R | 6-0 | 200 | 9-22-68 | 1990 | San Diego, Calif. |
| Bruno, Julio | .273 | 80 | 297 | 36 | 81 | 16 | 1 | 2 | 30 | 17 | 33 | 6 | 5 | R | R | 5-11 | 190 | 10-15-72 | 1990 | Puerta Plata, D.R. |
| Bush, Homer | .362 | 32 | 116 | 24 | 42 | 11 | 1 | 2 | 3 | 3 | 33 | 3 | 5 | R | R | 5-11 | 180 | 11-11-72 | 1991 | East St. Louis, Ill. |
| Colbert, Craig | .250 | 65 | 200 | 18 | 50 | 8 | 0 | 5 | 19 | 8 | 48 | 3 | 1 | R | R | 6-0 | 214 | 2-13-65 | 1986 | Pearland, Texas |
| Dascenzo, Doug | .284 | 86 | 320 | 48 | 91 | 17 | 3 | 0 | 20 | 32 | 38 | 15 | 13 | S | L | 5-8 | 160 | 6-30-64 | 1985 | Labelle, Pa. |
| Deer, Rob | .224 | 84 | 259 | 43 | 58 | 14 | 2 | 20 | 47 | 56 | 118 | 5 | 1 | R | R | 6-3 | 225 | 9-29-60 | 1978 | Scottsdale, Ariz. |
| Ingram, Riccardo | .249 | 124 | 409 | 54 | 102 | 21 | 1 | 8 | 51 | 49 | 64 | 6 | 6 | R | R | 6-0 | 198 | 9-10-66 | 1988 | Douglas, Ga. |
| Lopez, Luis | .206 | 18 | 68 | 4 | 14 | 3 | 0 | 1 | 12 | 2 | 15 | 0 | 0 | S | R | 5-11 | 175 | 9-4-70 | 1988 | Cidra, P.R. |
| Mulligan, Sean | .288 | 102 | 358 | 55 | 103 | 24 | 3 | 19 | 75 | 30 | 68 | 1 | 2 | R | R | 6-2 | 205 | 4-25-70 | 1991 | Diamond Bar, Calif. |
| Prieto, Chris | .000 | 5 | 7 | 1 | 0 | 0 | 0 | 0 | 0 | 0 | *0 | 0 | 0 | L | L | 5-11 | 180 | 8-24-72 | 1993 | Carmel, Calif. |
| Ready, Randy | .324 | 35 | 105 | 19 | 34 | 7 | 0 | 3 | 11 | 23 | 13 | 0 | 1 | R | R | 5-11 | 180 | 1-8-60 | 1980 | Cardiff, Calif. |
| Rossy, Rico | .252 | 130 | 413 | 56 | 104 | 21 | 2 | 4 | 35 | 70 | 63 | 6 | 6 | R | R | 5-10 | 175 | 2-16-64 | 1985 | Bayamon, P.R. |
| Russo, Paul | .252 | 80 | 226 | 16 | 57 | 15 | 2 | 4 | 33 | 23 | 53 | 2 | 1 | R | R | 5-11 | 215 | 8-26-69 | 1990 | Tampa, Fla. |
| Schwenke, Matt | .250 | 11 | 16 | 0 | 4 | 0 | 0 | 0 | 2 | 0 | 7 | 0 | 0 | R | R | 6-2 | 210 | 8-12-72 | 1993 | Loomis, Calif. |
| Scott, Gary | .272 | 65 | 217 | 24 | 59 | 16 | 2 | 2 | 27 | 31 | 47 | 0 | 2 | R | R | 6-0 | 175 | 8-22-68 | 1989 | Pelham, N.Y. |
| Sharperson, Mike | .304 | 32 | 112 | 17 | 34 | 8 | 0 | 1 | 21 | 20 | 11 | 1 | 0 | R | R | 6-3 | 190 | 10-4-61 | 1982 | Stone Mountain, Ga. |
| Shipley, Craig | .000 | 1 | 2 | 1 | 0 | 0 | 0 | 0 | 0 | 0 | 1 | 0 | 0 | R | R | 6-0 | 168 | 1-7-63 | 1984 | Jupiter, Fla. |
| Smith, Ira | .242 | 72 | 252 | 37 | 61 | 16 | 1 | 5 | 25 | 20 | 27 | 3 | 3 | R | R | 5-11 | 185 | 8-4-67 | 1990 | Chestertown, Md. |
| Steverson, Todd | .239 | 100 | 301 | 42 | 72 | 16 | 3 | 12 | 50 | 47 | 87 | 6 | 5 | R | R | 6-2 | 185 | 11-15-71 | 1992 | Inglewood, Calif. |
| Tatum, Jim | .343 | 64 | 233 | 40 | 80 | 20 | 1 | 12 | 56 | 23 | 53 | 4 | 0 | R | R | 6-2 | 200 | 10-9-67 | 1985 | Lakeside, Calif. |
| Thompson, Jason | .300 | 111 | 387 | 80 | 116 | 27 | 0 | 21 | 57 | 51 | 93 | 7 | 5 | L | L | 6-4 | 200 | 6-13-71 | 1993 | Laguna Hills, Calif. |
| Tredaway, Chad | .224 | 76 | 196 | 26 | 44 | 10 | 2 | 5 | 19 | 17 | 25 | 4 | 1 | S | R | 6-0 | 193 | 6-18-72 | 1992 | Mission, Texas |

| PITCHING | W | L | ERA | G | GS | CG | SV | IP | H | R | ER | BB | SO | B | T | HT | WT | DOB | 1st Yr | Resides |
|---|---|---|---|---|---|---|---|---|---|---|---|---|---|---|---|---|---|---|---|---|
| Abbott, Paul | 4 | 2 | 4.18 | 28 | 0 | 0 | 7 | 28 | 27 | 14 | 13 | 12 | 37 | R | R | 6-3 | 195 | 9-15-67 | 1985 | Fullerton, Calif. |
| Berumen, Andres | 4 | 7 | 6.11 | 50 | 0 | 0 | 1 | 71 | 73 | 53 | 48 | 58 | 59 | R | R | 6-1 | 205 | 4-5-71 | 1989 | Banning, Calif. |
| Dishman, Glenn | 6 | 8 | 5.57 | 26 | 26 | 3 | 0 | 155 | 177 | 103 | 96 | 43 | 115 | R | L | 6-1 | 195 | 11-5-70 | 1993 | Fremont, Calif. |
| Drahman, Brian | 1 | 0 | 1.00 | 9 | 0 | 0 | 0 | 9 | 4 | 1 | 1 | 4 | 10 | R | R | 6-3 | 231 | 11-7-66 | 1986 | Fort Lauderdale, Fla. |
| Freitas, Mike | 0 | 1 | 3.18 | 3 | 0 | 0 | 0 | 6 | 8 | 2 | 2 | 1 | 1 | R | R | 6-1 | 160 | 9-22-69 | 1989 | Sacramento, Calif. |
| Harriger, Denny | 10 | 7 | 4.22 | 26 | 25 | 1 | 0 | 164 | 183 | 91 | 77 | 51 | 102 | R | R | 5-11 | 185 | 7-21-69 | 1987 | Ford City, Pa. |
| Harris, Greg W. | 0 | 1 | 18.00 | 1 | 1 | 0 | 0 | 4 | 11 | 9 | 8 | 3 | 2 | R | R | 6-2 | 195 | 12-1-63 | 1985 | Las Vegas, Nev. |
| Hermanson, Dustin | 1 | 4 | 3.13 | 42 | 0 | 0 | 21 | 46 | 41 | 20 | 16 | 27 | 54 | R | R | 6-3 | 195 | 12-21-72 | 1994 | Springfield, Ohio |
| Lewis, Scott | 3 | 9 | 5.34 | 29 | 21 | 2 | 0 | 150 | 174 | 96 | 89 | 36 | 109 | R | R | 6-3 | 178 | 12-5-65 | 1988 | Tustin, Calif. |
| Long, Joey | 3 | 3 | 4.24 | 32 | 0 | 0 | 1 | 34 | 39 | 21 | 16 | 23 | 23 | R | L | 6-2 | 215 | 7-15-70 | 1991 | Rosewood, Ohio |
| Oquist, Mike | 9 | 4 | 2.89 | 27 | 20 | 2 | 1 | 140 | 136 | 55 | 45 | 44 | 110 | R | R | 6-2 | 170 | 5-30-68 | 1989 | La Junta, Colo. |
| Osuna, Al | 1 | 0 | 2.30 | 11 | 0 | 0 | 0 | 16 | 9 | 6 | 4 | 5 | 17 | R | L | 6-3 | 200 | 8-10-65 | 1987 | Houston, Texas |
| Schmitt, Todd | 0 | 0 | 4.50 | 4 | 0 | 0 | 0 | 4 | 2 | 2 | 2 | 6 | 6 | R | R | 6-2 | 170 | 2-12-70 | 1992 | Clinton Township, Mich. |
| Smith, Pete | 11 | 9 | 4.95 | 26 | 26 | 2 | 0 | 169 | 192 | 106 | 93 | 42 | 95 | R | R | 6-2 | 200 | 2-27-66 | 1984 | Smyrna, Ga. |
| Swan, Russ | 5 | 6 | 5.08 | 25 | 20 | 1 | 0 | 126 | 148 | 80 | 71 | 47 | 71 | L | L | 6-4 | 210 | 1-3-64 | 1986 | Kent, Wash. |
| Veras, Dario | 6 | 2 | 2.90 | 19 | 1 | 0 | 1 | 40 | 41 | 17 | 13 | 6 | 30 | R | R | 6-2 | 165 | 3-13-73 | 1991 | Villa Vasquez, D.R. |
| Villone, Ron | 2 | 1 | 1.64 | 23 | 0 | 0 | 3 | 22 | 13 | 5 | 4 | 9 | 29 | L | L | 6-3 | 235 | 1-16-70 | 1992 | Bergenfield, N.J. |
| Walker, Pete | 5 | 1 | 6.83 | 26 | 0 | 0 | 0 | 28 | 37 | 22 | 21 | 14 | 23 | R | R | 6-2 | 184 | 4-8-69 | 1990 | East Lyme, Conn. |
| Weber, Weston | 2 | 1 | 6.30 | 7 | 0 | 0 | 0 | 10 | 12 | 7 | 7 | 8 | 4 | R | R | 6-0 | 175 | 1-5-64 | 1986 | Dodge Center, Minn. |

### FIELDING

| Catcher | PCT | G | PO | A | E | DP | PB |
|---|---|---|---|---|---|---|---|
| Colbert | .986 | 54 | 307 | 33 | 5 | 2 | 3 |
| Mulligan | .989 | 90 | 582 | 58 | 7 | 3 | 14 |
| Schwenke | .962 | 5 | 22 | 3 | 1 | 0 | 0 |

| First Base | PCT | G | PO | A | E | DP |
|---|---|---|---|---|---|---|
| Deer | .986 | 16 | 132 | 10 | 2 | 12 |
| Ready | .909 | 1 | 10 | 0 | 1 | 0 |
| Russo | .986 | 9 | 68 | 3 | 1 | 13 |
| Scott | 1.000 | 1 | 4 | 0 | 0 | 0 |
| Tatum | 1.000 | 18 | 121 | 13 | 0 | 10 |
| Thompson | .992 | 109 | 952 | 62 | 8 | 88 |
| Tredaway | 1.000 | 2 | 9 | 1 | 0 | 0 |

| Second Base | PCT | G | PO | A | E | DP |
|---|---|---|---|---|---|---|
| Bruno | .976 | 71 | 127 | 195 | 8 | 39 |
| Bush | .969 | 31 | 67 | 88 | 5 | 21 |
| Lopez | .983 | 13 | 32 | 26 | 1 | 7 |
| Ready | .962 | 12 | 24 | 27 | 2 | 9 |

| | PCT | G | PO | A | E | DP |
|---|---|---|---|---|---|---|
| Scott | .000 | 1 | 0 | 0 | 0 | 0 |
| Sharperson | .000 | 1 | 0 | 0 | 0 | 0 |
| Tredaway | .957 | 27 | 49 | 63 | 5 | 15 |

| Third Base | PCT | G | PO | A | E | DP |
|---|---|---|---|---|---|---|
| Bruno | .889 | 3 | 2 | 6 | 1 | 0 |
| Colbert | .000 | 1 | 0 | 0 | 0 | 0 |
| Ready | .500 | 1 | 1 | 0 | 1 | 0 |
| Rossy | 1.000 | 1 | 1 | 1 | 0 | 0 |
| Russo | .943 | 47 | 31 | 68 | 6 | 11 |
| Scott | .918 | 57 | 29 | 106 | 12 | 8 |
| Sharperson | .941 | 29 | 21 | 75 | 6 | 8 |
| Tatum | 1.000 | 4 | 0 | 4 | 0 | 0 |
| Tredaway | .915 | 22 | 13 | 30 | 4 | 3 |

| Shortstop | PCT | G | PO | A | E | DP |
|---|---|---|---|---|---|---|
| Lopez | .960 | 9 | 7 | 17 | 1 | 3 |
| Rossy | .969 | 127 | 163 | 405 | 18 | 76 |

| | PCT | G | PO | A | E | DP |
|---|---|---|---|---|---|---|
| Scott | 1.000 | 2 | 1 | 0 | 0 | 0 |
| Shipley | 1.000 | 1 | 0 | 2 | 0 | 0 |
| Tredaway | .944 | 11 | 9 | 25 | 2 | 4 |

| Outfield | PCT | G | PO | A | E | DP |
|---|---|---|---|---|---|---|
| Barry | .923 | 4 | 12 | 0 | 1 | 0 |
| Colbert | 1.000 | 1 | 1 | 0 | 0 | 0 |
| Dascenzo | .994 | 85 | 168 | 6 | 1 | 0 |
| Deer | .956 | 58 | 83 | 3 | 4 | 0 |
| Ingram | 1.000 | 106 | 198 | 10 | 0 | 3 |
| Prieto | 1.000 | 5 | 12 | 2 | 0 | 2 |
| Ready | 1.000 | 1 | 2 | 0 | 0 | 0 |
| Scott | .000 | 1 | 0 | 0 | 0 | 0 |
| Smith | .984 | 64 | 124 | 1 | 2 | 0 |
| Steverson | .980 | 86 | 140 | 9 | 3 | 2 |
| Tatum | .960 | 45 | 64 | 8 | 3 | 0 |

## SOUTHERN LEAGUE

| BATTING | AVG | G | AB | R | H | 2B | 3B | HR | RBI | BB | SO | SB | CS | B | T | HT | WT | DOB | 1st Yr | Resides |
|---|---|---|---|---|---|---|---|---|---|---|---|---|---|---|---|---|---|---|---|---|
| Alvarez, Gabe | .247 | 104 | 368 | 58 | 91 | 23 | 1 | 8 | 40 | 64 | 87 | 2 | 3 | R | R | 6-1 | 185 | 3-6-74 | 1995 | El Monte, Calif. |
| Barry, Jeff | .243 | 91 | 226 | 29 | 55 | 7 | 0 | 3 | 25 | 29 | 48 | 3 | 7 | S | R | 6-0 | 200 | 9-22-68 | 1990 | San Diego, Calif. |
| Briggs, Stoney | .274 | 133 | 452 | 72 | 124 | 24 | 6 | 12 | 80 | 62 | 123 | 28 | 11 | R | R | 6-3 | 215 | 12-26-71 | 1991 | Seaford, Del. |
| Brinkley, Darryl | .296 | 60 | 203 | 36 | 60 | 9 | 0 | 9 | 29 | 22 | 33 | 13 | 5 | R | R | 5-11 | 205 | 12-23-68 | 1994 | Stamford, Conn. |
| Bruno, Julio | .238 | 27 | 84 | 11 | 20 | 8 | 1 | 0 | 9 | 6 | 18 | 1 | 2 | R | R | 5-11 | 190 | 10-15-72 | 1990 | Puerta Plata, D.R. |
| Johnson, Earl | .252 | 82 | 337 | 50 | 85 | 10 | 6 | 2 | 33 | 18 | 59 | 15 | 13 | S | R | 5-9 | 163 | 10-3-71 | 1991 | Detroit, Mich. |
| Keefe, Jamie | .176 | 12 | 17 | 2 | 3 | 0 | 0 | 0 | 3 | 5 | 0 | 0 | R | R | 5-11 | 180 | 8-29-73 | 1992 | Rochester, N.H. |
| Killeen, Tim | .259 | 83 | 224 | 44 | 58 | 10 | 6 | 11 | 51 | 27 | 57 | 0 | 2 | L | R | 6-0 | 195 | 7-26-70 | 1992 | Phoenix, Ariz. |
| LaRocca, Greg | .274 | 128 | 445 | 66 | 122 | 22 | 5 | 6 | 42 | 51 | 58 | 5 | 9 | R | R | 5-11 | 185 | 11-10-72 | 1994 | Bedford, N.H. |
| Lee, Derrek | .280 | 134 | 500 | 98 | 140 | 32 | 3 | 34 | 104 | 65 | 170 | 13 | 6 | R | R | 6-5 | 200 | 9-6-75 | 1993 | Folsom, Calif. |
| Massarelli, John | .263 | 65 | 205 | 26 | 54 | 16 | 3 | 2 | 15 | 13 | 32 | 9 | 4 | R | R | 6-2 | 200 | 1-23-66 | 1987 | Canton, Ohio |
| Moore, Vince | .206 | 44 | 141 | 24 | 29 | 11 | 2 | 1 | 11 | 20 | 47 | 7 | 4 | L | L | 6-1 | 190 | 9-22-71 | 1991 | Houston, Texas |
| Prieto, Chris | .333 | 7 | 12 | 1 | 4 | 0 | 1 | 0 | 0 | 1 | 2 | 2 | 0 | L | L | 5-11 | 180 | 8-24-72 | 1993 | Carmel, Calif. |

| BATTING | AVG | G | AB | R | H | 2B | 3B | HR | RBI | BB | SO | SB | CS | B | T | HT | WT | DOB | 1st Yr | Resides |
|---|---|---|---|---|---|---|---|---|---|---|---|---|---|---|---|---|---|---|---|---|
| Rohrmeier, Dan ........... | .344 | 134 | 471 | 98 | 162 | 29 | 2 | 28 | 95 | 77 | 76 | 2 | 5 | R | R | 6-0 | 185 | 9-27-65 | 1987 | Woodridge, Ill. |
| Romero, Mandy .......... | .269 | 88 | 297 | 40 | 80 | 15 | 0 | 10 | 46 | 41 | 52 | 3 | 1 | R | R | 5-11 | 196 | 10-19-67 | 1988 | Miami, Fla. |
| Velandia, Jorge ........... | .240 | 122 | 392 | 42 | 94 | 19 | 0 | 9 | 48 | 31 | 65 | 3 | 7 | R | R | 5-9 | 160 | 1-12-75 | 1992 | Caracas, Venez. |
| Woodridge, Dickie ....... | .154 | 34 | 65 | 10 | 10 | 0 | 0 | 0 | 11 | 16 | 6 | 1 | 0 | L | R | 5-9 | 180 | 1-24-71 | 1993 | Jordan, N.Y. |

| PITCHING | W | L | ERA | G | GS | CG | SV | IP | H | R | ER | BB | SO | B | T | HT | WT | DOB | 1st Yr | Resides |
|---|---|---|---|---|---|---|---|---|---|---|---|---|---|---|---|---|---|---|---|---|
| Clark, Dera ................. | 4 | 3 | 3.13 | 9 | 9 | 0 | 0 | 46 | 47 | 24 | 16 | 13 | 42 | R | R | 6-1 | 204 | 4-14-65 | 1987 | Lindsay, Texas |
| Clayton, Craig .............. | 0 | 0 | 5.59 | 5 | 0 | 0 | 0 | 10 | 14 | 12 | 6 | 5 | 9 | R | R | 6-0 | 185 | 11-29-70 | 1991 | Anaheim, Calif. |
| Cole, Victor ................ | 1 | 0 | 1.20 | 8 | 1 | 0 | 1 | 15 | 11 | 3 | 2 | 8 | 13 | S | R | 5-10 | 160 | 1-23-68 | 1988 | Monterey, Calif. |
| Dennis, Shane ............. | 9 | 1 | 2.27 | 19 | 19 | 1 | 0 | 115 | 83 | 35 | 29 | 45 | 131 | R | L | 6-3 | 200 | 7-3-71 | 1994 | Uniontown, Kan. |
| Dixon, Bubba .............. | 2 | 3 | 4.12 | 42 | 0 | 0 | 3 | 63 | 53 | 32 | 29 | 28 | 77 | L | L | 5-10 | 165 | 1-7-72 | 1994 | Lucedale, Miss. |
| Fesh, Sean ................. | 1 | 1 | 5.63 | 7 | 0 | 0 | 0 | 8 | 7 | 5 | 5 | 7 | 5 | L | L | 6-2 | 165 | 11-3-72 | 1991 | Bethel, Conn. |
| Freitas, Mike .............. | 3 | 0 | 5.11 | 44 | 0 | 0 | 0 | 69 | 78 | 41 | 39 | 26 | 36 | R | R | 6-1 | 160 | 9-22-69 | 1989 | Sacramento, Calif. |
| Hernandez Fernando .11 | 10 | 4.64 | 27 | 27 | 0 | 0 | 147 | 128 | 83 | 76 | 85 | 161 | R | R | 6-2 | 185 | 6-16-71 | 1990 | Santiago, D.R. |
| Kaufman, Brad ........... | 12 | 10 | 3.63 | 29 | 29 | 3 | 0 | 178 | 161 | 84 | 72 | 83 | 163 | R | R | 6-2 | 210 | 4-26-72 | 1993 | Traer, Iowa |
| Kilgo, Rusty ............... | 1 | 4 | 3.65 | 48 | 0 | 0 | 2 | 74 | 80 | 35 | 30 | 18 | 53 | L | L | 6-0 | 175 | 8-9-66 | 1989 | Houston, Texas |
| Kroon, Marc ............... | 2 | 3 | 2.89 | 44 | 0 | 0 | 22 | 47 | 33 | 19 | 15 | 28 | 56 | S | R | 6-2 | 175 | 4-2-73 | 1991 | Phoenix, Ariz. |
| Long, Joey ................. | 2 | 0 | 2.00 | 10 | 0 | 0 | 0 | 18 | 16 | 4 | 4 | 11 | 14 | R | L | 6-2 | 215 | 7-15-70 | 1991 | Rosewood, Ohio |
| Mattson, Rob .............. | 13 | 8 | 4.33 | 27 | 27 | 3 | 0 | 164 | 172 | 87 | 79 | 54 | 88 | R | R | 6-1 | 190 | 11-18-66 | 1991 | Palm Beach Gardens, Fla. |
| Murray, Heath ............ | 13 | 9 | 3.21 | 27 | 27 | 1 | 0 | 174 | 154 | 83 | 62 | 60 | 156 | L | L | 6-4 | 205 | 4-19-73 | 1994 | Troy, Ohio |
| Schmitt, Todd .............. | 4 | 3 | 3.43 | 38 | 0 | 0 | 11 | 39 | 39 | 26 | 15 | 21 | 47 | R | R | 6-2 | 170 | 2-12-70 | 1992 | Clinton Township, Mich. |
| Veras, Dario ............... | 3 | 1 | 2.32 | 29 | 0 | 0 | 1 | 43 | 38 | 14 | 11 | 9 | 47 | R | R | 6-2 | 165 | 3-13-73 | 1991 | Villa Vasquez, D.R. |
| Yoda, Tsuyoshi ............ | 0 | 0 | 11.74 | 9 | 0 | 0 | 0 | 8 | 9 | 11 | 10 | 8 | 3 | R | R | 6-0 | 170 | 12-4-65 | 1996 | Aichi, Japan |

**FIELDING**

| Catcher | PCT | G | PO | A | E | DP | PB |
|---|---|---|---|---|---|---|---|
| Killeen ............ | .987 | 66 | 424 | 40 | 6 | 2 | 6 |
| Massarelli ...... | 1.000 | 9 | 32 | 5 | 0 | 0 | |
| Romero .......... | .983 | 78 | 657 | 52 | 12 | 5 | 12 |

| First Base | PCT | G | PO | A | E | DP |
|---|---|---|---|---|---|---|
| Barry ............... | .902 | 5 | 33 | 4 | 4 | 3 |
| Killeen ........... | 1.000 | 2 | 5 | 0 | 0 | 0 |
| Lee ................. | .991 | 133 | 1121 | 76 | 11 | 91 |
| Rohrmeier ..... | 1.000 | 2 | 13 | 0 | 0 | 1 |

| Second Base | PCT | G | PO | A | E | DP |
|---|---|---|---|---|---|---|
| Barry ............... | 1.000 | 1 | 1 | 0 | 0 | 0 |
| Bruno ............. | .958 | 19 | 25 | 44 | 3 | 9 |
| Keefe .............. | .944 | 7 | 3 | 14 | 1 | 3 |
| LaRocca ......... | .959 | 107 | 171 | 274 | 19 | 49 |

| | PCT | G | PO | A | E | DP |
|---|---|---|---|---|---|---|
| Woodridge ...... | .973 | 21 | 34 | 38 | 2 | 11 |
| Third Base | PCT | G | PO | A | E | DP |
| Alvarez .......... | .878 | 96 | 59 | 156 | 30 | 7 |
| Barry ............. | .915 | 42 | 21 | 76 | 9 | 5 |
| Bruno ............. | 1.000 | 6 | 4 | 7 | 0 | 1 |
| Keefe ............. | 1.000 | 3 | 0 | 1 | 0 | 1 |
| Lee ................ | 1.000 | 1 | 0 | 1 | 0 | |
| Massarelli ..... | .000 | 1 | 0 | 0 | 0 | 0 |
| Rohrmeier ..... | 1.000 | 1 | 1 | 0 | 0 | 0 |
| Woodridge ..... | .750 | 3 | 1 | 5 | 2 | 1 |
| Shortstop | PCT | G | PO | A | E | DP |
| Alvarez .......... | .889 | 3 | 3 | 5 | 1 | 1 |
| LaRocca ........ | .926 | 28 | 17 | 46 | 5 | 10 |

| | PCT | G | PO | A | E | DP |
|---|---|---|---|---|---|---|
| Velandia ......... | .943 | 121 | 173 | 368 | 33 | 66 |
| Outfield | PCT | G | PO | A | E | DP |
| Barry ............. | 1.000 | 30 | 35 | 1 | 0 | 0 |
| Briggs ............ | .963 | 133 | 217 | 15 | 9 | 3 |
| Brinkley ......... | .989 | 51 | 89 | 1 | 1 | 0 |
| Johnson ......... | .986 | 82 | 204 | 9 | 3 | 3 |
| Killeen ........... | .000 | 3 | 0 | 0 | 0 | 0 |
| Massarelli ...... | .978 | 47 | 84 | 6 | 2 | 1 |
| Moore ............ | .983 | 40 | 58 | 0 | 1 | 0 |
| Prieto ............. | 1.000 | 5 | 6 | 0 | 0 | 0 |
| Rohrmeier ...... | .990 | 63 | 93 | 9 | 1 | 2 |

---

## BAKERSFIELD
Class A/Co-Op

## CALIFORNIA LEAGUE

| BATTING | AVG | G | AB | R | H | 2B | 3B | HR | RBI | BB | SO | SB | CS | B | T | HT | WT | DOB | 1st Yr | Resides |
|---|---|---|---|---|---|---|---|---|---|---|---|---|---|---|---|---|---|---|---|---|
| Espinal, Juan ............... | .274 | 137 | 522 | 81 | 143 | 38 | 0 | 26 | 98 | 74 | 126 | 1 | 4 | R | R | 6-0 | 207 | 4-15-75 | 1992 | La Vega, D.R. |

**GAMES BY POSITION: OF**—Espinal 129.

---

# RANCHO CUCAMONGA
Class A

## CALIFORNIA LEAGUE

| BATTING | AVG | G | AB | R | H | 2B | 3B | HR | RBI | BB | SO | SB | CS | B | T | HT | WT | DOB | 1st Yr | Resides |
|---|---|---|---|---|---|---|---|---|---|---|---|---|---|---|---|---|---|---|---|---|
| Allen, Dusty ................. | .298 | 55 | 208 | 41 | 62 | 15 | 1 | 10 | 45 | 38 | 65 | 3 | 2 | R | R | 6-4 | 215 | 8-9-72 | 1995 | Oklahoma City, Okla. |
| Brinkley, Darryl ............ | .363 | 59 | 259 | 52 | 94 | 28 | 2 | 9 | 59 | 23 | 37 | 18 | 10 | S | R | 5-11 | 205 | 12-23-68 | 1994 | Stamford, Conn. |
| Bucci, Carmen .............. | .000 | 9 | 16 | 1 | 0 | 0 | 0 | 0 | 1 | 0 | 5 | 0 | 0 | S | R | 5-11 | 180 | 3-29-73 | 1995 | Oak Forest, Ill. |
| Cuevas, Eduardo ........ | .348 | 7 | 23 | 3 | 8 | 0 | 0 | 0 | 5 | 2 | 4 | 0 | 0 | R | R | 5-10 | 180 | 12-1-73 | 1992 | Haina, D.R. |
| Curtis, Randy ................ | .267 | 104 | 359 | 63 | 96 | 14 | 5 | 5 | 52 | 76 | 94 | 22 | 6 | L | L | 5-10 | 180 | 1-16-71 | 1991 | Norco, Calif. |
| Davis, Ben ................... | .201 | 98 | 353 | 35 | 71 | 10 | 1 | 6 | 41 | 31 | 89 | 1 | 1 | S | R | 6-4 | 205 | 3-10-77 | 1995 | Aston, Pa. |
| Eaddy, Keith ................ | .221 | 40 | 104 | 13 | 23 | 5 | 1 | 3 | 10 | 18 | 41 | 1 | 3 | R | R | 5-9 | 180 | 11-23-70 | 1992 | Newark, N.J. |
| 2-team (12 H.D.) ...... | .194 | 52 | 129 | 14 | 25 | 5 | 1 | 3 | 10 | 18 | 48 | 3 | 4 | | | | | | | |
| Fernandez, Antonio ........ | .308 | 121 | 471 | 77 | 145 | 27 | 0 | 9 | 73 | 43 | 96 | 2 | 2 | R | R | 6-0 | 195 | 5-24-73 | 1994 | Tucson, Ariz. |
| Gama, Rick ................. | .271 | 108 | 417 | 59 | 113 | 28 | 2 | 7 | 50 | 37 | 57 | 13 | 5 | R | R | 5-10 | 180 | 4-27-73 | 1995 | Mexico City, Mexico |
| Hunter, Andy ................ | .222 | 4 | 9 | 2 | 2 | 0 | 0 | 0 | 0 | 0 | 2 | 0 | 0 | R | R | 6-2 | 185 | 12-28-76 | 1995 | Mansfield, Texas |
| Joyner, Wally ............... | .300 | 3 | 10 | 1 | 3 | 1 | 0 | 0 | 2 | 1 | 1 | 0 | 0 | L | L | 6-2 | 200 | 6-16-62 | 1983 | Lee's Summit, Mo. |
| Keefe, Jamie ................ | .234 | 24 | 64 | 12 | 15 | 5 | 1 | 2 | 10 | 11 | 26 | 1 | 0 | R | R | 5-11 | 180 | 8-29-73 | 1992 | Rochester, N.H. |
| Massarelli, John ............ | .296 | 26 | 108 | 24 | 32 | 9 | 3 | 0 | 17 | 15 | 14 | 6 | 1 | R | R | 6-2 | 200 | 1-23-66 | 1987 | Canton, Ohio |
| Matthews, Gary ............ | .271 | 123 | 435 | 65 | 118 | 21 | 11 | 7 | 54 | 60 | 102 | 7 | 8 | S | R | 6-3 | 185 | 8-25-74 | 1994 | Canoga Oark, Calif. |
| McKinnis, Leroy ............ | .268 | 87 | 328 | 49 | 88 | 20 | 2 | 4 | 39 | 38 | 74 | 2 | 3 | R | R | 6-1 | 185 | 11-14-72 | 1993 | Irving, Texas |
| Melo, Juan .................. | .304 | 128 | 503 | 75 | 153 | 27 | 6 | 8 | 75 | 22 | 102 | 6 | 8 | S | R | 6-3 | 185 | 11-5-76 | 1994 | Bani, D.R. |
| Moore, Vince ................ | .288 | 63 | 219 | 49 | 63 | 13 | 2 | 8 | 38 | 42 | 78 | 12 | 1 | L | L | 6-1 | 190 | 9-22-71 | 1991 | Houston, Texas |
| Prieto, Chris ................ | .241 | 55 | 216 | 36 | 52 | 11 | 2 | 2 | 23 | 39 | 36 | 23 | 8 | L | L | 5-11 | 180 | 8-24-72 | 1993 | Carmel, Calif. |
| Roberts, John ............... | .164 | 23 | 73 | 11 | 12 | 4 | 1 | 2 | 6 | 11 | 27 | 4 | 1 | R | R | 5-9 | 185 | 9-30-73 | 1991 | Pine Bluff, Ark. |
| Rosario, Melvin ........... | .273 | 10 | 33 | 7 | 9 | 3 | 0 | 3 | 10 | 3 | 8 | 1 | 0 | S | R | 6-0 | 191 | 5-25-73 | 1992 | Miami, Fla. |
| Schwenke, Matt ........... | .207 | 10 | 29 | 2 | 6 | 0 | 0 | 1 | 2 | 2 | 13 | 0 | 0 | R | R | 6-2 | 210 | 8-12-72 | 1993 | Loomis, Calif. |
| Tredaway, Chad ............ | .250 | 21 | 84 | 13 | 21 | 3 | 0 | 2 | 13 | 7 | 7 | 1 | 0 | S | R | 6-0 | 193 | 6-18-72 | 1992 | Mission, Texas |
| Watkins, Sean ............. | .273 | 97 | 363 | 57 | 99 | 21 | 4 | 6 | 51 | 56 | 104 | 0 | 2 | L | L | 6-4 | 210 | 10-6-74 | 1995 | Peoria Heights, Ill. |
| Woodridge, Dickie ......... | .298 | 36 | 141 | 32 | 42 | 5 | 3 | 2 | 24 | 14 | 11 | 0 | 1 | L | R | 5-9 | 180 | 1-24-71 | 1993 | Jordan, N.Y. |

**GAMES BY POSITION: C**—Davis 77, McKinnis 53, Rosario 5, Schwenke 9. **1B**—Allen 44, Fernandez 3, Joyner 3, Keefe 1, McKinnis 3, Watkins 92. **2B**—Bucci 2, Cuevas 4, Gama 103, Keefe 5, Tredaway 5, Woodridge 28. **3B**—Bucci 3, Cuevas 2, Fernandez 118, Keefe 9, Massarelli 1, Tredaway 10, Woodridge 4. **SS**—Bucci 2, Fernandez 1, Keefe 8, Melo 128, Tredaway 6, Woodridge 1. **OF**—Allen 10, Brinkley 30, Curtis 96, Eaddy 27, Hunter 2, Massarelli 25, Matthews 122, Moore 46, Prieto 54, Roberts 21.

| PITCHING | W | L | ERA | G | GS | CG | SV | IP | H | R | ER | BB | SO | B | T | HT | WT | DOB | 1st Yr | Resides |
|---|---|---|---|---|---|---|---|---|---|---|---|---|---|---|---|---|---|---|---|---|
| Baron, Jim ................... | 6 | 3 | 3.00 | 54 | 0 | 0 | 1 | 87 | 87 | 44 | 29 | 35 | 85 | L | L | 6-3 | 230 | 2-22-74 | 1992 | Humble, Texas |
| Bussa, Todd ................ | 0 | 1 | 9.72 | 16 | 0 | 0 | 0 | 17 | 27 | 20 | 18 | 16 | 19 | R | R | 5-11 | 170 | 12-13-72 | 1991 | Palm Beach Gardens, Fla. |

| PITCHING | W | L | ERA | G | GS | CG | SV | IP | H | R | ER | BB | SO | B | T | HT | WT | DOB | 1st Yr | Resides |
|---|---|---|---|---|---|---|---|---|---|---|---|---|---|---|---|---|---|---|---|---|
| Clayton, Craig | 2 | 3 | 4.76 | 11 | 3 | 0 | 0 | 28 | 34 | 18 | 15 | 8 | 29 | R | R | 6-0 | 185 | 11-29-70 | 1991 | Anaheim, Calif. |
| Clement, Matt | 4 | 5 | 5.59 | 11 | 11 | 0 | 0 | 56 | 61 | 40 | 35 | 26 | 75 | R | R | 6-3 | 190 | 8-12-74 | 1994 | Butler, Pa. |
| Davis, Keith | 6 | 15 | 5.75 | 28 | 28 | 0 | 0 | 153 | 180 | 119 | 98 | 78 | 123 | R | R | 6-2 | 210 | 11-1-72 | 1994 | Vacherie, La. |
| Dennis, Shane | 4 | 2 | 3.20 | 9 | 9 | 1 | 0 | 59 | 57 | 22 | 21 | 19 | 54 | R | L | 6-3 | 200 | 7-3-71 | 1994 | Uniontown, Kan. |
| Dixon, Bubba | 0 | 3 | 7.16 | 11 | 0 | 0 | 0 | 16 | 20 | 16 | 13 | 4 | 20 | L | L | 5-10 | 165 | 1-7-72 | 1994 | Lucedale, Miss. |
| Erdos, Todd | 3 | 3 | 3.74 | 55 | 0 | 0 | 17 | 67 | 63 | 33 | 28 | 37 | 82 | R | R | 6-1 | 205 | 11-21-73 | 1992 | Meadville, Pa. |
| Garrett, Hal | 4 | 1 | 1.94 | 24 | 1 | 0 | 0 | 51 | 41 | 12 | 11 | 20 | 56 | R | R | 6-1 | 160 | 4-27-75 | 1993 | Mt. Juliet, Tenn. |
| Gaspar, Cade | 7 | 4 | 5.05 | 24 | 19 | 0 | 0 | 112 | 121 | 69 | 63 | 50 | 106 | R | R | 6-3 | 175 | 8-21-73 | 1994 | Mission Viejo, Calif. |
| Hammerschmidt, Andy | 6 | 4 | 5.25 | 35 | 7 | 0 | 2 | 82 | 102 | 59 | 48 | 20 | 59 | L | L | 6-1 | 220 | 6-21-72 | 1995 | New Ulm, Minn. |
| Harris, Greg W. | 1 | 3 | 5.94 | 13 | 4 | 0 | 0 | 33 | 44 | 28 | 22 | 11 | 34 | R | R | 6-2 | 195 | 12-1-63 | 1985 | Las Vegas, Nev. |
| Henderson, Kenny | 1 | 5 | 5.71 | 4 | 4 | 0 | 0 | 17 | 19 | 14 | 11 | 10 | 14 | R | R | 6-5 | 195 | 2-14-73 | 1995 | Ringgold, Ga. |
| Logan, Chris | 5 | 2 | 4.90 | 53 | 0 | 0 | 6 | 72 | 80 | 44 | 39 | 36 | 56 | R | R | 6-1 | 200 | 11-10-70 | 1994 | Hattiesburg, Miss. |
| Sak, James | 0 | 3 | 6.32 | 4 | 4 | 0 | 0 | 16 | 21 | 13 | 11 | 12 | 14 | R | R | 6-1 | 195 | 8-18-73 | 1995 | Chicago, Ill. |
| Schlutt, Jason | 0 | 0 | 5.63 | 7 | 0 | 0 | 0 | 8 | 10 | 5 | 5 | 2 | 6 | R | L | 6-0 | 190 | 1-21-72 | 1993 | Baroda, Mich. |
| Schmitt, Todd | 0 | 1 | 6.75 | 7 | 0 | 0 | 4 | 7 | 6 | 6 | 5 | 3 | 8 | R | R | 6-2 | 170 | 2-12-70 | 1992 | Clinton Township, Mich. |
| Thomas, Carlos | 1 | 1 | 11.42 | 9 | 0 | 0 | 0 | 9 | 13 | 12 | 11 | 10 | 10 | R | R | 6-4 | 225 | 8-6-70 | 1991 | Memphis, Tenn. |
| VanDeWeg, Ryan | 9 | 6 | 4.06 | 26 | 26 | 0 | 0 | 146 | 164 | 78 | 66 | 52 | 129 | R | R | 6-0 | 180 | 2-24-74 | 1995 | West Olive, Mich. |
| Walters, Brett | 9 | 9 | 4.32 | 24 | 24 | 0 | 0 | 135 | 150 | 73 | 65 | 39 | 88 | R | R | 6-1 | 185 | 9-30-74 | 1994 | Bateman, Australia |
| White, Darell | 1 | 1 | 6.50 | 38 | 0 | 0 | 0 | 54 | 76 | 48 | 39 | 25 | 43 | R | R | 6-2 | 200 | 4-16-72 | 1992 | Alexandria, La. |

# CLINTON — Class A

## MIDWEST LEAGUE

| BATTING | AVG | G | AB | R | H | 2B | 3B | HR | RBI | BB | SO | SB | CS | B | T | HT | WT | DOB | 1st Yr | Resides |
|---|---|---|---|---|---|---|---|---|---|---|---|---|---|---|---|---|---|---|---|---|
| Abernathy, Matt | .199 | 60 | 211 | 23 | 42 | 6 | 1 | 5 | 36 | 11 | 53 | 0 | 1 | L | R | 5-11 | 200 | 10-13-73 | 1995 | Jackson, Tenn. |
| Allen, Dusty | .267 | 77 | 243 | 46 | 65 | 10 | 3 | 10 | 46 | 67 | 59 | 4 | 7 | R | R | 6-4 | 215 | 8-9-72 | 1995 | Oklahoma City, Okla. |
| Amerson, Gordon | .203 | 116 | 394 | 47 | 80 | 14 | 4 | 9 | 48 | 60 | 113 | 9 | 5 | L | L | 6-1 | 185 | 10-10-76 | 1994 | San Bernardino, Calif. |
| Bucci, Carmen | .169 | 28 | 65 | 9 | 11 | 1 | 0 | 0 | 5 | 8 | 22 | 3 | 0 | S | R | 5-11 | 180 | 3-29-73 | 1995 | Oak Forest, Ill. |
| Carmona, Cesarin | .197 | 104 | 315 | 38 | 62 | 7 | 2 | 2 | 21 | 44 | 104 | 8 | 6 | S | R | 5-11 | 180 | 12-20-76 | 1994 | Bani, D.R. |
| Cuevas, Eduardo | .276 | 88 | 312 | 33 | 86 | 15 | 5 | 1 | 34 | 22 | 47 | 19 | 5 | R | R | 5-10 | 180 | 12-1-73 | 1992 | Haina, D.R. |
| Davis, Josh | .056 | 9 | 18 | 0 | 1 | 0 | 0 | 0 | 0 | 5 | 5 | 0 | 0 | R | R | 6-0 | 180 | 6-13-76 | 1994 | Locust Grove, Okla. |
| Dunn, Nathan | .253 | 50 | 166 | 20 | 42 | 11 | 2 | 0 | 23 | 29 | 44 | 10 | 1 | R | R | 6-0 | 190 | 10-17-74 | 1996 | Pell City, Ala. |
| Ebbert, Chad | .182 | 27 | 77 | 5 | 14 | 1 | 1 | 0 | 6 | 2 | 13 | 0 | 0 | R | R | 6-4 | 215 | 10-1-73 | 1994 | Lake Mary, Fla. |
| Hills, Rich | .249 | 124 | 433 | 42 | 108 | 34 | 0 | 7 | 58 | 50 | 69 | 4 | 4 | R | R | 6-0 | 195 | 7-28-73 | 1995 | Springdale, Ark. |
| Johnson, James | .252 | 118 | 428 | 67 | 108 | 13 | 3 | 0 | 26 | 53 | 67 | 44 | 15 | R | R | 5-11 | 160 | 6-25-73 | 1994 | Highland, Calif. |
| Keefe, Jamie | .302 | 32 | 106 | 23 | 32 | 5 | 0 | 3 | 15 | 34 | 18 | 8 | 1 | R | R | 5-11 | 180 | 8-29-73 | 1992 | Rochester, N.H. |
| Lindsey, Rodney | .161 | 23 | 87 | 11 | 14 | 2 | 0 | 0 | 4 | 11 | 30 | 12 | 8 | R | R | 5-8 | 175 | 1-28-76 | 1994 | Opelika, Ala. |
| Lowry, Curt | .186 | 32 | 70 | 9 | 13 | 2 | 1 | 1 | 7 | 8 | 21 | 0 | 1 | R | R | 6-0 | 170 | 9-22-72 | 1995 | Paris, Texas |
| Loyd, Brian | .297 | 10 | 37 | 3 | 11 | 2 | 0 | 0 | 2 | 0 | 6 | 0 | 0 | R | R | 6-2 | 195 | 12-3-73 | 1996 | Yorba Linda, Calif. |
| Martin, Mike | .175 | 77 | 206 | 16 | 36 | 7 | 0 | 1 | 23 | 29 | 33 | 1 | 0 | L | R | 6-1 | 175 | 2-19-73 | 1995 | Tallahassee, Fla. |
| Powers, John | .257 | 64 | 237 | 29 | 61 | 8 | 4 | 1 | 21 | 34 | 38 | 1 | 4 | L | R | 5-9 | 165 | 6-2-74 | 1996 | Scottsdale, Ariz. |
| Sanchez, Marcos | .203 | 42 | 123 | 14 | 25 | 6 | 1 | 3 | 13 | 15 | 49 | 2 | 0 | S | R | 6-0 | 190 | 9-25-74 | 1992 | Santo Domingo, D.R. |
| Schwenke, Matt | .151 | 28 | 86 | 4 | 13 | 3 | 0 | 0 | 2 | 6 | 28 | 0 | 1 | R | R | 6-2 | 210 | 8-12-72 | 1993 | Loomis, Calif. |
| Totman, Jason | .215 | 39 | 121 | 15 | 26 | 7 | 2 | 0 | 11 | 22 | 17 | 2 | 1 | R | R | 5-9 | 170 | 11-3-72 | 1995 | McPherson, Kan. |
| Watkins, Sean | .200 | 16 | 55 | 7 | 11 | 3 | 0 | 1 | 6 | 9 | 17 | 0 | 0 | L | L | 6-4 | 210 | 10-6-74 | 1995 | Peoria Heights, Ill. |
| Wulfert, Mark | .251 | 127 | 450 | 66 | 113 | 24 | 6 | 16 | 65 | 69 | 111 | 26 | 9 | R | R | 5-11 | 175 | 8-20-72 | 1995 | Farmington, N.M. |

**GAMES BY POSITION: C**—Davis 3, Ebbert 27, Loyd 10, Martin 73, Sanchez 16, Schwenke 28. **1B**—Allen 76, Davis 2, Dunn 34, Hills 4, Sanchez 6, Watkins 5, Wulfert 1. **2B**—Bucci 9, Cuevas 18, Keefe 27, Powers 52, Totman 32. **3B**—Bucci 6, Cuevas 3, Davis 2, Dunn 15, Hills 104, Martin 3, Powers 8, Totman 2. **SS**—Bucci 12, Carmona 104, Hills 19, Keefe 7. **OF**—Abernathy 50, Allen 3, Amerson 113, Johnson 114, Lindsey 23, Lowry 7, Wulfert 88.

| PITCHING | W | L | ERA | G | GS | CG | SV | IP | H | R | ER | BB | SO | B | T | HT | WT | DOB | 1st Yr | Resides |
|---|---|---|---|---|---|---|---|---|---|---|---|---|---|---|---|---|---|---|---|---|
| Bussa, Todd | 1 | 0 | 1.30 | 32 | 0 | 0 | 18 | 35 | 22 | 7 | 5 | 7 | 50 | R | R | 5-11 | 170 | 12-13-72 | 1991 | Palm Beach Gardens, Fla. |
| Campbell, Tim | 0 | 3 | 3.13 | 42 | 0 | 0 | 3 | 63 | 44 | 27 | 22 | 18 | 67 | R | R | 6-0 | 190 | 12-22-72 | 1995 | Seattle, Wash. |
| Carmody, Brian | 7 | 4 | 3.52 | 13 | 13 | 1 | 0 | 77 | 79 | 42 | 30 | 22 | 46 | L | L | 6-3 | 195 | 7-1-75 | 1996 | San Jose, Calif. |
| Clark, Chris | 3 | 8 | 5.05 | 24 | 11 | 0 | 1 | 82 | 96 | 58 | 46 | 51 | 74 | R | R | 6-1 | 180 | 10-29-74 | 1994 | Aurora, Colo. |
| Clayton, Craig | 2 | 1 | 1.45 | 27 | 0 | 0 | 9 | 37 | 27 | 10 | 6 | 8 | 29 | R | R | 6-0 | 185 | 11-29-70 | 1991 | Anaheim, Calif. |
| Clement, Matt | 8 | 3 | 2.80 | 16 | 16 | 1 | 0 | 96 | 66 | 31 | 30 | 52 | 109 | R | R | 6-3 | 190 | 8-12-74 | 1994 | Butler, Pa. |
| Garrett, Hal | 2 | 3 | 4.53 | 25 | 3 | 0 | 1 | 50 | 45 | 28 | 25 | 31 | 60 | R | R | 6-1 | 160 | 4-27-75 | 1993 | Mt. Juliet, Tenn. |
| Guzman, Domingo | 0 | 5 | 12.63 | 6 | 5 | 0 | 0 | 21 | 32 | 33 | 29 | 19 | 18 | R | R | 6-3 | 198 | 4-5-75 | 1994 | San Cristobal, D.R. |
| Henderson, Kenny | 0 | 3 | 2.33 | 7 | 7 | 0 | 0 | 27 | 30 | 13 | 7 | 5 | 26 | R | R | 6-5 | 195 | 2-14-73 | 1995 | Ringgold, Ga. |
| Kolb, Brandon | 16 | 9 | 3.42 | 27 | 27 | 3 | 0 | 181 | 170 | 84 | 69 | 76 | 138 | R | R | 6-1 | 190 | 11-20-73 | 1995 | Danville, Calif. |
| Leach, Jarman | 1 | 1 | 4.97 | 10 | 0 | 0 | 0 | 13 | 17 | 8 | 7 | 6 | 3 | L | L | 6-1 | 195 | 11-7-72 | 1994 | Novato, Calif. |
| Martinez, Uriel | 0 | 1 | 13.50 | 1 | 0 | 0 | 0 | 2 | 3 | 4 | 3 | 3 | 1 | R | R | 6-1 | 180 | 10-22-74 | 1995 | Mexico City, Mexico |
| Newman, Eric | 5 | 7 | 4.29 | 34 | 14 | 0 | 1 | 113 | 101 | 71 | 54 | 67 | 108 | R | R | 6-4 | 220 | 8-27-72 | 1995 | Fremont, Calif. |
| Remington, Jake | 6 | 7 | 5.19 | 27 | 7 | 1 | 0 | 85 | 98 | 60 | 49 | 25 | 59 | R | R | 6-4 | 175 | 8-26-75 | 1994 | Broken Arrow, Okla. |
| Sak, James | 3 | 4 | 3.56 | 21 | 7 | 0 | 0 | 66 | 46 | 31 | 26 | 45 | 72 | R | R | 6-1 | 195 | 8-18-73 | 1995 | Chicago, Ill. |
| Spear, Russell | 4 | 3 | 6.10 | 11 | 10 | 0 | 0 | 52 | 60 | 43 | 35 | 42 | 44 | R | R | 6-0 | 190 | 8-30-77 | 1995 | Albanvale, Australia |
| Torres, Luis | 2 | 2 | 5.08 | 35 | 1 | 0 | 1 | 67 | 76 | 46 | 38 | 26 | 65 | R | R | 6-2 | 228 | 1-13-76 | 1994 | Manati, P.R. |
| Walker, Kevin | 4 | 6 | 4.74 | 13 | 13 | 0 | 0 | 76 | 80 | 46 | 40 | 33 | 43 | L | L | 6-4 | 190 | 9-20-76 | 1995 | Glen Rose, Texas |

# IDAHO FALLS — Rookie

## PIONEER LEAGUE

| BATTING | AVG | G | AB | R | H | 2B | 3B | HR | RBI | BB | SO | SB | CS | B | T | HT | WT | DOB | 1st Yr | Resides |
|---|---|---|---|---|---|---|---|---|---|---|---|---|---|---|---|---|---|---|---|---|
| Boulo, Tyler | .260 | 35 | 127 | 15 | 33 | 8 | 1 | 3 | 33 | 15 | 24 | 1 | 0 | R | R | 6-2 | 210 | 6-19-74 | 1996 | Mobile, Ala. |
| Chavez, Steven | .325 | 69 | 277 | 55 | 90 | 19 | 2 | 7 | 50 | 49 | 52 | 5 | 3 | L | R | 5-11 | 190 | 7-30-75 | 1995 | Carlsbad, N.M. |
| Conroy, Danny | .278 | 23 | 54 | 11 | 15 | 3 | 1 | 1 | 5 | 6 | 8 | 5 | 3 | S | R | 5-11 | 175 | 6-14-73 | 1996 | Astoria, N.Y. |
| Davis, Josh | .188 | 32 | 101 | 12 | 19 | 2 | 0 | 2 | 13 | 21 | 39 | 5 | 0 | R | R | 6-0 | 180 | 6-13-76 | 1994 | Locust Grove, Okla. |
| Ebbert, Chad | .275 | 27 | 102 | 10 | 28 | 5 | 0 | 0 | 12 | 3 | 23 | 0 | 0 | R | R | 6-4 | 215 | 10-1-73 | 1994 | Lake Mary, Fla. |
| Hunter, Andy | .245 | 32 | 102 | 13 | 25 | 3 | 0 | 0 | 9 | 21 | 30 | 3 | 3 | R | R | 6-2 | 185 | 12-28-76 | 1995 | Mansfield, Texas |
| Jackson, Rod | .284 | 54 | 250 | 56 | 71 | 3 | 5 | 1 | 21 | 12 | 32 | 25 | 6 | R | R | 5-11 | 155 | 2-24-75 | 1994 | Camden, Ark. |
| Kent, Robbie | .309 | 47 | 181 | 40 | 56 | 14 | 0 | 2 | 25 | 21 | 28 | 4 | 1 | R | R | 5-10 | 185 | 1-8-74 | 1996 | Evansville, Ind. |
| Lindsey, Rodney | .303 | 48 | 185 | 45 | 56 | 4 | 6 | 5 | 17 | 23 | 53 | 16 | 3 | R | R | 5-8 | 175 | 1-28-76 | 1994 | Opelika, Ala. |

| BATTING | AVG | G | AB | R | H | 2B | 3B | HR | RBI | BB | SO | SB | CS | B | T | HT | WT | DOB | 1st Yr | Resides |
|---|---|---|---|---|---|---|---|---|---|---|---|---|---|---|---|---|---|---|---|---|
| Martinez, Obed | .245 | 28 | 110 | 14 | 27 | 4 | 1 | 0 | 10 | 10 | 27 | 1 | 2 | R | R | 6-1 | 180 | 7-19-75 | 1994 | Rio Piedras, P.R. |
| McClure, Brian | .321 | 72 | 308 | 62 | 99 | 18 | 6 | 6 | 45 | 38 | 63 | 10 | 2 | L | R | 6-0 | 170 | 1-15-74 | 1996 | Chatham, Ill. |
| Nova, Pascual | .190 | 15 | 58 | 2 | 11 | 2 | 3 | 0 | 10 | 4 | 32 | 0 | 0 | R | R | 5-11 | 185 | 12-25-74 | 1994 | Barrio San Geronimo, D.R. |
| Paciorek, Pete | .297 | 72 | 283 | 56 | 84 | 15 | 2 | 15 | 69 | 36 | 64 | 6 | 1 | S | L | 6-3 | 195 | 5-19-76 | 1995 | San Gabriel, Calif. |
| Reynoso, Ben | .345 | 72 | 284 | 45 | 98 | 26 | 0 | 4 | 50 | 26 | 42 | 20 | 7 | R | R | 5-9 | 165 | 9-12-74 | 1996 | Visalia, Calif. |
| Rutherford, Daryl | .303 | 46 | 175 | 29 | 53 | 9 | 1 | 2 | 23 | 20 | 30 | 4 | 5 | R | R | 6-0 | 175 | 10-30-75 | 1995 | Union, S.C. |

**GAMES BY POSITION: C**—Boulo 17, Davis 31, Ebbert 27. **1B**—Kent 8, Paciorek 65. **2B**—Davis 1, Kent 1, McClure 71. **3B**—Chavez 56, Kent 16. **SS**—Conroy 1, Reynoso 72. **OF**—Boulo 1, Conroy 19, Hunter 32, Jackson 53, Lindsey 44, Martinez 24, Nova 15, Rutherford 39.

| PITCHING | W | L | ERA | G | GS | CG | SV | IP | H | R | ER | BB | SO | B | T | HT | WT | DOB | 1st Yr | Resides |
|---|---|---|---|---|---|---|---|---|---|---|---|---|---|---|---|---|---|---|---|---|
| Adair, Scott | 2 | 3 | 7.71 | 23 | 3 | 0 | 1 | 47 | 73 | 42 | 40 | 21 | 29 | R | R | 6-0 | 190 | 11-10-75 | 1993 | Riverside, Calif. |
| Desabrais, Mark | 1 | 0 | 6.70 | 27 | 0 | 0 | 0 | 46 | 65 | 35 | 34 | 22 | 43 | R | R | 6-2 | 195 | 7-10-75 | 1994 | Casselberry, Fla. |
| Ervin, Kent | 2 | 5 | 6.50 | 22 | 4 | 0 | 0 | 54 | 72 | 52 | 39 | 18 | 35 | R | R | 6-3 | 195 | 1-12-74 | 1996 | Littleton, Colo. |
| Guzman, Domingo | 4 | 4 | 4.13 | 15 | 10 | 1 | 0 | 65 | 52 | 41 | 30 | 29 | 75 | R | R | 6-3 | 198 | 4-5-75 | 1994 | San Cristobal, D.R. |
| Lopez, Rodrigo | 4 | 4 | 5.70 | 15 | 14 | 0 | 1 | 71 | 76 | 52 | 45 | 34 | 72 | R | R | 5-11 | 170 | 12-14-75 | 1995 | Thalnepantla, Mexico |
| Schroeder, Scott | 5 | 5 | 4.63 | 20 | 9 | 0 | 0 | 58 | 71 | 39 | 30 | 29 | 58 | R | R | 6-6 | 235 | 9-8-74 | 1994 | Portland, Ore. |
| Smith, Josh | 2 | 1 | 4.91 | 17 | 0 | 0 | 1 | 15 | 11 | 9 | 8 | 11 | 11 | L | L | 5-11 | 185 | 8-26-77 | 1995 | Houston, Texas |
| Sullivan, Brendan | 2 | 1 | 5.23 | 33 | 0 | 0 | 5 | 43 | 41 | 25 | 25 | 27 | 41 | R | R | 6-3 | 190 | 12-15-74 | 1996 | Washington, D.C. |
| Szymborski, Tom | 7 | 3 | 3.94 | 16 | 14 | 0 | 1 | 80 | 80 | 39 | 35 | 30 | 65 | R | R | 6-3 | 210 | 3-7-75 | 1996 | Chicago, Ill. |
| Thomas, Ryan | 4 | 3 | 5.20 | 30 | 4 | 0 | 4 | 62 | 54 | 44 | 36 | 32 | 44 | R | R | 6-0 | 190 | 10-18-72 | 1996 | Houston, Texas |
| Walker, Kevin | 1 | 0 | 3.00 | 1 | 1 | 0 | 0 | 6 | 4 | 3 | 2 | 2 | 4 | L | L | 6-4 | 190 | 9-20-76 | 1995 | Glen Rose, Texas |
| Witte, Nick | 0 | 2 | 6.14 | 21 | 0 | 0 | 0 | 29 | 39 | 23 | 20 | 5 | 19 | R | R | 6-0 | 200 | 11-25-73 | 1996 | Richmond, Ind. |
| Workman, Widd | 4 | 5 | 6.79 | 14 | 13 | 0 | 0 | 56 | 77 | 48 | 42 | 31 | 42 | R | R | 6-1 | 195 | 5-23-74 | 1996 | Gilbert, Ariz. |

## PEORIA — Rookie

### ARIZONA LEAGUE

| BATTING | AVG | G | AB | R | H | 2B | 3B | HR | RBI | BB | SO | SB | CS | B | T | HT | WT | DOB | 1st Yr | Resides |
|---|---|---|---|---|---|---|---|---|---|---|---|---|---|---|---|---|---|---|---|---|
| Cronin, Shane | .327 | 54 | 208 | 40 | 68 | 13 | 0 | 9 | 54 | 12 | 32 | 4 | 1 | R | R | 6-1 | 210 | 2-26-76 | 1996 | Renton, Wash. |
| Dunham, Traylor | .273 | 32 | 77 | 13 | 21 | 1 | 0 | 0 | 9 | 13 | 23 | 2 | 2 | L | R | 6-1 | 175 | 9-8-77 | 1996 | Shattuck, Okla. |
| Garcia, Sandro | .291 | 53 | 189 | 29 | 55 | 6 | 4 | 1 | 17 | 8 | 27 | 11 | 6 | R | R | 5-10 | 180 | 11-22-77 | 1996 | Deerfield Beach, Fla. |
| Gonzalez, Santos | .290 | 38 | 131 | 27 | 38 | 5 | 3 | 1 | 17 | 5 | 20 | 10 | 2 | S | R | 5-11 | 170 | 6-25-77 | 1994 | Bani, D.R. |
| Halloran, Matt | .261 | 39 | 134 | 22 | 35 | 7 | 4 | 0 | 15 | 10 | 22 | 2 | 1 | R | R | 6-2 | 185 | 3-3-78 | 1994 | Fredericksburg, Va. |
| Jacobo, Roberto | .216 | 40 | 111 | 18 | 24 | 4 | 2 | 0 | 12 | 12 | 27 | 6 | 2 | S | L | 6-4 | 174 | 6-7-76 | 1994 | Haina, D.R. |
| Jacobus, Brian | .264 | 50 | 193 | 29 | 51 | 8 | 7 | 0 | 24 | 9 | 33 | 2 | 3 | L | L | 6-0 | 190 | 6-8-76 | 1995 | Puyallup, Wash. |
| Maxwell, Vernon | .251 | 55 | 191 | 41 | 48 | 6 | 4 | 0 | 17 | 31 | 45 | 15 | 4 | R | R | 6-3 | 195 | 10-22-76 | 1996 | Midwest City, Okla. |
| Nieves, Wilbert | .345 | 43 | 113 | 23 | 39 | 5 | 0 | 2 | 22 | 13 | 19 | 3 | 4 | R | R | 5-10 | 160 | 9-25-77 | 1996 | Santurce, P.R. |
| Pernell, Brandon | .333 | 53 | 174 | 38 | 58 | 9 | 10 | 1 | 33 | 18 | 30 | 14 | 4 | R | R | 6-2 | 180 | 4-11-77 | 1995 | Torrance, Calif. |
| Rodriguez, John | .225 | 43 | 120 | 11 | 27 | 2 | 1 | 0 | 11 | 4 | 24 | 1 | 1 | R | R | 6-0 | 180 | 11-25-75 | 1996 | Corpus Christi, Texas |
| Ruotsinoja, Jacob | .291 | 52 | 172 | 37 | 50 | 14 | 3 | 6 | 40 | 40 | 38 | 2 | 2 | L | R | 6-2 | 195 | 11-11-76 | 1996 | Seminole, Fla. |
| Shipley, Craig | .714 | 3 | 7 | 4 | 5 | 1 | 0 | 0 | 1 | 0 | 0 | 0 | 1 | R | R | 6-0 | 168 | 1-7-63 | 1984 | Jupiter, Fla. |
| Soto, Luis | .203 | 28 | 69 | 9 | 14 | 2 | 0 | 2 | 10 | 8 | 19 | 0 | 0 | R | R | 6-0 | 170 | 7-9-74 | 1995 | Bani, D.R. |
| Stewart, Adrian | .100 | 22 | 50 | 4 | 5 | 0 | 0 | 1 | 7 | 13 | 20 | 1 | 1 | L | L | 6-0 | 200 | 4-11-77 | 1996 | Claremont, Calif. |

**GAMES BY POSITION: C**—Dunham 19, Nieves 37, Soto 18. **1B**—Cronin 20, Dunham 1, Jacobo 36, Stewart 16. **2B**—Garcia 42, Gonzalez 16, Gonzalez 1, Jacobo 1, Maxwell 1, Nieves 1, Rodriguez 25, Shipley 1. **SS**—Gonzalez 27, Halloran 38, Rodriguez 6, Shipley 2. **OF**—Garcia 6, Jacobo 3, Jacobus 36, Maxwell 49, Nieves 1, Pernell 43, Rodriguez 2, Ruotsinoja 44, Stewart 6.

| PITCHING | W | L | ERA | G | GS | CG | SV | IP | H | R | ER | BB | SO | B | T | HT | WT | DOB | 1st Yr | Resides |
|---|---|---|---|---|---|---|---|---|---|---|---|---|---|---|---|---|---|---|---|---|
| Alarcon, James | 0 | 0 | 6.16 | 14 | 0 | 0 | 0 | 19 | 25 | 20 | 13 | 17 | 14 | R | R | 6-3 | 188 | 7-14-76 | 1996 | Jupiter, Fla. |
| Gonzalez, Francisco | 6 | 2 | 4.32 | 25 | 4 | 0 | 2 | 50 | 65 | 33 | 24 | 6 | 32 | R | R | 6-4 | 190 | 3-21-78 | 1996 | Bajaderos, P.R. |
| Hite, Kevin | 5 | 5 | 3.62 | 13 | 12 | 2 | 0 | 77 | 86 | 44 | 31 | 15 | 65 | R | R | 6-1 | 155 | 7-23-74 | 1996 | Hermitage, Tenn. |
| Hoff, Steve | 8 | 2 | 2.85 | 16 | 13 | 0 | 0 | 85 | 66 | 37 | 27 | 36 | 104 | L | L | 6-4 | 205 | 7-1-77 | 1996 | San Bruno, Calif. |
| Jones, Travis | 0 | 2 | 6.21 | 14 | 9 | 0 | 0 | 42 | 52 | 38 | 29 | 37 | 29 | L | L | 6-3 | 180 | 12-3-77 | 1996 | Asher, Okla. |
| Marino, Dominic | 1 | 1 | 6.51 | 20 | 0 | 0 | 1 | 28 | 28 | 20 | 20 | 17 | 27 | R | R | 6-3 | 175 | 2-5-78 | 1996 | Walnut, Calif. |
| Nash, Damond | 5 | 3 | 3.05 | 22 | 4 | 0 | 5 | 59 | 45 | 30 | 20 | 36 | 78 | L | R | 6-2 | 200 | 3-7-76 | 1995 | Texarkana, Ark. |
| Precinal, Huilberto | 0 | 0 | 0.00 | 14 | 0 | 0 | 0 | 2 | 1 | 0 | 0 | 0 | 2 | R | R | 6-6 | 190 | 9-8-77 | 1995 | Bani, D.R. |
| Schlutt, Jason | 0 | 1 | 3.60 | 3 | 0 | 0 | 0 | 5 | 6 | 3 | 2 | 0 | 7 | R | L | 6-0 | 190 | 1-21-72 | 1993 | Baroda, Mich. |
| Sellers, Justin | 1 | 0 | 2.25 | 26 | 0 | 0 | 6 | 32 | 31 | 14 | 8 | 14 | 36 | R | R | 6-4 | 210 | 2-22-77 | 1996 | Vancouver, Wash. |
| Smith, Josh | 2 | 1 | 0.43 | 10 | 0 | 0 | 2 | 21 | 12 | 3 | 1 | 3 | 22 | L | L | 5-11 | 185 | 8-26-77 | 1995 | Houston, Texas |
| Thompson, Josef | 8 | 2 | 2.65 | 13 | 12 | 0 | 0 | 75 | 67 | 33 | 22 | 22 | 50 | L | L | 6-1 | 195 | 9-2-72 | 1996 | North Platte, Neb. |
| Walker, Pete | 0 | 1 | 2.25 | 2 | 2 | 0 | 0 | 4 | 4 | 1 | 1 | 0 | 5 | R | R | 6-2 | 184 | 4-8-69 | 1990 | East Lyme, Conn. |

# SAN FRANCISCO GIANTS

**Manager:** Dusty Baker.    **1996 Record:** 68-94, .420 (4th, NL West).

| BATTING | AVG | G | AB | R | H | 2B | 3B | HR | RBI | BB | SO | SB | CS | B | T | HT | WT | DOB | 1st Yr | Resides |
|---|---|---|---|---|---|---|---|---|---|---|---|---|---|---|---|---|---|---|---|---|
| Aurilia, Rich | .239 | 105 | 318 | 27 | 76 | 7 | 1 | 3 | 26 | 25 | 52 | 4 | 1 | R | R | 6-0 | 170 | 9-2-71 | 1992 | Hazlet, N.J. |
| Batiste, Kim | .208 | 54 | 130 | 17 | 27 | 6 | 0 | 3 | 11 | 5 | 33 | 3 | 3 | R | R | 6-0 | 193 | 3-15-68 | 1987 | Prairieville, La. |
| Benard, Marvin | .248 | 135 | 488 | 89 | 121 | 17 | 4 | 5 | 27 | 59 | 84 | 25 | 11 | L | L | 5-10 | 180 | 1-20-71 | 1992 | Cudahy, Calif. |
| Bonds, Barry | .308 | 158 | 517 | 122 | 159 | 27 | 3 | 42 | 129 | 151 | 76 | 40 | 7 | L | L | 6-1 | 185 | 7-24-64 | 1985 | Murrietta, Calif. |
| Canizaro, Jay | .200 | 43 | 120 | 11 | 24 | 4 | 1 | 2 | 8 | 9 | 38 | 0 | 2 | R | R | 5-10 | 175 | 7-4-73 | 1993 | Orange, Texas |
| Carreon, Mark | .260 | 81 | 292 | 40 | 76 | 22 | 3 | 9 | 51 | 22 | 33 | 2 | 3 | R | L | 6-0 | 195 | 7-9-63 | 1981 | Tucson, Ariz. |
| Cruz, Jacob | .234 | 33 | 77 | 10 | 18 | 3 | 0 | 3 | 10 | 12 | 24 | 0 | 1 | L | L | 6-0 | 175 | 1-28-73 | 1994 | Oxnard, Calif. |
| Decker, Steve | .230 | 57 | 122 | 16 | 28 | 1 | 0 | 1 | 12 | 15 | 26 | 0 | 0 | R | R | 6-3 | 205 | 10-25-65 | 1988 | Keizer, Ore. |
| Delgado, Wilson | .364 | 6 | 22 | 3 | 8 | 0 | 0 | 0 | 2 | 1 | 5 | 1 | 0 | S | R | 5-11 | 165 | 7-15-75 | 1993 | Santo Domingo, D.R. |
| Dunston, Shawon | .300 | 82 | 287 | 27 | 86 | 12 | 2 | 5 | 25 | 13 | 40 | 8 | 0 | R | R | 6-1 | 175 | 3-21-63 | 1982 | Fremont, Calif. |
| Hall, Mel | .120 | 25 | 25 | 3 | 3 | 0 | 0 | 0 | 5 | 1 | 4 | 0 | 0 | L | L | 6-1 | 215 | 9-18-60 | 1978 | Parkland, Fla. |
| Hill, Glenallen | .280 | 98 | 379 | 56 | 106 | 26 | 0 | 19 | 67 | 33 | 95 | 6 | 3 | R | R | 6-2 | 210 | 3-22-65 | 1983 | Boca Raton, Fla. |
| Hubbard, Trenidad | .207 | 10 | 29 | 3 | 6 | 0 | 1 | 1 | 2 | 2 | 5 | 0 | 0 | R | R | 5-8 | 180 | 5-11-66 | 1986 | Houston, Texas |
| 2-team (45 Colorado) | .213 | 55 | 89 | 15 | 19 | 5 | 2 | 2 | 14 | 11 | 27 | 2 | 0 | | | | | | | |
| Javier, Stan | .270 | 71 | 274 | 44 | 74 | 25 | 0 | 2 | 22 | 25 | 51 | 14 | 2 | S | R | 6-0 | 185 | 1-9-64 | 1981 | Santo Domingo, D.R. |
| Jensen, Marcus | .211 | 9 | 19 | 4 | 4 | 1 | 0 | 0 | 4 | 8 | 7 | 0 | 0 | S | R | 6-4 | 195 | 12-14-72 | 1990 | Oakland, Calif. |
| Jones, Dax | .172 | 34 | 58 | 7 | 10 | 0 | 2 | 1 | 7 | 8 | 12 | 2 | 2 | R | R | 6-0 | 170 | 8-4-70 | 1991 | Waukegan, Ill. |
| Lampkin, Tom | .232 | 66 | 177 | 26 | 41 | 8 | 0 | 6 | 29 | 20 | 22 | 1 | 5 | L | R | 5-11 | 183 | 3-4-64 | 1986 | Boring, Ore. |
| Manwaring, Kirt | .234 | 49 | 145 | 9 | 34 | 6 | 0 | 1 | 14 | 16 | 24 | 0 | 1 | R | R | 5-11 | 203 | 7-15-65 | 1986 | Scottsdale, Ariz. |
| McCarty, Dave | .217 | 91 | 175 | 16 | 38 | 3 | 0 | 6 | 24 | 18 | 43 | 2 | 1 | R | L | 6-5 | 207 | 11-23-69 | 1991 | Houston, Texas |
| Mirabelli, Doug | .222 | 9 | 18 | 2 | 4 | 1 | 0 | 0 | 1 | 3 | 4 | 0 | 0 | R | R | 6-1 | 205 | 10-18-70 | 1992 | Las Vegas, Nev. |
| Mueller, Bill | .330 | 55 | 200 | 31 | 66 | 15 | 1 | 0 | 19 | 24 | 26 | 0 | 0 | S | R | 5-11 | 173 | 3-17-71 | 1993 | Maryland Heights, Mo. |
| Peltier, Dan | .254 | 31 | 59 | 3 | 15 | 2 | 0 | 0 | 9 | 7 | 9 | 0 | 0 | L | L | 6-1 | 200 | 6-30-68 | 1989 | Eden Prairie, Minn. |
| Phillips, J.R. | .200 | 15 | 25 | 3 | 5 | 0 | 0 | 2 | 5 | 1 | 13 | 0 | 0 | L | L | 6-1 | 185 | 4-29-70 | 1988 | Moreno Valley, Calif. |
| Scarsone, Steve | .219 | 105 | 283 | 28 | 62 | 12 | 1 | 5 | 23 | 25 | 91 | 2 | 3 | R | R | 6-2 | 170 | 4-11-66 | 1986 | Anaheim, Calif. |
| Thompson, Robby | .211 | 63 | 227 | 35 | 48 | 11 | 1 | 5 | 21 | 24 | 69 | 2 | 2 | R | R | 5-11 | 173 | 5-10-62 | 1983 | Tequesta, Fla. |
| Wilkins, Rick | .293 | 52 | 157 | 19 | 46 | 10 | 0 | 8 | 36 | 21 | 40 | 0 | 2 | L | R | 6-2 | 210 | 6-4-67 | 1987 | Jacksonville, Fla. |
| Williams, Keith | .250 | 9 | 20 | 0 | 5 | 0 | 0 | 0 | 0 | 0 | 6 | 0 | 0 | R | R | 6-0 | 190 | 4-21-72 | 1993 | Bedford, Pa. |
| Williams, Matt | .302 | 105 | 404 | 69 | 122 | 16 | 1 | 22 | 85 | 39 | 91 | 1 | 2 | R | R | 6-2 | 205 | 11-28-65 | 1986 | Scottsdale, Ariz. |
| Wilson, Desi | .271 | 41 | 118 | 10 | 32 | 2 | 0 | 2 | 12 | 12 | 27 | 0 | 2 | L | L | 6-7 | 230 | 5-9-68 | 1991 | Glen Cove, N.Y. |

| PITCHING | W | L | ERA | G | GS | CG | SV | IP | H | R | ER | BB | SO | B | T | HT | WT | DOB | 1st Yr | Resides |
|---|---|---|---|---|---|---|---|---|---|---|---|---|---|---|---|---|---|---|---|---|
| Barton, Shawn | 0 | 0 | 9.72 | 7 | 0 | 0 | 0 | 8 | 19 | 12 | 9 | 1 | 3 | R | L | 6-3 | 195 | 5-14-63 | 1984 | Reading, Pa. |
| Bautista, Jose | 3 | 4 | 3.36 | 37 | 1 | 0 | 0 | 70 | 66 | 32 | 26 | 15 | 28 | R | R | 6-2 | 207 | 7-25-64 | 1981 | Cooper City, Fla. |
| Beck, Rod | 0 | 9 | 3.34 | 63 | 0 | 0 | 35 | 62 | 56 | 23 | 23 | 10 | 48 | R | R | 6-1 | 236 | 8-3-68 | 1986 | Scottsdale, Ariz. |
| Bourgeois, Steve | 1 | 3 | 6.30 | 15 | 5 | 0 | 0 | 40 | 60 | 35 | 28 | 21 | 17 | R | R | 6-1 | 220 | 8-4-72 | 1993 | Paulina, La. |
| Carlson, Dan | 1 | 0 | 2.70 | 5 | 0 | 0 | 0 | 10 | 13 | 6 | 3 | 2 | 4 | R | R | 6-1 | 185 | 1-26-70 | 1990 | Portland, Ore. |
| Creek, Doug | 0 | 2 | 6.52 | 63 | 0 | 0 | 0 | 48 | 45 | 41 | 35 | 32 | 38 | L | L | 5-10 | 205 | 3-1-69 | 1991 | Martinsburg, W.Va. |
| DeLucia, Rich | 3 | 6 | 5.84 | 56 | 0 | 0 | 0 | 62 | 62 | 44 | 40 | 31 | 55 | R | R | 6-0 | 185 | 10-7-64 | 1986 | Columbia, S.C. |
| Dewey, Mark | 6 | 3 | 4.21 | 78 | 0 | 0 | 0 | 83 | 79 | 40 | 39 | 41 | 57 | R | R | 6-0 | 216 | 1-3-65 | 1987 | Jenison, Mich. |
| Estes, Shawn | 3 | 5 | 3.60 | 11 | 11 | 0 | 0 | 70 | 63 | 30 | 28 | 39 | 60 | R | L | 6-2 | 200 | 2-28-73 | 1991 | Gardnerville, Nev. |
| Fernandez, Osvaldo | 7 | 13 | 4.61 | 30 | 28 | 2 | 0 | 172 | 193 | 95 | 88 | 57 | 106 | R | R | 6-2 | 190 | 11-4-68 | 1996 | Santo Domingo, D.R. |
| Gardner, Mark | 12 | 7 | 4.42 | 30 | 28 | 4 | 0 | 179 | 200 | 105 | 88 | 57 | 145 | R | R | 6-1 | 190 | 3-1-62 | 1985 | Fresno, Calif. |
| Hook, Chris | 0 | 1 | 7.43 | 10 | 0 | 0 | 0 | 13 | 16 | 13 | 11 | 14 | 4 | S | R | 6-5 | 195 | 8-4-68 | 1989 | Florence, Ky. |
| Juden, Jeff | 4 | 0 | 4.10 | 36 | 0 | 0 | 0 | 42 | 39 | 23 | 19 | 20 | 35 | R | R | 6-7 | 245 | 1-19-71 | 1989 | Salem, Mass. |
| Leiter, Mark | 4 | 10 | 5.19 | 23 | 22 | 1 | 0 | 135 | 151 | 93 | 78 | 50 | 118 | R | R | 6-3 | 210 | 4-13-63 | 1983 | West Caldwell, N.J. |
| Poole, Jim | 2 | 1 | 2.66 | 35 | 0 | 0 | 0 | 24 | 15 | 7 | 7 | 13 | 19 | L | L | 6-2 | 203 | 4-28-66 | 1988 | Ellicott City, Md. |
| Rueter, Kirk | 1 | 2 | 1.93 | 4 | 3 | 0 | 0 | 23 | 18 | 6 | 5 | 5 | 16 | L | L | 6-3 | 190 | 12-1-70 | 1991 | Hoyleton, Ill. |
| 2-team (16 Montreal) | 6 | 8 | 3.97 | 20 | 19 | 0 | 0 | 102 | 109 | 50 | 45 | 27 | 46 | | | | | | | |
| Scott, Tim | 2 | 2 | 8.24 | 20 | 0 | 0 | 0 | 20 | 24 | 18 | 18 | 9 | 10 | R | R | 6-2 | 205 | 11-16-66 | 1984 | Hanford, Calif. |
| 2-team (45 Montreal) | 5 | 7 | 4.64 | 65 | 0 | 0 | 1 | 66 | 65 | 36 | 34 | 30 | 47 | | | | | | | |
| Soderstrom, Steve | 2 | 0 | 5.27 | 3 | 3 | 0 | 0 | 14 | 16 | 11 | 8 | 6 | 9 | R | R | 6-3 | 215 | 4-3-72 | 1994 | Turlock, Ca. |
| VanLandingham, Bill | 9 | 14 | 5.40 | 32 | 32 | 0 | 0 | 182 | 196 | 123 | 109 | 78 | 97 | R | R | 6-2 | 210 | 7-16-70 | 1991 | Franklin, Tenn. |
| Watson, Allen | 8 | 12 | 4.61 | 29 | 29 | 2 | 0 | 186 | 189 | 105 | 95 | 69 | 128 | L | L | 6-3 | 195 | 11-18-70 | 1991 | Middle Village, N.Y. |

## FIELDING

| Catcher | PCT | G | PO | A | E | DP | PB |
|---|---|---|---|---|---|---|---|
| Decker | 1.000 | 30 | 183 | 12 | 0 | 4 | 5 |
| Jensen | .955 | 7 | 37 | 5 | 2 | 1 | 1 |
| Lampkin | .992 | 53 | 342 | 27 | 3 | 4 | 0 |
| Manwaring | .993 | 49 | 268 | 26 | 2 | 5 | 3 |
| Mirabelli | 1.000 | 8 | 29 | 2 | 0 | 0 | 0 |
| Wilkins | .991 | 42 | 188 | 29 | 2 | 4 | 4 |

| First Base | PCT | G | PO | A | E | DP |
|---|---|---|---|---|---|---|
| Carreon | .986 | 73 | 533 | 37 | 8 | 64 |
| McCarty | .990 | 51 | 269 | 16 | 3 | 30 |
| Peltier | 1.000 | 13 | 87 | 6 | 0 | 11 |
| Phillips | .981 | 10 | 49 | 2 | 1 | 4 |
| Scarsone | 1.000 | 1 | 1 | 0 | 0 | 0 |
| Wilkins | 1.000 | 7 | 52 | 5 | 0 | 4 |
| M. Williams | .990 | 13 | 90 | 12 | 1 | 10 |
| Wilson | .984 | 33 | 236 | 18 | 4 | 20 |

| Second Base | PCT | G | PO | A | E | DP |
|---|---|---|---|---|---|---|
| Aurilia | 1.000 | 11 | 16 | 18 | 0 | 8 |
| Canizaro | .972 | 35 | 60 | 79 | 4 | 16 |
| Scarsone | .973 | 74 | 161 | 161 | 9 | 44 |
| Thompson | .976 | 62 | 124 | 155 | 7 | 38 |

| Third Base | PCT | G | PO | A | E | DP |
|---|---|---|---|---|---|---|
| Batiste | .847 | 25 | 24 | 37 | 11 | 7 |
| Mueller | .966 | 45 | 34 | 79 | 4 | 10 |
| Scarsone | .913 | 14 | 5 | 16 | 2 | 3 |
| M. Williams | .951 | 92 | 74 | 179 | 13 | 18 |

| Shortstop | PCT | G | PO | A | E | DP |
|---|---|---|---|---|---|---|
| Aurilia | .973 | 93 | 126 | 228 | 10 | 44 |
| Batiste | 1.000 | 7 | 11 | 4 | 0 | 4 |
| Canizaro | .889 | 7 | 4 | 12 | 2 | 4 |
| Delgado | .960 | 6 | 12 | 12 | 1 | 3 |
| Dunston | .957 | 78 | 116 | 217 | 15 | 51 |

| | PCT | G | PO | A | E | DP |
|---|---|---|---|---|---|---|
| Scarsone | .000 | 1 | 0 | 0 | 0 | 0 |
| M. Williams | .000 | 1 | 0 | 0 | 0 | 0 |

| Outfield | PCT | G | PO | A | E | DP |
|---|---|---|---|---|---|---|
| Benard | .984 | 132 | 310 | 7 | 5 | 0 |
| Bonds | .980 | 152 | 286 | 10 | 6 | 1 |
| Carreon | 1.000 | 5 | 6 | 1 | 0 | 0 |
| Cruz | .977 | 23 | 41 | 1 | 1 | 0 |
| Hall | .000 | 4 | 0 | 0 | 0 | 0 |
| Hill | .959 | 98 | 159 | 6 | 7 | 3 |
| Hubbard | 1.000 | 9 | 19 | 1 | 0 | 0 |
| Javier | .984 | 71 | 180 | 2 | 3 | 0 |
| Jones | 1.000 | 33 | 46 | 1 | 0 | 0 |
| McCarty | 1.000 | 20 | 22 | 2 | 0 | 1 |
| Peltier | 1.000 | 1 | 0 | 0 | 0 | 0 |
| D. Williams | 1.000 | 4 | 8 | 0 | 0 | 0 |

Matt Williams was slowed by injuries, but hit .302 with 22 homers

Giants minor league Player of the Year Darin Blood

LES BALDWIN

LARRY GOREN

# GIANTS

## FARM SYSTEM

**Director of Player Development:** Jack Hiatt

| Class | Farm Team | League | W | L | Pct. | Finish* | Manager | First Yr |
|---|---|---|---|---|---|---|---|---|
| AAA | Phoenix (Ariz.) Firebirds | Pacific Coast | 69 | 75 | .479 | 8th (10) | Ron Wotus | 1966 |
| AA | Shreveport (La.) Captains | Texas | 73 | 66 | .525 | 3rd (8) | Frank Cacciatore | 1979 |
| #A | San Jose (Calif.) Giants | California | 89 | 51 | .636 | 1st (10) | Carlos Lezcano | 1988 |
| A | Burlington (Iowa) Bees | Midwest | 65 | 73 | .471 | 11th (14) | Glen Tufts | 1995 |
| A | Bellingham (Wash.) Giants | Northwest | 39 | 36 | .520 | 4th (8) | Ozzie Virgil Sr. | 1995 |

*Finish in overall standings (No. of teams in league)   #Advanced level

## ORGANIZATION LEADERS

### MAJOR LEAGUERS

**BATTING**
*AVG Barry Bonds ........... .308
   R Barry Bonds ........... 122
   H Barry Bonds ........... 159
  TB Barry Bonds ........... 318
  2B Barry Bonds ........... 27
  3B Marvin Benard ........... 4
  HR Barry Bonds ............. 42
 RBI Barry Bonds ........... 129
  BB Barry Bonds ........... 151
  SO Glenallen Hill............ 95
  SB Barry Bonds ........... 40

**PITCHING**
   W Mark Gardner........... 12
   L B. VanLandingham ... 14
#ERA Mark Dewey............ 4.21
   G Mark Dewey............. 78
  CG Mark Gardner............. 4
  SV Rod Beck ................. 35
  IP Allen Watson........... 186
  BB B. VanLandingham ... 78
  SO Mark Gardner......... 145

MORRIS FOSTOFF

**Mark Gardner.** 145 strikeouts

### MINOR LEAGUERS

**BATTING**
*AVG Desi Wilson, Phoenix ........................... .339
   R Tim Garland, San Jose......................... 96
   H Two tied at.............................................. 171
  TB Dante Powell, Shreve./Phoenix............. 240
  2B Jesse Ibarra, San Jose......................... 38
  3B Chris Singleton, Shreve./Phoenix............. 9
  HR Don Denbow, Burlington/San Jose ........ 27
 RBI Jesse Ibarra, San Jose......................... 95
  BB Benji Simonton, Shreve./Phoenix.......... 102
  SO Don Denbow, Burlington/San Jose ....... 153
  SB Tim Garland, San Jose........................... 51

**PITCHING**
   W Darin Blood, San Jose........................... 17
   L Three tied at ........................................... 10
#ERA Mike Villano, San Jose/Shreveport ........ 0.99
   G Santos Hernandez, Burlington ............... 61
  CG Keith Foulke, Shreveport.......................... 4
  SV Russ Ortiz, San Jose/Shreveport ........... 36
  IP Keith Foulke, Shreveport...................... 183
  BB Joe Fontenot, San Jose ......................... 74
  SO Darin Blood, San Jose......................... 193

*Minimum 250 At-Bats  #Minimum 75 Innings

## TOP 10 PROSPECTS

How the Giants Top 10 prospects, as judged by Baseball America prior to the 1996 season, fared in 1996:

**Shawn Estes**

| Player, Pos. | Club (Class—League) | AVG | AB | R | H | 2B | 3B | HR | RBI | SB |
|---|---|---|---|---|---|---|---|---|---|---|
| 3. Jacob Cruz, of | Phoenix (AAA—Pacific Coast) | .285 | 435 | 60 | 124 | 26 | 4 | 7 | 75 | 5 |
| | San Francisco | .234 | 77 | 10 | 18 | 3 | 0 | 3 | 10 | 0 |
| 4. Jay Canizaro, 2b | Phoenix (AAA—Pacific Coast) | .262 | 363 | 50 | 95 | 21 | 2 | 7 | 64 | 14 |
| | San Francisco | .200 | 120 | 11 | 24 | 4 | 1 | 2 | 8 | 0 |
| 5. Dante Powell, of | Phoenix (AAA—Pacific Coast) | .250 | 8 | 0 | 2 | 0 | 1 | 0 | 0 | 0 |
| | Shreveport (AA—Texas) | .280 | 508 | 92 | 142 | 27 | 2 | 21 | 78 | 43 |
| 7. Rich Aurilia, ss | Phoenix (AAA—Pacific Coast) | .433 | 30 | 9 | 13 | 7 | 0 | 0 | 4 | 1 |
| | San Francisco | .239 | 318 | 27 | 76 | 7 | 1 | 3 | 26 | 4 |
| 8. Marcus Jensen, c | Phoenix (AAA—Pacific Coast) | .264 | 405 | 41 | 107 | 22 | 4 | 5 | 53 | 1 |
| | San Francisco | .211 | 19 | 4 | 4 | 1 | 0 | 0 | 4 | 0 |
| 10. Jesse Ibarra, 1b | Shreveport (AA—Texas) | .283 | 498 | 74 | 141 | 38 | 0 | 17 | 95 | 5 |

| Player, Pos. | Club (Class—League) | W | L | ERA | G | SV | IP | H | BB | SO |
|---|---|---|---|---|---|---|---|---|---|---|
| 1. Shawn Estes, lhp | Phoenix (AAA—Pacific Coast) | 9 | 3 | 3.43 | 18 | 0 | 110 | 92 | 35 | 95 |
| | San Francisco | 3 | 5 | 3.60 | 11 | 0 | 70 | 63 | 39 | 60 |
| 2. Joe Fontenot, rhp | San Jose (A—California) | 9 | 4 | 4.44 | 26 | 0 | 144 | 137 | 74 | 124 |
| 6. Steve Soderstrom, rhp | Phoenix (AAA—Pacific Coast) | 7 | 8 | 4.41 | 29 | 0 | 171 | 178 | 58 | 80 |
| | San Francisco | 2 | 0 | 5.27 | 3 | 0 | 14 | 16 | 6 | 9 |
| 9. Russ Ortiz, rhp | San Jose (A—California) | 0 | 0 | 0.25 | 34 | 23 | 37 | 16 | 20 | 63 |
| | Shreveport (AA—Texas) | 1 | 2 | 4.05 | 26 | 13 | 27 | 22 | 21 | 29 |

## PACIFIC COAST LEAGUE

| BATTING | AVG | G | AB | R | H | 2B | 3B | HR | RBI | BB | SO | SB | CS | B | T | HT | WT | DOB | 1st Yr | Resides |
|---|---|---|---|---|---|---|---|---|---|---|---|---|---|---|---|---|---|---|---|---|
| Aurilia, Rich | .433 | 7 | 30 | 9 | 13 | 7 | 0 | 0 | 4 | 2 | 3 | 1 | 1 | R | R | 6-0 | 170 | 9-2-71 | 1992 | Hazlet, N.J. |
| Batiste, Kim | .297 | 42 | 165 | 32 | 49 | 8 | 3 | 14 | 44 | 6 | 25 | 1 | 1 | R | R | 6-0 | 193 | 3-15-68 | 1987 | Prairieville, La. |
| Benard, Marvin | .368 | 4 | 19 | 2 | 7 | 0 | 0 | 0 | 4 | 2 | 2 | 1 | 0 | L | L | 5-10 | 180 | 1-20-71 | 1992 | Cudahy, Calif. |
| Canizaro, Jay | .262 | 102 | 363 | 50 | 95 | 21 | 2 | 7 | 64 | 46 | 77 | 14 | 4 | R | R | 5-10 | 175 | 7-4-73 | 1993 | Orange, Texas |
| Cruz, Jacob | .285 | 121 | 435 | 60 | 124 | 26 | 4 | 7 | 75 | 62 | 77 | 5 | 9 | L | L | 6-0 | 175 | 1-28-73 | 1994 | Oxnard, Calif. |
| Delgado, Wilson | .140 | 12 | 43 | 1 | 6 | 0 | 1 | 0 | 1 | 3 | 7 | 0 | 1 | S | R | 5-11 | 165 | 7-15-75 | 1993 | Santo Domingo, D.R. |
| DeLeon, Roberto | .194 | 19 | 36 | 1 | 7 | 2 | 0 | 0 | 2 | 0 | 7 | 0 | 0 | R | R | 5-10 | 188 | 3-29-71 | 1992 | Missouri City, Texas |
| Duncan, Andres | .226 | 42 | 106 | 11 | 24 | 7 | 2 | 1 | 12 | 8 | 22 | 2 | 0 | S | R | 5-11 | 155 | 11-30-71 | 1989 | San Pedro de Macoris, D.R. |
| Ehmann, Kurt | .201 | 50 | 134 | 14 | 27 | 6 | 2 | 0 | 12 | 12 | 35 | 0 | 2 | R | R | 6-1 | 185 | 8-18-70 | 1992 | Ukiah, Calif. |
| Florez, Tim | .290 | 113 | 366 | 42 | 106 | 31 | 3 | 4 | 39 | 34 | 56 | 0 | 5 | R | R | 5-10 | 170 | 7-23-69 | 1991 | Goleta, Calif. |
| Glenn, Darrin | .056 | 12 | 18 | 3 | 1 | 0 | 0 | 0 | 1 | 1 | 8 | 0 | 0 | R | R | 6-0 | 195 | 1-4-71 | 1993 | El Paso, Texas |
| Hill, Glenallen | .353 | 5 | 17 | 4 | 6 | 1 | 0 | 2 | 2 | 0 | 3 | 1 | 0 | R | R | 6-2 | 210 | 3-22-65 | 1983 | Boca Raton, Fla. |
| Jensen, Marcus | .264 | 120 | 405 | 41 | 107 | 22 | 4 | 5 | 53 | 44 | 95 | 1 | 1 | S | R | 6-4 | 195 | 12-14-72 | 1990 | Oakland, Calif. |
| Jones, Dax | .309 | 74 | 298 | 52 | 92 | 20 | 6 | 6 | 41 | 19 | 21 | 13 | 8 | R | R | 6-0 | 170 | 8-4-70 | 1991 | Waukegan, Ill. |
| Kennedy, Darryl | .307 | 64 | 192 | 27 | 59 | 11 | 3 | 2 | 24 | 12 | 25 | 2 | 2 | R | R | 5-10 | 170 | 1-23-69 | 1991 | Davenport, Fla. |
| Manwaring, Kirt | .182 | 4 | 11 | 1 | 2 | 0 | 0 | 0 | 1 | 2 | 0 | 0 | 0 | R | R | 5-11 | 203 | 7-15-65 | 1986 | Scottsdale, Ariz. |
| McCarty, Dave | .400 | 6 | 25 | 4 | 10 | 1 | 1 | 1 | 7 | 2 | 4 | 0 | 0 | R | L | 6-5 | 207 | 11-23-69 | 1991 | Houston, Texas |
| Mirabelli, Doug | .298 | 14 | 47 | 10 | 14 | 7 | 0 | 0 | 7 | 4 | 7 | 0 | 0 | R | R | 6-1 | 205 | 10-18-70 | 1992 | Las Vegas, Nev. |
| Mueller, Bill | .302 | 106 | 440 | 73 | 133 | 14 | 6 | 4 | 36 | 44 | 40 | 2 | 5 | S | R | 5-11 | 173 | 3-17-71 | 1993 | Maryland Heights, Mo. |
| Murray, Calvin | .244 | 83 | 311 | 50 | 76 | 16 | 6 | 3 | 28 | 43 | 60 | 12 | 6 | R | R | 5-11 | 185 | 7-30-71 | 1992 | Dallas, Texas |
| Peltier, Dan | .285 | 70 | 267 | 40 | 76 | 8 | 3 | 0 | 27 | 28 | 39 | 0 | 2 | L | L | 6-1 | 200 | 6-30-68 | 1989 | Eden Prairie, Minn. |
| Powell, Dante | .250 | 2 | 8 | 0 | 2 | 0 | 1 | 0 | 0 | 2 | 3 | 0 | 1 | R | R | 6-2 | 185 | 8-25-73 | 1994 | Long Beach, Calif. |
| Simonton, Benji | .750 | 1 | 4 | 1 | 3 | 0 | 0 | 1 | 2 | 1 | 0 | 0 | 0 | R | R | 6-1 | 225 | 5-12-72 | 1992 | Tempe, Ariz. |
| Singleton, Chris | .125 | 9 | 32 | 3 | 4 | 0 | 0 | 0 | 0 | 1 | 2 | 0 | 0 | L | L | 6-2 | 195 | 8-15-72 | 1993 | Hercules, Calif. |
| Williams, Keith | .274 | 108 | 398 | 63 | 109 | 25 | 3 | 13 | 63 | 52 | 96 | 2 | 2 | R | R | 6-0 | 190 | 4-21-72 | 1993 | Bedford, Pa. |
| Wilson, Desi | .339 | 113 | 407 | 56 | 138 | 26 | 7 | 5 | 59 | 18 | 80 | 15 | 4 | L | L | 6-7 | 230 | 5-9-68 | 1991 | Glen Cove, N.Y. |
| Woods, Ken | .279 | 56 | 208 | 32 | 58 | 12 | 1 | 2 | 13 | 19 | 29 | 3 | 4 | R | R | 5-10 | 173 | 8-2-70 | 1992 | Los Angeles, Calif. |

| PITCHING | W | L | ERA | G | GS | CG | SV | IP | H | R | ER | BB | SO | B | T | HT | WT | DOB | 1st Yr | Resides |
|---|---|---|---|---|---|---|---|---|---|---|---|---|---|---|---|---|---|---|---|---|
| Barton, Shawn | 4 | 4 | 4.74 | 44 | 0 | 0 | 2 | 49 | 52 | 27 | 26 | 19 | 27 | R | L | 6-3 | 195 | 5-14-63 | 1984 | Reading, Pa. |
| Bautista, Jose | 2 | 2 | 4.35 | 6 | 6 | 0 | 0 | 39 | 41 | 19 | 19 | 5 | 18 | R | R | 6-2 | 207 | 7-25-64 | 1981 | Cooper City, Fla. |
| Bourgeois, Steve | 8 | 6 | 3.62 | 20 | 18 | 2 | 0 | 97 | 112 | 50 | 39 | 42 | 65 | R | R | 6-1 | 220 | 8-4-72 | 1993 | Paulina, La. |
| Brewington, Jamie | 6 | 9 | 7.02 | 35 | 17 | 0 | 1 | 110 | 130 | 93 | 86 | 72 | 75 | R | R | 6-4 | 180 | 9-28-71 | 1992 | Greenville, N.C. |
| Carlson, Dan | 13 | 6 | 3.44 | 33 | 15 | 2 | 1 | 147 | 135 | 61 | 56 | 46 | 123 | R | R | 6-1 | 185 | 1-26-70 | 1990 | Portland, Ore. |
| Carter, Andy | 1 | 5 | 5.54 | 37 | 8 | 0 | 0 | 80 | 98 | 61 | 49 | 36 | 50 | L | L | 6-5 | 190 | 11-9-68 | 1987 | Erdenheim, Pa. |
| Estes, Shawn | 9 | 3 | 3.43 | 18 | 18 | 0 | 0 | 110 | 92 | 43 | 42 | 63 | 95 | R | L | 6-2 | 200 | 2-28-73 | 1991 | Gardnerville, Nev. |
| Hancock, Lee | 0 | 2 | 4.33 | 17 | 3 | 0 | 0 | 35 | 42 | 19 | 17 | 12 | 19 | L | L | 6-4 | 215 | 6-27-67 | 1988 | Saratoga, Calif. |
|   2-team (9 Calgary) | 0 | 2 | 3.58 | 26 | 4 | 0 | 0 | 50 | 51 | 22 | 20 | 17 | 28 | | | | | | | |
| Heredia, Julian | 0 | 5 | 4.91 | 52 | 2 | 1 | 4 | 70 | 71 | 40 | 38 | 23 | 59 | R | R | 6-1 | 160 | 9-22-69 | 1989 | La Romana, D.R. |
| Hook, Chris | 7 | 10 | 4.78 | 32 | 20 | 0 | 0 | 128 | 139 | 75 | 68 | 51 | 70 | S | R | 6-5 | 195 | 8-4-68 | 1989 | Florence, Ky. |
| Mintz, Steve | 3 | 5 | 5.37 | 59 | 0 | 0 | 27 | 57 | 63 | 39 | 34 | 25 | 35 | L | R | 5-11 | 190 | 11-24-68 | 1990 | Leland, N.C. |
| Pickett, Ricky | 0 | 3 | 8.64 | 8 | 0 | 0 | 0 | 8 | 12 | 8 | 8 | 5 | 7 | L | L | 6-0 | 185 | 1-19-70 | 1992 | Fort Worth, Texas |
| Rueter, Kirk | 1 | 2 | 3.51 | 5 | 5 | 0 | 0 | 26 | 25 | 12 | 10 | 12 | 15 | L | L | 6-3 | 190 | 12-1-70 | 1991 | Hoyleton, Ill. |
| Soderstrom, Steve | 7 | 8 | 4.41 | 29 | 29 | 0 | 0 | 171 | 178 | 94 | 84 | 58 | 80 | R | R | 6-3 | 215 | 4-3-72 | 1994 | Turlock, Calif. |
| Valdez, Carlos | 4 | 3 | 4.98 | 44 | 0 | 0 | 5 | 60 | 63 | 38 | 33 | 34 | 38 | R | R | 5-11 | 165 | 12-26-71 | 1990 | Bani, D.R. |
| Vanderweele, Doug | 4 | 2 | 5.36 | 41 | 3 | 0 | 0 | 89 | 101 | 55 | 53 | 35 | 39 | R | R | 6-3 | 200 | 3-18-70 | 1991 | Las Vegas, Nev. |

### FIELDING

| Catcher | PCT | G | PO | A | E | DP | PB |
|---|---|---|---|---|---|---|---|
| Ehmann | .955 | 4 | 20 | 1 | 1 | 0 | 1 |
| Glenn | 1.000 | 2 | 5 | 0 | 0 | 0 | 1 |
| Jensen | .988 | 102 | 568 | 65 | 8 | 7 | 6 |
| Kennedy | .982 | 31 | 156 | 10 | 3 | 0 | 0 |
| Manwaring | 1.000 | 4 | 15 | 3 | 0 | 0 | 0 |
| Mirabelli | .982 | 14 | 97 | 10 | 2 | 1 | 0 |

| First Base | PCT | G | PO | A | E | DP |
|---|---|---|---|---|---|---|
| Batiste | 1.000 | 1 | 16 | 1 | 0 | 5 |
| Ehmann | 1.000 | 1 | 8 | 1 | 0 | 1 |
| Glenn | 1.000 | 2 | 3 | 0 | 0 | 1 |
| McCarty | 1.000 | 2 | 24 | 0 | 0 | 3 |
| Peltier | .993 | 46 | 407 | 33 | 3 | 46 |
| Simonton | 1.000 | 1 | 9 | 0 | 0 | 1 |
| Wilson | .991 | 98 | 842 | 52 | 8 | 92 |

| Second Base | PCT | G | PO | A | E | DP |
|---|---|---|---|---|---|---|
| Aurilia | .000 | 1 | 0 | 0 | 0 | 0 |
| Canizaro | .986 | 56 | 123 | 167 | 4 | 44 |
| DeLeon | .750 | 1 | 2 | 1 | 1 | 0 |

| | PCT | G | PO | A | E | DP |
|---|---|---|---|---|---|---|
| Florez | .982 | 87 | 186 | 256 | 8 | 74 |
| Mueller | 1.000 | 12 | 25 | 30 | 0 | 7 |

| Third Base | PCT | G | PO | A | E | DP |
|---|---|---|---|---|---|---|
| Batiste | .878 | 20 | 12 | 31 | 6 | 3 |
| Canizaro | .900 | 3 | 2 | 7 | 1 | 1 |
| DeLeon | .944 | 11 | 2 | 15 | 1 | 1 |
| Duncan | 1.000 | 2 | 1 | 4 | 0 | 0 |
| Ehmann | .957 | 9 | 5 | 17 | 1 | 0 |
| Florez | .957 | 16 | 13 | 31 | 2 | 5 |
| Kennedy | .750 | 12 | 3 | 15 | 6 | 3 |
| Mueller | .975 | 85 | 50 | 180 | 6 | 25 |
| Woods | 1.000 | 7 | 4 | 15 | 0 | 1 |

| Shortstop | PCT | G | PO | A | E | DP |
|---|---|---|---|---|---|---|
| Aurilia | .972 | 7 | 10 | 25 | 1 | 6 |
| Batiste | .894 | 12 | 16 | 26 | 5 | 8 |
| Canizaro | .958 | 41 | 69 | 134 | 9 | 30 |
| Delgado | .975 | 12 | 30 | 47 | 2 | 13 |
| Duncan | .906 | 30 | 33 | 83 | 12 | 12 |

| | PCT | G | PO | A | E | DP |
|---|---|---|---|---|---|---|
| Ehmann | .933 | 29 | 39 | 72 | 8 | 12 |
| Florez | 1.000 | 1 | 0 | 1 | 0 | 0 |
| Mueller | .919 | 16 | 17 | 40 | 5 | 10 |
| Woods | .913 | 14 | 22 | 41 | 6 | 9 |

| Outfield | PCT | G | PO | A | E | DP |
|---|---|---|---|---|---|---|
| Batiste | 1.000 | 10 | 4 | 0 | 0 | 0 |
| Benard | 1.000 | 4 | 10 | 0 | 0 | 0 |
| Cruz | .989 | 116 | 249 | 11 | 3 | 2 |
| Ehmann | 1.000 | 2 | 3 | 0 | 0 | 0 |
| Hill | 1.000 | 5 | 8 | 0 | 0 | 0 |
| Jones | 1.000 | 70 | 178 | 9 | 0 | 0 |
| McCarty | 1.000 | 4 | 5 | 1 | 0 | 0 |
| Murray | .991 | 79 | 207 | 3 | 2 | 2 |
| Peltier | 1.000 | 17 | 25 | 2 | 0 | 0 |
| Powell | 1.000 | 2 | 4 | 0 | 0 | 0 |
| Singleton | 1.000 | 8 | 18 | 1 | 0 | 0 |
| Williams | .988 | 96 | 160 | 6 | 2 | 2 |
| Wilson | 1.000 | 3 | 5 | 0 | 0 | 0 |
| Woods | 1.000 | 34 | 50 | 3 | 0 | 0 |

## TEXAS LEAGUE

| BATTING | AVG | G | AB | R | H | 2B | 3B | HR | RBI | BB | SO | SB | CS | B | T | HT | WT | DOB | 1st Yr | Resides |
|---|---|---|---|---|---|---|---|---|---|---|---|---|---|---|---|---|---|---|---|---|
| Alguacil, Jose | .208 | 13 | 24 | 2 | 5 | 0 | 0 | 0 | 0 | 3 | 9 | 0 | 0 | L | R | 6-2 | 185 | 8-9-72 | 1993 | Caracas, Venez. |
| Bess, Johnny | .246 | 57 | 175 | 25 | 43 | 10 | 3 | 7 | 30 | 19 | 63 | 1 | 1 | S | R | 6-1 | 190 | 4-6-70 | 1992 | Grand Junction, Colo. |
| DeLeon, Roberto | .236 | 85 | 263 | 30 | 62 | 11 | 4 | 4 | 34 | 23 | 43 | 0 | 2 | R | R | 5-10 | 188 | 3-29-71 | 1992 | Missouri City, Texas |
| Duncan, Andres | .264 | 68 | 193 | 33 | 51 | 6 | 2 | 2 | 10 | 20 | 38 | 8 | 3 | S | R | 5-11 | 155 | 11-30-71 | 1989 | San Pedro de Macoris, D.R. |
| Florez, Tim | .273 | 18 | 66 | 9 | 18 | 1 | 0 | 2 | 8 | 7 | 11 | 2 | 0 | R | R | 5-10 | 170 | 7-23-69 | 1991 | Goleta, Calif. |
| Glenn, Darrin | .182 | 7 | 11 | 1 | 2 | 0 | 0 | 1 | 4 | 1 | 3 | 0 | 0 | R | R | 6-0 | 195 | 1-4-71 | 1993 | El Paso, Texas |
| King, Brett | .233 | 127 | 459 | 61 | 107 | 23 | 4 | 7 | 48 | 49 | 116 | 19 | 9 | R | R | 6-1 | 190 | 7-20-72 | 1993 | Apopka, Fla. |
| Mayes, Craig | .400 | 10 | 40 | 5 | 16 | 2 | 0 | 0 | 3 | 5 | 2 | 0 | 1 | L | R | 5-10 | 195 | 5-8-70 | 1992 | Washington, Mich. |

LARRY GOREN

FRANK RAGSDALE

**Long Ball Leaders.** Outfielders Barry Bonds, left, and Don Denbow led Giants major leaguers and minor leaguers, respectively, in home runs in 1996. Bonds hit 42, Denbow hit 27 in Class A.

| BATTING | AVG | G | AB | R | H | 2B | 3B | HR | RBI | BB | SO | SB | CS | B | T | HT | WT | DOB | 1st Yr | Resides |
|---|---|---|---|---|---|---|---|---|---|---|---|---|---|---|---|---|---|---|---|---|
| Mirabelli, Doug | .295 | 115 | 380 | 60 | 112 | 23 | 0 | 21 | 70 | 76 | 49 | 0 | 1 | R | R | 6-1 | 205 | 10-18-70 | 1992 | Las Vegas, Nev. |
| Murray, Calvin | .260 | 50 | 169 | 32 | 44 | 7 | 0 | 7 | 24 | 25 | 33 | 6 | 5 | R | R | 5-11 | 185 | 7-30-71 | 1992 | Dallas, Texas |
| Phillips, Gary | .246 | 111 | 337 | 37 | 83 | 18 | 4 | 2 | 43 | 22 | 71 | 1 | 6 | R | R | 5-11 | 170 | 9-25-71 | 1992 | Tullahoma, Tenn. |
| Powell, Dante | .280 | 135 | 508 | 92 | 142 | 27 | 2 | 21 | 78 | 72 | 92 | 43 | 23 | R | R | 6-2 | 185 | 8-25-73 | 1994 | Long Beach, Calif. |
| Ramirez, Hiram | 1.000 | 1 | 3 | 2 | 3 | 1 | 0 | 0 | 4 | 0 | 0 | 0 | 0 | R | R | 6-2 | 200 | 9-10-72 | 1991 | Ensenada, P.R. |
| Reid, Derek | .246 | 30 | 118 | 16 | 29 | 4 | 0 | 4 | 18 | 11 | 18 | 2 | 2 | R | R | 6-3 | 195 | 2-4-70 | 1990 | Cincinnati, Ohio |
| Rios, Armando | .283 | 92 | 329 | 62 | 93 | 22 | 2 | 12 | 49 | 44 | 42 | 9 | 9 | L | L | 5-9 | 178 | 9-13-71 | 1994 | Carolina, P.R. |
| Sbrocco, Jon | .247 | 23 | 81 | 16 | 20 | 2 | 1 | 1 | 5 | 11 | 10 | 5 | 0 | L | R | 5-10 | 165 | 1-5-71 | 1993 | Willoughby Hills, Ohio |
| Schneider, Dan | .238 | 7 | 21 | 3 | 5 | 1 | 0 | 2 | 6 | 0 | 11 | 0 | 0 | R | R | 6-2 | 195 | 4-18-72 | 1994 | Greensboro, N.C. |
| Simonton, Benji | .249 | 137 | 469 | 86 | 117 | 25 | 1 | 23 | 76 | 101 | 144 | 6 | 4 | R | R | 6-1 | 225 | 5-12-72 | 1992 | Tempe, Ariz. |
| Singleton, Chris | .298 | 129 | 500 | 68 | 149 | 31 | 9 | 5 | 72 | 24 | 58 | 27 | 12 | L | L | 6-2 | 195 | 8-15-72 | 1993 | Hercules, Calif. |
| Weaver, Terry | .125 | 5 | 8 | 1 | 1 | 0 | 0 | 1 | 1 | 1 | 1 | 0 | 0 | R | R | 6-0 | 175 | 10-8-72 | 1995 | Harrisonburg, Va. |
| Woods, Kenny | .279 | 83 | 287 | 36 | 80 | 17 | 1 | 1 | 29 | 29 | 35 | 14 | 10 | R | R | 5-10 | 173 | 8-2-70 | 1992 | Los Angeles, Calif. |

| PITCHING | W | L | ERA | G | GS | CG | SV | IP | H | R | ER | BB | SO | B | T | HT | WT | DOB | 1st Yr | Resides |
|---|---|---|---|---|---|---|---|---|---|---|---|---|---|---|---|---|---|---|---|---|
| Brohawn, Troy | 9 | 10 | 4.60 | 28 | 28 | 0 | 0 | 157 | 163 | 99 | 80 | 49 | 82 | L | L | 6-1 | 190 | 1-14-73 | 1994 | Woolford, Md. |
| Castillo, Marino | 5 | 5 | 3.58 | 38 | 0 | 0 | 3 | 50 | 48 | 21 | 20 | 14 | 53 | R | R | 6-0 | 168 | 3-17-71 | 1990 | Boca Chica, D.R. |
| Corps, Edwin | 2 | 3 | 4.48 | 38 | 3 | 0 | 1 | 70 | 74 | 46 | 35 | 26 | 39 | R | R | 5-11 | 180 | 11-3-72 | 1994 | Carolina, P.R. |
| Foulke, Keith | 12 | 7 | 2.76 | 27 | 27 | 4 | 0 | 183 | 149 | 61 | 56 | 35 | 129 | R | R | 6-1 | 195 | 10-19-72 | 1994 | Huffman, Texas |
| Howry, Bobby | 10 | 8 | 4.65 | 27 | 27 | 0 | 0 | 157 | 163 | 90 | 81 | 56 | 57 | L | R | 6-5 | 215 | 8-4-73 | 1994 | Glendale, Ariz. |
| Hyde, Rich | 1 | 2 | 5.94 | 19 | 0 | 0 | 1 | 33 | 36 | 26 | 22 | 12 | 25 | R | R | 6-0 | 185 | 12-24-68 | 1991 | Mahomet, Ill. |
| Macey, Fausto | 10 | 7 | 4.30 | 27 | 26 | 1 | 0 | 157 | 165 | 86 | 75 | 47 | 62 | R | R | 6-4 | 185 | 10-9-75 | 1994 | Santo Domingo, D.R. |
| Ortiz, Russ | 1 | 2 | 4.05 | 26 | 0 | 0 | 13 | 27 | 22 | 14 | 12 | 21 | 29 | R | R | 6-1 | 200 | 6-5-74 | 1995 | Norman, Okla. |
| Peterson, Mark | 5 | 3 | 3.21 | 41 | 0 | 0 | 2 | 56 | 58 | 23 | 20 | 8 | 32 | L | L | 5-11 | 195 | 11-27-70 | 1992 | Kirkland, Wash. |
| Phillips, Randy | 1 | 4 | 3.23 | 35 | 2 | 0 | 4 | 70 | 77 | 34 | 25 | 21 | 31 | R | R | 6-3 | 210 | 3-18-71 | 1992 | Pine Bluff, Ark. |
| Pickett, Ricky | 4 | 1 | 2.77 | 29 | 0 | 0 | 2 | 49 | 35 | 21 | 15 | 35 | 51 | L | L | 6-0 | 185 | 1-19-70 | 1992 | Fort Worth, Texas |
| Purdy, Shawn | 5 | 4 | 3.10 | 54 | 0 | 0 | 16 | 52 | 46 | 23 | 18 | 16 | 23 | R | R | 6-0 | 205 | 7-30-68 | 1991 | St. Cloud, Fla. |
| Taulbee, Andy | 6 | 10 | 5.00 | 27 | 24 | 0 | 1 | 139 | 169 | 87 | 77 | 47 | 55 | R | R | 6-4 | 210 | 10-5-72 | 1994 | Tucker, Ga. |
| Villano, Mike | 2 | 0 | 3.00 | 2 | 2 | 0 | 0 | 12 | 6 | 4 | 4 | 8 | 7 | R | R | 6-1 | 200 | 8-10-71 | 1994 | Bay City, Mich. |

## FIELDING

| Catcher | PCT | G | PO | A | E | DP | PB |
|---|---|---|---|---|---|---|---|
| Bess | .984 | 23 | 106 | 14 | 2 | 3 | 1 |
| Glenn | .933 | 6 | 13 | 1 | 1 | 1 | 0 |
| Mayes | .981 | 10 | 48 | 3 | 1 | 1 | 0 |
| Mirabelli | .988 | 106 | 517 | 55 | 7 | 8 | 4 |
| Ramirez | 1.000 | 1 | 2 | 1 | 0 | 0 | 0 |
| Schneider | .971 | 7 | 33 | 0 | 1 | 0 | 0 |

| First Base | PCT | G | PO | A | E | DP |
|---|---|---|---|---|---|---|
| Mirabelli | 1.000 | 4 | 31 | 1 | 0 | 2 |
| Phillips | 1.000 | 2 | 11 | 0 | 0 | 1 |
| Simonton | .988 | 136 | 1171 | 79 | 15 | 109 |

| Second Base | PCT | G | PO | A | E | DP |
|---|---|---|---|---|---|---|
| Alguacil | 1.000 | 5 | 4 | 10 | 0 | 4 |
| DeLeon | .962 | 69 | 138 | 167 | 12 | 39 |
| Duncan | .964 | 30 | 45 | 63 | 4 | 8 |

| | PCT | G | PO | A | E | DP |
|---|---|---|---|---|---|---|
| Florez | .972 | 18 | 45 | 60 | 3 | 10 |
| Sbrocco | .960 | 23 | 49 | 46 | 4 | 14 |
| Woods | .968 | 13 | 39 | 21 | 2 | 5 |

| Third Base | PCT | G | PO | A | E | DP |
|---|---|---|---|---|---|---|
| Alguacil | 1.000 | 3 | 0 | 1 | 0 | 0 |
| Bess | 1.000 | 1 | 1 | 0 | 0 | 0 |
| DeLeon | 1.000 | 2 | 1 | 0 | 0 | 0 |
| Duncan | 1.000 | 8 | 6 | 14 | 0 | 3 |
| Glenn | 1.000 | 1 | 1 | 4 | 0 | 1 |
| Phillips | .947 | 93 | 66 | 183 | 14 | 14 |
| Weaver | 1.000 | 3 | 0 | 1 | 0 | 0 |
| Woods | .883 | 53 | 26 | 87 | 15 | 7 |

| Shortstop | PCT | G | PO | A | E | DP |
|---|---|---|---|---|---|---|
| Alguacil | 1.000 | 1 | 1 | 1 | 0 | 1 |

| | PCT | G | PO | A | E | DP |
|---|---|---|---|---|---|---|
| Duncan | .930 | 13 | 16 | 24 | 3 | 4 |
| Florez | 1.000 | 1 | 2 | 1 | 0 | 0 |
| King | .945 | 126 | 198 | 353 | 32 | 66 |
| Woods | .946 | 11 | 25 | 28 | 3 | 6 |

| Outfield | PCT | G | PO | A | E | DP |
|---|---|---|---|---|---|---|
| Alguacil | 1.000 | 3 | 3 | 0 | 0 | 0 |
| Bess | 1.000 | 6 | 7 | 1 | 0 | 0 |
| Duncan | .958 | 7 | 22 | 1 | 1 | 0 |
| Murray | .969 | 41 | 89 | 4 | 3 | 1 |
| Powell | .977 | 127 | 331 | 8 | 8 | 2 |
| Reid | 1.000 | 30 | 56 | 0 | 0 | 0 |
| Rios | .963 | 85 | 165 | 15 | 7 | 3 |
| Singleton | .986 | 123 | 262 | 10 | 4 | 2 |
| Woods | .967 | 12 | 28 | 1 | 1 | 0 |

## CALIFORNIA LEAGUE

| BATTING | AVG | G | AB | R | H | 2B | 3B | HR | RBI | BB | SO | SB | CS | B | T | HT | WT | DOB | 1st Yr | Resides |
|---|---|---|---|---|---|---|---|---|---|---|---|---|---|---|---|---|---|---|---|---|
| Alguacil, Jose | .265 | 79 | 272 | 53 | 72 | 11 | 3 | 1 | 31 | 24 | 53 | 18 | 7 | L | R | 6-2 | 185 | 8-9-72 | 1993 | Caracas, Venez. |
| Batiste, Kim | .167 | 2 | 6 | 0 | 1 | 0 | 0 | 0 | 0 | 0 | 2 | 0 | 0 | R | R | 6-0 | 193 | 3-15-68 | 1987 | Prairieville, La. |
| Bonds, Bobby | .248 | 110 | 420 | 65 | 104 | 16 | 5 | 11 | 51 | 43 | 126 | 21 | 5 | R | R | 6-4 | 180 | 3-7-70 | 1992 | Tampa, Fla. |
| Corujo, Rey | .271 | 57 | 188 | 26 | 51 | 12 | 1 | 4 | 28 | 19 | 43 | 1 | 0 | R | R | 5-11 | 185 | 10-19-71 | 1995 | Bayamon, P.R. |
| Delgado, Wilson | .268 | 121 | 462 | 59 | 124 | 19 | 6 | 2 | 54 | 48 | 89 | 8 | 2 | S | R | 5-11 | 165 | 7-15-75 | 1993 | Santo Domingo, D.R. |
| Denbow, Don | .371 | 26 | 97 | 19 | 36 | 8 | 3 | 6 | 19 | 17 | 30 | 1 | 1 | R | R | 6-4 | 215 | 4-30-73 | 1993 | Corsicana, Texas |
| DeLeon, Roberto | .091 | 3 | 11 | 0 | 1 | 0 | 0 | 0 | 0 | 0 | 2 | 0 | 1 | R | R | 5-10 | 188 | 3-29-71 | 1992 | Missouri City, Texas |
| Galarza, Joel | .289 | 81 | 291 | 39 | 84 | 17 | 0 | 8 | 50 | 25 | 60 | 10 | 3 | R | R | 5-11 | 198 | 10-14-73 | 1993 | Yabucoa, P.R. |
| Garland, Tim | .311 | 132 | 550 | 96 | 171 | 18 | 7 | 5 | 61 | 54 | 77 | 51 | 18 | R | R | 6-0 | 185 | 7-15-68 | 1989 | Danville, Va. |
| Glenn, Darrin | .222 | 3 | 9 | 2 | 2 | 0 | 0 | 1 | 1 | 2 | 4 | 0 | 0 | R | R | 6-0 | 195 | 1-4-71 | 1993 | El Paso, Texas |
| Guzman, Edwards | .270 | 106 | 367 | 41 | 99 | 19 | 5 | 1 | 40 | 39 | 60 | 3 | 5 | L | R | 5-11 | 192 | 9-11-76 | 1996 | Naranjito, P.R. |
| Ibarra, Jesse | .283 | 126 | 498 | 74 | 141 | 38 | 0 | 17 | 95 | 63 | 108 | 5 | 1 | S | R | 6-3 | 195 | 7-12-72 | 1994 | El Monte, Calif. |
| Javier, Stan | .400 | 3 | 5 | 1 | 2 | 0 | 0 | 0 | 1 | 1 | 1 | 0 | 0 | S | R | 6-0 | 185 | 1-9-64 | 1981 | Santo Domingo, D.R. |
| Lampkin, Tom | .286 | 2 | 7 | 2 | 2 | 0 | 1 | 0 | 2 | 1 | 0 | 0 | 0 | L | R | 5-11 | 183 | 3-4-64 | 1986 | Boring, Ore. |
| Marval, Raul | .234 | 39 | 137 | 19 | 32 | 6 | 0 | 0 | 19 | 9 | 13 | 0 | 0 | R | R | 6-2 | 170 | 12-13-75 | 1993 | Cabodare, Venez. |
| Mayes, Craig | .328 | 114 | 472 | 56 | 155 | 26 | 4 | 3 | 68 | 29 | 43 | 6 | 8 | L | R | 5-10 | 195 | 5-8-70 | 1992 | Washington, Mich. |
| McGuire, Matt | .333 | 4 | 6 | 1 | 2 | 1 | 0 | 0 | 0 | 1 | 0 | 0 | 0 | R | R | 6-1 | 180 | 7-29-75 | 1996 | Chesterfield, Mo. |
| Morales, Alex | .167 | 17 | 54 | 9 | 9 | 2 | 0 | 1 | 5 | 13 | 17 | 5 | 2 | R | R | 6-0 | 190 | 2-15-74 | 1995 | Palm Beach Gardens, Fla. |
| Reid, Derek | .343 | 88 | 350 | 71 | 120 | 15 | 4 | 14 | 58 | 35 | 68 | 23 | 2 | R | R | 6-3 | 195 | 2-4-70 | 1990 | Cincinnati, Ohio |
| Sbrocco, Jon | .310 | 95 | 358 | 76 | 111 | 12 | 5 | 2 | 48 | 67 | 36 | 29 | 11 | L | R | 5-10 | 165 | 1-5-71 | 1993 | Willoughby Hills, Ohio |
| Thielen, D.J. | .273 | 6 | 22 | 4 | 6 | 1 | 0 | 1 | 4 | 3 | 8 | 0 | 1 | R | R | 6-2 | 185 | 8-5-71 | 1991 | Portland, Ore. |
| Torrealba, Yolvit | .000 | 2 | 5 | 0 | 0 | 0 | 0 | 0 | 0 | 1 | 1 | 0 | 0 | R | R | 5-11 | 180 | 7-19-78 | 1995 | Guarenas, Venez. |
| Van Rossum, Chris | .258 | 11 | 31 | 7 | 8 | 2 | 0 | 0 | 4 | 6 | 10 | 1 | 2 | L | L | 6-2 | 180 | 2-15-74 | 1996 | Turlock, Calif. |
| Weaver, Terry | .214 | 6 | 14 | 1 | 3 | 0 | 0 | 0 | 1 | 1 | 0 | 0 | 0 | R | R | 6-0 | 175 | 10-8-72 | 1995 | Harrisonburg, Va. |
| Wilson, Todd | .305 | 90 | 318 | 50 | 97 | 18 | 1 | 5 | 40 | 18 | 47 | 3 | 2 | R | R | 6-0 | 210 | 11-20-69 | 1994 | San Diego, Calif. |

**GAMES BY POSITION: C**—Galarza 36, Glenn 1, Ibarra 6, Lampkin 2, Mayes 101, McGuire 3, Torrealba 2. **1B**—Alguacil 4, Galarza 3, Glenn 1, Ibarra 109, Wilson 33. **2B**—Alguacil 60, DeLeon 3, Marval 19, Sbrocco 61, Weaver 3. **3B**—Alguacil 2, Batiste 1, Guzman 105, Marval 4, Weaver 3, Wilson 35. **SS**—Alguacil 9, Batiste 1, Guzman 121, Marval 15. **OF**—Alguacil 5, Bonds 101, Corujo 43, Denbow 20, Galarza 7, Garland 130, Guzman 1, Javier 2, Mayes 1, Morales 17, Reid 88, Thielen 4, Van Rossum 11, Wilson 1.

| PITCHING | W | L | ERA | G | GS | CG | SV | IP | H | R | ER | BB | SO | B | T | HT | WT | DOB | 1st Yr | Resides |
|---|---|---|---|---|---|---|---|---|---|---|---|---|---|---|---|---|---|---|---|---|
| Bailey, Philip | 9 | 2 | 3.05 | 35 | 6 | 0 | 0 | 74 | 76 | 30 | 25 | 22 | 53 | L | L | 6-1 | 185 | 10-4-73 | 1995 | Benton, Ark. |
| Blood, Darin | 17 | 6 | 2.65 | 27 | 25 | 2 | 0 | 170 | 140 | 59 | 50 | 71 | 193 | L | R | 6-2 | 205 | 8-31-74 | 1995 | Post Falls, Idaho |
| Castillo, Marino | 3 | 0 | 0.79 | 10 | 0 | 0 | 1 | 11 | 8 | 1 | 1 | 0 | 19 | R | R | 6-0 | 168 | 3-17-71 | 1990 | Boca Chica, D.R. |
| DeLucia, Rich | 0 | 0 | 2.45 | 5 | 4 | 0 | 0 | 7 | 5 | 2 | 2 | 3 | 11 | R | R | 6-0 | 185 | 10-7-64 | 1986 | Columbia, S.C. |
| Fontenot, Joe | 9 | 4 | 4.44 | 26 | 23 | 0 | 0 | 144 | 137 | 87 | 71 | 74 | 124 | R | R | 6-2 | 185 | 3-20-77 | 1995 | Scott, La. |
| Fultz, Aaron | 9 | 5 | 3.96 | 36 | 12 | 0 | 1 | 105 | 101 | 52 | 46 | 54 | 103 | L | L | 6-0 | 196 | 9-4-73 | 1992 | Northport, Ala. |
| Gardner, Mark | 0 | 0 | 3.18 | 1 | 1 | 0 | 0 | 6 | 4 | 2 | 2 | 0 | 7 | R | R | 6-1 | 190 | 3-1-62 | 1985 | Fresno, Calif. |
| Gomez, Dennys | 1 | 0 | 6.99 | 22 | 0 | 0 | 0 | 28 | 30 | 28 | 22 | 16 | 27 | S | R | 6-0 | 195 | 6-21-71 | 1994 | Miami, Fla. |
|   2-team (10 Bakers.) | 4 | 1 | 5.44 | 32 | 0 | 0 | 0 | 51 | 52 | 39 | 31 | 28 | 38 | | | | | | | |
| Hartvigson, Chad | 4 | 7 | 3.23 | 36 | 10 | 0 | 2 | 103 | 94 | 46 | 37 | 30 | 114 | R | L | 6-2 | 195 | 12-15-70 | 1994 | Kirkland, Wash. |
| Martin, Jeff | 2 | 4 | 4.62 | 42 | 0 | 0 | 3 | 60 | 52 | 36 | 31 | 29 | 54 | R | R | 6-2 | 195 | 3-28-73 | 1991 | Renton, Wash. |
| Myers, Jason | 8 | 7 | 4.89 | 33 | 16 | 1 | 1 | 120 | 140 | 74 | 65 | 38 | 82 | L | L | 6-4 | 200 | 9-19-73 | 1993 | Butte Falls, Ore. |
| Ortiz, Russ | 0 | 0 | 0.25 | 34 | 0 | 0 | 23 | 37 | 16 | 2 | 1 | 20 | 63 | R | R | 6-1 | 200 | 6-5-74 | 1995 | Norman, Okla. |
| Rector, Bobby | 12 | 8 | 3.59 | 28 | 26 | 1 | 0 | 165 | 161 | 77 | 66 | 43 | 145 | R | R | 6-4 | 200 | 9-24-74 | 1994 | Imperial Beach, Calif. |
| Schramm, Carl | 7 | 3 | 3.45 | 39 | 0 | 0 | 1 | 70 | 64 | 31 | 27 | 25 | 66 | R | R | 6-4 | 200 | 6-10-70 | 1991 | Crete, Ill. |
| Tucker, Ben | 1 | 4 | 6.25 | 13 | 13 | 0 | 0 | 68 | 71 | 54 | 47 | 36 | 30 | R | R | 6-4 | 210 | 11-6-73 | 1995 | Fresno, Calif. |
| Villano, Mike | 7 | 1 | 0.72 | 39 | 2 | 0 | 8 | 88 | 48 | 12 | 7 | 33 | 133 | R | R | 6-1 | 200 | 8-10-71 | 1994 | Bay City, Mich. |
| Watson, Allen | 0 | 0 | 1.42 | 2 | 2 | 0 | 0 | 6 | 7 | 1 | 1 | 0 | 12 | L | L | 6-3 | 195 | 11-18-70 | 1991 | Middle Village, N.Y. |

## BAKERSFIELD · Class A/Co-Op

### CALIFORNIA LEAGUE

| PITCHING | W | L | ERA | G | GS | CG | SV | IP | H | R | ER | BB | SO | B | T | HT | WT | DOB | 1st Yr | Resides |
|---|---|---|---|---|---|---|---|---|---|---|---|---|---|---|---|---|---|---|---|---|
| Gomez, Dennys | 3 | 1 | 3.52 | 10 | 0 | 0 | 0 | 23 | 22 | 11 | 9 | 12 | 11 | S | R | 6-0 | 195 | 6-21-71 | 1994 | Miami, Fla. |

## MIDWEST LEAGUE

| BATTING | AVG | G | AB | R | H | 2B | 3B | HR | RBI | BB | SO | SB | CS | B | T | HT | WT | DOB | 1st Yr | Resides |
|---|---|---|---|---|---|---|---|---|---|---|---|---|---|---|---|---|---|---|---|---|
| Baeza, Art | .093 | 17 | 43 | 4 | 4 | 1 | 0 | 1 | 5 | 5 | 7 | 0 | 0 | R | R | 6-2 | 195 | 3-31-74 | 1996 | West Covina, Calif. |
| Bess, Johnny | .140 | 15 | 43 | 5 | 6 | 1 | 0 | 3 | 11 | 10 | 12 | 0 | 1 | S | R | 6-1 | 190 | 4-6-70 | 1992 | Grand Junction, Colo. |
| Calderon, Ricardo | .143 | 19 | 63 | 8 | 9 | 0 | 0 | 2 | 4 | 6 | 16 | 0 | 0 | L | L | 6-2 | 195 | 12-22-75 | 1994 | Carolina, P.R. |
| Cepeda, Malcolm | .158 | 82 | 209 | 20 | 33 | 9 | 1 | 0 | 15 | 41 | 73 | 1 | 2 | R | R | 6-1 | 190 | 11-3-72 | 1993 | Suisun City, Calif. |
| Cordero, Pablo | .089 | 33 | 79 | 5 | 7 | 3 | 0 | 0 | 4 | 6 | 17 | 2 | 0 | R | R | 6-0 | 189 | 6-24-73 | 1991 | El Seibo, D.R. |
| Cruz, Deivi | .294 | 127 | 517 | 72 | 152 | 27 | 2 | 9 | 64 | 35 | 49 | 12 | 5 | R | R | 6-0 | 175 | 6-11-75 | 1993 | Bani, D.R. |
| Denbow, Don | .278 | 92 | 302 | 64 | 84 | 17 | 2 | 21 | 62 | 81 | 123 | 19 | 5 | R | R | 6-4 | 215 | 4-30-73 | 1993 | Corsicana, Texas |
| Felix, Pedro | .265 | 93 | 321 | 36 | 85 | 12 | 2 | 5 | 36 | 18 | 65 | 5 | 2 | R | R | 6-1 | 180 | 4-27-77 | 1994 | Azua, D.R. |
| Gulseth, Mark | .262 | 125 | 423 | 61 | 111 | 35 | 4 | 5 | 41 | 89 | 95 | 4 | 2 | L | R | 6-4 | 200 | 11-12-71 | 1993 | Callaway, Minn. |
| Manning, Brian | .297 | 33 | 111 | 16 | 33 | 4 | 2 | 3 | 22 | 22 | 18 | 2 | 1 | R | R | 6-3 | 200 | 2-1-75 | 1996 | Hazlet, N.J. |
| Marval, Raul | .201 | 44 | 159 | 13 | 32 | 10 | 0 | 0 | 9 | 6 | 12 | 3 | 1 | R | R | 6-0 | 170 | 12-13-75 | 1993 | Cabodare, Venez. |
| Morales, Alex | .225 | 41 | 138 | 26 | 31 | 6 | 1 | 6 | 17 | 27 | 37 | 15 | 2 | R | R | 6-0 | 190 | 2-15-74 | 1995 | Palm Beach Gardens, Fla. |
| Oyola, Carlos | .160 | 7 | 25 | 1 | 4 | 2 | 0 | 0 | 3 | 0 | 5 | 0 | 0 | S | R | 6-2 | 175 | 12-6-77 | 1996 | Rio Piedras, P.R. |
| Poor, Jeff | .242 | 104 | 359 | 27 | 87 | 17 | 0 | 1 | 40 | 49 | 54 | 1 | 0 | R | R | 6-1 | 200 | 5-23-74 | 1994 | El Segundo, Calif. |
| Prospero, Teo | .167 | 10 | 24 | 0 | 4 | 0 | 0 | 0 | 2 | 2 | 9 | 0 | 0 | R | R | 5-11 | 170 | 2-12-77 | 1995 | San Pedro de Macoris, D.R. |
| Ramirez, Hiram | .245 | 101 | 327 | 42 | 80 | 17 | 0 | 11 | 55 | 52 | 94 | 2 | 1 | R | R | 6-2 | 200 | 9-10-72 | 1993 | Ensenada, P.R. |
| Sorrow, Michael | .241 | 61 | 224 | 30 | 54 | 7 | 1 | 0 | 13 | 42 | 33 | 0 | 1 | R | R | 6-0 | 185 | 4-2-74 | 1996 | Fayetteville, Ga. |
| Thompson, Bruce | .197 | 116 | 365 | 47 | 72 | 6 | 0 | 1 | 20 | 61 | 107 | 17 | 11 | L | R | 5-11 | 180 | 10-30-72 | 1995 | Brandon, Fla. |
| Topping, Dan | .229 | 45 | 131 | 16 | 30 | 4 | 0 | 4 | 22 | 19 | 24 | 0 | 1 | R | R | 6-0 | 210 | 1-18-76 | 1994 | St. Petersburg, Fla. |
| Torrealba, Yolvit | .000 | 1 | 4 | 0 | 0 | 0 | 0 | 0 | 0 | 0 | 1 | 0 | 0 | R | R | 5-11 | 180 | 7-19-78 | 1995 | Guarenas, Venez. |

| BATTING | AVG | G | AB | R | H | 2B | 3B | HR | RBI | BB | SO | SB | CS | B | T | HT | WT | DOB | 1st Yr | Resides |
|---|---|---|---|---|---|---|---|---|---|---|---|---|---|---|---|---|---|---|---|---|
| Watson, Jon | .261 | 81 | 318 | 46 | 83 | 15 | 2 | 0 | 25 | 31 | 38 | 23 | 5 | R | R | 6-0 | 185 | 12-18-73 | 1995 | Wallington, N.J. |
| Watson, Kevin | .115 | 32 | 78 | 8 | 9 | 1 | 1 | 5 | 11 | 10 | 34 | 0 | 0 | R | R | 6-3 | 200 | 9-8-72 | 1994 | Portland, Ore. |
| Weaver, Terry | .208 | 72 | 216 | 25 | 45 | 13 | 2 | 1 | 20 | 29 | 49 | 2 | 4 | R | R | 6-0 | 175 | 10-8-72 | 1995 | Harrisonburg, Va. |

**GAMES BY POSITION: C**—Bess 3, Poor 89, Ramirez 24, Topping 29, Torrealba 1. **1B**—Cepeda 1, Felix 2, Gulseth 121, Ramirez 16. **2B**—Cepeda 2, Marval 33, Prospero 1, Sorrow 7, J. Watson 44, Weaver 60. **3B**—Baeza 3, Cruz 7, Felix 91, Marval 8, Prospero 1, Sorrow 3, J. Watson 36. **SS**—Cruz 121, Marval 2, Oyola 7, Weaver 11. **OF**—Baeza 10, Bess 3, Calderon 18, Cepeda 30, Cordero 29, Denbow 92, Manning 33, Morales 40, Sorrow 53, Thompson 113, J. Watson 1, K. Watson 27.

| PITCHING | W | L | ERA | G | GS | CG | SV | IP | H | R | ER | BB | SO | B | T | HT | WT | DOB | 1st Yr | Resides |
|---|---|---|---|---|---|---|---|---|---|---|---|---|---|---|---|---|---|---|---|---|
| Barcelo, Lorenzo | 12 | 10 | 3.54 | 26 | 26 | 1 | 0 | 153 | 138 | 70 | 60 | 46 | 139 | R | R | 6-4 | 205 | 9-10-77 | 1994 | San Pedro de Macoris, D.R. |
| Bermudez, Manuel | 10 | 9 | 4.39 | 26 | 26 | 1 | 0 | 135 | 119 | 73 | 66 | 73 | 95 | R | R | 6-1 | 180 | 12-15-76 | 1995 | Antioch, Calif. |
| Blasingim, Joe | 1 | 4 | 4.86 | 27 | 4 | 0 | 0 | 67 | 54 | 39 | 36 | 35 | 60 | R | R | 6-4 | 190 | 2-16-73 | 1995 | Moro, Ill. |
| Brester, Jason | 10 | 9 | 3.96 | 27 | 27 | 0 | 0 | 157 | 139 | 78 | 69 | 64 | 143 | L | L | 6-3 | 190 | 12-7-76 | 1995 | Burlington, Wash. |
| Grote, Jason | 11 | 9 | 4.38 | 28 | 26 | 1 | 0 | 140 | 146 | 80 | 68 | 55 | 103 | R | R | 6-0 | 180 | 4-13-75 | 1994 | Gresham, Ore. |
| Hernandez, Santos | 3 | 3 | 1.89 | 61 | 0 | 0 | 35 | 67 | 39 | 15 | 14 | 13 | 79 | R | R | 6-1 | 172 | 11-3-72 | 1994 | Chiriqui, Panama |
| Hutzler, Jeff | 8 | 7 | 3.81 | 25 | 25 | 2 | 0 | 139 | 133 | 71 | 59 | 33 | 79 | R | R | 6-2 | 220 | 12-5-72 | 1995 | San Antonio, Texas |
| Keith, Jeff | 1 | 2 | 3.78 | 35 | 0 | 0 | 1 | 52 | 45 | 32 | 22 | 40 | 41 | L | L | 6-1 | 205 | 6-1-72 | 1994 | Troy, N.Y. |
| Knoll, Brian | 3 | 8 | 3.65 | 52 | 0 | 0 | 1 | 79 | 76 | 43 | 32 | 34 | 56 | R | R | 6-3 | 200 | 8-4-73 | 1995 | Corona, Calif. |
| Lake, Kevin | 3 | 7 | 4.45 | 43 | 4 | 0 | 0 | 97 | 107 | 57 | 48 | 38 | 85 | L | L | 6-0 | 180 | 6-28-73 | 1994 | Lompoc, Calif. |
| McMullen, Mike | 0 | 2 | 2.88 | 38 | 0 | 0 | 0 | 56 | 47 | 22 | 18 | 28 | 33 | R | R | 6-6 | 210 | 10-13-73 | 1993 | Granada Hills, Calif. |
| Stoops, Jim | 3 | 3 | 2.52 | 46 | 0 | 0 | 5 | 61 | 43 | 24 | 17 | 40 | 69 | R | R | 6-2 | 180 | 6-30-72 | 1995 | Somerset, N.J. |

# BELLINGHAM — Class A
## NORTHWEST LEAGUE

| BATTING | AVG | G | AB | R | H | 2B | 3B | HR | RBI | BB | SO | SB | CS | B | T | HT | WT | DOB | 1st Yr | Resides |
|---|---|---|---|---|---|---|---|---|---|---|---|---|---|---|---|---|---|---|---|---|
| Baeza, Art | .198 | 25 | 86 | 11 | 17 | 2 | 0 | 2 | 9 | 10 | 24 | 2 | 0 | R | R | 6-2 | 195 | 3-31-74 | 1996 | West Covina, Calif. |
| Calderon, Ricardo | .222 | 43 | 108 | 10 | 24 | 5 | 1 | 3 | 11 | 11 | 42 | 3 | 2 | L | L | 6-2 | 195 | 12-22-75 | 1994 | Carolina, P.R. |
| Caruso, Mike | .292 | 73 | 312 | 48 | 91 | 13 | 1 | 2 | 24 | 16 | 23 | 24 | 10 | S | R | 6-1 | 172 | 5-27-77 | 1996 | Coral Springs, Fla. |
| Galloway, Paul | .277 | 47 | 177 | 22 | 49 | 11 | 2 | 5 | 24 | 15 | 35 | 1 | 1 | R | R | 5-11 | 185 | 12-25-73 | 1996 | Camden, S.C. |
| Glendenning, Mike | .260 | 73 | 265 | 54 | 69 | 19 | 4 | 12 | 48 | 39 | 80 | 4 | 6 | R | R | 6-0 | 210 | 8-26-76 | 1996 | West Hills, Calif. |
| Kenna, David | .217 | 56 | 180 | 11 | 39 | 9 | 3 | 1 | 25 | 20 | 78 | 2 | 0 | L | R | 6-0 | 200 | 3-16-78 | 1996 | North Fort Myers, Fla. |
| Lopez, Luis | .000 | 1 | 2 | 0 | 0 | 0 | 0 | 0 | 0 | 0 | 2 | 0 | 0 | R | R | 6-3 | 175 | 4-13-78 | 1995 | San Felipe, Venez. |
| Manning, Brian | .297 | 35 | 138 | 26 | 41 | 6 | 2 | 3 | 22 | 13 | 27 | 0 | 3 | R | R | 6-3 | 200 | 2-1-75 | 1996 | Hazlet, N.J. |
| McGuire, Matt | .133 | 7 | 15 | 1 | 2 | 0 | 0 | 0 | 0 | 1 | 4 | 1 | 0 | R | R | 6-1 | 180 | 7-29-75 | 1996 | Chesterfield, Mo. |
| Minor, Damon | .242 | 75 | 269 | 44 | 65 | 11 | 1 | 12 | 55 | 47 | 86 | 0 | 2 | L | L | 6-7 | 230 | 1-5-74 | 1996 | Edmond, Okla. |
| Miskolczi, Levi | .214 | 57 | 187 | 19 | 40 | 6 | 0 | 0 | 17 | 3 | 36 | 4 | 2 | R | R | 6-2 | 205 | 3-25-75 | 1996 | Trenton, N.J. |
| Oliva, Osvaldo | .000 | 3 | 4 | 0 | 0 | 0 | 0 | 0 | 0 | 0 | 2 | 0 | 0 | R | R | 5-11 | 170 | 3-22-74 | 1993 | San Pedro de Macoris, D.R. |
| Prospero, Teo | .211 | 26 | 76 | 7 | 16 | 1 | 1 | 3 | 8 | 2 | 28 | 0 | 3 | R | R | 5-11 | 170 | 2-12-77 | 1995 | San Pedro de Macoris, D.R. |
| Rand, Ian | .215 | 53 | 149 | 23 | 32 | 3 | 1 | 1 | 8 | 8 | 48 | 5 | 1 | R | R | 6-4 | 200 | 1-30-77 | 1995 | La Mesa, Calif. |
| Rodriguez, Guillermo | .000 | 3 | 4 | 1 | 0 | 0 | 0 | 0 | 0 | 0 | 1 | 0 | 0 | R | R | 5-11 | 190 | 5-15-78 | 1996 | Barquisimeto, Venez. |
| Sorrow, Michael | .333 | 2 | 3 | 1 | 1 | 0 | 0 | 0 | 0 | 1 | 0 | 0 | 0 | R | R | 6-0 | 185 | 4-2-74 | 1996 | Fayetteville, Ga. |
| Topaum, Tom | .271 | 38 | 129 | 15 | 35 | 9 | 0 | 4 | 18 | 4 | 34 | 0 | 0 | R | R | 6-3 | 210 | 12-13-76 | 1996 | Gresham, Ore. |
| Torrealba, Yolvit | .267 | 48 | 150 | 23 | 40 | 4 | 0 | 1 | 10 | 9 | 27 | 4 | 1 | R | R | 5-11 | 180 | 7-19-78 | 1995 | Guarenas, Venez. |
| Van Rossum, Chris | .143 | 23 | 42 | 3 | 6 | 0 | 0 | 0 | 4 | 3 | 12 | 5 | 1 | L | L | 6-2 | 180 | 2-15-74 | 1996 | Turlock, Calif. |
| Zuniga, Tony | .299 | 69 | 264 | 36 | 79 | 11 | 1 | 2 | 35 | 34 | 47 | 0 | 5 | R | R | 6-0 | 185 | 1-13-75 | 1996 | Santa Ana, Calif. |

**GAMES BY POSITION: C**—Kenna 7, McGuire 7, Prospero 1, Topaum 30, Torrealba 36. **1B**—Calderon 1, Minor 75. **2B**—Galloway 4, Prospero 9, Zuniga 62. **3B**—Baeza 22, Galloway 41, Glendenning 10, Prospero 3. **SS**—Caruso 71, Galloway 1, Zuniga 3. **OF**—Calderon 31, Glendenning 64, Kenna 1, Lopez 1, Manning 33, Miskolczi 52, Prospero 1, Rand 50, Rodriguez 1, Sorrow 1, Van Rossum 16.

| PITCHING | W | L | ERA | G | GS | CG | SV | IP | H | R | ER | BB | SO | B | T | HT | WT | DOB | 1st Yr | Resides |
|---|---|---|---|---|---|---|---|---|---|---|---|---|---|---|---|---|---|---|---|---|
| Abreu, Jose | 1 | 0 | 4.20 | 8 | 0 | 0 | 0 | 15 | 15 | 8 | 7 | 14 | 14 | R | R | 6-2 | 194 | 5-4-75 | 1993 | Puerto Plata, D.R. |
| Blasingim, Joe | 1 | 1 | 0.78 | 4 | 0 | 0 | 0 | 23 | 16 | 5 | 2 | 5 | 23 | R | R | 6-4 | 190 | 2-16-73 | 1995 | Moro, Ill. |
| Castillo, Alberto | 3 | 0 | 1.88 | 9 | 7 | 0 | 0 | 24 | 20 | 5 | 5 | 12 | 18 | L | L | 6-3 | 205 | 7-5-75 | 1994 | New Port Richey, Fla. |
| Crabtree, Robby | 3 | 3 | 2.77 | 28 | 0 | 0 | 4 | 52 | 38 | 18 | 16 | 14 | 72 | R | R | 6-1 | 165 | 11-25-72 | 1996 | Anaheim, Calif. |
| Estrella, Luis | 4 | 0 | 1.79 | 23 | 0 | 0 | 1 | 55 | 35 | 13 | 11 | 22 | 52 | R | R | 6-2 | 215 | 10-7-74 | 1996 | Santa Ana, Calif. |
| Herrera, Luis | 0 | 1 | 12.71 | 6 | 0 | 0 | 0 | 6 | 10 | 11 | 8 | 4 | 0 | R | R | 6-6 | 215 | 12-16-76 | 1995 | Acarigua, Venez. |
| Jensen, Ryan | 2 | 4 | 4.98 | 13 | 11 | 0 | 0 | 47 | 35 | 30 | 26 | 38 | 31 | R | R | 6-0 | 200 | 9-17-75 | 1996 | West Valley, Utah |
| Larreal, Guillermo | 3 | 2 | 1.44 | 22 | 0 | 0 | 1 | 50 | 46 | 15 | 8 | 10 | 48 | R | R | 6-1 | 175 | 2-3-76 | 1995 | Maracaibo, Venez. |
| Leese, Brandon | 5 | 6 | 3.25 | 16 | 15 | 0 | 0 | 80 | 59 | 39 | 29 | 37 | 90 | R | R | 6-4 | 190 | 10-8-75 | 1996 | Lincolnshire, Ill. |
| Malloy, Bill | 2 | 3 | 5.82 | 15 | 7 | 0 | 0 | 34 | 34 | 27 | 22 | 15 | 41 | R | R | 6-2 | 210 | 5-22-75 | 1996 | Piscataway, N.J. |
| Pageler, Mick | 2 | 0 | 1.57 | 30 | 0 | 0 | 12 | 34 | 22 | 9 | 6 | 10 | 55 | R | R | 6-2 | 205 | 4-30-76 | 1996 | Mesa, Ariz. |
| Pohl, Jeff | 3 | 5 | 3.94 | 17 | 0 | 0 | 0 | 32 | 33 | 17 | 14 | 19 | 19 | R | R | 6-4 | 215 | 3-1-76 | 1996 | St. Charles, Mo. |
| Riley, Mike | 1 | 3 | 4.17 | 17 | 3 | 0 | 0 | 37 | 38 | 26 | 17 | 29 | 38 | L | L | 6-2 | 165 | 1-2-75 | 1996 | Seaford, Del. |
| Rodriguez, Luis | 0 | 0 | 0.00 | 1 | 0 | 0 | 0 | 0 | 1 | 0 | 0 | 0 | 0 | L | L | 6-3 | 205 | 3-3-76 | 1994 | Carolina, P.R. |
| Takahashi, Kurt | 1 | 2 | 4.00 | 16 | 6 | 0 | 1 | 54 | 45 | 25 | 24 | 20 | 55 | R | R | 6-4 | 215 | 2-22-74 | 1995 | Clovis, Calif. |
| Vining, Ken | 4 | 2 | 2.09 | 12 | 11 | 0 | 0 | 60 | 45 | 16 | 14 | 23 | 69 | L | L | 5-11 | 180 | 12-5-74 | 1996 | Hopkins, S.C. |
| Wells, Matt | 2 | 4 | 7.05 | 12 | 11 | 0 | 0 | 45 | 57 | 38 | 35 | 30 | 41 | R | R | 6-3 | 210 | 5-25-75 | 1996 | Quincy, Calif. |
| Woodrow, Jim | 2 | 0 | 3.96 | 17 | 0 | 0 | 0 | 25 | 26 | 16 | 11 | 14 | 25 | R | R | 6-6 | 240 | 5-4-73 | 1995 | Bradenton, Fla. |

# SEATTLE MARINERS

**Manager:** Lou Piniella.    **1996 Record:** 85-76, .528 (2nd, AL West).

| BATTING | AVG | G | AB | R | H | 2B | 3B | HR | RBI | BB | SO | SB | CS | B | T | HT | WT | DOB | 1st Yr | Resides |
|---|---|---|---|---|---|---|---|---|---|---|---|---|---|---|---|---|---|---|---|---|
| Amaral, Rich | .292 | 118 | 312 | 69 | 91 | 11 | 3 | 1 | 29 | 47 | 55 | 25 | 6 | R | R | 6-0 | 175 | 4-1-62 | 1983 | Seattle, Wash. |
| Bragg, Darren | .272 | 69 | 195 | 36 | 53 | 12 | 1 | 7 | 25 | 33 | 35 | 8 | 5 | L | R | 5-9 | 180 | 9-7-69 | 1991 | Wolcott, Conn. |
| Buhner, Jay | .271 | 150 | 564 | 107 | 153 | 29 | 0 | 44 | 138 | 84 | 159 | 0 | 1 | R | R | 6-3 | 210 | 8-13-64 | 1984 | League City, Texas |
| Cora, Joey | .291 | 144 | 530 | 90 | 154 | 37 | 6 | 6 | 45 | 35 | 32 | 5 | 5 | S | R | 5-8 | 155 | 5-14-65 | 1985 | Caguas, P.R. |
| Davis, Russ | .234 | 51 | 167 | 24 | 39 | 9 | 0 | 5 | 18 | 17 | 50 | 2 | 0 | R | R | 6-0 | 170 | 9-13-69 | 1988 | Hueytown, Ala. |
| Diaz, Alex | .241 | 38 | 79 | 11 | 19 | 2 | 0 | 1 | 5 | 2 | 8 | 6 | 3 | S | R | 5-11 | 180 | 10-5-68 | 1987 | San Sebastian, P.R. |
| Griffey, Ken | .303 | 140 | 545 | 125 | 165 | 26 | 2 | 49 | 140 | 78 | 104 | 16 | 1 | L | L | 6-3 | 205 | 11-21-69 | 1987 | Renton, Wash. |
| Hollins, Dave | .351 | 28 | 94 | 17 | 33 | 3 | 0 | 3 | 25 | 13 | 15 | 0 | 2 | S | R | 6-1 | 207 | 5-25-66 | 1987 | Orchard Park, N.Y. |
| 2-team (121 Minn.).. | .262 | 149 | 516 | 88 | 135 | 29 | 0 | 16 | 78 | 84 | 117 | 6 | 6 | | | | | | | |
| Hunter, Brian R. | .268 | 75 | 198 | 21 | 53 | 10 | 0 | 7 | 28 | 15 | 43 | 0 | 1 | R | L | 6-0 | 195 | 3-4-68 | 1987 | Anaheim, Calif. |
| Ibanez, Raul | .000 | 4 | 5 | 0 | 0 | 0 | 0 | 0 | 0 | 0 | 1 | 0 | 0 | L | R | 6-2 | 210 | 6-2-72 | 1992 | Miami, Fla. |
| Jordan, Ricky | .250 | 15 | 28 | 4 | 7 | 0 | 0 | 1 | 4 | 1 | 6 | 0 | 0 | R | R | 6-3 | 205 | 5-26-65 | 1983 | Gold River, Calif. |
| Manto, Jeff | .185 | 21 | 54 | 7 | 10 | 3 | 0 | 1 | 4 | 9 | 12 | 0 | 1 | R | R | 6-3 | 210 | 8-23-64 | 1985 | Bristol, Pa. |
| Martinez, Edgar | .327 | 139 | 499 | 121 | 163 | 52 | 2 | 26 | 103 | 123 | 84 | 3 | 3 | R | R | 5-11 | 190 | 1-2-63 | 1983 | Kirkland, Wash. |
| Martinez, Manny | .235 | 9 | 17 | 3 | 4 | 2 | 1 | 0 | 3 | 3 | 5 | 2 | 0 | R | R | 6-2 | 169 | 10-3-70 | 1988 | San Pedro de Macoris, D.R. |
| Marzano, John | .245 | 41 | 106 | 8 | 26 | 6 | 0 | 0 | 6 | 7 | 15 | 0 | 0 | R | R | 5-11 | 195 | 2-14-63 | 1985 | Philadelphia, Pa. |
| Pirkl, Greg | .190 | 7 | 21 | 2 | 4 | 1 | 0 | 1 | 1 | 0 | 3 | 0 | 0 | R | R | 6-5 | 225 | 8-7-70 | 1988 | Phoenix, Ariz. |
| Rodriguez, Alex | .358 | 146 | 601 | 141 | 215 | 54 | 1 | 36 | 123 | 59 | 104 | 15 | 4 | R | R | 6-2 | 190 | 7-27-75 | 1994 | Miami, Fla. |
| Sheets, Andy | .191 | 47 | 110 | 18 | 21 | 8 | 0 | 0 | 9 | 10 | 41 | 2 | 0 | R | R | 6-2 | 180 | 11-19-71 | 1992 | St. Amant, La. |
| Sojo, Luis | .211 | 77 | 247 | 20 | 52 | 8 | 1 | 1 | 16 | 10 | 13 | 2 | 2 | R | R | 5-11 | 174 | 1-3-66 | 1987 | Barquisimeto, Venez. |
| Sorrento, Paul | .289 | 143 | 471 | 67 | 136 | 32 | 1 | 23 | 93 | 57 | 103 | 0 | 2 | L | R | 6-2 | 220 | 11-17-65 | 1986 | Peabody, Mass. |
| Strange, Doug | .235 | 88 | 183 | 19 | 43 | 7 | 1 | 3 | 23 | 14 | 31 | 1 | 0 | S | R | 6-2 | 170 | 4-13-64 | 1985 | Scottsdale, Ariz. |
| Whiten, Mark | .300 | 40 | 140 | 31 | 42 | 7 | 0 | 12 | 33 | 21 | 40 | 2 | 1 | S | R | 6-3 | 215 | 11-25-66 | 1986 | Pensacola, Fla. |
| Widger, Chris | .182 | 8 | 11 | 1 | 2 | 0 | 0 | 0 | 0 | 0 | 5 | 0 | 0 | R | R | 6-3 | 195 | 5-21-71 | 1992 | Pennsville, N.J. |
| Wilson, Dan | .285 | 138 | 491 | 51 | 140 | 24 | 0 | 18 | 83 | 32 | 88 | 1 | 2 | R | R | 6-3 | 190 | 3-25-69 | 1990 | St. Louis Park, Ill. |

| PITCHING | W | L | ERA | G | GS | CG | SV | IP | H | R | ER | BB | SO | B | T | HT | WT | DOB | 1st Yr | Resides |
|---|---|---|---|---|---|---|---|---|---|---|---|---|---|---|---|---|---|---|---|---|
| Ayala, Bobby | 6 | 3 | 5.88 | 50 | 0 | 0 | 3 | 67 | 65 | 45 | 44 | 25 | 61 | R | R | 6-3 | 200 | 7-8-69 | 1988 | Oxnard, Calif. |
| Bosio, Chris | 4 | 4 | 5.93 | 18 | 9 | 0 | 0 | 61 | 72 | 44 | 40 | 24 | 39 | R | R | 6-3 | 225 | 4-3-63 | 1982 | Shingle Springs, Calif. |
| Carmona, Rafael | 8 | 3 | 4.28 | 53 | 1 | 0 | 1 | 90 | 95 | 47 | 43 | 55 | 62 | L | R | 6-2 | 185 | 10-2-72 | 1993 | Comerio, P.R. |
| Charlton, Norm | 4 | 7 | 4.04 | 70 | 0 | 0 | 20 | 76 | 68 | 37 | 34 | 38 | 73 | S | L | 6-3 | 205 | 1-6-63 | 1984 | Jamaica Beach, Texas |
| Davis, Tim | 2 | 2 | 4.01 | 40 | 0 | 0 | 0 | 43 | 43 | 21 | 19 | 17 | 34 | L | L | 5-11 | 165 | 7-14-70 | 1992 | Bristol, Fla. |
| Davison, Scott | 0 | 0 | 9.00 | 5 | 0 | 0 | 0 | 9 | 11 | 9 | 9 | 3 | 9 | R | R | 6-0 | 190 | 10-16-70 | 1988 | Redondo Beach, Calif. |
| Guetterman, Lee | 0 | 2 | 4.09 | 17 | 0 | 0 | 0 | 11 | 11 | 8 | 5 | 10 | 6 | L | L | 6-8 | 225 | 11-22-58 | 1981 | Lenoir City, Tenn. |
| Harikkala, Tim | 0 | 1 | 12.46 | 1 | 1 | 0 | 0 | 4 | 4 | 6 | 6 | 2 | 1 | R | R | 6-2 | 185 | 7-15-71 | 1992 | Lake Worth, Fla. |
| Hitchcock, Sterling | 13 | 9 | 5.35 | 35 | 35 | 0 | 0 | 197 | 245 | 131 | 117 | 73 | 132 | L | L | 6-1 | 195 | 4-29-71 | 1989 | Seffner, Fla. |
| Hurtado, Edwin | 2 | 5 | 7.74 | 16 | 4 | 0 | 2 | 48 | 61 | 42 | 41 | 30 | 36 | R | R | 6-2 | 225 | 2-1-70 | 1991 | Naguanagua, Venez. |
| Jackson, Mike | 1 | 1 | 3.63 | 73 | 0 | 0 | 6 | 72 | 61 | 32 | 29 | 24 | 70 | R | R | 6-2 | 223 | 12-22-64 | 1984 | Spring, Texas |
| Johnson, Randy | 5 | 0 | 3.67 | 14 | 8 | 0 | 1 | 61 | 48 | 27 | 25 | 25 | 85 | R | L | 6-10 | 225 | 9-10-63 | 1985 | Bellevue, Wash. |
| Klink, Joe | 0 | 0 | 3.86 | 3 | 0 | 0 | 0 | 2 | 3 | 1 | 1 | 1 | 2 | L | L | 5-11 | 170 | 2-3-62 | 1983 | Pembroke Pines, Fla. |
| McCarthy, Greg | 0 | 0 | 1.86 | 10 | 0 | 0 | 0 | 10 | 8 | 2 | 2 | 4 | 7 | L | L | 6-2 | 193 | 10-30-68 | 1987 | Shelton, Conn. |
| Meacham, Rusty | 1 | 1 | 5.53 | 15 | 5 | 0 | 1 | 42 | 57 | 27 | 26 | 13 | 25 | R | R | 6-2 | 175 | 1-27-68 | 1988 | Palm City, Fla. |
| Menhart, Paul | 2 | 2 | 7.29 | 11 | 6 | 0 | 0 | 42 | 55 | 36 | 34 | 25 | 18 | R | R | 6-2 | 190 | 3-25-69 | 1990 | Conyers, Ga. |
| Milacki, Bob | 1 | 4 | 6.86 | 7 | 4 | 0 | 0 | 21 | 30 | 20 | 16 | 15 | 13 | R | R | 6-4 | 230 | 7-28-64 | 1984 | Lake Havasu, Ariz. |
| Minor, Blas | 0 | 1 | 4.97 | 11 | 0 | 0 | 0 | 25 | 27 | 14 | 14 | 11 | 14 | R | R | 6-3 | 200 | 3-20-66 | 1988 | Gilbert, Ariz. |
| Moyer, Jamie | 6 | 2 | 3.31 | 11 | 11 | 0 | 0 | 71 | 66 | 36 | 26 | 19 | 29 | L | L | 6-0 | 170 | 11-18-62 | 1984 | Granger, Ill. |
| 2-team (23 Boston).. | 13 | 3 | 3.98 | 34 | 21 | 0 | 0 | 161 | 177 | 86 | 71 | 46 | 79 | | | | | | | |
| Mulholland, Terry | 5 | 4 | 4.67 | 12 | 12 | 0 | 0 | 69 | 75 | 38 | 36 | 28 | 34 | R | L | 6-3 | 200 | 3-9-63 | 1984 | Scottsdale, Ariz. |
| Suzuki, Mac | 0 | 0 | 20.25 | 1 | 0 | 0 | 0 | 1 | 2 | 3 | 3 | 2 | 1 | R | R | 6-4 | 195 | 5-31-75 | 1992 | Kobe, Japan |
| Torres, Salomon | 3 | 3 | 4.59 | 10 | 7 | 1 | 0 | 49 | 44 | 27 | 25 | 23 | 36 | R | R | 5-11 | 150 | 3-11-72 | 1990 | San Pedro de Macoris, D.R. |
| Wagner, Matt | 3 | 5 | 6.98 | 15 | 14 | 1 | 0 | 80 | 91 | 63 | 62 | 38 | 41 | R | R | 6-5 | 215 | 4-4-72 | 1994 | Cedar Falls, Iowa |
| Wells, Bob | 12 | 7 | 5.30 | 36 | 16 | 1 | 0 | 131 | 141 | 78 | 77 | 46 | 94 | R | R | 6-0 | 190 | 11-1-66 | 1989 | Cowiche, Wash. |
| Wolcott, Bob | 7 | 10 | 5.73 | 30 | 28 | 1 | 0 | 149 | 179 | 101 | 95 | 54 | 78 | R | R | 6-0 | 190 | 9-8-73 | 1992 | Medford, Ore. |

## FIELDING

| Catcher | PCT | G | PO | A | E | DP | PB |
|---|---|---|---|---|---|---|---|
| Marzano | .986 | 39 | 194 | 10 | 3 | 1 | 3 |
| Widger | .905 | 7 | 18 | 1 | 2 | 0 | 0 |
| Wilson | .996 | 135 | 834 | 58 | 4 | 5 | 5 |

| First Base | PCT | G | PO | A | E | DP |
|---|---|---|---|---|---|---|
| Amaral | 1.000 | 10 | 11 | 0 | 0 | 2 |
| Hollins | .000 | 1 | 0 | 0 | 0 | 0 |
| Hunter | .991 | 41 | 219 | 7 | 2 | 19 |
| Jordan | 1.000 | 9 | 40 | 1 | 0 | 5 |
| E. Martinez | .967 | 4 | 28 | 1 | 1 | 3 |
| Sorrento | .990 | 138 | 957 | 80 | 11 | 112 |
| Strange | 1.000 | 3 | 4 | 0 | 0 | 1 |

| Second Base | PCT | G | PO | A | E | DP |
|---|---|---|---|---|---|---|
| Amaral | 1.000 | 15 | 16 | 21 | 0 | 2 |
| Cora | .979 | 140 | 296 | 314 | 13 | 88 |

| | PCT | G | PO | A | E | DP |
|---|---|---|---|---|---|---|
| Sheets | .959 | 18 | 18 | 29 | 2 | 9 |
| Sojo | .981 | 27 | 42 | 59 | 2 | 15 |
| Strange | 1.000 | 3 | 0 | 1 | 0 | 0 |

| Third Base | PCT | G | PO | A | E | DP |
|---|---|---|---|---|---|---|
| Amaral | .000 | 1 | 0 | 0 | 0 | 0 |
| Cora | .000 | 1 | 0 | 0 | 0 | 0 |
| Davis | .933 | 51 | 31 | 67 | 7 | 5 |
| Hollins | .961 | 28 | 21 | 53 | 3 | 6 |
| Manto | .971 | 16 | 8 | 26 | 1 | 2 |
| E. Martinez | 1.000 | 2 | 1 | 0 | 0 | 0 |
| Sheets | .947 | 25 | 16 | 38 | 3 | 7 |
| Sojo | .940 | 33 | 24 | 55 | 5 | 7 |
| Strange | .961 | 39 | 11 | 38 | 2 | 3 |

| Shortstop | PCT | G | PO | A | E | DP |
|---|---|---|---|---|---|---|
| Hollins | .000 | 1 | 0 | 0 | 1 | 0 |
| Rodriguez | .977 | 146 | 238 | 403 | 15 | 92 |
| Sheets | 1.000 | 7 | 6 | 10 | 0 | 2 |
| Sojo | .987 | 19 | 31 | 44 | 1 | 10 |

| Outfield | PCT | G | PO | A | E | DP |
|---|---|---|---|---|---|---|
| Amaral | 1.000 | 91 | 168 | 3 | 0 | 0 |
| Bragg | .992 | 63 | 118 | 7 | 1 | 1 |
| Buhner | .989 | 142 | 251 | 9 | 3 | 1 |
| Diaz | .982 | 28 | 55 | 1 | 1 | 0 |
| Griffey | .990 | 137 | 376 | 10 | 4 | 1 |
| Hunter | .955 | 29 | 61 | 3 | 3 | 0 |
| M. Martinez | 1.000 | 8 | 12 | 2 | 0 | 0 |
| Strange | 1.000 | 11 | 11 | 0 | 0 | 0 |
| Whiten | .969 | 39 | 90 | 4 | 3 | 0 |

# MARINERS

**AL MVP Alex Rodriguez and Mariners' minor league Player of the Year Jose Cruz Jr.**

FRANK RAGSDALE

## FARM SYSTEM

**Director of Player Development:** Larry Beinfest

| Class | Farm Team | League | W | L | Pct. | Finish* | Manager | First Yr |
|---|---|---|---|---|---|---|---|---|
| AAA | Tacoma (Wash.) Rainiers | Pacific Coast | 69 | 73 | .486 | 7th (10) | Dave Myers | 1995 |
| AA | Port City (N.C.) Roosters | Southern | 56 | 84 | .400 | 10th (10) | Orlando Gomez | 1995 |
| #A | Lancaster (Calif.) Jethawks | California | 71 | 69 | .507 | 6th (10) | Dave Brundage | 1996 |
| A | Wisconsin Timber Rattlers | Midwest | 77 | 58 | .570 | 2nd (14) | Mike Goff | 1993 |
| A | Everett (Wash.) Aquasox | Northwest | 33 | 42 | .440 | 6th (8) | Roger Hansen | 1995 |
| R | Peoria (Ariz.) Mariners | Arizona | 29 | 27 | .518 | 3rd (6) | Tom LeVasseur | 1988 |

*Finish in overall standings (No. of teams in league)   #Advanced level

## ORGANIZATION LEADERS

### MAJOR LEAGUERS

**BATTING**
| | | |
|---|---|---|
| *AVG | Alex Rodriguez | .358 |
| R | Alex Rodriguez | 141 |
| H | Alex Rodriguez | 215 |
| TB | Alex Rodriguez | 379 |
| 2B | Alex Rodriguez | 54 |
| 3B | Joey Cora | 6 |
| HR | Ken Griffey | 49 |
| RBI | Ken Griffey | 140 |
| BB | Edgar Martinez | 123 |
| SO | Jay Buhner | 159 |
| SB | Rich Amaral | 25 |

**PITCHING**
| | | |
|---|---|---|
| W | Sterling Hitchcock | 13 |
| L | Bob Wolcott | 10 |
| #ERA | Norm Charlton | 4.04 |
| G | Mike Jackson | 73 |
| CG | Four tied at | 1 |
| SV | Norm Charlton | 20 |
| IP | Sterling Hitchcock | 197 |
| BB | Sterling Hitchcock | 73 |
| SO | Sterling Hitchcock | 132 |

**Ken Griffey.** 49 homers

THE SPORTS GROUP

### MINOR LEAGUERS

**BATTING**
| | | |
|---|---|---|
| *AVG | David Arias, Wisconsin | .322 |
| R | Shane Monahan, Lancaster | 107 |
| H | Shane Monahan, Lancaster | 164 |
| TB | Shane Monahan, Lancaster | 261 |
| 2B | Karl Thompson, Wisconsin | 36 |
| 3B | Shane Monahan, Lancaster | 12 |
| HR | James Bonnici, Tacoma | 26 |
| RBI | Jesus Marquez, Lancaster | 106 |
| BB | Jason Cook, Lancaster | 89 |
| SO | Scott Smith, Wisconsin/Lancaster | 148 |
| SB | Kyle Towner, Bakersfield | 53 |

**PITCHING**
| | | |
|---|---|---|
| W | Two tied at | 15 |
| L | Marino Santano, Lancaster | 15 |
| #ERA | Matt Wagner, Tacoma | 2.41 |
| G | Dean Crow, Port City | 60 |
| CG | Bob Milacki, Tacoma | 5 |
| SV | Dean Crow, Port City | 26 |
| IP | Ryan Franklin, Port City | 182 |
| BB | Ivan Montane, Lancaster/Port City | 75 |
| SO | Marino Santana, Lancaster | 167 |

*Minimum 250 At-Bats   #Minimum 75 Innings

## TOP 10 PROSPECTS

**How the Mariners Top 10 prospects, as judged by Baseball America prior to the 1996 season, fared in 1996:**

STEVE MOORE

**Jason Varitek**

| Player, Pos. | Club (Class—League) | AVG | AB | R | H | 2B | 3B | HR | RBI | SB |
|---|---|---|---|---|---|---|---|---|---|---|
| 1. Jose Cruz Jr., of | Port City (AA—Southern) | .282 | 181 | 39 | 51 | 10 | 2 | 3 | 31 | 5 |
| | Tacoma (AAA—Pacific Coast) | .237 | 76 | 15 | 18 | 1 | 2 | 6 | 15 | 1 |
| | Lancaster (A—California) | .325 | 203 | 38 | 66 | 17 | 1 | 6 | 43 | 7 |
| 2. Jason Varitek, c | Port City (AA—Southern) | .262 | 503 | 63 | 132 | 34 | 1 | 12 | 67 | 7 |
| 3. *Desi Relaford, 2b | Tacoma (AAA—Pacific Coast) | .205 | 317 | 27 | 65 | 12 | 0 | 4 | 32 | 10 |
| | Scranton (AAA—International) | .235 | 85 | 12 | 20 | 4 | 1 | 1 | 11 | 7 |
| | Philadelphia | .175 | 40 | 2 | 7 | 2 | 0 | 0 | 1 | 1 |
| 7. Chris Widger, c | Tacoma (AAA—Pacific Coast) | .304 | 352 | 42 | 107 | 20 | 2 | 13 | 48 | 7 |
| | Seattle | .182 | 11 | 1 | 2 | 0 | 0 | 0 | 0 | 0 |
| 8. Raul Ibanez, of | Tacoma (AAA—Pacific Coast) | .284 | 405 | 59 | 115 | 20 | 3 | 11 | 47 | 7 |
| | Port City (AA—Southern) | .368 | 76 | 12 | 28 | 8 | 1 | 1 | 13 | 3 |
| | Seattle | .000 | 5 | 0 | 0 | 0 | 0 | 0 | 0 | 0 |
| 9. Russ Davis, 3b | Seattle | .234 | 167 | 24 | 39 | 9 | 0 | 5 | 18 | 2 |

| Player, Pos. | Club (Class—League) | W | L | ERA | G | SV | IP | H | BB | SO |
|---|---|---|---|---|---|---|---|---|---|---|
| 4. Matt Wagner, rhp | Tacoma (AAA—Pacific Coast) | 9 | 2 | 2.41 | 15 | 0 | 93 | 89 | 30 | 82 |
| | Seattle | 3 | 5 | 6.86 | 15 | 0 | 80 | 91 | 38 | 41 |
| 5. Mac Suzuki, rhp | Port City (AA—Southern) | 3 | 6 | 4.72 | 16 | 0 | 74 | 69 | 32 | 66 |
| | Tacoma (AAA—Pacific Coast) | 0 | 3 | 7.25 | 13 | 0 | 22 | 31 | 12 | 14 |
| | Seattle | 0 | 0 | 20.25 | 1 | 0 | 1 | 2 | 2 | 1 |
| 6. Bob Wolcott, rhp | Seattle | 7 | 10 | 5.73 | 30 | 0 | 149 | 179 | 54 | 78 |
| | Tacoma (AAA—Pacific Coast) | 0 | 2 | 7.30 | 3 | 0 | 12 | 17 | 3 | 16 |
| | Lancaster (A—California) | 0 | 1 | 10.50 | 1 | 0 | 6 | 9 | 0 | 6 |
| 10. Rafael Carmona, rhp | Tacoma (AAA—Pacific Coast) | 0 | 0 | 1.42 | 4 | 0 | 6 | 5 | 5 | 9 |
| | Seattle | 8 | 3 | 4.28 | 53 | 1 | 90 | 95 | 55 | 62 |

*Traded to Phillies

## PACIFIC COAST LEAGUE

| BATTING | AVG | G | AB | R | H | 2B | 3B | HR | RBI | BB | SO | SB | CS | B | T | HT | WT | DOB | 1st Yr | Resides |
|---|---|---|---|---|---|---|---|---|---|---|---|---|---|---|---|---|---|---|---|---|
| Bonnici, James | .292 | 139 | 497 | 76 | 145 | 25 | 0 | 26 | 74 | 59 | 100 | 1 | 3 | R | R | 6-4 | 230 | 1-21-72 | 1991 | Ortonville, Mich. |
| Bragg, Darren | .282 | 20 | 71 | 17 | 20 | 8 | 0 | 3 | 8 | 14 | 14 | 1 | 0 | L | R | 5-9 | 180 | 9-7-69 | 1991 | Wolcott, Conn. |
| Bryant, Scott | .266 | 58 | 214 | 21 | 57 | 10 | 3 | 2 | 19 | 13 | 41 | 0 | 3 | R | R | 6-2 | 215 | 10-31-67 | 1989 | San Antonio, Texas |
| Cruz, Jose | .237 | 22 | 76 | 15 | 18 | 1 | 2 | 6 | 15 | 18 | 12 | 1 | 1 | S | R | 6-0 | 200 | 4-19-74 | 1995 | Houston, Texas |
| Diaz, Alex | .244 | 44 | 176 | 19 | 43 | 5 | 0 | 0 | 7 | 7 | 20 | 5 | 6 | S | R | 5-11 | 180 | 10-5-68 | 1987 | San Sebastian, P.R. |
| Diaz, Eddy | .280 | 107 | 422 | 63 | 118 | 28 | 4 | 13 | 58 | 15 | 38 | 3 | 4 | R | R | 5-10 | 160 | 9-29-71 | 1990 | Barquisimeto, Venez. |
| Drinkwater, Sean | .258 | 9 | 31 | 2 | 8 | 1 | 0 | 0 | 1 | 1 | 5 | 0 | 0 | R | R | 6-3 | 195 | 6-22-71 | 1992 | El Toro, Calif. |
| Friedman, Jason | .164 | 20 | 73 | 9 | 12 | 6 | 1 | 1 | 4 | 2 | 14 | 0 | 1 | L | L | 6-1 | 200 | 8-8-69 | 1989 | Cypress, Calif. |
| Hunter, Brian | .348 | 25 | 92 | 19 | 32 | 6 | 1 | 7 | 24 | 9 | 11 | 1 | 0 | R | L | 6-0 | 195 | 3-4-68 | 1987 | Anaheim, Calif. |
| Ibanez, Raul | .284 | 111 | 405 | 59 | 115 | 20 | 3 | 11 | 47 | 44 | 56 | 7 | 7 | L | R | 6-2 | 210 | 6-2-72 | 1992 | Miami, Fla. |
| Jordan, Ricky | .200 | 13 | 50 | 3 | 10 | 0 | 0 | 2 | 7 | 5 | 6 | 0 | 0 | R | R | 6-3 | 205 | 5-26-65 | 1983 | Gold River, Calif. |
| Knapp, Mike | .190 | 59 | 184 | 12 | 35 | 10 | 1 | 3 | 18 | 21 | 51 | 1 | 2 | R | R | 6-0 | 195 | 10-6-64 | 1986 | Sacramento, Calif. |
| Martinez, Manny | .314 | 66 | 277 | 54 | 87 | 15 | 1 | 4 | 24 | 23 | 41 | 14 | 10 | R | R | 6-2 | 169 | 10-3-70 | 1988 | San Pedro de Macoris, D.R. |
| Peguero, Julio | .280 | 100 | 328 | 41 | 92 | 15 | 1 | 1 | 21 | 20 | 47 | 7 | 7 | S | R | 5-11 | 160 | 9-7-68 | 1987 | Santo Domingo, D.R. |
| Pirkl, Greg | .302 | 88 | 348 | 50 | 105 | 22 | 2 | 21 | 75 | 14 | 58 | 1 | 1 | R | R | 6-5 | 225 | 8-7-70 | 1988 | Phoenix, Ariz. |
| Pozo, Arquimedez | .279 | 95 | 365 | 55 | 102 | 12 | 5 | 15 | 64 | 39 | 40 | 3 | 3 | R | R | 5-10 | 160 | 8-24-73 | 1991 | Santo Domingo, D.R. |
| Reimer, Kevin | .280 | 24 | 93 | 9 | 26 | 3 | 0 | 3 | 11 | 3 | 12 | 0 | 0 | L | R | 6-2 | 230 | 6-28-64 | 1985 | Enderby, B.C. |
| 2-team (54 Salt Lake) | .283 | 78 | 286 | 38 | 81 | 12 | 0 | 13 | 44 | 14 | 43 | 4 | 1 | | | | | | | |
| Relaford, Desi | .205 | 93 | 317 | 27 | 65 | 12 | 0 | 4 | 32 | 23 | 58 | 10 | 6 | S | R | 5-8 | 155 | 9-16-73 | 1991 | Jacksonville, Fla. |
| Rodriguez, Alex | .200 | 2 | 5 | 0 | 1 | 0 | 0 | 0 | 0 | 2 | 1 | 0 | 0 | R | R | 6-2 | 190 | 7-27-75 | 1994 | Miami, Fla. |
| Saunders, Doug | .252 | 40 | 131 | 16 | 33 | 6 | 0 | 3 | 13 | 19 | 22 | 1 | 0 | R | R | 6-0 | 172 | 12-13-69 | 1988 | Port St. Lucie, Fla. |
| Sheets, Andy | .358 | 62 | 232 | 44 | 83 | 16 | 5 | 5 | 33 | 25 | 56 | 6 | 4 | R | R | 6-2 | 180 | 11-19-71 | 1992 | St. Amant, La. |
| Vazquez, Ramon | .224 | 18 | 49 | 7 | 11 | 2 | 1 | 0 | 4 | 4 | 12 | 0 | 0 | L | R | 5-11 | 170 | 8-21-76 | 1995 | Cayey, P.R. |
| Wakamatsu, Don | .000 | 1 | 3 | 0 | 0 | 0 | 0 | 0 | 0 | 0 | 0 | 0 | 0 | R | R | 6-2 | 200 | 2-22-63 | 1985 | Hayward, Calif. |
| Widger, Chris | .304 | 97 | 352 | 42 | 107 | 20 | 2 | 13 | 48 | 27 | 62 | 7 | 1 | R | R | 6-3 | 195 | 5-21-71 | 1992 | Pennsville, N.J. |
| Yelding, Eric | .267 | 19 | 60 | 5 | 16 | 2 | 1 | 0 | 5 | 5 | 12 | 3 | 4 | R | R | 5-11 | 165 | 2-22-65 | 1984 | Daphne, Ala. |

| PITCHING | W | L | ERA | G | GS | CG | SV | IP | H | R | ER | BB | SO | B | T | HT | WT | DOB | 1st Yr | Resides |
|---|---|---|---|---|---|---|---|---|---|---|---|---|---|---|---|---|---|---|---|---|
| Ayala, Bobby | 0 | 0 | 0.00 | 1 | 1 | 0 | 0 | 1 | 0 | 0 | 0 | 1 | 1 | R | R | 6-3 | 200 | 7-8-69 | 1988 | Oxnard, Calif. |
| Bosio, Chris | 0 | 0 | 0.00 | 2 | 1 | 0 | 0 | 4 | 2 | 0 | 0 | 0 | 3 | R | R | 6-3 | 225 | 4-3-63 | 1982 | Shingle Springs, Calif. |
| Brosnan, Jason | 3 | 1 | 2.84 | 12 | 2 | 0 | 1 | 32 | 19 | 14 | 10 | 15 | 26 | L | L | 6-1 | 190 | 1-26-68 | 1989 | San Leandro, Calif. |
| Butcher, Mike | 1 | 4 | 11.79 | 14 | 8 | 0 | 0 | 42 | 70 | 59 | 55 | 27 | 42 | R | R | 6-1 | 200 | 5-10-65 | 1986 | Phoenix, Ariz. |
| Carmona, Rafael | 0 | 0 | 1.42 | 4 | 1 | 0 | 0 | 6 | 5 | 1 | 1 | 5 | 9 | R | R | 6-2 | 185 | 10-2-72 | 1993 | Comerio, P.R. |
| Davis, Tim | 0 | 1 | 5.29 | 8 | 1 | 0 | 0 | 17 | 19 | 12 | 10 | 10 | 19 | L | L | 5-11 | 165 | 7-14-70 | 1992 | Bristol, Fla. |
| Davison, Scott | 1 | 1 | 0.39 | 17 | 0 | 0 | 9 | 23 | 13 | 2 | 1 | 6 | 23 | R | R | 6-0 | 190 | 10-16-70 | 1988 | Redondo Beach, Calif. |
| Fernandez, Osvaldo | 0 | 0 | 5.40 | 1 | 1 | 0 | 0 | 3 | 4 | 2 | 2 | 0 | 4 | L | L | 6-2 | 193 | 4-15-70 | 1994 | San Fernando, Calif. |
| Gould, Clint | 0 | 1 | 4.50 | 1 | 1 | 0 | 0 | 4 | 4 | 3 | 2 | 2 | 2 | R | R | 6-2 | 230 | 8-18-71 | 1994 | Kent, Wash. |
| Guetterman, Lee | 2 | 2 | 3.77 | 25 | 0 | 0 | 0 | 29 | 27 | 14 | 12 | 10 | 28 | L | L | 6-8 | 225 | 11-22-58 | 1981 | Lenoir City, Tenn. |
| Guzman, Jose | 0 | 1 | 3.52 | 5 | 2 | 0 | 0 | 15 | 14 | 7 | 6 | 6 | 11 | R | R | 6-3 | 195 | 4-9-63 | 1981 | Arlington, Texas |
| Harikkala, Tim | 8 | 12 | 4.83 | 27 | 27 | 1 | 0 | 158 | 204 | 98 | 85 | 48 | 115 | R | R | 6-2 | 185 | 7-15-71 | 1992 | Lake Worth, Fla. |
| Hurtado, Edwin | 1 | 2 | 3.73 | 5 | 4 | 0 | 0 | 31 | 23 | 13 | 13 | 12 | 16 | R | R | 6-2 | 170 | 2-1-70 | 1991 | Naguanagua, Venez. |
| Klink, Joe | 1 | 0 | 4.05 | 7 | 0 | 0 | 0 | 7 | 9 | 3 | 3 | 3 | 4 | L | L | 5-11 | 170 | 2-3-62 | 1983 | Pembroke Pines, Fla. |
| Lowe, Derek | 6 | 9 | 4.54 | 17 | 16 | 1 | 0 | 105 | 118 | 64 | 53 | 37 | 54 | R | R | 6-6 | 170 | 6-1-73 | 1991 | Dearborn, Mich. |
| McCarthy, Greg | 4 | 2 | 3.29 | 39 | 0 | 0 | 4 | 68 | 58 | 31 | 25 | 53 | 90 | L | L | 6-2 | 193 | 10-30-68 | 1987 | Shelton, Conn. |
| Meacham, Rusty | 2 | 1 | 2.29 | 7 | 2 | 0 | 2 | 20 | 13 | 7 | 5 | 5 | 20 | R | R | 6-2 | 175 | 1-27-68 | 1988 | Palm City, Fla. |
| Menhart, Paul | 0 | 3 | 11.08 | 6 | 6 | 0 | 0 | 26 | 53 | 33 | 32 | 16 | 12 | R | R | 6-2 | 190 | 3-25-69 | 1990 | Conyers, Ga. |
| Milacki, Bob | 13 | 3 | 2.74 | 23 | 23 | 5 | 0 | 164 | 131 | 62 | 50 | 37 | 99 | R | R | 6-4 | 200 | 7-28-64 | 1984 | Lake Havasu, Ariz. |
| Minor, Blas | 1 | 2 | 8.38 | 7 | 0 | 0 | 1 | 10 | 15 | 11 | 9 | 3 | 8 | R | R | 6-3 | 200 | 3-20-66 | 1988 | Gilbert, Ariz. |
| Phillips, Tony | 1 | 3 | 6.40 | 21 | 3 | 0 | 1 | 52 | 70 | 40 | 37 | 9 | 24 | R | R | 6-4 | 195 | 6-9-69 | 1991 | Hattiesburg, Miss. |
| Pirkl, Greg | 0 | 0 | 0.00 | 2 | 0 | 0 | 0 | 6 | 1 | 0 | 0 | 0 | 2 | R | R | 6-5 | 225 | 8-7-70 | 1988 | Phoenix, Ariz. |
| Suzuki, Mac | 0 | 3 | 7.25 | 13 | 2 | 0 | 0 | 22 | 31 | 19 | 18 | 12 | 14 | R | R | 6-4 | 195 | 5-31-75 | 1992 | Kobe, Japan |
| Torres, Salomon | 7 | 10 | 5.29 | 22 | 21 | 3 | 0 | 134 | 150 | 87 | 79 | 52 | 121 | R | R | 5-11 | 150 | 3-11-72 | 1990 | San Pedro de Macoris, D.R. |
| Urso, Sal | 6 | 2 | 2.35 | 46 | 0 | 0 | 3 | 73 | 69 | 22 | 19 | 32 | 45 | R | L | 5-11 | 195 | 1-19-72 | 1990 | Tampa, Fla. |
| Wagner, Matt | 9 | 2 | 2.41 | 15 | 15 | 0 | 0 | 93 | 89 | 30 | 25 | 30 | 82 | R | R | 6-5 | 215 | 4-4-72 | 1994 | Cedar Falls, Iowa |
| Wertz, Bill | 0 | 3 | 5.01 | 16 | 2 | 0 | 0 | 32 | 46 | 21 | 18 | 23 | 25 | R | R | 6-6 | 220 | 1-15-67 | 1989 | Cleveland, Ohio |
| Witte, Trey | 2 | 2 | 2.15 | 35 | 0 | 0 | 7 | 46 | 47 | 12 | 11 | 13 | 22 | R | R | 6-1 | 190 | 1-15-70 | 1991 | Houston, Texas |
| Wolcott, Bob | 0 | 2 | 7.30 | 3 | 3 | 0 | 0 | 12 | 17 | 13 | 10 | 3 | 16 | R | R | 6-0 | 190 | 9-8-73 | 1992 | Medford, Ore. |
| Zimmerman, Mike | 1 | 1 | 9.17 | 13 | 0 | 0 | 0 | 18 | 23 | 19 | 18 | 13 | 13 | R | R | 6-0 | 180 | 2-6-69 | 1990 | Brooklyn, N.Y. |

### FIELDING

| Catcher | PCT | G | PO | A | E | DP | PB |
|---|---|---|---|---|---|---|---|
| Bonnici | 1.000 | 2 | 13 | 0 | 0 | 0 | 0 |
| Knapp | .988 | 57 | 369 | 32 | 5 | 3 | 9 |
| Wakamatsu | 1.000 | 1 | 8 | 1 | 0 | 0 | 0 |
| Widger | .988 | 89 | 622 | 41 | 8 | 9 | 3 |

| First Base | PCT | G | PO | A | E | DP |
|---|---|---|---|---|---|---|
| Bonnici | .989 | 90 | 777 | 35 | 9 | 75 |
| Diaz | 1.000 | 1 | 2 | 0 | 0 | 0 |
| Drinkwater | 1.000 | 1 | 11 | 0 | 0 | 1 |
| Friedman | 1.000 | 2 | 11 | 2 | 0 | 2 |
| Hunter | 1.000 | 4 | 22 | 2 | 0 | 3 |
| Ibanez | 1.000 | 2 | 4 | 0 | 0 | 0 |
| Pirkl | .990 | 46 | 385 | 32 | 4 | 37 |
| Reimer | .972 | 4 | 33 | 2 | 1 | 2 |

| Second Base | PCT | G | PO | A | E | DP |
|---|---|---|---|---|---|---|
| Diaz | .972 | 21 | 38 | 66 | 3 | 16 |
| Pozo | .989 | 18 | 29 | 62 | 1 | 12 |
| Relaford | .964 | 73 | 148 | 249 | 15 | 53 |

| | PCT | G | PO | A | E | DP |
|---|---|---|---|---|---|---|
| Sheets | 1.000 | 5 | 4 | 16 | 0 | 2 |
| Vazquez | 1.000 | 13 | 20 | 31 | 0 | 10 |
| Yelding | .909 | 17 | 35 | 25 | 6 | 6 |

| Third Base | PCT | G | PO | A | E | DP |
|---|---|---|---|---|---|---|
| Bonnici | .733 | 7 | 5 | 6 | 4 | 2 |
| Bryant | .889 | 5 | 1 | 7 | 1 | 0 |
| Diaz | 1.000 | 1 | 2 | 0 | 0 | 0 |
| Diaz | 1.000 | 2 | 10 | 18 | 0 | 1 |
| Drinkwater | .941 | 6 | 2 | 14 | 1 | 1 |
| Pozo | .930 | 74 | 44 | 115 | 12 | 17 |
| Saunders | .951 | 36 | 36 | 81 | 6 | 5 |
| Sheets | 1.000 | 2 | 3 | 7 | 0 | 0 |
| Yelding | .500 | 2 | 0 | 1 | 1 | 1 |

| Shortstop | PCT | G | PO | A | E | DP |
|---|---|---|---|---|---|---|
| Diaz | .962 | 65 | 87 | 193 | 11 | 37 |
| Drinkwater | 1.000 | 1 | 3 | 5 | 0 | 2 |
| Relaford | .943 | 19 | 26 | 57 | 5 | 13 |

| | PCT | G | PO | A | E | DP |
|---|---|---|---|---|---|---|
| Rodriguez | .833 | 2 | 1 | 4 | 1 | 2 |
| Sheets | .945 | 55 | 88 | 153 | 14 | 29 |
| Vazquez | .938 | 4 | 1 | 14 | 1 | 1 |

| Outfield | PCT | G | PO | A | E | DP |
|---|---|---|---|---|---|---|
| Bragg | 1.000 | 20 | 32 | 2 | 0 | 0 |
| Bryant | .976 | 49 | 80 | 3 | 2 | 0 |
| Cruz | 1.000 | 22 | 36 | 4 | 0 | 0 |
| Diaz | .975 | 42 | 74 | 5 | 2 | 0 |
| Diaz | 1.000 | 5 | 6 | 0 | 0 | 0 |
| Friedman | 1.000 | 2 | 3 | 0 | 0 | 0 |
| Hunter | .963 | 22 | 23 | 3 | 1 | 0 |
| Ibanez | .950 | 109 | 197 | 12 | 11 | 1 |
| Martinez | .975 | 65 | 181 | 11 | 5 | 3 |
| Peguero | .995 | 99 | 195 | 6 | 1 | 3 |
| Reimer | .957 | 14 | 21 | 1 | 1 | 0 |
| Yelding | .000 | 2 | 0 | 0 | 0 | 0 |

## SOUTHERN LEAGUE

| BATTING | AVG | G | AB | R | H | 2B | 3B | HR | RBI | BB | SO | SB | CS | B | T | HT | WT | DOB | 1st Yr | Resides |
|---|---|---|---|---|---|---|---|---|---|---|---|---|---|---|---|---|---|---|---|---|
| Barger, Mike | .205 | 108 | 366 | 45 | 75 | 17 | 4 | 0 | 26 | 26 | 47 | 19 | 4 | R | R | 6-0 | 165 | 4-6-71 | 1993 | Fenton, Mo. |
| Cardenas, John | .189 | 27 | 74 | 4 | 14 | 0 | 0 | 1 | 6 | 1 | 16 | 1 | 0 | R | R | 6-3 | 210 | 7-23-70 | 1993 | Fort Worth, Texas |
| Cruz, Jose | .282 | 47 | 181 | 39 | 51 | 10 | 2 | 3 | 31 | 27 | 38 | 5 | 0 | S | R | 6-0 | 200 | 4-19-74 | 1995 | Houston, Texas |
| Drinkwater, Sean | .267 | 32 | 101 | 10 | 27 | 9 | 0 | 1 | 13 | 13 | 18 | 1 | 3 | R | R | 6-3 | 195 | 6-22-71 | 1992 | El Toro, Calif. |
| Friedman, Jason | .188 | 45 | 133 | 7 | 25 | 5 | 3 | 1 | 11 | 8 | 16 | 0 | 0 | L | L | 6-1 | 200 | 8-8-69 | 1989 | Cypress, Calif. |
| Gipson, Charles | .268 | 119 | 407 | 54 | 109 | 12 | 3 | 1 | 30 | 41 | 62 | 26 | 15 | R | R | 6-0 | 188 | 12-16-72 | 1992 | Orange, Calif. |
| Griffey, Craig | .222 | 120 | 396 | 43 | 88 | 14 | 7 | 2 | 35 | 46 | 88 | 20 | 7 | R | R | 5-11 | 175 | 6-3-71 | 1991 | Westchester, Ohio |
| Guevara, Giomar | .266 | 119 | 414 | 60 | 110 | 18 | 2 | 2 | 41 | 54 | 102 | 21 | 7 | S | R | 5-9 | 158 | 10-23-72 | 1991 | Guarenas, Venez. |
| Hickey, Mike | .255 | 75 | 247 | 35 | 63 | 14 | 3 | 1 | 23 | 58 | 51 | 9 | 6 | S | R | 6-2 | 180 | 6-22-70 | 1992 | Honolulu, Hawaii |
| Ibanez, Raul | .368 | 19 | 76 | 12 | 28 | 8 | 1 | 1 | 13 | 8 | 7 | 3 | 2 | L | R | 6-2 | 210 | 6-2-72 | 1992 | Miami, Fla. |
| Jorgensen, Randy | .280 | 137 | 460 | 61 | 129 | 32 | 1 | 8 | 81 | 58 | 75 | 2 | 1 | L | L | 6-2 | 200 | 4-3-72 | 1993 | Snohomish, Wash. |
| Ladjevich, Rick | .283 | 115 | 414 | 44 | 117 | 23 | 1 | 7 | 48 | 35 | 58 | 1 | 4 | R | R | 6-3 | 220 | 2-17-72 | 1994 | West Middlesex, Pa. |
| Patel, Manny | .220 | 126 | 369 | 48 | 81 | 9 | 1 | 1 | 32 | 56 | 51 | 12 | 6 | L | R | 5-10 | 165 | 4-22-72 | 1993 | Tampa, Fla. |
| Rackley, Keifer | .158 | 6 | 19 | 0 | 3 | 1 | 0 | 0 | 1 | 1 | 5 | 0 | 0 | L | R | 6-1 | 200 | 2-27-71 | 1993 | Birmingham, Ala. |
| Ramirez, Roberto | .225 | 52 | 182 | 19 | 41 | 12 | 1 | 3 | 19 | 15 | 37 | 1 | 1 | R | R | 6-2 | 180 | 3-18-70 | 1989 | Phoenix, Ariz. |
| Sealy, Scot | .085 | 18 | 59 | 2 | 5 | 1 | 0 | 0 | 1 | 8 | 24 | 0 | 2 | R | R | 6-4 | 225 | 2-10-71 | 1992 | Saraland, Ala. |
| Sturdivant, Marcus | .284 | 63 | 243 | 34 | 69 | 11 | 4 | 2 | 23 | 26 | 33 | 13 | 7 | L | L | 5-10 | 150 | 10-29-73 | 1992 | Oakboro, N.C. |
| Varitek, Jason | .262 | 134 | 503 | 63 | 132 | 34 | 1 | 12 | 67 | 66 | 93 | 7 | 6 | S | R | 6-2 | 210 | 4-11-72 | 1995 | Longwood, Fla. |
| Wakamatsu, Don | .314 | 24 | 70 | 10 | 22 | 4 | 0 | 2 | 9 | 4 | 11 | 1 | 0 | R | R | 6-2 | 200 | 2-22-63 | 1985 | Hayward, Calif. |

| PITCHING | W | L | ERA | G | GS | CG | SV | IP | H | R | ER | BB | SO | B | T | HT | WT | DOB | 1st Yr | Resides |
|---|---|---|---|---|---|---|---|---|---|---|---|---|---|---|---|---|---|---|---|---|
| Apana, Matt | 3 | 8 | 5.33 | 18 | 18 | 0 | 0 | 96 | 86 | 58 | 57 | 69 | 55 | R | R | 6-0 | 195 | 1-16-71 | 1993 | Honolulu, Hawaii |
| Ayala, Bobby | 0 | 0 | 0.00 | 2 | 1 | 0 | 0 | 2 | 0 | 0 | 0 | 1 | 2 | R | R | 6-3 | 200 | 7-8-69 | 1988 | Oxnard, Calif. |
| Brosnan, Jason | 5 | 6 | 3.62 | 30 | 9 | 1 | 1 | 77 | 71 | 33 | 31 | 32 | 76 | L | L | 6-1 | 190 | 1-26-68 | 1989 | San Leandro, Calif. |
| Brumley, Duff | 0 | 1 | 3.86 | 6 | 5 | 0 | 0 | 28 | 27 | 13 | 12 | 21 | 17 | R | R | 6-4 | 195 | 8-25-70 | 1990 | Cleveland, Tenn. |
| Crow, Dean | 2 | 3 | 3.18 | 60 | 0 | 0 | 26 | 68 | 64 | 35 | 24 | 20 | 43 | L | R | 6-5 | 212 | 8-21-72 | 1993 | Houston, Texas |
| Franklin, Ryan | 6 | 12 | 4.01 | 28 | 27 | 2 | 0 | 182 | 186 | 99 | 81 | 37 | 127 | R | R | 6-3 | 160 | 3-5-73 | 1993 | Spiro, Okla. |
| Gipson, Charles | 0 | 1 | 1.93 | 4 | 0 | 0 | 0 | 5 | 3 | 1 | 1 | 4 | 3 | R | R | 6-0 | 188 | 12-16-72 | 1992 | Orange, Calif. |
| Gould, Clint | 0 | 1 | 3.38 | 11 | 0 | 0 | 0 | 21 | 17 | 11 | 8 | 6 | 9 | R | R | 6-2 | 230 | 8-18-71 | 1994 | Kent, Wash. |
| Gray, Dennis | 2 | 0 | 7.83 | 21 | 1 | 0 | 0 | 33 | 34 | 32 | 29 | 42 | 24 | L | L | 6-6 | 225 | 12-24-69 | 1991 | Banning, Calif. |
| Hanson, Craig | 0 | 0 | 3.86 | 5 | 0 | 0 | 0 | 9 | 5 | 4 | 4 | 6 | 9 | R | R | 6-3 | 190 | 9-30-70 | 1991 | Roseville, Minn. |
| Lowe, Derek | 5 | 3 | 3.05 | 10 | 10 | 0 | 0 | 65 | 56 | 27 | 22 | 17 | 33 | R | R | 6-6 | 170 | 6-1-73 | 1991 | Dearborn, Mich. |
| Montane, Ivan | 3 | 8 | 5.20 | 18 | 18 | 0 | 0 | 100 | 96 | 67 | 58 | 75 | 81 | R | R | 6-2 | 195 | 6-3-73 | 1992 | Miami, Fla. |
| Moore, Trey | 1 | 6 | 7.71 | 11 | 11 | 0 | 0 | 54 | 73 | 54 | 46 | 20 | 51 | L | L | 6-1 | 200 | 10-2-72 | 1994 | South Lake, Texas |
| Newton, Geronimo | 4 | 1 | 2.76 | 33 | 1 | 0 | 0 | 46 | 45 | 16 | 14 | 22 | 25 | L | L | 6-0 | 165 | 12-31-73 | 1992 | Christiansted, V.I. |
| Russell, LaGrande | 7 | 7 | 4.34 | 42 | 9 | 1 | 2 | 118 | 127 | 70 | 57 | 50 | 89 | R | R | 6-2 | 175 | 8-20-70 | 1990 | Hallsboro, N.C. |
| Simmons, Scott | 1 | 1 | 3.79 | 11 | 0 | 0 | 0 | 19 | 19 | 8 | 8 | 6 | 12 | R | L | 6-2 | 200 | 8-15-69 | 1991 | St. Charles, Mo. |
| Smith, Ryan | 6 | 9 | 3.13 | 50 | 0 | 0 | 2 | 98 | 92 | 42 | 34 | 37 | 65 | R | R | 6-3 | 215 | 11-11-71 | 1991 | Toledo, Ohio |
| Suzuki, Mac | 3 | 6 | 4.72 | 16 | 16 | 0 | 0 | 74 | 69 | 41 | 39 | 32 | 66 | R | R | 6-4 | 195 | 5-31-75 | 1992 | Kobe, Japan |
| Wertz, Bill | 2 | 2 | 2.57 | 6 | 5 | 1 | 0 | 28 | 28 | 10 | 8 | 9 | 26 | R | R | 6-6 | 220 | 1-15-67 | 1989 | Cleveland, Ohio |
| Worley, Robert | 2 | 5 | 3.93 | 35 | 1 | 0 | 0 | 66 | 66 | 40 | 29 | 39 | 40 | R | R | 6-3 | 185 | 2-15-71 | 1992 | Westerville, Ohio |
| Zimmerman, Mike | 4 | 4 | 6.94 | 14 | 8 | 0 | 0 | 48 | 56 | 40 | 37 | 33 | 25 | R | R | 6-0 | 180 | 2-6-69 | 1990 | Brooklyn, N.Y. |

### FIELDING

| Catcher | PCT | G | PO | A | E | DP | PB |
|---|---|---|---|---|---|---|---|
| Cardenas | .992 | 18 | 115 | 4 | 1 | 2 | 4 |
| Ibanez | 1.000 | 1 | 1 | 0 | 0 | 0 | 0 |
| Sealy | 1.000 | 8 | 57 | 4 | 0 | 0 | 4 |
| Varitek | .993 | 108 | 662 | 79 | 5 | 10 | 16 |
| Wakamatsu | .985 | 11 | 62 | 3 | 1 | 0 | 1 |

| First Base | PCT | G | PO | A | E | DP |
|---|---|---|---|---|---|---|
| Friedman | 1.000 | 5 | 30 | 2 | 0 | 4 |
| Ibanez | 1.000 | 1 | 9 | 1 | 0 | 1 |
| Jorgensen | .991 | 132 | 1118 | 106 | 11 | 116 |
| Ladjevich | 1.000 | 12 | 84 | 2 | 0 | 5 |
| Sealy | 1.000 | 1 | 1 | 0 | 0 | 0 |
| Wakamatsu | 1.000 | 7 | 35 | 2 | 0 | 0 |

| Second Base | PCT | G | PO | A | E | DP |
|---|---|---|---|---|---|---|
| Guevara | .971 | 24 | 44 | 57 | 3 | 16 |
| Hickey | .949 | 50 | 75 | 110 | 10 | 30 |
| Patel | .980 | 88 | 175 | 256 | 9 | 70 |

| Third Base | PCT | G | PO | A | E | DP |
|---|---|---|---|---|---|---|
| Drinkwater | .906 | 32 | 15 | 62 | 8 | 5 |
| Hickey | .928 | 36 | 22 | 55 | 6 | 7 |
| Ladjevich | .893 | 70 | 42 | 117 | 19 | 12 |
| Patel | .941 | 24 | 19 | 45 | 4 | 3 |
| Sealy | .000 | 1 | 0 | 0 | 0 | 0 |
| Varitek | .000 | 1 | 0 | 0 | 0 | 0 |

| Shortstop | PCT | G | PO | A | E | DP |
|---|---|---|---|---|---|---|
| Gipson | .945 | 43 | 71 | 151 | 13 | 21 |
| Guevara | .932 | 99 | 143 | 293 | 32 | 73 |

| | PCT | G | PO | A | E | DP |
|---|---|---|---|---|---|---|
| Patel | .894 | 13 | 14 | 28 | 5 | 7 |

| Outfield | PCT | G | PO | A | E | DP |
|---|---|---|---|---|---|---|
| Barger | 1.000 | 97 | 207 | 7 | 0 | 0 |
| Cruz | .990 | 46 | 90 | 6 | 1 | 2 |
| Friedman | 1.000 | 8 | 7 | 0 | 0 | 0 |
| Gipson | .987 | 75 | 139 | 11 | 2 | 4 |
| Griffey | 1.000 | 112 | 179 | 13 | 0 | 3 |
| Ibanez | .871 | 15 | 26 | 1 | 4 | 0 |
| Jorgensen | 1.000 | 4 | 1 | 0 | 0 | 0 |
| Rackley | 1.000 | 6 | 7 | 0 | 0 | 0 |
| Ramirez | .958 | 27 | 44 | 2 | 2 | 0 |
| Sturdivant | .986 | 61 | 136 | 8 | 2 | 0 |
| Varitek | 1.000 | 1 | 1 | 0 | 0 | 0 |

---

## BAKERSFIELD — Class A/Co-Op

### CALIFORNIA LEAGUE

| BATTING | AVG | G | AB | R | H | 2B | 3B | HR | RBI | BB | SO | SB | CS | B | T | HT | WT | DOB | 1st Yr | Resides |
|---|---|---|---|---|---|---|---|---|---|---|---|---|---|---|---|---|---|---|---|---|
| Carroll, Doug | .298 | 58 | 215 | 35 | 64 | 17 | 2 | 7 | 39 | 27 | 53 | 3 | 2 | L | R | 6-2 | 195 | 8-31-73 | 1994 | Holliston, Mass. |
| Towner, Kyle | .229 | 90 | 349 | 65 | 80 | 12 | 1 | 4 | 17 | 55 | 80 | 53 | 13 | S | R | 5-5 | 160 | 11-11-72 | 1994 | Saraland, Ala. |
| Watts, Josh | .313 | 34 | 134 | 24 | 42 | 6 | 1 | 6 | 23 | 12 | 36 | 2 | 2 | L | R | 6-1 | 205 | 3-24-75 | 1993 | Glendale, Ariz. |

GAMES BY POSITION: 1B—Carroll 11. 2B—Towner 2. OF—Carroll 35, Towner 88, Watts 33.

| PITCHING | W | L | ERA | G | GS | CG | SV | IP | H | R | ER | BB | SO | B | T | HT | WT | DOB | 1st Yr | Resides |
|---|---|---|---|---|---|---|---|---|---|---|---|---|---|---|---|---|---|---|---|---|
| Gould, Clint | 0 | 0 | 9.00 | 2 | 0 | 0 | 0 | 1 | 1 | 1 | 1 | 2 | 1 | R | R | 6-2 | 230 | 8-18-71 | 1994 | Kent, Wash. |

---

## LANCASTER — Class A

### CALIFORNIA LEAGUE

| BATTING | AVG | G | AB | R | H | 2B | 3B | HR | RBI | BB | SO | SB | CS | B | T | HT | WT | DOB | 1st Yr | Resides |
|---|---|---|---|---|---|---|---|---|---|---|---|---|---|---|---|---|---|---|---|---|
| Augustine, Andy | .278 | 41 | 115 | 16 | 32 | 5 | 1 | 0 | 12 | 22 | 40 | 2 | 0 | R | R | 5-10 | 190 | 11-13-72 | 1993 | Rothschild, Wis. |
| Buhner, Shawn | .209 | 69 | 239 | 28 | 50 | 19 | 1 | 3 | 25 | 20 | 55 | 0 | 0 | R | R | 6-2 | 205 | 8-29-72 | 1994 | League City, Texas |
| Carroll, Doug | .261 | 32 | 111 | 20 | 29 | 4 | 0 | 5 | 14 | 12 | 30 | 0 | 0 | L | R | 6-2 | 195 | 8-31-73 | 1994 | Holliston, Mass. |
| 2-team (58 Baker.) | .285 | 90 | 326 | 55 | 93 | 21 | 2 | 12 | 53 | 39 | 83 | 3 | 2 | | | | | | | |
| Clifford, Jim | .257 | 112 | 389 | 78 | 100 | 19 | 6 | 20 | 85 | 53 | 92 | 4 | 4 | L | L | 6-2 | 225 | 3-23-70 | 1992 | Seattle, Wash. |
| Cook, Jason | .289 | 124 | 450 | 95 | 130 | 22 | 4 | 5 | 58 | 89 | 68 | 5 | 2 | R | R | 6-0 | 180 | 12-9-71 | 1993 | Atlanta, Ga. |
| Cruz, Jose | .325 | 53 | 203 | 38 | 66 | 17 | 1 | 6 | 43 | 39 | 33 | 7 | 1 | S | R | 6-0 | 200 | 4-19-74 | 1995 | Houston, Texas |

| BATTING | AVG | G | AB | R | H | 2B | 3B | HR | RBI | BB | SO | SB | CS | B | T | HT | WT | DOB | 1st Yr | Resides |
|---|---|---|---|---|---|---|---|---|---|---|---|---|---|---|---|---|---|---|---|---|
| Dean, Chris | .276 | 48 | 174 | 30 | 48 | 10 | 1 | 5 | 22 | 16 | 31 | 7 | 1 | S | R | 5-10 | 178 | 1-3-74 | 1994 | Hayward, Calif. |
| Figueroa, Luis | .387 | 9 | 31 | 5 | 12 | 4 | 1 | 0 | 6 | 2 | 6 | 0 | 1 | R | R | 5-11 | 177 | 3-2-77 | 1995 | Carolina, P.R. |
| Harrison, Adonis | .350 | 16 | 40 | 7 | 14 | 4 | 0 | 0 | 5 | 8 | 13 | 4 | 1 | L | R | 5-9 | 165 | 9-28-76 | 1995 | Pasadena, Calif. |
| Jordan, Ricky | .323 | 7 | 31 | 7 | 10 | 1 | 0 | 1 | 4 | 2 | 5 | 0 | 0 | R | R | 6-3 | 205 | 5-26-65 | 1983 | Gold River, Calif. |
| Lanza, Mike | .263 | 109 | 380 | 53 | 100 | 12 | 6 | 3 | 42 | 18 | 73 | 3 | 4 | R | R | 6-1 | 170 | 10-22-73 | 1994 | Port Chester, N.Y. |
| Marquez, Jesus | .300 | 126 | 490 | 84 | 147 | 31 | 10 | 20 | 106 | 45 | 78 | 19 | 8 | L | L | 6-0 | 175 | 3-12-73 | 1990 | Caracas, Venez. |
| Molina, Luis | .254 | 37 | 122 | 13 | 31 | 4 | 0 | 0 | 10 | 14 | 24 | 3 | 2 | R | R | 6-0 | 185 | 3-22-74 | 1993 | Panama City, Panama |
| Monahan, Shane | .281 | 132 | 584 | 107 | 164 | 31 | 12 | 14 | 97 | 30 | 124 | 19 | 5 | L | R | 6-1 | 200 | 8-12-74 | 1995 | Marietta, Ga. |
| Sealy, Scot | .272 | 75 | 254 | 47 | 69 | 22 | 3 | 9 | 49 | 41 | 63 | 3 | 2 | R | R | 6-4 | 225 | 2-10-71 | 1992 | Saraland, Ala. |
| Smith, Scott | .298 | 61 | 252 | 52 | 75 | 19 | 0 | 10 | 52 | 16 | 74 | 9 | 2 | R | R | 6-3 | 215 | 10-14-71 | 1994 | Coppell, Texas |
| Steinmann, Scott | .200 | 5 | 10 | 2 | 2 | 0 | 0 | 0 | 0 | 0 | 4 | 0 | 0 | S | R | 6-2 | 185 | 7-17-73 | 1996 | Cincinnati, Ohio |
| Sturdivant, Marcus | .284 | 68 | 292 | 54 | 83 | 19 | 6 | 0 | 31 | 32 | 35 | 23 | 9 | L | L | 5-10 | 150 | 10-29-73 | 1992 | Oakboro, N.C. |
| Villalobos, Carlos | .292 | 111 | 415 | 69 | 121 | 21 | 5 | 5 | 63 | 50 | 89 | 9 | 4 | R | R | 6-0 | 170 | 4-5-74 | 1993 | Cartagena, Colombia |
| Wathan, Dusty | .260 | 74 | 246 | 41 | 64 | 10 | 1 | 8 | 40 | 26 | 65 | 1 | 1 | S | R | 6-5 | 215 | 8-22-73 | 1994 | Blue Springs, Mo. |
| Watts, Josh | .211 | 21 | 71 | 6 | 15 | 1 | 1 | 1 | 11 | 9 | 17 | 2 | 1 | L | R | 6-1 | 205 | 3-24-75 | 1993 | Glendale, Ariz. |
| 2-team (34 Baker.) | .278 | 55 | 205 | 30 | 57 | 7 | 2 | 7 | 34 | 21 | 53 | 4 | 3 | | | | | | | |

**GAMES BY POSITION: C**—Augustine 39, Sealy 49, Steinmann 3, Wathan 60. **1B**—Buhner 50, Clifford 93, Jordan 4, Sealy 1, Wathan 1. **2B**—Cook 76, Dean 48, Harrison 14, Lanza 11. **3B**—Buhner 1, Cook 31, Figueroa 9, Lanza 6, Sealy 1, Villalobos 100. **SS**—Cook 19, Lanza 90, Molina 37. **OF**—Carroll 14, Clifford 2, Cook 6, Cruz 4, Marquez 106, Monahan 127, Sealy 1, Smith 58, Sturdivant 63, Villalobos 2, Watts 13.

| PITCHING | W | L | ERA | G | GS | CG | SV | IP | H | R | ER | BB | SO | B | T | HT | WT | DOB | 1st Yr | Resides |
|---|---|---|---|---|---|---|---|---|---|---|---|---|---|---|---|---|---|---|---|---|
| Beck, Chris | 6 | 5 | 3.53 | 23 | 11 | 0 | 1 | 87 | 90 | 45 | 34 | 43 | 57 | R | R | 6-3 | 205 | 6-11-72 | 1994 | Garden Grove, Calif. |
| Bosio, Chris | 0 | 0 | 1.13 | 2 | 2 | 0 | 0 | 8 | 6 | 3 | 1 | 0 | 7 | R | R | 6-3 | 225 | 4-3-63 | 1982 | Shingle Springs, Calif. |
| Clifford, Eric | 0 | 0 | 5.25 | 11 | 0 | 0 | 1 | 24 | 21 | 14 | 14 | 5 | 11 | R | R | 6-1 | 210 | 9-18-74 | 1994 | Chandler, Ariz. |
| Cloude, Ken | 15 | 4 | 4.22 | 28 | 28 | 1 | 0 | 168 | 167 | 94 | 79 | 60 | 161 | R | R | 6-1 | 200 | 1-9-75 | 1994 | Baltimore, Md. |
| Daniels, John | 3 | 5 | 3.30 | 43 | 0 | 0 | 8 | 95 | 91 | 51 | 35 | 30 | 100 | S | R | 6-3 | 185 | 2-7-74 | 1993 | Litte Chute, Wis. |
| Gould, Clint | 3 | 2 | 3.21 | 24 | 0 | 0 | 2 | 34 | 35 | 22 | 12 | 17 | 19 | R | R | 6-2 | 230 | 8-18-71 | 1994 | Kent, Wash. |
| 2-team (2 Bakers.) | 3 | 2 | 3.38 | 26 | 0 | 0 | 2 | 35 | 36 | 23 | 13 | 19 | 18 | | | | | | | |
| Hinchliffe, Brett | 11 | 10 | 4.24 | 27 | 26 | 0 | 0 | 163 | 179 | 105 | 77 | 64 | 146 | S | R | 6-4 | 205 | 7-21-74 | 1992 | Detroit, Mich. |
| Montane, Ivan | 2 | 2 | 3.64 | 11 | 11 | 0 | 0 | 59 | 57 | 37 | 24 | 43 | 54 | R | R | 6-2 | 195 | 6-3-73 | 1992 | Miami, Fla. |
| Moore, Trey | 7 | 5 | 4.10 | 15 | 15 | 2 | 0 | 94 | 106 | 57 | 43 | 31 | 77 | L | L | 6-1 | 200 | 10-2-72 | 1994 | South Lake, Texas |
| Morgan, Eric | 0 | 1 | 4.26 | 10 | 0 | 0 | 1 | 13 | 13 | 7 | 6 | 12 | 5 | R | R | 6-0 | 190 | 10-24-72 | 1994 | Cocoa, Fla. |
| Niemeier, Todd | 0 | 0 | 4.65 | 41 | 0 | 0 | 0 | 41 | 42 | 30 | 21 | 30 | 30 | R | L | 6-1 | 165 | 1-28-73 | 1995 | Evansville, Ind. |
| Pearce, Jeff | 0 | 0 | 2.08 | 21 | 0 | 0 | 0 | 22 | 13 | 7 | 5 | 23 | 17 | L | L | 6-2 | 215 | 7-14-69 | 1990 | Sebastopol, Calif. |
| Santana, Marino | 8 | 15 | 5.03 | 28 | 28 | 1 | 0 | 157 | 164 | 105 | 88 | 57 | 167 | R | R | 6-1 | 188 | 5-10-72 | 1990 | Andres Boca Chica, D.R. |
| Soden, Chad | 0 | 1 | 10.64 | 9 | 0 | 0 | 0 | 11 | 17 | 14 | 13 | 9 | 8 | L | L | 6-1 | 195 | 9-7-73 | 1995 | Tuckerman, Ark. |
| Szimanski, Tom | 2 | 2 | 4.22 | 35 | 0 | 0 | 9 | 43 | 55 | 24 | 20 | 12 | 46 | R | R | 6-1 | 205 | 9-9-72 | 1994 | Baltimore, Md. |
| Thompson, John | 3 | 8 | 6.13 | 50 | 0 | 0 | 14 | 62 | 72 | 50 | 42 | 29 | 53 | R | R | 6-2 | 200 | 1-18-73 | 1992 | Spokane, Wash. |
| Trawick, Tim | 2 | 2 | 6.39 | 16 | 0 | 0 | 0 | 31 | 43 | 26 | 22 | 9 | 20 | R | R | 6-4 | 208 | 3-7-72 | 1995 | Columbus, Ga. |
| Wolcott, Bob | 0 | 1 | 10.50 | 1 | 1 | 0 | 0 | 6 | 9 | 7 | 7 | 0 | 6 | R | R | 6-0 | 190 | 9-8-73 | 1992 | Medford, Ore. |
| Wooten, Greg | 8 | 4 | 3.80 | 14 | 14 | 1 | 0 | 97 | 101 | 47 | 41 | 25 | 71 | R | R | 6-7 | 210 | 3-30-74 | 1996 | Vancouver, Wash. |
| Worley, Robert | 3 | 0 | 0.34 | 4 | 4 | 0 | 0 | 26 | 20 | 2 | 1 | 5 | 17 | R | R | 6-3 | 185 | 2-15-71 | 1992 | Westerville, Ohio |

# WISCONSIN — Class A
## MIDWEST LEAGUE

| BATTING | AVG | G | AB | R | H | 2B | 3B | HR | RBI | BB | SO | SB | CS | B | T | HT | WT | DOB | 1st Yr | Resides |
|---|---|---|---|---|---|---|---|---|---|---|---|---|---|---|---|---|---|---|---|---|
| Amado, Jose | .289 | 61 | 232 | 43 | 67 | 13 | 0 | 5 | 36 | 20 | 20 | 6 | 5 | R | R | 6-1 | 194 | 1-1-75 | 1994 | San Cristobal, Venez. |
| Arias, David | .322 | 129 | 485 | 89 | 156 | 34 | 2 | 18 | 93 | 52 | 108 | 3 | 4 | L | L | 6-4 | 230 | 11-18-75 | 1993 | Haina, D.R. |
| Carroll, Doug | .206 | 22 | 68 | 12 | 14 | 2 | 0 | 1 | 7 | 8 | 10 | 1 | 1 | L | R | 6-2 | 195 | 8-31-73 | 1994 | Holliston, Mass. |
| Castro, Jose | .216 | 37 | 111 | 12 | 24 | 3 | 0 | 0 | 10 | 9 | 22 | 2 | 5 | L | L | 5-11 | 192 | 12-19-73 | 1993 | Los Mina, D.R. |
| Darcuiel, Faruq | .213 | 74 | 211 | 28 | 45 | 6 | 3 | 0 | 30 | 18 | 46 | 6 | 4 | L | L | 5-11 | 180 | 11-28-72 | 1994 | Fresno, Calif. |
| Dean, Chris | .271 | 53 | 210 | 32 | 57 | 8 | 2 | 4 | 32 | 18 | 46 | 11 | 7 | S | R | 5-10 | 178 | 1-3-74 | 1994 | Hayward, Calif. |
| Figueroa, Luis | .290 | 37 | 138 | 18 | 40 | 9 | 0 | 2 | 19 | 6 | 14 | 1 | 1 | R | R | 5-11 | 177 | 3-2-77 | 1995 | Carolina, P.R. |
| Harrison, Adonis | .265 | 54 | 196 | 29 | 52 | 15 | 2 | 1 | 24 | 19 | 36 | 5 | 3 | L | R | 5-9 | 165 | 9-28-76 | 1995 | Pasadena, Calif. |
| Hickey, Mike | .329 | 26 | 85 | 15 | 28 | 7 | 0 | 0 | 11 | 23 | 20 | 0 | 1 | S | R | 6-2 | 180 | 6-22-70 | 1992 | Honolulu, Hawaii |
| Mathis, Joe | .285 | 126 | 473 | 79 | 135 | 19 | 8 | 5 | 47 | 36 | 7 | 19 | 6 | L | R | 5-10 | 180 | 8-10-74 | 1993 | Johnston, S.C. |
| Medrano, Teodoro | .203 | 63 | 172 | 20 | 35 | 9 | 1 | 4 | 22 | 15 | 58 | 3 | 3 | R | R | 5-11 | 190 | 9-17-75 | 1993 | Santo Domingo, D.R. |
| Ramirez, Jose | .239 | 110 | 364 | 53 | 87 | 14 | 0 | 1 | 52 | 30 | 45 | 5 | 6 | R | R | 5-10 | 155 | 8-17-73 | 1994 | Miami, Fla. |
| Randolph, Ed | .179 | 70 | 196 | 23 | 35 | 9 | 1 | 1 | 13 | 23 | 43 | 3 | 0 | S | R | 6-2 | 205 | 10-17-74 | 1993 | Dallas, Texas |
| Sheffer, Chad | .196 | 101 | 316 | 60 | 62 | 11 | 0 | 4 | 35 | 63 | 79 | 13 | 10 | S | R | 6-0 | 180 | 12-17-73 | 1995 | Dover, Fla. |
| Smith, Scott | .332 | 67 | 241 | 43 | 80 | 11 | 4 | 10 | 49 | 24 | 74 | 11 | 7 | R | R | 6-3 | 215 | 10-14-71 | 1994 | Coppell, Texas |
| Thompson, Karl | .290 | 119 | 441 | 76 | 128 | 36 | 1 | 9 | 66 | 35 | 79 | 1 | 2 | R | R | 6-0 | 180 | 12-30-73 | 1995 | Diamond Bar, Calif. |
| Tinoco, Luis | .313 | 120 | 431 | 71 | 135 | 31 | 5 | 12 | 71 | 53 | 85 | 4 | 9 | R | R | 6-2 | 200 | 7-24-74 | 1992 | Maracaibo, Venez. |
| Vazquez, Ramon | .300 | 3 | 10 | 1 | 3 | 1 | 0 | 0 | 1 | 2 | 2 | 0 | 0 | L | R | 5-11 | 170 | 8-21-76 | 1995 | Cayey, P.R. |
| Vickers, Randy | .249 | 51 | 181 | 27 | 45 | 12 | 0 | 7 | 31 | 12 | 63 | 1 | 4 | R | R | 6-3 | 200 | 7-21-75 | 1994 | West Covina, Calif. |

**GAMES BY POSITION: C**—Medrano 45, Randolph 7, Thompson 101. **1B**—Amado 1, Arias 121, Carroll 2, Castro 3, Randolph 2, Sheffer 1, Vickers 13. **2B**—Amado 1, Dean 51, Harrison 51, Ramirez 37. **3B**—Amado 58, Arias 1, Figueroa 36, Hickey 24, Sheffer 15, Tinoco 1, Vazquez 3, Vickers 9. **SS**—Ramirez 67, Sheffer 78. **OF**—Carroll 6, Castro 29, Darcuiel 68, Mathis 124, Randolph 21, Smith 65, Tinoco 116.

| PITCHING | W | L | ERA | G | GS | CG | SV | IP | H | R | ER | BB | SO | B | T | HT | WT | DOB | 1st Yr | Resides |
|---|---|---|---|---|---|---|---|---|---|---|---|---|---|---|---|---|---|---|---|---|
| Bonilla, Denys | 6 | 1 | 2.19 | 45 | 0 | 0 | 4 | 70 | 56 | 21 | 17 | 25 | 62 | L | L | 6-1 | 204 | 3-15-74 | 1992 | Santo Domingo, D.R. |
| Collett, Andy | 2 | 2 | 3.65 | 22 | 0 | 0 | 0 | 37 | 32 | 18 | 15 | 23 | 31 | L | R | 6-3 | 215 | 10-28-73 | 1995 | Arroyo Grande, Calif. |
| Gould, Clint | 1 | 0 | 3.48 | 6 | 0 | 0 | 1 | 10 | 8 | 4 | 4 | 5 | 10 | R | R | 6-2 | 230 | 8-18-71 | 1994 | Kent, Wash. |
| Gryboski, Kevin | 10 | 5 | 4.74 | 32 | 21 | 3 | 1 | 139 | 146 | 90 | 73 | 62 | 100 | R | R | 6-5 | 220 | 11-15-73 | 1995 | Plains, Pa. |
| Iddon, Brent | 11 | 4 | 2.78 | 50 | 0 | 0 | 11 | 97 | 82 | 32 | 30 | 41 | 114 | R | R | 6-2 | 180 | 2-4-76 | 1994 | Sydney, Australia |
| Jacobs, Russell | 4 | 4 | 5.27 | 24 | 10 | 0 | 2 | 68 | 67 | 48 | 40 | 53 | 63 | R | R | 6-6 | 225 | 1-2-75 | 1994 | Winter Haven, Fla. |
| Kurtz, Danny | 2 | 5 | 5.10 | 38 | 4 | 0 | 0 | 53 | 51 | 51 | 48 | 54 | 71 | R | R | 6-1 | 190 | 5-23-74 | 1995 | Highland, N.Y. |
| Marte, Damaso | 8 | 6 | 4.49 | 26 | 26 | 2 | 0 | 142 | 134 | 82 | 71 | 75 | 115 | L | L | 6-2 | 194 | 2-14-74 | 1993 | Santo Domingo, D.R. |
| Scheer, Greg | 3 | 1 | 6.79 | 35 | 0 | 0 | 0 | 54 | 60 | 43 | 41 | 33 | 55 | R | L | 6-5 | 205 | 2-23-72 | 1995 | Louisville, Ky. |
| Scheffer, Aaron | 8 | 1 | 3.72 | 45 | 1 | 0 | 14 | 68 | 55 | 31 | 28 | 34 | 89 | L | R | 6-1 | 190 | 8-15-75 | 1994 | Westland, Mich. |
| Smith, Roy | 6 | 13 | 5.12 | 27 | 27 | 0 | 0 | 146 | 164 | 113 | 83 | 73 | 99 | R | R | 6-7 | 210 | 5-18-76 | 1994 | Pinellas Park, Fla. |
| Soden, Chad | 3 | 0 | 1.57 | 19 | 1 | 0 | 0 | 29 | 26 | 10 | 5 | 10 | 21 | L | L | 6-1 | 195 | 9-7-73 | 1995 | Tuckerman, Ark. |
| Trawick, Tim | 5 | 5 | 4.29 | 15 | 13 | 1 | 0 | 80 | 87 | 42 | 38 | 34 | 89 | R | R | 6-4 | 208 | 3-7-72 | 1995 | Columbus, Ga. |
| Vanhof, John | 1 | 10 | 7.88 | 27 | 19 | 0 | 0 | 94 | 104 | 89 | 82 | 105 | 58 | L | L | 6-3 | 180 | 12-4-73 | 1992 | Southgate, Mich. |
| Wooten, Greg | 7 | 1 | 2.47 | 13 | 13 | 3 | 0 | 84 | 58 | 27 | 23 | 29 | 68 | R | R | 6-7 | 210 | 3-30-74 | 1996 | Vancouver, Wash. |

## NORTHWEST LEAGUE

| BATTING | AVG | G | AB | R | H | 2B | 3B | HR | RBI | BB | SO | SB | CS | B | T | HT | WT | DOB | 1st Yr | Resides |
|---|---|---|---|---|---|---|---|---|---|---|---|---|---|---|---|---|---|---|---|---|
| Burrows, Mike | .211 | 43 | 147 | 18 | 31 | 9 | 2 | 3 | 19 | 21 | 41 | 5 | 3 | L | L | 6-4 | 180 | 1-19-76 | 1994 | American Fork, Utah |
| Castro, Jose | .250 | 1 | 4 | 0 | 1 | 0 | 0 | 0 | 0 | 0 | 1 | 0 | 0 | L | L | 5-11 | 192 | 12-19-75 | 1993 | Los Mina, D.R. |
| Cruz, Cirilo | .270 | 44 | 163 | 12 | 44 | 6 | 0 | 0 | 21 | 8 | 34 | 1 | 5 | R | R | 6-0 | 185 | 5-29-75 | 1995 | Arroyo, P.R. |
| Figueroa, Luis | .462 | 4 | 13 | 4 | 6 | 1 | 1 | 0 | 3 | 2 | 1 | 0 | 0 | R | R | 5-11 | 177 | 3-2-77 | 1995 | Carolina, P.R. |
| Horner, Jim | .150 | 18 | 60 | 6 | 9 | 2 | 0 | 2 | 5 | 10 | 16 | 0 | 0 | R | R | 6-0 | 210 | 11-11-73 | 1996 | Twin Falls, Idaho |
| Johnson, Duan | .262 | 51 | 202 | 32 | 53 | 7 | 2 | 1 | 19 | 7 | 26 | 3 | 3 | R | R | 6-1 | 205 | 2-23-76 | 1995 | St. Pauls, N.C. |
| Jordan, Ricky | .357 | 3 | 14 | 2 | 5 | 1 | 0 | 0 | 5 | 1 | 4 | 0 | 0 | R | R | 6-3 | 205 | 5-26-65 | 1983 | Gold River, Calif. |
| Kokinda, Steven | .146 | 16 | 48 | 7 | 7 | 2 | 0 | 0 | 8 | 8 | 16 | 0 | 0 | L | R | 6-3 | 190 | 8-21-74 | 1996 | West Palm Beach, Fla. |
| Lindner, Brian | .206 | 64 | 248 | 27 | 51 | 8 | 1 | 2 | 27 | 42 | 67 | 6 | 1 | R | R | 6-1 | 185 | 3-14-74 | 1996 | Bloomfield, N.J. |
| Nelson, Brian | .184 | 30 | 98 | 11 | 18 | 5 | 0 | 1 | 11 | 19 | 32 | 0 | 0 | R | R | 6-1 | 185 | 5-11-74 | 1996 | Sarasota, Fla. |
| Regan, Jason | .210 | 40 | 124 | 17 | 26 | 11 | 0 | 3 | 22 | 25 | 47 | 3 | 3 | R | R | 5-10 | 170 | 6-30-76 | 1996 | Belton, Texas |
| Rowson, James | .221 | 53 | 181 | 30 | 40 | 9 | 2 | 4 | 24 | 26 | 68 | 4 | 2 | L | L | 5-11 | 190 | 9-12-76 | 1995 | Mount Vernon, N.Y. |
| Sachse, Matt | .236 | 67 | 237 | 24 | 56 | 9 | 1 | 5 | 27 | 14 | 94 | 4 | 2 | L | L | 6-4 | 205 | 6-29-76 | 1995 | Spokane, Wash. |
| Simonton, Cy Leon | .213 | 40 | 136 | 18 | 29 | 1 | 0 | 1 | 8 | 19 | 37 | 3 | 3 | L | L | 6-0 | 170 | 8-23-76 | 1994 | Pittsburg, Calif. |
| Skeels, David | .286 | 25 | 77 | 8 | 22 | 3 | 0 | 1 | 8 | 3 | 13 | 2 | 1 | R | R | 6-2 | 195 | 6-23-73 | 1995 | Thousand Oaks, Calif. |
| Steinmann, Scott | .140 | 30 | 100 | 13 | 14 | 4 | 1 | 0 | 4 | 15 | 33 | 0 | 0 | S | R | 6-2 | 185 | 7-17-73 | 1996 | Cincinnati, Ohio |
| Stewart, Keith | .144 | 32 | 90 | 13 | 13 | 1 | 0 | 2 | 6 | 8 | 47 | 3 | 2 | L | R | 6-0 | 170 | 9-26-73 | 1995 | Clay City, Ky. |
| Valera, Ramon | .229 | 50 | 166 | 28 | 38 | 3 | 3 | 0 | 12 | 35 | 48 | 11 | 2 | S | R | 5-11 | 160 | 8-21-75 | 1994 | Haina, D.R. |
| Vazquez, Ramon | .278 | 33 | 126 | 25 | 35 | 5 | 2 | 1 | 18 | 26 | 26 | 7 | 2 | L | R | 5-11 | 170 | 8-21-76 | 1995 | Cayey, P.R. |
| Zachmann, Rob | .291 | 74 | 285 | 49 | 83 | 13 | 1 | 19 | 64 | 30 | 87 | 4 | 0 | R | R | 6-1 | 205 | 8-13-73 | 1995 | Oakdale, N.Y. |

**GAMES BY POSITION; C**—Homer 8, Nelson 24, Skeels 14, Steinmann 29. **1B**—Cruz 1, Johnson 1, Kokinda 15, Simonton 2, Skeels 3, Zachmann 59. **2B**—Cruz 5, Figueroa 3, Lindner 8, Regan 15, Valera 46. **3B**—Cruz 9, Johnson 31, Lindner 11, Regan 25. **SS**—Lindner 39, Valera 4, Vazquez 32. **OF**—Burrows 42, Cruz 16, Rowson 49, Sachse 66, Simonton 37, Skeels 1, Stewart 27.

| PITCHING | W | L | ERA | G | GS | CG | SV | IP | H | R | ER | BB | SO | B | T | HT | WT | DOB | 1st Yr | Resides |
|---|---|---|---|---|---|---|---|---|---|---|---|---|---|---|---|---|---|---|---|---|
| Ayala, Julio | 1 | 3 | 3.48 | 12 | 6 | 0 | 0 | 44 | 43 | 20 | 17 | 10 | 28 | L | L | 6-3 | 203 | 4-20-75 | 1996 | Guaynabo, P.R. |
| Blanco, Roger | 1 | 7 | 6.16 | 11 | 11 | 0 | 0 | 50 | 62 | 46 | 34 | 28 | 35 | R | R | 6-6 | 220 | 8-29-76 | 1993 | La Sabana, Venez. |
| Bond, Jason | 1 | 0 | 1.87 | 20 | 0 | 0 | 4 | 43 | 24 | 10 | 9 | 12 | 52 | L | L | 5-11 | 175 | 11-11-74 | 1996 | Scottsdale, Ariz. |
| Bosio, Chris | 0 | 0 | 2.25 | 1 | 1 | 0 | 0 | 4 | 3 | 1 | 1 | 0 | 8 | R | R | 6-3 | 225 | 4-3-63 | 1982 | Shingle Springs, Calif. |
| Clifford, Eric | 0 | 0 | 6.00 | 2 | 0 | 0 | 0 | 3 | 4 | 2 | 2 | 1 | 4 | R | R | 6-1 | 210 | 9-18-74 | 1994 | Chandler, Ariz. |
| Davis, Tim | 0 | 0 | 0.00 | 1 | 1 | 0 | 0 | 2 | 0 | 0 | 0 | 1 | 5 | L | L | 5-11 | 165 | 7-14-70 | 1992 | Bristol, Fla. |
| Farnsworth, Jeff | 3 | 3 | 4.12 | 10 | 7 | 0 | 0 | 39 | 33 | 19 | 18 | 13 | 42 | R | R | 6-2 | 190 | 10-6-75 | 1996 | Pensacola, Fla. |
| Fitzgerald, Brian | 1 | 2 | 6.46 | 21 | 1 | 0 | 1 | 39 | 56 | 36 | 28 | 8 | 31 | L | L | 5-11 | 175 | 12-26-74 | 1996 | Woodbridge, Va. |
| Fuentes, Brian | 0 | 1 | 4.39 | 13 | 2 | 0 | 0 | 27 | 23 | 14 | 13 | 13 | 26 | L | L | 6-4 | 220 | 8-9-75 | 1996 | Merced, Calif. |
| Gutierrez, Javier | 4 | 1 | 5.56 | 7 | 7 | 0 | 0 | 34 | 43 | 25 | 21 | 12 | 35 | R | R | 6-2 | 205 | 8-26-74 | 1994 | Guanta, Venez. |
| Jimenez, Jhonny | 1 | 3 | 4.60 | 24 | 0 | 0 | 5 | 31 | 34 | 20 | 16 | 12 | 26 | R | R | 6-2 | 198 | 4-26-76 | 1996 | San Jose de los Llanos, D.R. |
| Johnson, Randy | 0 | 0 | 0.00 | 1 | 1 | 0 | 0 | 2 | 0 | 0 | 0 | 0 | 5 | R | L | 6-10 | 225 | 9-10-63 | 1985 | Bellevue, Wash. |
| Kennison, Kyle | 1 | 2 | 8.24 | 12 | 2 | 0 | 0 | 20 | 25 | 18 | 18 | 11 | 25 | R | R | 6-2 | 220 | 8-10-72 | 1996 | Bangor, Maine |
| Luce, Robert | 3 | 4 | 4.39 | 23 | 0 | 0 | 7 | 41 | 45 | 26 | 20 | 16 | 47 | S | R | 6-0 | 185 | 7-19-74 | 1996 | Rescue, Calif. |
| Mays, Joe | 4 | 4 | 3.08 | 13 | 10 | 0 | 0 | 64 | 55 | 33 | 22 | 22 | 56 | S | R | 6-1 | 160 | 12-10-75 | 1995 | Bradenton, Fla. |
| Morgan, Eric | 0 | 1 | 4.70 | 4 | 0 | 0 | 0 | 15 | 20 | 14 | 8 | 12 | 11 | R | R | 6-0 | 190 | 10-24-72 | 1994 | Cocoa, Fla. |
| Nogowski, Brandon | 0 | 0 | 4.44 | 19 | 0 | 0 | 1 | 26 | 27 | 18 | 13 | 25 | 31 | L | L | 6-0 | 172 | 5-13-76 | 1995 | Hood River, Ore. |
| Rivera, Rafael | 4 | 1 | 2.19 | 24 | 0 | 0 | 0 | 49 | 47 | 19 | 12 | 10 | 61 | R | R | 6-0 | 190 | 12-13-75 | 1996 | Vega Baja, P.R. |
| Stark, Denny | 1 | 3 | 4.45 | 12 | 4 | 0 | 0 | 30 | 25 | 19 | 15 | 17 | 49 | R | R | 6-2 | 210 | 10-27-74 | 1996 | Edgerton, Ohio |
| Victery, Joe | 5 | 4 | 3.14 | 13 | 8 | 0 | 1 | 52 | 43 | 22 | 18 | 15 | 45 | R | R | 6-2 | 185 | 4-26-75 | 1996 | Ninnekah, Okla. |
| Weymouth, Marty | 2 | 3 | 4.83 | 10 | 10 | 0 | 0 | 41 | 46 | 28 | 22 | 16 | 35 | R | R | 6-3 | 190 | 8-6-77 | 1995 | Romeo, Mich. |

## ARIZONA LEAGUE

| BATTING | AVG | G | AB | R | H | 2B | 3B | HR | RBI | BB | SO | SB | CS | B | T | HT | WT | DOB | 1st Yr | Resides |
|---|---|---|---|---|---|---|---|---|---|---|---|---|---|---|---|---|---|---|---|---|
| Barthelemy, Edy | .216 | 38 | 111 | 18 | 24 | 5 | 3 | 1 | 14 | 19 | 30 | 3 | 4 | S | R | 6-0 | 189 | 4-24-76 | 1996 | Hartford, Conn. |
| Eady, Gerald | .222 | 46 | 176 | 24 | 39 | 9 | 4 | 1 | 26 | 21 | 53 | 7 | 2 | R | R | 6-1 | 195 | 10-25-75 | 1996 | Jacksonville, Fla. |
| Guerrero, Wascar | .234 | 31 | 111 | 9 | 26 | 6 | 1 | 1 | 10 | 4 | 37 | 0 | 0 | R | R | 6-5 | 230 | 4-10-76 | 1994 | Santo Domingo, D.R. |
| Jimenez, Miguel | .266 | 44 | 158 | 22 | 42 | 9 | 0 | 4 | 18 | 6 | 44 | 6 | 2 | R | R | 6-0 | 185 | 1-16-76 | 1994 | Santo Domingo, D.R. |
| Maldonado, Carlos | .220 | 29 | 100 | 10 | 22 | 0 | 0 | 2 | 18 | 6 | 10 | 0 | 1 | R | R | 6-2 | 195 | 1-3-79 | 1996 | Maracaibo, Venez. |
| Martinez, Victor | .344 | 16 | 61 | 10 | 21 | 1 | 4 | 0 | 10 | 9 | 17 | 4 | 0 | R | R | 5-11 | 185 | 8-10-78 | 1996 | New York, N.Y. |
| Maynard, Scott | .280 | 47 | 164 | 20 | 46 | 7 | 1 | 1 | 17 | 15 | 53 | 1 | 3 | R | R | 6-1 | 215 | 8-28-77 | 1995 | Laguna Niguel, Calif. |
| McDougall, Matt | .203 | 28 | 79 | 18 | 16 | 3 | 2 | 1 | 2 | 10 | 22 | 9 | 2 | R | R | 6-0 | 192 | 7-29-76 | 1995 | Henley Beach, Australia |
| Moreno, Jose | .278 | 44 | 176 | 34 | 49 | 4 | 2 | 0 | 18 | 18 | 33 | 12 | 5 | R | R | 5-11 | 168 | 8-9-77 | 1995 | San Pedro de Macoris, D.R. |
| Pacheco, Domingo | .250 | 8 | 16 | 0 | 4 | 1 | 0 | 0 | 1 | 0 | 6 | 0 | 0 | S | R | 6-1 | 175 | 11-8-78 | 1996 | Santo Domingo, D.R. |
| Pinson, Brian | .409 | 10 | 22 | 2 | 9 | 0 | 0 | 1 | 0 | 0 | 6 | 0 | 1 | L | R | 5-7 | 160 | 6-12-78 | 1996 | Bremerton, Wash. |
| Rose, Carlos | .129 | 40 | 132 | 12 | 17 | 1 | 1 | 2 | 13 | 11 | 56 | 0 | 0 | R | R | 6-2 | 208 | 8-21-75 | 1995 | Cleveland, Miss. |
| Smith, Brian | .296 | 54 | 223 | 39 | 66 | 15 | 6 | 3 | 16 | 21 | 46 | 13 | 11 | S | R | 5-9 | 155 | 4-29-77 | 1996 | El Cajon, Calif. |
| Tolbert, Ernest | .212 | 52 | 179 | 22 | 38 | 6 | 1 | 2 | 15 | 11 | 46 | 9 | 4 | R | R | 6-1 | 210 | 1-29-76 | 1995 | San Diego, Calif. |
| Valera, Ramon | .444 | 4 | 18 | 2 | 8 | 1 | 0 | 0 | 3 | 1 | 1 | 4 | 1 | S | R | 5-11 | 160 | 8-21-75 | 1994 | Haina, D.R. |
| Williams, Marcus | .154 | 11 | 39 | 5 | 6 | 0 | 0 | 0 | 2 | 9 | 5 | 3 | 0 | R | R | 6-5 | 185 | 1-24-77 | 1995 | Detroit, Mich. |
| Williams, Patrick | .250 | 38 | 140 | 18 | 35 | 4 | 1 | 6 | 26 | 12 | 46 | 1 | 1 | R | R | 6-2 | 220 | 10-3-77 | 1996 | Nacogdoches, Texas |

**GAMES BY POSITION: C**—Barthelemy 26, Maldonado 22, Maynard 17, P. Williams 3. **1B**—Guerrero 30, Maynard 16, M. Williams 11, P. Williams 1. **2B**—Jimenez 1, Moreno 1, Pinson 7, Smith 53. **3B**—Barthelemy 4, Guerrero 1, Jimenez 38, Maldonado 1, Martinez 6, Pacheco 5. **SS**—Martinez 5, Moreno 48, Pacheco 9, Valera 4. **OF**—Barthelemy 10, Eady 46, Jimenez 2, Maynard 6, Rose 40, Smith 2, Tolbert 52, P. Williams 18.

| PITCHING | W | L | ERA | G | GS | CG | SV | IP | H | R | ER | BB | SO | B | T | HT | WT | DOB | 1st Yr | Resides |
|---|---|---|---|---|---|---|---|---|---|---|---|---|---|---|---|---|---|---|---|---|
| Brea, Lesli | 1 | 0 | 5.06 | 7 | 0 | 0 | 0 | 11 | 7 | 10 | 6 | 4 | 14 | R | R | 5-10 | 170 | 10-12-78 | 1996 | Jersey City, N.J. |
| Christianson, Robby | 5 | 1 | 3.76 | 14 | 9 | 0 | 2 | 65 | 63 | 30 | 27 | 13 | 36 | R | R | 6-2 | 185 | 8-29-75 | 1996 | Riverside, Calif. |
| Derenches, Albert | 3 | 3 | 3.13 | 20 | 3 | 1 | 3 | 60 | 57 | 31 | 21 | 19 | 73 | S | L | 6-3 | 190 | 8-17-76 | 1995 | Tampa, Fla. |
| DeJesus, Tony | 3 | 5 | 3.63 | 12 | 11 | 0 | 0 | 57 | 54 | 29 | 23 | 28 | 61 | R | L | 6-2 | 185 | 5-14-78 | 1996 | Havelock, N.C. |
| Garey, Daniel | 2 | 5 | 5.09 | 12 | 11 | 0 | 0 | 53 | 65 | 37 | 30 | 18 | 38 | R | R | 6-2 | 220 | 10-22-77 | 1996 | St. Joseph, Mich. |
| Gonzalez, Jose | 2 | 0 | 0.90 | 2 | 2 | 0 | 0 | 10 | 5 | 2 | 1 | 3 | 10 | R | R | 6-1 | 194 | 3-4-77 | 1994 | Maracaibo, Venez. |
| Hearns, Shane | 1 | 1 | 2.93 | 9 | 0 | 0 | 2 | 15 | 10 | 7 | 5 | 6 | 12 | R | R | 6-1 | 195 | 9-29-75 | 1995 | Lambertville, Mich. |
| Kawahara, Orin | 5 | 5 | 4.16 | 18 | 10 | 0 | 1 | 71 | 64 | 42 | 33 | 40 | 87 | R | R | 6-2 | 195 | 11-10-77 | 1996 | Hallimaile, Hawaii |
| Kaye, Justin | 3 | 2 | 3.62 | 20 | 0 | 0 | 3 | 32 | 34 | 23 | 13 | 19 | 36 | S | R | 6-4 | 185 | 6-9-76 | 1995 | Las Vegas, Nev. |
| Mahan, Dallas | 0 | 0 | 7.71 | 2 | 0 | 0 | 0 | 5 | 4 | 4 | 4 | 5 | 2 | L | L | 6-3 | 185 | 12-10-77 | 1996 | Greeley, Colo. |
| Mears, Chris | 1 | 2 | 3.60 | 6 | 5 | 0 | 0 | 25 | 23 | 11 | 10 | 5 | 27 | R | R | 6-4 | 180 | 1-20-78 | 1996 | Victoria, B.C. |
| Meche, Gil | 1 | 0 | 6.00 | 2 | 0 | 0 | 0 | 3 | 4 | 2 | 2 | 1 | 4 | R | R | 6-3 | 190 | 9-8-78 | 1996 | Scott, La. |
| Morgan, Eric | 2 | 0 | 0.00 | 3 | 0 | 0 | 0 | 5 | 6 | 3 | 0 | 3 | 4 | R | R | 6-0 | 190 | 10-24-72 | 1994 | Cocoa, Fla. |
| Noe, Matthew | 2 | 2 | 3.53 | 11 | 5 | 0 | 0 | 36 | 34 | 25 | 14 | 26 | 18 | L | L | 6-5 | 215 | 11-20-76 | 1996 | Highland, Calif. |
| Palki, Jeromy | 1 | 1 | 2.47 | 18 | 0 | 0 | 6 | 47 | 31 | 14 | 13 | 17 | 56 | R | R | 6-0 | 195 | 4-14-76 | 1995 | Oakland, Ore. |

# TAMPA BAY
## DEVIL RAYS

**Director of Personnel:** Bill Livesey

| Class | Farm Team | League | W | L | Pct. | Finish* | Manager | First Yr |
|---|---|---|---|---|---|---|---|---|
| A | Hudson Valley (N.Y.) Renegades@ | New York-Penn | 32 | 44 | .421 | 10th (14) | Bump Wills | 1996 |
| #R | Butte (Mon.) Copper Kings | Pioneer | 37 | 35 | .514 | 5th (8) | Tom Foley | 1996 |
| R | St. Petersburg (Fla.) Devil Rays | Gulf Coast | 24 | 35 | .407 | 13th (16) | Bill Evers | 1996 |

*Finish in overall standings (No. of teams in league)   #Advanced level   @Shared with Texas Rangers

### HUDSON VALLEY                                     Class A/Co-Op
#### NEW YORK-PENN LEAGUE

| BATTING | AVG | G | AB | R | H | 2B | 3B | HR | RBI | BB | SO | SB | CS | B | T | HT | WT | DOB | 1st Yr | Resides |
|---|---|---|---|---|---|---|---|---|---|---|---|---|---|---|---|---|---|---|---|---|
| Anderson, Chris | .147 | 52 | 156 | 17 | 23 | 4 | 1 | 5 | 18 | 15 | 70 | 2 | 0 | R | R | 6-5 | 215 | 9-29-74 | 1996 | Guthrie, Okla. |
| Barner, Doug | .218 | 46 | 147 | 21 | 32 | 7 | 0 | 2 | 17 | 30 | 42 | 3 | 3 | R | R | 6-0 | 195 | 12-1-74 | 1996 | Paris, Tenn. |
| Niethammer, Marc | .208 | 67 | 212 | 21 | 44 | 8 | 1 | 8 | 27 | 21 | 80 | 2 | 5 | L | R | 6-5 | 230 | 9-28-73 | 1992 | Lake Wales, Fla. |
| Owens-Bragg, Luke | .182 | 67 | 214 | 22 | 39 | 7 | 2 | 0 | 13 | 36 | 53 | 12 | 8 | S | R | 5-11 | 170 | 6-6-74 | 1996 | Orangevale, Calif. |
| Pomierski, Joe | .260 | 74 | 285 | 45 | 74 | 25 | 3 | 8 | 54 | 35 | 91 | 2 | 4 | L | R | 6-2 | 192 | 4-15-74 | 1992 | Biloxi, Miss. |
| Raymondi, Michael | .040 | 16 | 25 | 1 | 1 | 0 | 0 | 1 | 4 | 10 | 0 | 0 | 1 | R | R | 5-11 | 196 | 9-28-75 | 1994 | Watertown, S.D. |
| Vazquez, Manny | .240 | 73 | 258 | 41 | 62 | 5 | 4 | 1 | 21 | 24 | 41 | 27 | 7 | L | L | 6-1 | 187 | 2-13-75 | 1996 | Miami, Fla. |

**GAMES BY POSITION: C**—Anderson 23, Raymondi 16. **1B**—Niethammer 10, Pomierski 27. **2B**—Barner 1, Owens-Bragg 66. **3B**—Barner 32, Pomierski 36. **SS**—Owens-Bragg 1. **OF**—Anderson 28, Niethammer 26, Vazquez.67.

| PITCHING | W | L | ERA | G | GS | CG | SV | IP | H | R | ER | BB | SO | B | T | HT | WT | DOB | 1st Yr | Resides |
|---|---|---|---|---|---|---|---|---|---|---|---|---|---|---|---|---|---|---|---|---|
| Aquino, Julio | 3 | 1 | 2.60 | 22 | 0 | 0 | 3 | 45 | 36 | 16 | 13 | 7 | 46 | R | R | 6-1 | 173 | 12-12-72 | 1991 | Estorga de Guerra, D.R. |
| Berry, Jason | 4 | 7 | 5.50 | 28 | 0 | 0 | 4 | 38 | 41 | 28 | 23 | 20 | 48 | R | R | 6-4 | 220 | 4-2-74 | 1993 | Brockton, Mass. |
| Cain, Travis | 2 | 5 | 4.60 | 15 | 15 | 0 | 0 | 76 | 67 | 50 | 39 | 44 | 87 | L | R | 6-3 | 185 | 8-10-75 | 1993 | Anderson, S.C. |
| Fowler, Jered | 0 | 0 | 2.25 | 2 | 0 | 0 | 0 | 4 | 2 | 2 | 1 | 0 | 1 | R | R | 6-2 | 205 | 1-7-73 | 1996 | Everett, Wash. |
| Griffiths, Everard | 1 | 1 | 3.06 | 11 | 4 | 0 | 0 | 32 | 26 | 12 | 11 | 13 | 39 | R | R | 6-3 | 190 | 9-11-73 | 1996 | North Miami, Fla. |
| Horton, Aaron | 0 | 3 | 12.43 | 9 | 7 | 0 | 0 | 25 | 55 | 46 | 35 | 15 | 15 | L | L | 6-5 | 196 | 10-10-74 | 1995 | Cardington, Ohio |
| Leon, Scott | 3 | 5 | 4.70 | 15 | 15 | 1 | 0 | 88 | 82 | 54 | 46 | 36 | 73 | R | R | 6-4 | 180 | 9-8-74 | 1996 | Topeka, Kan. |
| Whitson, Eric | 3 | 0 | 2.86 | 19 | 2 | 0 | 0 | 44 | 31 | 17 | 14 | 16 | 34 | S | R | 6-0 | 180 | 8-15-72 | 1995 | Weaverville, N.C. |

### BUTTE                                                   Rookie
#### PIONEER LEAGUE

| BATTING | AVG | G | AB | R | H | 2B | 3B | HR | RBI | BB | SO | SB | CS | B | T | HT | WT | DOB | 1st Yr | Resides |
|---|---|---|---|---|---|---|---|---|---|---|---|---|---|---|---|---|---|---|---|---|
| Arrendondo, Hernando | .357 | 67 | 252 | 59 | 90 | 21 | 7 | 4 | 49 | 24 | 31 | 8 | 3 | R | R | 6-1 | 195 | 11-23-77 | 1996 | Guaymas, Mexico |
| Bain, Tyler | .309 | 61 | 233 | 45 | 72 | 11 | 5 | 3 | 29 | 31 | 33 | 13 | 6 | L | R | 6-1 | 185 | 10-11-74 | 1996 | Greeley, Colo. |
| Barner, Doug | .111 | 6 | 18 | 1 | 2 | 0 | 0 | 0 | 0 | 4 | 6 | 0 | 1 | R | R | 6-0 | 195 | 12-1-74 | 1996 | Paris, Tenn. |
| De los Santos, Eddy | .271 | 16 | 59 | 15 | 16 | 0 | 0 | 0 | 12 | 6 | 17 | 1 | 1 | R | R | 6-2 | 165 | 2-24-78 | 1996 | Santo Domingo, D.R. |
| DeCelle, Mike | .291 | 69 | 258 | 54 | 75 | 18 | 7 | 8 | 51 | 45 | 68 | 6 | 2 | L | R | 6-2 | 205 | 7-10-74 | 1996 | Citrus Heights, Calif. |
| Ebling, Jamie | .278 | 50 | 194 | 49 | 54 | 10 | 3 | 3 | 32 | 38 | 62 | 6 | 4 | R | R | 5-11 | 185 | 1-29-74 | 1996 | Bradenton, Fla. |
| Kastelic, Matt | .354 | 40 | 158 | 26 | 56 | 8 | 1 | 2 | 26 | 6 | 16 | 6 | 0 | L | L | 6-1 | 185 | 1-7-74 | 1996 | Orange, Calif. |
| Kerr, James | .153 | 32 | 98 | 9 | 15 | 3 | 0 | 2 | 6 | 10 | 32 | 3 | 1 | R | R | 6-1 | 180 | 4-28-75 | 1994 | Coral Springs, Fla. |
| King, Mike | .313 | 50 | 192 | 35 | 60 | 13 | 3 | 1 | 27 | 12 | 27 | 7 | 3 | R | R | 5-10 | 165 | 8-6-73 | 1996 | Columbus, Ohio |
| Martinez, Leonardo | .234 | 39 | 128 | 13 | 30 | 1 | 1 | 0 | 16 | 5 | 24 | 5 | 2 | S | R | 6-0 | 168 | 10-25-75 | 1991 | Santo Domingo, D.R. |
| McCain, Marcus | .379 | 55 | 256 | 66 | 97 | 9 | 4 | 1 | 27 | 16 | 21 | 34 | 10 | R | R | 5-7 | 150 | 3-3-74 | 1996 | Long Beach, Calif. |
| McGehee, Mike | .254 | 28 | 71 | 12 | 18 | 1 | 1 | 0 | 8 | 13 | 20 | 0 | 0 | S | R | 6-2 | 195 | 10-15-75 | 1994 | Phoenix, Ariz. |
| Quatraro, Matt | .344 | 59 | 244 | 53 | 84 | 16 | 4 | 1 | 59 | 25 | 29 | 3 | 1 | R | R | 6-2 | 205 | 11-14-73 | 1996 | Selkirk, N.Y. |
| Salinas, Trey | .301 | 67 | 279 | 44 | 84 | 15 | 4 | 8 | 52 | 19 | 43 | 4 | 3 | R | R | 6-1 | 190 | 6-29-75 | 1996 | Corpus Christi, Texas |
| Verrall, Jared | .306 | 57 | 206 | 51 | 63 | 17 | 4 | 9 | 46 | 15 | 78 | 1 | 1 | R | R | 6-4 | 230 | 4-19-74 | 1996 | Burlington, Wash. |
| Voita, Sam | .600 | 5 | 5 | 1 | 3 | 0 | 0 | 0 | 2 | 3 | 0 | 0 | 0 | S | R | 6-1 | 200 | 5-16-74 | 1996 | Calabasas, Calif. |

**GAMES BY POSITION: C**—McGehee 8, Quatraro 41, Salinas 26, Voita 3. **1B**—Arredondo 1, Barner 4, King 8, McGehee 17, Quatraro 15, Salinas 36, Verrall 1. **2B**—Bain 19, Ebling 34, Kerr 2, King 17, Martinez 10. **3B**—Arrendondo 66, Bain 3, Kerr 3, Martinez 2, Salinas 4. **SS**—De los Santos 16, Ebling 17, Kerr 26, Martinez 25. **OF**—Bain 37, DeCelle 68, Kastelic 36, King 24, McCain 55, Salinas 5, Verrall 2.

| PITCHING | W | L | ERA | G | GS | CG | SV | IP | H | R | ER | BB | SO | B | T | HT | WT | DOB | 1st Yr | Resides |
|---|---|---|---|---|---|---|---|---|---|---|---|---|---|---|---|---|---|---|---|---|
| Benesh, Edward | 3 | 0 | 7.98 | 17 | 0 | 0 | 1 | 38 | 55 | 37 | 34 | 20 | 31 | R | R | 6-2 | 185 | 12-18-74 | 1996 | Chicago Heights, Ill. |
| Brown, Trent | 0 | 0 | 12.46 | 3 | 0 | 0 | 0 | 4 | 9 | 6 | 6 | 2 | 4 | L | L | 6-3 | 220 | 2-4-76 | 1996 | San Manuel, Ariz. |
| Callaway, Mickey | 6 | 2 | 3.71 | 16 | 11 | 0 | 0 | 63 | 70 | 37 | 26 | 25 | 57 | R | R | 6-2 | 190 | 5-13-75 | 1996 | Germantown, Tenn. |
| Enders, Trevor | 0 | 1 | 4.88 | 19 | 0 | 0 | 1 | 28 | 34 | 22 | 15 | 13 | 24 | R | L | 6-1 | 205 | 12-22-74 | 1996 | Houston, Texas |
| Fowler, Jered | 1 | 2 | 6.97 | 9 | 0 | 0 | 0 | 10 | 17 | 13 | 8 | 8 | 4 | R | R | 6-2 | 205 | 1-7-73 | 1996 | Everett, Wash. |
| Griffiths, Everard | 0 | 2 | 8.03 | 7 | 0 | 0 | 0 | 12 | 18 | 17 | 11 | 15 | 12 | R | R | 6-3 | 190 | 9-11-73 | 1996 | North Miami, Fla. |
| Hale, Mark | 2 | 2 | 3.26 | 21 | 0 | 0 | 7 | 39 | 32 | 17 | 14 | 10 | 56 | R | R | 6-4 | 220 | 8-31-75 | 1996 | Carefree, Ariz. |
| Hinojosa, Joel | 3 | 4 | 5.27 | 27 | 0 | 0 | 1 | 43 | 49 | 31 | 25 | 25 | 32 | R | R | 6-0 | 190 | 4-6-74 | 1996 | Garland, Texas |
| Howerton, R.J. | 3 | 1 | 4.43 | 15 | 13 | 0 | 0 | 61 | 72 | 47 | 30 | 42 | 47 | R | R | 6-4 | 210 | 1-2-74 | 1996 | Burneyville, Okla. |
| Kaufman, John | 3 | 4 | 4.66 | 13 | 12 | 0 | 0 | 46 | 53 | 36 | 24 | 24 | 55 | L | L | 5-10 | 170 | 10-23-74 | 1996 | Tampa, Fla. |
| Kimbrell, Michael | 7 | 1 | 3.86 | 23 | 0 | 0 | 2 | 49 | 35 | 30 | 21 | 37 | 65 | L | L | 6-3 | 215 | 2-20-74 | 1996 | Greenwell Springs, La. |
| Madison, Scott | 0 | 1 | 11.74 | 2 | 2 | 0 | 0 | 8 | 17 | 11 | 10 | 3 | 5 | L | L | 6-2 | 190 | 9-12-74 | 1996 | Latham, N.Y. |
| Manias, James | 5 | 4 | 5.25 | 16 | 13 | 0 | 0 | 72 | 98 | 64 | 42 | 22 | 55 | L | L | 6-4 | 190 | 10-21-74 | 1996 | Florham Park, N.J. |
| McCreery, Rick | 0 | 1 | 2.25 | 8 | 0 | 0 | 1 | 16 | 14 | 5 | 4 | 7 | 12 | R | R | 6-1 | 195 | 1-27-76 | 1996 | Casa Grande, Ariz. |

| PITCHING | W | L | ERA | G | GS | CG | SV | IP | H | R | ER | BB | SO | B | T | HT | WT | DOB | 1st Yr | Resides |
|---|---|---|---|---|---|---|---|---|---|---|---|---|---|---|---|---|---|---|---|---|
| Pujals, Denis .............. | 2 | 7 | 5.15 | 15 | 15 | 0 | 0 | 87 | 110 | 65 | 50 | 19 | 82 | R | R | 6-4 | 215 | 2-5-73 | 1996 | Miami, Fla. |
| Stutz, Shawn .............. | 2 | 3 | 8.51 | 19 | 6 | 0 | 2 | 49 | 63 | 60 | 46 | 40 | 46 | R | R | 6-3 | 185 | 6-23-75 | 1996 | Fort Myers, Fla. |
| Whitley, Kyle ............. | 1 | 1 | 9.00 | 10 | 0 | 0 | 1 | 11 | 17 | 15 | 11 | 7 | 14 | R | R | 6-3 | 205 | 9-28-73 | 1996 | Pilot Point, Texas |

# ST. PETERSBURG — Rookie

## GULF COAST LEAGUE

| BATTING | AVG | G | AB | R | H | 2B | 3B | HR | RBI | BB | SO | SB | CS | B | T | HT | WT | DOB | 1st Yr | Resides |
|---|---|---|---|---|---|---|---|---|---|---|---|---|---|---|---|---|---|---|---|---|
| Arias, Jeison ............... | .258 | 19 | 66 | 7 | 17 | 4 | 1 | 0 | 4 | 3 | 31 | 3 | 1 | R | R | 6-1 | 195 | 9-27-78 | 1996 | San Jose de Ocoa, D.R. |
| Barner, Doug .............. | .200 | 1 | 5 | 1 | 1 | 0 | 0 | 0 | 0 | 0 | 1 | 0 | 0 | R | R | 6-0 | 195 | 12-1-74 | 1996 | Paris, Tenn. |
| Becker, Brian .............. | .271 | 52 | 199 | 31 | 54 | 12 | 0 | 2 | 27 | 13 | 28 | 3 | 1 | R | R | 6-7 | 220 | 5-26-75 | 1996 | Tempe, Ariz. |
| Blanco, Octavio ........... | .300 | 11 | 20 | 0 | 6 | 0 | 0 | 0 | 2 | 0 | 5 | 0 | 0 | R | R | 6-2 | 180 | 8-13-78 | 1996 | Caracas, Venez. |
| De los Santos, Eddy ... | .245 | 50 | 196 | 18 | 48 | 6 | 1 | 0 | 20 | 13 | 58 | 11 | 4 | R | R | 6-2 | 165 | 2-24-78 | 1996 | Santo Domingo, D.R. |
| Gonzalez, Melciades ... | .068 | 17 | 44 | 7 | 3 | 0 | 0 | 0 | 2 | 5 | 13 | 2 | 0 | R | R | 6-0 | 170 | 10-22-78 | 1996 | San Pedro de Macoris, D.R. |
| Guerrero, Francisco ..... | .043 | 11 | 23 | 1 | 1 | 0 | 0 | 0 | 1 | 5 | 10 | 0 | 1 | R | R | 6-2 | 190 | 8-28-79 | 1996 | Santo Domingo, D.R. |
| Gunner, Chie .............. | .176 | 44 | 131 | 8 | 23 | 2 | 0 | 0 | 8 | 10 | 45 | 2 | 1 | L | R | 6-2 | 183 | 7-22-78 | 1996 | Grandview, Mo. |
| Johnson, Doug ........... | .231 | 28 | 108 | 12 | 25 | 3 | 1 | 1 | 9 | 7 | 41 | 0 | 2 | R | R | 6-3 | 195 | 10-27-77 | 1996 | Gainesville, Fla. |
| McCladdie, Tony .......... | .295 | 50 | 166 | 21 | 49 | 7 | 4 | 0 | 21 | 9 | 27 | 14 | 1 | R | R | 5-10 | 185 | 10-11-75 | 1996 | Martinez, Ga. |
| Ramirez, Edgar ........... | .158 | 38 | 114 | 12 | 18 | 0 | 0 | 0 | 8 | 10 | 29 | 3 | 2 | R | R | 6-2 | 165 | 8-7-79 | 1996 | San Pedro de Macoris, D.R. |
| Sanchez, Alex ............. | .282 | 56 | 227 | 36 | 64 | 7 | 6 | 1 | 22 | 10 | 35 | 20 | 12 | L | L | 5-10 | 179 | 8-26-76 | 1996 | Miami, Fla. |
| Sandberg, Jared .......... | .169 | 22 | 77 | 6 | 13 | 2 | 1 | 0 | 7 | 9 | 26 | 1 | 0 | R | R | 6-3 | 185 | 3-2-78 | 1996 | Olympia, Wash. |
| Severence, Lance ....... | .174 | 9 | 23 | 0 | 4 | 0 | 0 | 0 | 2 | 4 | 1 | 0 | 0 | R | R | 6-3 | 220 | 4-28-76 | 1996 | Archbold, Ohio |
| Stephens, Jesus .......... | .224 | 33 | 76 | 12 | 17 | 1 | 0 | 0 | 10 | 11 | 26 | 3 | 2 | R | R | 6-0 | 185 | 4-10-78 | 1996 | San Pedro de Macoris, D.R. |
| Suriel, Miguel ............. | .243 | 49 | 181 | 21 | 44 | 4 | 2 | 1 | 25 | 8 | 25 | 5 | 2 | R | R | 6-0 | 165 | 11-15-76 | 1994 | Palmirito, D.R. |
| Voita, Sam .................. | .259 | 22 | 58 | 8 | 15 | 1 | 0 | 1 | 6 | 10 | 14 | 1 | 0 | S | R | 6-1 | 200 | 5-16-74 | 1996 | Calabasas, Calif. |
| Weber, Brad ................ | .247 | 37 | 81 | 8 | 20 | 2 | 0 | 0 | 11 | 11 | 24 | 1 | 0 | L | L | 6-2 | 195 | 7-7-76 | 1996 | Auburn, Ind. |
| Wilder, Paul ............... | .207 | 53 | 184 | 31 | 38 | 10 | 2 | 3 | 20 | 37 | 66 | 7 | 5 | L | R | 6-4 | 230 | 1-9-78 | 1996 | Raleigh, N.C. |

**GAMES BY POSITION: C**—Blanco 10, Severance 7, Suriel 36, Voita 17. **1B**—Becker 52, Stephens 8, Voita 1. **2B**—Johnson 1, McCladdie 18, Ramirez 21, Sandberg 21. **3B**—Johnson 27, McCladdie 19, Ramirez 3, Suriel 14. **SS**—De los Santos 50, Ramirez 13. **OF**—Arias 18, Gonzalez 15, Guerrero 3, Gunner 44, McCladdie 10, Ramirez 1, Sanchez 56, Stephens 15, Weber 34, Wilder 1.

| PITCHING | W | L | ERA | G | GS | CG | SV | IP | H | R | ER | BB | SO | B | T | HT | WT | DOB | 1st Yr | Resides |
|---|---|---|---|---|---|---|---|---|---|---|---|---|---|---|---|---|---|---|---|---|
| Arias, Jose ................... | 0 | 1 | 2.37 | 10 | 0 | 0 | 1 | 19 | 22 | 8 | 5 | 9 | 20 | L | L | 6-0 | 165 | 7-26-76 | 1994 | Santo Domingo, D.R. |
| Bowers, Cedrick .......... | 3 | 5 | 5.37 | 13 | 13 | 0 | 0 | 60 | 50 | 39 | 36 | 39 | 85 | R | L | 6-2 | 210 | 2-10-78 | 1996 | Chiefland, Fla. |
| Brown, Michael ........... | 0 | 0 | 11.57 | 3 | 1 | 0 | 0 | 5 | 7 | 9 | 6 | 8 | 2 | R | R | 6-4 | 200 | 10-13-76 | 1996 | Oliver Springs, Tenn. |
| Brown, Trent ............... | 3 | 2 | 2.18 | 15 | 3 | 0 | 1 | 45 | 37 | 18 | 11 | 14 | 53 | L | L | 6-3 | 220 | 2-4-76 | 1996 | San Manuel, Ariz. |
| Cafaro, Robert ............ | 0 | 0 | 0.00 | 2 | 0 | 0 | 0 | 3 | 0 | 0 | 0 | 0 | 3 | R | R | 6-3 | 175 | 8-8-75 | 1996 | Seymour, Conn. |
| Deckard, Edward ......... | 1 | 0 | 2.82 | 9 | 0 | 0 | 0 | 22 | 23 | 10 | 7 | 11 | 15 | R | R | 6-5 | 190 | 11-23-77 | 1996 | Springfield, Mo. |
| DeLeon, Julio ............. | 0 | 0 | 4.70 | 7 | 0 | 0 | 0 | 15 | 18 | 9 | 8 | 4 | 6 | R | R | 6-5 | 198 | 11-19-75 | 1994 | Santo Domingo, D.R. |
| Fowler, Jered .............. | 0 | 0 | 4.70 | 4 | 0 | 0 | 2 | 8 | 8 | 7 | 4 | 8 | 10 | R | R | 6-2 | 205 | 1-7-73 | 1996 | Everett, Wash. |
| Hinojosa, Joel ............. | 0 | 0 | 20.25 | 1 | 0 | 0 | 0 | 1 | 3 | 5 | 3 | 2 | 1 | R | R | 6-0 | 190 | 4-6-74 | 1996 | Garland, Texas |
| James, Delvin .............. | 2 | 8 | 8.87 | 11 | 11 | 1 | 0 | 48 | 64 | 52 | 47 | 21 | 40 | R | R | 6-3 | 215 | 1-3-78 | 1996 | Nacogdoches, Texas |
| Kofler, Ed .................. | 1 | 4 | 5.27 | 10 | 10 | 0 | 0 | 41 | 49 | 30 | 24 | 11 | 36 | R | R | 6-2 | 165 | 12-23-77 | 1996 | Palm Harbor, Fla. |
| Madison, Scott ............ | 0 | 0 | 27.00 | 1 | 0 | 0 | 0 | 1 | 5 | 3 | 3 | 0 | 0 | L | L | 6-2 | 190 | 9-12-74 | 1996 | Latham, N.Y. |
| McCreery, Rick ............ | 0 | 2 | 1.17 | 11 | 0 | 0 | 5 | 15 | 12 | 5 | 2 | 4 | 16 | R | R | 6-1 | 195 | 1-27-76 | 1996 | Casa Grande, Ariz. |
| Ortega, Pablo .............. | 4 | 6 | 1.97 | 13 | 13 | 1 | 0 | 82 | 61 | 24 | 18 | 12 | 86 | S | R | 6-2 | 170 | 11-7-76 | 1993 | Nuevo Laredo, Mex. |
| Rodriguez, Jose .......... | 3 | 1 | 5.06 | 11 | 2 | 0 | 0 | 27 | 28 | 17 | 15 | 7 | 19 | R | R | 6-2 | 160 | 2-27-78 | 1996 | Cotuy, D.R. |
| Rosario, Juan ............. | 0 | 0 | 0.00 | 3 | 0 | 0 | 0 | 3 | 0 | 3 | 0 | 3 | 3 | R | R | 6-4 | 195 | 11-3-75 | 1993 | Perth Amboy, N.J. |
| Ruhl, Nathan .............. | 2 | 2 | 2.33 | 16 | 0 | 0 | 0 | 27 | 18 | 9 | 7 | 11 | 25 | R | R | 6-4 | 200 | 7-16-76 | 1996 | Lee's Summit, Mo. |
| Salvevold, Greg ........... | 1 | 1 | 3.82 | 15 | 0 | 0 | 2 | 31 | 26 | 17 | 13 | 13 | 22 | R | R | 6-3 | 180 | 9-24-75 | 1996 | Moorhead, Minn. |
| Seberino, Ronni ........... | 4 | 2 | 3.46 | 18 | 6 | 0 | 1 | 52 | 50 | 22 | 20 | 15 | 49 | L | L | 6-1 | 177 | 5-27-79 | 1996 | San Pedro de Macoris, D.R. |
| Vail, Keith ................... | 0 | 0 | 11.88 | 5 | 0 | 0 | 0 | 8 | 12 | 13 | 11 | 7 | 4 | R | R | 6-9 | 245 | 9-13-75 | 1996 | Shelton, Conn. |
| Zambrano, Victor ......... | 0 | 0 | 8.10 | 1 | 0 | 0 | 0 | 3 | 4 | 4 | 3 | 0 | 6 | S | R | 6-1 | 170 | 8-6-74 | 1994 | Los Teques, Venez. |

# TEXAS RANGERS

**Manager:** Johnny Oates.   **1996 Record:** 90-72, .556 (1st, AL West).

| BATTING | AVG | G | AB | R | H | 2B | 3B | HR | RBI | BB | SO | SB | CS | B | T | HT | WT | DOB | 1st Yr | Resides |
|---|---|---|---|---|---|---|---|---|---|---|---|---|---|---|---|---|---|---|---|---|
| Brown, Kevin | .000 | 3 | 4 | 1 | 0 | 0 | 0 | 0 | 1 | 2 | 2 | 0 | 0 | R | R | 6-2 | 200 | 4-21-73 | 1994 | Winslow, Ind. |
| Buford, Damon | .283 | 90 | 145 | 30 | 41 | 9 | 0 | 6 | 20 | 15 | 34 | 8 | 5 | R | R | 5-10 | 170 | 6-12-70 | 1990 | Sherman Oaks, Calif. |
| Clark, Will | .284 | 117 | 436 | 69 | 124 | 25 | 1 | 13 | 72 | 64 | 67 | 2 | 1 | L | L | 6-1 | 196 | 3-13-64 | 1985 | New Orleans, La. |
| Elster, Kevin | .252 | 157 | 515 | 79 | 130 | 32 | 2 | 24 | 99 | 52 | 138 | 4 | 1 | R | R | 6-2 | 200 | 8-3-64 | 1984 | Huntington Beach, Calif. |
| Faneyte, Rikkert | .200 | 8 | 5 | 0 | 1 | 0 | 0 | 0 | 1 | 0 | 0 | 0 | 0 | R | R | 6-1 | 170 | 5-31-69 | 1991 | Amsterdam, Holland |
| Frazier, Lou | .260 | 30 | 50 | 5 | 13 | 2 | 1 | 0 | 5 | 8 | 10 | 4 | 2 | S | R | 6-2 | 175 | 1-26-65 | 1986 | St. Louis, Mo. |
| Gil, Benji | .400 | 5 | 5 | 0 | 2 | 0 | 0 | 0 | 1 | 1 | 1 | 0 | 1 | R | R | 6-2 | 180 | 10-6-72 | 1991 | San Diego, Calif. |
| Gonzales, Rene | .217 | 51 | 92 | 19 | 20 | 4 | 0 | 2 | 5 | 10 | 11 | 0 | 0 | R | R | 6-3 | 215 | 9-3-61 | 1982 | Newport Beach, Calif. |
| Gonzalez, Juan | .314 | 134 | 541 | 89 | 170 | 33 | 2 | 47 | 144 | 45 | 82 | 2 | 0 | R | R | 6-3 | 210 | 10-16-69 | 1986 | Vega Baja, P.R. |
| Greer, Rusty | .332 | 139 | 542 | 96 | 180 | 41 | 6 | 18 | 100 | 62 | 86 | 9 | 0 | L | L | 6-0 | 190 | 1-21-69 | 1990 | Albertville, Ala. |
| Hamilton, Darryl | .293 | 148 | 627 | 94 | 184 | 29 | 4 | 6 | 51 | 54 | 66 | 15 | 5 | L | R | 6-1 | 180 | 12-3-64 | 1986 | Sugar Land, Texas |
| McLemore, Mark | .290 | 147 | 517 | 84 | 150 | 23 | 4 | 5 | 46 | 87 | 69 | 27 | 10 | S | R | 5-11 | 207 | 10-4-64 | 1982 | Gilbert, Ariz. |
| Newson, Warren | .255 | 91 | 235 | 34 | 60 | 14 | 1 | 10 | 31 | 37 | 82 | 3 | 0 | L | L | 5-7 | 202 | 7-3-64 | 1986 | Newnan, Ga. |
| Ortiz, Luis | .286 | 3 | 7 | 1 | 2 | 0 | 1 | 1 | 1 | 0 | 1 | 0 | 0 | R | R | 6-0 | 195 | 5-25-70 | 1991 | Santo Domingo, D.R. |
| Palmer, Dean | .280 | 154 | 582 | 98 | 163 | 26 | 2 | 38 | 107 | 59 | 145 | 2 | 0 | R | R | 6-2 | 195 | 12-27-68 | 1986 | Tallahassee, Fla. |
| Rodriguez, Ivan | .300 | 153 | 639 | 116 | 192 | 47 | 3 | 19 | 86 | 38 | 55 | 5 | 0 | R | R | 5-9 | 205 | 11-30-71 | 1989 | Vega Baja, P.R. |
| Stevens, Lee | .231 | 27 | 78 | 6 | 18 | 2 | 3 | 3 | 12 | 6 | 22 | 0 | 0 | L | L | 6-4 | 205 | 7-10-67 | 1986 | Wichita, Kan. |
| Stillwell, Kurt | .273 | 46 | 77 | 12 | 21 | 4 | 0 | 1 | 4 | 10 | 11 | 0 | 0 | S | R | 5-11 | 185 | 6-4-65 | 1983 | Poway, Calif. |
| Tettleton, Mickey | .246 | 143 | 491 | 78 | 121 | 26 | 1 | 24 | 83 | 95 | 137 | 2 | 1 | S | R | 6-2 | 212 | 9-16-60 | 1981 | Farmington, Hills, Mich. |
| Valle, Dave | .302 | 42 | 86 | 14 | 26 | 6 | 1 | 3 | 17 | 9 | 17 | 0 | 0 | R | R | 6-2 | 220 | 10-30-60 | 1978 | Renton, Wash. |
| Voigt, Jack | .111 | 5 | 9 | 1 | 1 | 0 | 0 | 0 | 0 | 0 | 2 | 0 | 0 | R | R | 6-1 | 175 | 5-17-66 | 1987 | Venice, Fla. |
| Worthington, Craig | .158 | 13 | 19 | 2 | 3 | 0 | 0 | 1 | 4 | 6 | 3 | 0 | 0 | R | R | 6-0 | 200 | 4-17-65 | 1985 | Anaheim, Calif. |

| PITCHING | W | L | ERA | G | GS | CG | SV | IP | H | R | ER | BB | SO | B | T | HT | WT | DOB | 1st Yr | Resides |
|---|---|---|---|---|---|---|---|---|---|---|---|---|---|---|---|---|---|---|---|---|
| Alberro, Jose | 0 | 1 | 5.79 | 5 | 1 | 0 | 0 | 9 | 14 | 6 | 6 | 7 | 2 | R | R | 6-2 | 190 | 6-29-69 | 1991 | San Juan, P.R. |
| Brandenburg, Mark | 1 | 3 | 3.21 | 26 | 0 | 0 | 0 | 48 | 48 | 22 | 17 | 25 | 37 | R | R | 6-0 | 170 | 7-14-70 | 1992 | Humble, Texas |
| Burkett, John | 5 | 2 | 4.06 | 10 | 10 | 1 | 0 | 69 | 75 | 33 | 31 | 16 | 47 | R | R | 6-3 | 205 | 11-28-64 | 1983 | Scottsdale, Ariz. |
| Cook, Dennis | 5 | 2 | 4.09 | 60 | 0 | 0 | 0 | 70 | 53 | 34 | 32 | 35 | 64 | L | L | 6-3 | 190 | 10-4-62 | 1985 | Austin, Texas |
| Gross, Kevin | 11 | 8 | 5.22 | 28 | 19 | 1 | 0 | 129 | 151 | 78 | 75 | 50 | 78 | R | R | 6-5 | 215 | 6-8-61 | 1981 | Claremont, Calif. |
| Helling, Rick | 1 | 2 | 7.52 | 6 | 2 | 0 | 0 | 20 | 23 | 17 | 17 | 9 | 16 | R | R | 6-3 | 215 | 12-15-70 | 1992 | West Fargo, N.D. |
| Henneman, Mike | 0 | 7 | 5.79 | 49 | 0 | 0 | 31 | 42 | 41 | 28 | 27 | 17 | 34 | R | R | 6-4 | 205 | 12-11-61 | 1984 | Colleyville, Texas |
| Heredia, Gil | 2 | 5 | 5.89 | 44 | 0 | 0 | 1 | 73 | 91 | 50 | 48 | 14 | 43 | R | R | 6-1 | 190 | 10-26-65 | 1987 | Tucson, Ariz. |
| Hill, Ken | 16 | 10 | 3.63 | 35 | 35 | 7 | 0 | 251 | 250 | 110 | 101 | 95 | 170 | R | R | 6-2 | 175 | 12-14-65 | 1985 | Lynn, Mass. |
| Oliver, Darren | 14 | 6 | 4.66 | 30 | 30 | 1 | 0 | 174 | 190 | 97 | 90 | 76 | 112 | R | L | 6-0 | 170 | 10-6-70 | 1988 | Rio Linda, Calif. |
| Patterson, Danny | 0 | 0 | 0.00 | 7 | 0 | 0 | 0 | 9 | 10 | 4 | 0 | 3 | 5 | R | R | 6-0 | 168 | 2-17-71 | 1990 | Rosemead, Calif. |
| Pavlik, Roger | 15 | 8 | 5.19 | 34 | 34 | 7 | 0 | 201 | 216 | 120 | 116 | 81 | 127 | R | R | 6-2 | 220 | 10-4-67 | 1987 | Houston, Texas |
| Russell, Jeff | 3 | 3 | 3.38 | 55 | 0 | 0 | 3 | 56 | 58 | 22 | 21 | 22 | 23 | R | R | 6-3 | 205 | 9-2-61 | 1980 | Colleyville, Texas |
| Stanton, Mike | 0 | 1 | 3.22 | 22 | 0 | 0 | 0 | 22 | 20 | 8 | 8 | 4 | 14 | L | L | 6-1 | 190 | 6-2-67 | 1987 | Houston, Texas |
| 2-team (59 Boston) | 4 | 4 | 3.66 | 81 | 0 | 0 | 1 | 79 | 78 | 32 | 32 | 27 | 60 | | | | | | | |
| Vosberg, Ed | 1 | 1 | 3.27 | 52 | 0 | 0 | 8 | 44 | 51 | 17 | 16 | 21 | 32 | L | L | 6-1 | 190 | 9-28-61 | 1983 | Tucson, Ariz. |
| Whiteside, Matt | 0 | 1 | 6.68 | 14 | 0 | 0 | 0 | 32 | 43 | 24 | 24 | 11 | 15 | R | R | 6-0 | 185 | 8-8-67 | 1990 | Charleston, Mo. |
| Witt, Bobby | 16 | 12 | 5.41 | 33 | 32 | 2 | 0 | 200 | 235 | 129 | 120 | 96 | 157 | R | R | 6-2 | 205 | 5-11-64 | 1985 | Colleyville, Texas |

## FIELDING

| Catcher | PCT | G | PO | A | E | DP | PB |
|---|---|---|---|---|---|---|---|
| Brown | 1.000 | 2 | 11 | 1 | 0 | 0 | 0 |
| Rodriguez | .989 | 146 | 850 | 81 | 10 | 11 | 10 |
| Valle | .994 | 35 | 145 | 13 | 1 | 2 | 0 |

| First Base | PCT | G | PO | A | E | DP |
|---|---|---|---|---|---|---|
| Clark | .996 | 117 | 956 | 73 | 4 | 90 |
| Gonzales | .989 | 23 | 88 | 6 | 1 | 11 |
| Greer | 1.000 | 1 | 0 | 0 | 0 | 0 |
| Stevens | .994 | 18 | 152 | 14 | 1 | 21 |
| Stillwell | 1.000 | 1 | 3 | 0 | 0 | 0 |
| Tettleton | .977 | 23 | 161 | 11 | 4 | 14 |
| Valle | 1.000 | 5 | 5 | 0 | 0 | 1 |
| Worthington | 1.000 | 6 | 16 | 4 | 0 | 1 |

| Second Base | PCT | G | PO | A | E | DP |
|---|---|---|---|---|---|---|
| Frazier | .000 | 1 | 0 | 0 | 1 | 0 |
| Gonzales | 1.000 | 5 | 2 | 18 | 0 | 1 |
| McLemore | .985 | 147 | 313 | 473 | 12 | 115 |
| Stillwell | .964 | 21 | 24 | 29 | 2 | 4 |

| Third Base | PCT | G | PO | A | E | DP |
|---|---|---|---|---|---|---|
| Gonzales | 1.000 | 15 | 7 | 16 | 0 | 3 |
| Palmer | .953 | 154 | 105 | 220 | 16 | 17 |

| Shortstop | PCT | G | PO | A | E | DP |
|---|---|---|---|---|---|---|
| Stillwell | 1.000 | 6 | 0 | 1 | 0 | 1 |
| Voigt | 1.000 | 1 | 0 | 1 | 0 | 0 |
| Worthington | .917 | 7 | 2 | 9 | 1 | 1 |

| Shortstop | PCT | G | PO | A | E | DP |
|---|---|---|---|---|---|---|
| Elster | .981 | 157 | 285 | 441 | 14 | 103 |
| Gil | .923 | 5 | 5 | 7 | 1 | 0 |
| Gonzales | .971 | 10 | 12 | 21 | 1 | 5 |
| Stillwell | .923 | 9 | 3 | 9 | 1 | 0 |

| Outfield | PCT | G | PO | A | E | DP |
|---|---|---|---|---|---|---|
| Buford | 1.000 | 80 | 93 | 3 | 0 | 0 |
| Faneyte | 1.000 | 6 | 11 | 0 | 0 | 0 |
| Frazier | .971 | 15 | 31 | 3 | 1 | 0 |
| Gonzales | .000 | 1 | 0 | 0 | 0 | 0 |
| Gonzalez | .988 | 102 | 162 | 6 | 2 | 0 |
| Greer | .984 | 137 | 304 | 6 | 5 | 0 |
| Hamilton | 1.000 | 147 | 387 | 2 | 0 | 0 |
| McLemore | .000 | 1 | 0 | 0 | 0 | 0 |
| Newson | .992 | 66 | 122 | 5 | 1 | 2 |
| Stevens | 1.000 | 5 | 6 | 0 | 0 | 0 |
| Voigt | 1.000 | 3 | 5 | 0 | 0 | 0 |

**Rusty Greer**

Ivan Rodriguez had an all-star season, hitting .300 with 47 doubles

Rangers minor league Player of the Year Dan Kolb

LARRY GOREN

ROBERT GURGANUS

# RANGERS

## FARM SYSTEM

**Director of Player Development:** Reid Nichols

| Class | Farm Team | League | W | L | Pct. | Finish* | Manager | First Yr |
|---|---|---|---|---|---|---|---|---|
| AAA | Oklahoma City (Okla.) 89ers | American Assoc. | 74 | 70 | .514 | +5th (8) | Greg Biagini | 1983 |
| AA | Tulsa (Okla.) Drillers | Texas | 75 | 64 | .540 | 2nd (8) | Bobby Jones | 1977 |
| #A | Charlotte (Fla.) Rangers | Florida State | 63 | 76 | .453 | 11th (14) | Butch Wynegar | 1987 |
| A | Charleston (S.C.) RiverDogs | South Atlantic | 63 | 78 | .447 | 10th (14) | Gary Allenson | 1993 |
| A | Hudson Valley (N.Y.) Renegades@ | New York-Penn | 32 | 44 | .421 | 10th (14) | Bump Wills | 1994 |
| R | Port Charlotte (Fla.) Rangers | Gulf Coast | 37 | 23 | .617 | 3rd (16) | James Byrd | 1973 |

*Finish in overall standings (No. of teams)  #Advanced level  +Won league championship  @Shared with Devil Rays

## ORGANIZATION LEADERS

### MAJOR LEAGUERS

**BATTING**

| | | |
|---|---|---|
| *AVG | Rusty Greer | .332 |
| R | Ivan Rodriguez | 116 |
| H | Ivan Rodriguez | 192 |
| TB | Juan Gonzalez | 348 |
| 2B | Ivan Rodriguez | 47 |
| 3B | Rusty Greer | 6 |
| HR | Juan Gonzalez | 47 |
| RBI | Juan Gonzalez | 144 |
| BB | Mickey Tettleton | 95 |
| SO | Dean Palmer | 145 |
| SB | Mark McLemore | 27 |

**PITCHING**

| | | |
|---|---|---|
| W | Two tied at | 16 |
| L | Bobby Witt | 12 |
| #ERA | Ken Hill | 3.63 |
| G | Dennis Cook | 60 |
| CG | Two tied at | 7 |
| SV | Mike Henneman | 31 |
| IP | Ken Hill | 251 |
| BB | Bobby Witt | 95 |
| SO | Ken Hill | 170 |

**Ken Hill.** 170 strikeouts

THE SPORTS GROUP

### MINOR LEAGUERS

**BATTING**

| | | |
|---|---|---|
| *AVG | Lee Stevens, Oklahoma City | .325 |
| R | Mike Murphy, Charlotte/Okla. City | 95 |
| H | Luis Ortiz, Oklahoma City | 159 |
| TB | Lee Stevens, Oklahoma City | 277 |
| 2B | Lee Stevens, Oklahoma City | 37 |
| 3B | Hanley Frias, Tulsa | 12 |
| HR | Two tied at | 32 |
| RBI | Two tied at | 94 |
| BB | Jack Voigt, Charlotte/Okla. City | 79 |
| SO | Shawn Gallagher, Charleston/H.V. | 152 |
| SB | Juan Nunez, Charleston | 53 |

**PITCHING**

| | | |
|---|---|---|
| W | Ted Silva, Charlotte/Tulsa | 17 |
| L | Toure Knighton, Bakersfield | 17 |
| #ERA | Ken Raines, Hudson Valley/Charlotte | 2.50 |
| G | Ken Raines, Hudson Valley/Charlotte | 61 |
| CG | Jonathan Johnson, Tulsa/Okla. City | 7 |
| SV | Mike Venafro, Charleston | 19 |
| IP | Ted Silva, Charlotte/Tulsa | 189 |
| BB | Dan Kolb, Charleston/Charlotte | 82 |
| SO | Rob Kell, Bakersfield/Charlotte | 164 |

*Minimum 250 At-Bats  #Minimum 75 Innings

## TOP 10 PROSPECTS

**How the Rangers Top 10 prospects, as judged by Baseball America prior to the 1996 season, fared in 1996:**

STEVE MOORE

**Andrew Vessel**

| Player, Pos. | Club (Class—League) | AVG | AB | R | H | 2B | 3B | HR | RBI | SB |
|---|---|---|---|---|---|---|---|---|---|---|
| 1. Andrew Vessel, of | Charlotte (A—Florida State) | .229 | 484 | 63 | 111 | 25 | 6 | 3 | 67 | 1 |
| 3. Kevin Brown, c | Tulsa (AA—Texas) | .263 | 460 | 77 | 121 | 27 | 1 | 26 | 86 | 0 |
| | Texas | .000 | 4 | 1 | 0 | 0 | 0 | 0 | 0 | 0 |
| 4. Edwin Diaz, 2b | Tulsa (AA—Texas) | .264 | 500 | 70 | 132 | 36 | 6 | 16 | 65 | 8 |
| 6. Fernando Tatis, 3b | Okla. City (AAA—Amer. Assoc.) | .500 | 4 | 0 | 2 | 1 | 0 | 0 | 0 | 0 |
| | Charlotte (A—Florida State) | .286 | 325 | 46 | 93 | 25 | 0 | 12 | 53 | 9 |
| 8. Mike Bell, 3b | Tulsa (AA—Texas) | .267 | 484 | 62 | 129 | 31 | 3 | 16 | 59 | 3 |
| 9. Shawn Gallagher, 1b | Charleston (A—South Atlantic) | .224 | 303 | 29 | 68 | 11 | 4 | 7 | 32 | 6 |
| | Hudson Valley (A—N. Y.-Penn) | .273 | 176 | 15 | 48 | 10 | 2 | 4 | 29 | 8 |
| 10. Mark Little, of | Tulsa (AA—Texas) | .291 | 409 | 69 | 119 | 24 | 2 | 13 | 50 | 22 |

| Player, Pos. | Club (Class—League) | W | L | ERA | G | SV | IP | H | BB | SO |
|---|---|---|---|---|---|---|---|---|---|---|
| 2. Julio Santana, rhp | Okla. City (AAA—Amer. Assoc.) | 11 | 12 | 4.02 | 29 | 0 | 186 | 171 | 66 | 113 |
| 5. Jonathan Johnson, rhp | Okla. City (AAA—Amer. Assoc.) | 1 | 0 | 0.00 | 1 | 0 | 9 | 2 | 1 | 6 |
| | Tulsa (AA—Texas) | 13 | 10 | 3.56 | 26 | 0 | 174 | 176 | 41 | 97 |
| 7. *Ryan Dempster, rhp | Charleston (A—South Atlantic) | 7 | 11 | 3.30 | 23 | 0 | 144 | 120 | 58 | 141 |
| | Kane County (A—Midwest) | 2 | 1 | 2.73 | 4 | 0 | 26 | 18 | 18 | 16 |

*Traded to Marlins

## AMERICAN ASSOCIATION

### BATTING

| BATTING | AVG | G | AB | R | H | 2B | 3B | HR | RBI | BB | SO | SB | CS | B | T | HT | WT | DOB | 1st Yr | Resides |
|---|---|---|---|---|---|---|---|---|---|---|---|---|---|---|---|---|---|---|---|---|
| Bryant, Scott | .268 | 12 | 41 | 4 | 11 | 3 | 0 | 0 | 3 | 4 | 10 | 0 | 0 | R | R | 6-2 | 215 | 10-31-67 | 1989 | San Antonio, Texas |
| Cardenas, Johnny | .169 | 30 | 77 | 8 | 13 | 5 | 0 | 0 | 2 | 1 | 23 | 0 | 0 | R | R | 6-3 | 210 | 7-23-70 | 1993 | Fort Worth, Texas |
| Charles, Frank | .186 | 35 | 113 | 10 | 21 | 7 | 2 | 1 | 8 | 4 | 29 | 0 | 3 | R | R | 6-4 | 210 | 2-23-69 | 1991 | Anaheim, Calif. |
| Estrada, Osmani | .262 | 50 | 130 | 15 | 34 | 6 | 1 | 1 | 13 | 14 | 26 | 3 | 1 | R | R | 5-8 | 180 | 1-23-69 | 1993 | Woodland Hills, Calif. |
| Faneyte, Rikkert | .236 | 93 | 364 | 53 | 86 | 15 | 0 | 11 | 44 | 34 | 65 | 14 | 9 | R | R | 6-1 | 170 | 5-31-69 | 1991 | Amsterdam, Netherlands |
| Frazier, Lou | .245 | 58 | 208 | 28 | 51 | 8 | 3 | 3 | 16 | 14 | 42 | 13 | 4 | S | R | 6-2 | 175 | 1-26-65 | 1986 | St. Louis, Mo. |
| Frye, Jeff | .238 | 49 | 181 | 25 | 43 | 10 | 0 | 1 | 18 | 24 | 21 | 10 | 1 | R | R | 5-9 | 180 | 8-31-66 | 1988 | Las Vegas, Nev. |
| Gil, Benji | .223 | 84 | 292 | 32 | 65 | 15 | 1 | 6 | 28 | 21 | 90 | 4 | 6 | R | R | 6-2 | 180 | 10-6-72 | 1991 | San Diego, Calif. |
| Gonzales, Rene | .260 | 42 | 154 | 21 | 40 | 8 | 2 | 3 | 13 | 26 | 23 | 1 | 1 | R | R | 6-3 | 215 | 9-3-61 | 1982 | Newport Beach, Calif. |
| Kennedy, Darryl | .286 | 2 | 7 | 0 | 2 | 0 | 0 | 0 | 0 | 2 | 0 | 0 | 0 | R | R | 5-10 | 170 | 1-23-69 | 1991 | Davenport, Fla. |
| Lee, Derek | .301 | 120 | 409 | 59 | 123 | 32 | 2 | 13 | 62 | 50 | 69 | 6 | 9 | L | R | 6-1 | 200 | 7-28-66 | 1988 | Reston, Va. |
| McFarlin, Jason | .167 | 3 | 12 | 0 | 2 | 1 | 0 | 0 | 1 | 1 | 2 | 0 | 0 | L | L | 6-0 | 175 | 6-28-70 | 1989 | Pensacola, Fla. |
| Ortiz, Luis | .317 | 124 | 501 | 70 | 159 | 25 | 0 | 14 | 73 | 22 | 36 | 0 | 5 | R | R | 6-0 | 195 | 5-25-70 | 1991 | Santo Domingo, D.R. |
| Owen, Spike | .000 | 2 | 4 | 0 | 0 | 0 | 0 | 0 | 0 | 0 | 0 | 0 | 0 | S | R | 5-9 | 165 | 4-19-61 | 1982 | Austin, Texas |
| Pappas, Erik | .206 | 107 | 330 | 38 | 68 | 15 | 0 | 5 | 36 | 63 | 69 | 3 | 8 | R | R | 6-0 | 195 | 4-25-66 | 1984 | Chicago, Ill. |
| Pemberton, Rudy | .254 | 17 | 71 | 6 | 18 | 3 | 0 | 2 | 11 | 1 | 10 | 1 | 4 | R | R | 6-1 | 185 | 12-17-69 | 1987 | San Pedro de Macoris, D.R. |
| Sagmoen, Marc | .293 | 32 | 116 | 16 | 34 | 6 | 0 | 5 | 16 | 4 | 20 | 1 | 0 | L | L | 5-11 | 180 | 4-6-71 | 1993 | Seattle, Wash. |
| Shave, Jon | .266 | 116 | 414 | 54 | 110 | 20 | 2 | 7 | 41 | 41 | 97 | 8 | 6 | R | R | 6-0 | 180 | 11-4-67 | 1990 | Fernandina Beach, Fla. |
| Smith, Alex | .225 | 81 | 200 | 22 | 45 | 12 | 0 | 6 | 20 | 22 | 53 | 4 | 2 | R | R | 6-0 | 180 | 12-1-69 | 1992 | Piqua, Ohio |
| Stevens, Lee | .325 | 117 | 431 | 84 | 140 | 37 | 2 | 32 | 94 | 58 | 90 | 3 | 0 | L | L | 6-4 | 205 | 7-10-67 | 1986 | Wichita, Kan. |
| Stillwell, Kurt | .235 | 4 | 17 | 1 | 4 | 0 | 0 | 0 | 1 | 0 | 2 | 0 | 0 | S | R | 5-11 | 185 | 6-4-65 | 1983 | Poway, Calif. |
| Tatis, Fernando | .500 | 2 | 4 | 0 | 2 | 1 | 0 | 0 | 0 | 1 | 0 | 0 | 0 | R | R | 6-1 | 175 | 1-1-75 | 1993 | San Pedro de Macoris, D.R. |
| Thomas, Brian | .263 | 88 | 247 | 30 | 65 | 14 | 4 | 7 | 36 | 31 | 63 | 1 | 0 | L | R | 6-0 | 185 | 5-6-71 | 1993 | Portland, Ore. |
| Voigt, Jack | .297 | 127 | 445 | 77 | 132 | 26 | 1 | 21 | 80 | 76 | 103 | 5 | 5 | R | R | 6-1 | 175 | 5-17-66 | 1987 | Venice, Fla. |
| Worthington, Craig | .264 | 15 | 53 | 5 | 14 | 2 | 0 | 1 | 4 | 5 | 6 | 0 | 0 | R | R | 6-0 | 200 | 4-17-65 | 1985 | Anaheim, Calif. |

### PITCHING

| PITCHING | W | L | ERA | G | GS | CG | SV | IP | H | R | ER | BB | SO | B | T | HT | WT | DOB | 1st Yr | Resides |
|---|---|---|---|---|---|---|---|---|---|---|---|---|---|---|---|---|---|---|---|---|
| Alberro, Jose | 9 | 9 | 3.47 | 29 | 27 | 4 | 0 | 171 | 154 | 73 | 66 | 57 | 140 | R | R | 6-2 | 190 | 6-29-69 | 1991 | San Juan, P.R. |
| Anderson, Mike | 3 | 4 | 6.34 | 11 | 4 | 0 | 0 | 33 | 45 | 32 | 23 | 11 | 21 | R | R | 6-3 | 205 | 7-30-66 | 1988 | Georgetown, Texas |
| Curtis, Chris | 2 | 5 | 5.11 | 41 | 2 | 0 | 1 | 76 | 91 | 50 | 43 | 34 | 38 | R | R | 6-2 | 185 | 5-8-71 | 1991 | Duncanville, Texas |
| Davis, Clint | 0 | 0 | 3.46 | 8 | 0 | 0 | 0 | 13 | 14 | 5 | 5 | 6 | 16 | R | R | 6-3 | 205 | 9-26-69 | 1991 | Irving, Texas |
| Dreyer, Steve | 6 | 8 | 3.89 | 29 | 14 | 0 | 2 | 118 | 130 | 55 | 51 | 31 | 79 | R | R | 6-3 | 180 | 11-19-69 | 1990 | Cedar Falls, Iowa |
| Eversgerd, Bryan | 3 | 3 | 2.74 | 38 | 5 | 0 | 4 | 66 | 57 | 21 | 20 | 14 | 60 | R | L | 6-1 | 185 | 2-11-69 | 1989 | Centralia, Ill. |
| Gross, Kevin | 0 | 0 | 6.75 | 1 | 1 | 0 | 0 | 4 | 6 | 4 | 3 | 2 | 3 | R | R | 6-5 | 215 | 6-8-61 | 1981 | Claremont, Calif. |
| Helling, Rick | 12 | 4 | 2.96 | 23 | 22 | 2 | 0 | 140 | 124 | 54 | 46 | 38 | 157 | R | R | 6-3 | 215 | 12-15-70 | 1992 | West Fargo, N.D. |
| Heredia, Gil | 0 | 0 | 1.86 | 6 | 0 | 0 | 0 | 10 | 11 | 3 | 2 | 0 | 4 | R | R | 6-1 | 190 | 10-26-65 | 1987 | Tucson, Ariz. |
| Johnson, Jonathan | 1 | 0 | 0.00 | 1 | 1 | 1 | 0 | 9 | 2 | 0 | 0 | 1 | 6 | R | R | 6-0 | 180 | 7-16-74 | 1995 | Ocala, Fla. |
| Lacy, Kerry | 3 | 3 | 2.89 | 37 | 0 | 0 | 6 | 56 | 48 | 21 | 18 | 15 | 31 | R | R | 6-2 | 195 | 8-7-72 | 1991 | Higdon, Ala. |
| Manning, David | 0 | 0 | 5.40 | 1 | 1 | 0 | 0 | 5 | 6 | 3 | 3 | 2 | 1 | R | R | 6-3 | 205 | 8-14-71 | 1992 | Lantana, Fla. |
| Mauser, Tim | 1 | 1 | 2.16 | 8 | 0 | 0 | 0 | 8 | 8 | 3 | 2 | 2 | 11 | R | R | 6-0 | 185 | 10-4-66 | 1988 | Fort Worth, Texas |
| Nichting, Chris | 1 | 0 | 1.00 | 4 | 1 | 0 | 0 | 9 | 9 | 1 | 1 | 3 | 7 | R | R | 6-1 | 205 | 5-13-66 | 1988 | Cincinnati, Ohio |
| Patterson, Danny | 6 | 2 | 1.68 | 44 | 0 | 0 | 10 | 80 | 79 | 22 | 15 | 15 | 53 | R | R | 6-0 | 168 | 2-17-71 | 1990 | Rosemead, Calif. |
| Russell, Jeff | 1 | 0 | 1.04 | 5 | 1 | 0 | 2 | 9 | 8 | 2 | 1 | 1 | 5 | R | R | 6-3 | 205 | 9-2-61 | 1980 | Colleyville, Texas |
| Sanford, Mo | 6 | 10 | 3.97 | 30 | 24 | 0 | 0 | 143 | 155 | 77 | 63 | 49 | 130 | R | R | 6-6 | 225 | 12-24-66 | 1988 | Starkville, Miss. |
| Santana, Julio | 11 | 12 | 4.02 | 29 | 29 | 4 | 0 | 186 | 171 | 102 | 83 | 66 | 113 | R | R | 6-0 | 175 | 1-20-73 | 1990 | San Pedro de Macoris, D.R. |
| Smith, Dan | 0 | 2 | 9.00 | 5 | 5 | 0 | 0 | 15 | 27 | 19 | 15 | 7 | 12 | L | L | 6-5 | 190 | 8-20-69 | 1990 | Apple Valley, Minn. |
| Vierra, Joey | 0 | 1 | 9.64 | 4 | 0 | 0 | 0 | 5 | 7 | 7 | 5 | 2 | 4 | L | L | 5-7 | 170 | 1-31-66 | 1987 | Honolulu, Hawaii |
| Whiteside, Matt | 9 | 6 | 3.45 | 36 | 7 | 0 | 0 | 94 | 95 | 41 | 36 | 24 | 52 | R | R | 6-0 | 185 | 8-8-67 | 1990 | Charleston, Mo. |

### FIELDING

| Catcher | PCT | G | PO | A | E | DP | PB |
|---|---|---|---|---|---|---|---|
| Cardenas | .981 | 29 | 141 | 10 | 3 | 0 | 3 |
| Charles | .968 | 31 | 173 | 11 | 6 | 4 | 3 |
| Kennedy | 1.000 | 2 | 12 | 0 | 0 | 0 | 0 |
| Pappas | .992 | 100 | 656 | 51 | 6 | 4 | 2 |

| First Base | PCT | G | PO | A | E | DP |
|---|---|---|---|---|---|---|
| Cardenas | .800 | 1 | 4 | 0 | 1 | 1 |
| Charles | .947 | 2 | 15 | 3 | 1 | 2 |
| Estrada | 1.000 | 1 | 2 | 0 | 0 | 0 |
| Gonzales | 1.000 | 1 | 9 | 4 | 0 | 1 |
| Lee | 1.000 | 5 | 24 | 3 | 0 | 0 |
| Ortiz | .995 | 100 | 912 | 49 | 5 | 92 |
| Pappas | 1.000 | 2 | 23 | 1 | 0 | 5 |
| Stevens | .994 | 36 | 315 | 22 | 2 | 37 |
| Voigt | 1.000 | 4 | 9 | 0 | 0 | 0 |

| Second Base | PCT | G | PO | A | E | DP |
|---|---|---|---|---|---|---|
| Estrada | 1.000 | 3 | 1 | 2 | 0 | 1 |
| Frazier | .778 | 2 | 3 | 4 | 2 | 0 |

| | PCT | G | PO | A | E | DP |
|---|---|---|---|---|---|---|
| Frye | .972 | 39 | 86 | 124 | 6 | 22 |
| Shave | .982 | 65 | 97 | 176 | 5 | 36 |
| Smith | .984 | 48 | 77 | 110 | 3 | 28 |
| Stillwell | .900 | 4 | 9 | 9 | 2 | 4 |

| Third Base | PCT | G | PO | A | E | DP |
|---|---|---|---|---|---|---|
| Estrada | .971 | 36 | 10 | 58 | 2 | 8 |
| Frye | 1.000 | 2 | 0 | 1 | 0 | 0 |
| Gonzales | .852 | 8 | 7 | 16 | 4 | 2 |
| Shave | .899 | 39 | 33 | 65 | 11 | 6 |
| Smith | .844 | 11 | 9 | 18 | 5 | 3 |
| Tatis | 1.000 | 1 | 0 | 1 | 0 | 0 |
| Voigt | .917 | 59 | 35 | 109 | 13 | 11 |
| Worthington | .915 | 15 | 10 | 33 | 4 | 1 |

| Shortstop | PCT | G | PO | A | E | DP |
|---|---|---|---|---|---|---|
| Estrada | .964 | 11 | 13 | 41 | 2 | 11 |
| Frye | .935 | 5 | 6 | 23 | 2 | 3 |
| Gil | .949 | 83 | 121 | 267 | 21 | 57 |

| | PCT | G | PO | A | E | DP |
|---|---|---|---|---|---|---|
| Gonzales | .964 | 34 | 39 | 122 | 6 | 24 |
| Owen | 1.000 | 1 | 2 | 1 | 0 | 0 |
| Shave | .921 | 17 | 28 | 42 | 6 | 13 |

| Outfield | PCT | G | PO | A | E | DP |
|---|---|---|---|---|---|---|
| Bryant | 1.000 | 8 | 8 | 2 | 0 | 0 |
| Estrada | .000 | 1 | 0 | 0 | 0 | 0 |
| Faneyte | .970 | 86 | 186 | 9 | 6 | 2 |
| Frazier | .981 | 53 | 101 | 4 | 2 | 1 |
| Frye | 1.000 | 4 | 2 | 0 | 0 | 0 |
| Lee | .959 | 86 | 133 | 7 | 6 | 1 |
| Pappas | .667 | 6 | 4 | 0 | 2 | 0 |
| Pemberton | .939 | 15 | 29 | 2 | 2 | 0 |
| Sagmoen | .964 | 29 | 52 | 2 | 2 | 0 |
| Smith | 1.000 | 8 | 11 | 1 | 0 | 0 |
| Stevens | .972 | 24 | 33 | 2 | 1 | 0 |
| Thomas | .979 | 76 | 132 | 6 | 3 | 0 |
| Voigt | .973 | 74 | 105 | 4 | 3 | 0 |

## TEXAS LEAGUE

### BATTING

| BATTING | AVG | G | AB | R | H | 2B | 3B | HR | RBI | BB | SO | SB | CS | B | T | HT | WT | DOB | 1st Yr | Resides |
|---|---|---|---|---|---|---|---|---|---|---|---|---|---|---|---|---|---|---|---|---|
| Arnold, Ken | .138 | 28 | 58 | 9 | 8 | 1 | 0 | 0 | 7 | 5 | 24 | 0 | 0 | R | R | 6-1 | 180 | 5-10-69 | 1991 | Atco, N.J. |
| Bell, Mike | .267 | 128 | 484 | 62 | 129 | 31 | 3 | 16 | 59 | 42 | 75 | 3 | 1 | R | R | 6-2 | 185 | 12-7-74 | 1993 | Cincinnati, Ohio |
| Blair, Brian | .245 | 113 | 379 | 47 | 93 | 28 | 3 | 3 | 29 | 45 | 86 | 7 | 8 | L | L | 6-0 | 180 | 4-9-72 | 1993 | Belton, Texas |
| Brown, Kevin | .263 | 128 | 460 | 77 | 121 | 27 | 1 | 26 | 86 | 73 | 150 | 0 | 3 | R | R | 6-2 | 200 | 4-21-73 | 1994 | Winslow, Ind. |
| Charles, Frank | .265 | 41 | 147 | 18 | 39 | 6 | 0 | 5 | 15 | 10 | 28 | 2 | 0 | R | R | 6-4 | 210 | 2-23-69 | 1991 | Anaheim, Calif. |
| Clark, Will | .222 | 3 | 9 | 3 | 2 | 0 | 0 | 0 | 0 | 2 | 0 | 0 | 0 | L | L | 6-1 | 196 | 3-13-64 | 1985 | New Orleans, La. |
| Coolbaugh, Mike | .348 | 7 | 23 | 6 | 8 | 3 | 0 | 2 | 9 | 2 | 3 | 1 | 0 | R | R | 6-1 | 190 | 6-5-72 | 1990 | San Antonio, Texas |

## BATTING

| BATTING | AVG | G | AB | R | H | 2B | 3B | HR | RBI | BB | SO | SB | CS | B | T | HT | WT | DOB | 1st Yr | Resides |
|---|---|---|---|---|---|---|---|---|---|---|---|---|---|---|---|---|---|---|---|---|
| Cossins, Tim | .500 | 3 | 4 | 0 | 2 | 0 | 0 | 0 | 1 | 3 | 0 | 0 | 0 | R | R | 6-1 | 192 | 3-31-70 | 1993 | Windsor, Calif. |
| Diaz, Edwin | .265 | 121 | 499 | 70 | 132 | 33 | 6 | 16 | 65 | 25 | 122 | 8 | 9 | R | R | 5-11 | 170 | 1-15-75 | 1993 | Vega Alta, P.R. |
| Estrada, Osmani | .259 | 27 | 85 | 12 | 22 | 4 | 0 | 2 | 16 | 9 | 13 | 1 | 1 | R | R | 5-8 | 180 | 1-23-69 | 1993 | Woodland Hills, Calif. |
| Frias, Hanley | .287 | 134 | 505 | 73 | 145 | 24 | 12 | 2 | 41 | 30 | 73 | 9 | 9 | S | R | 6-0 | 160 | 12-5-73 | 1991 | Villa Altagracia, D.R. |
| Kennedy, Darryl | .302 | 15 | 43 | 11 | 13 | 3 | 1 | 1 | 10 | 4 | 5 | 0 | 1 | R | R | 5-10 | 170 | 1-23-69 | 1991 | Davenport, Fla. |
| Little, Mark | .291 | 101 | 409 | 69 | 119 | 24 | 2 | 13 | 50 | 48 | 88 | 22 | 10 | R | R | 6-0 | 200 | 7-11-72 | 1994 | Edwardsville, Ill. |
| McFarlin, Jason | .273 | 2 | 11 | 1 | 3 | 1 | 0 | 0 | 2 | 0 | 1 | 0 | 1 | L | L | 6-0 | 175 | 6-28-70 | 1989 | Pensacola, Fla. |
| Murphy, Mike | .231 | 34 | 121 | 22 | 28 | 7 | 2 | 4 | 16 | 21 | 29 | 1 | 0 | R | R | 6-2 | 185 | 1-23-72 | 1990 | Canton, Ohio |
| O'Neill, Doug | .307 | 20 | 75 | 8 | 23 | 3 | 0 | 5 | 15 | 11 | 19 | 1 | 2 | R | R | 5-10 | 200 | 6-29-70 | 1991 | Campbell, Calif. |
| Sagmoen, Marc | .282 | 96 | 387 | 58 | 109 | 21 | 6 | 10 | 62 | 33 | 58 | 5 | 8 | L | L | 5-11 | 180 | 4-6-71 | 1993 | Seattle, Wash. |
| Sanders, Tracy | .232 | 52 | 168 | 31 | 39 | 10 | 0 | 7 | 20 | 33 | 49 | 2 | 1 | L | R | 6-0 | 206 | 7-26-69 | 1990 | Dallas, N.C. |
| Smith, Bubba | .292 | 134 | 513 | 82 | 150 | 28 | 0 | 32 | 94 | 48 | 121 | 0 | 1 | R | R | 6-2 | 225 | 12-18-69 | 1991 | Riverside, Calif. |
| Texidor, Jose | .256 | 85 | 301 | 34 | 77 | 15 | 0 | 11 | 37 | 18 | 44 | 2 | 1 | R | R | 6-0 | 150 | 12-14-71 | 1989 | Juana Diaz, P.R. |
| Thomas, Brian | .222 | 3 | 9 | 0 | 2 | 0 | 0 | 0 | 0 | 0 | 5 | 0 | 1 | L | R | 6-0 | 185 | 5-6-71 | 1993 | Portland, Ore. |
| Unrat, Chris | .182 | 20 | 55 | 6 | 10 | 2 | 0 | 1 | 7 | 16 | 13 | 0 | 0 | L | R | 6-1 | 205 | 3-28-71 | 1993 | Kirkland, Quebec |

## PITCHING

| PITCHING | W | L | ERA | G | GS | CG | SV | IP | H | R | ER | BB | SO | B | T | HT | WT | DOB | 1st Yr | Resides |
|---|---|---|---|---|---|---|---|---|---|---|---|---|---|---|---|---|---|---|---|---|
| Brower, Jim | 3 | 2 | 3.78 | 5 | 5 | 1 | 0 | 33 | 35 | 16 | 14 | 10 | 16 | R | R | 6-2 | 205 | 12-29-72 | 1994 | Minnetonka, Minn. |
| Castillo, Juan | 6 | 6 | 5.04 | 19 | 17 | 0 | 0 | 89 | 94 | 64 | 50 | 49 | 37 | R | R | 6-4 | 216 | 6-23-70 | 1988 | Caracas, Venez. |
| Davis, Clint | 3 | 3 | 1.88 | 32 | 0 | 0 | 10 | 48 | 31 | 11 | 10 | 12 | 40 | R | R | 6-3 | 205 | 9-26-69 | 1991 | Irving, Texas |
| Davis, Jeff | 7 | 2 | 4.59 | 16 | 15 | 3 | 0 | 98 | 110 | 57 | 50 | 20 | 51 | R | R | 6-0 | 170 | 9-20-72 | 1993 | Somerset, Mass. |
| Geeve, Dave | 7 | 6 | 5.55 | 18 | 17 | 0 | 0 | 83 | 105 | 53 | 51 | 23 | 60 | R | R | 6-3 | 190 | 10-19-69 | 1991 | Niles, Ill. |
| Johnson, Jonathan | 13 | 10 | 3.56 | 26 | 25 | 6 | 0 | 174 | 176 | 86 | 69 | 41 | 97 | R | R | 6-0 | 180 | 7-16-74 | 1995 | Ocala, Fla. |
| Kell, Rob | 0 | 0 | 0.00 | 2 | 0 | 0 | 1 | 1 | 1 | 0 | 0 | 0 | 0 | R | L | 6-2 | 200 | 9-21-70 | 1993 | Hatfield, Pa. |
| Keusch, Joe | 0 | 0 | 17.18 | 8 | 0 | 0 | 0 | 11 | 25 | 21 | 21 | 5 | 8 | L | R | 6-1 | 175 | 1-20-72 | 1994 | Huntingburg, Ind. |
| Kolb, Danny | 1 | 0 | 0.77 | 2 | 2 | 0 | 0 | 12 | 5 | 1 | 1 | 8 | 7 | R | R | 6-4 | 190 | 3-29-75 | 1995 | Sterling, Ill. |
| Lacy, Kerry | 0 | 0 | 0.00 | 2 | 0 | 0 | 2 | 4 | 3 | 0 | 0 | 0 | 1 | R | R | 6-2 | 195 | 8-7-72 | 1991 | Higdon, Ala. |
| Manning, David | 6 | 5 | 3.26 | 39 | 5 | 0 | 3 | 91 | 89 | 36 | 33 | 45 | 48 | R | R | 6-3 | 205 | 8-14-71 | 1992 | Lantana, Fla. |
| Martin, Jerry | 5 | 4 | 4.94 | 36 | 6 | 0 | 5 | 86 | 98 | 56 | 47 | 42 | 49 | R | R | 6-3 | 175 | 3-15-72 | 1992 | McMinnville, Tenn. |
| Martinez, Ramiro | 0 | 2 | 8.56 | 11 | 0 | 0 | 0 | 14 | 23 | 13 | 13 | 5 | 7 | L | L | 6-2 | 185 | 1-28-72 | 1992 | Los Angeles, Calif. |
| Moody, Eric | 8 | 4 | 3.57 | 44 | 5 | 0 | 16 | 96 | 92 | 40 | 38 | 23 | 80 | R | R | 6-6 | 185 | 1-6-71 | 1993 | Williamston, S.C. |
| Morvay, Joe | 2 | 2 | 6.26 | 24 | 1 | 0 | 2 | 46 | 55 | 32 | 32 | 20 | 27 | L | R | 6-4 | 210 | 2-8-71 | 1993 | Boardman, Ohio |
| O'Donoghue, John | 2 | 4 | 4.18 | 27 | 9 | 0 | 0 | 80 | 89 | 47 | 37 | 23 | 46 | L | L | 6-6 | 210 | 5-26-69 | 1990 | Elkton, Md. |
| Powell, John | 3 | 8 | 4.89 | 39 | 10 | 0 | 4 | 114 | 121 | 71 | 62 | 31 | 79 | R | R | 5-10 | 180 | 4-7-71 | 1994 | Snellville, Ga. |
| Russell, Jeff | 0 | 0 | 0.00 | 2 | 2 | 0 | 0 | 5 | 0 | 0 | 0 | 1 | 4 | R | R | 6-3 | 205 | 9-2-61 | 1980 | Colleyville, Texas |
| Shea, John | 0 | 1 | 13.97 | 9 | 0 | 0 | 0 | 10 | 23 | 15 | 15 | 5 | 4 | R | L | 6-6 | 210 | 6-23-66 | 1986 | Dunedin, Fla. |
| Silva, Ted | 7 | 2 | 2.99 | 11 | 11 | 2 | 0 | 75 | 72 | 27 | 25 | 16 | 27 | R | R | 6-0 | 170 | 8-4-74 | 1995 | Redondo Beach, Calif. |
| Smith, Dan | 2 | 3 | 4.29 | 9 | 9 | 0 | 0 | 50 | 53 | 27 | 24 | 21 | 29 | L | L | 6-5 | 190 | 8-20-69 | 1990 | Apple Valley, Minn. |

### FIELDING

| Catcher | PCT | G | PO | A | E | DP | PB |
|---|---|---|---|---|---|---|---|
| Brown | .982 | 104 | 541 | 66 | 11 | 3 | 8 |
| Charles | 1.000 | 7 | 31 | 2 | 0 | 0 | 0 |
| Cossins | 1.000 | 3 | 7 | 2 | 0 | 1 | 1 |
| Kennedy | .987 | 17 | 67 | 11 | 1 | 0 | 0 |
| Unrat | .956 | 17 | 101 | 8 | 5 | 1 | 1 |

| First Base | PCT | G | PO | A | E | DP |
|---|---|---|---|---|---|---|
| Arnold | .875 | 5 | 7 | 0 | 1 | 0 |
| Blair | 1.000 | 1 | 8 | 0 | 0 | 2 |
| Brown | .966 | 6 | 53 | 3 | 2 | 3 |
| Charles | 1.000 | 3 | 11 | 0 | 0 | 1 |
| Clark | 1.000 | 3 | 21 | 3 | 0 | 2 |
| Coolbaugh | 1.000 | 2 | 19 | 2 | 0 | 4 |
| Estrada | 1.000 | 1 | 2 | 0 | 0 | 0 |

| | PCT | G | PO | A | E | DP |
|---|---|---|---|---|---|---|
| Smith | .986 | 128 | 1193 | 100 | 18 | 121 |
| **Second Base** | | | | | | |
| Arnold | .966 | 10 | 14 | 14 | 1 | 3 |
| Coolbaugh | 1.000 | 5 | 12 | 21 | 0 | 4 |
| Diaz | .967 | 121 | 238 | 322 | 19 | 80 |
| Estrada | .961 | 8 | 22 | 27 | 2 | 8 |
| **Third Base** | PCT | G | PO | A | E | DP |
| Arnold | 1.000 | 8 | 4 | 10 | 0 | 0 |
| Bell | .936 | 126 | 90 | 277 | 25 | 28 |
| Estrada | .964 | 10 | 6 | 21 | 1 | 3 |
| Smith | .833 | 3 | 1 | 4 | 1 | 1 |

| Shortstop | PCT | G | PO | A | E | DP |
|---|---|---|---|---|---|---|
| Arnold | .889 | 4 | 8 | 8 | 2 | 1 |
| Estrada | 1.000 | 3 | 3 | 4 | 0 | 1 |
| Frias | .964 | 133 | 197 | 417 | 23 | 84 |
| **Outfield** | PCT | G | PO | A | E | DP |
| Blair | .981 | 111 | 195 | 10 | 4 | 2 |
| Estrada | .000 | 1 | 0 | 0 | 0 | 0 |
| Little | .968 | 94 | 263 | 9 | 9 | 3 |
| Murphy | .973 | 34 | 72 | 1 | 2 | 0 |
| O'Neill | .960 | 20 | 48 | 0 | 2 | 0 |
| Sagmoen | .981 | 93 | 198 | 7 | 4 | 0 |
| Sanders | 1.000 | 4 | 4 | 0 | 0 | 0 |
| Texidor | .986 | 65 | 139 | 2 | 2 | 1 |

## BAKERSFIELD — Class A/Co-Op
## CALIFORNIA LEAGUE

| PITCHING | W | L | ERA | G | GS | CG | SV | IP | H | R | ER | BB | SO | B | T | HT | WT | DOB | 1st Yr | Resides |
|---|---|---|---|---|---|---|---|---|---|---|---|---|---|---|---|---|---|---|---|---|
| Kell, Rob | 5 | 3 | 3.78 | 13 | 13 | 1 | 0 | 88 | 94 | 43 | 37 | 22 | 103 | R | L | 6-2 | 200 | 9-21-70 | 1993 | Hatfield, Pa. |
| Knighton, Toure | 5 | 15 | 6.54 | 25 | 24 | 1 | 0 | 150 | 197 | 134 | 109 | 67 | 108 | R | R | 6-3 | 180 | 7-4-75 | 1993 | Tucson, Ariz. |
| Perpetuo, Nelson | 0 | 5 | 5.75 | 8 | 7 | 0 | 0 | 41 | 35 | 31 | 26 | 38 | 45 | S | L | 5-10 | 170 | 7-6-72 | 1991 | Monroe, Conn. |

## CHARLOTTE — Class A
## FLORIDA STATE LEAGUE

| BATTING | AVG | G | AB | R | H | 2B | 3B | HR | RBI | BB | SO | SB | CS | B | T | HT | WT | DOB | 1st Yr | Resides |
|---|---|---|---|---|---|---|---|---|---|---|---|---|---|---|---|---|---|---|---|---|
| Adams, Tommy | .257 | 53 | 183 | 28 | 47 | 8 | 0 | 2 | 21 | 26 | 39 | 8 | 3 | R | R | 6-1 | 205 | 11-26-69 | 1991 | Mission Viejo, Calif. |
| Arnold, Ken | .243 | 52 | 144 | 23 | 35 | 4 | 1 | 0 | 12 | 16 | 42 | 2 | 3 | R | R | 6-1 | 180 | 5-10-69 | 1991 | Atco, N.J. |
| Barkett, Andy | .286 | 115 | 392 | 57 | 112 | 22 | 3 | 6 | 54 | 57 | 59 | 3 | 1 | L | L | 6-1 | 205 | 9-5-74 | 1995 | Raleigh, N.C. |
| Bokemeier, Matt | .274 | 131 | 503 | 74 | 138 | 31 | 4 | 2 | 62 | 28 | 81 | 18 | 2 | S | R | 6-2 | 190 | 8-7-72 | 1994 | Fresno, Calif. |
| Coolbaugh, Mike | .287 | 124 | 449 | 76 | 129 | 33 | 4 | 15 | 75 | 42 | 80 | 8 | 10 | R | R | 6-1 | 190 | 6-5-72 | 1990 | San Antonio, Texas |
| Cossins, Tim | .244 | 67 | 234 | 34 | 57 | 16 | 0 | 3 | 32 | 13 | 44 | 1 | 1 | R | R | 6-1 | 192 | 3-31-70 | 1993 | Windsor, Calif. |
| Ephan, Larry | .226 | 9 | 31 | 3 | 7 | 2 | 0 | 0 | 8 | 8 | 6 | 0 | 0 | R | R | 6-0 | 210 | 2-12-71 | 1993 | Kalaheo, Hawaii |
| Fenton, Cary | .272 | 87 | 290 | 47 | 79 | 9 | 1 | 0 | 22 | 31 | 49 | 21 | 11 | R | R | 5-9 | 165 | 10-18-72 | 1994 | Decatur, Ill. |
| Gil, Benji | .258 | 11 | 31 | 2 | 8 | 6 | 0 | 1 | 7 | 3 | 7 | 0 | 0 | R | R | 6-2 | 180 | 10-6-72 | 1991 | San Diego, Calif. |
| Gorecki, Ryan | .288 | 82 | 288 | 26 | 83 | 5 | 0 | 0 | 28 | 20 | 6 | 1 | 3 | L | R | 5-9 | 160 | 7-18-73 | 1995 | East Rockaway, N.Y. |
| Macon, Leland | .249 | 99 | 338 | 45 | 84 | 12 | 3 | 2 | 31 | 39 | 74 | 9 | 12 | R | R | 6-2 | 205 | 5-4-73 | 1993 | Kirkwood, Mo. |
| McAulay, John | .197 | 49 | 122 | 15 | 24 | 7 | 0 | 2 | 11 | 23 | 38 | 0 | 0 | R | R | 6-0 | 180 | 6-10-73 | 1995 | Lumberton, Miss. |
| Murphy, Mike | .332 | 87 | 358 | 73 | 119 | 20 | 7 | 7 | 52 | 32 | 94 | 22 | 9 | R | R | 6-2 | 185 | 1-23-72 | 1990 | Canton, Ohio |
| Parra, Jose | .333 | 3 | 6 | 1 | 2 | 0 | 0 | 1 | 3 | 0 | 0 | 0 | S | R | 6-0 | 155 | 4-23-77 | 1994 | Santiago, D.R. |
| Richards, Rowan | .162 | 34 | 117 | 10 | 19 | 3 | 1 | 1 | 10 | 5 | 33 | 2 | 1 | R | R | 6-0 | 195 | 5-17-74 | 1996 | Bloomfield, N.J. |
| Tatis, Fernando | .286 | 85 | 325 | 46 | 93 | 25 | 0 | 12 | 53 | 30 | 48 | 9 | 3 | S | R | 6-1 | 175 | 1-1-75 | 1993 | San Pedro de Macoris, D.R. |
| Unrat, Chris | .274 | 41 | 135 | 18 | 37 | 8 | 0 | 2 | 11 | 27 | 28 | 2 | 3 | L | R | 6-1 | 205 | 3-28-71 | 1993 | Kirkland, Quebec |

| BATTING | AVG | G | AB | R | H | 2B | 3B | HR | RBI | BB | SO | SB | CS | B | T | HT | WT | DOB | 1st Yr | Resides |
|---|---|---|---|---|---|---|---|---|---|---|---|---|---|---|---|---|---|---|---|---|
| Vasquez, Danny | .199 | 77 | 256 | 30 | 51 | 14 | 2 | 6 | 30 | 7 | 62 | 3 | 5 | R | R | 5-11 | 175 | 1-26-74 | 1994 | Bronx, N.Y. |
| Vessel, Andrew | .229 | 126 | 484 | 63 | 111 | 25 | 6 | 3 | 67 | 45 | 94 | 1 | 6 | R | R | 6-3 | 205 | 3-11-75 | 1993 | Richmond, Calif. |
| Voigt, Jack | .407 | 7 | 27 | 7 | 11 | 3 | 0 | 1 | 8 | 3 | 3 | 0 | 0 | R | R | 6-1 | 175 | 5-17-66 | 1987 | Venice, Fla. |

**GAMES BY POSITION:** C—Cossins 65, Gorecki 1, McAulay 48, Unrat 36. **1B**—Barkett 102, Bokemeier 4, Coolbaugh 36, Cossins 1, Unrat 1, Vasquez 1, Voight 5. **2B**—Arnold 2, Fenton 74, Gorecki 71, Parra 1. **3B**—Arnold 1, Bokemeier 35, Coolbaugh 28, Fenton 2, Parra 1, Tatis 81. **SS**—Arnold 50, Bokemeier 56, Coolbaugh 37, Fenton 7, Gil 10, Parra 1. **OF**—Adams 32, Coolbaugh 3, Macon 94, Murphy 84, Richards 26, Vasquez 70, Vessel 121, Voight 2.

| PITCHING | W | L | ERA | G | GS | CG | SV | IP | H | R | ER | BB | SO | B | T | HT | WT | DOB | 1st Yr | Resides |
|---|---|---|---|---|---|---|---|---|---|---|---|---|---|---|---|---|---|---|---|---|
| Brower, Jim | 9 | 8 | 3.79 | 23 | 21 | 2 | 0 | 145 | 148 | 67 | 61 | 40 | 86 | R | R | 6-2 | 205 | 12-29-72 | 1994 | Minnetonka, Minn. |
| Buckles, Bucky | 1 | 4 | 3.60 | 21 | 3 | 0 | 0 | 55 | 55 | 25 | 22 | 13 | 43 | R | R | 6-1 | 190 | 6-19-73 | 1994 | Victorville, Calif. |
| Chavarria, David | 1 | 6 | 3.09 | 38 | 4 | 0 | 7 | 82 | 76 | 46 | 28 | 43 | 76 | L | R | 6-7 | 195 | 5-19-73 | 1991 | Burnaby, B.C. |
| Cook, Rodney | 6 | 4 | 2.94 | 39 | 0 | 0 | 8 | 80 | 78 | 30 | 26 | 26 | 48 | R | R | 6-3 | 170 | 6-7-71 | 1994 | Atlanta, Texas |
| Escamilla, Jaime | 3 | 3 | 4.09 | 37 | 0 | 0 | 1 | 62 | 68 | 31 | 28 | 28 | 39 | R | L | 5-9 | 165 | 5-25-72 | 1994 | San Diego, Calif. |
| Kell, Rob | 6 | 4 | 3.81 | 11 | 11 | 3 | 0 | 78 | 71 | 39 | 33 | 17 | 61 | R | L | 6-2 | 200 | 9-21-70 | 1993 | Hatfield, Pa. |
| Knight, Brandon | 4 | 10 | 5.12 | 19 | 17 | 2 | 0 | 102 | 118 | 65 | 58 | 45 | 74 | L | R | 6-0 | 170 | 10-1-75 | 1995 | Oxnard, Calif. |
| Knighton, Toure | 0 | 2 | 2.82 | 5 | 2 | 0 | 0 | 22 | 15 | 11 | 7 | 11 | 11 | R | R | 6-3 | 180 | 7-4-75 | 1993 | Tucson, Ariz. |
| Kolb, Danny | 2 | 2 | 4.26 | 6 | 6 | 0 | 0 | 38 | 38 | 18 | 18 | 14 | 28 | R | R | 6-4 | 190 | 3-29-75 | 1995 | Sterling, Ill. |
| Link, Bryan | 5 | 4 | 4.10 | 15 | 10 | 1 | 0 | 75 | 79 | 41 | 34 | 18 | 62 | R | L | 6-1 | 170 | 4-6-73 | 1995 | Wylie, Texas |
| Moody, Ritchie | 1 | 1 | 4.05 | 18 | 1 | 0 | 1 | 33 | 34 | 17 | 15 | 22 | 25 | R | L | 6-1 | 185 | 2-22-71 | 1992 | Brookville, Ohio |
| Morillo, Donald | 2 | 3 | 4.76 | 32 | 0 | 0 | 2 | 51 | 51 | 33 | 27 | 40 | 34 | R | R | 6-0 | 185 | 9-1-73 | 1995 | Charleston, S.C. |
| O'Flynn, Gardner | 8 | 9 | 4.61 | 28 | 17 | 1 | 0 | 109 | 130 | 71 | 56 | 31 | 37 | S | L | 6-2 | 205 | 7-5-71 | 1993 | Ipswich, Mass. |
| Oliver, Darren | 0 | 1 | 3.00 | 2 | 1 | 0 | 0 | 12 | 8 | 4 | 4 | 3 | 9 | R | L | 6-0 | 170 | 10-6-70 | 1988 | Rio Linda, Calif. |
| Raines, Ken | 0 | 4 | 5.64 | 23 | 0 | 0 | 2 | 30 | 44 | 20 | 19 | 14 | 23 | R | L | 6-2 | 175 | 10-14-72 | 1994 | Freeland, Mich. |
| Russell, Jeff | 0 | 0 | 0.00 | 2 | 2 | 0 | 0 | 3 | 0 | 0 | 0 | 0 | 6 | R | R | 6-3 | 205 | 9-2-61 | 1980 | Colleyville, Texas |
| Silva, Ted | 10 | 2 | 2.86 | 16 | 16 | 4 | 0 | 113 | 98 | 39 | 36 | 27 | 95 | R | R | 6-0 | 170 | 8-4-74 | 1995 | Redondo Beach, Calif. |
| Smith, Dan | 3 | 7 | 5.07 | 18 | 18 | 1 | 0 | 87 | 100 | 61 | 49 | 38 | 55 | R | R | 6-2 | 175 | 9-15-75 | 1993 | Girard, Kan. |
| Smith, Danny | 0 | 1 | 2.74 | 5 | 5 | 0 | 0 | 23 | 21 | 7 | 7 | 8 | 16 | L | L | 6-5 | 190 | 8-20-69 | 1990 | Apple Valley, Minn. |
| Wiley, Chad | 2 | 1 | 2.03 | 5 | 5 | 0 | 0 | 27 | 19 | 7 | 6 | 4 | 14 | R | R | 5-11 | 175 | 11-20-71 | 1992 | Lenexa, Kan. |

## CHARLESTON — Class A
### SOUTH ATLANTIC LEAGUE

| BATTING | AVG | G | AB | R | H | 2B | 3B | HR | RBI | BB | SO | SB | CS | B | T | HT | WT | DOB | 1st Yr | Resides |
|---|---|---|---|---|---|---|---|---|---|---|---|---|---|---|---|---|---|---|---|---|
| Baker, Derek | .244 | 46 | 160 | 21 | 39 | 8 | 1 | 5 | 31 | 19 | 37 | 1 | 1 | L | R | 6-2 | 220 | 10-5-75 | 1996 | Tustin, Calif. |
| Briones, Chris | .190 | 26 | 79 | 10 | 15 | 4 | 1 | 0 | 10 | 2 | 39 | 0 | 1 | R | R | 5-11 | 205 | 6-5-73 | 1995 | Brea, Calif. |
| Brumbaugh, Cliff | .242 | 132 | 458 | 70 | 111 | 23 | 7 | 6 | 45 | 72 | 103 | 20 | 7 | R | R | 6-2 | 205 | 4-21-74 | 1995 | New Castle, Del. |
| Carrion, Jorge | .289 | 10 | 38 | 7 | 11 | 0 | 1 | 0 | 6 | 3 | 10 | 0 | 2 | R | R | 6-1 | 175 | 12-10-76 | 1995 | Brooklyn, N.Y. |
| De la Rosa, Miguel | .180 | 26 | 61 | 5 | 11 | 0 | 1 | 0 | 1 | 8 | 39 | 1 | 3 | R | R | 6-0 | 170 | 10-29-76 | 1994 | Santo Domingo, D.R. |
| Fisher, Tony | .234 | 30 | 111 | 10 | 26 | 4 | 0 | 3 | 13 | 3 | 45 | 4 | 3 | R | R | 6-1 | 180 | 1-8-75 | 1996 | Oakdale, Minn. |
| Gallagher, Shawn | .224 | 88 | 303 | 29 | 68 | 11 | 4 | 7 | 32 | 18 | 104 | 6 | 1 | R | R | 6-0 | 187 | 11-8-76 | 1995 | Wilmington, N.C. |
| Goodwin, Joe | .258 | 80 | 252 | 25 | 65 | 13 | 1 | 0 | 31 | 32 | 34 | 3 | 5 | R | R | 5-10 | 170 | 4-19-74 | 1995 | New Windsor, Md. |
| Jaramillo, Francisco | .191 | 45 | 131 | 14 | 25 | 5 | 0 | 1 | 7 | 10 | 41 | 2 | 0 | R | R | 5-11 | 170 | 11-28-74 | 1996 | Franksville, Wis. |
| Johnson, Jason | .217 | 116 | 391 | 40 | 85 | 18 | 4 | 1 | 38 | 43 | 115 | 11 | 7 | R | R | 6-2 | 190 | 2-1-76 | 1994 | Vallejo, Calif. |
| King, Cesar | .250 | 84 | 276 | 35 | 69 | 10 | 1 | 7 | 28 | 21 | 58 | 8 | 5 | R | R | 6-0 | 175 | 2-28-78 | 1994 | La Romana, D.R. |
| Mateo, Ruben | .260 | 134 | 496 | 65 | 129 | 30 | 8 | 8 | 58 | 26 | 78 | 30 | 9 | R | R | 6-0 | 170 | 2-10-78 | 1995 | San Cristobal, D.R. |
| McAulay, John | .167 | 5 | 12 | 2 | 2 | 0 | 0 | 0 | 1 | 7 | 1 | 1 | 1 | R | R | 6-0 | 180 | 6-10-73 | 1995 | Lumberton, Miss. |
| Monroe, Craig | .150 | 49 | 153 | 11 | 23 | 11 | 1 | 0 | 9 | 18 | 48 | 2 | 2 | R | R | 6-2 | 195 | 2-27-77 | 1995 | Texarkana, Texas |
| Nunez, Juan | .264 | 88 | 326 | 55 | 86 | 7 | 4 | 1 | 18 | 36 | 77 | 53 | 13 | S | R | 5-10 | 165 | 1-11-77 | 1994 | Esperanza, D.R. |
| Ortiz, Asbel | .216 | 88 | 310 | 23 | 67 | 11 | 3 | 1 | 32 | 13 | 94 | 1 | 3 | S | R | 5-10 | 155 | 6-20-76 | 1994 | Cidra, P.R. |
| Parra, Jose | .149 | 36 | 87 | 2 | 13 | 1 | 0 | 0 | 6 | 7 | 43 | 5 | 3 | S | R | 6-0 | 155 | 4-23-77 | 1994 | Santiago, D.R. |
| Santos, Jose | .199 | 37 | 136 | 15 | 27 | 4 | 2 | 4 | 13 | 13 | 48 | 3 | 3 | R | R | 5-11 | 165 | 3-1-78 | 1995 | Santiago, D.R. |
| Smella, Steve | .157 | 44 | 127 | 19 | 20 | 3 | 0 | 3 | 12 | 16 | 44 | 5 | 1 | R | R | 6-1 | 180 | 6-21-74 | 1996 | Toledo, Ohio |
| Vopata, Nate | .251 | 129 | 506 | 70 | 127 | 19 | 9 | 8 | 55 | 38 | 105 | 13 | 10 | L | R | 5-10 | 175 | 2-6-73 | 1995 | Visalia, Calif. |
| Zywica, Mike | .134 | 20 | 67 | 5 | 9 | 1 | 1 | 2 | 4 | 7 | 13 | 3 | 1 | R | R | 6-4 | 190 | 9-14-75 | 1996 | Richton Park, Ill. |

**GAMES BY POSITION:** C—Goodwin 75, King 66, McAulay 5. **1B**—Brumbaugh 47, Gallagher 88, Vopata 8. **2B**—Jaramillo 3, Ortiz 67, Santo 29, Vopata 36. **3B**—Baker 42, Brumbaugh 85, Parra 6, Vopata 11. **SS**—Briones 1, Carrion 6, Jaramillo 33, Ortiz 7, Parra 28, Vopata 75. **OF**—De la Rosa 21, Johnson 93, Mateo 127, Monroe 44, Nunez 83, Smella 43, Vopata 1, Zywica 20.

| PITCHING | W | L | ERA | G | GS | CG | SV | IP | H | R | ER | BB | SO | B | T | HT | WT | DOB | 1st Yr | Resides |
|---|---|---|---|---|---|---|---|---|---|---|---|---|---|---|---|---|---|---|---|---|
| Bauer, Chuck | 2 | 7 | 3.83 | 28 | 12 | 2 | 4 | 103 | 108 | 55 | 44 | 38 | 71 | R | R | 6-0 | 185 | 11-10-72 | 1995 | Rensselaer, N.Y. |
| Codd, Tim | 0 | 0 | 4.05 | 3 | 0 | 0 | 0 | 7 | 6 | 3 | 3 | 3 | 10 | R | R | 6-3 | 195 | 10-4-73 | 1995 | North Tonawanda, N.Y. |
| Dempster, Ryan | 7 | 11 | 3.30 | 23 | 23 | 2 | 0 | 144 | 120 | 71 | 53 | 58 | 141 | R | R | 6-2 | 195 | 5-3-77 | 1995 | Gibsons, B.C. |
| Draeger, Mark | 1 | 1 | 4.50 | 19 | 0 | 0 | 0 | 30 | 26 | 23 | 15 | 18 | 24 | R | R | 6-3 | 180 | 11-19-72 | 1995 | Lockport, Ill. |
| Glynn, Ryan | 8 | 7 | 4.54 | 19 | 19 | 2 | 0 | 121 | 118 | 70 | 61 | 59 | 72 | R | R | 6-3 | 200 | 11-1-74 | 1995 | Portsmouth, Va. |
| Hausman, Isaac | 0 | 0 | 3.00 | 1 | 1 | 0 | 0 | 6 | 3 | 2 | 2 | 1 | 8 | R | R | 6-4 | 170 | 6-27-76 | 1994 | Covina, Calif. |
| Kolb, Danny | 8 | 6 | 2.57 | 20 | 20 | 4 | 0 | 126 | 80 | 50 | 36 | 60 | 127 | R | R | 6-4 | 190 | 3-29-75 | 1995 | Sterling, Ill. |
| Martineau, Brian | 0 | 0 | 0.00 | 2 | 0 | 0 | 1 | 2 | 1 | 0 | 0 | 0 | 1 | R | R | 6-2 | 205 | 12-16-74 | 1995 | Riverside, Calif. |
| Martinez, Jose | 1 | 2 | 9.86 | 11 | 1 | 0 | 0 | 21 | 34 | 24 | 23 | 7 | 17 | R | R | 6-0 | 165 | 2-4-75 | 1995 | Santiago, D.R. |
| McHugh, Mike | 2 | 5 | 6.13 | 43 | 0 | 0 | 1 | 54 | 47 | 43 | 37 | 55 | 52 | L | L | 5-11 | 180 | 4-9-73 | 1995 | Pittsburgh, Pa. |
| Moore, Bobby | 11 | 11 | 4.06 | 25 | 25 | 2 | 0 | 142 | 128 | 82 | 64 | 45 | 125 | R | R | 6-5 | 217 | 3-27-73 | 1995 | Kalispell, Mon. |
| Morillo, Donald | 0 | 0 | 9.00 | 2 | 0 | 0 | 0 | 1 | 0 | 1 | 1 | 4 | 9 | R | R | 6-0 | 185 | 9-1-73 | 1995 | Charleston, S.C. |
| Mota, Henry | 7 | 5 | 2.78 | 32 | 10 | 2 | 2 | 97 | 71 | 39 | 30 | 28 | 68 | R | R | 5-11 | 170 | 5-13-78 | 1995 | Santo Domingo, D.R. |
| Mudd, Scott | 12 | 9 | 3.51 | 28 | 27 | 5 | 0 | 182 | 196 | 94 | 71 | 49 | 115 | R | R | 6-0 | 195 | 10-12-72 | 1995 | Louisville, Ky. |
| Nelson, Ron | 2 | 4 | 4.66 | 20 | 1 | 0 | 0 | 29 | 29 | 17 | 15 | 18 | 22 | R | R | 6-4 | 195 | 12-4-73 | 1996 | Niles, Ohio |
| Runion, Jeff | 0 | 1 | 3.75 | 5 | 1 | 0 | 1 | 12 | 13 | 5 | 5 | 5 | 9 | R | R | 6-5 | 185 | 8-29-74 | 1992 | Riverdale, Ga. |
| Simmons, Carlos | 3 | 7 | 5.08 | 33 | 1 | 0 | 4 | 57 | 56 | 43 | 32 | 33 | 34 | R | R | 6-1 | 200 | 1-22-74 | 1994 | Clinton, Md. |
| Venafro, Mike | 1 | 3 | 3.51 | 50 | 0 | 0 | 19 | 59 | 57 | 27 | 23 | 21 | 62 | L | L | 5-10 | 170 | 8-2-73 | 1995 | Chantilly, Va. |

## HUDSON VALLEY — Class A/Co-Op
### NEW YORK-PENN LEAGUE

| BATTING | AVG | G | AB | R | H | 2B | 3B | HR | RBI | BB | SO | SB | CS | B | T | HT | WT | DOB | 1st Yr | Resides |
|---|---|---|---|---|---|---|---|---|---|---|---|---|---|---|---|---|---|---|---|---|
| Dransfeldt, Kelly | .236 | 75 | 284 | 42 | 67 | 17 | 1 | 7 | 29 | 27 | 76 | 13 | 4 | R | R | 6-2 | 195 | 4-16-75 | 1996 | Morris, Ill. |

| BATTING | AVG | G | AB | R | H | 2B | 3B | HR | RBI | BB | SO | SB | CS | B | T | HT | WT | DOB | 1st Yr | Resides |
|---|---|---|---|---|---|---|---|---|---|---|---|---|---|---|---|---|---|---|---|---|
| Ellis, John | .244 | 64 | 221 | 22 | 54 | 13 | 2 | 1 | 23 | 5 | 45 | 2 | 1 | R | R | 6-1 | 195 | 8-4-75 | 1996 | Niantic, Conn. |
| Gallagher, Shawn | .273 | 44 | 176 | 15 | 48 | 10 | 2 | 4 | 29 | 7 | 48 | 8 | 5 | R | R | 6-0 | 187 | 11-8-76 | 1995 | Wilmington, N.C. |
| Majcherek, Matt | .188 | 40 | 80 | 16 | 15 | 4 | 1 | 0 | 9 | 20 | 24 | 5 | 1 | R | R | 5-10 | 170 | 11-9-74 | 1996 | Chicago, Ill. |
| Monroe, Craig | .276 | 67 | 268 | 53 | 74 | 16 | 6 | 5 | 29 | 23 | 63 | 21 | 7 | R | R | 6-2 | 195 | 2-27-77 | 1995 | Texarkana, Texas |
| Myers, Adrian | .169 | 54 | 142 | 22 | 24 | 5 | 4 | 1 | 15 | 17 | 44 | 19 | 2 | R | R | 5-10 | 175 | 5-10-75 | 1996 | Bassfield, Miss. |
| Richards, Rowan | .274 | 30 | 113 | 18 | 31 | 6 | 0 | 5 | 18 | 16 | 33 | 4 | 1 | R | R | 6-0 | 195 | 5-17-74 | 1996 | Bloomfield, N.J. |

GAMES BY POSITION: C—Ellis 56. 1B—Ellis 2, Gallagher 42. 2B—Majcherek 15. 3B—Majcherek 12. SS—Dransfeldt 75, Majcherek 7. OF—Ellis 1, Monroe 62, Myers 49, Richards 24.

| PITCHING | W | L | ERA | G | GS | CG | SV | IP | H | R | ER | BB | SO | B | T | HT | WT | DOB | 1st Yr | Resides |
|---|---|---|---|---|---|---|---|---|---|---|---|---|---|---|---|---|---|---|---|---|
| Dellamano, Anthony | 4 | 7 | 6.17 | 18 | 10 | 0 | 1 | 66 | 83 | 54 | 45 | 33 | 61 | R | R | 6-5 | 205 | 8-17-74 | 1996 | Thousand Oaks, Calif. |
| Draeger, Mark | 1 | 2 | 6.12 | 17 | 0 | 0 | 0 | 32 | 44 | 35 | 22 | 17 | 28 | R | R | 6-3 | 180 | 11-19-72 | 1995 | Lockport, Ill. |
| Knight, Brandon | 2 | 2 | 4.42 | 9 | 9 | 0 | 0 | 53 | 59 | 29 | 26 | 21 | 52 | L | R | 6-0 | 170 | 10-1-75 | 1995 | Oxnard, Calif. |
| Lee, Corey | 1 | 4 | 3.29 | 9 | 9 | 0 | 0 | 55 | 42 | 24 | 20 | 21 | 59 | S | L | 6-2 | 180 | 12-26-74 | 1996 | Clayton, N.C. |
| Martinez, Jose | 2 | 3 | 3.79 | 16 | 5 | 0 | 0 | 55 | 56 | 35 | 23 | 11 | 38 | R | R | 6-0 | 165 | 2-4-75 | 1995 | Santiago, D.R. |
| Raines, Ken | 6 | 2 | 1.07 | 38 | 0 | 0 | 5 | 67 | 51 | 19 | 8 | 21 | 64 | R | L | 6-2 | 175 | 10-14-72 | 1994 | Freeland, Mich. |
| Siegel, Justin | 0 | 1 | 5.68 | 5 | 0 | 0 | 0 | 6 | 8 | 5 | 4 | 5 | 8 | L | L | 6-0 | 170 | 9-3-75 | 1996 | Marina Del Ray, Calif. |

# PORT CHARLOTTE · Rookie
## GULF COAST LEAGUE

| BATTING | AVG | G | AB | R | H | 2B | 3B | HR | RBI | BB | SO | SB | CS | B | T | HT | WT | DOB | 1st Yr | Resides |
|---|---|---|---|---|---|---|---|---|---|---|---|---|---|---|---|---|---|---|---|---|
| Acevedo, Luis | .195 | 53 | 174 | 17 | 34 | 8 | 2 | 0 | 19 | 25 | 31 | 7 | 1 | R | R | 5-11 | 180 | 11-19-77 | 1996 | Isabella, P.R. |
| Barrera, Rafael | .294 | 40 | 136 | 20 | 40 | 4 | 2 | 1 | 13 | 10 | 24 | 14 | 2 | S | R | 6-2 | 170 | 10-10-76 | 1994 | Caracas, Venez. |
| Camacaro, Pedro | .190 | 36 | 121 | 8 | 23 | 5 | 1 | 0 | 13 | 7 | 29 | 6 | 1 | S | R | 5-11 | 165 | 9-18-77 | 1995 | Carabobo, Venez. |
| Carrion, Jorge | .309 | 19 | 55 | 13 | 17 | 2 | 0 | 0 | 8 | 3 | 6 | 9 | 1 | R | R | 6-1 | 175 | 12-10-76 | 1996 | Brooklyn, N.Y. |
| De la Rosa, Miguel | .140 | 16 | 43 | 4 | 6 | 1 | 0 | 0 | 1 | 4 | 20 | 1 | 0 | R | R | 6-0 | 170 | 10-29-76 | 1994 | Santo Domingo, D.R. |
| Fisher, Tony | .241 | 9 | 29 | 2 | 7 | 1 | 1 | 0 | 6 | 2 | 8 | 2 | 1 | R | R | 6-1 | 180 | 1-18-75 | 1996 | Oakdale, Minn. |
| Lina, Estivinson | .260 | 50 | 146 | 25 | 38 | 7 | 2 | 5 | 34 | 17 | 43 | 4 | 4 | R | R | 6-1 | 186 | 10-19-76 | 1994 | Santo Domingo, D.R. |
| Llibre, Brian | .306 | 33 | 108 | 18 | 33 | 5 | 0 | 8 | 24 | 2 | 29 | 3 | 1 | R | R | 6-4 | 201 | 9-16-77 | 1993 | West Covina, Calif. |
| Mercado, Julio | .215 | 42 | 107 | 18 | 23 | 4 | 1 | 3 | 7 | 10 | 24 | 10 | 4 | R | R | 6-0 | 180 | 5-11-77 | 1995 | Stafford, Va. |
| Parra, Jose | .258 | 15 | 31 | 4 | 8 | 0 | 0 | 1 | 3 | 3 | 8 | 4 | 1 | S | R | 6-0 | 155 | 4-23-77 | 1994 | Santiago, D.R. |
| Pena, Jose | .286 | 30 | 98 | 19 | 28 | 6 | 4 | 0 | 11 | 9 | 16 | 13 | 0 | R | R | 6-2 | 175 | 10-13-76 | 1994 | Santiago, D.R. |
| Piniella, Juan | .238 | 55 | 223 | 38 | 53 | 6 | 2 | 0 | 18 | 15 | 54 | 19 | 5 | R | R | 5-10 | 160 | 3-13-78 | 1996 | Stafford, Va. |
| Ramirez, Oscar | .195 | 56 | 195 | 21 | 38 | 12 | 2 | 2 | 23 | 16 | 59 | 3 | 3 | R | R | 6-1 | 155 | 7-6-76 | 1995 | San Pedro de Macoris, D.R. |
| Rivera, Juan | .282 | 26 | 78 | 14 | 22 | 5 | 1 | 2 | 7 | 6 | 30 | 6 | 0 | R | R | 6-2 | 184 | 4-30-77 | 1995 | Rio Grande, P.R. |
| Santos, Jose | .249 | 54 | 197 | 42 | 49 | 10 | 7 | 7 | 33 | 26 | 61 | 11 | 2 | R | R | 5-11 | 165 | 3-1-78 | 1995 | Santiago, D.R. |
| Schramm, Kevin | .330 | 23 | 88 | 16 | 29 | 8 | 1 | 3 | 16 | 4 | 22 | 2 | 2 | R | R | 6-2 | 210 | 7-24-74 | 1996 | Arcadia, Calif. |
| Seguro, Winston | .170 | 24 | 53 | 7 | 9 | 0 | 0 | 0 | 3 | 3 | 9 | 1 | 0 | R | R | 5-9 | 140 | 7-3-78 | 1996 | Valverde Mao, D.R. |
| Zywica, Mike | .273 | 33 | 110 | 18 | 30 | 7 | 1 | 3 | 22 | 14 | 24 | 3 | 0 | R | R | 6-4 | 190 | 9-14-75 | 1996 | Richton Park, Ill. |

GAMES BY POSITION: C—Lina 45, Llibre 4, Rivera 24. 1B—Camacaro 31, Llibre 1, Mercado 2, Schramm 22, Zywica 10. 2B—Camacaro 3, Santos 35, Seguro 11. 3B—Camacaro 1, Parra 9, Ramirez 55. SS—Acevedo 51, Parra 5, Seguro 12. OF—Barrera 38, De la Rosa 13, Lina 1, Mercado 39, Parra 1, Pena 29, Piniella 55, Zywica 19.

| PITCHING | W | L | ERA | G | GS | CG | SV | IP | H | R | ER | BB | SO | B | T | HT | WT | DOB | 1st Yr | Resides |
|---|---|---|---|---|---|---|---|---|---|---|---|---|---|---|---|---|---|---|---|---|
| Cook, Derrick | 2 | 1 | 4.70 | 6 | 5 | 1 | 0 | 23 | 25 | 14 | 12 | 11 | 13 | R | R | 6-3 | 198 | 11-19-77 | 1996 | Harrisonburg, Va. |
| Davis, Doug | 3 | 1 | 1.90 | 8 | 7 | 0 | 0 | 43 | 28 | 13 | 9 | 26 | 49 | R | L | 6-3 | 185 | 9-21-75 | 1996 | Sparks, Nev. |
| Fleming, Emar | 4 | 4 | 3.75 | 12 | 12 | 0 | 0 | 70 | 70 | 33 | 29 | 13 | 52 | R | R | 6-3 | 210 | 10-14-76 | 1996 | Baltimore, Md. |
| Hausman, Isaac | 7 | 3 | 2.89 | 12 | 11 | 2 | 0 | 81 | 85 | 38 | 26 | 14 | 48 | R | R | 6-4 | 170 | 6-27-76 | 1994 | Covina, Calif. |
| Henriquez, Jobannis | 2 | 3 | 4.10 | 13 | 6 | 0 | 0 | 42 | 42 | 22 | 19 | 19 | 29 | R | R | 6-2 | 175 | 6-2-77 | 1995 | Puerta Plata, D.R. |
| Kertis, John | 0 | 1 | 2.25 | 4 | 2 | 0 | 0 | 12 | 11 | 8 | 3 | 6 | 12 | S | R | 6-2 | 200 | 3-19-75 | 1996 | Miami, Fla. |
| Keusch, Joe | 0 | 0 | 3.00 | 2 | 0 | 0 | 0 | 3 | 1 | 1 | 1 | 0 | 3 | L | R | 6-1 | 175 | 1-20-72 | 1994 | Huntingburg, Ind. |
| Moody, Ritchie | 0 | 0 | 0.00 | 3 | 0 | 0 | 0 | 6 | 2 | 1 | 0 | 0 | 9 | R | L | 6-1 | 185 | 2-22-71 | 1992 | Brookville, Ohio |
| Ovalle, Bonelly | 2 | 1 | 2.23 | 18 | 0 | 0 | 7 | 44 | 36 | 17 | 11 | 13 | 38 | R | R | 5-11 | 164 | 7-30-78 | 1995 | Santiago, D.R. |
| Pauls, Matt | 1 | 0 | 0.00 | 1 | 0 | 0 | 0 | 1 | 0 | 1 | 0 | 1 | 0 | R | R | 6-1 | 190 | 7-26-74 | 1994 | Monahans, Texas |
| Pineda, Luis | 6 | 3 | 3.52 | 11 | 11 | 1 | 0 | 72 | 67 | 31 | 28 | 25 | 66 | R | R | 6-1 | 160 | 6-10-78 | 1995 | Santo Domingo, D.R. |
| Runion, Jeff | 1 | 0 | 2.37 | 7 | 2 | 0 | 0 | 19 | 14 | 8 | 5 | 12 | 19 | R | R | 6-5 | 185 | 8-29-74 | 1992 | Riverdale, Ga. |
| Seip, Rod | 0 | 0 | 0.00 | 1 | 0 | 0 | 0 | 1 | 1 | 0 | 0 | 1 | 0 | R | R | 6-2 | 190 | 3-12-74 | 1992 | Thebes, Ill. |
| Shourds, Tony | 3 | 2 | 2.31 | 20 | 0 | 0 | 0 | 35 | 27 | 12 | 9 | 12 | 28 | R | R | 6-3 | 185 | 10-9-76 | 1996 | Meriden, Conn. |
| Smith, Ryan | 2 | 0 | 4.68 | 14 | 0 | 0 | 0 | 25 | 18 | 15 | 13 | 24 | 24 | L | L | 6-4 | 215 | 9-4-74 | 1996 | Romana, Calif. |
| Styles, Bobby | 2 | 3 | 1.59 | 23 | 0 | 0 | 13 | 34 | 27 | 12 | 6 | 9 | 20 | R | R | 6-8 | 270 | 1-10-77 | 1995 | Hendersonville, N.C. |
| Wiley, Chad | 0 | 1 | 4.50 | 1 | 0 | 0 | 0 | 2 | 3 | 1 | 1 | 0 | 2 | R | R | 5-11 | 175 | 11-20-71 | 1992 | Lenexa, Kan. |

# TORONTO
# BLUE JAYS

**Manager:** Cito Gaston.     **1996 Record:** 74-88, .457 (4th, AL East).

| BATTING | AVG | G | AB | R | H | 2B | 3B | HR | RBI | BB | SO | SB | CS | B | T | HT | WT | DOB | 1st Yr | Resides |
|---|---|---|---|---|---|---|---|---|---|---|---|---|---|---|---|---|---|---|---|---|
| Brito, Tilson ................. | .238 | 26 | 80 | 10 | 19 | 7 | 0 | 1 | 7 | 10 | 18 | 1 | 1 | R | R | 6-0 | 170 | 5-28-72 | 1990 | Los Trinitarios, D.R. |
| Brumfield, Jacob ........... | .256 | 90 | 308 | 52 | 79 | 19 | 2 | 12 | 52 | 24 | 58 | 12 | 3 | R | R | 6-0 | 180 | 5-27-65 | 1983 | Atlanta, Ga. |
| Cairo, Miguel ................ | .222 | 9 | 27 | 5 | 6 | 2 | 0 | 0 | 1 | 2 | 9 | 0 | 0 | R | R | 6-1 | 160 | 5-4-74 | 1991 | Anaco, Venez. |
| Carter, Joe .................. | .253 | 157 | 625 | 84 | 158 | 35 | 7 | 30 | 107 | 44 | 106 | 7 | 6 | R | R | 6-3 | 215 | 3-7-60 | 1981 | Leawood, Kan. |
| Cedeno, Domingo ......... | .280 | 77 | 282 | 44 | 79 | 10 | 2 | 2 | 17 | 15 | 60 | 5 | 3 | S | R | 6-1 | 170 | 11-4-68 | 1988 | La Romana, D.R. |
| Crespo, Felipe ............. | .184 | 22 | 49 | 6 | 9 | 4 | 0 | 0 | 4 | 12 | 13 | 1 | 0 | S | R | 5-11 | 190 | 3-5-73 | 1991 | Caguas, P.R. |
| Delgado, Carlos ......... | .270 | 138 | 488 | 68 | 132 | 28 | 2 | 25 | 92 | 58 | 139 | 0 | 0 | L | R | 6-3 | 206 | 6-25-72 | 1989 | Aguadilla, P.R. |
| Gonzalez, Alex ........... | .235 | 147 | 527 | 64 | 124 | 30 | 5 | 14 | 64 | 45 | 127 | 16 | 6 | R | R | 6-0 | 182 | 4-8-73 | 1991 | Miami, Fla. |
| Green, Shawn ............. | .280 | 132 | 422 | 52 | 118 | 32 | 3 | 11 | 45 | 33 | 75 | 5 | 1 | L | L | 6-4 | 180 | 11-10-72 | 1992 | Santa Ana, Calif. |
| Huff, Mike ................... | .172 | 11 | 29 | 5 | 5 | 0 | 1 | 0 | 0 | 1 | 5 | 0 | 0 | R | R | 6-1 | 190 | 8-11-63 | 1985 | Chicago, Ill. |
| Martinez, Sandy ........... | .227 | 76 | 229 | 17 | 52 | 9 | 3 | 3 | 18 | 16 | 58 | 0 | 0 | L | R | 6-2 | 200 | 10-3-72 | 1990 | Villa Mella, D.R. |
| Mosquera, Julio ........... | .227 | 8 | 22 | 2 | 5 | 2 | 0 | 0 | 2 | 0 | 3 | 0 | 1 | R | R | 6-0 | 165 | 1-29-72 | 1991 | Panama City, Panama |
| Nixon, Otis .................. | .286 | 125 | 496 | 87 | 142 | 15 | 1 | 1 | 29 | 71 | 68 | 54 | 13 | S | R | 6-2 | 180 | 1-9-59 | 1979 | Alpharetta, Ga. |
| O'Brien, Charlie .......... | .238 | 109 | 324 | 33 | 77 | 17 | 0 | 13 | 44 | 29 | 68 | 0 | 1 | R | R | 6-2 | 205 | 5-1-61 | 1982 | Tulsa, Okla. |
| Olerud, John .............. | .274 | 125 | 398 | 59 | 109 | 25 | 0 | 18 | 61 | 60 | 37 | 1 | 0 | L | L | 6-5 | 218 | 8-5-68 | 1989 | Bellevue, Wash. |
| Perez, Robert ............. | .327 | 86 | 202 | 30 | 66 | 10 | 0 | 2 | 21 | 8 | 17 | 3 | 0 | R | R | 6-3 | 195 | 6-4-69 | 1990 | Bolivar, Venez. |
| Perez, Tomas ............. | .251 | 91 | 295 | 24 | 74 | 13 | 4 | 1 | 19 | 25 | 29 | 1 | 2 | R | R | 5-11 | 165 | 12-29-73 | 1991 | Santo Domingo, D.R. |
| Samuel, Juan ............. | .255 | 69 | 188 | 34 | 48 | 8 | 3 | 8 | 26 | 15 | 65 | 9 | 1 | R | R | 5-11 | 180 | 12-9-60 | 1980 | Santo Domingo, D.R. |
| Sprague, Ed ............... | .247 | 159 | 591 | 88 | 146 | 35 | 2 | 36 | 101 | 60 | 146 | 0 | 0 | R | R | 6-2 | 215 | 7-25-67 | 1989 | Lodi, Calif. |
| Stewart, Shannon ........ | .176 | 7 | 17 | 2 | 3 | 1 | 0 | 0 | 2 | 1 | 4 | 1 | 0 | R | R | 6-1 | 185 | 2-25-74 | 1992 | Miami, Fla. |

| PITCHING | W | L | ERA | G | GS | CG | SV | IP | H | R | ER | BB | SO | B | T | HT | WT | DOB | 1st Yr | Resides |
|---|---|---|---|---|---|---|---|---|---|---|---|---|---|---|---|---|---|---|---|---|
| Andujar, Luis ................ | 1 | 1 | 5.02 | 3 | 2 | 0 | 0 | 14 | 14 | 8 | 8 | 1 | 5 | R | R | 6-2 | 175 | 11-22-72 | 1991 | Bani, D.R. |
| 2-team (5 Chicago) | 1 | 3 | 6.99 | 8 | 7 | 0 | 0 | 37 | 46 | 30 | 29 | 16 | 11 | | | | | | | |
| Bohanon, Brian ............ | 0 | 1 | 7.77 | 20 | 0 | 0 | 1 | 22 | 27 | 19 | 19 | 11 | 9 | L | L | 6-3 | 220 | 8-1-68 | 1987 | Houston, Texas |
| Brow, Scott ................ | 1 | 0 | 5.59 | 18 | 1 | 0 | 0 | 39 | 45 | 25 | 24 | 25 | 23 | R | R | 6-3 | 200 | 3-17-69 | 1990 | Hillsboro, Ore. |
| Carrara, Giovanni ........ | 0 | 1 | 11.40 | 11 | 0 | 0 | 0 | 15 | 23 | 19 | 19 | 12 | 10 | R | R | 6-2 | 210 | 3-4-68 | 1990 | Anzoategui, Venez. |
| Castillo, Tony .............. | 2 | 3 | 4.23 | 40 | 0 | 0 | 1 | 72 | 72 | 38 | 34 | 20 | 48 | L | L | 5-10 | 190 | 3-1-63 | 1983 | Lara, Venez. |
| Crabtree, Tim .............. | 5 | 3 | 2.54 | 53 | 0 | 0 | 1 | 67 | 59 | 26 | 19 | 22 | 57 | R | R | 6-4 | 205 | 10-3-69 | 1992 | Jackson, Mich. |
| Flener, Huck ................ | 3 | 2 | 4.58 | 15 | 11 | 0 | 0 | 71 | 68 | 40 | 36 | 33 | 44 | S | L | 5-11 | 180 | 2-25-69 | 1990 | Fairfield, Calif. |
| Guzman, Juan ............. | 11 | 8 | 2.93 | 27 | 27 | 4 | 0 | 188 | 158 | 68 | 61 | 53 | 165 | R | R | 5-11 | 190 | 10-28-66 | 1985 | Manoguayabo, D.R. |
| Hanson, Erik ............... | 13 | 17 | 5.41 | 35 | 35 | 4 | 0 | 215 | 243 | 143 | 129 | 102 | 156 | R | R | 6-6 | 215 | 5-18-65 | 1986 | Kirkland, Wash. |
| Hentgen, Pat ............. | 20 | 10 | 3.22 | 35 | 35 | 10 | 0 | 266 | 238 | 105 | 95 | 94 | 177 | R | R | 6-2 | 200 | 11-13-68 | 1986 | Fraser, Mich. |
| Janzen, Marty ............. | 4 | 6 | 7.33 | 15 | 11 | 0 | 0 | 74 | 95 | 65 | 60 | 38 | 47 | R | R | 6-3 | 197 | 5-31-73 | 1991 | Gainesville, Fla. |
| Johnson, Dane ............ | 0 | 0 | 3.00 | 10 | 0 | 0 | 0 | 9 | 5 | 3 | 3 | 5 | 7 | R | R | 6-5 | 205 | 2-10-63 | 1993 | Miami, Fla. |
| Quantrill, Paul ............. | 5 | 14 | 5.43 | 38 | 20 | 0 | 0 | 134 | 172 | 90 | 81 | 51 | 86 | L | R | 6-1 | 185 | 11-3-68 | 1989 | Cobourg, Ontario |
| Risley, Bill ................ | 0 | 1 | 3.89 | 25 | 0 | 0 | 0 | 42 | 33 | 20 | 18 | 25 | 29 | R | R | 6-2 | 210 | 5-29-67 | 1987 | Farmington, N.M. |
| Robinson, Ken ............ | 1 | 0 | 6.00 | 5 | 0 | 0 | 0 | 6 | 9 | 4 | 4 | 3 | 5 | R | R | 5-9 | 175 | 11-3-69 | 1991 | Akron, Ohio |
| Silva, Jose .................. | 0 | 0 | 13.50 | 2 | 0 | 0 | 0 | 2 | 5 | 3 | 3 | 0 | 0 | R | R | 6-5 | 210 | 12-19-73 | 1991 | San Diego, Calif. |
| Spoljaric, Paul ............ | 2 | 2 | 3.08 | 28 | 0 | 0 | 1 | 38 | 30 | 17 | 13 | 19 | 38 | R | L | 6-3 | 205 | 9-24-70 | 1990 | Kelowna, B.C. |
| Timlin, Mike ............... | 1 | 6 | 3.65 | 59 | 0 | 0 | 31 | 57 | 47 | 25 | 23 | 18 | 52 | R | R | 6-4 | 210 | 3-10-66 | 1987 | Oldsmar, Fla. |
| Viola, Frank ................ | 1 | 3 | 7.71 | 6 | 6 | 0 | 0 | 30 | 43 | 28 | 26 | 21 | 18 | L | L | 6-4 | 209 | 4-19-60 | 1981 | Longwood, Fla. |
| Ware, Jeff .................. | 1 | 5 | 9.09 | 13 | 4 | 0 | 0 | 33 | 35 | 34 | 33 | 31 | 11 | R | R | 6-3 | 190 | 11-11-70 | 1991 | Virginia Beach, Va. |
| Williams, Woody .......... | 4 | 5 | 4.73 | 12 | 10 | 1 | 0 | 59 | 64 | 33 | 31 | 21 | 43 | R | R | 6-0 | 190 | 8-19-66 | 1988 | Houston, Texas |

## FIELDING

| Catcher | PCT | G | PO | A | E | DP | PB |
|---|---|---|---|---|---|---|---|
| Martinez ........ | .993 | 75 | 413 | 33 | 3 | 8 | 8 |
| Mosquera ...... | 1.000 | 8 | 48 | 1 | 0 | 0 | 3 |
| O'Brien .......... | .995 | 105 | 613 | 37 | 3 | 5 | 5 |

| First Base | PCT | G | PO | A | E | DP |
|---|---|---|---|---|---|---|
| Carter ......... | .992 | 41 | 248 | 16 | 2 | 31 |
| Crespo ......... | 1.000 | 2 | 3 | 1 | 0 | 0 |
| Delgado ........ | .983 | 27 | 221 | 13 | 4 | 21 |
| Olerud ......... | .998 | 101 | 781 | 56 | 2 | 107 |
| Samuel ......... | .979 | 17 | 90 | 2 | 2 | 7 |

| Second Base | PCT | G | PO | A | E | DP |
|---|---|---|---|---|---|---|
| Brito ............. | .956 | 18 | 36 | 50 | 4 | 14 |
| Cairo ............ | 1.000 | 9 | 22 | 18 | 0 | 5 |
| Cedeno ........ | .969 | 62 | 110 | 169 | 9 | 47 |
| Crespo ......... | .982 | 10 | 25 | 29 | 1 | 8 |
| T. Perez ....... | .970 | 75 | 133 | 226 | 11 | 64 |

| Third Base | PCT | G | PO | A | E | DP |
|---|---|---|---|---|---|---|
| Crespo ......... | 1.000 | 6 | 6 | 8 | 0 | 2 |

| | PCT | G | PO | A | E | DP |
|---|---|---|---|---|---|---|
| Huff ............... | 1.000 | 3 | 1 | 2 | 0 | 1 |
| T. Perez ........ | .882 | 11 | 1 | 14 | 2 | 0 |
| Sprague ......... | .956 | 148 | 109 | 216 | 15 | 29 |

| Shortstop | PCT | G | PO | A | E | DP |
|---|---|---|---|---|---|---|
| Brito ............. | 1.000 | 5 | 6 | 10 | 0 | 3 |
| Cedeno ........ | 1.000 | 5 | 12 | 16 | 0 | 4 |
| Gonzalez ....... | .973 | 147 | 279 | 466 | 21 | 122 |
| T. Perez ....... | .931 | 5 | 17 | 10 | 2 | 4 |

| Outfield | PCT | G | PO | A | E | DP |
|---|---|---|---|---|---|---|
| Brumfield ........ | .982 | 83 | 159 | 8 | 3 | 0 |
| Carter ............ | .961 | 115 | 167 | 7 | 7 | 1 |
| Green ............ | .992 | 127 | 254 | 10 | 2 | 3 |
| Huff ............... | 1.000 | 9 | 12 | 0 | 0 | 0 |
| Nixon ............ | .994 | 125 | 342 | 5 | 2 | 1 |
| R. Perez ........ | .994 | 79 | 114 | 3 | 2 | 0 |
| Samuel .......... | 1.000 | 24 | 27 | 0 | 0 | 0 |
| Stewart .......... | .800 | 6 | 4 | 0 | 1 | 0 |

MORRIS FOSTOFF

**Pat Hentgen**

CLIFF WELCH

Righthander Juan Guzman led American League pitchers with a 2.93 ERA

Blue Jays minor league Player of the Year Roy Halladay

RODGER WOOD

# BLUE JAYS

## FARM SYSTEM

**Director of Player Development:** Karl Kuehl

| Class | Farm Team | League | W | L | Pct. | Finish* | Manager | First Yr |
|-------|-----------|--------|---|---|------|---------|---------|----------|
| AAA | Syracuse (N.Y.) Chiefs | International | 67 | 75 | .472 | 7th (10) | Richie Hebner | 1978 |
| AA | Knoxville (Tenn.) Smokies | Southern | 75 | 65 | .536 | 4th (10) | Omar Malave | 1980 |
| #A | Dunedin (Fla.) Blue Jays | Florida State | 67 | 70 | .489 | 10th (14) | Dennis Holmberg | 1987 |
| A | Hagerstown (Md.) Suns | South Atlantic | 70 | 71 | .496 | 9th (14) | J.J. Cannon | 1993 |
| A | St. Catharines (Ont.) Stompers | New York-Penn | 44 | 32 | .579 | +4th (14) | Rocket Wheeler | 1986 |
| #R | Medicine Hat (Alta.) Blue Jays | Pioneer | 22 | 50 | .306 | 8th (8) | Marty Pevey | 1978 |

*Finish in overall standings (No. of teams in league)   #Advanced level   +Won league championship

## ORGANIZATION LEADERS

MIKE PONZINI

**Joe Carter.** 107 RBIs

### MAJOR LEAGUERS

**BATTING**
*AVG  Otis Nixon .............. .286
R  Ed Sprague................88
H  Joe Carter................158
TB  Joe Carter.............. 297
2B  Two tied at .............. 35
3B  Joe Carter................. 7
HR  Ed Sprague.............. 36
RBI  Joe Carter............. 107
BB  Otis Nixon ............... 71
SO  Ed Sprague............. 146
SB  Otis Nixon ............... 54

**PITCHING**
W  Pat Hentgen.............. 20
L  Erik Hanson ............. 17
#ERA  Juan Guzman ........ 2.93
G  Mike Timlin................ 59
CG  Pat Hentgen............ 10
SV  Mike Timlin................ 31
IP  Pat Hentgen............ 266
BB  Erik Hanson ........... 102
SO  Pat Hentgen............ 177

### MINOR LEAGUERS

**BATTING**
*AVG  Jeff Patzke, Knoxville .......................... .303
R  Anthony Sanders, Dunedin/Knoxville ...... 91
H  Anthony Sanders, Dunedin/Knoxville ... 144
TB  Anthony Sanders, Dunedin/Knoxville ... 231
2B  Craig Stone, Hagerstown/Dunedin......... 42
3B  Three tied at .............................................. 8
HR  Three tied at ............................................ 20
RBI  Ryan Jones, Knoxville ........................... 97
BB  Tom Evans, Knoxville........................... 115
SO  John Curl, Dunedin............................... 133
SB  Abraham Nunez, St. Catharines............. 37

**PITCHING**
W  Roy Halladay, Dunedin........................... 15
L  Three tied at ............................................ 12
#ERA  Beiker Graterol, St. Catharines ...........1.50
G  Carlos Almanzar, Knoxville .................... 54
CG  Mike Johnson, Hagerstown ..................... 5
SV  Dane Johnson, Syracuse ...................... 22
IP  Chris Carpenter, Knoxville.................... 171
BB  Two tied at ............................................. 91
SO  Joe Young, Hagerstown/Dunedin......... 193

*Minimum 250 At-Bats   #Minimum 75 Innings

## TOP 10 PROSPECTS

**How the Blue Jays Top 10 prospects, as judged by Baseball America prior to the 1996 season, fared in 1996:**

BILL SETLIFF

**Shannon Stewart**

| Player, Pos. | Club (Class—League) | AVG | AB | R | H | 2B | 3B | HR | RBI | SB |
|--------------|---------------------|-----|-----|---|-----|----|----|----|-----|----|
| 1. Shannon Stewart, of | Syracuse (AAA—International) | .298 | 420 | 77 | 125 | 26 | 8 | 6 | 42 | 35 |
| | Toronto | .176 | 17 | 2 | 3 | 1 | 0 | 0 | 2 | 1 |
| 7. Ryan Jones, 1b | Knoxville (AA—Southern) | .271 | 506 | 70 | 137 | 26 | 2 | 20 | 97 | 2 |
| 8. Tom Evans, 3b | Knoxville (AA—Southern) | .282 | 394 | 87 | 111 | 27 | 1 | 17 | 65 | 4 |
| 9. Felipe Crespo, 2b-3b | Syracuse (AAA—International) | .282 | 355 | 53 | 100 | 25 | 0 | 8 | 58 | 10 |
| | Toronto | .184 | 49 | 6 | 9 | 4 | 0 | 0 | 4 | 1 |
| 10. Kevin Witt, ss | Dunedin (A—Florida State) | .271 | 446 | 63 | 121 | 18 | 6 | 13 | 70 | 9 |

| Player, Pos. | Club (Class—League) | W | L | ERA | G | SV | IP | H | BB | SO |
|--------------|---------------------|---|---|-----|---|----|-----|----|----|----|
| 2. Marty Janzen, rhp | Syracuse (AAA—International) | 3 | 4 | 7.76 | 10 | 0 | 56 | 74 | 24 | 34 |
| | Toronto | 4 | 6 | 7.33 | 15 | 0 | 74 | 95 | 38 | 47 |
| 3. Chris Carpenter, rhp | Knoxville (AA—Southern) | 7 | 9 | 3.94 | 28 | 0 | 171 | 161 | 91 | 150 |
| 4. Jose Pett, rhp | Knoxville (AA—Southern) | 4 | 2 | 4.09 | 7 | 0 | 44 | 37 | 10 | 38 |
| | Syracuse (AAA—International) | 2 | 9 | 5.03 | 20 | 0 | 110 | 134 | 42 | 50 |
| 5. Jose Silva, rhp | Knoxville (AA—Southern) | 2 | 3 | 4.91 | 22 | 0 | 44 | 45 | 22 | 26 |
| | Toronto | 0 | 0 | 13.50 | 2 | 0 | 2 | 5 | 0 | 0 |
| 6. Roy Halladay, rhp | Dunedin (A—Florida State) | 15 | 7 | 2.73 | 27 | 0 | 165 | 158 | 46 | 109 |

## INTERNATIONAL LEAGUE

| BATTING | AVG | G | AB | R | H | 2B | 3B | HR | RBI | BB | SO | SB | CS | B | T | HT | WT | DOB | 1st Yr | Resides |
|---|---|---|---|---|---|---|---|---|---|---|---|---|---|---|---|---|---|---|---|---|
| Adriana, Sharnol | .281 | 90 | 292 | 48 | 82 | 12 | 5 | 10 | 37 | 24 | 72 | 18 | 7 | R | R | 6-1 | 185 | 11-13-70 | 1991 | Willemstad, Curacao |
| Amaro, Ruben | .240 | 16 | 50 | 8 | 12 | 1 | 0 | 0 | 2 | 10 | 11 | 6 | 2 | S | R | 5-10 | 175 | 2-12-65 | 1987 | Philadelphia, Pa. |
| Boston, D.J. | .247 | 26 | 85 | 12 | 21 | 7 | 0 | 4 | 12 | 14 | 23 | 0 | 1 | L | L | 6-7 | 230 | 9-6-71 | 1991 | Cincinnati, Ohio |
| Brito, Tilson | .278 | 108 | 400 | 63 | 111 | 22 | 8 | 10 | 54 | 38 | 65 | 11 | 10 | R | R | 6-0 | 170 | 5-28-72 | 1990 | Los Trinitarios, D.R. |
| Cairo, Miguel | .277 | 120 | 465 | 71 | 129 | 14 | 4 | 3 | 48 | 26 | 44 | 27 | 9 | R | R | 6-1 | 160 | 5-4-74 | 1991 | Anaco, Venez. |
| Chamberlain, Wes | .344 | 37 | 131 | 20 | 45 | 5 | 0 | 10 | 37 | 19 | 19 | 2 | 1 | R | R | 6-2 | 219 | 4-13-66 | 1987 | Chicago, Ill. |
| Cradle, Rickey | .200 | 40 | 130 | 22 | 26 | 5 | 3 | 8 | 22 | 14 | 39 | 1 | 0 | R | R | 6-2 | 180 | 6-20-73 | 1991 | Cerritos, Calif. |
| Crespo, Felipe | .282 | 98 | 355 | 53 | 100 | 25 | 0 | 8 | 58 | 56 | 39 | 10 | 11 | S | R | 5-11 | 190 | 3-5-73 | 1991 | Caguas, P.R. |
| Dismuke, Jamie | .167 | 19 | 42 | 3 | 7 | 1 | 0 | 0 | 5 | 5 | 5 | 1 | 0 | L | R | 6-1 | 210 | 10-17-69 | 1989 | Syracuse, N.Y. |
| Huff, Mike | .290 | 78 | 248 | 40 | 72 | 20 | 3 | 8 | 42 | 28 | 39 | 8 | 3 | R | R | 6-1 | 190 | 8-11-63 | 1985 | Chicago, Ill. |
| Jose, Felix | .257 | 88 | 327 | 47 | 84 | 14 | 2 | 16 | 61 | 32 | 63 | 3 | 0 | S | R | 6-1 | 220 | 5-8-65 | 1984 | Boca Raton, Fla. |
| 2-team (11 Paw.) | .253 | 99 | 359 | 50 | 91 | 17 | 2 | 18 | 66 | 35 | 73 | 3 | 0 | | | | | | | |
| Knorr, Randy | .278 | 12 | 36 | 1 | 10 | 5 | 0 | 0 | 5 | 5 | 8 | 0 | 0 | R | R | 6-2 | 212 | 11-12-68 | 1986 | Covina, Calif. |
| Kowitz, Brian | .241 | 34 | 108 | 14 | 26 | 6 | 3 | 1 | 19 | 9 | 20 | 2 | 2 | L | L | 5-10 | 175 | 8-7-69 | 1990 | Owings Mills, Md. |
| 2-team (24 Toledo) | .222 | 58 | 176 | 23 | 39 | 11 | 3 | 1 | 22 | 18 | 32 | 4 | 4 | | | | | | | |
| McGriff, Terry | .186 | 27 | 59 | 7 | 11 | 1 | 0 | 1 | 6 | 8 | 9 | 0 | 0 | R | R | 6-2 | 180 | 9-23-63 | 1981 | Fort Pierce, Fla. |
| Mosquera, Julio | .250 | 23 | 72 | 6 | 18 | 1 | 0 | 0 | 5 | 6 | 14 | 0 | 0 | R | R | 6-0 | 165 | 1-29-72 | 1991 | Panama City, Panama |
| Mummau, Bob | .000 | 4 | 3 | 1 | 0 | 0 | 0 | 0 | 0 | 0 | 1 | 0 | 0 | R | R | 5-11 | 180 | 8-21-71 | 1993 | Manheim, Pa. |
| Perez, Tomas | .276 | 40 | 123 | 15 | 34 | 10 | 1 | 1 | 13 | 7 | 19 | 8 | 1 | R | R | 5-11 | 165 | 12-29-73 | 1991 | Santo Domingo, D.R. |
| Pose, Scott | .272 | 113 | 419 | 71 | 114 | 11 | 6 | 0 | 39 | 58 | 71 | 30 | 16 | L | R | 5-11 | 165 | 2-11-67 | 1989 | West Des Moines, Iowa |
| Ramos, John | .243 | 89 | 317 | 38 | 77 | 16 | 0 | 8 | 42 | 41 | 51 | 1 | 1 | R | R | 6-0 | 190 | 8-6-65 | 1986 | Tampa, Fla. |
| Rowland, Rich | .226 | 96 | 288 | 43 | 65 | 24 | 2 | 8 | 45 | 50 | 79 | 1 | 1 | R | R | 6-1 | 215 | 2-25-64 | 1988 | Lakeland, Fla. |
| Stewart, Shannon | .298 | 112 | 420 | 77 | 125 | 26 | 8 | 6 | 42 | 54 | 61 | 35 | 8 | R | R | 6-1 | 185 | 2-25-74 | 1992 | Miami, Fla. |
| Turang, Brian | .172 | 37 | 93 | 13 | 16 | 2 | 1 | 1 | 8 | 9 | 14 | 3 | 0 | R | R | 5-10 | 170 | 6-14-67 | 1989 | Long Beach, Calif. |
| Weinke, Chris | .186 | 51 | 161 | 21 | 30 | 8 | 1 | 3 | 18 | 19 | 49 | 0 | 1 | R | R | 6-3 | 205 | 7-31-72 | 1991 | St. Paul, Minn. |

| PITCHING | W | L | ERA | G | GS | CG | SV | IP | H | R | ER | BB | SO | B | T | HT | WT | DOB | 1st Yr | Resides |
|---|---|---|---|---|---|---|---|---|---|---|---|---|---|---|---|---|---|---|---|---|
| Andujar, Luis | 0 | 0 | 2.25 | 2 | 2 | 0 | 0 | 12 | 17 | 7 | 3 | 2 | 10 | R | R | 6-2 | 175 | 11-22-72 | 1991 | Bani, D.R. |
| Baptist, Travis | 7 | 6 | 5.43 | 30 | 21 | 2 | 0 | 141 | 187 | 91 | 85 | 48 | 77 | S | L | 6-0 | 190 | 12-30-71 | 1990 | Aloha, Ore. |
| Bohanon, Brian | 4 | 3 | 3.86 | 31 | 0 | 0 | 0 | 58 | 56 | 29 | 25 | 17 | 38 | L | L | 6-3 | 220 | 8-1-68 | 1987 | Houston, Texas |
| Brandow, Derek | 8 | 7 | 4.28 | 24 | 20 | 2 | 0 | 124 | 118 | 64 | 59 | 57 | 103 | R | R | 6-1 | 200 | 1-25-70 | 1992 | London, Ontario |
| Brow, Scott | 5 | 4 | 4.93 | 18 | 11 | 0 | 0 | 77 | 84 | 49 | 42 | 26 | 52 | R | R | 6-3 | 200 | 3-17-69 | 1990 | Hillsboro, Ore. |
| Carrara, Giovanni | 4 | 4 | 3.58 | 9 | 6 | 1 | 0 | 38 | 37 | 16 | 15 | 12 | 28 | R | R | 6-2 | 210 | 3-4-68 | 1990 | Anzoategui, Venez. |
| Czajkowski, Jim | 6 | 4 | 3.83 | 48 | 2 | 0 | 1 | 89 | 85 | 52 | 38 | 37 | 71 | S | R | 6-4 | 215 | 12-18-63 | 1986 | Cary, N.C. |
| Flener, Huck | 7 | 3 | 2.28 | 14 | 14 | 0 | 0 | 87 | 73 | 27 | 22 | 23 | 62 | S | L | 5-11 | 180 | 2-25-69 | 1990 | Fairfield, Calif. |
| Horsman, Vince | 0 | 3 | 5.40 | 29 | 0 | 0 | 0 | 35 | 37 | 22 | 21 | 11 | 21 | R | L | 6-2 | 175 | 3-9-67 | 1985 | Dartmouth, N.S. |
| Janzen, Marty | 3 | 4 | 7.76 | 10 | 10 | 0 | 0 | 56 | 74 | 54 | 48 | 24 | 34 | R | R | 6-3 | 197 | 5-31-73 | 1991 | Gainesville, Fla. |
| Johnson, Dane | 3 | 2 | 2.45 | 43 | 0 | 0 | 22 | 51 | 37 | 14 | 14 | 17 | 51 | R | R | 6-5 | 205 | 2-10-63 | 1993 | Miami, Fla. |
| Pace, Scotty | 3 | 3 | 5.05 | 20 | 5 | 1 | 0 | 52 | 53 | 37 | 29 | 27 | 35 | L | L | 6-4 | 210 | 9-16-71 | 1994 | Cieba, P.R. |
| Pett, Jose | 2 | 9 | 5.83 | 20 | 18 | 1 | 0 | 110 | 134 | 81 | 71 | 42 | 50 | R | R | 6-6 | 190 | 1-8-76 | 1992 | Sao Paulo, Brazil |
| Risley, Bill | 0 | 0 | 0.00 | 2 | 0 | 0 | 0 | 1 | 0 | 1 | 0 | 1 | 0 | R | R | 6-2 | 210 | 5-29-67 | 1987 | Farmington, N.M. |
| Robinson, Ken | 3 | 7 | 4.64 | 47 | 0 | 0 | 1 | 64 | 52 | 37 | 33 | 39 | 78 | R | R | 5-9 | 175 | 11-3-69 | 1991 | Akron, Ohio |
| Rogers, Jimmy | 1 | 3 | 6.04 | 8 | 3 | 0 | 0 | 22 | 28 | 16 | 15 | 7 | 15 | R | R | 6-2 | 190 | 1-3-67 | 1987 | Tulsa, Okla. |
| Sievert, Mark | 2 | 5 | 5.93 | 10 | 10 | 1 | 0 | 55 | 62 | 40 | 36 | 33 | 46 | L | R | 6-4 | 180 | 2-16-73 | 1991 | Janesville, Wis. |
| Spoljaric, Paul | 3 | 0 | 3.27 | 17 | 0 | 0 | 4 | 22 | 20 | 9 | 8 | 6 | 24 | R | L | 6-3 | 205 | 9-24-70 | 1990 | Kelowna, B.C. |
| Ware, Jeff | 3 | 7 | 5.68 | 13 | 13 | 1 | 0 | 78 | 83 | 54 | 49 | 32 | 59 | R | R | 6-3 | 190 | 11-11-70 | 1991 | Virginia Beach, Va. |
| Williams, Woody | 3 | 1 | 1.41 | 7 | 7 | 1 | 0 | 32 | 22 | 5 | 5 | 7 | 33 | R | R | 6-0 | 190 | 8-19-66 | 1988 | Houston, Texas |

### FIELDING

| Catcher | PCT | G | PO | A | E | DP | PB |
|---|---|---|---|---|---|---|---|
| Knorr | 1.000 | 10 | 53 | 2 | 0 | 0 | 1 |
| McGriff | 1.000 | 25 | 95 | 6 | 0 | 1 | 2 |
| Mosquera | .983 | 23 | 164 | 9 | 3 | 0 | 1 |
| Ramos | .987 | 21 | 139 | 15 | 2 | 2 | 4 |
| Rowland | .994 | 83 | 476 | 38 | 3 | 5 | 6 |

| First Base | PCT | G | PO | A | E | DP |
|---|---|---|---|---|---|---|
| Adriana | 1.000 | 8 | 33 | 4 | 0 | 7 |
| Boston | .987 | 26 | 194 | 27 | 3 | 25 |
| Crespo | .981 | 7 | 50 | 2 | 1 | 5 |
| Dismuke | 1.000 | 15 | 114 | 20 | 0 | 10 |
| Huff | .973 | 17 | 98 | 11 | 3 | 15 |
| Pose | 1.000 | 1 | 1 | 0 | 0 | 0 |
| Ramos | .982 | 38 | 248 | 24 | 5 | 33 |
| Rowland | .976 | 8 | 37 | 4 | 1 | 6 |
| Weinke | .986 | 45 | 318 | 33 | 5 | 41 |

| Second Base | PCT | G | PO | A | E | DP |
|---|---|---|---|---|---|---|
| Adriana | 1.000 | 2 | 1 | 4 | 0 | 0 |
| Brito | .963 | 6 | 14 | 12 | 1 | 6 |
| Cairo | .963 | 84 | 165 | 222 | 15 | 64 |
| Crespo | .955 | 39 | 99 | 94 | 9 | 26 |
| Perez | .976 | 8 | 21 | 19 | 1 | 8 |
| Turang | .953 | 10 | 20 | 21 | 2 | 6 |

| Third Base | PCT | G | PO | A | E | DP |
|---|---|---|---|---|---|---|
| Adriana | .891 | 54 | 28 | 86 | 14 | 5 |
| Brito | .923 | 7 | 4 | 8 | 1 | 1 |
| Cairo | .925 | 32 | 24 | 62 | 7 | 6 |
| Crespo | .878 | 26 | 20 | 45 | 9 | 6 |
| Huff | 1.000 | 14 | 6 | 28 | 0 | 2 |
| Turang | .879 | 15 | 8 | 21 | 4 | 4 |
| Weinke | .600 | 3 | 3 | 3 | 4 | 1 |

| Shortstop | PCT | G | PO | A | E | DP |
|---|---|---|---|---|---|---|
| Adriana | .955 | 12 | 8 | 34 | 2 | 10 |
| Brito | .932 | 98 | 138 | 270 | 30 | 72 |

| | PCT | G | PO | A | E | DP |
|---|---|---|---|---|---|---|
| Cairo | .938 | 5 | 4 | 11 | 1 | 4 |
| Mummau | 1.000 | 1 | 1 | 2 | 0 | 0 |
| Perez | .958 | 32 | 59 | 78 | 6 | 20 |

| Outfield | PCT | G | PO | A | E | DP |
|---|---|---|---|---|---|---|
| Adriana | .951 | 17 | 39 | 0 | 2 | 0 |
| Amaro | .15 | 15 | 23 | 2 | 0 | 0 |
| Chamberlain | 1.000 | 15 | 23 | 0 | 0 | 0 |
| Cradle | .947 | 40 | 67 | 5 | 4 | 0 |
| Crespo | 1.000 | 31 | 51 | 2 | 0 | 0 |
| Dismuke | .000 | 2 | 0 | 0 | 0 | 0 |
| Huff | 1.000 | 51 | 99 | 3 | 0 | 2 |
| Jose | .923 | 7 | 10 | 2 | 1 | 0 |
| Kowitz | 1.000 | 33 | 60 | 0 | 0 | 0 |
| Mummau | .000 | 1 | 0 | 0 | 0 | 0 |
| Pose | .990 | 110 | 193 | 9 | 2 | 2 |
| Ramos | 1.000 | 12 | 12 | 1 | 0 | 0 |
| Stewart | .983 | 111 | 274 | 7 | 5 | 2 |
| Turang | 1.000 | 8 | 8 | 0 | 0 | 0 |

## SOUTHERN LEAGUE

| BATTING | AVG | G | AB | R | H | 2B | 3B | HR | RBI | BB | SO | SB | CS | B | T | HT | WT | DOB | 1st Yr | Resides |
|---|---|---|---|---|---|---|---|---|---|---|---|---|---|---|---|---|---|---|---|---|
| Candelaria, Ben | .278 | 55 | 162 | 16 | 45 | 11 | 2 | 3 | 14 | 18 | 40 | 3 | 3 | L | R | 5-11 | 167 | 1-29-75 | 1992 | Hatillo, P.R. |
| Cradle, Rickey | .282 | 92 | 333 | 59 | 94 | 23 | 2 | 12 | 47 | 55 | 65 | 15 | 11 | L | R | 6-2 | 180 | 6-20-73 | 1991 | Cerritos, Calif. |
| Cromer, Brandon | .277 | 98 | 318 | 56 | 88 | 15 | 8 | 7 | 32 | 60 | 84 | 3 | 6 | L | R | 6-2 | 175 | 1-25-74 | 1992 | Lexington, S.C. |
| De la Cruz, Lorenzo | .247 | 122 | 441 | 60 | 109 | 24 | 4 | 18 | 79 | 36 | 123 | 8 | 4 | R | R | 6-1 | 199 | 9-5-71 | 1991 | Santo Domingo, D.R. |
| Evans, Tom | .282 | 120 | 394 | 87 | 111 | 27 | 1 | 17 | 65 | 115 | 113 | 4 | 0 | R | R | 6-1 | 180 | 7-9-74 | 1992 | Kirkland, Wash. |
| Harmes, Kris | .213 | 44 | 122 | 16 | 26 | 8 | 1 | 2 | 8 | 13 | 17 | 1 | 0 | L | R | 6-2 | 190 | 6-13-71 | 1990 | Mount Joy, Pa. |
| Henry, Santiago | .270 | 110 | 371 | 37 | 100 | 15 | 7 | 3 | 32 | 19 | 66 | 11 | 7 | R | R | 5-11 | 156 | 7-27-72 | 1991 | San Pedro de Macoris, D.R. |
| Jones, Ryan | .271 | 134 | 506 | 70 | 137 | 26 | 3 | 20 | 97 | 60 | 88 | 2 | 2 | R | R | 6-3 | 220 | 11-5-74 | 1993 | Irvine, Calif. |

| BATTING | AVG | G | AB | R | H | 2B | 3B | HR | RBI | BB | SO | SB | CS | B | T | HT | WT | DOB | 1st Yr | Resides |
|---|---|---|---|---|---|---|---|---|---|---|---|---|---|---|---|---|---|---|---|---|
| Martinez, Angel | .188 | 4 | 16 | 2 | 3 | 0 | 0 | 0 | 0 | 0 | 5 | 0 | 0 | L | R | 6-2 | 200 | 10-3-72 | 1990 | Villa Mella, D.R. |
| Melhuse, Adam | .213 | 32 | 94 | 13 | 20 | 3 | 0 | 1 | 6 | 14 | 29 | 0 | 1 | S | R | 6-2 | 185 | 3-27-72 | 1990 | Stockton, Calif. |
| Mosquera, Julio | .230 | 92 | 318 | 36 | 73 | 17 | 0 | 2 | 31 | 29 | 55 | 6 | 5 | R | R | 6-0 | 165 | 1-29-72 | 1991 | Panama City, Panama |
| Mummau, Bob | .279 | 47 | 154 | 23 | 43 | 11 | 0 | 2 | 22 | 15 | 25 | 1 | 4 | R | R | 5-11 | 180 | 8-21-71 | 1993 | Manheim, Pa. |
| Patzke, Jeff | .303 | 124 | 429 | 70 | 130 | 31 | 4 | 4 | 66 | 80 | 103 | 6 | 5 | S | R | 6-0 | 170 | 11-19-73 | 1991 | Klamath Falls, Ore. |
| Ramirez, Angel | .281 | 102 | 392 | 64 | 110 | 25 | 7 | 5 | 51 | 15 | 69 | 16 | 6 | R | R | 5-10 | 166 | 1-24-73 | 1991 | Azua, D.R. |
| Roberts, Lonell | .291 | 58 | 237 | 35 | 69 | 1 | 0 | 1 | 12 | 32 | 39 | 24 | 14 | S | R | 6-0 | 172 | 6-7-71 | 1989 | Bloomington, Calif. |
| Sanders, Anthony | .271 | 38 | 133 | 16 | 36 | 8 | 0 | 1 | 18 | 7 | 33 | 1 | 3 | R | R | 6-2 | 180 | 3-2-74 | 1993 | Tucson, Ariz. |
| Weinke, Chris | .264 | 75 | 265 | 48 | 70 | 18 | 2 | 15 | 55 | 52 | 74 | 2 | 2 | L | R | 6-3 | 205 | 7-31-72 | 1991 | St. Paul, Minn. |

| PITCHING | W | L | ERA | G | GS | CG | SV | IP | H | R | ER | BB | SO | B | T | HT | WT | DOB | 1st Yr | Resides |
|---|---|---|---|---|---|---|---|---|---|---|---|---|---|---|---|---|---|---|---|---|
| Almanzar, Carlos | 7 | 8 | 4.85 | 54 | 0 | 0 | 9 | 95 | 106 | 58 | 51 | 33 | 105 | R | R | 6-2 | 166 | 11-6-73 | 1991 | Santo Domingo, D.R. |
| Bogott, Kurt | 2 | 2 | 5.33 | 33 | 0 | 0 | 3 | 54 | 64 | 34 | 32 | 29 | 56 | L | L | 6-4 | 195 | 9-30-72 | 1993 | Sterling, Ill. |
| Brandow, Derek | 1 | 2 | 7.71 | 5 | 1 | 0 | 2 | 12 | 11 | 10 | 10 | 5 | 6 | R | R | 6-1 | 200 | 1-25-70 | 1992 | London, Ontario |
| Brown, Chad | 2 | 4 | 4.06 | 46 | 0 | 0 | 7 | 64 | 72 | 33 | 29 | 23 | 63 | L | L | 6-0 | 185 | 12-9-71 | 1992 | Gastonia, N.C. |
| Carpenter, Chris | 7 | 9 | 3.94 | 28 | 28 | 1 | 0 | 171 | 161 | 94 | 75 | 44 | 150 | R | R | 6-6 | 220 | 4-27-75 | 1994 | Raymond, N.H. |
| Doman, Roger | 1 | 1 | 5.49 | 17 | 1 | 0 | 0 | 39 | 51 | 30 | 24 | 14 | 30 | R | R | 6-5 | 185 | 1-26-73 | 1991 | Cassville, Mo. |
| Duran, Roberto | 4 | 6 | 5.13 | 19 | 16 | 0 | 0 | 81 | 72 | 52 | 46 | 61 | 74 | L | L | 6-0 | 190 | 3-6-73 | 1990 | Moca, D.R. |
| Escobar, Kelvim | 3 | 4 | 5.10 | 10 | 10 | 0 | 0 | 54 | 61 | 36 | 32 | 24 | 44 | R | R | 6-1 | 195 | 4-11-76 | 1992 | La Guaira, Venez. |
| Freeman, Chris | 6 | 1 | 3.35 | 26 | 0 | 0 | 0 | 46 | 45 | 23 | 17 | 23 | 54 | R | R | 6-4 | 205 | 8-27-72 | 1994 | Knoxville, Tenn. |
| Halperin, Mike | 13 | 7 | 3.48 | 28 | 28 | 0 | 0 | 155 | 156 | 67 | 60 | 71 | 112 | L | L | 5-10 | 170 | 9-8-73 | 1994 | Naples, Fla. |
| Pace, Scotty | 2 | 0 | 3.00 | 4 | 1 | 0 | 0 | 12 | 8 | 4 | 4 | 5 | 6 | L | L | 6-4 | 210 | 9-16-71 | 1994 | Cieba, P.R. |
| Pett, Jose | 4 | 2 | 4.09 | 7 | 7 | 1 | 0 | 44 | 37 | 20 | 20 | 10 | 38 | R | R | 6-6 | 190 | 1-8-76 | 1992 | Sao Paulo, Brazil |
| Rhine, Kendall | 0 | 0 | 5.84 | 11 | 0 | 0 | 2 | 12 | 12 | 8 | 8 | 11 | 9 | R | R | 6-7 | 215 | 11-27-70 | 1992 | Lilburn, Ga. |
| Romano, Mike | 9 | 9 | 4.98 | 34 | 21 | 0 | 1 | 130 | 148 | 98 | 72 | 72 | 92 | S | R | 6-2 | 195 | 3-3-72 | 1992 | Chalmette, La. |
| Sievert, Mark | 9 | 2 | 2.58 | 17 | 17 | 0 | 0 | 101 | 79 | 32 | 29 | 51 | 75 | L | R | 6-4 | 200 | 2-16-73 | 1991 | Janesville, Wis. |
| Silva, Jose | 2 | 3 | 4.91 | 22 | 6 | 0 | 0 | 44 | 45 | 27 | 24 | 22 | 26 | R | R | 6-5 | 210 | 12-19-73 | 1991 | San Diego, Calif. |
| Smith, Brian | 3 | 5 | 3.81 | 54 | 0 | 0 | 16 | 76 | 76 | 42 | 32 | 31 | 58 | R | R | 5-11 | 185 | 7-19-72 | 1994 | Salisbury, N.C. |
| Viola, Frank | 0 | 0 | 1.64 | 7 | 4 | 0 | 0 | 22 | 16 | 4 | 4 | 3 | 15 | L | L | 6-4 | 209 | 4-19-60 | 1981 | Longwood, Fla. |

## FIELDING

| Catcher | PCT | G | PO | A | E | DP | PB |
|---|---|---|---|---|---|---|---|
| Harmes | .980 | 30 | 182 | 17 | 4 | 1 | 1 |
| Martinez | .950 | 3 | 17 | 2 | 1 | 1 | 0 |
| Melhuse | .989 | 31 | 162 | 15 | 2 | 2 | 6 |
| Mosquera | .991 | 92 | 679 | 63 | 7 | 6 | 19 |

| First Base | PCT | G | PO | A | E | DP |
|---|---|---|---|---|---|---|
| Evans | 1.000 | 1 | 6 | 0 | 0 | 0 |
| Harmes | 1.000 | 10 | 82 | 7 | 0 | 6 |
| Jones | .992 | 121 | 1054 | 76 | 9 | 116 |
| Mummau | 1.000 | 2 | 0 | 0 | | 1 |
| Weinke | 1.000 | 11 | 78 | 13 | 0 | 14 |

| Second Base | PCT | G | PO | A | E | DP |
|---|---|---|---|---|---|---|
| Cromer | 1.000 | 1 | 0 | 1 | 0 | 1 |

| | PCT | G | PO | A | E | DP |
|---|---|---|---|---|---|---|
| Henry | .966 | 26 | 47 | 65 | 4 | 16 |
| Patzke | .973 | 120 | 223 | 343 | 16 | 90 |

| Third Base | PCT | G | PO | A | E | DP |
|---|---|---|---|---|---|---|
| Cromer | .976 | 27 | 15 | 66 | 2 | 8 |
| Evans | .941 | 72 | 46 | 146 | 12 | 13 |
| Harmes | .500 | 2 | 0 | 2 | 2 | 0 |
| Mummau | .961 | 45 | 31 | 93 | 5 | 11 |
| Weinke | .000 | 1 | 0 | 0 | 0 | 0 |

| Shortstop | PCT | G | PO | A | E | DP |
|---|---|---|---|---|---|---|
| Cromer | .947 | 73 | 79 | 172 | 14 | 36 |
| Henry | .932 | 80 | 135 | 224 | 26 | 68 |
| Melhuse | .000 | 1 | 0 | 0 | 0 | 0 |

| Outfield | PCT | G | PO | A | E | DP |
|---|---|---|---|---|---|---|
| Candelaria | .962 | 38 | 47 | 3 | 2 | 0 |
| Cradle | .973 | 88 | 135 | 8 | 4 | 1 |
| DeLaCruz | .955 | 116 | 184 | 9 | 9 | 1 |
| Harmes | .000 | 1 | 0 | 0 | 0 | 0 |
| Henry | 1.000 | 3 | 4 | 0 | 0 | 0 |
| Ramirez | .979 | 95 | 180 | 5 | 4 | 1 |
| Roberts | .991 | 58 | 102 | 4 | 1 | 1 |
| Sanders | .957 | 38 | 66 | 1 | 3 | 0 |
| Weinke | 1.000 | 3 | 3 | 0 | 0 | 0 |

## BAKERSFIELD — Class A/Co-Op

### CALIFORNIA LEAGUE

| BATTING | AVG | G | AB | R | H | 2B | 3B | HR | RBI | BB | SO | SB | CS | B | T | HT | WT | DOB | 1st Yr | Resides |
|---|---|---|---|---|---|---|---|---|---|---|---|---|---|---|---|---|---|---|---|---|
| Moultrie, Pat | .209 | 48 | 158 | 19 | 33 | 4 | 0 | 3 | 15 | 29 | 37 | 15 | 5 | L | L | 5-10 | 170 | 4-27-73 | 1992 | Fresno, Calif. |

GAMES BY POSITION: OF—Moultrie 42.

| PITCHING | W | L | ERA | G | GS | CG | SV | IP | H | R | ER | BB | SO | B | T | HT | WT | DOB | 1st Yr | Resides |
|---|---|---|---|---|---|---|---|---|---|---|---|---|---|---|---|---|---|---|---|---|
| Lukasiewicz, Mark | 0 | 2 | 9.24 | 7 | 0 | 0 | 0 | 13 | 17 | 14 | 13 | 11 | 9 | L | L | 6-5 | 230 | 3-8-73 | 1994 | Secaucus, N.J. |

# DUNEDIN — Class A

### FLORIDA STATE LEAGUE

| BATTING | AVG | G | AB | R | H | 2B | 3B | HR | RBI | BB | SO | SB | CS | B | T | HT | WT | DOB | 1st Yr | Resides |
|---|---|---|---|---|---|---|---|---|---|---|---|---|---|---|---|---|---|---|---|---|
| Butler, Rich | .071 | 10 | 28 | 1 | 2 | 0 | 0 | 0 | 0 | 5 | 9 | 4 | 1 | L | R | 6-1 | 180 | 5-1-73 | 1991 | Toronto, Ontario |
| Candelaria, Ben | .200 | 39 | 125 | 13 | 25 | 5 | 0 | 1 | 6 | 12 | 25 | 1 | 4 | L | R | 5-11 | 167 | 1-29-75 | 1992 | Hatillo, P.R. |
| Crespo, Felipe | .324 | 9 | 34 | 3 | 11 | 1 | 0 | 2 | 6 | 2 | 3 | 1 | 3 | S | R | 5-11 | 190 | 3-5-73 | 1991 | Caguas, P.R. |
| Curl, John | .246 | 125 | 447 | 52 | 110 | 20 | 2 | 18 | 62 | 44 | 133 | 7 | 4 | L | R | 6-3 | 205 | 11-10-72 | 1995 | College Station, Texas |
| Davila, Vic | .269 | 122 | 398 | 54 | 107 | 26 | 2 | 8 | 72 | 33 | 76 | 1 | 3 | L | R | 6-0 | 185 | 10-27-72 | 1993 | New York, N.Y. |
| Freel, Ryan | .255 | 104 | 381 | 64 | 97 | 23 | 3 | 4 | 41 | 33 | 76 | 19 | 15 | R | R | 5-10 | 175 | 3-8-76 | 1995 | Jacksonville, Fla. |
| Gordon, Herman | .133 | 20 | 30 | 4 | 4 | 1 | 1 | 0 | 2 | 3 | 11 | 1 | 0 | S | R | 6-2 | 190 | 11-5-74 | 1994 | Oceanside, Calif. |
| Hayes, Chris | .236 | 32 | 106 | 14 | 25 | 6 | 0 | 1 | 12 | 11 | 21 | 1 | 2 | R | R | 6-2 | 190 | 12-23-73 | 1995 | Jacksonville, Fla. |
| King, Brion | .071 | 7 | 14 | 1 | 1 | 0 | 0 | 0 | 1 | 0 | 5 | 0 | 0 | R | R | 6-0 | 200 | 9-1-76 | 1995 | Oviedo, Fla. |
| Langaigne, Selwyn | .222 | 31 | 117 | 16 | 26 | 2 | 3 | 0 | 4 | 9 | 30 | 1 | 3 | L | L | 6-0 | 185 | 3-22-76 | 1994 | Las Acaias, Venez. |
| McCormick, Andrew | .214 | 55 | 126 | 15 | 27 | 3 | 1 | 0 | 7 | 20 | 36 | 4 | 0 | R | R | 5-11 | 190 | 6-21-73 | 1995 | Tempe, Ariz. |
| Melhuse, Adam | .248 | 97 | 315 | 50 | 78 | 23 | 2 | 13 | 56 | 69 | 68 | 3 | 1 | S | R | 6-2 | 185 | 3-27-72 | 1990 | Stockton, Calif. |
| Miller, Logan | .174 | 10 | 23 | 2 | 4 | 0 | 0 | 0 | 1 | 3 | 8 | 0 | 0 | R | R | 6-2 | 200 | 5-30-74 | 1996 | Fairfax, Calif. |
| Morgan, Dave | .261 | 39 | 88 | 13 | 23 | 3 | 1 | 4 | 15 | 18 | 24 | 0 | 1 | R | R | 6-4 | 215 | 11-19-71 | 1993 | Needham, Mass. |
| Mummau, Bob | .208 | 36 | 106 | 10 | 22 | 3 | 0 | 0 | 10 | 12 | 22 | 4 | 2 | R | R | 5-11 | 180 | 8-21-71 | 1993 | Manheim, Pa. |
| Rivers, Jonathan | .249 | 97 | 333 | 46 | 83 | 14 | 3 | 6 | 43 | 38 | 67 | 8 | 9 | R | R | 6-2 | 200 | 8-17-74 | 1992 | Tallassee, Ala. |
| Sanchez, Omar | .230 | 45 | 126 | 17 | 29 | 1 | 4 | 0 | 12 | 14 | 36 | 3 | 3 | S | R | 6-0 | 170 | 7-24-70 | 1991 | Guarico, Venez. |
| Sanders, Anthony | .259 | 102 | 417 | 75 | 108 | 25 | 0 | 17 | 50 | 34 | 93 | 16 | 12 | R | R | 6-2 | 180 | 3-2-74 | 1993 | Tucson, Ariz. |
| Stone, Craig | .263 | 61 | 228 | 26 | 60 | 25 | 4 | 0 | 22 | 20 | 55 | 0 | 0 | R | R | 6-2 | 190 | 7-12-75 | 1993 | Quaker Hill, Australia |
| Strange, Mike | .318 | 51 | 154 | 25 | 49 | 4 | 2 | 0 | 13 | 26 | 42 | 5 | 5 | R | R | 6-0 | 172 | 4-21-74 | 1994 | Melbourne, Fla. |
| Thompson, Andy | .282 | 129 | 425 | 60 | 120 | 26 | 5 | 11 | 50 | 60 | 108 | 16 | 4 | R | R | 6-3 | 210 | 10-8-75 | 1995 | Sun Prairie, Wis. |
| Umbria, Jose | .188 | 6 | 16 | 1 | 3 | 0 | 0 | 0 | 2 | 1 | 3 | 0 | 0 | R | R | 6-2 | 195 | 1-20-78 | 1996 | Barquisimeto, Venez. |
| Williams, Bryan | .000 | 6 | 17 | 0 | 0 | 0 | 0 | 0 | 0 | 0 | 9 | 0 | 0 | R | R | 6-1 | 195 | 2-9-74 | 1995 | Dickinson, Texas |
| Witt, Kevin | .271 | 124 | 446 | 63 | 121 | 18 | 6 | 13 | 70 | 39 | 96 | 9 | 4 | L | R | 6-4 | 185 | 1-5-76 | 1994 | |

**GAMES BY POSITION: C**—Melhuse 81, Miller 10, Morgan 29, Stone 27, Umbria 6, Williams 6. **1B**—Curl 108, Davila 3, Hayes 5, Melhuse 8, Mummau 2, Stone 17. **2B**—Crespo 9, Davila 3, Freel 94, Hayes 1, Mummau 12, Strange 30. **3B**—Davila 6, Freel 5, Hayes 1, Melhuse 2, Mummau 8, Strange 4, Thompson 114. **SS**—Mummau 13, Strange 11, Witt 119. **OF**—Candelaria 36, Davila 70, Gordon 14, Hayes 23, King 6, Langaigne 30, McCormick 48, Melhuse 1, Rivers 87, Sanchez 42, Sanders 100, Strange 1.

| PITCHING | W | L | ERA | G | GS | CG | SV | IP | H | R | ER | BB | SO | B | T | HT | WT | DOB | 1st Yr | Resides |
|---|---|---|---|---|---|---|---|---|---|---|---|---|---|---|---|---|---|---|---|---|
| Adkins, Tim | 7 | 9 | 3.92 | 39 | 11 | 0 | 2 | 103 | 88 | 68 | 45 | 73 | 91 | L | L | 6-0 | 195 | 5-12-74 | 1992 | Huntington, W.Va. |
| Bogott, Kurt | 1 | 1 | 1.78 | 19 | 0 | 0 | 4 | 30 | 22 | 16 | 6 | 20 | 41 | L | L | 6-4 | 195 | 9-30-72 | 1993 | Sterling, Ill. |
| Cornett, Brad | 0 | 1 | 8.59 | 4 | 0 | 0 | 0 | 7 | 15 | 7 | 7 | 3 | 5 | R | R | 6-3 | 190 | 2-4-69 | 1992 | Odessa, Texas |
| Doman, Roger | 0 | 1 | 3.30 | 18 | 0 | 0 | 0 | 30 | 36 | 22 | 11 | 14 | 19 | R | R | 6-5 | 185 | 1-26-73 | 1991 | Cassville, Mo. |
| Duran, Roberto | 3 | 1 | 1.12 | 8 | 8 | 1 | 0 | 48 | 31 | 9 | 6 | 19 | 54 | L | L | 6-0 | 190 | 3-6-73 | 1990 | Moca, D.R. |
| Escobar, Kelvim | 9 | 5 | 2.69 | 18 | 18 | 1 | 0 | 110 | 101 | 44 | 33 | 33 | 113 | R | R | 6-1 | 195 | 4-11-76 | 1992 | La Guaira, Venez. |
| Fitterer, Scott | 2 | 3 | 6.23 | 20 | 0 | 0 | 5 | 26 | 43 | 21 | 18 | 8 | 15 | R | R | 6-2 | 200 | 11-4-73 | 1995 | Kent, Wash. |
| Gomez, Miguel | 5 | 4 | 3.38 | 33 | 0 | 0 | 5 | 51 | 45 | 27 | 19 | 17 | 35 | R | R | 6-3 | 170 | 5-31-74 | 1992 | Panama City, Panama |
| Gordon, Mike | 3 | 12 | 3.44 | 24 | 24 | 0 | 0 | 133 | 127 | 70 | 51 | 64 | 102 | L | R | 6-2 | 195 | 11-30-72 | 1993 | Quincy, Fla. |
| Halladay, Roy | 15 | 7 | 2.73 | 27 | 27 | 2 | 0 | 165 | 158 | 75 | 50 | 46 | 109 | R | R | 6-6 | 200 | 5-14-77 | 1995 | Arvada, Colo. |
| Harris, D.J. | 4 | 3 | 5.19 | 35 | 0 | 0 | 6 | 43 | 49 | 30 | 25 | 19 | 31 | R | R | 5-10 | 190 | 4-11-71 | 1993 | Las Vegas, Nev. |
| Jarvis, Jason | 7 | 3 | 4.89 | 36 | 13 | 2 | 1 | 112 | 117 | 66 | 61 | 40 | 65 | R | R | 6-1 | 170 | 10-27-73 | 1994 | West Bountiful, Utah |
| Lee, Jeremy | 2 | 4 | 4.97 | 10 | 10 | 0 | 0 | 51 | 69 | 38 | 28 | 19 | 27 | R | R | 6-8 | 235 | 10-20-74 | 1993 | Galesburg, Ill. |
| Lukasiewicz, Mark | 2 | 1 | 4.60 | 23 | 0 | 0 | 1 | 31 | 28 | 20 | 16 | 22 | 31 | L | L | 6-5 | 230 | 3-8-73 | 1994 | Secaucus, N.J. |
| Meiners, Doug | 1 | 1 | 3.26 | 17 | 3 | 0 | 0 | 39 | 37 | 21 | 14 | 8 | 16 | R | R | 6-8 | 190 | 5-16-74 | 1992 | Staten Island, N.Y. |
| Pace, Scotty | 0 | 0 | 1.78 | 19 | 0 | 0 | 6 | 30 | 24 | 7 | 6 | 13 | 20 | L | L | 6-4 | 210 | 9-16-71 | 1994 | Cieba, P.R. |
| Rhine, Kendall | 1 | 0 | 3.91 | 20 | 0 | 0 | 3 | 23 | 20 | 11 | 10 | 11 | 25 | R | R | 6-7 | 215 | 11-27-70 | 1992 | Lilburn, Ga. |
| Sinclair, Steve | 0 | 1 | 3.38 | 3 | 0 | 0 | 0 | 3 | 4 | 2 | 1 | 1 | 1 | L | L | 6-2 | 172 | 8-2-71 | 1991 | Victoria, B.C. |
| Smith, Keilan | 0 | 3 | 5.04 | 23 | 1 | 0 | 2 | 45 | 50 | 32 | 25 | 22 | 37 | R | R | 6-4 | 175 | 12-20-73 | 1992 | Memphis, Tenn. |
| Veniard, Jay | 4 | 5 | 4.04 | 14 | 14 | 0 | 0 | 65 | 63 | 37 | 29 | 19 | 40 | L | L | 6-4 | 215 | 8-16-74 | 1995 | Jacksonville, Fla. |
| Williams, Woody | 0 | 2 | 8.22 | 2 | 2 | 0 | 0 | 8 | 9 | 7 | 7 | 2 | 11 | R | R | 6-0 | 190 | 8-19-66 | 1988 | Houston, Texas |
| Young, Joe | 1 | 3 | 5.88 | 6 | 6 | 0 | 0 | 34 | 30 | 24 | 22 | 17 | 36 | R | R | 6-4 | 205 | 4-28-75 | 1993 | Fort McMurray, Alberta |

# HAGERSTOWN — Class A
## SOUTH ATLANTIC LEAGUE

| BATTING | AVG | G | AB | R | H | 2B | 3B | HR | RBI | BB | SO | SB | CS | B | T | HT | WT | DOB | 1st Yr | Resides |
|---|---|---|---|---|---|---|---|---|---|---|---|---|---|---|---|---|---|---|---|---|
| Blake, Casey | .250 | 48 | 172 | 29 | 43 | 13 | 1 | 2 | 18 | 11 | 40 | 5 | 3 | R | R | 6-2 | 195 | 8-23-73 | 1996 | Indianola, Iowa |
| Farner, Matt | .154 | 11 | 26 | 10 | 4 | 1 | 0 | 0 | 3 | 8 | 11 | 0 | 1 | L | L | 6-4 | 185 | 10-15-74 | 1993 | Enola, Pa. |
| Gordon, Herman | .158 | 41 | 114 | 7 | 18 | 3 | 2 | 1 | 11 | 5 | 40 | 3 | 5 | S | R | 6-2 | 190 | 11-5-74 | 1994 | Oceanside, Calif. |
| Hampton, Robby | .203 | 19 | 69 | 9 | 14 | 3 | 1 | 1 | 8 | 4 | 28 | 1 | 0 | R | R | 6-3 | 200 | 2-21-76 | 1994 | Mount Pleasant, Texas |
| Hayes, Chris | .248 | 88 | 315 | 48 | 78 | 15 | 4 | 5 | 51 | 32 | 59 | 7 | 6 | R | R | 6-2 | 190 | 12-23-73 | 1995 | Jacksonville, Fla. |
| Johnson, Damon | .183 | 43 | 126 | 17 | 23 | 6 | 1 | 1 | 11 | 11 | 42 | 3 | 3 | R | R | 6-1 | 195 | 8-22-75 | 1993 | Crossett, Ark. |
| Kehoe, John | .272 | 117 | 383 | 66 | 104 | 24 | 2 | 6 | 47 | 73 | 92 | 16 | 9 | R | R | 6-0 | 185 | 1-9-73 | 1995 | South Bend, Ind. |
| Langaigne, Selwyn | .143 | 4 | 14 | 1 | 2 | 0 | 0 | 0 | 1 | 1 | 5 | 2 | 0 | L | L | 6-0 | 185 | 3-22-76 | 1994 | Las Acaias, Venez. |
| McCormick, Andrew | .176 | 33 | 102 | 11 | 18 | 2 | 0 | 0 | 5 | 20 | 39 | 3 | 1 | R | R | 5-11 | 190 | 6-21-73 | 1995 | Tempe, Ariz. |
| Moultrie, Pat | .271 | 39 | 129 | 25 | 35 | 5 | 1 | 1 | 12 | 12 | 24 | 10 | 1 | L | L | 5-10 | 190 | 4-27-73 | 1992 | Fresno, Calif. |
| Peck, Thomas | .333 | 19 | 48 | 7 | 16 | 2 | 0 | 0 | 7 | 10 | 11 | 1 | 1 | L | R | 6-1 | 160 | 7-2-74 | 1995 | Coral Gables, Fla. |
| Peeples, Michael | .235 | 74 | 268 | 30 | 63 | 15 | 1 | 3 | 31 | 37 | 55 | 15 | 5 | R | R | 5-11 | 160 | 9-3-76 | 1994 | Green Cove Springs, Fla. |
| Rodriguez, Luis | .207 | 79 | 256 | 19 | 53 | 8 | 1 | 1 | 25 | 24 | 58 | 6 | 4 | R | R | 5-9 | 160 | 1-3-74 | 1991 | Charallave, Venez. |
| Sanchez, Omar | .272 | 80 | 294 | 59 | 80 | 13 | 4 | 5 | 25 | 56 | 56 | 20 | 8 | S | R | 6-0 | 170 | 7-24-70 | 1991 | Guarico, Venez. |
| Shatley, Andy | .204 | 60 | 191 | 24 | 39 | 3 | 0 | 3 | 24 | 28 | 65 | 2 | 1 | R | R | 6-3 | 185 | 1-23-76 | 1994 | Jonesboro, Ark. |
| Solano, Fausto | .257 | 134 | 514 | 89 | 132 | 32 | 5 | 3 | 36 | 89 | 72 | 35 | 25 | R | S | 5-9 | 144 | 6-19-74 | 1992 | Santo Domingo, D.R. |
| Stone, Craig | .310 | 56 | 200 | 36 | 62 | 17 | 0 | 10 | 35 | 20 | 59 | 3 | 4 | R | R | 6-2 | 190 | 7-12-75 | 1993 | Quaker Hill, Australia |
| Whitlock, Mike | .252 | 131 | 424 | 72 | 107 | 22 | 1 | 20 | 91 | 108 | 132 | 1 | 4 | L | R | 6-3 | 200 | 12-14-76 | 1995 | Oakland, Calif. |
| Wilson, Craig | .261 | 131 | 495 | 66 | 129 | 27 | 5 | 11 | 70 | 32 | 120 | 17 | 11 | R | R | 6-0 | 190 | 11-30-76 | 1995 | Huntington Beach, Calif. |
| Woodward, Chris | .224 | 123 | 424 | 41 | 95 | 24 | 2 | 1 | 48 | 43 | 70 | 11 | 3 | R | R | 6-0 | 160 | 6-27-76 | 1995 | Covina, Calif. |

**GAMES BY POSITION: C**—Rodriguez 75, Stone 8, Wilson 67. **1B**—Blake 1, Hayes 7, Kehoe 2, Stone 17, Whitlock 126. **2B**—Kehoe 30, Solano 115. **3B**—Blake 47, Hayes 28, Kehoe 10, Rodriguez 4, Shatley 59, Stone 1. **SS**—Solano 20, Woodward 123. **OF**—Blake 1, Farner 11, Gordon 40, Hampton 19, Hayes 57, Johnson 41, Kehoe 66, Langaigne 4, McCormick 33, Moultrie 39, Peck 10, Sanchez 80, Stone 3, Wilson 48.

| PITCHING | W | L | ERA | G | GS | CG | SV | IP | H | R | ER | BB | SO | B | T | HT | WT | DOB | 1st Yr | Resides |
|---|---|---|---|---|---|---|---|---|---|---|---|---|---|---|---|---|---|---|---|---|
| Corral, Ruben | 1 | 5 | 5.53 | 14 | 4 | 0 | 1 | 42 | 52 | 32 | 26 | 21 | 36 | L | R | 6-5 | 200 | 5-1-76 | 1993 | El Monte, Calif. |
| Crowther, John | 2 | 3 | 3.22 | 41 | 0 | 0 | 10 | 67 | 59 | 33 | 24 | 43 | 61 | R | R | 6-5 | 231 | 9-23-73 | 1994 | Savannah, Ga. |
| Davey, Tom | 10 | 9 | 3.87 | 26 | 26 | 2 | 0 | 156 | 132 | 76 | 67 | 91 | 98 | R | R | 6-7 | 215 | 9-11-73 | 1994 | Canton, Mich. |
| Delgado, Ernie | 4 | 7 | 3.59 | 35 | 2 | 0 | 2 | 85 | 89 | 50 | 34 | 45 | 70 | R | R | 6-2 | 185 | 7-21-75 | 1993 | Tucson, Ariz. |
| Doman, Roger | 0 | 0 | 6.75 | 2 | 1 | 0 | 0 | 4 | 4 | 3 | 3 | 4 | 4 | R | R | 6-5 | 185 | 1-26-73 | 1991 | Cassville, Mo. |
| Fitterer, Scott | 1 | 0 | 9.00 | 2 | 0 | 0 | 0 | 3 | 5 | 3 | 3 | 0 | 4 | R | R | 6-2 | 200 | 11-4-73 | 1995 | Kent, Wash. |
| Halley, Allen | 1 | 0 | 0.00 | 2 | 0 | 0 | 0 | 4 | 0 | 0 | 0 | 4 | 6 | S | R | 6-1 | 195 | 9-7-71 | 1995 | St. Maarten, Neth. Antilles |
| Hartshorn, Tyson | 5 | 11 | 4.59 | 26 | 26 | 1 | 0 | 147 | 153 | 86 | 75 | 64 | 109 | R | R | 6-5 | 190 | 8-3-74 | 1993 | Lamar, Colo. |
| Horton, Eric | 1 | 2 | 4.91 | 13 | 1 | 0 | 1 | 22 | 21 | 14 | 12 | 13 | 17 | R | R | 6-2 | 180 | 8-9-70 | 1994 | Cedar Bluff, Ala. |
| Johnson, Mike | 11 | 8 | 3.13 | 29 | 23 | 5 | 0 | 163 | 157 | 74 | 57 | 39 | 155 | L | R | 6-2 | 175 | 10-3-75 | 1993 | Edmonton, Alberta |
| Lawrence, Clint | 3 | 1 | 1.98 | 6 | 6 | 0 | 0 | 36 | 26 | 12 | 8 | 10 | 27 | L | L | 6-4 | 200 | 10-19-76 | 1995 | Oakville, Ontario |
| Lee, Jeremy | 7 | 2 | 2.95 | 19 | 12 | 0 | 1 | 92 | 86 | 38 | 30 | 24 | 77 | R | R | 6-8 | 235 | 10-20-74 | 1993 | Galesburg, Ill. |
| Lowe, Ben | 2 | 3 | 2.33 | 46 | 1 | 0 | 9 | 66 | 40 | 24 | 17 | 13 | 48 | S | L | 5-10 | 185 | 6-13-74 | 1994 | Key West, Fla. |
| Lukasiewicz, Mark | 2 | 0 | 2.30 | 9 | 1 | 0 | 0 | 16 | 8 | 5 | 4 | 7 | 20 | L | L | 6-5 | 230 | 3-8-73 | 1994 | Secaucus, N.J. |
| McBride, Chris | 5 | 2 | 1.69 | 8 | 8 | 3 | 0 | 59 | 42 | 13 | 11 | 9 | 34 | L | R | 6-5 | 210 | 10-13-74 | 1994 | Leland, N.C. |
| Smith, Keilan | 2 | 3 | 3.72 | 19 | 1 | 0 | 2 | 29 | 32 | 19 | 12 | 8 | 34 | R | R | 6-4 | 175 | 12-20-73 | 1992 | Memphis, Tenn. |
| Veniard, Jay | 3 | 3 | 4.03 | 8 | 8 | 1 | 0 | 45 | 35 | 28 | 20 | 24 | 43 | L | L | 6-4 | 215 | 8-16-74 | 1995 | Jacksonville, Fla. |
| Volkert, Oreste | 1 | 3 | 2.84 | 38 | 0 | 0 | 2 | 63 | 53 | 28 | 20 | 19 | 44 | R | R | 6-6 | 187 | 1-16-75 | 1993 | La Habra, Calif. |
| Young, Joe | 9 | 9 | 3.84 | 21 | 21 | 3 | 0 | 122 | 101 | 64 | 52 | 63 | 157 | R | R | 6-4 | 205 | 4-28-75 | 1993 | Fort McMurray, Alberta |

# ST. CATHARINES — Class A
## NEW YORK-PENN LEAGUE

| BATTING | AVG | G | AB | R | H | 2B | 3B | HR | RBI | BB | SO | SB | CS | B | T | HT | WT | DOB | 1st Yr | Resides |
|---|---|---|---|---|---|---|---|---|---|---|---|---|---|---|---|---|---|---|---|---|
| Charles, Steve | .205 | 68 | 200 | 22 | 41 | 7 | 2 | 1 | 15 | 18 | 48 | 5 | 2 | L | R | 6-2 | 190 | 8-20-74 | 1994 | London, Ontario |
| Fortin, Blaine | .220 | 29 | 82 | 14 | 18 | 2 | 0 | 3 | 10 | 6 | 7 | 0 | 1 | R | R | 6-3 | 205 | 8-1-77 | 1995 | Lundar, Manitoba |

| BATTING | AVG | G | AB | R | H | 2B | 3B | HR | RBI | BB | SO | SB | CS | B | T | HT | WT | DOB | 1st Yr | Resides |
|---|---|---|---|---|---|---|---|---|---|---|---|---|---|---|---|---|---|---|---|---|
| Gordon, Herman | .150 | 13 | 40 | 5 | 6 | 2 | 0 | 1 | 9 | 3 | 9 | 1 | 0 | S | R | 6-2 | 190 | 11-5-74 | 1994 | Oceanside, Calif. |
| Hampton, Robby | .262 | 34 | 130 | 17 | 34 | 6 | 3 | 4 | 17 | 9 | 48 | 5 | 1 | R | R | 6-3 | 200 | 2-21-76 | 1994 | Mount Pleasant, Texas |
| Johnson, Damon | .241 | 19 | 58 | 12 | 14 | 6 | 0 | 0 | 3 | 3 | 17 | 0 | 1 | R | R | 6-1 | 195 | 8-22-75 | 1993 | Crossett, Ark. |
| Koehler, Jason | .230 | 47 | 135 | 21 | 31 | 6 | 0 | 4 | 18 | 19 | 40 | 2 | 1 | R | R | 6-0 | 220 | 9-15-74 | 1996 | Blandon, Pa. |
| Lawrence, Joe | .224 | 29 | 98 | 23 | 22 | 7 | 2 | 0 | 11 | 14 | 17 | 1 | 1 | R | R | 6-2 | 190 | 2-13-77 | 1996 | Lake Charles, La. |
| Lopez, Luis | .285 | 74 | 260 | 36 | 74 | 17 | 2 | 7 | 40 | 27 | 31 | 2 | 3 | R | R | 6-0 | 200 | 10-5-73 | 1996 | Spring Hill, Fla. |
| Maloney, Jeff | .250 | 1 | 4 | 0 | 1 | 0 | 0 | 0 | 1 | 0 | 2 | 0 | 0 | R | R | 6-4 | 190 | 11-27-76 | 1995 | Basking Ridge, N.J. |
| Nunez, Abraham | .279 | 75 | 297 | 43 | 83 | 6 | 4 | 3 | 26 | 31 | 43 | 37 | 14 | S | R | 5-11 | 160 | 3-16-76 | 1994 | Santo Domingo, D.R. |
| Rodriguez, Mike | .269 | 46 | 145 | 14 | 39 | 2 | 1 | 0 | 12 | 7 | 14 | 4 | 4 | R | R | 5-11 | 185 | 4-1-75 | 1996 | New York, N.Y. |
| Shatley, Andy | .281 | 76 | 256 | 34 | 72 | 17 | 2 | 5 | 36 | 21 | 64 | 4 | 3 | R | R | 6-3 | 185 | 1-23-76 | 1994 | Jonesboro, Ark. |
| Skett, Will | .276 | 75 | 272 | 47 | 75 | 13 | 1 | 15 | 52 | 33 | 73 | 13 | 3 | R | R | 5-11 | 190 | 5-22-74 | 1996 | Encino, Calif. |
| Snelling, Allen | .144 | 39 | 104 | 10 | 15 | 1 | 0 | 0 | 5 | 6 | 23 | 2 | 0 | R | R | 6-1 | 180 | 6-13-73 | 1995 | Newport, Ore. |
| Stewart, Paxton | .277 | 65 | 206 | 21 | 57 | 13 | 0 | 1 | 8 | 12 | 40 | 3 | 2 | L | R | 6-3 | 185 | 5-4-74 | 1995 | New York, N.Y. |
| Tucci, Peter | .254 | 54 | 205 | 28 | 52 | 8 | 7 | 7 | 33 | 23 | 58 | 5 | 3 | R | R | 6-2 | 205 | 10-8-75 | 1996 | Norwalk, Conn. |

**GAMES BY POSITION: C**—Fortin 24, Koehler 27, Rodriguez 35, Snelling 1. **1B**—Fortin 2, Koehler 1, Lopez 68, Shatley 3, Stewart 7. **2B**—Maloney 1, Nunez 24, Skett 38, Snelling 21. **3B**—Lawrence 2, Lopez 3, Shatley 74, Snelling 3. **SS**—Lawrence 22, Maloney 1, Nunez 52, Shatley 2. **OF**—Charles 64, Gordon 13, Hampton 30, Johnson 16, Lopez 1, Rodriguez 2, Skett 42, Snelling 10, Stewart 13, Tucci 54.

| PITCHING | W | L | ERA | G | GS | CG | SV | IP | H | R | ER | BB | SO | B | T | HT | WT | DOB | 1st Yr | Resides |
|---|---|---|---|---|---|---|---|---|---|---|---|---|---|---|---|---|---|---|---|---|
| Bale, John | 3 | 2 | 4.86 | 8 | 8 | 0 | 0 | 33 | 39 | 21 | 18 | 11 | 35 | L | L | 6-4 | 195 | 5-22-74 | 1996 | Crestview, Fla. |
| Bradford, Josh | 5 | 4 | 3.35 | 18 | 7 | 0 | 1 | 54 | 49 | 27 | 20 | 17 | 63 | R | R | 6-5 | 185 | 4-19-74 | 1996 | Sterling, Kan. |
| Davenport, Jon | 2 | 4 | 5.13 | 20 | 8 | 0 | 0 | 67 | 71 | 44 | 38 | 23 | 43 | R | R | 6-5 | 225 | 3-24-76 | 1994 | Santee, Calif. |
| Gaskill, Derek | 4 | 4 | 4.76 | 19 | 6 | 1 | 1 | 59 | 61 | 37 | 31 | 18 | 51 | R | R | 6-6 | 190 | 5-6-74 | 1992 | Portsmouth, Va. |
| Graterol, Beiker | 9 | 1 | 1.50 | 14 | 13 | 1 | 0 | 84 | 59 | 24 | 14 | 21 | 66 | R | R | 6-2 | 164 | 11-9-74 | 1993 | Lara, Venez. |
| Hueda, Alejandro | 0 | 3 | 8.71 | 12 | 5 | 0 | 0 | 31 | 41 | 33 | 30 | 16 | 17 | R | R | 6-2 | 180 | 2-28-76 | 1996 | San Jose, Costa Rica |
| LaChapelle, Yan | 0 | 0 | 0.00 | 3 | 0 | 0 | 0 | 4 | 0 | 0 | 0 | 0 | 8 | R | R | 5-10 | 190 | 10-26-75 | 1996 | Gatineau, Quebec |
| Lawrence, Clint | 4 | 1 | 2.50 | 9 | 8 | 2 | 0 | 58 | 53 | 18 | 16 | 11 | 25 | L | L | 6-4 | 200 | 10-19-76 | 1995 | Oakville, Ontario |
| Mann, James | 2 | 1 | 3.62 | 26 | 0 | 0 | 17 | 27 | 22 | 12 | 11 | 10 | 37 | R | R | 6-3 | 225 | 11-17-74 | 1994 | Holbrook, Mass. |
| McBride, Chris | 3 | 1 | 2.51 | 6 | 6 | 1 | 0 | 43 | 37 | 14 | 12 | 7 | 28 | R | R | 6-5 | 210 | 10-13-73 | 1994 | Leland, N.C. |
| Meyers, Ryan | 3 | 0 | 1.50 | 7 | 1 | 0 | 0 | 12 | 6 | 2 | 2 | 5 | 9 | R | R | 6-2 | 195 | 8-28-73 | 1996 | Brentwood, Tenn. |
| Needle, Chad | 0 | 1 | 5.13 | 20 | 0 | 0 | 0 | 26 | 24 | 22 | 15 | 28 | 26 | R | R | 6-3 | 180 | 5-17-79 | 1996 | Thornlie, Australia |
| Risley, Bill | 0 | 0 | 1.29 | 3 | 1 | 0 | 0 | 7 | 3 | 1 | 1 | 2 | 10 | R | R | 6-2 | 210 | 5-29-67 | 1987 | Farmington, N.M. |
| Rodriguez, Victor | 2 | 7 | 5.91 | 21 | 8 | 0 | 2 | 64 | 50 | 55 | 42 | 54 | 54 | R | R | 6-4 | 190 | 8-31-73 | 1994 | Pensacola, Fla. |
| Seabury, Jaron | 3 | 1 | 3.26 | 19 | 0 | 0 | 1 | 30 | 29 | 16 | 11 | 10 | 24 | R | R | 6-4 | 215 | 1-31-76 | 1995 | Mt. Vernon, Wash. |
| Spoljaric, Paul | 0 | 0 | 0.00 | 2 | 2 | 0 | 0 | 5 | 3 | 0 | 0 | 0 | 7 | R | L | 6-3 | 205 | 9-24-70 | 1990 | Kelowna, B.C. |
| Williams, Woody | 0 | 0 | 3.68 | 2 | 2 | 0 | 0 | 7 | 7 | 3 | 3 | 4 | 12 | R | R | 6-0 | 190 | 8-19-66 | 1988 | Houston, Texas |
| Zavershnik, Mike | 4 | 2 | 6.28 | 25 | 1 | 0 | 2 | 39 | 45 | 32 | 27 | 24 | 25 | R | L | 6-8 | 185 | 2-21-76 | 1994 | Mississauga, Ontario |

# MEDICINE HAT — Rookie
## PIONEER LEAGUE

| BATTING | AVG | G | AB | R | H | 2B | 3B | HR | RBI | BB | SO | SB | CS | B | T | HT | WT | DOB | 1st Yr | Resides |
|---|---|---|---|---|---|---|---|---|---|---|---|---|---|---|---|---|---|---|---|---|
| Albaral, Randy | .259 | 60 | 228 | 50 | 59 | 4 | 1 | 0 | 19 | 27 | 39 | 33 | 6 | R | R | 6-2 | 180 | 2-27-77 | 1996 | River Ridge, La. |
| Bagley, Lorenzo | .289 | 67 | 235 | 61 | 68 | 16 | 1 | 13 | 46 | 45 | 57 | 14 | 5 | R | R | 5-9 | 225 | 12-30-75 | 1996 | Citra, Fla. |
| Baston, Stanley | .280 | 68 | 271 | 45 | 76 | 14 | 1 | 5 | 45 | 36 | 58 | 10 | 3 | R | R | 6-2 | 180 | 2-12-77 | 1996 | Tallahassee, Fla. |
| Giles, Tim | .267 | 68 | 258 | 36 | 69 | 17 | 0 | 10 | 45 | 19 | 52 | 5 | 0 | L | R | 6-3 | 215 | 9-12-75 | 1996 | Gambrills, Md. |
| Langaigne, Selwyn | .260 | 32 | 100 | 19 | 26 | 4 | 1 | 2 | 11 | 17 | 20 | 8 | 2 | L | L | 6-0 | 185 | 3-22-76 | 1994 | Las Acaias, Venez. |
| Maloney, Jeff | .198 | 65 | 222 | 36 | 44 | 9 | 2 | 4 | 27 | 39 | 85 | 11 | 6 | R | R | 6-4 | 190 | 11-27-76 | 1995 | Basking Ridge, N.J. |
| Medina, Robert | .259 | 40 | 112 | 18 | 29 | 8 | 0 | 5 | 19 | 14 | 39 | 1 | 4 | R | R | 6-2 | 193 | 4-25-76 | 1996 | Caguas, P.R. |
| Moon, Brad | .176 | 34 | 51 | 5 | 9 | 1 | 0 | 0 | 1 | 2 | 15 | 0 | 1 | L | R | 6-3 | 180 | 4-18-78 | 1996 | Red Deer, Alberta |
| Phelps, Josh | .241 | 59 | 191 | 28 | 46 | 3 | 0 | 5 | 29 | 27 | 65 | 5 | 3 | R | R | 6-3 | 195 | 5-12-78 | 1996 | Rathdrum, Idaho |
| Rudolph, Jeremi | .250 | 12 | 28 | 4 | 7 | 1 | 0 | 0 | 3 | 4 | 13 | 1 | 1 | R | R | 5-8 | 170 | 12-7-76 | 1996 | Apopka, Fla. |
| Sencion, Pablo | .240 | 68 | 229 | 44 | 55 | 15 | 0 | 4 | 29 | 40 | 52 | 5 | 6 | R | R | 6-1 | 188 | 12-25-73 | 1994 | Santo Domingo, D.R. |
| Stromsborg, Ryan | .310 | 55 | 216 | 34 | 67 | 10 | 3 | 8 | 38 | 16 | 42 | 8 | 2 | R | R | 6-3 | 185 | 12-19-74 | 1996 | Encino, Calif. |
| Umbria, Jose | .189 | 36 | 122 | 9 | 23 | 3 | 0 | 0 | 10 | 7 | 23 | 1 | 2 | R | R | 6-2 | 195 | 1-20-78 | 1996 | Barquisimeto, Venez. |
| Willis, Symmion | .271 | 40 | 144 | 21 | 39 | 4 | 0 | 1 | 17 | 18 | 43 | 11 | 3 | R | R | 6-4 | 215 | 11-27-72 | 1996 | Atlanta, Ga. |

**GAMES BY POSITION: C**—Medina 16, Moon 1, Phelps 34, Umbria 31. **1B**—Bagley 1, Baston 1, Giles 56, Medina 9, Moon 1, Sencion 13, Umbria 1. **2B**—Baston 32, Maloney 23, Stromsborg 2. **3B**—Maloney 9, Medina 1, Sencion 54, Stromsborg 11, Umbria 1. **SS**—Baston 35, Maloney 33, Stromsborg 20, Willis 39. **OF**—Albaral 52, Bagley 60, Langaigne 8, Medina 8, Moon 21, Phelps 7, Sencion 1, Stromsborg 20, Willis 5.

| PITCHING | W | L | ERA | G | GS | CG | SV | IP | H | R | ER | BB | SO | B | T | HT | WT | DOB | 1st Yr | Resides |
|---|---|---|---|---|---|---|---|---|---|---|---|---|---|---|---|---|---|---|---|---|
| Andrews, Clayton | 2 | 4 | 7.36 | 8 | 4 | 0 | 0 | 26 | 37 | 23 | 21 | 10 | 14 | R | L | 6-0 | 175 | 5-15-78 | 1996 | Largo, Fla. |
| Bleazard, David | 0 | 0 | 4.56 | 20 | 0 | 0 | 10 | 24 | 29 | 16 | 12 | 14 | 31 | R | R | 6-0 | 175 | 3-7-74 | 1996 | Tooele, Utah |
| Bowles, Brian | 2 | 2 | 6.35 | 24 | 0 | 0 | 1 | 40 | 53 | 35 | 28 | 21 | 29 | R | R | 6-5 | 205 | 8-18-76 | 1995 | Manhattan Beach, Calif. |
| Burchart, Kyle | 4 | 7 | 6.59 | 15 | 15 | 0 | 0 | 72 | 75 | 69 | 53 | 67 | 33 | R | R | 6-5 | 190 | 8-18-76 | 1995 | Tulsa, Okla. |
| Glover, Gary | 3 | 12 | 7.75 | 15 | 15 | 2 | 0 | 84 | 119 | 94 | 72 | 29 | 54 | R | R | 6-5 | 200 | 12-3-76 | 1994 | DeLand, Fla. |
| Goure, Sam | 1 | 4 | 6.00 | 18 | 4 | 0 | 0 | 48 | 70 | 48 | 32 | 19 | 43 | S | L | 6-2 | 185 | 4-17-78 | 1996 | Pueblo, Colo. |
| Gourlay, Matt | 2 | 6 | 8.41 | 16 | 13 | 0 | 0 | 66 | 95 | 71 | 62 | 39 | 35 | R | R | 6-5 | 200 | 6-26-79 | 1996 | Melbourne, Australia |
| Herring, Jonathan | 0 | 0 | 13.95 | 20 | 0 | 0 | 0 | 20 | 30 | 35 | 31 | 27 | 14 | L | L | 6-3 | 190 | 6-28-76 | 1996 | Montgomery, Ala. |
| Higuchi, Roberto | 0 | 0 | 12.90 | 15 | 0 | 0 | 0 | 22 | 37 | 39 | 32 | 23 | 17 | R | R | 6-1 | 200 | 1-11-79 | 1996 | Sao Paulo, Brazil |
| Horton, Eric | 0 | 1 | 8.31 | 5 | 0 | 0 | 0 | 13 | 19 | 15 | 12 | 9 | 11 | R | R | 6-2 | 180 | 8-9-70 | 1994 | Cedar Bluff, Ala. |
| Keathley, Davan | 2 | 2 | 8.62 | 15 | 2 | 0 | 0 | 40 | 56 | 46 | 38 | 29 | 36 | R | L | 6-4 | 185 | 4-9-78 | 1996 | Turlock, Calif. |
| McClellan, Sean | 3 | 3 | 6.10 | 12 | 8 | 0 | 1 | 52 | 52 | 38 | 35 | 19 | 61 | R | R | 6-2 | 215 | 4-26-73 | 1996 | Seminole, Fla. |
| Satterfield, Jeremy | 0 | 3 | 6.12 | 14 | 0 | 0 | 0 | 32 | 39 | 31 | 22 | 27 | 25 | R | R | 6-3 | 200 | 12-2-75 | 1996 | Santa Barbara, Calif. |
| Seabury, Jaron | 0 | 0 | 4.50 | 5 | 0 | 0 | 3 | 6 | 4 | 4 | 3 | 5 | 5 | R | R | 6-4 | 215 | 1-31-76 | 1995 | Mt. Vernon, Wash. |
| Severino, Edy | 2 | 6 | 7.89 | 16 | 11 | 0 | 1 | 57 | 76 | 68 | 50 | 41 | 34 | R | R | 6-4 | 180 | 6-8-76 | 1994 | Yamasa, D.R. |

# INDEPENDENT/CO-OP
## TEAMS

## BAKERSFIELD — Class A
### CALIFORNIA LEAGUE

| | BATTING | AVG | G | AB | R | H | 2B | 3B | HR | RBI | BB | SO | SB | CS | B | T | HT | WT | DOB | 1st Yr | Resides |
|---|---|---|---|---|---|---|---|---|---|---|---|---|---|---|---|---|---|---|---|---|---|
| | Baugh, Gavin | .150 | 6 | 20 | 3 | 3 | 1 | 0 | 0 | 0 | 3 | 9 | 0 | 0 | S | R | 6-3 | 205 | 7-26-73 | 1992 | San Mateo, Calif. |
| 3 | Bazzani, Matt | .203 | 20 | 69 | 5 | 14 | 3 | 0 | 2 | 8 | 7 | 21 | 0 | 0 | R | R | 6-1 | 205 | 9-17-73 | 1994 | Foster City, Calif. |
| 4 | Bentley, Kevin | .274 | 22 | 84 | 19 | 23 | 3 | 1 | 5 | 21 | 9 | 30 | 7 | 1 | R | R | 6-2 | 210 | 9-21-72 | 1995 | Bedford, Texas |
| 4 | Cabrera, Alex | .281 | 89 | 345 | 45 | 97 | 18 | 1 | 15 | 53 | 14 | 80 | 0 | 1 | R | R | 6-2 | 217 | 12-24-71 | 1991 | El Tigre, Venez. |
| 9 | Carroll, Doug | .298 | 58 | 215 | 35 | 64 | 17 | 2 | 7 | 39 | 27 | 53 | 3 | 2 | L | R | 6-2 | 195 | 8-31-73 | 1994 | Holliston, Mass. |
| 3 | Collier, Dan | .274 | 56 | 212 | 22 | 58 | 15 | 1 | 5 | 40 | 6 | 63 | 9 | 3 | R | R | 6-3 | 200 | 8-13-70 | 1991 | Ozark, Ala. |
| 2 | Daedelow, Craig | .235 | 86 | 298 | 37 | 70 | 17 | 1 | 1 | 28 | 31 | 60 | 10 | 4 | R | R | 5-11 | 175 | 4-3-76 | 1994 | Huntington Beach, Calif. |
| 7 | Espinal, Juan | .274 | 137 | 522 | 81 | 143 | 38 | 0 | 26 | 98 | 74 | 126 | 1 | 4 | R | R | 6-0 | 207 | 4-15-75 | 1992 | La Vega, D.R. |
| | Gonzalez, Mauricio | .278 | 97 | 418 | 48 | 116 | 29 | 1 | 4 | 48 | 13 | 63 | 2 | 5 | S | R | 5-11 | 170 | 2-13-72 | 1990 | Santo Domingo, D.R. |
| | Greene, Eric | .222 | 2 | 9 | 1 | 2 | 0 | 0 | 0 | 0 | 0 | 3 | 0 | 0 | L | R | 5-10 | 180 | 8-27-71 | 1996 | Bakersfield, Calif. |
| | Greer, Ryan | .000 | 2 | 5 | 0 | 0 | 0 | 0 | 0 | 0 | 0 | 3 | 0 | 0 | R | R | 6-1 | 245 | 9-15-75 | 1996 | Bakersfield, Calif. |
| 2 | Hendricks, Ryan | .160 | 30 | 94 | 13 | 15 | 1 | 0 | 3 | 8 | 12 | 31 | 1 | 0 | L | R | 6-3 | 205 | 8-3-72 | 1994 | Randallstown, Md. |
| | 2-team (14 H.D.) | .179 | 44 | 123 | 16 | 22 | 3 | 0 | 3 | 12 | 17 | 42 | 2 | 0 | | | | | | | |
| 1 | Herider, Jeremy | .196 | 29 | 107 | 18 | 21 | 4 | 0 | 0 | 12 | 26 | 32 | 1 | 1 | S | R | 5-10 | 180 | 4-9-72 | 1995 | Lancaster, Calif. |
| | 2-team (49 Visalia) | .218 | 78 | 252 | 40 | 55 | 10 | 0 | 1 | 26 | 59 | 68 | 3 | 7 | | | | | | | |
| 1 | Johnson, Todd | .238 | 110 | 369 | 45 | 88 | 23 | 0 | 2 | 31 | 32 | 90 | 1 | 1 | R | R | 5-11 | 205 | 12-18-70 | 1993 | Fresno, Calif. |
| 1 | Kinard, Kirk | .198 | 37 | 116 | 16 | 23 | 3 | 2 | 0 | 5 | 13 | 44 | 3 | 1 | R | R | 6-0 | 175 | 3-7-74 | 1996 | Pascagoula, Miss. |
| 1 | Kliner, Josh | .308 | 43 | 156 | 37 | 48 | 6 | 1 | 5 | 33 | 37 | 25 | 0 | 3 | S | R | 5-11 | 180 | 12-27-72 | 1996 | Placentia, Calif. |
| 5 | Lewis, Andreaus | .244 | 62 | 205 | 40 | 50 | 13 | 0 | 3 | 16 | 22 | 78 | 9 | 2 | S | R | 6-2 | 215 | 1-22-74 | 1993 | Decatur, Ga. |
| 3 | Martin, Jeff | .182 | 5 | 22 | 2 | 4 | 0 | 0 | 0 | 1 | 0 | 10 | 0 | 0 | R | R | 6-3 | 230 | 7-14-70 | 1992 | Nashville, Tenn. |
| 11 | Moultrie, Pat | .209 | 48 | 158 | 19 | 33 | 4 | 0 | 3 | 15 | 29 | 37 | 15 | 5 | L | L | 5-10 | 170 | 4-27-73 | 1992 | Fresno, Calif. |
| 2 | Paxton, Chris | .249 | 85 | 269 | 30 | 67 | 14 | 0 | 11 | 39 | 35 | 89 | 0 | 0 | L | R | 6-2 | 195 | 12-11-76 | 1995 | Palmdale, Calif. |
| | Perez, Mickey | .176 | 6 | 17 | 1 | 3 | 0 | 0 | 0 | 3 | 8 | 0 | 0 | 0 | R | R | 5-10 | 165 | 6-2-72 | 1995 | San Antonio, Texas |
| 3 | Sheffield, Tony | .233 | 49 | 172 | 14 | 40 | 8 | 1 | 3 | 13 | 13 | 73 | 8 | 5 | L | L | 6-1 | 195 | 2-17-74 | 1992 | Tullahoma, Tenn. |
| 3 | Smith, Dave | .239 | 35 | 117 | 25 | 28 | 9 | 1 | 3 | 18 | 20 | 36 | 1 | 0 | R | R | 5-10 | 180 | 2-18-72 | 1993 | Cheektowaga, N.Y. |
| 1 | Stoner, Mike | .293 | 36 | 147 | 25 | 43 | 6 | 1 | 6 | 22 | 8 | 18 | 1 | 1 | R | R | 6-0 | 200 | 5-23-73 | 1996 | Simpsonville, Ky. |
| | Teasley, Ken | .158 | 21 | 57 | 4 | 9 | 1 | 0 | 0 | 2 | 4 | 19 | 0 | 0 | S | R | 6-0 | 220 | 11-16-72 | 1996 | Agoura Hills, Calif. |
| 9 | Towner, Kyle | .229 | 90 | 349 | 65 | 80 | 12 | 1 | 4 | 17 | 55 | 80 | 53 | 13 | S | R | 5-5 | 160 | 11-11-72 | 1994 | Saraland, Ala. |
| | Twist, Jeff | .115 | 7 | 26 | 0 | 3 | 0 | 0 | 0 | 1 | 1 | 8 | 0 | 0 | S | R | 6-3 | 220 | 6-17-73 | 1994 | Bakersfield, Calif. |
| 3 | Watts, John | .313 | 34 | 134 | 24 | 42 | 6 | 1 | 6 | 23 | 12 | 36 | 2 | 2 | L | R | 6-1 | 205 | 3-24-75 | 1993 | Glendale, Ariz. |
| | Wolger, Mike | .000 | 1 | 3 | 0 | 0 | 0 | 0 | 0 | 0 | 0 | 1 | 0 | 0 | L | L | 6-2 | 195 | 9-12-72 | 1995 | Redwood City, Calif. |

**GAMES BY POSITION: C**—Bazzani 10, Harmer 25, Johnson 73, Martin 5, Paxton 39, Teasley 4, Twist 7. **1B**—Cabrera 37, Carroll 11, Hendricks 26, Kliner 3, Paxton 20, Smith 18, Stoner 36. **2B**—Daedelow 1, Gonzalez 77, Greene 1, Herider 1, Johnson 6, Kinard 20, Kliner 24, Perez 6, Smith 9, Towner 2. **3B**—Espinal 129, Gonzalez 11, Herider 1, Kinard 2, Kliner 1. **SS**—Baugh 6, Daedelow 84, Gonzalez 7, Herider 24, Kinard 16, Smith 6. **OF**—Bazzani 6, Bentley 19, Cabrera 46, Carroll 35, Collier 46, Gonzalez 1, Greene 2, Greer 1, Herider 4, Johnson 1, Kliner 17, Lewis 38, Moultrie 42, Sheffield 39, Smith 2, Stoner 1, Teasley 12, Towner 88, Watts 33, Wolger 1.

| | PITCHING | W | L | ERA | G | GS | CG | SV | IP | H | R | ER | BB | SO | B | T | HT | WT | DOB | 1st Yr | Resides |
|---|---|---|---|---|---|---|---|---|---|---|---|---|---|---|---|---|---|---|---|---|---|
| 6 | Arffa, Steve | 5 | 6 | 6.81 | 15 | 11 | 1 | 0 | 73 | 98 | 61 | 55 | 22 | 71 | R | L | 6-2 | 195 | 1-26-73 | 1994 | Glendora, Calif. |
| 2 | Bates, Shawn | 1 | 1 | 12.60 | 4 | 0 | 0 | 0 | 5 | 13 | 8 | 7 | 4 | 1 | L | L | 6-3 | 202 | 2-27-75 | 1994 | Wichita Falls, Texas |
| 3 | Bazzani, Matt | 0 | 0 | 3.97 | 5 | 0 | 0 | 0 | 11 | 14 | 5 | 5 | 3 | 1 | R | R | 6-1 | 205 | 9-17-73 | 1994 | Foster City, Calif. |
| 2 | Bray, Chris | 0 | 2 | 12.68 | 17 | 0 | 0 | 1 | 22 | 28 | 34 | 31 | 38 | 15 | R | R | 6-4 | 200 | 10-28-74 | 1995 | Currituck, N.C. |
| 1 | Bush, Craig | 4 | 6 | 4.98 | 41 | 0 | 0 | 8 | 72 | 84 | 44 | 40 | 36 | 80 | R | R | 6-3 | 235 | 8-13-71 | 1991 | Lancaster, Ohio |
| 5 | Cabrera, Jose | 2 | 2 | 3.92 | 7 | 7 | 0 | 0 | 41 | 40 | 25 | 18 | 21 | 52 | R | R | 6-0 | 197 | 3-24-72 | 1991 | Santiago, D.R. |
| 9 | Carroll, Doug | 0 | 0 | 12.46 | 4 | 0 | 0 | 0 | 4 | 12 | 6 | 6 | 1 | 4 | L | R | 6-2 | 195 | 8-31-73 | 1994 | Holliston, Mass. |
| | Edwards, Wayne | 0 | 2 | 10.80 | 3 | 2 | 0 | 0 | 18 | 38 | 30 | 22 | 13 | 13 | L | L | 6-5 | 185 | 5-7-64 | 1985 | Sepulveda, Calif. |
| 8 | Gomez, Dennys | 3 | 1 | 3.52 | 10 | 0 | 0 | 0 | 23 | 22 | 11 | 9 | 12 | 11 | S | R | 6-0 | 195 | 6-21-71 | 1994 | Miami, Fla. |
| 9 | Gould, Clint | 0 | 0 | 9.00 | 2 | 0 | 0 | 0 | 1 | 1 | 1 | 1 | 2 | 1 | R | R | 6-2 | 230 | 8-18-71 | 1994 | Kent, Wash. |
| | Green, Blake | 0 | 1 | 16.20 | 1 | 1 | 0 | 0 | 2 | 4 | 3 | 3 | 1 | 1 | S | R | 6-1 | 225 | 8-17-51 | 1971 | Bakersfield, Calif. |
| 2 | Harmer, Frank | 0 | 0 | 1.80 | 4 | 0 | 0 | 0 | 5 | 3 | 1 | 1 | 0 | 4 | S | R | 6-3 | 210 | 5-21-75 | 1994 | Altamonte Springs, Fla. |
| 5 | Hritz, Derrick | 4 | 6 | 5.86 | 31 | 7 | 0 | 2 | 81 | 100 | 68 | 53 | 50 | 60 | L | L | 6-1 | 188 | 9-21-72 | 1993 | Gahanna, Ohio |
| 5 | Johnson, Todd | 1 | 1 | 5.30 | 21 | 1 | 0 | 3 | 36 | 54 | 28 | 21 | 15 | 9 | R | R | 5-11 | 205 | 12-18-70 | 1993 | Fresno, Calif. |
| 10 | Kell, Rob | 5 | 3 | 3.78 | 13 | 13 | 1 | 0 | 88 | 94 | 43 | 37 | 22 | 103 | R | L | 6-2 | 195 | 9-21-70 | 1993 | Hatfield, Pa. |
| 10 | Knighton, Toure | 5 | 15 | 6.54 | 25 | 24 | 1 | 0 | 150 | 197 | 134 | 109 | 67 | 108 | R | R | 6-3 | 180 | 7-4-75 | 1993 | Tucson, Ariz. |
| 2 | Lukasiewicz, Mark | 0 | 2 | 9.24 | 7 | 0 | 0 | 0 | 13 | 17 | 14 | 13 | 11 | 9 | L | L | 6-5 | 230 | 3-8-73 | 1994 | Secaucus, N.J. |
| 2 | Maine, Dalton | 2 | 3 | 3.23 | 23 | 2 | 0 | 6 | 47 | 42 | 25 | 17 | 14 | 58 | R | R | 6-3 | 185 | 3-22-72 | 1995 | Framingham, Mass. |
| 5 | Oldham, Bob | 2 | 10 | 9.69 | 41 | 17 | 0 | 0 | 143 | 224 | 187 | 154 | 105 | 107 | R | R | 6-5 | 220 | 4-4-74 | 1994 | Connellsville, Pa. |
| 5 | Oropeza, Igor | 1 | 14 | 6.80 | 23 | 21 | 4 | 0 | 138 | 160 | 113 | 104 | 92 | 104 | R | R | 6-4 | 183 | 7-11-72 | 1992 | La Guaira, Venez. |
| 5 | Palmer, Brett | 2 | 6 | 7.42 | 12 | 11 | 2 | 0 | 61 | 91 | 63 | 50 | 45 | 37 | L | L | 6-3 | 180 | 3-8-75 | 1993 | Idaho Falls, Idaho |
| 10 | Perpetuo, Nelson | 0 | 5 | 5.55 | 8 | 7 | 0 | 0 | 41 | 35 | 31 | 26 | 13 | 19 | S | L | 5-10 | 170 | 7-6-72 | 1991 | Monroe, Conn. |
| 2 | Reed, Dan | 2 | 4 | 5.00 | 20 | 7 | 0 | 0 | 68 | 83 | 52 | 38 | 36 | 48 | R | L | 6-4 | 210 | 10-20-74 | 1995 | McLean, Va. |
| 5 | Runion, Tony | 0 | 6 | 11.36 | 7 | 6 | 1 | 0 | 36 | 61 | 56 | 45 | 27 | 20 | R | R | 6-3 | 220 | 12-6-71 | 1993 | Florence, Ky. |
| 2 | Selleen, Aaron | 0 | 2 | 7.71 | 16 | 0 | 0 | 0 | 26 | 33 | 32 | 22 | 20 | 26 | L | R | 6-1 | 193 | 9-6-73 | 1994 | West Haven, Conn. |
| | Steinert, Rob | 0 | 1 | 27.00 | 4 | 1 | 0 | 0 | 3 | 4 | 9 | 9 | 14 | 5 | R | R | 6-2 | 195 | 9-29-71 | 1993 | Greenlawn, N.Y. |
| 3 | Symmonds, Maika | 0 | 2 | 8.88 | 7 | 2 | 1 | 0 | 24 | 34 | 32 | 24 | 21 | 3 | L | L | 5-9 | 180 | 3-13-75 | 1995 | Bellefonte, Pa. |

Property of Arizona (1), Baltimore (2), Boston (3), Chicago-NL (4), Cleveland (5), New York-NL (6), San Diego (7), San Francisco (8), Seattle (9), Texas (10), Toronto (11).

## VISALIA — Class A
### CALIFORNIA LEAGUE

| | BATTING | AVG | G | AB | R | H | 2B | 3B | HR | RBI | BB | SO | SB | CS | B | T | HT | WT | DOB | 1st Yr | Resides |
|---|---|---|---|---|---|---|---|---|---|---|---|---|---|---|---|---|---|---|---|---|---|
| 3 | Arano, Eloy | .229 | 43 | 140 | 19 | 32 | 6 | 0 | 0 | 16 | 17 | 30 | 4 | 2 | S | R | 5-11 | 170 | 3-5-74 | 1993 | Veracruz, Mexico |
| 1 | Barajas, Rod | .162 | 27 | 74 | 6 | 12 | 3 | 0 | 0 | 8 | 7 | 21 | 0 | 0 | R | R | 6-2 | 220 | 9-5-75 | 1996 | Norwalk, Calif. |

| # | BATTING | AVG | G | AB | R | H | 2B | 3B | HR | RBI | BB | SO | SB | CS | B | T | HT | WT | DOB | 1st Yr | Resides |
|---|---------|-----|---|----|---|---|----|----|----|-----|----|----|----|----|---|---|----|----|-----|--------|---------|
| 3 | Brissey, Jason | .226 | 83 | 234 | 32 | 53 | 15 | 3 | 7 | 34 | 18 | 80 | 2 | 4 | R | R | 5-8 | 165 | 8-7-72 | 1994 | Huntington Beach, Calif. |
| 3 | Danapilis, Eric | .257 | 105 | 377 | 58 | 97 | 29 | 1 | 10 | 64 | 66 | 122 | 2 | 1 | R | R | 6-2 | 220 | 6-11-71 | 1993 | St. Joseph, Mich. |
|   | Darnell, Bryce | .077 | 7 | 13 | 1 | 1 | 0 | 0 | 0 | 1 | 0 | 2 | 0 | 0 | L | R | 6-2 | 215 | 9-13-72 | 1996 | Brooklyn Center, Minn. |
| 3 | DeJesus, Malvin | .241 | 124 | 485 | 66 | 117 | 24 | 4 | 6 | 51 | 63 | 107 | 34 | 13 | R | R | 5-9 | 160 | 9-16-71 | 1992 | Carolina, P.R. |
| 3 | De la Rosa, Elvis | .221 | 69 | 204 | 33 | 45 | 10 | 1 | 6 | 27 | 24 | 76 | 2 | 2 | R | R | 5-11 | 210 | 5-5-75 | 1993 | Elias Pina, D.R. |
|   | Dunlop, Steve | .225 | 23 | 71 | 12 | 16 | 3 | 0 | 0 | 3 | 5 | 20 | 2 | 1 | R | R | 6-1 | 175 | 11-26-74 | 1996 | South Holland, Ill. |
| 1 | Durkac, Bo | .298 | 126 | 453 | 67 | 135 | 29 | 2 | 4 | 81 | 79 | 84 | 6 | 3 | S | R | 6-1 | 205 | 12-12-72 | 1995 | Kittanning, Pa. |
| 3 | Facione, Chris | .258 | 78 | 310 | 50 | 80 | 16 | 6 | 7 | 38 | 22 | 60 | 9 | 11 | S | R | 6-3 | 190 | 9-21-70 | 1993 | Millbrae, Calif |
| 1 | Herider, Jeremy | .234 | 49 | 145 | 22 | 34 | 6 | 0 | 1 | 14 | 33 | 36 | 2 | 6 | S | R | 5-10 | 180 | 4-9-72 | 1995 | Lancaster, Calif. |
| 3 | Kimsey, Keith | .274 | 99 | 394 | 64 | 108 | 17 | 3 | 21 | 72 | 43 | 140 | 13 | 4 | R | R | 6-7 | 200 | 8-15-72 | 1991 | Lakeland, Fla. |
| 3 | Lackey, Steve | .266 | 46 | 184 | 27 | 49 | 11 | 1 | 4 | 29 | 16 | 44 | 7 | 1 | R | R | 5-11 | 165 | 5-14-72 | 1992 | Riverside, Calif. |
| 3 | Landry, Lonny | .215 | 51 | 191 | 23 | 41 | 7 | 2 | 2 | 10 | 9 | 54 | 10 | 2 | R | R | 5-10 | 185 | 11-2-72 | 1993 | Broussard, La. |
| 3 | Lemonis, Chris | .278 | 126 | 482 | 69 | 134 | 27 | 3 | 14 | 82 | 35 | 99 | 12 | 5 | L | R | 5-11 | 185 | 8-21-73 | 1995 | New York, N.Y. |
| 3 | Marine, Del | .257 | 105 | 378 | 58 | 97 | 16 | 1 | 16 | 69 | 47 | 121 | 8 | 2 | R | R | 6-0 | 205 | 10-18-71 | 1992 | Woodland Hills, Calif. |
| 1 | Martinez, Tony | .193 | 31 | 83 | 7 | 16 | 6 | 0 | 0 | 11 | 7 | 20 | 0 | 0 | R | R | 6-2 | 185 | 11-27-73 | 1996 | Fullerton, Calif. |
| 3 | Neikirk, Derick | .148 | 9 | 27 | 3 | 4 | 0 | 0 | 0 | 2 | 2 | 9 | 0 | 0 | R | R | 5-9 | 170 | 9-5-74 | 1996 | Glendale, Ariz. |
| 3 | Roberts, Dave | .272 | 126 | 482 | 112 | 131 | 24 | 7 | 5 | 37 | 98 | 105 | 65 | 21 | L | L | 5-10 | 172 | 5-31-72 | 1994 | Oceanside, Calif. |
| 3 | Sanchez, Yuri | .237 | 18 | 59 | 9 | 14 | 1 | 0 | 3 | 6 | 7 | 19 | 1 | 1 | L | L | 6-1 | 165 | 11-11-73 | 1992 | Lynn, Mass. |

**GAMES BY POSITION: C**—Barajas 17, Darnell 5, De la Rosa 9, Marine 67, Neikirk 6. **1B**—Danapilis 96, Durkac 3, Herider 1, Marine 28, Martinez 23. **2B**—Arano 9, Brissey 3, Dunlop 13, Herider 17, Lackey 28, Lemonis 77. **3B**—Arano 6, Dunlop 1, Durkac 122, Herider 5, Lackey 4, Lemonis 3, Marine 2, Martinez 4. **SS**—Arano 20, Brissey 64, Dunlop 8, Herider 24, Lackey 14, Sanchez 17. **OF**—Arano 8, Brissey 3, Danapilis 3, DeJesus 85, Facione 7, Kimsey 99, Landry 51, Roberts 99.

| # | PITCHING | W | L | ERA | G | GS | CG | SV | IP | H | R | ER | BB | SO | B | T | HT | WT | DOB | 1st Yr | Resides |
|---|----------|---|---|-----|---|----|----|----|----|---|---|----|----|----|---|---|----|----|-----|--------|---------|
| 3 | Dalton, Brian | 1 | 1 | 5.40 | 13 | 0 | 0 | 0 | 27 | 26 | 16 | 16 | 19 | 19 | R | R | 6-1 | 190 | 6-24-72 | 1994 | Brooksville, Fla. |
|   | 2-team (6 Stock.) | 1 | 2 | 5.84 | 19 | 0 | 0 | 0 | 37 | 38 | 25 | 24 | 29 | 28 | | | | | | | |
| 1 | Duffy, Ryan | 0 | 0 | 1.17 | 15 | 0 | 0 | 0 | 15 | 6 | 3 | 2 | 6 | 9 | R | L | 6-3 | 185 | 6-1-73 | 1994 | Mooretown, Ontario |
| 1 | Goldsmith, Gary | 10 | 11 | 4.98 | 28 | 27 | 0 | 0 | 170 | 188 | 108 | 94 | 76 | 120 | R | R | 6-2 | 205 | 7-4-71 | 1993 | Alamogordo, N.M. |
| 1 | Gomez, Javier | 1 | 3 | 3.68 | 22 | 0 | 0 | 0 | 37 | 32 | 17 | 15 | 18 | 40 | R | R | 6-1 | 195 | 12-10-73 | 1995 | Miami, Fla. |
| 3 | Granger, Greg | 2 | 4 | 4.87 | 4 | 4 | 0 | 0 | 20 | 24 | 12 | 11 | 10 | 13 | R | R | 6-5 | 200 | 3-7-73 | 1993 | Ellettsville, Ind. |
| 3 | Harper, David | 0 | 0 | 19.73 | 12 | 0 | 0 | 0 | 9 | 15 | 19 | 19 | 10 | 5 | R | R | 6-3 | 185 | 9-14-74 | 1996 | Mansfield, Texas |
| 1 | Hernandez, Jeremy | 2 | 9 | 5.96 | 24 | 15 | 0 | 0 | 103 | 133 | 89 | 68 | 30 | 88 | R | R | 6-7 | 210 | 7-6-66 | 1987 | Yuma, Ariz. |
|   | Hoshiba, Takahisa | 1 | 8 | 4.43 | 21 | 16 | 0 | 1 | 126 | 151 | 77 | 62 | 39 | 108 | L | R | 6-1 | 180 | 1-12-72 | 1996 | Tokyo, Japan |
|   | Ito, Makoto | 0 | 1 | 3.94 | 34 | 0 | 0 | 0 | 32 | 34 | 16 | 14 | 12 | 26 | L | L | 6-0 | 177 | 7-26-69 | 1996 | Tokyo, Japan |
| 3 | Johnson, Carl | 3 | 5 | 15.55 | 15 | 5 | 0 | 0 | 22 | 35 | 44 | 38 | 35 | 16 | R | R | 6-4 | 195 | 9-8-70 | 1990 | Lacey, Wash. |
| 3 | Jordan, Jason | 6 | 10 | 4.85 | 30 | 20 | 1 | 0 | 145 | 175 | 89 | 78 | 54 | 110 | R | R | 6-3 | 220 | 10-2-72 | 1994 | Wichita, Kan. |
| 3 | Kelly, John | 2 | 10 | 7.13 | 19 | 18 | 1 | 1 | 96 | 115 | 100 | 76 | 63 | 89 | R | R | 6-2 | 205 | 11-26-71 | 1995 | Hillsboro, Ohio |
| 4 | Nartker, Mike | 1 | 1 | 6.75 | 3 | 0 | 0 | 0 | 12 | 12 | 10 | 9 | 7 | 11 | R | R | 6-5 | 240 | 3-15-75 | 1996 | Santo Domingo, D.R. |
| 1 | Nunez, Vladimir | 1 | 6 | 5.43 | 12 | 10 | 0 | 0 | 53 | 64 | 45 | 32 | 17 | 37 | R | R | 6-0 | 175 | 9-9-72 | 1993 | El Paso, Texas |
| 2 | Pena, Alex | 1 | 3 | 5.73 | 44 | 2 | 0 | 0 | 71 | 94 | 53 | 45 | 31 | 30 | R | R | 6-2 | 195 | 9-9-74 | 1996 | Santo Domingo, D.R. |
| 1 | Rodriguez, Larry | 2 | 5 | 5.24 | 13 | 10 | 0 | 0 | 57 | 72 | 49 | 33 | 19 | 37 | R | R | 6-3 | 205 | 7-5-72 | 1994 | Westville, Ill. |
| 2 | Ruch, Rob | 2 | 7 | 4.13 | 37 | 5 | 0 | 3 | 96 | 94 | 57 | 44 | 47 | 75 | R | R | 6-2 | 210 | 8-23-72 | 1995 | Gainesville, Fla. |
| 3 | Southall, Pete | 1 | 1 | 9.17 | 32 | 0 | 0 | 0 | 54 | 83 | 64 | 55 | 27 | 26 | L | L | 6-4 | 200 | 4-16-71 | 1993 | Clovis, Calif. |
| 1 | Salazar, Mike | 0 | 2 | 5.40 | 6 | 4 | 0 | 0 | 25 | 31 | 19 | 15 | 11 | 14 | L | L | 6-3 | 175 | 3-8-73 | 1991 | Spring, Texas |
| 3 | Thompson, Justin | 0 | 0 | 0.00 | 1 | 1 | 0 | 0 | 3 | 2 | 0 | 0 | 2 | 7 | L | L | 6-3 | 175 | 3-8-73 | 1991 | Spring, Texas |
| 3 | Tuttle, Dave | 7 | 9 | 3.71 | 55 | 0 | 0 | 21 | 70 | 71 | 39 | 29 | 33 | 56 | R | R | 6-3 | 190 | 9-29-69 | 1992 | Los Gatos, Calif. |

Property of Arizona (1), Baltimore (2), Detroit (3), Minnesota (4).

# HUDSON VALLEY                                        Class A

## NEW YORK-PENN LEAGUE

| # | BATTING | AVG | G | AB | R | H | 2B | 3B | HR | RBI | BB | SO | SB | CS | B | T | HT | WT | DOB | 1st Yr | Resides |
|---|---------|-----|---|----|---|---|----|----|----|-----|----|----|----|----|---|---|----|----|-----|--------|---------|
| 1 | Anderson, Chris | .147 | 52 | 156 | 17 | 23 | 4 | 1 | 5 | 18 | 15 | 70 | 2 | 0 | R | R | 6-5 | 215 | 9-29-74 | 1996 | Guthrie, Okla. |
| 1 | Barner, Doug | .218 | 46 | 147 | 21 | 32 | 7 | 0 | 2 | 17 | 30 | 42 | 3 | 3 | R | R | 6-0 | 195 | 12-1-74 | 1996 | Paris, Tenn. |
| 2 | Dransfeldt, Kelly | .236 | 75 | 284 | 42 | 67 | 17 | 1 | 7 | 29 | 27 | 76 | 13 | 4 | R | R | 6-2 | 195 | 4-16-75 | 1996 | Morris, Ill. |
| 1 | Ellis, John | .244 | 64 | 221 | 22 | 54 | 13 | 2 | 1 | 23 | 5 | 45 | 2 | 1 | R | R | 6-1 | 195 | 8-4-75 | 1996 | Niantic, Conn. |
| 2 | Gallagher, Shawn | .273 | 44 | 176 | 15 | 48 | 10 | 2 | 4 | 29 | 7 | 48 | 8 | 5 | R | R | 6-0 | 187 | 11-8-76 | 1995 | Wilmington, N.C. |
| 2 | Majcherek, Matt | .188 | 40 | 80 | 16 | 15 | 4 | 1 | 0 | 9 | 20 | 24 | 5 | 1 | R | R | 5-10 | 170 | 11-9-74 | 1996 | Chicago, Ill. |
| 2 | Monroe, Craig | .276 | 67 | 268 | 53 | 74 | 16 | 6 | 5 | 29 | 23 | 63 | 21 | 7 | R | R | 6-2 | 195 | 2-27-77 | 1995 | Texarkana, Texas |
| 1 | Myers, Adrian | .169 | 54 | 142 | 22 | 24 | 5 | 4 | 1 | 15 | 17 | 44 | 19 | 2 | R | R | 5-10 | 175 | 5-10-75 | 1996 | Bassfield, Miss. |
| 1 | Niethammer, Marc | .208 | 67 | 212 | 21 | 44 | 8 | 1 | 8 | 27 | 21 | 80 | 2 | 5 | L | R | 6-5 | 230 | 9-28-73 | 1992 | Lake Wales, Fla. |
| 1 | Owens-Bragg, Keith | .182 | 67 | 214 | 22 | 39 | 7 | 2 | 0 | 13 | 36 | 53 | 12 | 8 | S | R | 5-11 | 170 | 6-6-74 | 1996 | Orangevale, Calif. |
| 1 | Pomierski, Joe | .260 | 74 | 285 | 45 | 74 | 25 | 3 | 8 | 54 | 35 | 91 | 2 | 4 | L | R | 6-2 | 192 | 4-15-74 | 1993 | Biloxi, Miss. |
| 1 | Raymondi, Michael | .040 | 16 | 25 | 1 | 1 | 0 | 0 | 0 | 1 | 4 | 10 | 0 | 0 | R | R | 5-11 | 196 | 9-28-75 | 1994 | Watertown, S.D. |
| 2 | Richards, Rowan | .274 | 30 | 113 | 18 | 31 | 6 | 0 | 5 | 18 | 16 | 33 | 4 | 1 | R | R | 6-0 | 195 | 5-17-74 | 1996 | Bloomfield, N.J. |
| 1 | Vazquez, Manny | .240 | 73 | 258 | 41 | 62 | 5 | 4 | 1 | 21 | 24 | 41 | 27 | 7 | L | L | 6-1 | 187 | 2-13-75 | 1996 | Miami, Fla. |

**GAMES BY POSITION: C**—Anderson 23, Ellis 56, Raymondi 16. **1B**—Ellis 2, Gallagher 42, Niethammer 10, Pomierski 27. **2B**—Barner 9, Majcherek 6, Owens-Bragg 66. **3B**—Barner 32, Majcherek 12, Pomierski 36. **SS**—Dransfeldt 75, Majcherek 7, Owens-Bragg 1. **OF**—Anderson 28, Ellis 1, Monroe 62, Myers 49, Niethammer 26, Richards 24, Vazquez 67.

| # | PITCHING | W | L | ERA | G | GS | CG | SV | IP | H | R | ER | BB | SO | B | T | HT | WT | DOB | 1st Yr | Resides |
|---|----------|---|---|-----|---|----|----|----|----|---|---|----|----|----|---|---|----|----|-----|--------|---------|
| 1 | Aquino, Julio | 3 | 1 | 2.60 | 22 | 0 | 0 | 3 | 45 | 36 | 16 | 13 | 7 | 46 | R | R | 6-1 | 173 | 12-12-72 | 1991 | Estorga de Guerra, D.R. |
| 1 | Berry, Jason | 4 | 7 | 5.50 | 28 | 0 | 0 | 4 | 38 | 41 | 28 | 23 | 20 | 48 | R | R | 6-4 | 220 | 4-2-74 | 1993 | Brockton, Mass. |
| 1 | Cain, Travis | 2 | 5 | 4.60 | 15 | 15 | 0 | 0 | 76 | 67 | 50 | 39 | 44 | 87 | L | R | 6-3 | 185 | 8-10-75 | 1993 | Anderson, S.C. |
| 2 | Dellamano, Anthony | 4 | 7 | 6.17 | 18 | 10 | 0 | 1 | 66 | 83 | 54 | 45 | 33 | 61 | R | R | 6-5 | 205 | 8-17-74 | 1996 | Thousand Oaks, Calif. |
| 2 | Draeger, Mark | 1 | 2 | 6.12 | 17 | 0 | 0 | 0 | 32 | 44 | 35 | 22 | 17 | 28 | R | R | 6-3 | 180 | 11-19-72 | 1995 | Lockport, Ill. |
| 1 | Fowler, Jered | 0 | 0 | 2.25 | 2 | 0 | 0 | 0 | 4 | 2 | 2 | 1 | 0 | 1 | R | R | 6-2 | 205 | 1-7-73 | 1996 | Everett, Wash. |
| 1 | Griffiths, Everard | 1 | 1 | 3.06 | 11 | 4 | 0 | 0 | 32 | 26 | 12 | 11 | 13 | 39 | R | R | 6-3 | 190 | 9-11-73 | 1996 | North Miami, Fla. |
| 2 | Horton, Aaron | 3 | 0 | 12.43 | 9 | 7 | 0 | 0 | 25 | 55 | 46 | 35 | 15 | 15 | L | L | 6-5 | 196 | 10-10-74 | 1995 | Cardington, Ohio |
| 2 | Knight, Brandon | 2 | 2 | 4.42 | 9 | 9 | 0 | 0 | 53 | 59 | 29 | 26 | 21 | 52 | L | R | 6-0 | 170 | 12-26-74 | 1996 | Oxnard, Calif. |
| 1 | Lee, Corey | 1 | 4 | 3.29 | 9 | 9 | 0 | 0 | 55 | 42 | 24 | 20 | 21 | 59 | S | L | 6-2 | 180 | 12-26-74 | 1996 | Clayton, N.C. |
| 1 | Leon, Scott | 3 | 5 | 4.70 | 15 | 15 | 1 | 0 | 88 | 82 | 54 | 46 | 36 | 73 | R | R | 6-2 | 180 | 9-8-74 | 1994 | Topeka, Kan. |
| 2 | Martinez, Jose | 2 | 3 | 3.79 | 16 | 5 | 0 | 0 | 55 | 56 | 35 | 23 | 11 | 38 | R | R | 6-0 | 165 | 2-4-75 | 1995 | Santiago, D.R. |
| 2 | Raines, Ken | 6 | 2 | 1.07 | 38 | 0 | 0 | 5 | 67 | 51 | 19 | 8 | 15 | 64 | R | L | 6-2 | 175 | 10-14-72 | 1994 | Freeland, Mich. |
| 2 | Siegel, Justin | 0 | 1 | 5.68 | 5 | 0 | 0 | 0 | 6 | 8 | 5 | 4 | 5 | 8 | L | L | 6-0 | 170 | 9-3-75 | 1996 | Marina Del Rey, Calif. |
| 1 | Whitson, Eric | 3 | 0 | 2.86 | 19 | 2 | 0 | 0 | 44 | 31 | 17 | 14 | 16 | 34 | S | R | 6-0 | 180 | 8-15-72 | 1995 | Weaverville, N.C. |

Property of Tampa Bay (1), Texas (2).

# MINOR LEAGUES

# Attendance Passes 30 Million Again; Boom May Be Leveling Off

**By WILL LINGO**

Minor league attendance passed 30 million for the third straight year in 1996, but a three-year trend of flattening attendance continued as well.

Attendance in the American minor leagues climbed to 30,898,923 in 1996 from 30,709,738 in 1995. The average crowd was 3,426, up from 3,399 the year before.

The National Association includes Mexican League attendance in its official figures, and that raises the total to 33,289,278. That doesn't change the overall trend, though.

Overall minor league attendance in 1986 was 18,456,808, and it climbed to 30,022,761 by 1993. Attendance jumped by another three million in 1994, but it has held at about 33 million (30 million if you don't include Mexico) since then.

That may reflect a leveling off of the boom in the minor leagues, but it still shows a very healthy industry. The last three seasons are the three best attendance totals since 1949, when more than 400 teams fueled the minor leagues' postwar boom.

The Buffalo Bisons (American Association) drew 825,530 fans to lead the minors for the ninth straight season. But it also is the third straight year Buffalo hasn't drawn a million fans after the Bisons did so for six consecutive years.

That reflects the overall slowdown in Triple-A and Double-A attendance. The American Association and Pacific Coast League both saw their attendance increase 1 percent in 1996. The International League, which was plagued by bad weather, dropped 6 percent.

Every Double-A league was down in overall attendance, with the Southern League dropping by 7.5 percent. That

**First Pitch.** Chicken magnate Frank Perdue officially opens Delmarva's Perdue Stadium.

league should be helped a great deal by the move of the Port City Roosters to Mobile, Ala., for 1997. The Eastern League's Trenton Thunder was the Double-A attendance leader with 437,396 fans.

The real good news in the minor leagues in 1996 comes from Class A, where the California, Florida State and Midwest leagues showed double-digit percentage increases.

The Midwest League was the big winner as it continued to add successful new franchises. The league crossed the 3 million barrier, the first time that has happened in a Class A league, and the 3,168,632 fans represented an increase of more than 400,000 over 1995.

The hot new team for 1996 was the Lansing Lugnuts, who drew 538,325 fans to break the old Class A record. But that wasn't good enough to set a new record. The West Michigan Whitecaps, the team that held the old mark, did that with 547,401.

The California League drew almost 200,000 more fans than 1995, an increase of almost 12 percent, and its 1,875,387 fans set a league record. The Florida State League went back over 1 million in attendance with a 15 percent jump over 1995, and its 1,126,652 was also a league record.

The South Atlantic League held steady with 1.9 million fans, led by the first-year Delmarva Shorebirds, who drew a league record 315,011. The league will get a boost in 1997 when the Charleston RiverDogs move into a new ballpark and the Columbus RedStixx move back into their ballpark, which was renovated and used for the Olympic softball competition in 1996.

Only the Carolina League, another league plagued by bad weather all season, saw a sig-

## ORGANIZATION STANDINGS

| TEAM | W | 1996 L | Pct. | 1995 Pct | 1994 Pct | 1993 Pct |
|---|---|---|---|---|---|---|
| New York-NL (7) | 434 | 322 | .574 | .536 | .509 | .513 |
| Arizona (2) | 70 | 58 | .547 | — | — | — |
| Cleveland (6) | 384 | 324 | .542 | .544 | .521 | .579 |
| Montreal (6) | 372 | 320 | .539 | .462 | .529 | .522 |
| Oakland (6) | 371 | 321 | .536 | .507 | .556 | .526 |
| San Diego (6) | 361 | 320 | .530 | .456 | .458 | .446 |
| San Francisco (5) | 335 | 301 | .527 | .514 | .497 | .532 |
| New York-AL (6) | 364 | 329 | .525 | .507 | .512 | .527 |
| Milwaukee (6) | 367 | 334 | .524 | .550 | .507 | .479 |
| Kansas City (6) | 364 | 334 | .521 | .535 | .589 | .513 |
| Minnesota (6) | 357 | 329 | .520 | .514 | .502 | .503 |
| Baltimore (6) | 347 | 343 | .503 | .479 | .515 | .536 |
| Boston (6) | 348 | 344 | .503 | .493 | .485 | .423 |
| Detroit (6) | 347 | 345 | .501 | .521 | .454 | .494 |
| St. Louis (6) | 351 | 350 | .501 | .479 | .515 | .536 |
| Texas (6) | 312 | 311 | .501 | .429 | .450 | .499 |
| Chicago-NL (6) | 343 | 345 | .499 | .546 | .446 | .483 |
| Los Angeles (7) | 416 | 426 | .494 | .512 | .514 | .424 |
| Houston (6) | 338 | 347 | .493 | .515 | .501 | .473 |
| Philadelphia (6) | 345 | 355 | .493 | .533 | .475 | .456 |
| Toronto (6) | 345 | 363 | .487 | .453 | .498 | .497 |
| Seattle (6) | 335 | 353 | .487 | .469 | .518 | .479 |
| Pittsburgh (6) | 338 | 358 | .486 | .499 | .430 | .457 |
| Cincinnati (6) | 342 | 363 | .485 | .569 | .539 | .511 |
| California (6) | 331 | 354 | .483 | .566 | .507 | .479 |
| Colorado (6) | 329 | 359 | .478 | .510 | .477 | .451 |
| Tampa Bay (2) | 61 | 70 | .466 | — | — | — |
| Atlanta (7) | 354 | 407 | .465 | .453 | .485 | .528 |
| Florida (6) | 320 | 369 | .464 | .495 | .496 | .536 |
| Chicago-AL (7) | 355 | 470 | .430 | .473 | .524 | .527 |
| Co-op (3) | 121 | 235 | .340 | .383 | .383 | .429 |

Number of farm teams in parentheses

# PLAYER OF YEAR

## Jones Wins Again On Way To Atlanta

Andruw Jones is only 19, but already people are running out of ways to describe his amazing exploits.

He zipped through the Braves system, from Class A Durham to the big leagues, in less than a season. Then he became the youngest player to hit a postseason and a World Series home run.

The praise has been heaped on him. The Braves try desperately not to inflate their prospects, but even they had to admit that Jones is pretty doggone good.

"You know people are special," scouting and farm director Paul Snyder said. "You know they can overcome a lot of things. But if I said I knew this was going to happen so quickly, I'd be lying."

Those folks who were impressed by Jones' 1995 season (.277-25-100, 56 steals) at Class A Macon didn't look up when they noticed he batted .313 at Class A Durham, or .369 at Double-A Greenville, or even .378 at Triple-A Richmond in 1996.

Maybe they did finally notice when he batted .461 in July, which is illegal in some states. And when he got called up to Atlanta and hit .400 in the World Series, it was time to pay attention. And then he was Baseball America's Minor League Player of the Year for the second straight season.

**Andruw Jones**

MORRIS FOSTOFF

"I don't think anybody who's seen him hasn't thought he's been legit," Braves third baseman Chipper Jones says. "He's got the good face. You can just look at him and you can tell. He's got the smooth actions, the good body. He's the one that baseball comes easy to."

Andruw Jones talks a lot about adjustments. Coming to the United States from Curacao in the Netherlands Antilles. Learning to hit the curveball in 1995, and learning to hit consistent quality pitching in 1996. Life is all about adjustments. We all should be so well adjusted.

"Here everything is much harder, everyone is good," Jones says. "Other people have got to play; it's not just me. I'm used to playing every day, but they've got to play everybody."

A year earlier, the Braves' 18-year-old phenom was already the Minor League Player of the Year, and they had to worry about how to get him through the minor leagues without him going bad.

Jones solved that problem quite nicely, by blitzing through the system too quickly to pick up any bad habits.

Now he has to worry about becoming the best player on a team filled with all-stars. He's on his way.

When asked who the best Jones on the team is, Andruw points without hesitation toward Chipper: "Right now, he is. But maybe next year . . . "

Given what we've seen in the last 12 months, and the 12 before that, we wouldn't bet against it.

| PREVIOUS WINNERS |
| --- |
| 1981—Mike Marshall, 1b, Albuquerque (Dodgers) |
| 1982—Ron Kittle, of, Edmonton (White Sox) |
| 1983—Dwight Gooden, rhp, Lynchburg (Mets) |
| 1984—Mike Bielecki, rhp, Hawaii (Pirates) |
| 1985—Jose Canseco, of, Huntsville/Tacoma (Athletics) |
| 1986—Gregg Jefferies, ss, Columbia/Lynchburg/Jackson (Mets) |
| 1987—Gregg Jefferies, ss, Jackson/Tidewater (Mets) |
| 1988—Tom Gordon, rhp, Appleton/Memphis/Omaha (Royals) |
| 1989—Sandy Alomar, c, Las Vegas (Padres) |
| 1990—Frank Thomas, 1b, Birmingham (White Sox) |
| 1991—Derek Bell, of, Syracuse (Blue Jays) |
| 1992—Tim Salmon, of, Edmonton (Angels) |
| 1993—Manny Ramirez, of, Canton/Charlotte (Indians) |
| 1994—Derek Jeter, ss, Tampa/Albany/Columbus (Yankees) |
| 1995—Andruw Jones, of, Macon (Braves) |

nificant drop in attendance. The league dropped from 1.8 million to 1.7 million.

Short-season leagues also were about the same, with the Northwest League's Portland Rockies leading the way. They drew a record 249,995 fans, about the same as last year.

## Rangers Lose Musical Chairs

When major league and minor league teams change affiliates every couple of years, it usually resembles a junior high dance: Not everyone is ecstatic, but they all end up dancing together.

Following the 1996 season, it was more like musical chairs, with not enough affiliates to go around for 1997. Not only did organizations have to scramble for the last few teams, whether they were the right fit or not, but one sad sack, the Rangers, was left standing.

It happened because the expansion Devil Rays and Diamondbacks were in the Class A hunt for the first time. They each took two full-season Class A affiliates for 1997, but the minor leagues haven't expanded at the Class A level, meaning not enough clubs were available.

"I don't think anyone was taken by surprise," Devil Rays general manager Chuck LaMar said. "If you look at both organizations, you know we're both committed to scouting and player development. It's not just rhetoric."

The minor leagues have 32 high Class A teams in the California, Carolina and Florida State leagues, and 28 low Class A teams in the Midwest and South Atlantic leagues. That's 60 Class A clubs for 30 organizations.

The Dodgers complicated matters by having three Class A clubs, including two high A teams, but two high A teams in the Cal League have been co-ops for the last two seasons. The White Sox also had two low Class A teams in 1996, but abandoned South Bend of

# CLASSIFICATION ALL-STARS

Selected by Baseball America

## TRIPLE-A

| Pos. | Player, Club | B-T | Ht. | Wt. | Age | AVG | AB | R | H | 2B | 3B | HR | RBI | SB |
|---|---|---|---|---|---|---|---|---|---|---|---|---|---|---|
| C | Kelly Stinnett , New Orleans (Amer. Assoc.) | R-R | 5-11 | 195 | 26 | .287 | 334 | 63 | 96 | 21 | 1 | 27 | 70 | 3 |
| 1B | Dmitri Young, Louisville (American Assoc.) | S-R | 6-2 | 215 | 22 | .333 | 459 | 90 | 153 | 31 | 8 | 15 | 64 | 16 |
| 2B | Brian Raabe, Salt Lake (Pacific Coast) | R-R | 5-9 | 170 | 28 | .351 | 482 | 103 | 169 | 39 | 4 | 18 | 69 | 8 |
| 3B | Todd Walker, Salt Lake (Pacific Coast) | L-R | 6-0 | 180 | 23 | .339 | 551 | 94 | 187 | 41 | 9 | 28 | 111 | 13 |
| SS | Neifi Perez, Colorado Springs (Pacific Coast) | S-R | 6-0 | 175 | 21 | .316 | 570 | 77 | 180 | 28 | 12 | 7 | 72 | 16 |
| OF | Billy McMillon, Charlotte (International) | L-L | 5-11 | 172 | 24 | .352 | 347 | 72 | 122 | 32 | 2 | 17 | 70 | 5 |
| OF | Rudy Pemberton, Okla. City (AA)-Paw. (Inter.) | R-R | 6-1 | 185 | 26 | .315 | 467 | 83 | 147 | 31 | 3 | 29 | 103 | 17 |
| OF | Nigel Wilson, Buffalo (American Assoc.) | L-L | 6-1 | 170 | 26 | .299 | 482 | 88 | 144 | 23 | 6 | 30 | 95 | 4 |
| DH | Lee Stevens, Oklahoma City (Amer. Assoc.) | L-L | 6-4 | 205 | 29 | .325 | 431 | 84 | 140 | 37 | 2 | 32 | 94 | 3 |

| Pos. | Player, Club | B-T | Ht. | Wt. | Age | W | L | ERA | G | SV | IP | H | BB | SO |
|---|---|---|---|---|---|---|---|---|---|---|---|---|---|---|
| P | Mike Fyhrie, Norfolk (International) | R-R | 6-2 | 190 | 26 | 15 | 6 | 3.04 | 27 | 0 | 169 | 150 | 33 | 103 |
| P | Danny Graves, Buffalo (American Assoc.) | R-R | 5-11 | 200 | 23 | 4 | 3 | 1.48 | 43 | 19 | 79 | 57 | 24 | 46 |
| P | Rick Helling, Oklahoma City (Amer. Assoc.) | R-R | 6-3 | 215 | 25 | 12 | 4 | 2.96 | 23 | 0 | 140 | 124 | 38 | 157 |
| P | Bob Milacki, Tacoma (Pacific Coast) | R-R | 6-4 | 230 | 32 | 13 | 3 | 2.74 | 23 | 0 | 164 | 131 | 39 | 117 |
| P | Derek Wallace, Norfolk (International) | R-R | 6-3 | 200 | 25 | 5 | 2 | 1.72 | 49 | 26 | 58 | 37 | 17 | 52 |

**Player of the Year:** Todd Walker, 3b, Salt Lake. **Manager of the Year:** Gary Jones, Edmonton (Pacific Coast).

## DOUBLE-A

| Pos. | Player, Club | B-T | Ht. | Wt. | Age | AVG | AB | R | H | 2B | 3B | HR | RBI | SB |
|---|---|---|---|---|---|---|---|---|---|---|---|---|---|---|
| C | Eli Marrero, Arkansas (Texas) | R-R | 6-1 | 180 | 22 | .270 | 374 | 65 | 101 | 17 | 3 | 19 | 65 | 9 |
| 1B | Derek Lee, Memphis (Southern) | R-R | 6-5 | 220 | 20 | .280 | 500 | 98 | 140 | 39 | 2 | 34 | 104 | 13 |
| 2B | Luis Castillo, Portland (Eastern) | S-R | 5-11 | 146 | 20 | .317 | 420 | 83 | 133 | 15 | 7 | 1 | 35 | 51 |
| 3B | Aaron Boone, Chattanooga (Southern) | R-R | 6-2 | 190 | 23 | .288 | 548 | 86 | 158 | 44 | 7 | 17 | 95 | 21 |
| SS | Russ Johnson, Jackson (Texas) | R-R | 5-10 | 185 | 23 | .310 | 496 | 86 | 154 | 24 | 5 | 15 | 74 | 9 |
| OF | Mike Cameron, Birmingham (Southern) | R-R | 6-1 | 170 | 23 | .300 | 473 | 120 | 142 | 34 | 12 | 28 | 77 | 39 |
| OF | Vladimir Guerrero, Harrisburg (Eastern) | R-R | 6-2 | 160 | 20 | .360 | 417 | 84 | 150 | 32 | 8 | 19 | 78 | 17 |
| OF | Bubba Trammell, Jacksonville (Southern) | R-R | 6-2 | 205 | 24 | .328 | 311 | 63 | 102 | 23 | 2 | 27 | 75 | 3 |
| DH | Paul Konerko, San Antonio (Texas) | R-R | 6-3 | 210 | 20 | .300 | 470 | 78 | 141 | 23 | 2 | 29 | 86 | 1 |

| Pos. | Player, Club | B-T | Ht. | Wt. | Age | W | L | ERA | G | SV | IP | H | BB | SO |
|---|---|---|---|---|---|---|---|---|---|---|---|---|---|---|
| P | Curt Lyons, Chattanooga (Southern) | R-R | 6-5 | 230 | 21 | 13 | 4 | 2.41 | 24 | 0 | 142 | 113 | 52 | 176 |
| P | Sean Maloney, El Paso (Texas) | R-R | 6-7 | 210 | 25 | 3 | 2 | 1.43 | 51 | 38 | 57 | 49 | 12 | 57 |
| P | Brian Moehler, Jacksonville (Southern) | R-R | 6-3 | 195 | 24 | 15 | 6 | 3.48 | 28 | 0 | 173 | 186 | 50 | 120 |
| P | Carl Pavano, Trenton (Eastern) | R-R | 6-5 | 225 | 20 | 16 | 5 | 2.63 | 27 | 0 | 185 | 154 | 47 | 146 |
| P | Tony Saunders, Portland (Eastern) | L-L | 6-1 | 190 | 22 | 13 | 4 | 2.63 | 26 | 0 | 168 | 121 | 62 | 156 |

**Player of the Year:** Vladimir Guerrero, of, Harrisburg. **Manager of the Year:** Carlos Tosca, Portland (Eastern).

## CLASS A

| Pos. | Player, Club | B-T | Ht. | Wt. | Age | AVG | AB | R | H | 2B | 3B | HR | RBI | SB |
|---|---|---|---|---|---|---|---|---|---|---|---|---|---|---|
| C | Pat Cline, Daytona (Florida State) | R-R | 6-3 | 220 | 21 | .279 | 434 | 75 | 121 | 30 | 2 | 17 | 76 | 10 |
| 1B | Larry Barnes, Cedar Rapids (Midwest) | L-L | 6-1 | 195 | 22 | .317 | 489 | 84 | 155 | 36 | 5 | 27 | 112 | 9 |
| 2B | Richard Almanzar, Lakeland (Florida State) | R-R | 5-10 | 155 | 20 | .306 | 471 | 81 | 144 | 22 | 2 | 1 | 36 | 53 |
| 3B | Mike Berry, High Desert (California) | R-R | 5-10 | 185 | 26 | .361 | 463 | 109 | 167 | 44 | 5 | 13 | 113 | 7 |
| SS | Miguel Tejada, Modesto (California) | R-R | 5-10 | 180 | 20 | .279 | 458 | 97 | 128 | 12 | 5 | 20 | 72 | 27 |
| OF | Ben Grieve, Modesto (California) | L-R | 6-4 | 200 | 20 | .356 | 281 | 61 | 100 | 20 | 1 | 11 | 51 | 8 |
| OF | Jose Guillen, Lynchburg (Carolina) | R-R | 5-11 | 165 | 20 | .322 | 528 | 78 | 170 | 30 | 0 | 21 | 94 | 24 |
| OF | Andruw Jones, Durham (Carolina) | R-R | 6-1 | 170 | 19 | .313 | 243 | 65 | 76 | 14 | 3 | 17 | 43 | 16 |
| DH | D.T. Cromer, Modesto (California) | L-L | 6-2 | 205 | 25 | .329 | 505 | 100 | 166 | 40 | 10 | 30 | 130 | 20 |

| Pos. | Player, Club | B-T | Ht. | Wt. | Age | W | L | ERA | G | SV | IP | H | BB | SO |
|---|---|---|---|---|---|---|---|---|---|---|---|---|---|---|
| P | Darin Blood, San Jose (California) | L-R | 6-2 | 205 | 22 | 17 | 6 | 2.65 | 27 | 0 | 170 | 140 | 71 | 193 |
| P | Britt Reames, Peoria (Midwest) | R-R | 5-11 | 170 | 23 | 15 | 7 | 1.90 | 25 | 0 | 161 | 97 | 41 | 167 |
| P | Blake Stein, St. Petersburg (Florida State) | R-R | 6-7 | 210 | 23 | 16 | 5 | 2.15 | 28 | 1 | 172 | 122 | 54 | 159 |
| P | Jay Tessmer, Tampa (Florida State) | R-R | 6-3 | 190 | 23 | 12 | 4 | 1.48 | 68 | 35 | 97 | 68 | 19 | 104 |
| P | Mike Villano, San Jose (California) | R-R | 6-1 | 200 | 25 | 7 | 1 | 0.72 | 39 | 8 | 88 | 48 | 33 | 133 |

**Player of the Year:** Andruw Jones, of, Durham. **Manager of the Year:** Trey Hillman, Tampa (Florida State).

## SHORT-SEASON

| Pos. | Player, Club | B-T | Ht. | Wt. | Age | AVG | AB | R | H | 2B | 3B | HR | RBI | SB |
|---|---|---|---|---|---|---|---|---|---|---|---|---|---|---|
| C | Matt Curtis, Boise (Northwest) | S-R | 6-0 | 195 | 22 | .305 | 305 | 57 | 93 | 29 | 3 | 12 | 62 | 2 |
| 1B | Calvin Pickering, Bluefield (Appalachian) | L-L | 6-3 | 283 | 19 | .325 | 200 | 45 | 65 | 14 | 1 | 18 | 66 | 8 |
| 2B | Wylie Campbell, Billings (Pioneer) | S-R | 5-11 | 170 | 21 | .371 | 259 | 69 | 96 | 15 | 7 | 0 | 30 | 24 |
| 3B | Aramis Ramirez, Erie (New York-Penn) | R-R | 6-1 | 176 | 18 | .305 | 223 | 37 | 68 | 14 | 4 | 9 | 42 | 0 |
| SS | Ben Reynoso, Idaho Falls (Pioneer) | R-R | 5-9 | 170 | 21 | .345 | 284 | 45 | 98 | 26 | 0 | 4 | 50 | 20 |
| OF | Adam Johnson, Eugene (Northwest) | L-L | 6-0 | 185 | 21 | .314 | 318 | 58 | 100 | 22 | 9 | 7 | 56 | 4 |
| OF | Chris Stowers, Vermont (New York-Penn) | L-L | 6-3 | 200 | 22 | .319 | 282 | 58 | 90 | 21 | 9 | 7 | 44 | 16 |
| OF | Kevin Sweeney, Lethbridge (Pioneer) | L-L | 5-11 | 185 | 22 | .424 | 203 | 72 | 86 | 19 | 1 | 14 | 72 | 3 |
| DH | Rob Zachmann, Everett (Northwest) | R-R | 6-1 | 205 | 23 | .291 | 285 | 49 | 83 | 13 | 1 | 19 | 64 | 4 |

| Pos. | Player, Club | B-T | Ht. | Wt. | Age | W | L | ERA | G | SV | IP | H | BB | SO |
|---|---|---|---|---|---|---|---|---|---|---|---|---|---|---|
| P | Jared Camp, Watertown (New York-Penn) | R-R | 6-2 | 195 | 21 | 10 | 2 | 1.69 | 15 | 0 | 96 | 68 | 30 | 99 |
| P | Courtney Duncan, Williamsport (New York-Penn) | L-R | 5-11 | 175 | 21 | 11 | 1 | 2.19 | 15 | 0 | 90 | 58 | 34 | 91 |
| P | Brett Herbison, Kingsport (Appalachian) | R-R | 6-5 | 175 | 19 | 6 | 2 | 1.29 | 13 | 0 | 77 | 43 | 31 | 86 |
| P | Vladimir Nunez, Lethbridge (Pioneer) | R-R | 6-5 | 240 | 21 | 10 | 0 | 2.22 | 14 | 0 | 85 | 78 | 10 | 93 |
| P | Tim Young, Vermont (New York-Penn) | L-L | 5-9 | 160 | 22 | 1 | 0 | 0.37 | 27 | 18 | 29 | 14 | 4 | 46 |

**Player of the Year:** Vladimir Nunez, rhp, Lethbridge. **Manager of the Year:** Joe Vavra, Yakima (Northwest).

# MINOR LEAGUE ALL-STARS
Selected by Baseball America

| Pos. | Player, Club | B-T | Ht. | Wt. | Age | AVG | AB | R | H | 2B | 3B | HR | RBI | SB |
|------|--------------|-----|-----|-----|-----|-----|-----|-----|-----|-----|-----|-----|-----|-----|
| C | Mike Sweeney, Wichita/Omaha | R-R | 6-1 | 195 | 23 | .301 | 336 | 59 | 101 | 27 | 1 | 17 | 67 | 3 |
| 1B | Derrek Lee, Memphis | R-R | 6-5 | 220 | 20 | .280 | 500 | 98 | 140 | 39 | 2 | 34 | 104 | 13 |
| 2B | Brian Raabe, Salt Lake City | R-R | 5-9 | 170 | 28 | .351 | 482 | 103 | 169 | 39 | 4 | 18 | 69 | 8 |
| 3B | Todd Walker, Salt Lake City | L-R | 6-0 | 180 | 23 | .339 | 551 | 94 | 187 | 41 | 9 | 28 | 111 | 13 |
| SS | Neifi Perez, Colorado Springs | S-R | 6-0 | 175 | 21 | .316 | 570 | 77 | 180 | 28 | 12 | 7 | 72 | 16 |
| OF | Mike Cameron, Birmingham | R-R | 6-1 | 170 | 23 | .300 | 473 | 120 | 142 | 34 | 12 | 28 | 77 | 39 |
| OF | Vladimir Guerrero, West Palm/Harrisburg | R-R | 6-2 | 160 | 20 | .360 | 497 | 100 | 179 | 40 | 8 | 24 | 96 | 19 |
| OF | Andruw Jones, Durham/Greenville/Richmond | R-R | 6-1 | 170 | 19 | .339 | 445 | 115 | 151 | 27 | 5 | 34 | 92 | 30 |
| DH | D.T. Cromer, Modesto | L-L | 6-2 | 205 | 25 | .329 | 505 | 100 | 166 | 40 | 10 | 30 | 130 | 20 |

| Pos. | Player, Club | B-T | Ht. | Wt. | Age | W | L | ERA | G | SV | IP | H | BB | SO |
|------|--------------|-----|-----|-----|-----|-----|-----|-----|-----|-----|-----|-----|-----|-----|
| P | Rick Helling, Oklahoma City | R-R | 6-3 | 215 | 25 | 12 | 4 | 2.96 | 23 | 0 | 140 | 124 | 38 | 157 |
| P | Curt Lyons, Chattanooga | R-R | 6-5 | 230 | 21 | 13 | 4 | 2.41 | 24 | 0 | 142 | 113 | 52 | 176 |
| P | Sean Maloney, El Paso | R-R | 6-7 | 210 | 25 | 3 | 2 | 1.43 | 51 | 38 | 57 | 49 | 12 | 57 |
| P | Carl Pavano, Trenton | R-R | 6-5 | 225 | 20 | 16 | 5 | 2.63 | 27 | 0 | 185 | 154 | 47 | 146 |
| P | Jay Tessmer, Tampa | R-R | 6-3 | 190 | 23 | 12 | 3 | 1.48 | 68 | 35 | 97 | 68 | 19 | 104 |

**Player of the Year:** Andruw Jones, Durham/Greenville/Richmond.  **Manager of the Year:** Carlos Tosca, Portland (Eastern).

the Midwest League.

The two co-op clubs and the White Sox' cutbacks meant three Class A affiliates were available. Unfortunately, the expansion teams took four Class A clubs, setting off a wild scramble.

The Padres, who had looked to leave Clinton of the Midwest League, scurried back. The Reds, who left Winston-Salem of the Carolina League, grabbed Burlington of the Midwest League, even though that gave them two low-A teams. The Athletics got kicked out of West Michigan in the Midwest League and had to take Visalia, even though that gave them two teams in the California League. San Francisco, which abandoned Burlington, also ended up with a second Cal League, hooking on with Bakersfield.

That left the Rangers with only one full-season Class A affiliate, the team they own in the Florida State League.

Rangers farm director Reid Nichols wasn't excited, especially after he had been told that no team would be left in this position.

"In my mind I think it's a lack of foresight on the part of baseball," he said. "We were told it would be taken care of, and it wasn't."

## MINOR ADJUSTMENTS

**Several major league clubs changed affiliations following the 1996 season. The new look for 1997:**

| TRIPLE-A | League | 1996 | 1997 |
|----------|--------|------|------|
| New Orleans | American Assoc. | Brewers | Astros |
| Tucson | Pacific Coast | Astros | Brewers |
| **DOUBLE-A** | | | |
| Memphis | Southern | Padres | Mariners |
| Port City/Mobile | Southern | Mariners | Padres |
| **CLASS A** | | | |
| Bakersfield | California | Co-op | Giants |
| Burlington | Midwest | Giants | Reds |
| Charleston, S.C. | South Atlantic | Rangers | Devil Rays |
| Delmarva | South Atlantic | Expos | Orioles |
| Fayetteville | South Atlantic | Tigers | Expos |
| High Desert | California | Orioles | Diamondbacks |
| Prince William | Carolina | White Sox | Cardinals |
| St. Petersburg | Florida State | Cardinals | Devil Rays |
| South Bend | Midwest | White Sox | Diamondbacks |
| Visalia | California | Co-op | Athletics |
| West Michigan | Midwest | Athletics | Tigers |
| Winston-Salem | Carolina | Reds | White Sox |
| **ROOKIE** | | | |
| Butte | Pioneer | Devil Rays | Angels |
| Mesa | Arizona | Angels | None |
| Princeton | Appalachian | Reds | Devil Rays |

Jimmie Lee Solomon, who's in charge of minor league relations for Major League Baseball, said there was simply no good solution to the problem.

The expansion teams were not required to take two teams, but they did to get into good markets. And with the long-term trend pointing toward major league organizations shrinking their farm systems, Solomon said short-term expansion was not a good alternative.

The Rangers actually moved to cut back their farm system beginning in the 1995-96 offseason, when they split their Hudson Valley affiliation with the Devil Rays. That was

**Jimmie Lee Solomon**

done in anticipation of the Rays taking over the full affiliation in 1997.

Unfortunately for the Rangers, Marv Goldklang, who owns Hudson Valley and Charleston among other clubs, liked working with the Devil Rays. So Charleston dropped the Rangers and signed with Tampa Bay, leaving Texas with only four farm clubs.

"We wanted very badly to stay in Charleston, but they chose to go with Tampa Bay and we were left looking," Nichols said. "The opportunity was there to take a second high-A club, but I just didn't see where that fit our needs."

The Rangers will likely have to turn to the Rookie-level Appalachian League for another affiliate. That league had only nine teams in 1996 and needs another, but it hadn't found an acceptable city that's interested.

Nichols said he doesn't think this will devastate the Rangers' farm system, especially since the Rangers eventually wanted to have a team in the Appy League anyway. But he still wonders what the long-term solution will be.

"This is not going to hurt us that badly," he said. "We'll get through this year, and then I would hope something would get fixed for next year."

The assurances of baseball's leaders don't ease his mind, though. When asked if Organized Baseball has a plan for 1998 and beyond, he said, "I'm told they do, but I was told we wouldn't be in this situation."

# DEPARTMENT LEADERS
## MINOR LEAGUES

*Full-Season Teams Only

### TEAM

**WINS**
San Jose (California) ............................. 89
Trenton (Eastern).................................. 86
Columbus (International) ...................... 85
Asheville (South Atlantic) ....................84
Buffalo (American Association)............. 84
Edmonton (Pacific Coast) .................... 84
Tampa (Florida State).......................... 84

**LONGEST WINNING STREAK**
Trenton (Eastern).................................. 13
Memphis (Southern) ............................. 13
Stockton (California) ............................. 11
Stockton (California) ............................. 11
Wilmington (Carolina) .......................... 11
Kingsport (Appalachian) ...................... 11

**LOSSES**
Bakersfield (California) ........................ 101
Brevard County (Florida State)............. 92
Visalia (California) ................................ 90
Bowie (Eastern) .................................... 88
Greensboro (South Atlantic) ................ 86

**LONGEST LOSING STREAK**
Bakersfield (California) ......................... 22
Bristol (Appalachian)............................ 15
South Bend (Midwest) .......................... 14
Capital City (South Atlantic)................. 13
Hickory (South Atlantic) ....................... 12
Piedmont (South Atlantic) .................... 12
Bakersfield (California) ......................... 12
Bristol (Appalachian)............................ 12

**BATTING AVERAGE\***
Salt Lake (Pacific Coast) ................... .293
High Desert (California) ..................... .292
El Paso (Texas) ................................. .291
Calgary (Pacific Coast) ...................... .290
San Jose (California) ......................... .289

**RUNS**
Modesto (California) ........................... 952
High Desert (California) ...................... 924
Salt Lake (Pacific Coast) ................... 855
Lancaster (California) ......................... 852
Pawtucket (International) .................... 840

**HOME RUNS**
Pawtucket (International) .................... 209
Jacksonville (Southern) ...................... 200
Modesto (California) ........................... 187
Columbus (South Atlantic) ................. 167

**Vladimir Guerrero**
Minors-best .360 average

**Phil Hiatt**
Led minors with 42 homers

Charlotte (International) ..................... 165
Toledo (International) ......................... 165

**STOLEN BASES**
Macon (South Atlantic) ...................... 235
Modesto (California) ........................... 219
Winston-Salem (Carolina) ................. 219
Delmarva (South Atlantic) ................. 215
Rockford (Midwest) ............................ 211
Savannah (South Atlantic) ................. 211

**EARNED RUN AVERAGE\***
Capital City (South Atlantic) ............. 2.77
Delmarva (South Atlantic) ................ 2.85
St. Petersburg (Florida State) .......... 3.04
Asheville (South Atlantic) ................. 3.14
St. Lucie (Florida State) ................... 3.15
Tampa (Florida State)........................ 3.15

**STRIKEOUTS**
San Jose (California) ....................... 1236
Savannah (South Atlantic) .............. 1229
Capital City (South Atlantic) ........... 1168
San Bernardino (California) ............. 1165
Fayetteville (South Atlantic) ............ 1162

**FIELDING AVERAGE\***
St. Petersburg (Florida State) .......... .981
Iowa (American Association) ............. .978
Salt Lake (Pacific Coast) ................. .978
Buffalo (American Association) ......... .977
Las Vegas (Pacific Coast) ............... .977
Nashville (American Association) ..... .977
Ottawa (International) ....................... .977
Vancouver (Pacific Coast) ............... .977

### INDIVIDUAL BATTING

**BATTING AVERAGE\***
(Minimum 400 Plate Appearances)
Vladimir Guerrero, West Palm/Harr. . .360
Kerry Robinson, Peoria ..................... .359
Mike Berry, High Desert/Bowie ......... .354
Brian Raabe, Salt Lake ..................... .351
Brent Brede, Salt Lake ...................... .348
Dan Rohrmeier, Memphis ................. .344
Wilton Guerrero, Albuquerque .......... .344
Todd Dunn, El Paso .......................... .340
Todd Walker, Salt Lake ..................... .339
Desi Wilson, Phoenix ........................ .339
Andruw Jones, Durham/G'ville/Rich. . .339

**RUNS**
Mike Cameron, Birmingham .............. 120

Andruw Jones, Durham/G'ville/Rich. . . 115
Dave Roberts, Visalia/Jacksonville..... 112
Mike Berry, High Desert/Bowie........... 111
Eric Stuckenschneider, Savannah ..... 111

**HITS**
Todd Walker, Salt Lake .................... 187
Nelfi Perez, Colorado Springs .......... 180
Vladimir Guerrero, West Palm/Harr. .. 179
Rolando Avila, Bowie/Roch. .............. 174
Tim Garland, San Jose ..................... 171
Craig Mayes, San Jose/Shreve. ........ 171

**TOP HITTING STREAKS**
Jose Cepeda, Lansing ........................ 28
Jesus Hernaiz, Savannah ................... 26
Mike Rennhack, Stockton ................... 26
Jeff Ferguson, Hardware City ............. 25
Steven Chavez, Idaho Falls ............... 24

**MOST HITS, ONE GAME**
Neifi Perez, Colorado Springs ............. 7
Mike Berry, High Desert ...................... 6
Bobby Meyer, Yakima ......................... 6
Bob Mummau, Knoxville ...................... 6
Chris Stowers, Vermont ...................... 6

**TOTAL BASES**
Todd Walker, Salt Lake .................... 330
D.T. Cromer, Modesto ...................... 316
Vladimir Guerrero, West Palm/Harr. .. 307
Phil Hiatt, Toledo .............................. 304
Bubba Trammell, Jacksonville/Toledo . 297

**EXTRA-BASE HITS**
D.T. Cromer, Modesto ........................ 80
Todd Walker, Salt Lake ...................... 78
Derrek Lee, Memphis ......................... 75
Mike Cameron, Birmingham ............... 74
Bubba Trammell, Jacksonville/Toledo . 73

**DOUBLES**
Joe Urso, Lake Elsinore ..................... 47
Gabe Kapler, Fayetteville ................... 45
Aaron Boone, Chattanooga . .............. 44
Mike Berry, High Desert/Bowie .......... 44
Craig Stone, Hagerstown/Dunedin ...... 42

**TRIPLES**
Norm Hutchins, Cedar Rapids ............ 16
Bob Abreu, Tucson ............................ 16
Demond Smith, Huntsville/Edmonton .. 14

**D.T. Cromer**
Topped minors with 80 extra-base hits

Kerry Robinson, Peoria ........................ 14
Fletcher Bates, Capital City ................. 13
Chance Sanford, Carolina ................... 13

### HOME RUNS
Phil Hiatt, Toledo ................................... 42
Russ Branyan, Columbus .................... 40
Ron Wright, Durham/Green./Car. ........ 36
Chris Kirgan, High Desert .................... 35
Andruw Jones, Durham/Green./Rich. .. 34
Jerry Brooks, Charlotte (IL) ................. 34
Derrek Lee, Memphis .......................... 34

### RUNS BATTED IN
Chris Kirgan, High Desert .................. 131
D.T. Cromer, Modesto ...................... 130
Phil Hiatt, Toledo .............................. 119
Mike Berry, High Desert/Bowie ......... 116
Ron Wright, Durham/Green./Car. ...... 114

### MOST RBIs, ONE GAME
Freddy Diaz, Vancouver ......................... 9
Tal Light, Asheville ................................. 9
Mike Whitlock, Hagerstown ................... 9
Seven players tied with .......................... 8

### STOLEN BASES
Dave Roberts, Visalia/Jacksonville ...... 65
Kevin Gibbs, Vero Beach ..................... 60
Ramon Gomez, Hickory ........................ 57
Rod Smith, Greensboro .........................57
Richard Almanzar, Lakeland ................ 53
Kyle Towner, Bakersfield ...................... 53
Juan Nunez, Charleston, S.C. ............. 53

### HIT BY PITCHES
Mike Kinkade, Beloit ............................ 32
Jeremy Kendall, Clear./Reading .......... 30
Terrel Hansen, Toledo/Jacksonville .... 27
Scott Vieira, Rockford .......................... 26
Eric Schreimann, Piedmont ................. 26

### BASE ON BALLS
Tom Evans, Knoxville ......................... 115
Dana Walker, West Michigan ..............112
Eric Stuckenschneider, Savannah ..... 111
Mike Whitlock, Hagerstown ............... 108
Dusty Allen, Clinton/Rancho Cuca. .... 105

### STRIKEOUTS
Josh Booty, Kane County .................. 195
Keith Kimsey, Visalia/Jacksonville .... 190
Phil Hiatt, Toledo .............................. 180
Derrek Lee, Memphis ........................ 170
Nate Rolison, Kane County ............... 170

### SLUGGING PERCENTAGE*
Andruw Jones, Durham/Green./Rich. .652
Lee Stevens, Oklahoma City ............ .643
D.T. Cromer, Modesto ..................... .626
Vladimir Guerrero, West Palm/Harris. . .618
Adam Hydzu, Trenton ...................... .618

### ON-BASE PERCENTAGE*
Mike Berry, High Desert/Bowie ......... .471
Tom Evans, Knoxville ....................... .452
Scott Vieira, Rockford ...................... .451
Brent Brede, Salt Lake .................... .446
Don Denbow, San Jose .................... .446

### BATTING AVERAGE*
By Position
(Minimum 400 Plate Appearances)

### CATCHER
Craig Mayes, San Jose/Shreve. ....... .334
Mitch Meluskey, Kissimmee/Jackson .326
Doug Newstrom, High Desert ........... .313
Paul LoDuca, Vero Beach ................ .305
Walt McKeel, Trenton ...................... .302

### FIRST BASEMEN
Desi Wilson, Phoenix ...................... .339
Todd Helton, New Haven/Colo. Spr. . .336
Dmitri Young, Louisville ................... .333
Mario Valdez, South Bend/Birm. ....... .330
D.T. Cromer, Modesto ..................... .329

### SECOND BASEMEN
Brian Raabe, Salt Lake .................... .351
Wilson Guerrero, Albuquerque ......... .344
Kary Bridges, Jackson/Tuscon ......... .322
Dave Hajek, Tuscon ........................ .317

**Nelson Figueroa**
Led minors with 200 strikeouts

Luis Castillo, Portland (EL) .............. .317

### THIRD BASEMEN
Mike Berry, High Desert/Bowie ......... .354
Todd Walker, Salt Lake .................... .339
Pedro Castellano, Colo. Springs ....... .337
Scott Rolen, Scranton ..................... .324
Matt Franco, Norfolk ....................... .323

### SHORTSTOPS
Nelfi Perez, Colorado Springs .......... .316
Russ Johnson, Jackson ................... .310
Aaron Ledesma, Vancouver ............. .305
Juan Melo, Rancho Cucamonga ...... .304
Dave Berg, Portland (EL) ................. .302

### OUTFIELDERS
Vladimir Guerrero, West Palm/Harr. . .360
Kerry Robinson, Peoria .................... .359
Brent Brede, Salt Lake .................... .348
Todd Dunn, El Paso ........................ .340
Andruw Jones, Durham/Green./Rich. .339

## INDIVIDUAL PITCHING

### EARNED RUN AVERAGE*
(Minimum 112 Innings)
Britt Reames, Peoria ........................ 1.90
Nelson Figueroa, Capital City .......... 2.04
Blake Stein, St. Petersburg ............. 2.15
Randy Knoll, Piedmont/Clear. .......... 2.20
Nerio Rodriguez, Frederick/Roch. .... 2.21
Ethan McEntire, Capital City ............ 2.22
Tony Mounce, Kissimmee ................ 2.25
Chris Peters, Carolina/Calgary ........ 2.26
Andy Trumpour, Capital City ............ 2.29
Curt Lyons, Chattanooga ................. 2.41

### WINS
Ted Silva, Charlotte/Tulsa ................. 17
Elvin Hernandez, Augusta ................. 17
Darin Blood, San Jose ...................... 17
Carl Pavano, Trenton ........................ 16
Brian Bevil, Wichita/Omaha .............. 16
Bill King, Modesto ............................ 16
Billy Neal, Vero Beach ...................... 16
Blake Stein, St. Petersburg .............. 16
Brandon Kolb, Clinton ....................... 16

### LOSSES
Dan Lock, Kissimmee ........................ 18
Toure Knighton, Bakersfield/Char. (FSL) 17
Matt Beaumont, Midland .................... 16
Igor Oropeza, Bakersfield/Kinston ..... 16
Maximo Nunez, Hickory ..................... 16
Dan Elher, Brevard County ................ 16

### GAMES
Jay Tessmer, Tampa ......................... 68
Wayne Gomes, Reading .................... 67
Matt Arrandale, Louisville ................. 63

Tom Martin, Jackson/Tucson .............. 62
Dan Rios, Norwich/Columbus ............. 62
James Nix, Chattanooga .................... 62
Rick Trlicek, Norfolk .......................... 62
Joe Maskivish, Augusta/Lynchburg ..... 62
Jeff Matranga, Arkansas ................... 62

### COMPLETE GAMES
Jason Dickson, Midland/Vancouver ..... 10
Carlos Castillo, South Bend/Pr. Will. ..... 9
Nelson Figueroa, Capital City ............... 8
Jeff Suppan, Pawtucket ....................... 7
Jonathan Johnson, Tulsa/Okla. City ...... 7

### SAVES
Sean Maloney, El Paso ...................... 38
Russ Ortiz, San Jose/Shreveport ........ 36
Jay Tessmer, Tampa ......................... 35
Santos Hernandez, Burlington (MWL) . 35
Bryan Corey, Fayetteville ................... 34

### INNINGS PITCHED
Geoff Edsell, Midland/Vancouver ...... 193
Mark Redman, Ft. Myers/Hard. City/SL 193
Cory Lidle, Binghamton .................... 190
Jarrod Washburn, Lake Els./Mid./Van. . 189
Ted Silva, Charlotte/Tulsa ................ 188

### BASE ON BALLS
Ryan Creek, Jackson ....................... 121
Ivan Montane, Port City/Lancaster .... 118
Igor Oropeza, Bakersfield/Kinston ..... 110
Billy Blythe, Macon .......................... 107
Bob Oldham, Bakersfield .................. 105
Jon Vanhof, Wisconsin ..................... 105

### STRIKEOUTS
Nelson Figueroa, Capital City ........... 200
Joe Young, Hagerstown/Dunedin ...... 193
Darin Blood, San Jose ...................... 193
Ethan McEntire, Capital City ............ 190
Shane Dennis, Rancho Cuca./Memphis 185

### STRIKEOUTS/9 INNINGS*
(Starters)
Curt Lyons, Chattanooga ............... 11.18
Joe Young, Hagerstown/Dunedin ... 11.16
Matt Clement, Rancho Cuca./Clinton 10.85
Kerry Wood, Daytona ..................... 10.71
Eric Gagne, Savannah .................... 10.22
Darin Blood, San Jose .................... 10.22

### STRIKEOUTS/9 INNINGS*
(Relievers)
Ben Fleetham, Delmarva/WPB/Harr. . 14.06
Russ Ortiz, San Jose/Shreveport ... 13.07
Ken Glard, Macon/Durham ............. 12.46
Michael Walter, Quad City .............. 12.41
Ben Lowe, Hagerstown ................... 12.20

### BATTING AVERAGE AGAINST*
(Starters)
Britt Reames, Peoria ....................... .170
Kerry Wood, Daytona ...................... .179
Nelson Figueroa, Capital City .......... .181
Dan Kolb, Ch'ton/Charlotte/Tulsa ..... .197
Ethan McEntire, Capital City ........... .198

### BATTING AVERAGE AGAINST*
(Relievers)
Ben Fleetham, Delmarva/WPB/Harr. . .137
Dan Ricabal, Savannah/Vero Beach . .154
Chris Macca, Asheville/New Haven .. .157
Santos Hernandez, Burlington (MWL) . .169
Michael Walter, Quad City ............... .170

### MOST STRIKEOUTS IN ONE GAME
Bobby Rodgers, Lowell ..................... 16
Jack Cressand, Lowell ...................... 15
Steve Hoff, AZL Padres .................... 15
Joe Mays, Everett ............................ 15
Jeriome Robertson, GCL Astros ........ 15

## INDIVIDUAL FIELDING

### MOST ERRORS
Chad Hermansen, Augusta/Lynch. ...... 53
Rob Sasser, Macon ........................... 51
D'Angelo Jimenez, Greensboro .......... 50
Tal Light, Asheville/Salem ................. 50
Kevin Witt, Dunedin .......................... 48

MORRIS FOSTOFF

## Expansion Shakes Out

The Durham Bulls got back into the Triple-A expansion race after they hooked up with the Devil Rays, who will share some of the cost.

The Bulls pulled out of the process after being named one of the finalists, saying the $7.5 million expansion fee was too expensive.

But Bulls owner Jim Goodmon said he had worked out a deal in which the Bulls will own 75 percent of the Triple-A franchise and the Devil Rays will own 25 percent. The Devil Rays also will pay an unspecified portion of the expansion fee.

"We had some discussions with the people in Tampa Bay, and they said that they wanted their Triple-A team in Durham," Goodmon said.

"Durham is probably the most recognizable and successful minor league franchise in all baseball," Chuck LaMar said. LaMar is familiar with the Bulls from his days with the Braves, the Bulls' current parent club.

"This is a Triple-A market. We need to go ahead and do it," Goodmon said. "We are four or five years ahead of the curve of when I thought we would do it. I didn't want to be impatient, but when I had a major league team that wanted to invest in it and work with us, I thought we couldn't have a better situation if we waited."

The Bulls would expand Durham Bulls Athletic Park from 6,240 to 10,000 seats, and the Carolina League franchise would head out of town and get a new name.

John Carbray, the president of the Fresno Diamond Group, jumped on the Phoenix franchise when it became available, rather than waiting on the turbulent expansion process. The reported sale price was about $8 million.

"I thought since last December (1995) we were real close," Carbray said. "But it never happens until it happens. It was like a baseball game. It seems like nothing is going on, and then suddenly it all happened."

The team will be called the Fresno Grizzlies and is set to begin play in 1998, the same year the Diamondbacks begin their inaugural season in Phoenix.

The Double-A expansion committee decided at the 1995 Winter Meetings to push back the first year for the two new Double-A teams to 1999. That didn't do much, however, to settle the process down.

Cities came and went every week, and the committee extended the time for cities to make presentations. It finally settled on five finalists. Four were expected: Austin, Texas; Erie, Pa.; Springfield, Mass.; and Springfield, Mo. But a late-comer, Lexington, Ky., also made the cut.

Lexington turned away the Southern League franchise that will land in Mobile, Ala., in 1997. But a Lexington group led by real-estate developer Dudley Webb, made a presentation to the expansion committee in Boston and apparently turned some heads.

Erie and Springfield, Mass., would go into the Eastern League. Austin would go into the Texas League and Lexington into the Southern League. Springfield, Mo., could go into either of those leagues. The Texas League has eight teams; the Eastern and Southern leagues have 10.

"You'll never know how this thing will wash out," Webb said. "By the time politics and everybody's

# ORGANIZATION OF THE YEAR
## Braves Become Leaders In Finding, Shaping Talent

Since 1991, when what had been the game's most downtrodden franchise shocked the baseball world by going from worst to first and reaching the World Series, the Atlanta Braves have ranked among the game's elite. They have won a major league-best

550 regular-season games, captured division titles in each of the five completed seasons and participated in four Fall Classics.

No other team comes anywhere close to those accomplishments.

So does that rank the Braves among the game's all-time best? Nope, not yet, because more than one World Series championship is required for that distinction.

The decade's best team? Probably, though the next three years will better define such a label.

Baseball America's Organization of the Year for 1996? Absolutely, because no other team has done a better job of constantly rebuilding from within while getting stronger every year.

"Our farm system is the cornerstone and foundation of any success we have," general manager John Schuerholz says. "It's absolutely essential. We have been able to utilize our developed players to help our club get better each and every year."

As effective as the organization's scouting and coaching staffs have been, no one has done a better job of helping the prospects succeed in making the final step than manager Bobby Cox.

"He is the perfect manager for the Atlanta Braves," Schuerholz says. "Bobby's got a strong, varied background. He's been a player, coach, manager and general manager at the major league level. He understands the whole process. He understands how hard it is to play the game and the challenges involved. There's also not a lot of ranting and raving, and that creates an environment where everybody feels comfortable."

### PREVIOUS WINNERS

| | |
|---|---|
| 1982—Oakland Athletics | 1989—Texas Rangers |
| 1983—New York Mets | 1990—Montreal Expos |
| 1984—New York Mets | 1991—Atlanta Braves |
| 1985—Milwaukee Brewers | 1992—Cleveland Indians |
| 1986—Milwaukee Brewers | 1993—Toronto Blue Jays |
| 1987—Milwaukee Brewers | 1994—Kansas City Royals |
| 1988—Montreal Expos | 1995—New York Mets |

played their whole deal, you don't know who'll end up with the teams."

## Ejection Fever

In the year's most annoying trend, anything that wasn't nailed down got tossed.

It began in the California League, when High Desert Mavericks mascot Wooly Bully was thrown out after an umpire decided Wooly was mocking him. A local

# MANAGER OF THE YEAR

## Young Marlins Thrive Under Tosca

When the Florida Marlins hired John Boles as their manager midway through the 1996 season, much was made of his never having played professionally.

Now it looks as though the Marlins might produce another such manager for the big leagues. Carlos Tosca, who spent his third season at Double-A Portland in 1996, flatly says he wasn't good enough to play professionally.

He's proven he's good enough to manage professionally. His 15th season may have been his most successful yet.

Tosca made the Portland Sea Dogs one of the best teams in the Eastern League for the second straight year and continued to send prospects to the majors. For that reason, he earned Baseball

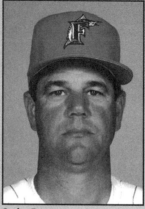

**Carlos Tosca**

America's Minor League Manager of the Year award.

"I've just been given a tremendous opportunity, and the Marlins have done things the correct way," said Tosca, who will skipper the Marlins' Triple-A affiliate at Charlotte in 1997. "If you can't develop a guy under the system we've developed here, he's probably not going to get developed."

Marlins general manager Dave Dombrowski said Tosca balances winning and developing individual players as well as any minor league manager.

"He's an outstanding baseball man," Dombrowski said. "He knows the game well and he communicates it well. He knows the balance between hav-

ing patience and when a player goes too far. He demands effort and will not tolerate repeated mistakes."

It's a philosophy Tosca has been working on since he got his first professional baseball job as a coach for the Yankees' short-season Oneonta affiliate in 1978. His first shot at managing came in the Rookie-level Gulf Coast League in 1980. Except for two seasons in the mid-1980s, he has been managing ever since.

Now, after 19 seasons working with minor leaguers, Tosca sees his career broken down into two phases.

"In the first, I was learning about the ins and outs of the game, learning all I could about strategy and fundamentals," he said. "I just did all I could to absorb information: watching, listening, reading, asking questions. Now I'm at the point where I want to concentrate on reaching people with the information I have."

Tosca said it's a bit strange that he's been managing long enough to have developed a managerial philosophy or to have had two big phases of his career. When he started as a minor league manager, he saw it as a way to get experience he could use to become a farm director or coordinator of instruction.

"But I've had some success," he said, "so I've decided I'm just going to see where this might lead me to go. If things happen,

wave of publicity ensued.

"This has all gone way too far," Wooly said. "I just went onto the field to have a little fun with the umpire. It was a very tense and heated moment, and I just wanted to lighten things up. Then the umpire goes and tosses me from the game."

In the Midwest League, Beloit clubhouse manager Jason DeZwarte was ejected after yelling about balls and strikes. Snappers manager Luis Salazar jokingly said he would suspend DeZwarte from doing laundry for three days.

Or maybe he wasn't even ejected. The umpires and league president George Spelius said DeZwarte hadn't been, and that they didn't appreciate all the publicity generated by the ejection.

The Snappers stood by their story.

"Jason claims he was given the heave-ho, our players say he was, so we say he was," public-relations director Brett Dolan said. "The umpires didn't write him up since he's the clubbie and he does the umpires' laundry. They probably didn't want a stack full of wet,

dirty jocks the next time they come to town.

"We're having fun with it, but George is upset. He doesn't want his guys to look bad, which doesn't take much in some of their cases."

Well put. In a similarly screwy situation in the South Atlantic League, Glenn Marr, the sound technician for the Savannah Sand Gnats, got tossed in two straight games for playing sound effects. In a game against Hickory, Marr played "Huh?" and "What?" over the loudspeakers after a Hickory runner was ruled safe on a play at third. Umpire James Thomas threw him out.

Marr played "What?" again the next night on a play at second, and umpire Wes Hamilton ejected him. Marr had played sound effects in the first two games of the series without incident.

"I felt that was really silly," he said. "It's part of baseball. But these guys are so touchy they go off on the smallest thing. They didn't even give me a warning."

Fortunately, some restraint was exercised in Calgary, where local disc jockeys who mocked Pacific

Coast League umpires in a between-innings promotion were just told to shut up.

## Chicks On The Move

David Hersh made news on another front as well in 1996. An attempt to keep his Southern League Chicks in Memphis fell through, so the team likely will move to Jackson, Tenn., for the 1998 season.

The move represents a sudden reversal of fortune for Memphis and Jackson, a city about 90 miles to the northeast. Jackson, which had remote hopes of landing a Double-A expansion franchise, now has an established team. Memphis, which has had a team in the Southern League since 1978, has to scramble to find another.

Hersh talked to Jackson because he was unsuccessful in getting a new ballpark built in Memphis. He said Tim McCarver Stadium, which opened in 1968 and went through a $3.1 million renovation in 1993, wasn't suitable for Double-A baseball.

Hersh has submitted the applications necessary to move his team. "It's in their court now," said Hersh, who mailed applications to both the Southern League and the National Association.

Both organizations had to approve the Chicks' move. That used to be considered nothing more than a formality, but a proposed move of the Harrisburg Senators (Eastern) to Springfield, Mass., in 1995 was delayed by the NA until the city of Harrisburg worked out a deal to buy the team and keep it there.

Jackson won't begin construction of an $8 million, 6,200-seat stadium until relocation has been approved.

The city and county governments in Memphis each offered to contribute $3 million to a stadium plan, but Hersh said that wouldn't be enough. Several weeks of negotiations ensued, with Memphis businessman Dean Jernigan stepping forward to possibly buy the team and keep it in town.

Jernigan reportedly offered close to $6 million for the team. He said he will continue looking for another team to play in Memphis.

"We may be without a team for a year or two," he said. "I will do everything in my power to bring professional baseball back to Memphis, and bring it back at the highest level possible and as soon as possible."

## Trappers Win Final Contest

**Joe Buzas**

It took awhile, but the Salt Lake Trappers finally won their last contest.

The Trappers were the Pioneer League team that played in Salt Lake City until the Pacific Coast League's Buzz came to town in 1994. The two parties argued for almost four years over how much Buzz owner Joe Buzas should pay the Trappers for taking over the Salt Lake territory.

The Trappers already had won a $1.35 million award from an arbitrator. The Utah Supreme Court decided unanimously Oct. 4, 1996, that Buzas had to pay an additional $400,000 as well.

# TEAM OF THE YEAR

## Gritty Trappers Cap Off Dream Season In Edmonton

Just a couple of years ago, it seemed baseball might never take off in Edmonton.

Then came manager Gary Jones, a good run of players and brand new TELUS Field. The pieces started to come together in 1996 was the

real payoff for the Trappers.

The team rewrote the franchise record book, winning a record 84 games, breaking another mark with a nine-game winning streak and putting together the first no-hitter in franchise history. To go with the on-field success, 463,684 fans came to the ballpark, breaking the record of 426,012 set a year earlier.

Then the Trappers topped it all off by charging through the Pacific Coast League playoffs to win their first league title since 1984, only their second overall. It was all good enough to be selected Baseball America's Minor League Team of the Year for 1996.

"There were a bit of growing pains in the first year, but in the second year things really worked out well," Trappers media-relations director Colin MacPhail said. "The team definitely responded."

In spite of a continual shuffle of players between Edmonton and the parent Athletics, Jones kept his team winning as the Trappers went wire-to-wire for their championship.

"All the way around it was a good year," Jones said. "The guys did a good job and worked hard. They didn't let too much faze them."

The crux of the case was a secret 1992 lease agreement between Buzas and Salt Lake City mayor Deedee Corrandini that prompted Buzas to move his team from Portland, Ore. The city and Buzas then announced that he was bringing a Triple-A team to town, old Derks Field would be torn down and Franklin Quest Field would be built. The Trappers were forced to leave and ended up in Ogden.

When baseball arbitrator George Nicolau heard the case, he ruled that the Buzz had to pay the Trappers $1.2 million for the territory.

He also ruled the secret deal violated baseball rules that require teams to negotiate with resident teams before they move in. He tacked on an additional $552,152 for tampering.

Buzas argued that $400,000 of that duplicated what Nicolau had already assessed as the value of the Trappers franchise, and he appealed the decision.

A Utah district court judge agreed with Buzas and threw out the $400,000. But the Utah Supreme Court said the judge improperly substituted his judgment for Nicolau's.

"This is precisely what a court reviewing an arbitration award may not do," the court's decision said.

# TOP 100 PROSPECTS

Through consultation with baseball's scouting and player development fraternity, Baseball America annually selects a list of the game's top 100 major league prospects. The list emphasizes long-range major league potential and considers only players in professional baseball who have not exhausted their major league rookie status.

The list, compiled prior to the 1996 season, identifies the highest level players attained in 1996.

1. Andruw Jones, of, Braves (Majors)
2. Paul Wilson, rhp, Mets (Majors)
3. Ruben Rivera, of, Yankees (Majors)
4. Darin Erstad, of, Angels (Majors)
5. Alan Benes, rhp, Cardinals (Majors)
6. Derek Jeter, ss, Yankees (Majors)
7. Karim Garcia, of, Dodgers (Majors)
8. Livan Hernandez, rhp, Marlins (Majors)
9. Vladimir Guerrero, of, Expos (Majors)
10. Ben Davis, c, Padres (A)
11. Jason Schmidt, rhp, Braves (Majors)
12. *Matt Drews, rhp, Yankees (AAA)
13. Derrick Gibson, of, Rockies (AA)
14. Billy Wagner, lhp, Astros (Majors)
15. Bartolo Colon, rhp, Indians (AAA)
16. Kerry Wood, rhp, Cubs (A)
17. Rey Ordonez, ss, Mets (Majors)
18. Chan Ho Park, rhp, Dodgers (Majors)
19. Rocky Coppinger, rhp, Orioles (Majors)
20. Richard Hidalgo, of, Astros (AA)
21. Jay Payton, of, Mets (AAA)
22. Todd Walker, 3b, Twins (Majors)
23. Jose Cruz Jr., of, Mariners (AAA)
24. Jim Pittsley, rhp, Royals (AAA)
25. Jeff D'Amico, rhp, Brewers (Majors)
26. Jason Kendall, c, Pirates (Majors)
27. Scott Rolen, 3b, Phillies (Majors)
28. Donnie Sadler, ss, Red Sox (AA)
29. Bob Abreu, of, Astros (Majors)
30. Jermaine Dye, of, Braves (Majors)
31. Jaime Jones, of, Marlins (A)
32. Todd Helton, 1b, Rockies (AAA)
33. Edgar Renteria, ss, Marlins (Majors)
34. Jaret Wright, rhp, Indians (A)
35. Jeff Suppan, rhp, Red Sox (Majors)

**Braves' Andruw Jones.** No.1

36. Nomar Garciaparra, ss, Red Sox (Majors)
37. Ben Grieve, of, Athletics (AA)
38. Jimmy Haynes, rhp, Orioles (Majors)
39. Trot Nixon, of, Red Sox (Majors)
40. Marty Janzen, rhp, Blue Jays (Majors)
41. Derrek Lee, 1b, Padres (AA)
42. Paul Konerko, 1b, Dodgers (AAA)
43. Alex Ochoa, of, Mets (Majors)
44. Todd Hollandsworth, of, Dodgers (Majors)
45. Andy Yount, rhp, Red Sox (A)
46. Shannon Stewart, of, Blue Jays (Majors)
47. Brooks Kieschnick, of, Cubs (Majors)
48. Ugueth Urbina, rhp, Expos (Majors)
49. Geoff Jenkins, of, Brewers (AA)
50. Richie Sexson, 1b, Indians (AA)
51. Jason Varitek, c, Mariners (AAA)
52. Chris Snopek, 3b, White Sox (Majors)
53. Dustin Hermanson, rhp, Padres (Majors)
54. Chad Hermansen, ss, Pirates (A)
55. Andrew Vessel, of, Rangers (A)
56. Matt Morris, rhp, Cardinals (AAA)
57. Roger Cedeno, of, Dodgers (Majors)
58. Jose Valentin, c, Twins (AA)
59. Todd Greene, c, Angels (Majors)
60. Pokey Reese, ss, Reds (AAA)
61. Wilton Guerrero, ss, Dodgers (Majors)
62. Mike Drumright, rhp, Tigers (AA)
63. Neifi Perez, ss, Rockies (Majors)
64. Terrell Wade, lhp, Braves (Majors)
65. Enrique Wilson, ss, Indians (AAA)
66. Jamey Wright, rhp, Rockies (Majors)
67. Jay Powell, rhp, Marlins (Majors)
68. Brad Fullmer, of, Expos (AA)
69. Doug Million, lhp, Rockies (AA)

70. LaTroy Hawkins, rhp, Twins (Majors)
71. Steve Gibralter, of, Reds (Majors)
72. Shawn Estes, lhp, Giants (Majors)
73. Hiram Bocachica, ss, Expos (A)
74. Carlos Guillen, ss, Astros (A)
75. Robert Smith, 3b, Braves (AAA)
76. Dan Serafini, lhp, Twins (Majors)
77. Scott Elarton, rhp, Astros (A)
78. Brian Rose, rhp, Red Sox (AA)
79. Luis Castillo, 2b, Marlins (Majors)
80. Julio Santana, rhp, Rangers (AAA)
81. Antone Williamson, 3b, Brewers (AAA)
82. Chris Carpenter, rhp, Blue Jays (AA)
83. Glendon Rusch, lhp, Royals (AAA)
84. John Wasdin, rhp, Athletics (Majors)
85. Brad Rigby, rhp, Athletics (AA)
86. Danny Graves, rhp, Indians (Majors)
87. Steve Cox, 1b, Athletics (AA)
88. Miguel Tejada, ss, Athletics (A)
89. *Desi Relaford, 2b, Mariners (Majors)
90. Trey Beamon, of, Pirates (Majors)
91. Jeff Abbott, of, White Sox (AAA)
92. Gabe Alvarez, 3b, Padres (AAA)
93. Jose Pett, rhp, Blue Jays (AAA)
94. Preston Wilson, of, Mets (A)
95. Damon Hollins, of, Braves (AAA)
96. Joe Fontenot, rhp, Giants (A)
97. John Frascatore, rhp, Cardinals (Majors)
98. Michael Coleman, of, Red Sox (A)
99. Billy Percibal, rhp, Orioles (Injured)
100. Josh Booty, 3b, Marlins (Marlins)

*Traded during 1996 season

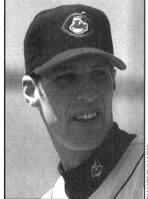

**Indians' Richie Sexson.** No.50

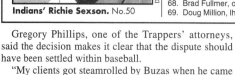

**Marlins' Josh Booty.** No.100

Gregory Phillips, one of the Trappers' attorneys, said the decision makes it clear that the dispute should have been settled within baseball.

"My clients got steamrolled by Buzas when he came to Salt Lake, and he figured he could steamroll us in court," Phillips said. "But we stuck it out, and they have now hit a grand slam."

## Best Game Of The Year

Sure there were plenty of 20-run blowouts and high-scoring shootouts in 1996, but the best game of the year was easily the Asheville Tourists' 2-1 win over the Augusta GreenJackets in 19 innings.

The South Atlantic League game featured great pitching from start to finish, starting with Asheville righthander Scott Randall, who pitched 11 innings of no-hit ball before he finally was relieved.

Randall pitched a perfect game for the first eight innings and allowed just two baserunners, both in the ninth. Elton Pollock reached on an error, and Freddy May was intentionally walked after Pollock was sacrificed to second.

Randall went out to the mound to start the 12th only to find reliever Heath Bost, who had trotted in from

# BOB FREITAS AWARDS
## Rejuvenated Indy, Wisconsin Clubs Feted

The recent success of minor league baseball has meant that many longtime franchises have been rejuvenated. Two of those were recognized by Baseball America as winners of the 1996 Bob Freitas Awards.

The Freitas Awards recognize and reward long-term success by minor league franchises. Freitas was a longtime operator, promoter and minor league ambassador who died in 1989, and the award named for him annually honors teams at Triple-A, Double-A, Class A and short-season levels.

Indianapolis, the Triple-A winner, has been in the American Association since 1902, except for a seven-year absence in the 1960s when it moved to the Pacific Coast League. The franchise has always been successful but took a major leap forward when it moved into Victory Field, a new downtown ballpark.

At Double-A, the Southern League had its first winner of the award, the Carolina Mudcats. The Mudcats have thrived since moving to Zebulon, N.C., in 1991 and playing a relay throw from the Durham Bulls, one of the most successful franchises in the minors.

Wisconsin won the Class A award, giving the Midwest League its fourth winner in the last five years. The Timber Rattlers have been in the league since 1962. After years as the Appleton Foxes, the team renamed itself two seasons ago and moved into a new ballpark in 1995, setting attendance records both years.

The Bluefield Orioles won the short-season award, becoming the first winner from the Appalachian League. Bluefield annually is one of the best draws in the Appy League, despite a population of less than 13,000.

the bullpen, on the mound ready to warm up. When the pitching change was announced, Randall received a loud ovation.

His no-hit stint was the longest in league history. No league pitcher ever had thrown a no-hitter longer than nine innings.

The teams set or tied six league records overall, and it was the longest game in Augusta history, both in innings and time (a pretty brisk five hours).

In order to stay in against Randall, the GreenJackets had to put up a good performance of their own. Starter Derek Bullock pitched six shutout innings, and he was followed by Jason Farrow, Craig Mattson, Joe Maskivish and Jose Reyes, who kept the shutout into the 16th inning.

Augusta catcher Wikelman Gonzalez hit a home run in the bottom of the 16th to tie the score 1-1. He also set a league record by throwing out seven Asheville runners attempting to steal.

After such a beautifully played game, the end came ugly. Asheville finally won when outfielder Efrain Alamo reached second on an error, advanced to third on a passed ball and scored on an infield hit by David Feuerstein in the top of the 19th.

## Prank For The Ages

The minor leagues were full of the usual zany antics, but one prank should be recorded for posterity.

San Antonio Missions broadcaster Roy Acuff pulled it off. With the Missions at home for a day game against Midland, no radio broadcast was scheduled. But Acuff, no relation to the late country singer, convinced Missions sales rep Bryan Beban the game would be on the air and asked Beban to fill in for his partner.

Beban, an aspiring broadcaster, eagerly took the bait and was on the hook for nine innings. Missions employees and local media listened on an in-house phone line as Acuff took Beban for a ride.

"I committed every broadcast sin I could, trying to break him," Acuff said. "But he stayed with the game and I was killing him."

Acuff said the Missions "sucked canal water" and blasted the players, team officials and even the mascot, Henry the Puffy Taco. By the fifth inning, Acuff took his shirt off, propped his feet on the desk, chugged beer and uttered words banned by the FCC.

Texas League president Tom Kayser, who along with everyone in Texas except Beban was in on the joke, came into the booth after Acuff criticized the umpires. As Kayser and Acuff argued loudly, Beban tried to call the game.

Between innings, Beban told Missions general manager Burl Yarbrough what was going on. Yarbrough finally went and pulled Acuff off the air.

"I was trying to save Roy's job," Beban said. "I thought, 'This guy is fired.' I was trying to save our radio contract. It was unbelievable."

But Acuff returned. "I was waiting for this guy to say, 'Hold it, stop,' " Acuff said, "but it never happened. I strung him out for nine innings. Beban would never let go. He stuck with it and he never understood he was being had."

Finally, as Beban tried to do the postgame show, Acuff lowered the boom and several Missions staff members entered the booth, shirtless and laughing.

"They nailed me," Beban said. "I was glad to get the chance to do the game, and then Roy was doing all these crazy things. It just blew me away. It was an all-timer."

# MINOR LEAGUES
## BEST TOOLS

| | American Association (AAA) | International League (AAA) | Pacific Coast League (AAA) | Eastern League (AA) | Southern League (AA) | Texas League (AA) | California League (A) | Carolina League (A) | Florida State League (A) | Midwest League (A) | South Atlantic League (A) |
|---|---|---|---|---|---|---|---|---|---|---|---|
| Best Batting Prospect | Jeff Abbott, Nashville | Alex Ochoa, Norfolk | Todd Walker, Salt Lake | Vladimir Guerrero, Harrisburg | Kevin Orie, Orlando | Richard Hidalgo, Jackson | Ben Grieve, Modesto | Andruw Jones, Durham | Daryle Ward, Lakeland | Jeff Liefer, South Bend | Adrian Beltre, Savannah |
| Best Power Hitter | Lee Stevens, Oklahoma City | Phil Hiatt, Toledo | James Bonnici, Tacoma | Vladimir Guerrero, Harrisburg | Bubba Trammell, Jacksonville | Paul Konerko, San Antonio | Keith Kimsey, Visalia | Ron Wright, Durham | Chris Durkin, Vero Beach | Jeff Liefer, South Bend | Adrian Beltre, Savannah |
| Best Baserunner | Curtis Goodwin, Indianapolis | Jim Buccheri, Ottawa | Mitch Simons, Salt Lake | Luis Castillo, Portland | Mike Cameron, Birmingham | Jeremy Carr, Wichita | Marcus Sturdivant, Lancaster | Sergio Nunez, Wilmington | Richard Almanzar, Lakeland | Elinton Jasco, Rockford | Orlando Cabrera, Delmarva |
| Fastest Baserunner | Curtis Goodwin, Indianapolis | Shannon Penn, Toledo | Terry Jones, Colorado Springs | Luis Castillo, Portland | Lonell Roberts, Knoxville | Dante Powell, Shreveport | Dave Roberts, Visalia | Eugene Kingsale, Frederick | Kevin Gibbs, Vero Beach | Elinton Jasco, Rockford | George Lombard, Macon |
| Best Pitching Prospect | Glendon Rusch, Omaha | Justin Thompson, Toledo | Billy Wagner, Tucson | Bartolo Colon, Canton-Akron | Mike Drumright, Jacksonville | Matt Morris, Arkansas | Ken Cloude, Lancaster | Jaret Wright, Kinston | Kerry Wood, Daytona | Britt Reames, Peoria | Dan Kolb, Charleston, S.C. |
| Best Fastball | Scott Ruffcorn, Nashville | Archie Corbin, Rochester | Dustin Hermanson, Las Vegas | Bartolo Colon, Canton-Akron | Marc Kroon, Memphis | Matt Morris, Arkansas | Russ Ortiz, San Jose | Jaret Wright, Kinston | Kerry Wood, Daytona | V. de los Santos, Beloit | Dan Kolb, Charleston, S.C. |
| Best BreakingPitch | Jaime Bluma, Omaha | Justin Thompson, Toledo | Shawn Estes, Phoenix | Wayne Gomes, Reading | Mike Drumright, Jacksonville | Dave Geeve, Tulsa | Francisco Saneaux, High Desert | Doug Million, Salem | Blake Stein, St. Petersburg | Britt Reames, Peoria | Frankie Sanders, Columbus |
| Best Control | Gabe White, Indianapolis | Mike Gardiner, Norfolk | Chris Holt, Tucson | Brian Rose, Trenton | Heath Murray, Memphis | Jeff D'Amico, El Paso | Brian Cooper, Lake Elsinore | Clint Koppe, Winston-Salem | Edgar Ramos, Kissimmee | Britt Reames, Peoria | Randy Knoll, Piedmont |
| Best Reliever | Danny Graves, Buffalo | Derek Wallace, Norfolk | Jeff Schmidt, Vancouver | Mike Welch, Binghamton | Marc Kroon, Memphis | Sean Maloney, El Paso | Mike Villano, San Jose | Steve Prihoda, Wilmington | Jay Tessmer, Tampa | Santos Hernandez, Burlington | Bryan Corey, Fayetteville |
| Best Defensive C | Henry Mercedes, Omaha | Alberto Castillo, Norfolk | A. Encarnacion, Calgary | Charlie Greene, Binghamton | Julio Mosquera, Knoxville | Eli Marrero, Arkansas | Bret Hemphill, Lake Elsinore | Justin Towle, Winston-Salem | Paul LoDuca, Vero Beach | Robinson Cancel, Beloit | James Davis, Charleston, W.Va. |
| Best Defensive 1B | Brant Brown, Iowa | Roberto Petagine, Norfolk | Jason Thompson, Las Vegas | Todd Helton, New Haven | Steve Cox, Huntsville | Larry Sutton, Wichita | D.T. Cromer, Modesto | Matt Smith, Wilmington | Chris Richard, St. Petersburg | David Arias, Wisconsin | Justin Drizos, Asheville |
| Best Defensive2B | Ramon Martinez, Omaha | Tony Graffanino, Richmond | Jay Canizaro, Phoenix | Luis Castillo, Portland | Marty Malloy, Greenville | Ronnie Belliard, El Paso | Jesse Garcia, High Desert | Mike Eaglin, Durham | Richard Almanzar, Lakeland | Carlos Febles, Lansing | Orlando Cabrera, Delmarva |
| Best Defensive 3B | Olmedo Saenz, Nashville | Scott McClain, Rochester | George Arias, Vancouver | Scott Rolen, Reading | Tom Evans, Knoxville | Mendy Lopez, Wichita | Antonio Fernandez, Rancho Cuca. | Wes Helms, Durham | Jose Lopez, St. Lucie | Cole Liniak, Michigan | Adrian Beltre, Savannah |
| Best Defensive SS | Pokey Reese, Indianapolis | Chris Martin, Ottawa | Neifi Perez, Colorado Springs | Enrique Wilson, Canton-Akron | Giomar Guevara, Port City | Hanley Frias, Tulsa | Juan Melo, Rancho Cuca. | Eddy Martinez, Frederick | Luis Ordaz, St. Petersburg | Deivi Cruz, Burlington | Chris Woodward, Hagerstown |
| Best Infield Arm | Pokey Reese, Indianapolis | Scott McClain, Rochester | Neifi Perez, Colorado Springs | Enrique Wilson, Canton-Akron | Lou Collier, Carolina | Mendy Lopez, Wichita | Juan Melo, Rancho Cuca. | Danny Magee, Durham | Luis Ordaz, St. Petersburg | Josh Booty, Kane County | Adrian Beltre, Savannah |
| Best Defensive OF | Kevin Koslofski, New Orleans | Jim Buccheri, Ottawa | J. Allensworth, Calgary | Vladimir Guerrero, Harrisburg | Earl Johnson, Memphis | Mark Little, Tulsa | M. Sturdivant, Lancaster | Andruw Jones, Durham | Ed Bady, West Palm Beach | Ramon Alvarez, Fort Wayne | Freddy May, Augusta |
| Best Outfield Arm | Darren Burton, Omaha | Alex Ochoa, Norfolk | Darin Erstad, Vancouver | Vladimir Guerrero, Harrisburg | Charles Peterson, Carolina | Armando Rios, Shreveport | Keith Kimsey, Visalia | Jose Guillen, Lynchburg | Juan Encarnacion, Lakeland | Osmel Garcia, Peoria | Ruben Mateo, Charleston, S.C. |
| Most Exciting Player | Dmitri Young, Louisville | Alex Ochoa, Norfolk | Todd Walker, Salt Lake | Vladimir Guerrero, Harrisburg | Mike Cameron, Birmingham | Dante Powell, Shreveport | Miguel Tejada, Modesto | Andruw Jones, Durham | Vladimir Guerrero, West Palm Beach | David Arias, Wisconsin | Adrian Beltre, Savannah |
| Best Umpire Prospect | Bennie Walton | Paul Nauert | Field Culbreth | Heath Jones | Marv Hudson | Dan Iassogna | Scott Higgins | Jeff Head | David Baldwin | Brian McCraw | James Thomas |
| Best Manager Prospect | Rick Renick, Nashville | Tom Runnells, Toledo | Ron Wotus, Phoenix | Pat Kelly, Harrisburg | Dick Scott, Huntsville | Ron Johnson, Wichita | Dave Brundage, Lancaster | Bill McGuire, Salem | Al LeBoeuf, Clearwater | Lynn Jones, Kane County | Doug Sisson, Delmarva |

Selected at midseason 1996 by minor league managers in consultation with Baseball America. Full-season leagues only.

# Rule V Draft Only Part Of Bartee's Baseball Travels

It was a strange year for Kimera Bartee, and his selection in the 1995 Rule V draft wasn't the end of his travels.

Bartee, a speedy outfield prospect, was picked up by the Orioles in the draft, an annual staple at baseball's Winter Meetings. He was one of 17 players selected in the major league portion of the draft, down from 24 the year before.

The Orioles were glad to get him back, it seemed, after reluctantly including him in a September 1995 deal with the Twins in which they acquired righthander Scott Erickson.

The Twins then left Bartee off their 40-man roster, and the Orioles quickly snapped him up again.

"There was a lot of reluctance to let him go," Orioles scouting director Gary Nickels said after the draft. "But it was a bargain to get him back for only $50,000."

Then the Orioles tried to get Bartee through waivers in the spring of 1996, and he was claimed by the Tigers. He finally appeared to find a home in Detroit, sticking with the big club all of the 1996 season to become the Tigers' center fielder of the future. He hit .253 in 110 games.

Though the Orioles waived him, Bartee was still under the requirements of the Rule V draft. Major league draft picks cost $50,000 each, and players must be kept on the team's 25-man major league roster all of the next season or be offered back to their old team for $25,000.

Three kinds of players, if not protected on organizations' 40-man winter rosters as filed on Nov. 20, are eligible for selection: players with major league experience; players who have played parts of three seasons in National Association-affiliated minor leagues who were 19 or older on June 5 preceding their first contract; and players who have played parts of four seasons and were 18 or younger on June 5 preceding their first contract.

As the American League club with the worst record in 1995, the Twins had the first pick in the

**Kimera Bartee.** Became a Tiger by way of the Orioles.

draft. They chose righthander Joe Jacobsen out of the Dodgers organization. Jacobsen had played at Class A in 1995. He failed to stick with the Twins, was offered back to the Dodgers and spent the 1996 season at Double-A San Antonio, going 1-4 with a 4.19 ERA in 38 games.

Cincinnati, Kansas City and St. Louis engaged in a trade immediately following the draft that involved two drafted players.

The Cardinals, picking fourth, selected outfielder Andre King from the White Sox with the understanding he would be traded to the Reds for infielder Luis Ordaz. Cincinnati didn't pick until 26th and feared King might not be available.

The Royals then took outfielder Miguel Mejia from Baltimore and immediately traded him to the Cardinals. The Reds completed the cycle by sending veteran lefthander Mike Remlinger to the Royals.

St. Louis wanted Mejia even though he spent most of 1995 in the Rookie-level Appalachian League and had to be kept on the Cardinals' 25-man roster all of 1996. He was and collected only two hits in 23 at-bats.

Bartee and Rodney Myers, drafted by the Cubs from the Royals, had the most successful 1996 seasons. Myers worked 45 games in relief for Chicago, compiling a 2-1 record and 4.68 ERA.

## 1995 RULE V DRAFT

**MAJOR LEAGUE DRAFT**
Selection Price: $50,000

**ROUND ONE**
Selecting Club, Player, Pos. (From)
Twins. *Joe Jacobsen, rhp (Dodgers)
Pirates. *Patricio Claudio, of (Indians)
Blue Jays. *Carey Paige, rhp (Braves)
Cardinals. Andre King, of (White Sox)
Tigers. Greg Keagle, rhp (Padres)
Expos. *Trey Witte, rhp (Mariners)
Brewers. *Tyrone Narcisse, rhp (Astros)
Phillies. B.J. Wallace, lhp (Expos)
Royals. Miguel Mejia, of (Orioles)
Orioles. Kimera Bartee, of (Twins)
Rangers. *Mark Mimbs, lhp (Dodgers)
Cubs. Rodney Myers, rhp (Royals)
Yankees. Marc Ronan, c (Brewers)
Red Sox. *Joe Crawford, lhp (Mets)

**ROUND TWO**
Tigers. *Jon Ratliff, rhp (Cubs)
Rangers. *Tim Rumer, lhp (Yankees)
    *Returned to original organization

**TRIPLE-A DRAFT**
Selection Price: $12,000

**ROUND ONE**
Selecting Club, Player, Pos. (From)
Twins. Phil Stidham, rhp (Mets)
Pirates. Keith Heberling, lhp (White Sox)
Blue Jays. Derek Gaskill, rhp (Brewers)
Tigers. Lamarr Robers, 2b (Rockies)
Expos. Jalal Leach, of (Yankees)
Brewers. Dennis Gray, lhp (Blue Jays)
Marlins. Keith Garagozzo, lhp (Yankees)
White Sox. M. Nunez, rhp (Blue Jays)
Phillies. Essex Burton, 2b (White Sox)
Royals. Jim Telgheder, rhp (Red Sox)
Mets. Jason Pierson, lhp (White Sox)
Orioles. Allen Plaster, rhp (Athletics)
Padres. Mike Basse, of (Brewers)
Rangers. M. Coolbaugh, 3b (Blue Jays)
Cubs. Joe Ciccarella, lhp (Red Sox)
Mariners. Terric McFarlin, rhp (Padres)
Rockies. J. Goligoski, ss (White Sox)
Yankees. Sandy Pichardo, 2b (Mets)
Dodgers. Scott Richardson, of (Brewers)
Reds. Billy Hall, 2b (Padres)
Indians. John Donati, 1b (Angels)
Braves. Eduard Cordero, ss (Tigers)

**ROUND TWO**
Blue Jays. Kurt Bogott, lhp (Red Sox)
Brewers. Mike Rennhack, of (Astros)
Phillies. Keith Troutman, rhp (Dodgers)
Royals. Steve Olsen, rhp (White Sox)
Mets. Jim Rosenbohm, rhp (Astros)
Orioles. Doug Newstrom, 1b (Dodgers)
Padres. George Glinatsis, rhp (Mariners)
Cubs. Rick Forney, rhp (Orioles)
Rockies. Zach Sawyer, rhp (Athletics)
Yankees. Kevin Northrup, of (Athletics)
Dodgers. D. Newman, rhp (Athletics)
Reds. Willie Canate, of (Blue Jays)

**ROUND THREE**
Mets. Pedro Grifol, c (Twins)
Padres. Melvin Rosario, c (White Sox)

**ROUND FOUR**
Mets. Angel Jaime, of (Dodgers)
Padres. Todd Bussa, rhp (Red Sox)

**ROUND FIVE**
Padres. Derek Hacopian, of (Tigers)

**DOUBLE-A DRAFT**
Selection Price: $4,000

**ROUND ONE**
Selecting Club, Player, Pos. (From)
Tigers. Sean Evans, rhp (Pirates)
Athletics. Brian Doughty, rhp (Mariners)
Mets. Rob Steinert, rhp (Blue Jays)
Padres. Derek Baker, rhp (Mets)
Angels. Mike Hermanson, rhp (Padres)
Mariners. Jared Baker, rhp (Padres)
Dodgers. Jamie Mackert, 1b (Pirates)

**ROUND TWO**
Tigers. Jerry Salzano, 3b (Cubs)
Mariners. Craig Hanson, rhp (Padres)

# AMERICAN
## ASSOCIATION

# 89ers Suddenly Strike Gold, Claim Title

**By PETER BARROUQUERE**

The Oklahoma City 89ers began the 1996 season looking like they were headed for their more-accustomed-than-not eighth-place finish, a spot they had occupied eight times in the last 13 years.

They were 20-40 at one point. Then they took off fast enough to get the bends. The 89ers played at a .643 clip (54-30) the last three months of the American Association season and hardly came up for air in the playoffs.

They defeated the Western Division champion Omaha Royals in four games, then took care of the scrappy Indianapolis Indians in similar fashion in the finals.

Oklahoma City experienced a similar worst-to-first roller coaster ride in 1992, when it won the championship with a 74-70 record after finishing last in 1991 with a 52-92 record.

In 1995, the 89ers were again on the bottom with a 54-89 record, only to enact another spectacular turnaround.

Manager Greg Biagini will be the first to say that championships are a lot more fun.

"I look good in champagne," he said, soaked to the skin in bubbly after the 89ers defeated the Indians, 4-2, in the championship game at Indianapolis' new Victory Field.

"This just feels great. I'm so happy for the players who stuck with it all year, even though there were a lot of changes here at the end. They still believed in themselves. They were on a mission, and they accomplished what they set out to do."

The Indians made Oklahoma City earn it, right to the last out. The 89ers led 4-0 after six innings of the championship game. When starter Steve Dreyer gave up two runs in the seventh, reliever Chris Nichting came on to pitch out of a bases-loaded, none-out situation.

Indians outfielder Steve Gibralter doubled off Danny Patterson to lead off the eighth. After Gibralter took his lead, 89ers second baseman Jon Shave, who was playing with a sore left wrist but had hit a two-run single in the fourth, caught him napping with a hidden-

**Lee Stevens.** Veteran Oklahoma City first baseman led the American Association in homers (32) and was second in RBIs (94).

ball trick. Steve Eddie followed with a double that would have cut the 89ers' lead to one run.

"I got the ball back from left field and held on to it," Shave said. "Nichting noticed I still had the ball. So he turned around to the plate, and I walked up to (Gibralter) and told him, 'Nice hit,' and asked him if I could clean the bag. And he stepped off.

"I felt bad for Steve, but it was a situation where we had nothing to lose. The game was on the line, and it worked. It was meant to be. For something like that to happen, it was meant to be."

## STANDINGS

| Page | EAST | W | L | PCT | GB | Manager | Attendance/Dates | Last Pennant |
|---|---|---|---|---|---|---|---|---|
| 110 | **Buffalo Bisons (Indians)** | 84 | 60 | .583 | — | Brian Graham | 825,530 (64) | None |
| 104 | **Indianapolis Indians (Reds)** | 78 | 66 | .542 | 6 | Dave Miley | 537,325 (67) | 1994 |
| 90 | **Nashville Sounds (White Sox)** | 77 | 67 | .535 | 7 | Rick Renick | 303,407 (70) | None |
| 204 | **Louisville Redbirds (Cardinals)** | 60 | 84 | .417 | 24 | Joe Pettini | 494,929 (68) | 1995 |
| Page | WEST | W | L | PCT | GB | Manager | Attendance/Dates | Last Pennant |
| 140 | **Omaha Royals (Royals)** | 79 | 65 | .549 | — | Mike Jirschele | 421,994 (66) | 1990 |
| 230 | **Oklahoma City 89ers (Rangers)** | 74 | 70 | .514 | 5 | Greg Biagini | 267,784 (66) | 1996 |
| 97 | **Iowa Cubs (Cubs)** | 64 | 78 | .451 | 14 | Ron Clark | 453,630 (70) | 1993 |
| 153 | **New Orleans Zephyrs (Brewers)** | 58 | 84 | .408 | 20 | Tim Ireland | 180,485 (71) | None |

**PLAYOFFS—Semifinals:** Indianapolis defeated Buffalo 3-1, and Oklahoma City defeated Omaha 3-1, in best-of-5 series. **Finals:** Oklahoma City defeated Indianapolis 3-1, in best-of-5 series.

**NOTE:** Team's individual batting and pitching statistics can be found on page indicated in lefthand column.

The Indians put runners on first and third with one out in the ninth when Patterson got first baseman Tim Belk to hit into a double play, setting off corks in the clubhouse.

## Stevens Named MVP

The Association's Most Valuable Player didn't even have a job when the 1996 season started. Lee Stevens, 28, had been released by the Japanese League's Kintetsu Buffaloes, and his baseball career was at the mercy of a telephone call.

The night before the season opener, Biagini got a call from Rangers farm director Reid Nichols, who told him Stevens was available.

"I had seen him earlier in his career," Biagini said. "He's a much different hitter now."

**Greg Biagini**

Stevens batted .325 with 94 RBIs, led the league in homers (32) and finished the season with the parent Rangers.

"Playing in Japan helped my mental approach," Stevens said. "I learned not to get down on myself like I always used to do."

Stevens also shortened his swing, quickening his batting stroke, which enabled him to handle fastballs and breaking pitches better.

"I'm a late bloomer," he said. "I feel like I've extended my career."

The league's top pitcher, righthander Rick Helling, also came from Oklahoma City. He led the league with a 2.96 ERA and 157 strikeouts, pitched a perfect game August 13 against Nashville and then finished the season in the majors after being traded to the Florida Marlins.

## Ballparks Up, Crowds Down

Attendance was down overall in the Association for the third straight season. But that downswing may

**Nigel Wilson.** Buffalo outfielder hit .299 with 30 homers and led the American Association with 95 RBIs.

reverse itself with the addition of several new playing facilities.

Indianapolis opened Victory Field, an $18-million, 15,500-seat downtown facility on July 11 after a final half-season in 65-year-old Bush Stadium.

The new park helped the Indians post the league's largest attendance gain. The Indians drew 537,325 for the season—an increase of 171,071—and attracted 267,525 in 26 dates at Victory Field with four sellouts, including the final two regular-season games.

The New Orleans Zephyrs were last for their fourth straight season at Privateer Park, but were two rainouts away from setting an attendance record there.

In 1997, they're scheduled to open a new $20-million, 10,000-seat facility in suburban Metairie, with the largest scoreboard in minor league baseball and a swimming pool. The stadium will have 16 skyboxes.

Oklahoma City started construction on its new downtown ballpark, scheduled to be completed in 1998. Cost is estimated between $28-$30 million, and the park will have 12,900 reserved seats, 18 skyboxes, 552 club seats and a hillside area with seating for 3,000-4,000 more fans.

### LEAGUE CHAMPIONS

**Last 25 Years**

| Year | Regular Season* | Pct. | Playoff |
|---|---|---|---|
| 1972 | Wichita (Cubs) | .621 | Evansville (Brewers) |
| 1973 | Iowa (White Sox) | .610 | Tulsa (Cardinals) |
| 1974 | Indianapolis (Reds) | .578 | Tulsa (Cardinals) |
| 1975 | Denver (White Sox) | .596 | Evansville (Tigers) |
| 1976 | Denver (Expos) | .632 | Denver (Expos) |
| 1977 | Omaha (Royals) | .563 | Denver (Expos) |
| 1978 | Indianapolis (Reds) | .578 | Omaha (Royals) |
| 1979 | Evansville (Tigers) | .574 | Evansville (Tigers) |
| 1980 | Denver (Expos) | .676 | Springfield (Cardinals) |
| 1981 | Omaha (Royals) | .581 | Denver (Expos) |
| 1982 | Indianapolis (Reds) | .551 | Indianapolis (Reds) |
| 1983 | Louisville (Cardinals) | .578 | Denver (White Sox) |
| 1984 | Indianapolis (Expos) | .591 | Louisville (Cardinals) |
| 1985 | Oklahoma City (Rangers) | .556 | Louisville (Cardinals) |
| 1986 | Indianapolis (Expos) | .563 | Indianapolis (Expos) |
| 1987 | Denver (Brewers) | .564 | Indianapolis (Expos) |
| 1988 | Indianapolis (Expos) | .627 | Indianapolis (Expos) |
| 1989 | Indianapolis (Expos) | .596 | Indianapolis (Expos) |
| 1990 | Omaha (Royals) | .589 | Omaha (Royals) |
| 1991 | Buffalo (Pirates) | .566 | Denver (Brewers) |
| 1992 | Buffalo (Pirates) | .604 | Oklahoma City (Rangers) |
| 1993 | Iowa (Cubs) | .590 | Iowa (Cubs) |
| 1994 | Indianapolis (Reds) | .601 | Indianapolis (Reds) |
| 1995 | Indianapolis (Reds) | .611 | Louisville (Cardinals) |
| 1996 | Buffalo (Indians) | .583 | Oklahoma City (Rangers) |

*Best overall record

### HONOR ROLL

**OFFICIAL ALL-STAR TEAM**

**C**—Kelly Stinnett, New Orleans. **1B**—Dmitri Young, Louisville. **2B**—Casey Candaele, Buffalo. **3B**—Eduardo Perez, Indianapolis. **SS**—Damian Jackson, Buffalo. **OF**—Jeff Abbott, Nashville; Brian Giles, Buffalo; Nigel Wilson, Buffalo. **DH**—Lee Stevens, Oklahoma City. **LHP**—Brian Anderson, Buffalo. **RHP**—Rick Helling, Oklahoma City. **RP**—Jaime Bluma, Omaha. **Most Valuable Player**—Lee Stevens, Oklahoma City. **Rookie of the Year**—Jeff Abbott, Nashville. **Manager of the Year**—Rick Renick, Nashville.

**TOP 10 PROSPECTS**

**1.** Dmitri Young, 1b, Louisville; **2.** Jose Rosado, lhp, Omaha; **3.** Jeff Abbott, of, Nashville; **4.** Brian Giles, of, Buffalo; **5.** Brant Brown, 1b, Iowa; **6.** Glendon Rusch, lhp, Omaha; **7.** Danny Graves, rhp, Buffalo; **8.** Albie Lopez, rhp, Buffalo; **9.** Pokey Reese, ss, Indianapolis; **10.** Robin Jennings, of, Iowa.

# AMERICAN ASSOCIATION
## 1996 BATTING, PITCHING STATISTICS

### CLUB BATTING

| | AVG | G | AB | R | H | 2B | 3B | HR | BB | SO | SB |
|---|---|---|---|---|---|---|---|---|---|---|---|
| Buffalo | .273 | 144 | 4870 | 723 | 1330 | 245 | 32 | 163 | 456 | 885 | 65 |
| Omaha | .266 | 144 | 4740 | 712 | 1263 | 258 | 28 | 148 | 497 | 887 | 106 |
| Oklahoma City | .266 | 144 | 4821 | 658 | 1282 | 271 | 20 | 139 | 516 | 952 | 77 |
| Indianapolis | .263 | 144 | 4806 | 689 | 1263 | 258 | 39 | 131 | 460 | 988 | 131 |
| Iowa | .262 | 142 | 4771 | 593 | 1250 | 226 | 25 | 121 | 362 | 820 | 64 |
| Nashville | .254 | 144 | 4708 | 624 | 1194 | 237 | 28 | 124 | 368 | 772 | 78 |
| Louisville | .250 | 144 | 4708 | 583 | 1178 | 215 | 37 | 145 | 387 | 912 | 100 |
| New Orleans | .244 | 142 | 4750 | 606 | 1160 | 217 | 28 | 142 | 465 | 999 | 79 |

### CLUB PITCHING

| | ERA | G | CG | SHO | SV | IP | H | R | ER | BB | SO |
|---|---|---|---|---|---|---|---|---|---|---|---|
| Indianapolis | 3.53 | 144 | 6 | 13 | 39 | 1245 | 1171 | 578 | 489 | 394 | 942 |
| Oklahoma City | 3.60 | 144 | 11 | 10 | 25 | 1250 | 1249 | 595 | 500 | 381 | 943 |
| Nashville | 3.77 | 144 | 13 | 12 | 40 | 1235 | 1167 | 590 | 517 | 472 | 880 |
| Buffalo | 3.97 | 144 | 11 | 9 | 40 | 1253 | 1198 | 632 | 552 | 454 | 935 |
| Omaha | 4.20 | 144 | 5 | 10 | 42 | 1245 | 1299 | 668 | 582 | 412 | 912 |
| New Orleans | 4.29 | 142 | 8 | 11 | 32 | 1253 | 1278 | 708 | 598 | 526 | 871 |
| Iowa | 4.46 | 142 | 8 | 7 | 36 | 1232 | 1261 | 676 | 611 | 405 | 837 |
| Louisville | 4.75 | 144 | 8 | 5 | 36 | 1234 | 1297 | 741 | 652 | 467 | 895 |

### CLUB FIELDING

| | PCT | PO | A | E | DP | | PCT | PO | A | E | DP |
|---|---|---|---|---|---|---|---|---|---|---|---|
| Iowa | .978 | 3697 | 1428 | 114 | 125 | Omaha | .972 | 3735 | 1423 | 147 | 147 |
| Nashville | .977 | 3704 | 1451 | 119 | 120 | New Orleans | .971 | 3759 | 1585 | 160 | 154 |
| Buffalo | .977 | 3758 | 1454 | 125 | 130 | Indianapolis | .971 | 3735 | 1398 | 156 | 119 |
| Louisville | .974 | 3702 | 1597 | 140 | 129 | Oklahoma City | .970 | 3751 | 1579 | 164 | 149 |

**Terry Bradshaw**
.303-12-44 for Louisville

**Scott Ruffcorn**
13-4, 3.87 for Nashville

### INDIVIDUAL BATTING LEADERS
(Minimum 389 Plate Appearances)

| | AVG | G | AB | R | H | 2B | 3B | HR | RBI | BB | SO | SB |
|---|---|---|---|---|---|---|---|---|---|---|---|---|
| Young, Dmitri, Louisville | .333 | 122 | 459 | 90 | 153 | 31 | 8 | 15 | 64 | 34 | 67 | 16 |
| Abbott, Jeff, Nashville | .325 | 113 | 440 | 64 | 143 | 27 | 1 | 14 | 60 | 32 | 50 | 12 |
| Stevens, Lee, Okla. City | .325 | 117 | 431 | 84 | 140 | 37 | 2 | 32 | 94 | 58 | 90 | 3 |
| Ortiz, Luis, Okla. City | .317 | 124 | 501 | 70 | 159 | 25 | 0 | 14 | 73 | 22 | 36 | 0 |
| Candaele, Casey, Buffalo | .311 | 94 | 392 | 66 | 122 | 22 | 2 | 6 | 37 | 27 | 35 | 3 |
| Glanville, Doug, Iowa | .308 | 90 | 373 | 53 | 115 | 23 | 3 | 3 | 34 | 12 | 35 | 15 |
| Bradshaw, Terry, Louisville | .303 | 102 | 389 | 56 | 118 | 23 | 1 | 12 | 44 | 42 | 64 | 21 |
| Lee, Derek, Okla. City | .301 | 120 | 409 | 59 | 123 | 32 | 2 | 13 | 62 | 50 | 69 | 6 |
| Mitchell, Keith, Indy | .300 | 112 | 357 | 60 | 107 | 21 | 3 | 16 | 66 | 64 | 68 | 9 |
| Wilson, Nigel, Buffalo | .299 | 128 | 482 | 88 | 144 | 23 | 6 | 30 | 95 | 50 | 117 | 4 |

### INDIVIDUAL PITCHING LEADERS
(Minimum 115 Innings)

| | W | L | ERA | G | GS | CG | SV | IP | H | R | ER | BB | SO |
|---|---|---|---|---|---|---|---|---|---|---|---|---|---|
| Helling, Rick, Okla. City | 12 | 4 | 2.96 | 23 | 22 | 2 | 0 | 140 | 124 | 54 | 46 | 38 | 157 |
| Givens, Brian, New Orleans | 10 | 9 | 3.02 | 29 | 22 | 3 | 1 | 137 | 124 | 60 | 46 | 57 | 117 |
| Roa, Joe, Buffalo | 11 | 8 | 3.27 | 26 | 24 | 5 | 0 | 165 | 161 | 66 | 60 | 36 | 82 |
| Fordham, Tom, Nashville | 10 | 8 | 3.45 | 22 | 22 | 3 | 0 | 141 | 117 | 60 | 54 | 69 | 118 |
| Alberro, Jose, Okla. City | 9 | 9 | 3.47 | 29 | 27 | 4 | 0 | 171 | 154 | 73 | 66 | 57 | 140 |
| Anderson, Brian, Buffalo | 11 | 5 | 3.59 | 19 | 19 | 2 | 0 | 128 | 125 | 57 | 51 | 28 | 85 |
| Ojala, Kirt, Indianapolis | 7 | 7 | 3.77 | 22 | 21 | 3 | 0 | 134 | 143 | 67 | 56 | 31 | 92 |
| Ruffcorn, Scott, Nashville | 13 | 4 | 3.87 | 24 | 24 | 2 | 0 | 149 | 142 | 71 | 64 | 61 | 129 |
| Swartzbaugh, Dave, Iowa | 8 | 11 | 3.88 | 44 | 13 | 0 | 0 | 118 | 106 | 61 | 51 | 33 | 103 |
| Dreyer, Steve, Okla. City | 6 | 8 | 3.89 | 29 | 14 | 0 | 2 | 118 | 130 | 55 | 51 | 31 | 79 |

---

# INTERNATIONAL LEAGUE

# Stump Puts His Stamp On IL Trophy

**By TIM PEARRELL**

Stump Merrill kept coming back for more. And after six tours of duty spanning 13 years, he finally left with his name etched on the International League's Governors' Cup.

The former New York Yankees manager led Columbus on a second-half surge that culminated with a rare sweep of the playoffs and the franchise's seventh Cup win in 20 years.

Merrill, the winningest manager in Columbus history at 424-321, had been to the IL playoffs twice before, losing in the semifinals in 1984 and in the final to Tidewater in 1985. His '90 club, which he left during the season to take over the Yankees, lost under Rick Down in the final to Rochester. The '93 and '94 Clipper ships Merrill piloted failed to make the playoffs.

"We've been to the dance with me a couple of times before and came up short," said Merrill, who went over the 1,000-win mark as a minor league manager during the season. "But this club was not to be denied, and the effort that they put forth showed just exactly what this club is made of.

**Stump Merrill**

"I have to take my hat off to this team. They are the ones that went out and got it done, and I'm just proud to be a part of it. They're the ones who deserve the credit, not me. They're the ones that played. All I did was put their names in the lineup and run them out there on a daily basis."

It was quite a run at the end of the season for the Clippers. They were puttering along at 48-40 at the Triple-A all-star break, five games behind Norfolk in the Western Division. But they caught the Tides with a

**Rudy Pemberton.** His 27 homers helped Pawtucket set an International League record of 209 homers.

37-17 finishing kick and ended up 2 ½ games ahead with a league-best 85-57 record.

Columbus then beat Norfolk three straight—11-5, 4-3 in 11 innings, and 8-3—in a best-of-5 semifinal series. Outfielder Matt Luke blasted a pair of three-run homers in the deciding game.

## Long Ball Bonanza

Pawtucket, meanwhile, was going, going, gone in the Eastern Division. Using a long-ball lineup led by Rudy Pemberton (27 homers) and Alan Zinter (26) and featuring nine others in double figures, the Pawsox

## STANDINGS

| Page | EAST | W | L | PCT | GB | Manager(s) | Attendance/Dates | Last Pennant |
|------|------|---|---|-----|-----|-----------|------------------|--------------|
| 76 | **Pawtucket Red Sox (Red Sox)** | 78 | 64 | .549 | — | Buddy Bailey | 461,181 (64) | 1984 |
| 69 | **Rochester Red Wings (Orioles)** | 72 | 69 | .511 | 5½ | Marv Foley | 375,781 (61) | 1990 |
| 191 | **Scranton/W-B Red Barons (Phillies)** | 70 | 72 | .493 | 8 | Hobson/Aviles | 458,033 (64) | None |
| 236 | **Syracuse Chiefs (Blue Jays)** | 67 | 75 | .472 | 11 | Richie Hebner | 300,410 (64) | 1976 |
| 165 | **Ottawa Lynx (Expos)** | 60 | 82 | .423 | 18 | Pete Mackanin | 347,050 (64) | 1995 |
| Page | WEST | W | L | PCT | GB | Manager(s) | Attendance/Dates | Last Pennant |
| 171 | **Columbus Clippers (Yankees)** | 85 | 57 | .599 | — | Stump Merrill | 526,599 (67) | 1996 |
| 178 | **Norfolk Tides (Mets)** | 82 | 59 | .582 | 2½ | Valentine/Benedict | 506,965 (68) | 1985 |
| 122 | **Toledo Mud Hens (Tigers)** | 70 | 72 | .493 | 15 | Tom Runnells | 316,126 (67) | 1967 |
| 62 | **Richmond Braves (Braves)** | 62 | 79 | .440 | 22½ | Bill Dancy | 500,035 (62) | 1994 |
| 128 | **Charlotte Knights (Marlins)** | 62 | 79 | .440 | 22½ | Sal Rende | 326,761 (68) | 1993 |

**PLAYOFFS—Semifinals:** Rochester defeated Pawtucket 3-1, and Columbus defeated Norfolk 3-0, in best-of-5 series. **Finals:** Columbus defeated Rochester 3-0, in best-of-5 series.

**NOTE:** Team's individual batting and pitching statistics can be found on page indicated in lefthand column.

smashed 209 homers, believed to be the first IL team to top the 200 barrier.

Pawtucket, under Manager of the Year Buddy Bailey, finished 78-64, 5½ games ahead of Rochester. The Red Wings surged past Scranton/Wilkes-Barre and Syracuse down the stretch to make the playoffs.

Rochester lost 2-1 in the first game of its semifinal series against Pawtucket, then reeled off three straight victories—3-0, 8-7 and 6-2—to advance to the final.

Columbus captured the first game of the Cup final 5-2. In the second game, Ramiro Mendoza and two relievers combined on a six-hitter as the Clippers marked the final game of Rochester's 67-year-old Silver Stadium with a 4-0 win. The Red Wings will move to newly constructed Frontier Field, which opened in July for professional soccer, in 1997.

Columbus returned home to complete its perfect run as shortstop Tim Barker hit a three-run homer in a 10-5 win. Tim McIntosh and Luke each drove in two runs.

Luke hit .333 with 10 RBIs during the playoffs, first baseman Ivan Cruz hammered three homers, and third baseman Tracy Woodson, a major cog during the second-half drive, hit .375 with two homers and six RBIs. The title was the second straight for the veteran Woodson, who was instrumental in Louisville's American Association championship in 1995.

## Banner Year For Hiatt

Toledo third baseman Phil Hiatt also had a season for the books, whacking 42 homers and driving in 119 runs in a league traditionally known more for its pitching than hitting.

**Phil Hiatt.** His 43 homers were IL's most since 1958.

JEFF GOLDEN

Hiatt's home run total was the highest since Toronto's Rocky Nelson smacked 43 in 1958. His RBI total was the highest since Rochester's Roger Freed knocked in 130 in 1970 and only the second time a player had topped 110 since 1959. Hiatt was a runaway choice for the league's MVP award.

Charlotte outfielder Billy McMillon, who won the batting crown with a .352 average, was named rookie of the year. Norfolk righthander Mike Fyhrie, the top winner (15-6) and ERA leader (3.04), was named the most valuable pitcher.

The IL's turnstile count dropped to just over 4.15 million in 1996, down from 4.4 million in 1995, though Mother Nature played a major factor. Poor weather early in the season, when several games were postponed because of snow, cost the league 62 openings—as opposed to 29 in '95—the most of any year since 1978, when such records began being compiled.

Traditional leader Columbus led the way with 526,599, and two other clubs—Norfolk and Richmond—topped the 500,000 mark. Only Toledo, however, had a higher attendance than in 1995.

## Hobson Arrested

Scranton/Wilkes-Barre manager Butch Hobson was arrested by Drug Enforcement Administration agents May 4 after receiving a Federal Express packet at his hotel room in Pawtucket, R.I.

Hobson, a former Boston Red Sox manager, was charged with possession of cocaine after agents said they found 2.5 grams of cocaine in Hobson's shaving kit. Hobson's attorney, Stephen Famiglietti, said Hobson denied any wrongdoing and said Hobson "issued his statement under trying circumstances." Hobson faced up to three years in jail and a $5,000 fine. He was fired by the Philadelphia Phillies and replaced by Ramon Aviles.

Syracuse began construction on its new stadium, which will replace 51-year-old MacArthur Stadium. The stadium is scheduled to be ready for Opening Day 1997.

### LEAGUE CHAMPIONS

**Last 25 Years**

| Year | Regular Season* | Pct. | Playoff |
|------|-----------------|------|---------|
| 1972 | Louisville (Red Sox) | .563 | Tidewater (Mets) |
| 1973 | Charleston (Pirates) | .586 | Pawtucket (Red Sox) |
| 1974 | Memphis (Expos) | .613 | Rochester (Orioles) |
| 1975 | Tidewater (Mets) | .607 | Tidewater (Mets) |
| 1976 | Rochester (Orioles) | .638 | Syracuse (Yankees) |
| 1977 | Pawtucket (Red Sox) | .571 | Charleston (Astros) |
| 1978 | Charleston (Astros) | .607 | Richmond (Braves) |
| 1979 | Columbus (Yankees) | .612 | Columbus (Yankees) |
| 1980 | Columbus (Yankees) | .593 | Columbus (Yankees) |
| 1981 | Columbus (Yankees) | .633 | Columbus (Yankees) |
| 1982 | Richmond (Braves) | .590 | Tidewater (Mets) |
| 1983 | Columbus (Yankees) | .593 | Tidewater (Mets) |
| 1984 | Columbus (Yankees) | .590 | Pawtucket (Red Sox) |
| 1985 | Syracuse (Blue Jays) | .564 | Tidewater (Mets) |
| 1986 | Richmond (Braves) | .571 | Richmond (Braves) |
| 1987 | Tidewater (Mets) | .579 | Columbus (Yankees) |
| 1988 | Tidewater (Mets) | .546 | Rochester (Orioles) |
|  | Rochester (Orioles) | .546 |  |
| 1989 | Syracuse (Blue Jays) | .572 | Richmond (Braves) |
| 1990 | Rochester (Orioles) | .614 | Rochester (Orioles) |
| 1991 | Columbus (Yankees) | .590 | Columbus (Yankees) |
| 1992 | Columbus (Yankees) | .660 | Columbus (Yankees) |
| 1993 | Charlotte (Indians) | .610 | Charlotte (Indians) |
| 1994 | Richmond (Braves) | .567 | Richmond (Braves) |
| 1995 | Norfolk (Mets) | .606 | Ottawa (Expos) |
| 1996 | Columbus (Yankees) | .599 | Columbus (Yankees) |

*Best overall record

### HONOR ROLL

**OFFICIAL ALL-STAR TEAM**

**C**—Jorge Posada, Columbus.
**1B**—Ivan Cruz, Columbus. **2B**—Jason Hardtke, Norfolk.
**3B**—Phil Hiatt, Toledo. **SS**—Clay Bellinger, Rochester.
**OF**—Phil Clark, Pawtucket; Billy McMillon, Charlotte; Rudy Pemberton, Pawtucket.
**DH**—Jerry Brooks, Charlotte.
**SP**—Mike Fyhrie, Norfolk. **RP**—Derek Wallace, Norfolk.
**Most Valuable Player**—Phil Hiatt, Toledo. **Pitcher of the Year**—Mike Fyhrie, Norfolk. **Rookie of the Year**—Billy McMillon, Charlotte. **Manager of the Year**—Buddy Bailey, Pawtucket.

**TOP 10 PROSPECTS**

**1.** Nomar Garciaparra, ss, Pawtucket; **2.** Alex Ochoa, of, Norfolk; **3.** Justin Thompson, lhp, Toledo; **4.** Billy McMillon, of, Charlotte; **5.** Shannon Stewart, of, Syracuse; **6.** Edgar Renteria, ss, Charlotte; **7.** Jeff Suppan, rhp, Pawtucket; **8.** Derek Wallace, rhp, Norfolk; **9.** Rocky Coppinger, rhp, Rochester; **10.** Ruben Rivera, of, Columbus.

# INTERNATIONAL LEAGUE
## 1996 BATTING, PITCHING STATISTICS

### CLUB BATTING

| | AVG | G | AB | R | H | 2B | 3B | HR | BB | SO | SB |
|---|---|---|---|---|---|---|---|---|---|---|---|
| Charlotte ................ | .284 | 142 | 4656 | 722 | 1320 | 271 | 15 | 165 | 391 | 832 | 99 |
| Pawtucket .............. | .282 | 142 | 4782 | 840 | 1350 | 301 | 36 | 209 | 497 | 932 | 84 |
| Rochester .............. | .281 | 141 | 4641 | 727 | 1304 | 258 | 56 | 131 | 488 | 855 | 117 |
| Columbus .............. | .272 | 142 | 4665 | 766 | 1268 | 298 | 46 | 151 | 483 | 858 | 100 |
| Ottawa .................... | .269 | 142 | 4618 | 606 | 1240 | 241 | 34 | 102 | 404 | 798 | 160 |
| Norfolk .................... | .267 | 141 | 4645 | 643 | 1238 | 258 | 42 | 110 | 437 | 900 | 109 |
| Richmond .............. | .264 | 142 | 4604 | 593 | 1215 | 253 | 20 | 100 | 360 | 966 | 92 |
| Syracuse .............. | .263 | 142 | 4624 | 694 | 1215 | 236 | 47 | 106 | 532 | 815 | 167 |
| Scranton/W-B .......... | .258 | 142 | 4692 | 640 | 1210 | 240 | 49 | 101 | 450 | 819 | 92 |
| Toledo .................... | .256 | 142 | 4675 | 716 | 1195 | 221 | 39 | 165 | 490 | 1086 | 130 |

### CLUB PITCHING

| | ERA | G | CG | SHO | SV | IP | H | R | ER | BB | SO |
|---|---|---|---|---|---|---|---|---|---|---|---|
| Norfolk .................... | 3.51 | 141 | 9 | 12 | 46 | 1221 | 1122 | 545 | 476 | 356 | 921 |
| Columbus .............. | 4.01 | 142 | 14 | 6 | 38 | 1210 | 1176 | 628 | 540 | 420 | 912 |
| Richmond .............. | 4.17 | 142 | 14 | 7 | 34 | 1196 | 1190 | 640 | 554 | 432 | 826 |
| Rochester .............. | 4.57 | 141 | 7 | 3 | 33 | 1179 | 1248 | 684 | 599 | 458 | 888 |
| Pawtucket .............. | 4.60 | 142 | 16 | 9 | 31 | 1215 | 1255 | 704 | 622 | 417 | 944 |
| Syracuse .............. | 4.64 | 142 | 10 | 4 | 28 | 1206 | 1265 | 709 | 622 | 470 | 890 |
| Scranton/W-B .......... | 4.67 | 142 | 6 | 4 | 36 | 1219 | 1271 | 712 | 633 | 509 | 860 |
| Toledo .................... | 4.95 | 142 | 9 | 4 | 34 | 1214 | 1317 | 761 | 668 | 457 | 920 |
| Ottawa .................... | 5.10 | 142 | 10 | 10 | 36 | 1201 | 1327 | 751 | 680 | 476 | 862 |
| Charlotte ................ | 5.48 | 142 | 7 | 3 | 41 | 1181 | 1384 | 813 | 720 | 537 | 838 |

### CLUB FIELDING

| | PCT | PO | A | E | DP | | PCT | PO | A | E | DP |
|---|---|---|---|---|---|---|---|---|---|---|---|
| Ottawa ........... | .977 | 3602 | 1461 | 117 | 117 | Rochester ...... | .975 | 3536 | 1402 | 128 | 111 |
| Toledo ........... | .976 | 3641 | 1609 | 128 | 149 | Norfolk ........... | .974 | 3663 | 1480 | 139 | 108 |
| Charlotte ........ | .976 | 3543 | 1493 | 125 | 110 | Pawtucket ...... | .973 | 3646 | 1406 | 140 | 117 |
| Scranton/W-B.. | .975 | 3656 | 1444 | 130 | 101 | Richmond ...... | .969 | 3587 | 1301 | 157 | 113 |
| Columbus ...... | .975 | 3631 | 1526 | 132 | 114 | Syracuse ....... | .969 | 3617 | 1411 | 162 | 155 |

**Billy McMillon**
.352 average

**Mike Fyhrie**
15-6, 3.04

**Mike Gardiner**
13-3, 3.21

### INDIVIDUAL BATTING LEADERS
(Minimum 383 Plate Appearances)

| | AVG | G | AB | R | H | 2B | 3B | HR | RBI | BB | SO | SB |
|---|---|---|---|---|---|---|---|---|---|---|---|---|
| McMillon, Billy, Charlotte........... | .352 | 97 | 347 | 72 | 122 | 32 | 2 | 17 | 70 | 36 | 76 | 5 |
| Pemberton, Rudy, Paw............... | .326 | 102 | 396 | 77 | 129 | 28 | 3 | 27 | 92 | 18 | 63 | 16 |
| Clark, Phil, Pawtucket ............... | .325 | 97 | 369 | 57 | 120 | 36 | 2 | 12 | 69 | 17 | 32 | 3 |
| Franco, Matt, Columbus ............. | .323 | 133 | 508 | 74 | 164 | 40 | 2 | 7 | 81 | 36 | 55 | 5 |
| Bieser, Steve, Ottawa ............... | .322 | 123 | 382 | 63 | 123 | 24 | 4 | 1 | 32 | 35 | 55 | 27 |
| Olmeda, Jose, Charlotte ........... | .320 | 115 | 375 | 52 | 120 | 26 | 1 | 9 | 49 | 21 | 58 | 7 |
| Barron, Tony, Ottawa............... | .320 | 105 | 394 | 58 | 126 | 29 | 2 | 14 | 59 | 20 | 74 | 9 |
| Zuber, Jon, Scranton ............... | .311 | 118 | 412 | 62 | 128 | 22 | 5 | 4 | 59 | 58 | 50 | 4 |
| Bellinger, Clay, Rochester ........ | .301 | 125 | 459 | 68 | 138 | 34 | 4 | 15 | 78 | 33 | 90 | 8 |
| Stewart, Shannon, Syracuse .... | .298 | 112 | 420 | 77 | 125 | 26 | 8 | 6 | 42 | 54 | 61 | 35 |

### INDIVIDUAL PITCHING LEADERS
(Minimum 114 Innings)

| | W | L | ERA | G | GS | CG | SV | IP | H | R | ER | BB | SO |
|---|---|---|---|---|---|---|---|---|---|---|---|---|---|
| Fyhrie, Mike, Norfolk ................ | 15 | 6 | 3.04 | 27 | 27 | 2 | 0 | 169 | 150 | 61 | 57 | 33 | 103 |
| Reed, Rick, Norfolk ................... | 8 | 10 | 3.16 | 28 | 28 | 1 | 0 | 182 | 164 | 72 | 64 | 33 | 128 |
| Gardiner, Mike, Norfolk ............. | 13 | 3 | 3.21 | 24 | 24 | 2 | 0 | 146 | 125 | 58 | 52 | 38 | 125 |
| Suppan, Jeff, Pawtucket .......... | 10 | 6 | 3.22 | 22 | 22 | 7 | 0 | 145 | 130 | 66 | 52 | 25 | 142 |
| Woodall, Brad, Richmond .......... | 9 | 7 | 3.38 | 21 | 21 | 5 | 0 | 133 | 124 | 59 | 50 | 36 | 74 |
| Sodowsky, Clint, Toledo........... | 6 | 8 | 3.94 | 19 | 19 | 1 | 0 | 119 | 128 | 67 | 52 | 51 | 90 |
| Boehringer, Brian, Col. ............. | 11 | 7 | 4.00 | 25 | 25 | 3 | 0 | 153 | 155 | 79 | 68 | 56 | 132 |
| Telford, Anthony, Ottawa .......... | 7 | 2 | 4.11 | 30 | 15 | 1 | 0 | 118 | 128 | 62 | 54 | 34 | 69 |
| Brandow, Derek, Syracuse ........ | 8 | 7 | 4.28 | 24 | 20 | 2 | 0 | 124 | 118 | 64 | 59 | 57 | 103 |
| Lomon, Kevin, Richmond........... | 9 | 8 | 4.33 | 26 | 26 | 2 | 0 | 141 | 151 | 82 | 68 | 44 | 102 |

### DEPARTMENT LEADERS

**BATTING**

| | | |
|---|---|---|
| G | Phil Hiatt, Toledo ...................... | 142 |
| AB | Phil Hiatt, Toledo ...................... | 555 |
| R | Phil Hiatt, Toledo ........................ | 99 |
| H | Matt Franco, Norfolk ................. | 164 |
| TB | Phil Hiatt, Toledo ...................... | 304 |
| XBH | Phil Hiatt, Toledo ...................... | 72 |
| 2B | Matt Franco, Norfolk ................. | 40 |
| 3B | Joe Hall, Rochester .................. | 10 |
| | Brad Tyler, Rochester .............. | 10 |
| HR | Phil Hiatt, Toledo ...................... | 42 |
| RBI | Phil Hiatt, Toledo ...................... | 119 |
| SH | Steve Bieser, Ottawa ................. | 23 |
| SF | Clay Bellinger, Rochester .......... | 11 |
| | Tracy Woodson, Louisville ........ | 11 |
| BB | Jorge Posada, Columbus ........... | 79 |
| IBB | Roberto Petagine, Norfolk ........... | 7 |
| HBP | Rudy Pemberton, Pawtucket ...... | 14 |
| | Shannon Penn, Toledo .............. | 14 |
| SO | Phil Hiatt, Toledo ...................... | 180 |
| SB | Shannon Stewart, Syracuse ....... | 35 |
| CS | Scott Pose, Syracuse ............... | 16 |
| GIDP | Jerry Brooks, Charlotte .............. | 17 |
| OB% | Billy McMillon, Charlotte ........... | .418 |
| SL% | Rudy Pemberton, Pawtucket .... | .616 |

**PITCHING**

| | | |
|---|---|---|
| G | Ricky Trlicek, Norfolk ................. | 62 |
| GS | Rick Reed, Norfolk ................... | 28 |
| CG | Jeff Suppan, Pawtucket .............. | 7 |
| ShO | Mike Gardiner, Norfolk ............... | 2 |
| | Mike Fyhrie, Norfolk ................... | 2 |
| GF | Rod Nichols, Richmond ............. | 51 |
| Sv | Derek Wallace, Norfolk .............. | 26 |
| | Dave Pavlas, Columbus ............ | 26 |
| W | Mike Fyhrie, Norfolk ................. | 15 |
| L | Chris Seelbach, Charlotte .......... | 13 |
| IP | Rick Reed, Norfolk ................... | 182 |
| H | Travis Baptist, Syracuse .......... | 187 |
| R | Chris Seelbach, Charlotte ......... | 123 |
| ER | Chris Seelbach, Charlotte ......... | 113 |
| HR | Chris Seelbach, Charlotte ........ | 26 |
| HB | Brian Boehringer, Columbus ....... | 11 |
| BB | Matt Whisenant, Charlotte ......... | 101 |
| SO | Jeff Suppan, Pawtucket ........... | 142 |
| WP | Matt Whisenant, Charlotte .......... | 30 |
| BK | Livan Hernandez, Charlotte ......... | 4 |

**FIELDING**

| | | | |
|---|---|---|---|
| C | AVG | Rich Rowland, Syracuse..... | .994 |
| | PO | Alberto Castillo, Norfolk ....... | 747 |
| | A | Alberto Castillo, Norfolk ....... | 72 |
| | E | Joe Ayrault, Richmond........... | 11 |
| | DP | Alberto Castillo, Norfolk .......... | 9 |
| | PB | Joe Ayrault, Richmond............ | 11 |
| 1B | AVG | Ivan Cruz, Columbus .......... | .996 |
| | PO | Ivan Cruz, Columbus ......... | 1028 |
| | A | Ivan Cruz, Columbus ......... | 94 |
| | E | Roberto Petagine, Norfolk ...... | 15 |
| | DP | Ivan Cruz, Columbus ............ | 88 |
| 2B | AVG | No qualifier | |
| | PO | Tony Graffanino, Rich.......... | 215 |
| | A | Steve Rodriguez, Paw. ........ | 252 |
| | E | Brad Tyler, Rochester............ | 19 |
| | DP | Miguel Cairo, Syracuse ......... | 64 |
| 3B | AVG | Tracy Woodson, Col. .......... | .956 |
| | PO | Scott McClain, Rochester ...... | 96 |
| | A | Phil Hiatt, Toledo ................. | 345 |
| | E | Phil Hiatt, Toledo ................. | 26 |
| | DP | Phil Hiatt, Toledo ................. | 39 |
| SS | AVG | Chris Martin, Ottawa........... | .965 |
| | PO | Chris Martin, Ottawa........... | 178 |
| | A | Chris Martin, Ottawa ........... | 341 |
| | E | Tilson Brito, Syracuse ......... | 30 |
| | DP | Tilson Brito, Syracuse ......... | 72 |
| OF | AVG | Scott Pose, Syracuse ......... | .990 |
| | PO | Shannon Stewart, Syr. ........ | 274 |
| | A | Joe Hall, Rochester ............. | 15 |
| | E | Juan Williams, Richmond ....... | 9 |
| | DP | Alex Ochoa, Norfolk............... | 3 |
| | | Raul Rodarte, Richmond ........ | 3 |

# PACIFIC COAST
## LEAGUE

# Edmonton Traps Best Year In Its History

**By JAVIER MORALES**

They set club records in victories and attendance. Their dominance covered both halves of the year. Their dream season included the Pacific Coast League's only no-hitter.

Winning the 1996 PCL championship could have been a foregone conclusion for the Edmonton Trappers, whose first title since 1984 was an exclamation point to what was the most memorable season in club history.

"I think we proved over the course of the season we were the best team in the PCL," Edmonton mananger Gary Jones said. "I'm just glad we pulled it out so we could definitely lay claim that we were the best team, no questions, no doubts."

Had they not defeated Southern Division champion Phoenix for the title, the Trappers, Oakland's Triple-A affiliate, would have been considered underachievers.

**Scott Spiezio**

Their 84-58 record was a franchise-best. Sweeping both half-season pennants in the Northern Division was a first.

Edmonton's attendance of 463,684 at two-year-old TELUS Field topped 1995's record total of 426,012. A hero to those fans was righthander Aaron Small, who threw a no-hitter against Vancouver on Aug. 10, another club first.

"It was just a dream season," said Scott Spiezio, who hit six home runs in eight playoff games and led the Trappers with 20 in the regular season. "I've never won anything like this before—except maybe in Little League or something.

"I was just hoping we could pull it off this year. I just wanted to win, to have that feeling."

Torey Lovullo and Scott Sheldon each hit three-run homers in the series-clinching, 8-6 win over the Firebirds. Lovullo, a journeyman, epitomized the make-up of the Trappers. Aside from prospects Bobby Chouinard and Spiezio, Edmonton featured veterans and others trying to make a name for themselves.

**Todd Walker.** PCL's all-star third baseman hit .339 with 28 homers and 111 RBIs for Salt Lake.

"Maybe we don't have the most talent in the world," Lovullo said, "but look at these guys. We've got a bunch of guys who hang together—that's a tough team to beat."

## Tragedy Strikes Stars

Phoenix's sweep of Las Vegas in the Southern Division playoffs was difficult for the Stars, but they learned to deal with adversity during the middle of the season. Veteran infielder Mike Sharperson, bestowed the role of team captain by manager Jerry Royster, died in an automobile accident in Las Vegas a day before he was scheduled to join the San Diego Padres in Montreal.

The Stars dedicated the remainder of the season to Sharperson, whose jersey hung in the dugout for every

## STANDINGS: OVERALL

| Page | | W | L | PCT | GB | Manager | Attendance/Dates | Last Pennant |
|------|------|----|----|------|------|---------|------------------|--------------|
| 185 | Edmonton Trappers (Athletics) | 84 | 58 | .592 | — | Gary Jones | 463,684 (62) | 1996 |
| 159 | Salt Lake Buzz (Twins) | 78 | 66 | .542 | 7 | Phil Roof | 621,027 (71) | 1979 |
| 210 | Las Vegas Stars (Padres) | 73 | 67 | .521 | 10 | Jerry Royster | 313,212 (67) | 1988 |
| 197 | Calgary Cannons (Pirates) | 74 | 68 | .521 | 10 | Trent Jewett | 273,545 (67) | None |
| 83 | Vancouver Canadians (Angels) | 68 | 70 | .493 | 14 | Don Long | 334,800 (68) | 1989 |
| 134 | Tucson Toros (Astros) | 70 | 74 | .486 | 15 | Tim Tolman | 307,091 (69) | 1993 |
| 222 | Tacoma Rainiers (Mariners) | 69 | 73 | .486 | 15 | Dave Myers | 338,500 (71) | 1978 |
| 216 | Phoenix Firebirds (Giants) | 69 | 75 | .479 | 16 | Ron Wotus | 267,649 (71) | 1977 |
| 146 | Albuquerque Dukes (Dodgers) | 67 | 76 | .469 | 17 ½ | Phil Regan | 307,445 (68) | 1994 |
| 116 | Colorado Springs Sky Sox (Rockies) | 58 | 83 | .411 | 25 ½ | Brad Mills | 237,826 (67) | 1995 |

**NOTE:** Team's individual batting and pitching statistics can be found on page indicated in lefthand column.

game.

"All the guys on the team respected Mike and his loss affected us a great deal," Royster said. "Hanging his jersey in the dugout was a genuine sign of our respect. His presence was still felt."

Salt Lake, which featured three of the four top hitters in the league in second baseman Brian Raabe (.351), outfielder Brent Brede (.348) and third baseman Todd Walker (.339), lost in four games to Edmonton in the Northern Division playoffs.

Walker finished 12 points shy of winning the league's Triple Crown. He led the league in homers (28) and RBIs (111), was selected the league's MVP and was voted the league's top prospect in a poll of managers.

## Attitude Counts

Albuquerque outfielder Karim Garcia and Vancouver lefthander Jim Abbott provided news of coming and going in 1996.

Garcia, a PCL all-star in 1995, was demoted to Double-A San Antonio shortly after the all-star break after complaining about not being promoted to Los Angeles. But after serving his brief punishment with San Antonio, he was back with Albuquerque and ended up with a .297 average, a 22-point drop from 1995. He joined the Dodgers as a September call-up.

"I have pride in myself," Garcia said. "I don't just want to be a good player. I want to be one of the best. I want an opportunity."

Abbott was assigned to Vancouver late in the 1996 season—his first stint in the minors after going directly to the California Angels in 1989. The Angels had no choice but to demote Abbott, who was 1-15 with a 7.79 ERA. Abbott, whose $7.8 million contract was not picked up by another major league team,

**Jim Abbott**

accepted his demotion.

"I always wondered what it would be like in the minors," he said. "I've always heard from guys how much fun it is, how much camaraderie there is. I was here to work on things, but I was also here to have fun, to take a look around and enjoy it."

Abbott rejoined the Angels in September after going 0-2 with a 3.41 ERA with the Canadians in 29 innings.

## Tucson Two-Step

Tucson's 17-year affiliation with Houston came to an end after the 1996 season, with the Astros relocating their Triple-A club to New Orleans of the American Association.

The Toros will become aligned in 1997 with the Milwaukee Brewers, who are expected to leave Tucson after a year to allow the Arizona Diamondbacks to field their Triple-A team there.

Although half of the PCL's franchises had an increase in attendance in 1996, the overall total was down from 1995. The total attendance was 3,464,779, down from 3,513,867 the previous year.

Despite making the playoffs, Phoenix's attendance decreased from 282,370 to 267,649. The Phoenix franchise will be displaced by the Diamondbacks in 1998, but the team's initial attempts to move the team to either Austin, Texas, or Fresno, Calif., fell through.

### STANDINGS: SPLIT SEASON

#### FIRST HALF

| NORTH | W | L | PCT | GB |
|---|---|---|---|---|
| Edmonton | 39 | 31 | .557 | — |
| Tacoma | 40 | 32 | .556 | — |
| Vancouver | 35 | 32 | .522 | 2½ |
| Calgary | 37 | 34 | .521 | 2½ |
| Salt Lake | 35 | 37 | .486 | 5 |

| SOUTH | W | L | PCT | GB |
|---|---|---|---|---|
| Phoenix | 39 | 33 | .542 | — |
| Tucson | 35 | 37 | .486 | 4 |
| Albuquerque | 33 | 39 | .458 | 6 |
| Las Vegas | 31 | 37 | .456 | 6 |
| Colo. Springs | 29 | 41 | .414 | 9 |

#### SECOND HALF

| NORTH | W | L | PCT | GB |
|---|---|---|---|---|
| Edmonton | 45 | 27 | .625 | — |
| Salt Lake | 43 | 29 | .597 | 2 |
| Calgary | 37 | 34 | .521 | 7½ |
| Vancouver | 33 | 38 | .465 | 11½ |
| Tacoma | 29 | 41 | .414 | 15 |

| SOUTH | W | L | PCT | GB |
|---|---|---|---|---|
| Las Vegas | 42 | 30 | .583 | — |
| Tucson | 35 | 37 | .486 | 7 |
| Albuquerque | 34 | 37 | .479 | 7½ |
| Phoenix | 30 | 42 | .417 | 12 |
| Colo. Springs | 29 | 42 | .408 | 12½ |

**PLAYOFFS—Semifinals:** Edmonton defeated Salt Lake 3-1, and Phoenix defeated Las Vegas 3-0, in best-of-5 series. **Finals:** Edmonton defeated Phoenix 3-1, in best-of-5 series.

### LEAGUE CHAMPIONS

**Last 25 Years**

| Year | Regular Season* | Pct. | Playoff |
|---|---|---|---|
| 1972 | Albuquerque (Dodgers) | .622 | Albuquerque (Dodgers) |
| 1973 | Tucson (Astros) | .583 | Spokane (Rangers) |
| 1974 | Spokane (Rangers) | .549 | Spokane (Rangers) |
| 1975 | Hawaii (Padres) | .611 | Hawaii (Padres) |
| 1976 | Salt Lake City (Angels) | .625 | Hawaii (Padres) |
| 1977 | Phoenix (Giants) | .579 | Phoenix (Giants) |
| 1978 | Tacoma (Yankees) | .584 | Tacoma (Yankees)# Albuquerque (Dodgers)# |
| 1979 | Albuquerque (Dodgers) | .581 | Salt Lake City (Angels) |
| 1980 | Tucson (Astros) | .595 | Albuquerque (Dodgers) |
| 1981 | Albuquerque (Dodgers) | .712 | Albuquerque (Dodgers) |
| 1982 | Albuquerque (Dodgers) | .594 | Albuquerque (Dodgers) |
| 1983 | Albuquerque (Dodgers) | .594 | Portland (Phillies) |
| 1984 | Hawaii (Pirates) | .621 | Edmonton (Angels) |
| 1985 | Hawaii (Pirates) | .587 | Vancouver (Brewers) |
| 1986 | Vancouver (Brewers) | .616 | Las Vegas (Padres) |
| 1987 | Calgary (Mariners) | .596 | Albuquerque (Dodgers) |
| 1988 | Albuquerque (Dodgers) | .605 | Las Vegas (Padres) |
| 1989 | Albuquerque (Dodgers) | .563 | Vancouver (White Sox) |
| 1990 | Albuquerque (Dodgers) | .641 | Albuquerque (Dodgers) |
| 1991 | Albuquerque (Dodgers) | .580 | Tucson (Astros) |
| 1992 | Colo. Springs (Indians) | .596 | Colo. Springs (Indians) |
| 1993 | Portland (Twins) | .608 | Tucson (Astros) |
| 1994 | Albuquerque (Dodgers) | .597 | Albuquerque (Dodgers) |
| 1995 | Tucson (Astros) | .608 | Colo. Springs (Rockies) |
| 1996 | Edmonton (Athletics) | .592 | Edmonton (Athletics) |

*Best overall record #Co-champions

### HONOR ROLL

**OFFICIAL ALL-STAR TEAM**

C—Angelo Encarnacion, Calgary. 1B—Jason Thompson, Las Vegas. 2B—Brian Raabe, Salt Lake. 3B—Todd Walker, Salt Lake. SS—Neifi Perez, Colorado Springs. OF—Jermaine Allensworth, Calgary; Brent Brede, Salt Lake; Ray Montgomery, Tucson. DH—James Bonnici, Tacoma. LHP—Shawn Estes, Phoenix. RHP—Bob Milacki, Tacoma. RP—Steve Mintz, Phoenix. **Most Valuable Player**—Steve Mintz, Phoenix. **Manager of the Year**—Gary Jones, Edmonton.

**TOP 10 PROSPECTS**

1. Todd Walker, 3b, Salt Lake; 2. Shawn Estes, lhp, Phoenix; 3. Billy Wagner, lhp, Tucson; 4. Neifi Perez, ss, Colorado Springs; 5. Bob Abreu, of, Tucson; 6. Karim Garcia, of, Albuquerque; 7. Darin Erstad, of, Vancouver; 8. Jermaine Allensworth, of, Calgary; 9. Willie Adams, rhp, Edmonton; 10. Dustin Hermanson, rhp, Las Vegas.

# PACIFIC COAST LEAGUE
## 1996 BATTING, PITCHING STATISTICS

### CLUB BATTING

| | AVG | G | AB | R | H | 2B | 3B | HR | BB | SO | SB |
|---|---|---|---|---|---|---|---|---|---|---|---|
| Salt Lake | .293 | 144 | 5085 | 855 | 1490 | 319 | 49 | 151 | 530 | 892 | 141 |
| Calgary | .290 | 143 | 4870 | 764 | 1413 | 288 | 40 | 96 | 390 | 844 | 119 |
| Tucson | .282 | 144 | 4893 | 742 | 1380 | 250 | 62 | 122 | 491 | 912 | 103 |
| Colorado Springs | .282 | 142 | 4863 | 719 | 1370 | 264 | 35 | 117 | 519 | 879 | 81 |
| Albuquerque | .278 | 143 | 4940 | 712 | 1372 | 237 | 46 | 113 | 474 | 1076 | 104 |
| Tacoma | .276 | 142 | 4852 | 665 | 1341 | 245 | 33 | 143 | 412 | 789 | 72 |
| Edmonton | .276 | 142 | 4728 | 785 | 1306 | 245 | 45 | 147 | 582 | 968 | 123 |
| Vancouver | .276 | 138 | 4732 | 677 | 1304 | 285 | 35 | 66 | 488 | 775 | 89 |
| Phoenix | .275 | 144 | 4984 | 700 | 1371 | 273 | 58 | 77 | 477 | 900 | 77 |
| Las Vegas | .264 | 140 | 4669 | 654 | 1232 | 272 | 24 | 126 | 531 | 949 | 74 |

### CLUB PITCHING

| | ERA | G | CG | SHO | SV | IP | H | R | ER | BB | SO |
|---|---|---|---|---|---|---|---|---|---|---|---|
| Edmonton | 4.03 | 142 | 6 | 9 | 28 | 1226 | 1259 | 628 | 549 | 406 | 840 |
| Vancouver | 4.10 | 138 | 25 | 5 | 29 | 1215 | 1175 | 639 | 554 | 530 | 840 |
| Tucson | 4.21 | 144 | 7 | 7 | 28 | 1247 | 1401 | 732 | 583 | 439 | 987 |
| Calgary | 4.30 | 143 | 4 | 6 | 31 | 1240 | 1397 | 691 | 593 | 461 | 788 |
| Tacoma | 4.36 | 142 | 10 | 8 | 28 | 1254 | 1344 | 699 | 608 | 485 | 978 |
| Las Vegas | 4.62 | 140 | 11 | 7 | 35 | 1221 | 1328 | 711 | 627 | 441 | 897 |
| Phoenix | 4.67 | 144 | 5 | 10 | 40 | 1277 | 1354 | 734 | 662 | 513 | 818 |
| Albuquerque | 4.81 | 143 | 5 | 6 | 30 | 1262 | 1409 | 799 | 675 | 598 | 981 |
| Salt Lake | 5.09 | 144 | 13 | 5 | 31 | 1285 | 1501 | 798 | 727 | 486 | 946 |
| Colorado Springs | 5.57 | 142 | 3 | 6 | 31 | 1226 | 1411 | 842 | 759 | 535 | 909 |

### CLUB FIELDING

| | PCT | PO | A | E | DP | | PCT | PO | A | E | DP |
|---|---|---|---|---|---|---|---|---|---|---|---|
| Salt Lake | .978 | 3855 | 1661 | 125 | 137 | Calgary | .973 | 3720 | 1625 | 146 | 128 |
| Las Vegas | .977 | 3664 | 1552 | 123 | 133 | Tacoma | .973 | 3763 | 1508 | 145 | 136 |
| Vancouver | .977 | 3646 | 1520 | 124 | 145 | Colo. Springs | .970 | 3677 | 1491 | 158 | 137 |
| Phoenix | .976 | 3830 | 1616 | 133 | 164 | Albuquerque | .966 | 3786 | 1674 | 193 | 156 |
| Edmonton | .974 | 3679 | 1581 | 141 | 125 | Tucson | .960 | 3742 | 1593 | 224 | 124 |

**Wilton Guerrero**
.344 average

**Brian Raabe**
.351 average

**Bob Milacki**
13-3, 2.74

### INDIVIDUAL BATTING LEADERS
(Minimum 389 Plate Appearances)

| | AVG | G | AB | R | H | 2B | 3B | HR | RBI | BB | SO | SB |
|---|---|---|---|---|---|---|---|---|---|---|---|---|
| Raabe, Brian, Salt Lake | .351 | 116 | 482 | 103 | 169 | 39 | 4 | 18 | 69 | 47 | 19 | 8 |
| Brede, Brent, Salt Lake | .348 | 132 | 483 | 102 | 168 | 38 | 8 | 11 | 86 | 87 | 87 | 14 |
| Guerrero, Wilton, Alb. | .344 | 98 | 425 | 79 | 146 | 17 | 12 | 2 | 38 | 26 | 48 | 26 |
| Walker, Todd, Salt Lake | .339 | 135 | 551 | 94 | 187 | 41 | 9 | 28 | 111 | 57 | 91 | 13 |
| Wilson, Desi, Phoenix | .339 | 113 | 407 | 56 | 138 | 26 | 7 | 5 | 59 | 18 | 80 | 15 |
| Echevarria, Angel, Colo. Spr. | .337 | 110 | 415 | 67 | 140 | 19 | 2 | 16 | 74 | 38 | 81 | 4 |
| Castellano, Pedro, Colo. Spr. | .337 | 94 | 362 | 56 | 122 | 30 | 3 | 13 | 59 | 40 | 46 | 0 |
| Allensworth, Jermain, Cal. | .330 | 95 | 352 | 77 | 116 | 23 | 6 | 8 | 43 | 39 | 61 | 25 |
| Ball, Jeff, Tucson | .324 | 116 | 429 | 64 | 139 | 31 | 2 | 19 | 73 | 34 | 83 | 10 |
| Hajek, Dave, Tucson | .317 | 121 | 508 | 81 | 161 | 31 | 5 | 4 | 64 | 25 | 36 | 9 |

### INDIVIDUAL PITCHING LEADERS
(Minimum 115 Innings)

| | W | L | ERA | G | GS | CG | SV | IP | H | R | ER | BB | SO |
|---|---|---|---|---|---|---|---|---|---|---|---|---|---|
| Milacki, Bob, Tacoma | 13 | 3 | 2.74 | 23 | 23 | 5 | 0 | 164 | 131 | 62 | 50 | 39 | 117 |
| Oquist, Mike, Las Vegas | 9 | 4 | 2.89 | 27 | 20 | 2 | 1 | 140 | 136 | 55 | 45 | 44 | 110 |
| Klingenbeck, Scott, Salt Lake | 9 | 3 | 3.11 | 22 | 22 | 5 | 0 | 151 | 159 | 64 | 52 | 41 | 100 |
| Carlson, Dan, Phoenix | 13 | 6 | 3.44 | 33 | 15 | 2 | 1 | 147 | 135 | 61 | 56 | 46 | 123 |
| Patrick, Bronswell, Tucson | 7 | 3 | 3.51 | 33 | 15 | 0 | 1 | 118 | 137 | 59 | 46 | 33 | 82 |
| Holt, Chris, Tucson | 7 | 9 | 3.63 | 26 | 27 | 4 | 0 | 186 | 209 | 87 | 77 | 38 | 137 |
| Dickson, Jason, Vancouver | 7 | 11 | 3.80 | 18 | 18 | 7 | 0 | 130 | 134 | 73 | 55 | 40 | 70 |
| Hawkins, LaTroy, Salt Lake | 9 | 8 | 3.92 | 20 | 20 | 4 | 0 | 138 | 138 | 66 | 60 | 31 | 99 |
| Bolton, Tom, Calgary | 12 | 5 | 4.02 | 40 | 14 | 0 | 2 | 116 | 121 | 64 | 52 | 47 | 92 |
| May, Darrell, Calgary | 7 | 6 | 4.10 | 23 | 22 | 1 | 0 | 132 | 146 | 64 | 60 | 36 | 75 |

## DEPARTMENT LEADERS

### BATTING

| | | |
|---|---|---|
| G | Scott Spiezio, Edmonton | 140 |
| AB | Neifi Perez, Colo. Springs | 570 |
| R | Brian Raabe, Salt Lake | 103 |
| H | Todd Walker, Salt Lake | 187 |
| TB | Todd Walker, Salt Lake | 330 |
| XBH | Todd Walker, Salt Lake | 78 |
| 2B | Todd Walker, Salt Lake | 41 |
| 3B | Bob Abreu, Tucson | 16 |
| HR | Todd Walker, Salt Lake | 28 |
| RBI | Todd Walker, Salt Lake | 111 |
| SH | Tony Womack, Calgary | 14 |
| SF | Jacob Cruz, Phoenix | 11 |
| BB | Kerwin Moore, Edmonton | 95 |
| IBB | Three tied at | 11 |
| HBP | Jason McDonald, Edmonton | 15 |
| | Tom Quinlan, Salt Lake | 15 |
| SO | Billy Lott, Albuquerque | 124 |
| SB | Kerwin Moore, Edmonton | 38 |
| CS | Bob Abreu, Tucson | 18 |
| GIDP | Aaron Ledesma, Vancouver | 18 |
| OB% | Brent Brede, Salt Lake | .446 |
| SL% | Todd Walker, Salt Lake | .599 |

### PITCHING

| | | |
|---|---|---|
| G | Steve Mintz, Phoenix | 59 |
| GS | Brett Roberts, Salt Lake | 30 |
| | Gary Rath, Albuquerque | 30 |
| CG | Jason Dickson, Vancouver | 7 |
| ShO | Three tied at | 2 |
| GF | Steve Mintz, Phoenix | 45 |
| Sv | Steve Mintz, Phoenix | 27 |
| W | Dan Carlson, Phoenix | 13 |
| | Bob Milacki, Tacoma | 13 |
| | Eric Bell, Tucson | 13 |
| L | Eric Bell, Tucson | 14 |
| IP | Chris Holt, Tucson | 186 |
| H | Brett Roberts, Salt Lake | 211 |
| R | Brett Roberts, Salt Lake | 115 |
| ER | Brett Roberts, Salt Lake | 101 |
| HR | Brett Roberts, Salt Lake | 28 |
| HB | Pete Janicki, Vancouver | 13 |
| BB | Gary Rath, Albuquerque | 89 |
| SO | Travis Miller, Salt Lake | 143 |
| WP | Andres Berumen, Las Vegas | 17 |
| BK | Sal Urso, Tacoma | 6 |

### FIELDING

| | | |
|---|---|---|
| C AVG | Tim Marx, Calgary | .994 |
| PO | Chris Widger, Tacoma | 622 |
| A | Damian Miller, Salt Lake | 70 |
| E | Jerry Goff, Tucson | 11 |
| DP | Ken Huckaby, Alb. | 11 |
| PB | Sean Mulligan, Las Vegas | 14 |
| 1B AVG | Chris Pritchett, Van. | .995 |
| PO | Chris Pritchett, Van. | 1107 |
| A | Chris Pritchett, Van. | 98 |
| E | Jeff Ball, Tucson | 12 |
| DP | Chris Pritchett, Van. | 107 |
| 2B AVG | P.J. Forbes, Vancouver | .986 |
| PO | Jason McDonald, Edm. | 254 |
| A | Jason McDonald, Edm. | 352 |
| E | Jason McDonald, Edm. | 24 |
| DP | Jason McDonald, Edm. | 75 |
| 3B AVG | Scott Spiezio, Edmonton | .970 |
| PO | Scott Spiezio, Edmonton | 91 |
| A | Scott Spiezio, Edmonton | 302 |
| E | Brian Richardson, Alb. | 25 |
| DP | Bill Mueller, Phoenix | 25 |
| SS AVG | Mitch Simons, Salt Lake | .970 |
| PO | Neifi Perez, Colo. Springs | 244 |
| A | Neifi Perez, Colo. Springs | 409 |
| E | Neifi Perez, Colo. Springs | 25 |
| DP | Neifi Perez, Colo. Springs | 91 |
| OF AVG | Riccardo Ingram, LV | 1.000 |
| PO | Kerwin Moore, Edmonton | 284 |
| A | Steve Hazlett, Salt Lake | 17 |
| E | Terry Jones, Colo. Springs | 16 |
| DP | Wm. Pennyfeather, Van. | 6 |

# Senators Return To Accustomed Place

**By ANDREW LINKER**

For most of the 1990s, the Harrisburg Senators have dominated headlines in the Eastern League because they were that good. From 1991 through 1994, they sent prospect after prospect to the parent Montreal Expos.

The headlines in the 1996 season again belonged to the Senators—not because they were good, but because they were so unusually bad in 1995.

As it was, the Senators were good enough in 1996 when it counted most. The EL's streakiest team finished the season with a playoff run that completed the league's first worst-to-first finish since 1987. Ironically, the Senators were the last franchise to accomplish the feat, winning the playoff title in their first year in Harrisburg in 1987 after an '86 season in which their predecessors, the Nashua Pirates, were the worst team in the league.

"To be honest," Harrisburg manager Pat Kelly said of his preseason prediction for the Senators, "I thought we'd be a .500 team."

He was not far off, considering the 74-68 Senators were 47-48 from June 1 through the end of the season before winning six of eight playoff games.

In wiping out Trenton and Portland—the EL's two winningest teams in 1996—a Harrisburg team that had the poorest record of the four playoff teams finished with its second title since 1993.

"We had a lot of ups-and-downs," said outfielder Jon Saffer, one of nine holdovers from a Harrisburg

**Vladimir Guerrero.** Top Expos prospect topped the Eastern League with a .360 average.

team that finished the 1995 season with the EL's worst record at 61-80. "A couple of times, we didn't know which way we were going."

The one Senator always pointed in the right direction was right fielder Vladimir Guerrero, who posted the league's highest batting average (.360) since Tommy Gregg hit .371 for Harrisburg's championship team in 1987.

Guerrero also hit 19 homers and threw out 10 runners from right field. He intimidated countless more from advancing.

Guerrero was named the league's MVP, joining Matt Stairs, Cliff Floyd and Mark Grudzielanek as other Montreal prospects to win the award since the Expos began their Double-A affiliation with Harrisburg in 1991. His franchise-record slugging percentage of .612 was second in the league to the .618 compiled by veteran Trenton outfielder Adam Hyzdu.

While Guerrero ignited the league's fourth-ranked offense, which was hitting .197 when he arrived from Class A West Palm Beach on May 1, the Senators again were blessed with some of Montreal's top pitching prospects.

Righthanders Jose Paniagua, Everett Stull and Neil Weber carried the Senators to the all-star break, from which point Tom Phelps, Mike Thurman and Steve Falteisek pitched the Senators through the playoffs, combining for four of Harrisburg's six victories and a 3.13 ERA.

The Senators also hit .303 against Trenton and

## STANDINGS

| Page | NORTH | W | L | PCT | GB | Manager(s) | Attendance/Dates | Last Pennant |
|------|-------|---|---|-----|-----|-----------|------------------|--------------|
| 128 | Portland Sea Dogs (Marlins) | 83 | 58 | .589 | — | Carlos Tosca | 408,503 (68) | None |
| 178 | Binghamton Mets (Mets) | 76 | 66 | .535 | 7½ | John Tamargo | 202,461 (67) | 1994 |
| 172 | Norwich Navigators (Yankees) | 71 | 70 | .504 | 12 | Jim Essian | 269,022 (65) | None |
| 116 | New Haven Ravens (Rockies) | 66 | 75 | .468 | 17 | Bill Hayes | 254,084 (62) | None |
| 159 | Hardware City Rock Cats (Twins) | 61 | 81 | .430 | 22½ | Al Newman | 160,765 (62) | 1983 |

| Page | SOUTH | W | L | PCT | GB | Manager(s) | Attendance/Dates | Last Pennant |
|------|-------|---|---|-----|-----|-----------|------------------|--------------|
| 77 | Trenton Thunder (Red Sox) | 86 | 56 | .606 | — | Ken Macha | 437,396 (69) | None |
| 165 | Harrisburg Senators (Expos) | 74 | 68 | .521 | 12 | Pat Kelly | 230,744 (64) | 1996 |
| 110 | Canton-Akron Indians (Indians) | 71 | 71 | .500 | 15 | Jeff Datz | 213,278 (65) | None |
| 192 | Reading Phillies (Phillies) | 66 | 75 | .468 | 19½ | Bill Robinson | 375,326 (69) | 1995 |
| 69 | Bowie Baysox (Orioles) | 54 | 88 | .380 | 32 | Miscik/Blackwell | 396,086 (64) | None |

**PLAYOFFS—Semifinals:** Portland defeated Binghamton 3-2, and Harrisburg defeated Trenton 3-1, in best-of-5 series. **Finals:** Harrisburg defeated Portland 3-1, in best-of-5 series.

**NOTE:** Team's individual batting and pitching statistics can be found on page indicated in lefthand column.

Portland, which went a combined 22-10 during the regular season against Harrisburg.

"Come playoff time, it's not really one guy who has to do the job," said Harrisburg outfielder-DH Brad Fullmer, who teamed with third baseman Jose Vidro to hit .459 with four homers and 19 RBIs in the postseason. "To win in the playoffs, you have to get production from everybody, and I think that's what we did."

## Record Setters

Guerrero, whose homer in his final at-bat in the playoffs clinched Harrisburg's 6-1 title victory in Portland, was not the only EL player to post some of the league's best offensive numbers in recent seasons.

Norwich outfielder Shane Spencer led the league with 29 homers, the most since Williamsport's Jeromy Burnitz hit 31 in 1991.

Binghamton third baseman Chris Saunders had 105 RBIs, the most in the EL since Buffalo's Jim Wilson had 105 in 1983.

Portland closer Bill Hurst finished with 30 saves, the EL's highest total since Al Reyes posted a league-record 35 for Harrisburg in 1994 and the second highest since the EL started in 1922.

Reading closer Wayne Gomes appeared in 67 games, a Phillies franchise record that matched the league record set in 1964 by Carlos Medrano of York.

## Rain And Change

For only the second time in 14 seasons, the EL did not have a franchise relocation or affiliation switch in

1996. That, however, will change in 1997, as the Canton-Akron Indians will abandon Canton after eight seasons for a new $30.7 million stadium in Akron.

Another change for 1997 will occur off the field as Bill Troubh begins a one-year term as the league's new president.

Troubh, who was hired just before the start of the playoffs, replaces John Levenda, who was fired after four seasons. Troubh, a former mayor of Portland, was instrumental in bringing the Sea Dogs to Portland in 1994.

All but one of the league's 10 franchises drew more than 200,000 fans in 1996. The exception was Hardware City, which played in a new stadium in New Britain and attracted 160,765.

Because of weather that forced 58 postponements, only three teams—Binghamton, Canton-Akron and Hardware City—improved on their attendance from a 1995 season in which the league suffered only 35 postponements.

## LEAGUE CHAMPIONS

### Last 25 Years

| Year | Regular Season* | Pct. | Playoff |
|------|-----------------|------|---------|
| 1972 | West Haven (Yankees) | .600 | West Haven (Yankees) |
| 1973 | Reading (Phillies) | .551 | Reading (Phillies) |
| | Pittsfield (Rangers) | .551 | |
| 1974 | Bristol (Red Sox) | .548 | Thetford Mines (Pirates) |
| 1975 | Reading (Phillies) | .613 | Bristol (Red Sox) |
| 1976 | Three Rivers (Reds) | .601 | West Haven (Yankees) |
| 1977 | West Haven (Yankees) | .623 | West Haven (Yankees) |
| 1978 | West Haven (Yankees) | .589 | Bristol (Red Sox) |
| 1979 | West Haven (Yankees) | .597 | None |
| 1980 | Bristol (Red Sox) | .568 | Holyoke (Brewers) |
| 1981 | Glens Falls (White Sox) | .615 | Bristol (Red Sox) |
| 1982 | West Haven (Athletics) | .614 | West Haven (Athletics) |
| 1983 | Reading (Phillies) | .686 | New Britain (Red Sox) |
| 1984 | Albany (Athletics) | .586 | Vermont (Reds) |
| 1985 | Albany (Yankees) | .589 | Vermont (Reds) |
| 1986 | Reading (Phillies) | .566 | Vermont (Reds) |
| 1987 | Pittsfield (Cubs) | .630 | Harrisburg (Pirates) |
| 1988 | Glens Falls (Tigers) | .583 | Albany (Yankees) |
| 1989 | Albany (Yankees) | .657 | Albany (Yankees) |
| 1990 | Albany (Yankees) | .568 | London (Tigers) |
| 1991 | Harrisburg (Expos) | .621 | Albany (Yankees) |
| 1992 | Canton-Akron (Indians) | .580 | Binghamton (Mets) |
| 1993 | Harrisburg (Expos) | .681 | Harrisburg (Expos) |
| 1994 | Harrisburg (Expos) | .633 | Binghamton (Mets) |
| 1995 | Portland (Marlins) | .606 | Reading (Phillies) |
| 1996 | Trenton (Red Sox) | .606 | Harrisburg (Expos) |

*Best overall record

DAVID SCHOFIELD

**Shane Spencer.** Norwich outfielder led the Eastern League with 29 home runs in 1996.

# EASTERN LEAGUE
## 1996 BATTING, PITCHING STATISTICS

### CLUB BATTING

| | AVG | G | AB | R | H | 2B | 3B | HR | BB | SO | SB |
|---|---|---|---|---|---|---|---|---|---|---|---|
| Canton-Akron | .280 | 142 | 4913 | 768 | 1377 | 248 | 46 | 142 | 431 | 896 | 105 |
| Portland | .275 | 141 | 4726 | 694 | 1301 | 260 | 38 | 106 | 476 | 907 | 153 |
| Trenton | .269 | 142 | 4677 | 751 | 1259 | 228 | 33 | 150 | 566 | 924 | 134 |
| Harrisburg | .261 | 142 | 4580 | 620 | 1195 | 233 | 29 | 110 | 515 | 881 | 72 |
| Norwich | .258 | 141 | 4619 | 675 | 1193 | 235 | 21 | 126 | 521 | 1016 | 82 |
| Hardware City | .255 | 142 | 4605 | 617 | 1174 | 227 | 26 | 137 | 446 | 950 | 71 |
| Binghamton | .253 | 142 | 4582 | 662 | 1160 | 204 | 27 | 103 | 572 | 867 | 109 |
| Bowie | .252 | 142 | 4730 | 582 | 1193 | 227 | 24 | 114 | 417 | 968 | 86 |
| Reading | .252 | 141 | 4686 | 684 | 1179 | 226 | 39 | 132 | 554 | 1056 | 130 |
| New Haven | .241 | 141 | 4502 | 510 | 1084 | 193 | 24 | 77 | 465 | 893 | 41 |

### CLUB PITCHING

| | ERA | G | CG | SHO | SV | IP | H | R | ER | BB | SO |
|---|---|---|---|---|---|---|---|---|---|---|---|
| Norwich | 3.63 | 141 | 11 | 11 | 33 | 1209 | 1154 | 633 | 488 | 523 | 979 |
| Harrisburg | 3.67 | 142 | 6 | 10 | 44 | 1219 | 1169 | 592 | 498 | 529 | 813 |
| Portland | 3.72 | 141 | 12 | 7 | 45 | 1233 | 1206 | 609 | 509 | 387 | 986 |
| New Haven | 3.84 | 141 | 7 | 14 | 37 | 1200 | 1151 | 609 | 512 | 496 | 1016 |
| Binghamton | 4.05 | 142 | 17 | 8 | 40 | 1225 | 1268 | 626 | 551 | 412 | 851 |
| Trenton | 4.11 | 142 | 15 | 8 | 39 | 1232 | 1170 | 644 | 563 | 494 | 896 |
| Canton-Akron | 4.15 | 142 | 8 | 4 | 33 | 1228 | 1190 | 663 | 566 | 530 | 1020 |
| Reading | 4.37 | 141 | 6 | 8 | 26 | 1236 | 1221 | 717 | 600 | 576 | 1026 |
| Hardware City | 4.61 | 142 | 13 | 7 | 24 | 1207 | 1278 | 726 | 619 | 513 | 886 |
| Bowie | 4.71 | 142 | 8 | 8 | 25 | 1234 | 1308 | 744 | 646 | 503 | 885 |

### CLUB FIELDING

| | PCT | PO | A | E | DP | | PCT | PO | A | E | DP |
|---|---|---|---|---|---|---|---|---|---|---|---|
| Binghamton | .976 | 3674 | 1684 | 133 | 137 | New Haven | .970 | 3599 | 1480 | 159 | 117 |
| Trenton | .972 | 3695 | 1510 | 148 | 135 | Reading | .969 | 3708 | 1482 | 165 | 129 |
| Bowie | .972 | 3703 | 1509 | 151 | 99 | Canton-Akron | .969 | 3684 | 1502 | 167 | 127 |
| Portland | .972 | 3698 | 1662 | 157 | 155 | Hardware City | .968 | 3622 | 1455 | 168 | 109 |
| Harrisburg | .971 | 3657 | 1587 | 158 | 137 | Norwich | .962 | 3626 | 1521 | 205 | 109 |

**Adam Hyzdu**
.337 for Trenton

**Carl Pavano**
16 wins, 2.63 ERA

### INDIVIDUAL BATTING LEADERS
(Minimum 383 Plate Appearances)

| | AVG | G | AB | R | H | 2B | 3B | HR | RBI | BB | SO | SB |
|---|---|---|---|---|---|---|---|---|---|---|---|---|
| Guerrero, Vladimir, Harr. | .360 | 118 | 417 | 84 | 150 | 32 | 8 | 19 | 78 | 51 | 42 | 17 |
| Hyzdu, Adam, Trenton | .337 | 109 | 374 | 71 | 126 | 24 | 3 | 25 | 80 | 56 | 75 | 1 |
| Ramirez, Alex, Canton | .329 | 131 | 513 | 79 | 169 | 28 | 12 | 14 | 85 | 16 | 74 | 18 |
| Millar, Kevin, Portland | .318 | 130 | 472 | 69 | 150 | 32 | 0 | 18 | 86 | 37 | 53 | 6 |
| Castillo, Luis, Portland | .317 | 109 | 420 | 83 | 133 | 15 | 7 | 1 | 35 | 66 | 68 | 51 |
| Woods, Tyrone, Trenton | .312 | 99 | 356 | 75 | 111 | 16 | 2 | 25 | 71 | 56 | 66 | 5 |
| Burton, Essex, Reading | .304 | 102 | 381 | 66 | 116 | 19 | 5 | 1 | 30 | 37 | 56 | 40 |
| Wilson, Enrique, Canton | .304 | 117 | 484 | 70 | 147 | 17 | 5 | 5 | 50 | 31 | 46 | 23 |
| Berg, Dave, Portland | .302 | 109 | 414 | 64 | 125 | 28 | 5 | 9 | 73 | 42 | 60 | 17 |
| McKeel, Walt, Trenton | .302 | 128 | 464 | 86 | 140 | 19 | 1 | 16 | 78 | 60 | 52 | 2 |

### INDIVIDUAL PITCHING LEADERS
(Minimum 114 Innings)

| | W | L | ERA | G | GS | CG | SV | IP | H | R | ER | BB | SO |
|---|---|---|---|---|---|---|---|---|---|---|---|---|---|
| Pavano, Carl, Trenton | 16 | 5 | 2.63 | 27 | 26 | 6 | 0 | 185 | 154 | 66 | 54 | 47 | 146 |
| Saunders, Tony, Portland | 13 | 4 | 2.63 | 26 | 26 | 2 | 0 | 168 | 121 | 51 | 49 | 62 | 156 |
| Pedraza, Rodney, NH | 7 | 3 | 2.95 | 19 | 18 | 3 | 0 | 122 | 115 | 49 | 40 | 21 | 74 |
| Saipe, Mike, New Haven | 10 | 7 | 3.07 | 32 | 19 | 1 | 3 | 138 | 114 | 53 | 47 | 42 | 126 |
| Beech, Matt, Reading | 11 | 6 | 3.17 | 21 | 21 | 0 | 0 | 133 | 108 | 57 | 47 | 32 | 132 |
| Maduro, Calvin, Bowie | 9 | 7 | 3.26 | 19 | 19 | 4 | 0 | 124 | 116 | 50 | 45 | 36 | 87 |
| Lidle, Cory, Binghamton | 4 | 10 | 3.31 | 27 | 27 | 6 | 0 | 190 | 186 | 78 | 70 | 49 | 141 |
| Brownson, Mark, NH | 8 | 13 | 3.50 | 37 | 19 | 1 | 3 | 144 | 141 | 73 | 56 | 43 | 155 |
| Guerra, Mark, Binghamton | 7 | 6 | 3.53 | 27 | 20 | 1 | 0 | 140 | 143 | 60 | 55 | 34 | 84 |
| Driskill, Travis, Canton | 13 | 7 | 3.61 | 29 | 24 | 4 | 0 | 172 | 169 | 89 | 69 | 63 | 148 |

## DEPARTMENT LEADERS

### BATTING
| | | |
|---|---|---|
| G | Chris Saunders, Binghamton | 141 |
| AB | Todd Dunwoody, Portland | 552 |
| R | Jon Saffer, Harrisburg | 96 |
| H | Alex Ramirez, Canton-Akron | 169 |
| TB | Todd Dunwoody, Portland | 267 |
| XBH | Todd Dunwoody, Portland | 60 |
| 2B | Todd Carey, Trenton | 34 |
| 3B | Alex Ramirez, Canton-Akron | 12 |
| HR | Shane Spencer, Norwich | 29 |
| RBI | Chris Saunders, Binghamton | 105 |
| SH | Essex Burton, Reading | 16 |
| SF | Chris Saunders, Binghamton | 11 |
| BB | Kevin Riggs, Norwich | 81 |
| IBB | Vladimir Guerrero, Harrisburg | 13 |
| HBP | Dan Held, Reading | 22 |
| SO | Todd Dunwoody, Portland | 149 |
| SB | Luis Castillo, Portland | 51 |
| CS | Luis Castillo, Portland | 28 |
| GIDP | Dan Donato, Norwich | 19 |
| OB% | Vladimir Guerrero, Harrisburg | .438 |
| SL% | Adam Hyzdu, Trenton | .618 |

### PITCHING
| | | |
|---|---|---|
| G | Wayne Gomes, Reading | 67 |
| GS | Jared Fernandez, Trenton | 29 |
| CG | Carl Pavano, Trenton | 6 |
| | Cory Lidle, Binghamton | 6 |
| ShO | Calvin Maduro, Bowie | 3 |
| GF | Wayne Gomes, Reading | 55 |
| Sv | William Hurst, Portland | 30 |
| W | Carl Pavano, Trenton | 16 |
| L | Three tied at | 13 |
| IP | Cory Lidle, Binghamton | 190 |
| H | Carlton Loewer, Reading | 191 |
| R | Carlton Loewer, Reading | 115 |
| | Jared Fernandez, Trenton | 115 |
| ER | Jared Fernandez, Trenton | 101 |
| HR | Carlton Loewer, Reading | 24 |
| HB | Tony Costa, Reading | 14 |
| BB | Tony Costa, Reading | 92 |
| SO | Tony Saunders, Portland | 156 |
| WP | Carlos Chavez, Bowie | 19 |
| BK | Four tied at | 4 |

### FIELDING
| | | |
|---|---|---|
| C AVG | Mike Redmond, Portland | .996 |
| PO | Mike Redmond, Portland | 814 |
| A | Bob Henley, Harrisburg | 92 |
| E | Einar Diaz, Canton-Akron | 15 |
| DP | Bob Henley, Harrisburg | 11 |
| | Walt McKeel, Trenton | 11 |
| PB | Walt McKeel, Trenton | 17 |
| 1B AVG | Tommy Davis, Bowie | .995 |
| PO | Tommy Davis, Bowie | 1158 |
| A | Brian Daubach, Bing. | 115 |
| E | Dan Held, Reading | 12 |
| DP | Dan Held, Reading | 111 |
| 2B AVG | Luis Castillo, Portland | .975 |
| PO | Howie Clark, Bowie | 249 |
| A | Luis Castillo, Portland | 326 |
| E | Chris Allison, Trenton | 21 |
| DP | Luis Castillo, Portland | 87 |
| 3B AVG | Todd Carey, Trenton | .941 |
| PO | Willis Otanez, Bowie | 106 |
| A | Chris Saunders, Bing. | 327 |
| E | Dan Donato, Norwich | 25 |
| | Chris Saunders, Bing. | 25 |
| DP | Jamie Taylor, New Haven | 30 |
| SS AVG | Kevin Morgan, Binghamton | .956 |
| PO | Juan Bautista, Bowie | 203 |
| A | Juan Bautista, Bowie | 354 |
| E | Juan Bautista, Bowie | 29 |
| DP | Enrique Wilson, Canton | 74 |
| OF AVG | Todd Dunwoody, Portland | .996 |
| PO | Bruce Aven, Canton-Akron | 280 |
| A | Trot Nixon, Trenton | 14 |
| E | Derrick Gibson, New Haven | 13 |
| DP | Trot Nixon, Trenton | 4 |
| | Scott Shores, Reading | 4 |

# SOUTHERN LEAGUE

## Jacksonville Wins Title In Weird Year

**By LARRY STARKS**

Jacksonville won its first-ever Southern League title, fast-charging Chattanooga advanced to the championship round of the playoffs for the second straight year and a permanent home finally was found for the league's vagabond franchise that was temporarily housed in Wilmington, N.C., in 1995-96.

On the field, 10 Southern Leaguers went on to play in the big leagues in 1996, including teenage phenom Andruw Jones of the Greenville Braves. Jones, Baseball America's two-time Minor League Player of the Year, made a 38-game cameo for Greenville, hitting .369 with 12 home runs.

In many regards, it should have been a giddy year in the Southern League in 1996. Instead, the focus shifted to an awkward schedule and the eventual relocation of two troubled franchises.

The unwieldy schedule took center stage from the outset. In a league that has some of the longest bus rides in the minor leagues, teams played 23 two-game series and three one-day doubleheader trips were mixed in.

In July, the Knoxville Smokies came off a six-game road swing, had a two-games series at home, then left for a two-game series in Huntsville, a two-game series in Jacksonville, and then doubled back to Huntsville for a two-game series—all without an off day.

A permanent home, meanwhile, was found in Mobile, Ala., for the nomadic Port City Roosters, who were housed in Wilmington for two years after previously operating on an interim basis for two years in Nashville.

The franchise originally lost its home in 1993, when Charlotte, N.C., then a member of the Southern League, was awarded a Triple-A expansion franchise. Since then, the league attempted to relocate the team in a number of cities—New Orleans; Lexington, Ky.; Springfield, Mo.; and San Juan, P.R., to name the most prominent—but to no avail.

In Wilmington, a last-place team attracted only

**Derrek Lee.** First baseman led Memphis to Southern League's best overall record on way to MVP award.

68,463 spectators—less than half the next least popular club in Double-A. The team will move to new Henry Aaron Stadium in Mobile for 1997 and be known as the BayBears.

The most shocking franchise development came two weeks after the title was decided. The Memphis Chicks, who have been an intregal part of the Southern League since 1978, signed a 15-year contract to play in Jackson, Tenn., beginning in 1998.

Despite posting the league's best overall record in 1996, the Chicks suffered their second consecutive downturn in attendance at rundown Tim McCarver Stadium, drawing 197,084. Two years earlier, the Chicks attracted 258,311.

The Chicks announced they would skip town because

## STANDINGS: OVERALL

| Page | | W | L | PCT | GB | Manager(s) | Attendance/Dates | Last Pennant |
|------|---|---|---|-----|----|-----------|--------|--------------|
| 210 | **Memphis Chicks (Padres)** | 81 | 58 | .583 | — | Ed Romero | 197,084 (66) | 1990 |
| 105 | **Chattanooga Lookouts (Reds)** | 81 | 59 | .579 | ½ | Mark Berry | 227,885 (67) | 1988 |
| 122 | **Jacksonville Suns (Tigers)** | 75 | 63 | .543 | 5 ½ | Plummer/Parrish | 219,947 (67) | 1996 |
| 236 | **Knoxville Smokies (Blue Jays)** | 75 | 65 | .536 | 6 ½ | Omar Malave | 142,537 (66) | 1978 |
| 90 | **Birmingham Barons (White Sox)** | 74 | 65 | .532 | 7 | Mike Heath | 296,131 (69) | 1993 |
| 198 | **Carolina Mudcats (Pirates)** | 70 | 69 | .504 | 11 | Marc Hill | 278,361 (66) | 1995 |
| 185 | **Huntsville Stars (Athletics)** | 66 | 74 | .471 | 15 ½ | Dick Scott | 255,139 (66) | 1994 |
| 97 | **Orlando Cubs (Cubs)** | 60 | 78 | .439 | 20 ½ | Bruce Kimm | 175,399 (67) | 1991 |
| 62 | **Greenville Braves (Braves)** | 58 | 82 | .414 | 23 ½ | Jeff Cox | 230,124 (66) | 1992 |
| 223 | **Port City Roosters (Mariners)** | 56 | 84 | .400 | 25 ½ | Orlando Gomez | 68,463 (67) | None |

**NOTE:** Team's individual batting and pitching statistics can be found on page indicated in lefthand column.

of the city of Memphis's refusal to help fund a new stadium. Jackson (pop. 50,000), which had been trying to lure a professional team since 1990 and once was a candidate for the since-relocated Mobile franchise, already had approved $8 million toward the building of a new stadium.

The stadium issue has plagued the Chicks for years. They had an agreement in 1995 to swap franchises with the Triple-A Nashville Sounds, but the American Association, of which Nashville is a member, required the Chicks to get a binding commitment for a new stadium before approving the switch. The Chicks were unable to secure a commitment. Jackson would become the smallest market in Double-A.

# Suns End Dry Spell

The most surprising on-field development was the success of the Jacksonville Suns, who won that city's first league title in 40 years.

The Suns won the the first half of the Eastern Division and promptly fired manager Bill Plummer, who was replaced by Detroit Tigers organization hitting instructor Larry Parrish. Despite promoting several players in the second half to Triple-A Toledo, including outfielder Bubba Trammell, who hit .328 with 27 homers in 83 games, and Mike Drumright, the league's top pitching prospect, the Suns managed to win the second-half title as well.

They beat defending champion Carolina in five games in the Eastern Division playoffs, lost the first game of the championship series to Chattanooga and swept the Lookouts in the next three games.

After a typically slow first-half performance, defending champion Chattanooga came alive in the second half and cruised to the second-half title in the West, posting a 48-22 record. The Lookouts won their second straight Western Division title, beating Memphis, 3-1.

Memphis raced to a 47-23 record in winning its second straight first-half Western Division title, but limped home with a sub-.500 record in the second half and was eliminated in the first round by Chattanooga.

The Chicks had five of San Diego's top 10 minor league prospects, including first baseman Derrek Lee, who homered in six straight games on his way to a league-high 34. He also led the league with 104 RBIs and was selected the Southern League MVP.

Veteran Memphis DH Dan Rohrmeier hit .344—the fourth time in his 11-year minor league career he has hit better than .300—to win the batting title. He also added a career-high 28 homers and 95 RBIs.

Birmingham outfielder Mike Cameron, who played briefly with the Chicago White Sox for the second straight season, finally became the offensive threat he was expected to be. He hit .300 with 28 homers and led the league in runs (120) and stolen bases (39).

Chattanooga third baseman Aaron Boone, whose grandfather Ray, father Bob and brother Bret have all played in the big leagues, had a breakthrough season, leading Chattanooga in six offensive categories, including a league-record 44 doubles.

**Mike Cameron**

# SOUTHERN LEAGUE
## 1996 BATTING, PITCHING STATISTICS

### CLUB BATTING

| | AVG | G | AB | R | H | 2B | 3B | HR | BB | SO | SB |
|---|---|---|---|---|---|---|---|---|---|---|---|
| Chattanooga | .273 | 140 | 4700 | 687 | 1284 | 270 | 32 | 104 | 469 | 897 | 139 |
| Knoxville | .270 | 140 | 4685 | 708 | 1264 | 263 | 41 | 113 | 620 | 1028 | 103 |
| Jacksonville | .266 | 138 | 4617 | 725 | 1227 | 238 | 35 | 200 | 451 | 1081 | 103 |
| Birmingham | .266 | 139 | 4676 | 670 | 1242 | 260 | 26 | 120 | 502 | 896 | 93 |
| Memphis | .265 | 139 | 4563 | 714 | 1208 | 245 | 35 | 136 | 550 | 981 | 107 |
| Huntsville | .262 | 140 | 4646 | 748 | 1219 | 229 | 31 | 120 | 584 | 993 | 98 |
| Greenville | .262 | 140 | 4625 | 667 | 1210 | 250 | 25 | 106 | 461 | 958 | 84 |
| Carolina | .259 | 139 | 4550 | 617 | 1178 | 220 | 40 | 69 | 540 | 968 | 175 |
| Orlando | .252 | 139 | 4593 | 643 | 1158 | 223 | 34 | 84 | 557 | 912 | 116 |
| Port City | .252 | 140 | 4717 | 591 | 1189 | 234 | 34 | 48 | 551 | 833 | 142 |

### CLUB PITCHING

| | ERA | G | CG | SHO | SV | IP | H | R | ER | BB | SO |
|---|---|---|---|---|---|---|---|---|---|---|---|
| Memphis | 3.69 | 139 | 8 | 11 | 40 | 1219 | 1125 | 599 | 500 | 510 | 1106 |
| Birmingham | 3.94 | 139 | 9 | 7 | 40 | 1222 | 1190 | 624 | 535 | 493 | 1017 |
| Chattanooga | 4.00 | 140 | 7 | 11 | 51 | 1218 | 1153 | 637 | 542 | 520 | 1013 |
| Jacksonville | 4.06 | 138 | 6 | 10 | 37 | 1198 | 1219 | 683 | 541 | 550 | 859 |
| Carolina | 4.18 | 139 | 1 | 10 | 35 | 1209 | 1226 | 641 | 562 | 456 | 969 |
| Knoxville | 4.22 | 140 | 2 | 12 | 40 | 1215 | 1223 | 673 | 570 | 582 | 1013 |
| Port City | 4.36 | 140 | 5 | 5 | 31 | 1239 | 1221 | 702 | 600 | 591 | 869 |
| Orlando | 4.37 | 139 | 6 | 5 | 27 | 1199 | 1259 | 699 | 582 | 503 | 910 |
| Huntsville | 4.58 | 140 | 8 | 9 | 22 | 1208 | 1257 | 743 | 615 | 526 | 950 |
| Greenville | 5.14 | 140 | 2 | 1 | 35 | 1192 | 1306 | 769 | 681 | 554 | 841 |

### CLUB FIELDING

| | PCT | PO | A | E | DP | | PCT | PO | A | E | DP |
|---|---|---|---|---|---|---|---|---|---|---|---|
| Knoxville | .972 | 3644 | 1508 | 148 | 152 | Greenville | .970 | 3577 | 1414 | 153 | 119 |
| Port City | .972 | 3717 | 1607 | 153 | 146 | Memphis | .968 | 3657 | 1407 | 169 | 107 |
| Chattanooga | .972 | 3655 | 1435 | 147 | 131 | Jacksonville | .967 | 3595 | 1645 | 177 | 147 |
| Birmingham | .972 | 3667 | 1452 | 148 | 109 | Orlando | .967 | 3598 | 1370 | 170 | 113 |
| Carolina | .970 | 3626 | 1499 | 156 | 131 | Huntsville | .966 | 3625 | 1529 | 182 | 128 |

**Phil Nevin**
.294-24-69

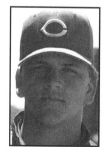

**Curt Lyons**
13-4, 2.41

**Brian Moehler**
15-6, 3.48

### INDIVIDUAL BATTING LEADERS
(Minimum 378 Plate Appearances)

| | AVG | G | AB | R | H | 2B | 3B | HR | RBI | BB | SO | SB |
|---|---|---|---|---|---|---|---|---|---|---|---|---|
| Rohrmeier, Dan, Memphis | .344 | 134 | 471 | 98 | 162 | 29 | 2 | 28 | 95 | 77 | 76 | 2 |
| Brown, Ray, Chattanooga | .327 | 115 | 364 | 68 | 119 | 26 | 5 | 13 | 52 | 52 | 62 | 2 |
| Malloy, Marty, Greenville | .312 | 111 | 429 | 82 | 134 | 27 | 2 | 4 | 36 | 54 | 50 | 11 |
| Santana, Ruben, Chatt. | .309 | 98 | 343 | 47 | 106 | 21 | 2 | 8 | 56 | 26 | 39 | 5 |
| Staton, T.J., Carolina | .308 | 112 | 386 | 72 | 119 | 24 | 3 | 15 | 57 | 58 | 99 | 17 |
| Patzke, Jeff, Knoxville | .303 | 124 | 429 | 70 | 130 | 31 | 4 | 4 | 66 | 80 | 103 | 6 |
| Cameron, Mike, Birm. | .300 | 123 | 473 | 120 | 142 | 34 | 12 | 28 | 77 | 71 | 117 | 39 |
| Catalanotto, Frank, Jax | .298 | 132 | 497 | 105 | 148 | 4 | 6 | 17 | 67 | 74 | 69 | 15 |
| Hall, Billy, Chattanooga | .295 | 117 | 461 | 80 | 136 | 24 | 3 | 2 | 43 | 57 | 72 | 34 |
| Bako, Paul, Chattanooga | .294 | 110 | 360 | 53 | 106 | 7 | 0 | 8 | 48 | 48 | 93 | 1 |
| Nevin, Phil, Jacksonville | .294 | 98 | 344 | 77 | 101 | 18 | 1 | 24 | 69 | 60 | 83 | 6 |

### INDIVIDUAL PITCHING LEADERS
(Minimum 112 Innings)

| | W | L | ERA | G | GS | CG | SV | IP | H | R | ER | BB | SO |
|---|---|---|---|---|---|---|---|---|---|---|---|---|---|
| Dennis, Shane, Memphis | 9 | 1 | 2.27 | 19 | 19 | 1 | 0 | 115 | 83 | 35 | 29 | 45 | 131 |
| Lyons, Curt, Chattanooga | 13 | 4 | 2.41 | 24 | 24 | 1 | 0 | 142 | 113 | 48 | 38 | 52 | 176 |
| Cruz, Nelson, Birmingham | 6 | 6 | 3.20 | 37 | 18 | 2 | 1 | 149 | 150 | 65 | 53 | 41 | 142 |
| Murray, Heath, Memphis | 13 | 9 | 3.21 | 27 | 27 | 1 | 0 | 174 | 154 | 83 | 62 | 60 | 156 |
| Beatty, Blaine, Carolina | 11 | 5 | 3.29 | 23 | 22 | 1 | 0 | 145 | 135 | 58 | 53 | 34 | 117 |
| Moehler, Brian, Jacksonville | 15 | 6 | 3.48 | 28 | 28 | 1 | 0 | 173 | 186 | 80 | 67 | 50 | 120 |
| Halperin, Mike, Knoxville | 13 | 7 | 3.48 | 28 | 28 | 0 | 0 | 155 | 156 | 67 | 60 | 71 | 112 |
| Kaufman, Brad, Memphis | 12 | 10 | 3.63 | 29 | 29 | 3 | 0 | 178 | 161 | 84 | 72 | 83 | 163 |
| Pratt, Rich, Birmingham | 13 | 9 | 3.86 | 27 | 27 | 5 | 0 | 177 | 180 | 87 | 76 | 40 | 122 |
| Tomko, Brett, Chattanooga | 11 | 7 | 3.88 | 27 | 27 | 0 | 0 | 158 | 131 | 73 | 68 | 54 | 164 |

# Generals Take Command Of Playoffs

**By GEORGE SCHROEDER**

The Jackson Generals were missing-in-action in the second half of the Texas League season, but got hot at the right time to capture the 1996 championship.

After winning the first-half Eastern Division title, the Generals faded to last place in the second half. To make matters worse, they lost standout players Richard Hidalgo and Melvin Mora to injuries in the same game just before the playoffs. And all-star shortstop Russ Johnson was hampered by a strained hamstring.

But the Generals overcame their adversity and raced to a 7-1 postseason record, including a four-game sweep of Western Division champion Wichita, for their second title in four years.

"It was one of the most complete team efforts I've ever been around in 19 years of pro ball," Jackson manager Dave Engle said. "It was a different hero every night. It was a very special thing, the Jackson Generals in the playoffs this year . . . This team realized it was probably undermanned, but there was no stopping these guys."

The Generals won with pitching. Jackson starters did not give up an earned run in 28 innings during their sweep of Wichita.

"They absolutely kept everybody off balance," Engle said.

Jackson won the final game, 7-3, at Wichita, behind righthander Scott Elarton, who spent all of the regular season at Class A Kissimmee before being recalled. He won two playoff games.

The Generals won the first-half division title when Tulsa backed out of the race. The Drillers went into the final weekend needing to win only one of three games against Shreveport to clinch, but lost all three.

"We just didn't get it done," Tulsa manager Bobby Jones said. "We couldn't do anything right. It was probably the worst baseball we've played the whole season, and we had to play it when the title was on the

**Paul Konerko.** San Antonio first baseman selected league's top prospect.

line. Maybe that was the reason."

But the Drillers took the division lead late in the second half after Arkansas, which led most of the way, faltered. The Travelers lost eight of their last nine games—including their last five at home to Shreveport—and Tulsa clinched on the next-to-last day of the regular season, setting up a best-of-5 series with Jackson. The Generals won in four games.

Wichita took a similar path to the championship series.

The Wranglers won the first-half title in the Western Division but hampered by promotions to key playes like catcher Mike Sweeney, second baseman Jed Hansen and pitchers Brian Bevil and Steve Olsen, they struggled in the second half.

## Impressive Staff

Arkansas failed to reach postseason play but had one of the strongest pitching rotations in recent league history.

Four starters—righthanders Manuel Aybar (8-6, 3.05 ERA, second), Brady Raggio (9-10, 3.22, fourth) and Matt Morris (12-12, 3.88, 10th), and lefthander Kris Detmers (12-8, 3.35, sixth)—finished among the Top 10 in ERA.

Led by Morris, the Cardinals' first-round draft pick in 1995, the Travs staff was dominant at times. Only a 28-2 spanking by Shreveport in the season finale dropped Arkansas from first place in the team ERA race.

"The only thing I can relate to it at any level is the Atlanta Braves," Engle said.

The league's top prospect, as judged by a poll of managers, was San Antonio slugger Paul Konerko, 20, the Los Angeles Dodgers' latest phenom.

Konerko began the 1996 season as the youngest player in Double-A and proved more than ready for the Texas League as he completed a move from catch-

## STANDINGS: OVERALL

| Page | | W | L | PCT | GB | Manager | Attendance/Dates | Last Pennant |
|---|---|---|---|---|---|---|---|---|
| 154 | **El Paso Diablos (Brewers)** | 76 | 63 | .547 | — | Dave Machemer | 292,074 (63) | 1994 |
| 230 | **Tulsa Drillers (Rangers)** | 75 | 64 | .540 | 1 | Bobby Jones | 343,196 (69) | 1988 |
| 216 | **Shreveport Captains (Giants)** | 73 | 66 | .525 | 3 | Frank Cacciatore | 179,584 (63) | 1995 |
| 140 | **Wichita Wranglers (Royals)** | 70 | 70 | .500 | 6½ | Ron Johnson | 186,084 (70) | 1992 |
| 135 | **Jackson Generals (Astros)** | 70 | 70 | .500 | 6½ | Dave Engle | 179,423 (65) | 1996 |
| 147 | **San Antonio Missions (Dodgers)** | 69 | 70 | .496 | 7 | John Shelby | 381,001 (69) | None |
| 204 | **Arkansas Travelers (Cardinals)** | 67 | 73 | .479 | 9½ | Rick Mahler | 209,535 (61) | 1989 |
| 84 | **Midland Angels (Angels)** | 58 | 82 | .414 | 18½ | Mario Mendoza | 203,011 (66) | 1975 |

**NOTE:** Team's individual batting and pitching statistics can be found on page indicated in lefthand column.

er to first base.

Playing in the unfriendly confines of San Antonio's Nelson Wolff Municipal Stadium, known for a fierce wind that blows in from center field, Konerko hit .300 with 29 homers and 86 RBIs.

"He's got the whole package," Dodgers farm director Charlie Blaney said. "Not only does he have the physical ability, but he has the make-up. He has the work habits and the professional attitude."

## The Bubba Factor

Konerko didn't lead the league in home runs or RBIs. Those honors went to Tulsa journeyman first baseman-DH Bubba Smith, who hit 32 home runs and had 94 RBIs. He became a fan favorite throughout the league for his hitting—and his name.

Playing for his fourth organization in six years, Smith, 26, found new life in the Texas League and was

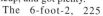

named the league's Player of the Year.

Smith had won consecutive Player of the Year honors in the Carolina League in 1992-93 for two different organizations, but had never played full-time at the Double-A level. The Texas Rangers signed Smith, hoping to add punch to the Drillers lineup, and got plenty.

**Matt Morris** The 6-foot-2, 225 pound Smith had 60 extra-base hits (second in the league), 150 hits (third), a .534 slugging percentage (third) and 82 runs (fifth).

"I knew my time was running out," Smith said. "I either had to go to Double-A and put up some numbers

### STANDINGS: SPLIT SEASON

#### FIRST HALF

| EAST | W | L | PCT | GB |
|---|---|---|---|---|
| Jackson | 37 | 31 | .544 | — |
| Tulsa | 36 | 32 | .529 | 1 |
| Shreveport | 36 | 32 | .529 | 1 |
| Arkansas | 30 | 38 | .441 | 7 |

| WEST | W | L | PCT | GB |
|---|---|---|---|---|
| Wichita | 38 | 30 | .559 | — |
| El Paso | 34 | 34 | .500 | 4 |
| Midland | 31 | 37 | .456 | 7 |
| San Antonio | 30 | 38 | .441 | 8 |

#### SECOND HALF

| EAST | W | L | PCT | GB |
|---|---|---|---|---|
| Tulsa | 39 | 32 | .549 | — |
| Shreveport | 37 | 34 | .521 | 2 |
| Arkansas | 37 | 35 | .514 | 2½ |
| Jackson | 33 | 39 | .458 | 6½ |

| WEST | W | L | PCT | GB |
|---|---|---|---|---|
| El Paso | 42 | 29 | .592 | — |
| San Antonio | 39 | 32 | .549 | 3 |
| Wichita | 32 | 40 | .444 | 10½ |
| Midland | 27 | 45 | .375 | 15½ |

**PLAYOFFS—Semifinals:** Jackson defeated Tulsa 3-1, and Wichita defeated El Paso 3-1, in best-of-5 series. **Finals:** Jackson defeated Wichita 4-0, in best-of-7 series.

or step aside and find another career . . . I think I may have bought myself another year."

Shreveport righthander Keith Foulke, 23, was named Pitcher of the Year after going 12-7 with a league-best 2.76 ERA in his second full professional season.

## Diablos Franchise Sold

Long-time El Paso owner Jim Paul sold the Diablos after 21 years.

Paul, 52, who bought the Diablos in 1975 for $1,000, said the offer was too good to pass up. He sold the team to Diamond Sports, Inc., of Boise, Idaho. Terms of the sale were not disclosed, but it was expected that the club went for in excess of $4 million.

"I'm financially secure for the rest of my life, really," said Paul, who will remain as the team's president and run day-to-day operations.

**Bubba Smith**

El Paso finished third in the league in attendance, behind San Antonio and Tulsa. The league finished with more than 1.97 million fans, a drop of more than 77,000 from the previous season.

### LEAGUE CHAMPIONS

**Last 25 Years**

| Year | Regular Season* | Pct. | Playoff |
|---|---|---|---|
| 1972 | Alexandria (Padres) | .600 | El Paso (Dodgers) |
| 1973 | San Antonio (Indians) | .589 | Memphis (Mets) |
| 1974 | Victoria (Mets) | .580 | Victoria (Mets) |
| 1975 | Midland (Cubs) | .604 | Midland (Cubs)# Lafayette (Giants)# |
| 1976 | Amarillo (Padres) | .600 | Amarillo (Padres) |
| 1977 | El Paso (Angels) | .600 | Arkansas (Cardinals) |
| 1978 | El Paso (Angels) | .592 | El Paso (Angels) |
| 1979 | Arkansas (Cardinals) | .571 | Arkansas (Cardinals) |
| 1980 | Arkansas (Cardinals) | .595 | Arkansas (Cardinals) |
| 1981 | San Antonio (Dodgers) | .571 | Jackson (Mets) |
| 1982 | El Paso (Brewers) | .568 | Tulsa (Rangers) |
| 1983 | El Paso (Brewers) | .544 | Beaumont (Padres) |
| 1984 | Beaumont (Padres) | .654 | Jackson (Mets) |
| 1985 | El Paso (Brewers) | .632 | Jackson (Mets) |
| 1986 | El Paso (Brewers) | .629 | El Paso (Brewers) |
| 1987 | Shreveport (Giants) | .577 | Wichita (Padres) |
| 1988 | El Paso (Brewers) | .552 | Tulsa (Rangers) |
| 1989 | Arkansas (Cardinals) | .585 | Arkansas (Cardinals) |
| 1990 | San Antonio (Dodgers) | .582 | Shreveport (Giants) |
| 1991 | Shreveport (Giants) | .632 | Shreveport (Giants) |
| 1992 | Shreveport (Giants) | .566 | Wichita (Padres) Tulsa (Rangers) | .566 |
| 1993 | El Paso (Brewers) | .560 | Jackson (Astros) |
| 1994 | El Paso (Brewers) | .647 | El Paso (Brewers) |
| 1995 | Shreveport (Giants) | .652 | Shreveport (Giants) |
| 1996 | El Paso (Brewers) | .547 | Jackson (Astros) |

*Best overall record   #Co-champions

### HONOR ROLL

#### OFFICIAL ALL-STAR TEAM

C—Eli Marrero, Arkansas.

**1B**—Paul Konerko, San Antonio. **2B**—Ronnie Belliard, El Paso. **3B**—Brad Seitzer, El Paso. **SS**—Russ Johnson, Jackson. **OF**—Todd Dunn, El Paso; Richard Hidalgo, Jackson; Bo Ortiz, Midland.

**DH**—Bubba Smith, Tulsa. **Util**—Jeff Berblinger, Arkansas; Jonas Hamlin, El Paso.

**P**—Kris Detmers, Arkansas; Keith Foulke, Shreveport; Jonathan Johnson, Tulsa; Sean Maloney, El Paso; Matt Morris, Arkansas; Brady Raggio, Arkansas; Eric Weaver, San Antonio.

**Player of the Year**—Bubba Smith, Tulsa. **Pitcher of the Year**—Keith Foulke, Shreveport. **Manager of the Year**—Dave Machemer, El Paso.

#### TOP 10 PROSPECTS

**1.** Paul Konerko, 1b, San Antonio; **2.** Matt Morris, rhp, Arkansas; **3.** Eli Marrero, c, Arkansas; **4.** Dante Powell, of, Shreveport; **5.** Richard Hidalgo, of, Jackson; **6.** Jeff D'Amico, rhp, El Paso; **7.** Mike Sweeney, c, Wichita; **8.** Ron Belliard, 2b, El Paso; **9.** Kevin Brown, c, Tulsa; **10.** Brian Bevil, rhp, Wichita.

# TEXAS LEAGUE
## 1996 BATTING, PITCHING STATISTICS

### CLUB BATTING

| | AVG | G | AB | R | H | 2B | 3B | HR | BB | SO | SB |
|---|---|---|---|---|---|---|---|---|---|---|---|
| El Paso | .291 | 139 | 4664 | 809 | 1356 | 265 | 68 | 117 | 504 | 871 | 129 |
| Jackson | .278 | 140 | 4753 | 647 | 1319 | 229 | 30 | 108 | 406 | 697 | 60 |
| Wichita | .277 | 140 | 4797 | 713 | 1331 | 279 | 32 | 124 | 423 | 669 | 124 |
| San Antonio | .273 | 139 | 4645 | 616 | 1267 | 244 | 43 | 93 | 376 | 773 | 112 |
| Tulsa | .268 | 139 | 4745 | 699 | 1274 | 271 | 36 | 156 | 478 | 1006 | 64 |
| Midland | .266 | 140 | 4711 | 670 | 1254 | 274 | 42 | 97 | 462 | 824 | 67 |
| Shreveport | .264 | 139 | 4622 | 692 | 1219 | 235 | 33 | 123 | 553 | 889 | 143 |
| Arkansas | .257 | 140 | 4495 | 610 | 1154 | 214 | 34 | 96 | 487 | 724 | 106 |

### CLUB PITCHING

| | ERA | G | CG | SHO | SV | IP | H | R | ER | BB | SO |
|---|---|---|---|---|---|---|---|---|---|---|---|
| Jackson | 3.78 | 140 | 5 | 10 | 36 | 1220 | 1199 | 631 | 513 | 513 | 894 |
| Arkansas | 3.80 | 140 | 10 | 8 | 28 | 1187 | 1180 | 597 | 501 | 470 | 888 |
| San Antonio | 3.87 | 139 | 6 | 5 | 37 | 1205 | 1229 | 625 | 518 | 534 | 764 |
| Shreveport | 4.01 | 139 | 5 | 6 | 43 | 1211 | 1211 | 635 | 540 | 395 | 675 |
| Tulsa | 4.38 | 139 | 12 | 8 | 42 | 1224 | 1306 | 677 | 596 | 403 | 721 |
| Wichita | 4.67 | 140 | 9 | 10 | 34 | 1225 | 1344 | 737 | 636 | 432 | 785 |
| El Paso | 4.74 | 139 | 9 | 2 | 47 | 1202 | 1353 | 746 | 633 | 465 | 872 |
| Midland | 5.06 | 140 | 11 | 2 | 28 | 1207 | 1352 | 808 | 679 | 477 | 854 |

### CLUB FIELDING

| | PCT | PO | A | E | DP | | PCT | PO | A | E | DP |
|---|---|---|---|---|---|---|---|---|---|---|---|
| Arkansas | .974 | 3562 | 1416 | 134 | 118 | San Antonio | .969 | 3616 | 1683 | 168 | 145 |
| Tulsa | .971 | 3672 | 1540 | 154 | 139 | Jackson | .966 | 3660 | 1607 | 185 | 137 |
| Wichita | .970 | 3676 | 1538 | 160 | 148 | Midland | .965 | 3620 | 1542 | 186 | 149 |
| Shreveport | .970 | 3633 | 1446 | 157 | 125 | El Paso | .962 | 3605 | 1550 | 202 | 152 |

**Eric Weaver**
10-5, 3.30 for San Antonio

**Brian Harrison**
9-2, 3.66 for Wichita

### INDIVIDUAL BATTING LEADERS
(Minimum 378 Plate Appearances)

| | AVG | G | AB | R | H | 2B | 3B | HR | RBI | BB | SO | SB |
|---|---|---|---|---|---|---|---|---|---|---|---|---|
| Dunn, Todd, El Paso | .340 | 98 | 359 | 72 | 122 | 24 | 5 | 19 | 78 | 45 | 84 | 13 |
| Bridges, Kary, Jackson | .325 | 87 | 338 | 51 | 110 | 12 | 2 | 4 | 33 | 32 | 14 | 4 |
| Seitzer, Brad, El Paso | .319 | 115 | 433 | 78 | 138 | 31 | 1 | 17 | 87 | 51 | 67 | 6 |
| Shockey, Greg, Midland | .317 | 98 | 325 | 58 | 103 | 26 | 6 | 7 | 49 | 47 | 56 | 2 |
| Johnson, Russ, Jackson | .310 | 132 | 496 | 86 | 154 | 24 | 5 | 15 | 74 | 56 | 50 | 9 |
| Christian, Eddie, Midland | .305 | 107 | 426 | 59 | 130 | 30 | 5 | 5 | 46 | 36 | 72 | 7 |
| Rupp, Brian, Arkansas | .303 | 114 | 353 | 46 | 107 | 17 | 2 | 4 | 41 | 33 | 44 | 5 |
| Konerko, Paul, San Antonio | .300 | 133 | 470 | 78 | 141 | 23 | 2 | 29 | 86 | 72 | 85 | 1 |
| Singleton, Chris, Shreveport | .298 | 129 | 500 | 68 | 149 | 31 | 9 | 5 | 72 | 24 | 58 | 27 |
| Sisco, Steve, Wichita | .297 | 122 | 462 | 80 | 137 | 24 | 1 | 13 | 74 | 40 | 69 | 4 |

### INDIVIDUAL PITCHING LEADERS
(Minimum 112 Innings)

| | W | L | ERA | G | GS | CG | SV | IP | H | R | ER | BB | SO |
|---|---|---|---|---|---|---|---|---|---|---|---|---|---|
| Foulke, Keith, Shreveport | 12 | 7 | 2.76 | 27 | 27 | 4 | 0 | 183 | 149 | 61 | 56 | 35 | 129 |
| Aybar, Manuel, Arkansas | 8 | 6 | 3.05 | 20 | 20 | 0 | 0 | 121 | 120 | 53 | 41 | 34 | 83 |
| Halama, John, Jackson | 9 | 10 | 3.21 | 27 | 27 | 0 | 0 | 163 | 151 | 77 | 58 | 59 | 110 |
| Raggio, Brady, Arkansas | 9 | 10 | 3.22 | 26 | 24 | 4 | 0 | 162 | 160 | 68 | 58 | 40 | 123 |
| Weaver, Eric, San Antonio | 10 | 5 | 3.30 | 18 | 18 | 1 | 0 | 123 | 106 | 51 | 45 | 44 | 69 |
| Detmers, Kris, Arkansas | 8 | 8 | 3.35 | 27 | 27 | 0 | 0 | 164 | 154 | 72 | 61 | 70 | 97 |
| Simons, Doug, Jackson | 8 | 7 | 3.48 | 20 | 19 | 1 | 0 | 127 | 132 | 53 | 49 | 30 | 75 |
| Johnson, Jonathan, Tulsa | 13 | 10 | 3.56 | 26 | 25 | 6 | 0 | 174 | 176 | 86 | 69 | 41 | 97 |
| Harrison, Brian, Wichita | 9 | 2 | 3.66 | 49 | 7 | 0 | 6 | 118 | 118 | 54 | 48 | 14 | 80 |
| Morris, Matt, Arkansas | 12 | 12 | 3.88 | 27 | 27 | 4 | 0 | 167 | 178 | 79 | 72 | 48 | 120 |

**BATTING**

| | | |
|---|---|---|
| G | Benji Simonton, Shreveport | 137 |
| AB | Keith Luuloa, Midland | 531 |
| R | Dante Powell, Shreveport | 92 |
| H | Russ Johnson, Jackson | 154 |
| TB | Bubba Smith, Tulsa | 274 |
| XBH | Jonas Hamlin, El Paso | 64 |
| 2B | Willie Romero, San Antonio | 36 |
| 3B | Hanley Frias, Tulsa | 12 |
| HR | Bubba Smith, Tulsa | 32 |
| RBI | Bubba Smith, Tulsa | 94 |
| | Jonas Hamlin, El Paso | 94 |
| SH | Brett King, Shreveport | 17 |
| SF | Jonas Hamlin, El Paso | 10 |
| BB | Benji Simonton, Shreveport | 101 |
| IBB | Chris Fick, Arkansas | 8 |
| HBP | Jeremy Carr, Wichita | 12 |
| SO | Kevin Brown, Tulsa | 150 |
| SB | Dante Powell, Shreveport | 43 |
| CS | Dante Powell, Shreveport | 23 |
| GIDP | Richard Hidalgo, Jackson | 24 |
| OB% | Doug Mirabelli, Shreveport | .419 |
| SL% | Todd Dunn, El Paso | .593 |

**PITCHING**

| | | |
|---|---|---|
| G | Jeff Matranga, Arkansas | 62 |
| GS | Troy Brohawn, Arkansas | 28 |
| | Matt Beaumont, Midland | 28 |
| CG | Jonathan Johnson, Tulsa | 6 |
| ShO | Matt Morris, Arkansas | 4 |
| GF | Manuel Barrios, Jackson | 53 |
| Sv | Sean Maloney, El Paso | 38 |
| W | Jonathan Johnson, Tulsa | 13 |
| L | Matt Beaumont, Midland | 16 |
| IP | Keith Foulke, Shreveport | 183 |
| H | Mike Bovee, Wichita | 223 |
| R | Matt Beaumont, Midland | 124 |
| ER | Matt Beaumont, Midland | 105 |
| HR | Troy Brohawn, Shreveport | 30 |
| HB | Matt Beaumont, Midland | 12 |
| BB | Ryan Creek, Jackson | 121 |
| SO | Matt Beaumont, Midland | 132 |
| WP | Jesus Martinez, SA | 20 |
| BK | Petie Roach, San Antonio | 4 |

**FIELDING**

| | | | |
|---|---|---|---|
| C | AVG | Eli Marrero, Arkansas | .996 |
| | PO | Eli Marrero, Arkansas | 675 |
| | A | Ben Molina, Midland | 81 |
| | E | Henry Blanco, San Antonio | 13 |
| | DP | Ben Molina, Midland | 9 |
| | PB | Henry Blanco, San Antonio | 17 |
| 1B | AVG | Larry Sutton, Wichita | .989 |
| | PO | Bubba Smith, Tulsa | 1193 |
| | A | Bubba Smith, Tulsa | 100 |
| | E | Dennis Colon, Jackson | 19 |
| | DP | Jonas Hamlin, El Paso | 122 |
| 2B | AVG | Jed Hansen, Wichita | .979 |
| | PO | Adam Riggs, San Antonio | 295 |
| | A | Adam Riggs, San Antonio | 395 |
| | E | Jeff Berblinger, Arkansas | 28 |
| | DP | Adam Riggs, San Antonio | 91 |
| 3B | AVG | Mike Bell, Tulsa | .936 |
| | PO | Mike Bell, Tulsa | 90 |
| | A | Mike Bell, Tulsa | 277 |
| | E | Tim Forkner, Jackson | 26 |
| | DP | Mike Bell, Tulsa | 28 |
| | | Mendy Lopez, Wichita | 28 |
| SS | AVG | Hanley Frias, Tulsa | .964 |
| | PO | Russ Johnson, Jackson | 219 |
| | A | Hanley Frias, Tulsa | 417 |
| | E | Anthony Medrano, Wichita | 36 |
| | DP | Russ Johnson, Jackson | 87 |
| OF | AVG | Joe McEwing, Arkansas | .993 |
| | PO | Dante Powell, Shreveport | 331 |
| | A | Armando Rios, Shreveport | 15 |
| | E | Nate Peterson, Jackson | 12 |
| | DP | Richard Hidalgo, Jackson | 6 |

# CALIFORNIA
## LEAGUE

# Storm Blows Away Giants In Upset

**By CINDY MARTINEZ RHODES**

Lake Elsinore pulled off a Giant upset in 1996, defeating the heavily-favored San Jose Giants to capture the California League championship. The Storm beat San Jose 3-2 in the best-of-5 final.

The Giants won more games (89) than any team in the minor leagues in 1996 and won the Northern Division title for the second year in a row. They also reached post-season play for the seventh time in nine seasons as an affiliate of the San Francisco Giants, yet failed again to win a league title. San Jose hasn't won a pennant since 1979.

Lake Elsinore, in its third year of existence, put together a strong second-half run to capture a wild card berth in the six team-playoffs. At 75-65, the Storm had only the fifth-best record in the league and won neither half of the Southern Division split-season schedule.

Lake Elsinore's road to the championship included beating 1994 champion Rancho Cucamonga, 2-1, in the first round and a 3-0 sweep of 1993 champion

**Bret Hemphill**

High Desert in the Southern Division final. The Storm also survived 50 roster moves during the course of the season by the parent California Angels.

San Jose earned a first-round bye in the North, while Stockton made quick work of the Modesto A's, sweeping the series in two games. San Jose then beat the Ports, 3-1, in the Northern Division title series.

The Storm won the deciding game over San Jose, 7-2, jumping on Giants starter Aaron Fultz for four runs in the fourth and three more off the league's Pitcher of the Year, Darin Blood, in the fifth and sixth. Storm catcher Bret Hemphill's three-run homer gave Lake Elsinore the lead and he homered a second time to lead off the sixth.

**Darin Blood.** San Jose righthander led Cal League in wins (17), ERA (2.65) and strikeouts (193).

Hemphill hit .417 with four homers and nine RBIs in 11 playoff games. After a dismal first half in which he hit .216 with four homers, Hemphill got hot in the second half, hitting .314 with eight homers in his final 40 games.

## Playing By The Numbers

Modesto DH D.T. Cromer had one of the best offensive seasons in recent California League history, but he was only one of several players to distinguish themselves in 1996.

Cromer had 80 extra-base hits, tops in the minors. It was the second-highest total in league history behind

## STANDINGS: OVERALL

| Page | | W | L | PCT | GB | Manager | Attendance/Dates | Last Pennant |
|---|---|---|---|---|---|---|---|---|
| 218 | San Jose Giants (Giants) | 89 | 51 | .636 | — | Carlos Lezcano | 144,782 (68) | 1979 |
| 186 | Modesto A's (Athletics) | 82 | 58 | .586 | 7 | Jim Colborn | 98,795 (70) | 1984 |
| 154 | Stockton Ports (Brewers) | 79 | 61 | .564 | 10 | Greg Mahlberg | 101,555 (67) | 1992 |
| 71 | High Desert Mavericks (Orioles) | 76 | 64 | .543 | 13 | Joe Ferguson | 143,852 (70) | 1993 |
| 85 | Lake Elsinore Storm (Angels) | 75 | 65 | .536 | 14 | Mitch Seoane | 360,392 (70) | 1996 |
| 223 | Lancaster Jet Hawks (Mariners) | 71 | 69 | .507 | 18 | Dave Brundage | 316,390 (70) | None |
| 147 | San Bernardino Stampede (Dodgers) | 70 | 70 | .500 | 19 | Del Crandall | 148,363 (70) | 1995 |
| 211 | Rancho Cucamonga Quakes (Padres) | 69 | 71 | .493 | 20 | Mike Basso | 410,214 (69) | 1994 |
| 240 | Visalia Oaks (Co-op) | 50 | 90 | .357 | 39 | Tim Torricelli | 67,798 (70) | 1978 |
| 240 | Bakersfield Blaze (Co-op) | 39 | 101 | .279 | 50 | Graig Nettles | 83,246 (70) | 1989 |

**NOTE:** Team's individual batting and pitching statistics can be found on page indicated in lefthand column.

Dick Wilson's 97 in 1951. Cromer hit .329 with 30 homers and 130 RBIs—none of which led the league—and was named the MVP.

Two of Cromer's teammates, shortstop Miguel Tejada and outfielder Ben Grieve, upstaged Cromer in the eyes of managers by being ranked the Nos. 1 and 3 prospects in the league. Cromer, 25, who hit .259 with 14 homers a year earlier for Modesto, did not crack the Top 10.

Tejada, the league's all-star shortstop, hit .279 with 20 homers and 72 RBIs, while Grieve, the second overall selection in the 1994 draft, hit .356 with 11 homers and 51 RBIs in a half season before being promoted to Double-A Huntsville.

San Jose's Blood, the No. 5-rated prospect, became the third pitcher to win the Cal League's version of a pitching Triple Crown, leading with 17 victories, a 2.65 ERA and 193 strikeouts. Blood's 17 wins tied for the minor league lead, while his 193 strikeouts were second.

Several other California Leaguers topped the minors in various categories.

High Desert first baseman Chris Kirgan garnered 131 RBIs, tying Visalia's Marty Cordova in 1991 for the most RBIs in the decade of the '90s. Teammate Mike Berry's .471 on-base percentage was the highest in the minors, and his .361 batting average the highest in the Cal League.

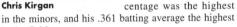

**Chris Kirgan**

Lake Elsinore second baseman Joe Urso led the minors with 47 doubles, while Visalia outfielder Dave Roberts was tops with 65 stolen bases.

## Changes Looming

San Francisco and Oakland left the Class A Midwest League after the 1996 season and elected to add second Cal League teams to their farm systems.

The Giants affiliated with Bakersfield, while

Oakland took on Visalia. Both Bakersfield and Visalia operated unsuccessfully as co-op clubs in 1995-96, with Bakersfield winning only 39 games in 1996. The Blaze ended the season with a 22-game losing streak.

Baltimore announced the termination of its player-development contract with High Desert, replacing the Mavericks with Delmarva of the South Atlantic League.

Within a week, Mavericks president Bobby Brett signed a four-year PDC with the expansion Arizona Diamondbacks.

The California League had an attendance explosion in 1996, reaching a league record of 1,875,387. That surpassed the previous record, set in 1994, by 11 percent.

The increase was facilitated, in part, by a new stadium in San Bernardino and the move of Riverside to Lancaster. The JetHawks drew 316,390 in their first season.

## STANDINGS: SPLIT SEASON

### FIRST HALF

| NORTH | W | L | PCT | GB |
|---|---|---|---|---|
| San Jose | 44 | 26 | .629 | — |
| Stockton | 40 | 30 | .571 | 4 |
| Modesto | 37 | 33 | .529 | 7 |
| Visalia | 27 | 43 | .386 | 17 |
| Bakersfield | 24 | 46 | .343 | 20 |

| SOUTH | W | L | PCT | GB |
|---|---|---|---|---|
| Rancho Cuca. | 38 | 32 | .543 | — |
| Lancaster | 36 | 34 | .514 | 2 |
| Lake Elsinore | 35 | 35 | .500 | 3 |
| High Desert | 35 | 35 | .500 | 3 |
| San Bern. | 34 | 36 | .486 | 4 |

### SECOND HALF

| NORTH | W | L | PCT | GB |
|---|---|---|---|---|
| San Jose | 45 | 25 | .643 | — |
| Modesto | 45 | 25 | .643 | — |
| Stockton | 39 | 31 | .557 | 6 |
| Visalia | 23 | 47 | .329 | 22 |
| Bakersfield | 15 | 55 | .214 | 30 |

| SOUTH | W | L | PCT | GB |
|---|---|---|---|---|
| High Desert | 41 | 29 | .586 | — |
| Lake Elsinore | 40 | 30 | .571 | 1 |
| San Bern. | 36 | 34 | .514 | 5 |
| Lancaster | 35 | 35 | .500 | 6 |
| Rancho Cuca. | 31 | 39 | .443 | 10 |

**PLAYOFFS—First Round:** Stockton defeated Modesto 2-0, and Lake Elsinore defeated Rancho Cucamonga 2-1, in best-of-3 series. **Semifinals:** San Jose defeated Stockton 3-1, and Lake Elsinore defeated High Desert 3-0, in best-of-5 series. **Finals:** Lake Elsinore defeated San Jose 3-2, in best-of-5 series.

## HONOR ROLL

### OFFICIAL ALL-STAR TEAM

**C**—Craig Mayes, San Jose.
**1B**—Chris Kirgan, High Desert. **2B**—Jason Cook, Lancaster.
**3B**—Mike Berry, High Desert. **SS**—Miguel Tejada, Modesto.
**OF**—Ben Grieve, Modesto; Mike Neill, Modesto; Mike Rennhack, Stockton.
**DH**—D.T. Cromer, Modesto.
**P**—Darin Blood, San Jose; Ken Cloude, Lancaster; Bill King, Modesto; Rich Linares, San Bernardino.
**Most Valuable Player**—D.T. Cromer, Modesto. **Pitcher of the Year**—Darin Blood, San Jose. **Rookie of the Year**—Darin Blood, San Jose. **Manager of the Year**—Carlos Lezcano, San Jose.

### TOP 10 PROSPECTS

**1.** Miguel Tejada, ss, Modesto; **2.** Jose Cruz, of, Lancaster; **3.** Ben Grieve, of, Modesto; **4.** Juan Melo, ss, Rancho Cucamonga; **5.** Darin Blood, rhp, San Jose; **6.** Mike Villano, rhp, San Jose; **7.** Ken Cloude, rhp, Lancaster; **8.** Russ Ortiz, rhp, San Jose; **9.** Adrian Beltre, 3b, San Bernardino; **10.** Ben Davis, c, Rancho Cucamonga.

## LEAGUE CHAMPIONS

### Last 25 Years

| Year | Regular Season* | Pct. | Playoff |
|---|---|---|---|
| 1972 | Bakersfield (Dodgers) | .629 | Modesto (Cardinals) |
| 1973 | Lodi (Orioles) | .550 | Lodi (Orioles) |
| | Salinas (Angels) | .550 | |
| 1974 | Fresno (Giants) | .607 | Fresno (Giants) |
| 1975 | Reno (Twins/Padres) | .614 | None |
| 1976 | Salinas (Angels) | .650 | Reno (Twins/Padres) |
| 1977 | Fresno (Giants) | .592 | Lodi (Dodgers) |
| 1978 | Visalia (Twins) | .697 | Visalia (Twins) |
| 1979 | San Jose (Mariners) | .636 | San Jose (Mariners) |
| 1980 | Stockton (Brewers) | .638 | Stockton (Brewers) |
| 1981 | Visalia (Twins) | .621 | Lodi (Dodgers) |
| 1982 | Modesto (Athletics) | .671 | Modesto (Athletics) |
| 1983 | Visalia (Twins) | .621 | Redwood (Angels) |
| 1984 | Redwood (Angels) | .654 | Modesto (Athletics) |
| 1985 | Salinas (Mariners) | .618 | Fresno (Giants) |
| 1986 | Palm Springs (Angels) | .612 | Stockton (Brewers) |
| 1987 | Stockton (Brewers) | .667 | Fresno (Giants) |
| 1988 | Stockton (Brewers) | .657 | Riverside (Padres) |
| 1989 | Stockton (Brewers) | .626 | Bakersfield (Dodgers) |
| 1990 | Visalia (Twins) | .638 | Stockton (Brewers) |
| 1991 | San Jose (Giants) | .676 | High Desert (Padres) |
| 1992 | Stockton (Brewers) | .604 | Stockton (Brewers) |
| 1993 | High Desert (Marlins) | .620 | High Desert (Marlins) |
| 1994 | Modesto (Athletics) | .706 | Rancho Cuca. (Padres) |
| 1995 | San Bern. (Dodgers) | .609 | San Bern. (Dodgers) |
| 1996 | San Jose (Giants) | .636 | Lake Elsinore (Angels) |

*Best overall record

# CALIFORNIA LEAGUE
## 1996 BATTING, PITCHING STATISTICS

### CLUB BATTING

| | AVG | G | AB | R | H | 2B | 3B | HR | BB | SO | SB |
|---|---|---|---|---|---|---|---|---|---|---|---|
| High Desert | .292 | 140 | 4957 | 924 | 1446 | 274 | 38 | 146 | 617 | 1034 | 119 |
| San Jose | .289 | 140 | 4950 | 771 | 1433 | 241 | 45 | 82 | 518 | 902 | 185 |
| Stockton | .286 | 140 | 4759 | 767 | 1359 | 225 | 42 | 102 | 536 | 894 | 147 |
| Modesto | .285 | 140 | 4858 | 952 | 1386 | 242 | 41 | 187 | 650 | 1192 | 219 |
| Lancaster | .278 | 140 | 4899 | 852 | 1362 | 275 | 59 | 115 | 544 | 1019 | 120 |
| San Bernardino | .278 | 140 | 4853 | 807 | 1349 | 243 | 22 | 152 | 456 | 1074 | 208 |
| Rancho Cuca. | .275 | 140 | 4826 | 779 | 1327 | 269 | 47 | 96 | 599 | 1096 | 124 |
| Lake Elsinore | .274 | 140 | 4846 | 805 | 1327 | 286 | 33 | 125 | 681 | 930 | 113 |
| Visalia | .254 | 140 | 4786 | 738 | 1216 | 254 | 34 | 106 | 598 | 1249 | 179 |
| Bakersfield | .250 | 140 | 4821 | 682 | 1205 | 256 | 15 | 114 | 517 | 1256 | 127 |

### CLUB PITCHING

| | ERA | G | CG | SHO | SV | IP | H | R | ER | BB | SO |
|---|---|---|---|---|---|---|---|---|---|---|---|
| San Jose | 3.54 | 140 | 4 | 16 | 40 | 1262 | 1154 | 594 | 497 | 494 | 1236 |
| Modesto | 4.22 | 140 | 0 | 6 | 39 | 1251 | 1318 | 749 | 587 | 487 | 1048 |
| Lancaster | 4.24 | 140 | 5 | 3 | 36 | 1241 | 1301 | 747 | 585 | 504 | 1070 |
| Lake Elsinore | 4.25 | 140 | 7 | 5 | 28 | 1250 | 1292 | 717 | 590 | 469 | 1111 |
| Stockton | 4.26 | 140 | 6 | 4 | 39 | 1228 | 1244 | 686 | 582 | 497 | 995 |
| Rancho Cuca. | 4.79 | 140 | 1 | 4 | 30 | 1229 | 1381 | 775 | 655 | 513 | 1112 |
| San Bernardino | 5.04 | 140 | 1 | 3 | 45 | 1248 | 1282 | 864 | 699 | 738 | 1165 |
| Visalia | 5.47 | 140 | 2 | 1 | 26 | 1242 | 1467 | 926 | 755 | 566 | 936 |
| High Desert | 5.54 | 140 | 3 | 3 | 29 | 1245 | 1372 | 881 | 766 | 702 | 965 |
| Bakersfield | 6.76 | 140 | 11 | 1 | 20 | 1238 | 1599 | 1138 | 931 | 746 | 1008 |

### CLUB FIELDING

| | PCT | PO | A | E | DP | | PCT | PO | A | E | DP |
|---|---|---|---|---|---|---|---|---|---|---|---|
| San Jose | .971 | 3787 | 1517 | 159 | 130 | Visalia | .961 | 3725 | 1561 | 216 | 120 |
| Stockton | .969 | 3684 | 1634 | 171 | 138 | San Bernardino | .961 | 3745 | 1491 | 214 | 104 |
| High Desert | .969 | 3734 | 1564 | 171 | 122 | Lancaster | .959 | 3723 | 1473 | 224 | 130 |
| Lake Elsinore | .968 | 3750 | 1520 | 173 | 105 | Modesto | .956 | 3753 | 1680 | 253 | 143 |
| Rancho Cuca. | .966 | 3687 | 1409 | 177 | 141 | Bakersfield | .954 | 3715 | 1386 | 246 | 111 |

**D.T. Cromer**
.329-30-130

**Eddie Oropesa**
11-6, 3.34

**Ken Cloude**
15-4, 4.22

### INDIVIDUAL BATTING LEADERS
(Minimum 378 Plate Appearances)

| | AVG | G | AB | R | H | 2B | 3B | HR | RBI | BB | SO | SB |
|---|---|---|---|---|---|---|---|---|---|---|---|---|
| Berry, Mike, High Desert | .361 | 121 | 463 | 109 | 167 | 44 | 5 | 13 | 113 | 99 | 67 | 7 |
| Reid, Derek, San Jose | .343 | 88 | 350 | 71 | 120 | 15 | 4 | 14 | 58 | 35 | 68 | 23 |
| Neill, Mike, Modesto | .339 | 114 | 442 | 101 | 150 | 20 | 6 | 19 | 78 | 68 | 123 | 28 |
| Cromer, D.T., Modesto | .329 | 124 | 505 | 100 | 166 | 40 | 10 | 30 | 130 | 32 | 67 | 20 |
| Mayes, Craig, San Jose | .328 | 114 | 472 | 56 | 155 | 26 | 4 | 3 | 68 | 29 | 43 | 6 |
| Wingate, Ervan, SB | .324 | 115 | 383 | 60 | 124 | 16 | 0 | 12 | 55 | 32 | 75 | 7 |
| Rennhack, Mike, Stockton | .320 | 121 | 456 | 67 | 146 | 32 | 4 | 17 | 103 | 53 | 66 | 8 |
| Bogle, Bryan, High Desert | .317 | 126 | 495 | 86 | 157 | 32 | 6 | 22 | 92 | 35 | 142 | 14 |
| Newstrom, Doug, HD | .313 | 122 | 403 | 84 | 126 | 30 | 3 | 11 | 75 | 73 | 62 | 15 |
| Garland, Tim, San Jose | .311 | 132 | 550 | 96 | 171 | 18 | 7 | 5 | 61 | 54 | 77 | 51 |

### INDIVIDUAL PITCHING LEADERS
(Minimum 112 Innings)

| | W | L | ERA | G | GS | CG | SV | IP | H | R | ER | BB | SO |
|---|---|---|---|---|---|---|---|---|---|---|---|---|---|
| Blood, Darin, San Jose | 17 | 6 | 2.65 | 27 | 25 | 2 | 0 | 170 | 140 | 59 | 50 | 71 | 193 |
| Oropesa, Eddie, SB | 11 | 6 | 3.34 | 33 | 19 | 0 | 1 | 156 | 133 | 74 | 58 | 77 | 133 |
| Rector, Bobby, San Jose | 12 | 8 | 3.59 | 28 | 26 | 1 | 0 | 165 | 161 | 77 | 66 | 43 | 145 |
| Woodard, Steve, Stockton | 12 | 9 | 4.02 | 28 | 28 | 3 | 0 | 181 | 201 | 89 | 81 | 33 | 142 |
| Van De Weg, Ryan, RC | 9 | 6 | 4.06 | 26 | 26 | 0 | 0 | 146 | 164 | 78 | 66 | 52 | 129 |
| Gardner, Scott, Stockton | 10 | 8 | 4.13 | 27 | 21 | 3 | 0 | 144 | 127 | 77 | 66 | 52 | 148 |
| Reyes, Dennis, SB | 11 | 12 | 4.17 | 29 | 28 | 0 | 0 | 166 | 166 | 106 | 77 | 77 | 176 |
| Perisho, Matt, Lake Elsinore | 7 | 5 | 4.20 | 21 | 18 | 1 | 0 | 129 | 131 | 72 | 60 | 58 | 97 |
| Cooper, Brian, Lake Elsinore | 7 | 9 | 4.21 | 26 | 23 | 1 | 0 | 162 | 177 | 100 | 76 | 39 | 155 |
| Cloude, Ken, Lake Elsinore | 15 | 4 | 4.22 | 28 | 28 | 1 | 0 | 168 | 167 | 94 | 79 | 60 | 161 |

# League Makes It Through Stormy Season

**By CHRIS WRIGHT**

For the most part, 1996 was a year to remember in the Carolina League. But in some ways, it was one league president John Hopkins would just as soon forget.

The season started and ended with wacky weather and saw several high-profile prospects come and go, most notably two-time Baseball America Minor League Player of the Year Andruw Jones. The 19-year-old outfielder started the season in Durham and, by fall, was starring for Atlanta in the World Series, homering twice for the Braves in Game One.

Jones hit .313 with 17 homers in only half a season, but that was plenty enough for league managers to rate him the circuit's best prospect. Hopkins said all the accolades should represent more than just the 1996 season.

"I'm not sure we had more prospects than usual," Hopkins said, "but we certainly had more high-profile prospects. Having Andruw start here was the highlight. His meteoric rise—he touched all the bases all the way up to Atlanta. And then Ron Wright. It was the last couple weeks of the season before anyone passed him in home runs."

But the biggest loss came in the months following the midseason promotion of four Bulls prospects—Jones, Wright, Wes Helms and Damian Moss—and it involved the storied Durham franchise itself.

After pulling out earlier in the running for a Triple-A club, Bulls officials announced after the break that they had signed a deal, after all, to become the Triple-A club of the expansion Tampa Bay Devil Rays, who agreed to pick up a portion of the expansion fee. The move isn't effective until 1998, but Hopkins said he can already feel the impact.

"That's the way most people on earth identify with the Carolina League," Hopkins said. "When I go out and represent the league in different cities, people say,

**Andruw Jones.** Minor League Player of the Year passed through Durham.

'Oh, you're in the same league as the Durham Bulls.' The value of that is almost incalculable. It will leave the league with quite a loss, but we'll deal with it."

## Repeat Champion

The league still is trying to find a way to deal with the Wilmington Blue Rocks, who made their fourth straight trip to the league championship series and won their second title.

The Blue Rocks breezed to the first half Northern Division title, and then held off a furious bid by Lynchburg to capture the second half. The season sweep automatically pushed them into the championship series, where they faced the Durham-Kinston winner.

The Indians won the opening game of the best-of-three series 6-4 at Grainger Stadium. Little did they know that might have been the last game played there. Two days later, Hurricane Fran, which ripped through the eastern part of North Carolina Sept. 5, damaged the old park's right field wall, grandstand roof, light towers and offices.

The two teams shifted to Durham for Game Two. Heavy rains not associated with the hurricane canceled that game, and Fran followed the next day, unleashing heavy winds and several more inches of rain. The damage wasn't as extensive to Durham Bulls Athletic Park, but the storm left the city without power for five days. In fact, 12 hours after Fran left, the field was deemed playable—for day games anyway.

"The second game in Durham," Hopkins said, "we discussed playing a day game. We had no power that Friday, but it was a beautiful day. The city said it didn't want to have a building open without power—and understandably so."

The series shifted farther west, to Winston-Salem, where the two teams settled the Southern Division title in a doubleheader before fewer than 100 fans. Durham won Game Two but fell in Game Three, 6-4, with the

## STANDINGS: OVERALL

| Page | | W | L | PCT | GB | Manager | Attendance/Dates | Last Pennant |
|------|---|---|---|-----|-----|---------|------------------|--------------|
| 141 | **Wilmington Blue Rocks (Royals)** | 80 | 60 | .571 | — | John Mizerock | 335,309 (69) | 1996 |
| 111 | **Kinston Indians (Indians)** | 76 | 62 | .551 | 3 | Jack Mull | 145,493 (66) | 1995 |
| 105 | **Winston-Salem Warthogs (Reds)** | 74 | 65 | .532 | 5 ½ | Phillip Wellman | 154,132 (67) | 1993 |
| 64 | **Durham Bulls (Braves)** | 73 | 66 | .525 | 6 ½ | Randy Ingle | 365,445 (66) | 1967 |
| 71 | **Frederick Keys (Orioles)** | 67 | 72 | .482 | 12 ½ | Tim Blackwell | 258,427 (63) | 1990 |
| 199 | **Lynchburg Hillcats (Pirates)** | 65 | 74 | .468 | 14 ½ | Jeff Banister | 100,016 (64) | 1984 |
| 117 | **Salem Avalanche (Rockies)** | 62 | 76 | .449 | 17 | Bill McGuire | 173,703 (66) | 1987 |
| 92 | **Prince William Cannons (White Sox)** | 58 | 80 | .420 | 21 | Dave Huppert | 190,055 (63) | 1989 |

**NOTE:** Team's individual batting and pitching statistics can be found on page indicated in lefthand column.

Indians scoring two runs in the top of the ninth inning. Kinston's victory set up a rematch of the 1995 championship series, which the Indians won.

"The Kinston club was worn out," Hopkins said. "They had been at the Red Roof Inn in Durham for three days without power and the next day after the series, they're playing in Wilmington (Del.) at 6 p.m. They lost the first game, understandably, and the second game."

Looking at being swept, Kinston rallied for two runs in the ninth to win Game Three. The Indians scored two in the ninth the next night to force extra innings, but Wilmington first baseman Matt Smith secured the title with a two-run homer in the 11th, leading the Blue Rocks to a 6-4 victory.

All games were played in Wilmington because of the damage done to Grainger Stadium.

## The Stars Come Out

Wilmington's victory was of the unheralded variety; the only two Blue Rocks named to the league all-star team were second baseman Sergio Nunez and shortstop Alejandro Prieto, both defensive whizzes who combined for just four home runs.

Durham, meanwhile, had no one selected to the team, even though it featured the four dominant players in the first half: Jones, Helms, Wright and Moss. All four were promoted by the parent Atlanta Braves to Double-A Greenville a day after playing for the Carolina League in the inaugural California League-Carolina League all-star game June 19 in Rancho Cucamonga,

Wes Helms

Calif.

Helms led the league with a .322 average at the time of his promotion. Wright had 20 homers and that total held up as the league lead until the final week when Lynchburg teammates Jose Guillen and Freddy Garcia surpassed him. Both players finished with 21.

Guillen, named the league's MVP, chased a triple crown before finishing second in hitting (.322) and RBIs (94).

## Trading Places

While Durham is scheduled to abandon the Braves, its parent club since 1980, when it hooks up with Tampa Bay in 1998, two switches in affiliation will take place in 1997. Prince William parted company with the White Sox in favor of the Cardinals, and the White Sox replaced the Reds in Winston-Salem.

Hopkins has been assured that Durham will stage the second Carolina League-California League all-star game in 1997, but the format will be different. For sure, there will be no five-day layoff to stage the battle of Class A leagues.

In 1997, California League players will take a red-eye, play in Durham that night and fly back to the West Coast the next day. After that, the game might be in jeopardy.

Several major league farm directors were not pleased with the problems created by the 1996 game, which ended in a 2-2, 10-inning tie when both teams ran out of pitching. The California League used a journeyman infielder, Joe Urso, as a pitcher to preserve the tie.

# CAROLINA LEAGUE
## 1996 BATTING, PITCHING STATISTICS

### CLUB BATTING

| | AVG | G | AB | R | H | 2B | 3B | HR | BB | SO | SB |
|---|---|---|---|---|---|---|---|---|---|---|---|
| Lynchburg | .283 | 139 | 4673 | 730 | 1323 | 253 | 34 | 105 | 405 | 965 | 155 |
| Durham | .262 | 139 | 4701 | 702 | 1232 | 245 | 30 | 152 | 425 | 1007 | 168 |
| Wilmington | .259 | 140 | 4609 | 637 | 1195 | 234 | 34 | 81 | 493 | 958 | 160 |
| Frederick | .259 | 139 | 4568 | 648 | 1184 | 226 | 25 | 93 | 495 | 819 | 150 |
| Kinston | .257 | 138 | 4529 | 635 | 1166 | 245 | 24 | 82 | 490 | 812 | 86 |
| Salem | .256 | 138 | 4539 | 585 | 1164 | 216 | 18 | 89 | 477 | 835 | 154 |
| Winston-Salem | .252 | 139 | 4493 | 641 | 1131 | 192 | 24 | 121 | 524 | 1070 | 219 |
| Prince William | .248 | 138 | 4583 | 603 | 1138 | 224 | 30 | 88 | 504 | 930 | 81 |

### CLUB PITCHING

| | ERA | G | CG | SHO | SV | IP | H | R | ER | BB | SO |
|---|---|---|---|---|---|---|---|---|---|---|---|
| Wilmington | 3.53 | 140 | 5 | 8 | 41 | 1221 | 1158 | 595 | 479 | 395 | 835 |
| Kinston | 3.56 | 138 | 3 | 14 | 37 | 1189 | 1095 | 566 | 470 | 534 | 869 |
| Durham | 3.82 | 139 | 6 | 12 | 36 | 1217 | 1178 | 630 | 517 | 499 | 1054 |
| Winston-Salem | 4.02 | 139 | 11 | 7 | 27 | 1203 | 1255 | 643 | 538 | 423 | 746 |
| Salem | 4.10 | 138 | 7 | 9 | 33 | 1205 | 1167 | 656 | 549 | 558 | 969 |
| Prince William | 4.15 | 138 | 14 | 9 | 19 | 1193 | 1194 | 668 | 550 | 479 | 923 |
| Lynchburg | 4.20 | 139 | 11 | 7 | 20 | 1193 | 1249 | 704 | 557 | 459 | 896 |
| Frederick | 4.41 | 139 | 6 | 9 | 37 | 1200 | 1237 | 719 | 588 | 466 | 1104 |

### CLUB FIELDING

| | PCT | PO | A | E | DP | | PCT | PO | A | E | DP |
|---|---|---|---|---|---|---|---|---|---|---|---|
| Kinston | .973 | 3566 | 1494 | 143 | 124 | Win.-Salem | .964 | 3609 | 1520 | 190 | 140 |
| Prince William | .967 | 3579 | 1445 | 173 | 111 | Salem | .964 | 3616 | 1607 | 195 | 113 |
| Durham | .966 | 3650 | 1397 | 180 | 116 | Frederick | .962 | 3600 | 1396 | 196 | 105 |
| Wilmington | .965 | 3663 | 1568 | 190 | 139 | Lynchburg | .959 | 3578 | 1511 | 220 | 111 |

**Jose Guillen**
.322-21-94 for Lynchburg

**Rick Short**
.312-3-54 for Frederick

### INDIVIDUAL BATTING LEADERS
(Minimum 378 Plate Appearances)

| | AVG | G | AB | R | H | 2B | 3B | HR | RBI | BB | SO | SB |
|---|---|---|---|---|---|---|---|---|---|---|---|---|
| Casey, Sean, Kinston | .331 | 92 | 344 | 62 | 114 | 31 | 3 | 12 | 57 | 36 | 47 | 1 |
| Guillen, Jose, Lynchburg | .322 | 136 | 528 | 78 | 170 | 30 | 0 | 21 | 94 | 20 | 73 | 24 |
| Short, Rick, Frederick | .312 | 126 | 474 | 68 | 148 | 33 | 0 | 3 | 54 | 29 | 44 | 12 |
| Garcia, Freddy, Lynchburg | .306 | 129 | 474 | 79 | 145 | 39 | 3 | 21 | 86 | 44 | 86 | 4 |
| Walker, Shon, Lynchburg | .303 | 97 | 323 | 61 | 98 | 19 | 3 | 14 | 70 | 49 | 99 | 3 |
| Magee, Danny, Durham | .299 | 95 | 344 | 59 | 103 | 19 | 3 | 12 | 40 | 20 | 70 | 17 |
| Thomas, Juan, PW | .299 | 134 | 495 | 88 | 148 | 28 | 6 | 20 | 71 | 54 | 129 | 9 |
| Gambill, Chad, Salem | .296 | 115 | 406 | 61 | 120 | 22 | 2 | 7 | 41 | 33 | 83 | 6 |
| Asche, Mike, Lynchburg | .295 | 129 | 498 | 79 | 147 | 25 | 6 | 7 | 54 | 38 | 92 | 26 |
| Mendez, Carlos, Wilmington | .293 | 109 | 406 | 40 | 119 | 25 | 3 | 4 | 59 | 22 | 39 | 3 |

### INDIVIDUAL PITCHING LEADERS
(Minimum 112 Innings)

| | W | L | ERA | G | GS | CG | SV | IP | H | R | ER | BB | SO |
|---|---|---|---|---|---|---|---|---|---|---|---|---|---|
| Najera, Noe, Kinston | 12 | 2 | 2.70 | 24 | 24 | 1 | 0 | 140 | 124 | 52 | 42 | 62 | 131 |
| Caldwell, David, Kinston | 13 | 9 | 3.30 | 23 | 23 | 0 | 0 | 139 | 142 | 66 | 51 | 37 | 80 |
| Herbert, Russ, PW | 6 | 10 | 3.38 | 25 | 25 | 1 | 0 | 144 | 129 | 73 | 54 | 62 | 148 |
| Brixey, Dustin, Wilmington | 10 | 5 | 3.44 | 34 | 12 | 1 | 1 | 115 | 109 | 58 | 44 | 41 | 38 |
| Moreno, Julio, Frederick | 9 | 10 | 3.50 | 28 | 26 | 0 | 0 | 162 | 167 | 80 | 63 | 38 | 147 |
| Halley, Allen, Prince William | 7 | 12 | 3.54 | 24 | 24 | 4 | 0 | 137 | 123 | 69 | 54 | 49 | 131 |
| Grundy, Phillip, Wilmington | 7 | 11 | 3.55 | 27 | 26 | 3 | 0 | 165 | 155 | 87 | 65 | 49 | 117 |
| Anderson, Eric, Wilmington | 12 | 5 | 3.69 | 27 | 26 | 1 | 0 | 158 | 161 | 81 | 65 | 44 | 69 |
| Dillinger, John, Lynchburg | 10 | 5 | 3.74 | 33 | 15 | 2 | 0 | 132 | 101 | 65 | 55 | 58 | 113 |
| Ebert, Derrin, Durham | 12 | 9 | 4.00 | 27 | 27 | 2 | 0 | 166 | 189 | 102 | 74 | 37 | 99 |

**BATTING**

| | | |
|---|---|---|
| G | Steve Eddie, Winston-Salem | 137 |
| AB | Jose Guillen, Lynchburg | 528 |
| R | Juan Thomas, Prince William | 88 |
| H | Jose Guillen, Lynchburg | 170 |
| TB | Jose Guillen, Lynchburg | 263 |
| XBH | Freddy Garcia, Lynchburg | 63 |
| 2B | Freddy Garcia, Lynchburg | 39 |
| 3B | Chip Glass, Kinston | 9 |
| HR | Jose Guillen, Lynchburg | 21 |
| | Freddy Garcia, Lynchburg | 21 |
| RBI | Johnny Isom, Frederick | 104 |
| SH | Guillermo Mercedes, Kinston | 14 |
| SF | Freddy Garcia, Lynchburg | 12 |
| | Marlon Allen, Winston-Salem | 12 |
| BB | Justin Towle, Winston-Salem | 93 |
| IBB | Shon Walker, Lynchburg | 6 |
| | John Giudice, Salem | 6 |
| HBP | Mike Eaglin, Durham | 18 |
| SO | Al Shirley, Wilmington | 149 |
| SB | Sergio Nunez, Wilmington | 44 |
| CS | Derek Swafford, Lynchburg | 18 |
| GIDP | Jose Guillen, Lynchburg | 16 |
| OB% | Justin Towle, Win.-Salem | .416 |
| SL% | Sean Casey, Kinston | .544 |

**PITCHING**

| | | |
|---|---|---|
| G | Matt Spade, Lynchburg | 53 |
| GS | Clay Caruthers, Win.-Salem | 28 |
| | Kevin Pickford, Lynchburg | 28 |
| CG | Three tied at | 4 |
| ShO | Phil Grundy, Wilmington | 2 |
| GF | Kerry Ligtenberg, Durham | 42 |
| Sv | Stephen Prihoda, Wilmington | 25 |
| W | David Caldwell, Kinston | 13 |
| L | Allen Halley, Prince William | 12 |
| IP | Kevin Pickford, Lynchburg | 172 |
| H | Kevin Pickford, Lynchburg | 195 |
| R | Teddy Warrecker, Kinston | 105 |
| ER | Teddy Warrecker, Kinston | 88 |
| HR | Clay Caruthers, Winston-Salem | 20 |
| HB | Clay Caruthers, Winston-Salem | 13 |
| BB | Teddy Warrecker, Kinston | 88 |
| SO | Russ Herbert, Prince William | 148 |
| WP | Todd Dyess, Frederick | 15 |
| BK | Allen Halley, Prince William | 4 |

**FIELDING**

| | | |
|---|---|---|
| C AVG | Jim Foster, Frederick | .999 |
| PO | Mike Mahoney, Durham | 674 |
| A | Justin Towle, Win.-Salem | 100 |
| E | Blake Barthol, Salem | 16 |
| DP | Jim Foster, Frederick | 8 |
| PB | Justin Towle, Win.-Salem | 20 |
| 1B AVG | Nate Holdren, Salem | .987 |
| PO | Matt Smith, Wilmington | 1039 |
| A | Juan Thomas, Pr. William | 76 |
| E | Marlon Allen, Win.-Salem | 18 |
| | Juan Thomas, Pr. William | 18 |
| DP | Matt Smith, Wilmington | 108 |
| 2B AVG | Mike Eaglin, Durham | .972 |
| PO | Mike Eaglin, Durham | 317 |
| A | Derek Swafford, Lynchburg | 281 |
| E | Derek Swafford, Lynchburg | 23 |
| DP | Mike Eaglin, Durham | 83 |
| 3B AVG | Tim Jorgensen, Kinston | .949 |
| PO | Tim Jorgensen, Kinston | 105 |
| A | Steve Eddie, Win.-Salem | 315 |
| E | Freddy Garcia, Lynchburg | 35 |
| DP | Freddy Garcia, Lynchburg | 29 |
| SS AVG | Guillermo Mercedes, Kin. | .978 |
| PO | Guillermo Mercedes, Kin. | 178 |
| A | Alejandro Prieto, Wilm. | 364 |
| E | Alejandro Prieto, Wilm. | 40 |
| DP | Alejandro Prieto, Wilm. | 79 |
| OF AVG | Erskine Kelley, Lynchburg | .988 |
| PO | Decomba Conner, W-S | 308 |
| A | Chip Glass, Kinston | 27 |
| E | Jose Guillen, Lynchburg | 13 |
| DP | Jose Guillen, Lynchburg | 6 |

# FLORIDA STATE LEAGUE

## St. Lucie Goes Long With Barry Short

**By SEAN KERNAN**

Thanks to the St. Lucie Mets, there was an amazing finish to the 1996 Florida State League season. The Mets' run to the title was nothing Short of miraculous.

The Mets won five of six postseason games, with four of the victories going to reliever Barry Short. St. Lucie swept the first two games of the Eastern Division series against Vero Beach, one a complete-game victory by Arnold Gooch.

After dropping the opener of the best-of-5 championship series against Clearwater, the Mets won three in a row to secure their second FSL title since joining the league in 1988. All the victories went to Short.

"We came together and I really can't describe it," Short said. "We got the job done and this is—by far—the highlight of my life."

With 24 days left in the season, it didn't look like the Mets would be involved in the playoffs. St. Lucie trailed the Daytona Cubs by eight games and not even manager John Gibbons, who had put up a sign in the St. Lucie clubhouse proclaiming the Mets as 1996 FSL champions in late July, thought his team had a chance.

"We didn't expect (to be in a pennant race) after we only split a four-game series with Daytona," Gibbons said. "Then we caught fire and they got on a losing streak. All of a sudden we were right back in it."

The Mets made up all eight games in just 16 days, tying the Cubs for first place on Aug. 21. While the Cubs became mired in a seven-game losing streak, the Mets, who had not won more than three games in a row all season, put together an eight-game winning streak.

"It was funny," Gibbons said. "I was talking with our pitching coach (Randy Niemann) and I told him I didn't think I ever was part of a team that didn't win five or six games in row, even if it was by accident. Then we ran off eight straight."

The Mets won the right to represent the Eastern Division as second-half champions, albeit by the slimmest of margins—a .002 advantage in winning percentage. Daytona won one more game, but finished

**Jay Tessmer.** Florida State League MVP had a 12-4 record and 35 saves for the Tampa Yankees.

second because its 40-29 record translated to a .580 winning percentage. The Mets were 39-28, a .582 mark. The issue was in doubt until the final night of the regular season.

After the defending champion Cubs took two games from the Mets Aug. 28-29 to move back into first place, St. Lucie showed its resolve on the next-to-last night of the season. Vero Beach beat the Cubs 4-2, giving the Mets a chance to regain first place. When word of Daytona's loss reached Port St. Lucie, the Mets trailed Brevard County 5-1 in the eighth inning. The Mets rallied for a 6-5 win.

On the last night, Daytona edged Vero Beach 4-3 to force St. Lucie into a must-win situation. The Mets needed 12 innings to end the suspense, triumphing 7-4 over Brevard County.

The Mets made the postseason on the strength of

## STANDINGS: OVERALL

| Page | | W | L | PCT | GB | Manager | Attendance/Dates | Last Pennant |
|------|---|---|---|-----|-----|---------|------------------|--------------|
| 173 | Tampa Yankees (Yankees) | 84 | 50 | .627 | — | Trey Hillman | 124,619 (61) | 1994 |
| 160 | Fort Myers Miracle (Twins) | 79 | 58 | .577 | 6 ½ | John Russell | 77,181 (63) | 1985 |
| 192 | Clearwater Phillies (Phillies) | 75 | 62 | .547 | 10 ½ | Al LeBoeuf | 75,118 (63) | 1993 |
| 205 | St. Petersburg Cardinals (Cardinals) | 75 | 63 | .543 | 11 | Chris Maloney | 124,174 (66) | 1986 |
| 179 | St. Lucie Mets (Mets) | 71 | 62 | .534 | 12 ½ | John Gibbons | 74,728 (64) | 1996 |
| 99 | Daytona Cubs (Cubs) | 71 | 66 | .518 | 14 ½ | Dave Trembley | 97,098 (63) | 1995 |
| 166 | West Palm Beach Expos (Expos) | 68 | 67 | .504 | 16 ½ | Rick Sofield | 76,172 (66) | 1991 |
| 148 | Vero Beach Dodgers (Dodgers) | 65 | 66 | .496 | 17 ½ | Jon Debus | 76,196 (67) | 1990 |
| 78 | Sarasota Red Sox (Red Sox) | 67 | 69 | .493 | 18 | DeMarlo Hale | 69,487 (67) | 1963 |
| 237 | Dunedin Blue Jays (Blue Jays) | 67 | 70 | .489 | 18 ½ | Dennis Holmberg | 66,567 (68) | None |
| 231 | Charlotte Rangers (Rangers) | 63 | 76 | .453 | 23 ½ | Butch Wynegar | 70,941 (66) | 1989 |
| 136 | Kissimmee Cobras (Astros) | 60 | 75 | .444 | 24 ½ | Alan Ashby | 29,482 (64) | None |
| 123 | Lakeland Tigers (Tigers) | 61 | 77 | .442 | 25 | Dave Anderson | 24,165 (64) | 1992 |
| 129 | Brevard County Manatees (Marlins) | 47 | 92 | .338 | 39 ½ | Fredi Gonzalez | 140,724 (63) | None |

NOTE: Team's individual batting and pitching statistics can be found on page indicated in lefthand column.

their pitching staff, which posted a 3.15 ERA, tied for second with Tampa, which posted the league's best overall record.

"(Niemann's) teams have always been near the top of the league in pitching," Gibbons said. "As a player, he got the most out of himself and found out what would work for him. He has been through the Mets organization as a coach at all levels. Our pitching (was) consistent all year."

## Tessmer Is Tops

Jay Tessmer, Tampa's side-arm relief ace, claimed the league's Most Valuable Player award after posting a 12-4 record and 35 saves in a league record-tying 68 appearances—a record originally set in 1955 by West Palm Beach's Bill Boyette.

Tampa nipped Fort Myers by a half-game for the Western Division second half title.

"We couldn't have been in that situation without Jay Tessmer," said Tampa skipper Trey Hillman, who was selected the league's Manager of the Year. "No possible way."

The Yankees posted an 84-50 record and Tessmer was involved in 47 of Tampa's victories.

"At first I wasn't real impressed with him," said one FSL manager. "But his fastball got better and his breaking ball got sharper. He's tough on righthanders. Hitters go up there thinking this guy's got nothing, then he gets them out. It will be interesting to see what happens when he gets to Double-A."

Daytona righthander Kerry Wood, voted the league's top prospect in a survey of managers, became only the third pitcher in league history to be involved in two no-hitters in the same season. Both came within a month of each other.

Wood, Chicago's first-round draft pick in 1995, struck out 10 batters in each no-hitter—a 5-1 win over Tampa on July 28 and a 3-0 shutout over Vero Beach on Aug. 24. He threw eight hitless frames against the

Yankees and seven hitless innings against the Dodgers.

Vero Beach's Sid Fernandez (1982) and Palatka's Mike Mattiace (1960) are the only other FSL pitchers to be involved in two no-hitters in the same season.

Vero Beach reliever Billy Neal set a franchise record with 16 wins, going 16-6 with a 2.28 ERA in 51 appearances. He tied St. Petersburg's Blake Stein (16-5) for the league lead in wins. Stein also paced the league with 159 strikeouts.

## Making Way For Expansion

A 30-year affiliation between St. Petersburg and the St. Louis Cardinals ended when the Tampa Bay Devil Rays purchased the club after the 1996 season. The Devil Rays will field an FSL club in 1997 at St. Pete's Al Lang Stadium, but are expected to move the club when the big league team begins play in 1998 just 12 blocks away.

Although no financial terms of the sale were revealed, it included territorial rights from Suncoast Baseball Inc., which purchased the franchise in 1989 for a reported $1.5 million.

Brevard County led the league in attendance, drawing 140,724 fans. On the field, the Manatees struggled with a record of 47-92, worst in the league.

---

## STANDINGS: SPLIT SEASON

### FIRST HALF

| EAST | W | L | PCT | GB |
|------|---|---|-----|----|
| Vero Beach | 39 | 24 | .619 | — |
| West Palm | 34 | 33 | .507 | 7 |
| St. Lucie | 32 | 34 | .485 | 8½ |
| Daytona | 31 | 37 | .456 | 10½ |
| Kissimmee | 28 | 38 | .424 | 12½ |
| Brevard | 25 | 45 | .357 | 17½ |

| WEST | W | L | PCT | GB |
|------|---|---|-----|----|
| Clearwater | 44 | 26 | .629 | — |
| Tampa | 41 | 25 | .621 | 1 |
| Dunedin | 40 | 29 | .580 | 3½ |
| Fort Myers | 36 | 32 | .529 | 7 |
| St. Pete. | 35 | 34 | .507 | 8½ |
| Lakeland | 33 | 36 | .478 | 10½ |
| Charlotte | 31 | 38 | .449 | 12½ |
| Sarasota | 25 | 43 | .368 | 18 |

### SECOND HALF

| EAST | W | L | PCT | GB |
|------|---|---|-----|----|
| St. Lucie | 39 | 28 | .582 | — |
| Daytona | 40 | 29 | .580 | — |
| West Palm | 34 | 34 | .500 | 5½ |
| Kissimmee | 32 | 37 | .464 | 8 |
| Vero Beach | 26 | 42 | .382 | 13½ |
| Brevard | 22 | 47 | .319 | 18 |

| WEST | W | L | PCT | GB |
|------|---|---|-----|----|
| Tampa | 43 | 25 | .632 | — |
| Fort Myers | 43 | 26 | .623 | ½ |
| Sarasota | 42 | 26 | .618 | 1 |
| St. Pete. | 40 | 29 | .580 | 3½ |
| Clearwater | 31 | 36 | .463 | 11½ |
| Charlotte | 32 | 38 | .457 | 12 |
| Lakeland | 28 | 41 | .406 | 15½ |
| Dunedin | 27 | 41 | .397 | 16 |

**PLAYOFFS—Semifinals:** St. Lucie defeated Vero Beach 2-0, and Clearwater defeated Tampa 2-0, in best-of-3 series. **Finals:** St. Lucie defeated Clearwater 3-1, in best-of-5 series.

---

## LEAGUE CHAMPIONS

### Last 25 Years

| Year | Regular Season | Pct. | Playoff |
|------|---------------|------|---------|
| 1972 | Daytona Beach (Dodgers) | .606 | Miami (Orioles) |
| 1973 | West Palm Beach (Expos) | .580 | St. Pete (Cardinals) |
| 1974 | Ft. Lauderdale (Yankees) | .626 | W. Palm Beach (Expos) |
| 1975 | St. Petersburg (Cardinals) | .651 | St. Pete (Cardinals) |
| 1976 | Tampa (Reds) | .559 | Lakeland (Tigers) |
| 1977 | Lakeland (Tigers) | .616 | Lakeland (Tigers) |
| 1978 | St. Petersburg (Cardinals) | .600 | Miami (~Orioles) |
| 1979 | Ft. Lauderdale (Yankees) | .643 | Winter Haven (Red Sox) |
| 1980 | Daytona Beach (Astros) | .627 | Ft. Lauderdale (Yankees) |
| 1981 | Ft. Lauderdale (Yankees) | .604 | Daytona Beach (Astros) |
| 1982 | Ft. Lauderdale (Yankees) | .621 | Ft. Lauderdale (Yankees) |
| 1983 | Daytona Beach (Astros) | .634 | Vero Beach (Dodgers) |
| 1984 | Fort Myers (Royals) | .574 | Ft. Lauderdale (Yankees) |
| 1985 | Ft. Myers (Royals) | .589 | Fort Myers (Royals) |
| 1986 | St. Petersburg (Cardinals) | .647 | St. Pete (Cardinals) |
| 1987 | Ft. Lauderdale (Yankees) | .615 | Ft. Lauderdale (Yankees) |
| 1988 | Osceola (Astros) | .605 | St. Lucie (Mets) |
| 1989 | St. Lucie (Mets) | .589 | Charlotte (Rangers) |
| 1990 | West Palm Beach (Expos) | .696 | Vero Beach (Dodgers) |
| 1991 | Clearwater (Phillies) | .623 | W. Palm Beach (Expos) |
| 1992 | Sarasota (White Sox) | .639 | Lakeland (Tigers) |
| 1993 | Charlotte (Rangers) | .632 | Clearwater (Phillies) |
| 1994 | Tampa (Yankees) | .606 | Tampa (Yankees) |
| 1995 | Daytona (Cubs) | .644 | Daytona (Cubs) |
| 1996 | Tampa (Yankees) | .627 | St. Lucie (Mets) |

*Best overall record

---

## HONOR ROLL

### OFFICIAL ALL-STAR TEAM

**C**—Pat Cline, Daytona; Paul LoDuca, Vero Beach. **1B**—Chris Richard, St. Petersburg. **2B**—Richard Almanzar, Lakeland. **3B**—Jose Lopez, St. Lucie. **SS**—Mike Coolbaugh, Charlotte. **Util INF**—Placido Polanco, St. Petersburg. **OF**—Aaron Fuller, Sarasota; Mike Murphy, Charlotte; Anthony Sanders, Dunedin. **Util OF**—Kurt Bierek, Tampa. **DH**—Daryle Ward, Lakeland. **LHP**—Tony Mounce, Kissimmee; Tommy Phelps, West Palm Beach. **RHP**—Roy Halladay, Dunedin; Blake Stein, St. Petersburg. **RP**—Curtis King, St. Petersburg; Jay Tessmer, Tampa.

**Most Valuable Player**—Jay Tessmer, Tampa. **Manager of the Year**—Trey Hillman, Tampa.

### TOP 10 PROSPECTS

**1.** Kerry Wood, rhp, Daytona; **2.** Kelvim Escobar, rhp, Dunedin; **3.** Roy Halladay, rhp, Dunedin; **4.** Pat Cline, c, Daytona; **5.** Hiram Bocachica, ss, West Palm Beach; **6.** Blake Stein, rhp, St. Petersburg; **7.** Jose Valentin, c, Fort Myers; **8.** Daryle Ward, 1b, Lakeland; **9.** Richard Almanzar, 2b, Lakeland; **10.** Arnold Gooch, rhp, St. Lucie.

# FLORIDA STATE LEAGUE
## 1996 BATTING, PITCHING STATISTICS

### CLUB BATTING

| | AVG | G | AB | R | H | 2B | 3B | HR | BB | SO | SB |
|---|---|---|---|---|---|---|---|---|---|---|---|
| Daytona | .267 | 137 | 4510 | 660 | 1205 | 234 | 36 | 92 | 404 | 795 | 181 |
| Charlotte | .264 | 139 | 4713 | 678 | 1246 | 253 | 32 | 65 | 456 | 890 | 110 |
| Sarasota | .262 | 136 | 4476 | 566 | 1171 | 215 | 42 | 64 | 439 | 915 | 159 |
| West Palm Beach | .260 | 135 | 4450 | 587 | 1156 | 214 | 34 | 49 | 428 | 815 | 142 |
| Lakeland | .257 | 138 | 4650 | 578 | 1197 | 233 | 42 | 63 | 379 | 919 | 144 |
| Tampa | .257 | 134 | 4407 | 587 | 1131 | 212 | 32 | 74 | 526 | 892 | 110 |
| Vero Beach | .255 | 131 | 4280 | 598 | 1092 | 171 | 41 | 52 | 490 | 859 | 139 |
| Kissimmee | .254 | 135 | 4348 | 500 | 1105 | 206 | 33 | 52 | 376 | 746 | 121 |
| St. Petersburg | .252 | 139 | 4508 | 533 | 1138 | 185 | 37 | 37 | 436 | 745 | 82 |
| Clearwater | .252 | 137 | 4534 | 629 | 1144 | 208 | 31 | 74 | 508 | 902 | 152 |
| Dunedin | .252 | 137 | 4500 | 629 | 1135 | 229 | 35 | 102 | 506 | 1056 | 102 |
| Fort Myers | .250 | 138 | 4538 | 641 | 1134 | 202 | 42 | 61 | 570 | 834 | 148 |
| St. Lucie | .249 | 133 | 4356 | 517 | 1083 | 161 | 31 | 51 | 378 | 863 | 177 |
| Brevard County | .246 | 139 | 4611 | 520 | 1134 | 192 | 36 | 40 | 467 | 896 | 128 |

### CLUB PITCHING

| | ERA | G | CG | SHO | SV | IP | H | R | ER | BB | SO |
|---|---|---|---|---|---|---|---|---|---|---|---|
| St. Petersburg | 3.04 | 139 | 5 | 13 | 44 | 1200 | 1111 | 474 | 406 | 451 | 892 |
| St. Lucie | 3.14 | 133 | 9 | 12 | 41 | 1156 | 1045 | 505 | 404 | 431 | 852 |
| Tampa | 3.15 | 134 | 4 | 8 | 49 | 1181 | 1123 | 522 | 413 | 337 | 912 |
| Clearwater | 3.48 | 137 | 7 | 8 | 37 | 1208 | 1149 | 568 | 468 | 478 | 837 |
| Fort Myers | 3.50 | 138 | 10 | 10 | 37 | 1213 | 1115 | 541 | 472 | 478 | 966 |
| Kissimmee | 3.54 | 135 | 11 | 9 | 30 | 1151 | 1125 | 603 | 453 | 491 | 793 |
| West Palm Beach | 3.55 | 135 | 5 | 9 | 35 | 1177 | 1170 | 581 | 464 | 420 | 841 |
| Vero Beach | 3.57 | 131 | 4 | 9 | 27 | 1124 | 1046 | 554 | 446 | 469 | 894 |
| Lakeland | 3.65 | 138 | 10 | 14 | 34 | 1200 | 1106 | 582 | 487 | 543 | 911 |
| Dunedin | 3.71 | 137 | 6 | 11 | 35 | 1187 | 1166 | 654 | 490 | 489 | 924 |
| Charlotte | 3.93 | 139 | 14 | 9 | 21 | 1228 | 1256 | 636 | 537 | 442 | 844 |
| Daytona | 4.01 | 137 | 6 | 7 | 38 | 1162 | 1146 | 648 | 518 | 488 | 912 |
| Brevard County | 4.14 | 139 | 5 | 5 | 23 | 1213 | 1277 | 669 | 558 | 364 | 715 |
| Sarasota | 4.39 | 136 | 8 | 10 | 35 | 1180 | 1236 | 686 | 576 | 482 | 834 |

### CLUB FIELDING

| | PCT | PO | A | E | DP | | PCT | PO | A | E | DP |
|---|---|---|---|---|---|---|---|---|---|---|---|
| St. Petersburg | .981 | 3601 | 1453 | 100 | 130 | Clearwater | .967 | 3625 | 1595 | 178 | 114 |
| Fort Myers | .975 | 3639 | 1612 | 134 | 141 | Brevard Cty. | .966 | 3638 | 1657 | 185 | 131 |
| Sarasota | .971 | 3540 | 1378 | 149 | 111 | Vero Beach | .964 | 3373 | 1458 | 179 | 112 |
| Charlotte | .970 | 3685 | 1541 | 161 | 118 | West Palm | .964 | 3528 | 1477 | 189 | 102 |
| Lakeland | .969 | 3600 | 1499 | 164 | 123 | Daytona | .961 | 3487 | 1405 | 198 | 104 |
| St. Lucie | .969 | 3468 | 1669 | 167 | 138 | Kissimmee | .958 | 3452 | 1467 | 213 | 115 |
| Tampa | .967 | 3542 | 1429 | 168 | 106 | Dunedin | .958 | 3562 | 1594 | 227 | 127 |

### INDIVIDUAL BATTING LEADERS
(Minimum 378 Plate Appearances)

| | AVG | G | AB | R | H | 2B | 3B | HR | RBI | BB | SO | SB |
|---|---|---|---|---|---|---|---|---|---|---|---|---|
| Murphy, Mike, Charlotte | .332 | 87 | 358 | 73 | 119 | 20 | 7 | 7 | 52 | 32 | 94 | 22 |
| Almanzar, Richard, Lake. | .306 | 124 | 471 | 81 | 144 | 22 | 2 | 1 | 36 | 49 | 49 | 53 |
| LoDuca, Paul, Vero Beach | .305 | 124 | 439 | 54 | 134 | 22 | 0 | 3 | 66 | 70 | 38 | 8 |
| Freeman, Ricky, Daytona | .304 | 127 | 477 | 70 | 145 | 36 | 6 | 13 | 64 | 36 | 72 | 10 |
| Fullmer, Brad, WPB | .303 | 102 | 380 | 52 | 115 | 29 | 1 | 5 | 63 | 32 | 43 | 4 |
| Fuller, Aaron, Sarasota | .300 | 115 | 434 | 74 | 130 | 20 | 5 | 5 | 49 | 63 | 60 | 33 |
| Reeves, Glenn, BC | .299 | 123 | 478 | 72 | 143 | 29 | 4 | 6 | 41 | 63 | 82 | 8 |
| Lopez, Jose, St. Lucie | .291 | 121 | 419 | 63 | 122 | 17 | 5 | 11 | 60 | 39 | 103 | 18 |
| Ward, Daryle, Lakeland | .291 | 128 | 464 | 65 | 135 | 29 | 4 | 10 | 68 | 57 | 77 | 1 |
| Polanco, Placido, St. Pete | .291 | 137 | 540 | 65 | 157 | 29 | 5 | 0 | 51 | 24 | 34 | 4 |
| Mientkiewicz, Doug, Ft. M. | .291 | 133 | 492 | 69 | 143 | 36 | 4 | 5 | 79 | 66 | 47 | 12 |

### INDIVIDUAL PITCHING LEADERS
(Minimum 112 Innings)

| | W | L | ERA | G | GS | CG | SV | IP | H | R | ER | BB | SO |
|---|---|---|---|---|---|---|---|---|---|---|---|---|---|
| Stein, Blake, St. Petersburg | 16 | 5 | 2.15 | 28 | 27 | 2 | 1 | 172 | 122 | 48 | 41 | 54 | 159 |
| Mounce, Tony, Kissimmee | 9 | 9 | 2.25 | 25 | 25 | 4 | 0 | 156 | 139 | 65 | 39 | 68 | 102 |
| Gooch, Arnold, St. Lucie | 12 | 12 | 2.58 | 26 | 26 | 2 | 0 | 168 | 131 | 74 | 48 | 51 | 141 |
| Cobb, Trevor, Ft. Myers | 7 | 3 | 2.64 | 31 | 14 | 1 | 0 | 126 | 101 | 44 | 37 | 43 | 98 |
| Halladay, Roy, Dunedin | 15 | 7 | 2.73 | 27 | 27 | 2 | 0 | 166 | 158 | 75 | 50 | 46 | 109 |
| Press, Gregg, Brevard Cty. | 9 | 9 | 2.75 | 28 | 23 | 0 | 0 | 150 | 134 | 62 | 46 | 37 | 90 |
| Silva, Ted, Charlotte | 10 | 2 | 2.86 | 16 | 16 | 4 | 0 | 113 | 98 | 39 | 36 | 27 | 95 |
| Roberts, Willis, Lakeland | 9 | 7 | 2.89 | 23 | 22 | 2 | 0 | 149 | 133 | 60 | 48 | 69 | 105 |
| Phelps, Tommy, WPB | 10 | 2 | 2.89 | 18 | 18 | 1 | 0 | 112 | 105 | 42 | 36 | 35 | 71 |
| Dixon, Tim, WPB | 5 | 11 | 2.90 | 37 | 16 | 0 | 2 | 124 | 126 | 55 | 40 | 35 | 87 |

# MIDWEST LEAGUE

# Athletics Players Win Title, Leave Town

**By CURT RALLO**

The West Michigan Whitecaps turned in a gutty effort to bring home a Midwest League championship in 1996. Then, those same Oakland Athletics' farmhands found out that West Michigan wasn't going to be home anymore.

The confetti from the celebration parade had hardly hit the ground in Grand Rapids when the Whitecaps announced they were replacing Oakland with the homestate Detroit Tigers.

"Coming back from Triple-A to spend a year with the kids was truly refreshing," said Whitecaps skipper Mike Quade, who managed at Scranton/Wilkes-Barre in the Phillies farm system in 1995. "I'm very happy for them. I am a little disappointed that we did so well, the kids played so hard, and we lost our home. I guess we gave the Tigers something to struggle to top."

West Michigan almost didn't make it out of the first round of the MWL's three-tiered playoff. The Whitecaps captured a 3-2 victory in extra innings against Lansing to advance to the second round, two games to one. West Michigan then beat Rockford, 2-0, and Wisconsin, 3-1, for the championship.

The title was the first for West Michigan, which joined the league in 1994.

"We just managed to survive and grind out a season and then did the exact same thing in the playoffs," said Quade, whose team had the third best record overall in the 14-team league. "We had good pitching all year. We were consistent. We didn't have a great deal of power or speed, but we managed to do a little of this and a little of that, and we managed to survive. I have to give the kids a ton of credit for having a great deal of character and wanting to win.

"I think all of our players knew there were tremendous demands made on all of them to be successful. I don't think anybody came in expecting to handle themselves well except Dane Walker, who had been in the league before."

Walker, moved from the outfield to second base, hit a team-high .277 and led the Whitecaps with 97 runs.

**Britt Reames.** Peoria righthander led the Midwest League with a 1.90 ERA and 167 strikeouts.

## Popular At The Gate

West Michigan also was a winner at the turnstiles in 1996, setting a Class A record by drawing 547,401— an average of 7,933 a game. It was the second straight year the Whitecaps topped the 500,000 mark, a feat never accomplished in Class A before 1995.

The Whitecaps were nearly beaten out in the attendance derby, however, by another Michigan team, the first-year Lansing Lugnuts, who drew 538,325 after moving from Springfield, Ill., following the 1995 season.

Kane County had another strong year at the gate,

## STANDINGS: OVERALL

| Page | | W | L | PCT | GB | Manager | Attendance/Dates | Last Pennant |
|------|---|---|---|-----|----|---------|------------------|--------------|
| 206 | Peoria Chiefs (Cardinals) | 79 | 57 | .581 | — | Roy Silver | 187,283 (63) | None |
| 224 | Wisconsin Timber Rattlers (Mariners) | 77 | 58 | .570 | 1½ | Mike Goff | 233,797 (62) | 1984 |
| 187 | West Michigan Whitecaps (Athletics) | 77 | 61 | .558 | 3 | Mike Quade | 547,401 (69) | 1996 |
| 136 | Quad City River Bandits (Astros) | 70 | 61 | .534 | 6½ | Jim Pankovits | 209,513 (56) | 1990 |
| 100 | Rockford Cubbies (Cubs) | 70 | 65 | .519 | 8½ | Steve Roadcap | 102,479 (63) | None |
| 161 | Fort Wayne Wizards (Twins) | 69 | 67 | .507 | 10 | Dan Rohn | 226,740 (68) | None |
| 155 | Beloit Snappers (Brewers) | 69 | 67 | .507 | 10 | Luis Salazar | 73,552 (64) | 1995 |
| 142 | Lansing Lugnuts (Royals) | 68 | 71 | .489 | 12½ | Brian Poldberg | 538,325 (69) | None |
| 130 | Kane County Cougars (Marlins) | 65 | 68 | .489 | 12½ | Lynn Jones | 436,076 (66) | None |
| 212 | Clinton Lumber Kings (Padres) | 64 | 70 | .478 | 14 | Mike Ramsey | 57,120 (62) | 1991 |
| 218 | Burlington Bees (Giants) | 65 | 73 | .471 | 15 | Glenn Tufts | 52,726 (64) | 1977 |
| 86 | Cedar Rapids Kernels (Angels) | 63 | 72 | .467 | 15½ | Tom Lawless | 127,379 (64) | 1994 |
| 79 | Michigan Battle Cats (Red Sox) | 60 | 78 | .435 | 20 | Tommy Barrett | 161,520 (68) | None |
| 92 | South Bend Silver Hawks (White Sox) | 54 | 82 | .397 | 25 | Dave Keller | 214,721 (61) | 1993 |

**NOTE:** Team's individual batting and pitching statistics can be found on page indicated in lefthand column.

drawing 436,076. That boosted the Cougars over the two million mark in their six years of existence, a feat not previously accomplished by another Class A team.

Wisconsin also set a franchise record with 233,797 fans.

Overall, the Midwest League attracted 3,168,632, the only time a minor league other than Triple-A had ever drawn more than 3 million fans.

Attendance could take another surge in the future as new parks are on the drawing board for Cedar Rapids, Rockford and Peoria. Quad City is talking major renovations.

At 52,726, the Burlington Bees were at the opposite end of the attendance scale,

**Larry Barnes**

and were one of three teams to lose working agreements following the 1996 season. San Francisco pulled out of Burlington, to be replaced by Cincinnati.

South Bend, which was plagued with the league's poorest overall record, also switched affiliations from the nearby Chicago White Sox to the expansion Arizona Diamonbacks.

## Barnes Top Performer

Cedar Rapids first baseman Larry Barnes led the league with 27 homers and 112 RBIs, and was named the league's MVP.

Peoria outfielder Kerry Robinson won the batting title with a .359 mark, the second highest average in the minor leagues. He also stole 50 bases, tying him

for the league lead.

Lansing third baseman Jose Cepeda, the nephew of former baseball great Orlando Cepeda, led the league in hits with 161. He also had a league-high 28-game hitting streak, four shy of the league record.

Peoria righthander Britt Reames led all minor leaguers with a 1.90 ERA, while going 17-7 with a league-high 167 strikeouts.

**Josh Booty**

Kane County boasted the Florida Marlins' three most recent first-round picks: third baseman Josh Booty (1994), and outfielders Jaime Jones (1995) and Mark Kotsay (1996). Booty set a league record with 195 strikeouts but also set a club record with 21 homers.

Beloit outfielder Tony Peters hit for the cycle May 19 against Wisconsin, the first Midwest League player to accomplish the trick since 1994.

## LEAGUE CHAMPIONS

**Last 25 Years**

| Year | Regular Season* | Pct. | Playoff |
|---|---|---|---|
| 1972 | Appleton (White Sox) | .598 | Danville (Brewers) |
| 1973 | Clinton (Tigers) | .588 | Wisconsin Rapids (Twins) |
| 1974 | Wisconsin Rapids (Twins) | .625 | Danville (Brewers) |
| 1975 | Waterloo (Royals) | .726 | Waterloo (Royals) |
| 1976 | Waterloo (Royals) | .600 | Waterloo (Royals) |
| 1977 | Waterloo (Indians) | .579 | Burlington (Brewers) |
| 1978 | Appleton (White Sox) | .708 | Appleton (White Sox) |
| 1979 | Waterloo (Indians) | .600 | Quad City (Cubs) |
| 1980 | Waterloo (Indians) | .609 | Waterloo (Indians) |
| 1981 | Wausau (Mariners) | .636 | Wausau (Mariners) |
| 1982 | Madison (Athletics) | .625 | Appleton (White Sox) |
| 1983 | Appleton (White Sox) | .635 | Appleton (White Sox) |
| 1984 | Appleton (White Sox) | .639 | Appleton (White Sox) |
| 1985 | Appleton (White Sox) | .611 | Kenosha (Twins) |
| 1986 | Springfield (Cardinals) | .621 | Waterloo (Indians) |
| 1987 | Springfield (Cardinals) | .671 | Kenosha (Twins) |
| 1988 | Cedar Rapids (Reds) | .621 | Cedar Rapids (Reds) |
| 1989 | South Bend (White Sox) | .643 | South Bend (White Sox) |
| 1990 | Cedar Rapids (Reds) | .656 | Quad City (Angels) |
| 1991 | Clinton (Giants) | .583 | Clinton (Giants) |
| 1992 | Quad City (Angels) | .664 | Cedar Rapids (Reds) |
| 1993 | Clinton (Giants) | .597 | South Bend (White Sox) |
| 1994 | Rockford (Royals) | .640 | Cedar Rapids (Angels) |
| 1995 | Beloit (Brewers) | .633 | Beloit (Brewers) |
| 1996 | Peoria (Cardinals) | .581 | West Michigan (A's) |
| *Best overall record | | | |

### HONOR ROLL

**OFFICIAL ALL-STAR TEAM**

**C**—Ramon Hernandez, West Michigan. **1B**—Larry Barnes, Cedar Rapids. **2B**—Andy Hall, Peoria. **3B**—Mike Kinkade, Beloit. **SS**—Deivi Cruz, Burlington. **OF**—Don Denbow, Burlington; Kerry Robinson, Peoria; Brian Simmons, South Bend. **DH**—Jeff Liefer, South Bend. **LHP**—Valerio de los Santos, Beloit. **RHP**—Britt Reames, Peoria. **LHRP**—Armando Almanza, Peoria. **RHRP**—Santos Hernandez, Burlington. **Most Valuable Player**—Larry Barnes, Cedar Rapids. **Manager of the Year**—Roy Silver, Peoria.

**TOP 10 PROSPECTS**

**1.** Valerio de los Santos, lhp, Beloit; **2.** Jeff Liefer, 3b-dh, South Bend; **3.** Brian Simmons, of, South Bend; **4.** Britt Reames, rhp, Peoria; **5.** Larry Barnes, 1b, Cedar Rapids; **6.** David Arias, 1b, Wisconsin; **7.** A.J. Pierzynski, c, Fort Wayne; **8.** Josh Booty, 3b, Kane County; **9.** Ramon Hernandez, c, West Michigan; **10.** Deivi Cruz, ss, Burlington.

# MIDWEST LEAGUE
## 1996 BATTING, PITCHING STATISTICS

### CLUB BATTING

| | AVG | G | AB | R | H | 2B | 3B | HR | BB | SO | SB |
|---|---|---|---|---|---|---|---|---|---|---|---|
| Wisconsin | .269 | 135 | 4561 | 731 | 1228 | 250 | 29 | 84 | 466 | 925 | 95 |
| Lansing | .266 | 139 | 4824 | 727 | 1285 | 233 | 41 | 71 | 528 | 893 | 161 |
| Quad City | .265 | 131 | 4391 | 629 | 1162 | 212 | 30 | 89 | 394 | 845 | 153 |
| Fort Wayne | .263 | 136 | 4552 | 632 | 1196 | 229 | 35 | 58 | 470 | 911 | 96 |
| Peoria | .261 | 136 | 4402 | 696 | 1148 | 214 | 45 | 40 | 561 | 933 | 159 |
| Michigan | .259 | 138 | 4693 | 638 | 1216 | 261 | 35 | 84 | 443 | 945 | 83 |
| Rockford | .256 | 135 | 4392 | 694 | 1126 | 207 | 43 | 56 | 561 | 979 | 211 |
| Cedar Rapids | .255 | 135 | 4491 | 645 | 1146 | 218 | 41 | 111 | 477 | 1049 | 153 |
| Beloit | .255 | 136 | 4434 | 637 | 1131 | 210 | 36 | 60 | 456 | 835 | 150 |
| West Michigan | .249 | 138 | 4559 | 603 | 1133 | 199 | 29 | 71 | 653 | 920 | 117 |
| South Bend | .245 | 136 | 4450 | 566 | 1090 | 213 | 34 | 71 | 445 | 947 | 117 |
| Kane County | .240 | 136 | 4280 | 580 | 1026 | 215 | 26 | 92 | 496 | 1137 | 101 |
| Burlington | .236 | 138 | 4479 | 572 | 1055 | 207 | 20 | 78 | 641 | 972 | 108 |
| Clinton | .230 | 134 | 4240 | 529 | 974 | 180 | 35 | 60 | 583 | 964 | 153 |

### CLUB PITCHING

| | ERA | G | CG | SHO | SV | IP | H | R | ER | BB | SO |
|---|---|---|---|---|---|---|---|---|---|---|---|
| Peoria | 3.30 | 136 | 7 | 13 | 31 | 1165 | 991 | 533 | 427 | 445 | 1065 |
| West Michigan | 3.42 | 138 | 0 | 9 | 45 | 1219 | 1121 | 561 | 463 | 495 | 1090 |
| Kane County | 3.65 | 133 | 12 | 7 | 30 | 1149 | 1099 | 596 | 466 | 459 | 941 |
| Beloit | 3.75 | 136 | 13 | 11 | 29 | 1179 | 1147 | 610 | 491 | 538 | 1000 |
| Burlington | 3.81 | 138 | 5 | 9 | 42 | 1203 | 1086 | 604 | 509 | 499 | 982 |
| Quad City | 3.87 | 131 | 3 | 5 | 36 | 1147 | 1068 | 599 | 493 | 502 | 948 |
| South Bend | 3.92 | 136 | 7 | 2 | 22 | 1177 | 1174 | 665 | 512 | 426 | 825 |
| Rockford | 4.02 | 135 | 11 | 4 | 31 | 1149 | 1170 | 663 | 513 | 457 | 886 |
| Fort Wayne | 4.08 | 136 | 7 | 8 | 28 | 1187 | 1224 | 661 | 539 | 440 | 969 |
| Clinton | 4.11 | 134 | 6 | 7 | 34 | 1144 | 1095 | 643 | 522 | 536 | 1013 |
| Cedar Rapids | 4.14 | 135 | 7 | 4 | 29 | 1172 | 1123 | 657 | 539 | 610 | 855 |
| Michigan | 4.16 | 138 | 13 | 4 | 26 | 1211 | 1147 | 675 | 560 | 573 | 901 |
| Lansing | 4.28 | 139 | 3 | 6 | 27 | 1239 | 1336 | 739 | 589 | 521 | 806 |
| Wisconsin | 4.61 | 135 | 9 | 4 | 33 | 1173 | 1135 | 709 | 601 | 673 | 974 |

### CLUB FIELDING

| | PCT | PO | A | E | DP | | PCT | PO | A | E | DP |
|---|---|---|---|---|---|---|---|---|---|---|---|
| Burlington | .972 | 3608 | 1573 | 147 | 121 | Peoria | .961 | 3495 | 1418 | 198 | 107 |
| Cedar Rapids | .969 | 3516 | 1461 | 159 | 137 | Kane County | .961 | 3446 | 1497 | 202 | 132 |
| Quad City | .963 | 3442 | 1447 | 186 | 128 | Wisconsin | .961 | 3518 | 1575 | 209 | 103 |
| Michigan | .963 | 3633 | 1511 | 197 | 117 | Clinton | .960 | 3431 | 1402 | 199 | 102 |
| Fort Wayne | .963 | 3561 | 1463 | 194 | 126 | Rockford | .960 | 3447 | 1427 | 203 | 125 |
| Beloit | .962 | 3536 | 1454 | 198 | 122 | West Michigan | .958 | 3657 | 1498 | 224 | 113 |
| Lansing | .962 | 3718 | 1743 | 218 | 171 | South Bend | .953 | 3530 | 1401 | 242 | 109 |

### INDIVIDUAL BATTING LEADERS
(Minimum 378 Plate Appearances)

| | AVG | G | AB | R | H | 2B | 3B | HR | RBI | BB | SO | SB |
|---|---|---|---|---|---|---|---|---|---|---|---|---|
| Robinson, Kerry, Peoria | .359 | 123 | 440 | 98 | 158 | 17 | 14 | 2 | 47 | 51 | 51 | 50 |
| Vieira, Scott, Rockford | .324 | 134 | 442 | 81 | 143 | 30 | 4 | 8 | 81 | 84 | 89 | 9 |
| Sapp, Damian, Michigan | .322 | 90 | 335 | 55 | 108 | 21 | 4 | 18 | 52 | 38 | 88 | 3 |
| Arias, David, Wisconsin | .322 | 129 | 485 | 89 | 156 | 34 | 2 | 18 | 93 | 52 | 108 | 3 |
| Amado, Jose, Wisc.-Lansing | .318 | 118 | 444 | 82 | 141 | 31 | 1 | 10 | 83 | 37 | 37 | 14 |
| Barnes, Larry, Cedar Rapids | .317 | 131 | 489 | 84 | 155 | 36 | 5 | 27 | 112 | 58 | 101 | 9 |
| Tinoco, Luis, Wisconsin | .313 | 120 | 431 | 71 | 135 | 31 | 5 | 12 | 71 | 53 | 85 | 4 |
| Joseph, Terry, Rockford | .305 | 128 | 449 | 98 | 137 | 23 | 6 | 9 | 94 | 69 | 88 | 28 |
| Kinkade, Mike, Beloit | .304 | 135 | 496 | 104 | 151 | 33 | 4 | 15 | 100 | 46 | 68 | 23 |
| Alvarez, Rafael, Ft. Wayne | .302 | 119 | 473 | 61 | 143 | 30 | 7 | 4 | 58 | 43 | 55 | 11 |
| Quinn, Mark, Lansing | .302 | 113 | 437 | 63 | 132 | 23 | 3 | 9 | 71 | 43 | 54 | 14 |

### INDIVIDUAL PITCHING LEADERS
(Minimum 112 Innings)

| | W | L | ERA | G | GS | CG | SV | IP | H | R | ER | BB | SO |
|---|---|---|---|---|---|---|---|---|---|---|---|---|---|
| Reames, Britt, Peoria | 15 | 7 | 1.90 | 25 | 25 | 2 | 0 | 161 | 97 | 43 | 34 | 41 | 167 |
| Politte, Cliff, Peoria | 14 | 6 | 2.59 | 25 | 25 | 0 | 0 | 150 | 108 | 50 | 43 | 47 | 151 |
| Mlodik, Kevin, West Mich. | 8 | 6 | 2.77 | 31 | 22 | 0 | 1 | 136 | 118 | 53 | 42 | 53 | 135 |
| Jimenez, Jose, Peoria | 12 | 9 | 2.92 | 28 | 27 | 3 | 0 | 172 | 158 | 75 | 56 | 53 | 129 |
| Pena, Juan, Michigan | 12 | 10 | 2.97 | 26 | 26 | 4 | 0 | 188 | 149 | 70 | 62 | 34 | 156 |
| Thorn, Todd, Lansing | 11 | 5 | 3.11 | 27 | 27 | 2 | 0 | 171 | 161 | 70 | 59 | 34 | 107 |
| Sikorski, Brian, Quad City | 11 | 8 | 3.13 | 26 | 25 | 1 | 0 | 167 | 140 | 79 | 58 | 70 | 150 |
| Mull, Blaine, Lansing | 15 | 8 | 3.25 | 28 | 28 | 1 | 0 | 175 | 186 | 91 | 63 | 40 | 114 |
| Hurtado, Victor, Kane County | 15 | 7 | 3.27 | 27 | 27 | 5 | 0 | 176 | 167 | 79 | 64 | 56 | 126 |
| O'Malley, Paul, Quad City | 11 | 9 | 3.34 | 26 | 26 | 1 | 0 | 178 | 173 | 80 | 66 | 51 | 111 |

# SOUTH ATLANTIC LEAGUE

## New Name, Same Success In Savannah

**By GENE SAPAKOFF**

They laughed at the nickname. The Sand Gnats. They laughed at one of the uniform colors. Tan. But only the Savannah Sand Gnats were smiling after Dan Ricabal finished off the Delmarva Shorebirds in the final inning of the 1996 South Atlantic League season.

Ricabal, a 24-year-old closer turned marathon man, got a win and a save as Savannah swept a doubleheader to win the SAL championship series three games to one. It was Savannah's third league title in four seasons but its first as a Los Angeles Dodgers affiliate—and its first as the Sand Gnats. The Savannah Cardinals, affiliated with St. Louis, won SAL crowns in 1993 and '94.

"Our club played as hard as it could the last six weeks of the season," Savannah manager John Shoemaker said. "In the playoffs, we didn't let up at all. This club really has something to be proud of."

After a 1-1 split in Savannah, the best-of-five series moved to Perdue Stadium in Salisbury, Md., where the first-year Shorebirds (Expos) drew an SAL record 315,011 fans during the regular season. Rain delayed the series for two days, forcing the teams to play a doubleheader.

Game Three, the first game of the decisive twinbill, went 13 innings and lasted 4:02. Savannah won 3-1 when season-long catalyst Eric Stuckenschneider hit a two-run triple over center fielder Jose Macias to drive in two runs.

The Dodgers added 1996 draft picks Peter Bergeron and Brian Sankey to the Savannah playoff roster and both came through with big hits in Savannah's 4-1 victory in Game Four. Bergeon had a pair of RBI singles. Sankey came through with an RBI double.

**Adrian Beltre.** Dominated the league in half a season

But Ricabal was the star. The 6-foot-1, 185-pound righthander pitched nine innings of the doubleheader—eight in Game Three (no runs, eight hits, two walks, eight strikeouts) and a scoreless ninth inning of Game Four. Ricabal was third in the SAL in saves with 24 but had been sent to Vero Beach (Florida State) before returning to Savannah in August.

Charlie Blaney, the Dodgers' director of minor league operations, marveled at Ricabal's sustained excellence.

"Ricabal was all guts and heart," Blaney said. "When did you ever see a closer close out both games of a doubleheader?"

### Beltin' Beltre

Savannah's title gets more impressive when considering the Sand Gnats downed Delmarva without Adrian Beltre, 18 and dominant. The league's top prospect, Beltre was promoted to San Bernardino (California) at midseason. But what a first half: .307-16-59.

In a midseason Baseball America poll, managers named Beltre the league's best batting prospect, best power prospect, infielder with the best arm and the most exciting player.

"Adrian adjusted as if he had been playing professionally for several years," Shoemaker said. "He was ready to hit every kind of pitch thrown to him. Of all the tools he has, his maturity may have been what stood out."

Columbus third baseman Russ Branyan made like Paul Bunyan. Branyan, 20, set an SAL single-season record with 40 home runs. That was 14 more than anyone else in the league hit in '96.

"He's a power prospect until he proves otherwise,"

## STANDINGS: OVERALL

| Page | | W | L | PCT | GB | Manager | Attendance/Dates | Last Pennant |
|---|---|---|---|---|---|---|---|---|
| 118 | Asheville Tourists (Rockies) | 84 | 52 | .618 | — | P.J. Carey | 145,798 (65) | 1984 |
| 180 | Capital City Bombers (Mets) | 82 | 57 | .590 | 3½ | Howie Freiling | 156,921 (65) | 1991 |
| 167 | Delmarva Shorebirds (Expos) | 83 | 59 | .585 | 4 | Doug Sisson | 315,011 (65) | None |
| 112 | Columbus RedStixx(Indians) | 79 | 63 | .556 | 8 | Joel Skinner | 45,110 (65) | None |
| 124 | Fayetteville Generals (Tigers) | 76 | 63 | .547 | 9½ | Dwight Lowry | 73,149 (66) | None |
| 193 | Piedmont Boll Weevils (Phillies) | 72 | 66 | .522 | 13 | Roy Majtyka | 102,983 (67) | None |
| 149 | Savannah Sand Gnats (Dodgers) | 72 | 69 | .511 | 14½ | John Shoemaker | 122,448 (68) | 1996 |
| 199 | Augusta GreenJackets (Pirates) | 71 | 70 | .504 | 15½ | Jay Loviglio | 157,487 (66) | 1989 |
| 238 | Hagerstown Suns (Blue Jays) | 70 | 71 | .496 | 16½ | J.J. Cannon | 102,765 (63) | None |
| 232 | Charleston, S.C., RiverDogs (Rangers) | 63 | 78 | .447 | 23½ | Gary Allenson | 100,428 (69) | None |
| 64 | Macon Braves (Braves) | 61 | 79 | .436 | 25 | Paul Runge | 117,042 (70) | None |
| 106 | Charleston, W. Va., Alley Cats (Reds) | 58 | 84 | .408 | 29 | T. Thompson/D. Scott | 87,189 (67) | 1990 |
| 174 | Greensboro Bats (Yankees) | 56 | 86 | .394 | 31 | R. Patterson/J. Johnson | 168,534 (67) | 1982 |
| 93 | Hickory Crawdads (White Sox) | 55 | 85 | .393 | 31 | Chris Cron | 207,069 (70) | None |

**NOTE:** Team's individual batting and pitching statistics can be found on page indicated in lefthand column.

Macon manager Paul Runge said. "We tried to pitch him various ways and the ball kept hitting the bat."

Branyan established quite a reputation in his native Georgia. The Warner Robins native hit 19 homers at Columbus in 1995.

Alas, not many fans saw Branyan's barrage. The RedStixx had to spend the 1996 season at Columbus College because their usual home, Golden Park, was touched up and booked for the Olympic Games softball competition. The RedStixx were not allowed to sell beer at Columbus College and drew an SAL-low 45,110 fans.

## No-Hitter Week

There were three SAL no-hitters in a one-week period of June. None went nine innings, but all three came with polish. Macon Braves righthander John Rocker blanked the Charleston RiverDogs, 2-0, over seven innings. Rocker, a Macon native, struck out nine and walked three.

Delmarva lefty Sean Leslie struck out two and walked one in a seven-inning no-hitter at Greensboro, winning 9-0. It was just the fourth start of Leslie's first pro season. The RiverDogs were on the fun side of a no-hitter when righthander Dan Kolb pitched a rain-shortened 5½-inning game against Columbus.

Asheville righthander Scott Randall outdid everyone with a pair of no-hitters—well, not officially. Randall pitched a nine-inning no-hitter at Fayetteville on July 17 in which he faced the minimum 27 batters. Fayetteville's Graham Koonce walked in the second inning and became a double-play victim.

On Aug. 14, Randall pitched 11 no-hit innings but did not get a decision in Asheville's 2-1, 19-inning win against Augusta. Before giving way to Heath Bost to start the 12th, Randall struck out 11 and walked one. He had a perfect game going into the ninth inning.

### STANDINGS: SPLIT SEASON

#### FIRST HALF

| NORTH | W | L | PCT | GB |
|---|---|---|---|---|
| Delmarva | 47 | 23 | .671 | — |
| Fayetteville | 35 | 33 | .515 | 11 |
| Hagerstown | 33 | 36 | .478 | 13½ |
| Char., W.Va. | 29 | 41 | .414 | 18 |
| **CENTRAL** | **W** | **L** | **PCT** | **GB** |
| Asheville | 47 | 20 | .701 | — |
| Capital City | 37 | 30 | .552 | 10 |
| Piedmont | 38 | 31 | .551 | 10 |
| Charleston, S.C. | 33 | 36 | .478 | 15 |
| Greensboro | 29 | 41 | .414 | 19½ |
| Hickory | 16 | 53 | .232 | 32 |
| **SOUTH** | **W** | **L** | **PCT** | **GB** |
| Augusta | 37 | 32 | .536 | — |
| Columbus | 36 | 34 | .514 | 1½ |
| Savannah | 34 | 36 | .486 | 3½ |
| Macon | 32 | 37 | .464 | 5 |

#### SECOND HALF

| NORTH | W | L | PCT | GB |
|---|---|---|---|---|
| Fayetteville | 41 | 30 | .577 | — |
| Hagerstown | 37 | 35 | .514 | 4½ |
| Delmarva | 36 | 36 | .500 | 5½ |
| Char., W.Va. | 29 | 43 | .403 | 12½ |
| **CENTRAL** | **W** | **L** | **PCT** | **GB** |
| Capital City | 45 | 27 | .625 | — |
| Hickory | 39 | 32 | .549 | 5½ |
| Asheville | 37 | 32 | .536 | 6½ |
| Piedmont | 34 | 35 | .493 | 9½ |
| Charleston, S.C. | 30 | 42 | .417 | 15 |
| Greensboro | 27 | 45 | .375 | 18 |
| **SOUTH** | **W** | **L** | **PCT** | **GB** |
| Columbus | 43 | 29 | .597 | — |
| Savannah | 38 | 33 | .535 | 4½ |
| Augusta | 34 | 38 | .472 | 9 |
| Macon | 29 | 42 | .408 | 13½ |

**PLAYOFFS—First Round:** Delmarva defeated Fayetteville 2-0, Asheville defeated Capital City 2-0, Columbus defeated Augusta 2-1, Savannah defeated Piedmont 2-0, in best-of-3 series. **Semifinals:** Savannah defeated Columbus 2-0, Delmarva defeated Asheville 2-1, in best-of-3 series. **Finals:** Savannah defeated Delmarva 3-1, in best-of-5 series.

The Greensboro Bats and Charleston Alley Cats changed managers during the 1996 season. The Yankees fired Greensboro manager Rick Patterson 26 games into the season citing "philosophical differences." Patterson, 14-12, was replaced by Jimmy Johnson, a coach at Triple-A Columbus.

The Yankees evidently were uncomfortable with Patterson's lineup tinkering. Johnson's first Greensboro lineup had three prospects at the top of the order: Second baseman Rod Smith, shortstop D'Angelo Jimenez and right fielder Shea Morenz. But Greensboro had the SAL's worst second-half record, 27-45.

The Reds canned Tommy Thompson with the Alley Cats at 34-50. Charleston slumped after an 18-12 start. Thompson was replaced by Donnie Scott, who had been working as the Reds' minor league field coordinator.

"I love a positive atmosphere and from what I understand there was some contradiction of that while Tommy was here," Scott said. He went on to a 24-34 record as Alley Cats manager.

### LEAGUE CHAMPIONS

**Last 25 Years**

| Year | Regular Season* | Pct. | Playoff |
|---|---|---|---|
| 1972 | Spartanburg (Phillies) | .674 | Spartanburg (Phillies) |
| 1973 | Charleston (Pirates) | .581 | Spartanburg (Phillies) |
| 1974 | Gastonia (Rangers) | .636 | None |
| 1975 | Spartanburg (Phillies) | .578 | None |
| 1976 | Asheville (Rangers) | .551 | Greenwood (Braves) |
| 1977 | Gastonia (Cardinals) | .589 | Gastonia (Cardinals) |
| 1978 | Greenwood (Braves) | .589 | None |
| 1979 | Greenwood (Braves) | .565 | Greenwood (Braves) |
| 1980 | Greensboro (Yankees) | .589 | Greensboro (Yankees) |
| 1981 | Greensboro (Yankees) | .695 | Greensboro (Yankees) |
| 1982 | Greensboro (Yankees) | .681 | Greensboro (Yankees) |
| 1983 | Columbia (Mets) | .619 | Gastonia (Expos) |
| 1984 | Columbia (Mets) | .589 | Asheville (Astros) |
| 1985 | Florence (Blue Jays) | .598 | Florence (Blue Jays) |
| 1986 | Columbia (Mets) | .681 | Columbia (Mets) |
| 1987 | Asheville (Astros) | .654 | Myrtle Beach (Blue Jays) |
| 1988 | Charleston, S.C. (Padres) | .615 | Spartanburg (Phillies) |
| 1989 | Gastonia (Rangers) | .657 | Augusta (Pirates) |
| 1990 | Columbia (Mets) | .580 | Charleston, W.Va. (Reds) |
| 1991 | Charleston, W.Va. (Reds) | .647 | Columbia (Mets) |
| 1992 | Columbia (Mets) | .572 | Myrtle Beach (Blue Jays) |
| 1993 | Savannah (Cardinals) | .662 | Savannah (Cardinals) |
| 1994 | Columbus (Indians) | .630 | Savannah (Cardinals) |
| 1995 | Fayetteville (Tigers) | .610 | Augusta (Pirates) |
| 1996 | Asheville (Rockies) | .618 | Savannah (Dodgers) |

*Best overall record

# SOUTH ATLANTIC LEAGUE
## 1996 BATTING, PITCHING STATISTICS

### CLUB BATTING

| | AVG | G | AB | R | H | 2B | 3B | HR | BB | SO | SB |
|---|---|---|---|---|---|---|---|---|---|---|---|
| Hickory | .251 | 140 | 4743 | 596 | 1191 | 200 | 27 | 57 | 433 | 1127 | 172 |
| Columbus | .250 | 142 | 4689 | 729 | 1170 | 216 | 25 | 167 | 535 | 1136 | 99 |
| Savannah | .247 | 141 | 4699 | 671 | 1162 | 202 | 42 | 103 | 479 | 1070 | 212 |
| Macon | .246 | 140 | 4596 | 589 | 1131 | 208 | 32 | 97 | 393 | 982 | 235 |
| Fayetteville | .244 | 139 | 4594 | 612 | 1123 | 238 | 19 | 80 | 510 | 963 | 163 |
| Asheville | .244 | 136 | 4498 | 612 | 1099 | 203 | 22 | 74 | 523 | 968 | 173 |
| Hagerstown | .244 | 141 | 4564 | 666 | 1115 | 235 | 31 | 74 | 624 | 1078 | 161 |
| Delmarva | .242 | 142 | 4621 | 673 | 1116 | 228 | 48 | 76 | 483 | 918 | 215 |
| Capital City | .239 | 139 | 4421 | 593 | 1057 | 182 | 37 | 59 | 479 | 1122 | 142 |
| Greensboro | .239 | 142 | 4758 | 586 | 1136 | 209 | 37 | 74 | 449 | 1229 | 160 |
| Piedmont | .235 | 138 | 4548 | 540 | 1070 | 197 | 25 | 49 | 408 | 1038 | 131 |
| Augusta | .234 | 141 | 4563 | 612 | 1066 | 178 | 30 | 55 | 568 | 964 | 147 |
| Charleston, S.C. | .229 | 141 | 4480 | 533 | 1028 | 183 | 49 | 57 | 412 | 1176 | 172 |
| Charleston, W.Va. | .226 | 142 | 4605 | 600 | 1043 | 200 | 28 | 65 | 625 | 1299 | 162 |

### CLUB PITCHING

| | ERA | G | CG | SHO | SV | IP | H | R | ER | BB | SO |
|---|---|---|---|---|---|---|---|---|---|---|---|
| Capital City | 2.77 | 139 | 16 | 18 | 33 | 1201 | 916 | 451 | 370 | 416 | 1168 |
| Delmarva | 2.84 | 142 | 14 | 17 | 38 | 1243 | 1031 | 534 | 393 | 441 | 1101 |
| Asheville | 3.13 | 136 | 6 | 11 | 41 | 1214 | 1039 | 526 | 423 | 461 | 1131 |
| Fayetteville | 3.20 | 139 | 8 | 7 | 46 | 1236 | 1067 | 582 | 439 | 511 | 1162 |
| Piedmont | 3.50 | 138 | 10 | 12 | 34 | 1219 | 1108 | 561 | 474 | 387 | 1088 |
| Hagerstown | 3.50 | 141 | 15 | 13 | 28 | 1220 | 1095 | 602 | 475 | 540 | 1072 |
| Augusta | 3.54 | 141 | 7 | 10 | 43 | 1233 | 1197 | 605 | 485 | 386 | 1106 |
| Savannah | 3.64 | 141 | 7 | 9 | 42 | 1241 | 1046 | 637 | 502 | 567 | 1229 |
| Columbus | 3.71 | 142 | 7 | 4 | 37 | 1219 | 1142 | 610 | 503 | 449 | 982 |
| Charleston, S.C. | 3.88 | 141 | 20 | 11 | 32 | 1193 | 1093 | 649 | 515 | 501 | 958 |
| Charleston, W.Va. | 3.92 | 142 | 3 | 8 | 34 | 1224 | 1194 | 674 | 533 | 518 | 954 |
| Hickory | 4.09 | 140 | 8 | 5 | 29 | 1245 | 1282 | 714 | 566 | 447 | 962 |
| Greensboro | 4.17 | 142 | 4 | 5 | 30 | 1246 | 1150 | 725 | 577 | 667 | 1080 |
| Macon | 4.31 | 140 | 5 | 9 | 29 | 1208 | 1147 | 742 | 579 | 630 | 1077 |

### CLUB FIELDING

| | PCT | PO | A | E | DP | | PCT | PO | A | E | DP |
|---|---|---|---|---|---|---|---|---|---|---|---|
| Capital City | .968 | 3603 | 1375 | 166 | 85 | Savannah | .959 | 3724 | 1461 | 222 | 95 |
| Asheville | .967 | 3642 | 1593 | 179 | 127 | Hickory | .958 | 3734 | 1530 | 230 | 104 |
| Hagerstown | .964 | 3660 | 1569 | 194 | 103 | Augusta | .958 | 3698 | 1400 | 224 | 88 |
| Piedmont | .964 | 3657 | 1382 | 187 | 86 | Fayetteville | .958 | 3707 | 1465 | 228 | 95 |
| Columbus | .962 | 3656 | 1590 | 207 | 108 | Greensboro | .955 | 3738 | 1564 | 250 | 94 |
| Char., W.Va. | .961 | 3673 | 1454 | 206 | 100 | Macon | .954 | 3625 | 1437 | 244 | 117 |
| Delmarva | .959 | 3729 | 1433 | 220 | 117 | Char., S.C. | .951 | 3579 | 1541 | 262 | 116 |

### INDIVIDUAL BATTING LEADERS
(Minimum 383 Plate Appearances)

| | AVG | G | AB | R | H | 2B | 3B | HR | RBI | BB | SO | SB |
|---|---|---|---|---|---|---|---|---|---|---|---|---|
| Mendoza, Carlos, Cap City | .336 | 85 | 304 | 61 | 102 | 10 | 2 | 0 | 37 | 57 | 47 | 31 |
| Lee, Carlos, Hickory | .313 | 119 | 480 | 65 | 150 | 23 | 6 | 8 | 70 | 23 | 50 | 18 |
| Stumberger, Darren, Col. | .310 | 129 | 471 | 77 | 146 | 30 | 3 | 22 | 89 | 53 | 72 | 0 |
| Raynor, Mark, Piedmont | .304 | 111 | 428 | 73 | 130 | 21 | 2 | 4 | 62 | 50 | 67 | 16 |
| Kapler, Gabe, Fayetteville | .300 | 138 | 524 | 81 | 157 | 45 | 0 | 26 | 99 | 62 | 73 | 14 |
| Long, Terrence, Cap City | .288 | 123 | 473 | 66 | 136 | 26 | 9 | 12 | 78 | 36 | 120 | 32 |
| Feuerstein, David, Asheville | .286 | 130 | 514 | 69 | 147 | 27 | 7 | 1 | 69 | 42 | 68 | 21 |
| Lowell, Mike, Greensboro | .282 | 113 | 433 | 58 | 122 | 33 | 0 | 8 | 64 | 46 | 43 | 10 |
| Cardona, Javier, Fayetteville | .282 | 97 | 348 | 42 | 98 | 21 | 0 | 4 | 28 | 28 | 53 | 1 |
| Hernaiz, Juan, Savannah | .278 | 132 | 492 | 68 | 137 | 19 | 8 | 14 | 73 | 21 | 96 | 42 |
| Brown, Roosevelt, Macon | .278 | 113 | 413 | 61 | 115 | 27 | 0 | 19 | 64 | 33 | 60 | 21 |
| Pimentel, Jose, Savannah | .278 | 123 | 461 | 66 | 128 | 21 | 4 | 7 | 54 | 28 | 100 | 50 |

### INDIVIDUAL PITCHING LEADERS
(Minimum 114 Innings)

| | W | L | ERA | G | GS | CG | SV | IP | H | R | ER | BB | SO |
|---|---|---|---|---|---|---|---|---|---|---|---|---|---|
| Figueroa, Nelson, Cap City | 14 | 7 | 2.04 | 26 | 25 | 8 | 0 | 185 | 119 | 55 | 42 | 58 | 200 |
| Knoll, Randy, Piedmont | 10 | 7 | 2.09 | 22 | 22 | 3 | 0 | 151 | 111 | 48 | 35 | 31 | 144 |
| McEntire, Ethan, Cap City | 9 | 6 | 2.22 | 27 | 27 | 1 | 0 | 174 | 123 | 51 | 43 | 61 | 190 |
| Trumpour, Andy, Cap City | 10 | 4 | 2.29 | 26 | 18 | 4 | 1 | 134 | 91 | 47 | 34 | 37 | 105 |
| Sanders, Frankie, Columbus | 9 | 3 | 2.52 | 22 | 22 | 0 | 0 | 121 | 103 | 52 | 34 | 37 | 109 |
| Kolb, Danny, Charleston, S.C. | 8 | 6 | 2.57 | 20 | 20 | 4 | 0 | 126 | 80 | 50 | 36 | 60 | 127 |
| Bruner, Clay, Fayetteville | 14 | 5 | 2.59 | 27 | 26 | 0 | 0 | 157 | 124 | 64 | 45 | 77 | 152 |
| Melendez, David, Fayetteville | 11 | 4 | 2.62 | 27 | 21 | 1 | 0 | 131 | 114 | 56 | 38 | 40 | 121 |
| Vazquez, Javier, Delmarva | 14 | 3 | 2.68 | 27 | 27 | 1 | 0 | 164 | 138 | 64 | 49 | 57 | 173 |
| Randall, Scott, Asheville | 14 | 4 | 2.74 | 24 | 24 | 1 | 0 | 154 | 121 | 53 | 47 | 50 | 136 |

## DEPARTMENT LEADERS

### BATTING

| | | |
|---|---|---|
| G | Derek Shumpert, Greensboro | 141 |
| AB | D'Angelo Jimenez, Gboro | 537 |
| R | Eric Stuckenschneider, Sav. | 111 |
| H | Gabe Kapler, Fayetteville | 157 |
| TB | Gabe Kapler, Fayetteville | 280 |
| XBH | Gabe Kapler, Fayetteville | 71 |
| 2B | Gabe Kapler, Fayetteville | 45 |
| 3B | Fletcher Bates, Cap City | 13 |
| HR | Russ Branyan, Columbus | 40 |
| RBI | Russ Branyan, Columbus | 106 |
| SH | Jeramie Simpson, Cap City | 12 |
| SF | Carlos Lee, Hickory | 11 |
| BB | Eric Stuckenschneider, Sav. | 111 |
| IBB | Mike Whitlock, Hagerstown | 8 |
| HBP | Eric Schreimann, Piedmont | 26 |
| SO | Bryon Gainey, Cap City | 169 |
| SB | Rod Smith, Greensboro | 57 |
| | Ramon Gomez, Hickory | 57 |
| CS | Fausto Solano, Hagerstown | 25 |
| GIDP | Boomer Whipple, Augusta | 18 |
| OB% | E. Stuckenschneider, Savannah | .424 |
| SL% | Russ Branyan, Columbus | .575 |

### PITCHING

| | | |
|---|---|---|
| G | Bryan Corey, Fayetteville | 60 |
| GS | Five tied at | 28 |
| CG | Nelson Figueroa, Cap City | 8 |
| ShO | Nelson Figueroa, Cap City | 4 |
| GF | Bryan Corey, Fayetteville | 53 |
| Sv | Bryan Corey, Fayetteville | 34 |
| W | Elvin Hernandez, Augusta | 17 |
| L | Maximo Nunez, Hickory | 16 |
| IP | Nelson Figueroa, Cap City | 185 |
| H | Scott Mudd, Charleston, S.C. | 196 |
| R | Billy Blythe, Macon | 98 |
| ER | David Coggin, Piedmont | 81 |
| HR | Dannon Atkins, Columbus | 19 |
| HB | Jason Baker, Delmarva | 16 |
| | David Melendez, Fayetteville | 16 |
| BB | Billy Blythe, Macon | 107 |
| SO | Nelson Figueroa, Cap City | 200 |
| WP | Three tied at | 22 |
| BK | David Melendez, Fayetteville | 8 |

### FIELDING

| | | |
|---|---|---|
| C AVG | Yohanny Valera, Cap City | .991 |
| PO | Yohanny Valera, Cap City | 857 |
| A | Yohanny Valera, Cap City | 123 |
| E | Wikleman Gonzalez, Aug. | 23 |
| DP | Fernando Lunar, Macon | 11 |
| PB | Brian Downs, Hickory | 23 |
| 1B AVG | Graham Koonce, Fay. | .993 |
| PO | Graham Koonce, Fay. | 1132 |
| A | Darren Stumberger, Col. | 92 |
| E | Cody Samuel, Greensboro | 20 |
| DP | Justin Drizos, Asheville | 102 |
| 2B AVG | Steven Goodhart, Char., W.Va. | .969 |
| PO | Rod Smith, Greensboro | 246 |
| A | Rod Smith, Greensboro | 302 |
| E | Rod Smith, Greensboro | 40 |
| DP | Fausto Solano, Hagerstown | 53 |
| 3B AVG | Mike Lowell, Greensboro | .926 |
| PO | Jose Fernandez, Delmarva | 102 |
| A | Mike Lowell, Greensboro | 301 |
| E | Rob Sasser, Macon | 45 |
| DP | Russ Branyan, Columbus | 24 |
| SS AVG | Mark Raynor, Piedmont | .965 |
| PO | Chris Woodward, Hag. | 214 |
| A | D'Angelo Jimenez, Gboro | 400 |
| E | D'Angelo Jimenez, Gboro | 50 |
| DP | Brett Elam, Asheville | 76 |
| OF AVG | S. Claybrook, Char., W.Va. | .996 |
| PO | Derek Shumpert, Greensboro | 297 |
| A | Derek Shumpert, Greensboro | 17 |
| E | Roosevelt Brown, Macon | 12 |
| | Jason Johnson, Char., S.C. | 12 |
| DP | Juan Hernaiz, Savannah | 5 |

# NEW YORK-PENN
## LEAGUE

# Vermont Completes Mission In 1996

**By HOWARD HERMAN**

The Vermont Expos compiled the best record in the New York-Penn League for the second consecutive year. In 1995, the Expos couldn't close the deal; in 1996, they did.

Vermont won the final two games of the league's best-of-3 championship series to beat the St. Catharines Stompers and claim its first New York-Penn League championship. Vermont had won consecutive championships in 1984-85-86 as members of the Double-A Eastern League.

The '96 championship series was a showdown of Canada's two major league organizations. Vermont is affiliated with Montreal, St. Catharines with Toronto.

"Nothing beats this right here. Nothing beats this championship game," Vermont shortstop Jamey Carroll said after the Expos thrilled an overflow crowd of 4,481 at Centennial Field in Burlington, Vt.

The McNamara Division champions beat the Stedler Division champion Stompers 4-3 in the deciding game, scoring the winning run on an seventh-inning passed ball.

The championship concluded another outstanding season for the Expos. In 1995, Vermont led the league with a 49-27 (.645) record, only to lose to Watertown in three games. In 1996, the Expos went 48-26, a near-identical .649 winning percentage.

**Top Prospect.** Erie third baseman Aramis Ramirez, the NYP's best talent.

St. Catharines defeated the Expos 2-0 in the first game of the series, but the Expos roared back to take Game Two, 5-3, on Paul Blandford's two-run bloop single which capped a three-run rally in the bottom of the eighth inning.

In the deciding game, the Expos used another late-inning rally to win the game and claim the title.

Left fielder Ethan Barlow, who played collegiately at Centennial Field for the University of Vermont, led off with an infield single. He stole second, took third on Blandford's ground out and scored on the passed ball.

Expos closer Tim Young pitched 1⅓ perfect innings in relief to get the victory. Young had a 0.31 ERA and 18 saves during the regular season.

The Expos reached the final by sweeping the Pittsfield Mets, the wild-card team, in two straight games. St. Catharines eliminated defending champion Watertown in the other series, also in two straight games.

"We took each game, game-by-game, pitch-by-pitch, inning-by-inning. That's how we got here," Blandford said. "We never quit."

## A Hit At Home

Home was definitely a sweet home for Vermont. Playing before 124,496 fans in 1996, the Expos

## STANDINGS: OVERALL

| Page | McNAMARA | W | L | PCT | GB | Manager | Attendance/Dates | Last Pennant |
|------|----------|---|---|-----|----|---------| -----------------|--------------|
| 167 | Vermont Expos (Expos) | 48 | 26 | .649 | — | Kevin Higgins | 124,496 (35) | 1996 |
| 181 | Pittsfield Mets (Mets) | 46 | 29 | .613 | 2½ | Doug Davis | 63,533 (33) | None |
| 79 | Lowell Spinners(Red Sox) | 33 | 41 | .446 | 15 | Billy Gardner Jr. | 95,986 (34) | None |
| 232 | H. V. Renegades (Rangers/Devil Rays) | 32 | 44 | .421 | 17 | Bump Wills | 152,626 (38) | None |
| 206 | New Jersey Cardinals(Cardinals) | 28 | 47 | .373 | 20½ | Scott Melvin | 172,314 (38) | 1994 |

| Page | PINCKNEY | W | L | PCT | GB | Manager | Attendance/Dates | Last Pennant |
|------|----------|---|---|-----|----|---------| -----------------|--------------|
| 112 | Watertown Indians (Indians) | 45 | 30 | .600 | — | Ted Kubiak | 40,681 (35) | 1995 |
| 100 | Williamsport Cubs (Cubs) | 43 | 32 | .573 | 2 | Ruben Amaro Sr. | 65.089 (36) | None |
| 137 | Auburn Doubledays (Astros) | 37 | 39 | .487 | 8½ | Manny Acta | 44,813 (37) | 1973 |
| 174 | Oneonta Yankees (Yankees) | 31 | 45 | .408 | 14½ | Gary Tuck | 50,509 (32) | 1990 |
| 130 | Utica Blue Marlins (Marlins) | 29 | 47 | .382 | 16½ | Steve McFarland | 51,432 (36) | 1983 |

| Page | STEDLER | W | L | PCT | GB | Manager | Attendance/Dates | Last Pennant |
|------|---------|---|---|-----|----|---------| -----------------|--------------|
| 238 | St. Catharines Stompers (Blue Jays) | 44 | 32 | .579 | — | Rocket Wheeler | 56,546 (36) | 1986 |
| 194 | Batavia Clippers (Phillies) | 42 | 33 | .560 | 1½ | Floyd Rayford | 39,025(34) | 1963 |
| 125 | Jamestown Jammers (Tigers) | 39 | 36 | .520 | 4½ | Bruce Fields | 60,114 (35) | 1991 |
| 200 | Erie SeaWolves (Pirates) | 30 | 46 | .395 | 14 | Jeff Richardson | 187,794 (38) | 1957 |

**PLAYOFFS—Semifinals:** Vermont defeated Pittsfield 2-0, and St. Catharines defeated Watertown 2-0, in best-of-3 series. **Finals:** Vermont defeated St. Catharines 2-1, in best-of-3 series.

**NOTE:** Team's individual batting and pitching statistics can be found on page indicated in lefthand column.

**Chris Stowers**          **Joe Freitas**

responded by going 29-9 in the regular season.

Vermont not only had the league's best record, but had the top batting average (.265) and ERA (3.07).

Expos outfielder Chris Stowers, a 17th-round draft pick from the University of Georgia, was named the league's MVP. He led the league in several offensive categories, but was edged out for the batting title on a technicality by New Jersey outfielder Joe Freitas, who hit .344. Stowers hit .319.

Freitas did not have the required number of plate appearances (205) to qualify for the title, but by adding 11 at-bats, as provided by section 10.23 (a) of the official scoring rules, his adjusted average of .322 still topped Stowers mark by three points.

Stowers led the league in runs (58), hits (90) and total bases (150).

## Emphasis On Youth

Stowers was one of several top prospects to grace the New York-Penn League in 1996.

Historically, the better prospects in the league have tended to be first-year players just out of college, like Stowers, but many of the top prospects in 1996 were teenagers.

The No. 1 prospect, as judged in a survey of managers was 18-year-old third baseman Aramis Ramirez of

the Erie SeaWolves. Ramirez, a product of the Dominican Republic, hit .305 with nine homers.

St. Catharines had two shortstops crack the Top 10—Abraham Nunez and Joe Lawrence. That should make for an interesting decision in Toronto in the next few years.

Lawrence was one of only two first-round picks from the 1996 draft to play in the New York-Penn League in 1996. And injuries limited the playing time of both Lawrence (29 games) and Watertown third baseman Danny Peoples (35 games), Cleveland's first-round selection. Lawrence hit only .224, Peoples .229.

## Attendance Increase

The league set an attendance record in 1996 by drawing 1,200,853 fans, topping the previous mark, set in 1995, by less than 20,000.

Erie drew 187,794 to set an individual club mark it established a year earlier.

**Joe Lawrence**

The SeaWolves' time in the New York-Penn League may not be long as they are a strong candidate for an expansion franchise at the Double-A level when that classification expands in 1999 to accomodate the Arizona Diamondbacks and Tampa Bay Devil Rays.

Tampa Bay made inroads on the NY-P in 1996 by sharing a working agreement with the Texas Rangers at Hudson Valley. The Devil Rays will have the Renegades all to themselves in 1997 as the Rangers have left the league.

Several clubs experienced drops in attendance. A big factor was inclement weather. Only Erie and New Jersey completed all 38 home dates, while Hudson Valley and Auburn had 37 openings. On the low end of the scale were Pittsfield and Oneonta, with 32 openings each.

The largest attendance gain was registered by the relocated Lowell Spinners, who extended the league's boundaries to the eastern Massachusetts city from Elmira, N.Y. The Spinners drew 88,515 to Alumni Field in 1996, double the previous year's total in Elmira.

## LEAGUE CHAMPIONS
### Last 25 Years

| Year | Regular Season* | Pct. | Playoff |
|---|---|---|---|
| 1972 | Niagara Falls (Pirates) | .686 | None |
| 1973 | Auburn (Phillies) | .667 | None |
| 1974 | Oneonta (Yankees) | .768 | None |
| 1975 | Newark (Brewers) | .701 | None |
| 1976 | Elmira (Red Sox) | .714 | None |
| 1977 | Oneonta (Yankees) | .671 | Oneonta (Yankees) |
| 1978 | Oneonta (Yankees) | .729 | Geneva (Cubs) |
| 1979 | Geneva (Cubs) | .725 | Oneonta (Yankees) |
| 1980 | Oneonta (Yankees) | .662 | Oneonta (Yankees) |
| 1981 | Oneonta (Yankees) | .658 | Oneonta (Yankees) |
| 1982 | Oneonta (Yankees) | .566 | Niagara Falls (White Sox) |
| 1983 | Utica (Independent) | .649 | Utica (Independent) |
|  | Newark (Orioles) | .649 |  |
| 1984 | Newark (Orioles) | .622 | Little Falls (Mets) |
| 1985 | Oneonta (Yankees) | .705 | Oneonta (Yankees) |
| 1986 | Oneonta (Yankees) | .766 | St. Catharines (Blue Jays) |
| 1987 | Geneva (Cubs) | .632 | Geneva (Cubs) |
| 1988 | Oneonta (Yankees) | .632 | Oneonta (Yankees) |
| 1989 | Pittsfield (Mets) | .697 | Jamestown (Expos) |
| 1990 | Oneonta (Yankees) | .667 | Oneonta (Yankees) |
| 1991 | Pittsfield (Mets) | .662 | Jamestown (Expos) |
| 1992 | Hamilton (Cardinals) | .737 | Geneva (Cubs) |
| 1993 | St. Catharines (Blue Jays) | .628 | Niagara Falls (Tigers) |
| 1994 | Watertown (Indians) | .649 | New Jersey (Cardinals) |
| 1995 | Vermont (Expos) | .645 | Watertown (Indians) |
| 1996 | Vermont (Expos) | .649 | St. Catharines (Blue Jays) |
| *Best overall record | | | |

# NEW YORK-PENN LEAGUE
## 1996 BATTING, PITCHING STATISTICS

### CLUB BATTING

| | AVG | G | AB | R | H | 2B | 3B | HR | BB | SO | SB |
|---|---|---|---|---|---|---|---|---|---|---|---|
| Vermont | .265 | 74 | 2406 | 373 | 637 | 116 | 26 | 20 | 268 | 437 | 95 |
| Erie | .256 | 76 | 2530 | 334 | 647 | 111 | 22 | 37 | 220 | 510 | 66 |
| Jamestown | .255 | 76 | 2491 | 391 | 634 | 117 | 29 | 55 | 318 | 609 | 91 |
| St. Catharines | .254 | 76 | 2493 | 347 | 634 | 113 | 24 | 51 | 232 | 535 | 84 |
| Batavia | .252 | 75 | 2516 | 348 | 635 | 116 | 26 | 32 | 207 | 510 | 57 |
| Pittsfield | .250 | 75 | 2401 | 360 | 600 | 82 | 26 | 40 | 301 | 593 | 93 |
| New Jersey | .250 | 75 | 2541 | 347 | 634 | 114 | 30 | 26 | 269 | 604 | 56 |
| Williamsport | .244 | 76 | 2482 | 342 | 606 | 96 | 20 | 24 | 238 | 582 | 104 |
| Watertown | .239 | 75 | 2424 | 359 | 580 | 105 | 13 | 27 | 358 | 581 | 75 |
| Auburn | .238 | 76 | 2499 | 308 | 596 | 123 | 21 | 33 | 221 | 522 | 80 |
| Lowell | .238 | 74 | 2458 | 306 | 586 | 108 | 9 | 38 | 233 | 575 | 51 |
| Oneonta | .236 | 76 | 2471 | 319 | 584 | 70 | 25 | 19 | 257 | 661 | 126 |
| Utica | .235 | 76 | 2426 | 299 | 570 | 112 | 18 | 22 | 308 | 641 | 64 |
| Hudson Valley | .228 | 76 | 2581 | 356 | 588 | 127 | 27 | 47 | 280 | 720 | 120 |

### CLUB PITCHING

| | ERA | G | CG | SHO | SV | IP | H | R | ER | BB | SO |
|---|---|---|---|---|---|---|---|---|---|---|---|
| Vermont | 3.07 | 74 | 7 | 7 | 20 | 630 | 541 | 256 | 215 | 194 | 575 |
| Watertown | 3.11 | 75 | 4 | 13 | 20 | 651 | 552 | 283 | 225 | 246 | 661 |
| Jamestown | 3.27 | 76 | 1 | 2 | 14 | 658 | 595 | 319 | 239 | 245 | 547 |
| Pittsfield | 3.37 | 75 | 6 | 8 | 19 | 635 | 575 | 274 | 238 | 221 | 559 |
| Batavia | 3.57 | 75 | 2 | 8 | 20 | 650 | 606 | 304 | 258 | 207 | 523 |
| Williamsport | 3.59 | 76 | 3 | 4 | 18 | 655 | 560 | 326 | 261 | 322 | 585 |
| Oneonta | 3.69 | 76 | 4 | 7 | 18 | 656 | 565 | 364 | 269 | 338 | 576 |
| Lowell | 3.91 | 74 | 4 | 3 | 18 | 637 | 603 | 372 | 277 | 297 | 592 |
| St. Catharines | 4.01 | 76 | 5 | 7 | 24 | 651 | 599 | 361 | 290 | 262 | 542 |
| Auburn | 4.01 | 76 | 2 | 4 | 24 | 661 | 639 | 371 | 295 | 317 | 519 |
| Erie | 4.10 | 76 | 4 | 2 | 13 | 659 | 670 | 373 | 300 | 272 | 573 |
| Utica | 4.19 | 76 | 4 | 2 | 15 | 647 | 648 | 360 | 301 | 236 | 567 |
| New Jersey | 4.25 | 75 | 0 | 3 | 16 | 654 | 692 | 399 | 309 | 270 | 608 |
| Hudson Valley | 4.31 | 76 | 1 | 2 | 13 | 688 | 686 | 427 | 330 | 283 | 653 |

### CLUB FIELDING

| | PCT | PO | A | E | DP | | PCT | PO | A | E | DP |
|---|---|---|---|---|---|---|---|---|---|---|---|
| Batavia | .969 | 1950 | 788 | 87 | 58 | Auburn | .961 | 1983 | 843 | 114 | 63 |
| Pittsfield | .969 | 1906 | 807 | 87 | 51 | New Jersey | .960 | 1962 | 778 | 114 | 46 |
| Vermont | .968 | 1890 | 734 | 86 | 65 | Williamsport | .957 | 1964 | 752 | 121 | 66 |
| Utica | .967 | 1940 | 721 | 90 | 38 | Erie | .957 | 1976 | 805 | 125 | 55 |
| Jamestown | .964 | 1975 | 845 | 106 | 60 | Hudson Valley | .952 | 2065 | 877 | 148 | 58 |
| Watertown | .962 | 1954 | 753 | 106 | 49 | Oneonta | .950 | 1967 | 797 | 147 | 53 |
| St. Catharines | .962 | 1953 | 811 | 109 | 57 | Lowell | .945 | 1912 | 692 | 151 | 57 |

### INDIVIDUAL BATTING LEADERS
(Minimum 205 Plate Appearances)

| | AVG | G | AB | R | H | 2B | 3B | HR | RBI | BB | SO | SB |
|---|---|---|---|---|---|---|---|---|---|---|---|---|
| Freitas, Joe, New Jersey | .344 | 45 | 163 | 29 | 56 | 10 | 3 | 4 | 37 | 25 | 35 | 0 |
| Stowers, Chris, Vermont | .319 | 72 | 282 | 58 | 90 | 21 | 9 | 7 | 44 | 21 | 37 | 16 |
| Manning, Nate, Williamsport | .317 | 62 | 240 | 28 | 76 | 14 | 1 | 4 | 32 | 14 | 62 | 4 |
| Hillenbrand, Shea, Lowell | .315 | 72 | 279 | 33 | 88 | 18 | 2 | 2 | 38 | 18 | 32 | 4 |
| Pratt, Wes, Auburn | .313 | 70 | 246 | 43 | 77 | 22 | 1 | 5 | 35 | 39 | 37 | 11 |
| Mazurek, Brian, NJ | .310 | 69 | 274 | 31 | 85 | 18 | 1 | 2 | 48 | 16 | 39 | 0 |
| Wakeland, Chris, James. | .309 | 70 | 220 | 38 | 68 | 14 | 5 | 10 | 49 | 43 | 83 | 8 |
| Ramirez, Aramis, Erie | .305 | 61 | 223 | 37 | 68 | 14 | 4 | 9 | 42 | 31 | 41 | 0 |
| Naples, Brandon, Pittsfield | .304 | 71 | 263 | 44 | 80 | 7 | 4 | 0 | 29 | 28 | 45 | 13 |
| Pond, Simon, Vermont | .300 | 69 | 253 | 37 | 76 | 16 | 1 | 3 | 40 | 26 | 26 | 9 |

### INDIVIDUAL PITCHING LEADERS
(Minimum 61 Innings)

| | W | L | ERA | G | GS | CG | SV | IP | H | R | ER | BB | SO |
|---|---|---|---|---|---|---|---|---|---|---|---|---|---|
| Raines, Ken, Hudson Valley | 6 | 2 | 1.07 | 38 | 0 | 0 | 5 | 67 | 51 | 19 | 8 | 21 | 64 |
| Graterol, Beiker, St. Cath. | 9 | 1 | 1.50 | 14 | 13 | 1 | 0 | 84 | 59 | 24 | 14 | 21 | 66 |
| Camp, Jared, Watertown | 10 | 2 | 1.69 | 15 | 15 | 1 | 0 | 96 | 68 | 29 | 18 | 30 | 99 |
| Rodgers, Bobby, Lowell | 7 | 4 | 1.90 | 14 | 14 | 2 | 0 | 90 | 60 | 33 | 19 | 31 | 108 |
| Miller, Brian, Batavia | 8 | 3 | 2.07 | 17 | 10 | 1 | 0 | 83 | 70 | 22 | 19 | 23 | 58 |
| Duncan, Courtney, Will. | 11 | 1 | 2.19 | 15 | 15 | 1 | 0 | 90 | 58 | 28 | 22 | 34 | 91 |
| Brittan, Corey, Pittsfield | 8 | 3 | 2.30 | 14 | 14 | 2 | 0 | 98 | 74 | 30 | 25 | 20 | 84 |
| Quezada, Edward, Vermont | 6 | 5 | 2.33 | 14 | 14 | 2 | 0 | 93 | 82 | 32 | 24 | 20 | 79 |
| Martinez, Willie, Watertwon | 6 | 5 | 2.40 | 14 | 14 | 1 | 0 | 90 | 79 | 25 | 24 | 21 | 92 |
| Yanez, Luis, Auburn | 5 | 5 | 2.45 | 15 | 15 | 2 | 0 | 99 | 85 | 38 | 27 | 31 | 73 |

# Bad News Bears Stage Late Comeback

**By SUSAN WADE**

Flying bananas always get their attention.

That's what Yakima Bears manager Joe Vavra figured Aug. 5, 1996, when his team was 17-30 and nine games out of first place in the Northwest League's North Division.

He smashed the postgame snack against the clubhouse wall in frustration after the team's 12th loss in 16 games.

"He was just trying to get something started," defended Bears righthander Blake Mayo.

Vavra got his team's attention. The Bad News Bears delivered a 10-game winning streak, won 23 of their last 29 games to capture the division title and swept the favored Eugene Emeralds in the NWL's best-of-3 championship series.

Mayo, the league leader with a 1.20 ERA, beat Bellingham 7-3 on the last day of the season to give Yakima the division title over the Giants by one-half game.

**Lonely At The Top.** Dodgers prospect Damian Rolls was the NWL's lone first-round pick in 1996.

He then pitched four shutout innings, striking out five, in the Bears' 9-2 championship game victory over Eugene, which went 49-27 and ran away with the Southern Division title.

Mayo's playoff stint came in relief of Kevin Culmo, his partner for most of the season in the Los Angeles Dodgers' piggyback pitching system. Culmo finished the regular season with a 2.27 ERA, second-best in the league.

**Joe Vavra**

Lefthander Ted Lilly, who went 4-0 with a 0.84 ERA (he was seven innings shy of qualifying for the ERA title), struck out eight in 6⅔ inning and allowed one run on two hits as Yakima opened the playoffs with a 2-1 victory at Eugene.

## Another Late-Season Surge

Like Yakima, Eugene made an impressive late-season run in the Southern Division, coming from six games back in mid-July for its first division title in 10 seasons. The Emeralds won 12 of 15 games in mid-August to grab first place for good, halting Boise's bid for a fourth straight league championship. Boise had started the season 20-3.

## STANDINGS

| Page | NORTH | W | L | PCT | GB | Manager(s) | Attendance/Dates | Last Pennant |
|---|---|---|---|---|---|---|---|---|
| 149 | **Yakima Bears (Dodgers)** | 40 | 36 | .526 | — | Joe Vavra | 82,313 (37) | 1996 |
| 218 | **Bellingham Giants (Giants)** | 39 | 36 | .520 | ½ | Ozzie Virgil, Shane Turner | 48,417 (36) | 1992 |
| 142 | **Spokane Indians (Royals)** | 37 | 39 | .487 | 3 | Bob Herold | 180,903 (38) | 1990 |
| 225 | **Everett AquaSox (Mariners)** | 33 | 42 | .440 | 6½ | Roger Hansen | 87,846 (38) | 1985 |
| **Page** | **SOUTH** | **W** | **L** | **PCT** | **GB** | **Manager** | **Attendance/Dates** | **Last Pennant** |
| 65 | **Eugene Emeralds (Braves)** | 49 | 27 | .645 | — | Jim Saul | 148,282 (37) | 1980 |
| 86 | **Boise Hawks (Angels)** | 43 | 33 | .566 | 6 | Tom Kotchman | 164,231 (38) | 1995 |
| 118 | **Portland Rockies (Rockies)** | 33 | 43 | .434 | 16 | Ron Gideon | 249,995 (38) | None |
| 187 | **Southern Oregon Timberjacks (A's)** | 29 | 47 | .382 | 20 | Tony DeFrancesco | 77,437 (38) | 1983 |

**PLAYOFFS**—Yakima defeated Eugene 2-0, in best-of-3 series.

**NOTE:** Team's individual batting and pitching statistics can be found on page indicated in lefthand column.

By the playoffs, Emeralds manager Jim Saul was caught in a revolving door of personnel changes. He lost middle infielders Adam Cross to injury and Mark DeRosa to a viral infection. The Braves also packaged outfielder Corey Pointer, who had 14 homers and 39 RBIs and hit well against Yakima, to Pittsburgh in a trade that netted Atlanta lefthander Denny Neagle.

The Braves sent Eugene six new players in one day just before the playoffs. Most were from Danville (Appalachian) and hadn't played in eight days. The Emeralds were not the same team that outscored Yakima 60-27 in their eight regular-season meetings.

**Adam Johnson**

Yakima third baseman Damian Rolls, the league's only first-round draft pick in 1996, said, "It was great to do the same thing they did to us all year. We played relaxed because we had nothing to lose."

Outfielder Adam Johnson, Atlanta's 55th-round pick in the 1996 draft, sparked Eugene in the regular season. He led the league in hitting (.314), runs (58) and hits (100).

Boise gave manager Tom Kotchman his 300th NWL victory July 20, but the Hawks faded after California promoted outfielder Rich Stuart and later second baseman Trent Durrington to Cedar Rapids (Midwest). When Stuart left, he and Durrington were tied for the league lead in runs scored (36) and Stuart was second in slugging percentage (.656).

Everett first baseman Rob Zachmann, who owned the league home run lead most of the season, sudden-

**Top Prospect.** NWL managers selected Bellingham shortstop Mike Caruso the league's No. 1 prospect. He hit .292 for the Giants.

ly turned cold in August and lost out to Eugene first baseman Steve Hacker. Hacker, who broke Bob Hamelin's club record for homers in a season, finished with 21 homers. Zachmann had an Everett franchise-best 19.

Bellingham shortstop Mike Caruso was the only unanimous pick in a managers' survey of the league's best prospects. He was San Francisco's second-round pick in the 1996 draft and drew as much attention for his league-high 38 fielding errors as his confidence and raw talent.

Boise catcher-infielder Matt Curtis set a new league record with 29 doubles, breaking the mark of 27 set by Victoria's Don Hyman in 1980.

## Prosperous League

Portland never threatened in the Southern Division, but came within five fans of becoming the first short-season club to hit the 250,000 mark in attendance. In the process, the Rockies broke their 1995 NWL record of 249,696 by less than 300 fans.

The Northwest League drew 1 million fans for the second year in a row. One of the most stable leagues in the National Association, the Northwest League had no new franchises or affiliation changes in 1996 and none was planned for 1997.

## LEAGUE CHAMPIONS

### Last 25 Years

| Year | Regular Season | Pct. | Playoff |
|---|---|---|---|
| 1972 | Lewiston (Orioles) | .675 | None |
| 1973 | Walla Walla (Padres) | .638 | None |
| 1974 | Bellingham (Dodgers) | .619 | Eugene (Independent) |
| 1975 | Eugene (Reds) | .684 | Eugene (Reds) |
| 1976 | Walla Walla (Padres) | .639 | Walla Walla (Padres) |
| 1977 | Portland (Independent) | .667 | Bellingham (Mariners) |
| 1978 | Grays Harbor (Independent) | .671 | Grays Harbor (Ind.) |
| 1979 | Bend (Phillies) | .606 | Bend (Phillies) |
| 1980 | Bellingham (Mariners) | .643 | Bellingham (Mariners)# |
| | | | Eugene (Reds)# |
| 1981 | Medford (Athletics) | .600 | Medford (Athletics) |
| 1982 | Medford (Athletics) | .757 | Salem (Angels) |
| 1983 | Medford (Athletics) | .735 | Medford (Athletics) |
| 1984 | Tri-Cities (Rangers) | .622 | Tri-Cities (Rangers) |
| 1985 | Everett (Giants) | .541 | Everett (Giants) |
| | Eugene (Royals) | .541 | |
| 1986 | Bellingham (Mariners) | .608 | Bellingham (Mariners) |
| | Eugene (Royals) | .608 | |
| 1987 | Spokane (Padres) | .711 | Spokane (Padres) |
| 1988 | Southern Oregon (A's) | .605 | Spokane (Padres) |
| 1989 | Southern Oregon (A's) | .600 | Spokane (Padres) |
| 1990 | Boise (Angels) | .697 | Spokane (Padres) |
| 1991 | Boise (Angels) | .650 | Boise (Angels) |
| 1992 | Bellingham (Mariners) | .566 | Bellingham (Mariners) |
| | Bend (Rockies) | .566 | |
| 1993 | Bellingham (Mariners) | .579 | Boise (Angels) |
| 1994 | Yakima (Dodgers) | .645 | Boise (Angels) |
| 1995 | Boise (Angels) | .640 | Boise (Angels) |
| 1996 | Eugene (Braves) | .645 | Yakima (Dodgers) |

*Best overall record  #Co-champions

# NORTHWEST LEAGUE
## 1996 BATTING, PITCHING STATISTICS

### CLUB BATTING

| | AVG | G | AB | R | H | 2B | 3B | HR | BB | SO | SB |
|---|---|---|---|---|---|---|---|---|---|---|---|
| Boise | .270 | 76 | 2764 | 477 | 747 | 149 | 25 | 53 | 347 | 561 | 79 |
| Eugene | .266 | 76 | 2669 | 447 | 710 | 150 | 28 | 86 | 273 | 607 | 51 |
| Spokane | .254 | 76 | 2623 | 433 | 667 | 122 | 18 | 72 | 326 | 563 | 122 |
| Bellingham | .252 | 75 | 2560 | 355 | 646 | 110 | 17 | 51 | 237 | 636 | 55 |
| Portland | .248 | 76 | 2628 | 367 | 653 | 128 | 23 | 30 | 250 | 544 | 59 |
| Yakima | .245 | 76 | 2597 | 337 | 635 | 120 | 20 | 43 | 266 | 703 | 79 |
| Southern Oregon | .244 | 76 | 2587 | 374 | 631 | 136 | 11 | 63 | 295 | 644 | 101 |
| Everett | .231 | 75 | 2519 | 344 | 581 | 100 | 16 | 45 | 319 | 738 | 56 |

### CLUB PITCHING

| | ERA | G | CG | SHO | SV | IP | H | R | ER | BB | SO |
|---|---|---|---|---|---|---|---|---|---|---|---|
| Bellingham | 3.41 | 75 | 0 | 5 | 19 | 673 | 575 | 318 | 255 | 316 | 691 |
| Yakima | 3.45 | 76 | 0 | 6 | 25 | 677 | 588 | 333 | 260 | 283 | 689 |
| Eugene | 3.67 | 76 | 0 | 4 | 33 | 687 | 634 | 365 | 280 | 272 | 682 |
| Portland | 4.10 | 76 | 0 | 4 | 18 | 678 | 656 | 386 | 309 | 250 | 585 |
| Everett | 4.19 | 75 | 0 | 4 | 19 | 657 | 658 | 390 | 306 | 254 | 657 |
| Boise | 4.42 | 76 | 2 | 2 | 16 | 699 | 695 | 440 | 344 | 334 | 585 |
| Spokane | 4.50 | 76 | 0 | 2 | 19 | 681 | 718 | 418 | 341 | 264 | 567 |
| Southern Oregon | 5.29 | 76 | 0 | 2 | 14 | 678 | 746 | 484 | 398 | 340 | 540 |

### CLUB FIELDING

| | PCT | PO | A | E | DP | | PCT | PO | A | E | DP |
|---|---|---|---|---|---|---|---|---|---|---|---|
| Bellingham | .962 | 2020 | 788 | 112 | 63 | Boise | .955 | 2098 | 885 | 139 | 68 |
| Yakima | .959 | 2032 | 801 | 120 | 55 | So. Oregon | .955 | 2033 | 862 | 138 | 51 |
| Everett | .959 | 1972 | 827 | 119 | 42 | Spokane | .954 | 2044 | 883 | 141 | 78 |
| Eugene | .958 | 2060 | 797 | 125 | 51 | Portland | .954 | 2035 | 763 | 136 | 52 |

### INDIVIDUAL BATTING LEADERS
(Minimum 205 Plate Appearances)

| | AVG | G | AB | R | H | 2B | 3B | HR | RBI | BB | SO | SB |
|---|---|---|---|---|---|---|---|---|---|---|---|---|
| Johnson, Adam, Eugene | .314 | 76 | 318 | 58 | 100 | 22 | 9 | 7 | 56 | 19 | 32 | 4 |
| Berger, Brandon, Spokane | .307 | 71 | 283 | 46 | 87 | 12 | 1 | 13 | 58 | 31 | 64 | 17 |
| Curtis, Matt, Boise | .305 | 75 | 305 | 57 | 93 | 29 | 3 | 12 | 62 | 37 | 47 | 2 |
| Meyer, Matt, Yakima | .302 | 66 | 235 | 40 | 71 | 14 | 6 | 4 | 28 | 27 | 73 | 6 |
| Zuniga, Jose, Bellingham | .299 | 69 | 264 | 36 | 79 | 11 | 1 | 2 | 35 | 34 | 47 | 0 |
| Livingston, Doug, Portland | .299 | 57 | 224 | 36 | 67 | 18 | 4 | 5 | 34 | 23 | 45 | 6 |
| Rodriguez, Juan, Boise | .297 | 52 | 192 | 24 | 57 | 9 | 0 | 2 | 28 | 12 | 52 | 3 |
| Sankey, Brian, Yakima | .294 | 72 | 255 | 40 | 75 | 19 | 2 | 11 | 52 | 34 | 53 | 2 |
| Caruso, Mike, Bellingham | .292 | 73 | 312 | 48 | 91 | 13 | 1 | 2 | 24 | 16 | 23 | 24 |
| Zachmann, Rob, Everett | .291 | 74 | 285 | 49 | 83 | 13 | 1 | 19 | 64 | 30 | 87 | 4 |

### INDIVIDUAL PITCHING LEADERS
(Minimum 61 Innings)

| | W | L | ERA | G | GS | CG | SV | IP | H | R | ER | BB | SO |
|---|---|---|---|---|---|---|---|---|---|---|---|---|---|
| Mayo, Blake, Yakima | 5 | 2 | 1.20 | 20 | 6 | 0 | 1 | 67 | 44 | 15 | 9 | 12 | 68 |
| Culmo, Kevin, Yakima | 4 | 2 | 2.27 | 17 | 5 | 0 | 2 | 63 | 47 | 18 | 16 | 22 | 60 |
| Chapman, Jake, Spokane | 7 | 1 | 2.37 | 19 | 7 | 0 | 1 | 68 | 44 | 19 | 18 | 20 | 71 |
| Calero, Enrique, Spokane | 4 | 2 | 2.52 | 17 | 11 | 0 | 1 | 75 | 77 | 34 | 21 | 18 | 61 |
| Hueston, Steve, Spokane | 3 | 2 | 3.08 | 13 | 13 | 0 | 0 | 64 | 54 | 27 | 22 | 31 | 60 |
| Mays, Joe, Everett | 4 | 4 | 3.08 | 13 | 10 | 0 | 0 | 64 | 55 | 33 | 22 | 22 | 56 |
| Leese, Brandon, Bellingham | 5 | 6 | 3.25 | 16 | 15 | 0 | 0 | 80 | 59 | 39 | 29 | 37 | 90 |
| Darrell, Tommy, Boise | 8 | 1 | 3.48 | 15 | 15 | 1 | 0 | 101 | 114 | 56 | 39 | 13 | 76 |
| Noriega, Ray, So. Oregon | 4 | 4 | 3.54 | 17 | 14 | 0 | 0 | 61 | 61 | 28 | 24 | 22 | 50 |
| Giuliano, Joe, Eugene | 4 | 5 | 3.55 | 26 | 1 | 0 | 3 | 66 | 61 | 39 | 26 | 26 | 58 |

## DEPARTMENT LEADERS

### BATTING
| | | |
|---|---|---|
| G | Adam Johnson, Eugene | 76 |
| AB | Adam Johnson, Eugene | 318 |
| R | Three tied at | 58 |
| H | Adam Johnson, Eugene | 100 |
| TB | Matt Curtis, Boise | 164 |
| XBH | Matt Curtis, Boise | 44 |
| 2B | Matt Curtis, Boise | 29 |
| 3B | Adam Johnson, Eugene | 9 |
| HR | Steve Hacker, Eugene | 21 |
| RBI | Kit Pellow, Spokane | 66 |
| SH | Dionys Cesar, So. Oregon | 7 |
| SF | Kit Pellow, Spokane | 7 |
| BB | Jeremy Giambi, Spokane | 61 |
| IBB | Damon Minor, Bellingham | 4 |
| | Corey Pointer, Eugene | 4 |
| HBP | Trent Durrington, Boise | 13 |
| SO | Matt Sachse, Everett | 94 |
| SB | Mike Caruso, Bellingham | 24 |
| | Trent Durrington, Boise | 24 |
| CS | Mike Caruso, Bellingham | 10 |
| GIDP | Mark DeRosa, Eugene | 10 |
| OB% | Jeremy Giambi, Spokane | .440 |
| SL% | Kit Pellow, Spokane | .559 |

### PITCHING
| | | |
|---|---|---|
| G | Mick Pageler, Bellingham | 30 |
| | Leonardo Patino, Boise | 30 |
| GS | Rob Bell, Eugene | 16 |
| | Brandon Leese, Bellingham | 16 |
| CG | Jerrod Riggan, Boise | 1 |
| | Tommy Darrell, Boise | 1 |
| ShO | Tommy Darrell, Boise | 1 |
| GF | Mick Pageler, Bellingham | 25 |
| Sv | Jeff Kubenka, Yakima | 14 |
| W | Tommy Darrell, Boise | 8 |
| L | Roger Blanco, Ever.-Eugene | 8 |
| | Keith Volkman, Boise | 8 |
| IP | Tommy Darrell, Boise | 101 |
| H | Tommy Darrell, Boise | 114 |
| R | Keith Volkman, Boise | 66 |
| ER | Keith Volkman, Boise | 50 |
| HR | Steve Matcuk, Portland | 11 |
| | Tommy Darrell, Boise | 11 |
| HB | Fernando De la Cruz, Boise | 13 |
| BB | Jeremy Blevins, Boise | 58 |
| SO | Brandon Leese, Bellingham | 90 |
| WP | Jeremy Blevins, Boise | 13 |
| BK | Matt Kramer, Yakima | 7 |

### FIELDING
| | | |
|---|---|---|
| C AVG | Dax Norris, Eugene | .994 |
| PO | Dax Norris, Eugene | 487 |
| A | Dax Norris, Eugene | 53 |
| E | Rogelio Arias, Portland | 10 |
| DP | Brian Ussery, Boise | 5 |
| PB | Dax Norris, Eugene | 18 |
| 1B AVG | Steve Hacker, Eugene | .995 |
| PO | Damon Minor, Bell. | 650 |
| A | T.R. Marcinczyk, So. Oregon | 48 |
| E | John Lindsey, Portland | 10 |
| DP | Damon Minor, Bell. | 56 |
| 2B AVG | Tony Zuniga, Bellingham | .967 |
| PO | Kenderick Moore, Spokane | 105 |
| A | Tony Zuniga, Bellingham | 167 |
| E | Kenderick Moore, Spokane | 44 |
| DP | Kenderick Moore, Spokane | 44 |
| 3B AVG | Aaron Myers, Portland | .913 |
| PO | Damian Rolls, Yakima | 58 |
| A | Damian Rolls, Yakima | 134 |
| E | Damian Rolls, Yakima | 23 |
| | Brian Rust, Eugene | 23 |
| DP | Brian Rust, Eugene | 9 |
| SS AVG | Eric Sees, Spokane | .943 |
| PO | Mike Caruso, Bellingham | 106 |
| A | Mike Caruso, Bellingham | 230 |
| E | John Clark, Portland | 38 |
| DP | Mike Caruso, Bellingham | 43 |
| OF AVG | Peter Bergeron, Yakima | .990 |
| PO | Adam Johnson, Eugene | 149 |
| A | Brandon Berger, Spokane | 10 |
| E | Jeremy Giambi, Spokane | 11 |
| DP | Adam Johnson, Eugene | 2 |
| | James Rowson, Bellingham | 2 |

# APPALACHIAN
## LEAGUE

# Bluefield Turns Tables On Kingsport

**By JOHN MANUEL**

The Bluefield Orioles enacted sweet revenge on the Kingsport Mets in 1996.

A year after posting the best record in professional baseball only to lose to the Mets in the Appalachian League championship series, the Orioles turned the tables on Kingsport, beating the Mets 2-1.

Just as Bluefield's .754 winning percentage was the best in 1995, Kingsport won 48 of 67 games in 1996 to finish with a minor league best .716. Yet neither team was able to follow up their success in the playoffs.

The Orioles won the final game 8-4 after trailing 3-0 through six innings. The comeback was highlighted by Orioles slugger Ryan Minor, the former University of Oklahoma baseball-basketball star who hit his second home run of the series in the eighth inning.

For the second straight year, Orioles and Mets players also dominated a managers' poll of the league's best prospects, occupying seven of the 10 places.

First baseman Calvin Pickering, a 6-foot-7, 275-pound giant who hit .325 and led the league with 18 homers and 66 RBIs, was the highest-rated Orioles prospect, at No. 4. He led all players in professional baseball by hitting 13 homers in August.

Mets righthander Andy Zwirchitz, who went 8-1, 1.55 in the regular season and shut out Bluefield 9-0 in Game Two of the playoffs, earned league Pitcher of the Year honors, but managers rated him only the third best pitching prospect on his own team behind righthanders Grant Roberts and Brett Herbison, who went 15-3 between them and ranked second and third, respectively.

The No. 1 spot was occupied by Danville righthander Kevin McGlinchy, who led the league with a 1.13 ERA. Under the tutelage of former Cy Young Award winner Steve Bedrosian, the Danville pitching coach, McGlinchy thrived.

**Kevin McGlinchy**

"He's the real thing," Kingsport manager John Stephenson said of the 1995 fifth-round pick, whose fastball was clocked consistently in the mid-90s. "As soon as he gets his other pitches down, he's going to be dangerous."

At the other end of the spectrum, Bristol brought up the rear with a .250 record, winning only 17 of 68 games. Thirteen of Bristol's players started the season with Hickory of the South Atlantic League, where they went 16-53 before being assigned to Bristol. For the year, the group's winning percentage was .241.

The Appalachian League operated with an awkward nine-team setup in 1996, after no major league team was willing to operate in Huntington, W. Va., after the 1995 season, forcing that club to fold.

## LEAGUE CHAMPIONS

**Last 25 Years**

| Year | Regular Season* | Pct. | Playoff |
|------|------|------|---------|
| 1972 | Bristol (Tigers) | .588 | None |
| 1973 | Kingsport (Royals) | .757 | None |
| 1974 | Bristol (Tigers) | .754 | None |
| 1975 | Johnson City (Cards) | .603 | None |
| 1976 | Johnson City (Cards) | .714 | None |
| 1977 | Kingsport (Braves) | .623 | None |
| 1978 | Elizabethton (Twins) | .594 | None |
| 1979 | Paintsville (Yankees) | .800 | None |
| 1980 | Paintsville (Yankees) | .657 | None |
| 1981 | Paintsville (Yankees) | .657 | None |
| 1982 | Bluefield (Orioles) | .681 | None |
| 1983 | Paintsville (Brewers) | .653 | None |
| 1984 | Elizabethton (Twins) | .580 | Elizabethton (Twins) |
| 1985 | Bristol (Tigers) | .638 | None |
| 1986 | Johnson City (Cards) | .667 | Pulaski (Braves) |
| 1987 | Burlington (Indians) | .725 | Burlington (Indians) |
| 1988 | Kingsport (Mets) | .644 | Kingsport (Mets) |
| 1989 | Elizabethton (Twins) | .691 | Elizabethton (Twins) |
| 1990 | Elizabethton (Twins) | .761 | None |
| 1991 | Pulaski (Braves) | .662 | Pulaski (Braves) |
| 1992 | Elizabethton (Twins) | .742 | Bluefield (Orioles) |
| 1993 | Burlington (Indians) | .647 | Burlington (Indians) |
| | Bluefield (Orioles) | .647 | |
| 1994 | Princeton (Reds) | .621 | Princeton (Reds) |
| 1995 | Bluefield (Orioles) | .754 | Kingsport (Mets) |
| 1996 | Kingsport (Mets) | .716 | Bluefield (Orioles) |

*Best overall record

## STANDINGS

| Page | EAST | W | L | PCT | GB | Manager | Attendance/Dates | Last Pennant |
|------|------|---|---|-----|-----|---------|------------------|--------------|
| 72 | Bluefield Orioles (Orioles) | 42 | 26 | .618 | — | Bobby Dickerson | 38,840 (30) | 1996 |
| 65 | Danville Braves (Braves) | 37 | 29 | .561 | 4 | Brian Snitker | 66,825 (31) | None |
| 113 | Burlington Indians (Indians) | 29 | 38 | .433 | 12½ | Harry Spilman | 43,596 (32) | 1993 |
| 106 | Princeton Reds (Reds) | 28 | 40 | .412 | 14 | Mark Wagner | 26,162 (30) | 1994 |
| 194 | Martinsville Phillies (Phillies) | 20 | 47 | .299 | 21½ | Ramon Henderson | 42,153 (32) | None |

| Page | WEST | W | L | PCT | GB | Manager | Attendance/Dates | Last Pennant |
|------|------|---|---|-----|-----|---------|------------------|--------------|
| 181 | Kingsport Mets (Mets) | 48 | 19 | .716 | — | John Stephenson | 33,100 (30) | 1995 |
| 207 | Johnson City Cardinals (Cardinals) | 42 | 26 | .618 | 6½ | Steve Turco | 47,375 (31) | 1976 |
| 161 | Elizabethton Twins (Twins) | 40 | 27 | .597 | 8 | Jose Marzan | 16,711 (28) | 1990 |
| 93 | Bristol White Sox (White Sox) | 17 | 51 | .250 | 31½ | Nick Capra | 25,262 (33) | 1985 |

**PLAYOFFS**—Bluefield defeated Kingsport 2-1, in best-of-3 series.

**NOTE:** Team's individual batting and pitching statistics can be found on page indicated in lefthand column.

# APPALACHIAN LEAGUE
## 1996 BATTING, PITCHING STATISTICS

### CLUB BATTING

| | AVG | G | AB | R | H | 2B | 3B | HR | BB | SO | SB |
|---|---|---|---|---|---|---|---|---|---|---|---|
| Johnson City | .291 | 68 | 2330 | 465 | 679 | 139 | 23 | 49 | 266 | 546 | 96 |
| Kingsport | .274 | 67 | 2240 | 412 | 613 | 94 | 23 | 38 | 279 | 418 | 82 |
| Bluefield | .261 | 68 | 2229 | 423 | 581 | 125 | 6 | 66 | 311 | 558 | 180 |
| Elizabethton | .260 | 67 | 2153 | 372 | 559 | 107 | 18 | 51 | 332 | 566 | 60 |
| Princeton | .246 | 68 | 2200 | 334 | 542 | 98 | 20 | 45 | 236 | 591 | 60 |
| Danville | .246 | 66 | 2189 | 348 | 539 | 104 | 34 | 37 | 292 | 526 | 123 |
| Martinsville | .237 | 67 | 2187 | 269 | 519 | 87 | 16 | 25 | 209 | 526 | 83 |
| Burlington | .228 | 67 | 2187 | 303 | 499 | 92 | 9 | 48 | 237 | 600 | 79 |
| Bristol | .226 | 68 | 2163 | 244 | 488 | 89 | 7 | 41 | 178 | 537 | 70 |

### CLUB PITCHING

| | ERA | G | CG | SHO | SV | IP | H | R | ER | BB | SO |
|---|---|---|---|---|---|---|---|---|---|---|---|
| Kingsport | 3.09 | 67 | 4 | 12 | 20 | 573 | 451 | 246 | 197 | 247 | 619 |
| Danville | 3.51 | 66 | 0 | 5 | 21 | 578 | 522 | 296 | 226 | 218 | 541 |
| Elizabethton | 4.12 | 67 | 4 | 4 | 14 | 555 | 553 | 323 | 254 | 209 | 545 |
| Bluefield | 4.28 | 68 | 3 | 6 | 14 | 575 | 514 | 335 | 273 | 286 | 602 |
| Burlington | 4.38 | 67 | 1 | 3 | 13 | 569 | 554 | 348 | 277 | 227 | 542 |
| Princeton | 4.53 | 68 | 8 | 4 | 13 | 565 | 532 | 370 | 285 | 279 | 572 |
| Johnson City | 4.73 | 68 | 1 | 2 | 20 | 585 | 606 | 360 | 308 | 307 | 505 |
| Bristol | 5.47 | 68 | 8 | 2 | 8 | 570 | 637 | 437 | 346 | 291 | 489 |
| Martinsville | 5.94 | 67 | 2 | 2 | 14 | 557 | 650 | 455 | 368 | 276 | 453 |

### CLUB FIELDING

| | PCT | PO | A | E | DP | | PCT | PO | A | E | DP |
|---|---|---|---|---|---|---|---|---|---|---|---|
| Johnson City | .963 | 1755 | 669 | 93 | 52 | Danville | .949 | 1734 | 667 | 129 | 53 |
| Kingsport | .963 | 1720 | 622 | 90 | 45 | Princeton | .947 | 1695 | 633 | 129 | 38 |
| Burlington | .954 | 1708 | 690 | 116 | 37 | Bristol | .943 | 1709 | 703 | 146 | 57 |
| Bluefield | .953 | 1724 | 649 | 118 | 48 | Martinsville | .942 | 1671 | 670 | 144 | 52 |
| Elizabethton | .949 | 1664 | 698 | 126 | 56 | | | | | | |

### INDIVIDUAL BATTING LEADERS
(Minimum 184 Plate Appearances)

| | AVG | G | AB | R | H | 2B | 3B | HR | RBI | BB | SO | SB |
|---|---|---|---|---|---|---|---|---|---|---|---|---|
| Harris, Rodger, JC | .369 | 44 | 168 | 38 | 62 | 12 | 2 | 5 | 30 | 10 | 28 | 16 |
| Hogan, Todd, JC | .344 | 47 | 183 | 38 | 63 | 7 | 3 | 0 | 32 | 20 | 41 | 18 |
| Butler, Brent, JC | .343 | 62 | 248 | 45 | 85 | 21 | 1 | 8 | 50 | 25 | 29 | 8 |
| Pickering, Calvin, Bluefield | .325 | 60 | 200 | 45 | 65 | 14 | 1 | 18 | 66 | 28 | 64 | 8 |
| Bishop, Tim, Kingsport | .325 | 61 | 237 | 47 | 77 | 6 | 4 | 4 | 29 | 20 | 42 | 23 |
| Reyes, Freddy, Elizabethton | .321 | 65 | 252 | 46 | 81 | 20 | 1 | 8 | 55 | 19 | 49 | 0 |
| Lopez, Pee Wee, Kingsport | .316 | 65 | 250 | 53 | 79 | 22 | 4 | 7 | 58 | 31 | 25 | 0 |
| Kritscher, Ryan, JC | .310 | 46 | 168 | 34 | 52 | 19 | 0 | 5 | 33 | 16 | 18 | 3 |
| Pendergrass, Tyrone, Dan. | .309 | 54 | 220 | 50 | 99 | 8 | 7 | 3 | 23 | 24 | 39 | 40 |
| Buczkowski, Matt, Mart. | .304 | 50 | 158 | 25 | 48 | 12 | 1 | 3 | 23 | 27 | 52 | 2 |

### INDIVIDUAL PITCHING LEADERS
(Minimum 54 Innings)

| | W | L | ERA | G | GS | CG | SV | IP | H | R | ER | BB | SO |
|---|---|---|---|---|---|---|---|---|---|---|---|---|---|
| McGlinchy, Kevin, Danville | 3 | 2 | 1.13 | 13 | 13 | 0 | 0 | 72 | 52 | 21 | 9 | 11 | 77 |
| Herbison, Brett, Kingsport | 6 | 2 | 1.29 | 13 | 12 | 0 | 0 | 77 | 43 | 18 | 11 | 31 | 86 |
| Zwirchitz, Andy, Kingsport | 8 | 1 | 1.55 | 12 | 11 | 1 | 0 | 75 | 51 | 22 | 13 | 19 | 76 |
| Shiell, Jason, Danville | 3 | 1 | 1.97 | 12 | 12 | 0 | 0 | 59 | 44 | 14 | 13 | 19 | 57 |
| Roberts, Grant, Kingsport | 9 | 1 | 2.10 | 13 | 13 | 2 | 0 | 69 | 43 | 18 | 16 | 37 | 92 |
| Bacsik, Mike, Bristol | 4 | 2 | 2.20 | 13 | 13 | 1 | 0 | 70 | 49 | 23 | 17 | 14 | 61 |
| McBride, Rodney, Eliz. | 3 | 2 | 2.43 | 12 | 12 | 1 | 0 | 74 | 60 | 29 | 20 | 28 | 83 |
| Pacheco, Delvis, Danville | 8 | 1 | 2.64 | 13 | 12 | 0 | 0 | 65 | 56 | 28 | 19 | 21 | 60 |
| Rosario, Ruben, JC | 7 | 3 | 3.28 | 13 | 13 | 1 | 0 | 71 | 53 | 30 | 26 | 37 | 72 |
| Spiers, Corey, Elizabethton | 6 | 5 | 3.34 | 17 | 8 | 0 | 0 | 59 | 69 | 45 | 22 | 26 | 67 |

# PIONEER LEAGUE

# Ogden Vs. Helena: Battle Of The Brewers

**By JOHN MANUEL**

Baseball's two newest expansion franchises spiced up the Pioneer League in 1996, but the Milwaukee Brewers were the big winners in the loop.

Two Brewers farm clubs, the Helena Brewers and Ogden Raptors, met in the league's best-of-3 championship series. Helena, which finished the regular season one game ahead of Ogden, earned bragging rights with a 5-3 victory in the rubber game.

It was Helena's second title in a row after not winning a league crown since 1984, a year before Milwaukee hooked up with Helena.

**Kevin Sweeney**

The Pioneer League had a full complement of eight working agreements for the first time since 1983. Three openings existed after the 1995 season but the Arizona Diamondbacks and Tampa Bay Devil Rays filled two of the spots, hooking on with Lethbridge and Butte respectively, while the Brewers moved their other rookie-level team from the Arizona League to Ogden. All three newly affiliated clubs advanced to the playoffs after posting sub-.500 records in 1995.

Lethbridge had the league's best record, going 50-22 overall, but lost to Helena in the Northern Division playoffs. Ogden beat Butte in the Southern Division.

Lethbridge had the most talent-laden team with three pitchers and outfielder Kevin Sweeney, whose

.424 average was the highest in professional baseball, ranked among the Top 10 prospects, as judged by managers.

Cuban-born pitchers Vladimir Nunez and Larry Rodriguez, who signed for $1.75 million and $1.25 million respectively, dominated the league. Nunez, the No. 1 prospect, went 10-0 and led the league in wins, ERA and strikeouts. Rodriguez also was effective, going 7-1 with a 3.83 ERA.

Sweeney, a 29th-round draft pick out of Division II Mercyhurst (Pa.) College, arrived with less fanfare than the Black Diamonds' pitchers but achieved stellar results. He led the league in hitting and RBIs and was named the MVP.

After posting the league's best regular-season record four years in a row, Billings experienced a down year by winning only 23 of 72 games, a .319 percentage. In the previous four years, the Mustangs won at a combined .689 clip.

## STANDINGS: SPLIT SEASON

**FIRST HALF**

| NORTH | W | L | PCT | GB |
|-------|---|---|-----|-----|
| Helena | 23 | 13 | .639 | — |
| Lethbridge | 21 | 15 | .583 | 2 |
| Great Falls | 21 | 15 | .583 | 2 |
| Medicine Hat | 12 | 24 | .333 | 11 |

| SOUTH | W | L | PCT | GB |
|-------|---|---|-----|-----|
| Ogden | 22 | 14 | .611 | — |
| Idaho Falls | 18 | 18 | .500 | 4 |
| Butte | 16 | 20 | .444 | 6 |
| Billings | 11 | 25 | .306 | 11 |

**SECOND HALF**

| NORTH | W | L | PCT | GB |
|-------|---|---|-----|-----|
| Lethbridge | 29 | 7 | .806 | — |
| Helena | 20 | 16 | .556 | 9 |
| Great Falls | 12 | 24 | .333 | 17 |
| Medicine Hat | 10 | 26 | .278 | 19 |

| SOUTH | W | L | PCT | GB |
|-------|---|---|-----|-----|
| Butte | 21 | 15 | .583 | — |
| Ogden | 20 | 16 | .556 | 1 |
| Idaho Falls | 20 | 16 | .556 | 1 |
| Billings | 12 | 24 | .333 | 9 |

**PLAYOFFS—Semifinals:** Helena defeated Lethbridge 2-0, and Ogden defeated Butte 2-1, in best-of-3 series. **Finals:** Helena defeated Ogden 2-0, in best-of-5 series.

## STANDINGS: OVERALL

| Page | | W | L | PCT | GB | Manager | Attendance/Dates | Last Pennant |
|------|--|---|---|-----|-----|---------|------------------|--------------|
| 58 | Lethbridge Black Diamonds (D'backs) | 50 | 22 | .694 | — | Chris Speier | 49,124 (35) | 1980 |
| 155 | Helena Brewers (Brewers) | 43 | 29 | .597 | 7 | Alex Morales | 44,935 (36) | 1996 |
| 156 | Ogden Raptors (Brewers) | 42 | 30 | .583 | 8 | Bernie Moncallo | 62,022 (36) | None |
| 212 | Idaho Falls Braves (Padres) | 38 | 34 | .528 | 12 | Don Werner | 54,475 (37) | 1974 |
| 226 | Butte Copper Kings (Devil Rays) | 37 | 35 | .514 | 13 | Tom Foley | 37,317 (36) | 1981 |
| 150 | Great Falls Dodgers (Dodgers) | 33 | 39 | .458 | 17 | Mickey Hatcher | 68,537 (34) | 1990 |
| 107 | Billings Mustangs (Reds) | 23 | 49 | .319 | 27 | Matt Martin | 83,586 (35) | 1994 |
| 239 | Medicine Hat Blue Jays (Blue Jays) | 22 | 50 | .306 | 28 | Marty Pevey | 41,942 (34) | 1982 |

**NOTE:** Team's individual batting and pitching statistics can be found on page indicated in lefthand column.

# PIONEER LEAGUE
## 1996 BATTING, PITCHING STATISTICS

### CLUB BATTING

| | AVG | G | AB | R | H | 2B | 3B | HR | BB | SO | SB |
|---|---|---|---|---|---|---|---|---|---|---|---|
| Lethbridge | .314 | 72 | 2583 | 637 | 811 | 133 | 25 | 88 | 407 | 579 | 93 |
| Butte | .309 | 72 | 2651 | 533 | 819 | 143 | 44 | 42 | 272 | 507 | 97 |
| Ogden | .302 | 72 | 2551 | 525 | 770 | 146 | 20 | 68 | 332 | 499 | 102 |
| Helena | .297 | 72 | 2544 | 543 | 755 | 122 | 19 | 68 | 362 | 464 | 80 |
| Idaho Falls | .295 | 72 | 2597 | 465 | 765 | 135 | 28 | 48 | 305 | 547 | 105 |
| Great Falls | .282 | 72 | 2490 | 440 | 702 | 113 | 35 | 56 | 252 | 597 | 140 |
| Billings | .266 | 72 | 2569 | 462 | 683 | 122 | 28 | 54 | 329 | 603 | 83 |
| Medicine Hat | .256 | 72 | 2412 | 410 | 617 | 109 | 9 | 57 | 311 | 605 | 113 |

### CLUB PITCHING

| | ERA | G | CG | SHO | SV | IP | H | R | ER | BB | SO |
|---|---|---|---|---|---|---|---|---|---|---|---|
| Lethbridge | 3.68 | 72 | 1 | 5 | 13 | 633 | 650 | 339 | 259 | 234 | 576 |
| Ogden | 4.83 | 72 | 1 | 1 | 19 | 637 | 654 | 441 | 342 | 326 | 627 |
| Butte | 5.33 | 72 | 0 | 1 | 16 | 638 | 767 | 516 | 378 | 323 | 602 |
| Idaho Falls | 5.48 | 72 | 1 | 1 | 13 | 633 | 717 | 452 | 386 | 291 | 538 |
| Helena | 5.64 | 72 | 1 | 1 | 20 | 631 | 727 | 479 | 396 | 338 | 602 |
| Great Falls | 6.46 | 72 | 1 | 0 | 18 | 624 | 729 | 544 | 448 | 348 | 486 |
| Billings | 6.77 | 72 | 2 | 1 | 9 | 634 | 875 | 603 | 477 | 323 | 521 |
| Medicine Hat | 7.51 | 72 | 2 | 3 | 16 | 609 | 803 | 641 | 509 | 387 | 449 |

### CLUB FIELDING

| | PCT | PO | A | E | DP | | PCT | PO | A | E | DP |
|---|---|---|---|---|---|---|---|---|---|---|---|
| Idaho Falls | .962 | 1900 | 812 | 106 | 66 | Ogden | .945 | 1912 | 720 | 154 | 58 |
| Lethbridge | .955 | 1898 | 790 | 127 | 55 | Butte | .944 | 1915 | 825 | 163 | 70 |
| Helena | .952 | 1893 | 765 | 133 | 63 | Billings | .943 | 1901 | 776 | 161 | 62 |
| Great Falls | .948 | 1871 | 793 | 147 | 63 | Medicine Hat | .934 | 1827 | 782 | 183 | 66 |

**Cuban Defectors.** Righthanders Vladimir Nunez, left, and Larry Rodriguez, who defected from Cuba in January 1996, went a combined 17-1 for Lethbridge.

### INDIVIDUAL BATTING LEADERS
(Minimum 194 Plate Appearances)

| | AVG | G | AB | R | H | 2B | 3B | HR | RBI | BB | SO | SB |
|---|---|---|---|---|---|---|---|---|---|---|---|---|
| Sweeney, Kevin, Lethbridge | .424 | 63 | 203 | 72 | 86 | 19 | 1 | 14 | 72 | 60 | 36 | 3 |
| Parent, Gerald, Ogden | .385 | 62 | 218 | 42 | 84 | 18 | 0 | 6 | 42 | 37 | 34 | 5 |
| McCain, Marcus, Butte | .379 | 55 | 256 | 66 | 97 | 9 | 4 | 1 | 27 | 16 | 21 | 34 |
| Campbell, Wylie, Billings | .371 | 70 | 259 | 69 | 96 | 15 | 7 | 0 | 30 | 45 | 29 | 24 |
| Conti, Jason, Lethbridge | .367 | 63 | 226 | 63 | 83 | 15 | 1 | 4 | 49 | 30 | 29 | 30 |
| Weekley, Jason, Great Falls | .366 | 64 | 238 | 35 | 87 | 12 | 5 | 7 | 43 | 18 | 63 | 18 |
| Arrendondo, Hernando, Butte | .357 | 67 | 252 | 59 | 90 | 21 | 7 | 4 | 49 | 24 | 31 | 8 |
| Walther, Chris, Ogden | .351 | 63 | 239 | 47 | 84 | 16 | 4 | 6 | 54 | 14 | 21 | 3 |
| Reynoso, Ben, Idaho Falls | .345 | 72 | 284 | 45 | 98 | 26 | 0 | 4 | 50 | 26 | 42 | 20 |
| Tucker, Jon, Great Falls | .345 | 48 | 174 | 39 | 60 | 12 | 1 | 12 | 54 | 15 | 30 | 13 |

### INDIVIDUAL PITCHING LEADERS
(Minimum 58 Innings)

| | W | L | ERA | G | GS | CG | SV | IP | H | R | ER | BB | SO |
|---|---|---|---|---|---|---|---|---|---|---|---|---|---|
| Nunez, Vladimir, Lethbridge | 10 | 0 | 2.22 | 14 | 13 | 0 | 0 | 85 | 78 | 25 | 21 | 10 | 93 |
| Tank, Travis, Helena | 7 | 3 | 3.22 | 29 | 0 | 0 | 3 | 64 | 65 | 38 | 23 | 30 | 74 |
| Passini, Brian, Helena | 7 | 2 | 3.48 | 15 | 14 | 1 | 0 | 78 | 91 | 37 | 30 | 27 | 71 |
| Callaway, Mickey, Butte | 6 | 2 | 3.71 | 16 | 11 | 0 | 0 | 63 | 70 | 37 | 26 | 25 | 57 |
| Allen, Craig, Great Falls | 4 | 2 | 3.84 | 13 | 12 | 0 | 0 | 61 | 52 | 38 | 26 | 31 | 46 |
| Szymborski, Tom, IF | 7 | 3 | 3.94 | 16 | 14 | 0 | 1 | 80 | 80 | 39 | 35 | 30 | 65 |
| O'Reilly, John, Ogden | 7 | 1 | 3.96 | 13 | 12 | 0 | 0 | 64 | 66 | 34 | 28 | 27 | 82 |
| Guzman, Domingo, IF | 4 | 2 | 4.13 | 15 | 10 | 1 | 0 | 65 | 52 | 41 | 30 | 29 | 75 |
| Howerton, R.J., Butte | 3 | 1 | 4.43 | 15 | 13 | 0 | 0 | 61 | 72 | 47 | 30 | 42 | 47 |
| Schroeder, Scott, Idaho Falls | 5 | 5 | 4.63 | 20 | 9 | 0 | 0 | 58 | 71 | 39 | 30 | 29 | 58 |

## DEPARTMENT LEADERS

### BATTING
| | | |
|---|---|---|
| G | Three tied at | 72 |
| AB | Brian McClure, Idaho Falls | 308 |
| R | Kevin Sweeney, Lethbridge | 72 |
| H | Brian McClure, Idaho Falls | 99 |
| TB | Ron Hartman, Lethbridge | 155 |
| XBH | Ron Hartman, Lethbridge | 39 |
| 2B | Ben Reynoso, Idaho Falls | 26 |
| 3B | Matt McCarty, Great Falls | 10 |
| HR | Three tied at | 17 |
| RBI | Ron Hartman, Lethbridge | 72 |
| | Kevin Sweeney, Lethbridge | 72 |
| SH | Adam Faurot, Ogden | 6 |
| | Jason Glover, Ogden | 6 |
| SF | David Hayman, Lethbridge | 9 |
| BB | Kevin Sweeney, Lethbridge | 60 |
| IBB | Josh Klimek, Helena | 5 |
| HBP | Jason Washam, Helena | 15 |
| SO | Darron Ingram, Billings | 88 |
| SB | Marcus McCain, Butte | 34 |
| CS | Jason Weekley, Great Falls | 12 |
| GIDP | Trey Salinas, Butte | 10 |
| OB% | Kevin Sweeney, Lethbridge | .552 |
| SL% | Kevin Sweeney, Lethbridge | .734 |

### PITCHING
| | | |
|---|---|---|
| G | Brendan Sullivan, Idaho Falls | 33 |
| GS | Three tied at | 15 |
| CG | Gary Glover, Medicine Hat | 2 |
| ShO | Domingo Guzman, Idaho Falls | 1 |
| | David Shepard, Billings | 1 |
| GF | Stephen Smith, Billings | 22 |
| Sv | David Bleazard, Med. Hat | 10 |
| W | Vladimir Nunez, Lethbridge | 10 |
| L | Gary Glover, Med. Hat | 12 |
| IP | Denis Pujals, Butte | 87 |
| H | Gary Glover, Med. Hat | 119 |
| R | Gary Glover, Med. Hat | 94 |
| ER | Gary Glover, Med. Hat | 72 |
| HR | Matt Gourlay, Med. Hat | 17 |
| HB | Bryan Zwemke, Billings | 13 |
| BB | Kyle Burchart, Med. Hat | 67 |
| SO | Vladimir Nunez, Lethbridge | 93 |
| WP | Bryan Zwemke, Billings | 19 |
| BK | Three tied at | 5 |

## HONOR ROLL

### OFFICIAL ALL-STAR TEAM
**C**—Matt Quatraro, Butte.
**1B**—Jonathan Tucker, Great Falls. **2B**—Wylie Campbell, Billings. **3B**—Steve Chavez, Idaho Falls. **SS**—Ben Reynoso, Idaho Falls.
**OF**—Kevin Sweeney, Lethbridge; Marcus McCain, Butte; Jason Weekley, Great Falls.
**DH**—Miguel Rodriguez, Ogden.
**LHP**—Brian Passini, Helena. **RHP**—Vladimir Nunez, Lethbridge. **RP**—David Bleazard, Medicine Hat.
**Most Valuable Player**—Kevin Sweeney, Lethbridge. **Manager of the Year**—Tom Foley, Butte.

### TOP 10 PROSPECTS
**1.** Vladimir Nunez, rhp, Lethbridge; **2.** Kevin Barker, 1b, Ogden; **3.** Nick Bierbrodt, lhp, Lethbridge; **4.** Larry Rodriguez, rhp, Lethbridge; **5.** Steve Chavez, 3b, Idaho Falls; **6.** Ben Reynoso, ss, Idaho Falls; **7.** Jon Tucker, 1b, Great Falls; **8.** Miguel Rodriguez, c-dh, Ogden; **9.** Kevin Sweeney, of, Lethbridge; **10.** Domingo Guzman, rhp, Idaho Falls.

# ARIZONA
## LEAGUE

# Arizona Launches Franchise In Style

**By JOHN MANUEL**

Rain doused the Lethbridge Black Diamonds' plans to host the first game in the history of the expansion Arizona Diamondbacks franchise.

So the honor went to the Diamondbacks' Arizona League affiliate, which attracted an opening-night crowd of 6,124 to Phoenix Municipal Stadium—unheard of for the cactus league, which plays most of its games early in the morning in relative solitude to beat Arizona's oppressive summer heat.

Diamondbacks owner Jerry Colangelo threw out the first pitch. In an omen of things to come, the Diamondbacks lost 15-7 to the Athletics and went on to finish with the league's poorest record.

Lethbridge, the Diamondbacks' other short-season affiliate, posted the best record in the Pioneer League.

The Diamondbacks replaced the Brewers in the six-team league. The Brewers, an original member, elected to place both of their short-season farm teams in the Pioneer League in 1996.

The Padres won the league crown with a 36-20 mark, three games better than the Athletics, who had won four of the previous five titles. It was the first victory for the Padres in the nine-year history of the league, which does not have a playoff.

The Padres were led by third baseman Shane Cronin, a 32nd-round draft pick in 1996 who led the league with nine home runs and 54 RBIs, and was named the league's MVP.

The Padres also featured the league's top starting pitcher in lefthander Steve Hoff, who won eight games and struck out 104, both league-best totals, and San Diego's two top draft picks, shortstop Matt Halloran and outfielder Vernon Maxwell. But no Padres player was rated among the league's five best prospects, according to a poll of managers.

In a season in which the talent level in the complex-based league was its best in years, managers were quick to identify Rockies righthanders Jake Westbrook, John Nicholson and Shawn Chacon as the cream of the crop. But no manager was willing to stick his neck out and say which of the

MEL BAILEY

**Impressive Debut.** Jake Westbrook, the Rockies' first-round draft pick in June, was rated the Arizona League's No. 1 prospect.

three had the greatest future.

"It's hard to differentiate them," Padres manager Larry See said. "They all have size, throw hard and throw strikes. They're very similar."

Westbrook, Nicholson and Chacon were drafted 1-2-3 in June by the Rockies. While Westbrook was the top pick, Nicholson earned all-star honors and Chacon led the Arizona League in ERA. Moreover, all had strikingly similar walk-strikeout ratios before being promoted on the same day to Class A Portland.

| LEAGUE CHAMPIONS | | | |
|---|---|---|---|
| **Last 25 Years** | | | |
| Year | Regular Season* | Pct. | Playoff |
| 1988 | Brewers | .690 | None |
| 1989 | Brewers | .727 | None |
| 1990 | Brewers | .679 | None |
| 1991 | Athletics | .650 | None |
| 1992 | Athletics | .604 | None |
| 1993 | Athletics | .636 | None |
| 1994 | Cardinals | .607 | None |
| 1995 | Athletics | .661 | None |
| 1992 | Padres | .643 | None |
| *Best overall record | | | |

## STANDINGS

| Page | | Complex Site | W | L | PCT | GB | Manager | Last Pennant |
|---|---|---|---|---|---|---|---|---|
| 213 | Padres | Peoria | 36 | 20 | .643 | — | Larry See | 1996 |
| 188 | Athletics | Phoenix | 33 | 23 | .589 | 3 | Juan Navarrete | 1995 |
| 225 | Mariners | Peoria | 29 | 27 | .518 | 7 | Tom LeVasseur | None |
| 119 | Rockies | Chandler | 26 | 30 | .464 | 10 | Jim Eppard | None |
| 87 | Angels | Mesa | 24 | 32 | .429 | 12 | Bruce Hines | None |
| 59 | Diamondbacks | Phoenix | 20 | 36 | .357 | 16 | Dwayne Murphy | None |

**PLAYOFFS**—None.

**NOTE:** Team's individual batting and pitching statistics can be found on page indicated in lefthand column.

# ARIZONA LEAGUE
## 1996 BATTING, PITCHING STATISTICS

### CLUB BATTING

| | AVG | G | AB | R | H | 2B | 3B | HR | BB | SO | SB |
|---|---|---|---|---|---|---|---|---|---|---|---|
| Padres | .277 | 56 | 1939 | 345 | 538 | 83 | 38 | 23 | 196 | 379 | 73 |
| Rockies | .254 | 56 | 1905 | 259 | 484 | 74 | 20 | 6 | 164 | 437 | 77 |
| Athletics | .250 | 56 | 1917 | 322 | 479 | 101 | 27 | 26 | 236 | 446 | 99 |
| Angels | .250 | 56 | 1909 | 276 | 477 | 100 | 29 | 16 | 191 | 436 | 124 |
| Mariners | .246 | 56 | 1905 | 265 | 468 | 72 | 26 | 24 | 173 | 512 | 72 |
| Diamondbacks | .241 | 56 | 1912 | 265 | 461 | 74 | 28 | 11 | 223 | 527 | 72 |

### CLUB PITCHING

| | ERA | G | CG | SHO | SV | IP | H | R | ER | BB | SO |
|---|---|---|---|---|---|---|---|---|---|---|---|
| Rockies | 3.51 | 56 | 2 | 6 | 14 | 489 | 489 | 269 | 191 | 158 | 451 |
| Padres | 3.57 | 56 | 2 | 2 | 16 | 499 | 488 | 276 | 198 | 203 | 471 |
| Mariners | 3.67 | 56 | 1 | 5 | 17 | 497 | 462 | 271 | 203 | 211 | 478 |
| Diamondbacks | 3.87 | 56 | 0 | 1 | 5 | 490 | 479 | 294 | 211 | 201 | 426 |
| Athletics | 4.29 | 56 | 0 | 2 | 15 | 496 | 498 | 293 | 236 | 195 | 468 |
| Angels | 4.63 | 56 | 4 | 5 | 12 | 487 | 491 | 329 | 251 | 215 | 443 |

### CLUB FIELDING

| | PCT | PO | A | E | DP | | PCT | PO | A | E | DP |
|---|---|---|---|---|---|---|---|---|---|---|---|
| Athletics | .955 | 1487 | 636 | 101 | 55 | Padres | .945 | 1496 | 570 | 121 | 41 |
| Mariners | .948 | 1491 | 562 | 113 | 38 | Diamondbacks | .944 | 1470 | 594 | 122 | 49 |
| Angels | .946 | 1461 | 589 | 118 | 35 | Rockies | .940 | 1468 | 612 | 133 | 39 |

### INDIVIDUAL BATTING LEADERS
(Minimum 151 Plate Appearances)

| | AVG | G | AB | R | H | 2B | 3B | HR | RBI | BB | SO | SB |
|---|---|---|---|---|---|---|---|---|---|---|---|---|
| Schwartzbauer, Brad, Rock. | .344 | 43 | 154 | 20 | 69 | 9 | 2 | 1 | 18 | 19 | 30 | 4 |
| Pernell, Brandon, Padres | .333 | 53 | 174 | 38 | 58 | 9 | 10 | 1 | 33 | 18 | 30 | 14 |
| Ortiz, Jose, Athletes | .330 | 52 | 200 | 43 | 66 | 12 | 8 | 4 | 25 | 20 | 34 | 16 |
| Rexrode, Jackie, D'backs | .329 | 48 | 140 | 28 | 46 | 2 | 0 | 1 | 17 | 44 | 27 | 8 |
| Cronin, Shane, Padres | .327 | 54 | 208 | 40 | 68 | 13 | 0 | 9 | 54 | 12 | 32 | 4 |
| Petersen, Mike, Rockies | .322 | 52 | 205 | 26 | 66 | 12 | 2 | 1 | 25 | 11 | 25 | 3 |
| Smith, Brian, Mariners | .296 | 54 | 223 | 39 | 66 | 15 | 6 | 3 | 16 | 21 | 46 | 13 |
| Garcia, Sandro, Padres | .291 | 53 | 189 | 29 | 55 | 6 | 4 | 1 | 17 | 8 | 27 | 11 |
| Ruotsinoja, Jacob, Padres | .291 | 52 | 172 | 37 | 50 | 14 | 3 | 6 | 40 | 40 | 38 | 2 |
| Knight, Marcus, Angels | .291 | 54 | 203 | 36 | 59 | 16 | 5 | 3 | 30 | 28 | 50 | 10 |
| Gordon, Gary, Rockies | .291 | 47 | 179 | 35 | 52 | 5 | 0 | 0 | 10 | 33 | 54 | 23 |

### INDIVIDUAL PITCHING LEADERS
(Minimum 45 Innings)

| | W | L | ERA | G | GS | CG | SV | IP | H | R | ER | BB | SO |
|---|---|---|---|---|---|---|---|---|---|---|---|---|---|
| Chacon, Shawn, Rockies | 1 | 2 | 1.60 | 11 | 11 | 1 | 0 | 56 | 46 | 17 | 10 | 15 | 64 |
| Nicholson, John, Rockies | 3 | 5 | 1.64 | 11 | 11 | 1 | 0 | 66 | 42 | 16 | 12 | 14 | 65 |
| Ortiz, Ramon, Angels | 5 | 4 | 2.12 | 16 | 8 | 2 | 1 | 68 | 55 | 28 | 16 | 27 | 78 |
| Penny, Bradley, D'backs | 2 | 2 | 2.36 | 11 | 8 | 0 | 0 | 50 | 36 | 18 | 13 | 14 | 52 |
| Palki, Jeromy, Mariners | 1 | 1 | 2.47 | 18 | 0 | 0 | 6 | 47 | 31 | 14 | 13 | 17 | 56 |
| Thompson, Josef, Padres | 8 | 2 | 2.65 | 13 | 12 | 0 | 0 | 75 | 67 | 33 | 22 | 22 | 50 |
| Hoff, Steve, Padres | 8 | 2 | 2.85 | 16 | 13 | 0 | 0 | 85 | 66 | 37 | 27 | 36 | 104 |
| Westbrook, Jake, Rockies | 4 | 2 | 2.87 | 11 | 11 | 0 | 0 | 63 | 66 | 33 | 20 | 14 | 57 |
| Nash, Damond, Padres | 5 | 3 | 3.05 | 22 | 4 | 0 | 5 | 59 | 45 | 30 | 20 | 36 | 78 |
| Derenches, Albert, Padres | 3 | 3 | 3.13 | 20 | 3 | 1 | 3 | 60 | 57 | 31 | 21 | 19 | 73 |

# GULF COAST LEAGUE

## From Top To Bottom, Yankees Are Best

By JOHN MANUEL

The Gulf Coast League Yankees followed the lead of their parent club and found their way back to post-season success in 1996.

The Yankees dominated the GCL's Northern Division and won three straight playoff games to win their first league title since back-to-back crowns in 1988-89. They upended the Expos, who posted the league's best record at 41-18 (.695), in a one-game semifinal, then swept the Rangers in a best-of-3 championshop series.

Yankees catcher-third baseman Donny Leon picked up where he left off in the regular season by hitting a pair of homers in the final series. Leon, 20, in his second stint in the GCL, won the batting title with a .361 average and led the league with 46 RBIs..

The Yankees led the league in hitting with a .287 average, 31 points higher than the second-best team and 52 points higher than the Expos, who relied on the starting pitching of righthander Joe Fraser (4-0, 1.81) and lefthander Peter Fortune (6-0, 1.96), to compile the league's best record.

Six first-round picks from the 1996 draft graced the GCL, but only Red Sox righthander Josh Garrett distinguished himself. He went 1-1 with a 1.67 ERA in seven appearances and was the only one of the six to warrant a spot on a list of the Top 10 prospects, as judged by the league's managers.

Tampa Bay's first-round pick, outfielder Paul Wilder, hit .207 and led the league with 66 strikeouts, while Atlanta's top pick, first baseman A.J. Zapp, hit only .149 with 58 strikeouts. Both were considered among the nation's top power-hitting prospects entering the draft.

The Braves got little production from any of their players and won only 14 of 59 games, the third straight year they've posted the league's poorest record.

The league's best prospect, according to managers, was 16-year-old Twins shortstop Luis Rivas, the youngest player in professional baseball in 1996. Rivas, a Venezuelan, hit .259 and tied for the league lead with 35 stolen bases.

Cubs third baseman Derrick Bly, a lowly 42nd-round pick, led the league with 13 homers.

### LEAGUE CHAMPIONS

**Last 25 Years**

| Year | Regular Season* | Pct. | Playoff |
|---|---|---|---|
| 1972 | Cubs | .651 | None |
| | Royals | .651 | |
| 1973 | Rangers | .732 | None |
| 1974 | Cubs | .702 | None |
| 1975 | Rangers | .774 | None |
| 1976 | Rangers | .704 | None |
| 1977 | White Sox | .731 | None |
| 1978 | Rangers | .600 | None |
| 1979 | Astros | .635 | None |
| 1980 | Royals Blue | .635 | None |
| 1981 | Royals Gold | .688 | None |
| 1982 | Yankees | .667 | None |
| 1983 | Rangers | .645 | Dodgers |
| 1984 | White Sox | .651 | Rangers |
| 1985 | Yankees | .705 | None |
| 1986 | Reds | .548 | Dodgers |
| 1987 | Dodgers | .683 | Dodgers |
| 1988 | Yankees | .714 | Yankees |
| 1989 | Yankees | .651 | Yankees |
| 1990 | Expos | .635 | Dodgers |
| 1991 | Orioles | .593 | Expos |
| 1992 | Royals | .695 | Royals |
| 1993 | Rangers | .667 | Rangers |
| 1994 | Royals | .797 | Astros |
| 1995 | Marlins | .714 | Royals |
| 1996 | Expos | .695 | Yankees |

*Best overall record

### STANDINGS

| Page | EASTERN | Complex Site | W | L | PCT | GB | Manager | Last Pennant |
|---|---|---|---|---|---|---|---|---|
| 168 | Expos | West Palm Beach | 41 | 18 | .695 | — | Jim Gabella | 1991 |
| 131 | Marlins | Melbourne | 34 | 25 | .576 | 7 | Juan Bustabad | None |
| 182 | Mets | Port St. Lucie | 29 | 30 | .492 | 12 | Mickey Brantley | None |
| 66 | Braves | West Palm Beach | 14 | 45 | .237 | 27 | Robert Lucas/Chino Cadahia | 1964 |
| Page | NORTHWEST | Complex Site | W | L | PCT | GB | Manager | Last Pennant |
| 233 | Rangers | Port Charlotte | 37 | 23 | .617 | — | James Byrd | 1993 |
| 73 | Orioles | Sarasota | 36 | 24 | .600 | 1 | Tommy Shields | None |
| 200 | Pirates | Bradenton | 28 | 31 | .475 | 8½ | Woody Huyke | None |
| 94 | White Sox | Sarasota | 20 | 40 | .333 | 17 | Hector Rincones | 1977 |
| Page | NORTHERN | Complex Site | W | L | PCT | GB | Manager | Last Pennant |
| 175 | Yankees | Tampa | 37 | 21 | .638 | — | Ken Dominguez | 1996 |
| 137 | Astros | Kissimmee | 31 | 28 | .525 | 6½ | Bobby Ramos | 1994 |
| 125 | Tigers | Lakeland | 26 | 34 | .433 | 12 | Kevin Bradshaw | None |
| 227 | Devil Rays | St. Petersburg | 24 | 35 | .407 | 13½ | Bill Evers | None |
| Page | SOUTHWEST | Complex Site | W | L | PCT | GB | Manager | Last Pennant |
| 101 | Cubs | Fort Myers | 34 | 26 | .567 | — | Sandy Alomar Sr. | None |
| 143 | Royals | Fort Myers | 30 | 29 | .508 | 3½ | Al Pedrique | 1992 |
| 162 | Twins | Fort Myers | 30 | 30 | .500 | 4 | Mike Boulanger | None |
| 80 | Red Sox | Fort Myers | 24 | 36 | .400 | 10 | Bob Geren | None |

**PLAYOFFS—Semifinals:** Yankees defeated Expos and Rangers defeated Cubs in one-game series. **Finals:** Yankees defeated Rangers 2-0, in best-of-3 series.

**NOTE:** Team's individual batting and pitching statistics can be found on page indicated in lefthand column.

# GULF COAST LEAGUE
## 1996 BATTING, PITCHING STATISTICS

### CLUB BATTING

| | AVG | G | AB | R | H | 2B | 3B | HR | BB | SO | SB |
|---|---|---|---|---|---|---|---|---|---|---|---|
| Yankees | .287 | 58 | 1948 | 345 | 560 | 101 | 21 | 17 | 190 | 387 | 32 |
| Pirates | .256 | 60 | 1995 | 284 | 510 | 82 | 27 | 20 | 186 | 367 | 63 |
| Red Sox | .254 | 60 | 2035 | 279 | 516 | 105 | 15 | 22 | 184 | 481 | 71 |
| Cubs | .253 | 60 | 1969 | 285 | 498 | 72 | 16 | 30 | 196 | 455 | 178 |
| Orioles | .248 | 60 | 1978 | 271 | 490 | 84 | 20 | 15 | 198 | 423 | 96 |
| Twins | .247 | 60 | 1917 | 262 | 473 | 86 | 22 | 18 | 183 | 389 | 103 |
| Royals | .246 | 60 | 1904 | 227 | 469 | 94 | 9 | 18 | 160 | 378 | 29 |
| Rangers | .244 | 60 | 1992 | 304 | 487 | 91 | 27 | 35 | 176 | 497 | 118 |
| White Sox | .244 | 60 | 1980 | 236 | 484 | 93 | 17 | 14 | 173 | 442 | 47 |
| Marlins | .244 | 60 | 1968 | 261 | 481 | 76 | 9 | 16 | 177 | 426 | 86 |
| Astros | .243 | 59 | 1898 | 263 | 462 | 92 | 18 | 20 | 171 | 469 | 85 |
| Mets | .243 | 59 | 1865 | 249 | 453 | 78 | 20 | 20 | 189 | 384 | 55 |
| Expos | .235 | 60 | 1909 | 303 | 449 | 76 | 25 | 11 | 207 | 358 | 82 |
| Devil Rays | .232 | 59 | 1979 | 240 | 460 | 61 | 18 | 9 | 175 | 505 | 76 |
| Tigers | .229 | 60 | 1918 | 264 | 439 | 91 | 19 | 15 | 204 | 513 | 91 |
| Braves | .211 | 59 | 1883 | 155 | 398 | 75 | 6 | 7 | 143 | 419 | 27 |

### CLUB PITCHING

| | ERA | G | CG | SHO | SV | IP | H | R | ER | BB | SO |
|---|---|---|---|---|---|---|---|---|---|---|---|
| Marlins | 2.73 | 60 | 5 | 11 | 11 | 524 | 402 | 214 | 159 | 182 | 421 |
| Cubs | 2.83 | 60 | 1 | 3 | 15 | 527 | 424 | 230 | 166 | 188 | 485 |
| Rangers | 2.98 | 60 | 4 | 4 | 20 | 527 | 467 | 232 | 175 | 196 | 431 |
| Expos | 3.15 | 60 | 3 | 7 | 16 | 515 | 436 | 225 | 180 | 152 | 348 |
| Orioles | 3.20 | 60 | 1 | 6 | 20 | 525 | 456 | 238 | 187 | 175 | 451 |
| Astros | 3.27 | 59 | 1 | 5 | 14 | 505 | 447 | 247 | 184 | 191 | 515 |
| Twins | 3.38 | 60 | 5 | 2 | 12 | 506 | 493 | 258 | 190 | 183 | 389 |
| Mets | 3.49 | 59 | 4 | 5 | 18 | 495 | 449 | 236 | 192 | 178 | 439 |
| Yankees | 3.60 | 58 | 2 | 9 | 13 | 485 | 452 | 256 | 194 | 178 | 453 |
| Red Sox | 3.68 | 60 | 0 | 3 | 10 | 527 | 546 | 308 | 216 | 173 | 423 |
| Pirates | 3.76 | 60 | 3 | 4 | 14 | 512 | 511 | 291 | 214 | 184 | 418 |
| Tigers | 3.88 | 60 | 0 | 2 | 10 | 505 | 527 | 305 | 218 | 172 | 405 |
| Royals | 4.05 | 60 | 3 | 4 | 14 | 495 | 495 | 279 | 223 | 165 | 427 |
| Braves | 4.08 | 59 | 0 | 1 | 6 | 505 | 494 | 293 | 229 | 204 | 379 |
| White Sox | 4.19 | 60 | 4 | 3 | 10 | 511 | 535 | 312 | 238 | 192 | 408 |
| Devil Rays | 4.22 | 59 | 2 | 0 | 12 | 517 | 495 | 304 | 243 | 199 | 501 |

### CLUB FIELDING

| | PCT | PO | A | E | DP | | PCT | PO | A | E | DP |
|---|---|---|---|---|---|---|---|---|---|---|---|
| Marlins | .963 | 1571 | 657 | 85 | 44 | Royals | .953 | 1486 | 673 | 107 | 41 |
| Rangers | .960 | 1582 | 621 | 92 | 44 | Cubs | .952 | 1582 | 699 | 115 | 53 |
| Astros | .958 | 1516 | 632 | 95 | 39 | Tigers | .947 | 1515 | 654 | 121 | 45 |
| Orioles | .957 | 1575 | 680 | 101 | 57 | Pirates | .946 | 1535 | 635 | 123 | 54 |
| Devil Rays | .956 | 1552 | 598 | 98 | 51 | Mets | .946 | 1485 | 611 | 119 | 36 |
| Yankees | .956 | 1454 | 584 | 94 | 43 | Red Sox | .945 | 1581 | 679 | 132 | 48 |
| Twins | .956 | 1518 | 719 | 104 | 60 | Braves | .944 | 1515 | 636 | 128 | 39 |
| Expos | .954 | 1544 | 654 | 107 | 48 | White Sox | .941 | 1532 | 661 | 138 | 55 |

### INDIVIDUAL BATTING LEADERS
(Minimum 162 Plate Appearances)

| | AVG | G | AB | R | H | 2B | 3B | HR | RBI | BB | SO | SB |
|---|---|---|---|---|---|---|---|---|---|---|---|---|
| Leon, Donny, Yankees | .361 | 53 | 191 | 30 | 69 | 14 | 4 | 6 | 46 | 9 | 30 | 1 |
| Bolivar, Ceasar, Twins | .342 | 41 | 155 | 30 | 53 | 7 | 1 | 1 | 18 | 8 | 32 | 26 |
| Figueroa, Frank, Orioles | .340 | 43 | 150 | 22 | 51 | 8 | 1 | 0 | 23 | 8 | 25 | 3 |
| Zapata, Alexis, Tigers | .333 | 51 | 189 | 34 | 63 | 13 | 5 | 6 | 41 | 12 | 35 | 8 |
| Alleyne, Roberto, Astros | .331 | 48 | 151 | 32 | 50 | 9 | 0 | 7 | 27 | 20 | 32 | 4 |
| Meran, Jorge, Tigers | .315 | 51 | 168 | 25 | 53 | 13 | 3 | 2 | 32 | 13 | 42 | 7 |
| Abreu, Dennis, Cubs | .313 | 56 | 192 | 32 | 60 | 5 | 0 | 0 | 15 | 21 | 20 | 35 |
| Polonia, Isreal, Marlins | .310 | 50 | 171 | 22 | 53 | 6 | 2 | 4 | 31 | 10 | 50 | 6 |
| Radcliff, Vic, Royals | .309 | 48 | 165 | 24 | 51 | 11 | 2 | 3 | 20 | 15 | 34 | 1 |
| Robertson, Dean, Orioles | .302 | 53 | 179 | 32 | 54 | 11 | 2 | 2 | 25 | 28 | 17 | 16 |

### INDIVIDUAL PITCHING LEADERS
(Minimum 48 Innings)

| | W | L | ERA | G | GS | CG | SV | IP | H | R | ER | BB | SO |
|---|---|---|---|---|---|---|---|---|---|---|---|---|---|
| Gholar, Antonio, Twins | 1 | 2 | 1.72 | 15 | 7 | 0 | 2 | 52 | 30 | 18 | 10 | 30 | 50 |
| Robertson, Jeriome, Astros | 5 | 3 | 1.72 | 13 | 13 | 1 | 0 | 78 | 51 | 20 | 15 | 15 | 98 |
| Fraser, Joe, Expos | 4 | 0 | 1.81 | 11 | 10 | 0 | 0 | 50 | 35 | 14 | 10 | 18 | 45 |
| Santana, Pedro, Red Sox | 5 | 3 | 1.89 | 13 | 8 | 0 | 0 | 71 | 59 | 24 | 15 | 12 | 33 |
| Fortune, Peter, Expos | 6 | 0 | 1.96 | 13 | 13 | 0 | 0 | 73 | 52 | 23 | 16 | 21 | 66 |
| Ortega, Pablo, Devil Rays | 4 | 6 | 1.97 | 13 | 13 | 1 | 0 | 82 | 61 | 24 | 18 | 12 | 86 |
| Santos, Victor, Tigers | 3 | 2 | 1.98 | 9 | 9 | 0 | 0 | 50 | 44 | 12 | 11 | 13 | 39 |
| Paraqueima, Jesus, Yankees | 3 | 2 | 2.01 | 11 | 9 | 0 | 0 | 49 | 43 | 24 | 11 | 15 | 49 |
| Jimenez, Ricardo, Orioles | 5 | 3 | 2.01 | 12 | 12 | 0 | 0 | 63 | 46 | 22 | 14 | 34 | 44 |
| Knotts, Gary, Marlins | 4 | 2 | 2.04 | 12 | 9 | 1 | 0 | 57 | 35 | 16 | 13 | 17 | 46 |

# Powerful Dodgers Stave Off Athletics

The Dodgers posted the Dominican Summer League's best record since 1992, when the Blue Jays set the professional baseball standard by going 68-2 (.971). Unlike the Jays four years before, the Dodgers completed the task of winning the league championship.

The La Romana-based club, one of two Dodgers entries in the DSL, went 59-10 to run away with the San Pedro de Macoris Division title by 12½ games over the Blue Jays. The Dodgers then disposed of the Tigers and Athletics in the playoffs.

In 1992, the high-flying Blue Jays were knocked out of the playoffs in two straight games by the A's, who in turn lost to the Dodgers in the finals. The Dodgers followed that up by winning again in 1993, giving them three titles in five years with their latest conquest.

The Dodgers finished a distant second in 1995 to Japan's Toyo Carp, who went 58-13 overall and proceeded to win the league title. The Carp did not field a team in the DSL in 1996 after a three-year run.

The Dodgers featured two 10-game winners in pitchers Pedro Hernandez (10-1) and Randy Galvez (10-2), while compiling a league best 2.52 ERA. Hernandez, who added two playoff wins, was selected the league's Pitcher of the Year.

The DSL fielded 25 clubs in 1996—the most ever. All but the Reds and Twins were involved in the league, though several clubs shared working agreements. The Dodgers were the only team to field two clubs.

**ALL-STAR TEAM: C**—Arnulfo Vasquez, Indians. **1B**—Danny Cabrera, Mets. **2B**—Luis Martinez, Dodgers II. **3B**—Melvin Olivares, Mets. **SS**—Pablo Ozuna, Cardinals. **OF**—Alex Fajardo, Phillies; Raul de la Cruz, Pirates; Frank Ventura, Indians. **DH**—Juan Silvestre, Mariners. **RHP**—Pablo Hernandez, Dodgers II. **LHP**—Bernardo Reyes, Cardinals.

**Player of the Year:** Frank Ventura, Indians. **Pitcher of the Year:** Pedro Hernandez, Dodgers II. **Manager of the Year:** Roberto Diaz, Cardinals.

## INDIVIDUAL BATTING LEADERS
(Minimum 170 Plate Appearances)

| | AVG | AB | R | H | 2B | 3B | HR | RBI | SB |
|---|---|---|---|---|---|---|---|---|---|
| De la Cruz, Raul, Pirates | .387 | 243 | 49 | 94 | 16 | 0 | 5 | 40 | 35 |
| Ventura, Frank, Indians | .382 | 225 | 55 | 86 | **24** | 2 | 4 | 42 | 26 |
| Martinez, Luis, Dodgers II | .378 | 286 | 68 | **108** | 12 | 3 | 0 | 45 | 8 |
| Fajardo, Alex, Phillies | .373 | 249 | 48 | 93 | 16 | 6 | 2 | 38 | 22 |
| Ozuna, Pablo, Cardinals | .363 | 295 | 57 | **107** | 12 | 4 | 6 | 60 | 18 |
| Perez, Edison, Mariners | .360 | 189 | 45 | 68 | 14 | 0 | 5 | 22 | 27 |
| Olivares, Melvin, Mets | .360 | 272 | 48 | 98 | 16 | 0 | 9 | 49 | 13 |
| Gutierrez, Victor, Pirates | .360 | 278 | 60 | 100 | 20 | 1 | 3 | 26 | 44 |
| Chavez, Endy, Mets | .354 | 164 | 42 | 58 | 11 | 1 | 7 | 29 | 3 |
| DeLeon, Raymundo, Cards | .348 | 282 | 51 | 98 | 17 | 7 | 5 | 46 | 8 |
| Vasquez, Arnulfo, Indians | .344 | 224 | 45 | 77 | 21 | 1 | 3 | 50 | 12 |
| Rodriguez, Miguel, Cards | .342 | 243 | 50 | 83 | 7 | 3 | 1 | 28 | **48** |
| Sanchez, Manuel, Braves | .342 | 228 | 47 | 78 | 9 | 9 | 4 | 48 | 22 |
| Cabrera, Danny, Mets | .338 | 213 | 44 | 72 | 15 | 0 | 14 | 43 | 3 |
| Garcia, Alfredo, Mets | .337 | 193 | 49 | 65 | 6 | 0 | 8 | 32 | 16 |
| Moreta, Ramon, Dodgers II | .330 | 270 | 69 | 89 | 13 | 2 | 1 | 29 | 17 |
| Valdez, Jean, Athletics | .328 | 177 | 34 | 58 | 9 | 2 | 4 | 20 | 7 |
| Mejia, Benato, Marlins | .327 | 254 | 38 | 83 | 9 | 1 | 5 | 36 | 9 |
| Espino, Fernando, Mariners | .327 | 165 | 23 | 54 | 10 | 2 | 3 | 20 | 4 |
| Ramirez, Frank, Dodgers I | .327 | 156 | 29 | 51 | 8 | 0 | 1 | 18 | 1 |
| Giron, Alex, Phillies | .326 | 273 | 31 | 89 | 15 | 4 | 1 | 37 | 10 |
| Lopez, J., Diamondbacks | .323 | 257 | 37 | 83 | 15 | 1 | 7 | 38 | 4 |
| Haad, Yamid, Pirates | .322 | 205 | 29 | 66 | 9 | 0 | 5 | 28 | 8 |
| Quero, Pedro, Expos | .322 | 273 | 34 | 88 | 12 | 0 | 7 | 48 | 7 |
| Juarez, Johnny, Blue Jays | .321 | 184 | 31 | 59 | 9 | 4 | 0 | 30 | 12 |
| Castro, Martires, Rangers | .320 | 231 | 30 | 74 | 16 | 3 | 7 | 38 | 8 |
| Guzman, Carlos, Tigers | .318 | 195 | 40 | 62 | 6 | 1 | 2 | 34 | 19 |
| Pena, Reynaldo, Tigers | .317 | 240 | 63 | 76 | 13 | **10** | 1 | 22 | 18 |
| Araujo, Orlany, Dodgers I | .316 | 174 | 22 | 55 | 6 | 0 | 0 | 13 | 7 |
| Rivera, Yorkis, Dodgers* | .315 | 232 | 47 | 73 | 17 | 2 | 5 | 42 | 10 |
| Silvestre, Juan, Mariners | .311 | 238 | 51 | 74 | 9 | 1 | **19** | **61** | 1 |
| Beatriz, R., Brewers/WhSox | .310 | 168 | 29 | 52 | 14 | 2 | 2 | 20 | 11 |
| Villar, Jose, Braves | .310 | 203 | 41 | 63 | 10 | 0 | 2 | 28 | 19 |
| Pichardo, Henry, Indians | .310 | 245 | 61 | 76 | 11 | 3 | 0 | 33 | 19 |
| #Araujo, Daniel, Cardinals | .303 | 261 | **77** | 79 | 9 | 2 | 1 | 22 | 36 |

## INDIVIDUAL PITCHING LEADERS
(Minimum 50 Innings)

| | W | L | ERA | G | SV | IP | H | BB | SO |
|---|---|---|---|---|---|---|---|---|---|
| Veras, Jovanny, Indians* | 2 | 1 | 0.34 | 34 | **13** | 52 | 30 | 18 | 56 |
| Villalobos, Noe, Red Sox | 4 | 2 | 1.13 | 16 | 1 | 64 | 41 | 12 | 50 |
| Jiron, Isabel, Blue Jays | 6 | 1 | 1.19 | 21 | 3 | 61 | 42 | 17 | 49 |
| Reyes, Bernardo, Cardinals | 8 | 1 | 1.18 | 16 | 0 | 76 | 52 | 37 | 56 |
| Mateo, Julio, Mariners | 4 | 2 | 1.74 | 14 | 1 | 52 | 42 | 19 | 23 |
| Hernandez, Pedro, Dodgers II | 10 | 1 | 1.87 | 14 | 0 | 87 | 65 | 25 | 62 |
| Paulino, Arison, Pirates | 3 | 0 | 1.95 | 21 | 0 | 60 | 40 | 21 | 42 |
| Guzman, Ambiorix, Rangers | 6 | 0 | 1.97 | 12 | 1 | 64 | 57 | 16 | 53 |
| Alcantara, Albin, Cardinals | 9 | 3 | 2.03 | 15 | 0 | 95 | 77 | 24 | 71 |
| Cepeda, Wellington, Dbacks | 7 | 2 | 3.09 | 16 | 0 | 82 | 72 | 20 | 70 |
| Rojas, Cesar, Rangers | 7 | 2 | 2.10 | 16 | 0 | 90 | 79 | 32 | 51 |
| Peguero, D., Astros/Red Sox | 3 | 4 | 2.14 | 12 | 0 | 59 | 38 | 29 | 52 |
| Montero, Agustin, Athletics | 2 | 8 | 2.21 | 17 | 1 | 86 | 64 | 58 | 71 |
| Rosario, Ramon, Athletics | 6 | 3 | 2.21 | 15 | 0 | 85 | 77 | 33 | 58 |
| Vega, Juan, Giants | 6 | 2 | 2.24 | 13 | 0 | 76 | 53 | 45 | 76 |
| Gonzalez, Luis, Athletics | 5 | 1 | 2.26 | 16 | 0 | 52 | 50 | 20 | 22 |
| Benoit, Joaquin, Rangers | 6 | 5 | 2.28 | 14 | 0 | 75 | 63 | 23 | 63 |
| Garcia, Jose, Indians | 5 | 4 | 2.35 | 24 | 6 | 54 | 47 | 11 | 54 |
| Anez, M., Brewers/WhSox | 5 | 3 | 2.42 | 13 | 0 | 74 | 74 | 28 | 34 |
| Baez, Miguel, Indians | 7 | 1 | 2.43 | 15 | 0 | 100 | 95 | 28 | 93 |
| #Galvez, Randy, Dodgers II | 10 | 2 | 2.53 | 13 | 0 | 75 | 63 | 21 | 54 |
| #Bello, Emerson, Mariners | 6 | 1 | 2.59 | 18 | 1 | 94 | 73 | 42 | **102** |
| #Nin, Daurin, Cardinals | 2 | 4 | 3.67 | 23 | **13** | 54 | 47 | 20 | 62 |

**Boldface** indicates league leader

## STANDINGS

| SANTO DOMINGO EAST | W | L | PCT | GB |
|---|---|---|---|---|
| Tigers | 47 | 25 | .653 | — |
| Cardinals | 47 | 27 | .635 | 1 |
| Yankees | 41 | 29 | .586 | 5 |
| Dodgers I | 39 | 28 | .582 | 5½ |
| Mariners | 35 | 34 | .507 | 10½ |
| Marlins | 20 | 50 | .286 | 26 |
| Expos | 19 | 52 | .268 | 27½ |

| SANTO DOMINGO WEST | W | L | PCT | GB |
|---|---|---|---|---|
| Athletics | 49 | 24 | .671 | — |
| Mets | 47 | 24 | .637 | 1 |
| Rangers | 43 | 28 | .606 | 5 |
| Diamondbacks | 36 | 36 | .500 | 12½ |
| Brewers/White Sox | 32 | 38 | .464 | 15½ |
| Pirates | 25 | 46 | .352 | 23 |
| Cubs/Padres | 17 | 56 | .233 | 32 |

| SAN PEDRO de MACORIS | W | L | PCT | GB |
|---|---|---|---|---|
| Dodgers II | 59 | 10 | .855 | — |
| Blue Jays | 47 | 23 | .671 | 12½ |
| Braves | 42 | 29 | .592 | 18 |
| Astros/Red Sox | 29 | 39 | .426 | 29½ |
| Giants | 26 | 40 | .394 | 31½ |
| Orioles | 27 | 42 | .391 | 32 |
| Devil Rays/Angels | 12 | 59 | .169 | 48 |

| CIBAO | W | L | PCT | GB |
|---|---|---|---|---|
| Indians | 50 | 21 | .704 | — |
| Phillies | 36 | 35 | .507 | 14 |
| Co-op* | 28 | 42 | .400 | 21½ |
| Royals/Rockies | 27 | 43 | .386 | 22½ |

**PLAYOFFS: Semifinals**— Dodgers II defeated Tigers 2-0, and Athletics defeated Indians 2-1, in best-of-3 series. **Finals**—Dodgers II defeated Athletics 3-2 in best-of-5 series.

# INDEPENDENT LEAGUES

# Attrition Hampers Independents But Northern League Thrives

By WILL LINGO

The giddy excitement from the early days of independent baseball's renaissance apparently has passed, with no sign of when or if it might be back.

After the Northern League and Frontier League blazed a new trail in 1993, independent leagues increased to five in 1994, followed by an explosion to 11 in 1995.

Open an independent baseball league. Make easy money. As it turns out, it's not that easy.

Just nine leagues came to the starting line in 1996—seven returners and two new leagues, the Big South and Heartland. They all completed their seasons, though many of their franchises will change in the offseason, as is the usual practice.

Plans for new leagues are also not as plentiful as before. Only one league, the Atlantic League, had made any tangible plans to field teams, and it postponed its debut for another year, to 1998.

On a much smaller scale, the independents are following the overall trend of the minor leagues after World War II. A postwar boom that saw 438 cities and 59 leagues in 1949 was followed by the inevitable bust, and only 10 years later there were just 21 minor leagues.

Even worse, the teams and leagues left debts behind, leaving a stain on minor league baseball that took years to wash away. Many cities that have welcomed independent baseball have seen the same problems.

More than any time in the short modern history of independent baseball, survival, much less success, is proving difficult. More leagues are getting smaller, looking for better markets or just trying to find stability.

Miles Wolff, the commissioner of the Northern League and president of Baseball America, began the craze when he suggested reopening the Northern League in 1993. He's not convinced independent baseball can be a long-term, large-scale success.

"The jury is still out. There's enough instability out there that it's hard to tell what's going to happen," he said. "When everything shakes out, there may be three or four that ultimately survive because there aren't enough good markets out there."

As always, the market is the key factor. The leagues have proven that they can always find players. Almost every league can find a former big leaguer to fill out a roster or manage a team.

"People have found out this is not an easy thing to do," said Norb Ecksl, executive vice president of the Big South League. "You can't just get your friends together and have a league."

Perhaps no other league better exemplifies that and the struggles at the bottom of the independent chain than the Heartland League. The new league was actually born out of the old Great Central League, which opened and closed in 1994.

Beset by financial and legal problems, the league

**Saints March In.** Former major leaguers Jack Morris, left, and Darryl Strawberry graced the roster of the St. Paul Saints in 1996.

sank only to be reformed in 1995 as the Mid-America League. The league staggered through the season, with only three teams finishing the schedule and no playoffs.

Those who survived came back and reformed a second time, as the Heartland League. The league made it through the season this time, but drew tiny crowds. The Dubois County franchise led the way with 33,203 for 30 home dates, but attendance dropped way off after that, with the other three teams combined drawing about 27,000 fans.

## NORTHERN LEAGUE

The St. Paul Saints continued their domination of the Northern League, sweeping past the Fargo-Moorhead RedHawks to win their third league championship in four years.

The Saints scored an unearned run in the ninth inning to win the decisive third game 4-3, the first time a team had swept the championship series.

With two out, Joe Biernat reached on an error and scored on a triple by Carlton Fleming. The rally spoiled a complete-game effort by Fargo-Moorhead's Jeff Bittiger, who struck out a playoff-record 10 batters.

This was the second straight championship for the Saints, who beat the Madison Black Wolf two games to none in the division playoffs. The RedHawks advanced to the finals by beating the Winnipeg Goldeyes two games to one.

Fleming, the Saints' leadoff hitter and second baseman, was the MVP of the championship series. He went 5-for-12 in the series with five runs, two RBIs and two stolen bases.

The RedHawks were led all season by outfielder-DH Darryl Motley, who batted .346 with 26 homers, 103 RBIs and 77 runs. Somehow he wasn't the Northern League MVP (that honor went to Winnipeg first baseman Terry Lee), but he was Baseball America's

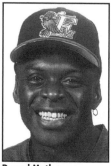

**Darryl Motley**          **Terry Lee**

first Independent League Player of the Year.

The Northern League continued to set itself apart from other independent leagues, with attendance and stability that are a quantum leap ahead of other leagues.

The league expanded for the first time, adding Fargo-Moorhead and Madison to give it eight teams. Those teams added to the league's success, as the league drew more than one million fans to far outpace all other leagues.

The Saints, in fact, drew 267,099 fans, more than most other leagues. And they were certainly the only team to be featured on a cable television program: "Baseball, Minnesota" was a 22-episode reality-based series on the fX network that sought to show baseball at its grass roots.

The Saints also attracted national attention by signing Jack Morris and Darryl Strawberry. Both performed well, with Morris going 5-1 with a no-hitter and Strawberry hitting .435 with 18 homers and 39 RBIs in 29 games. But while Strawberry got signed by the Yankees and went on to play in the World Series, Morris didn't create any interest, quit halfway through the season and went back to his farm. Morris' 2.61 ERA stood up as the league's best.

## STANDINGS

### FIRST HALF

| EAST | W | L | PCT | GB |
|---|---|---|---|---|
| St. Paul Saints | 23 | 20 | .535 | — |
| Madison Black Wolf | 22 | 21 | .512 | 1 |
| Duluth-Superior Dukes | 21 | 21 | .500 | 1½ |
| Thunder Bay Whiskey Jacks | 19 | 23 | .452 | 3½ |
| **WEST** | **W** | **L** | **PCT** | **GB** |
| Fargo-Moorhead RedHawks | 26 | 16 | .619 | — |
| Winnipeg Goldeyes | 25 | 17 | .595 | 1 |
| Sioux Falls Canaries | 20 | 22 | .476 | 6 |
| Sioux City Explorers | 13 | 29 | .310 | 13 |

### SECOND HALF

| EAST | W | L | PCT | GB |
|---|---|---|---|---|
| St. Paul Saints | 22 | 20 | .524 | — |
| Madison Black Wolf | 22 | 20 | .524 | — |
| Duluth-Superior Dukes | 21 | 21 | .500 | 1 |
| Thunder Bay Whiskey Jacks | 14 | 28 | .333 | 8 |
| **WEST** | **W** | **L** | **PCT** | **GB** |
| Fargo-Moorhead RedHawks | 27 | 15 | .643 | — |
| Winnipeg Goldeyes | 25 | 17 | .595 | 2 |
| Sioux Falls Canaries | 24 | 18 | .571 | 3 |
| Sioux City Explorers | 13 | 29 | .310 | 14 |

PLAYOFFS: **Semifinals**—St. Paul defeated Madison 2-0, and Fargo-Moorhead defeated Winnipeg 2-1, in best-of-3 series. **Finals**—St. Paul defeated Fargo-Moorhead 3-0 in best-of-5 series.

**MANAGERS:** Duluth-Superior—George Mitterwald. Fargo-Moorhead—Doug Simunic. Madison—Wayne Krenchicki. St. Paul—Marty Scott. Sioux City—Ed Nottle. Sioux Falls—John Zizzo. Thunder Bay—Jason Felice. Winnipeg—Hal Lanier.

**ATTENDANCE:** St. Paul, 267,099; Winnipeg, 171,351; Fargo-Moorhead, 155,052; Sioux City, 147,062; Sioux Falls, 100,958; Madison, 83,573; Duluth-Superior, 77,294; Thunder Bay, 50,429.

**ALL-STAR TEAM: C**—Mitch Lyden, Madison. **1B**—Terry Lee, Winnipeg. **2B**—Casey Waller, Thunder Bay. **3B**—Jose Peguero, Sioux City. **SS**—Matt Davis, Sioux Falls. **OF**—Sean Hearn, Thunder Bay; A.J. Johnson, Duluth-Superior; Darryl Motley, Fargo-Moorhead. **DH**—Kevin Garner, Sioux City. **RHP**—Jamie Ybarra, Winnipeg. **LHP**—Matt Jarvis, Winnipeg. **RP**—Paul Romanoli, St. Paul.

**Player of the Year:** Terry Lee, Winnipeg. **Pitcher of the Year:** Jamie Ybarra, Sioux Falls-Winnipeg. **Manager of the Year:** Doug Simunic, Fargo-Moorhead.

### INDIVIDUAL BATTING LEADERS
(Minimum 227 Plate Appearances)

| | AVG | AB | R | H | 2B | 3B | HR | RBI | SB |
|---|---|---|---|---|---|---|---|---|---|
| Peguero, Jose, SC | .366 | 333 | 49 | 122 | 17 | 10 | 6 | 59 | 21 |
| Lee, Terry, Winnipeg | .353 | 306 | 81 | 108 | 17 | 0 | 23 | 88 | 1 |
| Motley, Darryl, F-M | .346 | 324 | 77 | 112 | 23 | 1 | 26 | 103 | 7 |
| Reed, Darren, D-S | .345 | 206 | 42 | 71 | 18 | 0 | 7 | 40 | 1 |
| Marabella, Tony, Mad | .340 | 338 | 46 | 115 | 34 | 0 | 5 | 50 | 3 |
| Traxler, Brian, F-M | .335 | 328 | 73 | 110 | 16 | 2 | 16 | 75 | 0 |
| Davis, Matt, Sioux Falls | .328 | 317 | 72 | 104 | 20 | 0 | 7 | 64 | 4 |
| Johnson, Anthony, D-S | .327 | 315 | 59 | 103 | 29 | 2 | 20 | 65 | 6 |
| Neff, Marty, Sioux City | .323 | 353 | 53 | 114 | 29 | 1 | 19 | 74 | 3 |
| Kemp, Tim, D-S | .322 | 211 | 36 | 68 | 10 | 2 | 0 | 15 | 10 |
| Hearn, Sean, TB | .322 | 261 | 57 | 84 | 14 | 3 | 20 | 48 | 12 |

### INDIVIDUAL PITCHING LEADERS
(Minimum 67 Innings)

| | W | L | ERA | G | SV | IP | H | BB | SO |
|---|---|---|---|---|---|---|---|---|---|
| Morris, Jack, St. Paul | 5 | 1 | 2.61 | 10 | 0 | 72 | 66 | 16 | 43 |
| Hyde, Rich, Sioux Falls | 9 | 3 | 2.72 | 13 | 0 | 96 | 93 | 21 | 68 |
| Poeck, Chad, TB | 5 | 8 | 3.21 | 19 | 1 | 87 | 78 | 48 | 56 |
| Alkire, Jeff, St. Paul | 6 | 2 | 3.38 | 18 | 0 | 120 | 121 | 50 | 87 |
| Wise, Andy, Winnipeg | 4 | 0 | 3.45 | 23 | 1 | 76 | 84 | 13 | 48 |
| Devereux, Chad, TB | 4 | 2 | 3.48 | 14 | 0 | 83 | 72 | 27 | 75 |
| Kyslinger, Dan, Madison | 8 | 4 | 3.58 | 18 | 0 | 116 | 104 | 49 | 81 |
| Jarvis, Matt, Winnipeg | 11 | 3 | 3.58 | 17 | 0 | 103 | 99 | 55 | 63 |
| LaPlante, Michel, Mad | 10 | 7 | 3.62 | 19 | 0 | 129 | 134 | 41 | 82 |
| McGarity, Jeremy, D-S | 12 | 3 | 3.65 | 19 | 0 | 133 | 128 | 40 | 106 |

## DULUTH-SUPERIOR

| BATTING | AVG | AB | R | H | 2B | 3B | HR | RBI | SB |
|---|---|---|---|---|---|---|---|---|---|
| Barsoom, Alan, ss-2b | .288 | 104 | 18 | 30 | 7 | 2 | 1 | 15 | 0 |
| Briley, Greg, of | .303 | 330 | 69 | 100 | 22 | 2 | 5 | 51 | 25 |
| Brown, Ron, of | .264 | 231 | 36 | 61 | 16 | 0 | 7 | 35 | 4 |
| Champoux, Beau, of-3b | .164 | 55 | 7 | 9 | 3 | 0 | 1 | 4 | 0 |
| Chance, Tony, of-dh | .281 | 96 | 21 | 27 | 4 | 0 | 6 | 18 | 1 |
| Cruz, Paul, of | .357 | 14 | 2 | 5 | 1 | 0 | 0 | 3 | 0 |
| Dong, Tom, 2b | .273 | 139 | 21 | 38 | 3 | 2 | 2 | 13 | 5 |
| Jensen, Jeff, 1b | .295 | 261 | 36 | 77 | 15 | 1 | 4 | 40 | 5 |
| Johnson, Anthony, of-3b | .327 | 315 | 59 | 103 | 29 | 2 | 20 | 65 | 6 |
| Kemp, Tim, 2b-ss | .322 | 211 | 36 | 68 | 10 | 2 | 0 | 15 | 10 |
| Kuld, Pete, c | .287 | 310 | 44 | 89 | 24 | 0 | 17 | 75 | 4 |
| Lockwood, Brett, ss | .182 | 110 | 13 | 20 | 1 | 0 | 1 | 10 | 1 |
| Mitterwald, Bryan, c-1b | .253 | 182 | 23 | 46 | 13 | 0 | 1 | 13 | 1 |
| Nelson, Charlie, of | .298 | 228 | 46 | 68 | 9 | 2 | 3 | 17 | 29 |
| Reed, Darren, 3b | .345 | 206 | 42 | 71 | 18 | 0 | 7 | 40 | 1 |
| Thomas, Tim, ss | .273 | 99 | 16 | 27 | 4 | 2 | 2 | 14 | 2 |
| 2-team (5 St. Paul) | .265 | 117 | 18 | 31 | 4 | 2 | 4 | 20 | 2 |

| PITCHING | W | L | ERA | G | SV | IP | H | BB | SO |
|---|---|---|---|---|---|---|---|---|---|
| Ahearne, Pat | 0 | 0 | 12.46 | 1 | 0 | 4 | 10 | 1 | 1 |
| Butcher, Jason | 2 | 1 | 1.30 | 24 | 9 | 28 | 23 | 12 | 22 |
| Frascatore, Steve | 2 | 1 | 6.66 | 28 | 1 | 50 | 67 | 17 | 22 |
| Garcia, Jaime | 2 | 3 | 4.31 | 15 | 1 | 56 | 61 | 29 | 30 |
| Harvell, Pete | 1 | 2 | 5.32 | 30 | 4 | 46 | 52 | 37 | 39 |
| Hmielewski, Chris | 1 | 7 | 6.52 | 9 | 0 | 50 | 60 | 37 | 19 |
| Jersild, Aaron | 10 | 9 | 4.29 | 21 | 0 | 130 | 159 | 33 | 102 |
| Kummerfeldt, Jason | 8 | 9 | 5.25 | 20 | 0 | 123 | 133 | 67 | 83 |
| McGarity, Jeremy | 12 | 3 | 3.65 | 19 | 0 | 133 | 128 | 40 | 106 |
| Poehnelt, Vito | 0 | 2 | 13.50 | 4 | 0 | 8 | 14 | 8 | 6 |
| Reed, Jason | 0 | 0 | 18.00 | 4 | 0 | 4 | 7 | 6 | 1 |
| Wanke, Chuck | 3 | 1 | 3.21 | 21 | 2 | 34 | 31 | 18 | 34 |
| 2-team (6 Sioux Falls) | 4 | 1 | 3.89 | 27 | 3 | 42 | 38 | 22 | 40 |
| Weaver, Andy | 1 | 4 | 7.38 | 19 | 1 | 54 | 74 | 17 | 35 |

## FARGO-MOORHEAD

| BATTING | AVG | AB | R | H | 2B | 3B | HR | RBI | SB |
|---|---|---|---|---|---|---|---|---|---|
| Akers, Chad, ss | .273 | 330 | 84 | 90 | 11 | 0 | 5 | 41 | 13 |
| Carpenter, Jerry, c | .000 | 15 | 0 | 0 | 0 | 0 | 0 | 0 | 0 |

| BATTING | AVG | AB | R | H | 2B | 3B | HR | RBI | SB |
|---|---|---|---|---|---|---|---|---|---|
| Coste, Chris, c-2b | .314 | 315 | 40 | 99 | 30 | 0 | 6 | 56 | 2 |
| Crosby, Mike, c | .111 | 9 | 0 | 1 | 0 | 0 | 0 | 0 | 0 |
| Doty, Derrin, of | .190 | 58 | 11 | 11 | 1 | 0 | 3 | 4 | 1 |
| Iatarola, Aaron, of | .299 | 314 | 47 | 94 | 22 | 0 | 14 | 66 | 3 |
| Knott, John, 3b | .290 | 290 | 82 | 84 | 26 | 3 | 15 | 80 | 20 |
| Kunka, Tony, dh-1b | .213 | 108 | 22 | 23 | 4 | 0 | 3 | 13 | 1 |
| Mangual, Danny, 2b-ss | .216 | 37 | 7 | 8 | 0 | 0 | 0 | 5 | 2 |
| Migita, Lance, 2b-of | .267 | 255 | 40 | 68 | 11 | 2 | 1 | 31 | 4 |
| Motley, Darryl, of-dh | .346 | 324 | 77 | 112 | 23 | 1 | 26 | 103 | 7 |
| Powell, Chris, of | .250 | 88 | 22 | 22 | 6 | 2 | 2 | 9 | 14 |
| 3-team (3 Winn./36 SF) | .289 | 266 | 72 | 77 | 17 | 3 | 5 | 28 | 46 |
| Reams, Derek, c | .217 | 138 | 22 | 30 | 8 | 0 | 2 | 14 | 1 |
| Rundels, Matt, of | .272 | 305 | 71 | 83 | 19 | 4 | 12 | 64 | 14 |
| Traxler, Brian, 1b | .335 | 328 | 73 | 110 | 16 | 2 | 16 | 75 | 0 |

| PITCHING | W | L | ERA | G | SV | IP | H | BB | SO |
|---|---|---|---|---|---|---|---|---|---|
| Alamillo, Pete | 0 | 2 | 6.75 | 21 | 0 | 36 | 57 | 16 | 14 |
| Alazaus, Shawn | 1 | 2 | 4.32 | 26 | 1 | 33 | 30 | 25 | 26 |
| Antolick, Jeff | 0 | 2 | 7.89 | 6 | 0 | 22 | 29 | 5 | 20 |
| Bittiger, Jeff | 9 | 1 | 4.06 | 17 | 0 | 93 | 97 | 40 | 91 |
| Chandler, Jason | 0 | 1 | 12.34 | 5 | 0 | 12 | 20 | 8 | 5 |
| 2-team (16 Thunder Bay) | 1 | 6 | 7.84 | 21 | 0 | 60 | 82 | 32 | 33 |
| Fisher, Ernie | 5 | 1 | 4.73 | 24 | 5 | 53 | 64 | 17 | 36 |
| Isom, Jeff | 6 | 6 | 4.89 | 25 | 1 | 77 | 66 | 48 | 79 |
| Keenan, Brad | 0 | 0 | 19.50 | 6 | 0 | 6 | 13 | 4 | 3 |
| Lukas, Stephen | 9 | 1 | 1.93 | 36 | 11 | 56 | 43 | 29 | 51 |
| Shenk, Larry | 4 | 4 | 5.13 | 18 | 0 | 47 | 62 | 10 | 24 |
| Shoemaker, Steve | 7 | 6 | 4.86 | 19 | 0 | 128 | 149 | 48 | 79 |
| Smith, Tim | 11 | 3 | 4.01 | 19 | 0 | 121 | 114 | 58 | 108 |
| Valencia, Max | 1 | 0 | 7.24 | 11 | 0 | 14 | 21 | 6 | 8 |
| 3-team (19 SC/2 St. Paul) | 1 | 4 | 7.89 | 32 | 0 | 43 | 56 | 27 | 22 |
| Walters, Dwayne | 0 | 1 | 3.97 | 9 | 0 | 34 | 48 | 9 | 21 |
| Williams, Greg | 0 | 1 | 17.05 | 7 | 0 | 6 | 17 | 8 | 3 |

## MADISON

| BATTING | AVG | AB | R | H | 2B | 3B | HR | RBI | SB |
|---|---|---|---|---|---|---|---|---|---|
| Bruksch, Kurt, of | .000 | 4 | 0 | 0 | 0 | 0 | 0 | 0 | 0 |
| Connell, Lino, 2b | .298 | 339 | 57 | 101 | 17 | 6 | 3 | 46 | 31 |
| Cora, Manny, ss | .244 | 299 | 29 | 73 | 8 | 0 | 1 | 26 | 4 |
| Cullen, Geoff, of | .105 | 19 | 0 | 2 | 0 | 0 | 0 | 0 | 0 |
| Everson, Darin, 1b-c | .310 | 300 | 62 | 93 | 15 | 3 | 13 | 43 | 2 |
| Gibbons, Brian, of | .192 | 78 | 4 | 15 | 0 | 0 | 0 | 8 | 3 |
| Kimbler, Doug, 3b-ss | .255 | 243 | 34 | 62 | 19 | 0 | 5 | 24 | 10 |
| Lyden, Mitch, c-dh | .317 | 300 | 58 | 95 | 13 | 3 | 29 | 80 | 1 |
| Marabella, Tony, dh-3b | .340 | 338 | 46 | 115 | 34 | 0 | 5 | 50 | 3 |
| Meggers, Mike, of | .298 | 215 | 40 | 64 | 15 | 1 | 14 | 39 | 0 |
| Millam, Brandon, c | .204 | 54 | 8 | 11 | 2 | 0 | 0 | 4 | 3 |
| Powell, Corey, of | .304 | 335 | 66 | 102 | 19 | 1 | 17 | 63 | 3 |
| Reed, Curtis, of | .175 | 57 | 9 | 10 | 2 | 1 | 1 | 6 | 9 |
| Tsoukalas, John, 3b | .343 | 70 | 15 | 24 | 7 | 0 | 1 | 12 | 0 |
| 2-team (49 Thunder Bay) | .294 | 245 | 29 | 72 | 18 | 0 | 2 | 33 | 0 |
| Vatcher, Jim, of | .287 | 314 | 63 | 90 | 21 | 4 | 9 | 52 | 9 |

| PITCHING | W | L | ERA | G | SV | IP | H | BB | SO |
|---|---|---|---|---|---|---|---|---|---|
| Carter, Tommy | 0 | 3 | 7.50 | 7 | 0 | 18 | 30 | 5 | 12 |
| Cook, Will | 3 | 1 | 7.44 | 15 | 0 | 33 | 31 | 28 | 17 |
| Fischer, Tom | 6 | 6 | 5.09 | 17 | 0 | 97 | 108 | 52 | 61 |
| Harris, Phil | 0 | 0 | 4.91 | 17 | 0 | 18 | 22 | 14 | 12 |
| Hoyman, Adam | 0 | 0 | 3.38 | 11 | 0 | 21 | 19 | 9 | 11 |
| Kyslinger, Dan | 8 | 4 | 3.58 | 18 | 0 | 116 | 104 | 49 | 81 |
| LaPlante, Michel | 10 | 7 | 3.62 | 18 | 0 | 129 | 134 | 41 | 82 |
| Lott, Hank | 0 | 0 | 81.00 | 2 | 0 | 1 | 6 | 8 | 1 |
| Mosman, Marc | 2 | 7 | 6.14 | 20 | 0 | 59 | 70 | 29 | 57 |
| Rambo, Dan | 8 | 6 | 4.62 | 18 | 0 | 134 | 159 | 24 | 66 |
| Salamon, John | 3 | 1 | 2.31 | 37 | 7 | 51 | 47 | 38 | 40 |
| Salmon, Fabian | 4 | 6 | 6.79 | 25 | 3 | 57 | 73 | 32 | 42 |
| Zaikov, Craig | 0 | 0 | 4.50 | 2 | 0 | 2 | 5 | 0 | 3 |

## ST. PAUL

| BATTING | AVG | AB | R | H | 2B | 3B | HR | RBI | SB |
|---|---|---|---|---|---|---|---|---|---|
| Biernat, Joe, of-3b | .182 | 33 | 4 | 6 | 1 | 0 | 0 | 3 | 1 |
| Bruett, J.T., of | .320 | 206 | 48 | 66 | 9 | 2 | 0 | 14 | 13 |
| Cannaday, Aaron, c | .243 | 251 | 23 | 61 | 14 | 1 | 3 | 32 | 4 |
| D'Alexander, Greg, ss-3b | .290 | 276 | 38 | 80 | 17 | 2 | 6 | 36 | 3 |
| Dattola, Kevin, of | .271 | 107 | 21 | 29 | 6 | 0 | 2 | 17 | 10 |
| 2-team (54 Winnipeg) | .257 | 307 | 74 | 79 | 20 | 0 | 7 | 51 | 27 |
| Davis, Glenn, dh-1b | .265 | 155 | 24 | 41 | 5 | 0 | 9 | 50 | 3 |
| Evans, Chris, of-3b | .275 | 171 | 19 | 47 | 13 | 0 | 2 | 18 | 3 |
| Fleming, Carlton, 2b | .301 | 319 | 56 | 96 | 9 | 2 | 0 | 27 | 14 |
| Garner, Kevin, dh | .284 | 141 | 34 | 40 | 6 | 0 | 14 | 28 | 0 |
| Jackson, Chuck, 3b | .212 | 99 | 13 | 21 | 1 | 1 | 4 | 20 | 0 |
| Konigsmark, Dave, 3b-2b | .218 | 101 | 9 | 22 | 1 | 1 | 0 | 5 | 1 |
| Leary, Rob, of-1b | .286 | 147 | 35 | 42 | 6 | 0 | 9 | 30 | 0 |
| 2-team (42 Sioux City) | .296 | 307 | 64 | 91 | 18 | 0 | 15 | 53 | 2 |
| Lieder, Craig, 1b | .208 | 72 | 9 | 15 | 5 | 0 | 0 | 7 | 0 |
| McNally, Jason, c-3b | .239 | 67 | 12 | 16 | 6 | 0 | 2 | 7 | 0 |
| Neff, Marty, 1b-of | .342 | 187 | 29 | 64 | 18 | 0 | 8 | 41 | 2 |
| Robbins, Lance, ss-3b | .333 | 168 | 20 | 56 | 8 | 0 | 1 | 20 | 8 |

| | AVG | AB | R | H | 2B | 3B | HR | RBI | SB |
|---|---|---|---|---|---|---|---|---|---|
| 2-team (42 Sioux City) | .321 | 336 | 51 | 108 | 19 | 1 | 2 | 33 | 16 |
| Solomon, Steve, of | .303 | 333 | 63 | 101 | 15 | 5 | 6 | 44 | 17 |
| Strawberry, Darryl, of | .435 | 108 | 31 | 47 | 7 | 0 | 18 | 39 | 4 |
| Thomas, Tim, ss-2b | .222 | 18 | 2 | 4 | 0 | 0 | 2 | 6 | 0 |
| Villanueva, Hector, dh-c | .255 | 55 | 9 | 14 | 5 | 0 | 2 | 8 | 0 |

| PITCHING | W | L | ERA | G | SV | IP | H | BB | SO |
|---|---|---|---|---|---|---|---|---|---|
| Alkire, Jeff | 6 | 2 | 3.38 | 18 | 0 | 120 | 121 | 50 | 87 |
| Burgos, John | 2 | 0 | 2.12 | 3 | 0 | 17 | 15 | 5 | 18 |
| Cordeiro, Brian | 0 | 0 | 6.00 | 7 | 0 | 12 | 15 | 14 | 13 |
| Letourneau, Jeff | 1 | 5 | 6.85 | 7 | 0 | 45 | 59 | 24 | 31 |
| Manfred, Jim | 12 | 5 | 4.15 | 34 | 3 | 102 | 104 | 56 | 55 |
| Miller, Joe | 2 | 5 | 5.43 | 27 | 0 | 61 | 55 | 35 | 38 |
| Morris, Jack | 5 | 1 | 2.61 | 10 | 0 | 72 | 66 | 16 | 43 |
| Peterman, Ernie | 1 | 0 | 3.54 | 8 | 0 | 20 | 17 | 12 | 16 |
| Robinson, Scott | 1 | 2 | 12.60 | 3 | 0 | 10 | 19 | 5 | 2 |
| 2-team (9 Winnipeg) | 5 | 6 | 8.47 | 12 | 0 | 63 | 96 | 25 | 41 |
| Romanoli, Paul | 3 | 4 | 1.85 | 34 | 19 | 49 | 41 | 13 | 50 |
| Seip, Rod | 0 | 1 | 7.43 | 9 | 0 | 13 | 27 | 9 | 7 |
| Serna, Joe | 1 | 1 | 10.80 | 11 | 0 | 22 | 35 | 11 | 14 |
| Smith, Scott | 3 | 3 | 5.75 | 10 | 0 | 41 | 43 | 17 | 16 |
| Stewart, Scott | 6 | 8 | 5.84 | 19 | 0 | 86 | 121 | 42 | 54 |
| Thomson, Dan | 1 | 1 | 5.85 | 25 | 0 | 52 | 62 | 34 | 24 |
| Valencia, Max | 0 | 0 | 0.00 | 2 | 0 | 2 | 1 | 3 | 0 |
| Westfall, Joe | 1 | 2 | 8.16 | 20 | 0 | 32 | 43 | 21 | 25 |

## SIOUX CITY

| BATTING | AVG | AB | R | H | 2B | 3B | HR | RBI | SB |
|---|---|---|---|---|---|---|---|---|---|
| Dawson, Charles, c | .205 | 44 | 7 | 9 | 2 | 0 | 0 | 5 | 0 |
| Dreamer, Derek, c | .143 | 7 | 1 | 1 | 0 | 0 | 0 | 0 | 0 |
| Farlow, Kevin, ss | .261 | 299 | 37 | 78 | 14 | 1 | 8 | 44 | 2 |
| Garner, Kevin, dh | .257 | 144 | 23 | 37 | 8 | 1 | 12 | 26 | 1 |
| 2-team (39 St. Paul) | .270 | 285 | 57 | 77 | 14 | 1 | 26 | 54 | 1 |
| Griffiths, Kyle, c | .141 | 92 | 10 | 13 | 1 | 0 | 0 | 3 | 0 |
| Hoch, Cory, of | .211 | 19 | 2 | 4 | 0 | 0 | 0 | 1 | 0 |
| Irish, Cole, 3b-of | .189 | 122 | 17 | 23 | 4 | 1 | 0 | 10 | 3 |
| Kickul, Kory, c | .255 | 47 | 3 | 12 | 1 | 0 | 0 | 5 | 0 |
| Konigsmark, Dave, 2b-3b | .317 | 123 | 19 | 39 | 5 | 0 | 0 | 10 | 2 |
| 2-team (33 St. Paul) | .272 | 224 | 28 | 61 | 6 | 1 | 0 | 15 | 3 |
| Lane, Nolan, of | .271 | 306 | 54 | 83 | 20 | 1 | 10 | 38 | 26 |
| Leary, Rob, dh-1b | .306 | 160 | 29 | 49 | 12 | 0 | 6 | 23 | 2 |
| Neff, Marty, of | .301 | 166 | 24 | 50 | 11 | 1 | 11 | 33 | 1 |
| 2-team (43 St. Paul) | .323 | 353 | 53 | 114 | 29 | 1 | 19 | 74 | 3 |
| Peguero, Jose, 3b-2b | .366 | 333 | 49 | 122 | 17 | 10 | 6 | 59 | 21 |
| Proctor, Murph, 1b | .319 | 326 | 57 | 104 | 19 | 1 | 15 | 66 | 0 |
| Robbins, Lance, 2b-3b | .310 | 168 | 31 | 52 | 11 | 1 | 1 | 13 | 8 |
| Shwartzer, Mike, c | .154 | 91 | 6 | 14 | 2 | 0 | 0 | 7 | 1 |
| 2-team (1 Sioux Falls) | .149 | 94 | 6 | 14 | 2 | 0 | 0 | 7 | 1 |
| Williams, Dana, of | .254 | 122 | 8 | 31 | 3 | 0 | 0 | 12 | 4 |
| Young, Gerald, of | .317 | 293 | 49 | 93 | 25 | 1 | 4 | 27 | 21 |

| PITCHING | W | L | ERA | G | SV | IP | H | BB | SO |
|---|---|---|---|---|---|---|---|---|---|
| Boyd, Kevin | 0 | 1 | 9.42 | 5 | 0 | 14 | 17 | 12 | 9 |
| Brooks, Wes | 7 | 7 | 4.88 | 22 | 0 | 131 | 144 | 43 | 78 |
| Callahan, Brian | 0 | 3 | 13.78 | 8 | 0 | 16 | 29 | 18 | 10 |
| Corrigan, Cory | 2 | 8 | 6.75 | 21 | 1 | 95 | 139 | 27 | 46 |
| Drysdale, Brooks | 0 | 1 | 3.29 | 17 | 2 | 38 | 39 | 13 | 34 |
| Gogolewski, Chris | 2 | 11 | 5.79 | 20 | 0 | 93 | 105 | 48 | 45 |
| Greene, Danny | 0 | 5 | 9.82 | 13 | 1 | 33 | 52 | 14 | 22 |
| Murdaugh, Reese | 6 | 11 | 6.02 | 21 | 0 | 124 | 162 | 52 | 47 |
| Ortiz, Steve | 0 | 0 | 4.35 | 19 | 0 | 31 | 33 | 23 | 29 |
| Shanahan, Chris | 4 | 0 | 7.58 | 33 | 0 | 59 | 83 | 30 | 36 |
| Steinert, Bob | 1 | 4 | 8.00 | 5 | 0 | 18 | 13 | 31 | 8 |
| Valencia, Max | 0 | 4 | 8.78 | 19 | 0 | 28 | 34 | 18 | 14 |
| Wolfe, Don | 4 | 3 | 3.06 | 30 | 3 | 32 | 35 | 20 | 30 |

## SIOUX FALLS

| BATTING | AVG | AB | R | H | 2B | 3B | HR | RBI | SB |
|---|---|---|---|---|---|---|---|---|---|
| Allen, Matt, c-1b | .309 | 152 | 25 | 47 | 13 | 0 | 1 | 25 | 2 |
| Birk, Craig, 1b-dh | .283 | 113 | 15 | 32 | 7 | 1 | 4 | 23 | 0 |
| Carey, Paul, 1b | .385 | 104 | 24 | 40 | 11 | 1 | 5 | 36 | 1 |
| Castillo, Benny, of | .284 | 229 | 43 | 65 | 14 | 1 | 4 | 33 | 1 |
| Davis, Matt, ss | .328 | 317 | 72 | 104 | 20 | 0 | 7 | 64 | 4 |
| Dumas, Mike, 3b-of | .268 | 310 | 61 | 83 | 5 | 3 | 1 | 19 | 36 |
| Evans, Chris, of-3b | .304 | 92 | 12 | 28 | 5 | 0 | 3 | 20 | 0 |
| 2-team (47 St. Paul) | .285 | 263 | 31 | 75 | 18 | 0 | 5 | 38 | 3 |
| Guerrieri, P.J., 2b | .189 | 53 | 10 | 10 | 2 | 0 | 0 | 6 | 0 |
| Hosey, Steve, of-1b | .305 | 325 | 63 | 99 | 26 | 0 | 17 | 69 | 11 |
| Kessick, Chris, c | .000 | 8 | 2 | 0 | 0 | 0 | 0 | 0 | 0 |
| Lantigua, Eddie, of-3b | .308 | 146 | 23 | 45 | 10 | 0 | 7 | 34 | 2 |
| Lewis, Dan, dh | .284 | 81 | 20 | 23 | 5 | 0 | 5 | 16 | 0 |
| Loubier, Scott, c | .207 | 150 | 24 | 31 | 8 | 0 | 4 | 24 | 2 |
| Perez, Raidel, 2b | .263 | 266 | 30 | 70 | 11 | 1 | 6 | 36 | 2 |
| Powell, Chris, of | .333 | 132 | 38 | 44 | 8 | 1 | 3 | 15 | 26 |
| Ruckman, Steve, 3b | .288 | 73 | 6 | 21 | 2 | 0 | 0 | 8 | 1 |
| Saugstad, Mark, dh-1b | .304 | 46 | 4 | 14 | 4 | 0 | 0 | 3 | 0 |
| Schwartzer, Mike, c | .000 | 3 | 0 | 0 | 0 | 0 | 0 | 0 | 0 |
| Seal, Mike, of | .239 | 163 | 22 | 39 | 9 | 0 | 2 | 23 | 1 |

| | | | | | | | | |
|---|---|---|---|---|---|---|---|---|
| Serra, Joaquin, 2b | .000 | 3 | 0 | 0 | 0 | 0 | 0 | 0 |
| Slayton, Shane, 1b-c | .240 | 96 | 9 | 23 | 2 | 0 | 2 | 10 | 0 |
| Williams, Paul, c | .185 | 27 | 3 | 5 | 0 | 0 | 1 | 2 | 0 |
| Yelding, Eric, 2b | .324 | 68 | 16 | 22 | 2 | 0 | 2 | 6 | 1 |

| PITCHING | W | L | ERA | G | SV | IP | H | BB | SO |
|---|---|---|---|---|---|---|---|---|---|
| Andrakin, Rob | 5 | 5 | 5.34 | 30 | 5 | 61 | 67 | 42 | 48 |
| Dickens, John | 1 | 0 | 12.86 | 7 | 0 | 7 | 16 | 7 | 4 |
| Fontana, Mike | 4 | 4 | 5.40 | 10 | 0 | 55 | 63 | 27 | 36 |
| Frith-Smith, Chris | 1 | 3 | 3.25 | 30 | 2 | 53 | 58 | 14 | 13 |
| Hrepich, Jeff | 0 | 0 | 40.50 | 2 | 0 | 2 | 9 | 4 | 1 |
| Hyde, Rich | 9 | 3 | 2.72 | 13 | 0 | 96 | 93 | 21 | 68 |
| Jones, Cliff | 0 | 0 | 40.50 | 1 | 0 | 1 | 3 | 0 | 0 |
| Locklear, Jeff | 2 | 1 | 8.20 | 8 | 1 | 37 | 56 | 23 | 17 |
| Lovato, Nick | 1 | 2 | 9.87 | 18 | 0 | 31 | 50 | 28 | 18 |
| Magrini, Paul | 3 | 3 | 3.92 | 16 | 0 | 87 | 88 | 54 | 45 |
| 2-team (7 Winnipeg) | 3 | 4 | 4.63 | 23 | 0 | 101 | 106 | 67 | 51 |
| McRoberts, Brian | 1 | 5 | 7.04 | 26 | 3 | 38 | 47 | 19 | 22 |
| Mullikin, Jamie | 2 | 1 | 7.36 | 21 | 0 | 29 | 44 | 17 | 17 |
| Nickell, Jackie | 2 | 2 | 3.47 | 9 | 0 | 47 | 51 | 22 | 40 |
| Pollard, Chris | 0 | 0 | 19.29 | 2 | 0 | 2 | 6 | 4 | 2 |
| Post, Bobby | 10 | 5 | 5.67 | 19 | 0 | 121 | 148 | 35 | 54 |
| Seal, Mike | 0 | 1 | 3.29 | 7 | 0 | 14 | 18 | 8 | 12 |
| Sheets, Ryan | 0 | 0 | 11.25 | 8 | 1 | 8 | 14 | 6 | 6 |
| Shenk, Larry | 2 | 2 | 8.05 | 10 | 0 | 19 | 23 | 9 | 18 |
| 2-team (18 Fargo) | 6 | 6 | 5.97 | 28 | 0 | 66 | 85 | 19 | 42 |
| Wanke, Chuck | 0 | 0 | 6.75 | 6 | 1 | 8 | 7 | 4 | 6 |
| Wise, Andy | 0 | 1 | 3.31 | 8 | 1 | 16 | 16 | 2 | 8 |
| Ybarra, Jamie | 0 | 2 | 11.57 | 8 | 1 | 16 | 25 | 12 | 20 |

## THUNDER BAY

| BATTING | AVG | AB | R | H | 2B | 3B | HR | RBI | SB |
|---|---|---|---|---|---|---|---|---|---|
| Alvarez, Luis, dh | .281 | 32 | 5 | 9 | 2 | 0 | 0 | 4 | 1 |
| Brown, Jarvis, of | .300 | 160 | 27 | 48 | 7 | 1 | 4 | 20 | 9 |
| Fraraccio, Dan, 3b-1b | .295 | 132 | 19 | 39 | 11 | 2 | 2 | 17 | 0 |
| Grevengoed, Jayson, 1b-3b | .252 | 210 | 29 | 53 | 12 | 0 | 8 | 31 | 0 |
| Griffith, Tommy, of-1b | .261 | 157 | 25 | 41 | 3 | 4 | 4 | 19 | 3 |
| Hearn, Sean, of | .322 | 261 | 57 | 84 | 14 | 3 | 20 | 48 | 12 |
| Hernandez, Kiki, c | .236 | 246 | 25 | 58 | 8 | 0 | 7 | 30 | 1 |
| Hohman, Grant, 1b | .213 | 61 | 10 | 13 | 2 | 0 | 0 | 0 | 1 |
| LaGreca, Paul, of | .000 | 2 | 0 | 0 | 0 | 0 | 0 | 0 | 0 |
| Matos, Julius, ss | .275 | 295 | 33 | 81 | 13 | 0 | 3 | 32 | 8 |
| Palmer, Nate, c | .179 | 28 | 4 | 5 | 1 | 0 | 1 | 3 | 0 |
| Pierson, Paul, 1b-of | .241 | 58 | 6 | 14 | 8 | 0 | 0 | 7 | 1 |
| Ross, Jackie, of | .314 | 309 | 57 | 97 | 18 | 4 | 2 | 29 | 6 |
| Sawyer, Chris, of | .273 | 293 | 42 | 80 | 18 | 0 | 8 | 37 | 11 |
| Sturges, Brian, c-2b | .241 | 108 | 14 | 26 | 3 | 0 | 0 | 11 | 3 |
| Tsoukalas, John, 3b | .274 | 175 | 14 | 48 | 11 | 0 | 1 | 21 | 0 |
| Waller, Casey, 2b | .300 | 293 | 36 | 88 | 21 | 1 | 8 | 54 | 13 |

| PITCHING | W | L | ERA | G | SV | IP | H | BB | SO |
|---|---|---|---|---|---|---|---|---|---|
| Boynewicz, Jim | 2 | 9 | 6.44 | 32 | 2 | 81 | 104 | 34 | 51 |
| Browning, Mike | 0 | 0 | 10.29 | 6 | 2 | 7 | 8 | 7 | 2 |
| Chandler, Jason | 1 | 5 | 6.75 | 16 | 0 | 48 | 62 | 24 | 28 |
| De la Rosa, Francisco | 1 | 2 | 7.20 | 4 | 0 | 15 | 18 | 3 | 10 |
| Devereux, Charles | 4 | 2 | 3.48 | 14 | 0 | 83 | 72 | 27 | 75 |
| Englehart, Scott | 0 | 2 | 7.20 | 8 | 0 | 20 | 27 | 9 | 8 |
| Faino, Jeff | 0 | 2 | 8.18 | 3 | 0 | 11 | 13 | 9 | 4 |
| Jesperson, Bob | 3 | 5 | 7.56 | 19 | 2 | 86 | 100 | 44 | 67 |
| Knieper, Aaron | 0 | 0 | 9.39 | 5 | 0 | 8 | 10 | 12 | 3 |
| Loaiza, Sabino | 0 | 2 | 6.52 | 6 | 0 | 10 | 16 | 2 | 0 |
| McRoberts, Brian | 1 | 1 | 5.59 | 8 | 0 | 19 | 18 | 12 | 9 |
| 2-team (26 Sioux Falls) | 2 | 6 | 6.55 | 34 | 3 | 58 | 65 | 31 | 31 |
| Olmstead, Reed | 2 | 2 | 5.11 | 12 | 0 | 25 | 24 | 18 | 9 |
| Paskievitch, Tom | 1 | 2 | 6.85 | 5 | 0 | 22 | 32 | 12 | 15 |
| 2-team (2 Winnipeg) | 1 | 2 | 6.23 | 7 | 0 | 26 | 32 | 14 | 17 |
| Poeck, Chad | 5 | 8 | 3.21 | 19 | 1 | 87 | 78 | 48 | 56 |
| Quinn, Aaron | 4 | 5 | 4.03 | 46 | 2 | 67 | 68 | 20 | 54 |
| Rogers, Paul | 4 | 1 | 4.76 | 35 | 1 | 45 | 54 | 22 | 22 |
| Tilmon, Pat | 5 | 3 | 3.05 | 10 | 0 | 62 | 67 | 12 | 51 |
| Tipton, Shawn | 0 | 0 | 3.48 | 7 | 0 | 10 | 12 | 8 | 8 |

## WINNIPEG

| BATTING | AVG | AB | R | H | 2B | 3B | HR | RBI | SB |
|---|---|---|---|---|---|---|---|---|---|
| Castaldo, Gregg, ss | .236 | 276 | 39 | 65 | 10 | 3 | 7 | 44 | 3 |
| Castaldo, Vince, 3b | .361 | 97 | 23 | 35 | 9 | 1 | 3 | 14 | 2 |
| Dattola, Kevin, of | .250 | 200 | 53 | 50 | 14 | 0 | 5 | 34 | 17 |
| Duva, Brian, 2b-of | .282 | 323 | 55 | 91 | 8 | 1 | 4 | 34 | 29 |
| Geist, Jon, 2b | .000 | 13 | 2 | 0 | 0 | 0 | 0 | 1 | 0 |
| Halpenny, Andrew, c | .111 | 27 | 2 | 3 | 0 | 0 | 0 | 0 | 0 |
| Kokinda, Chris, 3b-of | .316 | 307 | 58 | 97 | 21 | 5 | 6 | 40 | 2 |
| Komminsk, Brad, dh-of | .278 | 277 | 47 | 77 | 16 | 1 | 16 | 66 | 1 |
| Lee, Terry, 1b | .353 | 306 | 81 | 108 | 17 | 0 | 23 | 88 | 1 |
| Manning, Henry, c | .264 | 307 | 40 | 81 | 14 | 0 | 7 | 48 | 1 |
| Martin, C.J., of | .262 | 195 | 31 | 51 | 10 | 2 | 6 | 27 | 7 |
| Pettiford, Torrey, 2b | .236 | 72 | 9 | 17 | 3 | 0 | 0 | 7 | 9 |
| Powell, Chris, of | .239 | 46 | 12 | 11 | 3 | 0 | 0 | 4 | 6 |

| | | | | | | | | |
|---|---|---|---|---|---|---|---|---|
| Saugstad, Mark, dh-3b | .256 | 82 | 9 | 21 | 3 | 0 | 3 | 12 | 0 |
| 2-team (15 Sioux Falls) | .273 | 128 | 13 | 35 | 7 | 0 | 3 | 15 | 0 |
| Watts, Brent, of | .287 | 317 | 69 | 91 | 14 | 2 | 16 | 42 | 23 |

| PITCHING | W | L | ERA | G | SV | IP | H | BB | SO |
|---|---|---|---|---|---|---|---|---|---|
| Atkinson, Neil | 0 | 1 | 18.00 | 1 | 0 | 3 | 4 | 2 | 0 |
| Bailey, Mike | 10 | 5 | 4.54 | 20 | 0 | 121 | 106 | 55 | 102 |
| Brewer, Nevin | 0 | 5 | 4.74 | 36 | 16 | 38 | 40 | 16 | 31 |
| Davis, Ray | 4 | 3 | 5.00 | 8 | 0 | 45 | 52 | 19 | 29 |
| Day, Steve | 1 | 1 | 14.21 | 7 | 0 | 6 | 13 | 5 | 9 |
| Futrell, Mark | 0 | 1 | 6.52 | 6 | 0 | 10 | 10 | 10 | 7 |
| Guehne, Dan | 2 | 1 | 4.30 | 31 | 3 | 38 | 45 | 12 | 36 |
| Jarvis, Matt | 11 | 3 | 3.58 | 17 | 0 | 103 | 99 | 55 | 63 |
| Lemp, Chris | 0 | 3 | 4.23 | 18 | 1 | 28 | 23 | 12 | 34 |
| Magrini, Paul | 0 | 1 | 9.22 | 7 | 0 | 14 | 18 | 13 | 6 |
| McClellan, Darren | 3 | 2 | 6.26 | 10 | 0 | 55 | 68 | 23 | 33 |
| McHugh, Pete | 0 | 0 | 5.87 | 12 | 0 | 15 | 13 | 13 | 10 |
| Paskievitch, Tom | 0 | 0 | 2.45 | 2 | 0 | 4 | 0 | 2 | 2 |
| Robinson, Scott | 4 | 4 | 7.69 | 9 | 0 | 53 | 77 | 20 | 39 |
| Smyth, Ken | 4 | 1 | 2.98 | 31 | 0 | 48 | 33 | 35 | 42 |
| Wise, Andy | 0 | 2 | 3.49 | 15 | 0 | 59 | 68 | 11 | 40 |
| 2-team (8 Sioux Falls) | 0 | 3 | 3.45 | 23 | 1 | 76 | 84 | 13 | 48 |
| Ybarra, Jamie | 11 | 1 | 3.18 | 14 | 0 | 93 | 72 | 46 | 99 |
| 2-team (8 Sioux Falls) | 11 | 3 | 4.43 | 22 | 1 | 110 | 97 | 58 | 119 |

## TEXAS-LOUISIANA LEAGUE

The Abilene Prairie Dogs completed a worst-to-first run by sweeping through the playoffs and taking the Texas-Louisana League championship.

The Prairie Dogs were 40-60 in 1995 as the league's worst team, but went 67-31 overall under new manager Phil Stephenson.

Abilene opened the playoffs against the Amarillo Dillas and knocked them out in two straight games, winning 7-4 and 5-2. Their opponents in the final were the Lubbock Crickets, who advanced with 11-2 and 10-1 victories over the Rio Grande Valley White-Wings.

The Prairie Dogs swept the Crickets as well, winning the first two games in Lubbock 5-4 and 8-2, then winning the championship at home, 12-8.

First baseman-DH Barry Jones and third baseman Manny Gagliano shared the award for series MVP. Jones went 6-for-21 with two home runs, six RBIs and two game-winning hits. Gagliano was 7-for-22 with seven RBIs.

The 1996 season was much better for the league's health as well. After an ill-fated attempt to expand to 10 teams in 1995, the league cut back to its six strongest franchises with good results. The league drew more than a half-million fans, and no team drew fewer than 50,000 fans.

### STANDINGS

| FIRST HALF | W | L | PCT | GB |
|---|---|---|---|---|
| Abilene Prairie Dogs | 35 | 15 | .700 | — |
| Rio Grande Valley WhiteWings | 29 | 21 | .580 | 6 |
| Lubbock Crickets | 27 | 23 | .540 | 8 |
| Amarillo Dillas | 25 | 25 | .500 | 10 |
| Alexandria Aces | 19 | 31 | .380 | 16 |
| Tyler WildCatters | 15 | 35 | .300 | 20 |

| SECOND HALF | W | L | PCT | GB |
|---|---|---|---|---|
| Abilene Prairie Dogs | 32 | 16 | .667 | — |
| Lubbock Crickets | 32 | 17 | .653 | ½ |
| Alexandria Aces | 23 | 27 | .460 | 10 |
| Rio Grande Valley WhiteWings | 21 | 27 | .438 | 11 |
| Tyler WildCatters | 21 | 28 | .429 | 11½ |
| Amarillo Dillas | 18 | 32 | .360 | 15 |

PLAYOFFS: Semifinals—Abilene defeated Amarillo 2-0, and Lubbock defeated Rio Grande Valley 2-0, in best-of-3 series. Finals: Abilene defeated Lubbock 3-0 in best-of-5 series.

**MANAGERS:** Abilene—Phil Stephenson. Alexandria—Stan Cliburn. Amarillo—Jim Nettles. Lubbock—Greg Minton. Rio Grande Valley—John Pacella. Tyler—Dave Hilton.

**ATTENDANCE:** Amarillo, 135,881; Rio Grande Valley, 81,884; Lubbock, 81,257; Alexandria, 76,414; Abilene, 68,297; Tyler, 58,572.

**ALL-STAR TEAM: C**—Jack Johnson, Abilene; **1B**—John O'Brien, Rio Grande Valley; **2B**—Jorge Alvarez, Amarillo. **3B**—Manny Gagliano, Abilene. **SS**—Lipso Nava, Rio Grande. **OF**—Rod Brewer, Abilene; Sean Collins, Tyler; Malvin Matos, Alexandria. **DH**—Joe Ronca, Alexandria. **Util**—Mike Hardge, Lubbock. **SP**—David Haas, Abilene; Kerry Knox, Abilene; Daren Brown, Amarillo; Steve Duda, Lubbock; Ron Gerstein, Lubbock. **RP**—Ken Winkle, Abilene.

**Most Valuable Player:** Rod Brewer, Abilene. **Most Valuable Pitcher:** David Haas, Abilene.

### INDIVIDUAL BATTING LEADERS
(Minimum 270 Plate Appearances)

| | AVG | AB | R | H | 2B | 3B | HR | RBI | SB |
|---|---|---|---|---|---|---|---|---|---|
| Alvarez, Jorge, Amarillo | .357 | 373 | 74 | 133 | 37 | 2 | 16 | 77 | 10 |
| Matos, Malvin, Alex | .341 | 299 | 63 | 102 | 18 | 1 | 13 | 44 | 19 |
| Coleman, Paul, Abilene | .334 | 356 | 64 | 119 | 31 | 2 | 9 | 59 | 12 |
| Nava, Lipso, Rio Grande | .331 | 360 | 66 | 119 | 20 | 2 | 17 | 72 | 29 |
| Brewer, Rod, Abilene | .325 | 348 | 67 | 113 | 23 | 3 | 19 | 87 | 10 |
| Ronca, Joe, Alex | .317 | 397 | 62 | 126 | 24 | 1 | 13 | 77 | 8 |
| Shade, Kyle, Tyler | .317 | 388 | 70 | 123 | 30 | 5 | 10 | 61 | 2 |
| Monroe, Darryl, Abilene | .316 | 320 | 67 | 101 | 18 | 4 | 12 | 54 | 26 |
| O'Brien, John, Rio | .315 | 368 | 60 | 116 | 17 | 0 | 25 | 63 | 1 |
| Collins, Sean, Tyler | .313 | 367 | 66 | 115 | 22 | 8 | 0 | 37 | 27 |

### INDIVIDUAL PITCHING LEADERS
(Minimum 80 Innings)

| | W | L | ERA | G | SV | IP | H | BB | SO |
|---|---|---|---|---|---|---|---|---|---|
| Haas, David, Abilene | 13 | 4 | 2.43 | 21 | 0 | 148 | 139 | 36 | 102 |
| Osuna, Al, Rio Grande | 8 | 2 | 2.86 | 14 | 0 | 104 | 74 | 42 | 115 |
| Johnson, Billy, Tyler | 4 | 5 | 2.97 | 17 | 0 | 109 | 91 | 42 | 83 |
| Schuermann, Lance, Abi | 12 | 0 | 3.46 | 24 | 1 | 109 | 121 | 38 | 69 |
| Gerstein, Ron, Lubbock | 14 | 4 | 3.56 | 23 | 0 | 149 | 143 | 66 | 109 |
| Knox, Kerry, Abilene | 10 | 3 | 3.61 | 20 | 0 | 120 | 124 | 23 | 85 |
| Duda, Steve, Lubbock | 11 | 8 | 3.76 | 24 | 0 | 160 | 182 | 43 | 120 |
| Arminio, Sam, Abilene | 11 | 7 | 3.81 | 23 | 0 | 149 | 183 | 35 | 73 |
| Brown, Daren, Amarillo | 11 | 9 | 3.89 | 23 | 0 | 160 | 180 | 50 | 143 |
| Rusciano, Chris, Tyler | 8 | 5 | 3.99 | 19 | 0 | 124 | 130 | 51 | 71 |

### ABILENE

| BATTING | AVG | AB | R | H | 2B | 3B | HR | RBI | SB |
|---|---|---|---|---|---|---|---|---|---|
| Arevalos, Ryan, 2b | .385 | 13 | 1 | 5 | 1 | 0 | 0 | 0 | 0 |
| Bethea, Scott, ss | .263 | 338 | 44 | 89 | 13 | 5 | 2 | 30 | 13 |
| Brewer, Rod, 1b-of | .325 | 348 | 67 | 113 | 23 | 3 | 19 | 87 | 10 |
| Coleman, Paul, of | .334 | 356 | 64 | 119 | 31 | 2 | 9 | 59 | 12 |
| Conkle, Troy, 3b-ss | .286 | 28 | 4 | 8 | 1 | 0 | 0 | 4 | 0 |
| 2-team (41 Tyler) | .223 | 148 | 14 | 33 | 4 | 0 | 1 | 12 | 1 |
| Gagliano, Manny, 3b | .290 | 293 | 48 | 85 | 17 | 1 | 3 | 43 | 3 |
| Gonzalez, Eric, 2b | .253 | 316 | 65 | 80 | 13 | 2 | 7 | 40 | 24 |
| Gonzalez, Paul, of-3b | .256 | 234 | 48 | 60 | 11 | 1 | 14 | 44 | 3 |
| Heller, Kyle, c | .167 | 18 | 0 | 3 | 0 | 0 | 0 | 2 | 0 |
| Hughes, Shawn, c | .222 | 9 | 1 | 2 | 0 | 0 | 0 | 0 | 0 |
| Johnson, Jack, c | .263 | 285 | 47 | 75 | 20 | 0 | 7 | 46 | 4 |
| Jones, Barry, dh-1b | .253 | 300 | 47 | 76 | 12 | 2 | 9 | 43 | 5 |
| Malone, Scott, 1b-of | .281 | 203 | 27 | 57 | 13 | 0 | 0 | 24 | 2 |
| McClure, Jason, of-c | .237 | 131 | 21 | 31 | 11 | 2 | 0 | 12 | 1 |
| Monroe, Darryl, of | .316 | 320 | 67 | 101 | 18 | 4 | 12 | 54 | 26 |
| Rich, Tony, 2b-ss | .219 | 64 | 14 | 14 | 7 | 0 | 0 | 7 | 1 |

| PITCHING | W | L | ERA | G | SV | IP | H | BB | SO |
|---|---|---|---|---|---|---|---|---|---|
| Arminio, Sam | 11 | 7 | 3.81 | 23 | 0 | 149 | 183 | 35 | 73 |
| Baker, Jared | 6 | 8 | 6.77 | 20 | 0 | 112 | 149 | 155 | 76 |
| Conkle, Troy | 1 | 0 | 2.11 | 16 | 1 | 21 | 14 | 6 | 18 |
| 2-team (1 Tyler) | 1 | 0 | 3.00 | 17 | 1 | 27 | 19 | 8 | 20 |
| Dunne, Brian | 6 | 2 | 3.12 | 38 | 5 | 49 | 54 | 24 | 34 |
| Haas, David | 13 | 4 | 2.43 | 21 | 0 | 148 | 139 | 36 | 102 |
| Hartung, Mike | 1 | 1 | 3.00 | 7 | 0 | 12 | 15 | 4 | 8 |
| Hirsch, Troy | 2 | 2 | 4.58 | 28 | 0 | 35 | 36 | 25 | 16 |
| Jones, Scott | 4 | 4 | 4.43 | 28 | 3 | 43 | 45 | 32 | 21 |
| Knox, Kerry | 10 | 3 | 3.61 | 20 | 0 | 120 | 124 | 23 | 85 |
| Schuermann, Lance | 12 | 0 | 3.46 | 24 | 1 | 109 | 121 | 38 | 69 |
| Winkle, Ken | 1 | 0 | 1.42 | 44 | 27 | 44 | 23 | 16 | 50 |

### ALEXANDRIA

| BATTING | AVG | AB | R | H | 2B | 3B | HR | RBI | SB |
|---|---|---|---|---|---|---|---|---|---|
| Andrews, Jay, of | .274 | 350 | 39 | 96 | 18 | 2 | 10 | 54 | 19 |
| Arntzen, Brian, c | .214 | 257 | 28 | 55 | 16 | 1 | 0 | 24 | 5 |
| Bender, Rick, ss | .238 | 323 | 45 | 77 | 9 | 4 | 5 | 38 | 20 |
| Colbert, Leighton, of | .231 | 13 | 0 | 3 | 0 | 0 | 0 | 0 | 1 |
| Cole, Marvin, 2b | .310 | 384 | 59 | 119 | 20 | 1 | 3 | 38 | 18 |

| | AVG | AB | R | H | 2B | 3B | HR | RBI | SB |
|---|---|---|---|---|---|---|---|---|---|
| Dando, Pat, 1b-dh | .268 | 123 | 12 | 33 | 7 | 0 | 2 | 23 | 1 |
| Glenn, Robby, 1b | .178 | 107 | 13 | 19 | 3 | 1 | 1 | 10 | 0 |
| Matos, Malvin, of | .341 | 299 | 63 | 102 | 18 | 1 | 13 | 44 | 19 |
| Motes, Jeff, 3b-2b | .222 | 36 | 6 | 8 | 1 | 0 | 0 | 5 | 1 |
| Ronca, Joe, of-dh | .317 | 397 | 62 | 126 | 24 | 1 | 13 | 77 | 8 |
| Rothe, Ryan, of-1b | .219 | 219 | 26 | 48 | 6 | 3 | 1 | 18 | 7 |
| Shade, Kyle, 3b-1b | .317 | 388 | 70 | 123 | 30 | 5 | 10 | 61 | 2 |
| Turco, Frank, dh-3b | .306 | 392 | 70 | 120 | 23 | 3 | 10 | 55 | 14 |
| Van Asselberg, Ricky, c | .238 | 63 | 6 | 15 | 1 | 0 | 0 | 4 | 0 |
| White, Darrin, c | .241 | 54 | 7 | 13 | 4 | 0 | 1 | 7 | 0 |
| Wilson, Mike, of | .208 | 24 | 2 | 5 | 1 | 0 | 0 | 2 | 0 |

| PITCHING | W | L | ERA | G | SV | IP | H | BB | SO |
|---|---|---|---|---|---|---|---|---|---|
| Fontenot, Lester | 0 | 0 | 7.07 | 8 | 0 | 14 | 22 | 2 | 10 |
| Hampton, Mark | 1 | 1 | 2.70 | 15 | 0 | 20 | 23 | 10 | 14 |
| Mack, Tony | 7 | 9 | 4.04 | 25 | 0 | 174 | 208 | 50 | 87 |
| Montgomery, Josh | 9 | 11 | 4.12 | 22 | 0 | 127 | 135 | 53 | 105 |
| Moran, Eric | 8 | 9 | 4.93 | 28 | 1 | 111 | 107 | 41 | 70 |
| Newman, Alan | 6 | 6 | 4.56 | 35 | 2 | 118 | 136 | 43 | 82 |
| Peters, Brannon | 8 | 10 | 4.32 | 24 | 0 | 154 | 180 | 54 | 132 |
| Santos, Jerry | 3 | 6 | 3.96 | 41 | 11 | 50 | 52 | 23 | 47 |
| Satre, Jason | 0 | 1 | 4.50 | 5 | 0 | 12 | 14 | 4 | 8 |
| 2-team (4 Rio Grande) | 1 | 2 | 3.66 | 9 | 0 | 39 | 42 | 11 | 19 |
| Stutz, Joe | 0 | 5 | 3.48 | 32 | 2 | 75 | 84 | 29 | 47 |

### AMARILLO

| BATTING | AVG | AB | R | H | 2B | 3B | HR | RBI | SB |
|---|---|---|---|---|---|---|---|---|---|
| Alvarez, Jorge, 2b | .357 | 373 | 74 | 133 | 37 | 2 | 16 | 77 | 10 |
| Bales, Taylor, c | .218 | 87 | 10 | 19 | 4 | 0 | 2 | 13 | 0 |
| Burd, Rob, of | .118 | 17 | 2 | 2 | 0 | 0 | 0 | 1 | 0 |
| Colbert, Leighton, of | .249 | 285 | 33 | 71 | 9 | 2 | 1 | 20 | 13 |
| 2-team (4 Alexandria) | .248 | 298 | 33 | 74 | 9 | 2 | 1 | 20 | 14 |
| Danford, Leroy, of | .218 | 87 | 14 | 19 | 2 | 0 | 0 | 7 | 7 |
| Holley, Battle, 3b | .279 | 154 | 16 | 43 | 3 | 2 | 0 | 16 | 5 |
| Howard, Tim, of | .329 | 152 | 24 | 50 | 10 | 3 | 0 | 22 | 6 |
| Keith, Jason, ss | .248 | 331 | 49 | 82 | 17 | 3 | 2 | 35 | 3 |
| Kiraly, Jeff, 1b | .236 | 331 | 41 | 78 | 16 | 5 | 9 | 60 | 1 |
| Maclin, Lonnie, of | .274 | 314 | 50 | 86 | 15 | 2 | 3 | 42 | 19 |
| Meza, Larry, 3b | .293 | 123 | 17 | 36 | 4 | 0 | 0 | 14 | 1 |
| Ornelaz, Michael, ss-dh | .246 | 211 | 36 | 52 | 5 | 2 | 0 | 14 | 8 |
| Prater, Andrew, c | .274 | 117 | 16 | 32 | 9 | 0 | 1 | 17 | 0 |
| Reese, Mat, of | .285 | 358 | 55 | 102 | 19 | 5 | 9 | 67 | 6 |
| Tahan, Kevin, c | .287 | 268 | 47 | 77 | 9 | 0 | 3 | 36 | 6 |
| Wollenberg, Doug, 3b-2b | .307 | 231 | 31 | 71 | 17 | 0 | 1 | 24 | 8 |
| 2-team (36 Tyler) | .280 | 361 | 45 | 101 | 21 | 0 | 2 | 34 | 14 |

| PITCHING | W | L | ERA | G | SV | IP | H | BB | SO |
|---|---|---|---|---|---|---|---|---|---|
| Bicknell, Greg | 4 | 6 | 6.26 | 14 | 0 | 82 | 117 | 22 | 49 |
| Brown, Daren | 11 | 9 | 3.89 | 23 | 0 | 160 | 180 | 50 | 143 |
| Burns, Todd | 0 | 0 | 0.00 | 1 | 0 | 1 | 0 | 0 | 0 |
| Gienger, Craig | 2 | 1 | 7.43 | 14 | 0 | 27 | 39 | 8 | 9 |
| Hampton, Mark | 2 | 2 | 6.33 | 16 | 0 | 54 | 63 | 26 | 34 |
| 2-team (15 Alexandria) | 3 | 3 | 5.35 | 31 | 0 | 74 | 86 | 36 | 48 |
| Holman, Brad | 0 | 3 | 11.68 | 3 | 0 | 12 | 17 | 11 | 3 |
| Kermode, Al | 8 | 12 | 4.45 | 24 | 0 | 156 | 174 | 27 | 107 |
| King, Kevin | 0 | 0 | 14.54 | 4 | 0 | 4 | 12 | 4 | 6 |
| Largusa, Levon | 4 | 7 | 5.31 | 18 | 1 | 95 | 92 | 52 | 85 |
| Montoya, Al | 1 | 2 | 2.76 | 40 | 3 | 62 | 60 | 23 | 34 |
| Perkins, Paul | 6 | 2 | 3.00 | 20 | 5 | 27 | 24 | 6 | 20 |
| Reyes, Michael | 0 | 2 | 7.50 | 6 | 0 | 6 | 8 | 9 | 2 |
| Swanson, David | 0 | 2 | 5.59 | 29 | 0 | 56 | 67 | 36 | 40 |
| Trice, Wally | 1 | 3 | 6.82 | 8 | 0 | 32 | 50 | 13 | 22 |
| Youngblood, Todd | 4 | 6 | 5.18 | 26 | 2 | 83 | 78 | 43 | 70 |

### LUBBOCK

| BATTING | AVG | AB | R | H | 2B | 3B | HR | RBI | SB |
|---|---|---|---|---|---|---|---|---|---|
| Bolick, Frank, 3b | .376 | 125 | 22 | 47 | 15 | 1 | 6 | 35 | 0 |
| Green, Ron, of | .199 | 141 | 23 | 28 | 8 | 2 | 1 | 11 | 8 |
| Hardge, Mike, 3b-of | .303 | 393 | 77 | 119 | 24 | 7 | 8 | 64 | 26 |
| Hoyes, Scott, of | .216 | 185 | 32 | 40 | 8 | 1 | 7 | 24 | 5 |
| Jones, Sy, c | .239 | 92 | 12 | 22 | 4 | 1 | 1 | 12 | 0 |
| Kim, Brett, of | .091 | 11 | 2 | 1 | 0 | 0 | 0 | 0 | 0 |
| King, Mitch, of-c | .227 | 22 | 5 | 5 | 1 | 0 | 0 | 0 | 1 |
| Lowery, David, 2b | .295 | 339 | 57 | 100 | 14 | 3 | 0 | 21 | 33 |
| Norton, Chris, 1b-c | .380 | 187 | 39 | 71 | 13 | 1 | 15 | 54 | 6 |
| Petrulis, Paul, ss | .285 | 337 | 59 | 96 | 17 | 3 | 6 | 40 | 2 |
| Ramirez, J.D., 3b-2b | .366 | 172 | 27 | 63 | 15 | 1 | 4 | 29 | 0 |
| Ramirez, Roberto, of | .306 | 180 | 35 | 55 | 14 | 1 | 11 | 45 | 1 |
| Sparks, Greg, 1b-of | .241 | 349 | 41 | 84 | 17 | 0 | 16 | 62 | 3 |
| Stratton, John, c | .233 | 236 | 30 | 55 | 11 | 1 | 9 | 33 | 1 |
| Sullivan, Glenn, dh | .280 | 250 | 37 | 70 | 16 | 1 | 2 | 18 | 8 |
| Vaughn, Derek, of | .298 | 322 | 44 | 96 | 20 | 3 | 4 | 42 | 17 |

| PITCHING | W | L | ERA | G | SV | IP | H | BB | SO |
|---|---|---|---|---|---|---|---|---|---|
| Baine, David | 4 | 8 | 4.41 | 21 | 0 | 104 | 118 | 42 | 76 |
| Bicknell, Greg | 5 | 1 | 2.23 | 17 | 4 | 40 | 29 | 13 | 24 |

| | | | | | | | | | |
|---|---|---|---|---|---|---|---|---|---|
| 2-team (14 Amarillo) .......... | 9 | 7 | 4.93 | 31 | 4 | 122 | 146 | 35 | 73 |
| Brewer, Ryan ............................ | 5 | 3 | 2.05 | 8 | 0 | 61 | 49 | 17 | 39 |
| Duda, Steve ............................. | 11 | 8 | 3.76 | 24 | 0 | 160 | 182 | 43 | 120 |
| Felix, Ruben ............................. | 0 | 5 | 6.61 | 20 | 0 | 31 | 39 | 17 | 24 |
| Forney, Rick ............................. | 9 | 7 | 4.50 | 22 | 0 | 142 | 151 | 56 | 123 |
| Gerstein, Ron ......................... | 14 | 4 | 3.56 | 23 | 0 | 149 | 143 | 66 | 109 |
| Huber, Jeff. ............................. | 0 | 0 | 0.49 | 17 | 11 | 18 | 9 | 6 | 19 |
| Landrum, Bill ........................... | 2 | 1 | 2.18 | 8 | 0 | 33 | 27 | 6 | 31 |
| Leiber, Zane ............................. | 2 | 0 | 7.88 | 26 | 1 | 40 | 48 | 31 | 29 |
| Madigan, Bob ........................... | 1 | 0 | 3.74 | 11 | 0 | 22 | 20 | 6 | 9 |
| Zongor, Steve ......................... | 6 | 3 | 3.43 | 31 | 8 | 42 | 44 | 16 | 27 |

## RIO GRANDE VALLEY

| BATTING | AVG | AB | R | H | 2B | 3B | HR | RBI | SB |
|---|---|---|---|---|---|---|---|---|---|
| Cantu, Mike, dh-1b ................ | .287 | 317 | 45 | 91 | 13 | 0 | 18 | 52 | 0 |
| Cedeno, Ramon, of ............. | .308 | 389 | 55 | 120 | 27 | 1 | 11 | 64 | 0 |
| Clark, Chalaco, c................... | .196 | 46 | 6 | 9 | 0 | 0 | 1 | 7 | 1 |
| Cooney, Jim, c-dh ............. | .308 | 65 | 2 | 20 | 3 | 0 | 0 | 4 | 0 |
| 2-team (37 Tyler) ............ | .304 | 181 | 14 | 55 | 11 | 0 | 4 | 21 | 0 |
| Gafford, Cory, c.................... | .197 | 188 | 22 | 37 | 4 | 0 | 3 | 22 | 2 |
| Grandizio, Steve, of............. | .254 | 169 | 28 | 43 | 9 | 1 | 2 | 20 | 17 |
| Kaczmar, Scott, of................ | .263 | 266 | 37 | 70 | 18 | 4 | 4 | 25 | 10 |
| Llanos, Bobby, 3b-of ......... | .268 | 314 | 48 | 84 | 11 | 1 | 13 | 39 | 12 |
| Martinez, Joey, of-ss ......... | .274 | 274 | 46 | 75 | 9 | 3 | 0 | 18 | 42 |
| Nava, Lipso, ss..................... | .331 | 360 | 66 | 119 | 20 | 2 | 17 | 72 | 29 |
| O'Brien, John, 1b................... | .315 | 368 | 60 | 116 | 17 | 0 | 25 | 63 | 1 |
| O'Connor, Pat, 2b.................. | .233 | 296 | 37 | 69 | 7 | 1 | 1 | 35 | 18 |
| Oglesby, Luke, of ................ | .237 | 156 | 28 | 37 | 5 | 1 | 0 | 13 | 22 |
| Ortiz, Alex, 3b ...................... | .182 | 55 | 6 | 10 | 2 | 0 | 3 | 9 | 0 |
| Shwartzer, Mike, c................ | .136 | 22 | 5 | 3 | 0 | 0 | 0 | 0 | 0 |
| Viegas, Clark, 3b-2b ......... | .211 | 57 | 10 | 12 | 1 | 0 | 0 | 4 | 0 |

| PITCHING | W | L | ERA | G | SV | IP | H | BB | SO |
|---|---|---|---|---|---|---|---|---|---|
| Allen, Harold.......................... | 0 | 3 | 8.10 | 9 | 0 | 27 | 48 | 13 | 14 |
| Bonelli, Ralph ........................ | 10 | 7 | 4.12 | 28 | 0 | 138 | 146 | 56 | 66 |
| Carranza, Javier.................... | 2 | 3 | 8.42 | 5 | 0 | 26 | 37 | 9 | 15 |
| Clough, Ricky ........................ | 9 | 6 | 4.91 | 27 | 1 | 117 | 111 | 44 | 121 |
| DeJesus, Javy......................... | 8 | 7 | 4.82 | 23 | 0 | 125 | 143 | 46 | 72 |
| Harrison, Brian ...................... | 4 | 3 | 3.18 | 13 | 0 | 71 | 68 | 41 | 70 |
| Hartman, Kelly ...................... | 1 | 2 | 4.23 | 29 | 2 | 38 | 40 | 22 | 29 |
| Hartung, Mike ........................ | 3 | 4 | 5.31 | 34 | 1 | 59 | 72 | 29 | 37 |
| 2-team (7 Abilene) ......... | 4 | 5 | 4.92 | 41 | 1 | 71 | 87 | 33 | 45 |
| Mallett, Lane. ........................ | 0 | 0 | 81.00 | 3 | 0 | 1 | 4 | 5 | 0 |
| Meador, Paul .......................... | 2 | 0 | 9.18 | 9 | 0 | 17 | 24 | 6 | 6 |
| 2-team (8 Tyler) ............ | 1 | 9 | 7.30 | 17 | 0 | 65 | 85 | 23 | 24 |
| Osuna, Al ............................. | 8 | 2 | 2.86 | 14 | 0 | 104 | 74 | 42 | 115 |
| Perkins, Scott ........................ | 0 | 0 | 7.27 | 6 | 0 | 9 | 7 | 12 | 3 |
| Piatt, Doug ............................. | 3 | 2 | 3.51 | 40 | 16 | 51 | 54 | 23 | 62 |
| Resendez, Oscar ................. | 0 | 1 | 10.64 | 4 | 0 | 11 | 12 | 7 | 7 |
| Rodriguez, Rene ................. | 0 | 1 | 9.64 | 2 | 0 | 5 | 10 | 4 | 2 |
| Satre, Jason ......................... | 1 | 1 | 3.29 | 4 | 0 | 27 | 28 | 7 | 11 |
| Spaulding, Scott ................. | 1 | 3 | 9.00 | 4 | 0 | 19 | 26 | 13 | 9 |
| Todd, Donovan ...................... | 0 | 1 | 10.80 | 8 | 0 | 8 | 18 | 4 | 3 |
| Wright, Scott........................... | 0 | 0 | 18.00 | 1 | 0 | 2 | 4 | 3 | 0 |

## TYLER

| BATTING | AVG | AB | R | H | 2B | 3B | HR | RBI | SB |
|---|---|---|---|---|---|---|---|---|---|
| Bowles, John, 1b-3b ............. | .278 | 126 | 16 | 35 | 6 | 0 | 3 | 15 | 2 |
| Collins, Sean, of-2b ........... | .313 | 367 | 66 | 115 | 22 | 8 | 0 | 37 | 27 |
| Conkle, Troy, 3b-ss ............. | .208 | 120 | 10 | 25 | 3 | 0 | 1 | 8 | 1 |
| Cooney, Jim, c-1b ............... | .302 | 116 | 12 | 35 | 8 | 0 | 4 | 17 | 0 |
| Hare, Richie, of.................... | .270 | 233 | 26 | 63 | 9 | 0 | 0 | 24 | 8 |
| Henderson, Derek, 3b ......... | .310 | 364 | 48 | 113 | 30 | 0 | 9 | 59 | 2 |
| Klam, Josef, c........................ | .243 | 115 | 13 | 28 | 3 | 0 | 0 | 12 | 1 |
| Koerick, Tom, c ..................... | .229 | 118 | 11 | 27 | 3 | 0 | 1 | 9 | 0 |
| Motes, Jeff, ss-2b................ | .246 | 57 | 4 | 14 | 1 | 0 | 0 | 5 | 1 |
| 2-team (18 Alexandria)...... | .237 | 93 | 10 | 22 | 2 | 0 | 0 | 10 | 2 |
| Motley, Jason, 1b ................ | .167 | 24 | 2 | 4 | 1 | 0 | 0 | 2 | 0 |
| Perez, Carlos, 1b-of .......... | .283 | 360 | 52 | 102 | 19 | 3 | 5 | 51 | 9 |
| Rich, Tony, 2b........................ | .271 | 177 | 19 | 48 | 10 | 0 | 0 | 15 | 5 |
| 2-team (25 Abilene) ......... | .257 | 241 | 25 | 62 | 17 | 0 | 0 | 22 | 6 |
| Shamburg, Ken, of-1b ......... | .289 | 357 | 65 | 103 | 25 | 3 | 15 | 49 | 5 |
| Smiga, Jason, ss ................. | .297 | 246 | 32 | 73 | 10 | 1 | 0 | 26 | 13 |
| Turner, Rocky, of................. | .248 | 274 | 36 | 68 | 8 | 4 | 0 | 16 | 11 |
| Weaver, Colby, c.................. | .221 | 97 | 7 | 17 | 3 | 1 | 0 | 6 | 0 |
| Williams, Lanny, c ............... | .226 | 31 | 3 | 7 | 1 | 0 | 1 | 5 | 1 |
| Wollenburg, Doug, 2b........... | .231 | 130 | 12 | 30 | 4 | 0 | 1 | 10 | 6 |

| PITCHING | W | L | ERA | G | SV | IP | H | BB | SO |
|---|---|---|---|---|---|---|---|---|---|
| Batchler, Rob ........................ | 1 | 7 | 5.16 | 27 | 2 | 89 | 111 | 24 | 33 |
| Brummett, Greg...................... | 4 | 9 | 4.37 | 13 | 0 | 78 | 83 | 47 | 68 |
| Carter, Tommy ...................... | 1 | 1 | 5.98 | 13 | 0 | 44 | 52 | 23 | 36 |
| Hancock, Chris...................... | 7 | 2 | 6.47 | 12 | 0 | 57 | 87 | 35 | 43 |
| Higgins, Ed. .......................... | 1 | 0 | 19.80 | 3 | 0 | 5 | 10 | 7 | 2 |
| Ingram, Todd ....................... | 1 | 3 | 6.68 | 5 | 0 | 32 | 43 | 15 | 26 |

| | | | | | | | | | |
|---|---|---|---|---|---|---|---|---|---|
| Johnson, Billy........................ | 4 | 5 | 2.97 | 17 | 0 | 109 | 91 | 42 | 83 |
| Kitchen, Ron........................... | 3 | 2 | 2.61 | 18 | 3 | 31 | 27 | 18 | 17 |
| Long, Steve ........................... | 3 | 6 | 4.96 | 19 | 0 | 78 | 92 | 31 | 33 |
| Meador, Paul ......................... | 1 | 7 | 6.66 | 8 | 0 | 49 | 61 | 17 | 18 |
| Mesewicz, Mark ................... | 1 | 4 | 5.64 | 15 | 0 | 22 | 31 | 7 | 6 |
| Patterson, Ken ...................... | 1 | 1 | 2.13 | 20 | 6 | 25 | 22 | 5 | 28 |
| Rusciano, Chris..................... | 8 | 5 | 3.99 | 19 | 0 | 124 | 130 | 51 | 71 |
| Simmons, John ..................... | 1 | 4 | 7.57 | 10 | 0 | 36 | 60 | 24 | 24 |
| Slattery, Alex ......................... | 4 | 1 | 4.53 | 33 | 2 | 56 | 48 | 42 | 43 |
| Williams, Brian ...................... | 0 | 1 | 10.13 | 3 | 0 | 3 | 1 | 8 | 0 |

# BIG SOUTH LEAGUE

As the fourth team in a six-team league to make the playoffs, the Greenville Bluesmen barely eked into the postseason and even finished the regular season a game below .500.

But they saved their best baseball for the playoffs, going 5-1 to win the first Big South League championship. The city of Greenville celebrated, erecting signs at the city limits and making the members of the team honorary citizens.

The Bluesmen, who finished 35-36 overall, met Pine Bluff in the first round and beat the Locomotives, who had been 42-30 in the regular season, two games to one. They moved on to face the Columbia Mules, who had beaten the Tennessee Tomahawks two games to one. Greenville swept the Mules in three games, winning 9-8, 10-7 and 6-1.

"I told the team in the second half that if we can make the playoffs, we'll be trouble," manager Lyle Yates said.

The league had a solid first season at the gate, with Tennessee drawing 57,086 fans and the other five teams drawing at least 30,000 fans each. Former Cubs pitcher Les Lancaster was the biggest star on the field, as he went 12-2 with a 3.03 ERA for Pine Bluff to win pitcher of the year and MVP honors.

The league also carved out a small place in baseball history when a player was traded for a blues album. First baseman Andre Keene was traded from Meridian to Greenville for cash and a Muddy Waters album. "We made it clear we were looking for an authentic vinyl record and not a tape or compact disc to make the deal complete," Meridian GM Gary Saunders said.

## STANDINGS

| FIRST HALF | W | L | PCT | GB |
|---|---|---|---|---|
| Tennessee Tomahawks | 22 | 12 | .629 | — |
| Pine Bluff Locomotives | 21 | 15 | .583 | 1½ |
| Columbia Mules | 18 | 16 | .529 | 3½ |
| Greenville Bluesmen | 16 | 19 | .457 | 6 |
| Clarksville Coyotes | 16 | 20 | .444 | 6½ |
| Meridian Brakemen | 12 | 22 | .353 | 9½ |

| SECOND HALF | W | L | PCT | GB |
|---|---|---|---|---|
| Pine Bluff Locomotives | 21 | 15 | .583 | — |
| Columbia Mules | 21 | 15 | .583 | — |
| Greenville Bluesmen | 19 | 17 | .528 | 2 |
| Tennessee Tomahawks | 18 | 18 | .500 | 3 |
| Clarksville Coyotes | 15 | 21 | .417 | 6 |
| Meridian Brakemen | 14 | 22 | .389 | 7 |

**PLAYOFFS: Semifinals**—Greenville defeated Pine Bluff 2-1, and Columbia defeated Tennessee 2-1, in best-of-3 series. **Finals**—Greenville defeated Columbia 3-0, in best-of-5 series.

**MANAGERS:** Clarksville—Nate Colbert. Columbia—Barry Lyons. Greenville—Lyle Yates. Meridian—Jose Santiago. Pine Bluff—Bobby Clark. Tennessee—Mike O'Berry.

**ATTENDANCE:** Tennessee, 57,086; Columbia, 39,229; Greenville, 36,532; Meridian, 37,339; Pine Bluff, 35,693; Clarksville, 31,287.

**ALL-STAR TEAM: C**—Tim Graham, Greenville; Jason Townley, Pine Bluff. **1B**—Andre Keene, Meridian/Greenville. **2B**—Jose Serra, Greenville. **3B**—Tony Gonzalez, Clarksville. **SS**—Jeff Michael, Tennessee. **OF**—Tony Bellinato, Meridian; Stanton Cameron, Meridian/Columbia; John Graham, Greenville; Tom McKinnon, Pine Bluff. **SP**—John Dopson, Tennessee; Les Lancaster, Pine Bluff; Shane Majors, Tennessee; John Mitchell, Columbia. **RP**—Charlie Mitchell, Columbia.

**Most Valuable Player:** Les Lancaster, Pine Bluff. **Pitcher of the Year:** Les Lancaster, Pine Bluff. **Manager of the Year:** Barry Lyons, Columbia.

### INDIVIDUAL BATTING LEADERS
(Minimum 189 Plate Appearances)

| | AVG | AB | R | H | 2B | 3B | HR | RBI | SB |
|---|---|---|---|---|---|---|---|---|---|
| Townley, Jason, PB | .362 | 246 | 49 | 89 | 18 | 0 | 15 | 65 | 2 |
| Graham, John, Green | .361 | 205 | 45 | 74 | 16 | 2 | 5 | 48 | 9 |
| Gonzalez, Tony, Clark | .359 | 220 | 48 | 79 | 25 | 3 | 3 | 47 | 9 |
| McKinnon, Tom, PB | .351 | 282 | 64 | 99 | 16 | 1 | 16 | 70 | 11 |
| Graham, Tim, Green | .347 | 202 | 40 | 70 | 16 | 3 | 6 | 50 | 2 |
| Rhein, Jeff, Clark | .341 | 229 | 58 | 78 | 19 | 2 | 2 | 30 | 31 |
| Bellinato, Tony, Mer | .340 | 241 | 36 | 82 | 18 | 1 | 15 | 46 | 6 |
| Preston, Doyle, PB | .340 | 241 | 54 | 82 | 22 | 2 | 6 | 42 | 6 |
| Hawkins, Wes, Mer | .340 | 253 | 52 | 86 | 17 | 3 | 9 | 52 | 17 |
| Felder, Mike, Tenn | .338 | 198 | 41 | 67 | 14 | 0 | 7 | 30 | 9 |
| Cameron, Stanton, Col-Mer | .333 | 243 | 62 | 81 | 17 | 3 | 21 | 78 | 11 |
| Smith, Kerby, Green | .329 | 237 | 43 | 78 | 11 | 1 | 3 | 43 | 8 |
| Vallero, Rich, Tenn | .322 | 174 | 28 | 56 | 11 | 1 | 3 | 27 | 1 |
| Underwood, Curtis, Clark | .319 | 260 | 38 | 83 | 12 | 0 | 7 | 50 | 3 |
| Russell, Jake, PB | .318 | 233 | 49 | 74 | 17 | 2 | 9 | 44 | 7 |
| Keene, Andre, Mer-Green | .317 | 208 | 50 | 66 | 14 | 0 | 16 | 49 | 11 |
| Stinson, Ryan, PB | .317 | 186 | 42 | 59 | 11 | 3 | 1 | 27 | 26 |
| Echols, Mandell, Col | .315 | 267 | 47 | 84 | 13 | 0 | 6 | 35 | 19 |
| Harris, Eric, Columbia | .311 | 222 | 40 | 69 | 14 | 1 | 7 | 39 | 3 |
| Corps, Erick, Green | .310 | 252 | 64 | 78 | 10 | 2 | 3 | 33 | 18 |
| Wilkerson, Willie, Tenn | .305 | 220 | 38 | 67 | 18 | 1 | 4 | 26 | 5 |
| Santiago, Arnold, Mer | .303 | 221 | 29 | 67 | 8 | 0 | 1 | 35 | 3 |
| Seals, Joey, Columbia | .303 | 218 | 37 | 66 | 16 | 0 | 13 | 48 | 0 |
| Murphy, Robby, Col | .302 | 291 | 59 | 88 | 11 | 7 | 1 | 27 | 18 |
| Rudolph, Gre, Clark | .295 | 288 | 43 | 85 | 13 | 1 | 4 | 44 | 13 |
| Hood, Dennis, Tenn | .295 | 261 | 59 | 77 | 19 | 3 | 4 | 38 | 42 |
| Gray, Danny, Clark | .295 | 200 | 28 | 59 | 16 | 1 | 1 | 27 | 4 |

### INDIVIDUAL PITCHING LEADERS
(Minimum 56 Innings)

| | W | L | ERA | G | SV | IP | H | BB | SO |
|---|---|---|---|---|---|---|---|---|---|
| #Mitchell, Charlie, Col | 3 | 2 | 1.17 | 27 | 12 | 31 | 23 | 8 | 35 |
| Dopson, John, Tenn | 6 | 5 | 2.95 | 14 | 0 | 95 | 93 | 19 | 99 |
| Mitchell, John, Col | 8 | 3 | 3.01 | 15 | 0 | 108 | 106 | 25 | 50 |
| Lancaster, Les, PB | 12 | 2 | 3.03 | 15 | 0 | 119 | 126 | 13 | 92 |
| Sepeda, Jamie, Tenn | 6 | 3 | 3.05 | 10 | 0 | 74 | 70 | 22 | 59 |
| Majors, Shane, Tenn | 5 | 1 | 3.56 | 12 | 0 | 61 | 48 | 43 | 43 |
| Porzio, Mike, Tenn | 7 | 4 | 3.65 | 15 | 0 | 99 | 94 | 30 | 54 |
| McCray, Eric, PB | 2 | 3 | 3.90 | 13 | 0 | 58 | 76 | 14 | 24 |
| Fronaberger, Brent, Col | 7 | 5 | 4.01 | 14 | 0 | 83 | 98 | 28 | 29 |
| Lovett, George, Clark | 7 | 4 | 4.31 | 14 | 0 | 94 | 101 | 32 | 56 |
| Borcherding, Mark, Clark | 5 | 6 | 4.46 | 15 | 0 | 101 | 103 | 39 | 48 |
| Scarpitti, Jeff, Clark | 4 | 4 | 4.52 | 13 | 0 | 76 | 89 | 31 | 34 |
| Conger, Bryan, PB | 6 | 4 | 4.64 | 17 | 0 | 76 | 85 | 28 | 44 |
| Williard, Brian, Green | 3 | 6 | 4.66 | 14 | 0 | 83 | 101 | 24 | 45 |
| Kirby, Wes, Meridian | 2 | 6 | 4.74 | 16 | 0 | 82 | 91 | 32 | 62 |
| Allison, Steve, PB | 6 | 2 | 4.88 | 15 | 0 | 72 | 71 | 39 | 46 |

# FRONTIER LEAGUE

The Springfield Capitals overcame two favored opponents to win the Frontier League title in their first season in the league.

The Capitals won their division in the first half of the season, but played below .500 in the second half. In the division playoffs against the Richmond Roosters, they lost the first game 10-8 before coming back to win the next two, 4-1 and 13-1.

In the finals the Capitals faced the Chillicothe Paints, who went 48-26 to finish with the league's best regular-season record. The Capitals beat the Johnstown Steal in three games to advance to the finals.

But Springfield dominated the series, sweeping the Paints 5-1 and 6-2 to win the series in two games.

Manager Mal Fichman guided an expansion team to the title for the third straight year. He did it with Erie in 1994 and Johnstown in 1995.

The continual expansion has moved the Frontier League to the upper echelon of independent leagues, with strong markets such as Evansville, Ind., and Kalamazoo, Mich. After almost dying in its first season in 1993, the league now thrives with only three of its original franchises.

The level of play also continued to improve. The league MVP was Richmond first baseman Morgan Burkhardt, who challenged for a triple crown and ended up hitting .357 with 17 homers and 64 RBIs.

## STANDINGS

### FIRST HALF

| EAST | W | L | PCT | GB |
|---|---|---|---|---|
| Chillicothe Paints | 23 | 14 | .622 | — |
| Johnstown Steal | 22 | 15 | .595 | 1 |
| Zanesville Greys | 20 | 17 | .541 | 3 |
| Ohio Valley Redcoats | 14 | 23 | .378 | 9 |

| WEST | W | L | PCT | GB |
|---|---|---|---|---|
| Springfield Capitals | 21 | 16 | .568 | — |
| Kalamazoo Kodiaks | 17 | 20 | .459 | 4 |
| Evansville Otters | 17 | 20 | .459 | 4 |
| Richmond Roosters | 15 | 22 | .405 | 6 |

### SECOND HALF

| EAST | W | L | PCT | GB |
|---|---|---|---|---|
| Chillicothe Paints | 25 | 12 | .676 | — |
| Zanesville Greys | 20 | 17 | .541 | 5 |
| Johnstown Steal | 19 | 18 | .514 | 6 |
| Ohio Valley Redcoats | 17 | 20 | .459 | 8 |

| WEST | W | L | PCT | GB |
|---|---|---|---|---|
| Richmond Roosters | 24 | 13 | .649 | — |
| Springfield Capitals | 18 | 19 | .486 | 6 |
| Evansville Otters | 17 | 20 | .459 | 7 |
| Kalamazoo Kodiaks | 8 | 29 | .216 | 16 |

**PLAYOFFS: Semifinals**—Springfield defeated Richmond 2-1, and Chillicothe defeated Johnstown 2-1, in best-of-3 series. **Finals**—Springfield defeated Chillicothe 2-0 in best-of-3 series.

**MANAGERS:** Chillicothe—Roger Hanners. Evansville—Fernando Arroyo. Johnstown—Jim Coffman. Kalamazoo—Glenn Gulliver. Ohio Valley—Jim Procopio. Richmond—John Cate. Springfield—Mal Fichman. Zanesville—Eric Welch.

**ATTENDANCE:** Evansville, 84,492; Kalamazoo, 62,331; Johnstown, 61,575; Richmond, 55,510; Chillicothe, 51,419; Springfield, 47,854; Ohio Valley, 30,248; Zanesville, 24,190.

**ALL-STAR TEAM: C**—Jorge Melendez, Springfield. **1B**—Morgan Burkhardt, Richmond. **2B**—Joe Pass, Richmond. **3B**—Mitch House, Chillicothe. **SS**—Matt Riemer, Chillicothe. **OF**—Gerald Bolden, Johnstown; Jackie Jempson, Chillicothe; Marty Watson, Evansville. **DH**—Scott Pinoni, Chillicothe. **SP**—Matt Baxter, Zanesville. **RP**—Terry Pearson, Zanesville.

**Most Valuable Player:** Morgan Burkhardt, Richmond. **Most Valuable Pitcher:** Matt Baxter, Zanesville. **Manager of the Year:** Roger Hanners, Chillicothe.

### INDIVIDUAL BATTING LEADERS
(Minimum 200 Plate Appearances)

| | AVG | AB | R | H | 2B | 3B | HR | RBI | SB |
|---|---|---|---|---|---|---|---|---|---|
| Pinoni, Scott, Chil | .384 | 281 | 59 | 108 | 19 | 2 | 11 | 65 | 1 |
| Burkhardt, Morgan, Rich | .357 | 266 | 60 | 95 | 27 | 1 | 17 | 64 | 22 |
| Holt, Kevin, John | .345 | 255 | 35 | 88 | 11 | 0 | 4 | 48 | 3 |
| Bolden, Gerald, John | .344 | 247 | 42 | 85 | 8 | 0 | 3 | 32 | 10 |
| Jempson, Jackie, Chil | .340 | 262 | 45 | 89 | 18 | 2 | 13 | 57 | 4 |
| Brown, Derek, John | .332 | 310 | 41 | 103 | 26 | 1 | 0 | 47 | 1 |
| Pass, Joe, Richmond | .330 | 297 | 43 | 98 | 15 | 1 | 1 | 30 | 2 |
| McDonnell, Tim, John | .329 | 228 | 33 | 75 | 18 | 0 | 4 | 32 | 4 |
| Watson, Marty, Evan | .324 | 296 | 66 | 96 | 26 | 4 | 8 | 55 | 15 |
| Johnson, Kevin, Evan | .320 | 206 | 34 | 66 | 17 | 1 | 4 | 37 | 2 |
| Beyna, Terry, Evan | .320 | 231 | 29 | 74 | 14 | 3 | 1 | 35 | 12 |
| Britt, Shane, Rich | .318 | 211 | 35 | 67 | 11 | 6 | 3 | 33 | 28 |
| Davenport, Shane, Evan | .317 | 287 | 38 | 91 | 14 | 1 | 6 | 53 | 1 |
| Harris, James, Spr | .315 | 260 | 33 | 82 | 12 | 0 | 1 | 56 | 1 |
| Wilcox, Troy, Chil | .314 | 210 | 33 | 66 | 6 | 4 | 1 | 35 | 23 |
| House, Mitch, Chil | .305 | 249 | 63 | 76 | 9 | 0 | 18 | 53 | 3 |

| | AVG | AB | R | H | 2B | 3B | HR | RBI | SB |
|---|---|---|---|---|---|---|---|---|---|
| Murphy, Sean, Evan | .304 | 237 | 43 | 72 | 9 | 3 | 2 | 25 | 23 |
| Fluck, Jessie, Chil | .298 | 312 | 56 | 93 | 9 | 6 | 1 | 33 | 20 |
| Surtaris, Tom, OV | .297 | 232 | 52 | 69 | 18 | 4 | 8 | 38 | 9 |
| Rockmore, thurston, John | .296 | 189 | 21 | 56 | 6 | 5 | 0 | 25 | 13 |
| Fatzinger, Darrell, OV | .296 | 247 | 27 | 73 | 10 | 1 | 10 | 42 | 3 |
| Baker, Curtis, Kal | .295 | 237 | 29 | 70 | 8 | 0 | 0 | 22 | 26 |
| Fitzmorris, Matt, Rich | .294 | 245 | 46 | 72 | 16 | **7** | 5 | 24 | 18 |
| Crothers, K.C., Zane | .292 | 212 | 31 | 62 | 16 | 1 | 2 | 27 | 11 |
| Wisely, Mike, Kalamazoo | .292 | 281 | 29 | 82 | 11 | 0 | 0 | 29 | 8 |
| Drabik, Jeff, Richmond | .289 | 270 | 47 | 78 | **27** | 0 | 10 | 51 | 3 |
| Benyo, Jason, Chil | .288 | 215 | 48 | 62 | 9 | 1 | 2 | 21 | 16 |
| Anderson, Patrick, Zane | .286 | 189 | 23 | 54 | 1 | 0 | 0 | 21 | 2 |
| Barrington, Roger, Zane | .286 | 182 | 37 | 52 | 5 | 1 | 1 | 23 | 24 |
| Counts, Justin, Zanesville | .285 | 207 | 23 | 59 | 13 | 0 | 0 | 28 | 4 |
| #Reimer, Matt, Chil | .272 | 254 | 42 | 69 | 17 | 2 | 1 | 37 | **42** |

### INDIVIDUAL PITCHING LEADERS
(Minimum 59 Innings)

| | W | L | ERA | G | SV | IP | H | BB | SO |
|---|---|---|---|---|---|---|---|---|---|
| Pearson, Terry, Zane | 4 | 1 | 0.50 | 31 | **20** | 36 | 30 | 8 | 43 |
| Baxter, Matt, Zanesville | 9 | 2 | 2.47 | 16 | 0 | 102 | 94 | 49 | 60 |
| House, Sean, Spr | 7 | 4 | 2.51 | 14 | 0 | 90 | 94 | 22 | 55 |
| Devries, Andrew, Spr | 7 | 2 | 2.73 | 16 | 0 | 102 | 97 | 33 | 54 |
| Edmondson, Reenn, Chil | 9 | 3 | 2.82 | 16 | 1 | 83 | 55 | 31 | 63 |
| Franek, Tom, Zanesville | 8 | 6 | 2.87 | 17 | 0 | 113 | 107 | 38 | 95 |
| Smith, Jarod, Evansville | 7 | 5 | 2.93 | 19 | 2 | 117 | 87 | 37 | 98 |
| Noblitt, Andy, Evan | 3 | 5 | 2.94 | 17 | 1 | 70 | 60 | 32 | 69 |
| Brantley, Jim, Spr | 4 | 3 | 2.97 | 31 | 1 | 67 | 63 | 28 | 41 |
| Crowley, Tom, Zane | 3 | 2 | 3.15 | 25 | 3 | 69 | 72 | 22 | 60 |
| Gieras, Kevin, John | 6 | 1 | 3.23 | 13 | 0 | 78 | 76 | 47 | 64 |
| Linder, Richie, Zane | 8 | 5 | 3.33 | 16 | 0 | 97 | 111 | 32 | 48 |
| Leystra, Jeff, Evansville | 7 | 4 | 3.50 | 15 | 0 | 103 | 100 | 24 | **109** |
| Williams, Larry, Zane | 4 | 7 | 3.51 | 14 | 0 | 59 | 62 | 24 | 48 |
| Cancel, Rob, Chil | 6 | 4 | 3.51 | 16 | 0 | 82 | 85 | 20 | 68 |
| Hacker, Scott, Rich | 6 | 8 | 3.68 | 16 | 0 | 93 | 119 | 10 | 47 |
| Sheridan, Tim, Chil | 4 | 3 | 3.69 | 11 | 0 | 63 | 61 | 34 | 40 |
| Abbott, Jim, OV | 6 | 2 | 3.70 | 17 | 0 | 90 | 73 | 41 | 76 |
| Hess, Christian, Evan | 7 | 4 | 3.81 | 15 | 0 | 78 | 79 | 41 | 61 |
| Hinkle, Jon, Chillicothe | 8 | 2 | 3.93 | 16 | 0 | 103 | 106 | 18 | 46 |
| Reeder, Russ, Spring | 0 | 5 | 3.97 | 13 | 0 | 66 | 75 | 19 | 54 |

# HEARTLAND LEAGUE

## STANDINGS

| TEAM | W | L | PCT | GB |
|---|---|---|---|---|
| Lafayette Leopards | 32 | 27 | .542 | — |
| Anderson Lawmen | 32 | 28 | .533 | ½ |
| Will County Cheetahs | 28 | 31 | .475 | 4 |
| Dubois County Dragons | 27 | 33 | .450 | 5½ |

**PLAYOFFS:** None.

**MANAGERS:** Anderson—Jay Walker. Dubois County—R.C. Lichtenstein. Lafayette—Bob Hallas. Will County—Gregg Slutsky.
**ATTENDANCE:** Dubois County, 33,203; Lafayette, 12,193; Anderson, 9,611; Will County, 6,378.
**ALL-STAR TEAM: C**—Chad Epperson, Lafayette. **1B**—Chris Webb, Anderson. **2B**—Ron D'Auteuil, Anderson. **3B**—Garry Kamphouse, Lafayette. **SS**—Kevin Jason, Will County. **OF**—Vincent Griffin, Dubois County; Kedrick Porter, Lafayette; Toby Ricard, Anderson. **DH**—Juan Price, Dubois County. **RHP**—Brian Sweeney, Lafayette. **LHP**—Dustin Riggs, Anderson. **RP**—Craig Shoobridge, Dubois County.
**Most Valuable Player:** Garry Kamphouse, Lafayette. **Most Valuable Pitcher:** Johnny Oestrich, Dubois County.

### INDIVIDUAL BATTING LEADERS
(Minimum 162 Plate Appearances)

| | AVG | AB | R | H | 2B | 3B | HR | RBI | SB |
|---|---|---|---|---|---|---|---|---|---|
| Stevenson, Mike, WC | **.361** | 147 | 27 | 53 | 10 | 2 | 5 | 26 | 5 |
| Griffin, Vincent, DC | .355 | 166 | 28 | 59 | 10 | 1 | 6 | 24 | 8 |
| Ricard, Toby, Anderson | .353 | 235 | **59** | **83** | 10 | 7 | 8 | 45 | 8 |
| Webb, Chris, Anderson | .351 | 191 | 37 | 67 | 17 | 2 | 6 | 48 | 0 |
| Kamphouse, Gary, Laf | .342 | 202 | 47 | 69 | 15 | 3 | 6 | **52** | 21 |
| Porter, Kedrick, Laf | .336 | 211 | 47 | 71 | 10 | 2 | 1 | 26 | 23 |
| Epperson, Chad, Laf | .336 | 217 | 46 | 73 | 15 | 4 | 10 | 49 | 9 |
| Delgado, Angel, DC-WC | .333 | 195 | 27 | 65 | 15 | 2 | 4 | 30 | 6 |
| Bailey, Heath, Anderson | .327 | 147 | 31 | 48 | 9 | 2 | 3 | 18 | 16 |
| D'Auteuil, Ron, And | .325 | 249 | 52 | 81 | 16 | 5 | 0 | 27 | 14 |
| Robinson, Eli, WC | .307 | 228 | 36 | 70 | 11 | 3 | 4 | 42 | 10 |
| Flood, Mike, Anderson | .306 | 206 | 40 | 63 | 4 | 3 | 3 | 32 | 13 |
| Jason, Kevin, WC | .305 | 164 | 25 | 50 | 12 | 0 | 3 | 22 | 8 |

| | | | | | | | | | |
|---|---|---|---|---|---|---|---|---|---|
| Santiago, Angel, DC | .305 | 220 | 31 | 67 | 15 | 2 | 2 | 37 | 7 |
| Diffenbaugh, Don, DC-And | .300 | 140 | 19 | 42 | 11 | 0 | 2 | 21 | 1 |
| Shirley, Mike, Anderson | .297 | 236 | 36 | 70 | 7 | 1 | 6 | 47 | 20 |
| #Green, Darrio, Laf-WC | .291 | 179 | 33 | 52 | 12 | 3 | 5 | 22 | **26** |
| #Staehle, Todd, WC | .286 | 210 | 47 | 60 | **18** | 2 | 5 | 24 | 5 |
| #Price, Juan, DC | .258 | 194 | 31 | 50 | 9 | 0 | **13** | 42 | 1 |

### INDIVIDUAL PITCHING LEADERS
(Minimum 48 Innings)

| | W | L | ERA | G | SV | IP | H | BB | SO |
|---|---|---|---|---|---|---|---|---|---|
| Olson, Mark, WC | 4 | 0 | **1.11** | 23 | 1 | 49 | 34 | 16 | 49 |
| Sweeney, Brian, Laf | 6 | 0 | 2.20 | 9 | 0 | 49 | 32 | 13 | 52 |
| Garcia, David, Lafayette | 6 | 4 | 2.88 | 15 | 0 | 91 | 79 | 28 | 60 |
| Wheeler, Ryan, DC | 5 | 3 | 3.02 | 9 | 0 | 63 | 56 | 19 | 49 |
| Oestreich, Johnny, DC | 8 | 2 | 3.18 | 12 | 0 | 76 | 58 | 19 | **96** |
| Barron, Josh, WC | 7 | 3 | 3.24 | 11 | 0 | 83 | 90 | 28 | 49 |
| Riggs, Dustin, Anderson | 7 | 5 | 3.59 | 13 | 0 | 98 | 89 | 41 | 71 |
| Shoobridge, Craig, DC | 4 | 2 | 3.60 | 31 | **11** | 60 | 64 | 25 | 45 |
| Smitherman, Jamie, And | 4 | 1 | 3.67 | 8 | 0 | 54 | 51 | 24 | 54 |
| Alleman, Derek, Laf | 5 | 5 | 4.04 | 12 | 0 | 89 | 101 | 11 | 56 |
| Rushford, Jim, DC | 4 | 4 | 4.35 | 21 | 1 | 62 | 58 | 33 | 51 |
| Gamble, Rob, Anderson | 4 | 4 | 4.37 | 10 | 0 | 68 | 75 | 21 | 29 |

# NORTH ATLANTIC LEAGUE

The Catskill Cougars, who got into the playoffs only after a successful protest, swept two games from the Massachusetts Mad Dogs to win the North Atlantic League title.

Catskill finished behind the Newark Barge Bandits in the league standings, but the Cougars protested a trade that the Bandits made after the league's trading deadline. The league ruled in Catskill's favor and ordered a four-game series, which the teams had split, forfeited to the Cougars. That put Catskill ahead of Newark and into the playoffs.

The Cougars squared off against Massachusetts, far and away the best team in the league during the regular season. The Mad Dogs finished 56-21, 13½ games ahead of the Cougars, and had the league's leading hitter (Doug Spofford) and pitcher (Jay Murphy), most valuable player (Roy Marsh) and manager of the year (George Scott).

But Catskill dominated the championship series, winning the first game 9-1 and then pulling out a win in the second game, 4-2 in 12 innings.

Massachusetts was also the biggest success at the gate, drawing 52,384 fans. Most of the other teams struggled to draw fans. The league vowed to expand, however, even after rumors that the league might merge with the Northeast League, with the strongest franchises surviving.

## STANDINGS

| | W | L | PCT | GB |
|---|---|---|---|---|
| Massachusetts Mad Dogs | 56 | 21 | .727 | — |
| Catskill Cougars | 43 | 35 | .551 | 13½ |
| Newark Barge Bandits | 41 | 37 | .526 | 15½ |
| Altoona Rail Kings | 36 | 42 | .462 | 20½ |
| Welland Aquaducks | 33 | 44 | .429 | 23 |
| Nashua Hawks | 23 | 53 | .303 | 32½ |

**PLAYOFFS:** Catskill defeated Massachusetts 2-0, in best-of-3 championship series.

**MANAGERS:** Altoona—Mike Richmond. Catskill—Al Lopez. Massachusetts—George Scott. Nashua—Ken Hairr. Newark—Ken Gardner. Welland—Ellis Williams.
**ATTENDANCE:** Massachusetts, 52,384; Altoona, 33,019; Catskill, 27,917; Nashua, 13,556; Newark, 12,676; Welland, 6,877.
**ALL-STAR TEAM: C**—Chris Hasty, Welland. **1B**—Doug Spofford, Massachusetts. **2B**—Billy Reed, Altoona. **3B**—Felix Colon, Massachusetts. **SS**—Karun Jackson, Altoona. **OF**—Jose DeLeon, Nashua; Dan Dillingham, Welland; Roy Marsh, Massachusetts.

RHP—Germaine Hunter, Newark; Jay Murphy, Massachusetts.
LHP—Ray Schmittle, Altoona; Tom Singer, Catskill. RP—Joe Nestor, Catskill.
**Most Valuable Player:** Roy Marsh, Massachusetts. **Manager of the Year:** George Scott, Massachusetts.

### INDIVIDUAL BATTING LEADERS
(Minimum 211 Plate Appearances)

| | AVG | AB | R | H | 2B | 3B | HR | RBI | SB |
|---|---|---|---|---|---|---|---|---|---|
| Spofford, Doug, Mass | .380 | 208 | 64 | 79 | 6 | 3 | 0 | 35 | 8 |
| Marsh, Roy, Mass | .364 | 294 | 87 | 107 | 10 | 7 | 2 | 40 | 45 |
| Dillingham, Dan, Wel | .356 | 239 | 46 | 85 | 11 | 4 | 4 | 46 | 39 |
| DeLeon, Jose, Nashua | .341 | 220 | 35 | 75 | 14 | 1 | 1 | 36 | 13 |
| Colon, Felix, Mass | .339 | 277 | 47 | 94 | 13 | 1 | 5 | 64 | 4 |
| Brown, Javier, Mass | .324 | 210 | 29 | 68 | 13 | 0 | 0 | 10 | 11 |
| Reed, Billy, Altoona | .323 | 257 | 46 | 83 | 18 | 4 | 2 | 32 | 15 |
| Smith, John, Altoona | .318 | 233 | 37 | 74 | 17 | 2 | 5 | 33 | 14 |
| Judy, Ray, Welland | .317 | 243 | 52 | 77 | 13 | 2 | 1 | 25 | 32 |
| Burrus, Daryl, Well.-Mass | .314 | 207 | 16 | 65 | 14 | 0 | 2 | 36 | 4 |
| Smith, Danny, Newark | .310 | 239 | 48 | 74 | 4 | 0 | 0 | 25 | 23 |
| Garcia, Manny, Cat | .308 | 227 | 42 | 70 | 15 | 1 | 8 | 53 | 6 |
| Burroughs, Eric, Alt | .306 | 288 | 57 | 88 | 10 | 5 | 0 | 24 | 37 |
| Cote, Steve, Nashua | .303 | 238 | 36 | 72 | 7 | 2 | 0 | 20 | 5 |
| Kurtz, Tony, Newark | .297 | 232 | 41 | 69 | 13 | 4 | 3 | 26 | 20 |
| Diaz, David, Newark | .291 | 275 | 62 | 80 | 5 | 1 | 1 | 24 | 45 |
| McWhite, Ray, Catskill | .284 | 225 | 37 | 64 | 9 | 2 | 6 | 40 | 8 |
| Mariucci, Rick, Catskill | .283 | 184 | 32 | 52 | 8 | 2 | 0 | 12 | 16 |
| Jackson, Karun, Altoona | .282 | 291 | 42 | 84 | 11 | 4 | 2 | 33 | 9 |
| Muckerheide, Troy, New | .275 | 247 | 36 | 68 | 13 | 1 | 2 | 36 | 25 |

### INDIVIDUAL PITCHING LEADERS
(Minimum 62 Innings)

| | W | L | ERA | G | SV | IP | H | BB | SO |
|---|---|---|---|---|---|---|---|---|---|
| Murphy, Jay, Mass | 12 | 3 | 1.11 | 17 | 1 | 122 | 97 | 18 | 108 |
| Hunter, Germaine, New | 12 | 3 | 1.76 | 16 | 0 | 123 | 84 | 35 | 116 |
| Rizzo, Nick, Nashua | 3 | 4 | 2.12 | 13 | 0 | 89 | 79 | 31 | 76 |
| #Collins, Larry, Newark | 3 | 2 | 2.16 | 26 | 13 | 33 | 28 | 3 | 16 |
| Martin, Mike, Welland | 2 | 2 | 2.59 | 18 | 0 | 66 | 61 | 34 | 39 |
| Scales, Stanley, Altoona | 6 | 3 | 2.85 | 16 | 0 | 107 | 92 | 43 | 51 |
| Holaren, Andy, Mass | 8 | 1 | 3.01 | 14 | 0 | 84 | 75 | 50 | 57 |
| Schmittle, Ray, Altoona | 7 | 3 | 3.18 | 26 | 0 | 65 | 70 | 34 | 56 |
| Tyner, Marcus, Catskill | 6 | 2 | 3.50 | 12 | 0 | 75 | 73 | 36 | 80 |
| Essery, Brian, Welland | 4 | 6 | 3.74 | 17 | 0 | 84 | 92 | 34 | 44 |
| Baum, Chris, Welland | 3 | 6 | 3.81 | 18 | 0 | 78 | 86 | 29 | 55 |
| Tidwell, Chris, Newark | 5 | 4 | 3.82 | 13 | 0 | 94 | 109 | 18 | 70 |
| Falcon, Jason, Mass | 7 | 5 | 4.19 | 19 | 0 | 97 | 116 | 35 | 48 |
| Ramagli, Matt, Catskill | 3 | 5 | 4.30 | 13 | 0 | 67 | 82 | 19 | 48 |
| Lynch, Joey, Newark | 3 | 7 | 4.34 | 14 | 0 | 93 | 106 | 34 | 54 |
| Dallas, Peter, Altoona | 1 | 6 | 4.48 | 18 | 0 | 64 | 65 | 38 | 20 |

# NORTHEAST LEAGUE

After making it to the finals and losing in 1995, the Albany Diamond Dogs made sure to get it right this time, winning the 1996 Northeast League title over Newburgh.

The Diamond Dogs had far and away the best record in the league a year earlier, but lost a three-game series to the Adirondack Lumberjacks in the league finals.

Albany again had the league's best record, at 55-25, but was just a half-game better than the Newburgh Nighthawks, who finished 54-25. Those two teams were at least eight games better than the rest of the league.

Though they were close in the standings, the Diamond Dogs and Night Hawks didn't play any close games in the championship series. Albany won the first two games, 9-0 and 7-3, then Newburgh came back to win the third game 9-1. Albany won the championship with a 14-3 blowout in the fourth game.

League batting champion and MVP Paul Reinisch also was the playoff MVP.

The league appeared to be gaining more solid footing after moving several struggling franchises after 1995. The Bangor Blue Ox were a success with Oil Can Boyd leading the way, but the Rhode Island franchise drew only 8,290 fans and wasn't expected to

return.

Bangor first baseman Corey Parker also became one of the few professional players ever to hit five home runs in five consecutive at-bats. He accomplished the feat in a June 20 doubleheader against Rhode Island. For the day he was 6-for-9 with 11 RBIs.

## STANDINGS

**FIRST HALF**

| | W | L | PCT | GB |
|---|---|---|---|---|
| Albany Diamond Dogs | 28 | 11 | .718 | — |
| Newburgh Night Hawks | 25 | 13 | .658 | 2½ |
| Bangor Blue Ox | 20 | 18 | .526 | 7½ |
| Adirondack Lumberjacks | 17 | 20 | .459 | 10 |
| Elmira Pioneers | 17 | 23 | .425 | 11½ |
| Rhode Island Tigersharks | 8 | 30 | .211 | 19½ |

**SECOND HALF**

| | W | L | PCT | GB |
|---|---|---|---|---|
| Newburgh Night Hawks | 29 | 12 | .707 | — |
| Albany Diamond Dogs | 27 | 14 | .659 | 2 |
| Bangor Blue Ox | 26 | 15 | .634 | 3 |
| Elmira Pioneers | 17 | 22 | .436 | 11 |
| Adirondack Lumberjacks | 13 | 30 | .302 | 17 |
| Rhode Island Tigersharks | 11 | 34 | .268 | 18 |

**PLAYOFFS:** Albany defeated Newburgh 2-1, in best-of-3 championship series.

**MANAGERS:** Adirondack—Dave LaPoint. Albany—John Wockenfuss. Bangor—Dick Phillips. Elmira—Ken Oberkfell. Newburgh—Dan Schwam. Rhode Island—Mike Palermo.

**ATTENDANCE:** Albany, 57,171; Adirondack, 56,341; Elmira, 41,501; Newburgh, 41,161; Bangor, 35,652; Rhode Island, 8,290.

**ALL-STAR TEAM:** C— 1B—Ron Lockett, Albany. 2B—Lonnie Goldberg, Bangor. 3B—Mike Miller, Newburgh. SS—Felix DeLeon, Albany. OF—Angelo Cox, Bangor; Rich Lemons, Newburgh; Timmie Morrow, Bangor; Jerome Tolliver, Albany. DH—John Mueller, Adirondack. RHP—Joel Bennett, Newburgh; Oil Can Boyd, Bangor. LHP—Gene Caruso, Newburgh.

**Most Valuable Player:** Paul Reinisch, Albany. **Pitcher of the Year:** Ed Riley, Albany. **Manager of the Year:** Dan Schwam, Newburgh.

### INDIVIDUAL BATTING LEADERS
(Minimum 216 Plate Appearances)

| | AVG | AB | R | H | 2B | 3B | HR | RBI | SB |
|---|---|---|---|---|---|---|---|---|---|
| Reinisch, Paul, Albany | .360 | 300 | 60 | 108 | 25 | 1 | 10 | 61 | 3 |
| Miller, Mike, RI-New | .355 | 276 | 62 | 98 | 13 | 7 | 9 | 49 | 11 |
| Tolliver, Jerome, Alb | .342 | 222 | 37 | 76 | 16 | 8 | 7 | 48 | 1 |
| Morrow, Timmie, Bangor | .337 | 249 | 47 | 84 | 16 | 1 | 11 | 43 | 8 |
| Lombardi, John, RI | .322 | 295 | 43 | 95 | 22 | 5 | 4 | 47 | 11 |
| Mercado, Rafael, Albany | .319 | 273 | 51 | 87 | 24 | 1 | 10 | 39 | 1 |
| Lockett, Ron, Albany | .314 | 274 | 53 | 86 | 22 | 3 | 5 | 46 | 16 |
| Cox, Angelo, Bangor | .309 | 307 | 59 | 95 | 17 | 6 | 5 | 36 | 50 |
| Lemons, Rich, New | .309 | 288 | 48 | 89 | 18 | 9 | 8 | 61 | 6 |
| Madden, Joey, New | .298 | 309 | 51 | 92 | 11 | 7 | 0 | 21 | 26 |
| DeLeon, Felix, Albany | .297 | 293 | 61 | 87 | 13 | 4 | 1 | 30 | 18 |
| Moeglin, Brian, Elm-Adir | .294 | 245 | 31 | 72 | 14 | 1 | 2 | 26 | 10 |
| Mariano, Joe, Albany | .294 | 218 | 28 | 64 | 9 | 0 | 1 | 31 | 2 |
| Piniero, Mike, New | .291 | 203 | 35 | 59 | 10 | 4 | 3 | 32 | 7 |
| Goldberg, Lonnie, Bangor | .284 | 317 | 51 | 90 | 20 | 1 | 3 | 37 | 49 |
| Gilliam, Sean, Albany | .284 | 261 | 45 | 74 | 12 | 6 | 12 | 47 | 3 |
| Simon, David, Albany | .283 | 237 | 37 | 67 | 9 | 3 | 2 | 20 | 5 |
| Mueller, Jon, Adir | .281 | 256 | 53 | 72 | 14 | 0 | 18 | 47 | 2 |
| Bifone, Pete, Elmira | .277 | 264 | 45 | 73 | 12 | 3 | 2 | 6 | 48 | 9 |
| Porzio, Nando, RI | .276 | 217 | 23 | 60 | 12 | 1 | 8 | 34 | 2 |
| Bellagamba, Mike, Elm | .272 | 268 | 35 | 73 | 18 | 1 | 2 | 38 | 1 |
| Mannino, Brian, RI | .267 | 258 | 30 | 69 | 13 | 0 | 6 | 24 | 0 |
| Woods, Byron, New | .267 | 240 | 42 | 64 | 7 | 5 | 9 | 45 | 22 |
| Cook, Jeff, Adirondack | .266 | 308 | 36 | 82 | 9 | 0 | 1 | 20 | 28 |

### INDIVIDUAL PITCHING LEADERS
(Minimum 64 Innings)

| | W | L | ERA | G | SV | IP | H | BB | SO |
|---|---|---|---|---|---|---|---|---|---|
| Hasler, Jerry, Albany | 5 | 0 | 1.72 | 32 | 6 | 68 | 68 | 15 | 57 |
| Riley, Ed, Albany | 11 | 1 | 1.78 | 14 | 0 | 86 | 68 | 17 | 90 |
| Reyes, Jose, Albany | 7 | 5 | 2.15 | 16 | 0 | 96 | 91 | 18 | 83 |
| Caruso, Gene, Newburgh | 8 | 8 | 2.28 | 17 | 0 | 110 | 94 | 34 | 121 |
| Hayes, Chris, Adirondack | 2 | 5 | 2.37 | 39 | 0 | 65 | 69 | 10 | 48 |
| Broome, John, New | 9 | 3 | 2.45 | 17 | 0 | 118 | 87 | 25 | 66 |
| Coleman, Raymond, RI | 3 | 6 | 2.89 | 29 | 5 | 65 | 54 | 45 | 58 |
| Maddalone, Vinny, Adir | 4 | 6 | 3.04 | 20 | 1 | 83 | 74 | 24 | 50 |
| Rapaglia, Stephan, Alb | 4 | 3 | 3.17 | 13 | 1 | 65 | 69 | 11 | 45 |

| | | | | | | | | | |
|---|---|---|---|---|---|---|---|---|---|
| Boyd, Oil Can, Bangor .......... | 10 | 0 | 3.23 | 16 | 0 | 95 | 93 | 10 | 62 |
| Lindemann, Wayne, New........ | 8 | 4 | 3.28 | 17 | 0 | 102 | 87 | 36 | 83 |
| Davis, Jamie, Bangor............ | 6 | 7 | 3.47 | 16 | 0 | 109 | 105 | 30 | 89 |
| Sullivan, Grant, Albany........... | 5 | 3 | 3.52 | 27 | 2 | 69 | 70 | 16 | 53 |
| Spang, R.J., Bangor.............. | 7 | 4 | 3.60 | 15 | 0 | 90 | 74 | 45 | 80 |
| Clark, Doug, Adir-Alb............ | 8 | 6 | 3.78 | 18 | 0 | 114 | 136 | 16 | 97 |
| Fryowicz, Travis, Elm............. | 5 | 7 | 3.87 | 17 | 0 | 109 | 134 | 34 | 51 |
| #Torres, Hiram, Elmira........... | 3 | 3 | 4.70 | 33 | 17 | 38 | 41 | 10 | 40 |

# PRAIRIE LEAGUE

The Minot Mallards completed a sensational one-season turnaround by winning the Prairie League championship series three games to one.

The Mallards not only had a 24-47 record in 1995, but the team also nearly folded in the offseason before being rescued by local owners.

Then Minot (54-26) had to face Aberdeen (54-24), the best team in the league for two years running, in the first round of the playoffs. The Mallards swept the series in two games to meet the Grand Forks Varmints, a first-year team that beat the Moose Jaw Diamond Dogs two games to one in the first round.

The Mallards were heavily favored in the finals but lost the first game 5-4. They came back to win the next two games, 7-4 and 10-1, before hammering the Varmints 17-4 for the championship.

Minot's Brad Strauss, the playoff MVP, led the way in the final game by going 3-for-4 with a home run and four RBIs. Strauss, who led the league with 27 homers in the regular season, had four in the championship series.

The league opened the season with 11 teams, but the Brainerd Bobcats franchise shut down early in the season after the league couldn't find a new ownership group when the old one couldn't pay the bills.

## STANDINGS

### FIRST HALF

| NORTH | W | L | PCT | GB |
|---|---|---|---|---|
| Moose Jaw Diamond Dogs | 24 | 12 | .667 | — |
| Grand Forks Varmints | 16 | 15 | .516 | 5½ |
| Regina Cyclones | 16 | 17 | .485 | 6½ |
| Saskatoon Smokin' Guns | 16 | 19 | .457 | 7½ |
| Brandon Grey Owls | 14 | 24 | .368 | 11 |

| SOUTH | W | L | PCT | GB |
|---|---|---|---|---|
| Minot Mallards | 23 | 12 | .657 | — |
| Aberdeen Pheasants | 20 | 12 | .625 | 1½ |
| Southern Minny Stars | 17 | 16 | .515 | 5 |
| *Brainerd Bobcats | 7 | 9 | .438 | 9½ |
| Dakota Rattlers | 12 | 19 | .387 | 9 |
| Green Bay Sultans | 10 | 20 | .333 | 10½ |

*Folded after first half.

### SECOND HALF

| NORTH | W | L | PCT | GB |
|---|---|---|---|---|
| Moose Jaw Diamond Dogs | 26 | 17 | .605 | — |
| Grand Forks Varmints | 29 | 19 | .604 | ½ |
| Regina Cyclones | 21 | 24 | .467 | 6 |
| Saskatoon Smokin' Guns | 14 | 28 | .333 | 11½ |
| Brandon Grey Owls | 12 | 29 | .293 | 13 |

| SOUTH | W | L | PCT | GB |
|---|---|---|---|---|
| Aberdeen Pheasants | 34 | 12 | .739 | — |
| Minot Mallards | 31 | 14 | .689 | 2½ |
| Dakota Rattlers | 21 | 25 | .457 | 13 |
| Green Bay Sultans | 18 | 26 | .409 | 15 |
| Southern Minny Stars | 17 | 29 | .370 | 17 |

**PLAYOFFS: Semifinals**—Minot defeated Aberdeen 2-0, and Grand Forks defeated Moose Jaw 2-1, in best-of-3 series. **Finals**—Minot defeated Grand Forks 3-1, in best-of-5 series.

**MANAGERS:** Aberdeen—Bob Flori. Bismarck—Bill Sharp. Brandon—L.J. Dupuis. Green Bay—Denny Ruh. Grand Forks—Mike Verdi. Minot—Mitch Zwolensky. Moose Jaw—Darryl Robinson. Regina—Daryl Boston. Saskatoon—Andre Johnson. Southern Minny—Greg Olson.

**ATTENDANCE:** Moose Jaw, 76,696; Grand Forks, 35,619; Regina, 33,370; Southern Minny, 31,548; Aberdeen, 29,552; Minot, 28,361; Dakota, 25,702; Saskatoon, 22,991; Green Bay, 16,038; Brandon, 10,967; Brainerd, 2,646.

**ALL-STAR TEAM: C**—Kevin Schula, Moose Jaw. **1B**—Ken Tirpack, Aberdeen. **2B**—Gordon Powell, Grand Forks. **3B**—Randy Kapano, Moose Jaw. **SS**—Sean McKamie, Southern Minny. **OF**—Gary Collum, Minot; Brian Cornelius, Moose Jaw; Ty Griffin, Grand Forks. **DH**—Lou List, Minot. **RHP**—Linc Mikkelsen, Minot. **LHP**—Leonel Vasquez, Aberdeen. **RP**—Mike Toney, Moose Jaw.

**Most Valuable Player:** Brian Cornelius, Moose Jaw. **Co-Managers of the Year:** Mike Verdi, Grand Forks; Mitch Zwolensky, Minot.

## INDIVIDUAL BATTING LEADERS
(Minimum 216 Plate Appearances)

| | AVG | AB | R | H | 2B | 3B | HR | RBI | SB |
|---|---|---|---|---|---|---|---|---|---|
| Tirpack, Ken, Aberdeen..... | .404 | 297 | 63 | 120 | 30 | 1 | 18 | 84 | 2 |
| Cornelius, Brian, MJ............. | .388 | 304 | 67 | 118 | 16 | 3 | 18 | 72 | 15 |
| Strauss, Brad, Minot............. | .365 | 288 | 85 | 105 | 16 | 2 | 27 | 60 | 17 |
| McKamie, Sean, SM............ | .355 | 287 | 61 | 102 | 18 | 3 | 8 | 58 | 14 |
| Weinheimer, Wayne, Br-Sask .354 | | 274 | 57 | 97 | 23 | 3 | 11 | 60 | 13 |
| Boston, Daryl, Regina .......... | .352 | 270 | 54 | 95 | 20 | 0 | 10 | 69 | 4 |
| Charbonnet, Mark, MJ-SM.... | .351 | 265 | 61 | 93 | 23 | 3 | 15 | 42 | 8 |
| Moon, Ray, Dakota............... | .348 | 267 | 53 | 93 | 17 | 2 | 2 | 41 | 20 |
| List, Lou, Minot..................... | .342 | 301 | 64 | 103 | 20 | 2 | 24 | 75 | 10 |
| Nalls, Kevin, Saskatoon....... | .341 | 211 | 24 | 72 | 7 | 0 | 7 | 43 | 1 |
| Smith, Luke, Aberdeen......... | .341 | 223 | 44 | 76 | 19 | 1 | 4 | 31 | 1 |
| Smith, Tom, Green Bay ........ | .340 | 241 | 51 | 82 | 14 | 3 | 18 | 49 | 6 |
| Billingsley, Kyle, Sask ......... | .338 | 228 | 36 | 77 | 24 | 2 | 5 | 36 | 2 |
| Gerald, Ed, Aberdeen.......... | .335 | 316 | 86 | 106 | 17 | 3 | 22 | 81 | 18 |
| Johnson, Andre, Sask.......... | .326 | 279 | 56 | 91 | 21 | 1 | 15 | 63 | 11 |
| Griffin, Ty, Grand Forks........ | .326 | 267 | 62 | 87 | 24 | 0 | 10 | 55 | 25 |
| Schula, Kevin, MJ................. | .325 | 203 | 35 | 66 | 12 | 0 | 11 | 46 | 1 |
| Witmer, Cory, Sask ............. | .324 | 287 | 44 | 93 | 16 | 0 | 0 | 39 | 6 |
| Cann, John, Moose Jaw........ | .323 | 235 | 49 | 76 | 15 | 0 | 10 | 41 | 1 |
| Wright, Pat, SM .................... | .322 | 273 | 60 | 88 | 13 | 2 | 13 | 52 | 9 |
| Collum, Gary, Minot.............. | .322 | 311 | 67 | 100 | 11 | 4 | 7 | 31 | 49 |
| Hoffner, Jamie, GF................ | .321 | 324 | 58 | 104 | 20 | 0 | 5 | 48 | 6 |
| Steele, Mack, Moose Jaw .... | .320 | 278 | 59 | 89 | 11 | 1 | 1 | 20 | 17 |
| Giles, Brian, Minot............... | .320 | 194 | 55 | 62 | 13 | 1 | 16 | 37 | 6 |
| Powell, Gordon, Reg-GF....... | .318 | 311 | 67 | 99 | 23 | 7 | 7 | 49 | 20 |
| Tovar, Edgar, Aberdeen........ | .316 | 269 | 52 | 85 | 17 | 2 | 7 | 48 | 2 |
| Dunn, Bill, Moose Jaw.......... | .315 | 248 | 55 | 78 | 9 | 0 | 8 | 34 | 21 |
| Kapano, Randy, MJ............... | .310 | 268 | 58 | 83 | 17 | 1 | 18 | 72 | 5 |
| Halpern, Dan, Dakota........... | .306 | 314 | 49 | 96 | 18 | 3 | 8 | 53 | 11 |
| Wooten, Shawn, MJ.............. | .305 | 292 | 44 | 89 | 17 | 0 | 12 | 57 | 2 |
| Sosa, Andre, MJ-Dakota....... | .304 | 230 | 40 | 70 | 18 | 3 | 4 | 54 | 6 |
| Martin, Ariel, SM.................. | .304 | 309 | 44 | 94 | 21 | 1 | 9 | 47 | 2 |
| Wearing, Mel, Reg-MJ.......... | .303 | 221 | 58 | 67 | 15 | 2 | 19 | 49 | 8 |
| Hisle, Larry, GF.................... | .303 | 175 | 48 | 53 | 14 | 0 | 13 | 35 | 11 |
| Gerteisen, Aaron, Aber........ | .302 | 298 | 49 | 90 | 16 | 4 | 5 | 38 | 15 |
| Christenson, Bryce, Reg ...... | .302 | 285 | 62 | 86 | 13 | 6 | 3 | 33 | 28 |
| Castro, Ernest, SM .............. | .302 | 295 | 52 | 89 | 21 | 0 | 11 | 55 | 1 |
| Vanek, Todd, Minot.............. | .300 | 310 | 49 | 93 | 18 | 2 | 16 | 61 | 7 |
| Sanchez, Ismael, Minot........ | .297 | 219 | 36 | 65 | 7 | 2 | 6 | 39 | 11 |
| Quintana, Alberto, GB .......... | .296 | 297 | 24 | 88 | 17 | 0 | 2 | 37 | 4 |
| Wiezorek, Ted, Brandon........ | .296 | 247 | 34 | 73 | 10 | 3 | 4 | 33 | 0 |
| Mitchell, Rivers, Dak............ | .295 | 220 | 34 | 65 | 11 | 4 | 3 | 30 | 6 |

## INDIVIDUAL PITCHING LEADERS
(Minimum 64 Innings)

| | W | L | ERA | G | SV | IP | H | BB | SO |
|---|---|---|---|---|---|---|---|---|---|
| Mikkelsen, Linc, Minot....... | 12 | 3 | 1.26 | 17 | 0 | 122 | 83 | 28 | 118 |
| Vasquez, Leonel, Aber......... | 11 | 2 | 2.22 | 19 | 0 | 105 | 79 | 39 | 106 |
| Matthews, Mark, Minot.......... | 7 | 1 | 2.29 | 16 | 0 | 75 | 76 | 23 | 56 |
| Brincks, Mark, MJ................ | 13 | 3 | 2.48 | 17 | 0 | 123 | 108 | 34 | 107 |
| Kerley, Collin, Minot............. | 14 | 4 | 2.86 | 18 | 0 | 132 | 115 | 15 | 117 |
| #Toney, Mike, Moose Jaw ..... | 2 | 0 | 2.95 | 31 | 17 | 37 | 19 | 34 | 49 |
| Wiesner, Chad, SM .............. | 5 | 5 | 2.99 | 36 | 0 | 90 | 93 | 33 | 85 |
| Ard, Johnny, Aberdeen.......... | 9 | 4 | 3.37 | 17 | 0 | 120 | 108 | 19 | 104 |
| Prosser, David, Dakota ......... | 8 | 9 | 3.59 | 21 | 0 | 143 | 154 | 32 | 88 |
| Gamble, James, Saskatoon.... | 5 | 6 | 3.70 | 15 | 0 | 90 | 92 | 18 | 49 |
| Basteyns, Brian, MJ.............. | 5 | 1 | 3.76 | 15 | 1 | 67 | 67 | 29 | 63 |
| Foshie, Josh, Brandon .......... | 6 | 7 | 3.92 | 19 | 0 | 122 | 116 | 60 | 95 |
| Wagner, Rick, Brandon .......... | 3 | 4 | 3.98 | 18 | 1 | 75 | 72 | 34 | 39 |
| Draper, Trey, Dakota-MJ........ | 4 | 4 | 4.10 | 13 | 0 | 79 | 89 | 27 | 33 |
| DuBois, Brian, Aber.............. | 8 | 3 | 4.25 | 18 | 0 | 112 | 132 | 21 | 107 |

| | | | | | | | | | | | |
|---|---|---|---|---|---|---|---|---|---|---|---|
| Gaiko, Rob, Saskatoon-GF | 6 | 4 | 4.26 | 31 | 3 | 68 | 65 | 19 | 40 |
| Spurgeon, Steve, SM-GF | 6 | 2 | 4.34 | 14 | 0 | 77 | 83 | 19 | 62 |
| Berenguer, Juan, SM | 3 | 7 | 4.35 | 35 | 9 | 72 | 83 | 13 | 80 |
| Shoemaker, John, Brai-Bran | 2 | 12 | 4.51 | 20 | 0 | 126 | 144 | 50 | 58 |
| Cota, Troy, Green Bay | 4 | 3 | 4.55 | 13 | 0 | 83 | 100 | 17 | 52 |
| Bretza, John, Brandon | 3 | 8 | 4.59 | 19 | 1 | 102 | 112 | 57 | 77 |
| Arambula, Mario, Regina | 5 | 4 | 4.61 | 24 | 2 | 96 | 115 | 39 | 74 |
| McDonald, Marty, Dakota | 6 | 9 | 4.61 | 19 | 0 | 121 | 128 | 45 | 59 |
| Richardson, Mike, MJ | 8 | 7 | 4.67 | 22 | 0 | 135 | 150 | 21 | 89 |
| Lehoisky, Russ, SM | 4 | 7 | 4.68 | 19 | 0 | 98 | 113 | 61 | 56 |
| Huss, Brian, Grand Forks | 3 | 7 | 4.80 | 21 | 2 | 86 | 104 | 24 | 51 |

# WESTERN LEAGUE

In the Western League's second season, the same teams met for the championship, and the same team won it in the same number of games as 1995.

The Long Beach Riptide beat the Tri-City Posse three games to one to take their second straight championship. The Riptide came back from a mediocre first half to finish 32-13 in the second half, and it continued that roll through the playoffs.

After dropping a game to Salinas, Long Beach came back to win two straight to advance to the finals against Tri-City, which swept two games from Reno.

The teams split the first two games, but Long Beach came back to win 8-5 and 13-1 to take the title.

The Riptide's Alan Burke, who played third base and the outfield, was the championship series MVP after going 6-for-17 with four RBIs.

The league held on to its solid beginning, with one new franchise, Reno, that drew 52,113 fans. The Grays Harbor and Palm Springs franchises saw significant drops in attendance, and Palm Springs resorted to a come-to-the-ballpark-naked promotion (which was cancelled) and a transvestite night to draw fans.

## STANDINGS

### FIRST HALF

| NORTH | W | L | PCT | GB |
|---|---|---|---|---|
| Reno Chukars | 24 | 21 | .533 | — |
| Grays Harbor Gulls | 23 | 22 | .511 | 1 |
| Bend Bandits | 22 | 22 | .500 | 1½ |
| Tri-City Posse | 19 | 25 | .432 | 4½ |

| SOUTH | W | L | PCT | GB |
|---|---|---|---|---|
| Salinas Peppers | 26 | 19 | .578 | — |
| Palm Springs Suns | 23 | 22 | .511 | 3 |
| Long Beach Riptide | 22 | 23 | .489 | 4 |
| Sonoma County Crushers | 20 | 25 | .444 | 6 |

### SECOND HALF

| NORTH | W | L | PCT | GB |
|---|---|---|---|---|
| Tri-City Posse | 25 | 20 | .556 | — |
| Reno Chukars | 24 | 21 | .533 | 1 |
| Grays Harbor Gulls | 17 | 28 | .378 | 8 |
| Bend Bandits | 17 | 28 | .378 | 8 |

| SOUTH | W | L | PCT | GB |
|---|---|---|---|---|
| Long Beach Riptide | 32 | 13 | .711 | — |
| Salinas Peppers | 28 | 17 | .622 | 4 |
| Palm Springs Suns | 23 | 22 | .511 | 9 |
| Sonoma County Crushers | 14 | 31 | .311 | 18 |

**PLAYOFFS: Semifinals**—Long Beach defeated Salinas 2-1, and Tri-Cities defeated Reno 2-0, in best-of-3 series. **Finals**—Long Beach defeated Tri-Cities 3-1 in best-of-5 series.

**MANAGERS:** Bend—Al Gallagher. Grays Harbor—Charley Kerfeld. Long Beach—Jeff Burroughs. Palm Springs—Jamie Nelson. Reno—Butch Hughes. Salinas—Dave Holt. Sonoma County—Dick Dietz. Tri-City—Bobo Brayton.

**ATTENDANCE:** Tri-City, 96,061; Sonoma County, 92,020; Long Beach, 74,440; Bend, 52,946; Reno, 52,113; Salinas, 47,363; Grays Harbor, 37,045; Palm Springs, 31,241.

**ALL-STAR TEAM: C**—Carl Nichols, Reno. **1B**—Todd Pridy, Salinas. **2B**—Chris Grubb, Grays Harbor. **3B**—Frank Valdez, Palm Springs. **SS**—Ryan Rutz, Tri-City. **OF**—Ray Harvey, Grays Harbor; Shawn Scott, Tri-City; Sam Taylor, Salinas. **DH**—David Mowry, Sonoma County. **Util**—Rick Prieto, Salinas. **P**—Paul Anderson, Long Beach; Tim Gower, Salinas; Jose Salcedo, Tri-City; Mark Tranberg, Long Beach; Ben Weber, Salinas.

**Player of the Year:** Rick Prieto, Salinas. **Pitcher of the Year:** Paul Anderson, Long Beach. **Manager of the Year:** Butch Hughes, Reno.

## INDIVIDUAL BATTING LEADERS
(Minimum 243 Plate Appearances)

| | AVG | AB | R | H | 2B | 3B | HR | RBI | SB |
|---|---|---|---|---|---|---|---|---|---|
| Grubb, Chris, GH | .365 | 282 | 42 | 103 | 14 | 4 | 4 | 30 | 8 |
| Harvey, Ray, GH | .363 | 273 | 62 | 99 | 22 | 3 | 11 | 55 | 5 |
| Pridy, Todd, Salinas | .346 | 315 | 63 | 109 | 16 | 3 | 21 | 63 | 3 |
| Valdez, Frank, PS | .345 | 325 | 47 | 112 | 25 | 2 | 8 | 62 | 19 |
| Miller, Roy, Reno | .344 | 262 | 60 | 90 | 19 | 10 | 8 | 53 | 3 |
| Prieto, Rick, Salinas | .338 | 364 | 83 | 123 | 27 | 10 | 5 | 49 | 30 |
| Cooper, Tim, Reno | .331 | 350 | 75 | 116 | 21 | 10 | 12 | 65 | 4 |
| Nunez, Bernie, PS-Bend | .329 | 307 | 60 | 101 | 21 | 1 | 13 | 44 | 3 |
| Burke, Alan, LB | .327 | 312 | 57 | 102 | 20 | 3 | 13 | 53 | 4 |
| Mowry, David, SC | .327 | 346 | 53 | 113 | 30 | 0 | 20 | 76 | 1 |
| Comeaux, Eddie, Reno | .326 | 331 | 65 | 108 | 7 | 8 | 4 | 54 | 20 |
| Paul, Corey, T-C | .326 | 267 | 40 | 87 | 17 | 1 | 5 | 43 | 4 |
| Taylor, Sam, Salinas | .325 | 372 | 63 | 121 | 25 | 5 | 11 | 68 | 10 |
| Turlais, John, T-C | .321 | 280 | 47 | 90 | 24 | 3 | 11 | 36 | 2 |
| Nichols, Carl, Reno | .317 | 347 | 60 | 110 | 29 | 1 | 20 | 89 | 4 |
| Casey, John, Long Beach | .315 | 346 | 57 | 109 | 26 | 2 | 0 | 43 | 5 |
| Nadeau, Mike, Bend | .312 | 292 | 53 | 91 | 17 | 1 | 5 | 39 | 11 |
| Lewis, Dan, SC | .311 | 228 | 38 | 71 | 15 | 0 | 13 | 54 | 0 |
| Smiley, Reuben, LB | .311 | 312 | 63 | 97 | 17 | 3 | 8 | 59 | 27 |
| Wallace, Tim, Tri City -PS | .311 | 322 | 52 | 100 | 15 | 0 | 5 | 46 | 16 |
| Reams, Ron, GH-Salinas | .309 | 359 | 53 | 111 | 17 | 2 | 7 | 59 | 6 |
| DeLeon, Ray, GH-Salinas | .309 | 343 | 49 | 106 | 22 | 2 | 8 | 83 | 11 |
| Scott, Shawn, Tri-Cities | .305 | 390 | 58 | 119 | 21 | 6 | 4 | 48 | 43 |
| Washington, Kyle, SC | .301 | 312 | 61 | 94 | 19 | 4 | 13 | 53 | 10 |
| Funderburk, Levi, Reno | .299 | 241 | 41 | 72 | 18 | 1 | 1 | 28 | 0 |
| Williams, Paul, Bend | .299 | 231 | 34 | 69 | 10 | 0 | 9 | 33 | 0 |
| Barbara, Don, Long Beach | .299 | 278 | 36 | 83 | 23 | 0 | 9 | 55 | 1 |
| Murphy, Jim, T-C | .295 | 237 | 30 | 70 | 11 | 0 | 5 | 40 | 5 |
| Villalona, Kadir, PS | .295 | 302 | 37 | 89 | 12 | 1 | 3 | 25 | 11 |
| Harris, Donald, Bend | .294 | 360 | 58 | 106 | 21 | 7 | 14 | 64 | 7 |
| Davis, Kendrick, Bend | .294 | 252 | 39 | 74 | 11 | 4 | 5 | 44 | 8 |
| Rendina, Mike, Reno | .294 | 235 | 34 | 69 | 17 | 1 | 10 | 39 | 4 |
| Pfeifer, Scott, Reno | .293 | 208 | 36 | 61 | 9 | 6 | 0 | 21 | 19 |
| Kooiman, Brian, Salinas | .293 | 362 | 60 | 106 | 18 | 4 | 13 | 76 | 7 |
| Rutz, Ryan, T-C | .293 | 352 | 57 | 103 | 9 | 7 | 0 | 34 | 20 |
| Brooks, Eric, Long Beach | .292 | 253 | 32 | 74 | 11 | 1 | 7 | 38 | 2 |
| Koehler, Jim, Bend | .292 | 322 | 49 | 94 | 24 | 1 | 17 | 67 | 0 |
| Vasquez, Chris, T-C | .289 | 308 | 38 | 89 | 16 | 2 | 9 | 47 | 1 |

## INDIVIDUAL PITCHING LEADERS
(Minimum 72 Innings)

| | W | L | ERA | G | SV | IP | H | BB | SO |
|---|---|---|---|---|---|---|---|---|---|
| #Gower, Tim, Salinas | 4 | 3 | 1.53 | 52 | 24 | 65 | 45 | 6 | 68 |
| Salcedo, Jose, T-C | 7 | 3 | 2.11 | 18 | 0 | 111 | 77 | 42 | 97 |
| Burcham, Tim, PS | 5 | 7 | 2.56 | 18 | 1 | 102 | 98 | 21 | 95 |
| Anderson, Paul, LB | 12 | 4 | 2.68 | 16 | 0 | 117 | 112 | 13 | 83 |
| Tranberg, Mark, LB | 9 | 3 | 2.93 | 19 | 0 | 135 | 128 | 38 | 113 |
| Rolish, Chad, PS | 10 | 7 | 3.37 | 28 | 1 | 139 | 140 | 58 | 94 |
| Weber, Ben, Salinas | 12 | 6 | 3.46 | 22 | 0 | 148 | 138 | 42 | 102 |
| Kotes, Chris, GH | 9 | 4 | 3.56 | 19 | 0 | 121 | 106 | 62 | 128 |
| Walania, Al, GH | 5 | 4 | 3.62 | 28 | 1 | 99 | 106 | 31 | 82 |
| Gogos, Keith, LB-T-C | 5 | 8 | 3.73 | 15 | 0 | 94 | 104 | 21 | 44 |
| Renko, Steve, Salinas | 4 | 3 | 3.75 | 14 | 0 | 72 | 75 | 22 | 44 |
| Smith, Mike, Long Beach | 11 | 5 | 3.77 | 18 | 0 | 124 | 117 | 31 | 85 |
| Coscia, Tony, SC | 7 | 6 | 3.86 | 19 | 0 | 117 | 118 | 33 | 108 |
| Sheehan, Chris, Tri-Cities | 8 | 8 | 3.87 | 19 | 0 | 126 | 146 | 27 | 135 |
| Alexander, Jordy, T-C | 5 | 4 | 3.90 | 22 | 1 | 90 | 89 | 39 | 74 |
| Patterson, Jim, PS | 3 | 4 | 3.90 | 30 | 3 | 88 | 109 | 24 | 50 |
| Niebla, Ruben, PS | 8 | 9 | 3.90 | 24 | 0 | 141 | 166 | 38 | 68 |
| Goedhart, Darrell, PS-GH | 8 | 3 | 3.93 | 15 | 0 | 85 | 98 | 27 | 79 |
| Baker, Derek, Salinas-Reno | 9 | 6 | 4.05 | 23 | 1 | 109 | 113 | 61 | 78 |
| Singleton, Scott, LB | 6 | 7 | 4.15 | 18 | 0 | 126 | 123 | 51 | 68 |
| Knudsen, Kurt, SC | 5 | 4 | 4.19 | 19 | 0 | 103 | 112 | 36 | 96 |
| Doughty, Brian, Reno | 11 | 3 | 4.27 | 18 | 0 | 133 | 143 | 44 | 73 |
| White, Chris, Bend | 6 | 8 | 4.28 | 20 | 0 | 132 | 126 | 38 | 90 |
| Reardon, Kevin, Bend | 6 | 5 | 4.44 | 15 | 0 | 95 | 103 | 21 | 72 |
| Deremer, Brent, SC-Bend | 3 | 3 | 4.44 | 28 | 2 | 77 | 87 | 42 | 41 |
| Carl, Todd, Reno | 9 | 5 | 4.57 | 20 | 0 | 130 | 162 | 48 | 76 |

# FOREIGN
# LEAGUES

# MEXICAN LEAGUE

## Mexico's Baseball Capital: Monterrey

**By JOHN MANUEL**

The two biggest baseball stories in Mexico in 1996 focused on the northern industrial city of Monterrey. One had little to do with the Mexican League, the other had plenty.

A weekend visit by the San Diego Padres and New York Mets to Monterrey in August made headlines because it represented the first major league regular-season games ever played outside the U.S. or Canada.

The series spotlighted the possibility of major league expansion into Mexico. The games did not sell out, despite an appearance in the opener by Padres lefthander and Mexican hero Fernando Valenzuela.

Monterrey also was the center of attention during the regular Mexican League season, where the Monterrey Sultans loomed large.

The Sultans made a mockery of the league, posting an 82-33 overall record and whipping the Mexico City Reds in the playoffs for the second year in a row.

It took the Sultans four games to win the 1995 championship series and five to repeat as champions in 1996. It was the third crown in six years and the seventh in franchise history.

Former big league first baseman Guillermo Velasquez and outfielder Jose Gonzalez represented the heart of the Monterrey batting order. Velasquez led the league with 112 RBIs while Gonzalez hit .354, third in the league. The Sultans' .297 team batting average was tops in the league.

But it was a Mexican native, outfielder Juan Carlos Canizales, who won the MVP award during the championship series against the Reds, winners of seven league titles in the past 25 years.

Canizales drove in four runs in Game Five, a 6-2

**Guillermo Velasquez**

win before 20,000 fans in Mexico City, and had the game-winning hit in the ninth inning of Game Two. Garcia also added a 4-for-5 performance with three RBIs and three runs in a 5-2 Game Four victory.

The Reds, who won the 1994 title, were in the championship series for the third straight season.

Led by defending Triple Crown winner Ty Gainey (.345-19-61) and fellow American Drew Denson (.314-14-50), the Reds jumped to a 15-3 start in the second half and ran away with the Central Zone title.

The league went to a three-zone format for the first time in 1996, splitting into the Central, North and South zones, and retained a 116-game schedule adopted in 1995.

The league lopped 16 games off its schedule because of Mexico's general economic troubles and the lack of available American players because of the players' strike in the U.S., when a number of players went to spring training as replacement players.

Three new teams joined the fold, with Poza Rica replacing Puebla, Oaxaca replacing Jalisco and Quintana Roo (Cancun) replacing Veracruz.

Former Marlins outfielder Matias Carrillo of the Mexico City Tigers won the batting title at .368, becoming the first native Mexican to win the batting crown in 23 seasons. Former Red Sox slugger Sam Horn of Torreon hit 30 homers to lead the circuit.

Gerardo Sanchez, meanwhile, became the Cal Ripken of Mexico. The Nuevo Laredo outfielder eclipsed the Mexican League record of 1,166 consecutive games played in a home game against Union Laguna.

The old record was held by Rolando Camaera when he played for Poza Rica, Aguascalientes and Tampico from 1968-1976.

Jesus Sommers of Poza Rica reached a different milestone. The 47-year-old notched his 3,000th hit early in the second half of the season. The next day, Sommers replaced Bernardo Calvo as manager. Calvo had already replaced Raul Cano in that role.

That was emblematic of the managerial musical chairs the league experienced in 1996. Half of the league's 16 teams fired their field leaders in the first half of the season, and a ninth manager, Aurelio Rodriguez, was suspended the rest of the season.

Rodriguez, a former major league third baseman who was managing Reynosa, struck umpire Alejandro Villalpando during an argument over a call at second base and was suspended.

## LEAGUE CHAMPIONS

**Last 25 Years**

| Year | Regular Season* | | Playoff |
|------|------|------|------|
| 1972 | Saltillo | .636 | Cordoba |
| 1973 | Saltillo | .656 | Mexico City Reds |
| 1974 | Jalisco | .627 | Mexico City Reds |
| 1975 | Cordoba | .649 | Tampico |
| 1976 | Cordoba | .595 | Mexico City Reds |
| 1977 | Puebla | .640 | Nuevo Laredo |
| 1978 | Cordoba | .655 | Aguascalientes |
| 1979 | Saltillo | .704 | Puebla |
| 1980 | Puebla | .716 | None |
| 1981 | Mexico City Reds | .615 | Reynosa |
| 1982 | Poza Rica | .623 | Ciudad Juarez |
| 1983 | Mexico City Reds | .667 | Campeche |
| 1984 | Mexico City Reds | .647 | Yucatan |
| 1985 | Mexico City Reds | .606 | Mexico City Reds |
| 1986 | Puebla | .682 | Puebla |
| 1987 | Mexico City Reds | .604 | Mexico City Reds |
| 1988 | Mexico City Reds | .646 | Mexico City Reds |
| 1989 | Laredo | .621 | Laredo |
| 1990 | Laredo | .618 | Leon |
| 1991 | Monterrey Sultans | .683 | Monterrey Sultans |
| 1992 | Mexico City Tigers | .594 | Mexico City Tigers |
| 1993 | Mexico City Reds | .633 | Tabasco |
| 1994 | Mexico City Reds | .646 | Mexico City Reds |
| 1995 | Mexico City Reds | .708 | Monterrey |
| 1996 | Monterrey | .713 | Monterrey |

*Best Overall Record

# STANDINGS

## CENTRAL ZONE

| | W | L | PCT | GB |
|---|---|---|---|---|
| Mexico City Reds (14.75) | 70 | 43 | .619 | — |
| Mexico City Tigers (14.5) | 68 | 45 | .602 | 2 |
| Poza Rica Oilers (13) | 63 | 50 | .558 | 7 |
| Aguascalientes Railroadmen (12.25) | 58 | 57 | .504 | 13 |
| Oaxaca Warriors (11.5) | 46 | 64 | .418 | 22½ |

## NORTH ZONE

| | W | L | PCT | GB |
|---|---|---|---|---|
| Monterrey Sultans (16) | 82 | 33 | .713 | — |
| Monclova Steelers (13) | 58 | 56 | .509 | 23½ |
| Reynosa Broncos (13) | 56 | 56 | .500 | 24½ |
| Union Laguna Cotton Pickers (12) | 50 | 62 | .446 | 30½ |
| Nuevo Laredo Owls (11.5) | 48 | 65 | .424 | 33 |
| Saltillo Sarape Makers (10.5) | 41 | 70 | .369 | 39 |

## SOUTH ZONE

| | W | L | PCT | GB |
|---|---|---|---|---|
| Yucatan Lions (15) | 58 | 56 | .509 | — |
| Quintana Roo Lobsters (13.5) | 55 | 55 | .500 | 1 |
| Campeche Pirates (14.5) | 53 | 59 | .473 | 4 |
| Tabasco Olmecas (12) | 48 | 63 | .432 | 8½ |
| Minatitlan Colts (11) | 45 | 65 | .409 | 11 |

**NOTE:** League played a split-season schedule. Points were awarded on basis of finish in each half (8 for first, 7 for second, 6.5 for third, 6 for fourth, 5.5 for fifth, 5 for sixth) to determine playoff pairings.

**PLAYOFFS—Quarterfinals:** Mexico City Reds defeated Aguascalientes 4-3, Monterrey defeated Monclova 4-2, Mexico City Tigers defeated Poza Rica 4-1, and Yucatan defeated Campeche 4-1, in best-of-7 series. **Semifinals:** Monterrey defeated Yucatan 4-1, and Mexico City Reds defeated Mexico City Tigers 4-2, in best-of-7 series. **Finals:** Monterrey defeated Mexico City Reds 4-1, in best-of-7 series.

**REGULAR-SEASON ATTENDANCE:** Monclova 290,994; Monterrey 211,333; Oaxaca 201,719; Poza Rica 200,226; Yucatan 199,433; Mexico City Tigers 154,764; Tabasco 149,328; Mexico City Reds 144,618; Quintana Roo 139,736; Aguascalientes 125,371; Reynosa 125,371; Campeche 113,785; Saltillo 100,736; Union Laguna 83,594; Nuevo Laredo 80,522; Minatitlan 64,673.

## INDIVIDUAL BATTING LEADERS
(Minimum 313 Plate Appearances)

| | AVG | AB | R | H | 2B | 3B | HR | RBI | SB |
|---|---|---|---|---|---|---|---|---|---|
| Carrillo, Matias, Tigers | .368 | 391 | 77 | 144 | 31 | 1 | 21 | 86 | 11 |
| Tellez, Alonso, Reynosa | .365 | 293 | 54 | 107 | 19 | 1 | 7 | 49 | 1 |
| Gonzalez, Jose, Monterrey | .354 | 384 | 84 | 136 | 21 | 5 | 10 | 71 | 34 |
| Garcia, Cornelio, Monterrey | .345 | 374 | 87 | 129 | 21 | 6 | 0 | 50 | 30 |
| Chance, Tony, Monclova | .338 | 435 | 84 | 147 | 31 | 0 | 13 | 78 | 4 |
| Magallanes, Ever, Monterrey | .338 | 287 | 60 | 97 | 16 | 2 | 2 | 46 | 7 |
| Chimelis, Joel, Oaxaca | .327 | 416 | 72 | 136 | 33 | 3 | 7 | 51 | 4 |
| Stark, Matt, Reynosa | .321 | 358 | 66 | 115 | 24 | 0 | 14 | 72 | 2 |
| Martinez, Domingo, Reynosa | .320 | 413 | 75 | 132 | 22 | 4 | 18 | 91 | 1 |
| Felix, Junior, Reynosa | .319 | 335 | 73 | 107 | 20 | 3 | 19 | 50 | 3 |

## INDIVIDUAL PITCHING LEADERS
(Minimum 93 Innings)

| | W | L | ERA | G | SV | IP | H | BB | SO |
|---|---|---|---|---|---|---|---|---|---|
| Baez, Sixto, Poza Rica | 7 | 5 | 1.54 | 41 | 9 | 105 | 79 | 59 | 30 |
| Jimenez, Isaac, Poza Rica | 10 | 6 | 1.70 | 20 | 1 | 127 | 96 | 43 | 68 |
| Gonzalez, Arturo, Mont. | 12 | 2 | 1.78 | 20 | 0 | 121 | 86 | 35 | 42 |
| Lopez, Emigdio, Tabasco | 15 | 4 | 2.15 | 25 | 0 | 159 | 135 | 41 | 68 |
| Valdez, Efrain, QR | 11 | 5 | 2.23 | 20 | 6 | 149 | 123 | 44 | 69 |
| Diaz, Rafael, Monterrey | 14 | 1 | 2.41 | 22 | 0 | 135 | 108 | 78 | 68 |
| Villarreal, Antonio, Yucatan | 10 | 6 | 2.45 | 22 | 0 | 143 | 141 | 53 | 67 |
| Campos, Francisco, Cam. | 10 | 3 | 2.49 | 23 | 0 | 145 | 120 | 52 | 60 |
| Perez, Vladimir, Aguas. | 8 | 5 | 2.59 | 55 | 3 | 101 | 92 | 50 | 52 |
| Miranda, Julio, Yucatan | 9 | 4 | 2.66 | 49 | 12 | 102 | 79 | 26 | 56 |

## AGUASCALIENTES

### BATTING

| | AVG | AB | R | H | 2B | 3B | HR | RBI | SB |
|---|---|---|---|---|---|---|---|---|---|
| Aguilar, Enrique, dh | .277 | 328 | 41 | 91 | 13 | 0 | 5 | 40 | 2 |
| Arevalo, Guadalupe, 3b-2b | .255 | 165 | 15 | 42 | 10 | 1 | 0 | 20 | 0 |
| Arredondo, Jesus, ss | .262 | 317 | 53 | 83 | 3 | 3 | 1 | 20 | 11 |
| Bowie, Jim, of-1b | .309 | 262 | 33 | 81 | 12 | 0 | 3 | 37 | 3 |
| Enriquez, Graciano, 3b-ss | .144 | 97 | 3 | 14 | 1 | 3 | 0 | 3 | 1 |
| Espino, Daniel, dh | .091 | 11 | 0 | 1 | 0 | 0 | 0 | 0 | 0 |
| Guerrero, Javier, 1b | .186 | 70 | 5 | 13 | 2 | 0 | 1 | 4 | 0 |
| Machiria, Pablo, 1b-of | .289 | 401 | 36 | 116 | 15 | 3 | 3 | 61 | 1 |
| Mendez, Ramon, c | .200 | 50 | 3 | 10 | 1 | 0 | 0 | 1 | 0 |
| Orantes, Ramon, 3b-of | .255 | 212 | 29 | 54 | 9 | 4 | 1 | 19 | 1 |
| Ramirez, Efren, c | .226 | 310 | 38 | 70 | 12 | 1 | 7 | 34 | 5 |

| | AVG | AB | R | H | 2B | 3B | HR | RBI | SB |
|---|---|---|---|---|---|---|---|---|---|
| Valencia, Carlos, of | .267 | 329 | 34 | 88 | 13 | 0 | 2 | 21 | 1 |
| Vizcarra, Roberto, 2b | .299 | 435 | 70 | 130 | 28 | 1 | 12 | 60 | 10 |
| Wood, Ted, of | .299 | 398 | 82 | 119 | 27 | 4 | 13 | 55 | 3 |
| Zambrano, Eduardo, of-3b | .288 | 427 | 56 | 123 | 34 | 0 | 16 | 74 | 2 |

### PITCHING

| | W | L | ERA | G | SV | IP | H | BB | SO |
|---|---|---|---|---|---|---|---|---|---|
| Antunez, Martin | 2 | 3 | 5.40 | 30 | 0 | 23 | 35 | 12 | 11 |
| Austin, James | 3 | 4 | 3.29 | 48 | 18 | 52 | 48 | 38 | 43 |
| DeLeon, Danilo | 1 | 2 | 6.57 | 12 | 0 | 12 | 15 | 8 | 13 |
| Enriquez, Martin | 2 | 10 | 5.70 | 21 | 0 | 77 | 102 | 35 | 37 |
| Franklin, Jay | 9 | 6 | 3.52 | 22 | 0 | 123 | 127 | 57 | 60 |
| Garza, Alejandro | 0 | 1 | 6.41 | 17 | 1 | 27 | 31 | 27 | 14 |
| Jimenez, German | 10 | 5 | 3.38 | 17 | 0 | 91 | 104 | 24 | 32 |
| Lopez, Jonas | 8 | 6 | 3.83 | 23 | 1 | 125 | 122 | 54 | 38 |
| Palacios, Vicente | 2 | 1 | 3.77 | 11 | 2 | 14 | 13 | 4 | 15 |
| Perez, Leonardo | 4 | 6 | 5.81 | 16 | 0 | 74 | 85 | 49 | 39 |
| Perez, Vladimir | 8 | 5 | 2.59 | 55 | 3 | 101 | 92 | 50 | 52 |
| Quiroz, Jose | 0 | 2 | 6.97 | 22 | 1 | 21 | 30 | 7 | 11 |
| Quinones, Enrique | 9 | 2 | 3.20 | 23 | 0 | 110 | 115 | 29 | 42 |
| Sanchez, Hector | 6 | 3 | 3.09 | 27 | 0 | 108 | 98 | 24 | 37 |
| Vazquez, Aguedo | 5 | 6 | 4.50 | 15 | 0 | 92 | 114 | 30 | 45 |
| Villanueva, Luis | 1 | 0 | 3.18 | 15 | 0 | 6 | 6 | 4 | 4 |
| Villegas, Jose | 2 | 6 | 3.22 | 31 | 3 | 95 | 99 | 25 | 31 |

## CAMPECHE

### BATTING

| | AVG | AB | R | H | 2B | 3B | HR | RBI | SB |
|---|---|---|---|---|---|---|---|---|---|
| Arvizu, Javier, 1b | .087 | 23 | 1 | 2 | 0 | 0 | 0 | 1 | 0 |
| Cervera, Francisco, ss | .265 | 302 | 39 | 80 | 19 | 1 | 7 | 54 | 12 |
| Espinoza, Javier, of | .250 | 168 | 23 | 42 | 1 | 1 | 3 | 19 | 3 |
| Gonzalez, Jesus, 1b-c | .292 | 308 | 38 | 90 | 21 | 0 | 6 | 37 | 9 |
| Gonzalez, Mauricio, ss | .143 | 14 | 0 | 2 | 0 | 0 | 0 | 0 | 0 |
| Guizar, Hector, ss | .226 | 305 | 25 | 69 | 15 | 0 | 0 | 29 | 5 |
| Hernandez, Martin, dh-1b | .304 | 69 | 6 | 21 | 3 | 1 | 0 | 7 | 1 |
| Herrera, Isidro, c | .246 | 349 | 51 | 86 | 11 | 0 | 0 | 23 | 18 |
| Hurtado, Hector, c | .157 | 198 | 11 | 31 | 5 | 0 | 5 | 26 | 0 |
| Leal, Guadalupe, of-1b | .260 | 231 | 28 | 60 | 6 | 1 | 3 | 28 | 5 |
| Loredo, Jorge, 2b | .244 | 344 | 48 | 84 | 14 | 1 | 3 | 22 | 5 |
| Medina, Ramon, of | .255 | 161 | 28 | 41 | 0 | 2 | 1 | 8 | 6 |
| Michel, Domingo, 1b-of | .280 | 350 | 63 | 98 | 19 | 2 | 17 | 55 | 15 |
| Ortiz, Raymond, dh-of | .269 | 312 | 38 | 84 | 14 | 1 | 5 | 43 | 5 |
| Payro, Edison, of | .249 | 350 | 36 | 87 | 12 | 1 | 0 | 23 | 6 |
| Ruiz, Demetrio, c | .091 | 33 | 0 | 3 | 0 | 0 | 0 | 1 | 0 |
| Sanchez, Roque, 3b-2b | .189 | 127 | 9 | 24 | 4 | 1 | 0 | 8 | 1 |
| Silverio, Nelson, c | .218 | 101 | 9 | 22 | 2 | 0 | 2 | 14 | 0 |
| Tiburico, Freddy, c | .305 | 311 | 44 | 95 | 11 | 5 | 7 | 35 | 3 |
| Villaescusa, Fernando, dh-of | .182 | 11 | 1 | 2 | 0 | 0 | 0 | 0 | 0 |

### PITCHING

| | W | L | ERA | G | SV | IP | H | BB | SO |
|---|---|---|---|---|---|---|---|---|---|
| Barron, Avelino | 3 | 6 | 4.65 | 30 | 4 | 50 | 45 | 29 | 19 |
| Campos, Francisco | 10 | 3 | 2.49 | 23 | 0 | 145 | 120 | 52 | 60 |
| Cuervo, Bernardo | 7 | 5 | 2.68 | 19 | 0 | 121 | 117 | 47 | 42 |
| De la Rosa, Francisco | 4 | 8 | 2.32 | 23 | 4 | 81 | 62 | 38 | 51 |
| Dominguez, Herminio | 3 | 0 | 1.86 | 20 | 1 | 19 | 20 | 5 | 5 |
| Lizarraga, Hugo | 1 | 4 | 9.69 | 10 | 0 | 26 | 43 | 24 | 11 |
| Loaiza, Sabino | 5 | 2 | 3.75 | 18 | 0 | 70 | 83 | 33 | 23 |
| Martinez, Jose A. | 0 | 2 | 2.42 | 22 | 1 | 48 | 46 | 8 | 21 |
| Maysey, Matt | 2 | 3 | 3.05 | 15 | 2 | 41 | 40 | 16 | 25 |
| Montalvo, Rafael | 4 | 2 | 4.00 | 16 | 1 | 18 | 23 | 5 | 6 |
| Sanchez, Efrain | 0 | 3 | 2.89 | 14 | 0 | 44 | 38 | 18 | 25 |
| Sierra, Abel | 8 | 12 | 3.53 | 23 | 0 | 156 | 158 | 50 | 75 |
| Tejeda, Juan | 1 | 1 | 5.14 | 12 | 1 | 7 | 6 | 4 | 1 |
| Tinoco, Ruben | 0 | 0 | 11.37 | 8 | 0 | 6 | 12 | 3 | 1 |
| Vazquez, Adrian | 6 | 7 | 4.02 | 19 | 0 | 112 | 100 | 68 | 48 |

## MEXICO CITY REDS

### BATTING

| | AVG | AB | R | H | 2B | 3B | HR | RBI | SB |
|---|---|---|---|---|---|---|---|---|---|
| Aguilera, Tony, of | .276 | 387 | 61 | 107 | 11 | 2 | 4 | 55 | 7 |
| Armenta, Guallermo, 2b | .247 | 81 | 9 | 20 | 2 | 0 | 0 | 8 | 3 |
| Arredondo, Luis, of | .292 | 418 | 75 | 122 | 19 | 7 | 4 | 47 | 32 |
| Bojorquez, Victor, of | .417 | 24 | 16 | 10 | 0 | 2 | 1 | 7 | 1 |
| Carranza, Pedro, 3b | .400 | 10 | 2 | 4 | 1 | 0 | 0 | 2 | 0 |
| Denson, Drew, dh-1b | .314 | 277 | 41 | 87 | 18 | 1 | 14 | 50 | 0 |
| Fernandez, Daniel, of | .313 | 402 | 84 | 126 | 17 | 6 | 3 | 27 | 2 |
| Figueroa, Bien, 3b | .364 | 33 | 8 | 12 | 3 | 1 | 0 | 4 | 0 |
| Gainey, Ty, dh | .345 | 235 | 54 | 81 | 17 | 0 | 19 | 61 | 3 |
| Magallanes, Roberto, 3b-ss | .282 | 411 | 59 | 116 | 24 | 1 | 12 | 71 | 8 |
| Ojeda, Miguel, c-of | .311 | 251 | 43 | 78 | 10 | 1 | 8 | 29 | 3 |
| Paez, Raul, 1b | .284 | 102 | 11 | 29 | 5 | 2 | 2 | 17 | 0 |
| Perez, Francisco, of | .302 | 139 | 17 | 42 | 10 | 0 | 7 | 35 | 2 |
| Renteria, Rich, 3b | .256 | 86 | 13 | 22 | 4 | 2 | 2 | 16 | 0 |
| Rojas, Homar, c-1b | .247 | 287 | 34 | 71 | 14 | 1 | 0 | 34 | 2 |
| Sandoval, Jose, ss | .261 | 352 | 39 | 92 | 12 | 1 | 8 | 45 | 4 |
| Vazquez, Felipe, c | .226 | 93 | 7 | 21 | 1 | 0 | 1 | 10 | 1 |
| Verdugo, Vicente, 2b-ss | .316 | 370 | 33 | 117 | 10 | 3 | 2 | 45 | 10 |

| PITCHING | W | L | ERA | G | SV | IP | H | BB | SO |
|---|---|---|---|---|---|---|---|---|---|
| Dessens, Elmer | 7 | 0 | 1.26 | 7 | 0 | 50 | 44 | 10 | 17 |
| Fajardo, Hector | 1 | 0 | 5.87 | 4 | 0 | 15 | 25 | 7 | 7 |
| Garcia, Francisco | 3 | 5 | 5.05 | 20 | 0 | 52 | 53 | 29 | 26 |
| Holman, Shawn | 14 | 6 | 3.30 | 35 | 3 | 142 | 165 | 48 | 61 |
| Loaiza, Esteban | 2 | 0 | 2.43 | 5 | 0 | 33 | 28 | 14 | 16 |
| Menendez, Tony | 1 | 3 | 4.40 | 28 | 4 | 29 | 33 | 13 | 30 |
| Moreno, Leobardo | 6 | 7 | 2.93 | 25 | 0 | 129 | 111 | 48 | 99 |
| Nunez, Edwin | 2 | 0 | 2.25 | 14 | 6 | 16 | 18 | 4 | 12 |
| Pina, Rafael | 7 | 4 | 3.09 | 39 | 4 | 84 | 72 | 49 | 56 |
| Ramirez, Roberto | 14 | 9 | 2.84 | 28 | 0 | 190 | 179 | 74 | 132 |
| Rincon, Ricardo | 5 | 3 | 2.97 | 50 | 10 | 79 | 58 | 27 | 60 |
| Rivera, Oscar | 0 | 0 | 3.60 | 11 | 0 | 20 | 21 | 3 | 5 |
| Soto, Daniel | 0 | 1 | 9.16 | 8 | 0 | 19 | 24 | 10 | 8 |
| Williams, Jeff | 5 | 1 | 2.28 | 12 | 2 | 51 | 45 | 16 | 23 |

## MEXICO CITY TIGERS

| BATTING | AVG | AB | R | H | 2B | 3B | HR | RBI | SB |
|---|---|---|---|---|---|---|---|---|---|
| Carrillo, Matias, of-1b | .368 | 391 | 77 | 144 | 31 | 1 | 21 | 86 | 11 |
| Castaneda, Rafael, 3b-c | .295 | 352 | 34 | 104 | 12 | 2 | 3 | 41 | 3 |
| Diaz, Luis, of-dh | .300 | 360 | 58 | 108 | 18 | 1 | 16 | 62 | 9 |
| Gastelum, Sergio, 2b-of | .238 | 80 | 14 | 19 | 1 | 0 | 0 | 4 | 1 |
| Grijak, Kevin, dh-1b | .288 | 323 | 41 | 93 | 13 | 0 | 11 | 42 | 3 |
| Hernandez, Gerardo, of | .282 | 206 | 32 | 58 | 11 | 2 | 3 | 18 | 2 |
| Howell, Pat, of | .300 | 293 | 52 | 88 | 7 | 4 | 1 | 19 | 13 |
| Montalvo, Ivan, 3b | .260 | 389 | 50 | 101 | 13 | 2 | 7 | 42 | 8 |
| Ochoa, Edgar, c | .257 | 152 | 17 | 39 | 6 | 0 | 2 | 9 | 2 |
| Perezchica, Tony, 2b | .274 | 179 | 27 | 49 | 9 | 0 | 2 | 15 | 0 |
| Robles, Javier, ss | .272 | 427 | 64 | 116 | 18 | 1 | 20 | 72 | 16 |
| Romero, Marco, 1b | .258 | 256 | 34 | 66 | 15 | 0 | 8 | 48 | 3 |
| Sandoval, Octavio, of | .239 | 142 | 22 | 34 | 6 | 0 | 0 | 12 | 2 |
| Trapaga, Julio, 2b | .259 | 270 | 28 | 70 | 11 | 1 | 3 | 27 | 7 |
| Vargas, Jose, dh | .200 | 25 | 1 | 5 | 0 | 0 | 0 | 1 | 0 |
| Vega, Edgar, c | .232 | 228 | 26 | 53 | 3 | 0 | 0 | 23 | 3 |

| PITCHING | W | L | ERA | G | SV | IP | H | BB | SO |
|---|---|---|---|---|---|---|---|---|---|
| Alvarez, Juan | 6 | 5 | 2.73 | 23 | 0 | 142 | 131 | 41 | 84 |
| Barraza, Ernesto | 9 | 7 | 4.21 | 21 | 0 | 115 | 119 | 58 | 62 |
| Burgos, John | 5 | 2 | 2.66 | 46 | 3 | 74 | 56 | 26 | 53 |
| Couoh, Enrique | 9 | 6 | 4.03 | 24 | 0 | 132 | 143 | 66 | 74 |
| Duncan, Chip | 5 | 2 | 2.95 | 27 | 1 | 55 | 51 | 22 | 32 |
| Garibay, Daniel | 2 | 4 | 4.98 | 20 | 0 | 60 | 64 | 32 | 36 |
| Harrison, Brian | 1 | 1 | 5.16 | 8 | 0 | 23 | 22 | 21 | 10 |
| Lynch, David | 7 | 5 | 4.32 | 17 | 0 | 98 | 93 | 51 | 84 |
| Manzano, Adrian | 0 | 1 | 5.48 | 11 | 0 | 21 | 26 | 7 | 9 |
| Marquez, Isidro | 9 | 4 | 3.46 | 48 | 23 | 68 | 55 | 21 | 44 |
| Moreno, Angel | 10 | 6 | 2.90 | 23 | 0 | 152 | 134 | 60 | 88 |
| Munoz, Jaime | 3 | 3 | 3.69 | 23 | 0 | 39 | 35 | 18 | 19 |
| Saldana, Edgardo | 4 | 2 | 2.89 | 39 | 1 | 72 | 63 | 27 | 23 |
| Thomas, Royal | 1 | 1 | 5.25 | 3 | 0 | 12 | 18 | 4 | 4 |
| Zavala, Marcos | 0 | 0 | 6.23 | 6 | 0 | 9 | 10 | 5 | 4 |

## MINATITLAN

| BATTING | AVG | AB | R | H | 2B | 3B | HR | RBI | SB |
|---|---|---|---|---|---|---|---|---|---|
| Armenta, Fernando, of | .273 | 11 | 0 | 3 | 1 | 0 | 0 | 2 | 0 |
| Avila, Roberto, 3b-ss | .095 | 42 | 1 | 4 | 0 | 0 | 0 | 7 | 0 |
| Balderas, Abelardo, 2b-ss | .192 | 78 | 8 | 15 | 0 | 0 | 0 | 11 | 1 |
| Beltran, Gerardo, of-1b | .264 | 250 | 31 | 66 | 7 | 3 | 6 | 21 | 0 |
| Beristain, Gregorio, 2b | .265 | 34 | 5 | 9 | 1 | 0 | 0 | 3 | 0 |
| Cabreja, Alexis, dh-of | .313 | 67 | 11 | 21 | 3 | 0 | 0 | 8 | 4 |
| Castaneda, Hector, c | .237 | 257 | 28 | 61 | 13 | 1 | 2 | 28 | 2 |
| Castro, Eddie, dh-1b | .285 | 319 | 43 | 91 | 18 | 0 | 6 | 46 | 1 |
| Cueto, Raul, c | .173 | 52 | 3 | 9 | 2 | 0 | 0 | 5 | 0 |
| Delima, Rafael, of | .228 | 101 | 14 | 23 | 3 | 1 | 0 | 9 | 4 |
| Gavia, Jesus, c-1b | .176 | 74 | 3 | 13 | 1 | 1 | 0 | 7 | 0 |
| Hinzo, Tommy, 2b | .235 | 204 | 31 | 48 | 9 | 1 | 0 | 7 | 7 |
| Marrujo, Hector, 3b | .200 | 10 | 2 | 2 | 0 | 0 | 0 | 1 | 0 |
| Romero, Oscar, 3b | .261 | 352 | 38 | 92 | 16 | 0 | 7 | 31 | 5 |
| Rusell, Omar, c | .167 | 12 | 0 | 2 | 0 | 0 | 0 | 0 | 0 |
| Santana, Miguel, of | .282 | 117 | 18 | 33 | 2 | 1 | 0 | 11 | 4 |
| Valdez, Ramon, of | .239 | 92 | 9 | 22 | 3 | 1 | 0 | 1 | 0 |
| Valle, Jose, ss | .275 | 374 | 38 | 103 | 10 | 3 | 2 | 31 | 3 |
| Vargas, Hector, of-3b | .267 | 344 | 41 | 92 | 12 | 2 | 0 | 32 | 11 |
| Yuriar, Jesus, of | .254 | 307 | 36 | 78 | 14 | 0 | 1 | 36 | 0 |
| Zambrano, Jose, of | .281 | 178 | 19 | 50 | 8 | 0 | 4 | 21 | 3 |

| PITCHING | W | L | ERA | G | SV | IP | H | BB | SO |
|---|---|---|---|---|---|---|---|---|---|
| Alvarez, Juan | 2 | 6 | 3.86 | 27 | 0 | 84 | 86 | 25 | 20 |
| Cabrales, Gabriel | 1 | 2 | 5.85 | 26 | 0 | 32 | 41 | 7 | 9 |
| Calderon, Manaces | 1 | 0 | 4.82 | 4 | 0 | 9 | 7 | 10 | 3 |
| Camara, Pedro | 0 | 0 | 5.56 | 15 | 0 | 11 | 13 | 11 | 8 |
| Delahoya, Javier | 4 | 4 | 3.05 | 13 | 0 | 65 | 62 | 42 | 48 |
| Garcia, Miguel | 4 | 8 | 3.87 | 29 | 0 | 102 | 93 | 56 | 33 |
| Gomez, Martin | 2 | 6 | 5.22 | 29 | 0 | 79 | 104 | 47 | 27 |
| Orozco, Jaime | 6 | 8 | 5.31 | 23 | 0 | 102 | 125 | 36 | 49 |
| Reyes, Flavio | 0 | 0 | 5.03 | 20 | 0 | 20 | 23 | 10 | 11 |
| Salgado, Eduardo | 0 | 0 | 5.71 | 20 | 0 | 35 | 40 | 17 | 13 |

| | W | L | ERA | G | SV | IP | H | BB | SO |
|---|---|---|---|---|---|---|---|---|---|
| Sandoval, Carlos | 1 | 0 | 5.66 | 25 | 1 | 21 | 25 | 17 | 11 |
| Solarte, Jose | 8 | 2 | 1.39 | 54 | 15 | 84 | 67 | 24 | 65 |
| Vargas, Ignacio | 1 | 2 | 5.16 | 31 | 0 | 45 | 58 | 22 | 22 |
| Velazquez, Israel | 7 | 13 | 4.19 | 29 | 0 | 150 | 147 | 73 | 83 |

## MONCLOVA

| BATTING | AVG | AB | R | H | 2B | 3B | HR | RBI | SB |
|---|---|---|---|---|---|---|---|---|---|
| Aganza, Ruben, 1b | .277 | 452 | 67 | 125 | 19 | 0 | 20 | 80 | 1 |
| Cabrera, Francisco, dh | .262 | 130 | 11 | 34 | 5 | 0 | 0 | 14 | 1 |
| Chan, Armando, dh-of | .305 | 190 | 25 | 58 | 7 | 2 | 2 | 26 | 1 |
| Chance, Tony, of | .338 | 435 | 84 | 147 | 31 | 0 | 13 | 78 | 4 |
| Espinoza, Jose, of | .200 | 10 | 1 | 2 | 0 | 0 | 0 | 2 | 0 |
| Gastelum, Carlos, c | .283 | 212 | 21 | 60 | 9 | 0 | 0 | 25 | 0 |
| Leyva, German, 3b | .267 | 409 | 62 | 109 | 14 | 3 | 4 | 37 | 3 |
| Lopez, Gonzalo, ss | .167 | 12 | 0 | 2 | 0 | 0 | 0 | 0 | 0 |
| Martinez, Grimaldo, 2b | .265 | 370 | 67 | 98 | 13 | 3 | 2 | 33 | 13 |
| Moreno, David, of | .171 | 35 | 2 | 6 | 0 | 0 | 0 | 3 | 0 |
| Olvera, Sergio, ss | .286 | 14 | 3 | 4 | 1 | 0 | 0 | 3 | 0 |
| Ramirez, Enrique, ss | .249 | 353 | 52 | 88 | 11 | 0 | 0 | 17 | 3 |
| Saenz, Ricardo, of | .326 | 224 | 40 | 73 | 18 | 1 | 7 | 47 | 0 |
| Samaniego, Manuel, c | .174 | 23 | 0 | 4 | 1 | 0 | 0 | 1 | 0 |
| Torres, Eduardo, of | .199 | 342 | 52 | 68 | 12 | 2 | 15 | 50 | 4 |
| Villanueva, Hector, dh-c | .287 | 394 | 69 | 113 | 16 | 1 | 25 | 94 | 1 |
| Wong, Julian, 2b-ss | .302 | 149 | 21 | 45 | 11 | 0 | 3 | 18 | 0 |

| PITCHING | W | L | ERA | G | SV | IP | H | BB | SO |
|---|---|---|---|---|---|---|---|---|---|
| Alicea, Miguel | 1 | 6 | 6.00 | 27 | 9 | 33 | 42 | 21 | 17 |
| Bauer, Matt | 1 | 1 | 3.57 | 14 | 0 | 23 | 23 | 20 | 18 |
| Cazares, Juan | 0 | 1 | 8.10 | 17 | 0 | 10 | 16 | 5 | 3 |
| Herrera, Calixto | 4 | 3 | 3.13 | 44 | 2 | 63 | 52 | 44 | 48 |
| Jimenez, Danilo | 3 | 1 | 2.48 | 5 | 0 | 29 | 21 | 10 | 12 |
| Kelly, Rich | 6 | 10 | 3.74 | 23 | 0 | 125 | 116 | 86 | 52 |
| Lara, Jorge | 2 | 4 | 5.28 | 31 | 3 | 44 | 55 | 21 | 35 |
| Leal, Gerardo | 3 | 1 | 3.74 | 33 | 1 | 67 | 77 | 37 | 40 |
| Montano, Francisco | 7 | 7 | 7.04 | 25 | 0 | 110 | 149 | 61 | 47 |
| Murillo, Felipe | 5 | 4 | 4.53 | 39 | 15 | 46 | 54 | 17 | 19 |
| Patterson, Kent | 0 | 1 | 1.42 | 6 | 0 | 6 | 4 | 6 | 2 |
| Pimental, Roberto | 0 | 2 | 6.98 | 43 | 0 | 40 | 50 | 35 | 23 |
| Rios, Jesus | 6 | 6 | 4.50 | 24 | 0 | 140 | 127 | 66 | 104 |
| Rodriguez, Raul | 13 | 8 | 3.15 | 26 | 0 | 172 | 148 | 71 | 121 |
| Valdez, Rodolfo | 3 | 2 | 4.37 | 27 | 0 | 56 | 69 | 31 | 28 |
| Velazquez, Ernesto | 0 | 0 | 8.53 | 6 | 0 | 6 | 17 | 4 | 4 |

## MONTERREY

| BATTING | AVG | AB | R | H | 2B | 3B | HR | RBI | SB |
|---|---|---|---|---|---|---|---|---|---|
| Canizalez, Juan, of | .313 | 422 | 71 | 132 | 25 | 7 | 9 | 62 | 3 |
| Contreras, Jose, 3b | .300 | 20 | 3 | 6 | 0 | 0 | 0 | 1 | 0 |
| Diaz, Remigio, ss-3b | .290 | 307 | 41 | 89 | 6 | 2 | 1 | 35 | 12 |
| Flores, Miguel, 2b | .280 | 407 | 81 | 114 | 18 | 4 | 2 | 41 | 27 |
| Garcia, Cornelio, of | .345 | 374 | 87 | 129 | 21 | 6 | 0 | 50 | 30 |
| Gonzalez, Jose, of | .354 | 384 | 84 | 136 | 21 | 5 | 10 | 71 | 34 |
| Magallanes, Ever, 3b-ss | .338 | 287 | 60 | 97 | 16 | 2 | 2 | 46 | 7 |
| Meza, Alfredo, c | .272 | 232 | 24 | 63 | 8 | 0 | 2 | 33 | 0 |
| Quintero, Guillermo, ss-2b | .272 | 158 | 23 | 43 | 6 | 1 | 0 | 13 | 4 |
| Reyes, Gilberto, c | .173 | 98 | 8 | 17 | 5 | 0 | 0 | 10 | 0 |
| Sanchez, Armando, 2b-3b | .258 | 124 | 15 | 32 | 5 | 1 | 0 | 23 | 0 |
| Santana, Mario, c | .182 | 44 | 3 | 8 | 2 | 0 | 0 | 3 | 1 |
| Tolentino, Jose, 1b-dh | .288 | 306 | 44 | 88 | 17 | 2 | 9 | 67 | 2 |
| Velazquez, Guillermo, dh-1b | .286 | 423 | 78 | 121 | 30 | 1 | 21 | 112 | 3 |
| Zamudio, Rafael, of-1b | .305 | 164 | 26 | 50 | 12 | 2 | 3 | 22 | 3 |

| PITCHING | W | L | ERA | G | SV | IP | H | BB | SO |
|---|---|---|---|---|---|---|---|---|---|
| Diaz, Rafael | 14 | 1 | 2.41 | 22 | 0 | 135 | 108 | 78 | 68 |
| Elvira, Narciso | 4 | 1 | 1.16 | 8 | 0 | 31 | 22 | 18 | 21 |
| Esquer, Mercedes | 7 | 6 | 4.09 | 18 | 0 | 92 | 97 | 39 | 37 |
| Federico, Gustavo | 2 | 3 | 5.80 | 15 | 2 | 36 | 43 | 29 | 6 |
| Gamez, Francisco | 2 | 2 | 5.47 | 28 | 0 | 54 | 62 | 36 | 19 |
| Gonzalez, Arturo | 12 | 2 | 1.78 | 20 | 0 | 121 | 86 | 35 | 42 |
| Green, Ottis | 5 | 3 | 2.01 | 40 | 10 | 49 | 28 | 37 | 52 |
| Heredia, Hector | 4 | 5 | 5.64 | 23 | 1 | 97 | 133 | 29 | 39 |
| Hurst, Jonathan | 4 | 2 | 2.28 | 45 | 18 | 55 | 41 | 28 | 42 |
| Munoz, Leonardo | 3 | 0 | 1.84 | 37 | 0 | 49 | 43 | 26 | 18 |
| Olague, Jesus | 3 | 2 | 4.24 | 32 | 1 | 64 | 60 | 52 | 37 |
| Orea, Flavio | 0 | 0 | 6.75 | 13 | 0 | 13 | 17 | 8 | 1 |
| Perez, David | 13 | 4 | 2.68 | 21 | 0 | 128 | 126 | 48 | 58 |
| Powell, Dennis | 5 | 1 | 1.53 | 38 | 4 | 47 | 30 | 21 | 48 |

## NUEVO LAREDO

| BATTING | AVG | AB | R | H | 2B | 3B | HR | RBI | SB |
|---|---|---|---|---|---|---|---|---|---|
| Arano, Wilfredo, of-dh | .320 | 172 | 22 | 55 | 6 | 3 | 0 | 11 | 4 |
| Carrasco, Ernesto, 2b-3b | .245 | 367 | 43 | 90 | 13 | 0 | 0 | 28 | 3 |
| Cruz, Marco, c | .265 | 238 | 21 | 63 | 9 | 0 | 4 | 27 | 0 |
| Delanuez, Rex, of-dh | .269 | 227 | 60 | 61 | 14 | 0 | 10 | 33 | 2 |
| Estrada, Ruben, 1b-of | .289 | 38 | 3 | 11 | 1 | 0 | 0 | 5 | 0 |
| Mack, Quinn, of | .318 | 421 | 53 | 134 | 24 | 2 | 9 | 78 | 14 |
| Mendoza, Omar, 2b | .205 | 132 | 14 | 27 | 7 | 1 | 1 | 10 | 1 |
| Montanez, Daniel, 3b | .188 | 16 | 2 | 3 | 0 | 0 | 0 | 0 | 0 |

| | AVG | AB | R | H | 2B | 3B | HR | RBI | SB |
|---|---|---|---|---|---|---|---|---|---|
| Morales, Florentino, dh-2b | .255 | 314 | 39 | 80 | 17 | 2 | 0 | 26 | 3 |
| Perez, Alejandro, 2b-3b | .092 | 65 | 6 | 6 | 1 | 0 | 0 | 3 | 0 |
| Pulido, Jesus, c | .192 | 52 | 7 | 10 | 0 | 0 | 3 | 4 | 0 |
| Robles, Trinidad, ss | .223 | 386 | 46 | 86 | 12 | 0 | 6 | 39 | 13 |
| Rodriguez, Boi, of-1b | .302 | 397 | 79 | 120 | 23 | 1 | 21 | 82 | 2 |
| Romero, Israel, c | .169 | 89 | 7 | 15 | 1 | 0 | 1 | 11 | 0 |
| Sanchez, Gerardo, of-1b | .288 | 406 | 57 | 117 | 17 | 2 | 9 | 69 | 6 |
| Villarreal, Alejandro, 1b-dh | .233 | 215 | 21 | 50 | 10 | 1 | 1 | 10 | 1 |

| PITCHING | W | L | ERA | G | SV | IP | H | BB | SO |
|---|---|---|---|---|---|---|---|---|---|
| Barfield, John | 4 | 1 | 4.81 | 22 | 8 | 24 | 26 | 10 | 12 |
| Campos, Frank | 9 | 3 | 5.20 | 38 | 0 | 71 | 91 | 55 | 24 |
| Cruz, Miguel | 2 | 1 | 4.50 | 19 | 0 | 22 | 25 | 12 | 10 |
| Diaz, Cesar | 2 | 2 | 4.56 | 43 | 1 | 71 | 72 | 32 | 38 |
| Drahman, Brian | 2 | 1 | 2.65 | 22 | 8 | 34 | 22 | 10 | 29 |
| Galvez, Rosario | 3 | 13 | 5.53 | 31 | 0 | 85 | 97 | 69 | 42 |
| Garcia, Jose | 1 | 4 | 4.02 | 36 | 2 | 65 | 65 | 18 | 35 |
| Garza, Roberto | 2 | 4 | 6.50 | 30 | 1 | 64 | 87 | 38 | 24 |
| Hernandez, Manny | 4 | 10 | 4.00 | 27 | 0 | 124 | 160 | 43 | 47 |
| Navarro, Luis | 0 | 0 | 9.45 | 6 | 0 | 7 | 12 | 4 | 3 |
| Osuna, Roberto | 6 | 5 | 4.24 | 51 | 3 | 121 | 130 | 49 | 70 |
| Quintanilla, Enrique | 6 | 7 | 5.64 | 41 | 1 | 107 | 120 | 40 | 58 |
| Quiroz, Aaron | 4 | 6 | 3.82 | 18 | 0 | 68 | 65 | 34 | 45 |
| Rodriguez, Rene | 0 | 0 | 7.88 | 5 | 0 | 8 | 13 | 2 | 4 |
| Vega, Obed | 1 | 3 | 5.50 | 25 | 0 | 52 | 66 | 33 | 22 |

## OAXACA

| BATTING | AVG | AB | R | H | 2B | 3B | HR | RBI | SB |
|---|---|---|---|---|---|---|---|---|---|
| Abrego, Jesus, of-c | .206 | 238 | 23 | 49 | 9 | 0 | 3 | 28 | 1 |
| Barrera, Nelson, dh-1b | .304 | 398 | 48 | 121 | 23 | 0 | 11 | 78 | 7 |
| Bolick, Frank, 3b-dh | .308 | 299 | 56 | 92 | 19 | 1 | 9 | 64 | 1 |
| Castaldo, Vince, 3b | .211 | 57 | 9 | 12 | 3 | 0 | 0 | 6 | 0 |
| Chimelis, Joel, 2b | .327 | 416 | 72 | 136 | 33 | 3 | 7 | 51 | 4 |
| Cobos, Rogelio, c | .257 | 202 | 25 | 52 | 10 | 1 | 2 | 17 | 0 |
| Duran, Felipe, ss | .272 | 364 | 32 | 99 | 10 | 5 | 2 | 34 | 4 |
| Espy, Cecil, of | .195 | 123 | 9 | 24 | 1 | 1 | 0 | 10 | 3 |
| Hecht, Steve, 3b | .227 | 22 | 3 | 5 | 0 | 0 | 0 | 1 | 0 |
| Herrera, Isidro, of | .275 | 385 | 79 | 106 | 7 | 2 | 1 | 16 | 21 |
| Lopez, Fabian, 3b | .244 | 78 | 8 | 19 | 4 | 2 | 0 | 10 | 0 |
| Lopez, Victor, c-of | .266 | 158 | 15 | 42 | 4 | 1 | 1 | 16 | 2 |
| Mendez, Roberto, of | .266 | 335 | 30 | 89 | 16 | 1 | 5 | 38 | 12 |
| Milligan, Randy, dh | .214 | 42 | 4 | 9 | 2 | 0 | 0 | 5 | 1 |
| Moreno, Leonardo, of | .279 | 219 | 30 | 61 | 6 | 4 | 0 | 14 | 4 |
| Naveda, Edgar, 3b-of | .246 | 126 | 8 | 31 | 0 | 0 | 0 | 10 | 0 |
| Nunez, Jose, ss | .200 | 45 | 5 | 9 | 2 | 0 | 0 | 1 | 1 |
| Pardo, Victor, 1b-2b | .200 | 225 | 20 | 45 | 3 | 0 | 0 | 9 | 1 |
| Valverde, Raul, of-dh | .240 | 50 | 2 | 12 | 2 | 1 | 0 | 4 | 1 |

| PITCHING | W | L | ERA | G | SV | IP | H | BB | SO |
|---|---|---|---|---|---|---|---|---|---|
| Carrasco, Alejandro | 4 | 10 | 3.50 | 30 | 1 | 139 | 135 | 53 | 66 |
| Castro, Leonel | 0 | 0 | 4.24 | 6 | 0 | 17 | 19 | 9 | 9 |
| Chapa, Javier | 7 | 12 | 3.23 | 24 | 0 | 151 | 145 | 63 | 72 |
| Conde, Ricardo | 0 | 0 | 5.40 | 9 | 0 | 8 | 9 | 9 | 1 |
| Diaz, Alejandro | 4 | 3 | 3.34 | 31 | 0 | 59 | 63 | 17 | 23 |
| Flynt, Will | 11 | 8 | 3.11 | 22 | 0 | 168 | 149 | 89 | 137 |
| Garcia, Zenon | 1 | 2 | 5.50 | 27 | 0 | 34 | 42 | 13 | 7 |
| Guereca, Guillermo | 1 | 4 | 5.92 | 15 | 0 | 38 | 47 | 20 | 14 |
| Kutzler, Jerry | 0 | 1 | 1.50 | 1 | 0 | 6 | 7 | 0 | 1 |
| Lancaster, Les | 2 | 4 | 6.26 | 6 | 0 | 42 | 57 | 19 | 15 |
| Lopez, Jose | 4 | 8 | 5.07 | 38 | 9 | 66 | 89 | 27 | 41 |
| Metoyer, Tony | 4 | 2 | 1.64 | 29 | 8 | 38 | 24 | 23 | 31 |
| Moreno, Ricardo | 0 | 1 | 14.66 | 9 | 0 | 12 | 18 | 10 | 7 |
| Nunez Avina, Jose | 0 | 0 | 7.62 | 19 | 2 | 13 | 14 | 17 | 14 |
| Picota, Len | 6 | 5 | 3.66 | 19 | 0 | 120 | 123 | 59 | 67 |
| Pineda, Gabriel | 5 | 3 | 3.66 | 27 | 2 | 71 | 55 | 50 | 39 |
| Sangeado, Juan | 1 | 5 | 8.64 | 12 | 0 | 33 | 44 | 27 | 17 |
| Vazquez, Lioner | 0 | 2 | 18.00 | 2 | 0 | 5 | 6 | 10 | 3 |

## POZA RICA

| BATTING | AVG | AB | R | H | 2B | 3B | HR | RBI | SB |
|---|---|---|---|---|---|---|---|---|---|
| Arauz, Ignacio, c | .193 | 57 | 5 | 11 | 3 | 0 | 1 | 4 | 0 |
| Azocar, Oscar, of | .312 | 443 | 52 | 138 | 15 | 7 | 10 | 56 | 4 |
| Basse, Mike, of | .259 | 85 | 15 | 22 | 3 | 1 | 0 | 6 | 8 |
| Campos, Oscar, c | .143 | 14 | 1 | 2 | 0 | 0 | 0 | 0 | 0 |
| Colon, Cris, 2b-3b | .249 | 229 | 26 | 57 | 11 | 3 | 0 | 15 | 2 |
| Dominguez, Fausto, c | .280 | 25 | 1 | 7 | 1 | 0 | 0 | 2 | 0 |
| Fox, Eric, of | .235 | 238 | 30 | 56 | 6 | 3 | 2 | 19 | 2 |
| Garcia, Heriberto, ss | .252 | 361 | 33 | 91 | 9 | 3 | 0 | 32 | 7 |
| Guerrero, Jaime, 3b-ss | .168 | 125 | 12 | 21 | 4 | 0 | 0 | 9 | 2 |
| Hernandez, Miguel, c | .195 | 159 | 9 | 31 | 2 | 1 | 0 | 11 | 0 |
| Malpica, Enrique, 3b | .167 | 54 | 13 | 9 | 2 | 2 | 0 | 3 | 1 |
| Martinez, Carlos, 3b-dh | .282 | 330 | 34 | 93 | 9 | 1 | 8 | 53 | 1 |
| Mendez, Jesus, 1b | .264 | 435 | 42 | 115 | 16 | 2 | 1 | 35 | 2 |
| Mere, Pedro, 2b | .257 | 377 | 52 | 97 | 15 | 4 | 0 | 28 | 6 |

| | AVG | AB | R | H | 2B | 3B | HR | RBI | SB |
|---|---|---|---|---|---|---|---|---|---|
| Morones, Martin, of | .244 | 180 | 24 | 44 | 6 | 2 | 2 | 19 | 4 |
| Motley, Darryl, of | .253 | 162 | 27 | 41 | 6 | 0 | 4 | 24 | 0 |
| Ramirez, Jesus, of | .278 | 194 | 18 | 54 | 3 | 2 | 1 | 16 | 8 |
| Sommers, Jesus, dh | .237 | 194 | 9 | 46 | 7 | 0 | 1 | 26 | 0 |
| Thomas, Keith, of | .270 | 89 | 16 | 24 | 2 | 1 | 2 | 14 | 0 |

| PITCHING | W | L | ERA | G | SV | IP | H | BB | SO |
|---|---|---|---|---|---|---|---|---|---|
| Baez, Sixto | 7 | 5 | 1.54 | 41 | 9 | 105 | 79 | 59 | 30 |
| Felix, Leopoldo | 1 | 1 | 5.70 | 14 | 0 | 24 | 25 | 13 | 8 |
| Gonzalez, Victor | 3 | 0 | 1.69 | 36 | 2 | 64 | 56 | 21 | 35 |
| Hernandez, Encarnacion | 2 | 0 | 4.54 | 21 | 0 | 36 | 42 | 7 | 9 |
| Hernandez, Julio | 6 | 3 | 2.81 | 22 | 0 | 118 | 109 | 60 | 48 |
| Jimenez, Isaac | 10 | 6 | 1.70 | 20 | 1 | 127 | 96 | 43 | 68 |
| Lara, Hugo | 7 | 5 | 3.38 | 26 | 0 | 117 | 108 | 46 | 54 |
| Lopez, Gilberto | 0 | 2 | 8.10 | 6 | 0 | 13 | 20 | 5 | 5 |
| Lopez, Rodrigo | 1 | 1 | 3.54 | 7 | 1 | 20 | 15 | 16 | 22 |
| Luevano, Juan | 5 | 3 | 2.23 | 34 | 6 | 73 | 67 | 26 | 25 |
| Meza, Leobardo | 0 | 2 | 4.50 | 3 | 0 | 12 | 14 | 6 | 6 |
| Mora, Eleazar | 5 | 7 | 3.34 | 30 | 1 | 102 | 118 | 36 | 56 |
| Neri, Eduardo | 6 | 5 | 2.70 | 53 | 5 | 87 | 70 | 37 | 36 |
| Raygoza, Martin | 7 | 8 | 3.18 | 22 | 0 | 130 | 136 | 33 | 56 |
| Rodriguez, Rosario | 1 | 0 | 3.71 | 11 | 0 | 17 | 13 | 11 | 3 |
| Solano, Julio | 1 | 3 | 5.06 | 20 | 2 | 21 | 30 | 10 | 12 |

## QUINTANA ROO

| BATTING | AVG | AB | R | H | 2B | 3B | HR | RBI | SB |
|---|---|---|---|---|---|---|---|---|---|
| Alvarez, Hector, of | .253 | 363 | 39 | 92 | 15 | 1 | 5 | 38 | 5 |
| Arias, Everardo, ss | .186 | 43 | 5 | 8 | 2 | 0 | 0 | 2 | 1 |
| Barrera, Jesus, 3b-ss | .171 | 76 | 8 | 13 | 2 | 0 | 0 | 5 | 0 |
| Cantu, Gerardo, c-dh | .121 | 33 | 2 | 4 | 0 | 0 | 0 | 1 | 0 |
| Castillo, Juan, 3b | .191 | 47 | 3 | 9 | 0 | 0 | 0 | 4 | 0 |
| Castro, Arnoldo, 2b | .230 | 404 | 49 | 93 | 10 | 0 | 1 | 30 | 4 |
| Estrada, Hector, of | .264 | 409 | 32 | 108 | 20 | 0 | 5 | 41 | 3 |
| Guerrero, Francisco, ss | .290 | 317 | 43 | 92 | 12 | 2 | 2 | 30 | 14 |
| Guerrero, Jose, c | .000 | 11 | 0 | 0 | 0 | 0 | 0 | 0 | 0 |
| Guzman, Marco, c | .210 | 62 | 5 | 13 | 3 | 0 | 0 | 2 | 0 |
| Martinez, Abel, 3b | .154 | 26 | 8 | 4 | 1 | 0 | 0 | 2 | 0 |
| O'Halloran, Greg, of-1b | .271 | 365 | 44 | 99 | 17 | 3 | 8 | 51 | 3 |
| Ortiz, Alejandro, 3b | .226 | 327 | 26 | 74 | 9 | 1 | 8 | 34 | 1 |
| Quintana, Carlos, 1b | .280 | 218 | 25 | 61 | 7 | 0 | 4 | 26 | 1 |
| Rodriguez, Jose, dh | .190 | 21 | 2 | 4 | 0 | 0 | 0 | 1 | 0 |
| Rodriguez, Serafin, of | .242 | 215 | 36 | 52 | 5 | 1 | 0 | 9 | 8 |
| Sanchez, Raul, of | .216 | 37 | 8 | 8 | 0 | 0 | 0 | 2 | 0 |
| Soto, Emison, c-of | .211 | 256 | 31 | 54 | 8 | 0 | 2 | 22 | 3 |
| Zambrano, Roberto, of | .278 | 352 | 44 | 98 | 14 | 4 | 13 | 52 | 1 |

| PITCHING | W | L | ERA | G | SV | IP | H | BB | SO |
|---|---|---|---|---|---|---|---|---|---|
| Garibay, Roberto | 9 | 5 | 2.54 | 45 | 11 | 64 | 48 | 34 | 28 |
| Hernandez, Martin | 9 | 5 | 3.02 | 20 | 0 | 128 | 120 | 41 | 63 |
| Linares, Efrain | 2 | 2 | 3.49 | 11 | 2 | 28 | 20 | 21 | 23 |
| Neri, Braulio | 1 | 3 | 3.58 | 42 | 0 | 28 | 31 | 21 | 12 |
| Ortega, Roberto | 0 | 0 | 4.22 | 35 | 2 | 21 | 16 | 20 | 22 |
| Ramos, Jorge | 1 | 2 | 2.04 | 38 | 3 | 57 | 52 | 18 | 24 |
| Renteria, Hilario | 5 | 8 | 3.01 | 22 | 0 | 140 | 139 | 28 | 52 |
| Saenz, Alfredo | 5 | 3 | 3.11 | 21 | 0 | 133 | 131 | 44 | 57 |
| Soto, Fernando | 10 | 12 | 3.51 | 26 | 1 | 159 | 176 | 33 | 73 |
| Soto, Antonio | 2 | 8 | 4.29 | 31 | 1 | 63 | 52 | 41 | 53 |
| Valdez, Efrain | 11 | 5 | 2.23 | 20 | 0 | 149 | 123 | 44 | 69 |
| Valenzuela, Saul | 8 | 7 | 3.61 | 21 | 0 | 122 | 118 | 42 | 44 |

## REYNOSA

| BATTING | AVG | AB | R | H | 2B | 3B | HR | RBI | SB |
|---|---|---|---|---|---|---|---|---|---|
| Cruz, Luis, of | .269 | 357 | 34 | 96 | 14 | 1 | 5 | 48 | 0 |
| Esquer, Ramon, 2b | .263 | 399 | 64 | 105 | 17 | 6 | 1 | 40 | 8 |
| Felix, Junior, of | .319 | 335 | 73 | 107 | 20 | 3 | 19 | 50 | 3 |
| Fernandez, Fabian, 2b-3b | .246 | 57 | 6 | 14 | 1 | 2 | 0 | 6 | 0 |
| Fornes, Daniel, of | .174 | 23 | 3 | 4 | 0 | 0 | 0 | 2 | 0 |
| Martinez, Ray, ss-3b | .303 | 353 | 60 | 107 | 21 | 5 | 6 | 44 | 7 |
| Martinez, Domingo, 1b | .320 | 413 | 75 | 132 | 22 | 4 | 18 | 91 | 1 |
| Monroy, Victor, c-dh | .219 | 73 | 4 | 16 | 3 | 0 | 0 | 3 | 1 |
| Munoz, Noe, c | .333 | 168 | 24 | 56 | 11 | 3 | 4 | 35 | 0 |
| Noris, Rogelio, of | .224 | 245 | 33 | 55 | 14 | 0 | 2 | 20 | 5 |
| Ortega, Antonio, c | .250 | 16 | 4 | 4 | 1 | 0 | 0 | 0 | 0 |
| Robles, Gerardo, 3b | .176 | 51 | 11 | 9 | 0 | 0 | 0 | 4 | 0 |
| Rodriguez, Hector, 3b | .195 | 267 | 35 | 52 | 8 | 1 | 3 | 32 | 1 |
| Stark, Matt, dh | .321 | 358 | 66 | 115 | 24 | 0 | 14 | 72 | 2 |
| Tellez, Alonso, of | .365 | 293 | 54 | 107 | 19 | 1 | 7 | 49 | 1 |
| Valdez, Francisco, c-of | .266 | 237 | 27 | 63 | 9 | 1 | 1 | 24 | 3 |
| Valenzuela, Armando, ss | .213 | 61 | 4 | 13 | 1 | 0 | 0 | 4 | 2 |

| PITCHING | W | L | ERA | G | SV | IP | H | BB | SO |
|---|---|---|---|---|---|---|---|---|---|
| Acosta, Gerardo | 7 | 6 | 5.00 | 39 | 5 | 76 | 80 | 43 | 39 |
| Bennett, Chris | 13 | 6 | 3.78 | 26 | 0 | 181 | 189 | 66 | 106 |
| Brummett, Greg | 1 | 6 | 5.87 | 8 | 0 | 38 | 59 | 14 | 17 |

| | W | L | ERA | G | SV | IP | H | BB | SO |
|---|---|---|---|---|---|---|---|---|---|
| Carranza, Javier | 1 | 3 | 7.81 | 18 | 0 | 28 | 39 | 24 | 14 |
| Cerros, Juan | 4 | 1 | 4.22 | 28 | 0 | 79 | 78 | 47 | 34 |
| Corbin, Archie | 0 | 0 | 9.31 | 9 | 2 | 10 | 10 | 7 | 13 |
| Cruz, Javier | 10 | 7 | 4.79 | 29 | 0 | 150 | 161 | 69 | 103 |
| Del Toro, Miguel | 1 | 1 | 4.11 | 32 | 7 | 46 | 45 | 36 | 29 |
| Draper, Mike | 0 | 3 | 5.79 | 10 | 1 | 9 | 16 | 3 | 4 |
| Guerrero, Omar | 1 | 2 | 4.43 | 22 | 2 | 61 | 64 | 26 | 24 |
| Lopez, Jesus | 1 | 1 | 5.60 | 5 | 0 | 18 | 16 | 13 | 8 |
| Mendez, Luis | 6 | 6 | 5.73 | 20 | 0 | 93 | 95 | 49 | 64 |
| Purata, Julio | 11 | 11 | 3.37 | 25 | 0 | 152 | 148 | 68 | 97 |
| Rojo, Oscar | 0 | 3 | 3.71 | 15 | 2 | 17 | 25 | 10 | 4 |

## SALTILLO

| BATTING | AVG | AB | R | H | 2B | 3B | HR | RBI | SB |
|---|---|---|---|---|---|---|---|---|---|
| Aguilera, Armando, c | .225 | 182 | 15 | 41 | 5 | 2 | 0 | 10 | 2 |
| Almeida, Shammar, 1b | .214 | 131 | 16 | 28 | 1 | 0 | 3 | 18 | 0 |
| Aviles, Alejandro, ss-3b | .162 | 37 | 3 | 6 | 0 | 0 | 0 | 2 | 0 |
| Camacho, Adulfo, 2b-3b | .214 | 210 | 35 | 45 | 8 | 2 | 0 | 18 | 0 |
| Clark, Tim, 1b-of | .280 | 411 | 68 | 115 | 26 | 4 | 15 | 85 | 1 |
| Escalante, Marcelo, of-dh | .209 | 86 | 7 | 18 | 2 | 1 | 0 | 6 | 0 |
| Guerrero Juan, 3b-of | .290 | 442 | 56 | 128 | 26 | 3 | 4 | 69 | 5 |
| Jimenez, Houston, ss | .286 | 378 | 68 | 108 | 22 | 2 | 3 | 39 | 13 |
| Luna, Jose, c | .186 | 172 | 8 | 32 | 4 | 0 | 0 | 17 | 1 |
| Martinez, Raul, 1b-dh | .301 | 136 | 12 | 41 | 9 | 0 | 3 | 15 | 0 |
| Munoz, Jose, of | .203 | 69 | 6 | 14 | 1 | 0 | 0 | 5 | 0 |
| Peralta, Amado, 1b | .203 | 128 | 15 | 26 | 4 | 1 | 1 | 12 | 1 |
| Precichi, Jorge, 2b | .205 | 73 | 17 | 15 | 1 | 0 | 0 | 4 | 1 |
| Robinson, Don, dh-of | .259 | 81 | 10 | 21 | 4 | 0 | 3 | 13 | 1 |
| Robles, Ricardo, dh | .147 | 34 | 4 | 5 | 0 | 1 | 0 | 1 | 1 |
| Valenzuela, Eduardo, c-dh | .313 | 339 | 31 | 106 | 15 | 0 | 1 | 43 | 1 |
| Villegas, Fernando, of | .300 | 243 | 32 | 73 | 7 | 5 | 2 | 32 | 3 |
| Vizcarra, Marco, 2b-ss | .284 | 345 | 51 | 98 | 11 | 2 | 0 | 24 | 4 |
| Wright, George, of | .309 | 356 | 61 | 110 | 17 | 2 | 6 | 82 | 8 |

| PITCHING | W | L | ERA | G | SV | IP | H | BB | SO |
|---|---|---|---|---|---|---|---|---|---|
| Cecena, Jose | 5 | 11 | 5.67 | 33 | 2 | 86 | 87 | 59 | 64 |
| Cota, Marino | 2 | 2 | 6.67 | 34 | 1 | 55 | 71 | 27 | 30 |
| Delfin, Adolfo | 1 | 1 | 7.34 | 23 | 0 | 38 | 46 | 33 | 15 |
| Flores, Ignacio | 5 | 10 | 5.09 | 26 | 0 | 141 | 144 | 108 | 82 |
| Gracia, Edmundo | 0 | 1 | 5.36 | 21 | 0 | 42 | 46 | 39 | 12 |
| Huerta, Luis | 4 | 12 | 4.87 | 24 | 0 | 133 | 160 | 58 | 50 |
| Johnson, Joe | 0 | 0 | 14.40 | 8 | 1 | 5 | 4 | 12 | 4 |
| Lupercio, Hector | 1 | 0 | 6.00 | 12 | 0 | 25 | 33 | 11 | 11 |
| Martinez, Mauricio | 0 | 0 | 6.75 | 16 | 0 | 21 | 30 | 13 | 12 |
| Serna, Ramon | 2 | 4 | 4.83 | 19 | 0 | 63 | 73 | 35 | 21 |
| Sombra, Francisco | 5 | 12 | 4.28 | 31 | 0 | 109 | 126 | 46 | 50 |
| Strange, Don | 4 | 5 | 2.91 | 38 | 12 | 53 | 41 | 28 | 58 |
| Valencia, Jorge | 2 | 8 | 5.97 | 36 | 0 | 75 | 93 | 55 | 25 |
| Zappelli, Mark | 7 | 4 | 3.92 | 14 | 0 | 96 | 96 | 61 | 32 |

## TABASCO

| BATTING | AVG | AB | R | H | 2B | 3B | HR | RBI | SB |
|---|---|---|---|---|---|---|---|---|---|
| Almendra, Gregorio, of | .158 | 19 | 6 | 3 | 0 | 0 | 0 | 1 | 0 |
| Armas, Marcos, dh | .247 | 81 | 6 | 20 | 5 | 0 | 1 | 6 | 0 |
| Castillo, Braulio, of | .260 | 173 | 23 | 45 | 9 | 1 | 5 | 28 | 0 |
| Dominguez, David, of-dh | .277 | 365 | 44 | 101 | 16 | 0 | 2 | 46 | 2 |
| Duarte, Rene, c | .282 | 188 | 23 | 53 | 11 | 1 | 1 | 25 | 2 |
| Elvira, Honorio, c | .256 | 43 | 2 | 11 | 1 | 0 | 0 | 4 | 0 |
| Fentanes, Oscar, of-3b | .288 | 375 | 42 | 108 | 11 | 4 | 2 | 38 | 3 |
| Garzon, Eliseo, c | .261 | 253 | 20 | 66 | 10 | 1 | 2 | 21 | 0 |
| Gomez, Ever, ss | .154 | 13 | 1 | 2 | 0 | 0 | 0 | 0 | 1 |
| Infante, Alexis, ss-2b | .290 | 303 | 26 | 88 | 3 | 0 | 1 | 24 | 1 |
| Iturbe, Pedro, of-1b | .236 | 347 | 38 | 82 | 16 | 1 | 4 | 34 | 28 |
| Landrum, Ced, of | .259 | 201 | 28 | 52 | 5 | 3 | 2 | 14 | 9 |
| Mercedes, Luis, of | .235 | 85 | 10 | 20 | 1 | 0 | 0 | 8 | 6 |
| Rivera, German, 3b | .252 | 206 | 28 | 52 | 7 | 0 | 3 | 27 | 0 |
| Rojas, Francisco, ss-3b | .229 | 105 | 8 | 24 | 3 | 0 | 0 | 7 | 2 |
| Sasser, Mackey, 1b | .177 | 124 | 9 | 22 | 4 | 0 | 0 | 10 | 0 |
| Scott, Bryant, 1b | .226 | 53 | 5 | 12 | 3 | 0 | 1 | 6 | 0 |
| Tiquet, Lazaro, of | .250 | 216 | 16 | 54 | 7 | 1 | 0 | 27 | 1 |
| Valenzuela, Horacio | .111 | 36 | 1 | 4 | 0 | 0 | 0 | 3 | 0 |
| Valenzuela, Jose, of | .379 | 29 | 8 | 11 | 0 | 0 | 1 | 2 | 0 |
| Vargas, Trinidad, ss | .212 | 113 | 4 | 24 | 1 | 0 | 0 | 8 | 0 |
| Zazueta, Juan, 2b | .206 | 262 | 22 | 54 | 1 | 0 | 1 | 8 | 0 |

| PITCHING | W | L | ERA | G | SV | IP | H | BB | SO |
|---|---|---|---|---|---|---|---|---|---|
| Aguilar, Miguel | 1 | 5 | 2.18 | 23 | 0 | 58 | 43 | 16 | 23 |
| Aguirre, Gaudencio | 4 | 4 | 4.25 | 21 | 0 | 42 | 40 | 17 | 12 |
| Cazares, Rosario | 4 | 3 | 1.64 | 54 | 5 | 66 | 41 | 27 | 39 |
| Herrera, Enrique | 1 | 1 | 1.93 | 19 | 0 | 33 | 35 | 17 | 18 |
| Lopez, Emigdio | 15 | 4 | 2.15 | 25 | 0 | 159 | 135 | 41 | 68 |
| Mauser, Tim | 1 | 6 | 2.72 | 47 | 25 | 56 | 46 | 24 | 56 |
| Munoz, Ricardo | 7 | 10 | 3.17 | 24 | 1 | 145 | 154 | 37 | 56 |
| Osuna, Ricardo | 2 | 7 | 3.58 | 14 | 0 | 78 | 83 | 30 | 32 |
| Retes, Lorenzo | 2 | 2 | 5.66 | 31 | 0 | 21 | 27 | 14 | 8 |

| | W | L | ERA | G | SV | IP | H | BB | SO |
|---|---|---|---|---|---|---|---|---|---|
| Rivera, Hector | 1 | 4 | 5.20 | 26 | 0 | 64 | 76 | 29 | 27 |
| Romero, Juan | 2 | 6 | 4.70 | 27 | 0 | 59 | 76 | 19 | 20 |
| Ruiz, Cecilio | 8 | 9 | 3.06 | 23 | 0 | 144 | 137 | 36 | 82 |
| Vargas, Joel | 0 | 2 | 2.78 | 12 | 0 | 36 | 29 | 17 | 18 |

## TORREON

| BATTING | AVG | AB | R | H | 2B | 3B | HR | RBI | SB |
|---|---|---|---|---|---|---|---|---|---|
| Avila, Ruben, 1b | .278 | 335 | 46 | 93 | 13 | 1 | 9 | 51 | 1 |
| Espinoza, Ramon, c | .300 | 10 | 2 | 3 | 0 | 0 | 0 | 3 | 0 |
| Garcia, Hector, of | .308 | 354 | 58 | 109 | 6 | 4 | 2 | 29 | 7 |
| Garza, Gerardo, c | .276 | 352 | 35 | 97 | 11 | 2 | 3 | 54 | 0 |
| Horn, Sam, dh | .265 | 359 | 78 | 95 | 19 | 0 | 30 | 90 | 1 |
| Jimenez, Ulises, of-1b | .275 | 40 | 9 | 11 | 1 | 0 | 2 | 9 | 0 |
| Perez, Juan, c | .170 | 47 | 7 | 8 | 0 | 1 | 0 | 4 | 0 |
| Rodriguez, Fernando, of | .303 | 320 | 44 | 97 | 25 | 3 | 6 | 50 | 1 |
| Ruiz, Juan, 3b-2b | .244 | 242 | 40 | 59 | 6 | 1 | 1 | 30 | 3 |
| Salas, Heriberto, ss | .301 | 415 | 62 | 125 | 19 | 4 | 4 | 53 | 2 |
| Snider, Van, of-1b | .239 | 352 | 40 | 84 | 14 | 1 | 7 | 37 | 3 |
| Soriano, Ricardo, of | .171 | 41 | 5 | 7 | 0 | 0 | 0 | 4 | 1 |
| Valenzuela, Joel, 2b | .125 | 16 | 4 | 2 | 0 | 0 | 0 | 0 | 0 |
| Valle, Jorge, 3b-ss | .284 | 285 | 40 | 81 | 7 | 3 | 2 | 31 | 3 |
| Zazueta, Mauricio, 2b | .279 | 391 | 50 | 109 | 17 | 8 | 0 | 45 | 2 |

| PITCHING | W | L | ERA | G | SV | IP | H | BB | SO |
|---|---|---|---|---|---|---|---|---|---|
| Acosta, Aaron | 4 | 8 | 4.16 | 22 | 0 | 119 | 120 | 60 | 64 |
| Castillo, Felipe | 0 | 1 | 7.00 | 7 | 1 | 9 | 15 | 3 | 5 |
| Diaz, Marco | 3 | 3 | 6.19 | 26 | 0 | 57 | 77 | 38 | 26 |
| Figueroa, Fernando | 15 | 4 | 2.98 | 25 | 0 | 184 | 170 | 73 | 93 |
| Flores, Ignacio | 1 | 1 | 5.83 | 18 | 0 | 29 | 24 | 27 | 21 |
| Gonzalez, Gilberto | 5 | 5 | 3.86 | 16 | 0 | 65 | 71 | 40 | 30 |
| Grajales, Norberto | 6 | 2 | 5.60 | 42 | 2 | 63 | 84 | 28 | 22 |
| Jimenez, Jesus | 1 | 1 | 8.80 | 22 | 0 | 31 | 46 | 29 | 12 |
| Juarez, Fernando | 1 | 1 | 5.40 | 32 | 0 | 18 | 21 | 6 | 9 |
| Leon, Juan | 0 | 0 | 4.05 | 5 | 0 | 7 | 7 | 5 | 2 |
| Marquez, Jose | 0 | 1 | 9.00 | 17 | 0 | 17 | 26 | 13 | 7 |
| Molina, Joaquin | 0 | 0 | 1.93 | 7 | 0 | 9 | 6 | 7 | 4 |
| Palafox, Juan | 7 | 11 | 4.16 | 24 | 0 | 167 | 190 | 54 | 58 |
| Perschke, Greg | 3 | 5 | 2.81 | 23 | 7 | 32 | 33 | 16 | 22 |
| Puig, Benny | 0 | 1 | 9.95 | 1 | 0 | 6 | 12 | 3 | 2 |
| Quijada, Mario | 3 | 8 | 4.59 | 32 | 1 | 98 | 88 | 73 | 55 |
| Rivera, Francisco | 1 | 1 | 6.37 | 15 | 0 | 30 | 31 | 23 | 14 |
| Romo, Guillermo | 1 | 3 | 9.89 | 16 | 1 | 34 | 46 | 24 | 16 |

## YUCATAN

| BATTING | AVG | AB | R | H | 2B | 3B | HR | RBI | SB |
|---|---|---|---|---|---|---|---|---|---|
| Alvarez, Luis, of | .273 | 33 | 2 | 9 | 4 | 0 | 0 | 4 | 2 |
| Cazarin, Manuel, c | .260 | 335 | 36 | 87 | 14 | 0 | 2 | 37 | 2 |
| Felix, Arturo, 2b-of | .228 | 298 | 23 | 68 | 12 | 0 | 1 | 23 | 3 |
| Franco, Manuel, 3b | .250 | 164 | 15 | 41 | 8 | 0 | 2 | 20 | 6 |
| Jimenez, Eduardo, of-dh | .244 | 271 | 34 | 66 | 12 | 0 | 10 | 35 | 4 |
| Lopez, Miguel, 2b | .242 | 95 | 13 | 23 | 1 | 0 | 0 | 8 | 3 |
| Lopez, Salvador, of | .165 | 97 | 10 | 16 | 2 | 1 | 0 | 4 | 1 |
| Magana, Gabriel, ss-2b | .250 | 12 | 4 | 3 | 1 | 0 | 0 | 1 | 0 |
| Osuna, Hector, c | .259 | 54 | 8 | 14 | 1 | 0 | 0 | 2 | 0 |
| Pacho, Juan, ss | .260 | 393 | 31 | 102 | 9 | 2 | 0 | 36 | 5 |
| Pena, Carlos, c | .051 | 39 | 0 | 2 | 0 | 0 | 0 | 2 | 0 |
| Pena, Luis, 1b | .148 | 155 | 5 | 23 | 4 | 0 | 0 | 8 | 0 |
| Quintero, Alan, of | .267 | 15 | 0 | 4 | 0 | 0 | 0 | 1 | 0 |
| Raven, Luis, 1b | .256 | 90 | 7 | 23 | 5 | 0 | 1 | 9 | 1 |
| Rubio, Sergio, of | .269 | 271 | 36 | 73 | 8 | 3 | 1 | 23 | 11 |
| Salinas, Rogelio, 1b | .259 | 205 | 15 | 53 | 9 | 0 | 4 | 23 | 0 |
| Sherman, Darrell, of | .305 | 266 | 40 | 81 | 10 | 1 | 0 | 20 | 17 |
| Sievers, Carlos, 1b | .180 | 50 | 2 | 9 | 1 | 0 | 0 | 1 | 0 |
| Tatis, Bernando, 3b-of | .269 | 416 | 48 | 112 | 11 | 5 | 4 | 46 | 27 |
| Torres, Raymundo, dh-of | .221 | 258 | 35 | 57 | 14 | 2 | 10 | 34 | 2 |
| Trafton, Todd, of-dh | .279 | 359 | 54 | 100 | 19 | 1 | 7 | 42 | 0 |
| Valdez, Jesus, 1b | .263 | 19 | 2 | 5 | 0 | 0 | 0 | 0 | 0 |

| PITCHING | W | L | ERA | G | SV | IP | H | BB | SO |
|---|---|---|---|---|---|---|---|---|---|
| Cano, Jose | 4 | 6 | 2.46 | 13 | 0 | 84 | 58 | 45 | 19 |
| Cruz, Juan | 0 | 0 | 5.40 | 12 | 0 | 8 | 9 | 10 | 4 |
| Garcia, Apolinar | 4 | 4 | 3.99 | 13 | 0 | 68 | 69 | 36 | 33 |
| Llanes, Emeterio | 0 | 1 | 1.99 | 6 | 0 | 23 | 14 | 11 | 12 |
| Melendez, Jose | 5 | 4 | 1.65 | 35 | 11 | 82 | 61 | 27 | 63 |
| Miranda, Julio | 9 | 4 | 2.66 | 49 | 12 | 102 | 79 | 26 | 56 |
| Ortega, Wilbert | 0 | 0 | 3.73 | 26 | 0 | 31 | 22 | 23 | 22 |
| Osuna, Gabriel | 4 | 5 | 2.53 | 20 | 5 | 32 | 35 | 8 | 20 |
| Rodriguez, Salavdor | 4 | 0 | 3.23 | 28 | 0 | 75 | 83 | 43 | 44 |
| Sandoval, Guillermo | 4 | 8 | 4.17 | 23 | 0 | 123 | 149 | 52 | 44 |
| Solis, Ricardo | 9 | 8 | 2.83 | 20 | 0 | 115 | 122 | 41 | 47 |
| Toliver, Fred | 1 | 3 | 5.31 | 8 | 0 | 41 | 40 | 32 | 32 |
| Uribe, Juan | 5 | 4 | 4.97 | 33 | 1 | 54 | 59 | 25 | 25 |
| Valenzuela, Lorenzo | 1 | 2 | 9.82 | 7 | 0 | 11 | 17 | 13 | 5 |
| Verdugo, Orlando | 0 | 0 | 1.27 | 9 | 0 | 21 | 13 | 11 | 3 |
| Villareal, Antonio | 10 | 6 | 2.45 | 22 | 0 | 143 | 141 | 53 | 67 |

**Batters:** 10 or more at-bats
**Pitchers:** 5 or more innings

# JAPANESE
## LEAGUES

# Earthquake-Ravaged City Celebrates

**By WAYNE GRACZYK**

The Orix BlueWave, representing the earthquake-ravaged city of Kobe in western Japan, cheered up their still-recovering fans by winning the 1996 Japan Series championship. The BlueWave won their first Japan title under the Orix banner after the leasing company bought the franchise from Hankyu Railways in 1988.

Manager Akira Ogi led his Pacific League champion Wave to a convincing five-game Japan Series victory over the Central League's Yomiuri Giants, clinching the title before a hometown crowd at Green Stadium Kobe on Oct. 24. Most of those fans were among those still suffering from the aftermath of the 7.2 magnitude Great Hanshin Earthquake of Jan. 17, 1995, which left 6,310 dead and hundreds of thousands homeless.

Orix had won the PL pennant in 1995 but lost a five-game Japan Series to the Yakult Swallows.

The Orix charge was led once again by Japan's most remarkable player, 22-year-old outfielder Ichiro Suzuki, who won a third consecutive batting title with a .356 average, along with a third straight MVP award. American DH-first baseman Troy Neel, a former Oakland Athletics player, led the Pacific League with 32 home runs and 111 RBIs during his second season in Japan.

**Top Hitter.** Ichiro Suzuki led Japanese hitters with a .355 average.

The BlueWave won the pennant after languishing in second place most of the season, behind the Nippon Ham Fighters of Tokyo. Orix finally passed the Fighters on Aug. 26 and coasted to the flag, clinching on Sept. 23.

Fighters righthander Kip Gross led the Pacific League in wins for the second straight year, posting a 17-9 record, while Chiba Lotte Marines righthander Hideki Irabu, who desires to pitch in the U.S. major leagues, led the PL in ERA. Irabu's ERA was 2.402, which narrowly topped teammate Eric Hillman's 2.404.

While Yomiuri lost the Japan Series to the BlueWave, the Giants can be proud to have come back from an 11½ game deficit as late as July 6 to overtake the Hiroshima Carp and win their second pennant in three years. The Giants defeated the Seibu Lions 4-2 in the 1994 Japan Series.

Leading the Giants was Central League MVP Hideki Matsui, who blasted 38 homers with 99 RBIs and a .314 average. On the mound, Yomiuri boasted twin 16-game-winning righthanders in Masaki Saito (16-4) and Dominican Balvino Galvez (16-6). Saito took the ERA title with a 2.36 figure.

Chunichi outfielder Alonzo Powell made it three CL batting titles in a row, hitting .340. His teammate, slugger Takeshi Yamasaki, led all of Japan with 39 homers. Another U.S. player, Hiroshima Carp first baseman Luis Lopez was the top RBI man with 109.

The Pacific League's Chiba Lotte Marines, who were managed in 1995 by Bobby Valentine and finished a strong second, dropped to fifth in the six-team league. Valentine was fired in favor of Japanese manager Akira Ejiri, who ousted Valentine. Lotte general manager Tatsuro Hirooka, was himself dismissed by club owners disappointed in the team's 1996 result.

## JAPAN SERIES

**Last 25 Years**

| Year | Champion | Manager | Runner-Up | Result | MVP |
|------|----------|---------|-----------|--------|-----|
| 1972 | Yomiuri (CL) | Tetsuharu Kawakami | Hankyu (PL) | 4-1 | Tsuneo Horiuchi, Yomiuri |
| 1973 | Yomiuri (CL) | Tetsuharu Kawakami | Nankai (PL) | 4-1 | Tsuneo Horiuchi, Yomiuri |
| 1974 | Lotte (PL) | Masaichi Kaneda | Chunichi (CL) | 4-2 | Sumio Hirota, Lotte |
| 1975 | Hankyu (PL) | Toshiharu Veda | Hiroshima (CL) | 4-0-2 | Takashi Yamuguchi, Hankyu |
| 1976 | Hankyu (PL) | Toshiharu Veda | Yomiuri (CL) | 4-3 | Yutaka Fukumoto, Hankyu |
| 1977 | Hankyu (PL) | Toshiharu Veda | Yomiuri (CL) | 4-1 | Hisashi Yamada, Hankyu |
| 1978 | Yakult (CL) | Tatsuro Hirooka | Hankyu (PL) | 4-3 | Katsuo Osugi, Yakult |
| 1979 | Hiroshima (CL) | Takeshi Koba | Kintetsu (PL) | 4-3 | Yoshihiko Takahashi, Hiroshima |
| 1980 | Hiroshima (CL) | Takeshi Koba | Kintetsu (PL) | 4-3 | Jim Lyttle, Hiroshima |
| 1981 | Yomiuri (CL) | Motoshi Fujita | Nippon (PL) | 4-2 | Takashi Nishimoto, Yomiuri |
| 1982 | Seibu (PL) | Tatsuro Hirooka | Chunichi (CL) | 4-2 | Osamu Higashio, Seibu |
| 1983 | Seibu (PL) | Tatsuro Hirooka | Yomiuri (CL) | 4-3 | Takuji Ota, Seibu |
| 1984 | Hiroshima (CL) | Toshiharu Ueda | Hankyu (PL) | 4-3 | Kiyoyuki Nagashima, Hiroshima |
| 1985 | Hanshin (CL) | Yoshio Yoshida | Seibu (PL) | 4-2 | Randy Bass, Hanshin |
| 1986 | Seibu (PL) | Masaaki Mori | Hiroshima (CL) | 4-3-1 | Kimiyasu Kudo, Seibu |
| 1987 | Seibu (PL) | Masaaki Mori | Yomiuri (CL) | 4-2 | Kimiyasu Kudo, Seibu |
| 1988 | Seibu (PL) | Masaaki Mori | Chunichi (CL) | 4-1 | Hiromichi Ishige, Seibu |
| 1989 | Yomiuri (CL) | Motoshi Fujita | Kintetsu (PL) | 4-3 | Norihiro Komada, Yomiuri |
| 1990 | Seibu (PL) | Masaaki Mori | Yomiuri (CL) | 4-0 | Orestes Destrade, Seibu |
| 1991 | Seibu (PL) | Masaaki Mori | Hiroshima (CL) | 4-3 | Koji Akiyama, Seibu |
| 1992 | Seibu (PL) | Masaaki Mori | Yakult (CL) | 4-3 | Takehiro Ishii, Seibu |
| 1993 | Yakult (CL) | Katsuya Nomura | Seibu (PL) | 4-3 | Kenjiro Kawasaki, Yakult |
| 1994 | Yomiuri (CL) | Shigeo Nagashima | Seibu (PL) | 4-2 | Hiromi Makihara, Yomiuri |
| 1995 | Yakult (CL) | Katsuya Nomura | Orix (PL) | 4-1 | Tom O'Malley, Yakult |
| 1996 | Orix (PL) | Akira Ogi | Yomiuri (CL) | 4-1 | Troy Neel, Orix |

# CENTRAL LEAGUE

## STANDINGS

| | W | L | PCT | T | GB |
|---|---|---|---|---|---|
| Yomiuri Giants | 77 | 53 | .592 | 0 | — |
| Chunichi Dragons | 72 | 58 | .554 | 0 | 5 |
| Hiroshima Carp | 71 | 59 | .546 | 0 | 6 |
| Yakult Swallows | 61 | 69 | .469 | 0 | 16 |
| Yokohama BayStars | 55 | 75 | .423 | 0 | 22 |
| Hanshin Tigers | 54 | 76 | .415 | 0 | 23 |

### INDIVUDUAL BATTING LEADERS
(Minimum 350 Plate Appearances)

| | AVG | AB | R | H | 2B | 3B | HR | RBI | SB |
|---|---|---|---|---|---|---|---|---|---|
| Powell, Alonzo, Dragons ... | .340 | 518 | 63 | 176 | 42 | 2 | 14 | 67 | 1 |
| Tsuji, Hatsuhiko, Swallows | .333 | 400 | 59 | 133 | 9 | 2 | 2 | 41 | 9 |
| Tatsunami, K., Dragons..... | .323 | 511 | 91 | 165 | 39 | 2 | 10 | 62 | 2 |
| Yamasaki, Takeshi, Dragons | .322 | 453 | 83 | 146 | 20 | 0 | 39 | 107 | 1 |
| O'Malley, Tom, Swallows .. | .315 | 461 | 56 | 145 | 23 | 0 | 18 | 97 | 3 |
| Eto, Akira, Carp ............... | .314 | 388 | 93 | 122 | 19 | 1 | 32 | 79 | 8 |
| Matsui, Hideki, Giants ...... | .314 | 487 | 97 | 153 | 34 | 1 | 38 | 99 | 7 |
| Nishiyama, Shuji, Carp...... | .314 | 411 | 45 | 129 | 18 | 2 | 3 | 41 | 4 |
| Maeda, Tomonori, Carp .... | .313 | 396 | 54 | 124 | 20 | 2 | 19 | 65 | 0 |
| Lopez, Luis, Carp ............. | .312 | 503 | 66 | 157 | 29 | 1 | 25 | 109 | 2 |
| Atsunori, Inaba, Swallows . | .310 | 436 | 63 | 135 | 26 | 3 | 11 | 53 | 9 |
| Rose, Bobby, BayStars .... | .304 | 483 | 62 | 147 | 21 | 6 | 16 | 86 | 1 |
| Coles, Darnell, Dragons .... | .302 | 513 | 77 | 155 | 15 | 1 | 29 | 79 | 0 |
| Ochiai, Hiromitsu, Giants... | .301 | 376 | 60 | 113 | 18 | 0 | 21 | 86 | 3 |
| Kanemoto, Tomoaki, Carp | .300 | 423 | 84 | 127 | 18 | 2 | 27 | 72 | 18 |
| Tanishige, M., BayStars .... | .300 | 380 | 36 | 114 | 25 | 3 | 8 | 54 | 2 |
| Komada, Narihiro, BayStars | .299 | 485 | 57 | 145 | 22 | 1 | 10 | 63 | 1 |
| Suzuki, Takanori, BayStars . | .299 | 355 | 66 | 106 | 15 | 0 | 13 | 62 | 6 |
| Wada, Yutaka, Tigers ........ | .298 | 520 | 66 | 155 | 22 | 3 | 5 | 44 | 2 |
| Taiho, Yasuaki, Dragons ... | .294 | 462 | 69 | 136 | 19 | 1 | 38 | 89 | 3 |
| Mack, Shane, Giants ......... | .293 | 484 | 71 | 142 | 28 | 0 | 22 | 75 | 12 |
| Nomura, Kenjiro, Carp....... | .292 | 514 | 77 | 150 | 30 | 3 | 12 | 68 | 8 |
| Iida, Tetsuya, Swallows ..... | .290 | 424 | 62 | 123 | 19 | 3 | 6 | 37 | 13 |
| Saeki, Takahiro, BayStars... | .290 | 390 | 49 | 113 | 23 | 5 | 6 | 59 | 3 |
| Ishii, Takuro, BayStars ....... | .282 | 496 | 94 | 140 | 19 | 3 | 1 | 29 | 45 |
| Braggs, Glenn, BayStars..... | .281 | 356 | 55 | 100 | 20 | 1 | 13 | 56 | 6 |
| Ogata, Kaichi, Carp ........... | .279 | 516 | 95 | 144 | 25 | 6 | 23 | 71 | 50 |

(Other Foreign Players)

| | AVG | AB | R | H | 2B | 3B | HR | RBI | SB |
|---|---|---|---|---|---|---|---|---|---|
| Perez, Timoniel, Carp........ | .278 | 54 | 8 | 15 | 1 | 0 | 1 | 7 | 0 |
| Worthington, Craig, Tigers | .267 | 75 | 15 | 20 | 2 | 1 | 3 | 12 | 1 |
| Meulens, H., Swallows ...... | .246 | 439 | 47 | 108 | 14 | 3 | 25 | 67 | 1 |
| Maas, Kevin, Tigers........... | .245 | 241 | 23 | 59 | 8 | 1 | 8 | 42 | 1 |
| Davis, Glenn, Tigers........... | .237 | 114 | 10 | 27 | 7 | 0 | 5 | 18 | 1 |
| Coolbaugh, Scott, Tigers.... | .210 | 167 | 14 | 35 | 4 | 1 | 2 | 16 | 1 |
| Manto, Jeff, Giants ............ | .111 | 27 | 1 | 3 | 1 | 0 | 0 | 1 | 0 |
| Perdomo, Felix, Carp ......... | .083 | 12 | 1 | 1 | 0 | 0 | 0 | 0 | 0 |

### INDIVIDUAL PITCHING LEADERS
(Minimum 133 Innings)

| | W | L | ERA | G | SV | IP | H | BB | SO |
|---|---|---|---|---|---|---|---|---|---|
| Saito, Masaki, Giants .......... | 16 | 4 | 2.36 | 25 | 0 | 187 | 172 | 44 | 158 |
| Galvez, Balvino, Giants........ | 16 | 6 | 3.05 | 28 | 0 | 204 | 186 | 59 | 112 |
| Yoshii, Masato, Swallows .... | 10 | 7 | 3.24 | 25 | 0 | 180 | 177 | 47 | 145 |
| Kawajiri, Tetsuro, Tigers ...... | 13 | 9 | 3.26 | 37 | 1 | 157 | 159 | 41 | 127 |
| Saito, Takashi, BayStars ...... | 10 | 10 | 3.29 | 28 | 0 | 197 | 157 | 63 | 206 |
| Imanaka, Shinji, Dragons...... | 14 | 8 | 3.31 | 25 | 0 | 180 | 175 | 57 | 133 |
| Yamazaki, Ken, Carp ........... | 9 | 6 | 3.38 | 28 | 0 | 133 | 134 | 19 | 68 |
| Tabata, Kazuya, Swallows | 12 | 12 | 3.51 | 33 | 1 | 177 | 154 | 60 | 109 |
| Bross, Terry, Swallows ......... | 7 | 12 | 3.61 | 23 | 0 | 137 | 115 | 43 | 97 |
| Yamamoto, M., Dragons........ | 7 | 9 | 3.67 | 26 | 0 | 155 | 159 | 38 | 119 |

(Other Foreign Players)

| | W | L | ERA | G | SV | IP | H | BB | SO |
|---|---|---|---|---|---|---|---|---|---|
| Brito, Mario, Giants................. | 3 | 2 | 3.33 | 39 | 19 | 49 | 50 | 18 | 43 |
| Checo, Robinson, Carp.......... | 4 | 1 | 4.80 | 9 | 0 | 51 | 52 | 24 | 36 |
| Birkbeck, Mike, BayStars ....... | 0 | 2 | 11.81 | 4 | 0 | 11 | 19 | 5 | 3 |

# PACIFIC LEAGUE

## STANDINGS

| | W | L | PCT | T | GB |
|---|---|---|---|---|---|
| Orix BlueWave | 74 | 50 | .597 | 6 | — |
| Nippon Ham Fighters | 68 | 58 | .540 | 4 | 7 |
| Seibu Lions | 62 | 64 | .492 | 4 | 13 |
| Kintetsu Buffaloes | 62 | 67 | .481 | 1 | 14½ |
| Chiba Lotte Marines | 60 | 67 | .472 | 3 | 15½ |
| Fukuoka Daiei Hawks | 54 | 74 | .422 | 2 | 22 |

**Top Americans.** Troy Neel, left, led the Pacific League in homers (32), while Alonzo Powell led the Central League in hitting (340).

### INDIVIDUAL BATTING LEADERS
(Minimum 350 Plate Appearances)

| | AVG | AB | R | H | 2B | 3B | HR | RBI | SB |
|---|---|---|---|---|---|---|---|---|---|
| Suzuki, Ichiro, BlueWave .. | .356 | 542 | 104 | 193 | 24 | 4 | 16 | 84 | 35 |
| Kataoka, Atsushi, Fighters | .315 | 416 | 60 | 131 | 20 | 3 | 15 | 51 | 3 |
| Hori, Koichi, Marines ......... | .312 | 465 | 70 | 145 | 28 | 3 | 16 | 68 | 8 |
| Suzuki, Ken, Lions............. | .302 | 354 | 47 | 107 | 17 | 1 | 21 | 60 | 1 |
| Akiyama, Koji, Hawks......... | .300 | 466 | 53 | 140 | 27 | 0 | 9 | 66 | 13 |
| Yoshinaga, Koichiro, Hawks | .295 | 390 | 59 | 115 | 21 | 2 | 20 | 72 | 1 |
| Rhodes, Tuffy, Buffaloes.... | .293 | 501 | 80 | 147 | 29 | 1 | 27 | 97 | 11 |
| Muramatsu, Akihito, Hawks | .293 | 406 | 56 | 119 | 14 | 9 | 0 | 38 | 58 |
| Matsui, Kazuo, Lions.......... | .283 | 473 | 51 | 134 | 22 | 5 | 1 | 29 | 50 |
| Mizuguchi, Eiji, Buffaloes... | .281 | 442 | 53 | 124 | 18 | 2 | 8 | 28 | 5 |
| Taguchi, So, BlueWave...... | .279 | 509 | 74 | 142 | 24 | 1 | 7 | 44 | 10 |
| Tanaka, Yukio, Fighters ..... | .277 | 513 | 73 | 142 | 29 | 3 | 22 | 82 | 3 |
| Neel, Troy, BlueWave........ | .274 | 430 | 77 | 118 | 24 | 0 | 32 | 111 | 1 |
| Nakamura, N., Buffaloes.... | .273 | 411 | 60 | 112 | 15 | 1 | 26 | 67 | 4 |
| Suzuki, Takahisa, Buffaloes | .268 | 426 | 45 | 114 | 21 | 1 | 9 | 50 | 3 |
| Jackson, Darrin, Lions........ | .266 | 489 | 42 | 130 | 21 | 3 | 19 | 64 | 10 |
| Hatsushiba, K., Marines ..... | .264 | 469 | 52 | 124 | 23 | 5 | 17 | 61 | 2 |
| Minamibuchi, T., Marines.... | .264 | 439 | 41 | 116 | 22 | 1 | 5 | 38 | 7 |
| Kaneko, Makoto, Fighters .. | .261 | 395 | 50 | 103 | 14 | 2 | 4 | 33 | 15 |
| Kiyohara, Kazuhiro, Lions .. | .257 | 487 | 67 | 125 | 30 | 0 | 31 | 84 | 0 |
| Hirose, Tetsuro, Fighters.... | .256 | 390 | 40 | 100 | 21 | 3 | 3 | 34 | 8 |
| Oshima, Koichi, BlueWave.. | .254 | 397 | 62 | 101 | 11 | 3 | 4 | 37 | 8 |
| Ide, Tetsuya, Fighters......... | .254 | 414 | 44 | 105 | 13 | 5 | 7 | 38 | 11 |
| Hamana, Chihiro, Hawks.... | .254 | 485 | 65 | 123 | 16 | 8 | 3 | 47 | 33 |
| Kakiuchi, Tetsuya, Lions .... | .253 | 387 | 57 | 98 | 19 | 3 | 28 | 57 | 16 |
| Brito, Bernardo, Fighters .... | .253 | 470 | 61 | 119 | 17 | 0 | 29 | 83 | 1 |
| Hirai, Mitsuchika, Marines .. | .249 | 357 | 38 | 89 | 16 | 2 | 5 | 33 | 4 |

(Other Foreign Players)

| | AVG | AB | R | H | 2B | 3B | HR | RBI | SB |
|---|---|---|---|---|---|---|---|---|---|
| Donnels, Chris, Buffaloes.. | .281 | 324 | 50 | 91 | 20 | 2 | 20 | 53 | 3 |
| Lydy, Scott, Hawks....... | .281 | 249 | 29 | 70 | 11 | 1 | 7 | 29 | 11 |
| Whitmore, Darrell, Marines | .266 | 229 | 27 | 61 | 9 | 0 | 12 | 29 | 12 |
| Chamberlain, Wes, Marines | .253 | 261 | 26 | 66 | 11 | 0 | 11 | 38 | 7 |
| Ducey, Rob, Fighters......... | .246 | 427 | 68 | 105 | 17 | 5 | 26 | 59 | 3 |
| Cooper, Scott, Lions..... | .243 | 276 | 27 | 67 | 13 | 0 | 7 | 27 | 1 |
| Jennings, Doug, BlueWave | .220 | 241 | 29 | 53 | 7 | 1 | 15 | 47 | 1 |
| Ready, Randy, Marines . . | .200 | 90 | 3 | 18 | 4 | 0 | 1 | 11 | 4 |
| Daugherty, Jack, Marines. | .119 | 42 | 1 | 5 | 2 | 0 | 0 | 4 | 0 |

### INDIVIDUAL PITCHING LEADERS
(Minimum 133 Innings)

| | W | L | ERA | G | SV | IP | H | BB | SO |
|---|---|---|---|---|---|---|---|---|---|
| Irabu, Hideki, Marines .......... | 12 | 6 | 2.40 | 23 | 0 | 157 | 108 | 59 | 167 |
| Hillman, Eric, Marines .......... | 14 | 9 | 2.40 | 29 | 0 | 213 | 179 | 46 | 119 |
| Watanabe, Hidekazu, Hawks.. | 9 | 5 | 2.54 | 21 | 0 | 145 | 141 | 36 | 99 |
| Nishizaki, Yukihiro, Fighters.. | 14 | 7 | 2.87 | 26 | 0 | 182 | 152 | 89 | 139 |
| Hoshino, N., BlueWave.......... | 13 | 5 | 3.05 | 22 | 0 | 145 | 137 | 38 | 85 |
| Noda, Koji, BlueWave ........... | 8 | 7 | 3.14 | 27 | 0 | 180 | 170 | 70 | 144 |
| Nishiguchi, Fumiya, Lions .... | 16 | 10 | 3.17 | 31 | 1 | 210 | 172 | 74 | 173 |
| Imazeki, Masaru, Fighters .... | 11 | 9 | 3.22 | 24 | 0 | 159 | 123 | 49 | 122 |
| Sakai, Hiroki, Buffaloes......... | 8 | 15 | 3.30 | 26 | 0 | 183 | 151 | 84 | 149 |
| Shintani, Hiroshi, Lions ........ | 11 | 5 | 3.41 | 30 | 2 | 145 | 134 | 56 | 121 |

(Other Foreign Players)

| | W | L | ERA | G | SV | IP | H | BB | SO |
|---|---|---|---|---|---|---|---|---|---|
| Fraser, Willie, BlueWave...... | 10 | 2 | 3.07 | 18 | 0 | 100 | 88 | 37 | 51 |
| Nunez, Jose, Hawks .............. | 6 | 9 | 3.13 | 42 | 16 | 104 | 117 | 28 | 79 |
| Gross, Kip, Fighters ............. | 17 | 9 | 3.62 | 28 | 0 | 194 | 201 | 53 | 79 |
| Aquino, Luis, Buffaloes......... | 11 | 9 | 4.04 | 25 | 0 | 156 | 158 | 55 | 58 |
| Bolton, Rod, Hawks .............. | 2 | 2 | 6.39 | 11 | 0 | 31 | 36 | 23 | 18 |

**Boldface** type indicates league leader

# WINTER
# LEAGUES

# Upstart Mexico Wins CWS Crown As Dominican Dream Team Falters

**By JOHN MANUEL**

In 1995, the "Dream Team" concept worked for Puerto Rico at the Caribbean World Series. A team that included major league stars Roberto Alomar, Carlos Baerga, Juan Gonzalez, Edgar Martinez, Ruben Sierra and Bernie Williams stormed to the CWS title, electrifying an entire nation.

But when the Dominican Republic tried the same concept in 1996, when the series shifted to Santo Domingo, the plan exploded in the team's face. To the dismay of a rabid national following, the Dominican squad never got untracked and finished 2-4, a badly beaten third in the four-nation competition.

Mexico's Culiacan Tomatogrowers emerged as the surprise champion, winning five of six games.

"The ugly ducklings are the belle of the ball," said manager Francisco Estrada, who was Mexico's catcher in 1986, the last time it won the Series. "No one gave us a chance. Everyone talked about the Dominican dream team and Puerto Rico, but we showed what a little heart can do."

All three titles for Mexico have been won by Culiacan, coming in 1976, 1986 and 1996.

"There's no explanation for that," Estrada said. "Let's just say I like our chances in 2006. Hopefully we'll have some titles between now and then."

A group of Dominican stars that included pitchers Juan Guzman (Blue Jays), Pedro Martinez (Expos), Jose Mesa (Indians) and Mel Rojas (Expos), first baseman Julio Franco (Indians) and outfielder Raul Mondesi (Dodgers) could

**Terry Francona**

not overcome a lack of chemistry. Or the Mexicans.

Terry Francona had managed the Dominican title, earning the right to manage that nation's CWS entry. But he had a difficult time incorporating 13 new players. The Dominicans lost twice to Culiacan: 7-6 in the opening round and 2-1 in the fourth, killing their chances.

"No excuses. We just got outplayed," Francona said. "There was a lot of pressure on this team. The fans expected nothing less than a title, and that probably had some bearing on the way we performed, especially at the outset."

The Tomatogrowers lost only once, a second-round setback against Arecibo of Puerto Rico. But in Round Five of the double round-robin series, Culiacan returned the favor, winning 9-6. The Mexicans then defeated Magallanes of Venezuela 5-4 to clinch the championship.

Puerto Rico manager Pat Kelly summed up the series, saying, "You can have the stars, but it's the guys with the heart who usually come out on top."

## 1996 CARIBBEAN WORLD SERIES

Santo Domingo, Dominican Republic
Feb. 3-8, 1996

| ROUND ROBIN STANDINGS | W | L | PCT. | GB |
|---|---|---|---|---|
| Mexico (Culiacan) | 5 | 1 | .833 | — |
| Puerto Rico (Arecibo) | 4 | 2 | .667 | 1 |
| Domincan Republic (Aguilas) | 2 | 4 | .333 | 3 |
| Venezuela (Magallanes) | 1 | 5 | .167 | 4 |

### INDIVIDUAL BATTING LEADERS
(Minimum 16 Plate Appearances)

| | AVG | AB | R | H | 2B | 3B | HR | RBI |
|---|---|---|---|---|---|---|---|---|
| Tony Barron, PR | .500 | 24 | 6 | 12 | 5 | 2 | 0 | 4 |
| Julio Franco, DR | .471 | 17 | 3 | 8 | 3 | 0 | 0 | 1 |
| Leo Gomez, PR | .458 | 24 | 4 | 11 | 2 | 0 | 3 | 9 |
| Bernie Williams, PR | .400 | 20 | 6 | 8 | 3 | 0 | 0 | 4 |
| Darrel Brinkley, Mexico | .350 | 20 | 5 | 7 | 0 | 0 | 0 | 5 |
| Ivan Rodriguez, PR | .333 | 27 | 4 | 9 | 1 | 1 | 0 | 3 |
| Luis Polonia, DR | .333 | 24 | 3 | 8 | 3 | 0 | 0 | 1 |
| Jose Vizcaino, DR | .318 | 22 | 1 | 7 | 0 | 0 | 0 | 1 |
| Tony Aguilera, Mexico | .316 | 19 | 5 | 6 | 3 | 0 | 1 | 3 |
| Rey Sanchez, PR | .313 | 16 | 1 | 5 | 0 | 0 | 0 | 1 |

### INDIVIDUAL PITCHING LEADERS
(Minimum 5 Innings)

| | W | L | ERA | G | SV | IP | H | BB | SO |
|---|---|---|---|---|---|---|---|---|---|
| Pedro Martinez, DR | 1 | 0 | 0.00 | 1 | 0 | 8 | 2 | 2 | 8 |
| Luis Mendez, Mexico | 0 | 0 | 0.00 | 2 | 0 | 7 | 6 | 4 | 7 |
| Robinson Checo, DR | 1 | 0 | 0.00 | 1 | 0 | 6 | 3 | 1 | 3 |
| Jose Melendez, PR | 1 | 0 | 1.29 | 1 | 0 | 7 | 2 | 0 | 8 |
| Juan Guzman, DR | 0 | 0 | 1.50 | 1 | 0 | 6 | 3 | 2 | 7 |
| Felipe Murillo, Mexico | 2 | 0 | 1.50 | 4 | 0 | 6 | 3 | 0 | 5 |
| Juan Palafox, Mexico | 1 | 0 | 1.50 | 1 | 0 | 6 | 1 | 1 | 3 |
| Kris Ralston, PR | 1 | 0 | 1.50 | 1 | 0 | 6 | 5 | 5 | 5 |
| Robert Toth, PR | 2 | 0 | 2.40 | 2 | 0 | 15 | 16 | 2 | 9 |
| Jose Lopez, Mexico | 0 | 0 | 2.70 | 3 | 1 | 7 | 3 | 6 | 5 |

**Most Valuable Player—Darrel Brinkley, Mexico.**

Mexico's roster included only two major leaguers—shortstop Benji Gil (Rangers) and righthander Esteban Loaiza (Pirates). The heroes of the team were minor leaguers and a player who had never played professionally in the U.S., series MVP Darrel Brinkley.

A 26-year-old outfielder, Brinkley hit .350 in the series, scoring five runs and knocking in five more. He led the Mexican Pacific League with 29 steals and hit .342 in the regular season while playing for Mexicali. He was picked up by

**Darrel Brinkley**

Culiacan for the CWS.

Brinkley graduated from Connecticut's Sacred Heart University in 1991 but never got a shot with a major league organization. He played in Holland in 1991-92, in Italy in 1993, in Canada with the independent Northern League's Winnipeg Goldeyes in 1994, and with Campeche of the Mexican League in the summer of 1995. He finally earned a chance with the Padres, who signed him just before the CWS.

His play at the series typified that of his team, traditional also-rans at the CWS.

"We were like gutter rats," Mexican DH Matt Stark said. "As usual, we didn't get much respect, but we played as a team and scrapped for everything we got. We weren't all-stars like the Dominicans."

## Strawberry, Gooden Suit Up

Winter baseball in the traditional Latin America strongholds experienced a dip in talent from 1995, a season fortified by major leaguers looking for a place to play during the strike.

Two of the more unlikely players to don winter league uniforms were former New York Mets teammates Darryl Strawberry and Dwight Gooden, who became reunited with the crosstown Yankees in 1996.

The two fallen stars were sent to Puerto Rico by the Yankees to get in some much-needed playing time, a result of off-field problems and suspensions. Strawberry had played sparingly with the Yankees in 1995 while Gooden did not play at all. As it turned out, neither player stuck around Puerto Rico for long.

Strawberry decided to jump ship when his $1.8 million option for the 1996 season was not picked up by the Yankees, though he later was signed as a free agent by the Yankees after a stint in the Northern League. He hit six homers in the seven games he played in Puerto Rico.

Gooden, who had only recently signed a contract with the Yankees before joining San Juan, was late arriving because he had to fulfill a court-ordered community service obligation in New York, his penalty for testing positive for drug use that led to a 16-month suspension from the game. He failed to win any of three starts, and was promptly called home by Yankees owner George Steinbrenner.

## The Cuban Factor

The 1995-96 off-season featured a wave of defections from Cuba's national team, which impacted the Domini-

can League. In order to be signed on the open market by major league clubs and not be subject to the draft, the Cuban players were required to take up residency in a foreign country and declare asylum.

At the behest of Miami-based agent Joe Cubas, it was decided that the players would be temporarily relocated in the Dominican Republic, where they would showcase their talent for scouts of major league teams lining up for their services.

The biggest contract, and the largest ever awarded an international free agent, was signed by righthander Livan Hernandez, 20, who was signed by the Florida Marlins to a four-year major league contract that included a $2.5 million bonus. Hernandez, a former Cuban junior star, went 1-1 with a 4.15 ERA for Escogido of the Dominican League.

Righthander Osvaldo Fernandez, 29, went 4-3 with a 2.30 ERA for Licey and shortly thereafter inked a contract with San Francisco that provided for a $1.3 million bonus and a three-year major league contract.

| CARIBBEAN WORLD SERIES | | |
|---|---|---|
| **Last 25 Years** | | |
| Years | Site | Champion |
| 1971-72 | Santo Domingo, D.R. | Ponce (Puerto Rico) |
| 1972-73 | Caracas, Venez. | Licey (Dominican Republic) |
| 1973-74 | Hermosillo, Mexico | Caguas (Puerto Rico) |
| 1974-75 | San Juan, P.R. | Bayamon (Puerto Rico) |
| 1975-76 | Santo Domingo, D.R. | Hermosillo (Mexico) |
| 1976-77 | Caracas, Venez. | Licey (Dominican Republic) |
| 1977-78 | Mazatlan, Mexico | Mayaguez (Puerto Rico) |
| 1978-79 | San Juan, P.R. | Magallanes (Venezuela) |
| 1979-80 | Santo Domingo, D.R. | Licey (Dominican Republic) |
| 1980-81 | No Series | |
| 1981-82 | Hermosillo, Mexico | Caracas (Venezuela) |
| 1982-83 | Caracas, Venez. | Arecibo (Puerto Rico) |
| 1983-84 | San Juan, P.R. | Zulia (Venezuela) |
| 1984-85 | Mazatlan, Mexico | Licey (Dominican Republic) |
| 1985-86 | Maracaibo, Venez. | Mexicali (Mexico) |
| 1986-87 | Hermosillo, Mexico | Caguas (Puerto Rico) |
| 1987-88 | Santo Domingo, D.R. | Escogido (Dominican Republic) |
| 1988-89 | Mazatlan, Mexico | Zulia (Venezuela) |
| 1989-90 | Miami | Escogido (Dominican Republic) |
| 1990-91 | Miami | Licey (Dominican Republic) |
| 1991-92 | Hermosillo, Mexico | Mayaguez (Puerto Rico) |
| 1992-93 | Mazatlan, Mexico | Santurce (Puerto Rico) |
| 1993-94 | Puerto La Cruz, Venez. | Licey (Dominican Republic) |
| 1994-95 | San Juan, P.R. | San Juan (Puerto Rico) |
| 1995-96 | Santo Domingo, D.R. | Culiacan (Mexico) |

# 1995-96 WINTER ALL-STAR TEAM
### Selected by Baseball America

| Player, Club (League) | Organiz. | PCT | AB | R | H | 2B | 3B | HR | RBI | SB |
|---|---|---|---|---|---|---|---|---|---|---|
| C Mike Matheny, Arecibo, (Puerto Rico) | Brewers | .264 | 208 | 29 | 55 | 9 | 0 | 6 | 30 | 2 |
| 1B Dmitri Young, Hermosillo (Mexico) | Cardinals | .351 | 205 | 42 | 72 | 17 | 1 | 8 | 45 | 7 |
| 2B Roberto Alomar, San Juan-Arecibo (Puerto Rico) | Orioles | .326 | 196 | 34 | 64 | 15 | 2 | 5 | 26 | 11 |
| 3B Domingo Cedeno, Azucareros-Aguilas (D.R.) | Blue Jays | .400 | 130 | 18 | 52 | 6 | 4 | 1 | 13 | 6 |
| SS Rey Ordonez, Santurce (Puerto Rico) | Mets | .348 | 158 | 12 | 55 | 6 | 0 | 0 | 21 | 1 |
| OF Darrel Brinkley, Mexicali-Culiacan (Mexico) | Padres | .341 | 267 | 58 | 91 | 20 | 1 | 8 | 25 | 37 |
| OF Doug Glanville, Mayaguez (Puerto Rico) | Cubs | .327 | 263 | 42 | 86 | 12 | 2 | 4 | 18 | 18 |
| OF Sherman Obando, Aguilas (Dom. Republic) | Expos | .376 | 221 | 39 | 83 | 21 | 1 | 11 | 47 | 6 |
| DH Eduardo Jiminez, Mexicali-Culiacan (Mexico) | None | .308 | 254 | 55 | 78 | 22 | 0 | 24 | 64 | 3 |

**Domingo Cedeno**

| | | W | L | ERA | G | SV | IP | H | BB | SO |
|---|---|---|---|---|---|---|---|---|---|---|
| P Jose Alberro, Arecibo (Puerto Rico) | Rangers | 3 | 2 | 1.66 | 39 | 20 | 54 | 38 | 20 | 39 |
| P Alan Benes, Sun Cities (Arizona) | Cardinals | 6 | 1 | 1.78 | 10 | 0 | 56 | 40 | 16 | 62 |
| P Mario Brito, Escogido (Domincan Republic) | Marlins | 1 | 0 | 0.51 | 31 | 21 | 35 | 20 | 9 | 39 |
| P Omar Daal, Caracas (Venezuela) | Expos | 10 | 2 | 1.68 | 15 | 0 | 102 | 81 | 31 | 80 |
| P Bronswell Patrick, Santurce (Puerto Rico) | Astros | 7 | 0 | 1.68 | 14 | 0 | 96 | 73 | 33 | 38 |

Statistics include regular-season, playoff and Caribbean World Series games

**Omar Daal**

# DOMINICAN LEAGUE

Unfulfilled expectations plagued the Dominican Winter League in post-season play in 1995-96.

Not only did the Dominican Dream Team stumble badly at the Caribbean World Series, going only 2-4 on home soil in Santo Domingo, but Escogido, which ran away with the regular-season title and set a league record for victories, also fell flat on its face.

Escogido won 34 games and played at a record .708 clip during the season but collapsed in the playoffs, winning five of 18 games in the four-team, round-robin to finish dead last.

That left the door open for Aguilas to win its 12th Dominican League championship. Aguilas beat Estrellas 4-1 in a best-of-5 series and represented the Dominican Republic in the Caribbean Series, though its roster was bolstered by the addition of native major leaguers like Julio Franco (Indians), Juan Guzman (Blue Jays), Pedro Martinez (Expos), Jose Mesa (Indians), Raul Mondesi (Dodgers) and Carlos Perez (Expos).

**Sherman Obando**

Aguilas got a strong season-long performance from outfielder Sherman Obando (Expos), who led the league in home runs (7) and RBIs·(31) and missed winning the league's second Triple Crown by finishing second in hitting (.370). He continued his hot hitting in the round-robin, hitting .362 with 10 RBIs helping Aguilas tie Estrellas with 11-7 records. Obando then hit .500 with two homers and six RBIs as Aguilas subdued Estrellas in the final.

Outfielder Luis Polonia (Braves), who played only five regular-season games for Aguilas, was a unanimous choice as MVP of the final. He had 14 hits, seven runs and a .560 average in the five-game series.

Shortstop Manny Alexander (Orioles), who hit only .217 in the regular season, shone in the playoffs for Estrellas, hitting .404 in the round-robin and .500 in the final.

**Mario Brito**

Escogido stormed to the league's best record behind righthanders Amaury Telemaco (Cubs), the league ERA leader at 1.31, and Mario Brito, who allowed one earned run in 28 innings and set a league record with 19 saves.

Third baseman Domingo Cedeno (Blue Jays) of Azucareros led the league with a .419 average. He became only the fourth player in Dominican history to hit .400, joining Ralph Garr (.457 in 1970-71), Angel Gonzalez (.434 in 1989-90) and Pedro Hernandez (.408 in 1981-82). On his way to that mark, Cedeno broke a 44-year-old record Dominican record held by

former Negro Leagues star Alonzo Perry by hitting in 30 straight games, three more than Perry.

## STANDINGS

| REGULAR SEASON | W | L | PCT | GB |
|---|---|---|---|---|
| Escogido | 34 | 14 | .708 | — |
| Aguilas | 26 | 21 | .553 | 7 ½ |
| Licey | 23 | 24 | .489 | 10 ½ |
| Estrellas | 19 | 29 | .396 | 15 |
| Azucareros | 17 | 31 | .354 | 17 |

| PLAYOFFS | W | L | PCT | GB |
|---|---|---|---|---|
| Estrellas | 11 | 7 | .611 | — |
| Aguilas | 11 | 7 | .611 | — |
| Licey | 9 | 9 | .500 | 2 |
| Escogido | 5 | 13 | .278 | 6 |

**Championship Series:** Aguilas defeated Estrellas, 4-1, in best-of-7 final.

## INDIVIDUAL BATTING LEADERS
(Minimum 96 Plate Appearances)

| | AVG | AB | R | H | 2B | 3B | HR | RBI | SB |
|---|---|---|---|---|---|---|---|---|---|
| Cedeno, Domingo, Azucareros | .419 | 117 | 15 | 49 | 5 | **4** | 1 | 13 | 6 |
| Obando, Sherman, Aguilas | .370 | 138 | 22 | 51 | 10 | 1 | **7** | **31** | 5 |
| Martinez, Manny, Licey | .353 | 139 | 23 | 49 | 9 | 3 | 2 | 19 | **13** |
| Johnson, Mark, Escogido | .345 | 84 | 12 | 29 | 1 | 0 | 2 | 9 | 3 |
| Batista, Tony, Aguilas | .336 | 122 | 16 | 41 | 10 | 0 | 4 | 20 | 1 |
| Ochoa, Alex, Licey | .333 | 174 | 20 | **58** | 9 | 1 | 2 | 25 | 0 |
| Espinosa, Ramon, Escogido | .321 | 134 | 14 | 43 | 11 | 1 | 1 | 12 | 5 |
| Pemberton, Rudy, Escogido | .315 | 92 | 12 | 29 | 4 | **4** | 2 | 14 | 1 |
| Bruno, Julio, Aguilas | .312 | 141 | 18 | 44 | 4 | 1 | 1 | 19 | 4 |
| Martin, Norberto, Estrellas | .302 | 139 | 20 | 42 | 5 | 1 | 1 | 15 | 5 |
| Fermin, Felix, Aguilas | .300 | 90 | 8 | 27 | 4 | 0 | 0 | 7 | 1 |
| Mercedes, Luis, Estrellas | .298 | 151 | **27** | 45 | 4 | 3 | 0 | 13 | 3 |
| Williams, Gerald, Estrellas | .297 | 158 | 24 | 47 | **14** | 2 | 3 | 20 | 9 |
| Encarnacion, Angelo, Esc | .297 | 91 | 18 | 27 | 7 | 1 | 1 | 17 | 1 |
| Jose, Felix, Licey | .295 | 129 | 16 | 38 | 5 | 1 | 2 | 16 | 2 |
| Leiper, Tim, Aguilas | .283 | 113 | 21 | 32 | 10 | 0 | 0 | 8 | 0 |
| Perez, Neifi, Escogido | .281 | 160 | 18 | 45 | 6 | 3 | 1 | 19 | 3 |
| Cruz, Fausto, Escogido | .280 | 93 | 14 | 26 | 3 | 1 | 0 | 5 | 0 |
| Gonzalez, Denny, Estrellas | .278 | 97 | 12 | 27 | 4 | 1 | 0 | 22 | 2 |
| Williams, Reggie, Azu | .277 | 83 | 8 | 23 | 4 | 2 | 1 | 8 | 6 |
| Frazier, Lou, Escogido | .274 | 113 | 17 | 31 | 6 | 2 | 1 | 10 | 9 |
| Cabrera, Francisco, Est | .273 | 99 | 16 | 27 | 3 | 0 | 4 | 19 | 0 |
| Pozo, Arquimedes, Escogido | .272 | 143 | 16 | 39 | 8 | 0 | 2 | 26 | 3 |
| Tavarez, Jesus, Escogido | .269 | 119 | 23 | 32 | 6 | 2 | 0 | 12 | 7 |
| Bell, Juan, Licey | .266 | 117 | 23 | 31 | 3 | 1 | 3 | 18 | 0 |
| Floyd, Cliff, Estrellas | .265 | 148 | 19 | 39 | 3 | 1 | 3 | 23 | 5 |
| Robertson, Mike, Aguilas | .262 | 168 | 25 | 44 | 10 | 0 | 4 | 17 | 1 |
| Matos, Francisco, Licey | .256 | 90 | 9 | 23 | 2 | 0 | 0 | 8 | 1 |
| Rodriguez, Henry, Licey | .255 | 141 | 14 | 36 | 7 | 2 | 3 | 22 | 0 |
| Carvajal, Jovino, Azucareros | .252 | 155 | 19 | 39 | 2 | 0 | 1 | 12 | 4 |
| Hollandsworth, Todd, Azu | .245 | 151 | 13 | 37 | 8 | 1 | 0 | 11 | 5 |
| Andrews, Shane, Estrellas | .240 | 146 | 18 | 35 | 4 | 1 | 6 | 23 | 2 |
| Herrera, Jose, Escogido | .237 | 97 | 12 | 23 | 3 | 0 | 0 | 13 | 3 |

## INDIVIDUAL PITCHING LEADERS
(Minimum 32 Innings)

| | W | L | ERA | G | SV | IP | H | BB | SO |
|---|---|---|---|---|---|---|---|---|---|
| #Brito, Mario, Escogido | 1 | 0 | 0.32 | 25 | **19** | 28 | 17 | 7 | 34 |
| Telemaco, Amaury, Escogido | 3 | 1 | **1.31** | 8 | 0 | 41 | 31 | 10 | 33 |
| Wilson, Gary, Escogido | 4 | 2 | 1.77 | 8 | 0 | 46 | 48 | 8 | 17 |
| Perez, Carlos, Licey | 4 | 1 | 1.88 | 11 | 0 | 72 | 68 | 15 | **74** |
| Fernandez, Osvaldo, Licey | 4 | 3 | 2.30 | 11 | 1 | 55 | 43 | 10 | 52 |
| Heredia, Julian, Estrellas | 4 | 2 | 2.30 | 26 | 6 | 47 | 45 | 16 | 31 |
| Morel, Ramon, Escogido | **5** | 1 | 2.33 | 10 | 0 | 46 | 45 | 6 | 29 |
| Hernandez, Fernando, Aguilas | 4 | 1 | 2.38 | 12 | 0 | 45 | 26 | 33 | 36 |
| Martinez, Jose, Aguilas | 4 | 3 | 2.72 | 9 | 0 | 53 | 49 | 14 | 31 |
| De la Rosa, Francisco, Est | 1 | 0 | 2.81 | 8 | 0 | 32 | 33 | 12 | 22 |
| Baxter, Bob, Estrellas | 3 | 3 | 2.89 | 14 | 0 | 44 | 42 | 15 | 12 |
| Heredia, Wilson, Azucareros | 2 | 2 | 2.93 | 12 | 0 | 68 | 56 | 41 | 42 |
| Linton, Doug, Escogido | 1 | 3 | 3.06 | 11 | 0 | 50 | 44 | 10 | 42 |
| Alfonseca, Antonio, Azu | 3 | 3 | 3.13 | 12 | 0 | **75** | 59 | 29 | 45 |
| Galvez, Balvino, Licey | 2 | 3 | 3.17 | 12 | 0 | 54 | 50 | 14 | 28 |
| Garcia, Apolinar, Aguilas | 3 | 3 | 3.39 | 12 | 0 | 72 | 69 | 18 | 48 |
| O'Donoghue, John, Azu | 0 | 2 | 3.41 | 13 | 0 | 37 | 34 | 23 | 23 |
| Eischen, Joey, Azucareros | 2 | 5 | 3.45 | 16 | 0 | 44 | 43 | 22 | 30 |
| Carrasco, Hector, Estrellas | 3 | 3 | 3.45 | 12 | 0 | 47 | 48 | 39 | 27 |
| Torres, Salomon, Licey | 4 | 1 | 4.00 | 13 | 0 | 36 | 27 | 19 | 28 |

Statistics in **boldface** indicate league leader.
#Indicates league leader in category other than batting/pitching.

# MEXICAN PACIFIC LEAGUE

The Culiacan Tomatogrowers were one of the most unlikely success stories of the 1995-96 winter league season.

Culiacan eased to a 29-27 record during the regular season, good for a fourth-place tie in the Mexican Pacific League standings. The Tomatogrowers then fell behind 3-0 in their best-of-7 quarter-final playoff series against Mexicali, only to enact the most miraculous turnaround in league history.

They rallied to beat Mexicali four games in a row to become the first team in 50 years to recover from a 3-0 deficit. From there, fate was on their side. The Tomatogrowers proceeded to beat Navojoa in six games and Mazatlan in five to capture their first MPL title since 1985 and sixth overall.

The rampaging Tomatogrowers didn't stop there. Despite being prohibitive underdogs, they won the Caribbean World Series to become the first Mexican team in 10 years to win the four-nation competition.

The Tomatogrowers won with pitching, sporting a league-best 2.55 ERA during the regular season. Luis Mendez was the club's top starter, going 5-4 with a 2.35 ERA in the regular season and 2-0 with a 1.80 ERA in post-season play, during which he allowed only eight hits in 25 innings.

For the final series against Mazatlan, the Tomatogrowers were permitted to add Mexicali slugger Eduardo Jimenez, the league leader in homers and RBIs. He hit three homers in five games.

**Dmitri Young**

Jimenez hit 18 homers and had 49 RBIs and missed winning the league's Triple Crown by finishing fourth in batting average, at .311. He also led the league in total bases (132), doubles (19) and slugging percentage (.695).

Outfielder Darrel Brinkley set the table for Jimenez. He hit .342, second in the league, and finished first in runs (46), hits (76) and stolen bases (29).

Hermosillo first baseman Dmitri Young (Cardinals) won the batting title with a .356 average, becoming the 12th American in 13 seasons to win Mexico's winter silver bat.

Hermosillo finished first in the regular season, but the two-time defending champions failed twice in the playoffs. The Orangegrowers were upset in seven games by sixth-place Navojoa, but by being the team with the best record to lose in the first round they advanced to the next round. They lost again, in six games to Mazatlan.

The Orangegrowers featured fireballer Antonio Osuna (Dodgers), the league's top reliever. Osuna appeared in 17 games during the regular season, picking up 16 saves and posting a 0.00 ERA. He was a major contributor, however, to his team's demise in the playoffs as he went 0-2 with a 10.19 ERA in five appearances.

## STANDINGS

| REGULAR SEASON | W | L | PCT | GB |
|---|---|---|---|---|
| Hermosillo Orangegrowers | 34 | 24 | .586 | — |
| Los Mochis Sugarcane Growers | 33 | 25 | .569 | 1 |
| Mazatlan Deer | 31 | 27 | .534 | 3 |
| Mexicali Eagles | 29 | 27 | .518 | 4 |
| Culiacan Tomatogrowers | 29 | 27 | .518 | 4 |
| Navojoa Mayos | 27 | 29 | .482 | 6 |
| Guasave Cottoneers | 23 | 35 | .397 | 11 |
| Obregon Yaquis | 22 | 34 | .393 | 11 |

**PLAYOFFS—Quarterfinals:** Culiacan defeated Mexicali 4-3; Mazatlan defeated Los Mochis, 4-3; Navojoa defeated Hermosillo, 4-3, in best-of-7-series. **Semifinals:** Culiacan defeated Navojoa, 4-2; Mazatlan defeated Hermosillo, 4-2, in best-of-7 series. **Finals:** Culiacan defeated Mazatlan 4-1, in best-of-7 series.

### INDIVIDUAL BATTING LEADERS
(Minimum 116 Plate Appearances)

| | AVG | AB | R | H | 2B | 3B | HR | RBI | SB |
|---|---|---|---|---|---|---|---|---|---|
| Young, Dmitri, Hermosillo | .356 | 163 | 29 | 58 | 15 | 1 | 5 | 34 | 5 |
| Brinkley, Darrel, Mexicali | .342 | 222 | 46 | 76 | 17 | 1 | 6 | 20 | 29 |
| Garcia, Cornelio, Hermosillo | .315 | 219 | 38 | 69 | 7 | 2 | 1 | 16 | 13 |
| Jimenez, Eduardo, Mexicali | .311 | 190 | 40 | 59 | 19 | 0 | 18 | 49 | 2 |
| Stairs, Matt, Navojoa | .311 | 132 | 24 | 41 | 6 | 0 | 6 | 27 | 5 |
| Myers, Roderick, Los Mochis | .309 | 217 | 43 | 67 | 10 | 1 | 9 | 28 | 16 |
| Magallanes, Ever, Culiacan | .299 | 177 | 24 | 53 | 7 | 1 | 1 | 19 | 6 |
| Selby, Bill, Navojoa | .295 | 176 | 25 | 52 | 8 | 0 | 9 | 28 | 1 |
| Carrillo, Matias, Mexicali | .293 | 205 | 36 | 60 | 10 | 1 | 8 | 39 | 1 |
| Arredondo, Luis, Hermosillo | .291 | 158 | 13 | 46 | 4 | 2 | 1 | 15 | 11 |
| Horn, Sam, Mazatlan | .291 | 110 | 19 | 32 | 9 | 0 | 4 | 17 | 3 |
| Hinzo, Tommy, Mazatlan | .283 | 127 | 17 | 36 | 4 | 1 | 2 | 17 | 4 |
| Gil, Benji, Culiacan | .281 | 114 | 17 | 32 | 3 | 0 | 3 | 15 | 7 |
| Robles, Oscar, Guasave | .280 | 157 | 21 | 44 | 0 | 1 | 0 | 7 | 8 |
| Fernandez, Daniel, Mazatlan | .278 | 205 | 38 | 57 | 11 | 0 | 5 | 14 | 13 |
| Wood, Ted, Obregon | .278 | 162 | 22 | 45 | 11 | 0 | 2 | 18 | 0 |
| Aguilera, Tony, Navojoa | .276 | 210 | 33 | 58 | 13 | 0 | 8 | 21 | 1 |
| Flores, Miguel, Hermosillo | .275 | 211 | 29 | 58 | 12 | 0 | 0 | 30 | 14 |
| Verdugo, Vicente, Mexicali | .273 | 194 | 14 | 53 | 6 | 0 | 3 | 18 | 4 |
| Sherman, Darrell, Culiacan | .272 | 206 | 38 | 56 | 4 | 1 | 1 | 11 | 21 |
| Stark, Matt, Culiacan | .272 | 114 | 20 | 31 | 6 | 0 | 6 | 24 | 0 |
| Estrada, Hector, Los Mochis | .270 | 174 | 18 | 47 | 9 | 0 | 6 | 25 | 1 |
| Romero, Marco, Mexicali | .265 | 185 | 24 | 49 | 9 | 0 | 7 | 29 | 2 |
| O'Halloran, Greg, Guasave | .263 | 190 | 17 | 50 | 5 | 1 | 3 | 25 | 0 |
| Vizcarra, Roberto, Obregon | .263 | 198 | 31 | 52 | 12 | 1 | 2 | 18 | 9 |
| Telles, Alonso, Guasave | .255 | 216 | 17 | 55 | 9 | 2 | 2 | 25 | 2 |
| Cameron, Mike, Los Mochis | .254 | 224 | 34 | 57 | 11 | 2 | 7 | 28 | 24 |
| Renteria, Rich, Guasave | .254 | 134 | 12 | 34 | 3 | 0 | 1 | 15 | 1 |
| Montalvo, Ivan, LM | .252 | 127 | 13 | 32 | 6 | 0 | 2 | 15 | 2 |
| Diaz, Remigio, Navojoa | .250 | 136 | 14 | 34 | 4 | 0 | 0 | 12 | 2 |
| Ramirez, Enrique, Guasave | .249 | 185 | 17 | 46 | 6 | 0 | 0 | 17 | 1 |
| Felix, Lauro, Los Mochis | .249 | 177 | 31 | 44 | 9 | 4 | 4 | 22 | 7 |
| Rojas, Homer, Navojoa | .248 | 141 | 13 | 35 | 6 | 0 | 2 | 20 | 3 |
| Gainey, Ty, Los Mochis | .246 | 195 | 29 | 48 | 11 | 1 | 14 | 49 | 2 |
| Mendez, Roberto, LM | .246 | 134 | 20 | 33 | 6 | 1 | 4 | 19 | 2 |
| Phillips, J.R., Culiacan | .243 | 136 | 13 | 33 | 7 | 0 | 5 | 21 | 0 |
| McGuire, Ryan, Navojoa | .241 | 133 | 15 | 32 | 7 | 0 | 0 | 12 | 2 |
| Bradshaw, Terry, Hermosillo | .240 | 196 | 34 | 47 | 5 | 2 | 1 | 22 | 16 |

### INDIVIDUAL PITCHING LEADERS
(Minimum 39 Innings)

| | W | L | ERA | G | SV | IP | H | BB | SO |
|---|---|---|---|---|---|---|---|---|---|
| #Osuna, Antonio, Hermosillo | 0 | 1 | 0.00 | 17 | 16 | 19 | 10 | 5 | 26 |
| Hernandez, Jose, Culiacan | 2 | 1 | 1.25 | 24 | 3 | 43 | 37 | 18 | 16 |
| Palafox, Juan, Mazatlan | 7 | 3 | 1.29 | 14 | 1 | 98 | 82 | 30 | 28 |
| Barraza, Ernesto, Mexicali | 3 | 1 | 1.45 | 6 | 0 | 43 | 23 | 28 | 25 |
| Quiroz, Aaron, Navojoa | 7 | 0 | 1.81 | 11 | 0 | 60 | 49 | 30 | 35 |
| Elvira, Narciso, Hermosillo | 5 | 1 | 1.92 | 11 | 0 | 70 | 55 | 23 | 56 |
| Sierra, Abel, Culiacan | 4 | 2 | 1.98 | 15 | 0 | 59 | 44 | 21 | 31 |
| Flores, Ignacio, Navojoa | 1 | 2 | 1.98 | 23 | 1 | 41 | 29 | 22 | 39 |
| Lopez, Emigdio, Los Mochis | 7 | 2 | 2.01 | 12 | 0 | 85 | 63 | 25 | 40 |
| Heredia, Hector, Navojoa | 2 | 3 | 2.08 | 9 | 0 | 61 | 54 | 14 | 35 |
| Sanchez, Hector, Guasave | 1 | 0 | 2.23 | 18 | 0 | 40 | 39 | 11 | 15 |
| Diaz, Rafel, Los Mochis | 5 | 1 | 2.30 | 13 | 1 | 78 | 57 | 51 | 59 |
| Soto, Fernando, Obregon | 4 | 0 | 2.34 | 27 | 0 | 42 | 42 | 13 | 20 |
| Mendez, Luis, Culiacan | 5 | 4 | 2.35 | 14 | 0 | 50 | 52 | 25 | 42 |
| Solis, Ricardo, Guasave | 5 | 3 | 2.47 | 12 | 0 | 77 | 64 | 21 | 33 |
| Munoz, Miguel, Culiacan | 4 | 5 | 2.55 | 11 | 0 | 67 | 62 | 15 | 24 |
| Osuna, Roberto, Herm. | 2 | 5 | 2.57 | 26 | 0 | 42 | 32 | 20 | 27 |
| Couoh, Enrique, Mexicali | 4 | 2 | 2.69 | 13 | 2 | 77 | 46 | 32 | 73 |
| Martinez, Cesar, Navojoa | 1 | 1 | 2.75 | 25 | 0 | 39 | 30 | 24 | 31 |
| Moreno, Angel, Hermosillo | 7 | 1 | 2.76 | 12 | 0 | 75 | 66 | 22 | 29 |
| Acosta, Aaron, Mazatlan | 4 | 5 | 2.95 | 13 | 0 | 73 | 66 | 32 | 44 |

| | | | | | | | | | |
|---|---|---|---|---|---|---|---|---|---|
| Higuera, Ted, Los Mochis | 3 | 3 | 2.97 | 10 | 0 | 61 | 49 | 26 | 40 |
| Villegas, Jose, Los Mochis | 4 | 1 | 3.02 | 25 | 0 | 42 | 31 | 21 | 19 |
| Purata, Julio, Guasave | 3 | 2 | 3.09 | 9 | 0 | 58 | 42 | 28 | 45 |
| Rios, Jesus, Guasave | 2 | 8 | 3.10 | 12 | 0 | 73 | 73 | 35 | 47 |
| Ruiz, Cecilio, Obregon | 2 | 3 | 3.10 | 13 | 0 | 70 | 60 | 23 | 26 |
| Orozco, Jaime, Obregon | 1 | 4 | 3.20 | 11 | 0 | 45 | 43 | 18 | 26 |
| Moreno, Jesus, Culiacan | 3 | 3 | 3.36 | 12 | 0 | 59 | 51 | 31 | 31 |
| Garibay, Daniel, Hermosillo | 5 | 5 | 3.38 | 13 | 0 | 59 | 63 | 27 | 30 |
| Esquer, Mercedes, Obregon | 2 | 2 | 3.41 | 12 | 0 | 63 | 65 | 24 | 36 |
| Jimenez, Isaac, Mexicali | 2 | 5 | 3.43 | 18 | 0 | 58 | 57 | 27 | 34 |
| Cuervo, Bernardo, Obregon | 2 | 2 | 3.59 | 22 | 1 | 43 | 36 | 17 | 23 |
| Pina, Rafael, Mexicali | 5 | 2 | 3.60 | 13 | 0 | 55 | 56 | 34 | 50 |
| Brosnan, Jason, Herm. | 4 | 1 | 3.80 | 15 | 1 | 43 | 40 | 20 | 36 |
| Renteria, Hilario, Guasave | 0 | 2 | 3.91 | 16 | 1 | 48 | 42 | 21 | 30 |

# PUERTO RICAN LEAGUE

Darryl Strawberry and Dwight Gooden stole the headlines with brief, early-season appearances, and native son and major league all-star Roberto Alomar garnered most of the attention down the stretch by staging a furious rally to win the batting title.

But in the end, the team with the fewest stars on its roster prevailed as the 1995-96 Puerto Rican League champion.

The Arecibo Wolves, perennial league also-rans, defeated Mayaguez 5-3 in the league's best-of-9 championship series to advance to the Caribbean World Series for only the second time in club history.

Arecibo relied on the arms of Angel Miranda (Brewers), who tied for the league lead in victories with six, and reliever Jose Alberro (Rangers), who tied for the lead with 13 saves. The Wolves got a late-season boost from outfielder Bernie Williams (Yankees), but otherwise relied primarily on second-line talent.

Williams played in only 16 games during the regular season, and hit .339. He hit .320 as Arecibo knocked off Santurce 4-2 in the semifinals and a team-high .400 in the win over Mayaguez, the regular-season champion.

Manager Pat Kelly (Expos), who managed Harrisburg to an Eastern League championship during the summer of 1996, used his bullpen well in the post-season. Alberro had seven saves in the playoffs and nailed down all five victories in the championship series.

Mayaguez edged Arecibo by one game in the regular season as outfielder Doug Glanville (Cubs) hit .325 and led the league in runs, hits and total bases to win the league's MVP award. The Indians then defeated defending Caribbean World Series champion San Juan 4-1 in the semifinals, winning the series with a 2-1 win in 21 innings in Game Five.

The Arecibo-Mayaguez series marked only the fourth time in league history that two non-San Juan teams reached the final.

San Juan, the league's two-time defending champion, expected Gooden to bolster its starting staff but the former Mets star, pitching for the first time in 16 months, failed to win a game and promptly left the team, apparently on the order of Yankees owner George Steinbrenner. Gooden, who had recently signed with the Yankees, started three games for San Juan and had a 1.26 ERA, but his record was 0-1.

The Senators also suffered through an off season from first baseman-outfielder Carlos Delgado (Blue Jays), who hit .177 with seven homers. A year earlier, Delgado hit .323 with a league-high 12 homers and was selected winter baseball's Player of the Year.

The Senators' on-field struggle led to the dismissal

**Breakthrough Winter.** Cubs outfield prospect Doug Glanville enjoyed a big season for Mayaguez, winning league MVP honors.

DAVID GREENE

of manager Luis Melendez 34 games into the season.

With two games left in the regular season, San Juan was mired in fifth place, two games out of the last playoff position. But the Senators beat Santurce twice to force a one-game playoff with Ponce for the final playoff position.

Alomar (Orioles), trailing by 19 points in the batting race to Santurce shortstop Rey Ordonez (Mets), went 7-for-12 in the final three games, while Ordonez went 0-for-8. Alomar finished at .362, Ordonez .351.

## STANDINGS

| REGULAR SEASON | W | L | PCT | GB |
|---|---|---|---|---|
| Mayaguez Indians | 28 | 21 | .571 | — |
| Arecibo Wolves | 27 | 22 | .551 | 1 |
| Santurce Crabbers | 26 | 24 | .520 | 2½ |
| San Juan Senators | 26 | 25 | .510 | 3 |
| Ponce Lions | 25 | 26 | .490 | 4 |
| Caguas Criollos | 18 | 32 | .360 | 10½ |

**PLAYOFFS—Semifinals:** Arecibo defeated Santurce, 4-2, in best-of-7 series. Mayaguez defeated San Juan, 4-1, in best-of-7 series. **Finals:** Arecibo defeated Mayaguez, 5-3, in best-of-9 final.

### INDIVIDUAL BATTING LEADERS
(Minimum 100 Plate Appearances)

| | AVG | AB | R | H | 2B | 3B | HR | RBI | SB |
|---|---|---|---|---|---|---|---|---|---|
| Alomar, Roberto, San Juan | .362 | 152 | 26 | 55 | 14 | 2 | 4 | 21 | 10 |
| Ordonez, Rey, Santurce | .351 | 134 | 7 | 47 | 4 | 0 | 0 | 21 | 1 |
| Vargas, Hector, Arecibo | .336 | 140 | 25 | 47 | 6 | 3 | 1 | 16 | 4 |
| McMillon, Billy, Ponce | .333 | 168 | 31 | 56 | 7 | 4 | 4 | 22 | 2 |
| Glanville, Doug, Mayaguez | .325 | 203 | 33 | 66 | 10 | 2 | 4 | 15 | 16 |
| Valdes, Pedro, San Juan | .321 | 140 | 16 | 45 | 7 | 0 | 2 | 19 | 1 |
| Renteria, Edgar, Ponce | .318 | 107 | 15 | 34 | 5 | 2 | 0 | 17 | 5 |
| Martinez, Carmelo, San Juan | .306 | 144 | 16 | 44 | 9 | 0 | 2 | 17 | 0 |
| Cora, Joey, Caguas | .302 | 86 | 12 | 26 | 4 | 1 | 0 | 6 | 4 |
| Munoz, Pedro, Mayaguez | .302 | 96 | 14 | 29 | 6 | 0 | 4 | 16 | 2 |
| Merced, Orlando, Santurce | .291 | 148 | 20 | 43 | 9 | 1 | 4 | 23 | 10 |
| Correa, Miguel, Ponce | .290 | 200 | 32 | 58 | 14 | 5 | 3 | 19 | 2 |

| | AVG | AB | R | H | 2B | 3B | HR | RBI | SB |
|---|---|---|---|---|---|---|---|---|---|
| Crespo, Felipe, Caguas | .287 | 129 | 21 | 37 | 7 | 0 | 1 | 16 | 6 |
| Echevarria, Angel, Arecibo | .283 | 113 | 15 | 32 | 4 | 0 | 2 | 10 | 0 |
| Olmeda, Jose, Santurce | .281 | 139 | 23 | 39 | 5 | 2 | 4 | 15 | 5 |
| Ortiz, Nick, Arecibo | .280 | 100 | 12 | 28 | 5 | 0 | 1 | 9 | 1 |
| Otero, Ricky, Arecibo | .279 | 197 | 27 | 55 | 5 | 2 | 1 | 20 | **17** |
| Diaz, Alex, Mayaguez | .278 | 158 | 21 | 44 | 8 | 0 | 4 | 25 | 13 |
| Rodriguez, Ivan, Caguas | .276 | 116 | 15 | 32 | 4 | 1 | 2 | 15 | 0 |
| Gomez, Leo, Santurce | .273 | 99 | 18 | 27 | 4 | 0 | 3 | 18 | 1 |
| Villanueva, Hector, Santurce | .268 | 179 | 23 | 48 | 10 | 0 | **8** | **30** | 0 |
| Munoz, Jose, Santurce | .265 | 170 | **33** | 45 | 13 | 1 | 2 | 23 | 3 |
| Texidor, Jose, Ponce | .265 | 113 | 16 | 30 | 3 | 0 | 2 | 7 | 0 |
| Matheny, Mike, Arecibo | .264 | 159 | 22 | 42 | 6 | 0 | 3 | 19 | 1 |
| Silvestri, Dave, Sant-Are. | .263 | 95 | 14 | 25 | 5 | 3 | 2 | 11 | 0 |
| Montoyo, Charlie, May. | .259 | 81 | 8 | 21 | 1 | 0 | 0 | 10 | 1 |
| Benitez, Yamil, Caguas | .258 | 163 | 25 | 42 | 10 | 1 | 5 | 16 | 10 |
| Kieschnick, Brooks, May. | .255 | 94 | 10 | 24 | 2 | 0 | 3 | 15 | 1 |
| Chimelis, Joel, Arecibo | .254 | 185 | 20 | 47 | 7 | 0 | 6 | 25 | 3 |
| Pappas, Erik, Ponce | .250 | 88 | 14 | 22 | 3 | 1 | 3 | 9 | 0 |
| Bragg, Darren, Caguas | .247 | 190 | 28 | 47 | 13 | 0 | 1 | 12 | 11 |
| Posada, Jorge, Santurce | .247 | 150 | 14 | 37 | 8 | 0 | 2 | 11 | 1 |
| Hubbard, Trinidad, San Juan | .246 | 187 | 29 | 46 | 9 | 3 | 3 | 21 | 7 |
| Nieves, Melvin, Santurce | .245 | 155 | 28 | 38 | 10 | 2 | 7 | 20 | 2 |
| #Timmons, Ozzie, Caguas | .212 | 156 | 21 | 33 | 13 | 1 | 3 | **30** | 3 |

### INDIVIDUAL PITCHING LEADERS
(Minimum 33 Innings)

| | W | L | ERA | G | SV | IP | H | BB | SO |
|---|---|---|---|---|---|---|---|---|---|
| Alicea, Miguel, Mayaguez | 3 | 2 | 1.59 | 27 | 0 | 40 | 32 | 10 | 17 |
| Patrick, Bronswell, Santurce | **6** | 0 | **1.66** | 12 | 0 | 81 | 59 | 29 | 33 |
| Olivares, Omar, Caguas | 2 | 3 | 2.10 | 11 | 0 | 64 | 42 | 30 | 37 |
| Rivera, Roberto, May. | 3 | 1 | 2.11 | 18 | 3 | 38 | 26 | 8 | 23 |
| Brock, Chris, Santurce | 4 | 2 | 2.29 | 10 | 0 | 51 | 42 | 24 | 36 |
| Miller, Kurt, Ponce | 5 | 5 | 2.31 | 12 | 0 | 74 | 56 | 31 | 46 |
| Mercado, Hector, Ponce | 2 | 3 | 2.36 | 21 | 0 | 34 | 24 | 14 | 26 |
| Alberro, Jose, Arecibo | 2 | 2 | 2.48 | 28 | **13** | 36 | 33 | 16 | 27 |
| Bowen, Ryan, San Juan | 5 | 3 | 2.62 | 11 | 0 | 58 | 48 | 33 | 49 |
| Burgos, John, SJ-May. | 5 | 1 | 2.67 | 26 | 2 | 34 | 27 | 11 | 22 |
| #Shuey, Paul, San Juan | 0 | 0 | 2.78 | 23 | **13** | 23 | 17 | 19 | 21 |
| Johnstone, John, Ponce | 2 | 1 | 2.83 | 27 | 1 | 35 | 25 | 12 | 27 |
| Mirando, Angel, Arecibo | **6** | 2 | 3.18 | 11 | 0 | 57 | 48 | 26 | 37 |
| Rosado, Jose, Mayaguez | 3 | 2 | 3.24 | 11 | 0 | 50 | 58 | 21 | 38 |
| DeLeon, Luis, Mayaguez | 1 | 2 | 3.25 | 13 | 0 | 36 | 34 | 9 | 26 |
| Abbott, Paul, Mayaguez | 5 | 5 | 3.28 | 13 | 0 | 58 | 52 | 30 | 47 |
| Ward, Bryan, Arecibo | 2 | 3 | 3.30 | 12 | 0 | 60 | 63 | 17 | 39 |
| Groom, Buddy, Ponce | 3 | 5 | 3.33 | 12 | 0 | 70 | 65 | 22 | 52 |
| Woodall, Brad, San Juan | 5 | 5 | 3.44 | 14 | 0 | 73 | 63 | 27 | 41 |
| Reyes, Carlos, San Juan | 4 | 6 | 3.47 | 13 | 0 | 70 | 77 | 23 | 49 |
| Valera, Julio, Mayaguez | **6** | 4 | 3.54 | 12 | 0 | 61 | 60 | 19 | 30 |
| Shepherd, Keith, Caguas | 1 | 5 | 3.56 | 25 | 6 | 48 | 38 | 20 | **63** |
| Grott, Matt, Santurce | 3 | 4 | 3.61 | 11 | 0 | 57 | 50 | 21 | 31 |
| Vasquez, Marcos, Arecibo | 1 | 3 | 3.67 | 18 | 0 | 34 | 36 | 23 | 16 |
| Oquist, Mike, Caguas | 4 | 4 | 3.99 | 13 | 0 | 65 | 70 | 30 | 54 |
| Telford, Anthony, San Juan | 5 | 4 | 4.02 | 17 | 0 | 53 | 52 | 17 | 29 |

# VENEZUELAN LEAGUE

The Lara Cardinals had everything in their favor. They posted the league's best record in the regular season, the best record in the five-team, round-robin playoff and, with a 3-1 edge, held the upper hand in the league's best-of-7 championship series.

All they needed was one more win to earn their second-ever berth in the Caribbean World Series. They never got it.

The underdog Magallanes Navigators stormed back to win the final three games of the series to beat Lara 4-3 and earn their second trip to the Series in three years under the direction of manager Tim Tolman. The Navigators fared poorly at the CWS, winning only one of six games.

Magallanes, stocked heavily with Houston Astros prospects, finished with a sub-.500 record in the regular season and for the fourth straight season placed second in their division to Caracas.

But the Navigators had a hero during the round robin, which was expanded from four to five teams. Right-hander Donne Wall (Astros), who joined the team late and didn't win a game during the regular season, went 3-0 with a 1.40 ERA and combined on a no-hitter as Magallanes went 10-6 to finish second behind Lara.

Righthander Juan Castillo then stepped up in the final series against Lara, winning two starts while posting a 0.60 ERA. Outfielder Jose Malave (Red Sox) hit .370 with three homers and 10 RBIs.

Tolman left the club after the first game of the series to fly home to attend to his son, who was hospitalized with appendicitis. He returned in time to lead his team's comeback.

**Robert Perez**

Lara, stocked primarily with Toronto Blue Jays prospects, earned the league's best regular-season record largely off the play of outfielder Robert Perez (Blue Jays), who hit .318 and finished second in the league in homers (6) and RBIs (35). He was selected the league's MVP.

Veteran Lara third baseman Luis Sojo (Mariners) failed to win a batting title for the first time in four years, but contributed a .329 average—third in the league.

Outfielder Roger Cedeno (Dodgers) helped traditional power Caracas win the other division title by hitting a league-best .340. He also led the loop in stolen bases (22) before crashing with a .173 average in the 16-game round-robin. Constant player shuffling and bickering between players and coaches during the post-season did in Caracas, which went a dismal 3-13.

Zulia claimed the league's first wild-card berth by beating Occidental 1-0 in a one-game playoff as left-hander Wilson Alvarez (White Sox) worked eight innings, allowing five hits.

Occidental reliever Tony Phillips (Mariners) recorded his 20th save on the final day of the regular season, which forced the sudden-death playoff between Zulia and Occidental. Phillips broke a record held for 12 years by Porfirio Altamirano.

## STANDINGS

| ORIENTAL | W | L | PCT | GB |
|---|---|---|---|---|
| Caracas Lions | 32 | 28 | .533 | — |
| Magallanes Navigators | 29 | 31 | .483 | 3 |
| Oriente Caribbeans | 27 | 33 | .450 | 5 |
| La Guaira Tiburones | 25 | 35 | .417 | 7 |

| OCCIDENTAL | W | L | PCT | GB |
|---|---|---|---|---|
| Lara Cardinals | 36 | 24 | .600 | — |
| Aragua Tigers | 31 | 29 | .517 | 5 |
| Zulia Eagles | 31 | 30 | .508 | 5½ |
| Occidental Pastora | 30 | 31 | .492 | 6½ |

| PLAYOFFS | W | L | PCT | GB |
|---|---|---|---|---|
| Lara Cardinals | 11 | 5 | .688 | — |
| Magallanes Navigators | 10 | 6 | .625 | 1 |
| Zulia Eagles | 9 | 7 | .563 | 2 |
| Aragua Tigers | 7 | 9 | .438 | 4 |
| Caracas Lions | 3 | 13 | .188 | 8 |

**Championship Series:** Magallanes defeated Lara 4-3, in best-of-7 final.

### INDIVIDUAL BATTING LEADERS
(Minimum 120 Plate Appearances)

| | AVG | AB | R | H | 2B | 3B | HR | RBI | SB |
|---|---|---|---|---|---|---|---|---|---|
| Espinoza, Alvaro, Mag. | .377 | 107 | 11 | 40 | 5 | 1 | 3 | 21 | 1 |
| Cedeno, Roger, Caracas | .340 | 144 | 29 | 49 | 10 | 2 | 0 | 13 | 22 |
| Azocar, Oscar, Aragua | .332 | 193 | 20 | 64 | 11 | 2 | 2 | 30 | 1 |
| Sojo, Luis, Lara | .329 | 161 | 20 | 53 | 11 | 4 | 3 | 27 | 2 |
| Cairo, Miguel, Lara | .318 | 239 | 39 | 76 | 6 | 2 | 1 | 16 | 19 |
| Perez, Robert, Lara | .318 | 233 | 31 | 74 | 12 | 3 | 6 | 35 | 2 |
| Carter, Michael, Aragua | .317 | 120 | 23 | 38 | 5 | 0 | 0 | 5 | 2 |
| Stewart, Shannon, Lara | .311 | 183 | 39 | 57 | 9 | 1 | 1 | 20 | 12 |
| Becker, Rich, Aragua | .311 | 90 | 15 | 28 | 3 | 1 | 1 | 10 | 2 |
| Ashley, Billy, Caracas | .305 | 95 | 15 | 29 | 8 | 2 | 5 | 17 | 2 |
| Marcano, Raul, Oriente | .303 | 178 | 15 | 54 | 4 | 2 | 3 | 24 | 1 |
| Zambrano, Roberto, Aragua | .303 | 185 | 16 | 56 | 11 | 0 | 1 | 23 | 1 |
| Ramos, Jairo, La Guaira | .301 | 173 | 27 | 52 | 6 | 0 | 0 | 15 | 3 |
| Diaz, Eddy, Magallanes | .297 | 229 | 31 | 68 | 17 | 0 | 2 | 14 | 12 |
| Infante, Alexis, Lara | .293 | 208 | 13 | 61 | 12 | 2 | 1 | 20 | 0 |
| Garcia, Jose, Aragua | .292 | 202 | 28 | 59 | 8 | 1 | 0 | 12 | 6 |
| Manrique, Marco, Oriente | .286 | 119 | 7 | 34 | 4 | 0 | 1 | 12 | 0 |
| Machado, Robert, Occ. | .285 | 193 | 23 | 55 | 11 | 1 | 1 | 15 | 8 |
| Abreu, Bob, Caracas | .280 | 186 | 29 | 52 | 10 | 4 | 3 | 25 | 8 |
| Spiezio, Scott, Oriente | .279 | 208 | 28 | 58 | 10 | 0 | 6 | 20 | 0 |
| Colon, Cris, Zulia | .277 | 206 | 19 | 57 | 9 | 1 | 2 | 26 | 0 |
| Cabrera, Alex, La Guaira | .277 | 112 | 10 | 31 | 7 | 2 | 3 | 14 | 1 |
| Raven, Luis, Magallanes | .276 | 221 | 26 | 61 | 7 | 0 | 7 | 26 | 3 |
| Querecuto, Juan, Lara | .275 | 178 | 18 | 49 | 7 | 1 | 0 | 18 | 0 |
| Amaro, Ruben, Zulia | .274 | 135 | 22 | 37 | 7 | 6 | 0 | 16 | 6 |
| Hajek, Dave, Magallanes | .273 | 161 | 18 | 44 | 8 | 0 | 0 | 22 | 4 |
| Petagine, Roberto, Caracas | .273 | 183 | 21 | 50 | 14 | 1 | 2 | 15 | 1 |
| Martinez, Carlos, La Guaira | .272 | 217 | 20 | 59 | 14 | 0 | 7 | 37 | 8 |
| Ordonez, Magglio, Oriente | .271 | 203 | 32 | 55 | 13 | 2 | 4 | 29 | 9 |
| Huckaby, Ken, Caracas | .271 | 170 | 11 | 46 | 7 | 1 | 0 | 18 | 0 |
| Mora, Melvin, Magallanes | .271 | 144 | 20 | 39 | 7 | 2 | 2 | 16 | 8 |
| Marquez, Edwin, Oriente | .271 | 107 | 11 | 29 | 7 | 0 | 1 | 14 | 0 |
| Arias, George, Aragua | .269 | 212 | 22 | 57 | 11 | 3 | 4 | 26 | 1 |
| Matos, Malvin, Occidental | .269 | 160 | 19 | 43 | 10 | 1 | 3 | 18 | 4 |
| Benard, Marvin, La Guaira | .263 | 175 | 32 | 46 | 9 | 3 | 2 | 13 | 16 |
| Lis, Joe, Lara | .253 | 190 | 24 | 48 | 12 | 0 | 0 | 20 | 4 |
| Mendez, Jesus, Aragua | .252 | 202 | 16 | 51 | 11 | 2 | 0 | 18 | 1 |

### INDIVIDUAL PITCHING LEADERS
(Minimum 40 Innings)

| | W | L | ERA | G | SV | IP | H | BB | SO |
|---|---|---|---|---|---|---|---|---|---|
| Crabtree, Tim, Lara | 3 | 1 | 0.60 | 22 | 7 | 45 | 28 | 13 | 33 |
| Bencomo, Omar, Zulia | 5 | 1 | 1.02 | 14 | 0 | 79 | 61 | 14 | 52 |
| Alvarez, Wilson, Zulia | 4 | 1 | 1.26 | 7 | 0 | 43 | 33 | 7 | 33 |
| Sorzano, Ronnie, Caracas | 5 | 2 | 1.36 | 19 | 0 | 53 | 48 | 23 | 23 |
| Villa, Jose, Occidental | 1 | 3 | 1.42 | 37 | 0 | 51 | 36 | 22 | 26 |
| Carrara, Giovanni, Lara | 7 | 2 | 1.65 | 13 | 0 | 87 | 72 | 18 | 45 |
| Daal, Omar, Caracas | 2 | 2 | 1.68 | 14 | 0 | 97 | 77 | 31 | 73 |
| Sanford, Mo, La Guaira | 2 | 7 | 2.01 | 12 | 0 | 72 | 57 | 29 | 46 |
| Holt, Chris, Magallanes | 2 | 1 | 2.06 | 9 | 0 | 48 | 33 | 14 | 47 |
| Farrell, Mike, Occidental | 10 | 2 | 2.07 | 16 | 0 | 100 | 73 | 15 | 48 |
| Baptist, Travis, Lara | 7 | 1 | 2.10 | 11 | 0 | 69 | 44 | 12 | 25 |
| Ruffcorn, Scott, Oriente | 7 | 6 | 2.18 | 13 | 0 | 87 | 65 | 26 | 53 |
| #Phillips, Tony, Occidental | 0 | 2 | 2.21 | 26 | 20 | 37 | 35 | 11 | 14 |
| Hurtado, Edwin, Lara | 4 | 3 | 2.38 | 11 | 0 | 72 | 65 | 30 | 52 |
| Pulido, Carlos, Magallanes | 5 | 4 | 2.40 | 15 | 0 | 86 | 90 | 26 | 36 |
| Banks, Willie, Caracas | 5 | 4 | 2.42 | 11 | 0 | 74 | 60 | 42 | 33 |
| Lopez, Johann, Caracas | 5 | 3 | 2.44 | 14 | 0 | 77 | 73 | 26 | 40 |
| Steenstra, Kennie, Zulia | 2 | 3 | 2.49 | 9 | 0 | 51 | 54 | 12 | 28 |
| Aldred, Scott, Zulia | 8 | 3 | 2.60 | 13 | 0 | 69 | 58 | 21 | 37 |
| Pett, Jose, Lara | 3 | 3 | 2.64 | 12 | 1 | 48 | 47 | 7 | 17 |
| Holzemer, Mark, Aragua | 4 | 3 | 2.82 | 13 | 0 | 77 | 67 | 22 | 35 |
| Springer, Dennis, La Guaira | 7 | 6 | 2.87 | 13 | 0 | 88 | 85 | 18 | 36 |
| Mlicki, Doug, Magallanes | 3 | 1 | 3.00 | 9 | 0 | 48 | 46 | 15 | 22 |
| Mejias, Fernando, Aragua | 2 | 3 | 3.07 | 12 | 0 | 56 | 47 | 19 | 35 |
| Gonzalez, Jeremy, Zulia | 5 | 6 | 3.09 | 15 | 0 | 76 | 69 | 26 | 37 |
| Castillo, Juan, Magallanes | 2 | 3 | 3.21 | 10 | 0 | 53 | 43 | 23 | 20 |
| Salazar, Luis, Occidental | 2 | 5 | 3.29 | 10 | 0 | 41 | 40 | 12 | 17 |
| Ganote, Joe, Occidental | 5 | 7 | 3.30 | 15 | 0 | 93 | 83 | 35 | 40 |
| Garcia, Ramon, Magallanes | 2 | 8 | 3.47 | 13 | 0 | 70 | 81 | 12 | 35 |
| Sirotka, Mike, Oriente | 3 | 3 | 3.53 | 9 | 0 | 59 | 61 | 18 | 44 |

# ARIZONA FALL LEAGUE

The 1995 Arizona Fall League did not have a drawing card like Michael Jordan, who caused attendance to soar the previous season, but it did have plenty of players who had an impact on major league teams in the 1996 season.

Righthander Alan Benes, the AFL's top starting pitcher and No. 1 prospect, went on to win 13 games for the National League Central Division champion St. Louis Cardinals.

Benes had a dominating AFL campaign with the Sun Cities Solar Sox, leading the league in wins (6) and ERA (1.78), and setting a league record with 62 strikeouts in 55 innings. He also won the first game of the playoffs for Sun Cities, 13-4 over eventual champion Mesa.

**Alan Benes**

"He's the best pitching prospect out here," Sun Cities manager Jamie Quirk said. "He's a big, strong, dominating hard thrower. He has a good slider, an excellent change, and he can sink the fastball against lefthanded batters to give a different look occasionally."

In its fourth season, the AFL proved a finishing school for other top prospects.

Outfielder Jermaine Dye (Braves) led the AFL with 41 RBIs and went on to sub admirably for the injured David Justice during Atlanta's bid to repeat as World Series champions. The Angels unveiled outfielder Darin Erstad after he narrowly missed winning the AFL batting title, finishing four points behind Mesa outfielder Robin Jennings (Cubs). Erstad had only 29 games of prior minor league experience before competing in the AFL.

The league boasted 25 former first-round draft picks in 1995.

The talent rush was due in part to relaxed eligibility rules, allowing players with as much as one year of major league experience to play. It was an effort to keep interest high in the post-Jordan era. Attendance in 1995 was up compared to non-Jordan games in 1994, from 223 to 258.

The Mesa Saguaros, winners of the Southern Division by a commanding 9½-game margin and winner of a league record 33 games, won the best-of-3 championship series, 2-1, over Sun Cities.

In the third and deciding game, Mesa snapped a 3-3 tie by scoring four runs in the eighth inning. Catcher Bobby Hughes (Brewers) had four RBIs in the game, three on a second-inning home run.

### STANDINGS

| NORTH | W | L | PCT | GB |
|---|---|---|---|---|
| Sun Cities Solar Sox | 30 | 21 | .588 | — |
| Peoria Javelinas | 28 | 23 | .549 | 2 |
| Scottsdale Scorpians | 15 | 35 | .300 | 14½ |

| SOUTH | W | L | PCT | GB |
|---|---|---|---|---|
| Mesa Saguaros | 33 | 18 | .647 | — |
| Tempe Rafters | 23 | 27 | .460 | 9½ |
| Phoenix Devil Dogs | 23 | 28 | .451 | 10 |

**Championship Series:** Mesa defeated Sun City, 2-1, in best-of-3 final.

### INDIVIDUAL BATTING LEADERS
(Minimum 138 Plate Appearances)

| | AVG | AB | R | H | 2B | 3B | HR | RBI | SB |
|---|---|---|---|---|---|---|---|---|---|
| Jennings, Robin, Mesa | .348 | 158 | 34 | 55 | 15 | 3 | 6 | 30 | 6 |
| Erstad, Darin, Tempe | .344 | 154 | 26 | 53 | 8 | 3 | 4 | 24 | 6 |
| Ledesma, Aaron, Tempe | .335 | 164 | 21 | 55 | 9 | 1 | 1 | 17 | 6 |
| McCracken, Quinton , Scott. | .324 | 188 | 29 | 61 | 11 | 2 | 0 | 15 | 10 |
| Walker, Todd, Peoria | .322 | 143 | 21 | 46 | 9 | 4 | 3 | 22 | 3 |

| | AVG | AB | R | H | 2B | 3B | HR | RBI | SB |
|---|---|---|---|---|---|---|---|---|---|
| Lawton, Matt, Peoria | .317 | 161 | 27 | 51 | 8 | 3 | 5 | 31 | 11 |
| Brown, Brant, Mesa | .312 | 154 | 21 | 48 | 15 | 1 | 3 | 29 | 8 |
| Norton, Greg, Phoenix | .303 | 175 | 30 | 53 | 11 | 5 | 2 | 23 | 6 |
| Bell, David, Peoria | .303 | 142 | 26 | 43 | 4 | 1 | 4 | 21 | 0 |
| Doster, David, Tempe | .302 | 149 | 18 | 45 | 12 | 0 | 1 | 25 | 7 |

## INDIVIDUAL PITCHING LEADERS
(Minimum 41 Innings)

| | W | L | ERA | G | SV | IP | H | BB | SO |
|---|---|---|---|---|---|---|---|---|---|
| Benes, Alan, Sun Cities | 6 | 1 | 1.78 | 10 | 0 | 56 | 40 | 16 | 62 |
| Brandow, Derek, Tempe | 2 | 2 | 1.89 | 10 | 0 | 48 | 37 | 17 | 30 |
| Person, Robert, Tempe | 1 | 2 | 2.15 | 11 | 0 | 46 | 33 | 18 | 48 |
| Wade, Terrell, Sun Cities | 5 | 3 | 2.66 | 9 | 0 | 44 | 43 | 14 | 46 |
| Park, Chan Ho, Peoria | 3 | 1 | 2.74 | 9 | 0 | 43 | 31 | 23 | 38 |
| Stull, Everett, Mesa | 2 | 1 | 2.79 | 10 | 0 | 42 | 29 | 23 | 38 |
| Whisenant, Matt, Mesa | 2 | 1 | 2.89 | 10 | 0 | 44 | 40 | 25 | 36 |
| Lowe, Derek, Peoria | 2 | 3 | 3.02 | 10 | 0 | 48 | 58 | 10 | 32 |
| Ratliff, Jon, Mesa | 2 | 2 | 3.07 | 10 | 0 | 41 | 38 | 17 | 24 |
| Helling, Rick, Peoria | 5 | 3 | 3.33 | 10 | 0 | 49 | 54 | 11 | 38 |

## MESA

### BATTING

| | | AVG | AB | R | H | 2B | 3B | HR | RBI | SB |
|---|---|---|---|---|---|---|---|---|---|---|
| 3 | Bako, Paul, c | .224 | 67 | 9 | 15 | 4 | 1 | 0 | 5 | 1 |
| 1 | Banks, Brian, of | .195 | 82 | 10 | 16 | 6 | 1 | 1 | 10 | 1 |
| 1 | Belk, Tim, 1b-3b | .254 | 122 | 18 | 31 | 5 | 1 | 3 | 23 | 4 |
| 3 | Boone, Aaron, 3b-ss | .282 | 110 | 18 | 31 | 6 | 0 | 2 | 13 | 3 |
| 2 | Brown, Brant, 1b | .312 | 154 | 21 | 48 | 15 | 1 | 3 | 29 | 8 |
| 1 | Dunn, Todd, of | .261 | 111 | 13 | 29 | 8 | 0 | 2 | 13 | 2 |
| 2 | Hubbard, Mike, c | .333 | 48 | 8 | 16 | 1 | 0 | 0 | 7 | 2 |
| 1 | Hughes, Bobby, c | .176 | 74 | 4 | 13 | 4 | 0 | 1 | 8 | 1 |
| 2 | Jennings, Robin, of | .348 | 158 | 34 | 55 | 15 | 3 | 6 | 30 | 6 |
| 2 | Maxwell, Jason, ss-3b | .375 | 16 | 5 | 6 | 2 | 0 | 0 | 0 | 6 |
| 4 | Milliard, Ralph, 2b | .268 | 179 | 40 | 48 | 11 | 3 | 3 | 11 | 9 |
| 3 | Reese, Pokey, ss | .267 | 168 | 31 | 43 | 8 | 2 | 3 | 26 | 15 |
| 4 | Sheff, Chris, of | .241 | 145 | 26 | 35 | 6 | 2 | 2 | 18 | 8 |
| 5 | Stovall, Darond, of | .230 | 126 | 15 | 29 | 3 | 0 | 2 | 12 | 6 |
| 1 | Unroe, Tim, 3b | .313 | 96 | 12 | 30 | 4 | 1 | 4 | 24 | 2 |
| 1 | Williamson, Antone, 3b | .186 | 43 | 5 | 8 | 1 | 1 | 0 | 5 | 2 |

### PITCHING

| | | W | L | ERA | G | SV | IP | H | BB | SO |
|---|---|---|---|---|---|---|---|---|---|---|
| 5 | Aucoin, Derek | 1 | 1 | 2.66 | 19 | 8 | 24 | 15 | 10 | 28 |
| 1 | Boze, Marshall | 2 | 3 | 6.08 | 18 | 4 | 24 | 30 | 11 | 20 |
| 3 | Fox, Chad | 3 | 2 | 3.23 | 9 | 0 | 39 | 34 | 24 | 33 |
| 4 | Hurst, Bill | 0 | 1 | 2.70 | 14 | 0 | 17 | 14 | 9 | 11 |
| 4 | Juelsgaard, Jarod | 4 | 0 | 2.03 | 16 | 0 | 27 | 16 | 15 | 17 |
| 1 | Lidle, Cory | 1 | 2 | 4.15 | 13 | 0 | 22 | 24 | 12 | 12 |
| 3 | Nix, James | 6 | 1 | 1.78 | 15 | 1 | 30 | 24 | 9 | 25 |
| 2 | Ratliff, Jon | 2 | 2 | 3.07 | 10 | 0 | 41 | 38 | 17 | 24 |
| 4 | Small, Aaron | 3 | 2 | 3.94 | 16 | 1 | 32 | 32 | 6 | 18 |
| 5 | Stull, Everett | 2 | 1 | 2.79 | 10 | 0 | 42 | 29 | 23 | 38 |
| 2 | Sturtze, Tanyon | 4 | 0 | 3.41 | 17 | 2 | 29 | 35 | 10 | 19 |
| 2 | Walker, Wade | | 1 | 6.11 | 12 | 1 | 28 | 39 | 14 | 18 |
| 5 | Weber, Neil | 2 | 1 | 4.09 | 10 | 0 | 44 | 42 | 21 | 40 |
| 4 | Whisenant, Matt | 2 | 1 | 2.89 | 10 | 0 | 44 | 40 | 25 | 36 |

Property of Brewers (1), Cubs (2), Reds (3), Marlins (4), Expos(5).

## PEORIA

### BATTING

| | | AVG | AB | R | H | 2B | 3B | HR | RBI | SB |
|---|---|---|---|---|---|---|---|---|---|---|
| 1 | Bell, David, 2b | .303 | 142 | 26 | 43 | 4 | 1 | 4 | 21 | 0 |
| 4 | Brown, Kevin, c-1b | .248 | 109 | 17 | 27 | 6 | 0 | 2 | 19 | 1 |
| 2 | Fonville, Chad, 2b | .303 | 76 | 18 | 23 | 1 | 0 | 0 | 6 | 9 |
| 1 | Gulan, Mike, 3b-1b | .242 | 132 | 12 | 32 | 5 | 0 | 4 | 18 | 0 |
| 1 | Holbert, Aaron, ss | .367 | 90 | 19 | 33 | 4 | 0 | 1 | 8 | 9 |
| 2 | Latham, Chris, of | .329 | 85 | 17 | 28 | 4 | 6 | 1 | 10 | 9 |
| 7 | Lawton, Matt, of | .317 | 161 | 27 | 51 | 8 | 3 | 5 | 31 | 11 |
| 4 | Lowery, Terrell, of | .238 | 160 | 26 | 38 | 6 | 0 | 0 | 22 | 9 |
| 2 | Martin, James, of | .235 | 34 | 5 | 8 | 2 | 1 | 1 | 4 | 0 |
| 5 | Nunnally, Jon, of-dh | .180 | 111 | 16 | 20 | 4 | 2 | 3 | 16 | 3 |
| 2 | Ogden, Jamie, 1b | .278 | 18 | 3 | 5 | 0 | 0 | 1 | 1 | 0 |
| 2 | Riggs, Adam, 2b | .200 | 30 | 8 | 6 | 1 | 1 | 1 | 6 | 2 |
| 7 | Simons, Mitch, ss-of | .271 | 85 | 14 | 23 | 4 | 1 | 0 | 9 | 4 |
| 1 | Sweeney, Mark, 1b-of | .236 | 144 | 25 | 34 | 8 | 2 | 0 | 20 | 5 |
| 8 | Tremie, Chris, c | .148 | 81 | 2 | 12 | 1 | 0 | 0 | 4 | 0 |
| 3 | Varitek, Jason, c | .281 | 89 | 12 | 25 | 5 | 2 | 1 | 11 | 0 |
| 7 | Walker, Todd, 3b | .322 | 143 | 21 | 46 | 9 | 3 | 4 | 21 | 9 |

### PITCHING

| | | W | L | ERA | G | SV | IP | H | BB | SO |
|---|---|---|---|---|---|---|---|---|---|---|
| 4 | Brandenburg, Mark | 2 | 3 | 2.64 | 16 | 0 | 31 | 30 | 8 | 29 |
| 1 | Frascatore, John | 1 | 0 | 2.35 | 20 | 6 | 23 | 22 | 11 | 33 |
| 7 | Hawkins, LaTroy | 3 | 2 | 6.18 | 9 | 0 | 39 | 54 | 14 | 35 |
| 4 | Helling, Rick | 5 | 3 | 3.33 | 10 | 0 | 49 | 54 | 11 | 38 |
| 6 | Keagle, Greg | 1 | 1 | 5.63 | 6 | 0 | 8 | 5 | 3 | 7 |
| 3 | Lowe, Derek | 2 | 3 | 3.02 | 10 | 0 | 48 | 58 | 10 | 32 |
| 7 | Naulty, Dan | 3 | 2 | 4.88 | 18 | 2 | 31 | 27 | 13 | 42 |

| | | W | L | ERA | G | SV | IP | H | BB | SO |
|---|---|---|---|---|---|---|---|---|---|---|
| 7 | Ohme, Kevin | 0 | 1 | 4.50 | 17 | 1 | 26 | 29 | 8 | 16 |
| 2 | Park, Chan Ho | 3 | 1 | 2.74 | 9 | 0 | 43 | 31 | 23 | 38 |
| 4 | Patterson, Danny | 4 | 0 | 4.38 | 17 | 1 | 25 | 28 | 8 | 28 |
| 2 | Rath, Gary | 0 | 3 | 4.50 | 10 | 0 | 48 | 60 | 15 | 33 |
| 3 | Suzuki, Makoto | 2 | 2 | 6.05 | 14 | 0 | 39 | 44 | 10 | 32 |
| 1 | Urso, Sal | 1 | 1 | 2.08 | 19 | 0 | 17 | 14 | 8 | 17 |
| 3 | Witte, Trey | 1 | 1 | 3.13 | 18 | 3 | 23 | 28 | 7 | 14 |

Property of Cardinals (1), Dodgers (2), Mariners (3), Rangers (4), Royals (5), Tigers (6), Twins (7), White Sox (8).

## PHOENIX

### BATTING

| | | AVG | AB | R | H | 2B | 3B | HR | RBI | SB |
|---|---|---|---|---|---|---|---|---|---|---|
| 4 | Allensworth, Jermaine, of. | .255 | 137 | 14 | 35 | 7 | 0 | 0 | 13 | 9 |
| 7 | Brady, Doug, 2b | .297 | 145 | 25 | 43 | 8 | 3 | 2 | 14 | 5 |
| 4 | Collier, Lou, ss | .305 | 59 | 6 | 18 | 4 | 1 | 0 | 4 | 2 |
| 8 | Eenhoorn, Robert, ss | .177 | 62 | 4 | 11 | 2 | 1 | 0 | 7 | 0 |
| 8 | Kendall, Jason, c | .268 | 97 | 13 | 26 | 4 | 2 | 2 | 13 | 1 |
| 8 | Knowles, Eric, ss | .180 | 50 | 8 | 9 | 3 | 0 | 0 | 3 | 1 |
| 6 | Merloni, Lou, 2b-ss | .217 | 106 | 12 | 23 | 5 | 1 | 1 | 16 | 0 |
| 2 | Molina, Izzy, c | .250 | 68 | 8 | 17 | 4 | 0 | 0 | 10 | 1 |
| 2 | Moore, Kerwin, of | .162 | 117 | 19 | 19 | 3 | 0 | 0 | 10 | 16 |
| 6 | Nixon, Trot, of | .259 | 158 | 26 | 41 | 6 | 3 | 2 | 26 | 1 |
| 3 | Norton, Greg, 3b | .303 | 175 | 30 | 53 | 11 | 5 | 2 | 23 | 6 |
| 4 | Polcovich, Kevin, 2b | .125 | 24 | 4 | 3 | 0 | 0 | 0 | 2 | 1 |
| 3 | Saffer, Jon, of | .262 | 141 | 22 | 37 | 13 | 1 | 0 | 15 | 5 |
| 8 | Seefried, Tate, 1b | .226 | 146 | 14 | 33 | 8 | 2 | 2 | 18 | 1 |
| 7 | Vollmer, Scott, c-1b | .309 | 110 | 14 | 34 | 5 | 0 | 0 | 16 | 0 |
| 2 | Young, Ernie, of | .285 | 123 | 22 | 35 | 10 | 0 | 5 | 25 | 0 |

### PITCHING

| | | W | L | ERA | G | SV | IP | H | BB | SO |
|---|---|---|---|---|---|---|---|---|---|---|
| 6 | Bakkum, Scott | 1 | 0 | 2.31 | 20 | 1 | 35 | 40 | 8 | 16 |
| 7 | Christman, Scott | 2 | 3 | 5.45 | 18 | 1 | 36 | 39 | 13 | 22 |
| 6 | Ciccarella, Joe | 1 | 0 | 5.68 | 4 | 0 | 6 | 9 | 0 | 6 |
| 8 | Cumberland, Chris | 2 | 3 | 4.27 | 11 | 0 | 46 | 44 | 14 | 27 |
| 5 | Curtis, Chris | 2 | 2 | 4.19 | 19 | 1 | 39 | 38 | 17 | 27 |
| 1 | Harris, Bryan | 0 | 0 | 4.91 | 4 | 0 | 7 | 7 | 6 | 7 |
| 4 | Hmielewski, Chris | 0 | 0 | 2.84 | 6 | 0 | 6 | 8 | 3 | 7 |
| 2 | Hollins, Stacy | 0 | 0 | 0.00 | 1 | 0 | 1 | 1 | 1 | 2 |
| 1 | Holtz, Mike | 0 | 1 | 2.38 | 10 | 0 | 11 | 9 | 7 | 11 |
| 2 | Looney, Brian | 0 | 0 | 3.38 | 4 | 0 | 11 | 14 | 1 | 13 |
| 7 | Lorraine, Andrew | 3 | 3 | 5.59 | 15 | 0 | 37 | 48 | 12 | 24 |
| 2 | Maurer, Mike | 2 | 2 | 2.08 | 17 | 6 | 17 | 17 | 6 | 17 |
| 2 | Pote, Lou | 1 | 0 | 6.00 | 2 | 0 | 3 | 3 | 1 | 0 |
| 2 | Reubel, Matt | 2 | 5 | 4.31 | 11 | 1 | 40 | 48 | 16 | 33 |
| 4 | Rychel, Kevin | 2 | 2 | 2.55 | 19 | 0 | 35 | 32 | 13 | 30 |
| 4 | Shouse, Kevin | 1 | 0 | 1.59 | 19 | 1 | 34 | 26 | 6 | 14 |
| 2 | Wengert, Don | 2 | 2 | 4.81 | 10 | 0 | 39 | 38 | 10 | 26 |
| 2 | Wojciechowski, Steve | 2 | 5 | 4.27 | 11 | 0 | 46 | 51 | 12 | 45 |

Property of Angels (1), Athletics (2), Expos (3), Pirates (4), Rangers (5), Red Sox (6), White Sox (7), Yankees (8).

## SCOTTSDALE

### BATTING

| | | AVG | AB | R | H | 2B | 3B | HR | RBI | SB |
|---|---|---|---|---|---|---|---|---|---|---|
| 2 | Aurilia, Rich, ss | .270 | 159 | 17 | 43 | 10 | 6 | 1 | 30 | 3 |
| 1 | Ball, Jeff, 3b-1b | .266 | 143 | 28 | 38 | 9 | 1 | 6 | 16 | 5 |
| 3 | Berrios, Harry, of | .244 | 82 | 8 | 20 | 2 | 0 | 2 | 9 | 3 |
| 1 | Bridges, Kary, 3b-2b | .140 | 57 | 3 | 8 | 1 | 0 | 0 | 4 | 0 |
| 4 | Brown, Randy, of-3b | .180 | 100 | 13 | 18 | 4 | 0 | 0 | 5 | 2 |
| 5 | Counsell, Craig, 2b-ss | .284 | 169 | 16 | 48 | 7 | 5 | 0 | 24 | 6 |
| 6 | Delvecchio, Nick, of | .190 | 79 | 9 | 15 | 4 | 0 | 3 | 5 | 0 |
| 3 | Fox, Andy, 3b | .353 | 34 | 2 | 12 | 2 | 0 | 1 | 4 | 1 |
| 5 | Hinds, Robert, 2b | .216 | 51 | 7 | 11 | 3 | 0 | 0 | 7 | 1 |
| 2 | Jensen, Marcus, c | .239 | 92 | 11 | 22 | 4 | 0 | 0 | 7 | 1 |
| 3 | Jones, Terry, of | .297 | 148 | 17 | 44 | 4 | 2 | 0 | 14 | 16 |
| 3 | McClain, Scott, 3b | .000 | 1 | 0 | 0 | 0 | 0 | 0 | 0 | 0 |
| 5 | McCracken, Quinton, of | .324 | 188 | 29 | 61 | 11 | 2 | 0 | 15 | 10 |
| 1 | Montgomery, Ray, of | .250 | 20 | 1 | 5 | 0 | 0 | 0 | 3 | 0 |
| 1 | Nelson, Bry, of-3b | .282 | 131 | 19 | 37 | 4 | 2 | 5 | 21 | 0 |
| 1 | Owens, Billy, 1b | .246 | 179 | 16 | 44 | 6 | 0 | 2 | 13 | 2 |
| 3 | Waszgis, B.J., c | .247 | 93 | 10 | 23 | 3 | 0 | 3 | 11 | 0 |

### PITCHING

| | | W | L | ERA | G | SV | IP | H | BB | SO |
|---|---|---|---|---|---|---|---|---|---|---|
| 5 | Alston, Garvin | 0 | 0 | 6.75 | 7 | 0 | 9 | 8 | 12 | 7 |
| 2 | Brewington, Jamie | 0 | 2 | 7.85 | 5 | 0 | 18 | 18 | 16 | 11 |
| 5 | Brownson, Mark | 2 | 0 | 2.63 | 7 | 0 | 14 | 14 | 0 | 21 |
| 2 | Conner, Scott | 0 | 3 | 6.52 | 11 | 0 | 19 | 21 | 21 | 14 |
| 1 | Creek, Ryan | 1 | 1 | 4.13 | 7 | 0 | 24 | 26 | 11 | 15 |
| 6 | DeJean, Mike | 2 | 1 | 6.49 | 19 | 2 | 26 | 39 | 14 | 23 |
| 2 | Estes, Shawn | 2 | 5 | 4.47 | 10 | 0 | 50 | 44 | 28 | 46 |
| 1 | Gallaher, Kevin | 1 | 6 | 7.13 | 10 | 0 | 42 | 47 | 37 | 42 |
| 1 | Grzanich, Mike | 0 | 0 | 40.50 | 1 | 0 | 1 | 4 | 1 | 0 |
| 5 | Jones, Bobby | 2 | 2 | 6.75 | 16 | 0 | 35 | 37 | 25 | 21 |
| 3 | Lane, Aaron | 1 | 2 | 3.12 | 22 | 0 | 40 | 43 | 23 | 34 |
| 2 | Pickett, Ricky | 0 | 2 | 6.82 | 20 | 0 | 32 | 33 | 36 | 33 |

| | | | | | | | | | | |
|---|---|---|---|---|---|---|---|---|---|---|
| 2 Rosselli, Joe | 0 | 1 | 3.60 | 5 | 0 | 10 | 9 | 0 | 6 |
| 2 Soderstrom, Steve | 0 | 6 | 8.53 | 13 | 0 | 38 | 56 | 21 | 31 |
| 3 Stephenson, Garrett | 1 | 2 | 3.47 | 11 | 1 | 47 | 40 | 15 | 42 |
| 5 Viano, Jacob | 3 | 2 | 4.72 | 23 | 2 | 34 | 37 | 13 | 28 |

Property of Astros (1), Giants (2), Orioles (3), Red Sox (4), Rockies (5), Yankees (6).

## SUN CITIES

| BATTING | AVG | AB | R | H | 2B | 3B | HR | RBI | SB |
|---|---|---|---|---|---|---|---|---|---|
| 4 Bush, Homer, ss-2b | .275 | 120 | 17 | 33 | 6 | 6 | 0 | 11 | 1 |
| 8 Catalanotto, Frank, 2b | .292 | 144 | 19 | 42 | 4 | 3 | 0 | 12 | 2 |
| 7 Damon, Johnny, of | .333 | 48 | 12 | 16 | 2 | 0 | 0 | 3 | 3 |
| 1 Dye, Jermaine, of | .250 | 184 | 26 | 46 | 14 | 3 | 5 | 41 | 1 |
| 4 Fasano, Sal, c | .279 | 129 | 19 | 36 | 6 | 0 | 3 | 19 | 0 |
| 1 Giovanola, Ed, ss-3b | .299 | 77 | 17 | 23 | 1 | 1 | 0 | 10 | 1 |
| 4 Lee, Derrek, 1b-of | .235 | 98 | 13 | 23 | 6 | 0 | 1 | 24 | 3 |
| 1 Malloy, Marty, ss | .336 | 116 | 14 | 39 | 7 | 0 | 0 | 13 | 2 |
| 6 McKeel, Walt, c | .220 | 50 | 3 | 11 | 3 | 1 | 0 | 4 | 0 |
| 3 Melendez, Dan, 1b | .209 | 134 | 18 | 28 | 5 | 2 | 2 | 15 | 0 |
| 4 Mulligan, Sean, c-dh | .281 | 96 | 13 | 27 | 3 | 1 | 2 | 11 | 0 |
| 7 Norman, Les, of | .333 | 87 | 22 | 29 | 10 | 0 | 4 | 15 | 1 |
| 7 Randa, Joe, 3b | .275 | 149 | 24 | 41 | 4 | 2 | 0 | 23 | 1 |
| 1 Smith, Bobby, 3b | .280 | 25 | 3 | 7 | 3 | 0 | 0 | 3 | 0 |
| 8 Steverson, Todd, of | .250 | 116 | 24 | 29 | 3 | 2 | 4 | 22 | 2 |
| 7 Tucker, Michael, of | .288 | 160 | 24 | 46 | 3 | 1 | 1 | 18 | 6 |

| PITCHING | W | L | ERA | G | SV | IP | H | BB | SO |
|---|---|---|---|---|---|---|---|---|---|
| 2 Benes, Alan | 6 | 1 | 1.78 | 10 | 0 | 56 | 40 | 16 | 62 |
| 5 Blazier, Ron | 3 | 3 | 3.71 | 20 | 1 | 34 | 33 | 9 | 13 |
| 8 Blomdahl, Ben | 1 | 0 | 5.56 | 12 | 0 | 23 | 29 | 11 | 15 |
| 8 Bluma, Jaime | 3 | 1 | 3.57 | 21 | 8 | 23 | 26 | 6 | 17 |
| 1 Daniels, Lee | 2 | 0 | 1.95 | 15 | 1 | 28 | 20 | 17 | 27 |
| 8 Greene, Rick | 0 | 0 | 2.87 | 8 | 0 | 16 | 15 | 7 | 10 |
| 4 Hermanson, Dustin | 2 | 3 | 4.64 | 10 | 0 | 43 | 36 | 24 | 39 |
| 4 Kroon, Marc | 0 | 2 | 4.50 | 11 | 1 | 26 | 24 | 21 | 22 |
| 4 Long, Joey | 1 | 0 | 1.38 | 13 | 0 | 13 | 8 | 4 | 14 |
| 1 May, Darrell | 1 | 0 | 2.70 | 2 | 0 | 10 | 8 | 2 | 9 |
| 8 Miller, Trever | 2 | 2 | 5.40 | 9 | 0 | 35 | 43 | 14 | 23 |
| 8 Moehler, Brian | 0 | 3 | 9.00 | 5 | 0 | 20 | 28 | 7 | 11 |
| 8 Myers, Mike | 0 | 0 | 4.35 | 10 | 1 | 10 | 9 | 3 | 13 |
| 1 Potts, Mike | 1 | 1 | 1.13 | 9 | 0 | 8 | 5 | 7 | 6 |
| 8 Tuttle, Dave | 0 | 1 | 5.75 | 5 | 0 | 20 | 22 | 14 | 14 |
| 1 Wade, Terrell | 5 | 3 | 2.66 | 9 | 0 | 44 | 43 | 14 | 46 |
| 4 Weaver, Eric | 3 | 1 | 2.17 | 20 | 1 | 37 | 26 | 21 | 26 |

Property of Braves (1), Cardinals (2), Dodgers (3), Padres (4), Phillies (5), Red Sox (6), Royals (7), Tigers (8).

## TEMPE

| BATTING | AVG | AB | R | H | 2B | 3B | HR | RBI | SB |
|---|---|---|---|---|---|---|---|---|---|
| 3 Bryant, Pat, of | .252 | 107 | 9 | 27 | 4 | 1 | 1 | 16 | 6 |
| 5 Doster, David, 3b-2b | .302 | 149 | 18 | 45 | 12 | 0 | 1 | 25 | 7 |
| 1 Erstad, Darin, of | .344 | 154 | 26 | 53 | 8 | 3 | 4 | 24 | 6 |
| 5 Estalella, Bobby, c | .231 | 104 | 9 | 24 | 12 | 0 | 3 | 22 | 0 |
| 4 Greene, Charlie, c | .206 | 68 | 8 | 14 | 1 | 0 | 0 | 7 | 1 |
| 1 Greene, Todd, c-dh | .196 | 107 | 12 | 21 | 3 | 0 | 2 | 16 | 0 |
| 4 Hardtke, Jason, 2b | .163 | 104 | 15 | 17 | 4 | 0 | 0 | 8 | 0 |
| 1 Harkrider, Tim, 2b-ss | .216 | 37 | 6 | 8 | 0 | 0 | 0 | 2 | 1 |
| 3 Jackson, Damian, ss | .252 | 163 | 28 | 41 | 8 | 3 | 0 | 21 | 14 |
| 4 Ledesma, Aaron, 3b-1b | .335 | 164 | 21 | 55 | 9 | 1 | 1 | 17 | 6 |
| 4 Luuloa, Keith, 2b | .294 | 34 | 3 | 10 | 4 | 0 | 0 | 3 | 1 |
| 5 Magee, Wendell, of | .265 | 155 | 26 | 41 | 9 | 3 | 1 | 14 | 3 |
| 3 McCall, Rod, 1b | .261 | 142 | 12 | 37 | 4 | 0 | 2 | 16 | 1 |
| 1 Riley, Marquis, of | .242 | 120 | 17 | 29 | 1 | 1 | 0 | 4 | 12 |
| 2 Roberts, Lonell, of | .237 | 93 | 15 | 22 | 3 | 1 | 0 | 4 | 2 |

| PITCHING | W | L | ERA | G | SV | IP | H | BB | SO |
|---|---|---|---|---|---|---|---|---|---|
| 2 Brandow, Derek | 2 | 2 | 1.89 | 10 | 0 | 48 | 37 | 17 | 30 |
| 2 Brow, Scott | 2 | 1 | 2.39 | 18 | 0 | 26 | 23 | 10 | 12 |
| 4 Edmondson, Brian | 1 | 2 | 6.69 | 14 | 0 | 39 | 55 | 14 | 25 |
| 2 Flener, Huck | 3 | 1 | 5.17 | 14 | 0 | 25 | 23 | 10 | 18 |
| 5 Gomes, Wayne | 0 | 2 | 5.97 | 12 | 0 | 35 | 36 | 22 | 29 |
| 3 Harris, Pep | 3 | 1 | 3.13 | 18 | 2 | 23 | 19 | 11 | 13 |
| 3 Kline, Steve | 1 | 3 | 4.88 | 14 | 0 | 28 | 33 | 20 | 18 |
| 5 Loewer, Carlton | 3 | 4 | 4.87 | 10 | 0 | 44 | 56 | 12 | 20 |
| 2 Lukasiewicz, Mark | 1 | 1 | 5.01 | 15 | 0 | 23 | 22 | 15 | 12 |
| 4 Person, Robert | 1 | 2 | 2.15 | 11 | 0 | 46 | 33 | 18 | 48 |
| 1 Schmidt, Jeff | 2 | 1 | 4.35 | 17 | 1 | 21 | 25 | 14 | 17 |
| 1 Sexton, Jeff | 0 | 2 | 7.06 | 14 | 2 | 29 | 29 | 14 | 18 |
| 4 Wallace, Derek | 4 | 2 | 1.69 | 17 | 1 | 27 | 22 | 15 | 20 |
| 2 Ware, Jeff | 0 | 3 | 5.77 | 9 | 0 | 34 | 37 | 19 | 13 |

Property of Angels (1), Blue Jays (2), Indians (3), Mets (4), Phillies (5).

# HAWAII WINTER BASEBALL

For the third time in Hawaii Winter Baseball's three-year existence, the team with the most wins did not win the title.

The loop's four squads were divided into two-team divisions—the Outrigger and Volcano—for the first time in 1995 with the two division winners meeting in a one-game playoff for the championship. The Honolulu Sharks (29-23), the Outrigger champion, had the league's best record but fell to the Maui Stingrays (25-28), the Volcano champion, 4-3.

A year earlier, when no playoff was held, Maui had the most wins in the league, but finished three percentage points behind Kauai, which relocated to West Oahu for the 1995 season. The discrepancy resulted from rained-out games not made up.

Maui went to its ace, righthander Joey Vierra (White Sox), a native Hawaiian, in the playoff. Vierra, the game's MVP, worked 7⅓ innings and turned it over to relief ace Alvie Shepherd, the Orioles' first-round draft pick in 1995 who nailed down his fifth save. Shortstop David Lamb (Orioles) had the big hit for Maui, a two-run double.

**D.J. Boston**

Outfielder Derrick Gibson (Rockies) went 0-for-4 in the playoff, but swung a big stick for Maui during the season. Coming off a 30-homer, 30-stolen base season with the Rockies' Class A Asheville affiliate he opened more eyes by leading HWB with eight homers.

Honolulu first baseman D.J. Boston (Blue Jays), one of only two .300 hitters, led the league with a .347 average.

Originally stocked equally with players from Japan and Korea, as the United States, the Hawaiian league continues to gain acceptance with major league clubs. It has evolved into a popular retreat for mid-level prospects from the U.S. More than 20 organizations sent prospects to Hawaii in 1995, with Japan sending only 15.

## STANDINGS

| OUTRIGGER | W | L | PCT | GB |
|---|---|---|---|---|
| Honolulu Sharks | 29 | 23 | .558 | — |
| West Oahu Cane Fires | 28 | 24 | .538 | 1 |
| VOLCANO | W | L | PCT | GB |
| Maui Stingrays | 25 | 28 | .472 | — |
| Hilo Stars | 23 | 30 | .434 | 2 |

**PLAYOFFS:** Maui defeated Honolulu in one-game playoff.

### INDIVIDUAL BATTING LEADERS
(Minimum 78 Plate Appearances)

| | AVG | AB | R | H | 2B | 3B | HR | RBI | SB |
|---|---|---|---|---|---|---|---|---|---|
| Boston, D.J., Honolulu | .347 | 118 | 29 | 41 | 6 | 1 | 7 | 25 | 5 |
| Wells, Forey, Maui | .310 | 71 | 8 | 22 | 6 | 1 | 2 | 7 | 1 |
| Medrano, Anthony, Honolulu | .309 | 188 | 20 | 58 | 4 | 3 | 1 | 12 | 7 |
| Neff, Marty, West Oahu | .304 | 112 | 16 | 34 | 7 | 0 | 5 | 21 | 0 |
| Taneda, Hitoshi, West Oahu | .300 | 80 | 12 | 24 | 7 | 3 | 0 | 12 | 3 |
| Truby, Chris, West Oahu | .297 | 158 | 26 | 47 | 11 | 0 | 3 | 20 | 9 |
| Maness, Dwight, Maui | .292 | 144 | 41 | 42 | 9 | 1 | 6 | 21 | 12 |

| | AVG | AB | R | H | 2B | 3B | HR | RBI | SB |
|---|---|---|---|---|---|---|---|---|---|
| Helton, Todd, Maui | .291 | 179 | 22 | 52 | 7 | 0 | 3 | 22 | 2 |
| Gibson, Derrick, Maui | .288 | 184 | 24 | 53 | 7 | 0 | 8 | 27 | 3 |
| Spencer, Shane, Hilo | .287 | 167 | 27 | 48 | 15 | 0 | 3 | 19 | 8 |
| Cruz, Jacob, West Oahu | .286 | 133 | 19 | 38 | 8 | 5 | 5 | 28 | 1 |
| Jackson, Ryan, Honolulu | .285 | 158 | 19 | 45 | 6 | 0 | 0 | 15 | 10 |
| Takayoshi, Todd, Hilo | .282 | 117 | 14 | 33 | 6 | 0 | 5 | 14 | 1 |
| Harrison, Ken, Honolulu | .282 | 110 | 14 | 31 | 6 | 0 | 3 | 11 | 0 |
| Agbayani, Benny, WO | .281 | 153 | 26 | 43 | 9 | 3 | 1 | 30 | 5 |
| Wilson, Preston, Maui | .278 | 198 | 29 | 55 | 9 | 3 | 5 | 30 | 11 |
| Conner, Decomba, Hilo | .276 | 87 | 12 | 24 | 7 | 0 | 0 | 6 | 0 |
| Staton, T.J., Honolulu | .273 | 165 | 22 | 45 | 6 | 3 | 3 | 19 | 4 |
| Marrero, Eli, West Oahu | .272 | 125 | 21 | 34 | 5 | 1 | 4 | 21 | 7 |
| Hiyama, Shinjiro, Hilo | .271 | 192 | 27 | 52 | 8 | 2 | 2 | 20 | 3 |
| Lamb, David, Maui | .271 | 181 | 18 | 49 | 12 | 0 | 3 | 19 | 1 |
| Cox, Steve, West Oahu | .264 | 125 | 19 | 33 | 4 | 0 | 5 | 22 | 0 |
| Thomas, Greg, Hilo | .261 | 165 | 23 | 43 | 15 | 1 | 5 | 29 | 1 |
| Canizaro, Jay, West Oahu | .261 | 119 | 23 | 31 | 5 | 0 | 4 | 14 | 9 |
| Motoki, Daisuke, Honolulu | .259 | 116 | 15 | 30 | 5 | 3 | 2 | 12 | 6 |
| Hamilton, Joe, Hilo | .256 | 117 | 18 | 30 | 6 | 0 | 3 | 16 | 1 |
| Konigsmark, David, Hilo | .256 | 94 | 16 | 24 | 2 | 0 | 0 | 9 | 1 |
| DeKneef, Mike, West Oahu | .252 | 143 | 20 | 36 | 8 | 0 | 0 | 11 | 2 |
| #Peterson, Charles, Honolulu | .235 | 162 | 25 | 38 | 5 | 5 | 1 | 22 | 14 |
| #Powell, Dante, West Oahu | .234 | 192 | 44 | 45 | 5 | 3 | 7 | 28 | 16 |

### INDIVIDUAL PITCHING LEADERS
(Minimum 34 Innings)

| | W | L | ERA | G | SV | IP | H | BB | SO |
|---|---|---|---|---|---|---|---|---|---|
| Kashiwada, Takashi, Hon. | 2 | 2 | 1.78 | 18 | 2 | 35 | 26 | 14 | 20 |
| Najera, Noe, Honolulu | 5 | 4 | 1.87 | 12 | 0 | 53 | 36 | 25 | 46 |
| Vierra, Joey, Maui | 3 | 3 | 1.95 | 11 | 0 | 60 | 47 | 18 | 59 |
| #Wolff, Bryan, Honolulu | 2 | 1 | 1.97 | 24 | 8 | 32 | 21 | 23 | 35 |
| Hancock, Ryan, West Oahu | 5 | 1 | 2.42 | 11 | 0 | 52 | 53 | 16 | 50 |
| Farmer, Mike, Maui | 4 | 2 | 2.45 | 14 | 0 | 51 | 43 | 23 | 55 |
| Sauerbeck, Scott, Maui | 1 | 3 | 2.83 | 13 | 0 | 51 | 49 | 38 | 32 |
| Blyleven, Todd, Honolulu | 4 | 1 | 2.93 | 13 | 0 | 46 | 42 | 16 | 26 |
| Winslett, Dax, Hilo | 1 | 3 | 2.98 | 11 | 0 | 57 | 61 | 16 | 47 |
| Price, Tom, Maui | 3 | 4 | 3.07 | 19 | 3 | 41 | 44 | 14 | 32 |
| Shepherd, Alvie, Maui | 4 | 2 | 3.08 | 20 | 4 | 38 | 24 | 22 | 37 |
| Teramoto, Hirofumi, Maui | 3 | 1 | 3.22 | 11 | 0 | 45 | 31 | 14 | 46 |
| Smith, Dan, West Oahu | 3 | 3 | 3.32 | 10 | 0 | 43 | 47 | 21 | 29 |
| Murdaugh, Reese, West Oahu | 1 | 2 | 3.38 | 16 | 0 | 45 | 48 | 12 | 20 |
| Harris, David, West Oahu | 1 | 2 | 3.46 | 10 | 0 | 39 | 36 | 13 | 36 |
| Shenk, Larry, Honolulu | 2 | 2 | 3.67 | 16 | 0 | 34 | 33 | 7 | 25 |
| Brown, Mike, Honolulu | 1 | 5 | 3.74 | 12 | 0 | 43 | 34 | 33 | 50 |
| Sebach, Kyle, West Oahu | 3 | 4 | 3.83 | 12 | 0 | 54 | 44 | 20 | 50 |
| Doorneweerd, Dave, Hilo | 3 | 4 | 3.99 | 17 | 1 | 38 | 30 | 14 | 45 |
| #Edsell, Geoff, West Oahu | 6 | 4 | 5.79 | 13 | 0 | 51 | 59 | 29 | 52 |

# AUSTRALIAN LEAGUE

In a series that had a distinct red, white and blue flavor, the Sydney Blues won their first Australian Baseball League title in 1995-96.

Veteran Australian catcher Gary White, the league's MVP, hit two homers as the Blues beat the Melbourne Reds two straight in the best-of-3 championship series.

White, 27, became the first player in the league's seven-year history to win both the series and league MVP trophies. He hit .357 with a league-best 17 homers and 49 RBIs during the season, but missed out on the batting title to Perth's Jason Hewitt, a native Australian who hit .396.

White wasn't the only hero for the Blues, whose roster included four members of the Toronto Blue Jays organization. The most effective Blue Jay was righthander Doug Meiners, who went 7-2 with a 4.10 ERA.

Each of the league's eight teams was affiliated with a major league club. League rules allow four imports per team.

Imports have played a significant role in the seven-year-old league's development, but imports were largely upstaged by White and other native Australians in the 1995-96 season.

"There's no doubt in my mind that Australians have improved dramatically," said Reds lefthander Jon Deeble,

the league ERA leader and a hitting coach in the Florida Marlins system.

Frankie Rodriguez (Brewers), a righthander with Double-A experience, was the top import. He led the league with seven wins, posted a 2.69 ERA and struck out 67 in 74 innings.

Defending champion Melbourne, previously the Waverley Reds, advanced to the title series despite a fourth-place regular-season finish.

The Reds started slowly, but picked up steam with the addition of veteran sluggers Dave Nilsson (Brewers) and Greg Jelks.

Nilsson, the best player in league history and the defending batting champion, had signed a five-year contract with the Reds and was a part-owner of the club, but he became embroiled in a six-month dispute that centered on his desire to play in his native Queensland. He refused to play for the Reds. It was eventually resolved that Nilsson would finish out the season but would be released from the three remaining years on his contract.

## STANDINGS

**REGULAR SEASON**

| | W | L | PCT | GB |
|---|---|---|---|---|
| Brisbane Bandits | 29 | 16 | .644 | — |
| Sydney Blues | 28 | 19 | .596 | 2 |
| Perth Heat | 26 | 20 | .565 | 3½ |
| Melbourne Reds | 27 | 21 | .563 | 3½ |
| Gold Coast Cougars | 23 | 21 | .527 | 5½ |
| Melbourne Monarchs | 24 | 24 | .500 | 6½ |
| Adelaide Giants | 21 | 25 | .457 | 8½ |
| Hunter Eagles | 7 | 39 | .152 | 22½ |

**PLAYOFFS—Semifinals:** Sydney defeated Perth, 2-1, and Melbourne defeated Brisbane, 2-0, in best-of-3 series. **Finals:** Sydney defeated Melbourne, 2-0, in best-of-3 series.

### INDIVIDUAL BATTING LEADERS
(Minimum 173 Plate Appearances)

| | AVG | AB | R | H | 2B | 3B | HR | RBI | SB |
|---|---|---|---|---|---|---|---|---|---|
| Hewitt, Jason, Perth | .396 | 144 | 38 | 57 | 15 | 2 | 2 | 23 | 10 |
| Dunn, Michael, Adelaide | .388 | 178 | 41 | 69 | 14 | 5 | 5 | 29 | 13 |
| Scott, Andrew, Adelaide | .363 | 171 | 32 | 62 | 19 | 2 | 6 | 36 | 2 |
| White, Gary, Sydney | .357 | 154 | 35 | 55 | 16 | 1 | 17 | 49 | 0 |
| Hammer, Ben, Monarchs | .351 | 154 | 34 | 54 | 8 | 2 | 2 | 28 | 5 |
| Thompson, Stuart, GC | .340 | 153 | 27 | 52 | 12 | 1 | 6 | 38 | 0 |
| Tunkin, Scott, Sydney | .328 | 177 | 41 | 58 | 12 | 0 | 12 | 31 | 5 |
| Watts, Craig, Adelaide | .327 | 116 | 36 | 56 | 10 | 0 | 17 | 49 | 3 |
| White, Darren, Adelaide | .325 | 163 | 38 | 53 | 12 | 0 | 15 | 41 | 8 |
| Buckley, Matt, Gold Coast | .316 | 158 | 31 | 50 | 19 | 1 | 1 | 27 | 3 |
| Metcalf, Scott, Perth | .311 | 164 | 30 | 51 | 9 | 1 | 14 | 44 | 0 |
| Dandridge, Brad, Adelaide | .309 | 152 | 30 | 47 | 8 | 1 | 4 | 26 | 5 |
| Vegg, Richard, Monarchs | .308 | 156 | 30 | 48 | 5 | 1 | 1 | 30 | 5 |
| Edmondson, Gavin, Perth | .307 | 163 | 33 | 50 | 7 | 3 | 8 | 33 | 2 |
| Harvey, Aaron, Reds | .301 | 176 | 35 | 53 | 10 | 2 | 2 | 20 | 21 |
| Davison, Nathan, Adelaide | .301 | 163 | 41 | 49 | 12 | 0 | 4 | 25 | 3 |
| Kingman, Brendan, Sydney | .292 | 161 | 33 | 47 | 6 | 3 | 9 | 40 | 1 |
| Johnson, Ron, Brisbane | .290 | 155 | 41 | 45 | 9 | 0 | 10 | 34 | 2 |

### INDIVIDUAL PITCHING LEADERS
(Minimum 51 Innings)

| | W | L | ERA | G | SV | IP | H | BB | SO |
|---|---|---|---|---|---|---|---|---|---|
| Deeble, Jon, Monarchs | 3 | 2 | 2.68 | 9 | 0 | 54 | 59 | 11 | 33 |
| Rodriguez, Frankie, Brisbane | 7 | 0 | 2.69 | 13 | 0 | 74 | 51 | 49 | 67 |
| Sheldon-Collins, Simon, Reds | 7 | 4 | 3.40 | 13 | 0 | 77 | 66 | 26 | 43 |
| Moss, Damian, Reds | 4 | 6 | 3.86 | 13 | 0 | 68 | 51 | 38 | 58 |
| Byrne, Earl, Monarchs | 6 | 3 | 3.89 | 14 | 0 | 69 | 64 | 33 | 72 |
| Feledyk, Kristian, Brisbane | 7 | 1 | 3.93 | 11 | 1 | 55 | 47 | 26 | 29 |
| Howell, Stuart, Gold Coast | 4 | 6 | 4.01 | 15 | 1 | 83 | 69 | 23 | 49 |
| Brunson, William, Adelaide | 5 | 1 | 4.08 | 12 | 0 | 57 | 62 | 25 | 51 |
| Meiners, Doug, Sydney | 7 | 2 | 4.10 | 12 | 0 | 68 | 81 | 13 | 39 |
| Challinor, John, Adelaide | 5 | 8 | 4.41 | 17 | 0 | 100 | 98 | 39 | 77 |
| Dale, Phil, Reds | 4 | 5 | 4.46 | 16 | 2 | 75 | 90 | 9 | 37 |
| Cederblad, Brett, Gold Coast | 9 | 2 | 4.54 | 13 | 0 | 83 | 83 | 15 | 54 |
| Hiljus, Erik, Monarchs | 6 | 3 | 4.58 | 12 | 0 | 75 | 81 | 26 | 58 |

# COLLEGE BASEBALL

# Dramatic Last-Inning Home Run By Morris Powers LSU To Title

**By JIM CALLIS**

Warren Morris is the poster boy for everything good about college baseball.

Morris came to Louisiana State in 1992 on a full academic scholarship. He was 5-foot-11 and 150 pounds when he attended his first team meeting as an unrecruited walk-on. "I looked around," Morris said, "and the only person I was bigger than was the equipment manager."

He spent the 1993 season as a redshirt behind Tigers All-American second baseman Todd Walker before becoming a three-year starter at that position. He worked hard to add 20 pounds and put just as much effort in the classroom, carrying a 3.57 GPA with a zoology (pre-med) major.

**We Are The Champions.** Louisiana State celebrates its third College World Series title in six years. The Tigers beat Miami 8-7 in the championship game.

BILL SETLIFF

That humble background is why Skip Bertman called what happened to Morris early in 1996 the saddest thing he's seen at Louisiana State in his 13 seasons as head coach. Morris was bothered by wrist problems that limited him to 14 regular-season starts before a broken hamate bone finally was discovered in his right hand.

He had surgery to remove the bone April 24, jeopardizing his prospects for the postseason and possibly the Olympics. Morris missed just 28 days before returning to earn all-tournament honors at the NCAA South II Regional.

As Morris strode to the plate in the bottom of the ninth on June 8, someone in the Tigers dugout said loud enough for all to hear, "Warren hasn't hit a home run all season."

Miami freshman closer Robbie Morrison had just struck out catcher Tim Lanier, stranding Brad Wilson at third base to preserve an 8-7 lead and bring the Hurricanes within one out of the College World Series championship.

There have been any number of dramatic hits in CWS play, but it took 50 years for a home run to end a game and determine the national championship. Morris lined Morrison's first pitch, a curveball, just over the right-field fence, screaming as he rounded first base and realizing that he had just led LSU to a heart-stopping 9-8 victory and the national title. Miami players lay prone on the infield as if they had been shot.

"I hadn't hit a home run in so long, I didn't know what one looked like," Morris said. "It's been a tough year, but it's all worth it now."

There hasn't been a more clutch home run in World Series history, be it college or the major leagues.

Bill Mazeroski? The game was tied. Kirk Gibson? It came in the first game of the Series. Joe Carter? If he doesn't take Mitch Williams deep, the Blue Jays come back the next day with another chance to win the championship.

"Isn't it ironic that Warren Morris would be there to hit his first home run of the year?" Bertman asked. "That shows you that the kids who are the greatest always come through."

## Don't Stop Believing

Louisiana State's championship left no doubt as to which is the premier program in college baseball. The Tigers also won the CWS in 1991 and 1993, and are just the fourth team to win three titles in six years. The others were Southern California (1958, '61, '63), Arizona State (1965, '67, '69) and Southern Cal again (1970, '71, '72, '73, '74).

Nothing can compare to the Trojans' five straight championships, but Louisiana State is dominating in an era of increased parity, scholarship reductions and greater competition with professional baseball for players. The Tigers have made nine trips to Omaha in the last 11 years, going 13-0 in regional and CWS championship games.

"Personally, this is the greatest championship I've ever been associated with," said Bertman, who also

**Ecstacy.** LSU's Warren Morris celebrates his dramatic last-inning homer that lifts Tigers to CWS title.

BILL SETLIFF

# COLLEGE WORLD SERIES
Omaha, Nebraska
May 31-June 8, 1996

## STANDINGS

| BRACKET 1 | W | L | RF | RA |
|---|---|---|---|---|
| Louisiana State | 4 | 0 | 29 | 21 |
| Florida | 2 | 2 | 16 | 16 |
| Florida State | 1 | 2 | 13 | 15 |
| Wichita State | 0 | 2 | 12 | 17 |

Bracket 1 Final: Louisiana State 2, Florida 1.

| BRACKET 2 | W | L | RF | RA |
|---|---|---|---|---|
| Miami | 3 | 1 | 44 | 18 |
| Clemson | 2 | 2 | 30 | 39 |
| Alabama | 1 | 2 | 21 | 34 |
| Oklahoma State | 0 | 2 | 10 | 15 |

Bracket 2 Final: Miami 14, Clemson 5.
CHAMPIONSHIP GAME: Louisiana State 9, Miami 8.

### INDIVIDUAL BATTING LEADERS
(Minimum 12 At-Bats)

| | AVG | AB | R | H | 2B | 3B | HR | RBI | SB |
|---|---|---|---|---|---|---|---|---|---|
| Moller, Chris, Alabama | .692 | 13 | 4 | 9 | 1 | 0 | 2 | 6 | 0 |
| Gomez, Rudy, Miami | .529 | 17 | 6 | 9 | 3 | 0 | 0 | 4 | 2 |
| Burrell, Pat, Miami | .500 | 14 | 7 | 7 | 2 | 0 | 2 | 8 | 1 |
| Bultmann, Kurt, Clem | .471 | 17 | 8 | 8 | 2 | 0 | 1 | 4 | 0 |
| Cora, Alex, Miami | .471 | 17 | 5 | 8 | 2 | 1 | 0 | 4 | 1 |
| DeCelle, Michael, Miami | .467 | 15 | 2 | 7 | 2 | 0 | 0 | 7 | 1 |
| Faurot, Adam, FSU | .462 | 13 | 2 | 6 | 1 | 0 | 0 | 0 | 1 |
| Morris, Warren, LSU | .462 | 13 | 5 | 6 | 2 | 0 | 1 | 5 | 1 |
| Galloway, Paul, Clemson | .438 | 16 | 4 | 7 | 2 | 0 | 1 | 3 | 1 |
| Bowles, Justin, LSU | .429 | 14 | 5 | 6 | 1 | 0 | 1 | 2 | 2 |

### INDIVIDUAL PITCHING LEADERS
(Minimum 7 Innings)

| | W | L | ERA | G | SV | IP | H | BB | SO |
|---|---|---|---|---|---|---|---|---|---|
| Kaufman, John, Florida | 1 | 1 | 2.08 | 2 | 0 | 13 | 9 | 6 | 12 |
| Chavez, Chris, FSU | 0 | 0 | 2.16 | 3 | 0 | 8 | 5 | 3 | 6 |
| Koch, Billy, Clemson | 0 | 0 | 2.45 | 2 | 1 | 7 | 8 | 4 | 9 |
| Arteaga, J.D., Miami | 1 | 0 | 2.63 | 2 | 0 | 14 | 15 | 5 | 12 |
| Yarnall, Eddie, LSU | 2 | 0 | 2.70 | 2 | 0 | 13 | 16 | 10 | 13 |

### ALL-TOURNAMENT TEAM
**C**—Tim Lanier, Louisiana State. **1B**—Chris Moller, Alabama. **2B**—Rudy Gomez, Miami. **3B**—Pat Burrell, Miami. **SS**—Alex Cora, Miami. **OF**—Justin Bowles, Louisiana State; Michael DeCelle, Miami; Brad Wilkerson, Florida. **DH**—Chuck Hazzard, Florida. **P**—J.D. Arteaga, Miami; Eddie Yarnall, Louisiana State.
**Most Outstanding Player**—Pat Burrell, 3b, Miami.

## CHAMPIONSHIP GAME
### Tigers 9, Hurricanes 8

| MIAMI | ab | r | h | bi | LSU | ab | r | h | bi |
|---|---|---|---|---|---|---|---|---|---|
| Grimmett cf | 3 | 2 | 0 | 0 | J. Williams ss | 4 | 0 | 1 | 0 |
| Gomez 2b | 5 | 1 | 3 | 0 | Koerner cf | 4 | 1 | 2 | 2 |
| Burrell 3b | 4 | 1 | 1 | 1 | Dunn 3b | 4 | 1 | 2 | 2 |
| Rivero rf-lf | 3 | 1 | 1 | 1 | Furniss 1b | 4 | 0 | 2 | 1 |
| DeCelle lf | 4 | 0 | 2 | 3 | Cooley lf | 5 | 0 | 1 | 0 |
| T. Moore rf | 0 | 0 | 0 | 0 | Wilson dh | 5 | 1 | 1 | 0 |
| Marcinczyk 1b | 5 | 2 | 2 | 0 | Bowles rf | 5 | 0 | 2 | 0 |
| Cora ss | 5 | 0 | 3 | 3 | Lanier c | 3 | 2 | 1 | 0 |
| Saggese dh | 5 | 0 | 2 | 0 | Morris 2b | 4 | 4 | 3 | 2 |
| Gargiulo c | 3 | 1 | 0 | 0 | | | | | |
| **Totals** | 37 | 8 | 14 | 8 | **Totals** | 38 | 9 | 15 | 7 |

| | | |
|---|---|---|
| **Miami** | | 200 032 001—8 |
| **Louisiana State** | | 003 000 222—9 |

Two out when winning run scored

**E**—Burrell (21), Rivero (5), Dunn (21), Furniss (7). **DP**—None. **LOB**—Miami 9, Louisiana State 10. **2B**—Marcinczyk (14), Cora (8), Saggese (12), Wilson (12), Bowles (13), Morris (3). **3B**—Cora (4). **HR**—Morris (11). **SB**—Gomez (28), Koerner (24), Lanier (2). **CS**—Koerner. **SH**—Grimmett, Morris. **SF**—Burrell, Rivero, DeCelle, Koerner, Dunn.

| Miami | ip | h | r | er | bb | so | LSU | ip | h | r | er | bb | so |
|---|---|---|---|---|---|---|---|---|---|---|---|---|---|
| Arteaga | 6⅔ | 10 | 5 | 3 | 2 | 7 | Shipp | 5⅔ | 11 | 7 | 5 | 3 | 3 |
| Morrison L. | 2 | 5 | 4 | 4 | 2 | 2 | Coogan W | 3⅓ | 3 | 1 | 1 | 0 | 1 |

**WP**—Morrison. **T**—3:19. **A**—23, 905.

won titles as an assistant at Miami (1982) and on the U.S. Olympic team (1988). "This is the most competitive team I've ever had. We had every opportunity not to win."

For the second time in four years, Louisiana State was ranked No. 1 in the preseason by Baseball America before winning the CWS. Despite that experience and the presence of eight seniors on the roster, this was the Tigers' most difficult championship.

Righthanders Kevin Shipp (shoulder tendinitis) and Joey Painich (elbow tenderness, shoulder tendinitis) missed four and eight weeks, respectively. First baseman Eddy Furniss (sprained ankle), the Division I home run and RBI leader, third baseman Nathan Dunn (pulled hamstring) and left fielder Chad Cooley (bad wrist) all were less than 100 percent in Omaha, as was Morris.

Not that the rash of injuries lessened the expectations of Louisiana State fans, more than 1,000 of whom made the trip to the CWS. Anything less than a national championship won't suffice in Baton Rouge.

"I remember in 1994, when we lost our first two games out here, we got home and it was like, 'God, what happened? Why didn't you win it all?'" Cooley said. "A team comes out here for the first time, and it can lose two games and go home and have a parade. It's not like that at LSU. If you don't win it all, you don't get a parade."

The local media ripped the Tigers when they made five errors and dropped three fly balls in a 12-11 loss to Kentucky in the Southeastern Conference tournament. One columnist called it "an exhibition of baseball such as few amateurs and no pros have ever seen, much less played" and questioned whether Louisiana State had what it took to win a regional.

The turning point came in the second round of the South II Regional at Baton Rouge. The Tigers spotted Nevada-Las Vegas a 6-0 lead before winning 7-6, with right fielder Justin Bowles saving the victory with a sprawling catch to end the game.

The comeback helped them regain the confidence they lost at the SEC tournament. More often than not, belief overrides skill in Omaha.

"I think who wins this thing is not the most talented guys, it's the guys who have the heart to win the national championship," Lanier said. "Even when things aren't going your way, you've got to keep fighting and believing in the guy behind you and the guy in front of you."

As Lanier walked back to the dugout after striking out against Morrison, he told Morris, "Don't stop believing." Morris had never stopped believing he could make it back from the hamate injury. With one swing, he became the poster boy for everything good about the College World Series.

## Coaching Carousel

After a year of coaching stability in 1995, college baseball saw perhaps more big-name changes in 1996 than ever before. When all was said and done, three coaches who have won CWS championships were out of work and another had switched addresses.

Here's how it all unfolded:

■ May 13: One day after Georgia's season ended, Steve Webber resigned under pressure.

Webber, 48, was Baseball America's Coach of the Year in 1990, when the Bulldogs became the first SEC school ever to win the College World Series. But in the next six seasons, the Bulldogs finished above .500 just twice and made only one regional playoff appearance.

Webber, who at 500-403 in 16 seasons was the winningest coach in school history, was replaced by former Bulldogs second baseman Robert Sapp as head coach June 5. Sapp, 55, won four Junior College World Series championships in 20 years at Middle Georgia JC.

# COLLEGE WORLD SERIES
## CHAMPIONS, 1947-96

| Year | Champion | Coach | Record | Runner-Up | MVP |
|------|----------|-------|--------|-----------|-----|
| 1947 | California* | Clint Evans | 31-10 | Yale | None selected |
| 1948 | Southern Cal | Sam Barry | 40-12 | Yale | None selected |
| 1949 | Texas* | Bibb Falk | 23-7 | Wake Forest | Charles Teague, 2b, Wake Forest |
| 1950 | Texas | Bibb Falk | 27-6 | Washington St. | Ray VanCleef, of, Rutgers |
| 1951 | Oklahoma* | Jack Baer | 19-9 | Tennessee | Sid Hatfield, 1b-p, Tennessee |
| 1952 | Holy Cross | Jack Berry | 21-3 | Missouri | Jim O'Neill, p, Holy Cross |
| 1953 | Michigan | Ray Fisher | 21-9 | Texas | J.L. Smith, p, Texas |
| 1954 | Missouri | Hi Simmons | 22-4 | Rollins | Tom Yewcic, c, Michigan St. |
| 1955 | Wake Forest | Taylor Sanford | 29-7 | W. Michigan | Tom Borland, p, Oklahoma St. |
| 1956 | Minnesota | Dick Siebert | 33-9 | Arizona | Jerry Thomas, p, Minnesota |
| 1957 | California* | George Wolfman | 35-10 | Penn State | Cal Emery, 1b-p, Penn State |
| 1958 | Southern Cal | Rod Dedeaux | 35-7 | Missouri | Bill Thom, p, Southern Cal |
| 1959 | Oklahoma St. | Toby Greene | 27-5 | Arizona | Jim Dobson, 3b, Oklahoma St. |
| 1960 | Minnesota | Dick Siebert | 34-7 | Southern Cal | John Erickson, 2b, Minnesota |
| 1961 | Southern Cal* | Rod Dedeaux | 43-9 | Oklahoma St. | Littleton Fowler, p, Oklahoma St. |
| 1962 | Michigan | Don Lund | 31-13 | Santa Clara | Bob Garibaldi, p, Santa Clara |
| 1963 | Southern Cal | Rod Dedeaux | 37-16 | Arizona | Bud Hollowell, c, Southern Cal |
| 1964 | Minnesota | Dick Siebert | 31-12 | Missouri | Joe Ferris, p, Maine |
| 1965 | Arizona State | Bobby Winkles | 54-8 | Ohio State | Sal Bando, 3b, Arizona State |
| 1966 | Ohio State | Marty Karow | 27-6 | Oklahoma St. | Steve Arlin, p, Ohio State |
| 1967 | Arizona State | Bobby Winkles | 53-12 | Houston | Ron Davini, c, Arizona State |
| 1968 | Southern Cal* | Rod Dedeaux | 45-14 | S. Illinois | Bill Seinsoth, 1b, Southern Cal |
| 1969 | Arizona State | Bobby Winkles | 56-11 | Tulsa | John Dolinsek, of, Arizona State |
| 1970 | Southern Cal | Rod Dedeaux | 51-13 | Florida State | Gene Ammann, p, Florida St. |
| 1971 | Southern Cal | Rod Dedeaux | 53-13 | S. Illinois | Jerry Tabb, 1b, Tulsa |
| 1972 | Southern Cal | Rod Dedeaux | 50-13 | Arizona State | Russ McQueen, p, Southern Cal |
| 1973 | Southern Cal* | Rod Dedeaux | 51-11 | Arizona State | Dave Winfield, of-p, Minnesota |
| 1974 | Southern Cal | Rod Dedeaux | 50-20 | Miami (Fla.) | George Milke, p, Southern Cal |
| 1975 | Texas | Cliff Gustafson | 56-6 | South Carolina | Mickey Reichenbach, 1b, Texas |
| 1976 | Arizona | Jerry Kindall | 56-17 | E. Michigan | Steve Powers, dh-p, Arizona |
| 1977 | Arizona State | Jim Brock | 57-12 | South Carolina | Bob Horner, 3b, Arizona State |
| 1978 | Southern Cal* | Rod Dedeaux | 54-9 | Arizona State | Rod Boxberger, p, Southern Cal |
| 1979 | CS Fullerton | Augie Garrido | 60-14 | Arkansas | Tony Hudson, p, CS Fullerton |
| 1980 | Arizona | Jerry Kindall | 45-21 | Hawaii | Terry Francona, of, Arizona |
| 1981 | Arizona State | Jim Brock | 55-13 | Oklahoma St. | Stan Holmes, of, Arizona State |
| 1982 | Miami (Fla.)* | Ron Fraser | 57-18 | Wichita State | Dan Smith, p, Miami (Fla.) |
| 1983 | Texas* | Cliff Gustafson | 66-14 | Alabama | Calvin Schiraldi, p, Texas |
| 1984 | CS Fullerton | Augie Garrido | 66-20 | Texas | John Fishel, of, CS Fullerton |
| 1985 | Miami (Fla.)* | Ron Fraser | 64-16 | Texas | Greg Ellena, dh, Miami (Fla.) |
| 1986 | Arizona | Jerry Kindall | 49-19 | Florida State | Mike Senne, of, Arizona |
| 1987 | Stanford | Mark Marquess | 53-17 | Oklahoma St. | Paul Carey, of, Stanford |
| 1988 | Stanford | Mark Marquess | 46-23 | Arizona State | Lee Plemel, p, Stanford |
| 1989 | Wichita State | Gene Stephenson | 68-16 | Texas | Greg Brummett, p, Wichita St. |
| 1990 | Georgia | Steve Webber | 52-19 | Oklahoma St. | Mike Rebhan, p, Georgia |
| 1991 | Louisiana St.* | Skip Bertman | 55-18 | Wichita State | Gary Hymel, c, Louisiana St. |
| 1992 | Pepperdine* | Andy Lopez | 48-11 | CS Fullerton | Phil Nevin, 3b, CS Fullerton |
| 1993 | Louisiana St. | Skip Bertman | 53-17 | Wichita State | Todd Walker, 2b, Louisiana St. |
| 1994 | Oklahoma* | Larry Cochell | 50-17 | Georgia Tech | Chip Glass, of, Oklahoma |
| 1995 | CS Fullerton* | Augie Garrido | 57-9 | Southern Cal | Mark Kotsay, of-lhp, CS Fullerton |
| 1996 | Louisiana State* | Skip Bertman | 52-15 | Miami (Fla.) | Pat Burrell, 3b, Miami |

*Undefeated

**June Raines**

■ May 15: If there was any doubt the SEC was college baseball's toughest conference on coaches, there shouldn't have been two days later when South Carolina's June Raines

# BOWING OUT

**Several big-name coaches left the game after the 1996 season**

**Cliff Gustafson**

**Jerry Kindall**

**Gary Ward**

**Steve Webber**

**John Winkin**

also stepped down under pressure.

Raines, 57, was an instant success at South Carolina. In his first year he took the Gamecocks to the 1977 CWS championship game, where they lost 2-1 to Arizona State.

South Carolina reached the NCAA playoffs in eight of the next 11 seasons, but just twice in the last eight years. Raines finished as the Gamecocks' winningest coach at 763-380 in 20 seasons.

South Carolina pulled a coup by hiring North Carolina State coach Ray Tanner June 14. Tanner, 38, is considered one of college baseball's brightest young coaches and spent the summer as an assistant on the U.S. Olympic team.

North Carolina State hired New Mexico State's Elliot Avent on Aug. 14.

■ May 21: One of the most successful college coaches ever called it quits when Jerry Kindall, who led Arizona to three national championships in 24 years, decided he no longer had what it took to lead the Wildcats to prominence.

Kindall, 61, won national championships in 1976, 1980 and 1986, and went 861-580 in 24 years as the winningest coach in Wildcats history. But Kindall, the only man to play for and coach a CWS champion, couldn't keep the magic going. The Wildcats have had three straight losing seasons and finished last in the Pacific-10 Conference Southern Division each year.

Arizona promoted Jerry Stitt to head coach July 3. Stitt, 49, was an all-America outfielder for the Wildcats in 1968 and an assistant for 18 years.

■ May 25: Another SEC coach bit the dust when former Chicago Cubs all-star shortstop Don Kessinger resigned as Mississippi head coach.

Kessinger, 53, took a position as an assistant to Rebels athletic director Pete Boone. In six years as Mississippi's coach, he went 185-153, posting five winning seasons before going 24-30 in 1996.

Mississippi lured Pat Harrison away from Pepperdine June 12. Harrison, 49, went 69-38 in two years with the Waves. After playing second base for Southern California's 1968 CWS champions, he won three more CWS titles as an assistant at Southern Cal and Oklahoma.

■ June 13: Maine fired coaching legend John Winkin, who took the Black Bears to five CWS from 1981-86.

Maine hasn't been back to Omaha since and has had four losing seasons in the last five years. After the Black Bears finished 19-36 in 1996, university president Fred Hutchinson and AD Sue Tyler agreed not to renew the 76-year-old Winkin's contract. Tyler said she discussed the idea of giving him one more year as a "celebration season," but Winkin rejected the offer.

Winkin, the winningest coach in Maine history at 642-430 in 22 years and 934-670 overall in 42 years of college coaching, found another job 12 miles away. Husson (Maine) College hired him as an assistant coach June 26.

Maine replaced Winkin with Providence coach Paul Kostacopoulos Aug. 16.

■ July 17: The biggest bombshell of the summer was dropped when Cliff Gustafson, the winningest coach in Division I history, resigned abruptly at Texas.

Gustafson, 65, led the Longhorns to CWS championships in 1975 and 1983 and went 1,466-377 in 29 seasons. But he was undone by a scandal involving his summer baseball camps.

Gustafson retired hours before the university detailed how he had broken university rules by diverting $285,000 from his camps into an unauthorized bank account. The money belonged to Gustafson, but he was supposed to report the revenue and route it

**Augie Garrido.** Texas-bound

# PLAYER OF THE YEAR

## No. 1 Pick Benson Shackles Hitters

In June 1995, Kris Benson sat in the outfield at USA Stadium in Millington, Tenn., trying to figure out why he wasn't good enough to make the U.S. national team.

He never had been cut from a team before, and he thought he had pitched well during the try-out camp. That night, he called home to suburban Atlanta and told his parents, "I'm outta here."

A year later, Benson realized Team USA head coach Skip Bertman had done him a favor.

"Once I realized what they were doing, they were right," Benson said. "It gave me time off to go work out in the weight room. That's probably my main point of success this year. It gave

**Kris Benson**

ROBERT GURGANUS

### PREVIOUS WINNERS

1981—**Mike Sodders**, 3b, Arizona State
1982—**Jeff Ledbetter**, of-lhp, Florida State
1983—**Dave Magadan**, 1b, Alabama
1984—**Oddibe McDowell**, of, Arizona State
1985—**Pete Incaviglia**, of, Oklahoma State
1986—**Casey Close**, of, Michigan
1987—**Robin Ventura**, 3b, Oklahoma State
1988—**John Olerud**, 1b-lhp, Washington State
1989—**Ben McDonald**, rhp, Louisiana State
1990—**Mike Kelly**, of, Arizona State
1991—**David McCarty**, 1b, Stanford
1992—**Phil Nevin**, 3b, Cal State Fullerton
1993—**Brooks Kieschnick**, dh-rhp, Texas
1994—**Jason Varitek**, c, Georgia Tech
1995—**Todd Helton**, 1b-lhp, Tennessee

me 15 pounds of muscle, and I'm a lot more aggressive this year."

And he was a lot more effective. Benson, Baseball America's 1996 College Player of the Year, went 14-2, 2.02 with 204 strikeouts and just 27 walks in 156 innings. He ranked first in Division I in innings, second in strikeouts, fourth in wins and sixth in ERA.

"We call him The Messiah," teammate Billy Koch said. "We joke around with him, saying he floats out to the mound and stands out there and twirls the ball on

his finger. He's phenomenal. I wish I could watch every one of his starts from here on out."

The Pittsburgh Pirates hope Koch is correct and that Benson has savior potential. Pittsburgh selected Benson with the No. 1 overall pick in the draft and gave him a $2 million bonus after he finished pitching with the Olympic team.

Benson opened the 1996 season with a three-hit shutout of South Florida, striking out 14 and walking none. It was one of six times in 1996 that he would reach double digits in strikeouts without a walk, including a 17-whiff two-hitter against Virginia Tech.

His package of stuff, command and makeup was so dominant that by March the Pirates pretty much knew they would select him with the first overall pick, even if they wouldn't tip their hand. The last two players who were such certain No. 1 overall picks also were college righthanders—Louisiana State's Ben McDonald (1989) and Florida State's Paul Wilson (1994).

"He's just the very best that I've ever seen in terms of consistency, focus and concentration," Clemson coach Jack Leggett said. "He has tremendous mental attributes that separate him from any other pitcher that I've ever seen at the college level. I know that's strong, but that's the way he is."

**—JIM CALLIS**

---

through the athletic department.

"It's not exactly the way I wanted to go out," Gustafson said. "My conscience is clear on the way I handled the camp situation and the so-called extra account.

"I felt that at this stage of my career and at my age, why put yourself through this kind of situation? Let's get on and live the rest of my life. That's what I'm going to do."

Any thought that Texas would have a difficult time filling its coaching void was quelled when the Long-horns hired Augie Garrido July 31. Garrido, 57, won three national championships at Cal State Fullerton and has a career record of 1,152-523 in 28 seasons at four schools.

Fullerton also found a capable replacement in George Horton, who had been the associate head coach under Garrido. Horton, 42, one of college baseball's top pitching coaches and recruiters, was promoted Sept. 4.

■ Sept. 9: Nevada-Las Vegas' Fred Dallimore went

out on his own terms, resigning and getting replaced by Rebels hitting coach Rod Soesbe.

Dallimore, 51, went 794-558 in 23 seasons with the Rebels. He had become fed up with the Rebels' athletic department and said the final straw came last November, when he was told that $24,000 in donor funds earmarked for the baseball team would be used to help offset the department's $800,000 deficit. He almost resigned immediately, but stayed on and led Vegas to a 43-17 record and the Big West Conference tournament championship.

■ Oct. 23: Another coaching giant left the game when Gary Ward retired at Oklahoma State.

Ward, 56, guided the Cowboys to a record seven straight CWS from 1981-87 and reached three CWS championship games, but never won a national title. At 953-313 in 19 seasons he was the winningest coach in Oklahoma State history, and he closed his career with 16 consecutive Big Eight Conference titles.

The Cowboys hoped to name a replacement by mid-December.

# 1996 COLLEGE ALL-AMERICA TEAM

Selected by Baseball America

**Illinois shortstop Josh Klimek**
.400 average, 26 homers

**LSU first baseman Eddy Furniss**
26 homers, 103 RBIs

**CS Northridge catcher Robert Fick**
.420 average, 96 RBIs

## FIRST TEAM

| Pos | Player, School | YR | HT | WT | B-T | Hometown | AVG | AB | R | H | 2B | 3B | HR | RBI | SB |
|-----|----------------|----|----|----|-----|----------|-----|----|---|---|----|----|----|-----|----|
| C | Robert Fick, Cal State Northridge | Jr. | 6-1 | 190 | L-R | Thousand Oaks, Calif. | .420 | 283 | 79 | 119 | 24 | 5 | 25 | 96 | 22 |
| 1B | Travis Lee, San Diego State | Jr. | 6-3 | 205 | L-L | Olympia, Wash. | .355 | 220 | 57 | 78 | 14 | 2 | 14 | 60 | 33 |
| 2B | Josh Kliner, Kansas | Sr. | 5-11 | 180 | B-R | Placentia, Calif. | .438 | 208 | 66 | 91 | 28 | 6 | 10 | 85 | 7 |
| 3B | Pat Burrell, Miami | Fr. | 6-4 | 220 | R-R | Boulder Creek, Calif. | .484 | 192 | 76 | 93 | 18 | 1 | 23 | 64 | 8 |
| SS | Josh Klimek, Illinois | Jr. | 6-1 | 175 | L-R | St. Louis | .400 | 215 | 86 | 73 | 22 | 1 | 26 | 94 | 1 |
| OF | J.D. Drew, Florida State | So. | 6-1 | 195 | L-R | Hahira, Ga. | .386 | 241 | 90 | 93 | 17 | 5 | 21 | 94 | 10 |
| OF | Chad Green, Kentucky | Jr. | 5-10 | 182 | B-R | Mentor, Ohio | .352 | 256 | 71 | 90 | 15 | 7 | 12 | 44 | 55 |
| OF | Mark Kotsay, Cal State Fullerton | Jr. | 6-0 | 180 | L-R | Santa Fe Springs, Calif. | .402 | 243 | 78 | 97 | 27 | 4 | 20 | 91 | 20 |
| DH | Eddy Furniss, Louisiana State | So. | 6-4 | 205 | L-L | Nacogdoches, Texas | .374 | 238 | 68 | 89 | 21 | 1 | 26 | 103 | 1 |

| Pos | Player, School | YR | HT | WT | B-T | Hometown | W | L | ERA | G | SV | IP | H | BB | SO |
|-----|----------------|----|----|----|-----|----------|---|---|-----|---|----|----|----|----|----|
| P | Kris Benson, Clemson | Jr. | 6-4 | 190 | R-R | Kennesaw, Ga. | 14 | 2 | 2.02 | 19 | 0 | 156 | 109 | 27 | 204 |
| P | Seth Greisinger, Virginia | Jr. | 6-4 | 195 | R-R | McLean, Va. | 12 | 2 | 1.76 | 16 | 0 | 123 | 78 | 36 | 141 |
| P | Braden Looper, Wichita State | Jr. | 6-5 | 220 | R-R | Mangum, Okla. | 4 | 1 | 2.09 | 26 | 12 | 56 | 37 | 15 | 64 |
| P | Evan Thomas, Fla. International | Sr. | 5-10 | 170 | R-R | Pembroke Pines, Fla. | 10 | 3 | 1.78 | 20 | 1 | 147 | 102 | 58 | 220 |
| P | Eddie Yarnall, Louisiana State | Jr. | 6-4 | 220 | L-L | Coral Springs, Fla. | 11 | 1 | 2.38 | 19 | 0 | 125 | 89 | 52 | 156 |

## SECOND TEAM

| Pos | Player, School | YR | HT | WT | B-T | Hometown | AVG | AB | R | H | 2B | 3B | HR | RBI | SB |
|-----|----------------|----|----|----|-----|----------|-----|----|---|---|----|----|----|-----|----|
| C | A.J. Hinch, Stanford | Sr. | 6-1 | 200 | R-R | Midwest City, Okla. | .381 | 210 | 60 | 80 | 19 | 3 | 11 | 59 | 18 |
| 1B | Lance Berkman, Rice | So. | 6-1 | 205 | B-L | New Braunfels, Texas | .398 | 241 | 76 | 96 | 16 | 4 | 20 | 92 | 8 |
| 2B | Travis Young, New Mexico | Jr. | 6-1 | 175 | R-R | Albuquerque, N.M. | .442 | 215 | 56 | 95 | 13 | 10 | 2 | 32 | 39 |
| 3B | Clint Bryant, Texas Tech | Sr. | 6-0 | 181 | R-R | Lubbock, Texas | .382 | 262 | 89 | 100 | 26 | 2 | 18 | 100 | 37 |
| SS | Kip Harkrider, Texas | So. | 5-11 | 170 | L-R | Carthage, Texas | .381 | 260 | 75 | 99 | 17 | 5 | 4 | 43 | 8 |
| OF | Kevin Barker, Virginia Tech | Jr. | 6-2 | 195 | L-L | Mendota, Va. | .361 | 202 | 63 | 73 | 9 | 9 | 20 | 62 | 3 |
| OF | Matt Kastellic, Texas Tech | Sr. | 6-1 | 185 | L-L | Anaheim, Calif. | .424 | 269 | 78 | 114 | 19 | 4 | 8 | 70 | 51 |
| OF | Jeremy Morris, Florida State | Jr. | 6-2 | 200 | R-R | Quincy, Fla. | .371 | 256 | 76 | 95 | 36 | 1 | 13 | 87 | 23 |
| DH | Casey Blake, Wichita State | Sr. | 6-3 | 195 | R-R | Indianola, Iowa | .360 | 247 | 79 | 89 | 21 | 2 | 22 | 101 | 19 |

| Pos | Player, School | YR | HT | WT | B-T | Hometown | W | L | ERA | G | SV | IP | H | BB | SO |
|-----|----------------|----|----|----|-----|----------|---|---|-----|---|----|----|----|----|----|
| P | Brian Carmody, Santa Clara | Jr. | 6-3 | 170 | L-L | San Jose | 10 | 3 | 1.81 | 17 | 0 | 120 | 84 | 57 | 118 |
| P | Eric DuBose, Mississippi State | So. | 6-2 | 217 | L-L | Jacksonville, Fla. | 10 | 4 | 3.11 | 17 | 1 | 133 | 127 | 55 | 174 |
| P | Seth Etherton, Southern Calif. | So. | 6-1 | 195 | R-R | Laguna Niguel, Calif. | 12 | 3 | 3.94 | 17 | 0 | 112 | 103 | 34 | 104 |
| P | Robbie Morrison, Miami | Fr. | 5-11 | 205 | R-R | Loxahatchee, Fla. | 4 | 2 | 1.68 | 38 | 14 | 59 | 35 | 27 | 88 |
| P | Jeff Weaver, Fresno State | Fr. | 6-5 | 175 | R-R | Simi Valley, Calif. | 12 | 5 | 2.51 | 19 | 1 | 143 | 107 | 30 | 136 |

## THIRD TEAM

**C**—Brian Loyd, Jr., Cal State Fullerton. **1B**—Danny Peoples, Jr., Texas. **2B**—Rudy Gomez, Jr., Miami. **3B**—Chris Heintz, Sr., South Florida. **SS**—Jason Grabowski, So., Connecticut. **OF**—Jeff Guiel, Jr., Oklahoma State; Jacque Jones, Jr., Southern Calif.; Brad Wilkerson, Fr., Florida. **DH**—Aaron Jaworowski, So., Missouri. **P**—Julio Ayala, Jr., Georgia Southern; Ryan Brannan, Jr., Long Beach State; Randy Choate, So., Florida State; R.A. Dickey, Jr., Tennessee; Ken Vining, Jr., Clemson.

# COACH OF THE YEAR
## Bertman Wins Difficult Championship

Louisiana State has had its share of memorable baseball coaches, though not always for the right reasons.

Harry Rabenhorst liked to practice his flycasting at practice. Jim Smith doubled as the football team's equipment manager. Jack Lamabe pitched in the major leagues for seven years, two more than he lasted in Baton Rouge.

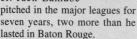
**Skip Bertman**

Enter Skip Bertman, who took over the Tigers in the fall of 1983. He'll be remembered as a winner.

Louisiana State won the College World Series for the third time in six years in 1996, further cementing the Tigers as college baseball's premier program. For the second time in four seasons, they backed up a preseason No. 1 ranking by Baseball America with a national championship.

It may have been Bertman's best coaching job yet, and for that reason he was named BA's College Coach of the Year. He became the third two-time winner of the award.

The Tigers went 52-15 despite getting hit with a rash of injuries, most notably to second baseman Warren Morris. Bertman, 58, said it was tough to inspire his 1996 team, which featured eight seniors.

"This team was not as easy to motivate as the other teams I've had," Bertman said. "This team is hip to my videos, my stories, my moments.

"Every time I turn left and every time I turn right, they know what I want from them. Every time I want to instill fear in them, they go, 'Here he goes again, the old goat.'"

Bertman, known as a master motivator, still was able to work some magic. After Louisiana State was eliminated from the Southeastern Conference tournament with an embarrassing 12-11 loss to Kentucky, he turned to an unlikely source: yellow uniform tops. His players were fired up when they found the garish uniforms and went 8-0 wearing yellow at the South II Regional and CWS.

Bertman is a hero in Baton Rouge after going 628-235 and taking the Tigers to Omaha nine times in 13 years. His legacy extends much further, throughout the SEC. Copying the blueprint he saw Ron Fraser use at Miami when Bertman was the Hurricanes' pitching coach, Bertman showed Louisiana State how to make money on college baseball.

The Tigers led college baseball in total (226,805) and average (5,816) attendance in 1996. The model built by Bertman and by Ron Polk at Mississippi State was borrowed throughout the SEC, where 10 of the 12 schools have renovated or built new stadiums in the last few years. When Auburn dedicated its refurbished Plainsman Park in 1996, coach Hal Baird thanked Bertman and Polk for making it possible.

**—JIM CALLIS**

### PREVIOUS WINNERS
1981—**Ron Fraser**, Miami
1982—**Gene Stephenson**, Wichita State
1983—**Barry Shollenberger**, Alabama
1984—**Augie Garrido**, Cal State Fullerton
1985—**Ron Polk**, Mississippi State
1986—**Skip Bertman**, Louisiana State
      **Dave Snow**, Loyola Marymount
1987—**Mark Marquess**, Stanford
1988—**Jim Brock**, Arizona State
1989—**Dave Snow**, Long Beach State
1990—**Steve Webber**, Georgia
1991—**Jim Hendry**, Creighton
1992—**Andy Lopez**, Pepperdine
1993—**Gene Stephenson**, Wichita State
1994—**Jim Morris**, Miami
1995—**Rod Delmonico**, Tennessee

---

## Fabulous Feats

Not all the coaching news was made off the field. On March 1, San Diego State's Jim Dietz became the 24th college coach to reach 1,000 wins.

Dietz, 56, reached the milestone with an 8-1 victory over Toledo in his 25th year with the Aztecs. He was mobbed by his players and couldn't hold back his emotions.

"This sends a message to younger coaches that if you keep at it, success will come your way," said Dietz, whose players have included Mark Grace and Tony Gwynn. "This isn't something I set out to do. I really didn't think about it until everyone made a big fuss.

"I want to thank all the people who are a part of this. From my assistant coaches to the players to the boosters to my friends, they've all given a lot of support."

Dietz has needed that support because he has received little from

**Jim Dietz**

the San Diego State administration. He and his players built the clubhouse, press box and bleachers and put up the lights at the Aztecs' Charlie Smith Field.

Other major accomplishments during the 1996 season:

■ Cal State Northridge set a Division I record with 13 homers in one game, a 29-3 rout of Fresno State on March 2. Catcher Robert Fick went deep three times, including the blast that tied the record. Second baseman Cesar Martinez and left fielder Ryan Hurd hit Nos. 12 and 13, respectively, in the eighth inning.

■ In what is believed to be a first in college baseball, every starter in the Nevada-Las Vegas lineup hit a homer in a 24-8 victory over San Jose State March 22. Doing the honors were Chris Adolph, Paul Tanner, Ryan Hankins, Brian Anthony, Stacy Kleiner, Scott Vincent, Ted Wilkes, Kevin Eberwein and Sean Campbell.

■ Troy State righthander Dean Cordova threw two no-hitters, March 4 against Valparaiso and March 31 against C.W. Post. Northeastern righthander John Forneiro matched him with no-hitters against Florida Atlantic on March 23 and Hofstra on May 11, but lost his first gem 1-0.

■ Connecticut shortstop Jason Grabowski turned an unassisted triple play in a 7-2 win over Yale on March 27. Baylor shortstop Scott Morrison did the same April 27 in a 7-0 victory over Rice.

■ Austin Peay State shortstop Chuck Abbott hit safely in 42 consecutive games, the fourth-longest streak in Division I history, before going 0-for-4 in an 8-4 loss to Western Kentucky on April 17.

**Chuck Abbott.** 42-game hitting streak

# FRESHMAN OF THE YEAR
## Miami's Burrell Becomes First Frosh To Win Batting Title

The question was asked again and again and again at the 1996 College World Series: Why wasn't Pat Burrell invited to try out for the U.S. Olympic team?

Louisiana State coach Skip Bertman, who also was in charge of Team USA, was on the receiving end of those queries. He patiently replied, time and time again, that he didn't want to send freshmen to battle against much older international teams.

But no freshman ever has hit the ball like Burrell. The Miami

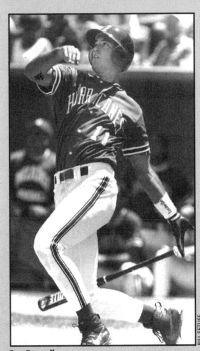

**Pat Burrell**

third baseman batted .484 in 1996, becoming the first freshman to lead Division I in hitting, and set additional Hurricanes freshman records with 23 home runs and 64 RBIs.

Few players ever have been as torrid in the postseason. At the Central I Regional at Texas, Burrell earned MVP honors by going 13-for-18 with four doubles and four homers. He followed up with an MVP performance at the CWS, going 7-for-14 with two homers and eight RBIs.

Those accomplishments made Burrell an easy choice for Baseball America's Freshman of the Year. But they weren't enough to garner Burrell a tryout for the Olympic team.

Miami coach Jim Morris, who ran the U.S. national team in 1990, was diplomatic about the omission.

"It's very, very difficult to select the top players in the country," Morris said. "But I will tell you I've never, ever seen a player hit the ball as hard as Pat Burrell has for 60-something games this year. He's been phenomenal."

For his part, Burrell wasn't bothered by the snub. In fact, he didn't even realize Bertman was the Olympic coach until a reporter told him.

"The way I look at it, I

know I'm young and I know the guys they have at third base have put up great numbers," Burrell said. "I'd like to be there. I'd like to get a tryout. But it's up to them."

After choosing Miami over Cal State Fullerton, Burrell had modest goals for the 1996 season. He never dreamed of the Olympics. He thought hitting .300 with 10 homers would make for a nice year.

Burrell, a 6-foot-4, 220-pound native of Boulder Creek, Calif., punished pitchers much more than that. Against Kris Benson, the Clemson righthander drafted No. 1 overall by the Pittsburgh Pirates, he more than held his own in Omaha. Burrell went 2-for-6 with a double and two walks.

Now the question becomes: What can he possibly do as an encore?

BA's 1996 Freshman All-America first team:

**C**—Chad Sutter, Tulane (.297-16-67). **1B**—Kevin Eberwein, Nevada-Las Vegas (.367-10-55). **2B**—Brian Oliver, California (.335-5-32, 21 SB). **3B**—Pat Burrell, Miami (.484-23-64). **SS**—Jay Hood, Georgia Tech (.276-8-46).

**OF**—Bubba Crosby, Rice (.318-12-64); Clinton Johnson, Vanderbilt (.328-13-53); Jason Tyner, Texas A&M (.407-0-29, 41 SB).

**DH**—Rick Saggese, Miami (.339-14-51).

**UT**—Brad Wilkerson, Florida (.407-9-68, 14 SB; 5-2, 2.97, 6 SV).

**P**—Jeff Austin, Stanford (6-4, 3.81); Chuck Crowder, Georgia Tech (10-5, 4.30); Chad Hutchinson, Stanford (7-2, 3.51); Robbie Morrison, Miami (4-2, 1.68, 14 SV); Jeff Weaver, Fresno State (12-5, 2.51).

**—JIM CALLIS**

■ Texas and Texas Christian attracted an NCAA-record regular-season crowd of 21,403 for a May 4 doubleheader at The Ballpark in Arlington, home of the Texas Rangers.

## Colgate, Wyoming Bow Out

Colgate and Wyoming played their last baseball games in 1996, bringing the total of Division I schools without the national pastime to 37.

Colgate's final games were to come in an April 29 doubleheader against Niagara, but rain canceled the contests. Instead, the Red Raiders capped a 3-20 season with a 16-0 loss to SUNY Oswego on April 25.

Colgate, which started playing baseball in 1886, played in the 1955 CWS but hadn't fielded a winning team in more than two decades. School officials originally planned to drop the sport after the 1993 season, but relented to allow the freshmen in their program to complete their careers.

Red Raiders baseball was a victim primarily of the enforcement of Title IX, federal law requiring equal opportunity for men and women in education. Many colleges have reacted by dropping men's sports while increasing opportunities for women.

The Wyoming program was more a victim of politics. The university's board of trustees voted Jan. 26 to cut baseball even though the team got 5,000 signatures on a petition to save the program. Interim athletic director Dan Viola devised a plan that would have spared baseball by trimming all sports, a measure that would have saved the school an additional $82,000 in 1997 and 1998.

In 1993, the Cowboys athletic department decided to drop men's track. Two members of the board have clients with sons in that program, so that sport was restored. Wyoming president Terry Roark feared this time around that the athletic department would again recommend to do away with men's track, so he didn't allow it to determine how its budget cuts would be made.

The Cowboys concluded a 36-20 season by sweeping Grand Canyon in a May 7 doubleheader, 12-10 and 24-5, and finished as the Division I leader in batting average at .363.

# NCAA TOURNAMENT

## PLAY-IN SERIES

(Best-of-3)

Cal State Northridge (Western Athletic) def. Santa Clara (West Coast)

Georgia Southern (Southern) def. Bethune-Cookman (Mid-Eastern Athletic)

Northeastern Illinois (Mid-Continent) def. Northern Illinois (Midwestern)

Austin Peay State (Ohio Valley) def. Southern (Southwestern Athletic)

Princeton (Ivy) def. Rider (Northeast)

Bucknell (Patriot) def. Siena (Metro Atlantic)

## REGIONALS

(Double elimination)

### ATLANTIC

**Site:** Clemson, S.C.
**Participants:** No. 1 Clemson (45-15, at large), No. 2 Tennessee (40-18, at large), No. 3 Georgia Southern (45-12, Southern), No. 4 Old Dominion (39-15, Colonial), No. 5 West Virginia (31-23, Big East), No. 6 Charleston Southern (30-22, Big South).
**Champion:** Clemson (4-0).
**Runner-Up:** Tennessee (3-2).
**Outstanding Player:** Jerome Robinson, of, Clemson.
**Attendance:** 20,797.

### CENTRAL I

**Site:** Austin.
**Participants:** No. 1 Miami (43-12, at large), No. 2 Long Beach State (34-24, at large), No. 3 Texas (38-22, at large), No. 4 UCLA (33-26, at large), No. 5 Southwest Missouri State (30-23, Missouri Valley), No. 6 Sam Houston State (30-27, Southland).
**Champion:** Miami (4-1).
**Runner-Up:** UCLA (3-2).
**Outstanding Player:** Pat Burrell, 3b, Miami.
**Attendance:** 36,495.

### CENTRAL II

**Site:** Lubbock, Texas.
**Participants:** No. 1 Southern California (41-14, Pacific-10), No. 2 Texas Tech (47-13, at large), No. 3 Oklahoma State (41-19, Big Eight), No. 4 Arkansas (39-18, at large), No. 5 Fresno State (35-22, at large), No. 6 Akron (37-21, Mid-American).
**Champion:** Oklahoma State (4-0).
**Runner-Up:** Southern California (3-2).
**Outstanding Player:** Tripp MacKay, ss, Oklahoma State.
**Attendance:** 26,575.

### EAST

**Site:** Gainesville, Fla.
**Participants:** No. 1 Florida (44-16, at large), No. 2 Central Florida (42-20, Trans America), No. 3 North Carolina State (42-17, at large), No. 4 South Florida (45-17, at large), No. 5 Massachusetts (37-11, Atlantic 10), No. 6 Bucknell (24-21, Patriot).
**Champion:** Florida (4-0).
**Runner-Up:** Massachusetts (3-2).
**Outstanding Player:** Brad Wilkerson, of-p, Florida
**Attendance:** 19,727.

### MIDWEST

**Site:** Wichita.
**Participants:** No. 1 Wichita State (50-9, at large), No. 2 Cal State Fullerton (43-14, at large), No. 3 Rice (39-21, Southwest), No. 4 Missouri (39-17, at large), No. 5 Delaware (44-10, North Atlantic), No. 6 Indiana (42-16, Big Ten).
**Champion:** Wichita State (4-0).
**Runner-Up:** Rice (3-2).
**Outstanding Player:** Brandon Baird, p, Wichita State.
**Attendance:** 31,683.

### SOUTH I

**Site:** Tuscaloosa, Ala.
**Participants:** No. 1 Alabama (45-17, Southeastern), No. 2 Virginia (41-19, Atlantic Coast), No. 3 South Alabama (42-15, Sun Belt), No. 4 Stetson (40-21, at large), No. 5 Notre Dame (43-16, at large), No. 6 Princeton (26-19, Ivy).
**Champion:** Alabama (4-0).
**Runner-Up:** Virginia (3-2).
**Outstanding Player:** Joel Colgrove, p, Alabama.
**Attendance:** 17,931.

### SOUTH II

**Site:** Baton Rouge.
**Participants:** No. 1 Louisiana State (44-15, at large), No. 2 Georgia Tech (37-22, at large), No. 3 Nevada-Las Vegas (43-15, Big West), No. 4 Tulane (42-18, Conference USA), No. 5 New Orleans (41-19, at large), No. 6 Austin Peay State (44-20, Ohio Valley).
**Champion:** Louisiana State (4-0).
**Runner-Up:** Georgia Tech (3-2).
**Outstanding Player:** Jason Williams, ss, Louisiana State.
**Attendance:** 35,164.

### WEST

**Site:** Stanford, Calif.
**Participants:** No. 1 Florida State (47-15, at large), No. 2 Stanford (39-17, at large), No. 3 Mississippi State (37-22, at large), No. 4 UC Santa Barbara (32-18, at large), No. 5 Cal State Northridge (49-16, Western Athletic), No. 6 Northeastern Illinois (31-27, Mid-Continent).
**Champion:** Florida State (4-0).
**Runner-Up:** Cal State Northridge (3-2).
**Outstanding Player:** Scooby Morgan, p-dh, Florida State
**Attendance:** 19,498.

# COLLEGE BASEBALL
## NCAA DIVISION I LEADERS

| FIELDING AVERAGE | G | AVG |
|---|---|---|
| Jacksonville State | 51 | .973 |
| Pepperdine | 52 | .973 |
| Ohio State | 56 | .972 |
| Alabama | 69 | .971 |
| Providence | 50 | .971 |
| Chicago State | 48 | .970 |
| Tulane | 63 | .970 |
| South Alabama | 59 | .969 |
| Florida | 68 | .968 |
| Cal State Fullerton | 61 | .968 |
| Arkansas State | 59 | .968 |
| Illinois | 59 | .968 |

### TEAM BATTING

| BATTING AVERAGE | G | AVG |
|---|---|---|
| Wyoming | 56 | .363 |
| Brigham Young | 57 | .361 |
| Texas Tech | 65 | .347 |
| Delaware | 56 | .346 |
| Miami (Fla.) | 64 | .343 |
| Nevada | 49 | .339 |
| Arizona State | 56 | .338 |
| Texas A&M | 58 | .337 |
| Southern Cal | 61 | .335 |
| Ohio State | 56 | .335 |

| RUNS SCORED | G | R |
|---|---|---|
| Oklahoma State | 66 | 750 |
| Texas Tech | 65 | 648 |
| Louisiana State | 67 | 640 |
| Cal State Northridge | 70 | 623 |
| Wichita State | 65 | 598 |
| Florida State | 69 | 596 |
| South Florida | 66 | 586 |
| Miami (Fla.) | 64 | 577 |
| Brigham Young | 57 | 568 |
| Arizona State | 56 | 552 |

| DOUBLES | G | 2B |
|---|---|---|
| Texas Tech | 65 | 181 |
| Wichita State | 65 | 161 |
| Alabama | 69 | 159 |
| Delaware | 56 | 156 |
| Bradley | 62 | 156 |

| TRIPLES | G | 3B |
|---|---|---|
| Texas | 63 | 37 |
| Arizona | 56 | 33 |
| Arkansas | 59 | 31 |
| The Citadel | 59 | 31 |
| Oklahoma State | 68 | 31 |

| HOME RUNS | G | HR |
|---|---|---|
| Louisiana State | 67 | 131 |
| Cal State Northridge | 70 | 129 |
| Brigham Young | 57 | 113 |
| Oklahoma State | 66 | 112 |
| Georgia Tech | 64 | 97 |
| Texas Tech | 65 | 97 |
| Miami (Fla.) | 64 | 91 |
| South Florida | 66 | 91 |
| Southwest Missouri State | 57 | 86 |
| Nevada-Las Vegas | 60 | 84 |

| STOLEN BASES | G | SB | ATT |
|---|---|---|---|
| Wichita State | 65 | 187 | 226 |
| Texas Tech | 65 | 185 | 227 |
| Evansville | 55 | 182 | 272 |
| California | 56 | 162 | 203 |
| Northeast Louisiana | 60 | 157 | 177 |
| The Citadel | 59 | 143 | 187 |
| Kentucky | 59 | 142 | 199 |
| UNC Charlotte | 59 | 137 | 164 |
| Texas Christian | 67 | 134 | 180 |
| Pittsburgh | 46 | 131 | 179 |

### TEAM PITCHING

| W-L PERCENTAGE | W | L | PCT |
|---|---|---|---|
| Wichita State | 54 | 11 | .831 |
| Southern | 34 | 7 | .829 |
| Delaware | 44 | 12 | .786 |
| Miami (Fla.) | 50 | 14 | .781 |
| Louisiana State | 52 | 15 | .776 |
| Georgia Southern | 46 | 14 | .767 |
| Texas Tech | 49 | 15 | .766 |
| Troy State | 41 | 13 | .759 |
| Massachusetts | 40 | 13 | .755 |
| Florida State | 52 | 17 | .754 |

| EARNED RUN AVERAGE | G | ERA |
|---|---|---|
| Clemson | 68 | 3.03 |
| Pepperdine | 52 | 3.16 |
| San Diego State | 59 | 3.31 |
| Wichita State | 65 | 3.32 |
| Louisiana State | 67 | 3.38 |
| Florida International | 59 | 3.51 |
| Tennessee | 63 | 3.51 |
| Santa Clara | 62 | 3.52 |
| Rutgers | 54 | 3.53 |
| Troy State | 54 | 3.55 |
| Florida State | 69 | 3.55 |

### INDIVIDUAL BATTING
#### BATTING AVERAGE
(Minimum 125 At-Bats)

| | AVG | G | AB | R | H | 2B | 3B | HR | RBI | BB | SO | SB |
|---|---|---|---|---|---|---|---|---|---|---|---|---|
| Pat Burrell, Miami (Fla.) | .484 | 60 | 192 | 75 | 93 | 18 | 1 | 23 | 64 | 61 | 40 | 8 |
| Marlon Stewart, Grambling | .449 | 41 | 138 | 42 | 62 | 6 | 4 | 14 | 49 | 14 | 25 | 9 |
| Mike Shannon, Penn | .444 | 37 | 142 | 37 | 63 | 18 | 2 | 6 | 30 | 11 | 9 | 5 |
| Travis Young, New Mexico | .442 | 51 | 215 | 56 | 95 | 13 | 10 | 2 | 32 | 20 | 30 | 39 |
| Alex Eckelman, Ohio State | .439 | 55 | 205 | 70 | 90 | 16 | 1 | 13 | 54 | 19 | 19 | 2 |
| Keith Finnerty, St. John's | .439 | 44 | 155 | 45 | 68 | 11 | 3 | 6 | 42 | 33 | 12 | 22 |
| Josh Kliner, Kansas | .438 | 56 | 208 | 66 | 91 | 28 | 6 | 10 | 85 | 44 | 24 | 7 |
| Matt Stringham, Brigham Young | .438 | 46 | 128 | 45 | 56 | 16 | 1 | 8 | 29 | 9 | 24 | 8 |
| Kevin Penwell, Boston College | .428 | 41 | 145 | 37 | 62 | 13 | 5 | 2 | 23 | 22 | 18 | 17 |
| Alex Tolbert, West. Carolina | .424 | 57 | 217 | 58 | 92 | 25 | 1 | 11 | 66 | 35 | 35 | 5 |
| Francis Collins, Nebraska | .424 | 55 | 217 | 60 | 92 | 10 | 2 | 1 | 37 | 42 | 21 | 19 |
| Matt Kastelic, Texas Tech | .424 | 65 | 269 | 78 | 114 | 19 | 4 | 8 | 70 | 31 | 15 | 51 |
| Steve Cote, Rhode Island | .422 | 39 | 135 | 34 | 57 | 10 | 5 | 6 | 37 | 10 | 13 | 13 |
| Robert Fick, Cal State Northridge | .420 | 69 | 283 | 79 | 119 | 24 | 5 | 25 | 96 | 33 | 44 | 22 |
| Rudy Gomez, Miami (Fla.) | .420 | 64 | 224 | 86 | 94 | 22 | 3 | 13 | 59 | 52 | 22 | 28 |
| Mark McNelly, New Mexico St. | .419 | 52 | 210 | 60 | 88 | 15 | 4 | 4 | 46 | 23 | 37 | 16 |
| Brian McClure, Illinois | .418 | 59 | 213 | 80 | 89 | 14 | 4 | 16 | 66 | 35 | 19 | 6 |
| Paul Tinelli, C.W. Post | .417 | 40 | 132 | 27 | 55 | 12 | 1 | 3 | 23 | 21 | 6 | 5 |
| Matt Quatraro, Old Dominion | .416 | 56 | 209 | 57 | 87 | 26 | 4 | 13 | 55 | 25 | 35 | 13 |
| Greg Taylor, Ark.-Little Rock | .415 | 51 | 207 | 62 | 86 | 31 | 3 | 4 | 51 | 29 | 24 | 14 |
| Muchie Dagliere, Massachusetts | .415 | 51 | 195 | 60 | 81 | 13 | 4 | 5 | 53 | 25 | 16 | 12 |
| Brian Schaller, LaSalle | .415 | 45 | 171 | 46 | 71 | 7 | 2 | 10 | 41 | 18 | 24 | 13 |
| Terrance Daniel, Jackson State | .415 | 42 | 135 | 23 | 56 | 12 | 1 | 1 | 27 | 13 | 16 | 20 |
| Marty Crawford, Baylor | .414 | 59 | 232 | 54 | 96 | 24 | 2 | 10 | 67 | 37 | 8 | 2 |
| Steve Dunlop, East. Illinois | .414 | 47 | 174 | 52 | 72 | 15 | 4 | 5 | 36 | 17 | 24 | 16 |
| Bryan Hobbs, Yale | .414 | 42 | 162 | 44 | 67 | 10 | 2 | 1 | 22 | 8 | 16 | 4 |
| Eric McDowell, Brigham Young | .412 | 51 | 194 | 56 | 80 | 11 | 4 | 3 | 46 | 26 | 17 | 4 |
| Mike Laskofski, William & Mary | .412 | 44 | 148 | 37 | 61 | 12 | 3 | 5 | 43 | 36 | 7 | 7 |
| Tyson Dowdell, Brigham Young | .412 | 55 | 187 | 68 | 77 | 21 | 0 | 17 | 71 | 47 | 28 | 3 |
| Carlos Licon, New Mexico State | .410 | 49 | 195 | 40 | 80 | 16 | 4 | 2 | 57 | 10 | 14 | 5 |
| Tom Stein, Fordham | .410 | 43 | 139 | 35 | 57 | 10 | 0 | 4 | 28 | 19 | 12 | 5 |
| Dan Thompson, Yale | .410 | 42 | 144 | 44 | 59 | 15 | 4 | 7 | 54 | 3 | 20 | 14 |
| Lincoln Williams, Southern | .410 | 41 | 144 | 39 | 59 | 11 | 2 | 6 | 39 | 24 | 17 | 8 |
| Don DeDonatis, East. Michigan | .409 | 56 | 186 | 38 | 76 | 11 | 1 | 3 | 38 | 25 | 8 | 28 |
| Mike Sharp, Air Force | .408 | 54 | 184 | 65 | 75 | 20 | 5 | 4 | 39 | 29 | 28 | 11 |
| Ryan Bennett, Austin Peay | .407 | 64 | 243 | 50 | 99 | 29 | 0 | 5 | 58 | 25 | 35 | 10 |
| Brad Wilkerson, Florida | .407 | 41 | 241 | 73 | 98 | 22 | 3 | 9 | 68 | 76 | 34 | 14 |
| Jason Tyner, Texas A&M | .407 | 58 | 246 | 74 | 100 | 7 | 0 | 0 | 29 | 22 | 10 | 41 |
| Danny Singletary, Coppin State | .404 | 39 | 146 | 43 | 59 | 10 | 5 | 7 | 49 | 24 | 15 | 17 |
| Paul Blandford, Kentucky | .403 | 54 | 233 | 60 | 94 | 15 | 4 | 11 | 51 | 24 | 29 | 30 |
| Mark Mortimer, Georgia State | .403 | 53 | 176 | 44 | 71 | 19 | 0 | 7 | 43 | 34 | 19 | 5 |
| Morgan Walker, Lamar | .403 | 55 | 206 | 51 | 83 | 18 | 2 | 15 | 50 | 21 | 30 | 5 |
| Mark Kotsay, Cal State Fullerton | .402 | 61 | 241 | 78 | 97 | 27 | 4 | 20 | 91 | 50 | 22 | 20 |
| Freddie Jackson, Grand Canyon | .402 | 55 | 214 | 48 | 86 | 17 | 4 | 8 | 50 | 26 | 52 | 21 |
| Rob Coddington, Wyoming | .401 | 43 | 147 | 27 | 59 | 9 | 1 | 4 | 30 | 14 | 19 | 3 |
| Joey Anderson, UNC Charlotte | .401 | 59 | 222 | 64 | 89 | 13 | 8 | 13 | 57 | 48 | 45 | 26 |
| Josh Klimek, Illinois | .400 | 59 | 215 | 73 | 86 | 22 | 1 | 26 | 94 | 28 | 21 | 1 |
| Mark Fischer, Georgia Tech | .400 | 63 | 260 | 60 | 104 | 23 | 5 | 14 | 66 | 20 | 34 | 8 |
| Travis Wyckoff, Wichita State | .400 | 63 | 235 | 90 | 94 | 29 | 2 | 3 | 68 | 59 | 30 | 25 |
| Mark Chonko, Ohio State | .400 | 55 | 195 | 58 | 78 | 11 | 1 | 14 | 61 | 31 | 22 | 2 |
| Chris Heintz, South Florida | .400 | 66 | 265 | 63 | 106 | 21 | 4 | 16 | 95 | 26 | 39 | 3 |
| Dan Olson, Indiana State | .399 | 53 | 188 | 52 | 75 | 15 | 4 | 9 | 46 | 35 | 51 | 9 |
| Lance Berkman, Rice | .398 | 65 | 241 | 76 | 96 | 16 | 4 | 20 | 92 | 57 | 27 | 8 |
| Chris Webb, SW Louisiana | .398 | 58 | 221 | 49 | 88 | 23 | 1 | 10 | 62 | 29 | 38 | 1 |
| Mike Pike, Fairfield | .397 | 40 | 151 | 43 | 60 | 20 | 1 | 8 | 51 | 19 | 14 | 11 |
| Jeff Berman, Maryland-Balt. Cty. | .397 | 36 | 126 | 28 | 50 | 5 | 1 | 2 | 20 | 13 | 14 | 5 |
| Brent Sachs, West. Michigan | .397 | 51 | 179 | 41 | 71 | 13 | 2 | 4 | 21 | 17 | 30 | 11 |
| Ryan Kritscher, UC Santa Barbara | .397 | 37 | 146 | 40 | 58 | 11 | 2 | 5 | 33 | 13 | 14 | 5 |
| Mike Ciminiello, Princeton | .396 | 46 | 159 | 46 | 63 | 11 | 0 | 13 | 48 | 32 | 27 | 4 |
| D.G. Nelson, Brigham Young | .396 | 56 | 207 | 63 | 82 | 10 | 1 | 19 | 68 | 16 | 45 | 10 |
| Jeremy Keller, Winthrop | .396 | 58 | 197 | 47 | 78 | 15 | 2 | 14 | 58 | 28 | 27 | 9 |
| Jeremy Giambi, Cal State Fullerton | .396 | 61 | 225 | 70 | 89 | 20 | 1 | 6 | 58 | 59 | 27 | 25 |
| Randall Brooks, Notre Dame | .396 | 60 | 225 | 42 | 89 | 16 | 4 | 4 | 27 | 22 | 35 | 15 |
| Ryan Roberts, Brigham Young | .395 | 56 | 220 | 82 | 87 | 8 | 2 | 23 | 50 | 30 | 27 | 10 |

## RUNS SCORED

| | G | R |
|---|---|---|
| Rusty McNamara, Okla. State | 66 | 100 |
| Stubby Clapp, Texas Tech | 62 | 97 |
| Tripp MacKay, Okla. State | 66 | 96 |
| Nathan Dunn, Louisiana St. | 66 | 95 |
| Adam Kennedy, CS Northridge | 70 | 94 |
| Travis Wyckoff, Wichitta St. | 63 | 90 |
| J.D. Drew, Florida State | 69 | 90 |
| Clint Bryant, Texas Tech | 65 | 89 |
| Randy Young, Wichita St. | 63 | 86 |
| Rudy Gomez, Miami (Fla.) | 64 | 86 |
| Gio Cafaro, South Florida | 66 | 86 |
| Matt Nivens, Missouri | 58 | 85 |
| Jeff Guiel, Okla. State | 61 | 84 |
| Ryan Fry, Missouri | 58 | 83 |
| Ross Gload, South Florida | 66 | 83 |
| Ryan Roberts, BYU | 56 | 82 |
| Brian McClure, Illinois | 59 | 80 |
| Casey Blake, Wichita State | 65 | 79 |
| Jason Williams, Louisiana St. | 67 | 79 |
| Robert Fick, CS Northridge | 69 | 79 |
| Eric Gillespie, CS Northridge | 69 | 79 |
| Brooks Badeaux, Fla. State | 69 | 79 |

## HITS

| | G | H |
|---|---|---|
| Adam Kennedy, CS Northridge | 70 | 121 |
| Robert Fick, CS Northridge | 69 | 119 |
| Matt Kastelic, Texas Tech | 65 | 114 |
| Chris Heintz, South Florida | 66 | 106 |
| Dax Norris, Alabama | 69 | 105 |
| Mark Fischer, Ga. Tech | 63 | 104 |
| David Eckstein, Florida | 68 | 102 |
| Joe Caruso, Alabama | 69 | 102 |
| Rusty McNamara, Okla. St. | 66 | 101 |
| Jason Tyner, Texas A&M | 58 | 100 |
| Nate Manning, Austin Peay | 65 | 100 |
| Clint Bryant, Texas Tech | 65 | 100 |
| Tripp MacKay, Okla. State | 66 | 100 |

## SLUGGING PERCENTAGE

| (Minimum 125 At-Bats) | G | PCT |
|---|---|---|
| Pat Burrell, Miami (Fla.) | 60 | .948 |
| Josh Klimek, Illinois | 59 | .874 |
| Marlon Stewart, Grambling | 41 | .855 |
| Robert Fick, CS Northridge | 69 | .806 |
| Eddy Furniss, Louisiana St. | 66 | .798 |
| Tyson Dowdell, BYU | 55 | .797 |
| Mark Kotsay, CS Fullerton | 61 | .797 |
| Kevin Barker, Va. Tech | 59 | .792 |
| Andy Tracy, Bowling Green | 50 | .777 |
| Josh Kliner, Kansas | 56 | .774 |

## TOTAL BASES

| | G | TB |
|---|---|---|
| Robert Fick, CS Northridge | 69 | 228 |
| Adam Kennedy, CS Northridge | 70 | 203 |
| Mark Kotsay, CS Fullerton | 61 | 192 |
| Nate Manning, Austin Peay | 65 | 191 |
| Eddy Furniss, Louisiana St. | 66 | 190 |
| Josh Klimek, Illinois | 59 | 188 |
| Tommy Peterman, Ga. South | 60 | 187 |
| Clint Bryant, Texas Tech | 65 | 184 |
| Chris Heintz, So. Florida | 66 | 183 |
| J.D. Drew, Fla. State | 69 | 183 |
| Pat Burrell, Miami (Fla.) | 60 | 182 |

**Adam Kennedy.** 121 hits

| | | |
|---|---|---|
| Nathan Dunn, Louisiana St. | 66 | 182 |
| Eric Gillespie, CS Northridge | 69 | 182 |
| Lance Berkman, Rice | 65 | 180 |
| Casey Blake, Wichita St. | 65 | 180 |
| Dion Ruecker, Texas Tech | 60 | 179 |
| Mark Fischer, Ga. Tech | 63 | 179 |
| Ross Gload, South Florida | 66 | 178 |
| B.J. Huff, Ala.-Birmingham | 58 | 173 |
| Rusty McNamara, Okla. St. | 66 | 173 |
| Joe Caruso, Alabama | 69 | 173 |

## DOUBLES

| | G | 2B |
|---|---|---|
| Jeremy Morris, Fla. State | 69 | 36 |
| Greg Taylor, Ark.-L.R. | 51 | 31 |
| Scott Schroeffel, Tennessee | 63 | 29 |
| Ryan Bennett, Austin Peay | 64 | 29 |
| Travis Wyckoff, Wichita St. | 63 | 29 |
| Josh Kliner, Kansas | 56 | 28 |
| Aaron Jaworowski, Missouri | 58 | 28 |
| Stubby Clapp, Texas Tech | 62 | 28 |
| Jacob Schaffer, Bradley | 62 | 28 |
| Jason Fitzgerald, Tulane | 63 | 28 |
| Mark Kotsay, CS Fullerton | 61 | 27 |
| Matt Quatraro, Old Dominion | 56 | 26 |
| Adam Platt, Miss. State | 61 | 26 |
| Clint Bryant, Texas Tech | 65 | 26 |
| Nate Manning, Austin Peay | 65 | 26 |
| John Musachio, Bradley | 65 | 25 |
| Alex Tolbert, West. Car. | 57 | 25 |
| Adam Johnson, Cent. Fla. | 65 | 25 |

## TRIPLES

| | G | 3B |
|---|---|---|
| Brig Taylor, McNeese State | 50 | 12 |
| B.J. Huff, Ala.-Birmingham | 58 | 11 |
| Travis Young, New Mexico | 51 | 10 |
| Justin Beasley, Butler | 46 | 9 |
| Kevin Barker, Va. Tech | 59 | 9 |
| Jake Weber, N.C. State | 61 | 9 |
| George Restovich, Notre Dame | 62 | 9 |

## HOME RUNS

| | G | HR |
|---|---|---|
| Josh Klimek, Illinois | 59 | 26 |
| Tommy Peterman, Ga. South. | 60 | 26 |
| Eddy Furniss, Louisiana St. | 66 | 26 |
| Robert Fick, CS Northridge | 69 | 25 |
| Ryan Roberts, Brigham Young | 56 | 23 |
| Pat Burrell, Miami (Fla.) | 60 | 23 |
| Eric Gillespie, CS Northridge | 69 | 23 |
| Justin Bowles, Louisiana St. | 64 | 22 |
| Casey Blake, Wichita State | 65 | 22 |
| Michael Rivers, Troy State | 54 | 21 |
| Bryan Britt, UNC Wilmington | 58 | 21 |
| J.J. Thomas, Ga. Tech | 63 | 21 |
| Nathan Dunn, Louisiana St. | 66 | 21 |
| Ross Gload, South Florida | 66 | 21 |
| J.D. Drew, Fla. State | 69 | 21 |
| Jason Glover, Georgia State | 53 | 20 |
| Michael Stoner, No. Carolina | 56 | 20 |
| Kevin Barker, Va. Tech | 59 | 20 |
| Dion Ruecker, Texas Tech | 60 | 20 |
| Mark Kotsay, CS Fullerton | 61 | 20 |
| Lance Berkman, Rice | 65 | 20 |
| Tony Hausladen, St. Louis | 48 | 19 |
| Doug Barner, Mid. Tenn. | 54 | 19 |

| | | |
|---|---|---|
| D.G. Nelson, Brigham Young | 56 | 19 |
| Jason Dellaero, South Florida | 61 | 19 |
| Jacques Landry, Rice | 64 | 19 |
| Nate Manning, Austin Peay | 65 | 19 |
| Rusty McNamara, Okla. State | 66 | 19 |
| Jason Grabowski., Conn. | 47 | 18 |
| Lance Burkhart, SW Mo. | 57 | 18 |
| Tim DeCinces, UCLA | 64 | 18 |
| Clint Bryant, Texas Tech | 65 | 18 |
| Chuck Hazzard, Florida | 66 | 18 |

## RUNS BATTED IN

| | G | RBI |
|---|---|---|
| Eddy Furniss, Louisiana St. | 66 | 103 |
| Casey Blake, Wichita St. | 65 | 101 |
| Aaron Jaworowski, Missouri | 68 | 101 |
| Clint Bryant, Texas Tech | 65 | 100 |
| Robert Fick, CS Northridge | 69 | 96 |
| Chris Heintz, South Florida | 66 | 95 |
| Josh Klimek, Illinois | 59 | 94 |
| J.D. Drew, Fla. State | 69 | 94 |
| Lance Berkman, Rice | 65 | 92 |
| Mark Kotsay, CS Fullerton | 61 | 91 |
| Rusty McNamara, Okla. St. | 66 | 89 |
| Jeremy Morris, Fla. State | 69 | 87 |
| Danny Peoples, Texas | 61 | 86 |
| Josh Kliner, Kansas | 56 | 85 |
| Ross Gload, South Florida | 66 | 83 |
| Tommy Peterman, Ga. South . | 60 | 82 |
| Dion Ruecker, Texas Tech | 60 | 82 |
| Jacques Landry, Rice | 64 | 81 |
| Nate Manning, Austin Peay | 65 | 81 |
| Nathan Dunn, Louisiana St. | 66 | 81 |
| Adam Kennedy, CS Northridge | 70 | 81 |
| Jeff Guiel, Okla. State | 61 | 80 |
| Jason Stephens, Texas A&M | 52 | 79 |

## BASE ON BALLS

| | G | BB |
|---|---|---|
| Tripp MacKay, Okla. State | 66 | 76 |
| Brad Wilkerson, Florida | 67 | 76 |
| Ross Gload, So. Florida | 66 | 68 |
| Stubby Clapp, Texas Tech | 62 | 66 |
| Pat Burrell, Miami (Fla.) | 60 | 61 |
| Gary Burnham, Clemson | 68 | 61 |
| Jose Miranda, CS Northridge | 70 | 61 |

## STRIKEOUTS

| | G | SO |
|---|---|---|
| Kurt Airoso, CS Northridge | 69 | 79 |
| Grant Hohman, CS Northridge | 70 | 76 |
| Ross Gload, South Florida | 66 | 68 |
| John Hanson, Mercer | 66 | 66 |
| Chip Rhea, Kentucky | 59 | 65 |
| Jeff Bell, Ala.-Birmingham | 57 | 65 |
| Willy Kingsbury, Campbell | 56 | 65 |

## TOUGHEST TO STRIKE OUT

| (Minimum 125 At-Bats) | AB | SO | Ratio |
|---|---|---|---|
| Dan O'Neill, Illinois | 166 | 2 | 83.0 |
| Kris Doiron, Drexel | 163 | 3 | 54.3 |
| Darren Case, Portland St. | 130 | 3 | 43.3 |
| Leonard Beltran, Wyom. | 196 | 6 | 32.7 |
| Vic Boccarossa, LeMoyne | 128 | 4 | 32.0 |

## STOLEN BASES

| | G | SB | ATT |
|---|---|---|---|
| Randy Young, Wichita St. | 63 | 68 | 75 |
| Maleke Fowler, Nich. State | 51 | 60 | 64 |
| Chad Green, Kentucky | 59 | 55 | 67 |
| Scott Sollmann, Notre Dame | 62 | 52 | 58 |
| Joe DiSalvo, New Orleans | 64 | 51 | 57 |
| Matt Kastelic, Texas Tech | 65 | 51 | 69 |
| Gio Cafaro, South Florida | 66 | 50 | 53 |
| Antoine Moran, Ga. South . | 59 | 50 | 55 |
| Ivan Lewis, California | 55 | 44 | 46 |
| Cordell Farley, Va. Comm. | 56 | 44 | 54 |
| Wylie Campbell, Texas | 60 | 43 | 47 |
| John Penatello, Iona | 46 | 42 | 52 |
| Kalin Foulds, San Diego St. | 59 | 42 | 53 |
| Jason Tyner, Texas A&M | 58 | 41 | 46 |
| Travis Young, New Mexico | 51 | 39 | 47 |
| Clint Bryant, Texas Tech | 65 | 37 | 41 |
| David Beckley, Citadel | 54 | 37 | 47 |
| Ryan Dillon, Indiana | 55 | 36 | 49 |
| Mandell Marsh, Md.-East Sh. | 49 | 36 | 44 |

## HIT BY PITCH

| | G | HBP |
|---|---|---|
| Corey Miller, Nebraska | 46 | 24 |
| Brett Casper, Oral Roberts | 51 | 22 |
| Brandon Walters, So. Carolina | 51 | 21 |
| Mason Hibbard, Santa Clara | 55 | 21 |
| Rusty McNamara, Okla. St. | 66 | 21 |

**Tommy Peterman.** 26 homers

## EARNED RUN AVERAGE
(Minimum 60 Innings)

| | W | L | ERA | G | GS | CG | SV | IP | H | R | ER | BB | SO |
|---|---|---|---|---|---|---|---|---|---|---|---|---|---|
| Steve Boyles, South Florida | 2 | 4 | 1.41 | 40 | 0 | 0 | 6 | 64 | 49 | 15 | 10 | 13 | 60 |
| Seth Greisinger, Virginia | 12 | 2 | 1.76 | 16 | 16 | 6 | 0 | 123 | 78 | 30 | 24 | 36 | 141 |
| Evan Thomas, Fla. International | 10 | 3 | 1.78 | 20 | 17 | 9 | 1 | 147 | 102 | 38 | 29 | 58 | 220 |
| Brian Carmody, Santa Clara | 10 | 3 | 1.81 | 17 | 16 | 3 | 0 | 120 | 84 | 29 | 24 | 57 | 118 |
| Brad Brasser, Northwestern | 6 | 2 | 1.93 | 11 | 11 | 4 | 0 | 65 | 51 | 27 | 14 | 20 | 55 |
| Kris Benson, Clemson | 14 | 2 | 2.02 | 19 | 19 | 7 | 0 | 156 | 109 | 47 | 35 | 27 | 204 |
| Randy Wolf, Pepperdine | 7 | 3 | 2.02 | 14 | 14 | 4 | 0 | 98 | 68 | 27 | 22 | 27 | 111 |
| Don Martin, Temple | 5 | 5 | 2.06 | 13 | 11 | 8 | 2 | 79 | 74 | 32 | 18 | 32 | 74 |
| Paul Rigdon, Florida | 9 | 2 | 2.19 | 42 | 0 | 0 | 10 | 74 | 64 | 21 | 18 | 28 | 66 |
| Brandon Allen, Ill.-Chicago | 7 | 2 | 2.22 | 15 | 12 | 3 | 1 | 65 | 52 | 21 | 16 | 26 | 62 |
| Darin Schmalz, Notre Dame | 9 | 4 | 2.23 | 14 | 14 | 6 | 0 | 85 | 82 | 29 | 21 | 18 | 56 |
| Dan Stutzman, Appalachian State | 5 | 1 | 2.24 | 18 | 7 | 2 | 0 | 64 | 58 | 24 | 16 | 28 | 54 |
| Dennis Healy, Geo. Washington | 7 | 3 | 2.25 | 17 | 12 | 4 | 0 | 76 | 81 | 37 | 19 | 14 | 53 |
| Brian Stegen, Rutgers | 5 | 4 | 2.28 | 15 | 10 | 4 | 0 | 79 | 77 | 31 | 20 | 29 | 48 |
| Marcus Jones, Long Beach St. | 9 | 5 | 2.29 | 16 | 15 | 4 | 0 | 110 | 90 | 36 | 28 | 37 | 118 |
| Scott Madison, Rutgers | 8 | 3 | 2.33 | 13 | 13 | 8 | 0 | 93 | 84 | 28 | 24 | 18 | 49 |
| Aaron Houdeshell, Ohio | 11 | 2 | 2.38 | 15 | 15 | 9 | 0 | 95 | 99 | 33 | 25 | 27 | 51 |
| Eddie Yarnall, Louisiana St. | 11 | 1 | 2.38 | 19 | 17 | 3 | 0 | 125 | 89 | 37 | 33 | 52 | 156 |
| Bryan Williamson, Jacksonville St. | 7 | 3 | 2.39 | 16 | 7 | 4 | 1 | 72 | 54 | 25 | 19 | 26 | 61 |
| Craig Zaikov, Virginia | 8 | 1 | 2.48 | 19 | 9 | 1 | 0 | 75 | 63 | 36 | 21 | 24 | 69 |
| Jeff Weaver, Fresno State | 12 | 5 | 2.51 | 19 | 16 | 12 | 1 | 143 | 107 | 50 | 40 | 30 | 136 |
| Gary Gubanich, Youngstown St. | 5 | 4 | 2.59 | 15 | 9 | 5 | 1 | 63 | 62 | 21 | 18 | 12 | 33 |
| Tom McLemore, Navy | 9 | 7 | 2.60 | 17 | 16 | 10 | 0 | 93 | 97 | 44 | 27 | 14 | 43 |
| Corey Lee, N.C. State | 10 | 3 | 2.62 | 18 | 17 | 3 | 0 | 103 | 84 | 41 | 30 | 49 | 99 |
| Kevin Shipp, Louisiana St. | 5 | 4 | 2.63 | 17 | 11 | 4 | 2 | 86 | 75 | 34 | 25 | 32 | 75 |
| Jimmy Hollifield, Jackson State | 6 | 3 | 2.63 | 11 | 9 | 7 | 0 | 65 | 58 | 35 | 19 | 36 | 45 |
| Andy Bernard, Alabama | 6 | 3 | 2.65 | 23 | 5 | 2 | 1 | 71 | 65 | 27 | 21 | 18 | 76 |
| Ryan Rademacker, St. Bona. | 4 | 5 | 2.71 | 12 | 10 | 7 | 1 | 70 | 57 | 38 | 21 | 36 | 44 |
| Tim Young, Alabama | 11 | 3 | 2.73 | 23 | 9 | 1 | 2 | 99 | 93 | 40 | 30 | 26 | 90 |
| R.A. Dickey, Tennessee | 9 | 4 | 2.76 | 27 | 12 | 5 | 3 | 127 | 114 | 51 | 39 | 33 | 137 |
| Randy Choate, Florida State | 15 | 4 | 2.76 | 22 | 21 | 6 | 1 | 150 | 129 | 59 | 46 | 44 | 130 |
| Ryan Harber, Butler | 4 | 2 | 2.80 | 12 | 9 | 4 | 0 | 61 | 58 | 28 | 18 | 18 | 54 |
| Ben Mann, NE Louisiana | 7 | 4 | 2.81 | 15 | 15 | 3 | 0 | 77 | 77 | 38 | 24 | 20 | 47 |
| Brian Murphy, Michigan State | 3 | 9 | 2.81 | 14 | 13 | 8 | 0 | 80 | 79 | 40 | 25 | 23 | 53 |

### WINS
| | W | L |
|---|---|---|
| Julio Ayala, Ga. South. | 15 | 3 |
| Clint Weibl, Miami (Fla.) | 15 | 3 |
| Randy Choate, Fla. State | 15 | 4 |
| Erasmo Ramirez, CS Northridge | 14 | 1 |
| Kris Benson, Clemson | 14 | 2 |
| Robby Crabtree, CS Northridge | 13 | 8 |
| J.D. Arteaga, Miami (Fla.) | 12 | 1 |
| Dean Cordova, Troy State | 12 | 1 |
| Matt Miller, Texas Tech | 12 | 2 |
| Seth Greisinger, Virginia | 12 | 2 |
| Brett Black, N.C. State | 12 | 3 |
| Doug Robertson, Bradley | 12 | 3 |
| Kirk Irvine, CS Fullerton | 12 | 3 |
| Scooby Morgan, Fla. State | 12 | 3 |
| Jason Norton, South Alabama | 12 | 3 |
| Seth Etherton, USC | 12 | 3 |
| Scott Glaser, South Florida | 12 | 4 |
| Jeff Williams, SE Louisiana | 12 | 4 |
| Jeff Weaver, Fresno State | 12 | 5 |

### LOSSES
| | W | L |
|---|---|---|
| Ryan Henderson, Md.-East. Shore | 0 | 14 |
| Chris Holt, Cincinnati | 0 | 11 |
| Brian Hedley, St. Mary's | 1 | 11 |

### APPEARANCES
| | G |
|---|---|
| Paul Rigdon, Florida | 42 |
| Joe Cali, Fla. Atlantic | 41 |
| Steve Boyles, So. Florida | 40 |
| Tod Lee, Ga. Southern | 38 |
| Robbie Morrison, Miami (Fla.) | 38 |
| Allan Westfall, Miami (Fla.) | 38 |

### COMPLETE GAMES
| | GS | CG |
|---|---|---|
| Doug Robertson, Bradley | 14 | 12 |
| Jeff Weaver, Fresno State | 16 | 12 |
| Jamie Puerto, NE Illinois | 16 | 12 |
| Eric DuBose, Miss. State | 16 | 11 |
| Jason Divin, SW Texas St. | 15 | 10 |
| Justin Burgess, Texas-S.A. | 15 | 10 |
| Tom McLemore, Navy | 16 | 10 |
| Jeff Williams, SE Louisiana | 17 | 10 |

### SAVES
| | G | SV |
|---|---|---|
| Mike Lyons, Stetson | 37 | 15 |
| Charlies Gillian, Va. Tech | 31 | 14 |
| Ryan Brannan, Long Beach St. | 32 | 14 |

| Robbie Morrison, Miami (Fla.) | 38 | 14 |
|---|---|---|
| Joe Cali, Fla. Atlantic | 40 | 14 |
| Jack Krawczyk, USC | 25 | 12 |
| Nick Witte, Ball State | 26 | 12 |
| Braden Looper, Wichita St. | 26 | 12 |
| Tod Lee, Ga. Southern | 38 | 11 |
| Skip Ames, Alabama | 21 | 11 |
| Andy Noblitt, Evansville | 29 | 11 |
| Paul Rigdon, Florida | 42 | 10 |
| David Darwin, Duke | 35 | 10 |
| Greg Ziesemer, Northwestern | 19 | 10 |
| Ron Walker, Old Dominion | 21 | 10 |
| Corey Richardson, No. Carolina | 24 | 10 |
| Mike McDonald, Santa Clara | 28 | 10 |

### INNINGS PITCHED
| | G | IP |
|---|---|---|
| Kris Benson, Clemson | 19 | 156 |
| Julio Ayala, Ga. South. | 22 | 152 |
| Randy Choate, Fla. State | 22 | 150 |
| Evan Thomas, Fla. International | 20 | 147 |
| Jeff Weaver, Fresno State | 19 | 143 |
| Robby Crabtree, CS Northridge | 29 | 139 |
| Eric DuBose, Miss. State | 17 | 133 |
| Chris Dooley, Oral Roberts | 20 | 130 |

### BASES ON BALLS
| | IP | BB |
|---|---|---|
| Clint Cortez, Nicholls State | 91 | 108 |
| Joshua Farrow, Florida A&M | 65 | 81 |

JEFF GOLDEN

**Seth Greisinger.** 1.76 ERA

| Tom Fontaine, Kent | 75 | 73 |
|---|---|---|
| Peter Moore, Temple | 92 | 71 |
| Zack Frachiseur, Georgia | 113 | 68 |

### STRIKEOUTS
| | IP | SO |
|---|---|---|
| Evan Thomas, Fla. Int. | 147 | 220 |
| Kris Benson, Clemson | 156 | 204 |
| Eric DuBose, Miss. State | 133 | 174 |
| Eddie Yarnall, Louisiana St. | 125 | 156 |
| Bill Koch, Clemson | 112 | 152 |
| Julio Ayala, Ga. South. | 152 | 143 |
| Seth Greisinger, Virginia | 123 | 141 |
| R.A. Dickey, Tennessee | 127 | 137 |
| Jeff Weaver, Fresno State | 143 | 136 |
| Jason Ramsey, UNC Wilmington | 98 | 135 |
| Ken Vining, Clemson | 115 | 135 |
| Mark Johnson, Hawaii | 119 | 132 |
| Donald Rushing, New Orleans | 103 | 126 |
| Sean McClellan, Okla. State | 110 | 125 |
| Donovan Harrison, Char. So | 111 | 125 |
| Jeff Williams, SE Louisiana | 129 | 125 |
| Chris Dooley, Oral Roberts | 130 | 124 |
| Jack Cressend, Tulane | 103 | 123 |
| David Elder, Ga. Tech | 106 | 123 |
| Eric Milton, Maryland | 90 | 118 |
| Marcus Jones, Long Beach St. | 119 | 118 |
| Brian Carmody, Santa Clara | 120 | 118 |
| Robby Crabtree, CS Northridge | 139 | 118 |

### STRIKEOUTS/9 INNINGS
| (Minimum 50 Innings) | IP | SO | AVG |
|---|---|---|---|
| Evan Thomas, Fla. Int. | 147 | 220 | 13.5 |
| Jason Ramsey, UNC Wilm. | 98 | 135 | 12.4 |
| Bill Koch, Clemson | 112 | 152 | 12.3 |
| Eric Milton, Maryland | 90 | 118 | 11.8 |
| Kris Benson, Clemson | 156 | 204 | 11.8 |
| Eric DuBose, Miss. State | 133 | 174 | 11.7 |
| Eddie Yarnall, LSU | 125 | 156 | 11.3 |
| Donald Rushing, UNO | 103 | 126 | 11.0 |
| Tom Szymborski, Ill.-Chi. | 70 | 85 | 10.9 |
| Tim Hudson, Auburn | 75 | 90 | 10.8 |
| Jack Cressend, Tulane | 103 | 123 | 10.8 |

**Evan Thomas.** 220 strikeouts

# Baseball America's

# COLLEGE TOP 25

BATTERS: 10 or more at-bats
PITCHERS: 5 or more innings

**Boldface** indicates selected in 1996 draft

## 1 LOUISIANA STATE

Coach: Skip Bertman     Record: 52-15

| BATTING | AVG | AB | R | H | 2B | 3B | HR | RBI | SB |
|---|---|---|---|---|---|---|---|---|---|
| Polozola, Keith, ss | .421 | 19 | 3 | 8 | 1 | 0 | 0 | 6 | 0 |
| **Morris, Warren, 2b** | .400 | 75 | 24 | 30 | 3 | 0 | 1 | 19 | 4 |
| Furniss, Eddy, 1b | .374 | 238 | 68 | 89 | 21 | 1 | 26 | 103 | 1 |
| **Dunn, Nathan, 3b** | .358 | 257 | 95 | 92 | 19 | 4 | 21 | 81 | 18 |
| Cooley, Chad, of | .348 | 253 | 61 | 88 | 16 | 1 | 14 | 66 | 16 |
| **Williams, Jason, ss** | .340 | 268 | 79 | 91 | 16 | 1 | 6 | 35 | 7 |
| Wilson, Brad, dh | .328 | 201 | 56 | 66 | 12 | 2 | 9 | 45 | 6 |
| Koerner, Mike, of | .315 | 238 | 71 | 75 | 15 | 3 | 12 | 47 | 24 |
| **Bowles, Justin, of** | .306 | 232 | 57 | 71 | 13 | 1 | 22 | 73 | 12 |
| Moore, Jeramie, 1b | .298 | 57 | 16 | 17 | 4 | 0 | 6 | 12 | 2 |
| Cuntz, Casey, 2b | .270 | 63 | 13 | 17 | 2 | 0 | 1 | 9 | 2 |
| **Lanier, Tim, c** | .258 | 198 | 48 | 51 | 6 | 2 | 5 | 36 | 2 |
| McClure, Trey, 2b | .250 | 100 | 19 | 25 | 7 | 0 | 2 | 19 | 2 |
| Bernhardt, Tom, of | .243 | 111 | 23 | 27 | 6 | 2 | 6 | 27 | 3 |
| Ward, Kevin, c | .222 | 18 | 5 | 4 | 2 | 0 | 0 | 1 | 0 |
| Hemphill, James, of | .182 | 11 | 2 | 2 | 0 | 1 | 0 | 0 | 0 |
| Horton, Conan, c | .136 | 44 | 8 | 6 | 0 | 0 | 0 | 6 | 0 |

| PITCHING | W | L | ERA | G | SV | IP | H | BB | SO |
|---|---|---|---|---|---|---|---|---|---|
| Painich, Joey | 3 | 0 | 0.46 | 7 | 0 | 20 | 18 | 11 | 15 |
| Leonardi, Antonio | 0 | 0 | 0.55 | 7 | 3 | 16 | 14 | 4 | 21 |
| Yarnall, Eddie | 11 | 1 | 2.38 | 19 | 0 | 125 | 89 | 52 | 156 |
| Shipp, Kevin | 5 | 4 | 2.63 | 17 | 2 | 86 | 75 | 32 | 75 |
| Daugherty, Brian | 2 | 0 | 3.09 | 20 | 0 | 35 | 26 | 14 | 38 |
| Laxton, Brett | 8 | 2 | 3.54 | 14 | 0 | 56 | 50 | 28 | 55 |
| Esteves, Jake | 5 | 3 | 3.58 | 23 | 2 | 65 | 71 | 12 | 67 |
| **Coogan, Patrick** | 6 | 0 | 4.13 | 26 | 1 | 81 | 88 | 28 | 95 |
| Demouy, Chris | 10 | 3 | 4.50 | 29 | 2 | 66 | 65 | 23 | 55 |
| Albritton, Jason | 1 | 1 | 5.25 | 16 | 2 | 24 | 18 | 14 | 30 |
| Guillory, Dan | 1 | 1 | 5.79 | 14 | 1 | 19 | 24 | 9 | 19 |
| Tyson, Jeremy | 0 | 0 | 10.00 | 4 | 0 | 9 | 11 | 6 | 9 |

## 2 MIAMI

Coach: Jim Morris     Record: 50-14

| BATTING | AVG | AB | R | H | 2B | 3B | HR | RBI | SB |
|---|---|---|---|---|---|---|---|---|---|
| Burrell, Pat, 3b | .484 | 192 | 75 | 93 | 18 | 1 | 23 | 64 | 8 |
| **Gomez, Rudy, 2b** | .420 | 224 | 86 | 94 | 22 | 3 | 13 | 59 | 28 |
| Rivero, Eddie, of | .364 | 209 | 51 | 76 | 12 | 2 | 8 | 54 | 7 |
| DeCelle, Michael, of | .358 | 151 | 40 | 54 | 14 | 1 | 4 | 41 | 5 |
| **Marcinczyk, T.R., 1b** | .354 | 229 | 53 | 81 | 14 | 0 | 12 | 69 | 15 |
| Saggese, Rick, dh-1b | .339 | 186 | 41 | 63 | 12 | 0 | 14 | 51 | 0 |
| **Gargiulo, Jim, c** | .326 | 218 | 47 | 71 | 16 | 0 | 8 | 57 | 4 |
| Lopez-Cao, Mike, c | .308 | 26 | 7 | 8 | 2 | 0 | 0 | 3 | 0 |
| Nykoluk, Kevin, dh-c | .306 | 134 | 24 | 41 | 9 | 0 | 3 | 25 | 2 |
| **Grimmett, Ryan, of** | .306 | 242 | 68 | 74 | 14 | 4 | 3 | 34 | 27 |
| **Cora, Alex, ss** | .304 | 224 | 46 | 68 | 8 | 4 | 0 | 33 | 12 |
| Beasley, Sean, inf | .300 | 20 | 1 | 6 | 1 | 0 | 0 | 5 | 0 |
| Bundrick, Brian, p-of | .300 | 10 | 4 | 3 | 2 | 0 | 0 | 2 | 0 |
| Reif, Derek, inf | .222 | 18 | 7 | 4 | 0 | 0 | 0 | 2 | 0 |
| Moore, Tris, of | .206 | 126 | 20 | 26 | 7 | 4 | 3 | 19 | 0 |
| **Lang, Kenard, dh** | .182 | 11 | 1 | 2 | 0 | 0 | 0 | 2 | 0 |
| Cannizzaro, Frank, of | .133 | 15 | 6 | 2 | 1 | 0 | 0 | 2 | 2 |

| PITCHING | W | L | ERA | G | SV | IP | H | BB | SO |
|---|---|---|---|---|---|---|---|---|---|
| Morrison, Robbie | 4 | 2 | 1.68 | 38 | 14 | 59 | 35 | 27 | 88 |
| Westfall, Allan | 5 | 2 | 2.45 | 38 | 2 | 51 | 40 | 23 | 62 |
| Spassoff, Darin | 2 | 0 | 3.14 | 9 | 0 | 29 | 27 | 8 | 17 |
| Bundrick, Brian | 1 | 1 | 3.57 | 19 | 0 | 23 | 23 | 11 | 22 |
| Weibl, Clint | 15 | 3 | 3.58 | 19 | 0 | 121 | 109 | 24 | 108 |

**Ace Lefthander.** Eddie Yarnall went 11-1 with a 2.38 ERA for national champion Louisiana State, earning All-America honors.

| | | | | | | | | | |
|---|---|---|---|---|---|---|---|---|---|
| Arteaga, J.D. | 12 | 1 | 3.82 | 18 | 0 | 111 | 112 | 34 | 96 |
| Petretta, Bob | 0 | 1 | 4.50 | 23 | 0 | 14 | 22 | 13 | 10 |
| Pujals, Denis | 9 | 2 | 4.52 | 17 | 0 | 82 | 85 | 25 | 68 |
| Gutierrez, Lazaro | 0 | 0 | 4.61 | 17 | 0 | 14 | 14 | 7 | 7 |
| Burton, Tim | 1 | 1 | 4.63 | 8 | 0 | 23 | 23 | 16 | 21 |
| Tosca, Carlos | 0 | 0 | 5.40 | 7 | 0 | 5 | 6 | 3 | 3 |
| Hoff, Eddie | 1 | 0 | 5.59 | 10 | 0 | 19 | 19 | 14 | 21 |
| Mastrolonardo, David | 0 | 1 | 5.59 | 10 | 0 | 10 | 10 | 5 | 10 |

## 3 FLORIDA

Coach: Andy Lopez     Record: 50-18

| BATTING | AVG | AB | R | H | 2B | 3B | HR | RBI | SB |
|---|---|---|---|---|---|---|---|---|---|
| Wilkerson, Brad, of-1b | .407 | 241 | 71 | 98 | 22 | 3 | 9 | 68 | 14 |
| **Hazzard, Chuck, dh** | .366 | 265 | 52 | 97 | 13 | 0 | 18 | 67 | 6 |
| Ellis, Mark, 3b | .351 | 205 | 48 | 72 | 9 | 0 | 1 | 26 | 19 |
| Eckstein, David, 2b | .338 | 302 | 76 | 102 | 19 | 9 | 9 | 60 | 24 |
| Chism, Chris, of | .337 | 169 | 34 | 57 | 7 | 1 | 4 | 32 | 14 |
| **Tamargo, John, ss** | .322 | 267 | 65 | 86 | 20 | 1 | 4 | 41 | 15 |
| Castaldo, Eric, c | .317 | 230 | 43 | 73 | 14 | 1 | 8 | 39 | 4 |
| Duncan, Matt, 3b-1b | .299 | 167 | 35 | 50 | 5 | 0 | 5 | 29 | 3 |
| Andre, Travis, 1b | .258 | 93 | 11 | 24 | 5 | 1 | 1 | 20 | 0 |
| Walsh, Sean, of | .246 | 240 | 35 | 59 | 14 | 1 | 5 | 45 | 4 |
| Medina, Octavio, c | .231 | 13 | 3 | 3 | 0 | 0 | 0 | 3 | 1 |
| Johannes, Todd, c | .231 | 13 | 2 | 3 | 0 | 0 | 0 | 2 | 0 |
| Ogle, Brian, of | .215 | 79 | 21 | 17 | 3 | 0 | 2 | 7 | 6 |
| Eckstein, Rick, of | .200 | 75 | 14 | 15 | 2 | 0 | 0 | 6 | 0 |
| Haught, Brian, of | .185 | 65 | 13 | 12 | 3 | 0 | 3 | 16 | 2 |

| PITCHING | W | L | ERA | G | SV | IP | H | BB | SO |
|---|---|---|---|---|---|---|---|---|---|
| Rigdon, Paul | 9 | 2 | 2.19 | 42 | 10 | 74 | 64 | 28 | 66 |
| Wilkerson, Brad | 5 | 2 | 2.97 | 30 | 6 | 64 | 59 | 28 | 67 |
| Bond, Tommy | 4 | 0 | 3.44 | 38 | 0 | 65 | 67 | 33 | 38 |
| Rodriguez, Sergio | 4 | 1 | 3.79 | 21 | 0 | 57 | 53 | 23 | 31 |
| Kaufman, John | 11 | 5 | 4.25 | 21 | 0 | 125 | 109 | 47 | 101 |
| Brewer, Thomas | 7 | 2 | 4.46 | 14 | 0 | 73 | 69 | 35 | 45 |
| Wheeler, Danny | 3 | 1 | 5.24 | 13 | 0 | 55 | 71 | 6 | 30 |
| Fogg, Josh | 4 | 2 | 6.29 | 22 | 1 | 54 | 71 | 11 | 38 |
| Roll, Jacob | 1 | 1 | 6.49 | 14 | 0 | 26 | 34 | 19 | 21 |
| Knollin, Chris | 2 | 2 | 7.59 | 11 | 0 | 19 | 27 | 6 | 14 |

## 4 ALABAMA

Coach: Jim Wells     Record: 50-19

| BATTING | AVG | AB | R | H | 2B | 3B | HR | RBI | SB |
|---|---|---|---|---|---|---|---|---|---|
| **Norris, Dax, c** | .370 | 284 | 50 | 105 | 21 | 0 | 7 | 49 | 3 |
| **Caruso, Joe, 2b** | .367 | 278 | 76 | 102 | 19 | 5 | 14 | 63 | 12 |
| Moller, Chris, 1b | .350 | 257 | 46 | 90 | 17 | 0 | 13 | 54 | 0 |
| Davis, Heath, ss | .333 | 15 | 11 | 5 | 1 | 0 | 0 | 1 | 1 |
| Bounds, Drew, of-dh | .316 | 114 | 26 | 36 | 8 | 2 | 1 | 27 | 3 |
| Tidwell, David, of | .310 | 245 | 49 | 76 | 16 | 5 | 5 | 30 | 27 |

| Mohr, Dustan, of | .306 | 252 | 52 | 77 | 21 | 1 | 10 | 55 | 3 |
|---|---|---|---|---|---|---|---|---|---|
| **Spiers, Corey, dh-p** | .297 | 148 | 31 | 44 | 7 | 1 | 8 | 39 | 2 |
| Hall, Doug, of | .296 | 206 | 40 | 61 | 10 | 3 | 2 | 26 | 18 |
| Tucker, Robbie, dh-1b | .288 | 66 | 11 | 19 | 4 | 0 | 1 | 10 | 0 |
| Loflin, Rusty, dh-c | .284 | 88 | 14 | 25 | 6 | 0 | 3 | 18 | 0 |
| **Taft, Brett, ss** | .283 | 212 | 42 | 60 | 19 | 2 | 7 | 35 | 3 |
| Duncan, Nate, 3b-ss | .241 | 174 | 28 | 42 | 5 | 1 | 2 | 21 | 2 |
| Phillips, Andy, 3b | .238 | 101 | 18 | 24 | 5 | 0 | 3 | 13 | 1 |
| Watson, Brandon, dh | .077 | 13 | 1 | 1 | 0 | 0 | 0 | 1 | 0 |

| PITCHING | W | L | ERA | G | SV | IP | H | BB | SO |
|---|---|---|---|---|---|---|---|---|---|
| Ames, Skip | 2 | 1 | 2.36 | 21 | 11 | 50 | 36 | 20 | 44 |
| Bernard, Andy | 6 | 3 | 2.65 | 23 | 1 | 71 | 65 | 18 | 76 |
| **Young, Tim** | 11 | 3 | 2.73 | 23 | 2 | 99 | 93 | 26 | 90 |
| Colgrove, Joel | 10 | 3 | 3.32 | 19 | 0 | 111 | 121 | 24 | 104 |
| Torres, Manny | 5 | 1 | 4.40 | 17 | 0 | 57 | 58 | 13 | 61 |
| Duman, Buster | 1 | 0 | 4.55 | 14 | 2 | 30 | 26 | 7 | 25 |
| **Tribe, Byron** | 4 | 0 | 4.58 | 10 | 0 | 35 | 37 | 27 | 41 |
| Collins, John | 2 | 1 | 4.72 | 16 | 0 | 48 | 49 | 13 | 42 |
| Eilers, Chris | 5 | 5 | 4.73 | 16 | 1 | 72 | 74 | 22 | 64 |
| **Spiers, Corey** | 4 | 2 | 5.36 | 16 | 2 | 49 | 47 | 17 | 30 |

## 5 CLEMSON

**Coach:** Jack Leggett    **Record:** 51-17

| BATTING | AVG | AB | R | H | 2B | 3B | HR | RBI | SB |
|---|---|---|---|---|---|---|---|---|---|
| Embler, Jason, 1b | .357 | 238 | 51 | 85 | 17 | 1 | 10 | 57 | 2 |
| Borgert, Derek, c | .353 | 17 | 3 | 6 | 2 | 0 | 1 | 3 | 0 |
| **Livingston, Doug, 2b** | .341 | 223 | 62 | 76 | 15 | 1 | 9 | 39 | 24 |
| LeCroy, Matthew, c-dh | .316 | 244 | 61 | 77 | 18 | 0 | 14 | 57 | 3 |
| Broome, Nathan, c | .306 | 36 | 7 | 11 | 0 | 0 | 0 | 6 | 1 |
| Bultmann, Kurt, ss | .304 | 194 | 34 | 59 | 10 | 0 | 5 | 27 | 2 |
| Robinson, Jerome, of | .303 | 241 | 38 | 73 | 13 | 6 | 6 | 55 | 2 |
| **Galloway, Paul, 3b** | .294 | 252 | 51 | 74 | 22 | 2 | 5 | 36 | 10 |
| **Burnham, Gary, of** | .290 | 241 | 62 | 70 | 24 | 4 | 6 | 56 | 2 |
| Duffie, Will, dh-c | .265 | 219 | 48 | 58 | 12 | 1 | 6 | 36 | 0 |
| DeMoura, Eric, 2b | .263 | 80 | 12 | 21 | 0 | 0 | 0 | 7 | 4 |
| Rhodes, Rusty, of | .260 | 96 | 10 | 25 | 3 | 0 | 0 | 13 | 3 |
| McCray, Ontrell, of | .234 | 77 | 12 | 18 | 2 | 0 | 1 | 9 | 7 |
| Padgett, Matt, of | .224 | 98 | 14 | 22 | 6 | 2 | 1 | 21 | 0 |
| Roper, Doug, ss | .109 | 46 | 6 | 5 | 1 | 0 | 0 | 3 | 3 |

| PITCHING | W | L | ERA | G | SV | IP | H | BB | SO |
|---|---|---|---|---|---|---|---|---|---|
| **Benson, Kris** | 14 | 2 | 2.02 | 19 | 0 | 156 | 109 | 27 | 204 |
| Werner, Brian | 1 | 1 | 2.37 | 11 | 0 | 19 | 8 | 4 | 8 |
| **Shepard, David** | 3 | 2 | 2.83 | 27 | 5 | 29 | 20 | 13 | 33 |
| Vining, Ken | 10 | 3 | 2.97 | 19 | 0 | 115 | 92 | 38 | 135 |
| Koch, Billy | 10 | 5 | 3.14 | 19 | 1 | 112 | 73 | 60 | 152 |
| Hauser, Scott | 6 | 2 | 3.15 | 22 | 0 | 71 | 64 | 20 | 42 |
| Williams, Rodney | 2 | 1 | 3.45 | 21 | 0 | 29 | 32 | 12 | 16 |
| White, Matt | 0 | 0 | 3.52 | 6 | 0 | 8 | 9 | 7 | 9 |
| Scott, Ray | 1 | 1 | 4.09 | 11 | 0 | 22 | 23 | 7 | 19 |
| **Matz, Brian** | 4 | 0 | 4.88 | 18 | 4 | 52 | 59 | 21 | 44 |

## 6 FLORIDA STATE

**Coach:** Mike Martin    **Record:** 52-17

| BATTING | AVG | AB | R | H | 2B | 3B | HR | RBI | SB |
|---|---|---|---|---|---|---|---|---|---|
| Drew, J.D., of | .386 | 241 | 90 | 93 | 17 | 5 | 21 | 94 | 10 |
| **Morris, Jeremy, of** | .371 | 256 | 76 | 95 | 36 | 1 | 13 | 87 | 23 |
| Badeaux, Brooks, ss | .355 | 279 | 79 | 99 | 16 | 3 | 0 | 44 | 15 |
| Zech, Scott, 2b | .347 | 245 | 62 | 85 | 17 | 2 | 6 | 59 | 26 |
| **Faurot, Adam, 3b-dh** | .335 | 233 | 66 | 78 | 9 | 3 | 5 | 46 | 14 |
| Sprague, Geoff, 1b | .320 | 153 | 37 | 49 | 14 | 2 | 2 | 33 | 9 |
| Morgan, Scooby, dh-p | .306 | 144 | 28 | 44 | 7 | 1 | 13 | 41 | 3 |
| Nedeau, Steve, of | .287 | 167 | 33 | 48 | 5 | 2 | 0 | 17 | 14 |
| Klosterman, Jeremiah, c | .286 | 63 | 10 | 18 | 1 | 1 | 1 | 12 | 0 |
| Salazar, Jeremy, c | .280 | 200 | 32 | 56 | 13 | 2 | 5 | 36 | 0 |
| Woodward, Matt, 1b | .278 | 115 | 24 | 32 | 3 | 0 | 0 | 25 | 3 |
| Brown, Billy, dh | .247 | 77 | 19 | 19 | 8 | 0 | 0 | 14 | 2 |
| Zabala, Jose, 3b-2b | .218 | 87 | 19 | 19 | 4 | 0 | 0 | 10 | 3 |
| Senior, Bryan, of | .214 | 28 | 14 | 6 | 2 | 0 | 0 | 6 | 2 |
| Mayfield, Henry, c | .143 | 21 | 7 | 3 | 0 | 0 | 1 | 0 | 0 |

| PITCHING | W | L | ERA | G | SV | IP | H | BB | SO |
|---|---|---|---|---|---|---|---|---|---|
| **Davis, Mike** | 6 | 1 | 2.26 | 20 | 0 | 60 | 43 | 43 | 56 |
| Neill, Stephen | 0 | 0 | 2.41 | 16 | 0 | 19 | 12 | 10 | 17 |
| Chavez, Chris | 4 | 0 | 2.68 | 28 | 1 | 50 | 32 | 36 | 60 |
| Choate, Randy | 15 | 4 | 2.76 | 22 | 1 | 150 | 129 | 44 | 130 |
| Howell, Chuck | 9 | 3 | 3.59 | 26 | 6 | 90 | 97 | 34 | 79 |
| Morgan, Scooby | 12 | 3 | 3.62 | 21 | 0 | 112 | 113 | 39 | 60 |
| Niles, Randy | 4 | 1 | 5.27 | 24 | 3 | 43 | 49 | 25 | 52 |
| Diaz, Zach | 2 | 4 | 5.44 | 30 | 1 | 48 | 51 | 18 | 31 |
| Davis, Josh | 0 | 1 | 5.79 | 10 | 0 | 9 | 6 | 11 | 16 |
| Proctor, Scott | 0 | 0 | 7.41 | 16 | 0 | 17 | 17 | 20 | 22 |

## 7 SOUTHERN CALIFORNIA

**Coach:** Mike Gillespie    **Record:** 44-16

| BATTING | AVG | AB | R | H | 2B | 3B | HR | RBI | SB |
|---|---|---|---|---|---|---|---|---|---|
| Ticehurst, Brad, of | .455 | 11 | 2 | 5 | 2 | 0 | 0 | 6 | 0 |
| **Inglin, Jeff, of** | .392 | 222 | 56 | 87 | 15 | 2 | 14 | 72 | 11 |
| Walbridge, Greg, 1b | .385 | 205 | 62 | 79 | 14 | 1 | 8 | 45 | 4 |
| Cruz, Paul, of-dh | .376 | 170 | 38 | 64 | 5 | 1 | 4 | 34 | 8 |
| Jones, Jacque, of | .375 | 248 | 58 | 93 | 16 | 3 | 10 | 56 | 11 |
| **Stromsborg, Ryan, 2b-3b** | .354 | 192 | 40 | 68 | 16 | 0 | 7 | 35 | 12 |
| Ensberg, Morgan, 3b | .354 | 161 | 37 | 57 | 9 | 2 | 10 | 35 | 8 |
| Montoya, Alfonso, of | .316 | 76 | 21 | 24 | 3 | 0 | 0 | 10 | 7 |
| Brown, Jason, dh-c | .314 | 86 | 15 | 27 | 5 | 1 | 2 | 21 | 1 |
| Mirizzi, Marc, ss | .304 | 224 | 38 | 68 | 17 | 0 | 2 | 37 | 8 |
| **Moeller, Chad, c** | .301 | 206 | 38 | 62 | 12 | 2 | 3 | 35 | 8 |
| Gorr, Robb, of | .295 | 44 | 8 | 13 | 3 | 0 | 1 | 9 | 0 |
| Rachels, Wes, 2b | .294 | 136 | 29 | 40 | 3 | 1 | 0 | 23 | 4 |
| Hanoian, Greg, of | .250 | 60 | 13 | 15 | 4 | 0 | 0 | 10 | 2 |
| Valdez, David, inf | .250 | 28 | 3 | 7 | 1 | 0 | 0 | 3 | 0 |
| Ponchak, Brian, p-dh | .176 | 34 | 5 | 6 | 2 | 0 | 0 | 4 | 2 |
| Diaz, Ernie, 3b | .083 | 36 | 9 | 3 | 2 | 0 | 0 | 4 | 1 |

| PITCHING | W | L | ERA | G | SV | IP | H | BB | SO |
|---|---|---|---|---|---|---|---|---|---|
| Henderson, Scott | 8 | 1 | 3.19 | 17 | 0 | 87 | 98 | 21 | 63 |
| **Flores, Randy** | 9 | 1 | 3.50 | 18 | 0 | 118 | 115 | 32 | 74 |
| Parle, Justin | 0 | 2 | 3.69 | 21 | 2 | 32 | 25 | 6 | 19 |
| Etherton, Seth | 12 | 3 | 3.94 | 17 | 0 | 112 | 103 | 34 | 104 |
| **Mejia, Javier** | 2 | 1 | 4.08 | 18 | 0 | 29 | 31 | 17 | 17 |
| Immel, Steve | 4 | 1 | 4.53 | 18 | 0 | 48 | 52 | 19 | 26 |
| Krawczyk, Jack | 4 | 1 | 4.55 | 25 | 12 | 32 | 41 | 8 | 34 |
| Jones, Craig | 0 | 2 | 6.75 | 12 | 0 | 13 | 11 | 10 | 10 |
| Penney, Mike | 3 | 1 | 6.83 | 15 | 0 | 28 | 28 | 16 | 17 |
| Ponchak, Brian | 1 | 2 | 8.72 | 16 | 0 | 22 | 31 | 15 | 20 |
| Sanchez, Paul | 1 | 1 | 9.75 | 9 | 0 | 12 | 23 | 3 | 11 |
| Saenz, Jason | 0 | 0 | 11.81 | 6 | 0 | 5 | 9 | 6 | 6 |

## 8 WICHITA STATE

**Coach:** Gene Stephenson    **Record:** 54-11

| BATTING | AVG | AB | R | H | 2B | 3B | HR | RBI | SB |
|---|---|---|---|---|---|---|---|---|---|
| **Wyckoff, Travis, of-p** | .400 | 235 | 90 | 94 | 29 | 2 | 3 | 68 | 25 |
| Ryan, Jeff, ss-3b | .391 | 87 | 23 | 34 | 7 | 1 | 5 | 22 | 0 |
| **Blake, Casey, 3b** | .360 | 247 | 79 | 89 | 21 | 2 | 22 | 101 | 19 |
| **Davis, Casey, of** | .353 | 17 | 4 | 6 | 2 | 0 | 0 | 2 | 0 |
| Stine, Jerry, of | .340 | 235 | 52 | 80 | 22 | 0 | 7 | 57 | 17 |
| Reese, Nathan, c | .340 | 159 | 23 | 54 | 9 | 0 | 5 | 33 | 0 |
| McCullough, Adam, 1b | .337 | 255 | 56 | 86 | 19 | 1 | 15 | 75 | 6 |
| Patrick, Matt, 1b | .333 | 12 | 4 | 4 | 2 | 1 | 0 | 3 | 0 |
| Thomas, Ben, p-1b | .331 | 124 | 32 | 41 | 7 | 0 | 2 | 28 | 4 |

**Terrific Trojan.** Outfielder Jacque Jones had a fabulous junior season for Southern Cal, hitting .375 with 10 homers.

LARRY GOREN

| BATTING | AVG | AB | R | H | 2B | 3B | HR | RBI | SB |
|---|---|---|---|---|---|---|---|---|---|
| Hooper, Kevin, 2b | .321 | 190 | 47 | 61 | 6 | 2 | 1 | 30 | 13 |
| Sorensen, Zach, ss | .307 | 225 | 40 | 69 | 13 | 4 | 4 | 31 | 15 |
| Ficken, Jason, 2b | .304 | 46 | 14 | 14 | 5 | 0 | 0 | 7 | 3 |
| Young, Randy, of | .295 | 271 | 86 | 80 | 11 | 7 | 4 | 36 | 68 |
| Preston, Brian, c | .269 | 93 | 22 | 25 | 5 | 1 | 3 | 22 | 5 |
| Blue, Joey, 3b-1b | .263 | 19 | 6 | 5 | 0 | 0 | 1 | 5 | 0 |
| Adams, John, of | .260 | 50 | 14 | 13 | 0 | 0 | 1 | 17 | 4 |
| Kempton, Curtis, of | .182 | 11 | 3 | 2 | 0 | 0 | 0 | 3 | 0 |

| PITCHING | W | L | ERA | G | SV | IP | H | BB | SO |
|---|---|---|---|---|---|---|---|---|---|
| Bauer, Chris | 1 | 0 | 1.46 | 11 | 4 | 25 | 25 | 8 | 19 |
| Looper, Braden | 4 | 1 | 2.09 | 26 | 12 | 56 | 37 | 15 | 64 |
| Thomas, Ben | 9 | 1 | 2.56 | 11 | 0 | 53 | 46 | 19 | 49 |
| Edwards, Tony | 0 | 0 | 2.89 | 10 | 0 | 9 | 9 | 4 | 5 |
| Brandley, Mike | 1 | 0 | 3.00 | 10 | 1 | 24 | 24 | 16 | 28 |
| Wyckoff, Travis | 5 | 0 | 3.38 | 23 | 6 | 59 | 55 | 17 | 56 |
| Foral, Steve | 11 | 1 | 3.63 | 18 | 0 | 92 | 87 | 32 | 79 |
| Krafft, Jason | 4 | 0 | 3.72 | 8 | 0 | 39 | 39 | 19 | 30 |
| Baird, Brandon | 7 | 6 | 3.74 | 19 | 0 | 101 | 112 | 39 | 94 |
| Bluma, Marc | 5 | 1 | 4.03 | 23 | 4 | 51 | 51 | 16 | 58 |
| Dobson, Matt | 6 | 1 | 4.24 | 12 | 0 | 47 | 50 | 26 | 39 |
| Drumright, Greg | 1 | 0 | 4.50 | 4 | 0 | 10 | 11 | 2 | 8 |

## 9 STANFORD

**Coach:** Mark Marquess **Record:** 41-19

| BATTING | AVG | AB | R | H | 2B | 3B | HR | RBI | SB |
|---|---|---|---|---|---|---|---|---|---|
| Flikke, Sean, of | .400 | 15 | 2 | 6 | 1 | 0 | 0 | 0 | 0 |
| Hinch, A.J., c-dh | .381 | 210 | 60 | 80 | 19 | 3 | 11 | 59 | 18 |
| Quaccia, Luke, 1b | .359 | 141 | 25 | 52 | 16 | 3 | 2 | 27 | 1 |
| Kilburg, Joe, of | .358 | 243 | 65 | 87 | 10 | 3 | 5 | 45 | 23 |
| Dallimore, Brian, 2b | .335 | 224 | 44 | 76 | 16 | 2 | 2 | 37 | 8 |
| Gerut, Jody, of | .321 | 246 | 55 | 79 | 15 | 6 | 6 | 46 | 9 |
| Kent, Troy, 1b-3b | .304 | 191 | 33 | 58 | 14 | 1 | 11 | 39 | 6 |
| Schaeffer, Jon, c-dh | .292 | 208 | 44 | 61 | 18 | 0 | 11 | 44 | 3 |
| Clark, Chris, of | .289 | 76 | 16 | 22 | 1 | 0 | 1 | 9 | 2 |
| Sees, Eric, ss | .280 | 175 | 33 | 49 | 10 | 0 | 3 | 31 | 7 |
| Salter, John, c | .276 | 29 | 3 | 8 | 2 | 0 | 0 | 5 | 1 |
| Hochgesang, Josh, 3b | .236 | 89 | 16 | 21 | 3 | 1 | 2 | 11 | 4 |
| Carter, Cale, of | .224 | 165 | 24 | 37 | 7 | 2 | 2 | 24 | 6 |
| Pecci, Jay, 3b-ss | .194 | 103 | 16 | 20 | 2 | 0 | 1 | 11 | 3 |

| PITCHING | W | L | ERA | G | SV | IP | H | BB | SO |
|---|---|---|---|---|---|---|---|---|---|
| Koons, Josh | 0 | 0 | 0.69 | 7 | 0 | 13 | 6 | 5 | 17 |
| Reimers, Tom | 4 | 4 | 2.92 | 27 | 5 | 71 | 58 | 27 | 64 |
| Iglesias, Mario | 10 | 1 | 3.00 | 21 | 2 | 57 | 58 | 12 | 27 |
| Hutchinson, Chad | 7 | 2 | 3.51 | 16 | 0 | 85 | 86 | 38 | 70 |
| Peterson, Kyle | 10 | 5 | 3.71 | 17 | 0 | 112 | 105 | 41 | 95 |
| Middlebrook, Jason | 1 | 1 | 3.72 | 2 | 0 | 10 | 4 | 6 | 7 |
| Sullivan, Brendan | 2 | 0 | 3.77 | 23 | 0 | 31 | 24 | 12 | 26 |
| Austin, Jeff | 6 | 4 | 3.81 | 16 | 1 | 90 | 94 | 36 | 88 |
| Cogan, Tony | 1 | 0 | 4.76 | 17 | 0 | 28 | 32 | 9 | 19 |
| Brammer, J.D. | 0 | 2 | 4.78 | 17 | 0 | 26 | 21 | 12 | 31 |
| Hoard, Brent | 0 | 0 | 11.57 | 6 | 0 | 5 | 7 | 10 | 8 |

## 10 CAL STATE NORTHRIDGE

**Coach:** Mike Batesole **Record:** 52-18

| BATTING | AVG | AB | R | H | 2B | 3B | HR | RBI | SB |
|---|---|---|---|---|---|---|---|---|---|
| Fick, Robert, c | .420 | 283 | 79 | 119 | 24 | 5 | 25 | 96 | 22 |
| Kennedy, Adam, ss | .393 | 308 | 94 | 121 | 19 | 6 | 17 | 81 | 15 |
| Gillespie, Eric, 3b | .357 | 263 | 79 | 94 | 15 | 2 | 23 | 70 | 12 |
| Miranda, Jose, of | .341 | 223 | 65 | 76 | 17 | 3 | 3 | 46 | 12 |
| Stevenson, David, dh-1b | .304 | 148 | 34 | 45 | 8 | 0 | 8 | 36 | 1 |
| Hohman, Grant, 1b-2b | .282 | 255 | 59 | 72 | 15 | 2 | 15 | 64 | 3 |
| Airoso, Kurt, of | .281 | 253 | 65 | 71 | 19 | 1 | 12 | 61 | 14 |
| Conrad, Jeremy, of | .268 | 112 | 25 | 30 | 3 | 0 | 3 | 21 | 4 |
| Martinez, Cesar, 2b | .250 | 156 | 30 | 39 | 5 | 1 | 5 | 29 | 6 |
| Cheshier, Casey, dh-1b | .247 | 174 | 29 | 43 | 9 | 0 | 7 | 28 | 2 |
| Hurd, Ryan, of | .244 | 176 | 46 | 43 | 4 | 2 | 9 | 31 | 7 |
| Anderson, Matt, 1b | .196 | 46 | 15 | 9 | 1 | 0 | 1 | 11 | 1 |
| McElwee, Heath, of | .167 | 18 | 2 | 3 | 0 | 0 | 0 | 0 | 0 |

| PITCHING | W | L | ERA | G | SV | IP | H | BB | SO |
|---|---|---|---|---|---|---|---|---|---|
| Settle, Andrew | 1 | 0 | 2.84 | 25 | 2 | 25 | 22 | 8 | 25 |
| Rice, Nathan | 6 | 2 | 3.02 | 23 | 0 | 51 | 40 | 28 | 29 |
| Ramirez, Erasmo | 14 | 1 | 3.74 | 24 | 1 | 123 | 119 | 26 | 94 |
| Flores, Benny | 7 | 2 | 3.75 | 21 | 0 | 84 | 83 | 34 | 63 |
| Crabtree, Robby | 13 | 8 | 3.89 | 29 | 5 | 139 | 133 | 35 | 118 |
| Cole, Jason | 3 | 0 | 4.10 | 16 | 1 | 48 | 43 | 14 | 28 |
| Stephenson, Gary | 4 | 3 | 4.27 | 24 | 2 | 53 | 60 | 14 | 36 |
| Velazquez, Juan | 1 | 0 | 4.50 | 22 | 0 | 24 | 34 | 9 | 17 |
| Howland, Evan | 3 | 0 | 5.76 | 14 | 0 | 25 | 25 | 12 | 26 |
| Nickens, Brandon | 0 | 0 | 5.93 | 12 | 1 | 14 | 18 | 11 | 9 |
| Yeomans, Jesse | 0 | 2 | 10.71 | 12 | 0 | 21 | 32 | 3 | 19 |

**Shocking Season.** Third baseman Casey Blake led Wichita State to a 54-11 record by hitting .360 with 22 homers and 101 RBIs.

## 11 OKLAHOMA STATE

**Coach:** Gary Ward **Record:** 45-21

| BATTING | AVG | AB | R | H | 2B | 3B | HR | RBI | SB |
|---|---|---|---|---|---|---|---|---|---|
| DiPace, Danny, of | .422 | 102 | 28 | 43 | 8 | 2 | 7 | 38 | 1 |
| Guiel, Jeff, of | .394 | 246 | 84 | 97 | 17 | 6 | 15 | 80 | 27 |
| Kent, Dean, of | .365 | 52 | 15 | 19 | 4 | 0 | 1 | 28 | 0 |
| McNamara, Rusty, 2b-of | .362 | 279 | 100 | 101 | 11 | 2 | 19 | 89 | 7 |
| MacKay, Tripp, ss-2b | .360 | 278 | 96 | 100 | 17 | 7 | 3 | 61 | 17 |
| Roossien, Tony, 3b-1b | .344 | 163 | 54 | 56 | 9 | 3 | 6 | 49 | 1 |
| Steelmon, Wyley, dh-1b | .337 | 175 | 51 | 59 | 13 | 2 | 14 | 56 | 0 |
| Wood, Jamey, dh-1b | .333 | 96 | 24 | 32 | 5 | 1 | 6 | 31 | 0 |
| Holliday, Josh, c-3b | .320 | 228 | 62 | 73 | 15 | 0 | 6 | 52 | 1 |
| McCullough, Jay, of-1b | .303 | 66 | 12 | 20 | 11 | 1 | 2 | 15 | 0 |
| Salhani, Ted, of | .296 | 189 | 60 | 56 | 8 | 2 | 16 | 58 | 3 |
| Cook, Jamie, 1b | .290 | 93 | 18 | 27 | 6 | 0 | 4 | 22 | 0 |
| Aylor, Brian, of | .277 | 148 | 40 | 41 | 6 | 1 | 9 | 35 | 11 |
| Folmar, Ryan, c | .259 | 112 | 40 | 29 | 3 | 1 | 2 | 20 | 1 |
| Hartsburg, Steve, 3b-ss | .237 | 114 | 38 | 27 | 5 | 1 | 2 | 18 | 1 |
| Smith, Cory, ss | .205 | 73 | 23 | 15 | 3 | 2 | 0 | 14 | 3 |

| PITCHING | W | L | ERA | G | SV | IP | H | BB | SO |
|---|---|---|---|---|---|---|---|---|---|
| McClellan, Sean | 8 | 3 | 4.49 | 19 | 0 | 110 | 103 | 66 | 125 |
| Thomas, Brian | 2 | 1 | 4.87 | 25 | 2 | 41 | 39 | 28 | 43 |
| Adkins, Jon | 5 | 3 | 5.35 | 24 | 4 | 76 | 90 | 29 | 47 |
| Maurer, David | 6 | 3 | 5.72 | 23 | 3 | 57 | 60 | 28 | 50 |
| Graves, Ryan | 10 | 2 | 5.86 | 20 | 0 | 114 | 133 | 55 | 104 |
| Askew, Heath | 7 | 4 | 5.88 | 20 | 0 | 41 | 52 | 25 | 32 |
| Smith, Larry | 3 | 0 | 6.49 | 15 | 0 | 43 | 58 | 33 | 22 |
| Forsythe, Neil | 2 | 1 | 8.58 | 13 | 0 | 36 | 53 | 15 | 29 |
| Kirby, Shane | 1 | 2 | 9.00 | 17 | 1 | 27 | 40 | 13 | 16 |
| Cunneen, Ryan | 1 | 0 | 10.66 | 10 | 0 | 13 | 18 | 12 | 10 |
| Nina, Elvin | 0 | 2 | 11.72 | 12 | 0 | 18 | 23 | 22 | 15 |

## 12 CAL STATE FULLERTON

**Coach:** Augie Garrido **Record:** 45-16

| BATTING | AVG | AB | R | H | 2B | 3B | HR | RBI | SB |
|---|---|---|---|---|---|---|---|---|---|
| Kotsay, Mark, of-p | .402 | 241 | 78 | 97 | 27 | 4 | 20 | 91 | 20 |
| Giambi, Jeremy, of | .396 | 225 | 70 | 89 | 20 | 1 | 6 | 58 | 25 |
| Alviso, Jerome, 2b-ss | .338 | 151 | 41 | 51 | 13 | 0 | 2 | 21 | 1 |

| BATTING | AVG | AB | R | H | 2B | 3B | HR | RBI | SB |
|---|---|---|---|---|---|---|---|---|---|
| Kiil, Skip, of | .337 | 101 | 32 | 34 | 9 | 3 | 6 | 21 | 11 |
| Martinez, Tony, 3b | .326 | 224 | 46 | 73 | 14 | 1 | 8 | 54 | 2 |
| Seal, Scott, dh | .326 | 86 | 13 | 28 | 8 | 0 | 2 | 21 | 0 |
| Lamb, Mike, c-inf | .324 | 179 | 35 | 58 | 14 | 0 | 5 | 30 | 0 |
| Loyd, Brian, c | .317 | 243 | 53 | 77 | 13 | 1 | 8 | 64 | 8 |
| Chatham, Steve, of | .316 | 171 | 50 | 54 | 13 | 1 | 2 | 38 | 4 |
| Ankrum, C.J., 1b | .312 | 231 | 51 | 72 | 13 | 1 | 5 | 60 | 2 |
| Jones, Jack, ss | .276 | 199 | 46 | 55 | 9 | 2 | 5 | 23 | 4 |
| Hill, Nakia, 2b | .250 | 20 | 7 | 5 | 1 | 0 | 0 | 1 | 2 |
| Rowand, Aaron, of-3b | .147 | 34 | 5 | 5 | 0 | 0 | 0 | 6 | 0 |

| PITCHING | W | L | ERA | G | SV | IP | H | BB | SO |
|---|---|---|---|---|---|---|---|---|---|
| Billingsley, Brent | 11 | 2 | 3.02 | 17 | 0 | 113 | 99 | 52 | 114 |
| White, Dan | 0 | 0 | 3.27 | 11 | 0 | 11 | 10 | 0 | 9 |
| Chavez, Mark | 2 | 3 | 3.45 | 31 | 9 | 57 | 45 | 19 | 52 |
| Estrella, Luis | 3 | 1 | 3.54 | 27 | 5 | 56 | 56 | 24 | 33 |
| Singelyn, Todd | 1 | 0 | 3.71 | 11 | 0 | 17 | 19 | 11 | 7 |
| Spencer, Dustin | 1 | 0 | 3.75 | 7 | 0 | 12 | 14 | 7 | 6 |
| Irvine, Kirk | 12 | 3 | 3.86 | 20 | 0 | 110 | 116 | 42 | 74 |
| Hild, Scott | 9 | 4 | 4.66 | 22 | 1 | 93 | 108 | 30 | 72 |
| Greenlee, Mike | 3 | 2 | 4.97 | 15 | 0 | 29 | 26 | 12 | 23 |
| Wise, Matt | 3 | 0 | 5.61 | 8 | 0 | 26 | 25 | 18 | 19 |
| Kotsay, Mark | 0 | 1 | 9.00 | 12 | 3 | 13 | 17 | 9 | 19 |
| Cardona, Steve | 0 | 0 | 9.64 | 4 | 0 | 5 | 4 | 7 | 4 |

## 13 TENNESSEE

Coach: Rod Delmonico   Record: 43-20

| BATTING | AVG | AB | R | H | 2B | 3B | HR | RBI | SB |
|---|---|---|---|---|---|---|---|---|---|
| Greene, Clay, of | .356 | 191 | 49 | 68 | 7 | 4 | 4 | 26 | 33 |
| Cortez, Sonny, of | .355 | 228 | 60 | 81 | 14 | 4 | 12 | 58 | 12 |
| Pickler, Jeff, 2b | .341 | 226 | 28 | 77 | 11 | 3 | 1 | 40 | 4 |
| Schroeffel, Scott, of-p | .340 | 256 | 58 | 87 | 29 | 0 | 14 | 58 | 15 |
| Lewis, Ed, 2b | .331 | 245 | 51 | 81 | 19 | 4 | 7 | 52 | 9 |
| Moore, Baker, ss-3b | .329 | 85 | 14 | 28 | 6 | 0 | 1 | 12 | 0 |
| Ojeda, Augie, ss | .317 | 199 | 51 | 63 | 11 | 3 | 1 | 24 | 12 |
| Ross, Justin, of-dh | .314 | 172 | 23 | 54 | 4 | 1 | 2 | 28 | 10 |
| Folkers, Ken, 3b | .294 | 238 | 42 | 70 | 12 | 1 | 6 | 47 | 0 |
| Espinosa, Ray,c | .275 | 178 | 30 | 49 | 11 | 0 | 4 | 24 | 0 |
| Copley, Travis, dh-1b | .227 | 110 | 22 | 25 | 6 | 1 | 2 | 20 | 2 |
| Fritz, Jim, c | .215 | 79 | 19 | 17 | 7 | 0 | 3 | 13 | 1 |

| PITCHING | W | L | ERA | G | SV | IP | H | BB | SO |
|---|---|---|---|---|---|---|---|---|---|
| Abell, Joe | 1 | 0 | 2.57 | 17 | 1 | 28 | 24 | 13 | 16 |
| Dickey, R.A. | 9 | 4 | 2.76 | 27 | 3 | 127 | 114 | 33 | 137 |
| Meyers, Ryan | 5 | 2 | 3.07 | 12 | 0 | 76 | 67 | 26 | 59 |
| Myers, Matt | 7 | 1 | 3.20 | 18 | 2 | 56 | 60 | 14 | 31 |
| Lincoln, Mike | 6 | 4 | 3.33 | 14 | 2 | 70 | 64 | 30 | 76 |
| Hudson, Luke | 5 | 0 | 3.91 | 12 | 0 | 53 | 40 | 22 | 57 |
| Schroeffel, Scott | 4 | 4 | 4.24 | 15 | 1 | 70 | 64 | 28 | 71 |
| Alkire, John | 6 | 4 | 4.50 | 26 | 4 | 70 | 52 | 31 | 62 |
| Hessler, Landon | 0 | 1 | 5.11 | 8 | 1 | 12 | 19 | 5 | 9 |

## 14 VIRGINIA

Coach: Dennis Womack   Record: 44-21

| BATTING | AVG | AB | R | H | 2B | 3B | HR | RBI | SB |
|---|---|---|---|---|---|---|---|---|---|
| Robinson, Adam, ss | .336 | 232 | 55 | 78 | 13 | 3 | 10 | 40 | 19 |
| Galloway, John, of | .335 | 239 | 55 | 80 | 11 | 4 | 6 | 38 | 20 |
| Kirkeide, Kyle, of | .318 | 22 | 5 | 7 | 2 | 0 | 1 | 10 | 1 |
| Sherlock, Brian, 3b | .299 | 174 | 25 | 52 | 11 | 0 | 3 | 25 | 2 |
| Schenk, Jonathan, dh | .286 | 21 | 4 | 6 | 1 | 0 | 2 | 5 | 0 |
| Willis, Symmion, of | .285 | 207 | 30 | 59 | 13 | 1 | 6 | 35 | 3 |
| Gilleland, Ryan, 2b | .283 | 230 | 38 | 65 | 10 | 2 | 8 | 43 | 10 |
| Counts, Justin, c | .274 | 219 | 46 | 60 | 17 | 0 | 6 | 37 | 11 |
| Bransford, Pat, 1b | .274 | 179 | 30 | 49 | 13 | 0 | 4 | 32 | 1 |
| Kinsman, Ted, of | .229 | 48 | 7 | 11 | 0 | 0 | 0 | 5 | 2 |
| Anderson, E.J., dh | .227 | 154 | 28 | 35 | 6 | 1 | 14 | 34 | 1 |
| McGettigan, Brian, 3b | .226 | 106 | 17 | 24 | 3 | 2 | 0 | 12 | 0 |
| Seward, Donnie, of | .226 | 195 | 32 | 44 | 6 | 2 | 1 | 17 | 6 |
| Post, Mark, 1b | .185 | 27 | 12 | 5 | 0 | 0 | 1 | 5 | 3 |
| Ford, Kevin, 1b-dh | .157 | 83 | 7 | 13 | 2 | 0 | 0 | 6 | 2 |
| Meadows, Jerry, c | .000 | 10 | 0 | 0 | 0 | 0 | 0 | 0 | 0 |

| PITCHING | W | L | ERA | G | SV | IP | H | BB | SO |
|---|---|---|---|---|---|---|---|---|---|
| Greisinger, Seth | 12 | 2 | 1.76 | 16 | 0 | 123 | 78 | 36 | 141 |
| Zaikov, Craig | 8 | 1 | 2.48 | 19 | 0 | 76 | 63 | 24 | 69 |
| Lee, Andy | 1 | 3 | 3.03 | 25 | 3 | 30 | 33 | 14 | 35 |
| Canady, Joel | 3 | 1 | 3.82 | 12 | 0 | 31 | 27 | 13 | 15 |
| Sekany, Jason | 6 | 4 | 3.86 | 28 | 5 | 77 | 67 | 41 | 79 |
| Daneker, Pat | 8 | 5 | 4.21 | 18 | 1 | 98 | 105 | 36 | 71 |
| Lopez, Javier | 4 | 2 | 4.72 | 18 | 0 | 53 | 56 | 35 | 36 |
| Robinson, Robby | 2 | 3 | 5.60 | 19 | 1 | 45 | 56 | 24 | 38 |
| Zawatski, Geoff | 0 | 0 | 5.96 | 16 | 0 | 26 | 28 | 10 | 19 |

**Tech Terror.** Third baseman Clint Bryant sparked Texas Tech to a 49-15 record, hitting .382 with 18 homers and 100 RBIs.

## 15 TEXAS TECH

Coach: Larry Hayes   Record: 49-15

| BATTING | AVG | AB | R | H | 2B | 3B | HR | RBI | SB |
|---|---|---|---|---|---|---|---|---|---|
| Kastelic, Matt, of | .424 | 269 | 78 | 114 | 19 | 4 | 8 | 70 | 51 |
| Bryant, Clint, 3b | .382 | 262 | 89 | 100 | 26 | 2 | 18 | 100 | 37 |
| Clapp, Stubby, 2b | .372 | 215 | 97 | 80 | 28 | 8 | 7 | 51 | 21 |
| Ruecker, Dion, ss | .350 | 260 | 69 | 91 | 22 | 3 | 20 | 82 | 18 |
| Davis, Brad, of | .347 | 202 | 56 | 70 | 11 | 3 | 4 | 39 | 17 |
| Fox, Brian, c | .333 | 66 | 10 | 22 | 3 | 1 | 2 | 11 | 0 |
| Chiprez, Chris, dh | .333 | 111 | 19 | 37 | 12 | 0 | 1 | 22 | 1 |
| Leonard, Neal, of | .333 | 21 | 3 | 7 | 3 | 1 | 1 | 10 | 0 |
| Lindstrom, David, c | .332 | 229 | 67 | 76 | 19 | 0 | 16 | 60 | 1 |
| Dillon, Joe, 1b | .326 | 267 | 56 | 87 | 16 | 2 | 10 | 70 | 18 |
| Bennett, Marshall, of | .292 | 154 | 42 | 45 | 10 | 1 | 4 | 26 | 16 |
| Martinez, Sergio, of | .289 | 159 | 44 | 46 | 11 | 1 | 5 | 30 | 3 |
| Price, Duane, of | .250 | 20 | 10 | 5 | 1 | 0 | 0 | 1 | 1 |
| Bledsoe, Roger, 2b | .212 | 33 | 6 | 7 | 0 | 0 | 0 | 3 | 1 |

| PITCHING | W | L | ERA | G | SV | IP | H | BB | SO |
|---|---|---|---|---|---|---|---|---|---|
| Stewart, Zack | 1 | 1 | 2.28 | 13 | 1 | 24 | 18 | 9 | 11 |
| Ralston, Brad | 3 | 0 | 3.16 | 20 | 2 | 43 | 37 | 28 | 40 |
| Brewer, Ryan | 10 | 3 | 3.53 | 17 | 1 | 105 | 114 | 23 | 69 |
| Frush, Jimmy | 10 | 6 | 3.70 | 23 | 4 | 100 | 92 | 34 | 116 |
| Miller, Matt | 12 | 2 | 3.98 | 18 | 0 | 111 | 114 | 56 | 113 |
| Reynolds, Chad | 0 | 0 | 4.05 | 7 | 0 | 7 | 9 | 3 | 1 |
| Ulrich, Kirk | 0 | 0 | 4.09 | 7 | 0 | 11 | 7 | 5 | 12 |
| Peck, Jeff | 7 | 1 | 4.89 | 15 | 0 | 70 | 83 | 32 | 38 |
| Ward, Monty | 5 | 1 | 5.80 | 21 | 1 | 76 | 69 | 35 | 88 |
| Kemp, Zane | 0 | 1 | 7.71 | 6 | 0 | 5 | 2 | 2 | 3 |
| Davidson, Tim | 1 | 0 | 9.00 | 7 | 0 | 9 | 12 | 7 | 6 |
| Bowman, James | 0 | 0 | 9.00 | 3 | 0 | 2 | 1 | 3 | 2 |

## 16 SOUTH FLORIDA

Coach: Eddie Cardieri   Record: 47-19

| BATTING | AVG | AB | R | H | 2B | 3B | HR | RBI | SB |
|---|---|---|---|---|---|---|---|---|---|
| Heintz, Chris, 3b | .400 | 265 | 63 | 106 | 21 | 4 | 16 | 95 | 3 |
| Gload, Ross, 1b | .376 | 250 | 83 | 94 | 15 | 3 | 21 | 83 | 8 |
| Pilger, Mike, of | .363 | 193 | 52 | 70 | 12 | 1 | 1 | 20 | 20 |
| Cafaro, Gio, of | .358 | 254 | 86 | 91 | 10 | 7 | 5 | 32 | 50 |
| DeLeon, Jorge, 2b-ss | .347 | 190 | 55 | 66 | 12 | 2 | 2 | 39 | 4 |
| Boles, Kevin, c | .337 | 101 | 16 | 34 | 9 | 0 | 2 | 20 | 1 |
| Michonski, Jason, of | .333 | 66 | 12 | 22 | 5 | 1 | 1 | 15 | 0 |
| Lentz, Bobby, of | .321 | 56 | 21 | 18 | 5 | 0 | 0 | 17 | 5 |
| Bland, Will, of | .317 | 82 | 19 | 26 | 7 | 3 | 3 | 18 | 1 |
| Braunstein, Aaron, of | .308 | 26 | 7 | 8 | 1 | 0 | 0 | 4 | 0 |
| Ribinski, Bob, c | .293 | 215 | 44 | 63 | 16 | 1 | 11 | 52 | 1 |
| Mason, John, dh-1b | .291 | 165 | 38 | 48 | 14 | 2 | 5 | 27 | 2 |
| Dellaero, Jason, ss | .284 | 243 | 40 | 69 | 12 | 2 | 19 | 61 | 2 |
| Alaimo, Jason, c | .262 | 42 | 2 | 11 | 2 | 0 | 0 | 8 | 0 |
| Lynch, Sean, of | .250 | 152 | 21 | 38 | 4 | 0 | 4 | 24 | 0 |
| West, Shawn, 2b | .194 | 108 | 20 | 21 | 2 | 1 | 1 | 9 | 6 |
| Peters, Bryan, 2b | .182 | 22 | 6 | 4 | 1 | 0 | 0 | 3 | 0 |
| Wolcott, Matt, 2b | .118 | 17 | 1 | 2 | 1 | 0 | 0 | 0 | 0 |

| PITCHING | W | L | ERA | G | SV | IP | H | BB | SO |
|---|---|---|---|---|---|---|---|---|---|
| Boyles, Steven | 2 | 4 | 1.41 | 40 | 6 | 64 | 49 | 13 | 60 |
| Ramos, Luis | 1 | 2 | 2.32 | 29 | 3 | 54 | 41 | 20 | 42 |
| Glaser, Scott | 12 | 4 | 3.52 | 23 | 1 | 100 | 92 | 28 | 61 |
| **Roberts, Mark** | 11 | 4 | 3.70 | 18 | 0 | 119 | 117 | 49 | 105 |
| Blank, Dave | 4 | 1 | 3.74 | 23 | 2 | 43 | 50 | 12 | 31 |
| **Danner, Adam** | 7 | 1 | 4.15 | 15 | 0 | 95 | 105 | 31 | 53 |
| Ryan, Pat | 9 | 3 | 5.76 | 17 | 1 | 91 | 108 | 39 | 54 |
| Busch, Eric | 1 | 0 | 9.16 | 13 | 0 | 19 | 27 | 18 | 7 |

## 17 RICE

**Coach:** Wayne Graham     **Record:** 42-23

| BATTING | AVG | AB | R | H | 2B | 3B | HR | RBI | SB |
|---|---|---|---|---|---|---|---|---|---|
| Berkman, Lance, 1b-of | .395 | 241 | 76 | 96 | 16 | 4 | 20 | 91 | 8 |
| **Venghaus, Jeff, of** | .360 | 250 | 77 | 90 | 18 | 4 | 5 | 42 | 18 |
| Ford, William, of | .322 | 239 | 53 | 77 | 13 | 2 | 6 | 46 | 18 |
| Cathey, Joseph, 2b-ss | .320 | 178 | 31 | 57 | 9 | 1 | 0 | 16 | 7 |
| Richards, Jason, ss-2b | .319 | 216 | 74 | 69 | 10 | 3 | 7 | 35 | 17 |
| Crosby, Bubba, of | .318 | 198 | 55 | 63 | 13 | 6 | 12 | 64 | 6 |
| McLaughlin, Tim, of | .310 | 187 | 25 | 58 | 19 | 0 | 2 | 41 | 3 |
| **Landry, Jacques, 3b-dh** | .284 | 236 | 61 | 67 | 19 | 3 | 19 | 81 | 5 |
| Doyle, Paul, dh-of | .282 | 174 | 39 | 49 | 9 | 1 | 3 | 38 | 8 |
| Joseph, Kevin, ss-3b | .269 | 156 | 27 | 42 | 12 | 3 | 0 | 20 | 3 |
| Herndon, Adam, of-p | .244 | 45 | 10 | 11 | 2 | 0 | 1 | 5 | 2 |
| Fuller, Brandon, c | .200 | 20 | 3 | 4 | 2 | 0 | 0 | 1 | 0 |
| Berg, Justin, c | .194 | 31 | 5 | 6 | 0 | 0 | 1 | 3 | 0 |
| Lorenz, Matt, dh | .190 | 21 | 1 | 4 | 1 | 0 | 0 | 3 | 0 |
| **Davis, Dana, p-dh** | .158 | 19 | 3 | 3 | 0 | 0 | 0 | 1 | 0 |
| Bess, Stephen, p-of | .071 | 14 | 1 | 1 | 0 | 1 | 0 | 4 | 0 |

| PITCHING | W | L | ERA | G | SV | IP | H | BB | SO |
|---|---|---|---|---|---|---|---|---|---|
| Kurtz-Nicholl, Jesse | 1 | 1 | 1.93 | 9 | 0 | 19 | 13 | 7 | 10 |
| **Davis, Dana** | 4 | 2 | 3.98 | 14 | 1 | 63 | 65 | 27 | 47 |
| **Taylor, Mark** | 5 | 2 | 4.06 | 18 | 0 | 64 | 40 | 60 | 64 |
| Anderson, Matt | 9 | 3 | 4.37 | 25 | 4 | 78 | 68 | 55 | 70 |
| Doyle, Paul | 1 | 1 | 4.50 | 11 | 2 | 16 | 20 | 12 | 18 |
| **Onley, Shawn** | 7 | 3 | 4.86 | 18 | 0 | 100 | 95 | 47 | 95 |
| Shaddix, Jeff | 5 | 4 | 5.02 | 26 | 2 | 61 | 64 | 24 | 32 |
| Herndon, Adam | 2 | 3 | 5.57 | 16 | 1 | 42 | 52 | 14 | 37 |
| Bess, Stephen | 7 | 2 | 5.79 | 18 | 1 | 78 | 86 | 49 | 53 |
| Brown, Allen | 1 | 2 | 6.17 | 21 | 4 | 35 | 45 | 13 | 24 |
| Baker, Jacob | 0 | 0 | 13.50 | 5 | 0 | 5 | 7 | 6 | 4 |

## 18 TEXAS

**Coach:** Cliff Gustafson     **Record:** 39-24

| BATTING | AVG | AB | R | H | 2B | 3B | HR | RBI | SB |
|---|---|---|---|---|---|---|---|---|---|
| Davis, Blake, of | .402 | 107 | 16 | 43 | 8 | 1 | 2 | 21 | 0 |
| Harkrider, Kip, ss | .381 | 260 | 75 | 99 | 17 | 5 | 4 | 43 | 8 |
| Byers, MacGregor, of-3b | .375 | 232 | 77 | 87 | 15 | 3 | 6 | 66 | 23 |
| **Peoples, Danny, 1b** | .375 | 216 | 67 | 81 | 18 | 5 | 17 | 86 | 7 |
| Klam, Josef, c | .375 | 56 | 9 | 21 | 2 | 1 | 1 | 8 | 0 |
| Scarborough, Mike, of | .333 | 15 | 2 | 5 | 1 | 1 | 0 | 3 | 1 |
| Layne, Jason, of-dh | .319 | 213 | 51 | 68 | 14 | 4 | 13 | 74 | 4 |
| **Salinas, Trey, 3b-c** | .306 | 196 | 41 | 60 | 12 | 5 | 5 | 46 | 2 |
| Campbell, Wylie, 2b | .284 | 232 | 66 | 66 | 14 | 4 | 0 | 35 | 43 |
| Braswell, Sean, 3b | .269 | 52 | 11 | 14 | 3 | 0 | 0 | 9 | 2 |
| **Escamilla, Roman, c** | .266 | 188 | 52 | 50 | 8 | 2 | 4 | 38 | 6 |
| Edelstein, Chris, of | .255 | 137 | 35 | 35 | 5 | 4 | 0 | 20 | 4 |
| Kiernsteadt, Clint, of | .240 | 150 | 26 | 36 | 7 | 2 | 5 | 32 | 3 |
| **Cridland, Mark, of** | .192 | 26 | 6 | 5 | 1 | 0 | 3 | 5 | 0 |
| Loeffler, Brett, of | .171 | 35 | 4 | 6 | 1 | 0 | 0 | 6 | 1 |
| Keith, Benji, of | .136 | 22 | 9 | 3 | 0 | 0 | 0 | 2 | 2 |

| PITCHING | W | L | ERA | G | SV | IP | H | BB | SO |
|---|---|---|---|---|---|---|---|---|---|
| Hinojosa, JoJo | 3 | 0 | 3.32 | 23 | 0 | 38 | 36 | 20 | 32 |
| **O'Dell, Jake** | 8 | 3 | 4.15 | 18 | 0 | 117 | 111 | 38 | 82 |
| Clements, Kelly | 1 | 1 | 4.32 | 21 | 1 | 25 | 31 | 12 | 11 |
| French, Eric | 2 | 2 | 4.33 | 27 | 9 | 35 | 23 | 22 | 48 |
| Adare, Kendal | 3 | 0 | 4.82 | 18 | 1 | 47 | 53 | 20 | 34 |
| Weaver, Rad | 3 | 2 | 4.95 | 16 | 1 | 40 | 53 | 19 | 23 |
| Lopez, Joe Luis | 4 | 4 | 4.96 | 20 | 0 | 53 | 51 | 37 | 32 |
| **Leon, Scott** | 7 | 5 | 4.96 | 20 | 1 | 74 | 69 | 49 | 60 |
| Zamarripa, Tony | 1 | 1 | 6.00 | 16 | 0 | 24 | 34 | 17 | 12 |
| McKinney, Brian | 0 | 1 | 6.00 | 4 | 1 | 6 | 6 | 5 | 4 |
| **Barker, Donny** | 5 | 5 | 6.03 | 18 | 1 | 63 | 74 | 52 | 47 |
| Smith, Chad | 1 | 0 | 7.62 | 8 | 0 | 13 | 20 | 5 | 5 |
| Powell, Dax | 1 | 0 | 11.57 | 15 | 0 | 14 | 31 | 13 | 10 |

## 19 MASSACHUSETTS

**Coach:** Mike Stone     **Record:** 40-13

| BATTING | AVG | AB | R | H | 2B | 3B | HR | RBI | SB |
|---|---|---|---|---|---|---|---|---|---|
| Dagliere, Muchie, 2b | .415 | 195 | 60 | 81 | 13 | 4 | 5 | 53 | 12 |

**On The Warpath.** Texas first baseman Danny Peoples became Cleveland's first-round draft pick by hitting .375 with 17 homers.

| | AVG | AB | R | H | 2B | 3B | HR | RBI | SB |
|---|---|---|---|---|---|---|---|---|---|
| Murphy, Nate, of | .390 | 195 | 50 | 76 | 17 | 4 | 10 | 66 | 10 |
| **Gorrie, Brad, ss** | .359 | 170 | 61 | 61 | 12 | 2 | 5 | 36 | 33 |
| Jette, Ryan, of | .358 | 212 | 60 | 76 | 12 | 3 | 3 | 25 | 31 |
| Samela, Brian, c | .322 | 87 | 19 | 28 | 4 | 0 | 0 | 17 | 0 |
| Clark, Doug, of-dh | .318 | 198 | 37 | 63 | 9 | 1 | 2 | 40 | 19 |
| Kelly, Justin, 1b | .307 | 166 | 31 | 51 | 7 | 0 | 2 | 38 | 2 |
| Kiah, Andy, c | .298 | 121 | 16 | 36 | 7 | 0 | 1 | 24 | 1 |
| Thistle, Ryan, 3b | .275 | 91 | 15 | 25 | 1 | 1 | 0 | 19 | 4 |
| Mazzaferro, Bryan, 3b | .261 | 92 | 21 | 24 | 5 | 0 | 0 | 10 | 4 |
| Gautreau, Pete, of | .248 | 129 | 31 | 32 | 4 | 1 | 3 | 22 | 7 |
| Giglio, David, ss | .214 | 28 | 4 | 6 | 0 | 1 | 0 | 4 | 0 |
| Hodgson, Ryan, 1b | .143 | 21 | 6 | 3 | 1 | 0 | 0 | 5 | 0 |
| Barnsby, Scott, p-dh | .100 | 10 | 2 | 1 | 0 | 0 | 0 | 1 | 0 |

| PITCHING | W | L | ERA | G | SV | IP | H | BB | SO |
|---|---|---|---|---|---|---|---|---|---|
| Levy, Steve | 2 | 0 | 1.66 | 15 | 4 | 22 | 16 | 4 | 5 |
| Barnsby, Scott | 4 | 0 | 3.60 | 8 | 0 | 30 | 31 | 18 | 29 |
| **Paronto, Chad** | 5 | 4 | 3.72 | 12 | 1 | 68 | 70 | 27 | 45 |
| Dart, David | 5 | 1 | 3.77 | 12 | 0 | 60 | 55 | 33 | 32 |
| Puleri, Jeff | 4 | 2 | 4.12 | 10 | 0 | 44 | 42 | 18 | 25 |
| Cooke, Bill | 6 | 2 | 4.26 | 12 | 0 | 51 | 59 | 16 | 34 |
| Bennett, Jason | 6 | 3 | 4.35 | 12 | 0 | 60 | 71 | 12 | 33 |
| Sullivan, Chad | 5 | 1 | 4.74 | 11 | 0 | 49 | 53 | 23 | 20 |
| Robinson, Adam | 2 | 0 | 5.96 | 8 | 0 | 26 | 24 | 17 | 22 |
| Cameron, Ryan | 1 | 0 | 8.03 | 7 | 0 | 12 | 16 | 9 | 10 |

## 20 TULANE

**Coach:** Rick Jones     **Record:** 43-20

| BATTING | AVG | AB | R | H | 2B | 3B | HR | RBI | SB |
|---|---|---|---|---|---|---|---|---|---|
| Fitzgerald, Jason, of | .353 | 252 | 58 | 89 | 28 | 1 | 9 | 56 | 20 |
| Graffagnini, Keith, 1b | .348 | 244 | 47 | 85 | 15 | 2 | 5 | 53 | 11 |
| Hughes, Brian, of | .344 | 241 | 65 | 83 | 17 | 1 | 4 | 45 | 33 |
| Bivalacqua, Trinity, c | .308 | 52 | 8 | 16 | 3 | 1 | 0 | 13 | 0 |
| Wilson, Scott, 3b | .305 | 223 | 50 | 68 | 16 | 3 | 6 | 32 | 6 |
| Sutter, Chad, c | .297 | 229 | 46 | 68 | 7 | 1 | 16 | 67 | 2 |
| Johns, Michael, ss | .280 | 218 | 30 | 61 | 8 | 2 | 2 | 25 | 8 |
| Brown, Craig, of | .275 | 233 | 57 | 64 | 14 | 4 | 1 | 24 | 15 |
| Boudreaux, Paul, dh | .274 | 84 | 10 | 23 | 6 | 0 | 1 | 15 | 2 |
| Pursell, Mike, 2b | .267 | 176 | 31 | 47 | 8 | 4 | 3 | 27 | 7 |
| Guillot, Trey, of | .262 | 42 | 11 | 11 | 1 | 0 | 0 | 5 | 3 |
| Lontayo, Alex, p-dh | .262 | 65 | 8 | 17 | 5 | 0 | 1 | 10 | 0 |
| Williams, Anthony, 1b | .250 | 12 | 4 | 3 | 1 | 0 | 1 | 3 | 0 |
| Bosio, Nate, of | .219 | 32 | 13 | 7 | 2 | 1 | 0 | 1 | 2 |
| Llorente, Marcelo, 3b | .214 | 14 | 3 | 3 | 1 | 0 | 1 | 5 | 0 |
| Bridgers, Land, 2b | .171 | 41 | 8 | 7 | 0 | 0 | 0 | 4 | 5 |
| Escudier, Mike, inf | .111 | 27 | 5 | 3 | 2 | 0 | 0 | 2 | 1 |

| PITCHING | W | L | ERA | G | SV | IP | H | BB | SO |
|---|---|---|---|---|---|---|---|---|---|
| Echeverez, Raul | 2 | 0 | 2.25 | 7 | 0 | 12 | 4 | 7 | 7 |
| Navarro, Jason | 11 | 0 | 3.30 | 17 | 0 | 93 | 85 | 48 | 110 |
| Ardoin, Todd | 1 | 2 | 3.53 | 25 | 5 | 36 | 43 | 23 | 41 |
| Bell, Scott | 9 | 2 | 3.84 | 19 | 0 | 96 | 111 | 28 | 79 |
| Cressend, Jack | 8 | 6 | 3.86 | 29 | 4 | 103 | 96 | 33 | 123 |
| Williamson, Anthony | 5 | 2 | 4.31 | 19 | 0 | 86 | 83 | 34 | 84 |
| Lontayo, Alex | 7 | 6 | 4.35 | 19 | 0 | 93 | 90 | 41 | 92 |
| Brown, Craig | 0 | 1 | 7.20 | 15 | 3 | 20 | 20 | 18 | 21 |
| Robinson, Jared | 0 | 1 | 7.84 | 4 | 1 | 10 | 12 | 12 | 4 |
| Frazine, Ryan | 0 | 0 | 11.88 | 6 | 0 | 8 | 13 | 7 | 4 |

## 21 UCLA

**Coach:** Gary Adams    **Record:** 36-28

| BATTING | AVG | AB | R | H | 2B | 3B | HR | RBI | SB |
|---|---|---|---|---|---|---|---|---|---|
| Ammirato, Zak, 3b-dh | .354 | 161 | 45 | 57 | 15 | 3 | 6 | 42 | 6 |
| Glaus, Troy, ss-3b | .352 | 216 | 65 | 76 | 17 | 1 | 16 | 50 | 12 |
| DeCinces, Tim, c | .341 | 232 | 66 | 79 | 16 | 0 | 18 | 67 | 6 |
| Byrnes, Eric, of | .338 | 225 | 32 | 76 | 21 | 1 | 8 | 56 | 14 |
| Theodorou, Nick, of-dh | .314 | 137 | 46 | 43 | 10 | 2 | 1 | 25 | 10 |
| Heinrichs, Jon, of | .296 | 250 | 55 | 74 | 13 | 5 | 3 | 40 | 21 |
| Valent, Eric, of | .289 | 228 | 56 | 66 | 12 | 0 | 12 | 55 | 6 |
| Green, Jason, c | .278 | 18 | 4 | 5 | 0 | 0 | 0 | 3 | 0 |
| Santora, Jack, ss-2b | .270 | 163 | 31 | 44 | 4 | 0 | 0 | 13 | 4 |
| Olson, Cass, 1b | .265 | 113 | 21 | 30 | 4 | 1 | 2 | 13 | 0 |
| Matoian, Chad, 2b | .258 | 97 | 17 | 25 | 7 | 0 | 1 | 14 | 1 |
| Nista, Brett, 2b | .251 | 179 | 24 | 45 | 6 | 2 | 2 | 31 | 4 |
| Zamora, Pete, 1b-p | .234 | 167 | 23 | 39 | 10 | 0 | 6 | 30 | 0 |
| Craig, Benny, dh | .176 | 34 | 7 | 6 | 0 | 0 | 2 | 9 | 0 |
| Schult, Rob, 3b | .091 | 11 | 1 | 1 | 0 | 0 | 0 | 1 | 0 |
| Edwards, Kamau, of | .091 | 11 | 2 | 1 | 1 | 0 | 0 | 1 | 0 |

| PITCHING | W | L | ERA | G | SV | IP | H | BB | SO |
|---|---|---|---|---|---|---|---|---|---|
| Meyer, Jake | 1 | 2 | 2.64 | 13 | 0 | 31 | 28 | 21 | 38 |
| Parque, Jim | 9 | 3 | 3.72 | 18 | 0 | 126 | 142 | 38 | 116 |
| Jacquez, Tom | 1 | 1 | 4.50 | 5 | 0 | 8 | 9 | 1 | 11 |
| Sheredy, Kevin | 4 | 2 | 4.59 | 24 | 8 | 49 | 41 | 34 | 55 |
| Keller, Dan | 7 | 3 | 4.79 | 20 | 1 | 68 | 74 | 29 | 40 |
| Zamora, Pete | 6 | 1 | 4.89 | 14 | 0 | 74 | 87 | 25 | 46 |
| O'Toole, Ryan | 2 | 3 | 5.45 | 12 | 0 | 33 | 47 | 14 | 22 |
| Klein, Matt | 1 | 2 | 5.57 | 14 | 3 | 32 | 38 | 16 | 19 |
| St. George, Nick | 2 | 3 | 6.04 | 19 | 0 | 45 | 68 | 14 | 29 |
| Heineman, Rick | 1 | 6 | 6.35 | 26 | 1 | 62 | 78 | 32 | 41 |
| Lynch, Ryan | 2 | 2 | 6.88 | 12 | 0 | 35 | 43 | 17 | 14 |

## 22 GEORGIA TECH

**Coach:** Danny Hall    **Record:** 40-24

| BATTING | AVG | AB | R | H | 2B | 3B | HR | RBI | SB |
|---|---|---|---|---|---|---|---|---|---|
| Fischer, Mark, of | .400 | 260 | 60 | 104 | 23 | 5 | 14 | 66 | 8 |
| Sorrow, Michael, 3b-of | .369 | 249 | 66 | 92 | 18 | 2 | 11 | 47 | 3 |
| Leggett, Adam, 2b | .339 | 230 | 58 | 78 | 17 | 2 | 13 | 46 | 15 |
| Thomas, J.J., of-dh | .338 | 228 | 67 | 77 | 17 | 1 | 21 | 68 | 5 |
| Honeycutt, Heath, inf | .333 | 42 | 7 | 14 | 2 | 0 | 0 | 7 | 0 |
| Byers, Scott, 1b | .324 | 262 | 60 | 85 | 20 | 1 | 15 | 62 | 1 |
| Easterling, Adam, of | .299 | 177 | 33 | 53 | 6 | 2 | 1 | 25 | 12 |
| Barr, Tucker, c | .297 | 219 | 54 | 65 | 13 | 1 | 12 | 42 | 5 |
| Byrd, Marlon, of-3b | .288 | 198 | 30 | 57 | 10 | 0 | 1 | 27 | 10 |
| Hood, Jay, ss | .276 | 268 | 43 | 74 | 11 | 1 | 8 | 46 | 2 |
| Stuetzer, Ryan, dh | .269 | 26 | 4 | 7 | 0 | 0 | 0 | 5 | 2 |
| McQueen, Eric, c | .255 | 47 | 7 | 12 | 2 | 0 | 1 | 7 | 1 |
| Donaghey, Stephen, 1b | .212 | 33 | 7 | 7 | 0 | 0 | 0 | 4 | 0 |
| Shannon, Lance, of | .191 | 47 | 8 | 9 | 4 | 0 | 0 | 4 | 0 |

| PITCHING | W | L | ERA | G | SV | IP | H | BB | SO |
|---|---|---|---|---|---|---|---|---|---|
| Wrigley, Jase | 4 | 4 | 3.41 | 25 | 2 | 74 | 67 | 39 | 57 |
| Crowder, Chuck | 10 | 5 | 4.30 | 22 | 0 | 92 | 87 | 39 | 98 |
| McGill, Shane | 3 | 4 | 4.62 | 21 | 1 | 74 | 71 | 36 | 57 |
| Wilson, Kris | 5 | 3 | 5.03 | 21 | 0 | 98 | 127 | 24 | 66 |
| Elder, David | 9 | 5 | 5.25 | 21 | 0 | 106 | 111 | 56 | 123 |
| Barr, Tucker | 1 | 1 | 5.79 | 7 | 3 | 5 | 4 | 3 | 3 |
| Prather, Scott | 5 | 2 | 5.89 | 21 | 1 | 44 | 52 | 27 | 56 |
| Yankosky, L.J. | 2 | 0 | 6.38 | 17 | 2 | 18 | 12 | 18 | 20 |
| Thieme, Rich | 1 | 0 | 7.82 | 15 | 0 | 13 | 23 | 9 | 14 |
| Cason, Carlos | 0 | 0 | 8.76 | 10 | 0 | 12 | 16 | 2 | 12 |
| Duncan, Geoff | 0 | 0 | 9.72 | 16 | 1 | 17 | 25 | 11 | 14 |

## 23 NEVADA-LAS VEGAS

**Coach:** Fred Dallimore    **Record:** 43-17

| BATTING | AVG | AB | R | H | 2B | 3B | HR | RBI | SB |
|---|---|---|---|---|---|---|---|---|---|
| Eberwein, Kevin, 1b-dh | .367 | 207 | 60 | 76 | 19 | 1 | 10 | 55 | 2 |
| Hankins, Ryan, 3b | .367 | 229 | 60 | 84 | 17 | 1 | 12 | 66 | 6 |
| Kleiner, Stacy, c | .364 | 250 | 78 | 91 | 18 | 1 | 13 | 61 | 1 |
| Vincent, Scott, of | .361 | 216 | 54 | 78 | 15 | 3 | 13 | 69 | 11 |
| Anthony, Brian, dh-1b | .349 | 235 | 53 | 82 | 10 | 2 | 13 | 72 | 3 |
| Tanner, Paul, ss | .337 | 267 | 74 | 90 | 9 | 0 | 6 | 34 | 28 |
| Campbell, Sean, 2b | .324 | 179 | 37 | 58 | 11 | 0 | 1 | 33 | 7 |
| Adolph, Chris, of | .315 | 222 | 44 | 70 | 10 | 1 | 5 | 40 | 3 |
| Wilkes, Ted, of | .279 | 208 | 54 | 58 | 9 | 0 | 10 | 48 | 11 |
| Miller, Zac, of | .261 | 69 | 11 | 18 | 2 | 1 | 0 | 6 | 2 |
| Jones, Henry, 2b | .246 | 61 | 15 | 15 | 1 | 0 | 0 | 12 | 1 |
| Novak, John, of | .095 | 21 | 10 | 2 | 1 | 0 | 1 | 2 | 0 |

| PITCHING | W | L | ERA | G | SV | IP | H | BB | SO |
|---|---|---|---|---|---|---|---|---|---|
| LaRosa, Tom | 9 | 2 | 3.80 | 19 | 0 | 128 | 125 | 52 | 103 |
| Luce, Rob | 6 | 3 | 3.86 | 32 | 9 | 40 | 37 | 15 | 37 |
| Barry, Chad | 4 | 2 | 4.27 | 19 | 0 | 46 | 38 | 29 | 46 |
| Perri, Tista | 7 | 3 | 4.38 | 18 | 0 | 103 | 107 | 30 | 48 |
| Bauder, Mike | 8 | 4 | 5.01 | 22 | 1 | 101 | 111 | 45 | 70 |
| Koehne, Fred | 6 | 1 | 5.13 | 24 | 1 | 53 | 63 | 26 | 32 |
| Zipser, Mike | 0 | 0 | 5.40 | 4 | 0 | 5 | 3 | 7 | 2 |
| Yeskie, Nate | 2 | 2 | 7.42 | 6 | 0 | 30 | 43 | 13 | 21 |
| Scheffels, Bill | 1 | 0 | 8.80 | 12 | 0 | 30 | 45 | 23 | 20 |

## 24 GEORGIA SOUTHERN

**Coach:** Jack Stallings    **Record:** 46-14

| BATTING | AVG | AB | R | H | 2B | 3B | HR | RBI | SB |
|---|---|---|---|---|---|---|---|---|---|
| Peterman, Tommy, 1b | .382 | 246 | 66 | 94 | 10 | 0 | 26 | 82 | 2 |
| Hamlin, Mark, of | .370 | 219 | 56 | 81 | 17 | 6 | 8 | 41 | 18 |
| Jones, Sy, of | .340 | 203 | 53 | 69 | 16 | 3 | 5 | 55 | 16 |
| Killimett, Kevin, of | .333 | 21 | 5 | 7 | 2 | 0 | 0 | 1 | 2 |
| Coe, Donnie, 2b | .329 | 207 | 48 | 68 | 14 | 2 | 2 | 40 | 10 |
| Moran, Antoine, of | .302 | 252 | 61 | 76 | 7 | 4 | 2 | 23 | 50 |
| Walson, Steve, dh | .296 | 206 | 46 | 61 | 14 | 2 | 12 | 45 | 1 |
| Andrews, Jason, ss | .289 | 204 | 27 | 59 | 15 | 0 | 1 | 31 | 1 |
| Wilson, Steve, c | .281 | 210 | 37 | 59 | 15 | 0 | 10 | 46 | 10 |
| Whitley, Tyson, 3b | .269 | 242 | 44 | 65 | 11 | 4 | 5 | 44 | 6 |
| Fussell, Chad, of | .222 | 18 | 11 | 4 | 2 | 0 | 0 | 2 | 4 |
| Olvey, Jamie, 3b | .214 | 14 | 5 | 3 | 0 | 0 | 0 | 1 | 1 |
| Holder, Michael, c | .171 | 41 | 4 | 7 | 2 | 0 | 1 | 8 | 0 |
| Aldridge, Kyle, ss | .136 | 22 | 3 | 3 | 1 | 0 | 1 | 5 | 0 |

| PITCHING | W | L | ERA | G | SV | IP | H | BB | SO |
|---|---|---|---|---|---|---|---|---|---|
| Lee, Tod | 7 | 4 | 1.18 | 38 | 11 | 53 | 35 | 21 | 88 |
| Washburn, Danny | 4 | 0 | 2.47 | 16 | 0 | 44 | 35 | 17 | 37 |
| Ayala, Julio | 15 | 3 | 3.49 | 22 | 0 | 152 | 145 | 42 | 143 |
| Sauls, Clint | 7 | 2 | 4.80 | 19 | 0 | 90 | 98 | 32 | 47 |
| Hall, Brian | 3 | 2 | 4.89 | 16 | 0 | 42 | 58 | 13 | 39 |
| Cummings, Ryan | 8 | 2 | 5.38 | 19 | 0 | 102 | 134 | 33 | 92 |
| Phillips, Jon | 2 | 0 | 7.27 | 20 | 0 | 26 | 35 | 11 | 27 |
| Davis, Kelvin | 0 | 1 | 8.84 | 14 | 0 | 19 | 26 | 20 | 19 |

## 25 ARIZONA STATE

**Coach:** Pat Murphy    **Record:** 35-21

| BATTING | AVG | AB | R | H | 2B | 3B | HR | RBI | SB |
|---|---|---|---|---|---|---|---|---|---|
| Tommasini, Kevin, 1b | .389 | 90 | 26 | 35 | 9 | 0 | 3 | 22 | 3 |
| Grijalva, Mike, ss | .387 | 62 | 15 | 24 | 7 | 1 | 4 | 19 | 1 |
| McKinley, Dan, of | .386 | 254 | 73 | 98 | 17 | 3 | 9 | 57 | 11 |
| Moreno, Mikel, of | .378 | 238 | 75 | 90 | 22 | 2 | 11 | 53 | 18 |
| Kent, Robbie, 1b-2b | .357 | 227 | 66 | 81 | 18 | 2 | 12 | 68 | 5 |
| McKay, Cody, c | .335 | 221 | 55 | 74 | 13 | 1 | 9 | 47 | 1 |
| Gosewisch, Chip, 2b | .324 | 139 | 31 | 45 | 7 | 0 | 1 | 26 | 1 |
| Cermak, Jeff, of | .317 | 186 | 53 | 59 | 5 | 3 | 9 | 50 | 1 |
| Torti, Mike, 3b | .317 | 186 | 45 | 59 | 5 | 2 | 8 | 49 | 5 |
| Kolb, Damien, of | .291 | 79 | 27 | 23 | 4 | 2 | 2 | 12 | 8 |
| Bradley, Ryan, p-dh | .286 | 21 | 2 | 6 | 2 | 0 | 0 | 4 | 1 |
| Leon, Richy, ss-p | .273 | 22 | 5 | 6 | 0 | 0 | 0 | 3 | 0 |
| Collins, Michael, of | .230 | 174 | 29 | 40 | 5 | 0 | 0 | 27 | 1 |

| PITCHING | W | L | ERA | G | SV | IP | H | BB | SO |
|---|---|---|---|---|---|---|---|---|---|
| Leon, Richy | 3 | 1 | 3.42 | 13 | 1 | 26 | 19 | 9 | 23 |
| Bradley, Ryan | 2 | 2 | 3.88 | 34 | 3 | 58 | 63 | 21 | 51 |
| Molina, Gabe | 3 | 2 | 4.09 | 23 | 1 | 62 | 58 | 37 | 51 |
| Lowery, Phill | 5 | 1 | 4.71 | 9 | 0 | 50 | 42 | 28 | 56 |
| Spenser, Kaipo | 3 | 5 | 5.29 | 12 | 0 | 48 | 56 | 27 | 42 |
| Bond, Jason | 7 | 5 | 5.52 | 21 | 2 | 73 | 82 | 27 | 62 |
| Verdugo, Jason | 2 | 0 | 5.73 | 14 | 0 | 38 | 45 | 21 | 35 |
| Vasquez, Tim | 0 | 0 | 5.74 | 10 | 0 | 16 | 15 | 9 | 13 |
| Workman, Widd | 3 | 3 | 5.80 | 14 | 0 | 54 | 45 | 36 | 54 |
| Marietta, Ron | 4 | 2 | 6.13 | 23 | 0 | 47 | 50 | 33 | 50 |
| Wente, Jon | 1 | 0 | 6.60 | 9 | 1 | 15 | 23 | 8 | 7 |
| Mills, Ryan | 0 | 0 | 15.88 | 4 | 0 | 6 | 17 | 4 | 7 |

# CONFERENCE STANDINGS, LEADERS

## NCAA Division I Conferences

*Won conference tournament
**Boldface:** NCAA regional participant/conference department leader
#Conference department leader who does not qualify among batting/pitching leaders

### ATLANTIC COAST CONFERENCE

| | Conference | | Overall | |
|---|---|---|---|---|
| | W | L | W | L |
| **Florida State** | 19 | 5 | 52 | 17 |
| **Clemson** | 17 | 7 | 51 | 17 |
| **Georgia Tech** | 13 | 11 | 40 | 24 |
| **North Carolina State** | 13 | 11 | 42 | 19 |
| *Virginia | 11 | 13 | 44 | 21 |
| North Carolina | 11 | 13 | 33 | 25 |
| Duke | 9 | 14 | 39 | 18 |
| Wake Forest | 7 | 16 | 26 | 32 |
| Maryland | 7 | 17 | 24 | 27 |

**ALL-CONFERENCE TEAM: C**—Matt LeCroy, So., Clemson. **1B**—Michael Stoner, Sr., North Carolina. **2B**—Scott Zech, Jr., Florida State. **3B**—Michael Sorrow, Sr., Georgia Tech. **SS**—Brooks Badeaux, So., Florida State. **OF**—J.D. Drew, So., Florida State; Mark Fischer, So., Georgia Tech; Jeremy Morris, Jr., Florida State. **DH**—Mandy Jacomino, Jr., North Carolina State. **Util**—Mike King, Sr., Duke. **SP**—Kris Benson, Jr., Clemson. **RP**—David Darwin, Sr., Duke.

**Player of the Year**—Kris Benson, Clemson.

### INDIVIDUAL BATTING LEADERS
(Minimum 125 At-Bats)

| | AVG | AB | R | H | 2B | 3B | HR | RBI | SB |
|---|---|---|---|---|---|---|---|---|---|
| Fischer, Mark, Ga. Tech | .400 | 260 | 60 | **104** | 23 | 5 | 14 | 66 | 8 |
| Drew, J.D., Florida State | .386 | 241 | **90** | 93 | 17 | 5 | **21** | **94** | 10 |
| Jacomino, Mandy, NC State | .384 | 203 | 40 | 78 | 15 | 0 | 10 | 62 | 1 |
| Morris, Jeremy, Fla. State | .373 | 255 | 76 | 95 | **36** | 1 | 13 | 85 | 22 |
| Sorrow, Michael, Ga. Tech | .369 | 249 | 66 | 92 | 18 | 2 | 11 | 47 | 3 |
| Postell, Matt, NC State | .364 | 162 | 27 | 59 | 9 | 1 | 1 | 24 | 1 |
| Becker, Jeff, Duke | .364 | 220 | 58 | 80 | 12 | 3 | 7 | 41 | 2 |
| Neuberger, Steve, Maryland | .362 | 188 | 47 | 68 | 12 | 3 | 3 | 20 | 10 |
| Embler, Jason, Clemson | .357 | 238 | 51 | 85 | 16 | 1 | 10 | 57 | 2 |
| Badeaux, Brooks, Fla. State | .355 | 279 | 79 | 99 | 16 | 3 | 0 | 44 | 15 |
| Weber, Jake, N.C. State | .354 | 237 | 68 | 84 | 12 | **9** | 7 | 55 | 8 |
| Chiou, Frankie, Duke | .353 | 224 | 55 | 79 | 9 | 5 | 1 | 42 | 10 |
| Maluchnik, Gregg, Duke | .347 | 213 | 43 | 74 | 19 | 1 | 10 | 68 | 2 |
| Zech, Scott, Florida State | .347 | 245 | 62 | 85 | 17 | 2 | 6 | 59 | **26** |
| Stoner, Michael, UNC | .346 | 228 | 55 | 79 | 14 | 2 | 20 | 65 | 8 |
| King, Mike, Duke | .343 | 236 | 55 | 81 | 16 | 3 | 10 | 60 | 4 |
| Livingston, Doug, Clemson | .341 | 223 | 62 | 76 | 15 | 1 | 9 | 39 | 24 |
| Whitlock, Brian, UNC | .341 | 185 | 40 | 63 | 9 | 2 | 10 | 30 | 10 |
| Maddox, Garry, Maryland | .341 | 126 | 31 | 43 | 8 | 1 | 4 | 26 | 7 |
| Leggett, Adam, Ga. Tech | .339 | 230 | 58 | 78 | 17 | 2 | 13 | 46 | 15 |
| Thomas, J.J., Georgia Tech | .338 | 228 | 67 | 77 | 17 | 1 | **21** | 68 | 5 |
| Robinson, Adam, Virginia | .336 | 232 | 55 | 78 | 13 | 3 | 10 | 40 | 19 |
| Faurot, Adam, Florida State | .335 | 233 | 66 | 78 | 9 | 3 | 5 | 46 | 14 |
| Galloway, John, Virginia | .335 | 239 | 55 | 80 | 11 | 4 | 6 | 38 | 20 |
| Hartman, Ron, Maryland | .332 | 208 | 48 | 69 | 12 | 2 | 16 | 60 | 3 |
| Terhune, Mike, N.C. State | .327 | 245 | 57 | 80 | 19 | 3 | 3 | 45 | 10 |
| Itzoe, Josh, Wake Forest | .325 | 246 | 44 | 80 | 12 | 3 | 9 | 52 | 6 |
| Byers, Scott, Georgia Tech | .324 | 262 | 60 | 85 | 20 | 1 | 15 | 62 | 1 |
| Sprague, Geoff, Fla. State | .320 | 153 | 37 | 49 | 14 | 2 | 2 | 33 | 9 |
| Lardieri, Dave, Wake Forest | .319 | 229 | 43 | 73 | 19 | 0 | 15 | 52 | 1 |
| Lasater, Robby, N.C. State | .319 | 138 | 31 | 44 | 15 | 0 | 8 | 34 | 0 |
| Litrownik, Jordan, Duke | .318 | 217 | 55 | 69 | 13 | 1 | 1 | 28 | 10 |
| Sergio, Tom, N.C. State | .317 | 246 | 63 | 78 | 17 | 4 | 3 | 34 | 23 |
| LeCroy, Matt, Clemson | .316 | 244 | 61 | 77 | 18 | 0 | 14 | 57 | 3 |
| Morgan, Scooby, Fla. State | .306 | 144 | 28 | 44 | 7 | 1 | 13 | 41 | 3 |
| Bultmann, Kurt, Clemson | .304 | 194 | 34 | 59 | 10 | 0 | 5 | 27 | 2 |
| Marciano, John, Maryland | .304 | 161 | 44 | 49 | 12 | 0 | 6 | 39 | 0 |
| Haverbusch, Kevin, Md. | .304 | 158 | 31 | 48 | 12 | 2 | 4 | 36 | 0 |
| Robinson, Jerome, Clemson | .303 | 241 | 38 | 73 | 13 | 6 | 6 | 55 | 2 |
| Everett, Adam, NC State | .300 | 203 | 39 | 61 | 11 | 1 | 1 | 24 | 11 |
| Easterling, Adam, Ga. Tech | .299 | 177 | 33 | 53 | 6 | 2 | 1 | 25 | 12 |
| Sherlock, Brian, Virginia | .299 | 174 | 25 | 52 | 11 | 0 | 3 | 25 | 2 |
| Lawler, Scott, NC State | .299 | 127 | 23 | 38 | 13 | 3 | 3 | 33 | 0 |
| Barr, Tucker, Georgia Tech | .297 | 219 | 54 | 65 | 13 | 1 | 12 | 42 | 5 |
| Marino, Larry, Wake Forest | .297 | 175 | 35 | 52 | 9 | 1 | 6 | 19 | 0 |

**Slugging Seminole.** Outfielder J.D. Drew led Florida State to a regular season ACC title by hitting .386 with 21 homers and 94 RBIs.

| | AVG | AB | R | H | 2B | 3B | HR | RBI | SB |
|---|---|---|---|---|---|---|---|---|---|
| Galloway, Paul, Clemson | .294 | 252 | 51 | 74 | 22 | 2 | 5 | 36 | 10 |
| Burnham, Gary, Clemson | .290 | 241 | 62 | 70 | 24 | 4 | 6 | 56 | 2 |
| Shearin, Jarrett, UNC | .290 | 207 | 44 | 60 | 14 | 1 | 8 | 40 | 15 |
| Malloy, Pat, Wake Forest | .290 | 217 | 36 | 63 | 14 | 1 | 14 | 53 | 4 |
| Byrd, Marlon, Georgia Tech | .288 | 198 | 30 | 57 | 10 | 0 | 1 | 27 | 10 |

### INDIVIDUAL PITCHING LEADERS
(Minimum 50 Innings)

| | W | L | ERA | G | SV | IP | H | BB | SO |
|---|---|---|---|---|---|---|---|---|---|
| Greisinger, Seth, Virginia | 12 | 2 | **1.76** | 16 | 0 | 123 | 78 | 36 | 141 |
| Benson, Kris, Clemson | **14** | 2 | 2.02 | 19 | 0 | 156 | 109 | 27 | **204** |
| Davis, Mike, Florida State | 6 | 1 | 2.26 | 20 | 0 | 60 | 43 | 43 | 56 |
| Zaikov, Craig, Virginia | 8 | 1 | 2.48 | 19 | 0 | 76 | 63 | 24 | 69 |
| Lee, Corey, NC State | 10 | 3 | 2.62 | 18 | 0 | 103 | 84 | 49 | 99 |
| Chavez, Chris, Florida State | 4 | 0 | 2.68 | 28 | 1 | 50 | 32 | 36 | 60 |
| Darwin, David, Duke | 7 | 2 | 2.75 | 35 | **10** | 59 | 54 | 30 | 61 |
| Choate, Randy, Fla. State | 15 | 4 | 2.76 | 22 | 1 | 150 | 129 | 44 | 130 |
| Vining, Ken, Clemson | 10 | 3 | 2.97 | 19 | 0 | 115 | 92 | 38 | 135 |
| Koch, Billy, Clemson | 10 | 5 | 3.14 | 19 | 1 | 112 | 73 | 60 | 152 |
| Hauser, Scott, Clemson | 6 | 2 | 3.15 | 22 | 0 | 71 | 64 | 20 | 42 |
| Schoeneweis, Scott, Duke | 10 | 4 | 3.23 | 15 | 0 | 92 | 86 | 28 | 109 |
| Wrigley, Jase, Ga. Tech | 4 | 4 | 3.41 | 25 | 2 | 74 | 67 | 39 | 57 |
| Black, Brett, NC State | 12 | 3 | 3.54 | 20 | 1 | 125 | 112 | 18 | 112 |
| Dishman, Richard, Duke | 5 | 3 | 3.56 | 16 | 0 | 86 | 78 | 43 | 93 |
| Howell, Chuck, Fla. State | 9 | 3 | 3.59 | 26 | 6 | 90 | 97 | 34 | 79 |
| Morgan, Scooby, Fla. State | 12 | 3 | 3.62 | 21 | 0 | 112 | 113 | 39 | 60 |
| Rambusch, Mike, NC State | 5 | 4 | 3.71 | 17 | 0 | 63 | 56 | 17 | 52 |
| Wallace, Jim, UNC | 6 | 8 | 3.72 | 18 | 0 | 82 | 69 | 47 | 71 |
| Wood, Bobby, Wake Forest | 2 | 4 | 3.81 | 26 | 1 | 54 | 48 | 18 | 29 |
| Sekany, Jason, Virginia | 6 | 4 | 3.86 | 28 | 5 | 77 | 67 | 41 | 79 |
| Stein, Ethan, North Carolina | 5 | 2 | 4.08 | 25 | 1 | 88 | 90 | 22 | 53 |
| Milton, Eric, Maryland | 4 | 7 | 4.20 | 14 | 0 | 90 | 83 | 17 | 118 |
| Daneker, Pat, Virginia | 8 | 5 | 4.21 | 18 | 1 | 98 | 105 | 36 | 71 |
| #Richardson, Corey, UNC | 5 | 1 | 4.24 | 24 | **10** | 47 | 26 | 35 | 66 |
| Crowder, Chuck, Ga. Tech | 10 | 5 | 4.30 | 22 | 0 | 92 | 87 | 39 | 98 |
| Holmes, Michael, Wake Forest | 7 | 4 | 4.45 | 16 | 0 | 93 | 103 | 23 | 69 |

McAllister, Scott, UNC.............. 4 3 4.50 14 0 64 55 41 40
Yoder, A.Y., North Carolina........ 7 5 4.53 17 0 103 107 47 62
Ramseyer, Mike, Wake Forest... 3 2 4.61 27 0 53 56 23 46
McGill, Shane, Georgia Tech..... 3 4 4.62 21 1 74 71 36 57

## ATLANTIC-10 CONFERENCE

| | Conference | | Overall | |
|---|---|---|---|---|
| **EAST** | W | L | W | L |
| *Massachusetts | 15 | 5 | 40 | 13 |
| Temple | 12 | 8 | 28 | 23 |
| St. Bonaventure | 10 | 10 | 19 | 19 |
| Fordham | 8 | 11 | 18 | 27 |
| St. Joseph's | 8 | 11 | 19 | 32 |
| Rhode Island | 6 | 14 | 15 | 24 |
| **WEST** | | | | |
| Virginia Tech | 16 | 4 | 35 | 24 |
| Xavier | 11 | 8 | 27 | 27 |
| George Washington | 10 | 10 | 23 | 30 |
| Dayton | 8 | 11 | 25 | 29 |
| LaSalle | 8 | 12 | 17 | 28 |
| Duquesne | 6 | 14 | 19 | 29 |

**ALL-CONFERENCE TEAM:** C—Buddy, Dice, Sr., Duquesne. 1B—Collin Abels, Jr., Dayton. 2B—Muchie Dagliere, So., Massachusetts. 3B—Tom Stein, Fr., Fordham. SS—Brad Gorrie, Jr., Massachusetts. OF—Kevin Barker, Jr., Virginia Tech; Steve Cote, Sr., Rhode Island; Brian Schaller, Jr., LaSalle. DH—Mike Hartman, Jr., LaSalle. RHP—Josh Bradford, Sr., Xavier. LHP—Don Martin, Jr., Temple.

**Player of the Year**—Kevin Barker, Virginia Tech. **Pitcher of the Year**—Josh Bradford, Xavier.

### INDIVIDUAL BATTING LEADERS
(Minimum 100 At-Bats)

| | AVG | AB | R | H | 2B | 3B | HR | RBI | SB |
|---|---|---|---|---|---|---|---|---|---|
| Cote, Steve, Rhode Island .... | .422 | 135 | 34 | 57 | 10 | 5 | 6 | 37 | 13 |
| Dagliere, Muchie, UMass ...... | .415 | 195 | 60 | 81 | 13 | 4 | 5 | 53 | 12 |
| Schaller, Brian, LaSalle ......... | .415 | 171 | 46 | 71 | 7 | 2 | 10 | 41 | 13 |
| Andreana, Joe, St. Bona ....... | .414 | 111 | 34 | 46 | 9 | 2 | 5 | 26 | 15 |
| Stein, Tom, Fordham ............ | .410 | 139 | 35 | 57 | 10 | 0 | 4 | 28 | 5 |
| Tomlinson, Dean, Temple ..... | .395 | 147 | 41 | 58 | 8 | 1 | 0 | 38 | 17 |
| Murphy, Nate, UMass............ | .390 | 195 | 50 | 76 | 17 | 4 | 10 | 66 | 10 |
| Abels, Collin, Dayton ........... | .379 | 182 | 48 | 69 | 17 | 2 | 10 | 55 | 13 |
| Howell, Rob, Dayton............. | .370 | 200 | 40 | 74 | 23 | 1 | 8 | 39 | 5 |
| Crawley, Dwayne, GWU......... | .363 | 157 | 33 | 57 | 14 | 0 | 11 | 41 | 7 |
| Black, Bill, St. Joseph's ......... | .362 | 141 | 28 | 51 | 11 | 0 | 3 | 25 | 8 |
| Barker, Kevin, Va. Tech ........ | .361 | 202 | 63 | 73 | 9 | 9 | 20 | 62 | 3 |
| Gorrie, Brad, UMass............. | .359 | 170 | 61 | 61 | 12 | 2 | 5 | 36 | 33 |
| Jette, Ryan, UMass .............. | .358 | 212 | 60 | 76 | 12 | 3 | 3 | 25 | 31 |
| Hartman, Mike, LaSalle ........ | .355 | 110 | 24 | 39 | 11 | 1 | 7 | 36 | 1 |
| Whelan, John, St. Bona......... | .348 | 112 | 24 | 39 | 6 | 0 | 0 | 19 | 10 |
| Rothemich, Chris, RI ............ | .344 | 125 | 28 | 43 | 6 | 2 | 2 | 14 | 6 |
| Dice, Buddy, Duquesne......... | .336 | 140 | 37 | 47 | 5 | 5 | 14 | 41 | 10 |
| Hampson, Rodd, Xavier ........ | .336 | 107 | 21 | 36 | 8 | 0 | 4 | 16 | 3 |
| Gancasz, Michael, Temple..... | .335 | 158 | 41 | 53 | 13 | 1 | 10 | 41 | 7 |
| Herman, Josh, Va. Tech........ | .335 | 215 | 36 | 72 | 20 | 0 | 6 | 48 | 1 |
| Marchiano, Mike, Fordham..... | .335 | 155 | 52 | 52 | 7 | 3 | 16 | 41 | 17 |
| Rappe, Austin, Va. Tech ....... | .327 | 113 | 30 | 37 | 6 | 5 | 2 | 19 | 6 |
| Rojik, Jeff, Duquesne............ | .327 | 153 | 36 | 50 | 14 | 2 | 5 | 35 | 13 |
| Fleming, Ryan, Dayton.......... | .322 | 208 | 33 | 67 | 11 | 2 | 4 | 23 | 3 |

### INDIVIDUAL PITCHING LEADERS
(Minimum 40 Innings)

| | W | L | ERA | G | SV | IP | H | BB | SO |
|---|---|---|---|---|---|---|---|---|---|
| #Gillian, Charlie, Va. Tech ........ | 2 | 1 | 1.98 | 31 | 14 | 27 | 18 | 8 | 35 |
| Martin, Don, Temple.................. | 5 | 5 | 2.06 | 13 | 2 | 79 | 74 | 32 | 74 |
| Healy, Dennis, GWU.................. | 7 | 3 | 2.25 | 17 | 0 | 76 | 81 | 14 | 53 |
| Rademacker, Ryan, St. Bona.... | 4 | 5 | 2.71 | 12 | 1 | 70 | 57 | 36 | 44 |
| Bradford, Josh, Xavier............... | 8 | 4 | 2.87 | 16 | 1 | 94 | 80 | 50 | 85 |
| Johnson, Jed, St. Joseph's....... | 6 | 4 | 2.96 | 15 | 0 | 82 | 78 | 39 | 51 |
| Couch, Brian, Fordham............. | 4 | 5 | 3.24 | 12 | 0 | 67 | 58 | 29 | 47 |
| Krystofolski, Jay, RI.................. | 2 | 3 | 3.33 | 10 | 1 | 49 | 51 | 24 | 43 |
| Fitzgerald, Brian, Va. Tech........ | 7 | 5 | 3.35 | 15 | 0 | 97 | 91 | 23 | 86 |
| VonSossen, Ryan, Dayton........ | 5 | 4 | 3.48 | 13 | 1 | 62 | 45 | 33 | 49 |
| Hand, Jon, Virginia Tech........... | 7 | 4 | 3.69 | 14 | 0 | 90 | 92 | 17 | 78 |
| Kenkelen, Stephen, Temple...... | 5 | 1 | 3.71 | 13 | 1 | 53 | 56 | 30 | 29 |
| Paronto, Chad, UMass............. | 5 | 4 | 3.72 | 12 | 1 | 68 | 70 | 27 | 45 |
| Huss, Brian, Dayton................. | 5 | 1 | 3.75 | 13 | 1 | 50 | 59 | 22 | 34 |
| Dart, David, UMass.................. | 5 | 1 | 3.77 | 12 | 0 | 60 | 55 | 33 | 32 |
| Hummel, Sean, Va. Tech.......... | 7 | 4 | 3.92 | 14 | 0 | 83 | 86 | 18 | 61 |
| Moore, Peter, Temple .............. | 8 | 5 | 4.00 | 21 | 2 | 92 | 92 | 71 | 72 |
| Buob, Mike, Dayton................. | 6 | 8 | 4.06 | 17 | 1 | 89 | 98 | 39 | 60 |
| Puleri, Jeff, UMass.................. | 4 | 2 | 4.12 | 10 | 0 | 44 | 42 | 18 | 25 |
| Cote, Steve, Rhode Island ........ | 3 | 4 | 4.17 | 9 | 1 | 54 | 72 | 9 | 36 |

## BIG EAST CONFERENCE

| | Conference | | Overall | |
|---|---|---|---|---|
| **AMERICAN** | W | L | W | L |
| *West Virginia | 15 | 10 | 33 | 25 |
| Providence | 15 | 10 | 32 | 17 |
| St. John's | 14 | 10 | 26 | 18 |
| Connecticut | 13 | 12 | 24 | 23 |
| Pittsburgh | 9 | 13 | 24 | 20 |
| Boston College | 6 | 18 | 15 | 27 |
| **NATIONAL** | | | | |
| Villanova | 16 | 5 | 25 | 20 |
| Rutgers | 15 | 7 | 32 | 21 |
| **Notre Dame** | 13 | 7 | 44 | 18 |
| Georgetown | 6 | 18 | 18 | 34 |
| Seton Hall | 5 | 17 | 18 | 27 |

**ALL-CONFERENCE TEAM:** C—Scott Friedholm, So., Providence. 1B—Brian Fitzsimmons, Sr., St. John's. 2B—Randall Brooks, Jr., Notre Dame. 3B—Reuben Wilson, Sr., Connecticut. SS—Larry Kleinz, Sr., Villanova. OF—Kevin Penwell, Jr., Boston College; Scott Sollmann, Jr., Notre Dame; Pete Tucci, Jr., Providence. DH—Jeff Wagner, Fr., Notre Dame. Util—Jason Grabowski, So., Connecticut. P—Todd Incantalupo, So., Providence; Scott Madison, Jr., Rutgers; Brian O'Hare, Sr., Georgetown.

**Player of the Year**—Jason Grabowski, Connecticut. **Pitcher of the Year**—Brian O'Hare, Georgetown.

### INDIVIDUAL BATTING LEADERS
(Minimum 125 At-Bats)

| | AVG | AB | R | H | 2B | 3B | HR | RBI | SB |
|---|---|---|---|---|---|---|---|---|---|
| Finnerty, Keith, St. John's ..... | .439 | 155 | 45 | 68 | 11 | 3 | 6 | 42 | 22 |
| Penwell, Kevin, Bos. Coll. ...... | .428 | 145 | 37 | 62 | 13 | 5 | 2 | 23 | 17 |
| Brooks, Randall, Notre Dame .396 | | 225 | 42 | 89 | 16 | 4 | 4 | 27 | 15 |
| Kleinz, Larry, Villanova.......... | .382 | 165 | 38 | 63 | 18 | 0 | 12 | 66 | 0 |
| Friedholm, Scott, Prov............ | .381 | 176 | 45 | 67 | 18 | 3 | 7 | 52 | 7 |
| Grabowski, Jason, Conn......... | .380 | 184 | 48 | 70 | 14 | 1 | 18 | 59 | 10 |
| Manahan, Bryan, Bos. Coll..... | .377 | 154 | 43 | 58 | 8 | 4 | 2 | 20 | 15 |
| McDonald, John, Providence... | .364 | 206 | 66 | 75 | 23 | 4 | 8 | 46 | 22 |
| Tucci, Pete, Providence ......... | .363 | 193 | 55 | 70 | 22 | 1 | 16 | 59 | 19 |
| Hummel, Dan, Seton Hall....... | .358 | 165 | 32 | 59 | 13 | 1 | 2 | 35 | 1 |
| Harrington, Roger, Geo.......... | .357 | 182 | 40 | 65 | 12 | 4 | 2 | 37 | 33 |
| Bisson, Chris, Connecticut ..... | .352 | 182 | 39 | 64 | 11 | 2 | 12 | 40 | 5 |
| Duffy, Jim, Seton Hall............ | .351 | 188 | 49 | 66 | 10 | 5 | 5 | 31 | 8 |
| Mushorn, Matthew, St.J......... | .348 | 141 | 25 | 49 | 10 | 1 | 1 | 18 | 13 |
| Sankey, Brian, Bos. Coll......... | .342 | 152 | 34 | 52 | 14 | 2 | 2 | 33 | 3 |
| Lisanti, Bob, Notre Dame ...... | .344 | 160 | 31 | 55 | 7 | 0 | 3 | 37 | 2 |
| Seabol, Scott, West Virginia.. | .342 | 202 | 44 | 69 | 14 | 1 | 10 | 44 | 9 |
| Scott, Jeff, Connecticut ......... | .336 | 134 | 30 | 45 | 6 | 0 | 6 | 27 | 1 |
| Restovich, George, ND .......... | .336 | 217 | 50 | 73 | 19 | 9 | 7 | 68 | 5 |
| Neubart, Adam, Rutgers........ | .333 | 186 | 46 | 62 | 16 | 3 | 3 | 29 | 16 |
| Randall, Marvin, West Va....... | .333 | 189 | 31 | 63 | 8 | 0 | 2 | 29 | 8 |
| Fitzsimmons, Brian, St.J........ | .331 | 154 | 40 | 51 | 6 | 3 | 6 | 41 | 11 |
| Johnson, Mike, St. John's ...... | .331 | 145 | 27 | 48 | 10 | 1 | 5 | 45 | 5 |
| Wirta, Shane, Seton Hall ....... | .331 | 166 | 29 | 55 | 8 | 2 | 6 | 30 | 1 |
| Stetina, Jeff, Villanova........... | .329 | 149 | 32 | 49 | 9 | 2 | 4 | 27 | 2 |
| Carrero, J.J., Seton Hall ........ | .327 | 199 | 55 | 65 | 13 | 2 | 5 | 34 | 28 |
| Wilson, Reuben, Conn. ......... | .327 | 199 | 36 | 65 | 13 | 2 | 5 | 34 | 28 |
| Uccello, Jeff, Connecticut....... | .325 | 169 | 35 | 55 | 9 | 2 | 6 | 36 | 10 |
| #Sollmann, Scott, ND ............ | .311 | 225 | 61 | 70 | 3 | 6 | 2 | 25 | 52 |

### INDIVIDUAL PITCHING LEADERS
(Minimum 50 Innings)

| | W | L | ERA | G | SV | IP | H | BB | SO |
|---|---|---|---|---|---|---|---|---|---|
| Schmalz, Darin, Notre Dame ......9 | | 4 | 2.23 | 14 | 0 | 85 | 82 | 18 | 56 |
| Stegen, Brian, Rutgers.............. | 5 | 4 | 2.28 | 15 | 0 | 79 | 77 | 29 | 48 |
| Madison, Scott, Rutgers............ | 8 | 3 | 2.33 | 13 | 0 | 93 | 84 | 18 | 49 |
| Love, Jeff, St. John's ............... | 7 | 3 | 2.91 | 14 | 0 | 74 | 57 | 46 | 60 |
| Incantalupo, Todd, Prov........... | 10 | 2 | 3.06 | 13 | 1 | 85 | 76 | 26 | 51 |
| Stavisky, Dan, Notre Dame...... | 7 | 1 | 3.07 | 15 | 0 | 70 | 64 | 18 | 47 |
| #Klopp, John, Villanova............. | 3 | 1 | 3.41 | 23 | 7 | 34 | 28 | 11 | 18 |
| Kennedy, Rich, Rutgers ........... | 2 | 4 | 3.51 | 10 | 0 | 56 | 58 | 38 | 46 |
| O'Hare, Brian, Georgetown....... | 8 | 2 | 3.55 | 11 | 0 | 76 | 78 | 19 | 59 |
| Byron, Andy, Providence.......... | 6 | 3 | 3.87 | 15 | 1 | 77 | 81 | 29 | 41 |
| Hughes, Mike, St. John's ......... | 5 | 2 | 3.88 | 15 | 1 | 51 | 51 | 35 | 50 |
| Schuster, Vincent, St. John's.... | 5 | 2 | 3.99 | 14 | 2 | 59 | 59 | 22 | 33 |
| Shilliday, Alex, Notre Dame ..... | 5 | 4 | 4.06 | 18 | 2 | 51 | 55 | 21 | 44 |
| Parker, Christian, Notre Dame... | 8 | 3 | 4.24 | 14 | 0 | 81 | 81 | 41 | 56 |
| Grilli, Jason, Seton Hall............ | 5 | 4 | 4.25 | 13 | 1 | 72 | 63 | 29 | 68 |
| Enochs, Chris, West Virginia..... | 8 | 4 | 4.28 | 16 | 2 | 76 | 73 | 34 | 47 |
| #Rakaczewski, Jason, Pitt......... | 3 | 2 | 4.70 | 21 | 7 | 44 | 48 | 23 | 49 |
| #Riley, Mike, West Virginia ....... | 7 | 3 | 5.20 | 16 | 1 | 106 | 129 | 67 | 87 |

# BIG EIGHT CONFERENCE

| | Conference | | Overall | |
|---|---|---|---|---|
| | W | L | W | L |
| **Missouri** | 20 | 8 | 39 | 19 |
| *Oklahoma State | 17 | 9 | 45 | 21 |
| Oklahoma | 14 | 12 | 32 | 25 |
| Iowa State | 12 | 14 | 23 | 31 |
| Kansas State | 11 | 16 | 28 | 26 |
| Kansas | 11 | 17 | 26 | 30 |
| Nebraska | 8 | 17 | 27 | 27 |

**ALL-CONFERENCE TEAM: C**—Javier Flores, Jr., Oklahoma. **1B**—Aaron Jaworowski, So., Missouri. **2B**—Josh Kliner, Sr., Kansas. **3B**—Jay White, Sr., Missouri. **SS**—Joe DeMarco, Jr., Kansas. **OF**—Bobby Brown, Sr., Oklahoma; Isaac Byrd, Jr., Kansas; Ryan Fry, So., Missouri; Jeff Guiel, Jr., Oklahoma State. **DH**—Wyley Steelmon, Jr., Oklahoma State. **Util**—Rusty McNamara, Jr., Oklahoma State. **SP**—Jeremy Callier, So., Missouri; Matt Koeman, Sr., Kansas State; Sean McClellan, Sr., Oklahoma State; Nathan Teut, So., Iowa State. **RP**—Casey Barrett, So., Kansas; Justin Stine, Fr., Missouri.

**Co-Players of the Year**—Jeff Guiel, Oklahoma State; Josh Kliner, Kansas.

## INDIVIDUAL BATTING LEADERS
(Minimum 125 At-Bats)

| | AVG | AB | R | H | 2B | 3B | HR | RBI | SB |
|---|---|---|---|---|---|---|---|---|---|
| Kliner, Josh, Kansas | .438 | 208 | 66 | 91 | 28 | 6 | 10 | 85 | 7 |
| Collins, Francis, Nebraska | .424 | 217 | 60 | 92 | 10 | 2 | 1 | 37 | 19 |
| Guiel, Jeff, Okla. State | .394 | 246 | 84 | 97 | 17 | 6 | 15 | 80 | 27 |
| Byrd, Issac, Kansas | .393 | 242 | 68 | 95 | 14 | 4 | 5 | 51 | 24 |
| Fry, Ryan, Missouri | .387 | 238 | 83 | 92 | 21 | 2 | 5 | 70 | 2 |
| Brown, Bobby, Oklahoma | .384 | 232 | 71 | 89 | 17 | 4 | 7 | 51 | 15 |
| Sears, Todd, Nebraska | .380 | 216 | 60 | 82 | 18 | 0 | 6 | 62 | 5 |
| White, Jay, Missouri | .370 | 219 | 74 | 81 | 18 | 4 | 10 | 68 | 2 |
| Nivens, Matt, Missouri | .365 | 230 | 85 | 84 | 19 | 2 | 9 | 52 | 5 |
| McNamara, Rusty, Okla. St. | .362 | 279 | 100 | 101 | 11 | 2 | 19 | 89 | 7 |
| Fereday, Todd, Kansas St. | .362 | 218 | 54 | 79 | 12 | 2 | 9 | 56 | 16 |
| Gonzalez, Izzy, Oklahoma | .362 | 130 | 24 | 47 | 12 | 1 | 1 | 22 | 0 |
| Hill, Willy, Oklahoma | .361 | 202 | 41 | 73 | 12 | 4 | 0 | 41 | 15 |
| MacKay, Tripp, Okla. State | .360 | 278 | 96 | 100 | 17 | 7 | 3 | 61 | 17 |
| Vance, Scott, Iowa State | .357 | 171 | 26 | 61 | 10 | 2 | 1 | 21 | 12 |
| Minor, Damon, Oklahoma | .348 | 207 | 64 | 72 | 17 | 2 | 14 | 62 | 4 |
| Roossien, Tony, Okla. State | .344 | 163 | 54 | 56 | 9 | 3 | 6 | 49 | 1 |
| Schesser, Heath, Kansas St. | .344 | 209 | 57 | 72 | 20 | 2 | 6 | 49 | 6 |
| Meyer, Matt, Nebraska | .342 | 228 | 71 | 78 | 15 | 7 | 10 | 73 | 8 |
| Shackelford, Brian, Okla. | .342 | 219 | 54 | 75 | 13 | 4 | 11 | 60 | 6 |
| DeMarco, Joe, Kansas | .338 | 231 | 76 | 78 | 11 | 4 | 5 | 41 | 32 |
| Steelmon, Wyley, Okla. St. | .337 | 175 | 51 | 59 | 13 | 2 | 14 | 56 | 0 |
| DeReu, Darrin, Iowa State | .335 | 191 | 54 | 64 | 17 | 8 | 4 | 41 | 8 |
| Headley, Justin, Kansas | .333 | 222 | 63 | 74 | 21 | 4 | 2 | 49 | 19 |
| Motley, Mel, Nebraska | .332 | 217 | 49 | 72 | 13 | 4 | 6 | 51 | 8 |
| Poepard, Scott, Kansas St. | .329 | 216 | 53 | 71 | 12 | 2 | 9 | 57 | 7 |
| Jaworowski, Aaron, Mo. | .329 | 249 | 49 | 82 | 28 | 1 | 14 | 101 | 1 |
| Seymour, Brian, Missouri | .329 | 219 | 46 | 72 | 12 | 3 | 4 | 49 | 1 |
| Bahun, Mike, Iowa State | .327 | 171 | 54 | 56 | 14 | 0 | 3 | 24 | 31 |
| Dimmick, Josh, Kansas | .322 | 214 | 41 | 69 | 11 | 2 | 4 | 58 | 1 |
| Hendrix, David, Kansas St. | .322 | 199 | 52 | 64 | 15 | 1 | 12 | 55 | 3 |
| Holliday, Josh, Okla. State | .320 | 228 | 62 | 73 | 15 | 0 | 6 | 52 | 1 |
| Jenkins, Pete, Nebraska | .320 | 194 | 40 | 62 | 11 | 0 | 7 | 43 | 5 |
| Zepeda, Jesse, Oklahoma | .320 | 225 | 59 | 72 | 16 | 0 | 2 | 36 | 14 |
| Cox, Sammy, Iowa State | .316 | 190 | 39 | 60 | 17 | 1 | 7 | 47 | 3 |
| Flores, Javier, Oklahoma | .305 | 220 | 43 | 67 | 16 | 1 | 1 | 36 | 7 |
| Buchman, Tom, Missouri | .306 | 183 | 33 | 56 | 8 | 0 | 5 | 41 | 0 |
| Harmon, Ryan, Iowa State | .302 | 159 | 33 | 48 | 4 | 1 | 2 | 28 | 4 |
| Bichelmeyer, Jason, Kan. St. | .302 | 182 | 44 | 55 | 16 | 3 | 4 | 47 | 3 |
| Salhani, Ted, Okla. State | .296 | 189 | 60 | 56 | 8 | 2 | 16 | 58 | 3 |
| Jones, Clark, Iowa State | .298 | 188 | 33 | 56 | 14 | 2 | 6 | 32 | 2 |
| Hess, Chris, Kansas State | .295 | 220 | 54 | 65 | 16 | 2 | 4 | 39 | 8 |
| Bohannon, Cory, Iowa St. | .292 | 212 | 34 | 62 | 7 | 4 | 1 | 39 | 5 |
| Dean, Mike, Kansas | .291 | 175 | 37 | 51 | 8 | 2 | 6 | 31 | 9 |

## INDIVIDUAL PITCHING LEADERS
(Minimum 50 Innings)

| | W | L | ERA | G | SV | IP | H | BB | SO |
|---|---|---|---|---|---|---|---|---|---|
| Mead, Chad, Oklahoma | 3 | 3 | 3.40 | 19 | 2 | 53 | 59 | 49 | 48 |
| Haverty, Mike, Missouri | 5 | 3 | 4.24 | 17 | 1 | 74 | 88 | 26 | 35 |
| McClellan, Sean, Okla. State | 8 | 3 | 4.49 | 19 | 0 | 110 | 103 | 66 | 125 |
| #Barrett, Casey, Kansas | 2 | 6 | 4.85 | 24 | 8 | 39 | 34 | 24 | 23 |
| Koeman, Matt, Kansas State | 7 | 5 | 4.90 | 18 | 0 | 105 | 120 | 48 | 84 |
| Driscoll, Pat, Nebraska | 3 | 5 | 4.95 | 17 | 0 | 64 | 67 | 29 | 44 |
| Belovsky, Josh, Kansas | 7 | 6 | 4.93 | 16 | 0 | 99 | 118 | 40 | 68 |
| Victery, Joe, Oklahoma | 8 | 5 | 5.21 | 22 | 4 | 97 | 117 | 55 | 73 |

Adkins, Jon, Oklahoma State..... 5 3 5.35 24 4 76 90 29 47
Oiseth, Jon, Kansas State.......... 6 4 5.43 19 1 63 79 42 58
Fish, Steve, Nebraska................. 8 5 5.66 15 0 89 95 41 70
Maurer, Dave, Okla. State.......... 6 3 5.72 23 3 57 60 28 50
Akin, Aaron, Missouri ................ 8 5 5.76 17 0 86 95 50 55
Graves, Ryan, Okla. State ......... 10 2 5.86 20 0 114 133 55 104
Bell, Jay, Missouri ...................... 5 5 5.88 15 0 86 115 50 55
Yanz, Eric, Kansas State ............ 4 6 5.92 14 0 73 91 45 56
Teut, Natha, Iowa State .............. 4 5 6.12 14 0 78 93 30 59
Callier, Jeremy, Missouri............. 9 3 6.20 16 0 90 111 36 53
Baird, Clay, Kansas.................... 6 6 6.28 15 0 57 79 30 20
Traylor, Chris, Kansas St. .......... 4 2 6.30 15 0 50 69 28 38
Seifert, Ryan, Iowa State ........... 2 4 6.44 14 2 59 75 26 52

# BIG SOUTH CONFERENCE

| | Conference | | Overall | |
|---|---|---|---|---|
| | W | L | W | L |
| **Charleston Southern** | 17 | 4 | 30 | 24 |
| Winthrop | 14 | 5 | 41 | 16 |
| UNC Greensboro | 12 | 6 | 28 | 24 |
| Coastal Carolina | 11 | 10 | 24 | 29 |
| Radford | 9 | 12 | 20 | 30 |
| Liberty | 8 | 13 | 21 | 27 |
| UNC Asheville | 5 | 15 | 18 | 34 |
| Maryland-Baltimore County | 4 | 15 | 9 | 28 |

**ALL-CONFERENCE TEAM: C**—David Benham, So., Liberty. **1B**—Jeremy Keller, Sr., Winthrop. **2B**—Jeff Berman, Jr., Maryland-Baltimore County. **3B**—Pat Calabrese, Sr., UNC Greensboro. **SS**—Kelly Dampeer, Jr., Radford. **OF**—Chad Faircloth, Jr., UNC Asheville; Nicky Phillips, Jr., UNC Greensboro; Mark Cisar, So., Charleston Southern; Stephen Wright, So., Liberty. **DH**—Matt Ragan, Sr., Coastal Carolina. **SP**—Jonathan Jackson, Fr., UNC Greensboro; Mike Condon, Jr., Winthrop.

**Player of the Year**—Jeremy Keller, Winthrop.

## INDIVIDUAL BATTING LEADERS
(Minimum 100 At-Bats)

| | AVG | AB | R | H | 2B | 3B | HR | RBI | SB |
|---|---|---|---|---|---|---|---|---|---|
| Berman, Jeff, UMBC | .397 | 126 | 28 | 50 | 5 | 1 | 2 | 20 | 5 |
| Keller, Jeremy, Winthrop | .396 | 197 | 47 | 78 | 15 | 2 | 14 | 58 | 4 |
| Vindich, Jason, Co. Car. | .386 | 145 | 42 | 56 | 9 | 0 | 1 | 20 | 18 |
| Faircloth, Chad, UNCA | .384 | 185 | 47 | 71 | 13 | 3 | 10 | 41 | 10 |
| Wright, Stephen, Liberty | .370 | 146 | 26 | 54 | 7 | 3 | 11 | 39 | 4 |
| Pattie, Dominic, UNCG | .363 | 215 | 53 | 78 | 18 | 1 | 1 | 18 | 26 |
| Giles, Tim, UNCG | .360 | 197 | 43 | 71 | 20 | 1 | 17 | 68 | 17 |
| Calabrese, Pat, UNCG | .360 | 186 | 34 | 67 | 21 | 0 | 4 | 41 | 21 |
| Hungate, Eric, Radford | .360 | 136 | 29 | 49 | 16 | 0 | 5 | 34 | 2 |
| Phillips, Nicky, UNCG | .352 | 196 | 67 | 69 | 7 | 8 | 6 | 37 | 21 |
| Weisgerber, Chip, Co. Car. | .346 | 179 | 46 | 62 | 15 | 0 | 7 | 44 | 16 |
| Cisar, Mark, Char. South. | .344 | 186 | 42 | 64 | 11 | 3 | 3 | 31 | 11 |
| Barker, Ben, Liberty | .342 | 161 | 29 | 55 | 8 | 0 | 2 | 20 | 3 |
| Colameco, Joe, Winthrop | .340 | 188 | 45 | 64 | 12 | 1 | 6 | 46 | 11 |
| Trahan, Matt, Co. Car. | .340 | 141 | 43 | 48 | 13 | 0 | 8 | 37 | 2 |
| Derwin, Tom, Winthrop | .332 | 208 | 52 | 69 | 21 | 1 | 4 | 42 | 20 |
| Reed, Shane, Radford | .330 | 115 | 9 | 38 | 3 | 1 | 1 | 12 | 4 |
| Kobsik, Rick, Winthrop | .326 | 138 | 20 | 45 | 11 | 0 | 3 | 23 | 0 |
| Gilmore, Bryant, Char. So. | .326 | 190 | 52 | 62 | 10 | 2 | 0 | 24 | 12 |
| Coble, John, Winthrop | .322 | 211 | 39 | 68 | 11 | 3 | 8 | 46 | 14 |
| Harwood, Brett, Coastal Car. | .319 | 191 | 49 | 61 | 11 | 3 | 3 | 29 | 9 |
| Ragan, Matt, Coastal Car. | .318 | 170 | 38 | 54 | 8 | 0 | 9 | 53 | 7 |
| #Constantino, Tony, Win. | .313 | 211 | 62 | 66 | 8 | 1 | 1 | 24 | 31 |

## INDIVIDUAL PITCHING LEADERS
(Minimum 40 Innings)

| | W | L | ERA | G | SV | IP | H | BB | SO |
|---|---|---|---|---|---|---|---|---|---|
| #Richards, Mark, Winthrop | 8 | 1 | 1.37 | 24 | 8 | 39 | 29 | 13 | 31 |
| Condon, Mike, Winthrop | 8 | 1 | 2.98 | 16 | 1 | 91 | 76 | 40 | 65 |
| Evrick, Ben, UNCG | 3 | 4 | 3.07 | 23 | 1 | 59 | 72 | 17 | 40 |
| Bickers, Tim, Liberty | 3 | 5 | 3.20 | 9 | 0 | 51 | 48 | 19 | 21 |
| Sylvester, Anthony, UNCG | 3 | 5 | 3.68 | 17 | 1 | 78 | 79 | 23 | 68 |
| Parsons, Jason, UNCG | 4 | 1 | 3.73 | 26 | 4 | 82 | 97 | 26 | 65 |
| Jackson, Jonathan, UNCG | 11 | 4 | 3.79 | 20 | 0 | 78 | 72 | 30 | 74 |
| Booth, Jamie, Radford | 4 | 4 | 3.84 | 14 | 0 | 63 | 67 | 36 | 39 |
| Harris, Eric, Radford | 6 | 2 | 3.86 | 10 | 0 | 54 | 59 | 13 | 48 |
| Franklin, Wayne, UMBC | 2 | 7 | 3.88 | 15 | 0 | 70 | 75 | 33 | 60 |
| Santa, Jeff, Winthrop | 9 | 3 | 3.97 | 18 | 0 | 107 | 103 | 26 | 99 |
| James, Steve, UMBC | 1 | 4 | 4.29 | 13 | 1 | 47 | 55 | 29 | 23 |
| Finley, Eric, Char. South | 5 | 4 | 4.35 | 15 | 0 | 81 | 82 | 27 | 60 |
| Cecchini, Pat, Radford | 3 | 0 | 4.44 | 29 | 0 | 47 | 56 | 18 | 30 |
| Kuykendall, Jay, UNCG | 5 | 2 | 4.45 | 18 | 1 | 55 | 60 | 22 | 27 |
| Erwin, Scott, Char. South | 1 | 1 | 4.50 | 22 | 1 | 42 | 45 | 19 | 28 |
| #Harrison, Donovan, Char. So. | 7 | 8 | 5.12 | 22 | 0 | 111 | 98 | 43 | 125 |

# BIG TEN CONFERENCE

| | Conference | | Overall | |
|---|---|---|---|---|
| | W | L | W | L |
| Penn State | 19 | 8 | 32 | 24 |
| *Indiana | 18 | 8 | 43 | 18 |
| Illinois | 17 | 10 | 37 | 22 |
| Michigan | 17 | 11 | 24 | 30 |
| Minnesota | 15 | 12 | 30 | 26 |
| Ohio State | 15 | 13 | 36 | 20 |
| Iowa | 13 | 13 | 25 | 22 |
| Northwestern | 10 | 18 | 26 | 29 |
| Purdue | 8 | 19 | 22 | 32 |
| Michigan State | 4 | 24 | 14 | 41 |

**ALL-CONFERENCE TEAM: C**—Matt Braughler, Sr., Indiana. **1B**—Mark Chonko, Sr., Ohio State. **2B**—Brian McClure, Sr., Illinois. **3B**—Rob Smith, Sr., Minnesota. **SS**—Josh Klimek, Jr., Illinois. **OF**—Jason Alcaraz, Fr., Michigan; Jim Reeder, Jr., Northwestern; Danny Rhodes, So., Illinois. **DH**—Carl Albrecht, Jr., Penn State. **SP**—Nate Bump, So., Penn State; Dan Ferrell, Jr., Indiana; Brian Murphy, So., Michigan State; Mark Temple, Sr., Michigan; Brett Weber, So., Illinois. **RP**—Kevin Zaleski, Sr., Indiana.

**Player of the Year**—Josh Klimek, Illinois. **Pitcher of the Year**—Nathan Bump, Penn State.

## INDIVIDUAL BATTING LEADERS
(Minimum 125 At-Bats)

| | AVG | AB | R | H | 2B | 3B | HR | RBI | SB |
|---|---|---|---|---|---|---|---|---|---|
| Eckelman, Alex, Ohio State... | .439 | 205 | 70 | 90 | 16 | 1 | 13 | 54 | 2 |
| McClure, Brian, Illinois........... | .418 | 213 | 80 | 89 | 14 | 4 | 16 | 65 | 6 |
| Chonko, Mark, Ohio State...... | .400 | 195 | 58 | 78 | 11 | 1 | 14 | 61 | 2 |
| Klimek, Josh, Illinois............. | .400 | 215 | 73 | 86 | 22 | 1 | 26 | 94 | 1 |
| Riggins, Matt, Mich. State ...... | .375 | 192 | 36 | 72 | 11 | 1 | 16 | 49 | 3 |
| Reeder, Jim, Northwestern...... | .377 | 199 | 47 | 75 | 11 | 3 | 10 | 48 | 11 |
| Boruta, Scott, Penn State ...... | .374 | 163 | 37 | 61 | 11 | 1 | 0 | 22 | 5 |
| Kramer, Kyle, Indiana............. | .371 | 186 | 51 | 69 | 16 | 2 | 4 | 44 | 5 |
| Middleton, Matt, Ohio State... | .370 | 127 | 29 | 47 | 6 | 0 | 9 | 39 | 0 |
| Smith, Rob, Minnesota.......... | .368 | 152 | 37 | 56 | 6 | 0 | 8 | 44 | 7 |
| Guse, Bryan, Minnesota........ | .367 | 169 | 38 | 62 | 16 | 1 | 4 | 39 | 5 |
| McClure, Todd, Illinois........... | .357 | 196 | 53 | 70 | 8 | 2 | 7 | 39 | 8 |
| Alcaraz, Jason, Michigan ...... | .356 | 177 | 35 | 63 | 10 | 2 | 3 | 29 | 2 |
| Cervenak, Mike, Michigan...... | .344 | 180 | 32 | 62 | 16 | 0 | 4 | 36 | 7 |
| Braughler, Matt, Indiana........ | .343 | 198 | 41 | 68 | 14 | 0 | 9 | 49 | 2 |
| McDermott, Phil, Minn............ | .342 | 152 | 29 | 52 | 17 | 2 | 3 | 28 | 0 |
| Dransfeldt, Kelly, Michigan...... | .341 | 170 | 43 | 58 | 8 | 2 | 9 | 34 | 11 |
| Rhodes, Danny, Illinois.......... | .340 | 206 | 45 | 70 | 10 | 3 | 5 | 40 | 13 |
| Rhodes, Dusty, Illinois........... | .339 | 165 | 39 | 56 | 11 | 1 | 5 | 34 | 6 |
| Frese, Nate, Iowa.................. | .333 | 114 | 26 | 38 | 6 | 2 | 4 | 28 | 1 |
| Keeney, Bob, Minnesota ....... | .333 | 147 | 42 | 49 | 7 | 1 | 1 | 19 | 9 |
| Besco, Derek, Minnesota....... | .331 | 121 | 27 | 40 | 8 | 2 | 7 | 26 | 3 |
| Piacenti, Neil, Northwestern.... | .331 | 172 | 38 | 57 | 19 | 1 | 2 | 21 | 2 |
| Bertolotti, Phil, Penn State .... | .328 | 186 | 29 | 61 | 11 | 1 | 3 | 27 | 4 |
| Huls, Steve, Minnesota ......... | .325 | 212 | 55 | 69 | 12 | 2 | 9 | 40 | 7 |
| Quinlan, Robb, Minnesota...... | .325 | 194 | 32 | 63 | 9 | 6 | 2 | 34 | 7 |
| Schley, Jeff, Iowa.................. | .323 | 164 | 28 | 53 | 13 | 0 | 5 | 22 | 4 |
| Marshall, Chad, Mich. State ... | .319 | 188 | 26 | 60 | 14 | 0 | 3 | 27 | 3 |
| Dunn, Ollie, Northwestern...... | .317 | 180 | 44 | 57 | 6 | 0 | 3 | 24 | 1 |
| Thieleke, C.J., Iowa.............. | .316 | 171 | 42 | 54 | 12 | 3 | 5 | 30 | 4 |
| Seimetz, Dan, Ohio State...... | .315 | 181 | 40 | 57 | 18 | 0 | 8 | 52 | 2 |
| Crotty, Mike, Indiana ............ | .314 | 185 | 39 | 58 | 16 | 1 | 10 | 52 | 3 |
| Sadlowski, Jared, Penn State | .314 | 188 | 36 | 59 | 13 | 0 | 5 | 34 | 7 |
| Ramacher, Robb, Purdue....... | .313 | 179 | 32 | 56 | 6 | 3 | 6 | 41 | 6 |
| Albrecht, Carl, Penn State...... | .313 | 163 | 30 | 61 | 11 | 1 | 11 | 44 | 1 |
| #Dillon, Ryan, Indiana ........... | .260 | 200 | 52 | 52 | 9 | 0 | 7 | 20 | 36 |

## INDIVIDUAL PITCHING LEADERS
(Minimum 50 Innings)

| | W | L | ERA | G | SV | IP | H | BB | SO |
|---|---|---|---|---|---|---|---|---|---|
| Brasser, Brad, Northwestern...... | 6 | 2 | 1.93 | 11 | 0 | 65 | 51 | 20 | 55 |
| Murphy, Brian, Mich. State........ | 3 | 9 | 2.81 | 14 | 0 | 80 | 80 | 23 | 53 |
| Partenheimer, Brian, Indiana ...... | 9 | 2 | 3.05 | 20 | 0 | 97 | 101 | 32 | 67 |
| #Ziesemer, Greg, Northwestern. | 3 | 2 | 3.14 | 19 | 10 | 29 | 32 | 10 | 23 |
| Hedman, Mike, Purdue ............. | 8 | 5 | 3.39 | 14 | 0 | 93 | 97 | 33 | 53 |
| Fry, Justin, Ohio State.............. | 7 | 3 | 3.55 | 12 | 0 | 76 | 70 | 27 | 57 |
| Bump, Nate, Penn State ........... | 8 | 5 | 3.60 | 15 | 0 | 90 | 71 | 47 | 93 |
| Jaskowski, Jim, Penn State ...... | 7 | 4 | 3.69 | 13 | 0 | 68 | 73 | 27 | 40 |
| Weber, Brett, Illinois................ | 9 | 6 | 3.82 | 18 | 1 | 97 | 87 | 32 | 89 |
| Pederson, Justin, Minnesota...... | 7 | 4 | 4.20 | 22 | 4 | 86 | 81 | 45 | 82 |
| Graft, Ryan, Indiana................. | 4 | 6 | 4.21 | 18 | 0 | 68 | 69 | 22 | 49 |
| Temple, Mark, Michigan............ | 8 | 5 | 4.37 | 15 | 1 | 70 | 81 | 11 | 35 |
| Ferrell, Dan, Indiana ................ | 9 | 6 | 4.43 | 18 | 1 | 106 | 120 | 31 | 104 |
| Weimer, Matt, Penn State......... | 6 | 4 | 4.43 | 12 | 0 | 67 | 62 | 44 | 29 |
| Putz, J.J., Michigan................. | 5 | 5 | 4.47 | 14 | 0 | 52 | 35 | 35 | 45 |

| Biehle, Mike, Ohio State............ | 7 | 3 | 4.48 | 13 | 0 | 68 | 75 | 40 | 66 |
| Austin, Matt, Iowa..................... | 3 | 4 | 4.89 | 10 | 0 | 57 | 72 | 28 | 46 |
| Bloomer, Chris, Purdue.............. | 6 | 6 | 4.75 | 14 | 0 | 78 | 77 | 50 | 69 |
| Weeks, Josh, Mich. State........... | 2 | 7 | 4.92 | 13 | 0 | 60 | 67 | 27 | 37 |
| Steinbach, Brian, Michigan ........ | 4 | 3 | 5.00 | 13 | 0 | 54 | 56 | 27 | 26 |

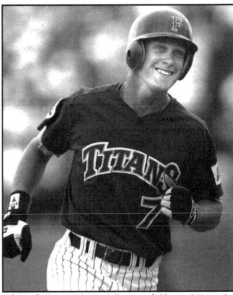

**Talented Titan.** Cal State Fullerton outfielder Mark Kotsay led the Big West Conference in homers (20) and RBIs (91).

# BIG WEST CONFERENCE

| | Conference | | Overall | |
|---|---|---|---|---|
| | W | L | W | L |
| Long Beach State | 15 | 6 | 34 | 26 |
| *Nevada-Las Vegas | 14 | 7 | 43 | 17 |
| UC Santa Barbara | 14 | 7 | 32 | 20 |
| Cal State Fullerton | 13 | 8 | 45 | 16 |
| Nevada | 8 | 13 | 30 | 19 |
| New Mexico State | 8 | 13 | 25 | 27 |
| San Jose State | 7 | 14 | 28 | 28 |
| Pacific | 5 | 16 | 24 | 25 |

**ALL-CONFERENCE TEAM: C**—Brian Loyd, Jr., Cal State Fullerton. **1B**—David Willis, Jr., UC Santa Barbara. **2B**—Mark McNelly, Jr., New Mexico State. **3B**—Ryan Hankins, So., Nevada-Las Vegas. **SS**—Jason Knupfer, Sr., Long Beach State. **OF**—Jeremy Giambi, Cal State Fullerton; Brett Hardy, Jr., UC Santa Barbara; Mark Kotsay, Jr., Cal State Fullerton. **DH**—Brian Anthony, Sr., Nevada-Las Vegas. **UT**—Andy Dominique, Jr., Nevada. **SP**—Brent Billingsley, So., Cal State Fullerton; Marcus Jones, So., Long Beach State; Tom LaRosa, Jr., Nevada-Las Vegas. **RP**—Ryan Brannan, Jr., Long Beach State.

**Player of the Year**—Mark Kotsay, Cal State Fullerton. **Pitcher of the Year**—Marcus Jones, Long Beach State.

## INDIVIDUAL BATTING LEADERS
(Minimum 125 At-Bats)

| | AVG | AB | R | H | 2B | 3B | HR | RBI | SB |
|---|---|---|---|---|---|---|---|---|---|
| McNelly, Mark, N. Mex. St... | .419 | 210 | 60 | 88 | 15 | 4 | 4 | 46 | 16 |
| Licon, Carlos, N. Mex. St...... | .410 | 195 | 40 | 80 | 16 | 4 | 2 | 57 | 5 |
| Kotsay, Mark, CS Fullerton... | .402 | 241 | 78 | 97 | 27 | 4 | 20 | 91 | 20 |
| Kritscher, Ryan, UCSB.......... | .397 | 146 | 40 | 58 | 11 | 2 | 5 | 33 | 5 |
| Giambi, Jeremy, CS Full....... | .396 | 225 | 70 | 89 | 20 | 1 | 6 | 58 | 25 |
| Walsh, Patrick, San Jose St.. | .379 | 224 | 42 | 85 | 15 | 3 | 2 | 41 | 19 |
| Jackson, Wade, Nevada ....... | .374 | 203 | 40 | 76 | 12 | 1 | 13 | 55 | 9 |
| Young, Mike, UCSB ............. | .373 | 169 | 40 | 63 | 10 | 4 | 5 | 38 | 6 |
| Slayton, Shane, Nevada........ | .371 | 175 | 55 | 65 | 15 | 3 | 12 | 46 | 0 |
| Eberwein, Kevin, UNLV......... | .367 | 207 | 60 | 76 | 19 | 1 | 10 | 55 | 2 |
| Hankins, Ryan, UNLV ........... | .367 | 229 | 60 | 84 | 17 | 1 | 12 | 66 | 6 |
| Kleiner, Stacy, UNLV............. | .364 | 250 | 78 | 91 | 18 | 1 | 13 | 61 | 1 |
| Pfeifer, Scott, Nevada ........... | .364 | 187 | 66 | 68 | 7 | 3 | 8 | 48 | 26 |
| Vincent, Scott, UNLV............. | .361 | 216 | 54 | 78 | 15 | 3 | 13 | 69 | 11 |
| Dominique, Andy, Nevada..... | .355 | 172 | 39 | 61 | 12 | 0 | 17 | 60 | 1 |

| Name | AVG | AB | R | H | 2B | 3B | HR | RBI | SB |
|---|---|---|---|---|---|---|---|---|---|
| Rooney, Shane, Pacific | .353 | 139 | 26 | 49 | 6 | 1 | 2 | 24 | 0 |
| Willis, David, UCSB | .353 | 207 | 57 | 73 | 16 | 1 | 16 | 66 | 1 |
| Carson, Glen, Nevada | .351 | 165 | 39 | 65 | 17 | 1 | 10 | 53 | 0 |
| Baugh, Darren, Nevada | .351 | 148 | 41 | 52 | 8 | 2 | 3 | 40 | 12 |
| Anthony, Brian, UNLV | .349 | 235 | 53 | 82 | 10 | 2 | 13 | 72 | 3 |
| Miller, Bob, New Mexico St. | .345 | 194 | 33 | 67 | 12 | 3 | 8 | 47 | 2 |
| Weitzman, Collin, UCSB | .344 | 192 | 40 | 66 | 7 | 1 | 4 | 35 | 7 |
| Hardy, Brett, UCSB | .344 | 195 | 54 | 67 | 9 | 5 | 8 | 43 | 8 |
| Knupfer, Jason, LBS | .339 | 221 | 38 | 75 | 6 | 5 | 1 | 24 | 14 |
| Alviso, Jerome, CSF | .338 | 151 | 41 | 51 | 13 | 0 | 2 | 21 | 1 |
| Tanner, Paul, UNLV | .337 | 267 | 74 | 90 | 9 | 0 | 6 | 34 | 28 |
| Johnson, Ryan, San Jose St. | .332 | 202 | 32 | 67 | 13 | 0 | 3 | 31 | 4 |
| Lewis, Ron, Pacific | .329 | 158 | 35 | 52 | 11 | 2 | 3 | 30 | 6 |
| Tapia, Lou, UCSB | .328 | 195 | 43 | 64 | 9 | 1 | 3 | 41 | 0 |
| Martinez, Tony, CS Fullerton | .326 | 224 | 46 | 73 | 14 | 1 | 8 | 54 | 2 |
| Berns, Robert, San Jose St. | .326 | 175 | 37 | 57 | 11 | 1 | 9 | 44 | 5 |
| Green, Dee, Pacific | .324 | 173 | 24 | 56 | 13 | 1 | 4 | 44 | 7 |
| Lamb, Mike, CS Fullerton | .324 | 179 | 35 | 58 | 14 | 0 | 5 | 30 | 0 |
| Campbell, Sean, UNLV | .324 | 179 | 37 | 58 | 11 | 0 | 1 | 33 | 7 |
| Phoenix, Wynter, UCSB | .322 | 205 | 47 | 66 | 10 | 5 | 8 | 52 | 5 |
| Loyd, Brian, CS Fullerton | .317 | 243 | 53 | 77 | 13 | 1 | 8 | 64 | 8 |
| Chatham, Steve, CS Full. | .316 | 171 | 50 | 54 | 13 | 1 | 2 | 38 | 4 |
| Adolph, Chris, UNLV | .315 | 222 | 44 | 70 | 10 | 1 | 5 | 40 | 3 |
| Ankrum, C.J., CS Fullerton | .312 | 231 | 51 | 72 | 13 | 1 | 5 | 60 | 2 |
| Champagne, Andre, NM St. | .311 | 180 | 37 | 56 | 11 | 2 | 0 | 31 | 11 |
| Skeet, Will, LBS | .310 | 229 | 55 | 71 | 23 | 0 | 5 | 28 | 13 |
| Kershner, Jake, NM St. | .310 | 145 | 31 | 45 | 6 | 0 | 0 | 17 | 13 |

### INDIVIDUAL PITCHING LEADERS
(Minimum 50 Innings)

| Name | W | L | ERA | G | SV | IP | H | BB | SO |
|---|---|---|---|---|---|---|---|---|---|
| Brannan, Ryan, LBS | 4 | 1 | 1.81 | 32 | 14 | 50 | 40 | 15 | 60 |
| Jones, Marcus, LBS | 9 | 5 | 2.29 | 16 | 0 | 110 | 90 | 37 | 118 |
| Billingsley, Brent, CS Fullerton | 11 | 2 | 3.02 | 17 | 0 | 113 | 99 | 52 | 114 |
| Hueston, Steve, LBS | 6 | 4 | 3.11 | 17 | 0 | 75 | 67 | 40 | 58 |
| Barrera, Iran, LBS | 4 | 4 | 3.44 | 26 | 0 | 55 | 61 | 17 | 30 |
| Chavez, Mark, CS Fullerton | 2 | 3 | 3.45 | 31 | 9 | 57 | 45 | 19 | 52 |
| Estrella, Luis, CS Fullerton | 3 | 1 | 3.54 | 27 | 5 | 56 | 56 | 24 | 33 |
| Flach, Jason, Pacific | 6 | 7 | 3.77 | 18 | 1 | 115 | 127 | 27 | 114 |
| LaRosa, Tom, UNLV | 9 | 2 | 3.80 | 19 | 0 | 128 | 125 | 52 | 103 |
| Irvine, Kirk, CS Fullerton | 12 | 3 | 3.86 | 20 | 0 | 110 | 116 | 42 | 74 |
| Hedquist, Lance, Pacific | 4 | 4 | 3.96 | 24 | 4 | 61 | 64 | 21 | 59 |
| Biddle, Rocky, LBS | 5 | 5 | 4.17 | 15 | 0 | 99 | 83 | 61 | 105 |
| Perri, Tista, UNLV | 7 | 3 | 4.38 | 18 | 0 | 103 | 107 | 30 | 48 |
| Wells, Matt, Nevada | 3 | 6 | 4.53 | 16 | 0 | 87 | 75 | 40 | 75 |
| Davis, Jason, San Jose State | 6 | 4 | 4.59 | 18 | 0 | 120 | 125 | 45 | 85 |
| Hild, Scott, CS Fullerton | 9 | 4 | 4.66 | 22 | 1 | 93 | 108 | 30 | 72 |
| Farias, Justin, San Jose State | 3 | 5 | 4.75 | 29 | 7 | 61 | 60 | 25 | 51 |
| Noyes, Bryan, UCSB | 5 | 4 | 4.78 | 16 | 1 | 87 | 92 | 39 | 42 |
| Garza, Chris, Nevada | 2 | 3 | 4.83 | 20 | 1 | 63 | 62 | 50 | 65 |
| Ledeit, Rich, San Jose State | 6 | 7 | 4.83 | 19 | 0 | 110 | 131 | 38 | 57 |
| Bauder, Mike, UNLV | 8 | 4 | 5.01 | 22 | 1 | 101 | 111 | 45 | 70 |

## COLONIAL ATHLETIC CONFERENCE

| | Conference | | Overall | |
|---|---|---|---|---|
| | W | L | W | L |
| *Old Dominion | 13 | 7 | 39 | 17 |
| Richmond | 13 | 7 | 27 | 25 |
| Virginia Commonwealth | 11 | 7 | 34 | 22 |
| George Mason | 12 | 9 | 25 | 29 |
| East Carolina | 10 | 11 | 22 | 24 |
| James Madison | 9 | 11 | 34 | 25 |
| UNC Wilmington | 9 | 11 | 28 | 30 |
| William & Mary | 2 | 16 | 23 | 25 |

**ALL-CONFERENCE TEAM: C**—Matt Quatraro, Sr., Old Dominion. **1B**—Greg White, So., James Madison. **2B**—Lamont Edwards, Sr., East Carolina. **3B**—Ron Walker, So., Old Dominion. **SS**—Ron Bush, So., William & Mary. **OF**—Bryan Britt, Jr., UNC Wilmington; Cordell Farley, Jr., Virginia Commonwealth; Brian Fiumara, Sr., Old Dominion. **DH**—Justin Lamber, So., Richmond. **LHP**—Jason Ramsey, Jr., UNC Wilmington. **RHP**—Patrick Dunham, So., East Carolina. **RP**—Brandon Inge, Fr., Virginia Commonwealth; Ron Walker, So., Old Dominion.
**Player of the Year**—Bryan Britt, UNC Wilmington.

### INDIVIDUAL BATTING LEADERS
(Minimum 125 At-Bats)

| Name | AVG | AB | R | H | 2B | 3B | HR | RBI | SB |
|---|---|---|---|---|---|---|---|---|---|
| Quatraro, Matt, Old Dominion | .416 | 209 | 57 | 87 | 26 | 4 | 13 | 55 | 13 |
| Laskopski, Mike, W&M | .412 | 148 | 37 | 61 | 12 | 3 | 5 | 43 | 7 |
| Edwards, Lamont, East Car. | .369 | 160 | 36 | 59 | 11 | 4 | 3 | 33 | 21 |
| Britt, Bryan, UNCW | .366 | 232 | 60 | 85 | 16 | 1 | 21 | 51 | 16 |

| Name | AVG | AB | R | H | 2B | 3B | HR | RBI | SB |
|---|---|---|---|---|---|---|---|---|---|
| Fiumara, Brian, ODU | .364 | 195 | 44 | 71 | 11 | 3 | 5 | 51 | 21 |
| Colangelo, Mike, George Mason | .361 | 155 | 40 | 56 | 12 | 7 | 5 | 38 | 5 |
| White, Greg, James Madison | .361 | 219 | 49 | 79 | 22 | 0 | 4 | 55 | 20 |
| Bush, Ron, William & Mary | .361 | 183 | 40 | 66 | 12 | 4 | 4 | 31 | 7 |
| Leek, Randy, William & Mary | .356 | 149 | 31 | 53 | 13 | 2 | 3 | 33 | 4 |
| Farley, Cordell, VCU | .348 | 224 | 64 | 78 | 14 | 4 | 1 | 33 | 44 |
| Ashcraft, Jay, VCU | .345 | 203 | 43 | 70 | 16 | 4 | 1 | 33 | 22 |
| Visconti, Rick, George Mason | .340 | 188 | 47 | 64 | 13 | 1 | 4 | 44 | 2 |
| Lamber, Justin, Richmond | .338 | 154 | 35 | 52 | 9 | 0 | 11 | 44 | 1 |
| Walker, Ron, Old Dominion | .335 | 197 | 54 | 66 | 21 | 4 | 11 | 55 | 3 |
| Lowery, Rusty, James Madison | .335 | 182 | 34 | 61 | 9 | 0 | 1 | 26 | 12 |
| Inge, Brandon, Va. Comm. | .333 | 204 | 34 | 68 | 15 | 3 | 4 | 41 | 6 |
| McGrory, P.J., Richmond | .328 | 174 | 34 | 57 | 14 | 0 | 7 | 38 | 3 |
| Dorman, John, Richmond | .323 | 192 | 63 | 62 | 21 | 0 | 1 | 38 | 24 |
| Virant, Adam, George Mason | .314 | 140 | 21 | 44 | 6 | 1 | 2 | 26 | 5 |
| Dorsey, Juan, JMU | .311 | 209 | 38 | 65 | 12 | 3 | 2 | 39 | 15 |
| #Snead, Brandon, VCU | .298 | 198 | 44 | 59 | 11 | 3 | 9 | 57 | 3 |

### INDIVIDUAL PITCHING LEADERS
(Minimum 50 Innings)

| Name | W | L | ERA | G | SV | IP | H | BB | SO |
|---|---|---|---|---|---|---|---|---|---|
| Hall, Brandon, UNCW | 4 | 0 | 2.64 | 20 | 1 | 58 | 59 | 22 | 33 |
| Gordon, Andrew, James Madison | 5 | 3 | 2.86 | 13 | 1 | 72 | 74 | 30 | 68 |
| Dunham, Patrick, East Carolina | 8 | 4 | 3.10 | 16 | 1 | 99 | 76 | 54 | 97 |
| Ramsey, Jason, UNCW | 4 | 9 | 3.13 | 15 | 1 | 98 | 79 | 40 | 135 |
| Camp, Shawn, George Mason | 6 | 2 | 3.16 | 18 | 4 | 63 | 55 | 21 | 73 |
| Craun, Brett, William & Mary | 4 | 7 | 3.35 | 21 | 2 | 78 | 82 | 38 | 59 |
| Harper, Travis, James Madison | 6 | 3 | 3.40 | 14 | 0 | 79 | 74 | 25 | 57 |
| Krieder, Justin, Old Dominion | 5 | 3 | 3.45 | 18 | 1 | 76 | 81 | 21 | 50 |
| Brookens, Casey, JMU | 3 | 4 | 3.62 | 18 | 5 | 50 | 50 | 15 | 39 |
| Luca, David, Richmond | 6 | 4 | 3.71 | 14 | 0 | 87 | 88 | 34 | 73 |
| #Walker, Ron, Old Dominion | 6 | 1 | 4.05 | 21 | 10 | 47 | 43 | 16 | 62 |
| Inge, Brandon, VCU | 6 | 2 | 4.19 | 21 | 8 | 62 | 59 | 24 | 55 |
| Plank, Marty, Old Dominion | 4 | 3 | 4.35 | 16 | 0 | 62 | 58 | 24 | 59 |
| Ketterman, Mike, Va. Comm. | 6 | 4 | 4.39 | 17 | 0 | 92 | 88 | 28 | 63 |
| Hafer, Jeff, James Madison | 6 | 4 | 4.44 | 15 | 0 | 79 | 88 | 21 | 59 |
| O'Reilly, John, Old Dominion | 11 | 2 | 4.50 | 17 | 0 | 98 | 97 | 45 | 97 |
| James, Jesse, Old Dominion | 6 | 4 | 4.61 | 18 | 0 | 92 | 104 | 31 | 72 |
| Mazur, Bryan, UNC Wilmington | 2 | 8 | 4.54 | 19 | 3 | 75 | 66 | 49 | 49 |
| Brown, Tim, UNC Wilmington | 4 | 3 | 4.59 | 13 | 0 | 51 | 65 | 21 | 39 |
| Burch, Matt, Va. Comm. | 6 | 8 | 4.66 | 17 | 0 | 87 | 91 | 57 | 65 |
| Lankford, Andy, Va. Comm. | 3 | 1 | 4.66 | 17 | 0 | 73 | 76 | 26 | 32 |
| Fulcher, John, George Mason | 6 | 5 | 4.86 | 13 | 0 | 70 | 78 | 23 | 62 |

## CONFERENCE USA

| | Conference | | Overall | |
|---|---|---|---|---|
| | W | L | W | L |
| South Florida | 20 | 4 | 47 | 19 |
| *Tulane | 18 | 6 | 43 | 20 |
| Southern Mississippi | 14 | 10 | 32 | 28 |
| Alabama-Birmingham | 13 | 11 | 33 | 25 |
| UNC Charlotte | 11 | 13 | 29 | 30 |
| Memphis | 9 | 11 | 26 | 28 |
| Saint Louis | 9 | 12 | 25 | 24 |
| Louisville | 6 | 15 | 18 | 36 |
| Cincinnati | 1 | 19 | 5 | 34 |

**ALL-CONFERENCE TEAM: C**—Jay Jones, Jr., Alabama-Birmingham. **INF**—Jason Dellaero, So., South Florida; Jorge DeLeon, Jr., South Florida; Ross Gload, So., South Florida; Chris Heintz, Sr., South Florida; Brian Jersey, Sr., Alabama-Birmingham. **OF**—Joey Anderson, Sr., UNC Charlotte; Gio Cafaro, Sr., South Florida; B.J. Huff, Jr., Alabama-Birmingham; Brian Hughes, So., Tulane. **DH**—Tony Hausladen, Jr., Saint Louis. **SP**—Jason Navarro, So., Tulane; Mark Roberts, Jr., South Florida. **RP**—Chad Harville, So., Memphis.
**Player of the Year**—Chris Heintz, South Florida. **Pitcher of the Year**—Mark Roberts, South Florida.

### INDIVIDUAL BATTING LEADERS
(Minimum 125 At-Bats)

| Name | AVG | AB | R | H | 2B | 3B | HR | RBI | SB |
|---|---|---|---|---|---|---|---|---|---|
| Anderson, Joey, UNCC | .401 | 222 | 64 | 89 | 13 | 8 | 13 | 57 | 26 |
| Heintz, Chris, South Florida | .400 | 265 | 63 | 106 | 21 | 4 | 16 | 95 | 3 |
| Barhorst, Steve, Cincinnati | .390 | 154 | 29 | 60 | 11 | 1 | 3 | 26 | 11 |
| Ray, Jeff, St. Louis | .378 | 185 | 45 | 70 | 12 | 2 | 3 | 31 | 19 |
| Gload, Ross, South Florida | .376 | 250 | 83 | 94 | 15 | 3 | 21 | 63 | 8 |
| Pilger, Mike, South Florida | .363 | 193 | 52 | 70 | 12 | 1 | 1 | 20 | 20 |
| Koettker, Eric, St. Louis | .362 | 185 | 37 | 67 | 8 | 1 | 0 | 17 | 7 |
| Barassi, Ronnie, Memphis | .360 | 139 | 36 | 50 | 7 | 0 | 12 | 40 | 7 |
| Cafaro, Gio, South Florida | .358 | 254 | 86 | 91 | 10 | 7 | 5 | 32 | 50 |
| Huff, B.J., Ala.-Birmingham | .355 | 248 | 53 | 88 | 24 | 11 | 13 | 74 | 3 |
| Jones, Jay, Ala.-Birmingham | .354 | 243 | 50 | 86 | 15 | 0 | 17 | 70 | 0 |

| | AVG | AB | R | H | 2B | 3B | HR | RBI | SB |
|---|---|---|---|---|---|---|---|---|---|
| Fitzgerald, Jason, Tulane | .353 | 252 | 58 | 89 | **28** | 1 | 9 | 56 | 20 |
| Graffagnini, Keith, Tulane | .348 | 244 | 47 | 85 | 15 | 2 | 5 | 53 | 11 |
| DeLeon, Jorge, South Florida | .347 | 190 | 55 | 66 | 12 | 2 | 2 | 39 | 4 |
| Reams, Derek, So. Miss. | .346 | 208 | 51 | 72 | 12 | 0 | 9 | 45 | 13 |
| Carnes, Shayne, Ala.-Birm. | .345 | 168 | 30 | 58 | 11 | 2 | 6 | 34 | 23 |
| Hughes, Brian, Tulane | .344 | 241 | 65 | 83 | 17 | 1 | 4 | 45 | 33 |
| Merrill, Jerry, Cincinnati | .342 | 152 | 32 | 52 | 11 | 0 | 1 | 24 | 4 |
| Wren, Cliff, So. Miss. | .339 | 227 | 36 | 77 | 16 | 0 | 9 | 56 | 1 |
| Jersey, Brian, Ala.-Birm. | .335 | 215 | 59 | 72 | 19 | 0 | 9 | 49 | 6 |
| Matan, James, UNCC | .330 | 230 | 40 | 76 | 15 | 0 | 10 | 64 | 1 |
| Huelsmann, Mike, St. Louis | .323 | 198 | 46 | 64 | 9 | 5 | 3 | 24 | 31 |
| Berger, Matt, Louisville | .317 | 186 | 39 | 59 | 8 | 0 | 14 | 43 | 2 |
| Hesse, Chris, So. Miss. | .315 | 232 | 59 | 73 | 13 | 2 | 6 | 27 | 32 |
| Rhodes, Nick, UNCC | .313 | 227 | 49 | 71 | 11 | 3 | 4 | 42 | 29 |
| Bredensteiner, Brett, St. L. | .313 | 198 | 41 | 62 | 15 | 4 | 3 | 37 | 6 |
| Albritton, Jeremy, So. Miss. | .311 | 161 | 20 | 50 | 12 | 0 | 2 | 36 | 6 |
| Weidemann, J., Louisville | .310 | 213 | 43 | 66 | 19 | 2 | 2 | 24 | 12 |
| Gabris, Adam, St. Louis | .309 | 188 | 39 | 58 | 12 | 0 | 10 | 41 | 4 |
| Bender, Heath, Memphis | .308 | 159 | 35 | 49 | 8 | 1 | 4 | 23 | 1 |
| Tompkins, John, Memphis | .306 | 157 | 36 | 48 | 10 | 2 | 6 | 31 | 9 |
| Wilson, Scott, Tulane | .305 | 223 | 50 | 68 | 16 | 3 | 6 | 32 | 6 |

## INDIVIDUAL PITCHING LEADERS
(Minimum 50 Innings)

| | W | L | ERA | G | SV | IP | H | BB | SO |
|---|---|---|---|---|---|---|---|---|---|
| Boyles, Steven, South Florida | 2 | 4 | **1.41** | 40 | 6 | 64 | 49 | 13 | 60 |
| Ramos, Luis, South Florida | 1 | 2 | 2.32 | 29 | 3 | 54 | 41 | 20 | 42 |
| Navarro, Jason, Tulane | 11 | 0 | 3.30 | 17 | 0 | 93 | 85 | 48 | 110 |
| Summey, Jesse, UNCC | 10 | 4 | 3.36 | 19 | 0 | 123 | 127 | 24 | 92 |
| Parker, Brandon, So. Miss. | 5 | 3 | 3.42 | 15 | 0 | 68 | 53 | 28 | 81 |
| Glaser, Scott, South Florida | **12** | 4 | 3.52 | 23 | 1 | 100 | 92 | 28 | 61 |
| Bradford, Chad, So. Miss. | 5 | 4 | 3.59 | 24 | 3 | 92 | 87 | 26 | 93 |
| Gray, Mark, Ala.-Birmingham | 6 | 5 | 3.63 | 14 | 0 | 84 | 86 | 25 | 80 |
| Roberts, Mark, South Florida | 11 | 4 | 3.70 | 18 | 0 | 119 | 117 | 49 | 105 |
| Harville, Chad, Memphis | 6 | 3 | 3.81 | 24 | **8** | 54 | 44 | 33 | 61 |
| Bell, Scott, Tulane | 9 | 2 | 3.84 | 19 | 0 | 96 | 111 | 28 | 79 |
| Wheat, Reggie, So. Miss. | 5 | 4 | 3.86 | 18 | 2 | 93 | 101 | 26 | 89 |
| Cressend, Jack, Tulane | 8 | 6 | 3.86 | 29 | 4 | 103 | 96 | 33 | **123** |
| Bale, John, So. Mississippi | 9 | 4 | 4.01 | 19 | 0 | 92 | 81 | 46 | 92 |
| Danner, Adam, South Florida | 7 | 1 | 4.15 | 15 | 0 | 95 | 105 | 31 | 53 |
| Williamson, Anthony, Tulane | 5 | 2 | 4.31 | 19 | 4 | 86 | 83 | 34 | 84 |
| Lontayo, Alex, Tulane | 7 | 6 | 4.35 | 19 | 0 | 93 | 90 | 41 | 92 |
| Beyer, Scott, Ala.-Birmingham | 6 | 2 | 4.39 | 23 | 1 | 68 | 74 | 23 | 39 |
| Tippett, Ray, St. Louis | 4 | 5 | 4.50 | 12 | 0 | 68 | 89 | 14 | 55 |
| Day, Collins, Memphis | 5 | 4 | 4.50 | 13 | 0 | 62 | 69 | 31 | 68 |
| McCrary, Scott, Ala.-Birm. | 8 | 4 | 4.63 | 17 | 0 | 95 | 107 | 16 | 56 |
| Mayo, Blake, Ala.-Birm. | 6 | 3 | 4.64 | 16 | 0 | 87 | 92 | 43 | 84 |
| Player, Brannon, UNCC | 8 | 5 | 4.65 | 17 | 0 | 112 | 118 | 41 | 83 |

## IVY LEAGUE

| | Conference | | Overall | |
|---|---|---|---|---|
| **GEHRIG** | W | L | W | L |
| *Princeton | 13 | 7 | 26 | 21 |
| Pennsylvania | 13 | 7 | 25 | 17 |
| Cornell | 8 | 12 | 17 | 27 |
| Columbia | 7 | 13 | 13 | 29 |
| **ROLFE** | | | | |
| Harvard | 14 | 6 | 23 | 17 |
| Yale | 11 | 9 | 24 | 18 |
| Dartmouth | 8 | 12 | 12 | 25 |
| Brown | 6 | 14 | 12 | 25 |

**ALL-CONFERENCE TEAM: C**—Mike Ciminiello, Sr., Princeton. **1B**—Mike Shannon, Sr., Penn. **2B**—Dave Ekelund, Sr., Princeton. **3B**—Tommy Hage, Sr., Princeton. **SS**—Bill Walkenbach, So., Cornell. **OF**—Dan Thompson, Sr., Yale; John Guilfoy, Sr., Columbia; Andrew Spencer, Jr., Dartmouth. **SP**—Dan Thompson, Sr., Yale; Frank Hogan, Jr., Harvard. **RP**—Jason Paul, So., Cornell.
**Player of the Year**—Mike Shannon, Penn.

## INDIVIDUAL BATTING LEADERS
(Minimum 100 At-Bats)

| | AVG | AB | R | H | 2B | 3B | HR | RBI | SB |
|---|---|---|---|---|---|---|---|---|---|
| Shannon, Mike, Penn | **.444** | 142 | 37 | 63 | 18 | 2 | 6 | 30 | 5 |
| Hobbs, Bryan, Yale | .414 | 162 | 44 | 67 | 10 | 2 | 1 | 22 | 4 |
| Thompson, Dan, Yale | .410 | 144 | 44 | 59 | 15 | **4** | 7 | **54** | 7 |
| Ciminiello, Mike, Princeton | .396 | 159 | **46** | 63 | 11 | 0 | **13** | 48 | 4 |
| Turner, Sean, Penn | .386 | 140 | 22 | 54 | 14 | 2 | 4 | 33 | 4 |
| Hage, Tommy, Princeton | .375 | 176 | 38 | **68** | **19** | 2 | 3 | 48 | 4 |
| Isler, Jake, Dartmouth | .369 | 122 | 17 | 45 | 3 | **4** | 2 | 28 | 3 |
| Spencer, Andrew, Dart. | .357 | 129 | 27 | 46 | 7 | 2 | 3 | 32 | 8 |

| | AVG | AB | R | H | 2B | 3B | HR | RBI | SB |
|---|---|---|---|---|---|---|---|---|---|
| Burt, Rick, Penn | .350 | 117 | 30 | 41 | 4 | 1 | 0 | 14 | 3 |
| Vankoski, Brett, Harvard | .340 | 103 | 19 | 35 | 4 | 1 | 2 | 19 | 5 |
| Doble, Dennis, Harvard | .339 | 124 | 29 | 42 | 8 | 0 | 4 | 31 | 4 |
| Mezzadri, Marc, Columbia | .338 | 133 | 29 | 45 | 9 | 1 | 4 | 26 | 1 |
| Malick, Ravi, Brown | .333 | 120 | 26 | 40 | 10 | 1 | 6 | 34 | 6 |
| Carey, Hal, Harvard | .329 | 143 | 39 | 47 | 12 | 1 | 0 | 20 | 10 |
| Keck, Michael, Princeton | .326 | 119 | 29 | 33 | 12 | 1 | 7 | 36 | 1 |
| Bird, Matthew, Yale | .324 | 142 | 27 | 46 | 9 | 2 | 6 | 26 | 14 |

## INDIVIDUAL PITCHING LEADERS
(Minimum 40 Innings)

| | W | L | ERA | G | SV | IP | H | BB | SO |
|---|---|---|---|---|---|---|---|---|---|
| Duffell, Andrew, Harvard | 5 | 2 | **2.49** | 11 | 0 | 43 | 32 | 17 | 21 |
| Schafer, Quinn, Harvard | 5 | 3 | 3.28 | 8 | 0 | 47 | 31 | 25 | 30 |
| Simonian, Armen, Penn | 5 | 2 | 3.29 | 9 | 1 | 52 | 37 | 25 | 31 |
| Thompson, Dan, Yale | 5 | 3 | 3.58 | 9 | 0 | 55 | 59 | 17 | 54 |
| Scarlata, Mike, Brown | 3 | 4 | 3.94 | 10 | 0 | 48 | 57 | 13 | 32 |
| Shannon, Mike, Penn | 4 | 1 | 3.89 | 7 | 0 | 44 | 36 | 13 | 40 |
| Griggs, Bobby, Yale | 5 | 2 | 4.05 | 17 | 2 | 47 | 48 | 18 | 35 |
| Volpp, Brian, Princeton | 5 | 2 | 4.14 | 12 | 0 | 63 | 69 | 20 | 29 |
| Greenwood, Mike, Penn | 3 | 3 | 4.22 | 10 | 0 | 49 | 48 | 30 | 26 |
| Yarbrough, Chris, Princeton | **8** | 3 | 4.26 | 12 | 0 | 89 | 89 | 19 | 45 |
| Walania, Eric, Dartmouth | 4 | 4 | 4.32 | 9 | 1 | 52 | 71 | 17 | 28 |
| Fischer, A.B., Penn | 5 | 4 | 4.57 | 9 | 0 | 45 | 45 | 20 | 18 |
| Ceterko, Steve, Columbia | 3 | 4 | 4.61 | 9 | 0 | 55 | 56 | 29 | 43 |
| #Smith, Ron, Princeton | 3 | 5 | 5.29 | 13 | 1 | 73 | 92 | 18 | **59** |

## METRO ATLANTIC CONFERENCE

| | Conference | | Overall | |
|---|---|---|---|---|
| **NORTH** | W | L | W | L |
| *Siena | 14 | 4 | 28 | 20 |
| Le Moyne | 10 | 8 | 17 | 19 |
| Niagara | 7 | 11 | 14 | 20 |
| Canisius | 5 | 13 | 13 | 22 |
| **SOUTH** | | | | |
| Iona | 11 | 7 | 26 | 21 |
| St. Peter's | 10 | 7 | 18 | 24 |
| Fairfield | 10 | 8 | 20 | 19 |
| Manhattan | 4 | 13 | 9 | 30 |

**MAAC North ALL-CONFERENCE TEAM: C**—Carm Panaro, Jr., Niagara. **1B**—John Geis, Sr., LeMoyne. **2B**—Dave Marek, So., Siena. **3B**—Dave Bunn, Sr., Niagara. **SS**—Tim Fleischman, Sr., Siena. **OF**—Kevin Glover, Jr., Canisius; Mike Horning, Jr., LeMoyne; Aaron Mindel, Fr., Niagara; Rob McShinsky, Sr., Siena. **DH**—Dave Bunn, Sr., Niagara. **P**—Tom Stepka, Jr. LeMoyne; Tim Christman, Jr., Siena; Ira Tilton, Jr., Siena.
**Co-Players of the Year**—Dave Bunn, Niagara; John Geis, LeMoyne.

**MAAC South ALL-CONFERENCE TEAM: C**—Kyran Connelly, So., Iona; Bill Moore, Sr., St. Peter's. **1B**—Brian Merkle, So., Iona; John Way, Sr., St. Peter's. **2B**—Adam Samuelian, Jr., Fairfield; Chris Nocera, Sr., St. Peter's. **3B**—Brian Hennessy, So., Iona; Mike Lucca, So., Iona. **SS**—Dave Filipkowski, Sr., Iona; Jeff Rowett, So., Manhattan. **OF**—Mike Pike, Sr., Fairfield; John Penatello, So., Iona; Dave Crane, Sr., Iona. **DH**—Jon Wilson, Jr., Fairfield; Elloid Alguila, So., Iona. **P**—Jared DeCore, So., Fairfield; Sean Breen, Sr., Iona; Ron Heusser, Sr., St. Peter's.
**Player of the Year**—Mike Pike, Fairfield.

## INDIVIDUAL BATTING LEADERS
(Minimum 100 At-Bats)

| | AVG | AB | R | H | 2B | 3B | HR | RBI | SB |
|---|---|---|---|---|---|---|---|---|---|
| Pike, Mike, Fairfield | .397 | 151 | 43 | 60 | **20** | 1 | 8 | **51** | 11 |
| Penatello, John, Iona | .386 | 145 | 54 | 56 | 9 | 3 | 2 | 44 | **42** |
| Kern, Justin, Fairfield | .380 | 129 | 38 | 49 | 4 | 0 | 1 | 25 | 14 |
| Giamone, Sal, Fairfield | .354 | 158 | 42 | 56 | 19 | 1 | 1 | 24 | 22 |
| Fleischman, Tim, Siena | .354 | 181 | 29 | **64** | 8 | 2 | 3 | 29 | 11 |
| Merkle, Brian, Iona | .352 | 145 | 30 | 51 | 11 | 0 | 11 | 45 | 1 |
| Filipkowski, Dave, Iona | .349 | 169 | 42 | 59 | 13 | 1 | 8 | 45 | 12 |
| Kline, Jason, Canisius | .347 | 124 | 24 | 43 | 9 | 2 | 1 | 15 | 4 |
| Rowett, Jeff, Manhattan | .339 | 118 | 22 | 40 | 8 | 1 | 2 | 26 | 6 |
| Boccarossa, Vic, LeMoyne | .336 | 128 | 22 | 43 | 4 | 2 | 2 | 19 | 1 |
| Herlong, Dave, Canisius | .333 | 108 | 17 | 36 | 7 | 0 | 8 | 27 | 1 |
| Larned, Andy, Fairfield | .331 | 145 | 21 | 48 | 12 | 2 | 2 | 31 | 2 |
| Nocera, Chris, St. Peter's | .329 | 158 | 41 | 52 | 12 | **5** | 1 | 20 | 28 |
| Wilson, Jon, Fairfield | .324 | 145 | 25 | 47 | 8 | 0 | 3 | 32 | 5 |
| Crane, David, Iona | .324 | 148 | 46 | 48 | 8 | 1 | 9 | 35 | 15 |
| Marek, Dave, Siena | .322 | 152 | 32 | 49 | 7 | 3 | 8 | 39 | 6 |
| Geis, John, LeMoyne | .316 | 114 | 25 | 36 | 9 | 0 | **12** | 37 | 0 |
| Hennesey, Bri, Canisius | .315 | 106 | 16 | 34 | 5 | 1 | 4 | 22 | 6 |

## INDIVIDUAL PITCHING LEADERS
(Minimum 40 Innings)

| | W | L | ERA | G | SV | IP | H | BB | SO |
|---|---|---|---|---|---|---|---|---|---|
| Christman, Tim, Siena | 4 | 2 | **2.25** | 9 | 1 | 40 | 23 | 13 | 53 |
| Cassidy, Scott, LeMoyne | 4 | 4 | 2.80 | 10 | 0 | 55 | 51 | 8 | 34 |
| Tilton, Ira, Siena | **7** | 3 | 3.09 | 11 | 0 | 76 | 67 | 40 | 55 |
| Bunn, Dave, Niagara | 3 | 3 | 3.11 | 10 | 1 | 46 | 34 | 26 | 44 |
| Stepka, Tom, LeMoyne | 3 | 5 | 3.15 | 10 | 1 | 66 | 50 | 13 | 53 |
| DeCore, Jared, Fairfield | 6 | 2 | 3.40 | 8 | 0 | 53 | 61 | 13 | 16 |
| Heusser, Ron, St. Peter's | 5 | 5 | 3.52 | 13 | 0 | 72 | 70 | 13 | 49 |
| Breen, Sean, Iona | 5 | 1 | 4.26 | 10 | 0 | 57 | 50 | 27 | 45 |
| Fields, Dave, Siena | 6 | 3 | 4.44 | 9 | 0 | 47 | 56 | 15 | 33 |
| Gannon, Joe, Canisius | 3 | 4 | 4.50 | 12 | 0 | 44 | 48 | 24 | 36 |
| #Manias, Jim, Fairfield | 4 | 5 | 5.20 | 13 | 0 | 64 | 62 | 41 | **64** |
| #Nesci, John, Manhattan | 2 | 0 | 5.48 | 7 | **3** | 10 | 7 | 13 | 8 |

## MID-AMERICAN CONFERENCE

| | Conference | | Overall | |
|---|---|---|---|---|
| | W | L | W | L |
| Kent | 21 | 7 | 30 | 20 |
| Ohio | 21 | 11 | 34 | 23 |
| Toledo | 18 | 14 | 27 | 27 |
| *Akron | 18 | 14 | 37 | 23 |
| Ball State | 16 | 14 | 32 | 20 |
| Central Michigan | 16 | 14 | 31 | 20 |
| Eastern Michigan | 16 | 16 | 26 | 29 |
| Bowling Green State | 14 | 17 | 28 | 22 |
| Western Michigan | 10 | 21 | 17 | 34 |
| Miami (Ohio) | 5 | 27 | 12 | 40 |

**ALL-CONFERENCE TEAM: C**—Bill Bronikowski, Jr., Toledo; Shannon Swaino, Jr., Kent. **1B**—Ed Farris, Jr., Ball State. **2B**—Jeff McGavin, Sr., Eastern Michigan. **3B**—Andy Tracy, Sr., Bowling Green. **SS**—Don DeDonatis, Jr., Eastern Michigan. **OF**—Jake Eye, Jr., Ohio; Brian Petrucci, Jr., Akron; Brent Sachs, Jr., Western Michigan. **DH**—Josh Sorge, Sr., Ohio. **UT**—Jason Armetta, Sr., Miami. **SP**—Aaron Houdeshell, Jr., Ohio; Todd Maynard, Jr., Akron; Ted Rose, Sr., Kent; Bruce Stanley, Jr., Ball State. **RP**—Nick Witte, Sr., Ball State.

**Player of the Year**—Ed Farris, Ball State. **Pitcher of the Year**—Ted Rose, Kent.

## INDIVIDUAL BATTING LEADERS
(Minimum 125 At-Bats)

| | AVG | AB | R | H | 2B | 3B | HR | RBI | SB |
|---|---|---|---|---|---|---|---|---|---|
| DeDonatis, Don, East. Mich. | .409 | 186 | 38 | 76 | 11 | 1 | 3 | 38 | **28** |
| Sachs, Brent, West. Mich. | .397 | 179 | 41 | 71 | 13 | 2 | 4 | 21 | 11 |
| Petrucci, Brian, Akron | .395 | 200 | **53** | **79** | 17 | 3 | 8 | **57** | 17 |
| Tracy, Andy, Bowling Green | .388 | 139 | 45 | 54 | 11 | 2 | 13 | 44 | 5 |
| Van Damme, Jude, CM | .386 | 140 | 32 | 54 | 10 | 1 | 5 | 26 | 12 |
| Eye, Jake, Ohio | .384 | 151 | 30 | 58 | 8 | 1 | 4 | 45 | 3 |
| Sorge, Josh, Ohio | .383 | 175 | 37 | 67 | 11 | 1 | 9 | 54 | 4 |
| Farris, Ed, Bowling Green | .377 | 183 | 41 | 69 | 18 | 0 | **15** | 47 | 1 |
| Swaino, Shannon, Kent | .372 | 148 | 37 | 55 | 8 | 0 | 8 | 36 | 1 |
| Bartos, Jay, Akron | .364 | 195 | 43 | 71 | 9 | 0 | 3 | 25 | 6 |
| Smetana, Steve, Kent | .356 | 177 | 40 | 63 | **22** | 1 | 8 | 38 | 4 |
| Peck, Tom, Miami | .356 | 163 | 24 | 58 | 14 | **4** | 3 | 27 | 7 |
| Burgei, Bill, Bowling Green | .355 | 166 | 43 | 59 | 10 | 0 | 3 | 17 | 13 |
| Marn, Kevin, Kent | .351 | 202 | 47 | 71 | 7 | 2 | 7 | 41 | 11 |
| Armetta, Jason, Miami | .350 | 163 | 31 | 57 | 9 | 2 | 3 | 17 | 12 |
| Fitzharris, Tim, Ball State | .346 | 156 | 26 | 54 | 8 | **4** | 3 | 25 | 1 |
| McGavin, Jeff, East. Mich. | .346 | 182 | 36 | 63 | 17 | 0 | 3 | 39 | 1 |
| Fails, Tim, Kent | .343 | 140 | 32 | 48 | 8 | 2 | 2 | 20 | 4 |
| Dorrmann, Brian, Ball State | .343 | 181 | 44 | 62 | 16 | 1 | 0 | 31 | 4 |
| Graham, Jason, Ohio | .338 | 148 | 23 | 50 | 10 | 0 | 4 | 33 | 6 |
| Lindsay, Derek, West. Mich. | .333 | 153 | 25 | 51 | 9 | 1 | 3 | 31 | 1 |
| Combs, Mike, Bowl. Green | .331 | 157 | 26 | 52 | 15 | 0 | 7 | 39 | 1 |

## INDIVIDUAL PITCHING LEADERS
(Minimum 50 Innings)

| | W | L | ERA | G | SV | IP | H | BB | SO |
|---|---|---|---|---|---|---|---|---|---|
| Witte, Nick, Ball State | 2 | 1 | 1.91 | 25 | **12** | 28 | 18 | 6 | 35 |
| Houdeshell, Aaron, Ohio | **11** | 2 | **2.38** | 15 | 0 | 95 | 99 | 27 | 51 |
| Chaney, Mike, Bowling Green | 7 | 4 | 2.75 | 15 | 0 | 59 | 56 | 21 | 48 |
| Coleman, Billy, West. Mich. | 5 | 6 | 3.13 | 14 | 0 | 83 | 77 | 28 | 66 |
| Simon, Ben, Easy. Michigan | 3 | 5 | 3.30 | 17 | 0 | 74 | 55 | 36 | 81 |
| Rose, Ted, Kent | 10 | 2 | 3.43 | 15 | 0 | 97 | 81 | 25 | 66 |
| Gardner, Lee, Cent. Mich. | 8 | 4 | 3.77 | 14 | 0 | 76 | 81 | 22 | 73 |
| Hoskins, Ashley, Ohio | 6 | 5 | 3.87 | 13 | 0 | 79 | 77 | 21 | 32 |
| Hughes, Greg, Miami | 0 | 5 | 3.93 | 14 | 0 | 53 | 67 | 15 | 40 |
| McConnell, Sam, Ball State | 6 | 6 | 3.95 | 15 | 0 | 66 | 69 | 28 | 57 |
| Stanley, Bruce, Ball State | 7 | 5 | 4.01 | 15 | 0 | 74 | 83 | 17 | 68 |
| Wirebaugh, Derek, Cent. Mich. | 5 | 6 | 4.23 | 13 | 0 | 62 | 69 | 13 | 50 |
| Stark, Denny, Toledo | 9 | 7 | 4.44 | 21 | 3 | 95 | 91 | 37 | **90** |

## MID CONTINENT CONFERENCE

| EAST | Conference | | Overall | |
|---|---|---|---|---|
| | W | L | W | L |
| Troy State | 16 | 2 | 41 | 13 |
| Pace | 10 | 10 | 20 | 28 |
| Youngstown State | 10 | 10 | 20 | 25 |
| New York Tech | 8 | 12 | 20 | 25 |
| C.W. Post | 7 | 11 | 15 | 24 |
| Central Connecticut State | 7 | 13 | 17 | 25 |
| **WEST** | | | | |
| Eastern Illinois | 15 | 3 | 25 | 22 |
| *Northeastern Illinois | 12 | 12 | 31 | 29 |
| Valparaiso | 9 | 11 | 18 | 29 |
| Western Illinois | 9 | 13 | 14 | 27 |
| Chicago State | 7 | 13 | 20 | 28 |

**EASTERN DIVISION ALL-CONFERENCE TEAM: C**—Michael Rivera, Jr., Troy State. **1B**—Chris Briller, Jr., New York Tech. **2B**—Travis Quesada, Sr., Troy State. **3B**—Peter Bezeredi, Sr., Troy State. **SS**—Michael Sidoti, Sr., Pace. **OF**—Rhodney Donaldson, Jr., Troy State; Reggie Hightower, Sr., Troy State; Jamie Palumbo, Sr., Youngstown State. **DH**—Fred Case, So., Troy State. **P**—Dean Cordova, Jr., Troy State; Jason Fawcett, Jr., Troy State; Gary Gubanich, Sr., Youngstown State.

**WESTERN DIVISION ALL-CONFERENCE TEAM: C**—Nolan Lofgren, Jr., Eastern Illinois. **1B**—Shane Hesse, Sr., Eastern Illinois. **2B**—James Renko, Sr., Chicago State. **3B**—Matt Dunne, Jr., Northeastern Illinois. **SS**—Steve Dunlop, Sr., Eastern Illinois. **OF**—Rob Bruce, Sr., Northeastern Illinois; Rob Hadrick, Jr., Valparaiso; Josh Zink, So., Eastern Illinois. **DH**—Andy Murphy, Sr., Western Illinois. **UT**—Brian Naese, Jr., Chicago State. **P**—Joe Lazewski, So., Valparaiso; Brian Neal, Sr., Eastern Illinois; Jamie Puorto, Jr., Northeastern Illinois.

**Player of the Year**—Reggie Hightower, Troy State. **Pitcher of the Year**—Dean Cordova, Troy State.

## INDIVIDUAL BATTING LEADERS
(Minimum 100 At-Bats)

| | AVG | AB | R | H | 2B | 3B | HR | RBI | SB |
|---|---|---|---|---|---|---|---|---|---|
| Tinelli, Paul, C.W. Post | .417 | 132 | 27 | 55 | 12 | 1 | 3 | 23 | 5 |
| Dunlop, Steve, East. Ill. | .414 | 174 | 52 | 72 | 15 | **4** | 5 | 36 | 16 |
| Hightower, Reggie, Troy St. | .391 | 207 | 56 | **81** | 16 | 3 | 13 | 62 | 9 |
| Hesse, Shane, East. Ill. | .389 | 131 | 38 | 51 | 13 | 1 | 10 | 48 | 1 |
| Graham, Dan, Cent. Conn. | .381 | 126 | 23 | 48 | 9 | 2 | 3 | 20 | 1 |
| Pruchnicki, Ken, Cent. Conn. | .380 | 142 | 24 | 54 | 3 | 3 | 1 | 28 | 2 |
| Rivera, Michael, Troy State | .376 | 205 | 48 | 77 | 12 | 0 | **21** | **63** | 11 |
| Sidoti, Michael, Pace | .374 | 187 | 37 | 70 | 16 | 2 | 9 | 55 | 0 |
| Donaldson, Rhodney, TS | .368 | 171 | 37 | 63 | 5 | 2 | 7 | 33 | 5 |
| Morsovillo, Jim, West. Ill. | .366 | 134 | 40 | 49 | 11 | 2 | 8 | 36 | 4 |
| Bishop, Steve, West. Ill. | .366 | 123 | 23 | 45 | 9 | 0 | 1 | 28 | 0 |
| Renko, James, Chi. State | .364 | 151 | 43 | 55 | 14 | 2 | 8 | 47 | 6 |
| Accardi, Bobby, Pace | .358 | 187 | 41 | 67 | 14 | 2 | 0 | 35 | 10 |
| Ciccone, Phillip, Pace | .352 | 128 | 34 | 45 | 5 | 3 | 3 | 25 | 5 |
| Quesada, Travis, Troy State | .351 | 174 | **61** | 61 | 11 | 1 | 8 | 39 | 14 |
| Mau, Eric, NE Illinois | .349 | 229 | 36 | 80 | 5 | 1 | 1 | 23 | 4 |
| Dunne, Matt, NE Illinois | .349 | 175 | 29 | 61 | 10 | 1 | 0 | 41 | 4 |
| Lofgren, Nolan, East. Ill. | .347 | 150 | 25 | 52 | 14 | 1 | 0 | 25 | 3 |
| Briller, Chris, New York Tech | .346 | 156 | 37 | 54 | 8 | 2 | 4 | 28 | 16 |
| Seifert, Kevin, West. Ill. | .343 | 140 | 37 | 48 | 20 | 1 | 7 | 24 | 5 |
| Case, Fred, Troy State | .342 | 158 | 37 | 54 | 16 | 0 | 7 | 33 | 1 |
| Meyer, Henry, Pace | .342 | 146 | 27 | 50 | 7 | 2 | 3 | 35 | 1 |
| Hadrick, Rob, Valparaiso | .342 | 161 | 44 | 55 | 7 | 2 | 7 | 36 | 20 |
| Bruce, Rob, NE Illinois | .340 | 194 | 49 | 66 | 8 | **4** | 9 | 51 | **25** |

## INDIVIDUAL PITCHING LEADERS
(Minimum 40 Innings)

| | W | L | ERA | G | SV | IP | H | BB | SO |
|---|---|---|---|---|---|---|---|---|---|
| Sommerfeld, Mike, East. Ill. | 5 | 1 | **2.48** | 29 | **4** | 40 | 42 | 9 | 32 |
| Gubanich, Gary, Young. State | 5 | 4 | 2.59 | 15 | 1 | 63 | 62 | 12 | 33 |
| Langford, Chris, Troy State | 5 | 3 | 3.03 | 15 | 0 | 77 | 64 | 22 | 59 |
| Fawcett, Jason, Troy State | 10 | 2 | 3.22 | 19 | 1 | 92 | 78 | 34 | **98** |
| Hitchcock, Scott, Young. State | 8 | 2 | 3.38 | 14 | 0 | 56 | 52 | 30 | 15 |
| Cordova, Dean, Troy State | **12** | 1 | 3.40 | 20 | 0 | 95 | 75 | 35 | 77 |
| Puorto, Jamie, NE Illinois | 9 | 6 | 3.41 | 19 | 1 | 111 | 111 | 37 | 92 |
| Neal, Brian, East. Illinois | 3 | 3 | 3.42 | 14 | 0 | 71 | 61 | 30 | 55 |
| Frowd, Ray, Pace | 2 | 3 | 3.47 | 11 | 0 | 47 | 50 | 25 | 23 |
| Mead, Shane, Young. State | 3 | 4 | 3.59 | 14 | 1 | 63 | 54 | 31 | 59 |
| Eason, Duane, Troy State | 7 | 1 | 3.62 | 15 | 2 | 50 | 39 | 29 | 44 |
| Jasper, Jim, NE Illinois | 3 | 3 | 3.80 | 15 | 3 | 47 | 49 | 17 | 37 |
| Lazewski, Joe, Valparaiso | 5 | 3 | 3.90 | 13 | 0 | 60 | 33 | 37 | 37 |
| Kvasnicka, Jay, NE Illinois | 4 | 2 | 3.98 | 12 | 2 | 41 | 36 | 19 | 30 |
| Callahan, Mike, Chicago State | 3 | 4 | 3.99 | 12 | 0 | 50 | 45 | 33 | 31 |

## MID-EASTERN CONFERENCE

| NORTH | Conference | | Overall | |
|---|---|---|---|---|
| | W | L | W | L |
| Coppin State | 13 | 5 | 19 | 21 |
| Howard | 11 | 7 | 14 | 35 |
| Delaware State | 9 | 9 | 11 | 24 |
| Maryland-Eastern Shore | 3 | 15 | 4 | 45 |
| **SOUTH** | | | | |
| *Bethune-Cookman | 8 | 1 | 28 | 25 |
| Florida A&M | 6 | 4 | 15 | 34 |
| North Carolina A&T | 1 | 10 | 4 | 38 |

**ALL-CONFERENCE TEAM: C**—Maurio Watkins, Sr., Florida A&M. **IF**—Freddie Little, Sr., Bethune-Cookman; Meryl Melendez, Sr., Bethune-Cookman; Brian Pisani, Jr., Coppin State; Terrance Johnson, Jr., Howard. **OF**—Theo Fefee, Jr., Bethune-Cookman; Danny Singletary, Jr., Coppin State; Rory Beauford, Jr., Bethune-Cookman. **DH**—Mike Rawls, So., Bethune-Cookman. **P**—Brian Pisani, Jr., Coppin State.
**Player of the Year**—Brian Pisani, Coppin State.

### INDIVIDUAL BATTING LEADERS
(Minimum 100 At-Bats)

| | AVG | AB | R | H | 2B | 3B | HR | RBI | SB |
|---|---|---|---|---|---|---|---|---|---|
| Beauford, Rory, Beth.-Cook. | .441 | 118 | 40 | 52 | 6 | 0 | 2 | 22 | 16 |
| Singletary, Danny, Coppin St. | .404 | 146 | 43 | 59 | 10 | 5 | 7 | 49 | 17 |
| Watkins, Maurio, Fla. A&M | .395 | 157 | 27 | 62 | 13 | 0 | 4 | 37 | 3 |
| Pisani, Brian, Coppin State | .387 | 124 | 26 | 48 | 9 | 1 | 5 | 32 | 1 |
| Melvin, Ernie, Delaware State | .368 | 125 | 27 | 46 | 10 | 1 | 4 | 17 | 15 |
| Lipsey, Leroy, Beth.-Cook. | .361 | 133 | 26 | 48 | 6 | 3 | 0 | 15 | 13 |
| Thornton, Travis, Coppin St. | .359 | 131 | 35 | 47 | 8 | 0 | 0 | 21 | 11 |
| Melendez, Meryl, Beth.-Cook. | .350 | 163 | 50 | 57 | 14 | 3 | 4 | 33 | 9 |
| Collins, Mike, Beth.-Cook. | .346 | 170 | 37 | 54 | 9 | 1 | 2 | 37 | 7 |
| Gilbert, Toriano, Beth.-Cook. | .341 | 173 | 42 | 59 | 7 | 1 | 1 | 20 | 14 |
| Beamon, Demetry, Fla. A&M. | .331 | 169 | 33 | 56 | 2 | 2 | 0 | 16 | 18 |
| Aiken, Chris, Delaware State | .330 | 100 | 17 | 33 | 8 | 0 | 3 | 21 | 0 |
| Rawls, Mike, Beth.-Cookman | .325 | 157 | 40 | 51 | 8 | 8 | 7 | 43 | 14 |
| Clark, Bob, Delaware State | .315 | 111 | 25 | 35 | 6 | 1 | 5 | 24 | 8 |
| Bell, Ruffin, Coppin State | .306 | 111 | 26 | 34 | 5 | 0 | 1 | 20 | 2 |

### INDIVIDUAL PITCHING LEADERS
(Minimum 40 Innings)

| | W | L | ERA | G | SV | IP | H | BB | SO |
|---|---|---|---|---|---|---|---|---|---|
| Barnes, Fred, Beth.-Cookman | 7 | 5 | 4.17 | 14 | 0 | 82 | 78 | 39 | 79 |
| Rawls, Mike, Beth.-Cookman | 7 | 3 | 4.31 | 12 | 1 | 71 | 55 | 32 | 81 |
| Moreland, Anthony, Fla. A&M | 4 | 6 | 4.64 | 14 | 1 | 76 | 101 | 36 | 44 |
| Gray, Wayne, UMES | 2 | 6 | 4.67 | 13 | 0 | 60 | 76 | 48 | 30 |
| Pisani, Brian, Coppin State | 7 | 4 | 4.71 | 15 | 0 | 86 | 94 | 33 | 58 |
| Jenkins, J.J., UMES | 0 | 3 | 5.50 | 17 | 0 | 50 | 64 | 41 | 23 |
| Thornton, Travis, Coppin State | 4 | 5 | 5.63 | 13 | 0 | 70 | 94 | 36 | 46 |
| Davis, Rodney, Beth.-Cook. | 5 | 4 | 5.85 | 14 | 1 | 80 | 87 | 44 | 58 |

## MIDWESTERN COLLEGIATE CONFERENCE

| | Conference | | Overall | |
|---|---|---|---|---|
| | W | L | W | L |
| Butler | 14 | 7 | 26 | 21 |
| Wisconsin-Milwaukee | 13 | 8 | 23 | 26 |
| Illinois-Chicago | 12 | 10 | 23 | 26 |
| *Northern Illinois | 12 | 10 | 27 | 30 |
| Detroit | 12 | 10 | 22 | 18 |
| Wright State | 10 | 12 | 20 | 28 |
| Cleveland State | 4 | 20 | 15 | 37 |

**ALL-CONFERENCE TEAM: C**—Justin Beasley, So., Butler. **1B**—Jak Kraus, Sr., Wisconsin-Milwaukee. **2B**—Phil Long, Sr., Wright State. **3B**—Matt Buczkowski, Sr., Butler. **SS**—Jason Wesemann, Sr., Wisconsin-Milwaukee. **OF**—Gerad Gast, Sr., Northern Illinois; Gerry Naughton, Sr., Illinois-Chicago; Michael Pesci, Jr., Detroit. **DH**—Clint McKoon, Sr., Cleveland State. **UT**—Chris Wallace, So., Wright State. **P**—Brandon Allen, Sr., Illinois-Chicago; Brandon Leese, Jr., Butler.
**Player of the Year**—Justin Beasley, Butler. **Pitcher of the Year**—Brandon Leese, Butler.

### INDIVIDUAL BATTING LEADERS
(Minimum 100 At-Bats)

| | AVG | AB | R | H | 2B | 3B | HR | RBI | SB |
|---|---|---|---|---|---|---|---|---|---|
| Ratliff, John, Wright State | .380 | 150 | 32 | 57 | 12 | 2 | 6 | 40 | 0 |
| Beasley, Justin, Butler | .379 | 153 | 36 | 58 | 8 | 9 | 6 | 41 | 11 |
| Wesemann, Jason, Wis.-Mil. | .365 | 192 | 51 | 70 | 17 | 0 | 8 | 37 | 10 |
| Kraus, Jak, Wisc.-Milwaukee | .364 | 151 | 48 | 55 | 15 | 3 | 10 | 48 | 12 |

---

| | AVG | AB | R | H | 2B | 3B | HR | RBI | SB |
|---|---|---|---|---|---|---|---|---|---|
| Gundry, Ed, Detroit | .362 | 152 | 25 | 55 | 13 | 1 | 6 | 39 | 2 |
| Gast, Gerad, No. Illinois | .360 | 189 | 41 | 68 | 14 | 0 | 0 | 22 | 16 |
| Wolsonovich, Mike, Cleve. St. | .357 | 140 | 27 | 50 | 10 | 1 | 8 | 33 | 5 |
| Long, Phil, Wright State | .354 | 161 | 40 | 57 | 10 | 4 | 2 | 35 | 4 |
| Tyree, Ryan, Wright State | .352 | 128 | 23 | 45 | 11 | 1 | 5 | 33 | 4 |
| Buczkowski, Matt, Butler | .343 | 137 | 24 | 47 | 15 | 1 | 6 | 33 | 8 |
| Holmes, J.C., No. Illinois | .340 | 159 | 31 | 54 | 7 | 1 | 3 | 38 | 9 |
| McKoon, Clint, Cleve. State | .339 | 171 | 45 | 58 | 12 | 2 | 11 | 38 | 5 |
| Aspeslet, Preston, Cleve. St. | .339 | 115 | 22 | 39 | 10 | 0 | 3 | 20 | 12 |
| Butcher, Ryan, No. Illinois | .333 | 159 | 32 | 53 | 14 | 1 | 6 | 38 | 2 |
| Kravarik, John, Ill.-Chicago | .331 | 175 | 39 | 58 | 18 | 4 | 5 | 48 | 13 |
| Zaun, Brian, Butler | .324 | 173 | 40 | 56 | 8 | 3 | 7 | 33 | 16 |
| Roberts, Robin, Detroit | .324 | 148 | 25 | 48 | 9 | 3 | 6 | 39 | 1 |
| #Wellbaum, Leyton, Butler | .305 | 141 | 39 | 43 | 11 | 1 | 3 | 20 | 26 |
| #Welsh, Eric, No. Illinois | .264 | 178 | 38 | 47 | 8 | 1 | 11 | 43 | 2 |

### INDIVIDUAL PITCHING LEADERS
(Minimum 40 Innings)

| | W | L | ERA | G | SV | IP | H | BB | SO |
|---|---|---|---|---|---|---|---|---|---|
| Allen, Brandon, Ill.-Chicago | 7 | 2 | 2.22 | 15 | 1 | 65 | 52 | 26 | 62 |
| Harber, Ryan, Butler | 4 | 2 | 2.80 | 12 | 0 | 61 | 58 | 19 | 54 |
| Szymborski, Tom, Ill.-Chicago | 5 | 3 | 2.82 | 14 | 0 | 70 | 57 | 21 | 85 |
| Sanford, Casey, Wright State | 3 | 3 | 3.25 | 9 | 0 | 44 | 48 | 11 | 28 |
| #Roman, Rob, Detroit | 2 | 4 | 3.38 | 16 | 8 | 32 | 33 | 16 | 21 |
| Leese, Brandon, Butler | 9 | 3 | 3.49 | 12 | 0 | 70 | 58 | 45 | 79 |
| Guler, Jeremy, Butler | 2 | 5 | 3.61 | 12 | 2 | 47 | 53 | 15 | 25 |
| Mroz, Gary, Detroit | 4 | 3 | 3.70 | 9 | 0 | 58 | 71 | 19 | 42 |
| Susalla, Dave, Detroit | 3 | 2 | 3.73 | 8 | 0 | 41 | 48 | 9 | 26 |
| Ellis, Corey, Wright State | 4 | 4 | 3.76 | 14 | 1 | 79 | 79 | 29 | 40 |
| Papp, Corey, Ill.-Chicago | 3 | 1 | 3.92 | 15 | 0 | 41 | 46 | 17 | 30 |
| Stringer, Justin, No. Illinois | 2 | 6 | 3.97 | 21 | 2 | 57 | 61 | 31 | 53 |

## MISSOURI VALLEY CONFERENCE

| | Conference | | Overall | |
|---|---|---|---|---|
| | W | L | W | L |
| **Wichita State** | 24 | 4 | 54 | 11 |
| ***Southwest Missouri State** | 18 | 11 | 32 | 25 |
| Southern Illinois | 18 | 12 | 29 | 26 |
| Evansville | 14 | 13 | 31 | 24 |
| Bradley | 14 | 16 | 40 | 22 |
| Northern Iowa | 13 | 19 | 26 | 32 |
| Creighton | 10 | 16 | 19 | 31 |
| Indiana State | 10 | 19 | 22 | 31 |
| Illinois State | 10 | 21 | 19 | 34 |

**ALL-CONFERENCE TEAM: C**—Nathan Reese, Jr., Wichita State. **1B**—Aaron Jones, Jr., Southern Illinois. **2B**—Ryan Brownlee, Jr., Evansville. **3B**—Casey Blake, Sr., Wichita State. **SS**—Jamey Carroll, Sr., Evansville. **OF**—Dan Kneeshaw, Sr., Southwest Missouri State; Dan Olson, Jr., Indiana State; Travis Wyckoff, Sr., Wichita State. **DH**—Kevin Frederick, So., Creighton. **UT**—Ben Thomas, So., Wichita State. **SP**—Brad Fisher, Jr., Indiana State; Jeff Johannsen, Sr., Northern Iowa; Doug Robertson, Jr., Bradley. **RP**—Braden Looper, Jr., Wichita State; Andy Noblitt, Sr., Evansville.
**Player of the Year**—Casey Blake, Wichita State. **Pitcher of the Year**—Doug Robertson, Bradley.

### INDIVIDUAL BATTING LEADERS
(Minimum 125 At-Bats)

| | AVG | AB | R | H | 2B | 3B | HR | RBI | SB |
|---|---|---|---|---|---|---|---|---|---|
| Wyckoff, Travis, Wichita St. | .400 | 235 | 90 | 94 | 29 | 2 | 3 | 68 | 25 |
| Olson, Dan, Indiana State | .399 | 188 | 52 | 75 | 15 | 4 | 9 | 46 | 9 |
| Carroll, Jamey, Evansville | .394 | 221 | 54 | 87 | 13 | 5 | 1 | 49 | 34 |
| Brownlee, Ryan, Evansville | .391 | 230 | 63 | 90 | 15 | 6 | 2 | 28 | 31 |
| Jones, Aaron, So. Illinois | .380 | 208 | 43 | 79 | 19 | 0 | 8 | 63 | 1 |
| Schaffer, Jacob, Bradley | .380 | 245 | 71 | 93 | 28 | 2 | 10 | 57 | 10 |
| Blake, Casey, Wichita State | .360 | 247 | 79 | 89 | 21 | 2 | 22 | 101 | 19 |
| Burkhart, Lance, SW Mo. | .358 | 229 | 52 | 82 | 19 | 1 | 18 | 64 | 5 |
| Kennedy, Brad, SW Missouri | .355 | 228 | 52 | 81 | 12 | 7 | 15 | 50 | 12 |
| Kneeshaw, Dan, SW Mo. | .354 | 237 | 64 | 84 | 13 | 3 | 11 | 49 | 9 |
| Russell, Mike, So. Illinois | .351 | 211 | 41 | 74 | 16 | 1 | 8 | 48 | 1 |
| Pembroke, Aaron, Evansville | .348 | 221 | 62 | 77 | 14 | 1 | 4 | 45 | 31 |
| Zywica, Mike, Evansville | .348 | 201 | 47 | 70 | 12 | 3 | 11 | 45 | 25 |
| Hodges, Bobby, Evansville | .347 | 190 | 35 | 66 | 16 | 0 | 2 | 33 | 16 |
| Frederick, Kevin, Creighton | .347 | 173 | 33 | 60 | 13 | 2 | 8 | 44 | 3 |
| Correa, Nelson, Bradley | .346 | 127 | 25 | 44 | 12 | 1 | 4 | 39 | 0 |
| Jergenson, Brian, No. Iowa | .343 | 178 | 27 | 61 | 8 | 2 | 7 | 40 | 7 |
| Stine, Jerry, Wichita State | .340 | 235 | 52 | 80 | 22 | 0 | 7 | 57 | 17 |
| Reese, Nathan, Wichita State | .340 | 159 | 23 | 54 | 9 | 0 | 5 | 33 | 0 |
| Hairston, Jerry, So. Illinois | .340 | 215 | 49 | 73 | 18 | 1 | 5 | 37 | 5 |
| Hart, Jason, SW Missouri | .338 | 237 | 54 | 80 | 20 | 1 | 15 | 52 | 1 |
| McCullough, Adam, Wichita St. | .337 | 255 | 56 | 86 | 15 | 0 | 8 | 55 | 5 |

| | AVG | AB | R | H | 2B | 3B | HR | RBI | SB |
|---|---|---|---|---|---|---|---|---|---|
| Musachio, John, Bradley | .333 | 180 | 54 | 60 | 25 | 0 | 5 | 47 | 7 |
| Mansavage, Jay, So. Illinois | .332 | 211 | 43 | 70 | 14 | 3 | 11 | 37 | 10 |
| Griak, Charlie, Bradley | .331 | 127 | 15 | 42 | 12 | 2 | 4 | 26 | 3 |
| Barrett, Ryan, Evansville | .330 | 194 | 32 | 64 | 18 | 1 | 1 | 51 | 6 |
| McCabe, Mike, Creighton | .328 | 186 | 33 | 61 | 12 | 4 | 8 | 37 | 5 |
| Thompson, Tyler, Indiana St. | .328 | 195 | 51 | 64 | 18 | 2 | 4 | 36 | 22 |
| Rocksvold, Andy, No. Iowa | .326 | 172 | 40 | 56 | 12 | 3 | 1 | 27 | 11 |
| Holst, Micah, SW Missouri | .325 | 200 | 48 | 65 | 9 | 3 | 8 | 42 | 6 |
| Saalfrank, Chad, Bradley | .322 | 236 | 56 | 76 | 14 | 3 | 8 | 43 | 21 |
| #Young, Randy, Wichita St. | .295 | 271 | 86 | 80 | 11 | **7** | 4 | 36 | **68** |

### INDIVIDUAL PITCHING LEADERS
(Minimum 50 Innings)

| | W | L | ERA | G | SV | IP | H | BB | SO |
|---|---|---|---|---|---|---|---|---|---|
| Looper, Braden, Wichita State | 4 | 1 | **2.09** | 26 | **12** | 56 | 37 | 15 | 64 |
| Thomas, Ben, Wichita State | 9 | 1 | 2.56 | 11 | 0 | 53 | 46 | 19 | 49 |
| Robertson, Doug, Bradley | **12** | 3 | 3.06 | 16 | 0 | 115 | 113 | 14 | 93 |
| Behrens, Brett, Bradley | 3 | 0 | 3.20 | 13 | 0 | 56 | 55 | 13 | 35 |
| McMahon, Kevin, Illinois State | 3 | 3 | 3.33 | 9 | 0 | 54 | 62 | 14 | 36 |
| Wyckoff, Travis, Wichita State | 5 | 0 | 3.38 | 23 | 6 | 59 | 55 | 17 | 56 |
| Lusk, Corey, Bradley | 6 | 1 | 3.59 | 12 | 0 | 68 | 70 | 38 | 67 |
| Foral, Steve, Wichita State | 11 | 1 | 3.63 | 18 | 0 | 92 | 87 | 32 | 79 |
| Baird, Brandon, Wichita State | 7 | 6 | 3.74 | 19 | 0 | 101 | 112 | 39 | **94** |
| Ritter, Kyle, Evansville | 7 | 2 | 3.90 | 14 | 0 | 88 | 91 | 27 | 62 |
| Bluma, Marc, Wichita State | 5 | 1 | 4.03 | 23 | 4 | 51 | 51 | 16 | 58 |
| Sterling, Christian, Creighton | 4 | 6 | 4.03 | 14 | 0 | 83 | 71 | 52 | 83 |
| Hattan, Tony, So. Illinois | 6 | 5 | 4.30 | 18 | 1 | 99 | 111 | 30 | 62 |
| Johannsen, Jeff, No. Iowa | 9 | 4 | 4.44 | 16 | 0 | 101 | 96 | 51 | **94** |
| Piazza, David, So. Illinois | 5 | 3 | 4.48 | 16 | 1 | 70 | 88 | 26 | 49 |
| Beck, Matt, Bradley | 6 | 8 | 4.55 | 16 | 0 | 93 | 109 | 25 | 66 |
| Klipowicz, Scott, Evansville | 5 | 4 | 4.58 | 13 | 0 | 77 | 87 | 35 | 52 |
| Finken, Brad, Indiana State | 8 | 4 | 4.82 | 17 | 0 | 93 | 103 | 33 | 68 |

## NORTH ATLANTIC CONFERENCE

| | Conference | | Overall | |
|---|---|---|---|---|
| | W | L | W | L |
| *Delaware | 19 | 5 | 44 | 12 |
| Maine | 12 | 8 | 19 | 36 |
| Drexel | 12 | 8 | 28 | 20 |
| Hofstra | 12 | 12 | 25 | 24 |
| Northeastern | 11 | 11 | 18 | 26 |
| Hartford | 10 | 14 | 18 | 30 |
| Vermont | 8 | 12 | 12 | 21 |
| Towson State | 8 | 14 | 17 | 29 |
| New Hampshire | 8 | 16 | 19 | 28 |

**ALL-CONFERENCE TEAM: C**—Lou Marchetti, Fr., Drexel. **1B**—Tim Mahony, Jr., Delaware. **2B**—Dan Colunio, Jr., Delaware. **3B**—Brian August, Jr., Delaware. **SS**—Dan Hammer, Sr., Delaware. **OF**—Ethan Barlow, Sr., Vermont; Kris Doiron, Sr., Drexel; Ethan Jack, Sr., Delaware. **DH**—James Vallillo, Sr., Towson State. **P**—Justin Romano, Sr., Hofstra; Matt Phillips, So., Delaware.

**Player of the Year**—James Vallillo, Towson State. **Pitcher of the Year**—Justin Romano, Hofstra.

### INDIVIDUAL BATTING LEADERS
(Minimum 100 At-Bats)

| | AVG | AB | R | H | 2B | 3B | HR | RBI | SB |
|---|---|---|---|---|---|---|---|---|---|
| Fleming, Mike, Towson St. | .398 | 123 | 18 | 49 | 11 | 1 | 3 | 18 | 0 |
| Snyder, Earl, Hartford | .391 | 169 | 47 | 66 | 14 | 0 | **15** | 58 | 5 |
| Vallillo, James, Towson St. | .389 | 167 | 39 | 65 | 11 | 1 | 14 | 49 | 5 |
| Hammer, Dan, Delaware | .389 | 211 | 74 | 82 | 20 | 2 | 10 | 68 | 11 |
| Eyman, Brad, Delaware | .387 | 186 | 49 | 72 | 17 | 1 | 7 | 47 | 5 |
| August, Brian, Delaware | .382 | 207 | 57 | 79 | **21** | 2 | 12 | **72** | 9 |
| Ardizzone, Matt, Delaware | .380 | 216 | 59 | **82** | 20 | 3 | 5 | 38 | 12 |
| O'Rourke, Keith, Hofstra | .375 | 128 | 24 | 48 | 8 | 0 | 6 | 44 | 0 |
| Doiron, Kris, Drexel | .374 | 163 | 33 | 61 | 9 | 0 | 5 | 48 | 2 |
| Friel, Pat, Hofstra | .364 | 107 | 28 | 39 | 5 | 2 | 1 | 23 | 0 |
| Colunio, Dan, Delaware | .348 | 230 | 78 | 80 | 21 | 2 | 3 | 42 | **24** |
| Tober, Dave, Hartford | .347 | 167 | 34 | 58 | 13 | 0 | 9 | 30 | 1 |
| McSherry, Jamie, Delaware | .341 | 129 | 33 | 44 | 11 | 0 | 0 | 22 | 0 |
| #Mahony, Tim, Delaware | .325 | 163 | 36 | 53 | 15 | 3 | **15** | 45 | 3 |
| #Valentine, Anthony, N. H. | .320 | 172 | 38 | 55 | 6 | 5 | 0 | 34 | 14 |

### INDIVIDUAL PITCHING LEADERS
(Minimum 40 Innings)

| | W | L | ERA | G | SV | IP | H | BB | SO |
|---|---|---|---|---|---|---|---|---|---|
| Gellert, Scott, Delaware | 5 | 1 | **2.45** | 16 | 7 | 59 | 54 | 14 | 41 |
| Phillips, Matt, Delaware | 7 | 1 | 2.82 | 10 | 0 | 54 | 55 | 24 | 50 |
| Lamanteer, Adam, Delaware | 6 | 3 | 2.82 | 12 | 0 | 83 | 76 | 25 | 49 |
| Ennico, Chris, Northeastern | 3 | 6 | 2.91 | 9 | 0 | 59 | 45 | 24 | 54 |
| Zack, Chris, Northeastern | 5 | 3 | 2.95 | 9 | 0 | 55 | 56 | 13 | 29 |
| Forneiro, John, Northeastern | 3 | 7 | 3.00 | 10 | 0 | 66 | 42 | 53 | 58 |
| Mayo, Erik, New Hampshire | 3 | 6 | 3.14 | 12 | 0 | 72 | 61 | 13 | 51 |
| Romano, Justin, Hofstra | **9** | 2 | 3.23 | 12 | 0 | 75 | 68 | 31 | **60** |
| Lynde, Jerry, Vermont | 2 | 3 | 3.31 | 10 | 0 | 54 | 43 | 15 | 45 |
| Chungu, Charlie, New Hamp. | 2 | 4 | 3.34 | 10 | 1 | 57 | 52 | 35 | 50 |
| Berger, Craig, Delaware | 6 | 1 | 3.44 | 12 | 1 | 65 | 51 | 21 | 33 |
| #Moore, Eric, Drexel | **9** | 2 | 4.71 | 19 | 0 | 63 | 75 | 16 | 35 |
| #Quinn, Garrett, Maine | 2 | 4 | 5.07 | 26 | **9** | 55 | 60 | 23 | 35 |

## NORTHEAST CONFERENCE

| | Conference | | Overall | |
|---|---|---|---|---|
| | W | L | W | L |
| *Rider | 15 | 6 | 28 | 22 |
| Monmouth | 15 | 6 | 25 | 22 |
| St. Francis | 12 | 8 | 21 | 20 |
| Long Island | 12 | 9 | 22 | 19 |
| Fairleigh Dickinson | 9 | 12 | 16 | 23 |
| Wagner | 8 | 12 | 14 | 24 |
| Marist | 8 | 13 | 16 | 24 |
| Mount St. Mary's | 4 | 17 | 6 | 24 |

**ALL-CONFERENCE TEAM: C**—Keith Montelbano, Jr., Fairleigh Dickinson. **1B**—Jon Manuelian, Sr., Long Island. **2B**—Nick DelGozzo, So., Monmouth. **3B**—Ryan Pandolfini, So., Rider. **SS**—George West, So., Monmouth. **OF**—Dan Conroy, Sr., Fairleigh Dickinson; Levi Miskolczi, Jr., Rider; Chris Novelli, Jr., Long Island. **DH**—Jason Irizarry, Sr., Fairleigh Dickinson. **P**—Joe Aragona, So., Monmouth; Mark Ciccarelli, Jr., Marist; Mike Liloia, Sr., Monmouth.

**Player of the Year**—Ryan Pandolfini, Rider. **Pitcher of the Year**—Joe Aragona, Monmouth.

### INDIVIDUAL BATTING LEADERS
(Minimum 100 At-Bats)

| | AVG | AB | R | H | 2B | 3B | HR | RBI | SB |
|---|---|---|---|---|---|---|---|---|---|
| DelGozzo, Nick, Monmouth | .376 | 157 | 45 | 59 | 13 | 1 | 1 | 25 | 8 |
| Novelli, Chris, Long Island | .372 | 148 | 43 | 55 | 10 | **6** | 4 | 27 | 13 |
| Montelbano, Kevin, FDU | .366 | 142 | 41 | 52 | 20 | 2 | **8** | 41 | 0 |
| Larrick, Chris, Mt. St. Mary's | .364 | 107 | 20 | 39 | 8 | 1 | 3 | 19 | 1 |
| Reina, Joe, Long Island | .362 | 127 | 26 | 46 | 6 | 3 | 4 | 33 | 8 |
| Conroy, Dan, FDU | .361 | 147 | 40 | 53 | 10 | 1 | 3 | 17 | 5 |
| Pandolfini, Ryan, Rider | .358 | 187 | 44 | **67** | 19 | 5 | 8 | **43** | 8 |
| Miskolczi, Levi, Rider | .355 | 183 | **48** | 65 | 11 | 1 | 8 | 37 | 16 |
| Williams, Rob, St. Francis | .352 | 117 | 20 | 41 | 9 | 0 | 1 | 19 | 3 |
| McCullough, Joe, Monmouth | .341 | 170 | 40 | 58 | 12 | 3 | 4 | 42 | **20** |
| DeStefano, Peter, Wagner | .339 | 109 | 21 | 37 | 5 | 0 | 2 | 20 | 2 |
| Dansky, Mike, Long Island | .338 | 148 | 26 | 50 | 18 | 1 | 3 | 29 | 6 |

### INDIVIDUAL PITCHING LEADERS
(Minimum 40 Innings)

| | W | L | ERA | G | SV | IP | H | BB | SO |
|---|---|---|---|---|---|---|---|---|---|
| Pesce, Donato, Long Island | 1 | 1 | **2.60** | 12 | 1 | 52 | 38 | 32 | 48 |
| McConnell, Chris, St. Francis | 3 | 4 | 2.73 | 10 | 0 | 59 | 53 | 14 | 48 |
| Lenko, Jared, Rider | 6 | 3 | 2.94 | 15 | **4** | 64 | 57 | 19 | 35 |
| Aragona, Joe, Monmouth | 7 | 2 | 3.00 | 11 | 0 | 69 | 48 | 47 | 58 |
| Rawa, Anthony, Rider | 6 | 1 | 3.35 | 12 | 0 | 51 | 55 | 21 | 26 |
| Gordon, Jim, Rider | 4 | 3 | 3.36 | 11 | 0 | 59 | 56 | 23 | 35 |
| Ciccarelli, Mark, Marist | 6 | 4 | 3.39 | 12 | 0 | 65 | 60 | 20 | **70** |
| Liloia, Mike, Monmouth | 6 | 5 | 3.39 | 12 | 1 | 77 | 64 | 37 | 67 |
| Doyle, Joe, Wagner | 2 | 6 | 3.98 | 11 | 1 | 63 | 69 | 24 | 33 |
| Giordano, James, St. Francis | 5 | 3 | 4.05 | 11 | 0 | 60 | 56 | 26 | 31 |

## OHIO VALLEY CONFERENCE

| | Conference | | Overall | |
|---|---|---|---|---|
| | W | L | W | L |
| *Austin Peay State | 13 | 7 | 44 | 22 |
| Middle Tennessee State | 13 | 7 | 28 | 26 |
| Tennessee Tech | 12 | 8 | 28 | 29 |
| Southeast Missouri State | 11 | 8 | 25 | 23 |
| Morehead State | 10 | 10 | 29 | 29 |
| Eastern Kentucky | 10 | 11 | 21 | 32 |
| Murray State | 6 | 14 | 20 | 31 |
| Tennessee-Martin | 5 | 15 | 14 | 30 |

**ALL-CONFERENCE TEAM: C**—Ryan Bennett, Sr., Austin Peay. **1B**—Jason Combs, Sr., Eastern Kentucky. **2B**—Josh Cox, So., Morehead State. **3B**—Nate Manning, Sr., Austin Peay. **SS**—Chuck Abbott, Jr., Austin Peay. **OF**—Jeremy Bonczynski, Jr., Tennessee Tech; Josh Williams, Jr., Eastern Kentucky; Jeff Matukewicz, Jr., Tennessee Tech. **DH**—Dave Sloan, So., Austin Peay. **Util**—Tom Breuer, Sr., Southeast Missouri. **P**—Craig Smith, Jr., Austin Peay; Michael Blount, So., Tennessee-Martin; Jason

Stanton, Sr., Middle Tennessee.
**Player of the Year**—Nate Manning, Austin Peay. **Pitcher of the Year**—Craig Smith, Austin Peay.

## INDIVIDUAL BATTING LEADERS
(Minimum 100 At-Bats)

| | AVG | AB | R | H | 2B | 3B | HR | RBI | SB |
|---|---|---|---|---|---|---|---|---|---|
| Bennett, Ryan, Austin Peay .. | .407 | 243 | 50 | 99 | 29 | 0 | 5 | 58 | 10 |
| Manning, Nate, Austin Peay.. | .394 | 254 | 70 | 100 | 26 | 4 | 19 | 81 | 18 |
| Cox, Josh, Morehead St........ | .393 | 201 | 47 | 79 | 13 | 3 | 8 | 41 | 3 |
| Bonczynski, Jeremy, Tenn. T. . | .385 | 182 | 48 | 70 | 15 | 2 | 12 | 48 | 2 |
| Abbott, Chuck, Austin Peay.... | .369 | 263 | 66 | 97 | 23 | 4 | 4 | 33 | 22 |
| Curran, Rusty, SE Mo. .......... | .358 | 179 | 43 | 64 | 10 | 2 | 0 | 25 | 1 |
| Milan, Brian, Morehead St..... | .352 | 210 | 49 | 74 | 15 | 2 | 3 | 22 | 5 |
| Combs, Jason, E. Kentucky .. | .351 | 185 | 27 | 65 | 10 | 0 | 7 | 31 | 7 |
| Mullins, Craig, Tenn. Tech ... | .351 | 205 | 44 | 72 | 22 | 0 | 2 | 33 | 8 |
| Oda, Daisuke, Tenn.-Martin .. | .346 | 159 | 26 | 55 | 14 | 1 | 7 | 28 | 0 |
| Maiser, Brock, Austin Peay ... | .343 | 236 | 43 | 81 | 16 | 1 | 8 | 48 | 6 |
| Allison, Brad, Morehead St.... | .342 | 190 | 35 | 65 | 22 | 0 | 10 | 48 | 2 |
| Sloan, Dave, Austin Peay...... | .341 | 223 | 49 | 76 | 13 | 2 | 13 | 53 | 1 |
| Quire, Jeremy, Murray St. ..... | .340 | 197 | 40 | 67 | 17 | 3 | 5 | 35 | 6 |
| Snellgrove, Clay. Mid. Tenn.. | .335 | 206 | 28 | 69 | 17 | 0 | 2 | 30 | 9 |
| Stoops, Russell, Tenn. Tech . | .332 | 187 | 30 | 62 | 7 | 1 | 5 | 33 | 4 |
| #Barner, Doug, Mid. Tenn..... | .315 | 178 | 43 | 56 | 12 | 0 | 19 | 53 | 2 |
| #Doyle, Eddie, Murray State . | .301 | 146 | 28 | 44 | 12 | 6 | 2 | 28 | 2 |
| #Brown, Kent, Austin Peay..... | .298 | 225 | 41 | 67 | 12 | 3 | 1 | 20 | 22 |
| #Zimmerman, Benji, Aus. Peay.. | .287 | 202 | 36 | 58 | 12 | 6 | 5 | 42 | 16 |

## INDIVIDUAL PITCHING LEADERS
(Minimum 40 Innings)

| | W | L | ERA | G | SV | IP | H | BB | SO |
|---|---|---|---|---|---|---|---|---|---|
| Witten, Joe, E. Kentucky ........... | 0 | 1 | 2.73 | 26 | 8 | 33 | 37 | 14 | 19 |
| Smith, Craig, Austin Peay ........ | 10 | 6 | 2.94 | 23 | 0 | 104 | 78 | 47 | 84 |
| Early, Brian, Mid. Tenn.............. | 5 | 3 | 3.13 | 14 | 0 | 72 | 60 | 25 | 52 |
| Blount, Michael, Tenn.-Martin .... | 5 | 6 | 3.21 | 12 | 0 | 67 | 67 | 25 | 42 |
| Stanton, Jason, Mid. Tenn. ........ | 7 | 2 | 3.28 | 15 | 0 | 74 | 82 | 17 | 50 |
| Longhurst, Glen, Austin Peay ... | 4 | 2 | 3.61 | 29 | 2 | 57 | 59 | 22 | 35 |
| Gallagher, Keith, Murray State... | 6 | 4 | 3.68 | 16 | 0 | 81 | 84 | 39 | 71 |
| Young, Troy, Morehead St......... | 6 | 4 | 3.69 | 28 | 2 | 76 | 83 | 27 | 41 |
| Hill, Jamie, Mid. Tenn................ | 3 | 5 | 3.77 | 12 | 0 | 57 | 53 | 28 | 51 |
| Eikenberry, Mike, Aus. Peay.... | 11 | 4 | 3.90 | 21 | 0 | 113 | 89 | 57 | 71 |
| Hedrick, Keith, Tenn. Tech........ | 5 | 6 | 3.90 | 16 | 1 | 88 | 106 | 31 | 92 |
| Sabel, Erik, Tenn. Tech............. | 7 | 5 | 4.09 | 18 | 2 | 94 | 94 | 27 | 70 |
| Kirby, Chad, Mid. Tenn. ............ | 4 | 4 | 4.09 | 18 | 1 | 51 | 50 | 12 | 47 |

# PACIFIC-10 CONFERENCE

| | Conference | | Overall | |
|---|---|---|---|---|
| **NORTH** | **W** | **L** | **W** | **L** |
| Washington | 16 | 8 | 30 | 28 |
| Oregon State | 14 | 10 | 32 | 16 |
| Washington State | 12 | 12 | 26 | 35 |
| Portland State | 6 | 18 | 14 | 37 |

**ALL-CONFERENCE TEAM: C**—David Schmidt, Jr., Oregon State. **1B**—Ryan Soules, So., Washington. **2B**—Ryan McDonald, Jr., Oregon State. **3B**—Matt Dorey, Sr., Portland State; Ryan Lipe, So., Oregon State. **SS**—Brandon Hageman, Sr., Oregon State; Kevin Miller, Fr., Washington. **OF**—Jim Horner, Sr., Washington State; Chris Magruder, Fr., Washington; Chris Wakeland, Sr., Oregon State. **DH**—Christian Shewey, Sr., Washington. **Util**—Jered Fowler, Sr., Washington State. **P**—Todd Belitz, So., Washington State; Eric Lovinger, Sr., Oregon State; Cody Morrison, So., Washington; Chris Pine, Fr., Oregon State; Matt Smith, Sr., Washington.
**Player of the Year**—Kevin Miller, Washington.

## INDIVIDUAL BATTING LEADERS
(Minimum 100 At-Bats)

| | AVG | AB | R | H | 2B | 3B | HR | RBI | SB |
|---|---|---|---|---|---|---|---|---|---|
| Wakeland, Chris, Oregon St....... | .368 | 182 | 51 | 67 | 17 | 3 | 9 | 49 | 6 |
| McDonald, Ryan, Oregon St. .. | .353 | 201 | 47 | 71 | 11 | 1 | 1 | 34 | 7 |
| Hageman, Brandon, Oregon St. .. | .348 | 178 | 25 | 62 | 6 | 1 | 0 | 26 | 4 |
| Leone, Mike, Oregon State ... | .338 | 160 | 32 | 54 | 15 | 1 | 4 | 39 | 1 |
| Horner, Jim, Wash. State ....... | .332 | 208 | 54 | 69 | 15 | 2 | 9 | 44 | 17 |
| Solomon, Ty, Wash. State...... | .330 | 103 | 25 | 34 | 6 | 3 | 2 | 16 | 3 |
| Lipe, Ryan, Oregon State....... | .324 | 139 | 39 | 45 | 6 | 1 | 4 | 34 | 8 |
| Schmidt, David, Oregon State .. | .321 | 162 | 41 | 52 | 11 | 1 | 12 | 47 | 0 |
| Marbut, Don, Portland State.. | .320 | 200 | 35 | 64 | 12 | 2 | 6 | 25 | 3 |
| Bundy, Ryan, Washington...... | .319 | 135 | 19 | 43 | 3 | 1 | 0 | 19 | 7 |
| Shewey, Christian, Wash....... | .317 | 123 | 21 | 39 | 12 | 0 | 2 | 28 | 3 |
| Schetzsle, Graham, Port. St.. | .316 | 190 | 31 | 60 | 8 | 0 | 5 | 32 | 0 |
| Magruder, Chris, Wash. ........ | .316 | 209 | 46 | 66 | 12 | 6 | 7 | 45 | 18 |
| Miller, Kevin, Washington...... | .313 | 214 | 46 | 67 | 10 | 3 | 6 | 36 | 8 |
| Fowler, Jered, Wash. State.... | .309 | 175 | 38 | 54 | 16 | 0 | 10 | 51 | 4 |
| Bowman, Mark, Wash. State.. | .308 | 104 | 19 | 32 | 5 | 1 | 3 | 23 | 1 |
| Wetmore, Mike, Wash. State.. | .307 | 228 | 49 | 70 | 14 | 4 | 7 | 33 | 32 |

**Stanford Standout.** Catcher A.J. Hinch enjoyed an excellent senior season for the Cardinal, hitting .381 with 11 homers.

| | AVG | AB | R | H | 2B | 3B | HR | RBI | SB |
|---|---|---|---|---|---|---|---|---|---|
| Soules, Ryan, Washington.... | .307 | 202 | 35 | 62 | 9 | 1 | 5 | 39 | 5 |

## INDIVIDUAL PITCHING LEADERS
(Minimum 40 Innings)

| | W | L | ERA | G | SV | IP | H | BB | SO |
|---|---|---|---|---|---|---|---|---|---|
| Pine, Chris, Oregon State ......... | 4 | 3 | 2.77 | 12 | 0 | 55 | 37 | 38 | 49 |
| Smith, Matt, Washington............ | 6 | 2 | 2.82 | 15 | 0 | 73 | 56 | 43 | 61 |
| Checketts, Andrew, Oregon St... | 6 | 2 | 3.47 | 12 | 1 | 73 | 72 | 27 | 61 |
| Smith, Jimmy, Port. State........... | 4 | 4 | 3.61 | 27 | 5 | 42 | 44 | 16 | 24 |
| Lovinger, Eric, Oregon State...... | 9 | 2 | 3.83 | 14 | 0 | 83 | 86 | 10 | 57 |
| Ramsay, Rob, Washington St.... | 2 | 7 | 3.93 | 14 | 0 | 94 | 78 | 60 | 94 |
| Harris, Ryan, Washington .......... | 4 | 3 | 4.01 | 19 | 1 | 43 | 44 | 23 | 28 |
| Kringen, Jake, Washington ....... | 4 | 7 | 4.78 | 16 | 0 | 85 | 105 | 34 | 89 |
| Percell, Brody, Oregon State ..... | 2 | 1 | 4.93 | 10 | 0 | 46 | 56 | 13 | 16 |
| Burkeen, Ryan, Portland St....... | 1 | 3 | 5.04 | 11 | 0 | 45 | 51 | 19 | 33 |
| #Morrison, Cody, Washington.... | 3 | 1 | 5.40 | 23 | 9 | 25 | 22 | 18 | 21 |

| | Conference | | Overall | |
|---|---|---|---|---|
| **SOUTH** | **W** | **L** | **W** | **L** |
| ***Southern California** | 24 | 6 | 44 | 16 |
| **Stanford** | 19 | 11 | 41 | 19 |
| UCLA | 16 | 14 | 36 | 28 |
| Arizona State | 14 | 16 | 35 | 21 |
| California | 10 | 20 | 27 | 29 |
| Arizona | 7 | 23 | 24 | 32 |

**ALL-CONFERENCE TEAM: C**—Tim DeCinces, Jr., UCLA; A.J. Hinch, Sr., Stanford; Chad Moeller, Jr., Southern California. **1B**—Greg Walbridge, Jr., Southern California. **2B**—Brian Dallimore, Sr., Stanford; Robbie Kent, Sr., Arizona State; John Powers, Sr., Arizona. **3B**—Troy Glaus, So., UCLA. **SS**—Dan Cey, Jr., California. **OF**—Jeff Inglin, Jr., Southern California; Jacque Jones, Jr., Southern California; Joe Kilburg, So., Stanford. **DH**—Jonathan Petke, Sr., California. **P**—Seth Etherton, So., Southern California; Randy Flores, Jr., Southern California; Jim Parque, So., UCLA; Kyle Peterson, So., Stanford.
**Player of the Year**—A.J. Hinch, Stanford. **Pitcher of the Year**—Seth Etherton, Southern California.

## INDIVIDUAL BATTING LEADERS
(Minimum 125 At-Bats)

| | AVG | AB | R | H | 2B | 3B | HR | RBI | SB |
|---|---|---|---|---|---|---|---|---|---|
| Powers, John, Arizona ......... | .393 | 229 | 47 | 90 | 18 | 8 | 4 | 37 | 9 |
| Inglin, Jeff, USC .................. | .392 | 222 | 56 | 87 | 15 | 2 | 14 | 72 | 11 |
| McKinley, Dan, Arizona St..... | .386 | 254 | 73 | 98 | 17 | 3 | 9 | 57 | 12 |

| Name | AVG | AB | R | H | 2B | 3B | HR | RBI | SB |
|---|---|---|---|---|---|---|---|---|---|
| Walbridge, Greg, USC | .385 | 205 | 62 | 79 | 14 | 1 | 8 | 45 | 4 |
| Hinch, A.J., Stanford | .381 | 210 | 60 | 80 | 19 | 3 | 11 | 59 | 18 |
| Moreno, Mikel, Ariz. St. | .378 | 238 | 75 | 90 | 22 | 2 | 11 | 53 | 18 |
| Cey, Dan, California | .377 | 162 | 34 | 61 | 11 | 1 | 3 | 23 | 22 |
| Cruz, Paul, USC | .376 | 170 | 38 | 64 | 5 | 1 | 4 | 34 | 8 |
| Jones, Jacque, USC | .375 | 248 | 58 | 93 | 16 | 3 | 10 | 56 | 11 |
| Gjerde, Jeff, Arizona | .364 | 225 | 48 | 82 | 16 | 6 | 8 | 65 | 4 |
| Beinbrink, Andrew, Ariz. St. | .362 | 152 | 44 | 55 | 8 | 7 | 5 | 41 | 0 |
| Quaccia, Luke, Stanford | .359 | 141 | 25 | 52 | 16 | 3 | 2 | 27 | 1 |
| Kilburg, Joe, Stanford | .358 | 243 | 65 | 87 | 10 | 3 | 5 | 45 | 23 |
| Kent, Robbie, Arizona St. | .357 | 227 | 66 | 81 | 18 | 2 | 12 | 68 | 5 |
| Corley, Kenny, Arizona | .355 | 152 | 37 | 54 | 14 | 1 | 11 | 46 | 2 |
| Stromsborg, Ryan, USC | .354 | 192 | 40 | 68 | 16 | 0 | 7 | 35 | 12 |
| Ammirato, Zak, UCLA | .354 | 161 | 45 | 57 | 15 | 3 | 6 | 42 | 6 |
| Ensberg, Morgan, USC | .354 | 161 | 37 | 57 | 9 | 2 | 10 | 35 | 8 |
| Glaus, Troy, UCLA | .352 | 216 | 65 | 76 | 17 | 1 | 16 | 50 | 12 |
| Becker, Brian, Arizona | .347 | 190 | 34 | 66 | 8 | 2 | 7 | 46 | 1 |
| DeCinces, Tim, UCLA | .341 | 232 | 66 | 79 | 16 | 0 | 18 | 67 | 6 |
| Byrnes, Eric, UCLA | .338 | 225 | 32 | 76 | 21 | 1 | 8 | 56 | 14 |
| Dallimore, Brian, Stanford | .335 | 224 | 44 | 75 | 16 | 2 | 2 | 37 | 8 |
| Oliver, Brian, California | .335 | 203 | 42 | 68 | 14 | 2 | 5 | 32 | 21 |
| McKay, Cody, Arizona St. | .335 | 221 | 55 | 74 | 13 | 1 | 9 | 47 | 1 |
| Gosewisch, Jeff, Arizona St. | .324 | 139 | 31 | 45 | 7 | 0 | 1 | 26 | 1 |
| Johnson, Gary, California | .324 | 207 | 46 | 67 | 18 | 1 | 5 | 46 | 11 |
| Rico, Diego, Arizona | .323 | 226 | 52 | 73 | 11 | 3 | 5 | 41 | 22 |
| Economos, Pete, California | .323 | 164 | 24 | 53 | 6 | 0 | 2 | 33 | 22 |
| Petke, Jonathan, California | .322 | 214 | 46 | 69 | 15 | 1 | 7 | 56 | 13 |
| Gerut, Jody, Stanford | .321 | 246 | 55 | 79 | 15 | 5 | 5 | 46 | 9 |
| Cermak, Jeff, Arizona St. | .317 | 186 | 53 | 59 | 10 | 3 | 9 | 50 | 1 |
| Torti, Mike, Arizona State | .317 | 186 | 45 | 59 | 5 | 2 | 8 | 49 | 5 |
| Theodorou, Nick, UCLA | .314 | 137 | 46 | 43 | 10 | 2 | 1 | 25 | 10 |
| Mattern, Erik, Arizona | .313 | 147 | 29 | 46 | 8 | 5 | 0 | 24 | 4 |
| Mirizzi, Marc, USC | .304 | 224 | 38 | 68 | 17 | 0 | 2 | 37 | 8 |
| Kent, Troy, Stanford | .304 | 191 | 33 | 58 | 14 | 1 | 11 | 39 | 6 |
| Moeller, Chad, USC | .301 | 206 | 38 | 62 | 12 | 2 | 3 | 35 | 8 |
| Lewis, Ivan, California | .300 | 227 | 45 | 68 | 12 | 1 | 0 | 27 | 44 |
| Heinrichs, Jon, UCLA | .296 | 250 | 55 | 74 | 13 | 5 | 3 | 40 | 21 |

## INDIVIDUAL PITCHING LEADERS
(Minimum 50 Innings)

| Name | W | L | ERA | G | SV | IP | H | BB | SO |
|---|---|---|---|---|---|---|---|---|---|
| Reimers, Tom, Stanford | 4 | 4 | 2.92 | 27 | 5 | 71 | 58 | 27 | 64 |
| Iglesias, Mario, Stanford | 10 | 1 | 3.00 | 21 | 2 | 57 | 58 | 12 | 27 |
| Henderson, Scott, USC | 8 | 1 | 3.19 | 17 | 0 | 87 | 98 | 21 | 63 |
| Flores, Randy, USC | 9 | 1 | 3.50 | 18 | 0 | 118 | 115 | 32 | 74 |
| Hutchinson, Chad, Stanford | 7 | 2 | 3.51 | 16 | 0 | 85 | 86 | 33 | 70 |
| Peterson, Kyle, Stanford | 10 | 5 | 3.71 | 17 | 0 | 112 | 105 | 41 | 96 |
| Parque, Jim, UCLA | 9 | 3 | 3.72 | 18 | 0 | 126 | 142 | 38 | 116 |
| Austin, Jeff, Stanford | 6 | 4 | 3.81 | 16 | 1 | 90 | 94 | 36 | 88 |
| Bradley, Ryan, Arizona St. | 2 | 2 | 3.88 | 34 | 3 | 58 | 63 | 21 | 51 |
| Etherton, Seth, USC | 12 | 3 | 3.94 | 17 | 0 | 112 | 103 | 34 | 104 |
| Vorhis, Jim, California | 5 | 6 | 3.99 | 19 | 0 | 86 | 95 | 23 | 20 |
| Molina, Gabe, Arizona State | 3 | 2 | 4.09 | 23 | 1 | 62 | 58 | 37 | 51 |
| #Krawczyk, Jack, USC | 4 | 1 | 4.55 | 25 | 12 | 32 | 41 | 8 | 34 |
| White, Ben, Arizona | 3 | 6 | 4.62 | 25 | 6 | 78 | 99 | 19 | 52 |
| Lowery, Phill, Arizona St. | 5 | 1 | 4.71 | 9 | 0 | 50 | 42 | 28 | 56 |
| Keller, Dan, UCLA | 7 | 3 | 4.79 | 20 | 1 | 68 | 74 | 29 | 40 |
| Zamora, Pete, UCLA | 6 | 1 | 4.89 | 14 | 0 | 74 | 87 | 25 | 46 |
| Evans, Keith, California | 4 | 7 | 4.90 | 16 | 0 | 105 | 76 | 32 | 70 |

# PATRIOT CONFERENCE

| | Conference | | Overall | |
|---|---|---|---|---|
| | W | L | W | L |
| *Bucknell | 14 | 6 | 24 | 23 |
| Lehigh | 12 | 8 | 18 | 20 |
| Navy | 11 | 9 | 24 | 28 |
| Army | 9 | 11 | 20 | 21 |
| Lafayette | 9 | 11 | 12 | 28 |
| Holy Cross | 5 | 15 | 7 | 26 |

**ALL-CONFERENCE TEAM: C**—Chad DeHart, Sr., Bucknell. **1B**—Bill Mullee, Sr., Army. **2B**—Tony Mauro, Fr., Navy; Bryan Price, So., Army. **3B**—Kevin Silverman, Sr., Bucknell. **SS**—Pete Gorski, Sr., Bucknell. **OF**—Brian Bernth, Sr., Navy; Alex Inclan, Jr., Bucknell; Heath Mathias, Sr., Bucknell. **DH**—Toph Lake, So., Navy. **P**—Tom McLemore, Jr., Navy; Mike Tomko, So., Bucknell. **RP**—John Ferri, Sr., Navy.
**Player of the Year**—Kevin Silverman, Bucknell. **Pitcher of the Year**—Mike Tomko, Bucknell.

## INDIVIDUAL BATTING LEADERS
(Minimum 100 At-Bats)

| Name | AVG | AB | R | H | 2B | 3B | HR | RBI | SB |
|---|---|---|---|---|---|---|---|---|---|
| Goria, Joe, Lehigh | .377 | 130 | 20 | 49 | 5 | 0 | 7 | 38 | 0 |
| Benke, Todd, Navy | .369 | 168 | 37 | 62 | 13 | 2 | 1 | 28 | 3 |

| Name | AVG | AB | R | H | 2B | 3B | HR | RBI | SB |
|---|---|---|---|---|---|---|---|---|---|
| McKernan, Bryan, Lafayette | .366 | 134 | 27 | 49 | 7 | 1 | 1 | 19 | 1 |
| Mullee, Bill, Army | .361 | 144 | 36 | 52 | 7 | 1 | 1 | 28 | 7 |
| Inclan, Alex, Bucknell | .359 | 145 | 39 | 52 | 10 | 4 | 6 | 25 | 2 |
| Johnson, Paul, Navy | .353 | 116 | 26 | 41 | 3 | 2 | 0 | 23 | 6 |
| Smith, Matt, Navy | .350 | 180 | 37 | 63 | 10 | 8 | 6 | 49 | 3 |
| Lake, Toph, Navy | .348 | 155 | 33 | 54 | 10 | 4 | 1 | 35 | 8 |
| Maher, Rob, Bucknell | .345 | 119 | 22 | 41 | 3 | 2 | 0 | 16 | 2 |
| Mauro, Tony, Navy | .345 | 113 | 25 | 39 | 6 | 2 | 0 | 30 | 2 |
| DeHart, Chad, Bucknell | .338 | 136 | 31 | 46 | 11 | 6 | 3 | 26 | 9 |
| Price, Bryan, Army | .338 | 148 | 43 | 50 | 10 | 0 | 0 | 20 | 7 |
| Paukovits, Nate, Navy | .336 | 152 | 40 | 51 | 14 | 0 | 2 | 32 | 0 |
| Scioletti, Mike, Army | .331 | 142 | 29 | 47 | 8 | 0 | 7 | 45 | 1 |
| Talbott, Ben, Lehigh | .328 | 116 | 27 | 38 | 7 | 1 | 5 | 23 | 1 |
| #Adams, Mike, Navy | .319 | 182 | 52 | 58 | 10 | 2 | 1 | 24 | 12 |
| #Silverman, Kevin, Buck. | .309 | 162 | 45 | 50 | 8 | 1 | 12 | 43 | 4 |

### INDIVIDUAL PITCHING LEADERS
(Minimum 40 Innings)

| Name | W | L | ERA | G | SV | IP | H | BB | SO |
|---|---|---|---|---|---|---|---|---|---|
| McLemore, Tom, Navy | 9 | 7 | 2.60 | 17 | 0 | 93 | 97 | 14 | 43 |
| King, Jason, Army | 4 | 1 | 3.31 | 11 | 0 | 54 | 68 | 17 | 22 |
| Fortune, Tim, Holy Cross | 1 | 5 | 3.56 | 9 | 0 | 48 | 51 | 9 | 29 |
| Anders, Mike, Bucknell | 8 | 3 | 3.61 | 15 | 0 | 92 | 97 | 18 | 44 |
| Angstreich, Dave, Lehigh | 4 | 5 | 4.14 | 14 | 4 | 63 | 70 | 31 | 38 |
| Kusko, Chad, Lehigh | 1 | 3 | 4.26 | 9 | 0 | 51 | 59 | 21 | 26 |
| Hoak, Ed, Navy | 2 | 2 | 4.64 | 15 | 0 | 52 | 59 | 20 | 26 |
| Smith, Travis, Army | 4 | 5 | 4.66 | 12 | 0 | 66 | 84 | 26 | 47 |
| Querns, Chris, Lehigh | 5 | 5 | 5.11 | 10 | 0 | 49 | 61 | 14 | 32 |
| Tomko, Mike, Bucknell | 6 | 6 | 5.60 | 13 | 0 | 71 | 73 | 49 | 47 |
| #Carlson, Kevin, Navy | 5 | 5 | 5.79 | 18 | 0 | 78 | 103 | 20 | 54 |

# SOUTHEASTERN CONFERENCE

| EAST | Conference | | Overall | |
|---|---|---|---|---|
| | W | L | W | L |
| Florida | 20 | 10 | 50 | 18 |
| Tennessee | 18 | 12 | 43 | 20 |
| Kentucky | 15 | 14 | 35 | 24 |
| Vanderbilt | 14 | 16 | 29 | 25 |
| South Carolina | 13 | 17 | 25 | 28 |
| Georgia | 8 | 21 | 24 | 30 |
| **WEST** | **W** | **L** | **W** | **L** |
| *Alabama | 20 | 10 | 50 | 19 |
| Louisiana State | 20 | 10 | 52 | 15 |
| Mississippi State | 17 | 13 | 38 | 24 |
| Arkansas | 15 | 15 | 39 | 20 |
| Auburn | 12 | 18 | 32 | 24 |
| Mississippi | 7 | 23 | 24 | 30 |

**ALL-CONFERENCE TEAM: C**—Dax Norris, Sr., Alabama. **1B**—Eddy Furniss, So., Louisiana State. **2B**—Kenderick Moore, Sr., Arkansas. **3B**—Nathan Dunn, Jr., Louisiana State. **SS**—Augie Ojeda, Jr., Tennessee. **OF**—Chad Green, Jr., Kentucky; Scott Schroeffel, Sr., Tennessee; Chris Stowers, Sr., Georgia. **DH**—Chuck Hazzard, Jr., Tennessee; Eric DuBose, So., Mississippi State; Eddie Yarnall, Jr., Louisiana State.
**Player of the Year**—Eddy Furniss, Louisiana State.

## INDIVIDUAL BATTING LEADERS
(Minimum 125 At-Bats)

| Name | AVG | AB | R | H | 2B | 3B | HR | RBI | SB |
|---|---|---|---|---|---|---|---|---|---|
| Wilkerson, Brad, Florida | .407 | 241 | 71 | 98 | 22 | 3 | 9 | 68 | 14 |
| Blandford, Paul, Kentucky | .403 | 233 | 60 | 94 | 15 | 4 | 11 | 51 | 30 |
| Erickson, Matt, Arkansas | .391 | 248 | 69 | 97 | 24 | 4 | 1 | 52 | 11 |
| Furniss, Eddy, LSU | .374 | 238 | 68 | 89 | 21 | 1 | 26 | 103 | 1 |
| Stowers, Chris, Georgia | .370 | 216 | 49 | 80 | 18 | 3 | 12 | 57 | 24 |
| Piatt, Adam, Miss. State | .370 | 227 | 51 | 84 | 26 | 0 | 4 | 34 | 6 |
| Norris, Dax, Alabama | .370 | 284 | 50 | 105 | 21 | 0 | 7 | 49 | 3 |
| Ruch, Dallan, Auburn | .369 | 187 | 34 | 69 | 17 | 1 | 1 | 45 | 2 |
| Caruso, Joe, Alabama | .367 | 278 | 76 | 102 | 19 | 5 | 14 | 63 | 12 |
| Hazzard, Chuck, Florida | .366 | 265 | 52 | 97 | 13 | 0 | 18 | 67 | 6 |
| Dunn, Nathan, LSU | .358 | 257 | 95 | 92 | 19 | 4 | 21 | 81 | 18 |
| Davis, Glenn, Vandy | .358 | 218 | 55 | 78 | 15 | 1 | 17 | 61 | 4 |
| Moore, Kenderick, Arkansas | .357 | 221 | 60 | 79 | 14 | 3 | 9 | 58 | 29 |
| Greene, Clay, Tennessee | .356 | 191 | 49 | 68 | 7 | 4 | 4 | 26 | 33 |
| Cortez, Sonny, Tennessee | .355 | 228 | 60 | 81 | 14 | 4 | 12 | 58 | 12 |
| Hauswald, Rob, Miss. State | .354 | 254 | 63 | 90 | 22 | 2 | 16 | 63 | 4 |
| Pellow, Kit, Arkansas | .352 | 213 | 48 | 75 | 16 | 2 | 7 | 65 | 9 |
| Green, Chad, Kentucky | .352 | 256 | 71 | 90 | 15 | 7 | 12 | 44 | 55 |
| Ellis, Mark, Florida | .351 | 205 | 48 | 72 | 9 | 0 | 1 | 26 | 19 |
| Moller, Chris, Alabama | .350 | 257 | 46 | 90 | 17 | 0 | 13 | 54 | 0 |
| Cooley, Chad, LSU | .348 | 253 | 61 | 88 | 16 | 1 | 14 | 66 | 16 |
| Curry, Mike, So. Carolina | .346 | 191 | 36 | 66 | 22 | 1 | 2 | 29 | 20 |

| | | | | | | | | | |
|---|---|---|---|---|---|---|---|---|---|
| Rhea, Chip, Kentucky | .344 | 250 | 62 | 86 | 21 | 0 | 10 | 61 | 17 |
| Pickler, Jeff, Tennessee | .341 | 226 | 28 | 77 | 11 | 3 | 1 | 40 | 4 |
| Williams, Jason, LSU | .340 | 268 | 79 | 91 | 16 | 1 | 6 | 35 | 7 |
| Schroeffel, Scott, Tenn. | .340 | 256 | 58 | 87 | 29 | 0 | 14 | 58 | 15 |
| Eckstein, David, Florida | .338 | 302 | 76 | 102 | 19 | 3 | 9 | 60 | 24 |
| Chism, Chris, Florida | .337 | 169 | 34 | 57 | 7 | 1 | 4 | 32 | 14 |
| Paul, Josh, Vanderbilt | .336 | 223 | 52 | 75 | 15 | 3 | 12 | 46 | 15 |
| Clark, Brian, Miss. State | .335 | 182 | 36 | 61 | 9 | 3 | 8 | 35 | 3 |
| Lewis, Ed, Tennessee | .331 | 245 | 51 | 81 | 19 | 4 | 7 | 52 | 9 |
| Urquhart, Derick, So. Car. | .331 | 130 | 28 | 43 | 6 | 1 | 5 | 24 | 3 |
| Hayes, Travis, Kentucky | .330 | 200 | 45 | 66 | 13 | 1 | 11 | 44 | 5 |
| McConnell, Jason, Arkansas | .329 | 255 | 78 | 84 | 12 | 7 | 1 | 38 | 14 |
| Macrory, Rob, Auburn | .328 | 204 | 58 | 67 | 11 | 1 | 0 | 33 | 24 |
| Wilson, Brad, LSU | .328 | 201 | 56 | 66 | 12 | 2 | 9 | 45 | 6 |
| Johnston, Clinton, Vandy | .328 | 204 | 39 | 67 | 21 | 1 | 13 | 53 | 4 |
| Tamargo, John, Florida | .322 | 267 | 65 | 86 | 20 | 1 | 4 | 41 | 15 |
| Arenas, Pete, Georgia | .322 | 202 | 42 | 65 | 12 | 3 | 3 | 32 | 2 |
| Lee, Richard, Miss. State | .322 | 239 | 49 | 77 | 15 | 1 | 6 | 55 | 4 |
| Hightower, Etienne, So. Car. | .321 | 224 | 48 | 72 | 17 | 1 | 1 | 36 | 34 |
| Etheredge, Josh, Auburn | .319 | 207 | 38 | 66 | 17 | 1 | 16 | 78 | 4 |
| Castaldo, Eric, Florida | .317 | 230 | 43 | 73 | 14 | 1 | 8 | 39 | 4 |
| Ojeda, Augie, Tennessee | .317 | 199 | 51 | 63 | 11 | 3 | 1 | 24 | 12 |
| Koerner, Mike, LSU | .315 | 238 | 71 | 75 | 15 | 3 | 12 | 47 | 24 |
| Sullivan, Adam, Auburn | .315 | 222 | 62 | 70 | 13 | 7 | 4 | 39 | 16 |
| Ross, Justin, Tennessee | .314 | 172 | 23 | 54 | 4 | 1 | 2 | 28 | 10 |
| Mensik, Todd, Mississippi | .314 | 194 | 37 | 61 | 14 | 1 | 9 | 43 | 2 |
| Mapes, Mark, So. Carolina | .313 | 176 | 31 | 55 | 8 | 0 | 9 | 53 | 2 |
| Anderson, Blake, Miss. State | .311 | 225 | 48 | 70 | 16 | 1 | 8 | 44 | 2 |
| Scioneaux, Damian, Miss. St. | .310 | 200 | 40 | 62 | 7 | 2 | 2 | 20 | 15 |
| Tidwell, David, Alabama | .310 | 245 | 49 | 76 | 16 | 5 | 5 | 30 | 27 |
| Hucks, Brian, So. Carolina | .309 | 149 | 30 | 46 | 6 | 0 | 12 | 37 | 0 |
| Minske, Eric, Arkansas | .309 | 139 | 33 | 43 | 10 | 2 | 4 | 26 | 0 |
| Huisman, Jason, Mississippi | .308 | 195 | 32 | 60 | 11 | 2 | 3 | 28 | 10 |
| Mohr, Dustan, Alabama | .306 | 252 | 52 | 77 | 21 | 1 | 10 | 55 | 3 |
| Bowles, Justin, LSU | .306 | 232 | 57 | 71 | 13 | 1 | 22 | 73 | 12 |
| Lewis, Keith, Mississippi | .302 | 202 | 42 | 61 | 8 | 1 | 5 | 30 | 13 |
| Pryor, Pete, Kentucky | .300 | 160 | 30 | 48 | 10 | 1 | 11 | 40 | 4 |
| Adeeb, Josh, Vanderbilt | .300 | 217 | 51 | 63 | 11 | 1 | 13 | 49 | 19 |
| Duncan, Matt, Florida | .299 | 167 | 35 | 50 | 5 | 0 | 5 | 29 | 3 |
| Spiers, Corey, Alabama | .297 | 148 | 31 | 44 | 7 | 1 | 8 | 39 | 2 |
| Bendix, Andy, Kentucky | .296 | 179 | 37 | 53 | 10 | 0 | 11 | 35 | 5 |
| Hall, Doug, Auburn | .296 | 206 | 40 | 61 | 10 | 3 | 2 | 26 | 18 |
| Weeks, Mark, Auburn | .296 | 196 | 30 | 58 | 11 | 2 | 2 | 17 | 2 |
| Folkers, Ken, Tennessee | .294 | 238 | 42 | 70 | 12 | 1 | 6 | 47 | 0 |
| Lundquist, Ryan, Arkansas | .294 | 177 | 30 | 52 | 8 | 4 | 5 | 40 | 5 |
| Bradley, Keith, Arkansas | .291 | 145 | 31 | 43 | 7 | 2 | 0 | 16 | 5 |
| Wilson, Andy, Arkansas | .289 | 128 | 30 | 37 | 11 | 3 | 1 | 37 | 7 |
| Meadows, Tydus, Vandy | .287 | 171 | 35 | 49 | 4 | 1 | 8 | 31 | 1 |
| Hopper, Shane, Georgia | .285 | 186 | 22 | 53 | 10 | 0 | 2 | 28 | 16 |
| Freeman, Brad, Miss. State | .285 | 239 | 37 | 68 | 13 | 1 | 4 | 43 | 9 |
| Taft, Brett, Alabama | .283 | 212 | 42 | 60 | 19 | 2 | 7 | 35 | 3 |
| Felston, Keith, Mississippi | .282 | 212 | 40 | 62 | 9 | 2 | 0 | 16 | 24 |
| Young, Todd, Kentucky | .280 | 161 | 32 | 45 | 8 | 0 | 3 | 28 | 5 |
| Knight, John, Mississippi | .280 | 143 | 19 | 40 | 8 | 2 | 0 | 15 | 8 |
| Harrelson, Richy, Miss. | .279 | 140 | 24 | 39 | 7 | 1 | 4 | 36 | 2 |
| Espinosa, Ray, Tennessee | .275 | 178 | 30 | 49 | 11 | 0 | 4 | 24 | 0 |
| Bachman, Ryan, Vandy | .275 | 131 | 20 | 36 | 5 | 1 | 5 | 23 | 4 |
| Stanton, Eric, So. Carolina | .274 | 190 | 33 | 52 | 14 | 0 | 8 | 36 | 3 |

## INDIVIDUAL PITCHING LEADERS
(Minimum 50 Innings)

| | W | L | ERA | G | SV | IP | H | BB | SO |
|---|---|---|---|---|---|---|---|---|---|
| Rigdon, Paul, Florida | 9 | 2 | 2.19 | 42 | 10 | 74 | 64 | 28 | 66 |
| Ames, Skip, Alabama | 2 | 1 | 2.36 | 21 | 11 | 50 | 36 | 20 | 44 |
| Yarnall, Eddie, LSU | 11 | 1 | 2.38 | 19 | 0 | 125 | 89 | 52 | 156 |
| Shipp, Kevin, LSU | 5 | 4 | 2.63 | 17 | 2 | 86 | 75 | 32 | 75 |
| Bernard, Andy, Alabama | 6 | 3 | 2.65 | 23 | 1 | 71 | 65 | 18 | 76 |
| Young, Tim, Alabama | 11 | 3 | 2.73 | 23 | 2 | 99 | 93 | 26 | 90 |
| Dickey, R.A., Tennessee | 9 | 4 | 2.76 | 27 | 3 | 127 | 114 | 33 | 137 |
| Franks, Lance, Arkansas | 9 | 3 | 2.93 | 26 | 1 | 71 | 60 | 15 | 61 |
| Wilkerson, Brad, Florida | 5 | 2 | 2.97 | 30 | 6 | 64 | 59 | 28 | 67 |
| Meyers, Ryan, Tennessee | 5 | 3 | 3.07 | 12 | 0 | 76 | 67 | 26 | 59 |
| Johnson, Van, Miss. State | 6 | 1 | 3.09 | 25 | 5 | 67 | 74 | 21 | 58 |
| DuBose, Eric, Miss. State | 10 | 4 | 3.11 | 17 | 1 | 133 | 127 | 55 | 174 |
| Milburn, Adam, Kentucky | 4 | 2 | 3.17 | 25 | 0 | 65 | 64 | 23 | 61 |
| Myers, Matt, Tennessee | 7 | 1 | 3.20 | 18 | 2 | 56 | 60 | 14 | 31 |
| Hudson, Tim, Auburn | 5 | 3 | 3.25 | 25 | 3 | 75 | 65 | 31 | 90 |
| Colgrove, Joel, Alabama | 10 | 3 | 3.32 | 19 | 0 | 111 | 121 | 24 | 104 |
| Lincoln, Mike, Tennessee | 6 | 4 | 3.33 | 14 | 2 | 70 | 64 | 30 | 76 |
| Haynie, Jason, So. Carolina | 7 | 6 | 3.43 | 17 | 0 | 108 | 108 | 39 | 86 |
| Bond, Tommy, Florida | 4 | 0 | 3.44 | 18 | 0 | 65 | 67 | 33 | 38 |
| Laxton, Brett, LSU | 8 | 2 | 3.54 | 14 | 0 | 56 | 50 | 28 | 55 |
| Esteves, Jake, LSU | 5 | 3 | 3.58 | 23 | 2 | 65 | 71 | 12 | 67 |
| Downs, Scott, Kentucky | 5 | 2 | 3.58 | 13 | 0 | 78 | 77 | 21 | 92 |
| Sexton, Patrick, So. Carolina | 2 | 0 | 3.60 | 24 | 0 | 50 | 60 | 12 | 27 |

| | | | | | | | | | |
|---|---|---|---|---|---|---|---|---|---|
| Rodriguez, Sergio, Florida | 4 | 1 | 3.79 | 21 | 0 | 57 | 53 | 23 | 31 |
| Frachiseur, Zach, Georgia | 6 | 5 | 3.82 | 18 | 0 | 113 | 95 | 68 | 81 |
| Brown, Elliot, Auburn | 6 | 3 | 3.90 | 26 | 2 | 65 | 54 | 37 | 77 |
| Hudson, Luke, Tennessee | 5 | 0 | 3.91 | 12 | 0 | 53 | 40 | 22 | 57 |
| Callaway, Mickey, Mississippi | 7 | 7 | 4.01 | 18 | 1 | 108 | 103 | 52 | 103 |
| Tidwell, Chad, Arkansas | 9 | 1 | 4.11 | 19 | 0 | 70 | 68 | 24 | 43 |
| Coogan, Patrick, LSU | 6 | 0 | 4.13 | 26 | 1 | 81 | 88 | 28 | 95 |
| Schroeffel, Scott, Tennessee | 4 | 4 | 4.24 | 15 | 1 | 70 | 64 | 28 | 71 |
| Kaufman, John, Florida | 11 | 5 | 4.25 | 21 | 0 | 125 | 109 | 47 | 101 |
| Halla, Ryan, Auburn | 5 | 4 | 4.29 | 13 | 0 | 65 | 56 | 28 | 63 |
| Carnes, Matt, Arkansas | 10 | 5 | 4.31 | 18 | 0 | 117 | 113 | 51 | 105 |
| Torres, Manny, Alabama | 5 | 1 | 4.40 | 17 | 0 | 57 | 58 | 13 | 61 |
| Brewer, Thomas, Florida | 7 | 2 | 4.46 | 14 | 0 | 73 | 69 | 35 | 45 |
| Demouy, Chris, LSU | 10 | 3 | 4.50 | 29 | 2 | 66 | 65 | 23 | 55 |
| Alkire, John, Tennessee | 6 | 4 | 4.50 | 26 | 4 | 70 | 52 | 31 | 62 |
| Bishop, Eric, Kentucky | 5 | 3 | 4.52 | 21 | 1 | 66 | 67 | 31 | 52 |
| Gandy, Josh, Georgia | 5 | 7 | 4.70 | 26 | 0 | 107 | 106 | 48 | 79 |
| Hoshour, Chad, So. Carolina | 3 | 4 | 4.70 | 21 | 2 | 61 | 71 | 34 | 49 |
| Nye, Richie, Arkansas | 3 | 5 | 4.71 | 16 | 0 | 78 | 68 | 42 | 72 |
| Eilers, Chris, Alabama | 5 | 5 | 4.73 | 16 | 1 | 72 | 74 | 22 | 64 |
| Woodward, Finley, Auburn | 5 | 4 | 4.76 | 26 | 2 | 81 | 80 | 51 | 62 |

# SOUTHERN CONFERENCE

| | Conference | | Overall | |
|---|---|---|---|---|
| | W | L | W | L |
| *Georgia Southern | 17 | 3 | 46 | 14 |
| Western Carolina | 17 | 7 | 32 | 24 |
| Furman | 15 | 9 | 26 | 29 |
| The Citadel | 13 | 10 | 33 | 26 |
| Appalachian State | 12 | 10 | 27 | 19 |
| East Tennessee State | 11 | 12 | 26 | 24 |
| Virginia Military | 7 | 16 | 17 | 29 |
| Davidson | 6 | 18 | 16 | 33 |
| Marshall | 4 | 17 | 7 | 35 |

**ALL-CONFERENCE TEAM: C**—Scott Garrett, Jr., Appalachian State. **1B**—Tommy Peterman, Jr., Georgia Southern. **2B**—Chris Rodriquez, Sr., Appalachian State. **3B**—Bo Betchman, Jr., The Citadel. **SS**—Bradley James, Jr., East Tennessee State. **OF**—Garrick Haltiwanger, Jr., The Citadel; Mark Hamlin, Sr., Georgia Southern; Antoine Moran, Jr., Georgia Southern. **DH**—Scott Musgrave, Sr., Appalachian State. **P**—Julio Ayala, Jr., Georgia Southern; Tod Lee, Sr., Georgia Southern.
**Player of the Year**—Tommy Peterman, Georgia Southern.
**Pitcher of the Year**—Julio Ayala, Georgia Southern.

## INDIVIDUAL BATTING LEADERS
(Minimum 100 At-Bats)

| | AVG | AB | R | H | 2B | 3B | HR | RBI | SB |
|---|---|---|---|---|---|---|---|---|---|
| Tolbert, Alex, West. Carolina | .424 | 217 | 58 | 92 | 25 | 1 | 11 | 66 | 5 |
| Peterman, Tommy, Ga. South. | .382 | 246 | 66 | 94 | 15 | 0 | 26 | 82 | 2 |
| Hagy, Mike, Marshall | .379 | 153 | 24 | 58 | 13 | 1 | 8 | 33 | 6 |
| Betchman, Bo, The Citadel | .378 | 209 | 53 | 79 | 16 | 3 | 2 | 47 | 21 |
| Moore, Chris, West. Carolina | .373 | 166 | 37 | 62 | 19 | 2 | 5 | 39 | 2 |
| Hamlin, Mark, Ga. Southern | .370 | 219 | 56 | 81 | 17 | 6 | 8 | 41 | 18 |
| Shepperson, Nate, VMI | .361 | 166 | 34 | 60 | 12 | 2 | 14 | 39 | 4 |
| Moore, Jason, West. Carolina | .354 | 206 | 46 | 73 | 12 | 1 | 2 | 30 | 15 |
| Polichnowski, A.J., ETSU | .347 | 190 | 45 | 66 | 15 | 2 | 9 | 39 | 0 |
| Rodriguez, Chris, ASU | .342 | 161 | 39 | 55 | 5 | 1 | 4 | 40 | 2 |
| Barrow, Martin, West. Car. | .340 | 147 | 40 | 50 | 6 | 3 | 3 | 27 | 5 |
| Jones, Sy, Ga. Southern | .340 | 203 | 53 | 69 | 16 | 3 | 5 | 55 | 16 |
| Beckley, David, The Citadel | .335 | 212 | 65 | 71 | 11 | 5 | 2 | 35 | 37 |
| Morrill, Jim, Furman | .332 | 202 | 42 | 67 | 14 | 2 | 3 | 30 | 6 |
| Puscian, Tim, ASU | .331 | 154 | 46 | 51 | 7 | 0 | 0 | 22 | 17 |
| Haltiwanger, Garrick, Citadel | .330 | 218 | 46 | 72 | 16 | 5 | 11 | 60 | 25 |
| Garrett, Scott, ASU | .329 | 170 | 38 | 56 | 14 | 1 | 8 | 48 | 3 |
| Coe, Donnie, Ga. Southern | .329 | 207 | 48 | 68 | 14 | 2 | 2 | 40 | 10 |
| #Moran, Antoine, Ga. South. | .302 | 252 | 61 | 76 | 7 | 4 | 2 | 23 | 50 |

## INDIVIDUAL PITCHING LEADERS
(Minimum 40 Innings)

| | W | L | ERA | G | SV | IP | H | BB | SO |
|---|---|---|---|---|---|---|---|---|---|
| Lee, Tod, Ga. Southern | 7 | 4 | 1.18 | 38 | 11 | 53 | 35 | 21 | 88 |
| Stutzman, Dan, ASU | 5 | 1 | 2.24 | 16 | 0 | 64 | 58 | 28 | 54 |
| Martin, Tom, The Citadel | 5 | 6 | 3.36 | 37 | 7 | 56 | 52 | 22 | 43 |
| Ayala, Julio, Ga. Southern | 15 | 3 | 3.49 | 22 | 0 | 152 | 145 | 42 | 143 |
| Noyce, David, Furman | 6 | 3 | 3.72 | 16 | 2 | 65 | 62 | 28 | 48 |
| Bain, Brian, West. Carolina | 5 | 2 | 3.99 | 15 | 2 | 70 | 60 | 26 | 56 |
| Rogers, Brian, The Citadel | 6 | 3 | 4.03 | 10 | 0 | 72 | 78 | 26 | 71 |
| Maxwell, Denny, ETSU | 4 | 7 | 4.04 | 18 | 2 | 91 | 106 | 34 | 83 |
| Price, John, The Citadel | 2 | 0 | 4.08 | 28 | 5 | 57 | 54 | 36 | 46 |
| Banks, Andrew, Furman | 5 | 5 | 4.19 | 14 | 0 | 88 | 104 | 24 | 54 |
| DiFelice, Mark, West. Carolina | 6 | 6 | 4.33 | 15 | 0 | 89 | 102 | 19 | 58 |

Davidson, Chris, West. Carolina 4   3  4.42  15   2  59  60  29  44
Hart, Len, ETSU........................ 3   3  4.50   7   0  42  46  15  41
Sica, Chris, The Citadel ............ 3   2  4.65  14   0  70  67  39  44

## SOUTHLAND CONFERENCE

| TEXAS | Conference | | Overall | |
|---|---|---|---|---|
| | W | L | W | L |
| Southwest Texas State | 19 | 11 | 27 | 32 |
| Texas-San Antonio | 17 | 13 | 26 | 26 |
| *Sam Houston State | 15 | 15 | 31 | 29 |
| Texas-Arlington | 13 | 17 | 23 | 35 |
| **LOUISIANA** | | | | |
| Northeast Louisiana | 21 | 9 | 41 | 19 |
| Northwestern State | 14 | 16 | 34 | 27 |
| Nicholls State | 11 | 19 | 17 | 36 |
| McNeese State | 10 | 20 | 23 | 31 |

**ALL-CONFERENCE TEAM: C**—Michael Harvey, So., Northeast Louisiana. **1B**—Ron Thames, Jr., Sam Houston State. **2B**—Mike Trahan, Jr., McNeese State. **3B**—Brian Keswick, Sr., Northeast Louisiana. **SS**—Brett Lockwood, Sr., Nicholls State. **OF**—Shannon Cooley, Sr., Northeast Louisiana; Marc Perez, Jr., Texas-San Antonio; Collin Wissen, Jr., Southwest Texas. **DH**—Nick Simokaitis, Sr., Northwestern State. **P**—Jason Divin, Jr., Southwest Texas; Ben Mann, Sr., Northeast Louisiana; Andy Weaver, Sr., Northeast Louisiana.
**Player of the Year**—Shannon Cooley, Northeast Louisiana.
**Pitcher of the Year**—Ben Mann, Northeast Louisiana.

### INDIVIDUAL BATTING LEADERS
(Minimum 100 At-Bats)

| | AVG | AB | R | H | 2B | 3B | HR | RBI | SB |
|---|---|---|---|---|---|---|---|---|---|
| Bubela, Brett, Sam Houston... | .382 | 131 | 28 | 50 | 10 | 0 | 3 | 27 | 2 |
| Lockwood, Brett, Nicholls St... | .376 | 210 | 39 | 79 | 16 | 1 | 5 | 45 | 7 |
| Wissen, Collin, SW Texas..... | .371 | 170 | 46 | 63 | 6 | 6 | 3 | 31 | 14 |
| Mott, Jeff, UTSA.................... | .358 | 190 | 57 | 68 | 9 | 4 | 0 | 33 | 20 |
| Simokatis, Nick, NW St......... | .352 | 182 | 41 | 64 | 11 | 1 | 8 | 52 | 5 |
| Cooley, Shannon, NE La....... | .345 | 229 | 55 | 79 | 24 | 1 | 7 | 57 | 28 |
| Trahan, Mike, McNeese St..... | .344 | 180 | 35 | 62 | 17 | 2 | 10 | 53 | 5 |
| Cotten, Nathan, Nicholls St... | .343 | 181 | 35 | 62 | 17 | 1 | 5 | 31 | 4 |
| Harvey, Michael, NE La......... | .343 | 199 | 35 | 68 | 11 | 1 | 6 | 42 | 6 |
| Thames, Ron, Sam Houston.. | .337 | 208 | 46 | 70 | 19 | 2 | 8 | 35 | 26 |
| Collins, Tim, Nicholls St........ | .335 | 185 | 27 | 62 | 16 | 3 | 3 | 37 | 13 |
| Perez, Marc, UTSA............... | .330 | 182 | 53 | 60 | 11 | 7 | 8 | 55 | 7 |
| Splawn, Matt, UTA............... | .330 | 182 | 27 | 60 | 10 | 4 | 9 | 56 | 0 |
| Taylor, Brig, McNeese St. ..... | .328 | 186 | 45 | 61 | 10 | 12 | 3 | 41 | 11 |
| Taylor, Corey, NE Louisiana . | .327 | 211 | 73 | 69 | 9 | 4 | 15 | 56 | 22 |
| Newkirk, Greg, SW Texas..... | .323 | 217 | 43 | 70 | 9 | 3 | 3 | 30 | 8 |
| Wilson, B.G., UTA ................ | .323 | 217 | 41 | 70 | 17 | 1 | 0 | 29 | 6 |
| Duvall, Jeremy, McNeese St.. | .321 | 162 | 41 | 52 | 7 | 6 | 4 | 19 | 23 |
| Fowler, Maleke, Nicholls St... | .319 | 191 | 54 | 61 | 4 | 1 | 2 | 15 | 60 |

### INDIVIDUAL PITCHING LEADERS
(Minimum 40 Innings)

| | W | L | ERA | G | SV | IP | H | BB | SO |
|---|---|---|---|---|---|---|---|---|---|
| Mann, Ben, NE La................ | 7 | 4 | 2.81 | 15 | 0 | 77 | 77 | 20 | 47 |
| Divin, Jason, SW Texas.......... | 10 | 3 | 3.55 | 17 | 0 | 106 | 132 | 24 | 62 |
| Hermes, Kevin, Sam Houston.... | 6 | 7 | 3.60 | 23 | 6 | 90 | 92 | 22 | 38 |
| Spencer, Bart, SW Texas....... | 4 | 7 | 3.73 | 15 | 0 | 66 | 69 | 21 | 47 |
| Weaver, Andy, NE La............ | 8 | 3 | 3.84 | 20 | 2 | 96 | 107 | 33 | 57 |
| Carter, Brian, NE La.............. | 4 | 3 | 3.90 | 15 | 0 | 99 | 93 | 39 | 72 |
| Renfrow, Daryl, UTSA............ | 4 | 3 | 3.95 | 15 | 0 | 66 | 87 | 22 | 38 |
| Martin, Zach, Northwestern St.. | 8 | 4 | 4.05 | 20 | 0 | 96 | 99 | 30 | 54 |
| Arrieta, Cory, NE La. ............ | 6 | 3 | 4.06 | 22 | 3 | 69 | 65 | 28 | 57 |
| Glaze, Randy, UTA ............... | 4 | 4 | 4.19 | 16 | 0 | 82 | 80 | 41 | 64 |
| Sanders, Kris, Northwestern St.. | 4 | 4 | 4.25 | 23 | 2 | 42 | 54 | 17 | 22 |
| Davis, Scott, Sam Houston ........ | 5 | 3 | 4.34 | 15 | 0 | 83 | 94 | 45 | 43 |
| Ehlers, Corey, SW Texas....... | 6 | 4 | 4.38 | 18 | 0 | 86 | 95 | 36 | 65 |
| Metcalfe, Rick, NW St. .......... | 8 | 4 | 4.55 | 16 | 0 | 89 | 91 | 33 | 63 |
| #Spencer, Stephen, SW Texas..... | 2 | 3 | 5.69 | 24 | 8 | 48 | 63 | 22 | 40 |
| #Cortez, Clint, Nicholls St....... | 6 | 10 | 6.60 | 23 | 1 | 91 | 87 | 108 | 109 |

## SOUTHWEST CONFERENCE

| | Conference | | Overall | |
|---|---|---|---|---|
| | W | L | W | L |
| **Texas** | 17 | 7 | 39 | 24 |
| **Texas Tech** | 15 | 9 | 49 | 15 |
| Texas A&M | 12 | 12 | 37 | 21 |
| Texas Christian | 11 | 13 | 34 | 33 |
| Baylor | 11 | 13 | 32 | 27 |
| *Rice | 9 | 15 | 42 | 23 |
| Houston | 9 | 15 | 29 | 28 |

**ALL-CONFERENCE TEAM: C**—David Lindstrom, Sr., Texas Tech. **1B**—Danny Peoples, Jr., Texas. **2B**—Marty Crawford, Sr., Baylor. **3B**—Clint Bryant, Sr., Texas Tech. **SS**—Kip Harkrider, So., Texas. **OF**—MacGregor Byers, Jr., Texas; Ryan Dunn, So., Texas Christian; Matt Kastelic, Sr., Texas Tech; Jeff McCurdy, Sr., Texas Christian; Jason Tyner, Fr., Texas A&M. **DH**—Jason Stephens, Jr., Texas A&M. **Util**—Jason Schreiber, Jr., Houston. **SP**—Jimmy Frush, Jr., Texas Tech; Kris Lambert, Jr., Baylor; Matt Miller, Jr., Texas Tech. **RP**—Scott Atchison, So., Texas Christian; Eric French, So., Rice; Mark Manbeck, Jr., Houston.
**Player of the Year**—Clint Bryant, Texas Tech.

### INDIVIDUAL BATTING LEADERS
(Minimum 125 At-Bats)

| | AVG | AB | R | H | 2B | 3B | HR | RBI | SB |
|---|---|---|---|---|---|---|---|---|---|
| Kastelic, Matt, Texas Tech..... | .424 | 269 | 78 | 114 | 19 | 4 | 8 | 70 | 51 |
| Crawford, Marty, Baylor......... | .414 | 232 | 54 | 96 | 24 | 2 | 10 | 67 | 2 |
| Tyner, Jason, Texas A&M...... | .407 | 246 | 74 | 100 | 7 | 0 | 0 | 29 | 41 |
| Berkman, Lance, Rice........... | .398 | 241 | 76 | 96 | 16 | 4 | 20 | 92 | 8 |
| Bryant, Clint, Texas Tech...... | .382 | 262 | 89 | 100 | 26 | 2 | 18 | 100 | 37 |
| Harkrider, Kip, Texas........... | .381 | 260 | 75 | 99 | 17 | 5 | 4 | 43 | 8 |
| Stephens, Jason, Texas A&M... | .380 | 187 | 37 | 71 | 10 | 2 | 11 | 79 | 1 |
| Byers, MacGregor, Texas...... | .375 | 232 | 77 | 87 | 15 | 3 | 6 | 66 | 23 |
| Peoples, Danny, Texas.......... | .375 | 216 | 67 | 81 | 18 | 5 | 17 | 86 | 7 |
| Clapp, Stubby, Texas Tech..... | .372 | 215 | 97 | 80 | 28 | 8 | 7 | 51 | 21 |
| Allen, Chad, Texas A&M........ | .367 | 196 | 67 | 72 | 11 | 4 | 5 | 41 | 23 |
| McCurdy, Jeff, TCU.............. | .365 | 192 | 49 | 70 | 21 | 3 | 3 | 35 | 28 |
| Huffman, Royce, TCU............ | .360 | 164 | 41 | 59 | 11 | 1 | 4 | 38 | 5 |
| Venghaus, Jeff, Rice ............. | .360 | 250 | 77 | 90 | 18 | 4 | 5 | 42 | 18 |
| Hunter, Johnny, Texas A&M .. | .359 | 170 | 52 | 61 | 11 | 6 | 9 | 39 | 9 |
| Milam, Brandon, Houston...... | .357 | 213 | 48 | 76 | 19 | 6 | 1 | 34 | 16 |
| Petru, Rich, Texas A&M........ | .351 | 188 | 29 | 66 | 10 | 3 | 4 | 39 | 11 |
| Johnson, David, TCU............ | .350 | 254 | 53 | 89 | 21 | 1 | 8 | 62 | 7 |
| Ruecker, Dion, Texas Tech..... | .350 | 260 | 69 | 91 | 22 | 3 | 20 | 82 | 18 |
| Dodson, Jeremy, Baylor........ | .349 | 146 | 34 | 51 | 13 | 3 | 2 | 29 | 6 |
| Davis, Brad, Texas Tech....... | .347 | 202 | 56 | 70 | 11 | 3 | 4 | 39 | 17 |
| Carr, Dustin, Houston........... | .347 | 199 | 46 | 69 | 10 | 1 | 5 | 33 | 15 |
| Schreiber, Jason, Houston..... | .347 | 225 | 38 | 78 | 10 | 0 | 7 | 57 | 1 |
| Huffman, Ryan, Texas A&M... | .341 | 164 | 43 | 56 | 9 | 3 | 9 | 48 | 14 |
| Yarbrough, Jeff, TCU............ | .341 | 211 | 59 | 72 | 13 | 1 | 2 | 36 | 22 |
| Dunn, Ryan, TCU................ | .340 | 235 | 47 | 80 | 18 | 4 | 11 | 64 | 1 |
| Lindstrom, David, Texas Tech.. | .332 | 229 | 67 | 76 | 19 | 0 | 16 | 60 | 1 |
| Nelson, Eric, Baylor.............. | .331 | 160 | 42 | 53 | 12 | 2 | 0 | 29 | 3 |
| Reintjes, Steve, Baylor.......... | .329 | 219 | 50 | 72 | 14 | 1 | 5 | 44 | 4 |
| Dillon, Joe, Texas Tech......... | .326 | 267 | 56 | 87 | 16 | 2 | 10 | 70 | 18 |
| Wallace, Brad, TCU.............. | .324 | 262 | 60 | 85 | 20 | 6 | 5 | 54 | 13 |
| Ford, William, Rice............... | .322 | 139 | 53 | 77 | 13 | 2 | 6 | 46 | 18 |
| Cathey, Joseph, Rice............ | .320 | 178 | 31 | 57 | 9 | 1 | 0 | 16 | 7 |
| Bailey, Jeff, Texas A&M......... | .320 | 125 | 30 | 40 | 9 | 0 | 5 | 28 | 0 |
| Richards, Jason, Rice........... | .319 | 216 | 74 | 69 | 10 | 3 | 7 | 35 | 17 |
| Topolski, Jon, Baylor............ | .319 | 238 | 68 | 76 | 9 | 6 | 3 | 26 | 16 |
| Layne, Jason, Texas............. | .319 | 213 | 51 | 68 | 14 | 4 | 13 | 74 | 4 |
| Crosby, Bubba, Rice............. | .318 | 198 | 55 | 63 | 13 | 6 | 12 | 64 | 6 |
| Howe, Matt, Texas Christian . | .318 | 255 | 49 | 81 | 12 | 1 | 5 | 50 | 8 |
| Lunsford, Sam, TCU............. | .317 | 230 | 77 | 73 | 16 | 1 | 4 | 49 | 32 |
| Hernandez, Dom, Houston..... | .316 | 228 | 62 | 72 | 17 | 3 | 7 | 28 | 14 |
| Morrison, Scott, Baylor.......... | .312 | 205 | 44 | 64 | 13 | 6 | 3 | 47 | 2 |
| McLaughlin, Tim, Rice........... | .310 | 187 | 25 | 58 | 19 | 0 | 2 | 41 | 3 |
| Martinez, Steve, Baylor......... | .308 | 130 | 19 | 40 | 6 | 1 | 5 | 34 | 6 |
| Salinas, Trey, Texas............. | .306 | 196 | 41 | 60 | 12 | 5 | 5 | 46 | 2 |
| Shiflett, William, Texas A&M . | .305 | 128 | 25 | 39 | 8 | 0 | 7 | 33 | 1 |
| Bennett, Marshall, Tex. Tech . | .292 | 154 | 42 | 45 | 10 | 1 | 4 | 26 | 16 |
| Matzke, J.J., Texas A&M....... | .292 | 154 | 32 | 45 | 6 | 0 | 7 | 25 | 1 |
| Martinez, Sergio, Texas Tech . | .289 | 159 | 44 | 46 | 11 | 1 | 5 | 30 | 3 |
| Medrano, Mike, Houston ....... | .289 | 152 | 24 | 44 | 10 | 1 | 0 | 20 | 5 |
| Ryden, Karl, Houston............ | .286 | 133 | 32 | 38 | 8 | 0 | 5 | 25 | 10 |
| Landry, Jacques, Rice........... | .284 | 236 | 61 | 67 | 19 | 3 | 19 | 81 | 5 |
| Campbell, Wylie, Texas......... | .284 | 232 | 66 | 66 | 14 | 4 | 0 | 35 | 43 |
| Doyle, Paul, Rice................. | .282 | 174 | 39 | 49 | 9 | 1 | 3 | 38 | 8 |
| Blair, James, Baylor ............. | .277 | 184 | 30 | 51 | 11 | 2 | 1 | 26 | 11 |
| Smith, Casey, TCU .............. | .277 | 166 | 32 | 46 | 7 | 4 | 5 | 34 | 10 |

### INDIVIDUAL PITCHING LEADERS
(Minimum 50 Innings)

| | W | L | ERA | G | SV | IP | H | BB | SO |
|---|---|---|---|---|---|---|---|---|---|
| Brewer, Ryan, Texas Tech...... | 10 | 3 | 3.53 | 17 | 1 | 105 | 114 | 23 | 69 |
| Lambert, Kris, Baylor............. | 10 | 5 | 3.60 | 21 | 1 | 108 | 101 | 41 | 81 |
| Frush, Jimmy, Texas Tech..... | 10 | 6 | 3.70 | 23 | 4 | 100 | 92 | 34 | 116 |
| Schreiber, Jason, Houston..... | 4 | 1 | 3.76 | 16 | 1 | 53 | 60 | 17 | 41 |
| Miller, Matt, Texas Tech......... | 12 | 2 | 3.98 | 18 | 0 | 111 | 114 | 56 | 113 |
| Davis, Dana, Rice................ | 4 | 2 | 3.98 | 14 | 1 | 63 | 65 | 27 | 47 |
| Taylor, Mark, Rice ............... | 5 | 2 | 4.06 | 18 | 0 | 64 | 40 | 60 | 64 |
| O'Dell, Jake, Texas.............. | 8 | 3 | 4.15 | 18 | 0 | 117 | 111 | 38 | 82 |
| #French, Eric, Texas............. | 2 | 2 | 4.33 | 27 | 9 | 35 | 23 | 22 | 48 |

| Name | W | L | ERA | G | SV | IP | H | BB | SO |
|---|---|---|---|---|---|---|---|---|---|
| Anderson, Matt, Rice | 9 | 3 | 4.37 | 25 | 4 | 78 | 68 | 55 | 70 |
| King, Shane, Texas A&M | 7 | 4 | 4.45 | 14 | 1 | 89 | 102 | 24 | 47 |
| Bergman, Brett, Baylor | 4 | 5 | 4.68 | 22 | 3 | 75 | 81 | 30 | 59 |
| Onley, Shawn, Rice | 7 | 3 | 4.86 | 18 | 0 | 100 | 95 | 47 | 95 |
| Peck, Jeff, Texas Tech | 7 | 1 | 4.89 | 15 | 0 | 70 | 83 | 32 | 38 |
| Smith, Jamie, Texas A&M | 4 | 4 | 4.92 | 20 | 0 | 53 | 64 | 24 | 45 |
| Lopez, Joe Luis, Texas | 4 | 4 | 4.96 | 20 | 0 | 53 | 51 | 37 | 32 |
| Leon, Scott, Texas | 7 | 5 | 4.96 | 20 | 1 | 74 | 69 | 49 | 60 |
| Shaddix, Jeff, Rice | 5 | 4 | 5.02 | 26 | 2 | 61 | 64 | 24 | 32 |
| Lee, Derek, TCU | 7 | 3 | 5.04 | 19 | 0 | 95 | 92 | 53 | 77 |
| Wallace, Flint, TCU | 10 | 5 | 5.10 | 20 | 1 | 109 | 114 | 48 | 84 |
| Blank, Matt, Texas A&M | 6 | 5 | 5.14 | 17 | 1 | 70 | 77 | 35 | 56 |
| Walter, Ryan, TCU | 4 | 4 | 5.21 | 22 | 2 | 57 | 60 | 22 | 35 |
| Crawford, Danny, Houston | 4 | 4 | 5.27 | 22 | 0 | 82 | 103 | 42 | 53 |
| Kirkland, Robb, Houston | 1 | 2 | 5.29 | 21 | 0 | 51 | 65 | 25 | 36 |
| Mitchell, Dean, Texas A&M | 3 | 2 | 5.66 | 18 | 1 | 62 | 73 | 35 | 41 |
| Atchison, Scott, TCU | 5 | 3 | 5.74 | 22 | 1 | 69 | 84 | 37 | 59 |
| Bess, Stephen, Rice | 7 | 2 | 5.79 | 18 | 1 | 78 | 86 | 49 | 53 |
| Ward, Monty, Texas Tech | 5 | 1 | 5.80 | 21 | 1 | 76 | 69 | 35 | 88 |
| Barker, Donny, Texas | 5 | | 6.03 | 18 | 1 | 63 | 74 | 52 | 47 |

# SOUTHWESTERN ATHLETIC CONFERENCE

| EAST | Conference W | L | Overall W | L |
|---|---|---|---|---|
| Jackson State | 16 | 2 | 23 | 20 |
| Alcorn State | 10 | 7 | 18 | 23 |
| Alabama State | 9 | 10 | 17 | 21 |
| Mississippi Valley St. | 3 | 19 | 5 | 31 |
| **WEST** | | | | |
| *Southern | 18 | 2 | 34 | 7 |
| Grambling State | 16 | 4 | 24 | 17 |
| Texas Southern | 6 | 15 | 12 | 27 |
| Prairie View A&M | 1 | 20 | 2 | 38 |

**ALL-CONFERENCE TEAM: C**—Shedrick Rodgers, Sr., Jackson State. **1B**—Lincoln Williams, So., Southern. **2B**—Terrance Daniel, Sr., Jackson State. **3B**—Timothy Stephney, Jr., Alcorn State. **SS**—Edwin Lawrence, Sr., Southern. **OF**—Andre Credit, Jr., Alcorn State; Kenneth Manuel, So., Southern; Marlon Stewart, Sr., Grambling State. **DH**—Kenyonn Gardner, Jr., Jackson State. **P**—Jimmy Hollifield, So., Jackson State; Craig Quintal, Jr., Southern; Berret Rey, Sr., Southern; Tyson Taplin, Jr., Alcorn State.
**Player of the Year**—Marlon Stewart, Grambling State.

## INDIVIDUAL BATTING LEADERS
(Minimum 100 At-Bats)

| Name | AVG | AB | R | H | 2B | 3B | HR | RBI | SB |
|---|---|---|---|---|---|---|---|---|---|
| Stewart, Marlon, Grambling | .449 | 138 | 42 | 62 | 6 | 4 | 14 | 49 | 9 |
| Daniel, Terrance, Jack. St. | .415 | 135 | 23 | 56 | 12 | 1 | 1 | 27 | 20 |
| Williams, Lincoln, Southern | .410 | 144 | 39 | 59 | 11 | 2 | 6 | 39 | 8 |
| Holloway, Victor, Ala. St. | .382 | 136 | 34 | 52 | 6 | 5 | 5 | 42 | 15 |
| Manuel, Kenneth, Southern | .381 | 118 | 41 | 45 | 12 | 0 | 9 | 26 | 8 |
| Harper, Gene, Jack. St. | .368 | 114 | 38 | 42 | 13 | 1 | 1 | 20 | 20 |
| Thompson, Alva, Southern | .362 | 127 | 38 | 46 | 5 | 0 | 11 | 38 | 8 |
| Credit, Andre, Alcorn State | .360 | 114 | 24 | 41 | 7 | 3 | 0 | 27 | 8 |
| Stephney, Tim, Alcorn State | .354 | 127 | 24 | 45 | 8 | 3 | 0 | 27 | 15 |
| Wooten, Corey, Alabama St. | .348 | 115 | 30 | 40 | 5 | 7 | 0 | 35 | 14 |
| Deleon, Ray, Texas Southern | .345 | 113 | 15 | 39 | 7 | 1 | 0 | 13 | 3 |
| Pierce, Johnny, Alcorn State | .341 | 123 | 21 | 42 | 8 | 0 | 0 | 19 | 1 |
| Gardner, Kenyonn, Jack. St. | .338 | 148 | 23 | 50 | 15 | 2 | 0 | 24 | 2 |
| Booker, Carlos, Alabama St. | .330 | 115 | 33 | 38 | 5 | 5 | 0 | 25 | 7 |
| Seastrunk, Gary, Texas South. | .328 | 125 | 22 | 41 | 11 | 0 | 1 | 26 | 12 |
| Johnson, Jason, Grambling | .326 | 132 | 32 | 43 | 10 | 7 | 3 | 31 | 4 |
| Mack, Torey, Alabama St. | .312 | 109 | 16 | 34 | 5 | 1 | 0 | 18 | 3 |
| Faul, Kurt, Southern | .310 | 116 | 24 | 36 | 7 | 3 | 2 | 30 | 8 |
| Smith, Doug, Southern | .307 | 127 | 45 | 39 | 6 | 4 | 2 | 12 | 11 |
| Ivy, Boris, Jackson State | .303 | 109 | 14 | 33 | 5 | 1 | 1 | 22 | 15 |
| #Coleman, Tony, Grambling | .250 | 128 | 39 | 32 | 6 | 1 | 0 | 13 | 32 |

## INDIVIDUAL PITCHING LEADERS
(Minimum 40 Innings)

| Name | W | L | ERA | G | SV | IP | H | BB | SO |
|---|---|---|---|---|---|---|---|---|---|
| Johnson, Jason, Grambling | 4 | 1 | 2.41 | 9 | 0 | 41 | 38 | 10 | 30 |
| Hollifield, Jimmy, Jackson State | 6 | 3 | 2.63 | 11 | 0 | 65 | 58 | 36 | 45 |
| Rey, Barret, Southern | 5 | 1 | 2.82 | 8 | 0 | 45 | 43 | 10 | 38 |
| #Williams, Thomas, Southern | 1 | 3 | 3.09 | 17 | 4 | 23 | 14 | 14 | 15 |
| Quintal, Craig, Southern | 8 | 2 | 3.18 | 11 | 0 | 65 | 44 | 11 | 76 |
| Taplin, Tyson, Alcorn State | 6 | 3 | 3.63 | 16 | 3 | 74 | 79 | 22 | 59 |
| Hill, Terrence, Southern | 7 | 1 | 4.14 | 11 | 0 | 59 | 43 | 29 | 49 |
| White, Kelcey, Jackson State | 2 | 3 | 4.19 | 10 | 0 | 54 | 63 | 22 | 28 |
| Washington, D., Southern | 2 | 4 | 4.30 | 8 | 0 | 46 | 56 | 23 | 34 |
| Moultry, Edrick, Texas Southern | 2 | 4 | 4.68 | 7 | 0 | 43 | 44 | 20 | 23 |
| Duncan, Courtney, Grambling | 4 | 7 | 4.90 | 12 | 0 | 73 | 62 | 32 | 70 |

# SUN BELT CONFERENCE

| | Conference W | L | Overall W | L |
|---|---|---|---|---|
| *South Alabama | 22 | 5 | 42 | 17 |
| New Orleans | 19 | 8 | 43 | 21 |
| Southwestern Louisiana | 15 | 12 | 25 | 33 |
| Arkansas State | 14 | 13 | 32 | 27 |
| Jacksonville | 12 | 14 | 23 | 34 |
| Texas-Pan American | 11 | 15 | 25 | 30 |
| Lamar | 11 | 16 | 26 | 29 |
| Arkansas-Little Rock | 10 | 15 | 29 | 22 |
| Louisiana Tech | 9 | 17 | 23 | 31 |
| Western Kentucky | 9 | 17 | 29 | 26 |

**ALL-CONFERENCE TEAM: C**—Jason Washam, Sr., New Orleans. **1B**—Morgan Walker, Sr., Lamar. **2B**—Hugh Lopes, Sr., South Alabama. **3B**—Sean Centeno, Sr., Arkansas-Little Rock. **SS**—Greg Taylor, Sr., Arkansas-Little Rock. **OF**—Shane Britt, Sr., South Alabama; Jason Klam, Jr., Lamar; C.J. Martin, Sr., Western Kentucky. **DH**—Chris Webb, Sr., Southwestern Louisiana. **SP**—Jason Norton, So., South Alabama; Donald Rushing, So., New Orleans. **RP**—Mike Nakamura, So., South Alabama.
**Player of the Year**—Greg Taylor, Arkansas-Little Rock.

## INDIVIDUAL BATTING LEADERS
(Minimum of 100 At-Bats)

| Name | AVG | AB | R | H | 2B | 3B | HR | RBI | SB |
|---|---|---|---|---|---|---|---|---|---|
| Taylor, Greg, Ark.-LR | .415 | 207 | 62 | 86 | 31 | 3 | 4 | 51 | 14 |
| Walker, Morgan, Lamar | .403 | 206 | 51 | 83 | 18 | 2 | 15 | 50 | 5 |
| Webb, Chris, SW La. | .398 | 221 | 49 | 88 | 23 | 1 | 10 | 62 | 1 |
| Martin, C.J., West. Ky. | .383 | 188 | 48 | 72 | 17 | 3 | 16 | 62 | 13 |
| Centeno, Sean, Ark.-LR | .367 | 188 | 48 | 69 | 22 | 1 | 11 | 58 | 5 |
| McBride, Kip, Ark.-LR | .364 | 195 | 56 | 71 | 11 | 0 | 1 | 25 | 20 |
| McKenzie, Shannon, West Ky. | .360 | 197 | 49 | 71 | 16 | 0 | 8 | 47 | 7 |
| Aguirre, Oswaldo, SW La. | .356 | 202 | 29 | 72 | 18 | 0 | 2 | 41 | 6 |
| Guidry, Greg, La. Tech | .352 | 179 | 40 | 63 | 9 | 2 | 2 | 27 | 20 |
| Loy, Chris, La. Tech | .349 | 192 | 30 | 67 | 17 | 0 | 8 | 42 | 0 |
| Dililo, Tony, Ark.-LR | .348 | 184 | 43 | 64 | 17 | 0 | 5 | 47 | 3 |
| Britt, Shane, So. Alabama | .347 | 245 | 58 | 85 | 11 | 2 | 10 | 63 | 16 |
| Washam, Jason, New Orleans | .347 | 193 | 43 | 67 | 17 | 0 | 7 | 39 | 4 |
| Francia, David, So. Alabama | .346 | 243 | 58 | 84 | 15 | 5 | 6 | 45 | 20 |
| Patton, Josh, West. Ky. | .346 | 211 | 39 | 73 | 14 | 1 | 4 | 45 | 4 |
| Klam, Jason, Lamar | .345 | 206 | 53 | 71 | 12 | 3 | 16 | 57 | 20 |
| Chabala, Chad, West. Ky. | .343 | 201 | 51 | 69 | 10 | 4 | 5 | 36 | 22 |
| Idlett, Matt, West. Ky. | .339 | 218 | 58 | 74 | 12 | 5 | 10 | 41 | 12 |
| Lawrence, Tony, La. Tech | .338 | 195 | 40 | 66 | 18 | 2 | 12 | 52 | 8 |
| Brownell, Scott, Ark.-LR | .337 | 175 | 48 | 59 | 10 | 4 | 1 | 28 | 26 |
| Nunnari, Talmadge, Jack. | .333 | 192 | 35 | 64 | 12 | 0 | 4 | 37 | 9 |
| Boulo, Tyler, So. Alabama | .332 | 208 | 48 | 69 | 12 | 1 | 6 | 47 | 7 |
| Nichol, John, Arkansas State | .332 | 211 | 39 | 70 | 19 | 2 | 2 | 39 | 4 |
| DiSalvo, Joe, New Orleans | .331 | 266 | 70 | 88 | 21 | 0 | 8 | 43 | 51 |
| Stacy, I.B., So. Alabama | .330 | 224 | 39 | 74 | 9 | 2 | 9 | 51 | 5 |
| Lopes, H.J., So. Alabama | .330 | 209 | 71 | 69 | 14 | 1 | 1 | 37 | 14 |
| Samples, Joe, Jacksonville | .327 | 214 | 42 | 70 | 18 | 3 | 2 | 38 | 9 |
| Carson, Scott, New Orleans | .325 | 154 | 30 | 50 | 14 | 0 | 6 | 25 | 1 |
| Siskowski, Matt, Tex.-Pan Am | .318 | 195 | 36 | 62 | 17 | 2 | 9 | 48 | 5 |
| Taylor, James, So. Alabama | .312 | 199 | 40 | 62 | 14 | 3 | 4 | 42 | 4 |
| #Powell, Chris, New Orleans | .246 | 232 | 50 | 57 | 9 | 6 | 3 | 40 | 22 |

## INDIVIDUAL PITCHING LEADERS
(Minimum 50 Innings)

| Name | W | L | ERA | G | SV | IP | H | BB | SO |
|---|---|---|---|---|---|---|---|---|---|
| Fisher, Mike, So. Alabama | 3 | 1 | 2.75 | 19 | 0 | 59 | 58 | 11 | 38 |
| Hegeman, Joel, Jacksonville | 6 | 3 | 3.21 | 25 | 0 | 56 | 64 | 30 | 48 |
| Rushing, Donald, New Orleans | 11 | 3 | 3.24 | 19 | 1 | 103 | 93 | 56 | 126 |
| Rowland, Carl, Ark.-LR | 6 | 5 | 3.40 | 14 | 0 | 82 | 85 | 18 | 52 |
| Akin, Jay, Arkansas State | 9 | 5 | 3.48 | 15 | 0 | 116 | 115 | 27 | 74 |
| Norton, Jason, So. Alabama | 12 | 3 | 3.49 | 17 | 0 | 108 | 106 | 37 | 101 |
| Karow, Mike, Texas-Pan Am | 7 | 5 | 3.52 | 16 | 0 | 100 | 94 | 51 | 77 |
| Kottmeyer, Matt, New Orleans | 3 | 2 | 3.78 | 18 | 2 | 50 | 51 | 28 | 34 |
| Methvin, Ian, SW La. | 7 | 3 | 3.83 | 20 | 0 | 115 | 126 | 44 | 92 |
| Trevino, Kiki, Texas-Pan Am | 6 | 4 | 3.94 | 15 | 1 | 89 | 108 | 43 | 45 |
| Wilkins, Jason, La. Tech | 5 | 6 | 3.99 | 24 | 4 | 97 | 106 | 23 | 59 |
| Dobson, Mark, Arkansas State | 7 | 3 | 4.04 | 26 | 6 | 62 | 54 | 35 | 57 |
| Lane, Kevin, Lamar | 4 | 3 | 4.18 | 19 | 0 | 67 | 77 | 15 | 50 |
| Cammack, Eric, Lamar | 7 | 5 | 4.23 | 18 | 1 | 83 | 81 | 31 | 68 |
| Williams, Randy, Lamar | 2 | 5 | 4.29 | 24 | 3 | 85 | 64 | 31 | 64 |
| Stanson, Steve, New Orleans | 5 | 5 | 4.31 | 19 | 0 | 94 | 114 | 35 | 83 |
| #Poche, Keane, New Orleans | 4 | 4 | 4.33 | 25 | 6 | 35 | 49 | 12 | 23 |
| Rayborn, Kenny, So. Alabama | 9 | 4 | 4.35 | 21 | 0 | 108 | 112 | 46 | 90 |
| Slaton, J.B., SW La. | 6 | 4 | 4.35 | 17 | 0 | 79 | 83 | 34 | 62 |
| Sordo, Eddie, Jacksonville | 9 | 8 | 4.46 | 20 | 0 | 105 | 122 | 30 | 92 |
| Stemle, Stephen, West. Ky. | 3 | 4 | 4.47 | 19 | 2 | 93 | 93 | 42 | 73 |
| Nakamura, Mike, So. Alabama | 6 | 3 | 4.48 | 29 | 3 | 78 | 76 | 26 | 77 |

## TRANS AMERICA CONFERENCE

| EAST | Conference W | L | Overall W | L |
|---|---|---|---|---|
| Georgia State | 12 | 6 | 21 | 32 |
| Campbell | 9 | 9 | 23 | 33 |
| Charleston | 8 | 10 | 28 | 23 |
| Mercer | 7 | 11 | 25 | 30 |
| **SOUTH** | | | | |
| Stetson | 12 | 6 | 42 | 23 |
| *Central Florida | 9 | 9 | 43 | 22 |
| Florida Atlantic | 9 | 9 | 39 | 23 |
| Florida International | 6 | 12 | 35 | 24 |
| **WEST** | | | | |
| Jacksonville State | 12 | 6 | 33 | 18 |
| Southeastern Louisiana | 11 | 7 | 34 | 24 |
| Centenary | 7 | 11 | 23 | 34 |
| Samford | 6 | 12 | 22 | 34 |

**ALL-CONFERENCE TEAM: C**—Mark Mortimer, So., Georgia State. **1B**—Ed Nodhturft, Jr., Southeastern Louisiana. **2B**—Kevin Connacher, So., Florida Atlantic. **3B**—Brian Batson, Jr., Charleston. **SS**—Kevin Nicholson, So., Stetson. **OF**—Shane Brister, Sr., Southeastern Louisiana; Jason Glover, Jr., Georgia State; John Hanson, Sr., Mercer. **DH**—Brock Crawford, Sr., Southeastern Louisiana. **SP**—Evan Thomas, Sr., Florida International; Jeff Williams, Sr., Southeastern Louisiana. **RP**—Mike Lyons, Jr., Stetson.

**Player of the Year**—Jason Glover, Georgia State. **Pitcher of the Year**—Evan Thomas, Florida International.

### INDIVIDUAL BATTING LEADERS
(Minimum 125 At-Bats)

| | AVG | AB | R | H | 2B | 3B | HR | RBI | SB |
|---|---|---|---|---|---|---|---|---|---|
| Mortimer, Mark, Ga. State | .403 | 176 | 44 | 71 | 19 | 0 | 7 | 43 | 5 |
| Moulder, Scott, Charleston | .378 | 201 | 50 | 76 | 11 | 3 | 1 | 20 | 31 |
| Batson, Brian, Charleston | .378 | 188 | 38 | 71 | 12 | 1 | 9 | 48 | 0 |
| Presto, Nick, Fla. Atlantic | .375 | 216 | 57 | 81 | 19 | 4 | 9 | 51 | 17 |
| Brooks, Roby, Jax. State | .358 | 151 | 34 | 54 | 15 | 1 | 4 | 40 | 4 |
| Garner, Mike, Jax. State | .356 | 188 | 53 | 67 | 22 | 2 | 12 | 50 | 1 |
| Nicholson, Kevin, Stetson | .351 | 251 | 66 | 88 | 15 | 8 | 13 | 71 | 21 |
| Henderson, Andy, Jax. State | .350 | 160 | 41 | 56 | 11 | 0 | 9 | 52 | 3 |
| Brister, Shane, SE Louisiana | .349 | 209 | 48 | 73 | 17 | 1 | 9 | 51 | 15 |
| Souders, Brooks, Samford | .349 | 192 | 28 | 67 | 13 | 1 | 7 | 42 | 3 |
| Hobbs, Jay, Jax. State | .345 | 142 | 32 | 49 | 9 | 2 | 6 | 29 | 2 |
| Glover, Jason, Ga. State | .345 | 194 | 38 | 67 | 11 | 1 | 20 | 62 | 5 |
| King, Brad, Central Florida | .345 | 197 | 41 | 68 | 15 | 1 | 5 | 32 | 19 |
| Henry, Jimmy, Samford | .342 | 196 | 44 | 67 | 13 | 3 | 0 | 25 | 1 |
| Nodhturft, Ed, SE Louisiana | .338 | 222 | 51 | 75 | 13 | 3 | 13 | 59 | 4 |
| Hannah, Neal, Mercer | .337 | 208 | 41 | 70 | 12 | 1 | 7 | 50 | 8 |
| Branz, Tim, Stetson | .333 | 201 | 45 | 67 | 8 | 3 | 0 | 37 | 7 |
| Brandon, Dustin, Centenary | .333 | 204 | 48 | 68 | 16 | 6 | 4 | 40 | 21 |
| Knight, Nathan, Ga. State | .333 | 138 | 27 | 46 | 4 | 0 | 4 | 16 | 12 |
| Ryan, B.J., Centenary | .330 | 209 | 36 | 69 | 6 | 1 | 7 | 43 | 12 |
| Florio, Jason, Mercer | .328 | 198 | 35 | 65 | 21 | 0 | 5 | 39 | 1 |
| Johnson, Adam, Central Fla. | .327 | 248 | 53 | 81 | 25 | 5 | 5 | 57 | 11 |
| Serrano, Sammy, Stetson | .326 | 221 | 39 | 72 | 11 | 2 | 1 | 36 | 4 |
| Reeves, Skip, Ga. State | .326 | 175 | 40 | 57 | 7 | 0 | 5 | 20 | 4 |
| Gainey, Chad, Jax. State | .326 | 173 | 48 | 57 | 17 | 3 | 7 | 36 | 10 |
| French, Ned, Stetson | .325 | 280 | 66 | 91 | 16 | 5 | 5 | 43 | 15 |
| Pacitti, Gregg, Central Fla. | .325 | 200 | 49 | 65 | 11 | 3 | 6 | 48 | 12 |
| Cox, Hunter, Charleston | .322 | 152 | 34 | 49 | 9 | 0 | 5 | 24 | 1 |

### INDIVIDUAL PITCHING LEADERS
(Minimum 50 Innings)

| | W | L | ERA | G | SV | IP | H | BB | SO |
|---|---|---|---|---|---|---|---|---|---|
| Thomas, Evan, Fla. Int. | 10 | 3 | 1.78 | 20 | 1 | 147 | 102 | 58 | 220 |
| Lyons, Mike, Stetson | 3 | 4 | 1.85 | 37 | 15 | 58 | 44 | 25 | 52 |
| Williamson, Bryan, Jax. State | 7 | 3 | 2.39 | 16 | 1 | 72 | 54 | 26 | 61 |
| Ramirez, Marco, Central Fla. | 6 | 0 | 2.68 | 20 | 2 | 54 | 46 | 18 | 53 |
| Buckley, Matt, Campbell | 6 | 6 | 2.87 | 16 | 0 | 75 | 64 | 37 | 46 |
| Lubozynski, Kevin, Central Fla. | 4 | 1 | 2.88 | 16 | 1 | 56 | 58 | 15 | 42 |
| Chrysler, Clint, Stetson | 4 | 2 | 3.11 | 31 | 3 | 55 | 48 | 13 | 51 |
| Williams, Jeff, SE Louisiana | 12 | 4 | 3.15 | 17 | 0 | 129 | 121 | 42 | 125 |
| Oliver, Scott, Charleston | 5 | 5 | 3.16 | 16 | 1 | 91 | 94 | 41 | 84 |
| Riegert, Tim, Central Fla. | 5 | 3 | 3.19 | 17 | 0 | 90 | 88 | 30 | 58 |
| Cali, Joe, Florida Atlantic | 5 | 3 | 3.19 | 40 | 14 | 62 | 42 | 29 | 58 |
| Argent, Ab, Samford | 4 | 5 | 3.26 | 21 | 4 | 86 | 70 | 40 | 83 |
| Schmidt, George, Central Fla. | 3 | 3 | 3.27 | 22 | 1 | 63 | 67 | 28 | 60 |
| Matcham, Marc, Stetson | 10 | 3 | 3.30 | 21 | 0 | 87 | 91 | 29 | 58 |
| Beale, Chuck, Stetson | 8 | 6 | 3.37 | 21 | 0 | 118 | 113 | 42 | 88 |

| | | | | | | | | | |
|---|---|---|---|---|---|---|---|---|---|
| Giancarlo, David, Ga. State | 8 | 8 | 3.63 | 19 | 0 | 109 | 110 | 38 | 115 |
| Dickinson, Rodney, Ga. State | 8 | 7 | 3.64 | 18 | 0 | 101 | 101 | 38 | 105 |
| Davis, Jamie, Campbell | 5 | 6 | 3.65 | 14 | 0 | 86 | 98 | 23 | 70 |
| Byars, Shane, Charleston | 4 | 5 | 3.65 | 15 | 1 | 69 | 76 | 20 | 54 |
| Piper, Robby, SE Louisiana | 5 | 4 | 3.66 | 17 | 0 | 76 | 81 | 19 | 46 |

## WEST COAST CONFERENCE

| | Conference W | L | Overall W | L |
|---|---|---|---|---|
| Santa Clara | 22 | 6 | 40 | 22 |
| Pepperdine | 19 | 6 | 33 | 19 |
| San Diego | 19 | 9 | 25 | 29 |
| Loyola Marymount | 14 | 14 | 22 | 38 |
| San Francisco | 12 | 16 | 27 | 28 |
| Gonzaga | 9 | 18 | 21 | 28 |
| St. Mary's | 8 | 20 | 13 | 38 |
| Portland | 5 | 19 | 14 | 32 |

**ALL-CONFERENCE TEAM: C**—Travis Wilson, Sr., Loyola Marymount. **1B**—Gerardo Gonzalez, Sr., Pepperdine. **2B**—Jermaine Clark, So., San Francisco. **3B**—Curt Fiore, Fr., Loyola Marymount. **SS**—Ross Parmenter, Sr., Santa Clara. **OF**—Jeb Dougherty, Jr., San Diego; Bill Mott, So., Santa Clara; Ikaika Hoopii, Sr., Loyola Marymount. **DH**—Peter Quittner, Jr., San Francisco. **Util**—Mike Frank, Jr., Santa Clara. **SP**—Brian Carmody, Jr., Santa Clara; Randy Wolf, So., Pepperdine; Brian Mazone, So., San Diego. **RP**—Mike McDonald, Jr., Santa Clara.

**Player of the Year**—Ross Parmenter, Santa Clara. **Pitcher of the Year**—Brian Carmody, Santa Clara.

### INDIVIDUAL BATTING LEADERS
(Minimum 125 At-Bats)

| | AVG | AB | R | H | 2B | 3B | HR | RBI | SB |
|---|---|---|---|---|---|---|---|---|---|
| Clark, Jermaine, USF | .375 | 184 | 44 | 69 | 10 | 2 | 2 | 30 | 30 |
| Parmenter, Ross, Santa Clara | .350 | 243 | 36 | 85 | 11 | 4 | 4 | 60 | 11 |
| Dougherty, Jeb, San Diego | .348 | 221 | 36 | 77 | 7 | 3 | 2 | 36 | 15 |
| Fiore, Curt, LMU | .348 | 184 | 37 | 64 | 6 | 1 | 2 | 21 | 4 |
| Wilson, Travis, LMU | .347 | 213 | 40 | 74 | 19 | 0 | 11 | 50 | 5 |
| Gonzalez, Gerardo, Pepp. | .338 | 160 | 30 | 54 | 17 | 1 | 7 | 46 | 0 |
| Schramm, Kevin, San Diego | .337 | 202 | 34 | 68 | 13 | 1 | 7 | 40 | 2 |
| Betancourt, Tony, San Diego | .337 | 208 | 31 | 70 | 10 | 1 | 6 | 43 | 3 |
| Wicher, Ken, Pepperdine | .335 | 167 | 32 | 56 | 10 | 1 | 4 | 26 | 12 |
| Pearsall, Rob, Gonzaga | .333 | 168 | 32 | 56 | 11 | 1 | 2 | 33 | 6 |
| Quittner, Peter, San Francisco | .329 | 146 | 24 | 48 | 8 | 0 | 5 | 32 | 1 |
| Oder, Josh, Pepperdine | .322 | 183 | 29 | 59 | 9 | 2 | 1 | 32 | 7 |
| Wong, Jerrod, Gonzaga | .315 | 184 | 34 | 58 | 14 | 2 | 8 | 46 | 3 |
| Montgomery, Kalalea, LMU | .311 | 135 | 26 | 42 | 11 | 1 | 3 | 29 | 2 |
| Hoopii, Ikaika, LMU | .310 | 252 | 56 | 78 | 13 | 4 | 9 | 44 | 21 |
| Konrady, Dennis, Pepp. | .309 | 181 | 41 | 56 | 11 | 0 | 1 | 20 | 10 |
| Frankel, Jeff, Santa Clara | .308 | 227 | 45 | 70 | 11 | 1 | 0 | 32 | 5 |
| Hueth, Jason, LMU | .306 | 183 | 34 | 56 | 5 | 0 | 5 | 27 | 0 |
| Hurlbut, Bryan, St. Mary's | .303 | 155 | 25 | 47 | 6 | 1 | 1 | 12 | 11 |

### INDIVIDUAL PITCHING LEADERS
(Minimum 50 Innings)

| | W | L | ERA | G | SV | IP | H | BB | SO |
|---|---|---|---|---|---|---|---|---|---|
| Carmody, Brian, Santa Clara | 10 | 3 | 1.80 | 17 | 0 | 120 | 84 | 57 | 118 |
| Wolf, Randy, Pepperdine | 7 | 3 | 2.02 | 14 | 0 | 98 | 68 | 27 | 111 |
| Nelson, Joe, San Francisco | 4 | 1 | 2.33 | 14 | 5 | 54 | 45 | 15 | 52 |
| Perry, Jeff, Santa Clara | 9 | 4 | 3.04 | 18 | 0 | 101 | 100 | 22 | 66 |
| Gregory, Greg, Pepperdine | 6 | 5 | 3.10 | 12 | 0 | 67 | 59 | 17 | 33 |
| Shibilo, Andrew, Pepperdine | 5 | 1 | 3.33 | 12 | 0 | 54 | 48 | 11 | 46 |
| Frank, Mike, Santa Clara | 7 | 3 | 3.48 | 15 | 1 | 72 | 71 | 33 | 57 |
| Mazone, Brian, San Diego | 5 | 5 | 3.74 | 17 | 1 | 99 | 113 | 36 | 64 |
| Marchbanks, Greg, USF | 4 | 3 | 3.77 | 10 | 0 | 62 | 66 | 22 | 40 |
| LeBlanc, Jason, Pepperdine | 6 | 2 | 3.79 | 11 | 0 | 62 | 64 | 16 | 39 |
| Bennett, Steve, Gonzaga | 3 | 4 | 4.09 | 14 | 0 | 66 | 69 | 41 | 47 |
| Crudale, Mike, Santa Clara | 6 | 2 | 4.45 | 17 | 0 | 55 | 41 | 31 | 44 |
| #McDonald, Mike, Santa Clara | 1 | 4 | 4.50 | 28 | 10 | 34 | 28 | 14 | 36 |
| Gilich, Denny, Portland | 5 | 7 | 4.59 | 16 | 1 | 80 | 78 | 31 | 59 |
| Porter, Aaron, St. Mary's | 1 | 5 | 4.71 | 16 | 0 | 71 | 72 | 42 | 47 |

## WESTERN ATHLETIC CONFERENCE

| EAST | Conference W | L | Overall W | L |
|---|---|---|---|---|
| Brigham Young | 20 | 8 | 38 | 19 |
| New Mexico | 19 | 9 | 27 | 24 |
| Utah | 15 | 15 | 30 | 22 |
| Wyoming | 15 | 15 | 36 | 20 |
| Grand Canyon | 10 | 19 | 23 | 32 |
| Air Force | 8 | 21 | 18 | 36 |

**ALL-CONFERENCE TEAM: C**—Rob Coddington, Jr., Wyoming. **1B**—Tyson Dowdell, So., Brigham Young. **2B**—Travis Young, Jr., New Mexico. **3B**—Ryan Roberts, Sr., Brigham Young. **SS**—Ron Cincera, Jr., Wyoming. **OF**—Rod Bair, Jr., Grand Canyon; Casey Child, So., Utah; Jeremy Schied, So., Wyoming. **DH**—Travis Flint, Jr., Utah. **P**—Dan Bell, Sr., Utah; Luis Gonzalez, Sr., New Mexico; Brett McDermaid, Fr., Brigham Young; Rob Price, So., Grand Canyon.

**Player of the Year**—Travis Young, New Mexico.

## INDIVIDUAL BATTING LEADERS
(Minimum 100 At-Bats)

| | AVG | AB | R | H | 2B | 3B | HR | RBI | SB |
|---|---|---|---|---|---|---|---|---|---|
| Young, Travis, New Mexico... | .442 | 215 | 56 | 95 | 13 | 10 | 2 | 32 | 39 |
| Stringham, Matt, BYU............ | .438 | 128 | 45 | 56 | 16 | 1 | 8 | 29 | 8 |
| McDowell, Eric, BYU ............ | .412 | 194 | 56 | 80 | 11 | 4 | 3 | 46 | 4 |
| Dowdell, Tyson, BYU ........... | .412 | 187 | 68 | 77 | 21 | 0 | 17 | 71 | 3 |
| Sharp, Mike, Air Force........ | .408 | 184 | 65 | 75 | 20 | 5 | 4 | 39 | 11 |
| Jackson, Freddie, Gr. Canyon .. | .402 | 214 | 48 | 86 | 17 | 4 | 8 | 50 | 21 |
| Coddington, Rob, Wyoming .. | .401 | 147 | 27 | 59 | 9 | 1 | 4 | 30 | 3 |
| Nelson, D.G., BYU .............. | .396 | 207 | 63 | 82 | 10 | 1 | 19 | 68 | 10 |
| Roberts, Ryan, BYU .............. | .395 | 220 | 82 | 87 | 8 | 2 | 23 | 50 | 10 |
| Child, Casey, Utah .............. | .392 | 143 | 37 | 56 | 20 | 2 | 10 | 45 | 8 |
| Winget, Brad, BYU .............. | .391 | 202 | 59 | 79 | 15 | 0 | 16 | 68 | 1 |
| Williams, Dan, Gr. Canyon .... | .390 | 195 | 74 | 76 | 17 | 4 | 16 | 44 | 4 |
| Cincera, Ron, Wyoming...... | .387 | 212 | 66 | 82 | 22 | 3 | 15 | 76 | 7 |
| Schied, Jeremy, Wyoming.... | .387 | 225 | 73 | 87 | 13 | 1 | 11 | 48 | 8 |
| Beltran, Leonard, Wyoming .... | .383 | 196 | 60 | 75 | 18 | 1 | 1 | 32 | 3 |
| Brasher, Wes, Wyoming........ | .378 | 209 | 53 | 79 | 15 | 1 | 4 | 48 | 8 |
| Norris, Lawrence, Wyoming.... | .377 | 191 | 43 | 72 | 13 | 2 | 4 | 46 | 3 |
| Sawser, Derek, Air Force ...... | .376 | 197 | 40 | 74 | 20 | 4 | 4 | 47 | 6 |
| Esterline, Brian, Wyoming .... | .376 | 149 | 49 | 56 | 13 | 0 | 8 | 43 | 5 |
| Bair, Rod, Grand Canyon ...... | .372 | 239 | 59 | 89 | 22 | 6 | 10 | 61 | 19 |
| Heidemann, Mike, Utah......... | .367 | 169 | 55 | 62 | 15 | 1 | 9 | 60 | 2 |

## INDIVIDUAL PITCHING LEADERS
(Minimum 40 Innings)

| | W | L | ERA | G | SV | IP | H | BB | SO |
|---|---|---|---|---|---|---|---|---|---|
| #Waites, David, BYU.............. | 1 | 1 | 3.05 | 18 | 5 | 21 | 23 | 11 | 23 |
| Mallard, Brandon, Utah .......... | 3 | 4 | 4.91 | 18 | 0 | 51 | 60 | 37 | 40 |
| Gonzalez, Luis, New Mexico.... | 10 | 3 | 5.00 | 15 | 0 | 108 | 127 | 40 | 94 |
| Williams, Gordon, Wyoming.... | 5 | 2 | 5.51 | 17 | 2 | 47 | 67 | 13 | 21 |
| Schwitzer, Kyle, Wyoming......... | 7 | 3 | 5.66 | 15 | 0 | 68 | 96 | 12 | 22 |
| Bell, Danny, Utah .................... | 5 | 1 | 5.74 | 8 | 0 | 42 | 53 | 30 | 29 |
| Henderson, Adam, New Mexico. | 3 | 2 | 5.86 | 13 | 1 | 58 | 71 | 34 | 45 |
| Markey, Ed, Utah ................... | 7 | 4 | 5.91 | 15 | 0 | 75 | 93 | 25 | 41 |
| Gmirk, Mark, Grand Canyon .... | 4 | 6 | 6.00 | 14 | 0 | 69 | 95 | 27 | 43 |
| Haws, Scott, Brigham Young ... | 8 | 4 | 6.15 | 15 | 0 | 89 | 96 | 44 | 93 |
| McDermaid, Brett, BYU.............. | 7 | 1 | 6.17 | 20 | 2 | 42 | 55 | 14 | 35 |

| WEST | Conference | | Overall | |
|---|---|---|---|---|
| | W | L | W | L |
| *Cal State Northridge | 21 | 9 | 52 | 18 |
| Fresno State | 20 | 10 | 36 | 24 |
| Cal Poly SLO | 18 | 12 | 30 | 23 |
| San Diego State | 16 | 14 | 32 | 25 |
| Hawaii | 12 | 18 | 29 | 26 |
| Sacramento State | 3 | 27 | 12 | 43 |

**ALL-CONFERENCE TEAM: C**—Robert Fick, Jr., Cal State Northridge. **1B**—Travis Lee, Jr., San Diego State. **2B**—Jody Napunoaa, Sr., Hawaii. **3B**—Eric Gillespie, Jr., Cal State Northridge. **SS**—Ben Reynoso, Sr., Fresno State. **OF**—Derek Feramisco, Jr., Fresno State; Jon Macalutas, Sr., Cal Poly SLO; Greg Millichap, Fr., Hawaii; Neal Honma, So., Hawaii; Jason Quintel, Jr., Cal State Northridge. **DH**—Robby Crabtree, Sr., Cal State Northridge; Erasmo Ramirez, So., Cal State Northridge; Jeff Weaver, Fr., Fresno State.

**Co-Players of the Year**—Robert Fick, Cal State Northridge; Travis Lee, San Diego State.

## INDIVIDUAL BATTING LEADERS
(Minimum 125 At-Bats)

| | AVG | AB | R | H | 2B | 3B | HR | RBI | SB |
|---|---|---|---|---|---|---|---|---|---|
| Fick, Robert, CS Northridge ... | .420 | 283 | 79 | 119 | 24 | 5 | 25 | 96 | 22 |
| Kennedy, Adam, CS North.... | .393 | 308 | 94 | 121 | 19 | 6 | 17 | 81 | 15 |
| Honma, Noel, Hawaii.......... | .359 | 156 | 41 | 56 | 8 | 3 | 2 | 23 | 22 |
| Gillespie, Eric, CS Northridge ... | .357 | 263 | 79 | 94 | 15 | 2 | 23 | 70 | 12 |
| Lee, Travis, San Diego State ... | .355 | 220 | 57 | 78 | 14 | 2 | 14 | 60 | 33 |
| Feramisco, Derek, Fresno St.... | .344 | 241 | 47 | 83 | 13 | 3 | 15 | 60 | 4 |
| Miranda, Jose, CS Northridge.... | .341 | 223 | 65 | 76 | 17 | 3 | 3 | 46 | 12 |
| Brennan, Ryan, Cal Poly SLO .. | .341 | 132 | 25 | 45 | 10 | 1 | 2 | 25 | 8 |
| Medeiros, Robert, Hawaii ...... | .338 | 210 | 43 | 71 | 13 | 4 | 2 | 46 | 26 |
| Hennecke, Pete, Fresno St. .. | .337 | 184 | 24 | 62 | 13 | 3 | 3 | 36 | 1 |

| | AVG | AB | R | H | 2B | 3B | HR | RBI | SB |
|---|---|---|---|---|---|---|---|---|---|
| Garnett, Chris, Hawaii .......... | .333 | 177 | 22 | 59 | 8 | 0 | 0 | 22 | 3 |
| Rohlmeier, Steve, CPSLO..... | .333 | 177 | 30 | 59 | 7 | 5 | 4 | 28 | 2 |
| Phillips, Jason, San Diego St. | .330 | 230 | 32 | 76 | 13 | 1 | 1 | 32 | 10 |
| Bevins, Andy, San Diego St.. | .330 | 215 | 36 | 71 | 8 | 2 | 5 | 40 | 3 |
| Smothers, Stewart, SD St. ..... | .330 | 176 | 26 | 58 | 11 | 2 | 1 | 25 | 8 |
| Macalutas, Jon, CPSLO....... | .328 | 201 | 47 | 66 | 15 | 1 | 8 | 41 | 11 |
| Marston, Jeff, Cal Poly SLO .. | .327 | 150 | 28 | 49 | 3 | 3 | 4 | 18 | 3 |
| Millichap, Greg, Hawaii......... | .322 | 177 | 37 | 57 | 10 | 3 | 1 | 25 | 6 |
| Brauning, Jay, Fresno State... | .321 | 159 | 30 | 51 | 3 | 1 | 5 | 20 | 6 |
| Napunoaa, Jody, Hawaii ....... | .316 | 206 | 35 | 65 | 14 | 2 | 0 | 32 | 4 |
| Maier, Taber, Cal Poly SLO ... | .313 | 192 | 37 | 60 | 11 | 4 | 5 | 22 | 4 |
| Curtis, Matt, Fresno State ..... | .311 | 228 | 47 | 71 | 19 | 1 | 5 | 45 | 3 |
| Neal, Rob, Cal Poly SLO....... | .310 | 168 | 34 | 52 | 13 | 1 | 7 | 34 | 10 |
| Trentine, David, San Diego St.. | .309 | 149 | 21 | 46 | 8 | 0 | 2 | 20 | 1 |
| Wakakuwa, Kenn, Hawaii...... | .306 | 170 | 27 | 52 | 12 | 4 | 2 | 25 | 1 |
| Hagins, Steve, San Diego St. | .305 | 187 | 33 | 57 | 8 | 6 | 5 | 31 | 5 |
| Reynoso, Ben, Fresno State . | .305 | 266 | 54 | 73 | 13 | 2 | 6 | 26 | 12 |
| Stevenson, David, CS North.. | .304 | 148 | 34 | 45 | 8 | 0 | 8 | 36 | 1 |
| Kaitfors, Josh, Fresno State .. | .303 | 241 | 54 | 73 | 13 | 2 | 6 | 26 | 12 |
| Roberts, Noel, Fresno State .. | .296 | 125 | 31 | 37 | 7 | 1 | 1 | 15 | 4 |
| #Foulds, Kalin, San Diego St.... | .269 | 238 | 47 | 64 | 9 | 1 | 0 | 28 | 42 |

## INDIVIDUAL PITCHING LEADERS
(Minimum 50 Innings)

| | W | L | ERA | G | SV | IP | H | BB | SO |
|---|---|---|---|---|---|---|---|---|---|
| Weaver, Jeff, Fresno State ........ | 12 | 5 | 2.51 | 19 | 1 | 143 | 107 | 30 | 136 |
| Scott, Brian, San Diego State ... | 5 | 5 | 2.93 | 16 | 0 | 98 | 91 | 28 | 87 |
| Rice, Nathan, CS Northridge...... | 6 | 2 | 3.02 | 23 | 0 | 51 | 40 | 28 | 29 |
| Stevens, Jody, San Diego State ... | 4 | 2 | 3.46 | 21 | 2 | 65 | 54 | 23 | 72 |
| Harriger, Mark, San Diego State... | 3 | 3 | 3.48 | 19 | 1 | 52 | 49 | 14 | 46 |
| Ramirez, Erasmo, CS North..... | 14 | 1 | 3.74 | 24 | 1 | 123 | 119 | 26 | 94 |
| Flores, Benny, CS Northridge .... | 7 | 2 | 3.75 | 21 | 3 | 84 | 83 | 34 | 63 |
| Novi, Jason, Cal Poly SLO ...... | 5 | 4 | 3.76 | 19 | 4 | 91 | 76 | 53 | 69 |
| Riggan, Jerrod, San Diego State ..... | 5 | 6 | 3.80 | 15 | 0 | 83 | 91 | 41 | 65 |
| Atterberry, Matt, Cal Poly SLO .. | 8 | 4 | 3.81 | 15 | 0 | 85 | 74 | 37 | 43 |
| Crabtree, Robby, CS Northridge... | 13 | 8 | 3.89 | 29 | 5 | 139 | 133 | 35 | 118 |
| Zirelli, Mike, Cal Poly SLO ........ | 7 | 3 | 3.96 | 16 | 0 | 91 | 98 | 22 | 44 |
| Stephenson, Gary, CS North. .... | 4 | 3 | 4.27 | 24 | 2 | 53 | 60 | 14 | 36 |
| Johnson, Mark, Hawaii............. | 6 | 5 | 4.60 | 17 | 0 | 119 | 114 | 40 | 132 |
| Ah Yat, Paul, Hawaii ................. | 10 | 6 | 4.66 | 19 | 1 | 112 | 122 | 37 | 87 |

# INDEPENDENTS

| | Overall | |
|---|---|---|
| | W | L |
| Miami | 50 | 14 |
| Oral Roberts | 32 | 24 |
| Hawaii-Hilo | 14 | 31 |
| Southern Utah | 9 | 34 |
| Wofford | 9 | 35 |
| Colgate | 3 | 20 |

## INDIVIDUAL BATTING LEADERS
(Minimum 100 At-Bats)

| | AVG | AB | R | H | 2B | 3B | HR | RBI | SB |
|---|---|---|---|---|---|---|---|---|---|
| Burrell, Pat, Miami ................. | .484 | 192 | 75 | 93 | 18 | 1 | 23 | 64 | 8 |
| Gomez, Rudy, Miami.............. | .420 | 224 | 86 | 94 | 22 | 3 | 13 | 59 | 28 |
| Dinsmore, Brian, Oral Roberts . | .376 | 181 | 44 | 68 | 14 | 1 | 7 | 38 | 2 |
| Rivero, Eddie, Miami ............. | .364 | 209 | 51 | 76 | 12 | 2 | 8 | 54 | 7 |
| DeCelle, Michael, Miami......... | .358 | 151 | 40 | 54 | 14 | 1 | 4 | 41 | 5 |
| Marcinczyk, T.R., Miami......... | .354 | 229 | 53 | 81 | 14 | 0 | 12 | 69 | 15 |
| Walton, Vernon, Wofford........ | .343 | 143 | 25 | 49 | 7 | 2 | 4 | 23 | 5 |
| Saggese, Rick, Miami............. | .339 | 186 | 41 | 63 | 12 | 0 | 14 | 51 | 0 |
| Paul, Tristan, Oral Roberts..... | .339 | 180 | 42 | 61 | 13 | 1 | 4 | 38 | 2 |
| Marsters, Brandon, ORU....... | .339 | 192 | 48 | 65 | 12 | 0 | 9 | 48 | 5 |
| Gargiulo, Jim, Miami............... | .326 | 218 | 47 | 71 | 16 | 0 | 8 | 57 | 4 |
| Rios, Brian, Oral Roberts........ | .323 | 189 | 38 | 61 | 9 | 1 | 2 | 30 | 23 |
| Jackson, Michael, Hawaii-Hilo .. | .319 | 135 | 23 | 43 | 5 | 0 | 0 | 21 | 3 |
| Caoili, Felipe, Hawaii-Hilo ...... | .317 | 142 | 20 | 45 | 7 | 0 | 2 | 26 | 26 |
| Nykoluk, Kevin, Miami........... | .306 | 134 | 24 | 41 | 9 | 0 | 3 | 25 | 2 |
| Grimmett, Ryan, Miami.......... | .306 | 242 | 68 | 74 | 14 | 4 | 3 | 34 | 27 |

## INDIVIDUAL PITCHING LEADERS
(Minimum 40 Innings)

| | W | L | ERA | G | SV | IP | H | BB | SO |
|---|---|---|---|---|---|---|---|---|---|
| Morrison, Robbie, Miami........... | 4 | 2 | 1.68 | 38 | 14 | 59 | 35 | 27 | 88 |
| Westfall, Allan, Miami................. | 5 | 2 | 2.45 | 38 | 2 | 51 | 40 | 23 | 62 |
| Weibl, Clint, Miami.................. | 15 | 3 | 3.58 | 19 | 0 | 121 | 109 | 24 | 108 |
| Sagara, Brendan, Hawaii-Hilo.... | 8 | 2 | 3.61 | 15 | 0 | 62 | 63 | 25 | 47 |
| Arteaga, J.D., Miami................. | 12 | 1 | 3.82 | 18 | 0 | 111 | 112 | 34 | 99 |
| Nakaahiki, Klay, Hawaii-Hilo .... | 2 | 6 | 4.13 | 12 | 0 | 59 | 71 | 45 | 32 |
| Dooley, Chris, Oral Roberts....... | 11 | 6 | 4.21 | 20 | 0 | 130 | 132 | 54 | 124 |
| Barrett, Dusty, Oral Roberts...... | 6 | 5 | 4.29 | 15 | 0 | 80 | 89 | 28 | 60 |
| Pujals, Denis, Miami................. | 9 | 2 | 4.52 | 17 | 0 | 82 | 85 | 25 | 68 |
| Fitch, Ray, Oral Roberts............ | 3 | 1 | 4.61 | 21 | 1 | 53 | 53 | 20 | 30 |

# Kennesaw State Wins Second Title

**By JIM CALLIS**

Kennesaw State (Ga.) won its second national championship in three years by winning the Division II College World Series in its first try, shutting down the powerful bats of St. Joseph's (Ind.) 4-0 in the finale June 1 in Montgomery, Ala.

The Fighting Owls (48-17) won the 1994 NAIA World Series before moving to Division II in 1995.

St. Joseph's (52-12) had hit .487 in the tournament before running into junior righthander Jason Childers in the championship game. Childers pitched a seven-hitter for his fourth shutout of the year, improving his season mark to 12-0 with a 2.01 ERA.

"It's the same thing he has done all year," Kennesaw State junior catcher Chris Halliday said. "He's got one of the nastiest curveballs around, and when he's got it working he's tough to beat."

Halliday, the tournament's MVP, provided all of the offense Childers needed with a three-run home run in the third inning. Halliday batted .467 with two homers and seven RBIs in four consecutive wins in the Series.

**David Townsend.**
Small College Player of the Year.

Kennesaw State also won the Division II softball championship, joining Cal State Northridge (1984) as the only school to achieve that double in the same season.

■ Delta State (Miss.) senior righthander Dave Townsend was named Baseball America's Small College Player of the Year. He won his first 16 decisions and finished the year 16-1 with a 2.33 ERA and 145 strikeouts in 124 innings. No Division II pitcher won more games.

Townsend was honored as the American Baseball Coaches Association's Division II player and pitcher of the year as well. After picking up a win and a save to help the Statesmen reach the semifinals of the Division II College World Series, he signed with the Florida Marlins as a sixth-round draft pick.

■ Columbus (Ga.) junior outfielder Brandon O'Hearn was the ABCA's Division II position player of the year after batting .364 with 16 homers and 58 RBIs. He was no slouch on the mound either, tying for the Division II lead with 13 saves and posting a 1.10 ERA.

| FINAL POLL | |
|---|---|
| **NCAA Division II** | |
| 1. Kennesaw State (Ga.) | 48-17 |
| 2. St. Joseph's (Ind.) | 52-12 |
| 3. Delta State (Miss.) | 53- 8 |
| 4. Tampa | 45-16 |
| 5. Missouri-St. Louis | 37- 9 |
| 6. Adelphi (N.Y.) | 29-16 |
| 7. Columbus (Ga.) | 43-13 |
| 8. Southern Colorado | 44-23 |
| 9. Florida Southern | 44-14 |
| 10. Mercyhurst (Pa.) | 37- 8 |

## NCAA DIVISION III

William Paterson (N.J.) staged a dramatic eighth-inning rally and then held on in the ninth to edge California Lutheran 6-5 for the Division III College World Series championship May 29 in Salem, Va.

The Pioneers (39-5) trailed 5-1 entering the eighth, and cut the gap to 5-4 on a three-run home run from sophomore center fielder Mark DeMenna. First baseman Greg Cimilluca delivered a two-run single with one out to give Paterson the lead over the Kingsmen (34-14).

Freshman righthander Eduardo Gomez saved the game with a scoreless ninth. He was a hero earlier in the tournament, pitching 10 innings to beat Upper Iowa 2-1 in a game won by a DeMenna RBI single. DeMenna was named tournament MVP after batting .462 in four straight victories.

Paterson's previous championship came in 1992, also in dramatic fashion against Cal Lutheran. That year, Ralph Perdomo hit a three-run homer in the top of the ninth inning for a 3-1 victory.

"It's a double-edged sword. I feel for Marty right now," said Paterson coach Jeff Albies, alluding to Lutheran counterpart Marty Slimak. "The last time we shocked them. This time had to shock them also."

■ Marietta (Ohio) junior first baseman-lefthander Joe Thomas was named the ABCA Division III player of the year. Thomas batted .418 with 13 homers and 67 RBIs, and went 4-3 with a 3.11 ERA on the mound.

■ Emory (Ga.) opened the 1996 season with consecutive no-hitters and threw three in its first 11 games.

Mike Garvis, Bill Ezell and Roy Smetana combined to beat Oglethorpe (Ga.) 3-1 in the seven-inning opener Feb. 10. Todd Stein, Andrew Rothenberg and Smetana matched the feat against Savannah Art & Design (Ga.) on Feb. 11, but lost 1-0 in seven innings on a hit batter, error, stolen base and wild pitch. Andy Atkins threw gem No. 3 on Feb. 25, an 8-0 win over Chowan (N.C.) called after five innings because of darkness.

■ Southern Maine, the 1991 Division III champion,

| FINAL POLL | |
|---|---|
| **NCAA Division III** | |
| 1. William Paterson (N.J.) | 39- 5 |
| 2. California Lutheran | 34-14 |
| 3. Bridgewater State (Mass.) | 31-10 |
| 4. Wisconsin-Oshkosh | 35- 6 |
| 5. Methodist (N.C.) | 35- 9 |
| 6. Upper Iowa | 37-14 |
| 7. Marietta (Ohio) | 35- 9 |
| 8. Rensselaer (N.Y.) | 29- 5 |
| 9. St. Thomas (Minn.) | 38- 5 |
| 10. Ferrum (Va.) | 35-11 |

# NCAA DIVISION II

**Site:** Montgomery, Ala.
**Participants:** Adelphi, N.Y. (26-14); Delta State, Miss. (51-6); Kennesaw, Ga, State (44-17); Missouri-St. Louis (37-7); St. Joseph's, Ind. (49-10); Shippensburg, Pa. (34-17); Southern Colorado (43-21); Tampa (44-14).
**Champion:** Kennesaw State (4-0).
**Runner-Up:** St. Joseph's (3-2).
**Outstanding Player:** Chris Halliday, c, Kennesaw State.

## ALL-AMERICA TEAM

| Pos. | Player, School | Yr. | AVG | HR | RBI |
|---|---|---|---|---|---|
| C | Jason Page, Sr., Delta State (Miss.) ... | Sr. | .383 | 5 | 61 |
| 1B | Rob Horgeshimer, St. Joseph's (Ind.) .... | Sr. | .381 | 13 | 81 |
| 2B | Greg Robertson, Mansfield (Pa.)......... | Sr. | .403 | 11 | 67 |
| 3B | Rick Moss, Lewis (Ill.) .................... | Jr. | .449 | 12 | 70 |
| SS | Brian Keck, Fort Hays (Kan.)............... | Sr. | .412 | 13 | 69 |
| INF | Darin Dagle, Bryant (R.I.) ................. | Sr. | .454 | 11 | 50 |
| OF | Brandon O'Hearn, Columbus (Ga.) ..... | Jr. | .364 | 16 | 58 |
|  | Mike Hill, Bentley (Mass.) .................... | Jr. | .417 | 19 | 68 |
|  | Tommy Keeling, Tarleton State (Texas) . | Jr. | .425 | 15 | 66 |
|  | Brian Gibbons, Lewis (Ill.) ................ | Sr. | .402 | 16 | 75 |
| DH | Jose Santos, St. Leo (Fla.) ................ | Jr. | .381 | 15 | 70 |
|  |  | Yr. | W | L | ERA |
| P | Ricky Burton, Tampa .................... | So. | 14 | 2 | 2.29 |
|  | Dave Townsend, Delta State (Miss.)... | Sr. | 16 | 1 | 2.33 |
|  | Eric LeBlanc, St. Rose (N.Y.) ............. | Sr. | 11 | 2 | 1.90 |
|  | Jason Childers, Kennesaw State (Ga.) ... | Jr. | 12 | 0 | 2.01 |
|  | George Wise, UC Riverside ............... | Sr. | 2 | 2 | 2.17 |

**Player/Pitcher of the Year**—Dave Townsend, lhp, Delta State (Miss.).

## NATIONAL LEADERS

### BATTING AVERAGE
(Minimum 125 At-Bats)

|  | AB | H | AVG |
|---|---|---|---|
| Sorrentino, Joe, So. Connecticut ...................... | 149 | 72 | .483 |
| Folkers, Brandon, St. Andrews (N.C.) ............. | 150 | 71 | .473 |
| Davis, Terry, So. Colorado........................ | 151 | 71 | .470 |
| Flores, Freddy, N.M. Highlands .................... | 150 | 70 | .467 |
| Dagle, Darin, Bryant (R.I.) ............................. | 163 | 74 | .454 |
| Stennett, Mike, Mo.-St. Louis ..................... | 159 | 72 | .453 |
| Irish, Cole, So. Dakota State ........................ | 167 | 75 | .449 |
| Moss, Rick, Lewis (Ill.) ............................ | 243 | 109 | .449 |
| Whitworth, Wade, No. Dakota St. .................. | 187 | 82 | .439 |
| Bordes, Cormac, Assumption (Mass.) ............. | 131 | 57 | .435 |
| Gifford, Matt, St. Leo (Fla.) ........................ | 201 | 87 | .433 |
| Rakers, Jason, Quincy (Ill.) ............................ | 163 | 70 | .429 |

### Department Leaders: Batting

| Dept. | Player, School | G | Total |
|---|---|---|---|
| R | Moss, Rick, Lewis (Ill.) ................................. | 62 | 80 |
| H | Moss, Rick, Lewis (Ill.) ................................. | 62 | 109 |
| TB | Moss, Rick, Lewis (Ill.) ................................. | 62 | 180 |
| 2B | Moss, Rick, Lewis (Ill.) ................................. | 62 | 29 |
| 3B | Funderburk, Jack, SW Baptist (Mo.) ............. | 51 | 10 |
| HR | Mosher, Willie, Mesa (Colo.) State ................ | 57 | 24 |
| RBI | Horgeshimer, Rob, St. Joseph's (Ind.) ........... | 64 | 81 |
| SB | Chancey, Bailey, Ala.-Huntsville.................... | 52 | 50 |

### EARNED RUN AVERAGE
(Minimum 60 Innings)

|  | IP | ER | ERA |
|---|---|---|---|
| Cline, Brian, New Haven (Conn.) ....................... | 64 | 6 | 0.84 |
| Rodriguez, Richie, St. Andrews (N.C.) ............... | 70 | 7 | 0.90 |
| Agard, Jeff, Armstrong (Ga.) State .................... | 78 | 9 | 1.04 |
| Rockwood, Mike, Adelphi (N.Y.) ....................... | 72 | 12 | 1.51 |
| Tavarnese, Sal, SUNY Stony Brook ................. | 88 | 15 | 1.53 |
| Herman, Jason, Emporia (Kan.) State ............... | 87 | 16 | 1.65 |
| Bivins, Donnie, Lynn (Fla.) ............................... | 108 | 20 | 1.67 |
| Falk, Nate, Florida Tech ................................ | 128 | 25 | 1.76 |

### Department Leaders: Pitching

| Dept. | Player, School | G | Total |
|---|---|---|---|
| W | Townsend, Dave, Delta State (Miss.) ............ | 22 | 16 |
| SV | O'Hearn, Brandon, Columbus (Ga.) .............. | 20 | 13 |
|  | Wise, George, UC Riverside ....................... | 27 | 13 |
| SO | Donaldson, Bo, Tampa ................................. | 19 | 172 |

---

# NCAA DIVISION III

**Site:** Salem, Va.
**Participants:** Bridgewater, Mass., State (28-8); California Lutheran (30-12); Marietta, Ohio (43-11); Methodist, N.C. (34-7); Rensselaer, N.Y. (29-3); Upper Iowa (36-12); William Paterson, N.J. (35-4); Wisconsin-Oshkosh (33-4).
**Champion:** William Paterson (4-1).
**Runner-Up:** California Lutheran (4-2).
**Outstanding Player:** Mark DeMenna, of, William Paterson.

## ALL-AMERICA TEAM

| Pos. | Player, School | Yr. | AVG | HR | RBI |
|---|---|---|---|---|---|
| C | Matt Jackson, Wooster (Ohio) ............. | Jr. | .411 | 15 | 56 |
| 1B | Mark Beyer, Carthage (Wis.) ............. | Jr. | .411 | 20 | 61 |
|  | Joe Thomas, Marietta (Ohio) ............. | Jr. | .417 | 12 | 66 |
| 2B | David Jones, Ferrum (Va.) ................. | Sr. | .387 | 3 | 41 |
| 3B | Tony Miner, Southern Maine .............. | Jr. | .382 | 6 | 39 |
| SS | Brian Lindner, Wm. Paterson (N.J.) .... | Sr. | .440 | 8 | 79 |
| OF | Shorty Flees, Carthage (Wis.) ............. | Jr. | .434 | 15 | 57 |
|  | Jason Nypaver, Allegheny (Pa.) ......... | Sr. | .439 | 16 | 61 |
|  | Eric Roepsch, Framingham (Mass.) St... | Sr. | .462 | 14 | 58 |
|  | Jeff Zappa, Wis.-Oshkosh .................. | Sr. | .482 | 17 | 72 |
| DH | Joe Musgrove, Allegheny (Pa.) ........... | Jr. | .503 | 10 | 74 |
|  |  | Yr. | W | L | ERA |
| P | Tim Adkins, Methodist (N.C.) ............. | Jr. | 10 | 0 | 1.77 |
|  | Bob Davies, Marietta (Ohio) ............. | So. | 13 | 4 | 2.24 |
|  | Jim Hamilton, Ferrum (Va.) ............. | Jr. | 12 | 2 | 2.73 |
|  | Dave Lohrman, Rensselaer (N.Y.)....... | Jr. | 8 | 0 | 1.50 |
|  | Joe Thomas, Marietta (Ohio) ............. | Jr. | 4 | 2 | 2.91 |

**Player of the Year**—Joe Thomas, 1b-lhp, Marietta (Ohio).

## NATIONAL LEADERS

### BATTING AVERAGE
(Minimum 100 At-Bats)

|  | AB | H | AVG |
|---|---|---|---|
| Akana, Jason, Worcester (Mass.) St. ............. | 105 | 54 | .514 |
| Scott, Jeremy, Maryville (Mo.) ........................ | 115 | 58 | .504 |
| Musgrove, Joe, Allegheny (Pa.)...................... | 159 | 80 | .503 |
| Barnes, Todd, William Penn (Ia.) .................... | 116 | 56 | .483 |
| Zappa, Jeff, Wis.-Oshkosh ............................ | 168 | 81 | .482 |
| Johnson, Dan, Centre (Ky.) ............................ | 100 | 48 | .480 |
| Krebs, Kurt, Albright (Pa.) .............................. | 124 | 59 | .476 |
| Mosier, Mark, Chicago ................................... | 129 | 61 | .473 |
| Ahrendt, Jay, Ill. Wesleyan ........................... | 103 | 48 | .466 |
| Clapp, Andrew, SUNY Oswego ....................... | 101 | 47 | .465 |

### Department Leaders: Batting

| Dept. | Player, School | G | Total |
|---|---|---|---|
| R | DeMenna, Mark, Willam Paterson (N.J.) ........ | 45 | 68 |
|  | Scher, Mike, William Paterson (N.J.) ............. | 45 | 68 |
| H | Martinez, Tommy, Upper Iowa ..................... | 51 | 87 |
| TB | Zappa, Jeff, Wis.-Oshkosh ............................ | 39 | 150 |
| 2B | Musgrove, Joe, Allegheny (Pa.) ..................... | 49 | 25 |
| 3B | Garret, Bret, Greensboro (N.C.) ..................... | 41 | 8 |
| HR | Beyer, Mark, Carthage (Wis.) ........................ | 44 | 20 |
| RBI | Lindner, Brian, William Paterson (N.J.) ........... | 45 | 79 |
| SB | Gunn, Brian, Christopher Newport (Va.) ........ | 39 | 49 |

### EARNED RUN AVERAGE
(Minimum 50 Innings)

|  | IP | ER | ERA |
|---|---|---|---|
| Snyder, Bill, Rensselaer (N.Y.) ....................... | 61 | 7 | 1.03 |
| Hinckley, Tim, Rensselaer (N.Y.) ................... | 50 | 7 | 1.26 |
| Lewis, Eric, Olivet (Mich.) ............................. | 80 | 12 | 1.36 |
| Guibord, Steve, Albion (Mich.) ...................... | 56 | 9 | 1.44 |
| Bailey, Geoff, Beloit (Wis.) ........................... | 56 | 9 | 1.46 |
| Strickler, Bob, Juniata (Pa.) .......................... | 56 | 9 | 1.46 |
| Larsen, Thor, Washington (Mo.) ..................... | 75 | 13 | 1.57 |

### Department Leaders: Pitching

| Dept. | Player, School | G | Total |
|---|---|---|---|
| W | Davies, Bob, Marietta (Ohio) ........................ | 19 | 13 |
| SV | Mohn, Stan, North Carolina Wesleyan .......... | 27 | 14 |
| SO | Davies, Bob, Marietta (Ohio) ........................ | 19 | 135 |

was rocked by a gambling scandal that resulted in suspensions for 11 players ranging from four games to the entire season. The penalties totaled 176 games.

Seventeen players, none of whose names were released, placed a total of $4,500 in bets on pro and college basketball and football games. None of the wagering involved Huskies teams. Only players who bet on college sports were suspended, though new NCAA rules that took effect Aug. 1 would have applied to the others.

The most active bettors were two players who wagered on as many as 50 games, called in bets for other students and delivered money to a bookmaker. One of the players placed bets totaling $1,000.

Southern Maine finished the season 27-11.

## NAIA

After a three-year absence, Lewis-Clark State (Idaho) returned to the pinnacle of the NAIA in 1996. The Warriors crushed St. Ambrose (Iowa) 9-0 May 31 at Sioux City, Iowa, to win their ninth NAIA World Series.

Lewis-Clark State (53-11) won five consecutive games for its first title since 1992. The Warriors captured six straight championships from 1987-92 and also won in 1984 and 1985.

Freshman righthander Matt Randel threw a four-hitter against the Fighting Bees (42-19) with 10 strikeouts to improve his season record to 8-0. First baseman Troy Silva added three hits and earned tournament MVP by batting .471 with a homer and five RBIs for the tournament. Silva was also MVP of the NAIA's Far West Regional after hitting .588-2-14 in four games.

■ Embry-Riddle (Fla.) senior righthander Frankie Thomas was selected as the ABCA's NAIA player of the year. He went 14-1 with a 1.40 ERA and 115 strikeouts in 109 innings.

■ What happens when a perennial NAIA power meets a program in its second year? On April 2, St. Francis (Ill.) pounded Robert Morris (Ill.) 71-1. Eagles coach Gerald McNamara surrendered after four innings.

The Saints, who have dual NCAA Division II and NAIA membership and won the NAIA World Series in 1993, broke 21 national records and tied six others in the blowout. They set marks at both levels for runs, runs in an inning (26 in the first), largest margin of victory, hits (44) and total bases (79).

Left fielder Mike Holcomb became the first NCAA or NAIA player to score nine runs in a game. DH Brian Mazurek hit for the cycle, including a double, triple and homer in the fourth inning alone.

When the Saints took a 48-1 lead after two innings, coach Tony Delgado offered McNamara the opportunity to end the game whenever he wanted. McNamara called Delgado gracious and said he didn't think St. Francis tried to humiliate his team.

"I just did not feel going out there for two innings and walking off the field was the thing to do," McNamara said. "We know we have to pay the price. We paid it. I think good things will come of it."

■ Lewis-Clark State coach Ed Cheff added more than another championship to his resume in 1996. He became the third NAIA coach to reach 1,000 victories with an 8-0, 6-0 doubleheader sweep of Central Wash-

# NAIA

## WORLD SERIES

**Site:** Sioux City, Iowa.
**Participants:** No. 1 Lewis-Clark State, Idaho (48-11); No. 2 St. Mary's, Texas (43-12); No. 3 Oklahoma Baptist (52-11); No. 4 Cumberland, Tenn. (41-19); No. 5 St. Thomas, Fla. (45-19); No. 6 Ohio Dominican (35-18); No. 7 St. Ambrose, Iowa (39-17); No. 8 Geneva, Pa. (24-19).
**Champion:** Lewis-Clark State (5-0).
**Runner-Up:** St. Ambrose (3-2).
**Outstanding Player:** Troy Silva, 1b, Lewis-Clark State.

## ALL-AMERICA TEAM

| Pos. | Player, School | Yr. | AVG | HR | RBI |
|---|---|---|---|---|---|
| C | Josh Robertson, Friends (Kan.) | Jr. | .500 | 24 | 83 |
| | Calvin Tanton, Briar Cliff (Iowa) | So. | .450 | 9 | 55 |
| 1B | Chris Shuffield, Lubbock Christian | Jr. | .391 | 18 | 82 |
| 2B | Ed Gillis, Oklahoma City | Sr. | .419 | 13 | 71 |
| 3B | Art Baeza, Lewis-Clark (Idaho) State | Sr. | .389 | 14 | 73 |
| SS | Ryan Andersen, Dallas Baptist | Sr. | .411 | 9 | 66 |
| INF | Jason Kinchen, Brewton-Parker (Ga.) | Jr. | .455 | 15 | 87 |
| OF | Johnny Goodrich, Embtry-Riddle (Fla.) | Sr. | .385 | 1 | 25 |
| | Scott Harp, Dallas Baptist | Jr. | .430 | 7 | 57 |
| | Bernard Hutchinson, Montevallo (Ala.) | Sr. | .409 | 2 | 18 |
| | Marcus McCain, Lubbock Christian | Jr. | .449 | 0 | 47 |
| DH | Jim Cannon, Illinois Tech | Jr. | .468 | 15 | 54 |

| | | Yr. | W | L | ERA |
|---|---|---|---|---|---|
| P | Aaron Carter, St. Mary's (Texas) | Jr. | 15 | 1 | 1.23 |
| | Kevin Hite, Cumberland (Tenn.) | Sr. | 13 | 2 | 2.30 |
| | Frankie Thompson, Embry-Riddle | Sr. | 14 | 1 | 1.40 |

**Player of the Year**—Frankie Thompson, rhp, Embry-Riddle (Fla.).

## NATIONAL LEADERS

### BATTING AVERAGE
(Minimum 100 At-Bats)

| | AB | H | AVG |
|---|---|---|---|
| Robertson, Josh, Friends (Kan.) | 144 | 72 | .500 |
| Dunbar, Jeff, McKendree (Ill.) | 112 | 55 | .491 |
| Cannon, Jim, Illinois Tech | 141 | 66 | .468 |
| Bly, Derrick, Concordia (Calif.) | 144 | 67 | .465 |
| Starkey, Chris, Southern Arkansas | 185 | 84 | .454 |
| Cadize, Mariano, McKendree (Ill.) | 113 | 51 | .451 |
| Tanton, Calvin, Briar Cliff (Iowa) | 189 | 85 | .450 |
| Boomsma, Kent, Kansas Newman | 143 | 64 | .448 |
| Horen, Gary, Nova Southeastern (Fla.) | 179 | 80 | .447 |
| Kaiser, Jason, Culver-Stockton (Mo.) | 119 | 53 | .445 |
| Reed, Chris, Friends (Kan.) | 152 | 67 | .441 |

### Department Leaders: Batting

| Dept. | Player, School | G | Total |
|---|---|---|---|
| R | Blessing, Chad, Houston Baptist | 54 | 76 |
| | Baeza, Art, Lewis-Clark (Idaho) State | 62 | 76 |
| H | Harp, Scott, Dallas Baptist | 72 | 107 |
| 2B | Starkey, Chris, Southern Arkansas | 56 | 29 |
| 3B | Bly, Derrick, Concordia (Calif.) | 43 | 9 |
| HR | Robertson, Josh, Friends (Kan.) | 42 | 24 |
| RBI | Robertson, Josh, Friends (Kan.) | 42 | 83 |
| SB | Hutchinson, Bernard, Montevallo (Ala.) | 61 | 55 |

### EARNED RUN AVERAGE
(Minimum 50 Innings)

| | IP | ER | ERA |
|---|---|---|---|
| Black, Randy, Southern Tech (Ga.) | 56 | 5 | 0.81 |
| Carter, Aaron, St. Mary's (Texas) | 110 | 15 | 1.23 |
| Cohen, Abe, Williamette (Ore.) | 72 | 10 | 1.24 |
| Thompson, Frankie, Embry-Riddle (Fla.) | 109 | 17 | 1.40 |
| Fuhrman, Devin, Grand View (Ill.) | 81 | 13 | 1.44 |
| Baugh, Frank, William Carey (Miss.) | 87 | 14 | 1.45 |
| Carbone, Marc, Dominican (N.Y.) | 53 | 9 | 1.54 |
| McInnish, Clay, Shorter (Ga.) | 93 | 16 | 1.54 |
| Harper, Lee, Birmingham-Southern | 92 | 16 | 1.57 |
| Pasley, Brian, Linfield (Ore.) | 97 | 17 | 1.58 |

### Department Leaders: Pitching

| Dept. | Player, School | G | Total |
|---|---|---|---|
| W | Carter, Aaron, St. Mary's (Texas) | 19 | 15 |
| SO | Kubenka, Jeff, St. Mary's (Texas) | 20 | 147 |

ington on May 10. Cheff finished the season with a 1,010-266 record in 20 seasons.

■ Lipscomb's (Tenn.) Ken Dugan, the winningest coach in NAIA history, retired after the season because of health problems. Dugan, 61, has calcified lungs which limit him to 50 percent of normal breathing capacity and are worsening slowly. Dugan finished his career with a 1,137-460 record and two NAIA championships.

## JUNIOR COLLEGE

In just its fourth year playing baseball, Northeast Texas won the Junior College World Series by beating Meridian (Miss.) 4-3 in an all-Eagles final on June 1 in Grand Junction, Colo.

Northeast Texas (48-18) had lost to Meridian (50-12) 13-4 in the semifinals, then beat Arizona Western 11-1 to force a rematch. That game was tied 3-3 in the eighth inning before catcher Kevin Fountain hit a solo home run to break the deadlock. Chuck Crumpton struck out Paul Phillips in the ninth with the tying run on base.

Northeast Texas center fielder Robert Vaz was named Series MVP after hitting .578 with four homers and 15 RBIs in six games.

■ Rancho Santiago became the first team to successfully defend its California community college championship in 21 years by beating Cypress 16-10 on May 27 in Fresno.

The Dons (39-12) won three straight games in the finals, including a previous 1-0 victory over the Chargers (41-14). Rancho Santiago has appeared in four consecutive California championship games, winning in 1993 over Sacramento City, losing in 1994 to Cypress and prevailing in 1995 over Cerritos.

Left fielder Ryan Fullerton and shortstop Tony Zuniga shared MVP honors. Fullerton went 7-for-14 with a homer, while Zuniga went 6-for-13 with two homers. Zuniga was the lone MVP in 1995.

■ Rancho Santiago sophomore third baseman Derek Baker was named Baseball America's Junior College Player of the Year after transferring from Southern California following an injury-plagued 1995 season.

Baker batted .363 with 16 homers and 53 RBIs and led California juco players with 63 runs and 48 walks. He signed with the Texas Rangers as a third-round draft pick in June.

■ Grand Rapids (Mich.) captured the National Junior College Athletic Association Division II World Series by winning four straight games, including the 18-10 finale over Northwest Mississippi May 24 in Millington, Tenn.

Third baseman Clint Balgera, who batted .615 as the tournament MVP, hit two doubles and drove in three runs to power the Raiders' attack in the championship contest. The 18 runs were a Series record.

■ Madison Area Tech (Wis.) repeated as NJCAA Division III World Series champion by besting Waubonsee (Ill.) 7-2 on May 24 in Batavia, N.Y.

Freshman Ian Lewellin, normally the Trojans' No. 4 starter, responded to the challenge when pressed into service in the finale by throwing a complete-game five-hitter. Madison, which beat Joliet (Ill.) twice on the final day in 1995, similarly had to rally against the Chiefs, who would have been champions with a win in either game.

In the opener, Carey Shrank threw a six-hitter and struck out 10 as Madison won 5-2. Schrank was named tournament MVP after batting .375 and going 2-0, 0.64 on the mound.

# JUNIOR COLLEGE

## NJCAA DIVISION I

### WORLD SERIES

**Site:** Grand Junction, Colo.
**Participants:** Allegany, Md. (43-4); Arizona Western (42-23); Indian Hills, Ia. (45-14); Indian River, Fla. (38-14); Jackson State, Tenn. (37-18); Meridian, Miss. (46-10); Middle Georgia (55-7); Northeast Texas (43-17); St. Louis-Meramec (43-12); Triton, Ill. (32-14);
**Champion:** Northeast Texas (5-1).
**Runner-Up:** Meridian (4-2).
**Outstanding Player:** Robert Vaz, of, Northeast Texas JC.

### ALL-AMERICA TEAM

**C**—Matt Frick, Yavapai (Ariz.). **INF**—Shawn Leimbeck, Des Moines Area (Iowa) CC; Andy Osbolt, Middle Georgia; John Summers, Trinidad State (Colo.); Jeremy Troutman, Butler County (Kan.) CC. **OF**—Mark Peer, St. Louis-Meramec; Greg Strickland, Volunteer State (Tenn.); Tyrone Wayne, Northwest Shoals (Ala.). **DH**—Jeff Hedrick, Anne Arundel (Md.). **P**—Chris Brown, Cowley County (Kan.); Ryan Channell, Manatee (Fla.); Jarrod Kingrey, Central Alabama.

### NATIONAL LEADERS

#### BATTING AVERAGE
(Minimum 100 At-Bats)

| | AB | H | AVG |
|---|---|---|---|
| Clemmer, Terry, New Mexico | 140 | 68 | .486 |
| Goodwin, David, Jackson State (Tenn.) | 143 | 69 | .483 |
| Summers, John, Trinidad State (Colo.) | 191 | 92 | .482 |
| Ziemann, Trevor, Colby (Kan.) | 109 | 50 | .459 |
| Moore, Jeff, Odessa (Texas) | 164 | 75 | .457 |

#### Department Leaders: Batting

| Dept. | Player, School | G | Total |
|---|---|---|---|
| HR | Dill, Justin, Connors State (Okla.) | 63 | 25 |
| RBI | Dill, Justin, Connors State (Okla.) | 63 | 106 |
| SB | Reiner, Brad, Lamar (Colo.) | 45 | 60 |

#### EARNED RUN AVERAGE
(Minimum 50 Innings)

| | IP | ER | ERA |
|---|---|---|---|
| Thompson, Doug, Mississippi Gulf Coast | 104 | 9 | 0.78 |
| Waller, Jerry, Hagerstown (Md.) | 57 | 6 | 0.95 |
| Lefever, Dan, Hagerstown (Md.) | 53 | 6 | 1.02 |
| Phillips, Randy, Olney Central (Ill.) | 80 | 11 | 1.24 |
| Kingrey, Jarrod, Central Alabama | 69 | 12 | 1.57 |

#### Department Leaders: Pitching

| Dept. | Player, School | G | Total |
|---|---|---|---|
| SV | Beasley, Ray, Lake City (Fla.) | 32 | 15 |
| SO | Hoerman, Jared, Eastern Oklahoma | 13 | 145 |

## NJCAA DIVISION II

### WORLD SERIES

**Site:** Millington, Tenn.
**Participants:** Dundalk (Md.); Grand Rapids (Mich.); Iowa Central; Lewis & Clark (Ill.); Mercer County (N.J.); Northwest Mississippi; Redlands (Okla.); Rhode Island.
**Champion:** Grand Rapids (4-0).
**Runner-Up:** Northwest Mississippi (3-2).
**Outstanding Player:** Clint Balgera, 3b, Grand Rapids.

## NJCAA DIVISION III

### WORLD SERIES

**Site:** Batavia, N.Y.
**Participants:** Columbia-Greene (N.Y.); Gloucester County (N.J.); Madison Area Tech (Wis.); Norwalk (Conn.); Owens (Ohio); Richland (Texas); Ulster (N.Y.); Waubonsee (Ill.).
**Champion:** Madison Area Tech (5-1).
**Runner-Up:** Waubonsee (3-2).
**Outstanding Player:** Carey Schrank, p-of, Madison Area Tech.

## CALIFORNIA JUCOS

### STATE CHAMPIONSHIP

**Site:** Fresno.
**Participants:** Cypress (39-12); Fresno City (34-15); Lassen (34-9); Rancho Santiago (36-12).
**Champion:** Rancho Santiago (3-0).
**Runner-Up:** Cypress (2-2).
**Most Valuable Players:** Ryan Fullerton, of, Rancho Santiago; Tony Zuniga, ss, Rancho Santiago.

# HIGH SCHOOL
# BASEBALL

# Westminster Survives Upset Bid To Capture Second National Title

**By CHRIS WRIGHT**

All season long, Miami Westminster Christian coach Rich Hofman dismissed talk that his 1996 team was his best ever. But with an unbeaten season finally in his grasp, there no longer was any denying it.

"I still can't fathom it," said Hofman. "This season has been a once-in-a-lifetime thing. I told the players before the championship that if they pulled this off, it would become more significant every day. It is awesome. This has to be one of the finest accomplishments ever."

The '96 Warriors did what the Alex Rodriguez-led Warriors of 1992 and 1993 couldn't: They ran the table. In recognition, Westminster was named national champion by Baseball America and the National High School Baseball Coaches Association. It's the second time in five years the Warriors have worn the crown.

The Warriors weren't exactly handed the title. Against the toughest schedule in school history, they beat then-No. 1-ranked Key West (Fla.) early, stopped two more nationally-ranked teams to win the prestigious Dole National Classic in Orange County, Calif., at midseason, and crushed seven state playoff opponents by a combined margin of 85-6. The Warriors' pitching staff threw six straight shutouts en route to the school's sixth state 2-A title.

"We've had some great teams," Hofman said, "but our schedule was a little easier in the late '80s. Now we're on a national schedule. Our players are better, but so is the competition. We feel pretty good about beating Key West, Kennedy (Granada Hills, Calif.) and Mater Dei (Santa Ana, Calif.). Another poll had them ranked second and third behind us. Nobody can argue the point. That's what makes it satisfying."

The lone blemish on Westminster Christian's 36-0-1 record was an error-marred tie with Southwest High of Miami.

While unbeatable, the Warriors weren't untouchable. Hofman said they had their share of close games.

They endured a tough two-week stretch sandwiched around the Dole Classic in which they trailed in six of eight games. But the biggest scare came during the final game of the season. With state and national titles at stake, Westminster's dream of an unbeaten season nearly ended in a nightmarish first inning of the 2-A state final.

**Rich Hofman**

Liberty County High of Bristol roughed up starter Keith Brice, taking a 4-0 lead with runners on the corners and no outs in the first. Hofman couldn't help but think back to 1994, when K.O. Wiegandt, then a sophomore, inherited a similar first-inning mess and threw seven innings of no-hit ball in relief to win the championship.

Looking for a similar miracle, Hofman called on Danny Rodriguez, a capable pitcher who earlier in the season threw a no-hitter in his first varsity start. Rodriguez got a double-play grounder on the first pitch he threw. The runner from third scored, but the leak was plugged. Rodriguez allowed two hits and one more run before turning the game over to Wiegandt in the seventh.

The Warriors rallied and Wiegandt went on to nail down a 10-6 victory to complete the perfect season.

"It was scary," Hofman said. "I think I realized the magnitude of the game a little more than the players. I knew what the difference between winning and losing meant as far as the national scope. A loss would have been devastating. I was thinking maybe it wasn't meant to be, but we held on. It was an unbelievable season."

## Repeat Champions

No. 2 Cherry Creek High (22-0) of Englewood slammed 43 homers on the season to easily win its second straight Colorado 5-A championship. Junior outfielder Darnell McDonald led Cherry Creek with 15 homers and 48 RBIs while hitting .581.

Kennedy High (31-3) of Granada Hills,

## HIGH SCHOOL TOP 25

Baseball America's final 1996 Top 25, selected in conjunction with the National High School Baseball Coaches Association:

| SCHOOL, CITY | W-L | Achievement |
|---|---|---|
| 1 Westminster Christian Academy, Miami | 36-0 | State 2-A champion |
| 2 Cherry Creek HS, Englewood, Colo. | 22-0 | State 5-A champion |
| 3 Kennedy HS, Granada Hills, Calif. | 31-3 | CIF sectional champion |
| 4 Monterey HS, Lubbock, Texas | 36-3 | State 5-A champion |
| 5 Horizon HS, Scottsdale, Ariz. | 32-2 | State 5-A champion |
| 6 Tottenville HS, Staten Island, N.Y. | 33-1 | Class A sectional champion |
| 7 Key West (Fla.) HS | 31-5 | State 4-A champion |
| 8 Fontana (Calif.) HS | 25-2 | |
| 9 Jesuit HS, Tampa | 32-4 | |
| 10 Mater Dei HS, Santa Ana, Calif. | 25-4 | |
| 11 George Washington HS, New York | 41-3 | |
| 12 Duncanville (Texas) HS | 29-4 | |
| 13 Green Valley HS, Henderson, Nev. | 32-5 | State 3-A champion |
| 14 Round Rock (Texas) HS | 28-3 | |
| 15 Glen Oak HS, Canton, Ohio | 25-2 | State Division I champion |
| 16 Mission Bay HS, San Diego | 29-5 | CIF sectional champion |
| 17 Sarasota (Fla.) HS | 26-7 | State 5-A champion |
| 18 Dr. Phillips HS, Orlando | 28-7 | State 6-A champion |
| 19 Klein Oak HS, Spring, Texas | 29-5 | |
| 20 Columbus (Ga.) HS | 30-4 | State 3-A champion |
| 21 F.W. Cox HS, Virginia Beach | 25-1 | State 3-A champion |
| 22 Center Grove HS, Greenwood, Ind. | 25-2 | |
| 23 Ralston (Neb.) HS | 26-1 | State champion |
| 24 New Hope (Miss.) HS | 43-0 | State 4-A champion |
| 25 Lee County HS, Sanford, N.C. | 26-2 | State 4-A champion |

# PLAYER OF THE YEAR

## White Meets High Expectations

**Great Expectations.** Pennsylvania schoolboy Matt White went 10-1 with a 0.66 ERA as the nation's top high school talent.

Since the summer of 1995, when Waynesboro (Pa.) High righthander Matt White dominated the Team One Showcase in Cincinnati and starred for the U.S. junior national team, he has carried the burden of great expectations.

When he struck out 10, fans wanted 15. When he allowed four hits, many wondered why someone who throws 96 mph couldn't throw no-hitters at will. One Waynesboro supporter even told coach Greg Chandler that the team shouldn't wear black jerseys when White pitched, because opponents could pick up the ball better.

"I tried not to think about that," said White, who was selected seventh overall in the 1996 draft by the San Francisco Giants. "Yeah, it was pretty pressure filled in order to perform up to my capability, but I worked hard to prepare for it."

White finished the 1996 season with a 10-1 record and 0.66 ERA and 131 strikeouts in 74 innings. The 6-foot-5, 230-pound power pitcher was selected Baseball America's high school

### PREVIOUS WINNERS

1992—**Preston Wilson**, ss-rhp, Bamberg-Ehrhardt (S.C.) High
1993—**Trot Nixon**, of-lhp, New Hanover High, Wilmington, N.C.
1994—**Doug Million**, lhp, Sarasota (Fla.) High
1995—**Ben Davis**, c, Malvern (Pa.) Prep

Player of the Year, the second straight player from Pennsylvania to win the award. Ben Davis, a catcher from Malvern Prep now with the Padres organization, was the 1995 winner.

White credits his health, not his fastball, for a successful senior season in which he pitched two no-hitters, led Waynesboro to the state playoffs and established a school record with 401 career strikeouts.

"Staying healthy enabled me to go out there with my best stuff consistently," he said. "I wanted to perform, show people what I could do. It was nice that I had pretty good velocity coming out. I've always pitched in cold weather, so that didn't bother me. I'm used to it."

---

Calif., won its second straight Los Angeles 4-A city championship to earn a No. 3 national ranking.

Lubbock's Monterey High earned a No. 4 ranking by winning the Texas 5-A title. It beat Klein Oak 5-4 in a game that was delayed five hours by rain and ended at 2:24 a.m.

It was the fourth state title for Monterey coach Bobby Moegle and the 1,038th win of his career.

**Talented Teammates.** Catcher Eric Munson, left, and Eric Chavez of pre-season No. 1-ranked Mt. Carmel High of San Diego.

Moegle is the nation's all-time winningest high school coach.

Lefthander Mark Martinez, who was the winning pitcher in Monterey's 4-3 win over Clear Creek in the semifinals, worked the final three innings against Klein Oak for his national-best 17th win. He struck out seven and allowed only two base runners.

No. 5 Horizon High won its second straight Arizona 5-A title, tying a state record with 32 wins in the process. Senior lefthander Jerod Berkowitz (16-0, 1.42) was selected the Arizona player of the year.

In a much anticipated showdown of New York City powers, Tottenville stopped George Washington 5-1 before 5,000 at Yankee Stadium to win its fifth straight New York city championship. No. 6 Tottenville, which had a 44-game winning streak stopped during the season, finished at 33-1, No. 11 George Washington at 41-3.

Righthander Jason Marquis, a supplemental first-round pick of the Atlanta Braves, struck out 15 and allowed just five hits in the victory. He finished with a 14-1 record and 0.71 ERA.

After having its 43-game winning streak broken, losing its showdown with West-

Selected by Baseball America       *Junior

### FIRST TEAM

| Pos. | Player, School | AVG | AB | R | H | 2B | 3B | HR | RBI | SB |
|---|---|---|---|---|---|---|---|---|---|---|
| C | Eric Munson, Mt. Carmel HS, San Diego | .432 | 88 | 29 | 38 | 6 | 0 | 10 | 30 | 18 |
| 1B | A.J. Zapp, Center Grove HS, Greenwood, Ind. | .507 | 69 | 43 | 35 | 8 | 0 | 14 | 46 | 3 |
| INF | Brent Abernathy, Lovett HS, Atlanta | .635 | 126 | 77 | 80 | 23 | 4 | 13 | 50 | 46 |
| | Eric Chavez, Mt. Carmel HS, San Diego | .458 | 96 | 37 | 44 | 8 | 3 | 11 | 24 | 33 |
| | Joe Lawrence, Barbe HS, Lake Charles, La. | .449 | 89 | 50 | 40 | 8 | 5 | 9 | 38 | 20 |
| OF | Dermal Brown, Marlboro (N.Y.) Central HS | .450 | 60 | 36 | 27 | 4 | 1 | 9 | 35 | 20 |
| | John Oliver, Lake-Lehman HS, Lehman, Pa. | .625 | 88 | 54 | 55 | 12 | 3 | 11 | 43 | 25 |
| | *Vicente Rosario, George Washington HS, New York | .583 | 120 | 54 | 70 | 14 | 6 | 13 | 72 | 96 |
| DH | *Darnell McDonald, Cherry Creek HS, Englewood, Colo. | .581 | 74 | 36 | 43 | 11 | 2 | 15 | 48 | 9 |

| Pos. | Player, School | W | L | ERA | G | SV | IP | H | BB | SO |
|---|---|---|---|---|---|---|---|---|---|---|
| P | Jason Marquis, Tottenville HS, Staten Island, N.Y. | 14 | 1 | 0.46 | 18 | 3 | 82 | 28 | 22 | 135 |
| | Sam Marsonek, Jesuit HS, Tampa | 12 | 1 | 0.93 | 14 | 0 | 93 | 47 | 25 | 153 |
| | John Patterson, West Orange (Texas) Stark HS | 7 | 2 | 0.77 | 14 | 1 | 72 | 35 | 36 | 142 |
| | Bobby Seay, Sarasota (Fla.) HS | 9 | 2 | 0.70 | 14 | 0 | 70 | 33 | 29 | 122 |
| | Jake Westbrook, Madison County HS, Danielsville, Ga. | 9 | 1 | 1.11 | 14 | 1 | 63 | 32 | 17 | 110 |
| | Matt White, Waynesboro (Pa.) Area HS | 10 | 1 | 0.66 | 12 | 0 | 74 | 21 | 16 | 131 |

### SECOND TEAM

| Pos. | Player, School | AVG | AB | R | H | 2B | 3B | HR | RBI | SB |
|---|---|---|---|---|---|---|---|---|---|---|
| C | Mark Osborne, Lee County HS, Sanford, N.C. | .469 | 81 | 30 | 38 | 12 | 1 | 4 | 31 | 10 |
| 1B | Nick Johnson, McClatchy HS, Sacramento | .367 | 79 | 36 | 29 | 5 | 3 | 6 | 30 | 13 |
| INF | Matt Halloran, Chancellor HS, Fredericksburg, Va. | .493 | 69 | 20 | 34 | 5 | 1 | 7 | 28 | 7 |
| | Jimmy Rollins, Encinal HS, Alameda, Calif. | .510 | 106 | 39 | 54 | 16 | 5 | 6 | 29 | 30 |
| | Damian Rolls, Schlagel HS, Kansas City, Kan. | .488 | 41 | 18 | 20 | 6 | 4 | 4 | 22 | 18 |
| OF | Dernell Stenson, LaGrange (Ga.) HS | .526 | 95 | 51 | 50 | 10 | 1 | 10 | 34 | 9 |
| | Robert Stratton, San Marcos HS, Santa Barbara, Calif. | .424 | 66 | 30 | 28 | 8 | 2 | 3 | 24 | 26 |
| | Paul Wilder, Cary (N.C.) HS | .438 | 73 | 25 | 32 | 3 | 2 | 10 | 24 | 13 |
| DH | Grant Sharpe, Watkins HS, Laurel, Miss. | .492 | 59 | 27 | 29 | 8 | 2 | 7 | 42 | 3 |

| Pos. | Player, School | W | L | ERA | G | SV | IP | H | BB | SO |
|---|---|---|---|---|---|---|---|---|---|---|
| P | Scott Comer, Mazama HS, Klamath Falls, Ore. | 13 | 0 | 0.90 | 15 | 1 | 95 | 28 | 5 | 135 |
| | Adam Eaton, Snohomish (Wash.) HS | 8 | 0 | 0.60 | 12 | 0 | 58 | 28 | 15 | 80 |
| | Casey Fossum, Midway HS, Waco, Texas | 13 | 1 | 0.53 | 16 | 1 | 105 | 31 | 39 | 210 |
| | Josh Garrett, South Spencer HS, Richland, Ind. | 8 | 0 | 0.42 | 13 | 0 | 67 | 26 | 14 | 102 |
| | Brent Schoening, Columbus (Ga.) HS | 12 | 2 | 0.87 | 20 | 4 | 84 | 6 | 20 | 137 |
| | Kris Stevens, Fontana (Calif.) HS | 10 | 0 | 0.86 | 10 | 0 | 65 | 32 | 22 | 93 |

minster Christian, 5-3, and dropping three of four games at the Dole National Classic, Key West (31-5) rebounded to win its second straight Florida 4-A title and earn a No. 7 ranking.

There were numerous other repeat champions.

No. 18 Sarasota (26-7), the 1994 national champion, reestablished its elite status by winning the Florida 5-A title, its third state title in four years.

No. 13 Green Valley High (32-5) of Henderson racked up its fourth straight Nevada 3-A state title while No. 20 Columbus High (30-4) won its third straight Georgia 3-A crown. Unranked Vestavia Hills High (31-6) won its second straight Alabama 6-A title and fifth championship in six years.

## High-Profile Teammates

Third baseman Eric Chavez and catcher Eric Munson of San Diego's Mt. Carmel High nearly became the second set of high school teammates to become first-round draft picks, joining Mike Ondina and ex-big leaguer Jerry Manuel of Rancho Cordova (Calif.) High in 1972. Chavez went in the first round to Oakland, while Munson ended up going in the second round to Atlanta.

Mt. Carmel began the 1996 season ranked No. 1 but won only two of its first nine games and quickly dropped from national contention. The Sun Devils rallied to finish 21-10 and won their second straight San Diego CIF sectional 2-A championship.

"It was a roller-coaster season," said Mt. Carmel coach Steve Edwards. "I guess it's not where you start but where you finish."

Chavez and Munson were selected to Baseball America's High School All-America team and were joined by junior outfielders Vicente Rosario of New York's George Washington High, who hit .583 with a national-record 92 stolen bases, and McDonald, who became the nation's most hotly-recruited two-sport star during the 1996-97 school year.

Nantucket (Mass.) High junior third baseman Aaron Hull tied Shawn Gallagher's national record by hitting five home runs in a 22-3 victory against New England Christian Academy. Hull drove in 12 runs, which is four shy of the national mark.

"I didn't think I'd ever be capable of getting five hits in a game," Hull said. "Five homers is beyond my belief."

Hull hit a grand slam in the second, a two-run shot in the third and solo homers in the fifth and sixth. A pair of two-out hits allowed him to bat once more in the seventh. He responded with a three-run blast. As he circled the bases, opposing players gave him high fives.

Another Massachusetts high school player, senior first baseman Josh Plosker of Somerset High hit a national-record tying three grand slams in a 21-20 loss to Dartmouth High. His slams came in his first, second and fourth at-bats.

# AMATEUR BASEBALL

# Cuba Runs Win Streak To 126, But Is Severely Tested At Olympics

**By JIM CALLIS**

Omar Linares and Cuba used the Olympic gold-medal game to yet again show why they're the class of international baseball. Surprisingly, Team USA wasn't around to prove otherwise.

Linares hit three of his team's eight home runs as Cuba defeated Japan 13-9 on Aug. 2 before a crowd of 44,221 at Atlanta-Fulton County Stadium. Cuba, which won the first official Olympic baseball tournament four years earlier in Barcelona, Spain, stretched its winning streak at major international tournaments to 126 games.

While the wins continued—as they have since Team USA defeated the Cubans in the round-robin at the 1987 Pan American Games—the 1996 Olympic championship wasn't nearly as easy as Cuba's first. Wracked by defections and injuries during the past year, Cuba had to escape close calls from Japan, the United States and Nicaragua during the round-robin, and Japan again in the final game.

Cuban head coach Jorge Fuentes conceded privately that he was surprised his team was able to go 9-0 in Atlanta.

"This is the most difficult championship of all," Fuentes said through a translator. "In fact, it doesn't have any comparison to Barcelona in 1992 or any other tournament we've won. We feel very fortunate to win this gold medal."

Part of Cuba's good fortune is having the services of Linares, who has been considered finest amateur player in the world since joining the Cuban national team in 1984 at age 16.

He put on a show in the gold-medal game, hitting an upper-deck homer to left in the first inning off starter Masanori Sugiura (who also started in the semifinals the day before), a screaming, line-drive shot to right in the sixth off Takeo Kawamura and a blast to dead center in the eighth off Masahiko Mori.

**Omar Linares**

"It is one of the greatest games of my career," Linares said. "I practically helped my team win the gold medal."

Said Fuentes: "Everyone will be so happy back in Cuba. It will be a big party. I'm sure everyone will be happy with this gold medal we worked so hard for."

## Stabbed In Heart

USA Baseball also worked hard, trying to erase its bitter memories of a fourth-place finish in Barcelona. Team USA general manager Mike Fiore devised a two-year plan that cost $5 million and was designed to win a gold medal. Nearly everything worked perfectly.

Before the Olympics, Fuentes said Cuba was the only team strong enough to defeat the United States. And with six wins in 10 games against Cuba during the last two years, including an unprecedented four-game sweep in 1995, Team USA was ready to take its chances.

Then the United States ran into an old nemesis in the semifinals.

Japan hit five home runs and rode the pitching of Sugiura to an improbably easy 11-2 victory over

## TEAM USA '96

### OVERALL STATISTICS

| BATTING | AVG | AB | R | H | 2B | 3B | HR | RBI | SB | College | Class |
|---|---|---|---|---|---|---|---|---|---|---|---|
| *Adam Kennedy, ss.. | .462 | 13 | 4 | 6 | 0 | 0 | 0 | 1 | 0 | Cal State Northridge | So. |
| Travis Lee, 1b .......... | .416 | 137 | 46 | 57 | 15 | 0 | 17 | 57 | 6 | San Diego State | Jr. |
| Jacque Jones, of....... | .404 | 151 | 38 | 61 | 11 | 3 | 15 | 49 | 2 | Southern California | Jr. |
| Chad Allen, of.......... | .403 | 124 | 30 | 50 | 11 | 4 | 6 | 29 | 1 | Texas A&M | Jr. |
| Jason Williams, ss..... | .398 | 103 | 28 | 43 | 8 | 0 | 5 | 23 | 1 | Louisiana State | Sr. |
| *Lance Berkman, of... | .364 | 11 | 1 | 4 | 2 | 0 | 0 | 4 | 0 | Rice | So. |
| Mark Kotsay, of ......... | .351 | 131 | 40 | 46 | 12 | 2 | 8 | 27 | 3 | Cal State Fullerton | Jr. |
| Troy Glaus, 3b.......... | .342 | 120 | 35 | 41 | 8 | 2 | 15 | 34 | 0 | UCLA | So. |
| A.J. Hinch, c............. | .337 | 89 | 21 | 30 | 7 | 0 | 3 | 15 | 1 | Stanford | Sr. |
| Kip Harkrider, 2b ....... | .333 | 51 | 10 | 17 | 4 | 0 | 1 | 8 | 3 | Texas | So. |
| Matt LeCroy, dh......... | .333 | 102 | 26 | 34 | 2 | 1 | 15 | 32 | 0 | Clemson | So. |
| Warren Morris, 2b...... | .327 | 101 | 31 | 33 | 4 | 0 | 8 | 29 | 4 | Louisiana State | Jr. |
| *Robert Fick, c.......... | .308 | 13 | 3 | 4 | 1 | 0 | 1 | 4 | 0 | Cal State Northridge | Jr. |
| Brian Loyd, c ............ | .290 | 62 | 11 | 18 | 2 | 0 | 6 | 15 | 0 | Cal State Fullerton | Jr. |
| *J.D. Drew, of........... | .268 | 41 | 14 | 11 | 2 | 0 | 6 | 9 | 0 | Florida State | So. |
| *Nathan Dunn, 3b...... | .250 | 12 | 2 | 3 | 1 | 0 | 0 | 1 | 0 | Louisiana State | Jr. |
| Chad Green, of.......... | .247 | 77 | 19 | 19 | 6 | 1 | 2 | 11 | 6 | Kentucky | Jr. |
| *Casey Blake, 3b....... | .233 | 30 | 7 | 7 | 3 | 0 | 0 | 1 | 0 | Wichita State | Sr. |
| Augie Ojeda, ss......... | .213 | 47 | 9 | 10 | 3 | 0 | 0 | 6 | 0 | Tennessee | Jr. |
| *Clint Bryant, 3b ........ | .000 | 4 | 1 | 0 | 0 | 0 | 0 | 0 | 0 | Texas Tech | Sr. |
| *Brian Dallimore, 2b .. | .000 | 5 | 1 | 0 | 0 | 0 | 0 | 0 | 0 | Stanford | Sr. |

| PITCHING | W | L | ERA | G | SV | IP | H | BB | SO | College | Class |
|---|---|---|---|---|---|---|---|---|---|---|---|
| *Matt Anderson........... | 0 | 0 | 0.00 | 1 | 0 | 1 | 0 | 0 | 1 | Rice | So. |
| *Ryan Brannan ........... | 0 | 0 | 0.00 | 2 | 0 | 2 | 1 | 2 | 1 | Long Beach State | Jr. |
| *Scott Downs ............. | 1 | 0 | 0.00 | 1 | 0 | 4 | 1 | 1 | 0 | Kentucky | So. |
| *Chad Harville............. | 0 | 0 | 0.00 | 1 | 0 | 1 | 1 | 0 | 1 | Memphis | So. |
| *Scott Schoeneweis..... | 0 | 0 | 0.00 | 1 | 0 | 2 | 1 | 2 | 3 | Duke | Sr. |
| Braden Looper........... | 1 | 0 | 2.25 | 18 | 4 | 24 | 20 | 8 | 23 | Wichita State | Jr. |
| Seth Greisinger........... | 9 | 0 | 2.98 | 10 | 0 | 57 | 45 | 15 | 55 | Virginia | Jr. |
| *Eric Milton................. | 0 | 0 | 3.00 | 1 | 0 | 3 | 2 | 1 | 2 | Maryland | Jr. |
| Jim Parque................. | 1 | 0 | 3.30 | 15 | 3 | 30 | 32 | 11 | 37 | UCLA | So. |
| R.A. Dickey ................ | 7 | 0 | 3.35 | 10 | 0 | 51 | 56 | 12 | 45 | Tennessee | Jr. |
| Jeff Weaver................. | 1 | 1 | 3.37 | 14 | 2 | 35 | 34 | 8 | 32 | Fresno State | Fr. |
| Kris Benson ............... | 7 | 1 | 4.12 | 9 | 0 | 55 | 55 | 12 | 53 | Clemson | Jr. |
| Billy Koch .................. | 5 | 2 | 4.25 | 9 | 0 | 42 | 42 | 28 | 45 | Clemson | Jr. |
| *Randy Wolf................ | 2 | 0 | 4.50 | 7 | 2 | 14 | 18 | 6 | 13 | Pepperdine | So. |
| *Mark Johnson............ | 0 | 1 | 6.55 | 7 | 0 | 11 | 14 | 5 | 8 | Hawaii | Jr. |
| *Eric DuBose ............. | 0 | 0 | 8.64 | 4 | 0 | 8 | 12 | 5 | 10 | Mississippi State | So. |
| *Evan Thomas ............ | 1 | 0 | 20.25 | 2 | 0 | 4 | 9 | 2 | 5 | Florida International | Sr. |
| *Matt White ................ | 0 | 0 | 40.50 | 1 | 0 | 1 | 6 | 0 | 1 | Waynesboro (Pa.) HS | Sr. |

*Did not make U.S. Olympic team roster

# OLYMPIC GAMES
## Atlanta, Georgia
July 20-August 2, 1996

### ROUND-ROBIN STANDINGS

| | W | L | RF | RA |
|---|---|---|---|---|
| Cuba | 7 | 0 | 97 | 49 |
| United States | 6 | 1 | 81 | 27 |
| Japan | 4 | 3 | 69 | 45 |
| Nicaragua | 4 | 3 | 44 | 30 |
| Netherlands | 2 | 5 | 32 | 76 |
| Italy | 2 | 5 | 33 | 71 |
| Australia | 2 | 5 | 47 | 86 |
| Korea | 1 | 6 | 40 | 59 |

**SEMIFINALS (August 1):** Cuba 8, Nicaragua 1; Japan 11, United States 2.
**GOLD MEDAL (August 2):** Cuba 13, Japan 9.
**BRONZE MEDAL:** United States 10, Nicaragua 3.

### INDIVIDUAL BATTING LEADERS
(Minimum 19 Plate Appearances)

| | AVG | AB | R | H | 2B | 3B | HR | RBI | SB |
|---|---|---|---|---|---|---|---|---|---|
| Luigi Carrozza, Italy | .571 | 21 | 6 | 12 | 3 | 0 | 0 | 1 | 0 |
| Luis Ulacia, Cuba | .556 | 27 | 10 | 15 | 5 | 1 | 3 | 6 | 3 |
| Yasuyuki Saigo, Japan | .481 | 27 | 12 | 13 | 2 | 1 | 1 | 5 | 1 |
| Omar Linares, Cuba | .476 | 42 | 21 | 20 | 1 | 0 | 8 | 16 | 0 |
| Eric de Bruin, Neth | .471 | 17 | 4 | 8 | 0 | 0 | 1 | 3 | 0 |
| David Hynes, Australia | .462 | 26 | 5 | 12 | 2 | 1 | 1 | 3 | 0 |
| Scott Tunkin, Australia | .462 | 13 | 2 | 6 | 0 | 0 | 1 | 3 | 0 |
| Orestes Kindelan, Cuba | .442 | 43 | 18 | 19 | 1 | 0 | 9 | 18 | 0 |
| Marcel Joost, Neth | .440 | 25 | 5 | 11 | 2 | 0 | 2 | 5 | 1 |
| Bayardo Davila, Nic | .435 | 23 | 2 | 10 | 0 | 0 | 0 | 7 | 0 |
| Makoto Imaoka, Japan | .435 | 23 | 6 | 10 | 2 | 0 | 2 | 7 | 0 |
| Tadahito Iguchi, Japan | .429 | 35 | 11 | 15 | 1 | 2 | 2 | 7 | 0 |
| Kang Hyuk, Korea | .429 | 28 | 7 | 12 | 4 | 0 | 1 | 6 | 0 |
| Marco Ubani, Italy | .429 | 21 | 5 | 9 | 2 | 0 | 1 | 7 | 1 |
| Juan Manrique, Cuba | .423 | 26 | 11 | 11 | 5 | 0 | 4 | 12 | 0 |
| Yoshitomo Tani, Japan | .421 | 38 | 8 | 16 | 3 | 1 | 4 | 11 | 2 |
| Warren Morris, USA | .409 | 22 | 9 | 10 | 1 | 0 | 5 | 11 | 1 |
| Jacque Jones, USA | .395 | 38 | 12 | 15 | 1 | 2 | 5 | 13 | 0 |
| Matt LeCroy, USA | .394 | 33 | 10 | 13 | 1 | 1 | 4 | 10 | 0 |
| R. Balentina, Neth | .389 | 18 | 1 | 7 | 0 | 1 | 0 | 1 | 0 |
| Choi Hyun-Ho, Korea | .385 | 26 | 6 | 10 | 0 | 1 | 2 | 6 | 1 |
| Travis Lee, USA | .382 | 34 | 9 | 13 | 4 | 0 | 2 | 10 | 1 |
| Henry Roa, Nicaragua | .382 | 34 | 9 | 13 | 2 | 1 | 0 | 5 | 0 |
| Chad Allen, USA | .375 | 32 | 9 | 12 | 3 | 1 | 3 | 8 | 0 |
| Lee Byoung-Kyu, Korea | .375 | 32 | 5 | 12 | 0 | 1 | 0 | 6 | 2 |
| Eduardo Paret, Cuba | .375 | 32 | 9 | 12 | 1 | 0 | 2 | 7 | 0 |
| Claudio Liverziani, Italy | .370 | 27 | 5 | 10 | 3 | 0 | 1 | 4 | 0 |
| Lee Dong, Korea | .368 | 19 | 3 | 7 | 0 | 0 | 0 | 0 | 0 |
| Jason Williams, USA | .367 | 30 | 10 | 11 | 0 | 0 | 3 | 9 | 0 |
| Tomoaki Sato, Japan | .364 | 33 | 8 | 12 | 3 | 0 | 2 | 7 | 0 |
| Antonio Pacheco, Cuba | .359 | 39 | 13 | 14 | 1 | 0 | 5 | 14 | 0 |
| F. Casolari, Italy | .357 | 28 | 2 | 10 | 5 | 0 | 2 | 9 | 0 |
| Marcel Kruyt, Neth | .353 | 17 | 4 | 6 | 4 | 0 | 0 | 2 | 0 |
| Jin Kab-Yong, Korea | .346 | 26 | 3 | 9 | 1 | 0 | 1 | 3 | 0 |
| Andrew Scott, Australia | .345 | 29 | 6 | 10 | 2 | 0 | 2 | 8 | 1 |
| Lazaro Vargas, Cuba | .343 | 35 | 7 | 12 | 3 | 0 | 0 | 4 | 1 |
| Peter Vogler, Australia | .333 | 21 | 5 | 7 | 2 | 0 | 0 | 2 | 1 |
| David Rigoli, Italy | .333 | 18 | 7 | 6 | 0 | 1 | 1 | 1 | 1 |
| N. Matsunaka, Japan | .333 | 33 | 7 | 11 | 0 | 0 | 5 | 16 | 0 |
| S. Moreno, Nicaragua | .321 | 28 | 7 | 9 | 1 | 0 | 0 | 1 | 2 |
| Miguel Caldes, Cuba | .324 | 34 | 10 | 11 | 1 | 0 | 3 | 13 | 0 |
| Jason Hewitt, Australia | .310 | 29 | 7 | 9 | 1 | 0 | 0 | 4 | 2 |
| Steve Hinton, Australia | .308 | 26 | 7 | 8 | 3 | 0 | 0 | 4 | 0 |
| E. Baca, Nicaragua | .306 | 36 | 5 | 11 | 3 | 0 | 1 | 6 | 0 |
| Jose Padilla, Nicaragua | .304 | 23 | 3 | 7 | 0 | 0 | 1 | 3 | 0 |
| Mark Kotsay, USA | .303 | 33 | 10 | 10 | 4 | 0 | 3 | 6 | 0 |

### INDIVIDUAL PITCHING LEADERS
(Minimum 6 Innings)

| | W | L | ERA | G | SV | IP | H | BB | SO |
|---|---|---|---|---|---|---|---|---|---|
| Braden Looper, USA | 0 | 0 | 0.00 | 4 | 1 | 6 | 3 | 1 | 6 |
| Paul Nanne, Neth | 0 | 0 | 0.00 | 5 | 1 | 7 | 4 | 2 | 3 |
| Shane Tonkin, Australia | 1 | 0 | 2.31 | 4 | 0 | 12 | 9 | 2 | 8 |
| R.A. Dickey, USA | 2 | 0 | 3.00 | 2 | 0 | 12 | 9 | 3 | 12 |
| Jose Luis Quiroz, Nic | 2 | 1 | 3.14 | 3 | 0 | 14 | 12 | 10 | 15 |
| Omar Obando, Nicaragua | 0 | 0 | 3.38 | 5 | 0 | 11 | 11 | 5 | 6 |

---

| | | | ERA | G | SV | IP | H | BB | SO |
|---|---|---|---|---|---|---|---|---|---|
| Roberto Cabalisti, Italy | 2 | 1 | 3.66 | 3 | 0 | 20 | 19 | 6 | 17 |
| Jeff Weaver, USA | 0 | 0 | 3.68 | 4 | 1 | 7 | 6 | 1 | 3 |
| Omar Ajete, Cuba | 0 | 0 | 4.00 | 3 | 1 | 9 | 8 | 1 | 11 |
| Rolando Cretis, Italy | 0 | 0 | 4.35 | 4 | 0 | 19 | 13 | 6 | 8 |
| Masahiko Mori, Japan | 0 | 0 | 4.50 | 6 | 0 | 8 | 10 | 4 | 10 |
| Masao Morinaka, Japan | 0 | 1 | 4.66 | 4 | 0 | 10 | 14 | 3 | 15 |
| Takeo Kawamura, Japan | 0 | 1 | 4.85 | 5 | 1 | 13 | 13 | 4 | 14 |
| Seth Greisinger, USA | 3 | 0 | 5.00 | 3 | 0 | 18 | 18 | 4 | 11 |
| Koichi Misawa, Japan | 1 | 1 | 5.06 | 4 | 0 | 11 | 10 | 1 | 13 |
| Mun Dong-Hwan, Korea | 0 | 1 | 5.14 | 4 | 0 | 14 | 19 | 2 | 15 |
| Asdrudes Flores, Nic | 1 | 2 | 5.21 | 4 | 0 | 19 | 17 | 12 | 17 |
| Jutaro Kimura, Japan | 2 | 1 | 5.27 | 6 | 0 | 14 | 15 | 2 | 19 |
| Pedro Luis Lazo, Cuba | 2 | 0 | 5.40 | 4 | 1 | 13 | 11 | 6 | 22 |
| Oswaldo Mairena, Nic | 0 | 0 | 5.40 | 4 | 0 | 8 | 12 | 2 | 1 |
| Jeon Seung-Nam, Korea | 0 | 2 | 5.59 | 3 | 0 | 10 | 13 | 1 | 7 |
| Omar Luis, Cuba | 3 | 0 | 5.71 | 4 | 0 | 17 | 13 | 5 | 18 |
| Kris Benson, USA | 2 | 1 | 5.82 | 3 | 0 | 17 | 20 | 5 | 17 |
| Oh Chul-Min, Korea | 1 | 0 | 6.00 | 3 | 0 | 9 | 13 | 6 | 9 |
| Jose Contreras, Cuba | 1 | 0 | 6.23 | 3 | 0 | 13 | 17 | 3 | 16 |
| Billy Koch, USA | 0 | 1 | 6.23 | 3 | 0 | 9 | 8 | 5 | 4 |
| Fredy Corea, Nicaragua | 1 | 2 | 6.57 | 3 | 0 | 12 | 17 | 7 | 15 |
| E. Bojorge, Nicaragua | 0 | 0 | 6.75 | 1 | 0 | 7 | 8 | 4 | 2 |
| Rob Cordemans, Neth | 2 | 0 | 6.94 | 2 | 0 | 12 | 13 | 7 | 11 |

### GOLD-MEDAL GAME
#### Cuba 13, Japan 9

| JAPAN | ab | r | h | bi | CUBA | ab | r | h | bi |
|---|---|---|---|---|---|---|---|---|---|
| Takabayashi rf | 3 | 1 | 0 | 0 | Estrada cf | 5 | 1 | 1 | 1 |
| Nakamura cf | 1 | 1 | 1 | 0 | Ulacia rf | 5 | 3 | 4 | 2 |
| Saigo lf-rf | 3 | 2 | 1 | 1 | Linares 3b | 4 | 3 | 3 | 6 |
| Kuroso ph | 1 | 0 | 0 | 0 | Kindelan dh | 5 | 1 | 1 | 1 |
| Tani cf-lf | 5 | 3 | 3 | 3 | Pacheco 2b | 4 | 1 | 1 | 1 |
| Matsunaka, 1b | 5 | 1 | 2 | 5 | Vargas 1b | 4 | 0 | 0 | 0 |
| Okubo c | 5 | 0 | 1 | 0 | Caldes lf | 4 | 2 | 3 | 1 |
| Sato dh | 3 | 0 | 0 | 0 | Manrique c | 3 | 0 | 0 | 0 |
| Kuwamoto ph | 1 | 0 | 0 | 0 | Paret ss | 3 | 2 | 1 | 1 |
| Iguchi ss | 4 | 0 | 1 | 0 | | | | | |
| Imaoka 2b | 3 | 0 | 0 | 0 | | | | | |
| Fukudome 3b | 2 | 1 | 0 | 0 | | | | | |
| Totals | 36 | 9 | 9 | 9 | Totals | 37 | 13 | 14 | 13 |

Japan 000 150 102— 9
Cuba 330 004 12x—13

**E**—Fukudome. **DP**—Cuba 1. **LOB**—Japan 6, Cuba 3. **2B**—Ulacia 2, Estrada. **HR**—Linares 3, Kindelan, Ulacia, Matsunaka, Caldes, Paret, Tani 2, Pacheco. **SB**—Nakamura.

| Japan | ip | h | r | er | bb | so | Cuba | ip | h | r | er | bb | so |
|---|---|---|---|---|---|---|---|---|---|---|---|---|---|
| Sugiura | 1⅔ | 5 | 5 | 5 | 0 | 1 | Luis | 4⅔ | 5 | 6 | 6 | 2 | 4 |
| Kimura L | 3⅓ | 3 | 2 | 2 | 2 | 7 | Lazo W | 4⅓ | 4 | 3 | 3 | 3 | 7 |
| Kawamura | ⅔ | 3 | 3 | 3 | 0 | 1 | | | | | | | |
| Morinaka | 1 | 2 | 1 | 1 | 0 | 1 | | | | | | | |
| Mori | 1 | 1 | 2 | 2 | 1 | 2 | | | | | | | |
| Misawa | ⅓ | 0 | 0 | 0 | 0 | 1 | | | | | | | |

Kimura pitched to one batter in 6th.
**HBP**—Fukudome (by Luis).
**T**—2:57. **A**—44,221.

### TEAM USA
#### OLYMPIC STATISTICS

| BATTING | AVG | AB | R | H | 2B | 3B | HR | RBI | SB |
|---|---|---|---|---|---|---|---|---|---|
| Warren Morris, 2b | .409 | 22 | 9 | 10 | 1 | 0 | 5 | 11 | 1 |
| Jacque Jones, of | .395 | 38 | 12 | 15 | 1 | 2 | 5 | 13 | 0 |
| Matt LeCroy, dh | .394 | 33 | 10 | 13 | 1 | 1 | 4 | 10 | 0 |
| Travis Lee, 1b | .382 | 34 | 9 | 13 | 4 | 0 | 2 | 10 | 1 |
| Chad Allen, of | .375 | 32 | 9 | 12 | 3 | 1 | 3 | 8 | 0 |
| Jason Williams, ss | .367 | 30 | 10 | 11 | 0 | 0 | 3 | 9 | 0 |
| Mark Kotsay, of | .303 | 33 | 10 | 10 | 4 | 0 | 3 | 6 | 0 |
| Brian Loyd, c | .267 | 15 | 4 | 4 | 0 | 0 | 2 | 8 | 0 |
| Kip Harkrider, 2b | .250 | 8 | 0 | 2 | 1 | 0 | 0 | 0 | 0 |
| A.J. Hinch, c | .238 | 21 | 6 | 5 | 2 | 0 | 1 | 3 | 0 |
| Troy Glaus, 3b | .219 | 32 | 7 | 9 | 1 | 0 | 4 | 5 | 0 |
| Augie Ojeda, ss | .200 | 5 | 2 | 1 | 0 | 0 | 0 | 1 | 0 |
| Chad Green, of | .143 | 7 | 2 | 1 | 0 | 0 | 1 | 1 | 1 |

| PITCHING | W | L | ERA | G | SV | IP | H | BB | SO |
|---|---|---|---|---|---|---|---|---|---|
| Braden Looper, rhp | 0 | 0 | 0.00 | 4 | 1 | 6 | 3 | 1 | 6 |
| R.A. Dickey, rhp | 2 | 0 | 3.00 | 2 | 0 | 12 | 9 | 3 | 12 |
| Jeff Weaver, rhp | 0 | 0 | 3.68 | 4 | 1 | 7 | 6 | 1 | 3 |
| Seth Greisinger, rhp | 3 | 0 | 5.00 | 3 | 0 | 18 | 18 | 4 | 11 |
| Kris Benson, rhp | 2 | 1 | 5.82 | 3 | 0 | 17 | 20 | 5 | 17 |
| Billy Koch, rhp | 0 | 1 | 6.23 | 3 | 0 | 9 | 8 | 3 | 5 |
| Jim Parque, lhp | 0 | 0 | 9.00 | 4 | 0 | 4 | 6 | 1 | 4 |

a U.S. team that had crushed the Japanese three times earlier in the year. When the teams met in the Olympic round-robin, Team USA hit five first-inning home runs, including four in a row, during a 15-5 game that was called after seven innings because of international baseball's mercy rule.

"The script was not written like this," Stanford catcher A.J. Hinch said. "The script was written for us to play Cuba in a one-game playoff for the gold medal. This feels like they stabbed me in the heart."

Sugiura did most of the knifework. After missing the first half of the Olympics with an injury to his right thigh, he kept Team USA scoreless until Clemson catcher Matt LeCroy hit a two-run homer with two out in the sixth. By then Japan had established a 6-0 lead on a U.S. team that had averaged nearly 12 runs and four homers per game in the round-robin.

**Victory Lap.** Cuba's gold-medal winning Olympic team celebrates its 13-9 win over Japan, its 126th straight victory in international play.

Such a performance was nothing new for Sugiura. He beat the United States in the bronze-medal game in Barcelona, and dealt Team USA its last shutout, a 17-strikeout gem at the 1994 World Championships in Managua, Nicaragua.

Japan's hitters had no such trouble with Clemson righthander Kris Benson, Baseball America's College Player of the Year and the No. 1 overall draft pick by the Pittsburgh Pirates. Catcher Hideaki Okubo and second baseman Makota Imaoka homered off Benson in a three-run second, and Takabayashi nailed him for another as Japan chased Benson in a three-run fifth.

"If I had the chance to turn in all the 21 wins I had this year for this one, I would," said Benson, who went 14-2 for Clemson and 7-1 for the Olympic team. His three losses came in the three biggest games of his amateur career—two at the College World Series and one at the Olympics.

Though this was one of the best U.S. national teams ever assembled, going 71-11 in two years, the fact remains that it lost in the most significant game it played during the previous two years as well. Team USA head coach Skip Bertman of Louisiana State bristled when asked if the pressure of a must-win game got to his team.

"If you're a football writer, you've got to ask those kinds of questions," Bertman said. "I don't mean to be snide. But if you're a baseball man . . . It's a baseball game.

"If it was nuclear war and we were playing Grenada, we'd win every single time. But a baseball game is different. There are many ways to lose."

But the loss left USA Baseball executive director Dick Case looking at a harsher truth.

"Maybe America isn't the No. 1 country in amateur baseball," Case said while Team USA was beating Nicaragua 10-3 for the bronze medal, "if this tournament is the realization of that."

## The Pros Are Coming

USA Baseball will have to overhaul its plans again, though not because it came up short in 1996. After twice rejecting proposals to open its baseball competitions to professional players, the International Baseball Association finally abandoned its amateurs-only policy Sept. 21 in a vote at its Lausanne, Switzerland headquarters.

A two-thirds majority of the 65 member nations present was required to remove the word "amateur" from IBA's constitution and bylaws. Fifty-six nations, including the United States, voted in favor; seven, including two-time Olympic champion Cuba, voted against; and Hong Kong and Nicaragua abstained.

International Olympic Committee president Juan Antonio Samaranch had set three conditions for baseball remaining an Olympic sport. The first two were met at the Atlanta Olympics, where Team USA won a medal (a bronze) after failing to do so four years earlier in Barcelona and fan support (920,000 for 32 games) was much stronger than in Spain.

**Dejection.** Team USA outfielder Jacque Jones shows his frustration at winning only a bronze medal at the 1996 Olympics.

# GOLDEN SPIKES AWARD

## Lee Wins Amateur Prize

It would be understandable if Travis Lee hoped that 1996 would never end.

In the spring, he capped three years of stardom at San Diego State by batting .355 with 14 homers, 60 RBIs and 33 steals. During the summer, he led Team USA with a .416 batting average, 17 home runs, 57 RBIs and six stolen bases.

**Travis Lee**

The No. 2 overall pick in the draft by the Minnesota Twins, Lee was declared a free agent because the team failed to tender him a contract within 15 days of the draft. In October, Lee signed a stunning $10 million deal with the Arizona Diamondbacks.

Then in November, Lee added amateur baseball's highest honor. He was named the 18th winner of the Golden Spikes Award.

A gifted athlete with tremendous power potential, Lee should fit right in with the previous winners, most of whom have gone on to become major league stars. Amazingly, he wasn't drafted or recruited out of Capitol High in Olympia, Wash. He put together a videotape and sent it to Aztecs coach Jim Dietz, who watched only two swings before calling Lee.

"Two swings is all it took," Dietz said. "You could tell right away Travis was something special."

USA Baseball annually gives the award, college baseball's Heisman Trophy, to the nation's top amateur player. Other finalists were: Clemson righthander Kris Benson; Miami third baseman Pat Burrell; Florida State outfielder J.D. Drew; Virginia righthander Seth Greisinger; Stanford catcher A.J. Hinch; Southern California outfielder Jacque Jones; Cal State Fullerton outfielder Mark Kotsay, the 1995 winner; and Wichita State righthander Braden Looper.

### PREVIOUS WINNERS

1978—**Bob Horner**, 3b, Arizona State
1979—**Tim Wallach**, 1b, Cal State Fullerton
1980—**Terry Francona**, of, Arizona
1981—**Mike Fuentes**, of, Florida State
1982—**Augie Schmidt**, ss, New Orleans
1983—**Dave Magadan**, 1b, Alabama
1984—**Oddibe McDowell**, of, Arizona State
1985—**Will Clark**, 1b, Mississippi State
1986—**Mike Loynd**, rhp, Florida State
1987—**Jim Abbott**, lhp, Michigan
1988—**Robin Ventura**, 3b, Oklahoma State
1989—**Ben McDonald**, rhp, Louisiana State
1990—**Alex Fernandez**, rhp, Miami-Dade CC South
1991—**Mike Kelly**, of, Arizona State
1992—**Phil Nevin**, 3b, Cal State Fullerton
1993—**Darren Dreifort**, rhp-dh, Wichita State
1994—**Jason Varitek**, c, Georgia Tech
1995—**Mark Kotsay**, of-lhp, Cal State Fullerton

The final hurdle was making a way for major league dream teams to take a place in future Olympics. Samaranch long has advocated opening the Olympics to the best athletes, regardless of amateur status, and was not pleased when IBA voted down such a measure in June 1994. That vote was 48-28, three shy of the needed two-thirds majority.

The new ruling took effect immediately. Professional players will be eligible for the next IBA-sanctioned competition, the Intercontinental Cup in Barcelona from Aug. 1-10, 1997. California head coach Bob Milano has been selected to guide Team USA at that competition.

But getting pros to international competitions will require more than simply changing a rule, especially for the 2000 Olympics in Sydney, Australia. Those Games are scheduled from Sept. 16-Oct. 1, a direct conflict with major league pennant races. Both Major League Baseball Players Association executive director Donald Fehr and acting MLB commissioner Bud Selig have said there's virtually no chance major leaguers will compete in Sydney.

"The problem of the major league players is separate from today's decision," IBA president Aldo Notari said. "At the moment, this federation has no power over the major leagues. We'll start to work and reach an agreement with everybody as soon as possible. Our goal was to succeed in having the best players in international competition."

## Cuba Also Wears Junior Crown

While the U.S. Olympic team learned that it takes just one bad game to destroy a summer of promise, the U.S. national junior team learned that it can take as little as one bad inning.

The script for the World Junior Championships for 16- to 18-year-olds, held in Sancti Spiritus, Cuba, played out similar to the Olympics. Cuba won the championship game 6-5 on Aug. 16 for its eighth title after not qualifying for the medal round in 1995 in Boston.

Chinese Taipei scored five runs in the bottom of the second off two Cuban pitchers, but reliever Angel Pena entered and provided 7⅓ innings of shutout relief. Taipei turned to tournament MVP

**Matt White**

Huang Chin-Chih after Cuba tied the game 5-5 in the fifth, and the Cubans beat him with a run in the sixth that closed the scoring.

Huang finished the tournament as the leading hitter (.563) and went 3-1 with 28 strikeouts in 27 innings.

After allowing three runs in five preliminary games, Team USA faced Taipei in the semifinals. The United States saw its hope of defending its 1995 world title evaporate in the second inning.

Taipei manufactured six runs on just two singles, aided by two misplayed bunts, four walks, a wild pitch, a passed ball and a sacrifice fly off lefthanders Geoff Goetz (Lutz, Fla.) and Bobby Seay (Sarasota, Fla.). Huang pitched shutout ball into the bottom of the eighth, when Team USA rallied with three runs. Chi-

# SUMMER PLAYER OF THE YEAR
## Greisinger Upstages Bigger-Name U.S. Olympic Stars

Seth Greisinger finished the 1996 college season with a flourish. Then he never cooled down all summer.

Greisinger won all nine of his starts for the U.S. Olympic team, becoming the first Team USA pitcher ever to record nine victories. Jim Abbott (1987 and 1988), Ben McDonald (1988) and John Powell (1993) had shared the previous record of eight.

His performance earned Greisinger Baseball America's Summer Player of the Year award. That was just the latest in a string of accomplishments for a righthander who entered his junior season at Virginia with a 9-12 career record.

Greisinger blossomed in the spring, going 12-2 with a Division I-best 1.76 ERA and 141 strikeouts in 123 innings. His last three starts were complete-game wins in the postseason: a four-hitter against North Carolina State and a two-hitter against Florida State in the Atlantic Coast Conference tournament, and a six-hit-

**Seth Greisinger**

ter against Notre Dame in the South I Regional.

The Detroit Tigers made him the sixth overall pick in the June draft, but Greisinger put his pro plans on hold to pitch in the Olympics. He was sparkling all summer, leading Team USA with a 2.98 ERA, 55 strikeouts and 57 innings.

The highlight was a seven-inning performance against powerful Cuba, allowing just five hits, one run and no walks while striking out six. After that gem, U.S. coach Skip Bertman set up his pitching rotation so Greisinger could face Cuba in a rematch for the Olympic gold-medal.

That didn't come to pass, because Japan beat Team USA in the semifinals. Greisinger delivered the bronze medal with a seven innings of two-hit ball in a 10-3 victory over Nicaragua.

Greisinger's top competition for the Summer Player of the Year award came from U.S. Olympic first baseman Travis Lee, the 1995 winner. Lee, a San Diego State star drafted second overall by the Minnesota Twins, led Team USA with a .416 batting average, 46 hits, 15 doubles, 17 home runs, 57 RBIs and six stolen bases. He joined Olympic teammates Jacque Jones and Braden Looper, and Cape Cod League batting champion Lance Berkman as repeaters from 1995's first team.

The complete Summer All-America first team:

**C**—A.J. Hinch, Team USA (Stanford), .337-3-15.
**1B**—Travis Lee, Team USA (San Diego State), .416-17-57. **2B**—Scott Kidd, Anchorage Glacier Pilots/Alaska Central (Cal Poly San Luis Obispo), .378-14-53. **3B**—Troy Glaus, Team USA (UCLA), .342-15-34. **SS**—Kevin Nicholson, Wareham/Cape Cod (Stetson), .315-3-23.
**OF**—Chad Allen, Team USA (Texas A&M), .403-6-29; Lance Berkman, Wareham/Cape Cod (Rice), .352-1-19; Jacque Jones, Team USA (Southern California), .404-15-49.
**DH**—Matt LeCroy, Team USA (Clemson), .333-15-32.
**P**—Clint Chrysler, Wareham/Cape Cod (Stetson), 3-2, 0.36, 13 SV; Billy Coleman, Harwich/Cape Cod (Western Michigan), 6-3, 1.77; Seth Greisinger, Team USA (Virginia), 9-0, 2.98; Braden Looper, Team USA (Wichita State), 1-0, 2.25, 4 SV; Eric Milton, Falmouth/Cape Cod (Maryland), 5-1, 0.21.

### PREVIOUS WINNERS

1984—**Will Clark**, 1b, Team USA
—**Rafael Palmeiro**, of, Hutchinson/Jayhawk
1985—**Jeff King**, 3b, Team USA
—**Bob Zupcic**, of, Liberal/Jayhawk
1986—**Jack Armstrong**, rhp, Wareham/Cape Cod
—**Mike Harkey**, rhp, Fairbanks/Alaska
1987—**Cris Carpenter**, rhp, Team USA
1988—**Ty Griffin**, 2b, Team USA
—**Robin Ventura**, 3b, Team USA
1989—**John Olerud**, 1b-lhp, Palouse/Alaska
1990—**Calvin Murray**, of, Anchorage Bucs/Alaska
1991—**Chris Roberts**, of, Team USA
1992—**Jeffrey Hammonds**, of, Team USA
1993—**Geoff Jenkins**, of, Anchorage Bucs/Alaska
1994—**Steve Carver**, 1b, Glacier Pilots/Alaska Central
1995—**Travis Lee**, 1b, Team USA

nese Taipei added two more runs in the ninth to win 8-3.

"One inning out of 61, you can't fault anybody," said U.S. head coach Ron Davini, the coach at Tempe (Ariz.) Corona del Sol High and an assistant on the 1995 junior team. "I wouldn't change a thing."

With the gold medal no longer a possibility, Team USA focused on extending its streak of medaling throughout the 16-year history of the tournament. The United States succeeded, riding the pitching of San Francisco Giants first-round draft pick Matt White (Waynesboro, Pa.) to a 5-2 victory over Korea. Catcher Dane Sardinha (Iolani, Hawaii) hit a three-run homer in the fourth inning.

For his efforts, White was named USA Baseball's junior player of the year. Earlier in the summer, he made it through the walk-on tryouts for the Olympic

team. Attempting to become the first high school player ever to make Team USA, he was cut after getting shelled by Australia.

## Second No More

The Chatham A's finished second in the Cape Cod League playoffs in 1995 and second in the Western Division in 1996. After returning to the postseason, they finally came out on top.

Chatham swept through four playoff games, defeating the Falmouth Commodores two games to none in the finals for its first championship since 1992. California righthander Keith Evans threw a 6-2 six-hitter in the Aug. 14 finale, allowing just one hit after the second inning.

It was the second straight impressive postseason outing for Evans, who joined Chatham after negotia-

# SUMMER BASEBALL
## CHAMPIONS

### INTERNATIONAL

| LEAGUE (Age Group) | Site | Champion | Runner-Up |
|---|---|---|---|
| Olympics | Atlanta | Cuba | Japan |
| AAA World Junior Championships (16-18) | Sancti Spiritus, Cuba | Cuba | Chinese Taipei |
| AA World Junior Championships (13-15) | Chiba, Japan | South Korea | Cuba |
| Junior Pan American Games (16 & under) | Fairview Heights, Ill. | United States | Brazil |

### NATIONAL

| LEAGUE (Age Group) | Site | Champion | Runner-Up |
|---|---|---|---|
| AAABA (21 & under) | Johnstown, Pa. | Balti. Corrigan Insurance | Washington, D.C. |
| National Baseball Congress (open) | Wichita | El Dorado (Kan.) Broncos | Tacoma (Wash.) Timbers |
| USA Jr. Olympic Championships (16 & under) | Fort Myers, Fla. | California-Riverside ABD | Nor-Cal |
| National Amateur All-Star Tournament (HS) | Pine Bluff, Ark. | AABC | Dixie Baseball |
| Sunbelt Baseball Classic (HS players) | Shawnee, Okla. | Georgia | Oklahoma |

### AMATEUR ATHLETIC UNION
**HEADQUARTERS:** Lake Buena Vista, Fla.

| Age Group | Site | Champion | Runner-Up |
|---|---|---|---|
| 9 & under | Sherwood, Ark. | Crieve Hall (Nashville) | Mississippi Heat |
| 10 & under | Kansas City, Mo. | Columbus (Ohio) Sharks | Tampa Bay Angels |
| 11 & under | West Des Moines | Hawaii | Spring (Texas) Panthers |
| 12 & under | Burnsville, Minn. | Carson (Calif.) Reds | Virginia Blasters |
| 13 & under | Chickasha, Okla. | Dallas Hurricanes | Westlake (Calif.) Senators |
| 14 & under | Kingsport, Tenn. | Southern Nevada Bulldogs | St. Louis Comets |
| 15 & under | Concord, N.C. | East Cobb Stallions (Marietta, Ga.) | Florida Braves (Orlando) |
| 16 & under | New Orleans | East Cobb Astros (Marietta, Ga.) | Florida Storm |
| 17 & under | Norman, Okla. | Oklahoma Outlaws | San Diego Sting |
| 18 & under | Fort Myers, Fla. | Austin Slam Sox | Oakland, Mich. |

### AMERICAN AMATEUR BASEBALL CONGRESS
**HEADQUARTERS:** Marshall, Mich.

| Age Group | Site | Champion | Runner-Up |
|---|---|---|---|
| Roberto Clemente (8 & under) | Wheatridge, Colo. | Bayamon, P.R. | Dallas Texans |
| Willie Mays (9-10) | Collierville, Tenn. | Houston Cougars | Montebello (Calif.) Stars |
| Pee Wee Reese (11-12) | Toa Baja, P.R. | Houston Jaybirds | Adefaico, P.R. |
| Sandy Koufax (13-14) | Jersey City, N.J. | Houston Baseball Academy | Michigan Bulls |
| Mickey Mantle (15-16) | McKinney, Texas | Encinitas (Calif.) Reds | Dallas |
| Connie Mack (17-18) | Farmington, N.M. | Dallas Mustangs | Memphis Tigers |
| Stan Musial (open) | Battle Creek, Mich. | Chicago Prairie Gravel | Toledo Fifth Third Bank |

### BABE RUTH BASEBALL
**HEADQUARTERS:** Trenton, N.J.

| Age Group | Site | Champion | Runner-Up |
|---|---|---|---|
| Bambino (11-12) | Henderson, Ky. | Oakland | Henderson, Ky. |
| 13 prep | Dickinson, N.D. | Nederland, Texas | Lompoc, Calif. |
| 13-15 | Lebanon, Mo. | Vancouver, Wash. | Nederland, Texas |
| 16 | Gulfport, Miss. | West Torrance, Calif. | Nashville |
| 16-18 | Manteo, N.C. | Nashville | Alacosta, Calif. |

### CONTINENTAL AMATEUR BASEBALL ASSOCIATION
**HEADQUARTERS:** Westerville, Ohio

| Age Group | Site | Champion | Runner-Up |
|---|---|---|---|
| 9 & under | Charles City, Iowa | Honolulu Rainbows | Marysville (Ohio) Mets |
| 10 & under | Aurelia, Iowa | Columbus (Ohio) Sharks | Houston Red Sox |
| 11 & under | Tarkio, Mo. | Germantown (Tenn.) Giants | Denver Rawlings |
| 12 & under | Omaha | Carolina (P.R.) Indians | Atlanta Yellow Jackets |
| 13 & under | Broken Arrow, Okla. | Dallas Horns | Greenwood (Ill.) Brewers |
| 14 & under | Dublin, Ohio | Encinitas (Calif.) Reds | Maryland Orioles |
| 15 & under | Crystal Lake, Ill. | Hawaii All-Stars | Crystal Lake (Ill.) Travelers |
| 16 & under | Waukesha, Wis. | Paramount (Calif.) Orioles | Kansas City Monarchs |
| High school | Euclid, Ohio | Brooklyn Bergen Beach | Honolulu |
| 18 & under | Reynoldsburg, Ohio | Wisconsin Playmaker Rebels | Lombard (Ill.) Orioles |
| College | Chicago | Glen Ellyn, Ill. | Springfield (Ohio) Warhawks |
| Open | Eau Claire, Wis. | Eau Claire (Wis.) Cavaliers | New Rochelle (N.Y.) Robins |

### DIXIE BASEBALL
**HEADQUARTERS:** Lookout Mountain, Tenn.

| Age Group | Site | Champion | Runner-Up |
|---|---|---|---|
| Youth (12 & under) | Dothan, Ala. | Murfreesboro, Tenn. | Columbia County, Ga. |
| Youth (13 & under) | Alexandria, La. | Philadelphia, Miss. | Decatur, Ala. |
| Boys (13-14) | Cleveland, Miss. | Valdosta, Ga. | Florence, S.C. |
| Pre-Majors (15-16) | Salem, Va. | Auburn Univ.-Montgomery | Vinton, Va. |
| Majors (15-18) | Montgomery, Ala. | Columbia County, Ga. | Lufkin, Texas |

### DIZZY DEAN BASEBALL
**HEADQUARTERS:** Hixson, Tenn.

| Age Group | Site | Champion | Runner-Up |
|---|---|---|---|
| Minor (9-10) | Vicksburg, Miss. | St. Bernard Parish, La. | Northport, Ill. |
| Freshmen (11-12) | Greneda, Miss. | St. Bernard Parish, La. | Rock Spring, Ga. |
| Sophomore (13-14) | Baton Rouge | Jackson, Miss. | Ohio |
| Junior (15-16) | Shelby County, Ala. | Vestavia, Ala. | Rome, Ga. |
| Senior (17-18) | Johnson City, Tenn. | Hammond, La. | None |

## HAP DUMONT BASEBALL
**HEADQUARTERS:** Wichita.

| | | | |
|---|---|---|---|
| 10 & under | Casper, Wyo. | Houston Patriots | Topeka (Kan.) Yankees |
| 12 & under | Harrison, Ark. | Southhaven (Miss.) White Sox | Wichita Hurricanes |
| 14 & under | Brainerd, Minn. | Fort Worth Blackhawks | Wichita Rangers |
| 16 & under | Arlington, Texas | Topeka (Kan.) Bandits | Wichita Polecats |

## LITTLE LEAGUE BASEBALL
**HEADQUARTERS:** Williamsport, Pa.

| | | | |
|---|---|---|---|
| Little League (11-12) | Williamsport, Pa. | Chinese Taipei | Cranston, R.I. |
| Junior League (13) | Taylor, Mich. | Spring, Texas | Aiea, Hawaii |
| Senior League (13-15) | Kissimmee, Fla. | Maracaibo, Venez. | Thousand Oaks, Calif. |
| Big League (16-18) | Fort Lauderdale | Chinese Taipei | Burbank, Ill. |

## NATIONAL AMATEUR BASEBALL FEDERATION
**HEADQUARTERS:** Bowie, Md.

| | | | |
|---|---|---|---|
| Freshman (11-12) | Sylvania, Ohio | Columbus (Ohio) Raiders | Nashville Pirates |
| Sophomore (13-14) | Miamisburg, Ohio | Oklahoma Sooners (Norman) | Miamisburg (Ohio) Postmen |
| Junior (15-16) | Northville, Mich. | Bayside (N.Y.) Yankees | Mobile (Ala.) Bears |
| Senior (17-18) | Indianapolis | Jackson (Miss.) 96ers | New Lenox, Ill. |
| High School | Hopkinsville, Ky. | Indiana Bulls | Apopka (Fla.) Bears |
| College (22 & under) | Oshkosh, Wis. | Mid-South Braves (Rome, Ga.) | Melrose Park, Ill. |
| Major (open) | Louisville | Stratford (Conn.) Ale House | Louisville Star Drywall |

## POLICE ATHLETIC LEAGUE
**HEADQUARTERS:** North Palm Beach, Fla.

| | | | |
|---|---|---|---|
| 16 & under | Salinas, Calif. | St. Petersburg, Fla. | Metro Dade, Fla. |

## PONY BASEBALL
**HEADQUARTERS:** Washington, Pa.

| | | | |
|---|---|---|---|
| Mustang (9-10) | Irving, Texas | Miami | Humble, Texas |
| Bronco (11-12) | Monterey, Calif. | Anaheim | Seoul, Korea |
| Pony (13-14) | Washington, Pa. | Chinese Taipei | Evansville, Ind. |
| Colt (15-16) | Lafayette, Ind. | Corona, Calif. | West Cicero, Ill. |
| Palomino (17-18) | Greensboro, N.C. | Suffolk, Va. | Long Island, N.Y. |

## REVIVING BASEBALL IN INNER CITIES (RBI)
**HEADQUARTERS:** New York.

| | | | |
|---|---|---|---|
| Junior (13-15) | Cleveland | San Juan, P.R. | Atlanta |
| Senior (16-17) | Cleveland | San Juan, P.R. | Richmond |

## U.S. AMATEUR BASEBALL FEDERATION
**HEADQUARTERS:** Edmonds, Wash.

| | | | |
|---|---|---|---|
| 11 & under | Bountiful, Utah | Taylorsville, Utah | Muller Park, Utah |
| 12 & under | Mesquite, Nev. | Portland, Ore. | Marysville, Wash. |
| 13 & under | Tigard, Ore. | Portland, Ore. | Canby, Ore. |
| 14 & under | St. Albert, Alberta | Lake County (Ill.) Chiefs | Los Angeles |
| 15 & under | Tigard, Ore. | San Gabriel (Calif.) Fighting Irish | Vacaville, Calif. |
| 16 & under | Fresno | Taylorsville, Utah | Spokane |
| 17 & under | West Jordan, Utah | Fresno | Portland, Ore. |
| 18 & under | Edmonds, Wash. | Oregon | Bothell (Wash.) Pirates |
| 19 & under | Tacoma | Seattle | British Columbia |

---

tions stalled with the Montreal Expos, who drafted him in the eighth round in June. In the A's playoff opener, Evans threw a four-hitter for 11 innings in a game Chatham won 5-2 in the 12th on Providence catcher Scott Friedholm's three-run homer.

**Kevin Nicholson**

Evans, who struck out 12 and didn't walk a batter in 20 postseason innings, shared playoff MVP honors with Chatham second baseman Jermaine Clark (San Francisco). Clark went 8-for-17 with three runs, three RBIs and four stolen bases in four games, and sparkled defensively.

Wareham Gatemen shortstop Kevin Nicholson (Stetson) was named the Cape Cod League MVP after batting .315 with three homers, 23 RBIs, 12 steals and a league-best 18 doubles. The Cape's pitcher of the year

was Harwich Mariners righthander Billy Coleman (Western Michigan), who went 6-3 with a 1.77 ERA and led the Cape with 94 strikeouts in 81 innings. He walked just eight batters.

Big league scouts chose Chatham righthander Matt Anderson (Rice) as the Cape's top pro prospect. He went 1-2 with a 1.50 ERA and struck out 30 in 24 innings as his fastball was clocked at 97 mph. In an earlier Baseball America survey of league managers, Falmouth lefthander Eric Milton (Maryland) was selected as the best prospect. A first-round pick of the New York Yankees, Milton set a Cape record with an 0.21 ERA and went 5-1 with 61 whiffs in 43 innings.

## Broncos Win NBC Title

The El Dorado (Kan.) Broncos, a National Baseball Congress World Series power, didn't fare too well in their first season since relocating from Wichita, finishing in a fourth-place tie in the Jayhawk League. But when they returned to Wichita for the NBC tournament, so did their winning ways.

The Broncos surprised everyone, including themselves, and won the NBC World Series by beating the

# WORLD JUNIOR CHAMPIONSHIPS

Sancti Spiritus, Cuba
August 9-16, 1996

## ROUND-ROBIN STANDINGS

| POOL A | W | L | RF | RA |
|---|---|---|---|---|
| United States | 5 | 0 | 31 | 3 |
| Korea | 4 | 1 | 42 | 22 |
| Venezuela | 2 | 3 | 27 | 19 |
| Panama | 2 | 3 | 21 | 24 |
| Brazil | 2 | 3 | 35 | 27 |
| Italy | 0 | 5 | 17 | 78 |

| POOL B | W | L | RF | RA |
|---|---|---|---|---|
| Cuba | 4 | 0 | 44 | 9 |
| Chinese Taipei | 3 | 1 | 40 | 11 |
| Mexico | 2 | 2 | 28 | 43 |
| Netherlands | 1 | 3 | 25 | 38 |
| Nicaragua | 0 | 4 | 8 | 44 |

**SEMIFINALS:** Chinese Taipei 8, United States 3; Cuba 6, Korea 4. **GOLD MEDAL:** Cuba 6, Chinese Taipei 5. **BRONZE MEDAL:** United States 5, Korea 2. **FIFTH-SIXTH PLACE GAME:** Venezuela 8, Mexico 7. **SEVENTH-EIGHTH PLACE GAME:** Netherlands 3, Panama 0. **NINTH-TENTH PLACE GAME:** Brazil 13, Nicaragua 0.

**ALL-STAR TEAM: C**—Josh Bard, United States. **1B**—Marcio Suzuki, Brazil. **2B**—Manuel Moerjon, Mexico. **3B**—Eliecer O'Connor, Cuba. **SS**—Michel Tamayo, Cuba. **LF**—Lee Hung-Yu, Chinese Taipei. **CF**—Geoff Goetz, United States. **RF**—Chuang Ming-Che, Chinese Taipei. **P**—Huang Chin-Chih, Chinese Taipei; Lee Dong-Chul, Korea. **MVP**—Huang Chin-Chih, lhp-off, Chinese Taipei.

## INDIVIDUAL BATTING LEADERS
(Minimum 12 Plate Appearances)

| PLAYER, TEAM | AVG | AB | R | H | 2B | 3B | HR | RBI | SB |
|---|---|---|---|---|---|---|---|---|---|
| Huang Chin-Chih, CT.... | .563 | 16 | 4 | 9 | 2 | 0 | 0 | 3 | 0 |
| E. Candanedo, Panama | .500 | 14 | 3 | 7 | 2 | 0 | 2 | 6 | 0 |
| Giacomo Falciani, Italy.. | .500 | 18 | 4 | 9 | 3 | 1 | 1 | 2 | 1 |
| Marcio Suzuki, Brazil..... | .500 | 20 | 8 | 10 | 2 | 0 | 4 | 11 | 4 |
| Josh Bard, USA............. | .462 | 13 | 5 | 6 | 2 | 0 | 1 | 2 | 0 |
| Chuang Ming-Che, CT.. | .458 | 24 | 5 | 11 | 1 | 1 | 2 | 6 | 0 |
| Elieser O'Connor, Cuba | .458 | 24 | 7 | 11 | 3 | 2 | 0 | 6 | 0 |
| Giacomo Bettati, Italy.... | .455 | 11 | 1 | 5 | 0 | 0 | 0 | 1 | 0 |
| Patrick Beljaards, Neth.. | .444 | 18 | 4 | 8 | 3 | 0 | 0 | 4 | 0 |
| Daniel Overbeek, Neth.. | .429 | 14 | 4 | 6 | 1 | 1 | | 3 | 0 |
| Yosvani Peraza, Cuba .. | .429 | 21 | 7 | 9 | 1 | 2 | 2 | 8 | 0 |
| Pedro Diaz, Mexico ....... | .412 | 17 | 5 | 7 | 0 | 1 | 0 | 2 | 0 |
| Geoff Goetz, USA ......... | .412 | 17 | 2 | 7 | 3 | 0 | 0 | 3 | 3 |
| Son Ji-Hwan, Korea ...... | .407 | 27 | 2 | 11 | 1 | 2 | 0 | 5 | 3 |
| Kin Jae-Goo, Korea....... | .400 | 15 | 6 | 6 | 1 | 1 | 0 | 3 | 0 |
| Fidel Garza, Mexico ...... | .400 | 15 | 1 | 6 | 1 | 0 | 0 | 0 | 0 |

## INDIVIDUAL PITCHING LEADERS
(Minimum 5 Innings)

| PITCHING | W | L | ERA | G | SV | IP | H | BB | SO |
|---|---|---|---|---|---|---|---|---|---|
| Lee Dong-Chul, Korea ....... | 4 | 0 | 0.00 | 5 | 0 | 18 | 15 | 2 | 11 |
| David Mendez, Panama .... | 1 | 0 | 0.00 | 2 | 0 | 16 | 9 | 8 | 9 |
| Angel Pena, Cuba ............ | 1 | 0 | 0.00 | 3 | 0 | 8 | 8 | 1 | 7 |
| Bobby Seay, USA ............. | 1 | 0 | 0.82 | 2 | 0 | 11 | 7 | 5 | 14 |
| Norberto Gonzalez, Cuba .. | 0 | 0 | 0.96 | 3 | 0 | 9 | 2 | 3 | 5 |
| Rich Ankiel, USA................ | 1 | 0 | 1.29 | 1 | 0 | 7 | 4 | 5 | 5 |
| Pat Collins, USA................. | 1 | 0 | 1.50 | 1 | 0 | 6 | 3 | 3 | 7 |
| Modesto Luis, Cuba .......... | 1 | 0 | 1.50 | 1 | 0 | 6 | 6 | 3 | 5 |
| Matt White, USA................. | 2 | 0 | 1.72 | 2 | 0 | 16 | 9 | 6 | 16 |
| Douglas Matumoto, Brazil.. | 3 | 1 | 1.83 | 4 | 0 | 20 | 13 | 1 | 17 |

## TEAM USA
### WORLD CHAMPIONSHIP STATISTICS

| BATTING | AVG | AB | R | H | 2B | 3B | HR | RBI | SB |
|---|---|---|---|---|---|---|---|---|---|
| Tom Graham, p ......... | 1.000 | 1 | 0 | 1 | 0 | 0 | 0 | 0 | 0 |
| Josh Bard, c-1b ............. | .462 | 13 | 5 | 6 | 2 | 0 | 1 | 2 | 0 |
| Rich Ankiel, lh-of-p....... | .417 | 12 | 2 | 5 | 0 | 0 | 0 | 1 | 0 |
| Geoff Goetz, of-p........... | .412 | 17 | 2 | 7 | 3 | 0 | 0 | 3 | 3 |
| Michael Cuddyer, of-3b .. | .367 | 30 | 5 | 11 | 1 | 0 | 1 | 5 | 0 |
| Pat Collins, p ................. | .333 | 3 | 1 | 1 | 0 | 0 | 0 | 1 | 0 |
| Casey Myers, 1b-dh ...... | .313 | 16 | 1 | 5 | 3 | 0 | 0 | 1 | 0 |
| Tim Drew, of-p-3b .......... | .310 | 29 | 4 | 9 | 2 | 0 | 0 | 3 | 0 |
| Dane Sardinha, c ........... | .308 | 13 | 3 | 4 | 1 | 0 | 2 | 6 | 0 |
| Matt White, p ................. | .286 | 7 | 1 | 2 | 0 | 0 | 0 | 3 | 0 |
| Bobby Seay, p................ | .250 | 4 | 0 | 1 | 0 | 0 | 0 | 0 | 0 |
| K. DeRenne, 3b-ss-2b.... | .231 | 26 | 4 | 6 | 2 | 0 | 0 | 2 | 2 |
| Matt Kata, 2b-ss ............ | .211 | 19 | 4 | 4 | 1 | 0 | 0 | 1 | 1 |
| Brett Groves, ss ............ | .188 | 16 | 3 | 3 | 0 | 0 | 2 | 0 | 0 |
| Jeff Deardoff, of............. | .100 | 10 | 2 | 1 | 0 | 0 | 0 | 1 | 1 |
| Mike Kolbach, of-1b ...... | .083 | 12 | 2 | 1 | 0 | 0 | 0 | 1 | 0 |
| K.O. Wiegandt, p........... | .000 | 1 | 0 | 0 | 0 | 0 | 0 | 0 | 0 |

| PITCHING | W | L | ERA | G | SV | IP | H | BB | SO |
|---|---|---|---|---|---|---|---|---|---|
| Tim Drew, rhp................ | 1 | 0 | 0.00 | 2 | 0 | 3 | 0 | 0 | 4 |
| Tom Graham, rhp........... | 0 | 0 | 0.00 | 3 | 1 | 3 | 2 | 1 | 4 |
| K.O. Wiegandt, rhp......... | 0 | 0 | 0.00 | 3 | 1 | 4 | 3 | 0 | 3 |
| Bobby Seay, lhp ............ | 1 | 0 | 0.82 | 2 | 0 | 11 | 7 | 5 | 14 |
| Rich Ankiel, lhp ............. | 1 | 0 | 1.29 | 1 | 0 | 7 | 4 | 5 | 5 |
| Pat Collins, rhp.............. | 1 | 0 | 1.50 | 1 | 0 | 6 | 3 | 3 | 7 |
| Matt White, rhp.............. | 2 | 0 | 1.72 | 2 | 0 | 16 | 9 | 6 | 16 |
| Ryan Anderson, lhp......... | 0 | 0 | 5.40 | 3 | 0 | 3 | 1 | 4 | 5 |
| Geoff Goetz, lhp ............ | 0 | 0 | 5.63 | 2 | 0 | 8 | 4 | 5 | 9 |

---

Tacoma Timbers twice on Aug. 10.

Tacoma, a team of mostly college-age players from schools in Washington, had won its first six tournament games by an average of nearly seven runs. The Timbers seemed invincible, and had beaten El Dorado 13-5 earlier in the double-elimination tournament.

Then the Broncos used a 20-hit attack to beat Tacoma 13-8 in the first championship game. Pitching made the difference in the second game, which ended well after midnight. Broncos lefthander Nate Robertson (Wichita State) pitched five shutout innings and El Dorado breezed 6-2 before 4,114 fans.

The Broncos, who arrived in Wichita with a 26-22 record, went 9-1 in the NBC World Series.

"Honestly, we just didn't want to be remembered as the worst team in Broncos history," said El Dorado

**Kevin Frederick**

third baseman Kevin Frederick (Creighton), who was named World Series MVP after batting .500 and leading the tournament in runs (15), hits (18) and RBIs (19).

The Broncos, who moved to El Dorado from Wichita after the 1995 season, won back-to-back NBC championships in 1989 and 1990, but never got hot during the 1996 regular season. They made the NBC World Series only because of an automatic bid earned from their third-place performance in the 1995 tournament.

## Bear Carries Chinese Taipei

Hsieh Chin-Hsiung set a Little League World Series record with his seventh home run in leading Chinese Taipei to a 13-3 championship-game victory over Cranston, R.I. on Aug. 24 in Williamsport, Pa.

Hsieh, a 4-foot-11, 95-pound outfielder whose nickname is "Bear," broke the record set a year earlier by Chinese Taipei's Lin Chih-Hsiang. He finished with a .706 batting average.

Chinese Taipei won the series, which was celebrating its 50th anniversary, for the 12th time in 23 years and fourth time in the 1990s.

# COLLEGE SUMMER LEAGUES

## NCAA-AFFILIATED

### ARIZONA SUMMER COLLEGIATE

| | W | L | PCT | GB |
|---|---|---|---|---|
| Braves | 19 | 11 | .633 | — |
| Giants | 18 | 12 | .600 | 1 |
| Royals | 16 | 14 | .533 | 3 |
| Marlins | 16 | 14 | .533 | 3 |
| Yankees | 15 | 15 | .500 | 4 |
| Angels | 11 | 19 | .367 | 8 |
| Athletics | 10 | 20 | .333 | 9 |

**PLAYOFFS:** Braves defeated Marlins 2-1 and Giants defeated Royals 2-0 in best-of-3 semifinals. Giants defeated Braves 1-0 in one-game final.

### INDIVIDUAL BATTING LEADERS
(Minimum 75 Plate Appearances)

| | AVG | AB | R | H | 2B | 3B | HR | RBI | SB |
|---|---|---|---|---|---|---|---|---|---|
| Upshaw, Ryan, Braves | .457 | 92 | 30 | 42 | 3 | 5 | 7 | 28 | 10 |
| Maddox, Gary, Marlins | .450 | 100 | 33 | 45 | 9 | 2 | 4 | 25 | 24 |
| Hannah, Josh, Yankees | .402 | 87 | 23 | 35 | 6 | 2 | 0 | 16 | 11 |
| Flowers, Travis, Braves | .389 | 90 | 32 | 35 | 11 | 0 | 5 | 26 | 11 |
| Mahler, D.J., Giants | .380 | 108 | 20 | 41 | 5 | 2 | 0 | 14 | 10 |
| Theodorou, Nick, Yankees | .375 | 72 | 20 | 27 | 1 | 3 | 0 | 6 | 6 |
| Grijalva, Mike, Yankees | .374 | 107 | 24 | 40 | 12 | 0 | 8 | 33 | 3 |
| Kahl, Chris, Royals | .358 | 95 | 22 | 34 | 10 | 2 | 2 | 22 | 0 |
| Swintzenberg, Ty, Giants | .353 | 102 | 21 | 36 | 1 | 4 | 2 | 20 | 7 |
| Coats, David, Angels | .351 | 74 | 12 | 26 | 11 | 0 | 0 | 16 | 1 |

### INDIVIDUAL PITCHING LEADERS
(Minimum 20 Innings)

| | W | L | ERA | G | SV | IP | H | BB | SO |
|---|---|---|---|---|---|---|---|---|---|
| Byrd, Ben, Giants | 5 | 0 | 1.66 | 8 | 0 | 38 | 35 | 15 | 29 |
| Boop, Clayton, Royals | 3 | 2 | 1.71 | 12 | 3 | 21 | 20 | 10 | 13 |
| Ortiz, Jon, Braves | 3 | 1 | 2.03 | 7 | 0 | 40 | 28 | 22 | 46 |
| Rohn, Grady, Giants | 1 | 2 | 2.25 | 10 | 1 | 20 | 15 | 13 | 17 |
| Taylor, Anthony, A's | 2 | 1 | 2.53 | 6 | 0 | 21 | 13 | 16 | 18 |

### ATLANTIC COLLEGIATE LEAGUE

| BELSON | W | L | PCT | GB |
|---|---|---|---|---|
| Quakertown Blazers | 19 | 17 | .528 | — |
| West Deptford Storm | 15 | 21 | .417 | 4 |
| Delaware Gulls | 10 | 26 | .278 | 9 |

| KAISER | W | L | PCT | GB |
|---|---|---|---|---|
| New York Generals | 21 | 15 | .583 | — |
| Nassau Collegians | 20 | 16 | .556 | 1 |
| Metro New York Cadets | 15 | 21 | .417 | 6 |

| WOLFF | W | L | PCT | GB |
|---|---|---|---|---|
| Sussex Colonels | 30 | 6 | .833 | — |
| Jersey Pilots | 17 | 19 | .472 | 13 |
| Scranton/Wilkes-Barre Twins | 15 | 21 | .417 | 15 |

**PLAYOFFS:** Sussex defeated Nassau 2-0 and New York defeated Quakertown 2-0 in best-of-3 semifinals. Sussex defeated New York 1-0 in one-game final.

### INDIVIDUAL BATTING LEADERS
(Minimum 75 Plate Appearances)

| | AVG | AB | R | H | 2B | 3B | HR | RBI | SB |
|---|---|---|---|---|---|---|---|---|---|
| Speckhardt, Mike, New York | .392 | 102 | 21 | 40 | 6 | 2 | 1 | 15 | 8 |
| Marchiano, Mike, Sussex | .387 | 111 | 33 | 43 | 8 | 3 | 1 | 25 | 10 |
| McCorkle, Shawn, Sussex | .360 | 100 | 17 | 36 | 7 | 3 | 3 | 20 | 1 |
| Munkittrick, Mark, Scranton | .350 | 103 | 16 | 36 | 9 | 1 | 3 | 25 | 11 |
| Duffie, Andre, Delaware | .342 | 79 | 10 | 27 | 2 | 0 | 0 | 12 | 0 |
| Spano, Joe, Metro | .342 | 76 | 3 | 26 | 5 | 1 | 1 | 11 | 0 |
| Busch, Chad, Sussex | .336 | 128 | 28 | 43 | 6 | 1 | 1 | 23 | 21 |
| Dinkelacker, Billy, Nassau | .333 | 82 | 11 | 28 | 8 | 0 | 2 | 17 | 0 |
| Fili, Brian, Delaware | .329 | 70 | 21 | 23 | 5 | 0 | 2 | 7 | 0 |
| Rooney, Mike, New York | .325 | 77 | 15 | 25 | 1 | 0 | 0 | 11 | 3 |

### INDIVIDUAL PITCHING LEADERS
(Minimum 35 Innings)

| | W | L | ERA | G | SV | IP | H | BB | SO |
|---|---|---|---|---|---|---|---|---|---|
| Stabile, Paul, Metro | 2 | 3 | 1.30 | 7 | 0 | 42 | 30 | 14 | 25 |
| Lenko, Jared, Quakertown | 4 | 2 | 1.41 | 10 | 0 | 57 | 36 | 14 | 52 |

| Gordon, Jim, Jersey | 3 | 1 | 1.51 | 9 | 0 | 48 | 37 | 22 | 27 |
|---|---|---|---|---|---|---|---|---|---|
| Giancola, Jim, New York | 4 | 2 | 1.59 | 7 | 0 | 45 | 24 | 16 | 32 |
| Antico, Matt, Metro | 3 | 3 | 1.64 | 9 | 0 | 49 | 36 | 12 | 32 |

### CAPE COD LEAGUE

| EAST | W | L | T | PCT | PTS |
|---|---|---|---|---|---|
| Brewster Whitecaps | 23 | 20 | 1 | .534 | 47 |
| Chatham A's | 22 | 21 | 1 | .511 | 45 |
| Harwich Mariners | 20 | 22 | 1 | .477 | 42 |
| Orleans Cardinals | 20 | 22 | 1 | .477 | 41 |
| Yarmouth-Dennis Red Sox | 13 | 29 | 2 | .318 | 28 |

| WEST | W | L | T | PCT | PTS |
|---|---|---|---|---|---|
| Wareham Gatemen | 29 | 15 | 0 | .659 | 58 |
| Falmouth Commodores | 26 | 17 | 0 | .605 | 52 |
| Cotuit Kettleers | 23 | 19 | 2 | .545 | 48 |
| Hyannis Mets | 20 | 24 | 0 | .455 | 40 |
| Bourne Braves | 18 | 25 | 1 | .420 | 37 |

**PLAYOFFS:** Chatham defeated Brewster 2-0 and Falmouth defeated Wareham 2-0 in best-of-3 semifinals. Chatham defeated Falmouth 2-0 in best-of-3 finals.

**ALL-STAR TEAM:** C—Jon Schaeffer, Cotuit (Stanford). 1B—C.J. Ankrum, Brewster (Cal State Fullerton). 2B—Jermaine Clark, Chatham (San Francisco). 3B—Ryan Hankins, Orleans (Nevada-Las Vegas). SS—Kevin Nicholson, Wareham (Stetson). OF—Lance Berkman, Wareham (Rice); Mike Colangelo, Chatham (George Mason); Jody Gerut, Harwich (Stanford). Util—Brian Benefield, Wareham (Texas A&M). SP—Billy Coleman, Harwich (Western Michigan); Seth Etherton, Chatham (Southern California); Eric Milton, Falmouth (Maryland); Randy Niles, Hyannis (Florida State). RP—Drew Fischer, Brewster (California).

**MVP:** Kevin Nicholson, ss, Wareham (Stetson). **Pitcher of the Year:** Billy Coleman, Harwich (Western Michigan).

### INDIVIDUAL BATTING LEADERS
(Minimum 119 Plate Appearances)

| | AVG | AB | R | H | 2B | 3B | HR | RBI | SB |
|---|---|---|---|---|---|---|---|---|---|
| Berkman, Lance, Wareham | .352 | 145 | 26 | 51 | 9 | 2 | 1 | 19 | 12 |
| McKinley, Dan, Wareham | .328 | 116 | 28 | 38 | 4 | 4 | 1 | 10 | 12 |
| Colangelo, Mike, Chatham | .317 | 120 | 9 | 38 | 10 | 2 | 0 | 12 | 4 |
| Benefield, Brian, Wareham | .316 | 136 | 17 | 43 | 7 | 0 | 2 | 22 | 12 |
| Nicholson, Kevin, Wareham | .315 | 149 | 22 | 47 | 18 | 1 | 3 | 23 | 12 |
| Schaeffer, Jon, Cotuit | .310 | 145 | 25 | 45 | 10 | 3 | 5 | 20 | 3 |
| Ankrum, C.J., Brewster | .308 | 172 | 18 | 53 | 11 | 1 | 1 | 25 | 11 |
| Burnham, Gary, Falmouth | .301 | 123 | 14 | 37 | 7 | 0 | 3 | 16 | 3 |
| Fitzgerald, Jason, Chatham | .296 | 135 | 18 | 40 | 7 | 1 | 1 | 16 | 6 |
| Mohr, Dustan, Wareham | .294 | 136 | 21 | 40 | 6 | 0 | 3 | 26 | 2 |
| Walker, Ron, Cotuit | .293 | 150 | 25 | 44 | 13 | 0 | 2 | 24 | 3 |
| Lunsford, Sam, Wareham | .293 | 123 | 20 | 36 | 3 | 0 | 0 | 9 | 8 |
| Rowand, Aaron, Brewster | .292 | 154 | 23 | 45 | 10 | 1 | 4 | 18 | 11 |
| Clark, Jermaine, Chatham | .291 | 158 | 30 | 46 | 6 | 1 | 0 | 14 | 17 |
| Hauswald, Rob, Falmouth | .289 | 142 | 20 | 41 | 3 | 2 | 4 | 20 | 5 |
| Gerut, Jody, Harwich | .283 | 159 | 20 | 45 | 14 | 1 | 2 | 19 | 4 |
| Sergio, Tom, Y-D | .282 | 149 | 18 | 42 | 4 | 2 | 2 | 11 | 12 |
| Hairston, Jerry, Bourne | .281 | 139 | 16 | 39 | 7 | 3 | 0 | 11 | 3 |
| Weber, Jake, Orleans | .280 | 164 | 15 | 46 | 6 | 2 | 2 | 19 | 12 |
| Seimetz, Dan, Falmouth | .278 | 126 | 13 | 35 | 12 | 0 | 2 | 17 | 1 |
| Cutshall, Pat, Harwich | .277 | 155 | 12 | 43 | 8 | 0 | 1 | 18 | 4 |
| Hankins, Ryan, Orleans | .272 | 151 | 22 | 41 | 5 | 1 | 6 | 24 | 0 |
| Fischer, Mark, Falmouth | .270 | 141 | 21 | 38 | 6 | 0 | 0 | 9 | 12 |
| Freeman, Ryan, Harwich | .262 | 141 | 18 | 37 | 3 | 0 | 1 | 18 | 14 |
| Davis, Glenn, Cotuit | .262 | 168 | 27 | 44 | 7 | 4 | 5 | 30 | 9 |
| Chiaramonte, Gino, Cotuit | .260 | 127 | 13 | 33 | 6 | 1 | 5 | 13 | 0 |
| Pratt, Scott, Brewster | .259 | 147 | 17 | 38 | 3 | 1 | 1 | 10 | 18 |

### INDIVIDUAL PITCHING LEADERS
(Minimum 35 Innings)

| | W | L | ERA | G | SV | IP | H | BB | SO |
|---|---|---|---|---|---|---|---|---|---|
| Milton, Eric, Falmouth | 5 | 1 | 0.21 | 7 | 0 | 43 | 15 | 11 | 61 |
| Niles, Randy, Hyannis | 5 | 2 | 0.83 | 10 | 1 | 65 | 44 | 21 | 62 |
| Immel, Steve, Brewster | 2 | 1 | 1.06 | 8 | 0 | 42 | 25 | 18 | 37 |
| Bess, Stephen, Wareham | 1 | 1 | 1.11 | 10 | 0 | 41 | 27 | 12 | 24 |
| Hild, Scott, Brewster | 5 | 2 | 1.33 | 10 | 0 | 61 | 54 | 11 | 31 |
| Adair, Derek, Orleans | 1 | 2 | 1.46 | 8 | 0 | 56 | 44 | 6 | 37 |
| Husted, Brent, Bourne | 3 | 0 | 1.46 | 19 | 10 | 37 | 21 | 3 | 24 |
| Incantalupo, Todd, Harwich | 1 | 1 | 1.50 | 5 | 0 | 36 | 30 | 9 | 21 |
| Fry, Justin, Wareham | 4 | 2 | 1.63 | 8 | 0 | 55 | 42 | 10 | 32 |
| Crowder, Chuck, Falmouth | 5 | 3 | 1.67 | 10 | 0 | 59 | 47 | 17 | 66 |
| Carnes, Matt, Wareham | 4 | 2 | 1.68 | 9 | 0 | 59 | 46 | 16 | 45 |
| Bivens, Donnie, Y-D | 1 | 3 | 1.73 | 27 | 6 | 57 | 36 | 10 | 57 |
| Anderson, Jason, Falmouth | 4 | 1 | 1.75 | 9 | 0 | 36 | 32 | 17 | 31 |
| Coleman, Billy, Harwich | 6 | 3 | 1.77 | 10 | 0 | 81 | 50 | 8 | 94 |
| Cressend, Jack, Cotuit | 7 | 0 | 1.89 | 7 | 0 | 48 | 22 | 14 | 49 |

| | W | L | ERA | G | SV | IP | H | BB | SO |
|---|---|---|---|---|---|---|---|---|---|
| Thomas, Brian, Orleans | 2 | 5 | 1.96 | 17 | 0 | 37 | 25 | 14 | 28 |
| Etherton, Seth, Chatham | 4 | 2 | 1.98 | 8 | 0 | 50 | 39 | 5 | 68 |
| Rushing, Donald, Y-D | 1 | 5 | 2.04 | 10 | 0 | 66 | 47 | 46 | 61 |
| Quarnstrom, Rob, Wareham | 4 | 3 | 2.07 | 10 | 4 | 65 | 62 | 14 | 53 |
| Jacquez, Tom, Cotuit | 2 | 1 | 2.14 | 15 | 2 | 42 | 39 | 14 | 35 |

## CENTRAL ILLINOIS LEAGUE

| FIRST | W | L | PCT | GB | SECOND | W | L | PCT | GB |
|---|---|---|---|---|---|---|---|---|---|
| Danville | 15 | 5 | .750 | — | Danville | 14 | 6 | .700 | — |
| Twin City | 14 | 6 | .700 | 1 | Quincy | 10 | 8 | .556 | 3 |
| Quincy | 12 | 8 | .600 | 3 | Twin City | 11 | 9 | .550 | 3 |
| Springfield | 11 | 9 | .550 | 4 | Springfield | 9 | 11 | .450 | 5 |
| Champaign | 6 | 14 | .300 | 9 | Champaign | 8 | 12 | .400 | 6 |
| Decatur | 2 | 18 | .100 | 14 | Decatur | 6 | 12 | .333 | 7 |

**PLAYOFF TOURNAMENT:** Quincy 3-0, Danville 1-1, Springfield 1-1, Champaign County 0-1, Decatur 0-1, Twin City 0-1.

**ALL-STAR TEAM: C**—Tim Richardson, Springfield (Western Illinois). **INF**—Heath Bender, Quincy (Memphis); Todd Burke, Champaign County (Central Michigan); Doug Ferguson, Springfield (Lincoln Land, Ill., CC); Mark Mosier, Twin City (Chicago); Tyler Turnquist, Twin City (Illinois State); Brian Yaeger, Quincy (Missouri Baptist). **OF**—Tom Bernhardt, Danville (Louisiana State); Aaron Sapp, Springfield (Lincoln Land, Ill., CC); Corey Taylor, Danville (Northeast Louisiana); Scott Vance, Springfield (Iowa State). **DH**—Justin Beasley, Danville (Butler). **SP**—Mike Brown, Danville (Liberty); Brian Carter, Danville (Northeast Louisiana); Billy Cusack, Twin City (St. Francis, Ill.); Cory Lusk, Springfield (Bradley); Tony Pena, Quincy (Lewis, Ill.); Roy Tippett, Quincy (Saint Louis). **RP**—Jason Albritton, Danville (Louisiana State); Brian Wiese, Danville (Mississippi State).

**MVP:** Aaron Sapp, of, Springfield (Lincoln Land, Ill., CC). Pitchers of the Year: Mike Brown, Danville (Liberty); Brian Carter, Danville (Northeast Louisiana).

### INDIVIDUAL BATTING LEADERS
(Minimum 100 Plate Appearances)

| | AVG | AB | R | H | 2B | 3B | HR | RBI | SB |
|---|---|---|---|---|---|---|---|---|---|
| Ferguson, Doug, Springfield | .360 | 114 | 16 | 41 | 10 | 1 | 1 | 21 | 3 |
| Sapp, Aaron, Springfield | .353 | 150 | 32 | 53 | 13 | 4 | 3 | 26 | 4 |
| Taylor, Corey, Danville | .336 | 134 | 35 | 45 | 7 | 1 | 5 | 13 | 17 |
| Yaeger, Brian, Quincy | .333 | 126 | 22 | 42 | 8 | 0 | 0 | 18 | 6 |
| Beasley, Justin, Danville | .319 | 138 | 29 | 44 | 11 | 1 | 5 | 26 | 4 |
| Turnquist, Tyler, Twin City | .318 | 157 | 30 | 50 | 5 | 3 | 2 | 15 | 5 |
| Mosier, Mark, Twin City | .316 | 155 | 19 | 49 | 10 | 1 | 2 | 32 | 10 |
| Gaffney, Brian, Champaign | .314 | 153 | 24 | 48 | 8 | 0 | 1 | 18 | 7 |
| Bender, Heath, Quincy | .307 | 140 | 29 | 43 | 7 | 0 | 5 | 31 | 3 |
| Burke, Todd, Champaign | .301 | 143 | 15 | 43 | 5 | 1 | 2 | 13 | 10 |
| Carlon, Joe, Twin City | .300 | 150 | 45 | 45 | 13 | 3 | 2 | 15 | 12 |
| Vance, Scott, Springfield | .299 | 147 | 25 | 44 | 7 | 3 | 2 | 23 | 18 |

### INDIVIDUAL PITCHING LEADERS
(Minimum 40 Innings)

| | W | L | ERA | G | SV | IP | H | BB | SO |
|---|---|---|---|---|---|---|---|---|---|
| Brown, Mike, Danville | 6 | 1 | 1.46 | 9 | 0 | 62 | 42 | 22 | 57 |
| Carter, Brian, Danville | 5 | 2 | 1.62 | 9 | 0 | 61 | 62 | 14 | 65 |
| Cusack, Billy, Twin City | 5 | 2 | 1.88 | 8 | 0 | 67 | 57 | 25 | 58 |
| Pena, Tony, Quincy | 5 | 3 | 1.95 | 14 | 4 | 60 | 47 | 14 | 41 |
| Tippett, Roy, Quincy | 6 | 1 | 2.02 | 11 | 1 | 71 | 68 | 6 | 45 |
| Brown, Jeremy, Twin City | 3 | 3 | 2.12 | 13 | 0 | 47 | 33 | 11 | 56 |
| Lusk, Cory, Springfield | 5 | 1 | 2.29 | 8 | 0 | 59 | 39 | 32 | 85 |
| Beck, Matt, Decatur | 0 | 5 | 2.45 | 8 | 0 | 48 | 41 | 12 | 26 |

## GREAT LAKES LEAGUE

| | W | L | PCT | GB |
|---|---|---|---|---|
| Grand Lake Mariners | 30 | 10 | .750 | — |
| Columbus All-Americans | 29 | 11 | .725 | 1 |
| Bexley | 18 | 22 | .450 | 12 |
| Sandusky Bay Stars | 17 | 23 | .425 | 13 |
| Euclid Admirals | 13 | 27 | .325 | 17 |
| Lima Locos | 13 | 27 | .325 | 17 |

**PLAYOFFS:** Grand Lake defeated Sandusky 2-1 and Columbus defeated Bexley 2-0 in best-of-3 semifinals. Columbus defeated Grand Lake 2-0 in best-of-3 final.

**ALL-STAR TEAM: C**—Bryan Guse, Grand Lake (Minnesota). **1B**—Jason Embler, Columbus (Clemson); Ed Farris, Grand Lake (Ball State). **2B**—Dominic Pattie, Columbus (UNC Greensboro). **3B**—Brian Smith, Euclid (Kent). **SS**—Will Otero, Bexley (Ohio Dominican). **OF**—Jake Eye, Bexley (Ohio); Rod Metzler, Grand Lake (Purdue); Mike Zerbe, Sandusky (Tampa). **DH**—Aaron Sledd, Columbus (Memphis). **Util**—Alex Eckelman, Bexley (Ohio State). **P**—Jake Eye, Bexley (Ohio); Mike Hedman, Grand Lake (Purdue);

Justin Pederson, Grand Lake (Minnesota); Andrew Smith, Columbus (Bowling Green State).
**MVP:** Dominic Pattie, 2b, Columbus (UNC Greensboro). Pitcher of the Year: Justin Pederson, Grand Lake (Minnesota).

### INDIVIDUAL BATTING LEADERS
(Minimum 100 At-Bats)

| | AVG | AB | R | H | 2B | 3B | HR | RBI | SB |
|---|---|---|---|---|---|---|---|---|---|
| Smith, Brian, Euclid | .402 | 107 | 15 | 43 | 6 | 0 | 3 | 12 | 3 |
| Eye, Jake, Bexley | .388 | 116 | 20 | 45 | 8 | 2 | 0 | 18 | 2 |
| McDonald, Corey, Columbus | .356 | 101 | 18 | 36 | 7 | 0 | 0 | 20 | 12 |
| Pattie, Dominic, Columbus | .352 | 128 | 40 | 45 | 5 | 2 | 2 | 13 | 26 |
| Besco, Bryan, Lima | .343 | 134 | 16 | 46 | 9 | 0 | 0 | 21 | 5 |
| Metzler, Rod, Grand Lake | .342 | 117 | 25 | 40 | 10 | 0 | 1 | 23 | 4 |
| Otero, William, Bexley | .331 | 139 | 26 | 46 | 4 | 0 | 1 | 11 | 13 |
| Embler, Jason, Columbus | .330 | 115 | 24 | 38 | 4 | 1 | 6 | 28 | 5 |
| Schwamel, Mike, Euclid | .325 | 120 | 15 | 39 | 7 | 0 | 2 | 16 | 4 |
| Fucile, Frank, Bexley | .325 | 117 | 16 | 38 | 7 | 0 | 1 | 16 | 8 |

### INDIVIDUAL PITCHING LEADERS
(Minimum 28 Innings)

| | W | L | ERA | G | SV | IP | H | BB | SO |
|---|---|---|---|---|---|---|---|---|---|
| Pederson, Justin, Grand Lake | 7 | 0 | 0.88 | 8 | 1 | 51 | 23 | 16 | 52 |
| Smith, Andrew, Columbus | 5 | 1 | 1.79 | 10 | 1 | 40 | 41 | 9 | 39 |
| Myers, Todd, Lima | 1 | 0 | 1.95 | 12 | 0 | 28 | 20 | 19 | 23 |
| Haverstick, David, Columbus | 5 | 2 | 2.16 | 8 | 0 | 33 | 28 | 12 | 32 |
| Eye, Jake, Bexley | 4 | 2 | 2.17 | 11 | 3 | 46 | 29 | 14 | 44 |
| Rowland, Doug, Bexley | 1 | 3 | 2.20 | 15 | 1 | 29 | 15 | 12 | 22 |
| Maynard, Todd, Euclid | 3 | 2 | 2.23 | 6 | 0 | 36 | 24 | 13 | 48 |
| Golden, Steve, Bexley | 3 | 5 | 2.49 | 13 | 0 | 51 | 43 | 21 | 43 |
| Finken, Brad, Grand Lake | 3 | 0 | 2.55 | 8 | 0 | 42 | 37 | 6 | 49 |
| Hedman, Mike, Grand Lake | 5 | 7 | 2.57 | 7 | 0 | 49 | 44 | 10 | 38 |

## NEW ENGLAND COLLEGIATE LEAGUE

| | W | L | PCT | GB |
|---|---|---|---|---|
| Central Massachusetts Collegians | 27 | 13 | .675 | — |
| Danbury Westerners | 25 | 13 | .658 | 1 |
| Rhode Island Reds | 21 | 17 | .553 | 5 |
| Middletown Giants | 21 | 18 | .538 | 5½ |
| Eastern Tides | 13 | 26 | .333 | 13½ |
| Waterbury Barons | 10 | 30 | .250 | 17 |

**PLAYOFFS:** Central Massachusetts defeated Middletown 2-1 and Danbury defeated Rhode Island 2-0 in best-of-3 semifinals. Central Massachusetts defeated Danbury 2-1 in best-of-3 final.

### INDIVIDUAL BATTING LEADERS
(Minimum 108 Plate Appearances)

| | AVG | AB | R | H | 2B | 3B | HR | RBI | SB |
|---|---|---|---|---|---|---|---|---|---|
| Crepeau, Jason, Danbury | .411 | 95 | 17 | 39 | 7 | 1 | 3 | 18 | 0 |
| Zorn, Steve, Waterbury | .379 | 124 | 16 | 47 | 4 | 1 | 1 | 18 | 1 |
| Rich, Bill, Middletown | .377 | 114 | 18 | 43 | 6 | 6 | 3 | 25 | 9 |
| Forsberg, Dana, Central | .375 | 128 | 26 | 48 | 11 | 7 | 0 | 23 | 1 |
| Woodfork, Peter, RI | .349 | 126 | 23 | 44 | 2 | 1 | 1 | 24 | 5 |
| Torre, Frank, Danbury | .336 | 122 | 22 | 41 | 6 | 2 | 2 | 21 | 7 |
| Zoccolillo, Pete, Danbury | .328 | 128 | 27 | 42 | 8 | 5 | 6 | 26 | 7 |
| MacDonald, Matt, RI | .325 | 126 | 29 | 41 | 4 | 2 | 2 | 17 | 16 |
| Lambert, Brian, Central | .317 | 101 | 18 | 32 | 3 | 2 | 0 | 19 | 7 |
| Riccio, John, Rhode Island | .317 | 120 | 33 | 38 | 7 | 2 | 7 | 28 | 6 |

### INDIVIDUAL PITCHING LEADERS
(Minimum 32 Innings)

| | W | L | ERA | G | SV | IP | H | BB | SO |
|---|---|---|---|---|---|---|---|---|---|
| Jenson, Jason, Central | 5 | 4 | 1.07 | 9 | 0 | 50 | 38 | 22 | 46 |
| Farrer, Nick, Danbury | 5 | 2 | 1.35 | 8 | 0 | 53 | 37 | 15 | 53 |
| Taglienti, Jeff, Central | 5 | 3 | 1.43 | 10 | 0 | 69 | 46 | 19 | 69 |
| Scarlata, Michael, RI | 4 | 3 | 2.03 | 9 | 0 | 67 | 53 | 17 | 60 |
| Puleri, Jeff, Central | 6 | 1 | 2.44 | 7 | 0 | 52 | 47 | 16 | 44 |

## NORTHEASTERN LEAGUE

| EAST | W | L | PCT | GB |
|---|---|---|---|---|
| Cooperstown Knickerbockers | 24 | 16 | .600 | — |
| Cortland Apples | 24 | 16 | .600 | — |
| Schenectady Mohawks | 22 | 18 | .550 | 2 |
| Utica/Rome Indians | 14 | 26 | .350 | 10 |

| WEST | W | L | PCT | GB |
|---|---|---|---|---|
| Ithaca Lakers | 28 | 12 | .700 | — |
| Cohocton Red Wings | 17 | 23 | .425 | 11 |
| Hornell Dodgers | 17 | 23 | .425 | 11 |
| Geneva Knights | 14 | 26 | .350 | 14 |

**PLAYOFF TOURNAMENT:** Ithaca 3-0, Cooperstown 2-2, Cortland 1-2, Cohocton 0-2.

## INDIVIDUAL BATTING LEADERS
(Minimum 80 Plate Appearances)

| | AVG | AB | R | H | 2B | 3B | HR | RBI | SB |
|---|---|---|---|---|---|---|---|---|---|
| Folkers, Ken, Hornell............ | .381 | 134 | 30 | 51 | 9 | 5 | 2 | 27 | 6 |
| Cannon, Brian, Ithaca .......... | .336 | 149 | 23 | 50 | 8 | 2 | 3 | 27 | 10 |
| Kaplan, Brett, Ithaca ........... | .331 | 124 | 21 | 41 | 5 | 1 | 3 | 27 | 8 |
| Larsen, Barry, Hornell........... | .330 | 106 | 19 | 35 | 11 | 1 | 2 | 22 | 0 |
| Henderson, Brad, Schenectady | .326 | 144 | 25 | 47 | 8 | 3 | 0 | 18 | 3 |
| Mahoney, Sean, Geneva ..... | .326 | 95 | 17 | 31 | 10 | 0 | 5 | 21 | 1 |
| Shannon, Lance, Cortland ..... | .326 | 89 | 9 | 29 | 2 | 0 | 0 | 18 | 1 |
| Granville, Earnie, Schenectady. | .314 | 121 | 18 | 38 | 3 | 2 | 0 | 16 | 4 |
| Satcher, John, Schenectady..... | .313 | 128 | 16 | 40 | 2 | 2 | 1 | 15 | 7 |
| Jaillet, Jason, Cohocoton..... | .310 | 158 | 25 | 49 | 7 | 7 | 0 | 21 | 6 |

## INDIVIDUAL PITCHING LEADERS
(Minimum 30 Innings)

| | W | L | ERA | G | SV | IP | H | BB | SO |
|---|---|---|---|---|---|---|---|---|---|
| Henebry, Gregg, Ithaca........... | 6 | 0 | 0.90 | 8 | 0 | 40 | 33 | 9 | 17 |
| Snyder, Billy, Schenectady ..... | 2 | 3 | 1.05 | 22 | 11 | 43 | 22 | 20 | 50 |
| Lidge, Brad, Ithaca................ | 1 | 1 | 1.15 | 14 | 5 | 31 | 8 | 16 | 48 |
| Brunette, Justin, Cooper. ........ | 6 | 2 | 1.18 | 9 | 0 | 69 | 50 | 10 | 90 |
| Houdeshell, Aaron, Ithaca........ | 3 | 0 | 1.18 | 5 | 0 | 38 | 29 | 14 | 17 |

## NORTHWEST COLLEGIATE LEAGUE

| FIRST | W | L | PCT | GB | SECOND | W | L | PCT | GB |
|---|---|---|---|---|---|---|---|---|---|
| Dukes | 10 | 3 | .769 | — | Toros | 10 | 5 | .667 | — |
| Toros | 8 | 7 | .533 | 3 | Bucks | 10 | 5 | .667 | — |
| Ports | 7 | 7 | .500 | 3½ | Lobos | 8 | 7 | .533 | 2 |
| Lobos | 7 | 8 | .467 | 4 | Dukes | 7 | 7 | .500 | 2½ |
| Stars | 7 | 8 | .467 | 4 | Ports | 6 | 8 | .429 | 3½ |
| Bucks | 4 | 10 | .286 | 6½ | Stars | 2 | 11 | .133 | 7 |

**PLAYOFFS:** Dukes defeated Toros 2-1 in best-of-3 final.

## INDIVIDUAL BATTING LEADERS
(Minimum 70 Plate Appearances)

| | AVG | AB | R | H | 2B | 3B | HR | RBI | SB |
|---|---|---|---|---|---|---|---|---|---|
| Burke, Mark, Toros............... | .389 | 95 | 16 | 37 | 8 | 0 | 1 | 25 | 6 |
| Bramble, Todd, Lobos........... | .365 | 74 | 14 | 27 | 5 | 1 | 1 | 14 | 6 |
| Bertrano, Ben, Dukes........... | .361 | 61 | 10 | 22 | 3 | 0 | 4 | 18 | 0 |
| Schiller, Todd, Bucks ........... | .354 | 65 | 11 | 23 | 8 | 0 | 0 | 13 | 1 |
| Heriford, Jimmy, Bucks ........ | .351 | 74 | 15 | 26 | 4 | 2 | 0 | 10 | 6 |
| Scott, Jeff, Ports.................. | .339 | 62 | 15 | 21 | 3 | 1 | 0 | 10 | 11 |
| Hageman, Brandon, Dukes.. | .329 | 82 | 13 | 27 | 2 | 0 | 0 | 14 | 2 |
| Munoz, Ryan, Stars.............. | .328 | 64 | 14 | 21 | 2 | 0 | 0 | 4 | 1 |
| Powell, Casey, Stars............ | .322 | 87 | 13 | 28 | 2 | 0 | 0 | 12 | 5 |
| Rohr, Bryan, Stars................ | .314 | 70 | 8 | 22 | 2 | 2 | 1 | 10 | 3 |

## INDIVIDUAL PITCHING LEADERS
(Minimum 25 Innings)

| | W | L | ERA | G | SV | IP | H | BB | SO |
|---|---|---|---|---|---|---|---|---|---|
| Miadich, Bart, Dukes.............. | 6 | 1 | 0.53 | 9 | 0 | 53 | 32 | 9 | 40 |
| Wingerd, Josh, Toros............. | 5 | 4 | 2.05 | 11 | 0 | 55 | 50 | 24 | 40 |
| Kosderka, Matt, Stars............ | 5 | 4 | 2.09 | 12 | 0 | 74 | 65 | 36 | 82 |
| Ellett, Justin, Ports ................ | 2 | 4 | 2.19 | 10 | 1 | 38 | 42 | 9 | 23 |
| Gregory, Josh, Lobos............. | 1 | 4 | 2.24 | 10 | 1 | 34 | 40 | 7 | 12 |

## SAN DIEGO COLLEGIATE LEAGUE

### FIRST HALF

| AMERICAN | W | L | PCT | GB | NATIONAL | W | L | PCT | GB |
|---|---|---|---|---|---|---|---|---|---|
| San Diego | 10 | 4 | .714 | — | El Cajon | 9 | 5 | .643 | — |
| East County | 7 | 8 | .467 | 3½ | Beach City | 8 | 7 | .533 | 1½ |
| South Bay | 5 | 10 | .333 | 5½ | North County | 5 | 10 | .333 | 4½ |

### SECOND HALF

| AMERICAN | W | L | PCT | GB | NATIONAL | W | L | PCT | GB |
|---|---|---|---|---|---|---|---|---|---|
| South Bay | 8 | 6 | .571 | — | El Cajon | 11 | 3 | .786 | — |
| East County | 6 | 9 | .400 | 2½ | Beach City | 10 | 5 | .667 | 1½ |
| San Diego | 4 | 11 | .267 | 4½ | North County | 5 | 10 | .333 | 6½ |

**PLAYOFFS:** Indians defeated Royals in one-game semifinal. Padres defeated Indians 2-1 in best-of-3 final.

## INDIVIDUAL BATTING LEADERS
(Minimum 72 Plate Appearances)

| | AVG | AB | R | H | 2B | 3B | HR | RBI | SB |
|---|---|---|---|---|---|---|---|---|---|
| Bolton, Jason, East County... | .471 | 85 | 17 | 40 | 4 | 3 | 1 | 17 | 9 |
| Waller, Derric, East County... | .443 | 79 | 20 | 35 | 4 | 3 | 3 | 21 | 6 |
| Brown, Barry, East County... | .393 | 84 | 12 | 33 | 6 | 6 | 0 | 18 | 14 |
| Smith, Chad, Beach City...... | .388 | 80 | 18 | 31 | 12 | 0 | 3 | 29 | 2 |
| Wright, Brad, Beach City...... | .387 | 93 | 25 | 36 | 8 | 4 | 1 | 25 | 5 |
| Hammons, Ryan, El Cajon.... | .381 | 84 | 33 | 32 | 6 | 2 | 8 | 35 | 3 |
| Altman, James, Beach City... | .359 | 64 | 12 | 23 | 4 | 1 | 1 | 14 | 3 |
| Cecil, Eli, North County....... | .344 | 93 | 20 | 32 | 5 | 0 | 0 | 7 | 12 |
| Pelaez, Alex, South Bay ...... | .344 | 93 | 23 | 32 | 9 | 0 | 0 | 18 | 0 |
| Ramos, Javier, El Cajon....... | .342 | 73 | 18 | 25 | 5 | 2 | 0 | 12 | 2 |

## INDIVIDUAL PITCHING LEADERS
(Minimum 30 Innings)

| | W | L | ERA | G | SV | IP | H | BB | SO |
|---|---|---|---|---|---|---|---|---|---|
| Adams, Seth, South Bay ......... | 2 | 0 | 1.25 | 8 | 1 | 34 | 31 | 12 | 21 |
| Dufek, Jeff, El Cajon .............. | 6 | 1 | 1.62 | 16 | 3 | 61 | 53 | 6 | 55 |
| Smythe, Stephen, San Diego... | 6 | 3 | 2.11 | 16 | 2 | 63 | 51 | 13 | 31 |
| Waterhouse, Cory, El Cajon..... | 6 | 2 | 2.33 | 12 | 0 | 33 | 20 | 21 | 25 |
| Uris, David, Beach City .......... | 6 | 1 | 2.46 | 10 | 1 | 43 | 53 | 16 | 45 |

## SHENANDOAH VALLEY LEAGUE

| | W | L | PCT | GB |
|---|---|---|---|---|
| Waynesboro Generals | 28 | 12 | .700 | — |
| Harrisonburg Turks | 22 | 18 | .550 | 6 |
| New Market Rebels | 22 | 18 | .550 | 6 |
| Winchester Royals | 18 | 22 | .450 | 10 |
| Staunton Braves | 16 | 24 | .400 | 12 |
| Front Royal Cardinals | 14 | 26 | .350 | 14 |

**PLAYOFFS:** BRACKET ONE—Staunton 3-1, Waynesboro 2-2, Front Royal 1-3. BRACKET TWO—Harrisonburg 3-1, New Market 2-2, Winchester 1-3. Staunton defeated Harrisonburg 3-1 in best-of-5 final.

## INDIVIDUAL BATTING LEADERS
(Minimum 100 Plate Appearances)

| | AVG | AB | R | H | 2B | 3B | HR | RBI | SB |
|---|---|---|---|---|---|---|---|---|---|
| Scioneaux, Damian, Harr..... | .372 | 94 | 29 | 35 | 5 | 3 | 0 | 22 | 17 |
| Eckstein, David, Harr. .......... | .352 | 105 | 32 | 37 | 5 | 0 | 1 | 14 | 27 |
| Eaton, Bill, Waynesboro....... | .350 | 140 | 25 | 49 | 8 | 0 | 1 | 18 | 15 |
| Tolbert, Alex, Staunton ........ | .331 | 139 | 29 | 46 | 7 | 0 | 14 | 40 | 1 |
| Cisar, Mark, New Market...... | .331 | 136 | 25 | 45 | 8 | 1 | 1 | 13 | 19 |
| Robinson, Adam, Staunton ... | .324 | 145 | 30 | 47 | 8 | 4 | 4 | 22 | 11 |
| Nunnari, Talmadge, Harr...... | .323 | 130 | 16 | 42 | 10 | 2 | 4 | 40 | 9 |
| Inge, Brandon, Wayne. ........ | .322 | 121 | 26 | 39 | 4 | 3 | 3 | 14 | 9 |
| Berman, Jeff, New Market.... | .314 | 140 | 20 | 44 | 13 | 3 | 4 | 25 | 10 |
| Visconti, Rick, Staunton ....... | .310 | 87 | 22 | 27 | 5 | 0 | 7 | 16 | 5 |
| Trott, Jason, Front Royal....... | .307 | 140 | 16 | 43 | 4 | 0 | 2 | 14 | 9 |
| Dunn, Casey, New Market .... | .305 | 118 | 12 | 36 | 7 | 1 | 0 | 18 | 0 |
| Corley, Kenny, Winchester... | .304 | 115 | 21 | 35 | 11 | 1 | 4 | 21 | 8 |
| Dill, Justin, Front Royal ....... | .302 | 139 | 35 | 42 | 11 | 0 | 8 | 26 | 6 |
| Johnson, Erik, Winchester ... | .300 | 100 | 17 | 30 | 6 | 0 | 2 | 13 | 3 |

## INDIVIDUAL PITCHING LEADERS
(Minimum 30 Innings)

| | W | L | ERA | G | SV | IP | H | BB | SO |
|---|---|---|---|---|---|---|---|---|---|
| Roach, Jason, Winchester ..... | 6 | 0 | 1.91 | 8 | 1 | 42 | 31 | 19 | 53 |
| Hanson, Matt, Waynesboro... | 5 | 0 | 2.13 | 8 | 0 | 42 | 34 | 16 | 26 |
| Maroth, Mike, Staunton ......... | 1 | 2 | 2.43 | 15 | 3 | 33 | 21 | 18 | 37 |
| Saylor, Ryan, Waynesboro .... | 3 | 1 | 2.51 | 21 | 8 | 32 | 14 | 12 | 53 |
| Malerich, Will, New Market.... | 3 | 1 | 2.72 | 8 | 0 | 53 | 40 | 25 | 65 |
| Wooten, Shane, Harrisonburg.. | 2 | 0 | 2.84 | 5 | 0 | 32 | 22 | 12 | 21 |
| Brewer, Tommy, Harrisonburg. | 5 | 3 | 3.04 | 9 | 0 | 56 | 52 | 19 | 44 |
| Knott, Eric, Wayneboro ......... | 4 | 3 | 3.08 | 13 | 2 | 61 | 53 | 21 | 57 |
| Combe, Chris, New Market.... | 3 | 2 | 3.57 | 10 | 0 | 35 | 38 | 8 | 28 |
| Buob, Mike, Winchester ........ | 4 | 1 | 3.75 | 10 | 0 | 58 | 58 | 29 | 46 |

# NON-AFFILIATED LEAGUES

## ALASKAN LEAGUES

| | | League | | | Overall | |
|---|---|---|---|---|---|---|
| **ALASKA** | W | L | PCT | GB | W | L |
| Anchorage Bucs | 12 | 4 | .750 | — | 33 | 21 |
| Alaska Goldpanners | 7 | 9 | .438 | 5 | 24 | 30 |
| Hawaii Island Movers | 5 | 11 | .313 | 7 | 21 | 19 |

| | | League | | | Overall | |
|---|---|---|---|---|---|---|
| **ALASKA CENTRAL** | W | L | PCT | GB | W | L |
| Anchorage Glacier Pilots | 27 | 15 | .643 | — | 32 | 18 |
| Mat-Su Miners | 22 | 20 | .524 | 5 | 23 | 20 |
| Kenai Peninsula Oilers | 21 | 21 | .500 | 6 | 27 | 25 |

**ALASKA BASEBALL FEDERATION STANDINGS:** Anchorage Glacier Pilots 19-9, Anchorage Bucs 15-13, Kenai Peninsula Oilers 15-13, Mat-Su Miners 13-15, Alaska Goldpanners 8-20.

**ALL-ALASKA TEAM: C**—Greg Halvorsen, Glacier Pilots (Arizona State). **1B**—Tyson Dowdell, Mat-Su (Brigham Young). **2B**—Scott Kidd, Glacier Pilots (Cal Poly San Luis Obispo). **3B**—Andrew Beinbrink, Bucs (Arizona State). **SS**—Clay Snellgrove, Mat-Su (Middle Tennessee State). **OF**—Santos Cortez, Mat-Su (Tennessee); John Heinrichs, Glacier Pilots (Arizona State); Kevin Tommasini, Glacier Pilots (Arizona State). **DH**—Keith Ginter, Mat-Su (Cypress, Calif., JC). **Util**—Adam Piatt, Bucs (Mississippi State);

Matt Schnabel, Bucs (Southwest Texas State). **P**—Jason Cole, Kenai (Cal State Fullerton); Jimmy Frush, Glacier Pilots (Texas Tech); Marcus Jones, Bucs (Long Beach State); Ryan Seifert, Glacier Pilots (Iowa State).

**Player of the Year:** Andrew Beinbrink, 3b, Bucs (Arizona State).

### INDIVIDUAL BATTING LEADERS
(Minimum 100 Plate Appearances)

| | AVG | AB | R | H | 2B | 3B | HR | RBI | SB |
|---|---|---|---|---|---|---|---|---|---|
| Hinske, Eric, Bucs | .422 | 116 | 25 | 49 | 7 | 2 | 4 | 26 | 4 |
| Ginter, Keith, Mat-Su | .416 | 113 | 31 | 47 | 13 | 0 | 6 | 39 | 4 |
| Gjerde, Jeff, Pilots | .400 | 170 | 49 | 68 | 12 | 2 | 8 | 39 | 1 |
| Snellgrove, Clay, M-S/Pilots | .393 | 211 | 53 | 83 | 22 | 1 | 8 | 38 | 4 |
| Heinrichs, Jon, Pilots | .386 | 166 | 46 | 64 | 15 | 1 | 4 | 26 | 9 |
| Kidd, Scott, Pilots | .378 | 180 | 39 | 68 | 15 | 0 | 14 | 53 | 2 |
| Gonzales, Israel, Ala/M-S | .368 | 190 | 40 | 70 | 16 | 0 | 5 | 42 | 5 |
| Nicholson, Derek, Kenai | .368 | 171 | 52 | 63 | 16 | 3 | 5 | 41 | 3 |
| Cortez, Santos, Mat-Su | .360 | 139 | 32 | 50 | 10 | 1 | 5 | 43 | 4 |
| Beinbrink, Andrew, Bucs | .359 | 198 | 47 | 71 | 19 | 4 | 10 | 55 | 12 |
| Mead, Chad, Kenai | .352 | 88 | 23 | 31 | 6 | 0 | 1 | 13 | 0 |
| Aloy, Jaime, Hawaii | .350 | 103 | 21 | 36 | 4 | 2 | 2 | 28 | 6 |
| Schnabel, Matt, Bucs | .349 | 192 | 54 | 67 | 18 | 1 | 6 | 39 | 11 |
| Thrower, Jake, Kenai | .348 | 198 | 44 | 69 | 20 | 4 | 1 | 47 | 11 |
| Dartt, Michael, Hawaii | .348 | 141 | 33 | 49 | 5 | 0 | 2 | 18 | 17 |
| Piatt, Adam, Bucs | .342 | 199 | 55 | 68 | 21 | 2 | 4 | 41 | 22 |
| Matranga, Dave, Kenai | .341 | 164 | 42 | 56 | 10 | 4 | 4 | 29 | 10 |
| Young, Michael, Alaska | .335 | 215 | 40 | 72 | 10 | 3 | 5 | 33 | 10 |
| McConnell, Jason, Pilots | .330 | 182 | 59 | 60 | 10 | 5 | 2 | 16 | 14 |
| Bernhard, John, Alaska | .327 | 101 | 26 | 33 | 6 | 5 | 0 | 21 | 22 |
| Murphy, Sean, Hawaii | .325 | 126 | 29 | 41 | 6 | 6 | 0 | 20 | 7 |
| Soules, Ryan, Alaska | .321 | 212 | 50 | 68 | 18 | 4 | 3 | 42 | 2 |
| Takamori, Sean, Hawaii | .318 | 85 | 20 | 27 | 3 | 2 | 0 | 15 | 10 |
| Voshell, Key, Hawaii | .314 | 105 | 19 | 33 | 5 | 4 | 0 | 17 | 2 |

### INDIVIDUAL PITCHING LEADERS
(Minimum 32 Innings)

| | W | L | ERA | G | SV | IP | H | BB | SO |
|---|---|---|---|---|---|---|---|---|---|
| Boulware, Brian, Hawaii | 1 | 2 | 2.16 | 15 | 1 | 42 | 28 | 14 | 21 |
| Krawczyk, Jack, Bucs | 4 | 2 | 2.61 | 21 | 7 | 38 | 26 | 10 | 41 |
| Picos, Humberto, Alaska | 5 | 1 | 2.66 | 8 | 0 | 47 | 46 | 21 | 36 |
| Sumner, Ryland, Hawaii | 2 | 4 | 2.84 | 8 | 0 | 38 | 33 | 18 | 27 |
| Scott, Brian, Alaska | 6 | 4 | 3.12 | 12 | 0 | 75 | 67 | 23 | 59 |
| Walker, Adam, Kenai | 2 | 2 | 3.18 | 10 | 0 | 45 | 47 | 19 | 53 |
| Kimball, Andy, Kenai | 7 | 2 | 3.27 | 12 | 0 | 77 | 78 | 25 | 87 |
| Lee, Fletcher, Hawaii | 6 | 0 | 3.30 | 13 | 0 | 57 | 61 | 19 | 38 |
| Jones, Marcus, Bucs | 5 | 3 | 3.39 | 9 | 0 | 58 | 49 | 18 | 66 |
| Klein, Matt, Bucs | 4 | 1 | 3.58 | 11 | 2 | 38 | 28 | 22 | 23 |
| Nakaahiki, Clay, Hawaii | 4 | 0 | 3.63 | 11 | 1 | 35 | 38 | 10 | 30 |
| Haddix, Tyler, Pilots | 4 | 4 | 3.76 | 9 | 0 | 52 | 53 | 22 | 26 |
| Jones, Craig, Alaska | 1 | 1 | 3.82 | 19 | 1 | 40 | 35 | 20 | 39 |
| Navarro, Scott, Bucs | 3 | 0 | 3.94 | 7 | 1 | 48 | 51 | 20 | 47 |
| Bromley, Randy, Mat-Su | 1 | 1 | 4.06 | 22 | 3 | 38 | 28 | 39 | 33 |
| French, Eric, Pilots | 1 | 2 | 4.13 | 17 | 2 | 32 | 33 | 8 | 32 |

## CLARK GRIFFITH COLLEGIATE LEAGUE

| FIRST | W | L | SECOND | W | L | THIRD | W | L |
|---|---|---|---|---|---|---|---|---|
| Prince William | 8 | 4 | Arlington | 9 | 3 | Arlington | 8 | 3 |
| Maryland | 8 | 4 | Maryland | 8 | 4 | Reston | 7 | 5 |
| Arlington | 6 | 6 | Reston | 6 | 6 | Prince William | 5 | 5 |
| Herndon | 4 | 8 | Prince William | 3 | 7 | Maryland | 5 | 7 |
| Reston | 4 | 8 | Herndon | 2 | 8 | Herndon | 3 | 8 |

**PLAYOFFS:** Arlington defeated Prince William in one-game final.

### INDIVIDUAL BATTING LEADERS
(Minimum 75 At-Bats)

| | AVG | AB | R | H | 2B | 3B | HR | RBI | SB |
|---|---|---|---|---|---|---|---|---|---|
| Herndon, Eric, Maryland | .414 | 116 | 24 | 48 | 12 | 2 | 1 | 20 | 22 |
| Whiting, Chris, Reston | .359 | 128 | 29 | 46 | 5 | 1 | 0 | 25 | 25 |
| Schenk, Jonathon, Maryland | .359 | 78 | 5 | 28 | 7 | 0 | 1 | 21 | 1 |
| Anderson, E.J., Arlington | .354 | 79 | 15 | 28 | 5 | 1 | 3 | 16 | 10 |
| Dour, Craig, Arlington | .341 | 126 | 25 | 43 | 7 | 2 | 8 | 27 | 5 |
| Kemmerer, Jon, Reston | .323 | 133 | 43 | 43 | 5 | 0 | 0 | 10 | 32 |
| Clements, Chad, Herndon | .307 | 75 | 8 | 23 | 0 | 0 | 0 | 7 | 7 |
| Haas, Trevor, Reston | .295 | 129 | 22 | 38 | 6 | 1 | 1 | 23 | 17 |
| Gauch, Barry, Prince William | .290 | 100 | 11 | 29 | 2 | 1 | 0 | 7 | 1 |
| Beck, Art, Reston | .289 | 97 | 14 | 28 | 4 | 0 | 1 | 15 | 2 |

### INDIVIDUAL PITCHING LEADERS
(Minimum 30 Innings)

| | W | L | ERA | G | SV | IP | H | BB | SO |
|---|---|---|---|---|---|---|---|---|---|
| Eason, Clay, Maryland | 4 | 3 | 1.27 | 12 | 0 | 64 | 30 | 36 | 78 |
| Busch, Eric, Arlington | 2 | 2 | 1.99 | 7 | 0 | 41 | 30 | 26 | 22 |

| Collins, Don, Prince William | 3 | 3 | 2.00 | 10 | 1 | 54 | 38 | 14 | 49 |
| Scott, Cory, Maryland | 5 | 2 | 2.18 | 10 | 1 | 54 | 35 | 38 | 51 |
| Cepeda, Victor, Arlington | 8 | 0 | 2.34 | 10 | 0 | 62 | 63 | 12 | 35 |

## JAYHAWK LEAGUE

| | W | L | PCT | GB |
|---|---|---|---|---|
| Liberal Bee Jays | 24 | 12 | .667 | — |
| Nevada Griffons | 23 | 13 | .639 | 1 |
| Topeka Capitals | 22 | 14 | .611 | 2 |
| El Doroado Broncos | 20 | 16 | .556 | 4 |
| Hays Larks | 20 | 16 | .556 | 4 |
| Elkhart Dusters | 12 | 24 | .333 | 12 |
| Kansas City Monarchs | 5 | 31 | .139 | 19 |

**PLAYOFFS:** None.

### INDIVIDUAL BATTING LEADERS
(Minimum 75 At-Bats)

| | AVG | AB | R | H | 2B | 3B | HR | RBI | SB |
|---|---|---|---|---|---|---|---|---|---|
| Gorr, Robb, Topeka | .413 | 104 | 18 | 43 | 8 | 2 | 3 | 29 | 10 |
| Feramisco, Derek, Nevada | .369 | 84 | 18 | 31 | 4 | 2 | 5 | 14 | 4 |
| Frederick, Kevin, El Dorado | .357 | 115 | 23 | 41 | 9 | 2 | 5 | 31 | 9 |
| Brown, Todd, Kansas City | .354 | 96 | 16 | 34 | 2 | 0 | 3 | 15 | 12 |
| Klam, Jason, Nevada | .353 | 102 | 20 | 36 | 7 | 2 | 7 | 26 | 9 |
| Carr, Dustin, Liberal | .351 | 97 | 29 | 34 | 5 | 0 | 2 | 18 | 5 |
| Oder, Josh, Nevada | .348 | 92 | 14 | 32 | 3 | 1 | 4 | 16 | 9 |
| Wheat, Ty, Kansas City | .346 | 78 | 10 | 27 | 2 | 1 | 1 | 17 | 3 |
| DeMarco, Joey, Topeka | .341 | 85 | 23 | 29 | 3 | 2 | 1 | 11 | 10 |
| Wren, Cliff, Liberal | .341 | 85 | 15 | 29 | 8 | 0 | 5 | 22 | 0 |
| Headley, Justin, Hays | .338 | 133 | 23 | 45 | 15 | 1 | 4 | 33 | 7 |
| Hunter, Johnny, Hays | .338 | 136 | 38 | 46 | 8 | 0 | 10 | 32 | 14 |
| Murse, Jeff, Elkhart | .328 | 119 | 27 | 39 | 7 | 0 | 8 | 30 | 4 |
| Phillips, Andy, Liberal | .321 | 84 | 16 | 27 | 2 | 0 | 2 | 17 | 7 |
| Troutman, Jeremy, El Dorado | .311 | 132 | 27 | 41 | 9 | 0 | 3 | 18 | 16 |

### INDIVIDUAL PITCHING LEADERS
(Minimum 20 Innings)

| | W | L | ERA | G | SV | IP | H | BB | SO |
|---|---|---|---|---|---|---|---|---|---|
| Rohrback, Mike, Hays | 2 | 1 | 0.78 | 13 | 4 | 23 | 11 | 6 | 28 |
| Wright, Shane, Topeka | 4 | 0 | 1.46 | 7 | 0 | 37 | 32 | 9 | 28 |
| McDonald, Jon, Topeka | 6 | 0 | 1.56 | 9 | 0 | 40 | 40 | 10 | 46 |
| Bradford, Mike, Liberal | 5 | 1 | 1.59 | 6 | 0 | 40 | 26 | 12 | 33 |
| Dickinson, Brady, Nevada | 1 | 2 | 1.67 | 7 | 1 | 27 | 18 | 11 | 32 |
| Richardson, Corey, Elkhart | 1 | 1 | 1.78 | 10 | 4 | 25 | 17 | 12 | 35 |
| Ralston, Brad, El Dorado | 3 | 0 | 1.86 | 11 | 0 | 29 | 15 | 13 | 32 |
| Stewart, Zack, Liberal | 1 | 0 | 1.99 | 14 | 1 | 23 | 15 | 8 | 27 |
| Key, Calvin, Nevada | 4 | 1 | 1.99 | 9 | 0 | 63 | 48 | 18 | 55 |
| Poland, Trey, Hays | 3 | 2 | 2.09 | 8 | 0 | 47 | 38 | 11 | 62 |

## NORTHWOODS LEAGUE

| FIRST | W | L | PCT | GB | SECOND | W | L | PCT | GB |
|---|---|---|---|---|---|---|---|---|---|
| Waterloo | 20 | 10 | .667 | — | Waterloo | 20 | 10 | .667 | — |
| Rochester | 19 | 11 | .633 | 1 | Kenosha | 19 | 11 | .633 | 1 |
| Wausau | 14 | 16 | .467 | 6 | Rochester | 16 | 13 | .552 | 3½ |
| Manitowoc | 13 | 16 | .448 | 6½ | Manitowoc | 14 | 16 | .467 | 6 |
| Kenosha | 12 | 17 | .414 | 7½ | Wausau | 12 | 18 | .400 | 8 |
| Dubuque | 11 | 19 | .367 | 9 | Dubuque | 8 | 21 | .276 | 11½ |

**PLAYOFFS:** Waterloo defeated Rochester 2-0 in best-of-3 final.

### INDIVIDUAL BATTING LEADERS
(Minimum 162 Plate Appearances)

| | AVG | AB | R | H | 2B | 3B | HR | RBI | SB |
|---|---|---|---|---|---|---|---|---|---|
| Pierre, Juan, Manitowoc | .360 | 136 | 32 | 49 | 7 | 2 | 0 | 16 | 15 |
| Quinlan, Robb, Dubuque | .357 | 230 | 47 | 82 | 16 | 2 | 7 | 44 | 1 |
| Lucas, Kevin, Rochester | .355 | 248 | 43 | 88 | 7 | 1 | 3 | 37 | 34 |
| Gibbons, Jay, Manitowoc | .351 | 202 | 37 | 71 | 11 | 0 | 11 | 53 | 7 |
| Poepard, Scott, Rochester | .342 | 184 | 42 | 63 | 18 | 2 | 7 | 29 | 9 |
| Huisman, Jason, Waterloo | .342 | 228 | 39 | 78 | 12 | 2 | 6 | 38 | 14 |
| Flees, Shorty, Kenosha | .335 | 209 | 45 | 70 | 24 | 1 | 7 | 47 | 8 |
| Gregory, Rich, Kenosha | .322 | 171 | 39 | 55 | 16 | 1 | 8 | 35 | 6 |
| Zander, Bryan, Dubuque | .318 | 214 | 41 | 68 | 14 | 5 | 2 | 27 | 6 |
| Byas, Mike, Waterloo | .309 | 243 | 45 | 75 | 12 | 1 | 0 | 34 | 30 |

### INDIVIDUAL PITCHING LEADERS
(Minimum 48 Innings)

| | W | L | ERA | G | SV | IP | H | BB | SO |
|---|---|---|---|---|---|---|---|---|---|
| Diebolt, Mike, Rochester | 5 | 0 | 1.48 | 15 | 5 | 67 | 52 | 18 | 74 |
| Faust, Jason, Waterloo | 7 | 2 | 2.19 | 11 | 0 | 74 | 60 | 26 | 51 |
| Brickman, Scott, Waterloo | 4 | 2 | 2.44 | 10 | 0 | 70 | 70 | 15 | 51 |
| Ballenger, Bryan, Kenosha | 4 | 5 | 2.45 | 12 | 2 | 59 | 47 | 26 | 49 |
| Drakulich, Luke, Kenosha | 3 | 2 | 2.59 | 27 | 7 | 49 | 46 | 22 | 43 |

# AMATEUR
# DRAFT

# Little-Known Draft Rule Enables Lee To Sign Staggering $10M Deal

**By ALAN SCHWARZ**

Baseball's amateur draft usually is known for how it doles out talent. In the 1990s, it has been known for doling out huge sums of money.

But in 1996, it became known for a once-innocuous paragraph buried in the Professional Baseball Agreement, one that wound up turning the entire process upside down and made some prospects rich beyond everyone's wildest dreams—and nightmares.

Because of four clubs' violations to Rule 4 (E) of the PBA, which requires that teams make a formal uniform contract offer to every pick within 15 days of the draft, Major League Baseball granted several premium players free agency and touched off unprecedented bidding wars for their services.

The four players were: San Diego State first baseman Travis Lee (No. 2 overall, Twins); Orange, Texas, righthander John Patterson (No. 5, Expos); Waynesboro, Pa., righthander Matt White (No. 7, Giants); and Sarasota, Fla., lefthander Bobby Seay (No. 12, White Sox).

It was generally agreed by scouts that Lee was the top position player available in the draft, and Patterson, White and Seay the top three high school pitchers.

**Expensive Taste.** Travis Lee showcases his Diamondbacks uniform after inking $10 million deal.

Hitting the open market offered all of those players the chance to sign for significantly more money than if they had remained bound to the clubs that drafted them. Lee wound up agreeing with the expansion Arizona Diamondbacks on a stunning $10 million contract; Patterson also came to terms with the Diamondbacks for $5 million, and Seay for $3 million with the Devil Rays. White remained unsigned in mid-November..

"It provided as unique an experience for a player as I can possibly imagine," said Jeff Moorad, the attorney representing Lee. "Not only to have free-market influences determine his initial signing packages, but also to choose his team."

Meanwhile, clubs that lost the rights to their first-round picks had to reconcile that they had been foiled by a rule that never had been challenged, enforced or barely recognized before.

"We'll live by the ruling," Twins scouting director Mike Radcliff said. "We can agree or disagree with it, but it doesn't matter anymore. We'll carry on."

Said Expos scouting director Ed Creech: "They found a chink in the armor, a technicality, that they could exploit and they took advantage of it. Baseball has shot itself in the foot again."

## White Sox Lead Off

Rule 4 (E) had been part of the PBA since at least 1990. But never before had players or agents made it an issue.

The rule first was challenged by Seay, his father and their attorney, Scott Boras. Though Seay's rights were relinquished voluntarily by the White Sox Aug. 15, the virtual precedent set the stage for others to file.

No hearing was held in the Seay case. Chicago officials claimed they were removing the lefthander from their negotiation list in part because Seay was demanding a $2 million contract and also because the club didn't want to participate in a formal investigation. Boras claimed that the team had supplied MLB with no evidence of making an offer to Seay within the 15 days.

"I still contend that the grievance would not have held up," White Sox vice president Larry Monroe said. "But it would have been a hol-

## TOP 10 SIGNING BONUSES

### DRAFTED PLAYERS

| Player, Pos. | Club, Year (Round) | Bonus |
|---|---|---|
| 1. Kris Benson, rhp | Pirates '96 (1) | $2,000,000 |
| 2. Braden Looper, rhp | Cardinals '96 (1) | 1,675,000 |
| 3. Josh Booty, ss | Marlins '94 (1) | 1,600,000 |
| 4. Darin Erstad, of | Angels '95 (1) | 1,575,000 |
| 5. Brien Taylor, lhp | Yankees '91 (1) | 1,550,000 |
| Paul Wilson, rhp | Mets '94 (1) | 1,550,000 |
| 7. Bill Koch, rhp | Blue Jays '96 (1) | 1,450,000 |
| 8. Seth Greisinger, rhp | Tigers '96 (1) | 1,415,000 |
| 9. Jaime Jones, of | Marlins '95 (1) | 1,337,000 |
| 10. Ben Davis, c | Padres '95 (1) | 1,300,000 |
| Darren Dreifort, rhp | Dodgers '93 (1) | 1,300,000 |

### FREE AGENTS

| Player, Pos., Country | Club, Year | Bonus |
|---|---|---|
| 1. Travis Lee, 1b, U.S. | Diamondbacks '96 | $10,000,000 |
| 2. John Patterson, rhp, U.S. | Diamondbacks '96 | 5,000,000 |
| 3. Bobby Seay, lhp, U.S. | Devil Rays '96 | 3,000,000 |
| 4. Livan Hernandez, rhp, Cuba | Marlins '96 | 2,500,000 |
| 5. Hideo Nomo, rhp, Japan | Dodgers '95 | 2,000,000 |
| 6. Vladimir Nunez, rhp, Cuba | Diamondbacks '96 | 1,750,000 |
| 7. Jackson Melian, of, Venezuela | Yankees '96 | 1,600,000 |
| 8. Katsuhiro Maeda, rhp, Japan | Yankees '96 | 1,500,000 |
| 9. Osvaldo Fernandez, rhp, Cuba | Giants '96 | 1,300,000 |
| 10. Larry Rodriguez, rhp, Cuba | Diamondbacks '96 | 1,250,000 |

low feeling to gather all the information for the hearing, go to New York and defend ourselves, win and find out that we still don't get the player. We're still very far apart on money and we don't think we'll get him signed anyway."

The White Sox' gesture was construed by some onlookers as an attempt to avoid a precedent-setting ruling by MLB. But it didn't stop six others from filing similar grievances, with three ultimately becoming free agents as well.

Three players who appealed for free agency signed before MLB made a decision. Wichita State righthander Braden Looper (No. 3, Cardinals) received a $1.675 million bonus and Maryland lefthander Eric Milton (No. 20, Yankees) got $775,000 in late August. Stanford catcher A.J. Hinch (third round, Athletics) signed for $125,000.

Lee, Patterson and White carried through with their grievances and came up big. They were declared free agents Sept. 24, becoming the first U.S. players ever to gain free agency during the summer in which they had been drafted. Previous snafus involving Tom Seaver (1966), Bill Bordley (1979) and Billy Cannon (1980) afforded those players either limited free agency or access to a special lottery.

## Evolution Of The Rule

By many estimates, at most only half of the 30 teams made offers to their first-round picks that threaded the needle of Rule 4 (E). And none of the four teams which lost picks claimed that it had followed the rule to the letter.

Radcliff said the Twins made a verbal offer to Lee within 15 days after the draft—which Moorad disputed—but in either case the rule mandates a written, uniform major or minor league contract. Both the Expos and Giants made written proposals, but didn't offer uniform contracts. The Seay camp claimed that no offer ever was made within the 15 days.

Rule 4 (E) was revised in December 1990 after previously requiring only that an offer—verbal or written, formal or informal—be made within 15 days. Virtually no teams changed their approach. Some baseball officials were unaware of the change, while others figured the rule wouldn't be enforced.

It might not have if the rule hadn't come to light in 1996. Two scenarios were given as to how it did.

After the Angels tendered major league lefthander Brian Anderson an incorrect contract during the 1995-96 offseason, negotiators for the owners and players discussed a rule that would cure incorrect tenders as part of the next Basic Agreement. That led to talk of another existing tender rule, Rule 4 (E) in the PBA. Union lawyers then brought Rule 4 (E) to the attention of several agents who specialize in the draft, and those agents were poised if any violations were made.

Boras, who represents White and Seay, said he noticed Rule 4 (E) when he was revising a draft guidebook he sends to his clients. Seay's father Robert brought up the rule after the White Sox failed to make his son an offer within 15 days.

The rule probably won't become an issue again, as major league teams certainly will adhere to it in the future. But the windfalls reaped by this crop of free agents will undoubtedly expose the restrictive effect of the draft on bonuses, and it's possible that a premium

**Top Dog.** Clemson righthander Kris Benson was the No. 1 pick in the 1996 draft, signing with Pittsburgh for a $2 million bonus.

talent in future years might decide to challenge the legality of the draft on the grounds that it unfairly restricts their earning power.

"Baseball has made an admission that they're not paying for talent, they're paying for jurisdiction," said Boras, noting that most foreign players can sign with any club while U.S. players are limited by the draft to one team. "That's where the draft is wrong."

Radcliff said he hoped the summer's momentous events won't lead anyone to contest the draft rules in the future.

"You could view this as the first step toward a major upheaval of the draft," Radcliff said. "The draft is designed to benefit all teams. I think you can show that it has."

## Open-Market Competition

In 1996, though, the draft benefited the free-agent foursome far more than ever before.

Lee and the Diamondbacks sent tremors throughout the industry with their historic, $10 million deal on Oct. 11. Club personnel all over baseball were left shaking their heads.

"I think it's insanity to pay that to an unproven college player," Orioles assistant GM Kevin Malone said. "It's another sign the game's in trouble, and another sign that the industry can't control spending."

The Diamondbacks won out in the bidding war for Lee by offering more than twice the largest contract ever for an amateur player.

Cuban righthander Livan Hernandez had commanded a $4.5 million deal from the Marlins during the previous offseason, including a $2.5 million bonus (see Page 8). The record for an American player was Clemson righthander Kris Benson's $2 million bonus from the Pirates two months before as the draft's No. 1 pick.

When he hit the open market, Lee found himself

# DRAFT '96
## TOP 50 PICKS

Signing bonuses do not include college scholarships, incentive bonus plans or salaries from a major league contract.

*Highest level attained
†Signed as free agent by Diamondbacks
•Signed as free agent by Devil Rays

| Team. Player, Pos. | School | Hometown | Bonus | B'date | Ht. | Wt. | B-T | AVG | AB | H | HR | RBI | SB | '96 Assignment* |
|---|---|---|---|---|---|---|---|---|---|---|---|---|---|---|
| 2. †Twins. Travis Lee, 1b | San Diego State U. | Olympia, Wash. | $10,000,000 | 5-26-75 | 6-3 | 210 | L-L | .355 | 220 | 78 | 14 | 60 | 33 | Team USA |
| 8. Brewers. Chad Green, of | U. of Kentucky | Mentor, Ohio | 1,060,000 | 6-28-75 | 5-10 | 185 | B-R | .352 | 256 | 90 | 12 | 44 | 55 | Ogden (R) |
| 9. Marlins. Mark Kotsay, of | Cal State Fullerton | Santa Fe Springs, Calif. | 1,125,000 | 12-02-75 | 6-0 | 180 | L-L | .402 | 243 | 97 | 20 | 91 | 20 | Kane County (A) |
| 10. Athletics. Eric Chavez, 3b | Mt. Carmel HS | San Diego | 1,140,000 | 12-07-77 | 6-1 | 190 | B-R | .458 | 96 | 44 | 11 | 24 | 33 | DNP—Signed late |
| 13. Mets. Robert Stratton, of | San Marcos HS | Santa Barbara, Calif. | 975,000 | 10-07-77 | 6-2 | 220 | R-R | .424 | 66 | 28 | 3 | 24 | 26 | GCL Mets (R) |
| 14. Royals. Dermal Brown, of | Marlboro Central HS | Marlboro, N.Y. | 1,000,000 | 3-27-78 | 6-1 | 210 | L-R | .450 | 60 | 27 | 9 | 35 | 20 | GCL Royals (R) |
| 15. Padres. Matt Halloran, ss | Chancellor HS | Fredericksburg, Va. | 1,000,000 | 3-3-78 | 6-2 | 190 | R-R | .493 | 69 | 34 | 7 | 28 | 7 | AZL Padres (R) |
| 16. Blue Jays. Joe Lawrence, ss | Barbe HS | Lake Charles, La. | 907,500 | 2-13-77 | 6-1 | 190 | R-R | .449 | 89 | 40 | 9 | 38 | 20 | St. Catharines (A) |
| 23. Dodgers. Damian Rolls, 3b | Schalgel HS | Kansas City, Kan. | 695,000 | 9-15-77 | 6-2 | 205 | R-R | .488 | 41 | 20 | 4 | 22 | 18 | Yakima (A) |
| 25. Reds. John Oliver, of | Lake-Lehman HS | Lehman, Pa. | 672,000 | 5-14-78 | 6-3 | 190 | R-R | .625 | 88 | 55 | 11 | 43 | 25 | Princeton (R) |
| 27. Braves. A.J. Zapp, 1b | Center Grove HS | Greenwood, Ind. | 650,000 | 4-24-78 | 6-3 | 190 | L-R | .507 | 69 | 35 | 14 | 46 | 3 | GCL Braves (R) |
| 28. Indians. Danny Peoples, 1b | U. of Texas | Round Rock, Texas | 400,000 | 1-20-75 | 6-0 | 210 | R-R | .375 | 216 | 81 | 17 | 86 | 7 | Watertown (A) |
| 29. Devil Rays. Paul Wilder, of | Cary HS | Cary, N.C. | 650,000 | 1-9-78 | 6-4 | 235 | L-R | .438 | 73 | 32 | 10 | 24 | 13 | GCL Devil Rays (R) |
| 31. Blue Jays. Pete Tucci, 1b-of | Providence College | Norwalk, Conn. | 400,000 | 10-8-75 | 6-2 | 195 | R-R | .363 | 193 | 70 | 16 | 59 | 19 | St. Catharines (A) |
| 37. Twins. Jacque Jones, of | U. of Southern Calif. | San Diego | 360,000 | 4-25-75 | 5-10 | 170 | L-L | .375 | 248 | 93 | 10 | 56 | 11 | Fort Myers (A) |
| 39. Red Sox. Gary LoCurto, 1b | University HS | San Diego | 375,000 | 5-25-78 | 6-2 | 200 | B-R | .470 | 100 | 47 | 3 | 39 | 8 | GCL Red Sox (R) |
| 40. Expos. Milton Bradley, of | Poly HS | Long Beach | 363,000 | 4-15-78 | 5-11 | 165 | B-R | .341 | 79 | 27 | 1 | 10 | 15 | GCL Expos (R) |
| 42. Giants. Mike Caruso, ss | Stoneman Douglas HS | Parkland, Fla. | 327,500 | 5-27-77 | 6-0 | 165 | B-R | .488 | 86 | 42 | 3 | 22 | 26 | Bellingham (A) |
| 44. Blue Jays. Brent Abernathy, ss | The Lovett School | Atlanta | 425,000 | 9-23-77 | 6-0 | 180 | R-R | .635 | 126 | 80 | 13 | 50 | 46 | DNP—Signed late |
| 45. Athletics. Josue Espada, ss | U. of Mobile (Ala.) | Carolina, P.R. | 265,000 | 8-30-75 | 5-10 | 175 | R-R | .446 | 166 | 74 | 5 | 39 | 38 | So. Oregon (A) |
| 46. Phillies. Jimmy Rollins, ss | Encinal HS | Alameda, Calif. | 340,000 | 11-27-78 | 5-9 | 165 | B-R | .510 | 106 | 54 | 6 | 39 | 30 | Martinsville (R) |
| 47. White Sox. Josh Paul, c-of | Vanderbilt U. | Buffalo Grove, Ill. | 285,000 | 5-19-75 | 6-1 | 185 | R-R | .336 | 223 | 75 | 12 | 46 | 15 | Hickory (A) |
| 50. Padres. Vernon Maxwell, of | Midwest City HS | Midwest City, Okla. | 425,000 | 10-22-76 | 6-3 | 225 | R-R | .364 | 107 | 39 | 5 | 31 | 18 | AZL Padres (R) |

| Team. Player, Pos. | School | Hometown | Bonus | B'date | Ht. | Wt. | B-T | W | L | ERA | IP | H | BB | SO | '96 Assignment |
|---|---|---|---|---|---|---|---|---|---|---|---|---|---|---|---|
| 1. Pirates. Kris Benson, p | Clemson U. | Kennesaw, Ga. | $2,000,000 | 11-7-74 | 6-4 | 190 | R-R | 14 | 2 | 2.02 | 156 | 109 | 27 | 204 | Team USA |
| 3. Cardinals. Braden Looper, p | Wichita State U. | Mangum, Okla. | 1,675,000 | 10-28-74 | 6-4 | 220 | R-R | 4 | 1 | 2.09 | 56 | 37 | 15 | 64 | Team USA |
| 4. Blue Jays. Bill Koch, p | Clemson U. | West Babylon, N.Y. | 1,450,000 | 12-14-74 | 6-3 | 195 | R-R | 10 | 5 | 3.14 | 112 | 73 | 60 | 152 | Team USA |
| 5. •Expos. John Patterson, p | West Orange Stark HS | Orange, Texas | 6,075,000 | 1-30-78 | 6-4 | 185 | R-R | 7 | 2 | 0.77 | 72 | 35 | 36 | 142 | Did not sign |
| 6. Tigers. Seth Greisinger, p | U. of Virginia | Falls Church, Va. | 1,415,000 | 7-29-75 | 6-4 | 190 | R-R | 12 | 2 | 1.76 | 123 | 78 | 16 | 131 | Team USA |
| 7. •Giants. Matt White, p | Waynesboro Area HS | Waynesboro, Pa. | 10,200,000 | 8-13-78 | 6-5 | 230 | R-R | 10 | 1 | 0.66 | 74 | 21 | 16 | 131 | Did not sign |
| 11. Phillies. Adam Eaton, p | Snohomish HS | Snohomish, Wash. | 1,100,000 | 11-23-77 | 6-2 | 190 | R-R | 8 | 0 | 0.60 | 58 | 28 | 15 | 80 | DNP—Signed late |
| 12. •White Sox. Bobby Seay, p | Sarasota HS | Sarasota, Fla. | 3,000,000 | 6-20-78 | 6-2 | 190 | L-L | 9 | 2 | 0.70 | 70 | 33 | 29 | 122 | Did not sign |
| 17. Cubs. Todd Noel, p | North Vermillion HS | Maurice, La. | 900,000 | 9-28-78 | 6-4 | 185 | R-R | 9 | 3 | 1.16 | 42 | 24 | 16 | 79 | GCL Cubs (R) |
| 18. Rangers. R.A. Dickey, p | U. of Tennessee | Nashville, Tenn. | 75,000 | 10-29-74 | 6-1 | 205 | R-R | 9 | 4 | 2.76 | 127 | 114 | 33 | 137 | Team USA |
| 19. Astros. Mark Johnson, p | U. of Hawaii | Lebanon, Ohio | 775,000 | 5-2-75 | 6-3 | 215 | R-R | 6 | 5 | 4.60 | 119 | 114 | 40 | 132 | Team USA |
| 20. Yankees. Eric Milton, p | U. of Maryland | Bellefonte, Pa. | 775,000 | 8-4-75 | 6-3 | 200 | L-L | 4 | 7 | 4.20 | 90 | 83 | 17 | 118 | DNP—Signed late |
| 21. Rockies. Jake Westbrook, p | Madison County HS | Danielsville, Ga. | 750,000 | 9-27-77 | 6-3 | 180 | R-R | 9 | 1 | 1.11 | 63 | 32 | 17 | 110 | Portland (A) |
| 22. Mariners. Gilbert Meche, p | Acadiana HS | Lafayette, La. | 820,000 | 9-8-78 | 6-3 | 185 | R-R | 6 | 4 | 2.30 | 42 | 32 | 32 | 34 | AZL Mariners (R) |
| 24. Rangers. Sam Marsonek, p | Jesuit HS | Tampa | 834,000 | 7-10-78 | 6-6 | 225 | R-R | 12 | 1 | 0.93 | 93 | 47 | 25 | 153 | DNP—Signed late |
| 26. Red Sox. Josh Garrett, p | South Spencer HS | Richland, Ind. | 665,000 | 1-12-78 | 6-6 | 190 | R-R | 8 | 0 | 0.42 | 67 | 26 | 14 | 102 | GCL Red Sox (R) |
| 30. †Diamondbacks. Nick Bierbrodt, p | Millikin HS | Long Beach | 525,000 | 5-16-78 | 6-6 | 200 | L-L | 10 | 3 | 2.53 | 70 | 33 | 16 | 80 | Lethbridge (A) |
| 32. Rangers. Corey Lee, p | North Carolina State U. | Clayton, N.C. | 385,000 | 12-26-74 | 6-5 | 200 | L-L | 10 | 2 | 2.62 | 78 | 58 | 28 | 122 | Hudson Valley (A) |
| 33. Reds. Matt McClendon, p | Dr. Phillips HS | Orlando | — | 10-13-77 | 6-3 | 187 | R-R | 10 | 2 | 1.09 | 72 | 70 | 15 | 80 | Did not sign |
| 34. Red Sox. Chris Reitsma, p | Calgary Christian HS | Calgary, Alberta | 425,000 | 12-31-77 | 6-3 | 180 | R-R | No high school team | | | | | | | Did not sign |
| 35. Braves. Jason Marquis, p | Tottenville HS | Staten Island, N.Y. | 600,000 | 8-21-78 | 6-1 | 180 | R-R | 14 | 1 | 0.46 | 82 | 28 | 22 | 135 | Danville (R) |
| 36. Pirates. Andy Prater, p | McCluer North HS | Florissant, Mo. | 415,000 | 9-27-77 | 6-3 | 175 | R-R | 4 | 2 | 1.76 | 56 | 36 | 16 | 85 | GCL Pirates (R) |
| 38. Reds. Buddy Carlyle, p | Bellevue East HS | Bellevue, Neb. | 270,000 | 12-21-77 | 6-3 | 175 | B-R | 4 | 3 | 0.92 | 53 | 32 | 12 | 74 | Princeton (R) |
| 41. Tigers. Matt Miller, p | Texas Tech | Lubbock, Texas | 352,500 | 8-2-74 | 6-4 | 195 | R-R | 12 | 2 | 3.98 | 111 | 114 | 56 | 113 | Jamestown (A) |
| 43. Brewers. Jose Garcia, p | Baldwin Park HS | Chino, Calif. | 325,000 | 4-29-78 | 6-1 | 215 | L-L | 6 | 7 | 2.92 | 72 | 71 | 30 | 98 | Helena (R) |
| 48. Mets. Brendan Behn, p | Merced (Calif.) JC | Merced, Calif. | 285,000 | 10-10-75 | 6-1 | 165 | L-L | Did not play | | | | | | | DNP—Signed late |
| 49. Royals. Taylor Myers, p | Green Valley HS | Henderson, Nev. | 320,000 | 11-9-77 | 6-1 | 165 | R-R | 9 | 1 | 1.74 | 72 | 43 | 20 | 102 | DNP—Injured |

KEN BABBITT

**Wealthy Youngsters.** John Patterson, left, and Matt White were drafted in the first round by the Expos and Giants, respectively. The pair opted for free agency. Patterson signed with the Diamondbacks for $5 million; White continued to entertain multimillion dollar offers.

wined and dined by many of baseball's power brokers. He said he finally chose Arizona, an expansion team not set to begin play until 1998, both because of the money offered and to be part of a building franchise.

"I know they're an expansion team, and that was one of the downsides at first," Lee said. "There's no tradition. But if I went to the Yankees, people would be always comparing me to Don Mattingly. I didn't want that. I didn't want to be Don Mattingly. I want to be Travis Lee."

Lee became a very rich Travis Lee with his historic contract. The deal specified that he would receive a $5 million bonus and $5 million in major league salary over three years, beginning when the Diamondbacks get their first 40-man roster in November 1997. Obscure major league rules later required that the payments be restructured, calling for almost all of the $10 million be paid before November 1997, but the monumental total value remained intact.

"Some might look at the expansion ownership and front office and think they are spending money foolishly," said Diamondbacks owner Jerry Colangelo, the longtime owner of the NBA's Phoenix Suns before his foray into baseball. "In some cases, it might be a legitimate gripe. What some people don't realize is that we have 30 years of experience, a lot more than most baseball owners do now. We understand how the system works."

"To the people who say we're ruining baseball," Arizona GM Joe Garagiola Jr. said, "there were other teams out there prepared to do what we did."

"We wish him good luck," said Twins GM Terry Ryan, who originally drafted Lee before losing him to free agency. "I'm not going to say anything negative about the situation, just good luck."

## Benson Emerges As Top Talent

Before the fervor over Rule 4 (E), the 1996 draft had unfolded like most others. One of its only notable

features was the consensus opinion that the talent wasn't as strong as it had been in previous years—particularly in position players.

The clear No. 1 choice was Benson, who emerged as the nation's top amateur talent during his stellar junior season. Baseball America's 1996 College Player of the Year, Benson went 14-2 with a 2.02 ERA and 204 strikeouts in 156 innings. His only two losses came at the College World Series.

Benson, armed with a 95-mph fastball and excellent command of a curveball for a power pitcher, later signed for a $2 million bonus, breaking the record of $1.6 million set by Marlins first-rounder Josh Booty in 1994. He immediately spurred hope in Pittsburgh that he could help that club's struggling pitching staff as early as Opening Day 1997.

"I think he will need at least some time in the minor leagues," Pirates general manager Cam Bonifay said. "He's a very advanced prospect, but you never know how players will react to professional baseball until they actually get there."

Said Benson: "I know people will expect a lot, me being the No. 1 pick and all. But I've had to deal with that this season, too. I put a lot of great expectations on myself. My goal was to be the top pitcher in the country and the No. 1 draft pick. I expect a lot out of myself, so it doesn't bother me if other people expect a lot from me."

The Twins followed the Pirates' selection of Benson by choosing Lee, considered by most clubs to be the best hitter in the draft by a considerable margin.

The Cardinals followed by drafting Looper, the Wichita State closer, with the No. 3 overall pick. Then came the biggest question of the draft at the time: Would the Blue Jays take White at No. 4 or gamble that he might be available when they selected again at No. 16?

A bigger question was why a player like White, who was regarded by some scouts as one of the best high school pitching prospects in the draft era, could last that long. The reason was that White's stated bonus demand of $2.5 million and aggressive approach turned away many clubs.

White, with Boras' help, told at least 10 teams that they shouldn't draft him, either because they didn't have the wherewithal to afford him the money he was seeking or for other reasons, such as the reputation of the club's minor league system. He said unless he received his demands he would accept his scholarship to Georgia Tech.

"It's got to stop," one scouting director said of White's strategy of trying to choose where he'd get drafted. "The draft is supposed to help the worst teams. Now agents are saying, 'Don't pick this guy.' We have to start calling their bluff."

The Blue Jays, intentionally or not, didn't. They chose Billy Koch, a hard-throwing Clemson righthander, making Koch and Benson the highest-drafted pitching teammates ever. Patterson then went to the Expos at No. 5. The Tigers chose University of Virginia righthander Seth Greisinger with the sixth selection before the Giants ended the suspense over White by making him the No. 7 overall pick.

"God hates a coward," Bob Quinn, the club's general manager before Brian Sabean replaced him in October, said hours after selecting White. "If we don't want to be aggressive, we shouldn't be in this business. We're not going to be afraid to fail."

It appeared as if the Giants would have failed to sign White even before he attained free agency. The two sides barely spoke all summer. In mid-September the Giants offered $1.625 million while the White camp asked for a four-year major league deal worth $4.75 million, comparable to what Hernandez received from the Marlins on the open market.

Sabean let his frustration show. "We're on different planets—except theirs is undiscovered," he said. White laughed and reassured reporters, "I am from Earth." That controversy ended with the MLB ruling which made White a free agent. If he was from Earth, he got his taste of heaven.

## Dickey Provides A Twist

In one of the most bizarre developments in the most bizarre draft ever, University of Tennessee righthander R.A. Dickey's hope for a large signing bonus was felled by a magazine cover.

**R.A. Dickey**

Dickey, chosen No. 18 overall by the Rangers, had agreed with Texas on a $810,000 bonus contract, but several subsequent physicals revealed that the pitcher's right elbow has no ulnar collateral ligament, which gives stability to the joint. The Rangers nixed the deal. Dickey finally signed for just $75,000 in hopes that he could avoid injury and reach the major leagues anyway.

The strange twist in the story came after a Rangers physician looked at the cover of Baseball America's July 22-Aug. 4 issue, which featured Dickey and four U.S. Olympic team pitchers. Dr. John Conway, Texas' orthopedic consultant, was bothered by the look of Dickey's right elbow in the picture. His arm didn't hang naturally like the others'. Conway's concerns and Dickey's subpar performance with Team USA

## NO. 1 DRAFT PICKS, 1965-96

| Year | Club, Player, Pos. | School | Hometown | Highest Level (G*) | '96 Team | Bonus |
|---|---|---|---|---|---|---|
| 1965 | A's. Rick Monday, of | Arizona State U. | Santa Monica, Calif. | Majors (1,996) | Out of Baseball | $104,000 |
| 1966 | Mets. Steve Chilcott, c | Antelope Valley HS | Lancaster, Calif. | Triple-A (2) | Out of Baseball | 75,000 |
| 1967 | Yankees. Ron Blomberg, 1b | Druid Hills HS | Atlanta | Majors (461) | Out of Baseball | 75,000 |
| 1968 | Mets. Tim Foli, ss | Notre Dame HS | Sherman Oaks, Calif. | Majors (1,696) | Out of Baseball | 75,000 |
| 1969 | Senators. Jeff Burroughs, of | Wilson HS | Long Beach, Calif. | Majors (1,689) | Out of Baseball | 88,000 |
| 1970 | Padres. Mike Ivie, c | Walker HS | Decatur, Ga. | Majors (857) | Out of Baseball | 80,000 |
| 1971 | White Sox. Danny Goodwin, c | Central HS | Peoria, Ill. | Majors (252) | Out of Baseball | DNS |
| 1972 | Padres. Dave Roberts, 3b | U. of Oregon | Corvallis, Ore. | Majors (709) | Out of Baseball | 60,000 |
| 1973 | Rangers. David Clyde, lhp | Westchester HS | Houston | Majors (84) | Out of Baseball | 125,000 |
| 1974 | Padres. Bill Almon, ss | Brown U. | Warwick, R.I. | Majors (1,236) | Out of Baseball | 90,000 |
| 1975 | Angels. Danny Goodwin, c | Southern U. | Peoria, Ill. | Majors (252) | Out of Baseball | 125,000 |
| 1976 | Astros. Floyd Bannister, lhp | Arizona State U. | Seattle | Majors (431) | Out of Baseball | 100,000 |
| 1977 | White Sox. Harold Baines, of | St. Michaels HS | St. Michaels, Md. | Majors (2,326) | White Sox | 40,000 |
| 1978 | Braves. Bob Horner, 3b | Arizona State U. | Glendale, Ariz. | Majors (1,020) | Out of Baseball | 175,000 |
| 1979 | Mariners. Al Chambers, of | Harris HS | Harrisburg, Pa. | Majors (57) | Out of Baseball | 60,000 |
| 1980 | Mets. Darryl Strawberry, of | Crenshaw HS | Los Angeles | Majors (1,447) | Yankees | 210,000 |
| 1981 | Mariners. Mike Moore, rhp | Oral Roberts U. | Eakly, Okla. | Majors (450) | Out of Baseball | 100,000 |
| 1982 | Cubs. Shawon Dunston, ss | Jefferson HS | New York | Majors (1,220) | Giants | 100,000 |
| 1983 | Twins. Tim Belcher, rhp | Mt. Vernon Naz. Coll. | Sparta, Ohio | Majors (295) | Royals | DNS |
| 1984 | Mets. Shawn Abner, of | Mechanicsburg HS | Mechanicsburg, Pa. | Majors (392) | Out of Baseball | 150,000 |
| 1985 | Brewers. B.J. Surhoff, c | U. of North Carolina | Rye, N.Y. | Majors (1,245) | Orioles | 150,000 |
| 1986 | Pirates. Jeff King, 3b | U. of Arkansas | Colorado Springs | Majors (894) | Pirates | 160,000 |
| 1987 | Mariners. Ken Griffey Jr., of | Moeller HS | Cincinnati | Majors (1,057) | Mariners | 169,000 |
| 1988 | Padres. Andy Benes, rhp | U. of Evansville | Evansville, Ind. | Majors (235) | Cardinals | 235,000 |
| 1989 | Orioles. Ben McDonald, rhp | Louisiana State U. | Denham Springs, La. | Majors (190) | Brewers | 350,000 |
| 1990 | Braves. Chipper Jones, ss | The Bolles School | Jacksonville | Majors (305) | Braves | 275,000 |
| 1991 | Yankees. Brien Taylor, lhp | East Carteret HS | Beaufort, N.C. | Double-A (27) | Yankees (A) | 1,550,000 |
| 1992 | Astros. Phil Nevin, 3b | Cal State Fullerton | Placentia, Calif. | Majors (85) | Tigers | 700,000 |
| 1993 | Mariners. Alex Rodriguez, ss | West. Christian HS | Miami | Majors (211) | Mariners | 1,000,000 |
| 1994 | Mets. Paul Wilson, rhp | Florida State U. | Orlando, Fla. | Majors (26) | Mets | 1,550,000 |
| 1995 | Angels. Darin Erstad, of | U. of Nebraska | Jamestown, N.D. | Majors (57) | Angels | 1,575,000 |
| 1996 | Kris Benson, rhp | Clemson U. | Kennesaw, Ga. | None | None | 2,000,000 |

*No. of games at that level     DNS—Did not sign

# YANKS SCORE BIG INTERNATIONALLY

## Maeda, Melian The Big Free Agent Catches

The presence of several Cubans on the open market (see Page 8) wasn't the only news on the international talent front in 1996. Several other amateur players became the subject of bidding wars too.

The deep-pocketed Yankees won out on the two most notable players, Japanese righthander Katsuhiro Maeda and Venezuelan outfielder Jackson Melian.

Maeda, 24, became a Yankee thanks to the first deal between a major league team and a Japanese League team in 32 years. While righthander Hideo Nomo used a loophole to sign with the Dodgers in 1995, Maeda had a contract dispute with the Seibu Lions and forced that club to trade him.

The Yankees won the competition for his services over the Giants and White Sox. They paid the Seibu organization $350,000 and gave Maeda a $1.5 million signing bonus.

"Players want to play in the United States, and the Japanese teams want something for them," said Don Nomura, Maeda's agent and interpreter.

Maeda, whose fastball had been clocked in the high 90s, spent most of his first summer in the United States playing for the Yankees' Double-A Norwich farm team. He went 3-2 with a 4.05 ERA there in nine starts. He became more known for dying his hair silver, hot pink and purple.

Melian was more of a conventional signing than Maeda. All Venezuelan players go on the open market essentially at age 16, and the Yankees won out with a $1.6 million bonus.

Melian's package of power and speed, which had

**Rich Get Richer.** The Yankees signed Japanese righthander Katsuhiro Maeda, left, and Venezuelan outfielder Jackson Melian.

been compared to that of top Yankees prospect Ruben Rivera, probably would have made him one of the first five players selected in the June draft had he been eligible.

"He hits the ball over fences with a wooden bat at age 16 with regularity," Yankees farm and scouting director Mark Newman said of Melian, who by major league rules couldn't begin his professional career until 1997. "That's the kind of power we're talking about. And he's athletic, a big, strong guy."

Melian's father Vincent is a longtime Yankees fan who named his son after Reggie Jackson. Because of the family's affinity for the Yankees and George Steinbrenner's wallet, most insiders expected the Blue Jays, Braves and Orioles, the other teams most interested in Melian, to have little chance at him.

A third top player on the international talent scene went to the Blue Jays. Toronto signed Diegomar Markwell, a 16-year-old lefthander from Curacao, for a $750,000 bonus.

**—ALAN SCHWARZ**

---

over the summer raised the Rangers' concerns.

An examination by Birmingham orthopedist James Andrews revealed that Dickey has no ulnar collateral ligament in his pitching elbow. He had either blown out the ligament so badly years before that it had vanished, or he was born without one.

"All this stuff was news to me," Dickey said. "I've never been to the doctor. I've never had an injury. I've never missed a start. The Rangers drafted me on my ability, and that's still there."

## Middlebrook Returns Rich

The way Padres general manager Kevin Towers viewed his team's signing of Stanford righthander Jason Middlebrook, the Padres didn't spend $750,000. They saved more than $1 million.

Middlebrook had a sensational freshman season in 1994, going 7-2 with a 2.34 ERA and throwing a no-hitter. His fastball was clocked at 97 mph, and he became a leading candidate to go No. 1 overall in the 1996 draft.

But a sore right elbow limited Middlebrook to nine appearances as a sophomore. He made two starts in

1996 before having surgery in March. The initial fear was that he would require Tommy John surgery, and one doctor told Middlebrook he never would pitch again.

It turned out that Middlebrook needed only to have excessive scar tissue removed. The Padres, after risking their ninth-round pick on him,

**Jason Middlebrook**

gave him a $750,000 bonus, blowing away the record for a drafted player who didn't go in the first round.

"Our doctors said the risk of injury was minimal and that he'll be throwing at 100 percent by the start of the '97 season," Towers said. "He has a terrific arm, and that's all we needed to hear.

"We took him in the ninth round but felt he was a first-rounder. He was projected as as a top-five pick this year had he not been injured."

# Draft Tidbit Plate

There were 1,740 players selected in the 1996 draft, over 100 rounds. That broke the record of 1,719, set in 1993. San Diego was the first team to drop out, in the 40th round, and the Yankees were the last..

■ The Arizona Diamondbacks and Tampa Bay Devil Rays, two expansion clubs slated to begin major league play in 1998, made their first-ever draft picks in 1996. The Devil Rays selected Cary (N.C.) High outfielder Paul Wilder with their first pick at No. 29, while the Diamondbacks selected Long Beach prep lefthander Nick Bierbrodt.

Tampa Bay's selection of Wilder was considered the most surprising pick in the draft's first round. Most clubs considered him a third-round pick.

Cleveland spent only $400,000 on its first-round pick, University of Texas first baseman Danny Peoples. The Indians, drafting 28th, did not feel there was a legitimate first-round pick still available and were not prepared to pay first-round money. They set their figure and took the first player on their list who would agree in advance to the devalued amount. Peoples signed the day he was selected.

■ Two sons of former major leaguers were taken 10 picks apart in the third round. Dan Cey, son of Ron and a shortstop at the University of California, went to the Twins at No. 67. Jimmy Terrell, whose father Jerry scouts for the Dodgers, was a high school shortstop from Blue Springs, Mo., and went to the White Sox at No. 77.

Arizona State catcher-third baseman Cody McKay, son of ex-big leaguer Dave McKay, was the only other son of a big leaguer drafted in the first 10 rounds. McKay was tabbed in the ninth round by the Athletics, the team his father served as first-base coach in 1995 before moving to St. Louis with manager Tony La Russa.

**Chris Reitsma**

■ For the third time in nine years, the Angels spent their top pick on an Abbott. In 1988 and 1989, they chose Jim Abbott and Kyle Abbott, both college lefthanders. In 1996 they didn't have a first-round pick—they forfeited it to the Yankees after signing utilityman Randy Vel-arde as a free agent in the offseason—but spent their second-rounder on Chuck Abbott, a shortstop from Austin Peay State.

■ Chris Reitsma, a righthander from Calgary Christian School, narrowly missed becoming Canada's first-ever first-round pick. He went in the supplemental first round, No. 34 overall, to the Red Sox.

■ In a startling replay of the events surrounding two-way sensation Frank Rodriguez in 1991, George Carrion, a righthander-shortstop from Northeast Texas Community College, looked to shake up the first round of the 1996 draft but signed hours beforehand with the Rangers. Carrion led his team to the National

Junior College World Series championship three days before the draft.

Texas had retained Carrion's rights as a draft-and-follow from 1995, when they had selected him in the seventh round out of DeWitt Clinton High in the Bronx, and inked him for $700,000.

Similar events surrounded Rodriguez, another New York product who starred as a righthander-shortstop at Howard (Texas) Junior College before signing with the Red Sox hours before the 1991 draft. He later was traded to the Twins.

Carrion's contract allowed him to pitch and DH during his first summer in the Rookie-level Gulf Coast League, though Texas officials believed his professional future lies on the mound.

**Ryan Minor**

■ The Orioles pulled off a coup by signing Ryan Minor, a second-round draft pick of the NBA's Philadelphia 76ers who appeared headed to a career exclusively in basketball. But Baltimore gambled its 33rd-round pick on Minor, an Oklahoma third baseman with considerable power potential, and signed him to a contract that allows him to pursue his basketball career.

Minor had starred at Oklahoma in baseball, where he led the Sooners to the 1994 College World Series championship, and in basketball.

# DRAFT '96
## CLUB-BY-CLUB SELECTIONS

### ARIZONA (30)
1. Nick Bierbrodt, lhp, Millikan HS, Long Beach.
2. Jerry Proctor, of, Muir HS, Pasadena, Calif.
3. Mark Osborne, c, Lee County HS, Sanford, N.C.
4. Josh McAffee, c, Farmington (N.M.) HS.
5. Brad Penny, rhp, Broken Arrow (Okla.) HS.
6. Eric Putt, rhp, Deltona (Fla.) HS.
7. Casey Fossum, lhp, Midway HS, Waco, Texas.
8. Joe Verplancke, rhp, Cal State Los Angeles.
9. Marc Van Wormer, rhp, Prescott (Ariz.) HS.
10. George Oleksik, rhp, Middle Tennessee State U.
11. Ron Hartman, 3b, U. of Maryland.
12. Michael Boughton, ss, Northwood (Texas) Institute.
13. Ben Norris, lhp, Westwood HS, Austin.
14. Jamie Gann, of, U. of Oklahoma.
15. Reggie Davis, c, Augusta (Ga.) College.
16. Kevin Johnson, ss, St. Joseph's HS, Alameda, Calif.
17. Jackie Rexrode, ss, Riverdale Baptist HS, Laurel, Md.
18. David Chapman, of, Alta Loma (Calif.) HS.
19. Jacob Brooks, rhp, East Lake HS, Palm Harbor, Fla.
20. John Fleming, rhp, Bonita Vista HS, Chula Vista, Calif.
21. Brian Crisorio, 3b, East Lake HS, Clearwater, Fla.
22. Jeffrey Nichols, rhp, Duncanville (Texas) HS.
23. Michael McCutchen, lhp, Modesto (Calif.) JC.
24. Eric Knott, lhp, Stetson U.
25. Scott Glasser, 2b, Rancho Santiago (Calif.) JC.
26. Rob Ryan, of, Washington State U.
27. Justin Bice, rhp, Grand Canyon U.
28. Beau Baltzell, c, Purdue U.
29. Kevin Sweeney, of, Mercyhurst (Pa.) College.
30. Michael Pesci, of, U. of Detroit.
31. Jose Nunez, 3b-2b, Northeast Texas CC.
32. Jason Conti, of, U. of Pittsburgh.
33. Dallas Anderson, rhp, Lethbridge (Alberta) CC.
34. Corey Hart, 2b, Connors State (Okla.) JC.
35. Brett Hardy, of, UC Santa Barbara.
36. Junior Spivey, 2b, Cowley County (Kan.) CC.
37. Jason Moore, c-1b, West Virginia State College.
38. Curtis Johnson, of, St. Joseph's HS, Oakland.
39. Bert Hudson, c, Jay (Fla.) HS.
40. Travis McCall, lhp, Ayala HS, Chino Hills, Calif.
41. Brad Allison, c, Morehead State U.
42. Eric Sable, rhp, Tennesse Tech.
43. Charles Chungu, rhp, U. of New Hampshire.
44. James Harrison, rhp, William Penn HS, New Castle, Del.
45. Brett DeBoer, lhp, Lakeland HS, Rathdum, Idaho.
46. Matt Bell, rhp, Joplin (Mo.) HS.
47. Ryan Evans, c, Tuscaloosa County HS, Northport, Ala.
48. Jorge Martinez, rhp, Newtown HS, New York.
49. Brent Wagler, rhp, Florida Southern College.
50. Casey Rowe, rhp, Bullard HS, Fresno.
51. Patrick Coogan, rhp, Louisiana State U.
52. Jeff Remillard, rhp, Memorial HS, Manchester, N.H.
53. David Harper, rhp, Lubbock Christian (Texas) U.
54. Jason Jennings, rhp, Poteet HS, Mesquite, Texas.
55. Blake Ricken, lhp, Fresno CC.
56. Andrew McCulloch, rhp, Western HS, Las Vegas.
57. Eric O'Brien, rhp, Alton (N.H.) HS.
58. Bryce Darnell, c, Missouri Southern State U.
59. Carmen Panaro, c, Niagara U.
60. Mark Chavez, rhp, Cal State Fullerton.
61. Brandon Duckworth, rhp, JC of Southern Idaho.
62. George Otero, 3b-c, Pace HS, Miami.

### ATLANTA (27)
1. A.J. Zapp, 1b, Center Grove HS, Greenwood, Ind.
1. Jason Marquis, rhp, Tottenville HS, Staten Island, N.Y. (Supplemental pick for failure to sign 1995 first-round pick Chad Hutchinson).
2. Eric Munson, c, Mount Carmel HS, San Diego.
3. Junior Brignac, of, Cleveland HS, Reseda, Calif.
4. Joe Nelson, rhp, U. of San Francisco.
5. Josh Pugh, c, Henry Clay HS, Lexington, Ky.
6. Shawn Onley, rhp, Rice U.
7. Mark DeRosa, 3b, U. of Pennsylvania.
8. A.D. Thorpe, ss, Southern HS, Durham, N.C.
9. Nathan Harden, rhp, Dripping Springs (Texas) HS.
10. Winston Lee, rhp, Glendale (Calif.) JC.
11. Aaron Taylor, rhp, Lowndes HS, Hahira, Ga.

12. Greg Ward, of, Avon (Conn.) HS.
13. Jason Ross, of, U. of Hawaii.
14. John Alkire, rhp, U. of Tennessee.
15. Mike Hessman, 1b-rhp, Mater Dei HS, Westminster, Calif.
16. Earl Beasley, lhp, Lake City (Fla.) CC.
17. Dana Davis, rhp, Rice U.
18. Donald Ceasar, rhp, LaGrange HS, Lake Charles, La.
19. Adam Milburn, lhp, U. of Kentucky.
20. John Arnold, c, Eastern New Mexico U.
21. Jesse Crespo, c, Camuy, P.R.
22. Aaron Melebeck, ss, Clear Brook HS, Webster, Texas.
23. Dax Norris, c, U. of Alabama.
24. Patrick Collins, rhp, Union (N.J.) HS.
25. Anthony Brooks, ss, Gulf Coast (Fla.) CC.
26. Jason Katz, ss, New Mexico JC.
27. Aaron Strangfeld, 1b, Grossmont (Calif.) JC.
28. Miguel Garcia, rhp, Cerritos (Calif.) JC.
29. Galen Reeder, lhp, DeKalb (Ga.) JC.
30. Fred Sanchez, ss, Burbank (Calif.) HS.
31. Adam Love, rhp, Westlake HS, Austin.
32. Dustin Franklin, lhp, Permian HS, Odessa, Texas.
33. Jerrod Wong, 1b, Gonzaga U.
34. Adam Springston, rhp, Oxnard (Calif.) JC.
35. Byron Embry, rhp, Indian Hills (Iowa) CC.
36. Scott Frawley, c, South Suburban (Ill.) JC.
37. Hunter Wenzel, lhp, Boerne HS, Fair Oaks Ranch, Texas.
38. Randy Phillips, lhp, Olney Central (Ill.) JC.
39. Jeff Lindemann, rhp, Andrew HS, Lockport, Ill.
40. Anthony Barrow, 1b, Blazer HS, Ashland, Ky.
41. Justin Willoughby, lhp, Princeton (N.C.) HS.
42. George Snead, rhp, Albany State (Ga.) U.
43. Cory Simpson, rhp, Sumner HS, Kentwood, La.
44. Nate Fernley, rhp, Long Beach CC.
45. John Zydowsky, ss, Portage HS, Pardeeville, Wis.
46. Joe Holzbauer, rhp, Palomar (Calif.) JC.
47. Patrick Fuentes, ss, Logan HS, South San Francisco.
48. Greg Dukeman, rhp, Millikan HS, Long Beach.
49. Michael Jones, lhp, UC Riverside.
50. Travis Richo, of, Fernandina Beach (Fla.) HS.
51. Daniel Bell, of, University HS, Los Angeles.
52. Brett Pierce, ss, Citrus (Calif.) JC.
53. Marcus Giles, 2b, Granite Hills HS, El Cajon, Calif.
54. Jeff Champion, of, Florida Memorial College.
55. Adam Johnson, of, U. of Central Florida.
56. Bradley Green, ss, South Pittsburg (Tenn.) HS.
57. Juan Galban, lhp, Miami.
58. Baylor Moore, lhp, Friendswood (Texas) HS.
59. Hector Gonzales, c, Scottsdale (Ariz.) CC.
60. Ray Plummer, lhp, Point Loma Nazarene (Calif.) College.

### BALTIMORE (16)
1. (Choice to Blue Jays as compensation for Type A free agent Roberto Alomar).
2. Brian Falkenborg, rhp, Redmond (Wash.) HS.
3. Daren Hooper, of, U. of Arizona.
4. Mark Seaver, rhp, Wake Forest U.
5. Frank Figueroa, 1b-of, Florida Bible HS, Hialeah, Fla.
6. Josh McNatt, lhp, Motlow State (Tenn.) CC.
7. Brent Schoening, rhp, Columbus (Ga.) HS.
8. Chad Paronto, rhp, U. of Massachusetts.
9. Luis Ramirez, 1b, Arroyo, P.R.
10. Luis Matos, of, Bayamon, P.R.
11. Bruce Stanley, rhp, Ball State U.
12. Simeon Theodile, rhp, Acadiana HS, Lafayette, La.
13. Augie Ojeda, ss, U. of Tennessee.
14. Ryan Kohlmeier, rhp, Butler County (Kan.) CC.
15. Josh Towers, rhp, Oxnard (Calif.) JC.
16. Josh Morris, ss, Motlow State (Tenn.) CC.
17. Tim DeCinces, c, UCLA.
18. Andrew Cheek, lhp, Beaver Creak HS, West Jefferson, N.C.
19. Gabe Crecion, rhp, Chaminade Prep, West Hills, Calif.
20. Ashanti Davison, of, St. Mary's HS, Stockton, Calif.
21. Gabe Molina, rhp, Arizona State U.
22. Mike MacDougal, rhp, Mesa (Ariz.) HS.
23. Jesse Perez, ss, Mayaguez, P.R.
24. Jay Gehrke, rhp, North HS, Fargo, N.D.
25. John Parrish, lhp, McCaskey HS, Lancaster, Pa.
26. Maleke Fowler, of, Nicholls State U.
27. Robert Baker, rhp, Westwood HS, Austin.
28. Cordell Lindsey, 3b, North Shore HS, Houston.
29. Jason Johnson, lhp, Sacred Heart Academy, Winn, Mich.
30. Johnny Morales, lhp, Central Arizona JC.
31. Jeff Phipps, rhp, San Joaquin Delta (Calif.) JC.
32. Todd Morgan, of, Deerfield Beach (Fla.) HS.

33. **Ryan Minor, 3b-1b, U. of Oklahoma.**
34. DeShawn Ziths, of, Columbia-Greene (N.Y.) CC.
35. **Jeremiah Johnson, rhp, Kellogg (Mich.) CC.**
36. Jaime Escalante, c, Hagerstown (Md.) JC.
37. **Craig Ratliff, rhp, Paintsville HS, West Van Plear, Ky.**
38. Randall Benge, lhp, Fort Vancouver HS, Yacolt, Wash.
39. Eric Drew, rhp, Montello (Wis.) HS.
40. Ben Christensen, rhp, Goddard HS, West Goddard, Kan.
41. Vanshan Renfroe, ss, McGavock HS, Hermitage, Tenn.
42. **Michael Kirkpatrick, of, St. Elizabeth HS, New Castle, Del.**
43. Tyson Martinez, rhp, Fort Madison (Iowa) HS.
44. Daniel Allen, of, Perry (Okla.) HS.
45. Josh Taylor, ss, Seminole (Okla.) JC.
46. Sean Gilchrist, of, Bigfork (Mont.) HS.
47. Chad Anderson, of, Bigfork (Mont.) HS.

## BOSTON (26)

1. **Josh Garrett, rhp, South Spencer HS, Richland, Ind.**
1. **Chris Reitsma, rhp, Calgary (Alberta) Christian HS**
(Supplemental pick for loss of Type A free agent Erik Hanson).
2. **Gary LoCurto, 1b, University HS, San Diego** (Choice from Blue Jays as compensation for Hanson).
2. **Jason Sekany, rhp, U. of Virginia.**
3. **Dernell Stenson, of, LaGrange (Ga.) HS.**
4. **John Barnes, of, Grossmont (Calif.) CC.**
5. **Bobby Brito, c, Cypress (Calif.) HS.**
6. **Mike Perini, of, Carlsbad (N.M.) HS.**
7. **Rob Ramsey, lhp, Washington State U.**
8. **Justin Duchscherer, rhp, Coronado HS, Lubbock, Texas.**
9. Marcus Martinez, lhp, Monterey HS, Lubbock, Texas.
10. **Shea Hillenbrand, ss, Mesa (Ariz.) CC.**
11. **Brian Musgrave, lhp, Appalachian State U.**
12. **Dion Ruecker, ss, Texas Tech.**
13. **Skipp Benzing, rhp, Indian Hills (Iowa) CC.**
14. Justin Lynch, rhp, Marina HS, Huntington Beach, Calif.
15. Mark Robbins, 3b, Derry (Kan.) HS.
16. **Jeff Keaveney, 1b-of, U. of Southern Maine.**
17. Justin Crisafulli, rhp, Arizona Western JC.
18. **Mike McKinley, of, Scottsdale (Ariz.) CC.**
19. **Mike Rupp, rhp, Monte Vista HS, Spring Valley, Calif.**
20. **Chuck Beale, rhp, Stetson U.**
21. **Javier Fuentes, ss-2b, Arizona State U.**
22. Aaron Harang, rhp, Patrick Henry HS, San Diego.
23. Paul McCurtain, rhp, Mesa (Ariz.) CC.
24. Robert Brandt, rhp, A&M Consolidated HS, College Station, Texas.
25. Dominic Barrett, of, Trimble Tech HS, Fort Worth, Texas.
26. **Chris Thompson, rhp, St. Leo (Fla.) College.**
27. Ryan Murray, rhp, Tampa Bay Tech HS, Tampa.
28. **Erik Metzger, c, Samford U.**
29. Josh Stewart, lhp, Livingston Central HS, Ledbetter, Ky.
30. William Whitaker, lhp, First Coast HS, Jacksonville.
31. Matt Frick, c, Yavapai (Ariz.) JC.
32. Mike Bynum, lhp, Middleburg (Fla.) HS.
33. Adam Roller, rhp, Lakeland (Fla.) HS.
34. Jaime Bonilla, lhp, Lake City (Fla.) CC.
35. Kasey Kuhlmeyer, lhp, San Pasqual HS, Escondido, Calif.
36. Ken Sarna, ss, Durango HS, Las Vegas.
37. Jeremy Swindell, lhp, Clear Lake HS, Houston.
38. Travis McRoberts, ss, El Capitan HS, El Cajon, Calif.
39. **Andre Thompson, of, Delta State U.**
40. Curtis Anthony, ss, Bishop Gorman HS, Las Vegas.
41. Selection voided
42. Wesley Warren, rf, Arcadia HS, Scottsdale, Ariz.
43. Jamaon Halbig, c, Southwestern (Calif.) JC.
44. Bart Vaughn, rhp, Manatee (Fla.) CC.

## CALIFORNIA (20)

1. (Choice to Yankees as compensation for Type B free agent Randy Velarde).
2. **Chuck Abbott, ss, Austin Peay State U.**
3. **Scott Schoeneweis, lhp, Duke U.**
4. **Brandon Steele, rhp, Huntington Beach (Calif.) HS.**
5. Bobby Hill, ss, Leland HS, San Jose.
6. Jason Verdugo, rhp, Arizona State U.
7. **Marcus Knight, of, Miramar HS, Pembroke Pines, Fla.**
8. **Jerrod Riggan, rhp, San Diego State U.**
9. **Jason Stephens, rhp, U. of Arkansas.**
10. **Eric Gillespie, 3b, Cal State Northridge.**
11. **Pat Johnson, c, Brigham Young U.**
12. Mark Richards, rhp, Winthrop U.
13. Ken Polk, c, Howard (Texas) JC.
14. Jaeme Leal, 1b, Poly HS, Riverside, Calif.
15. **Theo Fefee, of, Bethune-Cookman College.**
16. **Nate Murphy, of, U. of Massachusetts.**

17. Jason Cly, rhp, Arcadia (Calif.) HS.
18. **Mark Harriger, rhp, San Diego State U.**
19. Brian Ussery, c, U. of Tampa.
20. Cale Carter, of, Stanford U.
21. Scott Byers, 1b, Georgia Tech.
22. **Nathan Starkey, 3b-c, Modesto (Calif.) JC.**
23. **John Margaritis, of, Treasure Valley (Ore.) CC.**
24. **Eduardo Ferrer, 2b, Florida International U.**
25. **Jose Ortiz, rhp, Hayward (Calif.) HS.**
26. Jason Dewey, c, Indian River (Fla.) CC.
27. **Rob Neal, of, Cal Poly San Luis Obispo.**
28. **Matt Curtis, c, Fresno State U.**
29. **Wade Jackson, 2b, U. of Nevada.**
30. **James Leach, lhp, Gibbs HS, Pinellas Park, Fla.**
31. William Robbins, rhp, Gulf Breeze (Fla.) HS.
32. Greg Blum, c, Chino (Calif.) HS.
33. Richard Stegbauer, c, Seminole (Fla.) HS.
34. Kirk Asche, of, Edison (Fla.) CC.
35. **Eric Plooy, rhp, JC of The Sequoias (Calif.).**
36. Jeremy Freitas, of, Fresno CC.
37. Jack Taschner, lhp, Horlick HS, Racine, Wis.
38. Michael Carney, lhp, Indian River (Fla.) CC.
39. Gary Forrester, rhp, Centralia (Wash.) JC.
40. Dominic Repetti, ss, DeAnza (Calif.) JC.
41. Kris William, rhp, Brevard (Fla.) CC.
42. Greg Jones, c, Pasco-Hernando (Fla.) CC.
43. **Marc Collier, ss, Lower Dauphin HS, Hummelstown, Pa.**
44. Richard Shaw, rhp, Marquette U.
45. Nathan Burnett, rhp, Gulf Coast (Fla.) CC.
46. Michael Gauger, lhp, Tallahassee (Fla.) CC.
47. Adrian Merkey, ss, Polk (Fla.) CC.
48. Chris Finnegan, c, Millard North HS, Omaha.
49. Kenny Avera, rhp, Pensacola (Fla.) JC.
50. Anthony Lopresti, c, University HS, San Diego.
51. Michael Abate, of, Norwalk (Conn.) HS.
52. Elvis Hernandez, of, Aurora West HS, Montgomery, Ill.
53. William Snellings, lhp, Pasco-Hernando (Fla.) CC.
54. Paul Poplin, rhp, South Stanly HS, Norwood, N.C.
55. Kevin Davis, ss, South Spencer HS, Rockport, Ind.
56. Orlando Sloan, of, Santa Monica HS, Westchester, Calif.

## CHICAGO/AL (12)

1. Bobby Seay, lhp, Sarasota (Fla.) HS.
2. **Josh Paul, of, Vanderbilt U.**
3. **Jimmy Terrell, ss, Tri-City Christian HS, Blue Springs, Mo.**
4. **Mark Roberts, rhp, U. of South Florida.**
5. **Joe Crede, 3b, Fatima HS, Westphalia, Mo.**
6. **Dan Olson, of, Indiana State U.**
7. Kevin Knorst, rhp, Lake Howell HS, Winter Park, Fla.
8. Marcus Jones, rhp, Long Beach State U.
9. **Edwin Cochran, 2b, Arroyo, P.R.**
10. **Gene Forti, rhp, Del Valle HS, El Paso.**
11. **Steve Schorzman, rhp, Gonzaga U.**
12. **Darren Baugh, ss, U. of Nevada.**
13. **Chad Bradford, rhp, U. of Southern Mississippi.**
14. **Joe Farley, lhp, Susquehanna (Pa.) U.**
15. **Tom Reimers, rhp, Stanford U.**
16. **Jeff Inglin, of, U. of Southern California.**
17. **Derek Wallace, of, Bossier Parish (La.) CC.**
18. **Joe Sutton, c, West Virginia Wesleyan.**
19. **Chris Heintz, 3b, U. of South Florida.**
20. **Mario Iglesias, rhp, Stanford U.**
21. Kevin Sadowski, rhp, Joliet (Ill.) Catholic Academy.
22. **Reid Hodges, rhp, Columbus (Ga.) College.**
23. Mike Holmes, rhp, Wake Forest U.
24. **Sean Connolly, c, Rollins (Fla.) College.**
25. **Elvis Perez, lhp, Miami Lakes HS, Hialeah, Fla.**
26. **Pete Pryor, 1b, U. of Kentucky.**
27. Kenneth Ferguson, of, Issaquah (Wash.) HS.
28. **Eloy Tellez, rhp, El Paso CC.**
29. Robert Hatcher, lhp, Miami-Dade CC North.
30. Marcos Munoz, rhp, North Rockland HS, Pomona, N.Y.
31. Juan Mendoza, lhp, Miami-Dade CC Wolfson.
32. **Rick Heineman, rhp, UCLA.**
33. **Kevin Stinson, rhp, Bellevue (Wash.) CC.**
34. Chris Delgado, 1b, St. Thomas Aquinas HS, Fort Lauderdale.
35. Ray Goirigolzarri, 3b, Columbus HS, Miami.
36. Anthony Lofink, of, Salesianum HS, Bear, Del.
37. Tim McGhee, of, Crenshaw HS, Los Angeles.
38. Michael Lindgren, rhp, Sandpoint (Idaho) HS.
39. **Marcus Rodgers, lhp, Vigor HS, Saraland, Ala.**
40. Jose Arrieta, rhp, El Paso CC.
41. Marshall McDougall, 2b, Buchholz HS, Gainesville, Fla.
42. Ken Trapp, rhp, Texas City (Texas) HS.
43. Kenard Lang, 1b, U. of Miami.

44. Johnnie Thibodeaux, 3b, Barbe HS, Lake Charles, La.
45. **Allen Thomas, of, Wingate (N.C.) U.**
46. **Kirk Irvine, rhp, Cal State Fullerton.**
47. Matt Watson, 3b-2b, McCaskey HS, Lancaster, Pa.
48. Levy Duran, 3b, George Washington HS, New York.
49. Andres Martinez, c, St. Brendan HS, Miami.
50. Mario Gianfortune, of, Elmwood Park (Ill.) HS.
51. William Mauer, c, East HS, Mission Hills, Kan.
52. **Mike McDermott, 3b, U. of Idaho.**
53. Elio Borges, ss, American HS, Miami.

## CHICAGO/NL (17)

1. **Todd Noel, rhp, North Vermillion HS, Maurice, La.**
2. **Quincy Carter, of, Southwest DeKalb HS, Ellenwood, Ga.**
3. **Skip Ames, rhp, U. of Alabama.**
4. **Chris Gissell, rhp, Hudson's Bay HS, Vancouver, Wash.**
5. **Chad Meyers, 2b-of, Creighton U.**
6. **Doug Hall, of, U. of Alabama.**
7. **Jon Cannon, lhp, Canada (Calif.) JC.**
8. **Brian Connell, lhp, Dunedin (Fla.) HS.**
9. **Nate Manning, 3b, Austin Peay State U.**
10. **Phillip Norton, lhp, Texarkana (Texas) JC.**
11. Steve Sanberg, c, Midlothian (Texas) HS.
12. Mark Ernster, ss, Ironwood HS, Glendale, Ariz.
13. Johnny Whitesides, rhp, Sarasota (Fla.) HS.
14. Tim Lavery, lhp, Naperville (Ill.) Central HS.
15. Freddie Young, of, Lyman HS, Longwood, Fla.
16. **Byron Tribe, rhp, U. of Alabama.**
17. **Brad King, c, U. of Central Florida.**
18. **Jim Crawford, rhp, Cowley County (Kan.) CC.**
19. **Marcel Longmire, c-of, Vallejo (Calif.) HS.**
20. **Courtney Duncan, rhp, Grambling State U.**
21. **Ryan Anderson, 2b, Dallas Baptist U.**
22. **John Nall, lhp, U. of California.**
23. Jason Smith, ss, Meridian (Miss.) CC.
24. Ronald Payne, of, Pitt (N.C.) CC.
25. Douglas Young, rhp, Sierra (Calif.) College.
26. **Courteney Stewart, of, DeKalb (Ga.) JC.**
27. Matthew Perry, rhp, Allegheny (Pa.) CC.
28. Jeff Velez, rhp, U. of Connecticut.
29. Kyle Lohse, rhp, Hamilton Union HS, Glenn, Calif.
30. **Casey Brookens, rhp, James Madison U.**
31. **Randy Crane, rhp, Linn-Benton (Ore.) CC.**
32. Mike Miller, rhp-3b, Manatee (Fla.) CC.
33. Nicholas Lee, rhp, Brockton (Mass.) HS.
34. Richard Powalski, lhp, Central Catholic HS, Clearwater, Fla.
35. Keola Delatori, rhp, Schaumburg (Ill.) HS.
36. David Regan, of, Brockton (Mass.) HS.
37. **Lendon Hart, lhp, East Tennessee State U.**
38. Justin Lee, of, McLennan (Texas) CC.
39. Brad Ramsey, c, Gulf Coast (Fla.) CC.
40. Jeremy Smith, rhp, Needles (Calif.) HS.
41. **Daniel Hodges, lhp, Liberty U.**
42. **Derrick Bly, 3b, Concordia (Calif.) U.**
43. Cameron Newitt, rhp, Northwest Shoals (Ala.) CC.
44. John Guilmet, rhp, Merrimack (Mass.) College.
45. **Keith Lewis, 2b, U. of Mississippi.**
46. Mike Mainella, of, West Fairmont (W.Va.) HS.
47. Joseph Tillmon, ss, Chatsworth HS, Winnetka, Calif.
48. **Dax Kiefer, of, Texas Lutheran College.**
49. Jacob Sutter, rhp, Celina (Ohio) HS.
50. Rob Holmes, rhp, Creighton Prep, Omaha.
51. Rahman Corbett, of, Princeton HS, Cincinnati.
52. Harris Stanton, of, Spartanburg Methodist (S.C.) JC.
53. Chris Bentley, rhp, Molalla Union HS, Mulino, Ore.
54. Cory Cattaneo, lhp, Sequoia HS, Redwood City, Calif.
55. Shane Sullivan, rhp, Serrano HS, Pinon Hills, Calif.
56. Ryan Blackmum, c, Mater Dei HS, Garden Grove, Calif.
57. John Halliday, 1b, Clearwater (Fla.) HS.
58. Franklyn Bencosme, rhp, Miami-Dade CC North.
59. Gene Richardson, rhp, Edison (Fla.) CC.
60. Joseph Ortiz, c, Edison HS, San Antonio.
61. Daniel Zisk, 3b, Pine Crest HS, Lighthouse Point, Fla.
62. Michael Thomson, rhp, Sulphur (La.) HS.
63. Ryan Fien, rhp, U. of Idaho.

## CINCINNATI (25)

1. **John Oliver, of, Lake-Lehman HS, Lehman, Pa.**
1. **Matt McClendon, rhp, Dr. Phillips HS, Orlando** (Supplemental pick for loss of Type A free agent Ron Gant).
2. **Buddy Carlyle, lhp, Bellevue (Neb.) East HS** (Choice from Cardinals as compensation for Gant).
2. **Randi Mallard, rhp, Hillsborough (Fla.) CC.**
3. **David Shepard, rhp, Clemson U.**
4. **Phillip Merrell, rhp, Nampa (Idaho) HS.**

5. **Nick Presto, ss, Florida Atlantic U.**
6. **Carl Caddeii, ihp, Northwood (Texas) U.**
7. **Wylie Campbell, 2b, U. of Texas.**
8. **Kevin Marn, of, Kent U.**
9. **Desi Herrera, rhp, San Diego State U.**
10. Michael Vento, of, Cibola HS, Albuquerque.
11. Kris Lambert, rhp, Baylor U.
12. **Corey Price, ss, North Central Texas JC.**
13. **Chris Ward, c, Lubbock Christian (Texas) College.**
14. **Ted Rose, rhp, Kent U.**
15. Drew Roberts, lhp, Kent U.
16. **Jason Williams, ss, Louisiana State U.**
17. **Bubba Dresch, 1b-of, St. Mary's (Texas) U.**
18. Keith Dilgard, rhp, Mississippi State U.
19. **Bryan Zwemke, rhp, Trinidad State (Colo.) JC.**
20. **Gene Altman, rhp, Hudgens Academy, Lynchburg, S.C.**
21. Travis Young, 2b, U. of New Mexico.
22. **Kevin Needham, rhp, Northwestern State U.**
23. **Scott Garrett, c, Appalachian State U.**
24. **Jeremy Keller, 3b-1b, Winthrop U.**
25. **Matt Buckley, rhp, Campbell U.**
26. **Josh Harriss, rhp, Smithson Valley HS, Canyon Lake, Texas.**
27. **Doug Kirby, of, Victor Valley (Calif.) CC.**
28. **Daniel Jenkins, of, Sam Houston State U.**
29. **Demond Denman, 1b, Dallas Baptist U.**
30. **Rod Griggs, of, Lambuth (Tenn.) U.**
31. **Brian Hucks, c, U. of South Carolina.**
32. **Brian Horne, rhp, Limestone (S.C.) College.**
33. **Jeremy Skeens, of, Lakota HS, Middletown, Ohio.**
34. **Eric LeBlanc, rhp, College of St. Rose (N.Y.).**
35. Doug Devore, lhp, Dublin (Ohio) HS.
36. David Ferres, 2b, JC of the Redwoods (Calif.).
37. **John Clark, 2b, Jacksonville State U.**
38. **Brandon O'Hearn, of, Columbus (Ga.) College.**
39. **Stephan Smith, rhp, Southwest Texas State U.**
40. **Jon Phillips, rhp, Georgia Southern U.**
41. Nicholas Prater, c, Judson HS, Converse, Texas.

## CLEVELAND (28)

1. **Danny Peoples, 1b, U. of Texas.**
2. **Ryan McDermott, rhp, Alamogordo (N.M.) HS.**
3. **Jarrod Mays, rhp, Southwest Missouri State U.**
4. **J.D. Brammer, rhp, Stanford U.**
5. **Grant Sharpe, 1b, Watkins HS, Laurel, Miss.**
6. **Paul Rigdon, rhp, U. of Florida.**
7. **Jim Hamilton, lhp, Ferrum (Va.) College.**
8. **Rob Stanton, of, Rollins (Fla.) College.**
9. **Sean DePaula, rhp, Wake Forest U.**
10. **William Jackson, of, Collin County (Texas) CC.**
11. **Joe Horgan, lhp, Sacramento CC.**
12. **John McDonald, ss, Providence College.**
13. **Cody Allison, c, Arkansas State U.**
14. **Troy Kent, ss-3b, Stanford U.**
15. Tonayne Brown, of, Godby HS, Tallahassee, Fla.
16. **Kaipo Spenser, rhp, Arizona State U.**
17. **Mark Taylor, lhp, Rice U.**
18. **Mike Bacsik, rhp, Duncanville (Texas) HS.**
19. Danny Wright, rhp, Sullivan South HS, Kingsport, Tenn.
20. **Mike Huelsmann, of, Saint Louis U.**
21. Jamie Brown, rhp, Okaloosa-Walton (Fla.) CC.
22. Tim Palmer, c, Fresno CC.
23. **Adam Taylor, c, U. of New Mexico.**
24. **Aurelio Rodriguez, ss, Mesa State (Colo.) College.**
25. David Willis, c-1b, UC Santa Barbara.
26. **Dennis Konrady, ss, Pepperdine U.**
27. **Bob Reichow, rhp, Bowling Green State U.**
28. **Brian Whitlock, ss, U. of North Carolina.**
29. **Mel Motley, of, U. of Nebraska.**
30. **Matt Koeman, rhp, Kansas State U.**
31. Chad Darnell, rhp, Carthage (Texas) HS.
32. Jonathan McDonald, rhp, Edgewater HS, Orlando.
33. Mitch Johnson, rhp, Meridian (Miss.) CC.
34. Samuel Moses, rhp, Sacramento CC.
35. Humberto Vargas, rhp, Connors State (Okla.) JC.
36. Robert Aaron, rhp, McCallie HS, Chattanooga.
37. Josh Walker, rhp, Lassen (Calif.) JC.
38. Jeremy Jones, c, Mesa (Ariz.) CC.
39. Marcus Gwyn, rhp, McCullough HS, The Woodlands, Texas.
40. Byron Watson, of, North Central (Texas) JC.
41. Miles Bryant, of, Woodham HS, Pensacola, Fla.
42. Travis Veracka, lhp, Nashoba Regional HS, Stow, Mass.
43. Alfred Leatherwood, 1b, Woodham HS, Pensacola, Fla.
44. **Brian Bosch, c, U. of Washington.**
45. Scott Krause, 2b, Centralia (Wash.) HS.

46. Brad Brenneman, rhp, Lane (Ore.) CC.
47. Mark Zenk, ss, Mountlake Terrace HS, Edmonds, Wash.
48. **Ryan Siponmaa, c, U. of Massachusetts-Lowell.**
49. Chris Hesse, of, U. of Southern Mississippi.
50. Anthony Wright, of, Hooks (Texas) HS.
51. **Casey Smith, c, Hill (Texas) JC.**
52. Mark Cridland, of, U. of Texas.
53. Joey Cole, rhp, Nacogdoches (Texas) HS.
54. **Matt Minter, lhp, Lassen (Calif.) JC.**
55. Charles Roberson, rhp, Green River (Wash.) CC.
56. David Riske, rhp, Green River (Wash.) CC.
57. Randy Keisler, lhp, Navarro (Texas) JC.
58. Ovid Valentin, of, Oak Park-River Forest HS, Oak Park, Ill.

## COLORADO (21)

1. Jake Westbrook, rhp, Madison County HS, Danielsville, Ga.
2. **John Nicholson, rhp, Episcopal HS, Houston.**
3. **Shawn Chacon, rhp, Greeley (Colo.) Central HS.**
4. **Steve Matcuk, rhp, Indian River (Fla.) CC.**
5. **Jeff Sebring, lhp, Iowa State U.**
6. **Dean Brueggeman, lhp, Belleville Area (Ill.) CC.**
7. **Clint Bryant, 3b, Texas Tech.**
8. **Alvin Rivera, rhp, Yabucoa, P.R.**
9. **Ryan Kennedy, rhp, Jones County (Miss.) JC.**
10. **Tom Stepka, rhp, Le Moyne College.**
11. **Tim Christman, lhp, Siena College.**
12. **Travis Thompson, rhp, Madison (Wis.) Area Tech HS.**
13. **Don Schmidt, rhp, Portland State U.**
14. Denny Gilich, rhp, U. of Portland.
15. **Scott Schroeffel, rhp-of, U. of Tennessee.**
16. **Rod Bair, of, Grand Canyon U.**
17. **Doug Livingston, 2b, Clemson U.**
18. **Brian Keck, ss, Fort Hays State (Kan.) U.**
19. Steve Scarborough, rhp, Duncanville (Texas) HS.
20. Jonathan Storke, ss, Douglas HS, Minden, Nev.
21. **Brian Hinchy, rhp, Green River (Wash.) CC.**
22. **Bernard Hutchison, of, U. of Montevallo (Ala.).**
23. **Blake Anderson, c, Mississippi State U.**
24. **Mark Hamlin, of, Georgia Southern U.**
25. **Brian Anthony, 1b, U. of Nevada-Las Vegas.**
26. **Mike Petersen, 1b, San Jacinto North (Texas ) JC.**
27. Lucas Anderson, rhp, Green Valley HS, Henderson, Nev.
28. **Jason Ford, lhp, U. of Arizona.**
29. Melvin Rosario, of, Carolina, P.R.
30. Steven Iannacone, rhp, Washington Township HS, Sicklerville, N.J.
31. Les Graham, 3b, Latta HS, Ada, Okla.
32. Jake Kidd, rhp, Hesperia (Calif.) HS.
33. Josh Kalinowski, lhp, Indian Hills (Iowa) CC.
34. Emmett Giles, ss, North Side HS, Jackson, Tenn.
35. Brad Woodard, rhp, Palatka HS, San Mateo, Fla.
36. Alex Fernandez, of, Hope HS, Providence
37. Eric Burris, of-1b, Carson (Calif.) HS.
38. Adam Bernero, rhp, Sacramento CC.
39. Daniel Viveros, rhp, JC of the Sequoias (Calif.).
40. Ryan Price, rhp, Goddard HS, Roswell, N.M.
41. Robby Shoults, rhp, Chaffey (Calif.) JC.
42. Martin Rankin, lhp, Hill (Texas) JC.
43. James Carroll, rhp, North Shore HS, Houston.
44. David Christy, ss, Mount Hood (Ore.) CC.
45. Ben Cortez, rhp, Santa Fe Springs (Calif.) HS.
46. Jose Vasquez, lhp, Cerritos (Calif.) JC.
47. Chris Robert, c, Soquel HS, Capitola, Calif.
48. James Munday, rhp, Hudson's Bay HS, Vancouver, Wash.
49. Mathew Bobo, ss, Longview (Texas) HS.
50. Paul Thames, ss, San Jacinto North (Texas) JC.
51. Jeremiah Harrington, of, Lowry HS, Winnemucca, Nev.

## DETROIT (6)

1. **Seth Greisinger, rhp, U. of Virginia.**
2. **Matt Miller, lhp, Texas Tech.**
3. Antonio McKinney, of, Jefferson HS, Portland, Ore.
4. Kris Keller, rhp, Fletcher HS, Neptune Beach, Fla.
5. **Robert Fick, c, Cal State Northridge.**
6. **Chris Bauer, rhp, Wichita State U.**
7. **Scott Sollmann, of, U. of Notre Dame.**
8. **Craig Quintal, rhp, Southern U.**
9. **Keith Whitner, of, Los Angeles CC.**
10. Justin Hazleton, of, Philipsburg-Osceola HS, Philipsburg, Pa.
11. **Aaron Alvord, rhp, Canton-Galva HS, Canton, Kan.**
12. **Jacques Landry, 3b, Rice U.**
13. Jeff Heaverlo, rhp, Ephrata (Wash.) HS.
14. Dan Kelly, lhp, Niceville (Fla.) HS.

LISA PAOLERCIO

**Wasted Selection.** The White Sox chose lefthander Bobby Seay with their first-round pick, but failed to offer him a contract. Seay later signed a $3 million deal with the expansion Tampa Bay Devil Rays.

15. **Chris Wakeland, of, Oregon State U.**
16. **Rick Kirsten, rhp-of, Rolling Meadows (Ill.) HS.**
17. **George Restovich, c, U. of Notre Dame.**
18. **Brian Rios, ss, Oral Roberts U.**
19. **Derrick Neikirk, c, Mesa (Ariz.) CC.**
20. **Don DeDonatis, ss, Eastern Michigan U.**
21. **David Lindstrom, c, Texas Tech.**
22. **Jeff Tagliaferri, 1b, Long Beach State U.**
23. **Jesse Zepeda, 2b, U. of Oklahoma.**
24. **Chris Mitchell, rhp, Allentown (Pa.) College.**
25. **Tom Browning, lhp, Indiana State U.**
26. **David Darwin, lhp, Duke U.**
27. Matt Schuldt, rhp, Howard (Texas) JC.
28. Drew Topham, 2b, Barbe HS, Lake Charles, La.
29. **Kurt Airoso, of, Cal State Northridge.**
30. **Chad Schroeder, rhp, Northwestern U.**
31. **Nick Jamison, of, Center Grove HS, Greenwood, Ind.**
32. John Ogiltree, rhp, Kennedy HS, Mississauga, Ont.
33. Joe Kalczynski, c, Brother Rice HS, Farmington, Mich.
34. Daniel Cole, rhp, Monroe (Mich.) HS.
35. Greg Bauer, rhp-ss, Jenks HS, Tulsa.
36. Tom Runnells, ss, Greeley (Colo.) West HS.
37. Michael Garner, lhp, Fullerton (Calif.) HS.
38. K.O. Wiegandt, rhp, Westminster Christian HS, Miami.
39. Harry Kenoi, rhp, Los Angeles Pierce JC.
40. Brian Justine, lhp, Broward (Fla.) CC.
41. Bryan Houston, rhp, Lake City (Fla.) CC.
42. **Mike Seebode, lhp, Ichabod Crane HS, Valatie, N.Y.**
43. **Dave Malenfant, rhp, Central Michigan U.**
44. Ian Herweg, rhp, Redondo Union HS, Redondo Beach, Calif.
45. **Tris Moore, of, U. of Miami.**
46. **Mike Ciminiello, 1b, Princeton U.**

47. Kevin Robles, c, Dorado, P.R.
48. Durendell Daniels, of, Gulf Coast (Fla.) CC.
49. Greg Sprehn, rhp, Triton (Ill.) JC.
50. **Bruce Johnston, rhp, Nassau (N.Y.) CC.**
51. Brandon Wheeler, rhp, Countryside HS, Clearwater, Fla.

## FLORIDA (9)

1. **Mark Kotsay, of, Cal State Fullerton.**
2. (Choice to Blue Jays as compensation for Type B free agent Devon White).
3. (Choice to Blue Jays as compensation for Type B free agent Al Leiter).
4. **Blaine Neal, rhp, Bishop Eustace HS, Pennsauken, N.J.**
5. **Brent Billingsley, lhp, Cal State Fullerton.**
6. **David Townsend, rhp, Delta State (Miss.) U.**
7. **Chris Moore, rhp, Harlan Community HS, Chicago.**
8. **Quantaa Jackson, of, Wharton (Texas) HS.**
9. Vaughn Schill, ss, Audubon (N.J.) HS.
10. **Cory Washington, of, Westover HS, Fayetteville, N.C.**
11. **Travis Wyckoff, lhp, Wichita State U.**
12. Skip Browning, rhp, Lakeview HS, Fort Oglethorpe, Ga.
13. Ryan Owens, rhp, Sonora HS, La Habra, Calif.
14. Brian Tallet, lhp, Putnam City West HS, Bethany, Okla.
15. **David Wesolowski, rhp, Williamsville (N.Y.) North HS.**
16. Simon Tafoya, 1b, Pittsburg (Calif.) HS.
17. **Larry Kleinz, ss, Villanova U.**
18. Bryan Farkas, lhp, Varina HS, Sandston, Va.
19. **Shaw Casey, rhp, U. of Nevada-Las Vegas.**
20. **Steve Gagliano, rhp, Rolling Meadows (Ill.) HS.**
21. **Matt Braughler, c, Indiana U.**
22. **Dan Ferrell, lhp, Indiana U.**
23. **Stephen Morales, c, Mayaguez, P.R.**
24. **Brad Farizo, rhp, Shaw HS, Marrero, La.**
25. **Jeff Venghaus, 2b, Rice U.**
26. Scott Dunn, rhp, Churchill HS, San Antonio.
27. Brian Matzenbacher, rhp, Belleville Area (Ill.) CC.
28. Justin Linquist, rhp, Palma HS, Salinas, Calif.
29. **Pete Arenas, ss, U. of Georgia.**
30. **Scott Conway, 1b, Lenape HS, Mount Laurel, N.J.**
31. Josh Laxton, lhp, Audubon (N.J.) HS.
32. **Alain Diaz, of, Barry (Fla.) U.**
33. Rafael Rigueiro, rhp, Riverside (Calif.) CC.
34. **Zak Ammirato, 3b-c, UCLA.**
35. **Justin Foerter, 1b, Holy Cross HS, Bordentown, N.J.**
36. **Jay Jones, c, U. of Alabama-Birmingham.**
37. **Jason Alaimo, c, U. of South Florida.**
38. Jason Sharp, ss, Owen County HS, Owenton, Ky.
39. Jeff Bloomer, rhp, County HS, Pueblo, Colo.
40. Simon Young, lhp, West Hall HS, Flowery Branch, Ga.
41. Brian Forystek, lhp, Carl Sandburg HS, Palos Park, Ill.
42. Edwin Erickson, 1b, Eisenhower HS, Yakima, Wash.
43. Jimmy Frush, rhp, Texas Tech.
44. **Patrick Pass, of, Tucker (Ga.) HS.**
45. Mike Rose, rhp, Texarkana (Texas) CC.
46. Steven Merrill, lhp, Sandy Union HS, Gresham, Ore.
47. **Mike Evans, lhp-1b, Palm Beach (Fla.) JC.**
48. Harry Anderson, of, Virginia HS, Bristol, Va.
49. Kevin Kurilla, rhp, Virginia Tech.
50. Eric Abshor, of, Heritage HS, Littleton, Colo.
51. **Kevin Zaleski, rhp, Indiana U.**
52. Daniel Torres, ss, Lenape HS, Mount Laurel, N.J.
53. David White, of, Water of Life Christian HS, Douglasville, Ga .
54. Joseph Hart, lhp, Walkersville (Md.) HS.
55. Craig Lewis, rhp, Wallace State (Ala.) CC.
56. Reece Borges, rhp, Lassen (Calif.) JC.
57. Letarvius Copeland, of, Miami-Dade CC Wolfson.
58. Travis Johnson, rhp, Snowflake HS, Taylor, Ariz.
59. Israel Pope, ss, Virginia HS, Bristol, Va.
60. Clayton Thomas, of, Central Senior HS, Victoria, Va.
61. Darius Gill, rhp, Columbia HS, Decatur, Ga.
62. Charles Walter, c, Lansdowne HS, Baltimore.
63. Joel Sajiun, of, Miami-Dade CC North.
64. Devon Younger, rhp, Lakota HS, West Chester, Ohio.
65. Jorge Soto, c, Patillas, P.R.
67. Juan Torres, rhp, Isabel, P.R.
66. Dustin Brisson, 1b, Wellington Community HS, West Palm Beach, Fla.
68. Brian Partenheimer, lhp, Indiana U.
69. **Geoff Duncan, rhp, Georgia Tech.**
70. Joshua Hoffpauir, ss, Vidalia (La.) HS.
71. Gerald Perkins, 1b, Royalton Hartlant HS, Lockport, N.Y.
72. Dwayne Webb, of, Gallatin County HS, Warsaw, Ky.
73. Brian Pirazzi, ss, South San Francisco HS.
74. Matt Pidgeon, ss, JC of the Redwoods (Calif.).
75. Scott Eskra, 3b, Lassen (Calif.) JC.

## HOUSTON (19)

1. **Mark Johnson, rhp, U. of Hawaii.**
2. **John Huber, rhp, Lakota HS, Cincinnati.**
3. **Brandon Byrd, 3b, Trinity Presbyterian HS, Montgomery, Ala.**
4. **Bryan Braswell, lhp, U. of Toledo.**
5. **Tucker Barr, c, Georgia Tech.**
6. **Michael Wheeler, ss, Oak Hills HS, Cincinnati.**
7. **Esteban Maldonado, rhp, Lambuth (Tenn.) U.**
8. **Jason Hill, c, Mount San Antonio (Calif.) JC.**
9. **Brian Dallimore, 2b, Stanford U.**
10. **John Blackmore, rhp, Plainville (Conn.) HS.**
11. **Jay Mansavage, 2b, Southern Illinois U.**
12. Jeff Cermak, of, Arizona State U.
13. Joey Hart, c, Round Rock (Texas) HS.
14. Ryan Oase, 3b-rhp, Lake Stevens HS, Everett, Wash.
15. **Jim Reeder, rhp, Northwestern U.**
16. **Randy Young, of, Wichita State U.**
17. **Matt Hyers, ss, Middle Georgia U.**
18. **David Bernhard, rhp, U. of San Francisco.**
19. Jake Eye, rhp-of, Ohio U.
20. **Wade Miller, rhp, Topton, Pa.**
21. **Geoff Robertson, of, Landrum (S.C.) HS.**
22. Joe DiSalvo, of, U. of New Orleans.
23. Roy Oswalt, rhp, Holmes (Miss.) JC.
24. Matt Dailey, lhp, Castro Valley (Calif.) HS.
25. Paul Phillips, c, Meridian (Miss.) CC.
26. Brian Grace, rhp, Mississippi Delta JC.
27. Michael Meyers, rhp, Black Hawk (Ill.) JC.
28. Jurrian Lobbezoo, lhp, Indian River (Fla.) CC.
29. **Thomas Shearn, rhp, Briggs HS, Columbus, Ohio.**
30. Kevin Tillman, 3b, Leland HS, San Jose.
31. Jed Fuller, rhp, St. Joseph Catholic HS, Renfrew, Ont.
32. Trey Hodges, rhp, Klein Oak HS, Spring, Texas.
33. **Dru Nicely, 3b, Burley (Idaho) HS.**
34. Brian Bishop, rhp, Crescenta Valley HS, La Crescenta, Calif.
35. Kevin Duck, 1b, Rancho Santiago (Calif.) JC.
36. Eric Cooper, rhp, Chabot (Calif.) JC.
37. Jason Davis, c, Woodbury (N.J.) HS.
38. James Igo, rhp, West Columbia (Texas) HS.
39. Chris Youmans, c, Seminole HS, Lake Mary, Fla.
40. Matt Gawer, lhp, Sullivan (Mo.) HS.
41. James Hostetler, rhp, Fullerton (Calif.) JC.
42. Jason Sinatra, of, Silver Creek HS, San Jose.
43. Joseph Morrell, c, Elmira (N.Y.) Free Academy.
44. Randy Brunette, ss, South Dade HS, Homestead, Fla.
45. Brad Payne, ss, Leacock HS, Agincourt, Ont.
46. Bruce Sutton, of, Seminole (Okla.) JC.
47. Derrick Vargas, lhp, Chabot (Calif.) JC.
48. Chaz Eiguren, 1b, Seward County (Kan.) CC.
49. Nathan King, of, Livingston (Texas) HS.
50. Anthony Garcia, rhp, Belen Jesuit HS, Miami.
51. Jason Chaney, lhp, Sacramento CC.
52. Mark Burnett, ss, Texarkana (Texas) CC.
53. Resh Bondi, ss, Monterey HS, Seaside, Calif.
54. James Edelen, c, Eastern Oklahoma State JC.
55. Jerymaine Beasley, of, Kamiakin HS, Kennewick, Wash.
56. Richard Terwilliger, rhp, Corning (N.Y.) East HS.
57. Charles Harrington, rhp, Oxnard (Calif.) JC.
58. Ferdinand Rivera, ss, Ranger (Texas) JC.
59. Brian Jensen, lhp, St. Vincent's HS, Petaluma, Calif.
60. Steven Knotts, of, Parkway HS, Bossier City, La.
61. Stephen Neal, 1b, Pine Bluff (Ark.) HS.
62. Todd Uzzell, rhp, Coronado HS, El Paso.
63. Troy Norrell, c, Navarro (Texas) JC.
64. Alexander Stencel, of, Mount San Antonio (Calif.) JC.
65. Greg Peterson, of, CC of Morris (N.J.).
66. George Johnson, 1b-of, Conners State (Okla.) JC.
67. Ben Keats, c, Faulkner State (Ala.) CC.
68. Tyler Dunlap, ss, Pleasant Grove HS, Texarkana, Texas.
69. Chris Hargett, 1b, Rend Lake (Ill.) JC.
70. Johnnie Wheeler, rhp, Skiatook (Okla.) HS.
71. George Rosamond, ss, Madison (Miss.) Central HS.
72. Robbie White, lhp, Trinidad (Texas) HS.
73. Daniel Duke, c, Leland HS, San Jose.
74. Marcos Rios, c, Moreau HS, Hayward, Calif.
75. Jason Cox, c, Northeast Texas CC.
76. Richard Roberts, 2b, Texarkana (Texas) CC.
77. Michael Janssen, rhp, Phoenix JC.
78. Noah Sweeters, rhp, Los Gatos (Calif.) HS.
79. Robert Porter, lhp, Texarkana (Texas) JC.
80. Jeremy Cunningham, rhp, Monte Vista HS, Cupertino, Calif.
81. Tim Neumark, of, Allegany (Md.) CC.
82. Shawn Hancock, rhp, Monte Vista HS, Cupertino, Calif.
83. Luis Perez, rhp, Rancho Santiago (Calif.) JC.

## KANSAS CITY (14)

1. Dermal Brown, of, Marlboro (N.Y.) Central HS.
2. Taylor Myers, rhp, Green Valley HS, Henderson, Nev.
3. Chad Durbin, rhp, Woodlawn HS, Baton Rouge.
4. Corey Thurman, rhp, Texas HS, Wake Village, Texas.
5. Jeremy Hill, c, W.T. White HS, Dallas.
6. Jeremy Giambi, of, Cal State Fullerton.
7. Scott Mullen, lhp, Dallas Baptist U.
8. Javier Flores, c, U. of Oklahoma.
9. Jeremy Morris, of, Florida State U.
10. Steve Hueston, rhp, Long Beach State U.
11. Mike Brambilla, c, Rancho Santiago (Calif.) JC.
12. Ethan Stein, rhp, U. of North Carolina.
13. Cory Kyzar, rhp, South Jones HS, Ellisville, Miss.
14. Brandon Berger, of, Eastern Kentucky U.
15. Eric Sees, ss, Stanford U.
16. Mike Torres, rhp, Fontana (Calif.) HS.
17. Roman Escamilla, c, U. of Texas.
18. Kris Didion, 3b, Riverside, Calif.
19. Brett Taft, ss, U. of Alabama.
20. Aaron Lineweaver, rhp, Dallas Baptist U.
21. Jason Simontacchi, rhp, Albertson (Idaho) College.
22. Kit Pellow, of, U. of Arkansas.
23. Richard Benes, 2b, Columbus HS, Bronx.
24. Brandon Baird, lhp, Wichita State U.
25. Scott Harp, 2b, Dallas Baptist U.
26. Jake Chapman, lhp, St. Joseph's (Ind.) College.
27. Enrique Calero, rhp, St. Thomas (Fla.) U.
28. Gordon Alexander, lhp, Burnaby, B.C.
29. Robert Spangler, ss, Allegany (Md.) CC.
30. Bryan Bealer, lhp, North Medford (Ore.) HS.
31. Steven Walsh, rhp, Wilson HS, Orleans, Ont.
32. Donald Quigley, rhp, Sonoma State (Calif.) U.
33. Matt Guerrier, rhp, Shaker Heights (Ohio) HS.
34. Richard Boring, rhp, Texas A&M U.
35. Gus Ornstein, 1b, Michigan State U.
36. Ryan Rupe, rhp, Texas A&M U.
37. Bryan Welch, rhp, Central Catholic HS, Salem, Mass.
38. Caleb Parmenter, of, Dinuba (Calif.) HS.
39. John Janek, rhp, West HS, Abbott, Texas.
40. William Cornish, rhp, Lucas HS, London, Ont.
41. Brent Gutierrez, of, Clovis West HS, Fresno.
42. Brent Cook, rhp, Sprague HS, Salem, Ore.
43. Ken Thomas, c, Pennsauken (N.J.) HS.
44. George Kauffman, rhp, Stetson U.
45. William Ward, lhp, Rancho Santiago (Calif.) JC.
46. Dennis Melendi, of, Pace HS, Miami.
47. Daniel Fernandez, 3b, Braddock HS, Miami.
48. Mario Ramos, lhp, Pflugerville (Texas) HS.
49. Nikki Moses, of, Doyline HS, Minden, La.
50. Michael Bender, rhp, Vanden HS, Vacaville, Calif.
51. Tim Pittsley, rhp, Allegany (Md.) CC.
52. David Meliah, ss, Walla Walla (Wash.) CC.
53. Bret Halbert, lhp, Western HS, Buena Park, Calif.
54. James Blanchard, ss, Grants Pass (Ore.) HS.
55. Macey Brooks, of, James Madison U.
56. Daniel Williams, 2b, Grand Canyon U.

## LOS ANGELES (23)

1. Damian Rolls, 3b, Schlagel HS, Kansas City, Kan.
2. Josh Glassey, c, Mission Bay HS, San Diego.
3. Alex Cora, ss, U. of Miami.
4. Peter Bergeron, of, Greenfield (Mass.) HS.
5. Nick Leach, 1b, Madera (Calif.) HS.
6. Jack Jones, ss, Cal State Fullerton.
7. Ben Simon, rhp, Eastern Michigan U.
8. Chris Karabinus, lhp, Towson State U.
9. David Falcon, c, Bayamon, P.R.
10. Jeff Auterson, of, Norte Vista HS, Riverside, Calif.
11. Jason Walters, rhp, Meridian (Miss.) CC.
12. Randy Stearns, of, U. of Wisconsin-River Falls.
13. Derrick Peoples, of, Ryan HS, Denton, Texas.
14. Willie King, 1b, Roosevelt HS, Brooklyn.
15. Casey Snow, c, Long Beach State U.
16. Matt Kramer, rhp, Moorpark (Calif.) JC.
17. Mikal Richey, of, Columbia HS, Decatur, Ga.
18. Pedro Flores, lhp, East Los Angeles JC.
19. Mickey Maestas, rhp, George Mason U.
20. Ismael Gallo, ss, Mount San Antonio (Calif.) JC.
21. Kimani Newton, of, St. Joseph HS, St. Croix, V.I.
22. Elvis Correa, rhp, South Division HS, Milwaukee.
23. Ted Lilly, lhp, Fresno CC.
24. Pat Kelleher, of, Paradise Valley, Ariz.
25. Scott Morrison, ss, Baylor U.

26. Monte Marshall, 2b, Birmingham-Southern College.
27. Steve Wilson, c, Georgia Southern U.
28. Brian Zaun, of, Butler U.
29. Toby Dollar, rhp, Texas Christian U.
30. Rick Saitta, 2b-ss, Rutgers U.
31. Brian Foulks, of, Benedict (S.C.) College.
32. Brian Sankey, 1b, Boston College.
33. Brian Jacobson, lhp, California Baptist College.
34. Brad Cresse, c, Marina HS, Huntington Beach, Calif.
35. Donnie Thomas, lhp, Andrew (Ga.) JC.
36. Wayne Franklin, lhp, U. of Maryland.
37. Jim Fritz, c, U. of Tennessee.
38. Jeff Kubenka, lhp, St. Mary's (Texas) U.
39. Bryan Cranson, lhp, Bronson (Mich.) HS.
40. Frank Thompson, rhp, Embry-Riddle Aeronautical (Fla.) U.
41. Jason Weekley, of, St. Mary's College.
42. Jacob Allen, c, Southeastern Illinois JC.
43. Kevin Culmo, rhp, Cal State Sacramento.
44. Eddie Sordo, rhp, Jacksonville U.
45. Erik Lazerus, ss, Cal State Chico.
46. Bradley Turner, c, Belton (Texas) HS.
47. Eric Lovinger, rhp, Oregon State U.
48. Mike Hannah, rhp, Mercer U.
49. Peter Brinjak, rhp, Power St. Josephs HS, Etobicoke, Ont.
50. Brian Paluk, rhp, Saginaw Valley State (Mich.) U.
51. Doug Straight, rhp, Buckhannon-Upshur HS, Buckhannon, W.Va.
52. Dean Mitchell, rhp, Texas A&M U.
53. Blake Mayo, rhp, U. of Alabama-Birmingham.
54. James Jackson, of, Kankakee (Ill.) HS.
55. Adam Flohr, lhp, Spokane Falls (Wash.) CC.
56. Spencer Micunek, rhp, Kalamazoo Valley (Mich.) CC.
57. Ryan Anholt, 2b, Kwantlen (B.C.) College.
58. Brian Little, 3b, JC of the Sequoias (Calif.).
59. Juan Huguet, c, Coral Park HS, Miami.
60. Craig Jarvis, of, Claremont HS, Victoria, B.C.
61. Kevin Sullivan, c, Pacelli HS, Stevens Point, Wis.
62. Mark Paschal, of, Chaffey (Calif.) JC.
63. George Bailey, 3b, St. Joseph HS, St. Croix, V.I.
64. Joseph Thomas, rhp, Mount San Antonio (Calif.) JC.
65. Devin Helps, lhp, McClung Collegiate HS, Maniton, Man.
66. Travis Bolton, c, West Valley HS, Anderson, Calif.
67. Graig Merritt, c, Terry Fox Senior HS, Pitt Meadows, B.C.
68. Samuel Shelton, rhp, Durango (Colo.) HS.
69. Mike Meyer, ss, Sabino HS, Tucson, Ariz.
70. Matthew Mason, c, J.L. Crowe HS, Trail, B.C.
71. Kevin Huff, rhp, Horizon HS, Scottsdale, Ariz.
72. Eric Bruntlett, ss, Harrison HS, Lafayette, Ind.
73. Edwin Rodriguez, 1b, Ponce, P.R.
74. Ryan Withey, ss, Mainland HS, Daytona Beach, Fla.
75. Paul Sirant, rhp, River East Collegiate HS, Winnipeg, Man.
76. Chad Zaniewski, of, John Leonard HS, West Palm Beach, Fla.
77. Richard Garner, c, Wade Hampton HS, Taylors, S.C.
78. Jim Davis, 1b, Berrien County HS, Nashville, Ga.
79. Rabell Rivera, ss, Lake Land (Ill.) JC.

## MILWAUKEE (8)

1. Chad Green, of, U. of Kentucky.
2. Jose Garcia, rhp, Baldwin Park (Calif.) HS.
3. Kevin Barker, of, Virginia Tech.
4. Josh Hancock, rhp, Vestavia Hills (Ala.) HS.
5. Philip Kendall, c, Jasper (Ind.) HS.
6. Paul Stewart, rhp, Garner (N.C.) HS.
7. Mike Wetmore, ss, Washington State U.
8. Brian Passini, lhp, Miami (Ohio) U.
9. Doug Johnston, rhp, Millard South HS, Omaha.
10. Josh Klimek, ss, U. of Illinois.
11. Val Pascucci, rhp, Gahr HS, Cerritos, Calif.
12. Garret Osilka, 3b, Edison (Fla.) CC.
13. Allen Levrault, rhp, CC of Rhode Island.
14. Shawn Sonnier, rhp, Panola (Texas) JC.
15. Al Hawkins, rhp, Elizabeth (N.J.) HS.
16. John Fulcher, lhp, George Mason U.
17. Samone Peters, 1b, McKinleyville (Calif.) HS.
18. Maney Leshay, rhp, Palm Beach Atlantic College.
19. John Boker, rhp, Mount Vernon Nazarene (Ohio) College.
20. Jay Arnold, rhp, Glendale (Ariz.) CC.
21. Danny Bogeajis, rhp, Lyman HS, Longwood, Fla.
22. Dan Thompson, of, Yale U.
23. Monsantos Armstrong, of, Calhoun City (Miss.) HS.
24. Ross Parmenter, ss, Santa Clara U.
25. Jeremy Ward, rhp, CC of Rhode Island.
26. Gio Cafaro, of, U. of South Florida.
27. Derrick Lee, lhp, Texas Christian U.
28. Kevin Candelaria, c, Page (Ariz.) HS.

29. Tyler Vanpatten, c, Seabreeze HS, Ormond Beach, Fla.
**30. Jason Glover, of, Georgia State U.**
31. Antonio Garris, 3b-of, Anson County HS, Wadesboro, N.C.
**32. Travis Tank, rhp, U. of Wisconsin-Whitewater.**
33. Steven Truitt, 2b, Elkins HS, Missouri City, Texas.
**34. Brad Richardson, lhp, Hill (Texas) JC.**
**35. Mick Fieldbinder, rhp, U. of Montevallo (Ala.).**
36. Brandon Backe, ss, Ball HS, Galveston, Texas.
37. Jay Sitzman, of, Horizon HS, Scottsdale, Ariz.
**38. Adam Faurot, 3b-ss, Florida State U.**
**39. Brian Hedley, rhp, St. Mary's College.**
40. Greg Freetly, rhp, Orange Glen HS, San Marcos, Calif.
**41. Jason Washam, c, U. of New Orleans.**
**42. Ramon Fernandez, of, Cayey, P.R.**
43. Frank Valois,of, Good Counsel HS, Ashton, Md.
44. Michel Dubreuil, rhp, Miami-Dade CC North.
45. Todd Ludwig, c, Thomas More HS, Franklin, Wis.
46. James Morgan, rhp, Central HS, Chattanooga.
47. Jack Keene, rhp, Gulf Coast (Fla.) CC.
48. Brian Moon, c, Southern Union State (Ala.) JC.
49. Tim Boeth, 3b-ss, Tallahassee (Fla.) CC.
50. Brenton Kelley, rhp, Texarkana (Texas) JC.
51. Kelley Love, rhp, Laredo (Texas) JC.
52. Jose Camilo, ss, San Juan, P.R.
53. Daniel Prata, lhp, Seminole (Okla.) JC.
54. Brian Steinbach, rhp, U. of Michigan.
55. Robert Cornett, c, Young Harris (Ga.) JC.
56. John Cornette, rhp, Seabreeze HS, Ormond Beach, Fla.
57. Eric McMaster, 2b, Seward County (Kan.) CC.

## MINNESOTA (2)

1. Travis Lee, 1b, San Diego State U.
**2. Jacque Jones, of, U. of Southern California.**
**3. Dan Cey, ss, U. of California.**
**4. Chad Allen, of, Texas A&M U.**
**5. Michael Ryan, ss, Indiana (Pa.) HS.**
**6. Tommy LaRosa, rhp, U. of Nevada-Las Vegas.**
**7. Chad Moeller, c, U. of Southern California.**
**8. Corey Spiers, lhp, U. of Alabama.**
**9. Nate Yeskie, rhp, U. of Nevada-Las Vegas.**
**10. Joe Cranford, 2b, U. of Georgia.**
**11. Tommy Peterman, 1b, Georgia Southern U.**
**12. Ryan Lynch, lhp, UCLA.**
**13. Mike Lincoln, rhp, U. of Tennessee.**
**14. David Hooten, rhp, Mississippi State U.**
**15. Steve Huls, ss, U. of Minnesota.**
**16. Eric Brosam, 1b, Redwood Valley HS, Redwood Falls, Minn.**
17. William Gray, ss, Liberty Eylau HS, Texarkana, Texas.
**18. Chris Garza, lhp, U. of Nevada.**
19. Tyler Martin, ss, Melbourne (Fla.) HS.
20. Matt Kata, rhp-ss, St. Ignatius HS, Willoughby Hills, Ohio.
**21. Jake Jacobs, rhp, Pine Forest HS, Pensacola, Fla.**
**22. Mike Bauder, lhp, U. of Nevada-Las Vegas.**
**23. Richie Nye, rhp, U. of Arkansas.**
**24. Marcus Smith, of, Valencia (Fla.) CC.**
**25. Phil Haigler, rhp, Vanderbilt U.**
**26. Charlie Gillian, rhp, Virginia Tech.**
27. Shaun Berrow, lhp, Tumwater HS, Olympia, Wash.
**28. Brian Kennedy, of, Harrison HS, Lafayette, Ind.**
29. David Johnson, rhp, Kansas State U.
30. Dwayne Jones, c, Rockledge (Fla.) HS.
31. Mike Lamb, c, Cal State Fullerton.
**32. C.J. Thieleke, 2b, U. of Iowa.**
**33. Rick Loonam, rhp, Regis (Colo.) U.**
**34. Anthony Felston, of, U. of Mississippi.**
35. Josh Bard, c, Cherry Creek HS, Englewood, Colo.
36. Andrew Persby, 1b, Hill Murray HS, North St. Paul, Minn.
37. Richard Durrett, c, Farmington (N.M.) HS.
**38. Tom Buchman, c, U. of Missouri.**
39. Ryan Brown, rhp, Northeast Texas CC.
40. Anthony Denard, of, Emeryville HS, Oakland.
41. Chris Shores, rhp, Beardstown (Ill.) HS.
**42. Antonio Gholar, rhp, William Carey (Miss.) College.**
43. Clinton Bailey, of, Chemainus (B.C.) HS.
**44. Rick Moss, 3b, Lewis (Ill.) U.**
45. Barry Lunney, lhp, U. of Arkansas.
46. Craig Munroe, 1b, The Crescent School, Thornhill, Ont.
47. Toby Franklin, of, Westwood HS, Fort Pierce, Fla.
48. Justin Pederson, of, U. of Minnesota.
49. Ryan Ferrell, rhp, Daviess County HS, Philpot, Ky.
50. Jacob Schaffer, ss, Bradley U.
51. Wilson Romero, of, Miami HS.
52. Adam Robinson, 2b, U. of Virginia.
**53. Mario Opipari, rhp, U. of Kansas.**

**Brewers Showpiece.** Former University of Kentucky outfielder Chad Green became the top pick of Milwaukee in the 1996 draft.

54. Chris Alexander, rhp, Indian River (Fla.) CC.
**55. John Mundine, rhp, Luling (Texas) HS.**
56. Chris Adams, rhp, McGregor (Texas) HS.

## MONTREAL (5)

1. John Patterson, rhp, West Orange (Texas) Stark HS.
**2. Milton Bradley, of, Poly HS, Long Beach.**
3. Joe Fraser, rhp, Katella HS, Anaheim.
**4. Christian Parker, rhp, U. of Notre Dame.**
5. Tony Lawrence, of, Louisiana Tech.
**6. Karl Chatman, of, Dallas Baptist U.**
**7. Luis Rivera, c, Bayamon, P.R.**
**8. Keith Evans, rhp, U. of California.**
**9. Brian Matz, lhp, Clemson U.**
**10. Paul Blandford, 2b, U. of Kentucky.**
**11. Jeremy Salyers, rhp, Walters State (Tenn.) CC.**
12. Greg Workman, lhp, Saddleback (Calif.) CC.
13. Ray Casteel, rhp, Liberty Eylau HS, Texarkana, Texas.
**14. Jamey Carroll, ss, U. of Evansville.**
**15. Tripp MacKay, 2b, Oklahoma State U.**
**16. Andy Tracy, 1b, Bowling Green State U.**
**17. Chris Stowers, of, U. of Georgia.**
**18. Matt Buirley, c, Ohio State U.**
**19. Tim Young, lhp, U. of Alabama.**
**20. Rod Stevenson, rhp, Columbus (Ga.) College.**
21. Kevin Jordan, 2b-ss, Blinn (Texas) JC.
22. Jason Hoffman, of, Monte Vista HS, Danville, Calif.
23. Keith Dunn, rhp, Rosa Fort HS, Tunica, Miss.
**24. Shannon Swaino, c, Kent U.**
25. Thomas Pace, of, Mesa (Ariz.) HS.
**26. Ethan Barlow, of, U. of Vermont.**
27. Ryan Luther, ss, Olympic (Wash.) JC.
**28. Michael Rahilly, rhp, North Fort Myers HS, Cape Coral, Fla.**
29. Kevin Forbes, of, American River (Calif.) JC.
**30. Eric Sparks, lhp, SUNY Cortland.**
**31. Curtis Martin, lhp, Merritt Island HS, Melbourne, Fla.**
**32. Darrick Edison, rhp, Cal Poly Pomona.**
33. Michael Schwam, rhp, Edison HS, Huntington Beach, Calif.
**34. William Sadler, lhp, Taylor County HS, Perry, Fla.**
35. Eric Cyr, lhp, Montreal.
36. Rafael Erazo, rhp, Sabana Seca, P.R.
37. Joe Fretwell, c, Cardinal Gibbons HS, Overland Park, Fla.
38. Javier Sein, 1b, Aguadilla, P.R.
39. Jeremy Cook, rhp, Yuba City (Calif.) HS.
40. Nathan Cook, 3b, Oakland (Calif.) HS.
41. Robert Cope, rhp, JC of the Siskiyous (Calif.).

42. Daniel Custer, 3b, Dewey HS, Copar, Okla.
43. Jacob Smith, rhp, East Coweta HS, Newnan, Ga.
44. Jason Huth, ss, Howard (Texas) JC.
45. Michael Brown, of, Saguaro HS, Scottsdale, Ariz.
46. Mike Sikorski, of, Knoch HS, Saxonburg, Pa.

## NEW YORK/AL (24)

1. **Eric Milton, lhp, U. of Maryland** (Choice from Angels as compensation for Type B free agent Randy Velarde).
1. (Choice to Rangers as compensation for Type A free agent Kenny Rogers).
2. **Jason Coble, lhp, Lincoln County HS, Fayetteville, Tenn.**
3. **Nick Johnson, 1b, McClatchy HS, Sacramento.**
4. **Vidal Candelaria, c, Manati, P.R.**
5. **Zach Day, rhp, LaSalle HS, Cincinnati.**
6. **Brian Reith, rhp, Concordia Lutheran HS, Fort Wayne, Ind.**
7. **Brian Aylor, of, Oklahoma State U.**
8. **Allen Butler, 3b, Lincoln Memorial (Tenn.) U.**
9. Chris Fulbright, rhp, Libertyville (Ill.) HS.
10. **Rudy Gomez, 2b, U. of Miami.**
11. Brant Ust, ss, Eastlake HS, Redmond, Wash.
12. **Eric Krall, lhp, Birmingham-Southern College.**
13. Andrew Helmer, rhp, Bishop Dwenger HS, New Haven, Ind.
14. **Yoiset Valle, lhp, Pace HS, Miami Lakes, Fla.**
15. Nick Stocks, rhp, Jesuit HS, Tampa.
16. **Justin Rayment, lhp, San Diego State U.**
17. Matt Ginter, rhp, Clark HS, Winchester, Ky.
18. Chuck Hazzard, 1b, U. of Florida.
19. Brian Gilman, c-ss, Westview HS, Portland, Ore.
20. **Brandon Hendrixx, rhp, Rancho Santiago (Calif.) JC.**
21. Kyle Brunen, Delisle Composite HS, Vanscoy, Sask.
22. Joseph Pourron, rhp, Chattahoochee Valley (Ala.) CC.
23. Kevin Overcash, ss, Collierville (Tenn.) HS.
24. Fontella Jones, of, Mississippi Gulf Coast JC.
25. Adam Ramos, of, Lehman HS, Bronx.
26. Joshua Hawes, rhp, Toll Gate HS, Warwick, R.I.
27. **Jason McBride, rhp, Pensacola (Fla.) JC.**
28. Samuel Eavenson, rhp, Loganville, Ga.
29. Ryan Tack, rhp, Saddleback (Calif.) CC.
30. Marcus Thames, of, East Central (Miss.) CC.
31. **Ryan Huffman, of, Texas A&M U.**
32. **Ryan Wheeler, 2b, Lincoln Memorial (Tenn.) U.**
33. **Blaine Phillips, c, U. of Southwestern Louisiana.**
34. Jared Hoerman, rhp, Eastern Oklahoma State JC.
35. Dan Kerrigan, c, Northeast HS, St. Petersburg, Fla.
36. Noel Manley, c-1b, Louisburg (N.C.) JC.
37. Justin Carpenter, rhp, Seminole (Okla.) JC.
38. Jarvis Larry, of, Parkway HS, Bossier City, La.
39. Eunique Johnson, 3b, Centennial HS, Compton, Calif.
40. **Dennis Twombley, c, Pepperdine U.**
41. Gavin Hare, c, Eastlake HS, Redmond, Wash.
42. **Alain Cruz, 3b, Miami-Dade CC North.**
43. Migues Rodriguez, ss, Cypress (Calif.) JC.
44. William Pieper, 3b, Kamenameha HS, Honolulu.
45. Mark Hamilton, lhp, Bell HS, Hurst, Texas.
46. Daryl Grant, 1b-lhp, Florin HS, Sacramento.
47. Nathan Dighera, of-c, Southwestern (Calif.) JC.
48. Samuel Norris, 1b, San Francisco CC.
49. Robert Simpson, c, Christian HS, El Cajon, Calif.
50. Charles Armstrong, lhp, Oakland.
51. Caesar Castaneda, 3b, East Los Angeles JC.
52. Russ Chambliss, of, Washington (Pa.) U.
53. Felix Lopez, 1b, Plant HS, Tampa.
54. Jason Halper, of, Columbia U.
55. Derek Bauer, 2b, Clarkstown North HS, New City, N.Y.
56. **Bob Meier, c, Cinnaminson (N.J.) HS.**
57. Hector Rivera, 3b, Jesuit HS, Tampa.
58. Trevor Bishop, rhp, Lethbridge (Alb.) CC.
59. Jay Foster, rhp, Birch Hills Composite HS, Birch Hills, Sask.
60. Nathan Cadena, ss, Cerritos (Calif.) JC.
61. Cedrick Harris, of, Ashdown (Ark.) HS.
62. Jason Tisone, rhp, Seton Hall U.
63. Tony Gomes, rhp, Lodi HS, Galt, Calif.
64. Matt Wise, rhp, Cal State Fullerton.
65. Mitchell Roth, c, Cleveland HS, Reseda, Calif.
66. Fred Smith, of, Bryan Station HS, Lexington, Ky.
67. Craig Hann, c, Walshe HS, Fort MacLeod, Alberta.
68. Avante Rose, of, Centennial HS, Compton, Calif.
69. Ryan Suyama, ss, Sprague HS, Salem, Ore.
70. Amir Taylor, of, Lincoln HS, San Diego.
71. Adrian Mora, 2b-ss, Southwestern (Calif.) JC.
72. Aaron Kramer, rhp, Grand Canyon U.
73. **Harold Frazier, lhp, Northeastern Oklahoma State JC.**
74. William Duncan, c, Big Bend (Wash.) CC.
75. **Mike Biehle, lhp, Ohio State U.**

76. Adam Danner, rhp, U. of South Florida.
77. **Rhett Ingerick, rhp, Davidson College.**
78. Bryan Green, 1b, Jasper (Texas) HS.
79. Richard Bottomley, c, Ramona (Calif.) HS.
80. Garry Templeton, ss, Poway (Calif.) HS.
81. Nicholas Herz, c, Poway (Calif.) HS.
82. Corey Ward, of, Skyline HS, Dallas.
83. Gustavo Alonso, c, Jordan HS, Long Beach.
84. Chris Small, c, Punahou HS, Honolulu.
85. Matt Martinez, ss, Big Bend (Wash.) CC.
86. Adam Wilson, ss, Mission Bay HS, San Diego.
87. Nathan Kaup, 3b, Camarillo (Calif.) HS.
88. **Scott Seabol, 3b, West Virginia U.**
89. Damion Malott, of, Cosumnes River (Calif.) JC.
90. Brad Gorrie, ss, U. of Massachusetts.
91. Michael Myers, c, Allentown (Pa.) College.
92. Ben Hickman, rhp, Northeast Texas CC.
93. Errol Smith, of, St. Augustine HS, San Diego.
94. Clay Condrey, rhp, Angelina (Texas) CC.
95. Greg Donohue, c, Rockland (N.Y.) CC.
96. Jose Garcia, lhp, Southwestern (Calif.) JC.
97. Mark Copeland, rhp, Muscatine (Iowa) CC.
98. **Todd Trunk, rhp, North Central (Ill.) JC.**
99. Mike Amrhein, 3b, U. of Notre Dame.
100. Aron Amundson, 3b, Eastern Oklahoma State JC.

## NEW YORK/NL (13)

1. **Robert Stratton, of, San Marcos HS, Santa Barbara, Calif.**
2. **Brendan Behn, lhp, Merced (Calif.) JC.**
3. **Eddie Yarnall, lhp, Louisiana State U.**
4. **Jeromie Lovingood, lhp, McMinn County HS, Riceville, Tenn.**
5. **Patrick Burns, of, Ryan HS, Denton, Texas.**
6. **Tom Johnson, of, Brookdale (N.J.) CC**
7. Tony Milo, lhp, Laguna Hills (Calif.) HS.
8. **Pee Wee Lopez, c, Miami-Dade CC South.**
9. **Willie Suggs, rhp, Mount Vernon (Ill.) JC.**
10. **Scott Comer, lhp, Mazama HS, Klamath Falls, Ore.**
11. **Garrick Haltiwanger, of, The Citadel.**
12. Geoff Linville, rhp, Redmond (Wash.) HS.
13. David Walling, rhp, El Capitan HS, Lakeside, Calif.
14. **Tom Stanton, c, Florida CC.**
15. Jeff Rook, of, Badin HS, Fairfield, Ohio.
16. **Dicky Gonzalez, rhp, Toa Baja, P.R.**
17. Kregg Talburt, rhp, Tahlequah (Okla.) HS.
18. Eric Schmitt, rhp, Woodson HS, Fairfax, Va.
19. **Bailey Chancey, of, U. of Alabama-Huntsville.**
20. **Mike Lyons, rhp, Stetson U.**
21. **John Tamargo, ss, U. of Florida.**
22. **Jersen Perez, ss-2b, CC of Rhode Island.**
23. **Brandon Mulvehill, of, Pell City (Ala.) HS.**
24. Kendall Prather, rhp, Sweetwater HS, Erick, Okla.
25. **James Dougherty, lhp, Eastern HS, Voorhees, N.J.**
26. Dennis Anderson, c, Canyon Del Oro HS, Tucson.
27. Jason Navarro, lhp, Tulane U.
28. Paul Ciofrone, of, Stony Brook School, Nesconset, N.Y.
29. Todd Meldahl, lhp, Butte (Mont.) HS.
30. **Mike Queen, lhp, Gravette (Ark.) HS.**
31. Joaquin Montada, rhp, Hialeah (Fla.) Senior HS.
32. **Mike Meadows, 3b, Seminole (Fla.) HS.**
33. James Magrane, rhp, Ottumwa (Iowa) HS.
34. Aaron Vincent, rhp, Bakersfield (Calif.) JC.
35. **Tim Carr, rhp, Westlake HS, Westlake Village, Calif.**
36. Randy Ruiz, 1b, Monroe HS, Bronx.
37. **Adam Garmon, rhp, St. Augustine (Fla.) HS.**
38. **Jeff Hafer, rhp, James Madison U.**
39. Zackery Usry, 1b, Hokes Bluff HS, Piedmont, Ala.
40. Joshua Pearce, rhp, West Valley HS, Yakima, Wash.
41. Andrew Watt, of, St. Francis HS, Los Altos, Calif.
42. Daniel Nelson, rhp, Lackawanna (Pa.) CC.
43. John Mattson, rhp, Tacoma (Wash.) CC.
44. Tim Corcoran, rhp, Jackson HS, Slaughter, La.
45. Patrick Gorman, rhp, Rockland (N.Y.) CC.
46. **William Payne, lhp, Rutherford HS, Panama City, Fla.**
47. Brian Holden, lhp, Palm Beach Lakes HS, West Palm Beach, Fla.
48. **B.J. Huff, of, U. of Alabama-Birmingham.**
49. Jason Gronert, c, Lyman HS, Longwood, Fla.
50. Michael Fierro, rhp, Merritt Island (Fla.) HS.
51. **Mike Davis, rhp, Florida State U.**
52. Aaron Abram, of, Valley HS, West Des Moines, Iowa.
53. **Matt Splawn, rhp, U. of Texas-Arlington.**
54. Ryan O'Toole, rhp, UCLA.
55. **Jason Bohannon, lhp, Oklahoma City U.**

## OAKLAND (10)

1. Eric Chavez, 3b, Mount Carmel HS, San Diego.
2. Josue Espada, ss, U. of Mobile (Ala.).
3. A.J. Hinch, c, Stanford U.
4. Tom Graham, rhp, Beyer HS, Modesto, Calif.
5. Julian Leyva, rhp, Arlington HS, Riverside, Calif.
6. Nick Sosa, 1b, Lake Mary (Fla.) HS.
7. Mike Paradis, rhp, Auburn (Mass.) HS.
8. Brad Blumenstock, rhp, Southern Illinois U.
9. Cody McKay, c-3b, Arizona State U.
10. Eric Lee, of, Clear Lake HS, Houston.
11. Jake O'Dell, rhp, U. of Texas.
12. Todd Mensik, 1b, U. of Mississippi.
13. Doug Robertson, rhp, Bradley U.
14. Chad Hawkins, rhp, Grapevine HS, Euless, Texas.
15. Kevin Gregg, rhp, Corvallis (Ore.) HS.
16. Justin Bowles, of, Louisiana State U.
17. Derek Rix, 3b, Bishop Kenny HS, Jacksonville.
18. Joel Colgrove, rhp, U. of Alabama.
19. Joe Caruso, 2b, U. of Alabama.
20. Eric Faulk, rhp, New Hanover HS, Wilmington, N.C.
21. Brian Luderer, c, Crespi HS, Tarzana, Calif.
22. Scott Skeen, of, Mountain View HS, Bend, Ore.
23. Frankey Jacobs, rhp, Jordan HS, Durham, N.C.
24. Brett Laxton, rhp, Louisiana State U.
25. Randy Eversgerd, rhp, Kaskaskia (Ill.) CC.
26. Rico Lagattuta, lhp, U. of Nevada.
27. Flint Wallace, rhp, Texas Christian U.
28. T.R. Marcinczyk, 1b, U. of Miami.
29. Monte Davis, 3b, Indian Hills (Iowa) CC.
30. Peter Dellaratta, rhp, U. of South Alabama.
31. Ray Noriega, lhp, New Mexico Highland U.
32. Bryan Garcia, rhp, Quartz Hill (Calif.) HS.
33. Ryan Gill, rhp, Galveston (Texas) JC.
34. Joe Dusan, of, Bend (Ore) HS.
35. Ian Perio, lhp, Castle HS, Kaneohe, Hawaii.
36. Danny Chavers, ss, Riverview HS, Sarasota, Fla.
37. Brent Spooner, c, Godby HS, Tallahassee, Fla.
38. Bryan King, rhp, Yavapai (Ariz.) JC.
39. Anthony Taylor, rhp, Central Arizona JC.
40. Gary Burnham, of-1b, Clemson U.
41. Graeme Brown, rhp, Avon Old Farms (Conn.) Prep School.
42. Brent Miller, 3b, Butte (Calif.) JC.
43. Michael Knight, of, Oakland (Calif.) HS.

## PHILADELPHIA (11)

1. Adam Eaton, rhp, Snohomish (Wash.) HS.
2. Jimmy Rollins, ss, Encinal HS, Alameda, Calif.
3. Kris Stevens, lhp, Fontana (Calif.) HS.
4. Ryan Brannan, rhp, Long Beach State U.
5. Ira Tilton, rhp, Siena College.
6. Kevin Burford, of, Fountain Valley (Calif.) HS.
7. B.J. Schlicker, c-1b, North Montgomery HS, Crawfordsville, Ind.
8. David Francia, of, U. of South Alabama.
9. Brandon Marsters, c, Oral Roberts U.
10. Evan Thomas, rhp, Florida International U.
11. Salvatore Molta, rhp, Brookdale (N.J.) CC.
12. Jason Johnson, of, Chaffey (Calif.) JC.
13. Jason Knupfer, ss, Long Beach State U.
14. Mike Torti, 3b, Arizona State U.
15. Brett Egan, ss, Royal HS, Simi Valley, Calif.
16. Brandon Allen, lhp, U. of Illinois-Chicago.
17. Bob Van Iten, c, Truman HS, Independence, Mo.
18. Joe Cotton, rhp, Bowling Green State U.
19. Brad Crede, 1b, Central Missouri State U.
20. Jason Wesemann, ss, U. of Wisconsin-Milwaukee
21. Greg Gregory, lhp, Pepperdine U.
22. Rodney Batts, 2b, Delta State U.
23. Marty Crawford, 2b, Baylor U.
24. Shannon Cooley, of, Northeast Louisiana U.
25. Adam Shadburne, rhp, U. of Kentucky.
26. Javier Mejia, rhp, U. of Southern California.
27. Skip Kiil, of, Cal State Fullerton.
28. Kevin Nichols, 1b-3b, U. of Alabama.
29. Nick Thompson, c, Elon (N.C.) College.
30. Jason Davis, lhp, San Jose State U.
31. Terry Bishop, lhp, College of St. Rose (N.Y.).
32. Kirby Clark, c, Auburn U.
33. Brad Philley, of, Rogers HS, Puyallup, Wash.
34. Tommy Ferrand, of, Southeastern Louisiana U.
35. Richard Estep, rhp, Grand Canyon U.
36. Justin Fenus, rhp, U. of North Alabama.
37. Matt Buczkowski, c-3b, Butler U.

**Grade A Talent.** Oakland's first-round pick, third baseman Eric Chavez, was rated the best hitting talent in the 1996 draft.

38. Robert Voltz, 1b, Jesuit HS, Metairie, La.
39. Tommy Worthy, ss, Gadsden State (Ala.) CC.
40. Greg Taylor, ss, U. of Arkansas-Little Rock.
41. Jason Cafferty, rhp, Hastings (Neb.) College.
42. John Crane, lhp, Rider U.
43. Eddie Rivero, of, U. of Miami.
44. David Campos, lhp, Kerman (Calif.) HS.
45. Stephen Murphy, rhp, El Camino HS, South San Francisco
46. Lee Molaison, c, Terrebonne HS, Theriot, La.
47. Keith Shockley, lhp, Allen County (Kan.) CC.
48. Clarence Hargrave, ss, Southern Union State (Ala.) JC.
49. Chuck Crumpton, rhp, Northeast Texas CC.
50. Rich Rodrigues, c, DeAnza (Calif.) JC.

## PITTSBURGH (1)

1. Kris Benson, rhp, Clemson U.
2. Andy Prater, rhp, McCluer North HS, Florissant, Mo.
3. Luis Lorenzana, ss, Montgomery HS, San Diego.
4. Lee Evans, c, Tuscaloosa County HS, Northport, Ala.
5. Julian Redman, of, Tuscaloosa (Ala.) Academy.
6. Yustin Jordan, ss, Monticello (Ark.) HS.
7. Andrew Hohenstein, rhp, Norte Vista HS, Riverside, Calif.
8. Bobby Vogt, lhp, Armwood HS, Tampa.
9. Jess Siciliano, rhp, Rockland (N.Y.) CC.
10. Carlos Rivera, 1b, Rio Grande, P.R.
11. Jason Haynie, lhp, U. of South Carolina.
12. Jeremy Rockow, of, Fort Myers (Fla.) HS.
13. Xavier Burns, 3b, Central State U.
14. Ali Brooks, ss-of, Laney (Calif.) JC.
15. Nick Day, of, Green Valley HS, Las Vegas.
16. Michael Chaney, lhp, Bowling Green State U.
17. Michael Gonzalez, lhp, Faith Christian Academy, Pasadena, Texas.
18. George Elmore, rhp, Lucama, N.C.

19. Garrett Larkin, ss, Merrimack (Mass.) College.
20. Jacob Jensen, ss, Fresno CC.
21. Paul Ah Yat, lhp, U. of Hawaii.
22. Luis Gonzalez, rhp, U. of New Mexico.
23. Morgan Walker, 1b, Lamar U.
24. Mark Freed, lhp, Pennsville (N.J.) HS.
25. Michael Gresko, lhp, Mercer County (N.J.) CC.
26. Daniel Tobias, rhp, Oregon, Ohio.
27. Kendall Rhodes, rhp, Crockett (Texas) HS.
28. William Harris, 2b-ss, Cairo (Ga.) HS.
29. Ender Classen, ss, Arecibo, P.R.
30. Wyatt Brooks, lhp, U. of North Florida.
31. Makani Lum, c-3b, Kamehameha HS, Kaneohe, Hawaii.
32. Chad Ciccone, c, Hopewell HS, Aliquippa, Pa.
33. Carlton McKenzie, of-3b, Raritan Valley (N.J.) CC.
34. Ramonzo Douglas, 1b, Eureka HS, Glenco, Mo.
35. Joseph Hunt, of, Sante Fe (Fla.) CC.
36. Barry Johnson, lhp-1b, Hales Franciscan HS, Chicago.
37. Brandon Schliinz, 3b-c, Orono HS, Loretto, Minn.
38. Jamaal Strong, of-ss, Pasadena HS, Altadena, Calif.
39. Josh Bonifay, ss-2b, Roberson HS, Arden, N.C.
40. Jesse Daggett, c, Crescenta Valley HS, La Crescenta, Calif.
41. Scott May, c, Carson-Newman (Tenn.) College.
42. James McAuley, c, Plant HS, Tampa.
43. Jeremy Sickles, c, Millikan HS, Long Beach.
44. Robert Moore, 2b, Coffee HS, Douglas, Ga.
45. Chris Capuano, lhp, Cathedral HS, West Springfield, Mass.
46. Ricardo Finol, rhp, Navarro (Texas) JC.
47. Ian Rauls, of, Mercer County (N.J.) CC.
48. Duane Eason, Troy State U.
49. Kevin Chapman, of, Bernards HS, Peapack, N.J.
50. Tim Bowers, ss, Laurel Highlands HS, Uniontown, Pa.
51. Francisco Lebron, 1b, Florida International U.
52. Dwight Edge, of, Apopka (Fla.) HS.
53. Robert Mackowiak, ss-2b, South Suburban (Ill.) JC.
54. J.D. Arteaga, lhp, U. of Miami.
55. Nathan Shepperson, 1b, Virginia Military Institute.
56. Steven Yeager, c, Thousand Oaks (Calif.) HS.

## ST. LOUIS (3)

1. Braden Looper, rhp, Wichita State U.
2. (Choice to Reds as compensation for Type A free agent Ron Gant).
3. Brent Butler, ss, Scotland County HS, Laurinburg, N.C.
4. Bryan Britt, of, UNC Wilmington.
5. Jeff Rizzo, 3b, La Jolla (Calif.) HS.
6. Jim Gargiulo, c, U. of Miami.
7. Kevin Sheredy, rhp, UCLA.
8. Dave Schmidt, c, Oregon State U.
9. Shawn Hogge, rhp, Western HS, Las Vegas.
10. Cordell Farley, of, Virginia Commonwealth U.
11. Isaac Byrd, of, U. of Kansas.
12. Rodney Eberly, 3b, Highland Community (Kan.) JC.
13. Lance Smith, rhp, Dickinson (Texas) HS.
14. Steve Norris, lhp, Tyler (Texas) JC.
15. Greg Heffernan, rhp, St. Andrews Presbyterian (N.C.) College.
16. Stacy Kleiner, c, U. of Nevada-Las Vegas.
17. Keith Gallagher, rhp, Murray State U.
18. William Goodson, lhp, Troup County HS, LaGrange, Ga.
19. Keith Finnerty, 2b, St. John's U.
20. Ryan Darr, ss, Corona (Calif.) HS.
21. Randy Flores, lhp, U. of Southern California.
22. Paul Tanner, ss, U. of Nevada-Las Vegas.
23. Nathan Rice, lhp, Cal State Northridge.
24. Jason Pollock, rhp, West Liberty State (W.Va.) College.
25. Andrew Gordon, rhp, James Madison U.
26. Patrick Driscoll, lhp, U. of Nebraska.
27. Greg Montgomery, rhp, U. of Central Arkansas.
28. Tim Onofrei, rhp-of, Albertson (Idaho) College.
29. Mark Nussbeck, rhp, Bellevue (Neb.) College.
30. Orvin Matos, c, Utuado, P.R.
31. Brian Mazurek, 1b, College of St. Francis (Ill.).
32. Steven Doherty, ss, Los Angeles CC.
33. Brad Kennedy, 3b, Southwest Missouri State U.
34. Ryan Kritscher, 2b-of, UC Santa Barbara.
35. Paul Wilders, 3b, Siena College.
36. Stubby Clapp, 2b, Texas Tech.
37. Clint Weibl, rhp, U. of Miami.
38. Greg Johnson, rhp, Okeechobee (Fla.) HS.
39. Daniel Pierce, of, Jurupa Valley HS, Mira Loma, Calif.
40. Clay Hawkins, c-of, Seminole (Okla.) JC.
41. John Tuttle, rhp, San Marino (Calif.) HS.
42. Ryan Roberts, 3b, Brigham Young U.

## SAN DIEGO (15)

1. Matt Halloran, ss, Chancellor HS, Fredericksburg, Va,.
2. Vernon Maxwell, of, Midwest City (Okla.) HS.
3. Widd Workman, rhp, Arizona State U.
4. Nathan Dunn, 3b, Louisiana State U.
5. Brian Loyd, c, Cal State Fullerton.
6. Tom Szymborski, rhp, U. of Illinois-Chicago.
7. Brian Carmody, lhp, Santa Clara U.
8. Chance Capel, rhp, Carroll HS, Southlake, Texas.
9. Jason Middlebrook, rhp, Stanford U.
10. Tim Lanier, c, Louisiana State U.
11. Brian McClure, 2b, U. of Illinois.
12. Ben Reynoso, ss, Fresno State U.
13. Brennan Hervey, 1b, Florida Atlantic U.
14. Francisco Gonzalez, rhp, Arecibo, P.R.
15. Stephen Watkins, rhp, Lubbock (Texas) Christian HS.
16. Sandro Garcia, 2b, Pope John Paul II HS, Deerfield Beach, Fla.
17. Craig Patterson, c, El Dorado HS, Placentia, Calif.
18. Jacob Ruotsinoja, of, Manatee (Fla.) CC.
19. Kyle Holle, rhp, Blinn (Texas) JC.
20. James Alarcon, rhp, Jupiter, Fla.
21. John Powers, 2b, U. of Arizona.
22. Dominic Marino, rhp, Walnut (Calif.) HS.
23. Ryan Thomas, rhp, Houston Baptist U.
24. Jesse Cornejo, lhp, Seward County (Kan.) CC.
25. Chris Spieth, of, Garfield HS, Seattle.
26. Brendan Sullivan, rhp, Stanford U.
27. Nick Witte, rhp, Ball State U.
28. Trey Dunham, c, Shattuck (Okla.) HS.
29. Robbie Kent, 1b-2b, Arizona State U.
30. Rufus French, of, Amory (Miss.) HS.
31. Danny Conroy, of, Fairleigh Dickinson U.
32. Shane Cronin, 1b-3b, Green River (Wash.) CC.
33. Keith Kubiak, c, Giddings (Texas) HS.
34. Jake Epstein, 1b-c, Mount Carmel HS, San Diego.
35. Tyler Boulo, c, U. of South Alabama.
36. Rich Park, rhp, Norman (Okla.) HS.
37. Travis Jones, lhp, Asher (Okla.) HS.
38. Al Thielemann, lhp, Vista HS, Oceanside, Calif.
39. Davis Kile, rhp, Tacoma (Wash.) CC.
40. Paul Boykin, of, Odessa (Texas) JC.

## SAN FRANCISCO (7)

1. Matt White, rhp, Waynesboro (Pa.) Area HS.
2. Mike Caruso, ss, Stoneman Douglas HS, Parkland, Fla.
3. David Kenna, c, North Fort Myers (Fla.) HS.
4. Ken Vining, lhp, Clemson U.
5. Matt Wells, lhp, U. of Nevada.
6. Bill Malloy, rhp, Rutgers U.
7. Brandon Leese, rhp, Butler U.
8. Ryan Jensen, rhp, Southern Utah U.
9. Brian Manning, of, Allentown (Pa.) College.
10. Mike Glendenning, 3b, Los Angeles Pierce JC.
11. Tony Zuniga, ss, Rancho Santiago (Calif.) JC.
12. Damon Minor, 1b, U. of Oklahoma.
13. Wynter Phoenix, of, UC Santa Barbara.
14. Paul Galloway, 3b, Clemson U.
15. Mick Pageler, rhp, Odessa (Texas) JC.
16. Mike Riley, lhp, West Virginia U.
17. Eric Johnson, rhp, Mount Hood (Ore.) CC.
18. Jeff Munster, rhp, Fresno CC.
19. Levi Miskolczi, of, Rider College.
20. Luis Estrella, rhp, Cal State Fullerton.
21. Robby Crabtree, rhp, Cal State Northridge.
22. Kevin Tommasini, of, Arizona State U.
23. Tom Bartosh, of, Duncanville (Texas) HS.
24. Joel Fuentes, ss, Southeastern (Iowa) CC.
25. Lance Woodcock, ss, Ponderosa HS, Shingle Springs, Calif.
26. Chris Curry, c, Conway (Ark.) HS.
27. Art Baeza, 3b, Lewis-Clark State (Idaho) College.
28. Craig Cozart, rhp, U. of Central Florida.
29. Michael Sorrow, of, Georgia Tech.
30. Mark Hutchings, rhp, Mineral Area (Mo.) CC.
31. Richard Clark, of, Countryside HS, Clearwater, Fla.
32. Michael Wright, lhp, Crete-Monee HS, Crete, Ill.
33. Michael Stevenson, rhp, Orange Coast (Calif.) JC.
34. Jacob Joseph, rhp, San Juan HS, Citrus Heights, Calif.
35. Brad Garrett, of, Mountain View HS, Orem, Utah.
36. Billy Coleman, rhp, North Central Texas JC.
37. Donald Pearson, rhp, Foothill HS, Highlands, Calif.
38. Charles Lopez, of, Cerritos (Calif.) JC.
39. Matt Dempsey, 1b, Cypress (Calif.) JC.
40. Andrew Beattie, ss, Clearwater (Fla.) HS.

41. Chad Baum, c, Golden West (Calif.) JC.
42. Chaz Johnson, of, Dr. Phillips HS, Orlando.
43. Thomas Gessner, 3b, Thomas More HS, Milwaukee.
44. Brandon Larson, ss, Blinn (Texas) JC.
45. Don Gierke, of, Dr. Phillips HS, Orlando.
46. Richard Dishman, rhp, Duke U.
47. Mark Williams, rhp, Cal State Sacramento.
48. Justin Sherrod, ss, Santaluces HS, Lake Worth, Fla.
49. Robert Purvis, rhp, Tipton (Ind.) HS.
50. **Angel Melendez, of, Caguas, P.R.**

## SEATTLE (22)

1. **Gil Meche, rhp, Acadiana HS, Lafayette, La.**
2. **Jeff Farnsworth, rhp, Okaloosa-Walton (Fla.) CC.**
3. **Tony DeJesus, lhp, Havelock (N.C.) HS.**
4. **Denny Stark, rhp, U. of Toledo.**
5. **Chris Mears, rhp, Lord Byng HS, Vancouver, B.C.**
6. **Pat D. Williams, c, Nacogdoches (Texas) HS.**
7. **Danny Garey, rhp, St. Joseph (Mich.) HS.**
8. Willie Bloomquist, ss, South Kitsap HS, Port Orchard, Wash.
9. **Rob Luce, rhp, U. of Nevada-Las Vegas.**
10. **Matthew Noe, lhp, Riverside (Calif.) CC.**
11. **Julio Ayala, lhp, Georgia Southern U.**
12. **Joe Victery, rhp, U. of Oklahoma.**
13. **Orin Kawahara, rhp, Rancho Santiago (Calif.) JC.**
14. Dwayne Dobson, rhp, Manatee (Fla.) CC.
15. **Don Beaver, rhp, East Rowan HS, Rockwell, N.C.**
16. **Mark Carroll, c, Coxsackie-Athens HS, Athens, N.Y.**
17. **Jason Bond, lhp, Arizona State U.**
18. Allan Westfall, rhp, U. of Miami.
19. Larry Haynes, of, Nogales HS, West Covina, Calif.
20. **Brian Fitzgerald, lhp, Virginia Tech.**
21. **Kyle Kennison, rhp, U. of Southern Maine.**
22. **Brian Lindner, ss, William Paterson (N.J.) College.**
23. Devlon Davis, c, Pittsburg (Calif.) HS.
24. Jeremy Pierce, rhp, Ventura (Calif.) JC.
25. Matt Vincent, Floyd Central HS, Floyd's Knob, Ind.
26. Jacob Underwood, c, Hillsboro (Ore.) HS.
27. Josue Matos, rhp, Cabo Rojo, P.R.
28. Donovan Ross, 3b, Columbia State (Tenn.) CC.
29. Karmen Randolph, ss, Los Angeles CC.
30. Jason Wilson, rhp, Broward (Fla.) CC.
31. Chris McAdoo, rhp, Winnsboro (Texas) HS.
32. Kevin Stewart, 3b, Corona HS, Newport Beach, Calif.
33. Patrick J. Williams, of, Blinn (Texas) JC.
34. Joe Barnes, of, Old Mill HS, Severn, Md.
35. **Dallas Mahan, lhp, Greeley (Colo.) West HS.**
36. Scott Harrison, lhp, Dixie (Utah) JC.
37. Steven Rivera, lhp, Dundalk (Md.) CC.
38. Laron McGee, ss-2b, Morse HS, San Diego.
39. James McCoy, of, South Dade HS, Homestead, Fla.
40. **Sean Spencer, lhp, U. of Washington.**
41. William Allison, rhp, Central Florida CC.
42. Brett Anderson, rhp, University HS, San Diego.
43. Scott Starkey, lhp, Vista HS, Oceanside, Calif.
44. Noel Pelekoudas, 2b, Eastlake HS, Redmond, Wash.
45. Adam Walker, lhp, Yavapai (Ariz.) JC.
46. Michael Campbell, of, Mesa (Ariz.) CC.
47. Bret Nielsen, of, Grossmont HS, El Cajon, Calif.
48. Juan Pierre, of, Galveston (Texas) JC.
49. Richard Sundstrom, rhp, Cypress (Calif.) JC.
50. Jason Sutherland, c, Chuckey-Doak HS, Afton, Tenn.
51. **Jason Regan, 3b-2b, Blinn (Texas) JC.**
52. Michael Albert, of, Carlsbad (Calif.) HS.
53. Greg Dobbs, 3b, Canyon Springs HS, Moreno Valley, Calif.
54. Richard Snider, rhp, Byng HS, Ada, Okla.
55. Chad Schmidt, of, Skidmore (Texas) Tynan HS.
56. Brandon Barnaby, rhp, Citrus (Calif.) JC.
57. Tamar Turner, of, Liberty (Texas) HS.
58. Brian Beinfest, lhp, Clayton (Calif.) Valley HS.
59. Barry Zito, lhp, University HS, San Diego.
60. Ryan Grimmett, of, U. of Miami.

## TAMPA BAY (29)

1. **Paul Wilder, of, Cary (N.C.) HS.**
2. **Doug Johnson, 1b-ss, Buchholz HS, Gainesville, Fla.**
3. **Ed Kofler, rhp, Tarpon Springs HS, Palm Harbor, Fla.**
4. **Cedrick Bowers, lhp, Chiefland (Fla.) HS.**
5. **Alex Sanchez, of, Miami-Dade CC Wolfson.**
6. **Elliot Brown, rhp, Auburn U.**
7. **Mickey Callaway, rhp, U. of Mississippi.**
8. **Matt Quatraro, c, Old Dominion U.**
9. **Denis Pujals, rhp, U. of Miami.**
10. **Chie Gunner, of, Grand View (Mo.) HS.**
11. **Robert Cafaro, rhp, Southern Connecticut State U.**

12. **Scott Madison, lhp, Rutgers U.**
13. **Shawn Stutz, rhp, Florida International U.**
14. **Delvin James, rhp, Nacogdoches (Texas) HS.**
15. **John Kaufman, lhp, U. of Florida.**
16. **Jared Sandberg, 3b, Capital HS, Olympia, Wash.**
17. **Michael DeCelle, of, U. of Miami.**
18. **Brad Weber, lhp, Indiana U.**
19. Ryan Ledden, rhp, Parkview HS, Lilburn, Ga.
20. **Jamie Ebling, 2b, Florida Southern College.**
21. **Trey Salinas, c, U. of Texas.**
22. **Luke Owens-Bragg, 2b, UC Riverside.**
23. Russ Jacobson, c, Horizon HS, Scottsdale, Ariz.
24. **Matt Kastelic, of, Texas Tech.**
25. **James Manias, lhp, Fairfield U.**
26. Jeff Jankowiak, rhp, Wayzata HS, Plymouth, Minn.
27. Kyle Snyder, rhp, Riverview HS, Sarasota, Fla.
28. Donny Barker, rhp, U. of Texas.
29. **R.J. Howerton, rhp, Southeastern Oklahoma State U.**
30. **Kyle Whitley, rhp, Southeastern Oklahoma State U.**
31. **Mark Hale, rhp, Carefree, Ariz.**
32. **Michael Brown, rhp, Walters State (Tenn.) CC.**
33. Aaron Bouie, rhp, Albion (N.Y.) Central HS.
34. Daniel Wheeler, rhp, Central Arizona JC.
35. Brian Packin, 1b, Randolph HS, Mendham, N.J.
36. Kevin Kay, c, Forest Park HS, Morrow, Ga.
37. Derek Mann, ss, Columbus (Ga.) HS.
38. Walter Ward, of, Edison (Fla.) CC.
39. Ryan Mottl, rhp, McCluer North HS, Florissant, Mo.
40. **Jared Verrall, 1b, Eastern Oregon State College.**
41. **Lawrence Severence, c, Logan (Ill.) CC.**
42. Dayle Campbell, of, Lynwood HS, Carson, Calif.
43. Jason Smith, rhp, Palm Beach Lakes HS, West Palm Beach, Fla.
44. Jason Michaels, of, Okaloosa-Walton (Fla.) CC.
45. **Michael Kimbrell, lhp, Southeastern Louisiana U.**
46. Robert Henkel, rhp, Monte Vista HS, La Mesa, Calif.
47. Jeremy Robinson, lhp, St. Amant (La.) HS.
48. Michael Barraza, lhp, Gladstone HS, Azusa, Calif.
49. Edward Lubbers, lhp, Forest Hill HS, West Palm Beach, Fla.
50. Bret Stewart, lhp, Leesburg HS, Fruitland Park, Fla.
51. Jason Briggs, rhp, Smithville (Texas) HS.
52. Chris Lagrone, of, Seward County (Kan.) CC.
53. **Scott Leon, rhp, U. of Texas.**
54. L.J. Yankosky, rhp, Georgia Tech.
55. Ron Merrill, ss, Jesuit HS, Tampa.
56. Joel De los Santos, 2b, Burncoat HS, Worcester, Mass.
57. Adrian Yother, rhp, Middle Georgia JC.
58. Clint Kinsey, rhp, Fairland (Okla.) HS.
59. Nathan Hilton, rhp, Boone (Iowa) HS.
60. John Hensley, rhp, Fountain Central HS, Kingman, Ind.
61. **Nathan Ruhl, rhp, Johnson County (Kan.) CC.**
62. **Mike King, of-2b, Duke U.**
63. Tim Hill, rhp, St. Leo (Fla.) College.
64. **Tony McCladdie, 2b, Middle Georgia JC.**
65. Don Kivinemi, rhp, Bellevue (Neb.) College.
66. **Chris Anderson, c, Southeastern Oklahoma State U.**
67. Matt Hoffman, rhp, Seminole (Okla.) JC.
68. Spencer Young, rhp, Mingus Union HS, Cottonwood, Ariz.
69. Roger Carter, rhp, Fort Gibson (Okla.) HS.
70. Juan Cruz, 3b, Jefferson HS, Lafayette, Ind.
71. Jason Kirk, of, Altus (Okla.) HS.
72. Brad Smith, 1b, Edmond (Okla.) Memorial HS.
73. Nicholas Rhodes, c, Danbury (Conn.) HS.
74. Chad Pyle, ss, Christian County HS, Hopkinsville, Ky.
75. Michael O'Brien, 1b, Old Bridge (N.J.) HS.
76. Zachary Roper, 3b, Tarpon Springs (Fla.) HS.
77. Keith Brice, rhp, Westminster Christian HS, Miami.
78. Rashard Casey, rhp, Hoboken (N.J.) HS.
79. Emory Brock, of, Parkway West HS, St. Louis.
80. Adrian Espino, 1b-of, Laredo (Texas) JC.
81. David DeMarco, 1b, Marple Newtown HS, Newtown Square, Pa.
82. Victor Sauceda, 2b-ss, Laredo (Texas) JC.
83. Layne Meyer, rhp, Parkway West HS, Ballwin, Mo.
84. Scott Diorio, of, Seward County (Kan.) CC.
85. Justin Clements, ss, Manatee (Fla.) CC.
86. Scott Neuberger, of, Tallahassee (Fla.) CC.
87. David Taylor, rhp, Crossroads HS, Pacific Palisades, Calif.
88. Shannon Lovan, rhp, Christian County HS, Crofton, Ky.
89. Travis Phelps, rhp, Crowder (Mo.) JC.
90. Jack Koch, rhp, Miami-Dade CC North.
91. David Hoffman, lhp, Danville (Ill.) HS.
92. Brian Newton, lhp, Juanita HS, Kirkland, Wash.
93. Willie Marin, rhp, Coral Gables (Fla.) HS.
94. Blair Barbier, rhp, Brother Martin HS, Harvey, La.

95. Ryan Gripp, ss, Indianola (Iowa) HS.
96. Jerrod Harris, c, Labelle (Fla.) HS.
97. Michael Rose, of, Alter HS, Dayton, Ohio.

## TEXAS (18)

1. **R.A. Dickey, rhp, U. of Tennessee.**
1. **Sam Marsonek, rhp, Jesuit HS, Tampa** (Choice from Yankees as compensation for Type A free agent Kenny Rogers).
1. **Corey Lee, lhp, North Carolina State U.** (Supplemental pick for loss of Rogers).
2. **Derrick Cook, rhp, James Madison U.**
3. **Derek Baker, 3b, Rancho Santiago (Calif.) JC.**
4. **Kelly Dransfeldt, ss, U. of Michigan.**
5. **Warren Morris, 2b, Louisiana State U.**
6. **Tony Fisher, of, U. of St. Thomas (Minn.).**
7. **Juan Pinella, of, North Stafford (Va.) HS.**
8. **Luis Acevedo, ss, Isabella, P.R.**
9. Randy Rodriguez, lhp, Florida Air Academy HS, Melbourne, Fla.
10. **Doug Davis, lhp, CC of San Francisco.**
11. Quenten Patterson, rhp, Killeen (Texas) HS.
12. **Tony Dellamano, rhp, UC Davis.**
13. **Justin Siegel, lhp, Long Beach State U.**
14. Chris Combs, 1b, North Carolina State U.
15. Alex Vazquez, of, Westminster HS, Anaheim.
16. **Ron Nelson, rhp, Ohio State U.**
17. **John Kertis, rhp, Miami.**
18. Brian Jackson, rhp, San Diego Mesa JC.
19. Mark Hendrickson, lhp, Washington State U.
20. **John Ellis, c, U. of Maine.**
21. **Adrian Myers, of, William Carey (Miss.) College.**
22. **Tony Shourds, rhp, Norwalk (Conn.) CC.**
23. Casey Davis, of, Wichita State U.
24. **Mike Zywica, of, U. of Evansville.**
25. John Santos, rhp, Cuesta (Calif.) JC.
26. Ronald Beimel, lhp, Alleghany (Pa.) CC.
27. Todd Periou, lhp, Lassen (Calif.) JC.
28. **Steve Smella, of, Indiana U.**
29. Grant Dorn, rhp, Derry Area (Pa.) HS.
30. Aaron Bond, rhp, JC of Southern Idaho.
31. Travis Hafner, 3b, Cowley County (Kan.) CC.
32. Danny Meier, of, Northeast Texas CC.
33. **Ryan Smith, lhp, San Diego State U.**
34. Kevin Smith, rhp, James Martin Senior HS, Texas.
35. Ali Cepeda, of, Canada (Calif.) JC.
36. Ryan Christenson, rhp, Normandale (Minn.) CC.
37. Steven Wombacher, lhp, Mingus Union HS, Clarkdale, Ariz.
38. Scott Green, rhp, Navarro (Texas) JC.
39. Craig Petulla, rhp, Philipsburg-Osceola HS, Philipsburg, Pa.
40. Jesse Smith, ss-of, American River (Calif.) JC.
41. Fehlendt Lentini, of, Napa (Calif.) JC.
42. Kyle Skinner, ss, Mount St. Joseph's HS, Baltimore.
43. Justin Wise, of, Westbrook HS, Beaumont, Texas.
44. Jose Pimentel, 1b, Indio HS, Palm Springs, Calif.
45. **Francisco Jaramillo, ss, Southern Illinois U.**
46. **Rowan Richards, of, U. of Notre Dame.**
47. Curtis Young, of, Purvis (Miss.) HS.
48. David Wigley, c, Pensacola (Fla.) HS.
49. Kevin Colbourn, lhp, Hagerstown (Md.) JC.
50. Ron Chiavacci, rhp, Lackawanna (Pa.) CC.
51. Greg Horton, of, El Paso CC.
52. Anthony Perlozzo, 1b, Athens HS, Sayre, Pa.

## TORONTO (4)

1. **Billy Koch, rhp, Clemson U.**
1. **Joe Lawrence, ss, Barbe HS, Lake Charles, La.** (Choice from Orioles as compensation for Type A free agent Roberto Alomar).
1. **Pete Tucci, 1b-of, Providence College** (Supplemental pick for loss of Alomar).
2. (Choice to Red Sox as compensation for Type A free agent Erik Hanson).
2. **Brent Abernathy, ss, The Lovett School, Atlanta** (Choice from Marlins as compensation for Type B free agent Devon White).
3. **Yan Lachapelle, rhp, Montreal.**
3. **Clayton Andrews, lhp, Seminole HS, Largo, Fla.** (Choice from Marlins as compensation for Type B free agent Devon White).
4. **Ryan Stromsborg, 2b, U. of Southern California.**
5. **John Bale, lhp, U. of Southern Mississippi.**
6. **Mike Rodriguez, c, Tarleton State (Texas) U.**
7. **Casey Blake, 3b, Wichita State U.**
8. **Davan Keathley, lhp, Johansen HS, Turlock, Calif.**
9. **Sam Goure, lhp, County HS, Pueblo, Colo.**
10. **Josh Phelps, c, Lakeland HS, Rathdrum, Idaho.**

ROBERT GURGANUS

**Toronto Tornado.** Clemson righthander Billy Koch, who was clocked at 100 mph, became the Blue Jays' top draft pick.

11. **Stan Baston, ss, Tallahassee (Fla.) CC.**
12. **Ryan Meyers, rhp, U. of Tennessee.**
13. Lorenzo Ferguson, of, St. Martin de Porres HS, West Bloomfield, Mich.
14. **Sean McClellan, rhp, Oklahoma State U.**
15. **Josh Bradford, rhp, Xavier U.**
16. **Lorenzo Bagley, of, U. of Central Florida.**
17. **Jason Koehler, c, Rider College.**
18. Gary Johnson, of, East Los Angeles JC.
19. Jason Ball, rhp, Los Alamitos (Calif.) HS.
20. **Tim Giles, 1b, UNC Greensboro.**
21. **Will Skett, of, Long Beach State U.**
22. **David Bleazard, rhp, Oklahoma City U.**
23. **Brad Moon, of, Hunting Hills HS, Red Deer, Alberta.**
24. Darold Butler, 2b, Simeon HS, Chicago.
25. Stephen Wood, 1b, Bishop Amat HS, West Covina, Calif.
26. Lawrence Adams, 1b, Lake City (Fla.) JC.
27. Gary Peete, of, Munford HS, Brighton, Tenn.
28. Brian Leach, rhp, Palm Beach (Fla.) JC.
29. **Ryan Zeber, c, Foothill HS, Tustin, Calif.**
30. Ryan Webb, 3b, Upland (Calif.) HS.
31. Clarence Watley, ss, Redan HS, Stone Mountain, Ga.
32. Justin Brager, ss, Wenatchee Valley (Wash.) CC.
33. Orlando Hudson, ss, Darlington (S.C.) HS.
34. Mark Curtis, rhp, Pensacola (Fla.) JC.
35. James Landingham, of, Miami-Dade CC Wolfson.
36. Justin Montalbano, lhp, Mendocino (Calif.) CC.
37. Craig Lariz, 1b, Key West (Fla.) HS.
38. Cody Hartshorn, rhp, Lamar (Colo.) HS.
39. Kyle Adams, lhp, Allen County (Kan.) CC.
40. Orlando Woodard, rhp, Franklin HS, Stockton, Calif.
41. Anthony Novelli, rhp, Oak Grove HS, San Jose.
42. Michael Galati, rhp, U. of Connecticut.
43. Derek Hines, of, Yavapai (Ariz.) CC.
44. Greg Ferrell, of, Saddleback (Calif.) CC.
45. Kevin Covington, of, Cherokee County HS, Centre, Ala.
46. Robert Gonzales, c, Castle Park HS, Chula Vista, Calif.
47. Michael Duperron, lhp, South Grenville HS, Prescott, Ont.
48. Harold Betts, c, Lakewood (Calif.) HS.
49. Shaw Scovel, 3b, Foothill HS, Villa Park, Calif.
50. Joshua Glober, rhp, Upper Canada College, Toronto.
51. Steven Lacy, rhp, Alhambra HS, Glendale, Ariz.
52. Michael Lopez, ss, Maryvale HS, Phoenix.

# OBITUARIES/
# INDEX

# OBITUARIES

**Mel Allen**, voice of the Yankees and later "This Week In Baseball," died June 16 in Greenwich, Conn. He was 83. Allen, whose lilting Alabama drawl became one of the great signatures in baseball broadcasting, was known for his trademark "How about that?" He was a broadcaster for 58 years and was honored in the broadcast wing of the Hall of Fame in 1978.

**Al Barlick**, a Hall of Fame umpire, died of a heart attack Dec. 27 in Springfield, Ill. He was 80. Known for his hustle, toughness and booming ball-strike calls, Barlick umpired in the National League from 1940-70, working seven World Series and seven All-Star Games.

**Jim Baumer**, a former big league infielder and Phillies farm and scouting director from 1981-88, died July 8 in Paoli, Pa. He was 65. Baumer hit .206 in 18 big league games in 1949 and 1961.

**John Beradino**, a big league infielder who went on to star in the soap opera "General Hospital," died of cancer May 19 in Los Angeles. He was 79. Beradino batted .249-36-387 in 912 games from 1939-52.

**Ewell "The Whip" Blackwell**, who came within two outs of joining Johnny Vander Meer as the only big leaguers to pitch consecutive no-hitters, died Oct. 29 in Hendersonville, N.C. He was 74. Blackwell went 82-78, 3.30 in 236 games from 1942-55. In 1947, he no-hit the Boston Braves 6-0 on June 18th and held them hitless for 8⅓ innings four days later before Eddie Stanky's broken-bat single broke up the gem. That year, Blackwell set an NL record for righthanders by winning 16 consecutive games, and led the NL in wins (22), complete games (23) and strikeouts (193 in 273 innings).

**Willard Brown**, the first black player to hit an American League home run, died Aug. 8 in Houston. He was 85. An outfielder, Brown batted .179-1-6 in 21 games with the 1947 St. Louis Browns. He hit his homer with a borrowed bat from a teammate, who broke the bat rather than allow Brown to use it again. Brown was a six-time all-star in the Negro Leagues, and won three batting and three homer crowns in the Puerto Rican winter league.

**Billy Bruton**, an outfielder who won three NL stolen base titles, died of a heart attack Dec. 5 in Wilmington, Del. Bruton batted .273-94-545 with 207 steals in 1,610 big league games from 1953-64.

**Jim Busby**, a former all-star outfielder, died of a heart attack July 8 in Augusta, Ga. He was 69. Busby batted .262-48-438 in 1,352 games from 1950-62, earning all-star honors in 1951 by hitting .283-5-68 for the White Sox. A star quarterback in college, he led Texas Christian to the 1945 Cotton Bowl.

**Ajani Carter**, an outfielder at Laney (Calif.) Junior College, was shot to death April 7 in Oakland. He was 19.

**Irving Cooper**, a judge who once upheld baseball's reserve clause, died Sept. 17 in Manhattan, N.Y. He was 94. In 1972, Cooper presided over a $3 million lawsuit in federal court in New York from Cardinals outfielder Curt Flood, who challenged the reserve clause. Cooper didn't rule on the merits of the reserve system, but rejected Flood's claims and upheld baseball's antitrust exemption.

**Keith Cooper**, a righthander in the Braves organization, died in an automobile accident Nov. 14 in Sheldon, Vt. He was 23. Signed as a nondrafted free agent out of the University of Vermont, Cooper went 1-0, 1.65 with four saves in 17 games for Rookie-level Danville in 1995, his only pro season.

**Tony Cox**, majority owner of the California League's San Jose Giants since 1987, died of a heart attack Sept. 21 in Manhattan, N.Y. He was 55.

**Harry Coyle**, the father of televised baseball, died Feb. 19 in Des Moines. He was 74. Coyle directed the first televised World Series in 1947 and stayed with NBC Sports until retiring in 1989. He won Emmy Awards in 1975 and 1978 for his World Series coverage.

**Babe Dahlgren**, who replaced Lou Gehrig at first base for the Yankees, died Sept. 4 in Arcadia, Calif. He was 84.

Dahlgren batted .261-82-569 in 1,137 games from 1935-46 and was an all-star with the Phillies in 1943, when he batted .287. He ended Gehrig's consecutive-game streak at 2,130 when he replaced the ailing star in 1939.

**Jim Davis**, who tied a big league record with four strikeouts in one inning, died Dec. 26 in San Mateo, Calif. He was 71. A lefthander, Davis went 24-26, 4.01 in 154 games from 1954-57. In 1956, he fanned four Cardinals in one inning and also gave up the home run that started Pittsburgh's Dale Long's record streak of eight consecutive games with a homer.

**Randy Donisthorpe**, a lefthander in the Reds organization, died in his sleep March 20 in Plant City, Fla. Donisthorpe, who was at Cincinnati's spring-training base, had been signed as a nondrafted free agent in January.

**Thomas Eaton** and **Alfred Stell**, teammates at South Mountain (Ariz.) Community College were killed and 11 players were injured when a van wrecked March 29 en route to a game in Douglas, Ariz. Both Eaton and Stell were 19.

**Del Ennis**, a three-time all-star outfielder and the second-leading home run-hitter in Phillies history, died of complications from diabetes Feb. 8 in Huntington Valley, Pa. He was 70. Ennis hit .284-288-1,284 in 1,903 games from 1946-59. His 259 homers as a Phillies lasted as a club record until Mike Schmidt surpassed him in 1980.

**Charlie Finley**, the controversial and innovative former owner of the Kansas City/Oakland Athletics, died Feb. 19 in Chicago. He was 77. Finley came up with the idea for World Series night games, which took off, and orange baseballs,

**Charlie Finley**

which didn't. He added color to the game, having his A's wear green and gold uniforms with white shoes, encouraging his players to wear facial hair and introducing a mule—which he named after himself—as the team mascot. He also was known for a running feud with commissioner Bowie Kuhn. Finley's team won three straight World Series from 1972-74.

**Hugh Finnerty**, Texas League president from 1965-69, died Dec. 15 in Tulsa. He was 77.

**Roger Freed**, who won two minor league MVP awards, died of heart problems Jan. 9 in Chino, Calif. He was 49. Freed batted .245-22-109 in 344 big league games from 1970-79. He won three home run and three RBI titles in the minors, and was named International League MVP in 1970 and American Association MVP in 1976.

**Milt Gaston**, who had more Hall of Fame teammates and mangers than any player in baseball history, died April 26 in Hyannis, Mass. He was 100. A righthander, Gaston went 97-164, 4.55 in 355 games from 1924-34. He played with Babe Ruth, Lou Gehrig and 15 other Cooperstown honorees. In January, Gaston became the eighth former big leaguer to reach age 100.

**Gordon Goldsberry**, a longtime player-development executive, died Feb. 23 in Lake Forest, Calif. He was 68. A first baseman, Goldsberry hit .241-6-56 in 217 major league games from 1949-52. He worked in player-development jobs with the Cubs, Brewers, Phillies and Orioles.

**Bill Goodstein**, a player agent most notable for negotiating Darryl Strawberry's 1995 contract with the Yankees, died of a heart attack Jan. 13 in Manhattan, N.Y. He was 56.

**Bob Grim**, the 1954 AL rookie of the year, died of a heart attack Oct. 23 in Shawnee, Kan. He was 66. A righthander, Grim went 61-41, 3.61 in 268 games from 1954-62. The last AL rookie to win 20 games, Grim went 20-6, 3.26 for the Yankees in 1954. He was an all-star in 1957, when he went 12-8, 2.63 with an AL-best 19 saves.

**Joe Hoerner**, who recovered from a heart attack in the minors to become a big league all-star, died when he was run over by a tractor in a farming accident Oct. 4 in Hermann, Mo. He was 60. A lefthander, Hoerner went 39-34, 2.99 with 99 saves in 493 major league games from 1963-77 after having a heart attack in 1958 at Davenport in the old Class B Three-I League. He was an all-star with the Phillies in 1970, when he went 9-5, 2.65 with nine saves.

**Vic Janowicz**, a Heisman Trophy winner who played in the majors, died Feb. 27 in Columbus, Ohio. He was 66. A catcher/third baseman, Janowicz batted .214-2-10 in 83 games from 1953-54. The Heisman winner was a single-wing halfback and defensive back at Ohio State in 1950, he played in the NFL with the Washington Redskins from 1954-55. A serious automobile accident in 1956 ended his athletic career.

**Oscar Judd**, the first Canadian to make the AL all-star team, died Dec. 27 in Ingersoll, Ontario. He was 87. A lefthander, Judd went 40-51, 3.90 in 161 games from 1941-48. He was an all-star in 1943, when he went 11-6, 2.90 for the Red Sox.

**Alex Kellner**, who won 20 games and made the AL all-star team as a Philadelphia Athletics rookie in 1949, died May 3 in Tucson. He was 71. A lefthander, Kellner went 101-112, 4.41 in 321 games from 1948-59.

**John McSherry**, an NL umpire, died after suffering a massive heart attack during the Reds-Expos season opener April 1 in Cincinnati. McSherry, who made the majors in 1971, was considered one of the best umpires in the big leagues.

**Danny Monzon**, Latin American scouting coordinator for the Red Sox, died in an automobile accident Jan. 21 near Santo Domingo, Dominican Republic. He was 49. An infielder, Monzon hit .244 in 94 major leagues games from 1972-73.

**Walter "Moose" Moryn**, a former all-star outfielder, died July 21 in Winfield, Ill. He was 70. Moryn batted .266-101-354 in 785 games from 1955-61, earning all-star recognition in 1958, when he hit .264-26-77 for the Cubs.

**George "Red" Munger**, a three-time all-star righthander for the Cardinals, died July 23 in Houston. He was 77. Munger went 77-56, 3.83 in 273 major league games, earning all-star honors in 1944, 1947 and 1949.

**Bob Muncrief**, a former all-star righthander, died Feb. 7 in Dallas. He was 80. Muncrief went 80-82, 3.80 in 288 games from 1937-50. He was an all-star in 1944, when he went 13-8, 3.08 and helped the St. Louis Browns win their only pennant.

**Bill "Swish" Nicholson**, a four-time all-star outfielder, died March 8 in Chestertown, Md. He was 81. Nicholson batted .263-235-948 in 1,677 games from 1936-53. He won two home run and two RBI titles in the NL, and earned all-star honors in 1940, 1941, 1943 and 1944. In 1944, he tied a big league record by homering in four straight plate appearances and lost the NL MVP award by one point to Cardinals shortstop Marty Marion.

**Keane Poche**, a freshman lefthander at the University of New Orleans, died in an automobile accident May 21 near New Orleans. He was 19. Poche went 4-0, 4.33 with six saves in 25 games.

**Paul Pryor**, an NL umpire from 1961-81, died Dec. 15 in St. Petersburg, Fla. He was 68.

**Tom Racine**, general manager of the New York-Penn League's Vermont Expos, died Jan. 3 in Burlington, Vt. He was 65.

**Ralph Rowe**, who spent 44 years in professional baseball as a minor league player and manager and major league coach, died Feb. 29 in Newberry, S.C. He was 71.

**Connie Ryan**, a former all-star second baseman and big league manager, died Jan. 3 in Metairie, La. He was 75. Ryan hit .248-56-381 in 1,184 games from 1942-54, earning NL all-star honors in 1944 by hitting .295 for the Boston Braves. He briefly managed the 1975 Braves, going 9-18, and the 1977 Rangers, going 2-4. In between, he was the scout who discovered Vida Blue for the Athletics.

**Joe Ryan**, former general manager for three Triple-A teams

and a man instrumental in the revival of the American Association in 1969, died Aug. 10 in Miami. He was 80.

**Joe Schultz**, the only manager in Seattle Pilots history, died of heart failure Jan. 10 in St. Louis. He was 77. Schultz guided the Pilots to a 64-98 record in 1969, after which they became the Milwaukee Brewers. He also skippered the Tigers at the end of 1973, going 14-14. A catcher, he batted .259-1-46 in 240 big league games from 1939-48.

**Scott Seator**, director of communications for the Texas League's Midland Angels, died of cancer Sept. 3. He was 27.

**Bill Serena**, a former big league third baseman who had one of the most memorable minor league seasons ever, died of cancer April 17 in Hayward, Calif. He as 71. Serena hit .251-48-198 in 408 major league games form 1949-54. His claim to fame was his 1947 season in the old Class C West Texas-New Mexico League, when he hit .374 and led the league with 183 runs, 57 home runs and 190 RBIs in 137 games.

**Mike Sharperson**, a former all-star second baseman playing with Triple-A Las Vegas, died in an automobile accident May 26 in Las Vegas. He was 34. Sharperson batted .281-10-121 in  550 big league games from 1987-93, earning all-star recognition by hitting .300 for the Dodgers in 1992. He was scheduled to join the Padres the day he was killed.

**C. Arnholt Smith**, the original owner of the Padres, died June 8 in Del Mar, Calif. He was 97. Smith brought San Diego into the NL as an expansion team in 1969. He tried to move the franchise to Washington D.C., but

**Mike Sharperson**

when his plan fell through he sold the Padres to Ray Kroc in 1973.

**Al Stump**, whose second biography of Hall of Famer Ty Cobb was the basis for the 1994 film "Cobb," died Dec. 14 in Newport Beach, Calif. He was 79.

**William Suero**, a former big league second baseman who played in Taiwan in 1995, died in an automobile accident Nov. 30 in Santo Domingo, Dominican Republic. He was 29. Suero went 7-for-30 (.233) in 33 major league games from 1992-93.

**Charlie Teague**, the first player named Most Outstanding Player of the College World Series, died May 8 in Greensboro, N.C. He was 71. A second baseman, Teague earned all-America honors at Wake Forest in 1949 and 1950. He led the Demon Deacons to a runner-up finish at the CWS in 1949, the first year the MOP award was given.

**Joanne Winter**, a star pitcher in the All-American Girls Baseball League, died Sept. 22 in Scottsdale, Ariz. She was 72. Winter went 133-115, 2.06 in 287 games in eight seasons. She shares the AAGBL record for wins in a season (33 in 1946), holds the mark for consecutive shutout innings (63) and is the only pitcher to lead the league in wins during both its underhand and overhand eras. Winter was part of Racine Belles championship teams in 1943 and 1946. In the latter year, she clinched the championship with a 14-inning shutout against Rockford Peaches.

**Burnis "Wild Bill" Wright**, a star outfielder in the Negro Leagues and the Mexican League, died Aug. 3 in Aguascalientes, Mexico. He was 82. A seven-time all-star in the Negro Leagues, Wright led the Negro National League with a .488 batting average in 1939. He led Mexico in hitting in 1941 and won the Mexican triple crown in 1943.

**Landon Yelverton**, a freshman righthander at the University of South Alabama, died in an automobile accident Jan. 26 in Mobile, Ala. He was 19.

**Al "Zeke" Zarilla**, a former all-star outfielder, died Sept. 4 in Honolulu. He was 77. Zarilla batted .276-61-456 in 1,120 games from 1943-53. He was an all-star with the St. Louis Browns in 1948, when he hit .329-12-74.

# INDEX

## GENERAL INFORMATION

## MAJOR, MINOR LEAGUE CLUBS

# Here's The Pitch

## Pencil Yourself Into The Lineup. Subscribe Today!

Pitchers At The Plate
Gone South: Prospects Who Hit The Skids
AL Draft Report Cards
ESPN's Peter Gammons

Bottoms UP

HOW BARRY BONDS' GIANTS
AND OTHER LAST-PLACE TEAMS
ARE REGROUPING FOR THE FUTURE

We take the mound 26 times a year. And as a 16-year veteran, we've developed quite a repertoire. We paint the corners with our special reports and insightful examinations of trends of the game.

Our colorful features, both major and minor league, will entice you like a lollipop curve.

Our draft coverage and prospect lists are nothing but heat, right down the middle. And we may surprise you with an occasional knuckleball, just a tinge of humor and irreverence that helps weave the fabric of baseball.

We blaze the trail for you to follow your favorite prospects up the ladder to stardom, with complete minor league statistics and reports. And even before they sign their first professional contract, we've got our eye on them with college and amateur news.

From Lynchburg to Pittsburgh, Tokyo to Omaha, **Baseball America** keeps you in touch with the game.

## BaseBall america

"Baseball News You Can't Get Anywhere Else"

**BASEBALL AMERICA**
P.O. Box 6710 · Torrance, CA 90504-9933

# 1-800-845-2726